The World Book Atlas

The World Book

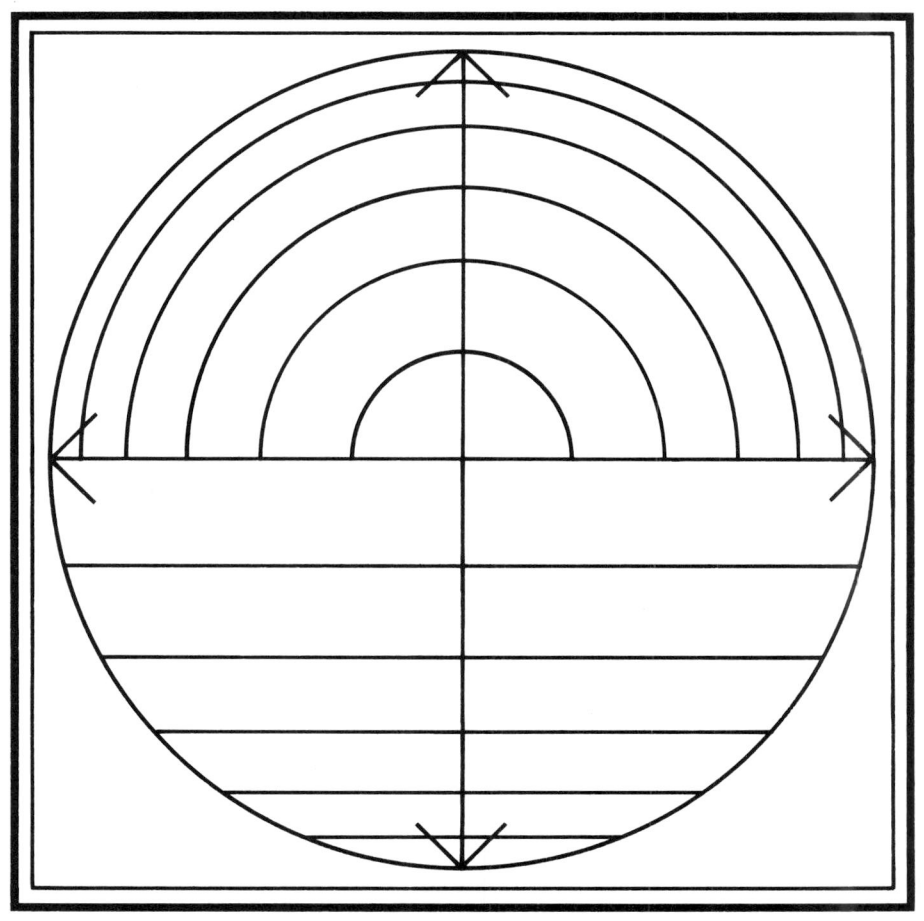

Atlas

World Book, Inc.
a Scott Fetzer company
Chicago

Staff

World Book Staff

President   *Tom Murphy*

Publisher   *William H. Nault*

Editorial

Editor in chief
Robert O. Zeleny

Executive editor
Dominic J. Miccolis

Associate editor
Maureen Mostyn Liebenson

Senior editor
Lisa Klobuchar

Rights and permissions
Janet T. Peterson

Art

Art director
Roberta Dimmer

Assistant art director
Joe Gound

Photography director
John S. Marshall

Designer
Chestnut House

Product production

Manufacturing
Sandra Van den Broucke, director

Pre-press services
Jerry Stack, director
Randi Park
Barbara Podczerwinski

Maps of the World credits

Cartographic and geographic director
Giuseppe Motta

Geographic research
G. Baselli
M. Colombo

Terrain illustration
S. Andenna
E. Ferrari

Cartographic production
F. Tosi
G. Capitini
A. Carnero

Coordination
S. Binda
L. Pasquali
G. Zanetta

Consultants

Lawrence C. Bliss, B.S., M.S., Ph.D.
Professor and Chairman
Department of Botany
University of Washington

Kempton E. Webb, A.B., M.A., Ph.D.
Professor and Chairperson
Department of Geography
and Anthropology
William Paterson College of New Jersey

James S. Sweitzer, B.S., M.S., Ph.D.
Astronomer
Chicago, Illinois

Mark Elison, M.S.
Department of Geological Sciences
Northwestern University

Rand McNally & Company Staff

Product director
Russell L. Voisin

Managing editor
Jon M. Leverenz

Geographic research
V. Patrick Healy

Research coordinator
Susan K. Hudson

Cartographic production
Ronald F. Peters

Acknowledgments

Illustration credits read from top to bottom and from left to right on each page. Illustrations that extend over two pages are credited to the left-hand page.

8, NASA. 9, John Shaw, Bruce Coleman Ltd.; © Marty Snyderman; Phil Degginger from E. R. Degginger. 10, Artwork © Mitchell Beazley Pub. Ltd. 1973 as The Good Earth. 11, © John Eastcott/ Yva Momatiuk, Woodfin Camp, Inc.; © Marty Snyderman; © Jeff Foott, Bruce Coleman Ltd. 12, © Leo Touchet, Woodfin Camp, Inc.; Henry Ausloss, World Wildlife Fund from Bruce Coleman Ltd. 13, WORLD BOOK diagrams; Terraphotographics/BPS; Carlos Elmer, Shostal; Robert Glaze; © Loren McIntyre. 14, Artwork Brian Delf. 15, Ronald Thompson/Frank W. Lane, Bruce Coleman Ltd.; © Jim Brandenburg, Woodfin Camp, Inc.; Charlie Ott, Bruce Coleman Ltd. 16, © David Muench; WORLD BOOK artwork. 17, © Dwight Kuhn; Artwork © Mitchell Beazley Pub. Ltd. 1973 as The Good Earth. 18, Norman Tomalin, Bruce Coleman Ltd. 19, © David Muench; © Jeff Foott. 20, Animals Coral Mula; trees Donald Myall. 21, E. R. Degginger; Mike Price, Bruce Coleman Ltd. 22, Hutchison Library; Artwork Bob Bampton/ The Garden Studio. 23, G. R. Plage, Bruce Coleman Ltd. 24, © Jodi Cobb, Woodfin Camp, Inc.; Artwork, Jim Robins. 26, © Dwight R. Kuhn; © J. Alsop, Bruce Coleman Inc.; © Dwight R. Kuhn. 27, E. R. Degginger; Artwork, Donald Myall. 28, W. E. Ruth, Bruce Coleman Inc. 29, Phil Degginger from E. R. Degginger; © Jim Brandenburg, Woodfin Camp, Inc.; Wolf Jean Hellmer for WORLD BOOK; other animals Coral Mula. 30, WORLD BOOK artwork; © B. and C. Alexander. 31, TSW/Chicago Ltd.; U.S. Naval Photographic Center; Artwork Jim Robins. 32, © Loren McIntyre, Woodfin Camp, Inc.

33, Hutchison Library; Photri; Shostal. 34, © Odyssey Productions. 35, Robert Glaze; © Odyssey Productions. 36, Cameramann International Ltd. 37, © Enrique Shore, Woodfin Camp, Inc.; © Steve Vidler, The Stock House Ltd.; Pedro Luis Roata, Shostal. 38, © DPA from Photoreporters. 39, Eric Carle, Shostal; © Alon Reininger, Woodfin Camp, Inc. 40, © Marc F. Bernheim, Woodfin Camp, Inc. 41, © Robert Azzi, Woodfin Camp, Inc.; © D. and J. Heaton, The Stock House Ltd.; © Malcolm Holmes, The Stock House Ltd. 42, © Robert Azzi, Woodfin Camp, Inc. 43, Masood Quereshi, Bruce Coleman Ltd.; S. Trevor/D. B., Bruce Coleman Inc.; © Carl Frank, Photo Researchers. 44, Fritz Prenzel, Bruce Coleman Ltd. 45, © Odyssey Productions; Shostal; © Robin Smith, The Stock House Ltd. 46, Cameramann International, Ltd. 47, Cameramann International, Ltd.; © N. Devore III, Bruce Coleman Inc. 48, TASS from Sovfoto. 49, Chris Bonington, Bruce Coleman Ltd.; David Falconer, © David R. Frazier Photolibrary. 50, NASA. 51, © Harold Sund; E. R. Degginger. 52, WORLD BOOK diagram. 53, WORLD BOOK diagrams; © David F. Malin, Anglo-Australian Telescope Board. 54, NASA. 55, WORLD BOOK diagrams. 56, WORLD BOOK diagram. 57, WORLD BOOK diagram; John S. Shelton. 58-59, Artwork © Mitchell Beazley Pub. Ltd. 1973 as The Good Earth. 59, © George Hall, Woodfin Camp, Inc. 60, Gene Ahrens; Artwork © Mitchell Beazley Pub Ltd. 1973 as The Good Earth. 61, © Odyssey Productions; John S. Shelton. 62-63, Map Librairie Hachette; Artwork © Mitchell Beazley Pub. Ltd. 1973 as The Good Earth. 64, Nicholas Devore III, Bruce Coleman Inc.; E. R. Degginger. 65, Smithsonian Collection from E. R. Degginger; WORLD BOOK photo; Smithsonian Collection from E. R. Degginger; Smithsonian Collection from E. R. Degginger; © Lee Boltin. 66, © Craig Aurness, West Light.

67, Map from Goode's World Atlas; G. R. Roberts. 73, NASA. 75, Jeff Foott; © Thomas Nebbia, Woodfin Camp, Inc. 77, E. R. Degginger; N. G. Blake, Bruce Coleman Ltd. 79, © Mike Yamashita, Woodfin Camp, Inc.; © Craig Aurness, Woodfin Camp, Inc.; © Tsang Yan-sau, The Stock House Ltd. 81, © Mike Yamashita, Woodfin Camp, Inc.; © William Strode, Woodfin Camp, Inc.; © Lincoln Potter, The Stock House Ltd. 82, © David J. Cross from Peter Arnold. 84, E. R. Degginger. 85, E. R. Degginger. 86, E. R. Degginger. 87, Standard Oil Company of California. 88, The Gas Council. 91, © Loren McIntyre, Woodfin Camp, Inc.; © Thomas Hopker, Woodfin Camp, Inc. 92, NASA. 93, © Scala, Art Resource; Hunting Surveys Ltd. 94, British Museum; Harvard Semitic Museum, Cambridge, Mass.; British Library. 95, Michael Holford, Science Museum, London; Diagrams Creative Cartography Ltd.; NASA. 96, Map Istituto Geografico De Agostini; WORLD BOOK diagram.

Locator maps on pages 20, 22, 25, 27, 28, 31, 34, 36, 38, 40, 42, 44, 46, 48 were created exclusively for The World Book Atlas.

Structure and Contents

Structure of The World Book Atlas

The World Book Atlas is arranged according to the structure that follows.

Contents of The World Book Atlas

Looking at Earth's

The earth in space

Mount McKinley, the highest summit in North America

Dolphins at play in the Atlantic Ocean

Gently rolling lowland cf New Jersey, U.S.

Features

EARTH POSSESSES a vast ocean of water, flowing rivers, bright lakes, great forests, green plains, towering mountains, windswept deserts, and snowy polar caps. This combination of features makes earth unique among all the planets and moons in the solar system.

The Ocean

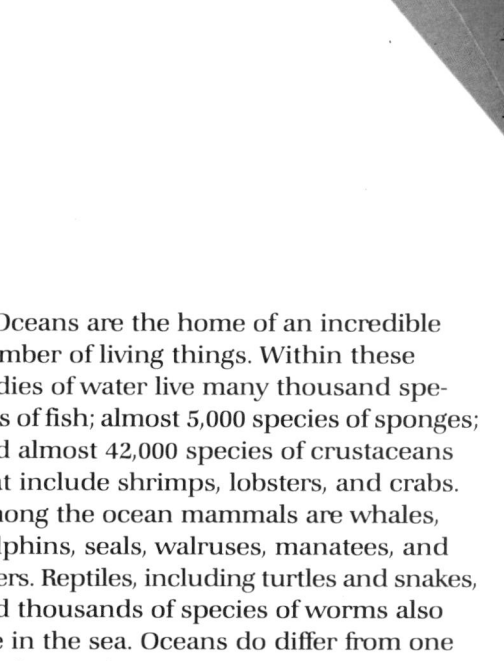

Ocean currents

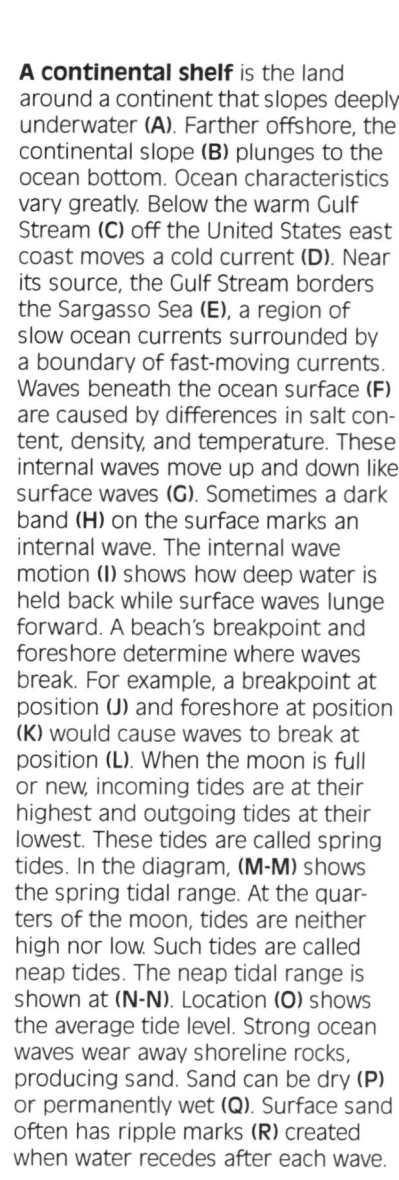

Internal waves

More than 70 per cent of the world's
surface is covered by oceans. Oceans have
been given different names, such as Atlantic and Pacific, but they are actually all one
large interconnected body of water, swept
by winds that create waves, and moved
by tides caused by the tug of the moon.

Oceans, often known as seas, are deep
as well as vast. The bottoms of some seas
lie more than 6 miles (10 kilometers) below
their surfaces. Great mountains can rise
from their floors and stick out above the
water as islands.

Oceans are very important parts of the
earth. The action of the sun's heat pouring
down on an ocean turns enormous amounts
of its surface into water vapor. This vapor
rises into the air, cools, and forms clouds,
which are carried by wind. When clouds
are cooled even more, much of the water
vapor forming them turns back into water
and falls as rain or snow. This moisture
creates the fresh water of rivers and lakes.
It also provides the ground water that
helps plants to grow, and thus animal life
to exist.

Ocean water moves constantly in streams
called currents. Currents are caused by a
combination of the wind, the sun's heat, the
salinity of the water, and the earth's rotation. The temperature of a current affects
the temperature of the air above it. Therefore, warm currents bring warm air and
water to some places, and cool currents
bring cool air and water to other places.
Without the help of the Equatorial Current,
the Gulf Stream, and other currents, the
air around the planet would be hotter both
day and night near the equator and cooler
both day and night at high latitudes.

Ocean water is salty. There is enough
salt in the sea to cover every bit of dry
land with a layer of salt 150 feet (45 meters)
high. Actually, much of this salt originally
came from the land. For countless millions of years, rivers that were supplied by
rainfall runoff moved down mountainsides
and across rolling lands. These rivers
washed millions of tons of minerals out of
the channels through which they flowed.
The minerals, mainly various kinds of salts,
were carried along by the rivers. Eventually, the rivers flowed into the ocean and
released their cargoes of mud and salt.
This accumulation of salt in its water keeps
the ocean salty. Only pure water evaporates from its surface when water vapor
forms.

Oceans are the home of an incredible
number of living things. Within these
bodies of water live many thousand species of fish; almost 5,000 species of sponges;
and almost 42,000 species of crustaceans
that include shrimps, lobsters, and crabs.
Among the ocean mammals are whales,
dolphins, seals, walruses, manatees, and
otters. Reptiles, including turtles and snakes,
and thousands of species of worms also
live in the sea. Oceans do differ from one
another in their species of plants and animals. That is because the seas vary in terms
of climate.

All these animals, together with ocean
plants, are members of complex ecological
systems. The ocean food chain begins with
microscopic plantlike organisms. These
organisms, called phytoplankton, drift in
masses near the sunlit surfaces and give
the water a greenish tint. Like green plants,
they use sunlight to manufacture food for
themselves. As a by-product of this process,
the phytoplankton produce tiny amounts
of oxygen. This oxygen is used by sea
animals and plants. It also helps replenish
the oxygen in the earth's air.

Floating among the phytoplankton are
trillions of microscopic animals called zooplankton. These creatures cannot make
their own food. Instead they feed on phytoplankton. Zooplankton themselves are
eaten by small fish and crustaceans, which
are eaten by bigger fish and other creatures. They, in turn, are food for still larger
animals, such as 60-foot-long sperm whales.
But without the tiny phytoplankton, the
earth's oceans could not support this
complex food chain.

A continental shelf is the land
around a continent that slopes deeply
underwater **(A)**. Farther offshore, the
continental slope **(B)** plunges to the
ocean bottom. Ocean characteristics
vary greatly. Below the warm Gulf
Stream **(C)** off the United States east
coast moves a cold current **(D)**. Near
its source, the Gulf Stream borders
the Sargasso Sea **(E)**, a region of
slow ocean currents surrounded by
a boundary of fast-moving currents.
Waves beneath the ocean surface **(F)**
are caused by differences in salt con-
tent, density, and temperature. These
internal waves move up and down like
surface waves **(G)**. Sometimes a dark
band **(H)** on the surface marks an
internal wave. The internal wave
motion **(I)** shows how deep water is
held back while surface waves lunge
forward. A beach's breakpoint and
foreshore determine where waves
break. For example, a breakpoint at
position **(J)** and foreshore at position
(K) would cause waves to break at
position **(L)**. When the moon is full
or new, incoming tides are at their
highest and outgoing tides at their
lowest. These tides are called spring
tides. In the diagram, **(M-M)** shows
the spring tidal range. At the quar-
ters of the moon, tides are neither
high nor low. Such tides are called
neap tides. The neap tidal range is
shown at **(N-N)**. Location **(O)** shows
the average tide level. Strong ocean
waves wear away shoreline rocks,
producing sand. Sand can be dry **(P)**
or permanently wet **(Q)**. Surface sand
often has ripple marks **(R)** created
when water recedes after each wave.

Wind action on the water produces surface waves. Waves travel forward in the direction of the wind.

In the ocean, fish often travel in schools—large groups of the same species. Here a school of grunts passes by coral formations. Grunts are known for making grunting sounds when taken from the water.

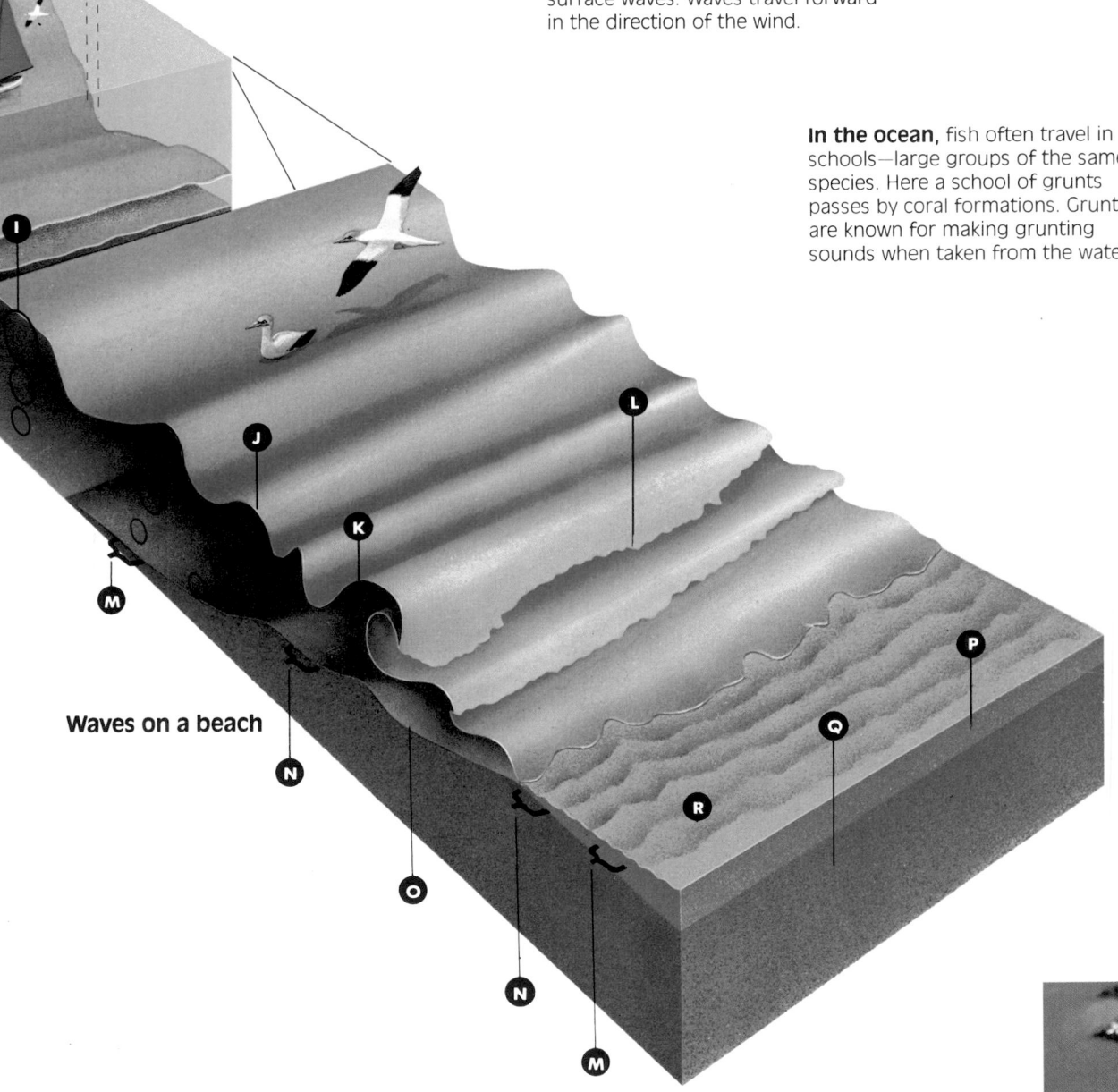

Waves on a beach

The sea otter swims, often on its back, in the North Pacific Ocean and near the shores of western North America and Siberia. This brown, furry animal floats in masses of seaweed called kelp.

Mountains

About one-fifth of the earth's land surface is made up of mountains. Mountains are composed of rock formations that rise 2,000 feet (610 meters) or more above the surrounding land. There are also mountains underwater. Those rock formations, called submarine mountains, form islands or are part of the ocean floor.

On land, mountains may be rocky and barren, or they may be green with vegetation. They may have high pointed peaks and narrow ridges. Their sides, or slopes, are long, broad, or slanting. Often mountains are cut by deep, wide indentations called canyons or valleys. Due to the decrease in temperature as elevation increases, mountainsides are made up of several different environments.

Mountains are formed over enormous amounts of time by movements of the earth's rocky crust. In some places, sideways shifts of the crust make huge wavelike wrinkles or folds. These movements result in fold mountains such as the Jura Mountains of Europe and the Appalachian Mountains of eastern North America. In other places, the crust is broken into gigantic blocks that are pushed upward along a fracture line called a fault to form fault-block mountains. The Sierra Nevada of California is an example of fault-block mountains. Dome mountains such as the Harlech Dome in Wales are created when molten rock called magma is forced upward under the surface rock to form a blister-like swelling. The volcanic mountains of Washington and Oregon were created by volcanic activity.

The top of a very high mountain is generally covered with ice and snow. But a little farther down the slope, melted snow can

Mount Saint Elias, Alaska, is one of the highest peaks in North America. It stands in the Saint Elias Mountains, a rugged series of the highest coastal mountains in the world.

An ibex climbs a rocky slope in the Italian Alps. The thinness of the forest shows that the animal is nearing the timber line.

provide moisture for lichens, mosses, and low-growing flowering plants that flourish where soil develops. This region is called the alpine zone. A number of species of insects, particularly springtails and bristletails, thrive in this region. Brightly colored butterflies flit among the flowers. The American Rocky Mountain goat and the European ibex live here too. Small animals such as conies, chipmunks, and mountain ground hogs also make their homes near a mountain's top.

The animals of the high mountain regions are especially fitted for their environment. Many have enlarged hearts and lungs, and their blood contains extra oxygen-bearing red corpuscles. These features help the animals survive in a mountaintop's thin air. When winter comes, most of the smaller creatures take shelter in burrows and live on seeds and hay stored during summer. Larger animals and even some birds simply move a short way down the mountainside. There the temperature is not as cold and food is still available.

A little below the alpine region is the timber line. This is the highest point at which a tree can survive without freezing. The tallest trees in this region are often bush-size dwarf willows, birches, aspens, spruces, firs, and pines. Each winter they are mostly covered by snow, which actually protects them from the terrible freezing wind of the mountaintop. These trees may, however, have some shoots that reach above the snow. At lower levels of mountains, the same kinds of trees can reach full size and form forests. Birds, squirrels, deer, and bears are at home in openings in these wooded areas.

The lower the elevation, the higher the temperature. If a mountain is in a place that gets plenty of rainfall, there will generally be a forest growing on its lower slopes. But if the mountain is in a dry region, its lower slopes will be covered with grassy meadow or maybe even desert. The animals that live here are not true "mountain animals." The same kinds of creatures may be found in other environments that feature similar conditions.

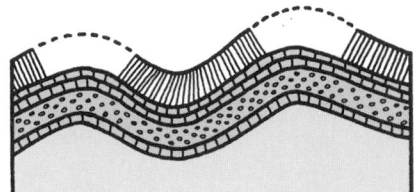

Fold mountains include the European Alps, *right*. The valleys and ridges that are characteristic of fold mountains are shown in the diagram above.

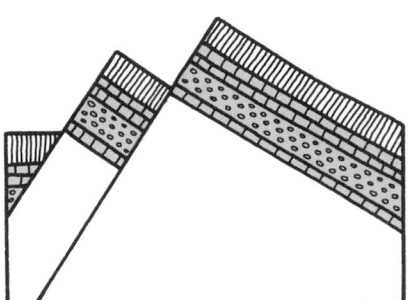

Fault-block mountains are found in the desert land near Las Vegas, Nevada, *right*. The diagram above shows the layers of cleanly broken sedimentary rock that are characteristic of fault-block mountains.

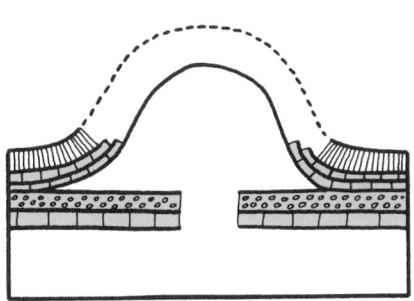

Dome mountains, such as Harlech Dome in Wales, *right*, are formed when the earth's crust rises into domes. The diagram above indicates that a dome's softer rock is eventually eroded.

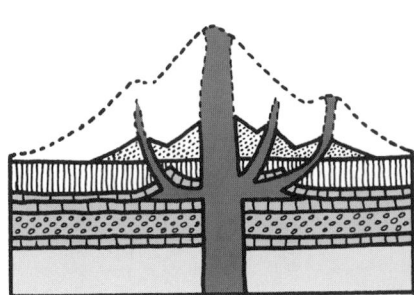

Volcanic mountains are the remains of volcanoes. The diagram above shows the pipeline vents through which lava moves inside a volcano. The material piles up and results in volcanic mountains such as the Cascade Mountains of Washington and Oregon, *right*.

Rivers and Streams

Rivers and streams are bodies of water that flow through land in long passages called channels. As they flow, always downhill, they are fed by other waters that enrich them and increase their size. Eventually they flow into another body of water, such as a larger river, a lake, or the ocean.

A river or stream channel is formed by the wearing away, or friction, of flowing water. The bottom of a channel is called the bed, and the sides are known as the banks. The channel of a small stream can be a few feet wide and less than a mile long. The channel of a large river, however, can be miles wide and extend for thousands of miles.

A river often begins high on a mountain. It can start as trickles of water from melting snow, as a spring bubbling out of rocks, or as a stream flowing from a mountain lake. As the water flows along, it is fed by streams and smaller rivers. It becomes deeper and wider, and its size is increased further by rainfall.

A river or stream is a habitat for plant and animal life. The character of that life depends upon the temperature, depth, and speed of the water. A swift-moving, shallow mountain stream is bare of most plant life. The exception is the jellylike algae that coat the rocky bottom. Black fly larvae use their tiny hooks to anchor themselves to the stream's rocks. These creatures have their food—microscopic plants and ani-

mals—delivered to them by the swift-flowing water. The larvae, in turn, are a source of nourishment for different species of birds such as dippers, or water ouzels, of western North America. These birds spend much of their time wading in swift streams and feeding on the insect life present.

A larger, slow-moving river that is far from its mountain beginnings is a very different environment. Unlike a swift-flowing stream that sweeps its floor clean, the bed of a slow-moving river is filled with mud and silt. These materials form soil for plant life. "Forests" of algae or eel-grass often cover a sluggish river's bottom. Cattails and bulrushes grow thickly along the banks. Water lilies and similar plants float on the surface. Fish such as pike and bass lurk among the bottom greenery and dart out to snap up frogs and smaller fishes. Muskrats use cattails and other plants both as food and to line the insides of riverbank burrows. Frogs attach their eggs to plants and rocks. Insects rely on the river plants as resting places.

Many kinds of insects lurk and burrow in the mud below the water. They are food for fish such as carp. Many kinds of predatory swimming insects, including dragonfly nymphs and diving beetles, often

thrive in surface waters where light is more plentiful. Small fish, frogs, otters, and birds such as kingfishers are also among the creatures that make these waters their regular hunting place. And in parts of Africa, warm, slow rivers are the natural habitat of hippopotamuses.

The place where a river empties into the sea is called the mouth. A low plain made up of clay, gravel, sand, and other sediments at a river's mouth is known as a delta, and a deep, broad mouth is called an estuary. In an estuary there is a mingling of fresh water and salt water. This mixing creates a new and different kind of environment for life. The most common kind of estuary animal is the oyster. Hundreds of thousands of oysters may cover an estuary's bottom. Shrimps, crabs, and fish such as flounder are typical dwellers of this environment. Sea plants such as turtle grass and sea lettuce can also thrive in the quiet, shallow, salty environment where a river and the ocean meet.

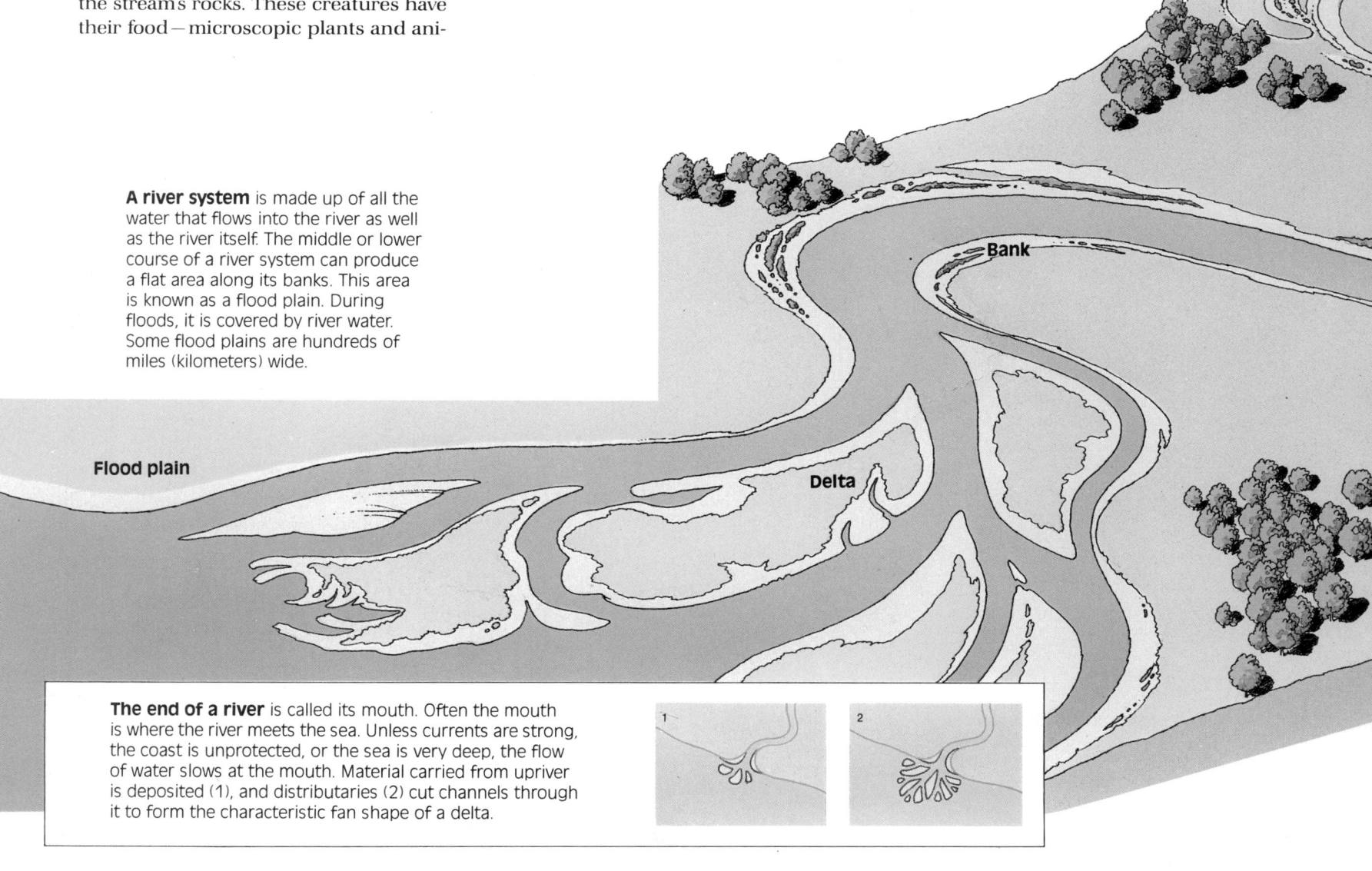

A river system is made up of all the water that flows into the river as well as the river itself. The middle or lower course of a river system can produce a flat area along its banks. This area is known as a flood plain. During floods, it is covered by river water. Some flood plains are hundreds of miles (kilometers) wide.

Flood plain

Bank

Delta

The end of a river is called its mouth. Often the mouth is where the river meets the sea. Unless currents are strong, the coast is unprotected, or the sea is very deep, the flow of water slows at the mouth. Material carried from upriver is deposited (1), and distributaries (2) cut channels through it to form the characteristic fan shape of a delta.

The flow of water in most rivers is fastest in the upper courses. Salmon have to fight to reach their upstream spawning grounds.

A river's slope tends to flatten near the mouth, and the water slows down. Painted turtles are at home in this environment.

Oxbow lake

The muddy Klamath River enters the clean, blue water of the Pacific Ocean north of Redwood National Park in northern California.

Lakes and Ponds

Lakes and ponds are bodies of standing water that are surrounded by land.

Lakes, which are larger than ponds, may be formed in many ways. Some lakes are made by stranded blocks of ice and blocked rivers that result when glaciers melt. Others are formed by the slow accumulation of rain water in volcanic craters. Still others are caused by the gradual filling in of sinkholes with ground water. Sinkholes are depressions in the earth caused by the collapse of underground rock.

Lakes can be fed in many ways. Some lakes are fed by rivers and mountain streams. Others are supplied by underground springs or streams, as well as ground water replenishment. Some lakes have inlets but no outlets. The excess waters of these kinds of lakes do not drain away. Instead, they slowly evaporate.

The presence of a large lake can affect weather conditions for the land around it. In summer, a lake will not get as warm as the surrounding land. Cool winds blowing off the water will help hold down the temperature. In winter, a lake will not cool off as fast as the land does. This will help keep the nearby land warmer, at least until the lake freezes. Then the lake acts the same way as a cold land surface.

Lake waters are divided into distinct layers, which are determined by the amount of penetrating sunlight. Each descending layer receives less sunlight than the one above it, unless the water is very clear. Therefore, the deeper a layer is, the colder and darker its waters.

The different layers of a lake are inhabited by distinct communities of animal and plant life. These communities depend on one another for food. For example, microscopic plants that drift in a lake's upper waters are eaten by microscopic animals. Both the tiny plants and the tiny animals are called plankton. Plankton is eaten by fish that live near a lake's surface.

Many kinds of insects live in the upper water of a lake. Whirligig beetles swim in this region. Their divided eyes look both above and below the water. Backswimmers, another type of insect, reside just at the surface, and they swim faceup. Water striders actually walk *upon* the water, which for them is like solid ground. All these insects feed on other insects that fall or alight upon the quiet surface water.

Many of a lake's plants and animals live near the shore, in what is called the littoral zone. Here snails and worms creep on plant stems, and predatory fish lurk among bulrushes and other water plants. In the shallows near the shore, water birds often hunt and use bits of plants as nesting material.

Few of the littoral zone animals or water animals are found on the lake bottom.

There is also little if any plant life there. The main inhabitants include snails and shrimplike crustaceans. These creatures eat the remains of dead plants and animals that drift down from the upper regions of the lake.

A pond is basically a miniature lake that is shallow enough for sunlight to reach the bottom and enable plants to grow there. Many ponds are formed naturally, but a great many are made by people. Most of the same creatures that are found in lakes are also found in ponds. Such creatures include fish, frogs, and water insects. In many cases, eggs and larvae of these animals are brought from one lake or pond to another by water birds. The birds carry the transported material on their feet or in their feathers. The wind is another transporter. It carries plant seeds from one water home to another. The seeds of water plants can also float to new locations.

Many ponds and small, shallow lakes are temporary features. Over time, the build-up of material on the water's floor and the spread of vegetation will fill in a small pond. Eventually it will become a marsh or swamp. Over many hundreds or many thousands of years, climate change, sediment accumulation, and vegetation growth will turn even a large, shallow lake into a wetland.

Crater Lake is located in an inactive volcano in the Cascade Mountains of Oregon. It is the deepest lake in the United States, measuring 1,932 feet (589 meters).

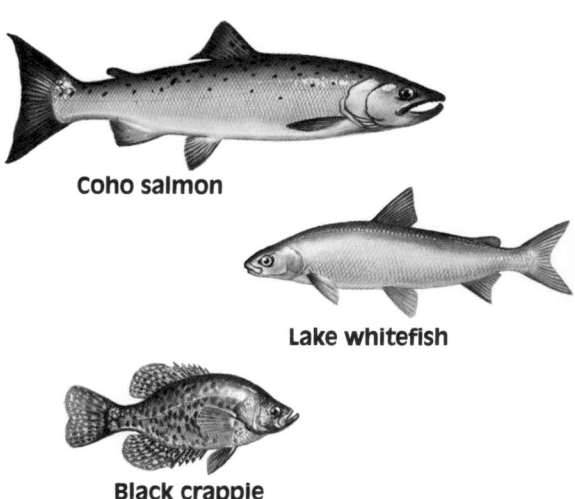

Many species of fish are found in lakes. If a lake freezes over in winter, the fish that live there can swim down to warmer water near the bottom until spring.

Coho salmon

Lake whitefish

Black crappie

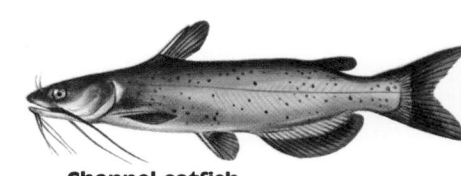

Channel catfish

Eutrophication is a process that destroys the delicate balance of water life. This dying pond is naturally eutrophic, but there are other ponds that are killed by pollution.

Pond animal and plant life

In a pond, the primary food producers are microscopic plants that use sunlight to make food for primary consumers, such as tadpoles. A fish (secondary consumer) may eat the tadpole. Decomposers complete the food chain by cleaning up the waste and producing chemicals that primary producers use to make food.

The pond environment

The pond environment
1 Common frog (male, x0.5)
2 Starwort (x0.5)
3 Water crowfoot (x0.25)
4 Aplecta hypnorum (x2)
5 Wandering snail (x0.75)
6 Keeled ramshorn snail (x0.5)
7 Curled pondweed (x0.25)
8 Bithynia (x1)
9 Ramshorn snail (x0.3)
10 Water lily root (x0.25)
11 Great pond snail (x0.8)

Near the surface
12 Pond skater (x0.5)
13 Whirligig beetle (x0.25)
14 Water boatman (x1)
15 Nonbiting midge (x5)
16 Mosquito pupa (x5)
17 Dragonfly (male, x0.65)
18 China-marks moth (x0.75)
19 Mayfly (female, x0.2)

Middle depths
20 Water flea (Daphnia, x2.5)
21 Smooth newt (male, x0.5)
22 Cyclops (typical of species, x8)
23 Flagellate (x650)
24 Great diving beetle (male, x1)
25 Hydra (x4)
26 Stickleback (male, x0.5)
27 Common frog tadpole (x1.5)
28 Flagellate (Euglena, x180)
29 Water mite (x5)

The bottom
30 Caddis-fly larva in case
31 Chaetonotus (x150)
32 Horny-orb shell (x1)
33 Tubifex worms (x0.2)
34 Midge larva (x3.5)
35 Pond sponge (x0.2)
36 Leech (Helobdella sp., x4)
37 Water hog-louse (x2.5)
38 Flatworm (x2)

Near the surface

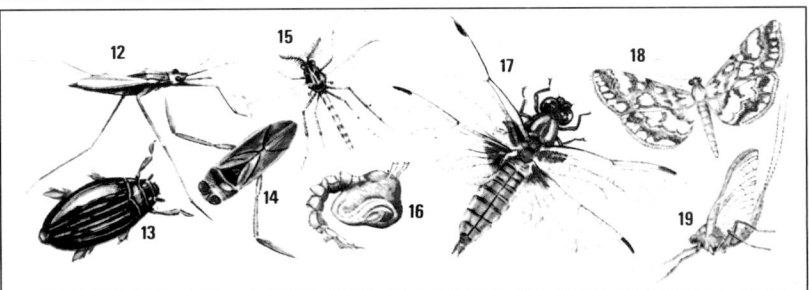

Middle depths

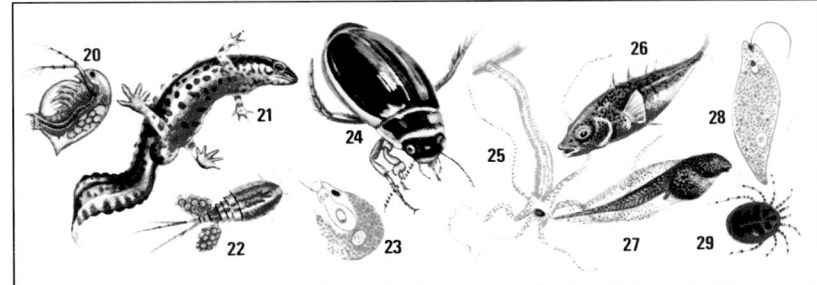

The bottom

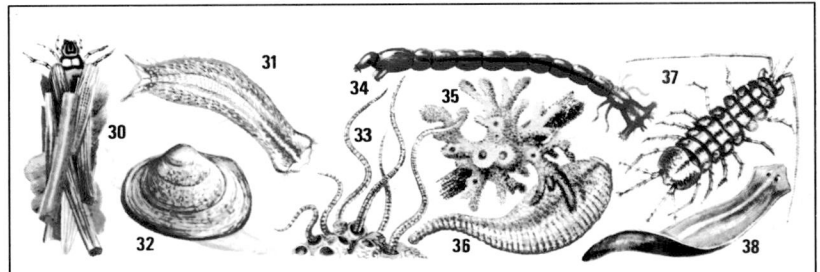

Swamps, Marshes, and Bogs

Okefenokee Swamp, in south-eastern Georgia and northeastern Florida, is the home of many animals, including deer, bears, wildcats, otters, raccoons, opossums, and alligators. About two-thirds of the swamp is a government wildlife preserve.

Swamps, marshes, and bogs are known as the earth's wetlands. A wetland is a land area where the water level remains near or above the surface of the ground for most of the year.

Swamps, the first type of wetland, are areas of muddy, watery land covered by trees and bushes. The major kinds of swamps are deepwater, shallow-water, and mangrove.

Deepwater swamps are near large, slow-flowing rivers that flood regularly. These floods spread water over adjoining land. Bald cypress and black gum trees, which thrive in muddy soil, grow easily in such areas. The thick foliage of these trees blocks out much of the sunlight. Thus, only certain kinds of plants can grow on the muddy ground.

Shallow-water swamps are usually found in areas where soil stays moist or water-covered for only part of the year. Bushes and trees such as willows, oaks, and maples, flourish there. Water lilies and similar plants cover the surface of the standing water in springtime.

Unlike the other deepwater and shallow-water swamps that have fresh water, mangrove swamps have salt water. These swamps lie along tropical seacoasts and are named for the mangrove shrubs that grow there.

Swamp water swarms with insects, frogs, and fish. These creatures are food for long-legged birds such as herons and egrets. The birds wade in the water and use their beaks to spear prey. In the tropics and subtropics, swamps are home to alligators, crocodiles, turtles, and snakes. Such animals prefer the combination of hot weather and watery conditions.

Many animals are equally at home in swamps and in inland marshes. Marshes, the second kind of wetland, are flat, tree-less areas covered with water. There are, however, animals such as American red-winged blackbirds and muskrats that prefer marshes. Blackbirds nest among the cattails, bulrushes, and other water plants that grow thickly in this environment. Those same plants are food for muskrats and also nesting places for many kinds of waterfowl. Like muskrats, these birds are prey for mink, which live on marshland edges.

An inland marsh is also a major source of food for animals that do not actually inhabit it. Raccoons visit marshes to hunt fish and crayfish in the shallow water. Raccoons also dig up nests of turtle eggs and search for the egg-filled nests of ducks and

other waterfowl. Deer also visit marshes. There, they browse on water lilies, marsh marigolds, grasses, and grasslike plants called sedges.

In addition to inland marshes, there are also saltwater marshes. These form where river deltas empty into the sea. Fish, crabs, oysters, and mussels flourish in salt marshes where salt grasses are abundant. Diving birds such as ospreys are salt marsh dwellers, and gulls are frequent visitors.

Bogs, the third type of wetland, are wet, spongy areas. They are filled with mosses and large amounts of partly decayed plant matter called peat. These environments are usually found in the colder, northern parts of the world. Bogs generally evolve from deep lakes that have become filled with dead, compacted plant material. Sphagnum moss and sedges form a thick mat on the surface of the water. There, wild cranberries, other berry bushes, and a few dwarf trees may grow. Other species of plants that thrive in and around bogs are carnivorous plants such as the sundew, pitcher plant, and Venus's-flytrap. Aside from insects and frogs, few animals live permanently in this type of wetland. But many animals, among them moose and bear, visit bogs in search of food.

In addition to supporting plant and animal communities, wetlands are ecologically valuable in other ways. They can store large amounts of water for long periods of time. And because they hold back water, they help prevent floods.

Bogs, with their acidic soil and water, favor the growth of mosses—especially sphagnum moss, which absorbs water like a sponge.

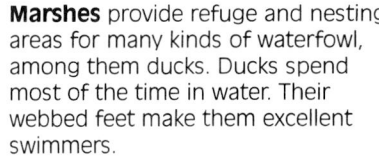

Marshes provide refuge and nesting areas for many kinds of waterfowl, among them ducks. Ducks spend most of the time in water. Their webbed feet make them excellent swimmers.

Tropical Forests

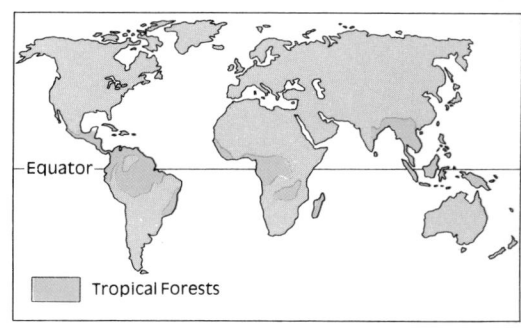

Tropical Forests

A broad band around the middle of the earth receives the planet's greatest amount of sunlight. This zone, known as the tropics, generally features year-round summer conditions. Humidity and temperatures are constantly high. Days are long and sunny, and many tropical regions are frequently rainy. In this climate, huge forests flourish. They are called tropical rain forests, and they almost always lie near the equator. These forests cover the tropical portions of Africa, Asia, Australia, Central and South America, and the Pacific islands.

Unlike a midlatitude forest, a tropical rain forest has few seasonal temperature changes. Because of the unending summer conditions, most trees in a tropical forest stay green all year. Such trees gradually lose old leaves as they grow new ones. However, there are some deciduous trees in tropical forests that shed all their leaves briefly during the dry season.

Generally all the trees in a tropical rain forest have tall, straight trunks with branches only at the very top. The tops of the trees are called the crowns, and they merge to form a covering of leaves high in the air. This covering is known as the upper canopy. Its thickness blocks most of the sunlight from reaching the forest floor. Because the floor is so dim, few plants can grow there. Mushrooms and other fungi that need little light flourish in this environment.

Orchids, wild pineapples, other flowering plants, and ferns grow high up on the trunks of tropical trees. These plants begin as seeds that are carried by the wind. The seeds lodge within crevices in the tree bark, and are warmed by sunlight. For water, the seeds soak up moisture from the air and rain that runs down the tree trunks.

Forest vines are rooted in the ground. Often they wind up tree trunks and other vines until they reach the treetops. There they can spread out among the leafy branches of the upper canopy. Extremely tall trees called emergents thrust through the upper canopy's vines and branches. Many kinds of insects and insect-eating birds live in the emergents. Large, predatory birds live there too. Such birds include harpy eagles, which prey on the monkeys that live below in the upper canopy.

Monkeys and many other creatures are attracted by the upper canopy's abundance of fruit and nuts. Fruit-eating birds, such as toucans, and leaf-eating mammals, such as sloths, also thrive in the crowns of tall trees. Hummingbirds and brilliantly colored butterflies flutter between the canopy's leaves and flowers. Tree frogs and lizards creep through the upper canopy branches, hunting insects. Snakes lurk among the leaves to capture these creatures. Other residents of the upper canopy include gliding animals such as large bats called flying foxes and flying dragons, a type of lizard.

Not all trees are tall enough to reach the upper canopy. Some full-grown trees can thrive at lower levels in the forest because they do not require an abundance of light. The crowns of these trees form one or two lower canopies that are generally quite sturdy. The lower canopies are inhabited by larger forest animals such as apes and leopards. These animals live both in trees and on the forest floor.

In many parts of a tropical rain forest, tree trunks are spread far apart and few plants grow on the ground. But in places where abundant sunlight is able to reach the ground, there is a thick, tangled growth of bushes and low plants. Such areas are called jungles, and they grow frequently in former clearings and along the banks of wide rivers in the tropical regions of the world.

Upper canopy
Abundant fruits and nuts at this level, from 100 to 150 feet (30 to 45 meters) high, provide food for monkeys, birds, leaf-eating mammals, snakes, tree frogs, and lizards. Well adapted to treetop life, they seldom touch the ground.

Royal python

Tree shrew

Sacred langur

Lower canopy
The crowns of shorter trees support larger creatures that also spend time on the ground. Plants such as orchids and mosses are abundant in the lower canopy, or understory, which rises from 16 to 100 feet (5 to 30 meters) from the forest floor.

Leopard

Orangutan

Pouched tree frog

Shrub layer
Woody shrubs at this layer rarely reach higher than 16 feet (5 meters). The plants spring up to fill the space available between larger, taller trees.

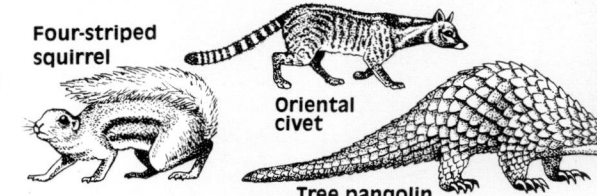

Four-striped squirrel

Oriental civet

Tree pangolin

Forest floor
The ground layer of the forest is dark. It receives less than 1 per cent of sunlight. Only ferns and other shade-loving plants can survive here. Animals that live here must be able to tolerate high humidity, so insects abound. Many ground-layer mammals have compact bodies that help them move through dense undergrowth.

Okapi

Forest buffalo

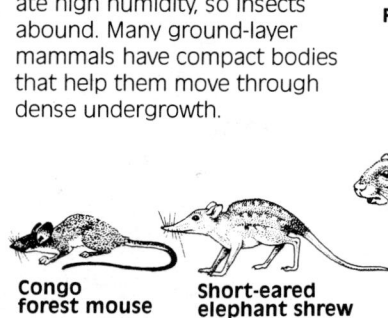

Congo forest mouse

Short-eared elephant shrew

Orange-rumped agouti

Mandrill

Indian tiger

Malayan tapir

Emergent layer

The tallest trees in a tropical forest form the emergent layer, up to 200 feet (61 meters) high. Animal life at this level is mostly birds and insects.

Demidoff's bushbaby

Flying fox

Gray parrot

Flying squirrel

Gold Coast turaco

Chameleon

Chimpanzee

Orchids, which thrive in humid conditions, abound in tropical forests. They range in size from small flowers to huge vines as long as 100 feet (30 meters).

In the dim light near the edge of a Sumatra rain forest, the forest floor is relatively free of plant life.

Layers of the forest

Living conditions at different heights determine what creatures inhabit different layers of the forest. The topmost layers are so high up that only birds and insects are found there. To survive in the dense canopy and middle layer, animals must be streamlined and adapted for climbing. In the high humidity and gloom of the ground layer, insects and fungi break down rotting fruit and leaves from above. These decomposers enrich the soil that feeds the forest.

Deserts

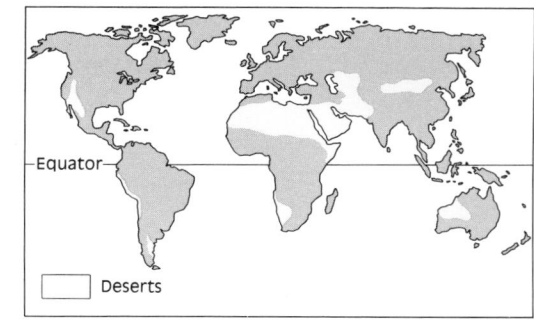

About one-seventh of the earth's land is covered by deserts. In general, deserts are any areas that have little rainfall, dry soil, and a limited amount of very special kinds of plants. But there is no "typical" desert. Some, such as parts of the Sahara, consist mainly of lifeless, rocky surfaces and smaller areas of shifting piles of sand called dunes. Others are limited to rocky, dry areas full of plant and animal life. Those deserts, located in the subtropics, remain searingly hot throughout the year. But others such as the Great Basin and the Gobi Desert are bitterly cold in winter and very hot in summer.

Often a desert will gradually merge with a fertile grassland. But unlike the neighboring grasses, desert plants must cope with a minimal supply of water. Some of these plants have long roots that probe far underground to find water. Others have shallow, widespread roots that absorb the tiniest amounts of dew and rain that soak down from the surface. The leaves of these plants are small, and they often fall off during the dry season.

Many types of desert vegetation flourish only when there is a little rain. After a rainfall, previously inactive seeds quickly germinate and grow into plants. These plants—known as annuals—flower, form more seeds, then die. The new seeds lie dormant until it rains again. The next rainfall, however, may be years away.

Desert plants vary in form from the prickly pear cactus to giant cacti. Many shrub and low tree species also grow in deserts. Such desert plants enable wildlife to live among them. They do this by providing animals with food and moisture. Some desert plants also provide animals with shelter. For example, North American Gila woodpeckers drill holes in giant cacti. In these hollows, the birds raise their families. When they leave, the holes are taken over by other kinds of birds or by lizards, rats, or mice.

Extreme heat can kill an animal. That is why desert creatures must be able to keep their bodies from becoming too hot. There are various ways animals can control their body temperatures. Small creatures, among them insects, snakes, and tiny mammals, hide from the heat. They dig down into the sand and stay there. Or they keep cool in underground burrows or dark crevices in the rocks. Some creatures pant to cool themselves. Others escape the heat by going into a kind of hibernation for days or weeks. During this time, their bodies stay cool. Some desert animals have special body features that help them lose heat. The big ears of a desert fox or jack rabbit are examples of these features. Blood carries body heat up into the thin skin of these animals' ears. From the ears, heat radiates into the dry, hot air of the desert. Thus the body temperature of the animals is lowered.

In addition to surviving the heat, desert animals must be adapted for an environment that has very little water. Desert larks of the Sahara, for example, can thrive for weeks without a drink. Camels and little furry dassies of South Africa can often live without drinking for months. These birds and mammals get moisture from the food they eat. They are also able to store this moisture in their bodies for a long time. There are also desert creatures, among them the kangaroo rat, that never need to drink. Their food gives them all the moisture they require.

Some desert dwellers, however, must find water each day. One such animal is the red kangaroo of the Australian Desert. This large mammal is known for grazing in the dry grasslands that border the desert. Each day, in search of water, the kangaroo must travel from the grasslands to one of the few watering holes in the almost waterless environment of the desert.

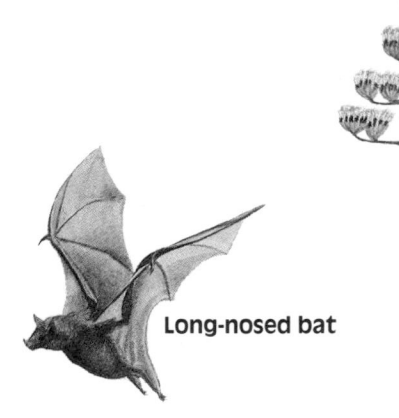

Long-nosed bat

Different deserts are home to different species of plants and animals. All desert creatures and vegetation, however, share the need to obtain and conserve water.

Scattered throughout the world's largest desert, the Sahara, are fertile areas known as oases. The water for Saharan oases comes mainly from springs or underground streams.

Agave

Esparto grass

Monument Valley, Jtah, gets bitterly cold in winter. Red sandstone
formations rise 1,000 feet (300
meters) from the desert floor.

Elf owl

Great horned owl

Gila monster

Fennec fox

Roadrunner

Desert hedgehog

Saguaro cactus

Kangaroo rat

Desert tortoise

Fat sand rat

Welwitschia

Dorcas gazelle

Addax antelope

Grasslands

Between humid forests and arid deserts lie the earth's sun-filled grasslands. These areas, which may be flat or hilly, are literally seas of grasses.

The three types of grasslands are steppes, prairies, and savannas. A grassland is classified into one of these three types according to the average height of the grass that grows there. Plant height depends upon the amount of rainfall received.

Steppes, which are the driest grassland, are covered mainly by short grasses. Most plants in a steppe do not grow over 1 foot (30 centimeters) high. In North America, steppes cover most of the Great Plains. In the Soviet Union, they reach from the southern Ukraine to central Asia.

Prairies, which receive moderate rainfall, are blanketed chiefly by tall grasses. In moist prairies, grass may grow 6 feet (1.8 meters) high or even taller. The North American prairie reaches from central Texas to southern Saskatchewan. Saskatchewan, Alberta, and Manitoba are called Canada's "Prairie Provinces." Other prairies include the Pampa of Argentina.

Savannas are grasslands with widely scattered trees and shrubs. Most savannas are in the tropics, but some are in temperate regions. This type of grassland covers more than two-fifths of Africa and large parts of Australia, South America, and India.

One of the main types of grassland animals is the grazer, or grass-eater. The larger grazers are generally animals that live in herds, such as the American bison and antelope and the African gnu and zebra. In many places, however, wild grazers have been replaced by domesticated grazers such as sheep and cattle. The herds of grass-eaters roam across a grassland, eating as they go. The area they move across looks like a mowed lawn for a time, but the grass quickly grows again unless it is the dry season.

Actually, there are many more small grazers than big ones. Small grazers include many kinds of grasshoppers, ants, aphids, leaf hoppers, and other insects. Just as large predators prey on large grazers, small predators such as birds and mice prey on small grazers.

Many kinds of flowering plants such as sunflowers, prairie clover, and cornflowers grow in grasslands. They produce seeds and leaves that are eaten by the region's wildlife, which includes jack rabbits and colonies of prairie dogs. There are many predators of these seed- and leaf-eaters. All grasslands contain snakes, which hunt for prey among the grass stems. But in addition to being the hunter, snakes are also the hunted. The sky over a grassland is the natural range for hawks and other birds of prey that will swoop down to seize snakes, as well as rabbits.

In tropical savannas, the temperature stays hot all year, so life goes on unchanged, except for alternating rainy and dry seasons. But the steppes and prairies have warm summers and cool to cold winters. In most of these regions the grassland life is curtailed by cold weather. The ground freezes and the grass stops growing. Much of the insect life dies or burrows underground. The insect-eating birds migrate to other regions. Most of the smaller animals hibernate or remain in burrows through the cold season, living on stored food. But with the coming of spring and the thawing of the ground, the grasslands quickly return to life.

Much of the world's grasslands have been turned into farmland where wheat and corn, which are actually grasses, are grown. Even in man-made grasslands, however, much of the same life which may be found in a natural grassland exists. Insects, birds, small mammals, and other creatures thrive among the cultivated grasses.

American buffalo, or bison, live in herds and graze on the grasses and small plants found on American prairies.

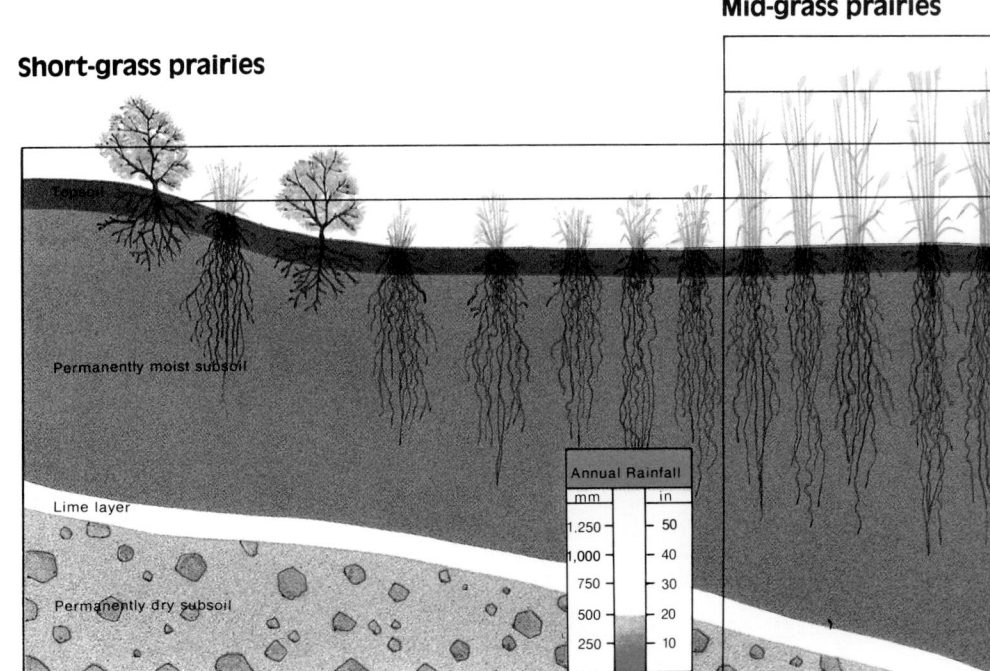

Mid-grass prairies

Short-grass prairies

Permanently moist subsoil

Lime layer

Permanently dry subsoil

Annual Rainfall	
mm	in
1,250	50
1,000	40
750	30
500	20
250	10

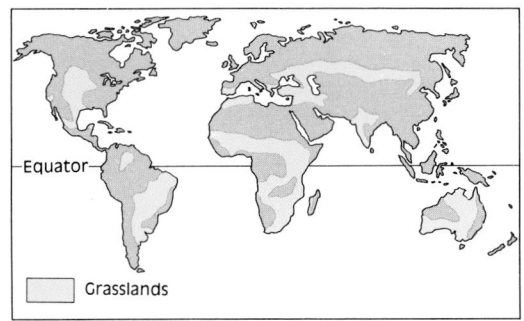

Grasslands

Red-tailed hawk

Western meadowlark

Burrowing owl

Grassland creatures solve the problem of survival by adapting to the environment in various ways. Many, such as small burrowing animals and certain invertebrates, seek protection underground. The marsupial mole lives almost entirely underground, while the prairie dog surfaces to eat. Snakes, of course, are well adapted for the pursuit of burrowing creatures. Small carnivores like the pampas cat often surprise their victims. Certain grassland predators rely on speed for catching prey—as do some of the creatures they hunt in the race for survival. The sharp-eyed hawk rides thermal winds in search of food, while the meadowlark adapts to a mostly treeless environment by singing to declare its territory. Camouflage protects many insects.

Saiga

American bison

European hare

Guanaco

Springhaas

Rainfall determines what grasses grow where on the North American prairies. In general, the drier the climate, the shorter the grasses. In regions where annual rainfall is no more than 20 inches (500 millimeters), only short grass—with short root systems—can survive in the relatively narrow layer of permanently moist subsoil. As the depth of the subsoil increases, it can support the longer root systems of mid-grass and tall-grass prairies. Tall bluestem and Indian grass predominate in the regions where annual rainfall measures 40 inches (1,000 millimeters). The North American prairie includes most of Oklahoma, Kansas, Nebraska, Iowa, Illinois, South Dakota, and North Dakota, and parts of neighboring states and provinces. Alberta, Saskatchewan, and Manitoba are the "Prairie Provinces" of Canada.

Marbled polecat

Pampas cat

Gopher snake

Marsupial mole

Prairie dog

European souslik

Viscacha

Lubber grasshopper

Praying mantis

Tumble bug

Tall-grass prairies

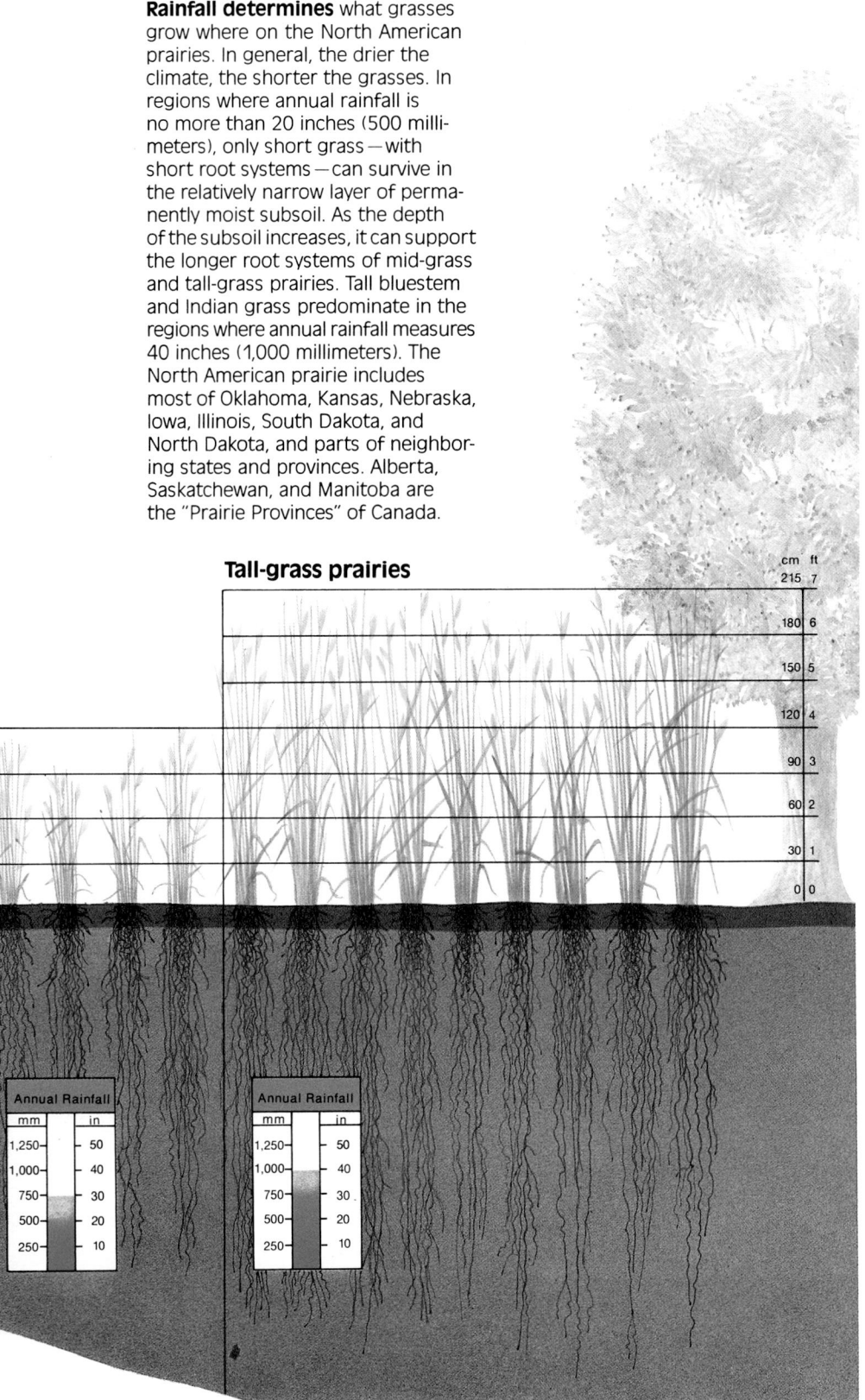

cm	ft
215	7
180	6
150	5
120	4
90	3
60	2
30	1
0	0

Annual Rainfall	
mm	in
1,250	50
1,000	40
750	30
500	20
250	10

Annual Rainfall	
mm	in
1,250	50
1,000	40
750	30
500	20
250	10

Midlatitude Forests

The earth's midlatitude regions lie between the polar circles and the tropics. Here, the seasonal climate ranges from warm summers to cold winters and, in some places, offers distinct dry and rainy seasons.

Deciduous trees, those with broad leaves that are shed annually, grow best in midlatitude regions where it is warm and moist at least four to five months a year. They are the main trees of most midlatitude forests, but many kinds of needle-leaved or broad-leaved evergreens also thrive in such a climate.

Midlatitude forests once covered eastern North America, western Europe, and eastern Asia. Changes in climate, together with activities such as forestry and farming, have reduced these forests to small areas.

Ground water generally freezes in midlatitude regions during winter. Thus, deciduous trees cannot draw up water into their leaves, and the leaves cannot tolerate freezing. This is why trees shed their leaves in autumn and stand bare during winter. However, evergreens can hold water in their needles throughout wintertime. This is how they can remain green all year.

In spring, when the ground begins to thaw, small flowers of the forest floor are first to bloom. Buds soon appear on trees and bushes and burst into pastel-colored flowers and tiny, pale-green leaves. Hibernating creatures stir. Birds return from the warm lands where they spent the winter. Insect and spider eggs, produced in autumn, now hatch by the millions.

Summer days are long and filled with sunshine and frequent rain. During this season, the tree leaves grow and become dark green with the substance called chlorophyll. Leaves are a tree's foodmakers. Using sunlight for power, their chlorophyll turns water absorbed by the roots and carbon dioxide from the air into sugars.

To get at this food in the leaves, leaf-eating insects, such as aphids, grasshoppers, and caterpillars, swarm among the upper branches of the trees. Many predatory insects and spiders live there too, preying on the leaf-eaters. And such a plentiful supply of insects and spiders attracts a variety of insect-eating birds.

The tops of the taller deciduous trees form the roof, or canopy, of the forest. The canopy is the home of insects, spiders, songbirds, squirrels, and nocturnal flying squirrels. Beneath the canopy is a second "layer" of trees called the understory. Some young trees in this layer must grow into the sunlight or they will die. Others are low-growing trees that do not need as much sunlight.

Beneath the understory is a layer of shrubs. These shrubs produce berries and seeds that are a source of food for mice and chipmunks. Under the bushes, upon the forest floor, are low-growing flowering plants, ferns, and mosses, which do not need much sunlight to make their food. Mushrooms also grow there. They need little sunlight, for they take their food from the rotting, decaying things on which they grow. Grouse, woodcocks, and pheasants feed on this vegetation. Deer also browse on the forest floor, and insects swarm there and are hunted by mice, frogs, and toads. They in turn are preyed upon by snakes, foxes, and raccoons.

In late summer, deciduous trees begin to prepare for winter. A layer of corklike substance grows where each leaf stem is attached to the branch. No more water can reach the leaves. Their green color fades, and their true color, generally yellow or orange, is seen. After chlorophyll breaks down, red or purple pigments form in a dying leaf.

With no water, the leaves die, turn brown, and wither. Autumn wind and rains tear them loose to swirl to the ground. There, they become food for mushrooms, other fungi, and tiny animals. These will help turn the leaves into the soil of the forest floor. The seasonal cycle is now complete, and winter is approaching.

Seasonal climate is an important feature of midlatitude forests. Deciduous trees, which lose their leaves each autumn, flourish in such an environment.

Mushrooms get their nourishment from dead matter, such as decaying bark.

A paper wasp makes its nest from chewed-up wood.

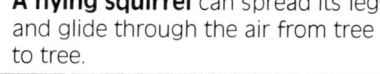

A flying squirrel can spread its legs and glide through the air from tree to tree.

Midlatitude forests provide food and shelter for many animals and for a variety of plants.

Hazel mouse

Acorn woodpecker

American black bear

European woodcock

Stag beetle

Bluebell

Hepatica

Equator

Midlatitude Forests

Subarctic Cold Lands

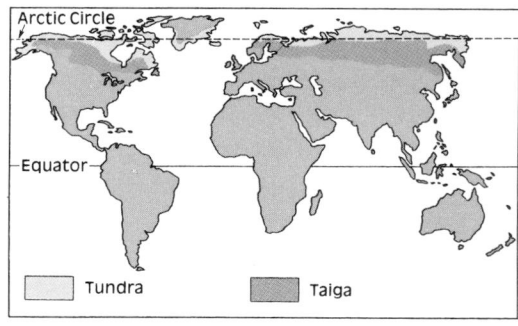

Tundra   Taiga

The transitional area between tundra and taiga is marked by shrubs, grasses, and the shoots of deciduous trees.

The dry, treeless, subarctic cold lands that lie near the Arctic Ocean are called arctic tundras. They include the northern parts of North America, Europe, and Asia. For three to four months a year, the sky over arctic tundras is dark both day and night. Beneath the darkened sky, snow blankets the frozen ground.

Change occurs on the tundra in spring, when the northern part of the earth is tilted toward the sun. This causes the tundra sky to lighten. Sunlight melts the snow and thaws the land's upper layer of soil, which is about one-foot (30 centimeters) deep. Below this layer is the perpetually frozen ground known as permafrost.

Plants that have been dormant through the months of darkness abruptly burst into bloom in springtime. These plants are tough, low-growing, and ground-hugging. They include mosses, lichens, grasses, and small flowering plants such as bilberries and bearberries. The very cold winters with strong winds prevent plants from growing higher than the depth of the protective snow. Therefore, no full-size trees can survive on the tundra. Some willow shrubs, however, grow 3 to 10 feet (91 to 305 centimeters) high on slopes and valleys where winter snows are deep.

In spring and summer, the many flowering plants of the tundra turn the region into a sea of color. Arctic foxes, ermines, and snowy owls prey on the little mouselike lemming and arctic hare that search the tundra for tender leaves. Birds such as the willow ptarmigan nest and raise their young among the flowers. Mosquitoes, midges, and black flies are everywhere. Polar bears may leave the icepack and come on land to find food. Caribou, reindeer, and musk oxen browse on plants and are hunted by packs of wolves.

When earth tilts away from the sun, winter returns suddenly. In late August or early September, the ground freezes and snow begins to fall. Most birds and animals migrate southward during winter, but some live year-round on the tundra. Lemmings spend the winter in nests of leaves and feed on the green shoots of flowering plants and mosses. In winter, herds of shaggy musk oxen use their broad hoofs to search for grasses buried beneath the snow in patches.

The tundra regions spread southward for hundreds of miles until they reach regions that are slightly warmer. There, where the ground thaws more in summer, short trees grow far apart from one anoth-

er. A little farther south, taller trees grow closer and closer together until they form vast, thick stretches of forest. This is the northern, boreal forest, or taiga. It covers much of Canada and the northern parts of the Scandinavian countries and the Soviet Union.

The trees of the taiga are mainly needle-leaf evergreens, such as the white spruce. A few species of hardy deciduous trees, among them birches, are also present. Mosses, lichens, and very few flowering plants cover the forest floor.

Throughout winter, trees in the taiga stand heaped with snow. Elk, caribou, reindeer, and moose graze through the forests. As they go, they eat shrubs, grasses, and shoots of deciduous trees. Snowshoe hare, squirrels, and ptarmigan are abundant and preyed on by lynxes, martins, and wolves. Bears spend their winters in the taiga in long periods of sleep or in complete hibernation.

In spring, the snow melts, soaking into the ground. This provides the taiga with a new supply of water for all the trees. Mosquitoes and horseflies swarm. Birds arrive. Hibernating animals become active. Like the tundra, the taiga teems with life through the short, warm summer.

With the spring thaws, bears emerge from their winter hibernation to forage along the banks of the McNeil River in Alaska.

Flowers, mosses, and lichens carpet the tundra when springtime relieves the long months of darkness. To survive, they must reproduce before the first snows come in September.

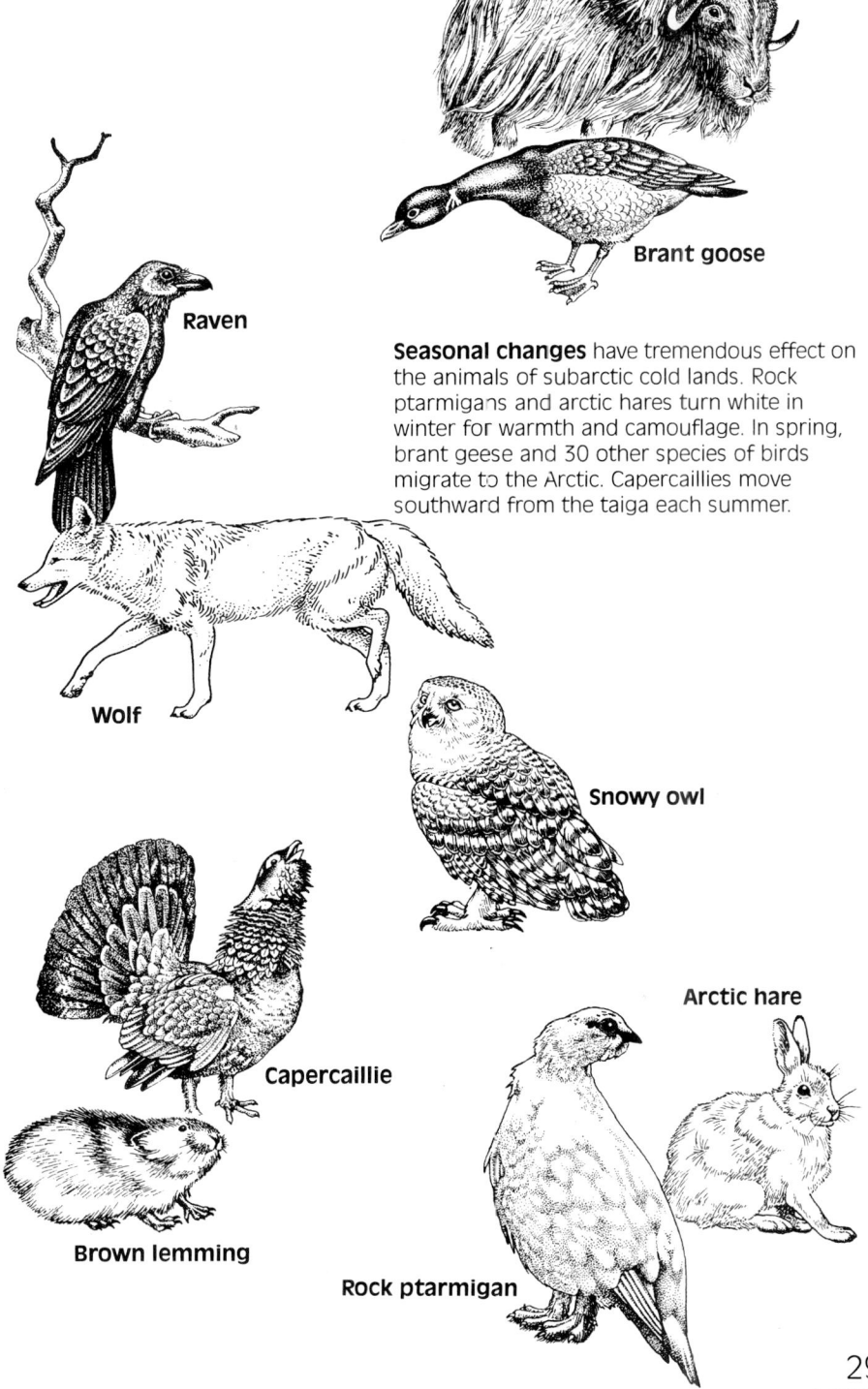

Raven

Musk ox

Brant goose

Seasonal changes have tremendous effect on the animals of subarctic cold lands. Rock ptarmigans and arctic hares turn white in winter for warmth and camouflage. In spring, brant geese and 30 other species of birds migrate to the Arctic. Capercaillies move southward from the taiga each summer.

Wolf

Snowy owl

Capercaillie

Arctic hare

Brown lemming

Rock ptarmigan

Polar Caps

The polar caps are regions of permanent ice and snow located at earth's North and South Poles. These regions are the parts of the planet that receive the least sunlight. During four months of winter, no sunlight touches either pole. In summer, much of the continuous light that does reach the poles is reflected into space by the glare of snow.

The two polar caps are very different from one another. The North Pole lies on a frozen sea, the Arctic Ocean. The South Pole sits upon the continent of Antarctica, which is covered by a layer of ice and snow at least a mile (1.6 kilometers) deep. The ice at the North Pole is frozen salty seawater, but the ice covering Antarctica is frozen fresh water — the largest concentration of fresh water in the world.

These frozen regions are deserts for plants. Animal life, however, does exist in the seas at both polar caps. Many kinds of fish, including the 8- to 14-foot (2.4- to 4.2-meter) long polar shark, live beneath the ice in the Arctic Ocean waters. Seals and walruses are also at home in the sea, and it is there that they find their food. Seals eat mainly fish, while walruses dive to the ocean floor to scoop up clams and other shellfish. Even in the coldest waters, these large mammals are kept warm by their extremely thick skin and layer of blubber. Of course, seals and walruses are air breathers. Thus, they must find or make openings in the ice so they can put their noses above water and breathe.

At the north polar cap, polar bears roam over the ice hunting for seals and other animals. These bears are excellent swimmers, and their thick, dense fur keeps them warm in freezing water. The fur's white color helps the animals blend in against their environment. Thus camouflaged, a bear can wait on ice near a seal's breathing hole and seize an unsuspecting victim when it comes up for air.

Several kinds of whales also make the Arctic Ocean their home. Such whales include the beluga, or white whale, and the narwhal. The narwhal is a small whale that has a maximum length of 18 feet (5.4 meters). Male narwhals have long, spiral tusks that jut from the mammals' upper jaw. The much larger bowhead whale is also an inhabitant of the Arctic Ocean.

The sea around Antarctica is the summer home of several species of whales that feed on small, shrimplike creatures called krill. These include blue, fin, humpback, and right whales. Southern bottlenose and southern fourtooth whales, which feed on squid and fish, are also Antarctic residents. Killer whales swim year-round in the cold Antarctic waters, preying on penguins, seals, and smaller whales in addition to fish and squid. A number of seal species, including krill-eating Antarctic fur seals and crabeater seals, aggressive leopard seals, and massive southern elephant seals, nest on the Antarctic coastline or on nearby islands.

The main creature found on land at the southern pole cap is the penguin, a flightless bird that walks with a clumsy waddle. One species of penguin, the emperor penguin, lays eggs and rears its young on the snow-covered slopes of Antarctica during winter. The birds' feathers and layers of fat keep them warm. To keep their eggs warm, the male birds hold them on their feet and cover them with their bellies.

Although they are at home on land for several months of the year, penguins are primarily sea creatures. Emperor penguins are superb swimmers that live on fish, and the birds spend months at a time in cold, polar waters.

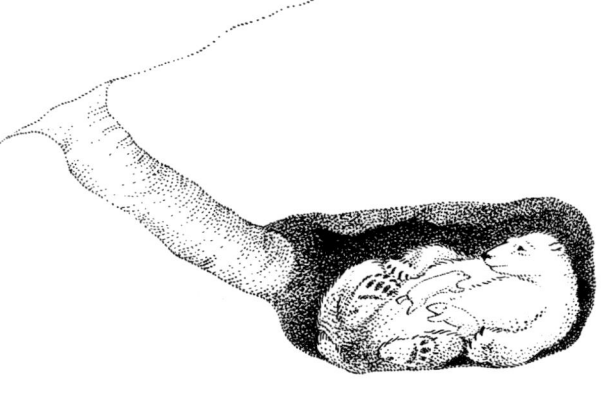

Polar bears live in underground shelters called dens during the colder months. Bears usually dig their dens in deep snowbanks.

A mother polar bear usually has twin cubs. Most cubs stay with their mother for about two years.

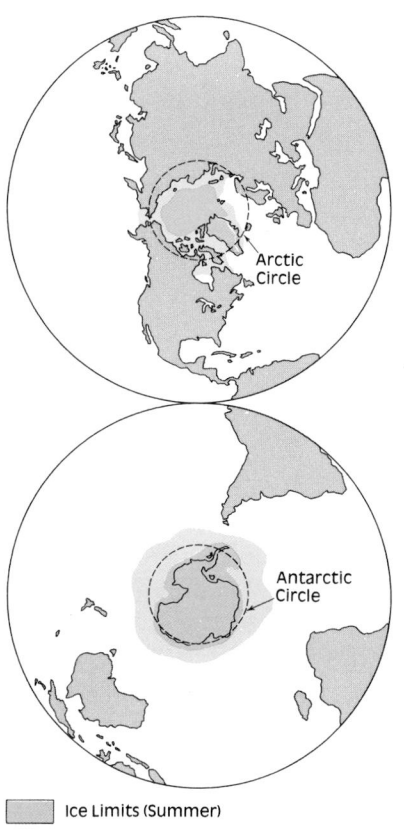

Ice Limits (Summer)
Ice Limits (Winter)

Penguins have adapted to Antarctic conditions with short, dense feathers, thick layers of fat, webbed feet, and wings that serve as flippers.

The Antarctic landscape is made up of mountains, glaciers, and dry valleys, like those shown at the left. A dry valley is an ice-free rocky area carved out by a glacier that has retreated. Wind sweeps away most of the snow that falls in dry valleys.

Blue whales and crabeater seals eat millions of tons of krill, the Antarctic's chief food source. Leopard seals and killer whales prey on penguins.

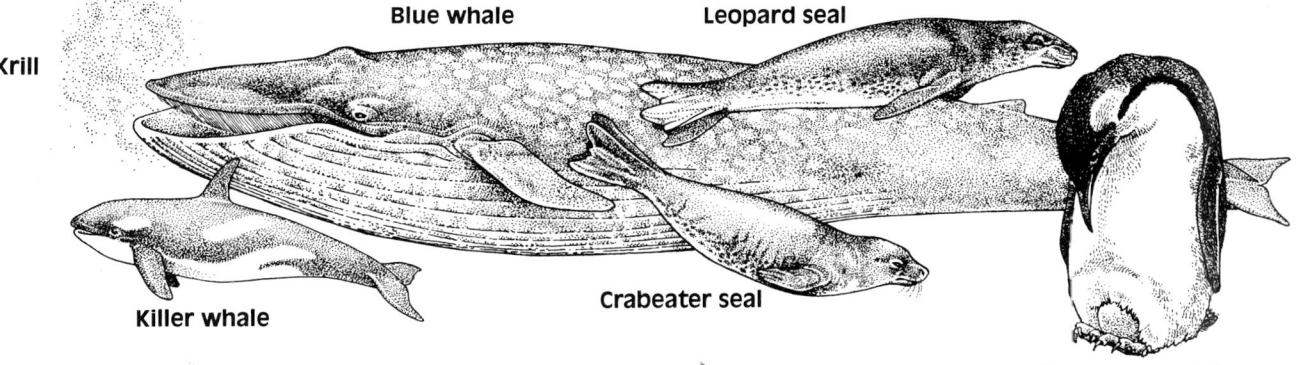

Krill
Blue whale
Leopard seal
Killer whale
Crabeater seal
Emperor penguin

31

Looking at Earth's

Highlands in Peru

Rockefeller Center Plaza in New York City, New York, U.S.

Rice fields in the Yangtze Valley, China

Supermarket in Luanda, Angola

People and Their Lands

Billions of people live on earth. They live on all the planet's land, from frozen polar caps to tropical regions. Their ways of life range from simple cultures to complex societies. People are the most adaptable of earth's creatures.

North America

The continent of North America extends from islands in the frozen Arctic Ocean southward to the tropical country of Panama, the connecting link to South America. North America includes Greenland, Canada, the United States, Mexico, Guatemala, Honduras, Nicaragua, Costa Rica, Panama, El Salvador, Belize, and the islands of the West Indies. These places are home to people who speak many different languages and have vastly different ways of life.

Greenland, the world's largest island, has been the home of Inuit people, or Eskimos, for about 5,000 years. Eric the Red, a Norse chieftain, discovered Greenland about A.D. 982. In 1721, Norwegians established a mission and trading center on the island. Today, Greenland is a province of Denmark, and Greenlanders are mostly a mixture of Danish and Inuit. They speak an Inuit language called Greenlandic, but many also speak Danish.

American Indians and Inuit were living in what is now Canada when the first European settlers arrived from France in the 1600's. For a time, Canada was a colony of France, but Great Britain gained control of most of it in 1763. Thousands of English, Scottish, and Irish colonists then began to arrive. In the late 1800's and in the 1900's, especially after World War II, people from other parts of Europe came to Canada.

Those people were chiefly from Germany, Italy, and Hungary. Today, about forty per cent of all Canadians are of British or Irish descent. About a fourth have French ancestry, and another fourth are from other parts of Europe. There are also still about 350,000 American Indians and 25,000 Inuit in Canada. The language most widely spoken in the world's second-largest country is English. French, however, is spoken by most people in the province of Quebec.

The United States has been called a "melting pot" because its people are a mixture from all over the world. The first permanent European settlement in what is now the United States was founded by Spaniards in 1565. In the 1600's and 1700's, many people from England, as well as some from the Netherlands, Sweden, and France, founded colonies on the east coast. Some of these people brought with them black slaves from Africa. During the 1600's, 1700's, and 1800's, many people from all parts of Europe migrated to the new land, but since most of the first colonists had been British, English became the main language. In the 1800's, many Chinese men were brought to help work on the railroads, and eventually they sent for their families. During the 1900's, immigrants from Japan, India, Pakistan, and other parts of Asia came to the United States. Also in the 1900's, people from Mexico and Latin America immigrated to the United States. And the country is

still the home of about 1,400,000 American Indians.

Mexico, Guatemala, Honduras, Nicaragua, Costa Rica, Panama, and El Salvador were all colonized in the 1500's and 1600's by people from Spain. The colonists intermarried with the American Indians who were already living there. Thus, the people of these countries are nearly all a mixture of Spanish and American Indian. There are also, however, some black people whose ancestors were from Africa.

The languages of all these countries settled by Spain is Spanish, but many people, especially in the small towns, still speak American Indian languages. English is the official language of Belize, another country that has a racially mixed population. About half the people have full or partial black African ancestry, about two-fifths have American Indian ancestry, and most of the rest of the people are of European, East Indian, Chinese, or Lebanese descent.

In the 1500's and 1600's, most of the West Indies islands were colonized by people from Spain, England, France, and the Netherlands. Most of the people now on many other islands are descendants of black Africans originally brought there as slaves. Others are descendants of European colonists. Depending on who were the original colonists of an island, the main spoken language is Spanish, English, or French.

A jungle village in Mexico's Chiapas Highlands climbs steeply up the mountainside. The area has great blocklike mountains cut by broad, deep valleys.

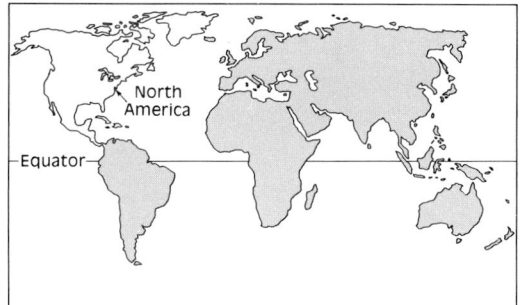

Schoolchildren in Chicago, Illinois, reflect the city's rich ethnic variety.

The city of Quebec is the capital of the province of Quebec, Canada. Street signs on Rue Champlain in the old section of the city are in French, the language of most of Quebec's residents.

South America

The continent of South America extends from a northernmost corner of land in the warm Caribbean Sea southward to a cold, tiny island only some 600 miles from the tip of snow-covered Antarctica. Between those points lie the continent's 12 independent countries. In order of size, those countries are: Brazil, Argentina, Peru, Colombia, Bolivia, Venezuela, Chile, Paraguay, Ecuador, Guyana, Uruguay, and Suriname. South America also includes French Guiana, an overseas department (administrative district) of France, and the Falkland Islands, a British dependency.

The equator runs through the northern part of South America, and more than three-fourths of the continent is in the tropics. A huge tropical rain forest covers more than one-third of the land mass, and the world's longest mountain range above sea level, the Andes, spans the entire west coast.

South America was inhabited by millions of American Indians for about 15,000 years before the first European explorers arrived. Some of the ancient peoples were quite primitive, but others achieved a fairly high degree of civilization. For example, the Inca established a great empire.

In the 1500's and 1600's, South America was explored and colonized by Europeans, chiefly from Spain and Portugal. For 300 years, the parts of South America that are now the nations of Argentina, Bolivia, Chile, Colombia, Ecuador, Paraguay, Peru, Uruguay, and Venezuela, were Spanish colonies. Many people in these countries today are descendants of Spanish colonists, and a great many are descended from Spaniards and American Indians who intermarried. The main language in these countries is Spanish. But there are still many American Indians, especially in Bolivia, Ecuador, and Peru, who speak their ancient languages. Peru, in fact, has two official languages. One is Spanish, and the other is Quechua, the country's chief Indian tongue.

Brazil covers almost half the continent. The country was settled by colonists from Portugal, and the main language of Brazil today is Portuguese. About half of South America's people live in Brazil. It is the world's sixth largest nation in population. Many Brazilians are descended from Portuguese colonists and other Europeans. Many others are descendants of Europeans and American Indians, or of Europeans and black African slaves. Still others are Asians, chiefly Japanese.

The small country of Suriname was ruled by the Netherlands during most of the period from 1667 until 1975, when it gained independence. Today Suriname is officially a Dutch-speaking country. Its population is made up of people of a great many backgrounds. Many of these people are Hindustanis, descendants of people from India. Others are of mixed European and black African ancestry. The population also includes blacks, Chinese, and Indonesians. A few American Indian tribes still live in the rain forests that cover much of the nation.

The country of Guyana was a British colony from 1831 to 1966, and its official language is English. But more than half of Guyana's population is made up of East Indians whose ancestors were brought from India to work on plantations. The rest of the country's people are blacks, American Indians, Europeans, and Chinese. Many of these people speak their own language, as well as English.

French Guiana became an overseas department of France in 1946. French is the district's official language. Most of the people's ancestors were black African, European, or both.

The Falkland Islands are a dependency of Great Britain, but the islands are also claimed by Argentina. Most of the islanders, however, are British people, and the main language is English.

A farmer inspects his sugar cane field in Brazil, one of the fastest-growing nations in the world.

Buenos Aires, Argentina, is the nation's capital and largest city, as well as its chief port and leading industrial center.

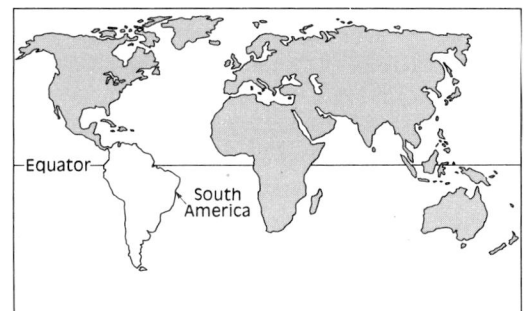

Markets like this one in the Peruvian highlands are a main source of both income and recreation for farmers. Conversation is exchanged along with goods and money.

Argentina's gauchos are typically people of mixed Amerindian and European ancestry. Gauchos chiefly work as ranch hands on estates or large ranches known as estancias.

Europe

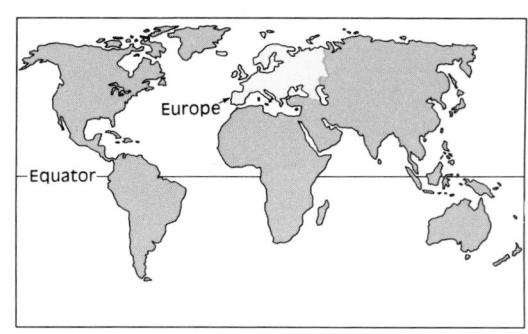

The land mass known as the continent of Europe is actually a huge peninsula — a piece of land nearly surrounded by water — that extends westward from the continent of Asia. Geographers say that Europe begins at the Ural Mountains in the Soviet Union and reaches into the Atlantic Ocean. There it includes the British Isles, Iceland, and a large number of small islands. From north to south, Europe extends from the Arctic Ocean to the Mediterranean Sea. In terms of area, Europe is smaller than any other continent, except Australia. In terms of population, it is packed with more people than any other continent, except Asia.

Europe currently includes 33 countries. These range in size from the world's biggest country, the Soviet Union, to its smallest one, Vatican City. Vatican City, which is the administrative center of the Roman Catholic Church, consists of only 0.17 of a square mile (0.44 square kilometer).

Europe is often called the birthplace of Western civilization. Most of the major scientific, philosophical, and political ideas affecting the Western world were developed by Europeans.

The majority of the people living in Europe today are descended from primitive tribes that lived there thousands of years ago. The members of these tribes and

their descendants did not always remain in the same areas. Throughout the centuries of European history, various groups of people have moved around and settled in different countries. As a result, many European countries are inhabited by several ethnic groups — people who share a common ancestry, language, religion, and way of life. For example, there are the Flemings and the Walloons in Belgium and the Czechs and the Slovaks in Czechoslovakia. The members of the various ethnic groups within a country may all think of themselves as citizens of the same country. Still, they are likely to associate mainly with the people of their own ethnic group and to marry members of that same group.

About 50 different languages are spoken in Europe. Often, people in various parts of a country speak a dialect of that country's language. Every dialect has its own pronunciation and sentence structure and may even have its own vocabulary. The same language, then, may be spoken differently in different parts of a country. There are more than 100 different dialects among the languages of Europe.

In many European countries, more than one language is spoken. Ireland, for example, has two official languages — English and Gaelic. Everyone in Ireland speaks English, and about 30 per cent of the Irish people can speak Gaelic too. Gaelic is a

form of the language spoken by the ancient Celts, from whom many of the Irish are descended. Switzerland has three official languages and four national languages. The official languages are German, French, and Italian. The national languages are the three official languages plus Romansh. Romansh, which is similar to Latin, is spoken by only about 1 per cent of the Swiss population.

Throughout Europe, many people can speak a second language, usually the language of the foreign country nearest to them. In the western part of Europe, a great number of people also speak English.

Europeans are generally light-skinned, and many are light-haired. However, in recent years, people of other racial groups from other continents have moved to Europe, chiefly to find jobs. Those people are now Europeans. Just as the Americas may be viewed as "melting pots," so has Europe become a place where people of various national and cultural backgrounds live together.

The Berlin Wall, built in 1961 to separate Communist East Berlin from West Berlin, was opened in November 1989 by the East German government. Thousands of Berliners gathered at the wall to celebrate East Germany's new freedom. Several other Eastern European countries began the process of democratic reform in 1989, and in 1990 East Germany and West Germany were reunified.

Crowds gather for the pope's weekly audience in the Square of Saint Peter in Vatican City. Vatican City is the world's smallest independent state. It lies entirely within the city of Rome, Italy.

Agriculture employs more Romanians than any other activity. Families work together on the nation's collective farms. To a large extent, the farmers rely on old-fashioned farm equipment.

Asia

The largest continent, Asia, includes almost one-third of all the earth's land. The northernmost part of the continent, which is the tip of Siberia in the Soviet Union, lies in the bitter cold of the Arctic Circle. The southernmost part, the islands of Indonesia, lies in the simmering tropics near the equator. From west to east, Asia stretches across the earth from Africa and Europe to the Pacific Ocean. Examples of every known kind of plant-and-animal habitat, from tundra to tropical rain forest, can be found in Asia.

This vast area is home to about 60 per cent of all the world's people. A variety of races and many different ethnic groups inhabit Asia. The population of the continent is divided among 41 independent nations and three other political units—the British dependency, Hong Kong; the Portuguese territory, Macao; and the Egyptian military administration, the Gaza Strip. The smallest unit is the Maldives, a group of islands in the Indian Ocean, with a population of about 227,000. The largest is gigantic China, with a population of more than one billion.

Few people live in large areas of Asia because those areas are either too cold, too hot, too mountainous, or too dry. The result is that Asians are jammed tightly into the places where the climate and the physical features of the land are more agreeable. Most of these people live in valleys, near rivers, or on the seacoast.

Different groups of Asians often differ greatly from each other in appearance. Most of the people in Southwest Asian countries such as Saudi Arabia and Turkey resemble Europeans. Some Asians, however, have darker skin and hair. People of southern India have dark skin and straight hair. Inhabitants of the Indonesian part of New Guinea and other islands of Southeast Asia have brown or yellow skin and curly hair. The people of most of East Asia, those who live in countries such as China and Japan, have yellowish to brownish skin and dark straight hair.

Numerous languages and dialects are spoken throughout Asia. Often, many different languages are spoken within the same country. In India alone, there are 16 major languages and more than 1,000 minor languages and dialects. Thus, the people of one village may not speak the same language as the people of the neighboring village. These language differences often cause serious problems in matters of education and commerce.

Ways of life, too, are often very different in various parts of Asia. In Southwest Asia, about half of the people are farmers. Most of them live, dress, and work in much the same way as their ancestors have always done. On the other hand, about 77 per cent of the people of Japan live and work in or near cities that resemble those of Western countries. Many of these urban dwellers work in tall office buildings and ride modern elevated and subway trains. But in Central Asian Mongolia, Sinkiang, and Tibet, life is simpler. Most people live by herding sheep, goats, cattle, horses, camels, or yaks on the vast dry plains. The few inhabitants of New Guinea also live uncomplicated lives in tiny primitive villages that lie within tropical rain forests. Most New Guineans supply all their own needs. Some live in isolated mountain valleys and never have contact with the outside world.

Asia has played an important part in human history. It was the ancient people of Southeast Asia who developed the world's first civilization some 5,500 years ago. Asia was also the site of a number of significant inventions, such as movable type and gunpowder. And it was in Asia that all the major religions of the world began—Christianity, Judaism, Islam, Buddhism, Hinduism, Shinto, and Taoism.

Raising livestock has long been the chief economic activity in Mongolia, though few Mongolians still follow the traditional nomadic way of life.

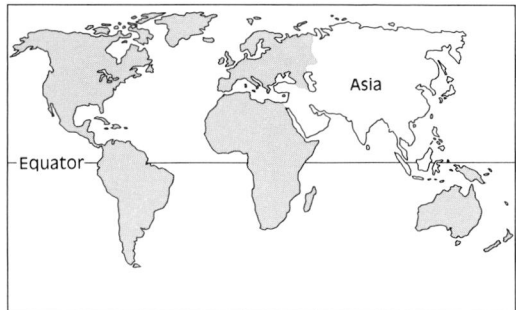

At floating markets in Bangkok, baskets of produce and other goods are exchanged from boat to boat.

At a used-car market in Saudi Arabia, a hawker sporting both Arab and Western dress uses a modern bullhorn to attract customers.

The Ganges River in India is sacred to Hindus. Each year, thousands of pilgrims climb down stairways called ghats to bathe in the river's waters.

Africa

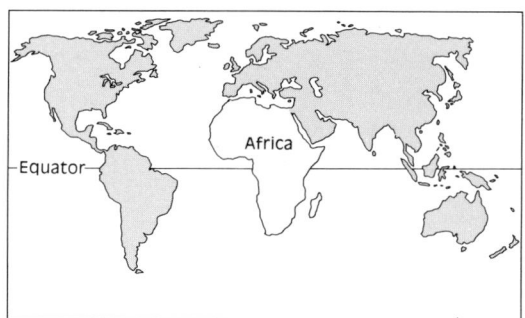

Africa, the second largest continent, occupies about one-fifth of the earth's land. The continent is an immense plateau, a region of striking contrasts. Less than one-fifth of the land is covered by great forests, most of them tropical rain forests. Although much of the continent is grassland, the world's largest desert, the Sahara, lies across 3½ million square miles (9 million square kilometers) of the northern region. The world's longest river, the Nile, flows through Africa's northeastern section.

The equator passes through almost the exact middle of the continent. Thus, about 90 per cent of Africa is in the tropic zones. The parts of the continent that lie at low elevations are hot all year long. Rain falls year-round in the Congo Basin and in some of the coastal areas, where the rain forests are located. But most of Africa has long, dry seasons with only one or two spells of heavy rainfall.

Many different kinds of people inhabit Africa. In northern Africa, mainly in Algeria and Morocco, live a group of people called Berbers. Most Berbers are light-skinned, dark-haired people. Their ancestors can be traced back thousands of years in Africa. Also living in this region are Arabs whose ancestors came from the Arabian Peninsula more than 1,300 years ago. Another group, people of European descent whose ancestors settled in Africa in the 1600's, live along the Mediterranean coast.

Black Africans make up about 70 per cent of all the African people. They are dark-skinned and have black, curly hair. Most of the people of the Sahara are black Africans.

Black African people also inhabit much of the land south of the Sahara. Their ancestors lived in the north many thousands of years ago, when the Sahara was a fertile grassland. Many began moving southward when the Sahara started to become a desert.

A group of small people called Pygmies dwell in the rain forests of central Africa. Pygmies have reddish-brown skin and tightly curled brown hair. They live primarily in small bands of fewer than 50 members. Each Pygmy band has its own territory in the forest. These people look on the forest as the giver of life, because it provides them with food, clothing, protection, and shelter.

In southwest Africa live two groups of people who have yellowish-brown skin and black, tightly coiled hair. These people, known as San (or Bushmen) and Khoikhoi,

The Nile River is the world's longest river. It flows northward from Burundi, through Sudan, Ethiopia, and Egypt to the Mediterranean Sea.

Nairobi, the capital of Kenya, is the most important commercial center in eastern Africa. The central area of the city has many modern buildings and tree-lined streets.

are members of the African Khoisan culture. Some of these Africans gather wild plant food and hunt animals. Others work on rural reserves, cattle ranches, or farms.

The major groups living in the far south are descendants of Europeans who came to Africa during the last four hundred years and of East Indians who came during the last century. The African island of Madagascar is home to many people whose ancestors came there from Indonesia about 2,000 years ago.

All these people make up hundreds of different ethnic groups, each with its own language or dialect. There are more than 800 different languages and many dialects in Africa. The fact that European nations had at one time established colonies throughout Africa is reflected in the official languages of a number of Africa's 52 nations. French is an official language of 20 nations; English of 18; and Portuguese of 3. Arabic is the official language of 7 African nations. While many citizens can speak their country's official language, most people speak mainly the language or dialect of their own ethnic group.

In Africa, as in Asia, a great many people still live in rural areas in exactly the same way that their ancestors lived for hundreds of years. However, some Africans lead very modern lives in large cities that are similar in many ways to ones in North America and Europe. Most urban dwellers have a higher standard of living than rural people. Better schools and medical facilities, as well as other attractions, lead more and more rural people to move into the cities.

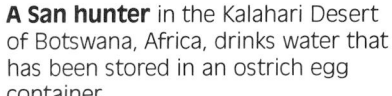

A San hunter in the Kalahari Desert of Botswana, Africa, drinks water that has been stored in an ostrich egg container.

Berber women perform a ceremonial dance in Morocco. About 20 million Berbers live in northwest Africa and the Sahara.

Australia and New Zealand

Australia, the smallest continent, lies entirely in the Southern Hemisphere between the Indian and the South Pacific oceans. The northern third of Australia is in the tropics and stays hot all year long. The other two-thirds have warm summers and mild winters. About one-third of the total land area of the continent is covered by desert.

All of Australia is a single nation, the Commonwealth of Australia, which is composed of six states. It is an independent nation with its own government, but it is a member of the Commonwealth of Nations. Australia regards the British monarch as its head of state.

Two groups of people make up most of Australia's population of about 17,000,000. Nearly all are European immigrants or descendants of European immigrants—mainly British—who came to Australia during the last 200 years. Some are more recent arrivals, having immigrated during the last 40 years. These people are all white-skinned, and many are fair-haired and have light-colored eyes. All speak English.

About 1 per cent of the Australian population is made up of a group of people known as Aborigines. Aborigines are descendants of a people who came to Australia at least 40,000 years ago, probably from somewhere in Southeast Asia. While all Aborigines are dark-skinned, some have dark brown hair and others have light brown or blond hair.

At one time, there were 300,000 Aborigines, separated into hundreds of tribes. Each of those tribes had its own language. Today, there are some 206,000 Australians who are classed as Aborigines. Most of them, however, are actually a mixture of Aborigine and European as a result of intermarriage among their ancestors. Aborigines now generally speak English, although many can also speak their ancient language.

Although these two groups make up most of Australia's population, several other groups are represented. Since the 1970's, an increasing number of immigrants from New Zealand and Southeast Asia have settled in Australia. There are also a small number of people from Canada and the United States.

Most Australians of European descent live in the southeastern quarter of the continent. They have settled largely in cities along the coast, where it is cooler and there is more rainfall. Some live along the extreme southwest coast. The way of life of these people is much like that of people in the United States and Canada. Although some Aborigines have moved into the cities, most live in the forested lands of central and northern Australia.

About 1,000 miles (1,600 kilometers) southeast of Australia in the Southwest Pacific Ocean lie two large islands and several dozen small ones. This cluster of islands forms the nation of New Zealand. Located far south of the equator, New Zealand has a mild climate with a good deal of rainfall. Much of the land is green and fertile, with numerous lakes, rivers, and snow-capped mountains.

Like Australia, New Zealand is a member of the Commonwealth of Nations and regards the British monarch as its head of state. Also like Australia, New Zealand's population, which is over 3 million, is made up primarily of two groups of people. Most of them are descendants of the British who settled in New Zealand during the 1800's. The other group, the Maoris, are descendants of a people who came to New Zealand about 1,000 years ago from some other South Pacific islands. Maoris, who belong to the Polynesian race, have light brown skin, dark hair, and dark eyes.

New Zealanders live much as people do in Great Britain. Their language is, of course, English. Many Maoris, however, can also speak the language of their ancestors.

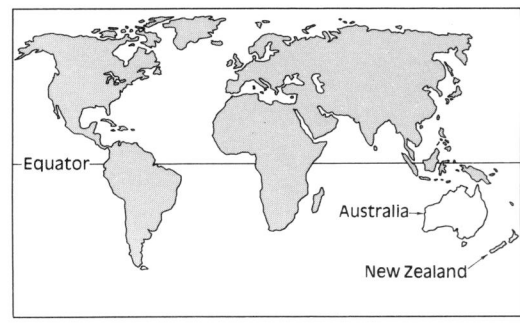

The Opera House in Sydney, Australia, has facilities for opera, concerts, and theater. The building, which is internationally known, was completed in 1973.

A sheep farmer in New Zealand uses a minibike to round up his herd. Lamb and wool are among the nation's chief exports.

The ancestors of these Aboriginal stockmen were the first people to live in Australia. Most Aborigines today live in the rural areas of the continent.

New Zealanders love outdoor sports and activities in all kinds of weather. Skiing is becoming increasingly popular.

Pacific Islands

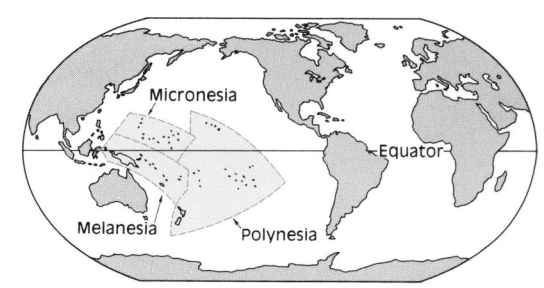

A vast portion of the Pacific Ocean is dotted with many thousands of big and little islands. This region of ocean and islands is known as the Pacific Islands, or Oceania. Not all islands in the Pacific Ocean, however, are a part of Oceania. For example, islands near the mainland of Asia are considered part of Asia, and islands near North and South America are grouped with those continents.

Geographers divide the Pacific Islands into three parts. Scattered across the central Pacific are thousands of islands that make up the portion called Polynesia, meaning "many islands." Polynesia includes Hawaii, New Zealand, and Midway Island. North and east of Australia lie groups of islands that form what is called Melanesia, meaning "black islands." Fiji, the Solomon Islands, and New Caledonia are Melanesian islands. Between Melanesia and Japan lie islands that form Micronesia, meaning "small islands." Some of the Micronesian islands are Guam, Wake Island, and the Caroline Islands.

All these islands fall into one of two types. High Islands, such as the main islands of Hawaii, are hilly and mountainous and often have volcanoes. Low Islands such as the Marshall Islands are formed of coral reefs that are generally just above sea level. Most of Oceania lies in the tropics. There-

fore, the weather on the islands is quite warm year-round. Although the area, in general, gets plenty of rainfall, some islands may receive little rain.

Generally, a different kind of people lives in each part of the Pacific Islands. In Melanesia, the people are rather short, with dark skin and coarse, curly black hair. They resemble the black people of Africa. Scientists believe that the ancestors of the Melanesians came from somewhere in Asia many thousands of years ago.

The people of Micronesia are a little taller than the Melanesians and have lighter skin. Most also have coarse, curly, or wavy black hair. Their ancestors, too, probably came from Asia, but at a later time than the ancestors of the Melanesians.

Polynesians are taller than both other groups. All have light brown skin, but some have wavy hair and others have straight hair. Their ancestors probably came from Melanesia or Micronesia.

There have been other influences on the people of the Pacific Islands. For example, many people from other lands have settled on the Polynesian islands in the past. Thus, many Polynesians have Asian and European ancestors. A large number of people living on Fiji are descended from East Indians who came there to work about 100 years ago. And people of European and Asian descent live on many of the other Pacific Islands.

The Melanesians, Micronesians, and Polynesians all have similar ways of life. There are, however, some differences in language, law, dress, and religion. Many hundreds of languages are spoken throughout Oceania. The people of Melanesia, particularly, speak a number of different languages. English is spoken on a great many of the islands that were once colonies of Great Britain or that are now governed by Great Britain or the United States. French is spoken on a number of islands that are governed by France.

Many of the islands of Oceania are independent and have their own governments. Hawaii, American Samoa, Guam, Midway Island, and Wake Island, however, belong to the United States. Pitcairn Island comes under the authority of Great Britain. France, Chile, and New Zealand all govern islands. And a part of New Guinea is governed by Indonesia.

Of all the Pacific Islands, only Hawaii and New Zealand have large, modern cities and towns. Most Pacific Islanders live in small villages and make their livings by farming or fishing, much as their ancestors have done for hundreds of years.

At a kava ceremony in Leone, American Samoa, a woman prepares a beverage called kava, which the participants will drink as they give thanks for their blessings. Such traditional ceremonies play a major role in Polynesian village life.

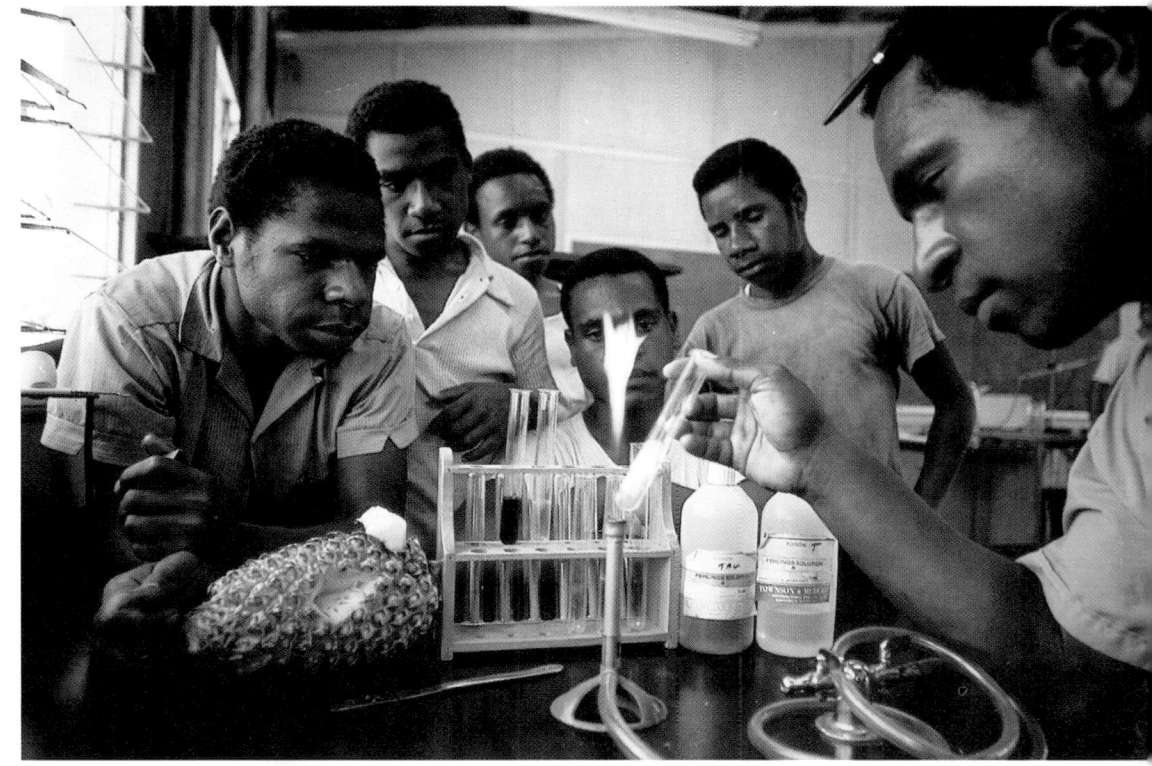

Off the Caroline Islands in Micronesia, some fishermen still travel in hand-hewn sailing canoes.

Melanesian students study pineapple extract in their school laboratory.

Polar Regions

The earth's north polar region, the Arctic, does not seem a likely place for people to live. Nevertheless, large numbers of people do live in the parts of North America, Europe, and Asia that lie within the Arctic Circle.

Large supplies of oil, uranium, titanium, and other valuable minerals have been found in the Arctic. This has caused the settlement of some areas by communities of scientists, technicians, miners, and oil field workers. Modern technology enables these settlements to survive in the Arctic's hostile environment.

Most Arctic residents, however, live simpler lives. Many follow the traditions of their ancestors.

In North America, about 117,000 of the people known as Inuit, or Eskimos, live in the northern parts of Greenland, Canada, and Alaska. Inuit are stocky people with short arms and legs. They resemble the Mongoloid people of Asia, and scientists believe they came to North America about 10,000 years ago via a land connection that once existed between Alaska and northeastern Asia. Inuit throughout the Arctic speak essentially the same language.

For thousands of years, Inuit followed a traditional way of life that had been developed to meet the needs of living in the Arctic. They lived mainly on the meat of seals and caribou, which they hunted with harpoons. During the short Arctic summer, they stayed in tents of sealskin or caribou skin, and they fished for arctic trout called char. In winter, the Inuit made temporary dome-shaped houses of snow. They traveled by means of dog sleds and boats made of wood, bone, and skins. Today, that way of life is largely gone. Most Inuit now hunt with rifles, travel by snowmobile and motorboat, and live in heated houses in settlements.

About 1,500 Inuit also live in Siberia, the Asian part of the Soviet Union. Several tribes of people who greatly resemble Amerindians of the Pacific Northwest live in northeastern Siberia. These tribes— the Kamchadals, the Koryaks, and the Chukchi—live by hunting and fishing. They number about 20,000 people. Tribes of Mongoloid people—the Yakuts, Tungus, and Samoyeds—reside in north-central Siberia and live mainly by raising reindeer. There are nearly 420,000 of these people.

The European part of the Arctic lies across the northern parts of the Soviet Union, Finland, Norway, and Sweden. In the Arctic part of the European Soviet Union, live some 250,000 people called

Zyrians. These people, who are related to modern Finlanders, are hunters, fishermen, and reindeer herders.

The Arctic part of Norway, Sweden, and Finland, together with a bit of the Soviet Union, has long been known as Lapland, the home of people called Lapps. Lapps are short and muscular, with slightly yellowish skin and straight black hair. Scientists think the Lapps may have come to Lapland from central Asia many thousands of years ago.

There are nearly 45,000 Lapps. Some are nomadic. They raise herds of reindeer that they follow from place to place as the animals search for edible vegetation. Other Lapps live near the sea and make their living mainly by fishing. Still others hunt, fish, and raise reindeer. All Lapps speak a language that is much like Finnish, but it is spoken with different dialects in different parts of Lapland.

People have never settled in the earth's south polar region, the Antarctic, as they have in the Arctic. People *do* live in Antarctica today, but they are mainly scientists studying the continent for various reasons. These people are really only visitors, however. They live in temporary housing, and their supplies are delivered by ship or by airplane.

Murmansk is the Soviet Union's chief port on the Arctic Ocean and the world's largest city north of the Arctic Circle.

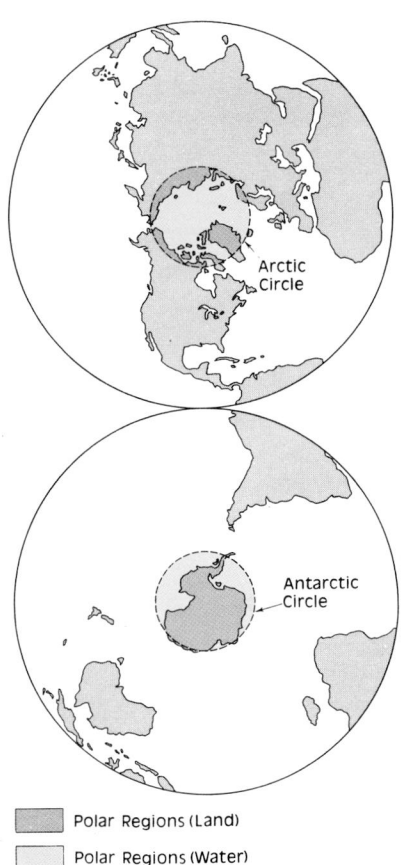

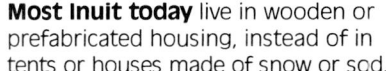
Polar Regions (Land)
Polar Regions (Water)

Most Inuit today live in wooden or prefabricated housing, instead of in tents or houses made of snow or sod.

Some Lapps support themselves by raising reindeer, which they sell for meat. These Lapps, mostly young men known as Mountain Lapps, live north in the summer and move south with their herds in winter.

Looking at Earth

Earthrise over the moon

Glaciers in southeastern Alaska, U.S.

Kilauea in southeastern Hawaii, U.S.

As a Planet

Eᴀʀᴛʜ ɪꜱ ᴏɴᴇ of the four rocky inner planets of the solar system. It is a ball of molten stone and metal enclosed by a shell of rock. The features of this active planet are in constant change from the action of volcanoes, earthquakes, water, and wind.

Earth in the Solar System

The planet Earth is a huge ball covered with water, rock, and soil. It travels in an orbit—an oval-shaped path—around a star, the sun. The sun, in turn, moves in an orbit around the center of a vast system of stars called a galaxy.

There are at least 100 billion galaxies scattered throughout the observable universe. Each consists of from less than a billion to a trillion or more stars. The galaxy in which Earth and the sun are located is known as the Milky Way.

The Milky Way is a spiral-shaped galaxy of hundreds of billions of stars. All these stars are at incredible distances from one another. The nearest star to the sun and to Earth is approximately 25 million million miles (40 million million kilometers) away.

All stars within a galaxy revolve around the center of the galaxy. The stars that are farthest from the center naturally take longer to make the journey. Both the sun and Earth are located far from the center of the Milky Way. It would take the sun and Earth about 250 million years to make one complete revolution around the center.

Earth is only one of a number of objects that orbit the sun. There are eight other major planets and their moons. There are also some very small minor planets, called asteroids. In addition, various-sized chunks of rock called meteoroids orbit the sun. And there are comets and clouds of dust and gas. All these things, together with the sun, make up what is known as the solar system.

The nine known planets of the solar system orbit the sun at various distances. In order of distance from the sun, these planets are Mercury, Venus, Earth, Mars, Jupiter, Saturn, Uranus, Neptune, and Pluto. Although Pluto is normally the outermost planet, it crossed inside Neptune's orbit in 1979 and will remain there until 1999.

Mercury, Venus, Earth, and Mars are essentially balls of rock and metal. Jupiter, Saturn, Uranus, and Neptune, called the giant planets, are made up chiefly of gases that are compressed into fluids and contain little iron and rock. Pluto's composition is still unknown. Scientists, however, believe Pluto is like a ball of ice, similar to the satellites of the giant planets.

Earth, the third planet from the sun, circles it at an average distance of 93 million miles (150 million kilometers). The closest planet to Earth is Venus, the second planet from the sun. Venus approaches to within 25.7 million miles (approximately 40 million kilometers) of Earth during its orbit.

But the closest to Earth of all solar-system bodies is its own moon. The moon's mean distance from Earth is only about 238,857 miles (384,403 kilometers). The moon is held in orbit around Earth by the pull of the planet's gravity. Earth's moon is a barren, airless ball of rock. It is about one-fourth the size of Earth. The moon's surface has mountains, valleys, and plains. It is pitted with billions of craters, caused by

The solar system, *below,* contains nine planets and their satellites, plus numerous comets, meteorites, and interplanetary dust. The planets orbit the sun, a rather ordinary star lying about 30,000 light years from the center of the Milky Way.

Distances from the sun (Figures in millions)

Sun	Mercury	Venus	Earth	Mars	Jupiter
	36 miles	67.2 miles	93 miles	141.6 miles	483.6 miles
	57.9 kilometers	109 kilometers	150 kilometers	228 kilometers	777 kilometers

Mercury is the planet closest to the sun. It also moves around the sun faster than any other planet—once every 88 Earth days. Like Venus, Mercury does not have a moon.

Venus is almost the same size and mass as Earth. But its atmosphere is mostly carbon dioxide, and its temperature is too high to allow life to exist.

Earth, like Pluto, has only one moon. The gravitational pull of Earth keeps the moon in its orbit. Without this pull from Earth, the moon would fly off into space.

Mars has surface conditions that are closer to Earth's than any other planet's. In spite of experiments conducted by space probes, scientists have not been able to determine whether life exists on Mars.

Jupiter, the largest planet, has the fastest spin in the solar system. It rotates once every 9 hours 55 minutes. The rapid spin flattens the planet at the poles. Jupiter has 16 known satellites.

the impact of pieces of rock that have smashed into its surface.

Earth's moon shines because sunlight reflects off its surface. The amount of light-reflecting surface visible from Earth varies when the moon is in different positions as it moves around the planet. These differences account for the phases of the moon, such as first quarter and full moon.

An eclipse of the moon occurs when Earth is directly between the sun and the full moon, casting its shadow on the moon's surface. An eclipse of the sun occurs when the moon passes directly between the sun and Earth, blocking off the sun's light and casting a shadow on Earth.

The spiral galaxy, *above,* like the Milky Way, resembles an enormous pinwheel. However, because of Earth's position in the Milky Way, its pinwheel shape cannot be seen from Earth. Instead, the galaxy appears as a broad, hazy band of starlight stretching across the sky.

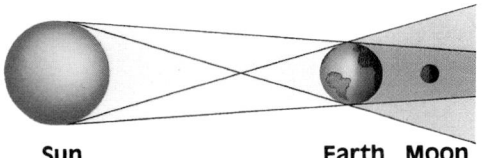

Sun   Earth   Moon

A lunar eclipse takes place when Earth passes between the sun and moon.

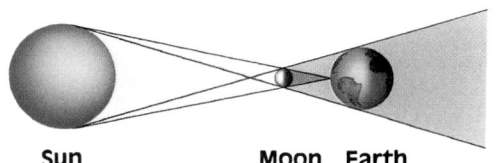

Sun   Moon   Earth

A solar eclipse occurs when the moon passes between the sun and Earth.

Saturn	Uranus	Neptune	Pluto
888.2 miles	1,786.4 miles	2,798.8 miles	3,666.2 miles
1,424 kilometers	2,869 kilometers	4,495 kilometers	5,890 kilometers

Neptune, like Pluto, cannot be seen without a telescope. Neptune has eight moons. One of them, Triton, is the only large satellite in the solar system that travels from east to west.

Saturn, the second largest planet, is circled by seven major rings. Jupiter, Neptune, and Uranus are the only other planets known to have rings, but theirs are much fainter than Saturn's.

Uranus is believed to be basically featureless and surrounded by clouds. Little is known about the planet's surface.

Pluto, which has a moon more than one-third its size, is the most distant planet from the sun. At some point in its oval-shaped orbit, Pluto enters Neptune's orbit and stays there for about 20 years. This event occurs every 248 years.

Earth's Atmosphere and Motion

Like the moon, Earth also glows with reflected sunlight. Seen from space, the planet appears to be a large, dark blue and brown ball covered with wispy white patches. The brown areas are Earth's continents, and the vast blue expanses are its oceans. Of all the planets in the solar system, only Earth has water in liquid form. Oceans, which contain most of Earth's water, cover about 70 per cent of the planet's surface. The white patches are the clouds that drift in Earth's atmosphere.

Earth's atmosphere is the layer of gases that surrounds the planet. The atmosphere of Earth is a mixture of 78 per cent nitrogen, 21 per cent oxygen, and small amounts of several other gases. The atmosphere extends 1,000 miles (1,600 kilometers) from the planet's surface. Earth's atmosphere is thickest within the first 50 miles (80 kilometers) of the planet, and it becomes progressively thinner thereafter.

Venus and Mars also have an atmosphere. The atmosphere of Venus is a thick mixture of mainly carbon dioxide and other gases. It is filled with clouds formed largely of droplets of sulfuric acid and sulfur. The atmosphere of Mars is a thin mixture of carbon dioxide and other gases.

Earth is fifth in size among all the planets and the largest of the rocky inner planets. The Earth's diameter, or distance from one side to the other through its center, is about 7,900 miles (12,713 kilometers) measured from North Pole to South Pole. Earth's circumference, or distance around the planet, is about 24,901.5 miles (40,075.16 kilometers) measured at the equator.

Venus is only slightly smaller than Earth. Mars is about half the size of Earth, and Mercury is about two-fifths as big. However, the diameter of Jupiter—the solar system's largest planet—is more than 11 times the length of Earth's.

Earth rotates on its axis, an imaginary line through the center of the planet from the North Pole to the South Pole. This

Earth is the only planet in the solar system that has enough oxygen surrounding it and enough water on its surface to support life as it is known today. About 70 per cent of Earth's surface is water; the rest is land. All Earth's animals and plants live on or close to the planet's surface.

rotation causes day and night on Earth. As the planet rotates, half of it faces the sun. There it is daytime. The other half faces away from the sun into the blackness of space, and on that half it is nighttime. The planet makes one complete rotation every 23 hours 56 minutes 4.09 seconds. This is the length of Earth's day.

As Earth rotates, it also moves in an orbit around the sun. Earth moves through space at an average speed of 66,600 miles (107,200 kilometers) an hour. One orbit, or revolution around the sun, takes 365 days 6 hours 9 minutes 9.54 seconds. This is the length of Earth's year.

Earth's axis is tilted, rather than straight up and down. This tilt and Earth's orbit around the sun cause the seasons. During part of the orbit, the northern half of the planet is tilted toward the sun. In this position, the northern half receives more light and heat than the southern half. This is summer for the northern portion of the planet and winter for the southern portion, which is tilted away from the sun. During another part of the orbit, the southern half of the planet is tilted toward the sun, and seasons are reversed.

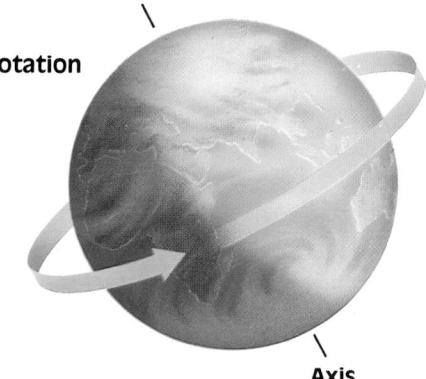

Rotation

Axis

Earth spins eastward around its axis once every 23 hours 56 minutes and 4.09 seconds. Earth circles the sun once every 365 days 6 hours 9 minutes and 9.54 seconds.

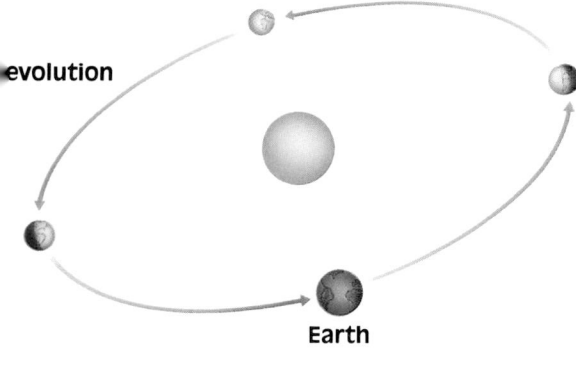

evolution

Earth

Altitude

Divisions of the Atmosphere

600 mi. (960 km)

550 mi. (890 km)

500 mi. (800 km)

450 mi. (720 km)

400 mi. (640 km)

350 mi. (560 km)

300 mi. (480 km)

250 mi. (400 km)

200 mi. (320 km)

150 mi. (240 km)

100 mi. (160 km)

50 mi. (80 km)

0 mi./km

Earth's atmosphere consists of four layers, the troposphere, the stratosphere, the mesosphere, and the thermosphere. The diagram on the right shows a detailed enlargement of the first three layers and the lower 70 miles (112 kilometers) of the thermosphere. More than 75 per cent of Earth's air and almost all its weather occurs in the troposphere. The stratosphere contains the ozone layer, which absorbs harmful rays from the sun. Meteor trails can be seen in the mesosphere. Auroral displays, or northern and southern lights, occur in the lower thermosphere.

120 mi. (200 km)

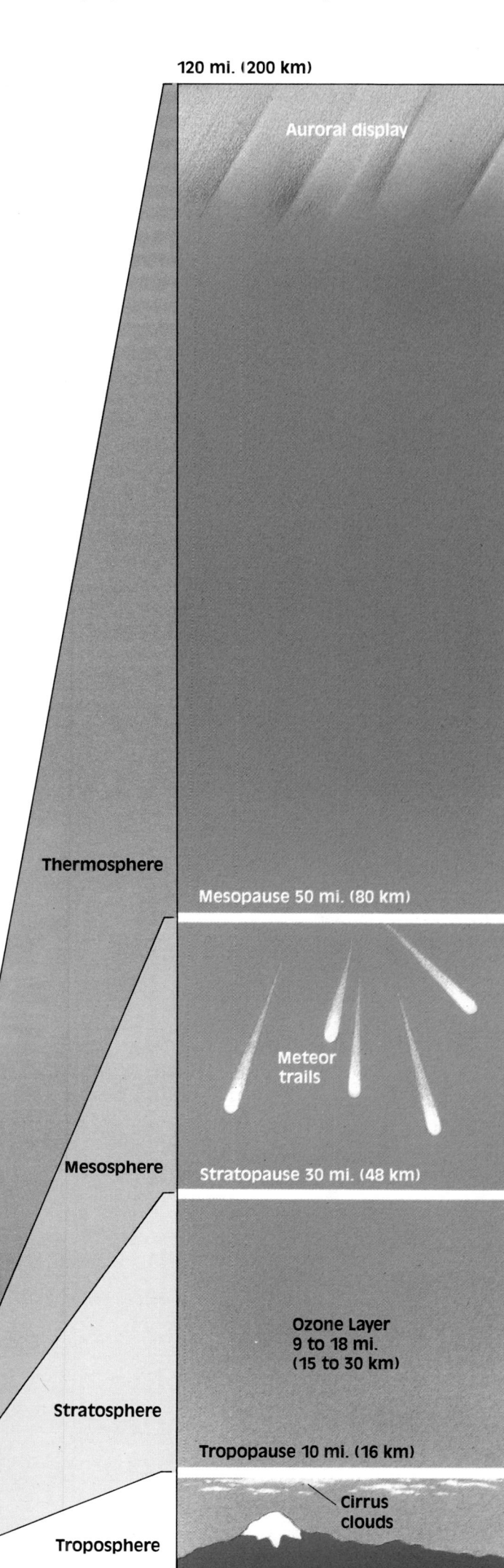

Auroral display

Thermosphere

Mesopause 50 mi. (80 km)

Meteor trails

Mesosphere

Stratopause 30 mi. (48 km)

Ozone Layer 9 to 18 mi. (15 to 30 km)

Tropopause 10 mi. (16 km)

Stratosphere

Cirrus clouds

Troposphere

Earth's Structure

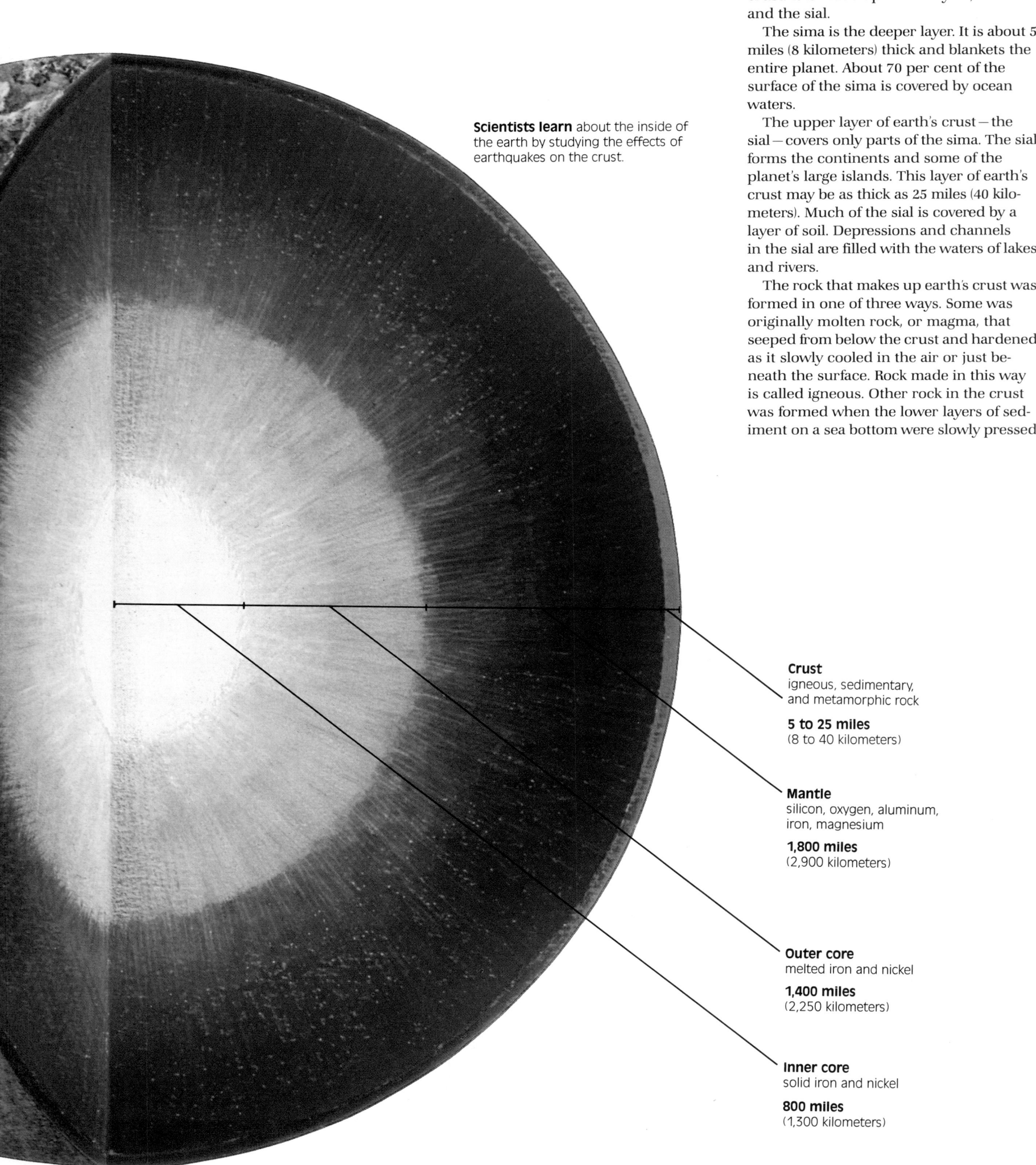

Scientists learn about the inside of the earth by studying the effects of earthquakes on the crust.

The earth is covered by a thin shell of cold, hard rock. This shell is called the crust. It is made up of two layers, the sima and the sial.

The sima is the deeper layer. It is about 5 miles (8 kilometers) thick and blankets the entire planet. About 70 per cent of the surface of the sima is covered by ocean waters.

The upper layer of earth's crust — the sial — covers only parts of the sima. The sial forms the continents and some of the planet's large islands. This layer of earth's crust may be as thick as 25 miles (40 kilometers). Much of the sial is covered by a layer of soil. Depressions and channels in the sial are filled with the waters of lakes and rivers.

The rock that makes up earth's crust was formed in one of three ways. Some was originally molten rock, or magma, that seeped from below the crust and hardened as it slowly cooled in the air or just beneath the surface. Rock made in this way is called igneous. Other rock in the crust was formed when the lower layers of sediment on a sea bottom were slowly pressed

Crust
igneous, sedimentary,
and metamorphic rock

5 to 25 miles
(8 to 40 kilometers)

Mantle
silicon, oxygen, aluminum,
iron, magnesium

1,800 miles
(2,900 kilometers)

Outer core
melted iron and nickel

1,400 miles
(2,250 kilometers)

Inner core
solid iron and nickel

800 miles
(1,300 kilometers)

together by the tremendous weight of sediment and water from above. This pressure formed the sediment into the kind of rock called sedimentary. Still other rock was formed when igneous and sedimentary rocks were changed by tremendous heat and pressure deep within earth's crust. Later, this rock was pushed to the surface. Such rock is called metamorphic.

Although much of the rock in earth's crust was formed long ago, the process of rock formation continues. Igneous rock is still formed by the cooling of magma. Sedimentary rock is still formed in shallow seas. Metamorphic rock is still pushed up from the lower layer of earth's crust.

Beneath the crust lies a layer of rock called the mantle. This layer extends to a depth of 1,800 miles (2,900 kilometers) thick. The temperatures of rock within the earth get progressively higher toward the center of the planet. The deepest part of the mantle reaches a temperature of 4000° F. (2200° C).

Beneath the mantle is the earth's outer core, which scientists believe is made of melted iron and nickel 1,400 miles (2,250 kilometers) thick. In the outer core, temperatures range from about 4000° F. (2200° C) at the upper level to about 9000° F. (5000° C) at the deepest level. Earth's magnetic field is generated by electricity in the outer core. It is the magnetic field that allows compasses to function.

At the very center of earth lies the inner core. Some scientists believe that this layer is a solid ball of iron and nickel about 800 miles (1,300 kilometers) thick. The temperature of the inner core is about 9000° F. (5000° C). Although the metal of the inner core is hot enough to be melted, the atoms of the metal are pressed together so tightly by gravity that melting is impossible.

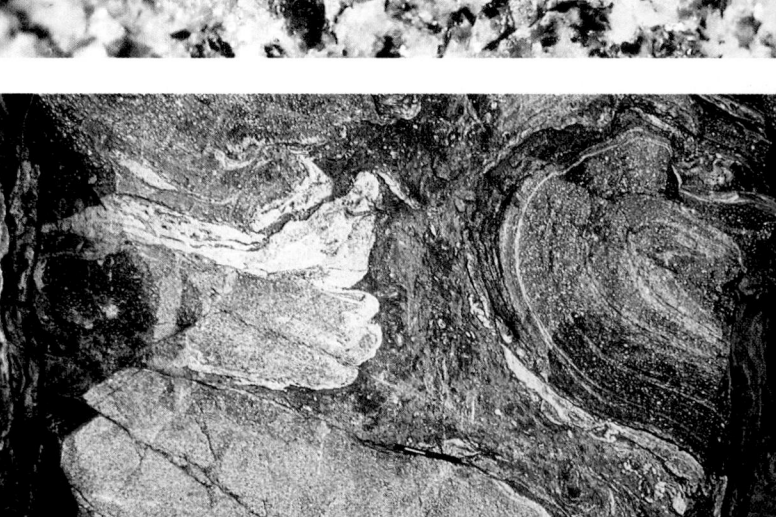

Igneous rocks are formed when melted rock deep inside the crust cools and hardens.

Metamorphic rocks are formed when igneous and sedimentary rocks are chemically and physically changed by heat and pressure.

Sedimentary rocks are developed from material worn away from the land. These rocks may contain fossils — shells, bones, and other remains of living things.

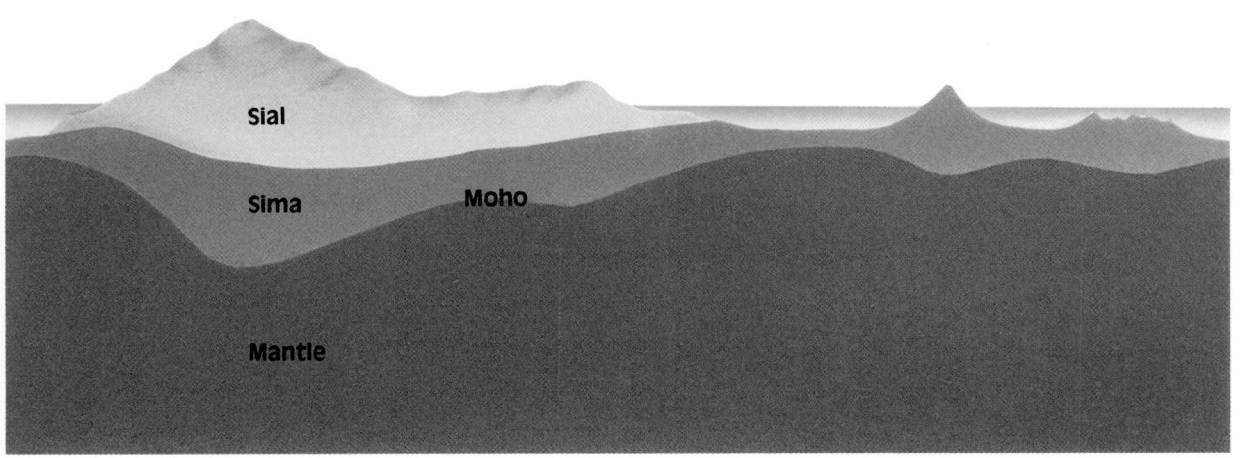

Sial

Sima   Moho

Mantle

The earth's crust has two layers — the sial, made up of granitelike rocks, and the sima, similar to hardened lava. The moho is the boundary between the crust and the mantle.

Earthquakes and Volcanoes

The earth's crust is continually changing. Most of the time, this change is so gradual that only the most sophisticated scientific equipment can detect it. But sometimes tremendous forces inside the earth unleash their power in sudden events that cause dramatic changes in the earth's surface. These events include volcanic eruptions and earthquakes.

An earthquake is the sometimes violent shaking of the earth's surface that happens as a result of the movement of the materials in the crust and mantle beneath it. The strongest earthquakes can tumble buildings, change the course of rivers, or shift parts of the ocean floor and send giant tidal waves charging across the sea. A volcano is an opening in the earth's surface where red-hot molten rock, called magma, escapes from deep inside the earth. Volcanic eruptions can create mountains and islands and cover hundreds of square miles (kilometers) with flowing lava or ash.

Most earthquakes and volcanoes occur at the boundaries between giant sections of the earth's outermost layer, called plates. These plates are in constant motion in relation to one another. They slowly glide over a zone of partially melted rock in the earth's mantle at a rate of ½ to 4 inches (1.3 to 10 centimeters) a year. Most earthquakes and volcanoes occur as a result of this movement.

Earthquakes occur along faults, which are breaks in the earth's crust. The rock that makes up the earth's crust is cold and rigid. As a result, it does not glide along smoothly as does the hot rock at deeper levels. The movement of the plates past each other combined with the resistance of the rock on each side of the fault create a build-up of stress at the fault. Eventually, the stress exceeds the rock's strength. Each side of the fault snaps to a new position to "catch up" with the plate it is attached to, and an earthquake occurs.

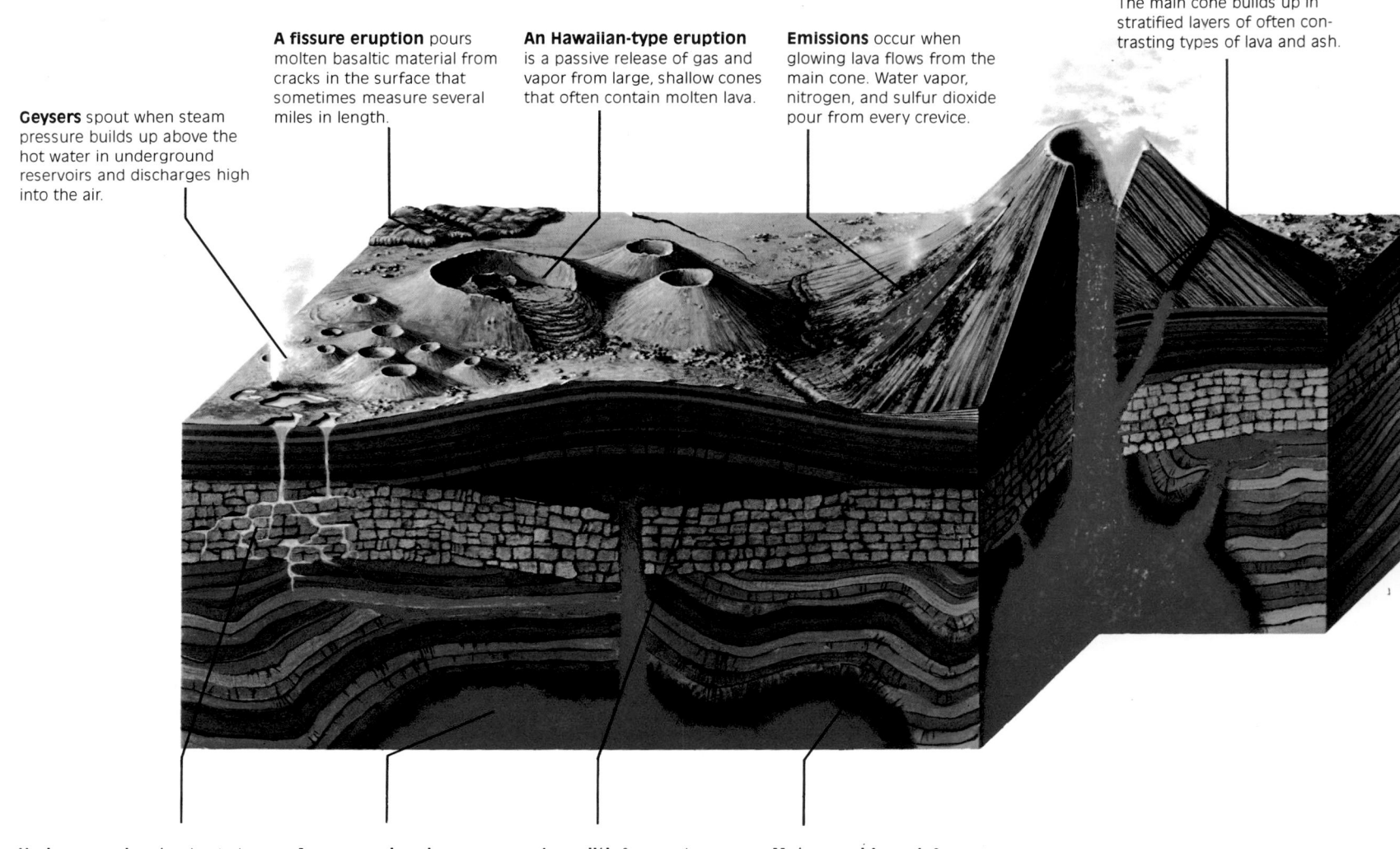

Layering is the product of millions of years of eruptions. The main cone builds up in stratified layers of often contrasting types of lava and ash.

A fissure eruption pours molten basaltic material from cracks in the surface that sometimes measure several miles in length.

An Hawaiian-type eruption is a passive release of gas and vapor from large, shallow cones that often contain molten lava.

Emissions occur when glowing lava flows from the main cone. Water vapor, nitrogen, and sulfur dioxide pour from every crevice.

Geysers spout when steam pressure builds up above the hot water in underground reservoirs and discharges high into the air.

Underground water, heated under pressure to beyond the normal boiling point, rushes out whenever pressure is relieved.

A magma chamber contains intensely hot magma under high pressure. Every volcano has one.

Laccolith forms a huge lens of cooled rock above the hot magma chamber.

Metamorphic rock forms near the magma chamber when heat and intense pressure create chemical and physical changes in sedimentary and igneous strata.

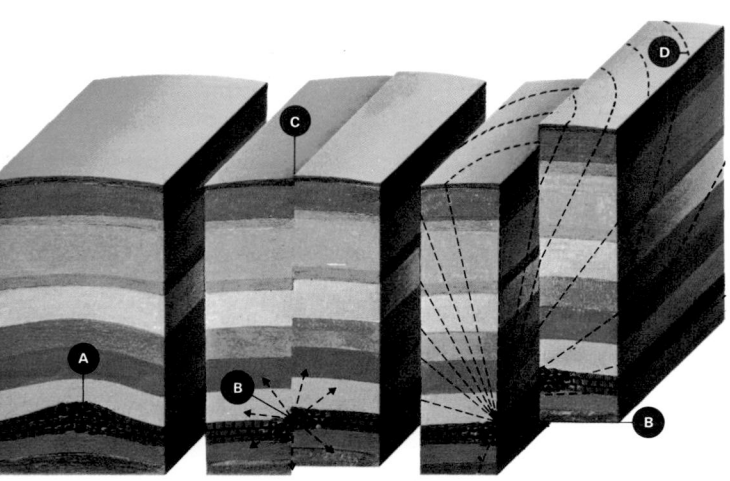

How earthquakes happen.
Stresses build over many years until the breaking strength of some part of the rock along a fault line or other line of potential movement is exceeded **(A)**. Shock waves move out in all directions **(B)**. The epicenter **(C)** is on the surface directly above the break. The most damage is done by the earthquake when the shock waves reach the surface **(D)**.

The San Andreas Fault, a major break in the earth's crust, extends more than 750 miles (1,210 kilometers) through California and produces a major quake every few hundred years.

The snapping of the rock causes vibrations called seismic waves to move out in all directions. The waves move like ripples in a pond after a stone is dropped into it. It is these waves that cause the damage to the earth's surface and to objects on it.

Earthquakes may occur at the surface of the earth or at depths of up to 400 miles (640 kilometers) below the surface. The point of an earthquake's origin is called its focus. The quake's epicenter is the place on the surface of the earth directly above the focus.

Many volcanoes form where the edge of one plate overlaps another and pushes it down into the mantle. There, portions of the plate melt to form magma and large amounts of gas. The mixture rises toward the surface and eventually collects in a magma chamber just beneath the earth's surface. The pressure of the surrounding rock forces the mixture in the magma chamber up through the surface of the earth, creating an opening called a central vent. Magma that has penetrated the earth's surface is called lava.

Lava builds up around the central vent. As the lava cools, it forms a cone-shaped volcanic mountain. Volcanic mountains can be either low and broad or tall and pointed.

Some volcanoes also form when the edges of two plates move apart from each other, allowing magma from the mantle to seep up between them. Most of this type of volcanic activity occurs on the ocean floor. The tops of some of these volcanoes become islands, such as Iceland.

A few volcanoes have developed near the center of plates far from the edges. Scientists think this happens when huge magma columns, called plumes, push up into the crust. The Hawaiian Islands were formed by this type of volcanic action, which continues today at Kilauea, a famous volcano on the island of Hawaii.

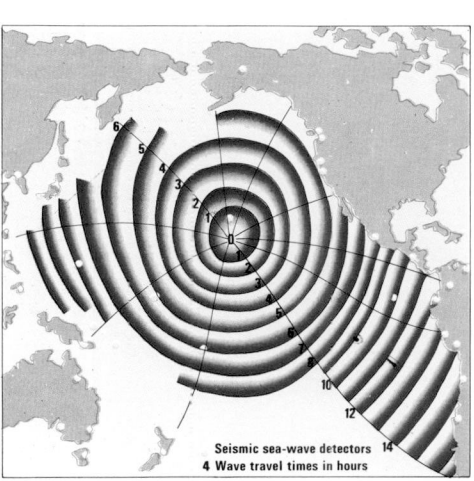

Seismographic stations throughout the Pacific watch for earthquake shocks and oceanic tidal waves that sometimes follow. Here concentric rings show the time necessary for a tidal wave to travel from the point above the earthquake's center in Hawaii.

Earth's Changing Surface

The earth's surface is constantly undergoing changes. Some changes are rapid, such as those caused by landslides, earthquakes, and volcanic eruptions. But other changes are slow and steady. Mountains are worn flat. Deep canyons are carved. Fertile lands lose their rich soil. Coastlines change shape.

One of the chief causes of the slow and steady changes in earth's surface is erosion, or the breaking down and movement of the planet's rock and soil by natural forces. A major factor in erosion is water, both in its liquid and in its solid form—ice.

Erosion begins with weathering, a process in which various environmental factors break down soil and rock and release them from earth's surface. Ice is a primary factor in weathering. Ice forms when water trapped inside the cracks of rocks freezes. As water becomes ice, it expands and can break the rock into fragments. Melting snow and rain that beats down on weathered rocks washes away billions of dust-sized particles. These bits of rock are carried into streams and rivers. As rivers move along, they tear more tiny bits of rock out of the channels through which they flow. After many thousands or millions of years, the action of flowing water can form a deep canyon or flatten a mountain.

Coastlines and lake shores are also altered by the force of water. Waves crashing against cliffs break away loose pieces of rock. The constant beating of the waves causes a crushing and grinding that breaks boulders into pebbles and pebbles into sand. In some places, the shoreline is slowly pushed back, and the sea takes its place. In other places, waves combine with wind, another major factor in erosion, to increase the land by moving sand from one location to another. This process helps build up beaches.

Wind can carry particles of earth great distances. If there are no trees or grasses to protect the land, wind may pick up tons of dry, dusty soil. This can rob farmland of rich soil. In time, the area may become almost a desert.

Wind that carries sand or sandy soil can also cause erosion in rocky places. A steady stream of wind-blown sand striking against stone can rub off or sandblast tiny particles and carry them away. Rocks that have been eroded in this way are common in many deserts.

The effects of water erosion can be as spectacular as the gooseneck canyons cut by the San Juan River in Utah.

Wind erosion: (1) parabolic blowout, (2) parabolic hairpin, (3) longitudinal ridge.

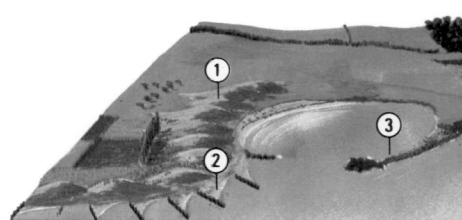

Sea erosion: (1) dunes, (2) deposition, (3) spit, (4) arch, (5) stack, (6) raised beach, (7) caves.

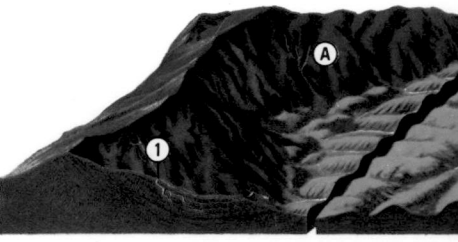

River erosion: (A) youthful stage, (B) mature stage, (C) old age stage, (1) pothole, (2) oxbow, (3) meander.

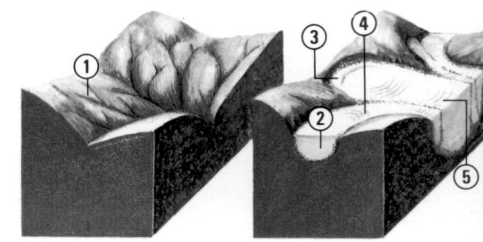

Glacial erosion: (1) preglacial rock, (2) valley, (3) bergschrund, (4) crevasses, (5) longitudinal moraine, (6) valley-floor moraines, (7) peaks and (8) valley carved by tributary, (9) terminal moraine.

Ice, in the form of glaciers, has been responsible for enormous changes on earth's surface in the past. Glaciers are huge rivers of ice that move at very slow rates and flow over anything in their paths. Some glaciers are still at work. They form when deep snow turns to ice on mountaintops. The ice, which can move slowly downward, may widen an old valley or gouge out a new one. It can also pick up and carry tons of soil or rock and deposit them hundreds of miles (kilometers) away. When a glacier melts, it can fill a depression with fresh water, thus creating a new lake. If the Antarctic icecap, which is a glacier, would melt, it could drastically raise the level of ocean waters. This would cause floods that could change the coastlines of continents.

The Australian rock formation, *above,* shows the sculptural effects of wind carrying sand and other debris.

Glaciated valleys and terraces such as those in Ortnevik, Norway, are typically formed over thousands of years.

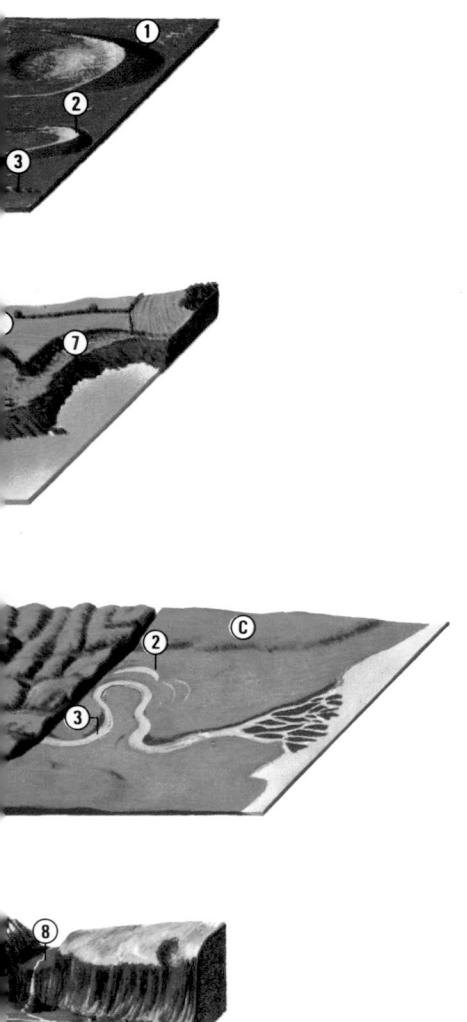

Beneath the Ocean

If all earth's ocean water would suddenly vanish, the planet would present a new landscape. There would be vast plains, slopes, deep valleys, and ranges of towering mountains never seen before. These features now lie beneath the water, forming the sea bottom.

Along the coasts of the continents, from the edges of the shores, the muddy or rocky ocean bottom slopes gently out beneath the water. This submerged land is known as the continental shelves. They are coated by thick layers of sediment that were carried to the coasts by rivers.

From the edges of the continental shelves, the ocean bottom slants downward more sharply, forming what are called the continental slopes. Deep canyons cut through the slopes in some places. Far below the surface of the water, the continental slopes merge with the abyss, or deep ocean bottom. The depth of the abyss ranges from 10,000 feet (3,040 meters) to 18,000 feet (5,486 meters). The abyssal plains are broad, almost completely flat areas that make up 30 per cent of earth's total surface. Most of the plains are covered with thick sediment.

A range of towering submarine mountains, known as the Mid-Atlantic Ridge, stretches north to south along the middle of the Atlantic Ocean bottom for 10,000 miles (16,000 kilometers). The peaks of a number of mountains in this range stick up above the water. They create islands in the Atlantic Ocean, such as the Azores

All submarine landscapes follow the same general pattern, although details vary from ocean to ocean. The layout includes a volcanic ridge, which may break the surface in places, broad abyssal plains with occasional deep trenches, and continents bordered by shallow slopes and shelves.

- **A** Volcano in midocean ridge
- **B** Deep oceanic trench
- **C** Continental shelf
- **D** Abyssal plain
- **E** Midocean ridge
- **F** Guyots
- **G** Oceanic islands
- **X1** Upper granitic crust and sediments
- **X2** Lower granitic crust
- **Y** Basaltic crust
- **S** Sediment
- **Z** Mantle

Features of the ocean floor

Aleutian Basin	B	8	Canada Plain	A	8	East Pacific Rise	E	9
Aleutian Trench	B	8	Canary Basin	C	2	Eltanin		
Angola Basin	D	3	Challenger			Fracture Zone	E	9
Arabian Basin	D	5	Fracture Zone	E	9	Emperor Seamounts	C	7
Argentine Basin	E	2	Clarion			Falkland Trough	E	2
Atlantic-Indian			Fracture Zone	C	9	Grand Banks	B	1
Basin	F	4	Clipperton			Hawaiian Ridge	C	8
Atlantic-Indian			Fracture Zone	D	9	Japan Trench	C	7
Ridge	F	4	Diamantina			Kerguelen		
Baffin Basin	A	1	Fracture Zone	E	6	Plateau	F	5
Bermuda Rise	C	1	Dogger Bank	B	3	Kermadec Trench	E	8

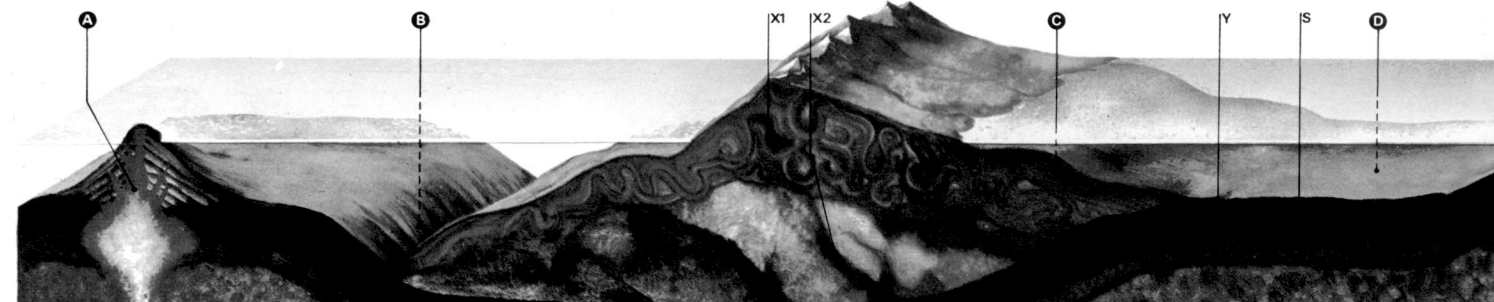
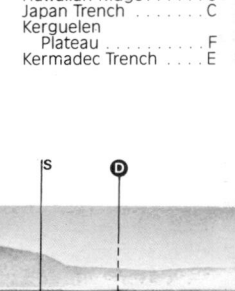

The ocean floor consists of narrow valleys, broad plains, and huge mountain ranges. Major undersea landforms are shown on the map, *below*. The map index indicates their locations.

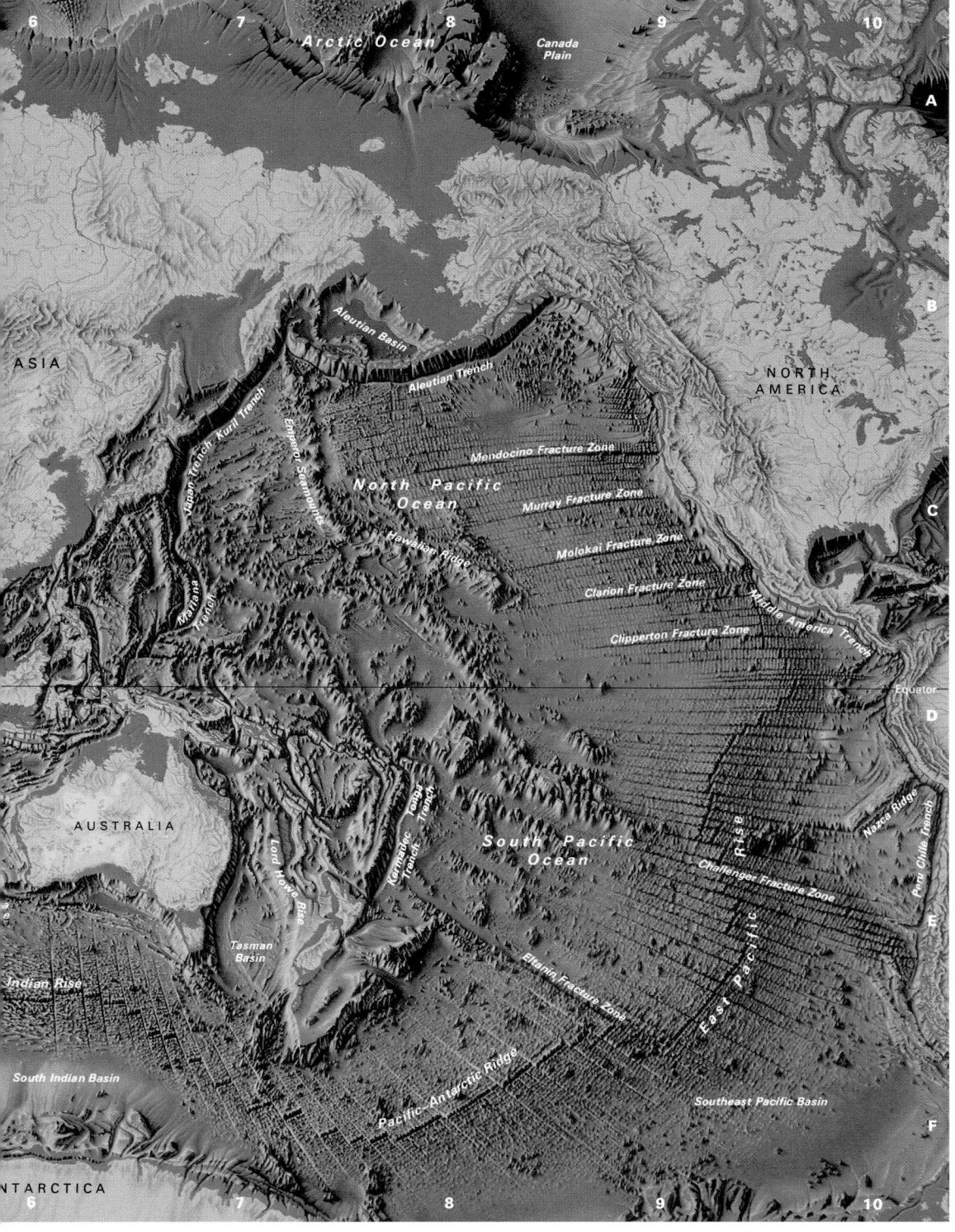

and Ascension. A continuation of the Mid-Atlantic Ridge circles the southern tip of Africa and extends beneath the Indian Ocean. Underwater mountains also extend between Australia and Antarctica, as well as beneath the Pacific Ocean to Mexico.

The deepest parts of the ocean bottom are long, narrow trenches, or valleys. These trenches are filled with sediment that is often hundreds of feet (meters) thick. The earth's deepest trench is the Mariana Trench. It is 43 miles (68.8 kilometers) wide and 1,580 miles (2,550 kilometers) long. Its bottom is 36,198 feet (11,033 meters) below the surface of the Pacific Ocean.

Many of earth's resources, such as minerals, oil, and gas, are found beneath the ocean waters. The continental shelves are particularly rich in oil. In fact, about 20 per cent of the world's oil supply comes from offshore drilling in modern or ancient river deltas. Rocks containing manganese, a mineral that is important in the production of steel, are scattered all over the ocean floor. There are large deposits of metals, among them nickel and cobalt, on some parts of the sea floor. It seems likely that additional deposits of minerals and other useful substances will be discovered beneath the sea. Exploration of the riches beneath earth's ocean water has really just begun.

Stages of a coral island are shown here from left to right. First, a volcanic peak on a submarine ridge starts to sink beneath the sea. Next, coral grows, forming a shallow saltwater lagoon. When the original island disappears, the coral continues its upward growth and fills in the lagoon. Eventually the coral atoll sinks beneath the surface. The submerged island is called a guyot.

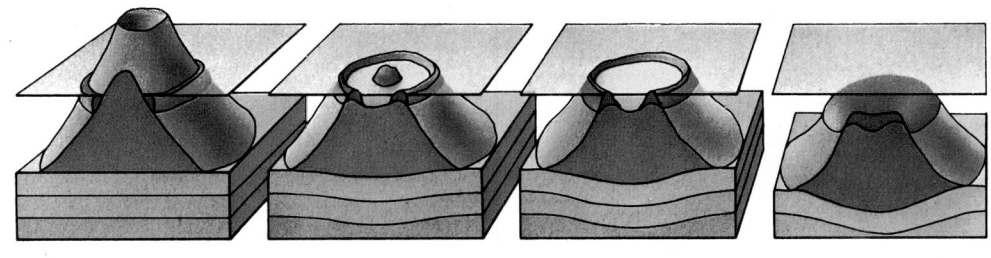

Earth's Minerals

All the rock on earth is formed of materials known as minerals. These substances are inorganic, which means they are made of matter that was never living. Some minerals such as gold are one single chemical element. Others are mixtures of elements. For example, hematite, also known as iron ore, consists of iron and oxygen.

The word "mineral" means something that is mined, or dug out of the earth. Nearly all minerals are formed inside the earth and can be removed only by mining. However, not all substances that are mined are minerals. Coal and oil are mined from the earth, but these substances are not minerals because they were formed from the remains of living things.

Atoms are incredibly tiny basic units of matter. In minerals, atoms are always arranged in repeated, three-dimensional patterns of flat surfaces and angles. These patterns of square or triangular shapes are called crystals. Its crystalline pattern determines one of the chief characteristics of a mineral—hardness. For example, a crystalline pattern formed of loosely packed atoms is softer than one formed of tightly packed atoms. Thus, some minerals, among them talc, are soft enough to be scratched by a fingernail. Other minerals, however, such as diamonds are extremely hard.

In addition to hardness, three other main characteristics of a mineral are its luster, cleavage, and color. The luster of a mineral may be shiny like metal, or it may be nonmetallic. A mineral's cleavage is the way it splits into pieces that have flat surfaces. The color of a mineral can result from its chemical composition or from chemical impurities in its crystals.

Minerals form in different ways. Many are brought into earth's crust in the hot, molten rock that seeps up from the mantle. The atoms of the various elements and compounds that make up the hot liquid are far apart and moving rapidly. As the liquid cools, the atoms slow down and come together, settling into crystalline patterns and forming minerals.

Some minerals form when hot gases erupt from volcanoes and vents in the earth's crust. The hot gases carry steam and particles of dust into the air. The gases cool suddenly when they reach the surface, and the atoms of certain elements join to form crystals that fall to the ground. Still other minerals form by the slow evaporation of water in which the minerals are dissolved. As some of the water evaporates, the atoms of mineral elements move together in the remaining waters. Finally the atoms form into their crystalline shape.

There are about 3,000 different minerals. Many are highly useful to people, and some are essential. Minerals are used in food preparation, art, manufacturing, building, agriculture, and medicine. Many countries make their coins out of the metal minerals silver and nickel. Gold is a highly valued mineral used as international currency. Other minerals form valuable gemstones such as emeralds, rubies, and sapphires.

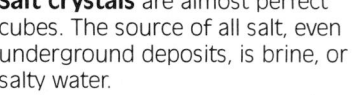

Copper, one of the world's most useful minerals, is used in products ranging from wiring for homes and machinery to pots and pans. Copper is mined throughout the world, often in large open-pit mines like the one shown here.

Salt crystals are almost perfect cubes. The source of all salt, even underground deposits, is brine, or salty water.

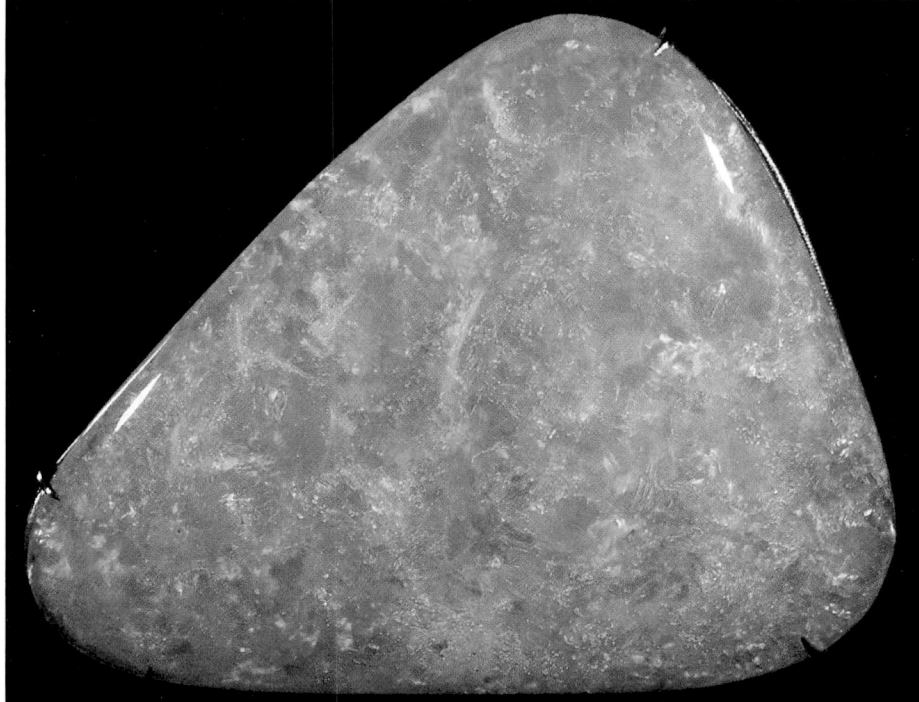

Opal is a gem made of silica that contains water. The water in an opal breaks the light that strikes it into brilliant internal colors.

An azure-blue color is characteristic of azurite, a copper mineral chiefly used as jewelry.

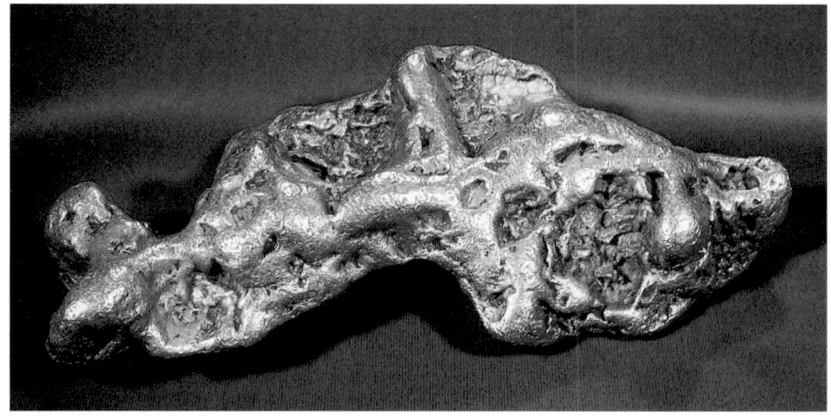

The metallic luster of gold does not tarnish. Gold, one of the first known metals, is prized for its beauty and scarcity.

Mica cleaves along specific planes — that is, it splits in one direction and forms thin sheets.

The hardest mineral is the diamond. It has a hardness of 10 on a hardness scale developed by Friedrich Mohs in 1822. A fingernail has a hardness of about 2 on the scale.

Natural vegetation in
New Mexico, U.S.

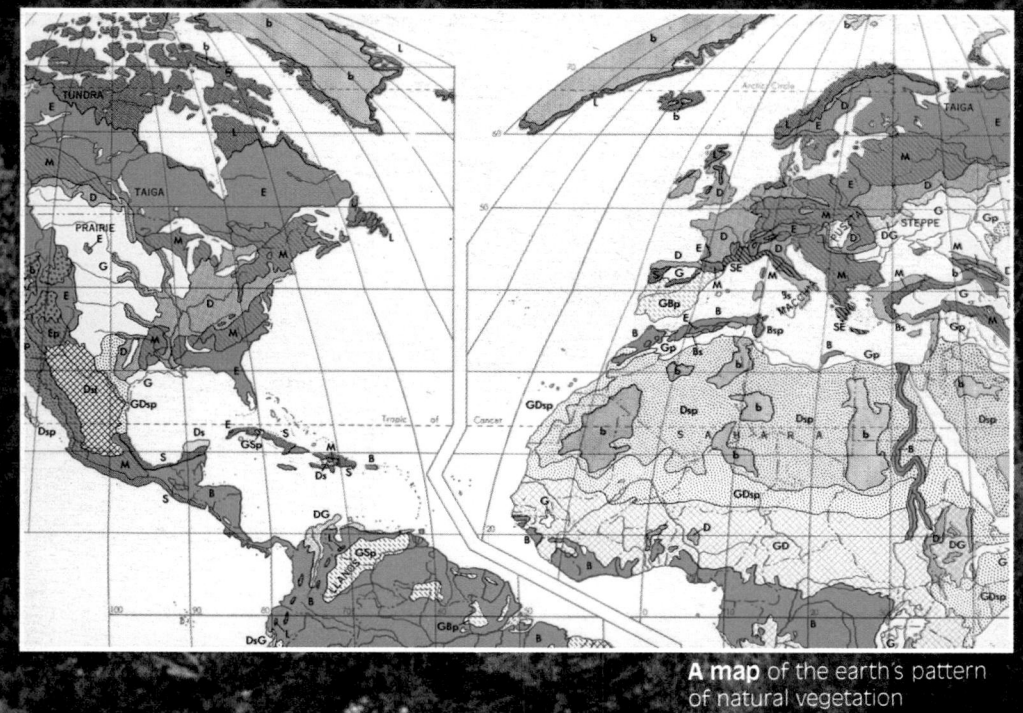

A map of the earth's pattern of natural vegetation

Natural vegetation in central Australia

Thematic Maps

THEMATIC MAPS graphically present and document information about aspects of the earth's land and its uses, and the earth's people and their cultures.

Births and Deaths

Birth and death rates are important measurements of population changes. Comparing the information in the two maps below provides an overview of the world's population growth. For example, in most of the inhabited areas of Africa, there are over 40 births for every 1,000 people every year. At the same time, although Africa's death rates are moderately high to high, they are still lower than its birth rates. Throughout the rest of the world, birth rates also remain higher than death rates. The combination of these factors shows that the world's population is growing rapidly.

The bar graphs give information on life expectancy and infant mortality in seven countries. Comparing the two graphs shows that in today's world the higher the infant mortality rate in a country, the lower the overall life expectancy.

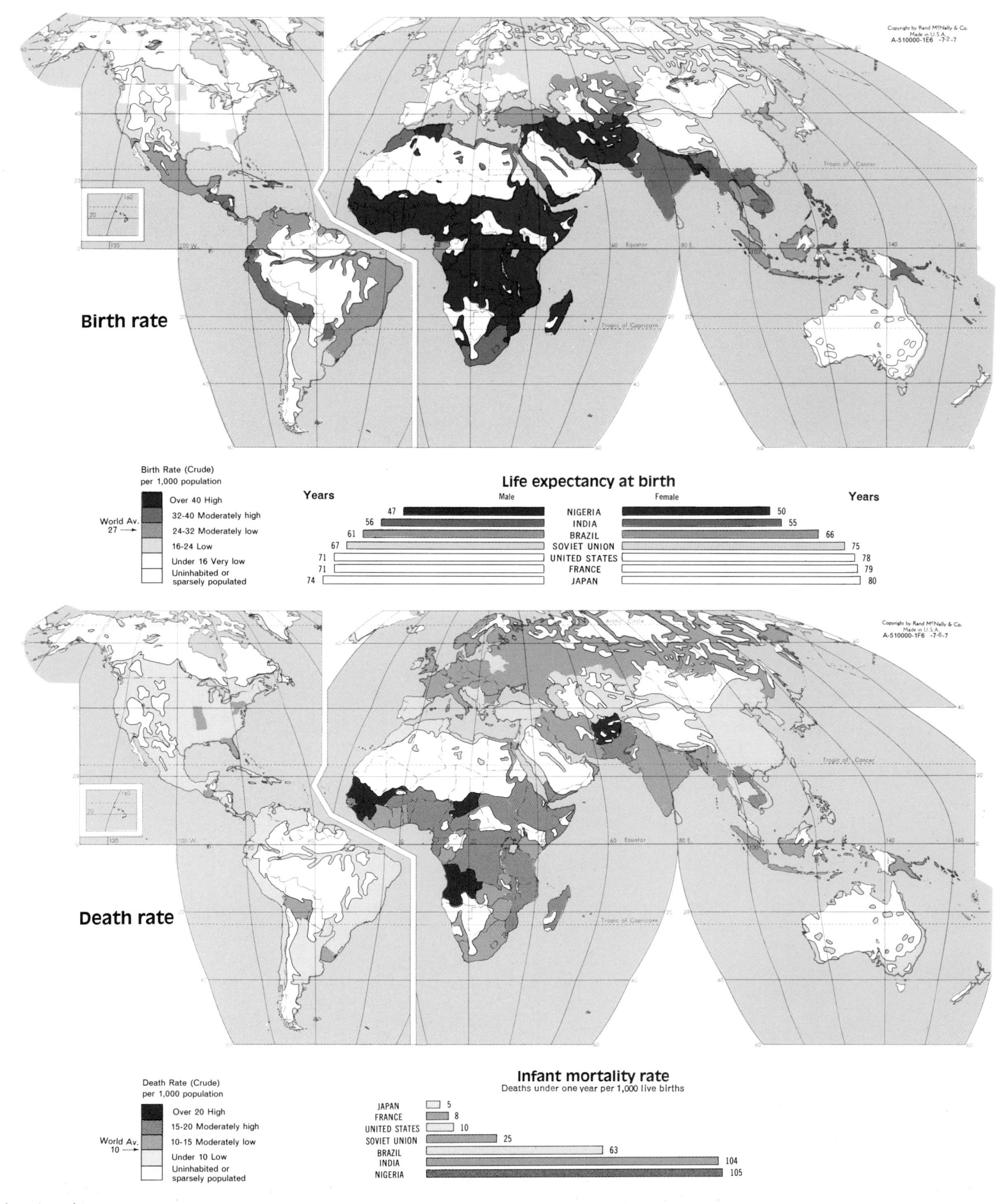

Birth rate

Birth Rate (Crude)
per 1,000 population

- Over 40 High
- 32-40 Moderately high
- 24-32 Moderately low
- 16-24 Low
- Under 16 Very low
- Uninhabited or sparsely populated

World Av. 27 →

Life expectancy at birth

Years — Male — Female — Years

	Male		Female	
NIGERIA	47		50	
INDIA	56		55	
BRAZIL	61		66	
SOVIET UNION	67		75	
UNITED STATES	71		78	
FRANCE	71		79	
JAPAN	74		80	

Death rate

Death Rate (Crude)
per 1,000 population

- Over 20 High
- 15-20 Moderately high
- 10-15 Moderately low
- Under 10 Low
- Uninhabited or sparsely populated

World Av. 10 →

Infant mortality rate
Deaths under one year per 1,000 live births

JAPAN	5
FRANCE	8
UNITED STATES	10
SOVIET UNION	25
BRAZIL	63
INDIA	104
NIGERIA	105

Economy and Literacy

The economic condition of a country is often expressed as its gross domestic product (GDP). The GDP is the total value of goods and services produced within a country each year. The colors on the map show countries' per capita GDP's in U.S. dollars. For example, countries colored dark green produce over $8,000 worth of goods and services each year for every person living there. The bar graph shows how wealth is distributed around the world.

The map at the bottom gives information on literacy rates throughout the world. Literacy is the ability to read and write. Countries that wish to grow economically place a high priority on increasing literacy among their people. Comparing the information on the two maps shows that in general, countries with high per capita GDP's also have high literacy rates.

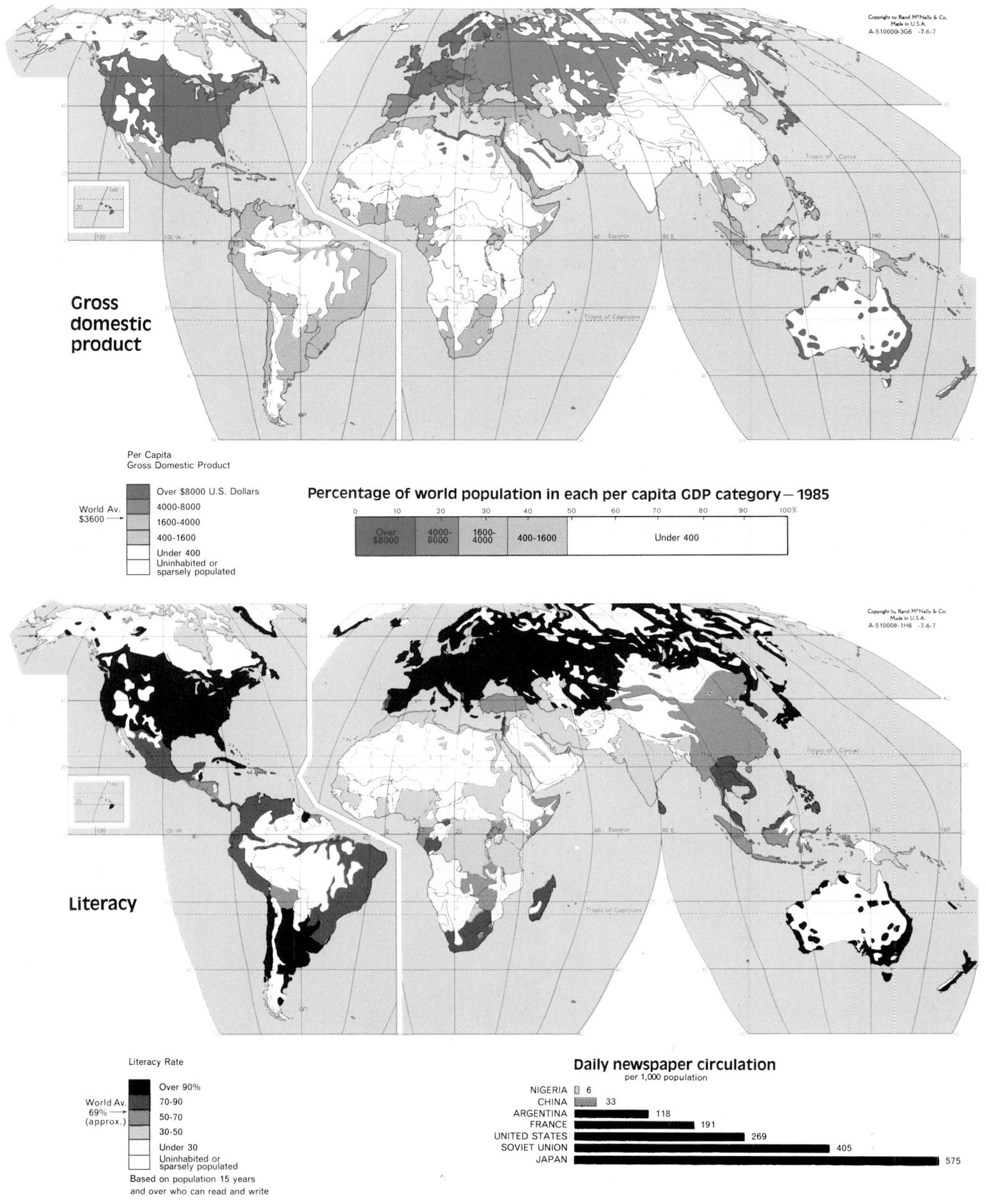

Gross domestic product

Copyright by Rand McNally & Co.
Made in U.S.A.
A-510000-3G6 -7-6-7

Per Capita
Gross Domestic Product

World Av.
$3600 →

- Over $8000 U.S. Dollars
- 4000-8000
- 1600-4000
- 400-1600
- Under 400
- Uninhabited or sparsely populated

Percentage of world population in each per capita GDP category — 1985

| 0 | 10 | 20 | 30 | 40 | 50 | 60 | 70 | 80 | 90 | 100% |

| Over $8000 | 4000-8000 | 1600-4000 | 400-1600 | Under 400 |

Literacy

Copyright by Rand McNally & Co.
Made in U.S.A.
A-510008-1H6 -7-6-7

Literacy Rate

World Av.
69%
(approx.) →

- Over 90%
- 70-90
- 50-70
- 30-50
- Under 30
- Uninhabited or sparsely populated

Based on population 15 years and over who can read and write

Daily newspaper circulation
per 1,000 population

NIGERIA	6
CHINA	33
ARGENTINA	118
FRANCE	191
UNITED STATES	269
SOVIET UNION	405
JAPAN	575

69

Temperature

In these maps, color is used to present general information about the temperatures in different parts of the world at different times of the year. As you can see from the map below, there are few parts of the earth where the temperature is always mild. The greatest swings in temperature are found in northeastern Siberia, where highs and lows may vary by more than 190°F. (106° C).

Surface temperature regions

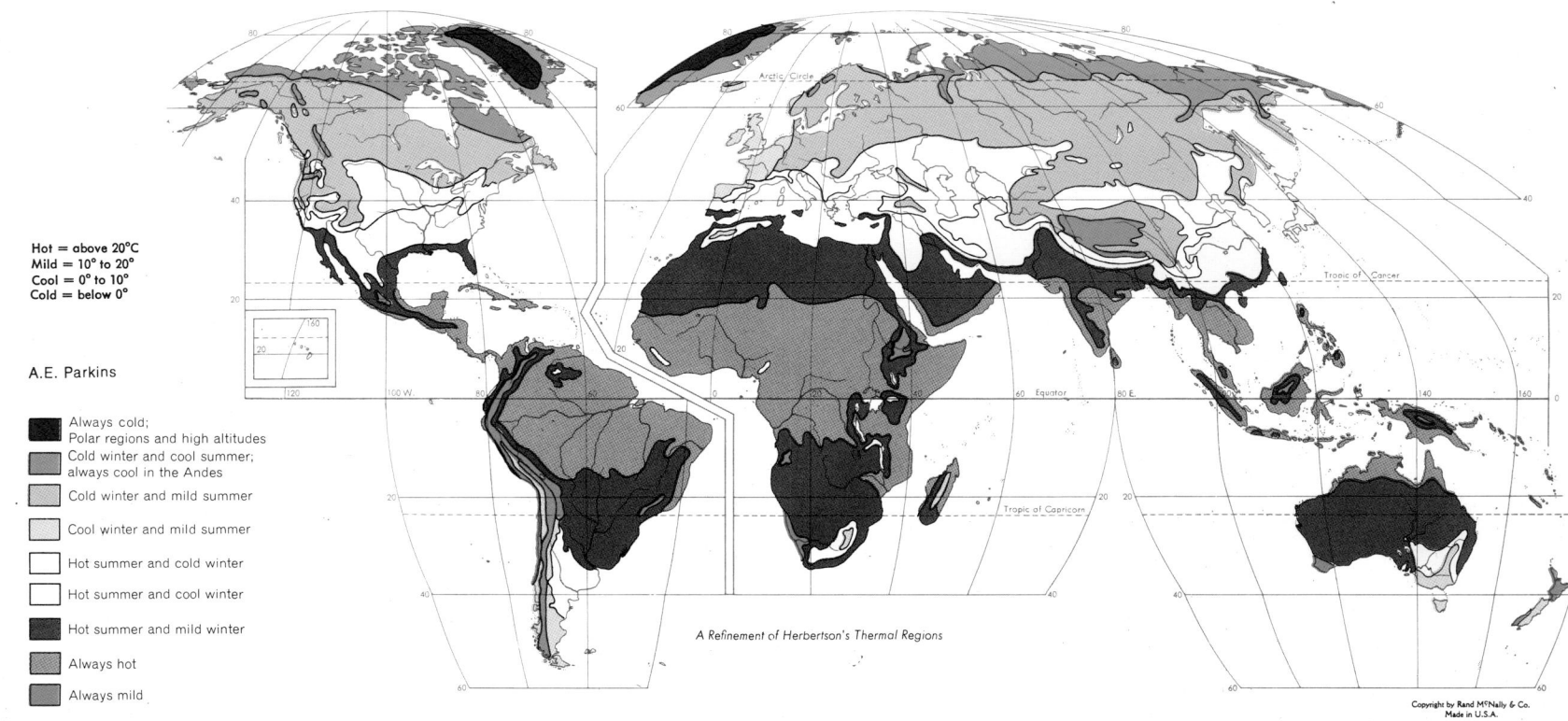

Hot = above 20°C
Mild = 10° to 20°
Cool = 0° to 10°
Cold = below 0°

A.E. Parkins

- Always cold;
  Polar regions and high altitudes
- Cold winter and cool summer;
  always cool in the Andes
- Cold winter and mild summer
- Cool winter and mild summer
- Hot summer and cold winter
- Hot summer and cool winter
- Hot summer and mild winter
- Always hot
- Always mild

A Refinement of Herbertson's Thermal Regions

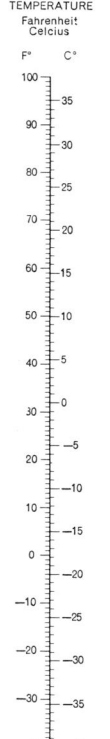

COMPARATIVE
TEMPERATURE
Fahrenheit
Celcius

F°   C°

The temperature of a region is determined by the total amount of sunlight that it receives. Temperature greatly affects a region's weather.

January normal temperature

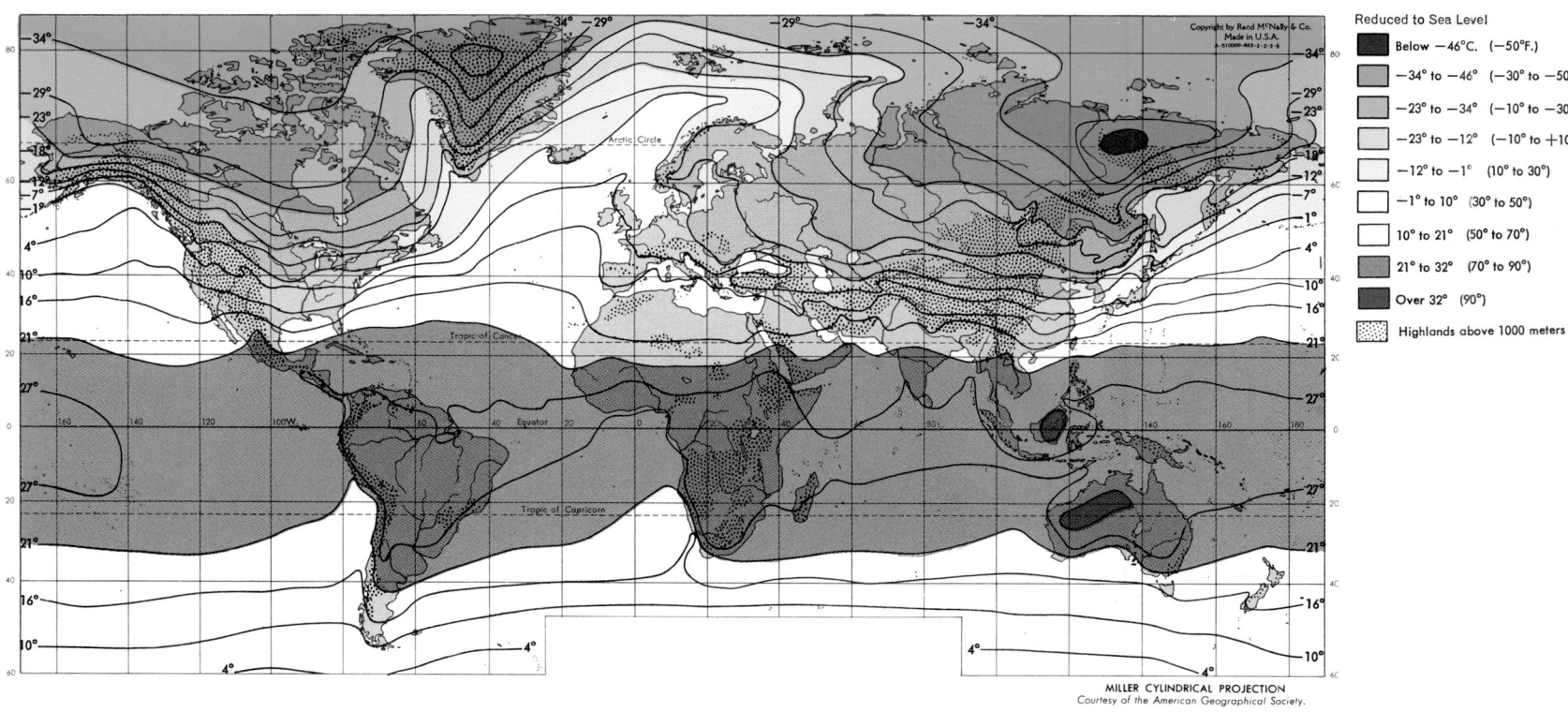

Reduced to Sea Level

- Below −46°C. (−50°F.)
- −34° to −46° (−30° to −50°)
- −23° to −34° (−10° to −30°)
- −23° to −12° (−10° to +10°)
- −12° to −1° (10° to 30°)
- −1° to 10° (30° to 50°)
- 10° to 21° (50° to 70°)
- 21° to 32° (70° to 90°)
- Over 32° (90°)
- Highlands above 1000 meters

MILLER CYLINDRICAL PROJECTION
Courtesy of the American Geographical Society.

July normal temperature

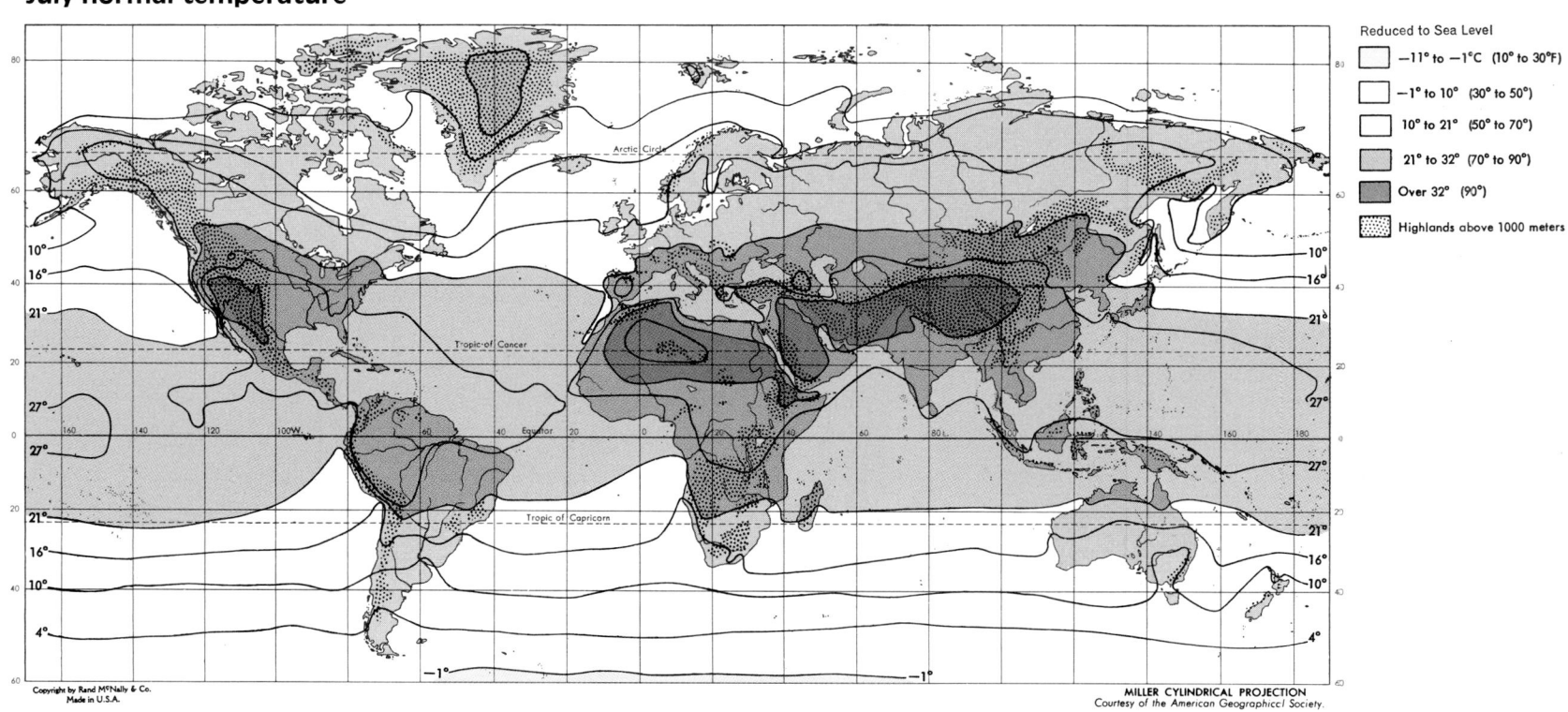

Reduced to Sea Level

- −11° to −1°C (10° to 30°F.)
- −1° to 10° (30° to 50°)
- 10° to 21° (50° to 70°)
- 21° to 32° (70° to 90°)
- Over 32° (90°)
- Highlands above 1000 meters

MILLER CYLINDRICAL PROJECTION
Courtesy of the American Geographical Society.

Normal annual range of temperature

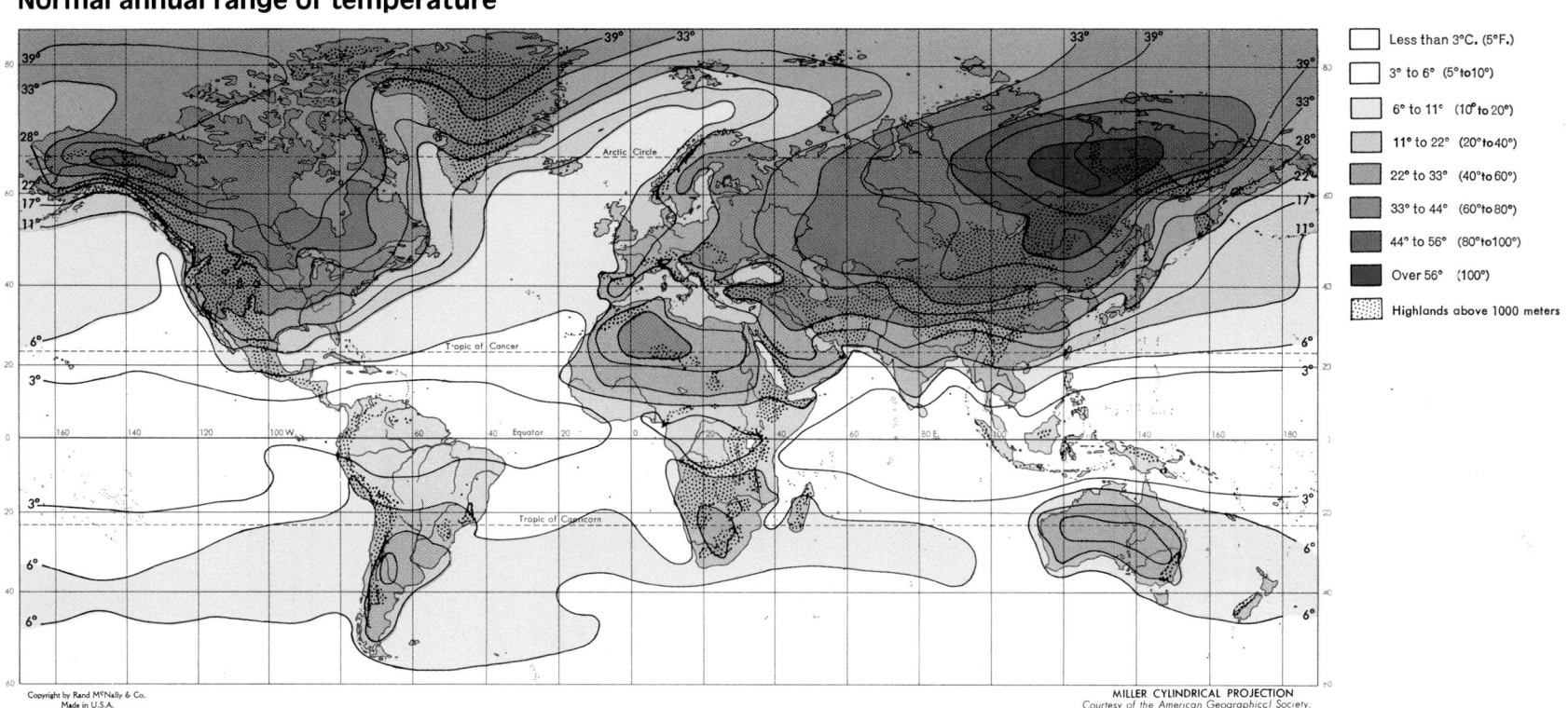

- Less than 3°C. (5°F.)
- 3° to 6° (5° to 10°)
- 6° to 11° (10° to 20°)
- 11° to 22° (20° to 40°)
- 22° to 33° (40° to 60°)
- 33° to 44° (60° to 80°)
- 44° to 56° (80° to 100°)
- Over 56° (100°)
- Highlands above 1000 meters

MILLER CYLINDRICAL PROJECTION
Courtesy of the American Geographical Society.

Precipitation, Atmospheric Pressure, and Winds

The precipitation maps on these pages show the amount of moisture—in the form of hail, rain, sleet, or snow—that falls in an area during a certain part of the year. Tan areas on the map are regions that get less than 5 inches (12.5 centimeters) of precipitation per year. Areas of extremely heavy rainfall—shown in blue and green—lie around the equator.

The maps at the bottom provide information on air pressure and predominant winds in January and July. Air pressure is the force of the atmosphere pressing on the earth. A high-pressure area has cool temperatures and relatively high atmospheric force. Skies tend to be clear. In a low-pressure area, the temperature is high and the force of the atmosphere is relatively

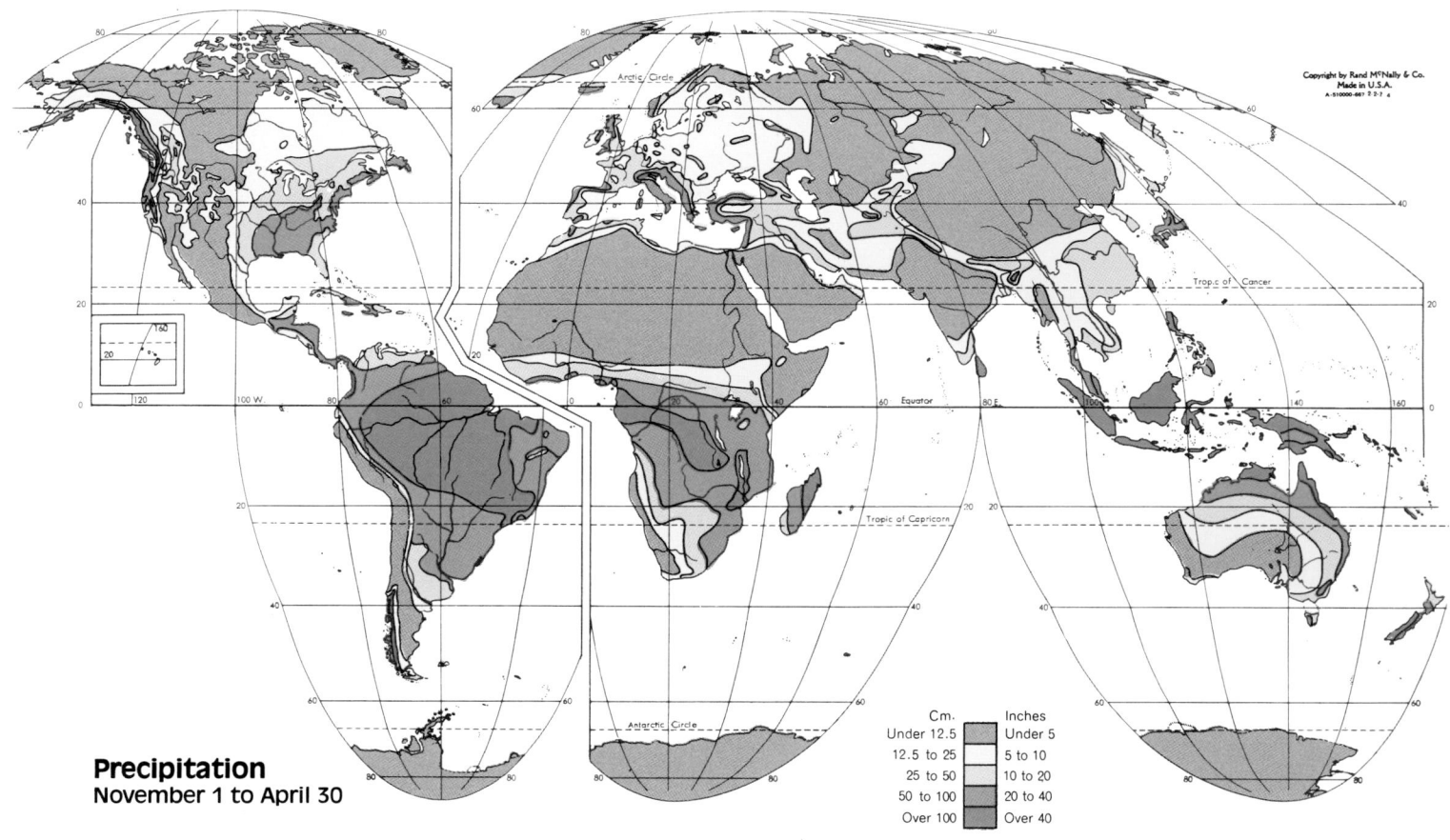

Precipitation
November 1 to April 30

Cm.	Inches
Under 12.5	Under 5
12.5 to 25	5 to 10
25 to 50	10 to 20
50 to 100	20 to 40
Over 100	Over 40

January pressure and predominant winds

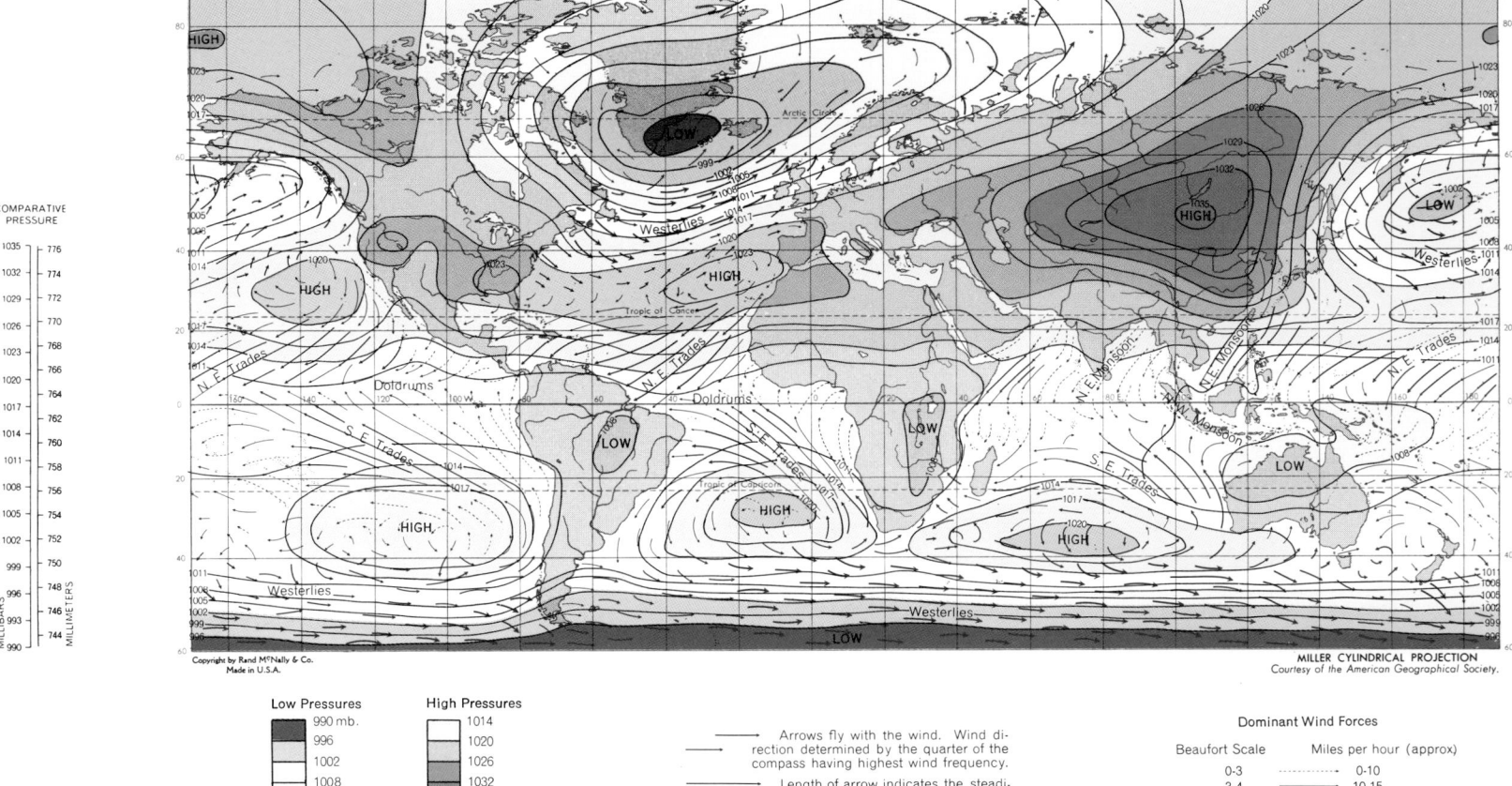

MILLER CYLINDRICAL PROJECTION
Courtesy of the American Geographical Society.

Low Pressures	High Pressures
990 mb.	1014
996	1020
1002	1026
1008	1032
1014	1038

Isobars on map at intervals of 3 millibars

Arrows fly with the wind. Wind direction determined by the quarter of the compass having highest wind frequency.

Length of arrow indicates the steadiness of the wind. Thickness of shaft indicates wind force.

Dominant Wind Forces

Beaufort Scale	Miles per hour (approx)
0-3	0-10
3-4	10-15
4-5½	15-25
Over 5½	Over 25

low. Skies tend to be cloudy, and storms are frequent.

Arrows on the map give information on winds. The longer the arrow, the steadier the wind; the thicker the arrow, the stronger the wind. Winds flow from high- to low-pressure areas. In the Northern Hemisphere, they move clockwise around a high and counterclockwise around a low. In the Southern Hemisphere, the opposite is true.

A hurricane's rain clouds swirl around the eye, a calm area in the center of the storm.

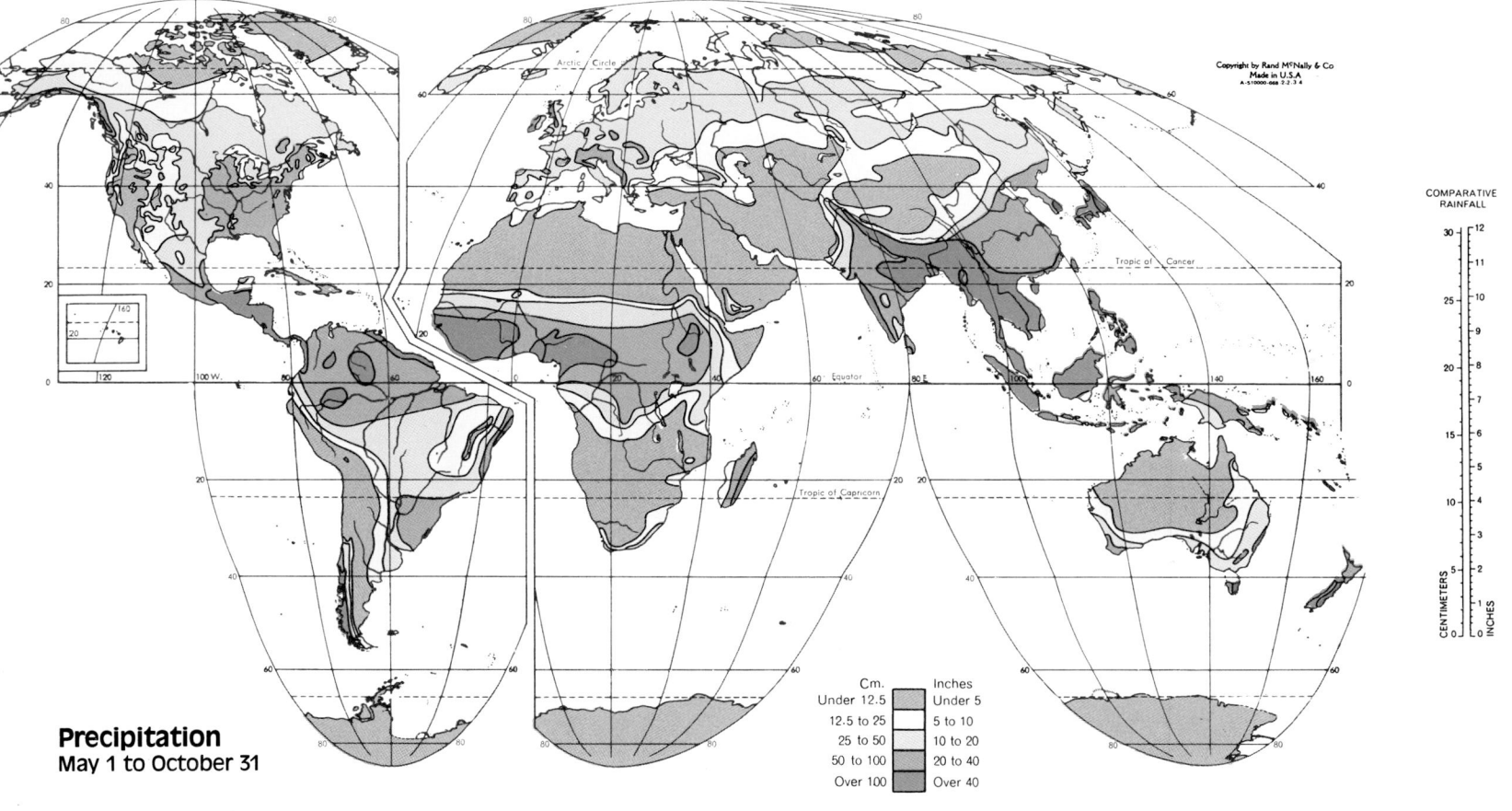

Precipitation
May 1 to October 31

Cm.	Inches
Under 12.5	Under 5
12.5 to 25	5 to 10
25 to 50	10 to 20
50 to 100	20 to 40
Over 100	Over 40

COMPARATIVE RAINFALL

July pressure and predominant winds

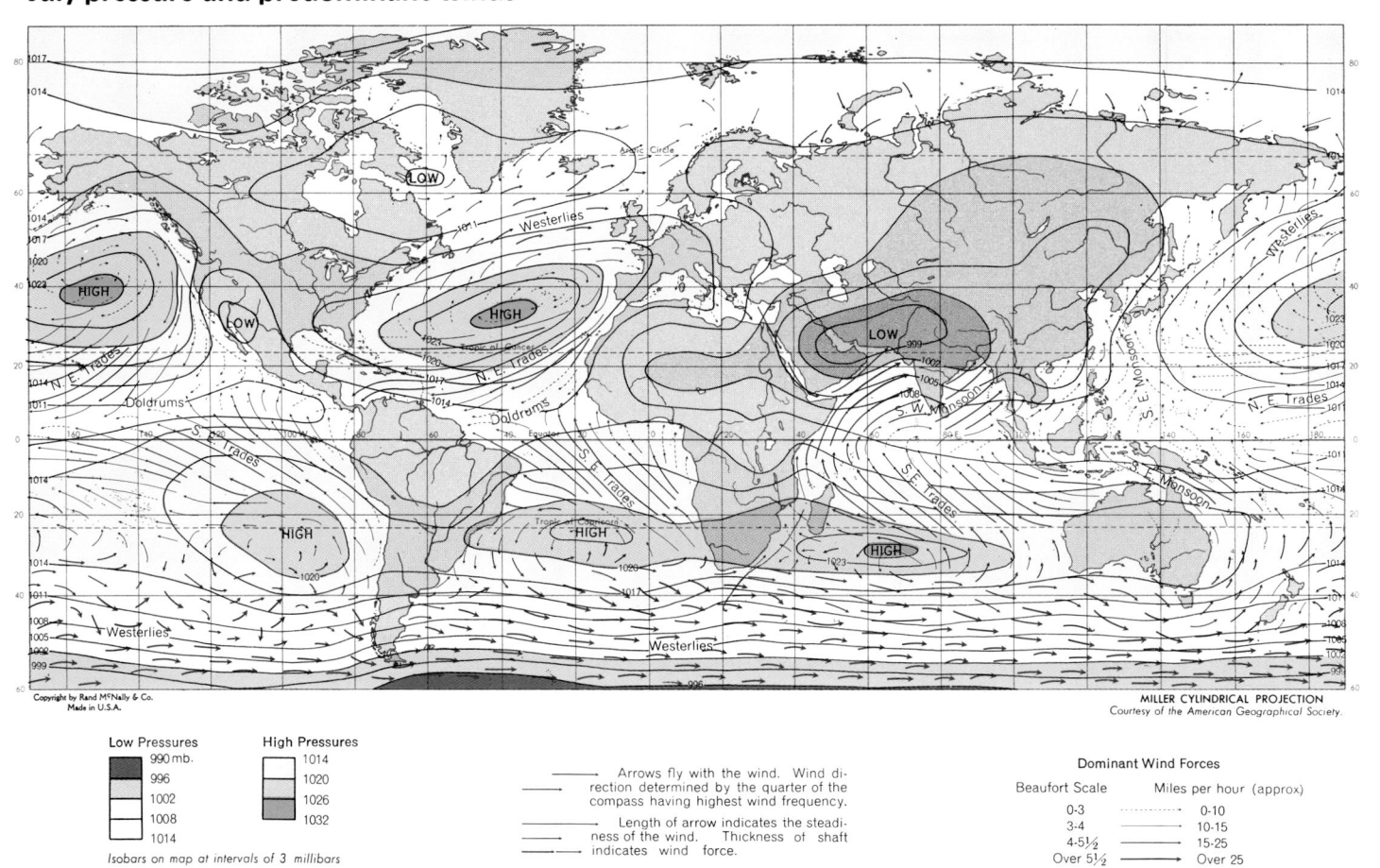

MILLER CYLINDRICAL PROJECTION
Courtesy of the American Geographical Society.

Low Pressures	High Pressures
990 mb.	1014
996	1020
1002	1026
1008	1032
1014	

Isobars on map at intervals of 3 millibars

Arrows fly with the wind. Wind direction determined by the quarter of the compass having highest wind frequency.

Length of arrow indicates the steadiness of the wind. Thickness of shaft indicates wind force.

Dominant Wind Forces

Beaufort Scale	Miles per hour (approx)
0-3	0-10
3-4	10-15
4-5½	15-25
Over 5½	Over 25

Climatic Regions

Interaction of temperature, winds, precipitation, and other forces create climates of the earth. Magenta and pink areas on this map show that most of the earth's hottest, wettest areas lie along the equator. More specific information about weather conditions is expressed by combinations of letters and colors. For example, "Caf" on light green indicates a subtropical climate in which the warmest month is above 71.6° F. (22° C), the coolest month is between 32° F. (0° C) and 64.4° F. (18° C), and rain falls throughout the year.

The graphs below provide a quick snapshot of the yearly weather at different places throughout the world. The colors and letter codes on the graphs correspond to those on the map. For example, Aswan, Egypt, gets no measurable rainfall, and the temperature is almost always hot. On the map, gold areas labeled "BWh" have similar climates. Dublin, Ireland, on the other hand, receives at least 2 inches (5 centimeters) of moisture per month, and the temperature is always moderate. Much of northern and central Europe has a similar climate.

Glenn T. Trewartha
The scheme of classification is modified and simplified from Köppen.

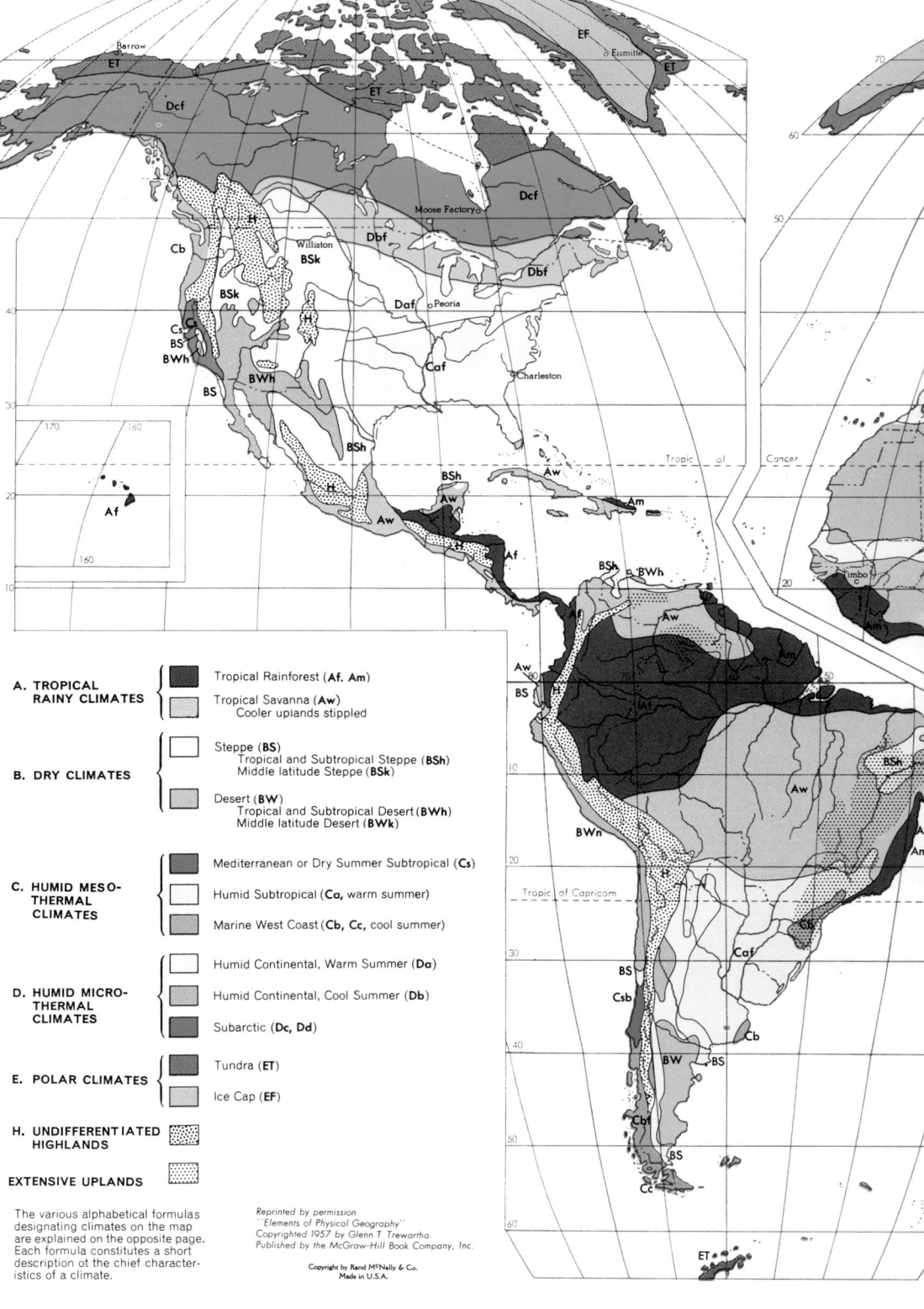

A. TROPICAL RAINY CLIMATES
- Tropical Rainforest (**Af, Am**)
- Tropical Savanna (**Aw**) Cooler uplands stippled

B. DRY CLIMATES
- Steppe (**BS**) Tropical and Subtropical Steppe (**BSh**) Middle latitude Steppe (**BSk**)
- Desert (**BW**) Tropical and Subtropical Desert (**BWh**) Middle latitude Desert (**BWk**)

C. HUMID MESO-THERMAL CLIMATES
- Mediterranean or Dry Summer Subtropical (**Cs**)
- Humid Subtropical (**Ca,** warm summer)
- Marine West Coast (**Cb, Cc,** cool summer)

D. HUMID MICRO-THERMAL CLIMATES
- Humid Continental, Warm Summer (**Da**)
- Humid Continental, Cool Summer (**Db**)
- Subarctic (**Dc, Dd**)

E. POLAR CLIMATES
- Tundra (**ET**)
- Ice Cap (**EF**)

H. UNDIFFERENTIATED HIGHLANDS

EXTENSIVE UPLANDS

The various alphabetical formulas designating climates on the map are explained on the opposite page. Each formula constitutes a short description of the chief characteristics of a climate.

Reprinted by permission.
"Elements of Physical Geography"
Copyrighted 1957 by Glenn T. Trewartha.
Published by the McGraw-Hill Book Company, Inc.

Copyright by Rand McNally & Co.
Made in U.S.A.

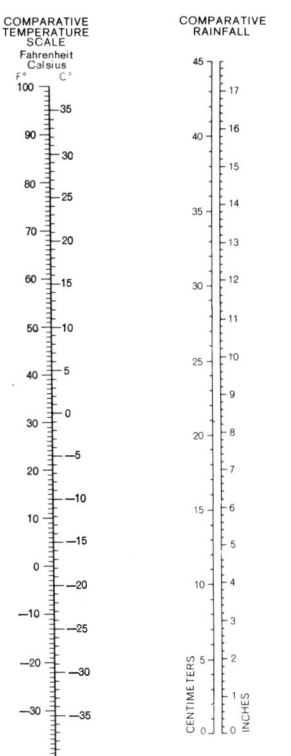

COMPARATIVE TEMPERATURE SCALE
Fahrenheit Celsius

COMPARATIVE RAINFALL

CURVES SHOW FAHRENHEIT TEMPERATURE
VERTICAL BARS SHOW RAINFALL IN INCHES

Af	Aw	BShs	BSk	BWh	BWk
SINGAPORE	TIMBO	BANGHĀZĪ	WILLISTON	ASWĀN	ASTRAKHAN
Tropical rainforest climate	Tropical savanna climate; with wet and dry seasons	Tropical and subtropical steppe climate	Middle latitude steppe climate	Tropical and subtropical desert climate	Middle latitude desert climate

The climate of a given region has a great effect on people's life style. Climate helps determine the kinds of crops that grow, the kinds of housing in which people live, and the kinds of clothes that are worn.

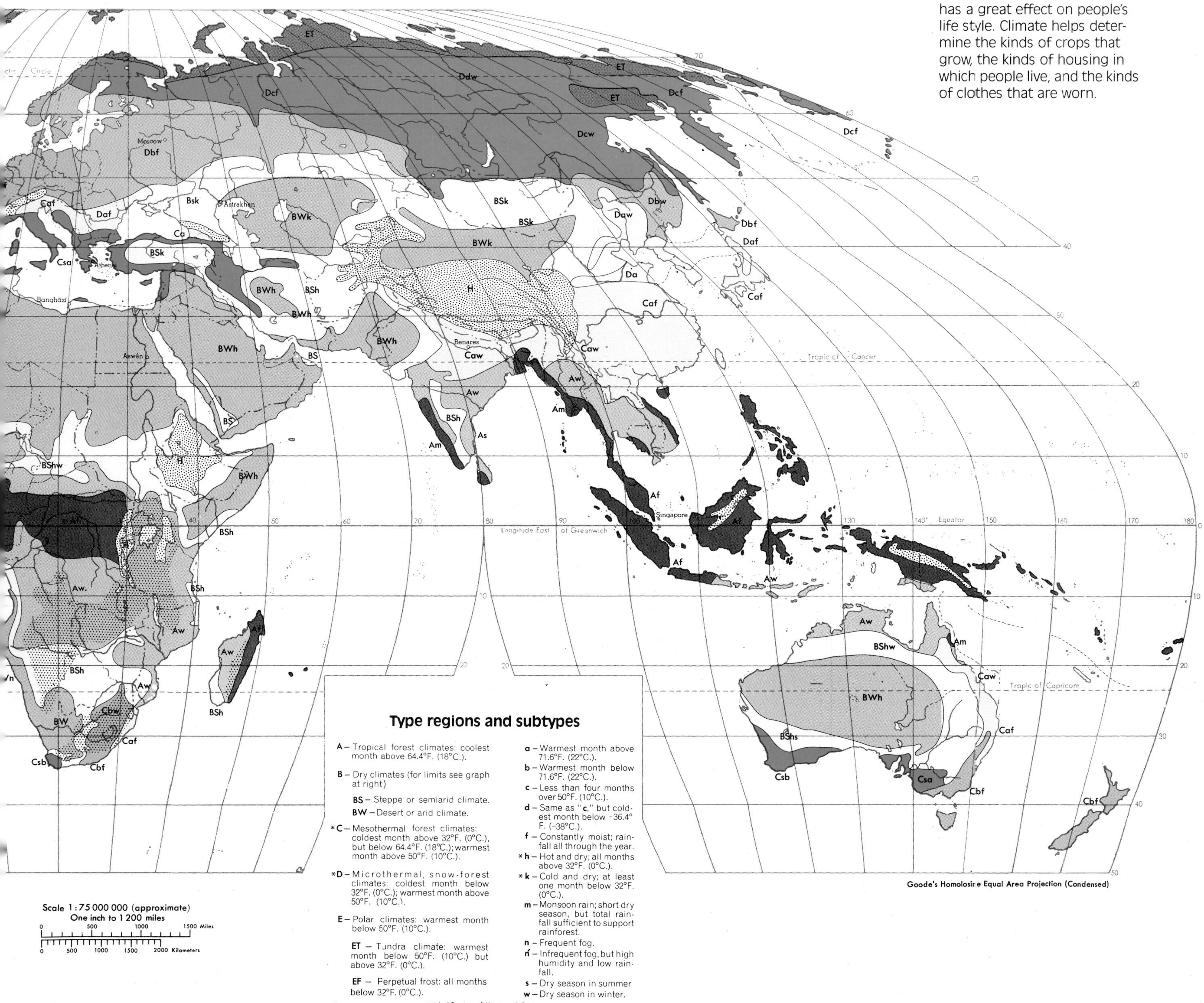

Type regions and subtypes

A – Tropical forest climates: coolest month above 64.4°F. (18°C.).

B – Dry climates (for limits see graph at right)

    BS – Steppe or semiarid climate.

    BW – Desert or arid climate.

***C** – Mesothermal forest climates: coldest month above 32°F. (0°C.), but below 64.4°F. (18°C.); warmest month above 50°F. (10°C.).

***D** – Microthermal, snow-forest climates: coldest month below 32°F. (0°C.); warmest month above 50°F. (10°C.).

E – Polar climates: warmest month below 50°F. (10°C.).

    ET – Tundra climate: warmest month below 50°F. (10°C.) but above 32°F.

    EF – Perpetual frost: all months below 32°F. (0°C.).

a – Warmest month above 71.6°F. (22°C.).

b – Warmest month below 71.6°F. (22°C.).

c – Less than four months over 50°F. (10°C.).

d – Same as "**c**," but coldest month below −36.4° F. (−38°C.).

f – Constantly moist; rainfall all through the year.

***h** – Hot and dry; all months above 32°F. (0°C.).

***k** – Cold and dry; at least one month below 32°F. (0°C.).

m – Monsoon rain; short dry season, but total rainfall sufficient to support rainforest.

n – Frequent fog.

n′ – Infrequent fog, but high humidity and low rainfall.

s – Dry season in summer

w – Dry season in winter.

* *Modification of Köppen definition*

Scale 1:75 000 000 (approximate)
One inch to 1 200 miles

Goode's Homolosine Equal Area Projection (Condensed)

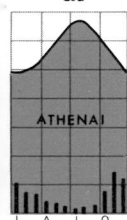
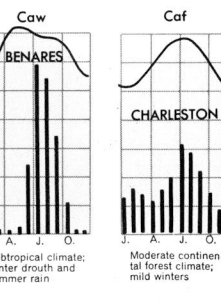
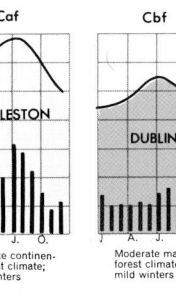
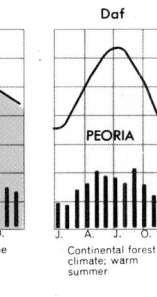
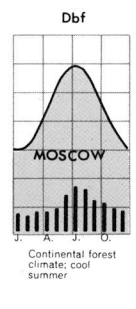
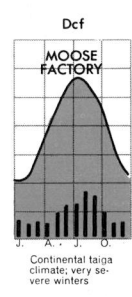
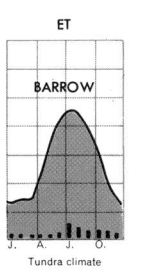
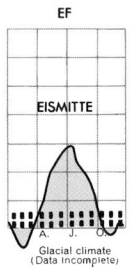

Csa	Caw	Caf	Cbf	Daf	Dbf	Dcf	ET	EF
ATHENAI	BENARES	CHARLESTON	DUBLIN	PEORIA	MOSCOW	MOOSE FACTORY	BARROW	EISMITTE
Mild climate; summer drouth and winter rain	Subtropical climate; winter drouth and summer rain	Moderate continental forest climate; mild winters	Moderate marine forest climate; mild winters	Continental forest climate; warm summer	Continental forest climate; cool summer	Continental taiga climate; very severe winters	Tundra climate	Glacial climate (Data incomplete)

Natural Vegetation

This map focuses on natural vegetation, found everywhere on earth except in the extreme Arctic and Antarctic regions. Areas of tundra are shown in purple on the map, indicating that the vegetation there consists of small herbaceous, or soft-stemmed, plants and no grass. Blue and green expanses south of the tundra are evergreen forests called taiga. Grasslands, generally shown in shades of yellow on this map, are another domi-

nant form of vegetation. Semiarid grasslands, including the short-grass prairies of western Canada and the Western United States, the Pampa of Argentina, and the eastern steppe of the Soviet Union, are well suited to grazing livestock. The prairies of midwestern Canada and the U.S. Midwest, and the western steppe in the Soviet Union receive enough moisture to allow farmers to grow crops.

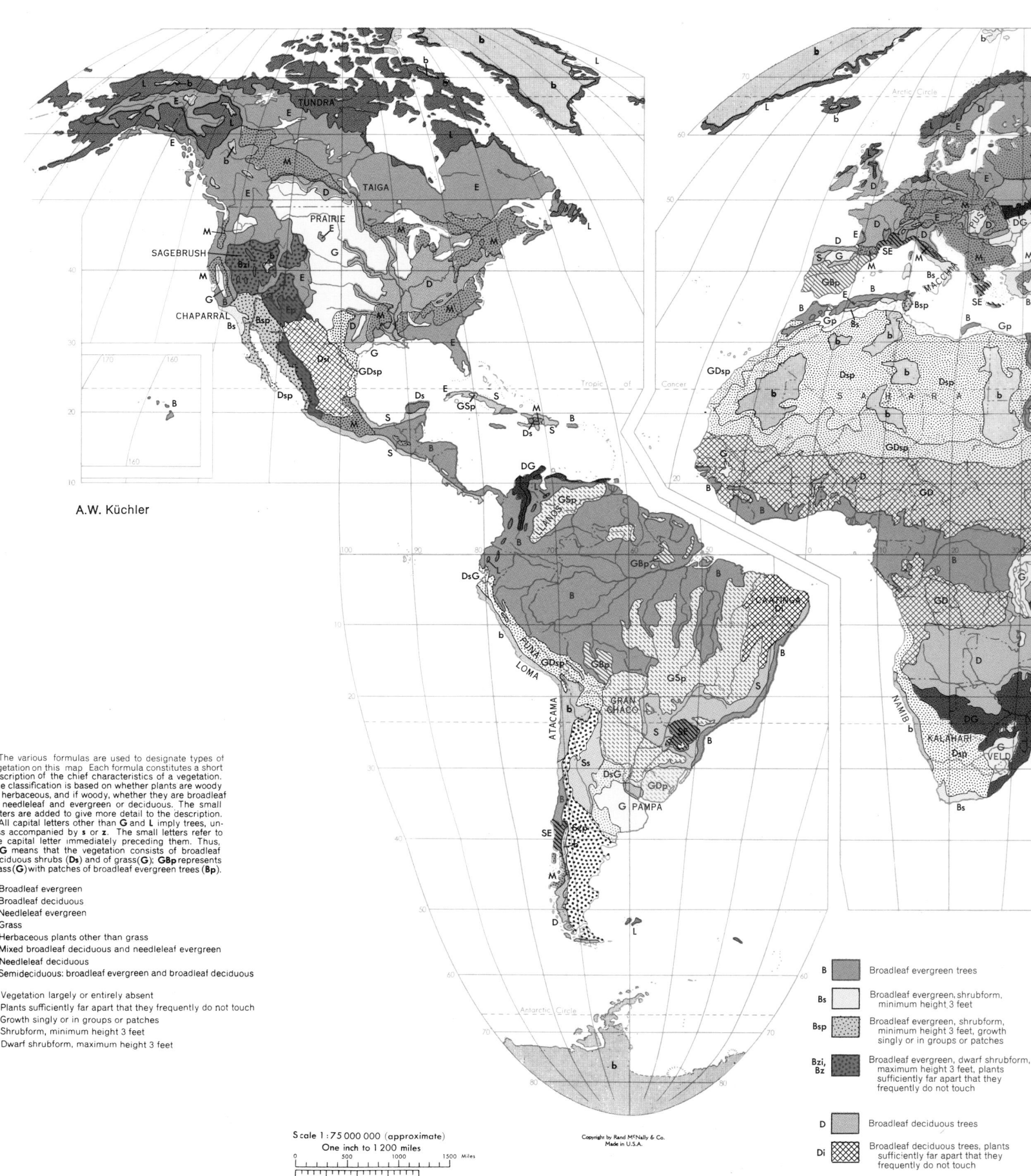

A.W. Küchler

The various formulas are used to designate types of vegetation on this map. Each formula constitutes a short description of the chief characteristics of a vegetation. The classification is based on whether plants are woody or herbaceous, and if woody, whether they are broadleaf or needleleaf and evergreen or deciduous. The small letters are added to give more detail to the description.

All capital letters other than **G** and **L** imply trees, unless accompanied by **s** or **z**. The small letters refer to the capital letter immediately preceding them. Thus, **DsG** means that the vegetation consists of broadleaf deciduous shrubs (**Ds**) and of grass(**G**); **GBp** represents grass(**G**) with patches of broadleaf evergreen trees (**Bp**).

B – Broadleaf evergreen
D – Broadleaf deciduous
E – Needleleaf evergreen
G – Grass
L – Herbaceous plants other than grass
M – Mixed broadleaf deciduous and needleleaf evergreen
N – Needleleaf deciduous
S – Semideciduous: broadleaf evergreen and broadleaf deciduous

b – Vegetation largely or entirely absent
i – Plants sufficiently far apart that they frequently do not touch
p – Growth singly or in groups or patches
s – Shrubform, minimum height 3 feet
z – Dwarf shrubform, maximum height 3 feet

B	Broadleaf evergreen trees
Bs	Broadleaf evergreen, shrubform, minimum height 3 feet
Bsp	Broadleaf evergreen, shrubform, minimum height 3 feet, growth singly or in groups or patches
Bzi, Bz	Broadleaf evergreen, dwarf shrubform, maximum height 3 feet, plants sufficiently far apart that they frequently do not touch
D	Broadleaf deciduous trees
Di	Broadleaf deciduous trees, plants sufficiently far apart that they frequently do not touch

Scale 1:75 000 000 (approximate)
One inch to 1 200 miles

0   500   1000   1500 Miles

0   500   1000   1500   2000 Kilometers

The Australian outback is dry most of the year and comes to life only after a heavy rain.

Broadleaf deciduous trees are the prevailing natural vegetation in much of Great Britain. Here, sunlight filters through the trees in Simonshyde Wood, Saint Albans.

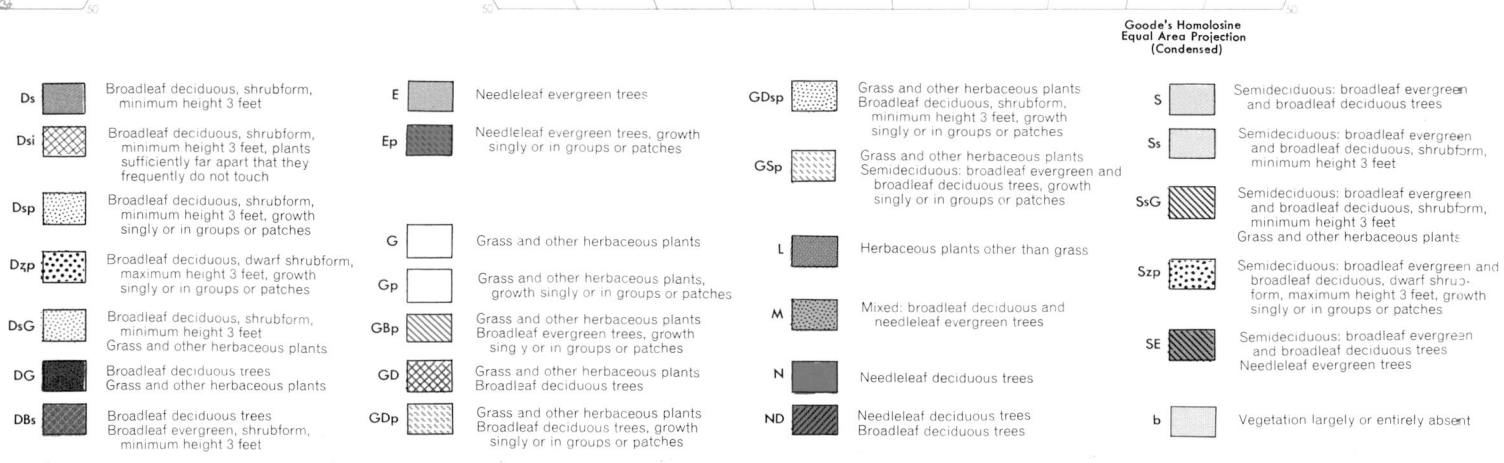

Goode's Homolosine
Equal Area Projection
(Condensed)

Ds	Broadleaf deciduous, shrubform, minimum height 3 feet	
Dsi	Broadleaf deciduous, shrubform, minimum height 3 feet, plants sufficiently far apart that they frequently do not touch	
Dsp	Broadleaf deciduous, shrubform, minimum height 3 feet, growth singly or in groups or patches	
Dzp	Broadleaf deciduous, dwarf shrubform, maximum height 3 feet, growth singly or in groups or patches	
DsG	Broadleaf deciduous, shrubform, minimum height 3 feet Grass and other herbaceous plants	
DG	Broadleaf deciduous trees Grass and other herbaceous plants	
DBs	Broadleaf deciduous trees Broadleaf evergreen, shrubform, minimum height 3 feet	

E	Needleleaf evergreen trees	
Ep	Needleleaf evergreen trees, growth singly or in groups or patches	
G	Grass and other herbaceous plants	
Gp	Grass and other herbaceous plants, growth singly or in groups or patches	
GBp	Grass and other herbaceous plants Broadleaf evergreen trees, growth singly or in groups or patches	
GD	Grass and other herbaceous plants Broadleaf deciduous trees	
GDp	Grass and other herbaceous plants Broadleaf deciduous trees, growth singly or in groups or patches	

GDsp	Grass and other herbaceous plants Broadleaf deciduous, shrubform, minimum height 3 feet, growth singly or in groups or patches	
GSp	Grass and other herbaceous plants Semideciduous: broadleaf evergreen and broadleaf deciduous trees, growth singly or in groups or patches	
L	Herbaceous plants other than grass	
M	Mixed: broadleaf deciduous and needleleaf evergreen trees	
N	Needleleaf deciduous trees	
ND	Needleleaf deciduous trees Broadleaf deciduous trees	

S	Semideciduous: broadleaf evergreen and broadleaf deciduous trees	
Ss	Semideciduous: broadleaf evergreen and broadleaf deciduous, shrubform, minimum height 3 feet	
SsG	Semideciduous: broadleaf evergreen and broadleaf deciduous, shrubform, minimum height 3 feet Grass and other herbaceous plants	
Szp	Semideciduous: broadleaf evergreen and broadleaf deciduous, dwarf shrubform, maximum height 3 feet, growth singly or in groups or patches	
SE	Semideciduous: broadleaf evergreen and broadleaf deciduous trees Needleleaf evergreen trees	
b	Vegetation largely or entirely absent	

Agricultural Regions

This thematic map describes the different agricultural methods practiced in various parts of the world. It contains no information on amount of agricultural output or specific types of products produced.

Nomadic herding—the movement of sheep, goats, or other animals from place to place for grazing—and livestock ranching together account for a large proportion of the world's agricultural activity. Shifting cultivation—also called slash-and-burn agriculture—is also widespread. In this type of agriculture, a farm community grows crops for only a year or two. Then the people move to a new location to start new farms, clearing land by cutting and burning grass and trees. In subsistence tillage, common throughout southern and southeastern Asia, farmers grow just enough food to meet their own needs.

Rudimental sedentary cultivation, which means permanent farming of small plots of land, is done in small parts of Central America, South America, and Africa. Plantation agriculture, in which such crops as cotton and sugar are grown on huge farms, characterizes portions of Central America, the Caribbean, and South America.

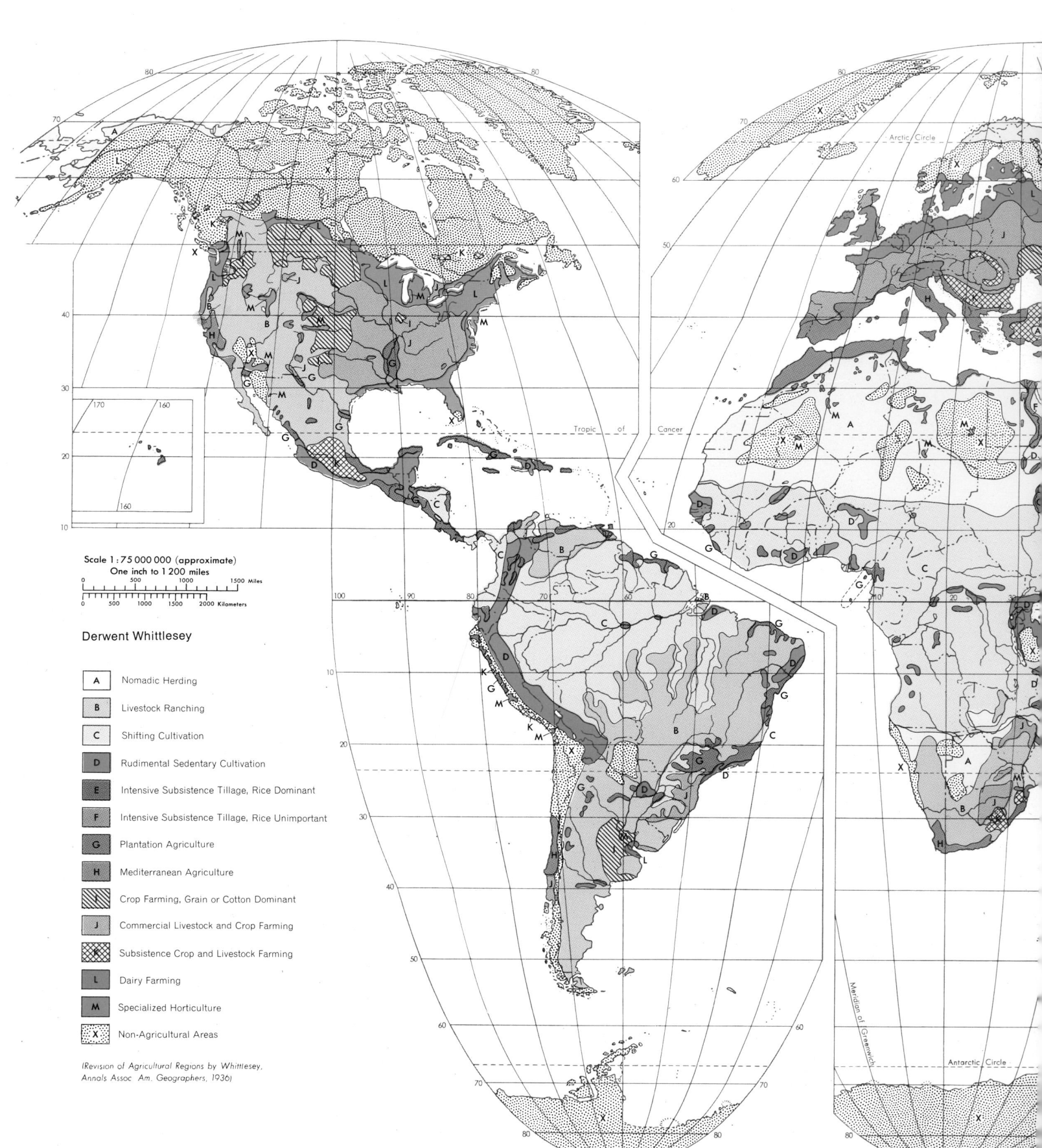

Scale 1 : 75 000 000 (approximate)
One inch to 1 200 miles

Derwent Whittlesey

A	Nomadic Herding
B	Livestock Ranching
C	Shifting Cultivation
D	Rudimental Sedentary Cultivation
E	Intensive Subsistence Tillage, Rice Dominant
F	Intensive Subsistence Tillage, Rice Unimportant
G	Plantation Agriculture
H	Mediterranean Agriculture
	Crop Farming, Grain or Cotton Dominant
J	Commercial Livestock and Crop Farming
	Subsistence Crop and Livestock Farming
L	Dairy Farming
M	Specialized Horticulture
X	Non-Agricultural Areas

(Revision of Agricultural Regions by Whittlesey,
Annals Assoc. Am. Geographers, 1936)

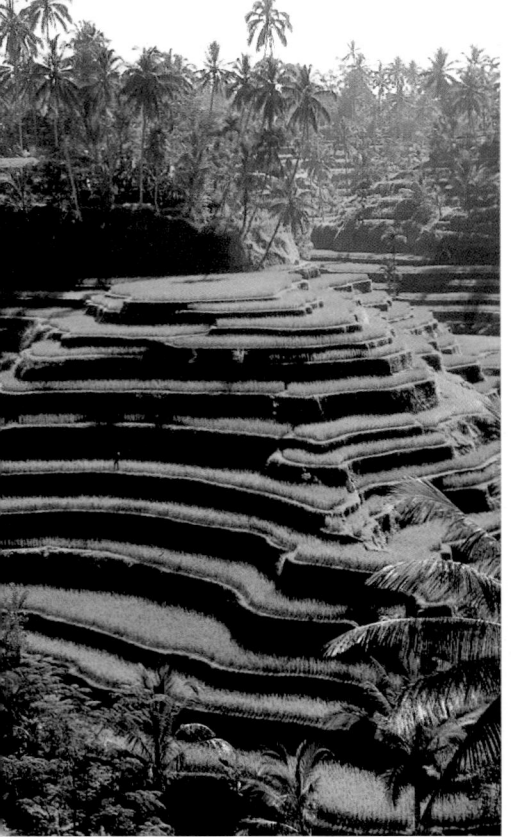

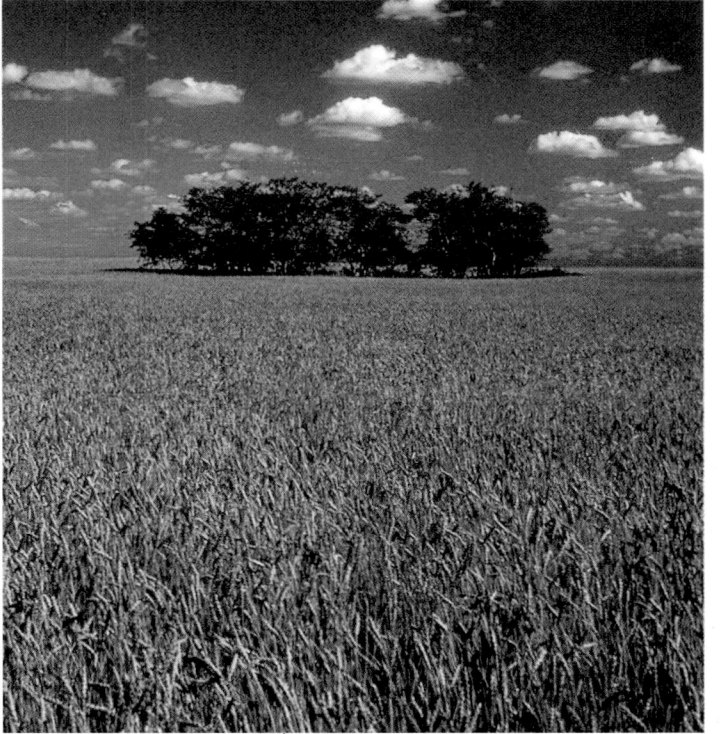

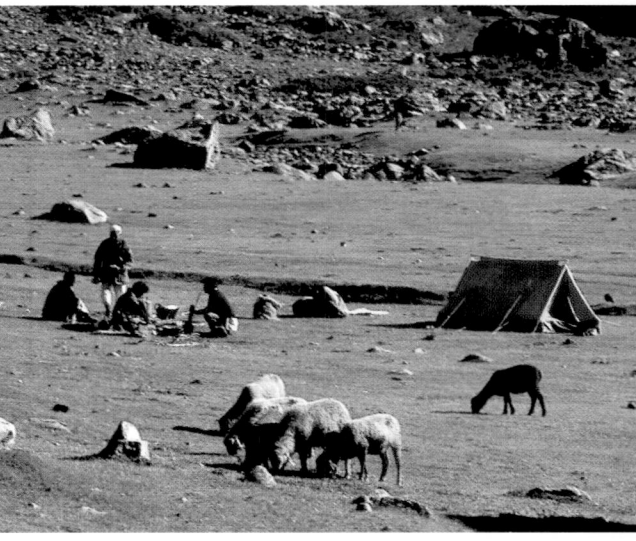

The type of agriculture in different parts of the world depends on conditions such as soil and climate. Terraced rice farming, *far left*, is seen in Bali; wheat farming in Saskatchewan, Canada; and nomadic herding in India.

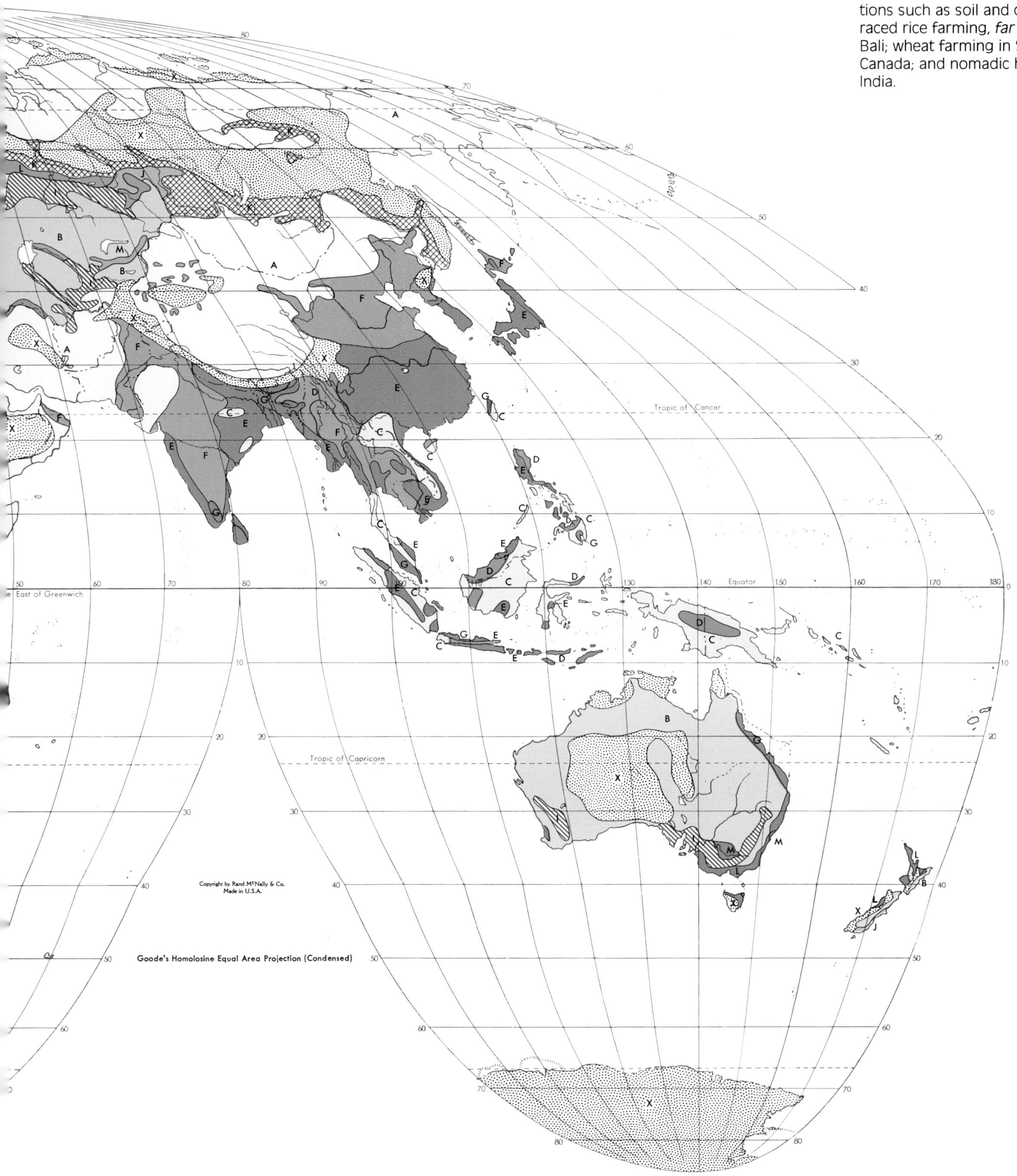

Tropic of Cancer
Equator
East of Greenwich
Tropic of Capricorn
Copyright by Rand McNally & Co. Made in U.S.A.
Goode's Homolosine Equal Area Projection (Condensed)

Land Use

The main economies of various regions are shown here through the use of color and symbols. This map makes it easy to draw comparisons between regions and to study the distribution of certain economic activities. For example, while mining sites are scattered over many parts of the United States, most mining in South America is found in the continent's western and northern regions. The pie charts below complement the map by offering occupational information.

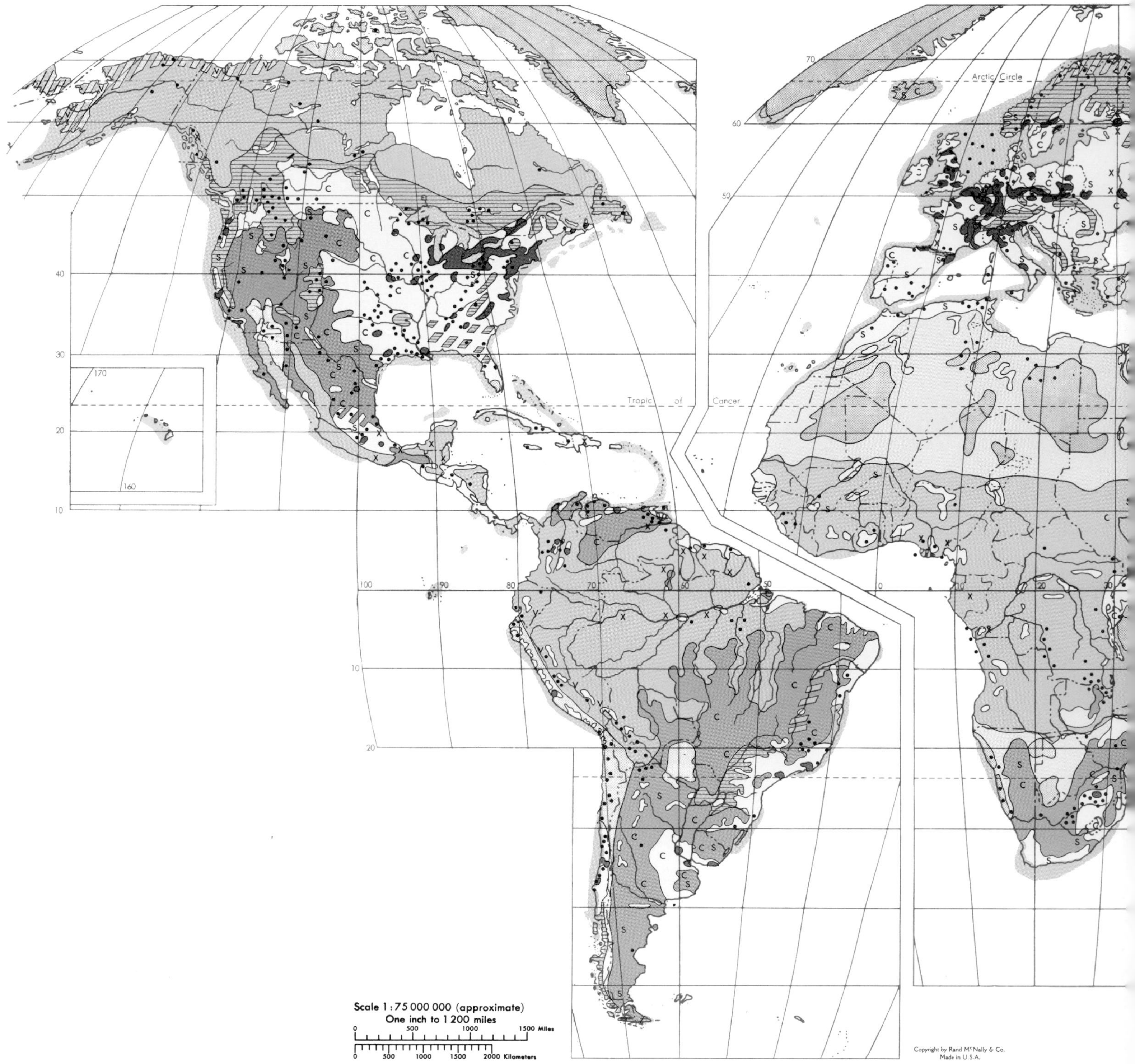

Arctic Circle
Tropic of Cancer
Scale 1 : 75 000 000 (approximate)
One inch to 1 200 miles
0 500 1000 1500 Miles
0 500 1000 1500 2000 Kilometers
Copyright by Rand McNally & Co.
Made in U.S.A.

Occupational structure of selected areas

A—Agriculture
B—Manufacturing
C—Mining
D—Construction
E—Trade and Commerce
F—Transportation and Communication
G—Service and Others

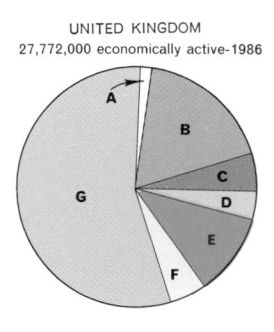

UNITED KINGDOM
27,772,000 economically active-1986

A
B
C
D
E
F
G

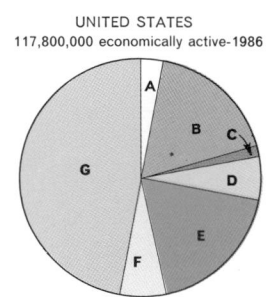

UNITED STATES
117,800,000 economically active-1986

A
B
C
D
E
F
G

CANADA
12,870,000 economically active-1986

A
B
C
D
E
F
G

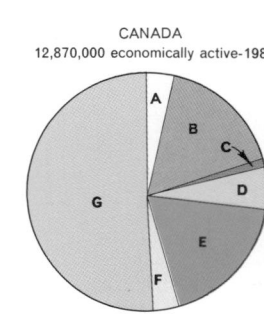

Most of the world's cultivated land is used to produce food, livestock, or forest products. Only in the last few centuries have mass-production methods become common.

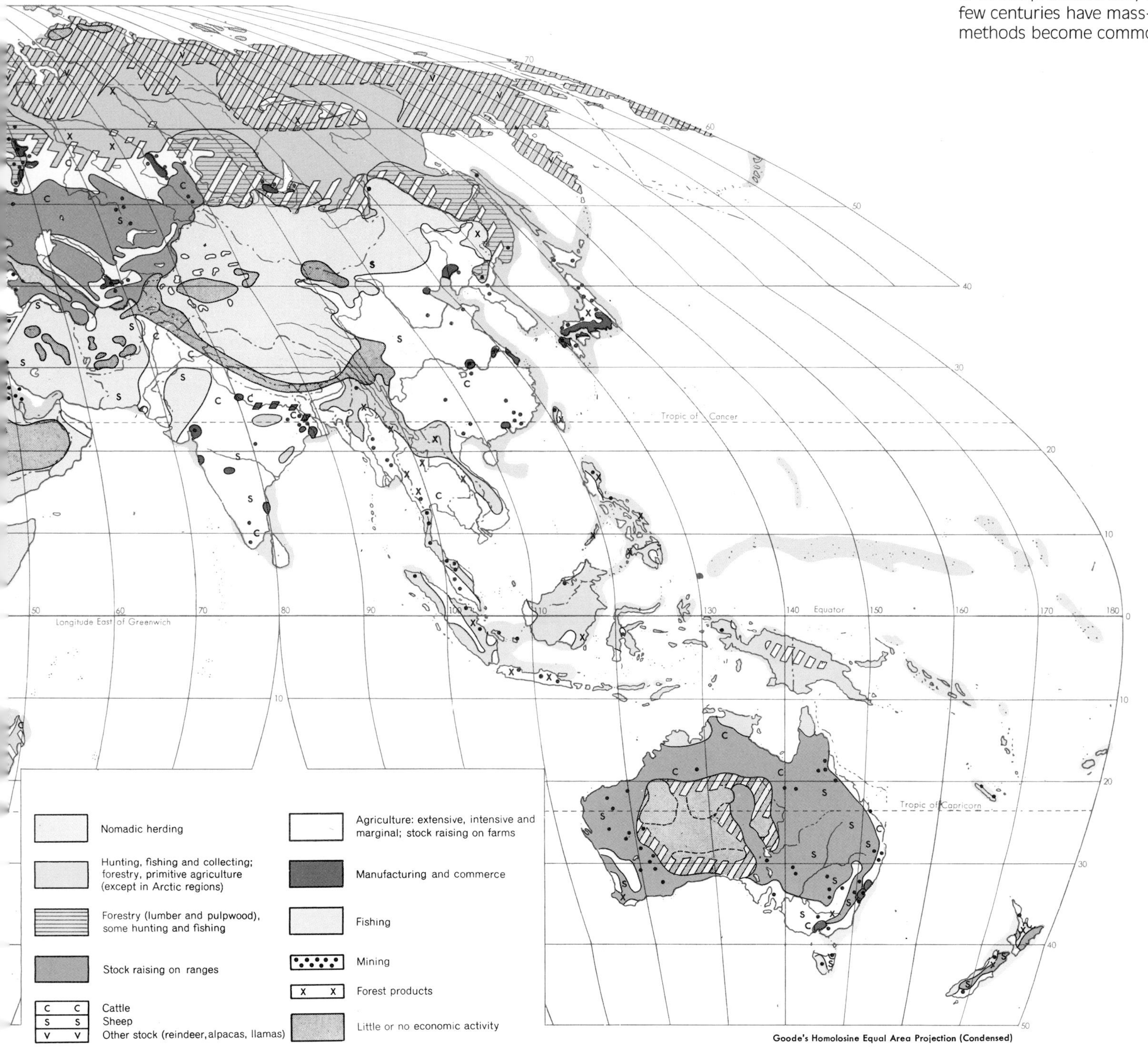

Nomadic herding

Hunting, fishing and collecting; forestry, primitive agriculture (except in Arctic regions)

Forestry (lumber and pulpwood), some hunting and fishing

Stock raising on ranges

C C Cattle
S S Sheep
V V Other stock (reindeer, alpacas, llamas)

Agriculture: extensive, intensive and marginal; stock raising on farms

Manufacturing and commerce

Fishing

Mining

X X Forest products

Little or no economic activity

Goode's Homolosine Equal Area Projection (Condensed)

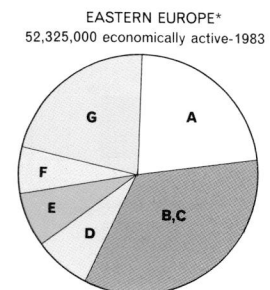

EASTERN EUROPE*
52,325,000 economically active-1983

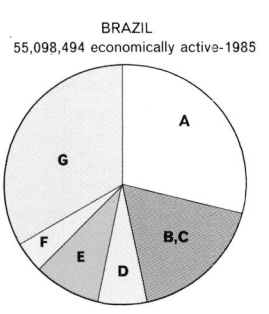

BRAZIL
55,098,494 economically active-1985

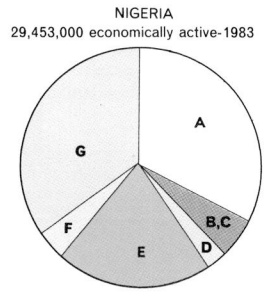

NIGERIA
29,453,000 economically active-1983

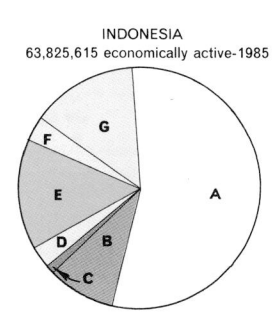

INDONESIA
63,825,615 economically active-1985

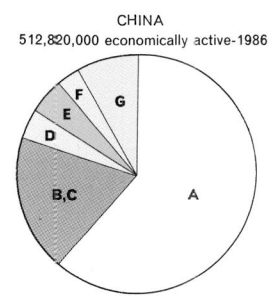

CHINA
512,820,000 economically active-1986

Distribution of Important Fuels

This thematic map uses color and symbols to show the distribution of the world's important mineral and fossil fuels: coal and lignite, petroleum, natural gas, and uranium. Arrows indicate the movement of petroleum from exporting to importing countries. The thicker the line, the heavier the flow of petroleum. It is easy to see that Japan, Europe, and the United States are the world's major importers of petroleum. The Middle East exports the most petroleum.

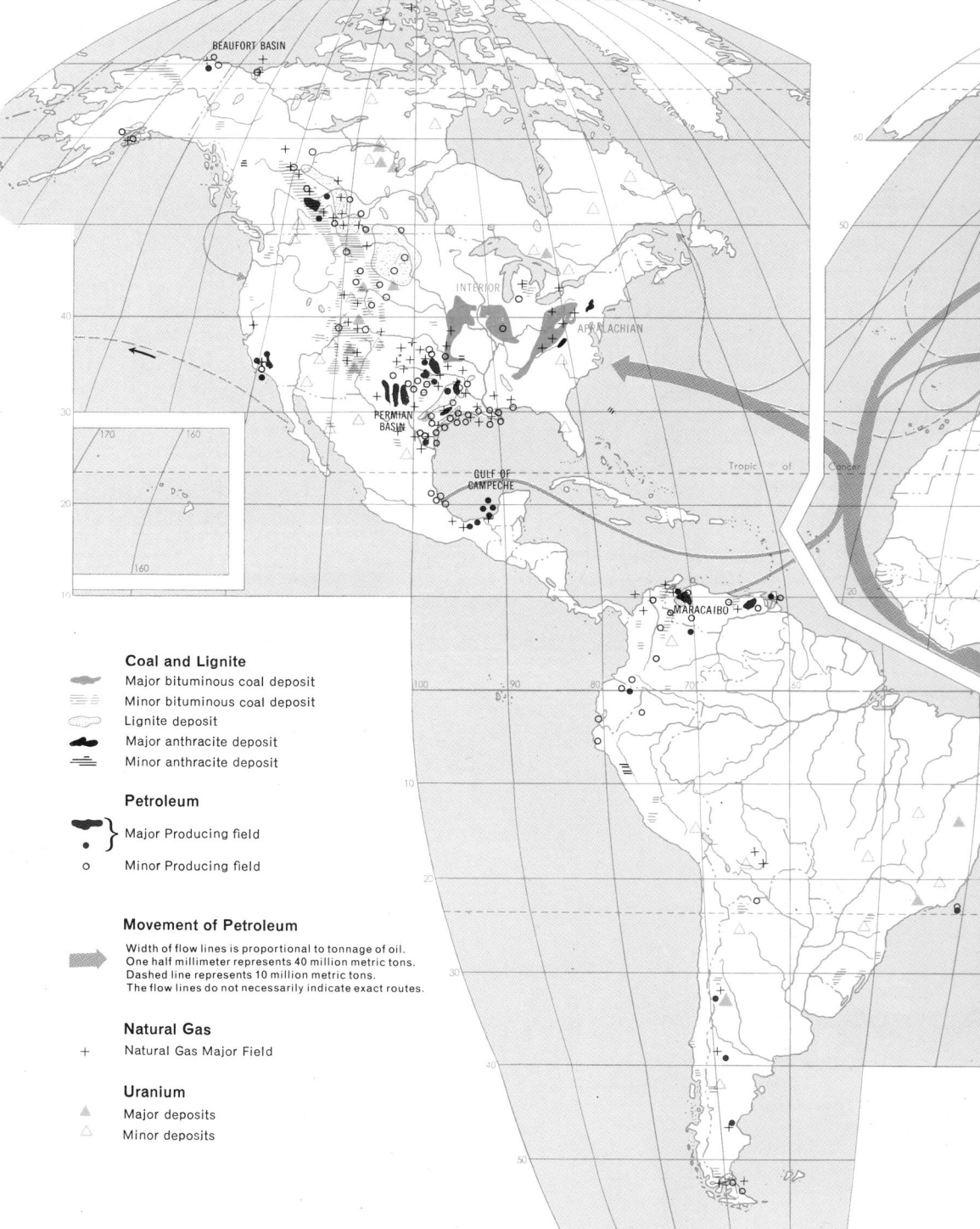

Coal and Lignite
- Major bituminous coal deposit
- Minor bituminous coal deposit
- Lignite deposit
- Major anthracite deposit
- Minor anthracite deposit

Petroleum
- Major Producing field
- Minor Producing field

Movement of Petroleum
Width of flow lines is proportional to tonnage of oil.
One half millimeter represents 40 million metric tons.
Dashed line represents 10 million metric tons.
The flow lines do not necessarily indicate exact routes.

Natural Gas
- + Natural Gas Major Field

Uranium
- ▲ Major deposits
- △ Minor deposits

Anthracite, *above,* is the hardest form of coal, a rock that can be ignited and burned.

Coal World Production-4,492,000,000* metric tons-Av. 1985-87

0	10	20	30	40	50	60	70	80	90	100%

CHINA 19.6%	INDIA 3.8	OTHER 3.4	UNITED STATES 18.1	SOVIET UNION 16.5	E. GER. 6.9	POL. 5.7	W. GER. 4.5	CZECH. 2.8	U.K. 2.3	OTHER 6.3	S. AFR. 3.9	AUSTL. 3.9

← ASIA → ← N. AMERICA → ← EUROPE → AF. OC.

Anthracite and Bituminous: World Total-3,278,000,000 metric tons-1986

Coal Reserves World Total-924,040,000,000* metric tons-1987

0	10	20	30	40	50	60	70	80	90	100%

UNITED STATES 28.6%	SOVIET UNION 26.5	CHINA 10.7	AUSTL. 7.1	W. GER. 6.4	POLAND 4.6	E. GER. 2.4	OTHER 4.4	S. AFR. 6.3

← NORTH AMERICA → ← ASIA → OC. ← EUROPE → AFR.

Anthracite and Bituminous: World Total-652,873,000,000 metric tons-1987
Includes anthracite, subanthracite, bituminous, subbituminous, lignite and brown coal

World Production-2,740,000,000** metric tons
Petroleum (20,153,000,000 barrels)-Av. 1985-87

0	10	20	30	40	50	60	70	80	90	100%

SOVIET UNION 20.8%	UNITED STATES 15.7	MEXICO 4.7	CANADA 2.7	SAUDI ARABIA 7.5	CHINA 4.7	IRAN 4.1	IRAQ 3.1	U.A.E. 3.2	INDON. 2.4	KUWAIT 2.3	OTHER 8.4	U.K. 4.6	OTHER 3.3	VENEZ. 3.2	OTHER 2.6	NIGERIA 2.8	OTHER 6.9

← NORTH AMERICA → ← ASIA → ← EUROPE.S. AM → AFRICA

World Total-115,083,200,000** metric tons
Petroleum Reserves (846,200,000,000 barrels)-1988

0	10	20	30	40	50	60	70	80	90	100%

SAUDI ARABIA 20.1%	IRAQ 11.8	KUWAIT 11.4	U.A.E. 9.1	IRAN 7.6	CHINA 2.4	OTHER 3.4	SOVIET UNION 7.0	VENEZ. 6.7	MEXICO 5.6	U.S.A. 3.2	LIBYA 2.6	OTHER 3.9	EUROPE 2.8

← ASIA → ← S. AM → ← N. AM → AFR.

**Crude Petroleum

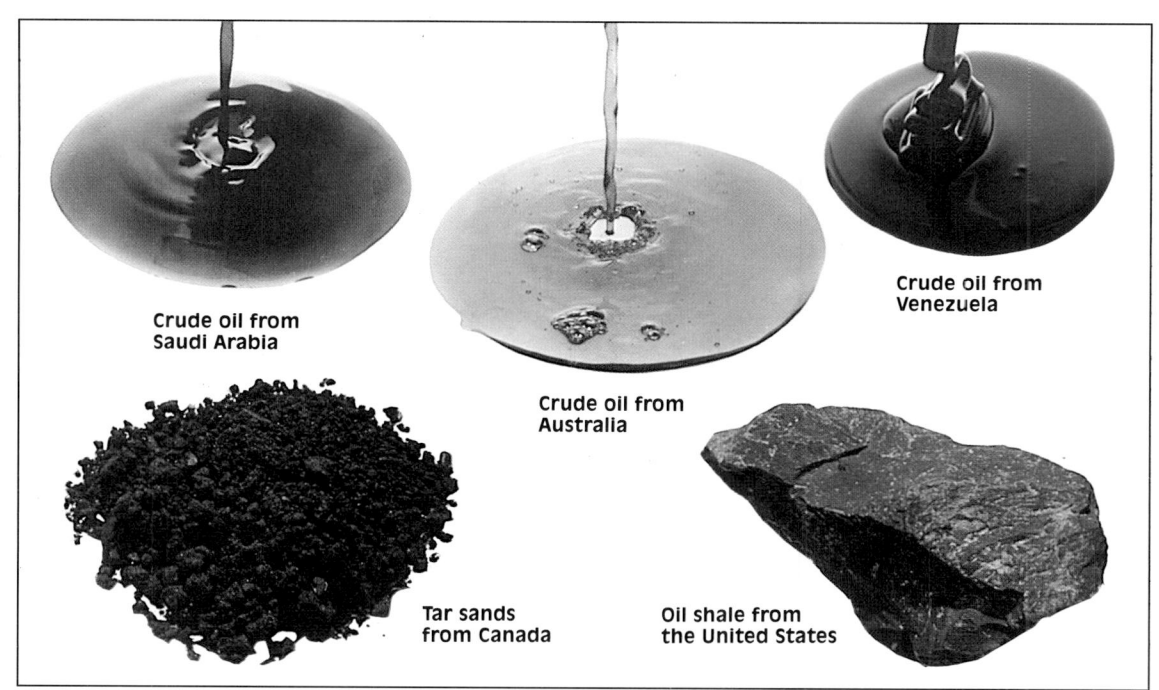

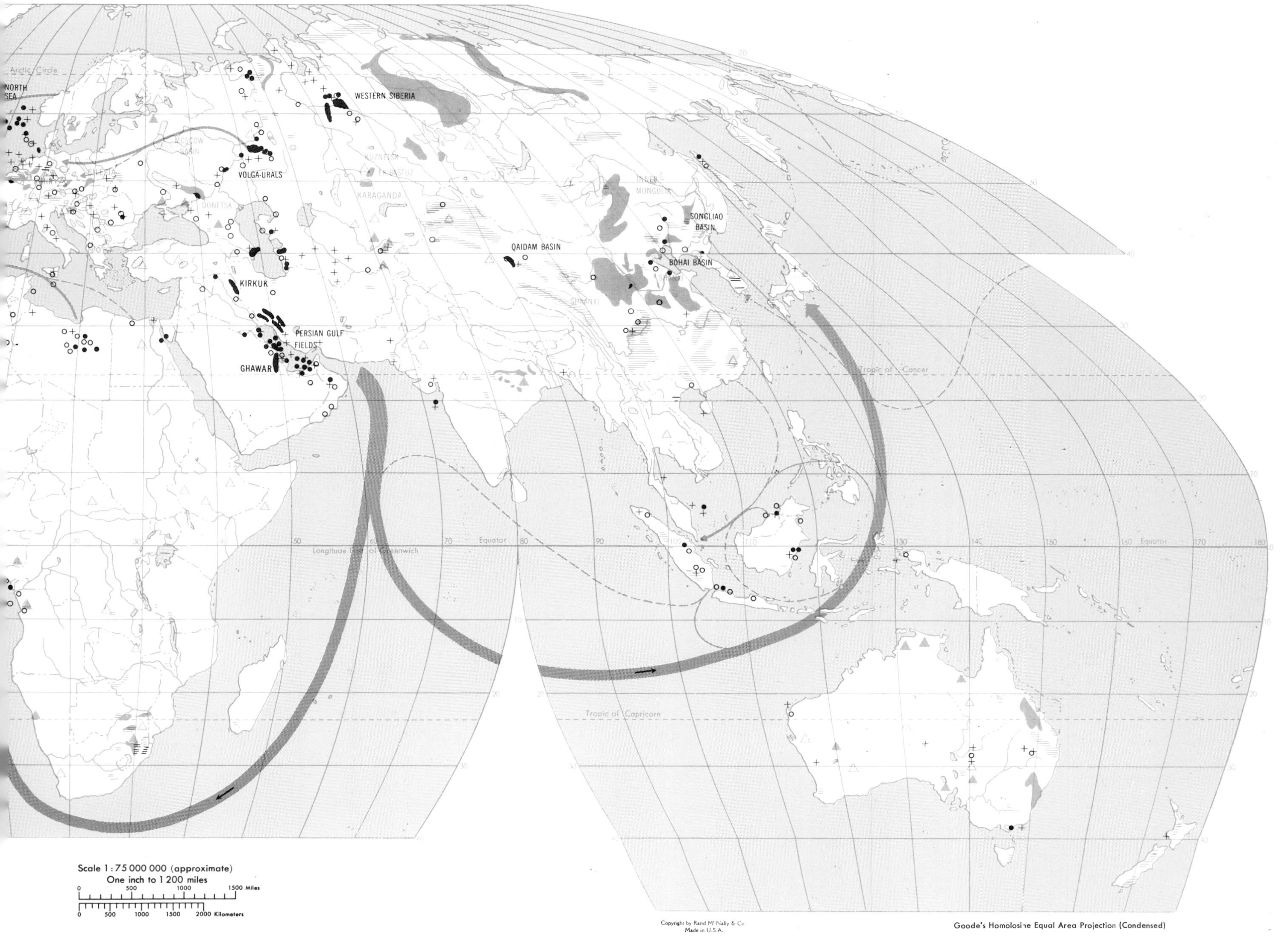

Crude oil from Saudi Arabia
Crude oil from Australia
Crude oil from Venezuela
Tar sands from Canada
Oil shale from the United States

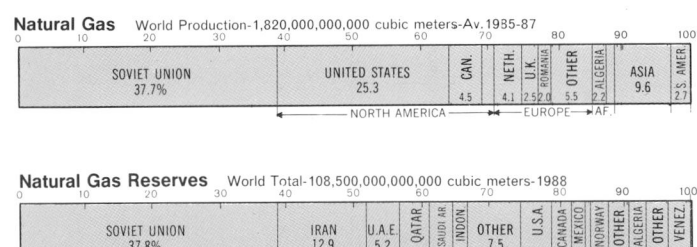

Petroleum has liquid and solid forms. Liquid crude oil occurs naturally in reservoirs. Tar sands and shale can be processed into oil.

NORTH SEA
Arctic Circle
WESTERN SIBERIA
VOLGA-URALS
KIRKUK
PERSIAN GULF FIELDS
GHAWAR
QAIDAM BASIN
SONGLIAO BASIN
BOHAI BASIN
Tropic of Cancer
Equator
Longitude East of Greenwich
Tropic of Capricorn
Scale 1 : 75 000 000 (approximate)
One inch to 1 200 miles
0 500 1000 1500 Miles
0 500 1000 1500 2000 Kilometers
Copyright by Rand McNally & Co.
Made in U.S.A.
Goode's Homolosine Equal Area Projection (Condensed)

Natural Gas World Production-1,820,000,000,000 cubic meters-Av. 1985-87

0 10 20 30 40 50 60 70 80 90 100%
SOVIET UNION
37.7%
UNITED STATES
25.3
CAN.
4.5
NETH.
4.1
U.K.
2.5
ROMANIA
2.0
OTHER
5.5
ALGERIA
2.2
ASIA
9.6
S. AMER.
2.7
NORTH AMERICA
EUROPE
AF.

Natural Gas Reserves World Total-108,500,000,000,000 cubic meters-1988

0 10 20 30 40 50 60 70 80 90 100%
SOVIET UNION
37.8%
IRAN
12.9
U.A.E.
5.2
QATAR
4.2
SAUDI AR.
3.8
INDON.
2.1
OTHER
7.5
U.S.A.
4.9
CANADA
2.7
MEXICO
2.0
NORWAY
2.9
OTHER
3.7
ALGERIA
2.8
OTHER
3.2
VENEZ.
2.5
ASIA
N. AMER.
EUR.
AFR.
SA

Uranium World Production-40,300† metric tons-Av. 1984-86

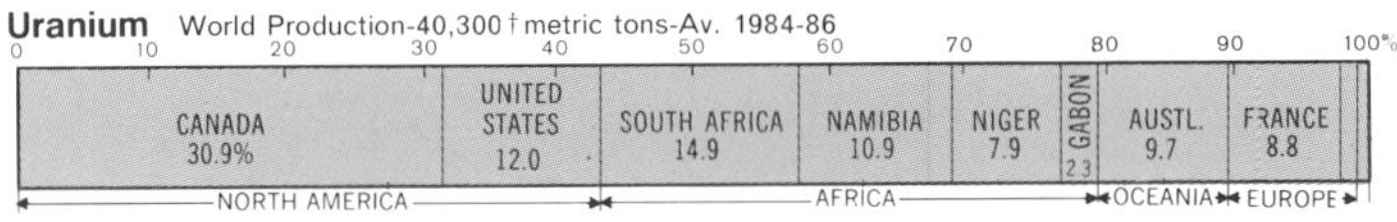

0 10 20 30 40 50 60 70 80 90 100%
CANADA
30.9%
UNITED STATES
12.0
SOUTH AFRICA
14.9
NAMIBIA
10.9
NIGER
7.9
GABON
2.3
AUSTL.
9.7
FRANCE
8.8
NORTH AMERICA
AFRICA
OCEANIA
EUROPE

†Excluding possible production in China, India, Israel, Soviet Union, and Eastern Europe

Uranium Reserves World Total-2,395,000 metric tons†† -1985

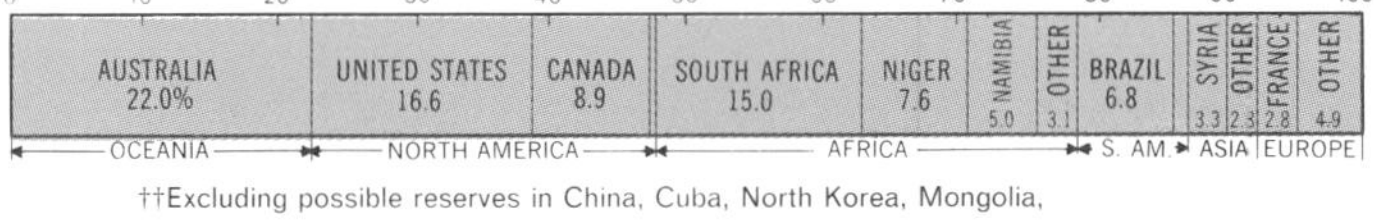

0 10 20 30 40 50 60 70 80 90 100%
AUSTRALIA
22.0%
UNITED STATES
16.6
CANADA
8.9
SOUTH AFRICA
15.0
NIGER
7.6
NAMIBIA
5.0
OTHER
3.1
BRAZIL
6.8
SYRIA
3.3
OTHER
2.3
FRANCE
2.8
OTHER
4.9
OCEANIA
NORTH AMERICA
AFRICA
S. AM.
ASIA
EUROPE

††Excluding possible reserves in China, Cuba, North Korea, Mongolia, Vietnam, Soviet Union, and Eastern Europe

Energy

The size of each circle on these maps is proportional to the volume of energy produced or consumed by the nation to which the circle corresponds. Colors in the circles show the types of energy produced or consumed. For example, magenta represents solid fuels, and green represents liquid fuels.

The energy consumption map gives information on countries' per capita energy consumption in addition to their total energy consumption. The bar graphs indicate that the United States and the Soviet Union together account for nearly 45 per cent of energy production and 44 per cent of consumption.

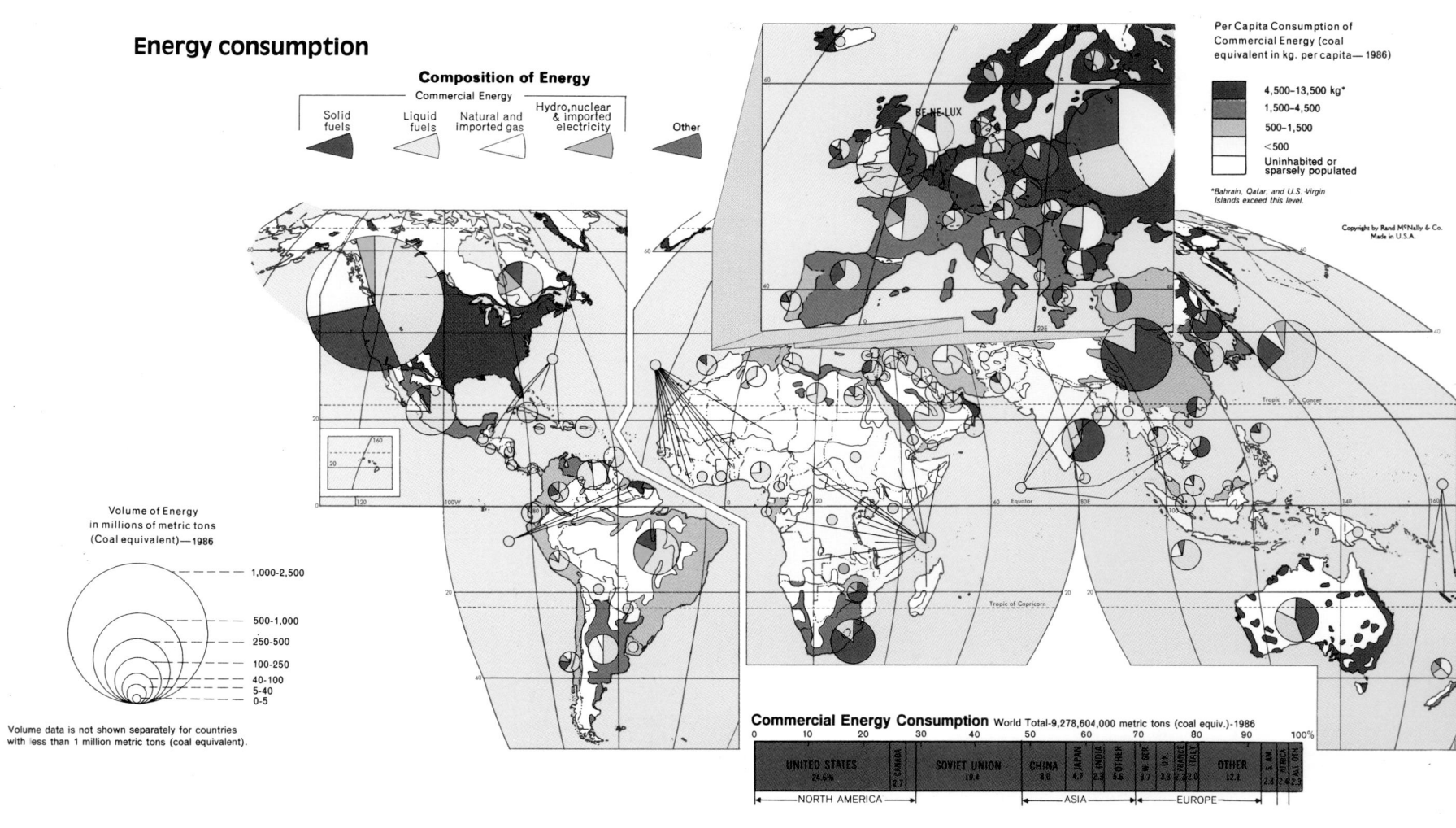

Energy production

Natural gas, often recovered from offshore wells, has many uses, from heating homes to supplying raw materials for manufacturing.

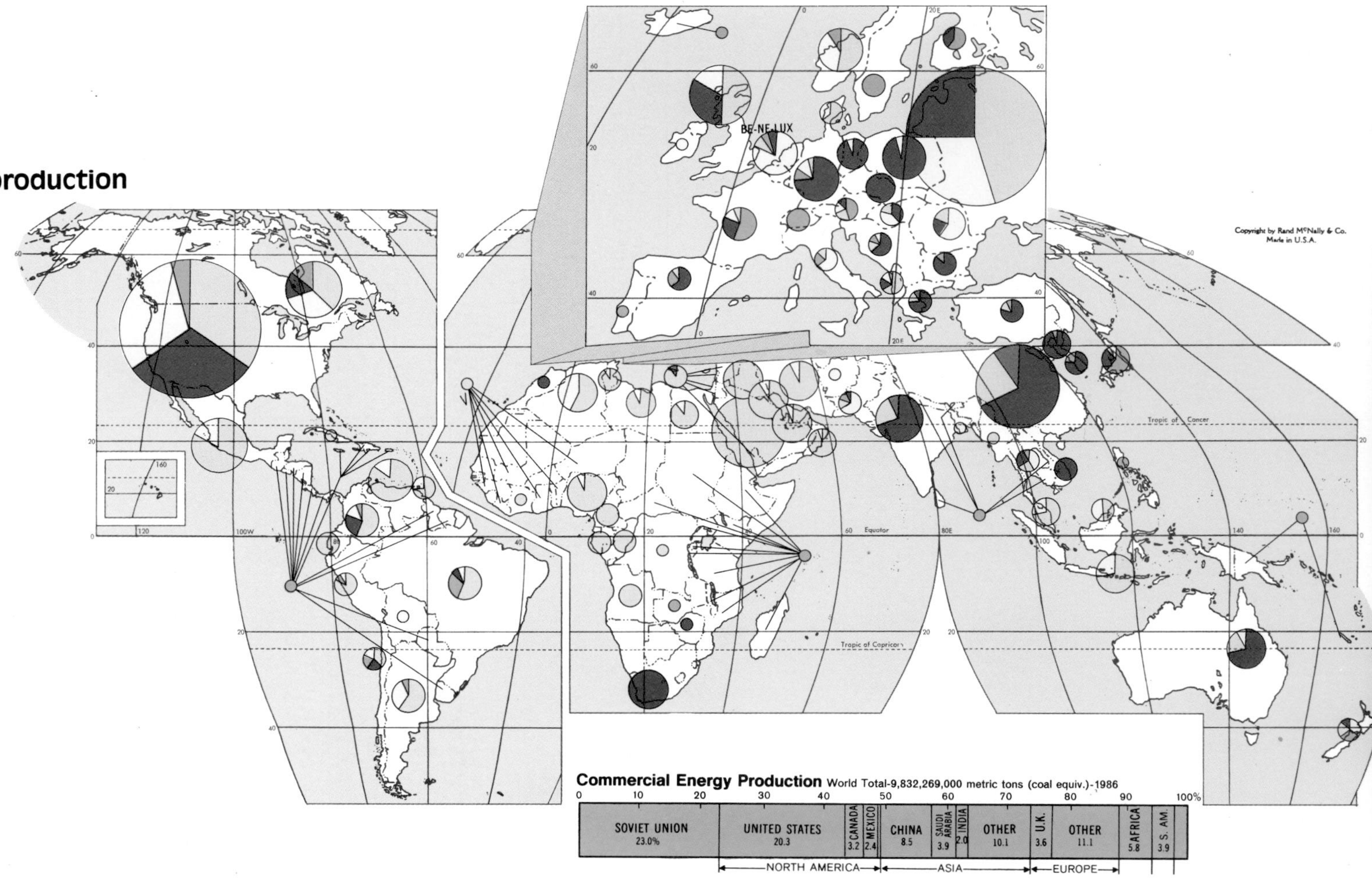

BE-NE-LUX

Copyright by Rand McNally & Co.
Made in U.S.A.

Commercial Energy Production World Total-9,832,269,000 metric tons (coal equiv.)-1986

0	10	20	30	40	50	60	70	80	90	100%

| SOVIET UNION 23.0% | UNITED STATES 20.3 | CANADA 3.2 | MEXICO 2.4 | CHINA 8.5 | SAUDI ARABIA 3.9 | INDIA 2.0 | OTHER 10.1 | U.K. 3.6 | OTHER 11.1 | AFRICA 5.8 | S. AM. 3.9 |

◄── NORTH AMERICA ──► ◄── ASIA ──► ◄── EUROPE ──►

Energy consumption

Composition of Energy
Commercial Energy

Solid fuels | Liquid fuels | Natural and imported gas | Hydro, nuclear & imported electricity | Other

BE-NE-LUX

Per Capita Consumption of Commercial Energy (coal equivalent in kg. per capita— 1986)

- 4,500–13,500 kg*
- 1,500–4,500
- 500–1,500
- <500
- Uninhabited or sparsely populated

*Bahrain, Qatar, and U.S. Virgin Islands exceed this level.

Copyright by Rand McNally & Co.
Made in U.S.A.

Volume of Energy in millions of metric tons (Coal equivalent)—1986

- 1,000–2,500
- 500–1,000
- 250–500
- 100–250
- 40–100
- 5–40
- 0–5

Volume data is not shown separately for countries with less than 1 million metric tons (coal equivalent).

Commercial Energy Consumption World Total-9,278,604,000 metric tons (coal equiv.)-1986

0	10	20	30	40	50	60	70	80	90	100%

| UNITED STATES 24.6% | CANADA 2.7 | SOVIET UNION 19.4 | CHINA 8.0 | JAPAN 4.7 | INDIA 2.6 | OTHER 5.6 | W. GER. 3.7 | U.K. 3.3 | FRANCE 2.6 | ITALY 2.6 | OTHER 12.1 | S. AM. 2.8 | AFRICA 2.4 | ALL OTH. 2.9 |

◄── NORTH AMERICA ──► ◄── ASIA ──► ◄── EUROPE ──►

Languages and Religions

These two thematic maps use color and pattern to indicate the different languages and religions that coexist in the world. Keys to major religions and 50 major languages appear directly beneath the maps. On the religions map, overlapping colors represent a mixture of two or more religions practiced in the same area. In some cases, religious groups in these areas share a number of characteristics and are not clearly distinguishable from one another. Such conditions exist between Sunni Muslims, Hindus, and practitioners of tribal religions in India, as well as between Muslims and followers of tribal and traditional Chinese religions in China.

Languages

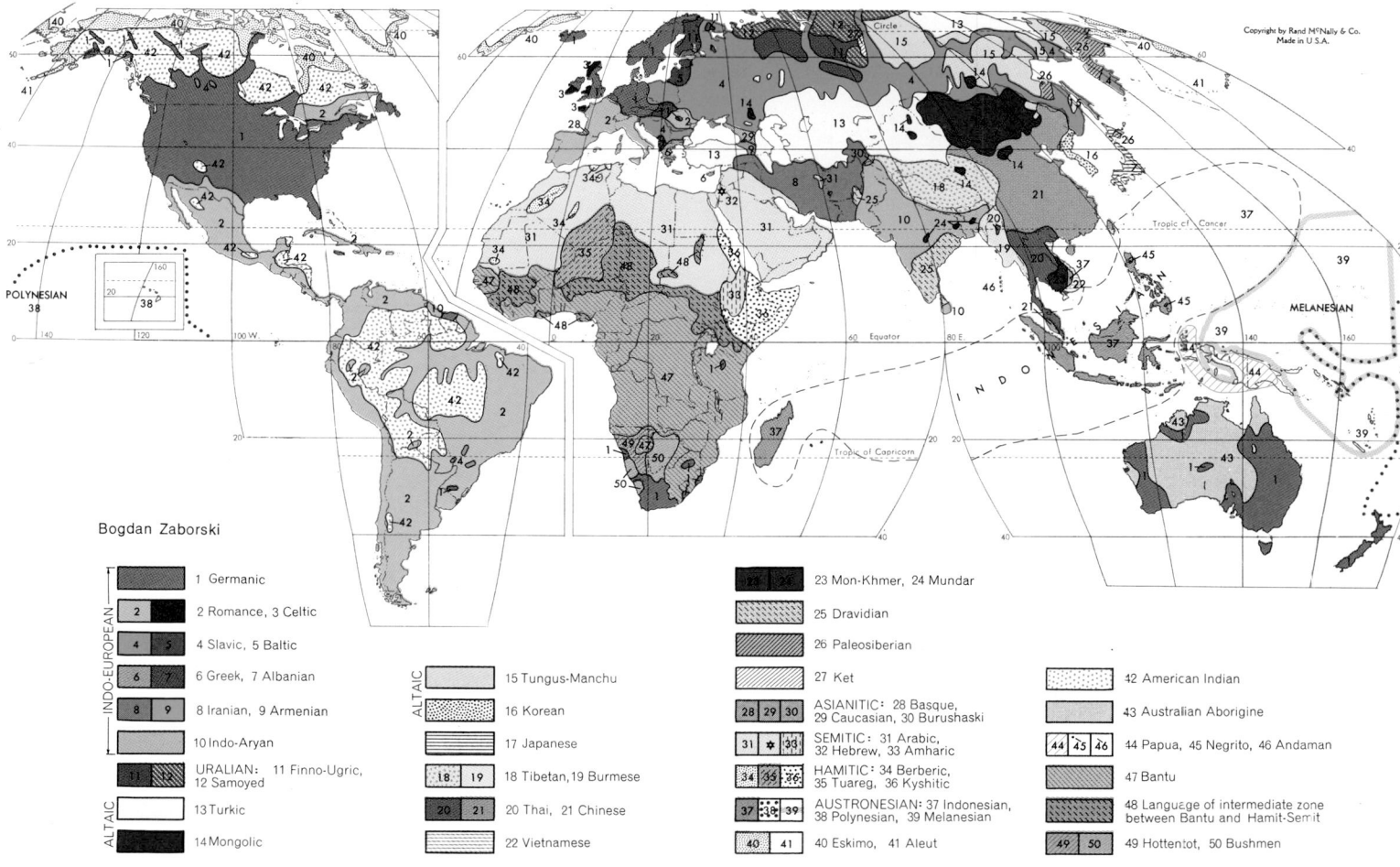

Bogdan Zaborski

INDO-EUROPEAN
- 1 Germanic
- 2 Romance, 3 Celtic
- 4 Slavic, 5 Baltic
- 6 Greek, 7 Albanian
- 8 Iranian, 9 Armenian
- 10 Indo-Aryan

- URALIAN: 11 Finno-Ugric, 12 Samoyed

ALTAIC
- 13 Turkic
- 14 Mongolic
- 15 Tungus-Manchu
- 16 Korean
- 17 Japanese
- 18 Tibetan, 19 Burmese
- 20 Thai, 21 Chinese
- 22 Vietnamese

- 23 Mon-Khmer, 24 Mundar
- 25 Dravidian
- 26 Paleosiberian
- 27 Ket
- ASIANITIC: 28 Basque, 29 Caucasian, 30 Burushaski
- SEMITIC: 31 Arabic, 32 Hebrew, 33 Amharic
- HAMITIC: 34 Berberic, 35 Tuareg, 36 Kyshitic
- AUSTRONESIAN: 37 Indonesian, 38 Polynesian, 39 Melanesian
- 40 Eskimo, 41 Aleut

- 42 American Indian
- 43 Australian Aborigine
- 44 Papua, 45 Negrito, 46 Andaman
- 47 Bantu
- 48 Language of intermediate zone between Bantu and Hamit-Semit
- 49 Hottentot, 50 Bushmen

Religions

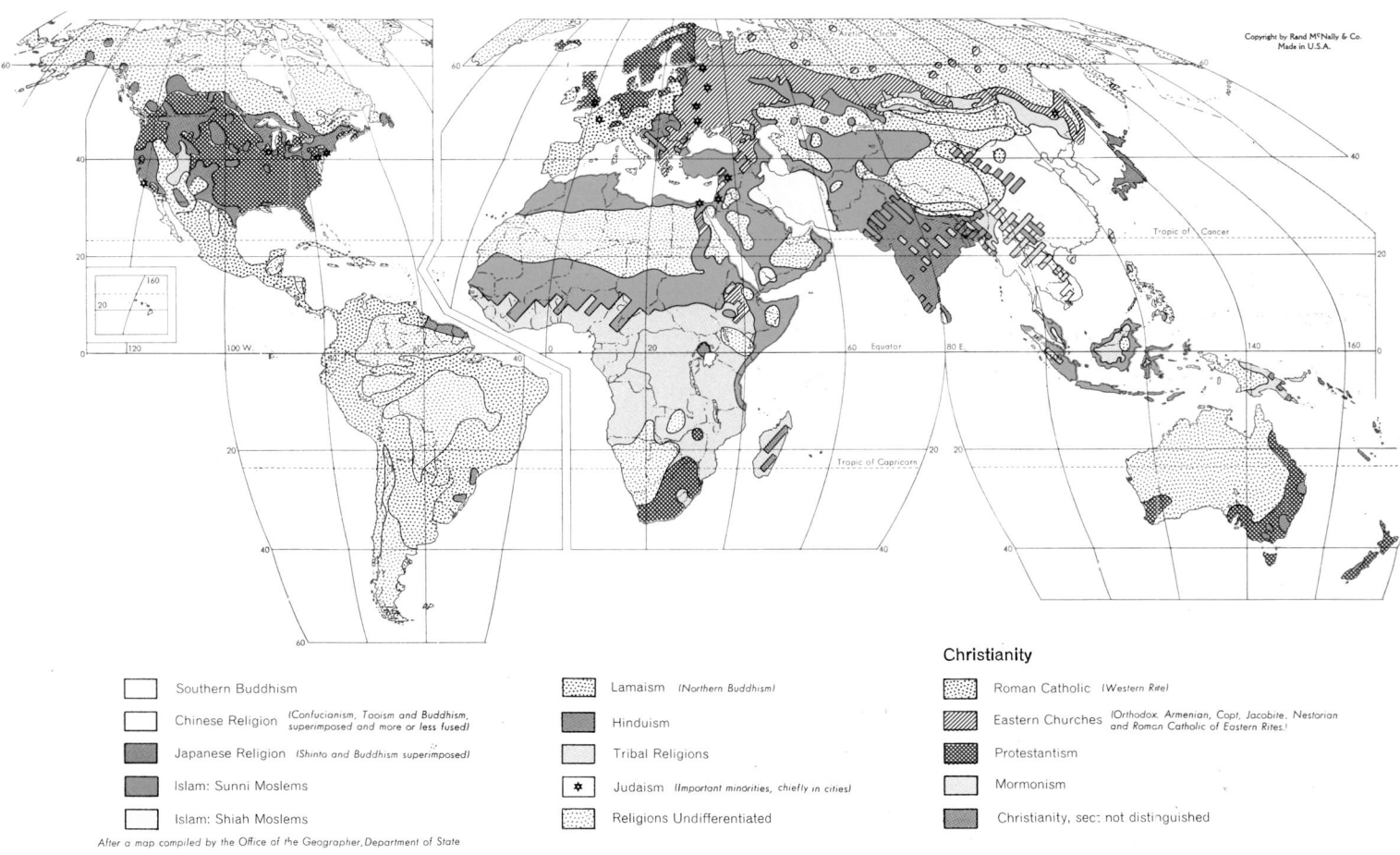

- Southern Buddhism
- Chinese Religion (Confucianism, Taoism and Buddhism, superimposed and more or less fused)
- Japanese Religion (Shinto and Buddhism superimposed)
- Islam: Sunni Moslems
- Islam: Shiah Moslems
- Lamaism (Northern Buddhism)
- Hinduism
- Tribal Religions
- Judaism (Important minorities, chiefly in cities)
- Religions Undifferentiated

Christianity
- Roman Catholic (Western Rite)
- Eastern Churches (Orthodox, Armenian, Copt, Jacobite, Nestorian and Roman Catholic of Eastern Rites.)
- Protestantism
- Mormonism
- Christianity, sect not distinguished

After a map compiled by the Office of the Geographer, Department of State

Population

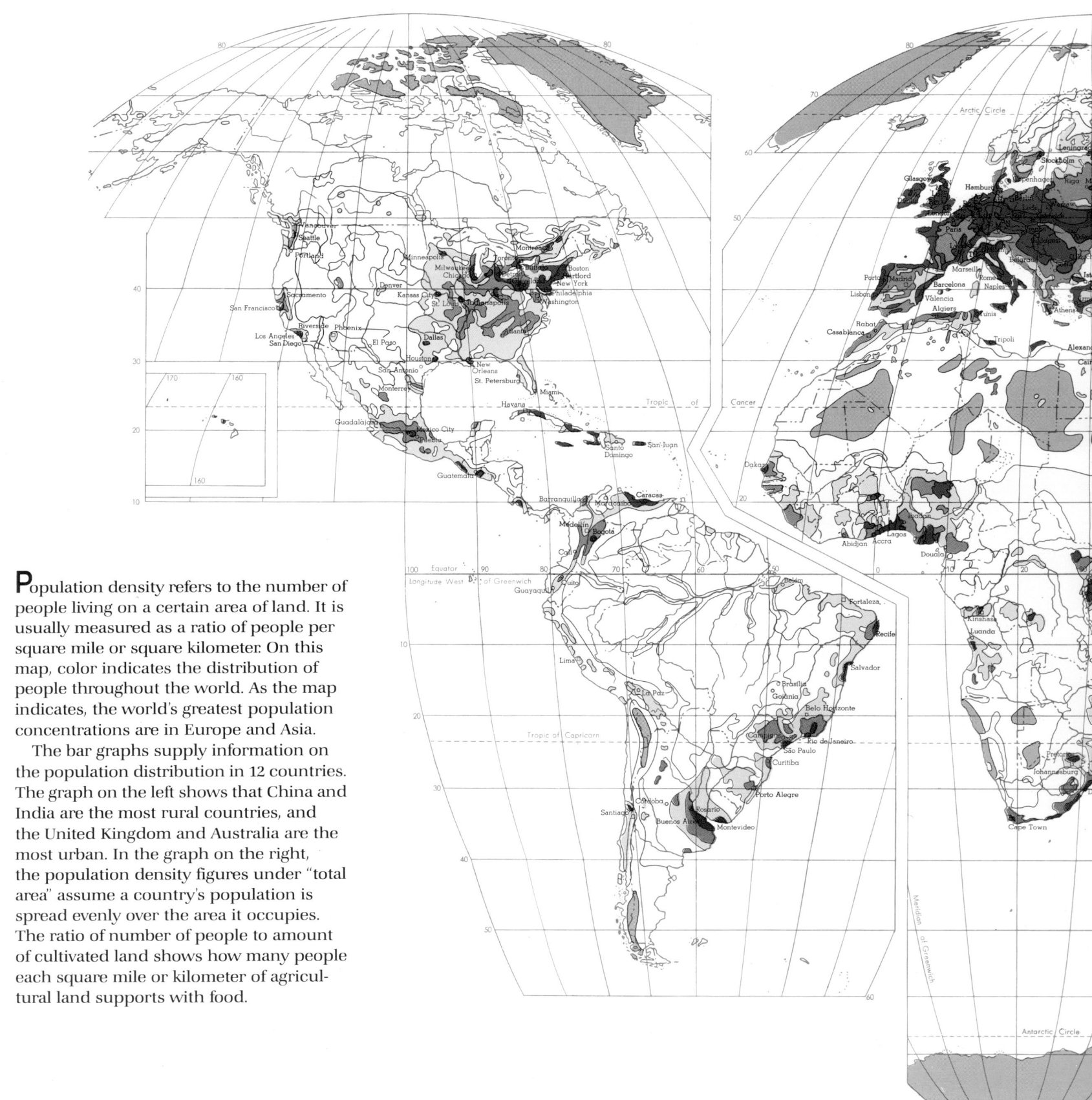

Population density refers to the number of people living on a certain area of land. It is usually measured as a ratio of people per square mile or square kilometer. On this map, color indicates the distribution of people throughout the world. As the map indicates, the world's greatest population concentrations are in Europe and Asia.

The bar graphs supply information on the population distribution in 12 countries. The graph on the left shows that China and India are the most rural countries, and the United Kingdom and Australia are the most urban. In the graph on the right, the population density figures under "total area" assume a country's population is spread evenly over the area it occupies. The ratio of number of people to amount of cultivated land shows how many people each square mile or kilometer of agricultural land supports with food.

Population density is not an issue among Amerindians of the Andes Mountains, *left*. But in Beijing (Peking), China, one of the world's largest cities, overcrowding is a problem. China has more people than any other country.

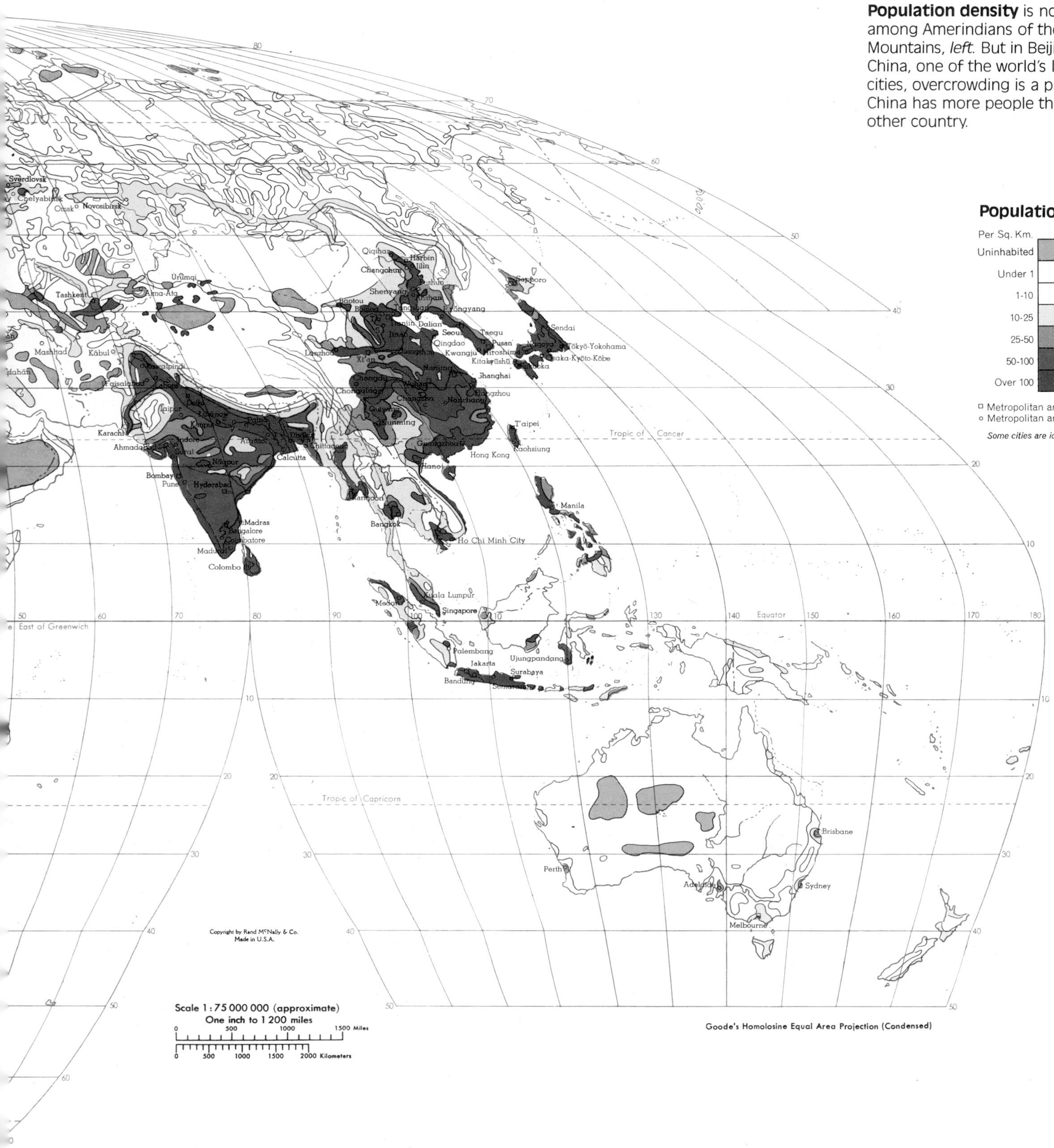

Population

Per Sq. Km.	Per Sq. Mile
Uninhabited	Uninhabited
Under 1	Under 2
1-10	2-25
10-25	25-60
25-50	60-125
50-100	125-250
Over 100	Over 250

▫ Metropolitan areas over 2,000,000 population
◦ Metropolitan areas 1,000,000 to 2,000,000 population

Some cities are identified by initial letter only.

Scale 1 : 75 000 000 (approximate)
One inch to 1 200 miles

0 500 1000 1500 Miles
0 500 1000 1500 2000 Kilometers

Goode's Homolosine Equal Area Projection (Condensed)

Copyright by Rand McNally & Co.
Made in U.S.A.

Rural/urban population ratios

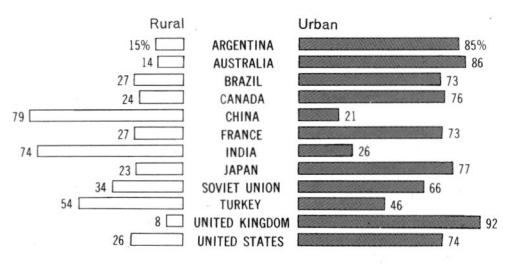

	Rural		Urban
ARGENTINA	15%		85%
AUSTRALIA	14		86
BRAZIL	27		73
CANADA	24		76
CHINA	79		21
FRANCE	27		73
INDIA	74		26
JAPAN	23		77
SOVIET UNION	34		66
TURKEY	54		46
UNITED KINGDOM	8		92
UNITED STATES	26		74

Population density

per square kilometer (per square mile)

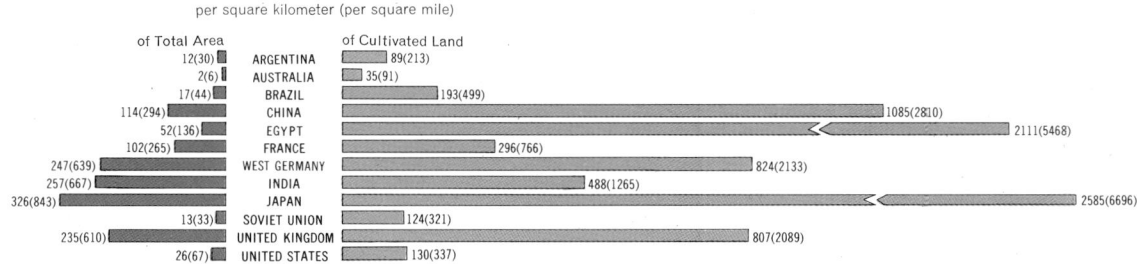

	of Total Area	of Cultivated Land
ARGENTINA	12(30)	89(213)
AUSTRALIA	2(6)	35(91)
BRAZIL	17(44)	193(499)
CHINA	114(294)	1085(2810)
EGYPT	52(136)	2111(5468)
FRANCE	102(265)	296(766)
WEST GERMANY	247(639)	824(2133)
INDIA	257(667)	488(1265)
JAPAN	326(843)	2585(6696)
SOVIET UNION	13(33)	124(321)
UNITED KINGDOM	235(610)	807(2089)
UNITED STATES	26(67)	130(337)

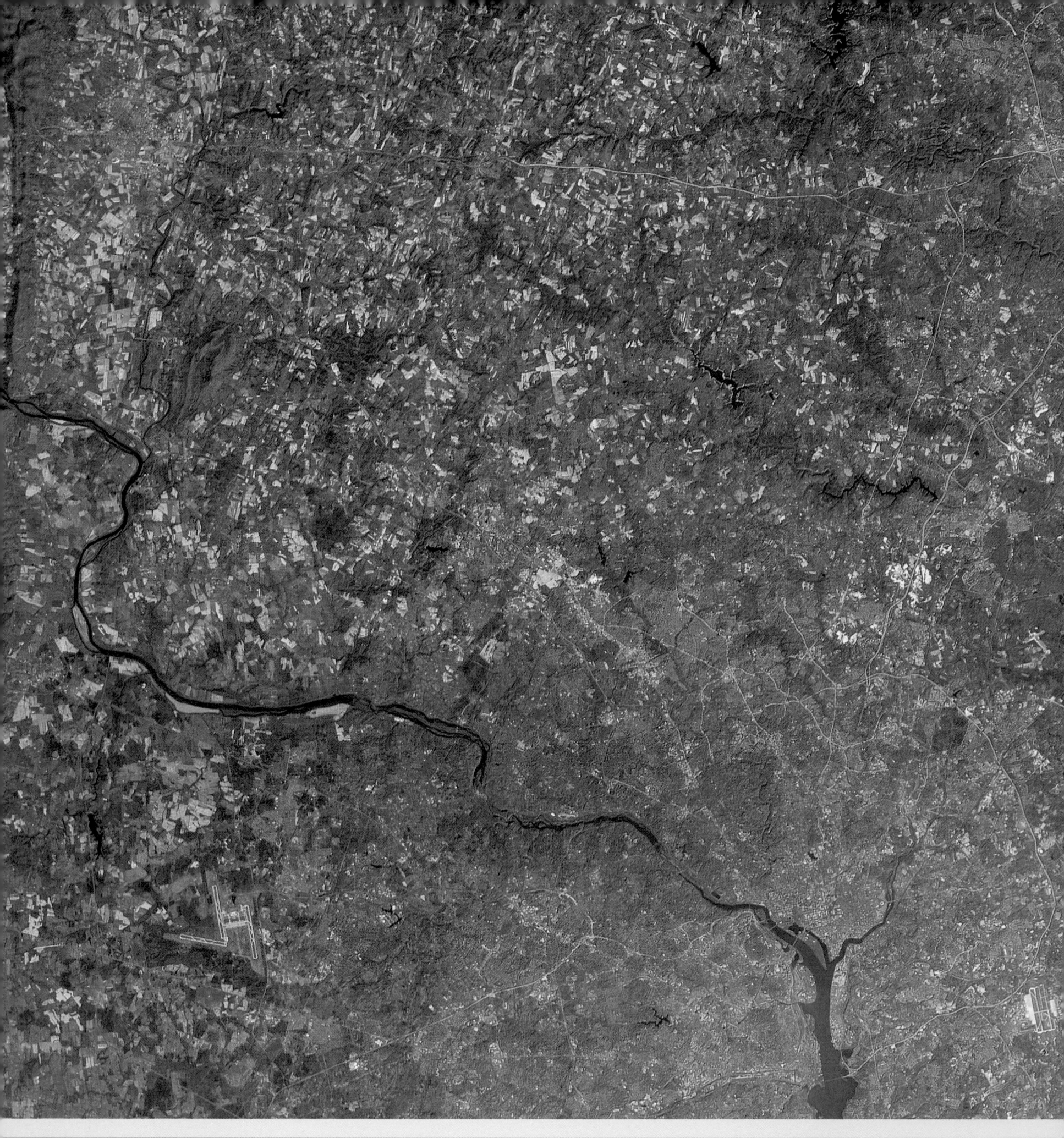

Satellite imagery of the
Washington, D.C., area, U.S.

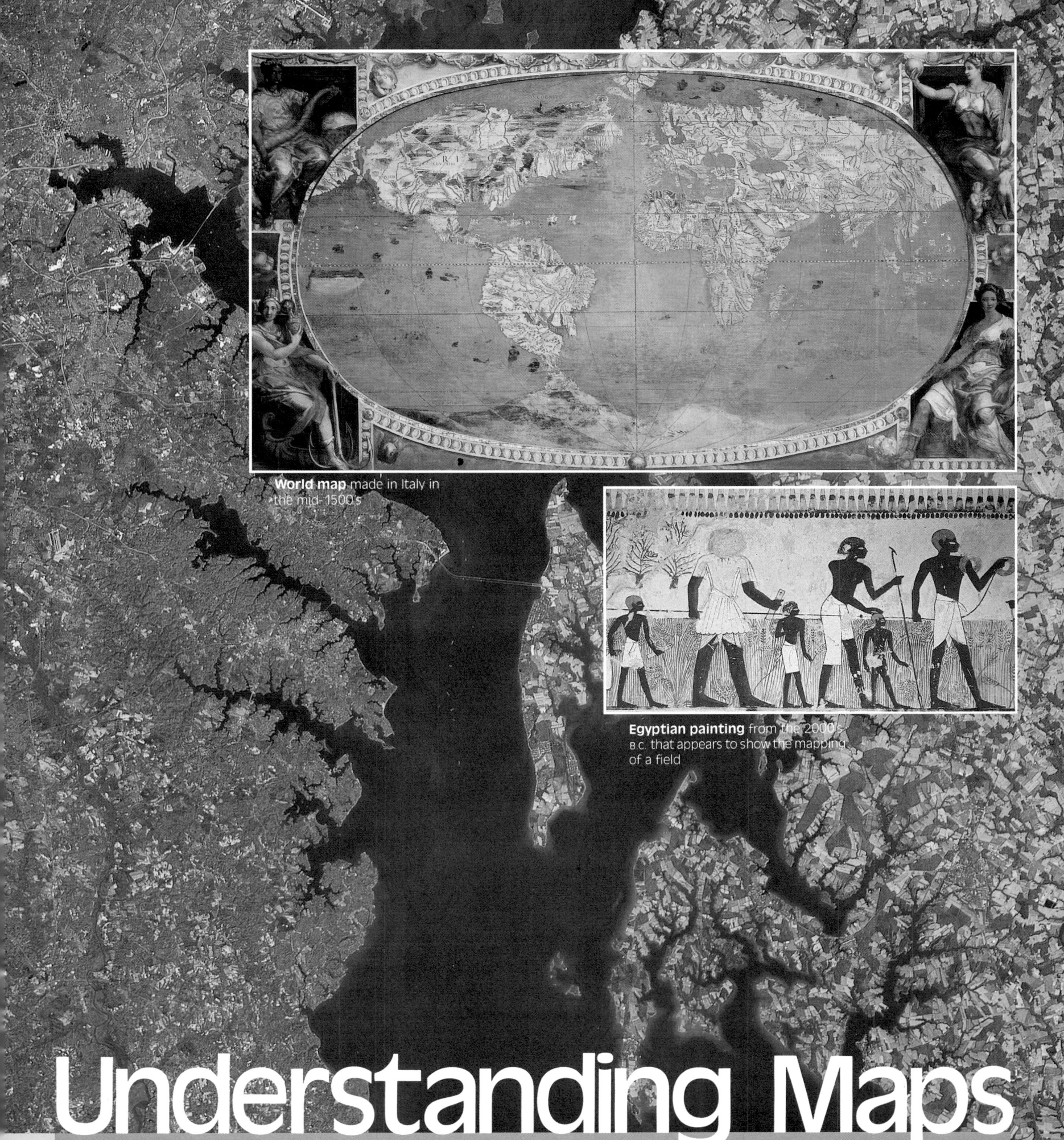

World map made in Italy in the mid-1500's

Egyptian painting from the 2000's B.C. that appears to show the mapping of a field

Understanding Maps

To UNDERSTAND the meanings of the lines, words, symbols, and colors on a map is to understand the distribution and arrangement of part or all of the earth's features.

The History of Maps

It is likely that, some forms of maps were made as long ago as prehistoric times. There are archaeologists who believe that certain markings in cave paintings and other marks scratched onto bone tablets could have shown game routes and hunting trails.

The earliest map in existence that clearly shows features of land is a Babylonian clay tablet. It dates back to about 2500 B.C. In 1300 B.C., the Egyptians were also making maps of their surrounding area. It was not until the time of the Greek philosophers and geographers that people began to think about the nature of the earth as a whole. It was the Greeks who first projected the idea that the earth was round. It was they who developed a system of parallels and meridians and a method of projecting them.

The greatest geographer and mapmaker of the ancient world was Claudius Ptolemy, who lived in Alexandria, Egypt, about A.D. 150. Ptolemy wrote the eight-volume *Geographia*. This work includes Ptolemy's map of the world, as well as instructions for making maps.

The earliest surviving globe was made in 1623 by Jesuit missionaries. The long legend on the globe contains one of the earliest known references to the force of gravity.

The oldest known map, made about 2500 B.C., is on a clay tablet found in Iraq that seems to show a valley estate.

A map carved in rock, showing the Val Camonica, Italy, dates from the second and first millennia B.C.

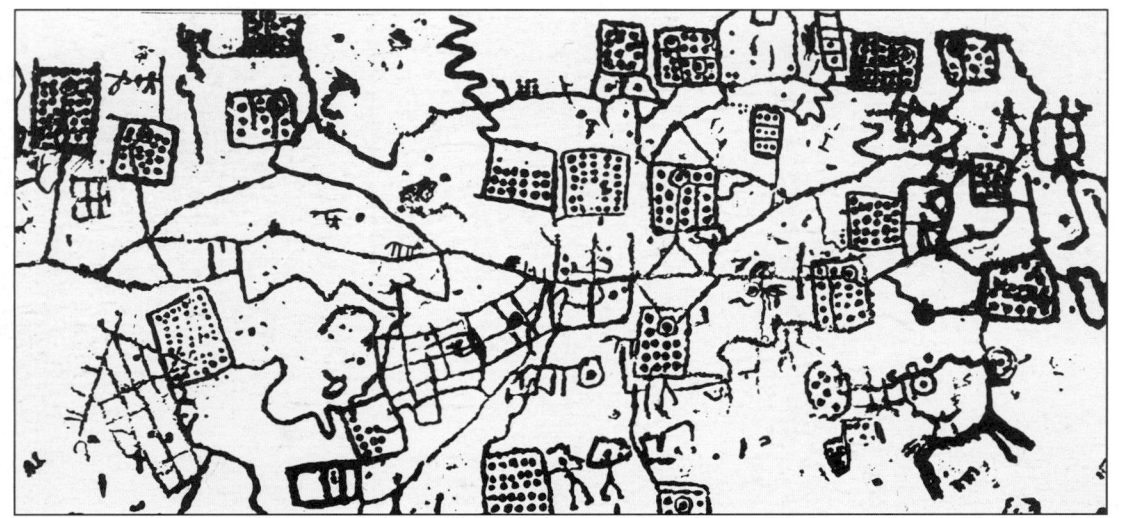

Ptolemy made one error that had far-reaching effects. He showed Europe and Asia as taking up half the globe and being much closer to each other than they actually are. Ptolemy's influence was so strong that about 1,700 years later, Columbus thought he had to sail only about 2,400 nautical miles (4,400 kilometers) to reach Asia from Spain. The actual distance is about 11,000 nautical miles (20,400 kilometers). Instead of reaching Cathay and India as he planned to do, Columbus discovered America.

The Middle Ages saw little progress in mapmaking. However, toward the end of that period, about the year 1300, the portolan chart came into being. Drawn on sheepskin, portolan charts were much in demand by people involved in trade and shipping. Ships' pilots and captains from cities such as Genoa, Pisa, Venice, and Barcelona contributed information about sailing routes, ports, and anchorages.

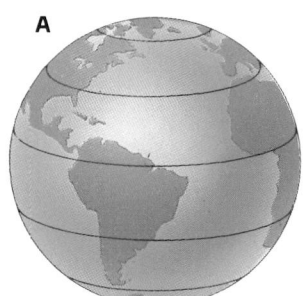 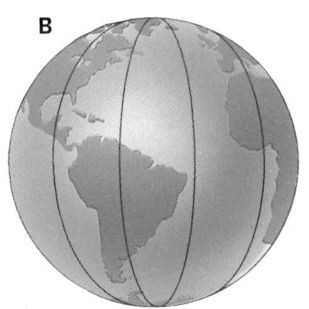 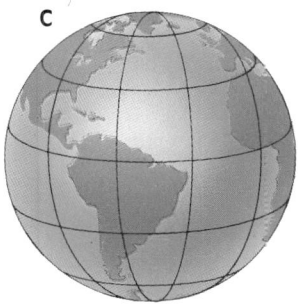

Lines of latitude (A) and longitude (B) are measured in degrees and enable every place on earth to be located by coordinates (C). The astrolabe, *left*, helped navigators in the Middle Ages establish latitude, or distance north and south from the equator, which has a latitude of 0 degrees. Longitude measures east-west distance from the prime meridian that passes through Greenwich, a borough of London, England. The longitude of the prime meridian is 0 degrees.

LandSat 1, a satellite, took the 46 infrared pictures that form this photomosaic of Italy.

Another thing that occurred in the Middle Ages also interested people in world maps and increased the sales of such maps. Marco Polo's travels to China gave people a desire to know the world. This desire probably helped lead to the great age of discovery and exploration.

The discoveries of explorers such as Columbus, da Gama, Vespucci, and Magellan changed the world maps during the 1400's and 1500's. The most important mapmaker of the period was Mercator of Flanders. He produced both globes and maps. Mercator also developed a map projection that was of great aid to sailors.

Mapmaking became more accurate and more scientific beginning in the 1700's. The use of new instruments such as the telescope and the chronometer—an instrument used in determining longitude at sea—made much more information available to mapmakers.

Great progress in mapping took place in the 1900's. Road maps for car travel first became widely used about 1910. Air travel, another form of transportation that developed in the early 1900's, required entirely different kinds of maps. Ever since World War I, aerial photography has played the major role in mapping. In 1940, after the U.S. Air Force reported that less than 10 per cent of the world was mapped sufficiently for the use of pilots, a major program was developed to map great areas of the world.

Much of the equipment still in use today had been developed by World War II. Since then, computers, satellites, and automation have made mapping even easier and more accurate.

How to Read Maps

Map language is a kind of code made up of elements such as scale, symbols, color, and grids. Understanding those elements allows the reader to break the map code.

Scale refers to the measurement on a map that represents a certain portion of the earth. A map scale may be shown as a representative fraction, in written form, or graphically.

As a representative fraction, a map scale might be written *1:3,300,000.* This means that one unit on the map represents 3,300,000 of the same units on the earth's surface (1 inch = 3,300,000 inches; 1 centimeter = 3,300,000 centimeters). In written form, the same proportion would be *1 inch = about 52 miles* or *1 centimeter = 33 kilometers.*

A graphic scale, also called a bar scale, is represented by a straight line on which distances have been marked off. Each mark represents a certain number of miles or kilometers.

Symbols allow mapmakers, or cartographers, to include a great deal of information clearly and concisely. Some symbols represent natural features of the land, such as mountains and lakes. Others represent cultural features such as cities and roads. Usually, a map contains a legend, which is a key that lists and explains the symbols used.

Color helps the map reader interpret what is shown. Mapmakers generally use blue for water, green for vegetation, and black or red for roads and place names.

Grid lines called meridians and parallels are used to mark longitude and latitude. Meridians are north-south lines drawn from pole to pole. Parallels are east-west lines drawn around a globe.

Learning to read maps is a skill. Like all skills, it requires practice. The ability to interpret a map will help the reader understand the earth, its features, and its people.

116
114
Colorado River
UNITED STATES OF AMERICA
San Luis Rio Colorado
114.47 W
MEXICO
Rio Colorado
32.29 N
32

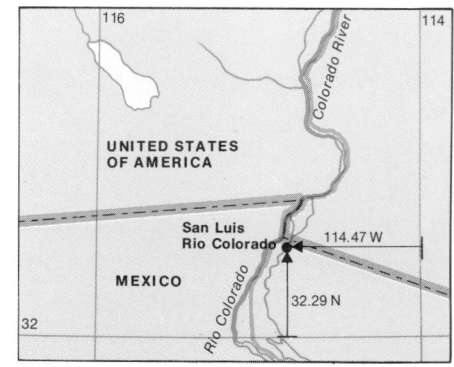

Any location can be expressed in terms of its latitude and longitude, the straight blue lines on the diagram above. San Luis on the Rio Colorado in Mexico is 32 degrees, 29 minutes (sixtieths of a degree) north of the equator and 114 degrees, 47 minutes west of Greenwich.

Maps often attempt to show what the surface of the earth looks like. For example, shading suggests that mountains rise above the land's surface. Detailed information about cities, boundaries, and roads can also appear on a map. The locations of various points of interest can be indicated as well.

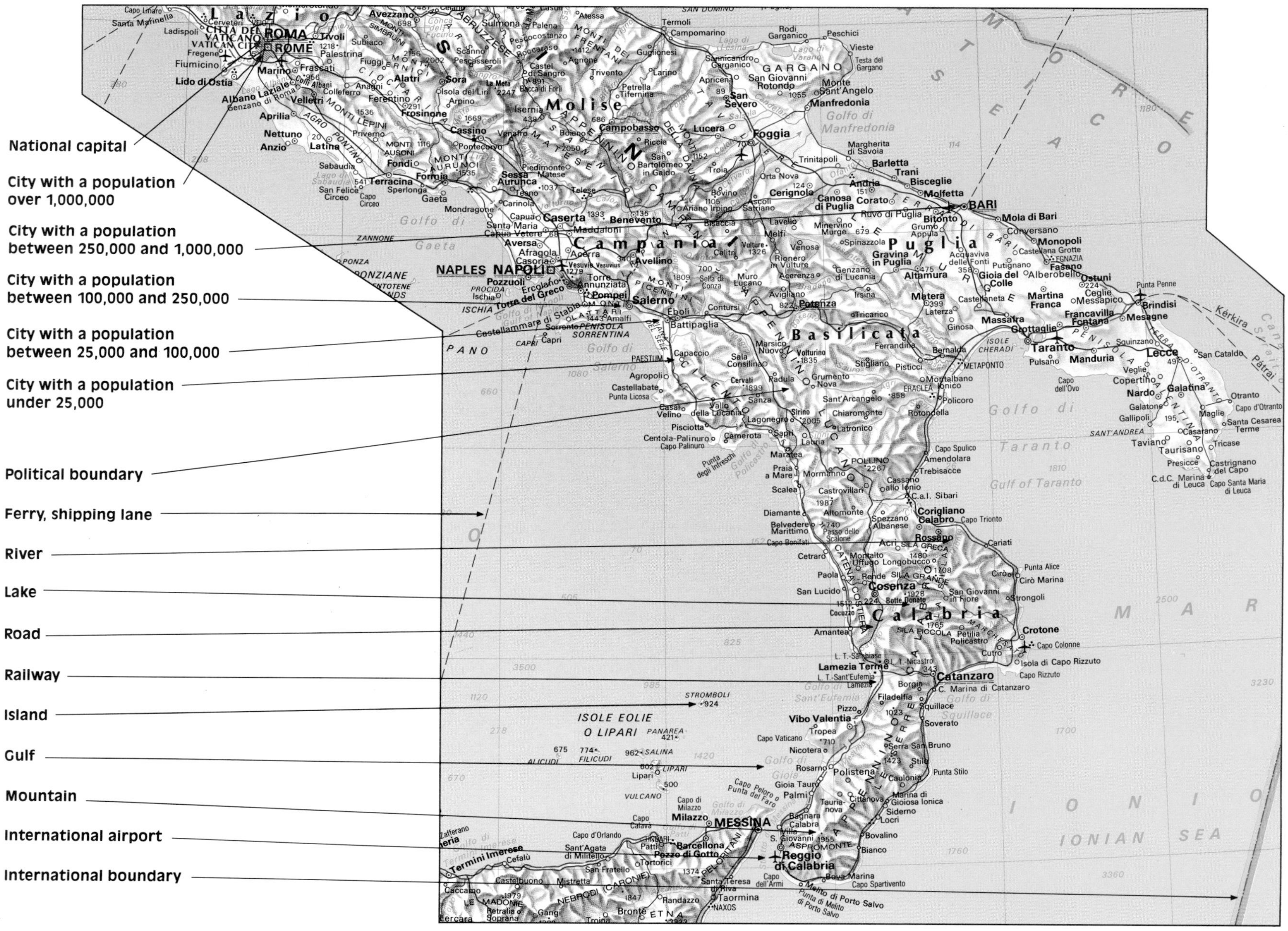

National capital
City with a population over 1,000,000
City with a population between 250,000 and 1,000,000
City with a population between 100,000 and 250,000
City with a population between 25,000 and 100,000
City with a population under 25,000
Political boundary
Ferry, shipping lane
River
Lake
Road
Railway
Island
Gulf
Mountain
International airport
International boundary

Maps of the World

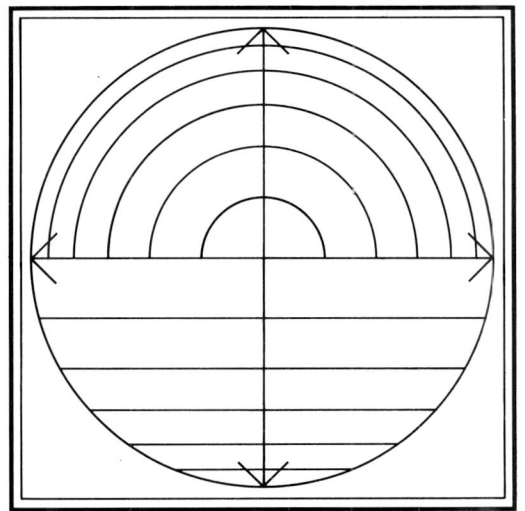

LEGEND

Hydrographic and Topographic Features
Symboles hydrographiques et morphologiques
Gewässer- und Geländeformen
Idrografia, Morfologia
Hidrografía y morfología

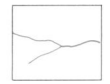

River, Stream
Cours d'eau permanent
Ständig wasserführender Fluß
Corso d'acqua perenne
Corriente de agua de régimen permanente

Lake
Lac d'eau douce
Süßwassersee
Lago d'acqua dolce
Lago de agua dulce

Rocks
Ecueils, Roches
Klippen, Felsriffe
Scogli, Rocce
Escollos, Rocas

Summer Limit of Pack-Ice
Limite du pack en été
Packeisgrenze im Sommer
Limite estivo del pack ghiacciato
Límite estival de banco de hielo

Intermittent Stream
Cours d'eau intermittent
Zeitweilig wasserführender Fluß
Corso d'acqua periodico
Corriente de agua intermitente

Intermittent Lake
Lac d'eau douce temporaire
Zeitweiliger Süßwassersee
Lago d'acqua dolce periodico
Lago de agua dulce intermitente

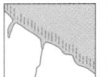

Reef, Atoll
Barrière, Atoll
Riff, Atoll
Barriera, Atollo
Barrera de arrecifes

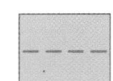

Winter Limit of Pack-Ice
Limite du pack en hiver
Packeisgrenze im Winter
Limite invernale del pack ghiacciato
Límite invernal de banco de hielo

Disappearing Stream
Perte de cours d'eau
Versickernder Fluß
Corso d'acqua che si inabissa
Corriente de agua que desaparece

Salt Lake
Lac d'eau salée
Salzsee
Lago d'acqua salata
Lago de agua salada

Mangrove
Mangrove
Mangrove
Mangrovie
Manglar

Limit of Icebergs
Limite des glaces flottantes
Treibeisgrenze
Limite dei ghiacci alla deriva
Limite de hielo a la deriva

Undefined or Fluctuating River Course
Cours d'eau incertain
Fluß mit veränderlichem Lauf
Fiume dal corso incerto
Corriente de agua incerta

Intermittent Salt Lake
Lac d'eau salée temporaire
Zeitweiliger Salzsee
Lago d'acqua salata periodico
Lago de agua salada intermitente

Continental Ice-cap
Glacier continental
Inlandeis. Gletscher
Ghiacciaio continentale
Glaciar continental

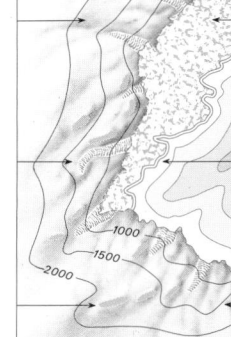

Ice Shelf
Banquise
Schelfeis oder Eisschelf
Banchisa polare (Ice-shelf)
Banquisa

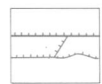

Waterfall, Rapids, Cataract
Chute, Rapide, Cataracte
Wasserfall, Stromschnelle, Katarakt
Cascata, Rapida, Cateratta
Cascada, Rapido, Catarata

Dry Lake Bed
Lac asséché
Trockener Seeboden
Alveo di lago asciutto
Lecho de lago seco

Glacial Tongue
Langue glaciaire
Gletscherzunge
Lingua di ghiaccio
Lengua de glaciar

Limit of Ice Shelf
Limite de la banquise
Schelfeisgrenze
Limite della banchisa
Límite de la banquisa

Canal
Canal
Kanal
Canale
Canal

Lake Surface Elevation
Cote du lac au-dessus du niveau de la mer
Höhe des Seespiegels
Altitudine del lago
Elevación de lago sobre el nivel del mar

Rocky Areas (Antarctica)
Région de roches (Antarctique)
Eisfreie Gebiete (Antarktika)
Aree rocciose (Antartide)
Area rocosa (Antártida)

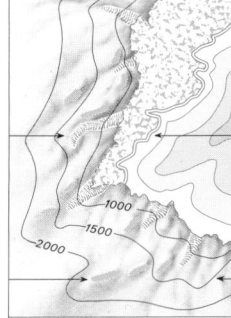

Contour Lines in Continental Ice
Courbes de niveau dans les régions glaciaires
Höhenlinien auf vergletschertem Gebiet
Curve altimetriche nelle aree ghiacciate
Curvas de nivel en áreas heladas

Navigable Canal
Canal navigable
Schiffbarer Kanal
Canale navigabile
Canal navegable

Lake Depth
Profondeur du lac
Seetiefe
Profondità del lago
Profundidad del lago

Defined Shoreline
Trait de côte définie
Küsten- oder Uferlinie
Linea di costa definita
Línea de costa definida

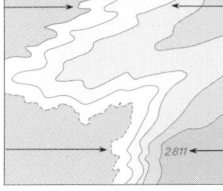

Bathymetric Contour
Courbe bathymétrique
Tiefenlinie
Curva batimetrica
Curva batimétrica

Swamp
Marais
Sumpf
Palude d'acqua dolce
Pantano

Sand Area
Région de sable, Désert
Sandgebiet, Sandwüste
Area sabbiosa, Deserto
Zona arenosa, desierto

Undefined or Fluctuating Shoreline
Trait de côte indéfinie
Unbestimmte oder veränderliche Uferlinie
Linea di costa indefinita
Línea de costa indefinida

Depth of Water
Valeur de sonde
Tiefenzahl
Quota batimetrica
Cota batimétrica

Salt Marsh
Marais d'eau salée
Salzsumpf
Palude d'acqua salata
Pantano de agua salada

Sandbank, Sandbar
Banc de sable
Sandbank
Bassofondo sabbioso
Banco submarino de arena

Mountain Range
Chaîne de montagnes
Bergkette
Catena di monti
Cadena montañosa

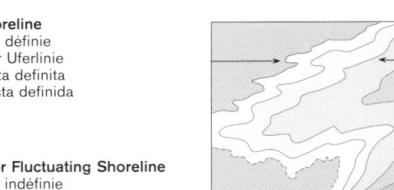

Mountain
Mont
Berg, Bergmassiv
Monte
Monte

Salt Pan
Marais salant
Salzpfanne
Salina
Salina

Port Facilities
Installations portuaires
Hafenanlagen
Impianti portuali
Instalaciones portuarias

Elevation
Cote, Altitude
Höhenzahl
Quota altimetrica
Cota altimétrica

Mountain Pass, Gap
Passage, Col, Port
Paß, Joch, Sattel
Passo, Colle, Valico
Paso, Collado, Puerto de montaña

Key to Elevation and Depth Tints
Hypsométrie, Bathymétrie
Höhenstufen, Tiefenstufen
Altimetria, Batimetria
Altimetría, Batimetría

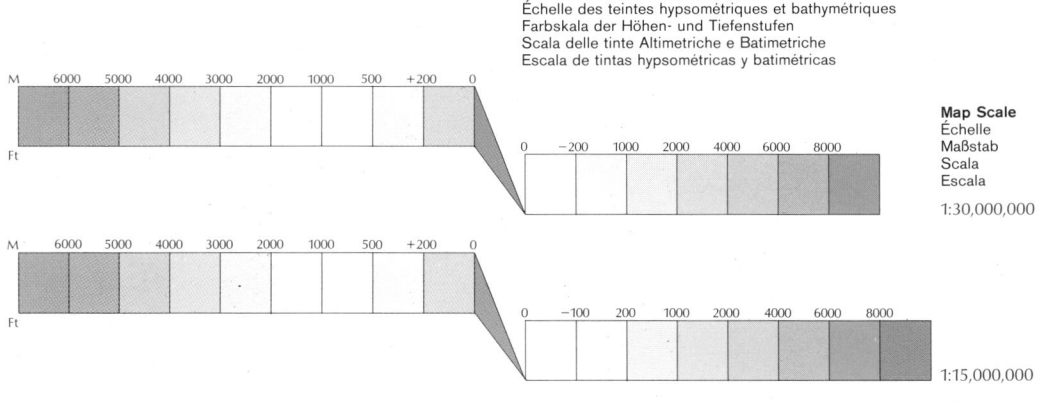

Scales in Metric and English Measures
Échelle des teintes hypsométriques et bathymétriques
Farbskala der Höhen- und Tiefenstufen
Scala delle tinte Altimetriche e Batimetriche
Escala de tintas hypsométricas y batimétricas

M 6000 5000 4000 3000 2000 1000 500 +200 0
Ft

0 −200 1000 2000 4000 6000 8000

Map Scale
Échelle
Maßstab
Scala
Escala

1:30,000,000

M 6000 5000 4000 3000 2000 1000 500 +200 0
Ft

0 −100 200 1000 2000 4000 6000 8000

1:15,000,000

Land Elevation Below Sea Level
−155
Dépression et cote au-dessous du niveau de la mer
Senke mit Tiefenzahl unter dem Meeresspiegel
Depressione e quota sotto il livello del mare
Depresión y elevación bajo el nivel del mar

The meanings of the symbols on the Legend pages are in English, French, German, Italian, and Spanish languages to permit the interpretation of the maps by a broad readership.

Map Projections
Projections cartographiques
Kartennetzentwürfe
Proiezioni cartografiche
Proyecciones cartográficas

The projections appearing in this atlas have been plotted by computer

Les réseaux des projections ont été obtenus par élaboration automatique à partir de formules mathématiques

Die Kartennetze aller im Atlas vorkommenden Abbildungen wurden mit Hilfe der Datenverarbeitung (EDV) völlig neu errechnet

I disegni delle proiezioni presenti in quest'opera sono stati realizzati interamente ex-novo con l'uso del computer e del plotter a partire dalle formule matematiche

El reticulado de las proyecciones (redes geográficas) incluidas en ésta obra han sido obtenidas por proceso automático a partir de las fórmulas matemáticas

Boundaries, Capitals
Frontières, Soulignements Confini, Sottolineature
Grenzen, Unterstreichungen Límites, Subrayados

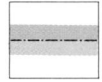

International Boundary
Frontière internationale
Staatsgrenze
Confine di Stato
Límite de Nación

Second-order Political Boundary
Frontière d'État fédéré, Région
Bundesstaats-, Regionsgrenze
Confine di Stato federato, Regione
Límite de Estado federado, Región

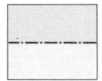

International Boundary (Continent Maps)
Frontière internationale (Continents)
Staatsgrenze (Erdteilkarten)
Confine di Stato (Carte dei Continenti)
Límite de Nación (Continentes)

Third-order Political Boundary
Frontière de Province, Comté, Bezirk
Provinz-, Grafschafts-, Bezirksgrenze
Confine di Provincia, Contea, Bezirk
Límite de Provincia, Condado, Bezirk

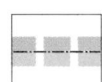

Undefined International Boundary
Frontière internationale indéfinie
Nicht genau festgelegte Staatsgrenze
Confine di Stato indefinito
Límite de Nación indefinido

Administrative District Boundary (U.S.S.R.)
Frontière de Circonscription
Kreisgrenze
Confine di Circondario
Límite de Circunscripción administrativa

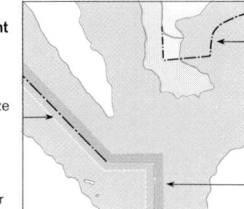

International Ocean Floor Boundary Defined by Treaty or Bilateral Agreement
Frontière d'état en mer définie par traités et conventions bilatéraux
Durch Verträge festgelegte Staatsgrenze im Meeresgebiet
Confine di Stato nel mare definito da trattati e convenzioni bilaterali
Límite de Nación en el Mar definido por los tratados bilaterales

International Ocean Floor Boundary
Frontière d'état en mer
Staatsgrenze im Meeresgebiet
Confine di Stato nel mare
Límite de Nación en el mar

Undefined Ocean Floor Boundary
Frontière indéfinie d'état tracée en mer
Unbestimmte Staatsgrenze im Meeresgebiet
Confine di Stato indefinito nel mare
Límite indefinido de Nación en el mar

ROMA **National Capital**
Capitale d'État
Hauptstadt eines unabhängigen Staates
Capitale di Stato
Capital de Nación

Kristiansand **Third - order Capital**
Capitale de Province, Comté, Bezirk
Provinz-, Grafschafts-, Bezirkshauptstadt
Capoluogo di Provincia, Contea, Bezirk
Capital de Provincia, Condado, Bezirk

RIGA **Dependency or Second-order Capital**
Capitale d'État fédéré, Région
Bundesstaats-, Regionshauptstadt
Capitale di Stato federato, Regione
Capital de Estado federado, Región

Anadyr **Administrative District Capital (U.S.S.R.)**
Capitale de Circonscription
Kreishauptstadt
Capoluogo di Circondario
Capital de Circunscripción administrativa

Other Symbols
Symboles divers Simboli vari
Sonstige Zeichen Signos varios

 LUTON AIRPORT **International Airport**
Aéroport international
Internationaler Flughafen
Aeroporto internazionale
Aeropuerto internacional

SANTAS CREUS **Church, Monastery, Abbey**
Monastère, Église, Abbaye
Kloster, Kirche, Abtei
Monastero, Chiesa, Abbazia
Monasterio, Iglesia, Abadía

 Lighthouse
Phare
Leuchtturm
Faro
Faro

DAMPIERRE **Castle**
Château
Burg, Schloß
Castello
Castillo

 BUI DAM **Dam**
Barrage
Staudamm, Staumauer
Diga artificiale, Sbarramento
Presa

PAESTUM **Ruin, Archeological Site**
Ruine, Centre archéologique
Ruine, Archäologisches Zentrum
Rovina, Zona archeologica
Ruina, Zona arqueológica

L.-GREENWICH · V.-IJmuiden **Section of a City**
Faubourg
Stadt- oder Ortsteil
Sobborgo urbano
Suburbio

MOLENS VAN KINDERDIJK **Monument, Historic Site, etc.**
Monument
Denkmal
Monumento
Monumento

Bidon V **Uninhabited Locality, Hamlet**
Ville inhabitée, Ferme, Hameau
Unbewohnte Stadt, Gehöft, Weiler
Città disabitata, Fattoria, Nucleo di case
Ciudad despoblada, Granja, Casar

HADRIAN'S WALL **Wall**
Muraille
Wall, Mauer
Vallo, Muraglia
Muralla

Bi'r Nāhid **Periodically Inhabited Oasis**
Oasis habitées périodiquement
Zeitweilig bewohnte Oase
Oasi periodicamente abitate
Oasis periodicamente habitados

★ GIANT'S CAUSEWAY **Point of Interest**
Curiosité
Sehenswürdigkeit
Curiosità
Curiosidad

Casey (Australia) **Scientific Station**
Base géophysique
Geophysikalische Beobachtungsstation
Base geofisica
Base geofísica

CUEVAS DE ARTÁ **Cave**
Grotte, Caverne
Höhle
Grotta, Caverna
Cueva, Gruta

Populated Places
Population Popolazione
Bevölkerung Población

 Continent Maps
Cartes des Continents Carte dei Continenti
Erdteilkarten Mapas de Continentes
○ < 25 000
◎ 25 000-100 000
◉ 100 000-250 000
◉ 250 000-1 000 000
□ > 1 000 000

Regional Maps
Cartes à plus grande échelle Carte di sviluppo
Karten größeren Maßstabs Mapas a gran escala
○ < 10 000
◎ 10 000-25 000
◉ 25 000-100 000
◉ 100 000-250 000
◉ 250 000-1 000 000
□ > 1 000 000

Symbols represent population of inhabited localities
Les symboles représentent le nombre d'habitants des localités
Die Signaturen entsprechen der Einwohnerzahl des Ortes
I simboli sono relativi al valore demografico dei centri abitati
Los símbolos son proporcionales a la población del lugar

Town area symbol represents the shape of the urban area
Le petit plan de la ville reproduit la configuration de l'aire urbaine
Die Plansignatur stellt die Gestalt des Stadtgebietes dar
La piantina della città rappresenta la configurazione dell'area urbana
El pequeño plano de la ciudad representa la forma del área urbana

Transportation
Communications Comunicazioni
Verkehrsnetz Comunicaciones

Primary Railway
Chemin de fer principal
Hauptbahn
Ferrovia principale
Ferrocarril principal

Road
Route de grande communication, Autres Routes
Fernverkehrsstraße, andere Straßen
Strada principale, Altre Strade
Carretera principal, Otras Carreteras

Secondary Railway
Chemin de fer secondaire
Sonstige Bahn
Ferrovia secondaria
Ferrocarril secundario

Trail, Caravan Route
Piste, Voie caravanière
Wüstenpiste, Karawanenweg
Pista nel deserto, Carovaniera
Pista en el desierto, Vía de Carabanas

Motorway, Expressway
Autoroute
Autobahn
Autostrada
Autopista

Ferry, Shipping Lane
Bac, Ligne maritime
Fähre, Schiffahrtslinie
Traghetto, Linea di navigazione
Transbordador (Ferry), Línea de navegación

Type Styles
Caractères utilisés pour la toponymie Caratteri usati per la toponomastica
Zur Namenschreibung verwendete Schriftarten Caracteres utilizados para la toponimia

ITALY
Hessen RIBE

Political Units
État, Dépendance, Division administrative
Staat, abhängiges Gebiet, Verwaltungsgliederung
Stato, Dipendenza, Divisione amministrativa
Nación, Dependencia, División administrativa

Ankaratra Monte Bianco
Tsiafajavona Ngorongoro Crater
Nevado del Tolima Kings Peak

Small Mountain Range, Mountain, Peak
Petit massif, Mont, Cime
Bergmassiv, Berg, Gipfel
Piccolo gruppo montuoso, Monte, Vetta
Macizo pequeño, Monte, Cima

LABRADOR SEA
Gulf of Alaska *Hudson Bay*
Estrecho de Magallanes

Sea, Gulf, Bay, Strait
Mer, Golfe, Baie, Détroit
Meer, Golf, Bucht, Meeresstraße
Mare, Golfo, Baia, Stretto
Mar, Golfo, Bahía, Estrecho

SAXONY
THRACE SUSSEX

Historical or Cultural Region
Région historique ou culturelle
Historische oder Kulturlandschaft
Regione storico-culturale
Región histórica y cultural

Cabo de São Vicente Land's End
Mizen Head Point Conception
Col de la Perche Passo della Cisa

Cape, Point, Pass
Cap, Pointe, Passe
Kap, Landspitze, Paß
Capo, Punta, Passo
Cabo, Punta, Paso

West Mariana Basin
Galapagos Fracture Zone
Mid-Atlantic Ridge

Undersea Features
Formes du relief sous-marin
Formen des Meeresbodens
Forme del rilievo sottomarino
Formas del relieve submarino

PATAGONIA
BASSIN DE RENNES
PENÍNSULA DE YUCATÁN

Physical Region (plain, peninsula)
Région physique (plaine, péninsule)
Landschaft (Ebene, Halbinsel)
Regione fisica (pianura, penisola)
Región natural (llanura, península)

MAHÉ ALDABRA ISLANDS
CORSE CHANNEL ISLANDS
SULU ARCHIPELAGO

Island, Archipelago
Ile, Archipel
Insel, Archipel
Isola, Arcipelago
Isla, Archipiélago

Tarfaya
Tombouctou
Agadir
Nouakchott
BRAZZAVILLE
CASABLANCA

Size of type indicates relative importance of inhabited localities
La dimension des caractères indique l'importance d'une localité
Die Schriftgröße entspricht der Gesamtbedeutung des Ortes
La grandezza del carattere è proporzionale all'importanza della località
La dimensión de los caracteres de imprenta indica la importancia de la localidad

PYRENEES
CUMBRIAN MOUNTAINS
SIERRA DE GÁDOR LA SILA

Mountain Range
Chaîne de montagnes
Bergkette, Gebirge
Catena di monti
Cadena montañosa

Thames Po Victoria Falls
Lotagipi Swamp Göta kanal
Lago Maggiore

River, Waterfall, Cataract, Canal, Lake
Fleuve, Chute d'eau, Cataracte, Canal, Lac
Fluß, Wasserfall, Katarakt, Kanal, See
Fiume, Cascata, Cateratta, Canale, Lago
Río, Cascada, Catarata, Canal, Lago

INDEX MAPS

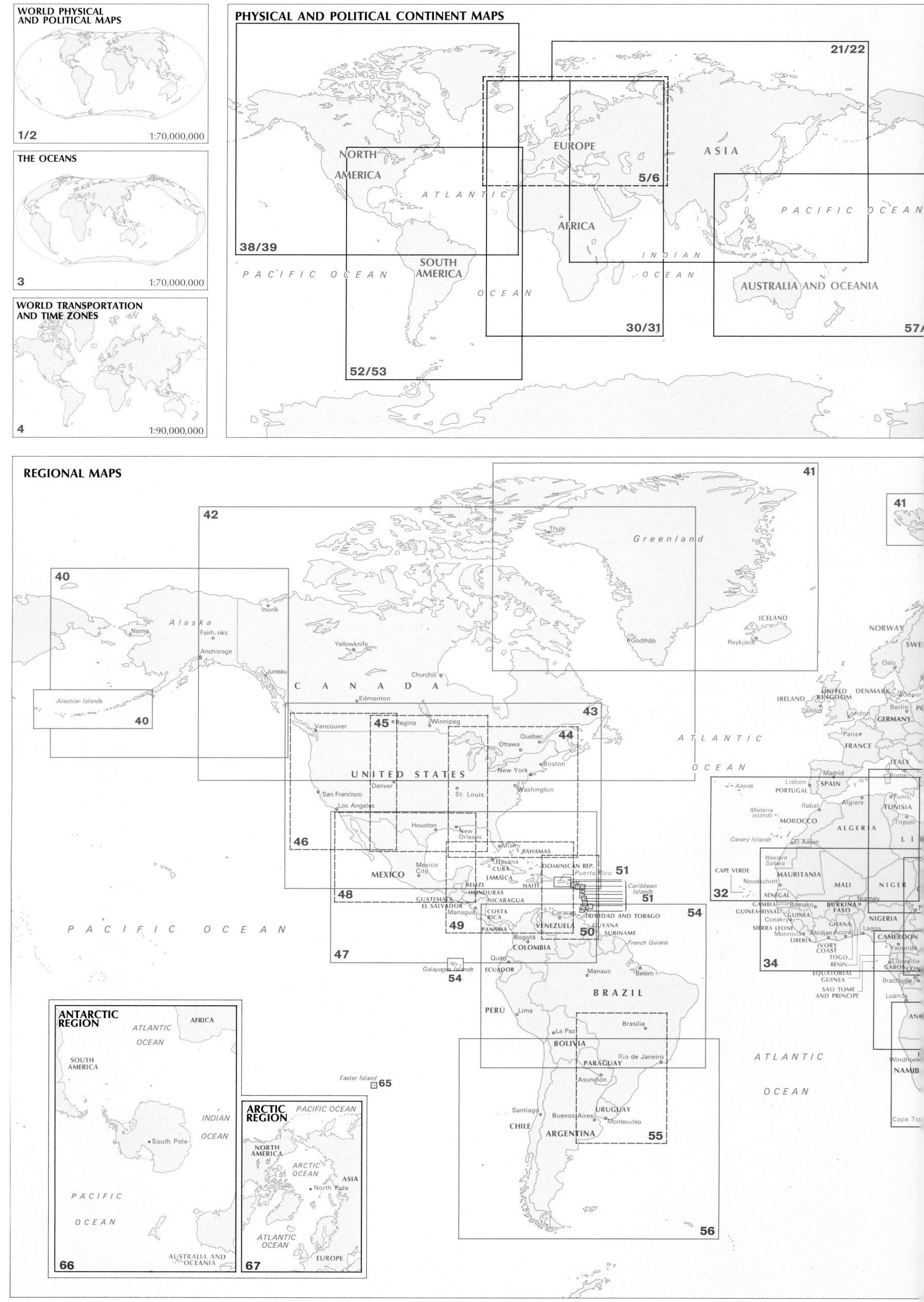

WORLD PHYSICAL AND POLITICAL MAPS

1/2   1:70,000,000

THE OCEANS

3   1:70,000,000

WORLD TRANSPORTATION AND TIME ZONES

4   1:90,000,000

PHYSICAL AND POLITICAL CONTINENT MAPS

21/22

EUROPE

ASIA

NORTH AMERICA

5/6

PACIFIC OCEAN

ATLANTIC OCEAN

AFRICA

INDIAN OCEAN

38/39

PACIFIC OCEAN

SOUTH AMERICA

AUSTRALIA AND OCEANIA

57/

30/31

52/53

REGIONAL MAPS

41

42

41

40

Greenland

Alaska

Nome
Inuvik
Fairbanks
Anchorage
Juneau
Yellowknife

ICELAND

Reykjavik
Godthåb
Thule

NORWAY

SWE

Oslo

40

Aleutian Islands

CANADA

Churchill
Edmonton

IRELAND
UNITED KINGDOM
DENMARK
Copen
Berlin
Dublin
London
GERMANY

ATLANTIC OCEAN

40

43

45

Regina
Winnipeg
Vancouver

Québec
Ottawa
Boston
New York

44

Paris
FRANCE

UNITED STATES

Denver
San Francisco
Los Angeles

St. Louis
Washington

ITALY
Rome

Lisbon
Madrid
PORTUGAL
SPAIN
Azores

46

Houston
New Orleans
Miami
BAHAMAS

Madeira Islands
Rabat
Algiers
TUNISIA
Tunis
Tripoli

MOROCCO
ALGERIA
LI

MEXICO

Mexico City
CUBA
Havana
JAMAICA
HAITI
DOMINICAN REP.
Puerto Rico

51

Canary Islands
El Aaiun
Western Sahara

CAPE VERDE

MAURITANIA
Nouakchott

MALI
NIGER

48

51

GUATEMALA
EL SALVADOR
BELIZE
HONDURAS
NICARAGUA
Managua
COSTA RICA
PANAMA

Caribbean Islands

54

32

SENEGAL
GAMBIA
Bamako
GUINEA-BISSAU
GUINEA
BURKINA FASO
Niamey
NIGERIA

PACIFIC OCEAN

49

Caracas
VENEZUELA
TRINIDAD AND TOBAGO
GUYANA
SURINAME
French Guiana

50

34

SIERRA LEONE
Monrovia
LIBERIA
IVORY COAST
Abidjan
GHANA
Accra
TOGO
BÉNIN
Lagos
CAMEROON
Yaoundé
Libreville
GABON

47

Bogotá
COLOMBIA
Quito
ECUADOR
Galapagos Islands

54

Manaus
Belém

EQUATORIAL GUINEA
SAO TOME AND PRINCIPE
Brazzaville
Luanda

BRAZIL

ANG

PERÚ
Lima

Brasilia

Windhoek

ATLANTIC OCEAN

NAMIB

ANTARCTIC REGION

AFRICA
ATLANTIC OCEAN
SOUTH AMERICA

INDIAN OCEAN

La Paz
BOLIVIA
PARAGUAY
Rio de Janeiro

Cape To

Asunción

Easter Island

65

ARCTIC REGION

PACIFIC OCEAN

Santiago
Buenos Aires
Montevideo
URUGUAY
CHILE
ARGENTINA

55

SOUTH POLE

South Pole

PACIFIC OCEAN

NORTH AMERICA
ARCTIC OCEAN
ASIA
North Pole

ATLANTIC OCEAN
EUROPE

56

66

AUSTRALIA AND OCEANIA

67

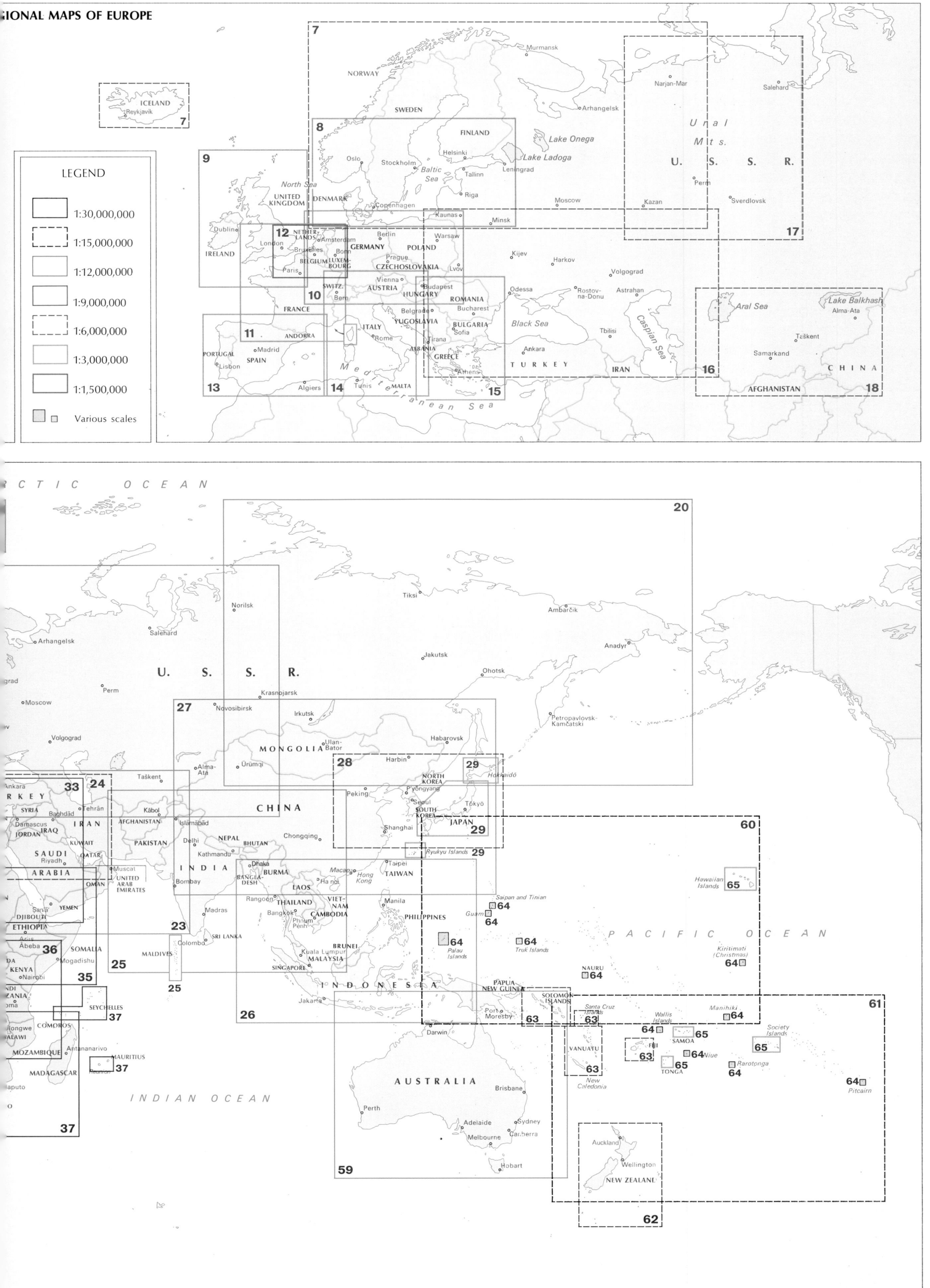

IONAL MAPS OF EUROPE

LEGEND

1:30,000,000

1:15,000,000

1:12,000,000

1:9,000,000

1:6,000,000

1:3,000,000

1:1,500,000

Various scales

Map 1 **WORLD, PHYSICAL**

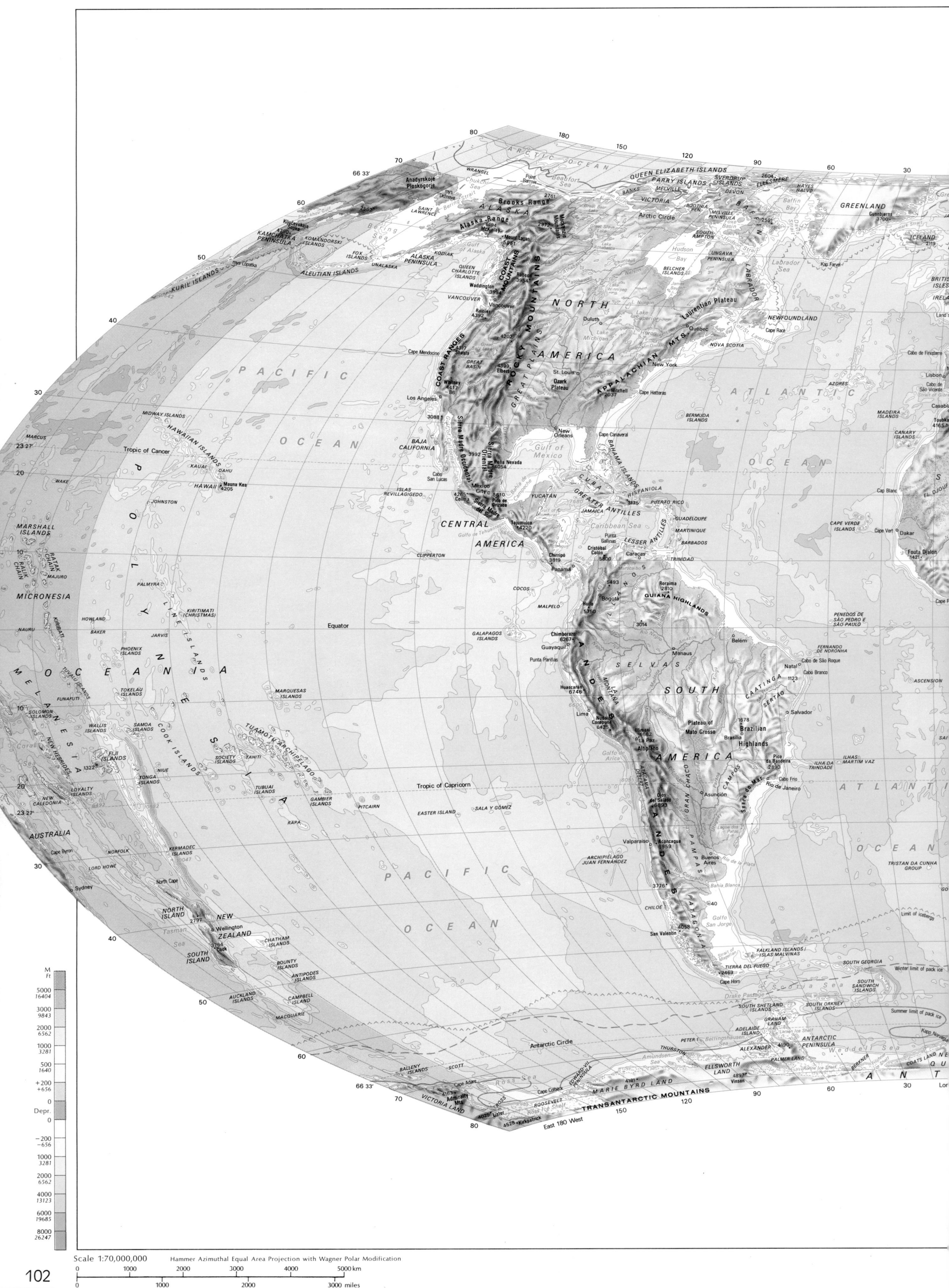

Scale 1:70,000,000   Hammer Azimuthal Equal Area Projection with Wagner Polar Modification

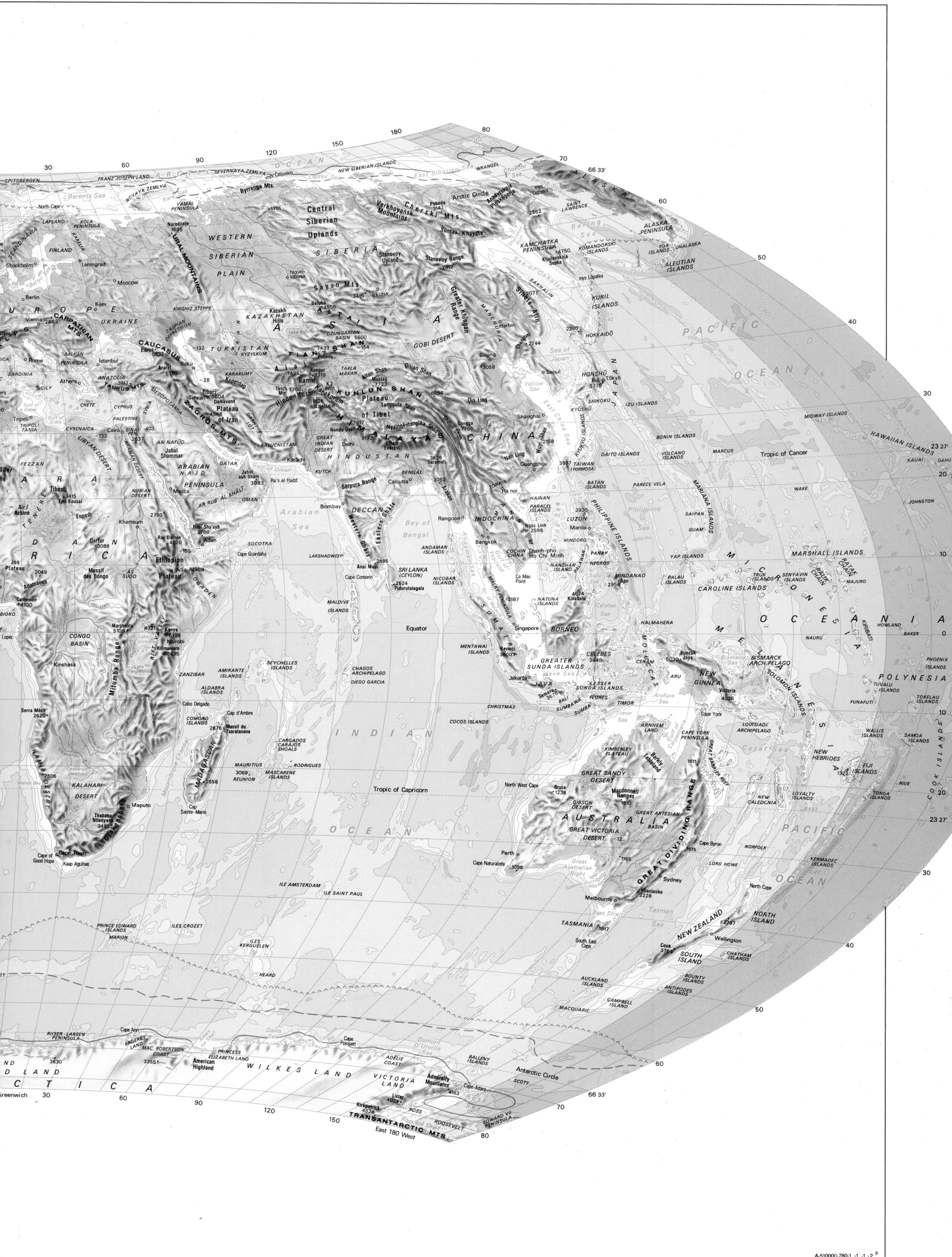

Map 2 **WORLD, POLITICAL**

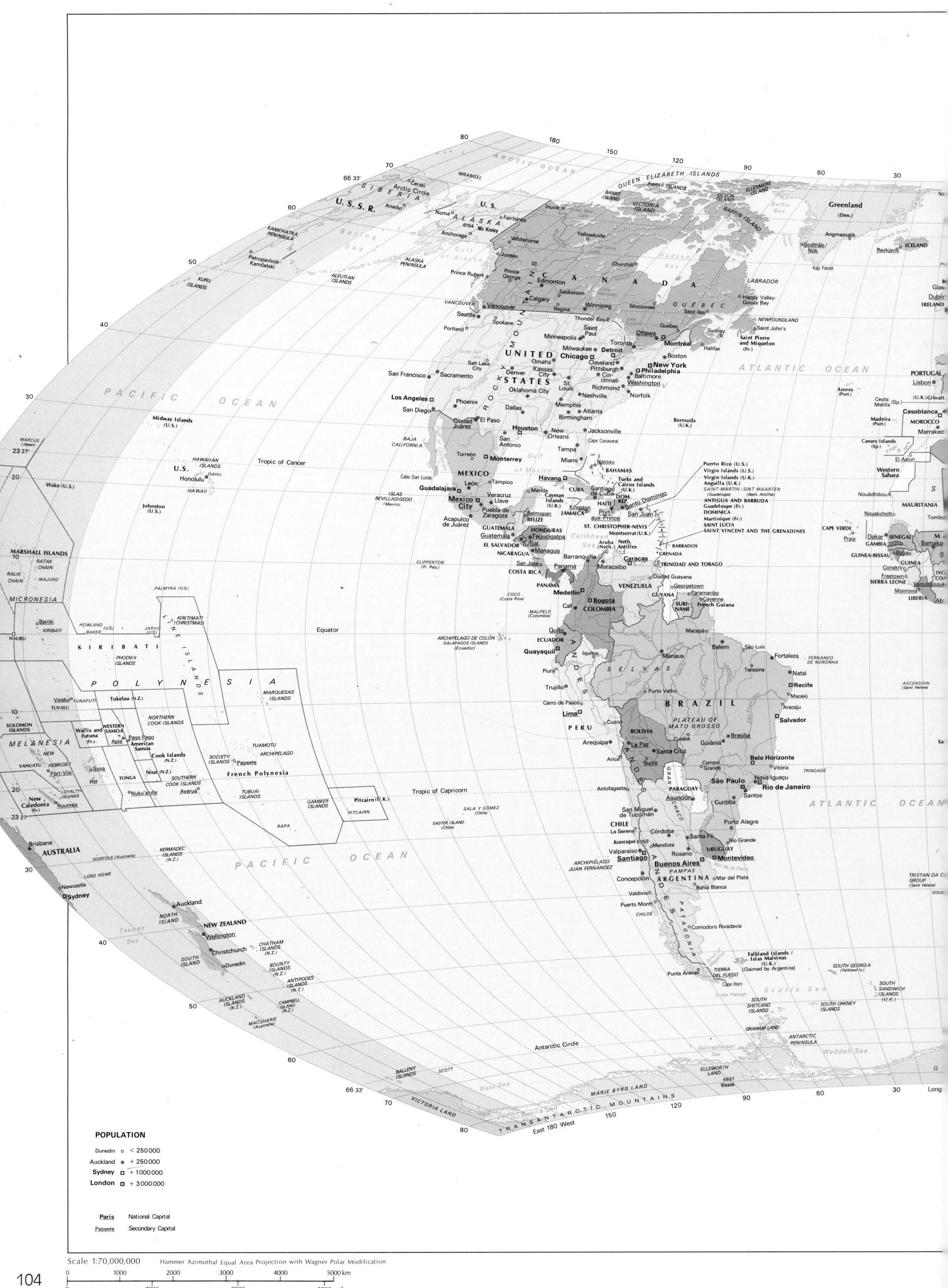

POPULATION

Dunedin ○	< 250 000
Auckland ◉	+ 250 000
Sydney ▫	+ 1000 000
London ◻	+ 3000 000

Paris   National Capital

Papeete   Secondary Capital

Scale 1:70,000,000   Hammer Azimuthal Equal Area Projection with Wagner Polar Modification

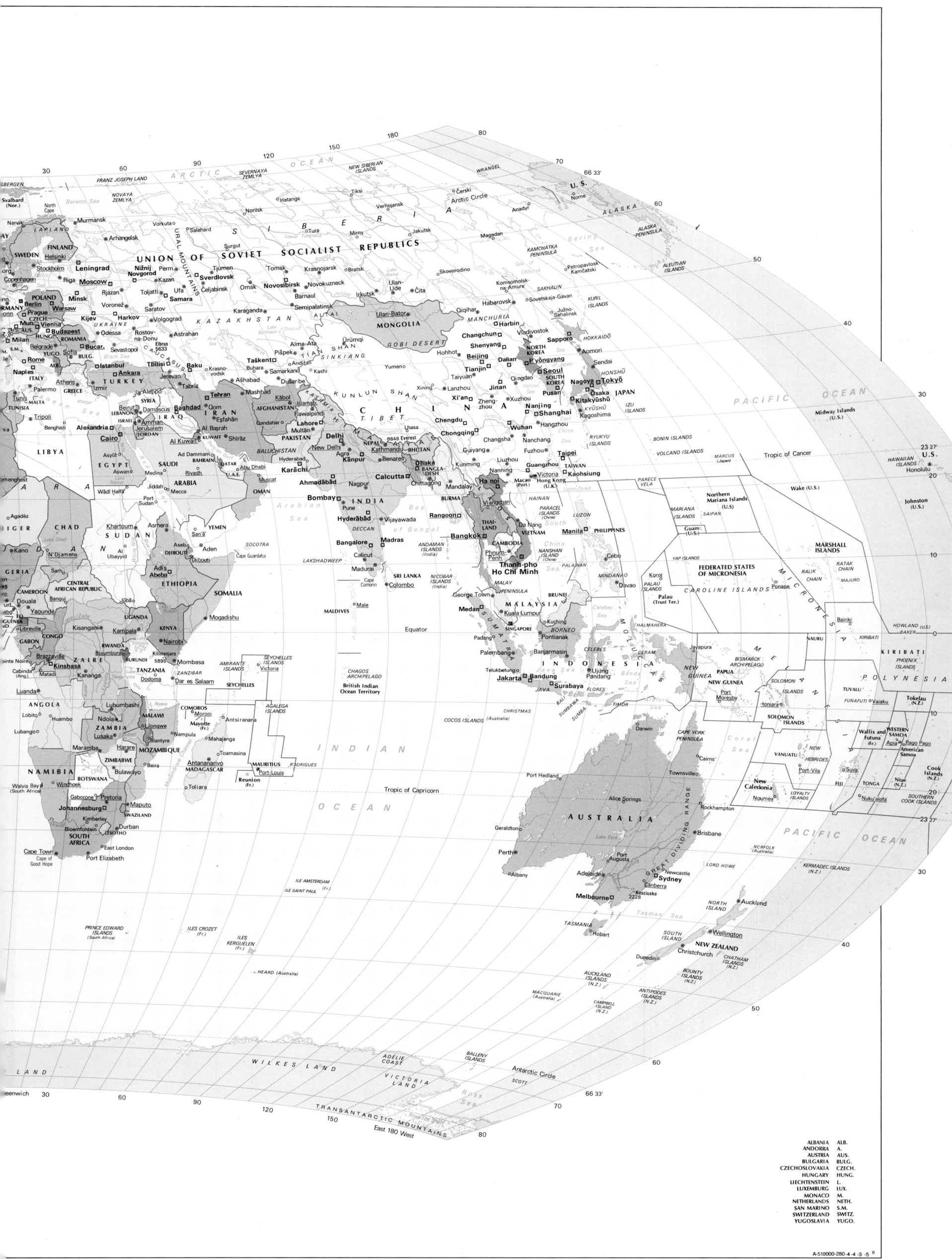

ALBANIA ALB.
ANDORRA A.
AUSTRIA AUS.
BULGARIA BULG.
CZECHOSLOVAKIA CZECH.
HUNGARY HUNG.
LIECHTENSTEIN L.
LUXEMBURG LUX.
MONACO M.
NETHERLANDS NETH.
SAN MARINO S.M.
SWITZERLAND SWITZ.
YUGOSLAVIA YUGO.

A-510000-280-4-4 -3 -5 ^{B}

Map 3 **THE OCEANS**

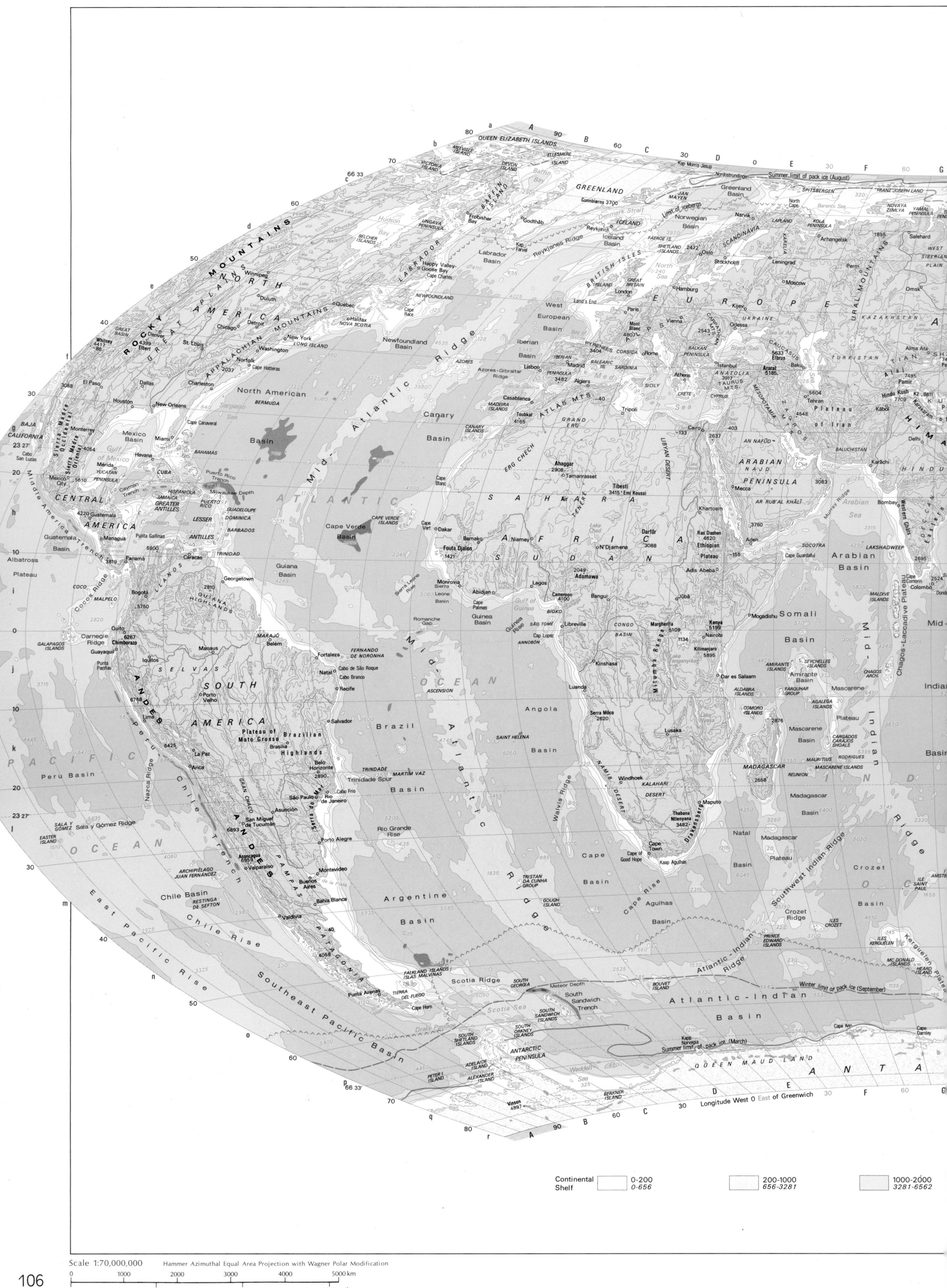

Scale 1:70,000,000   Hammer Azimuthal Equal Area Projection with Wagner Polar Modification

0   1000   2000   3000   4000   5000 km

0   1000   2000   3000 miles

| Continental Shelf | 0-200
0-656 | 200-1000
656-3281 | 1000-2000
3281-6562 |

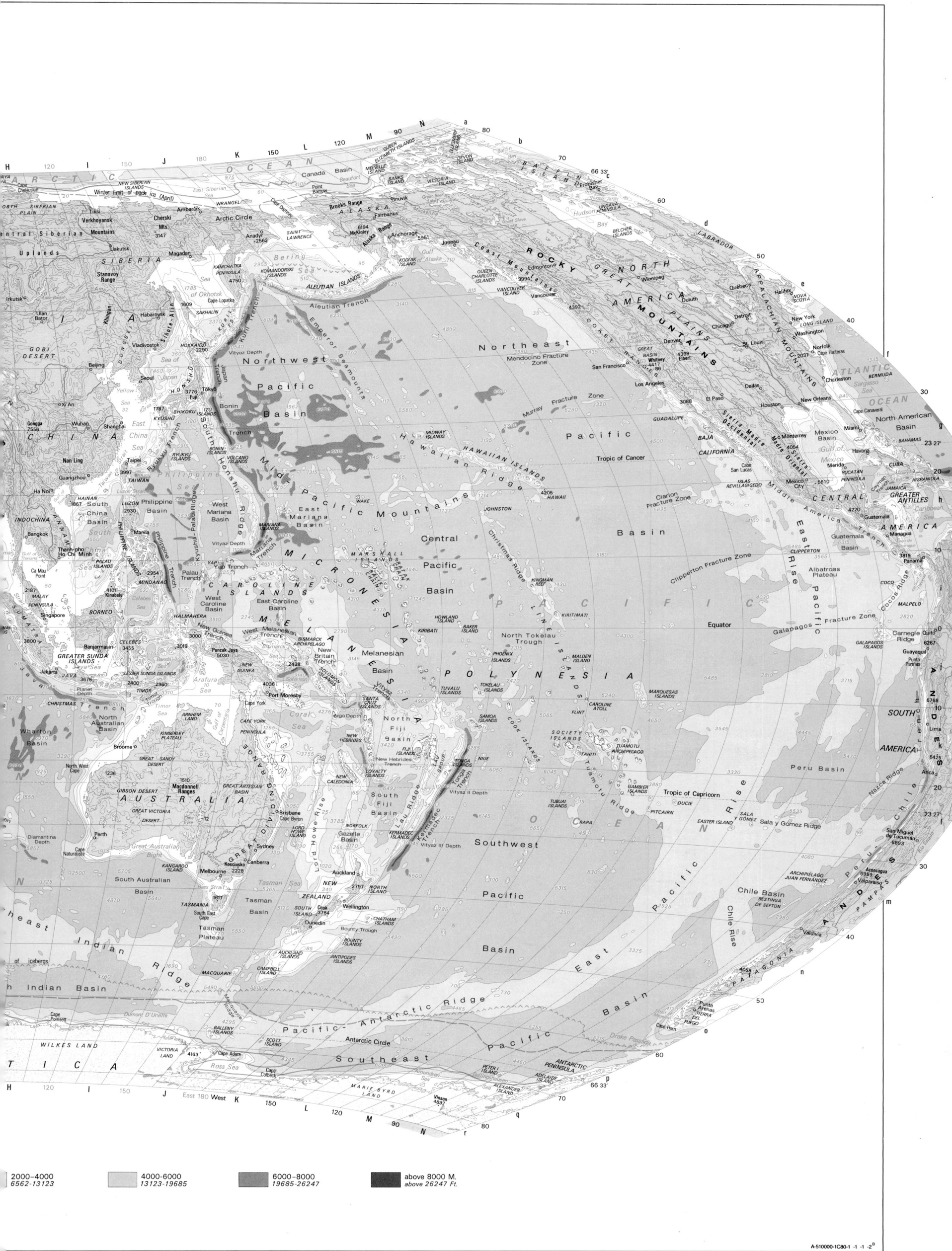

2000–4000 *6562-13123*	4000–6000 *13123-19685*	6000–8000 *19685-26247*	above 8000 M. *above 26247 Ft.*

A-510000-1C80-1 -1 -1 -2ᴮ

Map 4 **WORLD TRANSPORTATION AND TIME ZONES**

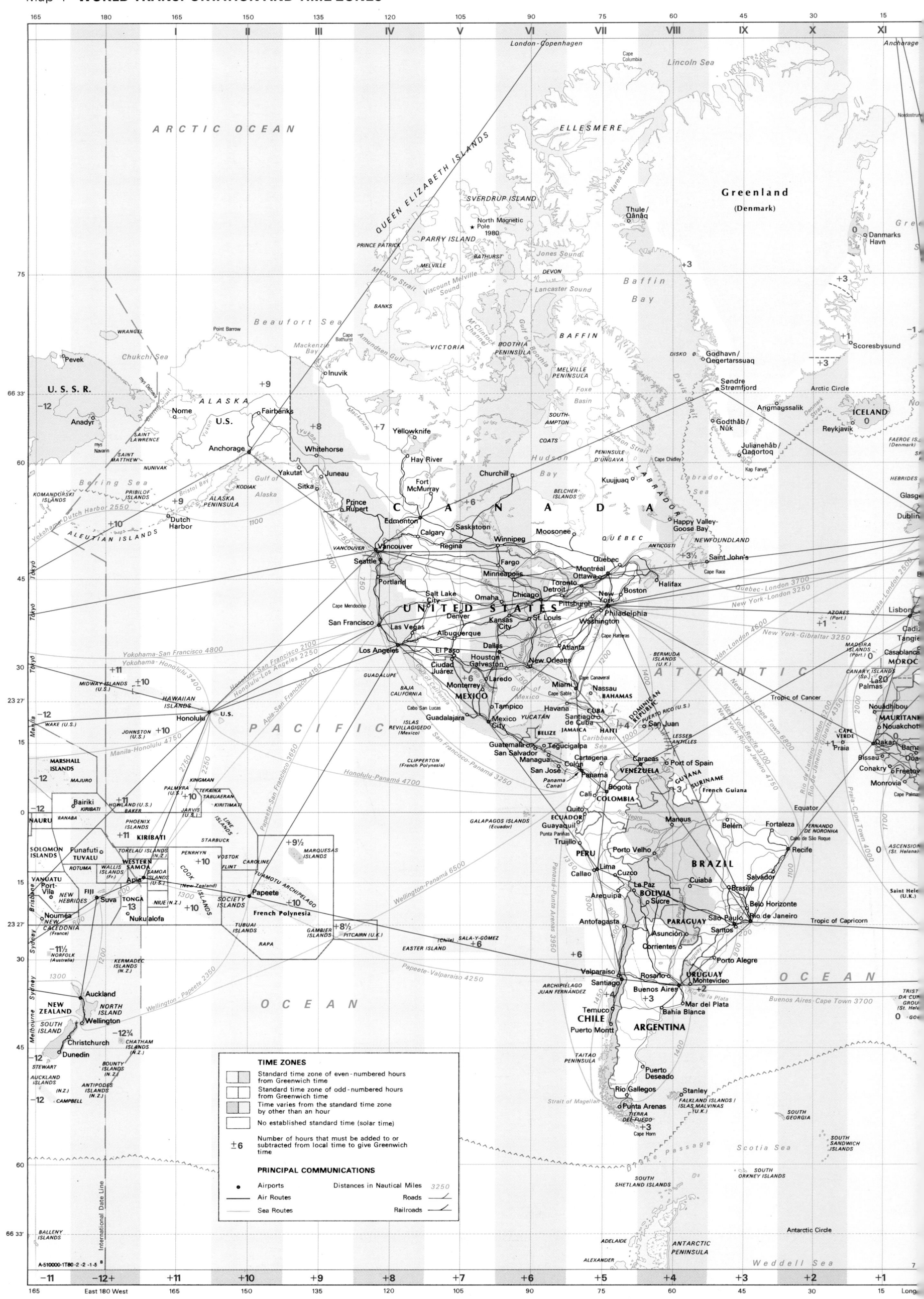

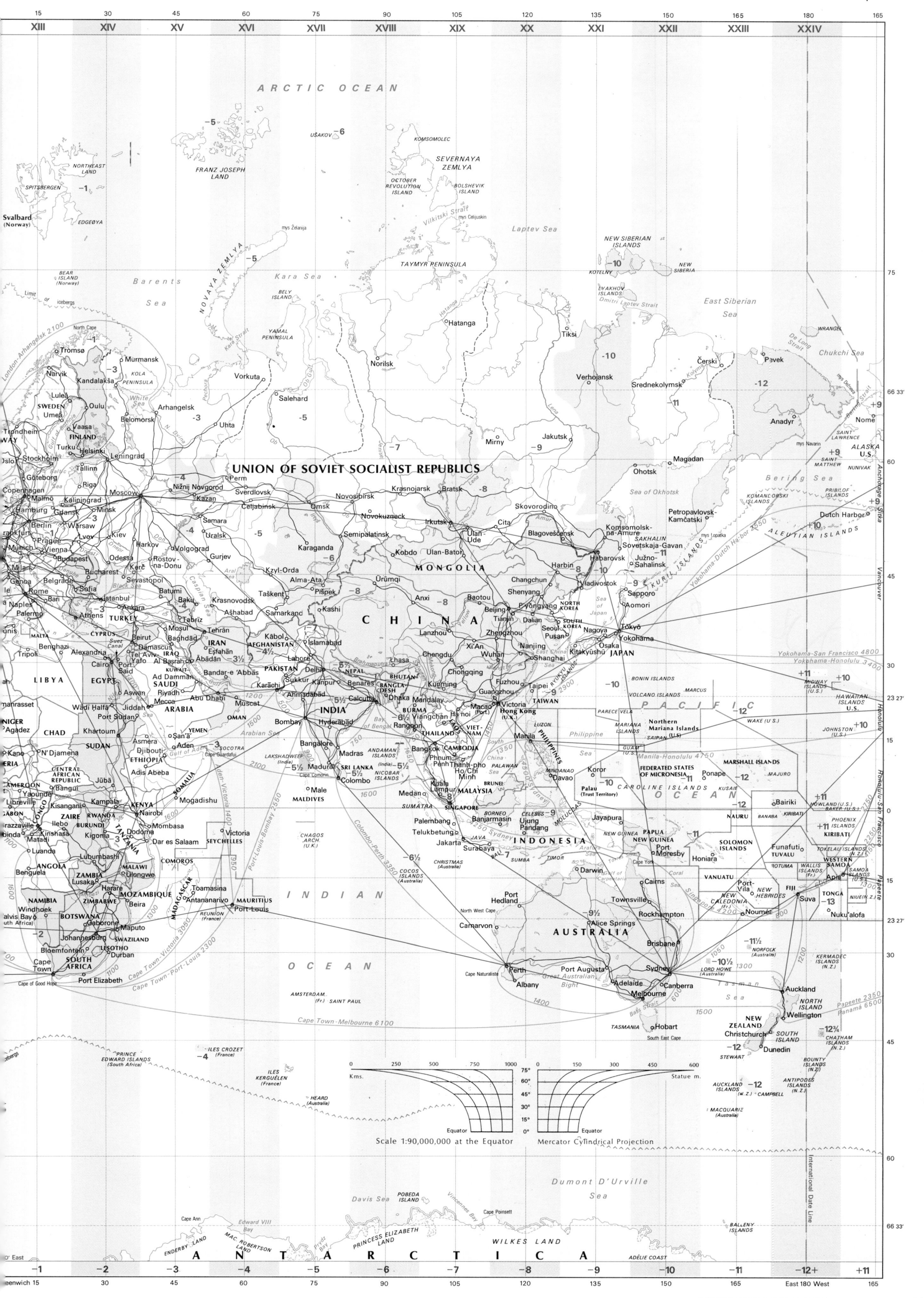

Map 5 **EUROPE, PHYSICAL**

G R E E N L A N D

KING CHRISTIAN IX LAND
KING FREDERIK VI COAST

GREENLAND SEA

JAN MAYEN

Mohns Ridge

Denmark Strait

Arctic Circle

ICELAND
Reykjavík
VATNAJÖKULL

NORWEGIAN SEA

Norwegian Basin

LOFOTEN
VESTERÅLEN

Reykjanes Ridge

Iceland Basin

Faeroe-Iceland Ridge

FAEROE ISLANDS

Limit of icebergs

Trondheim
Ålesund
Bergen
Oslo

A T L A N T I C   O C E A N

Mid-Atlantic Ridge

West European Basin

ROCKALL
Rockall Rise

Porcupine Bank

SHETLAND ISLANDS
ORKNEY ISLANDS

HEBRIDES

B R I T I S H   I S L E S

NORTH SEA

Göteborg
GÖTALAND

København
Copenhagen
JYLLAND

Hamburg
Berlin
GERMAN PLAIN
POMERANIA

SCOTLAND
Glasgow
Edinburgh
Southern Uplands
GREAT BRITAIN

IRELAND
Dublin
Cork

ENGLAND
Liverpool
Birmingham
London

WALES
Cambrian Mts.

CELTIC SEA

ENGLISH CHANNEL

Amsterdam
Rotterdam
FRIESLAND
FRISIAN ISLANDS
HOLLAND
Brussels
ARDENNES
Luxembourg
Frankfurt
HARZ
Leipzig
BOHEMIA
Praha
Prague
MORAVIA

AZORES
GRACIOSA
SÃO JORGE
PICO
TERCEIRA
SÃO MIGUEL
SANTA MARIA

Iberian Basin

Azores-Gibraltar Ridge

Josephine Seamount

Ampère Seamount

Seine Seamount

I B E R I A N   P E N I N S U L A

GALICIA
La Coruña
Cabo de Finisterre
CANTABRIAN MTS.
Bilbao
SUBMESETA NORTE
Duero
IBERIAN MOUNTAINS
Porto
SISTEMA CENTRAL
Lisboa
Lisbon
SIERRA MORENA
ANDALUSIA
Sevilla
Seville
SISTEMAS BÉTICOS
SIERRA NEVADA
Málaga
Cádiz
ALGARVE
SUBMESETA SUR
LA MANCHA
Valencia
ARAGÓN
PYRENEES
Zaragoza
CATALONIA
Barcelona
Madrid

Bay of Biscay

Bordeaux
AQUITAINE BASIN
Toulouse
LANGUEDOC
Marseille
PROVENCE
Gulf of Lions

FRENCH PLAIN
PARIS BASIN
Paris
Orléans
Loire
Nantes
BRITTANY
NORMANDY
Armorican Massif
BELLE ÎLE
ÎLE DE RÉ
ÎLE D'OLÉRON
Gironde

MASSIF CENTRAL
Lyon
JURA
VOSGES
BLACK FOREST
SWABIAN JURA
BAVARIA
München
Munich
BAVARIAN PLATEAU
Bern
A L P S
Genève
Milano
Milan
Torino
Turin
Genova
Genoa
PO VALLEY
Venezia
Venice
Gulf of Venice
SLOVENIA
Zagreb

LIGURIAN SEA

CORSICA
Ajaccio

SARDINIA
Cagliari

BALEARIC ISLANDS
MINORCA
MAJORCA
IBIZA
FORMENTERA
Palma

Gulf of Valencia

A P E N N I N E S
Bologna
Roma
Rome
ADRIATIC SEA
Ancona
Gran Sasso d'Italia
TUSCAN ARCHIPELAGO
ELBA
Napoli
Naples
Vesuvius
CAMPANIA
TYRRHENIAN SEA
Tyrrhenian Basin

M E D I T E R R A N E A N   S E A

Malta

Palermo
SICILY
Etna
Messina

Casablanca
Rabat
RIF
MIDDLE ATLAS
HIGH ATLAS
Marrakech
Agadir
ANTI ATLAS
ATLAS MOUNTAINS
SAHARAN ATLAS
HAUTS PLATEAUX
TELL ATLAS
Oran
Algiers
Constantine
Tunis
Cap Bon

CANARY ISLANDS
GRACIOSA
LANZAROTE
FUERTEVENTURA
GRAN CANARIA
TENERIFE
GOMERA
HIERRO
LA PALMA
Las Palmas
Santa Cruz de Tenerife

MADEIRA ISLANDS
PORTO SANTO
Funchal
ILHAS DESERTAS

GRAND ERG OCCIDENTAL
GRAND ERG ORIENTAL

TRIPOLITANIA
Tripoli

JBEL OUARKZIZ
HAMADA DU DRAA
HAMADA DU GUIR

Scale 1:15,000,000   Lambert Azimuthal Equal Area Projection

0   200   400   600   800   1000 km
0   250   500 miles

Longitude East 10 of Greenwich

BARENTS SEA

NOVAYA ZEMLYA
KARA SEA
YAMAL PENINSULA
Ob Gulf
WEST SIBERIAN PLAIN

PAJ-HOJ
POLAR URALS
SUBPOLAR URALS
NORTHERN URALS
URAL MOUNTAINS
CENTRAL URALS
SOUTHERN URALS

TIMAN RIDGE
KANIN PENINSULA
WHITE SEA
KOLA PENINSULA
Murmansk
VARANGER-HALVYA
RYBACHI PENINSULA
LAPLAND

Arhangelsk
Syktyvkar
ISHIM STEPPE
Tobolsk
Tjumen
Omsk

KARELIA
Oulu
Kuopio
Petrozavodsk
Lake Onega
Lake Ladoga
SALPAUSSELKÄ
Helsinki
Gulf of Finland
Tallinn
Leningrad
ESTONIA
INGERMANLAND
LIVONIA
Riga
Gulf of Riga

TURGAI UPLAND
TURGAI GATES
KAZAKHSTAN
KAZAKH HILLS
BETPAK DALA

VALDAI HILLS
MOSCOW UPLAND
Moskva Moscow
MOSCOW BASIN
SMOLENSK UPLAND
Smolensk
Vitebsk
Minsk
Vilnius
CENTRAL RUSSIAN UPLAND

VOLGA HILLS
Kazan
Gorkij
OBSCI SYRT
Kujbysev Reservoir
Samara
Orenburg
Uralsk
MUGODZARY

PRIPET MARSHES
VOLHYNIA
Kijev
UKRAINE
DNEPR UPLAND
PODOLIA
MOLDAVIA
DON UPLAND
Harkov
DONEC RIDGE
KIRGHIZ STEPPE
CASPIAN DEPRESSION
Aral Sea
PLATO USTJURT
WESTERN TURKISTAN
KYZYLKUM

CARPATHIAN MOUNTAINS
TRANSYLVANIAN ALPS
TRANSYLVANIA
APUSENI MTS.
Cluj Napoca
Bucuresti Bucharest
WALACHIA
DOBRUDJA
Constanta

Odessa
CRIMEA
Sevastopol
SEA OF AZOV
Kerc
Krasnodar
CISCAUCASIA
CAUCASUS
Elbrus
Groznyj
Mahackala
VOLGA DELTA
BUZACHI PENINSULA
MANGISTAU
CASPIAN SEA
APSHERON PENINSULA
Baku
KRASNOVODSKIJ PENINSULA
Krasnovodsk
KARAKUMY
HREBET KOPETDAG

BALKAN MTS.
Sofija
Plovdiv
RHODOPE MTS.
THRACE
BALKAN PENINSULA
Istanbul
SEA OF MARMARA
Bursa
Uludag
GEORGIA
LESSER CAUCASUS
Batumi
TRANSCAUCASIA
ARMENIA
AZERBAIJAN
Tbilisi
Yerevan
Mt. Ararat
Tabriz
ELBURZ MOUNTAINS
Tehran
Damavand
DASHT-E KAVIR

AEGEAN SEA
Thessaloniki
Salonika
CHALCIDICE
THASOS
LEMNOS
NORTHERN SPORADES
EUBOEA
Athens
ANDROS
CHIOS
SAMOS
CYCLADES
NAXOS
DODECANESE
Izmir
Smyrna

ANATOLIA
Ankara
KÖROGLU DAGLARI
Sivas
Erzurum
KURDISTAN
MESOPOTAMIA
Mosul
Kirkuk
Hamadan
PLATEAU OF IRAN
ZAGROS MTS.
DASHT-E LUT

TAURUS MOUNTAINS
Konya
Tuz
Adana
İskenderun
Gaziantep
Halab
Aleppo
Euphrates
Baghdad
Al Basrah
KHUZESTAN
LARESTAN

RHODES
KARPATHOS
CYPRUS
Nicosia
Bayrut
Beirut
Dimasq
Damascus
SYRIAN DESERT
LEBANON
AL JAZIRAH
AL WIDYAN
AL HAMAD

CRETE
Iraklion

NILE DELTA
Rosetta Mouth
Damietta Mouth
Port Said
Bur Sa'id
Al Iskandariyah
Alexandria
Al Qahirah
Cairo
As Suways
Suez
SINAI PENINSULA
EL TIH DESERT
Tel Aviv
Jerusalem
Amman
Jarusalaym

MARMARICA
CYRENAICA
QATTARA DEPRESSION
JARABUB OASIS
AN NAFUD
AL HASA
PERSIAN GULF
QATAR
BAHRAIN
Abu Zaby

BLACK SEA

MEDITERRANEAN SEA

M Ft
5000 16404
4000 13123
3000 9843
2000 6562
1000 3281
500 1640
+200 +656
0 Depr.
0
-100 -328
200 656
1000 3281
2000 6562
4000 13123

Map 6 **EUROPE, POLITICAL**

A 50 B 40 C 30 D 20 E 10 F 0 G 10

G r e e n l a n d
(Den.)

KING FREDERIK VI COAST
KING CHRISTIAN IX LAND

Greenland Sea

Denmark Strait

JAN MAYEN
(Norway)

ICELAND
Reykjavík
Akureyri
VATNAJÖKULL
Seydisfjördur

Arctic Circle

N o r w e g i a n   S e a

VESTERÅLEN
LOFOTEN
Bodø
Mo i Rana

NORWAY
SWEDEN
SCANDINAVIA

Faeroe Islands
(Den.)
FØROYAR / FÆRGENE
Thorshavn

SHETLAND ISLANDS

ROCKALL

ORKNEY ISLANDS
Thurso

HEBRIDES
Inverness
Aberdeen

North Sea

Kristiansund
Molde
Trondheim
Ålesund
Dombås
Glittertinden 2472

Bergen
Gjøvik
Oslo
Haugesund
Stavanger
Drammen
Skien
Kristiansand
Lindesnes

Falun
Östersund

Glasgow
Edinburgh
Dundee
Newcastle upon Tyne
Carlisle
Middlesbrough

IRELAND
Sligo
Galway
Belfast
Londonderry
Irish Sea

Limerick
Shannon
Dublin
Manchester
Liverpool
Leeds
UNITED KINGDOM
Kingston-upon-Hull

Waterford
Wexford
Fishguard
Sheffield
Nottingham
Leicester
Birmingham
Norwich

Mizen Head
Cork
Celtic Sea

Swansea
Cardiff
Oxford
Ipswich
Amsterdam
Gravenhage
Den Haag
Groningen

Bristol
London
Rotterdam
NETHERLANDS
Utrecht

Land's End
ISLES OF SCILLY
Penzance
Exeter
Southampton
Brighton
Dover
Antwerpen
Essen
Brussel
Bruxelles
BELGIUM
Lille
Köln Cologne
Bonn

Plymouth
English Channel
CHANNEL ISLANDS (U.K.)
Cherbourg
Le Havre
Amiens
Rouen
Liège
LUXEMBOURG

DENMARK
Herning
Esbjerg
Ålborg
Århus
København
Copenhagen
Odense
Flensburg
Kiel
Lübeck
Rostock

Helsingborg
Malmö
Trelleborg
BORNHOLM (Den.)
RÜGEN
Stralsund

GERMANY
Hamburg
Bremerhaven
Bremen
Hannover
Berlin
Magdeburg
Szczecin
Stettin

Dortmund
Düsseldorf
Leipzig
Dresden
Wrocław
Breslau

Wiesbaden
Frankfurt
Erfurt
Chemnitz
POLAND
Wałbrzych

Pointe de Saint-Mathieu
Brest
Saint-Malo
Caen
Reims
Saarbrücken
Mannheim
Würzburg
Nürnberg
Regensburg
Praha
Prague
Plzeň
CZECHOSLOVAKIA
Ostrava
Brno

Lorient
Rennes
Angers
Le Mans
Paris
Troyes
Nancy
Strasbourg
Stuttgart
Augsburg
München
Munich
Wien
Vienna

Nantes
Tours
Orléans
Bourges
Dijon
Mulhouse
Freiburg
Zürich
Innsbruck
Linz
Salzburg
Graz
Székesfehérvár
Győr

La Rochelle
Poitiers
FRANCE
Clermont-Ferrand
Monts Dore 1885
Besançon
Bern
SWITZERLAND
LIECHTENSTEIN
AUSTRIA
Klagenfurt
Balaton

Limoges
Lyon
Lausanne
Genève
Geneva
Bolzano
Ljubljana
Zagreb

Bordeaux
Gironde
Saint-Étienne
Grenoble
Milano
Milan
Brescia
Trieste
Rijeka

La Coruña
Cabo de Finisterre
Vigo
Oviedo
Gijón
Santander
San Sebastián
Bayonne
PYRENEES
Pico de Anету 3404
Toulouse
Montpellier
Nîmes
Avignon
Genova
Genoa
Torino
Turin
Nice
Parma
Verona
Venezia
Venice
Bologna
Zadar

Porto
Braga
León
Burgos
Pamplona
ANDORRA
Andorra la Vella
Perpignan
Marseille
Toulon
MONACO
La Spezia
Livorno
Leghorn
Firenze
Florence
Ancona
SAN MARINO
YUGOSLAVIA
Split

Coimbra
Valladolid
Duero
Zaragoza
Saragossa
Cabo de Creus
Barcelona
Tarragona
CORSICA (Fr.)
Bastia
Perugia
Pescara
Dubrovnik

PORTUGAL
Lisboa
Lisbon
Setúbal
Madrid
Toledo
Castellón de la Plana
Balearic Islands
MINORCA
Ajaccio
VATICAN CITY
Roma
Rome
ITALY
Foggia

Évora
Badajoz
SPAIN
Guadiana
Albacete
Valencia
IBIZA
MAJORCA
Palma
SARDINIA
Sassari
Nuoro
Olbia
Napoli
Naples
Bari
Brindisi

Cabo de São Vicente
Huelva
Córdoba
Guadalquivir
Júcar
Murcia
Alicante
Cagliari
Tyrrhenian Sea
Salerno
Taranto

Cádiz
Sevilla
Granada
Málaga
Almería
Cartagena
ISLA DE ALBORÁN (Spain)
Palermo
Trapani
Messina
Reggio di Calabria
Cosenza
Catanzaro

Algeciras
Gibraltar (U.K.)
Tanger
Ceuta (Spain)
Tétouan
Melilla (Spain)
Oran
Algiers
Al Jazā'ir
Bejaïa
Jijel
Skikda
Annaba
Bizerte
Tūnis
SICILY
Mt. Etna
Catania
Siracusa
Syracuse
Cabo delle Correnti
MALTA
Valletta

MADEIRA ISLANDS
Funchal
PORTO SANTO
ILHAS DESERTAS
Madeira
(Portugal)
ILHAS SELVAGENS

AZORES (Portugal)
GRACIOSA
SÃO JORGE
TERCEIRA
Angra do Heroísmo
PICO
FAIAL
SÃO MIGUEL
Ponta Delgada
SANTA MARIA

A T L A N T I C   O C E A N

Casablanca
Rabat
Kenitra
Ksar el Kebir
Larache
Meknès
Fès
Taza
Oujda
Sidi Bel Abbès
Relizane
Tiaret
Sétif
Constantine
Guelma
Tébessa
TUNISIA
Tarābulus
Tripoli

Canary Islands
(Spain)
LA PALMA
TENERIFE
Santa Cruz de Tenerife
GOMERA
HIERRO
GRAN CANARIA
Las Palmas de Gran Canaria
LANZAROTE
FUERTEVENTURA

MOROCCO
Marrakech
ATLAS   MOUNTAINS
ALGERIA
Agadir
Sidi Ifni
Tiznit

Western Sahara
El Aaiún

GRAND ERG OCCIDENTAL
GRAND ERG ORIENTAL
Ghardaïa
Ouargla
Touggourt
Qābis
DJERBA
Miṣrātah
TRIPOLITANIA
LIBYA
Gulf of

MEDITERRANEAN SEA
Ligurian Sea

Scale 1:15,000,000   Lambert Azimuthal Equal Area Projection
0   200   400   600   800   1000 km
0   250   500 miles

Longitude East 0 of Greenwich

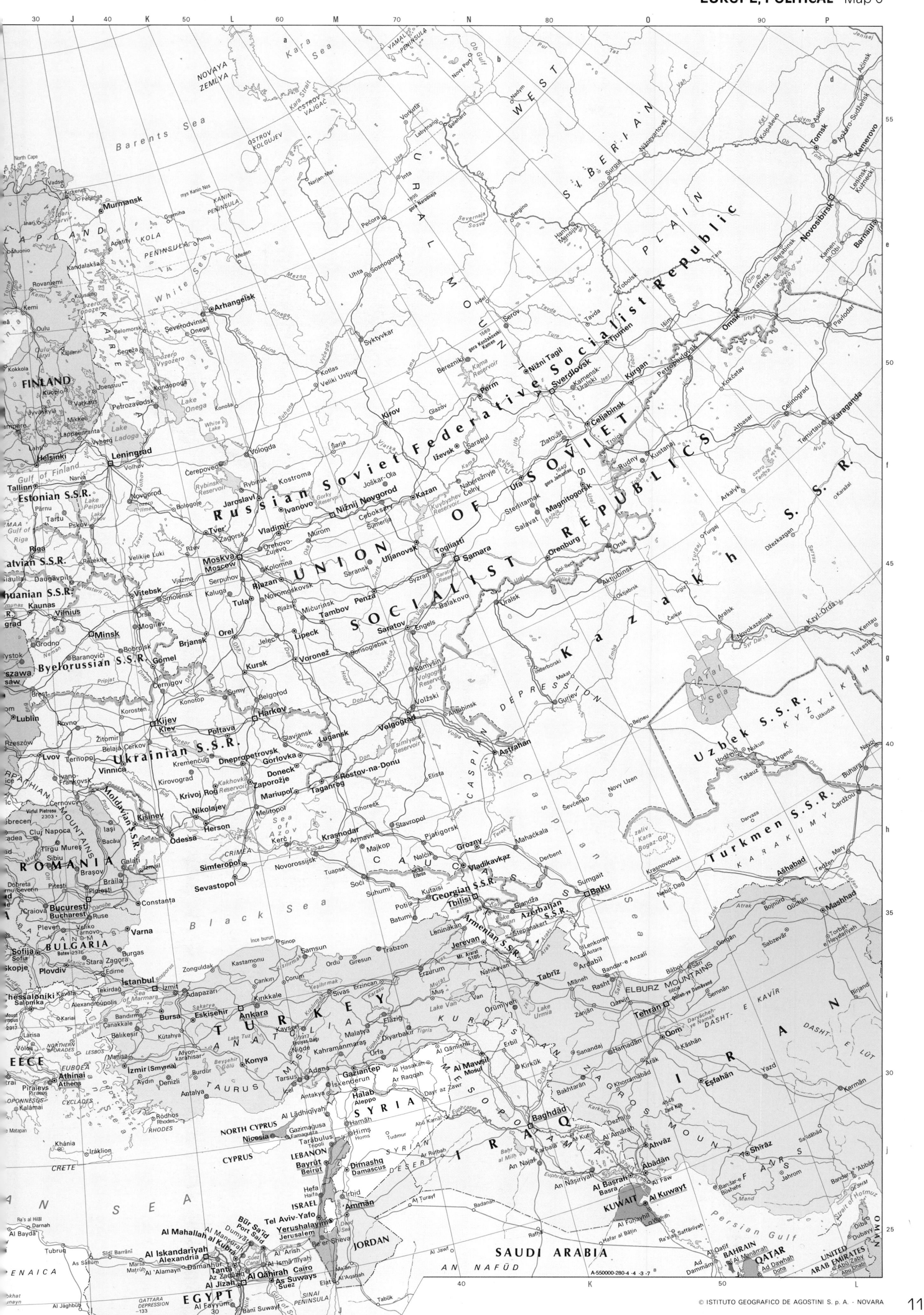

Map 7 **NORTHERN EUROPE**

ÍSLAND ICELAND

NORGE
NORWAY

SVERIGE
SWEDEN

SUOMI
FINLAND

DANMARK
DENMARK

DEUTSCHLAND
GERMANY

POLSKA
POLAND

Eesti SNSV
Estonian SSR

Latvijas PSR
Latvian SSR

Lietuvos TSR
Lithuanian SSR

Scale 1:6,000,000

Delisle Conic Equidistant Projection

Sojuz Sovetskich Socialističeskich Respublik (SSSR)

UNION OF SOVIET SOCIALIST REPUBLICS (USSR)

Rossijskaja Sovetskaja Federativnaja Socialističeskaja Respublika (RSFSR)

Russian Soviet Federative Socialist Republic (RSFSR)

8 Arhangelskaja oblast
8A Nanecki nac. okrug
11 Brjanskaja oblast
14 Gorkovskaja oblast
15 Ivanovskaja oblast
17 Jaroslavskaja oblast
18 Kaliningradskaja oblast
19 Kalininskaja oblast
20 Kalužskaja oblast
23 Kirovskaja oblast
24 Kostromskaja oblast
25 Kujbyševskaja oblast
28 Leningradskaja oblast
29 Lipeckaja oblast
31 Moskovskaja oblast
32 Murmanskaja oblast
33 Novgorodskaja oblast
36 Orenburgskaja oblast
37 Orlovskaja oblast
38 Penzenskaja oblast
39 Permskaja oblast
39A Komi-Permjacki nac. okrug

40 Pskovskaja oblast
42 Rjazanskaja oblast
44 Saratovskaja oblast
45 Smolenskaja oblast
47 Tambovskaja oblast
48A Tjumenskaja oblast
48A Hanty-Mansijski nac. okrug
50 Tulskaja oblast
51 Uljanovskaja oblast
52 Vladimirskaja oblast
54 Vologodskaja oblast

Belorusskaja SSR

Byelorussian SSR

3 Grodnenskaja oblast
4 Minskaja oblast
5 Mogilevskaja oblast
6 Vitebskaja oblast

Map 8 **BALTIC REGION**

Scale 1:3,000,000   Delisle Conic Equidistant Projection

0   50   100   150   200 km

0   50   100 miles

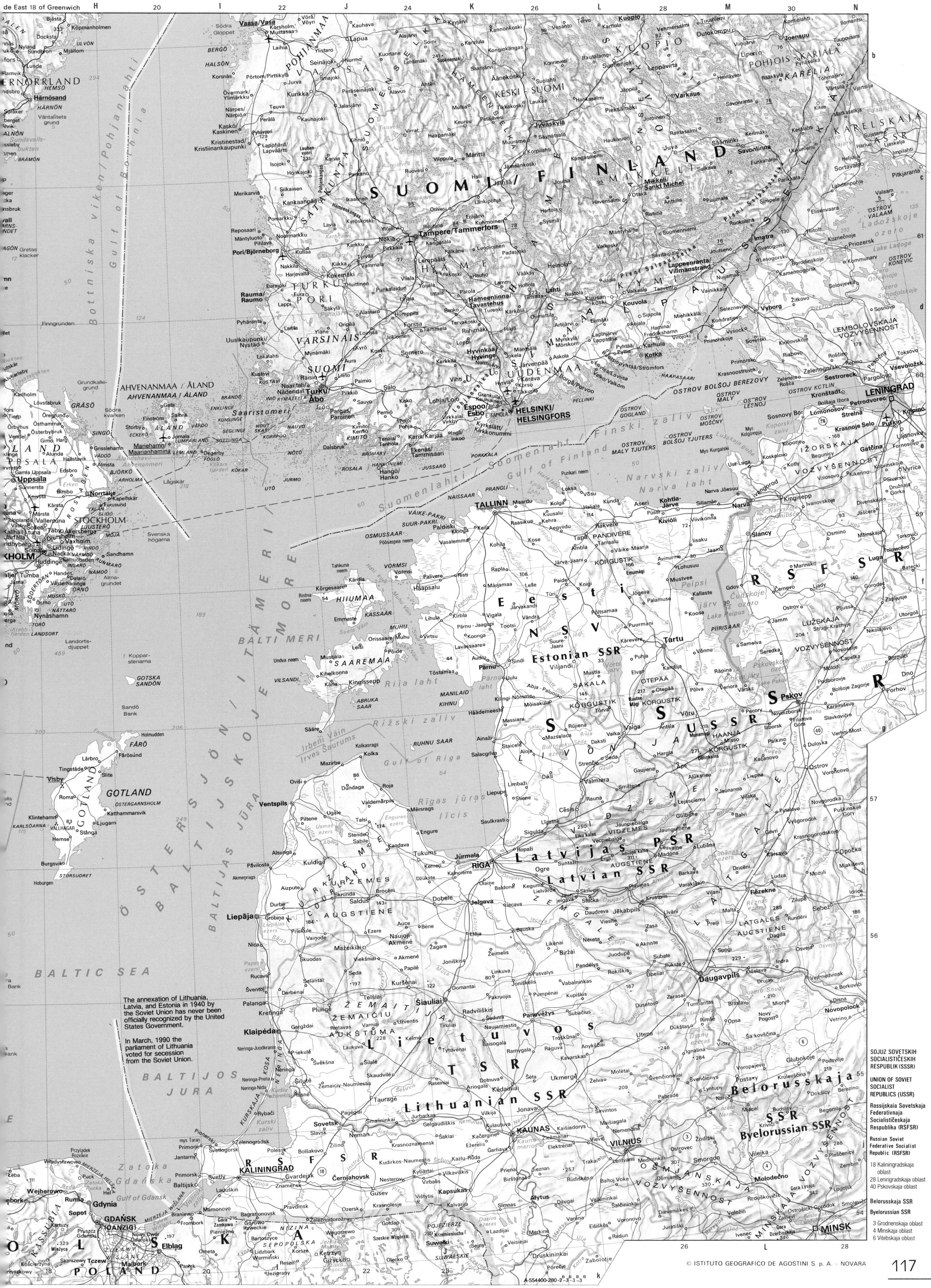

The annexation of Lithuania, Latvia, and Estonia in 1940 by the Soviet Union has never been officially recognized by the United States Government.

In March, 1990 the parliament of Lithuania voted for secession from the Soviet Union.

SOJUZ SOVETSKIH
SOCIALISTIČESKIH
RESPUBLIK (SSSR)

UNION OF SOVIET
SOCIALIST
REPUBLICS (USSR)

Rossijskaja Sovetskaja
Federativnaja
Socialističeskaja
Respublika (RSFSR)

Russian Soviet
Federative Socialist
Republic (RSFSR)

18 Kaliningradskaja
oblast
28 Leningradskaja oblast
40 Pskovskaja oblast

Belorusskaja SSR
Byelorussian SSR

3 Grodnenskaja oblast
4 Minskaja oblast
6 Vitebskaja oblast

© ISTITUTO GEOGRAFICO DE AGOSTINI S.p.A. - NOVARA

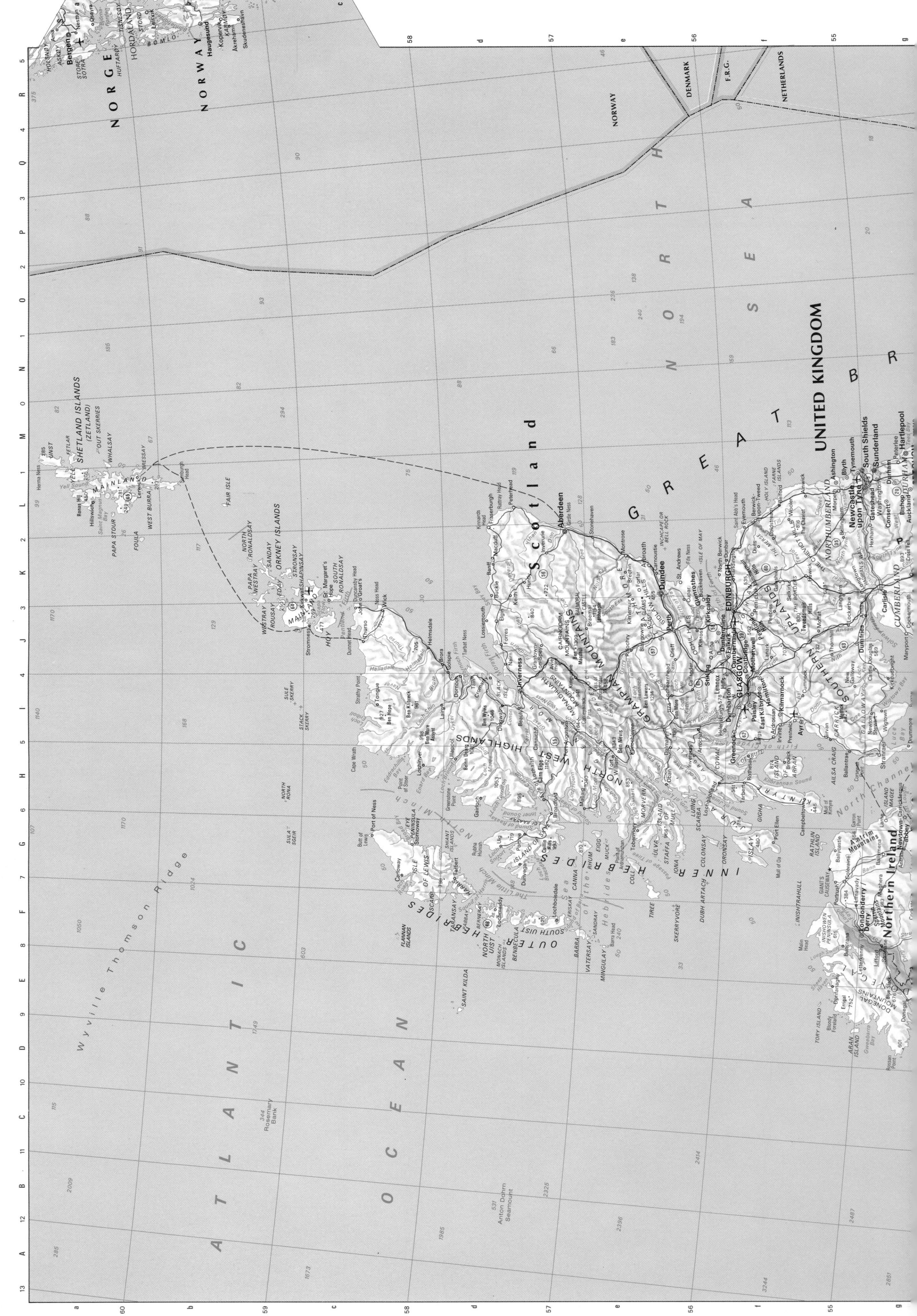

Scale 1:3,000,000

Delisle Conic Equidistant Projection

Longitude West 0 East of Greenwich

200 km

100 miles

GREAT BRITAIN

FORMER METROPOLITAN COUNTIES

England
1 Greater London
2 Greater Manchester
3 Merseyside
4 South Yorkshire
5 Tyne and Wear
6 West Midlands
7 West Yorkshire

NON-METROPOLITAN COUNTIES
8 Avon
9 Bedfordshire
10 Berkshire
11 Buckinghamshire
12 Cambridgeshire
13 Cheshire
14 Cleveland
15 Cornwall & Isles of Scilly
16 Cumbria
17 Derbyshire
18 Dorset
19 Devon
20 Durham
21 East Sussex
22 Essex
23 Gloucestershire
24 Hampshire
25 Hereford & Worcester
26 Hertfordshire
27 Humberside
28 Isle of Wight
29 Kent
30 Lancashire
31 Leicestershire
32 Lincolnshire
33 Norfolk
34 Northamptonshire
35 North Yorkshire
36 Nottinghamshire
37 Oxfordshire
38 Shropshire
39 Somerset
40 Staffordshire
41 Suffolk
42 Surrey
43 Warwickshire
44 West Sussex
45 Wiltshire

Wales
COUNTIES
46 Clwyd
47 Dyfed
48 Gwent
49 Gwynedd
50 Mid Glamorgan
51 Powys
52 South Glamorgan
53 West Glamorgan

Scotland
REGIONS
55 Highland
56 Grampian
57 Tayside
58 Fife
59 Lothian
60 Borders
61 Central
62 Strathclyde
63 Dumfries and Galloway

ISLANDS AREA
64 Orkney
65 Shetland
66 Western Isles

CROWN DEPENDENCY

Map 10 **CENTRAL EUROPE**

Scale 1:3,000,000   Delisle Conic Equidistant Projection

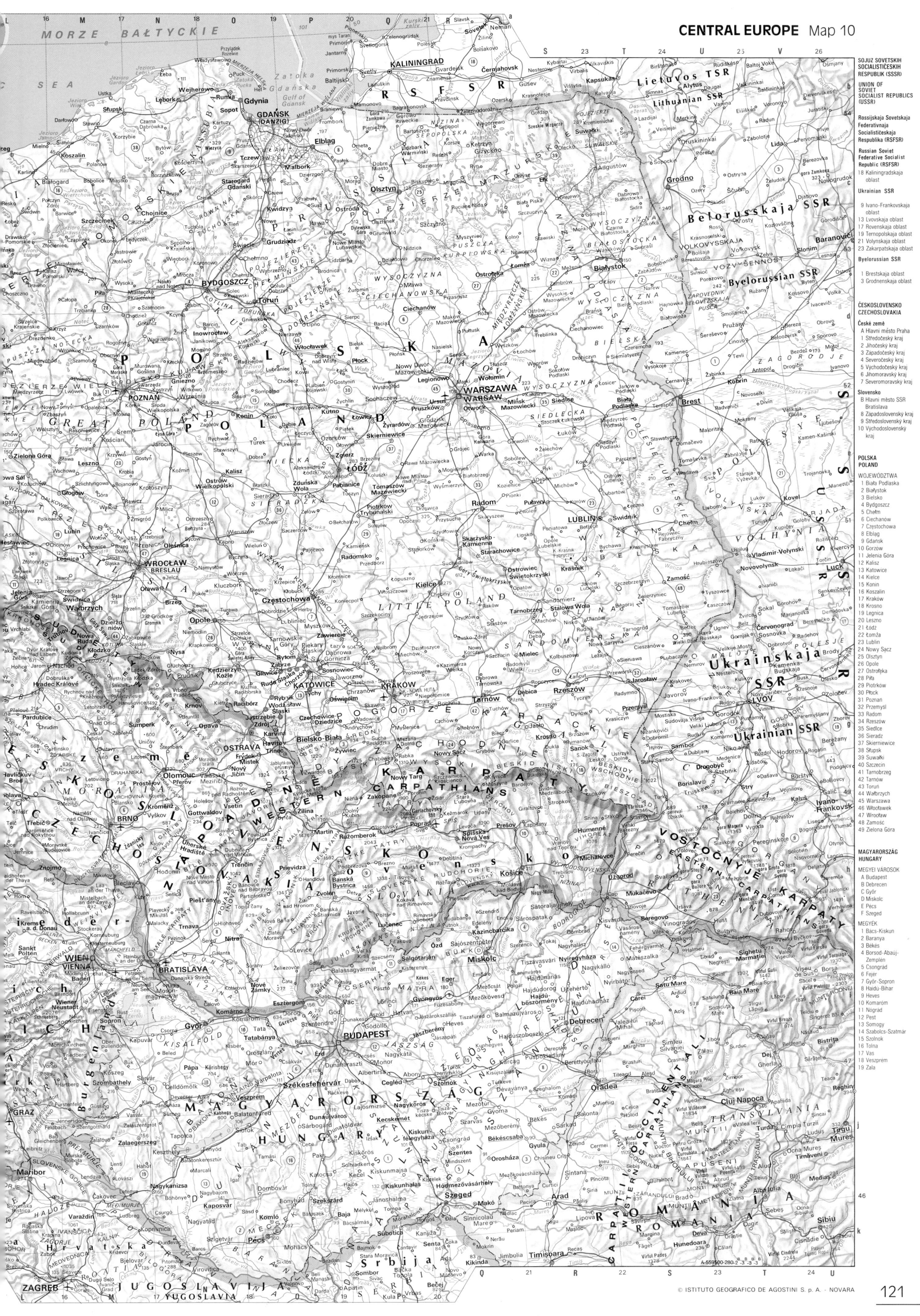

MORZE BAŁTYCKIE

C SEA

POLSKA
POLAND

GREAT POLAND

LITTLE POLAND

WESTERN CARPATHIANS

K A R P A T Y

EASTERN CARPATHIANS

SLOVENSKO
SLOVAKIA

MAGYARORSZÁG
HUNGARY

ROMÂNIA
ROMANIA

JUGOSLAVIJA
JUGOSLAVIA

KALININGRAD

R S F S R

Lietuvos TSR
Lithuanian SSR

Belorusskaja SSR
Byelorussian SSR

Ukrainskaja
SSR
Ukrainian SSR

WARSZAWA
WARSAW

POZNAN

BYDGOSZCZ

WROCŁAW
BRESLAU

KATOWICE

KRAKÓW

LUBLIN

LVOV

BRATISLAVA

WIEN
VIENNA

BRNO

BUDAPEST

ZAGREB

GRAZ

GDAŃSK
(DANZIG)

Gdynia

Olsztyn

Białystok

Grodno

Brest

Map 11 **FRANCE AND BENELUX**

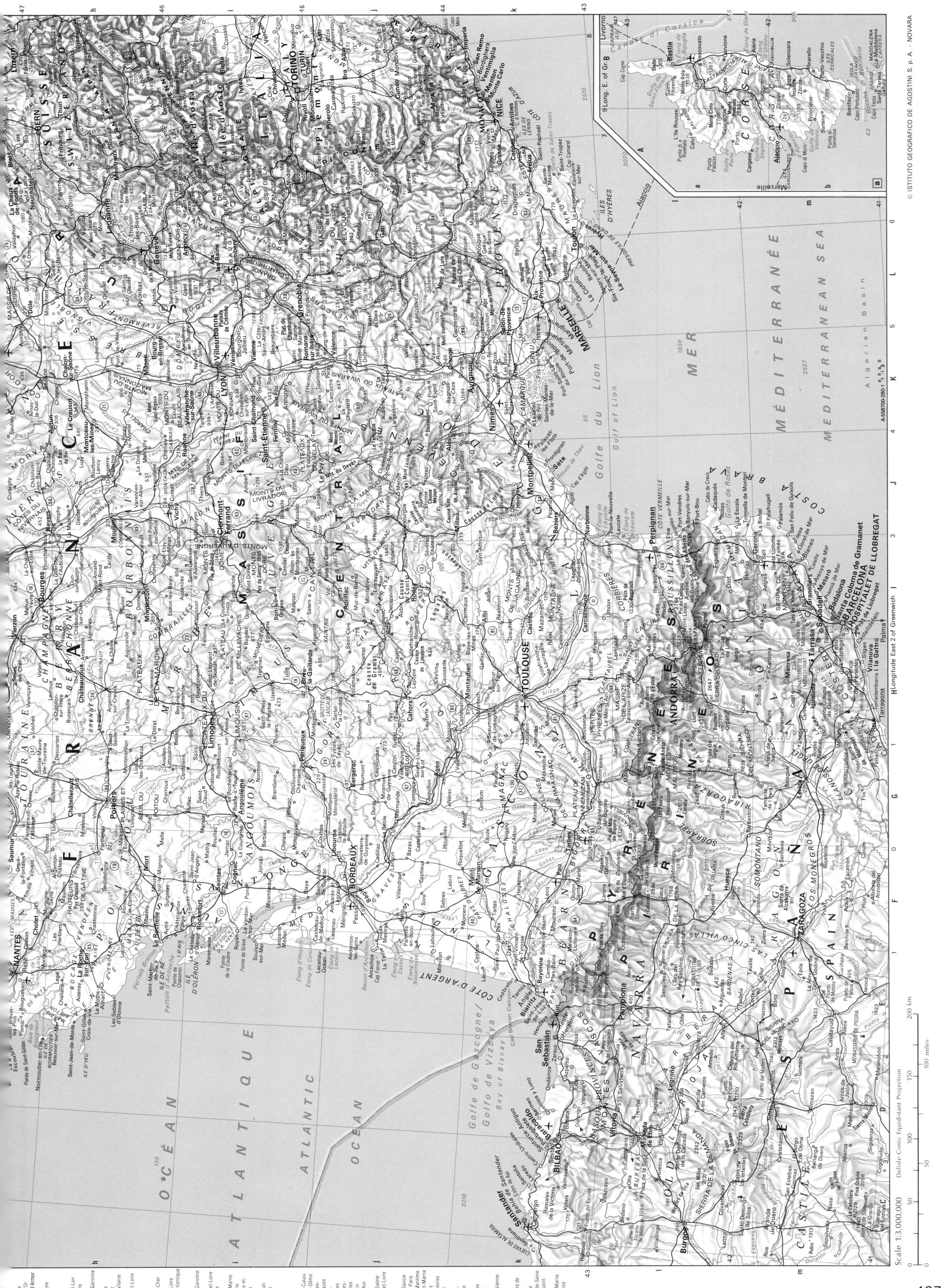

Map 12 **BELGIUM, NETHERLANDS AND LUXEMBOURG**

NORTH SEA / NOORDZEE / MER DU NORD

UNITED KINGDOM

England

ENGLISH CHANNEL / LA MANCHE

Baie de la Seine
Bay of the Seine

FRANCE

FRANCE
Départementos
75 Ville de Paris
92 Hauts-de-Seine
93 Seine-Saint-Denis
94 Val-de-Marne

Scale 1:1,500,000   Delisle Conic Equidistant Projection

0   25   50   75   100 km

0   25   50 miles

Map 12

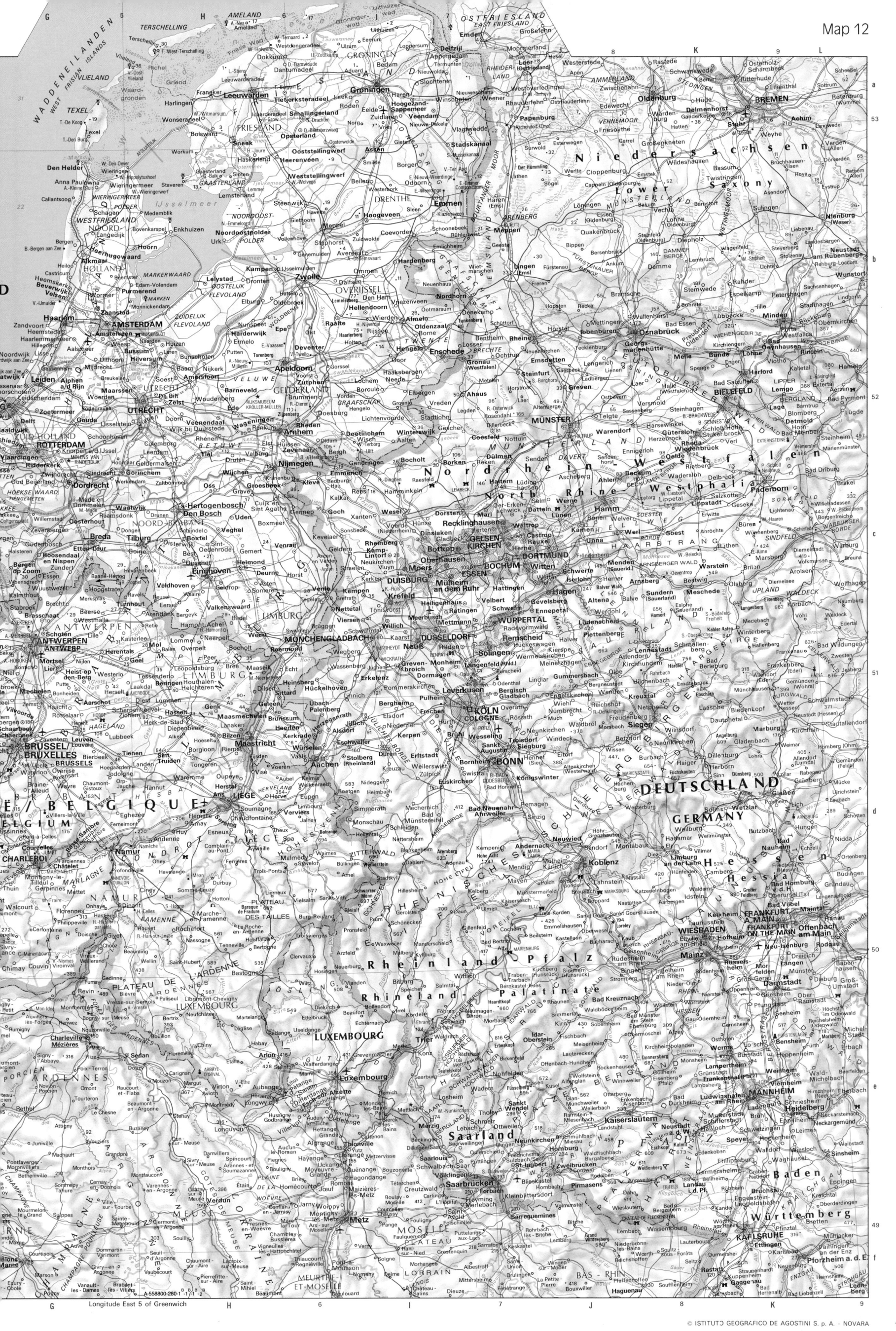

Map 13 **SPAIN AND PORTUGAL**

Scale 1:3,000,000   Delisle Conic Equidistant Projection

FRANCE
TOULOUSE
Montpellier
Nîmes
Avignon
MARSEILLE
Toulon
Perpignan
Golfe du Lion
Gulf of Lion
PYRÉNÉES
ANDORRA
Pamplona
NAVARRA
ARAGON
ZARAGOZA SARAGOSSA
Huesca
Lérida
CATALUÑA
GERONA
BARCELONA
Tarrasa
Sabadell
HOSPITALET DE LLOBREGAT
Tarragona
COSTA BRAVA
COSTA DORADA
Tortosa
Teruel
Castellón de la Plana
VALENCIA
Golfo de Valencia
ISLAS COLUMBRETES
ISLAS BALEARES
BALEARIC ISLANDS
MENORCA
MINORCA
MALLORCA
MAJORCA
PALMA
IBIZA
FORMENTERA
ISLA CABRERA
Alicante
Elche
MURCIA
Cartagena
Albacete
COSTA BLANCA
MEDITERRANEAN SEA
Algerian Basin
AL JAZĀ'IR
ALGIERS
ALGERIA
ORAN
Mostaganem
TELL ATLAS
Sétif
Béjaïa
TIZI OUZOU
KABYLIE
PLAINE DU HODNA
Chott el Hodna
TLEMCEN
SIDI BEL ABBES
MASCARA
Tiaret
Bou Saâda

Map 14 ITALY, AUSTRIA AND SWITZERLAND

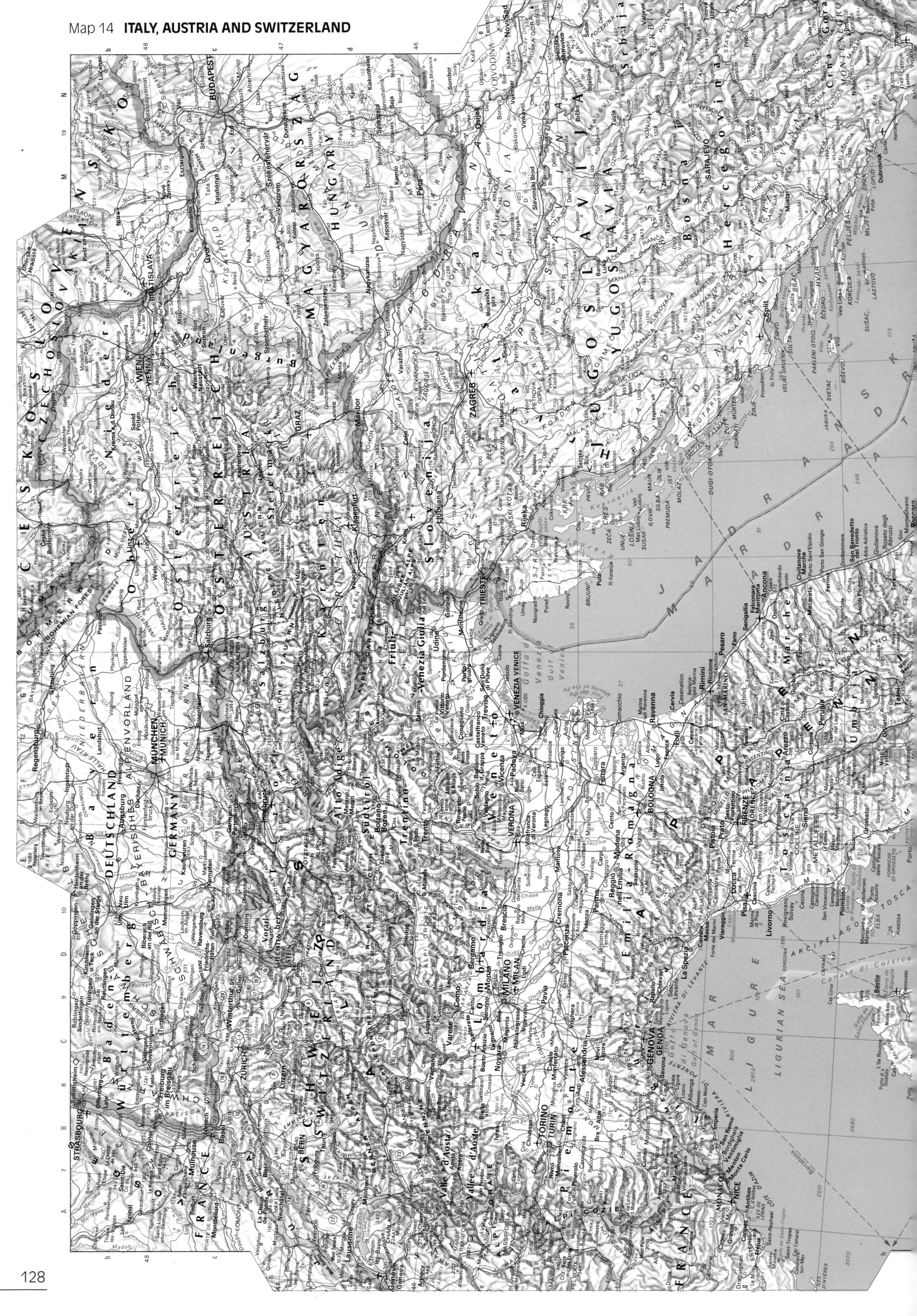

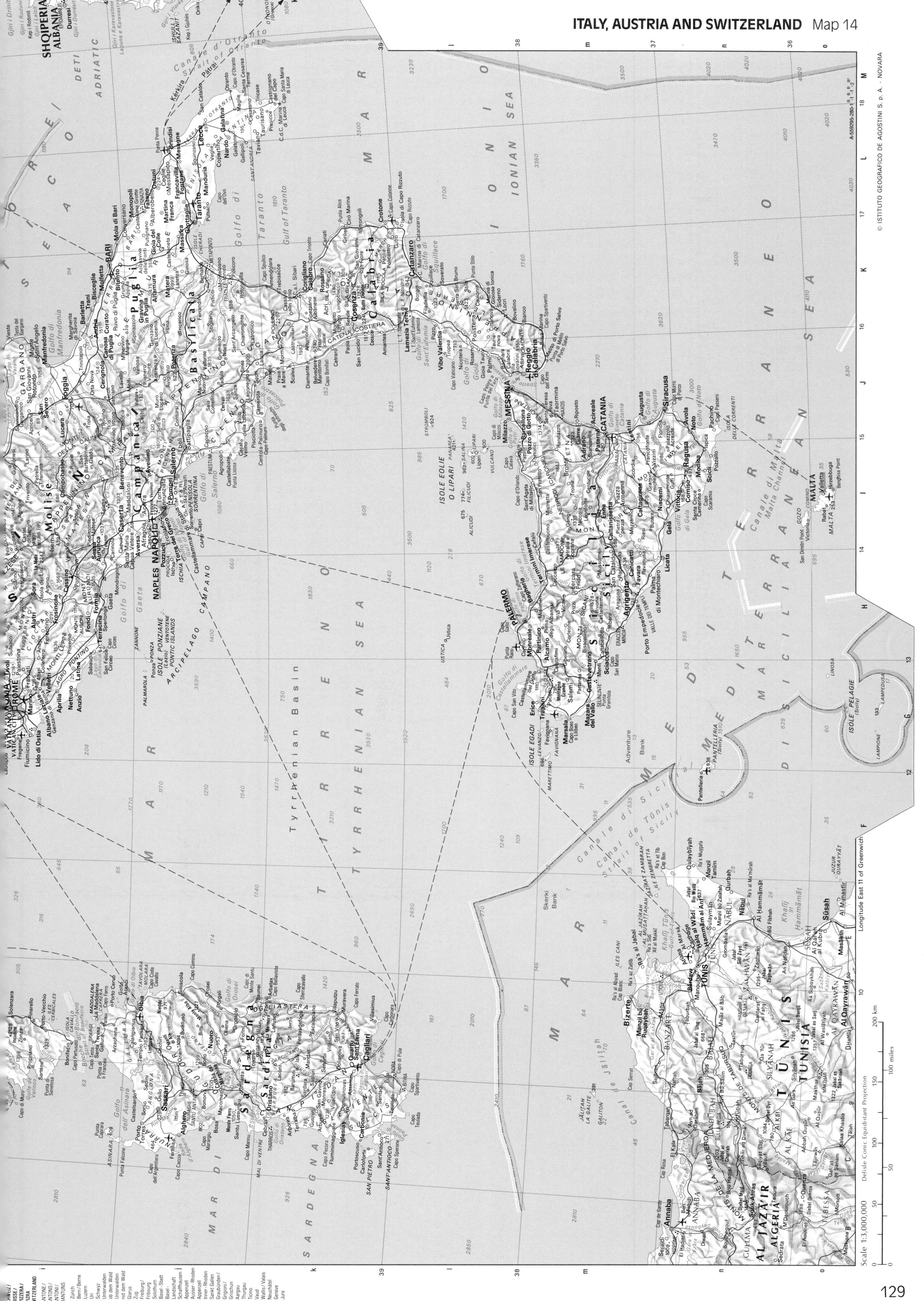

Map 15 SOUTHEASTERN EUROPE

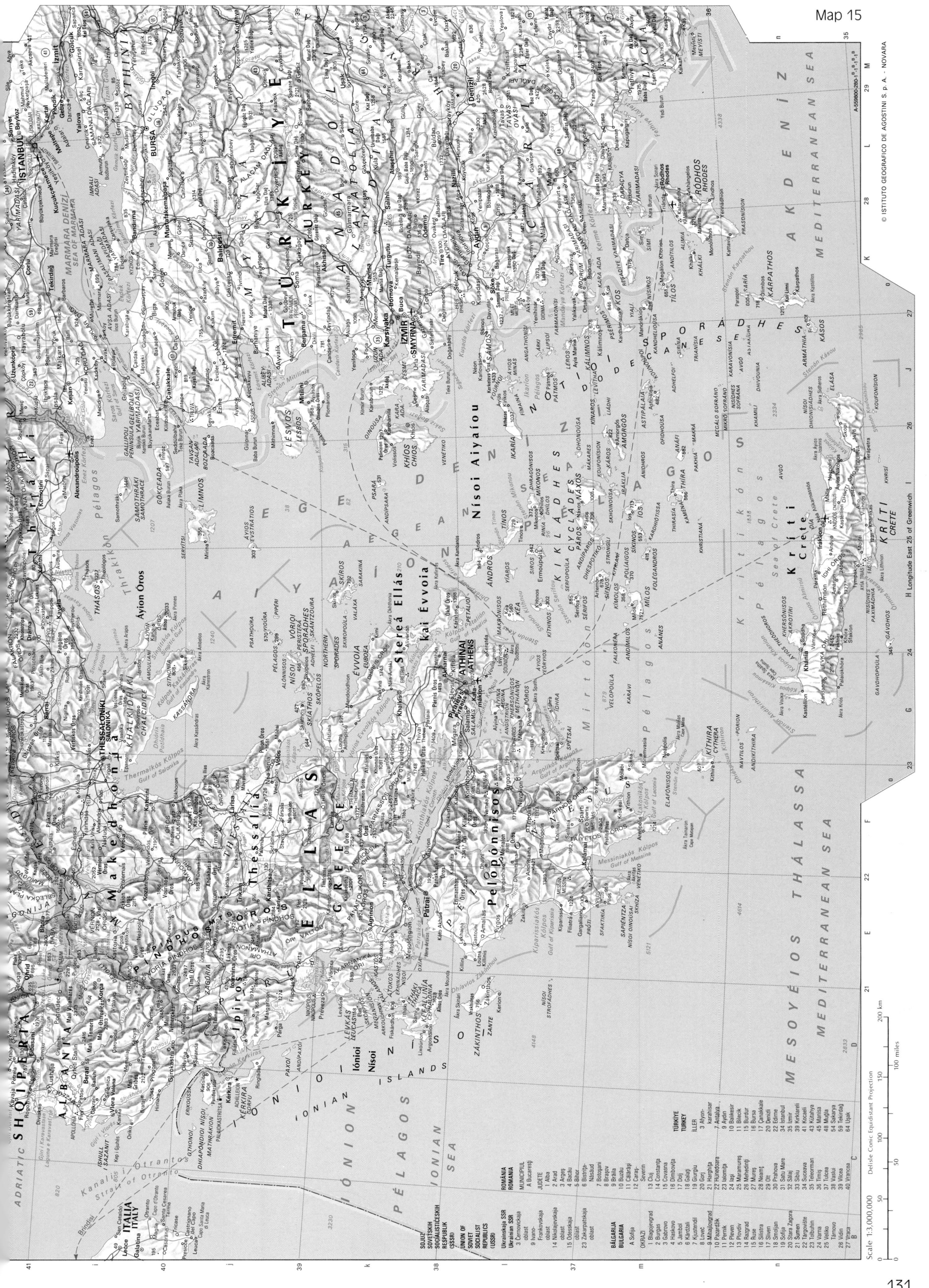

Map 15

Scale 1:3,000,000

Delisle Conic Equidistant Projection

200 km

100 miles

ROMANIA		TÜRKIYE	
ROMANIA		TURKEY	
MUNICIPIUL		ILLER	
A Bucareşti		3 Afyon-karahisar	
JUDETE		7 Aydın	
1 Alba		9 Balıkesir	
2 Arad		10 Bingöl	
3 Argeş		13 Burdur	
4 Bacău		15 Bursa	
5 Bihor		17 Çanakkale	
6 Bistriţa-		20 Denizli	
Năsăud		22 Edirne	
7 Botoşani		34 Istanbul	
8 Brăila		35 Kırklareli	
9 Braşov		41 Kocaeli	
10 Buzău		45 Kütahya	
11 Călăraşi		48 Manisa	
12 Caraş-		54 Muğla	
Severin		59 Tekirdağ	
13 Cluj		64 Uşak	
14 Constanţa			
15 Covasna			
16 Dîmboviţa			
17 Dolj			
18 Galaţi			
19 Giurgiu			
20 Gorj			
21 Harghita			
22 Hunedoara			
23 Ialomiţa			

SOJUZ
SOVETSKIH
SOCIALISTIČESKIH
RESPUBLIK (SSSR)
UNION OF
SOVIET
SOCIALIST
REPUBLICS (USSR)
1 Ukrainskaja SSR
2 Ukrainian SSR
3 Čornovickaja
   oblast
9 Frankovskaja
   oblast
14 Nikolajevskaja
   oblast
15 Odesskaja
   oblast
23 Zakarpatskaja
   oblast

BALGARIJA
BULGARIA
OKRAZI
A Sofija
1 Blagoevgrad
2 Burgas
3 Gabrovo
4 Haskovo
5 Kărdžali
6 Kjustendil
7 Lovec
8 Mihajlovgrad
9 Pazardžik
10 Pernik
11 Pleven
12 Plovdiv
13 Razgrad
14 Ruse
15 Silistra
16 Sliven
17 Smoljan
18 Sofija
19 Stara Zagora
20 Šumen
21 Tărgovište
22 Tolbuhin
23 Varna
24 Veliko
   Tărnovo
25 Vidin
26 Vraca

Map 16 **SOUTHWESTERN SOVIET UNION**

Scale 1:6,000,000   Delisle Conic Equidistant Projection

0   100   200   300   400 km

0   100   200 miles

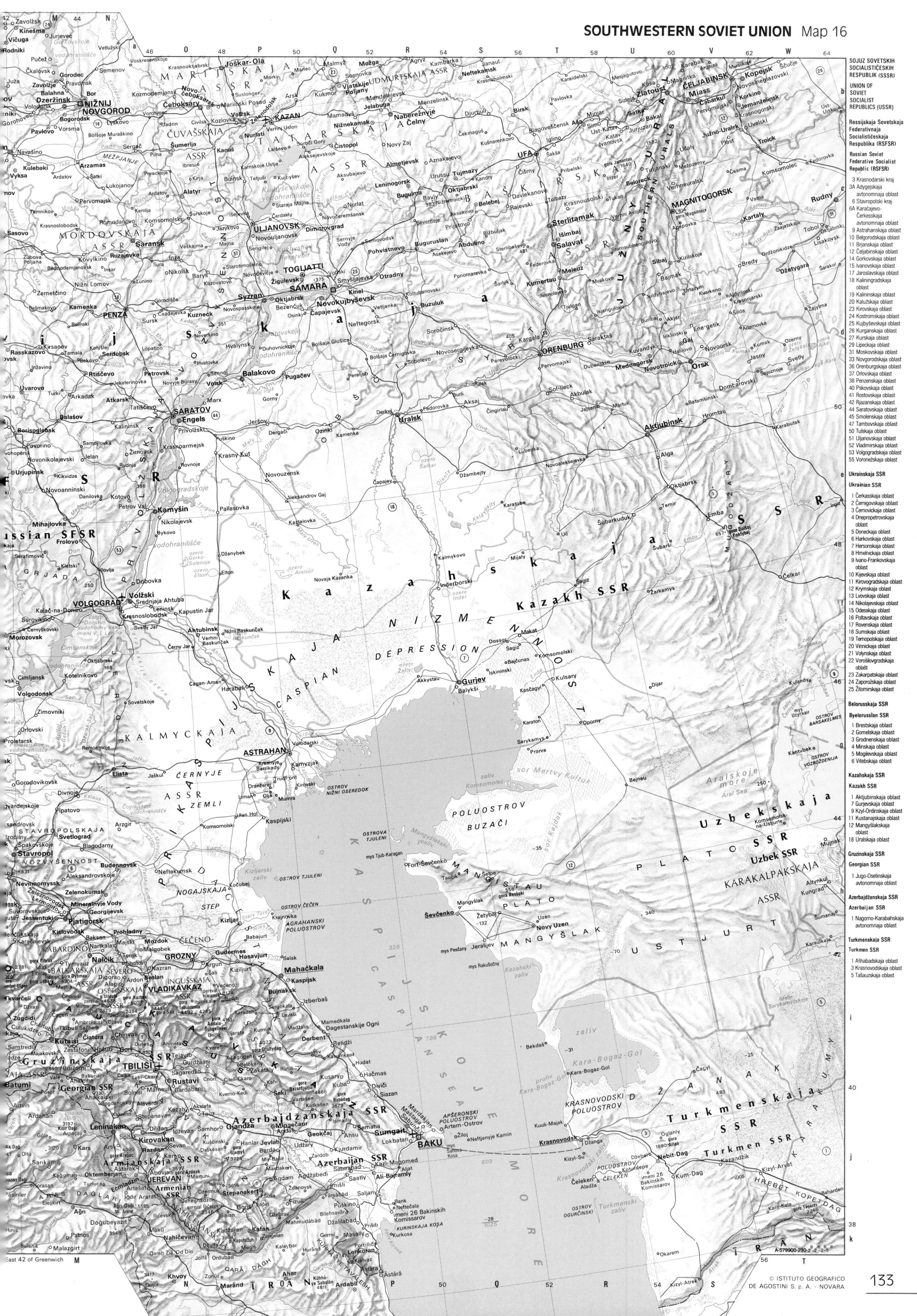

Map 17 **THE URALS**

SOJUZ SOVETSKIH
SOCIALISTIČESKIH
RESPUBLIK (SSSR)

UNION OF
SOVIET
SOCIALIST
REPUBLICS

Rossijskaja Sovetskaja
Federativnaja
Socialističeskaja
Respublika (RSFSR)

Russian Soviet
Federative Socialist
Republic

8 Arhangelskaja oblast
8A Nenecki nac. okrug
12 Čeljabinskaja oblast
14 Gorkovskaja oblast
23 Kirovskaja oblast
24 Kostromskaja oblast
25 Kujbēševskaja oblast
26 Kurganskaja oblast
35 Omskaja oblast
36 Orenburgskaja oblast
39 Permskaja oblast
39A Komi-Permjacki nac. okrug
44 Saratovskaja oblast
46 Sverdlovskaja oblast
48 Tjumenskaja oblast
48A Hanty-Mansijski nac. okrug
48B Jamalo-Nenecki nac. okrug
51 Uljanovskaja oblast
52 Vologodskaja oblast

Kazahskaja SSR

Kazakh SSR

3 Celinogradskaja oblast
10 Kokčetavskaja oblast
11 Kustanajskaja oblast
15 Severo-Kazahstanskaja oblast
17 Turgajskaja oblast

Pečorskoje more
Pechora Sea

OSTROV KOLGUJEV
OSTROV VAJGAČ
Arctic Circle

JUGORSKIJ POLUOSTROV
POLUOSTROV JAMAL
YAMAL PENINSULA

POLUOSTROV KANIN
KANIN PENINSULA

Narjan-Mar
Vorkuta
Pečora
Inta
Usinsk
Uhta
Sosnogorsk
Syktyvkar
Rossijskaja SFSR
Russian SFSR
Hanty-Mansijsk
WEST SIBERIAN PLAIN
RAVNINA
ZAPADNO SIBIRSKAJA

KOMI

UDMURTSKAJA ASSR
MARIJSKAJA ASSR
TATARSKAJA ASSR
BAŠKIRSKAJA ASSR

Kirov
Slobodskoj
Kirovo-Čepeck
Glazov
Votkinsk
IŽEVSK
Sarapul
Joškar-Ola
KAZAN
PERM
NIZNI TAGIL
SVERDLOVSK
Kamensk-Uralski
Serov
Solikamsk
Berezniki
Kizel
Kungur
Krasnokamsk
Lysva
TJUMEN
Tobolsk
KURGAN
Petropavlovsk

UFA
Zlatoust
Miass
ČELJABINSK
MAGNITOGORSK
Sterlitamak
Salavat
SAMARA
TOGLIATTI
ULJANOVSK
Naberežnyje Čelny
Nižnekamsk

KAZAHSKAJA SSR
KAZAKH SSR
Kustanaj
Rudny

POLARNYJ URAL
PRIPOLARNYJ URAL
SEVERNYJ URAL
NORTHERN URALS
SREDNIJ URAL
CENTRAL URALS
JUŽNYJ URAL
SOUTHERN URALS
URAL MOUNTAINS
URALSKIJ CHREBET

gora Narodnaja 1895
gora Telposiz 1617
gora Neroika 1648

Scale 1:6,000,000
Delisle Conic Equidistant Projection
0 100 200 300 400 km
0 100 200 miles

Longitude East 60 of Greenwich

A-570307-280-1-1-1-3

© ISTITUTO GEOGRAFICO DE AGOSTINI S.p.A. - NOVARA

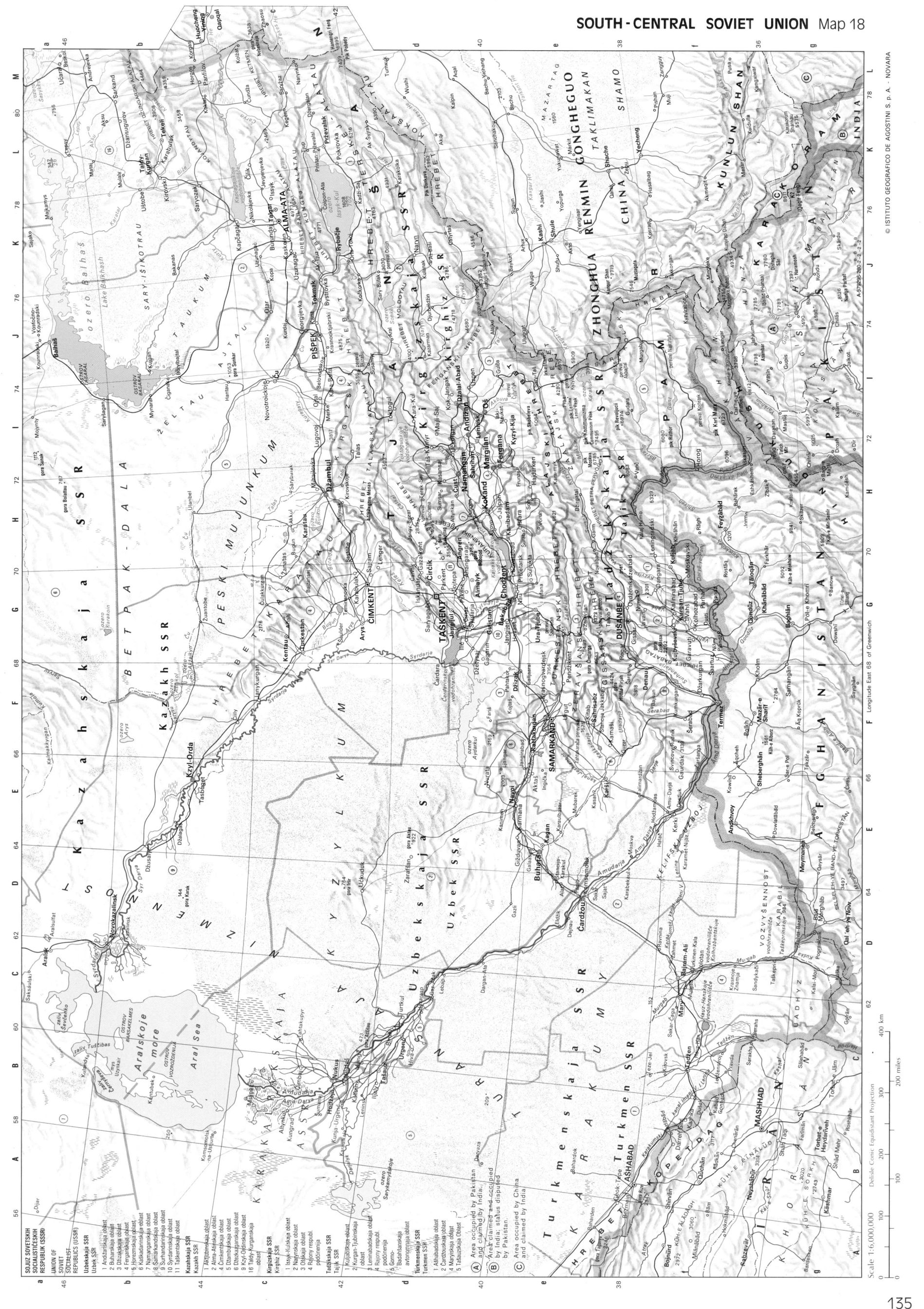

© ISTITUTO GEOGRAFICO DE AGOSTINI S. p. A. - NOVARA

Scale 1:6,000,000

Delisle-Conic Equidistant Projection

Map 19

SOJUZ SOVETSKIH
SOCIALISTIČESKIH
RESPUBLIK (SSSR)

UNION OF SOVIET
SOCIALIST
REPUBLICS (USSR)

Rossijskaja Sovetskaja
Federativnaja
Socialističeskaja
Respublika (RSFSR)

Russian Soviet
Federative Socialist
Republic (RSFSR)

3   Krasnodarski kraj
3A Adygejskaja
    avt. oblast
6   Stavropolski kraj
6A Karačajevo-
    Čerkesskaja
    avt. oblast
8   Arhangelskaja
    oblast
8A Nenecki nac. okr.
9   Astrahanskaja
    oblast
10 Belgorodskaja
    oblast
13 Brjanskaja obl.
16 Čeljabinskaja obl.
16 Gorkovskaja obl.
15 Ivanovskaja obl.
17 Jaroslavskaja obl.
18 Kaliningradskaja
    oblast
19 Kalininskaja obl.
20 Kalužskaja obl.
21 Kirovskaja obl.
22 Kostromskaja obl.
25 Kujbyševskaja
    oblast
26 Kurganskaja obl.
27 Kurskaja obl.
28 Leningradskaja
    oblast
29 Lipeckaja obl.
31 Moskovskaja obl.
32 Murmanskaja obl.
33 Novgorodskaja
    oblast
35 Omskaja obl.
36 Orenburgskaja
    oblast
37 Orlovskaja obl.
38 Penzenskaja obl.
39 Permskaja obl.
39A Komi-Permjacki
    nac. okr.
40 Pskovskaja obl.
41 Rostovskaja obl.
43 Rjazanskaja obl.
44 Saratovskaja obl.
45 Smolenskaja obl.
46 Sverdlovskaja obl.
47 Tambovskaja obl.
48 Tjumenskaja obl.
48A Hanty-Mansijski
    nac. okr.

50 Tulskaja obl.
51 Uljanovskaja obl.
52 Vladimirskaja obl.
53 Vologodskaja
    oblast
54 Vologodskaja obl.
55 Voronežskaja obl.

Ukrainskaja SSR
Ukrainian SSR

1   Čerkasskaja obl.
2   Černigovskaja obl.
3   Černovickaja obl.
4   Dnepropetrovskaja
    oblast
5   Doneckaja obl.
6   Harkovskaja obl.
7   Hersonskaja obl.
8   Hmelnickaja obl.
9   Ivano-Frankovskaja
    oblast
10 Kijevskaja obl.

Scale 1:12,000,000   Delisle Conic Equidistant Projection

Longitude East 55 of Greenwich

Ukrainskaja SSR
Ukrainian SSR

11 Kirovogradskaja oblast
12 Krymskaja obl.
13 Lvovskaja obl.
14 Nikolajevskaja obl.
15 Odesskaja obl.
16 Poltavskaja obl.
17 Rovenskaja obl.
18 Sumskaja obl.
19 Ternopolskaja obl.
20 Vinnickaja obl.
21 Volynskaja obl.
22 Vorošilovgradskaja oblast
23 Zakarpatskaja obl.
24 Zaporožskaja obl.
25 Žitomirskaja obl.

Belorusskaja SSR
Byelorussian SSR

1 Brestskaja obl.
2 Gomelskaja obl.
3 Grodnenskaja obl.
4 Minskaja obl.
5 Mogilevskaja obl.
6 Vitebskaja obl.

Uzbekskaja SSR
Uzbek SSR

1 Andižanskaja obl.
2 Buharskaja obl.
3 Džizakskaja obl.
4 Ferganskaja obl.
5 Horezmskaja obl.
6 Kaškadarinskaja oblast
7 Namanganskaja oblast
8 Samarkandskaja oblast
9 Surhandarinskaja oblast
10 Syrdarinskaja obl.
11 Taškentskaja obl.

Kazahskaja SSR
Kazakh SSR

1 Aktjubinskaja obl.
2 Alma-Atinskaja oblast
3 Celinogradskaja oblast
4 Čimkentskaja oblast
5 Džambulskaja obl.
6 Džezkazganskaja oblast
7 Gurjevskaja obl.
8 Karagandinskaja oblast
9 Kzyl-Ordinskaja oblast
10 Kokčetavskaja obl.
11 Kustanajskaja obl.
12 Mangyšlakskaja oblast
13 Pavlodarskaja obl.
14 Semipalatinskaja oblast
15 Severo-Kazahstanskaja oblast
16 Taldy-Kurganskaja obl.
17 Turgajskaja obl.
18 Uralskaja obl.
19 Vostočno-Kazahstanskaja obl.

Gruzinskaja SSR
Georgian SSR

1 Jugo-Osetinskaja avt. oblast

Azerbajdžanskaja SSR
Azerbaijan SSR

1 Nagorno-Karabahskaja avt. oblast

Kirgizskaja SSR
Kirghiz SSR

1 Issyk-Kulskaja oblast
2 Narynskaja obl.
3 Ošskaja obl.
4 Rajony respubl. podčinenija

Tadžikskaja SSR
Tajik SSR

1 Kuljabskaja obl.
2 Kurgan-Tjubinskaja obl.
3 Leninabadskaja oblast
4 Rajony respubl. podčinenija
5 Gorno-Badahšanskaja avt. oblast

Turkmenskaja SSR
Turkmen SSR

1 Ašhabadskaja obl.
2 Čardžouskaja obl.
3 Krasnovodskaja oblast
4 Maryjskaja obl.
5 Tašauzskaja obl.

Map 20

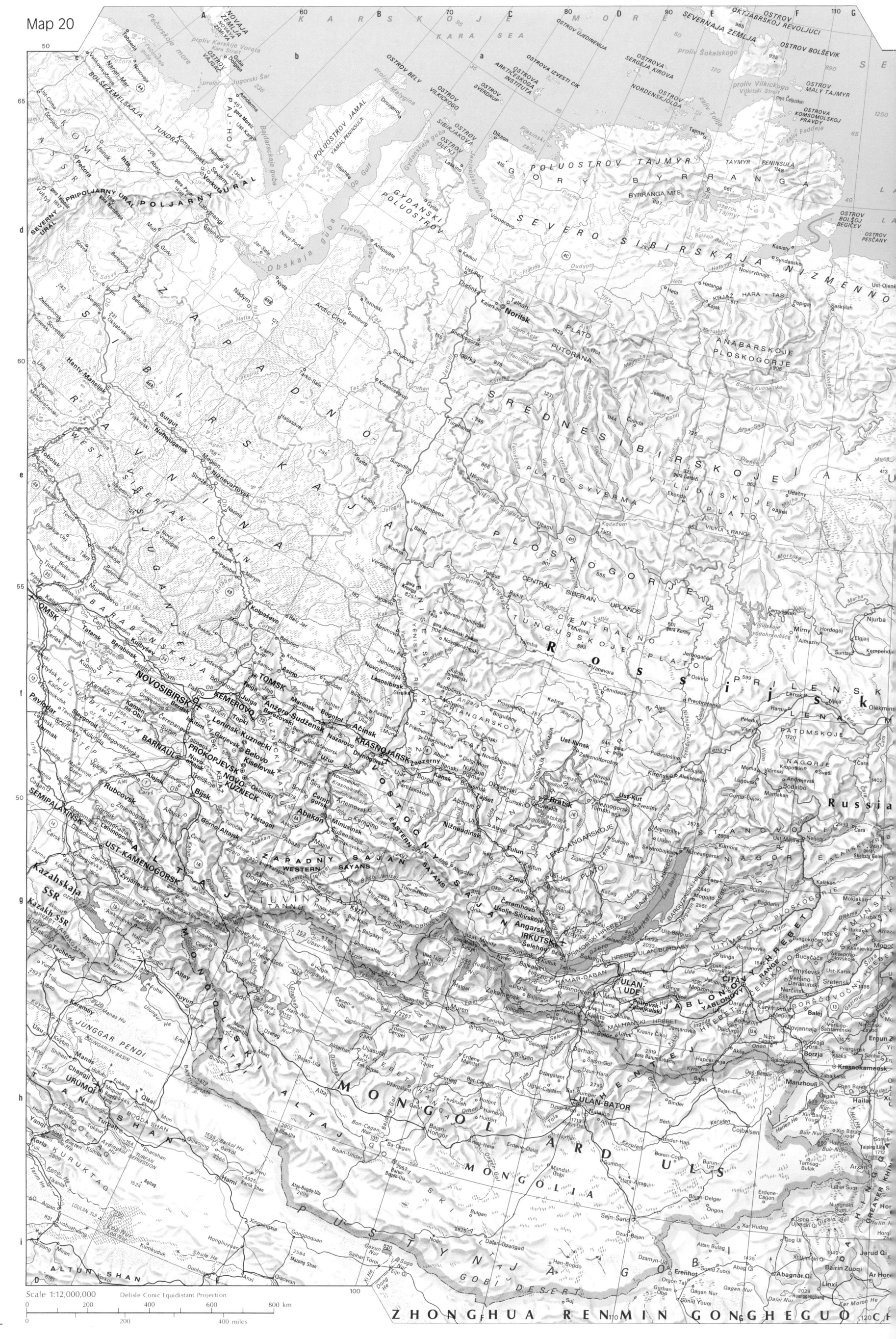

Scale 1:12,000,000   Delisle Conic Equidistant Projection

0   200   400   600   800 km

0   200   400 miles

ZHONGHUA RENMIN GONGHEGUO

SOJUZ SOVETSKIH
SOCIALISTIČESKIH
RESPUBLIK (SSSR)
UNION OF
SOVIET SOCIALIST
REPUBLICS (USSR)

Rossijskaja Sovetskaja
Federativnaja
Socialističeskaja
Respublika (RSFSR)

Russian Soviet
Federative Socialist
Republic (RSFSR)

1 Altajskij kraj
1A Gorno-Altajskaja
avtonomnaja oblast
2 Habarovskij kraj
2A Jevrejskaja
avtonomnaja oblast
4 Krasnojarskij kraj
4A Hakasskaja
avtonomnaja oblast
4B Evenkijskij nac.
okrug
4C Tajmyrskij (Dolgano-
Neneckij) nac. okrug
5 Primorskij kraj
7 Amurskaja oblast
8A Neneckij nac. okrug
13 Čitinskaja oblast
13A Aginskij Burjatskij
nac. okrug
16 Irkutskaja oblast
16A Ust-Ordynskij
Burjatskij nac. okrug
21 Kamčatskaja oblast
21A Korjakskij nac.
okrug
22 Kemerovskaja
oblast
30 Magadanskaja
oblast
30A Čukotski nac. okrug
34 Novosibirskaja
oblast
35 Omskaja oblast
43 Sahalinskaja oblast
48 Tjumenskaja oblast
48A Hanty-Mansijskij
nac. okrug
48B Jamalo-Neneckij
nac. okrug
49 Tomskaja oblast

Kazahskaja SSR

Kazakh SSR

13 Pavlodarskaja
oblast
14 Semipalatinskaja
oblast
19 Vostočno-
Kazahstanskaja
oblast

Ostrov Kunašir, ostrov Šikotan, ostrov
Iturup i Malaja Kurilskaja Grjada,
occupied by the U.S.S.R. since 1945,
are claimed by Japan pending a final
peace treaty.

Longitude East 150 of Greenwich

© ISTITUTO GEOGRAFICO DE AGOSTINI S. p A. - NOVARA

A-579395-280-1

139

Map 21 **ASIA, PHYSICAL**

Scale 1:30,000,000   Lambert Azimuthal Equal Area Projection

Map 22 **ASIA, POLITICAL**

PACIFIC OCEAN

ALEUTIAN ISLANDS

Bering Sea

Sea of Okhotsk

KURIL ISLANDS

KAMCHATKA PENINSULA

SAKHALIN

Chukchi Sea

East Siberian Sea

Laptev Sea

Kara Sea

ARCTIC OCEAN

North Pole

NOVAYA ZEMLYA

SEVERNAYA ZEMLYA

NEW SIBERIAN ISLANDS

FRANZ JOSEF LAND

Barents Sea

SVALBARD

Svalbard (Norway)

Spitsbergen

BEAR ISLAND (Norway)

JAN MAYEN (Norway)

Greenland Sea

Norwegian Sea

Greenland (Den.)

KNUD RASMUSSEN LAND

BAFFIN BAY

ELLESMERE

DEVON

QUEEN ELIZABETH ISLANDS

VICTORIA

BANKS

MELVILLE ISLAND

PRINCE PATRICK

Beaufort Sea

C A N A D A

A l a s k a (U.S.)

ALASKA RANGE

BROOKS RANGE

ALASKA PENINSULA

Gulf of Alaska

KODIAK

Anchorage

Fairbanks

Nome

Bristol Bay

ICELAND

Reykjavik

FAEROE ISLANDS (Den.)

SHETLAND ISLANDS (U.K.)

ORKNEY ISLANDS

HEBRIDES

ATLANTIC OCEAN

North Sea

IRELAND

Dublin

Cork

UNITED KINGDOM

Edinburgh

Glasgow

Belfast

Liverpool

Manchester

Birm.

London

Bristol

Plymouth

FRANCE

Paris

Nantes

Bordeaux

Lyon

Marseille

Le Havre

Brest

BELGIUM

Bruxelles

GERMANY

Hamburg

Bremen

Köln

Frankfurt

München

NORWAY

Oslo

Bergen

Trondheim

Tromsø

SWEDEN

Stockholm

Göteborg

Malmö

FINLAND

Helsinki

Turku

DENMARK

København

Baltic Sea

Gulf of Bothnia

POLAND

Warszawa

Kraków

Gdańsk

Szczecin

Wrocław

Łódź

CZECHOSLOVAKIA

Praha

AUSTRIA

Wien

HUNGARY

Budapest

ROMANIA

București

YUGOSLAVIA

Zagreb

Beograd

Sarajevo

Skopje

BULGARIA

Sofia

ALBANIA

GREECE

Athínai

Thessaloníki

ITALY

Roma

Napoli

Milano

Torino

Genova

Firenze

Bari

SARDINIA

CORSICA

SICILY

CRETE

CYPRUS

Adriatic Sea

Tyrrhenian Sea

Ionian Sea

Mediterranean Sea

Black Sea

Istanbul

Ankara

T U R K E Y

LEBANON

ISRAEL

EGYPT

Alexandria

Damascus

Baghdad

I R A N

Tehrān

CAUCASUS

UNION OF SOVIET SOCIALIST REPUBLICS

Moskva

Leningrad

Murmansk

Arhangelsk

Kiev

Harkov

Rostov

Volgograd

Astrahan

Baku

Tbilisi

Yerevan

Gorkiy

Kazan

Kuybyshev

Saratov

Perm

Sverdlovsk

Čeljabinsk

Ufa

Orenburg

Omsk

Novosibirsk

Tomsk

Krasnojarsk

Irkutsk

Kemerovo

Novokuznetsk

WEST SIBERIAN PLAIN

CENTRAL SIBERIAN UPLANDS

Norilsk

URAL MTS

KAZAKHSTAN

Karaganda

Alma-Ata

Taškent

Frunze

Aral Sea

Lake Balhaš

CHERSKI MOUNTAINS

VERKHOYANSK MOUNTAINS

STANOVOY RANGE

YABLONOVY RANGE

SIHOTE-ALIN

Vladivostok

Habarovsk

MONGOLIA

Ulan-Bator

GOBI DESERT

GREATER KHINGAN RANGE

MANCHURIA

Shenyang

Beijing

HOKKAIDO

Sapporo

HONSHU

Tokyo

Yokohama

Ōsaka

Kyōto

Nagoya

SHIKOKU

KYUSHU

KOREA

Sea of Japan

© ISTITUTO GEOGRAFICO DE AGOSTINI S.p.A. - NOVARA

A-515200-280 4 4 4 6

Scale 1:30,000,000

Lambert Azimuthal Equal Area Projection

Map 23 **SOUTHWESTERN ASIA**

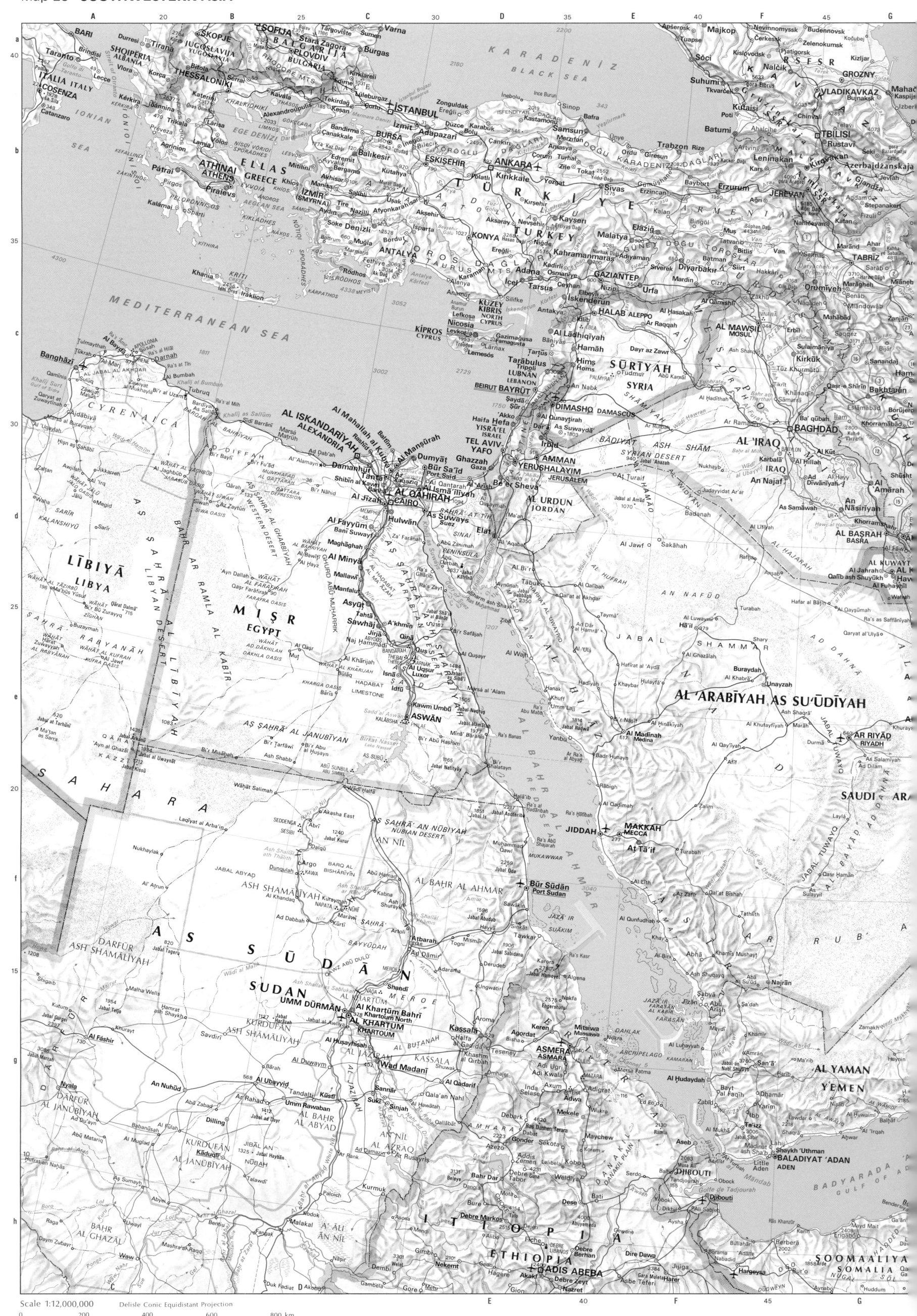

Scale 1:12,000,000

Delisle Conic Equidistant Projection

0   200   400   600   800 km

0   200   400 miles

AFGHANISTAN

VELĀYAT

1 Badakhshān
2 Bādghīsāt
3 Baghlān
4 Balkh
5 Bāmīān
6 Farāh
7 Fāryāb
8 Ghaznī
9 Ghowr
10 Helmand
11 Herāt
12 Jowzjān
13 Kābol
14 Kāpīsā
15 Konarhā
16 Laghmān
17 Lowgar
18 Nangarhār
19 Nīmrūz
20 Orūzgān
21 Paktīā
22 Parvān
23 Qandahār
24 Qondūz
25 Samangān
26 Takhār
27 Vardak
28 Zābol

ĪRĀN

OSTĀN

1 Āżarbāījān-e Gharbī
2 Āżarbāījān-e Sharqī
3 Bakhtarān
4 Boyer Ahmadī-e
  Kohkīlūyeh
5 Būshehr
6 Chahār Mahāl-e
  Bakhtīārī
7 Esfahān
8 Fārs
9 Gīlān
10 Hamadān
11 Hormozgān
12 Īlām
13 Kermān
14 Khorāsān
15 Khūzestān
16 Kordestān
17 Lorestān
18 Markazī
19 Māzandarān
20 Semnān
21 Sīstān-e
  Balūchestān
22 Yazd
23 Zanjān

Longitude East 55 of Greenwich

A Area occupied by Pakistan
  and claimed by India.

B Area claimed and occupied by India;
  status disputed by Pakistan.

C Area occupied by China
  and claimed by India.

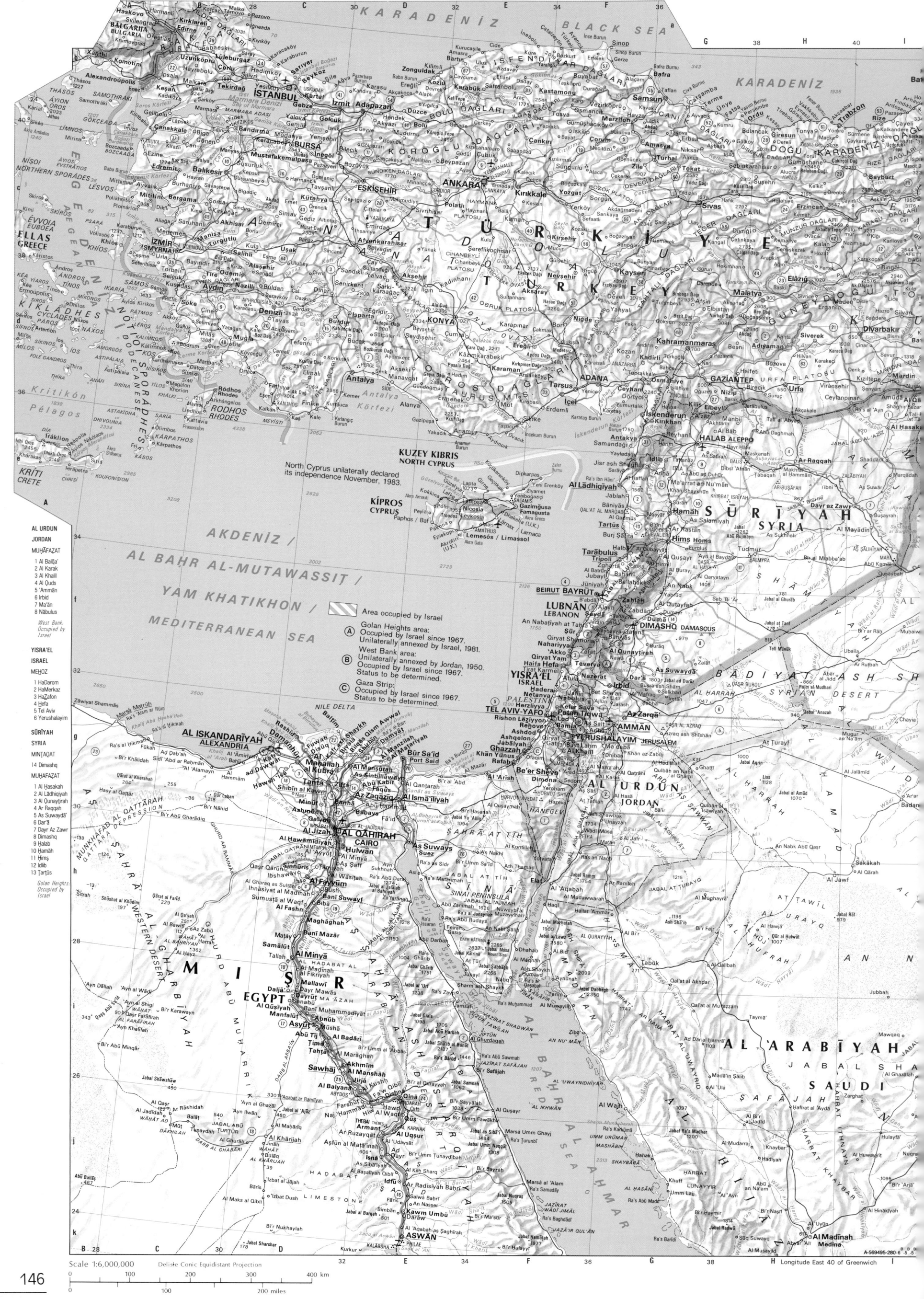

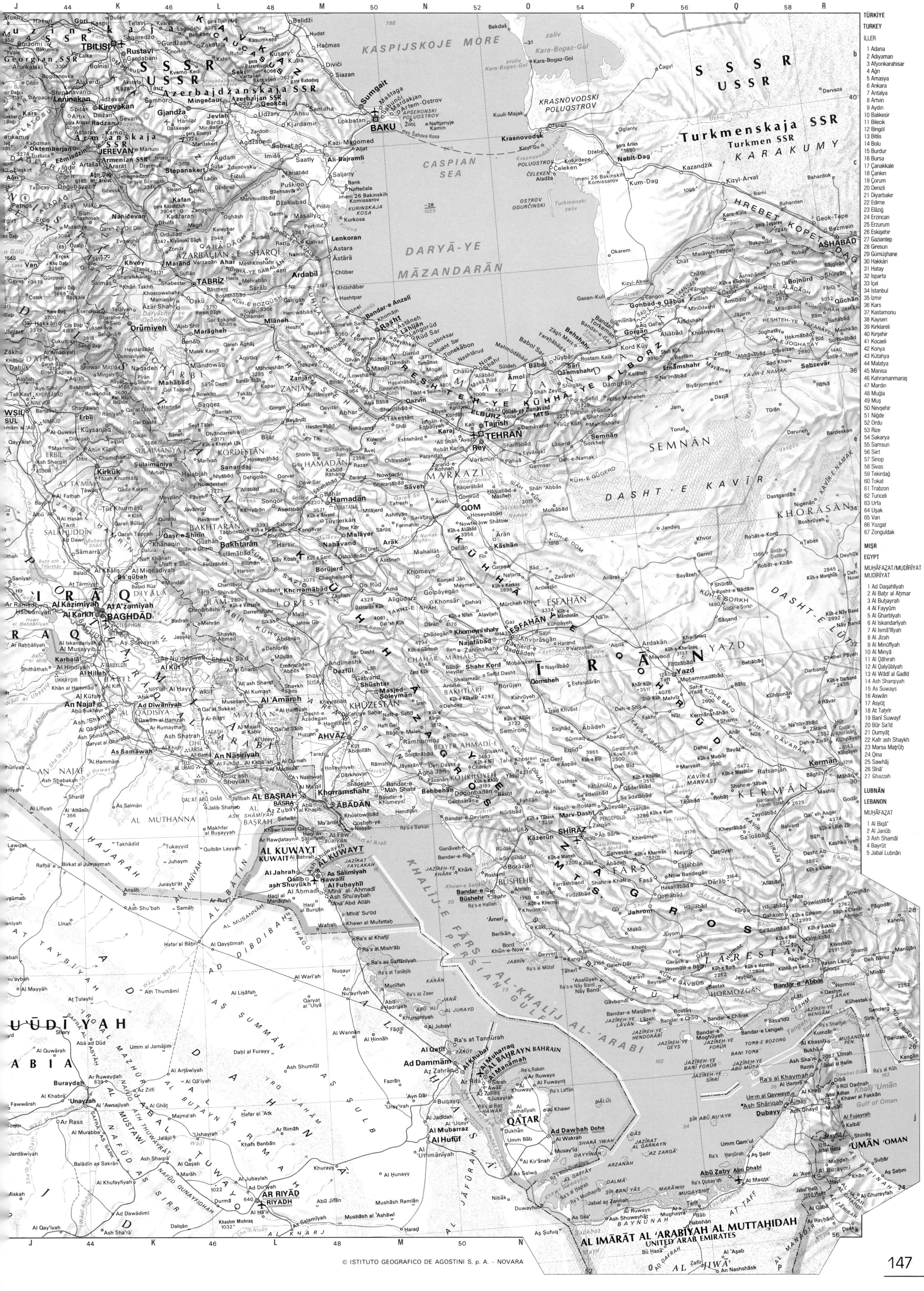

TÜRKIYE / TURKEY

İLLER

1 Adana
2 Adıyaman
3 Afyonkarahisar
4 Ağrı
5 Amasya
6 Ankara
7 Antalya
8 Artvin
9 Aydın
10 Balıkesir
11 Bilecik
12 Bingöl
13 Bitlis
14 Bolu
15 Burdur
16 Bursa
17 Çanakkale
18 Çankırı
19 Çorum
20 Denizli
21 Diyarbakır
22 Edirne
23 Elazığ
24 Erzincan
25 Erzurum
26 Eskişehir
27 Gaziantep
28 Giresun
29 Gümüşhane
30 Hakkâri
31 Hatay
32 Isparta
33 İçel
34 İstanbul
35 İzmir
36 Kars
37 Kastamonu
38 Kayseri
39 Kırklareli
40 Kocaeli
41 Konya
42 Kütahya
43 Malatya
44 Manisa
45 Kahramanmaraş
46 Mardin
47 Muğla
48 Muş
49 Nevşehir
50 Niğde
51 Ordu
52 Rize
53 Sakarya
54 Samsun
55 Siirt
56 Sinop
57 Sivas
58 Tekirdağ
59 Tokat
60 Trabzon
61 Tunceli
62 Urfa
63 Uşak
64 Van
65 Yozgat
66 Zonguldak

MIṢR / EGYPT

MUḤĀFAẒAT/MUDĪRĪYAT / MUDĪRIYAT

1 Ad Daqahlīyah
2 Al Baḥr al Aḥmar
3 Al Buḥayrah
4 Al Fayyūm
5 Al Gharbīyah
6 Al Iskandarīyah
7 Al Ismāʿīlīyah
8 Al Jīzah
9 Al Minūfīyah
10 Al Minyā
11 Al Qāhirah
12 Al Qalyūbīyah
13 Al Wādī al Gadīd
14 As Sharqīyah
15 As Suways
16 Aswān
17 Asyūṭ
18 Al Taḥrīr
19 Banī Suwayf
20 Būr Saʿīd
21 Dumyāṭ
22 Kafr ash Shaykh
23 Marsa Maṭrūḥ
24 Qinā
25 Sawhāj
26 Sīnāʾ
27 Ghazzah

LUBNĀN / LEBANON

MUḤĀFAẒAT

1 Al Biqāʿ
2 Al Janūb
3 Ash Shamāl
4 Bayrūt
5 Jabal Lubnān

Map 25

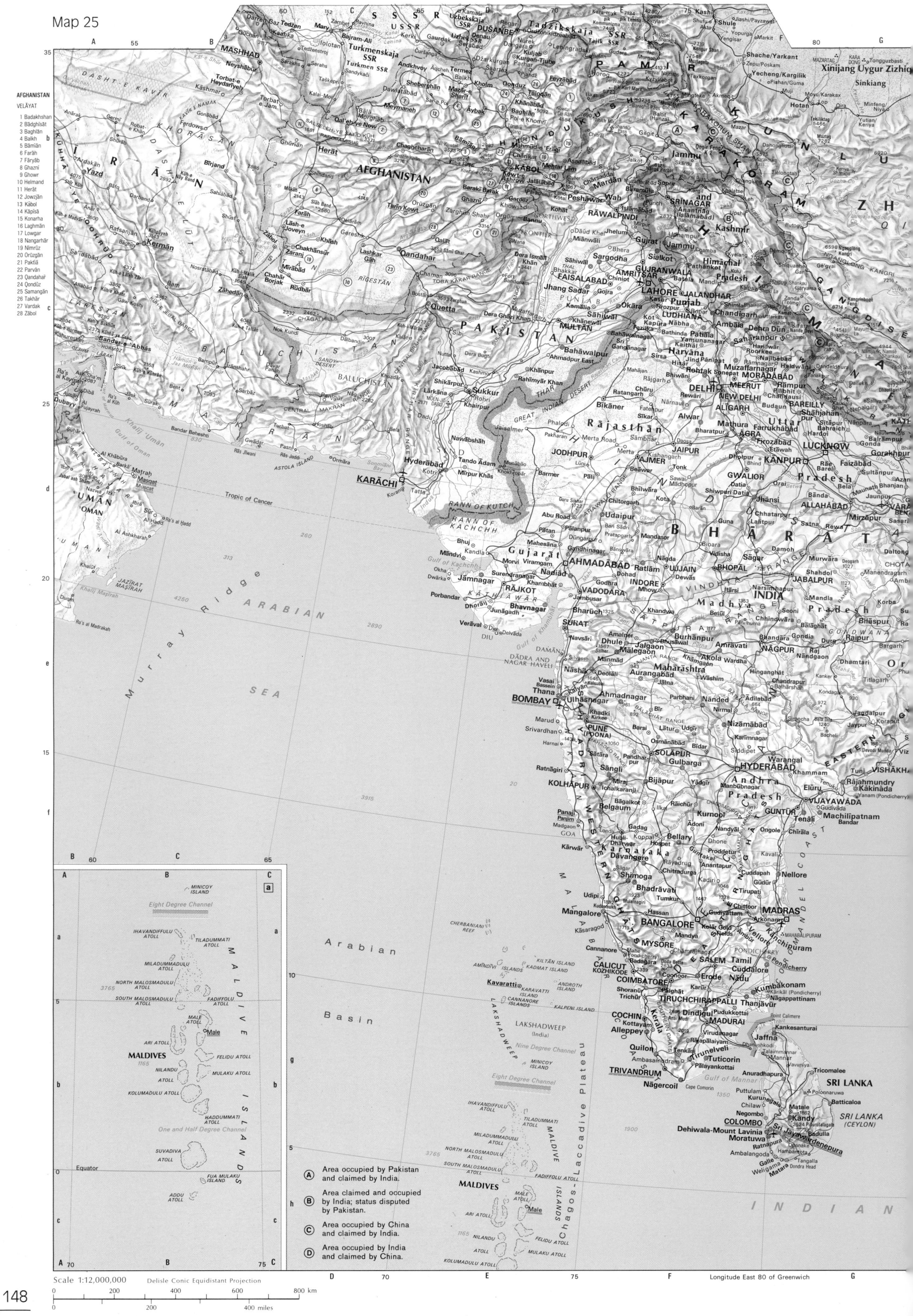

AFGHANISTAN
VELĀYAT
1 Badakhshān
2 Bādghīsāt
3 Baghlān
4 Balkh
5 Bāmīān
6 Farāh
7 Fāryāb
8 Ghazni
9 Ghowr
10 Helmand
11 Herāt
12 Jowzjān
13 Kābol
14 Kāpīsā
15 Konarha
16 Laghmān
17 Lowgar
18 Nangarhār
19 Nīmrūz
20 Orūzgān
21 Paktiā
22 Parvān
23 Qandahār
24 Qondūz
25 Samangān
26 Takhār
27 Vardak
28 Zābol

Ⓐ Area occupied by Pakistan
and claimed by India.

Ⓑ Area claimed and occupied
by India; status disputed
by Pakistan.

Ⓒ Area occupied by China
and claimed by India.

Ⓓ Area occupied by India
and claimed by China.

Scale 1:12,000,000   Delisle Conic Equidistant Projection   Longitude East 80 of Greenwich

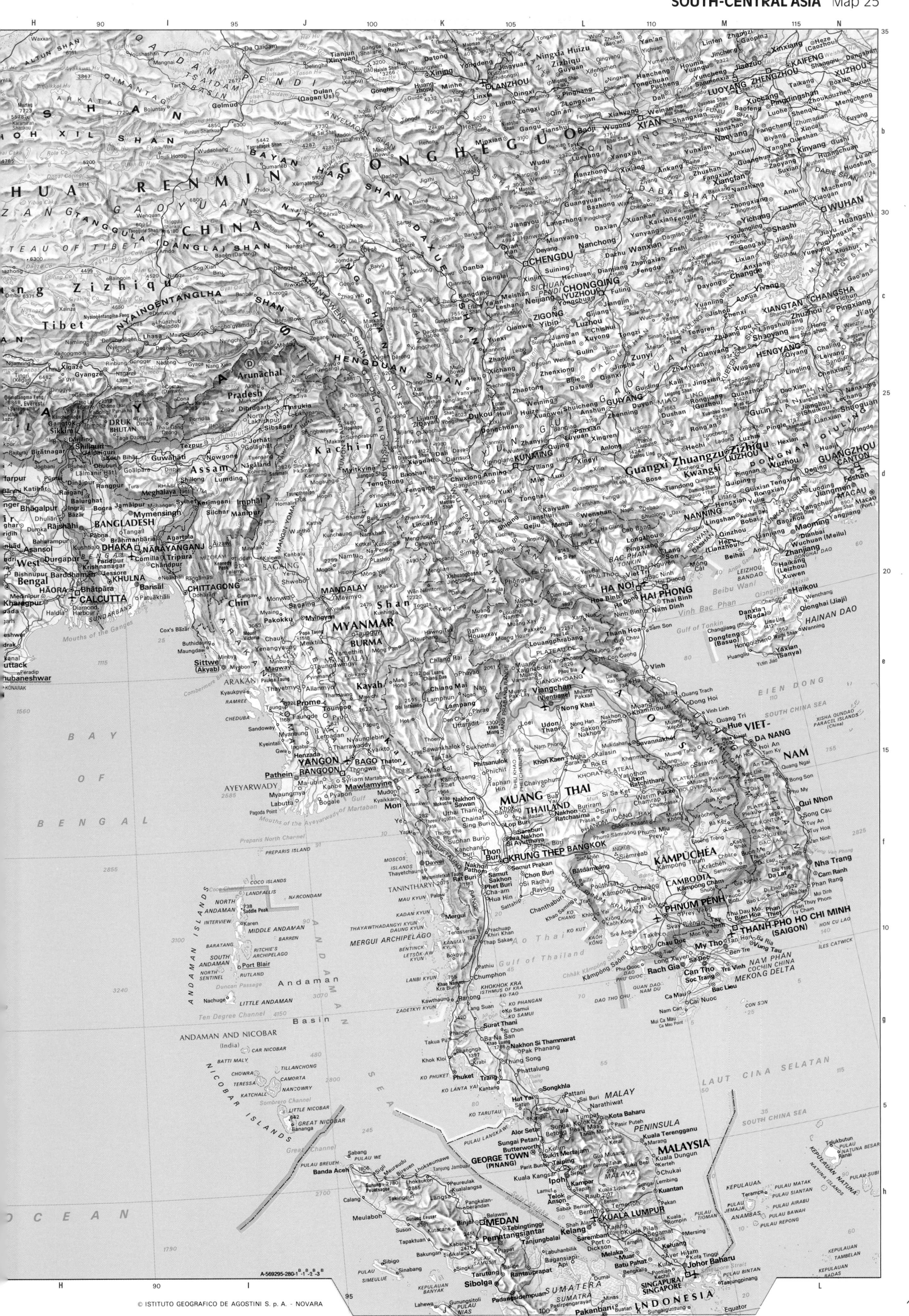

Map 26 **SOUTHEAST ASIA**

Scale 1:12,000,000 at the Equator   Mercator Cylindrical Projection

Longitude East 110 of Greenwich

A-569800-280-2-²-²-²-²

TAIWAN

KEELUNG
TAIPEI
Hsinchu
Ilan
Suao

TAICHUNG
CHIAYI
TAINAN
KAOHSIUNG
Pingtung

PHILIPPINE SEA

LUZON

MANILA
QUEZON CITY
PILIPINAS
PHILIPPINES

MINDORO

PANAY

NEGROS

CEBU

LEYTE

SAMAR

MASBATE

PALAWAN

SULU SEA

ZAMBOANGA

MINDANAO

DAVAO

General Santos

PACIFIC OCEAN

FEDERATED STATES
OF MICRONESIA

YAP ISLANDS

PALAU ISLANDS

CAROLINE ISLANDS

Palau

Belau

(Trust Territory)

West

Caroline

Basin

Sabah

CELEBES SEA

HALMAHERA

Manado
Tondano
Gorontalo

MOLUCCA SEA

SULAWESI

Samarinda

Ujung Pandang
(MAKASAR)

SULAWESI TENGGARA

SULAWESI SELATAN

INDONESIA

Ambon

SERAM CERAM

IRIAN JAYA

PEGUNUNGAN

PAPUA
NEW GUINEA

NEW GUINEA

Jayapura

MALUKU

BANDA SEA

FLORES

PULAU FLORES

NUSA TENGGARA TIMUR

SUMBA

TIMOR
TIMUR

LAUT TIMOR

TIMOR SEA

LAUT ARAFURA

ARAFURA SEA

AUSTRALIA

Darwin

Map 27 **CHINA AND MONGOLIA**

Area occupied by Pakistan
and claimed by India.

Area claimed and occupied by India;
status disputed by Pakistan.

Area occupied by China
and claimed by India.

Area occupied by India
and claimed by China.

Scale 1:12,000,000   Delisle Conic Equidistant Projection

0   200   400   600   800 km

0   200   400 miles

ZHONGHUA
RENMIN
GONGHEGUO

CHINA

1 Beijing Shi
2 Shanghai Shi
3 Tianjin Shi

Map 28 **NORTHEASTERN CHINA, KOREA AND JAPAN**

Scale 1:6,000,000   Delisle Conic Equidistant Projection

GJIANG

Shuangyashan
Yilan
Huanan
Baoqing
Dumur
Lučegorsk

Fangzheng
Dongfanghong
Hutou
He
Vostrecovo
Ust-Sobolevka
1730

Qitaihe
Hulin
Dalnerečensk
Amgu

Boli
Mishan
Lesozavodsk
Rakitnoje
Velikaja Kema

1185
Linkou
Didao
Hadagang
Lianzhushan
Novokačalinsk
Kirovskij
Plastun

Dazysui Shan
Hailin
Hengshan
Mashan
Jixi
Kamen-Rybolov
Gornyj Ključ
Anadnoje

S S S R
Muling (Bamiantong)
Kirovskij
Dalnegorsk
Kamenka
2495

MUDANJIANG
Hailin
Novokačalinsk
ozero Hanka
Rudnaja Pristan

Changting
Suiyang
Pogranичny
Horol
Vysokogornyj
Rudnaja Pristan

Ning'an
Dongning
Suifenhe
Spassk-Dalni
Svetlaja

Senlin Shan 1498
Grodekovo
Lipovcy
Sergeevka
Lazo
Olga

Wangqing
Tavričanka
Arseniev
Valentin

Caotougou
Tumen
Trudovoje
Preobraženije

Yanji
Chaoyangchuan
Hunchun
VLADIVOSTOK
Bolšoj Kamen
Nahodka

Helong
Posjet
zaliv Velikogo
Peter the Great Bay

Zhengfeng
Unggi
Partizansk

CH'ŎNGJIN
135

Japan Basin

CHOSŎN M.I.K.
NORTH KOREA
JAPONSKOJE MORE /
TONG-HAE / NIPPON-KAI

Yamato Rise

SEA OF JAPAN

NIPPON
JAPAN

TAEHAN-MIN'GUK
SOUTH KOREA

HONSHŪ

PUSAN

TSUSHIMA

KYŪSHŪ

PACIFIC OCEAN

T A I H E I Y Ō

Shikoku Basin

SHIKOKU

Nankai Trench

NIPPON
JAPAN
1 Hokkaidō Ken
2 Aomori Ken
3 Iwate Ken
4 Miyagi Ken
5 Akita Ken
6 Yamagata Ken
7 Fukushima Ken
8 Ibaraki Ken
9 Tochigi Ken
10 Gunma Ken
11 Saitama Ken
12 Chiba Ken
13 Tōkyō To
14 Kanagawa Ken
15 Niigata Ken
16 Toyama Ken
17 Ishikawa Ken
18 Fukui Ken
19 Yamanashi Ken
20 Nagano Ken
21 Gifu Ken
22 Shizuoka Ken
23 Aichi Ken
24 Mie Ken
25 Shiga Ken
26 Kyōto Fu
27 Ōsaka Fu
28 Hyōgo Ken
29 Nara Ken
30 Wakayama Ken
31 Tottori Ken
32 Shimane Ken
33 Okayama Ken
34 Hiroshima Ken
35 Yamaguchi Ken
36 Tokushima Ken
37 Kagawa Ken
38 Ehime Ken
39 Kōchi Ken
40 Fukuoka Ken
41 Saga Ken
42 Nagasaki Ken
43 Kumamoto Ken
44 Ōita Ken
45 Miyazaki Ken
46 Kagoshima Ken

CHOSŎN M.I.K.
NORTH KOREA
1 Chagang-Do
2 Ch'ŏngjin Si
3 Hamgyŏng-Namdo
4 Hamgyŏng-Pukto
5 Hwanghae-Namdo
6 Hwanghae-Pukto
7 Kaesŏng Si
8 Kangwŏn-Do
9 P'yŏngan-Namdo
10 P'yŏngan-Pukto
11 P'yŏngyang Si
12 Yanggang-Do

TAEHAN-MIN'GUK
SOUTH KOREA
1 Cheju-Do
2 Chŏlla-Namdo
3 Chŏlla-Pukto
4 Ch'ungch'ŏng-Namdo
5 Ch'ungch'ŏng-Pukto
6 Kangwŏn-Do
7 Kyŏnggi-Do
8 Kyŏngsang-Namdo
9 Kyŏngsang-Pukto
10 Pusan Si
11 Sŏul Si

ZHONGHUA RENMIN
GONGHEGUO
CHINA
1 Beijing Shi
2 Shanghai Shi
3 Tianjin Shi

Ⓐ Ostrov Kunašir, ostrov Sikotan,
ostrov Iturup and Malaja Kurilskaja
Grjada, occupied by the U.S.S.R.
since 1945, are claimed by Japan
pending a final peace treaty.

Map 29 **JAPAN**

NIPPON
JAPAN

1 Hokkaidō Ken
2 Aomori Ken
3 Iwate Ken
4 Miyagi Ken
5 Akita Ken
6 Yamagata Ken
7 Fukushima Ken
8 Ibaraki Ken
9 Tochigi Ken
10 Gunma Ken
11 Saitama Ken
12 Chiba Ken
13 Tōkyō To
14 Kanagawa Ken
15 Niigata Ken
16 Toyama Ken
17 Ishikawa Ken
18 Fukui Ken
19 Yamanashi Ken
20 Nagano Ken
21 Gifu Ken
22 Shizuoka Ken
23 Aichi Ken
24 Mie Ken
25 Shiga Ken
26 Kyōto Fu
27 Ōsaka Fu
28 Hyōgo Ken
29 Nara Ken
30 Wakayama Ken
31 Tottori Ken
32 Shimane Ken
33 Okayama Ken
34 Hiroshima Ken
35 Yamaguchi Ken
36 Tokushima Ken
37 Kagawa Ken
38 Ehime Ken
39 Kōchi Ken
40 Fukuoka Ken
41 Saga Ken
42 Nagasaki Ken
43 Kumamoto Ken
44 Ōita Ken
45 Miyazaki Ken
46 Kagoshima Ken
47 Okinawa Ken

Map 30 **AFRICA, PHYSICAL**

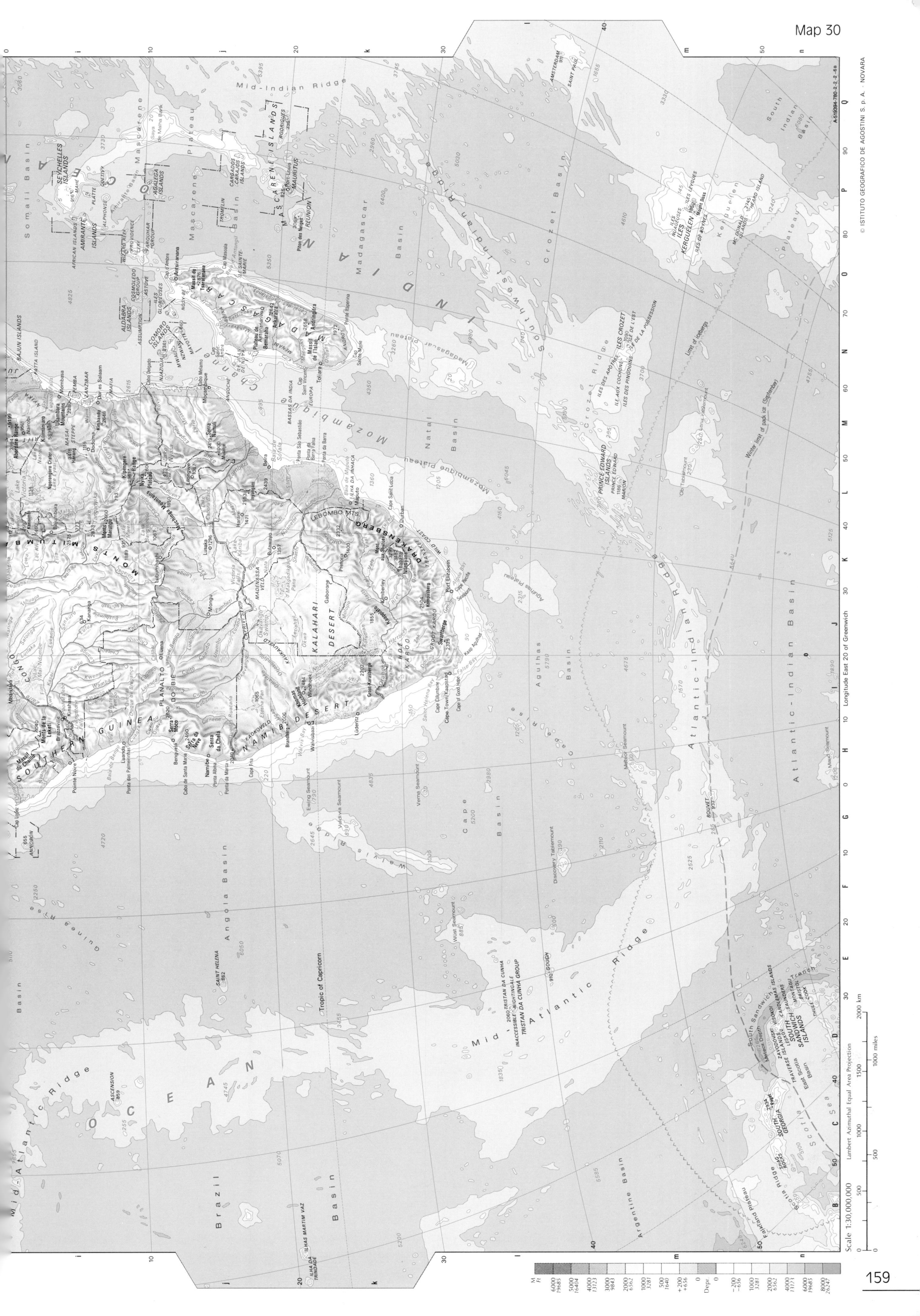

Map 30

Scale 1:30,000,000   Lambert Azimuthal Equal Area Projection

Map 31 **AFRICA, POLITICAL**

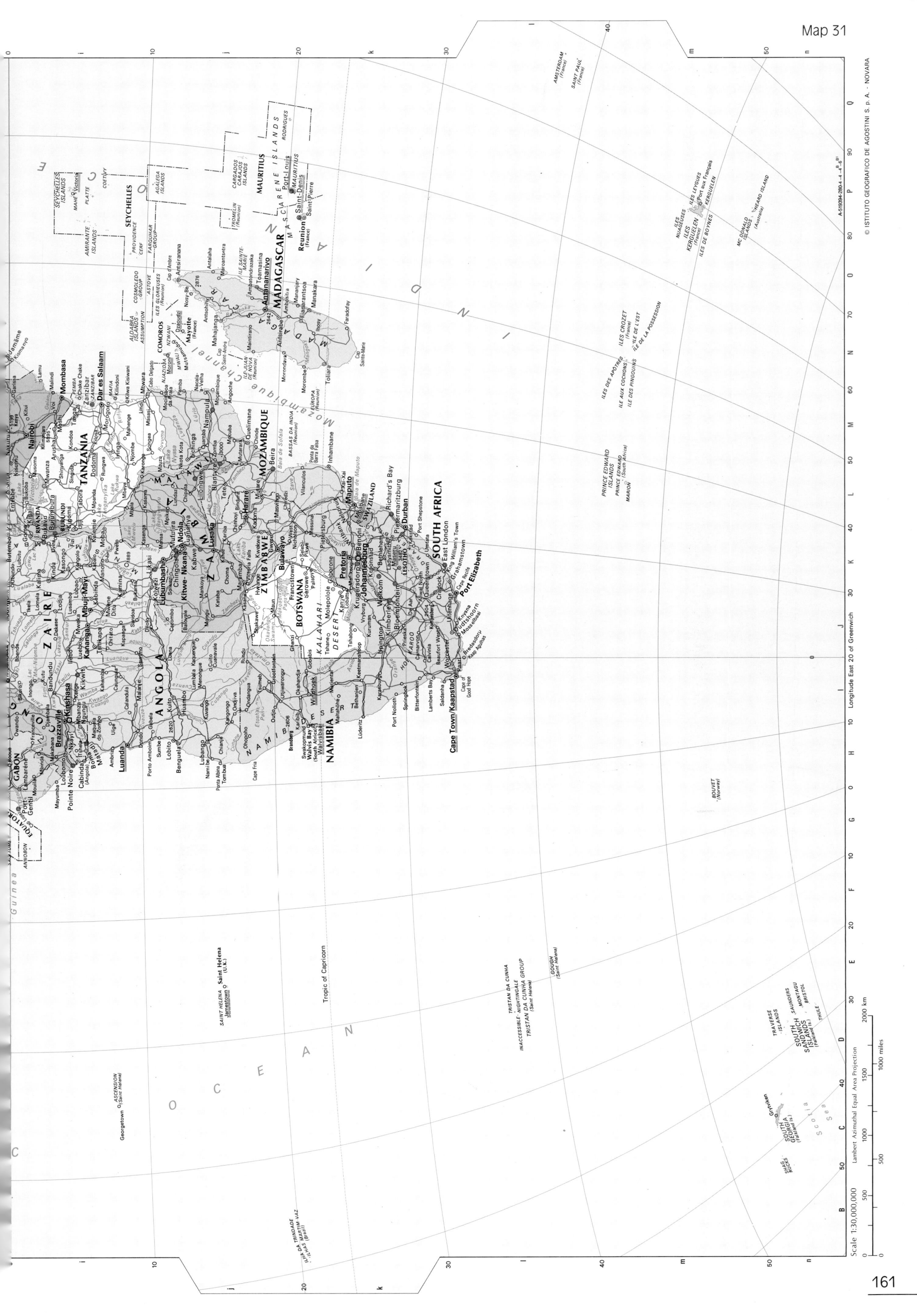

Map 31

Map 32

Scale 1:9,000,000   Lambert Azimuthal Equal Area Projection

A-589791-280-1

Ⓐ Western Sahara is occupied by Morocco.

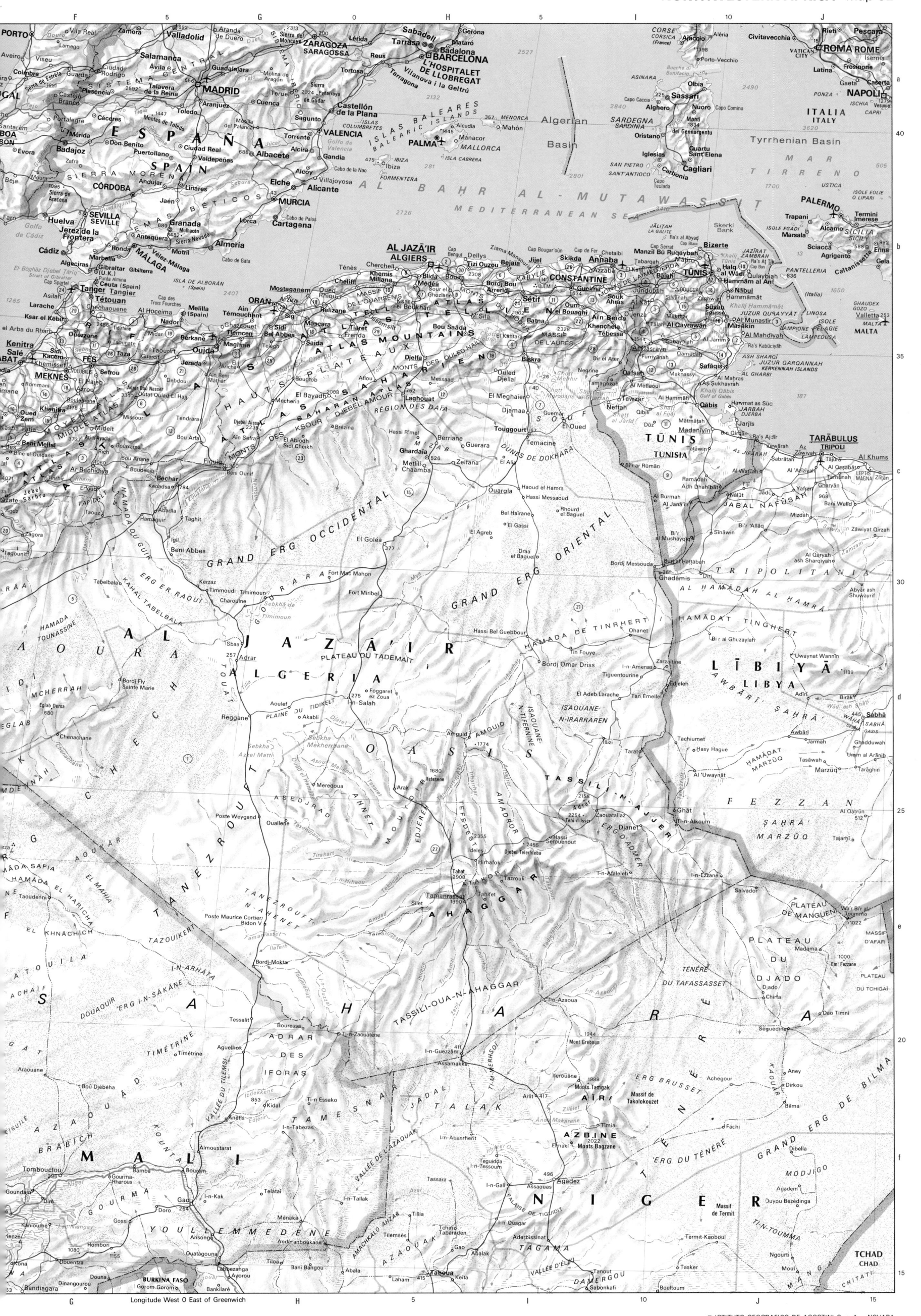

Map 33 **NORTHEASTERN AFRICA**

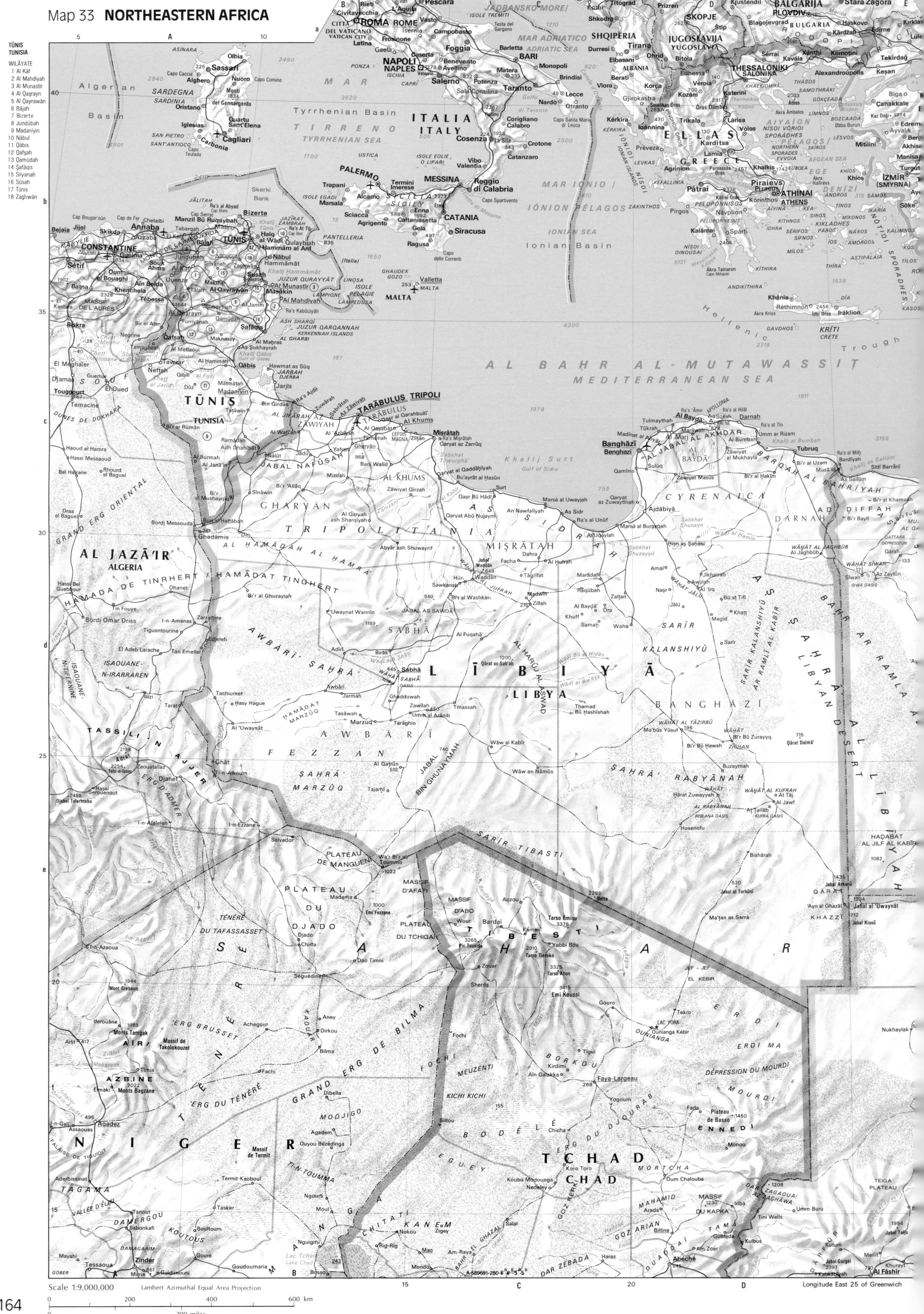

Scale 1:9,000,000   Lambert Azimuthal Equal Area Projection

Longitude East 25 of Greenwich

TŪNIS
TUNISIA
WILĀYATE
1 Al Kāf
2 Al Mahdīyah
3 Al Munastīr
4 Al Qaṣrayn
5 Al Qayrawān
6 Bājah
7 Bizerte
8 Jundūbah
9 Madanīyin
10 Nābul
11 Qābis
12 Qafṣah
13 Qamūdah
14 Ṣafāqis
15 Silyānah
16 Sūsah
17 Tūnis
18 Zaghwān

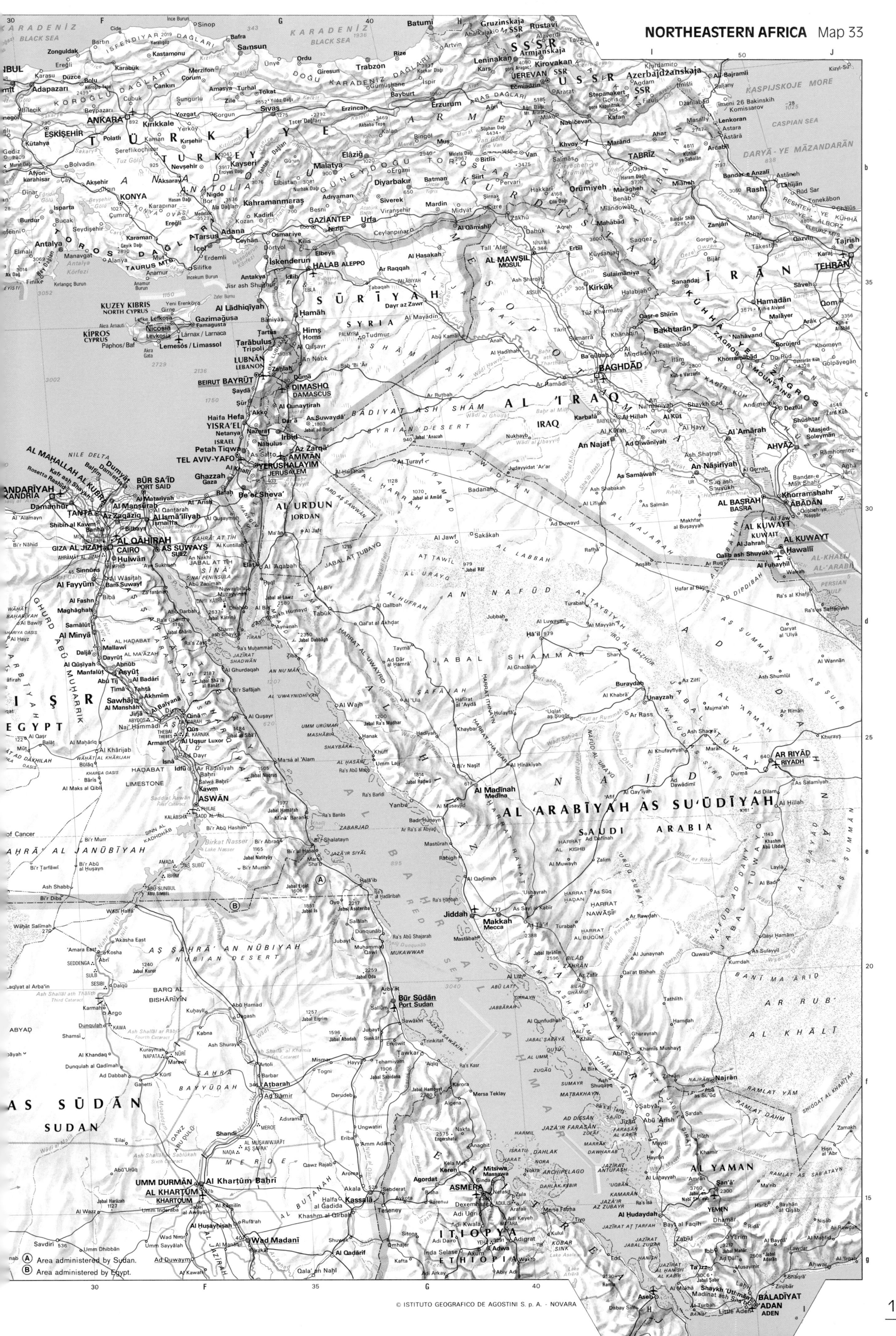

Ⓐ Area administered by Sudan.
Ⓑ Area administered by Egypt.

© ISTITUTO GEOGRAFICO DE AGOSTINI S.p.A. - NOVARA

Map 34 **WEST-CENTRAL AFRICA**

LIBERIA
COUNTIES
1 Bong
2 Cape Mount
3 Grand Bassa
4 Grand Gedeh
5 Lofa
6 Maryland
7 Montserrado
8 Nimba
9 Sinoe

CÔTE D'IVOIRE
IVORY COAST
DÉPARTEMENTS
1 Abengourou
2 Abidjan
3 Aboisso
4 Adzopé
5 Agboville
6 Biankouma
7 Bondoukou
8 Bongouanou
9 Bouaflé
10 Bouaké
11 Bouna
12 Boundiali
13 Dabakala
14 Daloa
15 Danané
16 Dimbokro
17 Divo
18 Ferkessédougou
19 Gagnoa
20 Guiglo
21 Issia
22 Katiola
23 Korhogo
24 Lakota
25 Man
26 Mankono
27 Odienné
28 Oumé
29 Sassandra
30 Séguéla
31 Soubré
32 Tengréla
33 Touba
34 Zuenoula

BURKINA FASO
DÉPARTEMENTS
1 Centre
2 Centre-Est
3 Centre-Nord
4 Centre-Ouest
5 Est
6 Hauts-Bassins
7 Komoé
8 Nord
9 Sahel
10 Sud-Ouest
11 Volta Noire

TOGO
RÉGIONS
1 Centre
2 Kara
3 Maritime
4 Plateaux
5 Savanes

BÉNIN
PROVINCES
1 Atakora
2 Atlantique
3 Borgou
4 Mono
5 Ouémé
6 Zou

Ⓐ Abuja is the future federal capital of Nigeria.

Ⓑ The political subdivisions shown for Guinea represent statistical areas and are not recognized for administrative purposes.

Scale 1:9,000,000   Lambert Azimuthal Equal Area Projection

0   200   400   600 km

0   200 miles

Longitude West 5 of Greenwich

A-589495-280-1

166

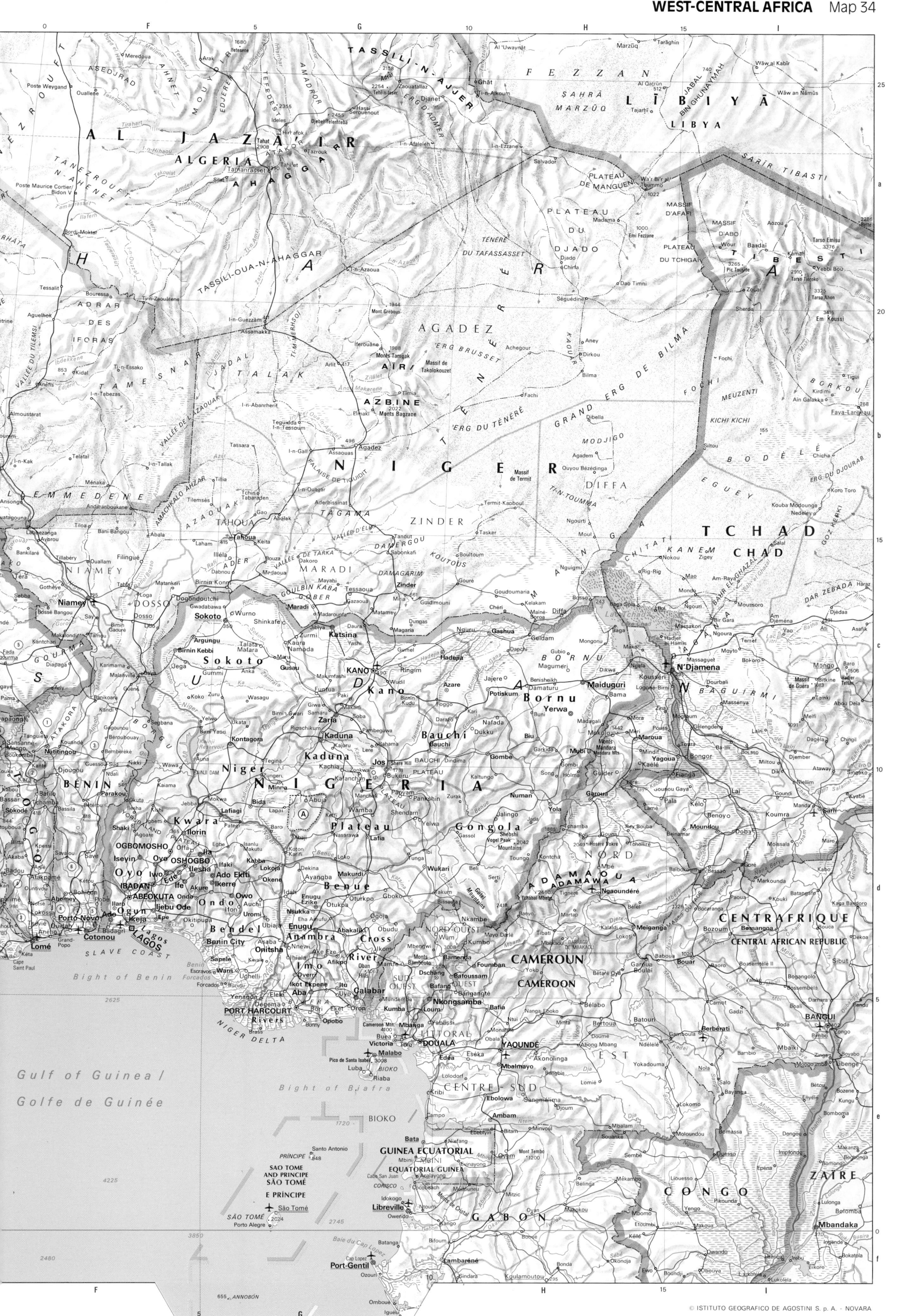

Map 35 **EAST-CENTRAL AFRICA**

Scale 1:9,000,000 Lambert Azimuthal Equal Area Projection

0   200   400   600 km

0   200 miles

Longitude East 30 of Greenwich

AL IMĀRĀT AL 'ARABĪYAH AL MUTTAHIDAH
UNITED ARAB EMIRATES

AL 'ARABĪYAH AS SUŪDĪYAH

SAUDI ARABIA

'UMĀN
OMAN

ERITREA

ASMERA

AL YAMAN

YEMEN

Gulf of Aden

SUQUTRĀ SOCOTRA

DJIBOUTI

Djibouti

TIGRAY

AMARA

GONDER

WELLO

ADEN

BALADĪYAT 'ADAN

Indian Ocean

SHEWA

ADIS ABEBA
(ADDIS ABABA)

ITIOPIA

ETHIOPIA

SOOMAALIYA

SOMALIA

ILUBABOR

KEFA

HARERGE

MUDUG

GAMO GOFA

SIDAMO

BALE

GAL GADUUD

BAKOOL

Somali Basin

KENYA

GEDO

SHABEELLAHA DHEXE

MUQDISHO MOGADISHU

Banaadir

SHABEELLAHA HOOSE

Marka

JUBBADA DHEXE

NAIROBI

JUBBADA HOOSE

Kismaayo

Equator

(A) Area administered by Sudan
(B) Area administered by Egypt

A-589395-280-2-2-1-2

Map 36 **EQUATORIAL AFRICA**

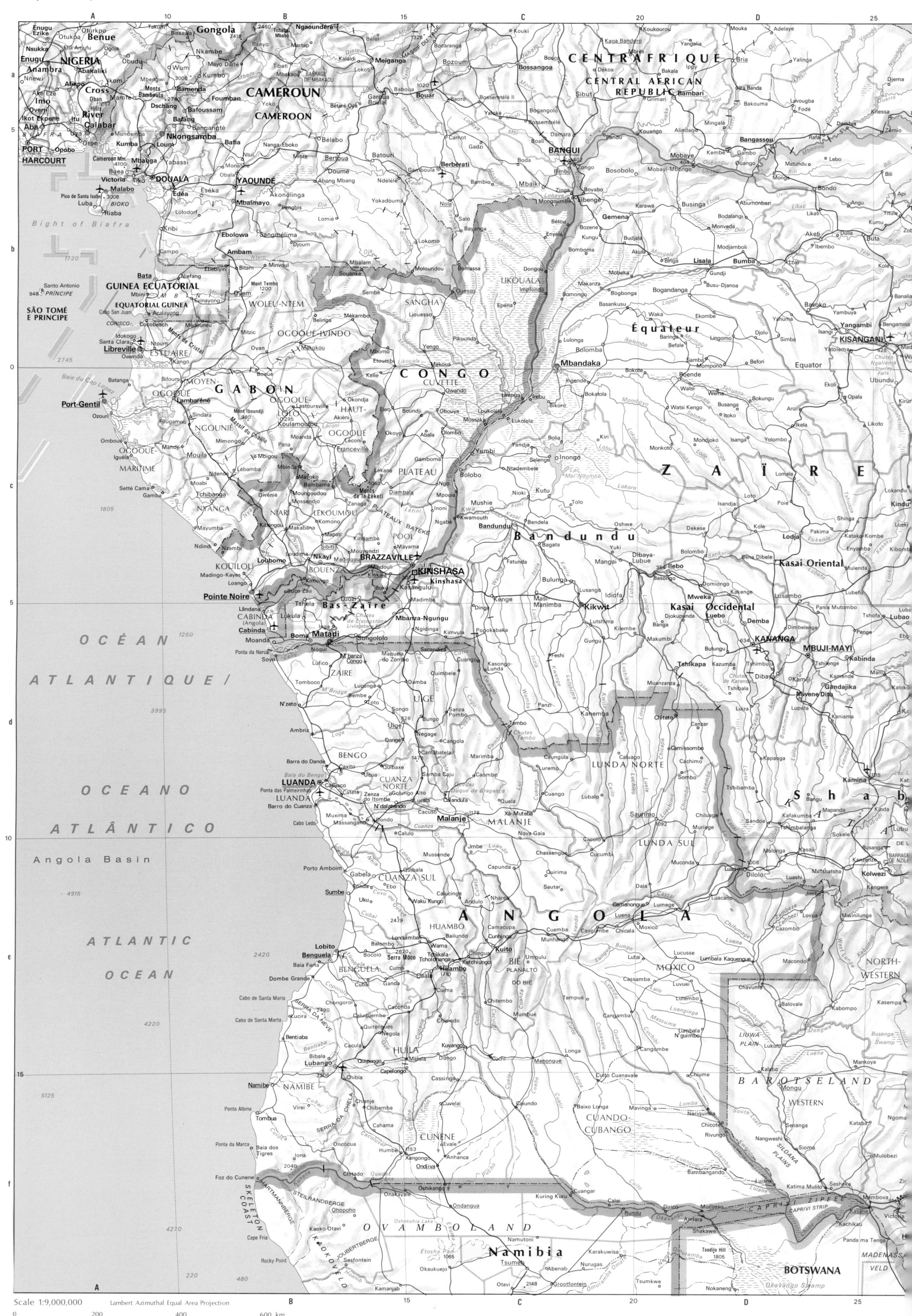

Scale 1:9,000,000   Lambert Azimuthal Equal Area Projection

0   200   400   600 km

0   200 miles

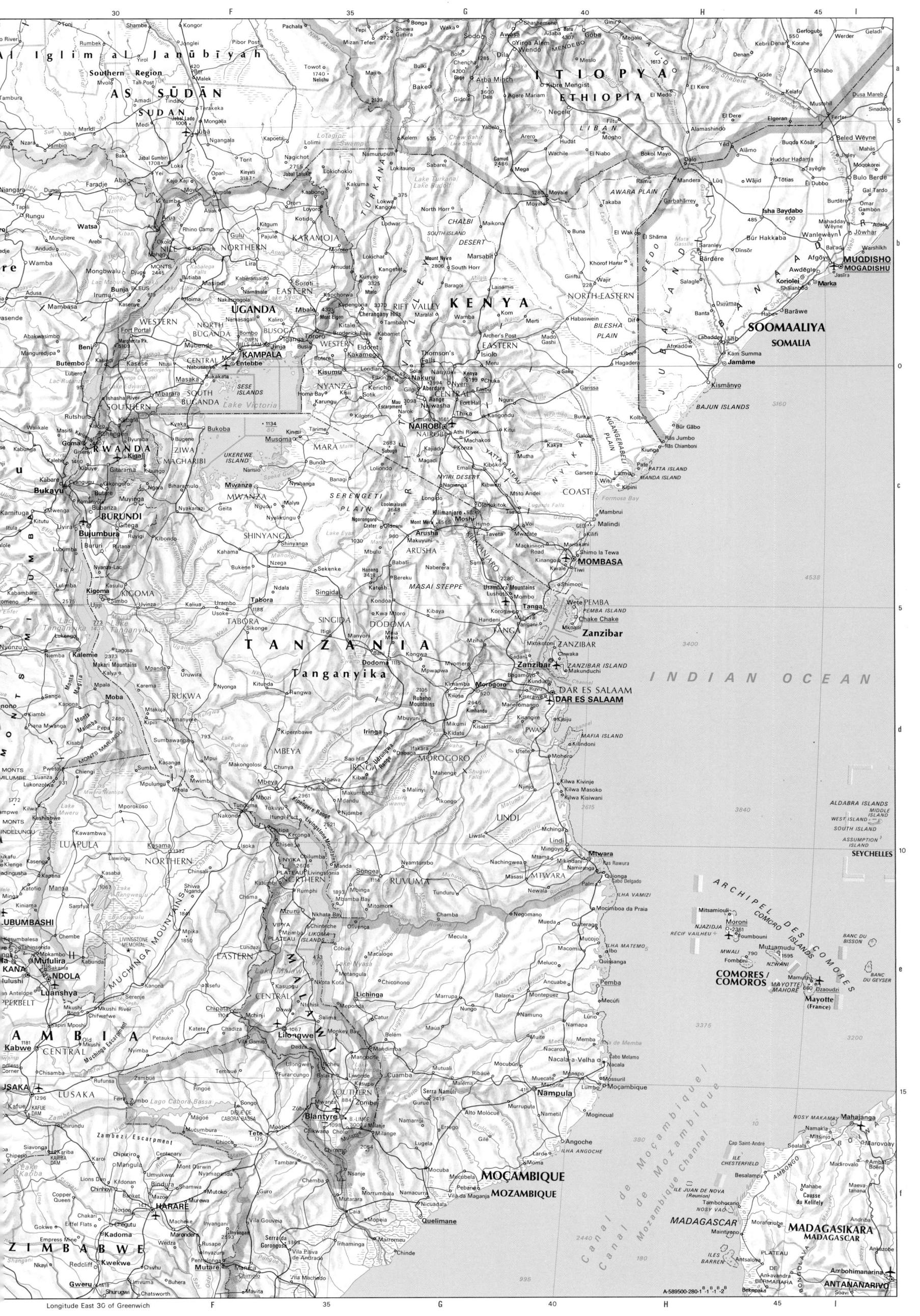

Map 37 SOUTHERN AFRICA

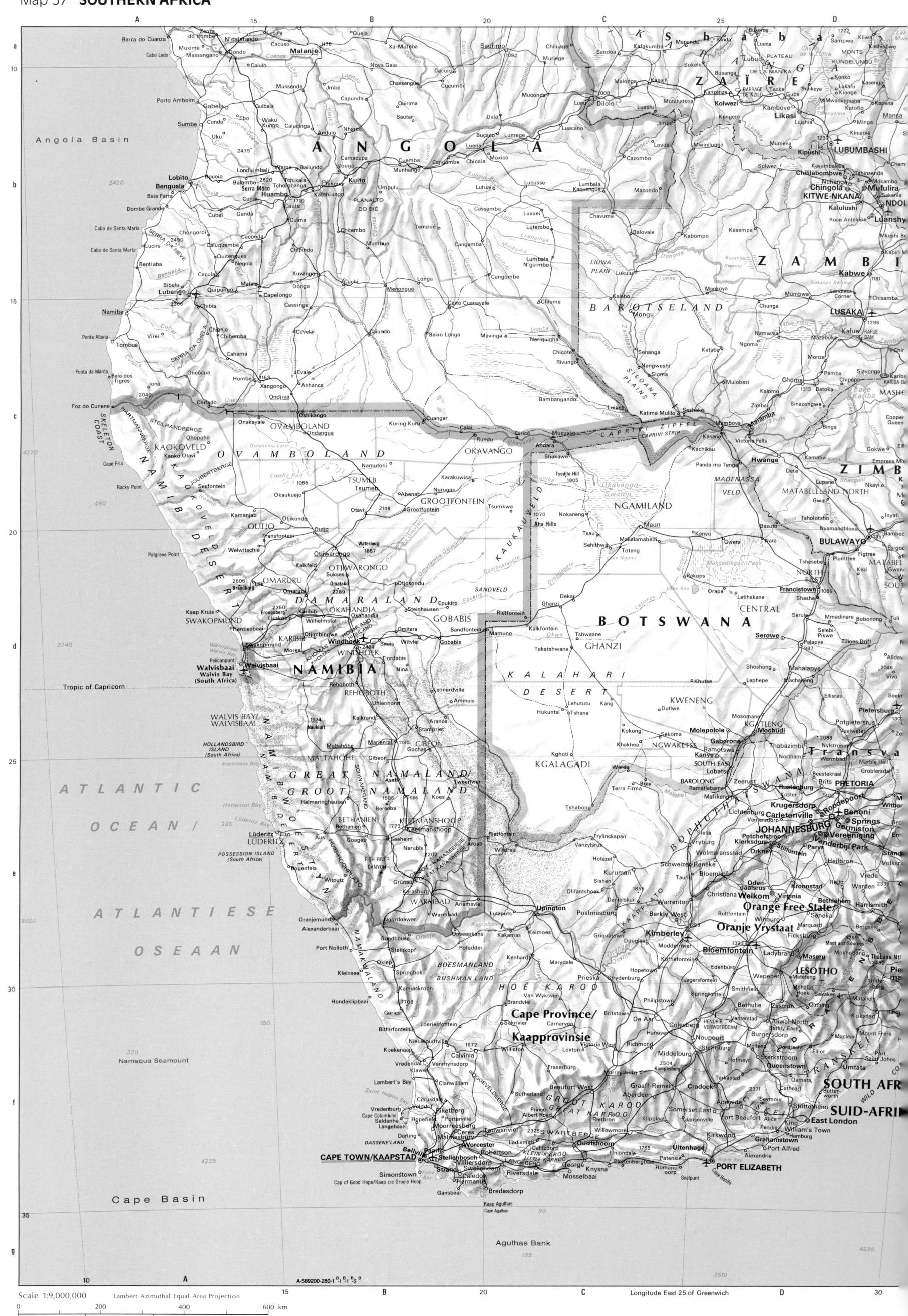

Scale 1:9,000,000   Lambert Azimuthal Equal Area Projection

Longitude East 25 of Greenwich

A-589200-280-1

0   200   400   600 km

0   200 miles

Map 38 **NORTH AMERICA, PHYSICAL**

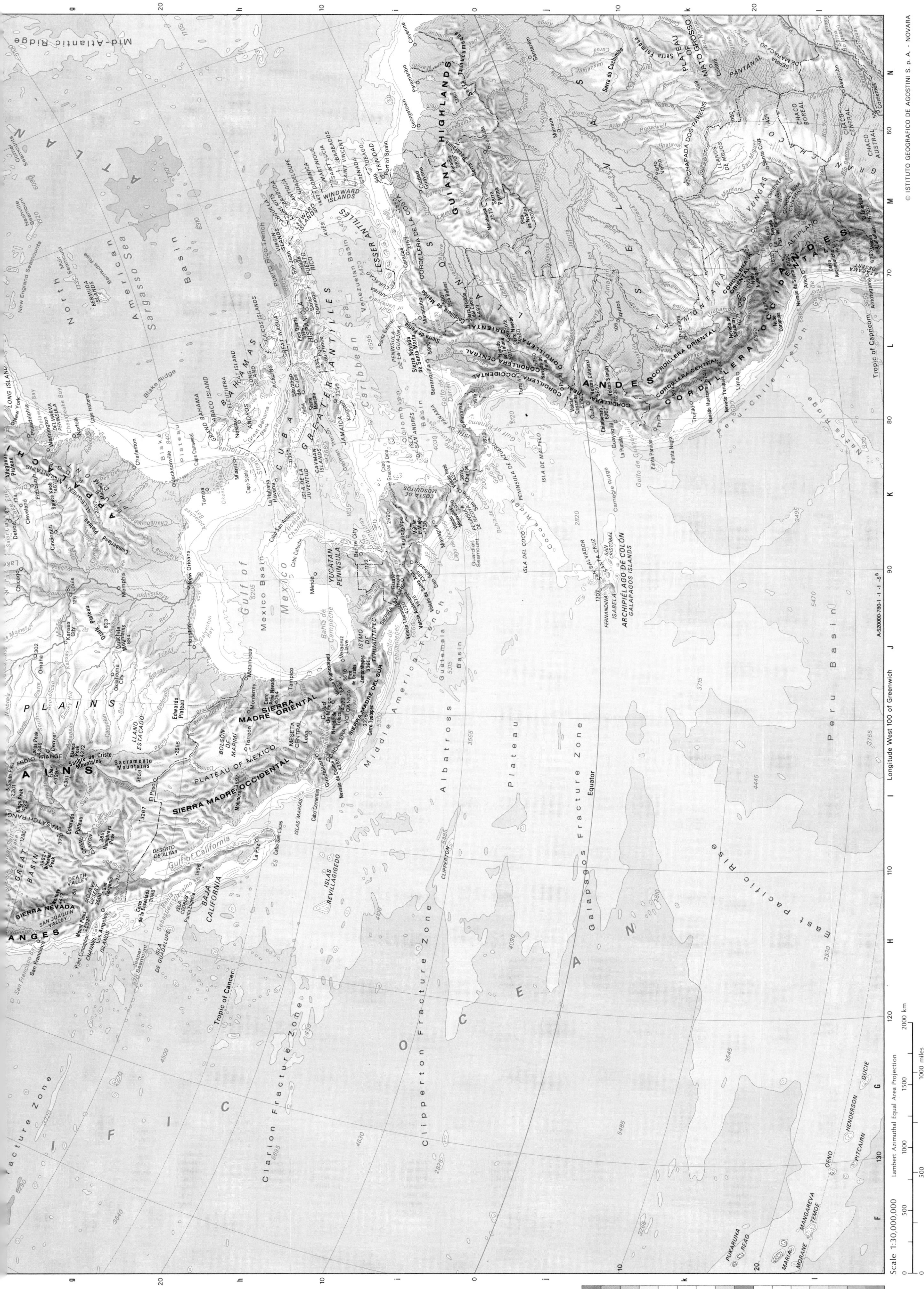

© ISTITUTO GEOGRAFICO DE AGOSTINI S. p. A. - NOVARA

Mid-Atlantic Ridge

ATLAN

North American Basin

Sargasso Sea

BERMUDA ISLANDS

New England Seamounts

GUIANA HIGHLANDS

PLATEAU DO MATO GROSSO

PANTANAL

CHACO BOREAL

CHACO CENTRAL

CHACO AUSTRAL

LLANOS

YUNGAS

ANDES

CORDILLERA OCCIDENTAL

CORDILLERA ORIENTAL

CORDILLERA CENTRAL

ALTIPLANO

Tropic of Capricorn

Peru-Chile Trench

WINDWARD ISLANDS

LEEWARD ISLANDS

LESSER ANTILLES

GREATER ANTILLES

CUBA

HISPANIOLA

JAMAICA

PUERTO RICO

Puerto Rico Trench

Caribbean Sea

Venezuelan Basin

Colombian Basin

PENINSULA DE LA GUAJIRA

Sierra Nevada de Santa Marta

CORDILLERA DE LA COSTA

APPALACHIANS

Allegheny Plateau

Cumberland Plateau

Blake Plateau

Cape Hatteras

Cape Canaveral

LONG ISLAND

DELMARVA PENINSULA

Chesapeake Bay

New York

Washington

Philadelphia

Baltimore

Richmond

Charleston

Jacksonville

BAHAMAS

GRAND BAHAMA ISLAND

ABACO ISLAND

ANDROS

GREAT INAGUA

ACKLINS

CAICOS ISLANDS

ELEUTHERA

Florida Strait

Miami

Tampa

La Habana / Havana

Yucatan Channel

ISLA DE LA JUVENTUD

CAYMAN ISLANDS

Gulf of Mexico

Mexico Basin

YUCATAN PENINSULA

Bahía de Campeche

Mérida

Belize City

New Orleans

Houston

Tampico

Veracruz

ISTMO DE TEHUANTEPEC

SIERRA MADRE ORIENTAL

SIERRA MADRE DEL SUR

SIERRA MADRE OCCIDENTAL

MESETA CENTRAL

PLATEAU OF MEXICO

BOLSÓN DE MAPIMÍ

LLANO ESTACADO

Edwards Plateau

GREAT PLAINS

PLAINS

Denver

Omaha

Kansas City

Oklahoma City

Des Moines

Memphis

Chicago

St. Louis

Ouachita Mountains

FRONT RANGE

Pikes Peak

Sangre de Cristo Mountains

Sacramento Mountains

El Paso

Monterrey

Torreón

DESIERTO DE ALTAR

GREAT BASIN

DEATH VALLEY

SIERRA NEVADA

SAN JOAQUIN VALLEY

RANGES

WASATCH RANGE

Colorado

CANYON

Sacramento

San Francisco

Los Angeles

Point Conception

CHANNEL ISLANDS

BAJA CALIFORNIA

Gulf of California

La Paz

Cabo San Lucas

ISLAS MARÍAS

Cabo Corrientes

ISLAS REVILLAGIGEDO

Tropic of Cancer

Middle America Trench

Guatemala Basin

SAN SALVADOR

COSTA DE MOSQUITOS

ISLA DEL COCO

Cocos Ridge

Carnegie Ridge

GALAPAGOS ISLANDS

ARCHIPIÉLAGO DE COLÓN

ISABELA

FERNANDINA

SAN CRISTÓBAL

SANTA CRUZ

Golfo de Guayaquil

Guayaquil

Lima

Callao

Nazca Ridge

Peru Basin

Equator

Galapagos Fracture Zone

Albatross Plateau

Clipperton Fracture Zone

CLIPPERTON

Clarion Fracture Zone

PACIFIC OCEAN

East Pacific Rise

DUCIE

HENDERSON

PITCAIRN

OENO

RÉAO

PUKARUHA

MARIA

MORANE

MANGAREVA

TEMOE

DE GUADALUPE

Mississippi

A500000-780-1 -1 -1 -5℠

Longitude West 100 of Greenwich

Lambert Azimuthal Equal Area Projection

Scale 1:30,000,000

| 0 | 500 | 1000 | 1500 | 2000 km |
| 0 | 500 | 1000 miles |

M Ft		
5000 16404		
4000 13123		
3000 9843		
2000 6562		
1000 3281		
500 1640		
+200 +656		
0 Depr. 0		
-200 -656		
1000 3281		
2000 6562		
4000 13123		
6000 19685		
6000 26247		

175

Map 39 **NORTH AMERICA, POLITICAL**

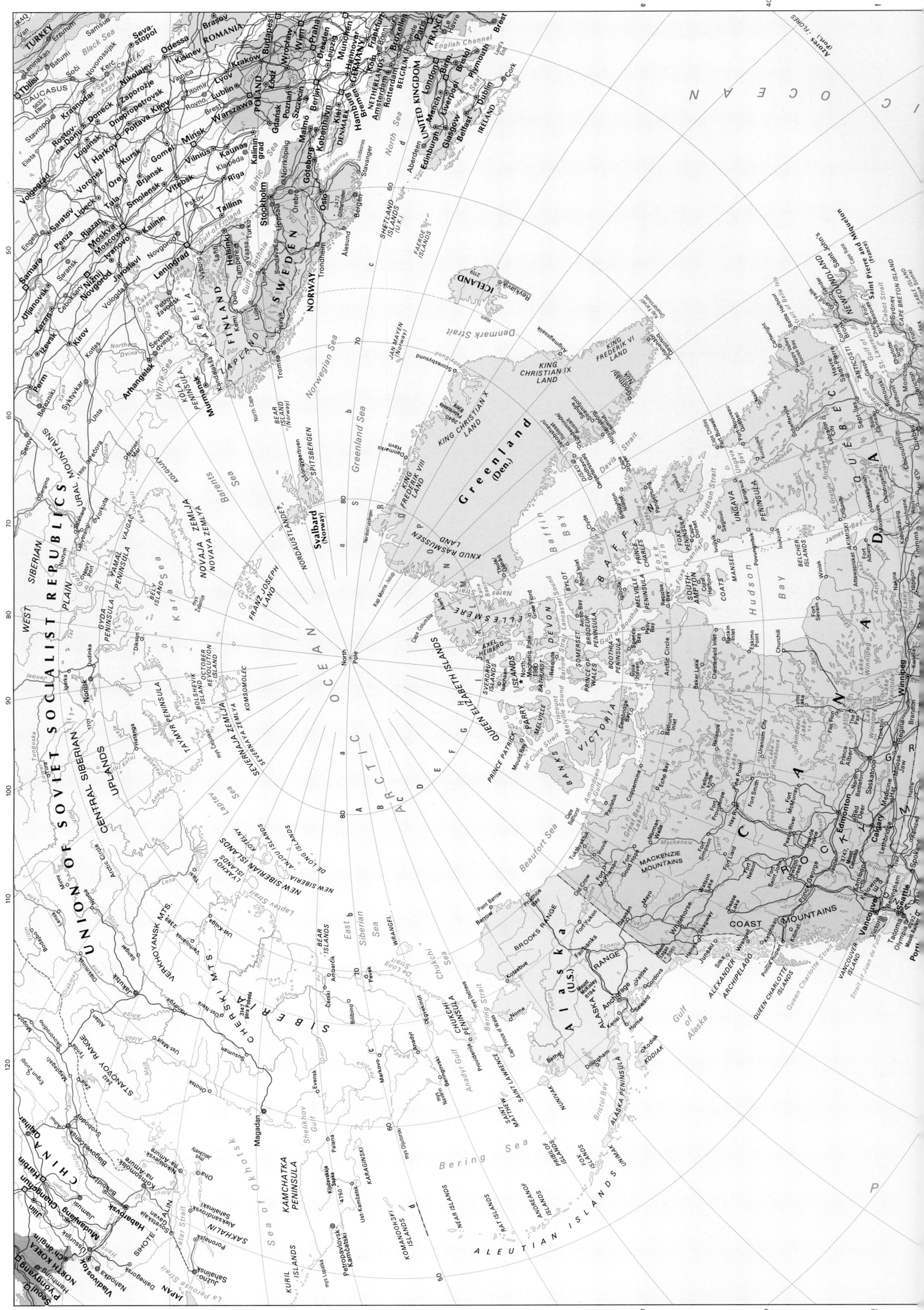

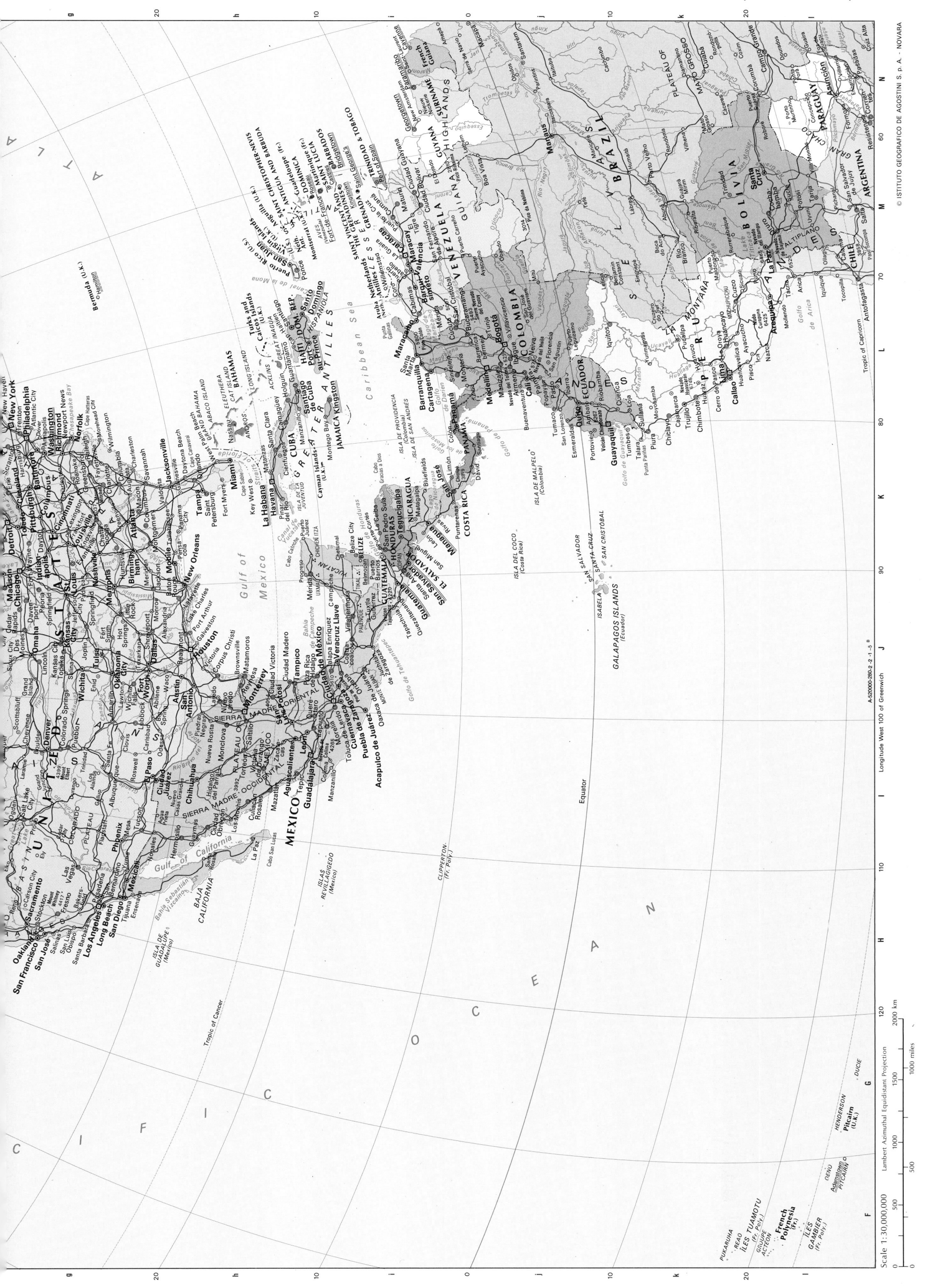

Scale 1:30,000,000

Lambert Azimuthal Equidistant Projection

© ISTITUTO GEOGRAFICO DE AGOSTINI S. p. A. · NOVARA

Map 40 **ALASKA**

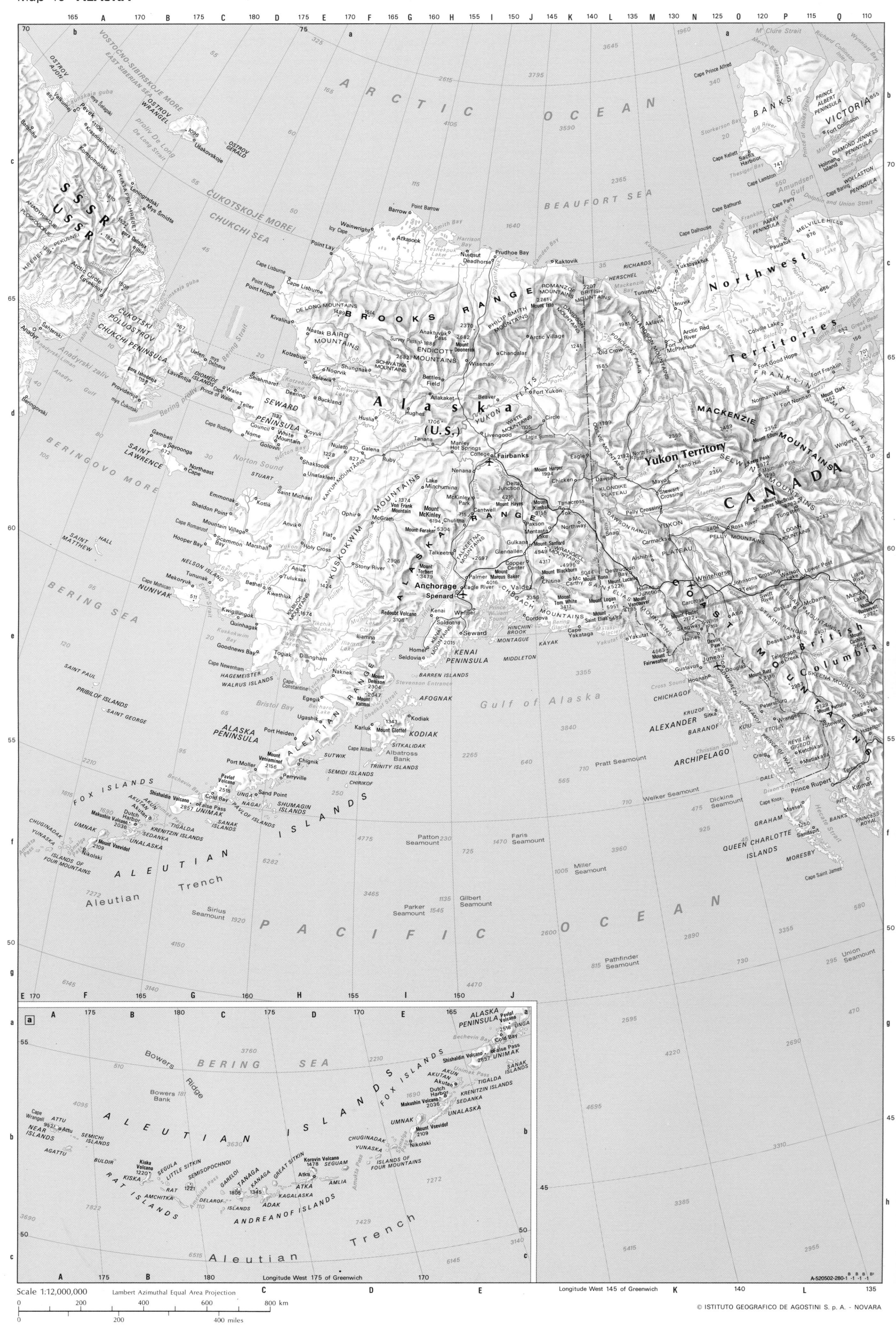

Scale 1:12,000,000 Lambert Azimuthal Equal Area Projection

© ISTITUTO GEOGRAFICO DE AGOSTINI S. p. A - NOVARA

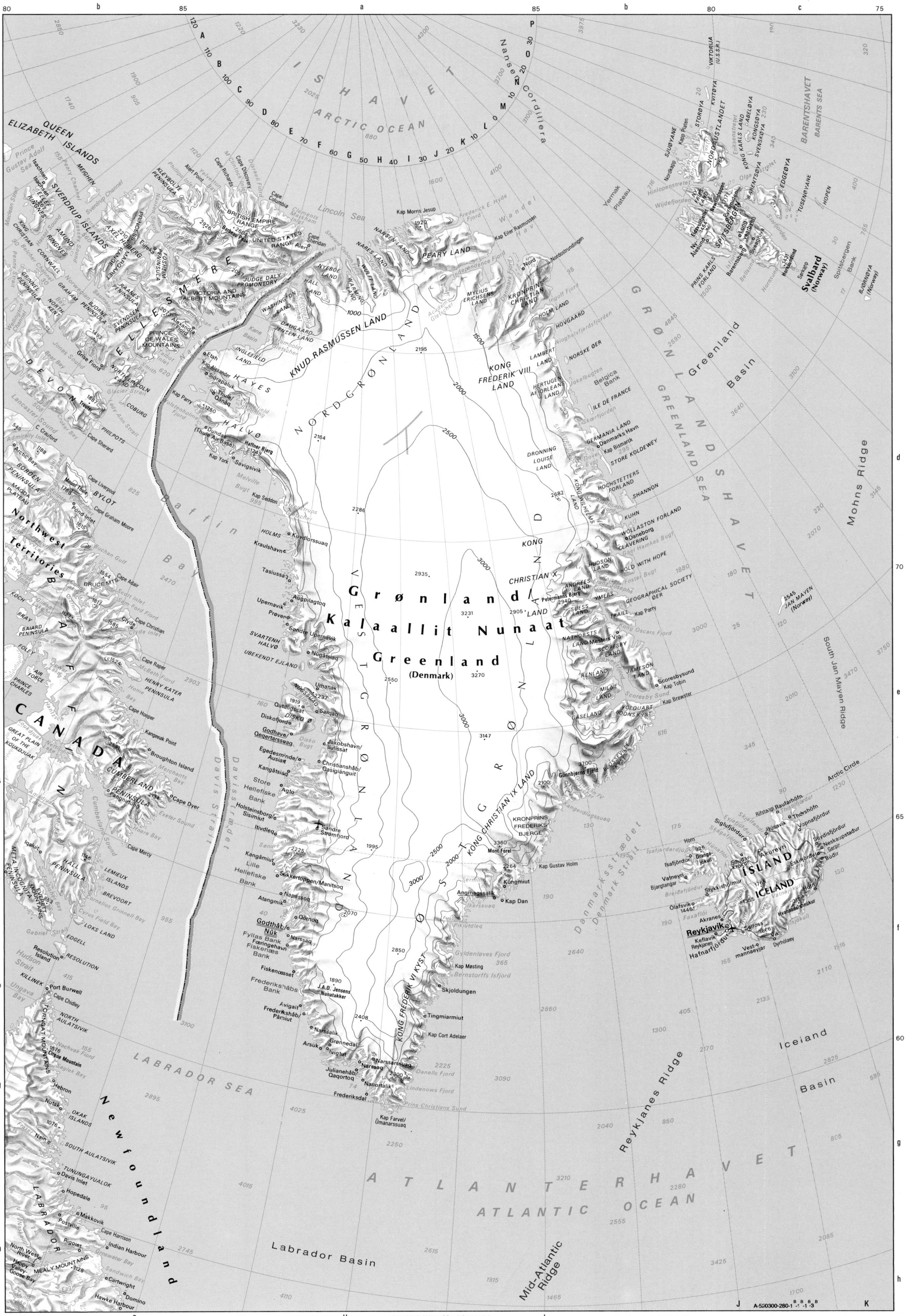

ARCTIC OCEAN
ISHAVET

QUEEN ELIZABETH ISLANDS

BARENTS SEA
BARENTSHAVET

Svalbard (Norway)

Lincoln Sea

PEARY LAND

ELLESMERE

KNUD RASMUSSEN LAND

NORDGRØNLAND

KONG FREDERIK VIII LAND

Greenland Basin

GRØNLANDSHAVET
GREENLAND SEA

Northwest Territories

Baffin Bay

DRONNING LOUISE LAND

KONG CHRISTIAN X LAND

Mohns Ridge

CANADA

Davis Strait
Davisstrædet

G r ø n l a n d /
K a l a a l l i t   N u n a a t
Greenland
(Denmark)

South Jan Mayen Ridge

(JAN MAYEN (Norway))

KONG CHRISTIAN IX LAND

Arctic Circle

KRONPRINS FREDERIKS BJERGE

Mont Forel

ISLAND
ICELAND

Reykjavik

Godthåb
Nuk

KONG FREDERIK VI KYST

Iceland Basin

Denmark Strait
Danmarkstrædet

Reykjanes Ridge

Newfoundland

LABRADOR SEA
LABRADORHAVET

Kap Farvel
Ûmanarssuaq

Labrador Basin

A T L A N T E R H A V E T

ATLANTIC OCEAN

Mid-Atlantic Ridge

Scale 1:12,000,000   Lambert Azimuthal Equal Area Projection

Longitude West 40 of Greenwich

| 0 | 200 | 400 | 600 | 800 km |
| 0 | | 200 | | 400 miles |

A-520300-280-1

Map 42 **CANADA**

Scale 1:12,000,000   Lambert Azimuthal Equal Area Projection

Longitude West 100 of Greenwich

0   200   400   600   800 km

0   200   400 miles

Map 43 **UNITED STATES**

Scale 1:12,000,000   Lambert Azimuthal Equidistant Projection

0   200   400   600   800 km

0   200   400 miles

Longitude West 100 of Greenwich

Map 44

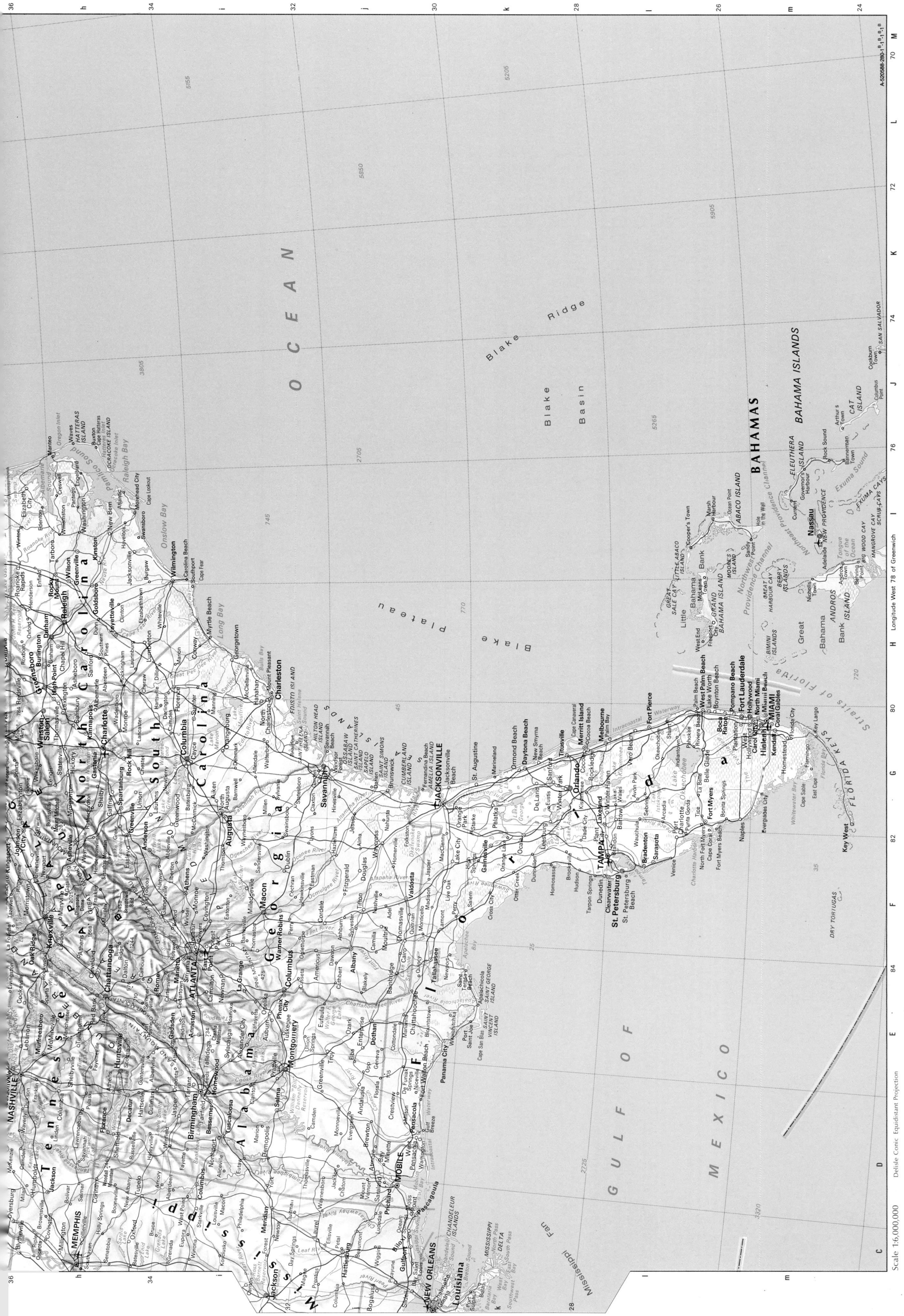

ATLANTIC OCEAN

Blake Ridge

Blake Basin

Blake Plateau

BAHAMAS

BAHAMA ISLANDS

GULF OF MEXICO

STRAITS OF FLORIDA

FLORIDA KEYS

Tennessee

North Carolina

South Carolina

Georgia

Alabama

Mississippi

Louisiana

Florida

NASHVILLE
MEMPHIS
Knoxville
Chattanooga
ATLANTA
Birmingham
Montgomery
MOBILE
NEW ORLEANS
Pensacola
Panama City
Tallahassee
JACKSONVILLE
Savannah
Charleston
Columbia
Charlotte
Greensboro
Winston Salem
Raleigh
Wilmington
Orlando
TAMPA
St. Petersburg
Fort Myers
MIAMI
Fort Lauderdale
West Palm Beach
Key West
Nassau

Longitude West 78 of Greenwich

Scale 1:6,000,000

Delisle Conic Equidistant Projection

0   100   200   300   400 km

0   100   200   miles

© ISTITUTO GEOGRAFICO DE AGOSTINI S.p.A. - NOVARA

A-520568-280-1-1-1-1-8

Map 45

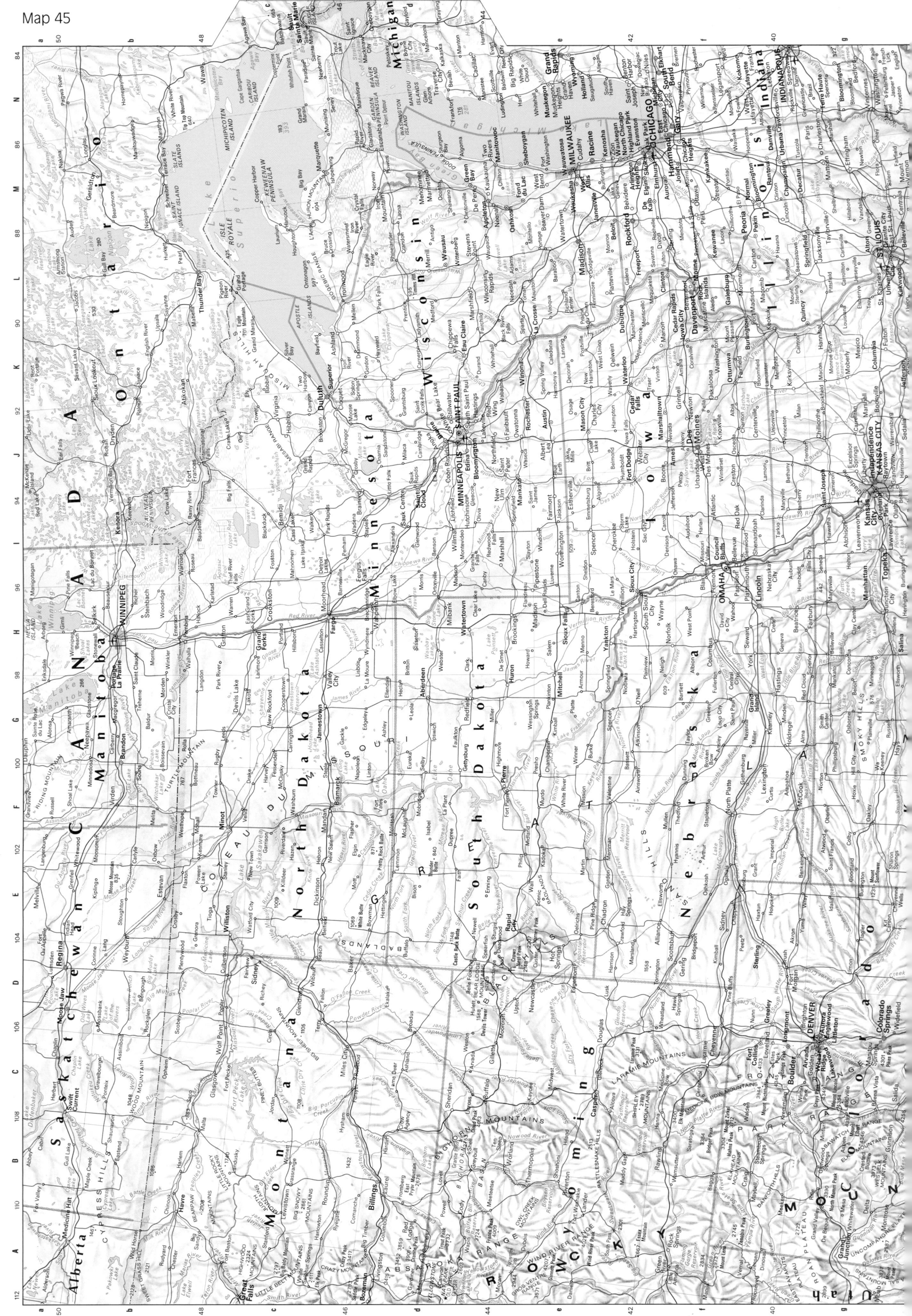

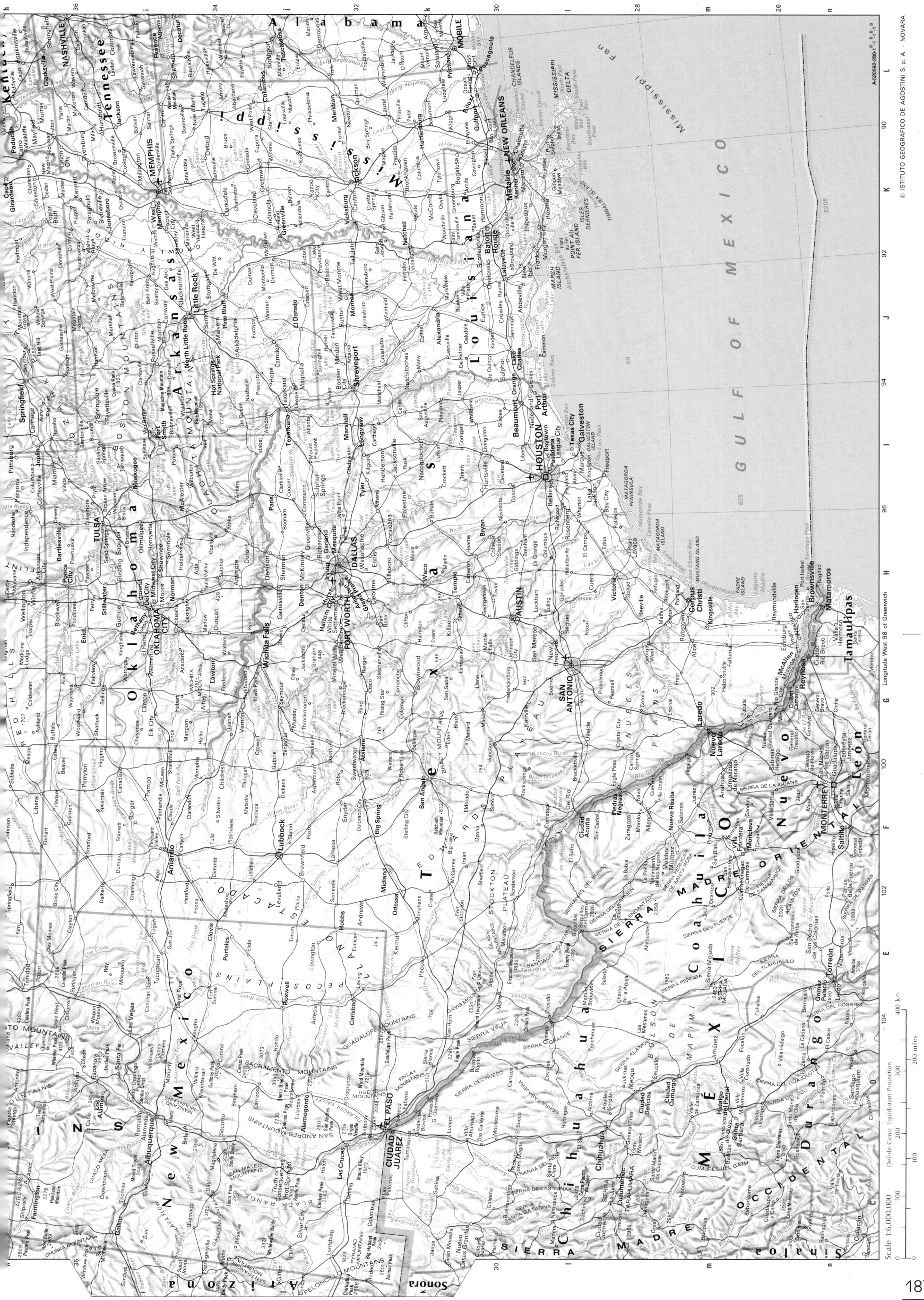
GULF OF MEXICO
Mississippi Fan
Tennessee
Alabama
Mississippi
Arkansas
Louisiana
Oklahoma
Texas
New Mexico
Arizona
Chihuahua
Coahuila
Nuevo León
Tamaulipas
Durango
Sonora
MÉXICO
SIERRA MADRE OCCIDENTAL
SIERRA MADRE ORIENTAL
NASHVILLE
MEMPHIS
MOBILE
NEW ORLEANS
Baton Rouge
Jackson
Little Rock
Shreveport
HOUSTON
DALLAS
FORT WORTH
AUSTIN
SAN ANTONIO
OKLAHOMA CITY
TULSA
Lubbock
Amarillo
EL PASO
CIUDAD JUÁREZ
Albuquerque
Santa Fe
Chihuahua
MONTERREY
Matamoros
Brownsville
Corpus Christi
Laredo
Nuevo Laredo
Torreón
Longitude West 98 of Greenwich
Scale 1:16,000,000
Delisle Conic Equidistant Projection
0 100 200 300 400 km
0 100 200 miles
A-520592-280-1

Map 46 **WESTERN UNITED STATES**

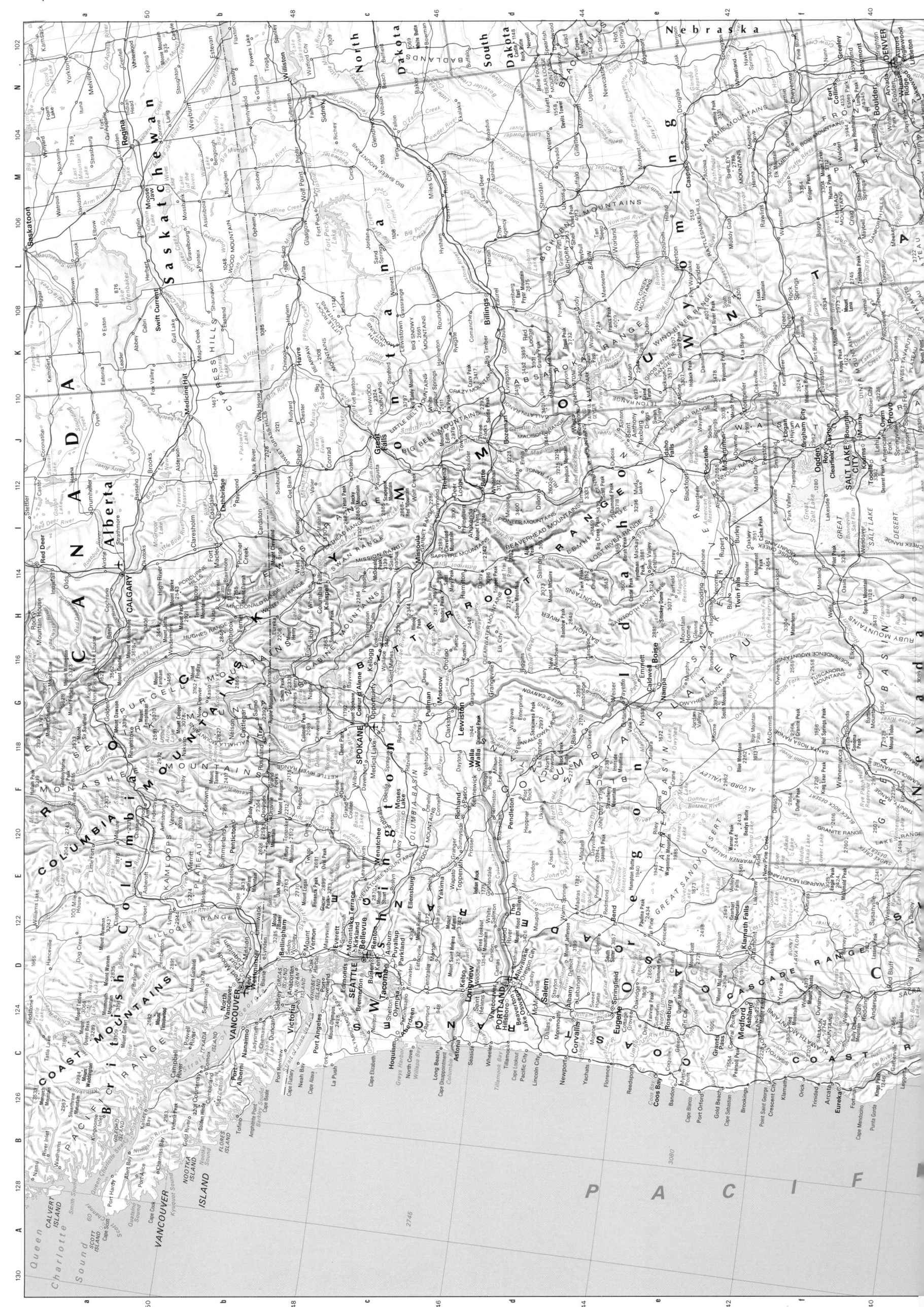

Map 47 **MIDDLE AMERICA**

MÉXICO

ESTADOS

D.F. Distrito Federal
1 Aguascalientes
2 Baja California Norte
3 Baja California Sur
4 Campeche
5 Coahuila
6 Colima
7 Chiapas
8 Chihuahua
9 Durango
10 Guanajuato
11 Guerrero
12 Hidalgo
13 Jalisco
14 México
15 Michoacán
16 Morelos
17 Nayarit
18 Nuevo León
19 Oaxaca
20 Puebla
21 Querétaro
22 Quintana Roo
23 San Luis Potosí
24 Sinaloa
25 Sonora
26 Tabasco
27 Tamaulipas
28 Tlaxcala
29 Veracruz
30 Yucatán
31 Zacatecas

Scale 1:12,000,000
Lambert Azimuthal Equal Area Projection

0   200   400   600   800 km
0   200   400 miles

A-530000-280-1 -1 -1 -1-2

Longitude West 90 of Greenwich

Scale 1:6,000,000   Delisle Conic Equidistant Projection

0   100   200   300   400 km

0   100   200 miles

Longitude West 104 of Greenwich

México

GOLFO DE MÉXICO

GULF OF MEXICO

Mexico Basin

Campeche Bank

Bahía de Campeche

Mississippi   Alabama   Florida

Louisiana

T e x a s

ATES

FORT WORTH   DALLAS

AUSTIN

SAN ANTONIO

HOUSTON

Corpus Christi

Laredo
Nuevo Laredo

MONTERREY

Tamaulipas

Nuevo León

TAMPICO
Ciudad Madero

Luis Potosí

Querétaro   Hidalgo

CIUDAD DE MÉXICO
MEXICO CITY
México D.F.   CUERNAVACA

Morelos   Puebla
PUEBLA DE ZARAGOZA

Veracruz

VERACRUZ LLAVE

Tlaxcala

Guerrero

ACAPULCO DE JUÁREZ

Oaxaca de Juárez

Oaxaca

ISTMO DE TEHUANTEPEC

Tabasco
Villahermosa

Coatzacoalcos
Minatitlán

Chiapas
Tuxtla Gutiérrez
San Cristóbal de las Casas

Tapachula

MÉRIDA

Yucatán

PENÍNSULA DE YUCATÁN

Campeche

Quintana Roo

Ciudad del Carmen

LLANOS DE TABASCO Y CAMPECHE

Chetumal

BELIZE
Belize City

GUATEMALA
GUATEMALA

HONDURAS

San Pedro Sula

NEW ORLEANS

Shreveport

MOBILE

Mississippi Fan

Map 49 **CENTRAL AMERICA AND WESTERN CARIBBEAN**

GOLFO DE MÉXICO

GULF OF MEXICO

UNITED STATES

Florida

MIAMI

CUBA

LA HABANA
HAVANA

Cayman Islands
(U.K.)

MÉXICO

Yucatán

Quintana Roo

Campeche

Tabasco

Chiapas

GUATEMALA

BELIZE

GUATEMALA

HONDURAS

EL SALVADOR

SAN SALVADOR

TEGUCIGALPA

NICARAGUA

MANAGUA

COSTA RICA

SAN JOSÉ

PANAMÁ

PANAMA

OCÉANO PACÍFICO

PACIFIC OCEAN

MAR

Scale 1:6,000,000   Delisle Conic Equidistant Projection

0   100   200   300   400 km

0   100   200 miles

A-533800-280-1 -1 -1 -1

Map 50 **EASTERN CARIBBEAN**

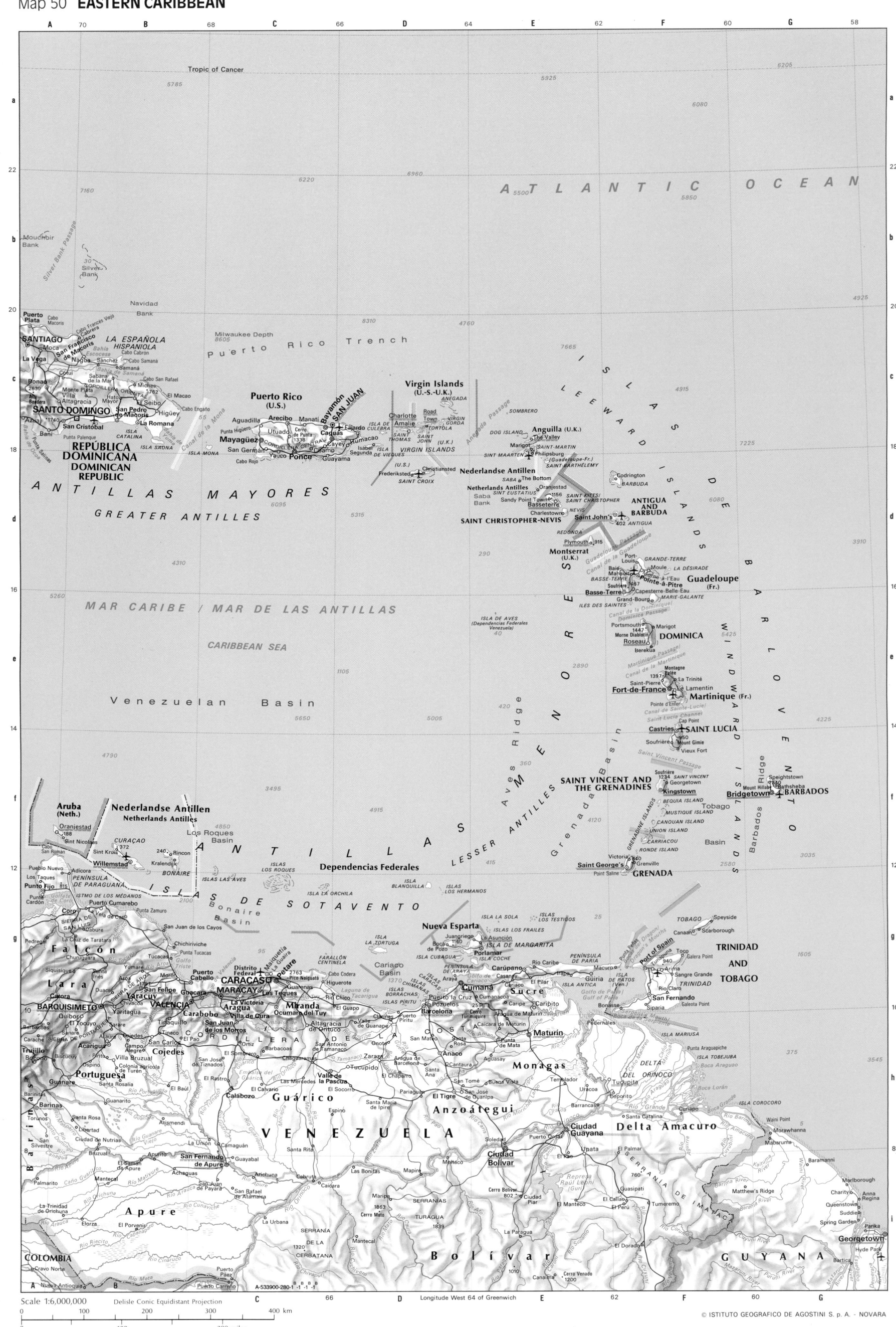

Scale 1:6,000,000   Delisle Conic Equidistant Projection

0   100   200   300   400 km

0   100   200 miles

Longitude West 64 of Greenwich

A-533900-280-1 -1 -1 -1

© ISTITUTO GEOGRAFICO DE AGOSTINI S. p. A. - NOVARA

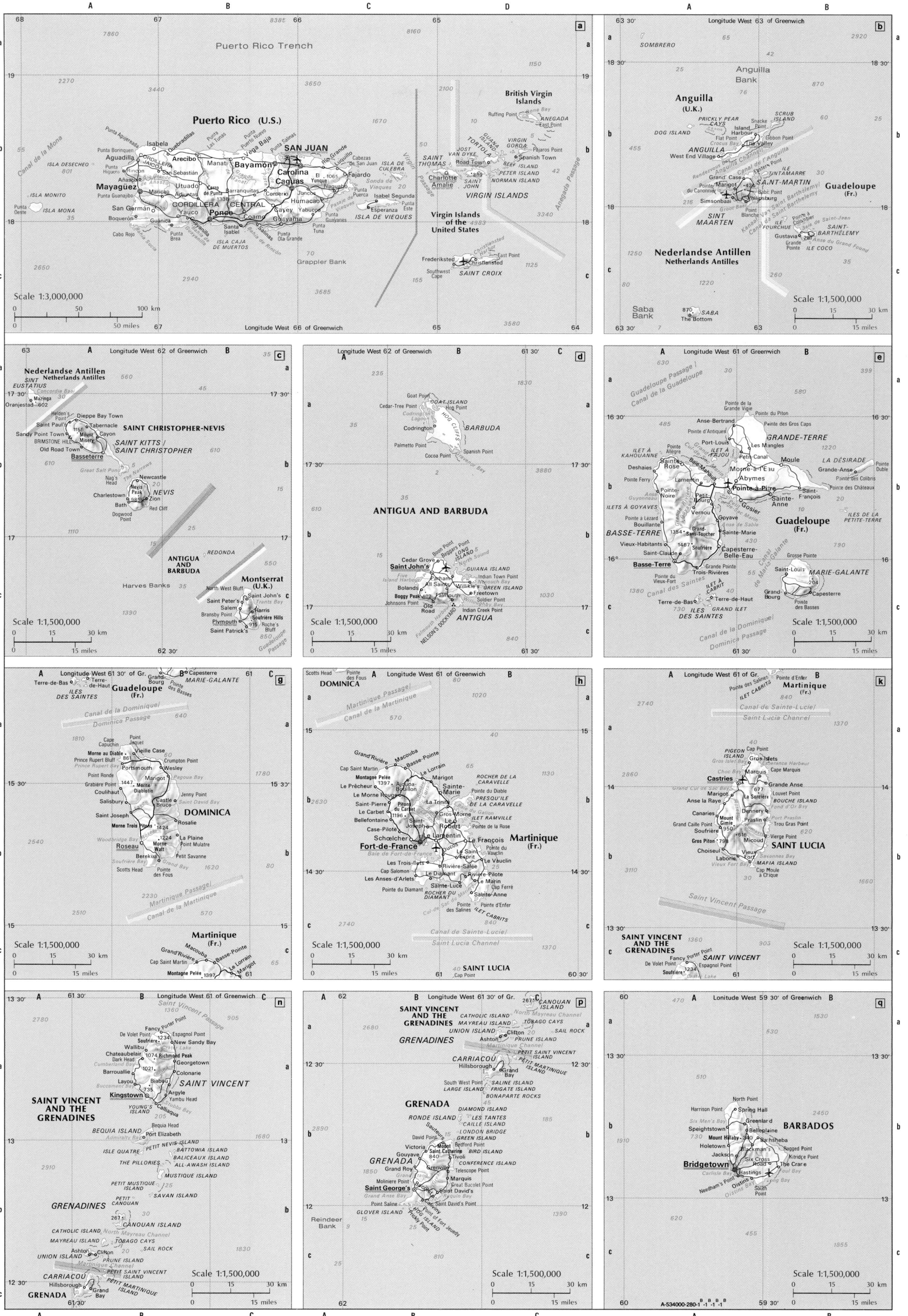

Mercator Cylindrical Projection

© ISTITUTO GEOGRAFICO DE AGOSTINI S.p.A. - NOVARA

Map 52

SOUTH AMERICA, PHYSICAL

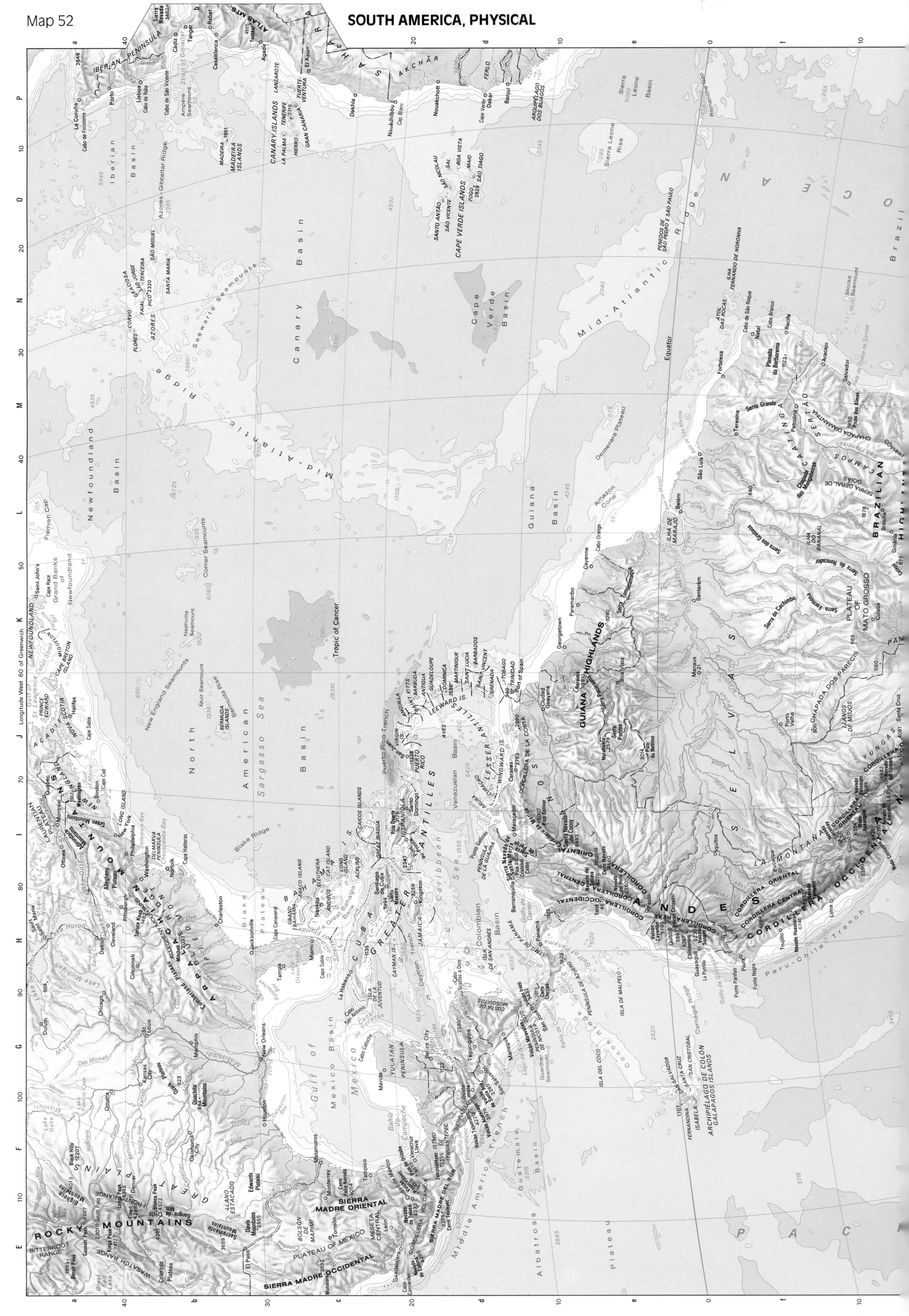

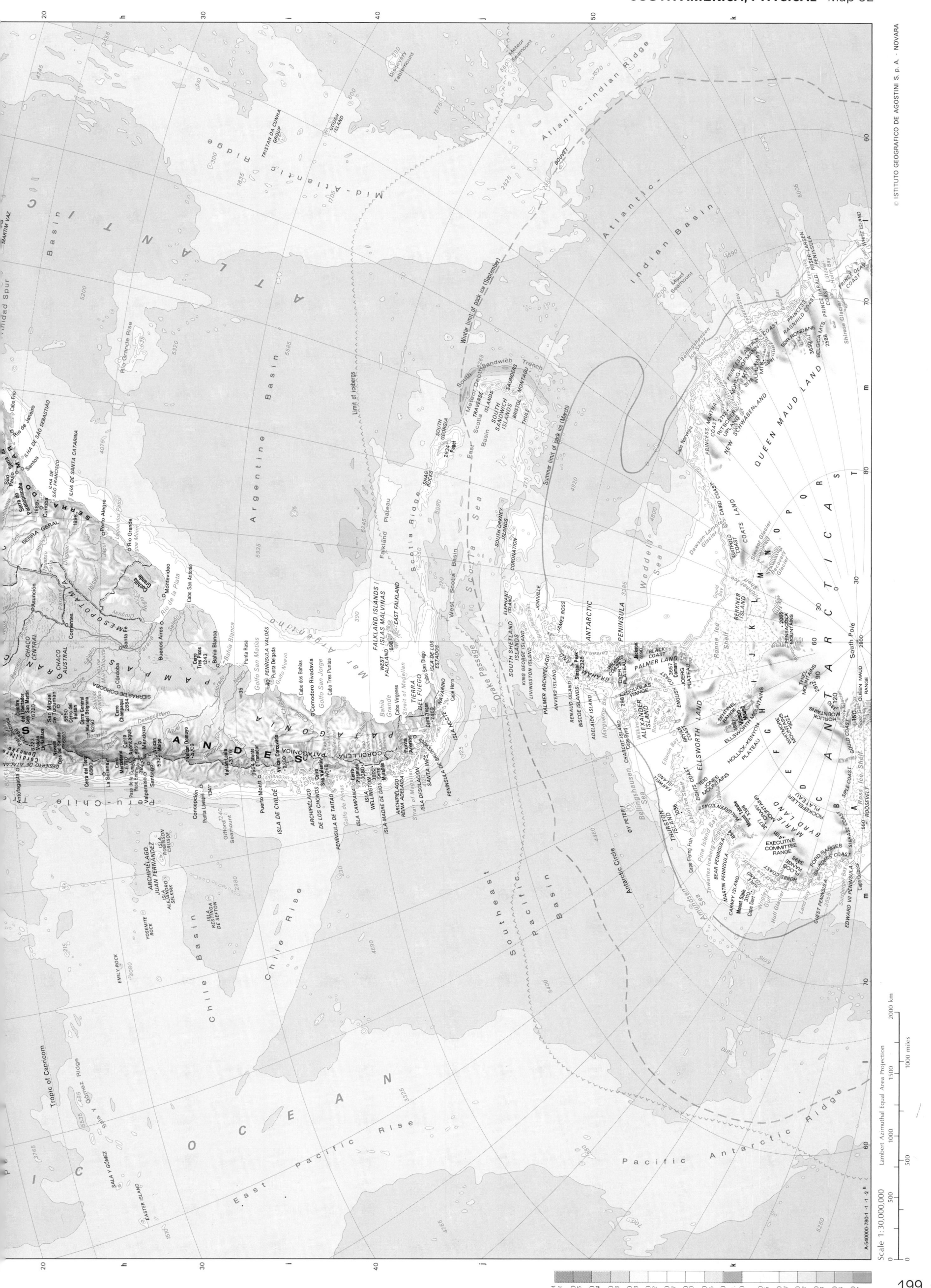

© ISTITUTO GEOGRAFICO DE AGOSTINI S. p. A. - NOVARA

Scale 1:30,000,000

Lambert Azimuthal Equal Area Projection

A-540000-780-1 -1 -1 -2°

M	6000	5000	4000	3000	2000	1000	500	+200	0	Depth	200	1000	2000	4000	6000	8000
Ft	19685	16404	13123	9843	6562	3281	1640	+656	0	0	-656	3281	6562	13123	19685	26247

Map 53

SOUTH AMERICA, POLITICAL

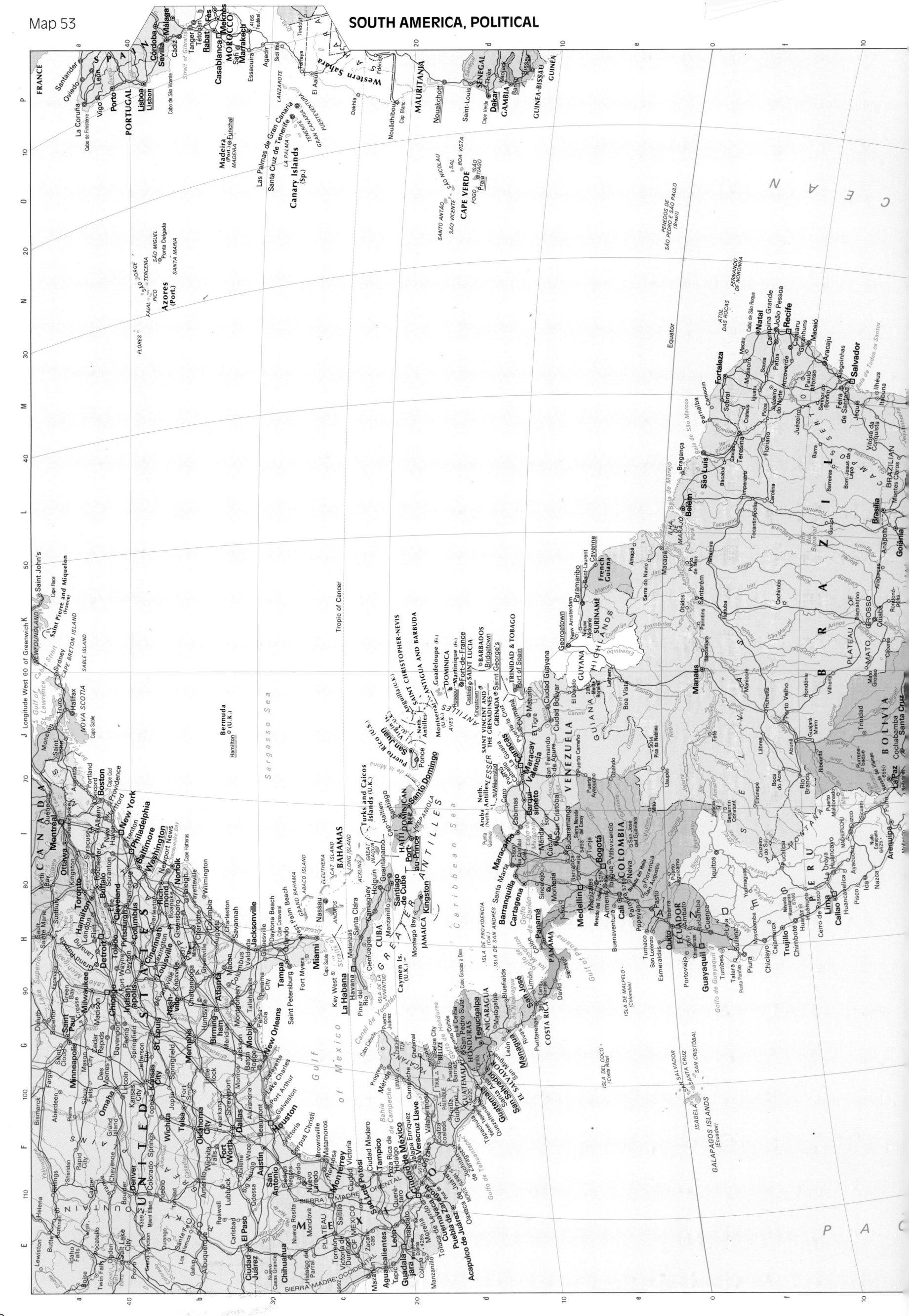

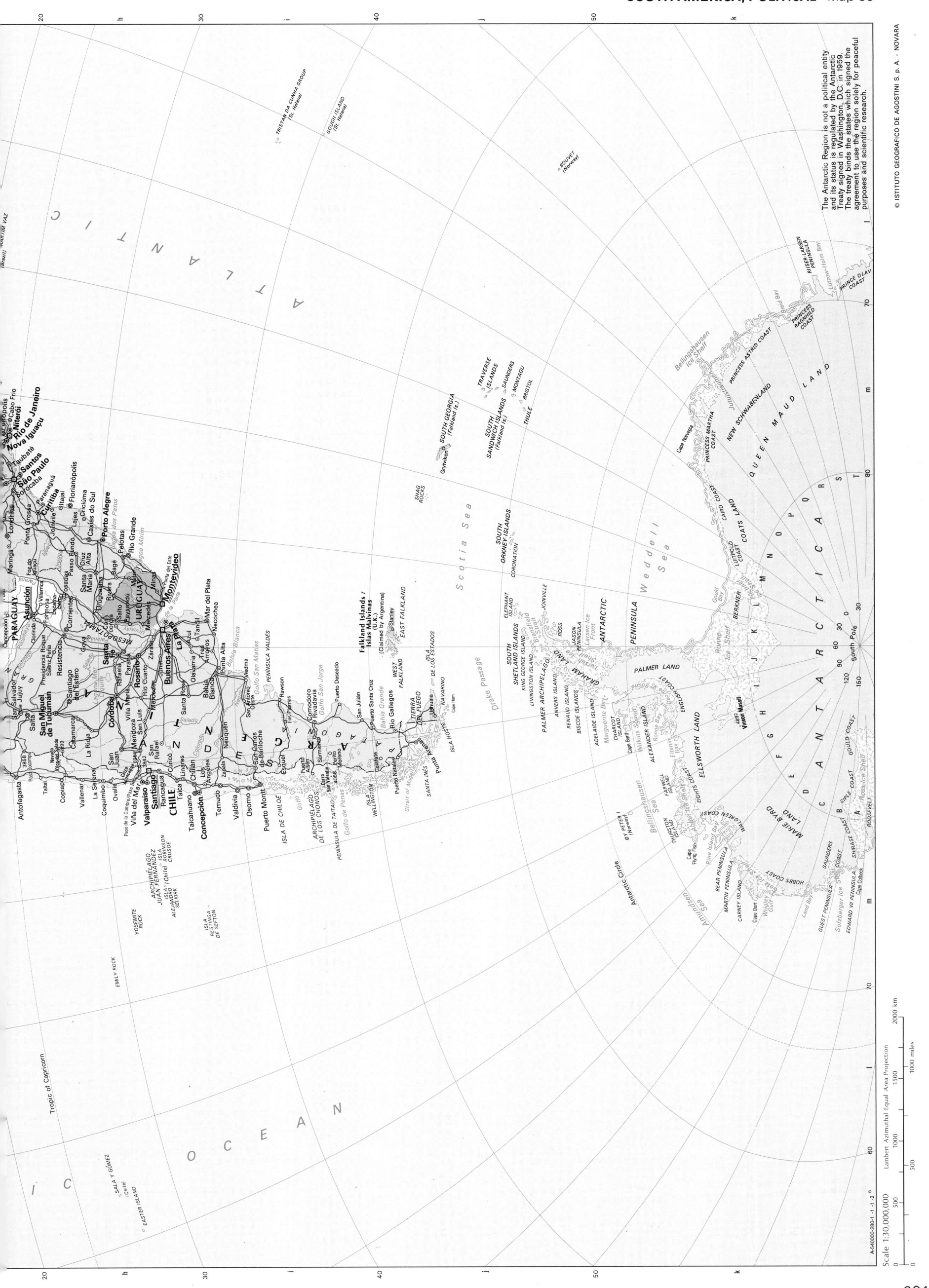

Scale 1:30,000,000

Lambert Azimuthal Equal Area Projection

A-540000-280-1 -1 -1 .2 ⑧

500	1000	1500	2000 km
500	1000		miles

VENEZUELA

DISTRITO FEDERAL

A Caracas

ESTADOS

1 Anzoátegui
2 Apure
3 Aragua
4 Barinas
5 Bolívar
6 Carabobo
7 Cojedes
8 Falcón
9 Guárico
10 Lara
11 Mérida
12 Miranda
13 Monagas
14 Nueva Esparta
15 Portuguesa
16 Sucre
17 Táchira
18 Trujillo
19 Yaracuy
20 Zulia

TERRITORIOS
FEDERALES

21 Amazonas
22 Delta Amacuro

23 DEPENDENCIAS
FEDERALES

Islas Los Monjes
Isla La Tortuga
Islas Los Frailes
Isla La Sola
Islas Los Testigos
Islas Las Aves
Islas Los Roques
Isla La Orchila
Isla Blanquilla
Islas Los Hermanos
Isla de Patos
Isla de Aves

Map 55 **EAST-CENTRAL SOUTH AMERICA**

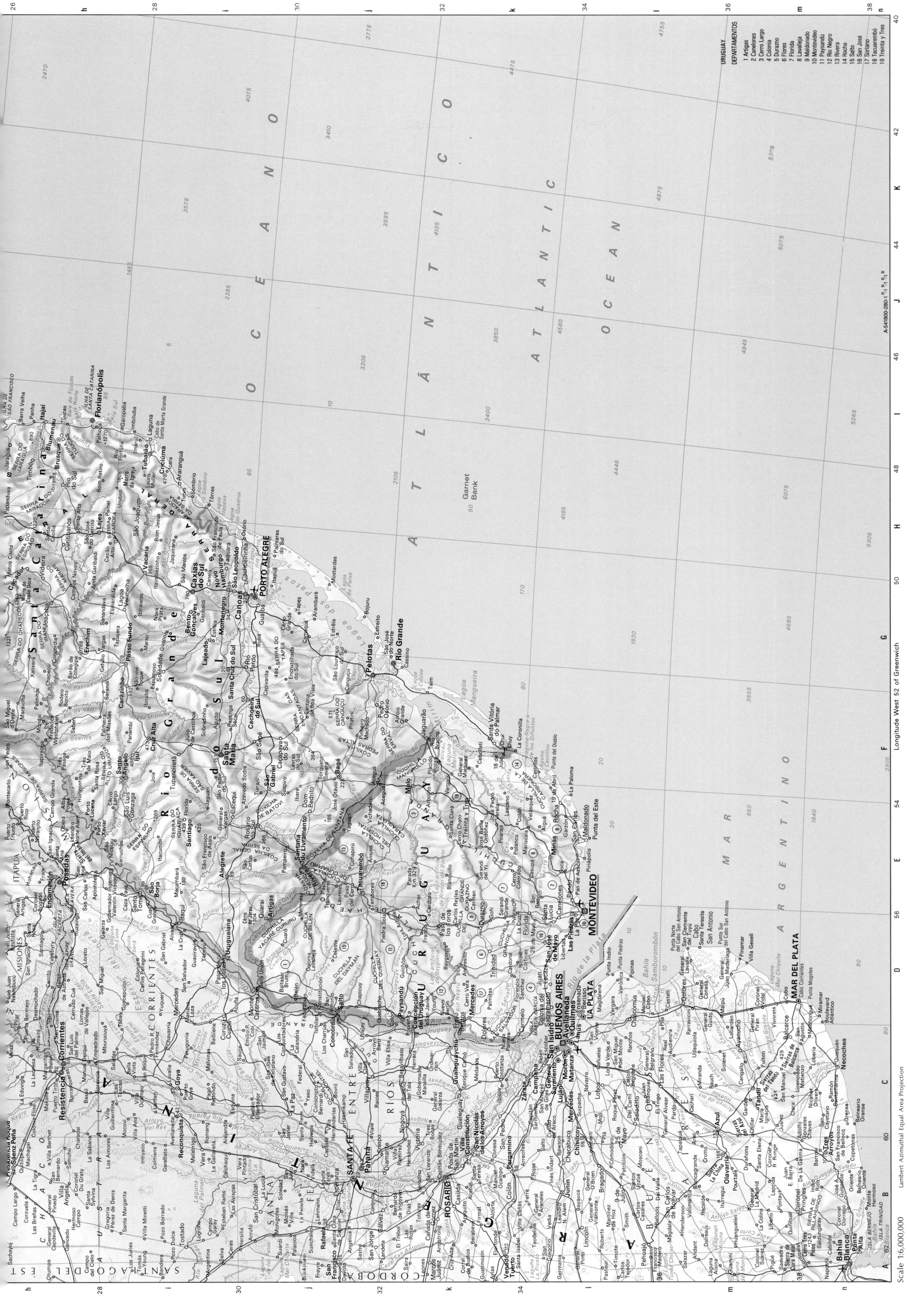

ATLANTIC OCEAN

MARINO ARGENTINO

Rio Grande do Sul

Santa Catarina

Florianópolis
Itajaí
Blumenau
Caxias do Sul
PORTO ALEGRE
Pelotas
Rio Grande
Santa Maria
Bagé

URUGUAY
MONTEVIDEO
Salto
Paysandú
Mercedes
Maldonado
Punta del Este
Rivera
Artigas
Tacuarembó
Durazno
Florida
Minas

CORRIENTES
Resistencia
Corrientes
Goya
Reconquista
Posadas
Encarnación

SANTA FE
Paraná
Rosario
ENTRE RIOS
Gualeguaychú
Concordia
Concepción del Uruguay

BUENOS AIRES
LA PLATA
Avellaneda
Quilmes
MAR DEL PLATA
Necochea
Azul
Tres Arroyos
Bahía Blanca

Río de la Plata

ITAPUA
MISIONES
CHACO
SANTIAGO DEL ESTERO
CÓRDOBA

URUGUAY (DEPARTAMENTOS)
1 Artigas
2 Canelones
3 Cerro Largo
4 Colonia
5 Durazno
6 Flores
7 Florida
8 Lavalleja
9 Maldonado
10 Montevideo
11 Paysandú
12 Río Negro
13 Rivera
14 Rocha
15 Salto
16 San José
17 Soriano
18 Tacuarembó
19 Treinta y Tres

Scale 1:6,000,000

Lambert Azimuthal Equal Area Projection

Longitude West 52 of Greenwich

0 100 200 300 400 km
0 100 200 miles

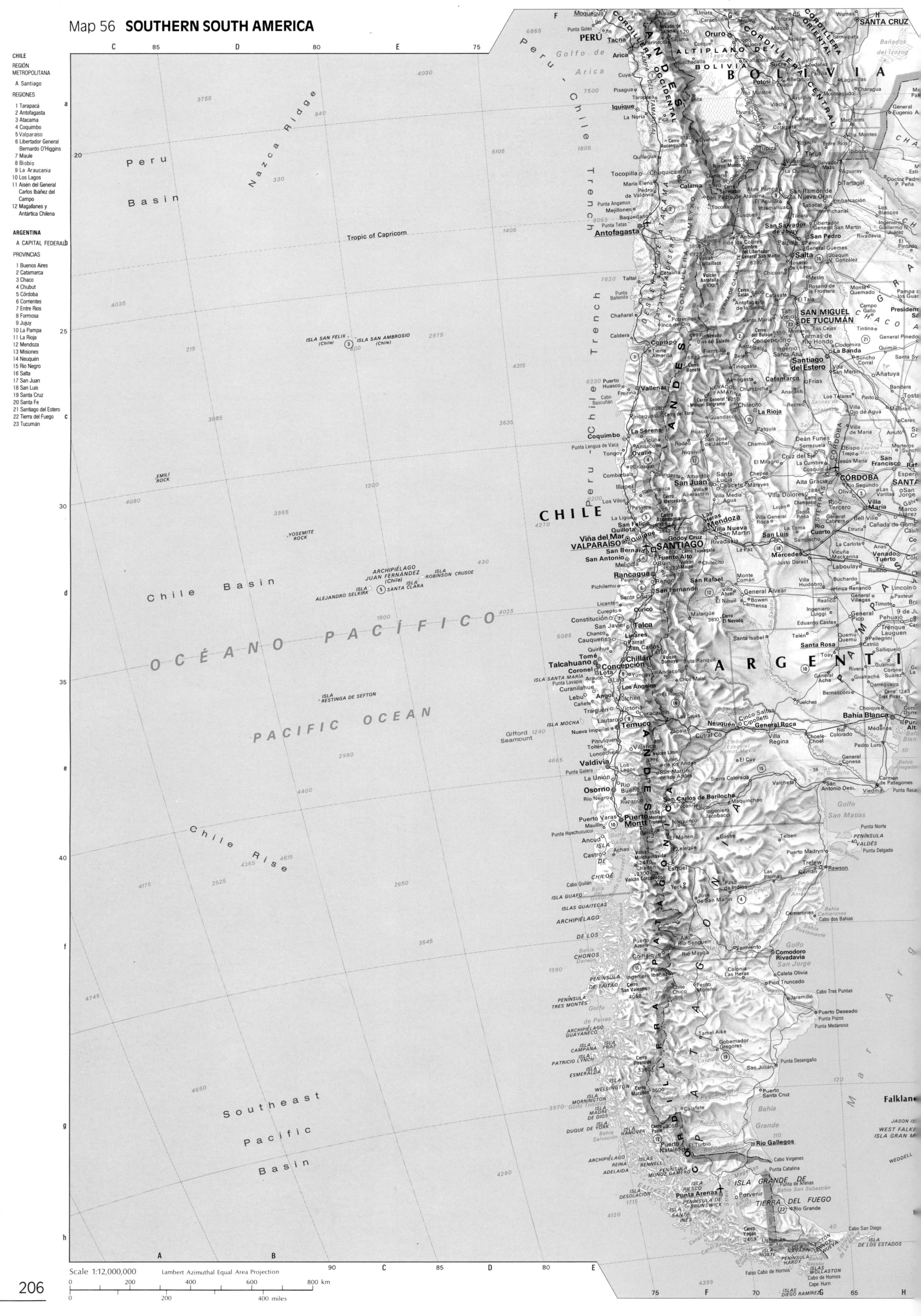

Map 56 **SOUTHERN SOUTH AMERICA**

© ISTITUTO GEOGRAFICO DE AGOSTINI S. p. A. - NOVARA

Map 57 **AUSTRALIA AND OCEANIA, PHYSICAL**

CHINA

QIN LING
NAN LING
WUYI SHAN
SICHUAN PENDI
DALOU SHAN
DA XUE SHAN
NAN SHAN

Yellow Sea
Sea of Japan
East China Sea
HONSHŪ
Tokyo
Fuji 3776
SHIKOKU
KYŪSHŪ
Nagasaki
Osaka
Pusan

Northwest Pacific Basin
Mid-Pacific Mountains
MARSHALL ISLANDS
WAKE
MICRONESIA

South China Sea
Philippine Basin
LUZON
Manila
MINDORO
PANAY
NEGROS
CEBU
SAMAR
LEYTE
MINDANAO
PALAWAN
SULU ARCHIPELAGO
SULU SEA
Davao

RYUKYU ISLANDS
OKINAWA ISLANDS
TAIWAN (FORMOSA)
HAINAN

Philippine Sea
West Mariana Basin
MARIANA ISLANDS
East Mariana Basin
GUAM
SAIPAN
TINIAN

Mariana Trench

CAROLINE ISLANDS
West Caroline Basin
East Caroline Basin
PALAU ISLANDS
YAP ISLANDS
TRUK ISLANDS
PONAPE

KIRIBATI
NAURU
BANABA

INDOCHINA
MEKONG DELTA
KHORAT PLATEAU
KALIMANTAN
BORNEO
CELEBES
HALMAHERA
MOLUCCAS
CERAM
BURU
NEW GUINEA
Puncak Jaya 5030
CENTRAL RANGE
Port Moresby
Jayapura

SUMATRA
JAVA
Jakarta
GREATER SUNDA ISLANDS
LESSER SUNDA ISLANDS
FLORES
TIMOR
BALI
SUMBAWA
SUMBA
Banda Sea
Flores Sea
Java Sea

BISMARCK ARCHIPELAGO
NEW BRITAIN
NEW IRELAND
SOLOMON ISLANDS
BOUGAINVILLE
GUADALCANAL
SAN CRISTOBAL
Solomon Sea
Coral Sea
Coral Sea Basin

MELANESIA
Melanesian Basin
TUVALU (ELLICE) ISLANDS
SANTA CRUZ ISLANDS
NEW HEBRIDES
FIJI ISLANDS
Fiji Basin
NEW CALEDONIA
LOYALTY ISLANDS

AUSTRALIA

ARNHEM LAND
KIMBERLEY PLATEAU
GREAT SANDY DESERT
TANAMI DESERT
GIBSON DESERT
GREAT VICTORIA DESERT
SIMPSON DESERT
MACDONNELL RANGES
MUSGRAVE RANGES
Alice Springs
Darwin
CAPE YORK PENINSULA
Gulf of Carpentaria
GREAT ARTESIAN BASIN
GREAT DIVIDING RANGE
Brisbane
Sydney
Canberra
Melbourne
NULLARBOR PLAIN
Great Australian Bight
Perth
Albany
Adelaide
EYRE PENINSULA
FLINDERS RANGES
Lake Eyre
Lake Torrens
Lake Gairdner

TASMANIA
Hobart
Bass Strait
Tasman Sea
Tasman Basin

NEW ZEALAND
NORTH ISLAND
SOUTH ISLAND
Auckland
Christchurch
Dunedin
Mount Cook 3764
STEWART ISLAND

INDIAN OCEAN
South Australian Basin

M
Ft
6000 19685
5000 16404
4000 13123
3000 9843
2000 6562
1000 3281
500 1640
+200 +656
Depr.
−200 −656
1000 3281
2000 6562
4000 13123
6000 19685
8000 26247

Scale 1:30,000,000
Lambert Azimuthal Equal Area Projection
0 500 1000 1500 2000 km
0 500 1000 miles

Longitude East 170 of Greenwich

Map 58 **AUSTRALIA AND OCEANIA, POLITICAL**

CHINA

SOUTH KOREA

JAPAN

Tōkyō
Yokohama
Ōsaka
Kyōto
Nagoya

East China Sea

Shanghai
Nanjing
Wuhan
Chongqing
Chengdu

Guangzhou
Hong Kong (U.K.)
Macao (Port.)
TAIWAN
Taipei
Kaohsiung

HAINAN

VIET-NAM
LAOS
THAI-LAND
CAMBODIA
Phnum Penh
Ho Chi Minh (Saigon)

South China Sea

Philippine Sea

PHILIPPINES
Manila
Quezon City
LUZON
MINDANAO
Davao

MALAYSIA
BRUNEI

KALIMANTAN / BORNEO

INDONESIA
SUMATRA
Jakarta
Bandung
Surabaya
CELEBES

Celebes Sea
Molucca Sea
Banda Sea
Flores Sea
Java Sea
Timor Sea
Arafura Sea

Northern Mariana Islands (U.S.)
MARIANA ISLANDS
Saipan
Guam (U.S.)

MARSHALL ISLANDS

Wake (U.S.)

FEDERATED STATES OF MICRONESIA
YAP ISLANDS
Palau
Belau (Trust Territory)
CAROLINE ISLANDS

M I C R O N E S I A

M E L A N E S I A

NAURU / NAOERO

KIRIBATI

NEW GUINEA
PAPUA NEW GUINEA
Port Moresby
BISMARCK ARCHIPELAGO
NEW BRITAIN
NEW IRELAND
Rabaul

SOLOMON ISLANDS
Honiara
GUADALCANAL

TUVALU

VANUATU
NEW HEBRIDES
Port-Vila

NEW CALEDONIA (France)
Nouméa

Coral Sea
Solomon Sea

FIJI ISL

Norfolk (Australia)

CAPE YORK PENINSULA
Gulf of Carpentaria
ARNHEM LAND
Darwin

KIMBERLEY
GREAT SANDY DESERT
TANAMI DESERT

A U S T R A L I A

GIBSON DESERT
GREAT VICTORIA DESERT
SIMPSON DESERT
Alice Springs

NULLARBOR PLAIN

Perth
Adelaide
Melbourne
Geelong

Brisbane
Gold Coast
Sydney
Wollongong
Canberra
Newcastle

Great Australian Bight

TASMANIA
Hobart
Bass Strait

Tasman Sea

NEW ZEALAND
NORTH ISLAND
Auckland
Manukau
Hamilton
New Plymouth

SOUTH ISLAND
Christch
Dunedin
Invercargill

I N D I A N   O C E A N

Scale 1:30,000,000 Lambert Azimuthal Equal Area Projection

0 500 1000 1500 2000 km
0 500 1000 miles

Longitude East 170 of Greenwich

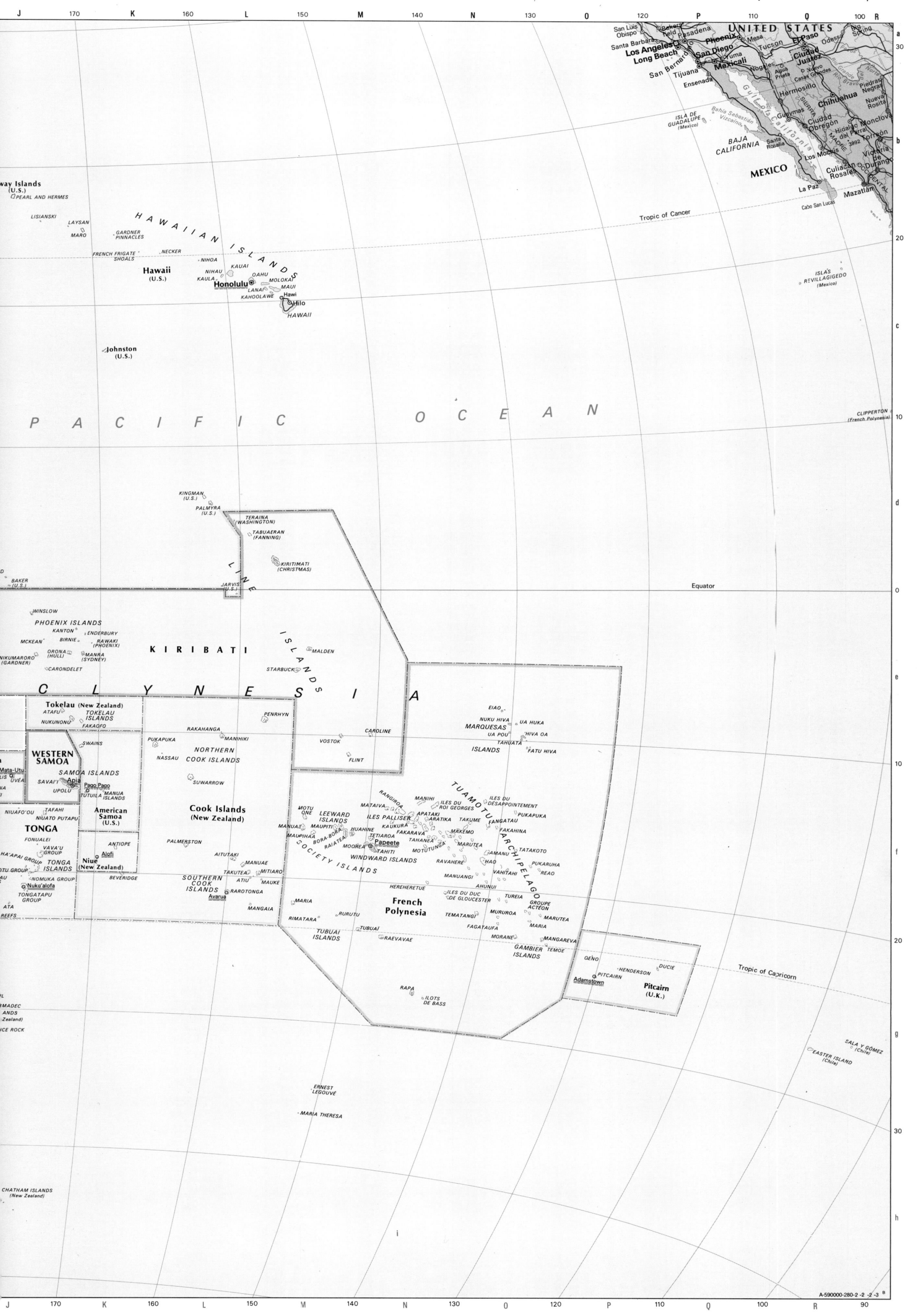

Map 59 **AUSTRALIA**

Scale 1:12,000,000   Delisle Conic Equidistant Projection

0   200   400   600   800 km

0   200   400 miles

PULAU IRIANI NEW GUINEA

PAPUA NEW GUINEA

NEW IRELAND ISLAND

BISMARCK ARCHIPELAGO

NEW BRITAIN

Solomon Sea

BOUGAINVILLE ISLAND

SOLOMON ISLANDS

PULAU DOLAK

Gulf of Papua

Port Moresby

Coral Sea Basin

CORAL SEA

SOLOMON ISLANDS

GUADALCANAL ISLAND

SANTA ISABEL ISLAND

MALAITA ISLAND

SAN CRISTOBAL ISLAND

Gulf of Carpentaria

CAPE YORK PENINSULA

GROOTE EYLANDT

GOVE PENINSULA

WELLESLEY ISLANDS

GREAT BARRIER REEF

Coral Sea Islands Territory

Coral Sea Basin

PACIFIC OCEAN

Nouvelle-Calédonie New Caledonia (France)

Tropic of Capricorn

TABLELAND

Mount Isa

Queensland

GREAT DIVIDING RANGE

Cairns

Townsville

Mackay

Rockhampton

Bundaberg

Maryborough

FRASER ISLAND

GREAT ARTESIAN BASIN

STURT DESERT

BRISBANE

Gold Coast

ralia

New South Wales

Broken Hill

Dubbo

Newcastle

ADELAIDE

SYDNEY

Wollongong

Canberra

Australian Capital Territory

Victoria

MELBOURNE

Geelong

Ballarat

KANGAROO ISLAND

Bass Strait

KING ISLAND

FLINDERS ISLAND

TASMAN SEA

Tasmania

Launceston

Hobart

Tasman Basin

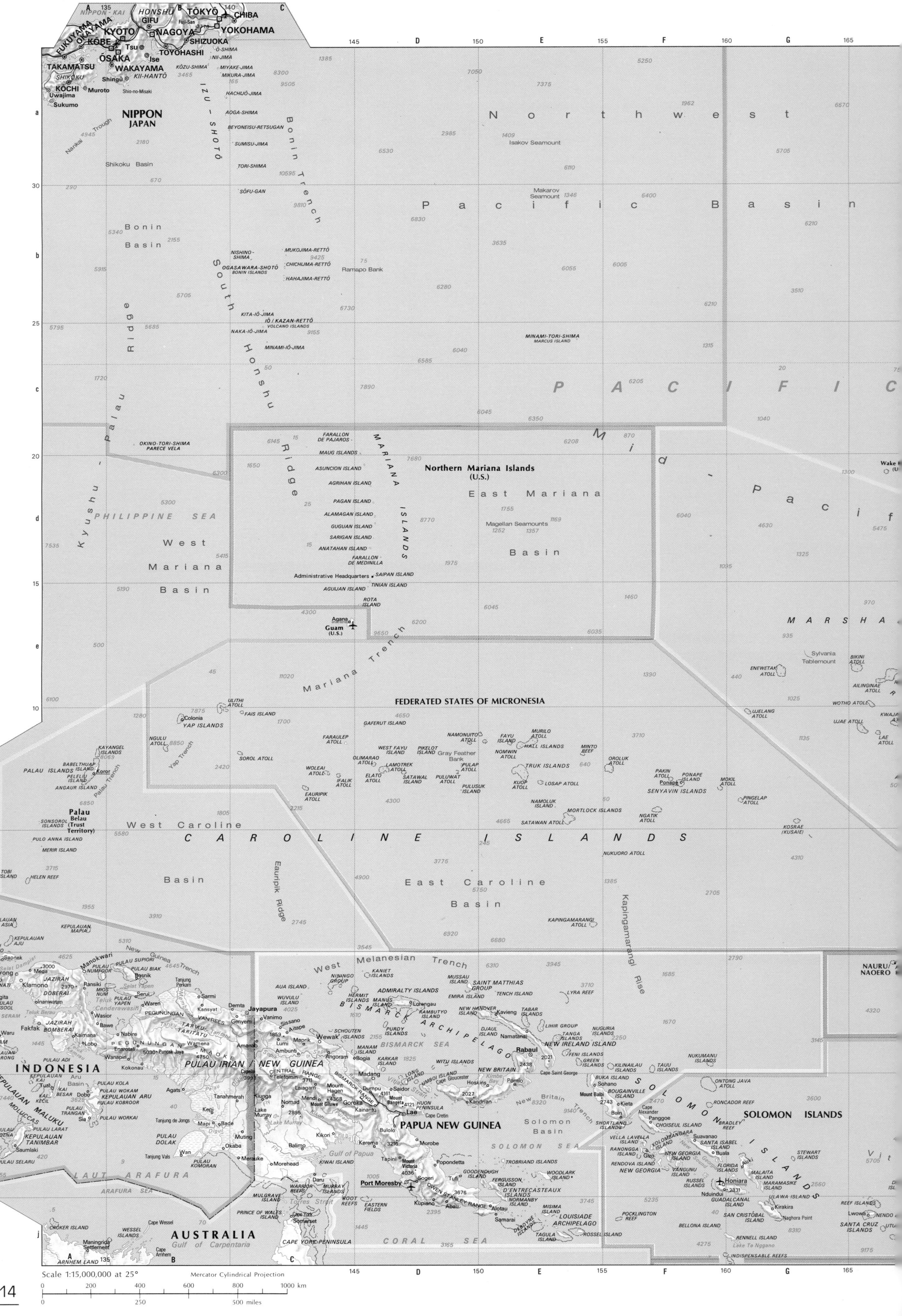

Scale 1:15,000,000 at 25°   Mercator Cylindrical Projection

O | I | 175 | J | 180 | K | 175 | L | 170 | M | 165 | N | 160 | O

Mellish Seamount 117

Milwaukee Seamounts 11

North east

Pacific Basin

1410

1020

5560

1900

6970

6185

5850

a

20

30

HAWAIIAN

Musicians Seamounts

795

6300

KURE ISLAND

Midway Islands (U.S.)

PEARL AND HERMES REEF

2195

b

6290

105

6145

Salmon Bank 54

LISIANSKI ISLAND 55

LAYSAN ISLAND

Raita Bank

930

1755

490

6365

Northampton Seamounts 31

MARO REEF

GARDNER PINNACLES

Saint Rogatien Bank
Brooks Banks 54

5055

ISLANDS

25

Tropic of Cancer

4960

FRENCH FRIGATE SHOALS

NECKER ISLAND

15

1465

6365

OCEAN

6100

1465

5560

2580

NIHOA

KAUAI Haena Kauai Channel
NIIHAU Mana Lihue OAHU Kaneohe
KAULA Wahiawa MOLOKAI
HONOLULU Kaunakakai MAUI Wailuku
LANAI Hana
Alenuihaha Channel Kauiki Head

c

1900

2085

1315

1714 Horizon Tablemount

1445

Hawaii (U.S.)

KAHOOLAWE Upolu Point Hawi
4205 Mauna Kea Hilo
HAWAII Cape Kumukahi
Ka Lae Naalehu

20

585

Mountains

815 1705

Hess Tablemount

5265

1510

731 Pensacola Seamount

1810

d

1955

1737 Cape Johnson Tablemount

Johnston Atoll (U.S.)

1050

1950

30

3110

15

ISLANDS

Central

6125

Vityaz Seamount 813

1445

5835

BIKAR ATOLL 1400

6220

Christmas Ridge

6000

5625

e

TIRIK TOLL
AILUK ATOLL

MARSHALL ISLANDS

6520

5890

1485

1070

1090

10

WOTJE ATOLL

RATAK CHAIN

Pacific

5 Wilder Seamount

1445

MALOELAP ATOLL 4840

AUR ATOLL

MAJURO ATOLL Uliga

KINGMAN REEF (U.S.)

1430

f

4540

MILI ATOLL

Keats Bank

3510

1830

3750

PALMYRA ATOLL (U.S.) 840

5

1245

Basin

2120

TERAINA (WASHINGTON)

5

2405

365

TABUAERAN (FANNING)

BUTARITARI ATOLL

420

LINE ISLANDS

g

ABAIANG ATOLL MARAKEI ATOLL

385

2815

KIRITIMATI (CHRISTMAS)

TARAWA ATOLL Bairiki

MAIANA ATOLL

4295

KIRIBATI

5340

HOWLAND ISLAND (U.S.)

2055

Equator

KURIA ISLAND ABEMAMA ATOLL

ARANUKA ATOLL

BAKER ISLAND (U.S.)

6000

0

NONOUTI ATOLL

1065

640

JARVIS ISLAND (U.S.)

BERU ISLAND NIKUNAU ISLAND

WINSLOW REEF

TABITEUEA ATOLL

3520

ONOTOA ATOLL

5770

5260

h

TAMANA ISLAND

KIRIBATI

ARORAE ISLAND

6250

KANTON ATOLL

7315 North Tokelau Trench

15

MCKEAN ISLAND 1570

BIRNIE ATOLL

ENDERBURY ATOLL

RAWAKI (PHOENIX)

2480

PHOENIX ISLANDS

NIKUMARORO (GARDNER)

ORONA (HULL)

MANRA (SYDNEY)

5

3705 5190

NANUMEA ATOLL

CARONDELET REEF

1700

STARBUCK ISLAND

4935

NANUMANGA ISLAND

NIUTAO ISLAND

TUVALU ISLANDS

6110

1095

5580

i

NUI ATOLL

VAITUPU ISLAND

7130

2420

TUVALU

NUKUFETAU ATOLL

FUNAFUTI Funafuti ATOLL

5590

Tokelau (New Zealand)

ATAFU ATOLL TOKELAU / UNION ISLANDS

1370

5520

FENRHYN ATOLL

5340

NUKULAELAE ATOLL

4935

NUKUNONU ATOLL

FAKAOFO ATOLL

4025

3110

Cook Islands (New Zealand)

RAKAHANGA ATOLL

10

NIULAKITA ISLAND

Robbie Bank 13

SWAINS ATOLL

PUKAPUKA ATOLL

NASSAU ISLAND

MANIHIKI ATOLL

NORTHERN COOK ISLANDS

20 18 Charlotte Bank 15

FIJI

ROTUMA ISLAND 29

Bayonnaise Seamount

4965

5400

American Samoa (U.S.)

5395

2450

5084

A-596591-280

I | 175 | J | Longitude East 180 West of Greenwich K | 175 | L | 170 | M | 165 | N | 160 | O

Map 61 **THE SOUTH PACIFIC**

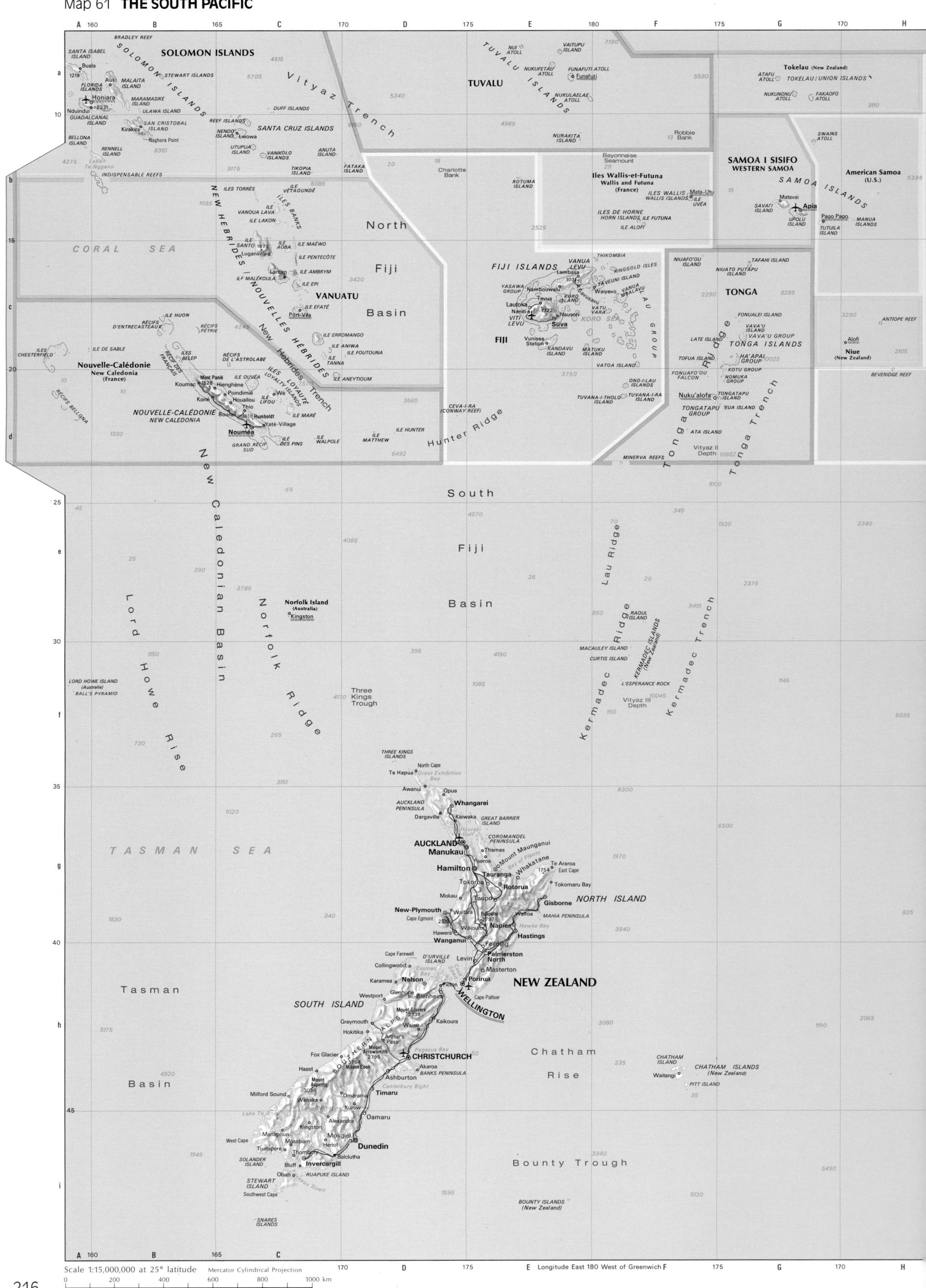

Scale 1:15,000,000 at 25° latitude   Mercator Cylindrical Projection

Longitude East 180 West of Greenwich

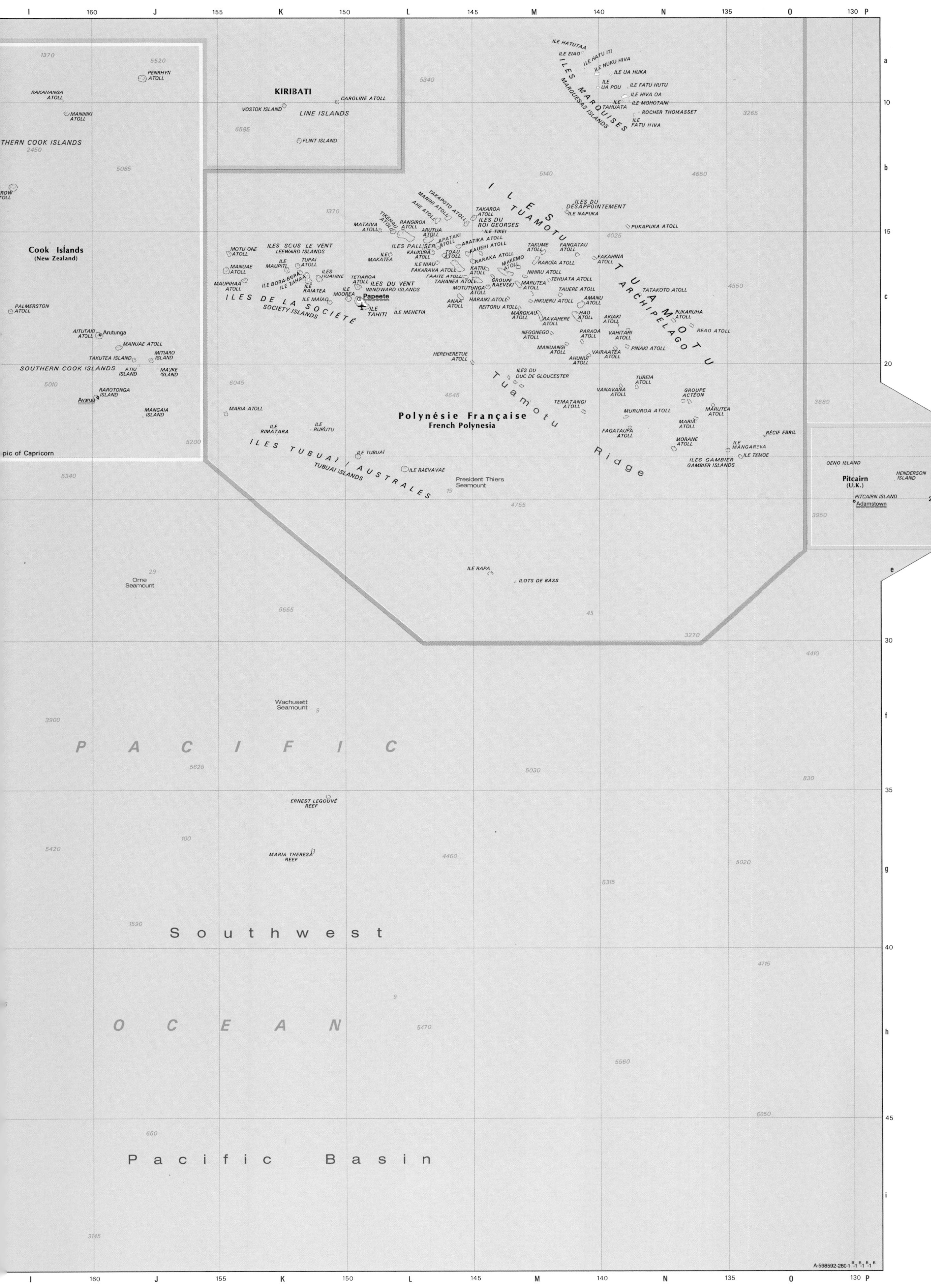

I 160 J 155 K 150 L 145 M 140 N 135 O 130 P

1370

5520

PENRHYN
ATOLL

RAKAHANGA
ATOLL

KIRIBATI

5340

ILE HATUTAA
ILE EIAO
ILE HATU ITI
ILE NUKU HIVA
ILE UA HUKA
ILE UA POU
ILE FATU HUTU
ILE HIVA OA
ILE MOHOTANI
TAHUATA
ROCHER THOMASSET
ILE
FATU HIVA

a

MANIHIKI
ATOLL

VOSTOK ISLAND

CAROLINE ATOLL

LINE ISLANDS

3265

10

THERN COOK ISLANDS
2450

6585

FLINT ISLAND

5140

4650

b

ROW
OLL

5085

1370

ILES
ILTUAMOTU

TAKAPOTO ATOLL
MANIHI ATOLL
AHE ATOLL
TIKEHAU RANGIROA
ATOLL
MATAIVA
ATOLL
ARUTUA
ATOLL
APATAKI

TAKAROA
ATOLL
ILES DU
ROI GEORGES
ILE DU
ILE TIKEI

ILES DU
DESAPPOINTEMENT
ILE NAPUKA

PUKAPUKA ATOLL

4025

15

Cook Islands
(New Zealand)

MOTU ONE
ATOLL

MANUAE
ATOLL

MAUPIHAA
ATOLL

ILES SCUS LE VENT
LEEWARD ISLANDS

ILE TUPAI
MAUPITI ATOLL

ILE BORA-BORA
ILE TAHAA
ILE
RAIATEA

ILES
HUAHINE

ARATIKA ATOLL
KAUKURA
ATOLL
ILE
MAKATEA
ILE NIAU
FAKARAVA ATOLL
TOAU
ATOLL
KATIU
ATOLL

TETIAROA
ATOLL ILES DU VENT

KAUEHI
ATOLL
RARAKA ATOLL
MAKEMO
ATOLL
NIHIRU ATOLL

TAKUME
ATOLL
FANGATAU
ATOLL

FAKAHINA
ATOLL

RAROÏA ATOLL

TATAKOTO ATOLL

4550

c

PALMERSTON
ATOLL

ILES DE LA SOCIÉTÉ
SOCIETY ISLANDS

ILE MAIAO

ILE MOOREA

FAAITE ATOLL
TAHANEA ATOLL
MOTUTUNGA
ATOLL

GROUPE
RAEVSKI
MARUTEA
ATOLL
TEHUATA ATOLL
TAUERE ATOLL

PUKARUHA
ATOLL

ARUTUNGA

AITUTAKI
ATOLL

MANUAE ATOLL

TAKUTEA ISLAND

MITIARO
ISLAND

ANAA
ATOLL
HARAIKI ATOLL
REITORU ATOLL
HIKUERU ATOLL
AMANU
ATOLL

REAO ATOLL

SOUTHERN COOK ISLANDS
5010

ATIU
ISLAND

MAUKE
ISLAND

6045

MAROKAU
ATOLL
RAVAHERE
ATOLL
HAO
ATOLL
AKIAKI
ATOLL

20

RAROTONGA
ISLAND

MANGAIA
ISLAND

MARIA ATOLL

4645

NEGONEGO
ATOLL
PARAOA
ATOLL
VAHITAHI
ATOLL

PINAKI ATOLL

Avarua

HEREHERETUE
ATOLL

MANUANGI
ATOLL
AHUNUI
ATOLL
VAIRAATEA
ATOLL

Polynésie Française
French Polynesia

ILES DU
DUC DE GLOUCESTER

Tuamotu Ridge

TUREIA
ATOLL

GROUPE
ACTÉON

3880

d

5200

pic of Capricorn

ILES TUBUAI / AUSTRALES
TUBUAI ISLANDS

ILE
RIMATARA
ILE
RURUTU
ILE TUBUAI

ILE RAEVAVAE

VANAVANA
ATOLL

TEMATANGI
ATOLL

MURUROA ATOLL

FAGATAUFA
ATOLL

MARUTEA
ATOLL

MARIA
ATOLL

MORANE
ATOLL

ILE
MANGAREVA
ILE TEMOE

RÉCIF EBRIL

OENO ISLAND

5340

President Thiers
Seamount
19

ILES GAMBIER
GAMBIER ISLANDS

Pitcairn
(U.K.)

HENDERSON
ISLAND

4755

PITCAIRN ISLAND
Adamstown

25

3950

Orne
Seamount

29

ILE RAPA

ILOTS DE BASS

e

5655

45

3270

30

4410

Wachusett
Seamount
9

f

3900

P   A   C   I   F   I   C

5625

5030

830

35

ERNEST LEGOUVÉ
REEF

g

5420

100

MARIA THERESA
REEF

4460

5315

5020

1590

S o u t h w e s t

40

O   C   E   A   N

9

h

5470

5560

6050

45

660

P a c i f i c   B a s i n

3145

i

Map 62 **NEW ZEALAND**

B 168 C 170 D 172 E 174 F 176 G 178 H 180 I

Norfolk Ridge

New Caledonia Basin

THREE KINGS ISLANDS

Cape Reinga North Cape
Cape Maria Te Hapua
van Diemen Te Kao
NINETY Cape Karikari
MILE Mangonui
BEACH CAVALLI ISLANDS
Awanui *Bay of Islands*
Tauroa Point Kaitaia Kaeo Cape Brett
Ahipara Okaihau Opua Russell
Herekino Kawakawa POOR KNIGHTS ISLANDS
Rawene Kaikohe
Hokianga Harbour Kamo Hikurangi

Northland Whangarei
Dargaville HEN AND CHICKENS ISLANDS
Te Koputu TARANGA ISLAND
Portland *MOKOHINAU ISLANDS*

NORTH ISLAND

Kaipara Harbour
AUCKLAND PENINSULA LITTLE BARRIER ISLAND GREAT BARRIER ISLAND
Wellsford Port Fitzroy
Warkworth Colville CUVIER ISLAND
Helensville Takapuna COROMANDEL THE ALDERMEN ISLANDS
Waitemata *PENINSULA* Whitianga MERCURY ISLANDS

Central Howick
AUCKLAND Manukau Mayor Island
Auckland Pukekohe Thames WHITE ISLAND
Waiuku Paeroa Tauranga *Bay of Plenty* Te Araroa
Pukemiro Te Aroha Mount Maunganui East Cape
Ngaruawahia Morrinsville MOTITI ISLAND MOTUHORA ISLAND Te Kaha
Raglan Cambridge Edgecumbe Whakatane Hicks Bay
Hamilton Whakatane Hikurangi

South Auckland- Putaruru **Tomaru Bay**
Bay of Plenty Te Kuiti **Rotorua** Kawerau Tikitiki Waipiro
Albatross Tokoroa Matawai
Point Manga Ruatoria

TASMAN SEA

North Taranaki Bight

Tirua Point Kawhia **East Coast**
Mokau Benneydale Taupo Tolaga Bay
New-Plymouth Urenui Ohakune **Gisborne** *Poverty Bay*
Okato Inglewood Turangi Waiotira
Taranaki Mount Egmont MAHIA PENINSULA
Cape Egmont Stratford Raurimu Makaroro PORTLAND ISLAND
Opunake Eltham Raetihi Wairoa Table Cape
Otakeho Waverley **Napier** Cape Kidnappers
Wanganui Hunter **Hastings** Havelock North
South Taranaki Bight Feilding Waipukurau **Hawke's Bay**

NEW ZEALAND

Cape Farewell Farewell Spit
Collingwood *Golden Bay* Cape Stephens **Wellington** **Palmerston North**
Kahurangi Point Takaka Separation D'URVILLE ISLAND Woodville Dannevirke
Point *Tasman* KAPITI ISLAND Foxton Norsewood
Nelson *Bay* French Shannon Weber
Karamea Motueka Pass Levin Pongaroa
Karamea Bight **Nelson** Paraparaumu Masterton
The Twins Richmond Upper Hutt Castlepoint
Seddonville Wakefield Picton Porirua Greytown
Millerton Glenhope Blenheim Lower Hutt Carterton
Waimangaroa Mount Owen **WELLINGTON** Cape Palliser
Westport Mount Richmond Seddon Ward
Cape Foulwind Murchison Cape Campbell

PACIFIC

Charleston Reefton
Marlborough
Barrytown Kaikoura
Runanga Hanmer Clarence
Greymouth Brunner Oaro
Kumara **Canterbury**
Hokitika Otira Waiau
Ross Arthur's Pass Cheviot
Westland Waipara *Chatham Rise*
Abut Head Oxford Amberley
Franz Josef Glacier Rangiora
Fox Glacier Mount Tasman Darfield **CHRISTCHURCH**
Hermitage Mount Cook Methven Lincoln BANKS PENINSULA
Jackson Head Mount Somers Akaroa *Pegasus Bay*
Cascade Point Lake Tekapo Ashburton
Jackson Bay Fairlie Rakaia
SOUTHERN ALPS Southbridge *Canterbury Bight*

OCEAN

Awarua Bay Lake **SOUTH ISLAND**
Milford Sound Pukaki Timaru
George Sound Mount Aspiring Temuka
Caswell Sound Omarama Geraldine
SECRETARY ISLAND Cromwell Studholme Junction
Thompson Sound Queenstown Waimate
Doubtful Sound Kingston Makikihi
Breaksea Sound Clyde Oamaru
RESOLUTION ISLAND Alexandra Maheno OTAGO PENINSULA
Dusky Sound Roxburgh Palmerston
West Cape **Otago** Mosgiel
Cape Providence Ranfurly Green Island
Chalky Inlet Middlemarch **Dunedin**
Puysegur Point Balclutha

Southland Lumsden Waitati
Te Anau Heriot Port Chalmers
Manapouri Beaumont Nugget Point
Tuatapere Mossburn Milton
Riversdale Clinton Kaitangata
Ohai Gore Owaka
Winton Mataura Kahakopa
Orepuki Clyde Wyndham
Colac Waikawa
Thornbury **Invercargill**
SOLANDER ISLAND Woodlands Waikawa
CODFISH ISLAND Bluff *Toetoes Bay*
Mount Anglem Ruapuke Island

STEWART ISLAND
Oban
MUTTON BIRD ISLANDS *Paterson Inlet*
Port Pegasus
NORTH TRAP *Shelter Point*
Southwest Cape SOUTH TRAP

SNARES ISLANDS

Campbell Plateau

AUCKLAND ISLANDS
(New Zealand)

CHATHAM ISLANDS
(New Zealand)

Bounty Trough

BOUNTY ISLANDS
(New Zealand)

ANTIPODES ISLANDS
(New Zealand)

The political subdivisions shown for New Zealand represent statistical areas and are not recognized for administrative purposes.

A 166 B 52 C 168 D 172 Longitude East 174 of Greenwich G 178 H

CAMPBELL ISLAND
(New Zealand)

Scale 1:6,000,000 Delisle Conic Equidistant Projection

0 100 200 300 km

0 100 miles

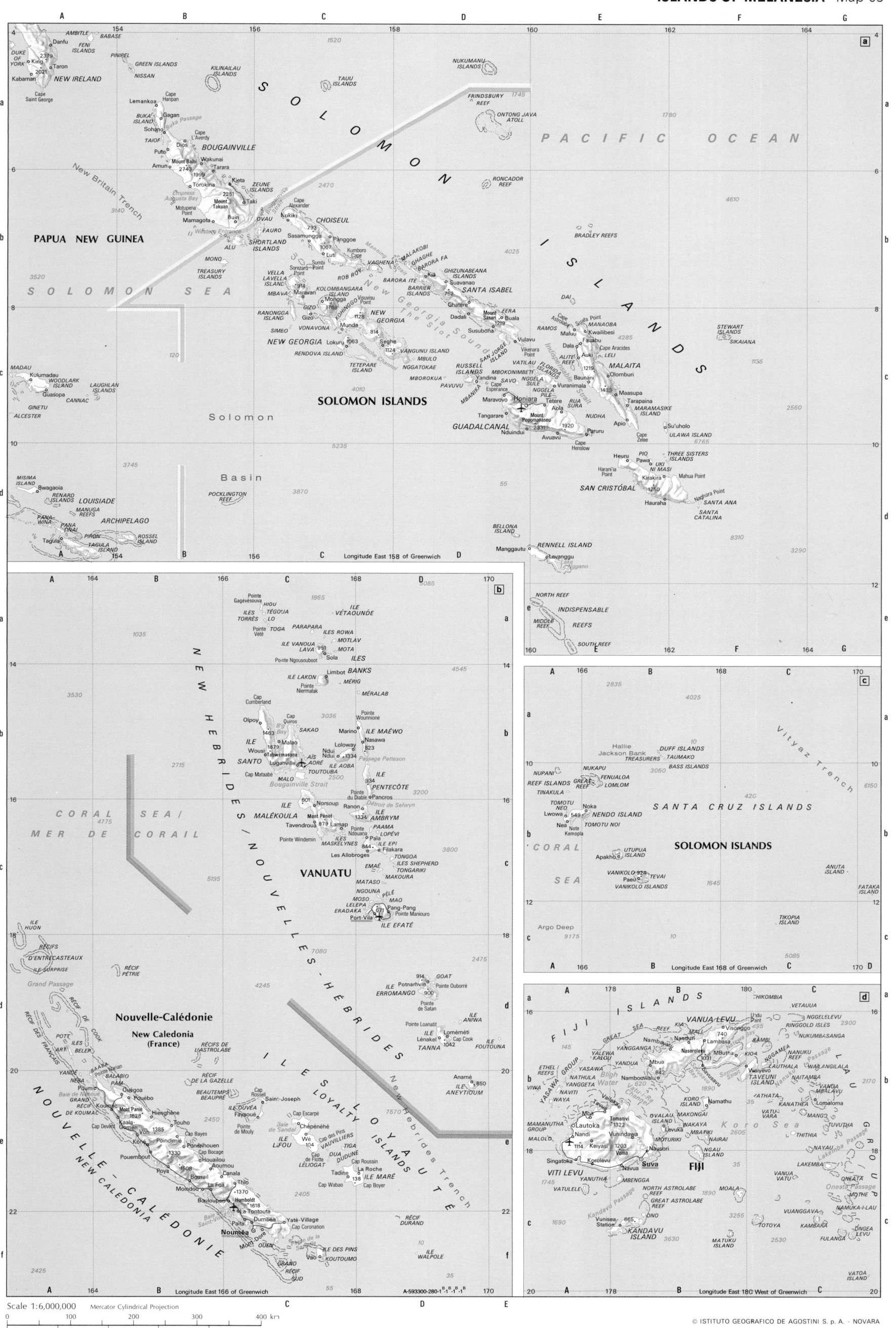

Map 64 **ISLANDS OF MICRONESIA-POLYNESIA**

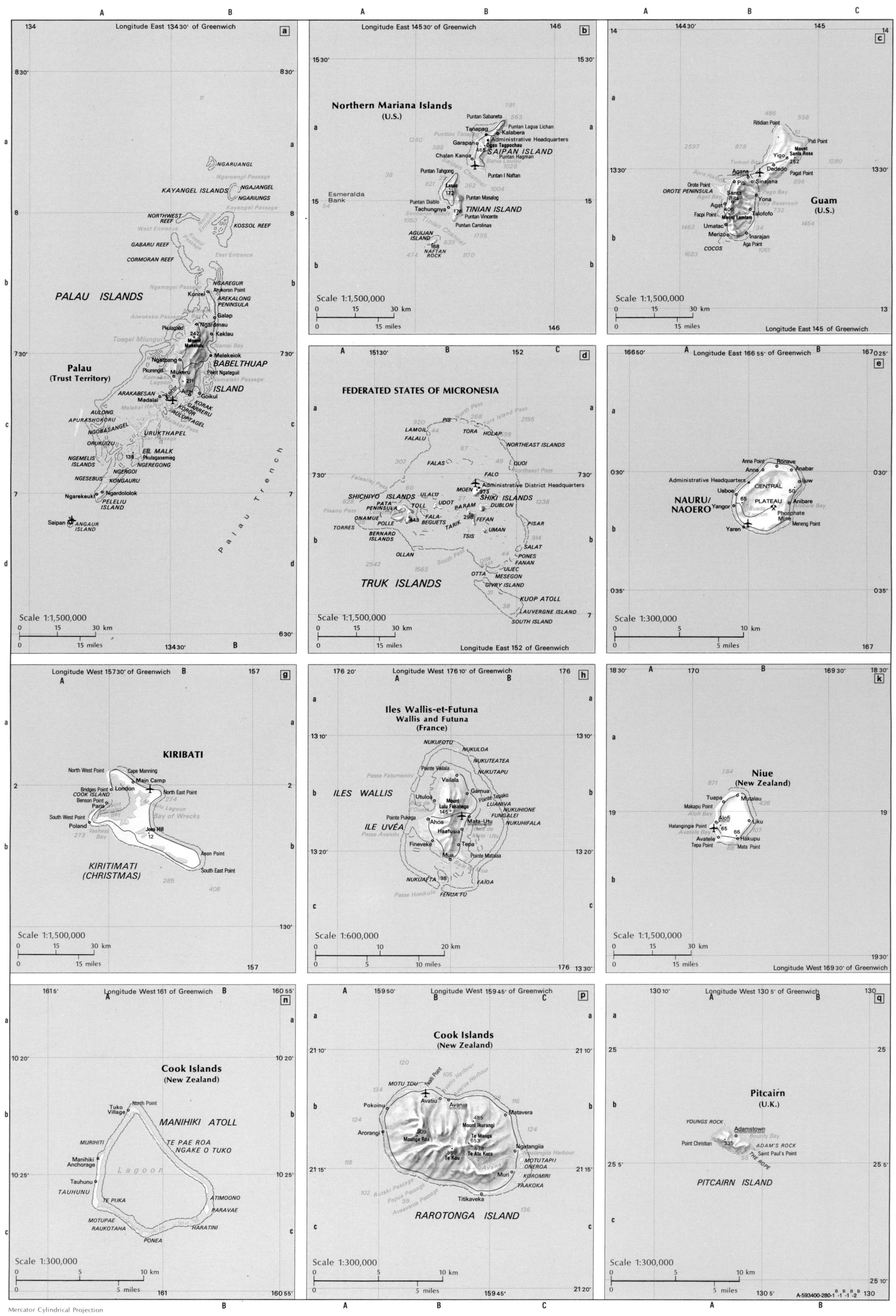

Mercator Cylindrical Projection

© ISTITUTO GEOGRAFICO DE AGOSTINI S. p. A. - NOVARA

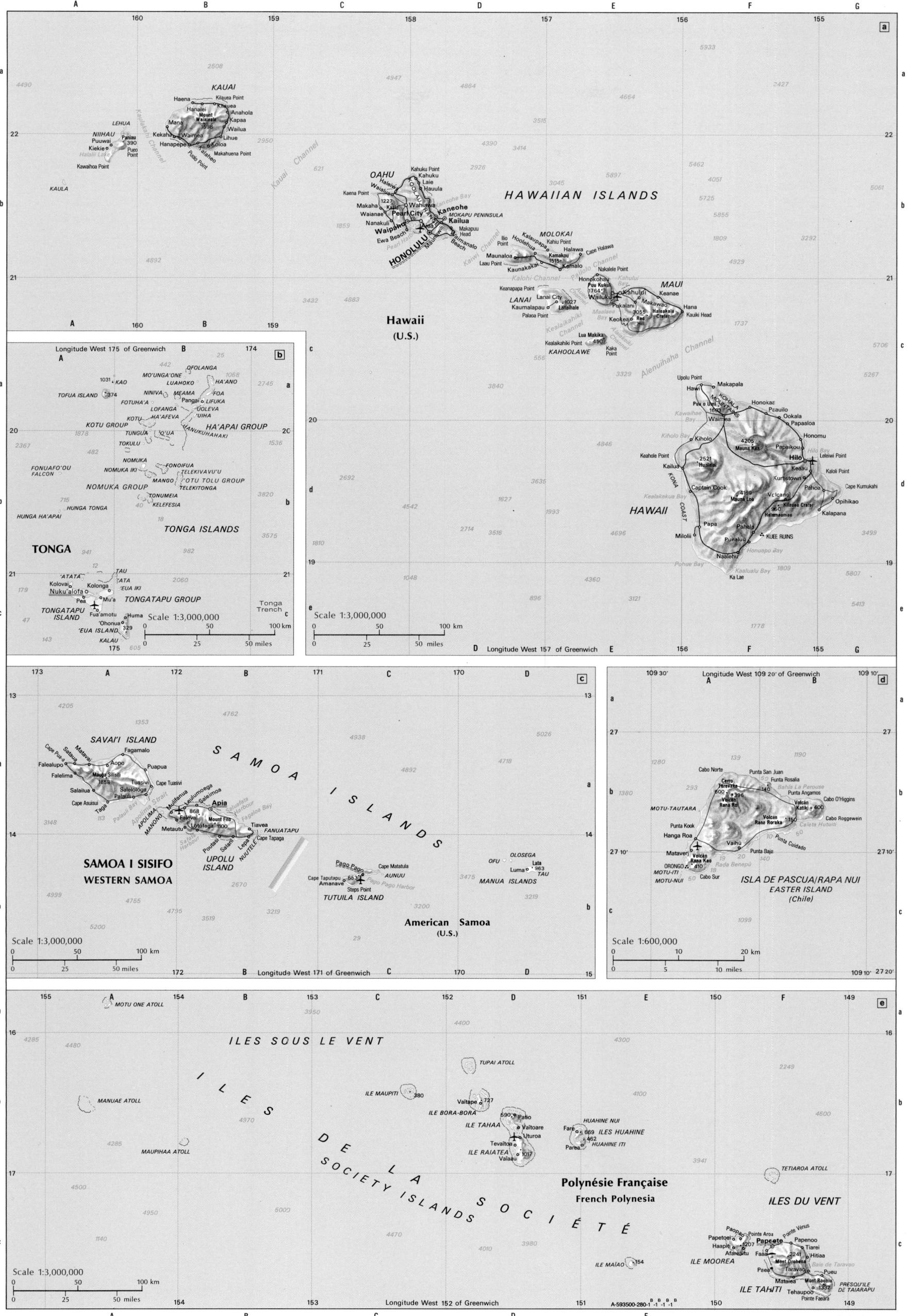

Map 66 **ANTARCTIC REGION, PHYSICAL**

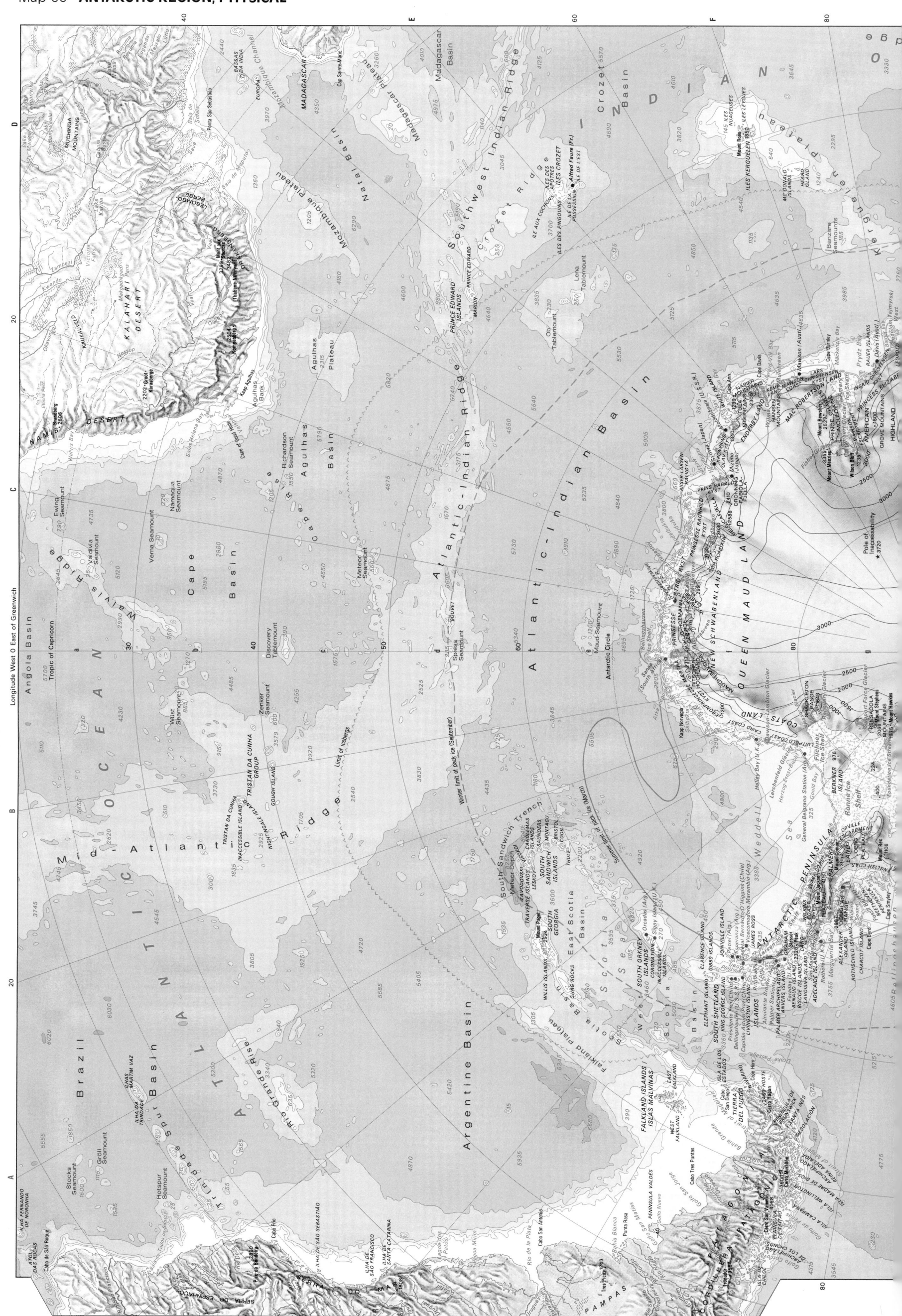

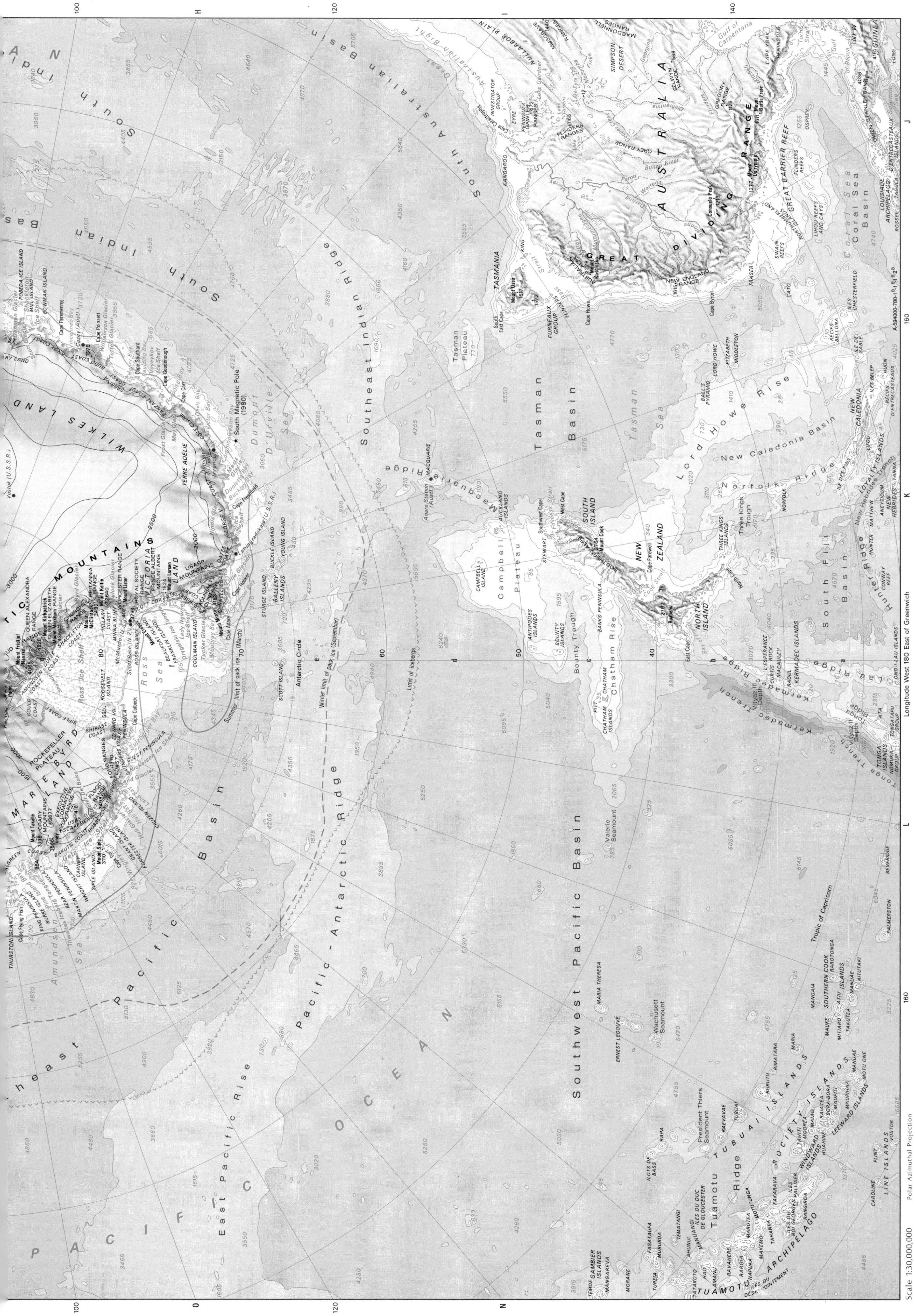

© ISTITUTO GEOGRAFICO DE AGOSTINI S. p. A. - NOVARA

The Antarctic region is not a political entity and its status is regulated by the Antarctic Treaty signed in Washington, D.C. in 1959. The treaty binds the states which signed the agreement to use the region solely for peaceful purposes and scientific research.

Longitude West 180 East of Greenwich

Scale 1:30,000,000   Polar Azimuthal Projection

2000 km
1500
1000
500

1000 miles
500

AUSTRALIA

TASMANIA

NEW ZEALAND

SOUTH ISLAND
NORTH ISLAND

Coral Sea

Tasman Sea

Tasman Basin

Lord Howe Rise

New Caledonia Basin

NEW CALEDONIA

Norfolk Ridge

Kermadec Trench

Kermadec Ridge

South Fiji Basin

SOUTHERN COOK ISLANDS

SOCIETY ISLANDS

TUAMOTU TUBUAI

TUAMOTU ARCHIPELAGO

Tropic of Capricorn

Southwest Pacific Basin

PACIFIC OCEAN

Pacific-Antarctic Ridge

East Pacific Rise

Pacific-Antarctic Basin

Amundsen Sea

Ross Sea

Ross Ice Shelf

WILKES LAND

MARIE BYRD LAND

VICTORIA LAND

TERRE ADÉLIE

South Magnetic Pole (1980)

Antarctic Circle

Southeast Indian Ridge

South Indian Basin

South Australian Basin

Great Australian Bight

Limit of icebergs

Summer limit of pack ice (March)

Winter limit of pack ice (September)

GREAT DIVIDING RANGE

223

Map 67 **ARCTIC REGION, PHYSICAL**

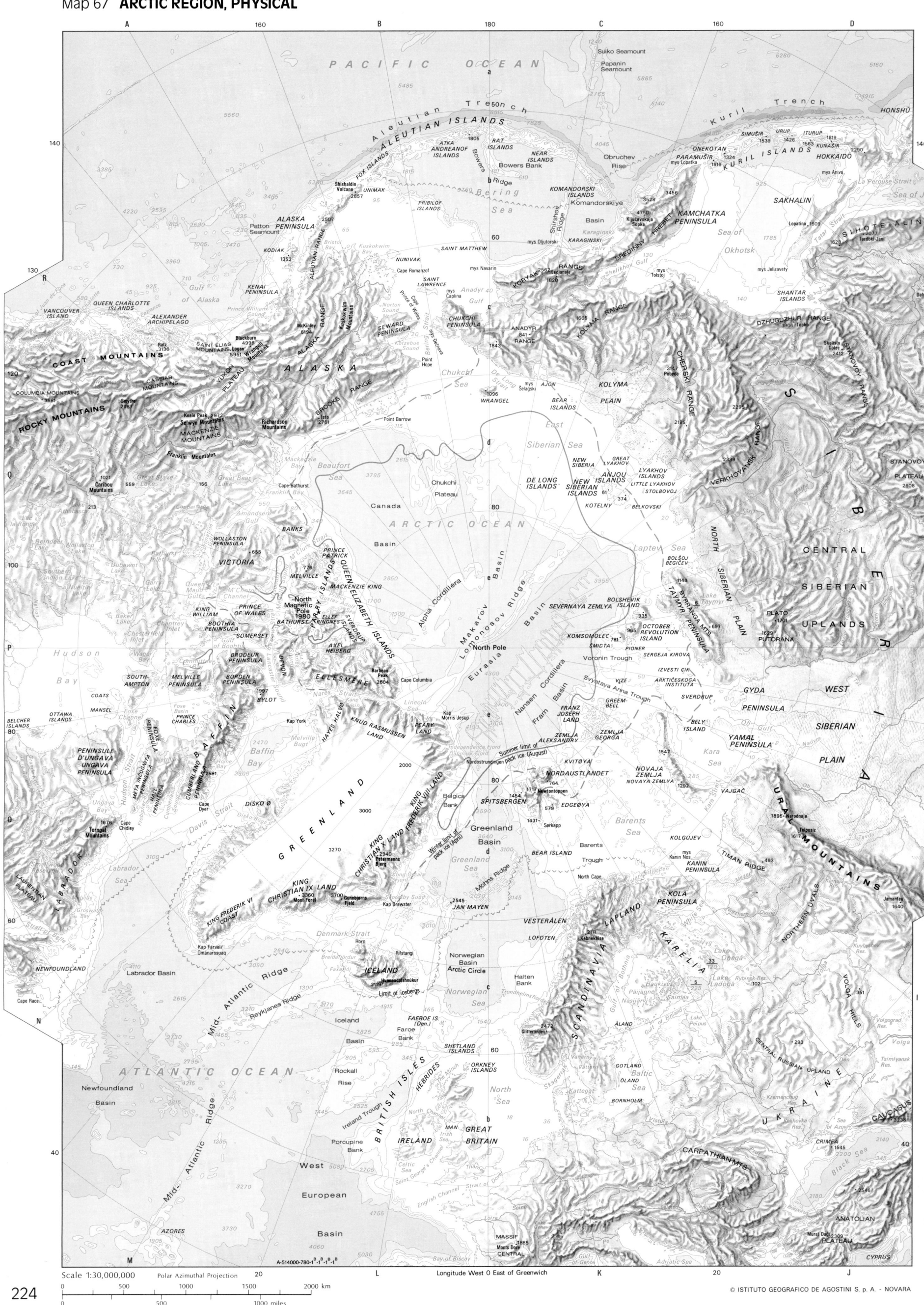

Scale 1:30,000,000   Polar Azimuthal Projection

Longitude West 0 East of Greenwich

© ISTITUTO GEOGRAFICO DE AGOSTINI S. p. A. - NOVARA

Maps of the United States and Canada

MAP LEGEND

CULTURAL FEATURES

Political Boundaries

 International

Secondary (State)

- - - - - - County

Populated Places

Cities, towns, and villages

•••••● Symbol size represents
population of the place

Chicago
Gary   Type size represents
Racine   relative importance of the place
Glenview
Edgewood

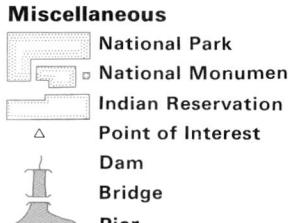 **Major Urban Areas**
Area of continuous commercial, industrial,
and residential development in and around
a major city

◦ Community within a city

⊛ Capital of major political unit

✪ Capital of U.S. state

◦ County Seat

▲ Military Installation

Transportation

———— Major Highway

———— Railroad

—+—·—+— Tunnel

Miscellaneous

▱ National Park

▱ National Monument

▱ Indian Reservation

△ Point of Interest

Dam

Bridge

Pier

LAND FEATURES

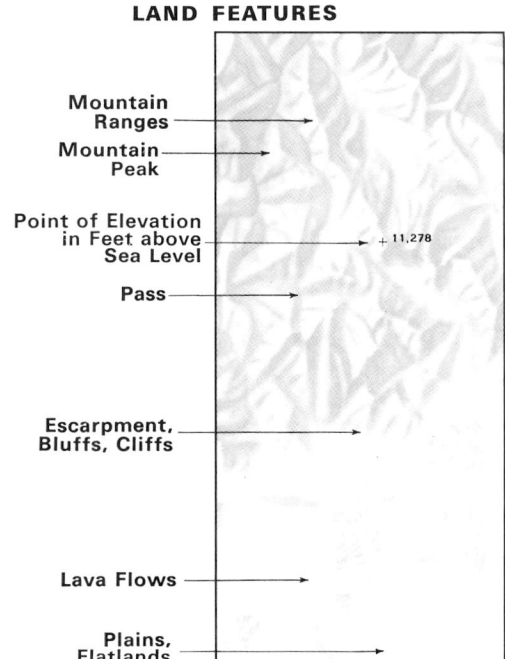

Mountain Ranges

Mountain Peak

Point of Elevation in Feet above Sea Level → + 11,278

Pass

Escarpment, Bluffs, Cliffs

Lava Flows

Plains, Flatlands

WATER FEATURES

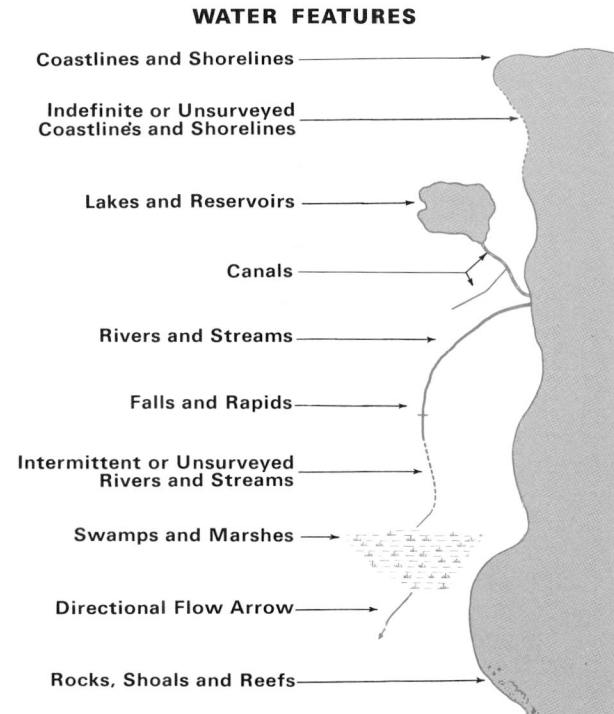

Coastlines and Shorelines

Indefinite or Unsurveyed Coastlines and Shorelines

Lakes and Reservoirs

Canals

Rivers and Streams

Falls and Rapids

Intermittent or Unsurveyed Rivers and Streams

Swamps and Marshes

Directional Flow Arrow

Rocks, Shoals and Reefs

TYPE STYLES USED TO NAME FEATURES

Note: Size of type varies according to importance and available space. Letters for names of major features are spread across the extent of the feature.

CANADA	Country, State, or Province	*U I N T A DESERT*	Major Terrain Features
Naval Air Station	Military Installation	MT. MORIAH	Individual Mountain
CROCKETT	County	*MESA VERDE SAN XAVIER*	National Park or Monument, Indian Res.

NUNIVAK   Island or Coastal Feature

Ocean
Lake   Hydrographic Features
River
Canal

Lambert Conformal Conic Projection
ALE 1:12,000,000 1 Inch = 189 Statute Miles

Cities and Towns

Albertville 14,507 A3
Alexander City 14,917 C4
Andalusia 9,269 D3
Anniston 26,623 B4
Arab 6,321 A3
Athens 16,901 A3
Atmore 8,046 D2
Auburn 33,830 C4
Bay Minette 7,168 E2
Bessemer 33,497 B3
Birmingham 265,968 B3
Bluff Park 8,000 g7
Boaz 6,928 A3
Brewton 5,885 D2
Center Point 22,000 f7
Childersburg 4,579 B3
Clanton 7,669 C3
Cullman 13,367 A3
Decatur 48,761 A3
Demopolis 7,512 C2
Dothan 53,589 D4
Enterprise 20,123 D4
Eufaula 13,220 C4
Fairfield 12,200 B3
Fayette 4,909 B2
Florence 36,426 A2
Fort Payne 11,838 A4
Gadsden 42,523 A3
Geneva 4,681 D4
Greenville 7,492 D3
Guntersville 7,038 A3
Haleyville 4,452 A2
Hamilton 5,787 A2
Hartselle 10,795 A3
Homewood 22,922 g7
Hueytown 15,280 g6
Huntsville 159,789 A3
Jackson 5,819 D2
Jacksonville 10,283 B4
Jasper 13,553 B2
Lanett 8,985 C4
Leeds 9,946 B3
Mobile 196,278 E1
Monroeville 6,993 D2
Montgomery 187,106 C3
Moundville 1,348 C2
Mountain Brook 19,810 g7
Muscle Shoals 9,611 A2
Northport 17,366 B2
Opelika 22,122 C4
Opp 6,985 D3
Ozark 12,922 D4
Pell City 8,118 B3
Phenix City 25,312 C4
Piedmont 5,288 B4
Prattville 19,587 C3
Prichard 34,311 E1
Roanoke 6,362 B4
Russellville 7,812 A2
Saraland 11,751 E1
Scottsboro 13,786 A3
Selma 23,755 C2
Sheffield 10,380 A2
Spanish Fort 3,732 E2
Sylacauga 12,520 B3
Talladega 18,175 B3
Tallassee 5,112 C4
Troy 13,051 D4
Tuscaloosa 77,759 B2
Tuscumbia 8,413 A2
Tuskegee 12,257 C4
Vestavia Hills 19,749 g7
Warrior 3,280 B3
Wetumpka 4,670 C3

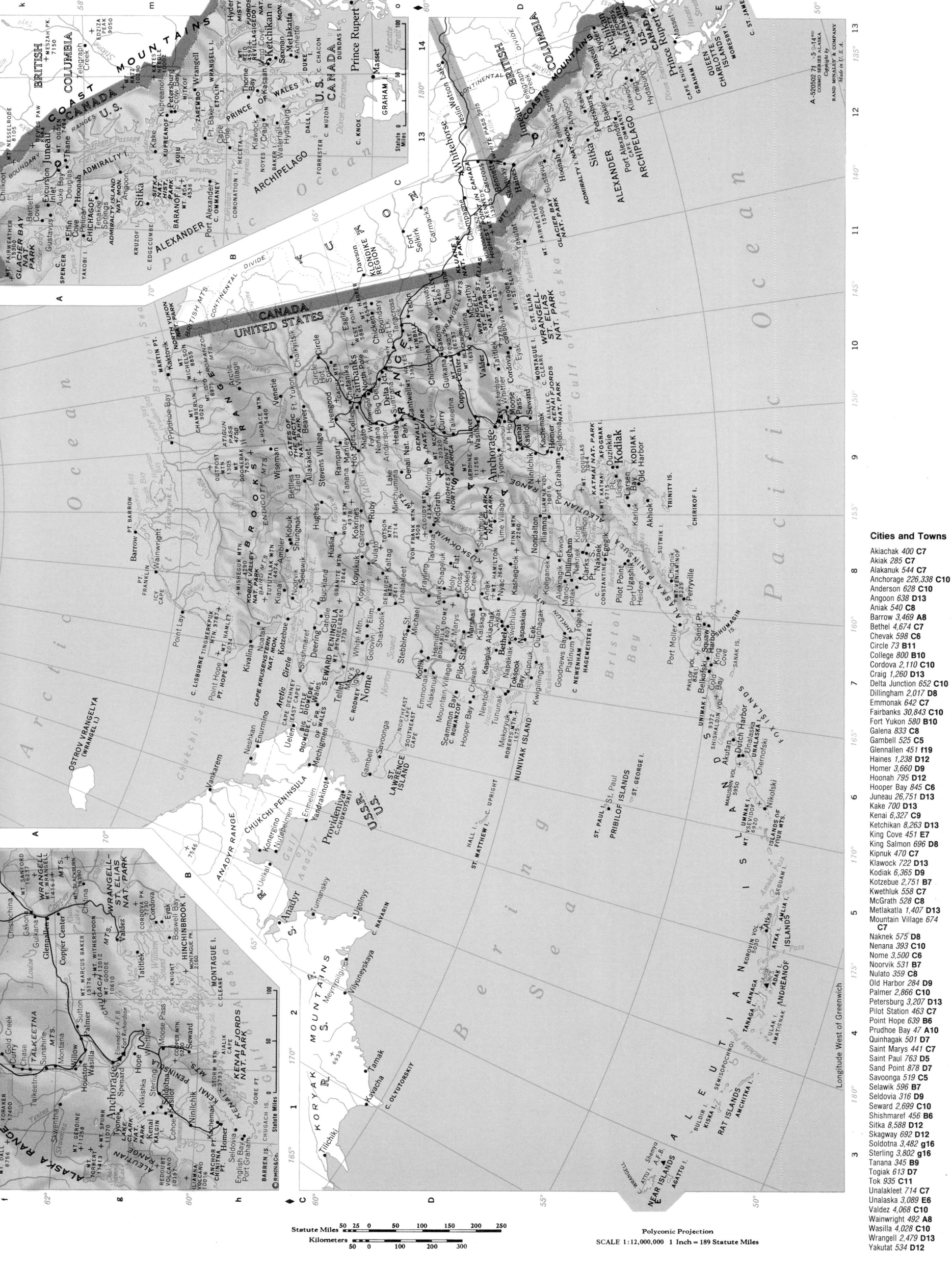

Cities and Towns

Akiachak *400* **C7**
Akiak *285* **C7**
Alakanuk *544* **C7**
Anchorage *226,338* **C10**
Anderson *628* **C10**
Angoon *638* **D13**
Aniak *540* **C8**
Barrow *3,469* **A8**
Bethel *4,674* **C7**
Chevak *598* **C6**
Circle *73* **B11**
College *800* **B10**
Cordova *2,110* **C10**
Craig *1,260* **D13**
Delta Junction *652* **C10**
Dillingham *2,017* **D8**
Emmonak *642* **C7**
Fairbanks *30,843* **C10**
Fort Yukon *580* **B10**
Galena *833* **C8**
Gambell *525* **C5**
Glennallen *451* **f19**
Haines *1,238* **D12**
Homer *3,660* **D9**
Hoonah *795* **D12**
Hooper Bay *845* **C6**
Juneau *26,751* **D13**
Kake *700* **D13**
Kenai *6,327* **C9**
Ketchikan *8,263* **D13**
King Cove *451* **E7**
King Salmon *696* **D8**
Kipnuk *470* **C7**
Klawock *722* **D13**
Kodiak *6,365* **D9**
Kotzebue *2,751* **B7**
Kwethluk *558* **C7**
McGrath *528* **C8**
Metlakatla *1,407* **D13**
Mountain Village *674*
  C7
Naknek *575* **D8**
Nenana *393* **C10**
Nome *3,500* **C6**
Noorvik *531* **B7**
Nulato *359* **C8**
Old Harbor *284* **D9**
Palmer *2,866* **C10**
Petersburg *3,207* **D13**
Pilot Station *463* **C7**
Point Hope *639* **B6**
Prudhoe Bay *47* **A10**
Quinhagak *501* **D7**
Saint Marys *441* **C7**
Saint Paul *763* **D5**
Sand Point *878* **D7**
Savoonga *519* **C5**
Selawik *596* **B7**
Seldovia *316* **D9**
Seward *2,699* **C10**
Shishmaref *456* **B6**
Sitka *8,588* **D12**
Skagway *692* **D12**
Soldotna *3,482* **g16**
Sterling *3,802* **g16**
Tanana *345* **B9**
Togiak *613* **D7**
Tok *935* **C11**
Unalakleet *714* **C7**
Unalaska *3,089* **E6**
Valdez *4,068* **C10**
Wainwright *492* **A8**
Wasilla *4,028* **C10**
Wrangell *2,479* **D13**
Yakutat *534* **D12**

Statute Miles 50 25 0 50 100 150 200 250

Kilometers 50 0 100 200 300

Polyconic Projection
SCALE 1:12,000,000 1 Inch = 189 Statute Miles

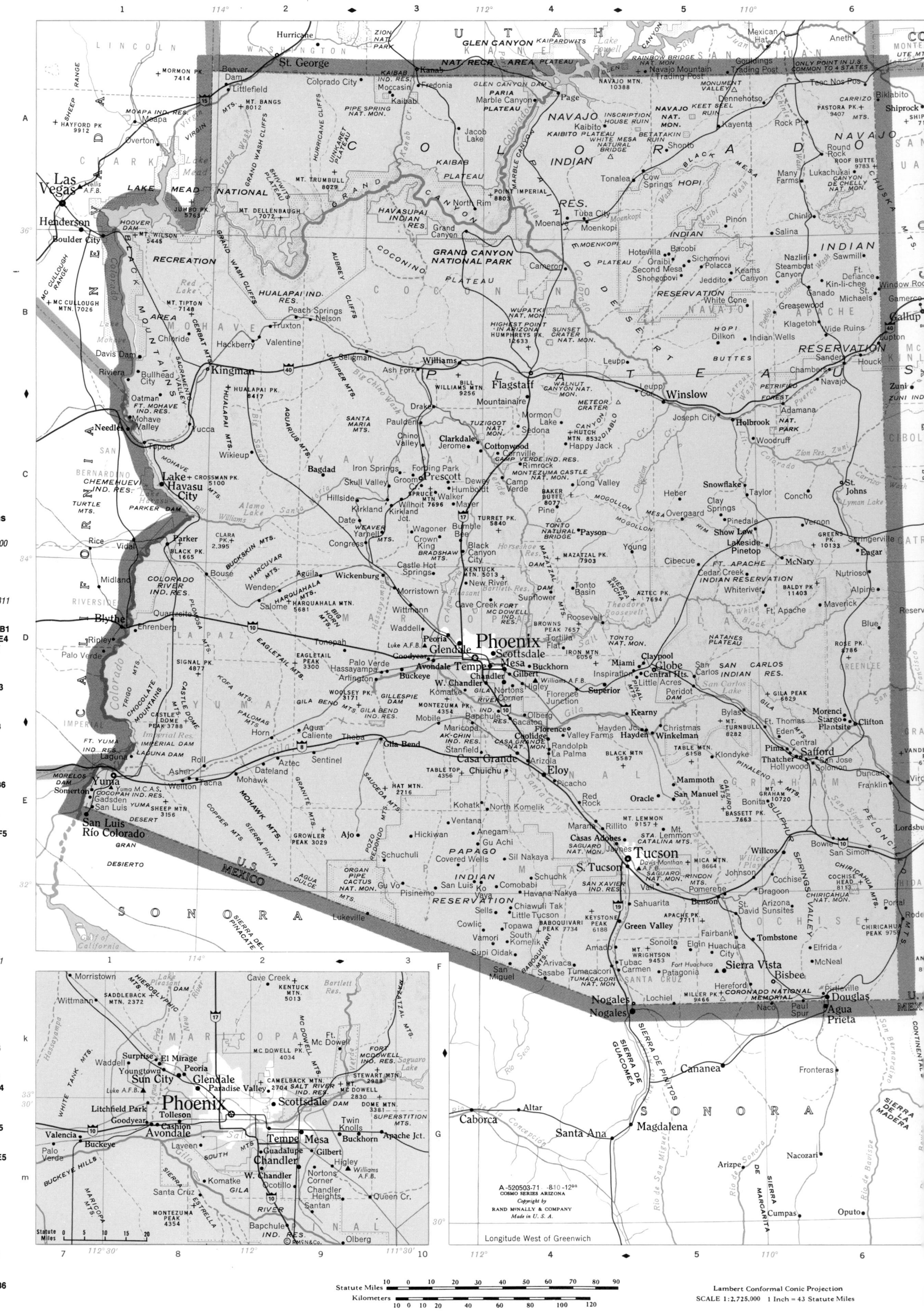

Cities and Towns

Ajo 2,919 **E3**
Apache Junction 18,100 **m9**
Avondale 16,169 **D3**
Bagdad 1,858 **C2**
Benson 3,824 **F5**
Bisbee 6,288 **F6**
Black Canyon City 1,811 **C3**
Buckeye 5,038 **D3**
Bullhead City 21,951 **B1**
Casa Grande 19,082 **E4**
Casas Adobes 12,155 **E5**
Chandler 90,533 **D4**
Chinle 5,059 **A6**
Chino Valley 4,837 **C3**
Claypool 1,942 **D5**
Clifton 2,840 **D6**
Coolidge 6,927 **E4**
Cottonwood 5,918 **C3**
Douglas 12,822 **F6**
Eagar 4,025 **C6**
Eloy 7,211 **E4**
Flagstaff 45,857 **B4**
Florence 7,510 **D4**
Fort Defiance 4,489 **B6**
Gila Bend 1,747 **E3**
Gilbert 29,188 **D4**
Glendale 148,134 **D3**
Globe 6,062 **D5**
Green Valley 13,231 **F5**
Holbrook 4,686 **C5**
Kayenta 4,372 **A5**
Kearny 2,262 **D5**
Kingman 12,722 **B1**
Lake Havasu City 24,363 **C1**
Mammoth 1,845 **E5**
Mesa 288,091 **D4**
Miami 2,018 **D5**
Nogales 19,489 **F5**
Oracle 3,043 **E5**
Page 6,598 **A4**
Paradise Valley 11,671 **k9**
Parker 2,897 **C1**
Payson 8,377 **C4**
Peoria 50,618 **D3**
Phoenix 983,403 **D3**
Prescott 26,455 **C3**
Sacaton 1,452 **D4**
Safford 7,359 **E6**
Saint Johns 3,294 **C6**
San Carlos 2,918 **D5**
San Luis 4,212 **E1**
San Manuel 4,009 **E5**
Scottsdale 130,069 **D4**
Sedona 7,720 **C4**
Sells 2,750 **F4**
Show Low 5,019 **C5**
Sierra Vista 32,983 **F5**
Snowflake 3,679 **C5**
Somerton 5,282 **E1**
South Tucson 5,093 **E5**
Sun City 38,126 **k8**
Superior 3,468 **D4**
Surprise 7,122 **k8**
Taylor 2,418 **C5**
Tempe 141,865 **D4**
Thatcher 3,763 **E6**
Tombstone 1,220 **F5**
Tuba City 7,323 **A4**
Tucson 405,390 **E5**
Wickenburg 4,515 **D3**
Willcox 3,122 **E6**
Williams 2,532 **B3**
Window Rock 3,306 **B6**
Winslow 8,190 **C5**
Yuma 54,923 **E1**

A-520503-71 · B10-12ªᵃ
COSMO SERIES ARIZONA
Copyright by
RAND MCNALLY & COMPANY
Made in U. S. A.

Longitude West of Greenwich

Statute Miles

Kilometers

Lambert Conformal Conic Projection
SCALE 1:2,725,000   1 Inch = 43 Statute Miles

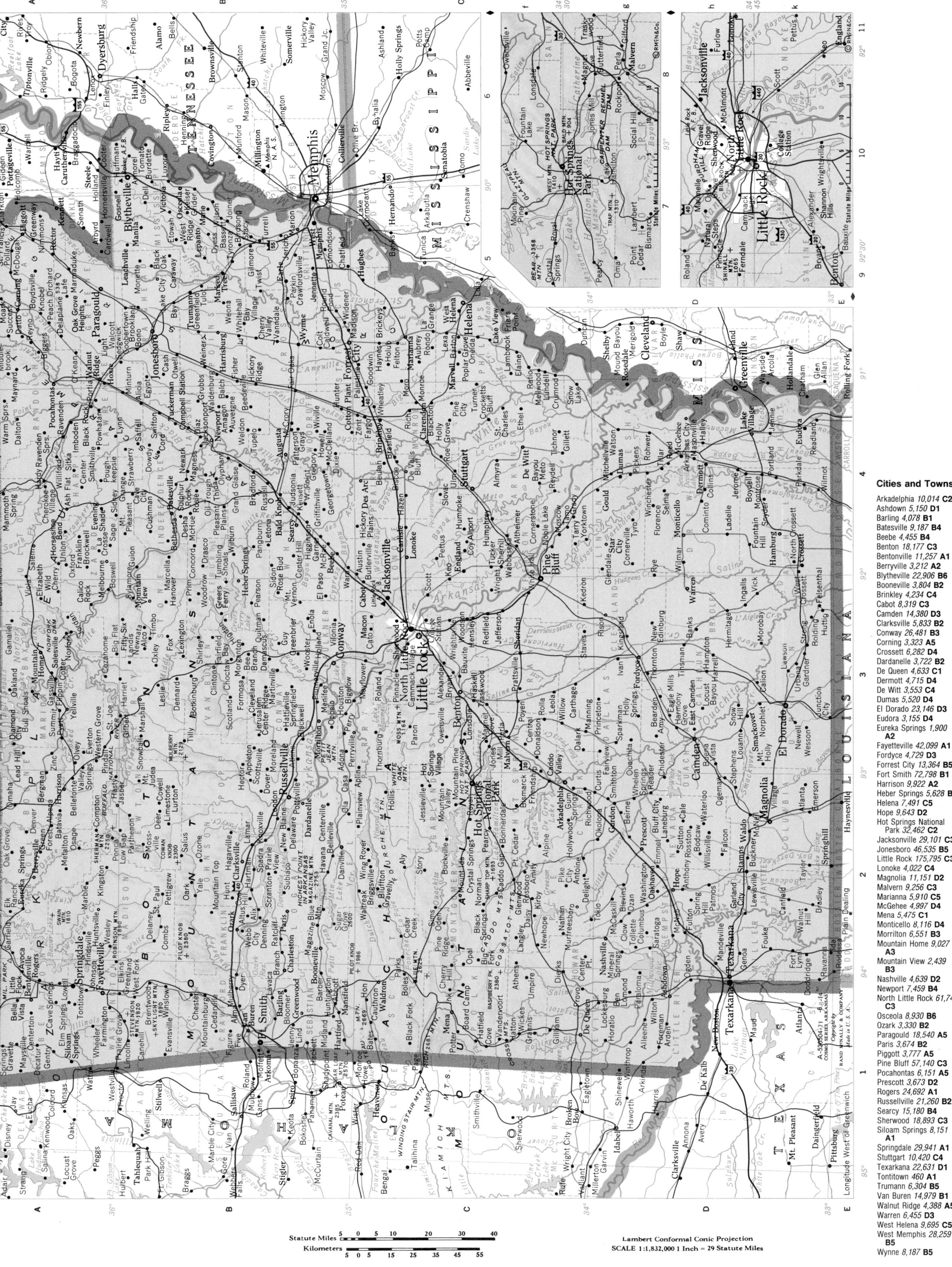

Cities and Towns

Arkadelphia *10,014* **C2**
Ashdown *5,150* **D1**
Barling *4,078* **B1**
Batesville *9,187* **B4**
Beebe *4,455* **B4**
Benton *18,177* **C3**
Bentonville *11,257* **A1**
Berryville *3,212* **A2**
Blytheville *22,906* **B6**
Booneville *3,804* **B2**
Brinkley *4,234* **C4**
Cabot *8,319* **C3**
Camden *14,380* **D3**
Clarksville *5,833* **B2**
Conway *26,481* **B3**
Corning *3,323* **A5**
Crossett *6,282* **D4**
Dardanelle *3,722* **B2**
De Queen *4,633* **C1**
Dermott *4,715* **D4**
De Witt *3,553* **C4**
Dumas *5,520* **D4**
El Dorado *23,146* **D3**
Eudora *3,155* **D4**
Eureka Springs *1,900*
   A2
Fayetteville *42,099* **A1**
Fordyce *4,729* **D3**
Forrest City *13,364* **B5**
Fort Smith *72,798* **B1**
Harrison *9,922* **A2**
Heber Springs *5,628* **B3**
Helena *7,491* **C5**
Hope *9,643* **D2**
Hot Springs National
   Park *32,462* **C2**
Jacksonville *29,101* **C3**
Jonesboro *46,535* **B5**
Little Rock *175,795* **C3**
Lonoke *4,022* **C4**
Magnolia *11,151* **D2**
Malvern *9,256* **C3**
Marianna *5,910* **C5**
McGehee *4,997* **D4**
Mena *5,475* **C1**
Monticello *8,116* **D4**
Morrilton *6,551* **B3**
Mountain Home *9,027*
   A3
Mountain View *2,439*
   B3
Nashville *4,639* **D2**
Newport *7,459* **B4**
North Little Rock *61,741*
   C3
Osceola *8,930* **B6**
Ozark *3,330* **B2**
Paragould *18,540* **A5**
Paris *3,674* **B2**
Piggott *3,777* **A5**
Pine Bluff *57,140* **C3**
Pocahontas *6,151* **A5**
Prescott *3,673* **D2**
Rogers *24,692* **A1**
Russellville *21,260* **B2**
Searcy *15,180* **B4**
Sherwood *18,893* **C3**
Siloam Springs *8,151*
   A1
Springdale *29,941* **A1**
Stuttgart *10,420* **C4**
Texarkana *22,631* **D1**
Tontitown *460* **A1**
Trumann *6,304* **B5**
Van Buren *14,979* **B1**
Walnut Ridge *4,388* **A5**
Warren *6,455* **D3**
West Helena *9,695* **C5**
West Memphis *28,259*
   B5
Wynne *8,187* **B5**

Statute Miles 5 0 5 10 20 30 40
Kilometers 5 0 5 15 25 35 45 55

Lambert Conformal Conic Projection
SCALE 1:1,832,000 1 Inch = 29 Statute Miles

231

CALIFORNIA

Statute Miles 5 0 5 10 20 30 40 50
Kilometers 5 0 5 15 25 35 45 55 65 75

Lambert Conformal Conic Projection
SCALE 1:2,186,000   1 Inch = 34.5 Statute Miles

CONNECTICUT

*Populations are for localities, not incorporated towns.

Statute Miles   5   0   5   10   15

Kilometers   5   0   5   10   15   20

Lambert Conformal Conic Projection
SCALE 1:545,000 1 Inch = 8.6 Statute Miles

A-520507-71 -7&.7°14'

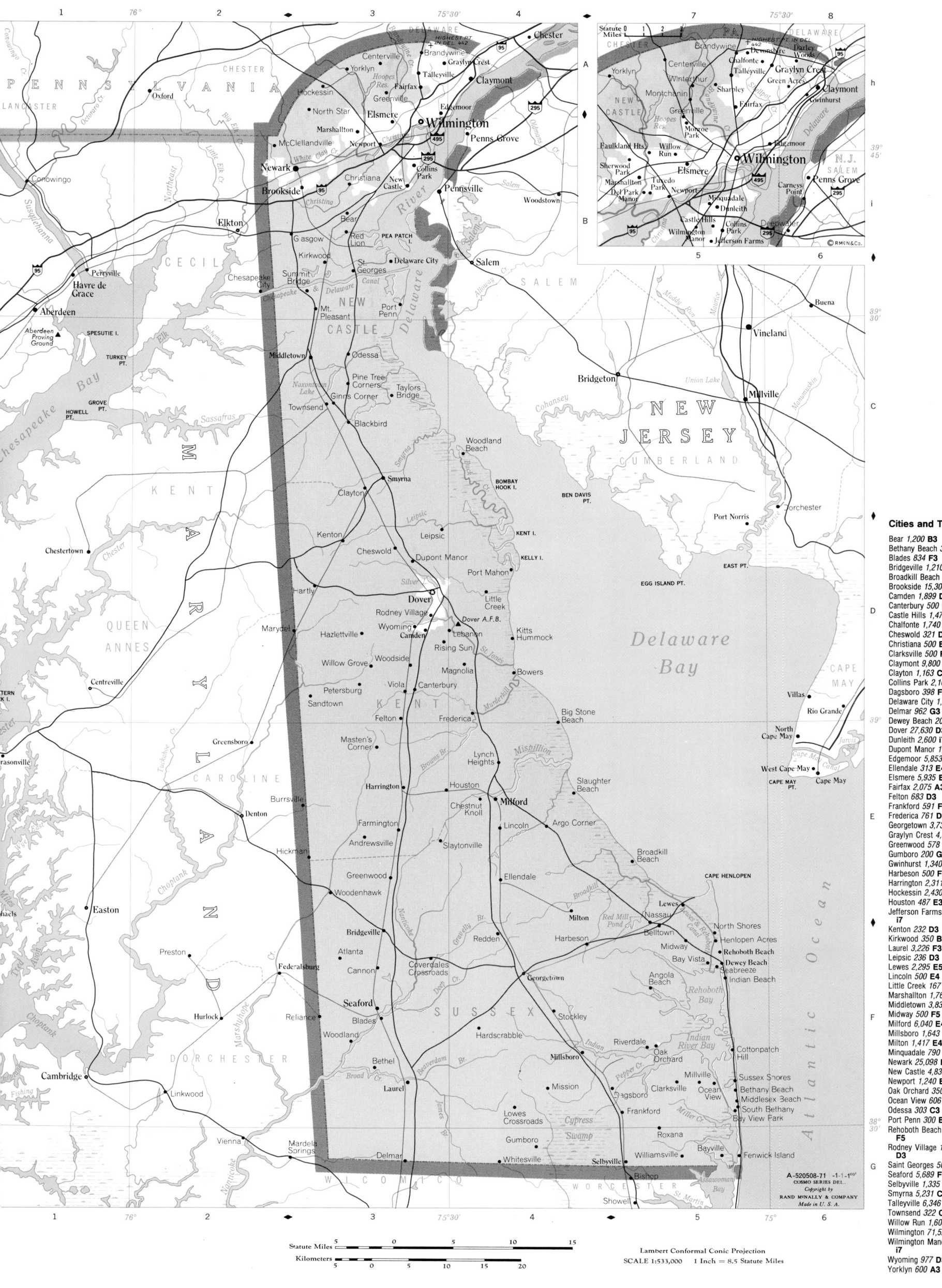

Cities and Towns

Bear 1,200 **B3**
Bethany Beach 326 **F5**
Blades 834 **F3**
Bridgeville 1,210 **F3**
Broadkill Beach 390 **E5**
Brookside 15,307 **B3**
Camden 1,899 **D3**
Canterbury 500 **D3**
Castle Hills 1,475 **i7**
Chalfonte 1,740 **h7**
Cheswold 321 **D3**
Christiana 500 **B3**
Clarksville 500 **F5**
Claymont 9,800 **A4**
Clayton 1,163 **C3**
Collins Park 2,100 **B3**
Dagsboro 398 **F5**
Delaware City 1,682 **B3**
Delmar 962 **G3**
Dewey Beach 204 **F5**
Dover 27,630 **D3**
Dunleith 2,600 **i7**
Dupont Manor 1,059 **D3**
Edgemoor 5,853 **A3**
Ellendale 313 **E4**
Elsmere 5,935 **B3**
Fairfax 2,075 **A3**
Felton 683 **D3**
Frankford 591 **F5**
Frederica 761 **D4**
Georgetown 3,732 **F4**
Graylyn Crest 4,380 **A3**
Greenwood 578 **E3**
Gumboro 200 **G4**
Gwinhurst 1,340 **h8**
Harbeson 500 **F4**
Harrington 2,311 **E3**
Hockessin 2,430 **A3**
Houston 487 **E3**
Jefferson Farms 3,100 **i7**
Kenton 232 **D3**
Kirkwood 350 **B3**
Laurel 3,226 **F3**
Leipsic 236 **D3**
Lewes 2,295 **E5**
Lincoln 500 **E4**
Little Creek 167 **D4**
Marshallton 1,765 **B3**
Middletown 3,834 **C3**
Midway 500 **F5**
Milford 6,040 **E4**
Millsboro 1,643 **F4**
Milton 1,417 **E4**
Minquadale 790 **i7**
Newark 25,098 **B3**
New Castle 4,837 **B3**
Newport 1,240 **B3**
Oak Orchard 350 **F5**
Ocean View 606 **F5**
Odessa 303 **C3**
Port Penn 300 **B3**
Rehoboth Beach 1,234 **F5**
Rodney Village 1,745 **D3**
Saint Georges 500 **B3**
Seaford 5,689 **F3**
Selbyville 1,335 **G5**
Smyrna 5,231 **C3**
Talleyville 6,346 **A3**
Townsend 322 **C3**
Willow Run 1,600 **i7**
Wilmington 71,529 **B3**
Wilmington Manor 8,568 **i7**
Wyoming 977 **D3**
Yorklyn 600 **A3**

A-520508-71 -1-1-1⁴⁰'
COSMO SERIES DEL.
Copyright by
RAND McNALLY & COMPANY
Made in U.S.A.

Lambert Conformal Conic Projection
SCALE 1:533,000   1 Inch = 8.5 Statute Miles

Statute Miles
Kilometers

FLORIDA

Statute Miles

Kilometers

Lambert Conformal Conic Projection
SCALE 1:2,425,000   1 Inch = 38 Statute Miles

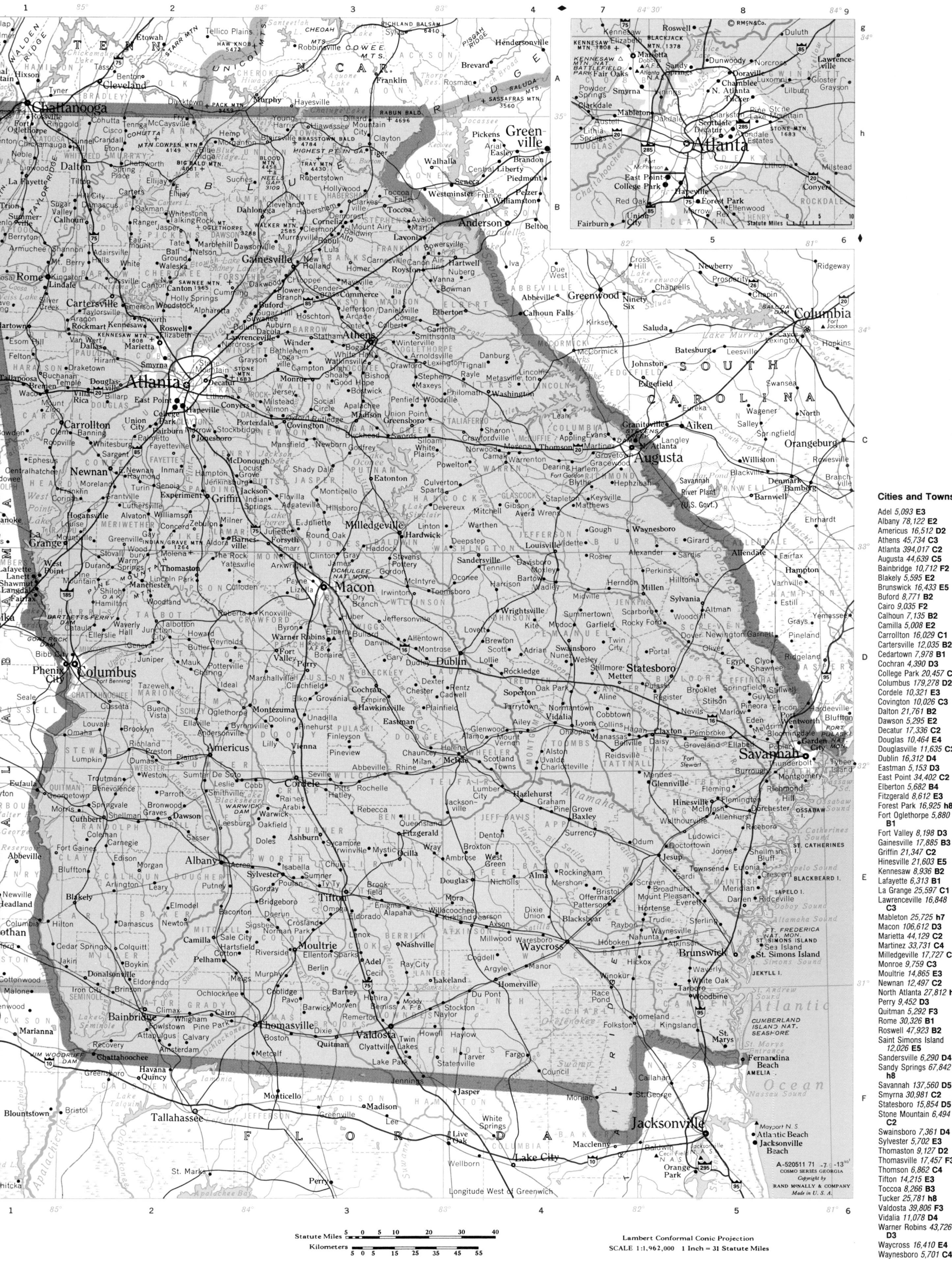

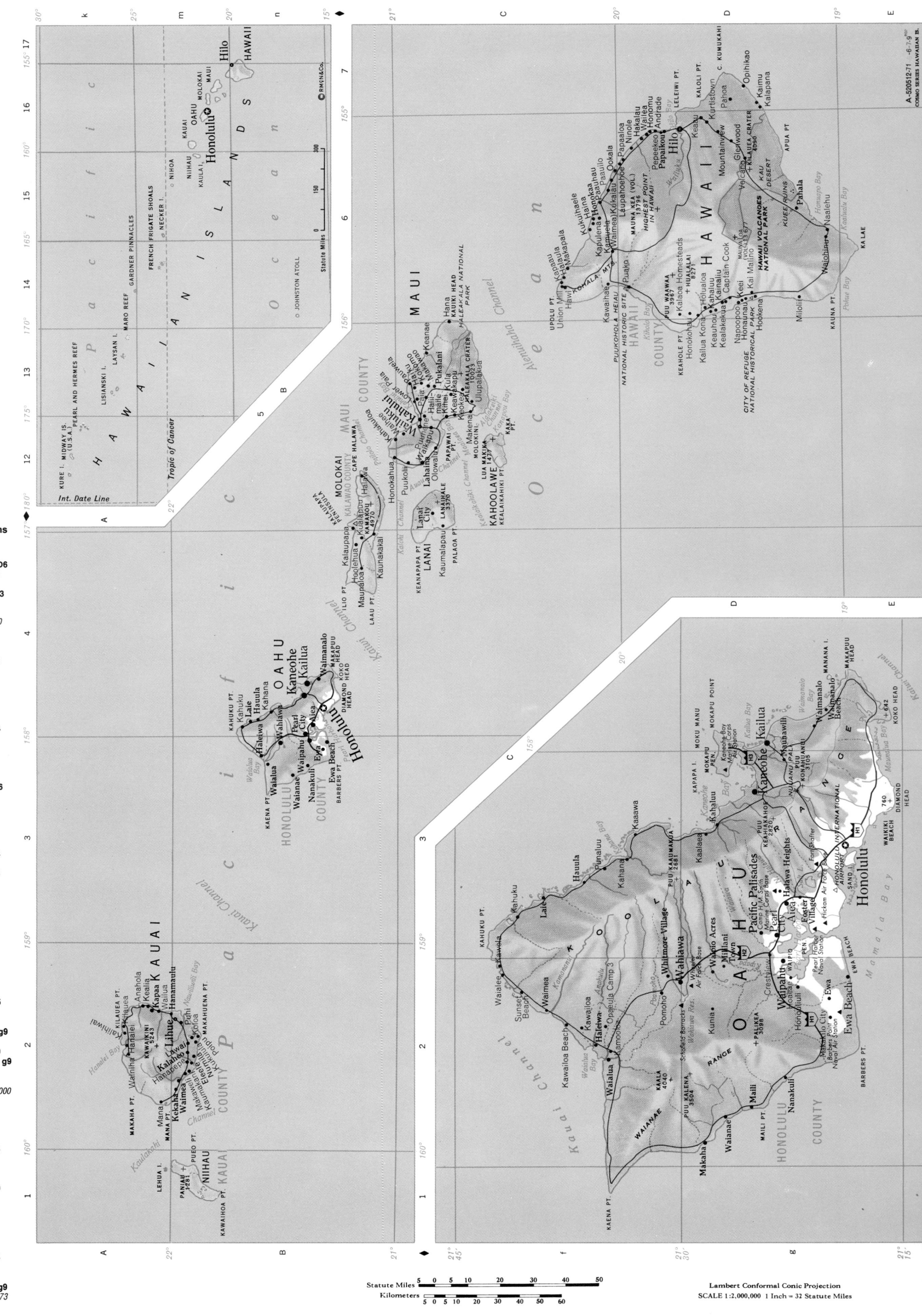

Cities and Towns

Aiea 8,906 **B4**
Anahola 1,181 **A2**
Captain Cook 2,696 **D6**
Crestview 1,000 **g10**
Ewa 3,780 **B3**
Ewa Beach 14,315 **B3**
Foster Village 3,700
  g10
Halawa Heights 7,000
  g10
Haleiwa 2,442 **B3**
Haliimaile 841 **C5**
Hanamaulu 3,611 **B2**
Hanapepe 1,395 **B2**
Hauula 3,479 **B4**
Hawi 924 **C6**
Hilo 37,808 **D6**
Holualoa 3,834 **D6**
Honokaa 2,186 **C6**
Honolulu 365,272 **B4**
Kaaawa 1,138 **f10**
Kahaluu 3,068 **g10**
Kahuku 2,063 **B4**
Kahului 16,889 **C5**
Kailua 36,818 **B4**
Kailua Kona 9,126 **D6**
Kalaheo 3,592 **B2**
Kamuela (Waimea)
  5,972 **C6**
Kaneohe 35,448 **B4**
Kapaa 8,149 **A2**
Kaumakani 803 **B2**
Kaunakakai 2,658 **B4**
Keaau 1,584 **D6**
Kealakekua 1,453 **D6**
Kekaha 3,506 **B2**
Keokea 900 **C5**
Kihei 11,107 **C5**
Kilauea 1,685 **A2**
Koloa 1,791 **B2**
Kula 1,300 **C5**
Kurtistown 910 **D6**
Lahaina 9,073 **C5**
Laie 5,577 **B4**
Lanai City 2,400 **C5**
Lawai 1,787 **B2**
Lihue 5,536 **B2**
Lower Paia 1,500 **C5**
Maili 6,059 **g9**
Makaha 7,990 **g9**
Makakilo City 9,828 **g9**
Makawao 5,405 **C5**
Maunawili 4,847 **g10**
Mililani Town 29,359 **g9**
Naalehu 1,027 **D6**
Nanakuli 9,575 **B3**
Pacific Palisades 10,000
  g10
Pahala 1,520 **D6**
Pahoa 1,027 **D7**
Paia 2,091 **C5**
Papaikou 1,634 **D6**
Pearl City 30,993 **B4**
Pepeekeo 1,813 **D6**
Puhi 1,210 **B2**
Pukalani 5,879 **C5**
Sunset Beach 800 **f9**
Volcano 1,516 **D6**
Wahiawa 17,386 **B3**
Waialua 3,943 **B3**
Waianae 8,758 **B3**
Wailua 2,018 **A2**
Wailuku 10,688 **C5**
Waimanalo 3,508 **B4**
Waimea 5,972 **B2**
Waipahu 31,435 **B3**
Waipio Acres 5,307 **g9**
Whitmore Village 3,373
  f9

Statute Miles
Kilometers

Lambert Conformal Conic Projection
SCALE 1:2,000,000 1 Inch = 32 Statute Miles

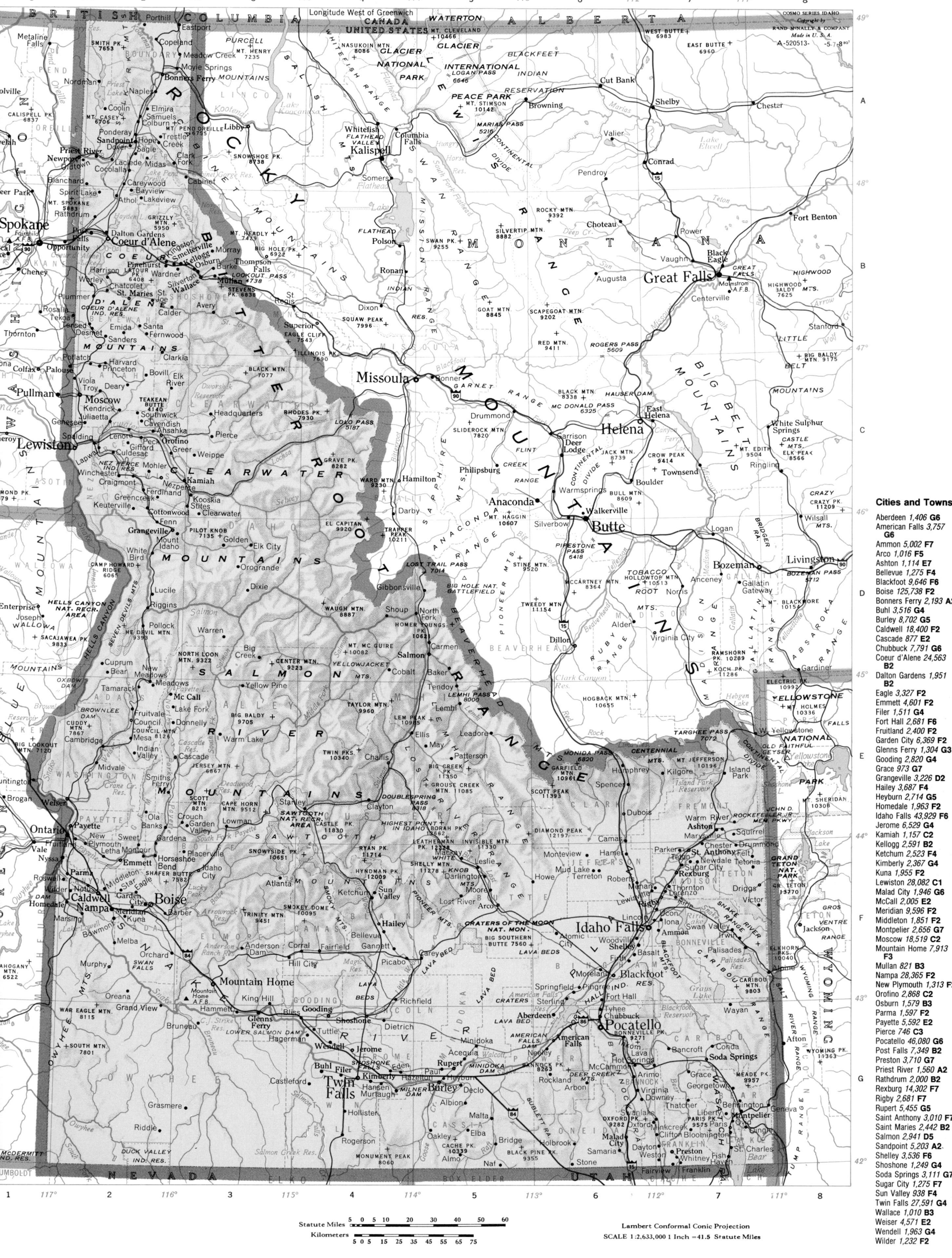

COSMO SERIES IDAHO
Copyright by
RAND McNALLY & COMPANY
Made in U. S. A.
A-520513-   -5-7-8-

Cities and Towns

Aberdeen 1,406 **G6**
American Falls 3,757 **G6**
Ammon 5,002 **F7**
Arco 1,016 **F5**
Ashton 1,114 **E7**
Bellevue 1,275 **F4**
Blackfoot 9,646 **F6**
Boise 125,738 **F2**
Bonners Ferry 2,193 **A2**
Buhl 3,516 **G4**
Burley 8,702 **G5**
Caldwell 18,400 **F2**
Cascade 877 **E2**
Chubbuck 7,791 **G6**
Coeur d'Alene 24,563 **B2**
Dalton Gardens 1,951 **B2**
Eagle 3,327 **F2**
Emmett 4,601 **F2**
Filer 1,511 **G4**
Fort Hall 2,681 **F6**
Fruitland 2,400 **F2**
Garden City 6,369 **F2**
Glenns Ferry 1,304 **G3**
Gooding 2,820 **G4**
Grace 973 **G7**
Grangeville 3,226 **D2**
Hailey 3,687 **F4**
Heyburn 2,714 **G5**
Homedale 1,963 **F2**
Idaho Falls 43,929 **F6**
Jerome 6,529 **G4**
Kamiah 1,157 **C2**
Kellogg 2,591 **B2**
Ketchum 2,523 **F4**
Kimberly 2,367 **G4**
Kuna 1,955 **F2**
Lewiston 28,082 **C1**
Malad City 1,946 **G6**
McCall 2,005 **E2**
Meridian 9,596 **F2**
Middleton 1,851 **F2**
Montpelier 2,656 **G7**
Moscow 18,519 **C2**
Mountain Home 7,913 **F3**
Mullan 821 **B3**
Nampa 28,365 **F2**
New Plymouth 1,313 **F2**
Orofino 2,868 **C2**
Osburn 1,579 **B3**
Parma 1,597 **F2**
Payette 5,592 **E2**
Pierce 746 **C3**
Pocatello 46,080 **G6**
Post Falls 7,349 **B2**
Preston 3,710 **G7**
Priest River 1,560 **A2**
Rathdrum 2,000 **B2**
Rexburg 14,302 **F7**
Rigby 2,681 **F7**
Rupert 5,455 **G5**
Saint Anthony 3,010 **F7**
Saint Maries 2,442 **B2**
Salmon 2,941 **D5**
Sandpoint 5,203 **A2**
Shelley 3,536 **F6**
Shoshone 1,249 **G4**
Soda Springs 3,111 **G7**
Sugar City 1,275 **F7**
Sun Valley 938 **F4**
Twin Falls 27,591 **G4**
Wallace 1,010 **B3**
Weiser 4,571 **E2**
Wendell 1,963 **G4**
Wilder 1,232 **F2**

Statute Miles 5 0 5 10 20 30 40 50 60
Kilometers 5 0 5 15 25 35 45 55 65 75

Lambert Conformal Conic Projection
SCALE 1:2,633,000 1 Inch = 41.5 Statute Miles

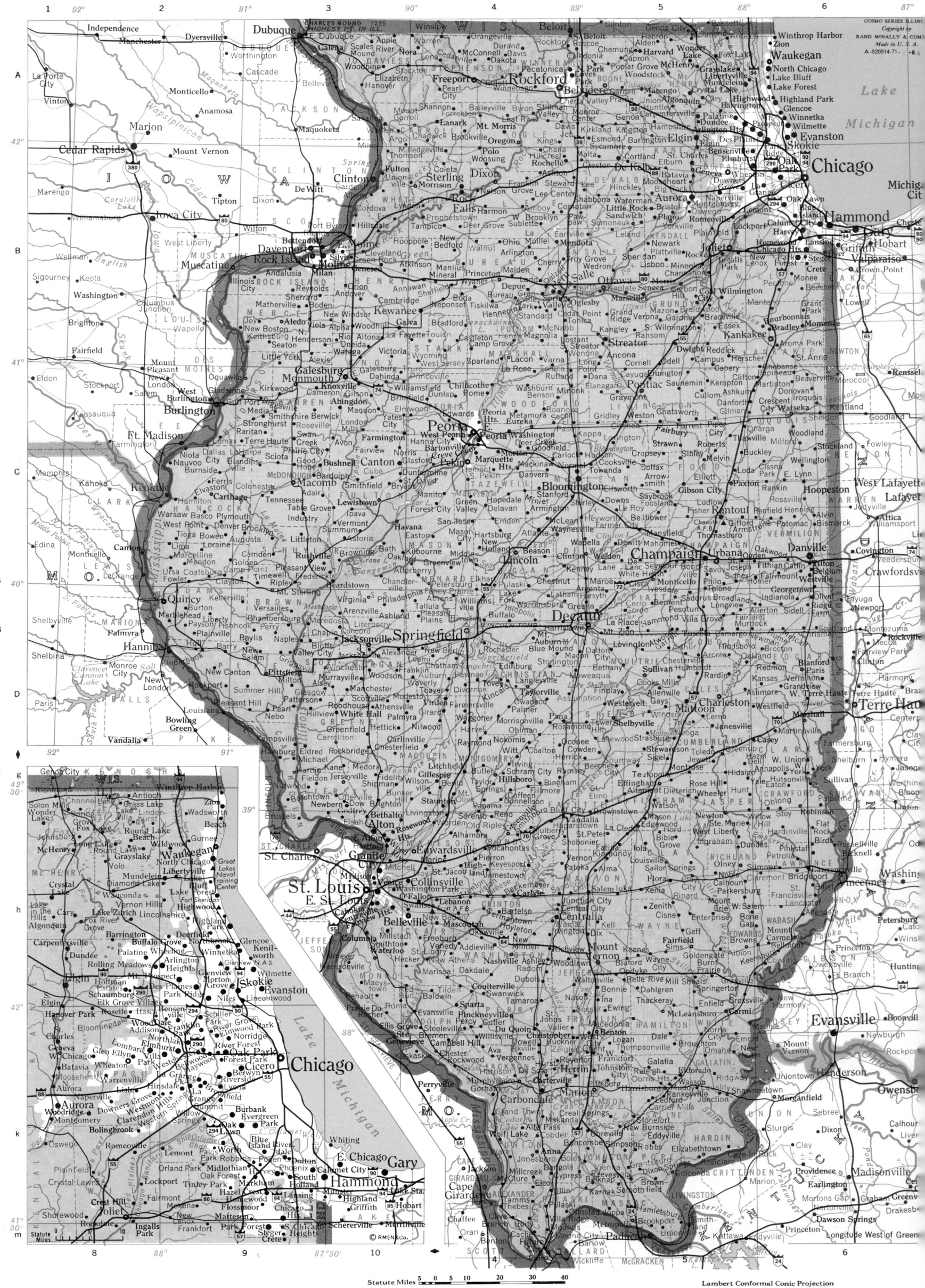

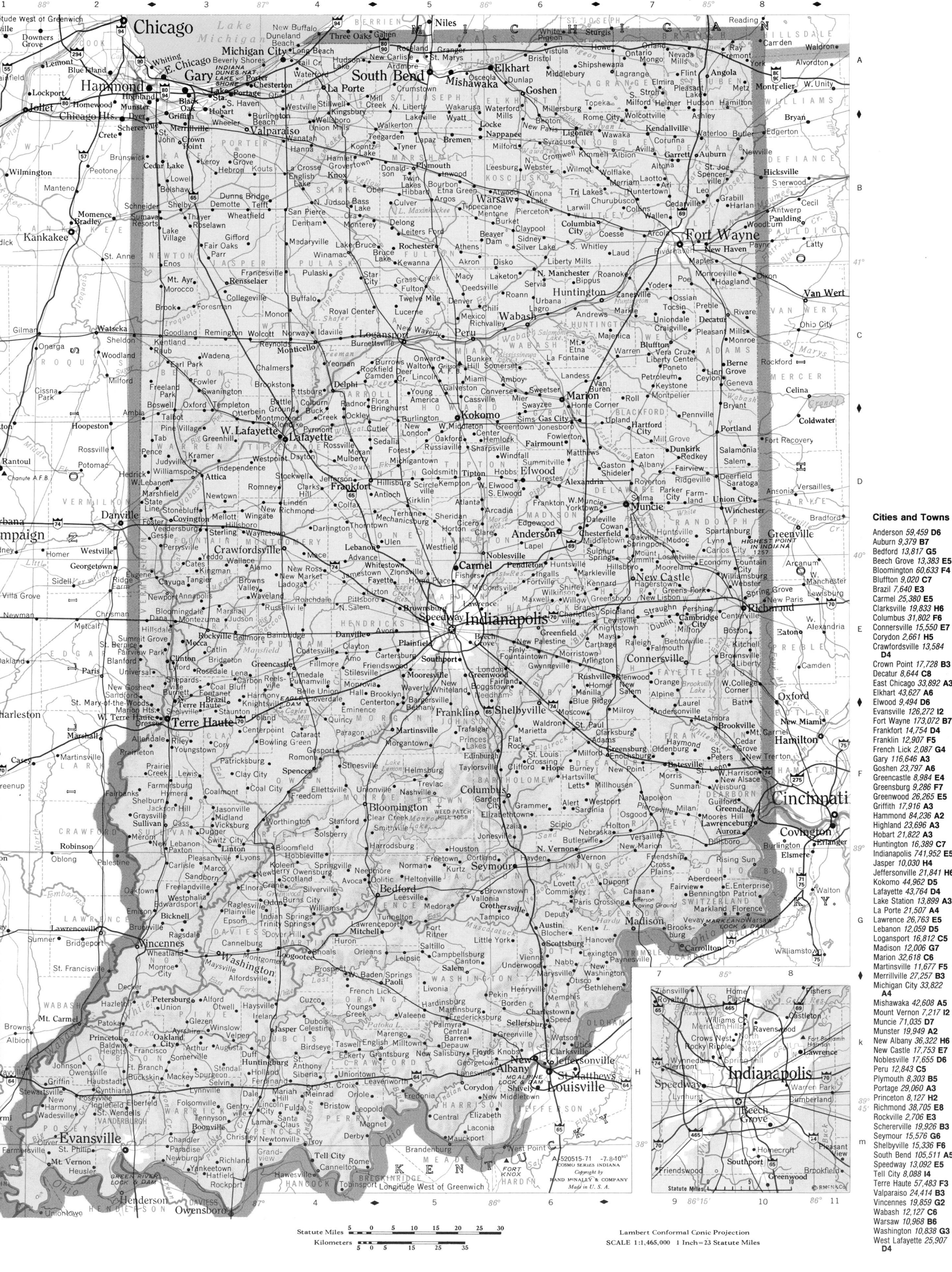

Cities and Towns

Anderson 59,459 **D6**
Auburn 9,379 **B7**
Bedford 13,817 **G5**
Beech Grove 13,383 **E5**
Bloomington 60,633 **F4**
Bluffton 9,020 **C7**
Brazil 7,640 **E3**
Carmel 25,380 **E5**
Clarksville 19,833 **H6**
Columbus 31,802 **F6**
Connersville 15,550 **E7**
Corydon 2,661 **H5**
Crawfordsville 13,584 **D4**
Crown Point 17,728 **B3**
Decatur 8,644 **C8**
East Chicago 33,892 **A3**
Elkhart 43,627 **A6**
Elwood 9,494 **D6**
Evansville 126,272 **I2**
Fort Wayne 173,072 **A7**
Frankfort 14,754 **D4**
Franklin 12,907 **F5**
French Lick 2,087 **G4**
Gary 116,646 **A3**
Goshen 23,797 **A6**
Greencastle 8,984 **E4**
Greensburg 9,286 **F7**
Greenwood 26,265 **E5**
Griffith 17,916 **A3**
Hammond 84,236 **A3**
Highland 23,696 **A3**
Hobart 21,822 **A3**
Huntington 16,389 **C7**
Indianapolis 741,952 **E5**
Jasper 10,030 **H4**
Jeffersonville 21,841 **H6**
Kokomo 44,962 **D5**
Lafayette 43,764 **D4**
Lake Station 13,899 **A3**
La Porte 21,507 **A4**
Lawrence 26,763 **E5**
Lebanon 12,059 **D5**
Logansport 16,812 **C5**
Madison 12,006 **G7**
Marion 32,618 **C6**
Martinsville 11,677 **F5**
Merrillville 27,257 **B3**
Michigan City 33,822 **A4**
Mishawaka 42,608 **A5**
Mount Vernon 7,217 **I2**
Muncie 71,035 **D7**
Munster 19,949 **A2**
New Albany 36,322 **H6**
New Castle 17,753 **E7**
Noblesville 17,655 **D6**
Peru 12,843 **C5**
Plymouth 8,303 **B5**
Portage 29,060 **A3**
Princeton 8,127 **H2**
Richmond 38,705 **E8**
Rockville 2,706 **E3**
Schererville 19,926 **A3**
Seymour 15,576 **G6**
Shelbyville 15,336 **F6**
South Bend 105,511 **A5**
Speedway 13,092 **E5**
Tell City 8,088 **I4**
Terre Haute 57,483 **F3**
Valparaiso 24,414 **B3**
Vincennes 19,859 **G2**
Wabash 12,127 **C6**
Warsaw 10,968 **B6**
Washington 10,838 **G3**
West Lafayette 25,907 **D4**

IOWA

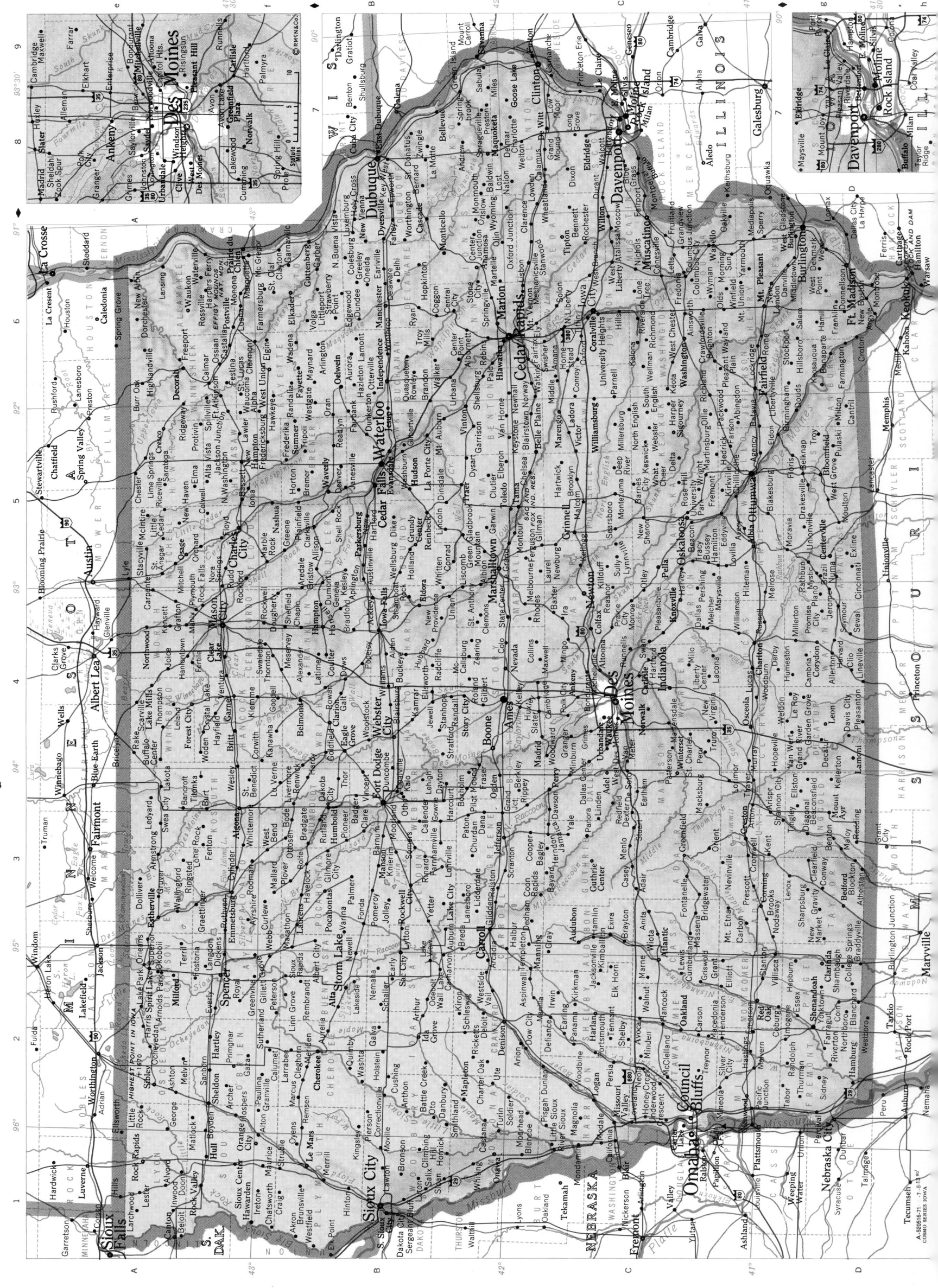

Cities and Towns

Algona 6,015 **A3**
Amana 540 **C6**
Ames 47,198 **B4**
Anamosa 5,100 **B6**
Ankeny 18,482 **C4**
Atlantic 7,432 **C2**
Bettendorf 28,132 **C7**
Boone 12,392 **B4**
Burlington 27,208 **D6**
Carroll 9,579 **B3**
Cedar Falls 34,298 **B5**
Cedar Rapids 108,751 **C6**
Centerville 5,936 **D5**
Chariton 4,616 **C4**
Charles City 7,878 **A5**
Cherokee 6,026 **B2**
Clarinda 5,104 **D2**
Clinton 29,201 **C7**
Council Bluffs 54,315 **C2**
Creston 7,911 **C3**
Davenport 95,333 **C7**
Decorah 8,063 **A6**
Denison 6,604 **B2**
Des Moines 193,187 **C4**
De Witt 4,514 **C7**
Dubuque 57,546 **B7**
Emmetsburg 3,940 **A3**
Estherville 6,720 **A3**
Fairfield 9,768 **C6**
Fort Dodge 25,894 **B3**
Fort Madison 11,618 **D6**
Glenwood 4,571 **C2**
Grinnell 8,902 **C5**
Guttenberg 2,257 **B6**
Hampton 4,133 **B4**
Harlan 5,148 **C2**
Humboldt 4,438 **B3**
Independence 5,972 **B6**
Indianola 11,340 **C4**
Iowa City 59,738 **C6**
Iowa Falls 5,424 **B4**
Jefferson 4,292 **B3**
Keokuk 12,451 **D6**
Knoxville 8,232 **C4**
Le Mars 8,454 **B1**
Manchester 5,137 **B6**
Maquoketa 6,111 **B7**
Marion 20,403 **B6**
Marshalltown 25,178 **B5**
Mason City 29,040 **A4**
Mount Pleasant 8,027 **D6**
Muscatine 22,881 **C6**
Newton 14,789 **C4**
Oelwein 6,493 **B6**
Orange City 4,940 **B1**
Oskaloosa 10,632 **C5**
Ottumwa 24,488 **C5**
Pella 9,270 **C5**
Perry 6,652 **C3**
Red Oak 6,264 **D2**
Sheldon 4,937 **A2**
Shenandoah 5,572 **D2**
Sioux Center 5,074 **A1**
Sioux City 80,505 **B1**
Spencer 11,066 **A2**
Storm Lake 8,769 **B2**
Urbandale 23,500 **C4**
Vinton 5,103 **B5**
Washington 7,074 **C6**
Waterloo 66,467 **B5**
Waverly 8,539 **B5**
Webster City 7,894 **B4**
West Branch 1,908 **C6**
West Des Moines 31,702 **C4**

Statute Miles 5 0 5 10 20 30 40
Kilometers 5 0 15 25 35 45 55

Lambert Conformal Conic Projection
SCALE 1:1,834,000   1 Inch = 29 Statute Miles

242

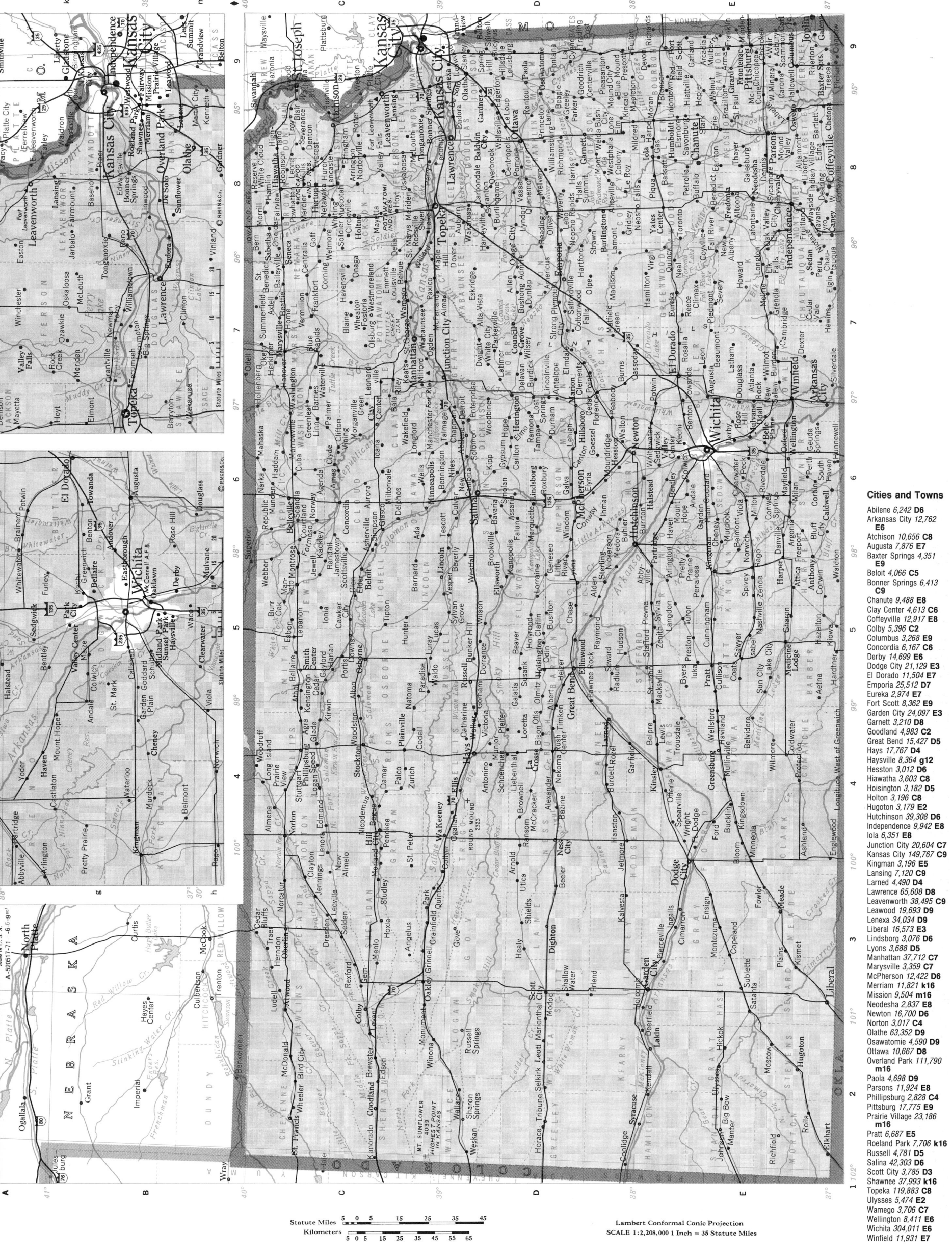

Lambert Conformal Conic Projection
SCALE 1:2,208,000 1 Inch = 35 Statute Miles

Statute Miles
Kilometers

Cities and Towns

Abilene 6,242 **D6**
Arkansas City 12,762 **E6**
Atchison 10,656 **C8**
Augusta 7,876 **E7**
Baxter Springs 4,351 **E9**
Beloit 4,066 **C5**
Bonner Springs 6,413 **C9**
Chanute 9,488 **E8**
Clay Center 4,613 **C6**
Coffeyville 12,917 **E8**
Colby 5,396 **C2**
Concordia 6,167 **C6**
Derby 14,699 **E6**
Dodge City 21,129 **E3**
El Dorado 11,504 **E7**
Emporia 25,512 **D7**
Eureka 2,974 **E7**
Fort Scott 8,362 **E9**
Garden City 24,097 **E3**
Garnett 3,210 **D8**
Goodland 4,983 **C2**
Great Bend 15,427 **D5**
Hays 17,767 **D4**
Haysville 8,364 **g12**
Hesston 3,012 **D6**
Hiawatha 3,603 **C8**
Hoisington 3,182 **D5**
Holton 3,196 **C8**
Hugoton 3,179 **E2**
Hutchinson 39,308 **D6**
Independence 9,942 **E8**
Iola 6,351 **E8**
Junction City 20,604 **C7**
Kansas City 149,767 **C9**
Kingman 3,196 **E5**
Lansing 7,120 **C9**
Larned 4,490 **D4**
Lawrence 65,608 **D8**
Leavenworth 38,495 **C9**
Leawood 19,693 **D9**
Lenexa 34,034 **D9**
Liberal 16,573 **E3**
Lindsborg 3,076 **D6**
Lyons 3,688 **D5**
Manhattan 37,712 **C7**
Marysville 3,359 **C7**
McPherson 12,422 **D6**
Merriam 11,821 **k16**
Mission 9,504 **m16**
Neodesha 2,837 **E8**
Newton 16,700 **D6**
Norton 3,017 **C4**
Olathe 63,352 **D9**
Osawatomie 4,590 **D9**
Ottawa 10,667 **D8**
Overland Park 111,790 **m16**
Paola 4,698 **D9**
Parsons 11,924 **E8**
Phillipsburg 2,828 **C4**
Pittsburg 17,775 **E9**
Prairie Village 23,186 **m16**
Pratt 6,687 **E5**
Roeland Park 7,706 **k16**
Russell 4,781 **D5**
Salina 42,303 **D6**
Scott City 3,785 **D3**
Shawnee 37,993 **k16**
Topeka 119,883 **C8**
Ulysses 5,474 **E2**
Wamego 3,706 **C7**
Wellington 8,411 **E6**
Wichita 304,011 **E6**
Winfield 11,931 **E7**

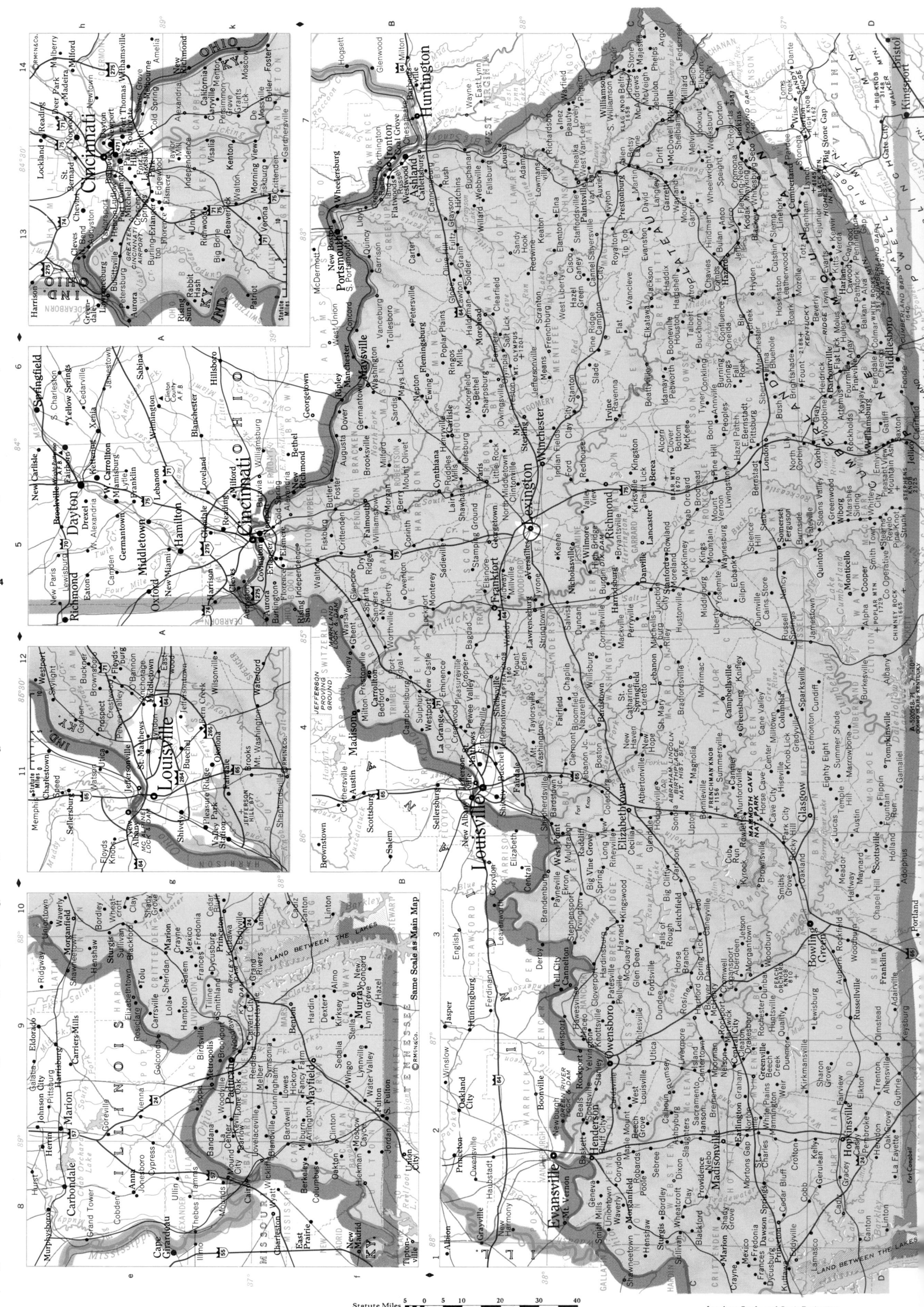

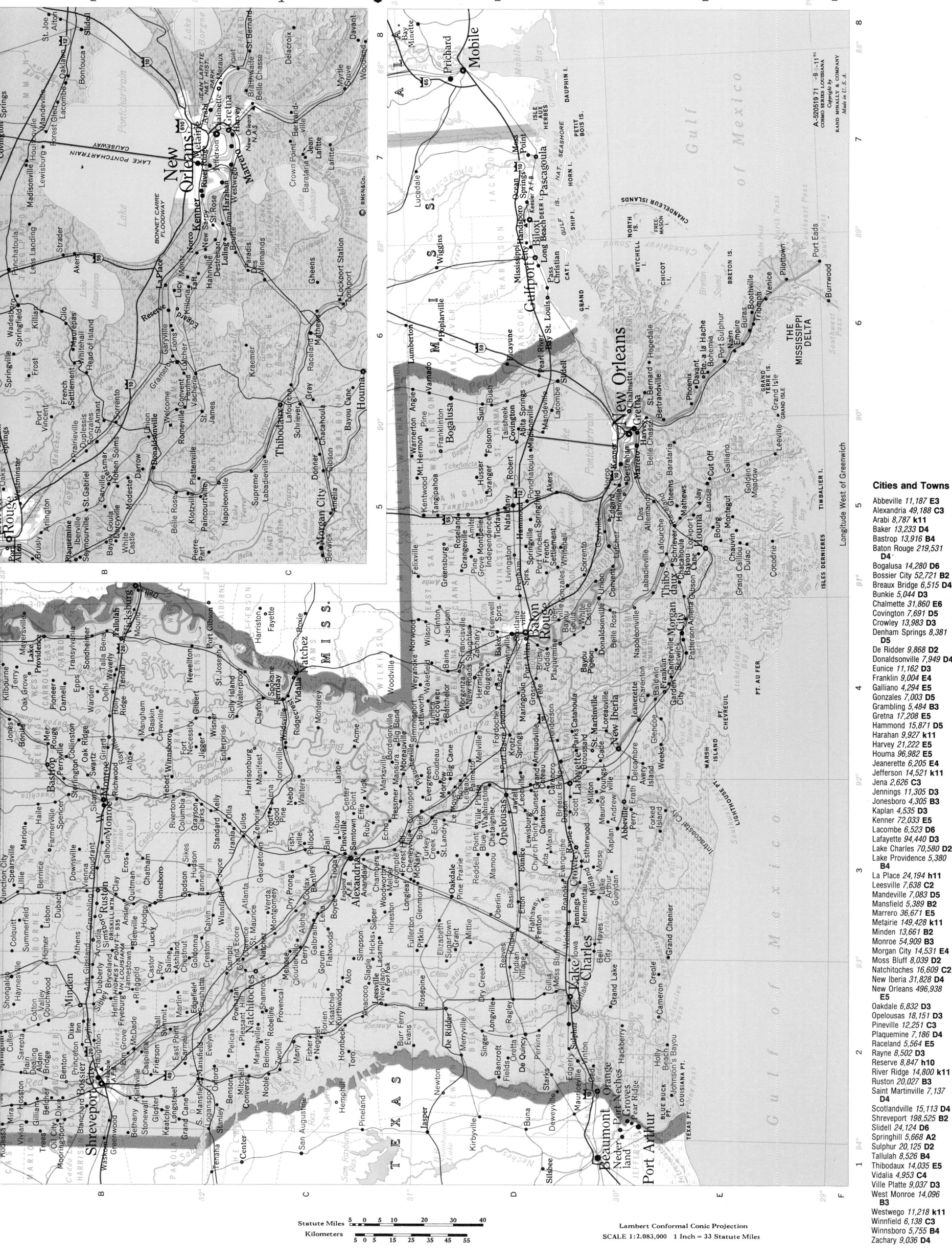

A-520519 71 —9—11²⁰
COSMO SERIES LOUISIANA
Copyright by
RAND M°NALLY & COMPANY
Made in U.S.A.

Lambert Conformal Conic Projection
SCALE 1:2,083,000   1 Inch = 33 Statute Miles

Statute Miles   5 0 5 10   20   30   40
Kilometers   5 0 5 15 25 35 45 55

Cities and Towns

Abbeville *11,187* **E3**
Alexandria *49,188* **C3**
Arabi *8,787* **k11**
Baker *13,233* **D4**
Bastrop *13,916* **B4**
Baton Rouge *219,531* **D4**
Bogalusa *14,280* **D6**
Bossier City *52,721* **B2**
Breaux Bridge *6,515* **D4**
Bunkie *5,044* **D3**
Chalmette *31,860* **E6**
Covington *7,691* **D5**
Crowley *13,983* **D3**
Denham Springs *8,381* **D5**
De Ridder *9,868* **D2**
Donaldsonville *7,949* **D4**
Eunice *11,162* **D3**
Franklin *9,004* **E4**
Galliano *4,294* **E5**
Gonzales *7,003* **D5**
Grambling *5,484* **B3**
Gretna *17,208* **E5**
Hammond *15,871* **D5**
Harahan *9,927* **k11**
Harvey *21,222* **E5**
Houma *96,982* **E5**
Jeanerette *6,205* **E4**
Jefferson *14,521* **k11**
Jena *2,626* **C3**
Jennings *11,305* **D3**
Jonesboro *4,305* **B3**
Kaplan *4,535* **D3**
Kenner *72,033* **E5**
Lacombe *6,523* **D6**
Lafayette *94,440* **D3**
Lake Charles *70,580* **D2**
Lake Providence *5,380*
  B4
La Place *24,194* **h11**
Leesville *7,638* **C2**
Mandeville *7,083* **D5**
Mansfield *5,389* **B2**
Marrero *36,671* **E5**
Metairie *149,428* **k11**
Minden *13,661* **B2**
Monroe *54,909* **B3**
Morgan City *14,531* **E4**
Moss Bluff *8,039* **D2**
Natchitoches *16,609* **C2**
New Iberia *31,828* **D4**
New Orleans *496,938*
  E5
Oakdale *6,832* **D3**
Opelousas *18,151* **D3**
Pineville *12,251* **C3**
Plaquemine *7,186* **D4**
Raceland *5,564* **E5**
Rayne *8,502* **D3**
Reserve *8,847* **h10**
River Ridge *14,800* **k11**
Ruston *20,027* **B3**
Saint Martinville *7,137*
  D4
Scotlandville *15,113* **D4**
Shreveport *198,525* **B2**
Slidell *24,124* **D6**
Springhill *5,668* **A2**
Sulphur *20,125* **D2**
Tallulah *8,526* **B4**
Thibodaux *14,035* **E5**
Vidalia *4,953* **C4**
Ville Platte *9,037* **D3**
West Monroe *14,096*
  B3
Westwego *11,218* **k11**
Winnfield *6,138* **C3**
Winnsboro *5,755* **B4**
Zachary *9,036* **D4**

MAINE

Cities and Towns*

Auburn 24,309 **D2**
Augusta 21,325 **D3**
Bangor 33,181 **D4**
Bar Harbor 2,768 **D4**
Bath 9,799 **E3**
Belfast 6,355 **D3**
Biddeford 20,710 **E2**
Boothbay Harbor 1,267 **E3**
Brewer 9,021 **D4**
Brunswick 14,683 **E3**
Bucksport 2,989 **D4**
Calais 3,963 **C5**
Camden 4,022 **D3**
Cape Elizabeth 8,854 **E2**
Caribou 9,415 **B5**
Cumberland Center 1,890 **g7**
Dexter 2,650 **C3**
Dover-Foxcroft 3,077 **C3**
East Millinocket 2,075 **C4**
Eastport 1,965 **D6**
Eliot 150 **E2**
Ellsworth 5,975 **D4**
Fairfield 2,794 **D3**
Falmouth 7,610 **E2**
Farmingdale 2,070 **D3**
Farmington 4,197 **D2**
Fort Fairfield 1,729 **B5**
Fort Kent 2,123 **A4**
Freeport 1,829 **E2**
Gardiner 6,746 **D3**
Gorham 3,618 **E2**
Hallowell 2,534 **D3**
Hampden 3,895 **D4**
Houlton 5,627 **B5**
Kennebunk 4,206 **E2**
Kittery 5,151 **E2**
Lewiston 39,757 **D2**
Lincoln 3,399 **C4**
Lisbon Falls 4,674 **E2**
Livermore Falls 1,935 **D2**
Madawaska 3,653 **A4**
Madison 2,956 **D3**
Mechanic Falls 2,388 **E2**
Mexico 2,302 **D2**
Millinocket 6,922 **C4**
Milo 2,129 **C4**
North Windham 4,077 **E2**
Norway 3,023 **D2**
Oakland 3,510 **D3**
Old Orchard Beach 7,789 **E2**
Old Town 8,317 **D4**
Orono 9,789 **D4**
Pittsfield 3,222 **D3**
Portland 64,358 **E2**
Presque Isle 10,550 **B5**
Rockland 7,972 **D3**
Rumford 5,419 **D2**
Saco 15,181 **E2**
Sanford 10,296 **E2**
Scarborough 2,586 **E2**
Skowhegan 6,990 **D3**
South Paris 2,320 **D2**
South Portland 23,163 **E2**
Thomaston 2,445 **D3**
Topsham 6,147 **E3**
Van Buren 2,759 **A5**
Waterville 17,173 **D3**
Westbrook 16,121 **E2**
Wilton 2,453 **D2**
Winslow 5,436 **D3**
Winthrop 2,819 **D3**
Yarmouth 3,338 **E2**
York 3,130 **E2**
York Harbor 2,555 **E2**

*Populations are for localities, not incorporated towns.

246

A-520520 71- -6-7-9
COSMO SERIES MAINE
Copyright by
RAND McNALLY & COMPANY
Made in U.S.A.

Longitude West of Greenwich

Statute Miles
Kilometers

Lambert Conformal Conic Projection
SCALE 1:1,581,000 1 Inch = 25 Statute Miles

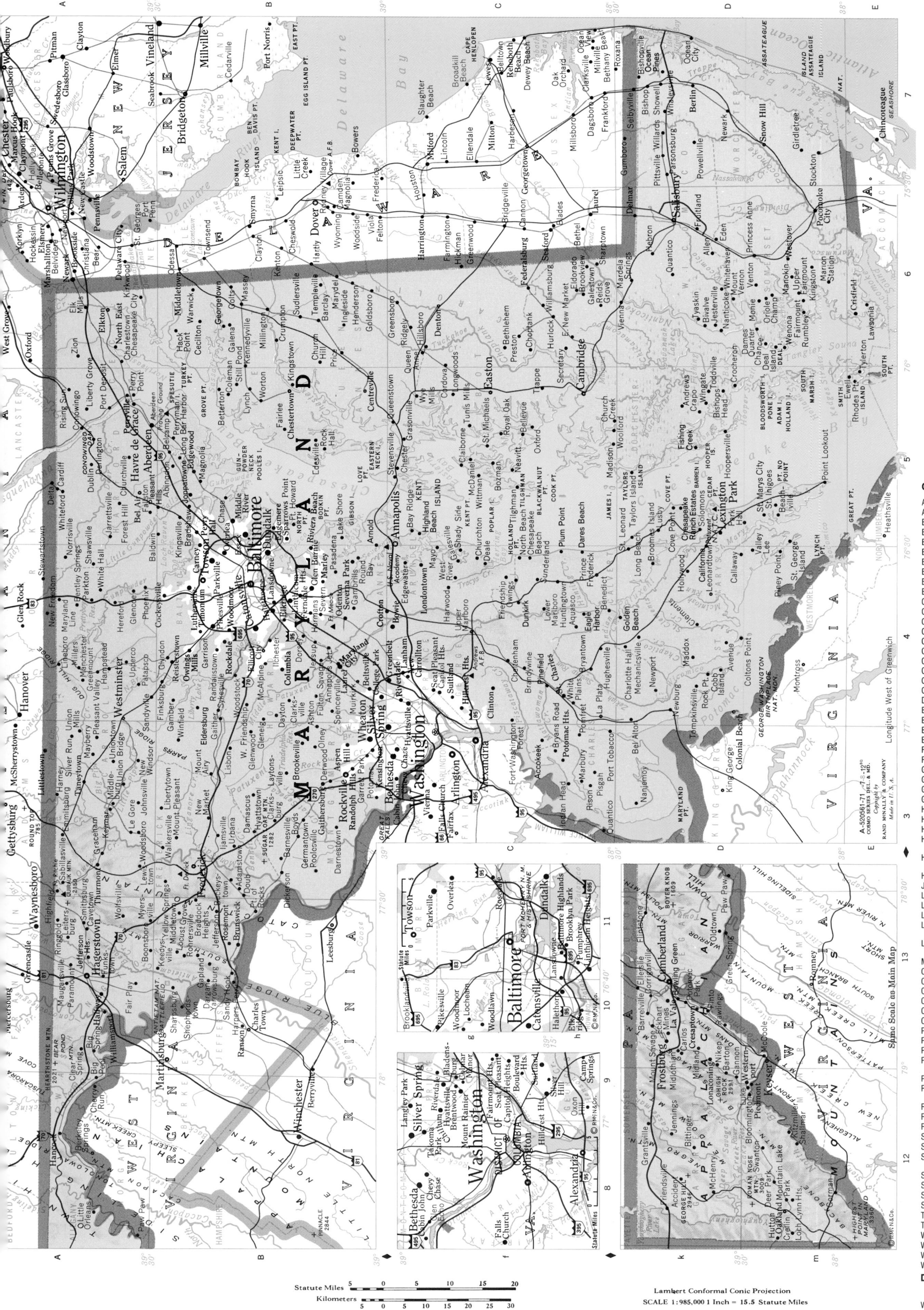

Statute Miles
Kilometers

Lambert Conformal Conic Projection
SCALE 1:985,000 1 Inch = 15.5 Statute Miles

Cities and Towns

Aberdeen 13,087 **A5**
Annapolis 33,187 **C5**
Baltimore 736,014 **B4**
Bel Air 8,860 **A5**
Beltsville 14,476 **B4**
Bethesda 62,936 **C3**
Bladensburg 8,064 **f9**
Bowie 37,589 **B4**
Brentwood 3,005 **f9**
Brunswick 5,117 **B2**
Cambridge 11,514 **C5**
Catonsville 35,233 **B4**
Chevy Chase 8,559 **C3**
Chillum 31,309 **f9**
Clinton 19,987 **C4**
Cockeysville 18,668 **B4**
College Park 21,927 **C4**
Columbia 75,883 **B4**
Crofton 12,781 **B4**
Cumberland 23,706 **k13**
Dundalk 65,800 **B4**
Easton 9,372 **C5**
Edgewood 23,903 **B5**
Elkton 9,073 **A6**
Essex 40,872 **B5**
Frederick 40,148 **B3**
Frostburg 8,075 **k13**
Gaithersburg 39,542 **B3**
Germantown 41,145 **B3**
Glen Burnie 37,305 **B4**
Greenbelt 21,096 **C4**
Hagerstown 35,445 **A2**
Halethorpe 19,750 **B4**
Halfway 8,873 **A2**
Havre de Grace 8,952 **A5**
Hillcrest Heights 17,136 **C4**
Hyattsville 13,864 **C4**
Joppatowne 11,084 **B5**
Langley Park 17,474 **f9**
Lansdowne 9,430 **B4**
Laurel 19,438 **B4**
Lexington Park 9,943 **D5**
Lutherville-Timonium 16,442 **B4**
Middle River 24,616 **B5**
Oakland 2,078 **m12**
Ocean City 5,146 **D7**
Olney 23,019 **B3**
Overlea 12,137 **B4**
Owings Mills 9,474 **B4**
Oxon Hill 3,730 **f9**
Parkville 31,617 **B4**
Perry Hall 22,723 **B5**
Pikesville 24,815 **B4**
Pocomoke City 3,922 **D6**
Potomac 45,634 **B3**
Randallstown 26,277 **B4**
Reisterstown 19,314 **B4**
Rockville 44,835 **B3**
Rosedale 18,703 **g11**
Salisbury 20,592 **D6**
Severn 24,499 **B4**
Severna Park 25,879 **B4**
Sharpsburg 659 **B2**
Silver Spring 76,046 **C3**
Snow Hill 2,217 **D7**
Suitland 35,400 **C4**
Takoma Park 16,700 **f8**
Towson 49,445 **B4**
Westminster 13,068 **A4**
Wheaton 58,300 **B3**
White Plains 3,560 **C4**
Woodlawn 5,329 **g10**

District of Columbia

Washington 606,900 **C3**

MASSACHUSETTS

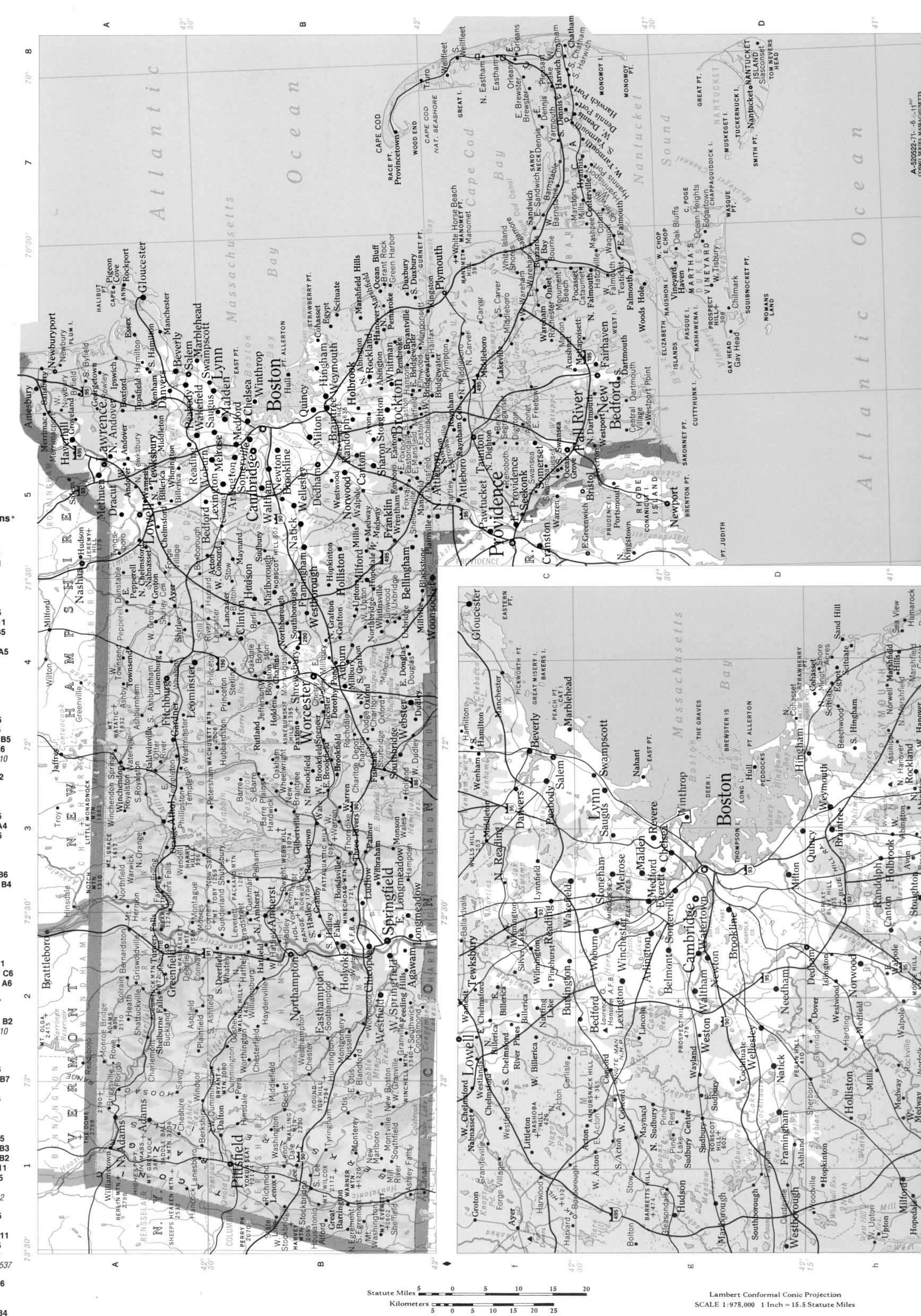

Cities and Towns*

Amherst 17,824 **B2**
Arlington 44,630 **B5**
Attleboro 38,383 **C5**
Belmont 24,720 **g11**
Beverly 38,195 **A6**
Boston 574,283 **B5**
Braintree 33,836 **B5**
Brockton 92,788 **B5**
Brookline 54,718 **B5**
Burlington 23,302 **f11**
Cambridge 95,802 **B5**
Chatham 1,922 **C8**
Chelmsford 32,383 **A5**
Chelsea 28,710 **B5**
Chicopee 56,632 **B2**
Concord 4,680 **B5**
Danvers 24,174 **A6**
Dedham 23,782 **B5**
Dracut 25,594 **A5**
Fall River 92,703 **C5**
Fitchburg 41,194 **A4**
Framingham 64,994 **B5**
Gloucester 28,716 **A6**
Great Barrington 2,810
  B1
Greenfield 14,016 **A2**
Haverhill 51,418 **A5**
Holyoke 43,704 **B2**
Hyannis 14,120 **C7**
Lawrence 70,207 **A5**
Leominster 38,145 **A4**
Lexington 28,974 **B5**
Lowell 103,439 **A5**
Lynn 81,245 **B6**
Malden 53,884 **B5**
Marblehead 19,971 **B6**
Marlborough 31,813 **B4**
Medford 57,407 **B5**
Melrose 28,150 **B5**
Methuen 39,990 **A5**
Milford 23,339 **B4**
Milton 25,725 **B5**
Nantucket 3,069 **D7**
Natick 30,100 **B5**
Needham 27,557 **g11**
New Bedford 99,922 **C6**
Newburyport 16,317 **A6**
Newton 82,585 **B5**
North Adams 16,797
  A1
Northampton 29,289 **B2**
North Attleboro 30,510
  C5
Peabody 47,039 **A6**
Pittsfield 48,622 **B1**
Plymouth 16,178 **C6**
Provincetown 3,374 **B7**
Quincy 84,985 **B5**
Randolph 30,093 **B5**
Reading 22,539 **A5**
Revere 42,786 **g11**
Salem 38,091 **A6**
Somerville 76,210 **B5**
Southbridge 13,631 **B3**
Springfield 156,983 **B2**
Stoneham 22,203 **g11**
Stoughton 26,777 **B5**
Taunton 49,832 **C5**
Vineyard Haven 1,762
  D6
Wakefield 24,825 **B5**
Waltham 57,878 **B5**
Watertown 33,284 **g11**
Wellesley 26,615 **B5**
Westfield 38,372 **B2**
West Springfield 27,537
  B2
Weymouth 54,063 **B6**
Winthrop 18,127 **B6**
Woburn 35,943 **B5**
Worcester 169,759 **B4**

*Populations are for localities, not incorporated towns.

Statute Miles
Kilometers

Lambert Conformal Conic Projection
SCALE 1:978,000   1 Inch = 15.5 Statute Miles

248

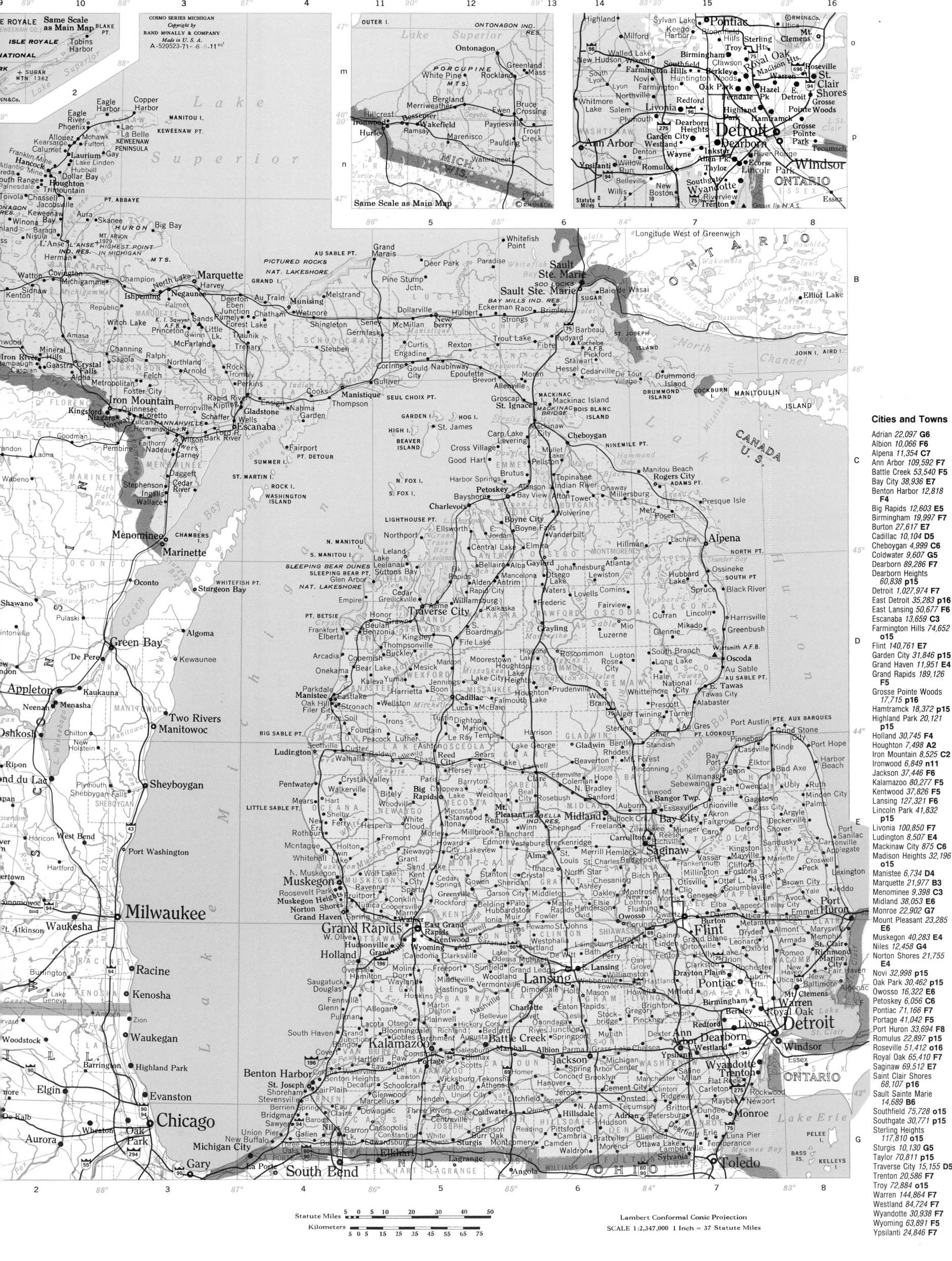

MINNESOTA

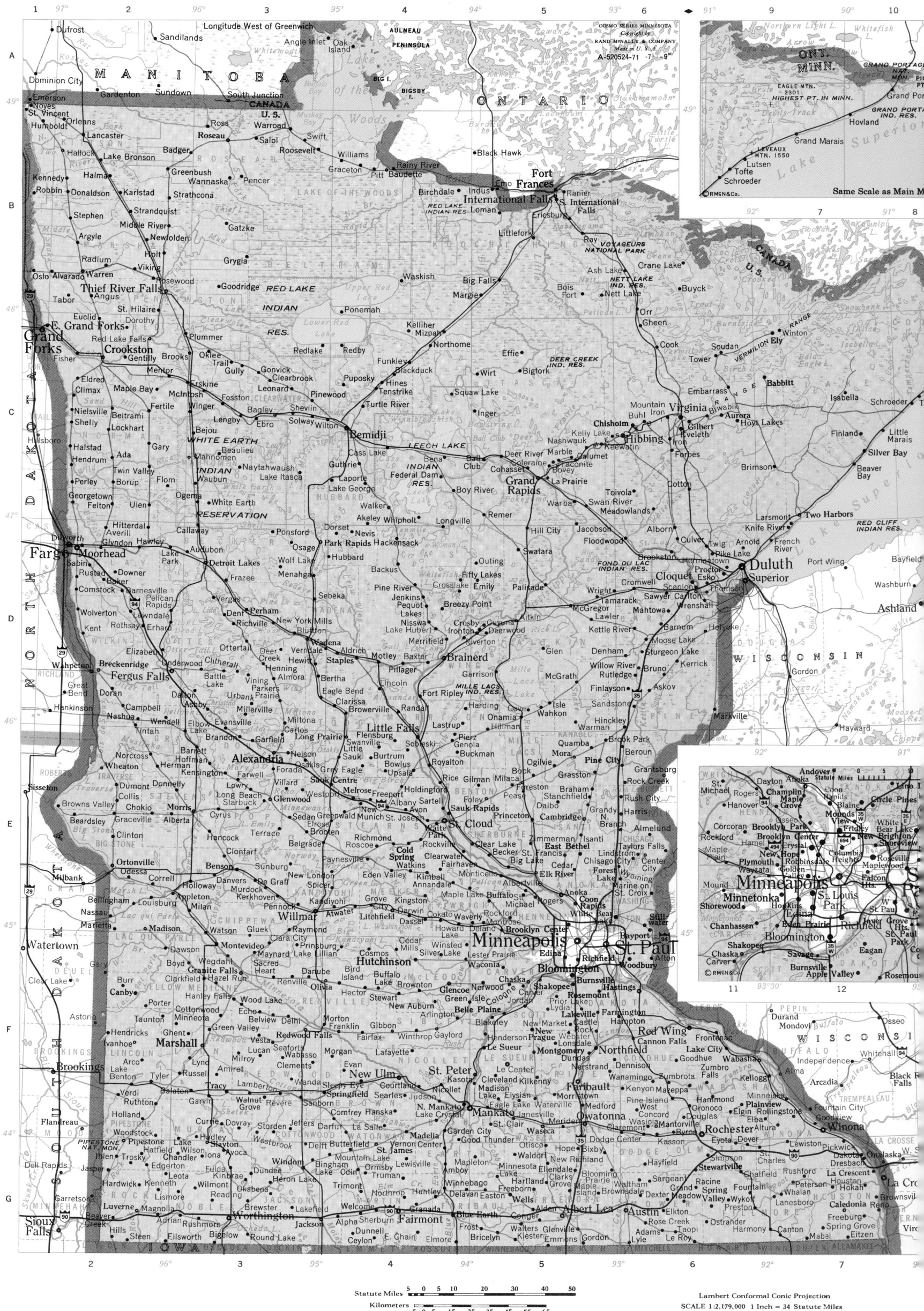

Statute Miles
Kilometers

Lambert Conformal Conic Projection
SCALE 1:2,179,000 1 Inch = 34 Statute Miles

250

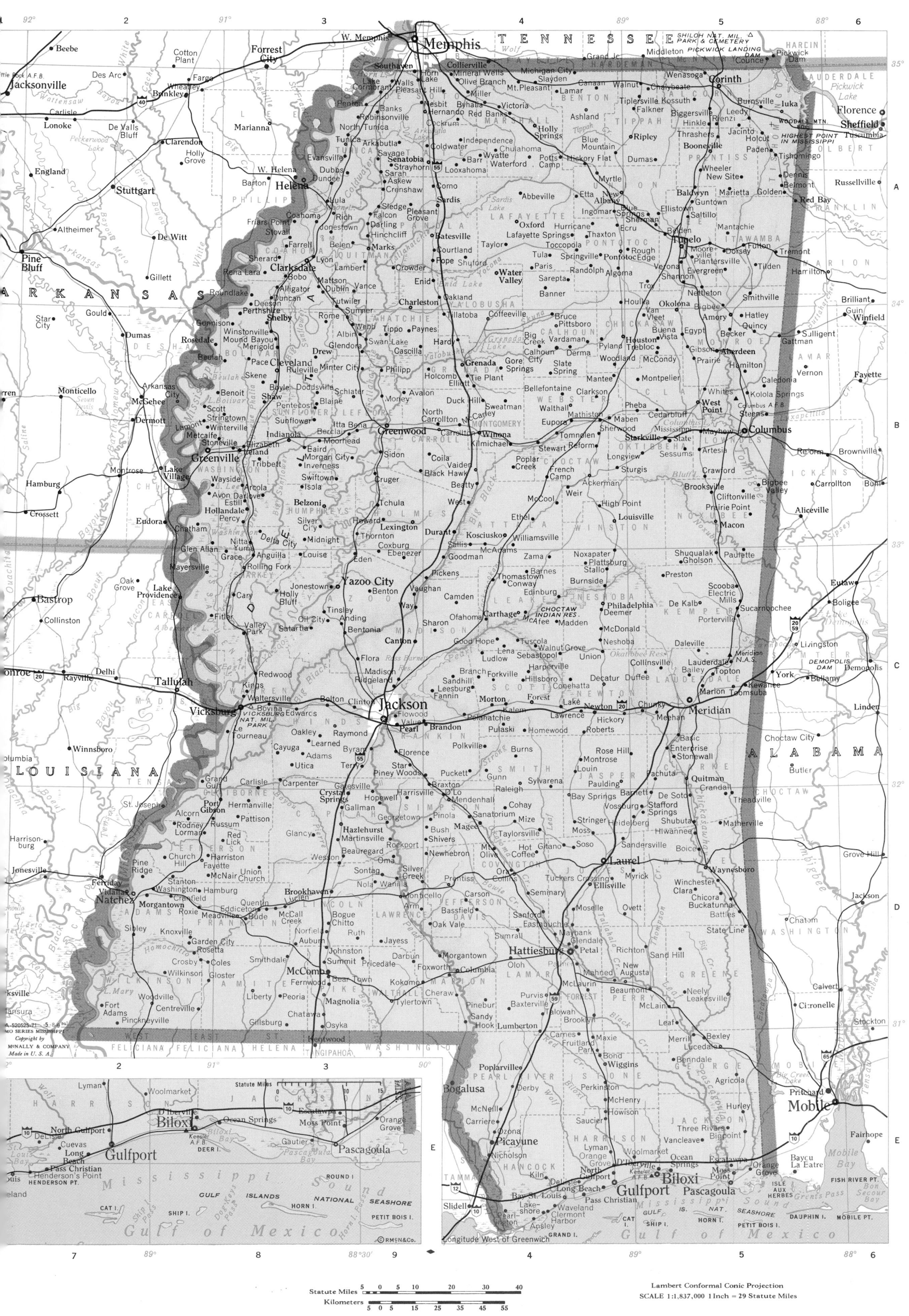

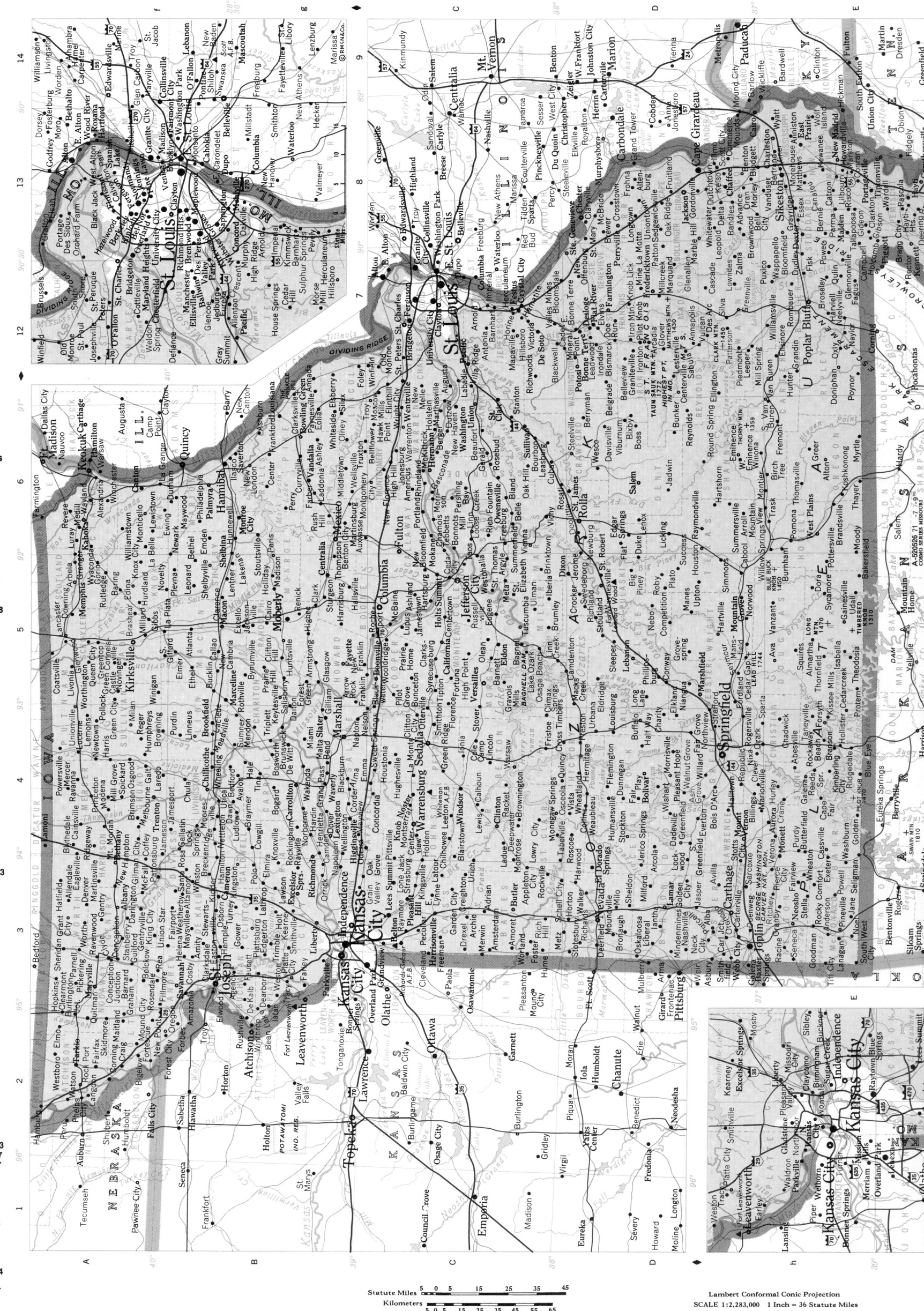

Cities and Towns

Arnold 18,828 **C7**
Aurora 6,459 **E4**
Ballwin 21,816 **f12**
Belton 18,150 **C3**
Berkeley 12,450 **f13**
Blue Springs 40,153
h11
Bolivar 6,845 **D4**
Boonville 7,095 **C5**
Branson 3,706 **E4**
Bridgeton 17,779 **C7**
Cape Girardeau 34,438
D8
Carthage 10,747 **D3**
Caruthersville 7,389 **E8**
Charleston 5,085 **E8**
Chillicothe 8,804 **B4**
Clayton 13,874 **f13**
Clinton 8,703 **C4**
Columbia 69,101 **C5**
Concord 19,859 **g13**
De Soto 5,993 **C7**
Dexter 7,559 **E8**
Eureka 4,683 **f12**
Excelsior Springs
10,354 **B3**
Farmington 11,598 **D7**
Ferguson 22,286 **C7**
Festus 8,105 **C7**
Florissant 51,206 **f13**
Fulton 10,033 **C6**
Gladstone 26,243 **h10**
Grandview 24,967 **C3**
Hannibal 18,004 **B6**
Independence 112,301
B3
Jackson 9,256 **D8**
Jefferson City 35,481
C5
Jennings 15,905 **f13**
Joplin 40,961 **D3**
Kansas City 435,146 **B3**
Kennett 10,941 **E7**
Kirksville 17,152 **A5**
Kirkwood 27,291 **f13**
Lebanon 9,983 **D5**
Lees Summit 46,418
C3
Liberty 20,459 **B3**
Malden 5,123 **E8**
Marshall 12,711 **B4**
Maryville 10,663 **A3**
Mehlville 27,557 **f13**
Mexico 11,290 **B6**
Moberly 12,839 **B5**
Monett 6,529 **E4**
Neosho 9,254 **E3**
Nevada 8,597 **D3**
Overland 17,987 **f13**
Perryville 6,933 **D8**
Poplar Bluff 16,996 **E7**
Raytown 30,601 **h11**
Richmond Heights
10,448 **f13**
Rolla 14,090 **D6**
Saint Charles 54,555
C7
Sainte Genevieve 4,411
D7
Saint Joseph 71,852 **B3**
Saint Louis 396,685 **C7**
Saint Peters 45,779 **C7**
Sappington 10,917 **f13**
Sedalia 19,800 **C4**
Sikeston 17,641 **E8**
Spanish Lake 20,322
f13
Springfield 140,494 **D4**
Sullivan 5,661 **C6**
Trenton 6,129 **A4**
University City 40,087
C7
Warrensburg 15,244 **C4**
Washington 10,704 **C6**
Webster Groves 22,987
f13
West Plains 8,913 **E6**

Statute Miles 5 0 5 15 25 35 45
Kilometers 5 0 5 15 25 35 45 55 65

Lambert Conformal Conic Projection
SCALE 1:2,283,000   1 Inch = 36 Statute Miles

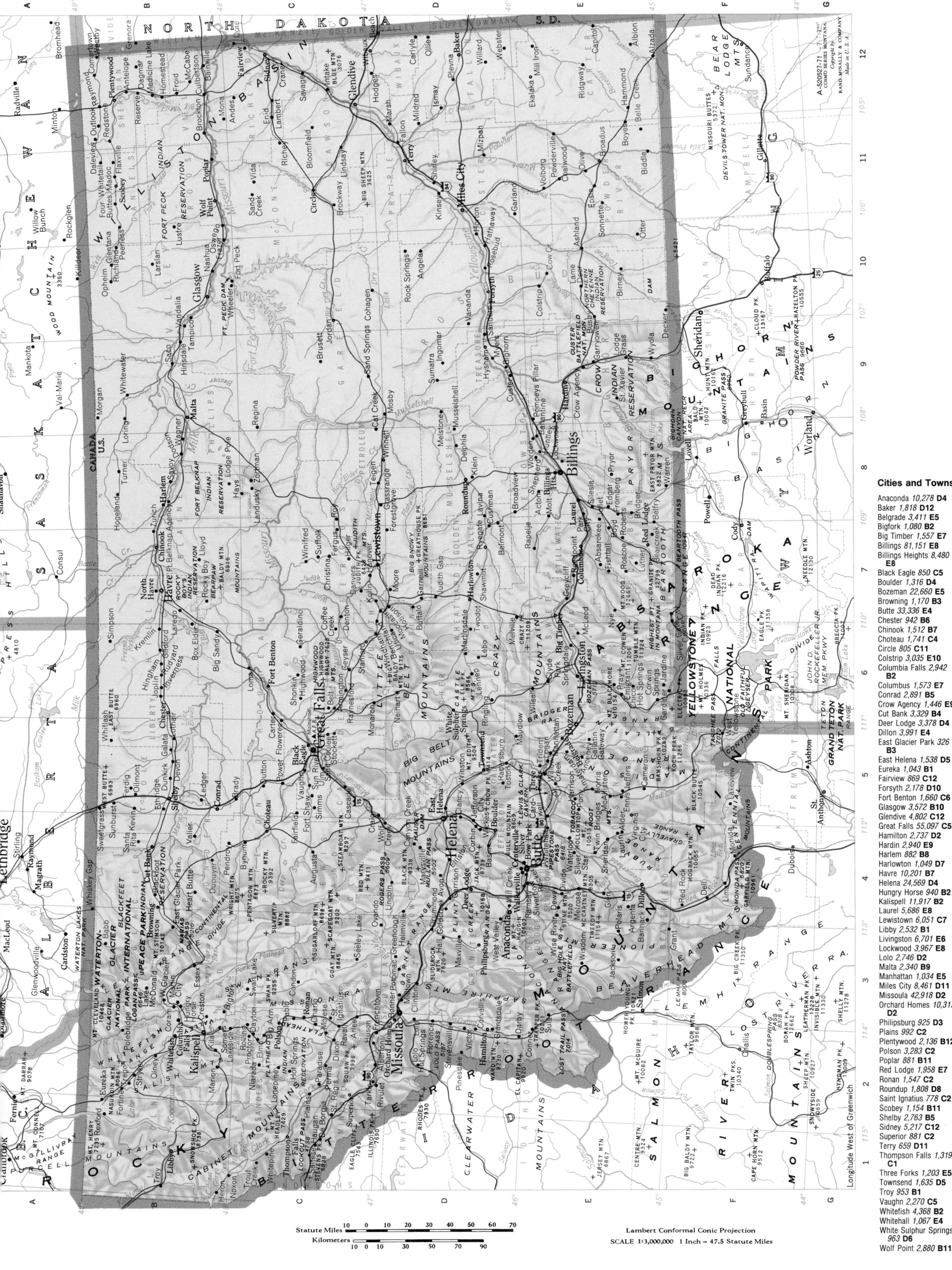

Statute Miles
Kilometers

Lambert Conformal Conic Projection
SCALE 1:3,000,000   1 Inch = 47.5 Statute Miles

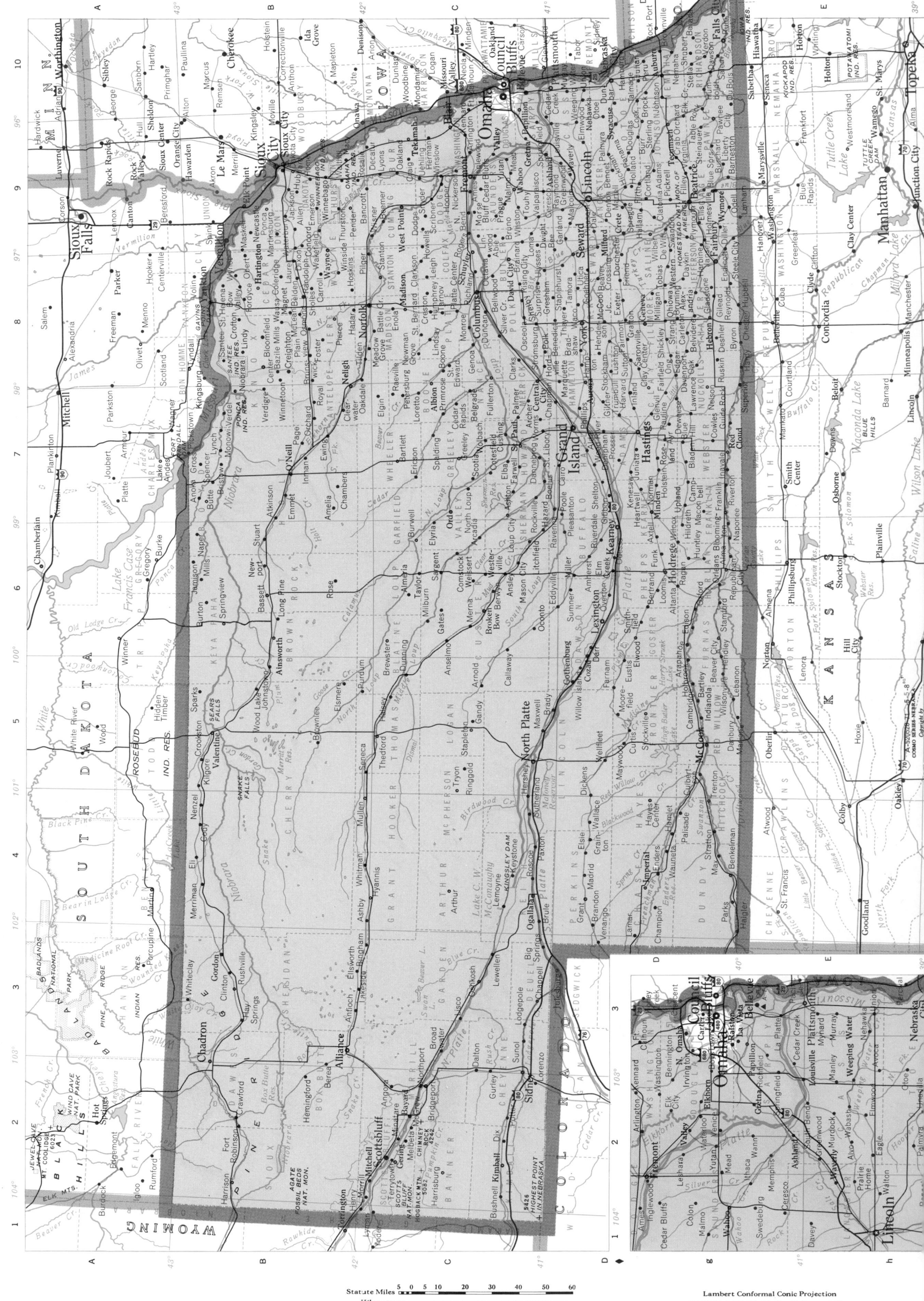

Statute Miles
Kilometers

Lambert Conformal Conic Projection
SCALE 1:2,460,000 1 Inch = 39 Statute Miles

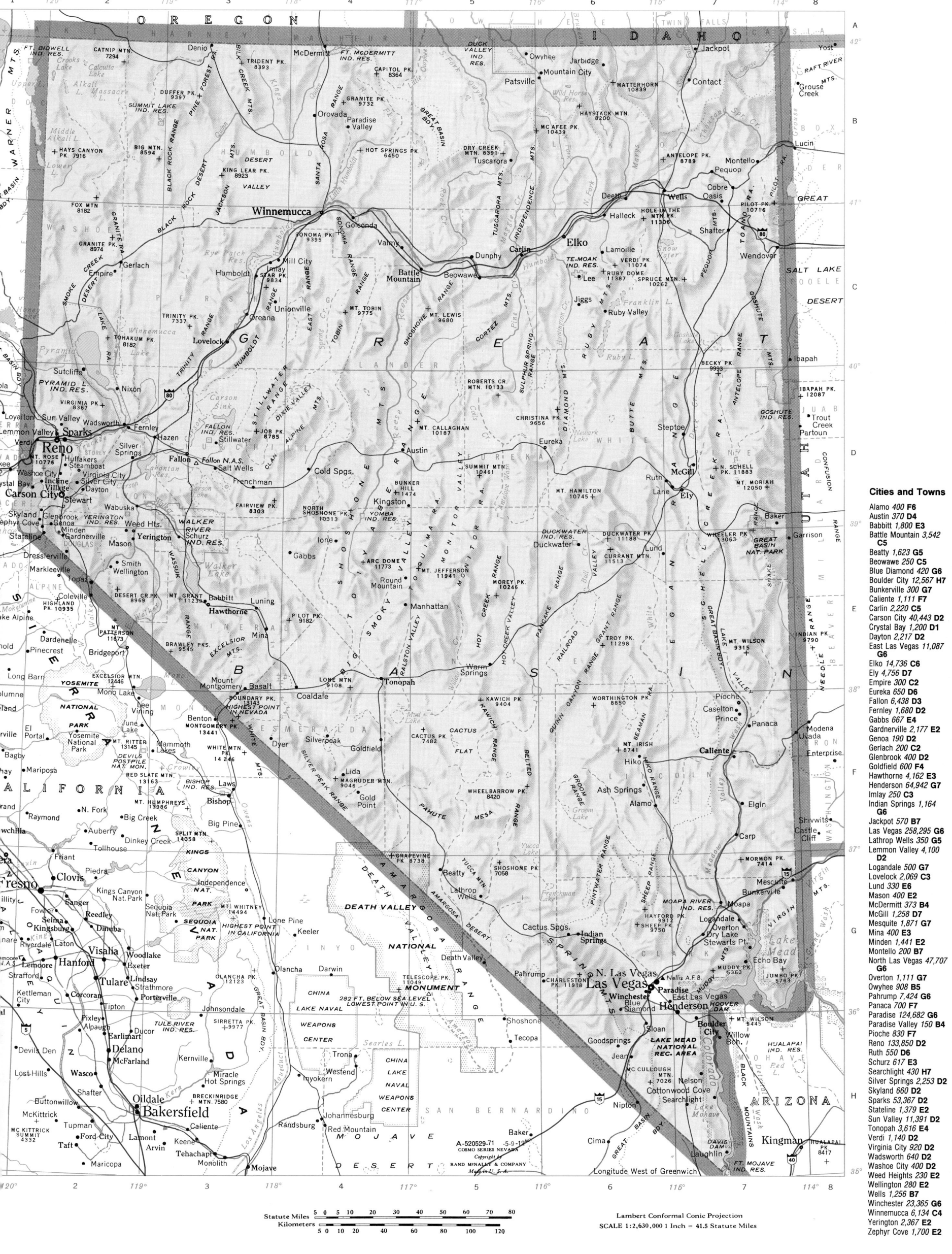

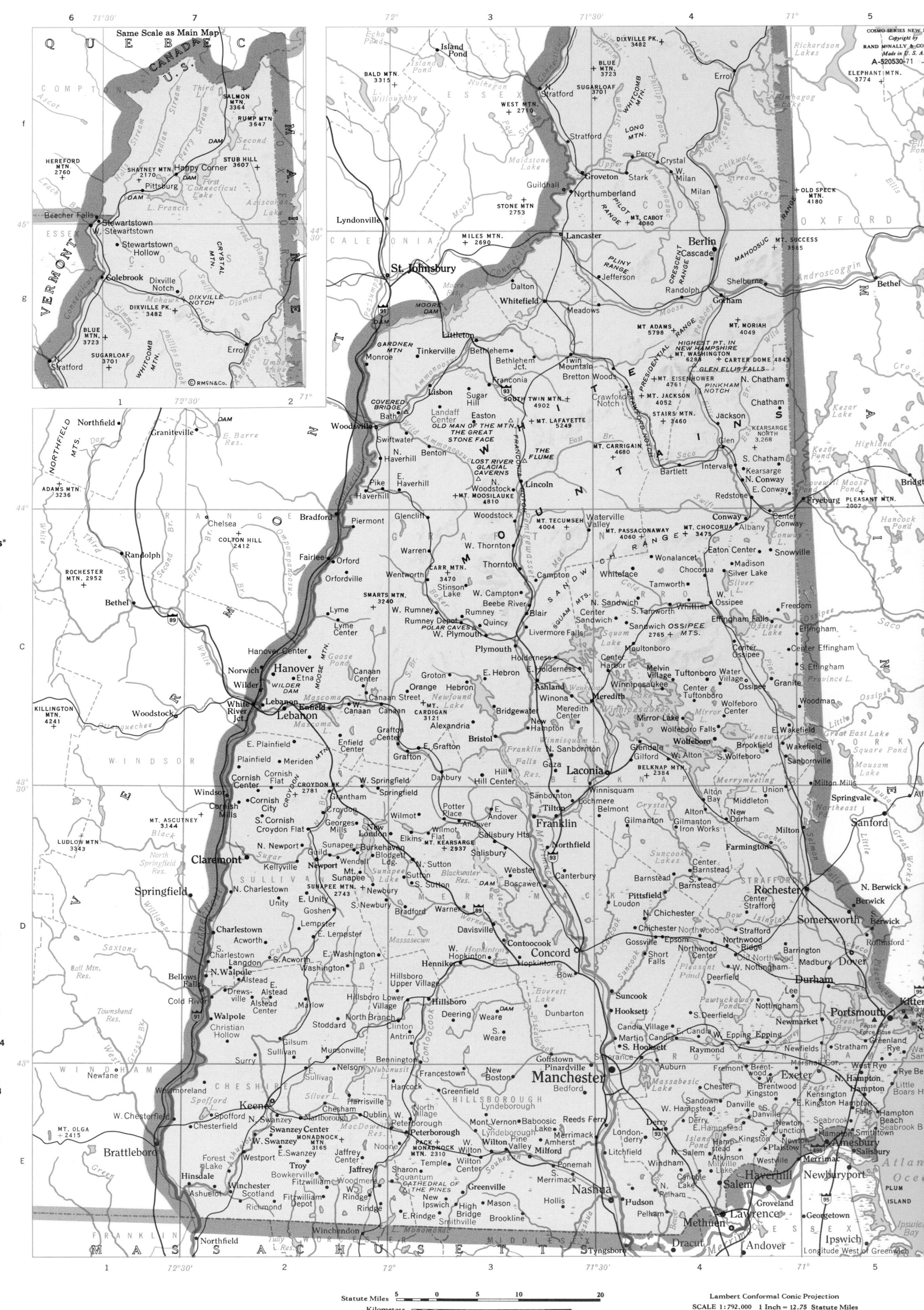

Cities and Towns*

Antrim 1,325 D3
Ashland 1,915 C3
Bedford 1,400 E3
Berlin 11,824 B4
Bristol 1,483 C3
Charlestown 1,173 D2
Claremont 13,902 D2
Colebrook 1,131 g7
Concord 36,006 D3
Contoocook 1,334 D3
Conway 1,604 C4
Derry 20,446 E4
Dover 25,042 D5
Durham 9,236 D5
Enfield 1,560 C2
Epping 1,384 D4
Exeter 9,556 E5
Farmington 3,567 D4
Franconia 811 B3
Franklin 8,304 D3
Goffstown 2,700 D3
Gorham 1,910 B4
Greenville 1,135 E3
Groveton 1,255 A3
Hampton 7,289 E5
Hanover 6,538 C2
Henniker 1,693 D3
Hillsboro 1,826 D3
Hinsdale 1,718 E2
Hooksett 2,573 D4
Hudson 7,626 E4
Jaffrey 2,558 E2
Keene 22,430 E2
Laconia 15,743 C4
Lancaster 1,859 B3
Lebanon 12,183 C2
Lisbon 1,246 B3
Littleton 4,633 B3
Manchester 99,567 E4
Marlborough 1,211 E2
Meredith 1,654 C3
Merrimack 1,300 E4
Milford 8,015 E3
Milton 1,000 D5
Nashua 79,662 E4
New Castle 400 D5
New London 1,335 D3
Newmarket 4,917 D5
Newport 3,772 D2
North Conway 2,032 B4
Northfield 1,375 D3
North Hampton 1,000 E5
North Walpole 980 D2
Peterborough 2,685 E3
Pinardville 4,684 E3
Pittsfield 1,717 D4
Plaistow 1,850 E4
Plymouth 3,967 C3
Portsmouth 25,925 D5
Raymond 2,516 D4
Rochester 26,630 D5
Rollinsford 1,173 D5
Salem 12,000 E4
Somersworth 11,249 D5
South Hooksett 3,638 D4
Suncook 5,214 D4
Tilton 1,380 D3
Troy 1,318 E2
West Swanzey 1,055 E2
Whitefield 1,041 B3
Wilton 1,165 E3
Winchester 1,735 E2
Wolfeboro 2,783 C4
Woodsville 1,122 B2

*Populations are for localities, not incorporated towns.

Statute Miles 5 0 5 10 20
Kilometers 5 0 5 10 15 20 25

Lambert Conformal Conic Projection
SCALE 1:792,000   1 Inch = 12.75 Statute Miles

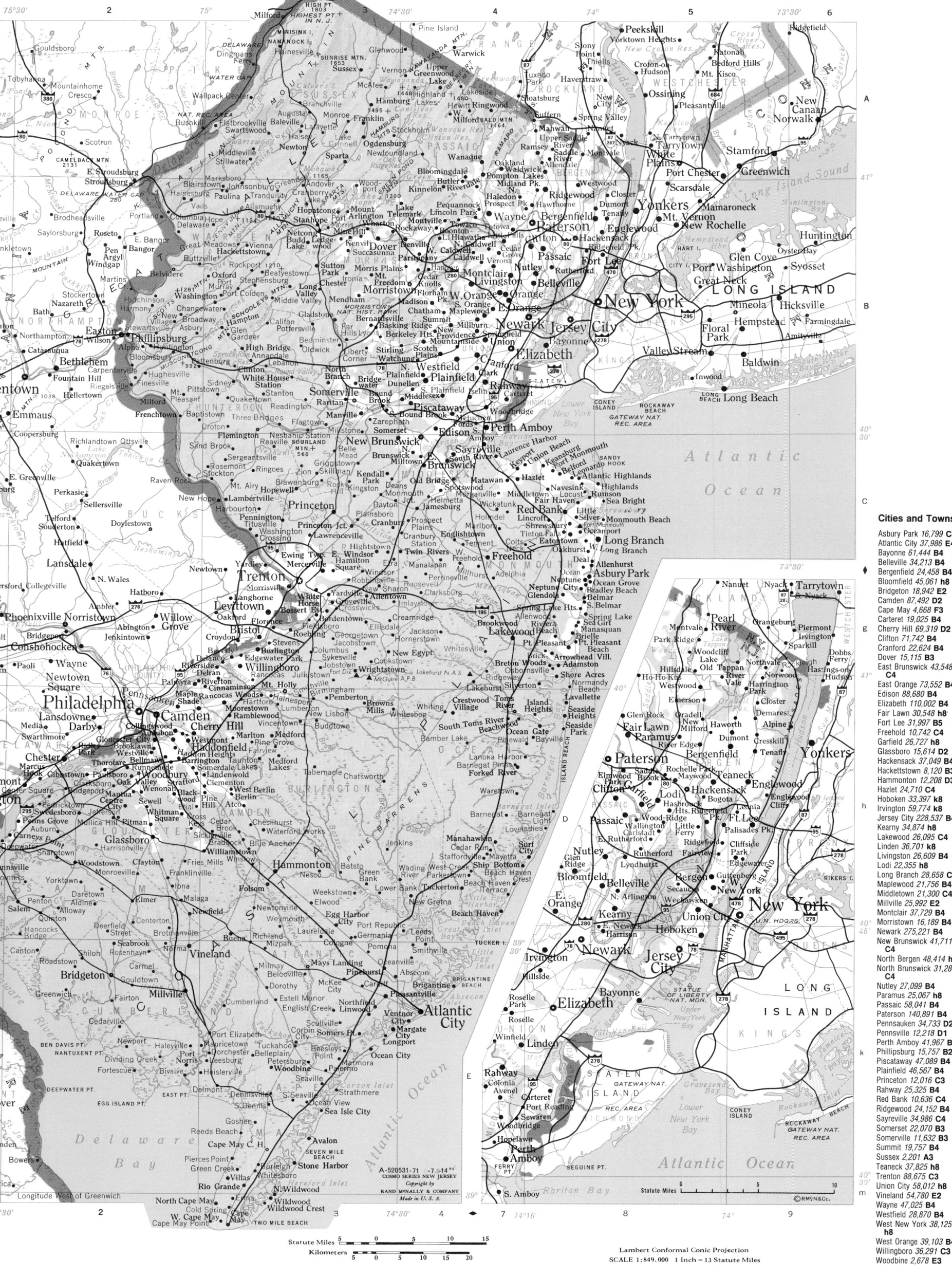

Cities and Towns

Asbury Park 16,799 **C4**
Atlantic City 37,986 **E4**
Bayonne 61,444 **B4**
Belleville 34,213 **B4**
Bergenfield 24,458 **B4**
Bloomfield 45,061 **h8**
Bridgeton 18,942 **E2**
Camden 87,492 **D2**
Cape May 4,668 **F3**
Carteret 19,025 **B4**
Cherry Hill 69,319 **D2**
Clifton 71,742 **B4**
Cranford 22,624 **B4**
Dover 15,115 **B3**
East Brunswick 43,548 **C4**
East Orange 73,552 **B4**
Edison 88,680 **B4**
Elizabeth 110,002 **B4**
Fair Lawn 30,548 **h8**
Fort Lee 31,997 **B5**
Freehold 10,742 **C4**
Garfield 26,727 **h8**
Glassboro 15,614 **D2**
Hackensack 37,049 **B4**
Hackettstown 8,120 **B3**
Hammonton 12,208 **D3**
Hazlet 24,710 **C4**
Hoboken 33,397 **k8**
Irvington 59,774 **k8**
Jersey City 228,537 **B4**
Kearny 34,874 **B4**
Lakewood 26,095 **C4**
Linden 36,701 **k8**
Livingston 26,609 **B4**
Lodi 22,355 **h8**
Long Branch 28,658 **C5**
Maplewood 21,756 **B4**
Middletown 21,300 **C4**
Millville 25,992 **E2**
Montclair 37,729 **B4**
Morristown 16,189 **B4**
Newark 275,221 **B4**
New Brunswick 41,711 **C4**
North Bergen 48,414 **h8**
North Brunswick 31,287 **C4**
Nutley 27,099 **B4**
Paramus 25,067 **h8**
Passaic 58,041 **B4**
Paterson 140,891 **B4**
Pennsauken 34,733 **D2**
Pennsville 12,218 **D1**
Perth Amboy 41,967 **B4**
Phillipsburg 15,757 **B2**
Piscataway 47,089 **B4**
Plainfield 46,567 **B4**
Princeton 12,016 **C3**
Rahway 25,325 **B4**
Red Bank 10,636 **C3**
Ridgewood 24,152 **B4**
Sayreville 34,986 **C4**
Somerset 22,070 **B3**
Somerville 11,632 **B3**
Summit 19,757 **B4**
Sussex 2,201 **A3**
Teaneck 37,825 **h8**
Trenton 88,675 **C3**
Union City 58,012 **h8**
Vineland 54,780 **E2**
Wayne 47,025 **B4**
Westfield 28,870 **B4**
West New York 38,125 **h8**
West Orange 39,103 **B4**
Willingboro 36,291 **C3**
Woodbine 2,678 **E3**

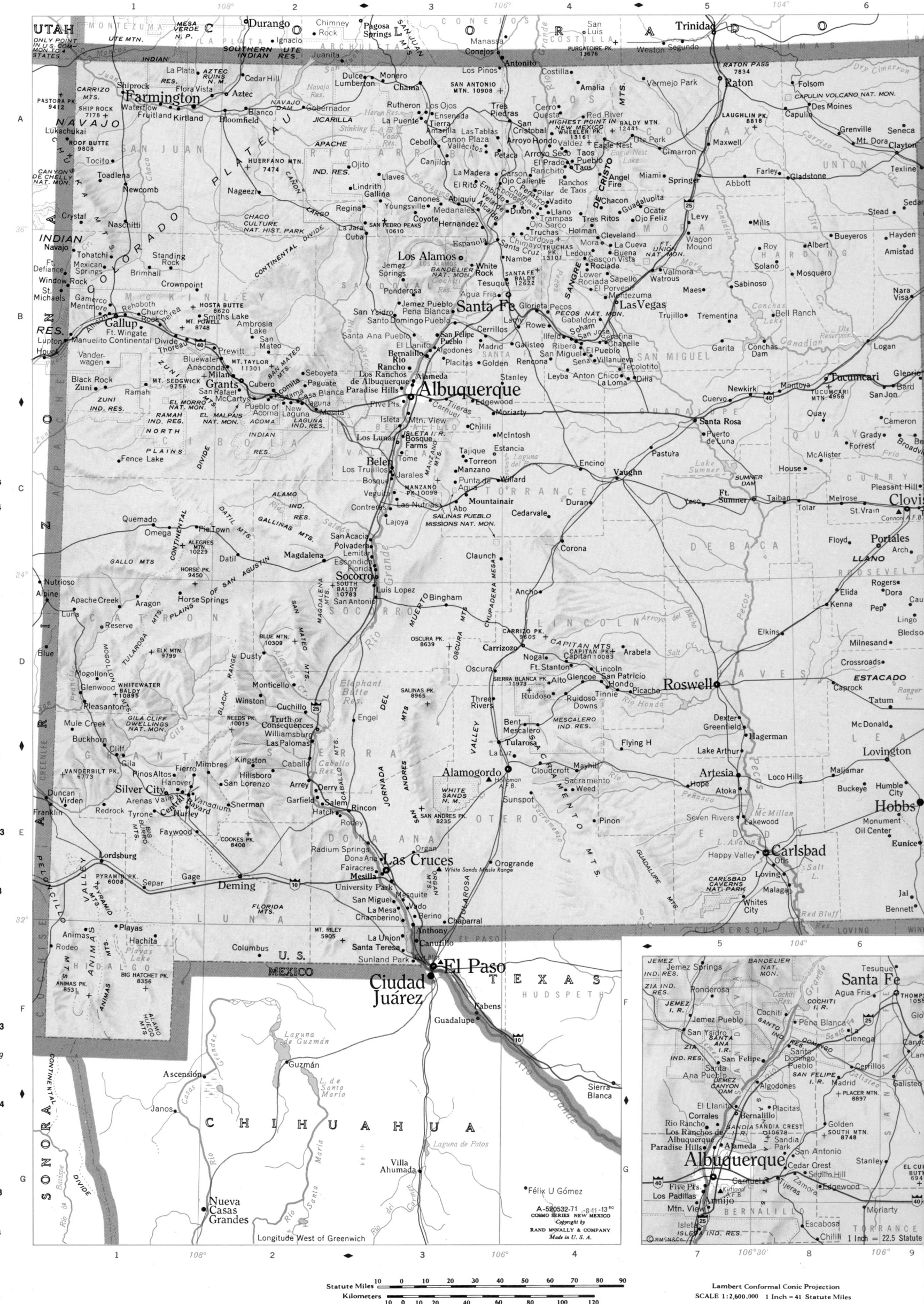

Cities and Towns

Alameda 5,900 **B3**
Alamogordo 27,596 **E4**
Albuquerque 384,736 **B3**
Anthony 5,160 **F3**
Armijo 14,600 **k7**
Artesia 10,610 **E5**
Aztec 5,479 **A2**
Bayard 2,598 **E1**
Belen 6,547 **C3**
Bernalillo 5,960 **B3**
Bloomfield 5,214 **A2**
Carlsbad 24,952 **E5**
Carrizozo 1,075 **D4**
Central 1,835 **E1**
Chama 1,048 **A3**
Chimayo 2,789 **A4**
Clayton 2,484 **A6**
Clovis 30,954 **C6**
Crownpoint 2,108 **B1**
Deming 10,970 **E2**
Dulce 2,438 **A2**
Espanola 8,389 **B3**
Eunice 2,676 **E6**
Farmington 33,997 **A1**
Five Points 4,200 **B3**
Fort Sumner 1,269 **C5**
Gallup 19,154 **B1**
Grants 8,626 **B2**
Hatch 1,136 **E2**
Hobbs 29,115 **E6**
Hurley 1,534 **E1**
Isleta 1,703 **C3**
Jal 2,156 **E6**
Jemez Pueblo 1,301 **B3**
Kirtland 3,552 **A1**
La Luz 1,625 **D4**
Las Cruces 62,126 **E3**
Las Vegas 14,753 **B4**
Lordsburg 2,951 **E1**
Los Alamos 11,455 **B3**
Los Lunas 6,013 **C3**
Los Ranchos de
  Albuquerque 3,955
  B3
Loving 1,243 **E5**
Lovington 9,322 **E6**
Magdalena 861 **C2**
Mescalero 1,159 **D4**
Mesilla 1,975 **E3**
Milan 1,911 **B2**
Moriarty 1,399 **C3**
Mountain View 2,300
  C3
Paradise Hills 5,513 **B3**
Portales 10,690 **C6**
Questa 1,707 **A4**
Ranchos de Taos 1,779
  A4
Raton 7,372 **A5**
Roswell 44,654 **D5**
Ruidoso 4,600 **D4**
Ruidoso Downs 920 **D4**
Santa Fe 55,859 **B4**
Santa Rosa 2,263 **C5**
Santo Domingo Pueblo
  2,866 **B3**
Shiprock 7,687 **A1**
Silver City 10,683 **E1**
Socorro 8,159 **C3**
Springer 1,262 **A5**
Sunland Park 8,179 **F3**
Taos 4,065 **A4**
Tesuque 1,490 **B4**
Thoreau 1,099 **B1**
Truth or Consequences
  (Hot Springs) 6,221
  D2
Tucumcari 6,831 **B6**
Tularosa 2,615 **D3**
University Park 4,520
  E3
Zuni (Zuni Pueblo)
  5,857 **B1**

Statute Miles

Kilometers

Lambert Conformal Conic Projection
SCALE 1:2,600,000   1 Inch = 41 Statute Miles

1 Inch = 22.5 Statute

A-520532-71   -8-41-13⁸⁰
COSMO SERIES NEW MEXICO
Copyright by
RAND M⁹NALLY & COMPANY
Made in U.S.A.

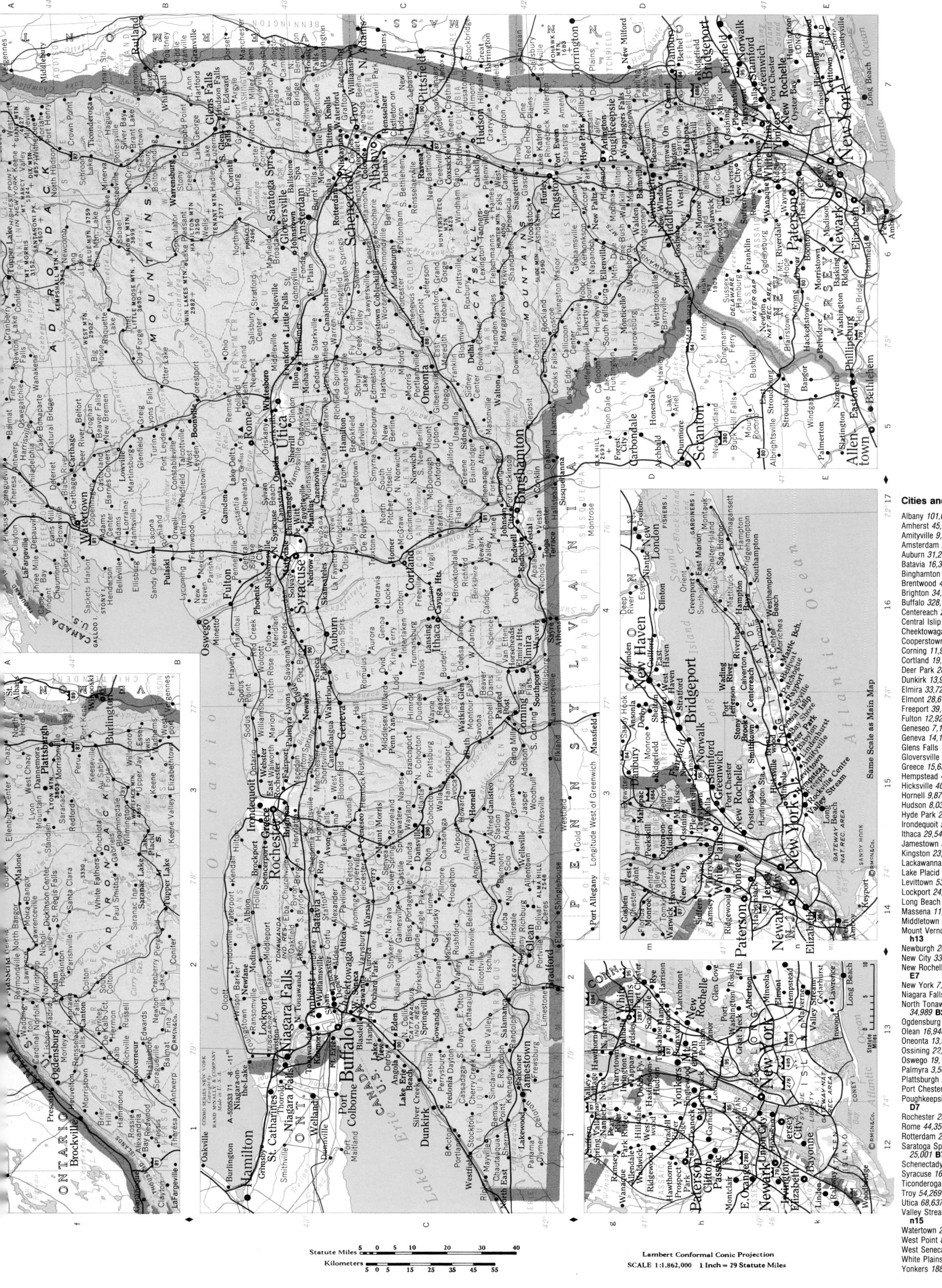

Statute Miles 5 0 5 10 20 30 40

Kilometers 5 0 5 15 25 35 45 55

Lambert Conformal Conic Projection
SCALE 1:1,862,000   1 Inch = 29 Statute Miles

Cities and Towns

Albany *101,082* **C7**
Amherst *45,600* **C2**
Amityville *9,286* **E7**
Amsterdam *20,714* **C6**
Auburn *31,258* **C4**
Batavia *16,310* **C2**
Binghamton *53,008* **C5**
Brentwood *45,218* **E7**
Brighton *34,455* **B3**
Buffalo *328,123* **C2**
Centereach *26,720* **n15**
Central Islip *26,028* **n15**
Cheektowaga *84,387* **C2**
Cooperstown *2,180* **C6**
Corning *11,938* **C3**
Cortland *19,801* **C4**
Deer Park *28,840* **n15**
Dunkirk *13,989* **C1**
Elmira *33,724* **C4**
Elmont *28,612* **k13**
Freeport *39,894* **n15**
Fulton *12,929* **B4**
Geneseo *7,187* **C3**
Geneva *14,143* **C4**
Glens Falls *15,023* **B7**
Gloversville *16,656* **B6**
Greece *15,632* **B3**
Hempstead *49,453* **n15**
Hicksville *40,174* **E7**
Hornell *9,877* **C3**
Hudson *8,034* **C7**
Hyde Park *2,550* **D7**
Irondequoit *52,322* **B3**
Ithaca *29,541* **C4**
Jamestown *34,681* **C1**
Kingston *23,095* **D6**
Lackawanna *20,585* **C2**
Lake Placid *2,485* **A7**
Levittown *53,286* **E7**
Lockport *24,426* **B2**
Long Beach *33,510* **E7**
Massena *11,719* **f10**
Middletown *24,160* **D6**
Mount Vernon *67,153*
h13
Newburgh *26,454* **D6**
New City *33,673* **D6**
New Rochelle *67,265*
E7
New York *7,322,554* **E7**
Niagara Falls *61,840* **B1**
North Tonawanda
34,989 **B2**
Ogdensburg *13,521* **f9**
Olean *16,946* **C2**
Oneonta *13,954* **C5**
Ossining *22,582* **D7**
Oswego *19,195* **B4**
Palmyra *3,566* **B3**
Plattsburgh *21,255* **f11**
Port Chester *24,728* **E7**
Poughkeepsie *28,844*
D7
Rochester *231,636* **B3**
Rome *44,350* **B5**
Rotterdam *21,228* **C6**
Saratoga Springs
25,001 **B7**
Schenectady *65,566* **C7**
Syracuse *163,860* **B4**
Ticonderoga *2,770* **C7**
Troy *54,269* **C7**
Utica *68,637* **B5**
Valley Stream *33,946*
n15
Watertown *29,429* **B5**
West Point *8,024* **D7**
West Seneca *47,866* **C2**
White Plains *48,718* **D7**
Yonkers *188,082* **E7**

72 17

16

15

14

13

Same Scale as Main Map

Longitude West of Greenwich

Cities and Towns

Albemarle 14,939 **B2**
Archdale 6,913 **B3**
Asheboro 16,362 **B3**
Asheville 61,607 **f10**
Boone 12,915 **A1**
Brevard 5,388 **f10**
Burlington 39,498 **A3**
Carrboro 11,553 **B3**
Chapel Hill 38,719 **B3**
Charlotte 395,934 **B2**
Clemmons 6,020 **A2**
Clinton 8,204 **C4**
Concord 27,347 **B2**
Dunn 8,336 **B4**
Durham 136,611 **B4**
Eden 15,238 **A3**
Edenton 5,268 **A6**
Elizabeth City 14,292 **A6**
Fayetteville 75,695 **B4**
Forest City 7,475 **B1**
Garner 14,967 **B4**
Gastonia 54,732 **B1**
Goldsboro 40,709 **B5**
Graham 10,426 **A3**
Greensboro 183,521 **A3**
Greenville 44,972 **B5**
Havelock 20,268 **C6**
Henderson 15,655 **A4**
Hendersonville 7,284 **f10**
Hickory 28,301 **B1**
High Point 69,496 **B2**
Jacksonville 30,013 **C5**
Kannapolis 29,696 **B2**
Kernersville 10,836 **A2**
Kings Mountain 8,763 **B1**
Kinston 25,295 **B5**
Laurinburg 11,643 **C3**
Lenoir 14,192 **B1**
Lexington 16,581 **B2**
Lincolnton 6,847 **B1**
Lumberton 18,601 **C3**
Monroe 16,127 **C2**
Mooresville 9,317 **B2**
Morehead City 6,046 **C6**
Morganton 15,085 **B1**
Mount Airy 7,156 **A2**
Mount Olive 4,582 **B4**
Nags Head 1,838 **B7**
Newton 9,304 **B1**
Oxford 7,913 **A4**
Plymouth 4,328 **B6**
Raleigh 207,951 **B4**
Reidsville 12,183 **A3**
Roanoke Rapids 15,722 **A5**
Rockingham 9,399 **C3**
Rocky Mount 48,997 **B5**
Roxboro 7,332 **A4**
Sanford 14,475 **B3**
Selma 4,600 **B4**
Shelby 14,669 **B1**
Smithfield 7,540 **B4**
Southern Pines 9,129 **B3**
Statesville 17,567 **B2**
Swannanoa 3,538 **f10**
Tarboro 11,037 **B5**
Thomasville 15,915 **B2**
Washington 9,075 **B5**
Whiteville 5,078 **C4**
Williamston 5,503 **B5**
Wilmington 55,530 **C5**
Wilson 36,930 **B5**
Winston-Salem 143,485 **A2**

Statute Miles 5 0 5 10 20 30 40
Kilometers 5 0 5 15 25 35 45 55

Lambert Conformal Conic Projection
SCALE 1:1,950,000 1 Inch = 31 Statute Miles

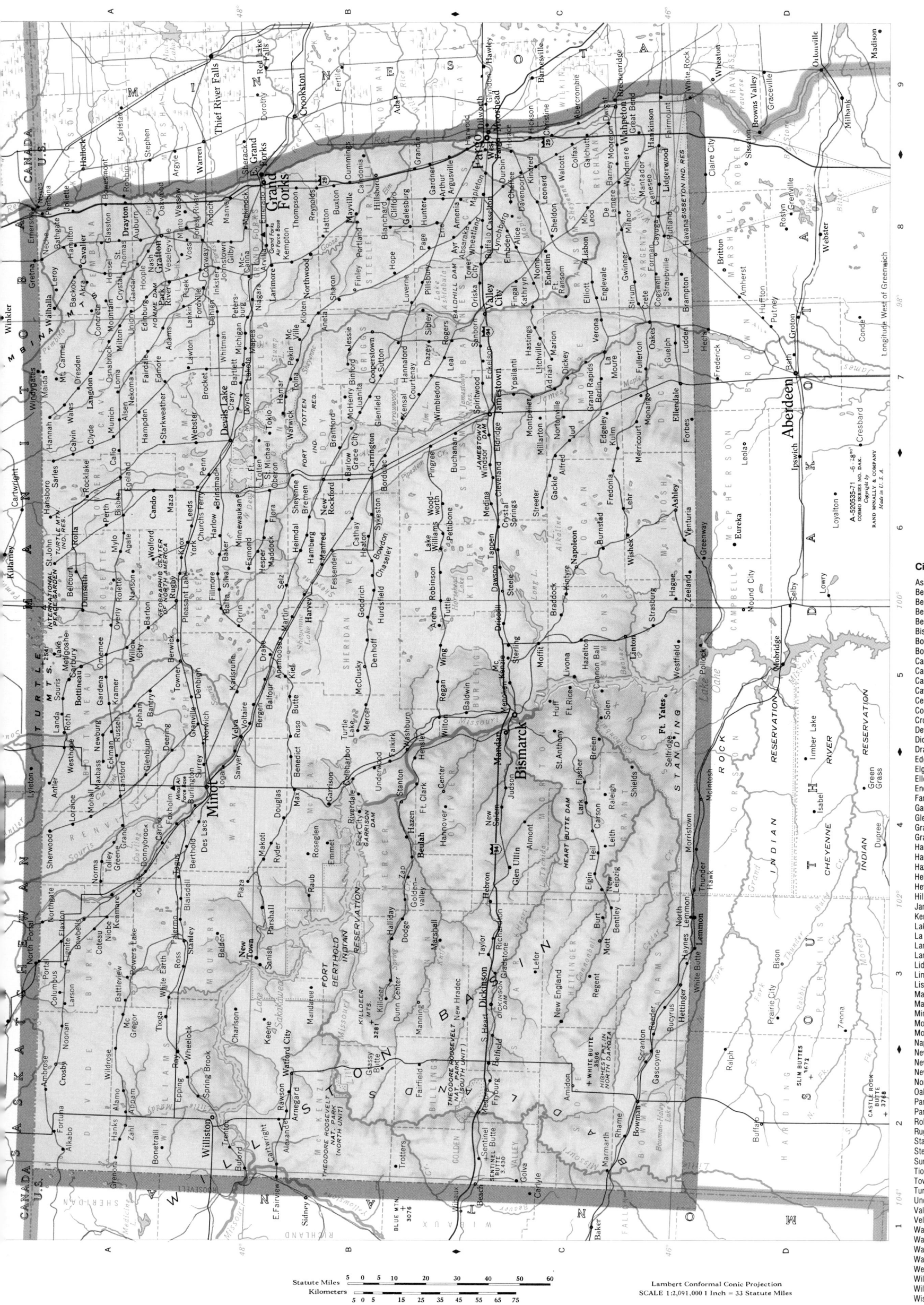

Cities and Towns

Ashley 1,052 **C6**
Beach 1,205 **C1**
Belcourt 2,458 **A6**
Belfield 887 **C2**
Beulah 3,363 **B4**
Bismarck 49,256 **C5**
Bottineau 2,598 **A5**
Bowman 1,741 **C2**
Cando 1,564 **A6**
Carrington 2,267 **B6**
Casselton 1,601 **C8**
Cavalier 1,508 **A8**
Center 826 **B4**
Cooperstown 1,247 **B7**
Crosby 1,312 **A2**
Devils Lake 7,782 **A7**
Dickinson 16,097 **C3**
Drayton 961 **A8**
Edgeley 680 **C7**
Elgin 765 **C4**
Ellendale 1,798 **C7**
Enderlin 997 **C8**
Fargo 74,111 **C9**
Garrison 1,530 **B4**
Glen Ullin 927 **C4**
Grafton 4,840 **A8**
Grand Forks 49,425 **B8**
Hankinson 1,038 **C9**
Harvey 2,263 **B6**
Hazen 2,818 **B4**
Hebron 888 **C3**
Hettinger 1,574 **D3**
Hillsboro 1,488 **B8**
Jamestown 15,571 **C7**
Kenmare 1,214 **A3**
Lakota 898 **A7**
La Moure 970 **C7**
Langdon 2,241 **A7**
Larimore 1,464 **B8**
Lidgerwood 799 **C8**
Linton 1,410 **C5**
Lisbon 2,177 **C8**
Mandan 15,177 **C5**
Mayville 2,092 **B8**
Minot 34,544 **A4**
Mohall 931 **A4**
Mott 1,019 **C3**
Napoleon 930 **C6**
New Rockford 1,604 **B6**
New Salem 909 **C4**
New Town 1,388 **B3**
Northwood 1,166 **B8**
Oakes 1,775 **C7**
Park River 1,725 **A8**
Parshall 943 **B3**
Rolla 1,286 **A6**
Rugby 2,909 **A6**
Stanley 1,371 **A3**
Steele 762 **C6**
Surrey 856 **A4**
Tioga 1,278 **A3**
Towner 669 **A5**
Turtle Lake 681 **B5**
Underwood 976 **B4**
Valley City 7,163 **C8**
Velva 968 **A5**
Wahpeton 8,751 **C9**
Walhalla 1,131 **A8**
Washburn 1,506 **B5**
Watford City 1,784 **B2**
West Fargo 12,287 **C9**
Williston 13,131 **A2**
Wilton 728 **B5**
Wishek 1,171 **C6**

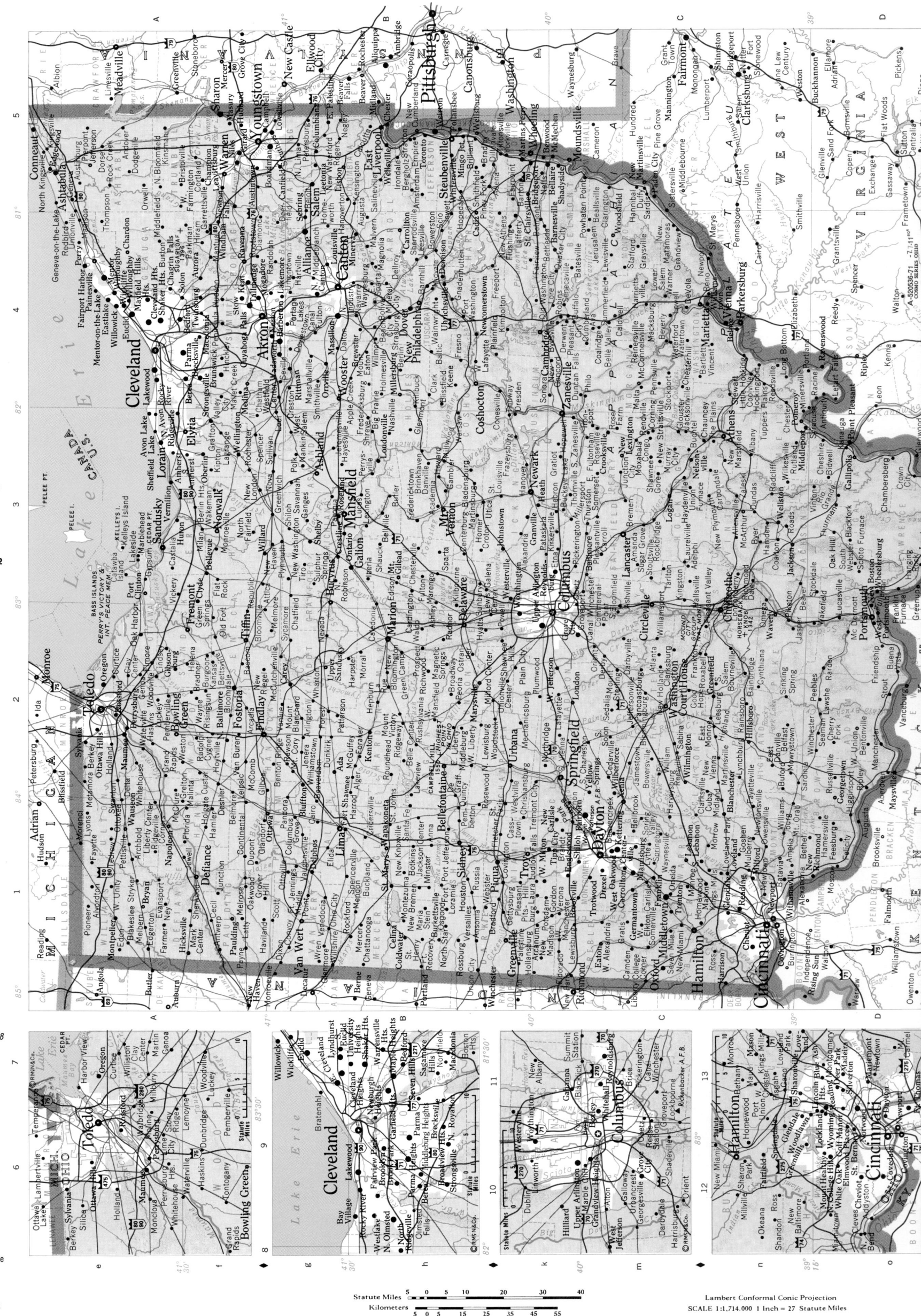

Cities and Towns

Akron 223,019 **A4**
Alliance 23,376 **B4**
Ashland 20,079 **B3**
Ashtabula 21,633 **A5**
Athens 21,265 **C3**
Barberton 27,623 **A4**
Bellefontaine 12,142 **B2**
Boardman 38,596 **A5**
Bowling Green 28,176 **A2**
Brunswick 28,230 **A4**
Bucyrus 13,496 **B3**
Cambridge 11,748 **B4**
Canton 84,161 **B4**
Chillicothe 21,923 **C3**
Cincinnati 364,040 **C1**
Circleville 11,666 **C3**
Cleveland 505,616 **A4**
Cleveland Heights 54,052 **A4**
Columbus 632,910 **C2**
Conneaut 13,241 **A5**
Coshocton 12,193 **B4**
Cuyahoga Falls 48,950 **A4**
Dayton 182,044 **C1**
Defiance 16,768 **A1**
Delaware 20,030 **B2**
East Cleveland 33,096 **g9**
East Liverpool 13,654 **B5**
Elyria 56,746 **A3**
Euclid 54,875 **A4**
Findlay 35,703 **A2**
Fostoria 14,983 **A2**
Fremont 17,648 **A2**
Greenville 12,863 **B1**
Hamilton 61,368 **C1**
Ironton 12,751 **D3**
Kettering 60,569 **C1**
Lakewood 59,718 **A4**
Lancaster 34,507 **C3**
Lima 45,549 **B1**
Lorain 71,245 **A3**
Mansfield 50,627 **B3**
Marietta 15,026 **C4**
Marion 35,703 **B2**
Massillon 31,007 **B4**
Medina 19,231 **A4**
Mentor 47,358 **A4**
Middletown 46,022 **C1**
Mount Vernon 14,550 **B3**
Newark 44,389 **B3**
New Philadelphia 15,698 **B4**
North Olmsted 34,204 **h9**
Norwalk 14,731 **A3**
Oxford 18,937 **C1**
Parma 87,876 **A4**
Piqua 20,612 **B1**
Portsmouth 22,676 **D3**
Salem 12,233 **B5**
Sandusky 29,764 **A3**
Shaker Heights 30,831 **A4**
Springfield 70,487 **C2**
Steubenville 22,125 **B5**
Strongsville 35,308 **A4**
Tiffin 18,604 **B2**
Toledo 332,943 **A2**
Upper Arlington 34,128 **B2**
Urbana 11,353 **B2**
Van Wert 10,891 **B1**
Warren 50,793 **A5**
Washington Court House 12,983 **C2**
Westerville 30,269 **B3**
Wooster 22,191 **B4**
Xenia 24,664 **C2**
Youngstown 95,732 **A5**
Zanesville 26,778 **C4**

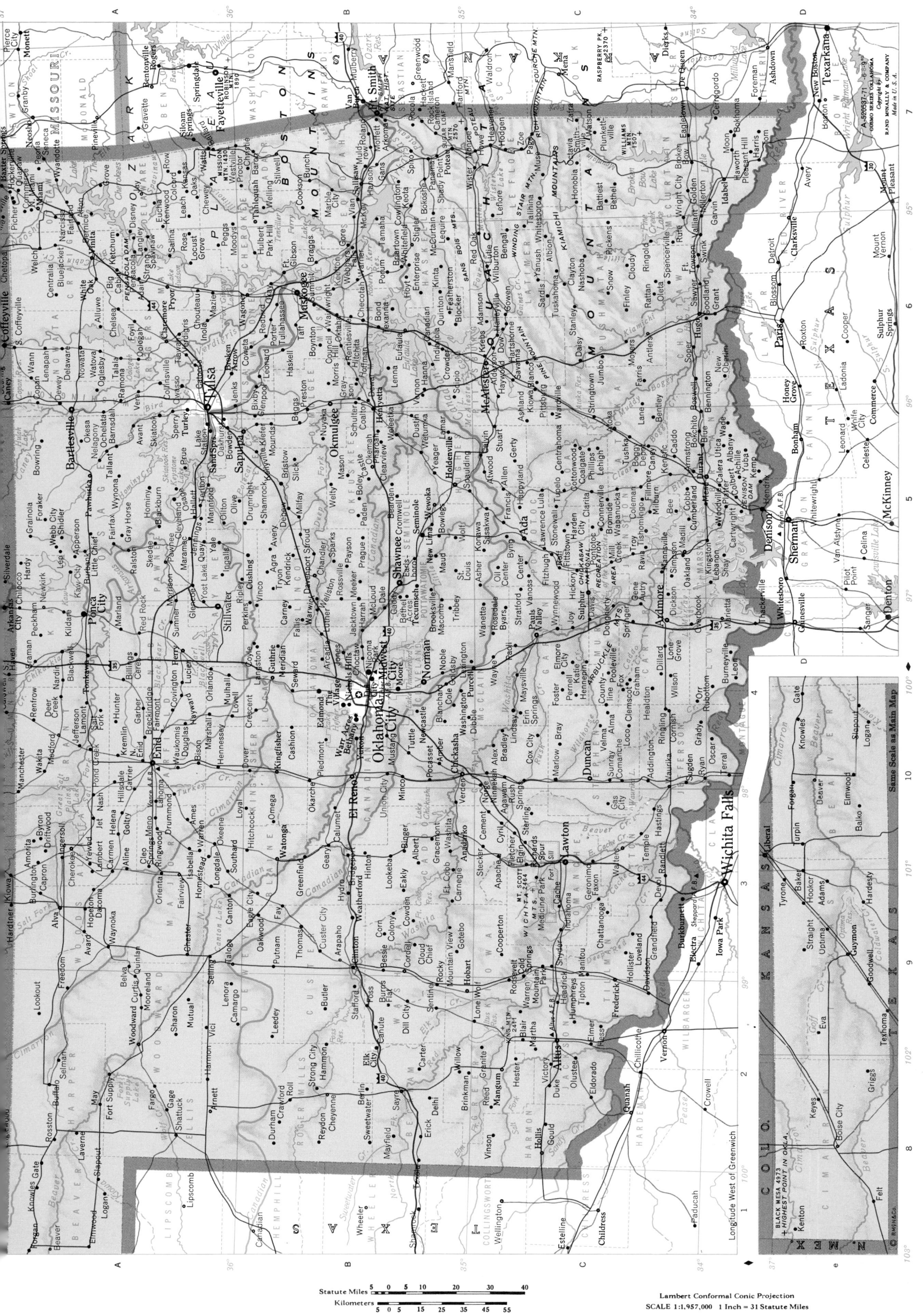

Lambert Conformal Conic Projection
SCALE 1:1,957,000 1 Inch = 31 Statute Miles

Statute Miles 5 0 5 10 20 30 40
Kilometers 5 0 5 15 25 35 45 55

Cities and Towns

Ada 15,820 **C5**
Altus 21,910 **C2**
Alva 5,495 **A3**
Anadarko 6,586 **B3**
Ardmore 23,079 **C4**
Bartlesville 34,256 **A6**
Bethany 20,075 **B4**
Bixby 9,502 **B6**
Blackwell 7,538 **A4**
Bristow 4,062 **B5**
Broken Arrow 58,043 **A6**
Broken Bow 3,961 **C7**
Chickasha 14,988 **B4**
Choctaw 8,545 **B4**
Claremore 13,280 **A6**
Clinton 9,298 **B3**
Coweta 6,159 **B6**
Cushing 7,218 **B5**
Del City 23,928 **B4**
Duncan 21,732 **C4**
Durant 12,823 **D5**
Edmond 52,315 **B4**
Elk City 10,428 **B2**
El Reno 15,414 **B4**
Enid 45,309 **A4**
Frederick 5,221 **C2**
Guthrie 10,518 **B4**
Guymon 7,803 **e9**
Henryetta 5,872 **B5**
Hobart 4,305 **B2**
Holdenville 4,792 **B5**
Hugo 5,978 **C6**
Idabel 6,957 **D7**
Kingfisher 4,095 **B4**
Lawton 80,561 **C3**
Madill 3,069 **C5**
Marlow 4,416 **C4**
McAlester 16,370 **C6**
Miami 13,142 **A7**
Midwest City 52,267 **B4**
Moore 40,318 **B4**
Muskogee 37,708 **B6**
Mustang 10,434 **B4**
Norman 80,071 **B4**
Nowata 3,896 **A6**
Oklahoma City 444,719 **B4**
Okmulgee 13,441 **B6**
Owasso 11,151 **A6**
Pauls Valley 6,150 **C4**
Pawhuska 3,825 **A5**
Perry 4,978 **A4**
Ponca City 26,359 **A4**
Poteau 7,210 **B7**
Pryor 8,327 **A6**
Purcell 4,784 **B4**
Sallisaw 7,122 **B7**
Sand Springs 15,346 **A5**
Sapulpa 18,074 **B5**
Seminole 7,071 **B5**
Shawnee 26,017 **B5**
Stillwater 36,676 **A4**
Sulphur 4,824 **C5**
Tahlequah 10,398 **B6**
Tecumseh 5,750 **B5**
The Village 10,353 **B4**
Tulsa 367,302 **A6**
Vinita 5,804 **A6**
Wagoner 6,894 **B6**
Warr Acres 9,288 **B4**
Watonga 3,408 **B3**
Weatherford 10,124 **B3**
Wewoka 4,050 **B5**
Woodward 12,340 **A2**
Yukon 20,935 **B4**

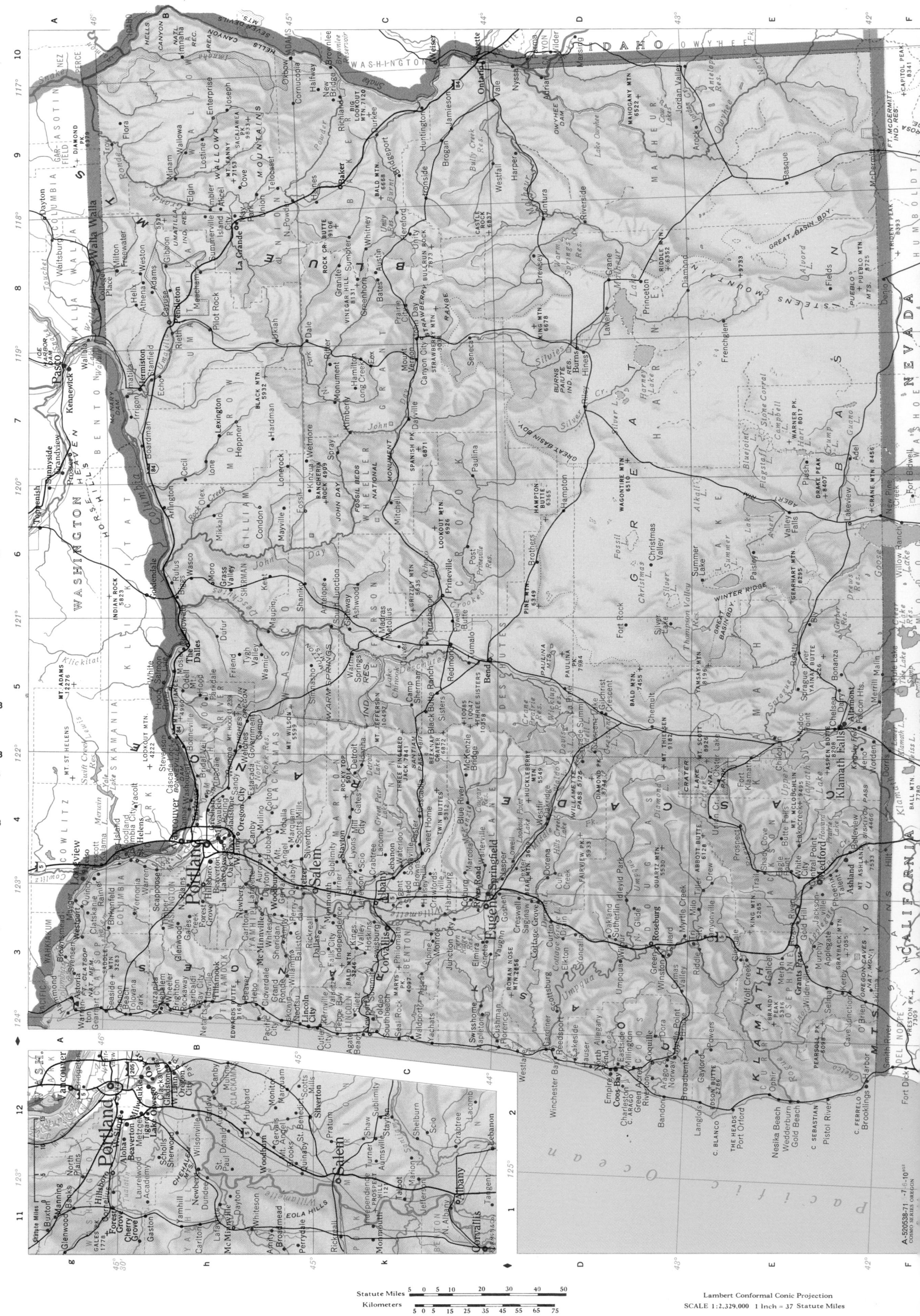

Cities and Towns

Albany 29,462 **C3**
Aloha 34,284 **h12**
Altamont 18,591 **E5**
Ashland 16,234 **E4**
Astoria 10,069 **A3**
Baker 9,140 **C9**
Beaverton 53,310 **B4**
Bend 20,469 **C5**
Burns 2,913 **D7**
Canby 8,983 **B4**
Central Point 7,509 **E4**
Coos Bay 15,076 **D2**
Coquille 4,121 **D2**
Corvallis 44,757 **C3**
Cottage Grove 7,402 **D3**
Crater Lake 25 **E4**
Dallas 9,422 **C3**
Eugene 112,669 **C3**
Florence 5,162 **D2**
Forest Grove 13,559 **B3**
Gladstone 10,152 **B4**
Grants Pass 17,488 **E3**
Gresham 68,235 **B4**
Hermiston 10,040 **B7**
Hillsboro 37,520 **B4**
Hood River 4,632 **B5**
Independence 4,425 **C3**
John Day 1,836 **C8**
Keizer 21,884 **C3**
Klamath Falls 17,737 **E5**
La Grande 11,766 **B8**
Lake Oswego 30,576 **B4**
Lakeview 2,526 **E6**
Lebanon 10,950 **C4**
Lincoln City 5,892 **C3**
McMinnville 17,894 **B3**
Medford 46,951 **E4**
Metzger 3,149 **h12**
Milton-Freewater 5,533 **B8**
Milwaukie 18,692 **B4**
Monmouth 6,288 **C3**
Myrtle Point 2,712 **D2**
Newberg 13,086 **B4**
Newport 8,437 **C2**
North Bend 9,614 **D2**
Oak Grove 12,576 **B4**
Ontario 9,392 **C10**
Oregon City 14,698 **B4**
Parkrose 21,108 **B4**
Pendleton 15,126 **B8**
Portland 437,319 **B4**
Prineville 5,355 **C6**
Redmond 7,163 **C5**
Reedsport 4,796 **D2**
River Road 9,443 **C3**
Roseburg 17,032 **D3**
Saint Helens 7,535 **B4**
Salem 107,786 **C4**
Scappoose 3,529 **B4**
Seaside 5,359 **B3**
Silverton 5,635 **C4**
Springfield 44,683 **C4**
Stayton 5,011 **C4**
Sutherlin 5,020 **D3**
Sweet Home 6,850 **C4**
The Dalles 11,060 **B5**
Tigard 29,344 **h12**
Tillamook 4,001 **B3**
Tri City 3,585 **E3**
Umatilla 3,046 **B7**
West Linn 16,367 **B4**
West Slope 7,959 **g12**
White City 5,891 **E4**
Woodburn 13,404 **B4**

Lambert Conformal Conic Projection
SCALE 1:2,329,000   1 Inch = 37 Statute Miles

Statute Miles
Kilometers

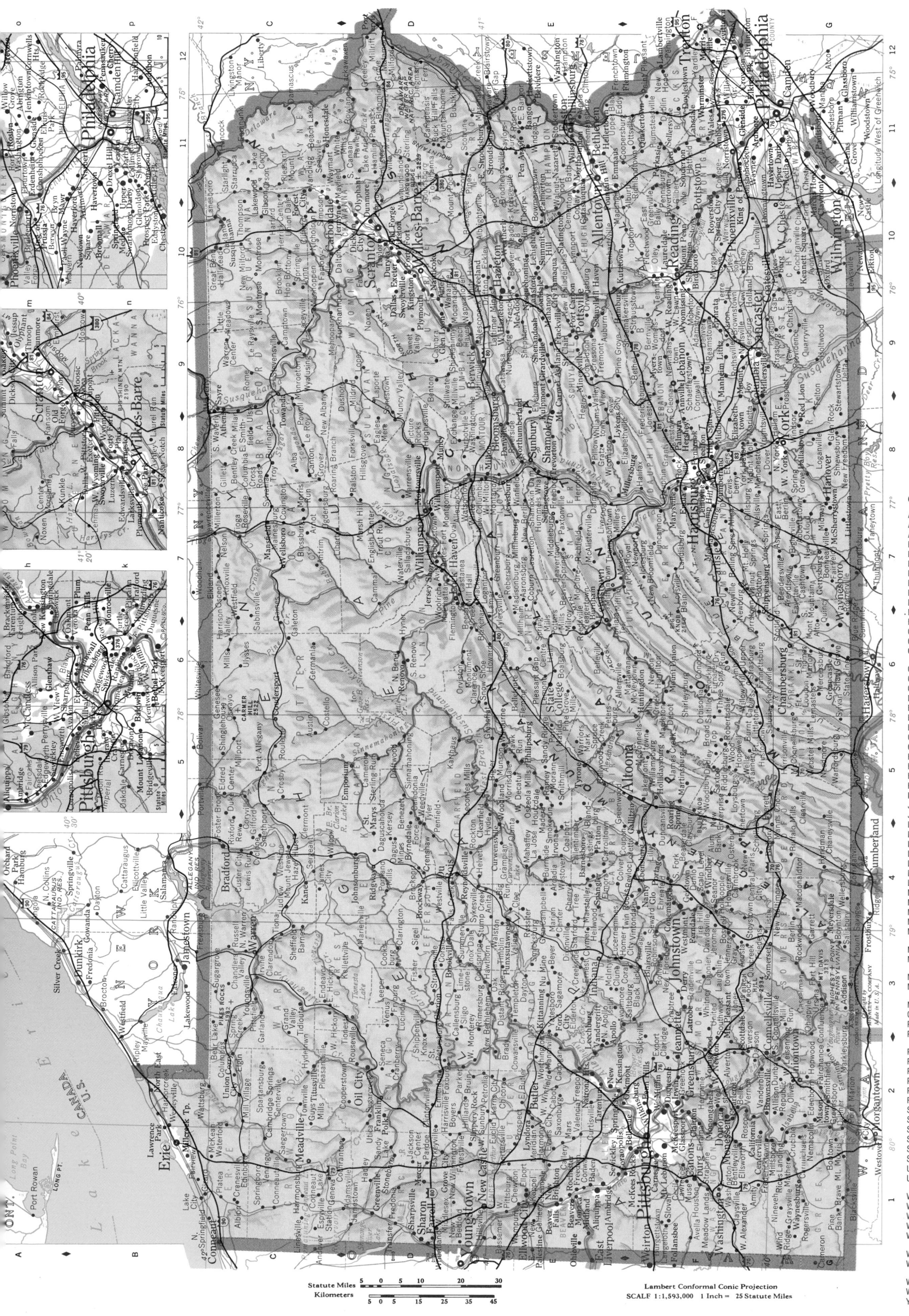

Statute Miles
Kilometers

Lambert Conformal Conic Projection
SCALE 1:1,593,000 1 Inch = 25 Statute Miles

Cities and Towns

Aliquippa 13,374 **E1**
Allentown 105,090 **E11**
Altoona 51,881 **E5**
Baldwin 21,923 **k14**
Beaver Falls 10,687 **E1**
Berwick 10,976 **D9**
Bethel Park 33,823 **k14**
Bethlehem 71,428 **E11**
Bloomsburg 12,439 **E9**
Bradford 9,625 **C4**
Broomall 10,930 **p20**
Butler 15,714 **E2**
Carbondale 10,664 **C10**
Carlisle 18,419 **F7**
Chambersburg 16,647
  G6
Chester 41,856 **G11**
Coatesville 11,038 **G10**
Connellsville 9,229 **D4**
Du Bois 8,286 **D4**
Easton 26,276 **E11**
Ephrata 12,133 **F9**
Erie 108,718 **B1**
Gettysburg 7,025 **G7**
Greensburg 16,318 **F2**
Hanover 14,399 **G8**
Harrisburg 52,376 **F8**
Hazleton 24,730 **E10**
Hershey 11,860 **F8**
Indiana 15,174 **E3**
Jeannette 11,221 **F2**
Johnstown 28,134 **F4**
Lancaster 55,551 **F9**
Lansdale 16,362 **F11**
Latrobe 9,265 **F3**
Lebanon 24,800 **F9**
Levittown 55,362 **F12**
Lewistown 9,341 **E6**
Lock Haven 9,230 **D7**
McCandless 28,781 **h13**
McKeesport 26,016 **F2**
Meadville 14,318 **C1**
Middletown 9,254 **F8**
Millcreek Township
  46,100 **B1**
Monroeville 29,169 **k14**
Mount Lebanon 33,362
  F1
New Castle 28,334 **D1**
New Kensington 15,894
  E2
Norristown 30,749 **F11**
Oil City 11,949 **D2**
Penn Hills 51,430 **k14**
Philadelphia 1,585,577
  G11
Pittsburgh 369,879 **F1**
Plum 25,609 **k14**
Pottstown 21,831 **F10**
Pottsville 16,603 **E9**
Punxsutawney 6,782 **E4**
Reading 78,380 **F10**
Scranton 81,805 **D10**
Shamokin 9,184 **E8**
Sharon 17,493 **D1**
Springfield 24,160 **p20**
State College 38,923 **E6**
Sunbury 11,591 **E8**
Uniontown 12,034 **G2**
Upper Darby 81,177
  G11
Warminster 32,832 **F11**
Warren 11,122 **C3**
Washington 15,864 **F1**
Waynesboro 9,578 **G6**
West Chester 18,041
  G10
West Mifflin 23,644 **F2**
Wilkes-Barre 47,523
  D10
Wilkinsburg 21,080 **F1**
Williamsport 31,933 **D7**
York 42,192 **G8**

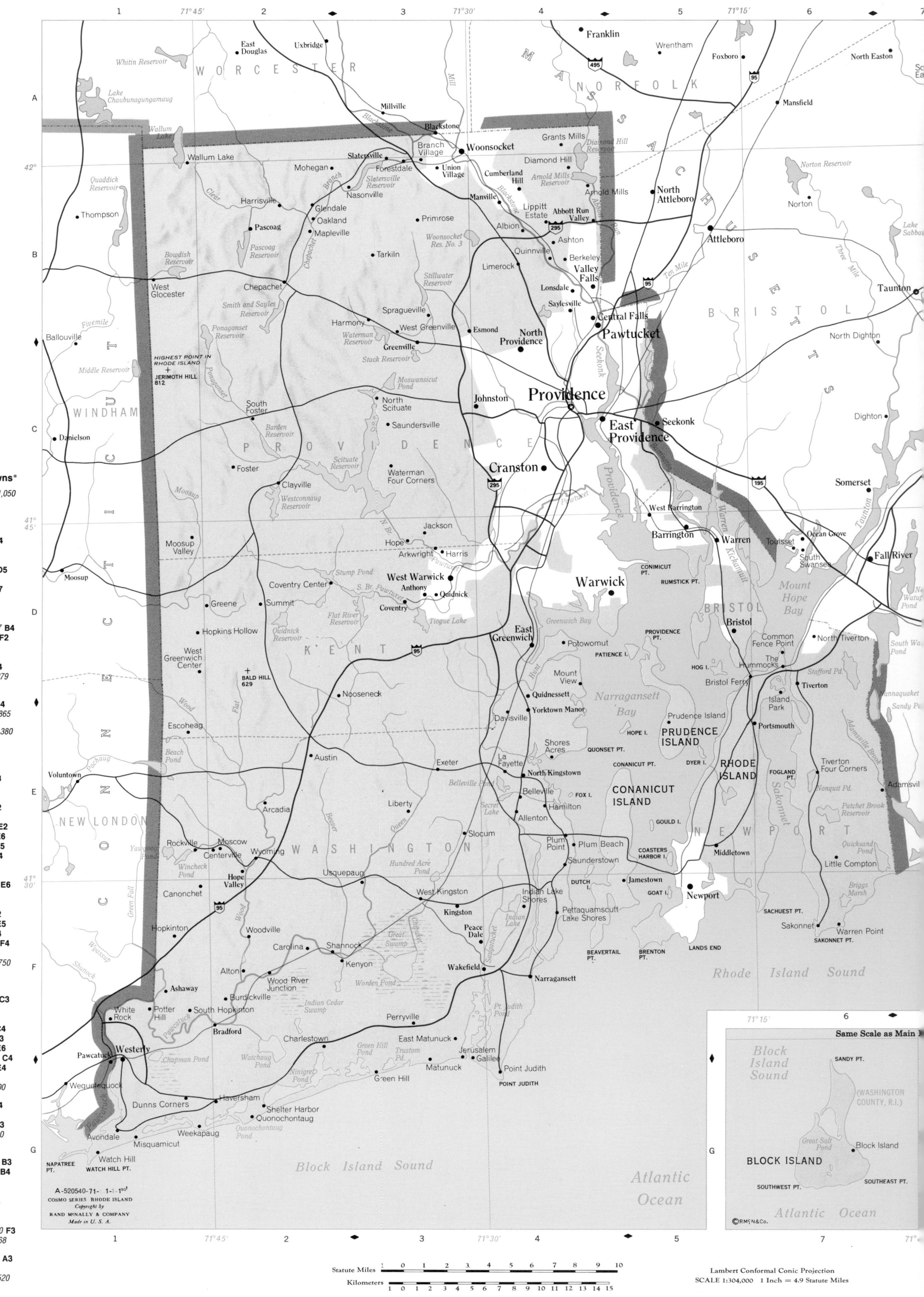

Cities and Towns*

Abbott Run Valley 1,050 **B4**
Albion 1,600 **B4**
Allenton 600 **E4**
Anthony 2,980 **D3**
Arnold Mills 600 **B4**
Ashaway 1,584 **F1**
Ashton 820 **B4**
Barrington 15,849 **D5**
Berkeley 830 **B4**
Block Island 620 **h7**
Bradford 1,604 **F2**
Bristol 21,625 **D5**
Carolina 650 **F2**
Central Falls 17,637 **B4**
Charlestown 1,500 **F2**
Chepachet 900 **B2**
Coventry 6,980 **D3**
Cranston 76,060 **C4**
Cumberland Hill 6,379 **B4**
Davisville 500 **E4**
Diamond Hill 810 **B4**
East Greenwich 11,865 **D4**
East Providence 50,380 **C4**
Esmond 4,320 **B4**
Forestdale 530 **B3**
Glendale 700 **B2**
Greenville 8,303 **C3**
Harmony 820 **B3**
Harris 1,050 **D3**
Harrisville 1,654 **B2**
Hope 270 **D3**
Hope Valley 1,446 **E2**
Island Park 1,240 **E6**
Jamestown 4,999 **F5**
Johnston 26,542 **C4**
Kingston 6,504 **F3**
La Fayette 640 **E4**
Little Compton 500 **E6**
Lonsdale 3,850 **B4**
Manville 3,030 **B4**
Mapleville 1,300 **B2**
Middletown 3,350 **E5**
Mount View 610 **D4**
Narragansett 3,721 **F4**
Newport 28,227 **F5**
North Kingstown 2,750 **E4**
North Providence 32,090 **C4**
North Scituate 350 **C3**
Oakland 600 **B2**
Pascoag 5,011 **B2**
Pawtucket 72,644 **C4**
Peace Dale 3,100 **F3**
Portsmouth 3,540 **E6**
Providence 160,728 **C4**
Quidnessett 3,300 **E4**
Quidnick 2,300 **D3**
Quonochontaug 1,500 **G2**
Saylesville 3,510 **B4**
Shannock 950 **F2**
Slatersville 2,330 **A3**
South Hopkinton 900 **F1**
Tiverton 7,259 **D6**
Union Village 2,150 **B3**
Valley Falls 11,175 **B4**
Wakefield 3,450 **F3**
Warren 11,385 **D5**
Warwick 85,427 **D4**
Watch Hill 500 **G1**
Westerly 16,477 **F1**
West Kingston 1,150 **F3**
West Warwick 29,268 **D3**
Woonsocket 43,877 **A3**
Wyoming 850 **E2**
Yorktown Manor 2,520 **E4**

*Populations are for localities, not incorporated towns.

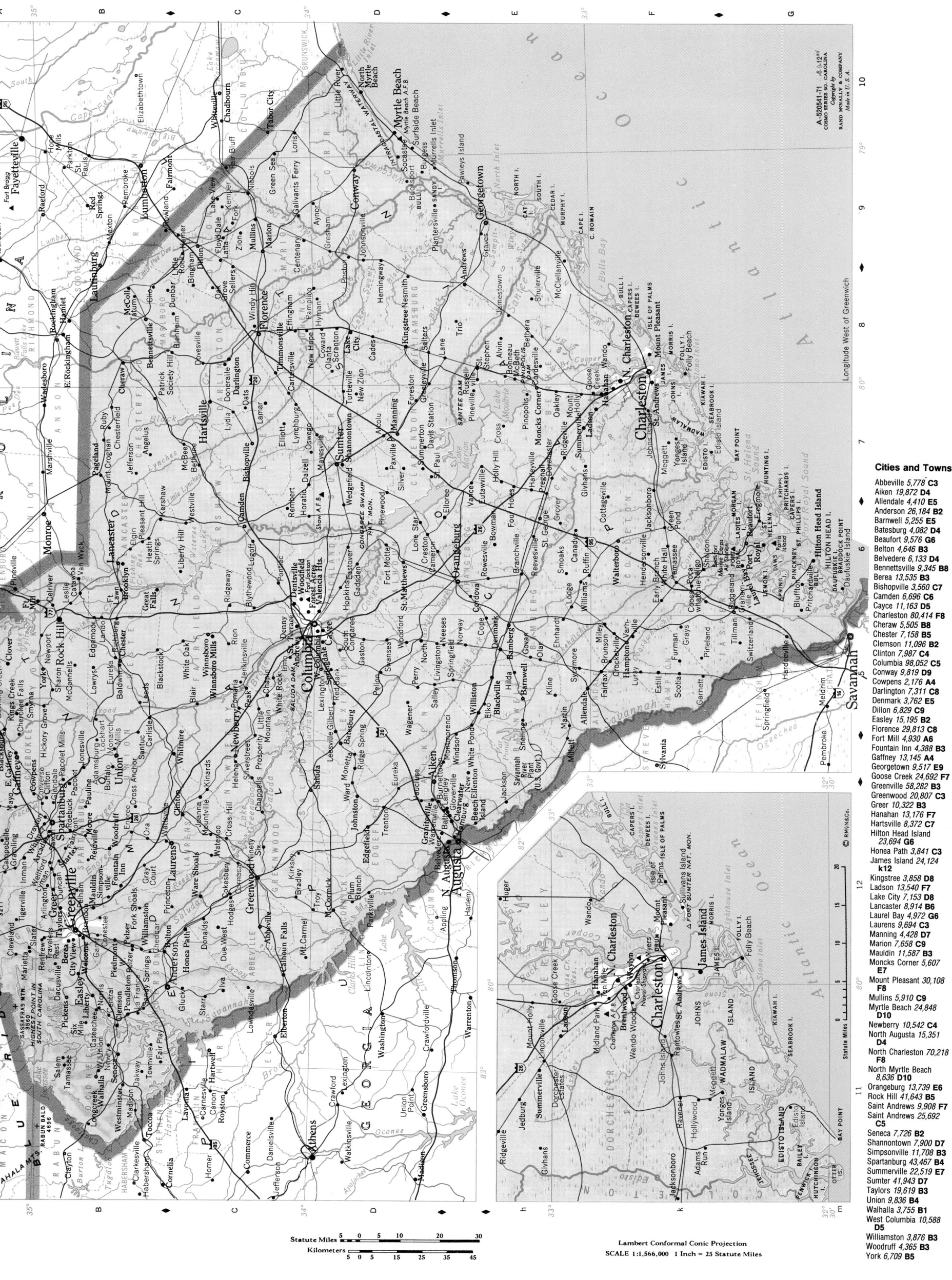

A-520541-71   -6 & 12nd
COSMO SERIES SO. CAROLINA
Copyright by
RAND M^cNALLY & COMPANY
Made in U.S.A.

Lambert Conformal Conic Projection
SCALE 1:1,566,000 1 Inch = 25 Statute Miles

Statute Miles 5 0 5 10 20 30
Kilometers 5 0 15 30 35 40 45

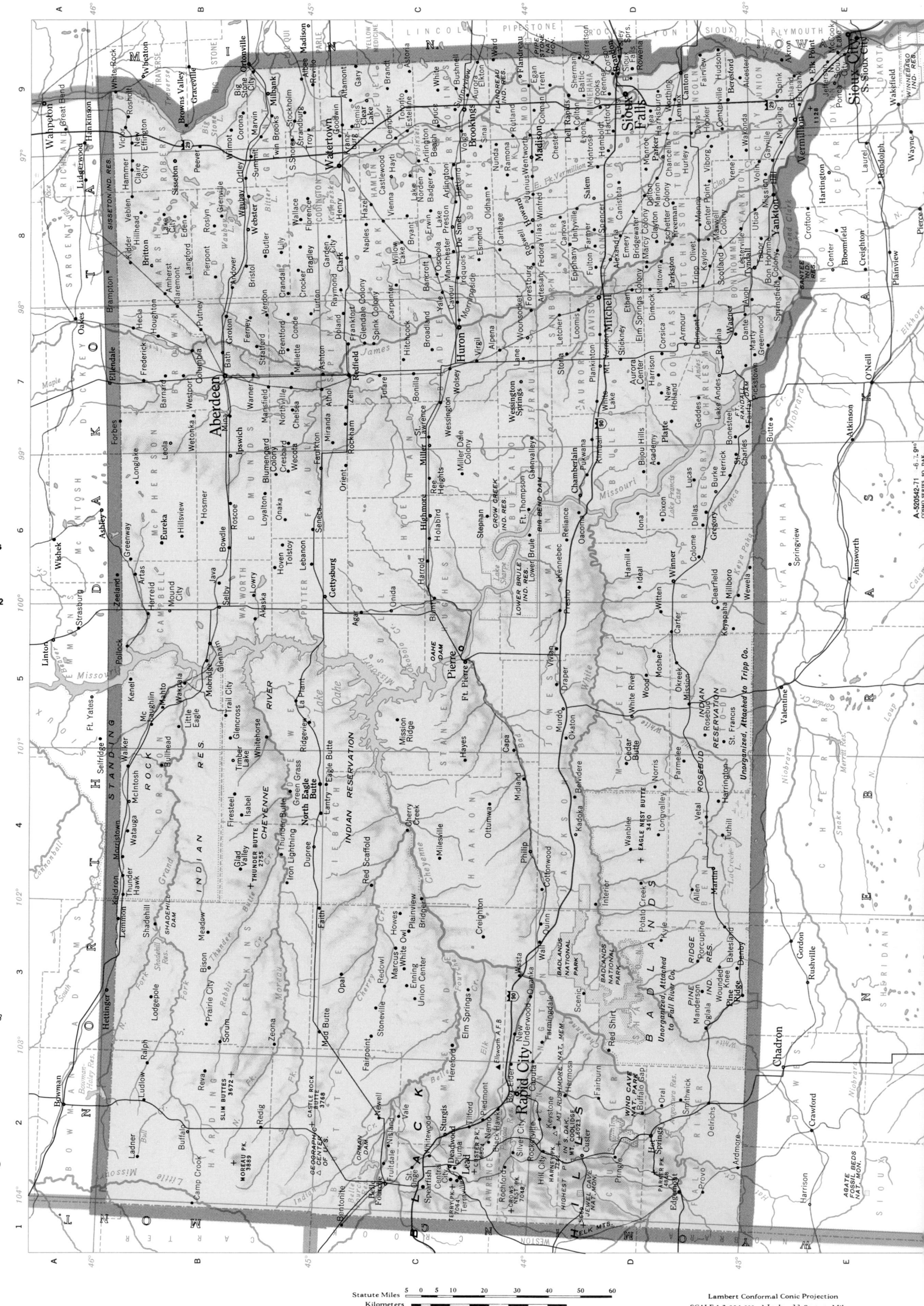

Cities and Towns

Aberdeen *24,927* **B7**
Alcester *843* **D9**
Arlington *908* **C8**
Armour *854* **D7**
Belle Fourche *4,335* **C2**
Beresford *1,849* **D9**
Black Hawk *1,955* **C2**
Box Elder *2,680* **C2**
Brandon *3,543* **D9**
Britton *1,394* **B8**
Brookings *16,270* **C9**
Burke *756* **D6**
Canton *2,787* **D9**
Centerville *887* **D9**
Chamberlain *2,347* **D6**
Clark *1,292* **C8**
Clear Lake *1,247* **C9**
Custer *1,741* **D2**
Deadwood *1,830* **C2**
De Smet *1,172* **C8**
Edgemont *906* **D2**
Elk Point *1,423* **E9**
Eureka *1,197* **B6**
Faulkton *809* **B6**
Flandreau *2,311* **C9**
Fort Pierre *1,854* **C5**
Freeman *1,293* **D8**
Garretson *924* **D9**
Gettysburg *1,510* **C6**
Gregory *1,384* **D6**
Groton *1,196* **B7**
Hartford *1,262* **D9**
Highmore *835* **C6**
Hot Springs *4,325* **D2**
Howard *1,156* **C8**
Huron *12,448* **C7**
Ipswich *965* **B6**
Lake Andes *846* **D7**
Lead *3,632* **C2**
Lemmon *1,614* **B3**
Lennox *1,767* **D9**
Martin *1,151* **D4**
Milbank *3,879* **B9**
Miller *1,678* **C7**
Mitchell *13,798* **D7**
Mobridge *3,768* **B5**
North Eagle Butte *1,423* **B4**
North Sioux City *2,019* **E9**
Parker *984* **D8**
Parkston *1,572* **D8**
Philip *1,077* **C4**
Pierre *12,906* **C5**
Pine Ridge *2,596* **D3**
Platte *1,311* **D7**
Rapid City *54,523* **C2**
Redfield *2,770* **C7**
Salem *1,289* **D8**
Scotland *968* **D8**
Selby *707* **B5**
Sioux Falls *100,814* **D9**
Sisseton *2,181* **B8**
Spearfish *6,966* **C2**
Springfield *834* **E8**
Sturgis *5,330* **C2**
Tyndall *1,201* **E8**
Vermillion *10,034* **E9**
Volga *1,263* **C9**
Wagner *1,462* **D7**
Wall *834* **D3**
Watertown *17,592* **C8**
Webster *2,017* **B8**
Wessington Springs *1,083* **C7**
Winner *3,354* **D6**
Yankton *12,703* **E8**

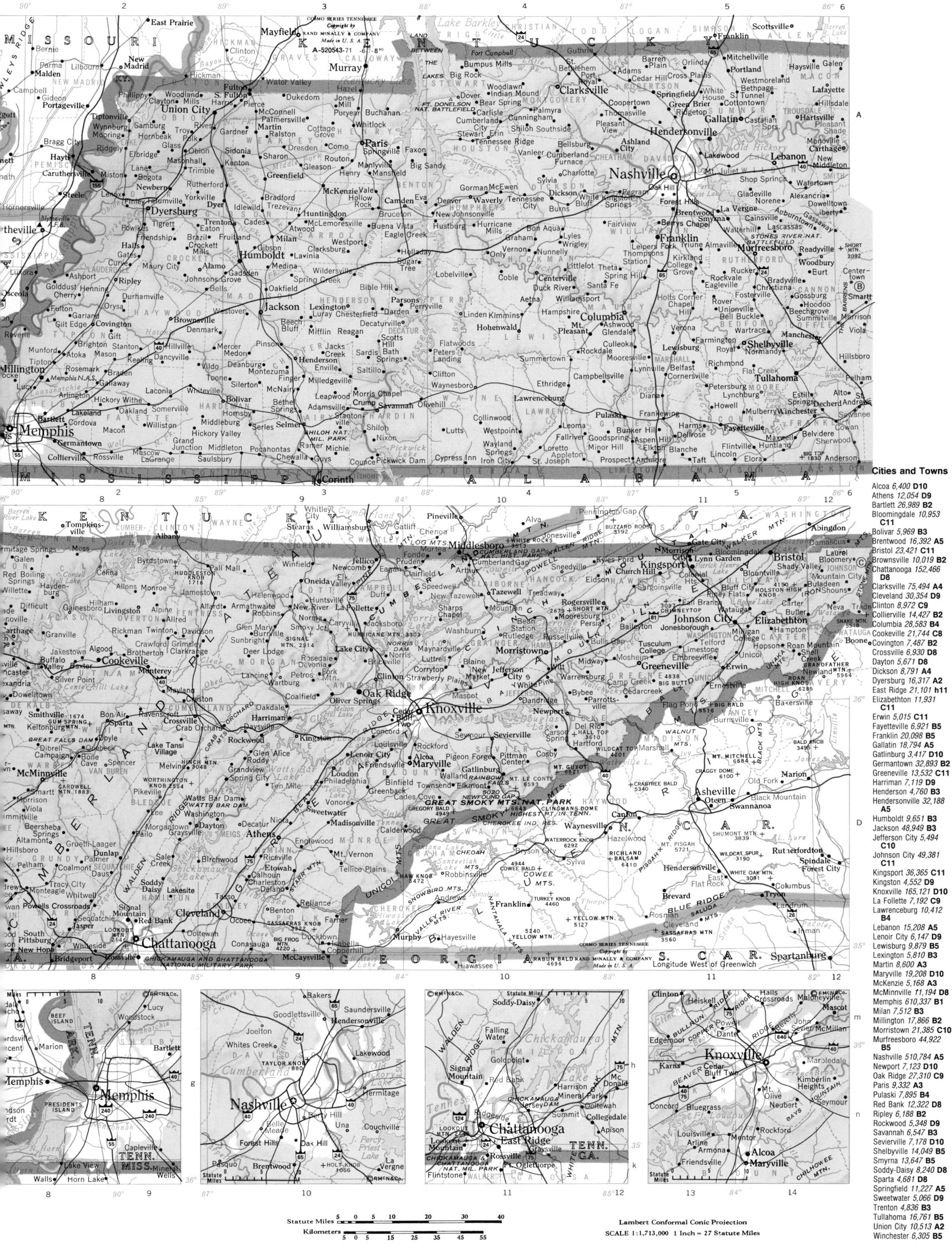

Statute Miles

Kilometers

Lambert Conformal Conic Projection
SCALE 1:1,713,000 1 Inch = 27 Statute Miles

Cities and Towns

Alcoa 6,400 **D10**
Athens 12,054 **D9**
Bartlett 26,989 **B2**
Bloomingdale 10,953 **C11**
Bolivar 5,969 **B3**
Brentwood 16,392 **A5**
Bristol 23,421 **C11**
Brownsville 10,019 **B2**
Chattanooga 152,466 **D8**
Clarksville 75,494 **A4**
Cleveland 30,354 **D9**
Clinton 8,972 **C9**
Collierville 14,427 **B2**
Columbia 28,583 **B4**
Cookeville 21,744 **C8**
Covington 7,487 **B2**
Crossville 6,930 **D8**
Dayton 5,671 **D8**
Dickson 8,791 **A4**
Dyersburg 16,317 **A2**
East Ridge 21,101 **h11**
Elizabethton 11,931 **C11**
Erwin 5,015 **C11**
Fayetteville 6,921 **B5**
Franklin 20,098 **B5**
Gallatin 18,794 **A5**
Gatlinburg 3,417 **D10**
Germantown 32,893 **B2**
Greeneville 13,532 **C11**
Harriman 7,119 **D9**
Henderson 4,760 **B3**
Hendersonville 32,188 **A5**
Humboldt 9,651 **B3**
Jackson 48,949 **B3**
Jefferson City 5,494 **C10**
Johnson City 49,381 **C11**
Kingsport 36,365 **C11**
Kingston 4,552 **D9**
Knoxville 165,121 **D10**
La Follette 7,192 **C9**
Lawrenceburg 10,412 **B4**
Lebanon 15,208 **A5**
Lenoir City 6,147 **D9**
Lewisburg 9,879 **B5**
Lexington 5,810 **B3**
Martin 8,600 **A3**
Maryville 19,208 **D10**
McKenzie 5,168 **A3**
McMinnville 11,194 **D8**
Memphis 610,337 **B1**
Milan 7,512 **B3**
Millington 17,866 **B2**
Morristown 21,385 **C10**
Murfreesboro 44,922 **B5**
Nashville 510,784 **A5**
Newport 7,123 **D10**
Oak Ridge 27,310 **C9**
Paris 9,332 **A3**
Pulaski 7,895 **B4**
Red Bank 12,322 **D8**
Ripley 6,188 **B2**
Rockwood 5,348 **D9**
Savannah 6,547 **B3**
Sevierville 7,178 **D10**
Shelbyville 14,049 **B5**
Smyrna 13,647 **B5**
Soddy-Daisy 8,240 **D8**
Sparta 4,681 **D8**
Springfield 11,227 **A5**
Sweetwater 5,066 **D9**
Trenton 4,836 **B3**
Tullahoma 16,761 **B5**
Union City 10,513 **A2**
Winchester 6,305 **B5**

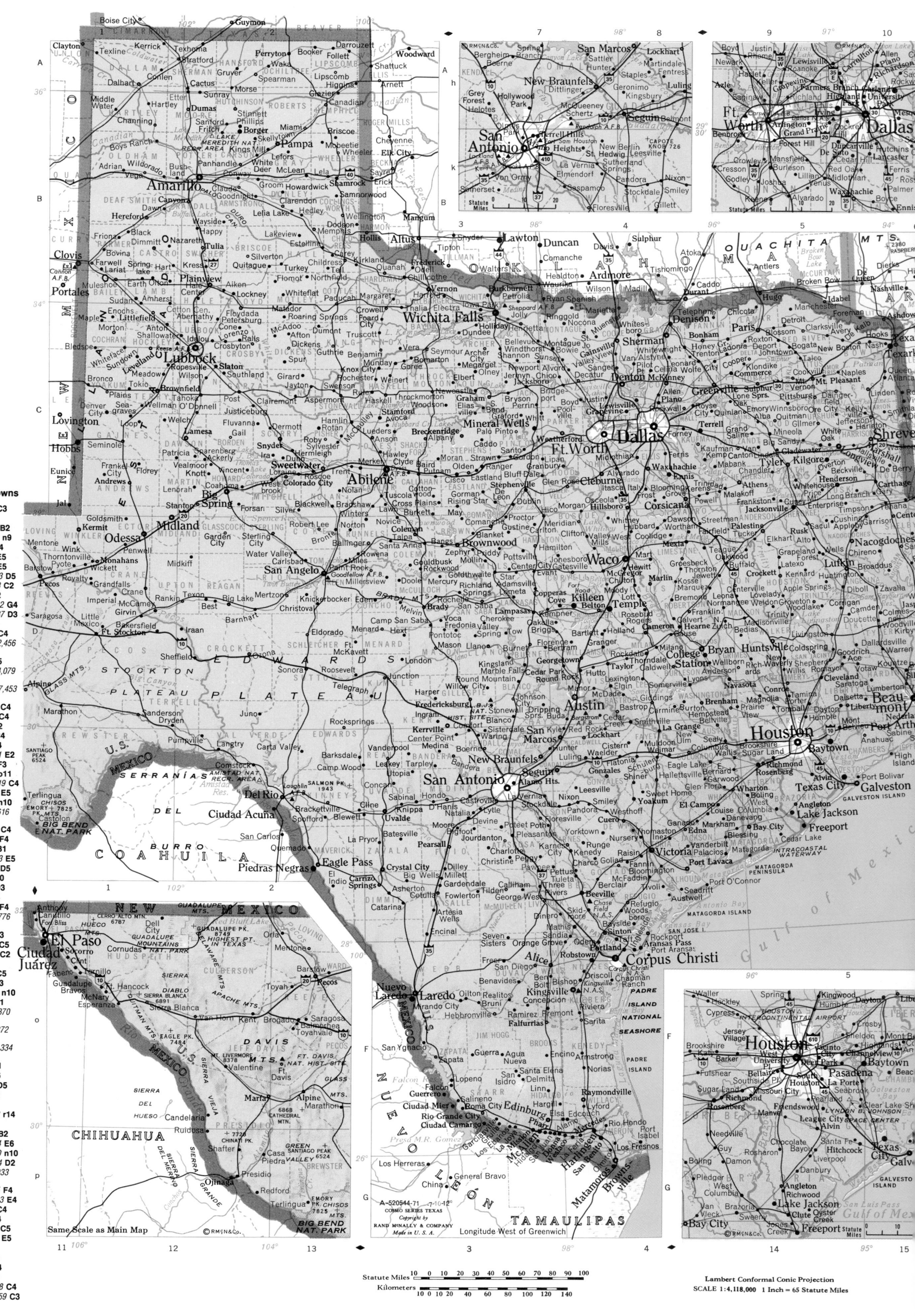

Cities and Towns

Abilene 106,654 **C3**
Alice 19,788 **F3**
Amarillo 157,615 **B2**
Arlington 261,721 **n9**
Austin 465,622 **D4**
Bay City 18,170 **E5**
Baytown 63,850 **E5**
Beaumont 114,323 **D5**
Big Spring 23,093 **C2**
Borger 15,675 **B2**
Brownsville 98,962 **G4**
Brownwood 18,387 **D3**
Bryan 55,002 **D4**
Cleburne 22,205 **C4**
College Station 52,456 **D4**
Conroe 27,610 **D5**
Copperas Cove 24,079 **D4**
Corpus Christi 257,453 **F4**
Corsicana 22,911 **C4**
Dallas 1,006,877 **C4**
Del Rio 30,705 **E2**
Denison 21,505 **C4**
Denton 66,270 **C4**
Eagle Pass 20,651 **E2**
Edinburg 29,885 **F3**
El Paso 515,342 **o11**
Fort Worth 447,619 **C4**
Galveston 59,070 **E5**
Garland 180,650 **n10**
Grand Prairie 99,616 **n10**
Greenville 23,071 **C4**
Harlingen 48,735 **F4**
Hereford 14,745 **B1**
Houston 1,630,553 **E5**
Huntsville 27,925 **D5**
Irving 155,037 **n10**
Kerrville 17,384 **D3**
Killeen 63,535 **D4**
Kingsville 25,276 **F4**
Lake Jackson 22,776 **E5**
Laredo 122,899 **F3**
Longview 70,311 **C5**
Lubbock 186,206 **C2**
Lufkin 30,206 **D5**
Marshall 23,682 **C5**
McAllen 84,021 **F3**
Mesquite 101,484 **n10**
Midland 89,443 **D1**
Mineral Wells 14,870 **C3**
Nacogdoches 30,872 **D5**
New Braunfels 27,334 **E3**
Odessa 89,699 **D1**
Orange 19,381 **D6**
Palestine 18,042 **D5**
Pampa 19,959 **B2**
Paris 24,699 **C5**
Pasadena 119,363 **r14**
Pecos 12,069 **D1**
Plainview 21,700 **B2**
Port Arthur 58,724 **E6**
Richardson 74,840 **n10**
San Angelo 84,474 **D2**
San Antonio 935,933 **E3**
San Benito 20,125 **F4**
San Marcos 28,743 **E4**
Sherman 31,601 **C4**
Temple 46,109 **D4**
Texarkana 31,656 **C5**
Texas City 40,822 **E5**
Tyler 75,450 **C5**
Uvalde 14,729 **E3**
Victoria 55,076 **E4**
Waco 103,590 **D4**
Waxahachie 18,168 **C4**
Wichita Falls 96,259 **C3**

Statute Miles 10 0 10 20 30 40 50 60 70 80 90 100
Kilometers   10 0 10 20 40 60 80 100 120 140

Lambert Conformal Conic Projection
SCALE 1:4,118,000 1 Inch = 65 Statute Miles

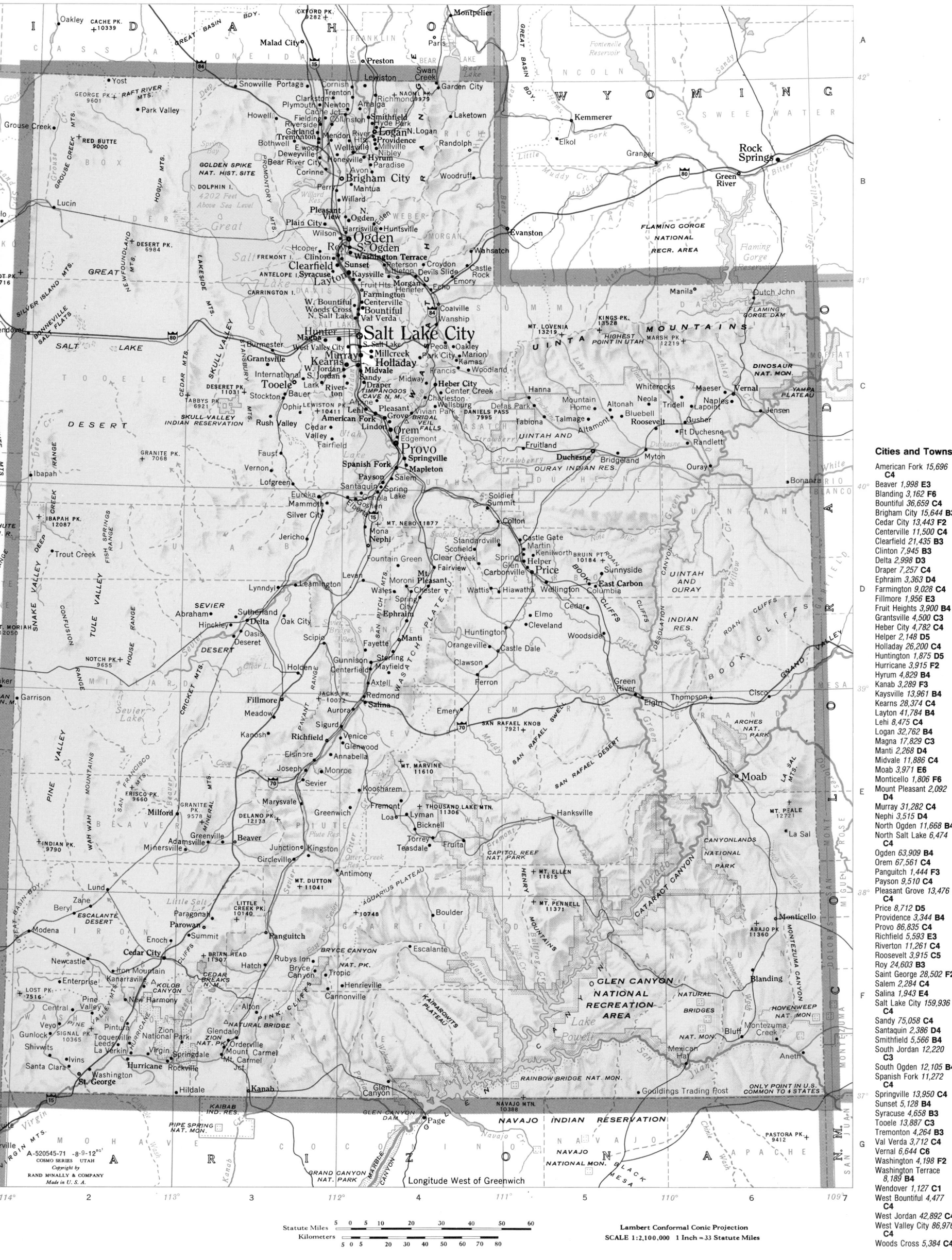

Cities and Towns

American Fork 15,696 **C4**
Beaver 1,998 **E3**
Blanding 3,162 **F6**
Bountiful 36,659 **C4**
Brigham City 15,644 **B3**
Cedar City 13,443 **F2**
Centerville 11,500 **C4**
Clearfield 21,435 **B3**
Clinton 7,945 **B3**
Delta 2,998 **D3**
Draper 7,257 **C4**
Ephraim 3,363 **D4**
Farmington 9,028 **C4**
Fillmore 1,956 **E3**
Fruit Heights 3,900 **B4**
Grantsville 4,500 **C3**
Heber City 4,782 **C4**
Helper 2,148 **D5**
Holladay 26,200 **C4**
Huntington 1,875 **D5**
Hurricane 3,915 **F2**
Hyrum 4,829 **B4**
Kanab 3,289 **F3**
Kaysville 13,961 **B4**
Kearns 28,374 **C4**
Layton 41,784 **B4**
Lehi 8,475 **C4**
Logan 32,762 **C3**
Magna 17,829 **C4**
Manti 2,268 **D4**
Midvale 11,886 **C4**
Moab 3,971 **E6**
Monticello 1,806 **F6**
Mount Pleasant 2,092 **D4**
Murray 31,282 **C4**
Nephi 3,515 **D4**
North Ogden 11,668 **B4**
North Salt Lake 6,474 **C4**
Ogden 63,909 **B4**
Orem 67,561 **C4**
Panguitch 1,444 **F3**
Payson 9,510 **C4**
Pleasant Grove 13,476 **C4**
Price 8,712 **D5**
Providence 3,344 **B4**
Provo 86,835 **C4**
Richfield 5,593 **E3**
Riverton 11,261 **C4**
Roosevelt 3,915 **C5**
Roy 24,603 **B3**
Saint George 28,502 **F2**
Salem 2,284 **C4**
Salina 1,943 **E4**
Salt Lake City 159,936 **C4**
Sandy 75,058 **C4**
Santaquin 2,386 **D4**
Smithfield 5,566 **B4**
South Jordan 12,220 **C3**
South Ogden 12,105 **C4**
Spanish Fork 11,272 **C4**
Springville 13,950 **C4**
Sunset 5,128 **B4**
Syracuse 4,658 **B3**
Tooele 13,887 **C3**
Tremonton 4,264 **B3**
Val Verda 3,712 **C4**
Vernal 6,644 **C6**
Washington 4,198 **F2**
Washington Terrace 8,189 **B4**
Wendover 1,127 **C1**
West Bountiful 4,477 **C4**
West Jordan 42,892 **C4**
West Valley City 86,976 **C4**
Woods Cross 5,384 **C4**

Statute Miles
Kilometers

Lambert Conformal Conic Projection
SCALE 1:2,100,000   1 Inch = 33 Statute Miles

VERMONT

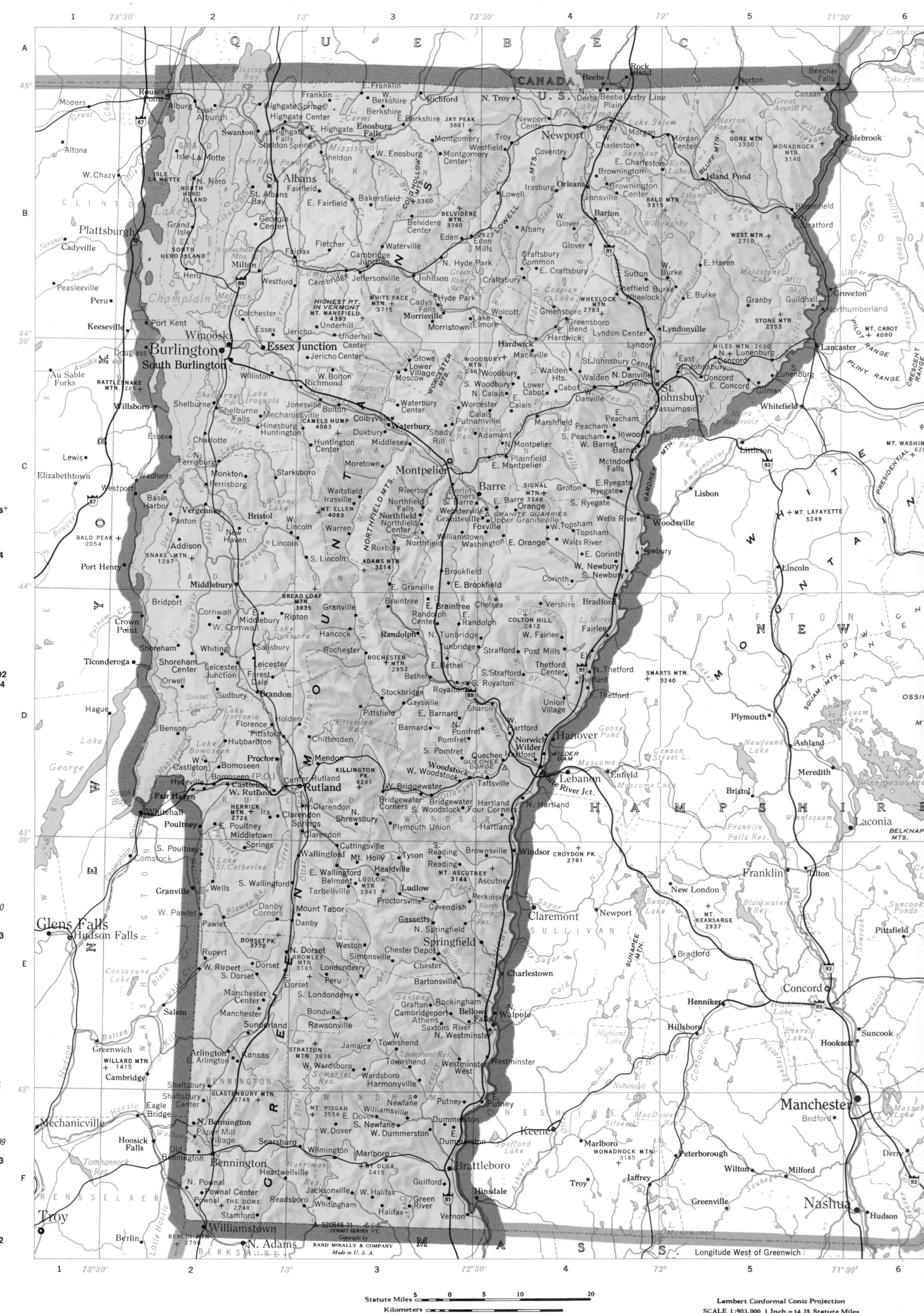

Statute Miles
Kilometers

Lambert Conformal Conic Projection
SCALE 1:903,000 1 Inch = 14.25 Statute Miles

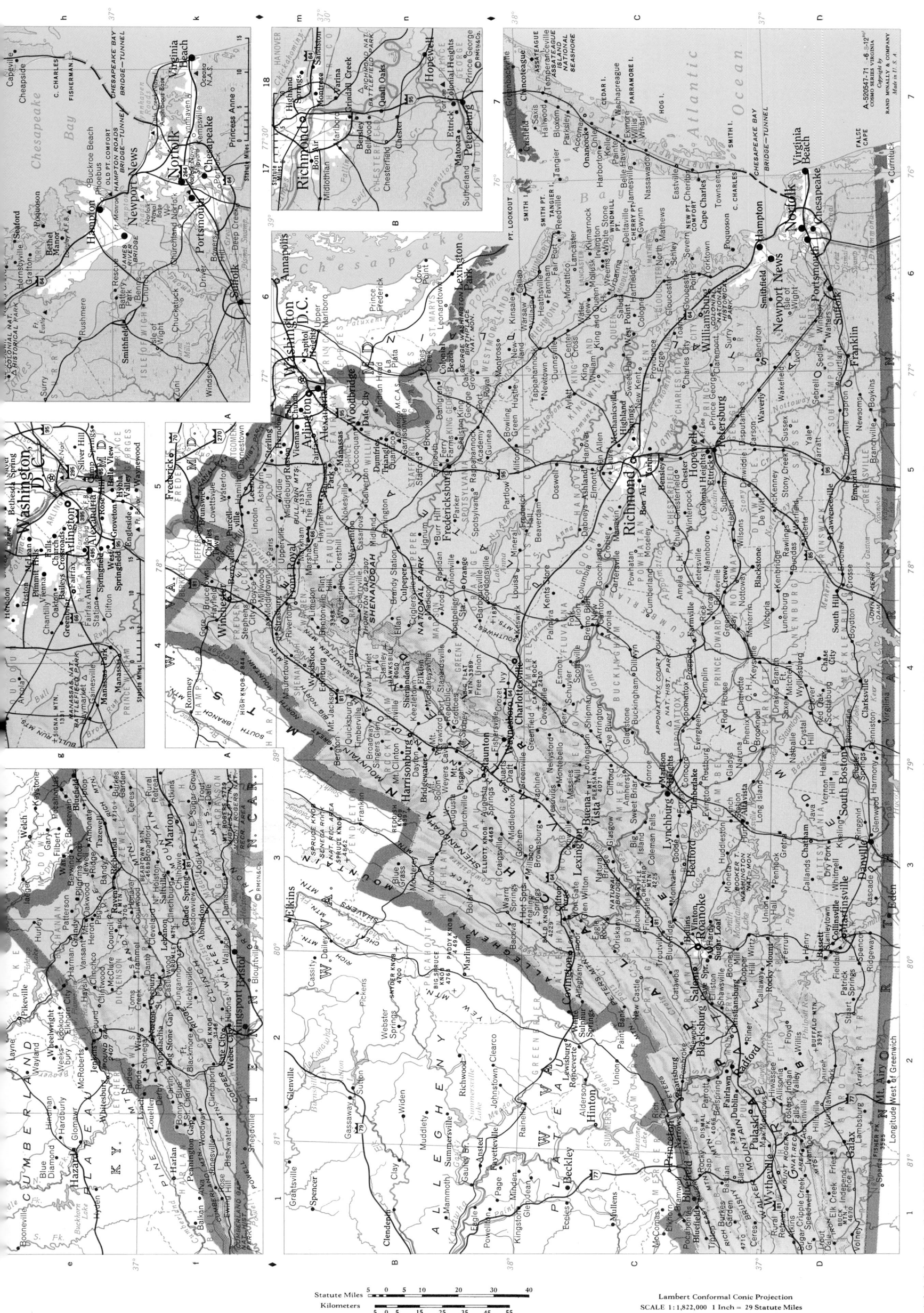

A-520547-71 -6 -5-12

COSMO SERIES VIRGINIA

RAND M⸱NALLY & COMPANY

Made in U.S.A.

Cities and Towns

Alexandria 111,183 **B5**
Annandale 50,975 **g12**
Appomattox 1,707 **C4**
Arlington 170,936 **B5**
Bedford 6,073 **C3**
Big Stone Gap 4,748 **f9**
Blacksburg 34,590 **C2**
Bluefield 5,363 **C1**
Bon Air 16,413 **C5**
Bristol 18,426 **f9**
Buena Vista 6,406 **C3**
Charlottesville 40,341 **B4**
Chesapeake 151,976 **D6**
Chester 14,896 **C5**
Chincoteague 3,572 **C7**
Christiansburg 15,004 **C2**
Clifton Forge 4,679 **C3**
Collinsville 7,280 **D3**
Colonial Heights 16,064 **C5**
Covington 6,991 **C3**
Culpeper 8,581 **B5**
Dale City 47,170 **B5**
Danville 53,056 **D3**
Emporia 5,306 **D5**
Engleside 27,485 **g12**
Fairfax 19,622 **B5**
Farmville 6,046 **C4**
Franklin 7,864 **D6**
Fredericksburg 19,027 **B5**
Front Royal 11,880 **B4**
Galax 6,670 **D2**
Hampton 133,793 **C6**
Harrisonburg 30,707 **B4**
Herndon 16,139 **B5**
Highland Springs 13,823 **C5**
Hollins 13,305 **C3**
Hopewell 23,101 **C5**
Leesburg 16,202 **A5**
Lexington 6,959 **C3**
Lynchburg 66,049 **C3**
Manassas 27,957 **B5**
Manassas Park 6,734 **B5**
Marion 6,630 **f10**
Martinsville 16,162 **g12**
McLean 38,168 **g12**
Mechanicsville 22,027 **C5**
Newport News 170,045 **D6**
Norfolk 261,229 **D6**
Norton 4,247 **f9**
Petersburg 38,386 **C5**
Poquoson 11,005 **C6**
Portsmouth 103,907 **D6**
Pulaski 9,985 **C2**
Radford 15,940 **C2**
Reston 48,556 **B5**
Richlands 4,456 **e10**
Richmond 203,056 **C5**
Roanoke 96,397 **C3**
Salem 23,756 **C2**
Shenandoah 2,213 **B4**
South Boston 6,997 **D4**
Springfield 23,706 **g12**
Staunton 24,461 **B3**
Sterling 20,512 **A5**
Suffolk 52,141 **D6**
Tazewell 4,176 **e10**
Vienna 14,852 **B5**
Vinton 7,665 **C3**
Virginia Beach 393,069 **D7**
Waynesboro 18,549 **B4**
West Springfield 28,126 **g12**
Williamsburg 11,530 **C6**
Winchester 21,947 **A4**
Woodbridge 26,401 **B5**
Wytheville 8,038 **D1**
Yorktown 270 **C6**

Statute Miles 5 0 5 10   20   30   40
Kilometers 5 0 5 15 25 35 45 55

Lambert Conformal Conic Projection
SCALE 1:1,822,000 1 Inch = 29 Statute Miles

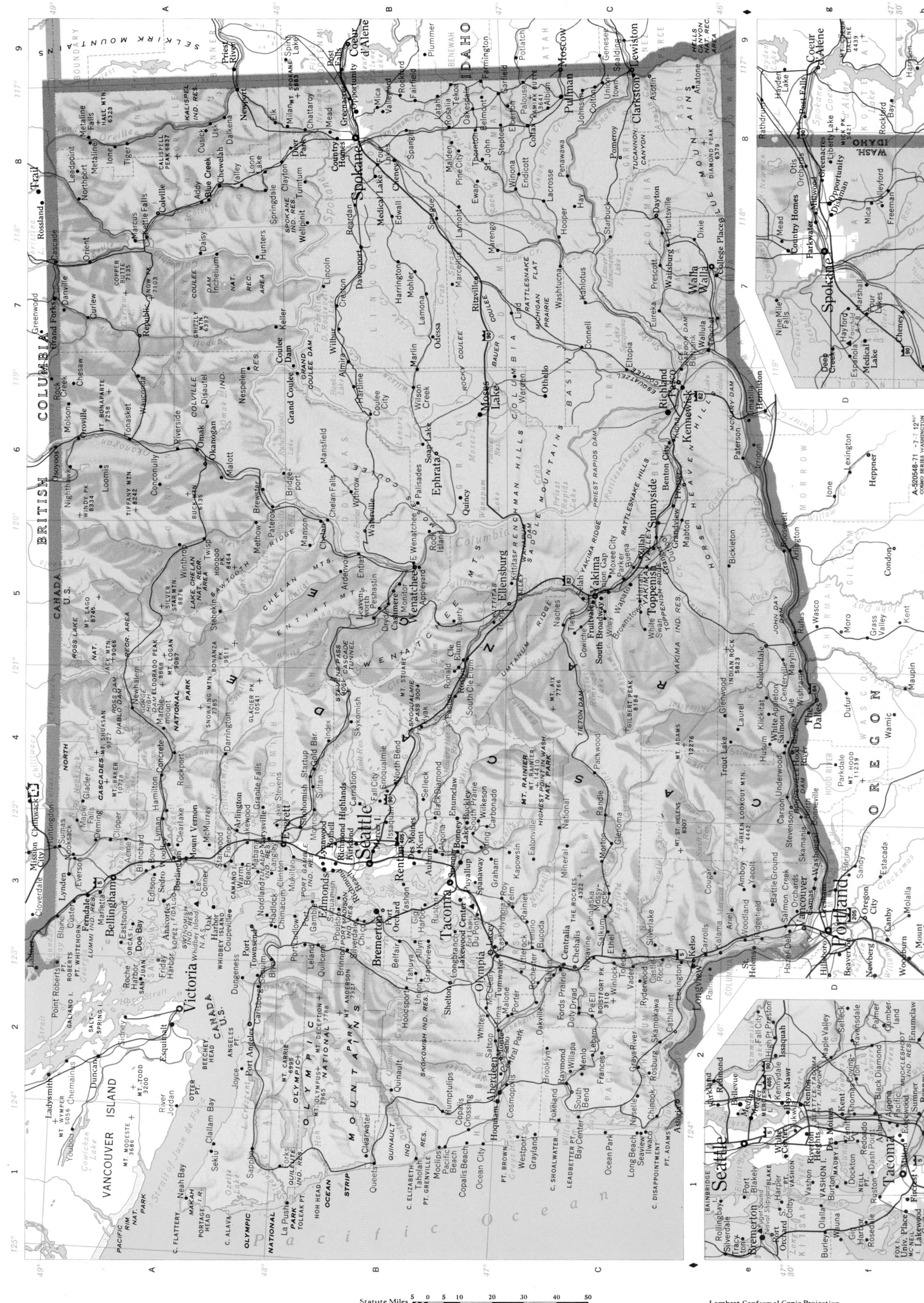

Cities and Towns

Aberdeen *16,565* **C2**
Anacortes *11,451* **A3**
Bellevue *86,874* **e11**
Bellingham *52,179* **A3**
Bonney Lake *7,494* **B3**
Bothell *12,345* **B3**
Bremerton *38,142* **B3**
Camas *6,442* **D3**
Centralia *12,101* **C3**
Chehalis *6,527* **C3**
Chelan *2,969* **B5**
Cheney *7,723* **B8**
Clarkston *6,753* **C8**
Colville *4,360* **A8**
Coulee Dam *1,087* **B7**
Des Moines *17,283* **B3**
Dishman *9,671* **g14**
Edmonds *30,744* **B3**
Ellensburg *12,361* **C5**
Enumclaw *7,227* **B4**
Ephrata *5,349* **B6**
Everett *69,961* **B3**
Ferndale *5,398* **A3**
Forks *2,862* **B1**
Goldendale *3,319* **D5**
Grandview *7,169* **C6**
Hoquiam *8,972* **C2**
Kelso *11,820* **C3**
Kennewick *42,155* **C6**
Kent *37,960* **B3**
Kirkland *40,052* **B3**
Lacey *19,279* **B3**
Lakewood Center
 62,000 **B3**
Longview *31,499* **C3**
Lynden *5,709* **A3**
Lynnwood *28,695* **B3**
Medical Lake *3,664* **B8**
Mercer Island *20,816*
 B3
Montesano *3,064* **C2**
Moses Lake *11,235* **B6**
Mount Vernon *17,647*
 A3
Oak Harbor *17,176* **A3**
Okanogan *2,370* **A6**
Olympia *33,840* **B3**
Omak *4,117* **A6**
Opportunity *22,326* **B8**
Othello *4,638* **C6**
Parkland *20,882* **f11**
Pasco *20,337* **C6**
Port Angeles *17,710* **A2**
Port Townsend *7,001*
 A3
Prosser *4,476* **C6**
Pullman *23,478* **C8**
Puyallup *23,875* **B3**
Quincy *3,738* **B6**
Redmond *35,800* **e11**
Renton *41,688* **B3**
Richland *32,315* **C6**
Richmond Highlands
 26,037 **B3**
Riverton Heights *14,182*
 f11
Seattle *516,259* **B3**
Sedro Woolley *6,031*
 A3
Shelton *7,241* **B2**
Snohomish *6,499* **B3**
Spokane *177,196* **B8**
Sunnyside *11,238* **C5**
Tacoma *176,664* **B3**
Toppenish *7,419* **C5**
Tumwater *9,976* **B3**
University Place *27,701*
 f10
Vancouver *46,380* **D3**
Walla Walla *26,478* **C7**
Wenatchee *21,756* **B5**
White Center *15,700*
 e11
Yakima *54,827* **C5**

Statute Miles
Kilometers

Lambert Conformal Conic Projection
SCALE 1:2,091,000 1 Inch = 33 Statute Miles

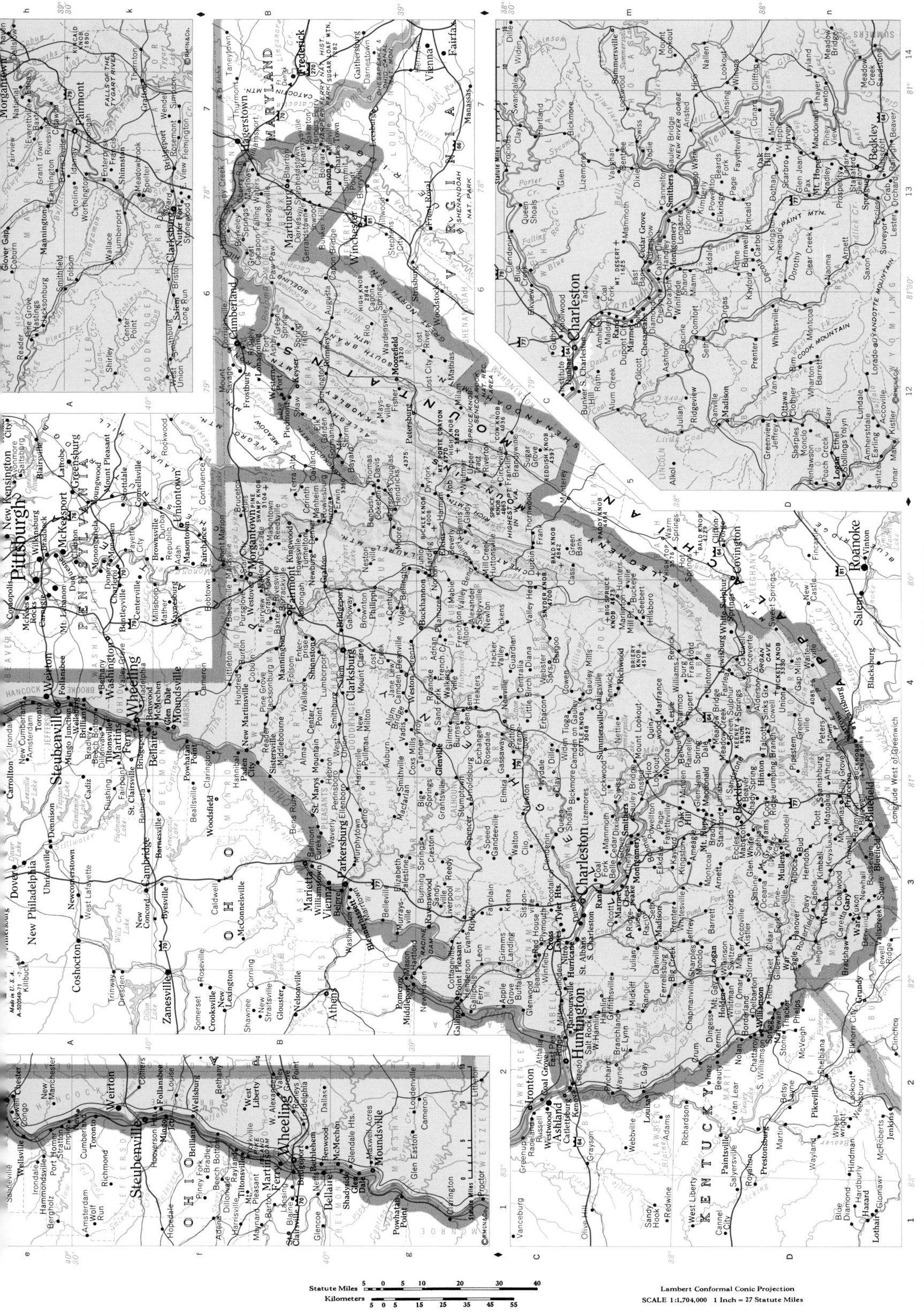

Statute Miles
Kilometers

Lambert Conformal Conic Projection
SCALE 1:1,704,000   1 Inch = 27 Statute Miles

Cities and Towns

Barboursville 2,774 **C2**
Beckley 18,296 **D3**
Bluefield 12,756 **D3**
Bridgeport 6,739 **B4**
Buckhannon 5,909 **C4**
Charleston 57,287 **C3**
Charles Town 3,122 **B7**
Chesapeake 1,896 **C3**
Chester 2,905 **A4**
Clarksburg 18,059 **B4**
Cross Lanes 10,878 **C3**
Dunbar 8,697 **C3**
Elkins 7,420 **C5**
Fairmont 20,210 **B4**
Fayetteville 2,182 **C3**
Follansbee 3,339 **A4**
Gary 1,355 **D3**
Grafton 5,524 **B4**
Harpers Ferry 308 **B7**
Hinton 3,433 **D4**
Huntington 54,844 **C2**
Hurricane 4,461 **C2**
Kenova 3,748 **C2**
Keyser 5,870 **B6**
Kingwood 3,243 **B5**
Lewisburg 3,598 **D4**
Logan 2,206 **D3**
Madison 3,051 **C3**
Mannington 2,184 **B4**
Martinsburg 14,073 **B7**
McMechen 2,130 **B4**
Montgomery 2,449 **C3**
Moorefield 2,148 **B6**
Morgantown 25,879 **B5**
Moundsville 10,753 **B4**
Mullens 2,006 **D3**
New Martinsville 6,705 **B4**
Nitro 6,851 **C3**
Oak Hill 6,812 **D3**
Oceana 1,791 **D3**
Paden City 2,862 **B4**
Parkersburg 33,862 **B3**
Petersburg 2,360 **B5**
Philippi 3,132 **B4**
Point Pleasant 4,996 **C2**
Princeton 7,043 **D3**
Rand 2,400 **C3**
Ranson 2,890 **B7**
Ravenswood 4,189 **C3**
Richwood 2,808 **C4**
Ripley 3,023 **C3**
Romney 1,966 **B6**
Ronceverte 1,754 **D4**
Saint Albans 11,194 **C3**
Saint Marys 2,148 **B3**
Salem 2,063 **B4**
Shinnston 2,543 **B4**
Sistersville 1,797 **B4**
South Charleston 13,645 **C3**
Spencer 2,279 **C3**
Stonewood 1,996 **k10**
Summersville 2,906 **C4**
Tyler Heights 4,070 **C3**
Vienna 10,862 **B3**
War 1,081 **D3**
Weirton 22,124 **A4**
Welch 3,028 **D3**
Wellsburg 3,385 **A4**
Weston 4,994 **B4**
Westover 4,201 **B5**
Wheeling 34,882 **A4**
White Sulphur Springs 2,779 **D4**
Williamson 4,154 **D2**
Williamstown 2,774 **B3**

WISCONSIN

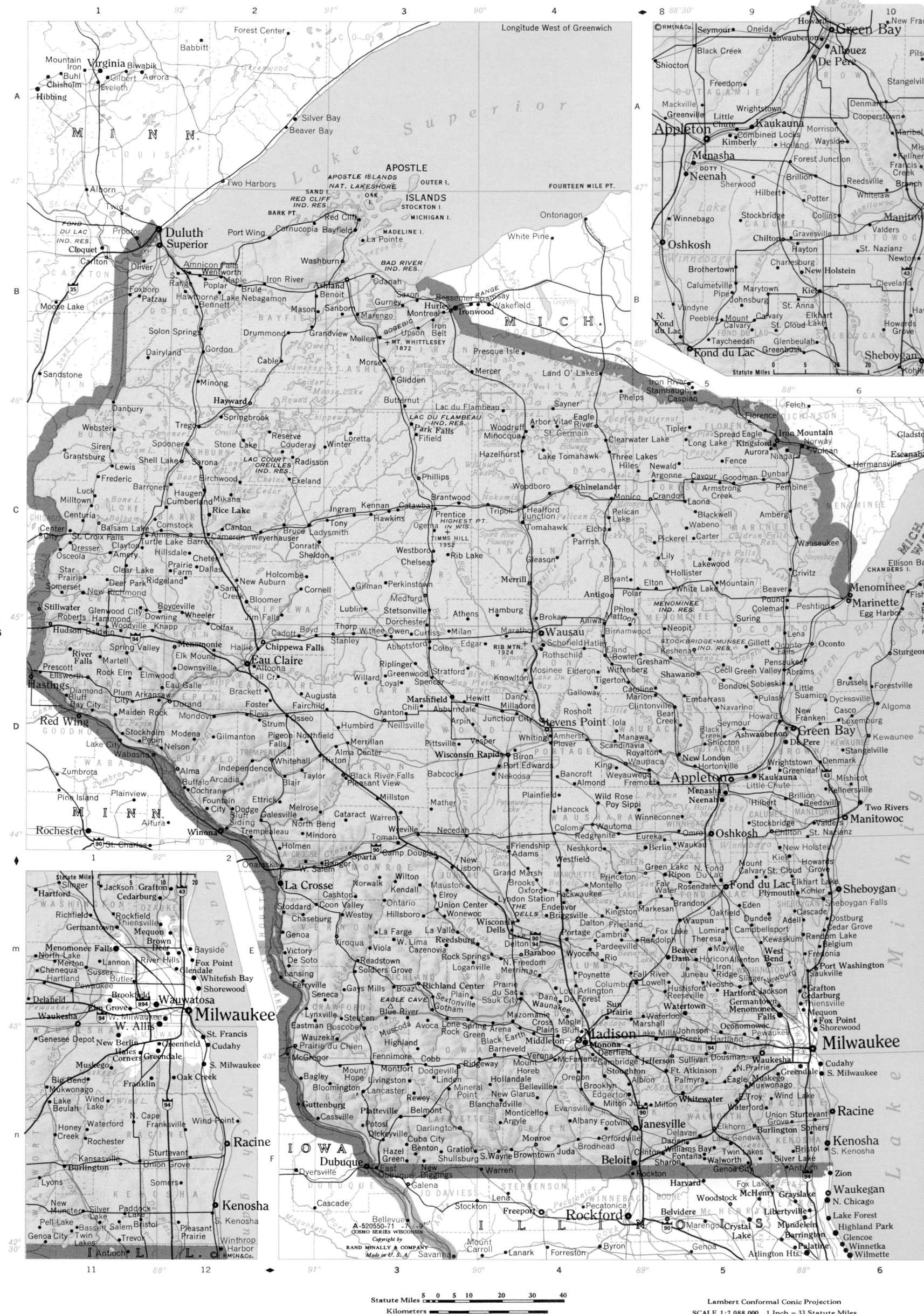

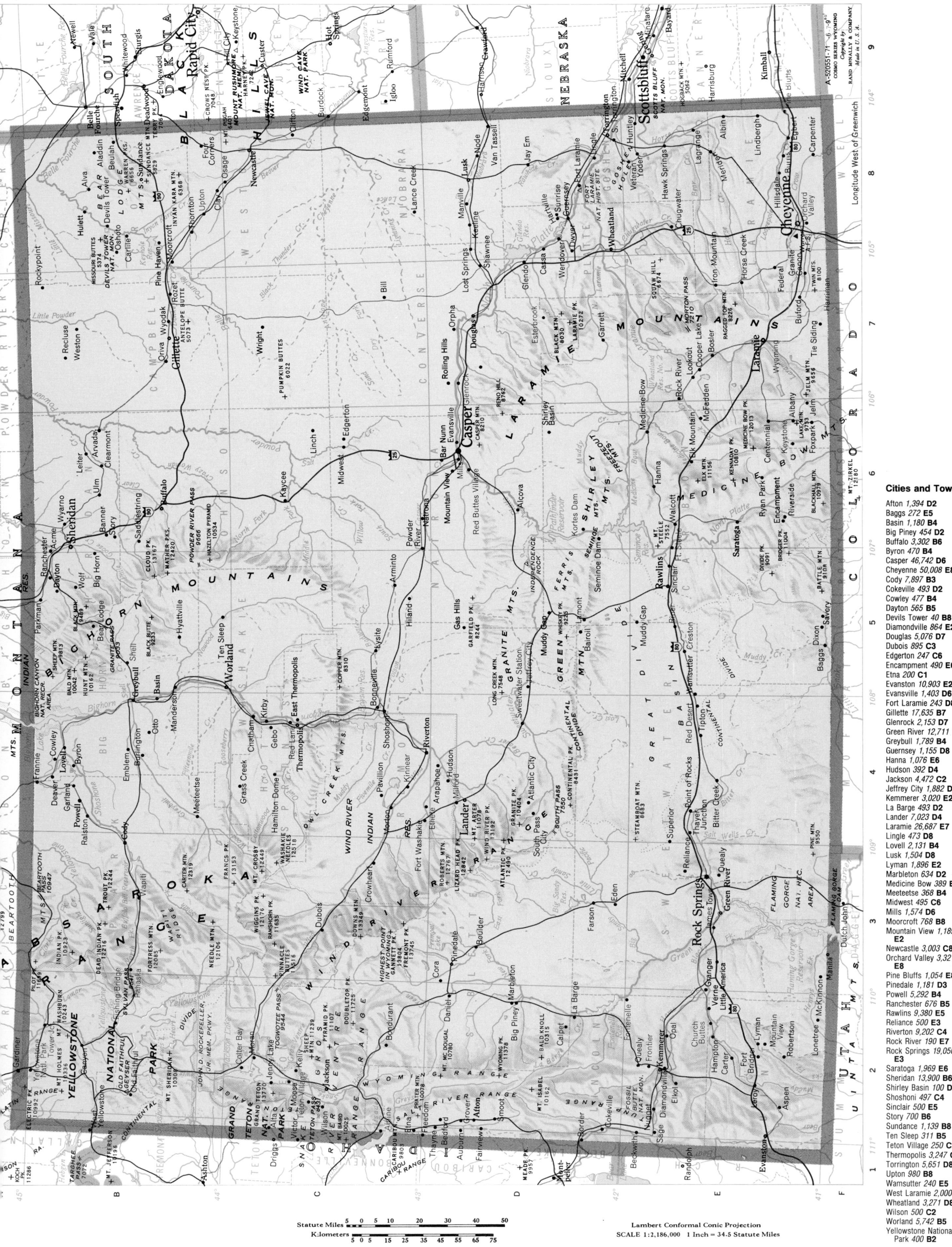

Cities and Towns

Afton *1,394* **D2**
Baggs *272* **E5**
Basin *1,180* **B4**
Big Piney *454* **D2**
Buffalo *3,302* **B6**
Byron *470* **B4**
Casper *46,742* **D6**
Cheyenne *50,008* **E8**
Cody *7,897* **B3**
Cokeville *493* **D2**
Cowley *477* **B4**
Dayton *565* **B5**
Devils Tower *40* **B8**
Diamondville *864* **E2**
Douglas *5,076* **D7**
Dubois *895* **C3**
Edgerton *247* **C6**
Encampment *490* **E6**
Etna *200* **C1**
Evanston *10,903* **E2**
Evansville *1,403* **D6**
Fort Laramie *243* **D8**
Gillette *17,635* **B7**
Glenrock *2,153* **D7**
Green River *12,711* **E3**
Greybull *1,789* **B4**
Guernsey *1,155* **D8**
Hanna *1,076* **E6**
Hudson *392* **D4**
Jackson *4,472* **C2**
Jeffrey City *1,882* **D5**
Kemmerer *3,020* **E2**
La Barge *493* **D2**
Lander *7,023* **D4**
Laramie *26,687* **E7**
Lingle *473* **D8**
Lovell *2,131* **B4**
Lusk *1,504* **D8**
Lyman *1,896* **E2**
Marbleton *634* **D2**
Medicine Bow *389* **E6**
Meeteetse *368* **B4**
Midwest *495* **C6**
Mills *1,574* **D6**
Moorcroft *768* **B8**
Mountain View *1,189* **E2**
Newcastle *3,003* **C8**
Orchard Valley *3,321* **E8**
Pine Bluffs *1,054* **E8**
Pinedale *1,181* **D3**
Powell *5,292* **B4**
Ranchester *676* **B5**
Rawlins *9,380* **E5**
Reliance *500* **E3**
Riverton *9,202* **C4**
Rock River *190* **E7**
Rock Springs *19,050* **E3**
Saratoga *1,969* **E6**
Sheridan *13,900* **B6**
Shirley Basin *100* **D6**
Shoshoni *497* **C4**
Sinclair *500* **E6**
Story *700* **B6**
Sundance *1,139* **B8**
Ten Sleep *311* **B5**
Teton Village *250* **C2**
Thermopolis *3,247* **C4**
Torrington *5,651* **D8**
Upton *980* **B8**
Wamsutter *240* **E5**
West Laramie *2,000* **E7**
Wheatland *3,271* **D8**
Wilson *500* **C2**
Worland *5,742* **B5**
Yellowstone National
  Park *400* **B2**

Statute Miles 5 0 5 10 20 30 40 50
Kilometers 5 0 5 15 25 35 45 55 65 75

Lambert Conformal Conic Projection
SCALE 1:2,186,000 1 Inch = 34.5 Statute Miles

277

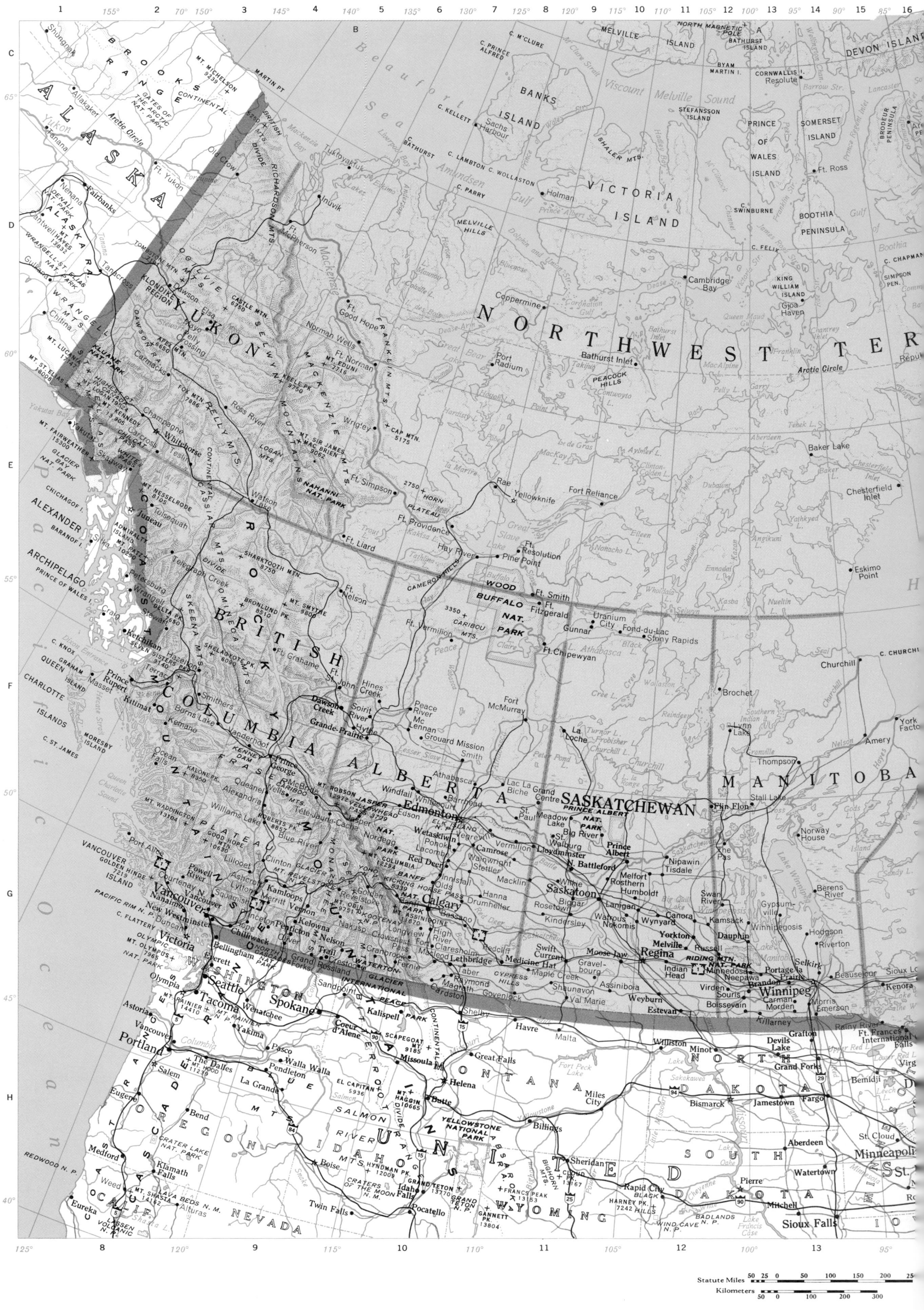

Northwest Territories

Cities and Towns

Alert *k39*
Arctic Bay *477* **B16**
Baker Lake *1,009* **D13**
Bathurst Inlet *16* **C11**
Cambridge Bay *1,002* **C12**
Cape Dorset *872* **D17**
Chesterfield Inlet *294* **C2**
Clyde *471* **B19**
Coppermine *888* **C9**
Eskimo Point *1,189* **D14**
Eureka *m34*
Fort Good Hope *562* **C7**
Fort Liard *395* **D8**
Fort McPherson *760* **C6**
Fort Norman *332* **D7**
Fort Providence *588* **D9**
Fort Resolution *447* **D10**
Fort Simpson *987* **D8**
Fort Smith *2,460* **D10**
Gjoa Haven *650* **C13**
Grise Fiord *114* **m35**
Hay River *2,964* **D9**
Inuvik *3,389* **C6**
Norman Wells *627* **C7**
Pine Point *1,558* **D10**
Pond Inlet *796* **A5**
Repulse Bay *420* **C15**

Yukon

Cities and Towns

Carcross *169* **D6**
Carmacks *280* **D5**
Champagne *57* **D5**
Dawson *896* **D5**
Elsa *294* **D5**
Mayo *317* **D5**
Old Crow *232* **C5**
Pelly Crossing *177* **D5**
Ross River *352* **D6**
Teslin *181* **D6**
Watson Lake *826* **D7**
Whitehorse *15,199* **D5**

Lambert Conformal Conic Projection
SCALE 1:12,000,000   1 Inch = 189 Statute Miles

ALBERTA

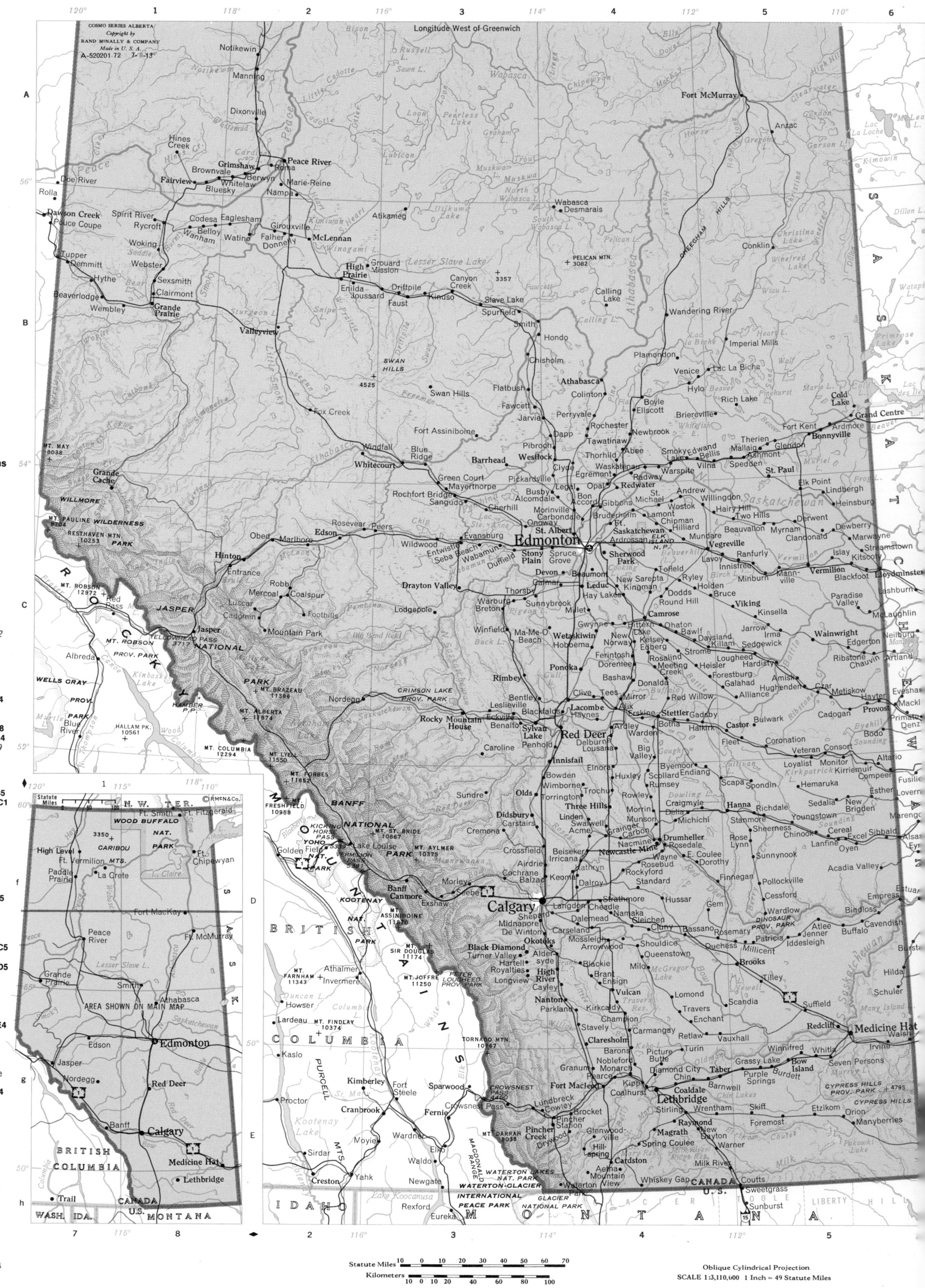

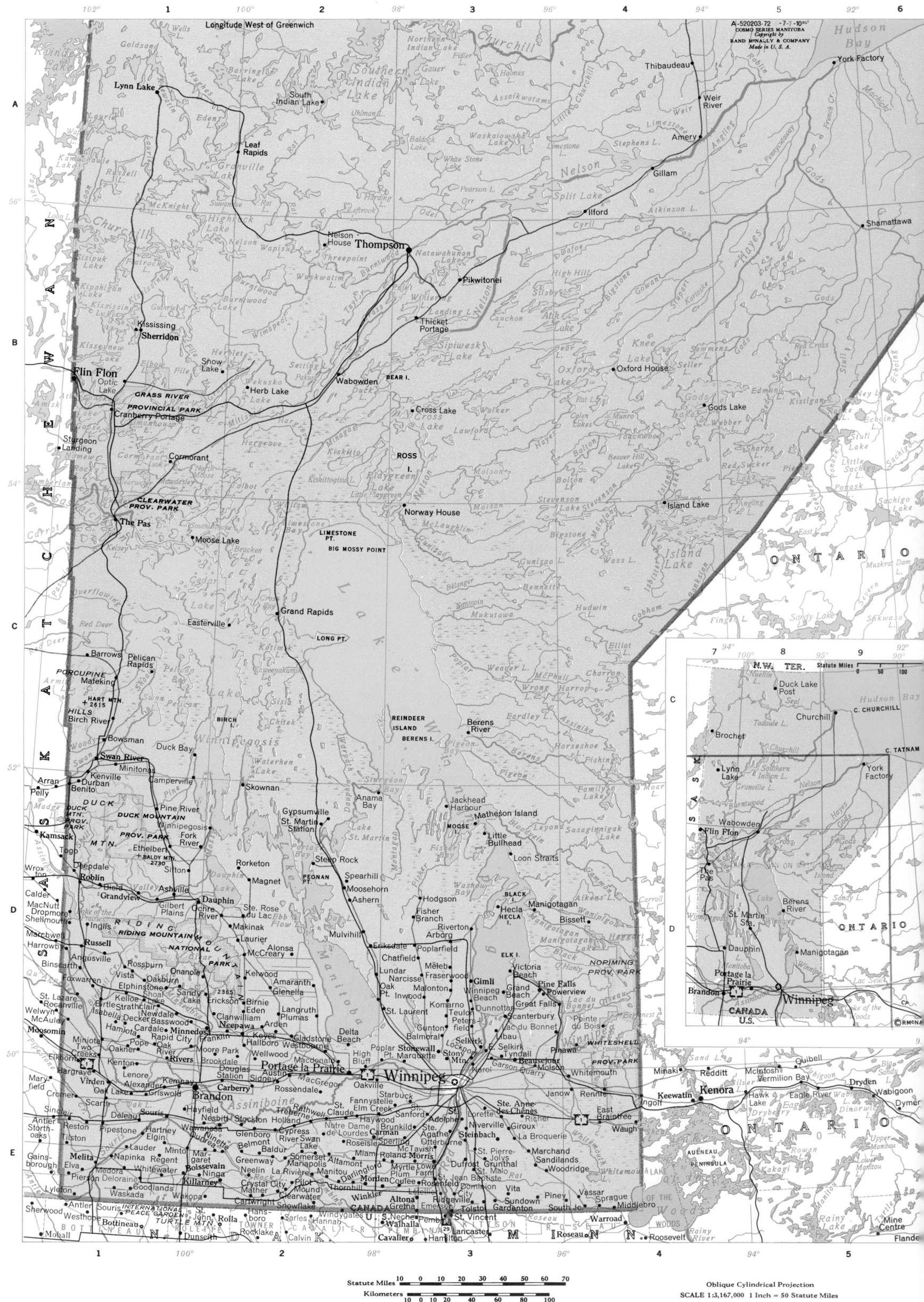

Cities and Towns

Altona *2,958* **E3**
Arborg *1,018* **D3**
Ashern *620* **D2**
Beausejour *2,535* **D3**
Birch River *509* **C1**
Birtle *850* **D1**
Boissevain *1,572* **E1**
Brandon *38,708* **E2**
Camperville *588* **D1**
Carberry *1,544* **E2**
Carman *2,500* **E2**
Churchill *1,109* **f9**
Cranberry Portage *849* **B1**
Cross Lake *580* **B3**
Dauphin *8,875* **D1**
Deloraine *1,134* **E1**
Duck Bay *559* **C1**
Easterville *675* **C2**
Emerson *725* **E3**
Flin Flon *7,591* **B1**
Gilbert Plains *816* **D1**
Gillam *1,909* **A4**
Gimli *1,681* **D3**
Gladstone *951* **D2**
Glenboro *719* **E2**
Grandview *941* **D1**
Grunthal *639* **E3**
Hamiota *815* **D1**
Killarney *2,318* **E2**
Lac du Bonnet *1,021* **D3**
Leaf Rapids *1,950* **A1**
Lorette *1,169* **E3**
MacGregor *854* **E2**
Manitou *856* **E2**
Melita *1,239* **E1**
Minnedosa *2,520* **D2**
Moose Lake *541* **C1**
Morden *5,004* **E2**
Morris *1,613* **E3**
Neepawa *3,314* **E2**
Niverville *1,452* **E3**
Norway House *633* **C3**
Pilot Mound *819* **E2**
Pine Falls *831* **D3**
Plum Coulee *677* **E3**
Portage la Prairie *13,198* **E2**
Powerview *724* **D3**
Reston *616* **E1**
Rivers *1,157* **D1**
Roblin *1,913* **D1**
Rossburn *664* **D1**
Russell *1,669* **D1**
Saint Adolphe *1,059* **E3**
Sainte Anne-des-Chênes *1,402* **E3**
Saint Claude *610* **E2**
Saint Malo *742* **E3**
Saint Pierre-Jolys *912* **E3**
Sainte Rose du Lac *1,030* **D2**
Selkirk *10,013* **D3**
Shoal Lake *832* **D1**
Snow Lake *1,837* **B1**
Souris *1,751* **E1**
South Indian Lake *743* **A2**
Steinbach *7,473* **E3**
Stonewall *2,349* **D3**
Swan River *3,946* **C1**
Teulon *953* **D3**
The Pas *6,283* **C1**
Thompson *14,701* **B3**
Treherne *762* **E2**
Virden *3,054* **E1**
Wabowden *571* **B2**
Winkler *5,926* **E3**
Winnipeg *594,551* **E3**
Winnipegosis *832* **D2**

Statute Miles 10 0 10 20 30 40 50 60 70

Kilometers 10 0 10 20 30 40 60 80 100

Oblique Cylindrical Projection
SCALE 1:3,167,000 1 Inch = 50 Statute Miles

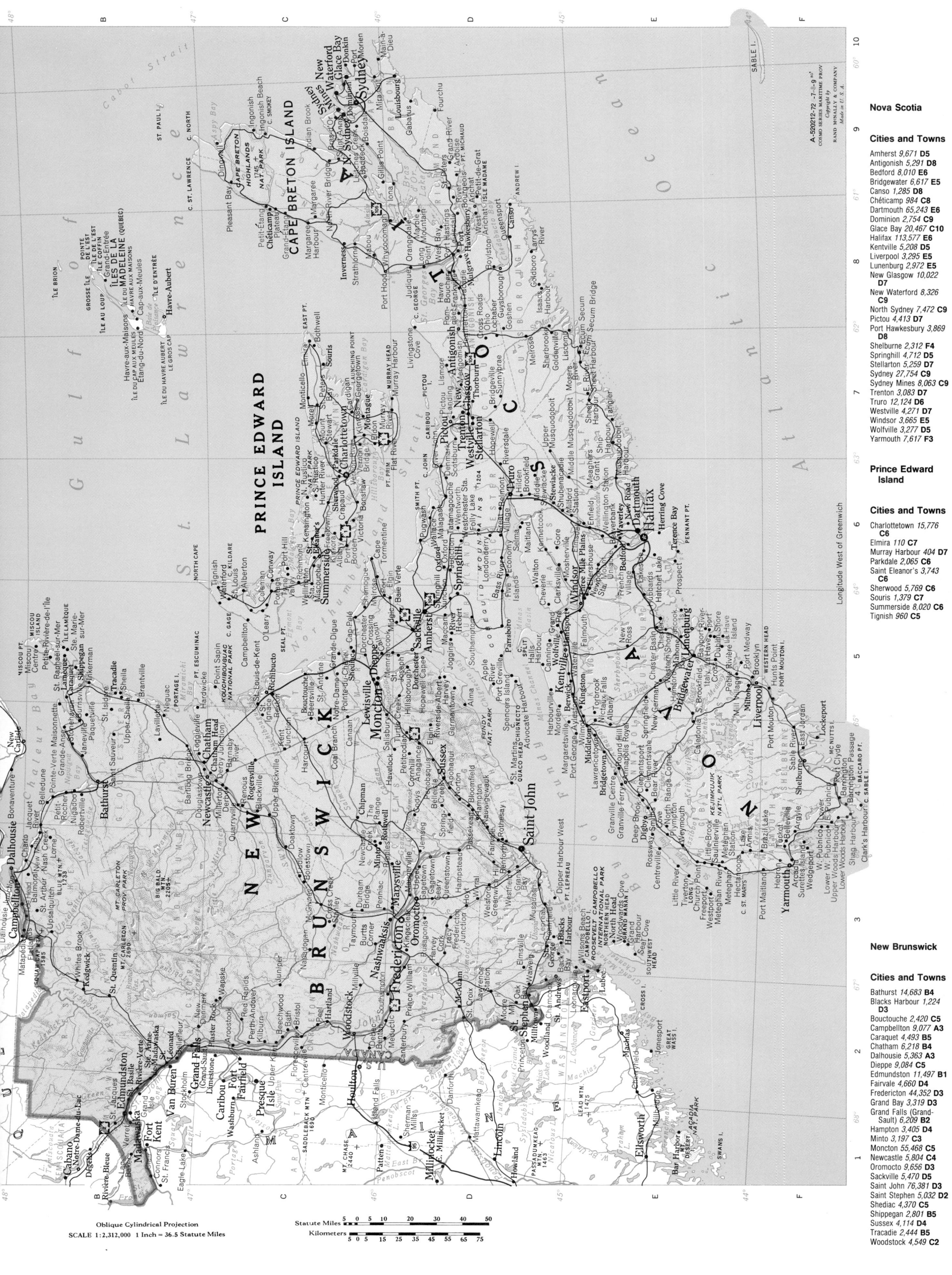

Nova Scotia

Cities and Towns

Amherst 9,671 **D5**
Antigonish 5,291 **D8**
Bedford 8,010 **E6**
Bridgewater 6,617 **E5**
Canso 1,285 **D8**
Chéticamp 984 **C8**
Dartmouth 65,243 **E6**
Dominion 2,754 **C9**
Glace Bay 20,467 **C10**
Halifax 113,577 **E6**
Kentville 5,208 **D5**
Liverpool 3,295 **E5**
Lunenburg 2,972 **E5**
New Glasgow 10,022 **D7**
New Waterford 8,326 **C9**
North Sydney 7,472 **C9**
Pictou 4,413 **D7**
Port Hawkesbury 3,869 **D8**
Shelburne 2,312 **F4**
Springhill 4,712 **D5**
Stellarton 5,259 **D7**
Sydney 27,754 **C9**
Sydney Mines 8,063 **C9**
Trenton 3,083 **D7**
Truro 12,124 **D6**
Westville 4,271 **D7**
Windsor 3,665 **E5**
Wolfville 3,277 **D5**
Yarmouth 7,617 **F3**

Prince Edward Island

Cities and Towns

Charlottetown 15,776 **C6**
Elmira 110 **C7**
Murray Harbour 404 **D7**
Parkdale 2,065 **C6**
Saint Eleanor's 3,743 **C6**
Sherwood 5,769 **C6**
Souris 1,379 **C7**
Summerside 8,020 **C6**
Tignish 960 **C5**

New Brunswick

Cities and Towns

Bathurst 14,683 **B4**
Blacks Harbour 1,224 **D3**
Bouctouche 2,420 **C5**
Campbellton 9,077 **A3**
Caraquet 4,493 **B5**
Chatham 6,218 **B4**
Dalhousie 5,363 **A3**
Dieppe 9,084 **C5**
Edmundston 11,497 **B1**
Fairvale 4,660 **D4**
Fredericton 44,352 **D3**
Grand Bay 3,319 **D3**
Grand Falls (Grand-Sault) 6,209 **B2**
Hampton 3,405 **D4**
Minto 3,197 **C3**
Moncton 55,468 **C5**
Newcastle 5,804 **C4**
Oromocto 9,656 **D3**
Sackville 5,470 **D5**
Saint John 76,381 **D3**
Saint Stephen 5,032 **D2**
Shediac 4,370 **C5**
Shippegan 2,801 **B5**
Sussex 4,114 **D4**
Tracadie 2,444 **B5**
Woodstock 4,549 **C2**

Oblique Cylindrical Projection
SCALE 1:2,312,000 1 Inch = 36.5 Statute Miles

Statute Miles
Kilometers

Oblique Cylindrical Projection
SCALE 1:2,226,000 1 Inch = 35 Statute Miles

Statute Miles 5 0 5 10   20   30   40   50
Kilometers 5 0 5 15 25 35 45 55 65 75

Cities and Towns

- Ajax 36,550 **D6**
- Barrie 48,287 **C5**
- Belleville 36,041 **C7**
- Brampton 188,498 **D5**
- Brantford 76,146 **D4**
- Brockville 20,880 **C9**
- Burlington 116,675 **D5**
- Cambridge 79,920 **D4**
- Chatham 42,211 **E2**
- Cobourg 13,197 **D6**
- Cornwall 46,425 **B10**
- Dryden 6,462 **o16**
- Dundas 20,118 **D5**
- East York 101,085 **D5**
- Etobicoke 302,973 **D5**
- Fergus 6,372 **D4**
- Fort Erie 23,253 **E6**
- Gloucester 89,810 **h12**
- Guelph 78,235 **D4**
- Haileybury 4,820 **p20**
- Hamilton 306,728 **D5**
- Hawkesbury 9,710 **B10**
- Kapuskasing 11,378 **o19**
- Kenora 9,621 **o16**
- Kingston 55,050 **C8**
- Kirkland Lake 11,604 **o19**
- Kitchener 150,604 **D4**
- Leamington 12,828 **E2**
- Lindsay 14,455 **C6**
- London 269,140 **E3**
- Markham 114,597 **D5**
- Midland 12,092 **C5**
- Milton 32,037 **D5**
- Mississauga 374,005 **D5**
- Moosonee 216 **o19**
- Nanticoke 20,202 **E4**
- Nepean 95,490 **h12**
- Newcastle 34,073 **D6**
- Newmarket 34,923 **C5**
- Niagara Falls 72,107 **D5**
- North Bay 50,623 **A5**
- North York 556,297 **D5**
- Oakville 87,107 **D5**
- Orillia 24,077 **C5**
- Oshawa 123,651 **D6**
- Ottawa 300,763 **B9**
- Owen Sound 19,804 **C4**
- Pembroke 14,131 **B7**
- Petawawa 5,580 **B7**
- Peterborough 61,049 **C6**
- Pickering 48,959 **D5**
- Port Colborne 18,281 **E5**
- Richmond Hill 46,766 **D5**
- Saint Catharines 123,455 **D5**
- Sarnia 49,033 **E2**
- Sault Sainte Marie 80,905 **p18**
- Scarborough 484,676 **m15**
- Sioux Lookout 3,098 **o17**
- Smiths Falls 9,163 **C8**
- Stratford 26,451 **D3**
- Sturgeon Falls 5,895 **A5**
- Sudbury 88,717 **A4**
- Tecumseh 7,731 **E2**
- Thunder Bay 112,072 **o17**
- Timmins 46,657 **o19**
- Toronto 612,289 **D5**

- Trenton 15,311 **C7**
- Vanier 18,426 **h12**
- Vaughan 65,058 **D5**
- Waterloo 58,718 **D4**
- Welland 45,054 **E5**
- Whitby 45,819 **D6**
- Windsor 193,111 **E1**
- Woodstock 26,386 **D4**
- York 135,401 **D5**

A-520206-72   -6.013'no"
CORPORATE   Made in U.S.A.
Rand McNally & Company

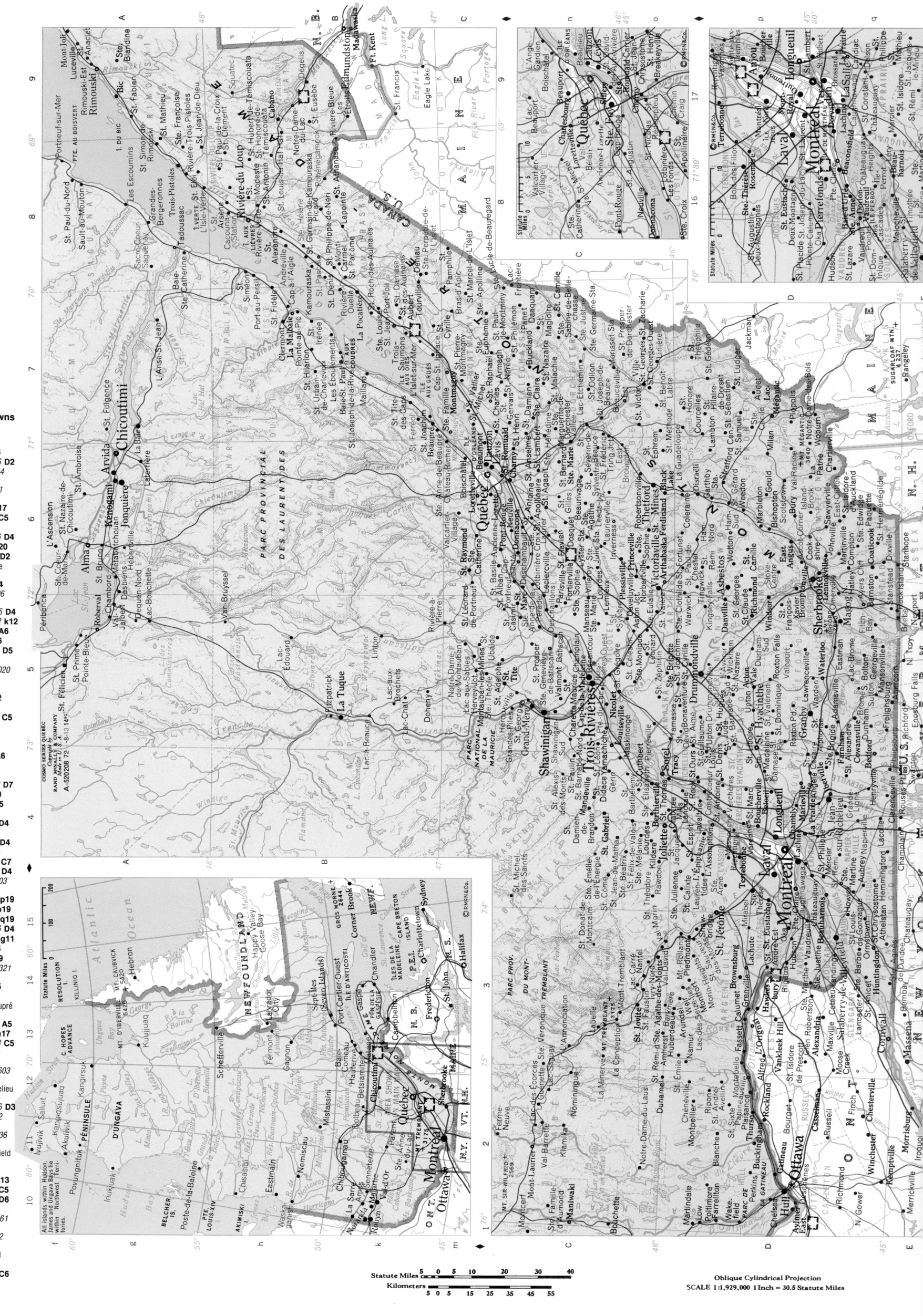

Statute Miles 5 0 5 10 20 30 40
Kilometers 5 0 5 15 25 35 45 55

Oblique Cylindrical Projection
SCALE 1:1,929,000 1 Inch = 30.5 Statute Miles

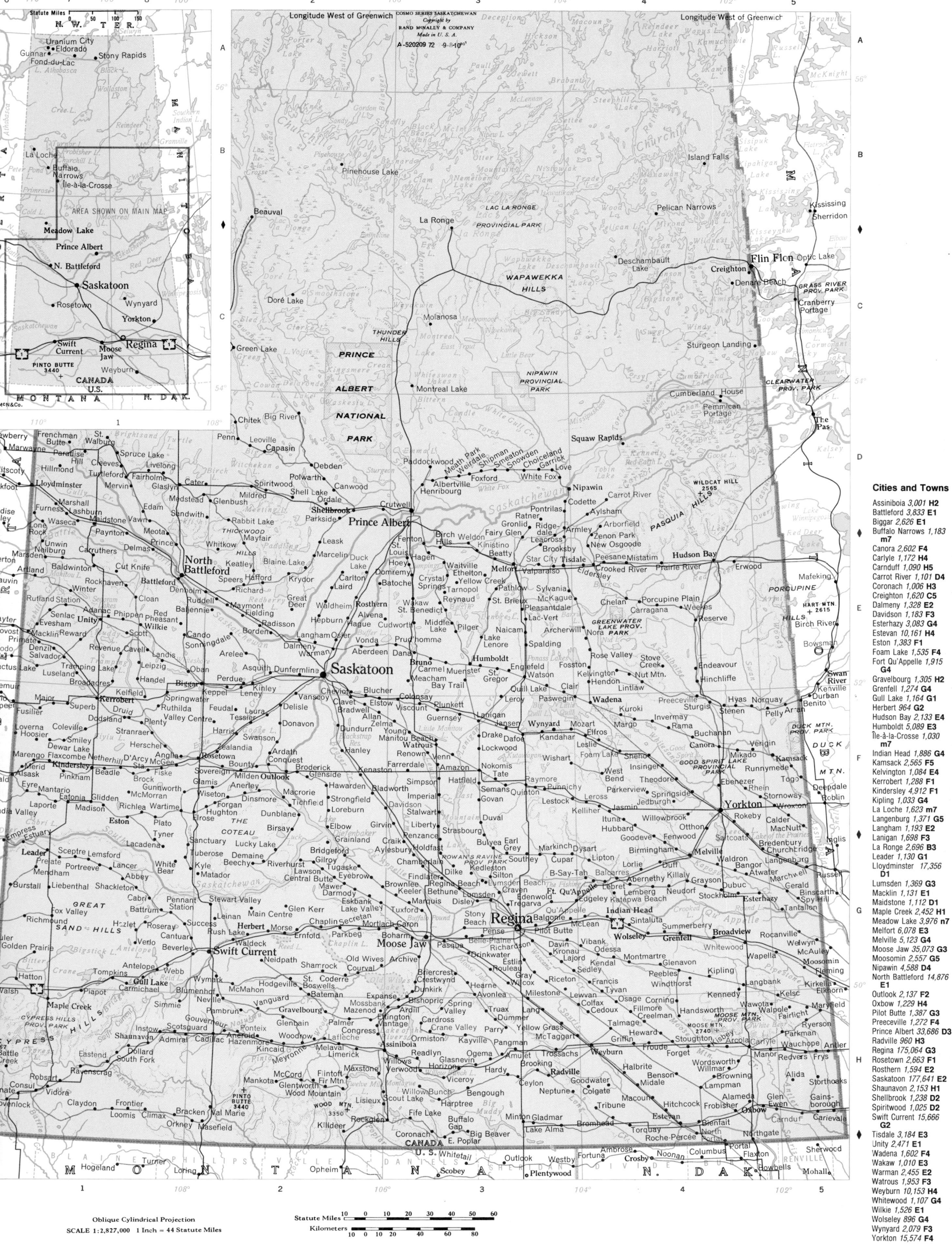

The United States and Canada / Facts in Brief

The table below provides a brief description of the United States and Canada. The chief products list includes the top products for each state, province, or territory in three major areas of production. The summary entry for each country indicates the national capital and the country's major products in agriculture, manufacturing, and mining.

The United States

CHIEF PRODUCTS

State	Entered Union	Capital	Agriculture	Manufacturing	Mining
Alabama	December 14, 1819, 22nd state	Montgomery	Broilers, beef cattle, soybeans	Paper prod., chemicals, textiles	Coal, natural gas, petroleum
Alaska	January 3, 1959, 49th state	Juneau	Milk, eggs, beef cattle, greenhouse and nursery prod.	Food, petroleum prod., paper prod.	Petroleum, natural gas, gold
Arizona	February 14, 1912, 48th state	Phoenix	Beef cattle, cotton, milk, lettuce	Elec. equip., trans. equip., elec. and nonelec. machinery	Copper, molybdenum, coal
Arkansas	June 15, 1836, 25th state	Little Rock	Broilers, soybeans, rice	Food, elec. equip., metal prod., paper prod.	Natural gas, petroleum, bromine
California	September 9, 1850, 31st state	Sacramento	Milk, beef cattle, cotton, grapes	Elec. equip., trans. equip., food	Petroleum, natural gas, boron
Colorado	August 1, 1876, 38th state	Denver	Beef cattle, wheat, corn	Instruments, food, trans. equip.	Petroleum, coal, natural gas
Connecticut	January 9, 1788, 5th state	Hartford	Eggs, milk, greenhouse and nursery prod.	Trans. equip., nonelec. machinery, metal prod.	Stone, sand and gravel
Delaware	December 7, 1787, 1st state	Dover	Broilers, soybeans, corn	Chemicals, food, trans. equip.	Magnesium compounds, sand and gravel
Florida	March 3, 1845, 27th state	Tallahassee	Oranges, sugar cane, beef cattle, greenhouse and nursery prod.	Elec. equip., food, printed materials, trans. equip.	Phosphate rock, petroleum, stone
Georgia	January 2, 1788, 4th state	Atlanta	Broilers, peanuts, peaches	Trans. equip., textiles, food, paper products	Clays, stone, sand and gravel
Hawaii	August 21, 1959, 50th state	Honolulu	Sugar cane, pineapples, flowers	Food, printed materials, refined petroleum	Stone, sand and gravel
Idaho	July 3, 1890, 43rd state	Boise	Potatoes, wheat, beef cattle	Food, lumber and wood prod., machinery	Silver, phosphate rock, gold
Illinois	December 3, 1818, 21st state	Springfield	Corn, soybeans, hogs	Nonelec. machinery, food, elec. equip., chemicals	Coal, petroleum, stone
Indiana	December 11, 1816, 19th state	Indianapolis	Corn, soybeans, tomatoes	Metals, trans. equip., elec. equip., chemicals	Coal, petroleum, stone
Iowa	December 28, 1846, 29th state	Des Moines	Corn, soybeans, hogs, beef cattle	Food, nonelec. machinery, elec. equip.	Stone, gypsum, sand and gravel
Kansas	January 29, 1861, 34th state	Topeka	Beef cattle, wheat, grain sorghum	Trans. equip., food, printed materials	Petroleum, natural gas, coal
Kentucky	June 1, 1792, 15th state	Frankfort	Tobacco, horses, beef cattle, milk	Trans. equip., chemicals, elec. equip., nonelec. machinery	Coal, natural gas, petroleum
Louisiana	April 30, 1812, 18th state	Baton Rouge	Soybeans, cotton, beef cattle	Chemicals, petroleum and coal prod., food	Natural gas, petroleum
Maine	March 15, 1820, 23rd state	Augusta	Milk, eggs, potatoes	Paper prod., wood prod., elec. equip.	Sand and gravel, stone
Maryland	April 28, 1788, 7th state	Annapolis	Broilers, milk, greenhouse and nursery prod.	Elec. equip., food, chemicals	Stone, coal, sand and gravel
Massachusetts	February 6, 1788, 6th state	Boston	Greenhouse and nursery prod., cranberries, milk	Elec. and nonelec. machinery, elec. equip., instruments, printed materials	Sand and gravel, stone
Michigan	January 26, 1837, 26th state	Lansing	Milk, beef cattle, corn, cherries	Trans. equip., elec. and nonelec. machinery, metal prod.	Natural gas, iron ore, petroleum
Minnesota	May 11, 1858, 32nd state	St. Paul	Milk, corn, soybeans, beef cattle	Elec. and nonelec. machinery, food	Iron ore, stone, clay
Mississippi	December 10, 1817, 20th state	Jackson	Broilers, cotton, soybeans	Trans. equip., elec. equip., food, clothing	Petroleum, natural gas
Missouri	August 10, 1821, 24th state	Jefferson City	Soybeans, beef cattle, hogs	Trans. equip., food, chemicals	Lead, stone, coal
Montana	November 8, 1889, 41st state	Helena	Beef cattle, wheat, hay, barley	Lumber and wood prod., food, printed materials	Coal, petroleum, copper, gold
Nebraska	March 1, 1867, 37th state	Lincoln	Beef cattle, corn, hogs, soybeans	Food, nonelec. machinery, elec. and electronic equip.	Petroleum, sand and gravel
Nevada	October 31, 1864, 36th state	Carson City	Beef cattle, milk, hay	Elec. machinery, printed materials, food	Gold, silver, diatomite
New Hampshire	June 21, 1788, 9th state	Concord	Milk, hay, beef cattle	Elec. and electronic equip., nonelec. machinery, plastic prod.	Sand and gravel, stone
New Jersey	December 18, 1787, 3rd state	Trenton	Greenhouse and nursery products, milk, tomatoes	Chemicals, food, elec. equip., printed materials	Stone, sand and gravel
New Mexico	January 6, 1912, 47th state	Santa Fe	Beef cattle, milk, chili peppers	Elec. equip., petroleum prod., food	Natural gas, petroleum, coal, potash
New York	July 26, 1788, 11th state	Albany	Milk, beef cattle, apples	Printed materials, instruments, elec. equip.	Stone, salt, sand and gravel
North Carolina	November 21, 1789, 12th state	Raleigh	Broilers, tobacco, hogs	Textiles, tobacco prod., chemicals	Stone, phosphate rock, sand and gravel
North Dakota	November 2, 1889, 39th state	Bismarck	Wheat, beef cattle, sunflower seeds	Food, nonelec. machinery, petroleum prod.	Petroleum, coal, natural gas
Ohio	March 1, 1803, 17th state	Columbus	Corn, soybeans, milk, hogs	Trans. equip., metal prod., nonelec. machinery	Coal, natural gas, stone
Oklahoma	November 16, 1907, 46th state	Oklahoma City	Beef cattle, wheat, hay	Trans. equip., elec. and nonelec. machinery, elec. equip.	Petroleum, natural gas, coal
Oregon	February 14, 1859, 33rd state	Salem	Timber, beef cattle, wheat	Lumber and wood prod., food, paper prod.	Sand and gravel, stone, pumice
Pennsylvania	December 12, 1787, 2nd state	Harrisburg	Milk, beef cattle, mushrooms	Food, chemicals, elec. and nonelec. machinery	Coal, stone, natural gas
Rhode Island	May 29, 1790, 13th state	Providence	Greenhouse and nursery prod., milk	Jewelry and silverware, metal prod., elec. equip.	Stone, sand and gravel
South Carolina	May 23, 1788, 8th state	Columbia	Tobacco, beef cattle, soybeans	Textiles, chemicals, paper prod.	Stone, clays
South Dakota	November 2, 1889, 40th state	Pierre	Beef cattle, hogs, corn	Food, nonelec. machinery	Gold, petroleum
Tennessee	June 1, 1796, 16th state	Nashville	Beef cattle, milk, soybeans	Chemicals, food, nonelec. machinery	Coal, stone, zinc
Texas	December 29, 1845, 28th state	Austin	Beef cattle, cotton, milk	Chemicals, food, elec. equip., petroleum prod.	Petroleum, natural gas, stone, magnesium
Utah	January 4, 1896, 45th state	Salt Lake City	Beef cattle, milk, hay	Elec. and nonelec. machinery, trans. equip., food	Petroleum, coal, uranium
Vermont	March 4, 1791, 14th state	Montpelier	Milk, beef cattle, maple syrup	Elec. equip., metal prod., printed materials, paper prod.	Stone, sand and gravel
Virginia	June 25, 1788, 10th state	Richmond	Beef cattle, tobacco, milk	Chemicals, tobacco prod., food	Coal, stone
Washington	November 11, 1889, 42nd state	Olympia	Timber, wheat, hops, apples	Trans. equip., food, paper and wood prod.	Coal, gold, magnesium
West Virginia	June 20, 1863, 35th state	Charleston	Beef cattle, milk, apples	Chemicals; metals; stone, clay, glass prod.	Coal, natural gas, petroleum
Wisconsin	May 29, 1848, 30th state	Madison	Milk, beef cattle, hogs	Nonelec. machinery, food, paper prod.	Stone, sand and gravel
Wyoming	July 10, 1890, 44th state	Cheyenne	Beef cattle, sheep, sugar beets	Chemicals, petroleum prod., nonelec. machinery	Petroleum, coal, natural gas
UNITED STATES	. . .	Washington, D.C.	Beef cattle, milk, corn	Trans. equip., food, chemicals	Petroleum, natural gas, coal

Canada

CHIEF PRODUCTS

Province/Territory	Entered Dominion	Capital	Agriculture	Manufacturing	Mining
Alberta	September 1, 1905, with Saskatchewan, 8th and 9th provinces	Edmonton	Beef cattle, wheat, canola	Chemicals, food, refined petroleum	Petroleum, natural gas, coal
British Columbia	July 20, 1871, 6th province	Victoria	Milk, apples, beef cattle	Wood prod., paper prod., food	Coal, copper, natural gas
Manitoba	July 15, 1870, 5th province	Winnipeg	Wheat, beef cattle, barley	Food, trans. equip., printed materials	Nickel, copper, zinc
New Brunswick	July 1, 1867, one of four original provinces	Fredericton	Milk, potatoes, beef cattle	Paper prod., food, wood prod.	Zinc, lead, potash
Newfoundland	March 31, 1949, 10th province	St. John's	Chickens, eggs, milk	Food, paper prod.	Iron ore, zinc, gold
Northwest Territories	—	Yellowknife		Food, petroleum prod., wood prod.	Zinc, gold, petroleum
Nova Scotia	July 1, 1867, one of four original provinces	Halifax	Milk, beef cattle, chickens	Food, paper prod., tires	Coal, gypsum, tin
Ontario	July 1, 1867, one of four original provinces	Toronto	Beef cattle, milk, hogs	Trans. equip., chemicals, food	Nickel, gold, copper
Prince Edward Island	July 1, 1873, 7th province	Charlottetown	Potatoes, milk, beef cattle	Food, printed materials, wood prod.	
Québec	July 1, 1867, one of four original provinces	Québec	Milk, hogs, corn	Paper prod., food, trans. equip.	Gold, iron ore, titanium
Saskatchewan	September 1, 1905, with Alberta, 8th and 9th provinces	Regina	Wheat, beef cattle, canola	Food, printed materials, elec. equip.	Petroleum, potash, uranium
Yukon Territory	—	Whitehorse	—	Lumber and wood prod., printed materials, food	Zinc, gold, lead
CANADA	. . .	Ottawa	Beef cattle, wheat, milk	Trans. equip., food, chemicals	Petroleum, natural gas, nickel, uranium

Abbreviations: elec. = electric; equip. = equipment; nonelec. = nonelectric; prod. = products; trans. equip. = transportation equipment

Geographical Information and Maps of the World Index

World Nations and Other Political Units

This table gives the area, population, population density, form of government, capital, and location of all the world's independent nations and other important political units.

Names of independent nations appear in **boldface type.** Continents are preceded by daggers.

Area figures include inland water.

The populations are either the estimates (E) or census figures (C) given in the 1992 edition of *The World Book Encyclopedia* or, where noted, estimates (RE) made by Rand McNally and Company on the basis of official data, United Nations estimates, and other available information. An asterisk (∗) following a population indicates that the figure is a 1992 or earlier estimate based on the latest figures from official government and United Nations sources.

Map plate numbers refer to the Maps of the World section of the atlas.

Political unit	Local name	Area sq. miles	Area km²	Population	Date	Population density per sq. mile	Population density per km²	Form of govt./ Political status	Capital	Continent	Map plate
Afghanistan	Afghanistan	251,773	652,090	18,850,000	1992E	75	29	Socialist Republic	Kabul	Asia	23
†Africa	—	11,678,000	30,246,000	692,000,000	1992E	59	23	—	—	Africa	30–31
Alabama, U.S.	Alabama	51,705	133,915	4,062,608	1990C	79	30	State (U.S.)	Montgomery	North America	44
Alaska, U.S.	Alaska	591,004	1,530,700	551,947	1990C	0.9	0.4	State (U.S.)	Juneau	North America	40
Albania	Shqipëri	11,100	28,748	3,346,000	1992E	301	116	Socialist People's Republic	Tiranë	Europe	15
Alberta, Can.	Alberta	251,870	662,330	2,375,278	1986C	9	4	Province (Canada)	Edmonton	North America	42
Algeria	Al Jaza'ir	919,595	2,381,741	26,851,000	1992E	29	11	Socialist Republic	Algiers	Africa	32
American Samoa	American Samoa	76	197	40,000	∗	526	203	U.S. Territory	Pago Pago	Oceania	65
Andaman and Nicobar Islands, India	Andaman and Nicobar	3,185	8,249	188,254	1981C	59	23	Territory of India	Port Blair	Asia	25
Andorra	Valls d'Andorra (Valleys of Andorra)	175	453	55,000	1992E	314	121	Principality; joint Spanish and French rule	Andorra	Europe	13
Angola	Angola	481,354	1,246,700	10,591,000	1992E	22	8	Communist	Luanda	Africa	36
Anguilla	Anguilla	37	96	7,000	—	189	73	British Dependency	The Valley	North America	51
Anhui, China	Anhwei	54,016	139,900	56,180,813	1990C	1,040	402	Province (China)	Hefei (Ho-fei)	Asia	28
†Antarctica	—	5,100,000	13,209,000	(1)	—	—	—	—	—	Antarctica	66
Antigua and Barbuda	Antigua and Barbuda	171	442	82,000	1992E	480	186	Constitutional Monarchy	St. John's	North America	51
Arabian Peninsula (2)	—	1,160,174	2,812,071	32,755,000	1992E	28	12	—	—	Asia	23
Argentina	Argentina	1,073,400	2,780,092	33,083,000	1992E	31	12	Republic; under military control	Buenos Aires	South America	56
Arizona, U.S.	Arizona	114,000	295,260	3,677,985	1990C	32	12	State (U.S.)	Phoenix	North America	46
Arkansas, U.S.	Arkansas	53,187	137,754	2,362,239	1990C	44	17	State (U.S.)	Little Rock	North America	45
Armenian Soviet Socialist Republic, U.S.S.R.	Armenia	11,506	29,800	3,267,000	1984E	284	110	Soviet Socialist Republic (U.S.S.R.)	Yerevan	Asia	16
Aruba	Aruba	75	193	63,000	∗	840	326	Self-governing	Oranjestad	North America	49
Ascension	Ascension	34	88	1,500	—	44	17	Belongs to Great Britain, under administration of St. Helena	Georgetown	Africa	30–31
†Asia	—	17,005,000	44,043,000	3,308,000,000	1992E	195	75	—	—	Asia	21–22
†**Australia**	Commonwealth of Australia	2,967,909	7,686,848	17,116,000	1992E	6	2	Constitutional Monarchy	Canberra	Australia	59
Australian Capital Territory (Canberra)	Australian Capital Territory	930	2,400	221,607	1981C	238	92	Territory (Australia)	Canberra	Australia	59
Austria	Österreich	32,376	83,853	7,486,000	1992E	231	89	Federal Republic	Vienna (Wien)	Europe	14
Azerbaijan Soviet Socialist Republic, U.S.S.R.	Azerbaijan	33,436	86,600	6,506,000	1984E	195	75	Soviet Socialist Republic (U.S.S.R.)	Baku	Europe	16
Azores	Açores	905	2,344	250,000	∗	276	107	Part of Portugal's territory	Ponta Delgada	Europe	32
Bahamas	Bahamas	5,385	13,878	267,000	1992E	47	18	Constitutional Monarchy	Nassau	North America	47
Bahrain	Al Baḥrayn	262	678	547,000	1992E	2,008	807	Emirate	Manama	Asia	24
Balearic Islands, Spain	Islas Baleares	1,936	5,014	685,088	1981C	354	137	Province of Spain	Palma	Europe	13
Baltic States, U.S.S.R.	Estonia, Latvia, Lithuania	67,182	174,000	7,644,000	1984E	114	44	Part of U.S.S.R. (3 republics) (6)	—	Europe	8
Bangladesh	Bangladesh	55,598	143,998	121,896,000	1992E	2,192	847	Republic	Dhaka	Asia	25
Barbados	Barbados	166	430	265,000	1992E	1,596	616	Constitutional Monarchy	Bridgetown	North America	51
Beijing (Peking), China	Beijing	6,873	17,800	10,819,407	1990C	1,574	608	Special Municipal District of China	—	Asia	28
Belgium	Belgique (French), België (Flemish)	11,783	30,519	9,954,000	1992E	845	326	Constitutional Monarchy	Brussels	Europe	12
Belize	Belize	8,867	22,965	189,000	1992E	21	8	Constitutional Monarchy	Belmopan	North America	49
Benin	Bénin	43,484	112,622	5,052,000	1992E	116	45	Republic	Porto-Novo	Africa	34
Bermuda	Bermuda	21	54	58,000	∗	2,762	1,074	British Dependency	Hamilton	North America	47
Bhutan	Druk	18,147	47,000	1,586,000	1992E	87	34	Monarchy	Thimphu	Asia	25
Bioko, Equat. Gui.	Bioko	785	2,034	94,000	1982RE	120	46	Territory of Equatorial Guinea	Malabo	Africa	34
Bolivia	Bolivia	424,165	1,098,581	7,732,000	1992E	18	7	Republic	Sucre (official); La Paz (actual)	South America	54
Borneo (3)	—	287,023	743,386	9,262,000	1992E	32	12	—	—	Asia	26
Botswana	Botswana	224,607	581,730	1,375,000	1992E	6	2	Republic	Gaborone	Africa	37
Brazil	Brasil	3,286,488	8,511,965	156,044,000	1992E	47	18	Federal Republic	Brasília	South America	54–56
British Columbia, Can.	British Columbia	365,900	947,800	2,889,207	1986C	8	3	Province (Canada)	Victoria	North America	42
British Honduras, see Belize	—	—	—	—	—	—	—	—	—		
British Indian Ocean Territory	British Indian Ocean Territory	30	78	2,000	—	67	26	British Dependency	—	Asia	22
British Solomon Islands, see Solomon Islands	—										
Brunei	Brunei	2,226	5,765	279,000	1992E	125	48	Monarchy	Bandar Seri Begawan	Asia	26
Bulgaria	Balgarija	42,823	110,912	9,021,000	1992E	211	81	People's Republic (Communist Dictatorship)	Sofia	Europe	15
Burkina Faso	Burkina Faso	105,869	274,200	9,526,000	1992E	90	35	Military Rule	Ouagadougou	Africa	34
Burma	Burma	261,228	676,578	43,435,000	1992E	166	64	Military Rule	Rangoon	Asia	25
Burundi	Burundi	10,747	27,834	5,771,000	1992E	537	207	Republic	Bujumbura	Africa	36
Byelorussian Soviet Socialist Republic, U.S.S.R.	Byelorussia	80,155	207,600	9,878,000	1984E	123	48	Soviet Socialist Republic (U.S.S.R.)	Minsk	Europe	16
California, U.S.	California	158 706	411,049	29,839,250	1990C	188	73	State (U.S.)	Sacramento	North America	46
Cambodia	Kâmpŭchéa	69,898	181,035	7,302,000	1992E	104	40	Communist Dictatorship	Phnom-Penh	Asia	26

Political unit	Local name	Area sq. miles	km²	Population	Date	Population density per sq. mile	km²	Form of govt./ Political status	Capital	Continent	Map plate
Cameroon	Cameroun	183,569	475,442	11,863,000	1992E	65	25	Republic	Yaounde	Africa	34
Canada	Canada	3,849,674	9,970,610	26,935,000	1992E	7	3	Constitutional Monarchy	Ottawa	North America	42
Canary Islands	Islas Canarias	2,796	7,242	1,444,626	1981C	517	199	Part of Spain (2 provinces)	Santa Cruz de Tenerife; Las Palmas de Gran Canaria	Africa	32
Cape Verde	Cabo Verde	1,557	4,033	403,000	1992E	259	100	Republic	Praia	Africa	32
Cayman Islands	Cayman Islands	100	259	24,000	*	240	93	British Dependency	Georgetcwn	North America	49
Celebes (Indonesia)	Sulawesi	73,057	189,216	10,409,533	1981C	142	55	Part of Indonesia	—	Asia	26
Central African Republic	Centrafrique	240,535	622,984	3,063,000	1992E	13	5	Republic	Bangui	Africa	35
Central America	—	202,000	523,000	30,674,000	1992E	152	59	—	—	North America	49
Ceylon, see Sri Lanka	—	—	—	—	—	—	—	—	—	—	—
Chad	Tchad	495,755	1,284,000	5,970,000	1992E	12	5	Republic	N'Djamena	Africa	35
Channel Islands	Channel Islands	75	195	136,000	*	1,813	697	British Crown Dependencies	St. Peter Port; St. Helier	Europe	9
Chile	Chile	292,258	756,945	13,585,000	1992E	46	18	Republic	Santiago	South America	56
China	Zhonghua Renmin Gongheguo	3.696,032	9,572,678	1,143,729,000	1992E	309	119	Communist Dictatorship	Beijing (Peking)	Asia	27
Christmas Island (Austl.)	Christmas Island	52	135	3,000	1980E	58	22	External Territory (Australia)	Flying Fish Cove	Oceania	26
Cocos (Keeling) Islands (Austl.)	Cocos (Keeling) Islands	5	13	1,000	1980E	200	77	External Territory (Australia)	—	Oceania	22
Colombia	Colombia	439,737	1,138,914	33,020,000	1992E	75	29	Republic	Bogotá	South America	54
Colorado, U.S.	Colorado	104,091	269,595	3,307,912	1990C	32	12	State (U.S.)	Denver	North America	45
Commonwealth of Nations	—	13,881,814	35,951,885	1,308,134,000	1989E	87	34	Association of 48 independent countries & 26 political units	—	—	—
Comoros	Comores	863	2,235	552,000	1992E	640	247	Republic	Moroni	Africa	37
Congo	Congo	132,047	342,000	2,106.000	1992E	16	6	Military Rule	Brazzaville	Africa	36
Connecticut, U.S.	Connecticut	5,018	12,997	3,295,669	1990C	657	254	State (U.S.)	Hartford	North America	44
Cook Islands	Cook Islands	93	240	17,000	*	183	71	Self-governing Dependency of New Zealand	Avarua	Oceania	61
Corsica	Corse	3,352	8,681	184,000	1982RE	55	21	Part of France (2 departments)	Ajaccio	Europe	11
Costa Rica	Costa Rica	19,730	51,100	3,152,000	1992E	160	62	Republic	San José	North America	49
Cuba	Cuba	42,804	110,861	10,655,000	1992E	249	96	Socialist State and a Republic; (Dictatorship)	Havana (La Habana)	North America	49
Curaçao	Curaçao	171	443	170,000	*	994	383	Largest Island of the Netherlands Antilles	Willemstad	North America	49
Cyprus	Kypros (Greek), Kibris (Turkish)	3,572	9,251	714,000	1992E	200	77	Republic	Nicosia	Asia	24
Czechoslovakia	Československo	49,373	127,876	15,749,000	1992E	319	123	Socialist Republic (Communist Dictatorship)	Prague (Praha)	Europe	10
Dahomey, see Benin	—	—	—	—	—	—	—	—	—	—	—
Delaware, U.S.	Delaware	2,044	5,295	668,696	1990C	327	126	State (U.S.)	Dover	North America	44
Denmark	Danmark	16,662	43,077	5,123,000	1992E	308	119	Constitutional Monarchy	Copenhagen (København)	Europe	8
District of Columbia (D.C.) [Washington, D.C., U.S.]	District of Columbia	69	179	609,909	1990C	8,839	3,407	U.S. Federal District	Washington D.C.	North America	44
Djibouti	Djibouti	8,958	23,200	431,000	1992E	48	19	Republic	Djibouti (city)	Africa	35
Dominica	Dominica	290	751	88,000	1992E	303	117	Republic	Roseau	North America	51
Dominican Republic	República Dominicana	18,816	48,734	7,457,000	1992E	396	153	Republic	Santo Domingo	North America	49
Dutch Guiana, see Suriname	—	—	—	—	—	—	—	—	—	—	—
Ecuador	Ecuador	109,484	283,561	11,363,000	1992E	104	40	Republic	Quito	South America	54
Egypt	Mişr	386,662	1,001,449	56,508,000	1992E	146	56	Republic	Cairo (Al Qahirah)	Africa	33
Ellice Islands, see Tuvalu	—	—	—	—	—	—	—	—	—	—	—
El Salvador	El Salvador	8,124	21,041	5,515,000	1992E	679	262	Republic	San Salvador	North America	49
England	England	50,363	130,439	48,078,000	1992E	955	369	Constitutional Monarchy	London	Europe	9
Equatorial Guinea	Guinea Ecuatorial	10,831	28,051	462,000	1992E	43	16	Military Rule	Malabo on Bioko	Africa	36
Estonian Soviet Socialist Republic, U.S.S.R.	Estonia	17,413	45,100	1,518,000	1984E	87	34	Soviet Socialist Republic (U.S.S.R.)	Tallinn	Europe	8
Ethiopia	Itiopya	471,800	1,221,900	49,263,000	1992E	104	40	Communist State	Addis Ababa	Africa	35
Eurasia	—	21,074,000	54,582,000	4,007,000,000	1992E	Europe: 172 Asia: 195	Europe: 66 Asia: 75	—	—	Europe and Asia	—
†Europe	—	4,069,000	10,539,000	699,000,000	1992E	172	66	—	—	Europe	5–6
Faeroe Islands	Føroyar (Faeroese) Færøerne (Danish)	540	1,399	46,000	*	85	33	Self-governing Community of Denmark	Tórshavn	Europe	6
Falkland Islands (Islas Malvinas— Argentina)	Falkland Islands	4,699	12,170	2,000	*	0.4	0.2	British Dependency; [claimed by Argentina]	Stanley	South America	56
Federated States of Micronesia, see Micronesia, Federated States of	—	—	—	—	—	—	—	—	—	—	—
Fiji	Fiji	7,056	18,274	767,000	1992E	109	42	Constitutional Monarchy	Suva	Oceania	63
Finland	Suomi (Finnish) Finland (Swedish)	130,559	338,145	4,997,000	1992E	38	15	Republic	Helsinki (Helsingfors)	Europe	7
Florida, U.S.	Florida	58,664	151,939	13,003,362	1990C	222	86	State (U.S.)	Tallahassee	North America	44
France	France	212,935	551,500	56,578,000	1992E	266	103	Republic	Paris	Europe	11
French Guiana	Guyane Française	35,135	91,000	73,000	*	2	1	Overseas Department (France)	Cayenne	South America	54
French Polynesia	Polynésie Française	1,544	4,000	203,000	*	131	51	Overseas Territory (France)	Papeete	Oceania	61
French West Indies	Guadaloupe and Martinique	1,083	2,806	657,000	*	607	234	2 Overseas Departments of France	Basse-Terre; Fort de France	North America	50
Fujian (Fukien), China	Fujian	47,529	123,100	30,048,224	1990C	632	244	Province (China)	Fuzhou (Fu-chóu)	Asia	27

Political unit	Local name	Area sq. miles	km²	Population	Date	Population density per sq. mile	km²	Form of govt./ Political status	Capital	Continent	Map plate
Gabon	Gabon	103,347	267,667	1,249,000	1992E	12	5	Republic	Libreville	Africa	36
Galapagos Islands, Ecuador	Archipiélago de Colón	3,029	7,844	6,200	1982C	2	0.8	Province of Ecuador: (Galapagos Islands)	Baquerizo Moreno	South America	54
Gambia	Gambia	4,361	11,295	905,000	1992E	208	80	Republic	Banjul	Africa	34
Gansu (Kansu), China	Gansu	141,500	366,500	22,371,141	1990C	158	61	Province (China)	Lanzhou (Lan-chou)	Asia	27
Gaza Strip	R'tzuat Aza	146	378	564,000	*	3,860	1,492	Occupied by Israel; formerly part of Egypt	Gaza	Asia	24
Georgia, U.S.	Georgia	58,910	152,576	6,508,419	1990C	110	43	State (U.S.)	Atlanta	North America	44
Georgian Soviet Socialist Republic, U.S.S.R.	Georgia	26,911	69,700	5,167,000	1984E	192	74	Soviet Socialist Republic (U.S.S.R.)	Tbilisi	Asia	16
Germany	Deutschland	137,804	356,910	77,042,000	1992E	559	216	Federal Republic	Berlin, Bonn	Europe	10
Ghana	Ghana	92,098	238,533	15,966,000	1992E	173	67	Military Rule	Accra	Africa	34
Gibraltar	Gibraltar	2.3	6.0	35,000	*	15,217	5,833	British Dependency	Gibraltar	Europe	13
Gilbert Islands	Gilbert Islands	105	272	52,000	—	495	191	part of Kiribati	—	Oceania	—
Golan Heights	Ramat ha-Golan	454	1,176	19,700	*	43	17	Occupied by Israel; formerly part of Syria	—	Asia	24
Great Britain	The United Kingdom of Great Britain and Northern Ireland	94,248	244,100	57,640,000	1992E	612	236	Constitutional Monarchy	London	Europe	9
Greece	Ellas	50,962	131,990	10,077,000	1992E	198	76	Republic	Athens (Athinai)	Europe	15
Greenland	Grønland (Danish) Kalaallit Nunaat (Eskimo)	840,004	2,175,600	57,000	1992E	0.07	0.03	Province of Denmark	Godthåb	North America	41
Grenada	Grenada	133	344	85,000	1992E	639	247	Parliamentary	St. George's	North America	51
Guadeloupe	Guadeloupe	658	1,704	328,000	*	498	192	Overseas Department (France)	Basse-Terre	North America	51
Guam	Guam	212	549	120,000	*	566	219	Territory of the United States	Agana	Oceania	64
Guangdong (Kwangtung), China	Guangdong	89,340	231,400	62,829,236	1990C	703	272	Province (China)	Guangzhou (Canton)	Asia	27
Guangxi (Kwangsi), China	Guangxi	85,100	220,400	42,245,765	1990C	496	192	Autonomous Region, China	Nanning (Nan-ning)	Asia	27
Guatemala	Guatemala	42,042	108,889	9,734,000	1992E	232	89	Republic	Guatemala City	North America	49
Guernsey	Guernsey	24	62	55,000	1982RE	1,833	714	British Crown Dependency	St. Peter Port	Europe	9
Guinea	Guinée	94,926	245,857	7,230,000	1992E	76	29	Military Rule	Conakry	Africa	34
Guinea-Bissau	Guiné-Bissau	13,948	36,125	1,032,000	1992E	74	29	Military Republic	Bissau	Africa	34
Guizhou (Kweichow), China	Guizhou	67,180	174,000	32,391,066	1990C	482	186	Province (China)	Guiyang (Kuei-yang)	Asia	27
Guyana	Guyana	83,000	214,969	819,000	1992E	10	4	Republic	Georgetown	South America	54
Haiti	Haïti	10,714	27,750	6,752,000	1992E	630	243	Military Republic	Port-au-Prince	North America	49
Hawaii, U.S.	Hawaii	6,471	16,759	1,115,274	1990C	172	67	State (U.S.)	Honolulu	Oceania	60
Hebei (Hopeh), China	Hebei	78,260	202,700	61,082,439	1990C	781	301	Province (China)	Shijiazhuang (Shih-chiachuang)	Asia	28
Heilongjiang (Heilungkiang), China	Heilongjiang	179,000	463,600	35,214,873	1990C	197	76	Province (China)	Harbin (Harbin)	Asia	27
Henan (Honan), China	Henan	64,480	167,000	85,509,535	1990C	1,326	512	Province (China)	Zheng-zhou (Cheng-chou)	Asia	27
Hispaniola	La Isla Española	29,530	76,484	14,209,000	1992E	481	186	Haiti; Dominican Republic	Port-au-Prince; Santo Domingo	North America	49
Holland, see Netherlands	—	—	—	—	—	—	—	—	—	—	—
Honduras	Honduras	43,277	112,088	5,451,000	1992E	126	49	Republic	Tegucigalpa	North America	49
Hong Kong	Hong Kong	400	1,045	5,965,000	1992E	14,801	5,700	British Dependency	Victoria	Asia	27
Hubei (Hupeh), China	Hubei	72,394	187,500	53,969,210	1990C	745	288	Province (China)	Wuhan (Wu-han)	Asia	27
Hunan, China	Hunan	81,275	210,500	60,659,754	1990C	746	288	Province (China)	Changsha (C'hang-sha)	Asia	27
Hungary	Magyarország	35,920	93,032	10,535,000	1992E	293	113	Republic	Budapest	Europe	10
Iceland	Ìsland	39,800	103,000	257,000	1992E	6	2	Republic	Reykjavík	Europe	7
Idaho, U.S.	Idaho	83,564	216,432	1,011,986	1990C	12	5	State (U.S.)	Boise	North America	46
Illinois, U.S.	Illinois	56,345	145,934	11,466,682	1990C	204	79	State (U.S.)	Springfield	North America	45
India	Bharat	1,269,346	3,287,590	889,417,000	1992E	701	271	Federal Republic	New Delhi	Asia	25
Indiana, U.S.	Indiana	36,185	93,720	5,564,228	1990C	154	59	State (U.S.)	Indianapolis	North America	44
Indonesia	Indonesia	741,101	1,919,443	186,043,000	1992E	251	97	Republic	Jakarta	Asia	26
Inner Mongolia, China	Nei Mongol	454,600	1,177,500	21,456,798	1990C	47	18	Autonomous Region (China)	Hohhot (Hu-ho-hao-t'e)	Asia	27
Iowa, U.S.	Iowa	56,275	145,753	2,787,424	1990C	50	19	State (U.S.)	Des Moines	North America	45
Iran	Īrān	636,300	1,648,000	59,601,000	1992E	94	36	Islamic Republic	Teheran	Asia	23
Iraq	Al'Irāq	169,235	438,317	18,048,000	1990E(4)	107	41	Republic	Baghdad	Asia	24
Ireland	Éire	27,137	70,284	3,791,000	1992E	140	54	Republic	Dublin	Europe	9
Israel	Yisra'el	8,019	20,770	4,713,000	1992E	588	227	Republic	Jerusalem	Asia	24
Italy	Italia	116,320	301,268	57,425,000	1992E	494	191	Republic	Rome (Roma)	Europe	14
Ivory Coast	Côte d'Ivoire	124,504	322,463	10,600,000	1992E	85	33	Republic	Abidjan	Africa	34
Jamaica	Jamaica	4,243	10,990	2,593,000	1992E	611	236	Constitutional Monarchy	Kingston	North America	49
Jammu and Kashmir	Jammu and Kashmīr	85,806	222,237	9,920,000	*	115	45	In dispute (India and Pakistan)	Srinagar and Jammu	Asia	25
Japan	Nippon	145,870	377,801	124,595,000	1992E	854	330	Constitutional Monarchy	Tokyo	Asia	29
Java (incl. Madura)	Jawa	51,038	132,187	91,269,528	1981C	1,787	690	Part of Indonesia	—	Asia	26
Jersey	Jersey	45	117	78,000	*	1,733	667	British Crown Dependency	St. Helier	Europe	9
Jiangsu (Kiangsu), China	Jiangsu	39,460	102,200	67,056,519	1990C	1,699	656	Province (China)	Nanjing (Nan-ching)	Asia	28
Jiangxi (Kiangsi), China	Jiangxi	63,630	164,800	37,710,281	1990C	593	229	Province (China)	Nanchang (Nan-ch'ang)	Asia	27
Jilin (Kirin), China	Jilin	72,200	187,000	24,658,721	1990C	342	132	Province (China)	Changchun (Ch'ang-ch'un)	Asia	27
Jordan	Al Urdun	35,475	91,880	3,510,000	1992E	91	35	Constitutional Monarchy	Amman	Asia	24
Kampuchea, see Cambodia	—	—	—	—	—	—	—	—	—	—	—
Kansas, U.S.	Kansas	82,277	213,098	2,485,600	1990C	30	12	State (U.S.)	Topeka	North America	45

Political unit	Local name	Area sq. miles	km²	Population	Date	Population density per sq. mile	km²	Form of govt./ Political status	Capital	Continent	Map plate
Kazakh Soviet Socialist Republic, U.S.S.R.	Kazakhstan	1,049,155	2,717,300	15,648,000	1984E	15	6	Soviet Socialist Republic (U.S.S.R.)	Alma-Ata	Asia	19
Kentucky, U.S.	Kentucky	40,409	104,660	3,698,969	1990C	92	35	State (U.S.)	Frankfort	North America	44
Kenya	Kenya	224,081	580,367	27,233,000	1992E	122	47	Republic	Nairobi	Africa	36
Kerguelen Island	Iles Kerguèlen	2,577	6,674	(1)	—	—	—	Part of French Southern and Antarctic Territories	—	Antarctica	30–31
Kirghiz Soviet Socialist Republic, U.S.S.R.	Kirghiz	76,641	198,500	3,886,000	1984E	51	20	Soviet Socialist Republic (U.S.S.R.)	Frunze	Asia	18
Kiribati	Kiribati	280	726	72,000	1992E	385	99	Republic	Tarawa	Oceania	60
Korea, see North Korea; South Korea	—	—	—	—	—	—	—	—	—	—	—
Kuwait	Al Kuwayt	6,880	17,818	2,096,000	1990E(4)	305	117	Emirate	Kuwait	Asia	24
Labrador (Can.)	Labrador	113,641	294,330	28,741	1986C	0.3	0.1	Part of Newfoundland Province (Canada)	—	North America	42
Laos	Laos	91,430	236,800	4,266,000	1992E	47	18	Socialist Republic (Communist)	Vientiane	Asia	26
Latin America	—	8,000,000	21,000,000	458,000,000	1992E	57	22	—	—	North America, South America	52–53
Latvian Soviet Socialist Republic, U.S.S.R.	Latvia	24,595	63,700	2,587,000	1984E	105	41	Soviet Socialist Republic (U.S.S.R.)	Riga	Europe	8
Lebanon	Lubnān	4,015	10,400	3,088,000	1992E	769	297	Republic	Beirut	Asia	24
Lesotho	Lesotho	11,720	30,355	1,876,000	1992E	160	62	Military Rule	Maseru	Africa	37
Liaoning (Liaoning), China	Liaoning	58,300	151,000	39,459,697	1990C	677	261	Province (China)	Shenyang (Shen-yang)	Asia	28
Liberia	Liberia	43,000	111,369	2,723,000	1992E	63	24	Republic/Military Rule	Monrovia	Africa	34
Libya	Lībiyā	679,362	1,759,540	4,879,000	1992E	7	3	Socialist Republic/ Military Rule	Tripoli	Africa	33
Liechtenstein	Liechtenstein	62	160	28,000	1992E	452	175	Constitutional Monarchy	Vaduz	Europe	14
Lithuanian Soviet Socialist Republic, U.S.S.R.	Lithuania	25,174	65,200	3,539,000	1984E	141	54	Soviet Socialist Republic (U.S.S.R.) (6)	Vilnius	Europe	8
Louisiana, U.S.	Louisiana	47,752	123,677	4,238,216	1990C	89	34	State (U.S.)	Baton Rouge	North America	45
Luxembourg	Luxembourg	998	2,586	367,000	1992E	368	142	Constitutional Monarchy	Luxembourg	Europe	12
Macao	Macau	6.5	16	436,000	*	67,077	27,250	Portuguese Territory	Macao	Asia	27
Macias Nguema Biyogo, see Bioko	—	—	—	—	—	—	—	—	—	—	—
Madagascar	Madagasikara	226,658	587,041	12,764,000	1992E	56	22	Republic	Antananarivo	Africa	37
Madeira Islands	Arquipélago da Madeira	308	797	258,200	1981C	838	324	District of Portugal	Funchal	Africa	32
Maine, U.S.	Maine	33,265	86,156	1,233,223	1990C	37	14	State (U.S.)	Augusta	North America	44
Malagasy Republic, see Madagascar											
Malawi	Malawi	45,747	118,484	9,399,000	1992E	205	79	Republic	Lilongwe	Africa	36
Malaya	Malaya	50,806	131,588	13,291,200	1988E	262	101	Part of Malaysia	—	Asia	26
Malaysia	Malaysia	127,317	329,749	18,047,000	1992E	142	55	Constitutional Monarchy	Kuala Lumpur	Asia	26
Maldives	Maldives	115	298	234,000	1992E	2,035	785	Republic	Male	Asia	34
Mali	Mali	478,841	1,240,192	8,818,000	1992E	18	7	Republic	Bamako	Africa	34
Malta	Malta	122	316	356,000	1992E	2,918	1,127	Republic	Valletta	Europe	14
Man, Isle of	Isle of Man	227	588	65,000	*	286	111	British Crown Dependency	Douglas	Europe	9
Manitoba, Can.	Manitoba	250,947	649,950	1,071,232	1986C	4	2	Province (Canada)	Winnipeg	North America	42
Marshall Islands	Marshall Islands	70	181	34,000	*	486	188	Self-governing area associated with U.S.	Majaro	Oceania	60
Martinique	Martinique	425	1,102	329,000	*	774	299	Overseas Department (France)	Fort-de-France	North America	51
Maryland, U.S.	Maryland	10,460	27,092	4,798,622	1990C	459	177	State (U.S.)	Annapolis	North America	44
Massachusetts, U.S.	Massachusetts	8,284	21,456	6,029,051	1990C	728	281	State (U.S.)	Boston	North America	44
Mauritania	Mūrītāniyā	395,956	1,025,520	2,139,000	1992E	5	2	Military Rule	Nouakchott	Africa	32
Mauritius	Mauritius	788	2,040	1,130,000	1992E	1,434	554	Constitutional Monarchy	Port Louis	Africa	37
Mayotte	Mayotte	144	374	54,000	*	375	144	French possession— claimed by Comoros	Dzaoudzi	Africa	37
Mexico	México	756,066	1,958,201	85,082,000	1992E	113	43	Republic	Mexico City	North America	48
Michigan, U.S.	Michigan	58,527	151,586	9,328,784	1990C	159	62	State (U.S.)	Lansing	North America	44
Micronesia, Federated States of	Federated States of Micronesia	271	702	88,000	*	325	125	Self-governing area associated with U.S.	Kolonia	Oceania	60
Midway Island	Midway Island	2	5	500	*	250	100	U.S. Possession	—	Oceania	60
Minnesota, U.S.	Minnesota	84,402	218,601	4,387,029	1990C	52	20	State (U.S.)	St. Paul	North America	45
Mississippi, U.S.	Mississippi	47,689	123,515	2,586,443	1990C	54	21	State (U.S.)	Jackson	North America	45
Missouri, U.S.	Missouri	69,697	180,516	5,137,804	1990C	74	28	State (U.S.)	Jefferson City	North America	45
Moldavian Soviet Socialist Republic, U.S.S.R.	Moldavia	13,012	33,700	4,080,000	1984E	314	121	Soviet Socialist Republic (U.S.S.R.)	Kishinev	Europe	16
Monaco	Monaco	0.58	1.49	30,000	1992E	51,724	20,000	Principality	Monaco	Europe	11
Mongolia	Mongol Ard Uls	604,829	1,566,500	2,229,000	1992E	4	1	People's Democracy (Communist)	Ulan Bator	Asia	27
Montana, U.S.	Montana	147,046	380,848	803,655	1990C	5	2	State (U.S.)	Helena	North America	46
Montserrat	Montserrat	38	98	12,000	1982RE	300	117	British Dependency	Plymouth	North America	51
Morocco	Al Maghrib	172,414	446,550	26,334,000	1992E	153	59	Constitutional Monarchy	Rabat	Africa	32
Mozambique	Moçambique	309,496	801,590	16,517,000	1992E	53	21	Socialist Republic	Maputo	Africa	37
Muscat and Oman, see Oman	—	—	—	—	—	—	—	—	—	—	—
Namibia	Namibia	317,827	823,168	1,994,000	1992E	6	2	Republic	Windhoek	Africa	37
Nationalist China, see Taiwan	—	—	—	—	—	—	—	—	—	—	—
Nauru	Nauru (English) Naoero (Nauruan)	8	21	9,000	1992E	1,125	429	Republic	—	Oceania	64
Nebraska, U.S.	Nebraska	77,355	200,350	1,584,617	1990C	20	8	State (U.S.)	Lincoln	North America	45
Nepal	Nepal	54,362	140,797	20,049,000	1992E	369	142	Constitutional Monarchy	Kathmandu	Asia	25
Netherlands	Nederland	16,163	41,863	14,852,000	1992E	1,134	438	Constitutional Monarchy	Amsterdam	Europe	12
Netherlands Antilles	Nederlandse Antillen	310	800	185,000	*	597	231	Self-governing; part of Kingdom of the Netherlands	Willemstad	North America	50

Political unit	Local name	Area sq. miles	km²	Population	Date	Population density per sq. mile	km²	Form of govt./ Political status	Capital	Continent	Map plate
Nevada, U.S.	Nevada	110,561	286,352	1,206,152	1990C	11	4	State (U.S.)	Carson City	North America	46
New Brunswick, Can.	New Brunswick	28,355	73,440	710,422	1986C	25	10	Province (Canada)	Fredericton	North America	42
New Caledonia	Nouvelle-Calédonie	7,366	19,079	165,000	*	22	9	Overseas Territory (France)	Nouméa	Oceania	63
Newfoundland, Can.	Newfoundland	156,649	405,720	568,349	1986C	4	1	Province (Canada)	St. John's	North America	42
Newfoundland (island of), (Can.)	Newfoundland	43,008	111,390	539,608	1986C	13	5	Part of Newfoundland Province, Canada	—	North America	42
New Guinea (7)	Pulau Irian	316,000	818,000	5,000,000	1992E	16	6	—	—	Oceania	60
New Hampshire, U.S.	New Hampshire	9,297	24,032	1,113,915	1990C	120	46	State (U.S.)	Concord	North America	44
New Hebrides Islands, see Vanuatu	—	—	—	—		—	—	—	—	—	—
New Jersey, U.S.	New Jersey	7,787	20,169	7,748,634	1990C	995	384	State (U.S.)	Trenton	North America	44
New Mexico, U.S.	New Mexico	121,593	314,295	1,521,779	1990C	13	5	State (U.S.)	Santa Fe	North America	45
New South Wales, Austl.	New South Wales	309,500	801,600	5,125,683	1981C	17	6	State (Australia)	Sydney	Australia	59
New York, U.S.	New York	49,108	127,189	18,044,505	1990C	367	142	State (U.S.)	Albany	North America	44
New Zealand	New Zealand	103,883	269,057	3,430,000	1992E	33	13	Constitutional Monarchy	Wellington	Oceania	62
Nicaragua	Nicaragua	50,200	130,000	4,122,000	1992E	82	32	Republic	Managua	North America	49
Niger	Niger	489,200	1,267,000	8,180,000	1992E	17	6	Military Republic	Niamey	Africa	34
Nigeria	Nigeria	356,669	923,768	120,972,000	1992E	339	131	Military Rule	Lagos	Africa	34
Ningxia (Ningsia), China	Ningxia	25,640	66,400	4,655,451	1990C	182	70	Autonomous Region (China)	Yinchaun	Asia	27
Niue Island	Niue	100	259	2,500	*	25	10	Self-governing area associated with New Zealand	—	Oceania	64
Norfolk Island (Austl.)	Norfolk Island	14	36	2,000	1980E	143	31	External Territory (Australia)	—	Australia	61
†North America	—	9,351,000	24,219,000	429,000,000	1992E	46	18	—	—	North America	38–39
North Borneo, see Sabah	—	—	—	—		—	—	—	—	—	—
North Carolina, U.S.	North Carolina	52,669	136,413	6,657,630	1990C	126	49	State (U.S.)	Raleigh	North America	44
North Dakota, U.S.	North Dakota	70,702	183,119	641,364	1990C	9	4	State (U.S.)	Bismarck	North America	45
North Korea	Choson-minjujuui-inmin-konghwaguk	46,540(5)	120,538(5)	23,939,000	1992E	514	199	Republic (Communist rule)	Pyongyang	Asia	28
Northern Ireland	Northern Ireland	5,452	14,121	1,601,000	1992E	294	113	Constitutional monarchy	Belfast	Europe	9
Northern Mariana Islands	Northern Mariana Islands	184	477	19,000	*	103	40	U.S. commonwealth	Saipan	Oceania	60
Northern Territory, Austl.	Northern Territory	519,800	1,346,200	123,333	1981C	0.2	0.09	Territory (Australia)	Darwin	Australia	59
Northwest Territories, Can.	Northwest Territories	1,332,910	3,426,320	52,238	1986C	0.04	0.02	Territory (Canada)	Yellowknife	North America	42
Norway	Norge	149,405	386,958	4,236,000	1992E	28	11	Constitutional Monarchy	Oslo	Europe	7
Nova Scotia, Can.	Nova Scotia	21,423	55,490	873,199	1986C	41	16	Province (Canada)	Halifax	North America	42
Oceania, see Pacific Islands	—	—	—	—		—	—	—	—	—	—
Ohio, U.S.	Ohio	41,330	107,044	10,887,325	1990C	263	102	State (U.S.)	Columbus	North America	44
Oklahoma, U.S.	Oklahoma	69,956	181,186	3,157,604	1990C	45	17	State (U.S.)	Oklahoma City	North America	45
Oman	'Umān	82,030	212,457	1,568,000	1992E	19	7	Sultanate	Muscat (Masqat)	Asia	23
Ontario, Can.	Ontario	412,581	1,068,580	9,113,515	1986C	22	9	Province (Canada)	Toronto	North America	42
Oregon, U.S.	Oregon	97,073	251,419	2,853,733	1990C	29	11	State (U.S.)	Salem	North America	46
Orkney Islands	Orkney Islands	377	976	19,351	1985E	51	20	Part of Scotland	Kirkwall	Europe	9
Pacific Islands		488,297	1,264,450	12,000,000	1992E	24	9	—	—	Oceania	57–58
Pacific Islands, Trust Territory of the (8)	Trust Territory of the Pacific Islands	192	497	13,000	*	73	28	Trust Territory administered by the U.S.	Saipan (island)	Oceania	60
Pakistan	Pākistān	307,374	796,095	129,808,000	1992E	422	163	Republic	Islamabad	Asia	25
Palau Islands, see Pacific Islands, Trust Territory of the	—	—	—	—		—	—	—	—	—	—
Panama	Panamá	30,193	78,200	2,511,000	1992E	83	32	Republic	Panama City	North America	49
Papua New Guinea	Papua New Guinea	178,704	462,840	4,217,000	1992E	24	9	Constitutional Monarchy	Port Moresby	Oceania	60
Paraguay	Paraguay	157,048	406,752	4,510,000	1992E	29	11	Republic	Asunción	South America	56
Pennsylvania, U.S.	Pennsylvania	45,302	117,348	11,924,710	1990C	263	102	State (U.S.)	Harrisburg	North America	44
Persia, see Iran	—	—	—	—		—	—	—	—	—	—
Peru	Peru	496,225	1,285,216	23,399,000	1992E	47	18	Republic	Lima	South America	54
Philippines	Pilipinas	116,000	300,000	65,275,000	1992E	563	218	Republic	Manila	Asia	26
Pitcairn Island	Pitcairn	2	5	60	*	30	12	Part of British Dependency: Pitcairn Islands Group	Adamstown	Oceania	61
Poland	Polska	120,725	312,677	38,793,000	1992E	321	124	Republic	Warsaw (Warszawa)	Europe	10
Portugal	Portugal	34,340	88,941	10,343,000	1992E	301	116	Republic	Lisbon (Lisboa)	Europe	13
Portuguese Guinea, see Guinea-Bissau	—	—	—	—		—	—	—	—	—	—
Prince Edward Island, Can.	Prince Edward Island	2,185	5,660	126,646	1986C	58	22	Province (Canada)	Charlottetown	North America	42
Puerto Rico	Puerto Rico	3,515	9,103	3,196,520	1980C	909	351	Commonwealth (U.S. Protection)	San Juan	North America	51
Qatar	Qaṭar	4,247	11,000	451,000	1992E	106	41	Emirate	Doha (Ad Dawhah)	Asia	24
Qinghai (Tsinghai), China	Qinghai	278,400	721,000	4,456,946	1990C	16	6	Province (China)	Xining (Hsi-ning)	Asia	27
Quebec, Can.	Québec	594,860	1,540,680	6,540,276	1986C	11	4	Province (Canada)	Quebec (Quebec City)	North America	42
Queensland, Austl.	Queensland	666,900	1,727,200	2,294,546	1981C	3	1	State (Australia)	Brisbane	Australia	59
Reunion	Réunion	970	2,512	564,000	*	581	225	Overseas Department (France)	Saint-Denis	Africa	37
Rhode Island, U.S.	Rhode Island	1,210	3,140	1,005,984	1990C	831	320	State (U.S.)	Providence	North America	44
Rhodesia, see Zimbabwe	—	—	—	—		—	—	—	—	—	—
Rodrigues	Rodrigues	42	109	32,000	1982RE	762	294	Part of Mauritius	—	Africa	30–31
Romania (Rumania)	România	91,700	237,500	23,487,000	1992E	256	99	Republic	Bucharest (Bucureşti)	Europe	15
Russian Soviet Federative Socialist Republic (R.S.F.S.R.), U.S.S.R.	Rossijskaja S.F.S.R.	6,592,849	17,075,400	142,117,000	1984E	22	8	Soviet Socialist Republic, U.S.S.R.	Moscow	Europe/Asia	19–20
Rwanda	Rwanda	10,169	26,338	7,735,000	1992E	761	294	Republic	Kigali	Africa	36
Sabah, Malaysia	Sabah	28,460	73,711	915,000	1982RE	31	12	State of Malaysia	Kota Kinabalu	Asia	26
Saint Christopher and Nevis	St. Christopher-Nevis	101	261	49,000	1992E	485	188	Constitutional Monarchy	Basseterre	North America	51

Political unit	Local name	Area sq. miles	km²	Population	Date	Population density per sq. mile	km²	Form of govt./ Political status	Capital	Continent	Map plate
St. Helena	St. Helena	160	414	8,000	*	50	19	British Dependency	Jamestown	Africa	31
Saint Lucia	Saint Lucia	240	622	161,000	1992E	671	259	Constitutional Monarchy	Castries	North America	51
Saint-Pierre and Miquelon	St.-Pierre et Miquelon	93	242	6,000	*	65	25	Territorial collectivity (France)	St.-Pierre	North America	42
Saint Vincent and the Grenadines	St. Vincent	150	388	114,000	1992E	760	294	Constitutional Monarchy	Kingstown	North America	50
Samoa, see American Samoa; Western Samoa	—	—	—	—	—	—	—	—	—	—	—
San Marino	San Marino	24	61	23,000	1992E	958	377	Republic	San Marino	Europe	14
São Tomé and Príncipe	São Tomé e Príncipe	372	964	132,000	1992E	355	137	Republic	São Tomé	Africa	34
Sarawak, Malaysia	Sarawak	48,050	124,450	1,345,000	1982RE	28	11	State of Malaysia	Kuching	Asia	26
Sardinia	Sardegna	9,301	24,090	1,585,959	1981C	171	66	Region of Italy	Cagliari	Europe	14
Saskatchewan, Can.	Saskatchewan	251,866	652,330	1,010,198	1986C	4	2	Province (Canada)	Regina	North America	42
Saudi Arabia	Al 'Arabīyah as Sa'ūdīyah	830,000	2,149,690	15,234,000	1992E	18	7	Monarchy	Riyadh (Ar Riyad)	Asia	23
Scandinavia	Denmark, Norway, Sweden	339,769	879,999	17,693,000	1992E	52	20	—		Europe	7
Scotland	Scotland	30,414	78,772	5,055,000	1992E	166	64	Constitutional Monarchy	Edinburgh	Europe	9
Senegal	Sénégal	75,955	196,722	7,661,000	1992E	101	39	Republic	Dakar	Africa	34
Senegambia	Senegambia	80,316	208,017	8,566,000	1992E	107	41	Confederation		Africa	34
Seychelles	Seychelles	176	455	70,000	1992E	398	154	Republic	Victoria	Africa	37
Shaanxi (Shensi), China	Shaanxi	75,599	195,800	32,882,403	1990C	435	168	Province (China)	Xi'an (Sian)	Asia	27
Shandong (Shantung), China	Shandong	59,189	153,300	84,392,827	1990C	1,426	551	Province (China)	Jinan (Tsinan)	Asia	28
Shanghai, China	Shanghai	2,240	5,800	13,341,896	1990C	5,956	2,300	Special Municipality (China)		Asia	28
Shanxi (Shansi), China	Shanxi	75,599	195,800	28,759,014	1990C	380	147	Province (China)	Taiyuan (Tai-yuan)	Asia	27
Shetland Islands	Shetland Islands	552	1,430	23,440	1985E	42	16	Region of Scotland; part of Great Britain	Lerwick	Europe	9
Siam, see Thailand	—	—	—	—	—	—	—	—	—	—	—
Sichuan (Szechwan), China	Sichuan	219,700	569,000	107,218,173	1990C	488	188	Province (China)	Chengdu (Ch'eng-tu)	Asia	27
Sicily	Sicilia	9,926	25,708	4,863,587	1981C	490	189	Region of Italy	Palermo	Europe	14
Sierra Leone	Sierra Leone	27,699	71,740	4,370,000	1992E	158	61	Republic	Freetown	Africa	34
Singapore	Singapore (English) Singapura (Malay)	239	618	2,755,000	1992E	11,527	4,458	Republic	Singapore	Asia	26
Solomon Islands	Solomon Islands	10,639	27,566	351,000	1992E	33	13	Constitutional Monarchy	Honiara	Oceania	63
Somalia	Soomaaliya	246,201	637,657	7,917,000	1992E	32	12	Military (Socialist) Rule	Mogadishu	Africa	35
South Africa (excludes Walvis Bay)	South Africa (English) Suid-Afrika (Afrikaans)	471,445	1,221,037	41,600,000	1992E	88	34	Republic	Cape Town, Pretoria, Bloemfontein	Africa	37
†South America	—	6,885,000	17,832,000	308,000,000	1992E	45	17	—	—	South America	52–53
South Australia, Austl.	South Australia	380,070	984,377	1,284,843	1981C	3	1	State (Australia)	Adelaide	Australia	59
South Carolina, U.S.	South Carolina	31,113	80,582	3,505,707	1990C	113	44	State (U.S.)	Columbia	North America	44
South Dakota, U.S.	South Dakota	77,116	199,730	699,999	1990C	9	4	State (U.S.)	Pierre	North America	45
South Georgia (3)	South Georgia	1,580	4,092	20	*	0.01	.005	Dependency of Falkland Islands (U.K.)	—	South America	56
South Korea	Taehan-Minguk	38,230 (5)	99,016 (5)	44,458,000	1992E	1,163	449	Republic	Seoul	Asia	28
South West Africa, see Namibia	—	—	—	—	—	—	—	—	—	—	—
Spain	España	194,885	504,750	39,625,000	1992E	203	79	Parliamentary Monarchy	Madrid	Europe	13
Spanish North Africa (9) (Sp.)	Plazas de Soberanía en el Norte de África	12	32	127,000	1982RE	10,583	3,969	Five Possessions (no central government)	—	Africa	13
Spanish Sahara, see Western Sahara	—	—	—	—	—	—	—	—	—	—	—
Sri Lanka	Sri Lanka	25,333	65,610	17,642,000	1992E	696	269	Republic	Colombo	Asia	25
Sudan	As Sūdān	967,500	2,505,813	26,672,000	1992E	28	11	Republic	Khartoum	Africa	35
Sumatra	Sumatera	182,860	473,606	28,016,160	1981C	153	59	Part of Indonesia	—	Asia	26
Suriname	Suríname	63,037	163,265	415,000	1992E	7	3	Republic	Paramaribo	South America	54
Swaziland	Swaziland	6,704	17,364	844,000	1992E	126	49	Monarchy	Mbabane and Lobamba	Africa	37
Sweden	Sverige	173,732	449,964	8,334,000	1992E	48	19	Constitutional Monarchy	Stockholm	Europe	7
Switzerland	Schweiz (German) Suisse (French) Svizzera (Italian)	15,943	41,293	6,534,000	1992E	410	158	Federal Republic	Bern	Europe	14
Syria	Sūrīyah	71,498	185,180	13,397,000	1992E	187	72	Republic	Damascus	Asia	24
Tajik Soviet Socialist Republic, U.S.S.R.	Takjikistan	55,251	143,100	4,365,000	1984E	79	31	Soviet Socialist Republic (U.S.S.R.)	Dushanbe (Stalinabad)	Asia	18
Taiwan	Taiwan	13,900	36,000	21,001,000	1992E	1,511	583	Republic	Taipei	Asia	27
Tanzania	Tanzania	364,900	945,087	29,393,000	1992E	81	31	Republic	Dar es Salaam	Africa	36
Tasmania, Austl.	Tasmania	26,200	67,800	418,956	1981C	16	6	State (Australia)	Hobart	Australia	59
Tennessee, U.S.	Tennessee	42,114	109,152	4,896,641	1990C	116	45	State (U.S.)	Nashville	North America	44
Texas, U.S.	Texas	266,807	691,030	17,059,805	1990C	64	25	State (U.S.)	Austin	North America	45
Thailand	Muang Thai	198,115	513,115	57,216,000	1992E	289	112	Constitutional Monarchy	Bangkok	Asia	26
Tianjin (Tientsin), China	Tianjin	4,250	11,000	8,758,402	1990C	2,061	796	Special Municipality (China)	—	Asia	28
Tibet, China	Xizang	471,662	1,221,600	2,196,010	1990C	5	2	Autonomous Region (China)	Lhasa	Asia	27
Togo	Togo	21,925	56,785	3,674,000	1992E	168	65	Presidential Regime	Lomé	Africa	34
Tokelau (N.Z.)	Tokelau	4	10	2,000	*	500	200	Territory of New Zealand		Oceania	61
Tonga	Tonga	290	750	99,000	1992E	341	132	Constitutional Monarchy	Nukualofa	Oceania	61
Trinidad and Tobago	Trinidad and Tobago	1,981	5,130	1,323,000	1992E	668	258	Republic	Port-of-Spain	North America	50
Tristan da Cunha	Tristan da Cunha	40	104	300	*	7.5	2.9	Dependency of St. Helena (U.K.)	Edinburgh	Africa	30–31
Trucial States, see United Arab Emirates	—	—	—	—	—	—	—	—	—	—	—
Tunisia	Tūnis	63,170	163,610	8,496,000	1992E	134	52	Republic	Tunis	Africa	32
Turkey	Türkiye	300,948	779,452	57,749,000	1992E	192	74	Republic	Ankara	Europe/Asia	24
Turkmen Soviet Socialist Republic, U.S.S.R.	Turkmenistan	188,456	488,100	3,118,000	1984E	17	6	Soviet Socialist Republic (U.S.S.R.)	Ashkhabad	Asia	19
Turks and Caicos Islands	Turks and Caicos Islands	156	430	11,000	*	66	26	British Dependency	Grand Turk	North America	49
Tuvalu	Tuvalu	10	26	9,000	1992E	900	346	Constitutional Monarchy	Funafuti	Oceania	60

Political unit	Local name	Area sq. miles	Area km²	Population	Date	Population density per sq. mile	Population density per km²	Form of govt./ Political status	Capital	Continent	Map plate
Uganda	Uganda	91,074	235,830	19,771,000	1992E	217	84	Republic	Kampala	Africa	36
Ukrainian Soviet Socialist Republic, U.S.S.R.	Ukraine	233,090	603,700	50,667,000	1984E	217	84	Soviet Socialist Republic (U.S.S.R.)	Kiev	Europe	16
Union of Soviet Socialist Republics U.S.S.R.	Soyuz Sovetskikh Sotsialisticheskikh Respublik	8,649,500	22,402,000	292,955,000	1992E	34	13	Communist Dictatorship	Moscow	Europe/Asia	19–20
United Arab Emirates	Al Imārāt al 'Arabīyah al Muttaḥidah	32,278	83,600	1,660,000	1992E	51	20	Federation	Abu Dhabi	Asia	23
United Arab Republic, *see* Egypt	—	—	—	—	—	—	—	—	—	—	—
United States	United States	3,618,770	9,372,571	253,190,000	1992E	70	27	Republic	Washington, D.C.	North America	43
Upper Volta, *see* Burkina Faso	—	—	—	—	—	—	—	—	—	—	—
Uruguay	Uruguay	68,500	177,414	3,174,000	1992E	46	18	Republic	Montevideo	South America	55
Utah, U.S.	Utah	84,899	219,889	1,727,784	1990C	20	8	State (U.S.)	Salt Lake City	North America	46
Uzbek Soviet Socialist Republic, U.S.S.R.	Uzbekistan	172,742	447,400	17,498,000	1984E	101	39	Soviet Socialist Republic (U.S.S.R.)	Tashkent	Asia	19
Vanuatu	Vanuatu	4,706	12,189	156,000	1992E	33	13	Republic	Port-Vila	Oceania	63
Vatican City	Città del Vaticano	0.17	0.44	1,000	1992E	5,882	2,273	Independent State	—	Europe	14
Venezuela	Venezuela	352,145	912,050	20,683,000	1992E	59	23	Federal Republic	Caracas	South America	54
Vermont, U.S.	Vermont	9,614	24,900	564,964	1990C	59	23	State (U.S.)	Montpelier	North America	44
Victoria, Austl.	Victoria	87,900	227,600	3,832,100	1981C	44	17	State (Australia)	Melbourne	Australia	59
Vietnam	Viet-nam Dan-chu Cong-hoa	128,066	331,689	68,777,000	1992E	537	207	Communist Dictatorship	Hanoi	Asia	26
Virgin Islands (U.S.)	Virgin Islands	132	342	111,000	*	841	325	Self-governing territory of U.S.	Charlotte Amalie	North America	51
Virgin Islands, British	British Virgin Islands	59	153	13,000	*	220	85	British Dependency	Road Town	North America	51
Virginia, U.S.	Virginia	40,767	105,586	6,216,568	1990C	152	59	State (U.S.)	Richmond	North America	44
Wake Island	Wake Island	3	8	300	*	100	38	Unincorporated possession (U.S.)	—	Oceania	60
Wales	Wales	8,019	20,768	2,906,000	1992E	362	140	Constitutional Monarchy	Cardiff	Europe	9
Wallis and Futuna Islands	Iles Wallis-et-Futuna	106	275	12,000	*	113	44	Overseas Territory (France)	Mata-Utu	Oceania	61
Washington, U.S.	Washington	68,139	176,479	4,887,941	1990C	72	28	State (U.S.)	Olympia	North America	46
West Bank	Yehuda v'Shomron (Judea and Samaria)	2,263	5,860	1,053,000		465	180	Occupied by Israel; formerly part of Jordan	—	Asia	24
West Indies	West Indies (English) Indias Occidentales (Spanish)	91,973	238,209	34,255,000	1992E	372	144	—	—	North America	47
West Virginia, U.S.	West Virginia	24,231	62,759	1,801,625	1990C	74	29	State (U.S.)	Charleston	North America	44
Western Australia, Austl.	Western Australia	975,100	2,525,500	1,273,420	1981C	1	0.5	State (Australia)	Perth	Australia	59
Western Sahara	—	102,700	266,000	180,000	*	2	1	Claimed by Morocco	—	Africa	32
Western Samoa	Samoa i Sisifo	1,093	2,831	173,000	1982E	158	61	Parliamentary	Apia	Oceania	65
White Russia, *see* Byelorussian S.S.R.	—	—	—	—	—	—	—	—	—	—	—
Wisconsin, U.S.	Wisconsin	56,153	145,436	4,906,745	1990C	87	34	State (U.S.)	Madison	North America	45
Wyoming, U.S.	Wyoming	97,809	253,326	455,975	1990C	5	2	State (U.S.)	Cheyenne	North America	46
Xinjiang (Sinkiang), China	Xinjiang	635,833	1,646,800	15,155,778	1990C	24	9	Autonomous Region (China)	Ürümqi (Urumchi)	Asia	27
Yemen	Al Yaman	203,877	528,038	11,199,000	1992E	55	22	Republic	Sana	Asia	23
Yugoslavia	Jugoslavija	98,766	255,804	24,093,000	1992E	244	94	Socialist Republic	Belgrade	Europe	14–15
Yukon Territory, Can.	Yukon Territory	186,661	483,450	23,504	1986C	0.13	0.05	Territory (Canada)	Whitehorse	North America	42
Yunnan, China	Yunnan	168,420	436,200	36,972,610	1992E	220	85	Province (China)	Kunming (K'un-ming)	Asia	27
Zaire	Zaïre	905,568	2,345,409	38,338,000	1992E	42	16	Presidential regime	Kinshasa	Africa	36
Zambia	Zambia	290,586	752,614	9,093,000	1992E	31	12	Republic	Lusaka	Africa	36
Zanzibar	Zanzibar	1,020	2,642	1,254,250	1988E	1,230	475	Part of Tanzania	Zanzibar	Africa	36
Zhejiang (Chekiang), China	Zhejiang	39,305	101,800	41,445,930	1990C	1,054	407	Province (China)	Hangzhou (Hang-chou)	Asia	27
Zimbabwe	Zimbabwe	150,804	390,580	10,333,000	1992E	69	26	Republic; Parliamentary	Harare	Africa	37
World	—	57,800,000	149,700,000	5,465,000,000	1992E	95	37	—	—	—	1–2

C = Census; E = Estimate; RE = Rand McNally estimate
† Continent
* Populations are 1992 and earlier estimates based on the latest figures from official government and United Nations sources.
— none, or not applicable
(1) No permanent population.
(2) Comprises Bahrain, Kuwait, Oman, Qatar, Saudi Arabia, United Arab Emirates, and Yemen
(3) Comprises Kalimantin (part of Indonesia), Sabah and Sarawak (states of Malaysia), and Brunei
(4) Prior to the Iraqi invasion of Kuwait in August 1990
(5) The 487 sq. mi. or 1,262 km² of the demilitarized zone are not included in either North Korea or South Korea.
(6) In March 1990, Lithuania declared its independence, a decision which the U.S.S.R. government did not accept.
(7) Comprises Papua New Guinea and Irian Jaya (part of Indonesia)
(8) Comprises the Palau Islands
(9) Comprises Ceuta, Melilla, and several small islands

World Geographical Tables

Earth: Land and Water

	Total area		Area of land			Area of water		
	sq. miles	sq. kilometers	sq. miles	sq. kilometers	per cent	sq. miles	sq. kilometers	per cent
Earth	196,951,000	510,100,000	57,259,000	148,300,000	30%	139,692,000	381,800,000	70%

Continents

Name	Area sq. miles/sq. kilometers	1988 population estimate	Population per sq. mile/sq. kilometer	Highest elevation place/feet/meters	Lowest elevation place/feet/meters (below sea level)	Highest recorded temperature place/°F./°C	Lowest recorded temperature place/°F./°C
Africa	11,694,000/30,330,000	600,000,000	51/20	Kilimanjaro, Tanzania 19,340/5,895	Lake Assal, Djibouti −509/−155	Al Aziziyah, Libya 136°F./58°C	Ifrane, Morocco −11°F./−24°C
Antarctica	5,100,000/13,209,000	(no permanent population)	—	Vinson Massif 16,864/5,140	sea level	Esperanza 58°F./14°C	Vostok Station −127°F./−88°C
Asia	16,968,000/43,947,000	3,069,000,000	181/70	Mount Everest, Nepal-Tibet 29,028/8,848	Dead Sea, Israel-Jordan −1,310/−399	Tirat Zevi, Israel 129°F./54°C	Verkhoyansk, Soviet Union −93°F./−69°C
Australia	2,966,150/7,682,300	16,297,000	5/2	Mount Kosciusko 7,310/2,228	Lake Eyre −52/−16	Cloncurry 128°F./53°C	Charlotte Pass −8°F./−22°C
Europe	4,066,000/10,532,000	692,000,000	170/66	Mount Elbrus 18,481/5,633	Caspian Sea, Soviet Union-Iran −92/−28	Seville, Spain 122°F./50°C	Ust-Ščugor, Soviet Union −67°F./−55°C
North America	9,363,000/24,249,000	418,000,000	45/17	Mount McKinley, U.S. 20,320/6,194	Death Valley, U.S. −282/−86	Death Valley, U.S. 134°F./57°C	North ce, Greenland −87°F./−66°C
South America	6,886,000/17,835,000	287,000,000	42/16	Mount Aconcagua, Argentina 22,831/6,959	Valdés Peninsula, Argentina −131/−40	Rivadavia, Argentina 120°F./49°C	Sarmiento, Argentina −27°F./−33°C
Earth	196,951,000/510,100,000	5,082,297,000	87/34	Mount Everest, Asia 29,028/8,848	Dead Sea, Asia −1,310/−399	Al Aziziyah, Africa 136°F./58°C	Vostok, Antarctica −127°F./−88°C

Historical Population of the World

Area	1650	1750	1800	1850	1900	1914	1920	1939	1950	1982	1992E
Europe	100,000,000	140,000,000	190,000,000	265,000,000	400,000,000	470,000,000	453,000,000	526,000,000	530,000,000	666,000,000	699,000,000
Asia	335,000,000	476,000,000	593,000,000	754,000,000	932,000,000	1,006,000,000	1,000,000,000	1,247,000,000	1,418,000,000	2,725,000,000	3,308,000,000
Africa	100,000,000	95,000,000	90,000,000	95,000,000	118,000,000	130,000,000	140,000,000	170,000,000	199,000,000	490,000,000	692,000,000
North America	5,000,000	5,000,000	13,000,000	39,000,000	106,000,000	141,000,000	147,000,000	186,000,000	219,000,000	379,000,000	429,000,000
South America	8,000,000	7,000,000	12,000,000	20,000,000	38,000,000	55,000,000	61,000,000	90,000,000	111,000,000	248,000,000	308,000,000
Oceania, incl. Australia	2,000,000	2,000,000	2,000,000	2,000,000	6,000,000	8,000,000	9,000,000	11,000,000	13,000,000	23,000,000	29,000,000
World	500,000,000	725,000,000	900,000,000	1,175,000,000	1,600,000,000	1,810,000,000	1,810,000,000	2,230,000,000	2,490,000,000	4,531,000,000	5,465,000,000

Figures are rounded to the nearest million.   Figures in italics represent very rough estimates.

Largest Countries: Population

	Name	Population 1992 estimate	1997 estimate
1.	China	1,143,729,000	1,217,861,000
2.	India	889,417,000	984,053,000
3.	Soviet Union	292,955,000	302,811,000
4.	United States	253,190,000	261,786,000
5.	Indonesia	186,043,000	200,067,000
6.	Brazil	156,044,000	170,643,000
7.	Pakistan	129,808,000	149,494,000
8.	Japan	124,595,000	127,433,000
9.	Bangladesh	121,896,000	139,184,000
10.	Nigeria	120,972,000	143,614,000
11.	Mexico	85,082,000	95,794,000
12.	Germany	77,042,000	76,663,000
13.	Vietnam	68,777,000	74,798,000
14.	Philippines	65,275,000	72,804,000
15.	Iran	59,601,000	68,269,000
16.	Turkey	57,749,000	63,260,000
17.	Great Britain	57,640,000	58,571,000
18.	Italy	57,425,000	57,706,000
19.	Thailand	57,216,000	61,189,000
20.	France	56,578,000	57,589,000
21.	Egypt	56,508,000	62,864,000
22.	Ethiopia	49,263,000	56,348,000
23.	South Korea	44,458,000	46,679,000
24.	Burma	43,435,000	48,145,000
25.	South Africa	41,600,000	47,334,000
26.	Spain	39,625,000	40,357,000
27.	Poland	38,793,000	39,760,000
28.	Zaire	38,338,000	44,915,000
29.	Argentina	33,083,000	35,036,000
30.	Colombia	33,020,000	36,123,000
31.	Tanzania	29,393,000	35,371,000
32.	Kenya	27,233,000	33,329,000
33.	Canada	26,935,000	27,938,000
34.	Algeria	26,851,000	30,802,000
35.	Sudan	26,672,000	30,811,000
36.	Morocco	26,334,000	29,457,000
37.	Yugoslavia	24,093,000	24,692,000
38.	North Korea	23,939,000	26,554,000
39.	Romania	23,487,000	24,026,000
40.	Peru	23,399,000	26,205,000
41.	Taiwan	21,001,000	22,182,000
42.	Venezuela	20,683,000	23,174,000
43.	Nepal	20,049,000	22,500,000
44.	Uganda	19,771,000	23,603,000
45.	Afghanistan	18,850,000	24,450,000

Smallest Countries: Population

	Name	Population 1992 estimate	1997 estimate
1.	Vatican City	1,000	1,000
2.	Tuvalu	9,000	10,000
3.	Nauru	9,000	10,000
4.	San Marino	23,000	24,000
5.	Liechtenstein	28,000	29,000
6.	Monaco	30,000	31,000
7.	Saint Christopher and Nevis	48,000	52,000
8.	Andorra	55,000	62,000
9.	Seychelles	70,000	73,000
10.	Kiribati	72,000	78,000
11.	Antigua and Barbuda	82,000	83,000
12.	Grenada	85,000	113,000
13.	Dominica	88,000	94,000
14.	Tonga	99,000	103,000
15.	Saint Vincent and the Grenadines	114,000	121,000
16.	São Tomé and Príncipe	132,000	153,000
17.	Vanuatu	156,000	178,000
18.	Saint Lucia	161,000	183,000
19.	Western Samoa	173,000	179,000
20.	Belize	189,000	209,000
21.	Maldives	234,000	281,000
22.	Iceland	257,000	268,000
23.	Barbados	265,000	277,000
24.	Bahamas	267,000	285,000
25.	Brunei	279,000	368,000
26.	Solomon Islands	351,000	415,000
27.	Malta	356,000	363,000
28.	Luxembourg	367,000	368,000
29.	Cape Verde	403,000	472,000
30.	Suriname	415,000	448,000
31.	Djibouti	431,000	503,000
32.	Qatar	451,000	529,000
33.	Equatorial Guinea	462,000	522,000
34.	Bahrain	547,000	632,000
35.	Comoros	552,000	645,000
36.	Cyprus	714,000	746,000

Largest Countries: Area

	Name	Area sq. miles	Area km²
1.	U.S.S.R.	8,649,500	22,402,000
2.	Canada	3,849,674	9,970,610
3.	China	3,696,032	9,572,678
4.	United States	3,618,770	9,372,571
5.	Brazil	3,286,488	8,511,965
6.	Australia	2,967,909	7,686,848
7.	India	1,269,346	3,287,590
8.	Argentina	1,073,400	2,780,092
9.	Sudan	967,500	2,505,813
10.	Algeria	919,595	2,381,741
11.	Zaire	905,568	2,345,409
12.	Saudi Arabia	830,000	2,149,690
13.	Mexico	756,066	1,958,205
14.	Indonesia	741,101	1,919,443
15.	Libya	679,362	1,759,540
16.	Iran	636,300	1,648,000
17.	Mongolia	604,829	1,566,300
18.	Peru	496,225	1,285,216
19.	Chad	495,755	1,284,000
20.	Niger	489,200	1,267,000
21.	Angola	481,354	1,246,700
22.	Mali	478,841	1,240,192
23.	Ethiopia	471,778	1,221,900
24.	South Africa	471,445	1,221,037
25.	Colombia	439,737	1,138,914
26.	Bolivia	424,165	1,098,581
27.	Mauritania	395,956	1,025,520
28.	Egypt	386,662	1,001,449
29.	Tanzania	364,900	945,087
30.	Nigeria	356,669	923,768
31.	Venezuela	352,145	912,050
32.	Namibia	317,827	823,158
33.	Mozambique	309,943	801,390
34.	Pakistan	307,374	796,095
35.	Turkey	300,948	779,452
36.	Chile	292,258	756,945
37.	Zambia	290,586	752,614
38.	Burma	261,228	676,578
39.	Afghanistan	251,773	652,090
40.	Somalia	246,201	637,657
41.	Central African Republic	240,535	622,984
42.	Madagascar	226,658	587,041
43.	Botswana	224,607	581,730
44.	Kenya	224,081	580,367
45.	France	212,935	551,500

Smallest Countries: Area

	Name	Area sq. miles	Area km²
1.	Vatican City	0.17	0.44
2.	Monaco	0.58	1.49
3.	Nauru	8	21
4.	Tuvalu	10	26
5.	San Marino	24	61
6.	Liechtenstein	62	160
7.	Saint Christopher and Nevis	101	261
8.	Maldives	115	298
9.	Malta	122	316
10.	Grenada	133	344
11.	Saint Vincent and the Grenadines	150	388
12.	Barbados	166	430
13.	Antigua and Barbuda	171	442
14.	Andorra	175	453
15.	Seychelles	176	455
16.	Singapore	239	618
17.	Saint Lucia	240	622
18.	Bahrain	262	678
19.	Kiribati	280	726
20.	Tonga	290	750
21.	Dominica	290	751
22.	São Tomé and Príncipe	372	964
23.	Mauritius	788	2,040
24.	Comoros	863	2,235
25.	Luxembourg	998	2,586
26.	Western Samoa	1,093	2,831
27.	Cape Verde	1,557	4,033
28.	Trinidad and Tobago	1,981	5,130
29.	Brunei	2,226	5,765
30.	Cyprus	3,572	9,251
31.	Lebanon	4,015	10,400
32.	Jamaica	4,243	10,990
33.	Qatar	4,247	11,000
34.	Gambia	4,361	11,295
35.	Vanuatu	4,706	12,189
36.	Bahamas	5,385	13,878
37.	Swaziland	6,704	17,363
38.	Kuwait	6,880	17,818
39.	Fiji	7,056	18,274
40.	Israel	8,019	20,770
41.	El Salvador	8,124	21,041
42.	Belize	8,867	22,965
43.	Djibouti	8,958	23,200
44.	Rwanda	10,169	26,338
45.	Solomon Islands	10,639	27,566

Highest Population Densities

	Country	Population density per sq. mile	Population density per km²
1.	Monaco	51,724	20,000
2.	Singapore	11,527	4,458
3.	Vatican City	5,882	2,273
4.	Malta	2,918	1,127
5.	Bangladesh	2,192	847
6.	Bahrain	2,088	807
7.	Maldives	2,035	785
8.	Barbados	1,596	616
9.	Taiwan	1,511	583
10.	Mauritius	1,434	554
11.	South Korea	1,163	449
12.	Netherlands	1,134	438
13.	Nauru	1,125	429
14.	San Marino	958	377
15.	Tuvalu	900	346
16.	Japan	854	330
17.	Belgium	845	326
18.	St. Vincent and the Grenadines	773	299
19.	Lebanon	769	297
20.	Rwanda	761	294
21.	India	701	271
22.	Sri Lanka	696	269
23.	El Salvador	679	262
24.	Saint Lucia	671	259
25.	Trinidad and Tobago	668	258
26.	Comoros	640	247
27.	Grenada	639	247
28.	Haiti	630	243

Lowest Population Densities

	Country	Population density per sq. mile	Population density per km²
1.	Mongolia	4	1
2.	Mauritania	5	2
3.	Australia	6	2
4.	Botswana	6	2
5.	Iceland	6	2
6.	Namibia	6	2
7.	Canada	7	3
8.	Libya	7	3
9.	Suriname	7	3
10.	Guyana	10	4
11.	Chad	12	5
12.	Gabon	12	5
13.	Central African Republic	13	5
14.	Congo	16	6
15.	Niger	17	6
16.	Bolivia	18	7
17.	Mali	18	7
18.	Saudi Arabia	18	7
19.	Oman	19	7
20.	Belize	21	8
21.	Angola	22	8
22.	Papua New Guinea	24	9
23.	Sudan	28	11
24.	Norway	28	11
25.	Algeria	29	11
26.	Paraguay	29	11
27.	Argentina	31	12
28.	Zambia	31	12

Principal Rivers

Name	Location	Length miles	Length km
Nile	Africa	4,145	6,671
Amazon	South America	4,000	6,437
Yangtze (Yangtze Kiang; Chang Jiang)	China	3,915	6,300
Huang He	China	2,903	4,672
Congo	Africa	2,900	4,667
Amur	Soviet Union	2,744	4,416
Lena	Soviet Union	2,734	4,400
Mekong	Asia (Indochinese Peninsula)	2,600	4,180
Niger	Africa	2,600	4,180
Yenisey	Soviet Union	2,543	4,093
Paraná	South America	2,485	3,999
Mississippi	United States	2,348	3,779
Missouri	United States	2,315	3,726
Murray-Darling	Australia	2,310	3,718
Ob	Soviet Union	2,268	3,650
Volga	Soviet Union	2,193	3,530
Purús	Peru-Brazil	2,100	3,380
Madeira	Brazil	2,000	3,200
São Francisco	Brazil	1,988	3,199
Yukon	Canada-United States	1,979	3,185
Rio Grande	United States-Mexico	1,885	3,034
Indus	Tibet-Pakistan	1,800	2,897
Danube	Europe	1,777	2,860
Darling	Australia	1,702	2,739
Euphrates	Asia	1,700	2,736
Zambezi	Africa	1,700	2,736
Brahmaputra	Asia	1,680	2,704
Murray	Australia	1,609	2,589
Paraguay	South America	1,584	2,549
Ural	Soviet Union	1,570	2,527
Amu Darya (Oxus)	Soviet Union-Afghanistan	1,560	2,511
Ganges	India-Bangladesh	1,540	2,478
Salween (Salwin)	Burma-Tibet	1,500	2,414
Arkansas	United States	1,459	2,348
Colorado	United States-Mexico	1,450	2,334
Dnepr (Dnieper)	Soviet Union	1,400	2,200
Orinoco	Venezuela-Colombia	1,284	2,066
Irrawaddy (Irawadi)	Burma	1,250	2,010
Saskatchewan	Canada	1,205	1,939
Mackenzie	Canada	1,071	1,724

Principal Mountains

Name	Height above sea level In feet	In meters	Location
Aconcagua	22,831	6,959	Andes in Argentina
Annapurna	26,504	8,078	Himalaya in Nepal
Ararat	17,011	5,185	Eastern Plateau in Turkey
Chimborazo	20,561	6,267	Andes in Ecuador
Cotopaxi	19,347	5,897	Andes in Ecuador
Ixtacihuatl	17,343	5,286	Plateau of Mexico
Jungfrau	13,642	4,158	Alps in Switzerland
Kilimanjaro	19,340	5,895	Isolated peak in Tanzania
Lassen Peak	10,457	3,187	Cascade in California
Matterhorn	14,692	4,478	Alps on Switzerland-Italy border
Mauna Kea	13,796	4,205	Island of Hawaii
Mauna Loa	13,677	4,169	Island of Hawaii
Mont Blanc	15,771	4,807	Alps on France-Italy-Switzerland border
Mount Cook	12,349	3,764	Southern Alps in New Zealand
Mount Elbrus	18,481	5,633	Caucasus in Soviet Union
Mount Etna	11,122	3,390	Island of Sicily
Mount Everest	29,028	8,848	Himalaya on Nepal-Tibet border
Mount Fuji	12,388	3,776	Island of Honshu in Japan
Mount Godwin Austen, or K2, or Dapsang	28,250*	8,611*	Karakoram, or Mustagh, in Kashmir
Mount Hood	11,239	3,426	Cascade in Oregon
Mount Kanchenjunga, or Kinchinjunga	28,208	8,598	Himalaya on Nepal-India border
Mount Kenya	17,058	5,199	Central Kenya
Mount Kosciusko	7,310	2,228	Australian Alps
Mount Logan	19,524	5,951	St. Elias in Canada
Mount Makalu	27,824	8,481	Himalaya on Nepal-Tibet border
Mount McKinley	20,320	6,194	Alaska Range in Alaska
Mount Rainier	14,410	4,392	Cascade in Washington
Mount Saint Helens	8,364	2,549	Cascade in Washington
Mount Shasta	14,162	4,317	Cascade in California
Mount Whitney	14,491	4,417	Sierra Nevada in California
Olympus	9,570	2,917	Greece
Orizaba, or Citlaltépetl	18,701	5,700	Plateau of Mexico
Pikes Peak	14,110	4,301	Front Range in Colorado
Popocatepetl	17,887	5,452	Plateau of Mexico
Vesuvius	4,190	1,277	Italy

*Traditional measurement.

Major Lakes

Name	Country	Area sq. miles	km²	Depth feet	meters
Caspian Sea	Iran-U.S.S.R.	143,630	372,000	3,363	1,025
Lake Superior	United States-Canada	31,700	82,103	1,333	406
Lake Victoria	Africa	26,828	69,484	270	82
Aral Sea	U.S.S.R.	25,660	66,459	223	68
Lake Huron	United States-Canada	23,050	59,699	750	229
Lake Michigan	United States	22,300	57,757	923	281
Lake Tanganyika	Africa	12,700	32,893	4,708	1,435
Great Bear Lake	Canada	12,275	31,732	1,350	411
Lake Baikal	U.S.S.R.	12,162	31,499	5,315	1,620
Lake Nyasa	Africa	11,100	28,749	2,300	701
Great Slave Lake	Canada	10,980	28,438	2,015	614
Lake Erie	United States-Canada	9,910	25,667	210	64
Lake Winnipeg	Canada	9,398	24,341	70	21
Lake Ontario	United States-Canada	7,550	19,554	802	244
Lake Ladoga	U.S.S.R.	6,835	17,703	738	225
Lake Balkhash	U.S.S.R.	6,670	17,275	85	26
Lake Chad	Africa	6,300	16,300	22	7
Lake Onega	U.S.S.R.	3,820	9,894	393	120
Lake Eyre	Australia	3,700	9,583	52	16

Name	Country	Area sq. miles	km²	feet below sea level	meters below sea level
Lake Titicaca	Peru-Bolivia	3,200	8,300	900	270
Lake Athabasca	Canada	3,120	8,081	407	124
Lake Nicaragua	Nicaragua	3,060	7,925	141	43
Lake Turkana (Lake Rudolf)	Kenya-Ethiopia	2,473	6,405	200	61
Reindeer Lake	Canada	2,444	6,330	720	219
Lake Torrens	Australia	2,230	5,776	shallow body of water	
Lake Vänern	Sweden	2,156	5,584	328	100
Lake Winnipegosis	Canada	2,013	5,214	38	12

Oceans, Seas, and Gulfs

Name	Area sq. miles	km²	Greatest depth feet	meters
Pacific Ocean	63,800,000	165,200,000	36,198	11,033
Atlantic Ocean	31,530,000	81,662,000	28,374	8,648
Indian Ocean	28,356,300	73,441,700	25,344	7,725
Arctic Ocean	3,662,000	9,485,100	17,880	5,450
Arabian Sea	1,492,000	3,863,000	19,029	5,800
South China Sea	1,300,000	3,370,000	18,241	5,560
Bering Sea	1,140,000	2,952,900	13,422	4,091
Caribbean Sea	1,105,000	2,877,000	24,720	7,535
Mediterranean Sea	969,100	2,510,000	16,302	5,093
Bay of Bengal	839,000	2,172,000	17,251	5,258
Gulf of Mexico	700,000	1,800,000	12,700	3,871
Norwegian Sea	597,000	1,547,000	13,189	4,020
Okhotsk, Sea of	589,800	1,527,600	11,063	3,372
Greenland Sea	465,000	1,205,000	15,899	4,846
Hudson Bay	316,500	819,731	850	259

Principal Islands

Name	Area sq. miles	km²	Highest point name	feet	meters
Greenland	840,004	2,175,600	Mount Gunnbjørn	12,139	3,700
New Guinea	311,737	807,396	Puncak Jaya	16,503	5,030
Borneo	288,151	746,308	Mount Kinabalu	13,455	4,101
Madagascar	226,658	587,041	Maromokotro	9,436	2,876
Baffin Island	195,927	507,449	(unnamed)	7,045	2,147
Sumatra (Sumatera)	182,860	473,606	Kerinci	12,484	3,805
Honshu	87,805	227,414	Mount Fuji	12,388	3,776
Great Britain	84,550	218,980	Ben Nevis	4,406	1,343
Victoria Island (N.W.T., Can.)	83,896	217,290	(unnamed)	2,150	655
Ellesmere Island	75,767	196,236	Barbeau Peak	8,534	2,616
Celebus (Sulawesi)	73,057	189,216	Rantekombola	11,335	3,455
South Island (New Zealand)	58,965	152,719	Mount Cook	12,349	3,764
Java (Djawa)	51,038	132,187	Semeru	12,060	3,676
North Island (New Zealand)	44,244	114,592	Mount Ruapehu	9,175	2,797
(island of) Newfoundland	43,008	111,390	Lewis Hills	2,672	814
Cuba	42,804	110,861	Pico Turquino	6,542	1,994
Luzon (Philippines)	40,420	104,688	Mount Pulog	9,606	2,928
Iceland	39,800	103,000	Hvannadalsh-núkur	6,952	2,119
Mindanao (Philippines)	36,537	94,630	Mount Apo	9,692	2,954
Ireland	32,588	84,404	Carrauntoohill	3,414	1,041
Hokkaido	30,144	78,073	Asahi Mountain	7,513	2,290
Hispaniola	29,418	76,192	Duarte Peak	10,417	3,175
Sakhalin (U.S.S.R.)	29,100	75,369	Lopatina	5,279	1,609
Tasmania	26,200	67,800	Mount Ossa	5,305	1,617
Sri Lanka	25,333	65,610	Pidurutalagala	8,281	2,524
Novaya Zemlya (northern island)	20,000	52,000	(unnamed)	5,075	1,574
Tierra del Fuego	19,280	49,935	Yogan	8,100	2,469
Kyushu	14,114	36,554	Kuju Mountain	5,866	1,788

Waterfalls

Name	Country	River	Height feet	meters
Angel	Venezuela	Churún	3,212	979
Yosemite	United States	Yosemite Creek	2,425	739
Tugela	South Africa	Tugela	2,014	614
Sutherland	New Zealand	Milford Sound	1,904	580
Gavarnie	France	Gave de Pau	1,385	422
Krimml	Austria	Krimml	1,312	400
Takakkaw	Canada	Yoho	1,200	366
Staubbach	Switzerland	Staubbach	984	300
Jog	India	—	830	253
Kaieteur	Guyana	Potaro	741	226

Drainage Basins

Name	Continent	Area sq. miles	km²
Amazon River	South America	2,700,000	7,000,000
Congo River	Africa	1,400,000	3,630,000
Mississippi River	North America	1,247,300	3,230,490
Ob River	Asia	1,125,200	2,914,250
Lena River	Asia	1,000,000	2,600,000
Yenisey River	Asia (Siberia)	1,000,000	2,600,000
Amur River	Asia	770,000	1,990,000
Yangtze River (Yangtze Kiang; Chang Jiang)	Asia	706,000	1,829,000
Mackenzie River system	North America	682,000	1,766,000
Niger River	Africa	580,000	1,500,000
Volga River	Europe	525,000	1,360,000
Saint Lawrence River	North America	498,500	1,291,100

Populations of Major Cities

The largest and most important of the world's major cities are listed in the following table. Also included are some smaller cities because of their regional significance.

Local official names have primarily been used throughout the table. When a commonly used conventional name exists, it has been featured. An alternate name follows in parentheses. A former name is identified in *italics*.

The population of each city has been dated, and is identified as either an official estimate (E) or a census figure (C).

City	Country	City population	Metropolitan area population	Date
Aachen	Germany	238,587	540,000	1985 E
Abidjan	Ivory Coast	1,850,000	—	1982 E
Acapulco (Acapulco de Juárez)	Mexico	409,335	—	1980 C
Accra	Ghana	964,879	1,420,065	1984 C
Addis Ababa	Ethiopia	1,412,577	—	1984 C
Adelaide	Australia	917,000	—	1986 C
Aden	Yemen	318,000	—	1984 E
Agra	India	723,676	770,352	1981 C
Ahmadabad	India	2,059,725	2,548,057	1981 C
Al Basrah (Basra)	Iraq	370,900	—	1970 E
Aleppo	Syria	961,000	—	1980 E
Alexandria (Al Iskandariyah)	Egypt	2,917,327	—	1986 C
Algiers (Alger)	Algeria	1,721,607	—	1983 E
Allahabad	India	609,232	642,420	1981 C
Alma-Ata	Soviet Union	1,046,000	—	1984 E
Amman	Jordan	900,000	—	1988 E
Amritsar	India	589,229	—	1981 C
Amsterdam	Netherlands	687,397	945,062	1983 E
Ankara	Turkey	2,235,035	—	1985 C
Anshan (An-shan)	China	1,260,000	—	1984 E
Antananarivo	Madagascar	662,585	—	1985 E
Antwerp (Antwerpen, Anvers)	Belgium	185,021	628,989	1983 E
Asansol	India	187,039	1,050,000	1981 C
Asunción	Paraguay	457,210	655,000	1982 C
Athens (Athinai)	Greece	885,737	3,027,331	1981 C
Atlanta	(Georgia) U.S.	394,017	2,833,511	1990 C
Auckland	New Zealand	820,754	—	1986 C
Augsburg	Germany	245,193	390,000	1985 E
Austin	(Texas) U.S.	465,622	781,572	1990 C
Baghdad	Iraq	2,969,000	—	1976 C
Baku	Soviet Union	1,084,000	1,661,000	1984 E
Baltimore	(Maryland) U.S.	736,014	2,382,172	1990 C
Bamako	Mali	404,022	—	1976 C
Bandung	Indonesia	1,462,637	1,525,000	1980 C
Bangalore	India	2,476,355	2,921,751	1981 C
Bangkok (Krung Thep)	Thailand	5,153,902	—	1980 C
Barcelona	Spain	1,694,064	—	1986 C
Barranquilla	Colombia	899,781	950,000	1985 C
Basel	Switzerland	174,606	361,809	1986 E
Beijing (Peking)	China	7,362,425	10,819,407	1990 C
Beirut	Lebanon	702,000	—	1974 E
Belém	Brazil	758,117	1,000,349	1980 C
Belfast	Northern Ireland	301,600	—	1985 E
Belgrade (Beograd)	Yugoslavia	1,455,046	—	1981 C
Belo Horizonte	Brazil	1,442,483	2,541,788	1980 C
Berlin	Germany	3,062,979	—	1985 E
Bern (Berne)	Switzerland	138,574	299,221	1986 E
Bhopal	India	672,329	—	1981 C
Bielefeld	Germany	299,727	525,000	1985 E
Bilbao	Spain	378,221	—	1986 E
Birmingham	England (Great Britain)	1,007,500	2,641,800	1985 E
Birmingham	(Alabama) U.S.	265,968	907,810	1990 C
Bogotá	Colombia	3,982,941	—	1985 C
Bologna	Italy	455,853	—	1981 C
Bombay	India	8,227,332	—	1981 C
Bonn	Germany	290,769	555,000	1985 E
Bordeaux	France	208,159	650,123	1982 C
Boston	(Massachusetts) U.S.	574,283	2,870,669	1990 C
Brasília	Brazil	411,305	—	1980 C
Brazzaville	Congo	596,200	—	1985 E
Bremen	Germany	526,377	800,000	1985 E
Bremerhaven	Germany	133,521	190,000	1985 E
Brisbane	Australia	1,037,815	—	1986 C
Bristol	England (Great Britain)	393,800	—	1985 E
Brussels (Brussel, Bruxelles)	Belgium	137,738	989,877	1983 E
Bucharest (Bucuresti)	Romania	1,961,189	2,227,568	1983 E
Budapest	Hungary	2,075,990	2,600,000	1986 E
Buenos Aires	Argentina	2,908,001	9,927,404	1980 C
Buffalo	(New York) U.S.	328,123	968,532	1990 C
Bulawayo	Zimbabwe	600,000	—	1990 E
Bursa	Turkey	612,510	—	1985 C
Cairo (Al Qahirah)	Egypt	6,052,836	8,500,000	1986 C
Calcutta	India	3,305,006	9,194,018	1981 C
Cali	Colombia	1,350,565	—	1985 C
Canberra	Australia	247,194	—	1986 C
Cape Town	South Africa	789,580	1,490,935	1980 C
Caracas	Venezuela	1,261,116	3,310,236	1988 E
Cardiff	Wales (Great Britain)	278,900	625,000	1985 E
Casablanca	Morocco	2,139,204	—	1982 C
Catania	Italy	378,521	—	1981 C
Cebu	Philippines	490,281	500,000	1980 C
Changchun (Ch'ang-ch'un)	China	1,810,000	—	1984 E
Changsha (Ch'ang-sha)	China	1,210,000	—	1984 E
Charleroi	Belgium	216,144	225,855	1983 E
Chelyabinsk	Soviet Union	1,086,000	—	1984 E
Chengdu (Ch'eng-tu)	China	2,540,000	—	1984 E
Chicago	(Illinois) U.S.	2,783,726	6,069,974	1990 C
Chittagong	Bangladesh	1,391,877	—	1981 C
Chongqing (Chungking, Ch'ung-ch'ing)	China	2,730,000	—	1984 E
Cincinnati	(Ohio) U.S.	364,040	1,452,645	1990 C
Cleveland	(Ohio) U.S.	505,616	1,831,122	1990 C
Cochin	India	513,081	552,408	1981 C
Coimbatore	India	700,923	965,000	1981 C
Cologne (Köln)	Germany	916,153	1,815,000	1985 E
Colombo	Sri Lanka	616,000	1,540,000	1977 E
Columbus	(Ohio) U.S.	632,910	1,377,419	1990 C
Copenhagen (København)	Denmark	472,729	1,358,540	1985 E
Córdoba	Argentina	968,664	982,018	1980 C
Coventry	England (Great Britain)	312,200	—	1985 E
Curitiba	Brazil	843,733	1,441,743	1980 C
Dakar	Senegal	978,523	—	1979 E
Dallas	(Texas) U.S.	1,006,877	2,533,362	1990 C
Damascus	Syria	1,200,000	—	1980 E
Dar es Salaam	Tanzania	870,000	—	1978 C
Dayton	(Ohio) U.S.	182,044	951,270	1990 C
Delhi	India	4,884,234	5,729,283	1981 C
Denver	(Colorado) U.S.	467,610	1,622,980	1990 C
Detroit	(Michigan) U.S.	1,027,974	4,382,299	1990 C
Dhaka (Dacca)	Bangladesh	2,365,695	—	1981 C
Dnepropetrovsk	Soviet Union	1,140,000	—	1984 E
Donetsk (Stalino)	Soviet Union	1,064,000	—	1984 E
Dortmund	Germany	572,094	—	1985 E
Douala	Cameroon	1,000,000	—	1984 E
Dresden	Germany	519,860	640,000	1985 E
Dublin	Ireland	502,749	983,683	1986 C
Duisburg	Germany	518,260	—	1985 E
Durban	South Africa	677,760	960,792	1980 C
Düsseldorf	Germany	561,686	1,225,000	1985 E
Edinburgh	Scotland (Great Britain)	439,672	—	1985 E
Edmonton	(Alberta) Canada	573,982	785,465	1986 C
El Paso	(Texas) U.S.	515,342	591,610	1990 C
Essen	Germany	619,991	5,125,000	1985 E
Florence (Firenze)	Italy	453,293	—	1981 C
Fortaleza	Brazil	648,815	1,581,588	1980 C
Frankfurt am Main	Germany	595,348	1,880,000	1985 E
Freetown	Sierra Leone	469,776	—	1985 C
Frunze	Soviet Union	590,000	—	1984 E
Fukuoka	Japan	1,160,402	1,575,000	1985 C
Fushun (Fu-shun)	China	1,220,000	—	1984 E
Gdańsk (German: Danzig)	Poland	468,600	820,000	1985 E
Geneva (Genève, Genf)	Switzerland	159,895	378,274	1986 C
Genoa (Genova)	Italy	760,300	—	1981 C
Ghent (Gent)	Belgium	236,540	—	1983 E
Giza (Al Jizah)	Egypt	1,870,508	—	1986 C
Glasgow	Scotland (Great Britain)	733,794	—	1985 E
Gorki (Gor'kiy)	Soviet Union	1,392,000	—	1984 E
Göteborg (Gothenburg)	Sweden	424,085	698,794	1984 E
Graz	Austria	243,405	—	1981 C
Guadalajara	Mexico	1,626,152	2,244,715	1980 C
Guangzhou (Canton)	China	3,220,000	—	1984 E
Guatemala City	Guatemala	754,243	—	1981 C
Guayaquil	Ecuador	1,199,344	—	1982 C
Guiyang (Kuei-yang)	China	1,360,000	—	1984 E
The Hague ('s Gravenhage)	Netherlands	449,338	677,962	1983 E
Hai Phong	Vietnam	1,448,000	—	1989 C
Haifa	Israel	266,100	374,950	1983 E
Hamburg	Germany	1,579,884	2,260,000	1985 E
Hangzhou (Hang-chou)	China	1,191,582	—	1984 E
Hannover (Hanover)	Germany	508,298	1,005,000	1985 E
Hanoi	Vietnam	3,057,000	—	1989 C
Harare (Salisbury)	Zimbabwe	656,100	—	1982 C
Harbin	China	2,590,000	—	1984 E
Hartford	(Connecticut) U.S.	139,739	767,841	1990 C
Havana (La Habana)	Cuba	1,924,886	—	1981 C
Helsinki (Helsingfors)	Finland	481,927	932,376	1984 C
Hiroshima	Japan	1,044,129	1,525,000	1985 C
Ho Chi Minh City (Saigon)	Vietnam	3,934,000	—	1989 C
Honolulu	(Hawaii) U.S.	365,272	836,231	1990 C
Houston	(Texas) U.S.	1,630,553	3,301,937	1990 C
Hyderabad	India	2,187,262	2,545,836	1981 C
Hyderabad	Pakistan	751,529	—	1981 C
Ibadan	Nigeria	885,300	—	1977 E
Inchon	South Korea	1,387,491	—	1985 C
Indianapolis	(Indiana) U.S.	741,952	1,249,822	1990 C
Innsbruck	Austria	116,100	—	1981 C
Irkutsk	Soviet Union	589,000	—	1984 E
Istanbul	Turkey	5,475,982	—	1985 C
Izmir (Smyrna)	Turkey	1,489,772	—	1985 C
Jacksonville	(Florida) U.S.	672,971	906,727	1990 C
Jaipur	India	966,677	1,025,000	1981 C
Jakarta	Indonesia	6,503,449	6,700,000	1980 C
Jerusalem	Israel	424,400	—	1983 E
Jidda (Jeddah, Juddah)	Saudi Arabia	1,210,000	—	1986 C
Jinan (Tsinan)	China	1,390,000	—	1984 E
Johannesburg	South Africa	703,980	1,726,073	1980 C
Juárez (Ciudad Juárez)	Mexico	567,365	—	1980 C
Kabul	Afghanistan	1,036,407	—	1982 C
Kananga	Zaire	460,091	—	1984 E
Kano	Nigeria	416,900	—	1977 E
Kanpur	India	1,481,789	1,639,064	1981 C
Kansas City	(Missouri) U.S.	435,146	1,566,280	1990 C
Kaohsiung	Taiwan	1,172,977	1,480,000	1977 E
Karachi	Pakistan	5,208,170	—	1981 C
Karaganda	Soviet Union	608,000	—	1984 E
Kathmandu	Nepal	150,402	215,000	1971 C
Katowice	Poland	363,300	2,590,000	1985 E
Kawasaki	Japan	1,088,611	—	1985 C
Kazan	Soviet Union	1,039,000	—	1984 E
Khabarovsk	Soviet Union	568,000	—	1984 E
Kharkov	Soviet Union	1,536,000	—	1984 E
Khartoum	Sudan	476,218	817,364	1983 C
Kiel	Germany	245,682	335,000	1985 E
Kiev	Soviet Union	2,409,000	—	1984 E
Kingston	Jamaica	104,041	524,638	1982 C
Kinshasa	Zaire	2,222,981	—	1984 E
Kishinev	Soviet Union	605,000	—	1984 E
Kitakyushu	Japan	1,056,400	—	1985 C
Kobe	Japan	1,410,843	—	1985 C

City	Country	City population	Metropolitan area population	Date
Kowloon	**Hong Kong**	799,123	—	1981 C
Kraków	**Poland**	740,100	—	1985 E
Krasnoyarsk	**Soviet Union**	859,000	—	1984 E
Kuala Lumpur	**Malaysia**	937,875	—	1980 C
Kunming (K'un-ming)	**China**	1,480,000	—	1984 E
Kuwait	**Kuwait**	78,116	780,000	1975 C
Kuybyshev	**Soviet Union**	1,250,000	—	1984 E
Kwangju	**South Korea**	906,129	—	1985 C
Kyoto	**Japan**	1,479,125	—	1985 C
Lagos	**Nigeria**	1,149,200	1,476,837	1977 E
Lahore	**Pakistan**	2,952,689	—	1981 C
Lanzhou (Lan-chou)	**China**	1,460,000	—	1984 E
La Paz	**Bolivia**	881,404	—	1982 E
Leeds	**England** (Great Britain)	710,500	2,052,800	1985 E
Leipzig	**Germany**	554,595	710,000	1985 E
Leningrad	**Soviet Union**	4,295,000	4,827,000	1984 E
León	**Mexico**	655,809	—	1980 C
Liège	**Belgium**	207,496	410,160	1983 E
Lille	**France**	168,424	945,572	1982 C
Lima	**Peru**	4,164,597	4,608,010	1981 C
Linz	**Austria**	197,962	—	1981 C
Lisbon (Lisboa)	**Portugal**	817,627	2,062,200	1981 C
Liverpool	**England** (Great Britain)	491,500	1,481,000	1985 E
Łódź	**Poland**	847,900	1,025,000	1985 E
London	**England** (Great Britain)	6,767,500	—	1985 E
Los Angeles	(California) **U.S.**	3,485,398	8,863,164	1990 C
Louisville	(Kentucky) **U.S.**	269,063	952,662	1990 C
Luanda	**Angola**	1,200,000	—	1988 E
Lubumbashi	**Zaire**	596,297	—	1984 E
Lucknow	**India**	895,947	1,060,000	1981 C
Lüda or **Dalian** (Lüta or Dairen)	**China**	1,590,000	—	1984 E
Ludhiana	**India**	606,250	—	1981 C
Lusaka	**Zambia**	818,994	—	1987 E
Lvov	**Soviet Union**	728,000	—	1984 E
Lyallpur	**Pakistan**	1,104,209	—	1981 C
Lyon	**France**	413,095	1,236,096	1982 C
Madras	**India**	3,276,622	4,289,347	1981 C
Madrid	**Spain**	3,123,713	—	1986 E
Madurai	**India**	817,562	—	1981 C
Managua	**Nicaragua**	677,680	—	1980 E
Manchester	**England** (Great Britain)	451,100	2,582,600	1985 E
Mandalay	**Burma**	472,512	—	1979 E
Manila	**Philippines**	1,630,485	5,926,000	1980 C
Mannheim	**Germany**	294,984	1,395,000	1985 E
Maputo (*Lourenço Marques*)	**Mozambique**	1,006,765	—	1987 E
Maracaibo	**Venezuela**	1,151,933	—	1988 E
Marseille	**France**	874,436	1,115,697	1982 C
Mecca (Makkah)	**Saudi Arabia**	463,000	—	1986 E
Medan	**Indonesia**	1,378,955	1,450,000	1980 C
Medellín	**Colombia**	1,468,089	—	1985 C
Melbourne	**Australia**	2,645,484	—	1986 C
Memphis	(Tennessee) **U.S.**	610,337	981,747	1990 C
Mexico City	**Mexico**	10,263,275	19,150,000	1988 E
Miami	(Florida) **U.S.**	358,548	1,937,094	1990 C
Milan (Milano)	**Italy**	1,634,638	—	1981 C
Milwaukee	(Wisconsin) **U.S.**	628,088	1,432,149	1990 C
Minneapolis	(Minnesota) **U.S.**	368,383	2,464,124	1990 C
Minsk	**Soviet Union**	1,442,000	—	1984 E
Mombasa	**Kenya**	341,148	—	1979 C
Monrovia	**Liberia**	421,058	—	1984 C
Monterrey	**Mexico**	1,090,009	1,916,472	1980 C
Montevideo	**Uruguay**	1,247,920	—	1985 C
Montreal	(Quebec) **Canada**	1,015,420	2,921,357	1986 C
Moscow	**Soviet Union**	8,769,000	8,967,000	1989 C
Multan	**Pakistan**	736,925	—	1981 C
Munich (München)	**Germany**	1,266,549	1,940,000	1985 E
Mysore	**India**	439,185	—	1981 C
Nagoya	**Japan**	2,116,350	3,700,000	1985 C
Nagpur	**India**	1,215,425	1,325,000	1981 C
Nairobi	**Kenya**	827,775	—	1979 C
Nanjing (Nan-ching) (Nanking)	**China**	2,210,000	—	1984 E
Nantes	**France**	240,539	474,068	1982 C
Naples (Napoli)	**Italy**	1,210,503	—	1981 C
Nashville	(Tennessee) **U.S.**	510,784	985,026	1990 C
New Delhi	**India**	271,990	—	1981 C
New Kowloon (Linked with Kowloon)	**Hong Kong**	1,651,064	—	1981 C
New Orleans	(Louisiana) **U.S.**	496,938	1,238,816	1990 C
Newcastle upon Tyne (Newcastle)	**England** (Great Britain)	282,200	1,139,900	1985 E
New York City	(New York) **U.S.**	7,322,564	8,546,846	1990 C
Niamey	**Niger**	360,000	—	1981 E
Norfolk	(Virginia) **U.S.**	261,229	1,396,107	1990 C
Nottingham	**England** (Great Britain)	279,400	—	1985 E
Novokuznetsk	**Soviet Union**	572,000	—	1984 E
Novosibirsk	**Soviet Union**	1,384,000	—	1984 E
Nuremberg (Nürnberg)	**Germany**	465,255	1,025,000	1985 E
Odessa	**Soviet Union**	1,113,000	—	1984 E
Okayama	**Japan**	572,423	—	1985 C
Oklahoma City	(Oklahoma) **U.S.**	444,719	958,839	1990 C
Omaha	(Nebraska) **U.S.**	335,795	618,262	1990 C
Omsk	**Soviet Union**	1,094,000	—	1984 E
Orlando	(Florida) **U.S.**	164,693	1,072,748	1990 C
Osaka	**Japan**	2,636,260	—	1985 C
Oslo	**Norway**	449,220	541,190	1987 E
Ostrava	**Czechoslovakia**	325,431	745,000	1985 E
Ottawa	(Ontario) **Canada**	300,763	819,263	1986 C
Palermo	**Italy**	699,691	—	1981 C
Panama City	**Panama**	389,172	794,300	1980 C
Paris	**France**	2,176,243	8,706,963	1982 C
Patna	**India**	773,720	—	1981 C
Perm	**Soviet Union**	1,048,000	—	1984 E
Perth	**Australia**	895,710	—	1986 C
Philadelphia	(Pennsylvania) **U.S.**	1,585,577	4,856,881	1990 C
Phnom Penh	**Cambodia**	700,000	—	1985 E
Phoenix	(Arizona) **U.S.**	983,403	2,122,101	1990 C
Pittsburgh	(Pennsylvania) **U.S.**	369,879	2,056,705	1990 C
Port-au-Prince	**Haiti**	738,342	—	1984 E
Portland	(Oregon) **U.S.**	437,319	1,239,842	1990 C
Porto (Oporto)	**Portugal**	330,199	1,550,800	1981 C
Pôrto Alegre	**Brazil**	1,108,883	2,232,370	1980 C
Portsmouth	**England** (Great Britain)	187,900	—	1985 E
Poznań	**Poland**	575,100	610,000	1985 E
Prague (Praha)	**Czechoslovakia**	1,189,828	—	1985 E
Pretoria	**South Africa**	435,100	739,040	1980 C
Providence	(Rhode Island) **U.S.**	160,728	654,854	1990 C
Puebla (Puebla de Zaragoza)	**Mexico**	835,759	—	1980 C
Pune	**India**	1,203,351	1,686,109	1981 C
Pusan	**South Korea**	3,516,807	—	1985 C
Pyongyang	**North Korea**	2,639,448	—	1984 E
Qingdao (Tsingtao)	**China**	1,230,000	—	1984 E
Quebec (Québec)	(Quebec) **Canada**	164,580	603,267	1986 C
Quezon City	**Philippines**	1,165,865	—	1980 C
Quito	**Ecuador**	866,472	—	1982 C
Rabat	**Morocco**	518,616	—	1982 C
Rangoon	**Burma**	1,315,964	2,452,881	1979 E
Rawalpindi	**Pakistan**	794,843	—	1981 C
Recife	**Brazil**	1,184,215	2,348,362	1980 C
Richmond	(Virginia) **U.S.**	203,056	865,640	1990 C
Riga	**Soviet Union**	875,000	—	1984 E
Rio de Janeiro	**Brazil**	5,093,232	9,018,637	1980 C
Riyadh (Ar Riyad)	**Saudi Arabia**	1,380,000	—	1986 E
Rochester	(New York) **U.S.**	231,636	1,002,410	1990 C
Rome (Roma)	**Italy**	2,830,569	—	1981 C
Rosario	**Argentina**	875,623	954,606	1980 C
Rostov-on-Don	**Soviet Union**	983,000	—	1984 E
Rotterdam	**Netherlands**	558,832	1,025,580	1983 E
Saarbrücken	**Germany**	186,229	390,000	1985 E
Sacramento	(California) **U.S.**	369,365	1,481,102	1990 C
Saint Louis	(Missouri) **U.S.**	396,685	2,444,099	1990 C
Saint Paul	(Minnesota) **U.S.**	272,235	—	1990 C
Saint Petersburg	(Florida) **U.S.**	238,629	—	1990 C
Sakai	**Japan**	818,368	—	1985 C
Salonika (Thessaloniki)	**Greece**	406,413	706,180	1981 C
Salt Lake City	(Utah) **U.S.**	159,936	1,072,227	1990 C
Salvador (Bahia)	**Brazil**	1,496,276	1,772,018	1980 C
Samarkand	**Soviet Union**	515,000	—	1984 E
Sana	**Yemen**	472,185	—	1986 E
San Antonio	(Texas) **U.S.**	935,933	1,302,099	1990 C
San Bernardino	(California) **U.S.**	164,164	—	1990 C
San Diego	(California) **U.S.**	1,110,549	2,498,016	1990 C
San Francisco	(California) **U.S.**	723,959	1,603,678	1990 C
San José	**Costa Rica**	241,464	560,000	1984 C
San Juan	**Puerto Rico**	424,600	1,086,376	1980 C
San Justo	**Argentina**	14,135	—	1980 C
San Salvador	**El Salvador**	452,614	—	1984 E
Santiago	**Chile**	4,225,299	—	1984 E
Santo Domingo	**Dominican Rep.**	1,313,172	—	1981 C
Santos	**Brazil**	411,023	—	1980 C
São Paulo	**Brazil**	7,033,529	12,588,439	1980 C
Sapporo	**Japan**	1,542,979	—	1985 C
Saragossa (Zaragoza)	**Spain**	596,080	—	1986 E
Saratov	**Soviet Union**	893,000	—	1984 E
Seattle	(Washington) **U.S.**	516,259	1,972,961	1990 C
Semarang	**Indonesia**	1,026,671	—	1980 C
Sendai	**Japan**	700,248	—	1985 C
Seoul	**South Korea**	9,645,932	—	1985 C
Seville (Sevilla)	**Spain**	668,356	—	1986 E
Shanghai	**China**	8,214,436	13,341,896	1990 C
Sheffield	**England** (Great Britain)	538,700	1,303,200	1985 E
Shenyang (Shen-yang)	**China**	4,130,000	—	1984 E
Shijiazhuang (Shih-chia-chuang)	**China**	1,130,000	—	1984 E
Singapore	**Singapore**	2,308,200	2 600,000	1978 E
Sofia	**Bulgaria**	1,056,945	1,142,582	1980 E
Southampton	**England** (Great Britain)	202,300	—	1985 E
Stockholm	**Sweden**	653,455	1,377,560	1984 E
Stuttgart	**Germany**	561,628	—	1985 E
Suez (As Suways)	**Egypt**	326,820	—	1986 C
Surabaya	**Indonesia**	2,027,913	2,150,000	1980 C
Surat	**India**	775,711	960,000	1981 C
Sverdlovsk	**Soviet Union**	1,286,000	—	1984 E
Sydney	**Australia**	2,989,070	—	1986 C
Taegu	**South Korea**	2,030,672	—	1985 C
Taichung	**Taiwan**	585,205	—	1977 E
Tainan	**Taiwan**	572,590	—	1977 E
Taipei	**Taiwan**	2,220,427	—	1980 C
Taiyuan (T'ai-yuan)	**China**	1,840,000	—	1984 E
Tallinn	**Soviet Union**	458,000	—	1984 E
Tampa	(Florida) **U.S.**	280,015	2,067,959	1990 C
Tashkent	**Soviet Union**	1,986,000	—	1984 E
Tbilisi (Tiflis)	**Soviet Union**	1,140,000	—	1984 E
Tegucigalpa	**Honduras**	576,661	—	1988 C
Teheran (Tehran)	**Iran**	5,734,199	—	1982 E
Tel Aviv-Yafo	**Israel**	325,700	1,350,000	1983 E
Tianjin (Tientsin)	**China**	5,855,068	8,785,402	1990 C
Tiranë (Tirana)	**Albania**	260,000	—	1983 E
Tokyo	**Japan**	8,353,674	11,618,281	1985 C
Toledo	(Ohio) **U.S.**	332,943	614,128	1990 C
Toronto	(Ontario) **Canada**	612,289	3,427,163	1986 C
Tripoli (Tarabulus)	**Libya**	990,697	—	1984 C
Tucson	(Arizona) **U.S.**	405,390	666,880	1990 C
Tula	**Soviet Union**	529,000	—	1984 E
Tulsa	(Oklahoma) **U.S.**	367,302	708,954	1990 C
Tunis	**Tunisia**	596,654		1984 C
Turin (Torino)	**Italy**	1,103,520	—	1981 C
Ufa	**Soviet Union**	1,048,000	—	1984 E
Ujung Pandang	**Indonesia**	709,038	—	1980 C
Ulan Bator (Urga)	**Mongolia**	402,900	—	1979 E
Vadodara	**India**	733,656	—	1981 C
Valencia	**Spain**	738,575	—	1986 E
Valparaíso	**Chile**	266,876	—	1984 E
Vancouver	(British Columbia) **Canada**	431,147	1,380,729	1986 C
Varanasi	**India**	708,647	—	1981 C
Venice (Venezia)	**Italy**	332,775	—	1981 C
Victoria	**Hong Kong**	1,183,621	—	1981 C
Vienna (Wien)	**Austria**	1,515,666	—	1981 C
Vladivostok	**Soviet Union**	590,000	—	1984 E
Volgograd (*Stalingrad*)	**Soviet Union**	969,000	—	1984 E
Voronezh	**Soviet Union**	840,000	—	1984 E
Warsaw (Warszawa)	**Poland**	1,659,400	2,080,000	1985 E
Washington, D.C.	**U.S.**	606,900	3,923,574	1980 C
Wellington	**New Zealand**	325,697	—	1986 C
Wiesbaden	**Germany**	266,623	795,000	1985 E
Winnipeg	(Manitoba) **Canada**	594,551	625,304	1986 C
Wrocław (Breslau)	**Poland**	637,200	—	1985 E
Wuhan (Wu-han)	**China**	3,340,000	—	1984 E
Wuppertal	**Germany**	376,579	870,000	1985 E
Xi'an (Sian)	**China**	2,280,000	—	1984 E
Xuzhou (Suchow)	**China**	779,289	—	1984 E
Yaoundé	**Cameroon**	313,706	—	1976 C
Yerevan	**Soviet Union**	1,114,000	—	1984 E
Yokohama	**Japan**	2,992,644	—	1985 C
Zagreb	**Yugoslavia**	763,293	—	1981 C
Zaporozhye	**Soviet Union**	844,000	—	1984 E
Zhdanov (Mariupol)	**Soviet Union**	520,000	—	1984 E
Zhengzhou (Cheng-chou)	**China**	1,550,000	—	1984 E
Zurich (Zürich)	**Switzerland**	351,545	834,299	1986 E

C = Census
E = Official Estimate

Sources

The maps in the Atlas have been compiled from diverse source materials, which are cited in the following lists. The citations are organized by continent and region or country. Within each regional or country group, atlases are listed alphabetically by title and then followed by maps, which are listed according to scale, from the smallest to the largest. Other sources, listed alphabetically by title, follow the map listings.

GENERAL SOURCES

Atlante dei confini sottomarini, *A. Giuffrè Editore, Milano 1979*
Atlante Internazionale del Touring Club Italiano, *TCI, Milano 1977*
Atlas Mira, *G.U.G.K. Moskva 1967*
Atlas Okeanov-Atlantičeski i Indijski Okeany, *Ministerstvo Oborony SSSR-Vojenno-Morskoj Flot, Moskva 1977*
Atlas Okeanov-Tihi Okean, *Ministerstvo Oborony SSSR-Vojenno-Morskoj Flot, Moska 1974*
Atlas of the World, *National Geographic Society (N.G.S.), Washington 1981*
Atlas zur Ozeanographie, *Bibliographisches Institut, Mannheim 1971*
Bertelsmann Atlas International, *C. Bertelsmann Verlag GmbH, München 1963*
Grande Atlante degli Oceani, *Instituto Geografico De Agostini (I.G.D.A.), Novara 1978*
Meyers Neuer Geographischer Handatlas, *Bibliographisches Institut, Mannheim 1966*
The New International Atlas, *Rand McNally & Company, Chicago 1980*
The Odyssey World Atlas, *Western Publishing Company Inc., New York 1966*
The Times Atlas of the World, *John Bartholomew & Son Ltd, Edinburgh 1980*
The World Book Atlas, *World Book Encyclopedia Inc, 1979*
The World Shipping Scene, *Weststadt-Verlag, München 1963*
Weltatlas Erdöl und Erdgas, *George Westermann Verlag, Braunschweig 1976*
Pacific Ocean Floor 1:36,432,000, *N.G.S., Washington 1969*
Atlantic Ocean Floor 1:30,580,000, *N.G.S., Washington 1973*
Indian Ocean 1:25,720,000, *N.G.S. Washington 1967*
Deutsche Meereskarte 1:25,000,000, *Kartographisches Institut Meyer*
Carte générale du Monde 1:10,000,000, *Institut Géographique National (I.G.N.), Paris*
Artic Ocean Floor 1:9,757,000, *N.G.S., Washington 1971*
Carte du Monde 1:5,000,000, *I.G.N., Paris*
Karta Mira 1:2,500,000, *G.U.G.K., Moskva*
Carte Internationale du Monde 1:1,000,000, *Geographical Survey Institute*
Carte Aéronautique du Monde 1:1,000,000, *I.G.N., Paris*
Calendario Atlante, *I.G.D.A., Novara 1982*
Cartactual, *Cartographia, Budapest*
Demographic Yearbook, *United Nations, New York, 1978*
Duden Wörterbuch Geographischer Namen, *Bibliographisches Institut, Mannheim 1966*
Gazetteers (Various), *U.S. Board on Geographical Names, Washington*
Meyers Enzyklopädisches Lexikon, *Bibliographisches Institut, Mannheim 1972–81*
Schtag nach!-Die Staaten der Erde, *Bibliographisches Institut, Mannheim 1977*
Statistical Yearbook, *United Nations, New York, 1978*
Statistik des Auslandes-Länderkurzberichte, *Statistisches Bundesamt, Wiesbaden*
The Columbia Lippincott Gazetteer of the World, *Columbia University Press, New York 1961*
The Europa Year Book 1981, *Europa Publication Ltd., London*
The Statesman's Yearbook 1981–82, *The Macmillan Press Ltd., London*
Webster's New Geographical Dictionary, *G & C Merriam Co, Springfield 1972*

EUROPE

ALBANIA
Shqiperia-Hartë Fizike 1:500,000, *MMS "Hamid Shijaku", Tirana 1970*
Shqiperia Politiko Administrative 1:500,000, *MMS "Hamid Shijaku", Tirana 1969*
Gjeografia e Shqiperise per shkollat e mesme, *Shtëpia Botuese e Librit Shkollor, Tirana 1970*

AUSTRIA
Neuer Schulatlas, *Freytag-Berndt und Artaria KG, Wien 1971*
Generalkarte Österreich 1:200,000, *Mairs Geographischer Verlag, Stuttgart 1974*
Gemeindeverzeichnis von Österreich, *Österreichischen Statistischen Zentralamt, Wien 1970*
Geographisches Namenbuch Österreichs, *Verlag der Österreichischen Akademie der Wissenschaften, Wien 1975*
Statistisches Handbuch für die Republik Österreich, *Österreichischen Statistischen Zentralamt, Wien 1978*

BELGIUM
Atlas de Belgique-Atlas van België, *Comité National de Géographie, Bruxelles 1974*
België, Luxemburg, Belgien 1:350,000, *Pneu. Michelin, Bruxelles 1976*
Belgique, Grand-Duché de Luxembourg, *Pneu. Michelin, Paris 1978*
Lista Alphabetique des Communes-fusion de 1963 à 1977, *Institut National de Statistique, Bruxelles*
Statistique Demographiques 1980, *Institut National de Statistique, Bruxelles*

BULGARIA
Atlas Narodna Republika Bulgarija, *Glavno Upravlenie po Geodezija i Kartografija, Sofija 1973*
Bulgaria 1:1,000,000, *PPWK, Warszawa 1977*
Statističeski Godišnik na Narodna Republika Bălgarija 1973, *Ministerstvo na Informacijata i Săobšenijata, Sofija*

CZECHOSLOVAKIA
Atlas ČSSR, *Kartografie, Praha 1972*
Školní Zeměpisný Atlas Československé Socialistické Republiky, *Kartografické* Nakladatelství, Praha 1970
Auto Atlas Č.S.S.R., *Kartografie, Praha 1971*
Č.S.S.R.-Fyzická Mapa 1:500,000, *Ústřední Správa Geodezie a Kartografie, Praha 1963*
Statistická Ročenka Č.S.S.R., *Federální Statistický Úřad, Praha 1980*

DENMARK
Haases Atlas, *P. Haase & Søns Forlag, København 1972*
Opgivne og Tilplantede Landbrugsarealer i Jylland, *Det Kongelige Danske Geografiske Selskab, København 1976*
Danmark 1:300,000, *Geodætisk Institut, København 1972*
Statistisk Årbog Danmark 1980, *Danmarks Statistik, København*

FINLAND
Oppikoulun Kartasto, *Werner Söderström Osakeyhtiö, Porvoo 1972*
Suomi-Finland 1:1,000,000, *Naanmittaushallituksen Kivipaino, Helsinki 1972*
Finland-Suomi 1:1,000,000, *Kümmerly & Frey, Bern 1981*
Suomen Tilastollinen Vuosikirja 1975, *Tilastokeskus, Helsinki*

FRANCE
Atlas Général Larousse, *Librairie Larousse, Paris 1976*
Atlas Général Bordas, *Bordas, Paris 1972*
Atlas Géographique Alpha, *I.G.D.A., Novara 1972*
Atlas Moderne Larousse, *Librairie Larousse-I.G.D.A., Paris 1976*
Carte Administrative de la France 1:1,400,000, *I.G.N., Paris 1977*
Carte de la France 1:1,000,000, *I.G.N., Paris 1971*
France: Routes-Autoroutes 1:1,000,000, *I.G.N., Paris 1978*
Carte Touristique 1:250,000, *I.G.N., Paris 1978*
France 1:200,000, *Pneu. Michelin, Paris*
Carte Touristique 1:100,000, *I.G.N., Paris*
Michelin 1977-France, *Pneu. Michelin, Paris*
Population de la France-Recensement 1975, *Institut National de la Statistique et des Études Économiques, Paris*

GERMAN DEMOCRATIC REPUBLIC
Haack Weltatlas, *V.E.B. Hermann Haack Geographisch-Kartographische Anstalt, Gotha-Leipzig 1972*
Weltatlas-Die Staaten der Erde und ihre Wirtschaft, *V.E.B. Hermann Haack Geographisch-Kartographische Anstalt, Gotha-Leipzig 1972*
Autokarte der D.D.R. 1:600,000, *V.E.B. Landkartenverlag, Berlin 1972*
Statistisches Jahrbuch der Deutschen Demokratischen Republik 1981, *Staatsverlag der D.D.R., Berlin*

GERMANY, FEDERAL REPUBLIC OF
Diercke Weltatlas, *Westermann Verlag, Braunschweig 1977*
Der Grosse Shell Atlas, *Mairs Geographischer Verlag, Stuttgart 1981–82*
Der Neue Weltatlas, *I.G.D.A., Novara 1977*
Deutschland-Strassenkarte 1:1,000,000, *Kümmerly & Frey, Bern 1981*
Bundesrepublik Deutschland-Übersichtskarte 1:500,000, *Institut für Angewandte Geodäsie, Frankfurt 1978*
Topographische Übersichtskarte 1:200,000, *Institut für Angewandte Geodäsie, Frankfurt*
Bevölkerung der Gemeinden, *Statistisches Bundesamt, Wiesbaden 1979*
Statistisches Jahrbuch für die B.R.D. 1980, *Statistisches Bundesamt, Wiesbaden*

GREECE
Greece-Autokarte 1:1,000,000, *Kümmerly & Frey, Bern*
Greece-Autokarte 1:650,000, *Freytag & Berndt, Wien*
Genikos Chartis tis Hellados 1:400,000, *Geografiki Hypiresia Stratoy, Athínai*
Etniki Statistiki Hypiresia tis Hellados 1:200,000, *E.S.Y.E., Athínai*
Statistiki Epetiris tis Hellados 1979, *E.S.Y.E., Athínai*

HUNGARY
Földrajzi Atlas a Középiskolák Számára, *Kartográfiai Vallalat, Budapest 1980*
A Magyar Népköztársaság 1:400,000, *Kartográfiai Vallalat, Budapest 1974*
Magyarorszag Domborzata és Vizei 1:350,000, *Kartográfiai Vallalat, Budapest 1961*
Megye Térképe, *Cartographia, Budapest 1979–80*
A Magyar Népköztársaság Helységnévtára 1973, *Statisztikai Kiadó Vállalat, Budapest*
Statistical Pocket Book of Hungary 1980, *Statistical Publishing House, Budapest*

ICELAND
Landabréfabok, *Rikisutgáfa Námsbóka, Reykjavik 1970*
Iceland-Road Guide, *Örn & Örlygur H.F., Reykjavik 1975*

IRELAND
Irish Student's Atlas, *Educational Company of Ireland, Dublin-Cork 1971*
Ireland 1:575,000, *Ordnance Survey Office, Dublin 1979*
Ireland 1:250,000, *Ordnance Survey Office, Dublin 1962*
Census of Population of Ireland 1979, *The Stationery Office, Dublin*

ITALY
Atlante Metodico, *I.G.D.A., Novara 1981*
Atlante Stradale d'Italia 1:200,000, *Touring Club Italiano, Milano*
Carta d'Italia 1:1,250,000, *Instituto Geografico Militare, Firenze 1972*
Carte batimetriche, *Istituto Idrografico della Marina, Genova*
Carta Generale d'Italia 1:500,000, *Touring Club Italiano, Milano 1979*
Carta Generale d'Italia 1:200,000, *I.G.M., Firenze*
Enciclopedia Italiana, *Istituto della Enciclopedia Italiana G. Treccani, Roma*
Il Mare, *I.G.D.A., Novara*
La Montagna, *I.G.D.A., Novara*
XI Censimento Generale della Popolazione 24 ottobre 1971, *Istituto Centrale di Statistica, Roma*
XII Censimento Generale della Popolazione 25 ottobre 1981, *Istituto Centrale di Statistica, Roma*

LUXEMBOURG
Grand-Duché de Luxembourg 1:100,000, *I.G.N., Paris 1970*
Annuaire Statistique-Luxembourg 1981–82, *Service Central de la Statistique et des Études Économiques, Paris*

NETHERLANDS
Atlas van Nederland, *Staatsdrukkerij-en Uitgeverijbedrijf,'s-Gravenhage*
De Grote Vara Gezinsatlas, *Vara Omroepvereniging, Hilversum 1975*
Der Kleine Bosatlas, *Wolter-Noordhoff, Groningen 1974*
Pays-Bas/Nederland 1:400,000, *Pneu. Michelin, Paris 1981*
Gegevens per Gemeente Betreffende de Loop der Bevolking in het Jaar 1980, *Centraal Bureau voor der Statistik, Amsterdam*

NORWAY
Atlas-Større Utgave for Gymnaset, *J. W. Cappelens Forlag A.S., Oslo 1969*
Bilkart Bok Road Atlas, *J. W. Cappelens Forlag A.S., Oslo 1967*
Norge-Bit-Og Turistkart 1:400,000, *J. W. Cappelens Forlag A.S., Oslo 1965*
Folketallet i Kommunene 1972–73, *Statistik Sentralbyraå, Oslo*
Statistisk Årbok 1981, *Statistik Sentralbyrå, Oslo*

POLAND
Atlas Geograficzny, *PPWK, Warszawa 1979*
Narodowy Atlas Polski, *Polska Akademia Nauk, Warszawa 1978*
Polska Kontynenty Świat, *P.P.W.K., Warszawa 1977*
Powszechny Atlas Świat, *P.P.W.K. Warszawa 1981*
Polska Rzeczpospolito. Ludowa-Mapa Administracyjna 1:500,000, *P.P.W.K., Warszawa 1980*
Rocznik Statystyczny 1978, *Glówny Urzad Statystyczny, Warszawa*

PORTUGAL
Portugal 1:1,500,000, *Pneu. Michelin, Paris 1981*
Mapa do Estado das Estradas de Portugal 1:550,000, *Automovel Club de Portugal, Lisboa 1979*
Carto. Corográfica de Portugal 1:400,000, *Instituto Geografico e Cadastral, Lisboa 1982*
Anuário Estatístico-Portugal 1974, *Instituto Nacional de Estatística, Lisboa*

ROMANIA
Atlas Geografic General, *Editura Didactica si Pedagogica, București 1974*
Atlasul Republicii Socialiste România, *Institutul de Geologie si Geofizica, București 1971*
Rumanien-Bulgarien 1:1,000,000, *Freytag-Berndt und Artaria K.G., Wien*
Anuarul Statistic al Republicii Socialiste România 1980, *Direcția Centrala de Statistică, București*

SPAIN
Atlas Bachillerato Universal y de España, *Aguilar, Madrid 1968*
Atlas Básico Universal, *I.G.D.A. Teide, Novara 1969*
Gran Atlas Aguilar, *Aguilar, Madrid 1969*
Peninsula Iberica, Baleares y Canarias 1:1,000,000, *Instituto Geografico y Catastral, Madrid 1966*
Mapa Militar de España 1:800,000, *Servicio Geografico del Ejercito, Madrid 1971*
España 1:500,000, *Firestone Hispania, Madrid*
España-Mapa Oficial de Carreteras 1:400,000 *Ministerio de Obras Publica, Madrid*
España-Anuario Estadistico 1979, *Instituto Nacional de Estadistica, Madrid*

SWEDEN
Atlas Över Välden, *Generalstabens Litografiska Anstalt, Stockholm 1972*
Atlas Över Välden, *Natur Miljö Befolkning, Stockholm 1974*
Kak Bil Atlas, *Generalstabens Litografiska Anstalt, Stockholm 1973*
Sverige-Bilkarta 1:625,000, *A.B. Kartlitografen, Stockholm 1972*
Statistisk Årsbok 1980, *Statistiska Centralbyrån, Stockholm*

SWITZERLAND
Atlas der Schweiz, *Verlag des Bundesamtes fur Landestopographie, Wabern-Bern*
Schweizerischer Mittelschulatlas, *Konferenz der Kantonalen Erziehungsdirektoren, Zürich 1976*
Switzerland 1:300,000, *Kümmerly & Frey, Bern 1979*
Carte Nazionale de la Suisse 1:200,000, *Service Topographique Federale, Wabern-Bern*

U.S.S.R.
Atlas Avtomobilnyh Dorog, *G.U.G.K., Moskva 1976*
Atlas Obrazovanie i Razvitie Sojuza S.S.R., *G.U.G.K., Moskva 1972*
Malyi Atlas S.S.S.R., *G.U.G.K., Moskva 1973*
SSSR 1:8,000,000, *G.U.G.K., Moskva 1980*
SSSR 1:4,000,000, *G.U.G.K., Moskva 1972*
Latvijskaja SSR 1:600,000, *G.U.G.K., Moskva 1967*
Litovskaja SSR 1:600,000, *G.U.G.K., Moskva 1969*
S.S.S.R. Administrativno-Territorialnoje Delenie Sojuznyh Respublik, *Prezidium Verhovnogo Soveta Sojuza Sovetskih Socialističeskih Respublik Moskva 1971*

UNITED KINGDOM
Philips' Modern School Economic Atlas, *George Philip & Son Ltd, London 1981*
Roads Atlas of Great Britain and Ireland, *George Philip & Son Ltd, London 1971*
The Atlas of Britain and Northern Ireland, *Clarendon Press, Oxford 1963*
Route Planning Map 1:625,000, *Ordnance Survey, Southampton 1973*
Cartes 1:400,000, *Michelin Tyre Co. Ltd., London 1981*

YUGOSLAVIA
Atlas, *Izrađenou u Oour Kartografiji Tlos "Učila", Zagreb 1980*
Jugoslavija-Auto Atlas, *Jugoslavenski Leksikografski Zavod, Zagreb 1972*
Školski Atlas, *Izrađenou u Oour Kartografiji Tlos "Učila", Zagreb 1975*
Jugoslavija 1:1,000,000, *Grafički Zavod Hrvatske, Zagreb 1980*
Statistički Godišnjak Jugoslavije 1975, *Savezni Zavod za Statistiku, Beograd*

ASIA

ARABIAN PENINSULA
The Oxford Map of Saudi Arabia 1:2,600,000, *GEO-projects, Beirut 1981*
Arabian Peninsula 1:2,000,000, *United States Geological Survey, Washington 1963*
Arabische Republik Jemen 1:1,000,000, *Deutsch-Jemenitische Gesellschaft e V, Schwaig 1976*
The United Arab Emirates 1:750,000, *GEO-projects, Beirut 1981*

MIDDLE EAST
Atlas of Iran, *"Sahab" Geographic & Drafting Institute, Tehrān 1971*
Modern Büyük Atlas, *Arkin Kitabevi-I.G.D.A., Istanbul 1981*
The New Israel Atlas-Zev Vilnay, *Israel Universities Press, Yerushalaym 1968*
Iran 1:2,500,000, *Imperial Government of Iran, Tehrān 1968*
Guide Map of Iran 1:2,250,000, *Gita Shenassi Co. Ltd, Tehrān*
Guide Map of Iraq 1:2,000,000, *"Sahab" Geographic & Drafting Institute, Tehrān 1971*
Türkiye 1:2,000,000, *Ravenstein Verlag GmbH, Frankfurt 1975*
Iran 1:1,500,000, *Imperial Government of Iran, Tehrān 1968*
Iraq Tourist Map 1:1,500,000, *Summer Resorts and Tourism Service, Baghdād 1967*
The Oxford Map of Syria 1:1,000,000, *GEO-projects, Beirut 1980*
Turkey-Road Map 1:1,000,000, *Kümmerly & Frey, Bern 1980*
Türkei und Naher Osten 1:800,000, *Reis und Verkehrsverlag, Berlin-Stuttgart 1977*
Israel und Angrenzende Länder-Strassenkarte 1:750,000, *Kümmerly & Frey, Bern 1981*
The Oxford Map of Jordan 1:730,000, *GEO-projects, Beirut 1979*
Map of Israel 1:500,000, *Survey of Israel, Yerushalaym 1979*
The Oxford Map of Kuwait 1:500,000, *GEO-projects, Beirut 1980*
The Oxford Map of Qatar 1:270,000, *GEO-projects, Beirut 1980*
Israel Map of the Cease-Fire Lines 1:250,000, *Survey of Israel, Yerushalaym 1973*
Qatar-Visitor's Map 1:250,000, *Ministry of Information, Doha 1979*
Carte Générale du Liban 1:200,000, *Ministère de la Défense Nationale, Beirut 1967*
Qatar 1:200,000, *Hunting Surveys Ltd., Borchamwood 1975*
Bahrain Islands 1:63,360, *Public Works Department, Al Manāmah 1968*
The Oxford Map of Bahrain 1:57,750, *GEO-projects, Beirut 1980*
Bahrain—A Map for Visitors 1:50,000, *Ministry of Information, Al Manāmah 1976*
Annual Abstract of Statistics 1978, *Central Statistical Organization, Baghdād*
Genel Nüfus Sayımı 12 ekim 1980, *Başbakanlik Devlet İstatistik Enstitüsü, Ankara*
Kuwait—Annual Statistical Abstract, *Central Statistical Office-Ministry of Planning, Al Kuwayt 1976*
List of Localities—Geographical Information and Population 1948–1961–1972–1975, *Central Bureau of Statistics, Yerushalaym*
Recueil de Statistiques Libanaises No. 8-1972, *Direction Centrale de la Statistique, Bayrūt*
Republic of Cyprus—Statistical Abstract 1973, *The Statistics and Research Department, Levkosia*
Statistical Abstract—Syrian Arab Republic 1973, *Central Bureau of Statistics, Dimashq*
Statistical Abstract of Israel 1979, *Central Bureau of Statistics, Yerushalaym*
The Hashemite Kingdom of Jordan, Statistical Yearbook 1976, *Department of Statistics, Ammān*
Türkiye İstatistik Yıllığı 1975, *Başbakanlik Devlet İstatistik Enstitüsü, Ankara*

SOUTH ASIA
National Atlas of India, *National Atlas & Thematic Mapping Organization, Calcutta*
Oxford School Atlas for Pakistan, *Oxford University Press—Pakistan Branch, Karachi 1973*
Tourist Atlas of India, *National Atlas Organization, Calcutta*
Physical Map of India 1:4,500,000, *Survey of India, Calcutta 1974*
Political Map of India 1:4,500,000, *Survey of India, Calcutta 1972*
Railway Map of India 1:3,500,000, *Government of India, Calcutta 1971*
Pākistān 1:3,168,000, *Survey of Pākistān, Rāwalpindi 1966*
Bangladesh 1:2,800,000, *Survey of Bangladesh, Dacca 1979*
Burma 1:2,000,000, *Army Map Service, Washington 1963*
Physical and Political Map of Afghanistan 1:1,500,000, *Afghan Cartographic Institute, Kabul 1968*
Ceylon Physical 1:1,000,000, *Survey Department, Colombo 1973*
New Map of Afghanistan 1:1,000,000, *"Sahab" Geographic & Drafting Institute, Tehrān*
Pākistān 1:1,000,000, *Survey of Pākistān, Rāwalpindi 1968*
Motor Map of Ceylon 1:506,880, *Survey Department, Colombo 1973*
Nepal 1:506,880, *Ministry of Defence, London 1967*
Nepal 1:408,000, *Kümmerly & Frey, Bern 1980*
Bangladesh Population Census Report 1974, *Statistics Division-Ministry of Planning, Dacca*
Geomedical Monograph Series—Afghanistan, *Springer-Verlag, Berlin 1968*
Pakistan Statistical Yearbook 1978, *Statistics Division, Karachi*
Statistical Pocket Book of the Democratic Socialist Republic of Sri Lanka 1979, *Department of Census and Statistics, Colombo*

SOUTHEAST ASIA
Atlas Indonesia, *Yayasan Dwidjendra, Denpasar-Jakarta 1977*
Atlas of Thailand, *Royal Thai Survey Department, Bangkok 1974*
Secondary Atlas for Malaysia and Singapore, *Niugini Press Pty. Ltd., Port Moresby 1975*
Secondary School Atlas for Malaysia, *McGraw-Hill Far Eastern Publishers Ltd., Singapore 1970*
Hành Chính Viet Nam 1:2,500,000, *Hô Chí Minh 1976*
Maluku dan Irian Jaya 1:2,250,000, *Pembina, Jakarta 1975–76*
Bàu-dô Viet Nam 1:2,000,000, *Saigon 1972*
Laos Administratif 1:2,000,000, *Service Géographique National du Laos, Vientiane 1968*
Malaysia 1:2,000,000, *Jabatanarah Pemetaan Negara, 1976*
Map of Thailand and Bangkok 1:2,000,000, *The Shell Company of Thailand Ltd., Bangkok*
Vietnam 1:2,000,000, *G.U.G.K., Moskva 1972*
Kalimantan 1:1,500,000, *Pembina, Jakarta 1975–76*
Philippines 1:1,500,000, *Philippine Coast and Geodetic Survey, Manila 1968*
Cambodia & South Vietnam—Southeast Asia 1:1,250,000, *Army Map Service, Washington 1966*
Carte Générale du Laos, *Service Géographique National du Laos, Vientiane 1968*
Sumatera 1:790,000, *Pembina, Jakarta 1975–76*
Malaysia Barat—West Malaysia 1:760,000, *Jabatanarah Pemetaan Negara, 1968*
Jawa Barat & D.K.I. Jakarta 1:500,000, *Pembina, Jakarta 1974–75*
Jawa Tengah & D.I. Yogyakarta 1:500,000, *Pembina, Jakarta 1974–75*
Jawa Timur 1:500,000, *Pembina, Jakarta 1974–75*

Sabah 1:500,000, *Jabatanarah Pemetaan Negara, 1976*
Nusa Tenggara Barat & Nusa Tenggara Timur 1:330,000, *Pembina, Jakarta 1975*
Jawa Madura 1:225,000, *Pembina, Jakarta 1975–76*
Sulawesi 1:220,000, *Pembina, Jakarta 1975–76*
Gulongan Masharakat-Banchi Pendudok dan Perumahan Malaysia 1970, *Jabatan Perangkaan, Kuala Lumpur*
Sensus Penduluk 1971, *Biro Pusat Statistik, Jakarta*
Statistical Summary of Thailand 1978, *Statistical Reports Division, Bangkok*
Statistik Indonesia 1974–75, *Biro Pusat Statistik, Jakarta*

CHINA, MONGOLIA
Zhonghua Renmin Gongheguo Fen Sheng Dituji, *Ditu Chubanshe, Beijing 1977*
Zhonghua Renmin Gongheguo Ditu 1:6,000,000, *Ditu Chubanshe, Beijing 1980*
China 1:5,500,000, *Cartographia, Budapest 1967*
Zhonghua Renmin Gongheguo Ditu 1:4,000,000, *Ditu Chubanshe, Beijing 1980*
Mongolskaja Narodnaja Respublika 1:3,000,000, *G.U.G.K., Moskva 1972*
Taiwan/Formosa 1:500,000, *Army Map Service, Washington 1964*
China's Changing Map, *Methuen & Co., London 1972*

JAPAN, KOREA
Japan—The Pocket Atlas, *Heibonsha Ltd., Tōkyō 1970*
The National Atlas of Japan, *Geographical Survey Institute, Tōkyō 1977*
Teikoku's Complete Atlas of Japan, *Teikoku Shoin Company Ltd., Tōkyō 1977*
Tourist Map of Japan 1:5,300,000, *Japan National Tourist Organisation, Tōkyō 1974*
Republic of Korea 1:1,000,000, *Chungang Map & Chart Service, Sŏul 1973*
Northern Korea—Road Map of Korea, *Republic of Korea Army Map Service, Sŏul 1971*
Southern Korea 1:700,000, *Republic of Korea Army Map Service, Sŏul 1977*

AFRICA
The Atlas of Africa, *Editions Jeune Afrique, Paris 1973*
Africa 1:14,000,000, *N.G.S., Washington 1980*
Africa 1:9,000,000, *V.E.B. Hermann Haack, Gotha-Leipzig 1977*
Afrique/Africa 1:4,000,000, *Pneu. Michelin, Paris-London*
Africa 1:2,000,000, *Army Map Service, Washington*

NORTH WEST AFRICA
Atlas International de l'Ouest Africain 1:2,500,000, *Organisation de l'Unité Africaine, Dakar 1971*
Mauritanie 1:2,500,000, *I.G.N., Paris 1978*
Algérie-Tunisie 1:1,000,000, *Pneu. Michelin, Paris 1975*
Maroc 1:1,000,000, *Pneu. Michelin, Paris 1975*
Generalkarte Gran Canaria-Tenerife 1:150,000, *Mairs Geographischer Verlag, Stuttgart 1979*
Annuaire Statistique du Maroc, *Direction de la Statistique, Rabat 1976*
Code Géographique National—Code des Communes, *Secretariat d'État au Plan, Alger 1975*
Recensement Général de la Population et des Logements 1975, *Institut National de la Statistique, Tūnis*

NORTH EAST AFRICA
Egypte 1:750,000, *Kummerly & Frey, Bern 1977*
Population Census 1973, *Census and Statistical Department, Tarābulus*

WEST AFRICA
Atlas de Côte d'Ivoire, *Institut de Géographie Tropicale-Université d'Abidjan, Abidjan 1971*
Atlas de Haute-Volta, *Centre Voltaïque de la Recherche Scientifique, Ouagadougou 1969*
Atlas du Cameroun, *Institut de Recherches Scientifiques du Cameroun, Yaoundé*
Atlas for the United Republic of Cameroon, *Collins-Longman, Glasgow 1977*
Ghana Junior Atlas, *E. A. Boateng-Thomas Nelson and Sons Ltd., London 1965*
Liberia in Maps, *Stefan von Gnielinski, Hamburg 1972*
Oxford Atlas for Nigeria, *Oxford University Press, London-Ibadan 1971*
School Atlas for Sierra Leone, *Collins-Longman, Glasgow 1975*
République du Mali 1:2,500,000, *I.G.N., Paris 1971*
Ghana-Administrative 1:2,000,000, *Survey of Ghana, Accra 1968*
Road Map of Nigeria 1:585,000, *Federal Surveys, Lagos 1969*
République Unie du Cameroun 1:1,000,000, *I.G.N., Paris 1972*
République de Haute-Volta-Carte Routière 1:1,000,000, *I.G.N., Paris 1968*
Philips' School Room Map of Ghana 1:1,000,000, *George Philip & Son Ltd., London 1963*
Sénégal 1:1,000,000, *I.G.N., Paris 1974*
Sénégal-Carte Administrative 1:1,000,000, *I.G.N., Paris 1966*
Physical Map of Nigeria 1:1,000,000, *Federal Surveys, Lagos 1965*
République du Côte d'Ivoire 1:1,000,000, *I.G.N., Paris 1970*
Côte d'Ivoire 1:800,000, *Pneu. Michelin, Paris 1978*
Mapa da Guiné 1:650,000, *J. R. Silva, Lisboa 1969*
République du Dahomey-Carte Routière et Touristique 1:500,000, *I.G.N., Paris 1968*
Road Map of Ghana 1:500,000, *Survey of Ghana, Accra 1970*
The Gambia Road Map 1:500,000, *Survey Department The Gambia, Banjul 1973*
Nigeria-Digest of Statistics 1973, *Federal Office of Statistics, Lagos*

EAST AND CENTRAL AFRICA
Atlas Pratique du Tchad, *Institut Tchadien pour les Sciences Humaines, Paris 1972*
Sudan Roads 1:4,000,000, *Sudan Survey Department, Khartoum 1976*
Äthiopie/Ethiopia 1:4,000,000, *Medizinische Länderkunde/Geomedical Monograph Series, Berlin 1972*
Carte de l'Afrique Centrale 1:2,500,000, *I.G.N., Paris 1968*
Highway Map of Ethiopia 1:2,000,000, *Imperial Ethiopian Government, Addis Ababa 1961*
République du Tchad-Carte Routière 1:1,500,000, *I.G.N., Paris 1968*
République Centrafricaine-Carte Routière 1:1,500,000, *I.G.N., Paris 1969*
Territoire Française des Afars et des Issas 1:400,000, *Office Developpement du Tourisme, Djibouti 1970*
Ethiopia-Statistical Abstract 1976, *Central Statistical Office, Addis Ababa*

EQUATORIAL AFRICA
Atlas du Congo, *Office de la Recherche Scientifique et Techique Outre-Mer, Brazzaville 1969*
Atlas for Malawi, *Collins-Longman, Glasgow 1969*
Atlas of Uganda, *Department of Lands and Surveys, Kampala 1967*
Malawi in Maps, *University of London Press Ltd., London 1972*
Tanzania in Maps, *University of London Press, Ltd., London 1975*
The First Kenya Atlas, *George Philip & Son Ltd., London 1973*
Carte de l'Afrique Centrale 1:2,500,000, *I.G.N., Paris 1968*
Carta Rodoviária de Angola 1:2,000,000, *Lello S.A.R.L., Luanda 1974*
Republic of Zambia 1:1,500,000, *Surveyor General, Ministry of Lands and Natural Resources, Lusaka 1972*
Tanzania 1:1,250,000, *Shell & B.P. Tanzania Ltd., Dar es Salaam 1973*
Malawi 1:1,000,000, *Malawi Government, Blantyre 1971*
Road Map of Kenya 1:1,000,000, *George Philip & Son Ltd., London 1972*
République Populaire du Congo 1:1,000,000, *I.G.N., Paris 1973*
Gabon 1:1,000,000, *I.G.N., Paris 1975*
Statistical Abstract 1979, *Central Bureau of Statistics, Nairobi*

SOUTHERN AFRICA
Large Print Atlas for Southern Africa, *George Philip & Son Ltd., London 1976*
Atlas de Madagascar, *Association des Géographes de Madagascar, Antananarivo 1971*
Atlas for Mauritius, *Macmillan Education Ltd., London 1971*
Ontwikkelingsatlas-Development Atlas, *Republic of South Africa-Department of Planning, Pretoria 1966*
Botswana Road Map and Climate Chart 1:6,000,000, *Department of Surveys and Lands, Gaborone 1980*
Madagascar et Comores 1:4,000,000, *I.G.N., Paris 1970*
Suidelike Afrika/Southern Africa 1:2,500,000, *The Government Printer, Pretoria 1973*
Roads of Zimbabwe 1:2,100,000, *Shell Zimbabwe Ltd., Salisbury, 1980*
Carta de Moçambique 1:2,000,000, *Ministerio do Ultramar, Lisboa 1971*
Mapa Rodoviário de Moçambique 1:2,000,000, *J.A.E.M. 1972*
The Black Homelands of South Africa 1:1,900,000, *Perskor Boeke Tekenkantoor, Johannesburg*
Road Map of Zimbabwe 1:1,800,000, *A.A. of Zimbabwe, Salisbury 1980*
Zimbabwe-Mobil 1:1,470,000, *M.O. Collins Ltd., Salisbury 1976*
Rhodesia Relief 1:1,000,000, *Surveyor General, Salisbury 1973*
Lafatsche La Botsvana/Republic of Botswana 1:1,000,000, *Department of Surveys and Lands, Gaborene 1970*
Suid Afrika/South Africa 1:500,000, *The Government Printer, Pretoria*
Lesotho, 1:250,000, *Government Overseas Surveys, Maseru 1969*

Île Maurice-Carte Touristique 1:100,000, *I.G.N., Paris 1978*
La Réunion-Carte Touristique 1:100,000, *I.G.N., Paris 1978*
Annual Statistical Bulletin 1973, *The Bureau of Statistics, Maseru*
Bi-Annual Digest of Statistics 1976, *Central Statistical Office, Port Louis*
Population Census 1970, *Department of Statistics, Pretoria*
Population de Madagascar au Ier Janvier 1972, *Direction Général du Gouvernement, Antananarivo*
South Africa 1980–81-Official Yearbook, *Chris van Rensburg Publications Ltd., Johannesburg*

NORTH AMERICA
CANADA
Atlas Larousse Canadien, *Les Editions Françaises Inc., Québec - Montréal 1971*
Oxford Regional Economic Atlas - United States & Canada, *Clarendon Press, Oxford 1967*
Road Atlas United States - Canada - Mexico, *Rand McNally & Co., Chicago 1981*
The National Atlas of Canada, *Department of Energy, Mines and Resources, Ottawa 1972*
Northwest Territories - Yukon Territory 1:4,000,000, *Department of Energy, Mines and Resources, Ottawa 1974*
Quebec and Newfoundland 1:3,700,000, *N.G.S., Washington 1980*
British Columbia, Alberta and the Yukon Territory 1:3,500,000, *N.G.S., Washington 1978*
Ontario 1:3,000,000, *N.G.S., Washington 1980*
Saskatchewan and Manitoba 1:2,600,000, *N.G.S., Washington 1979*
Canada Year Book 1978-79, *Minister of Industry, Trade and Commerce, Ottawa*

UNITED STATES
Oxford Regional Economic Atlas - United States & Canada, *Clarendon Press, Oxford 1967*
Road Atlas United States - Canada - Mexico, *Rand McNally & Co., Chicago 1981*
Transportation Map of the United States, *U.S. Department of Transportation, Washington 1976*
National Energy Transportation System 7,500,000, *U.S. Geological Survey, Reston, Virginia 1977*
Close-up: Alaska 1:3,295,000, *N.G.S., Washington 1975*
Close-up: The Southwest 1:2,124,000, *N.G.S., Washington 1977*
Close-up: The Northwest 1:2,000,000, *N.G.S., Washington 1973*
Close-up: The Southeast 1:1,780,000, *N.G.S., Washington 1975*
Close-up: California and Nevada 1:1,700,000, *N.G.S., Washington 1978*
Close-up: Florida 1:1,331,000, *N.G.S., Washington 1973*
Close-up: Illinois, Indiana, Ohio and Kentucky 1:1,267,000, *N.G.S., Washington 1977*
Close-up: The Northeast 1:1,215,000, *N.G.S., Washington 1978*
Close-up: The Mid-Atlantic States 1:886,000, *N.G.S., Washington 1973*
Topographic Maps 1:500,000, *U.S. Geological Survey, Washington*
Topographic Maps 1:250,000, *U.S. Geological Survey, Washington*
Topographic Maps 1:24,000, *U.S. Geological Survey, Washington*
Census of Population and Housing 1980, *Bureau of the Census, Washington*

MEXICO
Atlas of Mexico, *Bureau of Business Research, University of Texas, Austin 1975*
Road Atlas United States - Canada - Mexico, *Rand McNally & Co., Chicago 1981*
Mapas de los Estados-Serie Patria, *Libreria Patria S.A., México*
Carta Geografica de México 1:2,500,000, *Asociación Nacional Automovilística, Ciudad de México 1976*
Archeological Map of Middle America 1:2,250,000, *N.G.S., Washington 1968*

CENTRAL AMERICA AND THE CARIBBEAN
Atlas for Barbados, Windwards and Leewards, *Macmillan Education Ltd., London 1974*
Atlas for Guyana & Trinidad & Tobago, *Macmillan Education Ltd, London 1973*
Atlas for the Eastern Caribbean, *Collins-Longman, London 1977*
Atlas Nacional de Cuba, *Academia de Ciencias de Cuba, La Habana 1970*
Atlas of the Commonwealth of the Bahamas, *Kingston Publishers Ltd.-Ministry of Education, Kingston-Nassau 1976*
Jamaica in Maps, *University of London Press Ltd., London 1974*
West Indies and Central Amerika 1:4,500,000, *N.G.S., Washington 1981*
Mapa General-República de Honduras 1:1,000,000, *Instituto Geográfico Nacional, Tegucigalpa 1980*
Mapa Oficial de la República de Panamá 1:1,000,000, *Instituto Geográfico Nacional, Panamá 1979*
Mapa Preliminar de la República de Guatemala 1:1,000,000, *Instituto Geográfico Nacional, Guatemala 1976*
República de Nicaragua 1:1,000,000, *Instituto Geográfico Nacional, Managua 1975*
Belize 1:800,000, *Directorate of Overseas Surveys, London 1974*
Mapa de la República Dominicana 1:600,000, *Instituto Geográfico Universitario, Santo Domingo 1979*
Costa Rica - Mapa Fisico-Politico 1:500,000, *Instituto Geográfico de Costa Rica, San José 1974*
El Salvador 1:500,000, *Ministerio de Obras Públicas, San Salvador 1978*
Mapa Hipsométrico de la República de Guatemala 1:500,000, *Instituto Geográfico Nacional, Guatemala 1979*
Jamaica 1:280,000, *Fairey Surveys Ltd., Maidenhead 1974*
Mapa de Carreteras Estatales de Puerto Rico 1:250,000, *Autoridad de Carreteras Estatales, San Juan 1972*
Nicaragua-Costa Rica 1:250,000, *Instituto Geográfico Nacional, Managua 1972*
Puerto Rico e Islas Limitrofes 1:240,000, *U.S. Geological Survey, Washington 1970*
Turks & Caicos Islands 1:200,000, *Directorate of Overseas Surveys, London 1971*
Cayman Islands 1:150,000, *Directorate of Overseas Surveys, London 1972*
Trinidad 1:150,000, *Director of Surveys-Ministry of Defense, London 1970*
Guadeloupe-Carte Touristique 1:100,000, *I.G.N., Paris 1978*
Martinique-Carte Touristique 1:100,000, *I.G.N., Paris 1977*
Lesser Antilles-Antigua 1:50,000, *Directorate of Overseas Surveys, London 1973*
Tourist Map of Tobago 1:50,000, *Lands & Surveys Department, Port of Spain 1969*
Dominica 1:25,000, *Directorate of Overseas Surveys, London 1978*
Lesser Antilles-Barbuda 1:25,000, *Directorate of Overseas Surveys, London 1970*
Annuario Estadístico de Costa Rica 1977, *Direción General de Estadística, San José*
Annuario Estadístico de Cuba 1973, *Direción Central de Estadística, La Habana*
Caribbean Year Book 1978-80, *Caribook Ltd., Toronto*
Fact Sheets on the Commonwealth-Antigua, *British Information Services, London 1974*
Fact Sheets on the Commonwealth-Belize, *British Information Services, London 1976*
Guatemala-III Censo de Habitación 26 de marzo de 1973, *Direción General de Estadística, Guatemala*
Honduras-Annuario Estadístico 1978, *Direción General de Estadística, Censos, Tegucigalpa*
Nicaragua-Annuario Estadístico 1975, *Oficina Ejecutiva de Encuestas y Censos, Managua*
Statistical Yearbook for Latin America, *United Nations, New York 1976*
Zentralamerika-Karten zur Bevölkerungs und Wirtschaftsstruktur 1975, *H. Nuhn, P. Krieg & W. Schlick, Hamburg*

SOUTH AMERICA
NORTHERN SOUTH AMERICA
Atlas Basico de Colombia, *Instituto Geográfico Agustin Codazzi, Bogotá 1970*
Atlas de Colombia, *Instituto Geográfico Agustin Codazzi, Bogotá 1979*
Atlas de Venezuela, *Ministerio de Obras Públicas, Caracas 1970*
Atlas for Guyana, Trinidad & Tobago, *Macmillan Education Ltd., London 1973*
Atlas Histórico Geográfico y de Paisajes Peruanos, *Instituto Nacional de Planificación, Lima 1970*
Atlas Nacional do Brasil, *Instituto Brasileiro de Geografia*
Atlas Universal y del Perú, *Thomas Nelson & Sons Ltd., Sunbury on Thames 1968*
Brasil-Didáctico, Rodoviário, Turístico 1:5,000,000, *Gr. Editôra e Publicidade Ltda., Rio de Janeiro*
Mapa de la República de Bolivia 1:4,000,000, *Instituto Geográfico Militar, La Paz 1974*
Mapa Politico del Perú 1:2,400,000, *Editorial "Navarrete", Lima 1975*
Mapa de Carreteras del Perú 1:2,200,000, *Instituto Geográfico Militar, Lima 1979*
Mapa Fisico-Politico 1:2,000,000, *Instituto Geográfico Militar, Lima 1970*
Mapa Fisico de la República de Venezuela 1:2,000,000, *Ministerio de Obras Públicas, Bogotá 1975*
Brasil-Mapa Rodoviário 1:2,000,000, *Ministério dos Transportes, 1971*

Carte de la Guyane Française 1:1,500,000, *I.G.N., Paris 1973*
República de Colombia 1:1,500,000, *Ministerio de Hacienda y Credito Público, Bogotá 1979*
Ecuador 1:1,000,000, *Instituto Geográfico Militar, Quito 1971*
Kaart van Suriname 1:1,000,000, *C. Kersten & Co. N.V., Paramaribo*
Mapa de Bolivia 1:1,000,000, *Instituto Geográfico Militar, La Paz 1973*
Mapa Vial 1:1,000,000, *Ministerio de Obras Públicas, Caracas 1970*
República del Perú-Mapa Fisico-Politico, 1:1,000,000, *Instituto Geográfico Militar, Lima 1978*
Carte de la Guyane Française 1:500,000, *I.G.N., Paris 1976*
Suriname 1:500,000, *Uitgave Centraal Bureau Luchtkartering, 1969*
Guyana 1:500,000, *Ordnance Survey, Georgetown 1972*
Annuário Estatístico do Brasil 1978, *Fundacão Instituto Brasileiro de Geografia e Estatística, Rio de Janeiro*
Boletín Mensual de Estadística-agosto 1977, *D.A.N.E., Bogotá*
Dicionário Geográfico Brasileiro, *Editora Globo, Pôrto Alegre 1972*
Discover Bolivia, *Los Amigos del Libro, La Paz 1972*
Venezuela-Annuário Estadístico 1976, *Oficina Central de Estadística e Informatica, Caracas*

SOUTHERN SOUTH AMERICA
Atlas de la República Argentina, *Instituto Geográfico Militar, Buenos Aires 1972*
Atlas de la República Argentina, *Instituto Geográfico Militar, Santiago 1976*
Atlas de la República de Chile, *Instituto Geográfico Militar, Santiago 1970*
Atlas Escolar de Chile, *Instituto Geográfico Militar, Santiago 1978*
Atlas Universal y de la República Argentina, *Aguilar Argentina S.A. de Ediciones, Buenos Aires 1972*
Mapa de la República Argentina 1:5,000,000, *Instituto Geográfico Militar, Buenos Aires 1973*
Paraguay 1:1,000,000, *Instituto Geográfico Militar, Asuncion 1974*
República Oriental del Uruguay 1:500,000, *Servicio Geográfico Militar, Montevideo 1961*
Uruguay-Moyennes et Petites Villes 1972, *Institut des Hautes Etudes de l'Amerique Latine, Paris*

AUSTRALIA AND OCEANIA
Atlas of Australian Resources, *Division of National Mapping, Canberra 1980*
New Zealand-Mobil Travel Map, *Mobil Oil New Zealand Ltd., Wellington 1973*
New Zealand Atlas, *A.R. Shearer Government Printer, Wellington 1976*
The Jacaranda Atlas, *Jacaranda Press Pty. Ltd., 1971*
The Jacaranda Atlas For New Zealand, *Jacaranda Press Pty. Ltd., 1971*
Australia-Geographic Map 1:2,500,000, *Minister for National Development, Canberra 1967*
Territory of Papua and New Guinea 1:2,500,000, *Division of National Mapping, Canberra 1970*
Carte de l'Oceanie Française 1:2,000,000, *I.G.N., Paris 1971*
Îles Tuamotu-Îles Marquises 1:2,000,000, *I.G.N., Paris 1969*
New Zealand-Map Guide 1:1,900,000, *New Zealand Tourist and Publicity Department, Wellington 1978*
Mobil New Zealand Road Map, *Mobil Oil New Zealand Ltd., Wellington 1973*
Fiji Islands-World Aeronautical Chart 1:1,000,000, *Ordnance Survey, Southampton 1970*
Close-up: Hawaii 1:675,000, *N.G.S., Washington 1978*
Archipel des Nouvelles-Hébrides 1:500,000, *I.G.N., Paris 1976*
New Zealand 1:500,000, *Department of Lands and Survey, Wellington 1976*
Nouvelle Calédonie 1:500,000, *I.G.N., Paris 1978*
Palau Islands 1:165,000, *Defense Mapping Agency Hydrographic Center, Washington 1973*
General Map of Tokelau Islands 1:100,000, *Department of Lands & Survey, Wellington 1969*
Tahiti-Carte Touristique 1:100,000, *I.G.N., Paris 1977*
Christmas Islands - Gilbert and Ellice Islands Colony 1:50,000, *Directorate of Overseas Survey, London 1970*
Tuvalu, *Government of Tuvalu 1979*
Annual Statistical Abstract-Fiji 1970-71, *Bureau of Statistics, Suva*
Australia - Population and Dwellings in Local Government Areas and Urban Centres 1976, *Australian Bureau of Statistics, Canberra*
Fact Sheet - Pitcairn Islands Group, *British Information Services, London 1974*
Fact Sheet - The Gilbert Islands, *British Information Services, London 1977*
Fact Sheet - The New Hebrides, *British Information Services, London 1976*
Fact Sheet - The Solomon Islands, *British Information Services, London 1976*
Fact Sheet - Tuvalu, *British Information Services, London 1977*
New Zealand Pocket Digest of Statistics 1979, *Department of Statistics, Wellington*
New Zealand Official Yearbook 1978, *Department of Statistics, Wellington*

POLAR REGIONS
Antarctica 1:11,250,000, *U.S. Naval Oceanographic Office, Washington 1965*
Antarctica 1:10,000,000, *American Geographical Society, New York 1970*
Antarctica 1:10,000,000, *Division of National Mapping, Canberra 1979*
Antarctica 1:5,000,000, *American Geographical Society, New York 1970*
Map of the Artic Region 1:5,000,000, *American Geographical Society, New York 1975*

Transliteration Systems

Toponymy: Criteria Used for the Writing of Names on the Maps

The language of geography is a language which defines geographic features in universally recognized terms. In creating this language, toponymy experts and cartographers have confronted complex problems in finding terms which are universally acceptable. So that the reader can fully understand the maps in this atlas, here is a brief explanation of how the toponyms (place-names for geographic features) have been written, particularly those relating to regions or countries where the Roman alphabet is not used. Among these are the Slavic-speaking nations such as the Soviet Union, Yugoslavia and Bulgaria; and China and Japan, which use ideographic characters. Of the European countries, Greece has its own alphabet, which is totally different from the Roman alphabet. Many of the Islamic countries use Arabic, with variations derived from local dialects.

There are two basic systems for Romanizing writing. The first is by phonetic transcription, using combinations of different alphabetical signs for each language when the phonetic sound in other languages should be maintained. For example, the Italian sound "sc" (which must be followed by an "e" or "i" to remain soft) in French is "ch," in English is "sh," and in German is "sch."

The second system is transliteration, in which the words, letters or characters of one language are represented or spelled in the letters or characters of another language.

Chinese, Japanese and Arabic Languages

Various Asian and African countries use non-Roman forms in their writing. For example, the Chinese and Japanese languages use ideographic characters instead of an alphabet, and these ideographic characters are transformed into the Roman alphabet through phonetic transcription. Until recently, one of the methods used for transforming Chinese was the Wade-Giles system, named for its English authors. Used in this atlas is the Pinyin system, which was approved by the Chinese government in 1958 and has been incorporated into the official maps of the People's Republic of China. The Pinyin system also has been adopted by the United States Board on Geographic Names and is used in official United Nations documents. The Pinyin names, however, often are accompanied by the Wade-Giles form, as the latter was widely known.

In Japan, ideographic characters are used, although the Roman alphabet is used in many Japanese scientific works. Japan uses two principal systems for standardizing names. They are the Kunreisiki, used by the government in official publications, and the Hepburn method. Adopted for this atlas is the Hepburn method, the system used in international English-language publications and by the United States Board on Geographic Names.

Romanization of the Arabic alphabet, which is used in many Islamic countries, is by transliteration. Since English and French are still used as an international language in many Arab countries, the name forms proposed by the major English and French sources have been taken into consideration. Generally, the systems proposed by the United States Board on Geographic Names and the Permanent Committee on Geographical Names have been used for most Asian countries and Arab-speaking countries.

Greek, Russian and Other Slavic Languages

Practically all written languages in Europe use the Roman alphabet. The differences in phonetics and grammar are shown by the use of diacritical marks and by groupings of consonants, vocals and syllables which give meaning to the various tones in the language. According to a centuries-old tradition, each written language maintains its formal characters, using the translated form rather than the phonetic transcription when a geographical term must be given in another language. This system, therefore, makes it more a translation than a transliteration.

In the Aegean area, Greek and the Greek alphabet are particularly significant because of historical links to the beginning of European civilization. The 1962 United States Board on Geographic Names and the Permanent Committee on Geographical Names systems, based on modern Greek pronunciation, have been used in transcribing toponyms from official sources for these maps. (The table that follows has an example indicating essential norms for Romanizing the modern Greek alphabet.)

A different situation arises in countries using the Cyrillic alphabet. Six principal Slavic languages using this alphabet are Russian, Byelorussian, Ukrainian, Bulgarian, Serbian, and Macedonian. The Cyrillic alphabet also is used by the non-Slavic people of the central Soviet Union. The nomenclature of these regions has been transliterated in accordance with the system proposed by the International Organization for Standardization, taking into consideration sounds and letters and uses of the diacritical marks normal in Slavic languages. The International Organization for Standardization method is accepted and used in bibliographical works and international documents. (The table which follows gives the relationship between the letters of the Cyrillic and Roman alphabets for the above six languages.) An exception to this transliteration is made by the Soviet Balkan republics of Estonia, Latvia and Lithuania. Here the name forms deriving from the national languages have been adopted, using the Roman alphabet.

Special Cases: Conventional Forms and Multilinguals

Cartographic nomenclature generally derives from the official nomenclature of the sovereign and nonsovereign countries, although a number of cases need an explanation.

In numerous situations, English conventional forms are used along with the local or conventional name in referring to a geographical entity used outside the official language area. For example, Vienna, Prague, Copenhagen and Moscow are English forms for Wien, Praha, København and Moskva, respectively. There have been cases, however, where the conventional or historical form commonly used in English cartography has been applied with the same meaning. Thus, Peking and Nanking are the English conventional forms for Beijing and Nanjing, while Tsinan, Tientsin and Mukden are the former conventional spellings or names for Jinan, Tianjin and Shenyang, respectively. Other examples are Saigon, the former name for Ho Chi Minh, Vietnam; and Bangkok, the name for Krung Thep, which is used in Thailand.

The lack of reliable data for countries, especially ex-colonies without a firm national cartographic tradition, has made it necessary to utilize mapping skills of former colonist nations such as France, the United Kingdom and Belgium. A lack of data has led to the adoption of French and British forms in many areas, as these two languages are widely used for official purposes.

Another special case is that of the multilingual areas. Many countries and areas officially recognize two or more written and spoken languages; therefore, all of the principal written forms appear on the maps. This is true, for example, of Belgium where the official languages are French and Dutch (e.g. Bruxelles/Brussel) and of Italian regions such as Valle d'Aosta and Alto Adige, where French, German and Italian are used (e.g. Aosta/Aoste) (Bolzano/Bozen).

In preparing this atlas, each of these special cases has been taken into full consideration within the limits of the scale, space and readability of the maps.

Transliteration of the Cyrillic Alphabet
(International System—ISO)

Cyrillic Letter		Roman Letter		Cyrillic Letter		Roman Letter	
А	а	a		О	о	o	
Б	б	b		П	п	p	
В	в	v		Р	р	r	
Г	г	g		С	с	s	
Д	д	d		Т	т	t	
Е	е	e	initially, after a vowel or after the mute sign "Ъ", becomes "je"	У	у	u	
				Ф	ф	f	
				Х	х	h	
Ё	ё	ë		Ц	ц	c	
Ж	ж	ž		Ч	ч	č	
З	з	z		Ш	ш	š	
И	и	i		Щ	щ	šč	
Й	й	j	not written if preceded by "И" or "Ы"	Ъ	ъ	—	not written
				Ы	ы	y	
К	к	k		Ь	ь	—	not written
Л	л	l		Э	э	e	
М	м	m		Ю	ю	ju	
Н	н	n		Я	я	ja	

Transcription of Modern Greek
(U. S. B. G. N./P.C.G.N.)

Greek Letter (or combination)		Roman Letter (or combination)		Greek Letter (or combination)		Roman Letter (or combination)	
A	α	a			μπ	b	beginning a word
	αι	ai				mb	within a word
	αυ	av		N	ν	n	
B	β	v			ντ	d	beginning a word
Γ	γ	g				nd	within a word
	γγ	ng		Ξ	ξ	x	
	γκ	g	beginning a word	O	o	o	
		ng	within a word		οι	oi	
Δ	δ	d			ου	ou	
E	ε	e		Π	π	p	
	ει	i		P	ρ	r	
	ευ	ev		Σ	σ	s	
Z	ζ	z			ς	s	ending a word
H	η	i		T	τ	t	
	ηυ	iv			τζ	tz	
Θ	θ	th		Υ	υ	i	
					υι	i	
I	ι	i		Φ	φ	f	
K	κ	k		X	χ	kh	
Λ	λ	l		Ψ	ψ	ps	
M	μ	m		Ω	ω	o	

Geographical Glossary

The "Geographical Glossary" lists the principal geographical terms used on the maps. All of these terms, including abbreviations, prefixes and suffixes, appear in the cartographic table as they appear on the maps. Terms are listed in accordance with the English alphabet, without consideration of diacritical marks on letters or of particular groups of letters.

Prefixes and suffixes relating to principal names or forming part of geographical toponyms are followed or preceded by a dash and the language to which they refer: e.g. Chi-/*Dan.* (Chi, a Danish prefix, means large); -bor/*Slvn.* (-bor, a Slovakian suffix, means city). Suffixes can also appear as words in themselves. In this case, the suffix and primary word are coupled together: e.g. Berg, -berg (Berg, which means mountain, can be used alone or as part of another word, such as Hapsberg).

Certain terms are followed or preceded by their abbreviation used on the maps. Both instances are listed: e.g. Fjord, Fj. and Fj., Fjord.

All geographical terms are identified by the language or languages to which each belongs. The language or languages in italics follows the term: e.g. Abbey/*Eng.*; -bad/*Nor., Dut., Swed., Germ.* Each term is translated into a corresponding English term or terms.

Below is a table identifying the abbreviations of various language names used on the maps. Note that certain abbreviations represent a group of languages, instead of one language: e.g. Ural. is the abbreviation for Uralic, a group word for Udmurt, Komi, and Nenets.

Alt. = Altaic (Turkmen, Tatar, Bashkir, Kazakh, Karalpak, Nogai, Kirghiz, Uzbek, Uigur, Altaic, Yakut, Khakass)

Ban. = Bantu (KiSwahili, ChiLuba, Lingala, KiKongo)

Cauc. = Caucasian (Chechen, Ingush, Kalmuck, Georgian)

Iran. = Iranian (Baluchi, Tagus)

Mel. = Melanesian (Fijian, New Caledonian, Micronesian, Nauruan)

Mong. = Mongolian (Buryat, Khalka Mongol)

Poly. = Polynesian (Maori, Samoan, Tongan, Tahitian, Hawaiian)

Sah. = Saharan (Kanuri, Tubu)

Som. = Somalian (Somali, Galla)

Sud. = Sudanese (Peul, Ehoué, Mossi, Yoruba, Ibo)

Ural. = Uralic (Udmurt, Komi, Nenets).

Because of their technical application to geography, some geographical terms may not fully correspond with the meaning given for them in some dictionaries.

Abbreviations of Language Names

Abbreviations in English	English	Abbreviations in English	English	Abbreviations in English	English	Abbreviations in English	English	Abbreviations in English	English	Abbreviations in English	English
Afr.	Afrikaans	Bulg.	Bulgarian	Fr.	French	Khm.	Khmer	Pers.	Persian	Som.	Somalian
A.I.	American Indian	Burm.	Burmese	Gae.	Gaelic	Kor.	Korean	Pol.	Polish	Sp.	Spanish
Alb.	Albanian	Cat.	Catalan	Georg.	Georgian	K.S.	Khoi-San	Poly.	Polynesian	Sud.	Sudanese
Alt.	Altaic	Cauc.	Caucasian	Germ.	German	Laot.	Laotian	Port.	Portuguese	Swa.	Swahili
Amh.	Amharic	Chin.	Chinese	Gr.	Greek	Lapp.	Lappish	Prov.	Provençal	Swed.	Swedish
Ar.	Arabic	Cz.	Czech	Hebr.	Hebrew	Latv.	Latvian	Rmsh.	Romansh	Tam.	Tamil
Arm.	Armenian	Dan.	Danish	Hin.	Hindi	Lith.	Lithuanian	Rom.	Romanian	Thai	Thai
Az.	Azerbaidzhani	Dut.	Dutch	Hung.	Hungarian	Mal.	Malay	Rus.	Russian	Tib.	Tibetan
Ban.	Bantu	Eng.	English	Icel.	Icelandic	Malag.	Malagasy	Sah.	Saharan	Tur.	Turkish
Bas.	Basque	Esk.	Eskimo	Indon.	Indonesian	Mel.	Melanesian	S.C.	Serbo-Croatian	Ural.	Uralic
Beng.	Bengali	Est.	Estonian	Ir.	Irish	Mong.	Mongolian			Urdu	Urdu
Ber.	Berber	Far.	Faroese	Iran.	Iranian	Nep.	Nepalese	Sin.	Sinhalese	Viet.	Vietnamese
Br.	Breton	Finn.	Finnish	It.	Italian	Nor.	Norwegian	Slvk.	Slovak	Wall.	Walloon
		Fle.	Flemish	Jap.	Japanese	Pash.	Pashto	Slvn.	Slovene	Wel.	Welsh

Glossary of Geographical Terms

Local Form	English	Local Form	English	Local Form	English	Local Form	English
A		Ait / *Ar.; Ber.*	sons	Ard- / *Gae.*	high	Badwëynta / *Som.*	ocean
		Aivi, -aivi / *Lapp.*	mountain	Areg / *Ar.*	dune	Badyarada / *Som.*	gulf
A- / *Ban.*	people	Ak / *Tur.*	white	Areia / *Port.*	beach	Baeg / *Kor.*	white
A' / *Icel.*	river	'Aklé / *Ar.*	dunes	Arena / *Sp.*	beach	Bæk / *Dan.*	brook
Å / *Dan.; Nor.; Swed.*	stream	Akmeņs / *Latv.*	stone	Argent / *Fr.*	silver	Bælt / *Dan.*	strait
a., an / *Germ.*	on	Ákra / *Gr.*	point	Arhipelag / *Rus.*	archipelago	Bagni / *It.*	thermal springs
Aa / *Germ.*	stream	Akti / *Gr.*	coast	Arkhaios / *Gr.*	old, antique	Baharu / *Mal.*	new
Aache / *Germ.*	stream	Ala / *Malag.*	forest	Arm / *Eng.; Germ.*	branch	Bahia / *Port.*	bay
Aaiún / *Ar.*	springs	Ala / *Finn.*	low, lower	Arquipélago / *Port.*	archipelago	Bahia / *Sp.*	bay
Aan / *Dut.; Fle.*	on	Alan / *Tur.*	field	Arr., Arroyo / *Sp.*	stream	Bahir / *Ar.*	river, lake, sea
Āb / *Pers.*	stream	Alb / *Rom.*	white	Arrecife / *Sp.*	reef	Bahnhof / *Germ.*	railway station
Ābād / *Pers.*	city, town	Albo / *Sp.*	white	Arroio / *Port.*	stream	Bahr / *Ar.*	wadi
Abad, -abad / *Pers.*	city, town	Albufera / *Sp.*	lagoon	Art / *Tur.*	pass, watershed	Baḥr / *Ar.*	river, lake, sea
Ābār / *Ar.*	spring	Alcalà / *Sp.*	castle	Aru / *Sin.; Tam.*	river	Bahrat / *Ar.*	lake
Abbadia / *It.*	abbey	Alcázar / *Sp.*	castle	Ås / *Dan.; Nor.; Swed.*	hills	Bahri / *Ar.*	north, northern
Abbaye / *Fr.*	abbey	Aldea / *Sp.*	village	Asfar / *Ar.*	yellow	Baḥrī / *Ar.*	north
Abbazia / *It.*	abbey	Alföld / *Hung.*	lowland	Asif / *Ber.*	river	Bahrïyah / *Ar.*	northern
Abbi / *Amh.*	great	Ali / *Amh.*	mountain	Asky / *Alt.*	lower	Bai / *Chin.*	white
Abd / *Ar.*	servant	Alia / *Poly.*	stream	Áspros / *Gr.*	white	Bāi / *Rom.*	thermal springs
Abeba / *Amh.*	flower	Alin / *Mong.*	range	Assa / *Ber.*	wadi	Baia / *Port.*	bay
Aber / *Br.; Wel.*	estuary	Alm / *Germ.*	mountain	Atalaya / *Sp.*	frontier	Baie / *Fr.*	bay
Abhang / *Germ.*	slope		pasture	Áth / *Gae.*	ford	Baigne / *Fr.*	seaside resort
Abū / *Ar.*	father, master	Alor / *Mal.*	river	Átha / *Gae.*	ford	Baile / *Gae.*	city, town
Abyad / *Ar.*	white	Alp / *Germ.*	mountain	Atol / *Port.*	atoll	Bain / *Fr.*	thermal springs
Abyaḍ / *Ar.*	white		pasture	Au / *Germ.*	meadow	Bains / *Fr.*	thermal springs
Abyār / *Ar.*	well	Alpe / *Germ.; Fr.; It.*	mountain	Aue / *Germ.*	irrigated field	Baixo / *Port.*	low, lower
Abyss / *Eng.*	ocean depth, deep		pasture	Aust / *Nor.*	east	Bajan / *Mong.*	rich
Ach / *Germ.*	stream	Alps / *Eng.*	mountains	Austur / *Icel.*	east	Bajo / *Sp.*	low
Achaïf / *Ar.*	dunes	Alsó / *Hung.*	low, lower	Ava / *Poly.*	canal	Bajrak / *Alb.*	tribe
Ache / *Germ.*	stream	Alt / *Germ.*	old	Aven / *Fr.*	doline, sink	Bakhtïyärï / *Pers.*	western
Achter / *Afr.; Dut.; Fle.*	back	Altin / *Tur.*	lower	Awa / *Poly.*	bay	Bakki / *Icel.*	hill
Acqua / *It.*	water	Altiplano / *Sp.*	plateau	Áyios / *Gr.*	saint	Bālā / *Pers.*	high
Açu / *A.I.*	great	Alto / *Sp.; It.; Port.*	high	'Ayn / *Ar.*	spring, well	Bald / *Eng.*	peak
Açude / *Port.*	reservoir, dam	Altopiano / *It.*	plateau	'Ayoún / *Ar.*	springs, wells	Balka / *Rus.*	gorge
Ada / *Tur.*	island	Älv / *Swed.*	river	'Ayoûn / *Ar.*	spring	Balkan / *Bulg.; Tur.*	mountain range
Adalar / *Tur.*	archipelago	Am / *Kor.*	mountain, peak	Aza / *Ber.*	wadi	Ballin / *Gae.*	mouth
Adasr / *Tur.*	island	Amane / *Ber.*	water	Azraq / *Ar.*	light blue	Ballon / *Fr.*	dome
Addis / *Amh.*	new	Amba / *Amh.*	mountain	Azul / *Port.; Sp.*	light blue	Bally / *Gae.*	city, town
Adi / *Amh.*	village	Ambato / *Malag.*	rock	Azur / *Fr.*	light blue	Balta / *Rom.*	marsh
Adrar / *Ber.*	mount, mountains	An / *Gae.*	of			Báltos / *Gr.*	marsh
		An, a. / *Germ.*	on			Ban / *Laot.*	village
Aéroport / *Fr.*	airport	Ana / *Poly.*	grotto	**B**		Bana / *Jap.*	promontory
Aeroporto / *It.; Port.*	airport	Anatolikós / *Gr.*	eastern			Baña / *Slvk.*	mine
Aeropuerto / *Sp.*	airport	Äng / *Swed.*	meadow	B., Bay / *Eng.*	bay	Bañados / *Sp.*	marsh
Af / *Som.*	mouth, gorge	Angra / *Port.*	bay, anchorage	b., bei / *Germ.*	by	Banc / *Fr.*	bank
Afsluitdijk / *Dut.*	dam	Ani- / *Malag.*	center	B., Bucht / *Germ.*	bay	Banco / *It.; Sp.*	bank
Agadir / *Ber.*	castle	Áno / *Gr.*	upper	Ba / *Sud.*	river	Band / *Pers.*	dam, mountain range
Ağiz / *Tur.*	mouth	Ânou / *Ber.*	well	Ba- / *Ban.*	people	Bandao / *Chin.*	peninsula
Agro / *Sp.; It.*	plain	Anse / *Fr.*	inlet	Ba / *Mel.*	hill, mountain	Bandar / *Ar.; Mal.; Pers.*	port, market
Agua / *Sp.*	water	Ant- / *Malag.*	center	Baai / *Afr.*	bay	Bang / *Indon.; Mal.*	stream
Aguja / *Sp.*	needle	Ao / *Chin.; Khm.; Thai*	gulf	Bab / *Ar.*	gate	Bangou / *Sah.*	well
Agulha / *Port.*	needle, promontory	'Âouâna / *Ar.*	well	Bac / *Viet.*	north	Banhado / *Port.*	marsh
Ahal / *Georg.*	new	Apä / *Rom.*	water	Bach / *Germ.*	brook, torrent	Bani / *Ar.*	sons
Aḥmar / *Ar.*	red	'Aqabat / *Ar.*	pass	Bacino / *It.*	reservoir	Banja / *Bulg.; S.C.; Slvn.*	thermal springs
Ahrāmāt / *Ar.*	pyramids	Aqueduc / *Fr.*	aqueduct	Back / *Eng.*	ridge	Banjaran / *Mal.*	mountain range
Ahzar / *Ber.*	wadi	Ar / *Mong.*	north	Back / *Swed.*	brook	Banka / *Rus.*	sandbank
Aigialós / *Gr.*	coast	Ar / *Sin.; Tam.*	river	Bäck / *Swed.*	brook	Banke / *Dan.*	bank
Aigue / *Prov.*	water	'Arâguîb / *Ar.*	hills	Backe / *Swed.*	hill	Baño / *Sp.*	thermal springs
Aiguille / *Fr.*	needle	Arba / *Amh.*	mount	Bad, -bad / *Dan.; Germ.; Nor.; Swed.*	thermal springs	Banský / *Cz.*	upper
Ain / *Ar.*	spring	Arbore / *Rom.*	tree	Baden, -baden / *Germ.*	thermal springs	Bánya / *Hung.*	mine
		Archipiélago / *Sp.*	archipelago	Bādiyat / *Ar.*	desert	Bar / *Gae.*	peak
		Arcipelago / *It.*	archipelago			Bar / *Eng.*	sandbar
		Arḍ / *Ar.*	region				

Geographical Glossary

Local Form	English
Bar / *Hin.*	great
Bāra / *Hin.*	great
Bara / *S.C.*	pond
Barā / *Urdu*	great
Barajı / *Tur.*	dam
Barat / *Indon.; Mal.*	west, western
Barkas / *Lith.*	castle, city, town
Barlovento / *Sp.*	windward
Barq / *Ar.*	hill
Barra / *Port.; Sp.*	bar, bank
Barrage / *Fr.*	dam
Barragem / *Port.*	reservoir
Barranca / *Sp.*	gorge
Barranco / *Port.; Sp.*	gorge
Barre / *Fr.*	bar
Barun / *Mong.*	western
Bas / *Fr.*	low
-bas / *Rus.*	reservoir
Bassa / *Port.*	flat
Bassejn / *Rus.*	reservoir
Bassin / *Fr.*	basin
Bassure / *Fr.*	flat
Bassurelle / *Fr.*	flat
Bašta / *S.C.*	garden
Bataille / *Fr.*	battle
Batalha / *Port.*	battle
Batang / *Indon.; Mal.*	river
Batha / *Sah.*	stream
Baṭin / *Ar.*	depression
Bāṭlāq / *Pers.*	marsh
Batu / *Mal.*	rock
Bayan / *Mong.*	rich
Bayır / *Tur.*	mountain, slope
Bayou / *Fr.*	branch, stream
Bayt / *Ar.*	house
Bazar / *Pers.*	market
Be / *Malag.*	great
Beau / *Fr.*	beautiful
Becken / *Germ.*	basin
Bed / *Eng.*	river bed
Beek / *Dut.*	creek
Be'er / *Hebr.*	spring
Bei / *Chin.*	north
Bei, b. / *Germ.*	by
Beida / *Ar.*	white
Beinn / *Gae.*	mount
Bel / *Ar.*	son
Bel / *Bulg.*	white
Bel / *Tur.*	pass
Beled / *Ar.*	village
Belen / *Tur.*	mount
Belet / *Ar.*	village
Beli / *S.C.; Slvn.*	white
Beli / *Tur.*	pass
Bellah / *Sah.*	well
Belogorje / *Rus.*	mountains
Belt / *Dan.; Germ.*	strait
Bely / *Rus.*	white
Bělý / *Cz.*	white
Ben / *Ar.*	son
Ben / *Gae.*	mount
Bender / *Pers.*	port, market
Bendi / *Tur.*	dam
Beni / *Ar.*	son
Beo / *S.C.*	white
Bereg / *Rus.*	bank
Berg, -berg / *Afr.; Dut.; Fle.; Germ.; Nor.; Swed.*	mount
Berge / *Afr.*	mountain
Bergen / *Dut.; Fle.*	dunes
Bergland / *Germ.*	upland
Bermejo / *Sp.*	red
Besar / *Mal.*	great
Betsu / *Jap.*	river
Betta / *Tam.*	mountain
Bhani / *Hin.*	community
Bharu / *Mal.*	new
Bheag / *Gae.*	little
Biābān / *Pers.*	desert
Biały / *Pol.*	white
Bianco / *It.*	white
Bien / *Viet.*	lake
Bight / *Eng.*	bay
Bijeli / *S.C.*	white
Bill / *Eng.*	promontory
Bilo / *S.C.*	range
Bílý / *Cz.*	white
Binnen / *Dut.; Fle.; Germ.*	inner
Biqā' / *Ar.*	valley
Bir / *Ar.*	well
Bi'r / *Ar.*	well
Birkat / *Ar.*	pond
Bistrica / *Bulg.; S.C.; Slvn.*	stream
Bjarg / *Icel.*	rock
Bjerg / *Dan.*	mount
Bjeshkët / *Alb.*	mountain pasture
Blaauw / *Afr.*	blue
Blanc / *Fr.*	white
Blanco / *Sp.*	white
Blau / *Germ.*	blue
Bleu / *Fr.*	blue
Bluff / *Eng.*	cliff
Bo- / *Ban.*	people
Bo / *Chin.*	white
Bo / *Swed.*	habitation
Boca / *Sp.*	gap, mouth

Local Form	English
Bôca / *Port.*	gap, mouth
Bocage / *Fr.*	forest
Bocca / *It.*	gap, pass
Bocchetta / *It.*	gap, pass
Bodden / *Germ.*	bay, lagoon
Boden / *Germ.*	soil
Bœng / *Khm.*	lake, marsh
Bog / *Eng.*	marsh
Bogaz / *Alt.; Az.; Tur.*	strait
Boğāzi / *Tur.*	strait
Bogdo / *Mong.*	high
Bogen / *Nor.*	bay
Bois / *Fr.*	forest
Boka / *S.C.*	channel
Boloto / *Rus.*	marsh
Bolšoj / *Rus.*	great
Bolsón / *Sp.*	basin
Bom / *Port.*	good
Bong / *Kor.*	peak
Bongo / *Malag.*	upland
Bor / *Cz.; Rus.*	coniferous forest
Bór / *Pol.*	forest
-bor / *Slvn.*	city, town
Bóras / *Gr.*	north
Börde / *Germ.*	fertile plain
Bordj / *Ar.*	fort
Bóreios / *Gr.*	northern
Borg, -borg / *Dan.; Nor.; Swed.*	castle
Borgo / *It.*	village
Born / *Germ.*	spring
Bory / *Pol.*	forest
Bosch / *Dut.; Fle.*	forest
Bosco / *It.*	wood
Bosque / *Sp.*	forest
Bosse / *Fr.*	hill
Botn / *Nor.*	bay
Bou / *Ar.*	father, master
Bouche / *Fr.*	mouth
Boula / *Sud.*	well
Bourg / *Fr.*	city, town
Bourne, - bourne / *Eng.*	frontier
Boven / *Afr.*	upper
Boz / *Tur.*	grey
Bozorg / *Pers.*	great
Brána / *Cz.*	gate
Braña / *Sp.*	mountain pasture
Branche / *Fr.*	branch
Branco / *Port.*	white
Braṭul / *Rom.*	branch
Bravo / *Sp.*	wild
Brazo / *Sp.*	branch
Brdo / *Cz.; S.C.*	hill
Bre / *Nor.*	glacier
Bredning / *Dan.*	bay
Breg / *Alb.; Bulg.; S.C.*	hill, coast
Brjag / *Bulg.*	bank
Bro / *Dan.; Nor.; Swed.*	bridge
Brod / *Bulg.; Cz.; Rus.; S.C.; Slvk.; Slvn.*	ford
Bród / *Pol.*	ford
Bron / *Afr.*	spring
Bronn / *Germ.*	spring
Bru / *Nor.*	bridge
Bruch / *Germ.*	peat-bog
Bruchzone / *Germ.*	fracture zone
Bruck, -bruck / *Germ.*	bridge
Brücke / *Germ.*	bridge
Brug / *Dut.; Fle.*	bridge
Brugge / *Dut.; Fle.*	bridge
Bruk / *Nor.*	factory
Brunn / *Swed.*	spring
-brunn / *Germ.*	spring
Brunnen / *Germ.*	spring
Brygg / *Swed.*	bridge
Brzeg / *Pol.*	coast
Bū / *Ar.*	father, master
Bucht, B. / *Germ.*	bay
Bugt / *Dan.*	bay
Buḥayrat / *Ar.*	lake, lagoon
Bühel / *Germ.*	hill
Bühl / *Germ.*	hill
Buhta / *Rus.*	bay
Bukit / *Mal.*	mountain, peak
Bukt / *Nor.; Swed.*	bay
Buku / *Indon.*	hill, mountain
Bulag / *Mong.; Tur.*	spring
Bulak / *Mong.; Tur.*	spring
Būlāq / *Tur.*	spring
Bult / *Afr.*	hill
Bulu / *Indon.*	mountain
Bur / *Som.*	mount
Būr / *Ar.*	port
Burg, - burg / *Afr.; Ar.; Dut.; Eng.; Germ.*	castle
Burgh / *Eng.*	city, town
Burgo / *Sp.*	village
Burha / *Hin.*	old
Buri / *Thai*	city, town
Burj / *Ar.*	village
Burn / *Eng.*	stream
Burnu / *Tur.*	promontory
Burqat / *Ar.*	mount, marsh
Burun / *Tur.*	cape
Busen / *Germ.*	bay
Busu / *Ban.*	land
Būtat / *Ar.*	lake, pond
Butte / *Eng.; Fr.*	flat-topped hill

Local Form	English
Büyük / *Tur.*	great
By / *Eng.*	near
By, -by / *Dan.; Nor.; Swed.*	city, town
Bystrica / *Cz.; Slvk.*	stream
Bystrzyca / *Pol.*	stream

C

Local Form	English
C., Cap / *Cat.; Fr.; Rom.*	cape
C., Cape / *Eng.*	cape
C., Colle / *It.*	pass
Caatinga / *A.I.*	forest
Cabeça / *Port.*	peak
Cabeço / *Port.*	peak
Cabeza / *Sp.*	peak
Cabezo / *Sp.*	peak, mountain
Cabo / *Port.; Sp.*	cape
Cachoeira / *Port.*	waterfall, rapids
Cachopo / *Port.*	reef
Cadena / *Sp.*	range
Caer / *Wel.*	castle
Cagan / *Cauc.; Mong.*	white
Cairn / *Gae.*	hill
Čaj / *Az.; Tur.*	river
Cajdam / *Mong.*	salt marsh
Caka / *Chin.*	lake
Cala / *Sp.; It.*	inlet
Calar / *Sp.*	plateau
Caldas / *Sp.; Port.*	thermal springs
Caleta / *Sp.*	inlet
Camp / *Cat.; Fr.; Eng.*	field
Campagna / *It.*	plain
Campagne / *Fr.*	plain
Campo / *Sp.; It.; Port.*	field
Cañada / *Sp.*	gorge, ravine
Canale / *It.*	canal, channel
Caño / *Sp.*	branch
Cañón / *Sp.*	gorge
Canyon / *Eng.*	gorge
Cao / *Viet.*	mountain
Cap, C. / *Cat.; Fr.; Rom.*	cape
Car / *Gae.*	castle
Càrn / *Gae.*	peak
Carrera / *Sp.*	road
Carrick / *Gae.*	rock
Casale / *It.*	hamlet
Cascada / *Sp.*	waterfall
Cascata / *It.*	waterfall
Castel / *It.*	castle
Castell / *Cat.*	castle
Castello / *It.*	castle
Castelo / *Port.*	castle
Castillo / *Sp.*	castle
Castro / *Sp.; It.*	village
Catarata / *Sp.*	cataract
Catena / *It.*	mountain range
Catinga / *Port.*	degraded forest
Cauce / *Sp.*	river bed
Causse / *Fr.*	highland
Cava / *It.*	stone quarry
Çay / *Tur.*	river
Cay / *Eng.*	islet, island
Caye / *Fr.*	island
Cayo / *Sp.*	islet, island
Ceann / *Gae.*	promontory
Centralny / *Rus.*	middle
Čeren / *Alb.*	black
Černi / *Bulg.*	black
Černý / *Cz.*	black
Čërny / *Rus.*	black
Cerrillo / *Sp.*	hill
Cerrito / *Sp.*	hill
Cerro / *Sp.; Port.*	hill, mountain
Cêrro / *Port.*	hill, mountain
Červen / *Bulg.*	red
Červony / *Rus.*	red
Cetate / *Rom.*	city, town
Chaco / *Sp.*	scrubland
Chāh / *Pers.*	well
Chaïf / *Ar.*	dunes
Chaîne / *Fr.*	mountain range
Champ / *Fr.*	field
Chang / *Chin.*	highland
Chapada / *Port.*	highland
Chapadão / *Port.*	highland
Château / *Fr.*	castle
Châtel / *Fr.*	castle
Chāy / *Tur.*	river
Chedo / *Kor.*	archipelago
Chenal / *Fr.*	canal
Cheng / *Chin.*	city, town, wall
Cheon / *Kor.*	city, river
Chergui / *Ar.*	eastern
Cherry, -cherry / *Hin.; Tam.*	city, town
Chew / *Amh.*	salt mine, salt
Chhâk / *Khm.*	bay
Chhotla / *Hin.*	little
Chi- / *Ban.*	great
Chi / *Chin.*	marsh, lake
Chi / *Kor.*	lake, pond
Chi- / *Swa.*	land
Chiang / *Thai*	city, town
Chico / *Sp.*	little
Chine / *Eng.*	ridge
Ch'on / *Kor.*	station

Local Form	English
Ch'ŏn / *Kor.*	river
Chŏsuji / *Kor.*	reservoir
Chott / *Ar.*	salt marsh
Chu / *Chin.; Viet.*	mountain, hill
Chuŏr phnum / *Khm.*	mountain range
Chute / *Fr.*	waterfall
Chutes / *Fr.*	waterfalls
Cidade / *Port.*	city, town
Ciems / *Latv.*	village
Čierny / *Slvk.*	black
Cime / *Fr.*	peak
Cîmp / *Rom.*	field
Cîmpie / *Rom.*	plain
Cinco / *Sp.; Port.*	five
Citeli / *Georg.*	red
Città / *It.*	city, town
Ciudad / *Sp.*	city, town
Ckali / *Georg.*	water
Ckaro / *Georg.*	spring
Co / *Chin.*	lake
Col / *Cat.; Fr.*	pass
Colina / *Port.; Sp.*	hill
Coll / *Cat.*	hill
Collado / *Sp.*	pass
Colle, C. / *It.*	pass
Collina / *It.*	hill
Colline / *Fr.*	hill
Colonia / *Sp.; It.*	colony
Coma / *Sp.*	hill country
Comb / *Eng.*	basin
Comba / *Sp.*	basin
Combe / *Fr.*	basin
Comté / *Fr.*	county, shire
Con / *Viet.*	island
Conca / *It.*	depression
Condado / *Sp.*	county, shire
Cone / *Eng.*	volcanic cone
Cône / *Fr.*	volcanic cone
Contraforte / *Port.*	front range
Cordal / *Sp.*	crest
Cordilheira / *Port.*	mountain range
Cordillera / *Sp.*	mountain range
Coring / *Chin.*	lake
Corixa / *A.I.*	stream
Corno / *It.*	peak
Cornone / *It.*	peak
Corrente / *It.; Port.*	stream
Corriente / *Sp.*	stream
Costa / *Sp.; It.; Port.*	coast
Côte / *Fr.*	coast
Coteau / *Fr.*	height, slope
Coxilha / *Port.*	ridge
Craig / *Gae.*	rock
Cratère / *Fr.*	crater
Cresta / *Sp.; It.*	crest
Crêt / *Fr.*	crest
Crête / *Fr.*	crest
Crkva / *S.C.*	church
Crni / *S.C.; Slvn.*	black
Crven / *S.C.*	red
Csatorna / *Hung.*	canal
Cuchilla / *Sp.*	ridge
Cuenca / *Sp.*	basin
Cuesta / *Sp.*	escarpment
Cueva / *Sp.*	cave
Čuka / *Bulg.; S.C.*	peak
Çukur / *Tur.*	well
Cu Lao / *Viet.*	island
Cumbre / *Sp.*	peak
Cun / *Chin.*	village
Cura / *A.I.*	stone
Curr / *Alb.*	rock
Cy., City / *Eng.*	city, town
Czarny / *Pol.*	black

D

Local Form	English
Da / *Chin.*	great
Da / *Viet.*	mountain, peak
Daal / *Dut.; Fle.*	valley
Daba / *Mong.*	pass
Daba / *Som.*	hill
Daban / *Chin.; Mong.*	pass
Dae / *Kor.*	great
Dağ / *Tur.*	mountain
Dağ., Dağı / *Tur.*	mountain
Dāgh / *Pers.; Tur.*	mountain
Dağı, Dağ. / *Tur.*	mountain
Dağları / *Tur.*	mountain range
Dahar / *Ar.*	hill
Dahr / *Ar.*	plateau, escarpment
Dai / *Chin.; Jap.*	great
Daiet / *Ar.*	marsh
Dak / *Viet.*	stream
Dake / *Jap.*	mountain
Dakhla / *Ar.*	depression
Dakhlet / *Ar.*	depression, bay
Dal, -dal / *Afr.; Dan.; Dut.; Fle.; Nor.; Swed.*	valley
Dala / *Alt.*	steppe, plain
Dalaj / *Mong.*	lake, sea
Dalan / *Mong.*	wall
Dallol / *Sud.*	valley, torrent
Dalur / *Icel.*	valley
Damm / *Germ.*	dam
Dan / *Kor.*	point

Local Form	English
Danau / Indon.	lake
Danda / Nep.	mountains
Dao / Chin.	island, peninsula
Dao / Viet.	island
Dar / Ar.	house, region
Dar / Swa.	port
Dara / Tur.	torrent, valley
Darb / Ar.	track
Darja / Alt.	river, sea
Darya, Daryä / Pers.	river, sea
Daryächeh / Pers.	lake, sea
Daš / Alt.; Az.	rock
Dasht / Pers.	desert, plain
Dawḥat / Ar.	bay
Dayr / Ar.	convent
De / Sp.; Fr.	of
Deal / Rom.	hill
Dearg / Gae.	red
Debre / Amh.	hill, monastery
Dega / Som.	stone
Deh / Pers.	village
Dêḥ / Som.	stream
Deich / Germ.	dike
Dél / Hung.	south
Delft / Dut.; Fle.	deep
Delger / Mong.	wide, market
-den / Eng.	city, town
Deniz / Tur.	sea
Denizi / Tur.	sea
Dent / Fr.	peak
Deo / Laot.; Viet.	pass
Dépression / Fr.	depression
Depressione / It.	depression
Der / Som.	high
Dera / Hin.; Urdu	temple
Derbent / Tur.	gorge, pass
Dere / Tur.	river, valley
Désert / Fr.	desert
Desfiladero / Sp.	pass
Desh / Hin.	land, country
Desierto / Sp.	desert
Det / Alb.	sea
Détroit / Fr.	strait
Deux / Fr.	two
Dezh / Pers.	castle
Dhar / Ar.	heights, hills
Dhār / Hin.; Urdu	mountain
Dhitikós / Gr.	western
Dien / Khm.; Viet.	rice-field
Diep / Dut.; Fle.	deep, strait
Dijk, -dijk / Dut.; Fle.	dam
Ding / Chin.	mountain, peak
Dique / Sp.	dam
Di Sopra / It.	upper
Di Sotto / It.	lower
Distrito / Sp.; Port.	district
Diu / Hin.	island
Diz / Pers.	castle
Djebel / Ar.	mountain
Dji / Ban.	water
Djup / Swed.	deep
Do / Kor.	Island
Do / S.C.	valley
Dō / Jap.	island, administrative division
Dôho / Som.	valley
Doi / Thai	mountain, peak
Dol / Bulg.; Cz.; Rus.; S.C.	valley
Doł / Pol.	valley
Dolen / Bulg.	low
Dolgi / Rus.	long
Dolina / Bulg.; Cz.; Pol.; Rus.; S.C.; Slvn.	valley
Dolni / Bulg.	low
Dolni / Pol.	lower
Dolny / Pol.	lower
Domb / Hung.	hill
Dôme / Fr.	dome
Dong / Chin.; Viet.	east
Dong / Kor.	city, town
Dong / Thai	mountain
Dong / Viet.	marsh, plain
Donji / S.C.	low, lower
Dorf, -dorf / Germ.	village
Doroga / Rus.	road
Dorp, -dorp / Afr.; Dut.; Fle.	village
Dos / Rom.	ridge
Dos / Sp.	two
Douarn / Br.	land
Dougou / Sud.	settlement
Doukou / Sud.	settlement
Down / Eng.	hill
Drâa / Ar.	dunes, hills
Dracht / Germ.	sandbank
Draw / Eng.	ravine, valley
Drif / Afr.	ford
Drift / Afr.	ford
Droichead / Gae.	bridge
Droûs / Ar.	crest
Dry / Pash.	river
Dubh / Gae.	black
Dugi / S.C.	long
Dugu / Sud.	settlement
Dun / Gae.	castle
Duna / Sp.; It.	dune
Düne / Germ.	dune

Local Form	English
Dungar / Hin.	mountain
Düngar / Hin.	mountain
Duong / Viet.	stream
Durchbruch / Germ.	gorge
Ḍurg / Hin.	castle
-durga / Hin.	castle
Duży / Pol.	great
Dvor / Cz.	court
Dvorec / Rus.	castle
Dvůr / Cz.	castle
Dwór / Pol.	court
Džebel / Bulg.	mountain
Dzong / Tib.	fort, monastery

E

Local Form	English
Ea / Thai	river
Eau / Fr.	water
Ebe / Ban.	forest
Ebene / Germ.	plain
Eck / Germ.	point
Eclusa / Sp.	lock
Écluse / Fr.	lock
Écueil / Fr.	cliff
Edeien / Ber.	sand desert
Edjérir / Ber.	wadi
Egg / Germ.; Nor.	crest, point
Eglab / Ar.	hills
Ehi / Sah.	mountain
Eid / Nor.	isthmus
Eiland / Afr.	island
Eisen / Germ.	iron
Eisenerz / Germ.	iron ore
El / Amh.	well
Elv, -elv / Nor.	river
Embalse / Sp.	reservoir
Embouchure / Fr	mouth
Emi / Sah.	mountain
En / Fr.	in
Ende / Germ.	end
Enneri / Sah.	stream
Ennis / Gae.	island
Enseada / Port.	Bay, inlet
Ensenada / Sp.	bay, inlet
Ér / Hung.	stream
Erdö / Hung.	forest
Erg / Ar.	sand desert
Erz / Germ.	ore
Espigão / Port.	plateau
Ēstān / Pers.	land
Este / Sp.	east
Estero / Sp.	estuary, marsh
Estrecho / Sp.	strait
Estreito / Port.	strait
Estuaire / Fr.	estuary
Estuário / Port.	estuary
Estuario / Sp.; It.	estuary
Észak / Hung.	north
Étang / Fr.	pond
Ewaso / Ban.	river
Ey / Icel.	island
Eyja / Icel.	island
Eyjar / Icel.	islands
Eylandt / Dut.	island
Eżeras / Lith.	lake
Ezers / Latv.	lake

F

Local Form	English
Fa / Mel.	stream
Falaise / Fr.	cliff
Fall, -fall / Germ.; Eng.; Swed.	waterfall
Falls / Eng.	waterfall
Falu / Hung.	village
-falva / Hung.	village
Fan / Sah.	village
Faraglione / It.	cliff
Farallón / Sp.	cliff
Faro / Sp.; It.	lighthouse
Farvand / Dan.	strait
Fehér / Hung.	white
Fehn / Germ.	peat fen, peat-bog
Fekete / Hung.	black
Feld / Dan.; Germ.	field
Fell / Eng.	upland moor
Fell / Icel.	mountain
Fels / Germ.	rock
Fen / Eng.	marsh, peat-bog
Feng / Chin.	mountain, peak
Feste / Germ.	fort
Festung / Germ.	fort
Fier / Rom.	iron
Firn / Germ.	snow-field
Firth / Eng.	estuary, fjord
Fiume / It.	river
Fjäll / Swed.	mountain
Fjärd / Swed.	fjord
Fjell / Nor.	mountain
Fjöll / Icel.	mountain
Fjord, Fj. / Dan.; Nor.; Swed.	fjord
Fjörður / Icel.	fjord, bay
Fleuve / Fr.	river

Local Form	English
Fließ / Germ.	torrent
Fljót / Icel.	river
Flói / Icel.	bay, gulf
Floresta / Sp.; Port.	forest
Flow / Eng.	strait
Flughafen / Germ.	airport
Fluß / Germ.	river
Fo / Mel.	stream
Foa / Mel.	stream
Foa / Poly.	cove
Foce / It.	mouth
Föld / Hung.	plain
Fonn / Nor.	glacier
Fontaine / Fr.	fountain
Fonte / It.; Port.	spring
Fontein / Afr.; Dut.	spring
Foort / Afr.; Dut.	ford
Forca / It.	pass
Forcella / It.	defile
Ford / Rus.	fjord
Förde / Germ.	fjord, gulf
Foreland / Eng.	promontory
Foresta / It.	forest
Forêt / Fr.	forest
Fors / Swed.	rapids, waterfall
Forst / Germ.; Dut.	forest
Forte / It.; Port.	fort
Fortin / Sp.	fort
Fosa / Sp.	trench
Foss / Icel.; Nor.	rapids, waterfall
Fossé / Fr.	trench
Foum / Ar.	pass
Fourche / Fr.	pass
Foz / Sp.; Port.	mouth
Frei / Germ.	free
Fronteira / Port.	frontier
Frontera / Sp.	frontier
Frontón / Sp.	promontory
Fuente / Sp.	spring
Fuerte / Sp.	fort
Fuji / Jap.	mountain
Fülat / Ar.	marsh
Furt / Germ.	ford
Fushë / Alb.	plain

G

Local Form	English
G., Gora / Bulg.; Rus.; S.C.	mountain, hill
G., Gunung / Indon.	mountain
Ga / Jap.	bay
Ga / Mel.	mountain, peak
Gabel / Germ.	pass
Gaissa / Lapp.	mountain
Gala / Sin.; Tam.	mountain
Gam / Hin.; Urdu	village
Gamle / Nor.; Swed.	old
Gana / Sud.	little
Gang / Germ.	passage
Gang / Chin.	port, bay
Gang / Kor.	stream, bay
Gang / Tib.	glacier
Ganga / Hin.	river
Ganj / Hin.; Urdu	market
-gaon / Hin.	city, town
Gaoyuan / Chin.	plateau
Gap / Kor.	point
Gar / Hin.	house
Gara / Bulg.	station
Gara / Ar.	hills, range
Garā / Rom.	station
Garaet / Ar.	marsh, intermittent lake
Garam / Beng.; Hin.; Urdu	village
-gard / Pol.	city, town
Gård, -gård / Dan.; Nor.; Swed.	farmhouse
Gardaneh / Pers.	pass
Gare / Fr.	railway station
Garet / Ar.	hill
Garh, -garh / Hin.; Urdu	castle
Garhi / Hin.; Nep.; Urdu	fort
Garten / Germ.	garden
Gat / Dan.; Fle.; Dut.	strait
Gata / Jap.	bay, lake
Gau, -gau / Germ.	district
Gäu, -gäu / Germ.	district
Gavan / Rus.	port
Gave / Bas.	torrent
Gawa / Jap.	river
Geb., Gebirge / Germ.	mountain range
Gebergte / Afr.; Dut.	mountain range
Gebirge, Geb. / Germ.	mountain range
Geç., Geçit / Tur.	pass
Geçidi / Tur.	pass
Geçit, Geç. / Tur.	pass
Geysir / Icel.	geyser
Ghar / Hin.; Urdu	house
Ghar / Pash.	mountain, mountain range
Gharbīyah / Ar.	western
Ghat / Hin.; Nep.; Urdu	pass
Ghubbat / Ar.	bay
Ghurd / Ar.	dune
Gi / Kor.	peninsula
Giang / Viet.	stream
Giri / Hin.; Urdu	mountain, hill

Local Form	English
Girlo / Rus.	branch
Gjebel / Ar.	mountain
Gji / Alb	bay
Glace / Fr.	ice
Glaciar / Sp.	glacier
Glacier / Eng.; Fr.	glacier
Glen / Gae.	valley
Gletscher / Germ.	glacier
Gobi / Mong.	desert
Godär / Pers.	ford
Gok / Kor.	river
Gök / Tur.	blue
Gol / Cauc.; Mong.	river
Göl / Tur.	lake
Gola / It.	gorge
Gold / Germ.; Eng.	gold
Golet / S.C.	mountain
Golf / Germ.	gulf
Golfe / It.	gulf
Golfete / Sp.	inlet
Golfo / Sp.; It.; Port.	gulf
Goljam / Bulg.	great
Gölü / Tur.	lake
Gong / Tib.	high
Gonggar / Tib.	mountain
Gongo / Ban.	mountain
Góra / Pol.	mountain
Gora, G. / Bulg.; Rus.; S.C.	mountain, hill
Gorica / S.C.; Slvn.	hill
Gorje / S.C.	mountain range
Gorlo / Rus.	gorge
Gorm / Gae.	blue
Gorni / Bulg.; S.C.; Slvn.	upper
Gornji / S.C.; Slvn.	upper
Górny / Pol.	high
Gorod / Rus.	city, town
Gorodok / Rus.	village
Gorski / Bulg.	upper
Gory / Rus.	mountains
Goulbi / Sud.	river, lake
Goulbin / Sud.	wadi
Goulet / Fr.	gap
Gour / Ar.	hills, range
Gourou / Sud.	wadi
Goz / Sah.	dune
Graafschap / Dut.	county, shire
Graben / Germ.	ditch, canal
Gracht / Dut.	canal
Grad, -grad / Bulg.; Rus.; S.C.; Slvn.	city, town, castle
Gradac / S.C.	castle
Gradec / Bulg.	village
Gradec / Slvn.	castle
Græn / Icel.	green
Gran / Sp.; It.	great
Grande / Sp.; It.; Port.	great
Grao / Cat.; Sp.	gap
Grat / Germ.	crest
Grève / Fr.	beach
Grind / Germ.	peak
Grjada / Rus.	range
Gród, -gród / Pol.	castle, city, town
Grön / Icel.	green
Grond / Afr.	soil
Gronden / Dut.; Fle.	flat
Groot / Afr.; Dut.; Fle.	great
Groß / Germ.	great
Grotta / It.	grotto
Grotte / Fr.; Germ.	grotto
Grube / Germ.	mine
Grün / Germ.	green
Grunn / Nor.	ground
Gruppe / Germ.	mountain system
Gruppo / It.	mountain system
Gua / Mal.	cave
Guaçu / A.I.	great
Guan / Chin.	pass
Guazú / A.I.	great
Guba / Rus.	bay
Guchi / Jap.	strait
Guelb / Ar.	hill, mountain
Guelta / Ar.	well
Guic / Br.	village
Güney / Tur.	south, southern
Gunong / Mal.	mountain
Guntô / Jap.	archipelago
Gunung, G. / Indon.	mountain
Guo / Chin.	state, land
Gur / Rom.	mountain
Guri / Jap.	cliff
Gurud / Ar.	hills, dunes
Gyár / Hung.	factory

H

Local Form	English
Haag / Dut.; Fle.	hedge
-hâb / Dan.	port
Haḍabat / Ar.	highland
Hadd / Ar.	point
Hadjer / Ar.	hill, mountain
Hae / Kor.	bay, sea
Haehyeop / Kor.	strait

Geographical Glossary

Local Form	English	Local Form	English	Local Form	English	Local Form	English
Haf / Icel.	sea	Hora / Cz.; Slvk.	point	Jazā'ir / Ar.	islands	Kaupstadur / Icel.	city, town
Ḩafar / Ar.	well	Horn / Eng.; Germ.; Icel.; Nor.; Swed.	point	Jazīrat, J. / Ar.	island	Kaupunki / Finn.	city, town
Hafen / Germ.	port	Horni / Cz.	high	Jazovir / Bulg.	reservoir	Kavīr / Pers.	salt desert
Haff / Germ.	lagoon	Horný / Slvk.	upper	Jbel / Ar.	mountain	Kawa / Jap.	river
Hafir / Ar.	spring, ditch	Horst / Germ.	mountain	Jebel / Ar.	mountain	Kawm / Ar.	hill
Hafnar / Icel.	port	Horvot / Hebr.	ruins	Jedid / Ar.	new	Kebir / Ar.	great
Ḩāfūn / Som.	bay	Hory / Cz.; Slvk.	mountain range	Jedo / Kor.	archipelago	Kedi / Georg.	mountain range
Hage / Dan.	point	Hout / Dut.; Fle.	forest	Jezero / S.C.; Slvn.	lake	Kédia / Ar.	mountain, plateau
Hage / Dut.; Fle.	hedge	Hovd, -hovd / Dan.; Nor.	cape	Jezioro / Pol.	lake	Kedim / Ar.	old
Hågna / Swed.	peak	Ḩowz / Pers.	basin	Jhil / Hin.; Urdu	lake	Kef / Ar.	mountain
Hai / Chin.	sea, lake, bay	Hrad / Cz.; Slvk.	castle, city, town	Jian / Chin.	mountain	Kefála / Gr.	mountain, peak
Hain / Germ.	forest	Hradiště / Cz.	citadel	Jiao / Chin.	cape, cliff	Kefar / Hebr.	village
Haixia / Chin.	strait	Hřeben / Cz.	crest	Jibāl / Ar.	mountain	Kei / Jap.	river
Ḩajar / Ar.	hill, mountain	Hrebet / Rus.	mountain range	Jih / Cz.	south	Kelet / Hung.	east
Hajar / Ar.	hill country	Hu / Rmsh.	lake	Jima / Jap.	island	Ken / Gae.	cape
Halbinsel / Germ.	peninsula	Huang / Chin.	yellow	Jin / Kor.	cove	Kent / Alt.; Iran.; Tur.	city, town
Halma / Hung.	hill	Hude / Germ.	pasture	Jing / Chin.	spring	Kenya / Swa.	fog
Halom / Hung.	hill	Huerta / Sp.	market garden	Jisr / Ar.	bridge	Kep / Alb.	cape
Halq / Ar.	gap	Hügel / Germ.	hill	Joch / Germ.	pass	Kep., Kepulauan / Mal.	archipelago
Hals / Nor.	peninsula	Hügelland / Germ.	hill country	Jõgi / Est.	river	Kepulauan, Kep. / Mal.	archipelago
Halvø / Dan.	peninsula	Huis, -huis / Afr.; Dut.; Fle.	house	Jøkel / Nor.	glacier	Kereszt / Hung.	cross
Halvøy / Nor.	peninsula	Huisie / Afr.	house	Joki / Finn.	river	Kerk / Dut.; Fle.	church
Hama / Jap.	beach	Huizen, -huizen / Dut.	houses	Jokka / Lapp.	river	Keski / Finn.	middle
Hamāda / Ar.	rocky desert	Huk / Afr.; Dan.; Swed.	cape	Jökull / Icel.	glacier	Kette / Germ.	mountain range
Ḩamādah / Ar.	plateau	Hum / S.C.	hill	Jord, -jord / Nor.	earth	Keur / Sud.	village
Ḩamādat / Ar.	plateau	Hurst / Eng.	grove	Ju / Ural.	river	Key / Eng.	coral island
Hammam / Ar.	thermal springs	Hus / Dut.; Nor.; Swed.	house	Judeţ / Rom.	district	Kha / Tib.	valley
Ḩammām / Ar.	well	Huta / Pol.; Slvk.	hut	Jugan / Ural.	river	Khal / Hin.	canal
Hamn / Nor.; Swed.	port	Hütte / Germ.	hut	Jura / Lith.	sea	Khalīj / Ar.	gulf
Hamrā' / Ar.	red	Hver / Icel.	crater	Jūra / Latv.	sea	Khand / Hin.	district
Hāmūn / Jap.	salt lake	Hvit / Icel.	white	Jūras Līcis / Latv.	bay	Khao / Thai	hill, mountain
Hana / Jap.	cape	Hvost / Rus.	spit	Jūrmala / Latv.	beach	Kharābeh / Pers.	ruins
Hana / Poly.	bay			Jurt / Cauc.	village	Khashm / Ar.	promontory
Hane / Tur.	house	**I**		Južni / Bulg.; S.C.; Slvn.	southern	Khatt / Ar.	wadi
Hang / Kor.	port	I., Island / Eng.	island	Južny / Rus.	southern	Khawr / Ar.	mouth, bay
Hank / Ar.	escarpment, plateau	Ierós / Gr.	holy	Juzur / Ar.	islands	Khazzān / Ar.	dam
Hantō / Jap.	peninsula	Igarapé / A.I.	river			Khemis / Ar.	fifth
Har / Hebr.	mountain	Ighazer / Ber.	torrent	**K**		Khersónisos / Gr.	peninsula
Hara / Mong.	black	Ighil / Ber.	hill	Ka / Poly.	lake	Khirbat / Ar.	ruins
Harar / Swa.	well	Iguidi / Ber.	dunes	Kaap / Afr.	cape	Khlong / Thai	stream, mouth
Ḩarrah / Ar.	lava field	Ih / Mong.	great	Kabīr / Ar.	great	Khokhok / Thai	isthmus
Ḩarrat / Ar.	lava field	Ike / Jap.	pond	Kae / Kor.	inlet	Khor / Ar.	mouth, bay
Hasi / Ar.	well	Ile / Fr.	island	Kāf / Ar.	peak, mountain	Khóra / Gr.	land
Ḩasi / Ar.	well	Ilha / Port.	island	Kafr / Ar.	village	Khorion / Gr.	village
Hassi / Ar.	well	Iller / Tur.	administrative division	Kaga / Ban.	hills, mountain range	Khowr / Pers.	bay
Ḩasy / Ar.	well	Ilot / Fr.	islet	Kahal / Ar.	plateau, escarpment	Khrisós / Gr.	gold
Haug / Nor.	hill	Imi / Ar.	spring	Kai / Jap.	sea	Ki- / Ban.	little
Haupt- / Germ.	principal	I-n / Ber.	well	Kaikyō / Jap.	strait	Kibali / Sud.	river
Haure / Lapp.	lake	Inch / Gae.	island	Kaise / Lapp.	mountain	Kil / Gae.	church
Haus / Germ.	house	Inder / Dan.; Nor.	inner	Kal / Pers.	stream	Kilde / Dan.	spring
Hausen / Germ.	village	Indre / Nor.	inner	Kala / Az.; Kor.	fort	Kilima / Swa.	mountain
Haut / Fr.	high	Inferiore / It.	lower	Kala / Finn.	river	Kill / Gae.	strait
Hauteur / Fr.	hill	Inish / Gae.	island	Kala / Hin.	black	Kilwa / Ban.	lake
Hauts Plateaux / Fr.	highlands	Insel / Germ.	island	Kala / Tur.	castle	Kin / Gae.	cape
Hauz / Pers.	reservoir	Insulă / Rom.	island	Kalaa / Ar.	castle	Kinn / Nor.	cape, point
Hav / Dan.; Nor.; Swed.	sea, gulf	Inver / Gae.	mouth	Kalaki / Georg.	city, town	Kirche / Germ.	church
Haven / Eng.; Fle.; Dut.	port	Irhazér / Ber.	wadi	Kale / Tur.	castle	Kirk / Eng.	church
Havn / Dan.; Nor.	port	Irmak / Tur.	river	Kali / Hin.	black	Kis / Hung.	little
Havre / Fr.	port	'Irq / Ar.	dunes	Kali / Indon.; Mal.	bay, river	Kisiwa / Swa.	island
Hawr / Ar.	lake, marsh	Is / Nor.	glacier	Kallio / Finn.	rock	Kita / Jap.	north, northern
Ház / Hung.	house	Ís / Icel.	ice	Kaln / Latv.	mountain	Kızıl / Tur.	red
-háza / Hung.	house	Isblink / Dan.	glacier	Kalós / Gr.	beautiful, good	Klein / Afr.; Dut.; Germ.	little
Hazm / Ar.	height, mountain range	Ishi / Jap.	rock	Kamen / Bulg.; Rus.; S.C.; Slvn.	mountain, peak	Kliff / Afr.	cliff
He / Chin.	river	Iske / Alt.	old	Kámen / Cz.	rock	Klint / Dan.	reef
Head / Eng.	headland	Isla / Sp.	island	Kameň / Slvk.	rock	Klip / Afr.; Dut.	rock, cliff
Hed / Dan.; Swed.	heath	Iso / Finn.	great	Kami / Jap.	upper	Klit / Dan.	dune
Hegy / Hung.	mountain	Iso / Jap.	cliff	Kamień / Pol.	rock	Kloof / Afr.; Dut.	gorge
Hegység / Hung.	mountain	Isola / It.	island	Kamm / Germ.	crest	Kloster / Dan.; Germ.; Nor.; Swed.	convent
Hei / Nor.	heath	Isthmós / Gr.	isthmus	Kamp / Germ.	field	Knob / Eng.	mountain
Heide / Germ.	heath	Istmo / Sp.; It.	isthmus	Kâmpóng / Khm.	village	Knock / Gae.	mountain, hill
Heijde / Dut.; Fle.	heath	Ita / A.I.	stone	Kámpos / Gr.	field	Ko / Jap.	bay, lake, little
Heilig / Germ.	saint	Itä / Finn.	east	Kampung / Indon.; Mal.	village	Ko / Sud.	stream
Heim, -heim / Germ.; Nor.	house	Itivdleq / Esk.	isthmus	Kan., Kanal / Alb.; Dan.; Germ.; Nor.; Rus.; S.C.; Slvn.; Swed.; Tur.	canal, channel	Ko / Thai	island, point
Heiya / Jap.	plain	Iwa / Jap.	rock, cliff	Kanaal / Dut.; Fle.	canal	Købing / Dan.	town
-hely / Hung.	locality	Iztočni / Bulg.	eastern	Kanal / Pol.	canal	Kogel / Germ.	dome
Hem / Swed.	home	Izvor / Bulg.; Rom.; S.C.; Slvn.	spring	Kanal, Kan. / Alb.; Dan.; Germ.; Nor.; Rus.; S.C.; Slvn.; Swed.	canal, channel	Kōgen / Jap.	plateau
Hen / Br.	old			Kand, -kand / Pers.; Tur.	city, town	Koh / Hin.; Pers.	mountain, mountain range
Higashi / Jap.	east, eastern	**J**		Kang / Chin.; Kor.	bay, river	Kol / Alt.	river, valley
Hima / Hin.	ice	J., Jazirat / Ar.	island	Kangas / Fle.	heath	Kol / Alt.; Tur.	lake
Himal / Nep.	peak	J., Jiang / Chin.	river	Kange / Esk.	east	Koll / Nor.	peak
Hisar / Tur.	castle	Jabal / Ar.	mountain	Kangri / Tib.	snow-capped mountain	Kólpos / Gr.	gulf
Ho / Chin.	reservoir, river	Jaha / Ural.	river	Kantara / Ar.	bridge	Kong / Dan.; Nor.; Swed.	king
Ho / Kor.	river, reservoir	Jam / Ural.	lake, river	Kaôh / Khm.	island	Kong / Indon.; Mal.	mountain
Hō / Jap.	mountain	Jama / Rus.	cave	Kap / Dan.; Germ.	cape	Kong / Viet.	mountain, hill
Hoch / Germ.	high, upper	Jan / Alt.	great	Kapija / S.C.	gate, gorge	Konge / Ban.	river
Hochland / Germ.	highland	Janga / Tur.	north	Kapp / Nor.	cape	König / Germ.	king
Hochplato / Afr.	highland	Jangi / Alt.; Iran.	new	Kar / Tib.	white	Koog / Germ.	polder
Hodna / Afr.	highland	Janūbiyah / Ar.	southern	Kar / Ural.	city, town	Kop / Afr.	hill
Hoek / Dut.; Fle.	cape	Jar / Rus.	bank	Kara / Tur.	black	Kopec / Cz.; Slvk.	hill
Hof / Dut.; Germ.	court	Järv / Est.	lake	Karang / Indon.; Mal.	sandbank, cliff	Kopf / Germ.	peak
Höfn / Icel.	port	Järve / Finn.	lake	Kari / Finn.	cliff	Köping / Swed.	town
Høg / Nor.	peak	Järvi / Finn.	lake	Kariba / Ban.	gorge	Köprü / Tur.	bridge
Hög / Swed.	mountain	Jasiréd / Som.	island	Kariet / Ar.	village	Körfezi / Tur.	gulf
Hogna / Nor.	peak	Jaun / Latv.	new	Karki / Finn.	peninsula	Korfi / Tur.	rock
Höhe / Germ.	peak	Jaur / Lapp.	lake	Kastel / Germ.	castle	Koro / Mel.	mountain, island
Høj / Dan.	hill	Jaure / Lapp.	lake	Kástron / Gr.	fort, city, town	Koro / Sud.	old
Hoj / Ural.	mountain range	Javr / Lapp.	lake	Káto / Gr.	lower	Koru / Jap.	forest
Hok / Jap.	north	Javrre / Lapp.	lake			Kosa / Rus.	spit
Hoku / Jap.	north, northern					Koška / Rus.	cliff
Holm / Dan.; Nor.; Swed.	island					Koski / Finn.	rapids
Holz / Germ.	forest					Kosui / Jap.	lake
Hon / Viet.	island, point					Kot / Urdu	castle
Hong / Chin.; Viet.	red					Kota / Mal.	city, town
Hono / Poly.	bay, anchorage					Kotal / Pash.; Pers.	pass
Hoog / Afr.; Dut.; Fle.	high					Kotar / S.C.	cultivated area
Hook / Eng.	point					Kotlina / Pol.	basin
Hoorn / Afr.; Dut.; Fle.	cape, point						

Local Form	English
Kotlovina / Rus.	basin, plain
Kou / Chin.	mouth, pass
Kourou / Sud.	well
Kowr / Pers.	river
Kowtal / Pers.	pass
Koy / Tur.	bay
Köy / Tur.	village
Kraal / Afr.	village
Kraina / Pol.	land
Kraj / Rus.; S.C.	land
Kraj / Rus.	administrative division
Krajina / S.C.	land
Krak / Ar.	hill, castle
Krans / Afr.	mountain
Kras / S.C.; Slvn.	karst landscape
Krasny / Rus.	red
Kreb / Ar.	hills, mountain range
Kriaž / Ar.	mountain range
Krš / S.C.	karst area, limestone area
Krung / Thai	city, town
Ksar / Ar.	castle
Ksour / Ar.	fortified village
Ku- / Ban.	river branch
Kuala / Mal.	river, mouth
Kubra / Ar.	bridge
Küçük / Tur.	little
Kuduk / Tur.	spring
Küh / Pers.	mountain
Kūhhā / Pers.	mountain range
Kul / Alt.; Iran.; Tur.	lake
Kulam, -kulam / Hin.; Tam.	pond
Kulle / Swed.	hill
Kulm / Germ.	peak
Kultuk / Rus.	bay
Kum / Tur.	dunes, sand desert
Kuppe / Germ.	dome, seamount
Kurayb / Ar.	hill
Kurgan / Alt.	hill
Kurgan / Tur.	fort
Kuro / Jap.	black
Kurort / Bulg.; Germ.; Rus.	spa
Kust / Dut.; Fle.	coast
Kust- / Swed.	coast
Küste / Germ.	coast
Kút / Hung.	spring
Kuyu / Tur.	spring
Kvemo / Georg.	low, lower
Kwa / Ban.	village
Kylä / Finn.	village
Kyle / Gae.	strait, channel
Kyō / Jap.	strait
Kyrka / Swed.	church
Kyst / Dan.; Nor.	coast
Kyun / Burm.	island
Kyūryō / Jap.	hills, mountains
Kyzyl / Tur.	red
Kzyl / Tur.	red

L

Local Form	English
L., Lake, Lago / Eng.; It.; Port.; Sp.	lake
La / Tib.	pass
Laagte / Afr.	stream, valley
Labuan / Indon.; Mal.	bay, port
Lac / Fr.	lake
Lach / Som.	stream, wadi
Lacul / Rom.	lake
Lae / Poly.	cape, point
Laem / Thai	bay, port
Låg / Nor.; Swed.	low, lower
Lag / Swed.	stream, wadi
Läge / Swed.	beach
Lagh / Som.	stream, wadi
Lago, L. / It.; Port.; Sp.	lake
Lagoa / Port.	lagoon
Laguna / Alb.; It.; Rus.; Sp.	lagoon, lake
Lagune / Fr.	lagoon
Laht / Est.	bay
Lahti / Finn.	bay, gulf
Laks / Finn.	bay
Lalla / Ar.	saint
Lampi / Finn.	pond
Lande / Fr.	heath
Lang / Afr.; Dut.; Germ.	long
Lang / Viet.	village
Lao / Chin.	old
Lapa / Poly.	mountain range, peak
Largo / Port.; Sp.	basin
Las / Pol.	forest
Las, Läs / Som.	well
Laut / Mal.	sea
Law / Gae.	hill, mountain
Lázně / Cz.	thermal springs
Lednik / Rus.	glacier
Leite / Germ.	coast
Lekh / Nep.	mountain range

Local Form	English
Les / Bulg.; Cz.; Rus.; Slvk.	forest
Leso / Rus.	forested
Levante / It.; Sp.	eastern
Levkós / Gr.	white
Levy / Rus.	left
Lha / Tib.	temple
Lhari / Hin.; Nep.	mountain
Lho / Tib.	south
Lido / It.	sandbar
Liedao / Chin.	archipelago
Liehtao / Chin.	archipelago
Liels / Latv.	great
Lilla / Swed.	little
Lille / Dan.; Nor.	little
Liman / Alb.; Rus.; Tur.	lagoon, bay
Liman / Tur.	bay, port
Limin / Gr.	port
Limni / Gr.	lake
Ling / Chin.	mountain range, peak
Linna / Finn.	castle
Liqen / Alb.	lake
Lithos / Gr.	stone
Litoral / Port.; Sp.	littoral
Litorale / It.	littoral
Llan / Wel.	church
Llano / Sp.	plain
Llanura / Sp.	plain
Lo- / Ban.	river
Loch / Gae.	lake, inlet
Loch / Germ.	grotto
Loka / Slvn.	forest
Loma / Sp.	hill
Long / Indon.	stream
Loo / Dut.; Fle.	clearing
Lough / Gae.	lake
Loutrá / Gr.	thermal springs
Ložbina / Rus.	depression
Lu- / Ban.	river
Lua / Ban.	river
Lua / Mel.	island, reef
Lua / Poly.	crater
Luang / Thai	yellow
Luch / Germ.	peat-bog
Lücke / Germ.	pass
Lug / Rus.	meadow
Luka / S.C.; Slvn	port
Lule / Lapp.	east, eastern
Lum / Alb.	river
Lund / Dan.; Swed.	forest
Lung / Rom.	long
Lung / Tib.	valley
Luoto / Finn.	shoal
Lurg / Pers.	salt flat
Lut / Pers.	desert

M

Local Form	English
M., Monte / It.; Port.; Sp.	mountain
Ma / Ar.	water
Ma- / Ban.	people
Maa / Est.; Finn.	island, land
Ma'arrat / Ar.	height
Machi / Jap.	district
Macizo / Sp.	massif
Madhya / Hin.	central
Madīnah / Ar.	city, town
Mado / Swa.	well
Madu / Tam.	pond
Mae / Thai	stream
Mae nam / Thai	stream, mouth
Magh / Gae.	plain
Mägi / Est.	mountain
Măgura / Rom.	height
Mahā / Hin.	great
Mahal / Hin.; Urdu	palace
Mai / Amh.; Ban.	stream
Majdan / S.C.	quarry
Mäki / Finn.	mountain, hill
Makrós / Gr.	long
Mala / Hin.; Tam.	mountain
Malai / Hin.; Tam.	mountain
Malal / A.I.	fence
Malhão / Port.	dome
Mali / Alb.	mountain
Mali / S.C.; Slvn.	little
Malki / Bulg.	little
Malla / Tam.	mountain
Maly / Rus.	little
Malý / Cz.; Slvk.	little
Mały / Pol.	little
Man / Kor.	bay
Manastir / Bulg.; S.C.	monastery
Manche / Fr.	channel
Mar / It.; Port.; Sp.	sea
Mar / Tib.	red
Mar / Ural.	city, town
Marais / Fr.	marsh
Marché / Fr.	market
Mare / Fr.	pond
Mare / It.; Rom.	sea
Mare / Rom.	great
Marea / Rom.	sea
Marécage / Fr.	marsh
Marios / Lith.	reservoir

Local Form	English
Marisma / Sp.	marsh
Mark / Dan.; Nor.; Swed.	land
Markt / Germ.	market
Marsa / Ar.	anchorage, bay
Marsch / Germ.	marsh
Maru / Jap.	mountain
Mas / Prov.	farmhouse
Maşabb / Ar.	mouth
Mashra' / Ar.	landing, pier
Masívul / Rom.	massif
Massiv / Germ.; Rus.	massif
Mata / Poly.	point
Mata / Port.; Sp.	forest
Mata / Som.	waterfall
Mato / Port.; Sp.	forest
Matsu / Jap.	point
Mauna / Poly.	mountain
Mávros / Gr.	black
Mayo / Sud.	river
Maza / Lith.	little
Mazar / Pers.; Tur.	sanctuary
Mazs / Latv.	little
Me / Khm.	river
Me / Mel.	hill, mountain
Me / Thai	great
Medina / Ar.	city, town
Medjez / Ar.	ford
Meer / Dut.; Fle.	lake
Meer / Germ.	lake, sea
Megálos / Gr.	great
Mégas / Gr.	great
Megye / Hung.	district
Mélas / Gr.	black
Melkosopočnik / Rus.	hill country
Mellan / Swed.	central
Men / Chin.	gate, channel
Ménez / Br.	mountain
Menzel / Ar.	bivouac
Meos / Indon.	island
Mer / Fr.	sea
Mercato / It.	market
Merdja / Ar.	lagoon, marsh
Meri / Est.; Finn.	sea
Meridional / Rom.; Sp.	southern
Merin / A.I.	little
Merja / Ar.	lagoon, marsh
Mers / Ar.	port
Mersa / Ar.	port
Mesa / Sp.	mesa, tableland
Meseta / Sp.	plateau
Mésos / Gr.	central
Mesto / Bulg.; S.C.; Slvk.; Slvn.	city, town
Město / Cz.	city, town
Mestre / Port.	principal
Meydan / Tur.	square
Mezad / Hebr.	castle
Mező / Hung.	field
Mgne., Montagne / Fr.	mountain
Mgnes., Montagnes / Fr.	mountains
Miao / Chin.	temple
Miasto / Pol.	city, town
Mic / Rom.	little
Middel / Afr.; Dut.; Fle.	middle
Midi / Fr.	noon, south
Między / Pol.	central
Miedzyrzecze / Pol.	interfluve
Mierzeja / Pol.	sand spit
Mifraz / Hebr.	bay, gulf
Miftah / Ar.	gorge
Mikrós / Gr.	little
Mina / Port.; Sp.	mine
Mīnā' / Ar.	port
Minami / Jap.	south, southern
Minamoto / Jap.	spring
Minato / Jap.	port
Mine / Jap.	peak
Mirim / A.I.	little
Misaki / Jap.	cape
Mittel- / Germ.	middle
Mo / Chin.	sand desert
Mo / Nor.; Swed.	heath
Moana / Poly.	lake
Mogila / Bulg.; Rus.	hill
Moku / Poly.	island
Mølle / Dan.	mill
Monasterio / Sp.	monastery
Mond / Afr.; Dut.; Fle.	mouth
Mong / Burm.; Thai; Viet.	city, town
Moni / Gr.	monastery
Mont / Cat.; Fr.	mountain
Montagna / It.	mountain
Montagne, Mgne. / Fr.	mountain
Montagnes, Mgnes. / Fr.	mountains
Montaña / Sp.	mountain
Monte, M. / It.; Port.; Sp.	mountain
Monts, Mts. / Fr.	mountains
Moos / Germ.	moor
Mór / Gae.	great
More / Bulg.; Rus.; S.C.	sea
More / Gae.	great
Mori / Jap.	mountain, forest
Morne / Fr.	mountain
Moron / Mong.	river
Morro / Port.; Germ.	hill, peak
Morrón / Sp.	mountain
Morze / Pol.	sea

Local Form	English
Most / Bulg.; Cz.; Pol.; Rus.; S.C.; Slvn.	bridge
Moto / Jap.	spring
Motte / Fr.	hill
Motu / Mel.; Poly.	island, rock
Moutier / Fr.	monastery
Movilă / Rom.	hill
Moyen / Fr.	central
Mta / Georg.	mountain
Mts., Monts, Mountains / Eng.; Fr.	mountains
Muang / Laot.; Thai	city, town, land
Muara / Indon.; Mal.	mouth
Muela / Sp.	mountain
Mühle / Germ.	mill
Mui / Mel.	point
Mui / Viet.	point, cape
Muiden / Dut.; Fle.	mouth
Muir / Gae.	sea
Mukh / Hin.	mouth
Mull / Gae.	promontory
Münde / Germ.	mouth
Mündung / Germ.	mouth
Municipiul / Rom.	commune
Munkhafaḍ / Ar.	depression
Münster / Germ.	monastery
Munte / Rom	mountain
Muntele / Rom.	mountain
Munții / Rom.	mountain range
Muren / Mong.	river
Mushāsh / Ar.	spring
Muz / Tur.	ice
Muztagh / Tur.	snow-capped mountain
Mwambo / Ban.	rock, cliff
Myit / Burm.	stream
Mynydd / Wel.	mountain
Myo / Burm.	city, town
Mýri / Icel.	marsh
Mys / Rus.	cape

N

Local Form	English
Na / Cz.; Pol.; Rus.; S.C.; Slvn.	on
Nab / Ar.	spring
Nad / Cz.; Pol.; Rus.	on
Nada / Jap.	bay, sea
Nadi, -nadi / Hin.; Urdu	river
Næs / Dan.	point
Nafūd / Ar.	dunes
Nag / Tib.	black
Nagar, -nagar / Hin.; Tib.	city, town
Nagaram / Hin.; Tam.	city, town
Nagorje / Rus.	plateau, mountains
Nagy / Hung.	great
Nahr / Ar.	river
Naikai / Jap.	sea
Naka / Jap.	central
Nakhon / Thai	city, town
Nam / Burm.; Laot.; Thai	river
Nam / Kor.	south
Namakzar / Pers.	salt desert
Nan / Chin.	south
Narrows / Eng.	strait
Narssaq / Esk.	plain, valley
Näs / Swed.	cape
Nationalpark / Swed.; Germ.	national park
Nau / Lith.	new
Nauja / Lith.	new
Navolok / Rus.	cape, promontory
Ne / Jap.	cliff
Neder / Fle.; Dut.	low
Neem / Est.	cape
Negro / Port.; Sp.	black
Negru / Rom.	black
Nehir / Tur.	river
Nei / Chin.	inner
Nene, -nene / Ban.	great
Néos / Gr.	new
Nero / It.	black
Nes / Icel.; Nor.	cape
Ness / Gae.	promontory
Neu / Germ.	new
Neuf / Fr.	new
Nevado / Sp.	snow-capped mountain
Nez / Fr.	cape
Ngok / Viet.	mountain, peak
Ngolo / Ber.	great
Ni / Kor.	village
Niecka / Pol.	basin
Niemi / Finn.	peninsula
Nieuw / Fle.; Dut.	new
Nij / Dut.	new
Nil / Hin.	blue
Nishi / Jap.	west
Niski / Pol.	lower
Nisko / S.C.	low
Nisoi / Gr.	islands
Nisos / Gr.	island
Nizina / Pol.	lowland
Nižina / Cz.	depression
Nizký / Cz.	low, lower

Geographical Glossary

Local Form	English
Nizmennost / *Rus.*	lowland, depression
Nižni / *Rus.*	low, lower
Nižný / *Slvk.*	low, lower
No / *Mel.*	stream
Nock / *Gae.*	ridge
Noir / *Fr.*	black
Non / *Thai*	hill
Nong / *Thai*	lake, marsh
Noord / *Afr.; Fle.; Dut.*	north
Noordoost / *Afr.; Fle.; Dut.*	northeast
Nor / *Arm.*	new
Nord / *Fr.; It.; Germ.*	north
Nördlich / *Germ.*	northern
Nørdre / *Dan.; Nor.*	northern
Norra / *Swed.*	northern
Nørre / *Dan.*	northern
Norte / *Sp.*	north
Nos / *Bulg.; Rus.; S.C.; Slvn.*	cape
Nosy / *Malag.*	island
Nótios / *Gr.*	southern
Nou / *Rom.*	new
Novi / *Bulg.; S.C.; Slvn.*	new
Novo / *Port.*	new
Novy / *Rus.*	new
Nový / *Cz.; Slvk.*	new
Now / *Pers.*	new
Nowy / *Pol.*	new
Nudo / *Sp.*	mountain
Nuevo / *Sp.*	new
Nui / *Viet.*	mountain
Numa / *Jap.*	marsh, lake
Nummi / *Finn.*	heath
Nunatak / *Esk.*	peak
Nuovo / *It.*	new
Nur / *Chin.*	lake
Nusa / *Mal.*	island
Nut, -nut / *Nor.*	peak
Nuwara / *Sin.; Tam.*	city, town
Nuwe / *Afr.*	new
Nyanza / *Ban.*	water, river, lake
Nyasa / *Ban.*	lake
Nyeong / *Kor.*	pass
Nyika / *Ban.*	upland
Nyŏng / *Kor.*	mount, pass
Nyugat / *Hung.*	west

O

Local Form	English
Ō / *Jap.*	great
Ó / *Hung.*	old
Ö / *Swed.*	island
Ø, -ø / *Dan.; Nor.*	island
Öar / *Swed.*	islands
Ober / *Germ.*	upper
Oblast / *Rus.*	province
Obo / *Mong.*	mountain, hill
Occidental / *Fr.; Rom.; Sp.*	western
Océan / *Fr.*	ocean
Océano / *Sp.*	ocean
Oceano / *It.; Port.*	ocean
Ocnă / *Rom.*	salt mine
Odde / *Dan.; Nor.*	promontory
Oeste / *Port.; Sp.*	west
Oever / *Fle.; Dut.*	bank
Oewer / *Afr.*	bank
Oie / *Germ.*	islet
Ojos / *Sp.*	spring
Oka / *Jap.*	coast
Oke / *Sud.*	height
Okean / *Rus.*	ocean
Oki / *Jap.*	bay
Okrug / *Rus.*	district
Ola / *Alt.*	city, town
Omuramba / *K.S.*	stream
Onder / *Afr.*	under
Oni / *Malag.*	river
Oos / *Afr.*	east
Oost / *Fle.; Dut.*	east
Oostelijk / *Dut.*	eastern
Opatija / *Slvn.*	abbey
Or / *Fr.*	gold
Oraş / *Rom.*	city, town
Óri / *Gr.*	mountains
Oriental / *Fr.; Port.; Rom.; Sp.*	eastern
Orientale / *It.*	eastern
Orilla / *Sp.*	bank
Órmos / *Gr.*	bay
Óros / *Gr.*	mountain
Ország / *Hung.*	land
Ort / *Germ.*	cape
Orta / *Tur.*	central
Orto / *Alt.*	central
Oseaan / *Afr.*	ocean
Ōshima / *Jap.*	large island
Ost / *Dan.; Germ.*	east
Öst / *Swed.*	east
Ostān, -ostān / *Pers.*	province
Øster / *Dan.; Nor.*	east, eastern
Öster / *Swed.*	east, eastern
Östlich / *Germ.*	eastern
Ostrog / *Rus.*	castle
Ostrov / *Rus.*	island
Ostrovul / *Rom.*	island
Ostrów / *Pol.*	island
Ostrvo / *S.C.*	island
Otok / *S.C.; Slvn.*	island
Otrog / *Rus.*	front range (mountains)
Oua / *Mel.*	stream
Ouar / *Ar.*	rocky desert
Oud / *Fle.; Dut.*	old
Oued / *Ar.*	wadi
Ouest / *Fr.*	west
Ouled / *Ar.*	son
Oum / *Ar.*	mother
Ouro / *Port.*	gold
Outu / *Poly.*	cape
Ova / *Ban.*	people
Ova / *Tur.*	plain
Ovasi / *Tur.*	plain
Øver / *Nor.*	over
Över / *Swed.*	over
Övre / *Swed.*	over
Øy / *Dan.; Nor.*	island
oz., Ozero / *Rus.*	lake
Ozek / *Alt.*	hollow
Ozera / *Rus.*	lakes
Ozero, oz. / *Rus.*	lake

P

Local Form	English
P., Pulau / *Mal.; Indon.*	island
Pää / *Finn.*	principal
Pad / *Rus.*	valley
Padang / *Indon.*	plain
Padiş / *Rom.*	upland
Padół / *Pol.*	valley
Pădure / *Rom.*	forest
Pahorek / *Cz.*	hill
Pahorkatina / *Cz.*	plateau, hills
Pais / *Port.; Sp.*	land, country
Pak / *Thai*	mouth
Pala / *It.*	peak
Palaiós / *Gr.*	old
Palanka / *S.C.*	village
Pali / *Poly.*	cliff
-palli / *Hin.*	village
Pampa / *Sp.*	plain, prairie
Panda / *Swa.*	junction
Panev / *Cz.*	basin
Pantanal / *Sp.*	swamp
Pantano / *Sp.*	swamp, lake
Pao / *Mel.*	hill
Pará / *A.I.*	river
Paramera / *Sp.*	desert highland
Páramo / *Sp.*	moor
Paranā / *A.I.*	river
Parbat / *Hin.; Urdu*	mountain
Parc / *Fr.*	park
Parco / *It.*	park
Parco Nazionale / *It.*	national park
Pardo / *Port.*	grey
Parque / *Sp.*	park
Parque Nacional / *Sp.; Port.*	national park
Pas / *Fr.; Rom.*	pass, strait
Pasaje / *Sp.*	passage
Pasir / *Mal.*	sand, beach
Paso / *Sp.*	pass
Passágem / *Port.*	passage
Passe / *Fr.*	pass
Passo / *It.; Port.*	pass
Pasul / *Rom.*	pass
Patak / *Hung.*	stream
Patam, -patam / *Hin.*	city, town
Patnā / *Hin.*	city, town
Patnam, -patnam / *Hin.*	city, town
Pattinam, -pattinam / *Hin.*	city, town
Pays / *Fr.*	land, country
Pazar / *Tur.*	market
Pea / *Est.*	cape
Pech / *Cat.*	hill
Pedhiás / *Gr.*	plain
Pedra / *Port.*	rock, mountain
Peg., Pegunungan / *Mal.; Indon.*	mountain range
Pegunungan, Peg. / *Mal.; Indon.*	mountain range
Pélagos / *Gr.*	sea
Pele / *Poly.*	peak, hill
Pen / *Br.*	principal
Pen / *Br.; Gae.*	cape, mountain
Peña / *Sp.*	peak
Pendi / *Chin.*	basin
Pendiente / *Sp.*	slope
Penha / *Port.*	peak
Península / *Port.; Sp.*	peninsula
Péninsule / *Fr.*	peninsula
Penisola / *It.*	peninsula
Peñon / *Sp.*	rock, island
Pente / *Fr.*	slope
Perekop / *Rus.*	channel
Pereval / *Rus.*	pass
Perevoz / *Rus.*	ford
Pertuis / *Fr.*	strait
Peščara / *S.C.*	sandy soil
Peski / *Rus.*	sand desert
Petit / *Fr.*	little
Pétra / *Gr.*	rock
Phanom / *Thai; Khm.*	mountain range, mountain
Phau / *Laot.*	mountain
Phnum / *Khm.*	hill, mountain
Phu / *Viet.*	mountain, hill
Phum / *Thai*	forest
Phumĭ / *Khm.*	village
Pi / *Chin.*	cape
Piana, Pianura / *It.*	plain
Piano / *It.*	plain
Piatră / *Rom.*	stone
Pic / *Cat.; Fr.*	peak
Picacho / *Sp.*	peak
Piccolo / *It.*	little
Pico / *Port.; Sp.*	peak
Piedra / *Sp.*	rock, cliff
Pietra / *It.*	stone
Pieve / *It.*	parish
Pik / *Rus.*	peak
Pils / *Latv.*	city, town
Pinar / *Sp.*	pine forest
Pingyuan / *Chin.*	plain
Pioda / *It.*	crest
Pirgos / *Gr.*	tower, peak
Pīsh / *Pers.*	anterior, before
Pitkä / *Finn.*	great
Piton / *Fr.*	mountain, peak
Piz / *Rmsh.*	peak
Pizzo / *It.*	peak
Pjasăci / *Bulg.*	beach
Plaat / *Fle.; Dut.*	sandbank
Plage / *Fr.*	beach
Plaine / *Fr.*	plain
Plan / *Fr.*	plain
Planalto / *Port.*	plateau
Planina / *Bulg.*	mountain
Plano / *Sp.*	plain
Plas / *Dut.; Fle.*	lake, marsh
Plato / *Bulg.; Rus.*	plateau
Platosu / *Tur.*	plateau
Platte / *Germ.*	plain, plateau
Plav / *S.C.*	blue
Plavnja / *Rus.*	marsh
Playa / *Sp.*	beach
Ploskogorje / *Rus.*	plateau
Plou / *Br.*	church
Po / *Kor.*	port
Po / *Chin.*	lake, white
P'o / *Kor.*	bay, lake
Poa / *Mel.*	hill
Poarta / *Rom.*	pass
Poartă / *Rom.*	gate
Pobla / *Cat.*	village
Pobrzeże / *Pol.*	littoral, coast
Poço / *Port.*	well
Poço / *Port.*	point
Pod / *Cz.; Pol.; Rus.; S.C.; Slvn.*	bridge
Podkamenny / *Rus.*	stony
Poggio / *It.*	hill
Pohja / *Finn.*	north, northern
Pohjois- / *Finn.*	north
Pojezierze / *Pol.*	lake region
Pol / *Pers.*	bridge
Pol, -pol / *Rus.*	city, town
Pola / *Port.; Sp.*	village
Polder / *Fle.; Dut.*	reclaimed land
Pole / *Pol.*	field
Pólis / *Gr.*	city, town
Poljana / *Bulg.; Rus.; S.C.; Slvn.*	field, terrace
Poljarny / *Rus.*	polar
Polje / *S.C.; Slvn.*	valley, field, basin
Poluostrov / *Rus.*	peninsula
Pomorije / *Bulg.*	littoral
Pomorze / *Pol.*	littoral
Ponente / *It.*	western
Pont / *Cat.; Fr.*	bridge
Ponta / *Port.*	point
Ponte / *It.; Port.*	bridge
Pòntos / *Gr.*	sea
Poort / *Afr.; Fle.; Dut.*	pass
Pore, -pore / *Hin.; Urdu*	city, town
Porog / *Rus.*	rapids
Porte / *Fr.*	gate
Portile / *Rom.*	gorge
Portillo / *Sp.*	pass
Portiţa / *Rom.*	small gate
Porto / *It.*	port
Pôrto / *Port.*	port
Posht / *Pers.*	back, posterior
Potjo / *Indon.*	peak
Potok / *Bulg.; Cz.; Pol.; Rus.; S.C.; Slvn.*	stream
Póvoa / *Port.*	village
Pozo / *Sp.*	well
Pozzo / *It.*	well
Pradesh / *Hin.*	region, state
Prado / *Sp.*	meadow
Praia / *Port.*	beach
Prato / *It.*	meadow
Pré / *Fr.*	meadow
Prealpi / *It.*	prealps
Presa / *Sp.*	reservoir
Presqu'île / *Fr.*	peninsula
Prêto / *Port.*	black
Priehradní nádrž / *Cz.*	reservoir
Pripoljarny / *Rus.*	subpolar
Pristan / *Rus.*	port
Prohod / *Bulg.*	pass
Proliv / *Rus.*	strait
Promontoire / *Fr.*	promontory
Průchod / *Cz.*	pass
Przedgorze / *Pol.*	front range (mountains)
Przełęcz / *Pol.*	pass
Przemysł / *Pol.*	industry
Przylądek / *Pol.*	cape
Pua / *Mel.*	hill
Puebla / *Sp.*	village
Puente / *Sp.*	bridge
Puerto / *Sp.*	port, pass
Puig / *Cat.*	peak
Puits / *Fr.*	well
Pul / *Pash.*	bridge
Pulau, P. / *Mal.; Indon.*	island
Pulau Pulau / *Mal.*	islands
Pulo / *Mal.; Indon.*	island
Puna / *A.I.*	upland
Puncak / *Indon.*	mountain
Punjung / *Mal.; Indon.*	mountain
Punt / *Afr.*	point
Punta / *It.; Sp.*	point
Pur, -pur / *Hin.; Urdu*	city, town
-pura / *Hin.; Urdu*	city, town
Pura / *Indon.*	city, town, temple
Puri, -puri / *Hin.; Urdu*	city, town
Pus / *Alb.*	spring
Pušča / *Rus.*	forest
Pustynja / *Rus.*	desert
Puszcza / *Pol.*	heath
Puszta / *Hung.*	lowland
Put / *Afr.*	well
Put / *Rus.; S.C.*	road
Putra, -putra / *Hin.*	son
Puu / *Poly.*	mountain, volcano
Puy / *Fr.*	peak
Pwell / *Wel.*	pond
Pyeong / *Kor.*	plain
Pyhä / *Finn.*	saint

Q

Local Form	English
Qagan / *Mong.*	white
Qala / *Pash.*	fortified town
Qal'at / *Ar.*	castle
Qalb / *Ar.*	hill
Qalīb / *Ar.*	spring
Qalīq / *Ar.*	spring
Qanāt / *Ar.*	canal
Qantara / *Ar.*	bridge
Qaqortoq / *Esk.*	white
Qar / *Som.*	mountain
Qara / *Pers.*	black
Qarah / *Tur.*	black
Qārat / *Ar.*	height, mountain
Qāret / *Ar.*	village, hill
Qaryah / *Ar.*	village
Qaryat / *Ar.*	village
Qaşr / *Ar.*	castle
Qawz / *Ar.*	dunes
Qeqertarssuaq / *Esk.*	peninsula
Qezel / *Tur.*	red
Qi / *Chin.*	river
Qing / *Chin.*	blue, green
Qiryat / *Hebr.*	city, town
Qolleh / *Pers.*	mountain, peak
Qu / *Chin.*	river, canal
Quan dao / *Viet.*	islands
Quebracho / *Sp.*	stream
Quebrada / *Sp.*	gorge, stream
Quedas / *Port.*	waterfalls
Qulbān / *Ar.*	well
Qundao / *Chin.*	archipelago
Qūr / *Ar.*	height, hill
Qytet / *Alb.*	city, town
Qyteti / *Alb.*	city, town

R

Local Form	English
R., Rio, River / *Eng.; Sp.*	river
Rada / *It.; Sp.*	anchorage
Rade / *Fr.*	anchorage
Rags / *Latv.*	cape
Rahad / *Ar.*	lake, pond
Rajon / *Rus.*	district
Rak / *Fle.; Dut.*	strait
Rakai / *Poly.*	reef
Ramla / *Ar.*	sand
Rancho / *Port.; Sp.*	farm, ranch
Rand / *Afr.; Germ.*	escarpment
Range / *Eng.*	mountain range
Rann / *Urdu*	marsh
Rano / *Malag.*	water
Ranta / *Finn.*	bank, beach
Rapide / *Fr.*	rapids
Ras / *Amh.*	peak
Rās / *Ar.*	point, cape

Local Form	English
Ras, Rás / Ar.	promontory, peak
Rásiga / Som.	promontory
Rass / Ar.	promontory, peak
Rassa / Lapp.	mountain
Ráth / Gae.	castle
Raunina / Bulg.; Rus.	plain
Raz / Fr.	strait
Razliv / Rus.	flood plain
Récif / Fr.	reef
Recife / Port.	reef
Reede / Germ.; Dut.; Slvn.	anchorage
Reek / Afr.; Gae.	mountain range
Reg / Pash.	dunes
Région / Fr.	region
Rei / Port.	king
Reka / Bulg.; Rus.; S.C.; Slvn.	river
Řeka / Cz.	river
Réma / Gr.	torrent
Renne / Dan.; Nor.	deep
Represa / Port.	dam, reservoir
Represa / Sp.	dam, reservoir
República / Port.; Sp.	republic
République / Fr.	republic
Rês., Réservoir / Fr.	reservoir
Res., Reservoir / Eng.	reservoir
Réservoir, Rés. / Fr.	reservoir
Reshteh / Pers.	mountain range
Respublika / Rus.	republic
Restinga / Port.	cliff, sandbank
Retsugan / Jap.	reef
Rettō / Jap.	archipelago
Rev / Dan.; Nor.; Swed.	reef
Rey / Sp.	king
Ri / Tib.	mountain
Ria / Sp.	estuary
Riacho / Port.	stream
Rialto / It.	plateau
Rialto / It.	rise
Riba / Port.	bank
Ribeira / Port.	river
Ribeirão / Port.	stream
Ribeiro / Port.	stream
Ribera / Sp.	coast
Ribnik / Slvn.	pond
Rid / Bulg.	mountain range
Rif / Icel.	cliff
Riff / Germ.	reef
Rīg / Pash.	dunes
Rijeka / S.C.	river
Rimāl / Ar.	sand desert
Rincón / Sp.	peninsula between two rivers
Ring / Tib.	long
Rinne / Germ.	trench
Rio / Port.	river
Rio, R. / Sp.	river
Riu / Rom.	river
Riva / It.	bank
Rive / Fr.	bank
Rivera / Sp.	brook, stream
Rivier, -rivier / Afr.; Dut.; Fle.	river
Riviera / It.	coast
Rivière / Fr.	river
Roads / Eng.	anchorage
Roc / Fr.	rock
Roca / Port.; Sp.	rock
Rocca / It.	castle
Roche / Fr.	rock
Rocher / Fr.	rock
Rock / Eng.	rock
Rod / Pash.	river
Rode / Germ.	tilled soil
Rodnik / Rus.	spring
Rog / Rus.; S.C.; Slvn.	peak
Roi / Fr.	king
Rojo / Sp.	red
Roque / Sp.	rock
Rot / Germ.	red
Roto / Poly.	lake
Rouge / Fr.	red
Równina / Pol.	plain
Rt / S.C.; Slvn.	cape
Ru / Tib.	mountain
Ruck / Germ.	ridge
Rücken / Germ.	ridge
Rud / Pers.	river
Ruda / Cz.; Slvk.	mine
Ruda / Pol.	ore
Rūdbār / Pers.	river
Rudha / Gae.	point
Rudnik / Rus.; S.C.; Slvn.	mine
Rug / Fle.; Dut.	ridge
Ruggen / Afr.	ridge
Ruina / Sp.	ruins
Ruine / Fr.; Dut.; Germ.	ruins
Rujm / Ar.	hill
Run / Eng.	stream

S

Local Form	English
S., See / Germ.	lake, sea
Saar / Est.	island
Saari / Finn.	island
Sabbia / It.	sand
Sabkhat / Ar.	salt flat, salt marsh
Sable / Fr.; Eng.	beach
Sacca / It.	anchorage
Saco / Port.	bay
Sad / Cz.; Slvk.	park
Sad / Pers.	wall
Sadd / Ar.; Pers.	cataract, dam
Safid / Pash.; Urdu; Hin.	white
Şafrā' / Ar.	desert
Sāgar / Hin.	reservoir
Saguia / Ar.	irrigation canal
Sahara / Ar.	desert
Sahel / Ar.	plain, coast
Sahr / Iran.	city, town
Şaḥrā' / Ar.	desert
Said / Ar.	sweet
Saj / Alt.	stream, valley
Saki / Jap.	point
Sala / Latv.; Lith.	island
Saladillo / Sp.	salt desert
Salar / Sp.	salt lake
Sale / Ural.	village
Salina / It.; Sp.	salt flat, salt marsh
Saline / Dut.; Fr.; Germ.	salt flat, salt marsh
Salmi / Finn.	strait
Salseleh-ye Kūh / Pers.	mountain range
Salto / Port.; Sp.	waterfall, rapids
Salz / Germ.	salt
Samudera / Indon.	ocean
Samudra / Hin.	lake
Samut / Thai	sea
San / Jap.; Kor.	mountain
San / It.; Sp.	saint
Sanchi / Jap.	mountain range
Sand / Dan.; Eng.; Nor.; Swed.; Germ.	beach
Šand / Mong.	spring
Sandur / Icel.	sand
Sank / Pers.	rock
Sankt, St. / Germ.; Swed.	saint
Sanmaeg / Kor.	mountain range
Sanmyaku / Jap.	mountain range
Sansanné / Sud.	campsite
Santo / It.; Port.; Sp.	saint
Santuario / It.	sanctuary
São / Port.	saint
Sar / Pers.	cape; peak
Šar / Rus.; Tur.	strait
Saraf / Ar.	well
Sari / Finn.	island
Sari / Tur.	yellow
Sarīr / Ar.	rocky desert
Sary / Tur.	yellow
Sasso / It.	stone
Sat / Rom.	village
Sattel / Germ.	pass
Saurum / Latv.	strait
Schleuse / Germ.	lock
Schloß / Germ.	castle
Schlucht / Germ.	gorge
Schnee / Germ.	snow
Schwarz / Germ.	black
Scoglio / It.	cliff
Se / Jap.	bank, shoal
Sebkha / Ar.	salt flat
Sebkhet / Ar.	salt flat
Sed / Ar.	dam
Seda / Ural.	mountain
See, S. / Germ.	lake, sea
Sefra / Ar.	yellow
Segara / Indon.	lagoon
Şehir / Tur.	city, town
Seki / Jap.	dam
Selat / Mal.; Indon.	strait
Selatan / Indon.	southern
Selkä / Finn.	ridge, lake
Sella / It.	pass
Selo / Bulg.; Rus.; S.C.; Slvn.	village
Selsela Kohe / Pers.	mountain range
Selva / It.; Sp.	forest
Semenanjung / Mal	peninsula
Sen / Jap.	mountain
Seong / Kor.	castle
Sep / Alt.	canal
Serīr / Ar.	rocky desert
Serra / Cat.; Port.	mountain range
Serra / It.	mountain
Serrania / Sp.	mountain range
Sertão / Port.	steppe
Seto / Jap.	strait
Sett., Settentrionale / It.	northern
Settentrionale, Sett. / It.	northern
Seuil / Fr.	sill
Sev / Arm.	black
Sever / Rus.	north
Severny / Rus.	northern
Sfint / Rom.	saint
Sfintu / Rom.	saint
Sgeir / Gae.	cliff
Sha'b / Ar.	cliff
Shahr / Pers.; Hin.	city, town
Sha'īb / Ar.	stream
Shallāl / Ar.	cataract
Shām / Ar.	north; northern
Shamo / Chin.	sand desert
Shan / Chin.	mountain, mountain range
Shan / Gae.	old
Shand / Mong.	spring
Shankou / Chin.	pass
Shaqq / Ar.	wadi
Sharm / Ar.	bay
Sharqī / Ar.	east, eastern
Sharqīyah / Ar.	eastern
Shatt / Ar.	river, salt lake
Shatt / Tur.	stream
Shën / Alb.	saint
Sheng / Chin.	province
Shi / Chin.	city, town
Shibīn / Ar.	village
Shih / Chin.	rock
Shima / Jap.	island
Shimo / Jap.	lower
Shin / Jap.	new
Shō / Jap.	island
Shotō / Jap.	archipelago
Shū / Jap.	administrative division
Shui / Chin.	river
Shuiku / Chin.	reservoir
Shur / Pers.	salt
Sidhiros / Gr.	iron
Sidi / Ar.	master
Sieben / Germ.	seven
Sierra / Sp.	mountain range
Sikt / Ural.	village
Sillon / Fr.	furrow
Šine / Mong.	new
Sink / Eng.	depression
Sinn / Ar.	point
Sint / Dut.; Fle.	saint
Sirt / Tur.	mountain range
Sirtlar / Tur.	mountain range
Sistema / It.; Sp.	mountain system
Sīyāh / Pers.	black
Sjø / Nor.	lake
Sjö / Swed.	lake, sea
Skag / Icel.	peninsula
Skala / Bulg.; Rus.	rock
Skála / Slvk.	rock
Skar / Nor.	pass
Skär / Swed.	cliff
Skeir / Gae.	cliff
Skerry / Gae.	cliff
Skog / Nor.; Swed.	forest
Skóg / Icel.	forest
Skov / Dan.; Nor.	forest
Slatina / S.C.; Slvn.	mineral water
Slätt / Swed.	plain
Slieve / Gae.	mountain
Slot / Dut.; Fle.	castle
Slott / Nor.; Swed.	castle
Slough / Eng.	creek, pond, marsh
Sluis / Dut.; Fle.	sluice
Små / Swed.	little
Sne / Nor.	snow
Sneeuw / Afr.; Dut.	snow
Snežny / Rus.	snowy
Snø / Nor.	snow
So / Kor.	little
Sø / Dan.; Nor.	lake; sea
So / Ural.	passage
Söder / Swed.	south
Södra / Swed.	southern
Solončak / Rus.	salt flat
Sommet / Fr.	peak
Son / Viet.	mountain
Sønder / Dan.; Nor.	southern
Søndre / Dan.	southern
Sone / Jap.	bank
Song / Viet.	river
Sopka / Rus.	volcano
Sopočnik / Rus.	mountain system
Soprana / It.	upper
Šor, Sor / Alt.	salt marsh
Sos / Tur.	upon
Sotavento / Sp.	leeward
Sotoviento / Sp.	leeward
Sottana / It.	lower
Souk / Ar.	market
Souq / Ar.	market
Sour / Ar.	rampart
Source / Eng.; Fr.	spring
Souto / Port.	forest
Spitze / Germ.	peak
Spruit / Afr.	current
Sreden / Bulg.	central
Sredni / Rus.	central
Středni / Pol.	central
Srednji / S.C.; Slvn.	central
St., Saint, Sankt / Eng.; Fr.; Germ.; Swed.	saint
Stadhur / Icel.	city, town
Stadt, -stadt / Germ.	city, town
Stag / Eng.	city, town
Stagno / It.	pond
-stan / Hin.; Pers.; Urdu	land
Star / Bulg.	old
Stari / S.C.; Slvn.	old
Stary / Pol.; Rus.	old
Starý / Cz.; Slvk.	old
Stat / Afr.; Dan.; Fle.; Nor.; Dut.; Swed.	city, town
Stathmós / Gr.	railway station
Stausee / Germ.	reservoir
Stavrós / Gr.	cross
Sted / Dan.; Nor.	place
Stedt / Germ.	place
Stein, -stein / Nor.; Germ.	stone
Sten / Nor.; Swed.	stone
Stena / S.C.; Slvn.	rock
Stěna / Cz.	mountain range
Stenón / Gr.	strait, pass
Step / Rus.	steppe
-sthān / Hin.; Pers.; Urdu	land
Stift / Germ.	foundation
Štit / Cz.; Slvk.	peak
Stock / Germ.	massif
Stok / Pol.	slope
Stor / Dan.; Nor.; Swed.	great
Store / Dan	great
Stræde / Dan.	strait
Strana / Rus.	land
Strand / Germ.; Nor.; Swed.; Afr., Dan.	beach
Straße / Germ.	street, road
Strath / Gae.	valley
Straum / Nor.; Swed.	stream
Středni / Cz.	central
Středný / Slvk.	central
Strelka / Rus.	spit
Stret / Nor.	strait
Stretto / It.	strait
Strom / Germ.	stream
Strøm / Nor.	stream
Ström / Swed.	stream
Stroom / Dut.	stream
Su / Jap.	sandbank
Su / Tur.	river
Suando / Finn.	pond
Suid / Afr.	south
Suidō / Jap.	strait
Sul / Port.	south
Sund / Dan.; Nor.; Swed.; Germ.	strait
Sungai / Mal.	river
Sunn / Nor.	south
Süq / Ar.	market
Sur / Fr.	on
Sur / Sp.	south
Surkh / Pers.	red
Suu / Finn.	mouth, river mouth
Suur / Cat.	great
Svart / Nor.; Swed.	black
Sveti / S.C.; Slvn.	saint
Swa / Ban.	great
Swart / Afr.	black
Świety / Pol.	saint
Syrt / Alt.	ridge
Szállás / Hung.	village
Szczyt / Pol.	peak
Szeg / Hung.	bend
Székes / Hung.	residence
Szent / Hung.	saint
Sziget / Hung.	river island

T

Local Form	English
Tadi / Ban.	rock, cliff
Tae / Kor.	great
Tafua / Poly.	mountain
Tag / Alt.; Tur.	mountain
Tahta / Ar.	lower
Tahti / Ar.	lower
Tai / Chin.; Jap.	great
Taipale / Finn.	isthmus
Tajga / Rus.	forest
Take / Jap.	mountain
Tal / Germ.	valley
Tala / Mong.	plain, steppe
Tala / Ber.	spring
Tall / Ar.	hill
Talsperre / Germ.	dam
Tam / Viet.	stream
Tamgout / Ber.	peak
Tan / Chin.; Kor.	sandbank
Tana / Malag.	city, town
Tanana / Malag.	city, town
Tandjung / Mal.	cape, point
Tanezrouft / Ber.	desert
Tang / Tib.	upland
Tangeh / Pers.	strait
Tanjong / Mal.	cape, point
Tanjung, Tg. / Indon.	cape, point
Tanout / Ber.	well
Tao / Chin.	island
Taourirt / Ber.	peak
Targ / Pol.	market
Tărg / Bulg.	market
Tarn / Eng.	glacial lake
Tarso / Sah.	crater
Taš / Alt.	stone

Geographical Glossary

Local Form	English
Tassili / *Ber.*	upland
Tau / *Tur.*	mountain
Taung / *Burm.*	mountain
Ţawîl / *Ar.*	hill
Tégi / *Sah.*	hill
Teguidda / *Ber.*	well
Tehi / *Ber.*	pass, mountain
Teich / *Germ.*	pond
Tell / *Tur.*	hill
Telok / *Mal.*	bay, port
Teluk / *Mal.*	bay, port
Tempio / *It.*	temple
Ténéré / *Ber.*	rocky desert
Tengah / *Indon.; Mal.*	central
Tepe / *Tur.*	hill
Tepesi / *Tur.*	hill
Termas / *Sp.*	thermal springs
Terme / *It.*	thermal springs
Terra / *It.; Dut.*	land, earth
Terrazzo / *It.*	guyot, tablemount
Terre / *Fr.*	land, earth
Teso / *Cat.*	hill
Téssa / *Ber.*	wadi, depression
Testa / *It.*	point
Tête / *Fr.*	peak
Tetri / *Georg.*	white
Teu / *Poly.*	reef
Teze / *Alt.*	new
Tg., Tanjung / *Indon.*	cape, point
Thaba / *Ban.*	mountain
Thabana / *Ban.*	mountain
Thal / *Germ.*	valley
Thálassa / *Gr.*	sea
Thale / *Thai*	lagoon
Thamad / *Ar.*	well
Theós / *Gr.*	god
Thermes / *Fr.*	thermal springs
Thog / *Tib.*	high, upper
Tian / *Chin.*	field
Tiefe / *Germ.*	deep
Tierra / *Sp.*	land, earth
Timur / *Indon.; Mal.*	eastern
Tind / *Nor.*	mountain
Tinto / *Sp.*	black
Tirg / *Rom.*	market
Tis / *Amh.*	new
Tizgui / *Ber.*	forest
Tizi / *Ber.*	pass
Tjåkko / *Lapp.*	mountain
Tjärn / *Swed.*	tarn, glacial lake
Tji / *Mal.*	stream
To / *Kor.*	island
To / *Mel.*	stream
Tō / *Jap.*	island
Tó / *Hung.*	lake
To / *Ural.*	lake
Tobe / *Tur.*	hill
Tofua / *Poly.*	mountain
Tog / *Som.*	valley
Tōge / *Jap.*	pass
Tokoj / *Alt.*	forest
Tônle / *Khm.*	stream, lake
Tope / *Dut.*	peak
Toplice / *S.C.; Slvn.*	thermal springs
Topp / *Nor.*	peak
Tor / *Gae.*	rock
Tor / *Germ.*	gate
Torbat / *Pers.*	tomb
Törl / *Germ.*	pass
Torp / *Swed.*	hut
Torre / *Cat.; It.; Sp.; Port.*	tower
Torrente / *It.; Sp.*	torrent, stream
Tossa / *Cat.*	mountain, peak
Tota / *Sin.*	port
Tour / *Fr.*	tower
Traforo / *It.*	tunnel
Träsk / *Swed.*	lake
Trg / *S.C.*	market
Trog / *Germ.*	trough, trench
Trois / *Fr.*	three
Trung / *Viet.*	central
Tse / *Tib.*	peak, point
Tsi / *Chin.*	pond
Tskali / *Georg.*	river
Tsu / *Jap.*	bay
Tulül / *Ar.*	hills
Tünel / *Pers.*	tunnel
Tunturi / *Lapp.*	mountain, tundra
Tur'ah / *Ar.*	irrigation canal
Turm / *Germ.*	tower
Turn / *Rom.*	tower
Turó / *Cat.*	dome
Tuz / *Tur.*	salt
Týn / *Cz.*	fortress

U

Local Form	English
U., Unter-, Upon / *Eng.; Germ.*	under, lower
Uaimh / *Gae.*	cave
Uchi / *Jap.*	bay
Udde / *Swed.*	cape
Údolní nádrž / *Cz.*	reservoir
Uebi / *Som.*	river
Új- / *Hung.*	new
Ujście / *Pol.*	mouth
Ujung / *Indon.*	point, cape
Ul / *Chin.; Mong.*	mountain, mountain range
Ula / *Mong.*	mountain range
Ulan / *Mong.*	red
Uls / *Mong.*	state
Umi / *Jap.*	bay
Umm / *Ar.*	mother, spring
Umne / *Mong.*	south
Under / *Mong.*	mountain, peak
Ungur / *Alt.*	cave
Unter-, U. / *Germ.*	under, lower
Upar / *Hin.*	river
'Uqlat / *Ar.*	well
Ür / *Tam.*	city, town
Ura / *Jap.*	bay, coast
Ura / *Alt.*	depression
Urd / *Mong.*	south
Uru / *Tam.*	city, town
Ušće / *S.C.*	mouth
Uske / *Alt.*	upper
Ust / *Rus.*	mouth
Ústí / *Cz.*	mouth
Ustup / *Rus.*	terrace
Utan / *Indon.; Mal.*	forest
Utara / *Indon.*	north, northern
Uusi / *Finn.*	new
Uval / *Rus.*	height
Úval / *Cz.*	mountain
'Uwaynāt / *Ar.*	well
Uzboj / *Alt.*	river bed
Uzun / *Tur.*	long
Užurekis / *Lith.*	gulf

V

Local Form	English
Va / *Alb.*	ford
Va / *Ural.*	water, river
Vaara / *Finn.*	mountain
Väärti / *Finn.*	bay
Vad / *Rom.*	ford
Vær / *Nor.*	port
Våg / *Nor.*	bay
Vähä / *Finn.*	little
Väike / *Est.*	little
Väin / *Est.*	strait
Val / *Fr.; It.*	valley
Val / *Rom.; Rus.*	wall
Valico / *It.*	pass
Vall / *Cat.*	valley
Vall / *Swed.*	pasture
Valle / *It.; Sp.*	valley
Vallée / *Fr.*	valley
Vallei / *Afr.*	valley
Vallo / *It.*	wall
Valta / *Finn.*	cape
Váltos / *Gr.*	marsh
Valul / *Rom.*	wall
Vann / *Dan.; Nor.*	water, lake
Vanua / *Mel.*	land
Vár / *Hung.*	fort
Vara / *Finn.*	mountain
Varoš / *S.C.*	city, town
Város / *Hung.*	city, town
Varre / *Lapp.*	mountain
Vary / *Cz.*	spring
Vas / *S.C.; Slvn.*	village
Vásár / *Hung.*	market
Väst / *Swed.*	west
Väster / *Swed.*	western
Vatn / *Icel.; Nor.*	lake
Vatten / *Swed.*	water, lake
Vatu / *Mel.; Poly.*	island, reef
Vdhr., Vodohranilišče / *Rus.*	reservoir
Vechiu / *Rom.*	old
Vecs / *Latv.*	old
Veen / *Dut.; Fle.*	moor
Vega / *Sp.*	irrigated crops
Veld / *Afr.; Dut.; Fle.*	field
Veli / *S.C.; Slvn.*	great
Velik / *Bulg.*	great
Veliki / *Rus.; S.C.; Slvn.*	great
Veliký / *Cz.*	great
Velký / *Cz.*	great
Veľ'ky / *Slvk.*	great
Vella / *Cat.*	old
Ver / *Ural.*	forest
Verde / *It.; Sp.*	green
Verh / *Rus.*	peak
Verhni / *Rus.*	upper
Verk / *Swed.*	factory
Vermelho / *Port.*	red
Vert / *Fr.*	green
Ves / *Cz.*	village
Vesi / *Finn.*	water, lake
Vest / *Dan.; Nor.*	west
Vester / *Dan.; Nor.*	western
Vestur / *Icel.*	west
Vetta / *It.*	summit
Viaduc / *Fr.*	viaduct
Vidda / *Nor.*	upland
Vidde / *Nor.*	upland
Viejo / *Sp.*	old
Vier / *Germ.*	four
Viertel / *Germ.*	quarter
Vieux / *Fr.*	old
Vig / *Dan.*	bay
Vik / *Icel., Nor.; Swed.*	gulf, bay
Vila / *Port.*	city, town
Villa / *Sp.*	city, town
Ville, -ville / *Eng.; Fr.*	city, town
Vinh / *Viet.*	bay
Virful / *Rom.*	peak, mountain
Virta / *Finn.*	river
Višni / *Rus.*	high
Visok / *S.C.*	high
Viz / *Hung.*	water
Viztároló / *Hung.*	reservoir
Vlakte / *Dut.; Fle.*	plain
Vlei / *Afr.*	pond
Vliet / *Dut.; Fle.*	river
Vloer / *Afr.*	depression
Voda / *Bulg.; Cz.; Rus.; S.C.; Slvn.*	water
Vodny put / *Rus.*	stream, canal
Vodohranilišče, vdhr. / *Rus.*	reservoir
Vodopad / *Rus.*	waterfall
Volcan / *Fr.*	volcano
Volcán / *Sp.*	volcano
Voll / *Nor.*	meadow
Vórios / *Gr.*	northern
Vorota / *Rus.*	gate
Vorräs / *Gr.*	north
Vostočny / *Rus.*	eastern
Vostok / *Rus.*	east
Vötn / *Icel.*	lake, water
Vož / *Ural.*	mouth
Vozvyšennost / *Rus.*	upland
Vpadina / *Rus.*	depression
Vrah / *Bulg.*	peak
Vrata / *Bulg.; S.C.; Slvn.*	pass
Vrch / *Cz.; Slvk.*	mountain
Vrch / *S.C.; Slvn.*	peak
Vrchni / *Cz.*	upper
Vrchovina / *Cz.*	upland
Vulcan / *Rom.; Rus.*	volcano
Vulcano / *It.*	volcano
Vulkan / *Germ.; Rus.*	volcano
Vuopio / *Lapp.*	bend
Vuori / *Finn.*	rock
Východný / *Cz.*	eastern
Vyšný / *Slvk.*	upper
Vysoki / *Rus.*	high
Vysoky / *Cz.; Slvk.*	high
Vyšší / *Cz.*	high

W

Local Form	English
W., Wādī / *Ar.*	wadi
Wa / *Ban.*	people
Wabe / *Amh.*	stream
Wad / *Ar.*	wadi
Wad / *Dut.*	tidal flat
Wādī, W. / *Ar.*	wadi
Wāḥāt / *Ar.*	oasis
Wai / *Mel.; Poly.*	stream
Wal / *Afr.*	wall
Wala / *Hin.*	mountain range
Wald / *Germ*	forest
Wan / *Burm.*	village
Wan / *Chin.; Jap.*	bay
Wand / *Germ.*	bluff
War / *Som.*	pond
Wär / *Ar.*	desert
-waram / *Hin.; Tam.*	village
Wasser / *Germ.*	water
Wat / *Pol.*	wall
Wat / *Thai*	church
Waterval / *Afr.; Dut.*	waterfall
Watt / *Germ.*	tidal flat
Wāw / *Ar.*	oasis
Weald / *Eng.*	wooded country
Webi / *Som.*	stream
Weg / *Germ.*	way, road
Wei / *Chin.*	cape, point
Weide / *Germ.*	pasture
Weiler / *Germ.*	village
Weiß / *Germ.*	white
Weon / *Kor.*	field
Wer / *Som.*	pond
Werder / *Germ.*	river island
Werk / *Germ.*	factory
Wes / *Afr.*	west
Westlich / *Germ.*	western
Westr- / *Sca.*	western
Wēyn / *Som.*	great
Wēyne / *Som.*	great
Wick / *Eng.*	village
Wiek / *Germ.*	bay
Wielki / *Pol.*	great
Wieś / *Pol.*	village
Wijk / *Dut.; Fle.*	quarter, district
-willer / *Germ.*	village
Woda / *Pol.*	water
Woestyn / *Afr.*	desert
Wold / *Dut.; Fle.; Eng.*	forest
Wörth / *Germ.*	river island
Woud / *Dut.; Fle.*	forest
Wschodni / *Pol.*	eastern
Wysoczyzna / *Pol.*	upland
Wysoki / *Pol.*	upper
Wyspa / *Pol.*	island
Wyżyna / *Pol.*	highland
Wzgórze / *Pol.*	hill

X

Local Form	English
Xi / *Chin.*	west
Xia / *Chin.*	gorge, strait
Xian / *Chin.*	county, shire
Xiang / *Chin.*	village
Xiao / *Chin.*	little
Xin / *Chin.*	new
Xu / *Chin.*	island

Y

Local Form	English
Yam / *Hebr.*	lake, sea
Yama / *Jap.*	mountain
Yan / *Chin.*	mountain
Yang / *Chin.*	strait, ocean
Yani / *Tur.*	new
Yar / *Tur.*	gorge
Yarimada / *Tur.*	peninsula
Yazı / *Tur.*	plain
Yegge / *Sah.*	well
Yeni / *Tur.*	new
Yeon / *Kor.*	sea
Yeong / *Kor.*	mountain
Yeşil / *Tur.*	green
Ylä / *Finn.*	upper
Yli- / *Finn.*	upper
Yō / *Jap.*	ocean
Yobe / *Sud.*	great
Yōm / *Kor.*	island
Yoma / *Burm.*	mountain range
Yōn / *Kor.*	lake, pond
Yŏng / *Kor.*	mountain, peak
Ytter / *Nor.; Swed.*	outer
Yttre / *Swed.*	outer
Yu / *Chin.*	old
Yu / *Chin.*	island
Yu / *Jap.*	thermal spring
Yüan / *Chin.*	spring, river
Yunhe / *Chin.*	canal

Z

Local Form	English
Zāb / *Ar.*	river
Zachodni / *Pol.*	western
Zaki / *Jap.*	cape
Zalew / *Pol.*	gulf
Zaliv / *Bulg.; Rus.; S.C.; Slvn.*	gulf
Zaljev / *Slvn.*	bay
Zámek / *Cz.*	castle
Zan / *Jap.*	mountain
Zand / *Dut.; Fle.*	sand
Zandt / *Dut.; Fle.*	sand
Zangbo / *Chin.*	river
Zapad / *Rus.*	west
Zapaden / *Bulg.*	western
Zapadni / *S.C.; Slvn.*	western
Západní / *Cz.*	western
Zapadny / *Rus.*	western
Zapovednik / *Rus.*	reserve
Zatoka / *Pol.*	gulf
Zavod / *Rus.*	roadstead
Zāwiyat / *Ar.*	monastery
Zdrój / *Pol.*	thermal springs
Ze / *Jap.*	islet
Zee / *Dut.; Fle.*	sea
Zelěny / *Rus.*	green
Žem / *Lith.*	land, country
Země / *Cz.; Slvk.*	land, country
Zemlja / *Rus.*	land
Zen / *Jap.*	mountain
Zhan / *Chin.*	mountain
Zhen / *Chin.*	market
Zhong / *Chin.*	central
Zhou / *Chin.*	quarter, district
Zhuang / *Chin.*	village
Ziemia / *Pol.*	land
Zigos / *Gr.*	pass
Zipfel / *Germ.*	tip, point
Ziwa / *Swa.*	marsh
Zizhiqu / *Chin.*	autonomous region
Zlato / *Bulg.*	gold
Zuid / *Dut.; Fle.*	south
Zuidelijk / *Dut.*	southern
Żuława / *Pol.*	marsh
Zun / *Mong.*	east
Zwart / *Dut.*	black
Zwei / *Germ.*	two

Maps of the World Index

All of the toponyms (place-names) which appear on the maps are listed in the Maps of the World Index. Each entry includes the following: Place-name and, where applicable, other forms by which it is written or known; a symbol, where applicable, indicating what kind of feature it is; the page on which the map appears; and the map-reference letters and geographical coordinates indicating its location on the map.

Toponyms

Each toponym, or place-name, is written in full, with accents and diacritical marks. Since many countries have more than one official language, many of these forms are included on the maps. For example, many Belgian place-names are listed as follows: Bruxelles/Brussel; Antwerpen/Anvers, and vice versa, Brussel/Bruxelles; Anvers/Antwerpen. In Italy, certain regions have a special status — they are largely autonomous and officially bilingual. As a result, Index listings appears as follows: Aosta/Aoste; Alto Adige/Sud Tirol, and vice versa. One name, however, may be the only name on the map.

In China, the written forms of commonly used regional languages have been taken into account. These forms are enclosed in parenthesis following the official name: e.g. Xiangshan (Dancheng). However, when the regional is listed first, it is linked to the official name with an →: e.g. Dancheng→Xiangshan. The same style is used for former or historical name forms: e.g. Rhodesia→Zimbabwe and Zimbabwe (Rhodesia).

Place-names for major features (countries, major cities, and large physical features), where applicable, include the English conventional form identified by (EN) and linked in the local name or names with an = sign: e.g. Italia = Italy (EN), and vice versa, Italy (EN) = Italia. Former English names are linked in the Index to the conventional form by an →.

Symbols

The last component with the place-name is a symbol, where applicable, specifying the broad category of the feature named. A table preceding the Index lists all of the symbols used and their meanings; this information also appears as a footnote on each page of the Index. Place names without symbols are cities and towns.

Alphabetization

Place-names are listed in English alphabetical order — 26 letters, from A to Z — because of its international usage. Names including two or more words are listed alphabetically according to the first letter of the word: e.g. De Ruyter is listed under D; Le Havre is listed under L. Names with the prefix Mc are listed as if spelled Mac. The generic portion of a name (lake, sierra, mountain, etc.) is placed after the name: e.g. Lake Erie is listed as Erie, Lake; Sierra Morena is listed as Morena, Sierra. In Spanish, "ch" and "ll" groups and the letter "ñ" are included respectively under C, L, and N, without any distinction.

The same place-name sometimes is listed in the Index several times. It may because of the various translations of a name, or it may be that several places have the same name.

Various translations of a name appear as follows:

Danube (EN) = Dunav   Danube (EN) = Donau
Danube (EN) = Dunărea   Danube (EN) = Dunaj

Several places with the same name appear as follows; however, only in these cases is the location — abbreviated and enclosed in brackets — included. A table of these abbreviations precedes the Index.

Abbeville [U.S.]   Aberdeen [Scot.-U.K.]
Abbeville [Fr.]   Aberdeen [N.C.-U.S.]
Aberdeen [S. Afr.]

Page References

Page references to two-page maps always refer to the left-hand page. If a page contains several maps or insets, a lowercase letter identifies the specific map or inset.

Although a place-name may appear on one or more maps, it is indexed to only one map. Most places are indexed to the regional maps. However, if a place-name appears on either the physical or political continental maps, it is indexed to one of the two types of map. For example, a river or mountain would be indexed to a physical continental map; a city or state would be indexed to a political continental map.

Map-Reference Letters and Geographical Coordinates

The next elements in the Index listing are the map-reference letters and the geographical coordinates, respectively, locating the place on the map.

Map-reference letters consist of a capital and a lowercase letter. Capital letters are across the top and bottom of the maps; lowercase letters are down the sides. The map-reference letters assigned to each place-name refer to the location of the name within the area formed by grid lines connecting the geographical coordinates on either sides of the letters.

Geographical coordinates are the latitude (N for North, S for South) and longitude (E for East, W for West) expressed in degrees and minutes and based on the prime meridian, Greenwich.

Map-reference letters and coordinates for extensive geographical features, such as mountain ranges and countries, are given for the approximate central point of the area. Those for waterways, such as canals and rivers, are given for the mouth of the river, the point where it enters another river or where the feature reaches the map margin. On this page are sample maps showing points to which features are indexed according to map-reference letters and coordinates.

On most maps there is not enough space to place all the names of administrative subdivisions. In these cases the location of the place is shown on the map by a circled letter or number and the place-name and circled letter or number are listed in the map margin. The map-reference numbers and coordinates for these places refer to the location of the circled letter or number on the map.

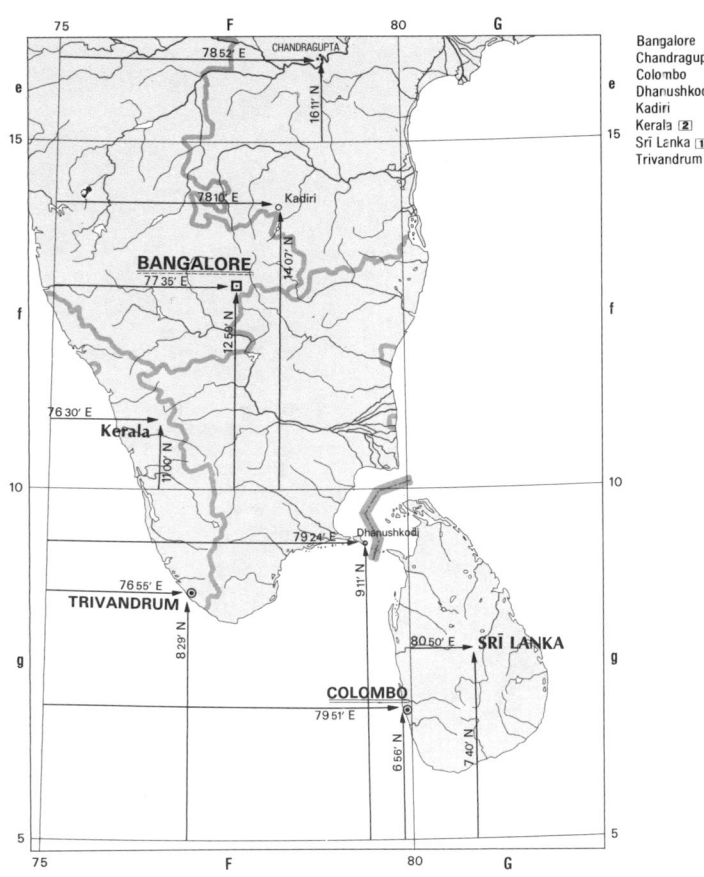

Bangalore	148	Ff	12°59'N 77°35'E
Chandragupta ⊡	148	Fe	16°11'N 78°52'E
Colombo	148	Fg	6°56'N 79°51'E
Dharushkodi	148	Fg	9°11'N 79°24'E
Kadiri	148	Ff	14°07'N 78°10'E
Kerala ⊡	148	Ff	11°00'N 76°30'E
Sri Lanka ⊡	148	Gg	7°40'N 80°50'E
Trivandrum	148	Fg	8°29'N 76°55'E

Alaska ⊡	174	Dc	65°00'N 153°00'W
Alaska, Gulf of- ⊡	174	Ed	58°00'N 146°00'W
Alexander Archipelago ⊡	174	Fd	56°30'N 134°00'W
Barrow, Point- ▶	174	Db	71°23'N 156°30'W
Bering Strait ⊟	174	Cc	65°30'N 169°00'W
Coast Mountains ⊡	174	Gd	55°00'N 129°00'W
Kodiak ⊡	174	Dd	57°30'N 153°30'W
Yukon ⊡	174	Cc	62°33'N 163°59'W

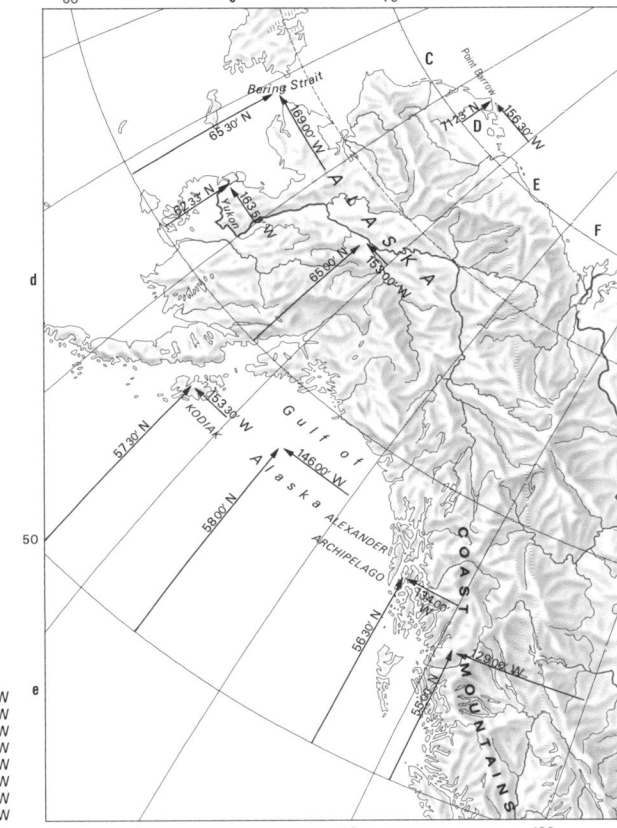

List of Abbreviations

Abz.-U.S.S.R.   Azerbaijan S.S.R., U.S.S.R.
Afg.   Afghanistan
Afr.   Africa
Agl.   Anguilla
Ak.-U.S.   Alaska, U.S.
Al.-U.S.   Alabama, U.S.
Alb.   Albania
Alg.   Algeria
Alta.-Can.   Alberta, Canada
Am. Sam.   American Samoa
And.   Andorra
Ang.   Angola
Ant.   Antarctica
Ar.-U.S.   Arkansas, U.S.
Arg.   Argentina
Arm.-U.S.S.R.   Armenian S.S.R., U.S.S.R.
Asia   Asia
Atg.   Antigua and Barbuda
Aus.   Austria
Austl.   Australia
Az.-U.S.   Arizona, U.S.
Azr.   Azores
Bah.   Bahamas
Bar.   Barbados
B.A.T.   British Antarctic Territory
B.C.-Can.   British Columbia, Canada
Bel.   Belgium
Ben.   Benin
Ber.   Bermuda
Bhr.   Bahrain
Bhu.   Bhutan
Blz.   Belize
Bnd.   Burundi
Bngl.   Bangladesh
Bol.   Bolivia
Bots.   Botswana
Braz.   Brazil
Bru.   Brunei
Bul.   Bulgaria
Bur.   Burma
Burkina   Burkina Faso
B.V.I.   British Virgin Islands
Bye.-U.S.S.R.   Byelorussian S.S.R., U.S.S.R.
Ca.-U.S.   California, U.S.
Cam.   Cameroon
C. Amer.   Central America
Can.   Canada
Can. Is.   Canary Islands
C.A.R.   Central African Republic
Cay. Is   Cayman Islands
Chad   Chad
Chan. Is.   Channel Islands
Chile   Chile
China   China
Co.-U.S.   Colorado, U.S.
Cocos Is.   Cocos Islands
Col.   Colombia
Con.   Congo
Cook   Cook Islands
Cor. Sea Is.   Coral Sea Islands
C.R.   Costa Rica
Ct.-U.S.   Connecticut, U.S.
Cuba   Cuba
C.V.   Cape Verde
Cyp.   Cyprus
Czech.   Czechoslovakia

D.C.-U.S.   District of Columbia, U.S.
De.-U.S.   Delaware, U.S.
Den.   Denmark
Dji.   Djibouti
Dom.   Dominica
Dom. Rep.   Dominican Republic
Ec.   Ecuador
Eg.   Egypt
El Sal.   El Salvador
Eng.-U.K.   England, U.K.
Eq. Gui.   Equatorial Guinea
Est.-U.S.S.R.   Estonian S.S.R., U.S.S.R.
Eth.   Ethiopia
Eur.   Europe
Falk. Is.   Falkland Islands
Far. Is.   Faeroe Islands
Fiji   Fiji
Fin.   Finland
Fl.-U.S.   Florida, U.S.
Fr.   France
Fr. Gui.   French Guiana
Fr. Poly.   French Polynesia
F.S.M.   Federated States of Micronesia
Ga.-U.S.   Georgia, U.S.
Gabon   Gabon
Gam.   Gambia
Geo.-U.S.S.R.   Georgian S.S.R., U.S.S.R.
Ger.   Germany
Ghana   Ghana
Gib.   Gibraltar
Grc.   Greece
Gren.   Grenada
Grld.   Greenland
Guad.   Guadeloupe
Guam   Guam
Guat.   Guatemala
Gui.   Guinea
Gui. Bis.   Guinea Bissau
Guy.   Guyana
Haiti   Haiti
Hi.-U.S.   Hawaii, U.S.
H.K.   Hong Kong
Hond.   Honduras
Hun.   Hungary
Ia.-U.S.   Iowa, U.S.
I.C.   Ivory Coast
Ice.   Iceland
Id.-U.S.   Idaho, U.S.
Il.-U.S.   Illinois, U.S.
In.-U.S.   Indiana, U.S.
India   India
Indon.   Indonesia
I. of M.   Isle of Man
Iran   Iran
Iraq   Iraq
Ire.   Ireland
Isr.   Israel
It.   Italy
Jam.   Jamaica
Jap.   Japan
Jor.   Jordan
Kam.   Cambodia
Kaz.-U.S.S.R.   Kazakh S.S.R., U.S.S.R.
Kenya   Kenya
Ker. Is.   Kermadec Islands
Kir.   Kiribati

Kirg.-U.S.S.R.   Kirghiz S.S.R., U.S.S.R.
Ks.-U.S.   Kansas, U.S.
Kuw.   Kuwait
Ky.-U.S.   Kentucky, U.S.
La.-U.S.   Louisiana, U.S.
Laos   Laos
Lat.-U.S.S.R.   Latvian S.S.R., U.S.S.R.
Lbr.   Liberia
Leb.   Lebanon
Les.   Lesotho
Lib.   Libya
Liech.   Liechtenstein
Lith.-U.S.S.R.   Lithuanian S.S.R., U.S.S.R.
Lux.   Luxembourg
Ma.-U.S.   Massachusetts, U.S.
Mac.   Macao
Mad.   Madagascar
Mala.   Malaysia
Mald.   Maldives
Mali   Mali
Malta   Malta
Man.-Can.   Manitoba, Canada
Mar. Is.   Marshall Islands
Mart.   Martinique
Maur.   Mauritius
May.   Mayotte
Mco.   Monaco
Md.-U.S.   Maryland, U.S.
Me.-U.S.   Maine, U.S.
Mex.   Mexico
Mi.-U.S.   Michigan, U.S.
Mid. Is.   Midway Islands
Mn.-U.S.   Minnesota, U.S.
Mo.-U.S.   Missouri, U.S.
Mold.-U.S.S.R.   Moldavian S.S.R., U.S.S.R.
Mong.   Mongolia
Mont.   Montserrat
Mor.   Morocco
Moz.   Mozambique
Ms.-U.S.   Mississippi, U.S.
Mt.-U.S.   Montana, U.S.
Mtna.   Mauritania
Mwi.   Malawi
Nam.   Namibia
N. Amer.   North America
Nauru   Nauru
N.B.-Can.   New Brunswick, Canada
Nb.-U.S.   Nebraska, U.S.
N.C.-U.S.   North Carolina, U.S.
N. Cal.   New Caledonia
N.D.-U.S.   North Dakota, U.S.
Nep.   Nepal
Neth.   Netherlands
Neth. Ant.   Netherlands Antilles
Newf.-Can.   Newfoundland, Canada
N.H.-U.S.   New Hampshire, U.S.
Nic.   Nicaragua
Nig.   Nigeria
Niger   Niger
N. Ire.-U.K.   Northern Ireland, U.K.

N.J.-U.S.   New Jersey, U.S.
N. Kor.   North Korea
N.M.-U.S.   New Mexico, U.S.
N. M. Is.   Northern Mariana Islands
Nor.   Norway
Nor. I.   Norfolk Island
N.S.-Canada   Nova Scotia, Canada
Nv.-U.S.   Nevada, U.S.
N.W.T.-Can.   Northwest Territories, Canada
N.Y.-U.S.   New York, U.S.
N.Z.   New Zealand
Ocn.   Oceania
Oh.-U.S.   Ohio, U.S.
Ok.-U.S.   Oklahoma, U.S.
Oman   Oman
Ont.-Ont.   Ontario, Canada
Or.-U.S.   Oregon, U.S.
Pa.-U.S.   Pennsylvania, U.S.
Pak.   Pakistan
Pal.   Palau
Pan.   Panama
Pap. N. Gui.   Papua New Guinea
Par.   Paraguay
Pas.   Pascua
P.E.I.-Can.   Prince Edward Island, Canada
Peru   Peru
Phil.   Philippines
Pit.   Pitcairn
Pol.   Poland
Port.   Portugal
P.R.   Puerto Rico
Qatar   Qatar
Que.-Can.   Quebec, Canada
Reu.   Reunion
R.I.-U.S.   Rhode Island, U.S.
Rom.   Romania
R.S.F.S.R.-U.S.S.R.   Russian Soviet Federative Socialist Republic, U.S.S.R.
Rwn.   Rwanda
S. Afr.   South Africa
S. Amer.   South America
Sao T.P.   Sao Tome and Principe
Sask.-Can.   Saskatchewan, Canada
Sau. Ar.   Saudi Arabia
S.C.-U.S.   South Carolina, U.S.
Scot.-U.K.   Scotland, U.K.
S.D.-U.S.   South Dakota, U.S.
Sen.   Senegal
Sey.   Seychelles
Sing.   Singapore
S. Kor.   South Korea
S.L.   Sierra Leone
S. Lan.   Sri Lanka
S.M.   San Marino
S.N.A.   Spanish North Africa
Sol. Is.   Solomon Islands
Som.   Somalia
Sp.   Spain
St. C.N.   Saint Christopher-Nevis
St. Hel.   Saint Helena
St. Luc.   Saint Lucia

St. P.M.   Saint Pierre and Miquelon
St. Vin.   Saint Vincent and the Grenadines
Sud.   Sudan
Sur.   Suriname
Sval.   Svalbard
Swe.   Sweden
Switz.   Switzerland
Syr.   Syria
Tad.-U.S.S.R.   Tajik S.S.R., U.S.S.R.
Tai.   Taiwan
Tan.   Tanzania
T.C. Is.   Turks and Caicos Islands
Thai.   Thailand
Tn.-U.S.   Tennessee, U.S.
Togo   Togo
Ton.   Tonga
Trin.   Trinidad and Tobago
T.T.P.I.   Trust Territory of the Pacific Islands
Tun.   Tunisia
Tur.   Turkey
Tur.-U.S.S.R.   Turkmen S.S.R., U.S.S.R.
Tuv.   Tuvalu
Tx.-U.S.   Texas, U.S.
U.A.E.   United Arab Emirates
Ug.   Uganda
U.K.   United Kingdom
Ukr.-U.S.S.R.   Ukrainian S.S.R., U.S.S.R.
Ur.   Uruguay
U.S.   United States
U.S.S.R.   Union of Soviet Socialist Republics
Ut.-U.S.   Utah, U.S.
Uzb.-U.S.S.R.   Uzbek S.S.R., U.S.S.R.
Va.-U.S.   Virginia, U.S.
Van.   Vanuatu
V.C.   Vatican City
Ven.   Venezuela
Viet.   Vietnam
V.I.U.S.   Virgin Islands of the U.S.
Vt.-U.S.   Vermont, U.S.
Wa.-U.S.   Washington, U.S.
Wake   Wake Island
Wales-U.K.   Wales, U.K.
W.F.   Wallis and Futuna
Wi.-U.S.   Wisconsin, U.S.
W. Sah.   Western Sahara
W. Sam.   Western Samoa
W.V.-U.S.   West Virginia, U.S.
Wy.-U.S.   Wyoming, U.S.
Yem.   Yemen
Yugo.   Yugoslavia
Yuk.-Can.   Yukon, Canada
Zaire   Zaire
Zam.   Zambia
Zimb.   Zimbabwe

List of Symbols

Plains and Associated Features
- Plain, Basin, Lowland
- Delta
- Salt Flat

Valleys and Depressions
- Valley, Gorge, Ravine, Canyon
- Cave, Crater, Quarry
- Karst Features
- Depression
- Polder, Reclaimed Marsh

Vegetational Features
- Desert, Dunes
- Forest, Woods
- Heath, Steppe, Tundra, Moor
- Oasis

Political/Administrative Units
- 1 Independent Nation
- 2 State, Canton, Region
- 3 Province, Department, County, Territory, District
- 4 Municipality
- 5 Colony, Dependency, Administered Territory

Geographical Regions
- Continent
- Physical Region
- Historical or Cultural Region

Mountain Features
- Mount, Mountain, Peak
- Volcano
- Hill
- Mountains, Mountain Range
- Hills, Escarpment
- Plateau, Highland, Upland
- Pass, Gap

Coastal Features
- Cape, Point
- Coast, Beach
- Cliff
- Peninsula, Promontory
- Isthmus
- Sandbank, Tombolo, Sandbar

Islands Rocks, Reefs
- Island
- Atoll
- Rock, Reef
- Islands, Archipelago
- Rocks, Reefs
- Coral Reef

Hydrographic Features
- Well, Spring
- Geyser, Fumarole
- River, Stream, Brook
- Waterfall, Rapids, Cataract
- River Mouth, Estuary
- Lake
- Salt Lake
- Intermittent Lake, Dry Lake Bed
- Reservoir, Artificial Lake
- Swamp, Marsh, Pond
- Irrigation Canal, Navigable Canal, Ditch, Aqueduct

Ice Features
- Glacier, Snowfield
- Ice Shelf, Pack Ice

Marine Features
- Ocean
- Sea
- Gulf, Bay
- Strait, Fjord, Sea Channel
- Lagoon, Anchorage

Submarine Features
- Bank, Shoal
- Seamount
- Rise, Plateau, Tablemount
- Seamount Chain, Ridge
- Platform, Shelf
- Basin, Depression
- Escarpment, Slope, Sea Scarp
- Fracture
- Trench, Abyss, Valley, Canyon

Other Features
- National Park, Nature Reserve
- Scenic Area, Point of Interest
- Recreation Site, Sports Arena
- Cave, Cavern
- Historic Site, Memorial, Mausoleum, Museum
- Ruins
- Wall, Walls, Tower, Castle, Fortress
- Church, Abbey, Cathedral, Sanctuary
- Temple, Synagogue, Mosque
- Research or Scientific Station
- Railway station
- Airport, Heliport
- Port, Dock
- Military installation
- Lighthouse
- Mine
- Tunnel
- Dam, Bridge

A

Å	114	Cc	67.53N	12.59 E
Aa [Eur.]	124	Ic	51.50N	6.25 E
Aa [Fr.]	122	Ic	51.01N	2.06 E
Aa [Fr.]	124	Dd	50.44N	2.18 E
Aa [Ger.]	124	Kb	52.07N	8.41 E
Aa [Ger.]	124	Jb	52.15N	7.18 E
Aa [Neth.]	124	Hc	51.42N	5.20 E
Aachen	120	Cf	50.46N	6.06 E
Aalen	120	Gh	48.50N	10.06 E
A'ālī an Nīl [3]	168	Ed	9.15N	33.00 E
Aalsmeer	124	Gb	52.15N	4.45 E
Aalst/Alost	122	Kd	50.56N	4.02 E
Aalten	124	Ic	51.55N	6.35 E
Aalter	124	Fc	51.05N	3.27 E
Äänekoski	114	Fe	62.36N	25.44 E
Aa of Weerijs	124	Gc	51.35N	4.46 E
Aar	124	Kd	50.23N	8.00 E
Aarau	128	Cc	47.25N	8.02 E
Aarbergen	124	Kd	50.13N	8.03 E
Aare	128	Cc	47.37N	8.13 E
Aargau [2]	128	Cc	47.30N	8.10 E
Aarlen/Arlon	122	Le	49.41N	5.49 E
Aarschot	122	Kd	50.59N	4.50 E
Aat/Ath	122	Jd	50.38N	3.47 E
Aazanèn	126	Ii	35.06N	3.02W
Āb	146	Md	36.00N	48.05 E
Aba [Nig.]	160	Hh	5.07N	7.22 E
Aba [Zaire]	160	Kh	3.52N	30.14 E
Aba/Ngawa	152	He	32.55N	101.45 E
Abā ad Dūd	146	Ki	27.02N	44.04 E
Abā as Su'ūd	144	Ff	17.28N	44.06 E
Abacaxis, Rio-	202	Gd	3.54 S	58.50W
Abaco Island	174	Lg	26.25N	77.10W
Abacou, Pointe l'-	194	Kd	18.03N	73.47W
Abadab, Jabal-	168	Fb	18.53N	35.59 E
Ābādān	142	Gf	30.10N	48.50 E
Ābādeh [Iran]	144	Hc	31.10N	52.37 E
Ābādeh [Iran]	146	Oh	29.08N	52.52 E
Abadiânia	204	Hc	16.06 S	48.48W
Abadla	160	Ge	31.01N	2.43W
Abaeté	204	Jd	19.09 S	45.27W
Abaeté, Rio-	204	Jd	18.02 S	45.12W
Abaetetuba	202	Id	1.42 S	48.54W
Abagnar Qi (Xilin Hot)	142	Ne	43.58N	116.08 E
Abag Qi (Xin Hot)	152	Jc	44.01N	114.59 E
Abaí	204	Eh	26.01 S	55.57W
Abaiang Atoll	208	Id	1.51N	172.58 E
Abaj	136	Hf	49.38N	72.50 E
Abaji	166	Gd	8.28N	6.57 E
Abajo Mountains	188	Kh	37.50N	109.25W
Abakaliki	166	Gd	6.20N	8.03 E
Abakan	142	Ld	53.43N	91.26 E
Abakan	138	Ef	53.43N	91.30 E
Abakwasimbo	170	Eb	0.36N	28.43 E
Abala [Con.]	170	Cc	1.21 S	15.30 E
Abala [Niger]	166	Fc	14.56N	3.26 E
Abalak	166	Gb	15.27N	6.17 E
Aban	138	Ee	56.40N	96.10 E
Abancay	202	Df	13.35 S	72.55W
Abancourt	124	De	49.42N	1.46 E
Abanga	170	Bb	0.13N	10.28 E
Abano Terme	128	Fe	45.21N	11.47 E
Ābār al Jidd	146	Hf	32.50N	39.50 E
Abarqū	144	Hc	31.08N	53.17 E
Abarqu, Kavīr-e-	146	Og	31.00N	53.50 E
Abashiri	152	Pc	44.01N	144.17 E
Abashiri-Gawa	156a	Db	43.56N	144.09 E
Abashiri-Ko	156a	Da	44.00N	144.10 E
Abashiri-Wan	156a	Da	44.00N	144.35 E
Abasolo	192	Je	24.04N	98.22W
Abatski	136	Hd	56.18N	70.28 E
Abau	214	Dj	10.11 S	148.42 E
Abava	114	Eh	57.06N	21.54 E
Abay=Blue Nile (EN)	158	Kg	15.38N	32.31 E
Abaya, Lake-	158	Kh	6.20N	37.55 E
Abaza	138	Ef	52.39N	90.06 E
Abbadia San Salvatore	128	Fh	42.53N	11.41 E
Abbah Quşūr	128	Co	35.57N	8.50 E
Āb Bārīk	146	Oh	29.45N	52.37 E
'Abbāsābād	146	Qd	36.20N	56.25 E
Abbekås	116	Ei	55.24N	13.36 E
Abberton Reservoir	124	Cc	51.50N	0.55 E
Abbeville [Fr.]	122	Hd	50.06N	1.50 E
Abbeville [La.-U.S.]	186	Jl	29.58N	92.08W
Abbeville [S.C.-U.S.]	184	Fh	34.10N	82.23W
Abbey	188	Ka	50.43N	108.45W
Abbeyfeale/Mainistir na Féile	118	Di	52.24N	9.18W
Abbiategrasso	128	Ce	45.24N	8.54 E
Abbot, Mount-	212	Jd	20.03 S	147.45 E
Abbot Ice Shelf	222	Pf	72.45 S	96.00W
'Abd Al 'Azīz, Jabal-	146	Id	36.25N	40.20 E
'Abd al Kurī	140	Hh	12.12N	52.13 E
Ābdānān	146	Lf	32.57N	47.26 E
Abdul Ghadir	168	Gc	10.42N	42.59 E
Abdulino	136	Fe	53.42N	53.38 E
Abe, Lake-	168	Gc	11.10N	41.45 E
Abéché	160	Jg	13.49N	20.49 E
Abeek	124	Hc	51.15N	6.00 E
Abe-Gawa	156	Fd	34.55N	138.22 E
Abeløya	179	Pc	79.00N	30.15 E
Abelvær	114	Cd	64.44N	11.11 E
Abemama Atoll	208	Id	0.21N	173.51 E
Abenab	172	Bc	19.12 S	18.06 E
Abengourou	160	Gh	6.44N	3.29W
Abengourou [3]	166	Ed	6.35N	3.25W
Åbenrå	114	Bi	55.02N	9.26 E
Åbenrå Fjord	116	Ci	55.05N	9.35 E
Abeokuta	160	Hh	7.09N	3.21 E
Aberaeron	118	Ii	52.15N	4.15W
Aberdare Range	158	Ki	0.25 S	36.38 E
Aberdeen [Id.-U.S.]	188	Ie	42.57N	112.50W
Aberdeen [Md.-U.S.]	184	If	39.30N	76.14W
Aberdeen [Ms.-U.S.]	186	Lj	33.49N	88.33W
Aberdeen [N.C.-U.S.]	184	Hh	35.08N	79.26W
Aberdeen [S.Afr.]	172	Cf	32.29 S	24.03 E
Aberdeen [Scot.-U.K.]	112	Fd	57.10N	2.04W
Aberdeen [S.D.-U.S.]	176	Je	45.28N	98.29W
Aberdeen [Wa.-U.S.]	182	Cb	46.59N	123.50W
Aberdeen Lake	180	Hd	64.28N	99.00W
Abergavenny	118	Kj	51.50N	3.00W
Aberystwyth	118	Ii	52.25N	4.05W
Abetone	128	Ef	44.08N	10.40 E
Abez	136	Gb	66.32N	61.46 E
Abhā	142	Gh	18.13N	42.30 E
Abhainn an Chláir/Clare	118	Dh	53.20N	9.03W
Abhainn an Lagáin/Lagan	118	Hg	54.37N	5.53W
Abhainn na Bandan/Bandon	118	Ej	51.40N	8.30W
Abhainn na Deirge/Derg	118	Fg	54.40N	7.25W
Abhar	144	Gb	36.09N	49.13 E
Abhar	146	Md	36.02N	49.45 E
Abhazskaja ASSR [3]	136	Eg	43.00N	41.10 E
Abibe, Serranía de-	202	Cb	8.00N	76.30W
Abidjan	160	Gh	5.19N	4.02W
Abidjan [3]	166	Ed	5.30N	4.30W
Abilene [Ks.-U.S.]	186	Hg	38.55N	97.13W
Abilene [Tx.-U.S.]	176	Jf	32.27N	99.44W
Abingdon	118	Lj	51.41N	1.17W
Abinsk	132	Kg	44.52N	38.10 E
Abiquiu	186	Ch	36.12N	106.19W
Abiquiu Reservoir	186	Ch	36.18N	106.32W
Abisko	114	Eb	68.20N	18.51 E
Abitibi	180	Jf	51.04N	80.55W
Abitibi, Lake-	174	Le	48.42N	79.45W
Abiy Adi	168	Fc	13.37N	39.01 E
Abiyata, Lake-	168	Fd	7.38N	38.36 E
Abja-Paluoja	116	Kf	58.02N	25.14 E
Abnūb	164	Fd	27.16N	31.09 E
Åbo/Turku	112	Ic	60.27N	22.17 E
Abo, Massif d'-	168	Ba	21.41N	16.08 E
Abóboras, Serra das-	204	Jc	16.12 S	44.35W
Abodo	168	Ed	7.50N	34.25 E
Aboisso	166	Ed	5.28N	3.12W
Aboisso [3]	166	Ed	5.28N	3.02W
Abomey	160	Hh	7.11N	1.59 E
Abong Mbang	166	He	3.59N	13.11 E
Abony	120	Pi	47.11N	20.00 E
Aborigen, pik-	138	Jd	62.05N	149.10 E
Aborlar	150	Ge	9.26N	118.33 E
Aborrebierg	116	Ej	54.59N	12.32 E
Abou Deïa	168	Bc	11.27N	19.17 E
Abou Goulem	168	Cc	13.37N	21.38 E
Abovjan	132	Ni	40.14N	44.37 E
Abraham's Bay	194	Kb	22.21N	72.55W
Abramovski bereg	114	Kc	66.25N	43.05 E
Abrántes	126	De	39.28N	8.12W
Abra Pampa	206	Gb	22.43 S	65.42W
Abrego	194	Ki	8.04N	73.14W
Abreojos, Punta-	190	Bc	26.42N	113.35W
Abrets, Les-	122	Li	45.32N	5.35 E
'Abrī	168	Ea	20.48N	30.20 E
Abrolhos, Arquipélago dos-	202	Kg	18.00 S	38.40W
Abrud	130	Gc	46.16N	23.04 E
Abruka, ostrov- / Abruka saar	116	Jf	58.08N	22.25 E
Abruka saar / Abruka, ostrov-	116	Jf	58.08N	22.25 E
Abruzzi [2]	128	Hh	42.20N	13.45 E
Absaroka Range	182	Fc	44.45N	109.50W
Abtenau	128	Hc	47.33N	13.21 E
Abū ad Duhūr	146	Ge	35.44N	37.02 E
Abū 'Alī	146	Mi	27.20N	49.33 E
Abū al Khaşīb	146	Lg	30.27N	47.59 E
Abū an Na'am	146	Hj	25.14N	38.49 E
Abū 'Arīsh	144	Ff	16.58N	42.50 E
Abū Ballaş	164	Ee	24.26N	27.39 E
Abū Daghmah	146	Hd	36.25N	38.15 E
Abū Darbah	164	Fd	28.29N	33.20 E
Abu Dhabi (EN)=Abū Z̧aby	142	Hg	24.28N	54.22 E
Abū Ḩād, Wādī-	146	Ei	27.46N	33.30 E
Abū Ḩadrīyah	146	Mi	27.20N	48.56 E
Abū Ḩamad	160	Kg	19.32N	33.19 E
Abū Ḩammād	146	Dg	30.32N	31.40 E
Abū Ḩarbah, Jabal-	146	Ei	27.17N	33.13 E
Abū Ḩashā'ifah, Khalīj-	146	Bg	31.16N	27.25 E
Abuja	160	Hh	9.10N	7.11 E
Abu Jābirah	168	Dc	11.04N	26.51 E
Abū Jifān	146	Lj	24.31N	47.43 E
Abū Kabīr	146	Dg	30.44N	31.40 E
Abū Kamāl	144	Fc	34.27N	40.55 E
Abukuma-Gawa	156	Gb	38.06N	140.52 E
Abukuma-Sanchi	156	Gc	37.20N	140.45 E
Abū Latt	164	Hf	19.58N	40.08 E
Abū Libdah, Khashm-	164	Ie	22.58N	46.13 E
Abū Madd, Ra's-	144	Ee	24.50N	37.12 E
Abū Maţāriq	168	Dc	10.58N	26.17 E
Abu Mendi	168	Fc	11.47N	35.42 E
Abumonbazi	170	Db	3.42N	22.10 E
Abū Muḩarrik, Ghurd-	164	Ed	27.00N	30.00 E
Abū Mūsa'	144	Hd	25.10N	59.00 E
Abū Musā, Jazīreh-ye-	144	Id	25.52N	55.03 E
Abunã	200	Jf	9.42 S	65.23W
Abuná, Rio-	198	Jf	9.41 S	65.23W
Abune Yosef	168	Fc	12.09N	39.12 E
Abū Qīr	146	Dg	31.19N	30.04 E
Abū Qīr, Khalīj-	146	Dg	31.20N	30.15 E
Abū Qumayyis, Ra's-	146	Nj	24.34N	51.30 E
Abu Road	148	Ed	24.29N	72.47 E
Abū Sawmah, Ra's-	146	Ei	26.51N	33.59 E
Abū Shanab	168	Dc	13.57N	27.47 E
Abu Simbel (EN) = Abū Sunbul	164	Fe	22.22N	31.38 E
Abū Şukhayr	146	Kg	31.52N	44.27 E
Abū Sunbul = Abu Simbel (EN)	164	Fe	22.22N	31.38 E
Abuta	154	Pc	42.31N	140.46 E
Abut Head	218	De	43.06 S	170.15 E
Abū Tij	164	Fd	27.02N	31.19 E
Abū Ţurţūr, Jabal-	146	Cj	25.20N	30.00 E
Abū'Urūq	168	Eb	15.54N	30.27 E
Abuyemeda	168	Fc	10.38N	39.43 E
Abū Zabad	168	Dc	12.21N	29.15 E
Abū Z̧aby=Abu Dhabi (EN)	142	Hg	24.28N	54.22 E
Abū Zanīmah	164	Fd	29.03N	33.06 E
Abwong	168	Ed	9.07N	32.12 E
Åby	116	Gf	58.40N	16.11 E
Abyaḑ	168	Dc	13.46N	26.28 E
Abyaḑ, Al Baḩr al-=White Nile (EN) [3]	168	Ec	12.40N	32.30 E
Abyaḑ, Al Baḩr al-=White Nile (EN)	158	Kg	15.38N	32.31 E
Abyaḑ, Ar Ra's al-	144	Ee	23.32N	38.32 E
Abyaḑ, Jabal-	168	Db	18.55N	28.40 E
Abyaḑ, Ra's al-=Blanc, Cape- (EN)	158	He	37.20N	9.50 E
Abyār Alī	146	Hj	24.25N	39.33 E
Abyār ash Shuwayrif	164	Bd	29.59N	14.16 E
Åbybro	114	Bh	57.09N	9.45 E
Abydos	164	Fd	26.11N	31.55 E
Abyei	168	Dd	9.36N	28.26 E
Ābyek	146	Nd	36.02N	50.31 E
Abymes	197e	Ab	16.16N	61.31W
Acacías	202	Dc	3.59N	73.47W
Academy Gletscher	179	Ib	81.45N	33.35W
Acadie	174	Me	46.00N	65.00W
Acaill/Achill	118	Dh	54.00N	10.00W
Acajutla	194	Cg	13.36N	89.50W
Acalayong	166	Ge	1.05N	9.40 E
Acámbaro	190	Dd	20.02N	100.44W
Acandí	202	Cb	8.31N	77.17W
Acaponeta	190	Cd	22.30N	105.22W
Acaponeta, Río-	192	Gf	22.20N	105.37W
Acapulco de Juárez	176	Jh	16.51N	99.55W
Acará	202	Id	1.57 S	48.11W
Acarai, Serra-	202	Gc	1.50N	57.40W
Acaraú	202	Jd	2.53 S	40.07W
Acaray, Río-	204	Eg	25.29 S	54.42W
Acari, Rio- [Braz.]	202	Ge	5.18 S	59.42W
Acari, Rio- [Braz.]	204	Jb	16.00 S	45.03W
Acarigua	202	Eb	9.33N	69.12W
Acatenango, Volcán-	174	Jh	14.30N	91.40W
Acatlán de Osorio	192	Jh	18.12N	98.03W
Acayucan	190	Fe	17.57N	94.55W
Accéglio	128	Af	44.28N	7.00 E
Aččitau, gora-	135	Cc	42.07N	60.31 E
Accomac	184	Jg	37.43N	75.40W
Accra	160	Gh	5.33N	0.13W
Acebal	204	Bk	33.14 S	60.50W
Acebuches	192	Hc	28.15N	102.43W
Aceguá [Braz.]	204	Ej	31.52 S	54.09W
Aceguá [Ur.]	204	Ej	31.52 S	54.12W
Aceh [3]	150	Cf	4.10N	96.50 E
Acerenza	128	Jj	40.48N	15.56 E
Acerra	128	Ij	40.57N	14.22 E
Achacachi	202	Eg	16.03 S	68.43W
Achaguas	202	Eb	7.46N	68.14W
Achaïf, 'Erg-	166	Ea	20.49N	4.34W
Achao	206	Ff	42.28 S	73.30W
Achar	204	Dk	32.25 S	56.10W
Achegour	166	Hb	19.03N	11.53 E
Acheng	152	Mb	45.32N	126.56 E
Acheux-en-Amiénois	124	Ed	50.04N	2.32 E
Achiet-le-Grand	124	Ed	50.08N	2.47 E
Achill/Acaill	118	Dh	54.00N	10.00W
Achílleion	130	Cj	39.34N	19.55 E
Achill Head/Ceann Acla	118	Ch	53.59N	10.13W
Achim	120	Fc	53.02N	9.01 E
Achim	168	Bb	15.53N	19.31 E
Achterwasser	120	Jb	54.00N	13.57 E
Acı Gölü	146	Cd	37.50N	29.54 E
Ačinsk	142	Ld	56.17N	90.30 E
Acıpayam	146	Cd	37.25N	29.22 E
Acireale	128	Jm	37.37N	15.10 E
Acîş	130	Fb	47.32N	22.47 E
Ačisaj	135	Gc	43.33N	68.53 E
Ačit	134	Hh	56.48N	57.54 E
Ačit-Nur	152	Fb	49.30N	90.30 E
Acklins	174	Lg	22.25N	74.00W
Acklins, The Bight of-	194	Jb	22.30N	74.15W
Acle	124	Db	52.38N	1.33 E
Acobamba	202	Df	12.48 S	74.34W
Acolin	122	Jh	46.49N	3.23 E
Aconcagua, Cerro-	198	Ji	32.39 S	70.00W
Açor, Serra de-	126	Ed	40.13N	7.48W
Açores=Azores (EN) [5]	160	Ee	38.30N	28.00W
Açores, Arquipélago dos-=Azores (EN)	158	Ee	38.30N	28.00W
Acorizal	204	Db	15.12 S	56.22W
Acoyapa	194	Eh	11.58N	85.10W
Acquapendente	128	Fh	42.44N	11.52 E
Acquasanta Terme	128	Hh	42.46N	13.24 E
Acquasparta	128	Gh	42.41N	12.33 E
Acquaviva delle Fonti	128	Kj	40.54N	16.50 E
Acqui Terme	128	Cf	44.41N	8.28 E
Acraman, Lake-	212	Hf	32.05 S	135.25 E
Acre [2]	202	Ee	9.00 S	70.00W
Acre, Rio-	198	Jf	8.45 S	67.22W
Acri	128	Kk	39.29N	16.23 E
A Cruña / La Coruña	112	Fg	43.22N	8.23W
Actéon, Groupe-	208	Ng	21.20 S	136.30W
Actopan	192	Jg	20.16N	98.56W
Açu	202	Ke	5.34 S	36.54W
Acuña	204	Di	29.55 S	57.58W
Ada [Ghana]	166	Fd	5.47N	0.38 E
Ada [Ok.-U.S.]	182	He	34.46N	96.41W
Ada [Yugo.]	130	Dd	45.48N	20.08 E
Adaba	168	Fd	7.03N	39.31 E
'Adad	168	Hd	8.23N	46.48 E
'Adādle	168	Gd	9.45N	44.41 E
Adair, Bahia-	192	Cb	31.30N	113.50W
Adair, Cape -	180	Kb	71.31N	71.24W
Adaja	126	Hc	41.32N	4.52W
Adak	178a	Cb	51.45N	176.40W
Adalar	130	Mi	40.52N	29.07 E
'Adale	168	He	2.46N	46.20 E
Ådalen	116	Ga	63.20N	17.30 E
Adalselv	116	Dd	60.04N	10.11 E
Adam, Mount-	206	Hh	51.34 S	60.04W
Adamantina	204	Ge	21.42 S	51.04W
Adamaoua=Adamawa (EN)	158	Ih	7.00N	15.00 E
Adamawa (EN)=Adamaoua	158	Ih	7.00N	15.00 E
Adamello	128	Ed	46.09N	10.30 E
Adamovka	132	Ud	51.32N	59.59 E
Adams	186	Le	43.58N	89.49W
Adams, Mount-	182	Cb	46.12N	121.28W
Adams Lake	188	Fa	51.13N	119.33W
Adams River	180	Ff	50.54N	119.33W
Adam's Rock	220q	Ab	25.04 S	130.05W
Adamstown	210	Ng	25.04 S	130.05W
Adamuz	126	Hf	38.02N	4.31W
Adana	142	Ff	37.01N	35.18 E
Adapazarı	146	Db	40.46N	30.24 E
Adarama	168	Eb	17.05N	34.54 E
Adarān, Jabal-	164	Ig	13.46N	45.08 E
Adare, Cape-	222	Kf	71.17 S	170.14 E
Adavale	212	Ie	25.55 S	144.36 E
Adda [It.]	110	Gf	45.08N	9.53 E
Adda [Sud.]	168	Cd	9.51N	24.50 E
Aḑ Ḑab'ah	164	Ec	31.02N	28.26 E
Ad Dabbah	168	Eb	18.03N	30.57 E
Ad Dafīnah	164	He	23.18N	41.58 E
Aḑ Ḑafrah	146	Ok	23.25N	53.25 E
Ad Dahnā'	140	Gg	24.30N	48.10 E
Addala-Šuhgelmeer, gora-	132	Oh	42.20N	46.15 E
Aḑ Ḑālī'	164	Hg	13.42N	44.44 E
Ad Damazin	168	Ec	11.49N	34.23 E
Ad 'Dāmir	168	Eb	17.35N	33.58 E
Ad Dammām	142	Hg	26.26N	50.07 E
Ad Dār al Ḩamrā'	144	Ed	27.19N	37.44 E
Ad Dawādimī	146	Kj	24.28N	44.18 E
Ad Dawḩah=Doha (EN)	142	Hg	25.17N	51.32 E
Ad Dawr	146	Je	34.27N	43.47 E
Ad Dayr	164	Fd	25.20N	32.35 E
Ad Dibdibah	146	Lh	28.00N	46.30 E
Aḑ Ḑiffah	164	Ec	30.30N	25.30 E
Ad Dikākah	168	Ib	19.25N	51.30 E
Ad Dilam	144	Ge	23.59N	47.10 E
Ad Dindar	168	Ec	13.20N	34.05 E
Ad Dir'īyah	146	Lj	24.48N	46.32 E
Addis Ababa (EN) = Adis Abeba	160	Kh	9.01N	38.46 E
Ad Dissān	164	Hf	16.56N	41.41 E
Addis Zemen	168	Fc	12.05N	37.44 E
Ad Dīwānīya	144	Fc	31.59N	44.56 E
Addu Atoll	140	Jj	0.25 S	73.10 E
Ad Du'ayn	168	Dc	11.26N	26.09 E
Ad Duwayd	146	Jg	30.13N	42.18 E
Ad Duwaym	168	Ec	14.00N	32.19 E
Adel [Ga.-U.S.]	184	Fj	31.18N	83.25W
Adel [Or.-U.S.]	188	Fe	42.11N	119.54W
Adelaide [Austl.]	210	Eh	34.56 S	138.36 E
Adelaide [Bah.]	184	Im	25.00N	77.31W
Adelaide [S.Afr.]	172	Df	32.42 S	26.20 E
Adelaide Island	222	Qe	67.15 S	68.30W
Adelaide Peninsula	180	Hc	68.05N	97.50W
Adelaide River	210	Ef	13.15 S	131.06 E
Adelaye	168	Cd	7.07N	22.49 E
Adelboden	128	Bd	46.30N	7.33 E
Adèle Island	212	Ec	15.30 S	123.10 E
Adélie, Terre-	222	Ie	67.00 S	139.00 E
Ademuz	126	Kd	40.04N	1.17W
Aden (EN) = Baladīyat 'Adan	142	Gh	12.46N	45.01 E
Aden, Gulf of-	158	Lg	12.00N	48.00 E
Aden, Gulf of- (EN) = 'Admēd, Badyarada-	158	Lg	12.00N	48.00 E
Adenau	124	Id	50.23N	6.56 E
Ader	158	Hg	14.10N	5.05 E
Aderbissinat	166	Gb	15.37N	7.52 E
Adhan, Jabal-	146	Qj	25.27N	56.13 E
Adh Dhahībāt	162	Jc	32.01N	10.42 E
Adh Dhayd	146	Pj	25.17N	55.53 E
Adhélfi	130	Gj	39.08N	23.59 E
Adhelfoi	130	Jm	36.25N	26.37 E
'Adhırīyāt, Jıbāl- al-	146	Gg	30.25N	36.48 E
Adi, Pulau-	150	Jg	4.18 S	133.26 E
Adiaké	166	Ed	5.16N	3.17W
Adi Arkay	168	Fc	13.31N	38.00 E
Adícora	202	Ea	11.57N	69.48W
Adi Dairo	168	Fc	14.21N	38.12 E
Adigala	168	Gc	10.24N	42.18 E
Adige/Etsch	110	Hf	45.10N	12.20 E
Adigrat	168	Fc	14.16N	39.28 E
Adi Keyeh	168	Fc	14.48N	39.23 E
Adi Kwala	168	Fc	14.37N	38.51 E
Ādilābād	148	Fe	19.40N	78.32 E
Adīrī	160	If	27.30N	13.16 E
Adirondack Mountains	174	Le	44.00N	74.00W
Adis Abeba = Addis Ababa (EN)	160	Kh	9.01N	38.46 E
Adis Alem	168	Fd	9.03N	38.24 E
Adi Ugri	168	Fc	14.53N	38.49 E
Adiyaman	144	Eb	37.46N	38.17 E
Adjud	130	Kc	46.06N	27.10 E
Adjuntas	197a	Bb	18.09N	66.43W
'Admēd, Badyarada- = Aden, Gulf of- (EN)	158	Lg	12.00N	48.00 E
Admer, Erg d'-	162	Ie	24.12N	9.10 E
Admiralty	178	Me	57.50N	134.30W
Admiralty Bay	197n	Ba	13.00N	61.16W
Admiralty Gulf	212	Fb	14.20 S	125.50 E
Admiralty Inlet	180	Ib	72.30N	86.00W
Admiralty Islands	208	Fe	2.10 S	147.00 E
Admiralty Mountains	222	Kf	71.45 S	168.30 E
Admont	128	Ic	47.34N	14.27 E
Ado	166	Fd	6.36N	2.56 E
Ado Ekiti	166	Gd	7.38N	5.13 E
Adok	168	Ed	8.11N	30.19 E
Adolfo Gonzales Chaves	204	Bn	38.02 S	60.06W
Adolfo López Mateos, Presa-	192	Fe	25.05N	107.20W
Adonara, Pulau-	150	Hh	8.20 S	123.10 E
Ādoni	148	Fe	15.38N	77.17 E
Adour	122	Ek	43.32N	1.32W
Adra	126	Ih	36.44N	3.01W
Adrano	128	Im	37.40N	14.50 E
Adrar	160	Gf	27.54N	0.17W
Adrar	158	Hf	25.12N	8.10 E
Adrar	158	Ff	20.30N	13.30W
Adrar [Alg.] [3]	162	Gd	27.00N	1.00W
Adrar [Mtna.] [3]	162	Fe	21.00N	11.00W
Adré	168	Cc	13.28N	22.12 E
Adria	128	Ge	45.03N	12.03 E
Adrian	184	Ee	41.54N	84.02W
Adrianópolis	204	Hg	24.41 S	48.50W
Adriatic, Deti-=Adriatic Sea (EN)	110	Hg	43.00N	16.00 E
Adriatico, Mar-=Adriatic Sea (EN)	110	Hg	43.00N	16.00 E
Adriatic Sea (EN)=Adriatic, Deti-	110	Hg	43.00N	16.00 E
Adriatic Sea (EN)=Adriatico, Mar-	110	Hg	43.00N	16.00 E
Adriatic Sea (EN)=Jadransko More	110	Hg	43.00N	16.00 E
Aduard	124	Ia	53.15N	6.25 E
Adula	128	Dd	46.30N	9.05 E
Adulis	168	Fb	15.15N	39.37 E
Adur	124	Bd	50.49N	0.16W
Adusa	170	Eb	1.23N	28.01 E
Adventure Bank (EN)	128	Gm	37.20N	12.10 E
Adwa	160	Kg	14.10N	38.55 E
Adyča	140	Pc	68.13N	135.03 E
Adygalah	138	Jd	62.57N	146.25 E
Adygejskaja avtonomnaja oblast [3]	136	Eg	44.30N	40.05 E
Adžarskaja ASSR [3]	136	Eg	41.40N	42.10 E
Adzopé	166	Ed	6.06N	3.52W
Adzopé [3]	166	Ed	6.15N	3.45W
Adzva	134	Ic	66.36N	59.28 E
Aegean Sea (EN)=Aiyaion Pélagos	110	Ih	39.00N	25.00 E
Aegean Sea (EN)=Ege Denizi	110	Ih	39.00N	25.00 E
Aegina (EN) = Aiyina	130	Gl	37.40N	23.30 E
Aegviidu	116	Ke	59.17N	25.37 E
Aeon Point	220g	Bb	1.46N	157.11W
Aerfort na Sionainne/Shannon	118	Ei	52.42N	8.57W
Ærø	116	Dj	54.55N	10.20 E
Ærøskøbing	116	Dj	54.53N	10.25 E
Aerzen	124	Lb	52.02N	9.16 E
Afafi, Massif d'-	166	Ha	22.15N	15.00 E
'Afak	146	Kf	32.04N	45.15 E
Afanasjevo	114	Mg	58.54N	53.16 E
Afareaitu	221e	Fc	17.33 S	149.47W
Afars and Issas (EN) → Djibouti [1]	160	Lg	11.30N	43.00 E
Aff	122	Dg	47.43N	2.07W
Affollé	158	Fg	16.55N	10.25W
Affrica, Scoglio d'-	128	Eh	42.20N	10.05 E
Afghānistān [1]	142	If	33.00N	65.00 E
Afgōye	168	He	2.09N	45.07 E
'Afīf	144	Fe	23.55N	42.56 E
Afikpo	166	Gd	5.53N	7.55 E
Afipski	132	Kg	44.52N	38.50 E
Aflou	162	Hc	34.07N	2.06 E
Afmadōw	168	Ge	0.29N	42.06 E
Afognak	178	Ie	58.15N	152.30W
Afonso Cláudio	202	Jh	20.05 S	41.08W
Afon Teifi	118	Ii	52.06N	4.43W
Afon Tywi	118	Ij	51.40N	4.15W
Afragola	128	Ij	40.55N	14.18 E
Afrērā, Lake-	168	Gc	13.20N	41.03 E
Africa (EN)	106	Eh	10.00N	22.00 E
African Islands	158	Mi	4.53 S	43.24 E
Afşin	146	Gc	38.36N	36.55 E
Afsluitdijk	122	La	53.00N	5.15 E
Afton	188	Je	42.44N	110.56W
Afuá	202	Hd	0.10 S	50.23W
'Afula	146	Ff	32.36N	35.17 E
Afyonkarahisar	142	Ff	38.45N	30.40 E
Agadem	160	Ig	16.50N	13.17 E
Agadez	160	Hg	16.58N	7.59 E
Agadez [2]	166	Hb	19.45N	10.15 E
Agadez, Irhazer Oua-n-	166	Gb	17.28N	6.26 E
Agadir	160	Ge	30.25N	9.37W
Agadir [3]	162	Fc	30.00N	9.00W
Agadyr	136	Hf	48.17N	72.53 E
Agalega Islands	158	Mj	10.24 S	56.30 E
Agalta, Sierra de-	190	Ge	15.00N	85.53W
Agan	136	Hc	61.23N	74.35 E
Agana	210	Fc	13.28N	144.45 E
Agano-Gawa	154	Of	37.57N	139.07 E
Aga Point	220c	Bb	13.14N	144.43 E
Agapovka	134	Ij	53.18N	59.10 E
Agaro	168	Fd	7.53N	36.36 E
Agartala	142	Lg	23.49N	91.16 E
Agassiz Pool	186	Ib	48.20N	95.58W
Agat	220c	Bb	13.23N	144.39 E
Agat Bay	220c	Bb	13.24N	144.39 E
Agats	210	Ee	5.33 S	138.08 E
Agattu	178a	Ab	52.25N	173.35 E
Agawa Bay	134	Eb	47.22N	84.33W
Agawa Bay	184	Eb	47.20N	84.42W
Agboville	166	Ed	5.56N	4.13W
Agboville [3]	166	Ed	6.00N	4.15W
Agdam	136	Eh	39.58N	46.57 E
Agdaš	132	Oi	40.38N	47.29 E
Agde	122	Jk	43.19N	3.28 E
Agde, Cap d'-	122	Jk	43.16N	3.30 E
Agder	116	Cf	58.25N	8.15 E
Agdz	162	Fc	30.27N	7.56W
Agdžabedi	132	Oi	40.03N	47.28 E
Agematsu	156	Ed	35.47N	137.41 E
Agen	122	Gj	44.12N	0.38 E
Ageo	156	Fd	35.58N	139.35 E
Agepsta, gora-	132	Lh	43.32N	40.30 E
Ager	128	Hb	48.05N	13.51 E
Agere Mariam	168	Fd	5.39N	38.15 E

Index Symbols

- [1] Independent Nation
- [2] State, Region
- [3] District, County
- [4] Municipality
- [5] Colony, Dependency
- Continent
- Physical Region
- Historical or Cultural Region
- Mount, Mountain
- Volcano
- Hill
- Mountains, Mountain Range
- Hills, Escarpment
- Plateau, Upland
- Pass, Gap
- Plain, Lowland
- Delta
- Salt Flat
- Valley, Canyon
- Crater, Cave
- Karst Features
- Depression
- Polder
- Desert, Dunes
- Forest, Woods
- Heath, Steppe
- Oasis
- Cape, Point
- Coast, Beach
- Cliff
- Peninsula
- Isthmus
- Sandbank
- Island
- Atoll
- Rock, Reef
- Islands, Archipelago
- Rocks, Reefs
- Coral Reef
- Well, Spring
- Geyser
- River, Stream
- Waterfall, Rapids
- River Mouth, Estuary
- Lake
- Salt Lake
- Intermittent Lake
- Reservoir
- Swamp, Pond
- Canal
- Glacier
- Ice Shelf, Pack Ice
- Ocean
- Sea
- Gulf, Bay
- Strait, Fjord
- Lagoon
- Bank
- Seamount
- Tablemount
- Ridge
- Shelf
- Basin
- Escarpment, Sea Scarp
- Fracture
- Trench, Abyss
- National Park, Reserve
- Point of Interest
- Recreation Site
- Cave, Cavern
- Historic Site
- Ruins
- Wall, Walls
- Church, Abbey
- Temple
- Scientific Station
- Railway station
- Airport
- Port
- Military installation
- Lighthouse
- Mine
- Tunnel
- Dam, Bridge

Agersø	116	Di	55.10N	11.10 E
Agger	124	Jd	50.48N	7.11 E
Āghā Jārī	144	Gc	30.42N	49.50 E
Aghireşu	130	Gc	46.53N	23.15 E
Agiabampo, Estero de-	192	Ed	26.15N	109.15W
Ağın	146	Hc	38.57N	38.43 E
Aginski Burjatski nacionalny okrug [3]	138	Gf	51.00N	114.30 E
Aginskoje	138	Gf	51.03N	114.33 E
Agnew	212	Ee	28.01 S	120.30 E
Agnibilékrou	166	Ed	7.08N	3.12W
Agnita	130	Hd	45.58N	24.37 E
Agno	128	Fe	45.32N	11.21 E
Agnone	128	Ii	41.48N	14.22 E
Ago	156	Ed	34.19N	136.50 E
Agoare	166	Fd	8.30N	3.25 E
Agogna	128	Ce	45.04N	8.54 E
Agön	116	Gc	61.35N	17.25 E
Agordat	160	Kg	15.32N	37.53 E
Ágordo	128	Gd	46.17N	12.02 E
Agout	122	Hk	43.47N	1.41 E
Āgra	142	Jg	27.11N	78.01 E
Agrahanski poluostrov	132	Oh	43.45N	47.35 E
Agramunt	126	Nc	41.47N	1.06 E
Agreda	126	Kc	41.51N	1.56W
Ağrı	144	Fb	39.44N	43.03 E
Agri	128	Kj	40.13N	16.44 E
Agričaj	132	Oi	41.17N	46.43 E
Ağrı Dağı = Ararat, Mount- (EN)	140	Gf	39.40N	44.24 E
Agrigento	112	Hh	37.19N	13.34 E
Agrihan Island	208	Fc	18.46N	145.40 E
Agrij	130	Gb	47.15N	23.16 E
Agrínion	130	Ek	38.38N	21.25 E
Agropoli	128	Ij	40.21N	14.59 E
Agro Pontino	128	Gi	41.25N	12.55 E
Agryz	114	Mh	56.31N	53.01 E
Agto	179	Ge	67.37N	53.49W
Agua Brava, Laguna-	192	Gf	22.10N	105.32W
Agua Caliente, Cerro-	190	Cc	26.27N	106.12W
Aguachica	202	Db	8.18N	73.38W
Agua Clara	204	Fe	20.27 S	52.52W
Aguada de Pasajeros	194	Gb	22.23N	80.51W
Aguadilla	194	Nd	18.26N	67.09W
Aguadulce	194	Gi	8.15N	80.33W
Agua Fria River	188	Ij	33.23N	112.21W
Agua Limpa, Rio-	204	Gb	14.58 S	51.20W
Aguán, Río-	194	Ef	15.57N	85.44W
Aguanaval, Río-	192	Hf	25.28N	102.53W
Aguapeí	204	Cc	16.12 S	59.43W
Aguapeí, Rio-	204	Cb	15.53 S	58.25W
Aguapeí, Rio-	206	Jb	21.03 S	51.47W
Aguapey, Río-	204	Di	29.07 S	56.36W
Agua Prieta	176	If	31.18N	109.34W
Aguaray	206	Hb	22.16 S	63.44W
Aguaray-Guazú, Río- [Par.]	204	Dg	24.05 S	56.40W
Aguaray-Guazú, Río- [Par.]	204	Dg	24.47 S	57.19W
Aguasay	196	Eh	9.25N	63.44W
Aguascalientes	176	Ig	21.53N	102.18W
Aguascalientes [2]	190	Dd	22.00N	102.30W
Aguasvivas	126	Lc	41.20N	0.25W
Água Verde, Rio-	204	Da	13.42 S	56.43W
Agua Vermelha, Reprêsa-	206	Ja	19.53 S	50.17W
Agudo [Braz.]	204	Fi	29.38 S	53.15W
Agudo [Sp.]	126	Hf	38.59N	4.52W
Águeda	126	Dd	40.34N	8.27W
Agueda	126	Fc	41.02N	6.56W
Aguelhok	166	Fb	19.28N	0.51 E
Agüenit	162	Ee	22.11N	13.08W
Aguerguer	158	Ff	23.09N	16.01W
Aguijan Island	208	Fc	14.51N	145.34 E
Aguilar de Campoo	126	Hb	42.48N	4.16W
Aguilar de la Frontera	126	Hg	37.31N	4.39W
Águilas	126	Kg	37.24N	1.35W
Aguililla	192	Hh	18.44N	102.44W
Aguirre, Río-	196	Fh	8.28N	61.02W
Aguja, Cabo de la-	202	Da	11.21N	73.59W
Agujereada, Punta-	197a	Ab	18.31N	67.08W
Agul	138	Ee	55.40N	95.45 E
Agulhas, Cape-(EN) = Agulhas, Kaap-	158	Jl	34.50 S	20.00 E
Agulhas, Kaap- = Agulhas, Cape-(EN)	158	Jl	34.50 S	20.00 E
Agulhas Basin (EN)	106	En	47.00 S	20.00 E
Agulhas Negras, Pico das-	198	Lh	22.23 S	44.38W
Agulhas Plateau (EN)	158	Jm	40.00 S	26.00 E
Agung, Gunung-	150	Gh	8.21 S	115.30 E
Aguni-Shima	152	Mf	26.35N	127.15 E
Ağva	146	Cb	41.05N	29.50 E
Ahaggar	158	Hf	23.10N	5.50 E
Ahaggar, Tassili-oua-n-	158	Hf	20.30N	5.00 E
Aha Hills	172	Cc	19.45 S	21.10 E
Ahalcihe	136	Eg	41.38N	42.59 E
Ahalkalaki	136	Eg	41.25N	43.29 E
Ahangaran	135	Gd	40.57N	69.37 E
Ahar	144	Gb	38.28N	47.04 E
Ahat	130	Mk	38.39N	29.47 E
Ahaus	120	Cd	52.04N	7.00 E
Ahe Atoll	208	Mf	14.30 S	146.18W
Ahenet, Tanezrouft-n-	162	He	22.00N	1.00 E
Ahini	138	Ff	53.18N	105.01 E
Ahipara	218	Ea	35.10 S	173.09 E
Ahja jõgi	116	Lf	58.19N	27.15 E
Ahlat	146	Jc	38.45N	42.29 E
Ahlen	120	De	51.45N	7.55 E
Ahmadābād	142	Jg	23.02N	72.37 E
Aḩmadī	146	Qi	27.56N	56.42 E
Ahmadnagar	148	Ee	19.05N	74.44 E
Ahmadpur East	148	Ec	29.09N	71.16 E
Ahmar	158	Lh	9.23N	41.13 E
Aḩmar, Al Baḩr al- = Red Sea (EN)	158	Kf	25.00N	38.00 E
Ahmeta	132	Nh	42.02N	45.11 E
Ahmetli	130	Kk	38.31N	27.57 E
Ahnet	162	He	24.35N	3.15 E
Ahoa	220h	Ab	13.17 S	176.12W
Ahome	192	Ee	25.55N	109.11W
Ahon, Tarso-	168	Ba	20.23N	18.18 E
Ahr	120	Df	50.33N	7.17 E
Ahram	146	Nh	28.52N	51.16 E
Ahrāmāt al Jīzah	164	Fd	29.55N	31.05 E
Ahrensburg	120	Gc	53.41N	10.15 E
Ahrgebirge	124	Id	50.31N	6.54 E
Ahse	124	Jc	51.42N	7.51 E
Ahsu	132	Pi	40.35N	48.26 E
Ähtäri	114	Ee	62.02N	21.20 E
Ähtärinjarvi	116	Kb	62.40N	24.05 E
Ähtävänjoki	114	Fe	63.38N	22.48 E
Ahtopol	130	Kg	42.06N	27.57 E
Ahtuba	110	Kf	46.42N	48.00 E
Ahtubinsk	112	Kf	48.14N	46.14 E
Ahtyrka	136	De	50.19N	34.55 E
Ahuacapán	194	Cg	13.55N	89.51W
Ahuazotepec	192	Jg	20.03N	98.09W
Ahunui Atoll	208	Mf	19.35 S	140.28W
Åhus	114	Di	55.55N	14.17 E
Ahvāz	142	Gf	31.19N	48.42 E
Ahvenanmaa/Åland [2]	114	Ef	60.15N	20.00 E
Ahvenanmaa/Åland	110	Hc	60.15N	20.00 E
Ahvenanmeri	116	Hd	60.00N	19.30 E
Aḩwar	144	Gg	13.31N	46.42 E
Aibag Gol	154	Ad	41.42N	110.24 E
Aibetsu	156a	Cb	43.55N	142.33 E
Aichach	120	Hh	48.28N	11.08 E
Aichi Ken [2]	154	Ng	35.00N	137.07 E
Aiea	221a	Db	21.23N	157.56W
Aigle	128	Ad	46.20N	6.59 E
Aigle, L'-	122	Gf	48.45N	0.38 E
Aigoual, Mont-	122	Jj	44.07N	3.35 E
Aiguá	204	El	34.12 S	54.45W
Aigues	122	Kj	44.07N	4.43 E
Aigues-Mortes	122	Kk	43.34N	4.11 E
Aiguilles	122	Mj	44.47N	6.52 E
Aiguillon	122	Gj	44.18N	0.21 E
Aigurande	122	Hh	46.26N	1.50 E
Ai He	154	Hd	40.13N	124.30 E
Aihui (Heihe)	142	Od	50.13N	127.26 E
Aikawa	156	Fb	38.02N	138.14 E
Aiken	182	Ke	33.34N	81.44W
Ailao Shan	152	Hg	23.15N	102.20 E
Ailette	124	Fe	49.35N	3.10 E
Ailinginae Atoll	208	Hc	11.08N	166.24 E
Aillte an Mhothair/Moher, Cliffs of-	118	Di	52.58N	9.27W
Ailly-le-Haut-Clocher	124	Dd	50.05N	1.59 E
Ailly-sur-Noye	124	Ee	49.45N	2.22 E
Ailsa Craig	118	Hf	55.16N	5.07W
Ailuk Atoll	208	Hc	10.20N	169.56 E
Aim	138	Ie	58.48N	134.12 E
Aimogasta	206	Gc	28.33 S	66.49W
Aimorés	202	Jg	19.30 S	41.04W
Ain [3]	122	Lh	46.10N	5.20 E
Ain	122	Li	45.48N	5.10 E
Ainaži/Ajnaži	114	Fh	57.52N	24.25 E
Aïn Beïda	162	Ib	35.48N	7.24 E
Aïn Beni Mathar	162	Gc	34.01N	2.01W
Aïn Bessem	126	Ph	36.18N	3.40 E
Aïn Boucif	126	Pi	35.53N	3.09 E
Aïn Defla	126	Nh	36.16N	1.58 E
Aïn el Berd	126	Li	35.21N	0.31W
Aïn el Hammam	126	Qh	36.34N	4.19 E
Aïn el Turck	126	Li	35.44N	0.46W
Aïn Galakka	168	Bb	18.05N	18.31 E
Ainos Óros	130	Dk	38.07N	20.40 E
Aïn Oulmene	126	Ri	35.55N	5.18 E
Aïn Oussera	126	Oi	35.27N	2.54 E
Aïn Sefra	160	Ge	32.45N	0.35W
Ainsworth	186	Ge	42.33N	99.52W
Aïn Taghrout	126	Rh	36.08N	5.05 E
Aïn Tedeles	126	Mh	36.00N	0.18 E
Ain Témouchent	162	Gb	35.18N	1.08W
Aïn Tolba	126	Ki	35.15N	1.15W
Aioi	156	Dd	34.49N	134.28 E
Aiquile	202	Eg	18.10 S	65.10W
Aïr/Azbine	158	Hg	18.00N	8.30 E
Airabu, Pulau-	150	Ef	2.46N	106.14 E
Airai	220a	Bc	7.21N	134.34 E
Airaines	124	De	49.58N	1.57 E
Airão	202	Fd	1.56 S	61.22W
Airbangis	150	Cf	0.12N	99.23 E
Airdrie	188	Ha	51.18N	114.02W
Aire	122	Id	50.38N	2.24 E
Aire [Eng.-U.K.]	118	Mh	53.44N	0.54W
Aire [Fr.]	122	Ke	49.19N	4.49 E
Aire, Canal d'-	122	Id	50.38N	2.25 E
Aire, Isla del-	126	Qe	39.47N	4.16 E
Aire-sur-l'Adour	122	Fk	43.42N	0.16W
Air Force	180	Kc	67.55N	74.05W
Airolo	128	Cd	46.33N	8.35 E
Aïs	219b	Cb	15.26 S	167.15 E
Aisch	120	Hg	49.46N	11.01 E
Aisén del General Carlos Ibáñez del Campo [2]	206	Fg	46.00 S	73.00W
Aishihik	180	Dd	61.34N	137.30W
Ai-Shima	156	Bd	34.30N	131.18 E
Aisne [3]	122	Je	49.30N	3.30 E
Aisne	122	Ie	49.26N	2.50 E
Aisne à la Marne, Canal de l'-	122	Je	49.24N	3.55 E
Aïssa, Djebel-	162	Gc	32.51N	0.30W
Aitana, Pico-	126	Lf	38.39N	0.16W
Aitape	214	Ch	3.08 S	142.21 E
Aitolikón	130	Ek	38.26N	21.21 E
Aitutaki Atoll	208	Lf	18.52 S	159.45W
Ait Youssef ou Ali	126	Ii	35.09N	3.55W
Aiud	130	Gc	46.18N	23.43 E
Aiviekste/Ajviekste	114	Fh	56.36N	25.44 E
Aiwokako Passage	220a	Bb	7.39N	134.33 E
Aix, Ile d'-	122	Eh	46.01N	1.10W
Aix-en-Provence	122	Lk	43.32N	5.26 E
Aixe-sur-Vienne	122	Hi	45.48N	1.08 E
Aix-les-Bains	122	Li	45.42N	5.55 E
Aiyaíon Pélagos = Aegean Sea (EN)	110	Ih	39.00N	25.00 E
Aiyina	130	Gl	37.45N	23.26 E
Aiyina = Aegina (EN)	130	Gl	37.40N	23.30 E
Aiyínion	130	Fi	40.30N	22.33 E
Aíyion	130	Fk	38.15N	22.05 E
Aizawl	148	Id	23.44N	92.43 E
Aizenay	122	Eh	46.44N	1.37W
Aizpute/Ajzpute	114	Eh	56.45N	21.39 E
Aizubange	156	Fc	37.34N	139.49 E
Aizutakada	156	Fc	37.29N	139.48 E
Aizuwakamatsu	154	Of	37.30N	139.56 E
Ajā', Jabal-	146	Ii	27.30N	41.30 E
'Ajab Shīr	146	Kd	37.28N	45.54 E
Ajaccio	112	Gg	41.55N	8.44 E
Ajaccio, Golfe d'-	122a	Ab	41.50N	8.41 E
Ajaguz	142	Ke	47.58N	80.27 E
Ajakli	138	Eb	70.13N	95.55 E
Ajan [R.S.F.S.R.]	138	Fe	59.38N	106.45 E
Ajan [R.S.F.S.R.]	138	Ie	56.27N	138.10 E
Ajanka	138	Ld	63.40N	167.30 E
Ajanta Range	148	Fd	20.30N	76.00 E
Ajat	134	Kj	52.54N	62.50 E
Ajax Peak	188	Id	45.20N	113.40W
Ajdābiyā	160	Je	30.46N	20.14 E
Ajdabul	136	Ge	52.42N	69.01 E
Ajdar	132	Ke	48.42N	39.13 E
Ajdar, Soloncak-	135	Fd	40.50N	66.50 E
Ajdovščina	128	He	45.53N	13.53 E
Ajdyrlinski	134	Ij	52.03N	59.50 E
Ajhal	138	Gc	66.00N	111.32 E
Ajigasawa	154	Pd	40.47N	140.12 E
Aji-Shima	156	Gb	38.15N	141.30 E
Ajjer, Tassili-n-	158	Hf	25.30N	9.00 E
Ajka	120	Ni	47.06N	17.34 E
Ajke, ozero-	132	Vd	50.55N	61.35 E
Ajkino	134	De	62.15N	49.56 E
'Ajlūn	146	Ff	32.20N	35.45 E
'Ajmah, Jabal al-	146	Fh	29.12N	34.02 E
'Ajmān	144	Id	25.25N	55.27 E
Ajmer	142	Jg	26.27N	74.38 E
Ajnaži/Ainaži	114	Fh	57.52N	24.25 E
Ajni	135	Ge	39.23N	68.36 E
Ajo	182	Ee	32.22N	112.52W
Ajo, Cabo de-	126	Ia	43.31N	3.35W
Ajon, ostrov-	140	Sc	69.50N	168.40 E
Ajoupa-Bouillon	197h	Ab	14.50N	61.08W
Ajsary	136	He	53.05N	71.00 E
Ajtos	130	Kg	42.42N	27.15 E
Aju, Kepulauan-	150	Jf	0.28N	131.03 E
'Ajūz, Jabal al-	146	Dj	25.49N	30.43 E
Ajviekste/Aiviekste	114	Fh	56.36N	25.44 E
Ajzpute/Aizpute	114	Eh	56.45N	21.39 E
Akaba	166	Fd	7.57N	1.03 E
Akabira	154	Qc	43.30N	142.04 E
Akabli	162	Hd	26.42N	1.22 E
Akademika Obručeva, hrebet-	138	Ef	51.30N	96.45 E
Akadomari	156	Fc	37.54N	138.24 E
Aka-Gawa	156	Fb	38.54N	139.50 E
Akagi-San	156	Fc	36.33N	139.11 E
Akaishi-Dake	156	Fd	35.27N	138.09 E
Akaishi-Sanmyaku	156	Fd	35.25N	138.10 E
Akajaure	114	Dc	67.42N	17.30 E
Aka-Jima	156b	Ab	26.14N	127.17 E
Akaki	168	Fd	8.51N	38.48 E
Akala	168	Fb	15.38N	36.12 E
Akan	156a	Db	43.08N	144.07 E
Akan-Gawa	156a	Db	43.00N	144.16 E
Akar	146	Dc	38.38N	31.06 E
Akarnaniká Óri	130	Dk	38.45N	21.00 E
Akaroa	216	Dh	43.48 S	172.59 E
Akasaki	156	Cd	35.31N	133.38 E
'Akasha East	168	Ea	21.05N	30.43 E
Akashi	154	Mg	34.38N	134.59 E
Akbaba Tepe	146	Hc	39.32N	39.33 E
Akbajtal, pereval-	136	Hh	38.31N	73.41 E
Akbou	126	Qh	36.28N	4.32 E
Akbulak	136	Fe	51.03N	55.37 E
Akbura	135	Id	40.34N	72.45 E
Akçaabat	146	Hb	40.59N	39.34 E
Akçadağ	146	Gc	38.21N	37.59 E
Akçakale	146	Hd	36.41N	38.56 E
Akçakara Dağı	146	Ic	38.40N	40.52 E
Akçakoca	146	Db	41.05N	31.09 E
Akçaova [Tur.]	130	Mh	41.03N	29.57 E
Akçaova [Tur.]	130	Ll	37.30N	28.02 E
Akčatau	136	Hf	47.59N	74.02 E
Akçay	130	Mm	36.36N	29.45 E
Akçay	130	Ll	37.50N	28.15 E
Akchâr	158	Ff	20.20N	14.28W
Akdağ [Tur.]	146	Gd	37.53N	37.56 E
Ak Dağ [Tur.]	146	Ib	40.35N	41.46 E
Akdağ [Tur.]	146	Fb	40.57N	35.55 E
Akdağ [Tur.]	146	Cc	39.15N	28.49 E
Akdağ [Tur.]	130	Mk	38.18N	29.58 E
Akdağ [Tur.]	130	Ll	37.42N	28.56 E
Akdağ [Tur.]	130	Jk	38.33N	26.30 E
Ak Dağ [Tur.]	144	Cb	36.32N	29.34 E
Ak Dağlar	146	Gc	39.30N	36.00 E
Ak Dağları	146	Ic	38.40N	40.12 E
Akdağmadeni	146	Fc	39.40N	35.54 E
Akdeniz = Mediterranean Sea (EN)	110	Hh	35.00N	20.00 E
Ak-Dovurak	138	Ef	51.10N	90.40 E
Akechi	156	Ed	35.18N	137.22 E
Ake Eze	166	Gd	5.55N	7.40 E
Akelamo	150	If	1.29N	128.39 E
Akera	132	Oj	39.09N	46.48 E
Åkersberga	116	He	59.29N	18.18 E
Akershus [2]	114	Cf	60.00N	11.10 E
Aketi	160	Jh	2.44N	23.46 E
Akharnai	130	Gk	38.05N	23.44 E
Akhḑar, Al Jabal al-	158	Je	32.30N	21.30 E
Akhḑar, Al Jabal al-	140	Hg	23.30N	57.00 E
Akhḑar, Wādī al-	146	Gh	28.35N	36.35 E
Akhelóös	130	Ej	38.18N	21.10 E
Akhisar	144	Cb	38.55N	27.51 E
Akhmīm	164	Fd	26.34N	31.44 E
Akhtarīn	146	Gd	36.31N	37.20 E
Aki	156	Ce	33.30N	133.53 E
Akiaki Atoll	216	Nc	18.30 S	139.12W
Akiéni	170	Bc	1.11 S	13.53 E
Akimiski	174	Kd	53.00N	81.20W
Akimovka	132	If	46.42N	35.09 E
Aki-Nada	156	Cd	34.05N	132.40 E
Åkirkeby	116	Fi	55.04N	14.56 E
Akita	142	Qf	39.43N	140.07 E
Akita Ken [2]	154	Pe	39.45N	140.20 E
Akjar	132	Ud	51.50N	58.14 E
Akjoujt	160	Fg	19.44N	14.22W
Akka	162	Fd	29.25N	8.15W
Akkanburluk	134	Mj	52.46N	66.35 E
'Akko	144	Ec	32.55N	35.05 E
Akkol	135	Hc	43.25N	70.47 E
Akköy	146	Bd	37.29N	27.15 E
Akkystau	136	Ff	47.17N	51.03 E
Aklavik	180	Dc	68.14N	135.02W
Aklé 'Âouâna	162	Ff	18.09N	5.40W
Aklé Mseïguîlé	166	Eb	16.20N	4.45W
Akmene/Akmenė	116	Jh	56.14N	22.43 E
Akmenė/Akmene	116	Jh	56.14N	22.43 E
Akmeņrags/Akmenrags	116	Ih	56.54N	20.55 E
Akmenrags/Akmeņrags	116	Ih	56.54N	20.55 E
Akmeqit	152	Cd	37.05N	76.55 E
Akniste	116	Kh	56.10N	25.54 E
Akō	156	Dd	34.45N	134.23 E
Akobo	160	Kh	7.47N	33.01 E
Akobo	168	Ed	7.48N	33.03 E
Akola	142	Jg	20.44N	77.00 E
Akonolinga	166	He	3.46N	12.15 E
Akosombo Dam	166	Fd	6.16N	0.03 E
Akpatok	180	Kd	60.24N	68.05W
Akqi	152	Cc	40.50N	78.01 E
Ákra Ámbelos	130	Gj	39.56N	23.56 E
Ákra Kambanós	130	Hl	37.59N	24.45 E
Akranes	114a	Ab	64.19N	22.06W
Ákra Spathí	130	Gl	37.27N	23.31 E
Åkrehamn	114	Ag	59.16N	5.11 E
Akrítas, Ákra- = Akritas, Cape- (EN)	130	Em	36.43N	21.53 E
Akritas Cape- (EN) = Akrítas, Ákra-	130	Em	36.43N	21.53 E
Akron [Co.-U.S.]	186	Ef	40.10N	103.13W
Akron [Oh.-U.S.]	182	Kc	41.04N	81.31W
Akrotiri	146	Ee	34.36N	32.57 E
Akša	138	Gf	50.17N	113.17 E
Aksaj	132	Oh	43.32N	46.55 E
Aksaj [Kaz.-U.S.S.R.]	136	Fe	51.13N	53.01 E
Aksaj [R.S.F.S.R.]	132	Kf	47.15N	39.52 E
Aksakal	130	Li	40.09N	28.07 E
Aksakovo	134	Gi	54.02N	54.09 E
Aksaray	144	Db	38.23N	34.03 E
Aksay	152	Fd	39.28N	94.15 E
Aksayqin Hu	152	Cd	35.12N	79.50 E
Akşehir	144	Db	38.21N	31.25 E
Akşehir Gölü	146	Dc	38.30N	31.28 E
Akseki	146	Dd	37.02N	31.48 E
Aksenovo-Zilovskoje	138	Gf	53.00N	117.35 E
'Aks-e Rostam	146	Ph	28.23N	54.52 E
Aksoran, gora-	136	Hf	48.25N	75.30 E
Akstafa	132	Ni	41.06N	45.28 E
Akstafa	132	Ni	41.13N	45.27 E
Aksu [China]	142	Ke	41.09N	80.15 E
Aksu [Kaz.-U.S.S.R.]	135	Lb	45.34N	79.30 E
Aksu [Kaz.-U.S.S.R.]	136	He	52.28N	71.59 E
Aksu [Kaz.-U.S.S.R.]	136	Hf	46.20N	78.15 E
Aksu [Tur.]	130	Ll	37.56N	28.56 E
Aksu [Tur.]	146	Dd	36.51N	30.54 E
Aksuat	136	If	47.48N	82.50 E
Aksubajevo	114	Mi	54.52N	50.50 E
Aksu He	140	Ke	40.28N	80.52 E
Aksum	168	Fc	14.07N	38.44 E
Ak-Šyjrak	135	Ld	41.49N	78.44 E
Aktag	152	Dd	36.45N	84.40 E
Aktaš [R.S.F.S.R.]	138	Df	50.18N	87.44 E
Aktaš [Uzb.-U.S.S.R.]	136	Gh	39.55N	65.53 E
Aktau	136	He	50.16N	73.07 E
Aktau, gora-	136	Gg	41.45N	64.30 E
Aktjubinsk	112	Le	50.17N	57.10 E
Aktjubinskaja oblast [3]	136	Ff	48.00N	58.00 E
Ak-Tjuz	135	Kc	42.50N	76.07 E
Akto	152	Cd	39.05N	76.02 E
Aktogaj	136	Hf	47.01N	79.40 E
Akula	170	Db	2.22N	20.11 E
Akun	178a	Eb	54.12N	165.35W
Akune	154	Kh	32.01N	130.11 E
Akure	166	Gd	7.15N	5.12 E
Akureyri	112	Eb	65.40N	18.06W
Akuseki-Jima	154	Jj	29.28N	129.33 E
Akutan	178a	Eb	54.08N	165.46W
Akutan	178a	Eb	54.10N	165.55W
Akyab → Sittwe	142	Lg	20.09N	92.54 E
Akyazı	146	Db	40.41N	30.37 E
Akžajkyn, ozero-	135	Fb	44.55N	67.45 E
Akžal	136	If	49.13N	81.30 E
Ål	116	Cd	60.38N	8.34 E
Alà, Monti di-	128	Dj	40.35N	9.16 E
Alabama [2]	182	Je	32.50N	87.30W
Alabama	174	Kf	31.08N	87.57W
Al'Abbāsīyah	168	Ec	12.10N	31.18 E
Alaca	146	Fb	40.10N	34.51 E
Alaçam	146	Fb	41.37N	35.37 E
Alaçam Dağları	130	Lj	39.20N	28.32 E
Alacant / Alicante	112	Fh	38.21N	0.29W
Alacant / Alicante [3]	126	Lf	38.30N	0.30W
Alacant, Golf d'- / Alicante, Golfo de-	126	Lf	38.20N	0.15W
Alaçati	130	Jk	38.16N	26.23 E
Aladağ	146	Jc	43.35N	39.20 E
Ala Dağ [Tur.]	146	Jb	40.11N	42.49 E
Ala Dağ [Tur.]	146	Ed	37.58N	32.04 E
Alādāgh, Kūh-e-	146	Qd	37.13N	57.30 E
Ala Dağları	146	Fd	37.55N	35.13 E
Aladža	132	Rj	39.21N	53.12 E
Aladža Manastir	130	Lf	43.17N	28.01 E
Alagir	132	Nh	43.01N	44.12 E
Alagna Valsesia	128	Be	45.51N	7.56 E
Alagnon	122	Ji	45.27N	3.19 E
Alagoas [2]	202	Ke	9.30 S	36.30W
Alagoas [2]	202	Ke	9.00 S	36.00W
Alagoinhas	200	Mg	12.07 S	38.26W
Alagón	126	Kc	41.46N	1.07W
Alagón	126	Fe	39.44N	6.53W
Ala Gou	152	Ec	42.42N	89.12 E
Alahanpanjang	150	Dg	1.05 S	100.47 E
Alahärmä	114	Fe	63.14N	22.51 E
Al Aḩmadī	146	Mh	29.05N	48.04 E
Alaid, vulkan-	138	Kf	50.50N	155.33 E
Alaior / Alayor	126	Qe	39.56N	4.08 E
Alajärvi	114	Fe	63.00N	23.49 E
Alajku	136	Hg	40.18N	74.29 E
Alajski hrebet	140	Jf	39.45N	72.30 E
Alajuela	190	Hf	10.01N	84.13W
Alajuela [3]	194	Eh	10.30N	84.30W
Alajuela, Lago-	194	Hi	9.05N	79.24W
Alakol, ozero-	140	Ke	46.05N	81.50 E
Alakurtti	114	Hc	66.59N	30.20 E
Alalakeiki Channel	221a	Ec	20.35N	156.30W
Al 'Alamayn	160	Je	30.49N	28.57 E
Alalau, Rio-	202	Fd	0.30 S	61.10W
Al Amādīyah	146	Jd	37.06N	43.29 E
Alamagan Island	208	Fc	17.36N	145.50 E
Al 'Amārah	144	Gc	31.50N	47.09 E
'Alam ar Rūm, Ra's-	146	Bg	31.22N	27.21 E
Alāmarvdasht	146	Oi	27.52N	52.34 E
Alamashindo	168	Ge	4.51N	42.04 E
Alamata	168	Fc	12.25N	39.37 E
Alameda	186	Ci	35.11N	106.37W
Alaminos	150	Gc	16.10N	119.59 E
Al 'Āmirīyah	146	Cg	31.01N	29.48 E
Alamito Creek	186	Dl	29.31N	104.17W
Alamitos, Sierra de los-	192	Hd	26.20N	102.15W
Alamo	188	Hh	37.22N	115.10W
'Alāmo	168	Ge	4.23N	43.09 E
Alamogordo	182	Fe	32.54N	105.57W
Álamos	190	Cc	27.01N	108.56W
Álamos, Sierra-	192	Gc	28.25N	105.00W
Alamosa	182	Fd	37.28N	105.52W
Al Anbār [3]	146	If	34.00N	42.00 E
Åland/Ahvenanmaa [2]	114	Ef	60.15N	20.00 E
Åland/Ahvenanmaa	110	Hc	60.15N	20.00 E
Älandsbro	116	Gb	62.40N	17.50 E
Ålandshav	116	Hd	60.00N	19.30 E
Alange	126	Ff	38.47N	6.15W
Alanje	194	Fi	8.24N	82.33W
Alanya	144	Db	36.33N	32.01 E
Alaotra, Lac-	172	Hc	17.30 S	48.30 E
Alapaha River	184	Fj	30.26N	83.06W
Alapajevsk	136	Gd	57.52N	61.42 E
Alaplı	146	Db	41.08N	31.25 E
Al 'Aqabah = Aqaba (EN)	144	Dd	29.31N	35.00 E
Al 'Aqabah aş Şaghīrah	146	Ej	24.14N	32.53 E
Al 'Arabīyah As-Su'ūdīyah = Saudi Arabia (EN) [1]	142	Gg	25.00N	45.00 E
Alarcón, Embalse de-	126	Je	39.45N	2.20W
Al 'Arīsh	164	Fc	31.08N	33.48 E
Al 'Armah	146	Lj	25.30N	46.30 E
Al Arţāwīyah	146	Ki	26.30N	45.20 E
Alas, Selat-	150	Gh	8.40 S	116.40 E
Al 'Aşab	146	Pk	23.20N	54.10 E
Alaşehir	146	Cc	38.21N	28.32 E
Al Ashkharah	144	Ie	21.47N	59.30 E
Al 'Āshūrīyah	146	Jg	31.02N	43.05 E
Alaska [2]	178	Ic	65.00N	153.00W
Alaska	174	Dc	65.00N	153.00W
Alaska, Gulf of-	174	Ed	58.00N	146.00W
Alaska Peninsula	174	Dd	57.00N	158.00W
Alaska Range	174	Ec	62.30N	150.00W
Alassio	128	Cf	44.00N	8.10 E
Alastaro	116	Jd	60.57N	22.51 E
Alat	135	De	39.26N	63.48 E
Alataw Shan	152	Cb	45.00N	80.00 E
Alataw Shankou = Dzungarian Gate (EN)	140	Ke	45.25N	82.25 E
Al 'Athāmīn	146	Jg	30.35N	43.40 E
Alatri	128	Hi	41.43N	13.21 E
Al 'Aţrun	160	Jg	18.11N	26.36 E
Alatyr	136	Ee	54.50N	46.36 E
Alatyr	114	Li	54.52N	46.36 E
Álava [3]	126	Jb	42.50N	2.45W
Alava, Cape-	188	Cb	48.10N	124.43W
Alaverdi	136	Eg	41.08N	44.37 E
Alavījeh	146	Nf	33.03N	51.05 E
Alavo/Alavus	114	Fe	62.35N	23.37 E
Alavus/Alavo	114	Fe	62.35N	23.37 E
Al 'Awāliq	144	Gg	14.15N	46.30 E
Al 'Awāriq	168	Ha	20.25N	48.40 E
Al 'Awsajīyah	146	Ki	26.04N	44.08 E
'Ālayh	146	Ff	33.48N	35.36 E
Al 'Ayn [Oman]	144	Ie	24.15N	55.45 E
Al 'Ayn [Sau.Ar.]	146	Hj	25.04N	38.06 E
Alayor / Alaior	126	Qe	39.56N	4.08 E
Al 'Ayyāţ	146	Dh	29.37N	31.15 E
Al A'ẓamīyah	146	Kf	33.23N	44.22 E
Alazani	132	Oi	41.03N	46.40 E
Alazeja	138	Kb	70.55N	153.40 E
Al'Azīzīyah	164	Bc	32.32N	13.01 E
Alazores, Puerto de los-	126	Hg	37.05N	4.15W
Alb [Ger.]	124	Ke	49.04N	8.20 E
Alb [Ger.]	120	Ei	47.35N	8.08 E
Alba	128	Cf	44.42N	8.02 E
Alba [2]	130	Gc	46.08N	23.30 E
Alba Adriatica	128	Hh	42.50N	13.56 E
Al Bāb	146	Gd	36.22N	37.31 E
Albac	130	Fc	46.27N	22.58 E
Albacete	112	Fh	38.59N	1.51W
Albacete [3]	126	Kf	38.50N	2.00W
Al Badārī	164	Fd	26.59N	31.25 E
Alba de Tormes	126	Gd	40.49N	5.31W
Al Bādi	146	Ie	35.56N	41.32 E
Al Badi	164	Ie	22.02N	46.34 E
Ålbæk	116	Dg	57.36N	10.25 E

Index Symbols

- [1] Independent Nation
- [2] State, Region
- [3] District, County
- [4] Municipality
- [5] Colony, Dependency
- Continent
- Physical Region
- Historical or Cultural Region
- Mount, Mountain
- Volcano
- Hill
- Mountains, Mountain Range
- Hills, Escarpment
- Plateau, Upland
- Pass, Gap
- Plain, Lowland
- Delta
- Salt Flat
- Valley, Canyon
- Crater, Cave
- Karst Features
- Depression
- Polder
- Desert, Dunes
- Forest, Woods
- Heath, Steppe
- Oasis
- Cape, Point
- Coast, Beach
- Cliff
- Peninsula
- Isthmus
- Sandbank
- Island
- Atoll
- Rock, Reef
- Islands, Archipelago
- Rocks, Reefs
- Coral Reef
- Well, Spring
- Geyser
- River, Stream
- Waterfall, Rapids
- River Mouth, Estuary
- Lake
- Salt Lake
- Intermittent Lake
- Reservoir
- Swamp, Pond
- Canal
- Glacier
- Ice Shelf, Pack Ice
- Ocean
- Sea
- Gulf, Bay
- Strait, Fjord
- Lagoon
- Bank
- Seamount
- Tablemount
- Ridge
- Shelf
- Basin
- Escarpment, Sea Scarp
- Fracture
- Trench, Abyss
- National Park, Reserve
- Point of Interest
- Recreation Site
- Cave, Cavern
- Historic Site
- Ruins
- Wall, Walls
- Church, Abbey
- Temple
- Scientific Station
- Railway station
- Airport
- Port
- Military installation
- Lighthouse
- Mine
- Tunnel
- Dam, Bridge

Alb-Alm

Name	Page	Grid	Lat.	Long.
Ålbæk Bugt	116	Dg	57.35N	10.30 E
Al Bahrah	146	Lh	29.40N	47.52 E
Al Baḩr al Aḩmar [3]	168	Fb	19.50N	35.30 E
Al Baḩrayn	140	Hg	26.00N	50.30 E
Al Baḩrayn = Bahrain (EN) [1]	142	Hg	26.00N	50.29 E
Albaida	126	Lf	38.51N	0.31W
Alba Iulia	130	Gc	46.04N	23.35 E
Albalate del Arzobispo	126	Lc	41.07N	0.31W
Al Balqā' [3]	146	Ff	31.50N	35.40 E
Al Balyanā	164	Fd	26.14N	32.00 E
Alban	122	Ik	43.54N	2.28 E
Albanel, Lac-	180	Kf	51.05N	73.05W
Albani, Colli-	128	Gi	41.45N	12.45 E
Albania (EN) = Shqiperia [1]	112	Hg	41.00N	20.00 E
Albano, Lago-	128	Gi	41.45N	12.40 E
Albano Laziale	128	Gi	41.44N	12.39 E
Albany	174	Kd	52.17N	81.31W
Albany [Austl.]	210	Ch	35.02S	117.53 E
Albany [Ga.-U.S.]	182	Ke	31.35N	84.10W
Albany [Ky.-U.S.]	184	Eg	36.42N	85.08W
Albany [N.Y.-U.S.]	176	Le	42.39N	73.45W
Albany [Or.-U.S.]	182	Cc	44.38N	123.06W
Alba Posse	204	Eh	27.33S	54.42W
Albardón	206	Gd	31.26S	68.32W
Albarracín	126	Kd	40.25N	1.26W
Albarracín, Sierra de-	126	Kd	40.30N	1.30W
Al Başalīyah Qiblī	146	Ej	25.06N	32.47 E
Al Başrah [3]	146	Lg	30.30N	47.27 E
Al Başrah = Basra (EN)	142	Gf	30.30N	47.47 E
Al Baṭḥā'	146	Kg	31.07N	45.54 E
Al Bāṭin	146	Lh	29.00N	46.35 E
Al Bāṭinah	140	Hg	23.45N	57.20 E
Albatross Bank (EN)	178	Ie	56.10N	152.20W
Albatross Bay	212	Ib	12.45S	141.43 E
Albatross Plateau (EN)	106	Mi	10.00N	103.00W
Albatross Point	218	Fc	38.07S	174.40 E
Al Batrūn	146	Fe	34.15N	35.39 E
Al Bawīṭī	164	Ed	28.21N	28.52 E
Al Bayāḑ	140	Gg	22.00N	47.00 E
Al Bayḑā'	160	Je	32.46N	21.43 E
Al Bayḑā' [3]	164	Dc	32.00N	21.30 E
Al Bayḑā' [Lib.]	164	Cd	28.21N	18.58 E
Al Bayḑā' [Yem.]	164	Ig	13.58N	45.35 E
Albegna	128	Fh	42.30N	11.11 E
Albemarle	184	Gh	35.21N	80.12W
Albemarle Sound	182	Ld	36.03N	76.12W
Albenga	128	Cf	44.03N	8.13 E
Alberche	126	He	39.58N	4.46W
Alberdi	206	Ic	26.10S	58.09W
Albères, Chaîne des-	122	Il	42.28N	2.56 E
Albères, Montes-/Les Alberes	122	Il	42.28N	2.56 E
Albergaria-a-Velha	126	Dd	40.42N	8.29W
Alberic / Alberique	126	Le	39.07N	0.31W
Alberique / Alberic	126	Le	39.07N	0.31W
Alberobello	128	Lj	40.47N	17.16 E
Albert	122	Id	50.00N	2.39 E
Albert, Canal-/Albert Kanaal = Albert Canal (EN)	122	Lc	51.10N	5.10 E
Albert, Lake- [Afr.]	158	Kh	1.40N	31.00 E
Albert, Lake- [Or.-U.S.]	188	Ee	42.38N	120.13W
Albert, Lake- (EN) = Mobuto Sese Seko, Lac-	158	Kh	1.40N	31.00 E
Alberta [2]	180	Gf	55.00N	115.00W
Albert Canal (EN) = Albert, Canal-/Albert Kanaal	122	Lc	51.10N	5.10 E
Albert Canal (EN) = Albert Kanaal/Albert, Canal-	122	Lc	51.10N	5.10 E
Albert Edward, Mount-	212	Ja	8.23S	147.27 E
Albert Edward Bay	180	Hc	69.35N	103.10W
Alberti	206	He	35.02S	60.16W
Albertirsa	120	Pi	47.15N	19.37 E
Albert Kanaal/Albert, Canal- = Albert Canal (EN)	122	Lc	51.10N	5.10 E
Albert Lea	182	Ic	43.39N	93.22W
Albert Nile	158	Kh	3.36N	32.02 E
Albertville [Al.-U.S.]	184	Dh	34.16N	86.12W
Albertville [Fr.]	122	Mi	45.41N	6.23 E
Albestroff	124	If	48.56N	6.51 E
Albi	122	Ik	43.56N	2.09 E
Albia	186	Jf	41.02N	92.48W
Al Bid'	146	Fh	28.28N	35.01 E
Albina	202	Hb	5.30N	54.03W
Albina, Ponta-	158	Ij	15.51S	11.44 E
Albino	128	De	45.46N	9.47 E
Albion [Mi.-U.S.]	184	Ed	42.15N	84.45W
Albion [Nb.-U.S.]	186	Hf	41.42N	98.00W
Albion [N.Y.-U.S.]	184	Hd	43.15N	78.12W
Al Biqā' [3]	146	Ge	34.00N	36.00 E
Al Biqa'	146	Ge	34.10N	36.10 E
Al Bi'r	144	Ed	28.51N	36.15 E
Al Bi'r al Jadīd	146	Hi	26.01N	38.29 E
Al Birk	144	Ff	18.13N	41.33 E
Albis	128	Cc	47.20N	8.30 E
Albo, Monte-	128	Dj	40.32N	9.35 E
Albocácer / Albocàsser	126	Md	40.21N	0.02 E
Albocàsser / Albocácer	126	Md	40.21N	0.02 E
Alborán, Isla de-	110	Fh	35.58N	3.02W
Alboran Basin (EN)	126	Ii	36.00N	4.00W
Ålborg	112	Gd	57.03N	9.56 E
Ålborg Bugt	114	Ch	56.45N	10.30 E
Alborz, Reshteh-ye Kūhhā-ye- = Elburz Mountains (EN)	140	Hf	36.00N	53.00 E
Albox	126	Jg	37.23N	2.08W
Albret, Pays d'-	122	Fj	44.10N	0.20W
Ālbū 'Alī	146	Je	34.49N	43.35 E
Albufeira	126	Dg	37.05N	8.15W
Albū Gharz, Sabkhat-	146	Ie	34.45N	41.15 E
Al Buheyrat [3]	168	Dd	7.00N	29.30 E
Al Bumbah	164	Dc	32.13N	23.00 E
Albuñol	126	Ih	36.47N	3.12W
Albuquerque [Braz.]	204	Dd	19.23S	57.26W
Albuquerque [N.M.-U.S.]	176	If	35.05N	106.40W
Albuquerque, Cayos de-	190	Hf	12.10N	81.50W
Al Burayj	146	Ge	34.15N	36.46 E
Al Burmah	162	Ic	31.45N	9.02 E
Alburquerque	126	Ee	39.13N	7.00W
Albury [Austl.]	210	Fh	36.05S	146.55 E
Albury [N.Z.]	218	Df	44.14S	170.53 E
Al Buṭanah	158	Kg	15.00N	35.00 E
Al Buṭayn	146	Kj	25.52N	45.50 E
Alby	116	Fb	62.30N	15.28 E
Alcácer do Sal	126	Df	38.22N	8.30W
Alcáçovas	126	Df	38.25N	8.13W
Alcalá de Chivert / Alcalà de Xivert	126	Md	40.18N	0.14 E
Alcalá de Guadaira	126	Gg	37.20N	5.50W
Alcalá de Henares	126	Id	40.29N	3.22W
Alcalá del Júcar	126	Ke	39.12N	1.26W
Alcalá de los Gazules	126	Gh	36.28N	5.44W
Alcalá del Río	126	Gg	37.31N	5.59W
Alcalà de Xivert / Alcalá de Chivert	126	Md	40.18N	0.14 E
Alcalá la Real	126	Ig	37.28N	3.56W
Alcamo	128	Gm	37.59N	12.58 E
Alcanadre	126	Mc	41.37N	0.12 E
Alcañices	126	Fc	41.42N	6.21W
Alcañiz	126	Lc	41.03N	0.08W
Alcantara	128	Jm	37.49N	15.16 E
Alcântara [Braz.]	202	Jd	2.24S	44.24W
Alcántara [Sp.]	126	Fe	39.43N	6.53W
Alcántara, Embalse de-	126	Fe	39.45N	6.48W
Alcantarilla	126	Kg	37.58N	1.13W
Alcaraz	126	Jf	38.40N	2.29W
Alcaraz, Sierra de-	126	Jf	38.35N	2.25W
Alcaudete	126	Hg	37.36N	4.05W
Alcázar de San Juan	126	Ie	39.24N	3.12W
Alcester	219a	Ac	9.33S	152.25 E
Alcira/Alzira	126	Le	39.09N	0.26W
Alcobaça [Braz.]	202	Kg	17.30S	39.13W
Alcobaça [Port.]	126	De	39.33N	8.59W
Alcobendas	126	Id	40.32N	3.38W
Alcoi/Alcoy	126	Lf	38.42N	0.28W
Alcolea del Pinar	126	Jc	41.02N	2.28W
Alcorta	204	Bk	33.32S	61.07W
Alcoutim	126	Eg	37.28N	7.28W
Alcova	188	Le	42.37N	106.36W
Alcoy/Alcoi	126	Lf	38.42N	0.28W
Alcubierre, Sierra de-	126	Lc	41.44N	0.29W
Alcudia / Alcúdia de Mallorca	126	Pe	39.52N	3.07 E
Alcúdia, Badia d'-/Alcudia, Bahía de-	126	Pe	39.48N	3.13 E
Alcudia, Bahía de-/Alcúdia, Badia d'-	126	Pe	39.48N	3.13 E
Alcudia, Sierra de-	126	Hf	38.35N	4.35W
Alcúdia de Mallorca / Alcudia	126	Pe	39.52N	3.07 E
Aldabra Group	172b	Ab	9.25S	46.22 E
Aldabra Islands	158	Li	9.25S	46.22 E
Aldama [Mex.]	190	Cc	28.51N	105.54W
Aldama [Mex.]	192	Jf	22.55N	98.04W
Aldan	142	Od	58.37N	125.24 E
Aldan	140	Oc	63.28N	129.35 E
Aldan Plateau (EN) = Aldanskoje nagorje	140	Od	57.30N	127.30 E
Aldanskoje nagorje = Aldan Plateau (EN)	140	Od	57.30N	127.30 E
Aldarhan	152	Gb	47.42N	96.36 E
Alde	124	Db	52.10N	1.32 E
Aldeburgh	118	Oi	52.09N	1.35 E
Aldeia	204	Ed	18.12S	55.10W
Aldeia, Serra da-	204	Ic	17.00S	46.50W
Alderney	118	Kl	49.43N	2.12W
Aldershot	124	Bc	51.15N	0.46W
Alderson	188	Ja	50.18N	111.26W
Aledo	186	Kf	41.12N	90.45W
Aleg	160	Fg	17.03N	13.53W
Alegranza	162	Ed	29.23N	13.30W
Alegre	202	Jh	20.46S	41.32W
Alegre, Rio-	204	Cb	15.14S	59.58W
Alegrete	206	Ic	29.46S	55.46W
Alej	138	Df	52.50N	83.35 E
Alejandra	204	Ci	29.54S	59.50W
Alejandro Selkirk, Isla-	198	Hi	33.45S	80.46W
Alejsk	138	Df	52.28N	82.45 E
Aleksandrija	132	He	48.40N	33.07 E
Aleksandrov	136	Dd	56.25N	38.42 E
Aleksandrov Gaj	136	Ee	50.08N	48.32 E
Aleksandrovka	132	He	48.59N	32.13 E
Aleksandrovsk	134	Hg	59.10N	57.35 E
Aleksandrovskoje	132	Mg	44.39N	43.00 E
Aleksandrovsk-Sahalinsk	142	Qd	50.54N	142.10 E
Aleksandrów Kujawski	120	Od	52.52N	18.42 E
Aleksandrów Łódzki	120	Pe	51.49N	19.19 E
Aleksandry, zemlja-	140	Ga	80.45N	46.00 E
Aleksejevka [Kaz.-U.S.S.R.]	136	If	48.26N	85.40 E
Aleksejevka [Kaz.-U.S.S.R.]	136	He	51.58N	70.59 E
Aleksejevka [Kaz.-U.S.S.R.]	134	Nj	53.31N	69.28 E
Aleksejevka [R.S.F.S.R.]	136	De	50.39N	38.42 E
Aleksejevsk	138	Fe	57.50N	108.23 E
Aleksejevskoje	114	Mi	55.19N	50.03 E
Aleksin	132	Jb	54.31N	37.07 E
Aleksinac	130	Ef	43.32N	21.43 E
Alem [Arg.]	206	Ic	27.31S	55.15W
Ålem [Swe.]	114	Dh	56.57N	16.23 E
Alem Maya	168	Gd	9.27N	41.58 E
Ålen	116	Db	62.51N	11.17 E
Alençon	122	Gf	48.26N	0.05 E
Alenquer	202	Hd	1.56S	54.46W
Alenuihaha Channel	214	Oc	20.26N	156.00W
Alépé	166	Ed	5.30N	3.39W
Aleppo (EN) = Ḩalab	142	Ff	36.12N	37.10 E
Aléria	122a	Ba	42.06N	9.31 E
Aléria, Plaine d'-	122a	Ba	42.05N	9.30 E
Alert	176	Ma	82.30N	62.00W
Alert Bay	188	Ba	50.35N	126.55W
Alès	122	Kj	44.08N	4.05 E
Aleşd	130	Fb	47.04N	22.25 E
Alessandria	128	Cf	44.54N	8.37 E
Ålestrup	116	Ch	56.42N	9.30 E
Ålesund	112	Gc	62.28N	6.09 E
Aleutian Basin (EN)	174	Ad	57.00N	177.00 E
Aleutian Islands	174	Bd	52.00N	176.00W
Aleutian Range	174	Dd	59.00N	155.00W
Aleutian Trench (EN)	106	Je	51.00N	179.00 E
Alexander, Cape-	214	Fi	6.35S	156.30 E
Alexander, Kap-	179	Ec	78.10N	72.45W
Alexander Archipelago	174	Fd	56.30N	134.00W
Alexanderbaai	172	Be	28.40S	16.30 E
Alexander City	182	Je	32.56N	85.57W
Alexander Island	222	Qe	71.00S	70.00W
Alexandra	216	Ci	45.15S	169.24 E
Alexandra Fiord	180	Ka	79.17N	75.00W
Alexandretta (EN) = İskenderun	142	Ff	36.37N	36.07 E
Alexandretta, Gulf of- (EN) = İskenderun Körfezi	144	Eb	36.30N	35.40 E
Alexándria	130	Fi	40.38N	22.27 E
Alexandria	172	Df	33.39S	26.24 E
Alexandria [Austl.]	212	Hc	19.05S	136.40 E
Alexandria [La.-U.S.]	176	Jf	31.18N	92.27W
Alexandria [Mn.-U.S.]	182	Hb	45.53N	95.22W
Alexandria [Rom.]	130	If	43.59N	25.20 E
Alexandria [Va.-U.S.]	184	If	38.49N	77.06W
Alexandria (EN) = Al Iskandarīyah [Eg.]	160	Je	31.12N	29.54 E
Alexandria Bay	184	Jc	44.20N	75.55W
Alexandrina, Lake-	212	Hg	35.25S	139.10 E
Alexandrita	202	Hg	19.42S	50.27W
Alexandroúpolis	112	Ig	40.51N	25.52 E
'Aleyak, Godār-e-	146	Qd	36.30N	57.45 E
Alf	120	Df	50.03N	7.07 E
Alfabia, Sierra de-	126	Oe	39.45N	2.48 E
Alfambra	126	Kd	40.21N	1.07W
Al Fardah	168	Hc	14.51N	48.26 E
Alfaro	126	Kb	42.11N	1.45W
Al Fāshir	160	Jg	13.38N	25.21 E
Al Fashn	164	Fd	28.49N	30.54 E
Alfatar	130	Kf	43.57N	27.17 E
Al Fathah	146	Je	35.04N	43.34 E
Al Fāw	144	Gd	29.58N	48.29 E
Al Fawwārah	146	Ji	26.03N	43.05 E
Al Fayyūm	160	Kf	29.19N	30.58 E
Alfbach	124	Jd	50.03N	7.08 E
Alfeld	120	Fe	51.59N	9.50 E
Alfenas	202	Ih	21.26S	45.57W
Al Fifi	168	Dc	10.03N	25.01 E
Alfiós	130	El	37.37N	21.27 E
Alföld	110	If	47.15N	20.25 E
Alfonsine	128	Gf	44.30N	12.03 E
Alford	124	Ca	53.15N	0.11 E
Ålfotbreen	116	Ac	61.45N	5.40 E
Alfreton	124	Aa	53.06N	1.23W
Alfta	114	Df	61.21N	16.05 E
Al Fuḩayḩīl	144	Gd	29.05N	48.08 E
Al Fuhūd	146	Lg	30.58N	46.43 E
Al Fujayrah	144	Id	25.06N	56.21 E
Al Fūlah	168	Dc	11.48N	28.24 E
Al Fuqahā'	164	Cd	27.50N	16.21 E
Al Furāt = Euphrates (EN)	140	Gf	30.00N	47.25 E
Al Fuwayriṭ	146	Ni	26.02N	51.22 E
Alga	136	Ff	49.55N	57.20 E
Algador	126	Ie	39.55N	3.53W
Algarås	116	Ff	58.48N	14.14 E
Ålgård	116	Af	58.46N	5.51 E
Algarrobo	194	Jh	10.12N	74.04W
Algarve	110	Fh	37.10N	8.15W
Algarve	126	Dg	37.10N	8.15W
Algeciras	112	Fh	36.08N	5.30W
Algeciras, Bahía de-	126	Gh	36.09N	5.25W
Algena	168	Fb	17.20N	38.34 E
Algeria (EN) = Al Jazā'ir [1]	160	Hf	28.00N	3.00 E
Algerian Basin (EN)	110	Gh	39.00N	5.00 E
Al Gharaq as Sulṭānī	146	Dh	29.08N	30.42 E
Al Gharbi	162	Jc	34.40N	11.13 E
Al Ghāṭ	146	Ki	26.00N	45.03 E
Al Ghaydah	144	Hf	16.12N	52.15 E
Al Ghazālah	144	Fd	26.47N	41.23 E
Alghero	128	Cj	40.33N	8.19 E
Alghero, Rada d'-	128	Cj	40.35N	8.20 E
Älghult	116	Fg	57.01N	15.34 E
Al Ghurāb	146	Dj	25.20N	30.20 E
Al Ghurayfah	146	Qk	23.59N	56.29 E
Al Ghurdaqah	164	Fd	27.14N	33.50 E
Algiers (EN) = Al Jazā'ir	160	He	36.47N	3.03 E
Algiers (EN) = Al Jazā'ir [3]	162	Hb	36.35N	3.00 E
Algoa Bay	158	Jl	33.50S	25.50 E
Algodoeiro, Serra do-	204	Jc	16.30S	44.45W
Algoma	186	Md	44.36N	87.27W
Algoma Uplands	184	Fb	47.00N	83.35W
Algona	186	Ie	43.04N	94.14W
Algonquin Park	184	Hc	45.27N	78.26W
Algrange	124	Ie	49.21N	6.03 E
Al Ḩabakah	146	Jh	29.51N	42.16 E
Al Ḩadd	144	Ie	22.29N	59.58 E
Al Ḩadīdah	168	Ia	21.31N	50.28 E
Al Ḩadithah	146	Gg	31.28N	37.08 E
Al Ḩadīthah	144	Fc	34.07N	42.23 E
Al Ḩaḑr	146	Je	35.35N	42.44 E
Al Haffah	146	Ge	35.35N	36.02 E
Al Ḩā'ir	146	Lj	24.23N	46.50 E
Al Ḩajar	168	Hb	16.08N	47.50 E
Al Ḩajarah	144	Fc	30.25N	44.30 E
Al Halfāyah	146	Lg	31.49N	47.26 E
Alhama	126	Kb	42.11N	1.45W
Al Ḩamād	140	Ff	32.00N	39.30 E
Alhama de Granada	126	Ih	37.00N	3.59W
Alhama de Murcia	126	Kg	37.51N	1.25W
Alhamilla, Sierra-	126	Jh	36.58N	2.20W
Al Ḩammāh	162	Ic	33.54N	9.48 E
Al Ḩammām [Eg.]	146	Cg	30.50N	29.23 E
Al Ḩammām [Iraq]	146	Kg	31.08N	44.04 E
Al Ḩamrā	146	Pj	25.42N	55.47 E
Al Hanīyah	146	Kh	29.10N	45.50 E
Al Ḩarrah	146	Ch	28.20N	29.07 E
Al Ḩarrah	146	Hg	31.00N	38.40 E
Al Ḩarrah	146	Gf	32.30N	37.45 E
Al Harūj al Aswad	158	If	27.00N	17.10 E
Al Ḩasā	146	Fg	30.49N	35.59 E
Al Hasā'	140	Gg	26.35N	48.10 E
Al Ḩasakah	144	Fb	36.29N	40.45 E
Al Ḩasan	146	Je	34.39N	43.43 E
Al Ḩasānī	146	Gj	24.58N	37.05 E
Alhaurín el Grande	126	Hh	36.38N	4.41W
Al Ḩawāmidīyah	146	Dh	29.54N	31.15 E
Al Ḩawātah	168	Ec	13.25N	34.38 E
Al Ḩawjā'	146	Hh	28.59N	38.34 E
Al Ḩawrah	168	Hc	13.49N	47.35 E
Al Hayy	144	Gc	32.10N	46.03 E
Al Ḩayyānīyah	146	Jh	28.42N	42.18 E
Al Ḩayz	164	Ed	28.02N	28.39 E
Al Hibāk	144	He	20.20N	53.10 E
Al Ḩijāz	140	Fg	24.30N	38.30 E
Al Ḩijāz	144	Ee	24.30N	38.30 E
Al Ḩillah [Iraq]	144	Fc	32.29N	44.25 E
Al Ḩillah [Sau.Ar.]	164	Ie	23.50N	46.51 E
Al Ḩinākīyah	144	Fe	24.51N	40.31 E
Al Hindiyah	146	Kf	32.32N	44.13 E
Al Ḩinnāh	146	Mi	26.56N	48.45 E
Al Hirmil	146	Ge	34.23N	36.23 E
Al Hoceima	162	Gb	35.15N	3.55W
Al Hoceima [3]	162	Gb	35.00N	4.15W
Alhucemas, Peñón de-	126	Ii	35.13N	3.53W
Al Ḩudaydah	142	Gh	14.48N	42.57 E
Al Ḩufrah	164	Cd	29.30N	17.55 E
Al Hufrah	144	Ed	28.49N	38.15 E
Al Hufūf	142	Gg	25.22N	49.34 E
Al Hūj	146	Hh	29.00N	38.25 E
Al Ḩunayy	146	Mj	24.48N	48.45 E
Al Ḩuşayḩişah	168	Ec	14.44N	33.18 E
Al Ḩuwaimī	144	Fg	13.58N	47.40 E
Al Ḩuwayyiṭ	146	Ij	25.36N	40.23 E
'Āli, Sadd al-	164	Fe	23.54N	32.52 E
Aliābād	146	Pd	36.56N	54.50 E
'Alīābād [Iran]	146	Nd	36.37N	51.33 E
'Alīābād [Iran]	146	Le	35.04N	46.58 E
'Alīābād [Iran]	144	Id	28.37N	55.51 E
Alīābād, Kūh-e-	144	Hc	34.13N	50.46 E
Aliaga	126	Ld	40.40N	0.42W
Aliağa	146	Bc	38.48N	26.59 E
Aliákmon	130	Fi	40.30N	22.40 E
'Alī al Gharbī	146	Lf	32.27N	46.41 E
'Alī ash Sharqī	146	Lf	32.07N	46.44 E
Ali-Bajramly	136	Eh	39.55N	48.57 E
Alibej, ozero-	130	Nd	45.50N	30.00 E
Alibey Adası	130	Jj	39.20N	26.38 E
Alibo	168	Fd	9.53N	37.05 E
Alibori	166	Fc	11.56N	3.17 E
Alibunar	130	Dd	45.04N	20.58 E
Alicante / Alacant	112	Fh	38.21N	0.29W
Alicante / Alacant [3]	126	Lf	38.30N	0.30W
Alicante, Golfo de- / Alacant, Golf d'-	126	Lf	38.20N	0.15W
Alice [S.Afr.]	172	Df	32.47S	26.50 E
Alice [Tx.-U.S.]	182	Hf	27.45N	98.04W
Alice, Punta-	128	Lk	39.12N	17.09 E
Alice Springs	210	Eg	23.42S	133.53 E
Aliceville	184	Ci	33.08N	88.09W
Alicudi	128	Il	38.30N	14.20 E
Alīgarh	142	Jg	28.02N	78.17 E
Al Iglim al Janūbīyah = Southern Region (EN) [2]	168	Dd	6.00N	30.00 E
Alīgūdarz	146	Mf	33.24N	49.41 E
Alihe → Oroqen Zizhiqi	152	La	50.35N	123.42 E
Alijó	126	Ec	41.16N	7.28W
Alijos, Rocas-	190	Ad	24.57N	115.44W
'Al Ijūq, Kūh-e-	146	Ng	31.30N	51.45 E
Al Ikhwān	146	Fi	26.19N	34.52 E
Al Ikhwan	140	Hh	12.08N	53.10 E
Alima	158	Ii	1.36S	16.36 E
Al Imārāt al 'Arabīyah al Muttaḩidah = United Arab Emirates (EN) [1]	142	Hg	24.00N	54.00 E
Alimiá	130	Km	36.16N	27.43 E
Alindao	168	Cd	5.02N	21.13 E
Alinglapalap Atoll	208	Hd	7.08N	168.16 E
Alingsås	114	Ch	57.56N	12.31 E
Aliquippa	184	Ge	40.38N	80.16W
Al 'Irāq = Iraq (EN) [1]	142	Gf	33.00N	44.00 E
Al'Irq	164	Dd	29.01N	21.31 E
Al 'Irqah	144	Gg	13.40N	47.18 E
Ali-Sabjeh	168	Gc	11.08N	42.43 E
'Alī Shāh 'Avaẕ	146	Ne	35.39N	51.04 E
Al Iskandarīyah [Eg.] = Alexandria (EN)	160	Je	31.12N	29.54 E
Al Iskandarīyah [Iraq]	146	Kf	32.53N	44.21 E
Aliskerovo	138	Lc	67.52N	167.40 E
Al Ismā'īlīyah = Ismailia (EN)	164	Fc	30.35N	32.16 E
Al Istiwā'īyah al Gharbīyah [3]	168	Dd	5.20N	28.30 E
Al Istiwā'īyah al Sharkīyah [3]	168	Ed	5.20N	33.50 E
Alistráti	130	Gh	41.04N	23.58 E
Alitak, Cape-	178	Ie	56.51N	154.21W
Alite Reef	219a	Ec	8.53S	160.38 E
Alitus/Alytus	136	Ce	54.25N	24.08 E
Alivérion	130	Hk	38.25N	24.02 E
Aliwal North	160	Jl	30.44S	26.40 E
Al Jabalayn	168	Ec	12.36N	32.48 E
Al Jadīdah [Eg.]	146	Cj	25.34N	28.51 E
Al Jadīdah [Sau.Ar.]	146	Mj	25.39N	49.32 E
Al Jafr	146	Gg	30.18N	36.13 E
Al Jāfūrah	146	Nj	25.00N	50.15 E
Al Jāfūrah	146	Nj	23.25N	50.17 E
Al Jaghbūb	160	Jf	29.45N	24.31 E
Al Jahrah	144	Gc	29.20N	47.40 E
Al Jalāmīd	146	Ig	31.17N	40.06 E
Al Jamalīyah	146	Nj	25.37N	51.05 E
Al Jamm	162	Jb	35.18N	10.43 E
Al Janā'in	162	Jc	31.44N	10.09 E
Al Janūb [3]	146	Ff	33.20N	35.30 E
Aljat	132	Pj	39.58N	49.27 E
Al Jawf [Lib.]	160	Jf	24.12N	23.18 E
Al Jawf [Sau.Ar.]	142	Fg	29.50N	39.52 E
Al Jazā'ir = Algeria (EN) [1]	160	Hf	28.00N	3.00 E
Al Jazā'ir = Algiers (EN)	160	He	36.47N	3.03 E
Al Jazā'ir = Algiers (EN) [3]	162	Hb	36.35N	3.00 E
Al Jazā'ir-El Harrach	126	Ph	36.43N	3.08 E
Al Jazīrah [3]	168	Ec	14.40N	33.30 E
Al Jazīrah [Asia]	140	Gf	35.10N	42.00 E
Al Jazīrah [Sud.]	158	Kg	14.25N	33.00 E
Aljezur	126	Dg	37.19N	8.48W
Aljibe	126	Gh	36.31N	5.37W
Al Jifārah	158	Ie	32.30N	11.45 E
Al Jiwā'	144	He	23.00N	54.00 E
Al Jīzah = Giza (EN)	160	Ke	30.01N	31.13 E
Al Jubayl	144	Gd	27.01N	49.40 E
Al Jubaylah	146	Lj	24.54N	46.27 E
Al Junaynah [Sau.Ar.]	164	He	20.17N	42.48 E
Al Junaynah [Sud.]	160	Jg	13.27N	22.27 E
Al Juraid	146	Mi	27.11N	49.52 E
Aljustrel	126	Dg	37.52N	8.10W
Al Kaba'ish	146	Lg	30.58N	47.00 E
Al Kāf	162	Ib	36.11N	8.43 E
Al Kāf [3]	162	Ib	36.00N	9.00 E
Alkali Lake	188	Ff	41.42N	119.50W
Al Kāmilīn	168	Eb	15.05N	33.11 E
Al Karak	146	Fg	31.11N	35.42 E
Al Karak [3]	146	Fg	31.11N	35.42 E
Al Karkh	146	Kf	33.20N	44.20 E
Al Karnak	164	Fd	25.43N	32.39 E
Al Kawah	168	Ec	13.44N	32.30 E
Al Kāẓimīyah	146	Kf	33.22N	44.20 E
Alken	124	Hd	50.52N	5.18 E
Al Khabrā'	144	Fd	26.04N	43.33 E
Al Khābūra	144	Ie	23.50N	57.18 E
Al-Khalīj al- 'Arabi = Persian Gulf (EN)	140	Hg	27.00N	51.00 E
Al Khalīl	146	Fg	31.32N	35.06 E
Al Khalīl [3]	146	Fg	31.30N	35.05 E
Al Khālis	146	Kf	33.51N	44.32 E
Al Khandaq	168	Eb	18.36N	30.34 E
Al Khārijah	160	Kf	25.26N	30.33 E
Al Kharj	146	Lj	24.10N	47.30 E
Al Kharṭūm = Khartoum (EN) [3]	168	Eb	15.50N	33.00 E
Al Kharṭūm = Khartoum (EN)	160	Kg	15.36N	32.32 E
Al Kharṭūm Baḩrī = Khartoum North (EN)	160	Kg	15.38N	32.33 E
Al Khaşab	146	Qi	26.12N	56.15 E
Al Khaṭṭ	146	Qk	25.37N	56.01 E
Al Khawr	144	Hd	25.40N	51.30 E
Al Khidr	146	Kg	31.12N	45.33 E
Al Khubar	144	Hd	26.17N	50.12 E
Al Khufayfīyah	144	Fe	24.55N	44.42 E
Al Khums	160	Ie	32.39N	14.16 E
Al Khums [3]	164	Bc	31.20N	14.10 E
Al Khunn	168	Ha	23.18N	49.15 E
Al Khuwayr	146	Ni	26.04N	51.05 E
Al Kidn	168	Ia	22.30N	54.00 E
Al Kifl	146	Kf	32.14N	44.22 E
Al Kilḩ Sharq	146	Ej	25.03N	32.52 E
Alkionidhon, Kólpos-	130	Fk	38.05N	23.00 E
Al Kır'ānah	146	Nj	25.00N	51.03 E
Alkmaar	122	Kb	52.37N	4.44 E
Al Kūfah	146	Kf	32.02N	44.24 E
Al Kumayt	146	Lf	32.02N	46.52 E
Al Kuntillah	164	Fc	30.00N	34.41 E
Al Kushḩ	146	Ei	26.14N	32.05 E
Al Kut	144	Gc	32.30N	45.49 E
Al Kuwayt = Kuwait (EN)	142	Gg	29.20N	47.59 E
Al Kuwayt = Kuwait (EN) [1]	142	Gg	29.30N	47.45 E
Al Labbah	146	Ih	29.20N	41.30 E
Al Lādhiqīyah = Latakia (EN)	142	Ff	35.31N	35.07 E
Allagash River	184	Mb	47.05N	69.20W
Al Lagowa	168	Dc	11.24N	29.08 E
Allahābād	142	Kg	25.27N	81.51 E
Allah-Jun	138	Id	61.08N	137.59 E
Allah-Jun	138	Id	60.27N	134.57 E
Allahüekber Dağı	146	Jb	40.35N	42.32 E
Allakaket	178	Ic	66.34N	152.41W
Allanmyo	148	Je	19.22N	95.13 E
'Allāqī, Wadī al-	164	Fe	23.07N	32.47 E
Allariz	126	Eb	42.11N	7.48W
All-Awash Island	197n	Bb	12.55N	61.10W
Alldays	172	Dd	22.41S	29.06 E
Ålleberg	116	Ef	58.08N	13.36 E
Allegan	184	Ed	42.32N	85.51W
Allegheny Mountains	174	Lf	38.30N	80.00W
Allegheny Plateau	174	Le	41.30N	78.00W
Allegheny Reservoir	184	He	42.00N	78.56W
Allegheny River	182	Lc	40.27N	80.00W
Allègre, Pointe-	197e	Ab	16.22N	61.45W
Allen	150	Hd	12.30N	124.17 E
Allen, Bog of-	118	Gh	53.20N	7.00W
Allen, Lough-/Loch Aillionn	118	Eg	54.08N	8.08W
Allendale	184	Gi	33.01N	81.19W
Allende	190	Dc	28.20N	100.51W
Allendorf (Eder)	124	Kc	51.02N	8.40 E
Allendorf (Lumda)	124	Kd	50.41N	8.50 E
Allentown	182	Lc	40.37N	75.30W
Alleppey	142	Ji	9.29N	76.19 E
Aller	120	Fd	52.57N	9.11 E
Allevard	122	Mi	45.24N	6.04 E
Allgäu	120	Gi	47.35N	10.10 E
Allgäuer Alpen	120	Gi	47.20N	10.25 E
Alliance [Nb.-U.S.]	182	Gc	42.06N	102.52W
Alliance [Oh.-U.S.]	184	Ge	40.56N	81.06W
Allier [3]	122	Ih	46.30N	3.00 E
Allier	110	Gf	46.57N	3.05 E
Al Līfīyah	144	Fc	30.35N	43.09 E
Al Lişāfah	146	Li	27.37N	46.52 E
Alliston	184	Hc	44.09N	79.52W
Al Līth	144	Fe	20.09N	40.16 E
Alloa	118	Je	56.07N	3.49W
Allonnes	122	Gg	47.58N	0.09 E
Allos	122	Mj	44.14N	6.38 E
All Saints	197d	Bb	17.03N	61.48W
Al Luḩayyah	144	Ff	15.43N	42.42 E
Al Luwaymī	144	Fd	27.54N	42.22 E
Alm	128	Hb	48.05N	13.55 E
Alma [Ga.-U.S.]	184	Fj	31.33N	82.28W
Alma [Mi.-U.S.]	184	Ed	43.23N	84.39W
Alma [Nb.-U.S.]	186	Gf	40.06N	99.22W

Index Symbols

- [1] Independent Nation
- [2] State, Region
- [3] District, County
- [4] Municipality
- [5] Colony, Dependency
- Continent
- Physical Region
- Historical or Cultural Region
- Mount, Mountain
- Volcano
- Hill
- Mountains, Mountain Range
- Hills, Escarpment
- Plateau, Upland
- Pass, Gap
- Plain, Lowland
- Delta
- Salt Flat
- Valley, Canyon
- Crater, Cave
- Karst Features
- Depression
- Polder
- Desert, Dunes
- Forest, Woods
- Heath, Steppe
- Oasis
- Cape, Point
- Coast, Beach
- Cliff
- Peninsula
- Isthmus
- Sandbank
- Island
- Atoll
- Rock, Reef
- Islands, Archipelago
- Rocks, Reefs
- Coral Reef
- Well, Spring
- Geyser
- River, Stream
- Waterfall, Rapids
- River Mouth, Estuary
- Lake
- Salt Lake
- Intermittent Lake
- Reservoir
- Swamp, Pond
- Canal
- Glacier
- Ice Shelf, Pack Ice
- Ocean
- Sea
- Gulf, Bay
- Strait, Fjord
- Lagoon
- Bank
- Seamount
- Tablemount
- Ridge
- Shelf
- Basin
- Escarpment, Sea Scarp
- Fracture
- Trench, Abyss
- National Park, Reserve
- Point of Interest
- Recreation Site
- Cave, Cavern
- Historic Site
- Ruins
- Wall, Walls
- Church, Abbey
- Temple
- Scientific Station
- Railway station
- Airport
- Port
- Military installation
- Lighthouse
- Mine
- Tunnel
- Dam, Bridge

Alma [Que.-Can.] 180 Kg 48.32N 71.40W
Al Ma'āniyah 146 Jg 30.44N 43.00 E
Alma-Ata 142 Je 43.15N 76.57 E
Alma-Atinskaja oblast [3] 136 Hg 44.00N 77.00 E
Almada 126 Cf 38.41N 9.09W
Almadén 126 Hf 38.46N 4.50W
Al Madīnah [Iraq] 146 Lg 30.57N 47.16 E
Al Madīnah [Sau.Ar.] = Medina (EN) 142 Fg 24.28N 39.36 E
Al Madīnah al Fikrīyah 146 Di 27.56N 30.49 E
'Al Madōw 168 Hc 10.59N 48.42 E
Al Mafraq 146 Gf 32.21N 36.12 E
Al Maghrib=Morocco (EN) [1] 160 Ge 32.00N 5.50W
Almagro 126 If 38.53N 3.43W
Almagrundet 116 He 59.06N 19.00 E
Al Maḩallah al Kubrá 164 Fc 30.58N 31.10 E
Al Maḩāriq 164 Fd 25.37N 30.39 E
Al Mahdīyah 162 Jb 35.30N 11.04 E
Al Mahdīyah [3] 162 Jb 35.35N 11.00 E
Al Maḩfid 164 Ig 14.03N 46.55 E
Al Mahrah 144 Hf 16.56N 52.15 E
Al Maḩras 162 Jc 34.32N 10.30 E
Al Majarr al Kabīr 146 Lg 31.34N 47.10 E
Almajului, Munţii- 130 Fe 44.43N 22.12 E
Al Maks al Qiblī 164 Fe 24.35N 30.38 E
Almalyk 136 Gg 40.49N 69.38 E
Al Manādir 146 Pk 23.10N 55.10 E
Al Manāmah=Manama (EN) 142 Hg 26.13N 50.35 E
Al Manāqil 168 Ec 14.15N 32.59 E
Almanor, Lake- 188 Ef 40.15N 121.08W
Almansa 126 Kf 38.52N 1.05W
Almansa, Puerto de- 126 Lf 38.49N 0.58W
Al Manshāh 164 Fd 26.28N 31.48 E
Almansor 126 Df 38.56N 8.54W
Al Manşūrah 164 Fc 31.03N 31.23 E
Al Manzilah 146 Dg 31.09N 31.56 E
Almanzora / Guadalmanzor 126 Kg 37.14N 1.46W
Al Ma'qil 146 Lg 30.33N 47.48 E
Al Maqnah 146 Fh 28.24N 34.45 E
Al Maqta' 146 Pj 24.25N 54.29 E
Almar 126 Gd 40.54N 5.29W
Al Marāghah 146 Di 26.42N 31.36 E
Al Marsá 128 En 36.53N 10.20 E
Al Mary 160 Je 32.30N 20.54 E
Almaş 130 Gb 47.14N 23.19 E
Almas, Picos das- 198 Lg 13.33S 41.56W
Almas, Rio das- 202 If 14.35S 49.02W
'Al Maskād 168 Hc 11.18N 49.41 E
Almassora / Almazora 126 Le 39.57N 0.03W
Al Maţarīyah 164 Fc 31.11N 32.02 E
Al Mawşil=Mosul (EN) 142 Gf 36.20N 43.08 E
Al Mayādīn 146 Ie 35.01N 40.27 E
Al Mayyāh 146 Ji 27.51N 42.47 E
Almazán 126 Jc 41.29N 2.32W
Al Mazār 146 Eg 31.23N 33.23 E
Almazny 138 Gd 62.19N 114.04 E
Almazora / Almassora 126 Le 39.57N 0.03W
Al Mazra'ah 146 Fg 31.16N 35.31 E
Alme, Brilon- 124 Kc 51.27N 8.37 E
Almeida 126 Fc 41.16N 6.04W
Almeirim [Braz.] 202 Hd 1.32S 52.34W
Almeirim [Port.] 126 De 39.12N 8.38W
Al Mellem 168 Dd 9.49N 28.45 E
Almelo 122 Mb 52.21N 6.39 E
Almenara, Sierra de la- 126 Kg 37.35N 1.31W
Almendra, Embalse de- 126 Fc 41.13N 6.10W
Almendralejo 126 Ff 38.41N 6.24W
Almeria 112 Fh 36.50N 2.27W
Almeria [3] 126 Jg 37.10N 2.20W
Almeria, Golfo de- 126 Jh 36.46N 2.30W
Almetjevsk 136 Fe 54.54N 52.20 E
Al Metlaoui 162 Ic 34.20N 8.24 E
Älmhult 114 Dh 56.33N 14.08 E
Almijara, Sierra de- 126 Ih 36.55N 3.55W
Almina, Punta- 126 Gi 35.54N 5.17W
Al Minyā [Eg.] 146 Dh 29.45N 31.18 E
Al Minyā [Eg.] 160 Kf 28.06N 30.45 E
Al Miqdādīyah 146 Kf 33.59N 44.56 E
Almirante 194 Fi 9.18N 82.24W
Almirante Brown 222 Qe 64.53S 62.53W
Almirós 130 Fj 39.11N 22.46 E
Almiroú, Órmos- 130 Hn 35.23N 24.20 E
Almodôvar 126 Dg 37.31N 8.04W
Almodóvar del Campo 126 Hf 38.43N 4.10W
Almodóvar del Rio 126 Gg 37.48N 5.01W
Almonte 126 Fg 37.15N 6.31W
Almonte 126 Fe 39.42N 6.28W
Almoustarat 166 Fb 17.22N 0.07 E
Älmsta 116 He 59.58N 18.48 E
Al Mubarraz 144 Gd 25.25N 49.35 E
Al Mudarraj 146 Hj 25.41N 38.40 E
Al Mudawwarah 146 Fh 29.19N 35.59 E
Al Mudhari, Rujm- 146 Hf 32.45N 39.08 E
Al Mughayrā' [Sau.Ar.] 146 Gh 29.17N 37.41 E
Al Mughayrā' [U.A.E.] 146 Oj 24.05N 53.32 E
Al Muglad 160 Jg 11.02N 27.44 E
Al Muḩarraq 146 Ni 26.16N 50.37 E
Al Mukallā 142 Gh 14.32N 49.08 E
Al Mukhā 164 Fg 13.19N 43.15 E
Al Munastīr 162 Jb 35.47N 10.50 E
Al Munastīr [3] 162 Jb 35.40N 10.50 E
Almuñécar 126 Ih 36.43N 3.41W
Al Murabba' 146 Kj 25.43N 44.18 E
Almus 146 Gb 40.23N 36.55 E
Al Musannāh 146 Lh 29.02N 47.12 E
Al Muşawwarāt aş Şafra' 168 Eb 16.25N 33.22 E
Al Musayjid 146 Hj 24.05N 39.06 E
Al Musayyib 146 Kf 32.47N 44.18 E
Al Mustawī 146 Kj 25.55N 44.40 E
Al Muthanna [3] 146 Kg 30.50N 45.20 E
Al Muwayh 164 He 22.45N 41.35 E
Al Muwaylih 146 Fi 27.41N 35.28 E
Alnön 116 Gb 62.25N 17.25 E
Alnwick 118 Lf 55.25N 1.42W
Ålö 116 Jd 60.20N 22.15 E
Aloândia 204 Hc 17.43S 49.29W
Alofi 210 Kf 19.03S 169.56W
Alofi, Ile- 208 Jf 14.19S 178.02W
Alofi Bay 220k Bb 19.01S 169.56W
Aloja 114 Fh 57.44N 24.59 E
Along 148 Ic 28.10N 94.46 E
Alónnisos 130 Gj 39.13N 23.55 E
Alonsa 186 Ga 50.47N 99.00W
Alonso, Rio- 204 Gg 24.05S 51.35W
Alor, Kepulauan- 150 Hh 8.15S 124.30 E
Alor, Pulau- 140 Oj 8.15S 124.45 E
Alora 126 Hh 36.48N 4.42W
Alor Setar 142 Mi 6.07N 100.22 E
Alost/Aalst 122 Kd 50.56N 4.02 E
Alotau 214 Ej 10.31S 150.43 E
Aloysius, Mount- 212 Fe 26.00S 128.34 E
Alpen = Alps (EN) 110 Gf 46.25N 10.00 E
Alpena 182 Kb 45.04N 83.26W
Alpera 126 Kf 38.58N 1.13W
Alpes=Alps (EN) 110 Gf 46.25N 10.00 E
Alpes Cottiennes 128 Af 44.45N 7.00 E
Alpes-de-Haute-Provence [3] 122 Mj 44.10N 6.10 E
Alpes Grées/Alpi Graie 128 Be 45.30N 7.10 E
Alpes Mancelles 122 Ff 48.25N 0.10W
Alpes-Maritimes [3] 122 Nk 44.00N 7.10 E
Alpes Maritimes 128 Bf 44.15N 7.10 E
Alpes Pennines/Alpi Pennine 128 Bd 46.05N 7.50 E
Alpes Valaisannes 128 Bd 46.10N 7.30 E
Alpha Cordillera (EN) 224 Re 85.30N 125.00W
Alphen aan de Rijn 124 Gb 52.08N 4.42 E
Alphonse Island 158 Mi 7.00S 52.45 E
Alpi=Alps (EN) 110 Gf 46.25N 10.00 E
Alpi Apuane 128 Ef 44.05N 10.20 E
Alpi Aurine 120 Hi 47.00N 11.55 E
Alpi Carniche 128 Gd 46.40N 13.00 E
Alpi Cozie 128 Af 44.45N 7.00 E
Alpi Graie/Alpes Grées 128 Be 45.30N 7.10 E
Alpi Lepontine 128 Cd 46.25N 8.40 E
Alpi Liguri 128 Cf 44.10N 8.05 E
Alpi Marittime 128 Bf 44.15N 7.10 E
Alpine [Az.-U.S.] 188 Kj 33.51N 109.09W
Alpine [Tx.-U.S.] 182 Ge 30.22N 103.40W
Alpine [Wy.-U.S.] 188 Je 43.15N 110.59W
Alpi Orobie 128 Dd 46.00N 10.00 E
Alpi Pennine/Alpes Pennines 128 Bd 46.05N 7.50 E
Alpi Retiche=Rhaetian Alps (EN) 128 Dd 46.30N 10.00 E
Alpi Venoste 128 Gj 46.45N 10.55 E
Alprech, Cap d'- 124 Dd 50.42N 1.34 E
Alps (EN) = Alpen 110 Gf 46.25N 10.00 E
Alps (EN)=Alpes 110 Gf 46.25N 10.00 E
Alps (EN)=Alpi 110 Gf 46.25N 10.00 E
Al Qa 'āmiyāt 168 Hb 18.50N 48.30 E
Al Qābil 146 Pk 23.56N 55.49 E
Al Qaḑārif 160 Kg 14.02N 35.24 E
Al Qaḑīmah 146 Ee 22.21N 39.09 E
Al Qādisīya 146 Kg 31.42N 44.28 E
Al Qādisīya [3] 146 Kg 31.50N 45.00 E
Al Qadmūs 146 Ge 35.05N 36.10 E
Al Qaffāy 146 Nj 24.35N 51.44 E
Al Qāhirah=Cairo (EN) 160 Ke 30.03N 31.15 E
Al Qāhirah-Imbabah 164 Fc 30.05N 31.13 E
Al Qāhirah-Mişr al Jadīdah 164 Fc 30.06N 31.20 E
Al Qā'īyah 146 Ki 26.27N 45.35 E
Al Qal'ah al Kubrá 126 Ei 35.52N 10.32 E
Al Qalibah 144 Ed 28.24N 37.42 E
Al Qāmishlī 144 Fb 37.02N 41.14 E
Al Qanţarah 164 Fc 30.52N 32.19 E
Al Qārah 146 Ih 29.52N 40.15 E
Al Qaryah ash Sharqīyah 164 Bc 30.24N 13.36 E
Al Qaryatayn 146 Ge 34.14N 37.14 E
Al Qaşab 146 Kj 25.18N 45.30 E
Al Qaşabāt 164 Bc 32.35N 14.03 E
Al Qa'şah 146 Ch 28.25N 28.56 E
Al Qaşr 164 Ed 25.42N 28.53 E
Al Qaşrayn 162 Ib 35.11N 8.48 E
Al Qaşrayn [3] 162 Ib 35.15N 9.00 E
Al Qaţīf 146 Mi 26.33N 50.00 E
Al Qaţrānī 146 Gg 31.15N 36.03 E
Al Qaţrūn 164 Be 24.56N 14.38 E
Al Qay'īyah 146 Ke 24.18N 43.30 E
Al Qayrawān 162 Jb 35.41N 10.07 E
Al Qayrawān [3] 162 Ib 35.30N 10.00 E
Al Qayşūmah [Sau.Ar.] 144 Gd 28.16N 46.03 E
Al Qayşūmah [Sau.Ar.] 146 Jh 29.11N 42.58 E
Alqōsh 146 Jd 36.44N 43.06 E
Al Qubayyāt 146 Ge 34.34N 36.17 E
Al Quds [3] 146 Fg 31.45N 35.20 E
Al Qunaytirah 144 Ec 33.07N 35.49 E
Al Qunfudhah 144 Ff 19.08N 41.05 E
Al Qurayyah 146 Gh 28.45N 36.12 E
Al Qurnah 146 Lg 31.00N 47.26 E
Al Quşaymah 164 Fc 30.40N 34.22 E
Al Quşayr [Eg.] 160 Kf 26.06N 34.17 E
Al Quşayr [Syr.] 146 Ge 34.31N 36.35 E
Al Qūşīyah 164 Fd 27.26N 30.49 E
Al Quşūr 128 Co 35.54N 8.53 E
Al Quţayfah 146 Gf 33.44N 36.36 E
Al Quwārah 146 Ji 26.47N 43.28 E
Al Quwayr 146 Jd 36.03N 43.30 E
Al Quzah 168 Hb 15.06N 49.08 E
Als 116 Ci 55.00N 9.55 E
Alsace 122 Nf 48.30N 7.30 E
Alsace, Ballon d'- 122 Mg 47.50N 6.51 E
Alsasua / Altsasu 126 Jb 42.54N 2.10W
Alsdorf 124 Id 50.53N 6.10 E
Alsea River 188 Cd 44.26N 124.05W
Alsenz 124 Je 49.49N 7.51 E
Alsfeld 120 Ff 50.45N 9.16 E
Alsina, Laguna- 204 Am 36.52S 62.07W
Alsten 114 Cd 65.57N 12.36 E
Alsterån 116 Gh 56.55N 16.26 E
Alsunga 116 Ig 57.02N 21.28 E
Alta 114 Fb 69.58N 23.14 E
Altaelva 114 Fb 69.58N 23.23 E
Altafjorden 114 Fa 70.12N 23.06 E
Altagracia 202 Da 10.07N 71.14W
Alta Gracia 206 Hd 31.40S 64.26W
Altagracia de Orituco 196 Ch 9.52N 66.23W
Altai (EN) = Altay Shan 140 Le 46.30N 93.00 E
Altaj 142 Le 46.20N 96.17 E
Altaj 140 Kd 51.30N 90.00 E
Altajskij 138 Df 51.58N 85.30 E
Altajskij kraj [3] 138 Df 52.00N 82.30 E
Altamaha River 182 Ke 31.19N 81.17W
Altamira 200 Kf 3.12S 52.12W
Altamira, Cuevas de- 126 Ha 43.23N 4.05W
Altamira, Sierra de- 126 Ge 39.35N 5.10W
Altamirano 192 Mi 16.53N 92.09W
Altamont 188 Ee 42.12N 121.44W
Altamura 128 Kj 40.49N 16.33 E
Altamura, Isla de- 192 Ee 25.00N 108.10W
Altan Bulag 152 Jc 44.19N 113.28 E
Altan-Emel → Xin Barag Youqi 152 Kb 48.41N 116.47 E
Altan Xiret → Ejin Horo Qi 152 Id 39.31N 109.45 E
Altar 192 Db 30.43N 111.44W
Altar, Desierto de- 174 Hf 31.50N 114.15W
Altar, Rio- 192 Db 30.39N 111.55W
Altar de los Sacrificios 194 Be 16.28N 90.32W
Altata 190 Cd 24.38N 107.55W
Alta Verapaz [3] 194 Bf 15.40N 90.00W
Altavista 184 Hg 37.07N 79.18W
Altay 142 Ke 47.52N 88.07 E
Altay Shan = Altai (EN) 140 Le 46.30N 93.00 E
Altdorf 128 Cd 46.53N 8.40 E
Altea 126 Lf 38.36N 0.03W
Altena 120 De 51.18N 7.40 E
Altenberge 124 Jb 52.03N 7.28 E
Altenburg 120 If 50.59N 12.27 E
Altenglan 124 Je 49.33N 7.28 E
Altenkirchen (Westerwald) 124 Jd 50.42N 7.39 E
Alter do Chão 126 Ee 39.12N 7.40W
Altevatnet 114 Eb 68.32N 19.30 E
Altındağ, Ankara- 146 Ec 39.56N 32.52 E
Altinoluk 130 Jj 39.34N 26.44 E
Altinova 130 Jj 39.13N 26.47 E
Altintas 146 Dc 39.04N 30.07 E
Altinyayla 130 Mm 36.59N 29.33 E
Altkirch 122 Ng 47.37N 7.15 E
Altmark 120 Hd 52.40N 11.20 E
Altmühl 120 Hh 48.55N 11.52 E
Alto, Morro- 204 Ib 13.46S 46.50W
Alto, Pico- 202 Kd 4.20S 39.00W
Alto Alentejo 126 Ef 38.50N 7.40W
Alto Araguaia 202 Hg 17.19S 53.12W
Alto Coité 204 Eb 15.47S 54.20W
Alto Garças 204 Fc 16.56S 53.32W
Alto Longá 202 Je 5.15S 42.12W
Alto Molócuè 172 Fc 15.38S 37.42 E
Altomonte 128 Kk 39.42N 16.08 E
Alton [Eng.-U.K.] 124 Bc 51.08N 0.59W
Alton [Il.-U.S.] 182 Id 38.54N 90.10W
Altona, Hamburg- 120 Fc 53.33N 9.57 E
Altoona 182 Lc 40.32N 78.23W
Alto Paraguai 202 Gf 14.30S 56.31W
Alto Paraguay [3] 204 Ce 21.00S 59.00W
Alto Paraiso de Goiás 204 Ib 14.12S 47.38W
Alto Paraná [3] 204 Eg 25.00S 54.50W
Alto Parnaiba 202 Ie 9.06S 45.57W
Alto Purús, Rio- 202 De 9.34S 70.36W
Alto Rio Senguerr 206 Fg 45.02S 70.50W
Altos 202 Jd 5.03S 42.28W
Alto Sucuriú 204 Fd 19.19S 52.47W
Altötting 120 Ih 48.14N 12.41 E
Alto Uruguai, Serra do- 204 Fh 27.35S 53.40W
Altsasu / Alsasua 126 Jb 42.54N 2.10W
Altun Ha 194 Ce 17.50N 88.20W
Altun Köpri 146 Ke 35.45N 44.09 E
Altun Shan 140 Kf 38.00N 88.00 E
Alturas 182 Cc 41.29N 120.32W
Alturitas 194 Ki 9.45N 72.25W
Altus 182 He 34.38N 99.20W
Altynkan 135 Hd 41.03N 70.43 E
Altynkul 135 Bc 43.07N 58.55 E
Alu 219a Bb 7.05S 155.47 E
Al 'Ubaylah 168 Ia 21.59N 50.57 E
Al Ubayyid 160 Kg 13.11N 30.13 E
Alucra 146 Hb 40.20N 38.46 E
Al 'Udaysāt 146 Ej 25.35N 32.29 E
Al Uḑayyah 168 Dc 12.03N 28.17 E
Alūksne/Aluksnes 114 Gh 57.26N 27.01 E
Alūksne/Alūksnes 114 Gh 57.26N 27.01 E
Aluksne ozero 116 Lg 57.22N 27.10 E
Aluksne ozero / Alūksnes ezers 116 Lg 57.22N 27.10 E
Alūksnes ezers / Aluksne ozero 116 Lg 57.22N 27.10 E
'Alūla 168 Ic 11.58N 50.48 E
Al 'Ulá 144 Ed 26.37N 37.52 E
Al Umm 168 Hf 18.18N 40.45 E
Alunda 116 Hd 60.04N 18.05 E
Alupka 136 Dg 44.24N 34.03 E
Al'Uqaylah 164 Cc 30.16N 19.12 E
Al 'Uqaylāt 146 Ii 26.43N 41.43 E
Al 'Uqayr 146 Nj 25.39N 50.13 E
Al Uqşur=Luxor (EN) 164 Fd 25.41N 32.39 E
Al Urayq 146 Hh 29.00N 39.10 E
Al Urdun=Jordan (EN) [1] 142 Ff 31.00N 36.00 E
Al 'Urūq al Mu'tariḑah 168 Ia 21.00N 54.00 E
Ālūs 146 Ie 34.02N 42.26 E
Alušta 136 Dg 44.42N 34.20 E
Al 'Uthmānīyah 146 Mj 25.15N 49.22 E
Al'Uwaynāt 164 Bd 25.48N 10.33 E
Al 'Uwaynidhīyah 146 Gi 26.38N 36.05 E
Al 'Uwayqīlah 146 Jg 30.21N 42.14 E
Al 'Uyūn 146 Ij 24.33N 39.35 E
Al Uzaym 146 Ke 34.02N 44.20 E
Al 'Uzayr 146 Lg 31.19N 47.25 E
Alva 182 Hd 36.48N 98.40W
Alva 126 Dd 40.18N 8.15W
Alvand, Kūh-e- 146 Me 34.41N 48.28 E
Älvängen 116 Eg 57.56N 12.09 E
Alvaro Obregón, Presa- 192 Ed 28.00N 109.45W
Alvdal 114 Ce 62.07N 10.39 E
Älvdalen 114 Df 61.14N 14.02 E
Älvdalen 116 Ed 60.30N 13.00 E
Alvear 204 Di 29.06S 56.33W
Alvelos, Serra de- 126 De 39.55N 8.01W
Alvesta 114 Dh 56.54N 14.33 E
Ålvik [Nor.] 114 Bf 60.26N 6.26 E
Alvik [Swe.] 116 Gb 62.25N 17.24 E
Alvin 186 Il 29.25N 95.15W
Älvkarleby 114 Df 60.34N 17.27 E
Alvord Valley 188 Fe 42.45N 118.25W
Alvøy 116 Ad 60.35N 4.50 E
Älvros 116 Fb 62.03N 14.39 E
Älvsborg [2] 114 Cg 58.00N 12.30 E
Älvsbyn 114 Ed 65.40N 21.00 E
Al Wāḩidī 144 Gg 14.20N 47.50 E
Al Wajh 142 Fg 26.14N 36.28 E
Al Wakrah 146 Nj 25.10N 51.36 E
Al Wannān 146 Mi 26.55N 48.24 E
Alwar 148 Fc 27.34N 76.36 E
Al Warī'ah 146 Li 27.50N 47.29 E
Al Wāsiţah 164 Fd 29.20N 31.12 E
Al Waslātīyah 128 Do 35.51N 9.35 E
Al Waţī'ah 164 Bc 32.28N 11.46 E
Al Wazz 168 Eb 15.01N 30.10 E
Al Widyān 140 Gf 31.10N 40.45 E
Alxa Youqi (Ehen Hudag) 152 Hd 39.12N 101.40 E
Alxa Zuoqi (Bayan Hot) 152 Id 38.50N 105.32 E
Al Yaman = Yemen (EN) 142 Gh 15.00N 44.00 E
Al Yaman ad Dīmuqrāţīyah → Yemen (EN) 142 Gh 15.00N 44.00 E
Alyangula 212 Hb 13.50S 136.25 E
Alygdžer 138 Ef 53.38N 98.16 E
Alymka 134 Ng 59.01N 68.40 E
Alytus/Alitus 136 Ce 54.25N 24.08 E
Alz 120 Ih 48.10N 12.48 E
Alzamaj 138 Ee 55.33N 98.39 E
Alzey 120 Eg 49.45N 8.07 E
Alzira/Alcira 126 Le 39.09N 0.26W
Amachkalo Ahzar 166 Fb 15.30N 3.20 E
Amacuro, Rio- 202 Fb 8.32N 60.28W
Amada 164 Fe 22.45N 32.10 E
Amadeus, Lake- 208 Eg 24.50S 130.45 E
Amadi [Sud.] 168 Ed 5.31N 30.20 E
Amadi [Zaire] 170 Eb 3.35N 26.47 E
Amadjuak Lake 180 Kd 64.55N 71.00W
Amadora 126 Cf 38.45N 9.14W
Amadror 162 Ie 24.50N 6.25 E
Amadror 162 Id 26.00N 5.21W
Amagasaki 156 Dd 34.42N 135.25 E
Amager 116 Ei 55.35N 12.35 E
Amagi [Jap.] 156b Bb 27.47N 128.52 E
Amagi [Jap.] 156 Be 33.26N 130.39 E
Amagi-San 156 Fd 34.51N 139.00 E
Amaha 156 Fd 35.13N 139.51 E
Amahai 150 Ig 3.20S 128.55 E
Amain, Monts d'- 122 Gf 48.39N 0.20 E
Amajac, Rio- 192 Jg 21.15N 98.46W
Amakusa-Nada 154 Jh 32.25N 129.40 E
Amakusa-Shotō 154 Kh 32.22N 130.12 E
Amal [Lib.] 164 Dd 29.25N 21.10 E
Åmål [Swe.] 114 Cg 59.03N 12.42 E
Amalfi 128 Ij 40.38N 14.36 E
Amaliás 130 El 37.48N 21.21 E
Amalner 148 Fd 21.03N 75.04 E
Amambai 202 Gh 23.05S 55.13W
Amambai, Rio- 204 Ff 23.22S 53.56W
Amambai, Serra de- 204 Ef 23.10S 55.30W
Amambay [3] 204 Df 23.00S 56.00W
Amami Islands (EN) = Amami-Shotō 140 Og 28.16N 129.21 E
Amami-Ō-Shima 152 Mf 28.15N 129.20 E
Amami-Shotō=Amami Islands (EN) 140 Og 28.16N 129.21 E
Amān 116 Fc 61.12N 14.45 E
Amana 186 Kf 41.45N 91.51W
Amanã, Lago- 202 Fd 2.35S 64.40W
Amana, Rio- 196 Eh 9.45N 62.39W
Amanab 214 Ch 3.38S 141.16 E
Amanave 221c Cb 14.19S 170.49W
Amandola 128 Hh 42.59N 13.21 E
Amangeldy 136 Ge 50.10N 65.13 E
Amankaragaj 134 Lj 52.27N 64.08 E
Amantea 128 Kk 39.07N 16.08 E
Amanu Atoll 208 Mf 17.48S 140.46W
Amanzimtoti 172 Ef 30.05S 30.53 E
Amapá 200 Ke 2.03N 50.48W
Amapá, Territorio do- [2] 202 Hc 1.30N 52.00W
Amapala 194 Dg 13.17N 87.40W
Amara 130 Ke 44.37N 27.19 E
Amara 158 Kg 11.30N 37.45 E
Amaradia 130 Ge 44.22N 23.43 E
Amara East 168 Ea 20.48N 30.23 E
Amarante [Braz.] 202 Je 6.14S 42.50W
Amarante [Port.] 126 Dc 41.16N 8.05W
Amaranth 186 Ga 50.36N 98.43W
Amargosa 188 Gh 36.18N 116.25W
Amargosa Desert 188 Gh 36.40N 116.30W
Amargosa Range 188 Gh 36.30N 116.45W
Amargosa River 188 Gh 36.13N 116.48W
Amarillo 176 If 35.13N 101.49W
Amárion 130 Hn 35.14N 24.39 E
Amarume 156 Fb 38.50N 139.54 E
Amasra 146 Eb 41.45N 32.34 E
Amasya 144 Ea 40.39N 35.51 E
Amathus 146 Ee 34.42N 33.08 E
Amatique, Bahia de- 194 Cf 15.55N 88.45W
Amatlán de Cañas 192 Gg 20.52N 104.27W
Amatrice 128 Hh 42.38N 13.17 E
Amaurilandia 204 Ff 22.10S 52.38W
Amay 124 Hd 50.33N 5.19 E
Amazar 138 Hf 53.54N 120.57 E
Amazon (EN)=Amazonas, Rio- (Solimões) 198 Lf 0.10S 49.00W
Amazon (EN) = Solimoes → Amazonas, Rio- 198 Lf 0.10S 49.00W
Amazon, Mouths of the- (EN) 198 Le 0.10S 49.00W
Amazonas [Braz.] [2] 202 Fd 5.00S 63.00W
Amazonas [Col.] [3] 202 Dd 1.00N 72.00W
Amazonas [Peru] [3] 202 Ce 5.00S 77.00W
Amazonas [Ven.] [2] 202 Ec 3.30N 66.00W
Amazonas, Rio- (Solimões) =Amazon (EN) 198 Lf 0.10S 49.00W
Amazon Cone (EN) 198 Le 4.30N 52.00W
Amba Ferit 168 Fc 10.55N 38.55 E
Ambāla 148 Fb 30.21N 76.50 E
Ambalangoda 148 Gg 6.14N 80.03 E
Ambalavao 172 Hd 21.50S 46.57 E
Ambam 166 He 2.23N 11.17 E
Ambanja 172 Hb 13.39S 48.27 E
Ambarčik 142 Sc 69.39N 162.20 E
Ambarès-et-Lagrave 122 Fj 44.55N 0.29W
Ambargasta, Salinas de- 206 Hc 29.20S 64.30W
Ambarny 136 Db 65.54N 33.41 E
Ambasamudram 148 Fg 8.42N 77.28 E
Ambato 200 If 1.15S 78.37W
Ambato-Boéni 172 Hc 16.28S 46.40 E
Ambatofinandrahana 172 Hd 20.33S 46.47 E
Ambatolampy 172 Hc 19.23S 47.25 E
Ambatondrazaka 160 Lj 17.48S 48.26 E
Ambatosoratra 172 Hc 17.36S 48.32 E
Ambelau, Pulau- 150 Ig 3.51S 127.12 E
Amberg 120 Hg 49.27N 11.52 E
Ambergris Cay 194 Dd 18.03N 87.56W
Ambergris Cays 194 Lc 21.18N 71.37W
Ambérieu-en-Bugey 122 Li 45.57N 5.21 E
Amberley [Eng.-U.K.] 124 Bd 50.55N 0.32W
Amberley [N.Z.] 218 Ee 43.09S 172.45 E
Ambert 122 Ji 45.33N 3.45 E
Ambikāpur 148 Gd 23.07N 83.12 E
Ambila 172 Hd 21.58S 47.59 E
Ambilobe 172 Hb 13.11S 49.03 E
Ambitle 219a Aa 4.05S 153.40 E
Ambjörby 116 Ed 60.30N 13.10 E
Ambla 116 Ke 59.10N 25.44 E
Amblève 122 Ld 50.28N 5.36 E
Amblève/Amel 124 Id 50.21N 6.09 E
Ambo 202 Cf 10.07S 76.10W
Amboasary Sud 172 He 25.01S 46.23 E
Ambodifototra 172 Hc 16.58S 49.52 E
Ambohimahasoa 172 Hd 21.08S 47.12 E
Ambohimanarina 172 Hc 18.49S 47.26 E
Ambohitralanana 172 Ic 15.15S 50.28 E
Amboise 122 Gg 47.25N 0.59 E
Ambon 210 De 3.43S 128.12 E
Ambon, Pulau- 150 Ig 3.40S 128.10 E
Ambongo 172 Gc 16.50S 45.00 E
Amboseli, Lake- 170 Gc 2.37S 37.08 E
Ambositra 160 Lk 20.30S 47.14 E
Ambovombe 172 He 25.09S 46.06 E
Ambre, Cap d'- = Ambre, Cape d'-(EN) 158 Lj 11.57S 49.17 E
Ambre, Cape d'-(EN) = Ambre, Cap d'- 158 Lj 11.57S 49.17 E
Ambre, Montagne d'- 172 Hb 12.30S 49.10 E
Ambriz 160 Ii 7.50S 13.08 E
Ambrolauri 132 Mh 42.31N 43.05 E
Ambrym, Ile- 208 Hf 16.15S 168.07 E
Ambunti 214 Ch 4.14S 142.50 E
Āmbūr 148 Ff 12.47N 78.42 E
Amchitka 178a Bb 51.30N 179.00 E
Amchitka Pass 178a Cb 51.30N 179.30W
Am Dafok 168 Cc 10.28N 23.17 E
Am Dam 168 Cc 12.46N 20.29 E
Amded 162 He 22.10N 3.15 E
Amderma 136 Gb 69.45N 61.39 E
Am Djéména 168 Bc 13.06N 17.19 E
Amdo 152 Fe 32.29N 91.47 E
Ameca 190 Dd 20.33N 104.02W
Ameca, Rio- 192 Gg 20.41N 105.18W
Amel/Amblève 124 Id 50.21N 6.09 E
Ameland 124 Ha 53.26N 5.48 E
Ameland 122 La 53.25N 5.45 E
Ameland- Nes 124 Ha 53.26N 5.48 E
Amelia Island 184 Gj 30.37N 81.27W
Amélie-les-Bains-Palalda 122 Il 42.28N 2.40 E
Amendolara 128 Kk 39.57N 16.35 E
'Āmeri 146 Nh 28.30N 51.05 E
Americana 204 If 22.45S 47.20W
American Falls 188 Ie 42.47N 112.51W
American Falls Reservoir 188 Ie 43.00N 113.00W
American Fork 188 Jf 40.23N 111.48W
American Highland 222 Ff 72.30S 78.00 E
American Samoa [5] 210 Kf 14.50S 170.00W
Americus 182 Ke 32.04N 84.14W
Amersfoort 122 Lb 52.09N 5.24 E
Amery Ice Shelf 222 Fe 69.30S 72.00 E
Ames 182 Ic 42.02N 93.37W
Ametlla de Mar 126 Md 40.54N 0.48 E
Amfilokhia 130 Ek 38.52N 21.10 E
Amfissa 130 Fk 38.32N 22.23 E
Amfreville-la-Campagne 124 Ce 49.13N 0.57 E
Amga 138 Id 60.52N 131.50 E
Amga 140 Pc 62.40N 134.59 E
Amgalang → Xin Barag Zuoqi 152 Kb 48.13N 118.14 E
Am Géréda 168 Cc 12.52N 21.10 E
Amgu 154 Nb 45.51N 137.41 E
Amguema 138 Nc 68.03N 177.55W
Amguid 160 Hf 26.26N 5.22 E
Amguid 162 Id 26.30N 5.36 E
Amgun 140 Pd 52.56N 139.40 E
Amherst 180 Lg 45.49N 64.14W
Amherst, Mount- 212 Fc 18.11S 126.59 E
Amherst Island 184 Ic 44.12N 76.42W
Amiata, Monte- 128 Fh 42.53N 11.37 E
Amiens 112 Gf 49.54N 2.18 E
Āmij, Wādī- 146 Ih 33.48N 41.46 E
Amik Gölü 146 Gd 36.22N 36.17 E
Amili 148 Jc 28.26N 95.52 E
Amīndīvi Islands 148 Ef 11.23N 72.23 E
Aminuis 172 Bd 23.43S 19.21 E
'Āmir, Ra's- 158 Je 32.57N 21.43 E

Index Symbols

[1] Independent Nation
[2] State, Region
[3] District, County
[4] Municipality
[5] Colony, Dependency
Continent
Physical Region
Historical or Cultural Region
Mount, Mountain
Volcano
Hill
Mountains, Mountain Range
Hills, Escarpment
Plateau, Upland
Pass, Gap
Plain, Lowland
Delta
Salt Flat
Valley, Canyon
Crater, Cave
Karst Features
Depression
Polder
Desert, Dunes
Forest, Woods
Heath, Steppe
Oasis
Cape, Point
Coast, Beach
Cliff
Peninsula
Isthmus
Sandbank
Island
Atoll
Rock, Reef
Islands, Archipelago
Rocks, Reefs
Coral Reef
Well, Spring
Geyser
River, Stream
Waterfall, Rapids
River Mouth, Estuary
Lake
Salt Lake
Intermittent Lake
Reservoir
Swamp, Pond
Canal
Glacier
Ice Shelf, Pack Ice
Ocean
Sea
Gulf, Bay
Strait, Fjord
Lagoon
Bank
Seamount
Tablemount
Ridge
Shelf
Basin
Escarpment, Sea Scarp
Fracture
Trench, Abyss
National Park, Reserve
Point of Interest
Recreation Site
Cave, Cavern
Historic Site
Ruins
Wall, Walls
Church, Abbey
Temple
Scientific Station
Railway station
Airport
Port
Military installation
Lighthouse
Mine
Tunnel
Dam, Bridge

Amirante Basin (EN)	158	Mi	7.00 S	55.00 E
Amirante Islands	158	Mi	6.00 S	53.10 E
Amirante Trench (EN)	172b	Bb	6.00 S	52.30 E
Amisk Lake	180	Hf	54.35N	102.15W
Amistad, Presa de la-	186	Fl	28.34N	101.15W
Amistad Reservoir	182	Gf	28.34N	101.15W
Amite	186	Kk	30.44N	90.30W
Amlekhganj	148	Gc	27.17N	84.59 E
Amlia	178a	Db	52.06N	173.30W
Amlwch	118	Ih	53.25N	4.20W
Amm Adām	168	Fb	16.22N	36.09 E
Ammān	142	Ff	31.57N	35.56 E
Ammān [3]	146	Gg	31.57N	35.56 E
Ammanford	118	Jj	51.48N	3.59W
Ammarnäs	114	Dd	65.58N	16.12 E
mmeberg	116	Ff	58.52N	15.00 E
Ammer	120	Hi	47.57N	11.08 E
Ammerån	116	Ga	63.09N	16.13 E
mmerland	120	Dc	53.15N	8.00 E
Ammersee	120	Hi	48.00N	11.08 E
mmi-Moussa	126	Ni	35.52N	1.07 E
mmokhostos → Famagusta (EN)	144	Dc	35.07N	33.57 E
Amnja	134	Me	63.45N	67.07 E
mnok-kang	152	Ld	39.55N	124.20 E
mol	144	Hb	36.23N	52.20 E
Amolar	204	Dd	18.01 S	57.30W
morgós	130	Im	36.50N	25.53 E
morgós	130	Im	36.50N	25.59 E
Amorinópolis	204	Gc	16.36 S	51.08W
mory	186	Lj	33.59N	88.29W
mos	180	Jg	48.34N	78.07W
mot [Nor.]	114	Bg	59.54N	9.54 E
mot [Nor.]	116	Be	59.35N	8.00 E
motfors	116	Ee	59.46N	12.22 E
moucha	126	Rh	36.23N	5.25 E
mouliani	130	Gi	40.20N	23.55 E
mour, Djebel-	162	Hc	33.45N	1.45 E
mourj	162	Ff	16.10N	7.35W
moy (EN) = Xiamen	142	Ng	24.32N	118.06 E
mpanihy	172	Gd	24.40 S	44.45 E
mparafaravola	172	Hc	17.36 S	48.12 E
mparo	204	If	22.42 S	46.47W
mpato, Nevado de-	198	Ig	15.50 S	71.52W
mper	120	Hh	48.10N	11.50 E
mpère Seamount (EN)	110	Eh	35.05N	12.13W
mphitrite Point	188	Cb	48.56N	125.35W
mposta	126	Md	40.43N	0.35 E
mpthill	124	Bb	52.02N	0.29W
mpurdán / Empordà	126	Ob	42.12N	2.45 E
mpurias / Empúries	126	Pb	42.10N	3.05 E
mqui	184	Na	48.28N	67.26W
Amrān	144	Ff	15.41N	43.55 E
mrāvati	142	Jg	20.56N	77.45 E
m-Raya	168	Bc	14.05N	16.30 E
mritsar	142	Jf	31.35N	74.53 E
mrum	120	Eb	54.40N	8.20 E
msaga	162	Ee	20.07N	14.10W
msittene, Jebel-	162	Fc	31.11N	9.40W
mstel	124	Gb	52.22N	4.56 E
mstelveen	124	Gb	52.18N	4.53 E
msterdam	158	Ol	37.57 S	77.40 E
msterdam [Neth.]	112	Ge	52.22N	4.54 E
msterdam [N.Y.-U.S.]	184	Jd	42.56N	74.12W
msterdam-Rijnkanaal	124	Hc	51.57N	5.25 E
mstetten	128	Ib	48.07N	14.52 E
m Timan	160	Jg	11.02N	20.17 E
mūd, Jabal al-	144	Ec	30.59N	39.20 E
mūdā	146	Id	37.05N	40.54 E
mu-Darja	135	Ef	37.57N	65.15 E
mudarja = Amu Darya (EN)	140	He	43.40N	59.01 E
mū Daryā = Amu Darya (EN)	140	He	43.40N	59.01 E
mu Darya (EN) = Amudarja	140	He	43.40N	59.01 E
mu Darya (EN) = Āmū Daryā	140	He	43.40N	59.01 E
mudat	170	Fb	1.58N	34.56 E
mukta Pass	178a	Db	52.25N	172.00W
mun	219a	Ba	5.57 S	154.45 E
mund Ringnes	180	Ha	78.15N	97.00W
mundsen Bay	222	Ee	66.55 S	50.00 E
mundsen Coast	222	Mg	85.30 S	159.00W
mundsen Glacier	222	Mg	85.35 S	159.00W
mundsen Gulf	174	Gb	71.00N	124.00W
mundsen-Scott Station	222	Bg	90.00 S	0.00
mundsen Sea (EN)	222	Of	72.30 S	112.00W
mungen	116	Fc	61.10N	15.40 E
muntai	142	Nj	2.26 S	115.15 E
mur	140	Qd	52.56N	141.10 E
mūr, Wādī-	168	Eb	18.56N	33.34 E
murang	150	Hf	1.11N	124.35 E
mursk	138	If	50.16N	136.55 E
murskaja oblast [3]	138	Hf	54.00N	128.00 E
murzet	138	Ig	47.41N	131.07 E
mvrakia, Gulf of- (EN) = Amvrakikós Kólpos	130	Dk	39.00N	21.00 E
mvrakikós Kólpos = Amvrakia, Gulf of- (EN)	130	Dk	39.00N	21.00 E
mvrosijevka	132	Kf	47.44N	38.31 E
m Zoer	168	Cc	14.13N	21.23 E
naa Atoll	216	Lc	17.25 S	145.30W
nabar	220e	Ba	0.29 S	166.57 E
nabar	140	Nb	73.08N	113.36 E
nabarskoje ploskogorje	140	Mc	70.00N	108.00 E
n Abhainn Dubh/ Blackwater	118	Gh	53.39N	6.43W
n Abhainn Mhór/ Blackwater [Ire.]	118	Fj	51.51N	7.50W
n Abhainn Mhór/ Blackwater [N.Ire.-U.K.]	118	Gg	54.30N	6.35W
nabuki	156	Dd	34.02N	134.11 E
nacasti	206	Gc	28.49 S	65.30W
naco	202	Fb	9.27N	64.28W
naconda	182	Eb	46.08N	112.57W
nacortes	188	Db	48.30N	122.37W
nadarko	186	Gi	35.04N	98.15W

Anadolu = Anatolia (EN)	140	Ff	39.00N	35.00 E
Anadyr	142	Tc	64.45N	177.29 E
Anadyr	140	Tc	64.55N	176.05 E
Anadyr Gulf (EN) = Anadyrski zaliv	140	Uc	64.00N	179.00W
Anadyr Range (EN) = Anadyrskoje ploskogorje	140	Tc	67.00N	174.00 E
Anadyrski liman	138	Md	64.30N	178.00 E
Anadyrski zaliv = Anadyr Gulf (EN)	140	Uc	64.00N	179.00W
Anadyrskoje ploskogorje = Anadyr Range (EN)	140	Tc	67.00N	174.00 E
Anáfi	130	Im	36.22N	25.47 E
Anaghit	168	Fb	16.20N	38.39 E
Anagni	128	Hi	41.44N	13.09 E
'Ānah	144	Fc	34.28N	41.56 E
Anaheim	188	Gj	33.51N	117.57W
Anahola	221a	Ba	22.09N	159.19W
Anáhuac	192	Id	27.14N	100.09W
Anáhuac, Meseta de-	190	Dd	21.30N	101.00W
An Aird/Ards Peninsula	118	Hg	54.30N	5.30W
Anaj Mudi	140	Jh	10.10N	77.04 E
Anaktuvuk Pass	178	Ic	68.10N	151.50W
Analalava	172	Hb	14.38 S	47.45 E
Analavelona	172	Gd	22.37 S	44.10 E
Ana María, Golfo de-	194	Hc	21.25N	78.40W
Anambas, Kepulauan- = Anambas Islands (EN)	140	Mi	3.00N	106.00 E
Anambas Islands (EN) = Anambas, Kepulauan-	140	Mi	3.00N	106.00 E
Anambra [2]	166	Gd	6.30N	7.30 E
Anamé	219b	De	20.08 S	169.49 E
Anamizu	154	Nf	37.14N	136.54 E
Anamur	144	Db	36.06N	32.50 E
Anamur Burun	144	Db	36.03N	32.48 E
Anan [Jap.]	156	Ed	35.19N	137.48 E
Anan [Jap.]	154	Mh	33.55N	134.39 E
Anane, Djebel-	126	Mi	35.12N	0.47 E
Anánes	130	Hm	36.31N	24.08 E
Ananjev	132	Ff	47.43N	29.59 E
Anankwin	148	Je	15.41N	97.59 E
Anantapur	148	Ff	14.41N	77.36 E
Anantnāg (Islāmābād)	148	Fb	33.44N	75.09 E
Anapa	136	Dg	44.53N	37.19 E
Anapo	128	Jm	37.03N	15.16 E
Anápolis	200	Lg	16.20 S	48.58W
Anapu, Rio-	202	Hd	2.15 S	51.30W
Anār	144	Ic	30.53N	55.18 E
Anārak	144	Hc	33.20N	53.42 E
Anare Station	222	Jd	54.30 S	158.55 E
Anaro, Rio-	194	Lj	7.48N	70.12W
Añasco	197a	Ab	18.17N	67.10W
Anatahan Island	208	Fc	16.22N	145.40 E
Anatolia (EN) = Anadolu	140	Ff	39.00N	35.00 E
Anatolikí Rodhópi	130	Ih	41.44N	25.31 E
Añatuya	206	Hc	28.28 S	62.50W
Anauá, Rio-	202	Fc	0.58N	61.21W
Anazah, Jabal-	146	Hf	32.12N	39.18 E
Anazarba	146	Fd	37.15N	35.45 E
An Baile Meánach/ Ballymena	118	Gg	54.52N	6.17W
An Bhanna/Bann	118	Gf	55.10N	6.46W
An Bhearú/Barrow	118	Gi	52.10N	7.00W
An Bhinn Bhuí/Benwee Head	118	Dg	54.21N	9.48W
An Bhograch/Boggeragh Mountains	118	Ei	52.05N	9.00W
Ån Bhóinn/Boyne	118	Gh	53.43N	6.15W
An Bhrosnach/Brosna	118	Fh	53.13N	7.58W
An Blascaod Mór/Great Blasket	118	Ci	52.05N	10.32W
Anbyŏn	154	Ie	39.02N	127.32 E
An Cabhán / Cavan	118	Fg	54.00N	7.21W
An Cabhán/Cavan [2]	118	Fh	53.55N	7.30W
An Caisleán Nua/Newcastle	118	Hg	54.12N	5.54W
An Caisleán Nua/Newcastle West	118	Di	52.27N	9.03W
An Caisleán Riabhach/ Castlerea	118	Eh	53.46N	8.29W
An Caoláire Rua/Killary Harbour	118	Dh	53.38N	9.55W
Ancares, Sierra de-	126	Fb	42.46N	6.54W
Ancash [3]	202	Ce	9.30 S	77.45W
Ancenis	122	Eg	47.22N	1.10W
An Chathair/Caher	118	Fi	52.22N	7.55W
An Cheacha/Caha Mountains	118	Dj	51.45N	9.45W
Anchorage	176	Ec	61.13N	149.53W
An Chorr Chríochach/ Cookstown	118	Gg	54.39N	6.45W
Anci (Langfang)	152	Kd	39.29N	116.40 E
An Clár/Clare [2]	118	Ei	52.50N	9.00W
An Cóbh/Cóbh	118	Ej	51.51N	8.17W
Ancohuma, Nevado-	202	Eg	15.51 S	68.36W
Ancona	112	Hg	43.38N	13.30 E
Ancón de Sardinas, Bahía de-	202	Cc	1.30N	79.50W
Ancre	122	Ie	49.54N	2.28 E
Ancuabe	172	Fb	12.58 S	39.51 E
Ancud	206	Ff	41.52 S	73.50W
Ancud, Golfo de-	206	Ff	42.05 S	73.00W
Anda	152	Mb	46.24N	125.20 E
Anda (Sartu)	154	Ha	46.35N	125.00 E
Andacollo [Arg.]	206	Fe	37.11 S	70.41W
Andacollo [Chile]	206	Fd	30.14 S	71.06W
Andahuaylas	202	Df	13.39 S	73.23W
An Daingean/Dingle	118	Ci	52.08N	10.15W
Andalgalá	206	Gc	27.36 S	66.19W
Åndalsnes	114	Be	62.34N	7.42 E
Andalucía = Andalusia (EN) [2]	126	Hg	37.30N	4.30W
Andalucía = Andalusia (EN)	110	Fh	37.30N	4.30W
Andalusia	182	Je	31.19N	86.29W
Andalusia (EN) = Andalucía [2]	126	Hg	37.30N	4.30W

Andalusia (EN) = Andalucía	110	Fh	37.30N	4.30W
Andaman and Nicobar [3]	148	If	12.30N	92.45 E
Andaman Basin (EN)	140	Lh	10.00N	94.00 E
Andaman Islands	140	Lh	12.30N	92.43 E
Andaman Sea (EN)	140	Lh	10.00N	95.00 E
Andamooka	212	Hf	30.27 S	137.12 E
'Andān, Wādī-	144	Ie	21.05N	58.23 E
Andant	204	Am	36.34 S	62.07W
Andapa	172	Hb	14.38 S	49.33 E
Andara	172	Cc	18.03 S	21.27 E
Andelle	124	De	49.19N	1.14 E
Andelys, Les-	122	He	49.15N	1.25 E
Andenes	114	Db	69.19N	16.08 E
Andenne	124	Hd	50.29N	5.06 E
Andenne-Namêche	124	Hd	50.28N	5.00 E
Andéranboukane	166	Fb	15.26N	3.02 E
Anderlecht	124	Gd	50.50N	4.18 E
Anderlues	124	Gd	50.24N	4.16 E
Andermatt	128	Cd	46.38N	8.37 E
Andernach	120	Df	50.26N	7.24 E
Andernos-les-Bains	122	Ej	44.44N	1.06W
Anderson	180	Ec	69.42N	129.01W
Anderson [Ca.-U.S.]	188	Df	40.27N	122.18W
Anderson [In.-U.S.]	182	Jc	40.10N	85.41W
Anderson [S.C.-U.S.]	182	Ke	34.30N	82.39W
Anderstorp	116	Eg	57.17N	13.38 E
Andes (EN) = Andes, Cordillera de los-	198	Jh	20.00 S	67.00W
Andes, Cordillera de los- = Andes (EN)	198	Jh	20.00 S	67.00W
Andevoranto	172	Hc	18.56 S	49.06 E
Andfjorden	114	Db	69.10N	16.20 E
Andhra Pradesh [3]	148	Fe	16.00N	79.00 E
Andía, Sierra de- / Andia, Sierra de-	126	Kb	42.45N	2.00W
Andia, Sierra de- / Andía, Sierra de-	126	Kb	42.45N	2.00W
Andikhásia Ōri	130	Ej	39.47N	21.55 E
Andikíra	130	Fk	38.23N	22.38 E
Andikíthira = Andikithira (EN)	130	Gn	35.52N	23.18 E
Andikithira (EN) = Andikíthira	130	Gn	35.52N	23.18 E
Andikithíron, Stenón-	130	Gn	35.45N	23.25 E
Andilamena	172	Hc	17.01S	48.32 E
Andilanatoby	172	Hc	17.56 S	48.14 E
Andīmeshk	146	Mf	32.27N	48.21 E
Andímilos	130	Hm	36.47N	24.14 E
Andíparos	130	Il	37.00N	25.03 E
Andípaxoi	130	Dj	39.08N	20.14 E
Andípsara	130	Ik	38.33N	25.24 E
Andir He	152	Dd	38.00N	83.36 E
Andırın	146	Gd	37.34N	36.20 E
Andirlangar	152	Dd	37.36N	83.50 E
Andírrion	130	Ek	38.20N	21.46 E
Andítilos	130	Km	36.22N	27.28 E
Andižan	142	Je	40.45N	72.22 E
Andižanskaja oblast [3]	136	Hg	40.45N	72.20 E
Andkhvoy	144	Kb	36.56N	65.08 E
Andŏng	152	Md	36.36N	128.44 E
Andorra (Valls d'Andorra) [1]	112	Gg	42.30N	1.30 E
Andorra la Vella	112	Gg	42.31N	1.31 E
Andover	118	Lj	51.13N	1.28W
Andøya	114	Db	69.08N	15.54 E
Andradas	204	If	22.05 S	46.35W
Andradina	206	Jb	20.54 S	51.23W
Andraitx / Andratx	126	Oe	39.35N	2.25 E
Andratx / Andraitx	126	Oe	39.35N	2.25 E
Andreanof Islands	174	Bd	52.00N	176.00W
Andreapol	114	Hh	56.39N	32.16 E
Andrées Land	179	Jd	73.20N	26.30W
Andrejevka [Kaz.-U.S.S.R.]	136	If	45.47N	80.35 E
Andrejevka [Ukr.-U.S.S.R.]	132	Je	49.32N	36.40 E
Andrejevo-Ivanovka	130	Nb	47.31N	30.21 E
Andrejevsk	138	Ge	58.10N	114.15 E
Andrelândia	204	Je	21.44 S	44.18W
Andresito	204	Dk	33.08 S	57.09W
Andrespol	120	Pe	51.43N	19.40 E
Andrews	186	Ej	32.19N	102.33W
Andria	128	Ki	41.13N	16.17 E
Andriamena	172	Hc	17.28 S	47.29 E
Andriba	172	Hc	17.36 S	46.53 E
Andrijevica	130	Cg	42.44N	19.48 E
Andringitra	158	Lk	22.20 S	46.55 E
Andrítsaina	130	El	37.29N	21.54 E
Androka	172	Gd	24.59 S	44.04 E
Androna, Plateau de l'-	172	Hc	15.30S	48.20 E
Andropov → Rybinsk	112	Jd	58.03N	38.52 E
Ándros	130	Hl	37.50N	24.56 E
Andros	110	Ih	37.50N	24.50 E
Androscoggin River	184	Md	43.55N	69.55W
Andros Island	174	Lg	24.25N	78.00W
Andros Town	190	Id	24.43N	77.47W
Androth Island	148	Ef	10.50N	73.41 E
Androy	158	Lk	25.00 S	45.40 E
Andruševka	132	Fe	49.59N	29.01 E
Andrychów	120	Pg	49.52N	19.21 E
Andselv	114	Eb	69.04N	18.30 E
Andudu	170	Eb	2.29N	28.41 E
Andújar	126	Hf	38.03N	4.04W
Andulo	170	Ce	11.28 S	16.43 E
Andu Tan	150	Fe	7.35N	114.15 E
Anduze	122	Jj	44.03N	3.59 E
An Ea agail/Errigal	118	Ef	55.02N	8.07W
Aneby	116	Fg	57.50N	14.48 E
Anéfis	166	Fb	18.03N	0.36 E
Anegada	190	Le	18.45N	64.20W
Anegada, Bahía-	206	Hf	40.15 S	62.15W
Anegada Passage	190	Le	18.30N	63.40W
Aného	166	Fd	6.14N	1.36 E
An Éirne/Erne	118	Eg	54.30N	8.15W
An Eithne/Inny	118	Fh	53.35N	7.50W
An Eoghanach/Annalee	118	Fg	54.02N	7.25W
Anet	124	Df	48.51N	1.26 E
Aneto, Pico de-	110	Gg	42.38N	0.40 E

Aney	166	Hb	19.24N	12.56 E
Aneytioum, Ile-	208	Hg	20.12 S	169.49 E
An Feabhal / Foyle	118	Ff	55.04N	7.15W
An Fhéil/Feale	118	Di	52.28N	9.40W
An Fheoir/Nore	118	Gi	52.25N	6.58W
Angamos, Punta- [Chile]	206	Fb	23.01 S	70.32W
Angamos, Punta- [Pas.]	221d	Bb	27.04 S	109.17W
Angara	140	Ld	58.06N	93.00 E
Angarsk	142	Md	52.34N	103.54 E
Angarski, pereval-	132	Ig	44.47N	34.25 E
Angarski krjaž	138	Fe	57.30N	103.00 E
Angathonisi	130	Jl	37.28N	27.00 E
Angaur Island	208	Ed	6.54N	134.09 E
Änge [Swe.]	116	Fa	63.27N	14.03 E
Ånge [Swe.]	114	De	62.31N	15.37 E
An Gearrán/Garron Point	118	Hf	55.05N	5.58W
Ángel, Cerro-	192	Hf	22.49N	102.34W
Angelburg	124	Kd	50.47N	8.25 E
Ángel de la Guarda, Isla-	190	Bc	29.20N	113.25W
Angeles	150	Hc	15.09N	120.35 E
Ángeles, Sierra de los-	192	Jf	23.10N	99.20W
Ángel Falls (EN) = Angel, Salto-/Churún Merú	198	Je	5.57N	62.30W
Ángel Falls (EN) = Churún Merú/Angel, Salto-	198	Je	5.57N	62.30W
Ångelholm	114	Ch	56.15N	12.51 E
Angélica	204	Bj	31.33 S	61.33W
Angeln	120	Fb	54.40N	9.45 E
Angel Salto-/Churún Merú = Ángel Falls (EN)	198	Je	5.57N	62.30W
Ängelsberg	116	Ge	59.58N	16.02 E
Anger	168	Fd	9.40N	36.06 E
Angereb	168	Fc	13.44N	36.28 E
Ångermanälven	110	Hc	62.48N	17.56 E
Angermünde	120	Jc	53.02N	14.00 E
Angers	112	Ff	47.28N	0.33W
Angikuni Lake	180	Hd	62.10N	99.55W
Angístrion	130	Gl	37.40N	23.20 E
Angkor	148	Kf	13.26N	103.52 E
Anglem, Mount-	218	Bg	46.44 S	167.54 E
Anglès	126	Oc	41.57N	2.39 E
Anglesey	110	Fe	53.18N	4.20W
Anglet	122	Ek	43.29N	1.32W
Angleton	186	Il	29.10N	95.26W
Anglin	122	Gh	46.42N	0.52 E
Anglona	128	Cj	40.45N	8.45 E
Anglo-Normandes, Iles- (F) = Channel Islands [5]	118	Kl	49.20N	2.20W
Angmagssalik	224	Mc	65.45N	37.30W
Ango	170	Eb	4.02N	25.52 E
Angoche	160	Kj	16.12 S	39.54 E
Angoche, Ilha-	158	Kj	16.20 S	39.51 E
Angol	206	Fe	37.48 S	72.43W
Angola	184	Ee	41.38N	85.00W
Angola [1]	160	Ij	12.30 S	18.30 E
Angola Basin (EN)	106	Ek	15.00 S	3.00 E
Angoram	214	Ch	4.04 S	144.04 E
Angostura	192	Ee	25.22N	108.11W
Angostura, Presa de la-	192	Mi	16.30N	92.30W
Angostura, Salto-	202	Dc	2.43N	70.57W
Angostura Reservoir	186	Ee	43.18N	103.27W
Angoulême	122	Gi	45.39N	0.09 E
Angoumois	122	Gi	45.30N	0.00
Angra do Héroísmo	160	Ee	38.39N	27.13W
Angra do Heroísmo [3]	162	Bb	38.42N	27.15W
Angra dos Reis	204	Jf	23.00 S	44.18W
Angren	136	Hg	41.03N	70.10 E
Angu	170	Db	3.33N	24.28 E
Anguang	154	Gb	45.36N	123.48 E
Anguilla [5]	176	Mh	18.15N	63.05W
Anguilla	174	Mh	18.15N	63.05W
Anguilla, Canal de l'- = Anguilla Channel (EN)	197b	Ab	18.09N	63.04W
Anguilla Bank (EN)	197b	Ab	18.30N	63.03W
Anguilla Cays	194	Hb	23.31N	78.33W
Anguilla Channel	197b	Ab	18.09N	63.04W
Anguilla Channel (EN) = Anguilla, Canal de l'-	197b	Ab	18.09N	63.04W
Anguli Nur	154	Cd	41.23N	114.30 E
Anguo	154	Ce	38.25N	115.20 E
Anhanca	170	Cf	16.47 S	15.33 E
Anhanguera	204	Hd	18.21 S	48.17W
An Hoa	148	Le	15.46N	108.03 E
Anholt	114	Ch	56.40N	11.35 E
Anhua (Dongping)	152	Jf	28.27N	111.15 E
Anhui Sheng (An-hui Sheng) = Anhwei (EN) [2]	152	Ke	32.00N	117.00 E
An-hui Sheng → Anhui Sheng = Anhwei (EN) [2]	152	Ke	32.00N	117.00 E
Anhwei (EN) = Anhui Sheng (An-hui Sheng) [2]	152	Ke	32.00N	117.00 E
Anhwei (EN) = An-hui Sheng → Anhui Sheng [2]	152	Ke	32.00N	117.00 E
Ani	156	Gb	39.59N	140.25 E
Aniak	178	Hd	61.34N	159.30W
An Iarmhí/Westmeath [2]	118	Fh	53.30N	7.30W
Anibare	220e	Bb	0.32 S	166.57 E
Anibare Bay	220e	Bb	0.32 S	166.57 E
Aniche	124	Fd	50.20N	3.15 E
Ánidhros	130	Im	36.37N	25.41 E
Anié	166	Fd	7.45N	1.12 E
Anie, Pic d'-	122	Fl	42.57N	0.43W
Aniene	128	Gi	41.56N	12.30 E
Anijangying → Luanping	154	Dd	40.55N	117.19 E
Anikščiaj/Anykščiai	114	Fi	55.31N	25.08 E
Animas Peak	186	Bk	31.35N	108.47W
Anina	130	Ed	45.05N	21.51 E
Anita Garibaldi	204	Gh	27.37 S	51.05W
Anittepe	130	Kh	41.21N	27.42 E
Aniva	138	Jg	46.41N	142.35 E
Aniva, mys-	138	Jg	46.00N	143.25 E
Aniva, zaliv-	138	Jg	46.20N	142.40 E
Anivorano Avaratra	172	Hb	12.43 S	49.12 E
Anivorano Nord	172	Hb	12.43 S	49.12 E
Aniwa, Ile-	208	Hf	19.16 S	169.35 E
Anizy-le-Château	124	Fe	49.30N	3.27 E
Anjala	114	Gf	60.41N	26.50 E
Anji	154	Ei	30.39N	119.41 E

Anjiang → Qianyang	152	Jf	27.19N	110.13 E
Anjō	156	Ed	34.57N	137.05 E
Anjou	122	Fg	47.20N	0.30W
Anjou, Val d'-	122	Fg	47.25N	0.15W
Anjouan/Nzwani	158	Lj	12.15 S	44.25 E
Anjou Islands (EN) = Anžu, ostrova-	140	Qb	75.30N	143.00 E
Anjozorobe	172	Hc	18.24 S	47.52 E
Anju	152	Md	39.37N	125.40 E
Anjuj	138	Ig	49.20N	136.20 E
Anjujski hrebet	138	Lc	67.20N	166.00 E
Anka	166	Gc	12.07N	5.55 E
Ankang (Xing an)	142	Mf	32.37N	109.03 E
Ankara	142	Ff	39.56N	32.52 E
Ankara-Altındağ	146	Ec	39.56N	32.52 E
Ankara-Çankaya	146	Ec	39.56N	32.52 E
Ankaratra	158	Lj	19.25 S	47.12 E
Ankara-Yenimahalle	146	Ec	39.56N	32.52 E
Ankarsrum	114	Dh	57.42N	16.19 E
Ankavandra	172	Hc	18.45 S	45.18 E
Ankazoabo	172	Gd	22.16 S	44.30 E
Ankazobe	172	Hc	18.17 S	47.05 E
Ankeny	186	Jf	41.44N	93.36W
'Ankhor	168	Hc	10.47N	46.18 E
Anklam	120	Jc	53.52N	13.42 E
Ankober	168	Fd	9.40N	39.44 E
Ankoro	170	Ed	6.45 S	26.57 E
Ankum	124	Jb	52.33N	7.53 E
An Laoi/Lee	118	Ej	51.55N	8.30W
Anlong	152	If	25.02N	105.30 E
An Longfort / Longford	118	Fh	53.44N	7.47W
An Longfort/Longford [2]	118	Fh	53.40N	7.40W
An Lorgain/Lurgan	118	Gg	54.28N	6.20W
Anlu	152	Je	31.12N	113.46 E
An Mhí/Meath [2]	118	Gh	53.35N	6.40W
An Mhuaidh/Moy	118	Dg	54.12N	9.08W
An Mhuir Cheilteach = Celtic Sea (EN)	110	Fe	51.00N	7.00W
An Muileann gCearr/ Mullingar	118	Fh	53.32N	7.20W
An Muirthead/Mullet Peninsula	118	Cg	54.15N	10.04W
Ånn	116	Ea	63.19N	12.33 E
Ånn	114	Ce	63.15N	12.35 E
Ann, Cape- [Ant.]	222	Ee	66.10 S	51.22 E
Ann, Cape- [Ma.-U.S.]	184	Ld	42.39N	70.38W
Anna [Il.-U.S.]	186	Lh	37.28N	89.15W
Anna [Nauru]	220e	Ba	0.29 S	166.56 E
Anna [R.S.F.S.R.]	136	Ee	51.29N	40.26 E
Annaba	160	He	36.54N	7.46 E
Annaba [3]	162	Ib	35.35N	8.00 E
An Nabaţiyah at Taḩtā	146	Gf	33.23N	35.29 E
Annaberg-Buchholz	120	If	50.34N	13.00 E
An Nabī Şāliḩ	146	Eh	28.38N	33.59 E
An Nabk	144	Ec	34.01N	36.44 E
An Nabk Abū Qaşr	146	Hg	30.21N	38.34 E
An Nafīḑah	128	En	36.08N	10.23 E
An Nafūd	140	Gg	28.30N	41.00 E
An Nāḩiyah	146	Ie	34.26N	41.33 E
An Najaf	142	Gf	31.59N	44.20 E
An Najaf [3]	146	Kg	31.20N	44.07 E
An Nakhl	164	Fd	29.55N	33.45 E
Annalee/An Eoghanach	118	Fg	54.02N	7.25W
Annam (EN) = Trung Phan	140	Mh	15.00N	108.00 E
Annamitique, Chaîne-	148	Le	17.00N	106.00 E
Annan	118	Jg	55.00N	3.16W
Annan	118	Jg	54.59N	3.16W
Anna Paulowna	124	Gb	52.52N	4.52 E
Anna Paulowna-Kleine Sluis	124	Gb	52.52N	4.52 E
Anna Point	220e	Ba	0.29 S	166.56 E
Annapolis	176	Lf	38.59N	76.30W
Annapolis Royal	184	Oc	44.45N	65.31W
Annapurna	140	Kg	28.34N	83.50 E
Ann Arbor	182	Kc	42.18N	83.45W
Anna Regina	196	Gi	7.16N	58.30W
An Nás/Naas	118	Gh	53.13N	6.39W
An Nashshāsh	146	Pk	23.05N	54.02 E
An Nashwah	146	Lg	30.49N	47.36 E
An Nāşirīyah	144	Gc	31.02N	46.16 E
An Nasser	146	Ej	24.36N	32.58 E
An Nawfalīyah	164	Cc	30.47N	17.50 E
Annecy	122	Mi	45.54N	6.07 E
Annecy, Lac d'-	122	Mi	45.51N	6.11 E
Annemasse	122	Mh	46.12N	6.15 E
Annevoie-Rouillon	124	Gd	50.21N	4.50 E
An Nīl [3]	168	Ea	20.10N	33.00 E
An Nīl al Azraq [3]	168	Ec	12.20N	34.15 E
Anning	152	Hg	24.58N	102.29 E
Anniston	182	Je	33.40N	85.50W
Annobón	158	Hi	1.32 S	5.38 E
Annonay	122	Ki	45.14N	4.40 E
Annotto Bay	194	Id	18.16N	76.46W
An Nu'ayrīyah	146	Mi	27.28N	48.27 E
An Nuhūd	160	Jg	12.42N	28.26 E
An Nu' Mān	146	Fi	27.06N	35.46 E
An Nu'mānīyah	146	Kf	32.32N	45.25 E
Annweiler am Trifels	124	Je	49.12N	7.58 E
Anoia/Noya	126	Nc	41.28N	1.56 E
Anoka	186	Jd	45.11N	93.23W
An Omaigh/Omagh	118	Fg	54.36N	7.18W
Anori	202	Fd	3.47 S	61.38W
Anosyennes, Chaînes-	172	Hd	24.20 S	47.00 E
Áno Viánnos	130	In	35.03N	25.25 E
Anóyia	130	Hn	35.15N	24.54 E
Anping [China]	154	Ce	38.13N	115.32 E
Anping [China]	154	Gd	41.10N	123.25 E
An Pointe/Warrenpoint	118	Gg	54.06N	6.15W
Anpu	152	Ig	21.30N	110.00 E
Anpu Gang	152	Ig	21.25N	109.40 E
Anqing	142	Nf	30.32N	116.59 E
Anqiu	154	Ef	36.25N	119.12 E
An Ráth/Ráth Luirc	118	Ei	52.21N	8.41W
An Ribhéar/Kenmare River	118	Dj	51.50N	9.50W
Anröchte	124	Kc	51.34N	8.20 E
Ans	124	Hd	50.39N	5.32 E
Anşāb	144	Fd	29.11N	44.43 E

Index Symbols

Independent Nation	Historical or Cultural Region	Pass, Gap	Depression	Coast, Beach	Rock, Reef	Waterfall, Rapids	Canal	Lagoon	Escarpment, Sea Scarp
State, Region	Mount, Mountain	Plain, Lowland	Polder	Cliff	Islands, Archipelago	River Mouth, Estuary	Glacier	Bank	Fracture
District, County	Volcano	Delta	Desert, Dunes	Peninsula	Rocks, Reefs	Lake	Ice Shelf, Pack Ice	Seamount	Trench, Abyss
Municipality	Hill	Salt Flat	Forest, Woods	Isthmus	Coral Reef	Salt Lake	Ocean	Tablemount	National Park, Reserve
Colony, Dependency	Mountains, Mountain Range	Valley, Canyon	Oasis	Sandbank	Well, Spring	Intermittent Lake	Sea	Ridge	Point of Interest
Continent	Hills, Escarpment	Crater, Cave	Oasis	Island	Geyser	Reservoir	Gulf, Bay	Shelf	Recreation Site
Physical Region	Plateau, Upland	Karst Features	Cape, Point	Atoll	River, Stream	Swamp, Pond	Strait, Fjord	Basin	Cave, Cavern

Historic Site · Ruins · Wall, Walls · Church, Abbey · Temple · Scientific Station · Railway station

Airport · Port · Military installation · Lighthouse · Mine · Tunnel · Dam, Bridge

Index Symbols

◻ Independent Nation	◨ Historical or Cultural Region	◢ Pass, Gap	◳ Depression
◻ State, Region	◮ Mount, Mountain	◮ Plain, Lowland	◳ Polder
◻ District, County	◮ Volcano	◢ Delta	◳ Desert, Dunes
◻ Municipality	◮ Hill	◳ Salt Flat	◮ Forest, Woods
◻ Colony, Dependency	◮ Mountains, Mountain Range	◢ Valley, Canyon	◮ Heath, Steppe
◼ Continent	◮ Hills, Escarpment	◳ Crater, Cave	◳ Oasis
◻ Physical Region	◮ Plateau, Upland	◳ Karst Features	▶ Cape, Point

◳ Coast, Beach	◳ Rock, Reef	◳ Waterfall, Rapids	◳ Canal
◳ Cliff	◳ Archipelago	◳ River Mouth, Estuary	◳ Glacier
◮ Peninsula	◳ Rocks, Reefs	◳ Lake	◳ Ice Shelf, Pack Ice
◮ Isthmus	◳ Coral Reef	◳ Salt Lake	◳ Ocean
◳ Sandbank	◳ Well, Spring	◳ Intermittent Lake	◳ Sea
◳ Island	◳ Geyser	◳ Reservoir	◳ Shelf
◉ Atoll	◢ River, Stream	◳ Swamp, Pond	◻ Strait, Fjord

◳ Lagoon	◳ Escarpment, Sea Scarp	◮ Historic Site	✈ Airport
◳ Bank	◳ Fracture	◳ Ruins	◳ Port
◳ Seamount	◳ Trench, Abyss	◳ Wall, Walls	◳ Military installation
◳ Tablemount	◳ National Park, Reserve	◨ Church, Abbey	◳ Lighthouse
◳ Ridge	◳ Point of Interest	◳ Temple	◳ Mine
◳ Shelf	◳ Recreation Site	◳ Scientific Station	◻ Tunnel
◳ Basin	◳ Cave, Cavern	◳ Railway station	◳ Dam, Bridge

Index Symbols

◧ Independent Nation	▲ Historical or Cultural Region	Pass, Gap	Depression	Coast, Beach	Rock, Reef
◫ State, Region	▲ Mount, Mountain	Plain, Lowland	Polder	Cliff	Islands, Archipelago
◫ District, County	▲ Volcano	Delta	Desert, Dunes	Peninsula	Rocks, Reefs
◫ Municipality	▲ Hill	Salt Flat	Forest, Woods	Isthmus	Coral Reef
◫ Colony, Dependency	▲ Mountains, Mountain Range	Valley, Canyon	Heath, Steppe	Sandbank	Well, Spring
■ Continent	▲ Hills, Escarpment	Crater, Cave	Oasis	Island	Geyser
◫ Physical Region	▲ Plateau, Upland	Karst Features	Cape, Point	Atoll	River, Stream

Waterfall, Rapids	Canal	Lagoon	Escarpment, Sea Scarp	Historic Site	Airport
River Mouth, Estuary	Glacier	Bank	Fracture	Ruins	Port
Lake	Ice Shelf, Pack Ice	Seamount	Trench, Abyss	Wall, Walls	Military installation
Salt Lake	Ocean	Tablemount	National Park, Reserve	Church, Abbey	Lighthouse
Intermittent Lake	Ridge		Point of Interest	Temple	Tunnel
Sea	Shelf		Recreation Site	Scientific Station	Dam, Bridge
Swamp, Pond	Strait, Fjord	Basin	Cave, Cavern	Railway station	

Ax-les-Thermes	122	Hl	42.43N	1.50 E
Ayabaca	202	Cd	4.38 S	79.43W
Ayabe	154	Mg	35.18N	135.15 E
Ayachi, Ari n'-	162	Gc	32.30N	4.50W
Ayacucho [3]	202	Df	14.00 S	74.00W
Ayacucho [Arg.]	206	Ie	37.09 S	58.29W
Ayacucho [Peru]	200	Ig	13.07 S	74.13W
Ayakita-Gawa	156	Bf	31.58N	131.23 E
Ayakkum Hu	152	Ed	37.30N	89.20 E
Ayamé	166	Ed	5.37N	3.11W
Ayamonte	126	Eg	37.13N	7.24W
Ayancık	146	Fb	41.57N	34.36 E
Ayangba	166	Gd	7.31N	7.08 E
Ayapel	202	Cb	8.18N	75.08W
Ayas	146	Eb	40.01N	32.21 E
Ayaviri	202	Df	14.52 S	70.35W
Āybak	144	Kb	36.16N	68.01 E
Aybastı	146	Gb	40.41N	37.24 E
Aycliffe	118	Lg	54.36N	1.34W
'Aydim, Wādī-	168	Ib	18.08N	53.08 E
Aydın	144	Cb	37.51N	27.51 E
Aydincik	146	Ed	36.08N	33.17 E
Aydın Dağları	146	Bc	38.00N	28.00 E
Aydingkol Hu	152	Ec	42.40N	89.15 E
Aydinkent	146	Dd	37.06N	31.36 E
Aydos Dağı	146	Fd	37.21N	34.22 E
Ayerbe	126	Lb	42.17N	0.41W
Ayer Hitam	150	Df	1.55N	103.11 E
Ayeyarwady	148	Ie	17.00N	95.00 E
Ayeyarwady = Irrawaddy (EN)	140	Lg	15.50N	95.06 E
Ayiá	130	Fj	39.43N	22.46 E
Ayia Marina	130	Jl	37.09N	26.52 E
Ayiásos	130	Jj	39.06N	26.22 E
Ayıon Oros=Athos, Mount- (EN) [2]	130	Hi	40.15N	24.15 E
Áyios Evstrátios	130	Ij	39.31N	25.00 E
Áyios Ioánnis, Ákra-	130	In	35.20N	25.46 E
Áyios Kírikos	130	Jl	37.35N	26.14 E
Áyios Minás	130	Jl	37.36N	26.34 E
Áyios Nikólaos	130	In	35.11N	25.43 E
Áyios Theódhoros	130	Gn	35.32N	23.56 E
Ayios Theódóros	146	Fe	35.20N	34.01 E
Áyios Yeóryios	130	Gl	37.28N	23.56 E
Aykota	168	Fb	15.10N	37.03 E
Aylesbury	118	Mj	51.50N	0.50W
Ayllón, Sierra de-	126	Ic	41.15N	3.25W
Aylmer Lake	180	Gd	64.05N	108.30W
Aylsham	124	Db	52.47N	1.15 E
Ayna	126	Jf	38.33N	2.05W
'Aynabo	168	Hd	8.57N	46.30 E
'Ayn ad Darāhim	128	Cn	36.47N	8.42 E
'Ayn al Baydā	146	Ge	34.32N	37.55 E
'Ayn al Ghazāl [Eg.]	146	Dj	25.46N	30.38 E
'Ayn al Ghazāl [Lib.]	160	Jf	21.50N	24.55 E
'Ayn al Shigi	146	Ci	27.01N	28.02 E
'Ayn al Wādī	146	Ci	27.23N	28.13 E
'Ayn Bū Sālim	128	Cn	36.37N	8.59 E
'Ayn Dāllah	164	Ed	27.19N	27.20 E
'Ayn Dār	146	Mj	25.58N	49.14 E
'Ayn Dīwār	146	Jd	37.17N	42.11 E
'Ayn Ilwān	146	Dj	25.44N	30.25 E
'Ayn Khalīfah	146	Bi	26.46N	27.47 E
'Ayn Sifnī	146	Jd	36.42N	43.21 E
'Ayn Sukhnah	164	Fd	29.30N	32.10 E
'Aynūnah	144	Ed	28.05N	35.08 E
Ayod	168	Ed	8.08N	31.24 E
Ayora	126	Ke	39.04N	1.03W
Ayorou	166	Fc	14.44N	0.55 E
'Ayoûn el 'Atroûs	160	Gg	16.38N	9.36W
Ayr	118	If	55.29N	4.28W
Ayr [Austl.]	212	Jc	19.35 S	147.24 E
Ayr [Scot.-U.K.]	118	If	55.28N	4.38W
Ayre, Point of-	118	Ig	54.26N	4.22W
Ayrolle, Étang de l'-	122	Jk	43.16N	3.30 E
Aysha	168	Gc	10.45N	42.35 E
Aytré	122	Eh	46.08N	1.06W
Ayutla	192	Gg	20.07N	104.22W
Ayutla de los Libres	192	Ji	16.54N	99.13W
Ayvacik	130	Jj	39.36N	26.24 E
Ayvacık	146	Gb	41.00N	36.45 E
Ayvalık	144	Cb	39.18N	26.41 E
Aywaille	124	Hd	50.28N	5.40 E
Āzādshahr	146	Pd	37.05N	55.08 E
Azahar, Costa del- / Tarongers, Costa dels-	126	Me	39.58N	0.01 E
Azaila	126	Lc	41.17N	0.29W
Azambuja	126	De	39.04N	8.52W
Azamgarh	148	Gc	26.04N	83.11 E
Azángaro	202	Df	14.55 S	70.13W
Azannes-et-Soumazannes	124	He	49.18N	5.28 E
Azaouâd=Azaouad (EN)	158	Gg	19.00N	3.00W
Azaouad (EN)=Azaouâd	158	Gg	19.00N	3.00W
Azaouak	158	Hg	13.48N	3.36 E
Azaouak	166	Fb	15.30N	3.18 E
Azaouak, Vallée de l'-	158	Hg	17.30N	3.40 E
Azar	166	Fb	16.02N	4.04 E
Āzarbāījān-e Gharbī [3]	144	Fb	37.00N	45.00 E
Āzarbāījān-e Sharqī [3]	144	Gb	37.00N	47.00 E
Azarbaijčan Sovet Socialistik Respublicasy/ Azerbajdžanskaja SSR [2]	136	Eg	40.30N	47.30 E
Azare	166	Hc	11.41N	10.12 E
Āzār Shahr	146	Kd	37.45N	45.59 E
Azay-le-Rideau	122	Gg	47.16N	0.28 E
A 'zāz	146	Gd	36.35N	37.03 E
Azazga	126	Qh	36.44N	4.22 E
Azbine/Aïr	158	Hg	18.00N	8.30 E
Azdaak, gora-	132	Ni	40.13N	44.59 E
Azdavay	146	Eb	41.39N	33.18 E
Azefal	158	Ff	21.00N	14.45W
Azeffoun	126	Qh	36.53N	4.25 E
Azemmour	162	Fc	33.17N	8.21W
Azerbaijan SSR (EN) = Azerbajdžanskaja SSR [2]	136	Eg	40.30N	47.30 E
Azerbajdžanskaja Sovetskaja Socialističeskaja Respublika [2]	136	Eg	40.30N	47.30 E
Azerbajdžanskaja SSR/ Azarbaijčan Sovet Socialistik Respublicasy [2]	136	Eg	40.30N	47.30 E
Azerbajdžanskaja SSR = Azerbaijan SSR (EN) [2]	136	Eg	40.30N	47.30 E
Azeri/Aseri	114	Gg	59.29N	26.51 E
Azevedo Sodré	204	Ej	30.04 S	54.36W
Azezo	168	Fc	12.33N	37.25 E
Azilal	162	Fc	31.58N	6.35W
Azilal [3]	162	Fc	32.09N	6.05W
Aznā	146	Mf	33.56N	49.24 E
Aznakajevo	114	Mi	54.56N	53.04 E
Azogues	202	Cd	2.44 S	78.48W
Azores (EN)=Açores [5]	160	Ee	38.30N	28.00W
Azores (EN)=Açores, Arquipélago dos-	158	Ee	38.30N	28.00W
Azores-Gibraltar Ridge (EN)	106	Df	37.00N	16.00W
Azoum, Bahr-	158	Jg	10.53N	20.15 E
Azov	136	Df	47.05N	39.25 E
Azov, Sea of- (EN) = Azovskoje more	110	Jf	46.00N	36.00 E
Azovskoje more = Azov, Sea of- (EN)	110	Jf	46.00N	36.00 E
Azpeitia	126	Ja	43.11N	2.16W
Azrak, Bahr-	168	Bc	10.50N	19.50 E
Azraq, Baḩr al- = Blue Nile (EN)	158	Kg	15.38N	32.31 E
Azraq ash Shīshān	146	Gg	31.50N	36.49 E
Azrou	162	Fc	33.26N	5.13W
Aztec	186	Ch	36.49N	107.59W
Aztec Ruins	188	Kh	36.51N	108.10W
Azua	194	Ld	18.27N	70.44W
Azuaga	126	Gf	38.16N	5.41W
Azuar	126	Ie	39.08N	3.36W
Azuero, Peninsula de-= Azuero Peninsula (EN)	174	Ki	7.40N	80.30W
Azuero Peninsula (EN)= Azuero, Peninsula de-	174	Ki	7.40N	80.30W
Azul	200	Ki	36.45 S	59.50W
Azul, Arroyo del-	204	Cm	36.15 S	59.07W
Azul, Cerro-	202a	Ab	0.54 S	91.21W
Azul, Cordillera-	202	Ce	8.30 S	76.00W
Azul, Rio-	192	Oi	17.54N	88.52W
Azul, Serra-	204	Eb	14.50 S	54.50W
Azul, Sierras del-	204	Cm	37.02 S	59.55W
Azūm	168	Cc	10.53N	20.15 E
Azuma-San	156	Gc	37.44N	140.08 E
Azur, Côte d'-	122	Nk	43.30N	7.00 E
Azurduy	202	Fg	19.59 S	64.29W
Azzaba	162	Ib	36.44N	7.06 E
Az Zāb al Kabīr	144	Fb	36.00N	43.21 E
Az Zāb aş Şaghīr	144	Fb	35.12N	43.25 E
Az Zabdānī	146	Gf	33.43N	36.05 E
Az Zabū	146	Ch	28.22N	28.56 E
Aẕ Ẕafīr	144	Ff	19.57N	41.30 E
Az Zaghāwa	168	Cb	15.15N	23.14 E
Aẕ Ẕāhirah	146	Qk	23.30N	56.15 E
Aẕ Ẕahrān	146	Ni	26.18N	50.05 E
Az Zallāq	146	Ni	26.03N	50.29 E
Az Zaqāzīq	164	Fc	30.35N	31.31 E
Az Zarqā'	146	Gf	32.05N	36.06 E
Az Zarqā'	146	Oj	24.53N	53.04 E
Az Zāwiyah	164	Bc	32.45N	12.44 E
Az Zāwiyah [3]	164	Bc	32.40N	12.10 E
Az Zaytūn	164	Ed	29.09N	25.47 E
Azzel Matti, Sebkha-	158	Hf	26.00N	0.55 E
Az Zilfī	146	Ki	26.18N	44.48 E
Az Zubayr	146	Lg	30.23N	47.43 E

B

Baa	150	Hi	10.43 S	123.03 E
Baaba	219b	Ae	20.03 S	163.58 E
Ba'ādwēyn	168	Hd	7.12N	47.24 E
Bá an Daingin/Dingle Bay	118	Ci	52.05N	10.15W
Baar	120	Ei	48.00N	8.30 E
Baarle-Hertog	124	Gc	51.27N	4.56 E
Baarn	124	Hb	52.14N	5.17 E
Baas, Bassure de-	124	Dd	50.30N	1.15 E
Bāb	146	Ok	23.55N	53.45 E
Baba	130	Ei	40.55N	21.10 E
Baba	168	Bd	6.25N	17.07 E
Baba Burun [Tur.]	146	Bc	39.29N	26.04 E
Baba Burun [Tur.]	146	Db	41.18N	31.26 E
Babadağ	130	Ll	37.48N	28.52 E
Babadag	130	Le	44.54N	28.43 E
Babadag, gora-	132	Pi	41.01N	48.29 E
Babaeski	146	Bb	41.26N	27.06 E
Bābā-Ḩeydar	146	Nf	32.20N	50.28 E
Babahoyo	202	Cd	1.50 S	79.30W
Babajevo	136	Dd	59.24N	35.55 E
Babajtag, gora-	135	Hd	41.13N	70.16 E
Babajurt	132	Oh	43.35N	46.47 E
Bāb al Māndab=Bab el Mandeb (EN)	158	Lg	12.35N	43.25 E
Babanūsah	168	Dc	11.20N	27.48 E
Babao → Qilian	152	Hd	38.14N	100.15 E
Babar, Kepulauan-	150	Ih	7.50 S	129.45 E
Babar, Pulau-	208	De	7.55 S	129.45 E
Babase	219a	Aa	4.01 S	153.42 E
Babatag, hrebet-	135	Ge	38.00N	68.10 E
Babati	170	Gc	4.13 S	35.45 E
Babbitt	186	Kc	47.43N	91.57W
B'abdā	146	Ff	33.50N	35.32 E
Bab el Mandeb (EN)=Bāb al Māndab	158	Lg	12.35N	43.25 E
Babelthuap Island	208	Ed	7.30N	134.36 E
Babenhausen [Ger.]	120	Gh	48.09N	10.15 E
Babenhausen [Ger.]	124	Ke	49.58N	8.57 E
Babeni	130	He	44.59N	24.15 E
Baberton	184	Ge	41.02N	81.38W
Bá Bheanntrai/Bantry Bay	118	Dj	51.38N	9.48W
Babian Jiang [Asia] = Black River (EN)	140	Mg	20.17N	106.34 E
Babil [3]	146	Kf	32.40N	44.50 E
Babine Lake	180	Ef	54.45N	126.00W
Babino Polje	128	Lh	42.43N	17.33 E
Babit Point	197b	Ab	18.03N	63.02W
Babo	150	Jg	2.33 S	133.25 E
Bābol	144	Hb	36.34N	52.42 E
Babol Sar	146	Od	36.43N	52.39 E
Baboquivari Peak	188	Jk	31.46N	111.35W
Babor, Djebel-	126	Rh	36.32N	5.28 E
Baborigame	192	Fd	26.27N	107.16W
Baboua	168	Ad	5.48N	14.49 E
Babozero, ozero-	114	Ic	66.30N	37.25 E
Babu → Hexian	152	Jg	24.28N	111.34 E
Babuna	130	Eh	41.30N	21.40 E
Babuyan	150	Gd	10.01N	118.58 E
Babuyan	150	Hc	19.32N	121.57 E
Babuyan Channel	150	Hc	18.44N	121.40 E
Babuyan Islands	140	Oh	19.15N	121.40 E
Babylon	144	Fc	32.32N	44.25 E
Bač	130	Cd	45.23N	19.14 E
Bacabachi	192	Ed	26.55N	109.24W
Bacabal	200	Lf	4.14 S	44.47W
Ba-Cagan	152	Gb	45.40N	99.30 E
Bacajá, Rio-	202	Hd	3.25 S	51.50W
Bacalar	192	Oh	18.43N	88.27W
Bacalar, Laguna de-	192	Oh	18.43N	88.22W
Bacalar Chico, Boca-	194	Dd	18.12N	87.53W
Bacan, Kepulauan-	150	Ig	0.35 S	127.30 E
Bacan, Pulau-	150	Ig	0.35 S	127.30 E
Bacău	112	If	46.34N	26.54 E
Bacău [2]	130	Jc	46.36N	27.00 E
Baccarat	122	Mf	48.27N	6.45 E
Bacchiglione	128	Ge	45.11N	12.14 E
Baceşti	130	Kc	46.51N	27.14 E
Bachaquero	194	Li	9.56N	71.08W
Bacharach	124	Jd	50.04N	7.46 E
Bacheli	148	Ge	18.40N	81.15 E
Bachiniva	192	Fc	28.45N	107.15W
Bachu/Maralwexi	152	Cd	39.46N	78.15 E
Bačka	130	Cd	45.50N	19.30 E
Bačka Palanka	130	Cd	45.15N	19.22 E
Bačka Topola	130	Cd	45.49N	19.39 E
Bäckefors	116	Ef	58.48N	12.10 E
Bäckhammar	116	Fe	59.10N	14.11 E
Backnang	120	Fh	48.57N	9.26 E
Bačkovski Manastir	130	Hh	41.56N	24.51 E
Back River	174	Jc	67.15N	95.15W
Bac Lieu	148	Lg	9.17N	105.43 E
Bac Ninh	148	Ld	21.11N	106.03 E
Bacolet	197p	Bb	12.02N	61.41W
Bacolod	142	Oh	10.40N	122.57 E
Bac-Phan=Tonkin (EN)	140	Mg	22.00N	105.00 E
Bacqueville, Lac-	180	Ke	58.00N	74.00W
Bacqueville-en Caux	124	Ce	49.47N	1.00 E
Bácsalmás	120	Pj	46.08N	19.20 E
Bács-Kiskun [2]	120	Pj	46.30N	19.25 E
Bacton	124	Db	52.51N	1.28 E
Bād	144	Hc	33.41N	52.01 E
Bada Dağı	130	Mm	36.32N	29.10 E
Badagara	148	Ff	11.36N	75.35 E
Badagri	166	Fd	6.25N	2.53 E
Badain Jaran Shamo	140	Me	40.20N	101.40 E
Badajós, Lago-	202	Fd	3.15 S	62.45W
Badajoz	112	Fh	38.53N	6.58W
Badajoz [3]	126	Ff	38.40N	6.10W
Badakhshan [3]	144	Lb	36.45N	72.00 E
Badalona	126	Oc	41.27N	2.15 E
Badanah	144	Fc	30.59N	41.02 E
Badaohao	154	Fd	41.50N	121.59 E
Badas, Kepulauan-	150	Ef	0.35N	107.06 E
Bad Aussee	128	Hc	47.36N	13.47 E
Bad Axe	184	Fd	43.48N	83.00W
Bad Bergzabern	120	Dg	49.06N	8.00 E
Bad Berleburg	124	Kc	51.04N	8.24 E
Bad Bertrich	124	Jd	50.03N	7.02 E
Bad Bramstedt	120	Fc	53.55N	9.53 E
Bad Brückenau	120	Ff	50.18N	9.45 E
Badda	168	Fd	7.55N	39.23 E
Baddo	148	Cc	27.59N	64.21 E
Bad Doberan	120	Hb	54.06N	11.54 E
Bad Driburg	124	Lc	51.44N	9.01 E
Bad Düben	120	Ie	51.36N	12.35 E
Bad Dürkheim	124	Ke	49.28N	8.12 E
Bade	150	Kh	7.10 S	139.35 E
Bademli	130	Lk	38.04N	28.04 E
Baden [Aus.]	128	Kb	48.01N	16.14 E
Baden [Switz.]	128	Cc	47.28N	8.18 E
Baden-Baden	120	Eh	48.45N	8.15 E
Badenoch	118	Je	56.50N	4.00W
Baden-Württemberg [2]	120	Eh	48.30N	9.00 E
Bad Essen	124	Kb	52.19N	8.20 E
Bad Freienwalde	120	Kd	52.47N	14.02 E
Badgastein	128	Hc	47.07N	13.08 E
Bādghīsat [3]	144	Jc	35.00N	63.45 E
Bad Gleichenberg	128	Jd	46.52N	15.54 E
Bad Godesberg, Bonn-Bad Hall	120	Df	50.41N	7.09 E
Bad Hall	128	Ib	48.02N	14.12 E
Bad Harzburg	120	Ge	51.53N	10.34 E
Bad Herrenalb	124	Kf	48.48N	8.25 E
Bad Hersfeld	120	Ff	50.52N	9.42 E
Bad Homburg von der Hoehe	120	Ef	50.13N	8.37 E
Bad Honnef	124	Jd	50.38N	7.12 E
Bá Dhún na nGall/Donegal Bay	110	Fe	54.30N	8.30W
Badhyz	135	Cg	35.50N	62.00 E
Badiraguato	192	Fe	25.22N	107.31W
Bad Ischl	128	Hc	47.43N	13.37 E
Bad Kissingen	120	Gf	50.12N	10.05 E
Bad Kreuznach	120	Dg	49.50N	7.52 E
Badlands	182	Gb	46.45N	103.30W
Bad Langensalza	120	Ge	51.06N	10.39 E
Bad Lauterberg am Harz	120	Ge	51.38N	10.28 E
Bad Liebenwerda	120	Je	51.31N	13.24 E
Bad Liebenzell	124	Kf	48.46N	8.44 E
Bad Mergentheim	120	Fg	49.29N	9.46 E
Bad Mondorf/Mondorf-les-Bains	124	Ie	49.30N	6.17 E
Bad Münster am Stein-Ebernburg	124	Je	49.49N	7.51 E
Bad Münstereifel	124	Id	50.34N	6.45 E
Bad Nauheim	124	Kd	50.22N	8.45 E
Bad Neuenahr-Ahrweiler	120	Df	50.33N	7.08 E
Bad Neustadt an der Saale	120	Gf	50.20N	10.13 E
Bad Oeynhausen	124	Kb	52.12N	8.48 E
Bad Oldesloe	120	Gc	53.49N	10.23 E
Badou [China]	154	Df	36.27N	117.56 E
Badou [Togo]	166	Fd	7.35N	0.36 E
Bad Pyrmont	120	Fe	51.59N	9.15 E
Bad Ragaz	128	Dc	47.00N	9.30 E
Badrah	146	Kf	33.06N	45.58 E
Bad Reichenhall	120	Ii	47.44N	12.53 E
Badr Ḩunayn	144	Ee	23.44N	38.46 E
Bad River	186	Fd	44.22N	100.22W
Bad Salzuflen	124	Kb	52.05N	8.46 E
Bad Salzungen	120	Gf	50.49N	10.14 E
Bad Schwartau	120	Gc	53.55N	10.42 E
Bad Segeberg	120	Gc	53.56N	10.19 E
Bad Tölz	120	Hi	47.46N	11.34 E
Badulla	148	Gg	6.59N	81.03 E
Bad Vilbel	124	Kd	50.11N	8.45 E
Bad Wildungen	120	Fe	51.07N	9.07 E
Bad Wimpfen	120	Fg	49.14N	9.08 E
Baena	126	Hg	37.37N	4.19W
Baeza [Ec.]	202	Cd	0.28 S	77.53W
Baeza [Sp.]	126	Ig	37.59N	3.28W
Baf/Paphos	146	Ee	34.50N	32.35 E
Bafa Gölü	146	Bd	37.30N	27.25 E
Bafang	166	Hd	5.09N	10.11 E
Bafatà	160	Fg	12.10N	14.40W
Bafélé	166	Cc	10.09N	10.08W
Baffin	174	Mc	68.00N	70.00W
Baffin Bay [N.Amer.]	174	Mb	73.00N	65.00W
Baffin Bay [Tx.-U.S.]	186	Hm	27.15N	97.30W
Bafia	166	He	4.45N	11.14 E
Bafilo	166	Fd	9.21N	1.16 E
Bafing [Afr.]	158	Fg	13.49N	10.50W
Bafing [I.C.]	166	Dd	7.52N	7.07W
Bafoulabé	166	Cc	13.48N	10.50W
Bafoussam	160	Ih	5.28N	10.25 E
Bāfq	144	Ic	31.35N	55.24 E
Bāfq, Kūh-e-	146	Pg	31.20N	55.10 E
Bafra	144	Ea	41.34N	35.56 E
Bafra Burnu	146	Fb	41.44N	35.58 E
Bāft	146	Qh	29.14N	56.38 E
Bafwaboli	170	Eb	0.39N	26.10 E
Bafwasende	170	Eb	1.05N	27.16 E
Baga	166	Hc	13.06N	13.50 E
Bagaces	194	Eh	10.31N	85.15W
Bagagem, Rio-	204	Ha	13.58 S	48.21W
Bagajevski	132	Lf	47.19N	40.25 E
Bāgalkot	148	Fe	16.11N	75.42 E
Bagamoyo	170	Gd	6.26 S	38.54 E
Bagansiapi-Api	150	Df	2.09N	100.49 E
Bağarasi	130	Kl	37.42N	27.33 E
Baga Sola	168	Ac	13.32N	14.19 E
Bagata	170	Cc	3.44 S	17.57 E
Bagdad	192	Ke	25.57N	97.09W
Bagdarin	138	Gf	54.30N	113.36 E
Bağdere	146	Ic	38.10N	40.45 E
Bagé	200	Ki	31.20 S	54.06W
Bages et de Sigean, Étang de-	122	Jk	43.05N	3.01 E
Baggs	188	Lf	41.02N	107.39W
Bágh Baile na Sgealg/ Ballinskelligs Bay	118	Cj	51.50N	10.15W
Baghdād	142	Gf	33.21N	44.23 E
Baghdād [3]	146	Kf	33.18N	44.36 E
Baghdādī, Ra's-	146	Fj	24.40N	35.06 E
Bāgh-e Chenār	146	Qh	28.11N	56.54 E
Bāgh-e-Malek	146	Mg	31.32N	49.55 E
Bagheria	128	Hl	38.05N	13.30 E
Bāghīn	144	Ic	30.12N	56.48 E
Baghlān	144	Kb	36.13N	68.46 E
Baghlān [3]	144	Kb	35.45N	69.00 E
Bāglung	148	Gc	28.16N	83.36 E
Bagn	116	Cd	60.49N	9.34 E
Bagnara Calabra	128	Jl	38.17N	15.48 E
Bagnères-de-Bigorre	122	Gk	43.04N	0.09 E
Bagnères-de-Luchon	122	Gl	42.47N	0.36 E
Bagni di Lucca	128	Ef	44.01N	10.35 E
Bagno di Romagna	128	Fg	43.50N	11.57 E
Bagnolo Mella	128	Ee	45.26N	10.10 E
Bagnols-sur-Cèze	122	Kj	44.10N	4.37 E
Bago	142	Lh	17.30N	96.30 E
Bagoé	158	Gg	12.36N	6.34W
Bagolino	128	Ee	45.49N	10.28 E
Bagrationovsk	116	Ij	54.23N	20.40 E
Bagrax/Bohu	152	Ec	41.58N	86.29 E
Bagrax Hu/Bosten	140	Ke	42.00N	87.00 E
Bagua	202	Ce	5.40 S	78.31W
Baguio	142	Oh	16.25N	120.36 E
Baguirmi	158	Ig	11.40N	16.20 E
Bagzane, Monts-	158	Hg	17.43N	8.45 E
Bahama Islands	174	Lg	24.15N	76.00W
Bahamas [1]	176	Lg	24.15N	76.00W
Bahamas, Canal Viejo de-= Old Bahama Channel (EN)	194	Ib	22.30N	78.05W
Bahār	146	Me	34.54N	48.26 E
Baharampur	148	Hd	24.06N	88.15 E
Baharden	136	Fh	38.28N	57.28 E
Bahardok	136	Fh	38.51N	58.24 E
Bahariya Oasis (EN)= Baḩarīyah, Wāḩāt al-	164	Ed	28.15N	28.57 E
Bahaur	150	Fg	3.20N	114.00 E
Bahāwalnagar	148	Ec	29.59N	73.16 E
Bahāwalpur	142	Jg	29.24N	71.41 E
Bahçe	146	Gd	37.14N	36.34 E
Bahčisaraj	132	Hg	44.45N	33.51 E
Bahi	170	Gd	5.39 S	35.19 E
Bahia [2]	202	Jf	12.00 S	42.00W
Bahía, Islas de la-	190	Ge	16.20N	86.30W
Bahía Blanca	200	Ji	38.44 S	62.16W
Bahía de Caráquez	202	Bd	0.37 S	80.25W
Bahía Kino	190	Bc	28.50N	111.55W
Bahia Negra	206	Ib	20.15 S	58.12W
Bahías, Cabo dos-	198	Jj	44.55 S	65.32W
Bahīj	146	Cg	30.56N	29.35 E
Bahinga	170	Ed	5.57 S	27.06 E
Bahi Swamp	170	Gd	6.05 S	35.10 E
Bahlui	130	Kb	47.08N	27.44 E
Bahmač	136	De	51.11N	32.50 E
Bahoruco, Sierra de-	194	Ld	18.10N	71.25W
Bahraich	148	Gc	27.35N	81.36 E
Bahrain (EN)=Al Baḩrayn [1]	142	Hg	26.00N	50.29 E
Baḩr al Ghazāl [3]	168	Dd	8.15N	26.50 E
Baḩr ar Ramla al Kabīr	164	Ed	27.00N	26.00 E
Baḩrayn, Khalij al-	146	Nj	25.45N	50.40 E
Bahr Dar	160	Kg	11.36N	37.22 E
Bahta	138	Dd	62.20N	89.15 E
Bahuşi	130	Jc	46.43N	26.42 E
Baia	130	Le	44.43N	28.40 E
Baia de Aramă	130	Fe	45.00N	22.50 E
Baia de Fier	130	Gd	45.10N	23.46 E
Baía dos Tigres	170	Bf	16.35 S	11.43 E
Baia Farta	170	Be	12.37 S	13.26 E
Baia Mare	130	Gb	47.40N	23.35 E
Baião	202	Id	2.41 S	49.41W
Baia Sprie	130	Gb	47.40N	23.42 E
Baibiene	204	Ci	29.36 S	58.10W
Baïbokoum	168	Bd	7.45N	15.41 E
Baicheng	142	Oe	45.34N	122.49 E
Baicheng/Bay	152	Dc	41.46N	81.52 E
Băicoi	130	Id	45.02N	25.51 E
Băiculeşti	130	Hd	45.04N	24.42 E
Baïdou	168	Cd	5.52N	20.41 E
Baie-Comeau	176	Me	49.13N	68.10W
Baie-Mahault	196	Fd	16.16N	61.35W
Baie-Saint-Paul	180	Kg	47.27N	70.30W
Baie-Trinité	184	Na	49.24N	67.19W
Baie Verte	180	Lg	49.55N	56.11W
Baiguan → Shangyu	154	Fi	30.01N	120.53 E
Baihe	152	Je	32.46N	110.06 E
Bai He [China]	154	Bh	32.10N	112.20 E
Bai He [China]	154	Dd	40.43N	116.33 E
Baikal Lake (EN) = Bajkal, ozero-	140	Md	53.00N	107.40 E
Baikal Range (EN) = Bajkalski hrebet	140	Md	55.00N	108.40 E
Baile an Chaistil/ Ballycastle	118	Gf	55.12N	6.15W
Baile an Róba/Ballinrobe	118	Dh	53.37N	9.13W
Baile Átha Cliath/Dublin	112	Fe	53.20N	6.15W
Baile Átha Cliath/Dublin [2]	118	Gh	53.20N	6.15W
Baile Átha Luain/Athlone	118	Fh	53.25N	7.56W
Baile Átha Troim/Trim	118	Gh	53.34N	6.47W
Băile Borşa	130	Hb	47.41N	24.43 E
Baile Brigín/Balbriggan	118	Gh	53.37N	6.11W
Băile Govora	130	Hd	45.05N	24.11 E
Baile Locha Riach/Loughrea	118	Eh	53.12N	8.34W
Baile Mhistéala/ Mitchelstown	118	Ei	52.16N	8.16W
Bailén	126	If	38.06N	3.46W
Baile na Mainistreach/ Newtownabbey	118	Hg	54.42N	5.54W
Baile Nua na hArda/ Newtownards	118	Hg	54.36N	5.41W
Băile Olăneşti	130	Hd	45.12N	24.14 E
Băileşti	130	Ge	44.01N	23.21 E
Bailleul	124	Ed	50.44N	2.44 E
Bailleul	124	Ce	49.12N	0.26 E
Ba Illi	168	Bc	10.31N	16.29 E
Bailong Jiang	152	Ie	32.42N	105.15 E
Bailundo	170	Ce	12.10 S	15.56 E
Baima	152	He	33.05N	100.29 E
Bain	124	Ba	53.04N	0.12W
Bainbridge	182	Ke	30.54N	84.34W
Bain-de-Bretagne	122	Eg	47.50N	1.41W
Baines Drift	172	Dd	22.30 S	28.43 E
Baing	150	Hi	10.14 S	120.34 E
Baingoin	152	Ee	31.36N	89.48 E
Baiona / Bayona	126	Db	42.07N	8.51W
Baiquan	152	Mb	47.38N	126.04 E
Bā'ir	146	Gg	30.46N	36.41 E
Bā'ir, Wādī-	146	Gg	31.12N	37.31 E
Baird	186	Gj	32.24N	99.24W
Baird Inlet	178	Gd	60.45N	164.00W
Baird Mountains	178	Gc	67.35N	161.30W
Baird Peninsula	180	Jc	69.00N	75.15W
Bairiki	210	Id	1.20N	173.01 E
Bairin Youqi (Daban)	152	Kc	43.30N	118.37 E
Bairin Zuoqi (Lindong)	152	Kc	43.59N	119.22 E
Bairnsdale	210	Fh	37.50 S	147.38 E
Bais	150	He	9.35N	123.07 E
Baiše	122	Gj	44.17N	0.18 E
Baisha → Jiande	152	Kf	29.31N	119.17 E
Bai Shan	152	Fc	40.53N	93.48 E
Baisogala/Bajsogala	116	Ji	55.35N	23.44 E
Baitou Shan	140	Oe	42.00N	128.00 E
Baitoushan Tian Chi	154	Jc	42.00N	128.03 E
Baixiang	154	Cf	37.29N	114.44 E
Baixo Alentejo	126	Dg	37.55N	8.10W
Baixo Guandu	202	Jg	19.31 S	41.01W
Baixo Longa	170	Cf	15.42 S	18.38 E
Baiyanghe	152	Ec	43.12N	88.28 E
Baiyü	152	Ge	31.13N	98.51 E
Baja	120	Oj	46.11N	18.58 E
Baja, Punta- [Mex.]	192	Dc	28.25N	111.45W
Baja, Punta- [Pas.]	221d	Ab	27.10 S	109.22W
Baja California, Peninsula de- = Lower California (EN)	174	Hg	28.00N	112.00W
Baja California Norte [2]	190	Ac	30.00N	115.00W
Baja California Sur [2]	190	Bd	25.50N	111.50W
Bājah	162	Ib	36.44N	9.11 E
Bājah [3]	162	Ib	36.30N	9.30 E

Index Symbols

[1] Independent Nation
[2] State, Region
[3] District, County
[4] Municipality
[5] Colony, Dependency
Continent
Physical Region
Historical or Cultural Region
Mount, Mountain
Volcano
Hill
Mountains, Mountain Range
Hills, Escarpment
Plateau, Upland
Pass, Gap
Plain, Lowland
Delta
Salt Flat
Valley, Canyon
Crater, Cave
Karst Features
Depression
Polder
Desert, Dunes
Forest, Woods
Heath, Steppe
Oasis
Cape, Point
Coast, Beach
Cliff
Peninsula
Isthmus
Sandbank
Island
Atoll
Rock, Reef
Islands, Archipelago
Rocks, Reefs
Coral Reef
Well, Spring
Geyser
River, Stream
Waterfall, Rapids
River Mouth, Estuary
Lake
Salt Lake
Intermittent Lake
Reservoir
Swamp, Pond
Canal
Glacier
Ice Shelf, Pack Ice
Ocean
Sea
Gulf, Bay
Strait, Fjord
Lagoon
Bank
Seamount
Tablemount
Ridge
Shelf
Basin
Escarpment, Sea Scarp
Fracture
Trench, Abyss
National Park, Reserve
Point of Interest
Recreation Site
Cave, Cavern
Historic Site
Ruins
Wall, Walls
Church, Abbey
Temple
Scientific Station
Railway station
Airport
Port
Military installation
Lighthouse
Mine
Tunnel
Dam, Bridge

Bajalān 146 Md 37.18N 48.47 E
Bajan 152 Jb 49.15N 111.58 E
Bajanaul 136 He 50.47N 75.42 E
Bajandaj 138 Ff 53.04N 105.30 E
Bajan-Delger 152 Jb 45.55N 112.15 E
Bajangol 138 Ff 50.40N 103.25 E
Bajan-Hongor 142 Me 46.20N 100.40 E
Bajan-Ula [Mong.] 152 Jb 49.07N 112.45 E
Bajan-Ula [Mong.] 152 Gb 47.05N 95.15 E
Bajan-Under 152 Gc 44.45N 98.45 E
Baja Verapaz [3] 194 Bf 15.05N 90.20W
Bajawa 150 Hh 8.47S 120.59 E
Bajčunas 132 Rf 47.17N 53.03 E
Bajdarackaja guba 138 Bc 69.00N 67.30 E
Bajdarata 134 Nb 68.12N 68.18 E
Bajdrag Gol 152 Hb 45.10N 100.45 E
Bājgīrān 146 Rd 37.36N 58.24 E
Baj-Haak 138 Ef 51.07N 94.34 E
Bajiazi 154 Jc 42.41N 129.13 E
Bajina Bašta 130 Cf 43.58N 19.34 E
Bajkal 138 Ff 51.53N 104.47 E
Bajkal, ozero- = Baikal Lake (EN) 140 Md 53.00N 107.40 E
Bajkalovo 134 Kh 57.24N 63.40 E
Bajkalsk 138 Ff 51.30N 104.05 E
Bajkalski hrebet = Baikal Range (EN) 140 Md 55.00N 108.40 E
Bajkit 138 Ed 61.41N 96.25 E
Bajkonur 136 Gf 47.50N 66.07 E
Bajmak 136 Fe 52.36N 58.19 E
Bajmba, Mount- 212 Ke 29.20S 152.05 E
Bajmok 130 Cd 45.58N 19.26 E
Bajo Baudó 202 Cc 4.58N 77.22W
Bajo Boquete 194 Fi 8.46N 82.26W
Bajo Nuevo 190 Ie 15.50N 78.40W
Bajram-Ali 136 Gh 37.39N 62.12 E
Bajram Curri 130 Dg 42.21N 20.04 E
Bajsogala/Baisogala 116 Ji 55.35N 23.44 E
Bajsun 135 Fe 38.14N 67.12 E
Bajun Islands 158 Li 0.50S 42.15 E
Bajžansaj 135 Gc 43.13N 69.56 E
Baka 168 Ee 4.33N 30.05 E
Bakacak 130 Ki 40.12N 27.05 E
Bakadžicite 130 Jg 42.25N 26.43 E
Bakal 136 Fe 54.56N 58.48 E
Bakala 168 Cd 6.11N 20.22 E
Bakanas 136 Hg 44.48N 76.15 E
Bakar 128 Ie 45.18N 14.32 E
Bakčar 138 De 57.01N 82.10 E
Bake 150 Dg 3.03S 100.16 E
Bakel 166 Cc 14.54N 12.27W
Baker [Ca.-U.S.] 188 Gi 35.15N 116.02W
Baker [La.-U.S.] 186 Kk 30.35N 91.10W
Baker [Mt.-U.S.] 182 Gb 46.22N 104.17W
Baker [Or.-U.S.] 182 Dc 44.47N 117.50W
Baker, Mount- 182 Cb 48.47N 121.49W
Baker Island 208 Jd 0.15N 176.27W
Baker Lake 176 Jc 64.10N 95.30W
Baker Lake 174 Jc 64.10N 95.30W
Bakersfield 176 Hf 35.23N 119.01W
Bå Kêv 148 Lf 13.42N 107.12 E
Bakhma 146 Kd 36.38N 44.17 E
Bakhtarān 142 Gf 34.19N 47.04 E
Bakhtarān [3] 144 Gc 34.15N 47.20 E
Bakhtegān, Daryācheh-ye- 146 Ph 29.20N 54.05 E
Bakhūn, Kūh-e- 144 Id 27.56N 56.18 E
Bakır 136 Bc 38.55N 27.00 E
Bakırköy, İstanbul- 130 Li 40.59N 28.52 E
Bakkaflói 114a Ca 66.10N 14.45W
Baklan 130 Ml 37.58N 29.36 E
Bako 168 Fd 7.19N 35.08 E
Bako [Eth.] 168 Fd 5.50N 36.37 E
Bako [Eth.] 168 Fd 9.05N 37.07 E
Bakony=Bakony Mountains (EN) 110 Hf 47.15N 17.50 E
Bakony Mountains (EN)= Bakony 110 Hf 47.15N 17.50 E
Bakool [3] 168 Ge 4.10N 43.50 E
Bakouma 168 Cd 5.42N 22.47 E
Bakoye 166 Cc 13.49N 10.50W
Bakpulād 146 Qc 38.10N 57.00 E
Baksan 132 Mh 43.40N 43.28 E
Baksan 132 Nh 43.42N 44.03 E
Baku 112 Kg 40.23N 49.51 E
Bakum 124 Kb 52.44N 8.11 E
Bakungan 150 Cf 2.56N 97.30 E
Bakuriani 132 Mi 41.43N 43.31 E
Bakutis Coast 222 Of 74.45S 120.00W
Balā 146 Ec 39.34N 33.08 E
Bala, Cerros de- 202 Ef 14.30S 67.40W
Balabac 150 Ge 7.59N 117.04 E
Balabac 150 Ge 7.57N 117.01 E
Balabac, Selat-=Balabac Strait (EN) 140 Ni 7.40N 117.00 E
Balabac Strait (EN)= Balabac, Selat- 140 Ni 7.40N 117.00 E
Ba'labakk 146 Ge 34.00N 36.12 E
Balabalangan, Kepulauan- 150 Gg 2.20S 117.25 E
Balaban Daği 146 Hb 40.28N 39.15 E
Balabanovo 132 Jb 55.11N 36.40 E
Balabio 219b Be 20.07S 164.11 E
Balaci 130 He 44.21N 24.55 E
Balad 146 Ke 34.01N 44.01 E
Bal'ad 168 He 2.22N 45.24 E
Balādīn as Sakrān 146 Kj 25.12N 44.37 E
Baladīyat 'Adan = Aden (EN) 142 Gh 12.46N 45.01 E
Balad Rūz 146 Kf 33.42N 45.05 E
Balagannoje 138 Je 59.43N 149.15 E
Balagansk 138 Ff 53.58N 103.02 E
Bālāghāt 148 Gd 21.48N 80.11 E
Bālāghāt Range 148 Fe 18.45N 76.30 E
Balagna 122a Aa 42.35N 8.50 E
Balaguer 126 Mc 41.47N 0.49 E
Balahna 136 Ed 56.31N 43.37 E
Balahta 138 Ee 55.24N 91.37 E
Balaka 170 Fe 14.59S 34.57 E
Balaklava 132 Hg 44.31N 33.34 E
Balakleja 136 Df 49.27N 36.52 E
Balakovo 112 Ke 52.02N 47.45 E
Balama 172 Fb 13.16S 38.36 E
Balambangan, Pulau- 150 Ge 7.17N 116.55 E
Bālā Morghāb 144 Jb 35.35N 63.20 E
Balan Daği 130 Lm 36.52N 28.20 E
Balankanche 192 Og 20.45N 88.30W
Balasan 150 Hd 11.28N 123.05 E
Balasore → Bāleshwar 148 Hd 21.30N 86.56 E
Balašov 136 Ee 51.33N 43.10 E
Balassagyarmat 120 Ph 48.05N 19.18 E
Balāṭ 164 Ed 25.33N 29.16 E
Balaton 110 Hf 46.50N 17.45 E
Balatonfüred 120 Nj 46.57N 17.53 E
Balatonkeresztúr 120 Nj 46.42N 17.23 E
Balaurin 150 Hh 8.15S 123.43 E
Bălăuşeri 130 Hc 46.24N 24.41 E
Balayan 150 Hd 13.57N 120.44 E
Balazote 126 Jf 38.53N 2.08W
Balbi, Mount- 214 Ei 5.55S 154.59 E
Balboa Heights 190 Ig 8.57N 79.33W
Balbriggan/Baile Brigin 118 Gh 53.37N 6.11W
Balcarce 206 Ie 37.50S 58.15W
Balcarce, Sierras de- 204 Cm 37.50S 58.40W
Bălceşti 130 Ge 44.37N 23.57 E
Balčik 130 Lf 43.25N 28.10 E
Balclutha 216 Ci 46.14S 169.44 E
Bald Eagle Mountain 184 Ie 41.00N 77.45W
Bald Head 212 Dg 35.07S 118.01 E
Bald Knob 186 Ki 35.19N 91.34W
Bald Knob 184 Hg 37.56N 79.51W
Baldo, Monte- 128 Ee 45.40N 10.50 E
Baldock 124 Bc 51.59N 0.11W
Baldone 116 Kh 56.41N 24.22 E
Baldur 186 Gb 49.23N 99.15W
Baldwin 184 Ed 43.54N 85.51W
Baldy Peak 182 Fe 33.55N 109.35W
Bale [3] 168 Gd 6.00N 41.00 E
Baleares / Balears [2] 126 Oe 39.30N 3.00 E
Baleares, Islas-/Balears, Illes-=Balearic Islands (EN) 110 Gh 39.30N 3.00 E
Balearic Islands (EN)= Baleares, Islas-/Balears, Illes- 110 Gh 39.30N 3.00 E
Balearic Islands (EN)= Balears, Illes-/Baleares, Islas- 110 Gh 39.30N 3.00 E
Balears / Baleares [2] 126 Oe 39.30N 3.00 E
Balears, Illes-/Baleares, Islas-=Balearic Islands (EN) 110 Gh 39.30N 3.00 E
Balease, Gunung- 150 Hg 2.24S 120.33 E
Baleia, Ponta da- 198 Mg 17.40S 36.07W
Baleine, Rivière à la- 180 Ke 58.15N 67.38W
Balej 138 Gf 51.35N 116.38 E
Balen 124 Hc 51.10N 5.09 E
Baler 150 Hc 15.46N 121.34 E
Bāleshwar 148 Hd 21.30N 86.56 E
Balezino 136 Fd 57.59N 53.02 E
Balfate 194 Df 15.48N 86.25W
Bălgarija=Bulgaria (EN) [1] 112 Ig 43.00N 25.00 E
Balgazyn 138 Ef 50.58N 95.12 E
Balguntay 152 Ec 42.45N 86.18 E
Balḥāf 144 Fg 13.58N 48.11 E
Balhārshāh 148 Fe 19.50N 79.22 E
Balhaš=Balkhash (EN) 142 Je 46.49N 74.59 E
Balhaš, ozero- = Balkhash, Lake- (EN) 140 Je 46.00N 74.00 E
Balho 168 Gc 12.00N 42.10 E
Balholm 114 Bf 61.12N 6.33 E
Bali [3] 150 Gh 8.30S 115.00 E
Bali, Laut-=Bali Sea (EN) 140 Nj 7.45S 115.30 E
Bali, Pulau- 140 Nj 8.20S 115.00 E
Bali, Selat-=Bali Strait (EN) 150 Fh 8.18S 114.25 E
Baliceaux Island 197n Bb 12.57N 61.08W
Baliem 150 Kg 4.25S 138.59 E
Balige 150 Cf 2.20N 99.04 E
Balikesir 144 Cb 39.39N 27.53 E
Balık Gölü 146 Jc 39.45N 43.36 E
Balīkh, Nahr- 146 He 35.53N 39.10 E
Balikpapan 142 Nj 1.17S 116.50 E
Balimbing 150 Dh 5.55S 104.34 E
Balimo 214 Ci 8.03S 142.56 E
Balingen 120 Eh 48.17N 8.51 E
Balinqiao 154 Ec 43.16N 118.38 E
Balintang Channel 150 Hc 19.49N 121.40 E
Bali Sea (EN)=Bali, Laut- 140 Nj 7.45S 115.30 E
Bali Strait (EN)=Bali, Selat- 150 Fh 8.18S 114.25 E
Baliza 204 Fc 16.15S 52.25W
Balk, Gaasterland- 124 Hb 52.54N 5.36 E
Balkan Mountains (EN) = Stara Planina 110 Ig 43.15N 25.00 E
Balkan Peninsula (EN) 110 Ig 41.30N 23.00 E
Balkašino 136 Ge 52.32N 68.46 E
Balkh 144 Kb 36.46N 66.54 E
Balkh [3] 144 Kb 36.30N 67.00 E
Balkhash (EN)=Balhaš 142 Je 46.49N 74.59 E
Balkhash, Lake- (EN) = Balhaš, ozero- 140 Je 46.00N 74.00 E
Balladonia 212 Ef 32.27S 123.51 E
Ballagen 114 Db 68.20N 16.50 E
Ballaghaderreen/Bealach an Doirin 118 Eh 53.55N 8.35W
Ballantrae 118 If 55.06N 5.00W
Ballantyne Strait 180 Ga 77.30N 115.00W
Ballarat 210 Fh 37.34S 143.52 E
Ballard, Lake- 212 Ee 29.25S 120.55 E
Ballé 166 Db 15.20N 8.36W
Ballenas, Bahía- 192 Cd 26.45N 113.25W
Ballenas, Canal de- 192 Cc 29.10N 113.25W
Ballenero, Canal- 206 Fh 54.50S 71.00W
Ballenita, Punta- 206 Fc 25.46S 70.44W
Balleny Islands 222 Ke 66.35S 162.50 E
Balleroy 124 Be 49.11N 0.50W
Balleza 192 Fd 26.57N 106.21W
Balli 130 Ki 40.50N 27.03 E
Ballia 148 Gc 25.45N 84.10 E
Ballina 212 Ke 28.52S 153.33 E
Ballina/Béal an Átha 118 Dg 54.07N 9.09W
Ballinasloe/Béal Átha na Sluaighe 118 Eh 53.20N 8.13W
Ballinger 186 Gk 31.44N 99.57W
Ballinrobe/Baile an Róba 118 Dh 53.37N 9.13W
Ballinskelligs Bay/Bágh Baile na Sgealg 118 Cj 51.50N 10.15W
Ballshi 130 Ci 40.36N 19.44 E
Ball's Pyramid 208 Gh 31.45S 159.15 E
Ballycastle/Baile an Chaistil 118 Gf 55.12N 6.15W
Ballyhaunis/Béal Átha hAmhnais 118 Eh 53.46N 8.46W
Ballymena/An Baile Meánach 118 Gg 54.52N 6.17W
Ballyshannon/Béal Átha Seanaidh 118 Eg 54.30N 8.11W
Balmaseda / Valmaseda 126 Ia 43.12N 3.12W
Balmazújváros 120 Ri 47.37N 21.21 E
Balmoral Castle 118 Jd 57.02N 3.15W
Balneario Orense 204 Cn 38.49S 59.46W
Balneario Oriente 204 Bn 38.55S 60.32W
Balombo 170 Be 12.21S 14.43 E
Balonne River 208 Fg 28.47S 147.56 E
Balota, Virful- 130 Gd 45.18N 23.53 E
Balovale 160 Jj 13.33S 23.07 E
Balrāmpur 148 Gc 27.26N 82.11 E
Balranald 212 If 34.38S 143.33 E
Balş 130 He 44.21N 24.06 E
Balsas [Braz.] 202 Ie 7.31S 46.02W
Balsas [Mex.] 192 Jh 18.00N 99.47W
Balsas, Depresión del- 192 Ih 18.00N 100.10W
Balsas, Rio- [Mex.] 174 Ih 17.55N 102.10W
Balsas, Rio- [Pan.] 194 Ii 8.15N 77.59W
Balsas, Rio das- [Braz.] 202 Ie 9.58S 47.52W
Balsas, Rio das- [Braz.] 202 Je 7.14S 44.33W
Bålsta 116 Ge 59.35N 17.30 E
Balsthal 128 Bc 47.19N 7.42 E
Balta 132 Ff 47.57N 29.38 E
Baltanás 126 Hc 41.56N 4.15W
Baltasar Brum 206 Id 30.44S 57.19W
Baltați 130 Kb 47.13N 27.09 E
Baltic Sea (EN) = Baltijas jūra 110 Hd 57.00N 19.00 E
Baltic Sea (EN) = Baltijos jura 110 Hd 57.00N 19.00 E
Baltic Sea (EN) = Baltijskoje more 110 Hd 57.00N 19.00 E
Baltic Sea (EN) = Balti meri 110 Hd 57.00N 19.00 E
Baltic Sea (EN)=Bałtyckie, Morze- 110 Hd 57.00N 19.00 E
Baltic Sea (EN)=Itämeri 110 Hd 57.00N 19.00 E
Baltic Sea (EN)= Östersjön 110 Hd 57.00N 19.00 E
Baltic Sea (EN)= Østersøen 110 Hd 57.00N 19.00 E
Baltic Sea (EN)=Ostsee 110 Hd 57.00N 19.00 E
Baltijas jūra = Baltic Sea (EN) 110 Hd 57.00N 19.00 E
Baltijos jura = Baltic Sea (EN) 110 Hd 57.00N 19.00 E
Baltijsk 136 Be 54.40N 19.58 E
Baltijskaja grjada 114 Fi 55.00N 25.00 E
Baltijskoje more = Baltic Sea (EN) 110 Hd 57.00N 19.00 E
Balṭīm 164 Fc 31.33N 31.05 E
Balti meri = Baltic Sea (EN) 110 Hd 57.00N 19.00 E
Baltimore 176 Lf 39.17N 76.37W
Baltit (Hunza) 148 Ea 36.20N 74.40 E
Baltoj Voke 116 Kj 54.24N 25.16 E
Baltrum 120 Dc 53.44N 7.23 E
Bałtyckie, Morze-=Baltic Sea (EN) 110 Hd 57.00N 19.00 E
Baluarte, Rio- 192 Ff 22.49N 106.02W
Baluchistān=Baluchistan (EN) [3] 148 Cc 28.00N 63.00 E
Baluchistān=Baluchistan (EN) 140 Ig 28.00N 63.00 E
Baluchistan (EN)= Baluchistān [3] 148 Cc 28.00N 63.00 E
Baluchistan (EN)= Baluchistān 140 Ig 28.00N 63.00 E
Balupe 116 Lh 56.54N 27.02 E
Balurghat 148 Hc 25.13N 88.46 E
Balvard 146 Qh 29.25N 56.06 E
Balve 124 Jc 51.20N 7.52 E
Balver Wald 124 Jc 51.21N 7.51 E
Balvi/Balvy 114 Gh 57.08N 27.20 E
Balvy/Balvi 114 Gh 57.08N 27.20 E
Balya 146 Bc 39.45N 27.35 E
Balygyčan 138 Kd 64.00N 154.10 E
Balykši 132 Qf 47.02N 51.55 E
Bām 146 Qd 36.58N 57.59 E
Bam 144 Id 29.06N 58.21 E
Bama 166 Hc 11.31N 13.41 E
Bamaji Lake 186 Ka 51.09N 91.25W
Bamako 160 Gg 12.38N 8.00W
Bamako [3] 166 Dc 13.00N 8.00W
Bamba 166 Eb 17.02N 1.24W
Bambama 170 Bc 2.32S 13.33 E
Bambana, Rio- 194 Fg 13.27N 83.50W
Bambangando 170 Df 16.59S 20.57 E
Bambari 160 Jh 5.45N 20.40 E
Bamberg 120 Gg 49.42N 10.52 E
Bambesa 170 Eb 3.28N 25.43 E
Bambesi 168 Ed 9.45N 34.44 E
Bambey 166 Bc 14.42N 16.28W
Bambezi 172 Dc 19.57S 28.55 E
Bambili 170 Eb 3.39N 26.07 E
Bambio 168 Be 3.54N 16.59 E
Bamboi 166 Ed 8.10N 2.02W
Bambouti 168 Dd 5.24N 27.12 E
Bambouto, Monts- 158 Ih 5.44N 10.04 E
Bambui 204 Je 20.01S 45.58W
Bam Co 152 Fe 31.15N 90.35 E
Bamenda 166 Hd 5.56N 10.10 E
Bāmīān 144 Kc 34.50N 67.50 E
Bāmīān [3] 144 Kc 34.45N 67.15 E
Bamiancheng 154 Gc 43.15N 124.00 E
Bamiantong → Muling 154 Kb 44.55N 130.32 E
Bamingui 168 Cd 7.34N 20.11 E
Bamingui 158 Ih 8.33N 19.05 E
Bamingui-Bangoran [3] 168 Cd 7.50N 20.15 E
Bampūr 144 Jd 27.12N 60.27 E
Bampūr 144 Id 27.18N 59.06 E
Banaadir [3] 168 He 2.00N 45.15 E
Banaadir 158 Lh 1.00N 44.00 E
Banaba Island 208 He 0.52S 169.35 E
Banabuiú, Açude- 202 Ke 5.20S 39.00W
Banagi 170 Fc 2.16S 34.51 E
Banalia 170 Eb 1.33N 25.20 E
Banamba 166 Dc 13.32N 7.27W
Bananal, Ilha do- [Braz.] 198 Kg 11.30S 50.15W
Bananal, Ilha do- [Braz.] 204 Dc 17.05S 56.25W
Bananga 148 Ig 6.57N 93.54 E
Banarli 130 Kh 41.04N 27.20 E
Banās, Ra's- 158 Kf 23.54N 35.48 E
Banat 110 If 45.30N 21.00 E
Banat 130 Dd 45.30N 21.00 E
Banaz 146 Cc 38.46N 29.46 E
Banaz 146 Cc 38.12N 29.14 E
Banbar 152 Fe 30.48N 94.52 E
Banbridge/Droichead na Banna 118 Gg 54.21N 6.16W
Banbury 118 Li 52.04N 1.20W
Banco, Punta- 194 Fi 8.23N 83.09W
Bancroft 184 Ic 45.03N 77.51W
Bānda 148 Gc 25.29N 80.20 E
Banda, Kepulauan-=Banda Islands (EN) 150 Ig 4.35S 129.55 E
Banda, Laut-=Banda Sea (EN) 208 De 5.00S 128.00 E
Banda, Punta- 192 Ab 31.45N 116.45W
Banda Aceh 142 Li 5.34N 95.20 E
Bandai-San 156 Gc 37.38N 140.04 E
Banda Islands (EN)=Banda, Kepulauan- 150 Ig 4.35S 129.55 E
Bandak 116 Ce 59.25N 8.15 E
Bandar → Machilipatnam 148 Ge 16.10N 81.08 E
Bandar Beheshtī 144 Jd 25.18N 60.37 E
Bandar-e 'Abbās 142 Hg 27.11N 56.17 E
Bandar-e Anzalī 144 Gb 37.28N 49.27 E
Bandar-e Būshehr 142 Hg 28.59N 50.50 E
Bandar-e Chārak 146 Pi 26.43N 54.16 E
Bandar-e Chīrū 146 Oi 26.43N 53.43 E
Bandar-e Deylam 144 Hg 30.05N 50.07 E
Bandar-e-Gaz 146 Od 36.47N 53.59 E
Bandar-e-Khomeynī 146 Mg 30.25N 49.08 E
Bandar-e Lengeh 144 Hd 26.33N 54.53 E
Bandar-e Māh Shahr 144 Gc 30.33N 49.12 E
Bandar-e Maqām 144 Hd 26.56N 53.29 E
Bandar-e Moghūyeh 146 Pi 26.35N 54.31 E
Bandar-e-Rīg 146 Nh 29.29N 50.38 E
Bandar-e Torkeman 144 Hb 36.56N 54.06 E
Bandar Seri Begawan 142 Ni 4.53N 114.56 E
Banda Sea (EN)=Banda, Laut- 208 De 5.00S 128.00 E
Bande 126 Eb 42.02N 7.58W
Bandeira, Pico da- 198 Lh 20.26S 41.47W
Bandeirantes 204 Ga 13.41S 50.48W
Bandeirantes, Ilha dos- 204 Ff 23.22S 53.50W
Bandera 206 Hc 28.54S 62.16W
Bandera, Alto- 194 Ld 18.49N 70.37W
Banderas, Bahía de- 190 Cd 20.40N 105.25W
Bandiagara 166 Ec 14.20N 3.37W
Bandiat 122 Gi 45.46N 0.20 E
Bandırma 144 Ca 40.20N 27.58 E
Bandirma Körfezi 130 Ki 40.25N 28.00 E
Bandol 122 Lk 43.08N 5.45 E
Bandon 188 Ce 43.07N 124.25W
Bandon/Abhainn na Bandan 118 Ej 51.40N 8.30W
Bandon/Droichead na Bandan 118 Ej 51.45N 8.45W
Ban Don, Ao- 148 Jg 9.20N 99.25 E
Bandundu 160 Ii 3.18S 17.20 E
Bandundu [2] 170 Cc 5.00S 17.00 E
Bandung 142 Mj 6.54S 107.36 E
Bāneh 146 Ke 35.59N 45.53 E
Banes 190 Id 20.58N 75.43W
Banff [Alta.-Can.] 180 Ff 51.10N 115.34W
Banff [Scot.-U.K.] 118 Kd 57.40N 2.31W
Banfora 166 Ec 10.38N 4.46W
Banga 170 Dd 5.57S 20.28 E
Bangalore 142 Jh 12.59N 77.35 E
Bangangté 166 Hd 5.09N 10.31 E
Bangar 150 Gf 4.43N 115.04 E
Bangassou 160 Jh 4.44N 22.49 E
Bangeta, Mount- 214 Di 6.16S 147.04 E
Banggai 150 Hg 1.34S 123.30 E
Banggai, Kepulauan-= Banggai Archipelago (EN) 208 De 1.30S 123.15 E
Banggai, Selat- 150 Hg 1.55S 124.00 E
Banggai Archipelago (EN)= Banggai, Kepulauan- 208 De 1.30S 123.15 E
Banggi, Pulau- 150 Ge 7.17N 117.12 E
Banghāzī=Benghazi (EN) 160 Je 32.07N 20.04 E
Banghāzī=Benghazi (EN) [3] 164 Dd 27.00N 20.30 E
Bangka, Pulau- [Indon.] 150 If 1.48N 125.09 E
Bangka, Pulau- [Indon.] 140 Mj 2.15S 106.00 E
Bangka, Selat- 150 Eg 2.30S 105.40 E
Bangka, Selat-=Bangka Strait (EN) 150 Eg 2.20S 105.45 E
Bangkalan 150 Fh 7.02S 112.44 E
Bangka Strait (EN)= Bangka, Selat- 150 Eg 2.20S 105.45 E
Bangkinang 150 Df 0.21N 101.02 E
Bangko 150 Dg 2.05S 102.17 E
Bangkok (EN)=Krung Thep 142 Mh 13.45N 100.31 E
Bangladesh [1] 142 Kg 24.00N 90.00 E
Bangli 150 Gh 8.27S 115.21 E
Bangolo 166 Dd 7.01N 7.09W
Bangong Co 152 Ce 33.45N 79.15 E
Bangor [Me.-U.S.] 182 Nc 44.49N 68.47W
Bangor [Wales-U.K.] 118 Ih 53.13N 4.08W
Bangor/Beanncharc 118 Hg 54.40N 5.40W
Bangoran 168 Bd 8.42N 19.06 E
Bangsund 114 Cd 64.24N 11.24 E
Bangu 170 Dd 9.05S 23.44 E
Bangued 150 Hc 17.36N 120.37 E
Bangui [C.A.R.] 160 Ih 4.22N 18.35 E
Bangui [Phil.] 150 Hc 18.32N 120.46 E
Bangweulu, Lake- 158 Jj 11.05S 29.45 E
Bangweulu Swamps 170 Fe 11.30S 30.15 E
Banhā 164 Fc 30.28N 31.11 E
Ban Houayxay 148 Kd 20.18N 100.26 E
Bani 190 Je 18.17N 70.20W
Bani 158 Gg 14.30N 4.12W
Bani, Jbel- 158 Gf 28.30N 9.00W
Bani Bangou 166 Fb 15.03N 2.42 E
Banie 120 Kc 53.08N 14.38 E
Banifing 166 Dc 12.43N 6.25W
Banī Forūr, Jazīreh-ye- 146 Pi 26.07N 54.28 E
Banihal Pass 148 Fb 33.15N 75.09 E
Banija 128 Ke 45.10N 16.10 E
Banikoara 166 Fc 11.18N 2.26 E
Banī ma 'Āriḍ 164 Ie 20.42N 47.42 E
Banī Mazār 164 Fd 28.30N 30.48 E
Banī Muḥammadīyāt 146 Di 27.17N 31.05 E
Banī Suwayf 164 Fd 29.05N 31.05 E
Banī Tonb 146 Pi 26.12N 54.56 E
Banī Walīd 164 Bc 31.46N 13.59 E
Bāniyās 144 Ec 33.15N 35.41 E
Banja 130 Hg 42.33N 24.50 E
Banja Koviljača 130 Ce 44.30N 19.11 E
Banja Luka 128 Lf 44.46N 17.10 E
Banjarmarsin 142 Nj 3.20S 114.35 E
Banjul 160 Fg 13.27N 16.35W
Bank 132 Pj 39.27N 49.14 E
Bankas 166 Ec 14.05N 3.31W
Bankeryd 116 Fg 57.51N 14.07 E
Banket 172 Ec 17.23S 30.24 E
Bankhead Lake 184 Di 33.30N 87.15W
Bankilaré 166 Fc 14.35N 0.44 E
Bankja 130 Gg 42.42N 23.08 E
Ban Kongmi 148 Lf 14.31N 106.55 E
Banks [Can.] 174 Gb 73.15N 121.30W
Banks [Can.] 180 Ef 53.25N 130.10W
Banks, Iles-=Banks Islands (EN) 208 Hf 13.50S 167.35 E
Banks Island 212 Ib 10.10S 142.15 E
Banks Islands (EN)=Banks, Iles- 208 Hf 13.50S 167.35 E
Banks Lake 188 Fc 47.45N 119.15W
Banks Peninsula 208 Ii 43.40S 172.40 E
Banks Strait 212 Jh 40.40S 148.10 E
Bann/An Bhanna 118 Gf 55.10N 6.46W
Ban Na San 148 Jg 8.53N 99.17 E
Bannerman Town 184 Im 24.09N 76.09W
Banning 188 Gj 33.56N 116.52W
Bannock Range 188 Ie 42.30N 112.20W
Bannu 148 Eb 32.59N 70.36 E
Bañolas / Banyoles 126 Ob 42.07N 2.46 E
Bánovce nad Bebravou 120 Oh 48.44N 18.15 E
Banqiao 152 Hf 25.28N 104.02 E
Banská Bystrica 120 Ph 48.44N 19.09 E
Banská Štiavnica 120 Oh 48.27N 18.55 E
Bansko 130 Gh 41.50N 23.29 E
Bānswāra 148 Ed 23.33N 74.27 E
Banta 168 Ge 1.13N 42.30 E
Bantenan, Tanjung- 150 Fh 8.47S 114.33 E
Bantry/Beanntrai 118 Dj 51.41N 9.27W
Bantry Bay/Bá Bheanntraí 118 Dj 51.38N 9.48W
Bañuela 126 Hf 38.24N 4.11W
Banyak, Kepulauan-= Banyak Islands (EN) 150 Cf 2.10N 97.15 E
Banyak Islands (EN)= Banyak, Kepulauan- 150 Cf 2.10N 97.15 E
Banyo 166 Hd 6.45N 11.49 E
Banyoles / Bañolas 126 Ob 42.07N 2.46 E
Banyuls-sur-Mer 122 Jl 42.29N 3.08 E
Banyuwangi 142 Nj 8.12S 114.21 E
Banzare Coast 222 Ie 67.00S 126.00 E
Banzare Seamounts (EN) 222 Fd 58.50S 77.44 E
Banzart, Buḥayrat- 128 Dm 37.11N 9.52 E
Bao'an 152 Jg 22.35N 114.10 E
Bao'an→Zhidan 152 Id 36.48N 108.46 E
Baochang→Taibus Qi 152 Kc 41.55N 115.22 E
Baode 152 Jd 38.59N 111.07 E
Baodi 154 De 39.43N 117.18 E
Baoding 142 Nf 38.47N 115.30 E
Baofeng 154 Bh 33.52N 113.04 E
Baoji 142 Mf 34.26N 107.12 E
Baokang 152 Je 31.49N 111.13 E
Baokang→Horqin Zuoyi Zhongqi 152 Lc 44.06N 123.19 E
Bao Loc 148 Lf 11.32N 107.48 E
Baoqing 152 Nb 46.20N 132.11 E
Baoro 168 Bd 5.40N 15.58 E
Baoshan 142 Lg 25.09N 99.12 E
Baotou 142 Me 40.38N 110.00 E
Baoulé [Afr.] 158 Gg 12.35N 6.34W
Baoulé [Mali] 158 Gg 13.33N 9.54W
Baoying 154 Eh 33.15N 119.18 E
Bapaume 122 Id 50.06N 2.51 E
Baqēn (Dartang) 152 Fe 31.58N 94.00 E
Bāqerābād 146 Ne 34.56N 50.50 E
Ba'qūbah 146 Fc 33.45N 44.38 E
Baquedano 206 Gb 23.20S 69.51W
Baquerizo Moreno 202a Bb 0.54S 89.37W
Bar 124 Gb 49.42N 4.50 E
Bar [Ukr.-U.S.S.R.] 132 Ee 49.02N 27.40 E
Bar [Yugo.] 130 Cg 42.05N 19.06 E

Index Symbols

[1] Independent Nation
[2] State, Region
[3] District, County
[4] Municipality
[5] Colony, Dependency
Continent
Physical Region
Historical or Cultural Region
Mount, Mountain
Volcano
Hill
Mountains, Mountain Range
Hills, Escarpment
Plateau, Upland
Pass, Gap
Plain, Lowland
Delta
Salt Flat
Valley, Canyon
Crater, Cave
Karst Features
Depression
Polder
Desert, Dunes
Forest, Woods
Heath, Steppe
Oasis
Cape, Point
Coast, Beach
Cliff
Peninsula
Isthmus
Sandbank
Island
Atoll
Rock, Reef
Islands, Archipelago
Rocks, Reefs
Coral Reef
Well, Spring
Geyser
River, Stream
Waterfall, Rapids
River Mouth, Estuary
Lake
Salt Lake
Intermittent Lake
Reservoir
Swamp, Pond
Canal
Glacier
Ice Shelf, Pack Ice
Ocean
Sea
Gulf, Bay
Strait, Fjord
Lagoon
Bank
Seamount
Tablemount
Ridge
Shelf
Basin
Escarpment, Sea Scarp
Fracture
Trench, Abyss
National Park, Reserve
Point of Interest
Recreation Site
Cave, Cavern
Historic Site
Ruins
Wall, Walls
Church, Abbey
Temple
Scientific Station
Railway station
Airport
Port
Military installation
Lighthouse
Mine
Tunnel
Dam, Bridge

Bar-Bay

Barabai	150	Gg	2.35 S	115.23 E
Barabinsk	142	Jd	55.21 N	78.21 E
Barabinskaja Step	138	Ce	55.00 N	79.00 E
Baraboo	186	Le	43.28 N	89.45 W
Baracaldo	126	Ja	43.18 N	2.59 W
Baracoa	190	Jd	20.21 N	74.30 W
Bărăganului, Cîmpia-	130	Ke	44.55 N	27.15 E
Baragoi	170	Gb	1.47 N	36.47 E
Bārah	168	Ec	13.42 N	30.22 E
Barahona	190	Je	18.12 N	71.06 W
Barak	146	Gd	36.51 N	37.59 E
Baraka	168	Fb	18.13 N	37.35 E
Barakah	168	Fb	18.13 N	37.35 E
Barakāt	168	Ec	14.20 N	33.36 E
Barakī Barak	144	Kc	33.58 N	68.58 E
Baram	150	Ff	4.36 N	113.58 E
Baram	150	Ff	4.36 N	113.59 E
Baramanni	196	Gi	7.50 N	59.13 W
Barama River	196	Gi	7.40 N	59.15 W
Bārāmūla	148	Eb	34.12 N	74.21 E
Baran	114	Hi	54.29 N	30.19 E
Bārān	148	Fc	25.06 N	76.31 E
Baraniha	138	Lc	68.31 N	168.25 E
Baranja	128	Me	46.00 N	18.30 E
Baranoa	194	Jh	10.49 N	75.03 W
Baranof	178	Le	57.00 N	135.00 W
Baranoviči	112	Ie	53.08 N	26.02 E
Baranovka	132	Ed	50.18 N	27.41 E
Baranya [2]	120	Oj	46.05 N	18.15 E
Barão de Capanema	204	Da	13.19 S	57.52 W
Barão de Cotegipe	204	Fh	27.37 S	52.23 W
Barão de Grajaú	202	Je	6.45 S	43.01 W
Barão de Melgaço	202	Gg	16.13 S	55.58 W
Baraque de Fraiture	122	Ld	50.16 N	5.45 E
Baratang	148	If	12.13 N	92.45 E
Barataria Bay	186	Li	29.22 N	89.57 W
Barat Daya, Kepulauan-	140	Oj	7.25 S	128.00 E
Barāwe	160	Lh	1.09 N	44.03 E
Barbacena	200	Lh	21.14 S	43.46 W
Barbacoas [Ven.]	194	Li	9.49 N	70.03 W
Barbacoas [Ven.]	196	Ch	9.29 N	66.58 W
Barbacoas, Bahia de-	194	Jh	10.10 N	75.35 W
Barbado, Rio-	204	Cb	15.12 S	58.58 W
Barbados [1]	176	Nh	13.10 N	59.32 W
Barbados	174	Nh	13.10 N	59.32 W
Barbados Ridge (EN)	196	Gf	12.45 N	59.35 W
Barbagia	128	Dj	40.10 N	9.10 E
Barbar	168	Eb	18.01 N	33.59 E
Bárbara	202	Dd	0.52 S	72.30 W
Barbaria, Cap de- / Berberia, Cabo-	126	Nf	38.38 N	1.23 E
Barbaros	130	Ki	40.54 N	27.27 E
Barbas, Cabo-	162	De	22.18 N	16.41 W
Barbastro	126	Mb	42.02 N	0.08 E
Barbate de Franco	126	Gh	36.12 N	5.55 W
Barbeau Peak	174	La	81.54 N	75.01 W
Barbeton	172	Ee	25.48 S	31.03 E
Barbezieux-Saint-Hilaire	122	Fi	45.28 N	0.09 W
Barbourville	184	Fg	36.52 N	83.53 W
Barboza Ferraz	204	Fg	24.04 S	52.03 W
Barbuda	174	Mh	17.38 N	61.48 W
Barcaldine	210	Fg	23.33 S	145.17 E
Barcarrota	126	Ff	38.31 N	6.51 W
Barcău	130	Ec	46.59 N	21.07 E
Barcellona Pozzo di Gotto	128	Jl	38.09 N	15.13 E
Barcelona [3]	126	Nc	41.40 N	2.00 E
Barcelona [Sp.]	112	Gg	41.23 N	2.11 E
Barcelona [Ven.]	202	Fa	10.08 N	64.42 W
Barcelonnette	122	Mj	44.23 N	6.39 E
Barcelos [Braz.]	202	Fd	0.58 S	62.57 W
Barcelos [Port.]	126	Dc	41.32 N	8.37 W
Barcin	120	Nd	52.52 N	17.57 E
Barcoo River	212	Ie	25.30 S	142.50 E
Barcs	120	Nk	45.58 N	17.28 E
Barda	132	Oi	40.25 N	47.05 E
Bardagé	168	Ba	22.06 N	16.28 E
Bardai	160	If	21.21 N	16.59 E
Bardār Shāh	146	Ld	36.45 N	47.15 E
Bārdaw	128	En	36.49 N	10.08 E
Barddhamān	148	Hd	23.15 N	87.51 E
Bardejov	120	Rg	49.18 N	21.16 E
Bārdēre	160	Lh	2.20 N	42.20 E
Bardeskan	146	Qe	35.12 N	57.58 E
Bardīyah	164	Ed	31.46 N	25.06 E
Bardonecchia	128	Ae	45.05 N	6.42 E
Bardsey	118	Ii	52.45 N	4.45 W
Bardstown	184	Eg	37.49 N	85.28 W
Barēda	160	Mg	11.52 N	51.03 E
Bareilly	142	Jg	28.25 N	79.23 E
Barencevo more = Barents Sea (EN)	224	Jd	74.00 N	36.00 E
Barentin	122	Ge	49.33 N	0.57 E
Barentsburg	224	Kd	78.04 N	14.14 E
Barentshavet = Barents Sea (EN)	224	Jd	74.00 N	36.00 E
Barentsøya	179	Oc	78.27 N	21.15 E
Barents Sea (EN) = Barencevo more	224	Jd	74.00 N	36.00 E
Barents Sea (EN) = Barentshavet	224	Jd	74.00 N	36.00 E
Barents Trough (EN)	110	Ia	73.00 N	29.00 E
Barentu	168	Fb	15.06 N	37.36 E
Barfleur	122	Ee	49.40 N	1.15 W
Barfleur, Pointe de-	122	Ee	49.42 N	1.16 W
Barga	142	Kf	30.48 N	81.17 E
Bārgāl	168	Ic	11.18 N	51.07 E
Bargarh	148	Gd	21.20 N	83.37 E
Barguelonne	122	Gj	44.07 N	0.50 E
Barguzin	138	Ff	53.27 N	108.58 E
Barguzinski hrebet	138	Ff	54.30 N	110.00 E
Bar Harbor	184	Mc	44.23 N	68.13 W
Barhi	148	Hd	24.18 N	85.25 E
Bari	112	Hg	41.08 N	16.51 E
Bari [3]	168	Hd	10.00 N	50.00 E
Bari, Terra di-	128	Kj	41.05 N	16.50 E
Ba Ria	148	Lf	10.30 N	107.10 E
Barīdī, Ra's-	146	Gj	24.17 N	37.31 E
Barika	126	Ri	35.22 N	5.05 E
Barīm	164	Hg	12.39 N	43.25 E
Barima, Rio-	196	Fh	8.35 N	60.25 W
Barima River	196	Fh	8.35 N	60.25 W
Barinas	202	Db	8.38 N	70.12 W
Barinas [2]	202	Eb	8.10 N	70.00 W
Baring, Cape-	180	Fb	70.01 N	117.28 W
Baringa	170	Db	0.45 N	20.52 E
Barinitas	194	Li	8.45 N	70.25 W
Baripāda	148	Hd	21.56 N	86.43 E
Bariri	204	Hf	22.04 S	48.44 W
Bariri, Represa-	204	Hf	22.21 S	48.39 W
Bāris	164	Fe	24.40 N	30.36 E
Bari Sādri	148	Ed	24.25 N	74.28 E
Barisāl	148	Id	22.42 N	90.22 E
Barisan, Pegunungan- = Barisan Mountains (EN)	140	Mj	3.00 S	102.15 E
Barisan Mountains (EN) = Barisan, Pegunungan-	140	Mj	3.00 S	102.15 E
Barito	140	Nj	3.32 S	114.29 E
Barjols	122	Lk	43.33 N	6.00 E
Barkā'	144	Ie	23.35 N	57.55 E
Barkam	152	He	31.45 N	102.32 E
Barkan, Ra's-e-	146	Mg	30.01 N	49.35 E
Barkava	116	Lh	56.40 N	26.45 E
Barkley, Lake-	182	Hf	36.40 N	87.55 W
Barkley Sound	188	Cb	48.53 N	125.20 W
Barkly East	172	Df	30.58 S	27.33 E
Barkly Tableland	208	Ef	19.00 S	138.00 E
Barkly West	172	Ce	28.05 S	24.31 E
Barkol	152	Fc	43.35 N	92.51 E
Barkol Hu	152	Fc	43.40 N	92.39 E
Barlavento [3]	162	Cf	16.10 N	24.40 W
Bar-le-Duc	122	Lf	48.47 N	5.10 E
Barlee, Lake-	208	Cg	29.10 S	119.30 E
Barlee Range	212	Dd	23.35 S	116.00 E
Barletta	128	Ki	41.19 N	16.17 E
Barlinek	120	Lc	53.00 N	15.12 E
Barlovento, Islas de- = Windward Islands (EN)	174	Mh	15.00 N	61.00 W
Barma	150	Jg	1.54 S	133.00 E
Barmer	148	Ec	25.45 N	71.23 E
Barmera	212	If	34.15 S	140.28 E
Barmouth	118	Ii	52.43 N	4.03 W
Barnard Castle	118	Lg	54.33 N	1.55 W
Barnaul	142	Kd	53.22 N	83.45 E
Barnes Ice Cap	180	Kc	70.00 N	73.30 W
Barnesville [Ga.-U.S.]	184	Ei	33.04 N	84.09 W
Barnesville [Mn.-U.S.]	186	Hc	46.39 N	96.25 W
Barnet, London-	124	Hb	51.39 N	0.12 W
Barneveld	124	Hb	52.08 N	5.34 E
Barneville-Carteret	122	Ee	49.23 N	1.47 W
Barnim	120	Jd	52.40 N	13.45 E
Barnsley	118	Lh	53.34 N	1.28 W
Barnstaple	118	Ij	51.05 N	4.04 W
Barnstaple (Bideford Bay)	118	Ij	51.05 N	4.20 W
Barnstorf	124	Kb	52.43 N	8.30 E
Barntrup	124	Lc	51.59 N	9.07 E
Barnwell	184	Gi	33.14 N	81.21 W
Baro	158	Kh	8.26 N	33.14 E
Baro [Chad]	168	Bc	12.12 N	18.58 E
Baro [Nig.]	166	Gd	8.36 N	6.25 E
Baroghil Pass	148	Ea	36.54 N	73.22 E
Baronnies	122	Lj	44.15 N	5.30 E
Barora Fa	219a	Db	7.30 S	158.20 E
Barora Ite	219a	Db	7.36 S	158.24 E
Barotseland	170	Df	15.05 S	24.00 E
Barqah = Cyrenaica (EN)	158	Je	31.00 N	23.00 E
Barqah = Cyrenaica (EN)	164	Dc	31.00 N	22.30 E
Barqah, Jabal al-	146	Ej	24.24 N	32.34 E
Barqah al Bahrīyah = Marmarica (EN)	158	Je	31.40 N	24.30 E
Barqū, Jabal-	128	Dn	36.04 N	9.37 E
Barques, Pointe aux-	184	Fc	44.04 N	82.58 W
Barquisimeto	200	Jd	10.04 N	69.19 W
Barr	122	Nf	48.24 N	7.27 E
Barr, Ra's al-	146	Nj	25.47 N	50.34 E
Barra	200	Lg	11.05 S	43.10 W
Barra	118	Fd	57.00 N	7.30 W
Barra, Ponta da-	172	Fd	23.47 S	35.32 E
Barra, Sound of-	118	Fd	57.10 N	7.20 W
Barraba	212	Kf	30.22 S	150.36 E
Barra Bonita, Represa-	204	Hf	22.38 S	48.20 W
Barra de Navidad	190	De	19.12 N	104.41 W
Barra do Bugres	202	Gg	15.05 S	57.11 W
Barra do Corda	202	Ie	5.30 S	45.15 W
Barra do Cuanza	170	Bd	9.18 S	13.09 E
Barra do Dande	170	Bd	8.28 S	13.22 E
Barra do Garças	202	Hg	15.53 S	52.15 W
Barra Falsa, Ponta da-	158	Kk	22.55 S	35.37 E
Barra Head	118	Fe	56.46 N	7.36 W
Barra Mansa	202	Jh	22.32 S	44.11 W
Barrāmīyah, Wādī al-	146	Ej	25.00 N	33.23 E
Barranca	202	Cd	4.50 S	76.42 W
Barrancabermeja	200	Ie	7.03 N	73.52 W
Barrancas [Col.]	194	Kh	10.57 N	72.50 W
Barrancas [Ven.]	202	Fb	8.42 N	62.11 W
Barrancas, Arroyo-	204	Cj	30.19 S	59.25 W
Barranco	204	Db	15.56 S	57.41 W
Barrancos	126	Ff	38.08 N	6.59 W
Barranqueras	206	Ic	27.29 S	58.56 W
Barranquilla	200	Id	10.59 N	74.48 W
Barranquitas	197a	Bb	18.12 N	66.23 W
Barra Patuca	194	Ef	15.50 N	84.17 W
Barras	202	Jd	4.15 S	42.18 W
Barra Velha	204	Hh	26.39 S	48.43 W
Barre	184	Kc	44.12 N	72.30 W
Barreira	204	Db	15.24 S	57.52 W
Barreiras	202	Jg	12.08 S	45.00 W
Barreirinha	202	Gd	2.47 S	57.03 W
Barreirinhas	202	Jd	2.45 S	42.50 W
Barreiro	126	Cf	33.40 N	9.04 W
Barreiro, Rio-	204	Fb	15.43 S	52.45 W
Barreiro Grande	204	Jd	13.12 S	45.10 W
Barreiros	202	Ke	3.49 S	35.12 W
Barren	148	If	12.16 N	93.51 E
Barren, Iles-	172	Gc	13.25 S	43.40 E
Barren Islands	178	Ie	58.55 N	152.15 W
Barretos	206	Kb	20.33 S	48.33 W
Barrie	180	Jh	44.24 N	79.40 W
Barrier Bay	222	Ge	67.45 S	81.10 E
Barrier Islands	219a	Db	7.44 S	158.32 E
Barrington Tops	212	Kf	32.00 S	151.28 E
Barro Alto	204	Hb	15.04 S	48.58 W
Barrois, Plateaux du-	122	Kf	48.45 N	5.00 E
Barros, Lagoa dos-	204	Gi	29.56 S	50.23 W
Barros, Tierra de-	126	Ff	38.40 N	6.25 W
Barroso	204	Ke	21.11 S	43.58 W
Barrouallie	197n	Ba	13.14 N	61.17 W
Barrow [Ak.-U.S.]	176	Db	71.17 N	156.47 W
Barrow [Arg.]	204	Bn	38.18 S	60.14 W
Barrow/An Bhearú	118	Gi	52.10 N	7.00 W
Barrow, Point-	174	Db	71.23 N	156.30 W
Barrow Creek	210	Eg	21.33 S	133.53 E
Barrow-in-Furness	118	Jg	54.07 N	3.14 W
Barrow Island	208	Cg	20.50 S	115.25 E
Barrow Range	212	Fe	26.05 S	127.30 E
Barrow Strait	174	Jb	74.21 N	94.10 W
Barru	150	Gg	4.25 S	119.37 E
Barry	118	Jj	51.24 N	3.18 W
Barrytown	218	De	42.14 S	171.20 E
Barsakelmes, ostrov-	135	Bb	45.40 N	59.55 E
Barsalogo	166	Ec	13.25 N	1.03 W
Barsatas	136	Hf	48.13 N	78.33 E
Baršč/Forst	120	Ke	51.44 N	14.38 E
Bārsi	148	Fe	18.14 N	75.42 E
Barsinghausen	120	Fd	52.18 N	9.27 E
Barstow	182	De	34.54 N	117.01 W
Bar-sur-Aube	122	Kf	48.14 N	4.43 E
Bar-sur-Seine	122	Kf	48.07 N	4.22 E
Baršyn	136	Gf	49.45 N	69.36 E
Barta/Bārta	116	Ih	56.57 N	20.57 E
Bārta/Barta	116	Ih	56.57 N	20.57 E
Barṭallah	146	Jd	36.23 N	43.25 E
Bartang	135	Hf	37.55 N	71.33 E
Barth	120	Ib	54.22 N	12.44 E
Bartholomew, Bayou-	186	Jj	32.43 N	92.04 W
Bartica	202	Gb	6.24 N	58.37 W
Bartın	146	Eb	41.38 N	32.21 E
Bartle Frere, Mount-	208	Ff	17.23 S	145.49 E
Bartlesville	182	Hd	36.45 N	95.59 W
Bartlett	186	Gf	41.53 N	98.33 W
Bartoszyce	120	Qb	54.16 N	20.49 E
Bartow	184	Gl	27.54 N	81.50 W
Barú, Isla-	194	Jh	10.26 N	75.35 W
Barú, Volcán	190	Hg	8.48 N	82.33 W
Barūd, Ra's-	146	Ei	26.47 N	33.39 E
Barumini	128	Dk	39.42 N	9.01 E
Barun-Bogdo-Ula	152	Hb	45.00 N	100.20 E
Bāruni	148	Hc	25.29 N	85.59 E
Barun-Šabartuj, gora-	138	Fg	49.43 N	109.58 E
Barun-Urt	152	Jb	46.40 N	113.12 E
Barwice	120	Mc	53.45 N	16.22 E
Barwon River	208	Fg	30.00 S	148.05 E
Barycz	120	Me	51.42 N	16.15 E
Baryš	114	Lj	53.40 N	47.08 E
Baryš	114	Li	54.35 N	46.47 E
Bāsa'idū	146	Pi	26.39 N	55.17 E
Basail	204	Ch	27.52 S	59.18 W
Basankusu	170	Cb	1.14 N	19.48 E
Basaral, ostrov-	135	Ib	45.25 N	73.45 E
Basauri	126	Ja	43.13 N	2.53 W
Basavilbaso	204	Ck	32.22 S	58.53 W
Bas Champs	124	Dd	50.10 N	1.41 E
Basco	150	Hb	20.27 N	121.58 E
Bascuñán, Cabo-	206	Fc	28.51 S	71.30 W
Basel	112	Gf	47.30 N	7.30 E
Basel-Landschaft [2]	128	Bc	47.30 N	7.45 E
Basel-Stadt [2]	128	Bc	47.35 N	7.40 E
Basentello	128	Kj	40.40 N	16.23 E
Basento	128	Kj	40.20 N	16.49 E
Başeu	130	Kb	47.44 N	27.15 E
Basey	150	Id	11.17 N	125.04 E
Bashi Channel (EN) = Bashi Haixia	152	Lg	22.00 N	121.00 E
Bashi Haixia = Bashi Channel (EN)	152	Lg	22.00 N	121.00 E
Bāsht	146	Ng	30.21 N	51.09 E
Ba Shui	154	Ci	30.25 N	115.02 E
Basilan	140	Oi	6.34 N	122.03 E
Basilan City (Isabela)	142	Oi	6.42 N	121.58 E
Basilan Strait	150	He	6.49 N	122.05 E
Basildon	118	Nj	51.34 N	0.25 E
Basilicata [2]	128	Kj	40.30 N	16.30 E
Basingstoke	118	Lj	51.16 N	1.05 W
Basjanovski	134	Jg	58.19 N	60.44 E
Başkale	146	Jc	38.02 N	44.00 E
Baskatong, Réservoir-	184	Jb	46.47 N	75.50 W
Baškaus	138	Df	51.09 N	87.43 E
Baskil	146	Hc	38.35 N	38.40 E
Baškirskaja ASSR [3]	136	Fe	55.00 N	56.00 E
Baskunčak, ozero-	132	Oe	48.10 N	46.55 E
Bašmakovo	132	Mc	53.12 N	43.03 E
Bāsmenj	146	Ld	37.59 N	46.29 E
Basoko	170	Db	1.14 N	23.36 E
Basongo	170	Dc	4.20 S	20.24 E
Basque Provinces (EN) = Euzkadi / Vascongadas	126	Ja	43.00 N	2.30 W
Basque Provinces (EN) = Vascongadas / Euzkadi	126	Ja	43.00 N	2.30 W
Basra (EN) = Al Başrah	142	Gf	30.30 N	47.47 E
Bas-Rhin [3]	122	Nf	48.35 N	7.40 E
Bass, Ilots de-	208	Mg	27.55 S	143.26 W
Bassano	188	Ia	50.47 N	112.28 W
Bassano del Grappa	128	Fe	45.46 N	11.44 E
Bassar	166	Fd	9.15 N	0.47 E
Bassas da India	158	Lk	21.25 S	39.42 E
Bassein → Pathein	142	Lh	16.47 N	94.44 E
Bassein → Vasai	148	Ee	19.21 N	72.48 E
Basse-Kotto [3]	168	Ce	5.00 N	21.30 E
Basse-Pointe	197h	Ab	14.52 N	61.07 W
Basses, Pointe des-	197e	Bc	15.52 N	61.17 W
Basse-Sambre	124	Gd	50.27 N	4.37 E
Basse Santa Su	166	Cc	13.19 N	14.13 W
Basse-Terre	190	Le	16.00 N	61.44 W
Basseterre	190	Le	17.18 N	62.43 W
Basse-Terre	196	Fd	16.10 N	61.40 W
Bassett	186	Ge	42.35 N	99.32 W
Bassigny	122	Lf	48.00 N	5.30 E
Bassikounou	162	Ff	15.52 N	5.58 W
Bassila	166	Fd	9.01 N	1.40 E
Bass Islands	219c	Ba	9.58 S	167.17 E
Basso, Plateau de-	158	Jg	17.20 N	22.40 E
Bass Strait	208	Fh	39.20 S	145.30 E
Bassum	124	Kb	52.51 N	8.44 E
Basswood Lake	186	Kb	48.05 N	91.35 W
Båstad	114	Ch	56.26 N	12.51 E
Bastak	146	Pi	27.14 N	54.22 E
Bastām	146	Pd	36.29 N	55.04 E
Bastenaken/Bastogne	122	Le	50.00 N	5.43 E
Bastia [Fr.]	112	Gg	42.42 N	9.27 E
Bastia [It.]	128	Gg	43.04 N	12.33 E
Bastogne/Bastenaken	122	Le	50.00 N	5.43 E
Bastrop	186	Kj	32.47 N	91.55 W
Basuo → Dongfang	152	Ih	19.14 N	108.39 E
Basuto	172	Dc	19.52 S	26.32 E
Bas-Zaïre [2]	170	Bd	5.30 S	14.30 E
Bata	160	Hh	1.51 N	9.45 E
Batabanó, Golfo de-	190	Hd	22.15 N	82.30 W
Batagaj	138	Ic	67.38 N	134.38 E
Batagaj-Alyta	138	Ic	67.53 N	130.31 E
Bataguaçu	202	Hh	21.42 S	52.22 W
Bataiporã	204	Ff	22.20 S	53.17 W
Batajnica	130	De	44.54 N	20.17 E
Batajsk	136	Df	47.05 N	39.46 E
Batak	130	Hh	41.57 N	24.13 E
Bataklık Gölü	146	Ed	37.42 N	33.07 E
Batala	148	Fb	31.48 N	75.12 E
Batalha	126	De	39.39 N	8.50 W
Batama	170	Eb	0.56 N	26.39 E
Batamaj	138	Hd	63.30 N	129.25 E
Batamšinski	136	Fe	50.36 N	58.17 E
Batan	150	Hb	20.30 N	121.50 E
Batang [China]	152	Ge	30.02 N	99.10 E
Batang [Indon.]	150	Eh	6.55 S	109.42 E
Batanga	170	Ac	0.21 S	9.18 E
Batangafo	168	Bd	7.18 N	18.18 E
Batangas	142	Oh	13.45 N	121.03 E
Batanghari	140	Mj	1.00 S	104.20 E
Batanghari	150	Mj	1.00 S	104.00 E
Batan Islands	140	Og	20.30 N	121.50 E
Batanta, Pulau-	150	Jg	0.50 S	130.40 E
Bátaszék	120	Oj	46.11 N	18.44 E
Batatais	204	Ie	20.53 S	47.37 W
Batavia	184	Hd	43.00 N	78.11 W
Bat-Cengel	152	Hb	47.47 N	101.58 E
Batchawana	184	Eb	46.58 N	84.34 W
Batchelor	212	Gb	13.04 S	131.01 E
Bătdâmbâng	142	Mh	13.06 N	103.12 E
Batecki	116	Nf	58.38 N	30.31 E
Batéké, Plateaux-	170	Cc	3.30 S	15.45 E
Batel, Esteros del-	204	Ci	28.30 S	58.20 W
Batemans Bay	212	Kg	35.43 S	150.11 E
Batesburg	184	Gi	33.56 N	81.33 W
Batesville [Ar.-U.S.]	186	Ki	35.46 N	91.39 W
Batesville [Ms.-U.S.]	186	Li	34.18 N	90.00 W
Bath [Eng.-U.K.]	118	Kj	51.23 N	2.22 W
Bath [Me.-U.S.]	184	Md	43.55 N	69.49 W
Bath [N.B.-Can.]	184	Nb	46.32 N	67.33 W
Bath [St.C.N.]	197c	Ab	17.08 N	62.37 W
Batha	168	Bc	14.00 N	19.00 E
Bathinda	148	Fb	30.12 N	74.57 E
Bá Thrá Lí/Tralee Bay	118	Di	52.15 N	9.59 W
Bathsheba	196	Gf	13.13 N	59.31 W
Bá Thuath Reanna/ Liscannor Bay	118	Di	52.55 N	9.25 W
Bathurst	174	Ib	76.00 N	100.30 W
Bathurst [Austl.]	212	Jf	33.25 S	149.35 E
Bathurst [N.B.-Can.]	176	Me	47.36 N	65.39 W
Bathurst, Cape-	174	Gb	70.35 N	128.00 W
Bathurst Inlet	176	Ic	66.50 N	108.01 W
Bathurst Inlet	174	Ic	68.10 N	108.50 W
Bathurst Island	208	Ef	11.35 S	130.25 E
Bati	168	Gc	11.13 N	40.01 E
Batié	166	Ed	9.53 N	2.55 W
Bāṭin, Wādī al-	144	Gc	30.25 N	47.35 E
Batman	144	Fb	37.52 N	41.07 E
Batman	146	Id	37.45 N	41.00 E
Batna	160	He	35.34 N	6.11 E
Batna [3]	162	Ib	35.10 N	6.00 E
Ba To	148	Lf	14.46 N	108.44 E
Bato Bato	150	Ge	5.06 N	119.50 E
Batoka	170	Ef	16.47 S	27.15 E
Baton Rouge	176	Jf	30.23 N	91.11 W
Batopilas	192	Fd	27.01 N	107.44 W
Batouri	166	He	4.26 N	14.22 E
Batovi	204	Fb	15.53 S	53.24 W
Batovi, Coxilha de-	204	Ej	30.33 S	54.27 W
Båtsfjord	114	Ga	70.38 N	29.44 E
Bat-Sumber	152	Ib	48.25 N	106.42 E
Batticaloa	148	Gg	7.43 N	81.42 E
Batti Maly	148	Ig	8.50 N	92.51 E
Battipaglia	128	Ij	40.37 N	14.58 E
Battle	124	Cd	50.55 N	0.30 E
Battle	180	Gf	52.42 N	108.15 W
Battle Creek	182	Jc	42.19 N	85.11 W
Battle Creek	188	Kb	48.36 N	109.11 W
Battle Harbour	176	Nd	52.17 N	55.35 W
Battle Mountain	182	Dc	40.38 N	116.56 W
Battonya	120	Rj	46.17 N	21.01 E
Battowia Island	197n	Bb	12.58 N	61.09 W
Batu	168	Fd	6.59 N	39.37 E
Batu, Kepulauan- = Batu Islands (EN)	140	Lj	0.18 S	98.28 E
Batuasa	150	Jg	3.32 S	130.08 E
Batuata, Pulau-	150	Hh	6.12 S	122.42 E
Batudaka, Pulau-	150	Hg	0.28 S	121.48 E
Batui	150	Hg	1.17 S	122.33 E
Batu Islands (EN) = Batu, Kepulauan-	140	Lj	0.18 S	98.28 E
Batumi	112	Kg	41.38 N	41.38 E
Batu Pahat	150	Df	1.51 N	102.56 E
Baturaja	150	Dg	4.08 S	104.10 E
Baturino	138	De	57.45 N	85.12 E
Baturité	202	Kd	4.20 S	38.53 W
Batz, Ile de-	122	Bf	48.45 N	4.01 W
Bau	150	Ff	1.25 N	110.09 E
Baubau	142	Oj	5.28 S	122.38 E
Baucau	150	Ih	8.27 S	126.27 E
Bauchi	160	Hg	10.19 N	9.50 E
Bauchi [2]	166	Hc	10.40 N	10.00 E
Bauchi Plateau	166	Gc	10.00 N	9.30 E
Baud	122	Cg	47.52 N	3.01 W
Baudette	186	Ib	48.43 N	94.36 W
Baudo, Serrania de-	202	Cb	6.00 N	77.05 W
Baudour, Saint-Ghislain-	124	Fd	50.29 N	3.49 E
Baugé	122	Fg	47.33 N	0.06 W
Bauges	122	Mi	45.38 N	6.10 E
Baúl, Cerro-	192	Ii	17.38 N	100.19 W
Baula	150	Hg	4.09 S	121.41 E
Bauld, Cape-	174	Nd	51.38 N	55.25 W
Baule-Escoublac, La-	122	Dg	47.17 N	2.24 W
Bauman Fiord	180	Ia	77.45 N	86.00 W
Baume-les-Dames	122	Mg	47.21 N	6.22 E
Baunach	120	Gg	49.59 N	10.51 E
Baunani	219a	Ec	9.08 S	160.51 E
Baunei	128	Dj	40.02 N	9.40 E
Baures	202	Ff	13.35 S	63.35 W
Bauru	200	Lh	22.19 S	49.04 W
Baús	204	Fd	18.19 S	53.10 W
Baús, Serra dos-	204	Fd	18.20 S	53.25 W
Bauska	114	Fh	56.24 N	24.13 E
Bautzen/Budyšin	120	Ke	51.11 N	14.26 E
Baux-de-Provence, Les-	122	Kk	43.45 N	4.48 E
Bavaria (EN) = Bayern [2]	120	Hg	49.00 N	11.30 E
Bavaria (EN) = Bayern	110	Hf	49.00 N	11.30 E
Bavarian Forest (EN) = Bayerischer Wald	120	Ig	49.00 N	12.55 E
Bavay	124	Fd	50.18 N	3.47 E
Båven	116	Ge	59.00 N	16.55 E
Bavispe	192	Eb	30.24 N	108.50 W
Bavispe, Rio de-	192	Ec	29.15 N	109.11 W
Bavly	114	Mi	54.26 N	53.18 E
Bawah, Pulau-	150	Ef	2.31 N	106.03 E
Bawal, Pulau-	150	Fg	2.44 S	110.06 E
Bawe	210	Ee	2.59 S	134.43 E
Bawean, Pulau-	150	Fh	5.46 S	112.40 E
Bawku	166	Ec	11.03 N	0.15 W
Baxian	152	Kd	39.03 N	116.24 E
Baxol	152	Ge	30.07 N	96.56 E
Bay [3]	168	Ge	2.50 N	43.30 E
Bay/Baicheng	152	Dc	41.46 N	81.52 E
Bayamo	190	Id	20.23 N	76.39 W
Bayamón	194	Nd	18.24 N	66.09 W
Bayan	154	Ia	46.05 N	127.24 E
Bayanbulak	152	Dc	43.05 N	84.05 E
Bayanga	168	Be	2.53 N	16.19 E
Bayan Gol	152	Gd	37.18 N	96.50 E
Bayan Gol → Dengkou	142	Me	40.25 N	106.59 E
Bayan Har Shan	140	Lf	34.20 N	97.00 E
Bayan Har Shankou	152	Ge	34.06 N	97.38 E
Bayan Hot → Alxa Zuoqi	152	Id	38.50 N	105.32 E
Bayan Hure → Chen Barag Qi	152	Kb	49.21 N	119.25 E
Bayan Huxu → Horqin Youyi Zhongqi	152	Lb	45.04 N	121.27 E
Bayano, Lago de-	194	Hi	9.00 N	78.30 W
Bayan Obo	152	Ic	41.50 N	109.58 E
Bayan Qagan	154	Ga	46.11 N	123.59 E
Bayan Qagan → Qahar Youyi Houqi	154	Bd	41.28 N	113.10 E
Bayan Ul Hot → Xi Ujimqin Qi	152	Kc	44.31 N	117.33 E
Bayas	192	Gf	23.32 N	104.50 W
Bayat	146	Fb	40.39 N	34.15 E
Bayauca	204	Bl	34.51 S	61.18 W
Bayawan	150	He	9.20 N	123.00 E
Bayāẕ	146	Pg	30.42 N	55.28 E
Bayāẕeh	146	Pf	30.42 N	55.28 E
Baybay	150	Hd	10.41 N	124.48 E
Bayburt	144	Fa	40.16 N	40.15 E
Bay City [Mi.-U.S.]	182	Kc	43.36 N	83.53 W
Bay City [Tx.-U.S.]	182	Hf	29.09 N	95.39 W
Bayerische Alpen	120	Hi	47.30 N	11.30 E
Bayerischer Wald = Bavarian Forest (EN)	120	Ig	49.00 N	12.55 E
Bayern = Bavaria (EN) [2]	120	Hg	49.00 N	11.30 E
Bayern = Bavaria (EN)	110	Hf	49.00 N	11.30 E
Bayes, Cap-	219b	Be	20.57 S	165.25 E
Bayeux	122	Fe	49.16 N	0.42 W
Bayfield	186	Kc	46.49 N	90.49 W
Bay Fiord	180	Ia	79.00 N	84.00 W
Baygorria	204	Dk	32.52 S	56.44 W
Baygorria, Lago Artificial de-	204	Dk	33.05 S	57.00 W
Bayḥān al Qişāb	164	Ig	14.48 N	45.44 E
Bayındır	146	Bc	38.13 N	27.40 E
Bayjī	146	Je	34.56 N	43.29 E
Bay Minette	184	Dj	30.53 N	87.47 W
Baynūnah	146	Ok	23.50 N	52.50 E
Bayombong	150	Hc	16.29 N	121.09 E
Bayona / Baiona	126	Db	42.07 N	8.51 W
Bayonnaise Seamount (EN)	208	Jf	12.00 S	179.30 W
Bayonne	112	Fg	43.29 N	1.29 W
Bayou Bodcau Lake	186	Jj	32.58 N	93.30 W
Bayou D'Arbonne Lake	186	Jj	32.45 N	92.27 W
Bayramiç	130	Jj	39.48 N	26.37 E
Bayreuth	120	Hg	49.57 N	11.35 E
Bayrūt [3]	146	Ff	33.56 N	35.30 E
Bayrūt = Beirut (EN)	142	Ff	33.53 N	35.30 E
Bay Saint Louis	186	Lk	30.19 N	89.20 W
Bay Springs	186	Lk	31.59 N	89.17 W
Bayt al Faqīh	144	Fg	14.31 N	43.17 E
Baytik Shan	152	Fb	45.15 N	90.50 E
Bayt Laḥm = Bethlehem (EN)	146	Fg	31.43 N	35.12 E
Baytown	182	If	29.44 N	94.58 W
Bayuda Desert (EN) = Bayyūḍah, Ṣaḥrā'-	158	Kg	18.00 N	33.00 E
Bayunglencir	150	Dg	2.03 S	103.41 E
Bayview	188	Gc	48.00 N	116.30 W
Bay View	218	Gc	39.26 S	176.52 E
Bayy al Kabīr	164	Cc	31.11 N	15.53 E

Index Symbols

[1] Independent Nation	Historical or Cultural Region	Pass, Gap	Depression	Coast, Beach	Rock, Reef	Waterfall, Rapids	Canal	Lagoon	Escarpment, Sea Scarp
[2] State, Region	Mount, Mountain	Plain, Lowland	Polder	Cliff	Islands, Archipelago	River Mouth, Estuary	Glacier	Bank	Fracture
[3] District, County	Volcano	Delta	Desert, Dunes	Peninsula	Rocks, Reefs	Lake	Ice Shelf, Pack Ice	Seamount	Trench, Abyss
[4] Municipality	Hill	Salt Flat	Forest, Woods	Isthmus	Coral Reef	Salt Lake	Ocean	Tablemount	National Park, Reserve
[5] Colony, Dependency	Mountains, Mountain Range	Valley, Canyon	Heath, Steppe	Sandbank	Well, Spring	Intermittent Lake	Sea	Ridge	Point of Interest
Continent	Hills, Escarpment	Crater, Cave	Oasis	Island	Geyser	Reservoir	Gulf, Bay	Shelf	Recreation Site
Physical Region	Plateau, Upland	Karst Features	Cape, Point	Atoll	River, Stream	Swamp, Pond	Strait, Fjord	Basin	Cave, Cavern

Historic Site	Airport
Ruins	Port
Wall, Walls	Military installation
Church, Abbey	Lighthouse
Temple	Mine
Scientific Station	Tunnel
Railway station	Dam, Bridge

Bayyūḑah, Şaḩrā'- = Bayuda Desert (EN) 158 Kg 18.00N 33.00 E
Baza 126 Jg 37.29N 2.46W
Baza, Sierra de- 126 Jg 37.15N 2.45W
Bazardjuzju, gora- 110 Kg 41.13N 47.51 E
Bazaruto, Ilha do- 172 Fd 21.40S 35.25 E
Bazas 122 Fj 44.26N 0.13W
Bazhong 152 Ie 31.54N 106.42 E
Bazoches-sur-Vesle 124 Fe 49.19N 3.37 E
Baztan / Baztán 126 Ka 43.09N 1.31 E
Baztán / Baztan 126 Ka 43.09N 1.31 E
Beach 182 Gb 46.55N 103.52W
Beachy Head 118 Nk 50.44N 0.16 E
Beacon 184 Ke 41.31N 73.59W
Beaconsfield [Austl.] 212 Jh 41.12S 146.48 E
Beaconsfield [Eng.-U.K.] 124 Bc 51.36N 0.38W
Beagle, Canal- 206 Gh 54.53S 68.10W
Beagle Gulf 212 Gb 12.00S 130.20 E
Bealach an Doirin/Ballaghaderreen 118 Eh 53.55N 8.35W
Béalanana 172 Hb 14.33S 48.44 E
Béal an Átha/Ballina 118 Dg 54.07N 9.09W
Béal an Bheara/Gweebarra Bay 118 Eg 54.52N 8.20W
Béal Átha Fhirdhia/Ardee 118 Gh 53.52N 6.33W
Béal Átha hAmhnais/Ballyhaunis 118 Eh 53.46N 8.46W
Béal Átha na Muice/Swinford 118 Eh 53.57N 8.57W
Béal Átha na Sluaighe/Ballinasloe 118 Eh 53.20N 8.13W
Béal Átha Seanaidh/Ballyshannon 118 Eg 54.30N 8.11W
Beale, Cape- 188 Cb 48.44N 125.20W
Béal Easa/Foxford 118 Dh 53.59N 9.07W
Béal Feirste/Belfast 112 Fe 54.35N 5.55W
Beal Range 212 Ie 25.30S 141.30 E
Béal Tairbirt/Belturbet 118 Fg 54.06N 7.26W
Beanna Boirche/Mourne Mountains 118 Gg 54.10N 6.04W
Beannchar/Bangor 118 Hg 54.40N 5.40W
Beanntrai/Bantry 118 Dj 51.41N 9.27W
Bear Bay 180 Ia 75.45N 86.30W
Beardmore 186 Mb 49.36N 87.57W
Beardstown 186 Kg 39.59N 90.26W
Bear Island (EN) = Bjørnøya 110 Ha 74.30N 19.00 E
Bear Islands (EN) = Medveži, ostrova- 180 Sb 70.52N 161.26 E
Bear Lake 182 Ec 42.00N 111.20W
Bear Lodge Mountains 186 Dd 44.35N 104.15W
Béarn 122 Fk 43.20N 0.45W
Bearpaw Mountains 188 Kb 48.15N 109.30W
Bear Peninsula 222 Of 74.36S 110.50W
Bear River 188 If 41.30N 112.08W
Bearskin Lake 180 If 53.57N 90.59W
Beās 148 Eb 31.10N 74.59 E
Beas de Segura 126 Jf 38.15N 2.53W
Beata, Cabo- 190 Je 17.36N 71.25W
Beata, Isla- 194 Le 17.35N 71.31W
Beata Ridge (EN) 190 Je 16.00N 72.30W
Beatrice 182 Hc 40.16N 96.44W
Beatrice, Cape- 212 Hb 14.15S 137.00 E
Beatton 180 Fe 56.06N 120.22W
Beatton River 180 Fe 56.10N 120.25W
Beatty 182 Dd 36.54N 116.46W
Beattyville 184 Ia 48.52N 77.10W
Beatys Butte 188 Fe 42.23N 119.20W
Beau-Bassin 172a Bb 20.13S 57.27 E
Beaucaire 122 Kk 43.48N 4.38 E
Beaucamps-le-Vieux 124 De 49.50N 1.47 E
Beaucanton 184 Ha 49.05N 79.15W
Beauce 122 Hf 48.22N 1.50 E
Beaudesert 212 Ke 27.59S 153.00 E
Beaufort [Mala.] 150 Ge 5.20N 115.45 E
Beaufort [S.C.-U.S.] 184 Gi 32.26N 80.40W
Beaufort/Befort 124 Ie 49.50N 6.18 E
Beaufort, Massif de- 122 Mi 45.50N 6.40 E
Beaufort Island 222 Kf 76.57S 166.56 E
Beaufort Sea 224 Ad 73.00N 140.00W
Beaufort West 160 Jl 32.20S 22.33 E
Beaugency 122 Hg 47.47N 1.38 E
Beaujolais, Monts du- 122 Kh 46.00N 4.22 E
Beauly 118 Id 57.29N 4.29W
Beaumesnil 124 Ce 49.01N 0.43 E
Beaumetz-lès-Loges 124 Ed 50.14N 2.39 E
Beaumont [Bel.] 124 Gd 50.14N 4.14 E
Beaumont [Fr.] 122 Gj 44.46N 0.46 E
Beaumont [Fr.] 122 Ee 49.40N 1.51W
Beaumont [Fr.] 124 Hf 48.51N 5.47 E
Beaumont [Ms.-U.S.] 186 Lk 31.11N 88.55W
Beaumont [N.Z.] 218 Cf 45.49S 169.32 E
Beaumont [Tx.-U.S.] 176 Jf 30.05N 94.06W
Beaumont-de-Lomagne 122 Gk 43.53N 0.59 E
Beaumont-en-Argonne 124 He 49.32N 5.03 E
Beaumont-le-Roger 124 Ce 49.05N 0.47 E
Beaumont-sur-Oise 124 Ee 49.08N 2.17 E
Beaumont-sur-Sarthe 122 Gf 48.13N 0.08 E
Beaune 122 Kg 47.02N 4.50 E
Beaupré 184 Lb 47.03N 70.53W
Beauraing 124 Gd 50.07N 4.48 E
Beaurepaire 122 Li 45.20N 5.03 E
Beausejour 180 Hf 50.04N 96.33W
Beautemps Beaupré 219b Ce 20.25S 166.08 E
Beauvais 122 Ie 49.26N 2.05 E
Beauval 124 Ed 50.06N 2.20 E
Beauvoir-sur-Mer 122 Dh 46.55N 2.03W
Beaver [Ak.-U.S.] 178 Jc 66.22N 147.24W
Beaver [Ok.-U.S.] 186 Fh 36.48N 100.30W
Beaver [Ut.-U.S.] 182 Ed 38.17N 112.38W
Beaver Creek [Co.-U.S.] 186 Ef 40.20N 103.33W
Beaver Creek [U.S.] 186 Gf 40.04N 99.20W
Beaver Creek [U.S.] 186 Ec 47.20N 103.39W
Beaver Creek [U.S.] 186 Ee 43.25N 103.59W
Beaver Dam 186 Le 43.28N 88.50W
Beaver Falls 184 Ge 40.45N 80.21W
Beaverhead Mountains 188 Id 45.00N 113.20W
Beaver Island 184 Ec 45.40N 85.31W
Beaver Lake 186 Jh 36.20N 93.55W
Beaver River [U.S.] 186 Gh 36.10N 98.45W
Beaver River [Ut.-U.S.] 188 Ig 39.10N 112.57W
Beaverton 188 Dd 45.29N 122.48W
Beāwar 148 Ec 26.06N 74.19 E
Bebedouro 206 Kb 20.56S 48.28W
Becan 192 Oh 18.37N 89.35W
Becanchén 192 Oh 19.50N 89.22W
Beccles 118 Oi 52.28N 1.34 E
Bečej 130 Dd 45.37N 20.03 E
Beceni 130 Jd 45.23N 26.47 E
Becerreá 126 Eb 42.51N 7.10W
Becerro, Cayos- 194 Ff 15.57N 83.17W
Béchar 160 Ge 31.37N 2.13W
Béchar [3] 162 Gd 30.00N 2.00W
Becharof Lake 178 He 58.00N 156.30W
Bechet 130 Gf 43.46N 23.57 E
Bechevin Bay 178 Ge 55.00N 163.27W
Bechyně 120 Kg 49.18N 14.28 E
Beckingen 124 Ie 49.24N 6.42 E
Beckley 182 Kd 37.46N 81.12W
Beckum 120 Ee 51.45N 8.02 E
Beckumer Berge 124 Kc 51.43N 8.10 E
Beclean 130 Hb 47.11N 24.11 E
Bédarieux 122 Jk 43.37N 3.09 E
Bedburg-Hau 124 Ic 51.46N 6.11 E
Bedele 168 Fd 8.27N 36.22 E
Bedesa 168 Gd 8.53N 40.46 E
Bedford 118 Mi 52.10N 0.50W
Bedford [Eng.-U.K.] 118 Mi 52.08N 0.29W
Bedford [In.-U.S.] 184 Df 38.52N 86.29W
Bedford [Pa.-U.S.] 184 He 40.00N 78.31W
Bedford [Va.-U.S.] 184 Hg 37.20N 79.31W
Bedford Level 118 Ni 52.30N 0.05 E
Bedford Point 197p Bb 12.13N 61.36W
Bedfordshire [3] 118 Mi 52.05N 0.20W
Bednja 128 Kd 46.18N 16.45 E
Bednodemjanovsk 132 Mc 53.55N 43.12 E
Bedourie 212 Hd 24.21S 139.28 E
Bedum 124 Ia 53.18N 6.39 E
Beech Grove 184 Df 39.43N 86.03W
Beecroft Head 212 Kg 35.01S 150.50 E
Beef Island 197a Db 18.27N 64.31W
Beelitz 120 Id 52.14N 12.58 E
Beemster 124 Gb 52.34N 4.56 E
Beerfelden 124 Ke 49.34N 8.59 E
Beernem 124 Fc 51.09N 3.20 E
Beerse 124 Gc 51.19N 4.52 E
Beersel 124 Gd 50.46N 4.18 E
Beersheba (EN) = Be'er Sheva' 144 Dc 31.14N 34.47 E
Be'er Sheva' = Beersheba (EN) 144 Dc 31.14N 34.47 E
Beerze 124 Hc 51.36N 5.19 E
Beeskow 120 Kd 52.10N 14.14 E
Beestekraal 172 De 25.23S 27.38 E
Beeston 118 Li 52.56N 1.12W
Beethoven Peninsula 222 Qf 71.40S 73.45W
Beetsterzwaag, Opsterland- 124 Ia 53.03N 6.04 E
Beeville 182 Hf 28.24N 97.45W
Befale 170 Db 0.28N 20.58 E
Befandriana Avaratra 172 Hc 15.15S 48.32 E
Befandriana Nord 172 Hc 15.15S 48.32 E
Befandriana Sud 172 Gd 22.06S 43.54 E
Befori 170 Db 0.06N 22.17 E
Befort/Beaufort 124 Ie 49.50N 6.18 E
Bega 210 Fh 36.40S 149.50 E
Bega 130 Dd 45.13N 20.19 E
Bégard 122 Cf 48.38N 3.18W
Begejski kanal 130 Dd 45.27N 20.27 E
Beggars Point 197d Bb 17.10N 61.48W
Bègles 122 Fj 44.48N 0.32W
Begna 114 Bf 60.35N 10.00 E
Begoml 116 Mj 54.46N 28.14 E
Begunicy 116 Me 59.31N 29.30 E
Behābād 146 Pg 31.52N 55.57 E
Behbehān 144 Hc 30.35N 50.14 E
Behring Point 194 Ia 24.27N 77.43W
Behshahr 144 Hb 36.43N 53.34 E
Bei'an 142 Oe 48.16N 126.29 E
Beibu Wan = Tonkin, Gulf of- (EN) 140 Mh 20.00N 108.00 E
Beida He 152 Gc 40.18N 99.01 E
Beihai 142 Mg 21.31N 109.07 E
Bei Hulsan Hu 152 Gd 36.55N 95.55 E
Bei Jiang 152 Jg 23.02N 112.58 E
Beijing = Peking (EN) 142 Nf 39.55N 116.23 E
Beijing Shi (Pei-ching Shih) [4] 152 Kc 40.15N 116.30 E
Beila 162 Df 18.10N 15.53W
Beilen 124 Ib 52.52N 6.32 E
Beilerstroom 124 Ib 52.41N 6.12 E
Beiliutang He 154 Eg 34.12N 119.33 E
Beilstein 124 Jd 50.07N 7.15 E
Beilu He 152 Fe 34.34N 94.00 E
Beinamar 168 Bd 8.40N 15.23 E
Beine-Nauroy 124 Ge 49.15N 4.13 E
Beipiao 152 Lc 41.49N 120.45 E
Beira 160 Kj 19.50S 34.52 E
Beira Alta 126 Ed 40.40N 7.35W
Beira Baixa 126 Ee 39.55N 7.30W
Beira Litoral 126 Dd 40.15N 8.25W
Beiru He 154 Bh 33.40N 113.35 E
Beirut (EN) = Bayrūt 142 Ff 33.53N 35.30 E
Bei Shan 140 Le 41.30N 96.00 E
Beitstad 114 Cd 64.05N 11.22 E
Beiuş 130 Fc 46.40N 22.21 E
Beiwei Tan 152 Kg 21.10N 116.10 E
Beizhen [China] 152 Kd 37.24N 117.59 E
Beizhen [China] 154 Fd 41.36N 121.47 E
Beja 126 Ef 38.01N 7.52W
Beja [2] 126 Eg 37.58N 7.50W
Bejaia 160 He 36.45N 5.05 E
Bejaia [3] 162 Ib 36.40N 5.10 E
Bejaia, Golfe de- 126 Rh 36.45N 5.20 E
Béjar 126 Gd 40.23N 5.46W
Beji 148 Dc 29.47N 67.58 E
Bejneu 136 Ff 45.15N 55.05 E
Bejsug 132 Kf 46.02N 38.35 E
Bejsugskij liman 132 Kf 46.05N 38.25 E
Bekabad 136 Gg 40.13N 69.14 E
Bekasi 150 Eh 6.14S 106.59 E
Bekdaš 136 Fg 41.31N 52.40 E
Békés 120 Rj 46.46N 21.08 E
Békés [2] 120 Qj 46.45N 21.00 E
Békéscsaba 120 Rj 46.41N 21.06 E
Bekilli 130 Mk 38.14N 29.26 E
Bekily 172 Hd 24.12S 45.18 E
Bekkai 156a Db 43.25N 145.07 E
Bekoji 168 Fd 7.32N 39.15 E
Bekopaka 172 Gc 19.08S 44.45 E
Bekovo 132 Mc 52.29N 43.45 E
Bela [India] 148 Gc 25.56N 81.59 E
Bela [Pak.] 148 Dc 26.14N 66.19 E
Bélabo 166 He 4.52N 13.10 E
Bela Crkva 130 Ee 44.54N 21.26 E
Bela Dila 148 Ge 18.40N 80.55 E
Bela Floresta 204 Ge 20.36S 51.16W
Belaga 150 Ff 2.42N 113.47 E
Belaja [R.S.F.S.R.] 110 Ld 56.00N 54.32 E
Belaja [R.S.F.S.R.] 132 Kg 45.03N 39.25 E
Belaja [R.S.F.S.R.] 138 Mc 65.30N 173.15 E
Belaja Cerkov 112 Jf 49.49N 30.07 E
Belaja Gora 138 Jc 68.30N 146.15 E
Belaja Holunica 136 Fd 58.53N 50.50 E
Belaja Kalitva 136 Ef 48.09N 40.49 E
Bela Krajina 128 Je 45.35N 15.15 E
Bela Lorena 204 Ib 15.13S 46.01W
Belang 150 Hf 0.57N 124.47 E
Bela Palanka 130 Ff 43.13N 22.19 E
Belarbi 126 Li 35.09N 0.27W
Belaruskaja Sovetskaja Socialistyčnaja Respublika /Belorusskaja SSR [2] 136 Ce 53.50N 28.00 E
Belau = Palau (EN) 128 Di 41.11N 9.23 E
Bela Vista [Braz.] 204 Dc 17.37S 57.01W
Bela Vista [Braz.] 202 Gh 22.06S 56.31W
Bela Vista [Moz.] 172 Ee 26.20S 32.40 E
Belawan 150 Cf 3.47N 98.41 E
Bela Woda/Weißwasser 120 Ke 51.31N 14.38 E
Belayan 150 Gg 0.14S 116.36 E
Belbo 128 Cf 44.54N 8.31 E
Belchatow 120 Pe 51.22N 19.21 E
Belcher Channel 180 Ia 77.20N 94.30W
Belcher Islands 174 Ld 56.20N 79.30W
Belchite 126 Lc 41.18N 0.45W
Belcy 136 Cf 47.46N 27.55 E
Belczyna 120 Ne 51.25N 17.50 E
Belebej 136 Fe 54.10N 54.07 E
Belecke, Warstein- 124 Kc 51.29N 8.20 E
Beled 120 Ni 47.28N 17.06 E
Beled Wëyne 160 Lh 4.47N 45.12 E
Bélel 166 Hd 7.03N 14.26 E
Belém [Braz.] 200 Lf 1.27S 48.29W
Belem [Mex.] 192 Dd 27.45N 110.28W
Belém [Moz.] 172 Fb 14.08S 35.58 E
Belém de São Francisco 202 Ke 8.46S 38.58W
Belen 182 Fe 34.40N 106.46W
Belén [Arg.] 206 Gc 27.39S 67.02W
Belén [Nic.] 194 Eh 11.30N 85.53W
Belén [Par.] 204 Df 23.30S 57.06W
Belén [Ur.] 204 Dj 30.47S 57.47W
Belén, Cuchilla de- 204 Dj 30.55S 56.30W
Belén de Escobar 204 Cl 34.21S 58.47W
Belene 130 If 43.39N 25.07 E
Bélep, Iles- 208 Hf 19.45S 163.40 E
Beles 168 Fc 10.55N 35.10 E
Belev 132 Jc 53.50N 36.10 E
Beleye 168 Fc 11.24N 36.10 E
Belfast [Me.-U.S.] 184 Mc 44.27N 69.01W
Belfast [S.Afr.] 172 Ee 25.43S 30.03 E
Belfast/Béal Feirste 112 Fe 54.35N 5.55W
Belfast Lough/Loch Lao 118 Hg 54.40N 5.50W
Belfield 186 Ec 46.53N 103.12W
Belford 118 Lf 55.36N 1.49W
Belfort 122 Mg 47.45N 7.00 E
Belgaum 142 Jh 15.52N 74.30 E
Belgica Bank (EN) 224 Ld 78.28N 15.00W
Belgicafjella 222 Df 72.35S 31.10 E
België/Belgique = Belgium (EN) [1] 112 Ge 50.30N 4.30 E
Belgique/België = Belgium (EN) [1] 112 Ge 50.30N 4.30 E
Belgium (EN) = België/Belgique [1] 112 Ge 50.30N 4.30 E
Belgium (EN) = Belgique/België [1] 112 Ge 50.30N 4.30 E
Belgorod 112 Je 50.36N 36.35 E
Belgorod-Dnestrovski 112 Df 46.12N 30.17 E
Belgorodskaja oblast [3] 136 De 50.45N 37.30 E
Belgrade (EN) = Beograd 112 Ig 44.50N 20.30 E
Bel Hairane 162 Ic 31.17N 6.20 E
Beli 166 Hd 7.52N 10.58 E
Belice 128 Gm 37.35N 12.52 E
Beli Drim 130 Dg 42.05N 20.20 E
Belidži 132 Pi 41.53N 48.20 E
Beli Lom 130 If 43.41N 26.00 E
Beli Manastir 128 Me 45.46N 18.37 E
Belimbegovo 130 Eh 42.00N 21.35 E
Belin-Béliet 122 Fj 44.30N 0.47W
Belinga 170 Bb 1.04N 13.12 E
Belinski 132 Mc 52.58N 43.29 E
Belinyu 150 Eg 1.38S 105.46 E
Beliş 130 Gc 46.39N 23.02 E
Beli Timok 130 Ff 43.55N 22.18 E
Belitung, Pulau- 140 Mj 2.50S 107.55 E
Belize [3] 194 Ce 17.35N 88.35W
Belize (British Honduras) [1] 176 Kh 17.15N 88.45W
Belize City 176 Kh 17.30N 88.12W
Belize River 194 Ce 17.32N 88.14W
Beljajevka 132 Gf 46.29N 30.14 E
Beljanica 130 Ee 44.07N 21.43 E
Belka 116 Mg 57.40N 29.47 E
Belkovski, ostrov- 138 Ia 75.30N 136.00 E
Bellac 122 Hh 46.07N 1.03 E
Bella Coola 180 Ef 52.22N 126.46W
Bellagio 128 De 45.59N 9.15 E
Bellaire [Oh.-U.S.] 184 Ge 40.02N 80.46W
Bellaire [Tx.-U.S.] 186 Il 29.43N 95.28W
Bellaria-Igea Marina 128 Gf 44.09N 12.28 E
Bellary 142 Jh 15.09N 76.56 E
Bella Unión 204 Dj 30.15S 57.35W
Bella Vista [Arg.] 206 Ic 28.30S 59.03W
Bella Vista [Par.] 204 Df 22.08S 56.31W
Bellavista, Capo- 128 Dk 39.56N 9.43 E
Bell Bay 180 Jb 71.10N 84.55W
Belle-Anse 194 Kd 18.14N 72.04W
Belledonne 122 Mi 45.18N 6.08 E
Bellefontaine [Mart.] 197h Ab 14.40N 61.10W
Bellefontaine [Oh.-U.S.] 184 Fe 40.22N 83.45W
Belle Fourche 182 Gc 44.40N 103.51W
Belle Fourche River 186 Ed 44.26N 102.19W
Bellegarde 122 Ig 47.59N 2.26 E
Bellegarde-sur-Valserine 122 Lh 46.06N 5.49 E
Belle Glade 184 Gl 26.41N 80.40W
Belle Ile 110 Ff 47.19N 3.11W
Belle Isle 180 Lf 51.55N 55.20W
Belle Isle, Strait of- 174 Nd 51.35N 56.30W
Bellencombre 124 De 49.42N 1.14 E
Belleplaine 197q Ab 13.15N 59.34W
Belleville [Fr.] 122 Kh 46.06N 4.45 E
Belleville [Il.-U.S.] 186 Lg 38.31N 90.00W
Belleville [Ks.-U.S.] 186 Hg 39.49N 97.38W
Belleville [Ont.-Can.] 180 Jh 44.10N 77.23W
Bellevue [Nb.-U.S.] 186 If 41.09N 95.54W
Bellevue [Wa.-U.S.] 188 Dc 47.37N 122.12W
Belley 122 Li 45.46N 5.41 E
Bellheim 124 Ke 49.12N 8.17 E
Bellingham [Eng.-U.K.] 118 Kf 55.09N 2.16W
Bellingham [Wa.-U.S.] 176 Ge 48.46N 122.29W
Bellingsfors 116 Ef 58.59N 12.15 E
Bellingshausen 222 Re 62.12S 58.56W
Bellingshausen Ice Shelf 222 Ce 71.00S 89.00W
Bellingshausen Sea (EN) 222 Pf 71.00S 85.00W
Bellinzona 128 Dd 46.11N 9.02 E
Bello 202 Cb 6.19N 75.34W
Bellocq 204 Bl 35.55S 61.32W
Bellona, Récifs- 208 Gg 21.00S 159.00 E
Bellona Island 214 Fj 11.17S 159.47 E
Bellot Strait 180 Ib 72.00N 94.30W
Bellow Falls 184 Kd 43.08N 72.28W
Bell Peninsula 180 Jd 63.45N 81.30W
Bell River 180 Jg 49.49N 77.39W
Bell Rock → Inchcape 118 Ke 56.26N 2.24W
Bellsund 179 Nc 77.39N 14.15 E
Belluno 128 Gd 46.09N 12.13 E
Bellville 172 Bf 33.53S 18.36 E
Bell Ville 206 Hd 32.37S 62.42W
Belmond 186 Je 42.51N 93.37W
Belmont 184 Hd 42.14N 78.02W
Belmonte [Braz.] 202 Kg 15.51S 38.54W
Belmonte [Port.] 126 Ed 40.21N 7.21W
Belmonte [Sp.] 126 Je 39.34N 2.42W
Belmopan 176 Kh 17.15N 88.46W
Belo 172 Gd 20.44S 44.00 E
Beloeil 124 Fd 50.35N 3.43 E
Belogorsk [R.S.F.S.R.] 142 Od 50.57N 128.25 E
Belogorsk [R.S.F.S.R.] 138 De 55.02N 88.28 E
Belogorsk [Ukr.-U.S.S.R.] 132 Ij 45.01N 34.33 E
Belogradčik 130 Ff 43.38N 22.41 E
Belogradčiški prohod 130 Ff 43.38N 22.28 E
Belo Horizonte 200 Lg 19.55S 43.56W
Beloit [Ks.-U.S.] 186 Gg 39.28N 98.06W
Beloit [Wi.-U.S.] 182 Jc 42.31N 89.02W
Belojarovo 138 Hf 51.35N 128.55 E
Belojarski 136 Gc 63.40N 66.45 E
Beloje more = White Sea (EN) 110 Kb 66.00N 44.00 E
Beloje ozero = White Lake (EN) 110 Jc 60.11N 37.35 E
Belokany 132 Oi 41.43N 46.28 E
Belomorsk 112 Jc 64.29N 34.43 E
Belomorsko-Baltijski kanal = White Sea-Baltic Canal (EN) 110 Jc 63.30N 34.48 E
Belomorsko-Kulojskoje plato 114 Jd 65.20N 41.50 E
Beloozersk 132 Dc 52.28N 25.13 E
Belopolje 136 De 51.09N 34.18 E
Belorečensk 132 Kg 44.43N 39.52 E
Beloreck 136 Fe 53.58N 58.24 E
Belorusskaja grjada 132 Ec 53.50N 27.00 E
Belorusskaja Sovetskaja Socialističeskaja Respublika [2] 136 Ce 53.50N 28.00 E
Belorusskaja SSR/Belaruskaja Sovetskaja Socialistyčnaja Respublika [2] 136 Ce 53.50N 28.00 E
Belorusskaja SSR = Byelorussian SSR (EN) [2] 136 Ce 53.50N 28.00 E
Belo-sur-Mer 172 Gd 20.44S 44.00 E
Belo-sur-Tsiribihina 172 Gc 19.39S 44.32 E
Belot, Lac- 180 Ec 66.50N 126.20W
Belo-Tsiribihina 172 Gc 19.39S 44.32 E
Belovežskaja Pušča, zapovednik- 120 Ud 52.45N 24.15 E
Belovo 138 Df 54.25N 86.18 E
Belovodsk 132 Ke 49.10N 39.33 E
Belovodskoe 135 Jc 42.47N 74.13 E
Belozersk 136 Dd 60.03N 37.48 E
Belper 124 Aa 53.02N 1.28W
Belted Range 188 Gh 37.25N 116.10W
Belton [Mo.-U.S.] 186 Ig 38.49N 94.32W
Belton [Tx.-U.S.] 186 Hk 31.04N 97.28W
Belton Lake 186 Hk 31.08N 97.32W
Belturbet/Beal Tairbirt 118 Fg 54.06N 7.26W
Beluha, gora- 140 Ke 49.48N 86.35 E
Belvedere Marittimo 128 Jk 39.37N 15.52 E
Belvidere 186 Le 42.15N 88.50W
Bely 114 Hi 55.50N 32.58 E
Bely, Island (EN) = Bely, ostrov- 140 Jb 73.10N 70.45 E
Bely, ostrov- = Bely, Island (EN) 140 Jb 73.10N 70.45 E
Belyando River 212 Jd 21.38S 146.50 E
Bely Čeremoš 130 Ia 48.06N 25.04 E
Bely Jar 138 De 58.26N 85.03 E
Belyje Berega 132 Ic 53.12N 34.42 E
Belz 132 Dd 50.23N 24.03 E
Bełżec 120 Tf 50.24N 23.26 E
Belzoni 186 Kj 33.11N 90.29W
Bełżyce 120 Se 51.11N 22.18 E
Bemaraha, Plateau de- 158 Lj 19.00S 45.15 E
Bembe 170 Bd 7.02S 14.18 E
Bembéréké 166 Fc 10.13N 2.40 E
Bembézar 126 Gg 37.45N 5.13W
Bembridge 124 Ad 50.41N 1.05W
Bemidji 182 Ib 47.29N 94.53W
Ben 146 Nf 32.32N 50.45 E
Benāb 144 Gb 37.18N 46.05 E
Benabarre / Benavarri 126 Mb 42.07N 0.29 E
Benaco → Garda, Lago di- 110 Hf 45.35N 10.35 E
Bena Dibele 170 Dc 4.07S 22.50 E
Benaize 122 Hh 46.34N 1.04 E
Benalla 212 Jg 36.33S 145.59 E
Benares → Vārānasi 142 Kg 25.20N 83.00 E
Benasc/Benasque 126 Mb 42.36N 0.32 E
Benasque/Benasc 126 Mb 42.36N 0.32 E
Benavarri / Benabarre 126 Mb 42.07N 0.29 E
Benavente 126 Gc 42.00N 5.41W
Benbecula 118 Fd 57.27N 7.20W
Bencheng → Luannan 154 Ee 39.30N 118.42 E
Ben-Chicao, Col de- 126 Oh 36.12N 2.51 E
Bend 182 Cc 44.03N 121.19W
Bendaja 166 Cd 7.10N 11.15W
Bendel [2] 166 Gd 6.00N 5.50 E
Bendela 170 Cc 3.18S 17.36 E
Bender Bäyla 160 Mh 9.30N 50.30 E
Bendersiyada 168 Hc 11.14N 48.57 E
Bendery 136 Cf 46.48N 29.22 E
Bendigo 210 Fh 36.46S 144.17 E
Bendorf 124 Jd 50.26N 7.34 E
Bēne/Bene 116 Jh 56.28N 23.01 E
Bene/Bēne 116 Jh 56.28N 23.01 E
Bénéna 166 Ec 13.06N 4.22W
Benepú, Rada- 221d Ac 27.10S 109.25W
Benešov 120 Kg 49.47N 14.40 E
Benevento 128 Ii 41.08N 14.45 E
Bengal 140 Kg 24.00N 90.00 E
Bengal, Bay of- (EN) 140 Kh 15.00N 90.00 E
Bengamisa 170 Eb 0.57N 25.10 E
Bengbis 166 He 3.27N 12.27 E
Bengbu 142 Nf 32.47N 117.23 E
Benghazi (EN) = Banghāzī 160 Je 32.07N 20.04 E
Benghazi (EN) = Banghāzī [3] 164 Dd 27.00N 20.30 E
Beng He 154 Eg 35.04N 118.22 E
Benghisa Point 128 Io 35.50N 14.35 E
Bengkalis 150 Df 1.28N 102.08 E
Bengkulu 142 Mj 3.48S 102.16 E
Bengkulu [3] 150 Dg 3.48S 102.16 E
Bengo [3] 170 Bd 8.30S 13.40 E
Bengo, Baia do- 158 Ii 8.43S 13.21 E
Bengough 188 Mb 49.24N 105.08W
Bengtsfors 114 Cg 59.02N 12.13 E
Benguela 160 Ij 12.35S 13.26 E
Benguela [3] 170 Be 12.00S 15.00 E
Benguerir 162 Fc 32.14N 7.57W
Benguérua, Ilha- 172 Fd 21.53S 35.26 E
Bengue Viejo 194 Ce 17.05N 89.08W
Bengut, Cap- 126 Hb 36.55N 3.54 E
Beni 160 Jh 0.30N 29.28 E
Beni [3] 202 Ef 14.00S 65.30W
Beni, Río- 198 Jg 10.23S 65.24W
Beni Abbes 162 Gc 30.08N 2.10W
Beni Boufrah 126 Hi 35.05N 4.18W
Benicarló 126 Md 40.25N 0.26 E
Benicasim / Benicàssim 126 Md 40.03N 0.04 E
Benicàssim / Benicasim 126 Md 40.03N 0.04 E
Beni Chougran, Monts des- 126 Mi 35.30N 0.15 E
Benidorm 126 Lf 38.32N 0.08W
Beni Enzar 126 Ji 35.14N 2.57W
Beni Haoua 126 Nh 36.32N 1.34 E
Beni Mellal 160 Ge 32.20N 6.21W
Beni Mellal [3] 162 Fc 32.30N 6.30W
Benin 166 Gd 5.45N 5.04 E
Bénin (Dahomey) [1] 160 Hh 9.30N 2.15 E
Benin, Bight of- 158 Hh 5.30N 4.00 E
Benin City 160 Hh 6.20N 5.38 E
Beni Ounif 162 Gc 32.03N 1.15W
Benisa / Benissa 126 Mf 38.43N 0.03 E
Beni Saf 126 Ki 35.19N 1.23W
Benisheikh 166 Hc 11.48N 12.29 E
Benissa / Benisa 126 Mf 38.43N 0.03 E
Benito Juárez 192 Mi 17.50N 92.32W
Benito Juárez, Presa- 192 Li 16.27N 95.30W
Benjamen Island 172b Bb 5.27S 53.21 E
Benjamin 186 Gj 33.35N 99.48W
Benjamin Aceval 204 Dg 24.58S 57.34W
Benjamin Constant 200 If 4.22S 70.02W
Benjamin Hill 192 Db 30.10N 111.10W
Benkei-Misaki 156a Bb 42.50N 140.11 E
Benkelman 186 Ff 40.03N 101.32W
Benkovac 128 Jf 44.02N 15.37 E
Ben Mehidi 126 Bn 36.46N 7.54 E
Bennett, Lake- 212 Gd 23.50S 131.00 E
Bennetta, ostrov- 138 Ja 76.45N 149.00 E
Benneydale 218 Fc 38.31S 175.21 E
Bennichab 162 Df 19.26N 15.21W
Bennington 184 Kd 42.53N 73.12W
Benom 150 Df 3.50N 102.06 E
Benoni 172 Jk 26.19S 28.27 E
Bénoué = Benue (EN) 158 Hh 7.48N 6.46 E
Benoy 168 Bd 8.59N 16.19 E
Benrath 124 Ic 51.10N 6.52 E
Bensekrane 126 Ki 35.04N 1.13W
Bensheim 120 Eg 49.41N 8.37 E
Ben Slimane 162 Fc 33.37N 7.07W
Benson [Az.-U.S.] 188 Jk 31.58N 110.18W

Index Symbols

[1] Independent Nation
[2] State, Region
[3] District, County
[4] Municipality
[5] Colony, Dependency
Continent
Physical Region
Historical or Cultural Region
Mount, Mountain
Volcano
Hill
Mountains, Mountain Range
Hills, Escarpment
Plateau, Upland
Pass, Gap
Plain, Lowland
Delta
Salt Flat
Valley, Canyon
Crater, Cave
Karst Features
Depression
Polder
Desert, Dunes
Forest, Woods
Heath, Steppe
Oasis
Cape, Point
Coast, Beach
Cliff
Peninsula
Isthmus
Sandbank
Island
Atoll
Rock, Reef
Islands, Archipelago
Rocks, Reefs
Coral Reef
Well, Spring
Geyser
River, Stream
Waterfall, Rapids
River Mouth, Estuary
Lake
Salt Lake
Intermittent Lake
Reservoir
Swamp, Pond
Canal
Glacier
Ice Shelf, Pack Ice
Ocean
Sea
Gulf, Bay
Strait, Fjord
Lagoon
Bank
Seamount
Tablemount
Ridge
Shelf
Basin
Escarpment, Sea Scarp
Fracture
Trench, Abyss
National Park, Reserve
Point of Interest
Recreation Site
Cave, Cavern
Historic Site
Ruins
Wall, Walls
Church, Abbey
Temple
Scientific Station
Railway station
Airport
Port
Military installation
Lighthouse
Mine
Tunnel
Dam, Bridge

Benson [Mn.-U.S.] 186 Id 45.19N 95.36W
Benson Point 220g Ab 1.56N 157.30W
Bent 144 Id 26.17N 59.31 E
Benteng [Indon.] 150 Hg 0.24S 121.59 E
Benteng [Indon.] 150 Hh 6.08N 120.27 E
Bentheim 120 Dd 52.19N 7.10 E
Bentiaba 170 Be 14.15S 12.24 E
Bentiaba 170 Be 14.29S 12.50 E
Bentinck 148 Jf 11.45N 98.03 E
Bentinck Island 212 Hc 17.05S 139.30 E
Bentiu 168 Dd 9.14N 29.50 E
Bento Gonçalves 206 Jc 29.10S 51.31W
Bento Gomes, Rio- 204 Dc 16.40S 57.12W
Benton [Ar.-U.S.] 186 Ji 34.34N 92.35W
Benton [Il.-U.S.] 186 Lg 38.01N 88.55W
Bentong 150 Df 3.32N 101.55 E
Benton Harbor 184 Dd 42.07N 86.27W
Bentonville 186 Ih 36.22N 94.13W
Ben Tre 148 Lf 10.14N 106.23 E
Benue [2] 166 Gd 7.15N 8.20 E
Benue 158 Hh 7.48N 6.46 E
Benue (EN)=Bénoué 158 Hh 7.48N 6.46 E
Benwee Head/An Bhinn Bhui 118 Dg 54.21N 9.48W
Benxi 142 Oe 41.16N 123.48 E
Bény-Bocage, Le- 124 Bf 48.56N 0.50W
Beo 150 If 4.15N 126.48 E
Beograd = Belgrade (EN) 112 Ig 44.50N 20.30 E
Beograd-Krnjača 130 De 44.52N 20.28 E
Beograd-Zemun 130 De 44.53N 20.25 E
Béoumi 166 Dd 7.40N 5.34W
Beppu 152 Ne 33.17N 131.30 E
Beppu-Wan 156 Be 33.20N 131.35 E
Bequia Head 197n Ba 13.03N 61.12W
Bequia Island 196 Ff 13.01N 61.13W
Berabevú 204 Bk 33.20S 61.52W
Beraketa 172 Hd 24.11S 45.42 E
Berati 130 Ci 40.42N 19.57 E
Beratus, Gunung- 150 Gg 1.02S 116.20 E
Berau, Teluk-=McCluer Gulf (EN) 150 Jg 2.30S 132.30 E
Berberá 160 Lg 10.25N 45.02 E
Berbérati 160 Ih 4.16N 15.47 E
Berberia, Cabo- / Barbaria, Cap de- 126 Nf 38.38N 1.23 E
Berbice River 202 Gb 6.17N 57.32W
Berca 130 Jd 45.17N 26.41 E
Berchères-sur-Vesgre 124 Df 48.51N 1.33 E
Berchtesgaden 120 Ii 47.38N 13.00 E
Berck 122 Hd 50.24N 1.36 E
Berck-Berck-Plage 124 Dd 50.24N 1.34 E
Berda 132 Jf 46.47N 36.52 E
Berdâle 168 Hd 7.04N 47.51 E
Berdičev 136 Cf 49.53N 28.36 E
Berdigestjah 138 Hd 62.03N 126.50 E
Berdjansk 136 Df 46.43N 36.48 E
Berdsk 138 Df 54.47N 83.05 E
Beregomet 130 Ia 48.10N 25.24 E
Beregovo 136 Cf 48.13N 22.41 E
Bereku 170 Gc 4.27S 35.44 E
Berekua 196 Fe 15.14N 61.19W
Berekum 166 Ed 7.27N 2.35W
Berens 180 Hf 52.21N 97.01W
Berens River 180 Hf 52.22N 97.02W
Beresford 186 He 43.05N 96.47W
Berestečko 120 Vf 50.16N 25.14 E
Bereşti 130 Kc 46.06N 27.53 E
Berettyó 130 Ec 46.59N 21.07 E
Berettyóújfalu 120 Ri 47.13N 21.33 E
Bereza 136 Ce 52.33N 24.58 E
Berezan 132 Gd 50.19N 31.31 E
Berežany 132 De 49.29N 25.00 E
Berezina [Bye.-U.S.S.R.] 132 Dc 53.48N 25.59 E
Berezina [U.S.S.R.] 110 Je 52.33N 30.14 E
Berezino [Bye.-U.S.S.R.] 132 Fc 53.51N 29.00 E
Berezino [Bye.-U.S.S.R.] 116 Mj 54.55N 28.16 E
Berezino [Ukr.-U.S.S.R.] 130 Mc 46.16N 29.11 E
Bereznegovatoje 132 Hf 47.20N 32.49 E
Bereznik 136 Ec 62.53N 42.42 E
Berezniki 112 Ld 59.24N 56.46 E
Berezno 132 Ed 51.01N 26.45 E
Berezovka [Bye.-U.S.S.R.] 120 Vc 53.40N 25.37 E
Berezovka [R.S.F.S.R.] 134 Hd 64.59N 56.29 E
Berezovka [Ukr.-U.S.S.R.] 136 Df 47.12N 30.56 E
Berezovka Višerka 134 Hf 60.55N 56.50 E
Berezovo 136 Gc 63.58N 65.00 E
Berezovski [R.S.F.S.R.] 138 De 55.39N 86.16 E
Berezovski [R.S.F.S.R.] 134 Jh 56.55N 60.50 E
Berezovy 138 If 51.41N 135.52 E
Berga [Sp.] 126 Nb 42.06N 1.51 E
Berga [Swe.] 116 Gg 57.13N 16.02 E
Bergama 144 Cb 39.07N 27.10 E
Bergamo 128 De 45.41N 9.43 E
Bergantiños 126 Da 43.20N 8.45W
Bergara / Vergara 126 Ja 43.07N 2.25W
Bergby 114 Df 60.56N 17.02 E
Bergen [Ger.] 120 Jb 54.25N 13.26 E
Bergen [Neth.] 124 Gb 52.40N 4.42 E
Bergen [Nor.] 112 Gc 60.23N 5.20 E
Bergen/Mons 122 Jd 50.27N 3.56 E
Bergen aan Zee, Bergen- 124 Gb 52.40N 4.38 E
Bergen-Bergen aan Zee 124 Gb 52.40N 4.38 E
Bergen op Zoom 122 Kc 51.30N 4.17 E
Bergerac 122 Gj 44.51N 0.29 E
Bergeyk 124 Hc 51.19N 5.22 E
Bergh 124 Ic 51.53N 6.16 E
Bergheim 120 Cf 50.58N 6.39 E
Bergh- 's Heerenberg 124 Ic 51.53N 6.16 E
Bergisches Land 120 De 51.15N 7.10 E
Bergisch Gladbach 120 Df 50.59N 7.08 E
Bergkvara 116 Gh 56.23N 16.05 E
Bergneustadt 124 Jc 51.02N 7.39 E
Bergö 116 Ib 62.55N 21.10 E
Bergsjö 114 Df 61.59N 17.04 E
Bergslagen 116 Fd 60.05N 14.30 E
Bergstraße 124 Ke 49.40N 8.40 E
Bergues 124 Ed 50.58N 2.26 E
Bergum, Tietjerksteradeel- 124 Ha 53.12N 6.00 E
Bergviken 116 Gc 61.10N 16.45 E
Bergville 172 De 28.52S 29.18 E
Berh 152 Jb 47.45N 111.07 E
Berhala, Selat- 150 Dg 0.48S 104.25 E
Berici, Monti- 128 Fe 45.26N 11.31 E
Berīkān 146 Nh 28.17N 51.14 E
Berikulski 138 De 55.32N 88.08 E
Beringa, ostrov- = Bering Island (EN) 138 Lf 55.00N 166.10 E
Beringen 124 Hc 51.03N 5.13 E
Bering Glacier 178 Kd 60.15N 143.30W
Bering Island (EN) = Beringa, ostrov- 138 Lf 55.00N 166.10 E
Beringovo more = Bering Sea (EN) 174 Bd 60.00N 175.00W
Beringovski 142 Tc 63.07N 179.19 E
Bering proliv = Bering Strait (EN) 174 Cc 65.30N 169.00W
Bering Sea 174 Bd 60.00N 175.00W
Bering Sea (EN) = Beringovo more 174 Bd 60.00N 175.00W
Bering Strait 174 Cc 65.30N 169.00W
Bering Strait (EN) = Bering proliv 174 Cc 65.30N 169.00W
Berislav 132 Hf 46.51N 33.29 E
Berisso 204 Dl 34.52S 57.53W
Berit Dağı 146 Gc 38.01N 36.52 E
Berizak 146 Qi 26.06N 57.15 E
Berja 126 Jh 36.51N 2.57W
Berkåk 114 Be 62.50N 10.00 E
Berkane 162 Gc 34.56N 2.20W
Berkel 120 Cd 52.09N 6.12 E
Berkeley 182 Cd 37.57N 122.18W
Berkhamsted 124 Bc 51.45N 0.33W
Berkner Island 222 Rf 79.30S 49.30W
Berkovica 130 Gf 43.14N 23.07 E
Berks 118 Lj 51.15N 1.20W
Berkshire [3] 118 Lj 51.30N 1.10W
Berkshire Downs 118 Lj 51.35N 1.25W
Berkshire Hills 184 Kd 42.20N 73.10W
Berlaimont 124 Fd 50.12N 3.49 E
Berlanga de Duero 126 Jc 41.28N 2.51W
Berlengas, Ilhas- 126 Ce 39.25N 9.30W
Berlevåg 114 Ga 70.51N 29.06 E
Berlin [N.H.-U.S.] 182 Mc 44.29N 71.10W
Berlin [Germany] 112 He 52.31N 13.24 E
Berlin (Ost) = Berlin 112 He 52.31N 13.24 E
Berlin (West) = Berlin 112 He 52.31N 13.24 E
Berlin-Pankow 120 Jd 52.34N 13.24 E
Bermeja, Sierra- 126 Gh 36.30N 5.15W
Bermejillo 190 Dc 25.53N 103.37W
Bermejito, Río- 204 Bg 25.39S 60.11W
Bermejo, Isla- 204 An 39.01S 62.01W
Bermejo, Paso del- 198 Ii 32.50S 70.05W
Bermejo, Río- [Arg.] 198 Ji 31.52S 67.22W
Bermejo, Río- [S.Amer.] 198 Kh 26.52S 58.23W
Bermen, Lac- 180 Kf 53.35N 68.55W
Bermeo 126 Ja 43.26N 2.43W
Bermillo de Sayago 126 Fc 41.22N 6.06W
Bermuda [5] 176 Mf 32.20N 64.45W
Bermuda Islands 174 Mf 32.20N 64.45W
Bermuda Rise (EN) 174 Mf 32.30N 65.00W
Bern/Berne 112 Gf 46.55N 7.30 E
Bern / Berne [2] 128 Bd 46.55N 7.40 E
Bernalda 128 Kj 40.24N 16.41 E
Bernalillo 186 Ci 35.18N 106.33W
Bernard Islands 220d Bb 7.18N 151.32 E
Bernardo de Irigoyen 204 Bk 32.10S 61.09W
Bernardo do Irigoyen 206 Jc 26.15S 53.39W
Bernasconi 206 He 37.54S 63.43W
Bernau bei Berlin 120 Jd 52.40N 13.35 E
Bernaville 124 Ed 50.08N 2.10 E
Bernay 122 Ge 49.06N 0.36 E
Bernburg 120 He 51.48N 11.44 E
Berndorf 128 Kc 47.57N 16.06 E
Berne [Ger.] 124 Ka 53.11N 8.29 E
Berne [In.-U.S.] 184 Ee 40.39N 84.57W
Berne/Bern 112 Gf 46.55N 7.30 E
Berne / Bern [2] 128 Bd 46.55N 7.40 E
Berner Alpen = Bernese Alps (EN) 128 Bd 46.25N 7.30 E
Berneray 118 Fd 57.43N 7.15W
Bernese Alps (EN) = Berner Alpen 128 Bd 46.25N 7.30 E
Bernesga 126 Gb 42.28N 5.31W
Bernesq 124 Be 49.16N 0.56W
Bernier Bay 180 Ib 71.08N 88.00W
Bernier Island 212 Cd 24.50S 113.10 E
Bernina 128 Dd 46.23N 9.54 E
Bernina 128 Ed 46.25N 10.01 E
Bernina, Piz- 128 Dd 46.23N 9.54 E
Berninapaß 128 Ed 46.25N 10.01 E
Bernissart 124 Fd 50.28N 3.38 E
Bernkastel-Kues 120 Dg 49.55N 7.04 E
Bernstorffs Isfjord 179 Hf 63.10N 40.45W
Berón de Astrada 204 Dh 27.33S 57.32W
Beroroha 172 Hd 21.39S 45.10 E
Béroubouay 166 Fc 10.32N 2.44 E
Beroun 120 Kg 49.58N 14.04 E
Berounka 120 Kg 50.00N 14.24 E
Berovo 130 Fh 41.43N 22.51 E
Berre, Étang de- 122 Lk 43.27N 5.08 E
Berriane 162 Hc 32.50N 3.46 E
Berrouaghia 126 Oh 36.08N 2.55 E
Berry 122 Hh 47.00N 2.00 E
Berry-au-Bac 124 Fe 49.24N 3.54 E
Berryessa, Lake- 188 Dg 38.37N 122.16W
Berry Head 118 Jk 50.24N 3.29W
Berry Islands 190 Ic 25.34N 77.45W
Berry River 188 Ja 50.50N 111.36W
Beršad 136 Cf 48.23N 29.33 E
Berseba 172 Be 26.01S 17.41 E
Bersenbrück 124 Jb 52.33N 7.56 E
Berthierville 184 Kb 46.05N 73.11W
Bertincourt 124 Ed 50.05N 2.59 E
Bertogne 124 Hd 50.05N 5.40 E
Bertolinia 202 Je 7.38S 43.57W
Bertoua 160 Ih 4.35N 13.41 E
Bertraghboy Bay 118 Dh 53.23N 9.50W
Bertrix 124 He 49.51N 5.15 E
Beru Island 208 Ie 1.20S 176.00 E
Berwick-upon-Tweed 118 Lf 55.46N 2.00W
Berwyn 118 Ji 52.53N 3.24W
Besalampy 172 Gc 16.44S 44.24 E
Besançon 112 Gf 47.15N 6.02 E
Besar, Gunung- 150 Gg 1.25S 115.39 E
Besbre 122 Jh 46.33N 3.44 E
Besed 132 Gc 52.38N 31.11 E
Besikama 150 Hh 9.36S 124.57 E
Beskid Mountains (EN) 110 Hf 49.40N 20.00 E
Beskid Niski 120 Rg 49.20N 21.30 E
Beskid Średni 120 Pg 49.45N 19.20 E
Beskid Wysoki 120 Pg 49.32N 20.00 E
Beskidy Wschodnie 120 Sg 49.20N 22.30 E
Beskidy Zachodnie 120 Pg 49.30N 19.30 E
Beskol 135 Ma 46.06N 81.01 E
Beslan 136 Eg 43.10N 44.35 E
Besna Kobila 130 Fg 42.32N 22.14 E
Besni 146 Gd 37.41N 37.52 E
Besparmak Dağ 130 Kl 37.30N 27.35 E
Bessao 168 Bd 7.53N 15.59 E
Bessarabia (EN) = Bessarabija 130 Lb 47.00N 28.30 E
Bessarabija = Bessarabia (EN) 130 Lb 47.00N 28.30 E
Bessarabka 132 Ff 46.20N 28.59 E
Bessèges 122 Kj 44.17N 4.06 E
Bessemer 182 Je 33.25N 86.57W
Bessin 122 Fe 49.10N 1.00W
Bessines-sur-Gartempe 122 Hh 46.06N 1.22 E
Besšoki, gora- 122 Rh 43.57N 52.30 E
Best 124 Hc 51.30N 5.24 E
Bestjah [R.S.F.S.R.] 138 Hc 66.00N 123.35 E
Bestjah [R.S.F.S.R.] 138 Hd 61.17N 128.50 E
Bestobe 136 He 52.30N 73.05 E
Bestwig 124 Kc 51.22N 8.24 E
Betafo 172 Hc 19.49S 46.50 E
Betanzos [Bol.] 202 Eg 19.34S 65.27W
Betanzos [Sp.] 126 Da 43.17N 8.12W
Betanzos, Ría de- 126 Da 43.23N 8.15W
Bétaré Oya 166 Hd 5.36N 14.05 E
Bétérou 166 Fd 9.12N 2.16 E
Beteta 126 Jd 40.34N 2.04W
Bethal 172 De 26.27S 29.28 E
Bethanien 160 Ik 26.32S 17.11 E
Bethanien [3] 172 Be 26.30S 17.00 E
Bethany [Mo.-U.S.] 186 If 40.16N 94.02W
Bethany [Ok.-U.S.] 186 Hi 35.31N 97.38W
Bethel 176 Cc 60.48N 161.46W
Béthéniville 124 Ge 49.18N 4.22 E
Bethlehem [Pa.-U.S.] 184 Je 40.36N 75.22W
Bethlehem [S.Afr.] 160 Jk 28.15S 28.15 E
Bethlehem (EN)=Bayt Laḥm 146 Fg 31.43N 35.12 E
Bethulie 172 Df 30.32S 25.59 E
Béthune 122 Id 50.32N 2.38 E
Béthune 122 He 49.53N 1.09 E
Béticas, Cordilleras- 110 Fh 37.35N 3.30W
Betioky 172 Gd 23.42S 44.22 E
Betong [Mala.] 150 Ff 1.26N 111.30 E
Betong [Thai.] 148 Kg 5.45N 101.05 E
Betor 168 Fc 11.37N 39.00 E
Bétou 170 Cb 3.03N 18.31 E
Betpak-Dala 140 Ie 46.00N 70.00 E
Betroka 172 Hd 23.15S 46.05 E
Bet She'an 146 Ff 32.30N 35.30 E
Betsiamites, Rivière- 180 Kg 48.56N 68.38W
Betsiboka 158 Lj 16.03S 46.36 E
Bette, Picco- 158 If 22.00N 19.12 E
Bettembourg/Bettemburg 124 Ie 49.31N 6.06 E
Bettemburg/Bettembourg 124 Ie 49.31N 6.06 E
Bettendorf 186 Kf 41.32N 90.30W
Bettles Field 178 Ic 66.53N 151.51W
Bettna 116 Gf 58.55N 16.38 E
Bettola 128 Df 44.47N 9.36 E
Betül 148 Fd 21.55N 77.54 E
Betuwe 122 Lc 51.55N 5.30 E
Betwa 148 Hc 25.55N 80.12 E
Betz 124 Ee 49.09N 2.57 E
Betzdorf 120 Df 50.47N 7.53 E
Beulah 184 Dc 44.38N 86.06W
Beult 124 Cc 51.13N 0.26 E
Beuvron 122 Hg 47.29N 1.15 E
Beuzeville 124 Ce 49.20N 0.21 E
Beveland 122 Jc 51.30N 3.40 E
Beveren 124 Gc 51.13N 4.15 E
Beveridge Reef 208 Kg 20.00S 168.00W
Beverley [Austl.] 212 Df 32.06S 116.56 E
Beverley [Eng.-U.K.] 118 Mh 53.51N 0.26W
Beverwijk 122 Kb 52.28N 4.40 E
Bewsher, Mount- 222 Ff 70.54S 65.28 E
Bexhill 118 Nk 50.50N 0.29 E
Bexley, London- 124 Cc 51.26N 0.09 E
Beyağaç 130 Ll 37.13N 28.57 E
Beyānlū 146 Ld 36.02N 47.53 E
Bey Dağı 146 Hc 38.15N 38.22 E
Bey Dağları 144 Db 36.40N 30.15 E
Beykoz 146 Cb 41.08N 29.05 E
Beyla 166 Dd 8.41N 8.38W
Beyoğlu, İstanbul- 130 Lh 41.02N 28.59 E
Beyoneisu-Retsugan 152 Oe 31.55N 139.55 E
Beypazari 146 Db 40.10N 31.55 E
Beyra 168 Hd 6.57N 47.19 E
Beyram 146 Oi 27.26N 53.31 E
Beyşehir 146 Dd 37.41N 31.43 E
Beyşehir Gölü 146 Dd 37.40N 31.30 E
Bezaha 172 Gd 23.29S 44.30 E
Bežanickaja vozvyšennost 114 Gh 56.45N 29.30 E
Bežanicy 114 Gh 56.58N 29.57 E
Bezdan 130 Bd 45.51N 18.56 E
Bezdež 120 Vd 52.18N 25.20 E
Bezděz 120 Kf 50.32N 14.43 E
Bežeck 136 Dd 57.50N 36.41 E
Bezenčuk 114 Lj 53.01N 49.24 E
Bezerra, Rio- 204 Ia 13.16S 47.33W
Bezerros 202 Ke 8.14S 35.45W
Béziers 122 Jk 43.21N 3.15 E
Bezmein 136 Fh 38.05N 58.12 E
Bežta 136 Eg 42.08N 46.08 E
Bhadrak 148 Hd 21.04N 86.30 E
Bhadrāvati 148 Ff 13.52N 75.43 E
Bhāgalpur 142 Kg 25.15N 87.00 E
Bhaironghati 148 Fb 31.01N 78.53 E
Bhakkar 148 Eb 31.38N 71.04 E
Bhamo 148 Jd 24.16N 97.14 E
Bhandāra 148 Fd 21.10N 79.39 E
Bhanjan 148 Gc 25.47N 83.36 E
Bhārat Juktarashtra=India (EN) [1] 142 Jh 20.00N 77.00 E
Bharatpur 148 Fc 27.13N 77.29 E
Bharūch 148 Ed 21.46N 72.54 E
Bhatinda → Bathinda 148 Eb 30.12N 74.57 E
Bhātpāra 148 Hd 22.52N 88.24 E
Bhavnagar 142 Jg 21.46N 72.09 E
Bhera 148 Eb 32.29N 72.55 E
Bheri 148 Gc 28.44N 81.16 E
Bhikhna-Thori 148 Gc 27.20N 84.38 E
Bhīlwāra 148 Ec 25.21N 74.38 E
Bhīma 140 Jh 16.25N 77.17 E
Bhind 148 Fc 26.34N 78.48 E
Bhiwāni 148 Fc 28.47N 76.08 E
Bhopāl 142 Jg 23.16N 77.24 E
Bhubaneshwar 142 Kg 20.14N 85.50 E
Bhuj 148 Dd 23.16N 69.40 E
Bhusāwal 148 Fd 21.03N 75.46 E
Bhutan (Druk-Yul) [1] 142 Lg 27.30N 90.30 E
Bia 166 Ed 5.21N 3.11W
Bia, Phou- 140 Mh 18.36N 103.01 E
Biá, Rio- 202 Ed 3.28S 67.23W
Biābān, Kūh-e- 146 Qi 26.30N 57.25 E
Biabou 197n Ba 13.12N 61.09W
Biafra 158 Hh 5.00N 7.30 E
Biafra, Bight of- 158 Hh 3.20N 9.20 E
Biak 150 Kg 1.10S 136.06 E
Biak, Pulau- 208 Ee 1.00S 136.00 E
Biała Piska 120 Sc 53.37N 22.04 E
Biała Podlaska 120 Td 52.02N 23.06 E
Biała Podlaska [2] 120 Td 52.00N 23.05 E
Białobrzegi 120 Qe 51.40N 20.57 E
Białogard 120 Lb 54.01N 16.00 E
Białostocka, Wysoczyzna- 120 Tc 53.23N 23.10 E
Białowieża 120 Td 52.41N 23.50 E
Białystok 112 Ie 53.09N 23.09 E
Białystok [2] 120 Tc 53.10N 23.10 E
Biancavilla 128 Im 37.38N 14.52 E
Bianco 128 Kl 38.05N 16.09 E
Bianco, Monte- / Blanc, Mont- 110 Gf 45.50N 6.52 E
Biankouma 166 Dd 7.44N 7.37W
Biankouma [3] 166 Dd 7.43N 7.40W
Bianzhuang → Cangshan 154 Eg 34.51N 118.03 E
Biaro, Pulau- 150 If 2.05N 125.20 E
Biarritz 122 Ek 43.29N 1.34W
Biasca 128 Cd 46.22N 8.57 E
Bibā 164 Fd 28.55N 30.59 E
Bibai 152 Pc 43.19N 141.52 E
Bibala 170 Be 14.50S 13.30 E
Biban, Chaine des- 126 Qh 36.12N 4.25 E
Bibbiena 128 Fg 43.42N 11.49 E
Biberach an der Riß 120 Fh 48.06N 9.48 E
Bibiani 166 Ed 6.28N 2.20W
Bic 184 Ma 48.22N 68.42W
Bicaj 130 Dh 41.59N 20.25 E
Bicas 204 Ke 21.43S 43.04W
Bicaz 130 Jc 46.55N 26.04 E
Bicaz, Pasul- 130 Ic 46.49N 25.52 E
Bičenekski, pereval- 132 Nj 39.33N 45.48 E
Bicester 118 Lj 51.54N 1.09W
Bichena 168 Fc 10.21N 38.14 E
Bickerton Island 212 Hb 13.45S 136.10 E
Bicske 120 Oi 47.29N 18.38 E
Bičura 138 Ff 50.36N 107.35 E
Bīd 146 Qd 36.33N 57.35 E
Bida 160 Hh 9.05N 6.01 E
Bīdar 148 Fe 17.54N 77.33 E
Bidasoa 126 Ka 43.22N 1.47W
Biddeford 182 Mc 43.30N 70.26W
Bideford 118 Ij 51.01N 4.13W
Bideford Bay → Barnstaple 118 Ij 51.05N 4.20W
Bidon V/Poste Maurice Cortier 162 Ee 22.18N 1.05 E
Bié [3] 170 Ce 13.00S 17.30 E
Bié, Planalto do- 158 Ij 13.00S 17.02 E
Biebrza 120 Sc 53.13N 22.28 E
Biecz 120 Rg 49.44N 21.14 E
Biedenkopf 120 Ef 50.55N 8.32 E
Biei 156a Cb 43.35N 142.28 E
Biel/Bienne 128 Bc 47.10N 7.15 E
Bielefeld 120 Ed 52.02N 8.32 E
Bielefeld-Brackwede 124 Kc 51.59N 8.31 E
Bielefeld-Sennestadt 124 Kc 51.57N 8.35 E
Biella 128 Ce 45.34N 8.03 E
Bielsk 120 Pd 52.40N 19.49 E
Bielsk, Wysoczyzna- 120 Sd 52.35N 23.00 E
Bielsko 120 Og 49.50N 19.00 E
Bielsko-Biała 120 Pg 49.49N 19.02 E
Bielsk Podlaski 120 Td 52.47N 23.12 E
Bien Dong = South China Sea (EN) 140 Ni 10.00N 113.00 E
Bien Hoa 148 Lf 10.57N 106.49 E
Bienne 122 Lh 46.20N 5.38 E
Bienne/Biel 128 Bc 47.10N 7.15 E
Bienvenida 126 Jd 40.30N 2.30W
Bienville, Lac- 180 Ke 55.20N 72.40W
Bierbeek 124 Gd 50.50N 4.46 E
Bieszczady 120 Sg 49.10N 22.35 E
Bièvre 124 He 49.56N 5.01 E
Biferno 128 Ji 41.59N 15.02 E
Bifoum 170 Bc 0.20S 10.23 E
Bifuka 154 Qb 44.29N 142.21 E
Biga 146 Bb 40.13N 27.14 E
Bigadiç 146 Cc 39.23N 28.08 E
Big Bald Mountain 184 Nb 47.37N 66.38W
Big Baldy Mountain 188 Jc 46.58N 110.37W
Big Bay [Mi.-U.S.] 184 Db 46.49N 87.44W
Big Bay [Van.] 219b Cb 15.05S 166.54 E
Big Beaver House 180 If 52.58N 89.57W
Big Belt Mountains 188 Jc 46.40N 111.25W
Big Black River 186 Kj 32.00N 91.05W
Big Blue River 182 Hd 39.11N 96.32W
Big Creek Peak 188 Id 44.28N 113.32W
Big Dry Creek 188 Lc 47.30N 106.19W
Big Falls 186 Jb 48.11N 93.46W
Biggar 180 Gf 52.04N 108.00W
Biggenden 212 Ke 25.30S 152.00 E
Biggleswade 118 Mi 52.05N 0.17W
Big Hatchet Peak 186 Bk 31.37N 108.20W
Big Hole River 188 Id 45.34N 112.20W
Bighorn Basin 182 Fc 44.15N 108.10W
Bighorn Lake 188 Kd 45.08N 108.10W
Bighorn Mountains 174 Ie 44.00N 107.30W
Bighorn River 182 Fb 46.09N 107.28W
Bight, Head of- 212 Gf 31.30S 131.10 E
Big Island 180 Kd 62.43N 70.40W
Big Lake 186 Fk 31.12N 101.28W
Big Lake 184 Nc 45.10N 67.40W
Big Lost River 188 Ie 43.50N 112.44W
Big Muddy Creek 188 Mb 48.08N 104.36W
Big Muddy Lake 188 Mb 49.08N 104.54W
Bignona 166 Bc 12.49N 16.14W
Bigorre 122 Gk 43.06N 0.05 E
Big Porcupine Creek 188 Lc 46.17N 106.47W
Big Quill Lake 180 Hf 51.51N 104.18W
Big Rapids 184 Ed 43.42N 85.29W
Big River 180 Gf 53.50N 107.01W
Big River 180 Fb 72.50N 125.00W
Big Sand Lake 180 He 57.45N 99.45W
Big Sandy 188 Jb 48.11N 110.07W
Big Sandy Creek 186 Eg 38.06N 102.29W
Big Sandy River [Az.-U.S.] 188 Ii 34.19N 113.31W
Big Sandy River [Wy.-U.S.] 188 Kf 41.50N 109.48W
Big Sheep Mountains 188 Mc 47.03N 105.43W
Big Sioux River 182 Hc 42.30N 96.25W
Big Smoky Valley 182 Dd 38.30N 117.15W
Big Snowy Mountains 188 Kc 46.50N 109.30W
Big Spring 176 If 32.15N 101.28W
Big Spruce Knob 184 Gf 38.16N 80.12W
Big Stone Lake 186 Hd 45.25N 96.40W
Big Timber 188 Kd 45.50N 109.57W
Big Trout Lake 180 If 53.45N 90.00W
Biguglia, Étang de- 122a Ba 42.36N 9.29 E
Big Wood Cay 194 Ia 24.21N 77.44W
Big Wood River 188 He 42.52N 114.55W
Bihać 128 Jf 44.49N 15.52 E
Bihār 148 Hc 25.11N 85.31 E
Bihār [3] 148 Hd 25.00N 86.00 E
Biharamulo 170 Fc 2.38S 31.20 E
Bihor [2] 130 Fc 47.00N 22.00 E
Bihoro 152 Pc 43.49N 144.07 E
Bihorului, Munţii- 130 Fc 46.40N 22.45 E
Bija 140 Kd 52.25N 85.05 E
Bijagós, Arquipélago dos- = Bijagos Islands (EN) 158 Fg 11.15N 16.05W
Bijagos Islands (EN) = Bijagós, Arquipélago dos- 158 Fg 11.15N 16.05W
Bijapur 148 Fe 16.50N 75.42 E
Bijār 144 Gb 35.52N 47.36 E
Bijeljina 128 Nf 44.45N 19.13 E
Bijelo Polje 130 Cf 43.02N 19.45 E
Bijiang (Zhiziluo) 152 Gf 26.39N 99.00 E
Bijie 152 If 27.15N 105.16 E
Bijlikol, ozero- 135 Hc 43.05N 70.40 E
Bijou Creek 186 Ef 40.17N 103.52W
Bijoutier Island 172b Bb 7.04S 52.45 E
Bijsk 142 Kd 52.34N 85.15 E
Bikāner 142 Jg 28.01N 73.18 E
Bikar Atoll 208 Ic 12.15N 170.06 E
Bikeqi 154 Ad 40.45N 111.17 E
Bikin 138 Ig 46.51N 134.02 E
Bikin 138 Ig 46.43N 134.02 E
Bikini Atoll 208 Hc 11.35N 165.23 E
Bikoro 160 Ii 0.45S 18.07 E
Bilād Ghāmid 164 Hf 19.58N 41.38 E
Bilād Zahrān 164 He 20.15N 41.15 E
Bilāspur 142 Kg 22.03N 82.10 E
Bilate 168 Fd 6.34N 38.01 E
Bilauktaung Range 140 Lh 13.00N 99.00 E
Bilbao 112 Fg 43.15N 2.58W
Bilbays 164 Fc 30.25N 31.34 E
Bileća 128 Mh 42.53N 18.26 E
Bilecik 144 Ca 40.09N 29.59 E
Bilehsavār 146 Mc 39.28N 48.20 E
Bilé Karpaty = White Carpathians (EN) 120 Nh 48.55N 17.50 E
Bilesha Plain 170 Hb 0.35N 40.45 E
Biłgoraj 120 Sf 50.34N 22.43 E
Bili 170 Eb 4.09N 25.10 E
Bili 170 Db 4.50N 22.29 E
Bilibino 142 Sc 68.03N 166.20 E
Biliran 150 Hd 11.35N 124.28 E
Bilishti 130 Di 40.37N 20.59 E
Biliu He 154 Ge 39.30N 122.36 E
Bill Baileys Bank (EN) 114 Ca 60.40N 10.20W
Billerbeck 124 Jc 51.58N 7.18 E
Billericay 124 Cc 51.37N 0.35 E
Billingen 116 Ef 58.24N 13.45 E
Billings 176 Ie 45.47N 108.27W
Billings, Represa- 204 If 23.45S 46.40W
Billingshurst 124 Bc 51.01N 0.27W
Bill Williams River 188 Hi 34.17N 114.03W
Billy Chinook, Lake- 188 Ed 44.33N 121.20W
Bilma 160 Ig 18.41N 12.56 E

Index Symbols

[1] Independent Nation
[2] State, Region
[3] District, County
[4] Municipality
[5] Colony, Dependency
Continent
Physical Region
Historical or Cultural Region
Mount, Mountain
Volcano
Hill
Mountains, Mountain Range
Hills, Escarpment
Plateau, Upland
Pass, Gap
Plain, Lowland
Delta
Salt Flat
Valley, Canyon
Crater, Cave
Karst Features
Depression
Polder
Desert, Dunes
Forest, Woods
Heath, Steppe
Oasis
Cape, Point
Coast, Beach
Cliff
Peninsula
Isthmus
Sandbank
Island
Atoll
Rock, Reef
Islands, Archipelago
Rocks, Reefs
Coral Reef
Well, Spring
Geyser
River, Stream
Waterfall, Rapids
River Mouth, Estuary
Lake
Salt Lake
Intermittent Lake
Reservoir
Swamp, Pond
Canal
Glacier
Ice Shelf, Pack Ice
Ocean
Sea
Gulf, Bay
Strait, Fjord
Lagoon
Bank
Seamount
Tablemount
Ridge
Shelf
Basin
Escarpment, Sea Scarp
Fracture
Trench, Abyss
National Park, Reserve
Point of Interest
Recreation Site
Cave, Cavern
Historic Site
Ruins
Wall, Walls
Church, Abbey
Temple
Scientific Station
Railway station
Airport
Port
Military installation
Lighthouse
Mine
Tunnel
Dam, Bridge

Biloela	212	Kd	24.24S	150.30 E
Bilo Gora ⛰	128	Le	45.50N	17.10 E
Biloku	202	Gc	1.46N	58.33W
Biloxi	182	Je	30.24N	88.53W
Bilqās Qism Awwal	146	Dg	31.13N	31.21 E
Bîlteni	130	Ge	44.52N	23.17 E
Biltine	168	Cc	14.32N	20.55 E
Biltine [3]	168	Cc	15.00N	21.00 E
Bilzen	124	Hd	50.51N	5.31 E
Bima ∿	170	Eb	3.23N	25.09 E
Bimbān	146	Ej	24.26N	32.53 E
Bimberi Peak ▲	212	Jg	35.40S	148.47 E
Bimbila	166	Fd	8.51N	0.04 E
Bimbo	168	Be	4.18N	18.33 E
Bimini Islands ◈	190	Ic	25.44N	79.15W
Bināb	146	Md	36.35N	48.41 E
Binačka Morava ∿	130	Eg	42.27N	21.47 E
Binaiya, Gunung- ▲	150	Ig	3.11S	129.26 E
Binatang	150	Ff	2.10N	111.38 E
Bınboğa Dağı ▲	146	Gc	38.21N	36.32 E
Binche	124	Gd	50.24N	4.10 E
Binder	152	Jb	48.35N	110.36 E
Bindura	160	Kj	17.17S	31.20 E
Bine el Ouidane	162	Fc	32.08N	6.28W
Binéfar	126	Mc	41.51N	0.18 E
Binem ∿	168	Bb	18.43N	19.40 E
Binga [Zaire]	170	Db	2.23N	20.30 E
Binga [Zimb.]	172	Dc	17.37S	27.20 E
Bingen	120	Dg	49.58N	7.54 E
Bingham [Me.-U.S.]	184	Mc	45.03N	69.53W
Bingham [N.M.-U.S.]	186	Cj	33.56N	106.17W
Binghamton	182	Lc	42.06N	75.55W
Bin Ghunaymah, Jabal- ⛰	158	If	25.00N	15.30 E
Bing Inlet	184	Gc	45.13N	80.30W
Bingöl	144	Fb	38.53N	40.29 E
Bingöl Dağları ⛰	146	Ic	39.20N	41.20 E
Binhai (Dongkan)	152	Ke	34.00N	119.52 E
Binjai	150	Cf	3.36N	98.30 E
Binkiliç	130	Lh	41.25N	28.11 E
Binongko, Pulau- ◆	150	Hh	5.57S	124.02 E
Bin Qirdān	162	Jc	33.08N	11.13 E
Bintan, Pulau-	150	Df	1.05N	104.30 E
Bintuhan	150	Dg	4.48S	103.22 E
Bintulu	150	Ff	3.10N	113.02 E
Bin Walīd, Jabal- ▲	128	En	36.52N	10.47 E
Binxian	154	Df	37.22N	117.57 E
Binxian (Binzhou) [China]	152	Mb	45.45N	127.27 E
Binxian (Binzhou) [China]	152	Id	35.02N	108.06 E
Binzhou → Binxian [China]	152	Id	35.02N	108.06 E
Binzhou → Binxian [China]	152	Mb	45.45N	127.27 E
Bioara	148	Fd	23.58N	76.55 E
Biobío [2]	206	Fe	37.45S	72.00W
Biobío ∿	206	Fe	36.49S	73.10W
Biograd na Moru	128	Jg	43.57N	15.27 E
Bioko [3]	166	Ge	3.00N	8.40 E
Bioko ◆	158	Hh	4.30N	9.30 E
Biokovo ⛰	128	Lg	43.18N	17.02 E
Biorra/Birr	118	Fh	53.05N	7.54W
Bippen	124	Jb	52.35N	7.44 E
Bīr	148	Fe	18.59N	75.46 E
Bira	138	Ig	49.03N	132.27 E
Bi'r Abraq	164	Fe	23.35N	34.48 E
Bi'r Abū al Ḩuşayn	164	Ee	22.53N	29.55 E
Bi'r Abū Gharādiq	146	Cg	30.06N	28.06 E
Bi'r Abū Hashim	164	Fe	23.42N	34.08 E
Bi'r Abū Minqat	164	Ed	26.30N	27.35 E
Bīrah Kaprah	146	Kd	36.52N	44.01 E
Birāk	164	Bd	27.39N	14.17 E
Birakan	138	Ig	49.02N	131.40 E
Bi'r al 'Abd	146	Eg	31.22N	32.58 E
Bi'r al Ghuzaylah	164	Bd	28.50N	10.45 E
Bi'r al Ḩakīm	164	Dc	31.36N	23.29 E
Bi'r al Hasa	168	Fa	22.58N	35.40 E
Bi'r al Khamsah	164	Ec	30.57N	25.46 E
Bi'r 'Allāq	164	Bc	31.10N	11.55 E
Bi'r al Mushayqīq	162	Jc	30.53N	10.18 E
Bi'r al Qurayyah	146	Ei	26.22N	33.01 E
Bi'r al Uzam	164	Dc	31.46N	23.59 E
Bi'r al Wa'r	160	If	22.39N	14.10 E
Bi'r al Washkah	164	Cd	28.52N	15.35 E
Birao	160	Jg	10.17N	22.47 E
Bi'r 'Arjā'	146	Ij	25.17N	40.58 E
Bi'r ar Rāh	146	If	33.27N	40.25 E
Bi'r ar Rūmān	162	Ic	32.31N	8.21 E
Birātnagar	148	Hc	26.29N	87.17 E
Biratori	154	Qc	42.35N	142.12 E
Bi'r Baylī	164	Ec	30.32N	25.08 E
Bi'r Bayzaḩ	146	Fj	25.10N	34.05 E
Bi'r Bū Ḩawsh	164	Dd	24.34N	22.07 E
Bi'r Bū Zurayyq	164	Dd	24.32N	22.38 E
Bîrca	130	Gf	43.58N	23.37 E
Birch ∿	180	Ge	58.28N	112.17W
Birch Mountains ⛰	180	Ge	57.20N	112.55W
Bird	180	Ie	56.30N	94.14W
Bi'r Dibs	164	Ee	22.12N	29.32 E
Bird Island [Gren.] ◆	197p	Bb	12.12N	61.33W
Bird Island [Sey.] ◆	172b	Ca	3.43S	55.12 E
Birdsville	212	He	25.54S	139.22 E
Birdum	212	Gc	15.39S	133.13 E
Birecik	146	Gd	37.02N	37.58 E
Bir El Ater	162	Ic	34.44N	8.03 E
Bīr el Mrabba'ab	146	He	34.30N	39.07 E
Bir Enzarán	162	Ee	23.53N	14.32W
Bireuen	150	Ce	5.12N	96.41 E
Bi'r Fajr	146	Gh	28.54N	37.54 E
Bi'r Fu'ād	164	Ec	30.27N	26.27 E
Bir Gandús	162	De	21.36N	16.30W
Bīrganj	148	Gc	27.00N	84.52 E
Bir Gara	168	Bc	13.11N	15.58 E
Bir-Ghbalou	126	Ph	36.16N	3.35 E
Birgi	130	Lk	38.15N	28.05 E
Bi'r Ḩasanah	146	Eg	30.28N	33.47 E
Bi'r Ḩaymir	146	Hj	24.41N	38.04 E
Bi'r Ḩulayyī	146	Fj	24.06N	34.32 E
Birigui	204	Ge	21.18S	50.19W
Biriliussy	138	Ee	57.07N	90.42 E
Bīrīn	146	Ge	35.01N	36.40 E
Birine	126	Pi	35.37N	3.13 E
Bīrjand	142	Hf	32.53N	59.13 E
Birjusa ∿	140	Ld	57.43N	95.24 E
Birjusinsk	138	Ee	55.55N	97.55 E
Bi'r Karawayn	146	Ci	27.06N	28.32 E
Birkeland	114	Bg	58.20N	8.14 E
Birkenfeld	120	Dg	49.39N	7.11 E
Birkenhead	118	Jh	53.24N	3.02W
Birkerød	116	Ei	55.50N	12.26 E
Bi'r Khālidah	146	Bg	30.50N	27.15 E
Birksgate Range ⛰	212	Fe	27.10S	129.45 E
Bîrlad	130	Kc	46.14N	27.40 E
Bîrlad ∿	130	Kc	45.36N	27.31 E
Bir Lehlú	162	Fd	26.21N	9.34W
Bi'r Ma'sūr	146	Fj	24.31N	34.12 E
Birmingham [Al.-U.S.]	176	Kf	33.31N	86.49W
Birmingham [Eng.-U.K.]	112	Fe	52.30N	1.50W
Bi'r Misāḩah	164	Ee	22.12N	27.57 E
Bi'r Murr	164	Fe	23.21N	30.05 E
Bi'r Murrah	164	Fe	22.32N	33.54 E
Bi'r Nāhid	164	Ec	30.13N	28.52 E
Bi'r Naşīf	144	Ee	24.51N	39.11 E
Birnie Atoll ◎	208	Je	3.35S	171.31W
Birnin Gaouré	166	Fc	13.05N	2.54 E
Birnin Gwari	166	Gc	11.02N	6.47 E
Birnin Kebbi	166	Fc	12.28N	4.12 E
Birni Nkonni	160	Hg	13.48N	5.15 E
Birnin Kudu	166	Gc	11.27N	9.30 E
Birni Yauri	166	Fc	10.47N	4.49 E
Bi'r Nukhaylah	146	Dj	24.01N	30.52 E
Birobidžan	142	Pe	48.48N	132.57 E
Birr/Biorra	118	Fh	53.05N	7.54W
Birs ∿	128	Bc	47.26N	7.33 E
Bi'r Safājah	164	Fd	26.50N	34.54 E
Bi'r Sayyālah	146	Ei	26.07N	33.56 E
Bi'r Shalatayn	164	Ge	23.08N	35.36 E
Birsk	136	Fd	55.25N	55.32 E
Birštonas	116	Kj	54.33N	24.07 E
Bi'r Ţarfāwī	164	Ee	22.55N	28.53 E
Biru	152	Fe	31.30N	93.50 E
Bi'r Umm al 'Abbās	146	Ei	26.57N	32.34 E
Bi'r Umm Fawākhīr	146	Ei	26.01N	33.38 E
Bi'r Umm Sa'īd	146	Eh	29.40N	33.34 E
Bi'r Umm Ţunayḑibah	146	Ej	25.16N	33.06 E
Biruni	136	Gg	41.42N	60.45 E
Biržai/Biržaj	136	Cd	56.12N	24.48 E
Biržaj/Biržai	136	Cd	56.12N	24.48 E
Bîrzava	130	Ec	46.07N	21.59 E
Bîrzava ∿	130	Dd	45.16N	20.49 E
Birzebbuga	128	Io	35.49N	14.32 E
Bisa, Pulau- ◆	150	Ig	1.15S	127.28 E
Bisaccia	128	Ji	41.01N	15.22 E
Bisacquino	128	Hm	37.42N	13.15 E
Bisan Shotō ◈	156	Cd	34.24N	134.00 E
Bisbee	182	Fe	31.27N	109.55W
Biscarrosse et de Parentis, Étang de- ᴡ	122	Ej	44.21N	1.10W
Biscay, Bay of- (EN) = Gascogne, Golfe de- ◧	110	Fg	44.00N	4.00W
Biscay, Bay of- (EN) = Gascogne, Golfe de- ◧	110	Fg	43.50N	2.30W
Biscay, Bay of- (EN) = Vizcaya, Golfo de- ◧	110	Fg	43.50N	2.30W
Bisceglie	128	Ki	41.14N	16.30 E
Bischofshofen	128	Hc	47.25N	13.13 E
Bischofswerda/Biskopicy	120	Ke	51.07N	14.11 E
Biscoe Islands ◈	222	Qe	66.00S	66.30W
Biscotasi Lake ≈	184	Fb	47.20N	82.05W
Biscucuy	196	Bh	9.22N	69.59W
Bisert	136	Fd	56.52N	59.03 E
Bisert ∿	134	Hh	56.39N	57.59 E
Biševo ◆	128	Kh	42.59N	16.01 E
Biševski kanal ≃	128	Kg	43.00N	16.03 E
Bisha	168	Fb	15.28N	37.33 E
Bishārah	164	De	22.58N	22.39 E
Bishārīyīn, Barq al- ⛰	168	Eb	19.26N	32.22 E
Bishnupur	148	Hd	23.05N	87.19 E
Bishop	182	Dd	37.22N	118.24W
Bishop Auckland	118	Lg	54.40N	1.40W
Bishop Rock ✱	118	Gl	49.53N	6.25W
Bishop's Falls	180	Lg	49.01N	55.30W
Bishop's Stortford	118	Nj	51.53N	0.09 E
Bishop's Waltham	124	Ad	50.57N	1.13W
Bishrī, Jabal- ⛰	146	He	35.20N	39.20 E
Bishui	152	La	52.07N	123.43 E
Biskopicy/Bischofswerda	120	Ke	51.07N	14.11 E
Biskra	160	He	34.51N	5.44 E
Biskra [3]	162	Ic	34.40N	6.00 E
Biskupiec	120	Qc	53.52N	20.27 E
Bislig	150	Ie	8.13N	126.19 E
Bismarck	176	Ie	46.48N	100.47W
Bismarck, Kap- ▶	179	Kc	76.40N	18.40W
Bismarck Archipelago ◈	208	Fe	5.00S	150.00 E
Bismarck Sea ☰	214	Dh	4.00S	147.30 E
Bismark Range ⛰	214	Ci	5.30S	144.45 E
Bismil	146	Id	37.51N	40.40 E
Bison	186	Ed	45.31N	102.28W
Bīsotūn	146	Le	34.23N	47.26 E
Bispfors	116	Ga	63.02N	16.37 E
Bissau	160	Fg	11.51N	15.35W
Bissaula	166	Hd	7.01N	10.27 E
Bisseca, Lach- ∿	168	Ge	0.45N	41.33 E
Bissett	184	Hb	46.13N	78.02W
Bisson, Banc du- ✾	172	Hb	12.00S	46.25 E
Bistcho Lake ≈	180	Fe	59.45N	118.50W
Bistineau, Lake- ≈	186	Jj	32.25N	93.22W
Bistra ⛰	130	Dh	41.37N	20.44 E
Bistra ∿	130	Fd	45.29N	22.11 E
Bistreţ	130	Gf	43.54N	23.30 E
Bistrica	130	Cf	43.28N	19.42 E
Bistrica ▲	130	Dg	42.09N	20.59 E
Bistriţa	130	Hb	47.08N	24.29 E
Bistriţa [Rom.] ∿	130	Hb	47.04N	24.25 E
Bistriţa [Rom.] ∿	130	Jc	46.30N	26.57 E
Bistriţa-Năsăud [2]	130	Hb	47.05N	24.35 E
Bitam	170	Bb	2.05N	11.29 E
Bitam ∿	126	Ri	35.15N	5.11 E
Bitburg	120	Cg	49.58N	6.32 E
Bitche	122	Ne	49.03N	7.26 E
Bitéa ∿	168	Cc	13.11N	20.10 E
Bithia ⁖	128	Cl	38.55N	8.52 E
Bithynia ▣	130	Mi	40.20N	29.30 E
Bitjug ∿	132	Kd	50.37N	39.55 E
Bitkine	168	Bc	11.59N	18.13 E
Bitlis	144	Fb	38.22N	42.06 E
Bitola	112	Ig	41.02N	21.20 E
Bitonto	128	Ki	41.06N	16.41 E
Bitterfeld	120	Ie	51.37N	12.19 E
Bitterfontein	160	Il	31.00S	18.32 E
Bitterroot Range ⛰	174	He	47.06N	115.10W
Bitterroot River ∿	188	Hc	46.52N	114.06W
Bitti	128	Dj	40.29N	9.23 E
Bitung	150	If	1.27N	125.11 E
Biu	160	Ig	10.37N	12.12 E
Bivolari	130	Kb	47.32N	27.26 E
Bivolu, Vîrful- ▲	130	Ib	47.15N	25.56 E
Bivona	128	Hm	37.37N	13.26 E
Biwa-Ko ≈	154	Ng	35.13N	136.05 E
Bixad [Rom.]	130	Ic	46.06N	25.52 E
Bixad [Rom.]	130	Gb	47.56N	23.24 E
Bixby	186	Ii	35.57N	95.53W
Biyalā	146	Dg	31.10N	31.13 E
Biyang	152	Je	32.40N	113.21 E
Biyārjomand	146	Pd	36.06N	55.53 E
Bižbuljak	134	Gj	53.43N	54.16 E
Biže ∿	135	Kb	45.10N	77.58 E
Bizen	154	Mg	34.44N	134.09 E
Bizerte	160	He	37.17N	9.52 E
Bizerte [3]	162	Ib	37.00N	9.30 E
Bizkaia / Vizcaya [3]	126	Ja	43.15N	2.55W
Bjala	130	If	43.27N	25.44 E
Bjala Slatina	130	Gf	43.28N	23.56 E
Bjargtangar ▶	110	Db	65.30N	24.32W
Bjärnå/Perniö	114	Ff	60.12N	23.08 E
Bjärnum	116	Eh	56.17N	13.42 E
Bjästa	116	Ha	63.12N	18.30 E
Bjelašnica [Yugo.] ⛰	128	Mh	42.51N	18.09 E
Bjelašnica [Yugo.] ⛰	128	Mg	43.09N	18.23 E
Bjelašnica [Yugo.] ⛰	128	Mg	43.43N	18.09 E
Bjelolasica ▲	128	Ie	45.16N	14.58 E
Bjelovar	128	Ke	45.54N	16.51 E
Bjerkvik	114	Db	68.33N	17.34 E
Bjerringbro	116	Ch	56.23N	9.40 E
Bjervamoen	116	Ce	59.25N	9.04 E
Bjeshkët e Nemuna ⛰	130	Cg	42.30N	19.50 E
Björbo	116	Fd	60.28N	14.42 E
Bjørkelangen	116	De	59.53N	11.34 E
Björkfors	116	Ff	58.01N	15.54 E
Björklinge	116	Gd	60.02N	17.33 E
Björkö ◆	114	Eg	59.55N	19.00 E
Björna	114	Ee	63.34N	18.33 E
Bjørnafjorden ≃	116	Ad	60.05N	5.20 E
Björneborg	116	Fe	59.15N	14.15 E
Björneborg/Pori	112	Ic	61.29N	21.47 E
Bjorne Peninsula ▀	180	Ia	77.30N	87.00W
Bjornesfjorden ≈	116	Bd	60.10N	7.40 E
Bjørnevatn	114	Gb	69.40N	30.00 E
Bjørnøya = Bear Island (EN) ◆	110	Ha	74.30N	19.00 E
Bjurholm	114	Ee	63.56N	19.13 E
Bjuröklubb ▶	114	Ed	64.28N	21.35 E
Bjuv	116	Eh	56.05N	12.54 E
Bla	166	Dc	12.56N	5.45W
Blace	130	Ef	43.18N	21.18 E
Blackall	210	Fg	24.25S	145.28 E
Black Bank (EN) = Zwarte Bank ▦	124	Fa	53.15N	3.55 E
Black Bay ◧	186	Lb	48.40N	88.30W
Blackburn	118	Kh	53.45N	2.29W
Blackburn, Mount- ▲	174	Ec	61.44N	143.26W
Black Butte Lake ≈	188	Dg	39.45N	122.20W
Black Coast ⌒	222	Qf	71.45S	62.00W
Black Down Hills	118	Jk	50.57N	3.09W
Blackduck	186	Ic	47.44N	94.33W
Blackfoot	182	Ec	43.11N	112.20W
Blackfoot Reservoir ⊟	188	Je	42.55N	111.35W
Black Forest (EN) = Schwarzwald ⛰	110	Gf	48.05N	8.15 E
Black Head ▶	118	Hk	50.01N	5.03W
Black Hills ⛰	174	Ie	44.00N	104.00W
Black Isle ▀	118	Id	57.35N	4.20W
Black Lake ≈	180	Ge	59.11N	105.20W
Blackman's	197q	Ab	13.11N	59.32W
Black Mesa ⛰	188	Jh	36.35N	110.20W
Blackmoor △	118	Ik	50.23N	4.50W
Black Mountain ▲	182	Kd	36.54N	82.54W
Black Mountains [U.S.] ⛰	188	Hi	35.30N	114.30W
Black Mountains [Wales-U.K.] ⛰	118	Jj	51.57N	3.08W
Blackpool	118	Jh	53.50N	3.03W
Black Range ⛰	182	Fe	33.20N	107.50W
Black River	194	Id	18.01N	77.51W
Black River [Az.-U.S.] ∿	188	Jj	33.44N	110.13W
Black River [Mi.-U.S.] ∿	184	Fd	43.00N	82.25W
Black River [N.Y.-U.S.] ∿	184	Id	43.59N	76.04W
Black River [U.S.] ∿	186	Ki	35.38N	91.19W
Black River [Wi.-U.S.] ∿	186	Ke	43.57N	91.22W
Black River (EN) = Babian Jiang [Asia] ∿	140	Mg	20.17N	106.34 E
Black River (EN) = Đà, Sông- [Asia] ∿	140	Mg	20.17N	106.34 E
Black River Falls	186	Kd	44.16N	90.52W
Black Rock ❋	206	Lh	53.39S	41.48W
Black Rock [Ire.] ✱	118	Cg	54.05N	10.20W
Black Rock [Phil.] ✱	150	Ge	8.48N	119.50 E
Black Rock Desert ◢	182	Dc	41.10N	119.00W
Blacksburg	184	Gg	37.15N	80.25W
Black Sea (EN) = Černoje more ☰	110	Jg	43.00N	35.00 E
Black Sea (EN) = Černo More ☰	110	Jg	43.00N	35.00 E
Black Sea (EN) = Karadeniz ☰	110	Jg	43.00N	35.00 E
Black Sea (EN) = Neagră, Marea- ☰	110	Jg	43.00N	35.00 E
Blacksod Bay ◧	118	Dg	54.08N	10.00W
Blacksod Bay/Cuan an Fhóid Duibh ◧	118	Dg	54.08N	10.00W
Blackstairs Mountains/Na Staighrí Dubha ▲	118	Ki	52.33N	6.49W
Blackstone	184	Hg	37.04N	78.01W
Blackville	184	Ob	46.47N	65.54W
Black Volta ∿	158	Gh	8.38N	1.30W
Black Volta (EN) = Volta Noire [3]	166	Ec	12.30N	4.00W
Black Volta (EN) = Volta Noire ∿	158	Gh	8.38N	1.30W
Blackwater ∿	124	Cc	51.43N	0.28 E
Blackwater/An Abhainn Dubh ∿	118	Gh	53.39N	6.43W
Blackwater/An Abhainn Mhór [Ire.] ∿	118	Fj	51.51N	7.50W
Blackwater/An Abhainn Mhór [N.Ire.-U.K.] ∿	118	Gg	54.30N	6.35W
Blackwell	186	Hh	36.48N	97.17W
Blackwood River ∿	212	Df	34.35S	115.02 E
Blagnac	122	Hk	43.38N	1.24 E
Blagodarny	132	Mg	45.04N	43.24 E
Blagojevgrad	130	Gg	42.01N	23.06 E
Blagojevgrad [2]	130	Gh	41.45N	23.25 E
Blagoveščenka	138	Cf	52.50N	79.55 E
Blagoveščensk [R.S.F.S.R.]	136	Fd	55.01N	55.59 E
Blagoveščensk [R.S.F.S.R.]	142	Od	50.17N	127.32 E
Blåhø ▲	116	Cb	62.45N	9.19 E
Blain	122	Eg	47.29N	1.45W
Blaine [Mn.-U.S.]	186	Jd	45.11N	93.14W
Blaine [Wa.-U.S.]	188	Db	48.59N	122.44W
Blair	186	Hf	41.33N	96.08W
Blair Athol	212	Jd	22.42S	147.33 E
Blairgowrie	118	Je	56.36N	3.21W
Blairmore	188	Hb	49.36N	114.26W
Blaise ∿	122	Kf	48.38N	4.43 E
Blaj	130	Gc	46.11N	23.55 E
Blake Basin (EN) ⊍	182	Mf	29.00N	76.00W
Blakely	184	Ej	31.23N	84.56W
Blakeney Point ▶	118	Ni	52.59N	1.00 E
Blake Plateau (EN) ⊓	174	Lf	31.00N	79.00W
Blakstad	114	Bg	58.30N	8.39 E
Blanc, Cap- / Blanco, Cabo- ▶	126	Oe	39.22N	2.46 E
Blanc, Cape- (EN) = Abyaḑ, Ra's al- ▶	158	He	37.20N	9.50 E
Blanc, Cape- (EN) = Nouâdhibou, Râs- ▶	158	Ff	20.46N	17.03W
Blanc, Lac- ⊟	184	Kb	47.45N	73.12W
Blanc, Le-	122	Hh	46.38N	1.04 E
Blanc, Mont- / Bianco, Monte- ▲	110	Gf	45.50N	6.52 E
Blanca, Bahía- ◧	198	Ji	38.55S	62.10W
Blanca, Cerro- △	194	Gi	8.40N	80.35W
Blanca, Cordillera- ⛰	202	Ce	9.10S	77.35W
Blanca, Costa- ⌒	126	Lg	37.38N	0.40W
Blanca, Isla- ◆	192	Pg	21.24N	86.50W
Blanca, Punta- ▶	192	Bc	29.05N	114.45W
Blancagrande	204	Bm	36.32S	60.53W
Blanca Peak ▲	174	If	37.35N	105.29W
Blanche, Lake- [Austl.] ≈	212	Ed	22.25S	123.15 E
Blanche, Lake- [Austl.] ≈	212	He	29.15S	139.40 E
Blanche, Point- ▶	197b	Ac	18.00N	63.03W
Blanche Channel ≃	219a	Cc	8.30S	157.30 E
Blanc-Nez, Cap- ▶	124	Dd	50.56N	1.42 E
Blanco, Cabo- ▶	190	Gg	9.33N	85.06W
Blanco, Cabo- / Blanc, Cap- ▶	126	Oe	39.22N	2.46 E
Blanco, Cape- ▶	182	Cc	42.50N	124.34W
Blanco, Cerro- ▲	192	Fe	25.43N	107.39W
Blanco, Río- ∿	202	Ff	12.30S	64.18W
Blanco del Sur, Cayo- ◆	194	Gb	22.02N	81.24W
Blanda ∿	114a	Bb	65.39N	20.18W
Blanding	188	Kh	37.37N	109.29W
Blanes	126	Oc	41.41N	2.48 E
Blangy-le-Château	124	Ce	49.14N	0.17 E
Blangy-sur-Bresle	122	He	49.56N	1.38 E
Blanice [Czech.] ∿	120	Kg	49.48N	14.58 E
Blanice [Czech.] ∿	120	Kg	49.17N	14.09 E
Blankaholm	116	Gg	57.35N	16.31 E
Blankenberge	122	Jc	51.19N	3.08 E
Blankenheim	124	Id	50.26N	6.39 E
Blanquilla, Isla- ◆	202	Fa	11.51N	64.37W
Blanquillo	204	Ek	32.55S	55.40W
Blansko	120	Mg	49.22N	16.39 E
Blantyre	160	Ki	15.47S	35.00 E
Blantyre-Limbe	170	Gf	15.49S	35.03 E
Blåskavlen ▲	116	Bd	60.58N	7.18 E
Błaszki	120	Oe	51.39N	18.27 E
Blatná	120	Jg	49.26N	13.53 E
Blato	128	Kh	42.56N	16.48 E
Blåvands Huk ▶	110	Gd	55.33N	8.05 E
Blavet ∿	122	Cg	47.46N	3.18W
Blaye	122	Fi	45.08N	0.40W
Blaye-les-Mines	122	Ij	44.01N	2.08 E
Bled	128	Id	46.22N	14.08 E
Blefjell ▲	116	Ce	59.48N	9.10 E
Bleialf	124	Id	50.14N	6.17 E
Blekinge [2]	114	Dh	56.20N	15.20 E
Blekinge ▣	116	Fh	56.20N	15.05 E
Blenheim	210	Ii	41.31S	173.57 E
Bletchley	118	Mj	52.00N	0.46W
Bleus, Monts- ⛰	170	Fb	1.30N	30.30 E
Blida	160	He	36.34N	2.55 E
Blida [3]	162	Hb	36.35N	2.30 E
Blidö ◆	116	He	59.35N	18.55 E
Blidsberg	116	Eg	57.56N	13.29 E
Blies ∿	124	Je	49.07N	7.04 E
Blieskastel	124	Je	49.14N	7.15 E
Bligh Water ≃	219d	Ab	17.00S	178.00 E
Blind River	180	Jg	46.10N	82.58W
Blitar	150	Fh	8.06S	112.09 E
Blitta	166	Fd	8.19N	0.59 E
Block Island ◆	184	Le	41.11N	71.35W
Bloemfontein	160	Jk	29.12S	26.07 E
Bloemhof	172	De	27.38S	25.32 E
Blois	122	Hg	47.35N	1.20 E
Blokhus	116	Cg	57.15N	9.35 E
Blomberg	124	Lc	51.56N	9.05 E
Blönduós	114a	Bb	65.40N	20.18W
Bloody Foreland/Cnoc Fola ▶	118	Ef	55.09N	8.17W
Bloomfield [Ia.-U.S.]	186	Jf	40.45N	92.25W
Bloomfield [In.-U.S.]	184	Df	39.01N	86.56W
Bloomington [Il.-U.S.]	182	Jc	40.29N	88.59W
Bloomington [In.-U.S.]	182	Jd	39.10N	86.32W
Bloomington [Mn.-U.S.]	186	Jd	44.50N	93.17W
Bloomsburg	184	Ie	41.01N	76.27W
Blosseville Kyst ⌒	179	Je	68.45N	27.25W
Blötberget	116	Fd	60.07N	15.04 E
Blountstown	184	Ej	30.29N	85.03W
Bludenz	128	Dc	47.09N	9.49 E
Blue Earth	186	Ie	43.38N	94.06W
Bluefield	182	Kd	37.14N	81.17W
Bluefields	176	Kh	12.00N	83.45W
Bluefields, Bahía de- ◯	194	Fg	12.02N	83.44W
Blue Mesa Reservoir ⊟	186	Cg	38.28N	107.15W
Blue Mountain ⛰	184	Ie	40.15N	77.30W
Blue Mountain [Or.-U.S.] ▲	188	Ge	42.25N	117.50W
Blue Mountain [U.S.] ▲	186	Ii	34.41N	94.03W
Blue Mountain Lake	184	Jd	43.53N	74.26W
Blue Mountain Pass ⋎	188	Ge	42.18N	117.45W
Blue Mountain Peak ▲	190	Ie	18.03N	76.35W
Blue Mountains [Austl.] ⛰	212	Kf	33.35S	150.15 E
Blue Mountains [U.S.] ⛰	182	Ec	44.35N	118.25W
Blue Mud Bay ◧	212	Hb	13.25S	135.55 E
Blue Nile (EN) = Abay ∿	158	Kg	15.38N	32.31 E
Blue Nile (EN) = Azraq, Baḩr al- ∿	158	Kg	15.38N	32.31 E
Bluenose Lake ≈	180	Fc	68.00N	121.00W
Blue Ridge	184	Eh	34.52N	84.20W
Blue Ridge ⛰	174	Kf	37.00N	82.00W
Blue Stack/Na Cruacha ▲	118	Eg	54.45N	8.06W
Bluestone Lake ≈	184	Gg	37.30N	80.50W
Bluff [N.Z.]	216	Ci	46.36S	168.21 E
Bluff [Ut.-U.S.]	188	Kh	37.17N	109.33W
Bluff Point ▶	212	Ce	27.50S	114.05 E
Bluffton	184	Ee	40.44N	85.11W
Blumberg	120	Ei	47.50N	8.32 E
Blumenau	206	Kc	26.56S	49.03W
Blyth	118	Lf	55.07N	1.30W
Blyth ∿	124	Db	52.19N	1.41 E
Blythe	182	Ee	33.37N	114.36W
Blytheville	182	Jd	35.56N	89.55W
Bø [Nor.]	114	Bg	59.25N	9.04 E
Bo [S.L.]	160	Fh	7.58N	11.45W
Boa ∿	166	Dd	8.26N	7.10W
Boac	150	Hd	12.28N	122.28 E
Boaco	194	Eg	12.28N	85.40W
Boaco [3]	194	Eg	12.35N	85.25W
Boa Esperança	204	Je	21.05S	45.34W
Boa Esperança, Represa- ⊟	202	Je	6.50S	44.00W
Boa Esperançao, Serra da- ⛰	204	Je	20.57S	45.40W
Bo'ai	154	Bg	35.10N	113.03 E
Boal	126	Fa	43.26N	6.49W
Boali	168	Be	4.48N	18.07 E
Boano, Pulau- ◆	150	Ig	2.56S	127.56 E
Boardman	188	Fd	45.51N	119.43W
Boa Sentença, Serra da- ⛰	204	Ed	19.13S	57.33W
Boa Vista ◆	158	Eg	16.05N	22.50W
Boa Vista [Braz.]	204	Ec	17.51S	54.13W
Boa Vista [Braz.]	200	Je	2.49N	60.40W
Boa Vista [Braz.]	204	Ia	12.40S	46.51W
Bobai	152	Ig	22.15N	109.58 E
Bobalí, Cerros de- ▲	194	Ki	8.53N	73.28W
Bobbio	128	Df	44.46N	9.23 E
Bobigny	122	If	48.54N	2.27 E
Böblingen	120	Fh	48.41N	9.01 E
Bobo Dioulasso	160	Gg	11.12N	4.18W
Bobojod, gora- ▲	135	Hd	40.50N	70.20 E
Bobolice	120	Mc	53.57N	16.36 E
Bobonong	172	Dd	21.58S	28.25 E
Bobovdol	130	Gg	42.22N	23.00 E
Bóbr ∿	120	Ld	52.04N	15.04 E
Bobrik ∿	132	Ec	52.08N	26.48 E
Bobrinec	132	He	48.04N	32.09 E
Bobrka	120	Ug	49.34N	24.20 E
Bobrov	136	Ee	51.06N	40.01 E
Bobrovica	132	Gd	50.43N	31.28 E
Bobrowniki	120	Tc	53.08N	23.50 E
Bobrujsk	112	Ie	53.09N	29.15 E
Bobures	202	Db	9.15N	71.11W
Boby, Pic- ▲	172	Hd	22.12S	46.55 E
Boca del Río	192	Ee	25.20N	108.25W
Boca de Pozo	196	Dg	11.00N	64.23W
Boca do Acre	200	Jf	8.45S	67.23W
Bocage, Cap- ▶	219b	Be	21.12S	165.37 E
Bocâina	204	Db	15.16S	56.45W
Bocaiúva	204	Kc	17.07S	43.49W
Bocajá	204	Ef	22.45S	55.13W
Bocaranga	168	Bd	6.59N	15.39 E
Boca Raton	182	Kf	26.21N	80.05W
Bocas del Toro	190	Hg	9.20N	82.15W
Bocas del Toro [3]	194	Fi	8.50N	82.10W
Bocas del Toro, Archipiélago de- ◈	194	Fi	9.20N	82.10W
Bocay	194	Ef	14.19N	85.10W
Bochaine ⧗	122	Lj	44.20N	5.50 E
Bochnia	120	Qg	49.58N	20.26 E
Bocholt [Bel.]	124	Hc	51.10N	5.35 E
Bocholt [Ger.]	120	Ce	51.50N	6.36 E
Bochum	120	De	51.29N	7.13 E
Bocognano	122a	Ba	42.05N	9.04 E
Bocoio	170	Be	12.28S	14.08 E
Boconó	194	Li	9.15N	70.16W
Bocşa	130	Ed	45.23N	21.47 E
Boda	168	Be	4.19N	17.28 E
Boda	116	Fc	61.01N	15.13 E
Böda	116	Gg	57.15N	17.03 E
Bodafors	116	Fg	57.30N	14.42 E
Bodajbo	142	Nd	57.51N	114.10 E
Bodalangi	170	Db	3.14N	22.14 E
Bode ∿	120	Hd	52.01N	11.12 E
Bödefeld-Freiheit, Schmallenberg-	124	Kc	51.15N	8.24 E

Index Symbols

[1] Independent Nation	▣ Historical or Cultural Region	⋎ Pass, Gap	⌣ Depression	⌒ Coast, Beach	✱ Rock, Reef	╲ Waterfall, Rapids	═ Canal	◯ Lagoon	⊿ Escarpment, Sea Scarp	♜ Historic Site	✈ Airport
[2] State, Region	▲ Mount, Mountain	▭ Plain, Lowland	▥ Polder	▌ Cliff	◈ Islands, Archipelago	⌔ River Mouth, Estuary	❄ Glacier	▦ Bank	⚡ Fracture	⁖ Ruins	⚓ Port
[3] District, County	⩘ Volcano	◣ Delta	◢ Desert, Dunes	▀ Peninsula	❋ Rocks, Reefs	≈ Lake	⧖ Ice Shelf, Pack Ice	⊼ Seamount	∨ Trench, Abyss	⊞ Wall, Walls	⊕ Military installation
[4] Municipality	△ Hill	▤ Salt Flat	♣ Forest, Woods	⋈ Isthmus	✾ Coral Reef	≊ Salt Lake	≋ Ocean	⊓ Tablemount	⚑ National Park, Reserve	✝ Church, Abbey	☼ Lighthouse
[5] Colony, Dependency	⛰ Mountains, Mountain Range	⋁ Valley, Canyon	⩛ Heath, Steppe	▁ Sandbank	⊙ Well, Spring	◌ Intermittent Lake	☰ Sea	⋀ Ridge	★ Point of Interest	⛩ Temple	⚒ Mine
■ Continent	⌓ Hills, Escarpment	◡ Crater, Cave	⚘ Oasis	◆ Island	⛲ Geyser	⊟ Reservoir	◧ Gulf, Bay	⊏ Shelf	☂ Recreation Site	⚗ Scientific Station	∩ Tunnel
⧗ Physical Region	◓ Plateau, Upland	✲ Karst Features	▶ Cape, Point	◎ Atoll	∿ River, Stream	ᴡ Swamp, Pond	≃ Strait, Fjord	⊍ Basin	◗ Cave, Cavern	⊶ Railway station	⌿ Dam, Bridge

Bodegraven 124 Gb 52.06N 4.44 E
Bodélé 158 Ig 16.30N 17.30 E
Boden 112 Ib 65.50N 21.42 E
Bodenheim 124 Ke 49.56N 8.18 E
Bodensee=Constance, Lake- (EN) 110 Gf 47.35N 9.25 E
Boderg, Lough- 118 Fh 53.52N 8.00W
Bodmin 118 Ik 50.29N 4.43W
Bodmin Moor 118 Ik 50.35N 4.40W
Bodø 112 Hb 67.17N 14.23 E
Bodoquena 204 De 20.12S 56.48W
Bodoquena, Serra da- 202 Gh 21.00S 56.50W
Bodrog 120 Rh 48.07N 21.25 E
Bodrogköz 120 Rh 48.15N 21.45 E
Bodrum 144 Cb 37.02N 27.06 E
Bodrum Yarımadası 130 Kl 37.05N 27.30 E
Bodva 120 Qh 48.12N 20.47 E
Boën 122 Ji 45.44N 4.00 E
Boende 160 Ji 0.13S 20.52 E
Boeo, Capo- (Lilibeo, Capo-) 128 Gm 37.34N 12.41 E
Boerne 186 Gl 29.47N 98.44W
Boesmanland=Bushmanland (EN) 172 Be 29.30S 19.00 E
Boffa 166 Cc 10.10N 14.02W
Boga 130 Cg 42.24N 19.38 E
Bogale 148 Je 16.17N 95.24 E
Bogalusa 186 Lk 30.47N 89.52W
Bogandé 166 Ec 12.59N 0.08W
Bogangolo 168 Bd 5.34N 18.15 E
Bogatić 130 Ce 44.51N 19.29 E
Bogatynia 120 Kf 50.55N 14.59 E
Boğazkale 146 Fb 40.01N 34.35 E
Boğazlıyan 146 Fc 39.12N 35.15 E
Bogbonga 170 Cb 1.35N 19.25 E
Bogcang Zangbo 152 Ee 31.56N 87.24 E
Bogda Feng 152 Ec 43.45N 88.32 E
Bogdan 130 Hg 42.37N 24.28 E
Bogdanovka 132 Mi 41.15N 43.36 E
Bogda Shan 140 Ke 43.35N 90.00 E
Bogen 114 Db 68.32N 17.00 E
Bogenfels 172 Be 27.23S 15.22 E
Bogense 116 Di 55.34N 10.06 E
Boggeragh Mountains/An Bhograch 118 Ei 52.05N 9.00W
Boggy Peak 197d Bb 17.03N 61.51W
Boghar 126 Oi 35.55N 2.43 E
Boghni 126 Ph 36.32N 3.57 E
Bogia 214 Ch 4.16S 144.58 E
Bognor Regis 124 Bd 50.47N 0.39W
Bogny-sur-Meuse 124 Ge 49.54N 4.43 E
Bogoduhov 132 Id 50.12N 35.31 E
Bogomila 130 Eh 41.36N 21.28 E
Bogor 142 Mj 6.35S 106.47 E
Bogoridick 136 De 53.50N 38.08 E
Bogorodčany 120 Uh 48.45N 24.40 E
Bogorodsk 114 Kh 56.09N 43.32 E
Bogorodskoje [R.S.F.S.R.] 114 Mh 57.51N 50.48 E
Bogorodskoje [R.S.F.S.R.] 138 Jf 52.22N 140.30 E
Bogotá 200 Ie 4.36N 74.05W
Bogotá [3] 202 Dc 4.20N 74.10W
Bogotol 138 De 56.17N 89.43 E
Bogøy 114 Dc 67.54N 15.11 E
Bogra 148 Hd 24.51N 89.22 E
Bogučany 138 Ee 58.23N 97.39 E
Bogučar 132 Le 49.57N 40.33 E
Bogué 162 Ef 16.36N 14.15W
Boguševsk 114 Hi 54.50N 30.13 E
Boguslav 136 Df 49.33N 30.54 E
Bo Hai=Chihli, Gulf of- (EN) 140 Nf 38.30N 120.00 E
Bohai Haixia 152 Ld 38.00N 121.30 E
Bohain-en-Vermandois 124 Fe 49.59N 3.27 E
Bohemia (EN)=Čechy 110 Hf 50.00N 14.30 E
Bohemia (EN)=Čechy [2] 120 Kf 50.00N 14.30 E
Bohemian Forest (EN)=Böhmerwald 110 Hf 49.00N 13.30 E
Bohemian Forest (EN)=Šumava 110 Hf 49.00N 13.30 E
Bohicon 166 Fd 7.12N 2.04 E
Böhmerwald=Bohemian Forest (EN) 110 Hf 49.00N 13.30 E
Bohmte 124 Kb 52.22N 8.19 E
Bohodoyou 166 Dd 9.46N 9.04W
Bohol 140 Oi 9.50N 124.10 E
Böhönye 120 Nj 46.24N 17.24 E
Bohor 128 Jd 46.04N 15.26 E
Bohu/Bagrax 152 Ec 41.58N 86.29 E
Bohus 116 Eg 57.51N 12.01 E
Bohuslän 116 Df 58.15N 11.50 E
Boiaçu 202 Fd 0.27S 61.46W
Boiano 128 Ii 41.29N 14.29 E
Boina 158 Lj 16.00S 46.30 E
Bois, Lac des- 180 Ec 66.50N 125.15W
Bois, Rio dos- [Braz.] 204 Gd 18.35S 50.02W
Bois, Rio dos- [Braz.] 204 Ha 13.55S 49.51W
Bois Blanc Island 184 Ec 45.45N 84.28W
Boischaut 122 Hh 46.40N 1.45 E
Boise 176 He 43.37N 116.13W
Boise City 186 Eh 36.44N 102.31W
Boise River 188 Ge 43.49N 117.01W
Boissay 124 De 49.31N 1.21 E
Boissevain 180 Hg 49.14N 100.03W
Boizenburg 120 Gc 53.23N 10.43 E
Bojador, Cabo- 158 Ff 26.08N 14.30W
Bojana 130 Ch 41.52N 19.22 E
Bojanowo 120 Me 51.42N 16.44 E
Bojarka 136 De 50.19N 30.20 E
Bojčinovci 130 Gf 43.28N 23.20 E
Bojnürd 144 Ib 37.28N 57.19 E
Bojonegoro 150 Fh 7.09S 111.52 E
Bojuru 204 Gj 31.38S 51.26W
Bokatola 170 Cc 0.38S 18.46 E
Boké 166 Cc 10.56N 14.13W
Bokhara River 212 Je 29.55S 146.42 E
Bokn 116 Ae 59.15N 5.25 E
Boknafjorden 110 Gd 59.10N 5.35 E
Boko 170 Bc 4.47S 14.38 E
Bokol Mayo 168 Ge 4.31N 41.32 E
Bokoro 168 Bc 12.23N 17.03 E
Bokote 170 Dc 0.05S 20.08 E
Bokpyin 148 Jf 11.16N 98.46 E
Boksitogorsk 136 Dd 59.29N 33.52 E
Bokungu 170 Dc 0.41S 22.19 E
Bol [Chad] 168 Ac 13.30N 14.41 E
Bol [Yugo.] 128 Kg 43.16N 16.40 E
Bola, Bahr- 168 Bd 9.50N 18.59 E
Bolama 166 Bc 11.35N 15.28W
Bolands 197d Bb 17.02N 61.53W
Bolaños, Rio- 192 Gg 21.14N 104.08W
Bolaños de Calatrava 126 If 38.54N 3.40W
Bolattau, gora- 135 Ha 46.44N 71.54 E
Bolayır 130 Ji 40.31N 26.45 E
Bolbec 122 Ge 49.34N 0.29 E
Bolda 132 Pg 45.58N 48.35 E
Bole [Eth.] 168 Fd 6.37N 37.22 E
Bole [Ghana] 166 Ed 9.02N 2.29W
Bole/Bortala 152 Dc 44.59N 81.57 E
Bolehov 132 Ce 49.03N 23.50 E
Bolesławiec 120 Le 51.16N 15.34 E
Bolgatanga 160 Gg 10.47N 0.51W
Bolgrad 132 Fg 45.40N 28.38 E
Bolhov 136 De 53.30N 36.01 E
Boli 152 Nb 45.46N 130.31 E
Bolia 170 Cc 1.36S 18.23 E
Boliden 114 Ed 64.52N 20.23 E
Bolinao, Cape- 150 Gc 16.22N 119.50 E
Bolintin Vale 130 Ie 44.27N 25.46 E
Bolivar [2] 202 Fb 6.20N 63.30W
Bolivar [3] 202 Db 9.00N 74.40W
Bolivar [Mo.-U.S.] 186 Jh 37.37N 93.25W
Bolivar [Tn.-U.S.] 184 Ch 35.15N 88.59W
Bolivar, Cerro- 202 Fb 7.28N 63.25W
Bolivar, Pico- 198 Ie 8.30N 71.02W
Bolivia [1] 200 Jg 17.00S 65.00W
Bolivia, Altiplano de- 198 Jg 18.00S 68.00W
Boljevac 130 Ef 43.50N 21.58 E
Bollendorf 124 Ie 49.51N 6.22 E
Bollène 122 Kj 44.17N 4.45 E
Bollnäs 114 Df 61.21N 16.25 E
Bollon 212 Je 28.02S 147.28 E
Bollstabruk 116 Ga 63.00N 17.41 E
Bollullos par del Condado 126 Fg 37.20N 6.32W
Bolmen 114 Ch 56.55N 13.40 E
Bolnisi 132 Ni 41.28N 44.31 E
Bolobo 170 Cc 2.10S 16.14 E
Bolodek 138 If 53.43N 133.09 E
Bologna 112 Hg 44.29N 11.20 E
Bolognesi 202 Df 10.01S 74.05W
Bologoje 112 Jd 57.54N 34.02 E
Bolohovo 132 Jb 54.05N 37.52 E
Bolomba 170 Cb 0.29N 19.12 E
Bolombo 170 Dc 3.59S 21.22 E
Bolon 138 Ig 49.58N 136.04 E
Bolotnoje 138 De 55.41N 84.33 E
Bolovens, Plateau des- 148 Le 15.20N 106.20 E
Bolšaja Balahnja 138 Fb 73.37N 107.05 E
Bolšaja Berestovica 120 Uc 53.09N 24.02 E
Bolšaja Černigovka 114 Mj 52.08N 50.48 E
Bolšaja Glušica 114 Mj 52.24N 50.29 E
Bolšaja Ižora 116 Me 59.55N 29.40 E
Bolšaja Kinel 114 Mj 53.14N 50.32 E
Bolšaja Koksaga 114 Lh 56.07N 47.48 E
Bolšaja Kuonamka 138 Gb 70.50N 113.20 E
Bolšaja Oju 134 Jb 69.42N 60.42 E
Bolšaja Rogovaja 134 Jc 66.30N 60.40 E
Bolšaja Synja 134 Id 65.58N 58.01 E
Bolšaja Tap 134 Lg 59.55N 65.42 E
Bolšaja Ussurka 138 Ig 46.00N 133.30 E
Bolšaja Vladimirovka 136 He 50.53N 79.30 E
Bolšakovo 116 Ij 54.50N 21.36 E
Bolsena 128 Fh 42.39N 11.59 E
Bolsena, Lago di- 128 Fh 42.35N 11.55 E
Bolšerečje 136 Hd 56.06N 74.38 E
Bolšereck 138 Kf 52.22N 156.24 E
Bolšeustikinskoje 134 Ii 55.57N 58.20 E
Bolševik 138 Jd 62.40N 147.30 E
Bolševik, ostrov- = Bolshevik Island (EN) 140 Mb 78.40N 102.30 E
Bolšezemelskaja tundra 136 Fb 67.30N 58.30 E
Bolshevik Island (EN) = Bolševik, ostrov- 140 Mb 78.40N 102.30 E
Bolšije Uki 136 Hd 56.57N 72.37 E
Bolšoj Anjuj 138 Lc 68.30N 160.50 E
Bolšoj Begičev, ostrov- 138 Gb 74.20N 112.30 E
Bolšoj Berezovy, ostrov- 116 Md 60.15N 28.35 E
Bolšoj Boktybaj, gora- 136 Ff 48.30N 58.20 E
Bolšoj Bolvanski Nos, mys- 134 Ia 70.27N 59.05 E
Bolšoj Čeremšan 114 Li 54.12N 49.40 E
Bolšoje Muraškino 114 Ki 55.47N 44.46 E
Bolšoje Vlasjevo 138 Jf 53.25N 140.55 E
Bolšoje Zagorje 116 Mg 57.47N 28.58 E
Bolšoj Gašun 132 Mf 47.22N 42.42 E
Bolšoj Ik 134 Hj 51.47N 56.20 E
Bolšoj Irgiz 136 Ee 52.01N 47.24 E
Bolšoj Jenisej 138 Ef 51.40N 94.26 E
Bolšoj Jugan 136 Hc 60.55N 73.40 E
Bolšoj Kamen 138 Ih 43.08N 132.28 E
Bolšoj Klimecki, ostrov- 114 Ie 62.00N 35.15 E
Bolšoj Kujalnik 132 Gf 46.46N 30.38 E
Bolšoj Kumak 132 Ud 51.22N 58.55 E
Bolšoj Ljahovski, ostrov- = Great Lyakhov (EN) 138 Jb 73.35N 142.00 E
Bolšoj Murta 138 Ee 56.55N 93.10 E
Bolšoj Nimnyr 138 He 58.08N 125.45 E
Bolšoj Pit 138 Ee 59.02N 91.40 E
Bolšoj Tjuters, ostrov- 116 Le 59.50N 27.10 E
Bolšoj Uluj 138 Ee 56.45N 90.46 E
Bolšoj Uvat, ozero- 134 Oh 57.35N 70.30 E
Bolšoj Uzen 110 Kf 48.50N 49.40 E
Bolsón, Cerro del- 198 Jh 27.13S 66.06W
Bolšovcy 120 Ug 49.08N 24.47 E
Bolsward 124 Ha 53.04N 5.30 E
Boltaña 126 Mb 42.27N 0.04 E
Bolton 118 Kh 53.35N 2.26W
Bolu 144 Da 40.44N 31.37 E
Bolu Dağları 146 Eb 41.05N 32.05 E
Bolungarvik 114a Aa 66.09N 23.15W
Boluntay 152 Fd 36.29N 92.18 E
Bolva 132 Ic 53.17N 34.20 E
Bolvadin 146 Dc 38.42N 31.04 E
Bolzano/Bozen 112 Hf 46.31N 11.22 E
Bom, Rio- 204 Gf 23.56S 51.44W
Boma 160 Ii 5.51S 13.03 E
Bomassa 170 Cb 2.12N 16.12 E
Bombala 212 Jg 36.54S 149.14 E
Bombarral 126 Ce 39.16N 9.09W
Bombay 142 Jh 18.58N 72.50 E
Bomberai, Jazirah- 150 Jg 3.00S 133.00 E
Bombo 170 Fb 0.35N 32.32 E
Bomboma 170 Cb 2.26N 18.57 E
Bom Comércio 202 Ee 9.45S 65.54W
Bom Conselho 202 Ke 9.10S 36.41W
Bom Despacho 202 Ig 19.43S 45.15W
Bomdila 148 Ic 27.16N 92.23 E
Bomi/Bowo 152 Ge 30.02N 95.39 E
Bomi Hills 160 Fh 6.52N 10.45W
Bomili 170 Eb 1.40N 27.01 E
Bom Jardim de Goiás 204 Fc 16.17S 52.07W
Bom Jardim de Minas 204 Je 21.57S 44.11W
Bom Jesus 204 Gi 28.42S 50.24W
Bom Jesus da Lapa 200 Lg 13.15S 43.25W
Bom Jesus de Goiás 204 Hd 18.12S 49.37W
Bømlafjorden 116 Ae 59.40N 5.20 E
Bømlo 114 Ag 59.45N 5.10 E
Bomokandi 170 Eb 3.30N 26.08 E
Bomongo 170 Cb 1.22N 18.21 E
Bom Retiro 204 Hh 27.48S 49.31W
Bom Sucesso 204 Je 21.02S 44.46W
Bomu 158 Jh 4.08N 22.26 E
Bomu (EN)=Mbomou [3] 168 Cd 5.30N 23.30 E
Bomu (EN)=Mbomou 158 Jh 4.08N 22.26 E
Bon, Cape- (EN) = Ţīb Ra's aţ- 158 Ie 37.05N 11.03 E
Bona, Mount- 178 Kd 61.20N 141.50W
Bonaire 202 Ea 12.10N 68.15W
Bonaire Basin (EN) 196 Cg 11.25N 67.30W
Bonampak 192 Ni 16.43N 91.05W
Bonanza 194 Ef 14.01N 84.35W
Bonanza Peak 188 Eb 48.14N 120.52W
Bonao 194 Ld 18.56N 70.25W
Bonaparte, Mount- 188 Fb 48.45N 119.08W
Bonaparte Archipelago 208 Df 14.20S 125.20 E
Bonaparte Lake 188 Ea 51.16N 120.35W
Bonaparte Rocks 197p Cb 12.24N 61.30W
Bonasse 196 Fg 10.05N 61.52W
Bonavista 180 Mg 48.39N 53.07W
Bonavista Bay 180 Mg 49.00N 53.20W
Bon-Cagan-Nur 152 Gb 45.35N 99.15 E
Bonda 170 Bc 0.49S 12.42 E
Bondeno 128 Ff 44.53N 11.25 E
Bondo 160 Jh 3.49N 23.40 E
Bondoukou 166 Ed 8.02N 2.48W
Bondoukou [3] 166 Ed 8.20N 2.55W
Bondowoso 150 Fh 7.55S 113.49 E
Bone, Gulf of- (EN)=Bone, Teluk- 140 Oj 4.00S 120.40 E
Bone, Teluk-=Bone, Gulf of- (EN) 140 Oj 4.00S 120.40 E
Bone Bay 197a Db 18.45N 64.22W
Bonelohe 150 Hh 5.48S 120.27 E
Bönen 124 Jc 51.36N 7.46 E
Bone Rate, Kepulauan- 150 Hh 7.00S 121.00 E
Bone Rate, Pulau- 150 Hh 7.22S 121.08 E
Bonete, Cerro- 206 Gc 27.51S 68.47W
Bong 166 Cd 6.49N 10.19W
Bong [3] 166 Dd 7.00N 9.40W
Bonga 168 Fd 7.16N 36.14 E
Bongabong 150 Hd 12.45N 121.29 E
Bongandanga 170 Db 1.30N 21.03 E
Bongo, Massif des- 158 Jh 8.40N 22.25 E
Bongolava 172 Hc 18.35S 45.20 E
Bongor 160 Ig 10.17N 15.22 E
Bongouanou 166 Ed 6.39N 4.12W
Bongouanou [3] 166 Ed 6.43N 4.12W
Bong Son 148 Lf 14.26N 109.01 E
Bonham 186 Hj 33.35N 96.11W
Bonheiden 124 Gc 51.02N 4.32 E
Bonhomme, Pic- 194 Kd 19.05N 72.15W
Bonifacio 122a Bb 41.23N 9.09 E
Bonifacio, Bocche di- = Bonifacio, Strait of- (EN) 110 Gg 41.18N 9.15 E
Bonifacio, Bouches de- = Bonifacio, Strait of- (EN) 110 Gg 41.18N 9.15 E
Bonifacio, Strait of- (EN) = Bonifacio, Bocche di- 110 Gg 41.18N 9.15 E
Bonifacio, Strait of- (EN) = Bonifacio, Bouches de- 110 Gg 41.18N 9.15 E
Bonifati, Capo- 128 Jk 39.33N 15.52 E
Bonin Basin (EN) 214 Bb 29.00N 137.00 E
Bonin Islands (EN)= Ogasawara-Shotō 140 Qg 27.00N 142.10 E
Bonin Trench (EN) 106 If 30.00N 145.00 E
Bonita Springs 184 Gl 26.21N 81.47W
Bonito [Braz.] 204 De 21.08S 56.28W
Bonito [Braz.] 204 Jb 15.20S 44.46W
Bonito, Pico- 190 Ge 15.38N 86.55W
Bonito, Rio- [Braz.] 204 Hb 15.18S 49.36W
Bonito, Rio- [Braz.] 204 Gc 16.31S 51.23W
Bonn 112 Ge 50.44N 7.06 E
Bonn-Bad Godesberg 120 Df 50.41N 7.09 E
Bonnebosq 124 Ce 49.12N 0.05 E
Bonnechère River 184 Ic 45.31N 76.33W
Bonners Ferry 188 Gb 48.41N 116.18W
Bonnet, Lac du- 186 Ia 50.22N 95.55W
Bonnétable 122 Gf 48.11N 0.26 E
Bonnet Plume 180 Ec 65.53N 134.58W
Bonneval 122 Hf 48.11N 1.24 E
Bonneville 122 Mh 46.05N 6.25 E
Bonneville Salt Flats 188 If 40.45N 113.50W
Bonnières-sur-Seine 124 De 49.02N 1.35 E
Bonningues-lès-Ardres 124 Ed 50.47N 2.01 E
Bonny 166 Ge 4.25N 7.10 E
Bono 128 Dj 40.25N 9.02 E
Bō-no-Misaki 156 Bf 31.15N 130.13 E
Bonorva 128 Cj 40.25N 8.46 E
Bontang 150 Gf 0.08N 117.30 E
Bonthain 150 Gh 5.32S 119.56 E
Bonthe 166 Cd 7.32N 12.30W
Bontoc 150 Hc 17.05N 120.58 E
Bonyhád 120 Oj 46.18N 18.32 E
Boo, Kepulauan- 150 Ig 1.12S 129.24 E
Boola 166 Dd 8.22N 8.43W
Booligal 212 If 33.52S 144.53 E
Boone [Ia.-U.S.] 186 Je 42.04N 93.53W
Boone [N.C.-U.S.] 184 Gg 36.13N 81.41W
Booneville [Ar.-U.S.] 186 Ji 35.08N 93.55W
Booneville [Ms.-U.S.] 186 Li 34.39N 88.34W
Boon Point 197d Bb 17.10N 61.50W
Boonville [In.-U.S.] 184 Df 38.03N 87.16W
Boonville [Mo.-U.S.] 186 Jg 38.58N 92.44W
Boos 124 De 49.23N 1.12 E
Boothia, Gulf of- 174 Jb 71.00N 91.00W
Boothia Peninsula 174 Jb 70.30N 95.00W
Boot Reefs 214 Cj 10.00S 144.35 E
Booué 160 Ii 0.06S 11.56 E
Bophuthatswana 172 De 26.00S 25.30 E
Bopolu 166 Cd 7.04N 10.29W
Boppard 124 Jd 50.14N 7.36 E
Boquerón 197a Ab 18.03N 67.09W
Boquerón [3] 204 Bf 23.00S 61.00W
Boquilla, Presa de la- 192 Gd 27.30N 105.30W
Boquillas del Carmen 192 Hc 29.17N 102.53W
Bor [Czech.] 120 Ig 49.43N 12.47 E
Bor [R.S.F.S.R.] 136 Ed 56.23N 44.07 E
Bor [Sud.] 160 Kh 6.12N 31.33 E
Bor [Swe.] 116 Fg 57.07N 14.10 E
Bor [Tur.] 146 Fd 37.54N 34.34 E
Bor [Yugo.] 130 Fe 44.06N 22.06 E
Bora-Bora, Ile- 208 Lf 16.30S 151.45W
Boraha, Nosy- 158 Lj 16.50S 49.55 E
Borah Peak 174 He 44.08N 113.14W
Boraldaj 135 Gc 42.30N 69.05 E
Bòramo 168 Gd 9.58N 43.07 E
Borås 114 Ch 57.43N 12.55 E
Borāzjān 146 Nh 29.16N 51.12 E
Borba [Braz.] 202 Gd 4.24S 59.35W
Borba [Port.] 126 Ef 38.48N 7.27W
Borborema, Planalto da- 198 Mf 7.00S 37.00W
Borca 130 Ib 47.11N 25.46 E
Borcea 130 Ke 44.20N 27.45 E
Borcea, Braţul- 130 Ke 44.40N 27.53 E
Borchgrevink Coast 222 Kf 73.00S 171.00 E
Borçka 146 Jb 41.22N 41.40 E
Borculo 124 Ib 52.07N 6.31 E
Borda da Mata, Serra- 204 Ie 21.18S 47.06W
Bordeaux 112 Fg 44.50N 0.34W
Borden 180 Ga 78.30N 110.30W
Borden Peninsula 174 Kb 73.00N 83.00W
Borders [3] 118 Kf 55.35N 3.00W
Bordertown 210 Fh 36.19S 140.47 E
Bordighera 128 Bg 43.46N 7.39 E
Bordj Bou Arreridj 162 Hb 36.04N 4.46 E
Bordj el Emir Abdelkader 126 Oi 35.52N 2.16 E
Bordj Fly Sainte Marie 162 Gd 27.18N 2.59W
Bordj Menaiel 126 Ph 36.44N 3.43 E
Bordj Messouda 162 Ic 30.12N 9.25 E
Bordj Moktar 160 Hf 21.20N 0.56 E
Bordj Omar Driss 160 Hf 28.09N 6.49 E
Bord Khūn-e Now 146 Nh 28.03N 51.28 E
Bordon Camp 124 Bc 51.07N 0.51W
Boreal, Chaco- 198 Kh 23.00S 60.00W
Boren 116 Ff 58.35N 15.10 E
Borensberg 116 Ff 58.34N 15.17 E
Borgå/Porvoo 116 Ff 60.24N 25.40 E
Borgarnes 114a Bb 64.32N 21.55W
Børgefjell 114 Cd 65.23N 13.50 E
Borgentreich 124 Lc 51.34N 9.15 E
Borger [Neth.] 124 Ib 52.55N 6.48 E
Borger [Tx.-U.S.] 182 Gd 35.39N 101.24W
Borgholm 114 Dh 56.53N 16.39 E
Borghorst, Steinfurt- 124 Jb 52.08N 7.25 E
Borgia 128 Kl 38.49N 16.30 E
Borgloon 124 Hd 50.48N 5.20 E
Borgomanero 128 Ce 45.42N 8.28 E
Borgorose 128 Hh 42.11N 13.15 E
Borgo San Dalmazzo 128 Bf 44.20N 7.30 E
Borgo San Lorenzo 128 Fg 43.57N 11.23 E
Borgosesia 128 Ce 45.43N 8.16 E
Borgou [3] 166 Fc 10.30N 2.50 E
Borgo Val di Taro 128 Df 44.29N 9.46 E
Borgo Valsugana 128 Fd 46.03N 11.27 E
Borgu 158 Hg 10.35N 3.40 E
Borgworm/Waremme 122 Ld 50.42N 5.15 E
Bori 166 Ge 4.42N 7.21 E
Borinquen, Punta- 197a Ab 18.30N 67.10W
Borislav 136 Cf 49.18N 23.27 E
Borisoglebsk 112 Ke 51.23N 42.06 E
Borisov 136 Ce 54.15N 28.30 E
Borisovka 132 Jd 50.36N 36.06 E
Borispol 136 De 50.23N 30.59 E
Bo River 168 Dd 6.48N 27.55 E
Borja 128 Lf 44.31N 17.44 E
Borja [Peru] 202 Cd 4.26S 77.33W
Borja [Sp.] 126 Kc 41.50N 1.32W
Borjas Blancas / les Borges Blanques 126 Mc 41.31N 0.52 E
Borken 120 Ce 51.51N 6.52 E
Borkou 158 Ig 18.15N 18.50 E
Borkou-Ennedi-Tibesti [3] 168 Bb 18.00N 19.00 E
Borkoviči 116 Mi 55.38N 28.23 E
Borkum 120 Cc 53.35N 6.41 E
Borlänge 114 Df 60.29N 15.25 E
Borlu 146 Cc 38.44N 28.27 E
Bormida 128 Cf 44.56N 8.40 E
Bormio 128 Ed 46.28N 10.22 E
Born 122 Ej 44.30N 1.00W
Borna 120 Ie 51.07N 12.30 E
Borndiep 124 Ha 53.25N 5.35 E
Borne 124 Ib 52.18N 6.45 E
Borneo/Kalimantan 140 Ni 1.00N 114.00 E
Bornheim 124 Id 50.46N 7.00 E
Bornholm [2] 116 Fi 55.10N 15.00 E
Bornholm 110 Hd 55.10N 15.00 E
Bornos 126 Gh 36.48N 5.44W
Bornova, İzmir- 146 Bc 38.27N 27.14 E
Bornu [2] 166 Hc 12.00N 12.40 E
Bornu 166 Ig 12.30N 13.00 E
Boro 158 Jh 8.52N 26.11 E
Borodino [R.S.F.S.R.] 114 Ii 55.32N 35.49 E
Borodino [R.S.F.S.R.] 138 Ee 55.57N 95.03 E
Borodinskoje 116 Md 61.00N 29.29 E
Borogoncy 138 Id 62.39N 131.08 E
Borohoro Shan 140 Ke 42.00N 85.00 E
Boromo 166 Ec 11.45N 2.56W
Borongan 150 Id 11.37N 125.26 E
Borotou 166 Dd 8.44N 7.30W
Borovan 130 Gf 43.26N 23.45 E
Borovec 130 Gg 42.16N 23.35 E
Boroviči 136 Dd 58.24N 33.56 E
Borovici 116 Mg 57.58N 29.47 E
Borovljanka 138 Df 52.38N 84.35 E
Borovo 128 Me 45.24N 18.59 E
Borovski 136 Gd 57.03N 65.44 E
Borovskoj 136 Ge 53.48N 64.17 E
Borrachas, Islas- 196 Dg 10.18N 64.44W
Borrān 168 Hc 10.11N 48.53 E
Borrby 116 Fi 55.27N 14.10 E
Borriana / Burriana 126 Le 39.53N 0.05W
Borroloola 210 Ef 16.04S 136.17 E
Borş 130 Eb 47.07N 21.49 E
Borşa 130 Hb 47.39N 24.40 E
Borščovočnyj hrebet = Borshchovochnyy Range (EN) 138 Gf 52.00N 118.30 E
Borsec 130 Ic 46.57N 25.34 E
Borshchovochnyy Range (EN) = Borščovočnyj hrebet 138 Gf 52.00N 118.30 E
Borsod-Abaúj-Zemplén [2] 120 Qh 48.15N 21.00 E
Bortala/Bole 152 Dc 44.59N 81.57 E
Bortala He 152 Dc 44.53N 82.45 E
Bort-les-Orgues 122 Ii 45.24N 2.30 E
Borūjen 146 Ng 31.59N 51.18 E
Borūjerd 144 Gc 33.54N 48.46 E
Borzja 142 Nd 50.24N 116.31 E
Borzna 132 Hd 51.15N 32.29 E
Boržomi 132 Mi 41.50N 43.25 E
Borzsöny 120 Oi 47.55N 19.00 E
Borzyszkowy 120 Nb 54.03N 17.22 E
Bosa 128 Cj 40.18N 8.30 E
Bosanska Dubica 128 Ke 45.11N 16.48 E
Bosanska Gradiška 128 Le 45.09N 17.15 E
Bosanska Krupa 128 Kf 44.53N 16.10 E
Bosanski Brod 128 Me 45.08N 18.01 E
Bosanski Novi 128 Ke 45.03N 16.22 E
Bosanski Petrovac 128 Kf 44.34N 16.21 E
Bosanski Šamac 128 Me 45.04N 18.28 E
Bosansko Grahovo 128 Kf 44.11N 16.22 E
Bōsāso 160 Lg 11.13N 49.08 E
Bosavi, Mount- 212 Ia 6.35S 142.50 E
Bosbeek 124 Hc 51.06N 5.48 E
Bose 142 Mg 24.01N 106.32 E
Boshan 152 Kd 36.30N 117.50 E
Boshrūyeh 146 Qf 33.53N 57.26 E
Bosilegrad 130 Fg 42.30N 22.28 E
Bosingfeld, Extertal- 124 Lb 52.04N 9.07 E
Bosna 130 Kg 42.11N 27.27 E
Bosna 128 Me 45.04N 18.28 E
Bosna=Bosnia (EN) 110 Hg 44.00N 18.00 E
Bosna = Bosnia (EN) 128 Lf 44.00N 18.00 E
Bosna i Hercegovina = Bosnia-Hercegovina (EN) [2] 128 Lf 44.15N 17.50 E
Bosnia (EN)=Bosna 110 Hg 44.00N 18.00 E
Bosnia (EN) = Bosna 128 Lf 44.00N 18.00 E
Bosnia-Hercegovina (EN) = Bosna i Hercegovina [2] 128 Lf 44.15N 17.50 E
Bosnik 150 Kg 1.10S 136.14 E
Bošnjakovo 138 Jg 49.41N 142.10 E
Bosobolo 170 Cb 4.11N 19.54 E
Bōsō-Hantō 154 Pg 35.20N 140.10 E
Bosporus (EN) = Instanbul Boğazi 110 Ig 41.00N 29.00 E
Bosque Bonito 192 Gb 30.42N 105.06W
Bossangoa 160 Ih 6.29N 17.27 E
Bossé Bangou 166 Fc 13.21N 1.18 E
Bossembélé 168 Bd 5.16N 17.39 E
Bossemtélé II 168 Bd 5.41N 16.38 E
Bossier City 182 Ie 32.31N 93.43W
Bosso 166 Hc 13.42N 13.19 E
Bosso, Dallol- 158 Hg 12.25N 2.50 E
Bossut, Cape- 212 Ec 18.43S 121.38 E
Bostān 148 Db 30.26N 67.02 E
Bostānābād 146 Ld 37.50N 46.50 E
Bosten/Bagrax Hu 140 Ke 42.00N 87.00 E
Boston [Eng.-U.K.] 118 Mi 52.59N 0.01W
Boston [Ma.-U.S.] 176 Le 42.21N 71.04W
Boston Bar 188 Eb 49.52N 121.26W
Boston Deeps 124 Ca 53.00N 0.15 E
Boston Mountains 182 Id 35.50N 93.20W
Botan 146 Id 37.44N 41.48 E
Botas, Ribeirão das- 204 Fe 20.26S 53.43W
Botesdale 124 Db 52.20N 1.01 E
Botev 110 Ig 42.43N 24.55 E
Botevgrad 130 Gg 42.54N 23.47 E
Bothnia, Gulf of- (EN)= Bottniska viken 110 Hc 63.00N 20.00 E
Bothnia, Gulf of- (EN)= Pohjanlahti 110 Hc 63.00N 20.00 E
Boticas 126 Ec 41.41N 7.40W
Botletle 172 Cd 21.07S 24.42 E
Botlih 132 Oh 42.41N 46.13 E
Botna 130 Mc 46.48N 29.30 E
Botoşani 130 Jb 47.45N 26.40 E
Botoşani [2] 130 Jb 47.40N 26.43 E
Botrange 122 Md 50.30N 6.08 E
Botswana [1] 160 Jk 22.00S 24.00 E

Index Symbols

[1] Independent Nation
[2] State, Region
[3] District, County
[4] Municipality
[5] Colony, Dependency
Continent
Physical Region
Historical or Cultural Region
Mount, Mountain
Volcano
Hill
Mountains, Mountain Range
Hills, Escarpment
Plateau, Upland
Pass, Gap
Plain, Lowland
Delta
Salt Flat
Valley, Canyon
Crater, Cave
Karst Features
Depression
Polder
Desert, Dunes
Forest, Woods
Heath, Steppe
Oasis
Cape, Point
Coast, Beach
Cliff
Peninsula
Isthmus
Sandbank
Island
Atoll
Rock, Reef
Islands, Archipelago
Rocks, Reefs
Coral Reef
Well, Spring
Geyser
River, Stream
Waterfall, Rapids
River Mouth, Estuary
Lake
Salt Lake
Intermittent Lake
Reservoir
Swamp, Pond
Canal
Glacier
Ice Shelf, Pack Ice
Ocean
Sea
Gulf, Bay
Strait, Fjord
Lagoon
Bank
Seamount
Tablemount
Ridge
Shelf
Basin
Escarpment, Sea Scarp
Fracture
Trench, Abyss
National Park, Reserve
Point of Interest
Recreation Site
Cave, Cavern
Historic Site
Ruins
Wall, Walls
Church, Abbey
Temple
Scientific Station
Railway station
Airport
Port
Military installation
Lighthouse
Mine
Tunnel
Dam, Bridge

Name	Page	Grid	Lat.	Long.
Botte Donato ▲	128	Kk	39.17N	16.27 E
Bottineau	182	Gb	48.50N	100.27W
Bottniska viken=Bothnia, Gulf of- (EN) ◁	110	Hc	63.00N	20.00 E
Bottrop	120	Ce	51.31N	6.55 E
Botucatu	206	Kb	22.52S	48.26W
Botucatu, Serra de- ▲	204	Hf	23.00S	48.20W
Botwood	180	Lg	49.08N	55.21W
Bouaflé	166	Dd	6.59N	5.45W
Bouaflé [3]	166	Dd	7.03N	5.48W
Bouaké	160	Gh	7.41N	5.02W
Bouaké [3]	166	Dd	7.45N	5.02W
Bou Anane	162	Gc	32.02N	3.03W
Bouar	160	Ih	5.57N	15.36 E
Bou Arfa	162	Gc	32.32N	1.57W
Boubin ▲	120	Jh	48.58N	13.50 E
Bouca	160	Ih	6.30N	18.17 E
Bouchain	124	Fd	50.17N	3.19 E
Bouchegouf	128	Bn	36.28N	7.44 E
Bouche Island ⟶	197k Bb	13.57N	60.53W
Bouches-du-Rhône [3]	122	Kk	43.30N	5.00 E
Boudenib	162	Gc	31.57N	3.36W
Boudeuse Cay ⟶	172b Bb	6.05S	52.51 E
Boû Djébéha	166	Eb	18.33N	2.45W
Bouenza [3]	170	Bc	3.00S	13.00 E
Boufarik	126	Oh	36.36N	2.54 E
Bougaa	126	Rh	36.20N	5.05 E
Bougainville Island ⟶	208	Ge	6.00S	155.00 E
Bougainville Reef ⟶	212	Jc	15.30S	147.05 E
Bougainville Strait [Ocn.] ⟶	219a Cb	6.40S	156.10 E
Bougainville Strait [Van.] ⟶	219b Cb	15.50S	167.10 E
Bougouni	160	Gg	11.25N	7.28W
Bougtob	162	Hc	34.02N	0.05 E
Bouguenais	122	Eg	47.11N	1.37W
Bouguirat	126	Mi	35.45N	0.15 E
Bougzoul	126	Oi	35.42N	2.51 E
Bou Hadjar	128	Cn	36.30N	8.06 E
Bouhalla, Jbel- ▲	126	Gi	35.06N	5.07W
Bou Hamed	126	Hi	35.19N	4.58W
Bouillante	197e Ab	16.08N	61.46W
Bouillon	122	Le	49.48N	5.04 E
Bouira	162	Hb	36.23N	3.54 E
Bouïra [3]	162	Hb	36.15N	4.10 E
Bou Ismail	126	Oh	36.38N	2.41 E
Bou Izakarn	162	Fd	29.10N	9.44W
Bou Kadir	126	Nh	36.04N	1.07 E
Boukombé	166	Fc	10.11N	1.06 E
Boû Lanouâr	162	De	21.16N	16.30W
Boulay-Moselle	124	Ie	49.11N	6.30 E
Boulder [Co.-U.S.]	176	Ie	40.01N	105.17W
Boulder [Mt.-U.S.]	188	Ic	46.14N	112.07W
Boulder City	188	Hi	35.59N	114.50W
Boulemane	162	Gc	33.22N	4.45W
Boulemane [3]	162	Gc	33.02N	4.04W
Boulevard Atlántico	204	Dn	38.19S	57.59W
Boulia	212	Hd	22.54S	139.54 E
Bouligny	122	Le	49.17N	5.45 E
Boulogne [3]	122	Eg	47.05N	1.40W
Boulogne-Billancourt	122	If	48.50N	2.15 E
Boulogne-sur-Mer	122	Hd	50.43N	1.37 E
Boulonnais ⟶	122	Hd	50.40N	1.40 E
Boulou, Le-	122	Il	42.31N	2.50 E
Bouloupari	219b Ce	21.52S	166.03 E
Boulsa	166	Ec	12.39N	0.34W
Boultoum	166	Hc	14.40N	10.18 E
Bou Maad, Djebel- ▲	126	Oh	36.26N	2.08 E
Boumba ⟶	166	Ie	2.02N	15.12 E
Boumdeïd	162	Ef	17.26N	11.21W
Boum Kabir	168	Bc	10.11N	19.24 E
Boumort ▲	126	Nb	42.14N	1.08 E
Bouna	160	Gh	9.16N	3.00W
Bouna [3]	166	Ed	9.15N	3.20W
Boû Nâga	162	Ef	19.00N	13.13W
Bou Nasser, Adrar- ▲	162	Gc	33.35N	3.53W
Boundary Peak ▲	188	Fh	37.51N	118.21W
Boundiali	166	Dd	9.31N	6.29W
Boundiali [3]	166	Dd	9.23N	6.32W
Boundji	170	Cc	1.03S	15.22 E
Boungou ⟶	168	Cd	6.45N	22.06 E
Bountiful	182	Ec	40.53N	111.53W
Bounty Bay ⟶	220q Ab	25.03S	130.05W
Bounty Islands ⟶	208	Ii	47.45S	179.05 E
Bounty Trough (EN) ⟶	106	Jn	46.00S	178.00 E
Bourail	216	Cd	21.34S	165.30 E
Bourbon-Lancy	122	Hg	46.37N	3.47 E
Bourbonnais ⟶	122	Ih	46.30N	3.00 E
Bourbonne-les-Bains	122	Lg	47.57N	5.45 E
Bourbourg	124	Ed	50.57N	2.12 E
Bourbre ⟶	122	Li	45.47N	5.11 E
Bourem	166	Eb	16.58N	0.21W
Bouressa	166	Fa	20.01N	2.18 E
Bourg-Achard	124	Ce	49.21N	0.49 E
Bourganeuf	122	Hi	45.57N	1.45 E
Bourg'ar'oün, Cap- ▶	162	Ib	37.06N	6.28 E
Bourg-de-Péage	122	Li	45.02N	5.03 E
Bourg-en-Bresse	122	La	46.12N	5.13 E
Bourges	112	Gf	47.05N	2.24 E
Bourget, Lac du- ⟶	122	Li	45.44N	5.52 E
Bourgneuf, Baie de- ⟶	122	Dg	47.05N	2.13W
Bourgogne	124	Ge	49.21N	4.04 E
Bourgogne=Burgundy (EN) ⟶	110	Gf	47.00N	4.30 E
Bourgogne=Burgundy (EN) ⟶	122	Kg	47.00N	4.30 E
Bourgogne, Canal de- ⟶	122	Kg	47.58N	3.30 E
Bourgogne, Porte de- ⟶	122	Mg	47.38N	6.52 E
Bourgoin-Jallieu	122	Li	45.35N	5.17 E
Bourgtheroulde-Infreville	124	Ce	49.18N	0.53 E
Bourguébus	124	Be	49.07N	0.18W
Boû Rjeïmat	162	Df	19.04N	15.08W
Bourke	210	Hg	30.05S	145.56 E
Bourne	124	Bb	52.46N	0.23W
Bournemouth	118	Lk	50.43N	1.54W
Bourtanger Moor ⟶	122	Jb	52.50N	7.06 E
Bourth	124	Cf	48.46N	0.49 E
Bou Saâda	160	Hb	35.12N	4.11 E
Bou Sellam ⟶	126	Qh	36.26N	4.34 E
Boussac	122	Ih	46.21N	2.13 E
Boussé	166	Ec	12.39N	1.53W
Boussens	122	Gk	43.11N	0.58 E
Bousso	168	Bc	10.29N	16.43 E
Bouthaleb, Djebel- ▲	126	Ri	35.48N	5.12 E
Boutilimit	162	Ef	17.33N	14.42W
Bou Tlelis	126	Li	35.34N	0.54W
Boutonne ⟶	122	Fi	45.55N	0.49W
Bouvet Øy ⟶	222	Cd	54.25S	3.24 E
Bouxwiller	124	Jf	48.49N	7.29 E
Bouza	166	Gc	14.25N	6.02 E
Bouzanne ⟶	122	Hh	46.38N	1.28 E
Bouzghaia	126	Mh	36.20N	1.15 E
Bouzonville	124	Ie	49.18N	6.32 E
Bovalino	128	Jm	38.09N	16.11 E
Bova Marina	128	Jm	37.56N	15.55 E
Bovec	128	Hd	46.20N	13.33 E
Bovenkarspel	124	Db	52.42N	5.17 E
Boves	124	Ee	49.51N	2.23 E
Bovino	128	Ji	41.15N	15.20 E
Bovril	204	Cj	31.21S	59.26W
Bowa → Muli	152	Hf	27.55N	101.13 E
Bowen [Arg.]	206	Ge	35.02S	67.31W
Bowen [Austl.]	210	Fg	20.01S	148.15 E
Bowers Bank (EN) ⟶	198	Mf	7.09S	34.47W
Bowers Ridge (EN) ⟶	178a Bb	54.00N	180.00
Bowie	186	Hj	33.34N	97.51W
Bowkān	146	Ld	36.31N	46.12 E
Bowland, Forest of- ⟶	118	Kh	54.00N	2.35W
Bowling Green [Ky.-U.S.]	182	Jd	37.00N	86.27W
Bowling Green [Oh.-U.S.]	184	Fe	41.22N	83.40W
Bowman	182	Gb	46.11N	103.24W
Bowman Bay ⟶	180	Kc	65.33N	73.40W
Bowman Island ⟶	222	He	65.17S	103.08 E
Bowman. Mount- ▲	188	Ea	51.10N	121.55W
Bowo/Bomi	152	Ge	30.02N	95.39 E
Bowokan, Kepulauan- ⟶	150	Hg	2.05S	123.35 E
Bowral	212	Kf	34.28S	150.25 E
Bow River ⟶	180	Gg	49.56N	111.42W
Box Elder Creek ⟶	188	Kc	46.57N	108.04W
Boxelder Creek ⟶	188	Md	45.59N	103.57W
Boxholm	114	Dg	58.12N	15.03 E
Boxian	152	Ke	33.46N	115.44 E
Boxing	152	Kd	37.07N	118.04 E
Boxmeer	124	Hc	51.39N	5.57 E
Boxtel	124	Gc	51.35N	5.20 E
Boyabat	146	Fh	41.28N	34.47 E
Boyabo	170	Cb	3.43N	18.46 E
Boyacá [3]	202	Db	5.30N	72.50W
Boyang	152	Kf	29.00N	116.41 E
Boyer, Cap- ▶	219b De	21.37S	168.07 E
Boyer Ahmadī-e Kohkīlūyeh [3]	144	Hc	31.00N	50.30 E
Boyle/Mainistir na Búille	118	Eh	53.58N	8.18W
Boyne/An Bhóinn ⟶	118	Gh	53.43N	6.15W
Boyne City	184	Ec	45.13N	85.01W
Boynes, Iles de- ⟶	158	Nm	49.58S	69.59 E
Boynton Beach	186	Jk	26.32N	80.03W
Boysen Reservoir ⟶	188	Ke	43.19N	108.11W
Boz, Küh-e- ▲	146	Pi	27.46N	55.54 E
Bozburun	130	Lm	36.41N	28.04 E
Bozburun ▲	130	Li	40.32N	28.46 E
Bozburun Dağı ▲	146	Dg	37.18N	31.03 E
Bozcaada	146	Bc	39.50N	26.04 E
Bozcaada ⟶	130	Ik	39.49N	26.03 E
Bozdağ	130	Lk	38.20N	28.00 E
Boz Dağı [Tur.] ▲	146	Cd	37.18N	29.12 E
Boz Dağı [Tur.] ▲	146	Cc	38.19N	28.08 E
Boz Dağları ▲	130	Kj	38.20N	27.45 E
Bozdoğan	130	Ll	37.40N	28.19 E
Bozeman	176	He	45.41N	111.02W
Bozen / Bolzano	112	Hf	46.31N	11.22 E
Bozene	170	Cb	2.56N	19.12 E
Bozhen	154	Be	38.04N	116.34 E
Bozkol, zaliv- ⟶	135	Cb	45.20N	61.45 E
Bozkurt	146	Fh	41.57N	34.01 E
Bozok Platosu ⟶	146	Fc	39.05N	35.05 E
Bozouls	122	Ij	44.28N	2.43 E
Bozoum	168	Ad	6.19N	16.23 E
Bozova	146	Hd	37.22N	38.31 E
Bozovici	130	Ha	44.56N	22.00 E
Bozqūsh, Küh-e- ▲	146	Ld	37.45N	47.40 E
Bozüyük	146	Dc	39.54N	30.03 E
Bra	128	Bf	44.42N	7.51 E
Braås	116	Fg	57.04N	15.03 E
Braathen, Cape- ▶	222	Pf	71.48S	96.05W
Brabant [3]	124	Gd	50.45N	4.30 E
Brabant [=]	124	Lc	51.00N	5.05 E
Brabant-les-Villers	124	Gf	48.51N	4.59 E
Brâbâich ⟶	116	Eb	17.30N	3.00W
Brač ⟶	128	Kg	43.19N	16.40 E
Bracadale, Loch- ⟶	118	Gd	57.20N	6.35W
Bracciano	128	Gh	42.06N	12.10 E
Bracciano, Lago di- ⟶	128	Gh	42.05N	12.15 E
Bräcke	114	De	62.43N	15.27 E
Brackettville	186	Fk	29.19N	100.24W
Brački kanal ⟶	128	Kg	43.24N	16.40 E
Brackley	118	Mj	52.02N	1.09W
Bracknell	118	Mj	51.26N	0.46W
Brackwede, Bielefeld-	124	Kc	51.59N	8.31 E
Brad	130	Fc	46.08N	22.47 E
Bradano ⟶	128	Kj	40.23N	16.51 E
Bradenton	182	Kf	27.29N	82.34W
Bradford [Eng.-U.K.]	118	Lh	53.48N	1.45W
Bradford [Pa.-U.S.]	184	He	41.57N	78.39W
Bradley Reef ⟶	214	Gg	6.52S	160.48 E
Brady	186	Gk	31.08N	99.20W
Brady Mountains ⟶	186	Gk	31.20N	99.40W
Brædstrup	116	Ci	55.58N	9.37 E
Braemar	118	Id	57.01N	3.24W
Braga	112	Fg	41.33N	8.25W
Braga [2]	126	Fc	41.35N	8.26W
Bragadiru	130	If	43.46N	25.31 E
Bragado	204	Cm	35.08S	60.30W
Bragança [Braz.]	202	Gd	1.03S	46.46W
Bragança [Port.]	126	Ec	41.49N	6.45W
Bragança Paulista	204	If	22.57S	46.34W
Brahestad/Raahe	114	Fd	64.41N	24.29 E
Brāhmanbāria	148	Id	23.59N	91.07 E
Brahmapur	142	Kh	19.19N	84.47 E
Brahmaputra	140	Lg	24.02N	90.59 E
Brăila	112	If	45.16N	27.59 E
Brăila	130	Kd	45.13N	27.48 E
Brăilei, Balta- ⟶	130	Ke	45.00N	28.00 E
Braine	124	Fe	49.20N	3.32 E
Braine-l'Alleud/Eigenbrakel	124	Gd	50.41N	4.22 E
Brainerd	182	Hb	46.21N	94.12W
Braintree	124	Cc	51.53N	0.34 E
Braithwaite Point ▶	212	Gb	11.58S	134.00 E
Brake (Unterweser)	120	Ec	53.20N	8.29 E
Brakel [Bel.]	124	Fd	50.47N	3.45 E
Brakel [Ger.]	124	Lc	51.43N	9.11 E
Brakna [3]	162	Ef	17.30N	13.30W
Brålanda	116	Ef	58.34N	12.22 E
Bralorne	188	Da	50.47N	122.49W
Bramming	116	Ci	55.28N	8.42 E
Bramön ⟶	116	Gb	62.10N	17.40 E
Brampton	184	Hd	43.41N	79.46W
Bramsche	120	Dd	52.24N	7.59 E
Bran, Pasul- ⟶	130	Id	45.26N	25.17 E
Branco, Cabo- ▶	198	Mf	7.09S	34.47W
Branco, Rio- [Braz.] ⟶	198	Jf	1.24S	61.51W
Branco, Rio- [Braz.] ⟶	204	De	21.00S	57.48W
Branco ou Cabixi, Rio- ⟶	204	Ba	13.55S	60.10W
Brandberg ▲	158	Ik	21.08S	14.35 E
Brandbu	114	Cf	60.26N	10.28 E
Brande	114	Bi	55.57N	9.07 E
Brandenburg	120	Ig	52.25N	12.33 E
Brandenburg [=]	120	Jd	52.10N	13.30 E
Brändö	116	Hf	60.25N	21.05 E
Brandon [Eng.-U.K.]	124	Cb	52.27N	0.37 E
Brandon [Fl.-U.S.]	184	Fl	27.56N	82.17W
Brandon [Man.-Can.]	176	Kd	49.50N	99.57W
Brandon [Vt.-U.S.]	184	Kd	43.47N	73.05W
Brandon Head/Na Machairí ▶	118	Ci	52.16N	10.15W
Brandon Mount/Cnoc Bréanainn ▲	118	Ci	52.14N	10.15W
Brandval	114	Cf	60.19N	12.02 E
Brandvlei	172	Cf	30.25S	20.30 E
Brandýs nad Labem-Stará Boleslav	120	Kf	50.11N	14.40 E
Brănești	130	Je	44.27N	26.20 E
Braniewo	120	Pb	54.24N	19.50 E
Bransby Point ▶	197c Bc	16.43N	62.14W
Bransfield Strait ⟶	222	Re	63.00S	59.00W
Brańsk	120	Sd	52.45N	22.51 E
Branson	186	Jh	36.39N	93.13W
Brantevik	116	Fi	55.31N	14.21 E
Brantford	180	Jh	43.08N	80.16W
Brantôme	122	Gi	45.22N	0.39 E
Bras d'Or Lake ⟶	180	Le	45.50N	60.50W
Brasil = Brazil (EN) [1]	200	Kf	9.00S	53.00W
Brasil, Planalto do- = Brazilian Highlands (EN)	198	Lg	17.00S	45.00W
Brasiléia	202	Ef	11.00S	68.44W
Brasilia	200	Lg	15.47S	47.55W
Brasilia de Minas	204	Jc	16.12S	44.26W
Brasla ⟶	116	Kg	57.08N	24.50 E
Braslav	114	Ss	55.37N	27.05 E
Braşov	112	If	45.38N	25.35 E
Braşov [2]	130	Id	45.40N	25.10 E
Brass	166	Ge	4.19N	6.14 E
Brassac	122	Ik	43.38N	2.30 E
Brasschaat	124	Gc	51.17N	4.27 E
Brasstown Bald ▲	184	Fh	34.52N	83.48W
Brastavăţu	130	Hf	43.55N	24.24 E
Brataj	130	Ci	40.16N	19.40 E
Bratca	130	Fc	46.56N	22.37 E
Brăte	116	De	59.43N	11.27 E
Bratislava	112	Hf	48.09N	17.07 E
Bratsk	142	Md	56.20N	101.48 E
Bratskoje vodohranilišče = Bratsk Reservoir (EN) ⟶	138	Fe	56.30N	102.00 E
Bratsk Reservoir (EN) = Bratskoje vodohranilišče ⟶	138	Fe	56.30N	102.00 E
Brattleboro	182	Mc	42.51N	72.36W
Brattvåg	116	Bg	62.36N	6.27 E
Braubach	124	Jd	50.17N	7.40 E
Braunau am Inn	128	Ha	48.16N	13.02 E
Braunschweig	120	Gd	52.16N	10.31 E
Brava	158	Ge	14.52N	24.43W
Brava, Costa- ⟶	126	Pc	41.45N	3.04 E
Bråviken ⟶	116	Gf	58.40N	16.30 E
Bravo del Norte, Rio-= Grande, Rio- (EN) ⟶	174	Jg	25.57N	97.09W
Brawley	188	Gj	32.59N	115.34W
Bray	172	Ce	26.23S	23.38 E
Bray	118	Jc	69.20N	77.00W
Bray/Bré	118	Jb	53.12N	6.06W
Bray, Pays de- ⟶	124	Ce	49.35N	1.40 E
Bray-Dunes	124	Ec	51.05N	2.31 E
Braye ⟶	122	Gg	47.45N	0.42 E
Bray Head ▶	118	Cj	51.52N	10.25W
Bray-sur-Somme	124	Ee	49.56N	2.43 E
Brazi	130	Je	44.56N	26.01 E
Brazil	184	Df	39.32N	87.08W
Brazil (EN) =Brasil [1]	200	Kf	9.00S	53.00W
Brazil Basin (EN) ⟶	106	Dk	15.00S	24.00W
Brazilian Highlands (EN) = Brasil, Planalto do- ⟶	198	Lg	17.00S	45.00W
Brazos ⟶	174	Jg	28.53N	95.23W
Brazos Santiago Pass ⟶	186	Gm	26.04N	97.09W
Brazzaville	160	Ii	4.16S	15.17 E
Brčko	128	Lf	44.52N	18.48 E
Brda ⟶	120	Nc	53.07N	18.08 E
Bré/Bray	118	Jb	53.12N	6.06W
Brea, Punta- ▶	197a Bc	17.54N	66.55W
Breaden, Lake- ⟶	212	Ee	25.45S	125.40 E
Breaksea Sound ⟶	218	Bf	45.35S	166.40 E
Breaza [Rom.]	130	Id	45.11N	25.40 E
Breaza [2]	130	Ib	47.30N	25.20 E
Breaza, Vîrful- ▲	130	Hb	47.22N	24.02 E
Brebes	150	Eh	6.53S	109.03 E
Brèche ⟶	124	Ee	49.16N	2.30 E
Brechin	118	Ke	56.44N	2.40W
Brecht	124	Gc	51.21N	4.38 E
Breckenridge [Mn.-U.S.]	186	Hc	46.16N	96.35W
Breckenridge [Tx.-U.S.]	186	Gj	32.45N	98.54W
Breckland ⟶	118	Ni	52.30N	0.35 E
Břeclav	120	Mh	48.46N	16.54 E
Brecon	118	Jj	51.57N	3.24W
Brecon Beacons ⟶	118	Jj	51.53N	3.31W
Breda	122	Kc	51.35N	4.46 E
Bredaryd	116	Eg	57.10N	13.44 E
Bredasdorp	160	Jl	34.32S	20.02 E
Brede ⟶	116	Ci	50.55N	0.43 E
Bredene	124	Ec	51.14N	2.58 E
Bredstedt	120	Eb	54.37N	8.59 E
Bredy	136	Gc	52.26N	60.21 E
Bree	124	Hc	51.08N	5.36 E
Breg ⟶	120	Ei	47.57N	8.31 E
Bregalnica ⟶	130	Eh	41.36N	21.56 E
Bregenz	112	Hf	47.30N	9.46 E
Bregovo	128	Nf	44.09N	22.39 E
Bréhat, Ile de- ⟶	122	Df	48.51N	3.00W
Breiðafjörður ⟶	110	Bb	65.15N	23.15W
Breidvika ⟶	222	Df	70.15S	24.15 E
Breisach am Rhein	120	Dh	48.02N	7.35 E
Breisgau ⟶	120	Di	47.50N	7.42 E
Breisund ⟶	116	Ab	63.00N	6.00 E
Breit Bridge ⟶	172	Dd	22.12S	29.59 E
Breivikbotn	114	Fa	70.37N	22.29 E
Brejão	204	Ce	12.59S	46.28W
Brekken	114	Ce	62.39N	11.53 E
Brekstad	114	Be	63.41N	9.41 E
Bremangerlandet ⟶	114	Af	61.50N	5.00 E
Bremberg, Val- ⟶	128	De	45.55N	9.40 E
Brembo ⟶	128	De	45.35N	9.32 E
Bremen [2]	120	Ec	53.05N	8.50 E
Bremen [Gar.]	112	Gd	53.05N	8.48 E
Bremen [In.-U.S.]	184	De	41.27N	86.09W
Bremerhaven	120	Ec	53.29N	9.08 E
Bremerton	182	Cb	47.34N	122.38W
Bremervörde	120	Fc	53.29N	9.08 E
Brendel	188	Kg	38.57N	109.50W
Brenham	186	Hk	30.10N	96.24W
Brenne ⟶	122	Hh	46.44N	1.14 E
Brenner, Passo del-= Brenner Pass (EN) ⟶	110	Hf	47.00N	11.30 E
Brennerpaß = Brenner Pass (EN) ⟶	110	Hf	47.00N	11.30 E
Brenner Pass (EN) = Brennero, Passo del- ⟶	110	Hf	47.00N	11.30 E
Brenner Pass (EN) = Brennerpaß ⟶	110	Hf	47.00N	11.30 E
Brenta ⟶	128	Ge	45.25N	12.18 E
Brentwood	118	Nj	51.38N	0.18 E
Brescia	112	Hf	45.33N	10.15 E
Breskens	124	Fc	51.24N	3.33 E
Breslau (EN) = Wrocław	112	Ne	51.06N	17.00 E
Bresle ⟶	122	Hd	50.04N	1.22 E
Bressanone / Brixen	128	Ga	46.43N	11.39 E
Bressay ⟶	118	La	60.08N	1.05W
Bresse ⟶	122	Kh	46.30N	5.15 E
Bressuire	122	Fh	46.51N	0.29W
Brest [Bye.-U.S.S.R.]	112	Ie	52.06N	23.42 E
Brest [Fr.]	112	Ff	48.24N	4.29W
Brestova	128	Ie	45.08N	14.14 E
Brestskaja oblast [3]	136	Ce	52.20N	25.30 E
Bretagne=Brittany (EN) [3]	110	Ff	48.00N	3.00W
Bretagne = Brittany (EN) [3]	122	Df	48.00N	3.00W
Bretcu	130	Jc	46.03N	26.18 E
Breteuil [Fr.]	124	Cf	48.50N	0.55 E
Breteuil [Fr.]	124	Ee	49.38N	2.18 E
Breton, Marais- ⟶	122	Eh	46.56N	2.00W
Breton, Pertuis- ⟶	122	Eh	46.16N	1.22W
Breton Sound ⟶	186	Ll	29.30N	89.30W
Brett ⟶	124	Cb	52.05N	0.53 E
Brett, Cape- ▶	218	Fa	35.10S	174.20 E
Bretten	124	Ke	49.03N	8.42 E
Bretteville-sur-Laize	124	Be	49.03N	0.20W
Breueh, Pulau- ⟶	150	Be	5.41N	95.05 E
Breuil-Cervinia	128	Bd	45.56N	7.38 E
Breukelen	124	Db	52.10N	5.01 E
Breuna	124	Lc	51.24N	9.11 E
Breves	202	Hd	1.40S	50.29W
Brevik	114	Bg	59.04N	9.42 E
Brevoort ⟶	180	Kd	63.30N	64.20W
Brewarrina	212	Je	29.57S	146.52 E
Brewerville	166	Cd	6.25N	10.47W
Brewster	188	Fa	48.06N	119.47W
Brewster, Kap- ▶	224	Md	70.10N	21.30W
Brewton	184	Dj	31.07N	87.04W
Brežiče	128	Je	45.54N	15.35 E
Brezina	162	Hc	33.05N	1.16 E
Březnice	120	Jg	49.33N	13.57 E
Brezno	120	Ph	48.49N	19.39 E
Brezoi	130	Hd	45.21N	24.15 E
Brezovo	130	Jg	42.21N	25.05 E
Bria	158	Jh	6.32N	21.59 E
Briançon	122	Mj	44.54N	6.39 E
Brianza ⟶	128	De	45.45N	9.15 E
Briare, Canal de- ⟶	122	If	48.02N	2.43 E
Bribie Island ⟶	212	Ke	27.04S	153.05 E
Bričany	130	Ka	48.18N	27.04 E
Brick's Point ▶	197a Bc	17.54N	66.55W
Bridgend	118	Jj	51.31N	3.35W
Bridgeport [Ca.-U.S.]	188	Fg	38.10N	119.14W
Bridgeport [Ct.-U.S.]	182	Mc	41.11N	73.11W
Bridgeport [Nb.-U.S.]	186	Ef	41.40N	103.06W
Bridge River ⟶	188	Da	50.45N	121.40W
Bridger Peak ▲	188	Lf	41.12N	107.02W
Bridges Point ▶	220q Bb	1.58N	157.28W
Bridgetor	184	Jf	39.26N	75.14W
Bridgetown [Austl.]	212	Df	33.57S	116.08
Bridgetown [Bar.]	176	Nh	13.06N	59.37W
Bridgewater	180	Lh	44.23N	64.31W
Bridgwater	118	Kj	51.08N	3.00W
Bridgwater Bay ⟶	118	Jj	51.16N	3.12W
Bridlington	118	Mg	54.05N	0.12W
Bridlington Bay ⟶	118	Mg	54.04N	0.08W
Bridport	118	Kk	50.44N	2.46W
Brie ⟶	122	Jf	48.40N	3.30
Brielle	124	Gc	51.54N	4.10
Brienzer See ⟶	128	Bd	46.45N	7.55
Briey	122	Le	49.15N	5.56
Brig	128	Bd	46.20N	8.00
Brigach ⟶	120	Ei	47.58N	8.30
Brigham City	182	Ed	41.31N	112.01W
Brighstone	124	Ad	50.38N	1.23W
Bright	212	Jg	36.44S	146.58 E
Brightlingsea	124	Dc	51.48N	1.02
Brighton [Co.-U.S.]	186	Dg	39.59N	104.49W
Brighton [Eng.-U.K.]	112	Fe	50.50N	0.10W
Brighton-Alme	124	Kc	51.24N	8.37
Brimstone Hill ⟶	197c Ab	17.21N	62.49W
Brindisi	112	Hg	40.38N	17.56
Brinje	186	Kk	34.53N	91.12W
Brinkmann	204	Aj	30.52S	62.02W
Brionne	124	Ce	49.12N	0.43
Brioude	122	Ji	45.18N	3.24
Brisbane	210	Gg	27.28S	153.02 E
Brisighella	128	Ff	44.13N	11.46
Bristol ⟶	222	Ad	59.02S	26.31W
Bristol [Eng.-U.K.]	112	Fe	51.27N	2.35W
Bristol [Tn.-U.S.]	184	Fg	36.36N	82.11W
Bristol Bay ⟶	174	Dd	58.00N	159.00W
Bristol Channel ⟶	110	Fe	51.20N	4.00W
Bristol Lake ⟶	188	Hi	34.28N	115.41W
Britannia Range ⟶	222	Jf	80.00S	158.00
British Columbia [2]	180	Fe	55.00N	125.00W
British Honduras → Belize [1]	176	Kh	17.15N	88.45W
British Indian Ocean Territory (EN) [5]	142	Jj	7.00S	72.00
British Isles ⟶	110	Fd	54.00N	4.00W
British Mountains ⟶	178	Kc	69.20N	140.20W
British Solomon Islands → Solomon Islands (EN) [1]	210	Ge	8.00S	159.00
British Virgin Islands [5]	176	Mh	18.20N	64.50W
Brits	172	De	25.40S	27.46
Britstown	172	Cf	30.37S	23.30
Brittany (EN) = Bretagne [3]	110	Ff	48.00N	3.00W
Brittany = Bretagne (EN) [3]	122	Df	48.00N	3.00W
Britton	186	Hc	45.48N	97.45W
Brive-la-Gaillarde	122	Hi	45.09N	1.32
Briviesca	126	Ja	42.33N	3.19W
Brixen / Bressanone	128	Ga	46.43N	11.39
Brixham, Torbay-	118	Jk	50.24N	3.30W
Brjansk	112	Ja	53.15N	34.22
Brjanskaja oblast [3]	136	Dd	53.00N	33.20
Brjuhovecka	132	Kg	45.46N	39.01
Brjukoviči	120	Tg	49.52N	24.00
Brno	112	Hf	49.12N	16.37
Broa, Ensenada de la- ⟶	194	Fb	22.35N	82.00W
Broadback ⟶	180	Jf	51.21N	78.53W
Broad Bay ⟶	118	Gc	58.15N	6.15W
Broadford	118	Gd	57.14N	5.54W
Broad Sound ⟶	212	Jd	22.10S	149.45
Broadstairs	124	Dc	51.22N	1.27
Broadus	186	Ed	45.27N	105.25W
Brocéni/Broceny	116	Ji	56.41N	22.30
Broceny/Brocéni	116	Ji	56.41N	22.30
Brochet	180	Hd	57.53N	101.40W
Brochu, Lac- ⟶	184	Ja	48.46N	74.15W
Brock ⟶	180	Ga	77.55N	114.30W
Brocken ▲	120	Ge	51.48N	10.36
Brockman, Mount- ▲	212	Dd	22.35S	117.18
Brockton	184	Ld	42.05N	71.01W
Brockville	184	Jd	44.35N	75.41W
Brod	130	Eh	41.31N	21.14
Brod/Bosanski Brod	128	Le	45.09N	18.00
Brodarevo	128	Mg	43.14N	19.43
Brodeur Peninsula ⟶	174	Kb	73.00N	88.00W
Brodnica	120	Pc	53.16N	19.23
Brody	132	Df	50.05N	25.12
Brogido	132	Dd	50.54N	25.16
Broglie	124	Ce	49.01N	0.32
Broken Arrow	186	Ih	36.03N	95.48W
Broken Bow	186	Gf	41.24N	99.38W
Broken Bow Lake ⟶	186	Ii	34.10N	94.40W
Broken Hill	210	Hf	31.57S	141.27
Broken Ridge (EN) ⟶	106	Hm	31.30S	95.00 E
Brokind	116	Ff	58.13N	15.40
Brokopondo	202	Hb	5.04N	55.00W
Bromarv	116	Hf	59.55N	23.03
Bromley, London-	110	Se	51.24N	0.01
Brömölla	116	Fi	56.04N	14.28
Brong-Ahafo [3]	166	Ed	7.45N	1.30W
Bronnikovo	134	Sg	58.29N	68.27
Bronnøysund	114	Cd	65.28N	12.13
Bronte	128	Im	37.47N	14.50
Brooke's Point	150	Gd	8.47N	117.50
Brookfield	186	Jg	39.47N	93.05W
Brookhaven	186	Kk	31.35N	90.26W
Brookings [Or.-U.S.]	188	Cd	42.03N	124.17W
Brookings [S.D.-U.S.]	182	Hc	44.19N	96.48W
Brooks	180	Gg	50.35N	111.53W
Brooks Banks (EN) ⟶	214	Mc	24.05N	166.55W
Brooks Range ⟶	174	Dc	68.00N	154.00W
Brookston	184	Jf	46.50N	92.36W

Index Symbols

[1] Independent Nation	Historical or Cultural Region	Pass, Gap	Depression	Coast, Beach	Rock, Reef	Waterfall, Rapids	Canal	Lagoon	Escarpment, Sea Scarp	Historic Site	Airport
[2] State, Region	Mount, Mountain	Plain, Lowland	Polder	Cliff	Islands, Archipelago	River Mouth, Estuary	Glacier	Bank	Fracture	Ruins	Port
[3] District, County	Volcano	Delta	Desert, Dunes	Peninsula	Rocks, Reefs	Lake	Ice Shelf, Pack Ice	Seamount	Trench, Abyss	Wall, Walls	Military installation
[4] Municipality	Hill	Salt Flat	Forest, Woods	Isthmus	Coral Reef	Salt Lake	Sea	Tableland	National Park, Reserve	Church, Abbey	Lighthouse
[5] Colony, Dependency	Mountains, Mountain Range	Valley, Canyon	Heath, Steppe	Sandbank	Well, Spring	Intermittent Lake	Gulf, Bay	Ridge	Point of Interest	Temple	Mine
■ Continent	Hills, Escarpment	Crater, Cave	Oasis	Island	Geyser	Reservoir	Shelf	Recreation Site	Scientific Station	Tunnel
⊃ Physical Region	Plateau, Upland	Karst Features	Cape, Point	Atoll	River, Stream	Swamp, Pond	Strait, Fjord	Basin	Cave, Cavern	Railway station	Dam, Bridge

Brooksville 184 Fk 28.33N 82.23W
Brookton 212 Df 32.22S 117.01 E
Brookville [In.-U.S.] 184 Ef 39.25N 85.01W
Brookville [Pa.-U.S.] 184 He 41.10N 79.06W
Broom 118 Hd 57.45N 5.05W
Broom, Loch- 118 Hd 57.55N 5.15W
Broome 210 Df 17.58S 122.14 E
Brora 118 Jc 58.01N 3.51W
Brora 118 Jc 58.00N 3.50W
Brosna/An Bhrosnach 118 Fh 53.13N 7.58W
Broşteni 130 Ib 47.14N 25.42 E
Brou 122 Hf 48.13N 1.11 E
Brough 118 Kg 54.32N 2.19W
Broughton Island 176 Mc 67.35N 63.50W
Broussard 186 Kk 30.09N 91.58W
Brovary 132 Gd 50.32N 30.48 E
Brovst 116 Cg 57.06N 9.32 E
Brown Bank (EN)=Bruine Bank 124 Fb 52.35N 3.20 E
Brownfield 182 Ge 33.11N 102.16W
Browning 188 Ib 48.34N 113.01W
Browns Bank (EN) 180 Kh 42.40N 66.05W
Brownsville [Tn.-U.S.] 184 Ch 35.36N 89.15W
Brownsville [Tx.-U.S.] 176 Jg 25.54N 97.30W
Brownwood 182 He 31.43N 98.59W
Browse Island 212 Eb 14.05S 123.35 E
Bruay-en-Artois 122 Id 50.29N 2.33 E
Bruay-sur-l'Escaut 124 Fd 50.23N 3.32 E
Bruce 186 Lj 33.59N 89.21W
Bruce, Mount- 208 Cg 22.36S 118.08 E
Bruce Crossing 184 Cb 46.32N 89.10W
Bruce Peninsula 180 Jh 44.59N 81.20W
Bruce Rock 212 Df 31.53S 118.09 E
Bruche 122 Nf 48.34N 7.43 E
Bruchhausen-Vilsen 124 Lb 52.50N 9.01 E
Bruchmühlbach-Miesau 124 Je 49.23N 7.28 E
Bruchsal 120 Eg 49.08N 8.36 E
Bruck an der Leitha 128 Kb 48.01N 16.46 E
Bruck an der Mur 128 Jc 47.25N 15.17 E
Brue 118 Kj 51.13N 3.00W
Bruges/Brugge 122 Jc 51.13N 3.14 E
Brugg 128 Cc 47.29N 8.12 E
Brugge/Bruges 122 Jc 51.13N 3.14 E
Brugge-Assebroek 124 Fc 51.12N 3.16 E
Brüggen 124 Ic 51.15N 6.11 E
Brugge-Sint-Andries 124 Fc 51.12N 3.10 E
Brühl [Ger.] 124 Ke 49.24N 8.32 E
Brühl [Ger.] 124 Id 50.50N 6.54 E
Bruine Bank = Brown Bank (EN) 124 Fb 52.35N 3.20 E
Bruin Point 182 Ed 39.39N 110.22W
Brule River 184 Cc 45.57N 88.12W
Brumado 202 Jf 14.13S 41.40W
Brummen 124 Ib 52.06N 6.10 E
Brummo 116 Ef 58.50N 13.40 E
Brumunddal 114 Cf 60.53N 10.56 E
Bruna 128 Eh 42.45N 10.53 E
Brune 124 Fe 49.45N 3.47 E
Bruneau 188 He 42.53N 115.48W
Bruneau River 188 He 42.57N 115.58W
Bruneck / Brunico 128 Fd 46.48N 11.56 E
Brunehamel 124 Ge 49.46N 4.11 E
Brunei 142 Ni 4.30N 114.40 E
Brunei, Teluk- 140 Ni 5.05N 115.18 E
Brunette Downs 212 Hc 18.38S 135.57 E
Brunflo 116 Fa 63.05N 14.49 E
Brunico / Bruneck 128 Fd 46.48N 11.56 E
Brunna 116 Ge 59.52N 17.25 E
Brunner 218 De 42.26S 171.19 E
Brunner, Lake- 218 De 42.35S 171.25 E
Brunnsberg 116 Ec 61.17N 13.55 E
Brunsbüttel 120 Fc 53.54N 9.07 E
Brunssum 124 Hd 50.57N 5.57 E
Brunswick [Ga.-U.S.] 182 Ke 31.10N 81.29W
Brunswick [Me.-U.S.] 182 Nc 43.55N 69.58W
Brunswick, Península- 198 Ik 53.30S 71.25W
Brunswick Lake 184 Fa 49.00N 83.23W
Bruntál 120 Ng 49.59N 17.28 E
Bruny Island 212 Jh 43.30S 147.05 E
Brus 130 Ef 43.23N 21.02 E
Brus, Laguna de- 194 Ef 15.50N 84.35W
Brush 182 Gc 40.15N 103.37W
Brus Laguna 194 Ef 15.47N 84.35W
Brusque 206 Kc 27.06S 48.56W
Brussel/Bruxelles=Brussels (EN) 112 Ge 50.50N 4.20 E
Brussels (EN)=Brussel/Bruxelles 112 Ge 50.50N 4.20 E
Brussels (EN)=Bruxelles/Brussel 112 Ge 50.50N 4.20 E
Brusset, 'Erg- 166 Hb 18.55N 10.30 E
Brusturi 130 Fb 47.09N 22.15 E
Brusy 120 Nc 53.53N 17.45 E
Bruxelles/Brussel=Brussels (EN) 112 Ge 50.50N 4.20 E
Bruzual 196 Bh 8.03N 69.19W
Bryan [Oh.-U.S.] 184 Ee 41.30N 84.34W
Bryan [Tx.-U.S.] 182 He 30.40N 96.22W
Bryan Coast 222 Pf 73.35S 84.00W
Bryne 114 Ag 58.44N 5.39 E
Brza Palanka 130 Fe 44.28N 22.27 E
Brzava kanal 130 Dd 45.16N 20.49 E
Brzeg 120 Nf 50.52N 17.27 E
Brzeg Dolny 120 Me 51.15N 16.40 E
Brzeziny 120 Pe 51.48N 19.46 E
Brzozów 120 Sg 49.42N 22.02 E
Bsharrī 146 Ge 34.15N 36.01 E
Bû 124 Df 48.48N 1.30 E
Bua 116 Eg 57.14N 12.07 E
Buada Lagoon 220e Ab 0.32S 166.54 E
Buala 210 Ge 8.10S 159.35 E
Bū al Ḩidān, Wādī- 164 Cd 27.25N 19.22 E
Buapinang 150 Hg 4.46S 121.34 E
Buatan 150 Df 0.44N 101.51 E
Bū aţ Tifl 164 Dd 28.54N 22.30 E
Bua Yai 148 Ke 15.34N 102.24 E
Bu'ayrāt al Ḩasūn 164 Cc 31.24N 15.44 E
Bubanza 170 Ec 3.06S 29.23 E
Bubaque 166 Bc 11.17N 15.50W
Būbīyan 146 Mh 29.45N 48.15 E
Bubu 170 Gd 6.03S 35.19 E
Bubye 172 Ed 22.20S 31.07 E
Buca 130 Kk 38.22N 27.11 E
Bučač 132 De 49.04N 25.23 E
Bucačača 138 Gf 52.59N 116.55 E
Bucak 146 Dd 37.28N 30.36 E
Bucaramanga 200 Ie 7.08N 73.09W
Bucas Grande 150 Ie 9.40N 125.58 E
Buccament Bay 197n Ba 13.12N 61.17W
Buccaneer Archipelago 212 Ec 16.17S 123.20 E
Bucecea 130 Jb 47.46N 26.26 E
Buchanan 160 Fh 5.53N 10.03W
Buchanan, Lake- [Austl.] 212 Jd 21.30S 145.50 E
Buchanan, Lake- [Tx.-U.S.] 186 Gk 30.48N 98.25W
Buchanan Bay 180 Ka 78.55N 75.00W
Buchan Gulf 180 Kb 71.48N 74.06W
Buchardo 206 Hd 34.43S 63.31W
Bucharest (EN)=Bucureşti 112 Ig 44.26N 26.06 E
Buchen 120 Fg 49.31N 9.20 E
Buchholz in der Nordheide 120 Fc 53.20N 9.52 E
Buchon, Point- 188 Ei 35.15N 120.54W
Buchs 128 Dc 47.10N 9.30 E
Buchy 124 De 49.35N 1.22 E
Bückeburg 124 Lb 52.16N 9.03 E
Buckeye 188 Ij 33.22N 112.35W
Buckhaven 118 Je 56.11N 3.03W
Buckie 118 Kd 57.40N 2.58W
Buckingham [Eng.-U.K.] 124 Bb 52.00N 0.59W
Buckingham [Que.-Can.] 184 Jc 45.35N 75.25W
Buckingham Bay 212 Hb 12.10S 135.46 E
Buckinghamshire 118 Mj 51.50N 0.55W
Buckland 178 Gc 66.16N 161.20W
Buckle Island 222 Ke 66.47S 163.14 E
Buckley Bay 222 Je 68.16S 148.12 E
Bucks 118 Mj 51.50N 0.55W
Bucksport 184 Mc 44.34N 68.48W
Buco Zau 170 Bc 4.50S 12.33 E
Bu Craa 162 Ed 26.17N 12.46W
Bucureşti 130 Je 44.30N 26.05 E
Bucureşti=Bucharest (EN) 112 Ig 44.26N 26.06 E
Bucy-lès-Pierrepont 124 Fe 49.39N 3.54 E
Bucyrus 184 Fe 40.47N 82.57W
Bud 114 Be 62.55N 6.55 E
Budacu, Vîrful- 130 Ib 47.07N 25.41 E
Buda-Koševelo 132 Gc 52.43N 30.39 E
Budapest 112 Hf 47.30N 19.05 E
Budapest 120 Pi 47.30N 19.05 E
Búðardalur 114a Bb 65.07N 21.46W
Budaun 148 Fc 28.03N 79.07 E
Budbud 168 He 4.13N 46.31 E
Budd Coast 222 He 66.30S 113.00 E
Buddusò 128 Dj 40.35N 9.15 E
Bude [Eng.-U.K.] 118 Ik 50.50N 4.33W
Bude [Ms.-U.S.] 186 Kk 31.28N 90.51W
Bude Bay 118 Ik 50.50N 4.37W
Budel 124 Hc 51.16N 5.30 E
Budennovsk 136 Eg 44.45N 44.08 E
Budeşti 130 Je 44.14N 26.27 E
Budia 126 Jd 40.38N 2.45W
Büdingen 120 Ff 50.18N 9.07 E
Búdir 114a Cb 64.56N 14.01W
Budjala 170 Cb 2.39N 19.42 E
Budkowiczanka 120 Nf 50.52N 17.33 E
Budogošč 114 Hg 59.19N 32.29 E
Budrio 128 Ff 44.32N 11.32 E
Budslav 116 Lj 54.49N 27.32 E
Budva 130 Bg 42.17N 18.51 E
Budyšin/Bautzen 120 Ke 51.11N 14.26 E
Budžjak 130 Lc 46.15N 28.45 E
Buea 166 Ge 4.09N 9.14 E
Buëch 122 Lj 44.12N 5.57 E
Buenaventura [Col.] 200 Ie 3.53N 77.04W
Buenaventura [Mex.] 190 Cc 29.51N 107.29W
Buenaventura, Bahia de- 202 Cc 3.45N 77.15W
Buena Vista 192 Bb 31.10N 115.40W
Buenavista 192 Ef 23.39N 109.42W
Buena Vista [Co.-U.S.] 186 Cg 38.50N 106.08W
Buena Vista [Mex.] 192 Mi 16.05N 93.00W
Buena Vista [Ven.] 196 Eh 9.02N 63.49W
Buena Vista, Bahía de- 194 Hb 22.30N 79.08W
Buendia, Embalse de- 126 Jd 40.25N 2.43W
Buenópolis 204 Jc 17.54S 44.11W
Buenos Aires 206 Ie 36.00S 60.00W
Buenos Aires [Arg.] 200 Ki 34.36S 58.27W
Buenos Aires [C.R.] 194 Fi 10.04N 84.26W
Buenos Aires, Lago- 198 Ij 46.30S 72.00W
Buffalo 180 Fe 60.52N 115.03W
Buffalo [N.Y.-U.S.] 176 Le 42.54N 78.53W
Buffalo [Ok.-U.S.] 186 Gh 36.50N 99.38W
Buffalo [S.D.-U.S.] 182 Gb 45.35N 103.33W
Buffalo [Tx.-U.S.] 186 Hk 31.28N 96.04W
Buffalo [Wy.-U.S.] 182 Fc 44.21N 106.42W
Buffalo Bill Reservoir 188 Kd 44.29N 109.13W
Buffalo Lake 180 Fd 60.12N 115.25W
Buffalo Narrows 180 Ge 55.51N 108.30W
Buffalo Pound Lake 188 Ma 50.38N 105.20W
Buffels 172 Be 29.41S 17.04 E
Bū Fīshah 128 En 36.18N 10.28 E
Buford 184 Fh 34.07N 84.00W
Buftea 130 Ie 44.34N 25.57 E
Bug 110 Ie 52.31N 21.05 E
Buga 202 Cc 3.55N 76.18W
Bugarach, Pech de- 122 Il 42.52N 2.23 E
Bugeat 122 Hi 45.36N 1.56 E
Bugene 170 Fc 1.35S 31.08 E
Bugey 122 Li 45.48N 5.30 E
Bugojno 128 Lf 44.03N 17.27 E
Bugøynes 114 Gb 69.58N 29.39 E
Bugrino 134 Db 68.48N 49.09 E
Bugsuk 150 Ge 8.15N 117.18 E
Bugt 152 Lb 48.47N 121.55 E
Bugulma 136 Fe 54.33N 52.48 E
Bugun 135 Hc 43.22N 70.10 E
Bugun 135 Gc 42.56N 68.36 E
Bügür/Luntai 152 Dc 41.46N 84.10 E
Buguruslan 136 Fe 53.39N 52.30 E
Buhara 142 If 39.49N 64.25 E
Buharskaja oblast 136 Gg 41.20N 64.20 E
Bū Ḩaşā' 146 Ok 23.20N 53.20 E
Buhera 172 Ec 19.18S 31.29 E
Buh He 152 Gd 36.58N 99.48 E
Buhl 188 He 42.36N 114.46W
Bühl 120 Eh 48.42N 8.09 E
Bühödle 168 Hd 8.15N 46.20 E
Buhtarminskoje vodohranilišče 136 If 49.10N 84.00 E
Bui Dam 166 Ed 8.22N 2.10W
Builth Wells 118 Ji 52.09N 3.24W
Buin [Chile] 206 Fd 33.44S 70.44W
Buin [Pap.N.Gui.] 214 Fi 6.50S 155.44 E
Buinsk 136 Ee 54.59N 48.17 E
Buir Nur 152 Kb 47.48N 117.42 E
Buitrago del Lozoya 126 Id 41.00N 3.38W
Buj 136 Ed 58.29N 41.31 E
Buj 134 Gh 56.15N 54.12 E
Bujalance 126 Hg 37.54N 4.22W
Bujanovac 130 Eg 42.28N 21.47 E
Bujaraloz 126 Lc 41.30N 0.09W
Buje 128 He 45.24N 13.40 E
Bujnaksk 136 Eg 42.49N 47.07 E
Bujukly 138 Jg 49.33N 142.55 E
Bujumbura 160 Ji 3.23S 29.22 E
Bujunda 138 Kd 62.00N 153.30 E
Bük 120 Mi 47.23N 16.45 E
Buk 120 Md 52.22N 16.31 E
Buka Island 208 Ge 5.15S 154.35 E
Bukakata 170 Fc 0.18S 32.02 E
Bukama 160 Ji 9.12S 25.51 E
Buka Passage 219a Ba 5.25S 154.41 E
Bukavu 160 Ji 2.30S 28.52 E
Bukene 170 Fc 4.14S 32.53 E
Bukhā 146 Qi 26.10N 56.09 E
Bukit Besi 150 Df 4.46N 103.12 E
Bukit Mertajam 150 De 5.22N 100.28 E
Bukittinggi 142 Mj 0.19S 100.22 E
Bükk 120 Qh 48.05N 20.30 E
Bukoba 160 Ki 1.20S 31.49 E
Bukovina 130 Ia 48.00N 25.30 E
Bukowiec 120 Ld 52.23N 15.20 E
Bukuru 166 Gd 9.48N 8.52 E
Būl, Kūh-e- 144 Hc 30.48N 52.45 E
Bulajevo 136 He 54.53N 70.26 E
Bulan 150 Hd 12.40N 123.52 E
Bulanaš 134 Kh 57.16N 62.02 E
Bulancak 146 Hb 40.57N 38.14 E
Bulanık 146 Jc 39.05N 42.15 E
Būlāq 164 Fd 25.12N 30.32 E
Bulawayo 160 Jk 20.09S 28.34 E
Buldan 146 Cc 38.03N 28.51 E
Buldir 178a Bb 52.21N 175.54 E
Bulgan [Mong.] 152 Fb 46.05N 91.34 E
Bulgan [Mong.] 152 Hb 48.45N 103.34 E
Bulgan [Mong.] 152 Hc 44.05N 103.32 E
Bulgaria (EN)=Bălgarija 112 Ig 43.00N 25.00 E
Buli 150 If 0.53N 128.18 E
Buli, Teluk- 150 If 0.45N 128.30 E
Bulilluyan, Cape- 150 Ge 8.20N 117.11 E
Bulki 168 Fd 6.01N 36.36 E
Bullahār 168 Gc 10.23N 44.27 E
Bullange/Büllingen 124 Id 50.25N 6.16 E
Bullaque 126 Hf 38.59N 4.17W
Bulla Regia 128 Cn 36.33N 8.45 E
Bullas 126 Kf 38.03N 1.40W
Bulle 128 Bd 46.37N 7.04 E
Buller 218 Dd 41.44S 171.35 E
Bullfinch 212 Df 30.59S 119.06 E
Büllingen/Bullange 124 Id 50.25N 6.16 E
Bullion Mountains 188 Hi 34.25N 116.00W
Bulloo River 208 Fg 28.43S 142.30 E
Bull Point [Eng.-U.K.] 118 Ij 51.12N 4.10W
Bull Point [Falk.Is.] 206 Ih 52.19S 59.18W
Bulls 218 Fd 40.10S 175.23 E
Bulls Bay 184 Hi 32.59N 79.33W
Bull Shoals Lake 186 Jh 36.30N 92.50W
Bully Choop Mountain 188 Df 40.35N 122.45W
Bully-les-Mines 124 Ed 50.26N 2.43 E
Bulo Berde 168 He 3.52N 45.40 E
Bulolo 214 Di 7.12S 146.39 E
Bulqiza 130 Dh 41.30N 20.21 E
Bulter 186 Ig 38.16N 94.20W
Bultfontein 172 De 28.20S 26.05 E
Bulukumba 150 Hh 5.33S 120.11 E
Bulungu [Zaire] 170 Cc 4.33S 18.36 E
Bulungu [Zaire] 170 Dd 6.04S 21.54 E
Bumba 160 Jh 2.11N 22.28 E
Bumbah, Khalīj al- 164 Dc 32.25N 23.06 E
Buna 170 Gb 2.47N 39.31 E
Buna 130 Ch 41.52N 19.22 E
Bunbury 210 Ch 33.19S 115.38 E
Buncrana/Bun Cranncha 118 Ff 55.08N 7.27W
Bun Crannch a/Buncrana 118 Ff 55.08N 7.27W
Bunda 170 Fc 2.03S 33.52 E
Bundaberg 210 Gg 24.52S 152.21 E
Bünde 120 Ed 52.12N 8.35 E
Bundesrepublik Deutschland = Germany 112 Ge 51.00N 10.00 E
Bun Dobhráin/Bundoran 118 Eg 54.28N 8.17W
Bundoran/Bun Dobhráin 118 Eg 54.28N 8.17W
Bungay 124 Db 52.27N 1.27 E
Bungku 150 Hg 2.33S 121.58 E
Bungo 170 Cd 7.26S 15.24 E
Bungo Strait (EN)=Bungo-Suidō 154 Lh 32.40N 132.18 E
Bungo-Suidō=Bungo Strait (EN) 154 Lh 32.40N 132.18 E
Bungotakada 156 Be 33.33N 131.27 E
Bungsberg 120 Gb 54.12N 10.43 E
Buni 166 Hc 11.12N 12.02 E
Bunja 160 Kh 1.34N 30.15 E
Bunji 148 Ea 35.40N 74.36 E
Bunker 186 Kh 37.27N 91.13W
Bunker Group 212 Kd 23.50S 152.20 E
Bunkeya 170 Ee 10.24S 26.58 E
Bunkie 186 Jk 30.57N 92.11W
Bunnerfjällen 116 Ea 63.10N 12.34 E
Buñol 126 Le 39.25N 0.47W
Bunschoten 124 Hb 52.14N 5.24 E
Buntingford 124 Bc 51.57N 0.01W
Buntok 150 Fg 1.42S 114.48 E
Bünyan 146 Fc 38.51N 35.52 E
Bunyu, Pulau- 150 Gf 3.30N 117.50 E
Buon Me Thuot 148 Lf 12.40N 108.03 E
Buor-Haja, guba- 138 Ib 71.00N 131.00 E
Buotama 138 Hd 61.17N 128.55 E
Buqayaq 144 Gd 25.56N 49.40 E
Buqda Kōsār 168 Ge 4.31N 44.49 E
Buqūm, Ḩarrat 164 He 20.54N 42.00 E
Bur 138 Hb 71.40N 123.40 E
Bura 170 Gc 1.06S 39.57 E
Buram 160 Jg 10.49N 25.10 E
Buran 136 If 48.04N 85.15 E
Burang 152 De 30.18N 81.08 E
Burāq 146 Gf 33.10N 36.29 E
Buras 186 Ll 29.21N 89.32W
Buraydah 142 Gg 26.20N 43.59 E
Burbach 124 Kd 50.43N 8.03 E
Būrdab 168 Hd 9.05N 46.30 E
Burdekin River 212 Jc 19.39S 147.30 E
Burdēre 168 He 3.30N 45.37 E
Burdur 144 Db 37.43N 30.17 E
Burdur Gölü 146 Dd 37.44N 30.12 E
Burdwood Bank (EN) 206 Ih 54.15S 59.00W
Bure 124 Db 52.38N 1.45 E
Bure [Eth.] 168 Fd 8.20N 35.08 E
Bure [Eth.] 168 Fc 10.43N 37.03 E
Bureå 114 Ed 64.37N 21.12 E
Bureinski hrebet = Bureya Range (EN) 140 Pd 50.40N 134.00 E
Bureja 138 Hg 49.43N 129.51 E
Bureja 140 Oe 49.25N 129.35 E
Büren 120 Ee 51.33N 8.34 E
Buren-Cogt 152 Jb 46.45N 111.30 E
Bureya Range (EN) = Bureinski hrebet 140 Pd 50.40N 134.00 E
Burfjord 114 Fb 69.56N 22.03 E
Būr Gābo 168 Gf 1.10S 41.50 E
Burgas 112 Ig 42.30N 27.28 E
Burgas 130 Kg 42.30N 27.20 E
Burgas, Gulf of- (EN)= Burgaski Zaliv 130 Kg 42.30N 27.33 E
Burgaski Zaliv=Burgas, Gulf of- (EN) 130 Kg 42.30N 27.33 E
Burg auf Fehmarn 120 Hb 54.26N 11.12 E
Burg auf Fehmarn-Puttgarden 120 Hb 54.30N 11.13 E
Burgaw 184 Ih 34.33N 77.56W
Burgaz Dağı 130 Mk 38.25N 29.46 E
Burg bei Magdeburg 120 Hd 52.16N 11.51 E
Burgdorf [Ger.] 120 Gd 52.27N 10.01 E
Burgdorf [Switz.] 128 Bc 47.04N 7.37 E
Burgenland 128 Kc 47.30N 16.25 E
Burgersdorp 172 Df 31.00S 26.20 E
Burgess Hill 124 Bd 50.58N 0.08W
Burgfjället 114 Dd 64.56N 15.03 E
Burghausen 120 Ih 48.10N 12.50 E
Burghūth, Sabkhat al- 146 Ie 34.58N 41.06 E
Burglengenfeld 120 Ig 49.12N 12.02 E
Burgos 126 Ib 42.20N 3.40W
Burgos [Mex.] 192 Je 24.57N 98.57W
Burgos [Sp.] 112 Fg 42.21N 3.42W
Burg-Reuland 124 Id 50.12N 6.09 E
Burgsvik 114 Eh 57.03N 18.16 E
Burgundy (EN)= Bourgogne 110 Gf 47.00N 4.30 E
Burgundy (EN)= Bourgogne 122 Kg 47.00N 4.30 E
Burgwald 124 Kd 50.57N 8.48 E
Būr Hakkaba 168 Ge 2.43N 44.10 E
Burhaniye 146 Bc 39.30N 26.58 E
Burhānpur 142 Jg 21.18N 76.14 E
Burias 150 Hd 12.57N 123.08 E
Buribaj 134 Ik 51.57N 58.11 E
Burica, Punta- 190 Hg 8.03N 82.53W
Burien 188 Dc 47.27N 122.21W
Burin Peninsula 180 Lg 47.00N 55.40W
Buriram 148 Kf 14.59N 103.08 E
Buriti, Rio- 204 Ca 12.50S 58.28W
Buriti Alegre 204 Hd 18.09S 49.03W
Buriti Bravo 202 Je 5.50S 43.50W
Buriti dos Lopes 202 Jd 3.10S 41.52W
Buritis 204 Ib 15.37S 46.26W
Burj al Ḩaţţābah 162 Ic 30.20N 9.30 E
Burjasot / Burjassot 126 Le 39.31N 0.25W
Burjassot / Burjasot 126 Le 39.31N 0.25W
Burjatskaja ASSR 138 Ff 53.00N 110.00 E
Burj Şāfitā 146 Ge 34.49N 36.07 E
Burkandja 138 Jd 63.27N 147.27 E
Burkburnett 186 Gi 34.06N 98.34W
Burke 186 Ge 43.11N 99.18W
Burke, Mount- 188 Ha 50.18N 114.30W
Burke Island 222 Of 73.08S 105.06W
Burke River 212 Hd 23.12S 139.33 E
Burkesville 184 Eg 36.48N 85.22W
Burketown 210 Ef 17.44S 139.22 E
Burkina Faso (Upper Volta) 160 Gg 13.00N 2.00W
Burley 182 Ec 42.32N 113.48W
Burli 132 Rd 51.28N 52.44 E
Burlingame 186 Ig 38.45N 95.50W
Burlington [Co.-U.S.] 182 Gd 39.18N 102.16W
Burlington [Ia.-U.S.] 182 Ic 40.49N 91.07W
Burlington [Ks.-U.S.] 186 Ig 38.12N 95.45W
Burlington [N.C.-U.S.] 184 Hg 36.06N 79.26W
Burlington [Ont.-Can.] 184 Hd 43.19N 79.43W
Burlington [Vt.-U.S.] 182 Mc 44.28N 73.14W
Burlington [Wi.-U.S.] 186 Le 42.41N 88.17W
Burma (Myanmar-Nainggan-Daw) 142 Lg 22.00N 98.00 E
Burnazului, Cîmpia- 130 Ie 44.10N 25.50 E
Burnett River 212 Kd 24.46S 152.25 E
Burney 188 Ef 40.53N 121.40W
Burnham Market 124 Cb 52.57N 0.44 E
Burnham-on-Crouch 124 Cc 51.37N 0.50 E
Burnie 212 Jh 41.04S 145.54 E
Burnley 118 Kh 53.48N 2.14W
Burns 182 Dc 43.35N 119.03W
Burnside 180 Gc 66.51N 108.04W
Burnside, Lake- 212 Ee 25.20S 123.10 E
Burns Lake 180 Ef 54.14N 125.46W
Burnsville 184 Fh 35.55N 82.18W
Burnt Lava Flow 188 Ef 41.35N 121.35W
Burnt River 184 Hc 44.35N 78.46W
Burntwood 180 He 56.08N 96.33W
Bur'o 160 Lh 9.30N 45.34 E
Burqin 152 Eb 47.43N 86.53 E
Burqin He 152 Eb 47.42N 86.50 E
Burra 212 Hf 33.40S 138.56 E
Burragorang Lake 212 Kf 34.00S 150.25 E
Burreli 130 Ch 41.37N 20.00 E
Burrendong Reservoir 212 Jf 32.40S 149.10 E
Burriana / Borriana 126 Le 39.53N 0.05W
Burro, Serranías del- 192 Ic 28.50N 101.35W
Burrow Head 118 Ig 54.41N 4.24W
Bursa 142 Ee 40.11N 29.04 E
Būr Sa'īd = Port Said (EN) 160 Ke 31.16N 32.18 E
Burscheid 124 Jc 51.06N 7.07 E
Bürstadt 124 Ke 49.38N 8.27 E
Burštyn 132 De 49.16N 24.37 E
Būr Sūdān=Port Sudan (EN) 160 Kg 19.37N 37.14 E
Burt Lake 184 Ec 45.27N 84.40W
Burtnieku, ozero- / Burtnieku ezers 116 Kg 57.35N 25.10 E
Burtnieku ezers / Burtnieku, ozero- 116 Kg 57.35N 25.10 E
Burton 184 Fd 43.02N 83.36W
Burton Latimer 124 Bb 52.21N 0.40W
Burton upon Trent 118 Li 52.49N 1.36W
Burträsk 114 Ed 64.31N 20.39 E
Buru, Pulau- 208 De 3.24S 126.40 E
Burullus, Buḩayrat al- 146 Dg 31.30N 30.50 E
Burultokay/Fuhai 152 Eb 47.06N 87.23 E
Burum Gana 166 Hc 13.00N 11.57 E
Burūn, Ra's- 146 Eg 31.14N 33.04 E
Burundaj 136 Hg 43.20N 76.49 E
Burundi 160 Ki 3.15S 30.00 E
Bururi 170 Ec 3.57S 29.37 E
Burutu 166 Gd 5.21N 5.31 E
Bury 118 Kh 53.36N 2.17W
Burylbajtal 135 Ib 44.56N 73.59 E
Buryn 132 Hd 51.13N 33.48 E
Bury Saint Edmunds 118 Ni 52.15N 0.43 E
Burzil Pass 148 Fb 34.54N 75.06 E
Busalla 128 Cf 44.34N 8.57 E
Busanga [Zaire] 170 Ee 10.12S 25.23 E
Busanga [Zaire] 170 Dc 0.51S 22.04 E
Busanga Swamp 170 Ee 14.10S 25.50 E
Buşayrah 146 Ie 35.09N 40.26 E
Būsh 146 Dh 29.09N 31.08 E
Būshehr 144 Hd 28.00N 52.00 E
Būshgān 146 Nh 28.48N 51.42 E
Bushimaie 158 Ji 6.02S 23.45 E
Bushmanland (EN)= Boesmanland 172 Be 29.30S 19.00 E
Busia 170 Fb 0.28N 34.06 E
Busigny 124 Fd 50.02N 3.28 E
Businga 170 Db 3.20N 20.53 E
Busira 158 Ii 0.15S 18.59 E
Busk 132 Dd 50.01N 24.37 E
Buskerud 114 Bf 60.30N 9.10 E
Busko-Zdrój 120 Qf 50.28N 20.44 E
Busoga 170 Fb 0.45N 33.30 E
Buşrá ash Shām 146 Gf 32.31N 36.29 E
Busselton 212 Df 33.39S 115.20 E
Bussum 122 Lb 52.16N 5.10 E
Bustamante, Bahía- 206 Gg 45.07S 66.27W
Buşteni 130 Id 45.24N 25.32 E
Busto Arsizio 128 Ce 45.37N 8.51 E
Buštyna 120 Th 48.03N 23.28 E
Busuanga 150 Hd 12.05N 120.05 E
Busu-Djanoa 170 Db 1.43N 21.23 E
Büsum 120 Eb 54.08N 8.51 E
Buta 160 Jh 2.48N 24.44 E
Butajira 168 Fd 8.08N 38.27 E
Buta Ranquil 206 Ge 37.03S 69.50W
Butare 170 Ec 2.36S 29.44 E
Butaritari Atoll 208 Id 3.03N 172.49 E
Bute, Island of- 118 Hf 55.50N 5.05W
Bute Inlet 188 Ca 50.37N 124.53W
Butembo 160 Jh 0.09N 29.17 E
Butera 128 Im 37.11N 14.11 E
Butere 170 Fb 0.13N 34.30 E
Butha Qi (Zalantum) 152 Lb 48.02N 122.42 E
Buthidaung 148 Id 20.52N 92.32 E
Butiá 206 Jd 30.07S 51.58W
Butiaba 170 Fb 1.49N 31.19 E
Butler 184 He 40.51N 79.55W
Butser Hill 124 Bd 50.57N 0.59W
Butte 176 He 46.00N 112.32W
Butterworth [Mala.] 150 Df 5.25N 100.24 E
Butterworth [S.Afr.] 172 Df 32.23S 28.04 E
Button Bay 180 Ie 58.45N 94.25W
Butuan 142 Oi 8.57N 125.33 E
Butung, Pulau- 140 Oj 5.00S 122.55 E
Buturlinovka 132 Ld 50.48N 40.45 E
Butzbach 124 Kd 50.26N 8.41 E
Bützow 120 Hc 53.50N 11.59 E
Buxtehude 120 Fc 53.27N 9.42 E
Buxton [Eng.-U.K.] 118 Lh 53.15N 1.55W
Buxton [N.C.-U.S.] 184 Jh 35.16N 75.32W
Buyo 166 Dd 6.16N 7.03W
Büyükanafarta 130 Ji 40.17N 26.22 E
Büyükçekmece 130 Lh 41.01N 28.34 E
Büyükkarıştıran 130 Kh 41.18N 27.32 E
Büyük Kemikli Burun 130 Ji 40.18N 26.14 E
Büyük Menderes 130 Kh 41.47N 27.36 E

Index Symbols

- Independent Nation
- State, Region
- District, County
- Municipality
- Colony, Dependency
- Continent
- Physical Region
- Historical or Cultural Region
- Mount, Mountain
- Volcano
- Hill
- Mountains, Mountain Range
- Hills, Escarpment
- Plateau, Upland
- Pass, Gap
- Plain, Lowland
- Delta
- Salt Flat
- Valley, Canyon
- Crater, Cave
- Karst Features
- Depression
- Polder
- Desert, Dunes
- Forest, Woods
- Heath, Steppe
- Oasis
- Cape, Point
- Coast, Beach
- Cliff
- Peninsula
- Isthmus
- Sandbank
- Island
- Atoll
- Rock, Reef
- Islands, Archipelago
- Rocks, Reefs
- Coral Reef
- Well, Spring
- Geyser
- River, Stream
- Waterfall, Rapids
- River Mouth, Estuary
- Lake
- Salt Lake
- Intermittent Lake
- Reservoir
- Swamp, Pond
- Canal
- Glacier
- Ice Shelf, Pack Ice
- Ocean
- Sea
- Gulf, Bay
- Strait, Fjord
- Lagoon
- Bank
- Seamount
- Tablemount
- Ridge
- Shelf
- Basin
- Escarpment, Sea Scarp
- Fracture
- Trench, Abyss
- National Park, Reserve
- Point of Interest
- Recreation Site
- Cave, Cavern
- Historic Site
- Ruins
- Wall, Walls
- Church, Abbey
- Temple
- Scientific Station
- Railway station
- Airport
- Port
- Military installation
- Lighthouse
- Mine
- Tunnel
- Dam, Bridge

Büyük Menderes 144 Cb 37.57N 28.58 E
Büyükorhan 130 Lj 39.45N 28.55 E
Buyun Shan 152 Lc 40.06N 122.42 E
Buzači, poluostrov- 110 Lf 45.00N 52.00 E
Buzan 132 Pf 46.18N 49.06 E
Buzançais 122 Hh 46.53N 1.25 E
Buzancy 124 Ge 49.25N 4.57 E
Buzău 130 Jd 45.09N 26.50 E
Buzău [2] 130 Jd 45.09N 26.50 E
Buzău 130 Kd 45.26N 27.44 E
Buzaymah 164 De 24.55N 22.02 E
Buzen 156 Be 33.37N 131.08 E
Buzet 128 He 45.24N 13.59 E
Būzhān 146 Le 34.09N 47.05 E
Búzi 172 Ec 19.51S 34.30 E
Búzi 172 Ec 19.52S 34.46 E
Buziaş 130 Ed 45.39N 21.36 E
Búzios, Ilha dos- 204 Jf 23.48S 45.08W
Bužora, gora- 120 Th 48.24N 23.15 E
Buzuluk 136 Fe 52.46N 52.17 E
Buzuluk [R.S.F.S.R.] 132 Rc 52.47N 52.16 E
Buzuluk [R.S.F.S.R.] 132 Md 50.13N 42.12 E
Buzzards Bay 184 Le 41.33N 70.47W
Bwagaoia 219a Ad 10.42S 152.50 E
Byälven 116 Ee 59.06N 12.54 E
Byam Martin 180 Ha 75.15N 104.15W
Byam Martin Channel 180 Ha 76.00N 105.00W
Bychawa 120 Se 51.01N 22.32 E
Byczyna 120 Oe 51.07N 18.11 E
Bydgoszcz 112 He 53.08N 18.00 E
Bydgoszcz [2] 120 Nc 53.10N 18.00 E
Byelorussian SSR (EN) = Belorusskaja SSR [2] 136 Ce 53.50N 28.00 E
Bygdin 116 Cc 61.20N 8.35 E
Bygland 114 Bg 58.51N 7.51 E
Byglandsfjord 116 Bf 58.41N 7.48 E
Byglandsfjorden 116 Bf 58.50N 7.50 E
Byhov 136 De 53.31N 30.15 E
Byk 130 Mc 46.55N 29.25 E
Bykovec 130 Lb 47.12N 28.18 E
Bykovo 132 Ne 49.47N 45.25 E
Bykovski 138 Hb 71.56N 129.05 E
Bylot 174 Lb 73.13N 78.34W
Byrd, Cape- 222 Qe 69.38S 76.07W
Byrdbreen 222 Df 71.35S 26.00 E
Byrd Glacier 222 Jg 80.15S 160.20 E
Byron, Cape- 208 Gg 28.39S 153.38 E
Byron Bay 212 Ke 28.39S 153.37 E
Byron Bay 180 Gc 68.55N 108.25W
Byrranga, gory- = Byrranga Mountains (EN) 140 Mb 75.00N 104.00 E
Byrranga Mountains (EN) = Byrranga, gory- 140 Mb 75.00N 104.00 E
Bystraja 138 Kf 52.40N 156.10 E
Bystreyca 120 Se 51.40N 22.33 E
Bystřice 120 Lf 50.11N 15.30 E
Bystrovka 135 Jc 42.45N 75.43 E
Bystrzyca [Pol.] 120 Se 51.16N 22.45 E
Bystrzyca [Pol.] 120 Me 51.13N 16.54 E
Bystrzyca Kłodzka 120 Mf 50.19N 16.39 E
Bytantaj 138 Ic 68.40N 134.50 E
Bytča 120 Og 49.14N 18.35 E
Byten 120 Vd 52.49N 25.33 E
Bytom 120 Of 50.22N 18.54 E
Bytów 120 Nb 54.11N 17.30 E
Byumba 170 Fc 1.35S 30.04 E
Byxelkrok 114 Dh 57.20N 17.00 E
Bzura 120 Qd 52.23N 20.09 E
Bzyb 132 Lh 43.12N 40.15 E

C

Cà, Sông- 148 Le 18.40N 105.40 E
Caacupé 206 Ic 25.23S 57.09W
Čaadajevka 132 Nc 53.09N 45.56 E
Caaguazú 206 Ic 25.26S 56.02W
Caaguazú [3] 204 Eg 25.00S 55.45W
Caála 170 Ce 12.55S 15.35 E
Caapucú 204 Dh 26.13S 57.12W
Caarapó 204 Ef 22.38S 54.48W
Caatinga 202 Ig 17.10S 45.53W
Caatinga 198 Lf 9.00S 42.00W
Caatinga, Rio- 204 Jc 17.10S 45.52W
Caazapá 206 Ic 26.09S 56.24W
Caazapá [3] 204 Dh 26.10S 56.00W
Cabaçal, Rio- 204 Db 16.00S 57.42W
Cabadbaran 150 Ie 9.10N 125.38 E
Cabaiguán 194 Hb 22.05N 79.30W
Caballeria, Cabo de- / Cavalleria, Cap de- 126 Qd 40.05N 4.05 E
Caballo Cocha 202 Dd 3.54S 70.32W
Caballo Reservoir 186 Cj 32.58N 107.18W
Cabañas 126 Jg 37.40N 3.00W
Cabanatuan 142 Oh 15.29N 120.58 E
Cabano 184 Mb 47.41N 68.54W
Čabar 128 Ie 45.36N 14.39 E
Cabeceira do Apa 204 Ef 22.01S 55.46W
Cabeceiras 204 Ib 15.48S 46.59W
Cabeceiras de Basto 126 Ec 41.31N 7.59W
Cabeza, Arrecife- 192 Lh 19.04N 95.50W
Cabeza de Buey 126 Gf 38.43N 5.13W
Cabildo 204 Bn 38.29S 61.54W
Cabimas 200 Id 10.23N 71.28W
Cabinda 160 Ii 5.35S 12.13 E
Cabinda [3] 170 Bd 5.00S 12.30 E
Cabinet Mountains 188 Hb 48.08N 115.46W
Cabixi, Rio- → Branco, Rio- 204 Ba 13.55S 60.10W
Cabo Bojador 162 Ed 26.08N 14.30W
Cabo Frio 200 Lh 22.53S 42.01W
Cabo Gracias a Dios 194 Ff 14.59N 83.10W
Cabonga, Réservoir- 180 Jg 47.20N 76.35W
Caboolture 212 Ke 27.05S 152.50 E
Cabora Bassa, Dique de- 172 Ec 15.34S 32.42 E
Cabora Bassa, Lago de- = Cabora Bassa, Lake- (EN) 158 Kj 15.40S 31.40 E
Cabora Bassa, Lake- (EN) = Cabora Bassa, Lago de- 158 Kj 15.40S 31.40 E
Caborca 190 Bb 30.37N 112.06W
Cabot Strait 174 Ne 47.20N 59.30W
Cabourg 122 Fe 49.17N 0.08W
Cabo Verde = Cape Verde (EN) [1] 160 Eg 16.00N 24.00W
Cabo Verde, Ilhas do- = Cape Verde Islands (EN) 158 Eg 16.00N 24.10W
Cabra 126 Hg 37.28N 4.27W
Cabral, Serra do- 204 Jc 17.45S 44.22W
Cabras 128 Ck 39.56N 8.32 E
Cabras, Stagno di- 128 Ck 39.55N 8.30 E
Cabreira 126 Dc 41.39N 8.04W
Cabrejas, Puerto de- 126 Jd 40.08N 2.25W
Cabrera 194 Md 19.38N 69.54W
Cabrera, Illa- / Cabrera, Isla- 126 Oe 39.09N 2.56 E
Cabrera, Isla- / Cabrera, Illa- 126 Oe 39.09N 2.56 E
Cabrera, Sierra de- 126 Fb 42.10N 6.25W
Cabri 188 Ka 50.37N 108.28W
Cabriel 126 Ke 39.14N 1.03W
Cabrit, Ilet à- 197e Ac 15.53N 61.36W
Cabrits, Ilet- 197h Bc 14.23N 60.52W
Cabrón, Cabo- 194 Md 19.22N 69.12W
Cabruta 196 Ci 7.38N 66.15W
Čabulja 128 Lg 43.30N 17.35 E
Cabure 194 Mh 11.08N 69.38W
Cacacas, Islas- 196 Dg 10.22N 64.26W
Caçador 206 Jc 26.47S 51.00W
Čačak 130 Df 43.54N 20.21 E
Caçapava do Sul 206 Jd 30.30S 53.30W
Caccamo 128 Hm 37.56N 13.40 E
Caccia, Capo- 128 Cj 40.34N 8.09 E
Cacequi 206 Ei 29.53S 54.49W
Cáceres [3] 126 Ge 39.40N 6.00W
Cáceres [Braz.] 200 Kg 16.04S 57.41W
Cáceres [Sp.] 126 Fe 39.29N 6.22W
Cáceres, Laguna- 204 Dd 18.56S 57.48W
Cachari 206 Ie 36.24S 59.32W
Cache Peak 188 Ie 42.11N 113.40W
Cacheu 166 Bc 12.10N 16.21W
Cachimbo 200 Kf 9.08S 55.10W
Cachimbo, Serra do- 198 Kf 8.30S 55.50W
Cachimo 170 Dd 8.20S 21.21 E
Cáchira 194 Kj 7.46N 73.03W
Cáchira, Rio- 194 Kj 7.52N 73.40W
Cachoeira 202 Kf 12.36S 38.58W
Cachoeira Alta 204 Gd 18.48S 50.58W
Cachoeira de Goiás 204 Gc 16.44S 50.38W
Cachoeira do Arari 202 Id 1.01S 48.58W
Cachoeira do Sul 206 Jc 29.58S 52.54W
Cachoeira Dourada, Represa de- 202 Ig 18.30S 49.00W
Cachoeirinha 204 Gi 29.57S 51.05W
Cachoeiro de Itapemirim 202 Jh 20.51S 41.06W
Cacinbinho 204 Ee 21.50S 55.43W
Căciulați 130 Je 44.38N 26.10 E
Cacolo 170 Ce 10.08S 19.18 E
Caconda 170 Ce 13.43S 15.05 E
Cacuaco 170 Bd 8.47S 13.21 E
Cacuchi 170 Ce 14.23S 16.59 E
Cacula 170 Be 14.29S 14.10 E
Caculé 202 Jf 14.30S 42.13W
Caculuvar 170 Bf 16.46S 14.56 E
Cacuso 170 Cd 9.26S 15.45 E
Čadan 138 Ef 51.17N 91.40 E
Cadaqués 126 Pb 42.17N 3.17 E
Čadca 120 Og 49.26N 18.48 E
Caddo Lake 186 Ij 32.42N 94.01W
Cadereyta Jiménez 192 Ie 25.36N 100.00W
Cadí, Serra de- / Cadí, Sierra del- 126 Nb 42.17N 1.42 E
Cadí, Sierra del- / Cadí, Serra de- 126 Nb 42.17N 1.42 E
Cadibarrawirracanna, Lake- 212 He 28.50S 135.25 E
Cadibona, Colle di- 128 Cf 44.20N 8.22 E
Cadillac [Fr.] 122 Fj 44.38N 0.19W
Cadillac [Mi.-U.S.] 182 Jc 44.15N 85.24W
Cádiz 112 Fh 36.32N 6.18W
Cadiz 184 Dg 36.52N 87.50W
Cádiz [3] 126 Gh 36.30N 5.45W
Cadiz [Ca.-U.S.] 188 Hi 34.30N 115.30W
Cadiz [Phil.] 150 Hd 10.57N 123.18 E
Cádiz, Bahía de- 126 Fh 36.32N 6.16W
Cádiz, Golfo de- 126 Fh 36.50N 7.10W
Cadiz Lake 188 Hi 34.18N 115.24W
Cadore 128 Gd 46.30N 12.20 E
Cadwell 182 Dc 43.40N 116.41W
Čadyr-Lunga 132 Ff 46.04N 28.52 E
Caen 112 Ff 49.11N 0.21W
Caen, Campagne de- 122 Fe 49.05N 0.20W
Caernarfon 118 Ih 53.08N 4.16W
Caernarfon Bay 118 Ih 53.05N 4.30W
Caerphilly 118 Jj 51.35N 3.14W
Caetité 202 Jf 14.04S 42.29W
Cafayate 206 Gc 26.05S 65.58W
Cafelândia [Braz.] 204 Fc 16.40S 53.25W
Cafelândia [Braz.] 204 He 21.49S 49.35W
Cafundó, Serra do- 204 Hb 14.40S 48.23W
Čagan 136 He 50.30N 79.10 E
Cagan-Aman 136 Ef 47.32N 46.43 E
Cagan-Nur [Mong.] 152 Eb 49.40N 89.55 E
Cagan-Nur [Mong.] 152 Ia 50.25N 105.15 E
Cagan-Ula 152 Gb 49.35N 98.25 E
Cagatá, Arroyo- 204 Df 23.26S 56.36W
Cagayan 150 Hc 18.22N 121.37 E
Cagayan de Oro 142 Oi 8.29N 124.39 E
Cagayan Islands 150 He 9.40N 121.16 E
Cagayan Sulu 150 Ge 7.01N 118.30 E
Čagda 138 Ie 58.42N 130.37 E
Cageri 132 Mh 42.39N 42.42 E
Çağiş 130 Lj 39.30N 28.01 E
Cagli 128 Gg 43.33N 12.39 E
Cagliari 112 Gh 39.13N 9.07 E
Cagliari, Golfo di- 128 Dk 39.10N 9.10 E
Cagliari, Stagno di- 128 Dk 39.15N 9.05 E
Čaglinka 134 Nj 53.59N 69.47 E
Cagnes-sur-Mer 122 Nk 43.40N 7.09 E
Čagoda 114 Ig 59.12N 35.13 E
Čagodošča 114 Ig 58.58N 36.37 E
Caguas 190 Ke 18.14N 66.02W
Çagyl 136 Fg 40.43N 55.25 E
Cahama 170 Bf 16.16S 14.17 E
Caha Mountains/An Cheacha 118 Dj 51.45N 9.45W
Caher/An Cathair 118 Fi 52.22N 7.55W
Cahersiveen/Cathair Saidhbhín 118 Cj 51.57N 10.13W
Cahore Point/Rinn Chathóir 118 Gi 52.34N 6.11W
Cahors 122 Hj 44.26N 1.26 E
Cai, Rio- 204 Gi 29.56S 51.16W
Caia 172 Fc 17.49S 35.20 E
Caia 126 Ef 38.50N 7.05W
Caiabis, Serra dos- 202 Gf 11.40S 56.30W
Caiapó, Rio- 204 Gb 15.49S 51.53W
Caiapó, Serra do- 198 Kg 17.00S 52.00W
Caiapônia 202 Gc 16.57S 51.49W
Caibarién 190 Id 22.31N 79.28W
Caiçara 204 Gb 15.34S 50.12W
Caicara 202 Eb 7.37N 66.10W
Caicara de Maturin 196 Eh 9.49N 63.36W
Caicó 202 Ke 6.27S 37.06W
Caicos Bank (EN) 190 Jd 21.35N 71.55W
Caicos Islands 174 Lg 21.45N 71.35W
Caicos Passage 190 Jd 22.00N 72.30W
Caille Island 197p Bb 12.17N 61.35W
Caimanera 194 Jd 19.59N 75.09W
Caine, Rio- 202 Eg 18.23S 65.21W
Cai Nuoc 148 Lg 8.56N 105.01 E
Caird Coast 222 Af 76.00S 24.30W
Cairngorm Mountains 118 Jd 57.06N 3.30W
Cairns 210 Ff 16.55S 145.46 E
Cairo [Ga.-U.S.] 184 Ej 30.53N 84.12W
Cairo [Il.-U.S.] 182 Jd 37.00N 89.11W
Cairo (EN) = Al Qāhirah 160 Ke 30.03N 31.15 E
Cairo Montenotte 128 Cf 44.24N 8.16 E
Caiseal/Cashel 118 Fi 52.31N 7.53W
Caisleán an Bharraigh/Castlebar 118 Dh 53.52N 9.17W
Caister-on-Sea 124 Db 52.40N 1.45 E
Caiundo 170 Cf 15.42S 17.27 E
Caiúva, Lagoa- 204 Fk 32.24S 52.30W
Caiyuanzhen → Shengsi 154 Gi 30.42N 122.29 E
Caizi Hu 154 Di 30.48N 117.05 E
Čaja 138 De 58.17N 82.45 E
Cajabamba 202 Ce 7.58S 77.59W
Caja de Muertos, Isla- 197a Bc 17.53N 66.31W
Cajamarca 200 If 7.10S 78.31W
Cajamarca [3] 202 Ce 6.15S 78.50W
Cajapió 202 Jd 2.58S 44.48W
Cajarc 122 Hj 44.29N 1.51 E
Cajatambo 202 Cf 10.29S 77.02W
Čajkovski 132 Fd 56.47N 54.09 E
Çakırgöl Dağ 146 Hb 40.34N 39.42 E
Cakmak 146 Fd 37.37N 34.19 E
Çakmak Dağı 146 Jc 39.46N 42.12 E
Čakor 130 Dg 42.40N 20.02 E
Čakovec 128 Kd 46.23N 16.26 E
Cakrani 130 Ci 40.36N 19.37 E
Çal 146 Cc 38.05N 29.24 E
Cal, Rio de la- 204 Cc 17.27S 58.15W
Calabar 160 Hh 4.57N 8.19 E
Calabozo 202 Eb 8.56N 67.26W
Calabozo, Ensenada de- 194 Lh 11.30N 71.45W
Calabria [2] 128 Kl 39.00N 16.30 E
Calaburras, Punta de- 126 Hh 36.30N 4.38W
Calacoto 202 Eg 17.18S 68.39W
Calacuccia 122a Ba 42.20N 9.01 E
Calaf 126 Nc 41.44N 1.31 E
Calafat 130 Ff 43.59N 22.56 E
Calafate 200 Ik 50.20S 72.16W
Cala Figuera, Cabo de- / Cala Figuera, Cap de- 126 Oe 39.22N 2.46 E
Cala Figuera, Cap de- / Cala Figuera, Cabo de- 126 Oe 39.22N 2.46 E
Calagua Islands 150 Hd 14.27N 122.55 E
Calahorra 126 Kb 42.18N 1.58W
Calai 170 Cf 17.50S 19.20 E
Calais [Fr.] 112 Ge 50.57N 1.50 E
Calais [Me.-U.S.] 184 Nc 45.11N 67.17W
Calais, Pas de- = Dover, Strait of- (EN) 110 Ge 51.00N 1.30 E
Calakmul 190 Oh 18.05N 89.55W
Calalaste, Sierra de- 206 Gc 25.30S 67.30W
Calama 200 Jh 22.28S 68.56W
Calamar 194 Jh 10.14N 74.56W
Calamian Group 140 Nh 12.00N 120.00 E
Calamocha 126 Kd 40.55N 1.18W
Călan 130 Fd 45.44N 22.59 E
Calanda 126 Ld 40.56N 0.14W
Calandula 160 Ii 9.06S 15.58 E
Calang 150 Cf 4.30N 95.40 E
Calangiánus 128 Dj 40.56N 9.11 E
Calapan 150 Hd 13.25N 121.10 E
Calar Alto 126 Jg 37.15N 2.25W
Călăraşi 130 Ke 44.12N 27.20 E
Călăraşi [2] 130 Je 44.15N 27.00 E
Cala Ratjada 126 Pe 39.42N 3.25 E
Calar del Mundo 126 Jf 38.31N 2.28W
Calatafimi 128 Gm 37.55N 12.52 E
Calatañazor 126 Jc 41.42N 2.49W
Calatayud 126 Kc 41.21N 1.38W
Calatrava 126 If 38.35N 3.48W
Calatrava, Campo de- 126 Hf 38.50N 4.05W
Calavà, Capo- 128 Il 38.10N 14.55 E
Calavon 122 Kk 43.53N 5.25 E
Calayan 150 Hc 19.20N 121.27 E
Calbayog 142 Oh 12.04N 124.36 E
Calchaquí 206 Hc 29.54S 60.18W
Calçoene 202 Hc 2.30N 50.57W
Calcutta 142 Kg 22.32N 88.22 E
Caldaro / Kaltern 128 Fd 46.25N 11.14 E
Caldas [3] 202 Cb 5.15N 75.30W
Caldas da Rainha 126 Ce 39.24N 9.08W
Caldas Novas 204 Hc 17.45S 48.38W
Caldeirão, Serra de- 126 Dg 37.19N 8.04W
Calder 118 Lh 53.44N 1.21W
Caldera 206 Fc 27.04S 70.50W
Calderina, Sierra de la- 126 Ie 39.19N 3.48W
Caldes de Montbui 126 Oc 41.38N 2.10 E
Caldwell 184 Gf 39.44N 81.32W
Căleanu, Vîrful- 130 Fd 45.19N 22.32 E
Caledon 172 Bf 34.12S 19.23 E
Caledon 158 Jl 30.32S 26.05 E
Caledonia [Blz.] 194 Cd 18.14N 88.29W
Caledonia [Mn.-U.S.] 186 Ke 43.38N 91.29W
Caledonian Canal 118 Id 57.20N 4.30W
Calella 126 Oc 41.37N 2.40 E
Caleta Olivia 206 Gg 46.26S 67.32W
Calexico 188 Hj 32.40N 115.30W
Çalgal Dağı 146 He 39.06N 38.05 E
Calgary 176 Hd 51.03N 114.05W
Calhoun 184 Eh 34.30N 84.57W
Cali 200 Ie 3.27N 76.31W
Calicut (Kozhikode) 142 Jh 11.19N 75.46 E
Caliente 182 Ed 37.37N 114.31W
California [2] 182 Dd 37.30N 119.30W
California, Golfo de- = California, Gulf of- (EN) 174 Hg 28.00N 112.00W
California, Gulf of- (EN) = California, Golfo de- 174 Hg 28.00N 112.00W
Căliman, Munții- 130 Ib 47.07N 25.03 E
Călimănești 130 Hd 45.14N 24.20 E
Calimere, Point- 148 Ff 10.18N 79.52 E
Calingasta 206 Gd 31.19S 69.25W
Calispell Peak 188 Gb 48.26N 117.30W
Calitri 128 Jj 40.54N 15.26 E
Calitzdorp 172 Cf 33.33S 21.42 E
Caliviny 197p Bb 12.01N 61.43W
Calixtlahuaca 192 Jh 19.15N 99.45W
Calka 132 Ni 41.35N 44.05 E
Calkini 192 Ng 20.22N 90.03W
Callabonna, Lake- 212 Ie 29.45S 140.05 E
Callac 122 Cf 48.24N 3.26W
Callaghan, Mount- 188 Gg 39.42N 116.57W
Callainn/Callan 118 Fi 52.33N 7.23W
Callan/Callainn 118 Fi 52.33N 7.23W
Callander [Ont.-Can.] 184 Hb 46.13N 79.23W
Callander [Scot.-U.K.] 118 Ie 56.15N 4.13W
Callantsoog 124 Gb 52.50N 4.41 E
Callao 200 Ig 12.02S 77.05W
Callao [3] 202 Cf 2.04S 77.09W
Calliaqua 197n Ba 13.08N 61.12W
Callosa de Ensarrià / Callosa d'eu Sarrià 126 Lf 38.39N 0.07W
Callosa de Segura 126 Lf 38.08N 0.52W
Callosa d'eu Sarrià / Callosa de Ensarrià 126 Lf 38.39N 0.07W
Calmalli 192 Cc 28.14N 113.33W
Călmățui [Rom.] 130 Ke 44.50N 27.50 E
Călmățui [Rom.] 130 If 43.46N 25.10 E
Calonne 124 Ce 49.17N 0.12 E
Calore 128 Ii 41.11N 14.28 E
Čalovo 120 Ni 47.52N 17.47 E
Calp / Calpe 126 Mf 38.39N 0.03 E
Calpe / Calp 126 Mf 38.39N 0.03 E
Caltabellotta 128 Hm 37.34N 13.13 E
Caltagirone 128 Im 37.14N 14.31 E
Caltanissetta 128 Im 37.29N 14.04 E
Caltilibük 130 Lj 39.57N 28.36 E
Čaltyr 132 Kf 47.17N 39.29 E
Caluago 170 Cd 8.21S 19.40 E
Calucinga 170 Ce 11.19S 16.13 E
Călugăreni 130 Ie 44.11N 25.59 E
Calulo 170 Bd 9.59S 14.54 E
Caluquembe 170 Be 13.46S 14.41 E
Calvados [3] 122 Fe 49.10N 0.30W
Calvados, Côte du- 122 Fe 49.22N 0.30W
Calvert Island 188 Ba 51.35N 128.00W
Calvert River 212 Hc 16.17S 137.44 E
Calvi 122a Aa 42.34N 8.45 E
Calvillo 192 Hg 21.51N 102.43W
Calvinia 160 Il 31.25S 19.45 E
Calvitero 126 Gd 40.20N 5.43W
Cam 118 Ni 52.21N 0.15 E
Camabatela 170 Cd 8.13S 15.23 E
Camacã 202 Kg 15.24S 39.30W
Camacupa 170 Ce 12.01S 17.22 E
Camaguán 196 Ch 8.06N 67.36W
Camagüey 176 Lg 21.23N 77.55W
Camagüey [3] 194 Ic 21.30N 78.10W
Camagüey, Archipiélago de- 190 Id 22.18N 78.00W
Camaiore 128 Eg 43.56N 10.18 E
Camajuani 194 Hb 22.28N 79.44W
Camamu 202 Kf 13.57S 39.07W
Camaná 202 Dg 16.37S 72.42W
Camanongue 170 De 11.27S 20.12 E
Camapuã 204 Ed 19.30S 54.05W
Camapuã, Sertão de- 198 Kg 19.00S 51.30W
Camaquã 206 Jd 30.51S 51.49W
Camaquã, Rio- 204 Gj 31.17S 51.47W
Camarat, Cap- 122 Mk 43.12N 6.41 E
Camargo [Bol.] 202 Eh 20.39S 65.13W
Camargo [Sp.] 126 Ia 43.24N 3.54W
Camargos, Represa- 204 Je 21.20S 44.30W
Camargue 122 Kk 43.31N 4.34 E
Camariñas 126 Ca 43.07N 9.10W
Camarón, Cabo- 190 He 16.00N 85.04W
Camarones 206 Gf 44.48S 65.42W
Camarones, Bahía- 206 Gf 44.45S 65.34W
Camas [Sp.] 126 Fg 37.24N 6.02W
Camas [Wa.-U.S.] 188 Dd 45.35N 122.24W
Ca Mau 148 Lg 9.11N 105.08 E
Ca Mau, Mui = Ca Mau Point (EN) 140 Mi 8.38N 104.44 E
Ca Mau Point (EN) = Ca
Mau, Mui- 140 Mi 8.38N 104.44 E
Cambados 126 Db 42.30N 8.48W
Camberg 124 Kd 50.18N 8.16 E
Camberley 124 Bc 51.21N 0.44W
Cambo 170 Cd 7.40S 17.17 E
Cambodia (EN) = Kampuchea 142 Mh 13.00N 105.00 E
Cambo-les-Bains 122 Ek 43.22N 1.24 E
Camboriú, Ponta- 204 Ig 25.10S 47.55W
Cambrai 122 Jd 50.10N 3.14 E
Cambremer 124 Ce 49.09N 0.03 E
Cambrésis 124 Fd 50.15N 3.05 E
Cambrian Mountains 110 Fe 52.35N 3.35W
Cambridge 118 Ni 52.25N 0.10 E
Cambridge [Eng.-U.K.] 118 Ni 52.12N 0.07 E
Cambridge [Id.-U.S.] 188 Gd 44.34N 116.41W
Cambridge [Ma.-U.S.] 184 Ld 42.22N 71.06W
Cambridge [Md.-U.S.] 184 If 38.34N 76.04W
Cambridge [Mn.-U.S.] 186 Jd 45.31N 93.14W
Cambridge [N.Z.] 218 Fb 37.53S 175.28 E
Cambridge [Oh.-U.S.] 184 Ge 40.02N 81.36W
Cambridge Airport 124 Cb 52.10N 0.08 E
Cambridge Bay 176 Ic 69.03N 105.05W
Cambridge Gulf 212 Fb 14.55S 128.15 E
Cambridgeshire [3] 118 Mi 52.25N 0.05W
Cambutal, Cerro- 194 Gj 7.16N 80.36W
Camden [Al.-U.S.] 184 Dj 32.00N 87.17W
Camden [Ar.-U.S.] 182 Ie 33.35N 92.50W
Camden [N.J.-U.S.] 184 Jf 39.57N 75.07W
Camden [S.C.-U.S.] 184 Gh 34.16N 80.36W
Camden [Tn.-U.S.] 184 Cg 36.04N 88.06W
Camden Bay 178 Kb 70.00N 145.00W
Camdenton 186 Jg 38.00N 92.45W
Camel 118 Ik 50.33N 4.55W
Çameli 146 Cd 37.05N 29.20 E
Camerino 128 Hg 43.08N 13.04 E
Cameron 180 Ha 76.15N 104.00W
Cameron [Az.-U.S.] 188 Ji 35.51N 111.25W
Cameron [La.-U.S.] 186 Jl 29.48N 93.19W
Cameron [Mo.-U.S.] 186 Ig 39.44N 94.14W
Cameron [Tx.-U.S.] 186 Hk 30.51N 96.59W
Cameron [Wi.-U.S.] 186 Kd 45.25N 91.44W
Cameron Hills 180 Fe 60.00N 118.00W
Cameron Mountains 218 Bf 46.00S 166.55 E
Cameroon (EN) = Cameroun [1] 160 Ih 6.00N 12.00 E
Cameroon Mountain 158 Hh 4.12N 9.11 E
Camerota 128 Jj 40.02N 15.22 E
Cameroun = Cameroon (EN) [1] 160 Ih 6.00N 12.00 E
Cametá 202 Id 2.15S 49.30W
Camiguin [Phil.] 150 He 9.11N 124.42 E
Camiguin [Phil.] 150 Hc 18.56N 121.55 E
Camiling 150 He 15.42N 120.24 E
Camilla 184 Ej 31.14N 84.12W
Caminha 126 Dc 41.52N 8.50W
Camissombo 170 Bd 8.10S 20.39 E
Camoapa 194 Eg 12.23N 85.31W
Camocim 200 Lf 2.54S 40.50W
Camonica, Val- 128 Ed 46.00N 10.20 E
Camooweal 212 Hc 19.55S 138.07 E
Camopi 202 Hc 3.13N 52.28W
Camorta 148 Ig 8.08N 93.30 E
Camotes Islands 150 Hd 11.00N 124.45 E
Campagne-lès-Hesdin 124 Dd 50.24N 1.52 E
Campana 204 Cl 34.10S 58.57W
Campana, Isla- 198 Ij 48.20S 75.15W
Campanario 126 Gf 38.52N 5.37W
Campanário 204 Ef 22.48S 55.03W
Campania [2] 128 Ii 41.00N 14.30 E
Campanquiz, Cerros- 202 Cd 4.30S 77.40W
Campbell, Cape- 218 Fd 41.44S 174.16 E
Campbell Island 218 Ci 52.30S 169.10 E
Campbell Plateau (EN) 208 Ij 51.00S 170.00 E
Campbell River 180 Ef 50.01N 125.15W
Campbellsville 184 Eg 37.21N 85.20W
Campbellton 180 Kg 48.00N 66.40W
Campbelltown, Sydney- 212 Kf 34.04S 150.49 E
Campbeltown 118 Hf 55.26N 5.36W
Campeche 176 Jh 19.51N 90.32W
Campeche [2] 190 Fe 19.00N 90.30W
Campeche, Bahía de- = Campeche, Gulf of- (EN) 174 Jg 20.00N 94.00W
Campeche, Gulf of- (EN) = Campeche, Bahía de- 174 Jg 20.00N 94.00W
Campeche Bank (EN) 190 Fd 22.00N 90.00W
Campechuela 194 Ic 20.14N 77.17W
Camperdown 212 Ig 38.14S 143.09 E
Campidano 128 Ck 39.30N 8.45 E
Campiglia Marittima 128 Eg 43.03N 10.37 E
Campillos 126 Hg 37.03N 4.51W
Campina Grande 200 Mf 7.13S 35.53W
Campinas 200 Lh 22.54S 47.05W
Campina Verde 204 Hd 19.31S 49.28W
Campine/Kempen 122 Lc 51.10N 5.20 E
Campinorte 204 Hb 14.20S 49.08W
Campione d'Italia 128 Ce 45.59N 8.59 E
Campo 166 Ge 2.22N 9.49 E
Campo Alegre 196 Bh 9.15N 68.25W
Campo Alegre de Goiás 204 Ic 17.36S 47.46W
Campobasso 128 Ii 41.34N 14.39 E
Campo Belo 204 Je 20.53S 45.16W
Campo de Criptana 126 Ie 39.24N 3.07W
Campo de la Cruz 194 Jh 10.23N 74.52W
Campo del Cielo 204 Bh 27.53S 61.49W
Campo Florido 204 Hd 19.46S 48.34W
Campo Formoso 202 Jf 10.31S 40.20W
Campo Gallo 206 Hc 26.35S 62.51W
Campo Garay 204 Bi 29.41S 61.37W
Campo Grande [Arg.] 204 Eh 27.13S 54.58W
Campo Grande [Braz.] 200 Kh 20.27S 54.37W
Campo Largo [Arg.] 204 Bh 26.48S 60.50W
Campo Largo [Braz.] 204 Hg 25.26S 49.32W
Campo Maior [Braz.] 202 Jd 4.49S 42.10W
Campo Maior [Port.] 126 Ee 39.01N 7.04W
Campomarino 128 Ji 41.57N 15.02 E
Campo Mourão 206 Jb 24.03S 52.22W

Index Symbols

[1] Independent Nation
[2] State, Region
[3] District, County
[4] Municipality
[5] Colony, Dependency
Continent
Physical Region
Historical or Cultural Region
Mount, Mountain
Volcano
Hill
Mountains, Mountain Range
Hills, Escarpment
Plateau, Upland
Pass, Gap
Plain, Lowland
Delta
Salt Flat
Valley, Canyon
Crater, Cave
Karst Features
Depression
Polder
Desert, Dunes
Forest, Woods
Heath, Steppe
Oasis
Cape, Point
Coast, Beach
Cliff
Peninsula
Isthmus
Sandbank
Island
Atoll
Rock, Reef
Islands, Archipelago
Rocks, Reefs
Coral Reef
Well, Spring
Geyser
River, Stream
Waterfall, Rapids
River Mouth, Estuary
Lake
Salt Lake
Intermittent Lake
Reservoir
Swamp, Pond
Canal
Glacier
Ice Shelf, Pack Ice
Ocean
Sea
Gulf, Bay
Strait, Fjord
Lagoon
Bank
Seamount
Tablemount
Ridge
Shelf
Basin
Escarpment, Sea Scarp
Fracture
Trench, Abyss
National Park, Reserve
Point of Interest
Recreation Site
Cave, Cavern
Historic Site
Ruins
Wall, Walls
Church, Abbey
Temple
Scientific Station
Railway station
Airport
Port
Military installation
Lighthouse
Mine
Tunnel
Dam, Bridge

ampos 200 Lh 21.45S 41.18W
ampos [Braz.] 198 Kh 21.00S 51.00W
ampos [Braz.] 198 Lg 15.00S 44.30W
ampos, Laguna- 204 Be 20.50S 61.31W
ampos, Tierra de- 126 Hb 42.10N 4.50W
ampos Altos 204 Id 19.41S 46.10W
ampos Belos 204 Ia 13.03S 46.53W
ampos do Jordão 204 Jf 22.44S 45.35W
ampos Novos 204 Gh 27.24S 51.12W
ampos Sales 202 Je 7.04S 40.23W
ampo Tures / Sand in Taufers 128 Fd 46.55N 11.57 E
amp Verde 182 Ee 34.34N 111.51W
am Ranh 148 Lf 11.54N 109.13 E
amrose 180 Gf 53.01N 112.50W
amseil 180 Fc 65.40N 118.07W
amsell Portage 180 Ge 59.38N 109.42W
an 146 Bb 40.02N 27.03 E
anaan [Ct.-U.S.] 184 Kd 42.02N 73.20W
anaan [Trin.] 196 Fg 11.09N 60.49W
anaan Mountain 188 Jh 37.45N 111.51W
ana Brava, Ribeirão- 204 Ic 16.35S 46.34W
ana Brava, Rio- [Braz.] 204 Ib 14.40S 47.07W
ana Brava, Rio- [Braz.] 204 Ha 12.12S 48.40W
ana Brava, Rio- [Braz.] 204 Ha 13.11S 48.11W
anada 176 Jc 60.00N 95.00W
añada 126 Fb 42.50N 6.05W
anada Basin (EN) 224 Ad 80.00N 145.00W
añada de Gómez 206 Hd 32.49S 61.24W
anadian 186 Fi 35.55N 100.23W
anadian River 174 Jf 35.27N 95.03W
anaguá, Rio- 194 Mj 7.57N 69.36W
anaima 202 Fb 6.07N 62.55W
anakkale bogazı = Dardanelles (EN) 110 Ig 40.15N 26.25 E
anala 219b Be 21.32S 165.57 E
anandaigua 184 Id 42.53N 77.19W
ananea 190 Bb 30.57N 110.18W
ananéia 204 Ig 25.01S 47.57W
anapolis 204 Hd 18.44S 49.13W
anarias, Islas-=Canary Islands (EN) 160 Ff 28.00N 15.30W
anarias, Islas-=Canary Islands (EN) 158 Ff 28.00N 15.30W
anaries 197k Ab 13.55N 61.04W
anaronero, Laguna- 192 Ff 23.00N 106.15W
anarreos, Archipiélago de los- 190 Hd 21.50N 82.30W
anary Basin (EN) 106 Dg 30.00N 25.00W
anary Islands (EN)= Canarias, Islas- 160 Ff 28.00N 15.30W
anary Islands (EN)= Canarias, Islas- 158 Ff 28.00N 15.30W
añas [C.R.] 194 Eh 10.25N 85.07W
añas [Pan.] 194 Gj 7.27N 80.16W
anastra, Serra da- 204 Ie 20.00S 46.20W
anatlán 192 Ge 24.31N 104.47W
añaveral 126 Fe 39.47N 6.23W
añaveral, Cape- 174 Kg 28.30N 80.35W
anavese 128 Be 45.20N 7.40 E
anavieiras 202 Kg 15.39S 38.57W
anazei 128 Fd 46.28N 11.46 E
anberra 210 Fh 35.17S 149.08 E
anby [Mn.-U.S.] 186 Hd 44.43N 96.16W
anby [Or.-U.S.] 188 Dd 45.16N 122.42W
ance 122 Ki 45.12N 4.48 E
anche 122 Hd 50.31N 1.39 E
ancon 122 Gj 44.32N 0.37 E
ancún 190 Gd 21.05N 86.46W
ancún, Isla- 192 Pg 21.05N 86.46W
andarli 130 Jk 38.56N 26.56 E
andarli Körfezi 130 Jk 38.52N 26.55 E
andé 122 Eg 47.34N 1.02W
andela 192 Id 26.50N 100.40W
andelaria 192 Nh 18.18N 91.21W
andelaria, Cerro- 192 Hf 23.25N 103.43W
andelaria, Rio- [Bol.] 204 Cc 17.17S 58.39W
andelaria, Rio- [Mex.] 192 Nh 18.38N 91.15W
andelaro 128 Ji 41.34N 15.53 E
ândido de Abreu 204 Gg 24.35S 51.20W
ândido Mendes 202 Id 1.27S 45.43W
andlemas Islands 222 Ad 57.03S 26.40W
andói 204 Fg 25.43S 52.11W
andyr 132 Sj 38.13N 55.44 E
anela 206 Jc 29.22S 50.50W
anelli 128 Cf 44.43N 8.17 E
anelones 204 Dl 34.32S 56.17W
anelones (3) 204 El 34.35S 56.00W
anendiyu 204 Eg 24.20S 55.00W
añete [Chile] 206 Fe 37.48S 73.24W
añete [Sp.] 126 Kd 40.03N 1.39W
angallo 204 Cm 37.13S 58.42W
angamba 170 Ce 13.44S 19.53 E
angas 126 Db 42.16N 8.47W
angas de Narcea 126 Fa 43.11N 6.33W
angas de Onis 126 Ga 43.21N 5.07W
angola 170 Cd 7.58S 15.53 E
angombe 170 Ce 14.24S 19.59 E
angshan (Bianzhuang) 154 Eg 34.51N 118.03 E
anguçu 204 Fj 31.24S 52.41W
anguçu, Serra do- 204 Fj 31.20S 52.40W
anguinha 204 Eb 14.42S 55.40W
angumbe 170 Ce 12.00S 19.09 E
angyuan 152 Gg 23.10N 99.15 E
angzhou 152 Kd 38.14N 116.58 E
ani, Iles- 128 Em 37.21N 10.07 E
aniapiscau 174 Md 57.40N 69.30W
aniapiscau, Lac- 180 Kf 54.00N 70.10W
anicatti 128 Hm 37.21N 13.51 E
anigou 122 Il 42.31N 2.27 E
anik Dağları 146 Gb 40.50N 37.10 E
anim Lake 188 Ea 51.52N 120.45W
anindé 202 Kd 4.22S 39.19W
anindé, Rio- 202 Je 6.15S 42.52W
añitas de Felipe Pescador 192 Hf 23.36N 102.43W
ankaya, Ankara- 146 Ec 39.56N 32.52 E
ankırı 144 Da 40.36N 33.37 E
anna 118 Gd 57.03N 6.33W
Cannac 219a Ac 9.15S 153.29 E
Çannakale 144 Ca 40.09N 26.24 E
Cannanore 148 Ff 11.51N 75.22 E
Cannanore Islands 148 Ef 10.05N 72.10 E
Cannes 122 Nk 43.33N 7.01 E
Cannich 118 Id 57.20N 4.45W
Canning Basin 212 Ed 20.10S 123.00 E
Cannobio 128 Cd 46.04N 8.42 E
Cannock 118 Ki 52.42N 2.01W
Cannonball River 186 Fc 46.26N 100.38W
Cann River 212 Jg 37.34S 149.10 E
Caño, Isla del- 194 Fi 8.44N 83.53W
Canoas 206 Jc 29.56S 51.11W
Canoas, Punta- 192 Bc 29.25N 115.10W
Canoas, Rio- 206 Jc 27.36S 51.25W
Canoeiros 202 Ig 18.02S 45.31W
Canoinhas 204 Gh 26.10S 50.24W
Canoinhas, Rio- 204 Gh 23.07S 50.22W
Cañoles / Cànyoles 126 Le 39.02N 0.29W
Canon City 182 Fd 38.27N 105.14W
Canon Fiord 180 Ja 80.15N 83.00W
Canonnier, Pointe du- 197b Ab 18.04N 63.10W
Canora 180 Hf 51.37N 102.26W
Canosa di Puglia 128 Ki 41.13N 16.04 E
Canouan Island 196 Ff 12.43N 61.20W
Canourgue, La- 122 Jj 44.25N 3.13 E
Canso, Strait of- 180 Lg 45.35N 61.23W
Canta 202 Cf 11.25S 76.38W
Cantabria (2) 126 Ha 43.15N 4.00W
Cantabrian Mountains (EN) =Cantábrica, Cordillera- 110 Fg 43.00N 5.00W
Cantábrica, Cordillera-= Cantabrian Mountains (EN) 110 Fg 43.00N 5.00W
Cantábrico, Mar- 126 Ha 44.00N 4.00W
Cantal (3) 122 Ii 45.05N 2.40 E
Cantal 110 Gf 45.10N 2.50 E
Cantalejo 126 Ic 41.15N 3.55W
Cantanhede 126 Dd 40.21N 8.36W
Cantaura 202 Fb 9.19N 64.21W
Cantavieja 126 Ld 40.32N 0.24W
Cantavir 130 Cd 45.55N 19.46 E
Canterbury 118 Oj 51.17N 1.05 E
Canterbury (2) 218 De 43.30S 171.50 E
Canterbury Bight 208 Ii 44.10S 172.00 E
Can Tho 142 Mi 10.02N 105.47 E
Cantiles, Cayo- 194 Fc 21.36N 82.02W
Canto do Buriti 202 Je 8.07S 42.58W
Canton [Il.-U.S.] 186 Kf 40.33N 90.02W
Canton [Mo.-U.S.] 186 Kf 40.08N 91.32W
Canton [Ms.-U.S.] 186 Kj 32.37N 90.02W
Canton [N.Y.-U.S.] 184 Jc 44.37N 75.11W
Canton [Oh.-U.S.] 182 Kc 40.48N 81.23W
Canton [S.D.-U.S.] 186 He 43.18N 96.35W
Canton (EN)=Guangzhou 142 Ng 23.07N 113.18 E
Canton Atoll 208 Je 2.50S 171.41W
Cantù 128 De 45.44N 9.08 E
Cantwell 178 Jd 63.23N 148.57W
Cañuelas 204 Cl 35.03S 58.44W
Canumã, Rio- 198 Kf 3.55S 59.10W
Canutama 202 Fe 6.32S 64.20W
Canvey Island 124 Cc 51.31N 0.36 E
Čany 138 Ce 55.19N 76.56 E
Čany, ozero- 140 Jd 54.50N 77.30 E
Cany-Barville 124 Ce 49.47N 0.38 E
Cànyoles / Cañoles 126 Le 39.02N 0.29W
Canyon [Mn.-U.S.] 186 Jc 47.02N 92.29W
Canyon [Tx.-U.S.] 182 Ge 34.59N 101.55W
Canyon [Wy.-U.S.] 188 Jd 44.44N 110.30W
Canyon Lake 186 Gl 29.52N 98.16W
Canzar 170 Dd 7.36S 21.33 E
Cao Bang 148 Ld 22.40N 106.15 E
Caojiahe → Qichun 154 Ci 30.15N 115.26 E
Caojian 152 Gf 25.38N 99.07 E
Caombo 170 Cd 8.42S 16.33 E
Caorle 128 Ge 45.36N 12.53 E
Caoxian 154 Cg 34.49N 115.33 E
Caozhou → Heze 152 Kd 35.14N 115.28 E
Capaccio 128 Jj 40.25N 15.05 E
Capajev 136 Fe 50.14N 51.08 E
Čapajevsk 136 Ee 53.01N 49.36 E
Capanaparo, Rio- 202 Eb 7.01N 67.07W
Capanema [Braz.] 204 Fg 25.40S 53.48W
Capanema [Braz.] 202 Id 1.12S 47.11W
Capanema, Serra do- 204 Fh 26.05S 53.16W
Capão Alto 204 Gh 27.56S 50.30W
Capão Bonito 204 Hf 24.01S 48.20W
Capão Doce, Morro do- 204 Gh 26.37S 51.28W
Caparo, Rio- 194 Lj 7.46N 70.23W
Capatárida 194 Lh 11.11N 70.37W
Capbreton 122 Ek 43.38N 1.26W
Cap Breton Canyon (EN) 122 Ek 43.40N 1.50W
Čapčama, pereval- 135 Hd 41.34N 70.50 E
Cap-Chat 184 Na 49.06N 66.42W
Capcir 122 Il 42.45N 2.10 E
Cap-de-la-Madeleine 180 Kg 46.22N 72.32W
Capdenac-Gare 122 Ij 44.34N 2.05 E
Cape Barren Island 212 Jh 40.25S 148.10 E
Cape Basin (EN) 105 Em 37.00S 7.00 E
Cape Breton Island 174 Me 46.00N 60.30W
Cape Charles 184 Jg 37.17N 76.00W
Cape Coast 160 Gh 5.06N 1.15W
Cape Cod Bay 184 Le 41.52N 70.22W
Cape Coral 184 Gl 26.33N 81.58W
Cape Dorset 176 Lc 64.14N 76.32W
Cape Dyer 176 Mc 66.30N 61.18W
Cape Fear River 184 Ii 33.53N 78.00W
Cape Girardeau 182 Jd 37.19N 89.32W
Cape Johnson Tablemount (EN) 238 Jc 17.08N 177.15W
Capel 124 Bc 51.08N 0.19W
Cape Lisburne 178 Fc 68.52N 166.05W
Capelka 116 Mf 58.02N 29.07 E
Capella 150 Lg 4.58S 141.06 E
Capelongo 170 Ce 14.54S 15.05 E
Capem 204 Ea 13.14S 55.14W
Cape May 184 Jf 38.56N 74.54W
Cape Mount (3) 166 Cd 7.05N 10.50W
Cape Province/ Kaapprovinsie (2) 172 Cf 32.00S 22.00 E
Cape Rise (EN) 106 En 42.00S 15.00 E
Cape Smith 180 Jd 60.44N 78.29W
Capesterre 197e Bc 15.54N 61.13W
Capesterre-Belle-Eau 196 Fd 16.03N 61.34W
Cape Town / Kaapstad 160 Il 33.55S 18.22 E
Cape Verde (EN)=Cabo Verde (1) 160 Eg 16.00N 24.00W
Cape Verde (EN)=Cap Vert (3) 166 Bc 14.45N 17.20W
Cape Verde Basin (EN) 106 Ch 15.00N 30.00W
Cape Verde Islands (EN)= Cabo Verde, Ilhas do- 158 Eg 16.00N 24.10W
Cape Verde Terrace (EN) 162 Cf 18.00N 20.00W
Cape Yakataga 178 Kd 60.04N 142.26W
Cape York Peninsula 208 Ff 14.00S 142.30 E
Cap-Haïtien 176 Lh 19.45N 72.15W
Capiibary, Arroyo- 204 Dg 24.06S 56.26W
Capiibary, Rio- 204 Eg 25.30S 55.33W
Capim, Rio- 198 Lf 1.40S 47.47W
Capinópolis 204 Hd 18.41S 49.35W
Capira 194 Hi 8.45N 79.53W
Capital Federal (2) 206 Id 34.36S 58.27W
Capitán Arturo Prat 222 Re 62.29S 59.39W
Capitán Bado 206 Ib 23.16S 55.32W
Capitán Bermúdez 204 Bk 32.49S 60.43W
Capitán Sarmiento 204 Cl 34.10S 59.48W
Capitão Noronha, Rio- 204 Ea 13.19S 54.36W
Capivara, Represa da- 204 Gf 22.40S 50.57W
Capivari, Rio- 204 Dd 19.16S 57.10W
Capivarita 204 Fj 30.18S 52.19W
Cap Lopez, Baie du- 170 Ac 0.40S 9.00 E
Čaplygin 132 Kc 53.17N 39.59 E
Cappelle, La- 122 Je 49.58N 3.55 E
Cappeln (Oldenburg) 124 Kb 52.49N 8.07 E
Cap Point 196 Fe 14.07N 60.57W
Capraia 128 Dg 43.05N 9.50 E
Caprara, Punta- 128 Ci 41.07N 8.19 E
Capreol 184 Gb 46.43N 80.56W
Caprera 128 Di 41.10N 9.30 E
Capri 128 Ij 40.33N 14.14 E
Capri 128 Ij 40.35N 14.15 E
Capricorn, Cape- 212 Kd 23.30S 151.15 E
Capricorn Channel 212 Kd 22.15S 151.30 E
Capricorn Group 208 Gg 23.30S 152.00 E
Caprivi Strip (EN) = Caprivizipfel 158 Jj 18.00S 23.00 E
Caprivizipfel = Caprivi Strip (EN) 158 Jj 18.00S 23.00 E
Captain Cook 221a Fd 19.30N 155.55W
Captains Flat 212 Jg 35.35S 149.27 E
Captieux 122 Fj 44.17N 0.15W
Capua 128 Ii 41.06N 14.12 E
Capuchin, Cape- 197g Ba 15.38N 61.28W
Capunda 170 Ce 10.41S 17.23 E
Cap Vert=Cape Verde (EN) (3) 166 Bc 14.45N 17.20W
Caquetá (3) 202 Dc 1.00N 74.00W
Caquetá, Rio- 198 Jf 3.08S 64.46W
Čara 140 Oc 60.17N 120.40 E
Čara [R.S.F.S.R.] 138 Ge 58.54N 118.12 E
Čara [R.S.F.S.R.] 138 Ge 56.58N 118.17 E
Carabobo (2) 202 Ea 10.10N 68.05W
Caracal 130 He 44.07N 24.21 E
Caracaraí 202 Fc 1.50N 61.08W
Caracas 200 Jd 10.30N 66.56W
Caracas (2) 202 Ea 10.15N 66.25W
Carache 194 Li 9.38N 70.14W
Caracol 204 De 21.59S 57.02W
Caracol, Rio- 204 Df 22.13S 57.03W
Caracollo 202 Eg 17.39S 67.10W
Caraguatá, Cuchilla- 204 Ek 32.05S 54.54W
Caraguatatuba 204 Jf 23.37S 45.25W
Caraïbe, Mer-/Antilles, Mer des-=Caribbean Sea (EN) 174 Lh 15.00N 73.00W
Carajas, Serra dos- 202 He 6.00S 51.20W
Caramoan Peninsula 150 Hd 13.48N 123.40 E
Caramulo, Serra do- 126 Dd 40.34N 8.11W
Caraná, Rio- 204 Ca 13.20S 59.17W
Carandai 204 Ke 20.57S 43.48W
Carandazal 204 Dd 19.50S 57.09W
Caransebeş 130 Fd 45.25N 22.13 E
Carapá, Rio- 204 Eg 24.30S 54.20W
Carapelle 128 Ji 41.30N 15.55 E
Caraquet 184 Ob 47.47N 64.57W
Caraş 130 Ee 44.49N 21.20 E
Caraş Severin (2) 130 Ed 45.20N 22.00 E
Caratasca, Cayo- 194 Fe 16.02N 83.20W
Caratasca, Laguna de- 190 He 15.20N 83.50W
Caratinga 202 Jg 19.47S 42.08W
Carauari 202 Ed 4.52S 66.54W
Caraúbas 202 Ke 5.47S 37.34W
Caravaca 126 Kf 38.06N 1.51W
Caravelas 200 Mg 17.45S 39.15W
Caraveli 202 Dg 15.46S 73.22W
Caravelle, Presqu'île de la- 197h Bb 14.45N 60.55W
Caravelle, Rocher de la- 197h Bb 14.48N 60.53W
Caràzinho 206 Jc 28.18S 52.48W
Carazo (3) 194 Dh 11.45N 86.15W
Carballino 126 Db 42.26N 8.04W
Carballo 126 Da 43.13N 8.41W
Carberry 186 Gb 49.52N 99.20W
Carbet, Pitons du- 197h Ab 14.42N 61.07W
Carbon, Cap- [Alg.] 126 Li 35.54N 0.20W
Carbon, Cap- [Alg.] 126 Rh 36.47N 5.06 E
Carbonara, Capo- 128 Dk 39.06N 9.31 E
Carbondale [Il.-U.S.] 182 Jd 37.44N 89.13W
Carbondale [Pa.-U.S.] 184 Je 41.35N 75.31W
Carbonera, Cuchilla de la- 204 El 34.10S 54.00W
Carboneras 126 Kh 36.59N 1.54W
Carboneras, Cerro- 192 Ih 18.10N 101.10W
Carbones 126 Gg 37.36N 5.39W
Carbonia 128 Ck 39.10N 8.31 E
Carcans, Étang de- 122 Ei 45.06N 1.07W
Carcar 150 Hd 10.06N 123.38 E
Carcarañá, Rio- 204 Bk 32.27S 60.48W
Carcassonne 122 Ik 43.13N 2.21 E
Carcross 180 Ed 60.10N 134.42W
Çardak [Tur.] 130 Ji 40.22N 26.43 E
Çardak [Tur.] 146 Cd 37.48N 29.40 E
Čardara 136 Gg 41.15N 68.01 E
Čardarinskoje vodohranilišče 135 Gd 41.05N 68.15 E
Cárdenas [Cuba] 190 Hd 23.02N 81.12W
Cárdenas [Mex.] 192 Mi 17.59N 93.22W
Cárdenas [Mex.] 190 Ed 22.00N 99.40W
Cárdenas, Bahía de- 194 Gb 23.05N 81.10W
Cardener/Cardoner 126 Nc 41.41N 1.51 E
Cardiel, Lago- 206 Fg 48.55S 71.15W
Cardiff 112 Fe 51.30N 3.13W
Cardigan 118 Ii 52.06N 4.40W
Cardigan Bay 110 Fe 52.30N 4.20W
Cardona [Sp.] 126 Nc 41.55N 1.41 E
Cardona [Ur.] 204 Dk 33.54S 57.22W
Cardoner/Cardener 126 Nc 41.41N 1.51 E
Cardozo 204 Dk 32.38S 56.21W
Cardston 180 Gg 49.12N 113.18W
Čardžou 142 If 39.06N 63.34 E
Čardžouskaja oblast (3) 136 Gh 39.00N 63.00 E
Carei 130 Fb 47.41N 22.28 E
Careiro 202 Gd 3.12S 59.45W
Carentan 122 Ee 49.18N 1.14W
Carey 188 Ie 43.20N 113.58W
Carey, Lake- 208 Dg 29.05S 122.15 E
Cargados Carajos Islands 158 Mj 16.35S 59.40 E
Cargèse 122a Aa 42.08N 8.35 E
Carhaix-Plouguer 122 Cf 48.17N 3.35W
Cari 128 Hi 41.23N 13.50 E
Caria 130 Ll 37.30N 29.00 E
Cariacica 202 Jh 20.16S 40.25W
Cariaco 196 Eg 10.29N 63.33W
Cariaco, Golfo de- 196 Eg 10.30N 64.00W
Cariaco Basin (EN) 196 Dg 10.37N 65.10W
Cariati 128 Kk 39.30N 16.57 E
Caribana, Punta- 194 Ii 8.37N 76.52W
Caribbean Sea 174 Lh 15.00N 73.00W
Caribbean Sea (EN)= Antillas, Mar de las-/ Caribe, Mar- 174 Lh 15.00N 73.00W
Caribbean Sea (EN)= Antilles, Mer des-/Caraïbe, Mer- 174 Lh 15.00N 73.00W
Caribbean Sea (EN)= Caraïbe, Mer-/Antilles, Mer des- 174 Lh 15.00N 73.00W
Caribbean Sea (EN)= Caribe, Mar-/Antillas, Mar de las- 174 Lh 15.00N 73.00W
Caribe, Mar-/Antillas, Mar de las-=Caribbean Sea (EN) 174 Lh 15.00N 73.00W
Cariboo Mountains 180 Ff 53.00N 121.00W
Caribou 184 Mb 46.52N 68.01W
Caribou 180 Ie 59.20N 94.45W
Caribou Island 184 Eb 47.22N 85.52W
Caribou Lake 186 La 50.25N 89.00W
Caribou Mountains 174 Hd 59.12N 115.40W
Caribou Range 188 Je 43.05N 111.15W
Caričin Grad 130 Eg 42.57N 21.45 E
Carignan 122 Le 49.38N 5.10 E
Carignano 128 Bf 44.55N 7.40 E
Cariñena 126 Kc 41.20N 1.13W
Carinhanha 202 Jf 14.08S 43.47W
Carinhanha, Rio- 204 Kb 14.20S 43.47W
Carini 128 Hl 38.08N 13.11 E
Carinola 128 Hi 41.11N 13.58 E
Carinthia (EN) = Kärnten (2) 128 Hd 46.45N 14.00 E
Carinthia (EN) = Kärnten 128 Hd 46.45N 14.00 E
Caripe 196 Eg 10.21N 63.29W
Caripito 202 Fa 10.08N 63.06W
Caris, Rio- 196 Eh 8.09N 63.46W
Carlet 126 Le 39.14N 0.31W
Carleton Place 184 Ic 45.07N 76.08W
Carletonville 172 De 26.23S 27.22 E
Carlin 188 Gf 40.43N 116.07W
Carling 124 Ie 49.10N 6.43 E
Carlingford Lough/Loch Cairlinn 118 Gg 54.05N 6.14W
Carlinville 186 Lg 39.17N 89.53W
Carlisle [Eng.-U.K.] 112 Fe 54.54N 2.55W
Carlisle [Pa.-U.S.] 184 Ie 40.12N 77.12W
Carlisle Bay 197q Ab 13.05N 59.37W
Carloforte 128 Ck 39.08N 8.18 E
Carlos Beguerie 204 Cl 35.29S 59.06W
Carlos Casares 206 He 35.38S 61.21W
Carlos Chagas 202 Jg 17.43S 40.45W
Carlos Reyles 204 Dk 33.03S 56.29W
Carlos Tejedor 204 Al 35.23S 62.25W
Carlow/Ceatharlach 118 Gi 52.50N 6.55W
Carlow/Ceatharlach (2) 118 Gi 52.50N 7.00W
Carloway 118 Gc 58.17N 6.47W
Carlsbad [Ca.-U.S.] 188 Gj 33.10N 117.21W
Carlsbad [N.M.-U.S.] 176 If 32.25N 104.14W
Carlyle 180 Hg 49.38N 102.16W
Carlyle Lake 186 Lg 38.40N 89.18W
Carmacks 180 Dd 62.05N 136.18W
Carmagnola 128 Bf 44.51N 7.43 E
Carmarthen 118 Ij 51.52N 4.19W
Carmarthen Bay 118 Ij 51.40N 4.30W
Carmaux 122 Ij 44.03N 2.09 E
Carmel Head 118 Ih 53.24N 4.34W
Carmelita 194 Be 17.21N 90.10W
Carmelo 206 Id 34.00S 58.17W
Carmen 204 Dk 33.15S 56.01W
Carmen, Isla- 190 Bc 25.57N 111.12W
Carmen, Isla del- 192 Nh 18.42N 91.40W
Carmen, Laguna del- 192 Mh 18.15N 93.50W
Carmen, Rio del- 192 Fb 30.42N 106.29W
Carmen, Sierra del- 192 Hc 29.00N 102.30W
Carmen de Patagones 206 Hf 40.48S 62.59W
Carmensa 206 Ge 35.08S 67.38W
Carmi 186 Lg 38.07N 88.10W
Carmichael 188 Eg 38.38N 121.19W
Carmo de Minas 204 Jf 22.07S 45.08W
Carmo do Paranaíba 204 Id 18.59S 46.21W
Carmona 126 Gg 37.28N 5.38W
Carnac 122 Cg 47.35N 3.05W
Carnamah 212 De 29.42S 115.53 E
Carnarvon [Austl.] 210 Cg 24.53S 113.40 E
Carnarvon [S.Afr.] 160 Jl 30.56S 22.08 E
Carnarvon Range 212 Ee 25.10S 121.00 E
Carnatic (EN) 140 Jh 10.30N 79.00 E
Carnegie, Lake- 208 Dg 26.10S 122.30 E
Carnegie Ridge (EN) 106 Nj 1.00S 85.00W
Carn Eige 118 Hd 57.30N 5.05W
Carney Island 222 Nf 73.57S 121.00W
Carnia 128 Gd 46.25N 13.00 E
Car Nicobar 148 Ig 9.10N 92.47 E
Carnot 168 Be 4.48N 16.03 E
Carnoustie 118 Ke 56.30N 2.44W
Carnsore Point/Ceann an Chairn 118 Gi 52.10N 6.22W
Carn Ui Neid/Mizen Head 110 Fe 51.27N 9.49W
Caro 184 Fd 43.29N 83.24W
Carol City 184 Gm 25.56N 80.16W
Carolina [Braz.] 200 Lf 7.20S 47.28W
Carolina [P.R.] 197a Cb 18.24N 65.57W
Carolina [S.Afr.] 172 Ee 26.05S 30.06 E
Carolina Beach 184 Ih 34.02N 77.54W
Carolinas, Puntan- 220b Bb 14.54N 145.38 E
Caroline Atoll 208 Le 9.58S 150.13W
Caroline Islands 208 Fd 8.00N 147.00 E
Carondelet Reef 208 Je 5.34S 173.51W
Caroni, Rio- 198 Je 8.21N 62.43W
Caronie → Nebrodi 128 Im 37.55N 14.35 E
Carora 202 Da 10.11N 70.05W
Carpathian Mountains (EN) 110 If 48.00N 24.00 E
Carpathian Mountains (EN) = Carpaţii Occidentali 130 Fc 46.30N 22.10 E
Carpathian Mountains (EN) =Carpaţii Orientali 130 Ib 47.30N 25.30 E
Carpaţii Meridionali= Transylvanian Alps (EN) 110 If 45.30N 24.15 E
Carpaţii Occidentali = Carpathian Mountains (EN) 130 Fc 46.30N 22.10 E
Carpaţii Orientali= Carpathian Mountains (EN) 130 Ib 47.30N 25.30 E
Carpen 130 Ge 44.20N 23.15 E
Carpentaria, Gulf of- 208 Ef 14.00S 139.00 E
Carpentras 122 Lj 44.03N 5.03 E
Carpi 128 Ef 44.47N 10.53 E
Carpina 202 Ke 7.51S 35.15W
Carr, Cape- 222 Ie 66.07S 130.51 E
Carraig Fhearghais/ Carrickfergus 118 Hg 54.43N 5.44W
Carraig na Siúire / Carrick on Suir 118 Fi 52.21N 7.25W
Carrara 128 Ef 44.05N 10.06 E
Carrauntoohil 110 Fe 5200N 9.45W
Carreiro, Rio- 204 Gi 29.07S 51.43W
Carreño 126 Ga 43.35N 5.46W
Carreta, Punta- 202 Cf 14.13S 76.18W
Carretero, Puerto- 126 Ig 37.28N 3.40W
Carriacou 196 Ff 12.30N 61.27W
Carrick 118 If 55.15N 4.40W
Carrickfergus/Carraig Fhearghais 118 Hg 54.43N 5.44W
Carrick on Shannon / Cora Droma Rúisc 118 Eh 53.57N 8.05W
Carrick on Suir / Carraig na Siúire 118 Fi 52.21N 7.25W
Carrington 182 Hb 47.27N 99.08W
Carrión 126 Hc 41.53N 4.32W
Carrión de los Condes 126 Hb 42.20N 4.36W
Carrizal 194 Kh 11.58N 72.12W
Carrizo Peak 186 Dj 33.20N 105.38W
Carrizos 192 Gc 29.58N 105.16W
Carrizo Springs 186 Gl 28.31N 99.52W
Carrizo Wash 186 Ki 34.36N 109.26W
Carrizozo 186 Dj 33.38N 105.53W
Carrol 186 Ie 42.04N 94.52W
Carrol Inlet 222 Qf 73.18S 78.30W
Carrollton [Ga.-U.S.] 184 Ei 33.35N 85.05W
Carrollton [Il.-U.S.] 186 Kg 39.18N 90.24W
Carrollton [Ky.-U.S.] 184 Ef 38.41N 85.11W
Carrollton [Mo.-U.S.] 186 Jg 39.22N 93.30W
Carron, Loch- 118 Hd 57.30N 5.40W
Carrot 180 Hf 53.50N 101.18W
Carrowmore Lough 118 Dg 54.12N 9.47W
Çarşamba 146 Gb 41.12N 36.44 E
Çarşamba 146 Ed 37.53N 32.37 E
Čaršanga 136 Gh 37.31N 66.03 E
Čarsk 136 If 49.35N 81.05 E
Carson 188 Ed 45.44N 121.49W
Carson City 176 Hf 39.10N 119.46W
Carson Lake 188 Fg 39.19N 118.43W
Carson Sink 188 Fg 39.45N 118.30W
Cartagena [Col.] 200 Id 10.25N 75.32W
Cartagena [Sp.] 112 Fh 37.36N 0.59W
Cartago (3) 194 Ei 9.50N 83.45W
Cartago [Col.] 202 Cc 4.46N 75.56W
Cartago [C.R.] 190 Hg 9.52N 83.55W
Cartaxo 126 De 39.09N 8.47W
Carter, Mount- 212 Ib 13.05S 143.15 E
Cartersville 184 Eh 34.10N 85.05W
Carterton 218 Fd 41.01S 175.31 E
Carthage [Mo.-U.S.] 186 Ih 37.11N 94.19W
Carthage [Tx.-U.S.] 186 Ij 32.09N 94.20W
Cartier 184 Gb 46.42N 81.32W
Cartier Island 208 Df 12.30S 123.30 E
Cartwright 176 Nd 53.50N 56.45W
Caruaru 200 Mf 8.17S 35.58W

ndex Symbols

Independent Nation
State, Region
District, County
Municipality
Colony, Dependency
Continent
Physical Region
Historical or Cultural Region
Mount, Mountain
Volcano
Hill
Mountains, Mountain Range
Hills, Escarpment
Plateau, Upland
Pass, Gap
Plain, Lowland
Delta
Salt Flat
Valley, Canyon
Crater, Cave
Karst Features
Depression
Polder
Desert, Dunes
Forest, Woods
Heath, Steppe
Oasis
Cape, Point
Coast, Beach
Cliff
Peninsula
Isthmus
Sandbank
Island
Atoll
Rock, Reef
Islands, Archipelago
Rocks, Reefs
Coral Reef
Well, Spring
Geyser
River, Stream
Waterfall, Rapids
River Mouth, Estuary
Lake
Salt Lake
Intermittent Lake
Reservoir
Swamp, Pond
Canal
Glacier
Ice Shelf, Pack Ice
Ocean
Sea
Gulf, Bay
Strait, Fjord
Lagoon
Bank
Seamount
Tablemount
Ridge
Shelf
Basin
Escarpment, Sea Scarp
Fracture
Trench, Abyss
National Park, Reserve
Point of Interest
Recreation Site
Cave, Cavern
Historic Site
Ruins
Wall, Walls
Church, Abbey
Temple
Scientific Station
Railway station
Airport
Port
Military installation
Lighthouse
Mine
Tunnel
Dam, Bridge

Carúpano 202 Fa 10.40N 63.14W
Carutapera 202 Id 1.13S 46.01W
Čarvak 135 Gd 41.38N 69.56 E
Carvin 124 Ed 50.29N 2.58 E
Carvoeiro, Cabo- 126 Ce 39.21N 9.24W
Čaryn 135 Lc 43.50N 79.12 E
Čaryš 138 Df 52.22N 83.45 E
Casablanca 160 Ge 33.36N 7.37W
Casablanca [2] 162 Fc 33.37N 7.35W
Casa Branca 204 Ie 21.46S 47.05W
Casa Grande 182 Ee 32.53N 111.45W
Casalbordino 128 Ih 42.09N 14.35 E
Casale Monferrato 128 Ce 45.08N 8.27 E
Casalmaggiore 128 Ef 44.59N 10.26 E
Casalvasco 204 Cb 15.19S 59.59W
Casal Velino 128 Jj 40.11N 15.06 E
Casamance [3] 166 Bc 12.50N 15.00W
Casamance 166 Bc 12.33N 16.46W
Casanare [3] 202 Db 5.20N 72.00W
Casanare, Rio- 202 Eb 6.02N 69.51W
Casanay 196 Eg 10.30N 63.25W
Casa Nova 202 Je 9.25S 41.08W
Casarano 128 Mj 40.00N 18.10 E
Casas Grandes, Rio- 192 Eb 30.22N 107.31W
Casas-Ibáñez 126 Ke 39.17N 1.28W
Casca, Rio da- 204 Eb 14.52S 55.52W
Cascade 188 Hd 44.31N 115.59W
Cascade Point 218 Cf 44.01S 168.22 E
Cascade Range 174 Ge 45.00N 121.30W
Cascais 126 Cf 38.42N 9.25W
Cascavel [Braz.] 202 Kd 4.07S 38.14W
Cascavel [Braz.] 206 Jb 24.57S 53.28W
Cascia 128 Hh 42.43N 13.01 E
Casciana Terme 128 Eg 43.32N 10.38 E
Cascina 128 Eg 43.41N 10.33 E
Casentino 128 Fg 43.40N 11.50 E
Case-Pilote 197h Ab 14.38N 61.08W
Caserta 128 Ii 41.04N 14.20 E
Casey 222 He 66.17S 110.32 E
Casey Bay 222 Ee 67.00S 48.00 E
Cashel/Caiseal 118 Fi 52.31N 7.53W
Casigua 194 Ki 8.46N 72.30W
Casilda 206 Hd 33.03S 61.10W
Casimcea 130 Le 44.24N 28.33 E
Casino 212 Ke 28.52S 153.03 E
Casiquiare, Brazo- 202 Ec 2.01N 67.07W
Čáslav 120 Lg 49.55N 15.25 E
Casma 202 Ce 9.28S 78.19W
Časnačorr, gora- 114 Hc 67.45N 33.29 E
Čašniki 114 Gi 54.52N 29.08 E
Casoli 128 Ih 42.07N 14.18 E
Casoria 128 Ij 40.54N 14.17 E
Caspe 126 Lc 41.14N 0.02W
Casper 176 Ie 42.51N 106.19W
Caspian Depression (EN) = Prikaspijskaja nizmennost 110 Lf 48.00N 52.00 E
Caspian Sea (EN) = Kaspijskoje more 110 Lg 42.00N 50.30 E
Caspian Sea (EN) = Māzandarān, Daryā-ye- 110 Lg 42.00N 50.30 E
Cassai 158 Ii 3.02S 16.57 E
Cassamba 170 De 13.04S 20.25 E
Cassange, Rio- 204 Dc 17.06S 57.23W
Cassano allo Ionio 128 Kk 39.47N 16.19 E
Cassano allo Ionio-Sibari 128 Kk 39.45N 16.27 E
Cass City 184 Fd 43.36N 83.10W
Cassel 124 Ed 50.47N 2.29 E
Casselton 186 Hc 46.54N 97.13W
Cássia 204 Ie 20.36S 46.56W
Cassiar 180 Ee 59.16N 129.40W
Cassiar Mountains 174 Gd 59.00N 129.00W
Cassilândia 202 Hg 19.09S 51.45W
Cassinga 170 Cf 15.06S 16.06 E
Cassino [Braz.] 204 Fk 32.11S 52.10W
Cassino [It.] 128 Hi 41.30N 13.49 E
Cassis 122 Lk 43.13N 5.32 E
Cass Lake 186 Ic 47.23N 94.36W
Cass River 184 Fd 43.23N 83.59W
Cassununga 204 Fc 16.03S 53.38W
Castagneto Carducci 128 Eg 43.10N 10.36 E
Castagniccia 122a Ba 42.25N 9.30 E
Castañar, Sierra del- 126 He 39.35N 4.10W
Castanhal 202 Id 1.18S 47.55W
Castaños 192 Id 26.47N 101.25W
Castelbuono 128 Im 37.56N 14.05 E
Castel di Sangro 128 Ii 41.47N 14.06 E
Castelfidardo 128 Hg 43.28N 13.33 E
Castelfranco Veneto 128 Fe 45.40N 11.55 E
Casteljaloux 122 Gj 44.19N 0.06 E
Castellabate 128 Ij 40.17N 14.57 E
Castellammare, Golfo di- 128 Gl 38.10N 12.55 E
Castellammare del Golfo 128 Gl 38.01N 12.53 E
Castellammare di Stabia 128 Ij 40.42N 14.29 E
Castellana Grotte 128 Lj 40.53N 17.10 E
Castellane 122 Mk 43.51N 6.31 E
Castellaneta 128 Kj 40.38N 16.56 E
Castelldefels 126 Nc 41.17N 1.58 E
Castelli [Arg.] 206 Hc 25.57S 60.37W
Castelli [Arg.] 204 Dm 36.06S 57.47W
Castelló de la Plana / Castellón [3] 126 Ld 40.10N 0.10W
Castelló de la Plana/ Castellón de la Plana 112 Fh 39.59N 0.02W
Castellón / Castelló de la Plana [3] 126 Ld 40.10N 0.10W
Castellón de la Plana/ Castelló de la Plana 112 Fh 39.59N 0.02W
Castellón de la Plana-El Grao 126 Me 39.58N 0.01 E
Castellote 126 Ld 40.48N 0.19W
Castelnaudary 122 Hk 43.19N 1.57 E
Castelnau-de-Médoc 122 Fi 45.02N 0.48W
Castelnovo ne' Monti 128 Ef 44.26N 10.24 E
Castelo Branco 126 Ee 39.49N 7.30W
Castelo Branco [2] 126 Ee 40.00N 7.30W
Castelo de Vide 126 Ee 39.25N 7.27W
Castelo do Piauí 202 Je 5.20S 41.33W
Castel San Giovanni 128 De 45.04N 9.26 E
Castelsardo 128 Cj 40.55N 8.43 E
Castelsarrasin 122 Hj 44.02N 1.06 E
Casteltermini 128 Hm 37.32N 13.39 E
Castelvetrano 128 Gm 37.41N 12.47 E
Castets 122 Ek 43.53N 1.09W
Castiglione del Lago 128 Gg 43.07N 12.03 E
Castiglione della Pescaia 128 Eh 42.46N 10.53 E
Castiglion Fiorentino 128 Fg 43.20N 11.55 E
Castilla-La Mancha [2] 126 Ie 39.30N 3.30W
Castilla la Nueva=New Castile (EN) 126 Id 40.00N 3.45W
Castilla la Vieja=Old Castile (EN) 126 Ic 41.30N 4.00W
Castilla-León [2] 126 Hc 41.30N 4.30W
Castillejo 126 Gc 41.14N 5.30W
Castillon-la-Bataille 122 Fj 44.51N 0.02W
Castillonnès 122 Gj 44.39N 0.36 E
Castillos 206 Jd 34.12S 53.50W
Castillos, Laguna de- 204 Fl 34.20S 53.54W
Castlebar/Caisleán an Bharraigh 118 Dh 53.52N 9.17W
Castle Bruce 197g Bb 15.26N 61.16W
Castle Dome Peak 188 Hj 33.05N 114.08W
Castle Douglas 118 Jg 54.57N 3.56W
Castlegar 180 Fg 49.19N 117.40W
Castleisland/Oileán Ciarrai 118 Di 52.14N 9.27W
Castlemaine 212 Ig 37.04S 144.13 E
Castle Peak 188 Hd 44.03N 114.32W
Castlepoint 218 Gd 40.55S 176.13 E
Castlepollard 118 Fh 53.41N 7.17W
Castlerea/An Caisleán Riabhach 118 Eh 53.46N 8.29W
Castlereagh Bay 212 Hb 12.10S 135.10 E
Castle Rock Butte 186 Ed 45.00N 103.27W
Castle Rock Lake 186 Le 43.56N 89.58W
Častoozerje 134 Mi 55.34N 67.53 E
Castor 188 Ja 52.13N 111.53W
Castres 122 Ik 43.36N 2.15 E
Castricum 124 Gb 52.33N 4.42 E
Castries 176 Mh 14.01N 61.00W
Castrignano del Capo 128 Mk 39.50N 18.20 E
Castrignano del Capo-Marina di Leuca 128 Mk 39.48N 18.21 E
Castro [Braz.] 206 Jb 24.47S 50.03W
Castro [Chile] 206 Ff 42.29S 73.46W
Castro Alves 202 Kf 12.45S 39.26W
Castrocaro Terme e Terra del Sole 128 Ff 44.10N 11.57 E
Castro Daire 126 Ed 40.54N 7.56W
Castro del Rio 126 Hg 37.41N 4.28W
Castrojeriz 126 Hb 42.17N 4.08W
Castropol 126 Eg 43.32N 7.02W
Castrop-Rauxel 124 Jc 51.33N 7.19 E
Castro-Urdiales 126 Ia 43.23N 3.13W
Castro Verde 126 Dg 37.42N 8.05W
Castrovillari 128 Kk 39.49N 16.12 E
Castrovirreyna 202 Cf 13.16S 75.19W
Castuera 126 Gf 38.43N 5.33W
Častyje 134 Gh 57.19N 54.59 E
Casupá 204 El 34.09S 55.38W
Caswell Sound 218 Bf 45.00S 167.10 E
Çat 146 Ic 39.40N 41.02 E
Čata 120 Oi 47.58N 18.40 E
Catacamas 194 Ef 14.54N 85.56W
Catahoula Lake 186 Jk 31.30N 92.06W
Çatak 146 Jc 38.01N 43.07 E
Çatak 146 Jd 37.53N 42.39 E
Catalan Coastal Range (EN) = Costero Catalana, Cadena- / Mediterrani Català, Sistema- 110 Gg 41.35N 1.40 E
Catalan Coastal Range (EN) = Mediterrani Català, Sistema- / Costero Catalana, Cadena- 110 Gg 41.35N 1.40 E
Catalão 202 Ig 18.10S 47.57W
Çatal Balkan 130 Jg 42.46N 27.00 E
Çatalca 130 Lh 41.09N 28.27 E
Çatal Dağ 130 Lj 39.51N 28.20 E
Catalina 206 Gc 25.13S 69.43W
Catalina, Isla- 194 Md 18.21N 69.00W
Catalina, Punta- 206 Gh 52.32S 68.47W
Catalonia (EN)=Cataluña/ Catalunya [2] 126 Nc 42.00N 2.00 E
Catalonia (EN)=Cataluña/ Catalunya 110 Gg 42.00N 2.00 E
Catalonia (EN)=Catalunya/ Cataluña [2] 126 Nc 42.00N 2.00 E
Catalonia (EN)=Catalunya/ Cataluña 110 Gg 42.00N 2.00 E
Cataluña/Catalunya= Catalonia (EN) [2] 126 Nc 42.00N 2.00 E
Cataluña/Catalunya= Catalonia (EN) 110 Gg 42.00N 2.00 E
Catalunya/Cataluña= Catalonia (EN) [2] 126 Nc 42.00N 2.00 E
Catalunya/Cataluña= Catalonia (EN) 110 Gg 42.00N 2.00 E
Çatalzeytin 146 Fb 41.57N 34.13 E
Catamarca [2] 206 Gc 27.00S 67.00W
Catanduanes 140 Oh 13.45N 124.15 E
Catanduva 206 Kb 21.08S 48.58W
Catanduvas 204 Fg 25.12S 53.08W
Catania 112 Hh 37.30N 15.06 E
Catania, Golfo di- 128 Jm 37.25N 15.10 E
Catania, Piana di- 128 Im 37.25N 14.50 E
Catanzaro 112 Hh 38.54N 16.35 E
Catanzaro-Marina di Catanzaro 128 Kl 38.49N 16.36 E
Catarman 150 Hd 12.30N 124.38 E
Catastrophe, Cape- 208 Eh 35.00S 136.00 E
Catatumbo, Rio- 194 Li 9.21N 71.45W
Catbalogan 150 Hd 11.46N 124.53 E
Catemaco, Lago- 192 Lh 18.25N 95.05W
Catete 170 Bd 9.07S 13.41 E
Cathair na Mart/Westport 118 Dh 53.48N 9.32W
Cathair Saidhbhín/ Cahersiveen 118 Cj 51.57N 10.13W
Cathcart 172 Df 32.18S 27.09 E
Catherine, Mount- 188 Ig 39.05N 112.04W
Catholic Island 197n Bb 12.40N 61.24W
Catio 166 Bc 11.17N 15.15W
Cat Island 174 Lg 24.30N 75.30W
Čatkal 135 Hd 41.36N 70.05 E
Čatkalski hrebet 136 Hg 41.30N 70.50 E
Cat Lake 180 If 51.40N 91.52W
Catoche, Cabo- 174 Kg 21.36N 87.07W
Cato Island 208 Gg 23.15S 155.35 E
Catolé do Rocha 202 Ke 6.21S 37.45W
Catoute 126 Fb 42.45N 6.20W
Catria 128 Gg 43.28N 12.42 E
Catriló 206 He 36.26S 63.24W
Catrimani, Rio- 202 Fc 0.28N 61.44W
Catskill Mountains 184 Jd 42.10N 74.30W
Cattenom 124 Ie 49.25N 6.15 E
Cattolica 128 Gg 43.58N 12.44 E
Catu 202 Kf 12.21S 38.23W
Catuane 172 Ee 26.48S 32.14 E
Catumbela 170 Be 12.27S 13.29 E
Catur 172 Fb 13.45S 35.37 E
Catwick, Iles- 148 Lg 10.00N 109.00 E
Catyrkël, ozero- 135 Jd 40.35N 75.20 E
Catyrtaš 135 Kd 40.52N 76.23 E
Cauca [3] 202 Cc 2.30N 77.00W
Cauca, Rio- 198 Ie 8.54N 74.28W
Caucasia 202 Cb 7.59N 75.13W
Caucasus (EN)=Kavkaz, Bolšoj- 110 Kg 42.30N 45.00 E
Caucete 206 Gd 31.38S 68.16W
Caudebec-en-Caux 124 Ce 49.32N 0.44 E
Caudete 126 Lf 38.42N 0.59W
Caudry 122 Jd 50.08N 3.25 E
Caulonia 128 Kl 38.23N 16.24 E
Caumont-l'Eventé 124 Be 49.05N 0.48W
Caungula 160 Ii 8.26S 18.37 E
Čaunskaja guba 138 Lc 69.30N 170.00 E
Caupolicán 202 Ef 13.30S 68.30W
Cauquenes 206 Fe 35.58S 72.21W
Caura, Rio- 198 Je 7.38N 64.53W
Causapscal 184 Na 48.22N 67.14W
Caussade 122 Hj 44.10N 1.32 E
Čausy 132 Gc 53.50N 30.59 E
Cauterets 122 Fl 42.53N 0.07W
Cauto, Rio- 194 Ic 20.33N 77.15W
Cauvery 140 Jh 11.09N 78.52 E
Caux, Pays de- 122 Ge 49.40N 0.40 E
Cávado 126 Dc 41.32N 8.48W
Cavaillon 122 Lk 43.50N 5.02 E
Cavalaire-sur-Mer 122 Mk 43.10N 6.32 E
Cavalcante 204 Ia 13.48S 47.30W
Cavalese 128 Fd 46.17N 11.27 E
Cavalleria, Cap de- / Caballeria, Cabo de- 126 Qd 40.05N 4.05 E
Cavalli Islands 218 Ea 35.00S 173.55 E
Cavallo, Isola- 122a Bb 41.22N 9.16 E
Cavallo Pass 186 Hl 28.25N 96.26W
Cavally 158 Gh 4.22N 7.32W
Cavan/An Cabhán 118 Fg 54.00N 7.21W
Cavan/An Cabhán [2] 118 Fh 53.55N 7.30W
Cavarzere 128 Ge 45.08N 12.05 E
Çavdarhisar 130 Mj 39.12N 29.37 E
Çavdir 130 Ml 37.09N 29.42 E
Caviana, Ilha- 202 Hc 0.10N 50.05W
Cavili 150 He 9.17N 120.50 E
Cavour, Canale- 128 Be 45.11N 7.54 E
Cavtat 128 Mh 42.35N 18.13 E
Caxambu 204 Je 21.59S 44.56W
Caxias 200 Lf 4.50S 43.21W
Caxias do Sul 206 Kh 29.10S 51.11W
Caxito 170 Bd 8.34S 13.40 E
Çay 146 Dc 38.35N 31.02 E
Cayambe 202 Cc 0.05N 78.08W
Cayambe, Volcán- 198 Ie 0.02N 77.59W
Cayastá 204 Bj 31.12S 60.10W
Cayce 184 Gi 33.59N 81.04W
Çaycuma 146 Eb 41.25N 32.05 E
Çayeli 146 Ib 41.05N 40.44 E
Cayenne 200 Ke 4.56N 52.20W
Cayeux-sur-Mer 124 Dd 50.11N 1.29 E
Cayey 194 Nd 18.07N 66.10W
Çayirli 146 Ic 39.48N 40.01 E
Çaykara 146 Ib 40.45N 40.19 E
Caylus 122 Hj 44.14N 1.47 E
Cayman Brac 190 Ie 19.43N 79.49W
Cayman Islands [5] 176 Kh 19.30N 80.30W
Cayman Islands 174 Kh 19.30N 80.30W
Cayman Ridge (EN) 190 He 19.30N 80.30W
Cayman Trench (EN) 106 Bh 19.00N 80.00W
Cayo [3] 194 Ce 17.10N 88.50W
Cayon 197c Ab 17.21N 62.43W
Cayones, Cayos- 194 Fe 16.05N 83.12W
Cay Sal Bank 190 Hd 23.45N 80.00W
Cayuga Lake 184 Id 42.45N 76.45W
Cazalla de la Sierra 126 Gg 37.56N 5.45W
Caza Pava 204 Di 28.17S 56.07W
Cazaux et de Sanguinet, Étang de- 122 Ej 44.29N 1.10W
Cazombo 160 Jj 11.54S 22.53 E
Cazorla 126 Jg 37.55N 3.00W
Cazorla, Sierra de- 126 Jf 37.55N 2.55W
Cea 126 Gb 42.00N 5.36W
Ceahlău 130 Ib 47.03N 25.58 E
Ceanannas Mór/Kells 118 Gh 53.44N 6.53W
Ceanna Cailllighe/Hags Head 118 Di 52.57N 9.28W
Ceann Acla/Achill Head 118 Ch 53.59N 10.13W
Ceann an Chairn/Carnsore Point 118 Gi 52.10N 6.22W
Ceann Chill Mhantáin/ Wicklow Head 118 Hi 52.58N 6.00W
Ceann Iorrais/Erris Head 110 Fe 54.19N 10.00W
Ceann Léime/Loop Head 118 Di 52.34N 9.56W
Ceann Ros Eoghain/Rossan Point 118 Eg 54.42N 8.48W
Ceann Sléibhe/Slea Head 118 Ci 52.06N 10.27W
Ceann Toirc/Kanturk 118 Ei 52.10N 8.55W
Ceará [2] 202 Kd 5.00S 39.30W
Ceará-Mirim 202 Ke 5.38S 35.26W
Ceatharlach/Carlow 118 Gi 52.50N 6.55W
Ceatharlach/Carlow [2] 118 Gi 52.50N 7.00W
Cébaco, Isla- 194 Gj 7.32N 81.09W
Ceballos 192 Gd 26.32N 104.09W
Čebarkul 134 Ji 54.58N 60.25 E
Čeboksary 112 Kd 56.09N 47.15 E
Cebollati 204 Fk 33.16S 53.47W
Cebollati, Rio- 204 Fk 33.09S 53.38W
Cebollera, La- 126 Ic 41.10N 3.32W
Cebollera, Sierra- 126 Jc 42.00N 2.40W
Ceboruco, Volcán- 192 Gg 21.09N 104.30W
Cebreros 126 Hd 40.27N 4.28W
Cebrikovo 130 Nb 47.09N 30.02 E
Cebu 142 Oh 10.18N 123.54 E
Cebu 140 Oh 10.20N 123.45 E
Cece 128 Oj 46.46N 18.39 E
Čečen, ostrov- 132 Og 44.00N 47.45 E
Čečeno-Ingušskaja ASSR [3] 136 Eg 43.15N 45.30 E
Cecen-Ula 152 Gb 48.45N 95.55 E
Cecerleg 142 Me 47.30N 101.27 E
Čečersk 132 Gc 52.56N 30.58 E
Čechy=Bohemia (EN) 110 Hf 50.00N 14.30 E
Čechy=Bohemia (EN) 120 Kf 50.00N 14.30 E
Cecina 128 Eg 43.19N 10.31 E
Cecina 128 Eg 43.18N 10.29 E
Čečuisk 138 Fe 58.07N 108.32 E
Cedar City 176 Hf 37.41N 113.04W
Cedar Creek 186 Fc 46.07N 101.18W
Cedar Creek Reservoir 186 Hj 32.20N 96.10W
Cedar Falls 182 Ic 42.32N 92.27W
Cedar Grove 197d Bb 17.10N 61.49W
Cedar Lake 180 Hf 53.25N 100.00W
Cedar Rapids 176 Je 41.59N 91.40W
Cedar River [Nb.-U.S.] 186 Hf 41.22N 97.57W
Cedar River [U.S.] 182 Ic 41.17N 91.20W
Cedartown 184 Eh 34.01N 85.15W
Cedar-Tree Point 197d Ba 17.42N 61.53W
Cedeira 126 Da 43.39N 8.03W
Cedral 192 If 23.48N 100.44W
Cedrino 128 Dj 40.23N 9.44 E
Cedro 202 Ke 6.36S 39.03W
Cedrón 126 Ie 39.48N 3.33W
Cedros, Isla-=Cedros Island (EN) 174 Hg 28.10N 115.15W
Cedros Island (EN)=Cedros, Isla- 174 Hg 28.10N 115.15W
Cedros Trench (EN) 190 Ac 27.45N 115.45W
Ceduna 212 Gf 32.07S 133.40 E
Cedynia 120 Kd 52.50N 14.14 E
Cefalù 128 Il 38.02N 14.01 E
Cega 126 Hc 41.33N 4.46W
Čegdomyn 142 Pd 51.07N 133.05 E
Čegem 132 Mh 43.36N 43.48 E
Cegléd 120 Pi 47.10N 19.48 E
Ceglie Messapico 128 Lj 40.39N 17.31 E
Cehegin 126 Kf 38.06N 1.48W
Čehotina 130 Bf 43.31N 18.45 E
Čehov [R.S.F.S.R.] 114 Ii 55.11N 37.29 E
Čehov [R.S.F.S.R.] 138 Jg 47.24N 142.05 E
Ceica 130 Fc 46.51N 22.11 E
Çekerek 146 Fb 40.04N 35.31 E
Çekerek 146 Fb 40.34N 35.46 E
Čekmaguš 134 Gi 55.10N 54.40 E
Celano 128 Hh 42.05N 13.33 E
Celaya 190 Dd 20.31N 100.37W
Čelbas 142 Kf 46.06N 38.59 E
Célé 122 Hj 44.28N 1.38 E
Celebes/Sulawesi 140 Oj 2.00S 121.10 E
Celebes Basin (EN) 150 Hf 4.00N 122.00 E
Celebes Sea (EN)= Sulawesi, Laut- 140 Oi 3.00N 122.00 E
Čeleken 136 Fh 39.27N 53.10 E
Čeleken, poluostrov- 132 Rj 39.25N 53.35 E
Celendin 202 Ce 6.52S 78.09W
Celerain, Punta- 192 Pg 20.16N 86.59W
Celeste 204 Dj 31.18S 57.04W
Celestún 192 Ng 20.52N 90.24W
Celinograd 142 Jd 51.10N 71.30 E
Celinogradskaja oblast [3] 136 Gh 51.00N 70.00 E
Čeljabinsk 142 Id 55.10N 61.24 E
Čeljabinskaja oblast [3] 136 Ge 54.00N 61.00 E
Celje 128 Jd 46.14N 15.16 E
Čeljuskin, mys- 140 Mb 77.45N 104.20 E
Čelkar 136 Ff 47.50N 59.29 E
Celldömölk 120 Ni 47.15N 17.09 E
Celle 120 Gd 52.37N 10.05 E
Celles 124 Fd 50.43N 3.27 E
Celles, Houyet- 124 Hd 50.19N 5.01 E
Cellina 128 Gd 46.02N 12.47 E
Celone 128 Ji 41.36N 15.41 E
Celorico da Beira 126 Ed 40.38N 7.23W
Celtic Sea 110 Fe 51.00N 7.00W
Celtic Sea (EN)=An Mhuir Cheilteach 118 Fe 51.00N 7.00W
Cemaes Head 118 Ii 52.07N 4.44W
Čemal 138 Df 51.25N 86.05 E
Čemdalsk 138 Fe 59.45N 103.18 E
Čemernica 128 Lf 44.30N 17.15 E
Čemerno 130 Df 43.36N 20.26 E
Çemişkezek 146 Hc 39.04N 38.55 E
Cenajo, Embalse de- 126 Kf 38.20N 1.55W
Cenderawasih, Teluk- 150 Kg 2.25S 135.10 E
Cengel 152 Eb 48.56N 89.10 E
Çengel Geçidi 146 Kc 39.45N 44.02 E
Ceno 128 Ef 44.41N 10.05 E
Centenary 172 Ec 16.44S 31.07 E
Centennial 188 Lf 41.51N 106.07W
Centennial Lake 184 Ic 45.15N 77.00W
Centennial Mountains 188 Jd 44.35N 111.55W
Center 186 Ik 31.48N 94.11W
Center Hill Lake 184 Eg 36.00N 85.45W
Centerville 186 Jf 40.43N 92.52W
Centinela, Farallón- 196 Cg 10.49N 66.05W
Centinela, Picacho del- 190 Dc 29.07N 102.27W
Cento 128 Ff 44.43N 11.17
Centola-Palinuro 128 Jj 40.02N 15.17
Centrafrique=Central African Republic (EN) [1] 160 Jh 7.00N 21.00
Central [Bots.] [3] 172 Dd 21.30S 26.00
Central [Ghana] [3] 166 Ed 5.30N 1.00W
Central [Kenya] [3] 170 Gc 0.45S 37.00
Central [Mwi.] [3] 170 Fe 13.30S 34.00
Central [Par.] [3] 204 Dg 25.30S 57.30W
Central [Scot.-U.K.] [3] 118 Ie 56.15N 4.10W
Central [Ug.] [3] 170 Fb 0.10N 32.05
Central [Zam.] [3] 170 Ee 14.30S 29.00
Central, Chaco- 198 Kh 25.00S 59.45W
Central, Cordillera- [Col.] 198 Ie 5.00N 75.00W
Central, Cordillera- [Dom.Rep.] 190 Je 18.45N 70.30W
Central, Cordillera- [P.R.] 194 Nd 18.10N 66.35W
Central, Massif- 110 Gf 45.00N 3.10
Central, Meseta- 174 Ig 23.00N 103.00W
Central, Sistema- 110 Fg 40.30N 5.00W
Central African Republic (EN)=Centrafrique [1] 160 Jh 7.00N 21.00
Central America (EN) 106 Bh 20.00N 100.00W
Central Auckland [2] 218 Fb 36.45S 174.40
Central Brāhui Range 148 Dc 29.20N 66.55
Central City 186 Hf 41.07N 98.00W
Centralia [Il.-U.S.] 186 Lg 38.31N 89.08W
Centralia [Wa.-U.S.] 182 Cb 46.43N 122.58W
Central Makrān Range 140 Ig 26.40N 64.30
Centralno Tungusskoje plato 138 Fd 61.15N 102.00
Centralny-Kospašski 134 Hg 59.03N 57.50
Central Pacific Basin (EN) 106 Ki 5.00N 175.00W
Central Plains 174 Ke 40.20N 90.00W
Central Plateau 220e Bb 0.32S 166.56
Central Point 188 De 42.23N 122.57W
Central Range 208 Fe 5.00S 142.30
Central Russian Uplands (EN) = Srednerusskaja vozvyšennost 110 Je 52.00N 38.00
Central Siberian Uplands (EN) = Srednesibirskoje ploskogorje 140 Mc 65.00N 105.00
Central Urals (EN)=Sredni Ural 110 Ld 58.00N 59.00
Centre [Burkina] [3] 166 Ec 12.00N 1.00W
Centre [Togo] [3] 166 Fd 9.15N 1.00
Centre, Canal du- 122 Jh 46.28N 3.59
Centre-Est [3] 166 Ec 11.30N 0.20W
Centre-Nord [3] 166 Ec 13.20N 0.55W
Centre-Ouest [3] 166 Ec 12.00N 2.20W
Centre-Sud [3] 166 He 3.30N 11.50
Centro, Cayo- 192 Ph 18.35N 87.20W
Centuripe 128 Im 37.37N 14.44
Čepca 136 Fd 58.35N 50.05
Čepelare 130 Hh 41.44N 24.41
Cephalonia (EN)= Kefallinia 110 Ih 38.15N 20.35
Čepin 128 Me 45.32N 18.34
Ceplenița 130 Jb 47.23N 26.58
Cepu 150 Fh 7.09S 111.35
Cer 130 Ce 44.37N 19.28
Ceram Sea (EN)=Seram, Laut- 208 De 2.30S 128.00
Cerbatana, Serrania de la- 202 Eb 6.50N 66.15W
Cerbicale, Iles- 122a Bb 41.33N 9.22
Cercal 126 Dg 37.47N 8.42W
Čerchov 120 Rg 49.10N 21.05
Čerdakly 114 Li 54.23N 48.51
Čerdyn 134 Hf 60.25N 56.29
Cère 122 Hj 44.55N 1.49
Čereha 114 Gh 57.47N 28.22
Čeremhovo 142 Md 53.09N 103.05
Čerepanovo 138 Df 54.13N 83.32
Čerepovec 112 Jd 59.08N 37.54
Ceres [Arg.] 206 Hc 29.53S 61.57W
Ceres [Braz.] 202 Ig 15.17S 49.35W
Ceres [S.Afr.] 172 Bf 33.21S 19.18
Ceresio→Lugano, Lago di- 128 Cd 46.00N 9.00
Céret 122 Il 42.29N 2.45
Cereté 202 Cb 8.53N 75.47W
Cerf Island 158 Mi 9.31S 51.01
Cerfontaine 124 Gd 50.10N 4.25
Cergy 124 Ee 49.02N 2.04
Cerignola 128 Ji 41.16N 15.54
Čerikov 132 Gc 53.35N 31.25
Cérilly 122 Ih 46.37N 2.50
Čerkasskaja oblast [3] 136 Df 49.15N 31.15
Čerkassy 136 Df 49.26N 32.04
Çerkeş 146 Eb 40.50N 32.54
Čerkessk 136 Eg 44.14N 42.04
Çerkezköy 130 Kh 41.17N 28.00
Čerlak 136 He 54.09N 74.58
Čerlakski 136 He 53.47N 74.31
Čermasan 134 Gi 55.10N 55.20
Cermei 130 Ec 46.33N 21.51
Čermenika 130 Dh 41.03N 20.20
Čermoz 134 Hg 58.47N 56.10
Cerna [Rom.] 130 Fe 45.53N 22.58
Cerna [Rom.] 130 Fd 44.42N 22.25
Cerna [Rom.] 130 Ge 44.37N 23.57
Čërnaja 134 Hb 68.35N 56.31
Čërnaja [R.S.F.S.R.] 134 Hb 68.35N 56.30
Čërnaja [Ukr.-U.S.S.R.] 130 Mb 47.39N 29.11
Černa Skala, prohod- 130 Fg 42.02N 22.47
Černatica 130 Hh 41.53N 24.33
Černavčicy 120 Td 52.11N 23.47
Cernavoda 130 Le 44.22N 28.01
Cernay 122 Ng 47.49N 7.10
Cernay-en-Dormois 124 Ge 49.13N 4.46
Černevo 116 Mf 58.35N 28.23
Černigov 136 Df 51.30N 31.18
Černigovskaja oblast [3] 136 De 51.20N 32.00
Černi Lom 130 If 43.33N 25.57
Černi vrăh 130 Gg 42.35N 23.15

Index Symbols

[1] Independent Nation
[2] State, Region
[3] District, County
[4] Municipality
[5] Colony, Dependency
Continent
Physical Region
Historical or Cultural Region
Mount, Mountain
Volcano
Hill
Mountains, Mountain Range
Hills, Escarpment
Plateau, Upland
Pass, Gap
Plain, Lowland
Delta
Salt Flat
Valley, Canyon
Crater, Cave
Karst Features
Depression
Polder
Desert, Dunes
Forest, Woods
Heath, Steppe
Oasis
Cape, Point
Coast, Beach
Cliff
Peninsula
Isthmus
Sandbank
Island
Atoll
Rock, Reef
Islands, Archipelago
Rocks, Reefs
Coral Reef
Well, Spring
Geyser
River, Stream
Waterfall, Rapids
River Mouth, Estuary
Lake
Salt Lake
Intermittent Lake
Reservoir
Swamp, Pond
Canal
Glacier
Ice Shelf, Pack Ice
Ocean
Sea
Gulf, Bay
Strait, Fjord
Lagoon
Bank
Seamount
Tablemount
Ridge
Shelf
Basin
Escarpment, Sea Scarp
Fracture
Trench, Abyss
National Park, Reserve
Point of Interest
Recreation Site
Cave, Cavern
Historic Site
Ruins
Wall, Walls
Church, Abbey
Temple
Scientific Station
Railway station
Airport
Port
Military installatio
Lighthouse
Mine
Tunnel
Dam, Bridge

ernjahovsk 136 Ce 54.38N 21.48 E
ernjanka 132 Jd 50.55N 37.49 E
ernobyl 136 De 51.17N 30.13 E
ernogorsk 138 Ef 53.45N 91.18 E
ernoje more = Black Sea (EN) 110 Jg 43.00N 35.00 E
erno More=Black Sea (EN) 110 Jg 43.00N 35.00 E
ernomorskoje 132 Hg 45.31N 32.42 E
ernovcy 112 If 48.18N 25.56 E
ernovickaja oblast [3] 136 Cf 48.20N 26.10 E
ernuška 136 Fd 56.31N 56.03 E
erny Jar 132 Oe 48.03N 46.05 E
ernyje Zemli 132 Nf 45.55N 46.00 E
ernyševa, grjada- 134 Ic 66.20N 59.45 E
ernyševa, zaliv- 135 Bb 45.50N 59.10 E
ernyševsk 138 Gf 52.35N 117.02 E
ernyševski 138 Gd 62.58N 112.15 E
ernyškovski 132 Me 48.27N 42.14 E
érou 122 Hj 44.08N 1.52 E
erralvo 192 Jd 26.06N 99.37W
erralvo, Isla- 190 Cd 24.15N 109.55W
erredo, Torre de- 126 Ha 43.13N 4.50W
erriku 130 Ch 41.02N 19.57 E
errito [Col.] 202 Db 6.51N 72.42W
errito [Par.] 204 Dh 27.19S 57.40W
erritos 190 Dd 22.26N 100.17W
érro Azul 206 Kb 24.50S 49.15W
erro Azul 192 Kg 21.12N 97.44W
erro Chato 204 Ek 33.06S 55.08W
erro Colorado 204 Ek 33.52S 55.33W
erro de las Mesas 192 Kh 18.47N 96.05W
erro de Pasco 200 Ig 10.41S 76.16W
érro Grande 204 Gj 30.36S 51.45W
erro Largo 206 Jc 28.09S 54.45W
erro Largo [3] 204 Ek 32.20S 54.20W
errón, Cerro- 194 Lh 10.19N 70.39W
erro San Valentin 198 Ij 46.36S 73.20W
erros Colorados, Embalse- 206 Ge 38.35S 68.40W
erro Vera 204 Dk 33.11S 57.28W
errudo Cué 204 Dh 27.34S 57.57W
erski 142 Sc 68.45N 161.45 E
erskogo, hrebet- [R.S.F.S.R.] 138 Gf 52.00N 114.00 E
erskogo, hrebet- [R.S.F.S.R.] = Cherski Mountains (EN) 140 Qc 65.00N 145.00 E
ertaldo 128 Fg 43.33N 11.02 E
ertkovo 132 Le 49.20N 40.12 E
ervaro 128 Ji 41.30N 15.52 E
ervati 128 Jj 40.17N 15.29 E
erven [Bul.] 130 Jf 43.37N 26.02 E
erven [Bye.-U.S.S.R.] 132 Fc 53.43N 28.29 E
erven brjag 130 Hf 43.16N 24.06 E
ervera 126 Nc 41.40N 1.17 E
ervera del Rio Alhama 126 Kb 42.01N 1.57W
ervera de Pisuerga 126 Hb 42.52N 4.30W
erveteri 128 Gh 42.00N 12.06 E
ervia 128 Gf 44.15N 12.22 E
ervin/Cervino 128 Be 45.58N 7.39 E
ervino/Cervin 128 Be 45.58N 7.39 E
ervione 122a Ba 42.20N 9.29 E
ervonoarmejsk 120 Vf 50.03N 25.18 E
ervonoarmejskoje 130 Ld 45.50N 28.38 E
ervonograd 126 Ce 50.24N 24.12 E
esano 128 Hg 43.45N 13.10 E
esar [3] 202 Db 9.50N 73.30W
esar, Rio- 194 Ki 9.00N 73.58W
esena 128 Gf 44.08N 12.15 E
esenatico 128 Gf 44.12N 12.24 E
ēsis/Cesis 136 Cd 57.18N 25.18 E
esis/Cēsis 136 Cd 57.18N 25.18 E
eská Lipa 120 Kf 50.42N 14.32 E
eská Třebová 120 Mg 49.54N 16.27 E
eské Budějovice 120 Kh 48.58N 14.29 E
eské středohoří 120 Jf 50.35N 14.00 E
eské země [2] 120 Kg 49.45N 15.00 E
eskomoravská Vrchovina= Moravian Upland (EN) 110 Hf 49.20N 15.30 E
eskoslovenská Socialistická Republika (ČSSR) [1] 112 Hf 49.30N 17.00 E
eskoslovensko= Czechoslovakia (EN) [1] 112 Hf 49.30N 17.00 E
eský Krumlov 120 Kh 48.49N 14.19 E
eský Les=North Bohemian Forest (EN) 120 Ig 49.50N 12.30 E
esma 134 Jj 53.50N 60.40 E
esma 128 Ke 45.35N 16.29 E
eşme 146 Bc 38.18N 26.19 E
eşme Yarımadası 130 Jk 38.30N 26.30 E
esskaja guba = Chesha Bay (EN) 110 Kb 67.20N 46.30 E
essnock 212 Kf 32.50S 151.21 E
estos 158 Gh 5.27N 9.35W
esvaine/Cesvajne 116 Lh 56.55N 26.20 E
esvajne/Cesvaine 116 Lh 56.55N 26.20 E
etate 204 Ge 44.06N 23.03 E
etina 128 Kg 43.27N 16.42 E
etinje 130 Bg 42.24N 18.55 E
etinkaya 146 Gc 39.15N 37.38 E
etraro 128 Jk 39.31N 15.56 E
etynia 120 Sd 52.33N 22.26 E
euta [5] 160 Ge 35.53N 5.19W
eva-i-Ra (Conway Reef) 208 Ig 21.45S 174.35 E
evedale/Zufallspitze 128 Ed 46.27N 10.37 E
evennes 110 Gg 44.20N 4.00 E
eyhan 144 Eb 37.04N 35.47 E
eyhan 144 Eb 36.45N 35.42 E
eylanpınar 146 Id 36.51N 40.02 E
eylon → Sri Lanka [1] 142 Ki 7.40N 80.50 E
ézallier 122 Ii 45.20N 3.00 E
èze 122 Kj 44.06N 4.42 E
haalis, Abbaye de- 124 Ee 49.10N 2.40 E
ha-am 148 Jf 12.48N 99.58 E
habanais 122 Gi 45.52N 0.43 E
habjuwardoo Bay 212 Cd 22.55S 113.50 E
Chablais 122 Mh 46.20N 6.30 E
Chāboksar 146 Nd 36.58N 50.34 E
Chabówka 120 Pg 49.34N 19.58 E
Chacabuco 206 Hd 34.38S 60.29W
Chachani, Nevado- 202 Dg 16.12S 71.33W
Chachapoyas 202 Ce 6.13S 77.51W
Chachoengsao 148 Kf 13.41N 101.03 E
Chaco [3] 206 Hc 26.00S 60.30W
Chaco [3] 204 Bd 20.00S 60.30W
Chaco Mesa 186 Ci 35.50N 107.35W
Chaco River 186 Bh 36.46N 108.39W
Chad (EN)=Tchad [1] 160 Ig 15.00N 19.00 E
Chad, Lake- (EN) = Tchad, Lac- 158 Ig 13.20N 14.00 E
Chādegān 146 Nf 32.46N 50.38 E
Chadileuvú, Rio- 206 Ge 38.49S 64.57W
Chadiza 170 Fe 14.04S 32.26 E
Chadron 182 Gc 42.50N 103.02W
Chaeryŏng 154 He 38.24N 125.37 E
Chafarinas, Islas- 126 Ji 35.11N 2.26W
Chāgai Hills 140 Ig 29.30N 64.15 E
Chagang-Do [2] 154 Ie 40.50N 126.30 E
Chaghcharān 142 If 34.31N 65.15 E
Chagny 122 Kh 46.55N 4.45 E
Chagos Archipelago 140 Jj 6.00S 72.00 E
Chagos-Laccadive Plateau (EN) 106 Gi 3.00N 73.00 E
Chagu, Serra do- 204 Fg 25.10S 52.40W
Chaguaramas 196 Ch 9.20N 66.16W
Chahār Borjak 144 Jc 30.17N 62.03 E
Chahār Mahāl-e Bakhtīārī [3] 144 Hc 32.00N 50.00 E
Chahbounia 126 Oi 35.33N 2.36 E
Ch'aho 154 Jd 40.12N 128.38 E
Chai Badan 148 Ke 15.05N 101.04 E
Chaibāsa 148 Hd 22.34N 85.49 E
Chaigoubu → Huai'an 154 Cd 40.40N 114.25 E
Chai He 154 Gc 42.20N 123.51 E
Chaillu, Massif du- 158 Ii 2.32S 11.10 E
Chainat 148 Ke 15.10N 100.10 E
Chaise-Dieu, La- 122 Ji 45.19N 3.42 E
Chaitén 206 Ff 42.55S 72.43W
Chaiyaphum 148 Ke 16.09N 102.02 E
Chajul 194 Bf 15.30N 91.02W
Chakari 172 Dc 18.09S 29.52 E
Chak Chak 168 Dd 8.40N 26.54 E
Chake Chake 160 Ki 5.15S 39.46 E
Chakhānsūr 144 Jc 31.10N 62.04 E
Chala 202 Dg 15.52S 74.16W
Chalais 122 Gi 45.17N 0.02 E
Chalaltenango 194 Cf 14.03N 88.56W
Chalan Kanoa 220b Ba 15.08N 145.43 E
Chalbi Desert 158 Kh 3.00N 37.20 E
Chalchuapa 194 Cg 13.59N 89.41W
Chalcidice (EN) = Khalkidhikí 110 Ig 40.25N 23.25 E
Chālesbān 146 Ne 35.18N 50.03 E
Chaleur Bay 180 Kg 47.50N 65.30W
Chalhuanca 202 Df 14.17S 73.15W
Chaling 152 Jf 26.47N 113.32 E
Chalky Inlet 218 Bg 46.05S 166.30 E
Challans 122 Eh 46.51N 1.53W
Challapata 202 Eg 18.54S 66.47W
Challis 188 Hd 44.30N 114.14W
Chalmette 186 Ll 29.56N 89.58W
Châlons-sur-Marne 122 Kf 48.57N 4.22 E
Chalon-sur-Saône 122 Kh 46.47N 4.51 E
Chalosse 122 Fk 43.45N 0.30W
Chaltubo 132 Mh 42.19N 42.34 E
Chālūs 144 Hb 36.38N 51.26 E
Châlus 122 Gi 45.39N 0.59 E
Cham 120 Ig 49.13N 12.40 E
Chama 170 Fe 11.12S 33.10 E
Chama, Rio- 194 Li 9.03N 71.37W
Chama, Rio- 186 Ch 33.03N 106.05W
Chaman 148 Db 30.55N 66.27 E
Chaman Bīd 146 Qd 37.25N 56.38 E
Chamba [India] 148 Fb 32.34N 76.08 E
Chamba [Tan.] 170 Ge 11.35S 36.58 E
Chambal 140 Jg 26.29N 79.15 E
Chambaran, Plateau de- 122 Li 45.10N 5.20 E
Chambas 194 Hb 22.12N 78.55W
Chamberlain 186 Ge 43.49N 99.20W
Chamberlain Lake 184 Mb 46.17N 69.20W
Chamberlain River 212 Fc 15.35S 127.51 E
Chambersburg 184 If 39.57N 77.40W
Chambéry 122 Li 45.34N 5.56 E
Chambeshi 158 Jj 11.53S 29.48 E
Chambley-Bussières 124 He 49.03N 5.54 E
Chambly 124 Ee 49.10N 2.15 E
Chambois 124 Cf 48.48N 0.07 E
Chambon, Lac de- 122 Hh 46.25N 1.35 E
Chambord 122 Hg 47.37N 1.31 E
Chamchamal 146 Ke 35.32N 44.50 E
Chame, Punta- 194 Hi 8.39N 79.42W
Chamela 192 Gh 19.32N 105.05W
Chamela, Bahía- 192 Gh 19.30N 105.10W
Chamelecón, Rio- 194 Df 15.51N 87.49W
Chamical 206 Gd 30.21S 66.19W
Chamiss Bay 188 Ba 50.07N 127.22W
Chamoli 148 Fb 30.24N 79.21 E
Chamonix-Mont-Blanc 122 Mi 45.55N 6.52 E
Chamouchouane, Rivière- 184 Ka 48.40N 72.20W
Champagne 110 Gf 49.00N 4.30 E
Champagne 122 Kf 49.00N 4.30 E
Champagne Berrichonne 122 Hh 47.00N 2.00 E
Champagne Humide 122 Kf 48.20N 4.30 E
Champagne Pouilleuse 122 Kf 48.40N 4.20 E
Champagnole 122 Lh 46.45N 5.55 E
Champaign 182 Jc 40.07N 88.14W
Champaqui, Cerro- 198 Ji 31.59S 64.56W
Champasak 148 Lf 14.53N 105.52 E
Champaubert 124 Ff 48.53N 3.47 E
Champdoré, Lac- 180 Ke 55.55N 65.45W
Champ du Feu, Le- 122 Nf 48.24N 7.15 E
Champeigne 122 Gg 47.15N 0.50 E
Champerico 194 Bf 14.18N 91.55W
Champlain, Lake- 182 Mc 44.45N 73.15W
Champlite 122 Lg 47.37N 5.31 E
Champotón 190 Fe 19.21N 90.43W
Champsaur 122 Mj 44.45N 6.10 E
Chāmrājnagar 148 Ff 11.55N 76.57 E
Chañaral 206 Fc 26.21S 70.37W
Chança 126 Eg 37.33N 7.31W
Chan Chan 202 Ce 8.07S 79.02W
Chanco 206 Fe 35.44S 72.32W
Chandalar 178 Jc 67.30N 148.30W
Chandalar 178 Jc 66.36N 145.48W
Chandausi 148 Fc 28.27N 78.46 E
Chandeleur Islands 182 Jf 29.48N 88.51W
Chandeleur Sound 186 Ll 29.55N 89.10W
Chandīgarh 142 Jf 30.44N 76.55 E
Chandler 180 Lg 48.21N 64.41W
Chandless, Rio- 202 Ee 9.08S 69.51W
Chāndpur 148 Id 23.13N 90.39 E
Chandragupta 148 Fe 16.11N 78.52 E
Chandrapur 142 Jh 19.57N 79.18 E
Chang, Ko- 148 Kf 12.00N 102.23 E
Changajn Nuruu = Khangai Mountains (EN) 140 Le 47.30N 100.00 E
Chang'an → Rong'an 152 If 25.10N 109.23 E
Changane 158 Kk 24.43S 33.32 E
Changbai 154 Jd 41.25N 128.11 E
Changbai Shan 140 Oe 42.00N 128.00 E
Changchun 142 Oe 43.51N 125.20 E
Changdao(Sihou) 154 Ff 37.56N 120.42 E
Changde 142 Ng 29.04N 111.42 E
Ch'angdo 154 Ie 38.30N 127.45 E
Changfeng (Shuijiahu) 154 Dh 32.29N 117.10 E
Changge 154 Bg 34.12N 113.45 E
Changhang 154 If 36.01N 126.42 E
Chang He 154 Ei 31.21N 118.21 E
Changhowŏn 154 If 37.07N 127.38 E
Changhua 152 Lg 24.05N 120.32 E
Changhŭng 154 Ig 34.40N 126.54 E
Changji 152 Ec 44.01N 87.16 E
Chang Jiang 154 Dj 28.59N 116.42 E
Changjiang (Shiliu) 152 Ih 19.20N 109.03 E
Chang Jiang (Yangtze Kiang) 140 Of 31.48N 121.10 E
Changjiang Kou 152 Le 31.24N 121.59 E
Changjin-gang 154 Id 40.30N 127.12 E
Changjin-ho 154 Id 40.30N 127.12 E
Changjin-ŭp 152 Mc 40.23N 127.15 E
Changli 154 Ee 39.43N 119.10 E
Changling 152 Lc 44.15N 123.58 E
Changlung 148 Fb 34.56N 77.29 E
Changping 154 Dd 40.14N 116.13 E
Changsha 142 Ng 28.12N 113.02 E
Changshan 154 Ej 28.55N 118.31 E
Changshan Qundao 154 Ge 39.10N 122.34 E
Changshu 154 Fi 31.38N 120.44 E
Changsŏng 154 Ig 35.19N 126.48 E
Changting 154 Jb 44.27N 128.50 E
Changtu 154 Hc 42.47N 124.08 E
Changuillo 202 Cf 14.40S 75.12W
Changuinola 194 Fi 9.26N 82.31W
Changwu 152 Id 35.17N 107.52 E
Changxing 154 Ei 31.01N 119.55 E
Changxing Dao 154 Fe 39.35N 121.42 E
Changyi 154 Ef 36.52N 119.25 E
Changyŏn 152 Md 38.15N 125.05 E
Changyuan 154 Cg 35.12N 114.40 E
Changzhi 152 Jd 36.07N 113.10 E
Changzhou 154 Ei 31.46N 119.56 E
Channel Islands [Chan.Is.] 110 Ff 49.20N 2.20W
Channel Islands [U.S.] 174 Hf 34.00N 120.00W
Channel Islands = Anglo-Normandes Iles- (F) [5] 118 Kl 49.20N 2.20W
Channel Port-aux-Basques 176 Ne 47.35N 59.11W
Channel Rock 194 Ib 23.00N 77.55W
Channing 186 Ei 35.41N 102.20W
Chantada 126 Eb 42.37N 7.46W
Chantengo, Laguna- 192 Ji 16.35N 99.10W
Chanthaburi 148 Kf 12.35N 102.06 E
Chantilly 122 Ie 49.12N 2.28 E
Chantonnay 122 Eh 46.41N 1.03W
Chantrey Inlet 174 Jc 67.48N 96.20W
Chanute 186 Ih 37.41N 95.27W
Chanza 126 Eg 37.33N 7.31W
Chao'an (Chaozhou) 152 Kg 23.41N 116.37 E
Chaobai Xinhe 154 De 39.07N 117.41 E
Chao He 154 Dd 40.36N 117.08 E
Chao Hu 154 Di 31.31N 117.33 E
Chao Phraya 140 Mh 13.32N 100.36 E
Chaor He 152 Lb 46.49N 123.45 E
Chaoxian 152 Ke 31.37N 117.49 E
Chaoyang [China] 152 Kg 23.17N 116.37 E
Chaoyang [China] 142 Oe 41.35N 120.26 E
Chaoyang → Huinan 154 Ic 42.41N 126.03 E
Chaoyang → Jiayin 152 Nb 48.52N 130.21 E
Chaoyangchuan 154 Jc 42.53N 129.23 E
Chaoyangcun 152 La 50.01N 124.22 E
Chaozhong 152 La 50.53N 121.23 E
Chaozhou → Chao'an 152 Kg 23.41N 116.37 E
Chapada dos Guimarães 202 Gg 15.26S 55.45W
Chapadinha 202 Jd 3.44S 43.21W
Chapais 184 Ja 49.47N 74.56W
Chapala 192 Hg 20.18N 103.12W
Chapala, Lago de- 174 Ig 20.15N 103.00W
Chaparral 202 Cc 3.43N 75.28W
Chapecó 206 Jc 27.06S 52.36W
Chapecó, Rio- 204 Fh 27.06S 53.01W
Chapecó, Serra do- 204 Gh 26.44S 51.54W
Chapel Hill 184 Hh 35.55N 79.04W
Chapicuy 204 Dj 31.40S 57.55W
Chapleau 180 Jg 47.50N 83.24W
Chaplin 188 La 50.28N 106.40W
Chaplin Lake 188 La 50.25N 106.35W
Chapman, Cape- 180 Ic 69.15N 89.27W
Chappell 186 Ef 41.06N 102.28W
Chāpra 148 Gc 25.46N 84.45 E
Chapultepec 192 Hf 23.27N 103.04W
Chaqui 202 Eg 19.36S 65.32W
Char 162 Ee 21.31N 12.51W
Charadai 204 Ch 27.38S 59.54W
Charagua 202 Fg 19.48S 63.13W
Charām 146 Ng 30.45N 50.44 E
Charaña 202 Eg 17.36S 69.28W
Charcas 192 If 23.08N 101.07W
Charco de la Aguja 192 Gc 28.25N 104.01W
Charcot Island 222 Qe 69.45S 75.15W
Chard [Alta.-Can.] 180 Ge 55.48N 111.10W
Chard [Eng.-U.K.] 118 Kk 50.53N 2.58W
Chardāvol 146 Lf 33.45N 46.38 E
Chardonnières 194 Jd 18.16N 74.10W
Charente [3] 122 Gi 45.40N 0.05 E
Charente 122 Ei 45.57N 1.05W
Charente-Maritime [3] 122 Fi 45.30N 0.45W
Charentonne 124 Ce 49.07N 0.44 E
Chari 158 Ig 12.58N 14.31 E
Chari-Baguirmi [3] 168 Bc 12.00N 17.00 E
Chārīkār 144 Kb 35.01N 69.11 E
Charing 124 Cc 51.12N 0.48 E
Charité-sur-Loire, La- 122 Jg 47.11N 3.01 E
Chariton 186 Jf 41.00N 93.19W
Chariton River 186 Jg 39.19N 92.57W
Charity 202 Gb 7.24N 58.36W
Charleroi 122 Kd 50.25N 4.26 E
Charleroi-Jumet 122 Kd 50.27N 4.26 E
Charleroi-Marcinelle 124 Gd 50.25N 4.28 E
Charles 180 Kd 62.38N 74.15W
Charles, Cape- [Can.] 174 Nd 52.13N 55.40W
Charles, Cape- [Va.-U.S.] 182 Ld 37.08N 75.58W
Charles, Peak- 212 Ef 32.52S 121.11 E
Charlesbourg 184 Lb 46.52N 71.16W
Charles City 182 Ic 43.04N 92.40W
Charles de Gaulle, Aéroport- = Charles de Gaulle, Airport- (EN) 124 Ee 49.02N 2.35 E
Charles de Gaulle, Airport- (EN) = Charles de Gaulle, Aéroport- 124 Ee 49.02N 2.35 E
Charleston [Il.-U.S.] 186 Lg 39.30N 88.10W
Charleston [Mo.-U.S.] 186 Lh 36.55N 89.21W
Charleston [Ms.-U.S.] 186 Ki 34.01N 90.04W
Charleston [N.Z.] 218 Dd 41.54S 171.27 E
Charleston [S.C.-U.S.] 176 Lf 32.48N 79.57W
Charleston [W.V.-U.S.] 176 Kf 38.21N 81.38W
Charleston Peak 182 Dd 36.16N 115.42W
Charles Town 184 If 39.18N 77.52W
Charlestown 196 Ed 17.12N 62.35W
Charleval 124 De 49.22N 1.23 E
Charleville 210 Fg 26.24S 146.15 E
Charleville-Mézières 122 Ke 49.46N 4.43 E
Charleville Mézières-Mohon 124 Ge 49.46N 4.43 E
Charlevoix 184 Ec 45.19N 85.16W
Charlieu 122 Kh 46.09N 4.11 E
Charlotte [Mi.-U.S.] 184 Ed 42.36N 84.50W
Charlotte [N.C.-U.S.] 176 Kf 35.14N 80.50W
Charlotte Amalie 190 Le 18.21N 64.56W
Charlotte Bank (EN) 208 If 11.47S 173.13 E
Charlotte Harbor 184 Fl 26.45N 82.12W
Charlottenberg 116 Ee 59.53N 12.17 E
Charlottesville 182 Ld 38.02N 78.29W
Charlottetown 176 Me 46.14N 63.08W
Charlton 212 Ig 36.16S 143.21 E
Charlton 180 Jf 52.00N 79.26W
Charly 124 Ff 48.58N 3.17 E
Charmes 122 Mf 48.22N 6.17 E
Charnley River 212 Ec 16.20S 124.53 E
Charny-sur-Meuse 124 He 49.12N 5.22 E
Charollais 122 Kh 46.26N 4.16 E
Charouine 162 Gd 29.01N 0.16W
Charroux 122 Gh 46.09N 0.24 E
Chārsadda 148 Eb 34.09N 71.44 E
Charters Towers 210 Fg 20.05S 146.16 E
Chartres 122 Hf 48.27N 1.30 E
Charzykowskie, Jezioro- 120 Nc 53.47N 17.30 E
Chascomus 206 Ie 35.34S 58.01W
Chase 188 Fa 50.49N 119.41W
Chasŏng 154 Id 41.25N 126.35 E
Chassengue 170 Ce 10.26S 18.32 E
Chassezac 122 Kj 44.26N 4.19 E
Chassiron, Pointe de- 122 Eh 46.03N 1.24W
Chat 146 Pd 37.59N 55.16 E
Châtaigneraie 122 Ij 44.45N 2.20 E
Chātāl 146 Pd 37.40N 55.45 E
Château-Arnoux 122 Lj 44.06N 6.00 E
Chateaubelair 197n Ba 13.17N 61.15W
Châteaubriant 122 Eg 47.43N 1.23W
Château-Chinon 122 Jg 47.04N 3.56 E
Château-d'Oléron, Le- 122 Ei 45.54N 1.12W
Château-du-Loir 122 Gg 47.42N 0.25 E
Châteaudun 122 Hf 48.05N 1.20 E
Château-Gontier 122 Fg 47.50N 0.42W
Châteaulin 122 Bf 48.12N 4.05W
Châteaulin, Bassin de- 122 Cf 48.18N 3.50W
Châteaumeillant 122 Ih 46.34N 2.12 E
Châteauneuf-de-Randon 122 Jj 44.39N 3.40 E
Châteauneuf-sur-Cher 122 Ih 46.51N 2.19 E
Châteauneuf-sur-Loire 122 Ig 47.52N 2.14 E
Château-Porcien 124 Ge 49.32N 4.15 E
Châteaurenard 122 Kk 43.53N 4.51 E
Château-Renault 122 Gg 47.35N 0.54 E
Châteauroux 122 Hh 46.49N 1.42 E
Château-Salins 122 Mf 48.49N 6.30 E
Château-Thierry 122 Je 49.03N 3.24 E
Châteaux, Pointe des- 197e Bb 16.15N 61.11W
Châtelaillon-Plage 122 Eh 46.04N 1.05W
Châtelet 124 Gd 50.24N 4.31 E
Châtelguyon 122 Ji 45.55N 3.04 E
Châtellerault 122 Gh 46.48N 0.32 E
Chatelodo 204 De 21.19S 57.28W
Chatham [Eng.-U.K.] 118 Nj 51.23N 0.32 E
Chatham [N.B.-Can.] 180 Kg 47.02N 65.26W
Chatham [Ont.-Can.] 180 Jh 42.24N 82.11W
Chatham [Va.-U.S.] 184 Hg 36.49N 79.26W
Chatham Island 208 Ji 44.00S 176.30W
Chatham Islands 208 Ji 44.00S 176.30W
Chatham Rise (EN) 208 Ii 43.30S 180.00
Chatham Strait 178 Me 57.30N 134.45W
Châtillon-en-Bazois 122 Jg 47.03N 3.40 E
Châtillon-sur-Indre 122 Hh 46.59N 1.10 E
Châtillon-sur-Marne 124 Fe 49.06N 3.45 E
Châtillon-sur-Seine 122 Kg 47.51N 4.33 E
Chatom 184 Cj 31.28N 88.16W
Châtre, La- 122 Hh 46.35N 1.59 E
Chatsworth 172 Ec 19.38S 30.50 E
Chattahoochee 184 Ej 30.42N 84.51W
Chattahoochee 174 Kf 30.52N 84.57W
Chattanooga 176 Kf 35.03N 85.19W
Chatteris 124 Cb 52.27N 0.03 E
Chaucas 204 Cc 16.46S 58.44W
Chaudfontaine 124 Hd 50.35N 5.38 E
Chaudière, Rivière- 184 Lb 46.43N 71.17W
Chau Doc 148 Lf 10.42N 105.07 E
Chauk 148 Id 20.53N 94.49 E
Chaulnes 124 Ee 49.49N 2.48 E
Chaumont 122 Lf 48.07N 5.08 E
Chaumont-en-Vexin 124 De 49.16N 1.53 E
Chaumont-Gistoux 124 Gd 50.41N 4.44 E
Chaumont-Porcien 124 Ge 49.39N 4.15 E
Chaumont-sur-Aire 124 Hf 48.56N 5.15 E
Chaumont-sur-Loire 122 Hg 47.29N 1.11 E
Chauny 122 Je 49.37N 3.13 E
Chausey, Iles- 122 Ef 48.53N 1.50W
Chauvigny 122 Gh 46.34N 0.39 E
Chavantina 202 Hf 14.40S 52.21W
Chavarria 204 Ci 28.57S 58.35W
Chaves [Braz.] 202 Id 0.10S 49.55W
Chaves [Port.] 126 Ec 41.44N 7.28W
Chavigny, Lac- 180 Je 58.00N 75.05W
Chavuma 170 De 13.05S 22.42 E
Chayia 146 If 32.09N 40.58 E
Chazelles-sur-Lyon 122 Ki 45.38N 4.23 E
Chbar 148 Lf 12.46N 107.10 E
Cheaha Mountain 184 Ei 33.30N 85.47W
Cheat River 184 Hf 39.45N 79.55W
Cheb 120 If 50.04N 12.23 E
Cheboygan 182 Kb 45.39N 84.29W
Chech, 'Erg- 158 Gf 25.00N 3.00W
Chechaouene 162 Fb 35.10N 5.16W
Chechaouene [3] 162 Fb 35.00N 5.00W
Checheng 152 Lg 22.05N 120.42 E
Che-Chiang Sheng → Zhejiang Sheng [2] 152 Kf 29.00N 120.00 E
Chech'ŏn 154 Jf 37.08N 128.12 E
Chęciny 120 Qf 50.48N 20.28 E
Cheddar Gorge 118 Kj 51.13N 2.47W
Cheduba 148 Ie 18.48N 93.38 E
Chée 124 Gf 48.45N 4.39 E
Cheektowaga 184 Hd 42.57N 78.38W
Chefu 172 Ed 22.27S 32.45 E
Chegga 160 Gf 25.22N 5.49W
Cheghelvandī 146 Mf 33.42N 48.25 E
Chegutu 172 Ec 18.07S 30.08 E
Chehel Pāyeh 146 Qg 31.54N 57.14 E
Cheju 152 Me 33.31N 126.32 E
Cheju-Do [2] 154 Ih 33.25N 126.30 E
Cheju-Do 140 Of 33.25N 126.30 E
Cheju-Haehyŏp 154 Ih 33.40N 126.28 E
Chela, Serra da- 158 Ij 16.00S 13.10 E
Chelan 188 Ec 47.51N 120.01W
Chelan, Lake- 188 Eb 48.05N 120.30W
Chelforó, Arroyo- 204 Cm 36.55S 58.12W
Cheliff 162 Hb 36.10N 1.20 E
Cheliff [3] 162 Hb 36.10N 1.45 E
Cheliff 158 He 36.02N 0.08 E
Cheliff, Plaine du- 126 Mi 35.57N 0.45 E
Chellalat el Adhaouara 126 Pi 35.56N 3.25 E
Chelleh Khāneh, Kūh-e- 146 Md 36.52N 48.36 E
Chełm 120 Te 51.10N 23.28 E
Chełm [2] 120 Te 51.10N 23.30 E
Chelmer 124 Cc 51.44N 0.42 E
Chełmińskie, Pojezierze- 120 Oc 53.20N 19.00 E
Chełmno 120 Oc 53.22N 18.26 E
Chelmsford 118 Nj 51.44N 0.28 E
Chełmża 120 Oc 53.12N 18.37 E
Cheltenham 118 Kj 51.54N 2.04W
Chelva 126 Ke 39.45N 0.59W
Chemainus 188 Db 48.55N 123.43W
Chemāmā 162 Ef 16.50N 14.00 E
Chemba 172 Ec 17.09S 34.53 E
Chembe 170 Ee 11.58S 28.45 E
Chemillé 122 Fg 47.13N 0.43W
Chemnitz = Karl-Marx-Stadt 112 He 50.50N 12.55 E
Chemult 188 Ee 43.13N 121.47W
Chenāb 140 Jg 29.13N 70.49 E
Chenachane 162 Gd 26.00N 4.15W
Chenachane 162 Gd 25.17N 3.10W
Chenārbāshi 146 Lf 33.20N 46.20 E
Chen Barag Qi (Bayan Hure) 152 Kb 49.21N 119.25 E
Chencha 168 Fd 6.17N 37.40 E
Chencoyi 192 Nh 19.48N 90.14W
Cheney 188 Gc 47.29N 117.34W
Cheney Reservoir 186 Hh 37.45N 97.50W
Cheng'an 154 Cf 36.27N 114.41 E
Chengde 152 Kc 41.00N 117.57 E
Chengdu 142 Mf 30.45N 104.04 E
Chengkou 152 Ie 31.54N 108.37 E
Chengmai 152 Ih 19.50N 109.59 E
Chengshan Jiao 152 Ld 37.24N 122.42 E
Chengxi Hu 154 Dh 32.22N 116.12 E
Chengzitan 154 Gd 39.31N 122.28 E
Chenisckali 132 Mh 42.06N 42.16 E
Chenjiagang 154 Eg 34.22N 119.48 E
Chenonceaux 122 Hg 47.20N 1.04 E
Chenxi 152 Jf 28.02N 110.15 E
Chenxian 152 Jf 25.49N 113.04 E
Chenying → Wannian 154 Dj 28.42N 117.04 E
Cheo Reo 148 Lf 13.24N 108.27 E
Chépénéhé 219b Ce 20.47S 167.09 E
Chepes 206 Gd 31.21S 66.36W
Chepo 194 Hi 9.10N 79.06W
Cher [3] 122 Ig 47.00N 2.30 E
Cher 110 Gf 47.21N 0.29 E

Index Symbols

[1] Independent Nation
[2] State, Region
[3] District, County
[4] Municipality
[5] Colony, Dependency
Continent
Physical Region
Historical or Cultural Region
Mount, Mountain
Volcano
Hill
Mountains, Mountain Range
Hills, Escarpment
Plateau, Upland
Pass, Gap
Plain, Lowland
Delta
Salt Flat
Valley, Canyon
Crater, Cave
Karst Features
Depression
Polder
Desert, Dunes
Forest, Woods
Heath, Steppe
Oasis
Cape, Point
Coast, Beach
Cliff
Peninsula
Isthmus
Sandbank
Island
Atoll
Rock, Reef
Islands, Archipelago
Rocks, Reefs
Coral Reef
Well, Spring
Geyser
River, Stream
Waterfall, Rapids
River Mouth, Estuary
Lake
Salt Lake
Intermittent Lake
Reservoir
Swamp, Pond
Canal
Glacier
Ice Shelf, Pack Ice
Ocean
Sea
Gulf, Bay
Strait, Fjord
Lagoon
Bank
Seamount
Tablemount
Ridge
Shelf
Basin
Escarpment, Sea Scarp
Fracture
Trench, Abyss
National Park, Reserve
Point of Interest
Recreation Site
Cave, Cavern
Historic Site
Ruins
Wall, Walls
Church, Abbey
Temple
Scientific Station
Railway station
Airport
Port
Military installation
Lighthouse
Mine
Tunnel
Dam, Bridge

Cheradi, Isole-→Coradi, Isole- 128 Lj 40.27N 17.09 E
Cherangany Hills 170 Gb 1.15N 35.27 E
Cheraw 184 Hh 34.42N 79.53W
Cherbaniani Reef 148 Ef 12.18N 71.53 E
Cherbourg 112 Ff 49.39N 1.39W
Cherchell 162 Hb 36.36N 2.12 E
Chère 122 Eg 47.42N 1.50W
Chergui, Chott Ech- 158 He 34.21N 0.30 E
Chéri 166 Hc 13.26N 11.21 E
Cherlen→Kerulen 140 Ne 48.48N 117.00 E
Cherokee 186 Ie 42.45N 95.33W
Cherokees, Lake O' the- 186 Ih 36.39N 94.49W
Cherski Mountains (EN) = Čerskogo, hrebet- [R.S.F.S.R.] 140 Qc 65.00N 145.00 E
Chertsey 124 Bc 51.23N 0.30W
Cherwell 118 Lj 51.44N 1.15W
Chesapeake 184 Ig 36.45N 76.15W
Chesapeake Bay 174 Lf 38.40N 76.25W
Chesapeake Bay Bridge-Tunnel 184 Ig 37.00N 76.02W
Chesha Bay (EN) = Čěšskaja guba 110 Kb 67.20N 46.30 E
Chesham 124 Bc 51.42N 0.36W
Cheshire [3] 118 Kh 53.15N 2.30W
Cheshire Plain 118 Kh 53.20N 2.40W
Cheshunt 124 Bc 51.42N 0.02W
Chesne, Le- 122 Ke 49.31N 4.46 E
Chester 118 Kh 53.10N 2.55W
Chester [Eng.-U.K.] 118 Kh 53.12N 2.54W
Chester [Il.-U.S.] 186 Lh 37.55N 89.49W
Chester [Mt.-U.S.] 188 Jb 48.31N 110.58W
Chester [Pa.-U.S.] 184 Jf 39.50N 75.23W
Chester [S.C.-U.S.] 184 Gh 34.40N 81.12W
Chesterfield 118 Lh 53.15N 1.25W
Chesterfield, Ile- 172 Gc 16.20S 43.58 E
Chesterfield, Récifs et Iles- =Chesterfield Reefs and Islands (EN) 208 Gf 20.00S 159.00 E
Chesterfield Inlet 176 Jc 63.21N 90.42W
Chesterfield Inlet 174 Jc 63.25N 90.45W
Chesterfield Reefs and Islands (EN)=Chesterfield, Récifs et Iles- 208 Gf 20.00S 159.00 E
Chesterton Range 212 Je 25.30S 147.30 E
Chestnut Ridge 184 He 40.10N 79.25W
Chesuncook Lake 184 Mb 46.00N 69.20W
Chetaibi 162 Ib 37.04N 7.23 E
Chetumal 176 Kh 18.35N 88.07W
Chetumal, Bahia de- 190 Ge 18.20N 88.05W
Cheviot 218 Ee 42.49S 173.16 E
Chew Bahir=Stefanie, Lake- (EN) 158 Kh 4.38N 36.50 E
Chewelah 188 Gb 48.17N 117.43W
Cheyenne [Ok.-U.S.] 186 Gi 35.37N 99.40W
Cheyenne [Wy.-U.S.] 176 Ie 41.08N 104.49W
Cheyenne River 182 Gc 44.40N 101.15W
Cheyenne Wells 186 Eg 38.51N 102.11W
Cheylard, Le- 122 Kj 44.54N 4.25 E
Cheyne Bay 212 Df 34.35S 118.50 E
Chhatarpur 148 Fd 24.54N 79.36 E
Chhindwāra 148 Fd 22.04N 78.56 E
Chi 148 Ke 15.11N 104.43 E
Chiamboni, Rās- 168 Gf 1.38S 41.36 E
Chiana, Val di- 128 Fg 43.15N 11.50 E
Chianciano Terme 128 Fg 43.02N 11.49 E
Chiange 160 Ij 15.45S 13.54 E
Chiang-hsi Sheng→Jiangxi Sheng [2] 152 Kf 28.00N 116.00 E
Chiang Mai 142 Lh 18.46N 98.58 E
Chiang Rai 142 Lh 19.54N 99.50 E
Chiang-su Sheng→Jiangsu Sheng=Kiangsu (EN) [2] 152 Ke 33.00N 120.00 E
Chiani 128 Gh 42.44N 12.07 E
Chianti 128 Fg 43.30N 11.25 E
Chiapa, Rio- 192 Mj 16.30N 93.10W
Chiapas [2] 190 Fe 16.30N 92.30W
Chiapas, Meseta de- 190 Fe 16.30N 92.00W
Chiaramonte Gulfi 128 Im 37.02N 14.42 E
Chiaravalle 128 Hg 43.36N 13.19 E
Chiaromonte 128 Kj 40.07N 16.13 E
Chiautla de Tapia 192 Jh 18.17N 98.36W
Chiavari 128 Df 44.19N 9.19 E
Chiavenna 128 Dd 46.19N 9.24 E
Chiayi 152 Lg 23.29N 120.27 E
Chiba 152 Pd 35.36N 140.07 E
Chiba Ken [2] 154 Pg 35.40N 140.20 E
Chibemba 170 Bf 15.45S 14.06 E
Chibia 170 Bf 15.11S 13.41 E
Chibougamau 176 Le 49.53N 74.21W
Chibougamau, Lac- 184 Ja 49.50N 74.15W
Chibougamau, Rivière- 184 Ja 49.50N 74.25W
Chiburi-Jima 154 Lf 36.00N 133.02 E
Chibuto 172 Ed 24.42S 33.33 E
Chicago 176 Ke 41.53N 87.38W
Chicago Heights 186 Mf 41.30N 87.38W
Chicala 170 Ce 11.59S 19.30 E
Chicapa 172 Ci 6.25S 20.48 E
Chic-Chocs, Monts- 184 Na 48.55N 66.45W
Chicha 168 Bb 16.52N 18.33 E
Chichagof 178 Le 57.30N 135.30W
Chichancanab, Laguna de- 192 Oh 19.54N 88.46W
Chichaoua 162 Fc 31.32N 8.46W
Chichas, Cordillera de- 202 Eh 20.30S 66.30W
Chicheng 152 Kc 40.55N 115.47 E
Chichén Itzá 176 Kg 20.40N 88.35W
Chichester 118 Mk 50.50N 0.48W
Chichester Range 212 Dd 22.20S 119.20 E
Chichibu 154 Og 35.59N 139.05 E
Chichigalpa 194 Dg 12.34N 87.02W
Chichijma-Rettō 214 Cb 27.06N 142.12 E
Chichilla de Monte Aragón 126 Kf 38.55N 1.43W
Chichiriviche 194 Mh 10.56N 68.16W
Chickasawhay River 186 Lk 31.00N 88.45W
Chickasha 182 Hd 35.02N 97.58W
Chicken 178 Kd 64.04N 141.56W
Chiclana de la Frontera 126 Fh 36.25N 6.08W
Chiclayo 200 If 6.46S 79.50W
Chico 182 Cd 39.44N 121.50W
Chico, Rio- [Arg.] 198 Jj 49.56S 68.32W
Chico, Rio- [Arg.] 198 Jj 43.48S 66.25W
Chicoana 206 Gc 25.06S 65.33W
Chicomo 172 Ed 24.31S 34.17 E
Chiconono 172 Fb 12.57S 35.45 E
Chicopee 184 Kd 42.10N 72.36W
Chicote 170 Df 16.01S 21.48 E
Chicoutimi 176 Le 48.26N 71.04W
Chicoutimi Nord 184 La 48.29N 71.02W
Chicualacuala 172 Ed 22.05S 31.42 E
Chidenguele 172 Ed 24.55S 34.10 E
Chidley, Cape- 174 Mc 60.25N 64.30W
Chiemsee 120 Ii 47.54N 12.29 E
Chiengi 170 Ed 8.39S 29.10 E
Chienti 128 Hg 43.18N 13.45 E
Chieri 128 Be 45.01N 7.49 E
Chiers 124 He 49.39N 5.00 E
Chiese 128 Ee 45.08N 10.25 E
Chieti 128 Ih 42.21N 14.10 E
Chièvres 124 Fd 50.35N 3.48 E
Chifeng/Ulanhad 152 Kc 42.16N 118.57 E
Chifumage 170 De 12.10S 22.30 E
Chifwefwe 170 Fe 13.35S 29.35 E
Chigasaki 156 Fd 35.19N 139.24 E
Chignik 178 He 56.18N 158.23W
Chigombe 172 Ed 23.26S 33.19 E
Chigorodó 194 Ij 7.41N 76.41W
Chigubo 172 Ed 22.50S 33.31 E
Chigu Co 152 Ff 28.40N 91.50 E
Chi He 154 Dh 32.51N 117.59 E
Chihli, Gulf of- (EN)=Bo Hai 140 Nf 38.30N 120.00 E
Chihuahua 176 Ig 28.38N 106.05W
Chihuahua [2] 190 Cc 28.30N 106.00W
Chii-san 154 Ig 35.20N 127.44 E
Chikaskia River 186 Hh 36.37N 97.15W
Chikugo 156 Be 33.13N 130.30 E
Chikugo-Gawa 156 Be 33.10N 130.21 E
Chikuma-Gawa 156 Fc 37.00N 138.35 E
Chikwana 170 Ff 16.03S 34.48 E
Chilapa de Álvarez 192 Ji 17.36N 99.10W
Chilās 148 Ea 35.26N 74.05 E
Chilaw 148 Fg 7.34N 79.47 E
Chilcotin 180 Ff 51.46N 122.22W
Childers 212 Ke 25.14S 152.17 E
Childress 182 Ge 34.25N 100.13W
Chile [1] 200 Ii 30.00S 71.00W
Chile Basin (EN) 106 Mm 33.00S 90.00W
Chile Chico 206 Fg 46.33S 71.44W
Chilecito [Arg.] 206 Gc 29.10S 67.30W
Chilecito [Arg.] 206 Gd 33.53S 69.03W
Chile Rise (EN) 106 Mm 40.00S 90.00W
Chili 168 Cb 16.44N 20.53 E
Chilia, Braţul- 130 Md 45.13N 29.43 E
Chililabombwe 170 Ee 12.22S 27.50 E
Chi-lin Sheng→Jilin Sheng =Kirin (EN) [2] 152 Mc 43.00N 126.00 E
Chilko Lake 188 Ca 51.20N 124.05W
Chilko River 188 Da 52.00N 123.40W
Chillán 200 Ii 36.36S 72.07W
Chillar 206 Ie 37.18S 59.59W
Chillicothe [Il.-U.S.] 186 Lf 40.55N 89.29W
Chillicothe [Mo.-U.S.] 186 Jg 39.48N 93.33W
Chillicothe [Oh.-U.S.] 182 Kd 38.20N 82.59W
Chilliwack 188 Eb 49.10N 121.57W
Chiloé, Isla de- 198 Ij 42.30S 73.55W
Chilón 192 Mi 17.14N 92.25W
Chiloquin 188 Ee 42.35N 121.52W
Chilpancingo de los Bravos 190 Ee 17.33N 99.30W
Chiltern Hills 118 Mj 51.42N 0.48W
Chilton 186 Ld 44.02N 88.10W
Chiluage 170 Dd 9.31S 21.46 E
Chilumba 170 Fe 10.27S 34.16 E
Chilwa, Lake- 170 Gf 15.12S 35.50 E
Chimala 170 Fd 8.51S 34.01 E
Chimaltenango 194 Bf 14.39N 90.49W
Chimaltenango [3] 194 Bf 14.40N 90.55W
Chimán 194 Hi 8.42N 78.37W
Chimanas, Islas- 196 Dg 10.17N 64.38W
Chimanimani 172 Ec 19.48S 32.50 E
Chimay 124 Gd 50.03N 4.19 E
Chimborazo, Volcán- 198 If 1.28S 78.48W
Chimbote 200 If 9.05S 78.36W
Chimichagua 194 Ki 9.16N 73.49W
Chimoio 172 Ec 19.00S 33.23 E
Chimorra 126 Hf 38.18N 4.53W
Chin [2] 148 Id 22.00N 93.30 E
China [Jap.] 156b Bb 27.20N 128.36 E
China [Mex.] 192 Je 25.42N 99.14W
China (EN) = Zhōngguó [1] 140 Mg 35.00N 105.00 E
China (EN)=Zhonghua Renmin Gongheguo [1] 142 Mf 35.00N 105.00 E
Chinacates 192 Ge 25.00N 105.13W
China Lake 188 Gi 35.46N 117.39W
Chinandega 190 Gf 12.37N 87.09W
Chinandega [3] 194 Dg 12.45N 87.05W
Chinati Peak 186 Dl 29.57N 104.29W
Chincha Alta 202 Cf 13.27S 76.08W
Chinchaga 180 Fe 58.52N 118.19W
Chinchilla 212 Ke 26.45S 150.38 E
Chinchón 126 Id 40.08N 3.25W
Chinchorro, Banco- 190 Ge 18.35N 87.20W
Chincoteague 184 Jg 37.55N 75.23W
Chinde 160 Kj 18.34S 36.27 E
Chin-Do 154 Ig 34.25N 126.15 E
Chindu 152 Ge 33.30N 96.31 E
Chindwinn 140 Lg 21.26N 95.15 E
Ch'ing-hai Sheng → Qinghai Sheng=Tsinghai (EN) [2] 152 Gd 36.00N 96.00 E
Chingil 168 Bc 10.33N 18.57 E
Chingola 160 Jj 12.32S 27.52 E
Chinguar 170 Ce 12.33S 16.22 E
Chinguetti 162 Ee 20.27N 12.21W
Chinguetti, Dahr de- 162 Ee 20.43N 12.20W
Chinhae 154 Jg 35.08N 128.40 E
Chinhoyi 160 Kj 17.22S 30.12 E
Chiniot 148 Eb 31.43N 72.59 E
Chinipas 192 Ed 27.23N 108.32W
Chinju 152 Md 35.11N 128.05 E
Chinko 158 Jh 4.50N 23.53 E
Chinle 188 Kh 36.09N 109.33W
Chinle Creek 188 Kh 37.12N 109.43W
Chinmen = Quemoy (EN) 152 Kg 24.25N 118.25 E
Chino 156 Fd 36.00N 138.09 E
Chinon 122 Gg 47.10N 0.15 E
Chinook 188 Kb 48.35N 109.14W
Chinquila 192 Pg 21.30N 87.25W
Chinsali 170 Fe 10.33S 32.04 E
Chinteche 170 Fe 11.50S 34.10 E
Chinú 202 Cb 9.06N 75.24W
Chinvali 136 Eg 42.13N 43.57 E
Chiny 124 He 49.44N 5.20 E
Chinyŏng 154 Jg 35.18N 128.44 E
Chioco 172 Ec 16.25S 32.50 E
Chioggia 128 Ge 45.13N 12.17 E
Chios (EN)=Khios 110 Ih 38.22N 26.00 E
Chipata 160 Kj 13.39S 32.40 E
Chipepo 170 Ef 16.49S 27.50 E
Chipindo 170 Ce 13.48S 15.48 E
Chiping 154 Df 36.35N 116.16 E
Chipinge 172 Ed 20.12S 32.38 E
Chipman 184 Ob 46.11N 65.53W
Chippenham 118 Kj 51.28N 2.07W
Chippewa, Lake- 186 Kd 45.56N 91.13W
Chippewa Falls 182 Ic 44.56N 91.24W
Chippewa River [Mn.-U.S.] 186 Id 44.56N 95.44W
Chippewa River [Wi.-U.S.] 186 Jd 44.25N 92.10W
Chipping Ongar 124 Cc 51.42N 0.15 E
Chiputneticook Lakes 184 Mc 45.45N 68.45W
Chiquián 202 Cf 10.09S 77.11W
Chiquimula 194 Cf 14.48N 89.33W
Chiquimula [3] 194 Cf 14.40N 89.25W
Chiquimulilla 194 Bf 14.05N 90.23W
Chiquinquirá 202 Db 5.37N 73.50W
Chiquitos, Llanos de- 202 Fg 18.00S 61.30W
Chirāla 148 Ge 15.49N 80.21 E
Chiran 156 Bf 31.22N 130.27 E
Chiredzi 160 Kk 21.03S 31.45 E
Chirfa 166 Ha 20.57N 12.21 E
Chirgua, Rio- 196 Bh 8.30N 68.01W
Chiricahua Peak 182 Fe 31.52N 109.20W
Chiriguaná 194 Ki 9.22N 73.37W
Chirikof 178 He 55.50N 155.35W
Chiriqui [3] 194 Fi 8.30N 82.00W
Chiriqui, Golfo de- 174 Ki 8.00N 82.20W
Chiriqui, Laguna de- 190 Hg 9.03N 82.00W
Chiriqui Grande 194 Fi 8.57N 82.07W
Chirnogi 130 Je 44.07N 26.34 E
Chiromo 170 Gf 16.33S 35.08 E
Chirripó, Cerro- 174 Ki 9.29N 83.29W
Chirripó, Rio- [C.R.] 194 Fh 10.41N 83.41W
Chirripó, Rio- [C.R.] 194 Fh 10.03N 83.16W
Chirundu 170 Ef 15.59S 28.54 E
Chisamba 170 Ee 14.59S 28.23 E
Chisāpāni Garhi 148 Hc 27.34N 85.08 E
Chisasibi 176 Ld 53.50N 79.00W
Chisenga 170 Fd 9.56S 33.26 E
Chishui 152 If 28.30N 105.44 E
Chişineu Criş 130 Ec 46.32N 21.31 E
Chisone 128 Bf 44.49N 7.25 E
Chitado 170 Bf 17.18S 13.54 E
Chita-Hantō 156 Ed 34.50N 136.50 E
Chitati 168 Ac 14.40N 14.30 E
Chitato 160 Ji 7.22S 20.49 E
Chitembo 170 Ce 13.31S 16.45 E
Chitina 178 Kd 61.31N 144.27W
Chitina 178 Kd 61.30N 144.28W
Chitipa 170 Fd 9.43S 33.16 E
Chitorgarh 148 Ed 24.53N 74.38 E
Chitose 154 Pc 42.49N 141.39 E
Chitradurga 148 Ff 14.14N 76.24 E
Chitrāl 148 Ea 35.51N 71.47 E
Chitré 190 Hg 7.58N 80.26W
Chittagong 142 Lg 22.20N 91.50 E
Chittoor 148 Ff 13.12N 79.07 E
Chiumbe 158 Ji 6.59S 21.12 E
Chiume 170 Df 15.08S 21.12 E
Chiusi 128 Fg 43.01N 11.57 E
Chiusi, Lago di- 128 Fg 43.05N 12.00 E
Chiva 126 Le 39.28N 0.43W
Chivacoa 196 Bg 10.10N 68.54W
Chivapuri, Rio- 196 Ci 6.25N 66.23W
Chivasso 128 Be 45.11N 7.53 E
Chivay 202 Dg 15.38S 71.36W
Chivhu 172 Ec 19.01S 30.53 E
Chivilcoy 206 Hd 34.53S 60.01W
Chizou → Guichi 152 Ke 30.38N 117.30 E
Chizu 156 Dd 35.15N 134.14 E
Chŏâm Khsant 148 Kf 14.13N 104.56 E
Choapa, Rio- 206 Dd 31.38S 71.34W
Chobe [3] 172 Cc 18.30S 25.00 E
Chobe 158 Jj 17.47S 25.10 E
Choc Bay 197k Ba 14.03N 60.59W
Choch'iwŏn 154 If 36.36N 127.18 E
Chocó [3] 202 Cb 6.00N 77.00W
Chocolate Mountains 188 Hj 33.25N 114.10W
Chodecz 120 Pd 52.24N 19.01 E
Chodov 120 If 50.15N 12.45 E
Chodžent = Leninabad 142 Ie 40.17N 69.37 E
Chodzież 120 Md 52.59N 16.56 E
Choele-Choel 206 Ge 39.16S 65.41W
Choique 206 He 38.28S 62.43W
Choiseul 197k Ab 13.47N 61.03W
Choiseul Island 208 Ge 7.00S 157.00 E
Choix 192 Ed 26.43N 108.17W
Chojna 120 Kd 52.58N 14.28 E
Chojnice 120 Nc 53.42N 17.34 E
Chojnów 120 Le 51.17N 15.56 E
Chōkai-San 140 Qf 39.10N 140.02 E
Choke 158 Kg 10.45N 37.35 E
Chókué 172 Ed 24.27S 32.55 E
Cho La 152 Ge 31.52N 98.51 E
Cholet 122 Fg 47.04N 0.53W
Chŏlla-Namdo [2] 154 Ig 34.45N 127.00 E
Chŏlla-Pukto [2] 154 Ig 35.45N 127.15 E
Cholo 170 Gf 16.04S 35.08 E
Cholula 192 Jh 19.04N 98.19W
Choluteca 190 Gf 13.18N 87.12W
Choluteca [3] 194 Dg 13.20N 87.10W
Choluteca, Rio- 194 Dg 13.07N 87.19W
Choma 160 Jj 16.49S 26.59 E
Chomo/Yadong 152 Ef 27.38N 89.03 E
Chomo Lhari 152 Ef 27.50N 89.16 E
Chomutov 120 Jf 50.28N 13.25 E
Ch'ŏnan 152 Md 36.48N 127.09 E
Chon Buri 148 Kf 13.22N 100.59 E
Chone 202 Bd 0.42S 80.07W
Ch'ŏngch'ŏn-gang 154 He 39.35N 125.28 E
Ch'ŏngjin 142 Oe 41.46N 129.49 E
Ch'ŏngjin Si [2] 154 Jd 41.45N 129.45 E
Ch'ŏngju 152 Md 36.38N 127.30 E
Chŏngju 152 Md 39.51N 125.15 E
Chongli (Xiwanzi) 154 Cd 40.57N 115.12 E
Chongming 154 Fi 31.38N 121.24 E
Chongming Dao 154 Fi 31.36N 121.33 E
Chongoroi 170 Be 13.34S 13.55 E
Chongqing (Chungking) 142 Mg 29.34N 106.27 E
Ch'ŏngsan-Do 154 Ig 34.11N 126.54 E
Chŏngŭp 154 Ig 35.34N 126.51 E
Chongyang 154 Cj 29.32N 114.02 E
Chongzuo 152 Ig 22.29N 107.22 E
Chŏnju 152 Md 35.49N 127.09 E
Chonos, Archipiélago de los- 198 Ij 45.00S 74.00W
Chontaleña, Cordillera- 194 Eh 11.50N 85.00W
Chontales [3] 194 Eg 12.05N 85.10W
Chopim, Rio- 204 Fg 25.35S 53.05W
Chopinzinho 204 Fg 25.51S 52.30W
Chorito, Sierra del- 126 He 39.25N 4.25W
Choroszcz 120 Sc 53.09N 22.59 E
Chorreras, Cerro- 192 Fd 26.02N 106.21W
Ch'ŏrwŏn 152 Md 38.15N 127.13 E
Chorzele 120 Qc 53.16N 20.55 E
Chorzów 120 Of 50.19N 18.57 E
Ch'osan 154 Hd 40.45N 125.50 E
Chośebuz/Cottbus 120 Ke 51.46N 14.20 E
Chōshi 154 Pg 35.44N 140.50 E
Chos Malal 206 Fe 37.23S 70.16W
Chosŏn M.I.K.=North Korea (EN) [1] 142 Oe 40.00N 127.30 E
Chosŏn Minjujŭi-Inmin-Konghwaguk [1] 142 Oe 40.00N 127.30 E
Choszczno 120 Lc 53.10N 15.26 E
Chota 202 Ce 6.33S 78.39W
Chotanāgpur Plateau 140 Kg 22.00N 86.00 E
Choteau 188 Ic 47.49N 112.11W
Chotla, Cerro de- 192 Ii 17.55N 101.31W
Choukchot, Djebel- 126 Qh 36.01N 4.11 E
Choum 162 Ee 21.18N 12.59W
Chovd→Kobdo 152 Fb 48.06N 92.11 E
Chövsgöl Nuur→Hubsugul Nur 140 Md 51.00N 100.30 E
Chowchilla 188 Eh 37.07N 120.16W
Chowra 148 Ig 8.27N 93.02 E
Chréa 126 Oh 36.25N 2.53 E
Chřiby 120 Ng 49.10N 17.20 E
Christchurch 210 Ii 43.32S 172.37 E
Christian, Cape- 180 Kb 70.32N 68.18W
Christian, Point- 220q Ab 25.04S 130.07W
Christiana 172 De 27.52S 25.08 E
Christian IV Gletscher 179 Ie 68.40N 30.20W
Christiansburg 184 Gg 37.07N 80.26W
Christiansfeld 116 Ci 55.21N 9.29 E
Christianshåb/Qasigiánguit 179 Ge 68.45N 51.30W
Christiansø 116 Fi 55.20N 15.10 E
Christian Sound 178 Me 55.56N 134.40W
Christiansted 196 Dd 17.45N 64.40W
Christiansted Harbor 197a Dc 17.46N 64.42W
Christie Bay 180 Gd 62.45N 110.15W
Christmas [5] 142 Mk 10.30S 105.40 E
Christmas→Kiritimati Atoll 208 Ld 1.52N 157.20W
Christmas Creek 212 Fc 18.53S 125.55 E
Christmas Creek 212 Fc 18.29S 125.23 E
Christmas Island 140 Mk 10.30S 105.40 E
Christmas Ridge (EN) 106 Ki 10.00N 165.00W
Chrudim 120 Lg 49.57N 15.47 E
Chrzanów 120 Pf 50.09N 19.24 E
Chrząstowa 120 Nc 53.35N 16.58 E
Chuansha 154 Fi 31.11N 121.42 E
Chúbar 146 Mc 38.11N 48.51 E
Chubut [2] 206 Gf 44.00S 69.00W
Chubut, Rio- 198 Jj 43.20S 65.03W
Chucunaque, Rio- 194 Ii 8.09N 77.44W
Chugach Mountains 178 Jd 61.00N 145.00W
Chuginadak 178 Ff 52.49N 169.50W
Chūgoku-Sanchi 140 Pf 35.15N 133.30 E
Chu He 154 Eh 32.15N 119.03 E
Chuhuichupa 192 Ec 29.38N 108.22W
Chui 204 Fk 33.41S 53.27W
Chuka 170 Gc 0.20S 37.39 E
Chukai 150 Df 4.15N 103.25 E
Chukchi Peninsula (EN) = Čukotski poluostrov 140 Uc 66.00N 175.00W
Chukchi Plateau (EN) 224 Bd 78.00N 165.00W
Chukchi Sea 224 Bd 69.00N 171.00W
Chukchi Sea (EN) = Čukotskoje more 224 Bd 69.00N 171.00W
Chula Vista 188 Gj 32.39N 117.05W
Chulitna 178 Jd 62.55N 149.39W
Chullo 126 Jg 37.10N 2.57W
Chulucanas 202 Be 5.06S 80.10W
Chumbicha 206 Gc 28.52S 66.14W
Chumphon 148 Jf 10.32N 99.13 E
Chumunjin 154 Jf 37.53N 128.49 E
Ch'unch'ŏn 152 Md 37.52N 127.44 E
Chunga 170 Ef 15.03S 26.00 E
Ch'ungch'ŏng-Namdo [2] 154 If 36.30N 127.00 E
Ch'ungch'ŏng-Pukto [2] 154 Jf 36.45N 128.00 E
Ch'ungju 152 Md 36.58N 127.56 E
Chungking → Chongqing 142 Mg 29.34N 106.27 E
Ch'ungmu 154 Jg 34.51N 128.26 E
Chunya 170 Fd 8.32S 33.25 E
Chuŏr Phnum Krâvanh 140 Mh 12.00N 103.15 E
Chuquibamba 202 Dg 15.50S 72.39W
Chuquibambilla 202 Df 14.07S 72.43W
Chuquicamata 206 Gb 22.19S 68.56W
Chuquisaca [3] 202 Fg 20.00S 64.20W
Chur/Cuera 128 Dd 46.50N 9.35 E
Churchill 176 Jd 58.46N 94.10W
Churchill [Can.] 174 Md 53.30N 60.10W
Churchill [Can.] 174 Jd 58.47N 94.12W
Churchill, Cape- 180 Ie 58.46N 93.12W
Churchill Falls 180 Lf 53.30N 64.10W
Churchill Lake 180 Ge 56.05N 108.15W
Churchill Peak 180 Ee 58.20N 125.02W
Churchill Range 222 Jg 81.30S 158.30 E
Chūru 148 Ec 28.18N 74.57 E
Churuguara 202 Ea 10.49N 69.32W
Churún Merú/Angel, Salto- =Ángel Falls (EN) 198 Je 5.57N 62.30W
Chuska Mountains 188 Kh 36.15N 108.50W
Chute-des-Passes 180 Kg 49.50N 71.00W
Chuxian 152 Ke 32.16N 118.15 E
Chuxiong 152 Hf 25.02N 101.32 E
Chuy 204 Fk 33.41S 53.27W
Ciamis 150 Eh 7.20S 108.21 E
Cianjur 150 Eh 6.49S 107.08 E
Ciarrai/Kerry [2] 118 Di 52.10N 9.30W
Čiatura 132 Mh 42.17N 43.15 E
Cibuta, Cerro- 192 Db 31.02N 110.58W
Čićarija 128 He 45.28N 13.54 E
Ćićevac 130 Ef 43.43N 21.27 E
Cicicleja 130 Nb 47.23N 30.50 E
Cicolano 128 Hh 42.15N 13.10 E
Cidacos 126 Kb 42.19N 1.55W
Cide 146 Eb 41.54N 33.00 E
Cidlina 120 Lf 50.09N 15.12 E
Ciechanów 120 Qd 52.53N 20.38 E
Ciechanów [2] 120 Qd 52.55N 20.40 E
Ciechanowiec 120 Sd 52.42N 22.31 E
Ciechanowska, Wysoczyzna- 120 Qc 53.10N 20.30 E
Ciego de Ávila 190 Id 21.51N 78.46W
Ciego de Ávila [3] 194 Hb 22.00N 78.40W
Ciénaga 202 Da 11.00N 74.14W
Ciénaga de Flores 192 Ie 25.57N 100.11W
Ciénaga de Oro 194 Ji 8.53N 75.38W
Cieneguita 192 Ff 27.57N 106.59W
Cienfuegos 176 Kg 22.09N 80.27W
Cienfuegos [3] 194 Gb 22.15N 80.30W
Cies, Islas- 126 Db 42.13N 8.54W
Cieszanów 120 Tf 50.16N 23.08 E
Cieza 126 Kf 38.14N 1.25W
Çifteler 146 Dc 39.22N 31.03 E
Cifuentes 126 Jd 40.47N 2.37W
Čiganak 136 Hf 45.05N 73.58 E
Čigirin 132 He 49.03N 32.42 E
Cigüela 126 Ie 39.08N 3.44W
Cihanbeyli 146 Ec 38.40N 32.56 E
Cihanbeyli Platosu 146 Ec 38.40N 32.45 E
Cihareşi 132 Mh 42.47N 43.02 E
Cihuatlán 192 Gh 19.14N 104.35W
Čiily 136 Gg 44.13N 66.46 E
Cijara, Embalse de- 126 He 39.18N 4.52W
Cijulang 150 Eh 7.44S 108.27 E
Čik 130 Dd 45.42N 20.04 E
Čikoj 138 Ff 51.02N 106.39 E
Čikurački, vulkan- 138 Kf 50.15N 155.29 E
Cilacap 150 Eh 7.44S 109.00 E
Çıldır 146 Jb 41.08N 43.07 E
Çıldır Gölü 146 Jb 41.04N 43.15 E
Cilento 128 Jj 40.20N 15.20 E
Čilik 136 Hg 43.35N 78.12 E
Čilik 135 Lc 43.42N 78.14 E
Cill Airne/Killarney 118 Di 52.03N 9.30W
Cill Chainnigh/Kilkenny 118 Fi 52.39N 7.15W
Cill Chainnigh/Kilkenny [2] 118 Fi 52.40N 7.20W
Cill Chaoi/Kilkee 118 Di 52.41N 9.38W
Cill Dara/Kildare 118 Gh 53.10N 6.55W
Cill Dara/Kildare [2] 118 Gh 53.15N 6.45W
Cill Mhantáin/Wicklow 118 Gi 52.59N 6.03W
Cill Mhantáin/Wicklow [2] 118 Gi 53.00N 6.30W
Cill Mocheallóg/Kilmallock 118 Ei 52.25N 8.35W
Cill Rois/Kilrush 118 Di 52.39N 9.29W
Cilma 134 Fd 65.25N 52.05 E
Cilo Daği 146 Kd 37.30N 44.00 E
Cimaltepec, Sierra- 190 Ee 16.00N 96.40W
Cimarron 186 Dh 36.31N 104.55W
Cimarron 174 Jf 36.10N 96.17W
Čimbaj 136 Fg 42.59N 59.47 E
Cimini, Monti- 128 Gh 42.24N 12.12 E
Čimišlija 132 Ff 46.32N 28.46 E
Čimkent 142 Ie 42.18N 69.36 E
Čimkentskaja oblast [3] 136 Gg 43.00N 68.40 E
Cimljansk 136 Ef 47.37N 42.04 E
Cimljanskoje vodohranilišče = Tsimlyansk Reservoir (EN) 110 Kf 48.00N 43.00 E
Cimone 110 Hg 44.12N 10.40 E
Cîmpeni 130 Gc 46.22N 23.03 E
Cîmpia Turzii 130 Gc 46.33N 23.53 E
Cîmpina 130 Id 45.08N 25.44 E
Cîmpulung 130 Id 45.16N 25.03 E
Cîmpulung Moldovenesc 130 Ib 47.32N 25.34 E
Čimtarga, gora- 135 Ge 39.14N 68.12 E
Cina, Tanjung- 150 Dh 5.55S 104.35 E
Çınar 146 Id 37.39N 40.06 E
Çınarcık 130 Mi 40.39N 29.06 E
Cinaruco, Rio- 196 Ci 6.41N 67.07W
Cina Selatan, Laut-=South China Sea (EN) 140 Ni 10.00N 113.00 E
Činaz 135 Gd 40.56N 68.45 E
Cinca 126 Mc 41.26N 0.21 E
Cincar 128 Lg 43.54N 17.04 E
Cincinnati 176 Kf 39.06N 84.31W

Index Symbols

[1] Independent Nation
[2] State, Region
[3] District, County
[4] Municipality
[5] Colony, Dependency
Continent
Physical Region
Historical or Cultural Region
Mount, Mountain
Volcano
Hill
Mountains, Mountain Range
Hills, Escarpment
Plateau, Upland
Pass, Gap
Plain, Lowland
Delta
Salt Flat
Valley, Canyon
Crater, Cave
Karst Features
Depression
Polder
Desert, Dunes
Forest, Woods
Heath, Steppe
Oasis
Cape, Point
Coast, Beach
Cliff
Peninsula
Isthmus
Sandbank
Island
Atoll
Rock, Reef
Islands, Archipelago
Rocks, Reefs
Coral Reef
Well, Spring
Geyser
River, Stream
Waterfall, Rapids
River Mouth, Estuary
Lake
Salt Lake
Intermittent Lake
Reservoir
Swamp, Pond
Canal
Glacier
Ice Shelf, Pack Ice
Ocean
Sea
Gulf, Bay
Strait, Fjord
Lagoon
Bank
Seamount
Tablemount
Ridge
Shelf
Basin
Escarpment, Sea Scarp
Fracture
Trench, Abyss
National Park, Reserve
Point of Interest
Recreation Site
Cave, Cavern
Historic Site
Ruins
Wall, Walls
Church, Abbey
Temple
Scientific Station
Railway station
Airport
Port
Military installation
Lighthouse
Mine
Tunnel
Dam, Bridge

Index Symbols

Symbol	Meaning
[1]	Independent Nation
[2]	State, Region
[3]	District, County
[4]	Municipality
[5]	Colony, Dependency
	Continent
	Physical Region
	Historical or Cultural Region
	Mount, Mountain
	Volcano
	Hill
	Mountains, Mountain Range
	Hills, Escarpment
	Plateau, Upland
	Pass, Gap
	Plain, Lowland
	Delta
	Salt Flat
	Valley, Canyon
	Crater, Cave
	Karst Features
	Depression
	Polder
	Desert, Dunes
	Forest, Woods
	Heath, Steppe
	Oasis
	Cape, Point
	Coast, Beach
	Cliff
	Peninsula
	Isthmus
	Sandbank
	Island
	Atoll
	Rock, Reef
	Islands, Archipelago
	Rocks, Reefs
	Coral Reef
	Well, Spring
	Geyser
	River, Stream
	Waterfall, Rapids
	River Mouth, Estuary
	Lake
	Salt Lake
	Intermittent Lake
	Reservoir
	Swamp, Pond
	Canal
	Glacier
	Ice Shelf, Pack Ice
	Ocean
	Sea
	Gulf, Bay
	Strait, Fjord
	Lagoon
	Bank
	Seamount
	Tablemount
	Ridge
	Shelf
	Basin
	Escarpment, Sea Scarp
	Fracture
	Trench, Abyss
	National Park, Reserve
	Point of Interest
	Recreation Site
	Cave, Cavern
	Historic Site
	Ruins
	Wall, Walls
	Church, Abbey
	Temple
	Scientific Station
	Railway station
	Airport
	Port
	Military installation
	Lighthouse
	Mine
	Tunnel
	Dam, Bridge

Cradock	160	Jl	32.08S	25.36 E
Craig [Ak.-U.S.]	178	Me	55.29N	133.09W
Craig [Co.-U.S.]	182	Fc	40.31N	107.33W
Craigmont	188	Gc	46.15N	116.28W
Craigs Range	212	Ke	26.40S	151.30 E
Crailsheim	120	Gg	49.09N	10.05 E
Craiova	112	Ig	44.19N	23.48 E
Cranbrook [Austl.]	212	Df	34.18S	117.32 E
Cranbrook [B.C.-Can.]	180	Fg	49.31N	115.46W
Cranbrook [Eng.-U.K.]	124	Cc	51.05N	0.32 E
Crandon	186	Ld	45.34N	88.54W
Crane [Or.-U.S.]	188	Fe	43.25N	118.35W
Crane [Tx.-U.S.]	186	Ek	31.24N	102.21W
Crane Lake	186	Jb	48.16N	92.28W
Crane Lake	188	Ka	50.06N	109.06W
Cranleigh	124	Bc	51.08N	0.29W
Craon	122	Fg	47.51N	0.57W
Craonne	124	Fe	49.26N	3.47 E
Crapaud, Puy-	122	Fh	46.40N	0.40W
Crary Mountains	222	Of	76.48S	117.40W
Crasna	130	Fa	48.09N	22.20 E
Crasna [Rom.]	130	Fb	47.10N	22.54 E
Crasna [Rom.]	130	Kc	46.31N	27.51 E
Crater Lake [Or.-U.S.]	182	Cc	42.56N	122.06W
Crater Lake [St.Vin.]	197n	Ba	13.19N	61.11W
Crateús	200	Lf	5.10S	40.40W
Crati	128	Kk	39.43N	16.31 E
Crato [Braz.]	202	Ke	7.14S	39.23W
Crato [Port.]	126	Ee	39.17N	7.39W
Crau	122	Kk	43.36N	4.50 E
Crauford, Cape -	180	Jb	73.44N	84.51W
Cravo Norte	202	Db	6.17N	70.12W
Crawford	186	Ee	42.41N	103.25W
Crawfordsville	184	De	40.02N	86.54W
Crawley	118	Mj	51.07N	0.12W
Crazy Mountains	188	Jc	46.08N	110.20W
Crazy Peak	182	Eb	46.01N	110.16W
Creciente, Isla-	192	De	24.23N	111.37W
Crécy-en-Ponthieu	124	Dd	50.15N	1.53 E
Crécy-la-Chapelle	124	Ef	48.51N	2.55 E
Crécy-sur-Serre	124	Fe	49.42N	3.37 E
Crediton	118	Jk	50.47N	3.39W
Cree [Sask.-Can.]	180	Ge	58.50N	105.40W
Cree [Scot.-U.K.]	118	Ig	54.52N	4.20W
Creede	186	Ch	37.51N	106.56W
Creel	190	Cc	27.45N	107.38W
Cree Lake	180	Ge	57.30N	106.30W
Creglingen	120	Gg	49.28N	10.02 E
Creil	122	Ie	49.16N	2.29 E
Crema	128	De	45.22N	9.41 E
Cremenea, Braţul-	130	Ke	44.57N	27.54 E
Crémieu, Plateau de-	122	Li	45.40N	5.30 E
Cremona	128	Ee	45.07N	10.02 E
Crepaja	130	Dd	45.01N	20.39 E
Crepori, Rio-	202	Ge	5.42S	57.08W
Crépy-en-Valois	122	Ie	49.14N	2.54 E
Cres	128	If	44.58N	14.24 E
Cres	128	If	44.40N	14.25 E
Crescent	188	Ee	43.29N	121.41W
Crescent City	182	Cc	41.45N	124.12W
Crescent Lake	184	Gk	29.28N	81.30W
Crespo	204	Bk	32.02S	60.19W
Crest	122	Lj	44.44N	5.02 E
Crested Butte	186	Cg	38.52N	106.59W
Creston [B.C.-Can.]	188	Gb	49.06N	116.31W
Creston [Ia.-U.S.]	182	Ic	41.04N	94.22W
Crestone Peak	186	Dh	37.58N	105.36W
Crestview	182	Je	30.46N	86.34W
Creswell	184	Ih	35.52N	76.23W
Creswell Bay	180	Ib	72.40N	93.30W
Creswell Creek	212	Hc	18.10S	135.11 E
Crete	186	Hf	40.38N	96.58W
Crete (EN) = Kriti [2]	130	Hn	35.35N	25.00 E
Crete (EN) = Kriti	110	Ih	35.15N	24.45 E
Crete, Sea of- (EN) = Kritikón Pélagos	130	Hn	36.00N	25.00 E
Créteil	122	If	48.47N	2.28 E
Cretin, Cape-	214	Di	6.40S	147.52 E
Creus, Cabo de-/Creus, Cap de-	110	Gg	42.19N	3.19 E
Creus, Cap de-/Creus, Cabo de-	110	Gg	42.19N	3.19 E
Creuse [3]	122	Hh	46.05N	2.00 E
Creuse	122	Gh	47.00N	0.34 E
Creusot, Le-	122	Kh	46.48N	4.26 E
Creutzwald	122	Me	49.12N	6.41 E
Crèvecoeur-en-Auge	124	Ce	49.07N	0.01 E
Crèvecoeur-le-Grand	124	Ee	49.36N	2.05 E
Crevillent / Crevillente	126	Lf	38.15N	0.48W
Crevillente / Crevillent	126	Lf	38.15N	0.48W
Crewe	118	Kh	53.05N	2.27W
Crézancy	124	Fe	49.03N	3.30 E
Criciúma	200	Lh	28.40S	49.23W
Cricket Mountains	188	Ig	38.50N	113.00W
Crieff	118	Je	56.23N	3.52W
Criel-sur-Mer	124	Dd	50.01N	1.19 E
Criel-sur-Mer-Mesnil-Val	124	Dd	50.03N	1.20 E
Crikvenica	128	Ie	45.11N	14.42 E
Crillon	124	De	49.31N	1.56 E
Crimea (EN) = Krymski poluostrov	110	Jf	45.00N	34.00 E
Crimean Mountains (EN) = Krymskije gory	110	Jg	44.45N	34.30 E
Crimmitschau	120	If	50.49N	12.23 E
Criquetot-l'Esneval	124	Ce	49.39N	0.16 E
Crissolo	128	Bf	44.42N	7.09 E
Cristal, Monts de-	170	Bb	0.30N	10.30 E
Cristal, Sierra del-	194	Jc	20.33N	75.31W
Cristalândia	202	If	10.36S	49.11W
Cristalina	202	Ig	16.45S	47.36W
Cristalino, Rio-	202	Hf	12.40S	50.40W
Cristallo	128	Gd	46.34N	12.12 E
Cristóbal Colón, Pico-	198	Id	10.50N	73.45W
Cristuru Secuiesc	130	Ic	46.17N	25.02 E
Crişu Alb	130	Ec	46.42N	21.16 E
Crişu Negru	130	Ec	46.42N	21.16 E
Crişu Repede	130	Dc	46.55N	20.59 E
Crixás	204	Hb	14.27S	49.58W
Crixás-Açu, Rio-	202	Hf	13.19S	50.36W
Crixás Mirim, Rio-	204	Ga	13.28S	50.36W
Crkvena Planina	130	Fg	42.48N	22.22 E
Crna Gora	130	Eg	42.16N	21.35 E
Crna Gora	130	Ce	44.05N	19.50 E
Crna Gora = Montenegro (EN) [2]	130	Cg	42.30N	19.18 E
Crna Gora=Montenegro (EN)	130	Cg	42.30N	19.18 E
Crna Reka	130	Ef	43.50N	21.55 E
Crna reka	130	Eh	41.33N	21.59 E
Crni Drim	130	Dg	42.05N	20.23 E
Crni Timok	130	Ff	43.55N	22.18 E
Črni vrh	128	Jd	46.29N	15.14 E
Črni vrh	128	Kf	44.36N	16.30 E
Črnomelj	128	Je	45.34N	15.12 E
Croatia (EN) = Hrvatska [2]	128	Jf	45.00N	15.30 E
Croatia (EN) = Hrvatska	110	Hf	45.00N	15.30 E
Croatia (EN) = Hrvatska	128	Je	45.00N	15.30 E
Crocker, Banjaran-	150	Ge	5.40N	116.20 E
Crockett	186	Ik	31.19N	95.28W
Crocq	122	Ii	45.52N	2.22 E
Crocus Bay	197b	Ab	18.13N	63.05W
Croisette, Cap-	122	Lk	43.13N	5.20 E
Croisic, Le-	122	Dg	47.18N	2.30W
Croisic, Pointe du-	122	Dg	47.17N	2.33W
Croisilles	124	Ed	50.12N	2.53 E
Croissy-sur-Celle	124	Ee	49.42N	2.11 E
Croix, Lac la-	186	Jb	48.21N	92.05W
Croix-Haute, Col de la-	122	Lj	44.43N	5.40 E
Croker, Cape-	212	Gb	10.58S	132.35 E
Croker Bay	180	Jb	74.38N	83.15W
Croker Island	212	Gb	11.10S	132.30 E
Cromarty	118	Id	57.40N	4.02W
Cromer	118	Oi	52.56N	1.18 E
Cromwell	218	Cf	45.03S	169.14 E
Crooked Island	190	Jd	22.45N	74.13W
Crooked Island Passage	190	Jd	22.55N	74.35W
Crooked River	188	Ed	44.34N	121.16W
Crookston	182	Hb	47.47N	96.37W
Crosby [Mn.-U.S.]	186	Jc	46.28N	93.57W
Crosby [N.D.-U.S.]	186	Eb	48.55N	103.18W
Cross	166	Ge	4.55N	8.15 E
Cross City	184	Fk	29.32N	83.07W
Crossett	186	Kj	33.08N	91.58W
Cross Fell	118	Kg	54.42N	2.29W
Cross Lake	180	Hf	54.47N	97.22W
Crossman Peak	188	Hi	34.32N	114.07W
Cross River [2]	166	Gd	5.40N	8.10 E
Cross Sound	178	Le	58.10N	136.30W
Crotone	128	Lk	39.05N	17.08 E
Crotto	204	Bm	36.35S	60.10W
Crouch	124	Cc	51.37N	0.53 E
Crow Agency	188	Ld	45.36N	107.27W
Crowborough	124	Cc	51.03N	0.09 E
Crow Creek	186	Df	40.23N	104.29W
Crowell	186	Gj	33.59N	99.43W
Crow Lake	186	Jb	49.12N	93.57W
Crowley	186	Jk	30.13N	92.22W
Crowley, Lake-	188	Fh	37.37N	118.44W
Crowley Ridge	186	Ki	35.45N	90.45W
Crownpoint	186	Bi	35.42N	108.07W
Crown Prince Frederik	180	Ic	70.05N	86.40W
Crowsnest Pass	180	Gg	49.40N	114.30W
Crows Nest Peak	186	Ed	44.03N	103.58W
Croydon	212	Ic	13.12S	142.14 E
Croydon, London-	118	Mj	51.23N	0.07W
Crozet, Iles- = Crozet Islands (EN)	222	Ec	46.30S	51.00 E
Crozet Basin (EN)	106	Gm	33.00S	60.00 E
Crozet Islands (EN) = Crozet, Iles-	222	Ec	46.30S	51.00 E
Crozet Ridge (EN)	106	Fn	45.00S	45.00 E
Crozon	122	Bf	48.15N	4.29W
Crozon, Presqu'île de-	122	Bf	48.15N	4.25W
Crucero, Cerro-	192	Gg	21.41N	104.25W
Cruces	194	Gb	22.21N	80.16W
Crump Lake	188	Fe	42.17N	119.50W
Crumpton Point	197g	Ba	15.35N	61.19W
Cruz, Cabo-	190	Ie	19.51N	77.44W
Cruz Alta [Arg.]	204	Bk	33.01S	61.49W
Cruz Alta [Braz.]	200	Kh	28.39S	53.36W
Cruz del Eje	206	Hd	30.44S	64.48W
Cruzeiro do Oeste	206	Jb	23.46S	53.04W
Cruzeiro do Sul	200	If	7.38S	72.36W
Cruzen Island	222	Mf	74.47S	140.42W
Cruz Grande	192	Ji	16.44N	99.08W
Crvanj	128	Mg	43.25N	18.11 E
Crvenka	130	Cd	45.39N	19.28 E
Crystal Brook	212	Hf	33.21S	138.13 E
Crystal City [Man.-Can.]	186	Gb	49.08N	98.57W
Crystal City [Tx.-U.S.]	186	Gl	28.41N	99.50W
Crystal Falls	184	Cb	46.06N	88.20W
Crystal Springs	186	Kk	31.59N	90.21W
Csákvár	120	Oi	47.24N	18.27 E
Cserhat	120	Pi	47.55N	19.30 E
Csongrád	120	Qj	46.42N	20.09 E
Csongrád [2]	120	Qj	46.25N	20.15 E
Csorna	120	Ni	47.37N	17.15 E
ČSSR → Československá Socialistická Republika [1]	112	Hf	49.30N	17.00 E
Csurgó	120	Nj	46.16N	17.06 E
Ctesiphon	146	Kf	33.05N	44.35 E
Ču	142	Je	43.33N	73.45 E
Ču	140	Ie	45.00N	67.44 E
Cuajinicuilapa	192	Ji	16.28N	98.25W
Cuale	170	Cd	7.40S	17.01 E
Cualiacán, Rio-	192	Fe	24.31N	107.41W
Cuamba	160	Kj	14.49S	36.33 E
Cuan an Fhóid Duibh	118	Dg	54.08N	10.00W
Cuan an Fhóid Duibh/Blacksod Bay	118	Dg	54.08N	10.00W
Cuanavale	170	Cf	15.07S	19.14 E
Cuan Bhaile Átha Cliath/Dublin Bay	118	Gh	53.20N	6.06W
Cuan Chill Ala/Killala Bay	118	Dg	54.15N	9.10W
Cuan Dhun Dealgan/Dundalk Bay	118	Gh	53.57N	6.17W
Cuan Dhún Droma/Dundrum Bay	118	Hg	54.13N	5.45W
Cuando	158	Jj	18.27S	23.32 E
Cuando-Cubango [3]	170	Df	16.00S	20.30 E
Cuan Eochaille/Youghal Harbour	118	Fj	51.52N	7.50W
Cuangar	170	Cf	17.36S	18.37 E
Cuango	158	Ii	3.14S	17.22 E
Cuango [Ang.]	170	Cd	9.07S	18.05 E
Cuango [Ang.]	170	Cd	6.17S	16.41 E
Cuan Loch Garman/Wexford Harbour	118	Gi	52.20N	6.25W
Cuan Mó/Clew Bay	118	Dh	53.50N	9.50W
Cuan na Gaillimhe/Galway Bay	110	Fe	53.10N	9.15W
Cuan na gCaorach/Sheep Haven	118	Ff	55.10N	7.52W
Cuan Phort Láirge/Waterford Harbour	118	Gi	52.10N	6.57W
Cuan Shligigh/Sligo Bay	118	Eg	54.20N	8.40W
Cuanza	158	Ii	9.19S	13.08 E
Cuanza Norte [3]	170	Bd	8.50S	14.30 E
Cuanza Sul [3]	170	Be	10.50S	14.50 E
Cuareim, Arroyo-	204	Dj	30.12S	57.36W
Cuaró	204	Dj	30.37S	56.54W
Cuaró Grande, Arroyo-	204	Dj	30.18S	57.12W
Cuarto, Rio-	206	Hd	33.25S	63.02W
Cuatir	170	Cf	17.01S	18.09 E
Cuatro Ciénegas de Carranza	192	Hd	26.59N	102.05W
Cuauhtémoc	190	Cc	28.25N	106.52W
Cuautitlán	192	Jh	19.40N	99.11W
Cuay Grande	204	Di	28.40S	56.17W
Cuba [1]	176	Lg	21.30N	80.00W
Cuba	174	Lg	21.30N	80.00W
Cuba [Mo.-U.S.]	186	Kg	38.04N	91.24W
Cuba [N.M.-U.S.]	186	Ch	36.01N	107.04W
Cuba [Port.]	126	Ef	38.10N	7.53W
Cubabi, Cerro-	192	Cb	31.42N	112.46W
Cubagua, Isla-	196	Dg	10.49N	64.11W
Cubal	170	Be	13.03S	14.15 E
Cubal [Ang.]	170	Be	11.19S	13.48 E
Cubal [Ang.]	170	Bf	15.22S	12.39 E
Cubango	158	Jj	18.53S	22.24 E
Çubuk	146	Eb	40.59N	32.05 E
Čubukulah, gora-	138	Kc	66.23N	153.59 E
Cucalón, Sierra de-	126	Kd	40.59N	1.10W
Cuchi	170	Ce	14.40S	16.52 E
Cuchi	158	Ij	15.28S	17.21 E
Cuchibi	170	De	15.00S	20.45 E
Cuchilla Águila, Cerro-	192	Ig	21.27N	101.03W
Cuchivero, Rio-	196	Di	7.40N	65.57W
Cuchumatanes, Sierra de los-	194	Bf	15.35N	91.25W
Cuckfield	124	Bc	51.01N	0.08W
Cuckmere	124	Cd	50.45N	0.09 E
Cucui	202	Ec	1.12N	66.50W
Cucumbi	170	Ce	10.17S	19.03 E
Cucurpe	192	Db	30.20N	110.43W
Cúcuta	200	Ie	7.54N	72.31W
Cudahy	186	Me	42.57N	87.52W
Cudalbi	130	Kd	45.47N	27.42 E
Cuddalore	142	Jh	11.45N	79.45 E
Cuddapah	148	Ff	14.28N	78.49 E
Čudovo	136	Dd	59.08N	31.41 E
Čudskoje ozero = Peipus, Lake- (EN)	110	Id	58.45N	27.30 E
Cue	212	De	27.25S	117.54 E
Cuebe	170	Cf	15.48S	17.30 E
Cuelei	170	Cf	15.33S	17.21 E
Cuéllar	126	Hc	41.29N	4.19W
Cuemba	170	Ce	12.09S	18.07 E
Cuenca [3]	126	Ke	40.00N	2.00W
Cuenca [Ec.]	200	If	2.53S	78.59W
Cuenca [Sp.]	126	Jd	40.04N	2.08W
Cuenca, Serrania de-	110	Fg	40.10N	1.55W
Cuencamé de Ceniceros	192	He	24.53N	103.42W
Cuera/Chur	128	Dd	46.50N	9.35 E
Cuerda del Pozo, Embalse de la-	126	Jc	41.51N	2.44W
Cuernavaca	176	Jh	18.55N	99.15W
Cuero	186	Hl	29.06N	97.18W
Cuevas del Almanzora	126	Kg	37.18N	1.53W
Cugir	130	Gd	45.50N	23.22 E
Cugo	170	Cd	7.22S	17.06 E
Čugujev	132	Je	49.50N	36.41 E
Čugujevka	154	Mb	44.08N	133.53 E
Čuhloma	136	Ed	58.47N	42.41 E
Cuiabá	200	Kg	15.35S	56.05W
Cuiabá, Rio-	198	Kg	17.05S	56.36W
Cuiabá Mirim, Rio-	204	Ec	16.20S	55.55W
Cuidado, Punta-	221d	Bb	27.08S	109.19W
Cuijk, Cuijk en Sint Agatha-	124	Hc	51.44N	5.52 E
Cuijk en Sint Agatha-Cuijk	124	Hc	51.44N	5.52 E
Cuilapa	194	Bf	14.17N	90.18W
Cuillin Hills	118	Gd	57.14N	6.15W
Cuilo [Afr.]	158	Ii	3.22S	17.22 E
Cuilo [Ang.]	170	Cd	5.52S	16.35 E
Cúil Raithin/Coleraine	118	Gf	55.08N	6.40W
Cuiluan	152	Mb	47.39N	128.34 E
Cuima	170	Ce	13.14S	15.38 E
Cuito	158	Jj	18.01S	20.48 E
Cuito Cuanavale	160	Ij	15.13S	19.08 E
Cuitzeo, Lago de-	192	Ih	19.55N	101.05W
Cuiuni, Rio-	202	Fd	0.45S	63.07W
Cujmir	130	Fe	44.13N	22.56 E
Čukata	130	Ih	41.50N	25.15 E
Čukotski nacionalny okrug [3]	138	Mc	66.00N	172.30 E
Čukotski poluostrov = Chukchi Peninsula (EN)	140	Uc	66.00N	175.00W
Čukotskoje more = Chukchi Sea (EN)	224	Bd	69.00N	171.00W
Çukurca	146	Jd	37.15N	43.37 E
Çukurdağı	130	Ll	37.58N	28.44 E
Čulakkurgan	136	Gg	43.48N	69.12 E
Culan	122	Ih	46.33N	2.21 E
Cu Lao, Hon-	148	Lf	10.30N	109.13 E
Culasi	150	Hd	11.26N	122.03 E
Culbertson	188	Mb	48.09N	104.31W
Culebra, Isla de-	194	Od	18.19N	65.17W
Culebra, Sierra de la-	126	Fc	41.55N	6.20W
Culebra Peak	186	Dh	37.06N	105.10W
Culemborg	124	Hc	51.57N	5.14 E
Culiacán Rosales	176	Ig	24.48N	107.24W
Culion	150	Hd	11.53N	120.01 E
Culion	150	Gd	11.50N	119.55 E
Culiseu, Rio-	202	Hf	12.14S	53.17W
Cullera	126	Le	39.10N	0.15W
Cullman	182	Je	34.11N	86.51W
Čulman	142	Od	56.52N	124.52 E
Culpeper	184	Hf	38.28N	78.01W
Culuene, Rio-	198	Kg	12.56S	52.51W
Culukidze	132	Mh	42.18N	42.25 E
Culver, Point-	212	Ef	32.54S	124.43 E
Culverden	218	Ee	42.46S	172.51 E
Čulym	138	De	55.06N	80.58 E
Čulym	140	Kd	57.40N	83.50 E
Čulyšman	138	Df	51.20N	87.45 E
Cuma	170	Ce	12.52S	15.04 E
Cumaná	200	Jd	10.28N	64.10W
Cumanacoa	196	Eg	10.15N	63.55W
Cumaovası	130	Kk	38.15N	27.09 E
Cumbal, Volcán-	202	Cc	0.57N	77.52W
Cumberland	118	Kg	54.40N	2.50W
Cumberland	174	Kf	37.09N	88.25W
Cumberland [B.C.-Can.]	188	Cb	49.37N	125.01W
Cumberland [Md.-U.S.]	182	Ld	39.39N	78.46W
Cumberland [Va.-U.S.]	184	Hg	37.31N	78.16W
Cumberland, Cap-	219b	Cb	14.39S	166.37 E
Cumberland, Lake-	184	Eg	36.57N	84.55W
Cumberland Bay	197n	Ba	13.16N	61.17W
Cumberland Island	184	Gj	30.51N	81.27W
Cumberland Islands	212	Jd	20.40S	149.10 E
Cumberland Lake	180	Hf	54.00N	102.20W
Cumberland Peninsula	174	Mc	66.50N	64.00W
Cumberland Plateau	174	Kf	36.00N	85.00W
Cumberland Sound	174	Mc	65.10N	65.30W
Cumbernauld	118	Jf	55.58N	3.59W
Cumbria [3]	118	Kg	54.35N	2.45W
Cumbrian Mountains	118	Jg	54.30N	3.05W
Čumerna	130	Ig	42.47N	25.58 E
Čumikan	138	If	54.42N	135.19 E
Cummins	212	Hf	34.16S	135.44 E
Cumnock	118	If	55.27N	4.16W
Cumpas	192	Eb	30.02N	109.48W
Çumra	146	Ed	37.34N	32.48 E
Čumyš	138	Df	53.30N	83.10 E
Čuna	140	Ld	57.42N	95.35 E
Cunagua	194	Hb	22.05N	78.20W
Cuñapirú	204	Ej	31.32S	55.35W
Cuñapirú, Arroyo-	204	Ej	31.12S	55.31W
Cuñapirú, Cuchilla de-	204	Ej	31.12S	55.36W
Cunaviche, Rio-	196	Ci	7.19N	67.11W
Cunderdin	212	Df	31.39S	117.15 E
Cundinamarca [3]	202	Db	5.00N	74.00W
Čundža	136	Hg	43.32N	79.28 E
Cunene [3]	170	Cf	16.30S	15.00 E
Cunene=Kunene (EN)	158	Ij	17.20S	11.50 E
Cuneo	128	Bf	44.23N	7.32 E
Cunhinga	170	Ce	12.14S	16.48 E
Cunillera, Isla- / Sa Conillera, Illa-	126	Nf	38.59N	1.12 E
Čunja	140	Lc	61.30N	96.20 E
Cunnamulla	210	Fg	28.04S	145.41 E
Čunski [R.S.F.S.R.]	138	Ee	57.23N	97.40 E
Čunski [R.S.F.S.R.]	138	Ee	56.03N	99.48 E
Cuorgnè	128	Be	45.23N	7.39 E
Čupa	136	Db	66.17N	33.01 E
Cupar	118	Je	56.19N	3.01W
Cupica, Golfo de-	202	Cb	6.35N	77.30W
Ćuprija	130	Ef	43.56N	21.22 E
Cúpula, Pico-	192	De	24.47N	110.50W
Čur	114	Mh	57.11N	53.01 E
Curaçá	202	Ke	8.59S	39.54W
Curaçao	198	Jd	12.11N	69.00W
Curacautín	206	Fe	38.26S	71.53W
Cura Malal, Sierra de-	204	Am	37.44S	62.16W
Curanilahue	206	Fe	37.28S	73.21W
Čurapča	138	Id	61.56N	132.18 E
Curaray, Rio-	202	Dd	2.20S	74.05W
Curdimurka	210	Eg	29.30S	137.10 E
Curé	204	De	21.25S	56.25W
Cure	122	Jg	47.40N	3.41 E
Curepipe	172a	Bb	20.19S	57.31 E
Curepto	206	Fe	35.05S	72.01W
Cureski prohod (Vitinja)	130	Gg	42.47N	23.45 E
Curiapo	202	Fb	8.33N	61.00W
Curicó	200	Ii	34.59S	71.14W
Curicuriari, Rio-	202	Ed	0.14S	66.48W
Curitabanos	206	Jc	27.18S	50.36W
Curitiba	200	Lh	25.25S	49.15W
Curoca	170	Bf	15.43S	11.55 E
Currais Novos	202	Ke	6.15S	36.31W
Curralinho	202	Id	1.48S	49.47W
Curral-Velho	162	Cf	15.59N	22.48W
Current	184	Im	25.27S	76.45W
Current River	186	Kh	36.15N	90.57W
Currie	212	Ig	39.56S	143.52 E
Curtea de Argeş	130	Hd	45.08N	24.41 E
Curtici	130	Ec	46.21N	21.18 E
Curtis	186	Ff	40.38N	100.31W
Curtis Channel	212	Kd	23.55S	152.05 E
Curtis Island [Austl.]	212	Kd	23.40S	151.10 E
Curtis Island [Ker.Is.]	208	Jh	30.35S	178.36W
Curuá, Rio- [Braz.]	198	Kf	5.23S	54.22W
Curuá, Rio- [Braz.]	204	Ga	13.26S	51.24W
Curuá, Rio- [Braz.]	202	Gd	1.55S	55.07W
Curuçá	202	Id	0.43S	47.50W
Curuça, Rio-	202	Dd	4.27S	71.23W
Curuguaty	206	Ib	24.31S	55.42W
Curuguaty, Arroyo-	204	Dg	24.06S	56.02W
Curup	150	Dg	3.28S	102.32 E
Curupira, Sierra de-	202	Fc	1.25N	64.30W
Cururupu	202	Jd	1.50S	44.52W
Curuzú Cuatia	206	Ic	29.47S	58.03W
Curvelo	202	Jg	18.45S	44.25W
Cushing	186	Hi	35.59N	96.46W
Cushing, Mount -	180	Ee	57.36N	126.51W
Cusio → Orta, Lago d'-	128	Ce	45.50N	8.25 E
Čusovaja	110	Ld	58.13N	56.30 E
Čusovoj	136	Fd	58.17N	57.50 E
Cusset	122	Jh	46.08N	3.28 E
Cusseta	184	Ei	32.18N	84.47W
Čust	135	Hd	41.00N	71.15 E
Custer	186	Ee	43.46N	103.36W
Cutato	170	Ce	10.33S	16.48 E
Cut Bank	182	Eb	48.38N	112.20W
Cutervo	202	Ce	6.22S	78.51W
Cuthbert	184	Ej	31.46N	84.48W
Cutral Có	206	Ge	38.56S	69.14W
Cutro	128	Kk	39.02N	16.59 E
Cuttack	142	Kg	20.30N	85.50 E
Čuvašskaja ASSR [3]	136	Ed	55.30N	47.10 E
Cuvelai	170	Cf	15.40S	15.47 E
Cuvette [3]	170	Cc	0.10S	15.30 E
Cuvier Basin (EN)	212	Cd	22.00S	111.00 E
Cuvier Island	218	Fb	36.25S	175.45 E
Cuvo ou Queve	158	Ij	10.50S	13.47 E
Cuxhaven	120	Ec	53.53N	8.42 E
Cuya	206	Fa	19.07S	70.08W
Cuyahoga Falls	184	Ge	41.08N	81.55W
Cuyo Islands	150	Hd	11.04N	120.57 E
Cuyubini, Rio-	196	Fh	8.20N	60.20W
Cuyuni, Rio-	198	Ke	6.23N	58.41W
Cuyuni River	198	Kf	6.23N	58.41W
Cuyutlán, Laguna-	192	Gh	19.00N	104.10W
Cuzco	200	Ig	13.31S	71.59W
Cuzco [3]	202	Df	12.30S	72.30W
Cuzna	126	Hf	38.04N	4.41W
Cvikov	120	Kf	50.48N	14.40 E
Čvrsnica	128	Lg	43.35N	17.35 E
Cyangugu	170	Ec	2.29S	28.54 E
Cybinka	120	Kd	52.12N	14.48 E
Cyclades (EN) = Kikládhes	110	Ih	37.00N	25.10 E
Čyjyrčyk, pereval-	135	Id	40.15N	73.20 E
Cypress Hills	174	Ie	49.40N	109.30W
Cypress Lake	188	Kb	49.28N	109.29W
Cyprus (EN)=Kıbrıs/Kypros [1]	142	Ff	35.00N	33.00 E
Cyprus (EN)=Kıbrıs/Kypros	140	Ff	35.00N	33.00 E
Cyprus (EN)=Kypros/Kıbrıs [1]	142	Ff	35.00N	33.00 E
Cyprus (EN)=Kypros/Kıbrıs	140	Ff	35.00N	33.00 E
Cyrenaica (EN)=Barqah	158	Je	31.00N	23.00 E
Cyrenaica (EN)=Barqah	164	Dc	31.00N	22.30 E
Cyrene	164	Dc	32.48N	21.59 E
Cyrus Field Bay	180	Ld	62.50N	65.00W
Cysoing	124	Fd	50.34N	3.13 E
Cythera (EN)=Kithira	130	Fm	36.09N	23.00 E
Czaplinek	120	Mc	53.34N	16.14 E
Czarna [Pol.]	120	Rf	50.30N	21.15 E
Czarna [Pol.]	120	Pe	51.12N	19.53 E
Czarna Białostocka	120	Tc	53.18N	23.19 E
Czarna Dąbrówka	120	Nb	54.20N	17.32 E
Czarna Hańcza	120	Tc	53.50N	23.47 E
Czarnków	120	Md	52.55N	16.34 E
Czchów	120	Qg	49.50N	20.39 E
Czechoslovakia (EN) = Československo [1]	112	Hf	49.30N	17.00 E
Czechowice-Dziedzice	120	Og	49.54N	19.00 E
Czeremcha	120	Td	52.32N	23.15 E
Czersk	120	Nc	53.48N	18.00 E
Częstochowa	112	He	50.49N	19.06 E
Częstochowa [2]	120	Pf	50.50N	19.05 E
Człopa	120	Mc	53.06N	16.08 E
Człuchów	120	Nc	53.41N	17.21 E

D

Đà, Sông- [Asia] = Black River (EN)	140	Mg	20.17N	106.34 E
Da'an (Dalai)	152	Lb	45.35N	124.16 E
Dabaga	170	Gd	8.07S	35.55 E
Dabakala	166	Ed	8.22N	4.26W
Dabakala [3]	166	Ed	8.27N	4.28W
Daban → Bairin Youqi	152	Kc	43.30N	118.37 E
Dabas	120	Pi	47.11N	19.19 E
Daba Shan	140	Mf	32.15N	109.00 E
Dabat	168	Fc	12.58N	37.45 E
Dabay Sima	168	Gc	12.43N	42.17 E
Dabba/Daocheng	152	Hf	29.01N	100.26 E
Dabbāgh, Jabal-	144	Ed	27.52N	35.45 E
Dabeiba	202	Cb	7.02N	76.16W
Dąbie	120	Od	52.06N	18.49 E
Dąbie, Jezioro-	120	Kc	53.29N	14.40 E
Dabie Shan	140	Nf	31.15N	115.00 E
Dabl, Wādī-	146	Gh	29.05N	36.14 E
Dabnou	166	Gc	14.09N	5.22 E
Dabola	166	Cc	10.45N	11.07W
Daborow	168	Hd	6.11N	48.22 E
Dabou	166	Ed	5.19N	4.23W
Dabqig → Uxin Qi	152	Id	38.27N	109.08 E
Dabraš	130	Gh	41.40N	23.50 E
Dąbrowa Białostocka	120	Tc	53.40N	23.20 E
Dąbrowa Górnicza	120	Pf	50.20N	19.11 E
Dąbrowa Tarnowska	120	Qf	50.11N	21.00 E
Dabsan Hu	152	Fd	36.58N	95.00 E
Dăbuleni	130	Hf	43.48N	24.05 E
Dabus	168	Fc	10.38N	35.10 E
Dacata	168	Gd	7.16N	42.15 E
Dacca → Dhaka	142	Lg	23.43N	90.25 E
Dachangzhen	154	Eh	32.13N	118.44 E
Dachau	120	Hh	48.16N	11.26 E
Dachen Dao	154	Fj	28.29N	121.53 E
Dachstein	128	Hc	47.30N	13.36 E
Dacia Seamount (EN)	110	Ei	31.10N	13.42W

Index Symbols

[1] Independent Nation; [2] State, Region; [3] District, County; [4] Municipality; [5] Colony, Dependency; Continent; Physical Region; Historical or Cultural Region; Mount, Mountain; Volcano; Hill; Mountains, Mountain Range; Hills, Escarpment; Plateau, Upland; Pass, Gap; Plain, Lowland; Delta; Salt Flat; Valley, Canyon; Crater, Cave; Karst Features; Depression; Polder; Desert, Dunes; Forest, Woods; Heath, Steppe; Oasis; Cape, Point; Coast, Beach; Cliff; Peninsula; Isthmus; Sandbank; Island; Atoll; Rock, Reef; Islands, Archipelago; Rocks, Reefs; Coral Reef; Well, Spring; Geyser; River, Stream; Waterfall, Rapids; River Mouth, Estuary; Lake; Salt Lake; Intermittent Lake; Reservoir; Swamp, Pond; Canal; Glacier; Ice Shelf, Pack Ice; Ocean; Sea; Gulf, Bay; Strait, Fjord; Lagoon; Bank; Seamount; Tablemount; Ridge; Shelf; Basin; Escarpment, Sea Scarp; Fracture; Trench, Abyss; National Park, Reserve; Point of Interest; Recreation Site; Cave, Cavern; Historic Site; Ruins; Wall, Walls; Church, Abbey; Temple; Scientific Station; Railway station; Airport; Port; Military installation; Lighthouse; Mine; Tunnel; Dam, Bridge

Dačice	120	Lg	49.05N	15.26 E
Dac Lac, Caonguyen-	148	Lf	12.50N	108.05 E
Dadali	219a	Dc	8.07 S	159.06 E
Dadanawa	202	Gc	2.50N	59.30W
Daday	146	Eb	41.28N	33.28 E
Dade City	184	Fk	28.22N	82.12W
Dadou	122	Hk	43.44N	1.49 E
Dādra and Nagar Haveli [3]	148	Ed	20.20N	72.50 E
Dadu	148	Dc	26.44N	67.47 E
Dadu He	140	Mg	29.32N	103.44 E
Dadukou	154	Di	30.30N	117.03 E
Dăeni	130	Le	44.50N	28.07 E
Daet	150	Hd	14.05N	122.55 E
Dafang	152	If	27.06N	105.32 E
Dafeng (Dazhongji)	154	Fh	33.11N	120.27 E
Dagana	166	Bb	16.31N	15.30W
Dagana	168	Bc	13.05N	16.00 E
Daga Post	168	Ed	9.13N	33.58 E
Dağardi	130	Lj	39.26N	29.00 E
Dagash	168	Eb	19.22N	33.24 E
Dagda	116	Lh	56.04N	27.36 E
Dagdan-Daba	152	Gb	48.20N	96.50 E
Dagéla	168	Bc	10.40N	18.26 E
Dagestanskaja ASSR [3]	136	Eg	43.00N	47.00 E
Dagestanskije Ogni	136	Eg	42.06N	48.12 E
Dagezhen → Fengning	154	Dd	41.12N	116.39 E
Dagu	154	De	38.58N	117.40 E
Daguan	152	Hf	27.48N	103.54 E
Dagu He	154	Ff	37.34N	121.17 E
Daguokui Shan	154	Jb	45.19N	129.50 E
Dagupan	150	Hc	16.03N	120.20 E
Dagxoi → Yidun	152	Ge	30.25N	99.28 E
Dagzê	152	Ff	29.41N	91.24 E
Dagzê Co	152	Ee	31.54N	87.29 E
Daheiding Shan	152	Mb	47.58N	129.10 E
Dahei He	154	Ad	40.34N	111.05 E
Da Hinggan Ling = Greater Khingan Range (EN)	140	Oe	49.00N	122.00 E
Dahlak Archipelago	158	Lg	15.40N	40.30 E
Dahlak Kebir	168	Gb	15.38N	40.11 E
Daḥl al Furayy	146	Li	26.45N	47.03 E
Dahlem	124	Id	50.23N	6.33 E
Dahlonega Plateau	184	Fh	34.30N	83.45W
Dahm, Ramlat-	164	If	16.25N	45.45 E
Dahme	120	Je	51.52N	13.26 E
Dahmouni	126	Ni	35.25N	1.29 E
Dahn	124	Je	49.09N	7.47 E
Dahomey → Bénin [1]	160	Hh	9.30N	2.15 E
Dahongliutan	152	Cd	36.00N	79.12 E
Dahra	126	Mh	36.18N	0.55 E
Dahra [Lib.]	164	Cd	29.40N	17.40 E
Dahra [Sen.]	166	Bb	15.21N	15.29W
Dahra, Massif de-	126	Oh	36.30N	2.05 E
Dahūk	146	Jd	36.52N	43.00 E
Dahūk [3]	146	Jd	36.57N	43.00 E
Dahushan	154	Gd	41.37N	122.09 E
Daḥy, Nafūd ad-	164	Ie	22.00N	45.25 E
Dai	219a	Eb	7.53 S	160.37 E
Daia	130	If	44.00N	25.59 E
Daïa, Région des-	162	Hc	33.30N	3.25 E
Daicheng	154	De	38.42N	116.37 E
Daigo	154	Pf	36.46N	140.21 E
Dai Hai	154	Bd	40.31N	112.43 E
Dailekh	148	Gc	28.50N	81.44 E
Daimanji-San	156	Cc	36.15N	133.19 E
Daimiel	126	Ie	39.04N	3.37W
Dainanji-San	156	Ec	36.36N	137.42 E
Dainichi-San	156	Ec	36.09N	136.30 E
Dainkog	152	Ge	32.31N	97.59 E
Daiō-Zaki	154	Ng	34.22N	136.53 E
Dairbhre/Valentia	118	Cj	51.55N	10.20W
Daireaux	204	Bm	36.36S	61.45W
Dairen → Dalian	142	Of	38.55N	121.39 E
Dai-Sen	156	Cd	35.24N	133.34 E
Daisengen-Dake	156a	Bc	41.35N	140.09 E
Daishan (Gaotingzhen)	154	Gi	30.15N	122.13 E
Daitō [Jap.]	156	Cd	35.19N	132.58 E
Daitō [Jap.]	156	Gb	39.02N	141.22 E
Daitō Islands (EN) = Daitō-Shotō	140	Pg	25.00N	131.15 E
Daitō-Shotō = Daito Islands (EN)	140	Pg	25.00N	131.15 E
Daitō-Zaki	156	Gd	35.18N	140.24 E
Daixian	154	Be	39.03N	112.57 E
Daiyue → Shanyin	154	Be	39.30N	112.48 E
Dajabón	194	Ld	19.33N	71.42W
Dajarra	210	Eg	21.42 S	139.31 E
Dajtit, Mali i-	130	Ch	41.22N	19.55 E
Daka	166	Ed	8.19N	0.13W
Dakar	160	Fg	14.40N	17.26W
Dākhilah, Wāḥāt ad- = Dakhla Oasis (EN)	158	Jf	25.30N	29.10 E
Dakhla	160	Ff	23.42N	15.56W
Dakhlet Nouâdhibou [3]	162	De	20.30N	16.00W
Dakla Oasis (EN) = Dākhilah, Wāḥāt ad-	158	Jf	25.30N	29.10 E
Dakoro	166	Gc	14.30N	6.25 E
Đakovica	130	Dg	42.23N	20.26 E
Đakovo	128	Me	45.19N	18.25 E
Daksti	116	Kg	57.38N	25.32 E
Dak To	148	Lf	14.42N	107.51 E
Dal	116	Dd	60.15N	11.12 E
Dal, Jökulsá á-	114a	Cb	65.40N	14.20W
Đala	130	Dc	46.09N	20.07 E
Dala [Ang.]	172	Dc	11.03 S	20.17 E
Dala [Sol.Is.]	219a	Ec	8.36 S	160.41 E
Dalaba	166	Cc	10.42N	12.15W
Dalai → Da'an	152	Lb	45.35N	124.16 E
Dalai Nur	152	Kc	43.18N	116.15 E
Dala-Järna	116	Fd	60.33N	14.21 E
Dalaki	146	Nh	29.19N	51.06 E
Dalälven	110	Hc	60.38N	17.27 E
Dalaman	130	Lm	36.44N	28.49 E
Dalaman	136	Cd	36.40N	28.45 E
Dalāmī	168	Ec	11.52N	30.28 E
Dalan-Dzadgad	142	Me	43.47N	104.29 E
Dalane	116	Bf	58.35N	6.20 E
Dalarna	116	Fd	61.00N	14.05 E
Dalarö	116	He	59.08N	18.24 E
Da Lat	142	Mh	11.56N	108.25 E
Dālbandin	148	Cc	28.53N	64.25 E
Dalbosjön	116	Ef	58.45N	12.50 E
Dalboslätten	116	Ef	58.35N	12.25 E
Dalby [Austl.]	212	Ke	27.11 S	151.16 E
Dalby [Swe.]	116	Ei	55.40N	13.20 E
Dale [Nor.]	114	Af	60.35N	5.49 E
Dale [Nor.]	114	Af	61.22N	5.25 E
Dale Hollow Lake	184	Eg	36.36N	85.19W
Dalen	116	Bg	59.27N	8.00 E
Dalfsen	124	Ib	52.30N	6.14 E
Dalgaranger, Mount-	212	De	27.51 S	117.06 E
Dălgopol	130	Kf	43.03N	27.21 E
Dalhart	182	Gd	36.04N	102.31W
Dalhousie	180	Kg	48.04N	66.23W
Dalhousie, Cape-	180	Eb	70.15N	129.41W
Dali [China]	152	Ie	34.55N	110.00 E
Dali [China]	142	Mg	25.43N	100.07 E
Dalian	142	Of	38.55N	121.39 E
Dalias	126	Jh	36.49N	2.52W
Dalizi	152	Mc	41.45N	126.50 E
Dalj	128	Me	45.29N	18.59 E
Daljā'	164	Fd	27.39N	30.42 E
Dalkowskie, Wzgórza-	120	Le	51.35N	15.50 E
Dall [Ak.-U.S.]	178	Mf	54.50N	132.55W
Dall [Can.]	178	Mf	55.00N	133.00W
Dallas [Or.-U.S.]	188	Dd	44.55N	123.19W
Dallas [Tx.-U.S.]	176	Jf	32.47N	96.48W
Dalmā'	146	Oj	24.30N	52.20 E
Dalmā', Qārat-	164	Dd	25.32N	23.57 E
Dalmacija = Dalmatia (EN)	110	Hg	43.00N	17.00 E
Dalmacija = Dalmatia (EN)	128	Kg	43.00N	17.00 E
Dalmaj, Hawr-	146	Kf	32.20N	45.28 E
Dalmally	118	Ie	56.24N	4.58W
Dalmatia (EN) = Dalmacija	110	Hg	43.00N	17.00 E
Dalmatia (EN) = Dalmacija	128	Kg	43.00N	17.00 E
Dalmatovo	134	Kh	56.16N	63.00 E
Dalnegorsk	142	Pe	44.31N	135.31 E
Dalnerečensk	142	Pe	45.55N	133.45 E
Dalni [R.S.F.S.R.]	138	Kf	53.15N	157.30 E
Dalni [R.S.F.S.R.]	138	Ih	44.57N	135.03 E
Dalnjaja, gora-	138	Mc	68.08N	179.53 E
Daloa	160	Gh	6.53N	6.27W
Daloa [3]	166	Dd	6.58N	6.23W
Dalou Shan	140	Mg	28.00N	106.40 E
Dalqān	146	Kj	24.15N	45.47 E
Dalqū	168	Ea	20.07N	30.35 E
Dalrymple, Mount-	208	Fg	21.02 S	148.38 E
Dalsbruk/Taalintendas	116	Jd	60.02N	22.31 E
Dalsfjorden	116	Ac	61.20N	5.05 E
Dalsjöfors	116	Eg	57.43N	13.05 E
Dalsland	116	Ef	58.35N	12.55 E
Dalslands kanal	116	Ef	58.50N	12.25 E
Dals Långed	114	Cg	58.55N	12.18 E
Dalton	184	Eh	34.47N	84.58W
Daltonganj	148	Gd	24.02N	84.04 E
Dalul	168	Gc	14.22N	40.21 E
Daluo	152	Hg	21.38N	100.15 E
Dalupiri	150	Hc	19.05N	121.12 E
Dalvik	114a	Bb	65.58N	18.32W
Dalwallinu	212	Df	30.17 S	116.40 E
Dalyan	130	Lm	36.50N	28.39 E
Daly Bay	180	Id	64.00N	89.40W
Daly City	188	Dh	37.42N	122.29W
Daly River	208	Ef	13.20 S	130.19 E
Daly Waters	212	Gc	16.15 S	133.22 E
Damā, Wādī-	146	Fi	27.09N	35.47 E
Damagarim	166	Gc	13.42N	9.00 E
Damān	148	Ed	20.10N	73.00 E
Damān [3]	148	Ed	20.10N	73.00 E
Damanhūr	164	Fc	31.02N	30.28 E
Damar, Pulau-	150	Ih	7.09 S	128.40 E
Damara	168	Be	4.58N	18.42 E
Damaraland	172	Bd	21.00 S	17.30 E
Damas Cays	194	Hb	23.58N	79.55W
Damascus (EN) = Dimashq	142	Ff	33.30N	36.15 E
Dāmāsh	146	Md	36.46N	49.46 E
Damaturu	166	Hc	11.45N	11.58 E
Damāvand	146	Oe	35.56N	52.08 E
Damāvand, Qolleh-ye-	140	Hf	35.59N	52.08 E
Damba	170	Cd	6.50 S	15.07 E
Dambaslar	130	Kh	41.13N	27.14 E
Dame Marie, Cap-	190	Je	18.36N	74.26W
Damergou	166	Hb	15.00N	9.00 E
Dāmghān	146	Pd	36.09N	54.22 E
Damianópolis	204	Ib	14.33 S	46.10W
Damiao	154	He	30.52N	104.38 E
Damietta (EN) = Dumyāṭ	160	Ke	31.25N	31.48 E
Daming	154	Cf	36.17N	115.09 E
Daming Shan	152	Ig	23.23N	108.30 E
Damīr Qābū	146	Id	36.54N	41.47 E
Dammartin-en-Goële	124	Ee	49.03N	2.41 E
Dammastock	128	Cd	46.38N	8.25 E
Damme [Bel.]	124	Fc	51.15N	3.17 E
Damme [Ger.]	124	Kb	52.31N	8.12 E
Dammer Berge	124	Kb	52.35N	8.17 E
Damoh	148	Fd	23.50N	79.27 E
Damongo	166	Ed	9.05N	1.49W
Damous	126	Nh	36.33N	1.42 E
Dampier	210	Cg	20.39 S	116.45 E
Dampier, Selat- = Dampier Strait (EN)	150	Jg	0.40 S	130.40 E
Dampier Archipelago	212	Dd	20.35 S	116.35 E
Dampier Land	212	Ec	17.30 S	122.55 E
Dampierre	124	Df	48.42N	1.59 E
Dampier Strait	212	Ja	5.36 S	148.12 E
Dampier Strait (EN) = Dampier, Selat-	150	Jg	0.40 S	130.40 E
Damqawt	144	Hf	16.34N	52.50 E
Damqog Kanbab/Maquan He	152	Df	29.36N	84.09 E
Dam Qu	152	Fe	33.56N	92.41 E
Damville	124	Df	48.52N	1.04 E
Damvillers	124	He	49.20N	5.24 E
Damwoude, Dantumadeel-	124	Ha	53.18N	5.59 E
Damxoi → Comai	152	Ff	28.26N	91.32 E
Damxung	152	Fe	30.34N	91.16 E
Danakil = Danakil Plain (EN)	158	Lg	12.25N	40.30 E
Danakil Plain (EN) = Danakil	158	Lg	12.25N	40.30 E
Danané	166	Dd	7.16N	8.09W
Danané [3]	166	Dd	7.25N	8.10W
Da Nang	142	Mh	16.04N	108.13 E
Danba/Rongzhag	152	He	30.48N	101.54 E
Danbury	184	Ke	41.23N	73.27W
Danby Lake	188	Hi	34.14N	115.07W
Dancheng	154	Ch	33.36N	115.14 E
Dancheng → Xiangshan	152	Lf	29.29N	121.52 E
Dandarah	164	Fd	26.10N	32.39 E
Dandeldhura	148	Gc	29.18N	80.35 E
Dandenong, Melbourne-	212	Jg	37.59 S	145.12 E
Dandong	142	Oe	40.10N	124.15 E
Daneborg	179	Jd	74.25N	20.10W
Danells Fjord	179	Hf	60.45N	42.45W
Daneţi	130	Hf	43.59N	24.03 E
Danfeng (Longjuzhai)	152	Je	33.44N	110.22 E
Danforth Hills	186	Cf	40.15N	108.00W
Danfu	219a	Aa	4.12 S	153.04 E
Dangara	136	Gh	38.09N	69.22 E
Dangchengwan → Subei	152	Fd	39.36N	94.58 E
Dange	170	Cd	7.56 S	15.03 E
Dang He	152	Fc	40.30N	94.42 E
Dangjin Shankou	140	Lf	39.15N	94.30 E
Dangla	168	Fc	11.16N	36.50 E
Dangla Shan → Tanggula Shan	140	Lf	33.00N	92.00 E
Dangoura, Mont-	168	.Dd	6.12N	26.27 E
Dangrek Range (EN) = Dong Rak, Phanom-	140	Mh	14.25N	104.30 E
Dangshan	152	Ke	34.22N	116.21 E
Dangtu	154	Ei	31.33N	118.30 E
Dangu	124	De	49.15N	1.42 E
Dangyang	154	Ai	30.49N	111.47 E
Dan He	154	Bg	35.05N	112.59 E
Daniel	188	Je	42.52N	110.04W
Daniel, Serra-	204	Ea	13.40 S	54.55W
Danielskuil	172	Ce	28.11 S	23.33 E
Danilov	136	Ed	58.12N	40.13 E
Danilovgrad	130	Cg	42.33N	19.07 E
Danilovka	132	Nd	50.21N	44.06 E
Daning	152	Jd	36.31N	110.45 E
Danjiang → Junxian	152	Je	32.31N	111.32 E
Danjiangkou Shuiku	152	Je	32.37N	111.30 E
Danjo-Guntō	152	Me	32.00N	128.20 E
Dank	146	Qk	23.33N	56.16 E
Dankov	132	Kc	53.16N	39.07 E
Dankova, Pik-	135	Kd	41.00N	77.37 E
Danli	194	Df	14.00N	86.35W
Danmark = Denmark (EN) [1]	112	Gd	56.00N	10.00 E
Danmark Fjord	224	Me	81.10N	23.20W
Danmarks Havn	224	Ld	76.50N	18.30W
Danmarksstrædet = Denmark Strait (EN)	110	Dc	67.00N	25.00W
Dannemora	114	Df	60.12N	17.49 E
Dannenberg (Elbe)	120	Hc	53.06N	11.06 E
Dannevirke	218	Gd	40.12 S	176.06 E
Danot	168	Hd	7.33N	45.17 E
Dantumadeel	124	Ha	53.18N	5.59 E
Dantumadeel-Damwoude	124	Ha	53.18N	5.59 E
Danube (EN) = Donau	110	If	45.20N	29.40 E
Danube (EN) = Duna	110	If	45.20N	29.40 E
Danube (EN) = Dunaj	110	If	45.20N	29.40 E
Danube (EN) = Dunărea	110	If	45.20N	29.40 E
Danube (EN) = Dunav	110	If	45.20N	29.40 E
Danube, Mouths of the- (EN) = Dunării, Delta-	110	If	45.30N	29.45 E
Danville [Ar.-U.S.]	186	Ji	35.03N	93.24W
Danville [Il.-U.S.]	182	Jc	40.08N	87.37W
Danville [In.-U.S.]	184	Df	39.46N	86.32W
Danville [Ky.-U.S.]	182	Kd	37.39N	84.46W
Danville [Va.-U.S.]	182	Ld	36.34N	79.25W
Danxian (Nada)	152	Ih	19.38N	109.32 E
Danyang	154	Eh	32.00N	119.33 E
Danzig → Gdańsk	112	He	54.23N	18.40 E
Dao	150	Hd	10.31N	121.57 E
Dão	126	Dd	40.20N	8.11W
Daocheng/Dabba	152	Hf	29.01N	100.26 E
Daokou → Huaxian	154	Cg	35.33N	114.30 E
Daosa	148	Fc	26.53N	76.20 E
Dao Shui	154	Ci	30.42N	114.40 E
Dao Timni	166	Ha	20.38N	13.39 E
Daoura	162	Gd	29.03N	4.33W
Dao Xian	152	Jf	25.37N	111.36 E
Dapaong	166	Fc	10.52N	0.12 E
Dapchi	166	Hc	12.29N	11.29 E
Da Qaidam	142	Lf	37.50N	95.18 E
Daqing Shan	154	Ad	41.00N	111.00 E
Daqin Tal → Naiman Qi	152	Lc	42.49N	120.38 E
Daquing Shan	154	Ed	40.30N	119.38 E
Dar'ā	144	Ec	32.37N	36.06 E
Dārāb	146	Ph	28.45N	54.34 E
Darabani	130	Ja	48.11N	26.35 E
Daraçya Yarımadası	130	Lm	36.40N	28.10 E
Darāfisah	168	Ec	13.23N	31.59 E
Dār al 'Umayrah	168	Gc	12.39N	44.07 E
Dārān	146	Nf	32.59N	50.24 E
Darasun	138	Gf	51.39N	113.59 E
Đaravica	130	Dg	42.32N	20.08 E
Darāw	146	Ej	24.25N	32.56 E
Darazo	166	Hc	11.00N	10.25 E
Darband	144	Ic	31.38N	57.02 E
Darband, Kūh-e-	146	Qg	31.34N	57.08 E
Darbandī Khān, Sad ad-	146	Ke	35.07N	45.50 E
Darbėnai/Darbenaj	116	Ih	56.02N	21.08 E
Darbenaj/Darbėnai	116	Ih	56.02N	21.08 E
Dar Ben Karriche el Bahri	126	Gi	35.51N	5.21W
Darbhanga	148	Hc	26.10N	85.54 E
Dārboruk	168	Gd	9.44N	44.31 E
Darby	188	Hc	46.01N	114.11W
Darchan → Darhan	142	Me	49.33N	106.21 E
Darda	128	Me	45.38N	18.42 E
Dardanelle Lake	186	Ji	35.25N	93.20W
Dardanelles (EN) = Çanakkale boğazı	110	Ig	40.15N	26.25 E
Dardo/Kangding	152	He	30.01N	101.58 E
Dar el Kouti	158	Jh	8.50N	21.50 E
Darende	146	Gc	38.34N	37.30 E
Dar es Salaam	160	Ki	6.48 S	39.17 E
Dar es Salaam [3]	170	Gd	6.50 S	39.02 E
Darfield	218	Ee	43.29 S	172.07 E
Darfo Boario Terme	128	Ee	45.53N	10.11 E
Dārfūr	158	Jg	13.30N	24.00 E
Dārfūr al Janūbīyah [3]	168	Dc	11.30N	25.10 E
Dārfūr ash Shamālīyah [3]	168	Db	16.00N	25.30 E
Dargan-Ata	136	Gg	40.29N	62.12 E
Dargaville	216	Dg	35.56 S	173.52 E
Darhan (Darchan)	142	Me	49.33N	106.21 E
Darhan Muminggan Lianheqi	152	Jc	41.45N	110.24 E
Darica [Tur.]	130	Mi	40.45N	29.23 E
Darica [Tur.]	130	Kj	40.00N	27.50 E
Darien	184	Gj	31.22N	81.26W
Darién [3]	194	Ii	8.10N	77.45W
Darién	190	Ig	8.30N	77.30W
Darién, Golfo de-	198	Ie	8.25N	76.53W
Darién, Serranía de-	190	Ig	8.30N	77.30W
Dariense, Cordillera-	194	Eg	12.55N	85.30W
Darja	135	Ee	38.13N	65.46 E
Darjeeling → Dārjiling	148	Hc	27.02N	88.16 E
Dārjiling	148	Hc	27.02N	88.16 E
Dar-Kebdani	126	Ii	35.07N	3.21W
Dark Head	197n	Ba	13.17N	61.17W
Dārkhovīn	146	Mg	30.45N	48.25 E
Darlag	152	Ge	33.49N	99.08 E
Darling	172	Bf	33.23 S	18.23 E
Darling Downs	212	Ke	27.30 S	150.30 E
Darling Range	208	Ch	32.00 S	116.30 E
Darling River	208	Fh	34.07 S	141.55 E
Darlington [Eng.-U.K.]	118	Lg	54.31N	1.34W
Darlington [S.C.-U.S.]	184	Hh	34.19N	79.53W
Darłowo	120	Mb	54.26N	16.23 E
Darmouth	118	Jk	50.21N	3.35W
Darmstadt	120	Eg	49.52N	8.39 E
Darnah	160	Je	32.46N	22.39 E
Darnah [3]	164	Dc	31.00N	23.40 E
Darnétal	124	De	49.27N	1.09 E
Darney	122	Mf	48.05N	6.03 E
Darnley, Cape-	222	Fe	67.43 S	69.30 E
Darnley Bay	180	Fc	69.45N	123.45W
Daroca	126	Kc	41.07N	1.25W
Darou Khoudos	166	Bb	15.06N	16.50W
Darovskoj	114	Lg	58.47N	47.59 E
Darrah, Mount-	188	Hb	49.28N	114.35W
Darregueira	206	Hf	37.42 S	63.10W
Darreh Gaz	144	Ib	37.27N	59.07 E
Darrehshahr	146	Lf	33.10N	47.18 E
D'Arros Island	172b	Bb	5.24 S	53.18 E
Dar Rounga	158	Jg	9.45N	22.20 E
Dar Sila	168	Cc	12.11N	21.21 E
Darß	120	Ib	54.25N	12.31 E
Darßer Ort	120	Ib	54.29N	12.31 E
Dart	118	Jk	50.20N	3.33W
Dart, Cape-	222	Nf	73.06 S	126.20W
D'Artagnan Bank (EN)	212	Eb	13.00 S	121.00 E
Dartang → Baqên	152	Fe	31.58N	94.00 E
Dartford	124	Cc	51.27N	0.13 E
Dartmoor	118	Jk	50.35N	4.00W
Dartmouth	180	Lh	44.40N	63.34W
Dartuch, Cabo- / Artrutx, Cap d'-	126	Pe	39.56N	3.48 E
Daru	214	Ci	9.04 S	143.12 E
Daruneh	146	Qe	35.10N	57.18 E
Daruvar	128	Le	45.35N	17.14 E
Darvaza	136	Fg	40.15N	58.24 E
Darvel, Teluk-	150	Gf	4.50N	118.30 E
Darwin	210	Ef	12.28 S	130.50 E
Darwin, Bahía-	206	Fg	45.27 S	74.40W
Darwin, Isla-	202a	Aa	1.39N	92.00W
Darwin, Port-	212	Gb	12.20 S	130.40 E
Daryā-ye Panj	144	Kb	37.06N	68.20 E
Dar Zagaoua	158	Cb	15.15N	23.14 E
Dar Zebada	168	Bc	13.45N	18.50 E
Dās	146	Oj	25.09N	52.53 E
Dašava	120	Ug	49.13N	24.05 E
Daš-Balbar	152	Jb	49.31N	114.21 E
Dasha He	154	Ce	38.27N	114.39 E
Dashengtang Shan	154	Dc	42.07N	117.12 E
Dashennongjia	154	Je	31.26N	110.18 E
Dashiqiao → Yingkou	154	Gd	40.39N	122.31 E
Dashitou	154	Jc	43.18N	128.29 E
Dasht	146	Qd	37.17N	56.04 E
Dasht Āb	146	Qh	28.59N	56.32 E
Dashtak	146	Og	30.23N	52.30 E
Dasht-e-Āzādegan	146	Mg	31.32N	48.10 E
Daškesan	132	Oi	40.30N	46.03 E
Dasseneiland	172	Bf	33.26 S	18.05 E
Dastgardān	146	Qe	34.19N	56.51 E
Dastjerd-e Qaddādeh	146	Nf	32.44N	51.32 E
Datça	146	Bd	36.45N	27.40 E
Date	154	Pc	42.27N	140.51 E
Dāth, Sha'īb ad-	146	Jj	25.45N	43.10 E
Datia	148	Fc	25.40N	78.28 E
Datian Ding	154	Jj	22.17N	111.13 E
Datil	186	Ci	34.09N	107.47W
Datong [China]	142	Ne	40.09N	113.17 E
Datong [China]	152	Hd	36.56N	101.40 E
Datteln	124	Jc	51.40N	7.23 E
Datteln-Hamm-Kanal	124	Jc	51.39N	7.21 E
Datu	140	Mi	2.05N	109.39 E
Datu, Teluk-	140	Ni	2.00N	111.00 E
Datu Plang	150	He	6.58N	124.40 E
Dāūd Khel	148	Eb	32.53N	71.34 E
Daudzeva	116	Kh	56.28N	25.18 E
Daugaard-Jensen Land	179	Fb	80.10N	63.30W
Daugai/Daugaj	116	Kj	54.20N	24.28 E
Daugaj/Daugai	116	Kj	54.20N	24.28 E
Daugava = Western Dvina (EN)	136	Cd	57.04N	24.03 E
Daugavpils	112	Id	55.53N	26.32 E
Daule	202	Cd	1.50 S	79.57W
Daun	120	Cf	50.12N	6.50 E
Daung Kyun	148	Jf	12.14N	98.05 E
Daunia, Monti della-	128	Ji	41.25N	15.05 E
Dauphin	180	Hf	51.09N	100.03W
Dauphiné	122	Lj	44.50N	6.00 E
Dauphin Lake	180	Hf	51.15N	99.45W
Daura	166	Gc	13.02N	8.18 E
Daurada, Costa- / Dorada, Costa-	126	Nc	41.08N	1.10 E
Dautphetal	124	Kd	50.52N	8.33 E
Dāvangere	148	Ff	14.28N	75.55 E
Davao	142	Oi	7.04N	125.36 E
Davao Gulf	140	Oi	6.40N	125.55 E
Dāvarān, Kūh-e-	146	Qg	30.40N	56.15 E
Dāvar Panāh	144	Jd	27.21N	62.21 E
Dāvarzan	146	Qd	36.23N	56.50 E
Đavat	130	Eh	41.04N	21.06 E
Davenport [Ia.-U.S.]	176	Je	41.32N	90.41W
Davenport [Wa.-U.S.]	188	Fc	47.39N	118.09W
Davenport Range	212	Gd	20.45 S	134.50 E
Daventry	124	Ab	52.15N	1.10W
Davert	124	Jc	51.51N	7.36 E
Davey, Port-	212	Jh	43.20 S	145.55 E
David	176	Ki	8.25N	82.27W
David City	186	Hf	41.15N	97.08W
David-Gorodok	132	Ec	52.03N	27.13 E
David Point	197p	Bb	12.14N	61.39W
Davidson	188	Ma	51.18N	105.59W
Davidson Mountains	178	Kc	68.45N	142.10W
Davies, Mount-	212	Fe	26.14 S	129.16 E
Davis	182	Cd	38.33N	121.44W
Davis	222	Fe	68.35 S	77.58 E
Davis, Cape-	222	Ee	66.24 S	56.50 E
Davis, Mount-	184	Hf	39.47N	79.10W
Davis Bay	222	Ie	66.08 S	134.05 E
Davis Inlet	180	Le	56.00N	61.30W
Davis Mountains	186	Ek	30.35N	104.00W
Davis Sea (EN)	222	Ge	66.00 S	92.00 E
Davisstrædet = Davis Strait (EN)	174	Nc	68.00N	58.00W
Davis Strait	174	Nc	68.00N	58.00W
Davis Strait (EN) = Davisstrædet	174	Nc	68.00N	58.00W
Davlekanovo	136	Fe	54.13N	55.03 E
Davo	166	Dd	5.00N	6.08W
Davos/Tavau	128	Dd	46.47N	9.50 E
Davutlar	130	Kl	37.43N	27.17 E
Dawa	154	Gd	40.58N	122.01 E
Dawanlē	168	Gc	11.06N	42.38 E
Dawei	142	Lh	14.05N	98.12 E
Dawen He	154	Dg	35.37N	116.23 E
Dawes Range	212	Kd	24.30 S	151.10 E
Dawḥarab	164	Hf	16.17N	41.57 E
Dawlatābād	144	Jb	36.30N	64.51 E
Dawson [Ga.-U.S.]	184	Ej	31.47N	84.26W
Dawson [Yuk.-Can.]	176	Fc	64.04N	139.25W
Dawson, Mount-	188	Ga	51.09N	117.25W
Dawson Creek	176	Gd	55.45N	120.07W
Dawson-Lambton Glacier	222	Af	76.15 S	27.30W
Dawson Range	180	Dd	65.15N	137.45W
Dawson River	212	Jd	23.38 S	149.46 E
Dawu	152	He	30.45N	101.11 E
Dawu (Erlangdian)	154	Ci	31.33N	114.07 E
Dawu → Maqên	152	He	34.29N	100.01 E
Dawukou → Shizuishan	152	Id	39.03N	106.24 E
Dax	122	Ek	43.43N	1.03W
Da Xi	152	Lf	28.10N	120.14 E
Daxian	152	Ie	31.15N	107.28 E
Daxin	152	Ig	22.52N	107.14 E
Daxing	154	De	39.45N	116.19 E
Daxinggou	154	Jc	43.23N	129.39 E
Daxue Shan	140	Mf	30.30N	101.30 E
Dayan → Lijiang	142	Mg	26.56N	100.15 E
Dayang He	154	Ge	39.52N	123.40 E
Dayao	152	Hf	25.49N	101.18 E
Daye	154	Ci	30.05N	114.58 E
Dayishan → Guanyun	154	Eg	35.19N	119.14 E
Daymán, Cuchilla del-	204	Dj	31.38 S	57.10W
Daymán, Río-	204	Dj	31.40 S	58.02W
Daym Zubayr	168	Dd	7.43N	26.13 E
Dayong	152	Jf	29.09N	110.30 E
Dayr, Jabal ad-	168	Ec	12.27N	30.45 E
Dayr az Zawr	142	Gf	35.20N	40.09 E
Dayr Ḥāfir	146	Gd	36.09N	37.42 E
Dayr Mawās	146	Di	27.38N	30.51 E
Dayrūṭ	164	Fd	27.33N	30.49 E
Dayton [Oh.-U.S.]	176	Kf	39.45N	84.15W
Dayton [Wa.-U.S.]	188	Gc	46.19N	117.59W
Daytona Beach	176	Kg	29.12N	80.59W
Dayu	152	Jf	25.29N	114.22 E
Da Yunhe = Grand Canal (EN)	140	Nf	39.54N	116.44 E
Dayville	188	Fd	44.28N	119.32W
Dayyīnah	146	Oj	24.57N	52.24 E
Dazhongji → Dafeng	154	Fh	33.11N	120.27 E
Dazhu	152	Ie	30.42N	107.12 E
Dazjā	146	Pe	35.50N	55.46 E
Dazkırı	146	Cd	37.54N	29.42 E
De Aar	160	Jl	30.39 S	24.00 E
Dead	118	Ei	52.40N	8.30W
Deadhorse	178	Jb	70.11N	148.27W
Deadmans Cay	194	Jb	23.14N	75.14W
Dead Sea (EN) = Mayyit, Al Baḥr al-	140	Ff	31.30N	35.30 E
Deadwood	186	Ed	44.23N	103.44W
Deal	118	Oj	51.13N	1.24 E
Dealu Mare	130	Jb	47.27N	26.40 E
De'an	154	Cj	29.18N	115.45 E
Deán Funes	206	Hd	30.26 S	64.21W
Dearborn	184	Fd	42.18N	83.10W
Dearg, Beinn-	118	Id	57.48N	4.57W
Deary	188	Gc	46.52N	116.31W
Dease	180	Ee	59.55N	128.29W
Dease Arm	180	Fc	66.50N	120.00W
Dease Lake	176	Fd	58.35N	130.02W
Dease Strait	180	Gc	69.00N	107.00W

Index Symbols

[1] Independent Nation · [2] State, Region · [3] District, County · [4] Municipality · [5] Colony, Dependency · Continent · Physical Region · Historical or Cultural Region · Mount, Mountain · Volcano · Hill · Mountains, Mountain Range · Hills, Escarpment · Plateau, Upland · Pass, Gap · Plain, Lowland · Delta · Salt Flat · Valley, Canyon · Crater, Cave · Karst Features · Depression · Polder · Desert, Dunes · Forest, Woods · Heath, Steppe · Oasis · Cape, Point · Coast, Beach · Cliff · Peninsula · Isthmus · Sandbank · Island · Atoll · Rock, Reef · Islands, Archipelago · Rocks, Reefs · Coral Reef · Well, Spring · Geyser · River, Stream · Waterfall, Rapids · River Mouth, Estuary · Lake · Salt Lake · Intermittent Lake · Reservoir · Swamp, Pond · Canal · Glacier · Ice Shelf, Pack Ice · Ocean · Sea · Gulf, Bay · Strait, Fjord · Lagoon · Bank · Seamount · Tablemount · Ridge · Shelf · Basin · Escarpment, Sea Scarp · Fracture · Trench, Abyss · National Park, Reserve · Point of Interest · Recreation Site · Cave, Cavern · Historic Site · Ruins · Wall, Walls · Church, Abbey · Temple · Scientific Station · Railway station · Airport · Port · Military installation · Lighthouse · Mine · Tunnel · Dam, Bridge

Index Symbols

[1] Independent Nation	Historical or Cultural Region	Pass, Gap	Depression	Coast, Beach	Rock, Reef	Waterfall, Rapids
[2] State, Region	Mount, Mountain	Plain, Lowland	Polder	Cliff	Islands, Archipelago	River Mouth, Estuary
[3] District, County	Volcano	Delta	Desert, Dunes	Peninsula	Rocks, Reefs	Lake
[4] Municipality	Hill	Salt Flat	Forest, Woods	Isthmus	Coral Reef	Salt Lake
[5] Colony, Dependency	Mountains, Mountain Range	Valley, Canyon	Heath, Steppe	Sandbank	Well, Spring	Intermittent Lake
■ Continent	Hills, Escarpment	Crater, Cave	Oasis	Island	Geyser	Reservoir
▨ Physical Region	Plateau, Upland	Karst Features	Cape, Point		River, Stream	Swamp, Pond

Canal	Lagoon	Escarpment, Sea Scarp	Historic Site	Airport
Glacier	Bank	Fracture	Ruins	Port
Ice Shelf, Pack Ice	Seamount	Trench, Abyss	Wall, Walls	Military installation
Ocean	Tablemount	National Park, Reserve	Church, Abbey	Lighthouse
Sea	Ridge	Point of Interest	Temple	Mine
Gulf, Bay	Shelf	Recreation Site	Scientific Station	Tunnel
Strait, Fjord	Basin	Cave, Cavern	Railway station	Dam, Bridge

Dila 168 Fd 6.23N 38.19 E
Dilbeek 124 Gd 50.51N 4.16 E
Dili 142 Oj 8.33S 125.34 E
Di Linh 148 Lf 11.35N 108.04 E
Diližan 132 Ni 40.46N 44.55 E
Dilj 128 Me 45.16N 18.01 E
Dill 124 Kd 50.33N 8.29 E
Dillenburg 120 Ef 50.44N 8.17 E
Dillia 158 Ig 14.09N 12.50 E
Dilling 160 Jg 12.03N 29.39 E
Dillingen (Saar) 124 Ie 49.21N 6.44 E
Dillingham 176 Dd 59.02N 158.29W
Dillon [Mt.-U.S.] 182 Eb 45.13N 112.38W
Dillon [S.C.-U.S.] 184 Hh 34.25N 79.22W
Dilly 166 Dc 14.57N 7.43W
Dilolo 160 Jj 10.42S 22.20 E
Dilsen 124 Hc 51.02N 5.44 E
Dimashq=Damascus (EN) 142 Ff 33.30N 36.15 E
Dimbelenge 170 Dd 5.30S 23.53 E
Dimbokro 166 Ed 6.39N 4.42W
Dimbokro [3] 166 Ed 6.50N 4.45W
Dimboola 212 Ig 36.27S 142.02 E
Dîmboviţa [2] 130 Ie 44.55N 25.30 E
Dîmboviţa 130 Je 44.14N 26.27 E
Dîmbovnic 130 Ie 44.20N 25.40 E
Dimitrovgrad [Bul.] 130 Ig 42.03N 25.36 E
Dimitrovgrad [R.S.F.S.R.] 136 Ee 54.14N 49.42 E
Dimitrovgrad [Yugo.] 130 Fg 43.01N 22.47 E
Dimmitt 186 Ei 34.33N 102.19W
Dimona 146 Fg 31.04N 35.02 E
Dimovo 130 Ff 43.44N 22.44 E
Dinagat 150 Id 10.12N 125.35 E
Dinājpur 148 Hc 25.38N 88.38 E
Dinan 122 Df 48.27N 2.02W
Dinangourou 166 Ec 14.27N 2.14W
Dinant 122 Kd 50.16N 4.55 E
Dinar 146 Dc 38.04N 30.10 E
Dīnār, Kūh-e- 146 Ng 30.50N 51.35 E
Dinara 128 Kf 44.04N 16.23 E
Dinara=Dinaric Alps (EN) 110 Hg 43.50N 16.35 E
Dinard 122 Df 48.38N 2.04W
Dinaric Alps (EN)= Dinara 110 Hg 43.50N 16.35 E
Dindar, Nahr ad- 168 Ec 14.06N 33.40 E
Dinder 168 Ec 14.06N 33.40 E
Dindigul 148 Ff 10.21N 77.57 E
Dindima 166 Hc 10.14N 10.09 E
Dinga 170 Cd 5.19S 16.34 E
Dingbian 152 Id 37.35N 107.37 E
Dingden, Hamminkeln- 124 Ic 51.46N 6.37 E
Dinggyê 152 Ef 28.25N 87.45 E
Dinghai 152 Le 30.05N 122.07 E
Dingle 116 Df 58.32N 11.34 E
Dingle/An Daingean 118 Ci 52.08N 10.15W
Dingle Bay/Bá an Daingin 118 Ci 52.05N 10.15W
Dingolfing 120 Ih 48.38N 12.30 E
Dingshuzhen 154 Ei 31.16N 119.50 E
Dingtao 154 Cg 35.04N 115.35 E
Dinguiraye 166 Cc 11.18N 10.43W
Dingwall 118 Id 57.35N 4.26W
Dingxi 152 Hd 35.33N 104.32 E
Dingxian 152 Jd 39.29N 115.00 E
Dingxiang 154 Be 38.32N 112.59 E
Dingxing 154 Cd 39.11N 115.48 E
Dingyuan 154 Dh 32.32N 117.41 E
Dingzi Gang 154 Ff 36.33N 120.59 E
Dinh, Mui- 140 Mh 11.22N 109.01 E
Dinkel 124 Ib 52.30N 6.58 E
Dinosaur 186 Bf 40.15N 109.01W
Dinskaja 132 Kg 45.09N 39.12 E
Dinslaken 124 Ic 51.34N 6.44 E
Dinsōr 168 Ge 2.23N 42.58 E
Dintel 124 Gc 51.39N 4.24 E
Dinuba 188 Fh 36.36N 119.27W
Dinwiddie 184 Ig 37.05N 77.35W
Dioïla 166 Dc 12.28N 6.47W
Diois, Massif du- 122 Lj 44.35N 5.20 E
Diomede Islands 178 Fc 65.53N 169.00W
Dion 166 Dc 10.12N 8.39W
Diorama 202 Gc 16.21S 51.14W
Dios 219a Ba 5.33S 154.58 E
Diosig 130 Eb 47.18N 22.00 E
Dioura 166 Dc 14.51N 5.15W
Diourbel 166 Bc 14.40N 16.15W
Diourbel [3] 166 Bc 14.45N 16.10W
Dipkarpas 146 Fe 35.36N 34.23 E
Dipolog 142 Oi 8.35N 123.20 E
Dīr 148 Ea 35.12N 71.53 E
Dira, Djebel- 126 Ph 36.05N 3.38 E
Diré 166 Eb 16.15N 3.24W
Dire Dawa 160 Lh 9.35N 41.53 E
Diriamba 194 Dh 11.51N 86.14W
Dirico 170 Df 17.58S 20.45 E
Dirj 164 Bc 30.09N 10.26 E
Dirk Hartog Island 212 Ce 25.45S 113.00 E
Dirkou 166 Hb 19.01N 12.53 E
Dirranbandi 210 Fg 28.35S 148.14 E
Dirty Devil River 188 Jh 37.53N 110.24W
Disappointment, Cape- [B.A.T.] 206 Mh 54.53S 36.07W
Disappointment, Cape- [U.S.] 188 Cc 46.18N 124.03W
Disappointment, Lake- 208 Dg 23.30S 122.50 E
Discovery Tablemount (EN) 158 Hm 42.00S 0.10 E
Dishna 164 Fd 26.07N 32.28 E
Disko Bay (EN)=Disko Bugt 224 Nc 69.15N 52.30W
Disko Bugt=Disko Bay (EN) 224 Nc 69.15N 52.30W
Diskofjord 179 Ge 69.39N 53.45W
Disko Ø 224 Nc 69.50N 53.30W
Disna 114 Gi 55.33N 28.12 E
Disna 114 Gi 55.34N 28.12 E
Disnaj, ozero- / Dysnų ežeras 114 Gi 55.35N 26.32 E
Dispur 148 Ic 26.07N 91.48 E
Diss 124 Db 52.23N 1.07 E
District of Columbia, [2] 182 Ld 38.54N 77.01W
Distrito Federal [Braz.] [2] 202 Ig 15.45S 47.45W
Distrito Federal [Mex.] [2] 190 Ee 19.15N 99.10W
Disūq 146 Dg 31.08N 30.39 E
Dithmarschen 120 Fb 54.10N 9.15 E
Ditrău 130 Ic 46.49N 25.31 E
Dittaino 128 Im 37.25N 15.00 E
Diu 148 Ed 20.42N 70.59 E
Dīvāndarreh 146 Le 35.55N 47.02 E
Divénié 170 Bc 2.41S 12.05 E
Divenskaja 116 Ne 59.09N 30.09 E
Dives [Fr.] 122 Fg 47.11N 0.05W
Dives [Fr.] 122 Fe 49.19N 0.05W
Dives-sur-Mer 124 Be 49.17N 0.06W
Diviaka 130 Ci 41.00N 19.32 E
Diviči 132 Pi 42.10N 49.01 E
Divin 120 Ue 51.57N 24.09 E
Divinópolis 200 Lh 20.09S 44.54W
Divion 124 Ed 50.28N 2.30 E
Divisões ou de Santa Marta, Serra das- 202 Hg 16.40S 50.50W
Divisor, Sierra de- 202 Dh 8.00S 73.50W
Divnogorsk 138 Ee 55.58N 92.32 E
Divnoje 136 Ef 45.53N 43.22 E
Divo 166 Dd 5.50N 5.22W
Divo [3] 166 Dd 5.57N 5.15W
Divoká Orlice 120 Mf 50.09N 16.06 E
Divor 126 Df 38.59N 8.29W
Divriği 146 Hc 39.23N 38.07 E
Dīvrūd 146 Nd 36.52N 49.34 E
Dixmude/Diksmuide 122 Ic 51.02N 2.52 E
Dixon [Il.-U.S.] 186 Lf 41.50N 89.29W
Dixon [N.M.-U.S.] 186 Dh 36.11N 105.53W
Dixon Entrance 174 Fd 54.25N 132.30W
Diyālā [3] 146 Kf 34.00N 45.00 E
Diyālā 140 Gf 33.14N 44.31 E
Diyarbakir 144 Fb 37.55N 40.14 E
Dizy 124 Fe 49.04N 3.58 E
Dizy-le-Gros 124 Ge 49.38N 4.01 E
Dja 158 Ih 2.02N 15.12 E
Djado 160 If 21.01N 12.18 E
Djado, Plateau du- 160 If 21.45N 12.50 E
Djakarta → Jakarta 142 Mj 6.10S 106.46 E
Djakovo 120 Th 48.03N 23.01 E
Djamaa 162 Ic 33.32N 6.00 E
Djambala 166 Ii 2.33S 14.45 E
Djanet 160 Hf 24.34N 9.29 E
Djaret 162 Hd 26.35N 1.38 E
Djatkovo 136 De 53.36N 34.20 E
Djatlovo 132 Dc 53.31N 25.24 E
Djaul Island 214 Eh 2.56S 150.55 E
Djebel Ṭāriq, El Bōghāz-= Gibraltar, Strait of- (EN) 110 Fh 35.57N 5.36W
Djédaa 168 Bc 13.31N 18.34 E
Djedi 158 He 34.39N 5.55 E
Djedoug, Djebel- 126 Qi 35.53N 4.20 E
Djelfa 160 He 34.40N 3.15 E
Djelfa [3] 162 Hc 34.15N 3.30 E
Djéma 160 Jh 6.03N 25.19 E
Djember 168 Bc 10.25N 17.50 E
Djemila 162 Ib 36.19N 5.44 E
Djenane 126 Pi 35.43N 3.59 E
Djenné 166 Ec 13.55N 4.33W
Djerem 166 Hd 5.20N 13.24 E
Dji 168 Cd 6.47N 22.14 E
Djibo 166 Ec 14.06N 1.38W
Djibouti 160 Lg 11.35N 43.08 E
Djibouti (Afars and Issas) [1] 160 Lg 11.30N 43.00 E
Djokupunda 170 Dd 5.27S 20.58 E
Djolu 170 Dh 0.37N 22.21 E
Djoua 170 Bb 1.13N 13.12 E
Djougou 166 Fd 9.42N 1.40 E
Djoum 166 He 2.40N 12.40 E
Djourab, Erg du- 168 Bb 16.40N 18.50 E
Djugu 170 Fb 1.55N 30.30 E
Djultydag, gora- 132 Oi 41.58N 46.56 E
Djup 116 Bd 60.50N 8.00 E
Djúpi vogur 114a Cb 64.39N 14.17W
Djurbeldžin 135 Jd 41.10N 74.59 E
Djurdjura, Djebel- 126 Qh 36.27N 4.15 E
Djurmo 116 Fd 60.33N 15.10 E
Djurö 116 Ef 58.50N 13.30 E
Djursholm 116 Hc 59.24N 18.05 E
Djursland 116 Dh 56.20N 10.45 E
Djurtjuli 136 Fd 55.29N 54.55 E
Dmitrija Lapteva, proliv- = Dmitri Laptev Strait (EN) 140 Qb 73.00N 142.00 E
Dmitrijev-Lgovski 132 Ic 52.08N 35.05 E
Dmitri Laptev Strait (EN) = Dmitrija Lapteva, proliv- 140 Qb 73.00N 142.00 E
Dmitrov 114 Ih 56.26N 37.31 E
Dmitrovsk-Orlovski 132 Ic 52.31N 35.09 E
Dnepr 110 Jf 46.30N 32.18 E
Dneprodzeržinsk 136 Df 48.30N 34.37 E
Dneprodzeržinskoje vodohranilišče 132 Ie 48.45N 34.10 E
Dnepropetrovsk 112 Jf 48.27N 34.59 E
Dnepropetrovskaja oblast [3] 136 Df 48.15N 35.00 E
Dneprorudnoje 132 If 47.23N 35.01 E
Dneprovski liman 132 Gf 46.35N 31.55 E
Dneprovsko-Bugski kanal 132 Dc 52.03N 25.10 E
Dnepr Upland (EN) = Pridneprovskaja vozvyšennost 110 Jf 49.00N 32.00 E
Dnestr 110 Jf 46.18N 30.17 E
Dnestrovsk 130 Mc 46.39N 29.48 E
Dnestrovski liman 132 Gf 46.15N 30.15 E
Dno 136 Cd 57.49N 29.59 E
Doany 172 Hb 14.22S 49.30 E
Doba 168 Bd 8.39N 16.51 E
Dobbiaco / Toblach 128 Gd 46.44N 12.14 E
Dobele 114 Fh 56.39N 23.16 E
Döbeln 120 Je 51.07N 13.07 E
Doberai, Jazirah- 150 Jg 1.30S 132.30 E
Dobo 150 Jh 5.46S 134.13 E
Doboj 128 Mf 44.44N 18.05 E
Dobra 120 Oe 51.54N 18.37 E
Dobre Miasto 120 Qc 53.59N 20.25 E
Dobreta Turnu Severin 112 Ig 44.38N 22.40 E
Dobrinka 132 Lc 52.08N 40.29 E
Dobříš 120 Kg 49.47N 14.10 E
Dobrjanka 136 Fd 58.29N 56.29 E
Dobrodzień 120 Of 50.44N 18.27 E
Dobrogea = Dobruja (EN) 110 Ig 44.00N 28.00 E
Dobrogea=Dobruja (EN) 130 Ke 44.00N 28.00 E
Dobrogean, Masivul- 130 Ke 44.50N 28.30 E
Dobromil 120 Sg 49.34N 22.49 E
Dobropolje 132 Je 48.28N 37.02 E
Dobroteşti 130 He 44.17N 24.53 E
Dobrotvor 120 Uf 50.10N 24.27 E
Dobrudžansko Plato 130 Kf 43.32N 27.50 E
Dobruja (EN) = Dobrogea 110 Ig 44.00N 28.00 E
Dobruja (EN)=Dobrogea 130 Ke 44.00N 28.00 E
Dobruš 132 Gc 52.26N 31.19 E
Dobruška 120 Mf 50.18N 16.10 E
Dobrzyń nad Wisłą 120 Pd 52.38N 19.20 E
Dobrzyńskie, Pojezierze- 120 Pc 53.00N 19.20 E
Dobšiná 120 Qh 48.49N 20.22 E
Doce, Rio- [Braz.] 204 Gd 18.28S 51.05W
Doce, Rio- [Braz.] 198 Mg 19.37S 39.49W
Doce Leguas, Cayos de las- 194 Hc 20.55N 79.05W
Doce Leguas, Laberinto de las- 194 Hc 20.39N 78.35W
Docker River 212 Fd 24.58S 129.03 E
Docksta 116 Ha 63.03N 18.20 E
Doctor Arroyo 192 If 23.40N 100.11W
Doctor Cecilio Báez 204 Dg 25.03S 56.19W
Doctor Pedro P. Peña 206 Hb 22.26S 62.22W
Doctor Petru Groza 130 Fc 46.37N 22.25 E
Doda 148 Fb 33.08N 75.34 E
Doda Betta 148 Ff 11.24N 76.44 E
Dodecanese (EN) = Dhodhekánisos 130 Jm 36.20N 27.00 E
Dodecanese (EN) = Nótioi Sporádhes 110 Ih 36.00N 27.00 E
Dodge City 182 Gd 37.45N 100.00W
Dodgeville 186 Ke 42.58N 90.08W
Dodman Point 118 Ik 50.13N 4.48W
Dodoma 160 Ki 6.11S 35.45 E
Dodoma [3] 170 Gd 6.00S 36.00 E
Dodona (EN) = Dhodhóni 130 Dj 39.33N 20.46 E
Dodurga 130 Mj 39.48N 29.55 E
Doesburg 124 Ib 52.01N 6.08 E
Doetinchem 122 Mc 51.58N 6.17 E
Dofa 150 Ig 1.47S 125.22 E
Dogai Coring 152 Ee 34.30N 89.10 E
Doğanbey 130 Jk 38.04N 26.53 E
Doğanşehir 146 Gc 38.06N 37.53 E
Dog Creek 188 Da 51.35N 122.15W
Dogger Bank 110 Ge 55.00N 3.00 E
Dog Island 196 Ec 18.15N 63.13W
Dog Lake [Man.-Can.] 186 Ga 51.02N 98.30W
Dog Lake [Ont.-Can.] 186 Lb 48.46N 89.32W
Dog Lake [Ont.-Can.] 184 Ea 48.18N 84.10W
Dogliani 128 Bf 44.32N 7.56 E
Dōgo 154 Lf 36.15N 133.17 E
Dogonbadān 144 Hc 30.21N 50.48 E
Dogondoutchi 166 Fc 13.38N 4.02 E
Dōgo-San 156 Cd 35.04N 133.14 E
Dog Rocks 194 Ha 24.05N 79.51W
Doğubayazıt 146 Kc 39.32N 44.08 E
Doğu Karadeniz Dağları 144 Ea 40.40N 40.00 E
Dogwood Point 197c Ab 17.06N 62.38W
Doha (EN)=Ad Dawḥah 142 Hg 25.17N 51.32 E
Dohad 148 Ed 22.50N 74.16 E
Dohāzāri 148 Id 22.10N 92.04 E
Doi Luang Chinag Dao 148 Je 19.23N 98.54 E
Doilungdêqên 152 Ff 29.47N 90.49 E
Doire Baltée/Dora Baltea 128 Ce 45.11N 8.03 E
Doische 124 Gd 50.08N 4.45 E
Dojransko jezero 130 Fh 41.13N 22.44 E
Doka 168 Fc 13.31N 35.46 E
Dokhara, Dunes de- 162 Ic 32.50N 6.00 E
Dokka 114 Cf 60.50N 10.05 E
Dokka 116 Dd 60.49N 10.05 E
Dokkum 122 La 53.19N 6.00 E
Dokšicy 114 Gi 54.56N 27.46 E
Doksy 120 Kf 50.34N 14.40 E
Dokučajevsk 132 Jf 47.43N 37.47 E
Dolak, Pulau- 208 Ee 7.50S 138.30 E
Dolbeau 180 Kg 48.52N 72.14W
Dol-de-Bretagne 122 Ef 48.33N 1.45W
Dôle 122 Lg 47.06N 5.30 E
Doleib Hill 168 Ed 9.22N 31.36 E
Dolenjsko 128 Je 45.50N 15.10 E
Dolgaja, kosa- 132 Jf 46.40N 37.45 E
Dolgellau 118 Ji 52.44N 3.53W
Dolgi, ostrov- 134 Ib 69.15N 59.05 E
Dolgi Most 138 Ee 56.45N 96.58 E
Dolianova 128 Dk 39.22N 9.10 E
Dolina 132 De 48.58N 24.01 E
Dolinsk 138 Jg 47.20N 142.50 E
Dolinskaja 136 Df 48.07N 32.44 E
Dolinskoje 130 Mb 47.33N 29.50 E
Dolj [2] 130 Ge 44.10N 23.40 E
Dollart 122 Na 53.17N 7.10 E
Dolly Cays 194 Ib 23.39N 77.22W
Dolni Dăbnik 130 Hf 43.24N 24.26 E
Dolní Dvořiště 120 Kh 48.39N 14.27 E
Dolnomoravský úval 120 Nh 49.00N 17.15 E
Dolnośląskie, Bory- 120 Le 51.25N 15.20 E
Dolný Kubín 120 Pg 49.12N 19.17 E
Dolo 160 Lh 4.11N 42.05 E
Dolomiten/Dolomiti = Dolomites (EN) 110 Hf 46.23N 11.51 E
Dolomites (EN) = Dolomiten/Dolomiti 110 Hf 46.23N 11.51 E
Dolomites (EN) = Dolomiti/Dolomiten 110 Hf 46.23N 11.51 E
Dolomiti/Dolomiten = Dolomites (EN) 110 Hf 46.23N 11.51 E
Dolon, pereval- 135 Jd 41.48N 75.45 E
Dolonnur/Duolun 152 Kc 42.10N 116.30 E
Dolores [Arg.] 206 Ie 36.20S 57.40W
Dolores [Guat.] 194 Ce 16.31N 89.25W
Dolores [Ur.] 206 Id 33.33S 58.13W
Dolores Hidalgo 192 Ig 21.10N 100.56W
Dolores River 188 Kg 38.49N 109.17W
Dolphin, Cape- 206 Ih 51.15S 58.58W
Dolphin and Union Strait 180 Gc 69.00N 115.00W
Dom, Kūh-e- 146 Of 33.52N 53.00 E
Domačevo 120 Te 51.46N 23.37 E
Domaniç 146 Cc 39.48N 29.37 E
Domantai/Domantaj 116 Ji 55.57N 23.19 E
Domantaj/Domantai 116 Ji 55.57N 23.19 E
Domart-en-Ponthieu 124 Ed 50.04N 2.07 E
Domaša, údolná nadrž- 120 Rg 49.05N 21.47 E
Domažlice 120 Ig 49.27N 12.56 E
Dombaj-Ulgen, gora- 132 Lh 43.14N 41.46 E
Dombarovski 136 Fe 50.47N 59.34 E
Dombås 112 Kc 62.05N 9.08 E
Dombe Grande 170 Be 12.56S 13.07 E
Dombes 122 Lh 46.00N 5.03 E
Dombóvár 120 Oj 46.23N 18.07 E
Dombrád 120 Rh 48.14N 21.56 E
Domburg 124 Fc 51.34N 3.30 E
Dôme, Monts- 122 Ii 45.45N 2.55 E
Dôme, Puy de- 122 Ii 45.47N 2.58 E
Domérat 122 Ih 46.21N 2.32 E
Domeyko, Cordillera- 198 Jh 24.30S 69.00W
Domfront 122 Ff 48.36N 0.39W
Domingo M. Irala 204 Eg 25.54S 54.43W
Domingos Martins 202 Jh 20.22S 40.40W
Dominica [1] 176 Mh 15.30N 61.20W
Dominica 174 Mh 15.30N 61.20W
Dominical 194 Fi 9.13N 83.51W
Dominicana, República- = Dominican Republic (EN) [1] 176 Lh 19.00N 70.40W
Dominican Republic (EN) = Dominicana, República- [1] 176 Lh 19.00N 70.40W
Dominica Passage 196 Fe 15.10N 61.15W
Dominica Passage (EN) = Dominique, Canal de la- 196 Fe 15.10N 61.15W
Dominion, Cape- 180 Kc 66.10N 74.30W
Dominique, Canal de la- = Dominica Passage (EN) 196 Fe 15.10N 61.15W
Domino 180 Lf 53.28N 55.46W
Domiongo 170 Dc 4.37S 21.15 E
Dommartin-Varimont 124 Gf 48.59N 4.46 E
Domme 122 Hj 44.48N 1.13 E
Dommel 124 Lc 51.40N 5.20 E
Domneşti 130 Hd 45.12N 24.50 E
Domo 168 Hd 7.57N 46.51 E
Domodedovo 114 Ii 55.27N 37.47 E
Domodossola 128 Cd 46.07N 8.17 E
Domont 124 Ee 49.02N 2.20 E
Dom Pedrito 206 Jd 30.59S 54.40W
Dom Pedro 202 Jd 5.00S 44.27W
Dompierre-sur-Besbre 122 Jh 46.31N 3.41 E
Dompu 150 Gh 8.32S 118.28 E
Domusnovas 128 Ck 39.19N 8.39 E
Domuyo, Volcán- 198 Ii 36.38S 70.26W
Don 192 Ed 26.26N 109.02W
Don [Eng.-U.K.] 118 Mh 53.39N 0.59W
Don [Fr.] 122 Eg 47.40N 1.56W
Don [R.S.F.S.R.] 110 Jf 47.04N 39.18 E
Don [Scot.-U.K.] 118 Kd 57.10N 2.04W
Donaldsonville 186 Kk 30.06N 90.59W
Donau=Danube (EN) 110 If 45.20N 29.40 E
Donaueschingen 120 Ei 47.57N 8.30 E
Donaumoos 120 Hh 48.40N 11.15 E
Donauried 120 Gh 48.35N 10.40 E
Donauwörth 120 Gh 48.42N 10.48 E
Don Benito 126 Gf 38.57N 5.52W
Doncaster 118 Lh 53.32N 1.07W
Dondjušany 130 Ka 48.11N 27.31 E
Dondo [Ang.] 160 Ii 9.40S 14.26 E
Dondo [Moz.] 172 Ec 19.36S 34.44 E
Dondra Head 140 Ki 5.55N 80.35 E
Donec 110 Kf 47.40N 40.50 E
Doneck [R.S.F.S.R.] 132 Ke 48.21N 39.59 E
Doneck [Ukr.-U.S.S.R.] 112 Jf 48.00N 37.48 E
Doneckaja oblast [3] 136 Df 48.00N 37.45 E
Donecki krjaž = Donec Ridge (EN) 110 Jf 48.15N 38.45 E
Donec Ridge (EN) = Donecki krjaž 110 Jf 48.15N 38.45 E
Donegal/Dún na nGall 118 Eg 54.39N 8.06W
Donegal/Dún na nGall [2] 118 Fg 54.50N 8.00W
Donegal Bay/Bá Dhún na nGall 110 Fe 54.30N 8.30W
Donegal Mountains 118 Eg 54.50N 8.10W
Donga 166 Hd 8.19N 10.01 E
Dongara 212 Ce 29.15S 114.56 E
Dongbei Pingyuan 154 Gc 44.00N 124.00 E
Dongchuan (Tangdan) 152 Hf 26.07N 103.05 E
Dongcun → Lanxian 154 Ae 38.17N 111.38 E
Dong Dao 150 Fc 16.45N 113.00 E
Donge 124 Gc 51.41N 4.49 E
Dong'e (Tongcheng) 154 Df 36.19N 116.14 E
Dongen 124 Gc 51.37N 4.57 E
Donges 122 Dg 47.18N 2.04W
Dongfang (Basuo) 154 Ih 19.14N 108.39 E
Dongfanghong 154 La 46.15N 133.07 E
Dongfeng 154 Hc 42.41N 125.33 E
Donggala 150 Gg 0.40S 119.44 E
Donggou 152 Ld 39.55N 124.08 E
Dongguang 154 Df 37.54N 116.32 E
Dong Hai = East China Sea (EN) 140 Og 29.00N 125.00 E
Donghai Dao 152 Jg 21.00N 110.25 E
Dong He 152 Hc 42.12N 101.10 E
Dong Hoi 148 Le 17.29N 106.36 E
Dong Jiang 140 Ng 23.02N 113.31 E
Dongkala 150 Hh 5.18S 122.03 E
Dongkan → Binhai 152 Ke 34.00N 119.52 E
Donglan 152 Ig 24.35N 107.22 E
Dongliao He 154 Gc 43.24N 123.42 E
Dongming 154 Cg 35.17N 115.04 E
Dongnan Qiuling 152 Jg 24.00N 113.00 E
Dongning 152 Nc 44.02N 131.06 E
Dongo 170 Ce 14.36S 15.43 E
Dongola (EN)=Dunqulah 160 Kg 19.10N 30.29 E
Dongou 170 Cb 2.02N 18.04 E
Dongoun → Haiyang 154 Ff 36.46N 121.09 E
Dongping 152 Kd 35.51N 116.15 E
Dongping → Anhua 152 Jf 28.27N 111.15 E
Dong Rak, Phanom- = Dangrek Range (EN) 140 Mh 14.25N 104.30 E
Dongsha Dao 152 Kg 20.45N 116.45 E
Dongsha Qundao 140 Ng 20.42N 116.43 E
Dongsheng 152 Id 39.48N 110.00 E
Dongtai 152 Le 32.47N 120.18 E
Dong Taijnar Hu 152 Fd 37.25N 94.00 E
Dongting Hu 140 Ng 29.18N 112.45 E
Dong Ujimqin Qi (Uliastai) 152 Kc 45.31N 116.58 E
Dongwe 170 De 13.56S 23.53 E
Dongxiang 152 Kf 28.15N 116.38 E
Dongyang 154 Fj 29.16N 120.14 E
Dongying 152 Kd 37.30N 118.30 E
Dongzhi (Yaodu) 154 Di 30.06N 117.01 E
Donington 124 Bb 52.54N 0.12W
Doniphan 186 Kh 36.37N 90.50W
Donja Brela 128 Kg 43.23N 16.55 E
Donji Miholjac 128 Me 45.45N 18.10 E
Donji Vakuf 128 Lf 44.08N 17.24 E
Donjon, Le- 122 Jh 46.21N 3.48 E
Dønna 114 Cc 66.06N 12.35 E
Donnacona 184 Lb 46.40N 71.47W
Donner Pass 182 Cd 39.19N 120.20W
Donnersberg 124 Je 49.38N 7.55 E
Donner und Blitzen River 188 Fe 43.17N 118.49W
Donnybrook 212 Df 33.35S 115.49 E
Donostia / San Sebastián 112 Fg 43.19N 1.59W
Donskaja grjada = Don Upland (EN) 110 Kf 49.10N 42.00 E
Donskoj 132 Kb 54.01N 38.20 E
Don Upland (EN) = Donskaja grjada 110 Kf 49.10N 42.00 E
Donuzlav, ozero- 132 Hg 45.25N 33.10 E
Doolette Bay 222 Je 67.55S 147.00 E
Doon 118 If 55.26N 4.38W
Doonerak, Mount- 178 Ic 67.56N 150.37W
Doorn 124 Hb 52.02N 5.19 E
Doornik/Tournai 122 Jd 50.36N 3.23 E
Door Peninsula 186 Md 44.55N 87.20W
Do Qu 152 He 31.48N 102.09 E
Dora, Lake- 212 Ed 22.05S 122.56 E
Dora Baltea/Doire Baltée 128 Ce 45.11N 8.03 E
Dorada, Costa- / Daurada, Costa- 126 Nc 41.08N 1.10 E
Dora Riparia 128 Be 45.05N 7.44 E
Dorat, Le- 122 Hh 46.13N 1.05 E
Dorbiljin/Emin 152 Db 46.32N 83.39 E
Dorchester 118 Kk 50.43N 2.26W
Dorchester, Cape - 180 Jc 65.28N 77.30W
Dordabis 172 Bd 22.52S 17.38 E
Dordogne [3] 122 Gi 45.10N 0.50 E
Dordogne 110 Ff 45.02N 0.35W
Dordrecht [Neth.] 122 Kc 51.49N 4.40 E
Dordrecht [S.Afr.] 172 Df 31.20S 27.03 E
Dore 122 Ji 46.00N 3.28 E
Dore, Monts- 110 Gf 45.30N 2.45 E
Doré Lake 180 Gf 54.45N 107.20W
Dores do Indaiá 202 Ig 19.27S 45.36W
Dorgali 128 Dj 40.17N 9.35 E
Dori 160 Gg 14.02N 0.02W
Doring 158 Il 31.52S 18.39 E
Dorking 124 Bc 51.13N 0.20W
Dormagen 124 Ic 51.06N 6.50 E
Dormans 122 Je 49.04N 3.38 E
Dormidontovka 138 Ig 47.45N 134.58 E
Dornbirn 128 Dc 47.25N 9.44 E
Dornoch 118 Id 57.52N 4.02W
Dornoch Firth 118 Id 57.52N 4.02W
Doro 166 Eb 16.09N 0.51W
Dorog 120 Oi 47.43N 18.44 E
Dorogobuž 132 Hb 54.56N 33.15 E
Dorohoi 130 Jb 47.57N 26.24 E
Dorotea 114 Dd 64.16N 16.24 E
Dorre Island 212 Ce 25.10S 113.05 E
Dorrigo 212 Kf 30.20S 152.45 E
Dorset [3] 118 Kk 50.50N 2.10W
Dorset 118 Kk 50.55N 2.15W
Dorsten 120 Ce 51.40N 6.58 E
Dortmund 118 Ge 51.31N 7.27 E
Dortmund-Ems-Kanal 120 De 51.42N 7.27 E
Dörtyol 146 Gd 36.52N 36.12 E
Do Rūd 144 Gc 33.28N 49.04 E
Doruma 170 Eb 4.44N 27.42 E
Dörverden 124 Lb 52.51N 9.14 E
Doséo, Bahr- 168 Bd 9.01N 19.38 E
Dos Hermanas 126 Gg 37.17N 5.55W
Dos Lagunas 194 Ce 17.42N 89.36W
Dospat 130 Hh 41.39N 24.10 E
Dospat 130 Hh 41.23N 24.05 E
Dos Picachos, Cerro- 192 Bc 29.25N 114.10W
Dosse 120 Ic 53.13N 12.20 E
Dosso 160 Hg 13.03N 3.12 E
Dosso [2] 166 Fc 13.30N 3.30 E
Dossor 136 Ff 47.32N 53.01 E
Dostluk 135 Ef 37.45N 65.22 E
Dothan 182 Je 31.13N 85.24W
Dotnuva 116 Ji 55.18N 23.55 E
Douai 122 Jd 50.22N 3.04 E
Douala 160 Hh 4.03N 9.42 E
Douaouir 166 Ea 20.45N 2.30W
Douarnenez 122 Bf 48.06N 4.20W
Douarnenez, Baie de- 122 Bf 48.10N 4.25W
Double Mountain Fork Brazos 186 Gj 33.15N 100.00W
Doubrava 120 Lf 50.03N 15.20 E

Index Symbols

[1] Independent Nation
[2] State, Region
[3] District, County
[4] Municipality
[5] Colony, Dependency
Continent
Physical Region
Historical or Cultural Region
Mount, Mountain
Volcano
Hill
Mountains, Mountain Range
Hills, Escarpment
Plateau, Upland
Pass, Gap
Plain, Lowland
Delta
Salt Flat
Valley, Canyon
Crater, Cave
Karst Features
Depression
Polder
Desert, Dunes
Forest, Woods
Heath, Steppe
Oasis
Cape, Point
Coast, Beach
Cliff
Peninsula
Isthmus
Sandbank
Island
Atoll
Rock, Reef
Islands, Archipelago
Rocks, Reefs
Coral Reef
Well, Spring
Geyser
River, Stream
Waterfall, Rapids
River Mouth, Estuary
Lake
Salt Lake
Intermittent Lake
Reservoir
Swamp, Pond
Canal
Glacier
Ice Shelf, Pack Ice
Ocean
Sea
Gulf, Bay
Strait, Fjord
Lagoon
Bank
Seamount
Tablemount
Ridge
Shelf
Basin
Escarpment, Sea Scarp
Fracture
Trench, Abyss
National Park, Reserve
Point of Interest
Recreation Site
Cave, Cavern
Historic Site
Ruins
Wall, Walls
Church, Abbey
Temple
Scientific Station
Railway station
Airport
Port
Military installation
Lighthouse
Mine
Tunnel
Dam, Bridge

Doubs [3] 122 Mg 47.10N 6.25 E
Doubs 122 Lh 46.54N 5.02 E
Doubtful Sound 218 Bf 45.15S 166.50 E
Doubtless Bay 218 Ea 34.55S 173.25 E
Douchy-les-Mines 124 Fd 50.18N 3.23 E
Doudeville 124 Ce 49.43N 0.48 E
Doué-la-Fontaine 122 Fg 47.12N 0.17W
Douentza 166 Eb 15.03N 2.57W
Douera 126 Oh 36.40N 2.57 E
Dougga 162 Ib 36.24N 9.13 E
Douglas [Ak.-U.S.] 178 Me 58.16N 134.26W
Douglas [Az.-U.S.] 182 Fe 31.21N 109.33W
Douglas [Ga.-U.S.] 184 Fj 31.31N 82.51W
Douglas [I. of M.] 118 Ig 54.09N 4.28W
Douglas [S.Afr.] 172 Ce 29.04S 23.46 E
Douglas [Wy.-U.S.] 182 Fc 42.45N 105.24W
Douglas Lake 184 Fh 36.00N 83.22W
Douglas Range 222 Qf 70.00S 69.35W
Doullens 122 Id 50.09N 2.21 E
Doumé 166 He 4.14N 13.27 E
Douna 166 Ec 14.39N 1.43W
Doupovské hory 120 Jf 50.13N 13.08 E
Dour 124 Fd 50.24N 3.47 E
Dourada, Serra- [Braz.] 204 Gb 16.00S 50.05W
Dourada, Serra- [Braz.] 204 Ha 13.10S 48.45W
Dourados 200 Kh 22.13S 54.48W
Dourados, Rio- [Braz.] 204 Ee 21.58S 54.18W
Dourados, Rio- [Braz.] 204 Id 18.17S 47.36W
Dourbali 168 Bc 11.49N 15.52 E
Dourdan 122 If 48.32N 2.01 E
Douro 110 Fg 41.08N 8.40W
Douro Litoral 126 Dc 41.05N 8.20W
Doushi → Gong'an 152 Je 30.05N 112.12 E
Douve 122 Ee 49.19N 1.44W
Douvres-la-Delivrande 124 Be 49.17N 0.23W
Douze 122 Fk 43.54N 0.30W
Douzy 124 He 49.40N 5.03 E
Dove 118 Li 52.50N 1.35W
Dove Bugt 179 Jc 76.25N 21.00W
Dove Creek 186 Bh 37.46N 108.54W
Dover [De.-U.S.] 176 Lf 39.10N 75.32W
Dover [Eng.-U.K.] 112 Ge 51.08N 1.19 E
Dover [N.H.-U.S.] 184 Ld 43.12N 70.55W
Dover [Oh.-U.S.] 184 Ge 40.32N 81.30W
Dover, Strait of- 110 Ge 51.00N 1.30 E
Dover, Strait of- (EN) = Calais, Pas de- 110 Ge 51.00N 1.30 E
Dover Foxcroft 184 Mc 45.11N 69.13W
Dovey 118 Ji 52.34N 3.59W
Dovre 116 Cc 61.59N 9.15 E
Dovrefjell 110 Gc 62.10N 9.25 E
Dowa 170 Fe 13.39S 33.56 E
Dowagiac 184 De 41.59N 86.06W
Dowlatābād 146 Qh 28.20N 57.13 E
Downey 188 Ie 42.26N 112.07W
Downham Market 124 Cb 52.36N 0.22 E
Downieville 188 Eg 39.34N 120.50W
Downpatrick/Dún Pádraig 118 Hg 54.20N 5.43W
Dow Sar 146 Me 35.06N 48.02 E
Dōzen 156 Cc 36.05N 132.59 E
Dozois, Reservoir- 184 Ib 47.30N 77.00W
Dozulé 124 Be 49.14N 0.03W
Drâa 158 Ff 28.40N 11.07W
Drâa, Cap- 162 Ed 28.44N 11.05W
Drâa, Hamada du- 158 Gf 28.30N 7.30W
Draâ Ben Khedda 126 Ph 36.44N 3.57 E
Draa el Baguel 162 Ic 30.17N 6.25 E
Draa el Mizan 126 Ph 36.32N 3.50 E
Drac 122 Li 45.13N 5.41 E
Drac, Cuevas del- 126 Pe 39.32N 3.15 E
Dracena 204 Ge 21.32S 51.29W
Dragalina 130 Ke 44.26N 27.19 E
Dragan 114 Dd 64.00N 15.21 E
Drăgănești-Olt 130 He 44.09N 24.42 E
Drăgănești-Vlașca 130 Ie 44.06N 25.36 E
Drăgășani 130 He 44.39N 24.16 E
Dragobia 130 Cg 42.26N 19.59 E
Dragón, Bocas del-/ Dragon's Mouths 202 Fa 10.45N 61.46W
Dragonera, Isla- / Sa Dragonera, Illa- 126 Oe 39.35N 2.19 E
Dragon's Mouths/Dragón, Bocas del- 202 Fa 10.45N 61.46W
Dragør 116 Ei 55.36N 12.41 E
Draguignan 122 Mk 43.32N 6.28 E
Drahanská vrchovina 120 Mg 49.30N 16.45 E
Drain 188 De 43.40N 123.19W
Drake 186 Fc 47.55N 100.23W
Drake, Paso- = Drake Passage (EN) 198 Jk 58.00S 70.00W
Drakensberg 158 Jk 29.00S 29.00 E
Drake Passage (EN) = Drake, Paso- 198 Jk 58.00S 70.00W
Dráma 130 Hh 41.09N 24.09 E
Drammen 112 Hd 59.44N 10.15 E
Dramselva 116 De 59.44N 10.14 E
Drangajökull 114a Aa 66.09N 22.15W
Dranse 122 Mh 46.24N 6.30 E
Drau = Drava (EN) 110 Hf 45.33N 18.55 E
Drava 110 Hf 45.33N 18.55 E
Dráva = Drava (EN) 110 Hf 45.33N 18.55 E
Drava (EN) = Drau 110 Hf 45.33N 18.55 E
Drava (EN) = Dráva 110 Hf 45.33N 18.55 E
Dravograd 128 Jd 46.35N 15.01 E
Drawa 120 Ld 52.52N 15.59 E
Drawno 120 Lc 53.13N 15.45 E
Drawsko, Jezioro- 120 Mc 53.33N 16.10 E
Drawsko Pomorskie 120 Lc 53.32N 15.48 E
Drayton Valley 180 Gf 53.13N 115.00W
Drean 128 Bn 36.41N 7.45 E
Dreieich 124 Ke 50.01N 8.43 E
Drenovci 128 Mf 44.55N 18.55 E
Drenthe [3] 124 Ib 52.45N 6.30 E
Dresden 112 He 51.03N 13.45 E
Dreux 122 Hf 48.44N 1.22 E
Drevsjø 114 Cf 61.54N 12.02 E
Drezdenko 120 Ld 52.51N 15.50 E
Dricēni/Driceni 116 Lh 56.39N 27.11 E
Driceni/Dricēni 116 Lh 56.39N 27.11 E
Driffield 118 Mg 54.01N 0.26W
Driggs 188 Je 43.44N 111.14W
Drina 110 Hg 44.53N 19.21 E
Drincea 130 Fe 44.07N 22.59 E
Drin Gulf (EN) = Drinit, Gjiri i- 130 Ch 41.45N 19.28 E
Drini 110 Hg 41.45N 19.34 E
Drini i Zi 130 Dg 42.05N 20.23 E
Drinit, Gjiri i- = Drin Gulf (EN) 130 Ch 41.45N 19.28 E
Drinjača 128 Nf 44.17N 19.10 E
Drinosi 130 Di 40.17N 20.02 E
Drissa 114 Gi 55.47N 27.57 E
Drisvjaty, ozero- / Drūkšiu ežeras 116 Li 55.37N 26.45 E
Driva 116 Cb 62.40N 8.34 E
Drjanovo 130 Ig 42.58N 25.28 E
Drniš 128 Kg 43.52N 16.09 E
Drøbak 114 Cg 59.39N 10.39 E
Drocea, Vîrful- 130 Fc 46.12N 22.14 E
Drogheda/Droichead Átha 118 Gh 53.43N 6.21W
Drogičin 132 Dc 52.13N 25.10 E
Drogobyč 132 Ce 49.22N 23.33 E
Drohiczyn 120 Sd 52.24N 22.41 E
Droichead Átha/Drogheda 118 Gh 53.43N 6.21W
Droichead na Bandan/ Bandon 118 Ej 51.45N 8.45W
Droichead na Banna/ Banbridge 118 Gg 54.21N 6.16W
Drokija 132 Ee 48.01N 27.53 E
Drôme [3] 122 Lj 44.35N 5.10 E
Drôme 124 Be 49.19N 0.45W
Drömling 120 Hd 52.29N 11.04 E
Dronero 128 Bf 44.28N 7.22 E
Dronne 122 Fi 45.02N 0.09W
Dronning Fabiolafjella 222 Df 71.30S 35.40 E
Dronning Louise Land 179 Jc 76.45N 24.00W
Dronten 122 Lb 52.31N 5.42 E
Dropt 122 Fj 44.35N 0.06W
Drovjanoj 138 Cb 72.25N 72.45 E
Drowning River 186 Na 50.55N 84.35W
Druja 114 Gi 55.47N 27.29 E
Drūkšiu ežeras / Drisvjaty, ozero- 116 Li 55.37N 26.45 E
Druk-Yul → Bhutan [1] 142 Lg 27.30N 90.30 E
Drulingen 124 Jf 48.52N 7.11 E
Drumheller 180 Gf 51.28N 112.42W
Drummond [Mt.-U.S.] 188 Ic 46.40N 113.09W
Drummond [Wi.-U.S.] 186 Kc 46.20N 91.15W
Drummond Island 184 Fb 46.00N 83.40W
Drummond Range 212 Jd 23.30S 147.15 E
Drummondville 180 Kg 45.50N 72.20W
Drummore 118 Ig 54.42N 4.54W
Drumochter, Pass of- 118 Ie 56.50N 4.12W
Drunen 124 Hc 51.41N 5.10 E
Druskininkai/Druskininkaj 114 Fi 54.04N 24.06 E
Druskininkaj/Druskininkai 114 Fi 54.04N 24.06 E
Drut 132 Gc 53.04N 30.35 E
Druten 124 Hc 51.54N 5.38 E
Družba [Kaz.-U.S.S.R.] 136 If 45.18N 82.29 E
Družba [Ukr.-U.S.S.R.] 132 Hc 52.02N 33.59 E
Družkovka 132 Je 48.36N 37.33 E
Družnaja Gorka 116 Ne 59.11N 30.10 E
Družnino 134 Ih 56.48N 59.29 E
Družno, Jezioro- 120 Pb 54.08N 19.30 E
Drvar 128 Kf 44.22N 16.23 E
Drvenik 128 Lg 43.09N 17.15 E
Drwęca 120 Oc 53.00N 18.42 E
Dryden 180 Ig 49.47N 92.50W
Dry Fork 188 Me 43.30N 105.24W
Drygalski Ice Tongue 222 Kf 75.24S 163.30 E
Drygalski Island 222 Ge 65.45S 92.30 E
Drysdale River 212 Fb 13.59S 126.51 E
Dry Tortugas 182 Kg 24.38N 82.55W
Drzewica 120 Qe 51.27N 20.28 E
Drzewiczka 120 Qe 51.33N 20.35 E
Dschang 166 Hd 5.27N 10.04 E
Dua 170 Db 3.20N 20.53 E
Duaca 202 Ea 10.18N 69.10W
Duancun → Wuxiang 154 Bf 36.50N 112.51 E
Duarte, Pico- 174 Lh 19.00N 71.00W
Duartina 204 Hf 22.24S 49.25W
Dubawnt 180 Hd 64.30N 100.06W
Dubawnt Lake 174 Ic 63.08N 101.30W
Dubay'ah, Ra's- 146 Pj 24.20N 54.09 E
Dubayy 142 Hg 25.18N 55.18 E
Dubbo 210 Fh 32.15S 148.36 E
Dübener Heide 120 Ie 51.40N 12.40 E
Dubenski 132 Td 51.29N 56.38 E
Dubh Artach 118 Ge 56.08N 6.39W
Dubica 128 Ke 45.13N 16.48 E
Dublin 182 Ke 32.32N 82.54W
Dublin/Baile Átha Cliath 112 Fe 53.20N 6.15W
Dublin/Baile Átha Cliath [2] 118 Gh 53.20N 6.15W
Dublin Bay/Cuan Bhaile Átha Cliath 118 Gh 53.20N 6.06W
Dubljany 120 Tg 49.26N 23.16 E
Dublon 220d Bb 7.23N 151.53 E
Dubna 136 Dd 56.47N 37.10 E
Dubna 116 Lh 56.20N 26.31 E
Dubnica nad Váhom 120 Oh 48.58N 13.10 E
Dubno 136 Ce 50.29N 25.46 E
Du Bois 184 He 41.06N 78.46W
Dubois [Id.-U.S.] 188 Id 44.10N 112.14W
Dubois [Wy.-U.S.] 188 Ke 43.33N 109.38W
Dubossary 132 Ff 47.17N 29.10 E
Dubovka 136 Ef 49.03N 44.50 E
Dubovoje 120 Th 48.08N 23.59 E
Dubreka 166 Cd 9.48N 13.31W
Dubrovica 132 Ed 51.34N 26.34 E
Dubrovnik 112 Hg 42.39N 18.07 E
Dubrovnoje 114 Hi 54.33N 30.41 E
Dubuque 136 Gd 57.58N 69.25 E
Dubysa 182 Ic 42.30N 90.41W
116 Ji 55.02N 23.27 E
Duc de Gloucester, Iles du- = Duke of Gloucester, Islands (En) 208 Mg 20.38S 143.20W
Duchang 154 Dj 29.16N 116.11 E
Duchesne 188 Jf 40.10N 110.24W
Duchess 212 Hd 21.22S 139.52 E
Ducie Atoll 208 Og 24.40S 124.47W
Duck River 184 Dg 36.02N 87.52W
Duckwater Peak 188 Hg 38.58N 115.26W
Duclair 124 Ce 49.29N 0.53 E
Duc Lap 148 Lf 12.27N 107.38 E
Ducos 197h Bb 14.34N 60.58W
Dudelange/Düdelingen 124 Ie 49.28N 6.06 E
Düdelingen/Dudelange 124 Ie 49.28N 6.06 E
Duderstadt 120 Ge 51.31N 10.16 E
Dudinka 142 Kc 69.25N 86.15 E
Dudley 118 Ki 52.30N 2.05W
Dūdo 168 Id 9.20N 50.14 E
Dudub 168 Hd 6.55N 46.42 E
Dudune 219b Ce 21.21S 167.44 E
Dudweiler, Saarbrücken- 124 Je 49.17N 7.02 E
Dūdwēyn 168 Gd 9.19N 44.53 E
Dudypta 138 Db 70.55N 89.50 E
Duékoué 166 Dd 6.45N 7.21W
Dueodde 116 Fj 54.59N 15.05 E
Duerna 126 Gb 42.19N 5.54W
Duero 110 Fg 41.08N 8.40W
Dufek Coast 222 Lg 84.30S 179.00W
Duffer Peak 188 Ff 41.40N 118.44W
Duff Islands 208 He 9.50S 167.10 E
Dugi Otok 128 Ig 44.00N 15.00 E
Dugo Selo 128 Ke 45.48N 16.15 E
Du Gué, Rivière- 180 Ke 57.20N 70.46W
Duhovnickoje 132 Pc 52.29N 48.15 E
Duijan Yan 152 He 31.01N 103.28 E
Duisburg 120 Ce 51.26N 6.45 E
Duitama 202 Db 5.50N 73.02W
Dujūma 168 Ge 1.14N 42.34 E
Dukagjini 130 Cg 42.18N 19.45 E
Dūkān 146 Ke 35.56N 44.58 E
Dūkān, Sad ad- 146 Kd 36.10N 44.56 E
Dukat 130 Fg 42.26N 22.21 E
Duke of Gloucester Islands (EN) = Duc de Gloucester, Iles du- 208 Mg 20.38S 143.20W
Duke of York 219a Aa 4.10S 152.28 E
Duke of York Bay 180 Jc 65.25N 84.50W
Duk Fadiat 168 Ed 7.45N 31.25 E
Duk Faiwil 168 Ed 7.30N 31.29 E
Dukhān 144 Hd 25.25N 50.48 E
Dukielska, Przełecz- 120 Rg 49.25N 21.42 E
Dukku 166 Hc 10.49N 10.46 E
Dukla 120 Rg 49.34N 21.41 E
Dukou 142 Mg 26.31N 101.44 E
Dūkštas/Dukštas 116 Li 55.32N 26.28 E
Dukštas/Dūkštas 116 Li 55.32N 26.28 E
Dulan (Qagan Us) 142 Lf 36.29N 98.29 E
Dulce, Bahia- 192 Ji 16.30N 98.50W
Dulce, Golfo- 190 Hg 8.36N 83.15W
Dulce, Rio- 198 Ji 30.31S 62.32W
Dulce Nombre de Culmí 194 Ef 15.09N 85.37W
Duldurga 138 Gf 50.38N 113.35 E
Dulgalah 140 Pc 67.30N 133.20 E
Dulia 170 Db 2.57N 24.08 E
Dülmen 120 De 51.50N 7.18 E
Dulovka 116 Mg 57.27N 28.29 E
Dulovo 130 Kf 43.49N 27.09 E
Duluth 176 Je 46.47N 92.06W
Dūmā 146 Gf 33.35N 36.24 E
Dumaguete 150 He 9.18N 123.18 E
Dumai 150 Df 1.41N 101.27 E
Dumaran 150 Gd 10.33N 119.51 E
Dumaresq River 212 Ke 28.40S 150.28 E
Dumas [Ar.-U.S.] 186 Kj 33.53N 91.29W
Dumas [Tx.-U.S.] 186 Fi 35.52N 101.58W
Dumayr 146 Gf 33.38N 36.40 E
Dumbarton 118 If 55.57N 4.35W
Dumbéa 219b Cf 22.09S 166.27 E
Dumbrăveni [Rom.] 130 Kd 45.31N 27.09 E
Dumbrăveni [Rom.] 130 Hc 46.14N 24.34 E
Dumbrăveni [Rom.] 130 Jb 47.39N 26.25 E
Dumfries 118 Jf 55.04N 3.37W
Dumfries and Galloway [3] 118 Jf 55.10N 3.35W
Dumka 148 Hd 24.16N 87.15 E
Dumlupinar 130 Mk 38.52N 30.00 E
Dümmer 120 Ed 52.31N 8.19 E
Dumoine, Lac- 184 Ib 46.52N 77.52W
Dumoine, Rivière- 184 Ib 46.13N 77.50W
Dumont d'Urville 222 Je 66.40S 140.01 E
Dumont D'Urville Sea (EN) 222 Je 63.00S 140.00 E
Dumpu 210 Fe 5.52S 145.46 E
Dümrek 130 Lk 38.40N 28.24 E
Dumuhe 154 La 46.21N 133.33 E
Dumyāţ = Damietta (EN) 160 Ke 31.25N 31.48 E
Dumyāţ, Maşabb- 146 Dg 31.27N 31.51 E
Duna = Danube (EN) 110 If 45.20N 29.40 E
Dunaföldvár 120 Oj 46.48N 18.56 E
Dunaharaszti 120 Pi 47.21N 19.05 E
Dunaj 138 Ih 42.57N 132.20 E
Dunaj = Danube (EN) 110 If 45.20N 29.40 E
Dunajec 120 Qf 50.15N 20.44 E
Dunajevcy 132 Ee 48.51N 26.44 E
Dunajská Streda 120 Ni 47.01N 17.38 E
Dunakeszi 120 Pi 47.38N 19.08 E
Dunántúl 120 Nj 47.00N 18.00 E
Dunărea = Danube (EN) 110 If 45.20N 29.40 E
Dunărea Veche 130 Ld 45.17N 28.02 E
Dunării, Delta- = Danube, Mouths of the- (EN) 110 If 45.30N 29.45 E
Duna-Tisza Köze 120 Pj 46.45N 19.30 E
Dunaújváros 120 Oj 46.58N 18.56 E
Dunav = Danube (EN) 110 If 45.20N 29.40 E
Dunavățu de Jos 130 Me 44.59N 29.13 E
Dunav-Tisa-Dunav kanal 130 Dd 45.10N 20.50 E
Dunback 218 Df 45.23S 170.38 E
Dunbar 118 Kf 56.00N 2.31W
Duncan [Az.-U.S.] 188 Kj 32.43N 109.06W
Duncan [B.C.-Can.] 188 Db 48.47N 123.42W
Duncan [Ok.-U.S.] 182 He 34.30N 97.57W
Duncan Passage 148 If 11.00N 92.00 E
Duncansby Head 110 Fd 58.39N 3.01W
Dundaga 116 Jg 57.31N 22.14 E
Dundalk 184 If 39.15N 76.31W
Dundalk/Dún Dealgan 118 Gg 54.01N 6.25W
Dundalk Bay/Cuan Dhun Dealgan 118 Gh 53.57N 6.17W
Dundas 184 Hd 43.16N 79.58W
Dundas (Thule Air Base) 179 Fc 76.30N 69.00W
Dundas, Lake- 212 Ef 32.35S 121.50 E
Dundas Peninsula 180 Gb 74.40N 113.00W
Dundas Strait 212 Gb 11.20S 131.35 E
Dún Dealgan/Dundalk 118 Gg 54.01N 6.25W
Dundee [S.Afr.] 172 Ee 28.12S 30.16 E
Dundee [Scot.-U.K.] 112 Fd 56.28N 3.00W
Dund Hot → Zhenglan Qi 154 Cc 42.14N 115.59 E
Dundrum Bay/Cuan Dhún Droma 118 Hg 54.13N 5.45W
Dunedin [Fl.-U.S.] 184 Fk 28.02N 82.47W
Dunedin [N.Z.] 210 Ii 45.53S 170.31 E
Dunfanaghy 118 Ff 55.11N 7.59W
Dunfermline 118 Je 56.04N 3.29W
Dungannon/Dún Geanainn 118 Gg 54.31N 6.46W
Dún Garbhán/Dungarvan 118 Fi 52.05N 7.37W
Dūngarpur 148 Ed 23.50N 73.43 E
Dungarvan/Dún Garbhán 118 Fi 52.05N 7.37W
Dungas 166 Gc 13.04N 9.20 E
Dungau 120 Ih 48.45N 12.30 E
Dún Geanainn/Dungannon 118 Gg 54.31N 6.46W
Dungeness 118 Nk 50.55N 0.58 E
Dungu 170 Eb 3.42N 28.40 E
Dungu 170 Eb 3.37N 28.34 E
Dunhua 152 Mc 43.22N 128.12 E
Dunhuang 152 Fc 40.10N 94.50 E
Dunkerque 122 Ic 51.03N 2.22 E
Dunkery Beacon 118 Jj 51.11N 3.35W
Dunkirk 182 Lc 42.29N 79.21W
Dunkwa 166 Ed 5.58N 1.47W
Dún Laoghaire 118 Gh 53.17N 6.08W
Dún Mánmhai/Dunmanway 118 Dj 51.43N 9.07W
Dunmanway/Dún Mánmhai 118 Dj 51.43N 9.07W
Dunn 184 Hh 35.19N 78.37W
Dún na nGall/Donegal 118 Eg 54.39N 8.06W
Dún na nGall/Donegal [2] 118 Fg 54.50N 8.00W
Dunnellon 184 Fk 29.03N 82.28W
Dunnet Head 118 Jc 58.39N 3.23W
Dunning 186 Ff 41.50N 100.06W
Dún Pádraig/Downpatrick 118 Hg 54.20N 5.43W
Dunqulah = Dongola (EN) 160 Kg 19.10N 30.29 E
Dunqulah al Qadīmah 168 Eb 18.13N 30.45 E
Dunqunāb 168 Fa 21.06N 37.05 E
Dunqunāb, Khalīj- 168 Fa 21.05N 37.08 E
Dunrankin 184 Fa 48.39N 83.04W
Duns 118 Kf 55.47N 2.20W
Dünsberg 124 Kd 50.39N 8.35 E
Dunsmuir 188 Df 41.13N 122.16W
Dunstable 124 Bc 51.53N 0.31W
Dunstan Mountains 218 Cf 44.55S 169.30 E
Dun-sur-Auron 122 Ih 46.53N 2.34 E
Dun-sur-Meuse 124 He 49.23N 5.11 E
Duntroon 218 Df 44.51S 170.41 E
Dunvegan 118 Gd 57.26N 6.35W
Duobukur 152 La 50.19N 124.57 E
Duolun/Dolonnur 152 Kc 42.10N 116.30 E
Dupree 186 Fd 45.03N 101.36W
Duqm 142 Hf 19.41N 57.32 E
Duque de Bragança, Quedas- 158 Ii 9.05S 16.10 E
Duque de Caxias 202 Jh 22.47S 43.18W
Duque de York, Isla- 206 Eh 50.40S 75.20W
Du Quoin 186 Lg 38.01N 89.14W
Durack Range 212 Fc 17.00S 128.00 E
Durack River 212 Fc 15.33S 127.52 E
Durağan 146 Fb 41.25N 35.04 E
Durance 110 Gg 43.55N 4.44 E
Durand 186 Kd 44.38N 91.58W
Durand, Récif- 219b Df 22.02S 168.39 E
Durango [2] 190 Dd 24.50N 104.50W
Durango [Co.-U.S.] 176 If 37.16N 107.53W
Durango [Sp.] 126 Ja 43.10N 2.37W
Durañona 204 Bm 37.15S 60.31W
Durant 182 He 33.59N 96.23W
Duras 122 Gj 44.40N 0.11 E
Duratón 126 Hc 41.37N 4.07W
Durazno 206 Id 33.22S 56.31W
Durazno [2] 204 Dk 33.05S 56.05W
Durazno, Cuchilla Grande del- 204 Dk 33.15S 56.15W
Durazzo (EN) = Durresi 130 Ch 41.19N 19.26 E
Durban 160 Kk 29.55S 30.56 E
Durbe 116 Ih 56.39N 21.14 E
Durbet-Daba, pereval- 152 Eb 49.37N 89.25 E
Durbo 168 Ic 11.30N 50.18 E
Durbuy 124 Hd 50.21N 5.28 E
Đurđevac 128 Ld 46.02N 17.04 E
Düren 120 Cf 50.48N 6.29 E
Durg 148 Gd 21.11N 81.17 E
Durgapūr 148 Hd 23.30N 87.15 E
Durgen-Nur 152 Fb 47.40N 93.30 E
Durham [3] 118 Lg 54.45N 1.40W
Durham 118 Lg 54.45N 1.45W
Durham [Eng.-U.K.] 118 Lg 54.47N 1.34W
Durham [N.C.-U.S.] 182 Ld 35.59N 78.54W
Durkee 188 Gd 44.36N 117.28W
Durlas/Thurles 118 Fi 52.41N 7.49W
Durmā 144 Ge 24.37N 46.08 E
Durmersheim 124 Kf 48.56N 8.16 E
Durmitor 110 Hg 43.09N 19.02 E
Durnford, Punta- 162 De 23.37N 16.00W
Durresi = Durazzo (EN) 130 Ch 41.19N 19.26 E
Durrësit, Gjiri- 130 Ch 41.16N 19.28 E
Dursey/Oiléan Baoi 118 Cj 51.36N 10.12W
Dursunbey 146 Cc 39.35N 28.38 E
Durtal 122 Fg 47.40N 0.15W
Duru → Wuchuan 152 If 28.28N 107.57 E
Duruksi 168 Hd 8.29N 45.38 E
Durusu Gölü 130 Lh 41.20N 28.38 E
Durūz, Jabal ad- 146 Gf 32.40N 36.44 E
D'Urville Island 216 Dh 40.50S 173.50 E
Dušak 135 Cf 37.15N 60.01 E
Dusa Mareb 168 Hd 5.31N 46.24 E
Dušanbe 142 If 38.35N 68.48 E
Dušeti 132 Nh 42.05N 44.42 E
Dusetos 116 Li 55.42N 26.02 E
Dushan 142 Mg 25.55N 107.36 E
Dushan Hu 154 Dg 35.06N 116.48 E
Dusios ežeras / Dusja, ozero- 116 Jj 54.15N 23.45 E
Dusja, ozero- / Dusios ežeras 116 Jj 54.15N 23.45 E
Dusky Sound 218 Bf 45.45S 166.30 E
Düsseldorf 112 Ge 51.13N 6.46 E
Dusti 135 Gf 37.22N 68.43 E
Dutch Harbor 178a Eb 53.53N 166.32W
Dutlwe 172 Cd 23.58S 23.54 E
Dutton, Mount- 188 Ig 38.01N 112.13W
Duved 116 Ea 63.24N 12.52 E
Duvergé 194 Ld 18.22N 71.31W
Düvertepe 130 Lj 39.14N 28.27 E
Duvno 128 Lg 43.43N 17.14 E
Duwayhin 144 He 24.16N 51.20 E
Duwayhin, Khawr- 146 Nj 24.20N 51.25 E
Duyfken Point 212 Ib 12.35S 141.40 E
Duyun 152 If 26.20N 107.28 E
Dūz 162 Ic 33.28N 9.01 E
Düzce 144 Da 40.50N 31.10 E
Dve Mogili 130 If 43.36N 25.52 E
Dvina Gulf (EN) = Dvinskaja guba 110 Jb 65.00N 39.45 E
Dvinskaja guba = Dvina Gulf (EN) 110 Jb 65.00N 39.45 E
Dvor 128 Ke 45.04N 16.23 E
Dvuh Cirkov, gora- 138 Lc 67.30N 168.20 E
Dvůr Králové nad Labem 120 Lf 50.26N 15.48 E
Dwārka 148 Dd 22.14N 68.58 E
Dworshak Reservoir 188 Hc 46.45N 116.00W
Dyer, Cape- 174 Mc 66.37N 61.18W
Dyero 166 Dc 12.50N 6.30W
Dyer Plateau 222 Qf 70.45S 65.30W
Dyersburg 182 Jd 36.03N 89.23W
Dyfed [3] 118 Ji 52.05N 4.00W
Dyhmau, gora- 132 Mh 43.05N 43.12 E
Dyje 120 Mh 48.37N 16.56 E
Dyjsko-Svratecký úval 120 Mh 48.56N 16.25 E
Dyle 124 Gd 50.57N 4.40 E
Dylewska Góra 120 Pc 53.34N 19.57 E
Dynów 120 Sg 49.49N 22.14 E
Dyr, Djebel- 128 Cn 36.13N 8.46 E
Dyrhólæy 110 Ec 63.24N 19.08W
Dysnų ežeras / Disnaj, ozero- 114 Gi 55.35N 26.32 E
Dytike Rodhópi 130 Hh 41.45N 24.05 E
Dzabhan 140 Le 48.54N 93.23 E
Džagdy, hrebet- 138 If 53.40N 131.00 E
Džalagaš 136 Gf 45.05N 64.40 E
Džalal-Abad 135 Id 40.56N 73.05 E
Džalilabad 136 Eh 39.12N 48.31 E
Džalinda 138 Hf 53.31N 123.59 E
Džambejty 132 Rd 50.14N 52.38 E
Džambul [Kaz.-U.S.S.R.] 136 Hf 47.17N 71.42 E
Džambul [Kaz.-U.S.S.R.] 142 Je 42.54N 71.22 E
Džambulskaja oblast [3] 136 Hg 44.30N 72.30 E
Dzamyn-Ud 152 Jb 43.50N 111.45 E
Džanak 132 Si 40.30N 55.35 E
Džanga 136 Fg 40.01N 53.10 E
Džankoj 136 Df 45.42N 34.22 E
Džansugurov 136 Hf 45.23N 79.29 E
Džanybek 136 Ef 49.24N 46.50 E
Dzaoudzi 160 Lj 12.47S 45.17 E
Džardžan 138 Hc 68.55N 124.05 E
Džargalant [Mong.] 152 Gb 47.20N 99.35 E
Džargalant [Mong.] 152 Ib 48.35N 105.50 E
Džarkurgan 136 Gh 37.29N 67.25 E
Džava 132 Mh 42.24N 43.53 E
Džebariki-Haja 138 Id 62.23N 135.50 E
Džebel [Bul.] 130 Ih 41.30N 25.18 E
Džebel [Tur.-U.S.S.R.] 132 Sj 39.37N 54.18 E
Džebrail 132 Oj 39.23N 47.01 E
Dzereg 152 Fb 47.03N 92.50 E
Džergalan 135 Lc 42.33N 79.02 E
Dzermuk 132 Nj 39.48N 45.39 E
Dzeržinsk [Bye.-U.S.S.R.] 132 Ec 53.44N 27.08 E
Dzeržinsk [R.S.F.S.R.] 136 Ed 56.16N 43.32 E
Dzeržinsk [Ukr.-U.S.S.R.] 132 Je 48.22N 37.50 E
Dzeržinskaja, gora- 116 Lk 53.53N 27.10 E
Dzeržinskoje 138 Ee 56.49N 95.18 E
Džetygara 142 Id 52.11N 61.12 E
Džetysaj 135 Gd 40.49N 68.20 E
Džezkazgan [Kaz.-U.S.S.R.] 142 Ie 47.47N 67.46 E
Džezkazgan [Kaz.-U.S.S.R.] 136 Gf 47.53N 67.27 E
Džezkazganskaja oblast [3] 136 Gf 47.30N 70.00 E
Dzhugdzhur Range (EN) = Džugdžur, hrebet- 140 Pd 58.00N 136.00 E
Działdówka 120 Qd 52.58N 20.05 E
Działdowo 120 Qc 53.15N 20.10 E
Działoszyce 120 Qf 50.22N 20.21 E
Dzibalchén 192 Oh 19.31N 89.45W
Dzibilchaltún 192 Og 21.05N 89.36W
Dzierzgoń 120 Pc 53.56N 19.21 E
Dzierżoniów 120 Mf 50.44N 16.39 E
Džirgatal 135 He 39.13N 71.12 E
Džizak 136 Gg 40.07N 67.52 E
Džizakskaja oblast [3] 136 Gg 40.20N 67.40 E
Džugdžur, hrebet- = Dzhugdzhur Range (EN) 140 Pd 58.00N 136.00 E
Džūkste/Džukste 116 Jh 56.45N 23.10 E
Džukste/Džūkste 116 Jh 56.45N 23.10 E
Džulfa 132 Nj 38.59N 45.35 E
Džuma 135 Fe 39.44N 66.39 E
Dzun-Bajan 152 Jc 44.26N 110.03 E
Dzungarian Basin (EN) = Junggar Pendi 140 Ke 45.00N 88.00 E

Index Symbols

[1] Independent Nation
[2] State, Region
[3] District, County
[4] Municipality
[5] Colony, Dependency
Continent
Physical Region
Historical or Cultural Region
Mount, Mountain
Volcano
Hill
Mountains, Mountain Range
Hills, Escarpment
Plateau, Upland
Pass, Gap
Plain, Lowland
Delta
Salt Flat
Valley, Canyon
Crater, Cave
Karst Features
Depression
Polder
Desert, Dunes
Forest, Woods
Heath, Steppe
Oasis
Cape, Point
Coast, Beach
Cliff
Peninsula
Isthmus
Sandbank
Island
Atoll
Rock, Reef
Islands, Archipelago
Rocks, Reefs
Coral Reef
Well, Spring
Geyser
River, Stream
Waterfall, Rapids
River Mouth, Estuary
Lake
Salt Lake
Intermittent Lake
Reservoir
Swamp, Pond
Canal
Glacier
Ice Shelf, Pack Ice
Ocean
Sea
Gulf, Bay
Strait, Fjord
Lagoon
Bank
Seamount
Tablemount
Ridge
Shelf
Basin
Escarpment, Sea Scarp
Fracture
Trench, Abyss
National Park, Reserve
Point of Interest
Recreation Site
Cave, Cavern
Historic Site
Ruins
Wall, Walls
Church, Abbey
Temple
Scientific Station
Railway station
Airport
Port
Military installation
Lighthouse
Mine
Tunnel
Dam, Bridge

Dzungarian Gate (EN) = Alataw Shankou	140	Ke	45.25N	82.25 E
Dzungarian Gate (EN) = Džungarskije vorota	140	Ke	45.25N	82.25 E
Džungarski Alatau, hrebet-	140	Ke	45.00N	81.00 E
Džungarskije vorota = Dzungarian Gate (EN)	140	Ke	45.25N	82.25 E
Dzun-Hara	152	Ib	48.40N	106.40 E
Dzun-Mod	152	Ib	47.50N	106.57 E
Džurak-Sal	132	Mf	47.18N	43.36 E
Džusaly	136	Gf	45.29N	64.05 E
Džvari	132	Mh	42.42N	42.02 E

E

Éadan Doire/Edenderry	118	Fh	53.21N	7.03W
Eads	186	Eg	38.29N	102.47W
Eagle	178	Kd	64.46N	141.16W
Eagle	180	Lf	53.35N	57.25W
Eagle Creek	188	La	52.22N	107.24W
Eagle Lake	184	Mb	47.02N	68.36W
Eagle Lake [Ca.-U.S.]	188	Ef	40.39N	120.44W
Eagle Lake [Me.-U.S.]	184	Mb	46.20N	69.20W
Eagle Lake [Ont.-Can.]	186	Jb	49.42N	93.13W
Eagle Mountain	186	Kc	47.54N	90.33W
Eagle Nest	186	Dh	36.35N	105.14W
Eagle Pass	182	Gf	28.43N	100.30W
Eagle Peak [Ca.-U.S.]	182	Cc	41.17N	120.12W
Eagle Peak [Tx.-U.S.]	186	Dk	30.56N	105.01W
Eagle River [Ak.-U.S.]	178	Jd	61.19N	149.34W
Eagle River [Wi.-U.S.]	186	Ld	45.55N	89.15W
Eagle Summit	178	Jc	65.30N	145.38W
Ealing, London-	124	Bc	51.30N	0.19W
Ear Falls	186	Ja	50.38N	93.13W
Earn	118	Je	56.25N	3.30W
Earn, Loch-	118	Ie	56.28N	4.10W
Earnslaw, Mount-	218	Cf	44.37S	168.25 E
Easley	184	Fh	34.50N	82.36W
East Alligator River	212	Gb	12.08S	132.42 E
East Anglia	118	Ni	52.25N	1.00 E
East Angus	184	Lc	45.29N	71.40W
East Bay [Can.]	180	Jd	64.05N	81.30W
East Bay [U.S.]	186	Ll	29.05N	89.15W
East Berlin = Berlin	112	He	52.31N	13.24 E
Eastbourne [Eng.-U.K.]	118	Nk	50.46N	0.17 E
Eastbourne [N.Z.]	218	Fd	41.17S	174.54 E
East Caicos	194	Lc	21.41N	71.30W
East Cape [Fl.-U.S.]	184	Gm	25.07N	81.05W
East Cape [N.Z.]	208	Ih	37.41S	178.33 E
East Caroline Basin (EN)	106	Ii	4.00N	146.45 E
East Chicago	184	De	41.38N	87.27W
East China Sea (EN) = Dong Hai	140	Og	29.00N	125.00 E
East China Sea (EN) = Higashi-Shina-Kai	140	Og	29.00N	125.00 E
East Coast [2]	218	Gc	38.20S	177.50 E
East Dereham	118	Ni	52.41N	0.56 E
Eastend	188	Kb	49.31N	108.48W
East Entrance	220a	Bb	7.50N	134.40 E
Easter Island (EN) = Pascua, Isla de- / Rapa Nui	208	Qg	27.07S	109.22W
Easter Island (EN) = Rapa Nui / Pascua, Isla de-	208	Qg	27.07S	109.22W
Eastern [Ghana] [3]	166	Ed	6.30N	0.30W
Eastern [Kenya] [3]	170	Gb	0.05N	38.00 E
Eastern [S.L.] [3]	166	Cd	8.15N	11.00W
Eastern [Ug.] [3]	170	Fb	1.30N	33.50 E
Eastern [Zam.] [3]	170	Fe	13.00S	32.15 E
Eastern Fields	214	Dj	10.03S	145.22 E
Eastern Ghats	140	Jh	14.00N	78.50 E
Eastern Point	197b	Ab	18.07N	63.01W
Eastern Sayans (EN) = Vostočny Sajan	140	Ld	53.00N	97.00 E
Eastern Siberia (EN)	140	Rc	65.00N	155.00 E
Eastern Sierra Madre (EN) = Madre Oriental, Sierra-	174	Jg	22.00N	99.30W
Eastern Turkistan (EN)	140	Jf	40.00N	80.00 E
East Falkland/Soledad, Isla-	198	Kk	51.45S	58.50W
East Fork	186	Ie	42.41N	94.12W
East Friesland (EN) = Ostfriesland	120	Dc	53.20N	7.40 E
East Frisian Islands (EN) = Ostfriesische Inseln	120	Dc	53.45N	7.25 E
East Grand Forks	186	Hc	47.56N	97.01W
East Grand Rapids	184	Ed	42.56N	85.35W
East Greenland (EN) = Østgrønland [2]	179	Id	72.00N	35.00W
East Grinstead	118	Mj	51.08N	0.01W
East Ilsley	124	Ac	51.32N	1.17W
East Kilbride	118	If	55.46N	4.10W
East Lansing	184	Ed	42.44N	84.29W
East Las Vegas	188	Hh	36.07N	115.01W
Eastleigh	118	Lk	50.58N	1.22W
East London	160	Jl	33.00S	27.55 E
East Lynn Lake	184	Ff	38.05N	82.20W
Eastmain	180	Jf	52.14N	78.31W
Eastmain	180	Jf	52.15N	78.34W
Eastman	184	Fi	32.12N	83.11W
East Mariana Basin (EN)	106	Jh	12.00N	153.00 E
East Midlands Airport	124	Ab	52.50N	1.20W
East Novaya Zemlya Trough (EN)	136	Fa	73.30N	61.00 E
Easton	184	Je	40.41N	75.13W
East Pacific Rise (EN)	106	Ml	20.00S	110.00W
East Point	184	Ei	33.40N	84.27W
East Point [B.V.I.]	197a	Db	18.43N	64.16W
East Point [V.I.U.S.]	197a	Dc	17.46N	64.33W
Eastport	184	Nc	44.54N	67.00W
East Pryor Mountain	188	Kd	45.14N	108.30W
East Retford	118	Mh	53.19N	0.56W
East Road	124	Cd	51.00N	1.02 E
East Schelde (EN) = Oosterschelde	122	Jc	51.30N	4.00 E
East Scotia Basin (EN)	198	Mk	57.00S	35.00W
East Siberian Sea (EN) = Vostočno Sibirskoje more	224	Cd	74.00N	166.00 E
East St. Louis	182	Id	38.38N	90.05W
East Sussex [3]	118	Nk	50.55N	0.15 E
East Tavaputs Plateau	188	Kg	39.45N	109.30W
East Wear Bay	124	Dc	51.08N	1.18 E
Eaton	184	Ef	39.44N	84.37W
Eatonia	188	Ka	51.13N	109.23W
Eatonton	184	Fi	33.20N	83.23W
Eatonville	188	Dc	46.51N	122.17W
Eau Claire	182	Ic	44.49N	91.31W
Eau-Claire, Lac à l' -	180	Ke	56.20N	74.00W
Eauripik Atoll	208	Fd	6.42N	143.03 E
Eauripik Ridge (EN)	214	Cg	3.00N	142.00 E
Eauze	122	Gk	43.52N	0.06 E
Ébano	192	Jf	22.13N	98.24W
Ebbegebirge	120	De	51.10N	7.45 E
Ebbw Vale	118	Jj	51.47N	3.12W
Ebebiyin	166	He	2.09N	11.20 E
Ebeltoft	116	Dh	56.12N	10.41 E
Ebensburg	184	He	40.28N	78.44W
Ebensee	128	Hc	47.48N	13.46 E
Eberbach	120	Eg	49.28N	8.59 E
Eber Gölü	146	Dc	38.38N	31.12 E
Ebersbach	120	Ke	51.01N	14.35 E
Eberswalde	120	Jd	52.50N	13.50 E
Ebetsu	154	Pc	43.07N	141.34 E
Ebino	154	Kh	32.02N	130.47 E
Ebinur Hu	140	Ke	44.55N	82.55 E
Ebla	144	Eb	35.42N	36.50 E
Ebo	170	Ce	11.02S	14.40 E
Ebola	170	Db	3.20N	20.57 E
Eboli	128	Jj	40.36N	15.04 E
Ebolowa	160	Ih	2.54N	11.09 E
Ebombo	170	Ed	5.42S	26.07 E
Ebon Atoll	208	Hd	4.38N	168.43 E
Ebre/Ebro	110	Gg	40.43N	0.54 E
Ebre, Delta de l'-/Ebro, Delta del- = Ebro, Delta of the- (EN)	126	Md	40.43N	0.54 E
Ebril, Récif-	216	Od	22.40S	133.30W
Ebro/Ebre	110	Gg	40.43N	0.54 E
Ebro, Delta del-/Ebre, Delta de l'- = Ebro, Delta of the- (EN)	126	Md	40.43N	0.54 E
Ebro, Delta of the- (EN) = Ebre, Delta de l'-/Ebro, Delta del-	126	Md	40.43N	0.54 E
Ebro, Delta of the- (EN) = Ebro, Delta del-/Ebre, Delta de l'-	126	Md	40.43N	0.54 E
Ebro, Embalse del-	126	Ia	43.00N	3.58W
Ebschloh	120	Ef	50.58N	8.15 E
Ecaussines	124	Gd	50.34N	4.10 E
Ecbatana	146	Me	34.48N	48.30 E
Eceabat	130	Ji	40.11N	26.21 E
Echdeiria	162	Ed	27.14N	10.27W
Echegarate, Puerto de-	126	Jb	42.57N	2.14W
Echeng [China]	152	Kd	36.10N	116.03 E
Echeng [China]	154	Ci	30.24N	114.52 E
Echez	122	Gk	43.28N	0.02 E
Echigo-Sanmyaku	156	Fc	37.30N	139.15 E
Echizen-Misaki	156	Dd	35.59N	135.57 E
Echo Bay	176	Hc	66.04N	118.00W
Echo Seamount (EN)	162	Dd	25.23N	19.25W
Echt	124	Hc	51.06N	5.52 E
Echternach	124	Ie	49.49N	6.25 E
Echuca	212	Ig	36.10S	144.45 E
Echzell	124	Kd	50.23N	8.52 E
Écija	126	Gg	37.32N	5.05W
Eckernförde	120	Fb	54.28N	9.50 E
Eckerö	114	Ef	60.15N	19.35 E
Eclipse Sound	180	Jb	72.40N	79.30W
Ečmiadzin	136	Eg	40.09N	44.18 E
Écommoy	122	Gg	47.50N	0.16 E
Ecos	124	De	49.10N	1.39 E
Ecouis	124	De	49.19N	1.26 E
Écouves, Forêt d'-	122	Gf	48.32N	0.04 E
Ecrins, Barre des-	122	Mj	44.55N	6.22 E
Ecuador [1]	200	If	2.00S	77.30W
Ecury-sur-Coole	124	Gf	48.54N	4.20 E
Ed [Eth.]	168	Gc	13.56N	41.40 E
Ed [Swe.]	114	Cg	58.54N	11.56 E
Edam-Volendam	124	Hb	52.30N	5.03 E
Edane	116	Ee	59.38N	12.49 E
Eday	118	Kb	59.11N	2.47W
Edchera	162	Ed	27.02N	13.04W
Eddrachillis Bay	118	Hc	58.19N	5.15W
Eddystone Point	212	Jh	41.00S	148.20 E
Eddystóne Rocks	118	Ik	50.15N	4.10W
Eddyville	184	Cg	37.03N	88.04W
Ede [Neth.]	122	Lb	52.03N	5.40 E
Ede [Nig.]	166	Fd	7.44N	4.26 E
Edéa	160	Ih	3.48N	10.08 E
Edefors	114	Ec	66.13N	20.54 E
Edéia	204	Hc	17.18S	49.55W
Edelény	120	Qh	48.18N	20.44 E
Eden	118	Jg	54.57N	3.01W
Eden [Austl.]	212	Jg	37.04S	149.54 E
Eden [Tx.-U.S.]	186	Gk	31.13N	99.51W
Edenburg	172	De	29.45S	25.56 E
Edenderry/Éadan Doire	118	Fh	53.21N	7.03W
Edenkoben	124	Ke	49.17N	8.09 E
Edenton	184	Ig	36.04N	76.39W
Eder	120	Fe	51.13N	9.27 E
Edersee	124	Lc	51.11N	9.03 E
Edertal	124	Lc	51.09N	9.09 E
Edewecht	124	Ja	53.08N	7.59 E
Edgar Ranges	212	Ec	18.43S	123.25 E
Edgartown	184	Le	41.23N	70.31W
Edgecumbe	218	Gb	37.58S	176.50 E
Edgeley	186	Gc	46.22N	98.43W
Edgell	180	Ld	61.50N	65.00W
Edgemont	186	Ee	43.18N	103.50W
Edgeøya	224	Jd	77.45N	22.30 E
Édhessa	130	Fi	40.48N	22.03 E
Edina	186	Jd	44.55N	93.20W
Edinburg	182	Hf	26.18N	98.10W
Edinburgh	112	Fd	55.57N	3.13W
Edinburgh, Arrecife-	194	Ff	14.50N	82.39W
Edincik	146	Bb	40.20N	27.51 E
Edingen/Enghien	124	Gd	50.42N	4.02 E
Edirne	146	Bb	41.40N	26.34 E
Edisto Island	184	Gi	32.35N	80.10W
Edisto River	184	Gi	32.39N	80.24W
Edith, Mount-	188	Jc	46.26N	111.11W
Edith Ronne Land (EN)	222	Rg	81.40S	50.00W
Edjeleh	162	Id	27.42N	9.53 E
Edjereh	162	He	24.35N	4.30 E
Édjérir	166	Fb	18.06N	0.50 E
Edmond	186	Hi	35.39N	97.29W
Edmonds	188	Dc	47.48N	122.22W
Edmonton	176	Hd	53.33N	113.28W
Edmundston	180	Kg	47.22N	68.20W
Edna	186	Hl	28.42N	96.39W
Edremit	144	Cb	39.35N	27.01 E
Edremit, Gulf of- (EN) = Edremit Körfezi	146	Bc	39.30N	26.45 E
Edremit Körfezi = Edremit, Gulf of- (EN)	146	Bc	39.30N	26.45 E
Edsbro	114	Eg	59.54N	18.29 E
Edsbruk	116	Gf	58.02N	16.28 E
Edsbyn	116	Fc	61.23N	15.49 E
Edson	180	Ff	53.35N	116.26W
Edsvalla	116	Ee	59.26N	13.13 E
Eduardo Castex	206	He	35.54S	64.18W
Eduni, Mount-	180	Ed	64.08N	128.10W
Edward, Lake-	158	Ji	0.25S	29.30 E
Edward, Lake- (EN) = Rutanzige, Lac-	158	Ji	0.25S	29.30 E
Edwards Creek	212	He	28.21S	135.51 E
Edwards Plateau	174	If	31.20N	101.00W
Edward VIII Bay	222	Ee	66.50S	57.00 E
Edward VII Peninsula	222	Mf	77.40S	155.00W
Edzo	180	Fd	62.47N	116.08W
Eeklo	122	Jc	51.11N	3.34 E
Eelde	124	Ia	53.08N	6.33 E
Eel River	182	Cc	40.40N	124.20W
Eem	124	Hb	52.16N	5.20 E
Eems	124	Ja	53.19N	7.03 E
Eemskanaal	124	Ia	53.19N	6.57 E
Eenrum	124	Ia	53.23N	6.25 E
Eersel	124	Hc	51.22N	5.19 E
Eesti Nõukogude Socialistik Vabarijk/Estonskaja SSR [2]	136	Cd	59.00N	26.00 E
Eesti NSV = Estonian SSR (EN) [2]	136	Cd	59.00N	26.00 E
Efaté, Ile-	208	Hf	17.40S	168.25 E
Eferding	128	Ib	48.19N	14.01 E
Efes = Ephesus (EN)	130	Kl	37.55N	27.20 E
Effingham	186	Lg	39.07N	88.33W
Eflâni	146	Eb	41.26N	32.57 E
Eforie	130	Le	44.01N	28.38 E
Ega	126	Kb	42.19N	1.55W
Egadi, Isole- = Egadi Islands (EN)	110	Hh	38.00N	12.15 E
Egadi Islands (EN) = Egadi, Isole-	110	Hh	38.00N	12.15 E
Egan Range	188	Hg	39.00N	115.00W
Eganville	184	Ic	47.33N	77.06W
Egbe	166	Gd	8.13N	5.31 E
Ege Denizi = Aegean Sea (EN)	110	Ih	39.00N	25.00 E
Egedesminde/Ausiait	224	Nc	68.50N	52.45W
Egegik	178	He	58.13N	157.22W
Egentliga Finland/Varsinais-Suomi	116	Jd	60.40N	22.30 E
Eger	120	Qi	47.54N	20.23 E
Eger	120	Kf	50.32N	14.08 E
Egersund	114	Ag	58.27N	6.00 E
Egerton, Mount-	212	Dd	24.45S	117.45 E
Egeskov	116	Di	55.10N	10.30 E
Eggegebirge	120	Ee	51.40N	8.55 E
Eggenfelden	120	Ih	48.24N	12.46 E
Eggenstein-Leopoldshafen	124	Ke	49.05N	8.23 E
Eggum	114	Cb	68.19N	13.42 E
Eghezée	124	Gd	50.36N	4.56 E
Egijn-Gol	152	Ha	49.24N	103.36 E
Égletons	122	Ii	45.24N	2.03 E
Eglinton	180	Fa	75.45N	118.50W
Egmont, Cape-	216	Dg	39.17S	173.45 E
Egmont, Mount-	218	Fc	39.18S	174.04 E
Egnazia	128	Lj	40.50N	17.25 E
Eğridir	146	Dd	37.52N	30.51 E
Eğridir Gölü	144	Db	38.02N	30.53 E
Eğrigöz Dağ	130	Mj	39.21N	29.07 E
Egtved	116	Ci	55.37N	9.18 E
Éguas ou Correntina, Rio das-	204	Ja	13.26S	44.14W
Eguey	158	Ig	16.10N	16.10 E
Egvekinot	142	Uc	66.19N	179.10W
Egypt (EN) = Mişr [1]	160	Jf	27.00N	30.00 E
Eha Amufu	166	Gd	6.40N	7.46 E
Ehen Hudag → Alxa Youqi	152	Hd	39.12N	101.40 E
Ehime Ken [2]	154	Lh	33.35N	132.40 E
Ehingen (Donau)	120	Fh	48.17N	9.44 E
Ehrang, Trier-	124	Ie	49.49N	6.41 E
Ehrwald	128	Ec	47.24N	10.55 E
Ei	156	Bf	31.13N	130.30 E
Eiao, Ile-	208	Me	8.00S	140.40W
Eibar	126	Ja	43.11N	2.28W
Eibergen	124	Ib	52.07N	6.40 E
Eichsfeld	120	Ge	51.25N	10.20 E
Eichstätt	120	Hh	48.53N	11.11 E
Eickelborn, Lippetal-	124	Kc	51.39N	8.13 E
Eide	116	Bb	62.55N	7.26 E
Eider	120	Eb	54.19N	8.58 E
Eiderstedt	120	Eb	54.22N	8.50 E
Eidet	114	Cd	64.27N	13.37 E
Eidfjord	114	Bf	60.28N	7.05 E
Eidfjorden	116	Bd	60.25N	6.45 E
Eidslandet	116	Ad	60.44N	5.45 E
Eidsvåg	114	Be	62.47N	8.03 E
Eidsvoll	114	Cf	60.19N	11.14 E
Eidsvollfjellet	179	Nc	79.00N	13.00 E
Eierlandse Gat	124	Ga	53.12N	4.52 E
Eifel	120	Cf	50.15N	6.45 E
Eiffel Flats	172	Dc	18.13S	29.48 E
Eigat, Jabal-	168	Fa	22.00N	35.01 E
Eigenbrakel/Braine-l'Alleud	124	Gd	50.41N	4.22 E
Eigerøya	116	Af	58.25N	5.55 E
Eigg	118	Ge	56.54N	6.10W
Eight Degree Channel	140	Ji	8.00N	73.00 E
Eights Coast	222	Pf	73.30S	96.00W
Eighty Mile Beach	212	Ec	19.45S	121.00 E
Eigrim, Jabal-	168	Fb	19.22N	35.18 E
Eijsden	124	Hd	50.46N	5.42 E
Eikeren	116	Ce	59.40N	10.00 E
Eikesdalsvatnet	116	Cb	62.35N	8.10 E
'Eilai	168	Eb	16.33N	30.54 E
Eildon, Lake-	212	Jg	37.10S	145.50 E
Eilenburg	120	Ie	51.28N	12.37 E
Eiler Rasmussen, Kap-	179	Kb	82.40N	20.00W
Eil Malk	220a	Ac	7.09N	134.22 E
Eina	116	Dd	60.38N	10.36 E
Einasleigh	212	Ic	18.31S	144.05 E
Einasleigh River	212	Ic	17.30S	142.17 E
Einbeck	120	Fe	51.49N	9.52 E
Eindhoven	122	Lc	51.26N	5.28 E
Einsiedeln	128	Cc	47.08N	8.45 E
Éire/Ireland [1]	112	Fe	53.00N	8.00W
Eiríksjökull	114a	Bb	64.46N	20.24W
Eirunepé	200	Jf	6.40S	69.52W
Eisack/Isarco	128	Fd	46.27N	11.18 E
Eisacktal/Isarco, Valle-	128	Fd	46.45N	11.35 E
Eisenach	120	Gf	50.59N	10.19 E
Eisenberg	120	Hf	50.58N	11.54 E
Eisenberg	124	Kc	51.15N	8.50 E
Eisenberg (Pfalz)	124	Ke	49.33N	8.06 E
Eisenerz	128	Ic	47.32N	14.53 E
Eisenerzer Alpen	128	Ic	47.30N	14.40 E
Eisenhüttenstadt	120	Kd	52.10N	14.42 E
Eisenstadt	128	Kc	47.51N	16.31 E
Eisenwurzen	128	Jc	47.56N	15.02 E
Eišiškės/Ejšiškes	114	Fi	54.14N	25.02 E
Eisleben	120	He	51.32N	11.33 E
Eitorf	124	Jd	50.46N	7.27 E
Eivissa/Ibiza = Iviza (EN)	110	Gh	39.00N	1.25 E
Eje, Sierra del-	126	Fb	42.20N	6.55W
Ejea de los Caballeros	126	Kb	42.08N	1.08W
Ejeda	172	Gd	24.19S	44.21 E
Ejido	202	Db	8.33N	71.14W
Ejido Insurgentes	192	De	25.12N	111.45W
Ejin Horo Qi (Altan Xiret)	152	Id	39.31N	109.45 E
Ejin Qi	142	Me	41.50N	100.50 E
Ejšiškes/Eišiškės	114	Fi	54.14N	25.02 E
Ejura	166	Ed	7.23N	1.22W
Ejutla de Crespo	190	Ee	16.34N	96.44W
Ekalaka	188	Md	45.53N	104.33W
Ekecek Dağı	146	Fc	38.39N	34.03 E
Ekenäs/Tammisaari	114	Fg	59.58N	23.26 E
Ekeren, Antwerpen-	122	Kc	51.17N	4.25 E
Eket	166	Ge	4.39N	7.56 E
Eketahuna	218	Fd	40.39S	175.44 E
Ekhinádhes Nísoi	130	Ek	38.25N	21.02 E
Ekiatapski hrebet	138	Mc	68.40N	177.50 E
Ekibastuz	136	He	51.42N	75.22 E
Ekimčan	138	If	53.07N	133.02 E
Ekoli	170	Dc	0.23S	24.16 E
Ekoln	116	Ge	59.45N	17.35 E
Ekombe	170	Db	1.16N	21.36 E
Ekonda	138	Fc	65.47N	105.17 E
Eksjö	114	Dh	57.40N	14.57 E
Ekuma	172	Bc	18.10S	15.47 E
Ekwan	180	Jf	53.12N	82.15W
El Aaiún	160	Ff	27.10N	13.12W
El Aargub	162	De	23.37N	15.52W
El Aatf	162	De	23.30N	15.30W
El Abadia	126	Nh	36.13N	1.40 E
El Abd	126	Mi	35.29N	0.42 E
El Abiodh Sidi Cheikh	162	Hc	32.53N	0.34 E
El 'Açâba [3]	162	Ef	16.30N	12.00W
El 'Açâba	162	Ef	16.49N	12.05W
El Adeb Larache	162	Id	27.22N	8.52 E
El Affroun	126	Oh	36.28N	2.37 E
Elafónisi Channel (EN) = Elafonisou, Stenon-	130	Fm	36.25N	23.00 E
Elafonisos	130	Fm	36.29N	22.58 E
Elafonisou Stenón- = Elafónisi Channel (EN)	130	Fm	36.25N	23.00 E
El Agreb	162	Ic	30.48N	5.30 E
El Aguilar	206	Gb	32.12S	65.42W
El Álamo	192	Ab	31.34N	116.02W
El Alia	162	Ic	32.42N	5.26 E
El Amria	126	Ki	35.32N	1.01W
Elan	130	Lc	46.06N	28.04 E
El Andévalo	126	Fg	37.40N	7.00W
El Aouinet	128	Bo	35.52N	7.54 E
El Arahal	126	Gg	37.16N	5.33W
El Aricha	162	Gc	34.13N	1.16W
Elása	130	Jn	35.17N	26.20 E
Elassón	130	Fj	39.54N	22.11 E
Elat	142	Fg	29.33N	34.57 E
Eláti	130	Dk	38.43N	20.39 E
Elato Atoll	208	Fd	7.28N	146.10 E
El Attaf	126	Nh	36.13N	1.40 E
Elâziğ	144	Eb	38.41N	39.14 E
El Azúcar, Presa de-	192	Jd	26.15N	99.00W
Elba	184	Dj	31.25N	86.04W
Elba	110	Hg	42.45N	10.15 E
Elban	138	If	50.05N	136.30 E
El Banco	202	Db	9.01N	73.58W
El Barco de Ávila	126	Gd	40.21N	5.31W
El Barco de Valdeorras	126	Fb	42.25N	6.59W
Elbasani	130	Dh	41.06N	20.05 E
El Baúl	202	Eb	8.57N	68.17W
El Bayadh	162	Hc	33.41N	1.01 E
Elbe	110	Ge	53.50N	9.00 E
Elbe (EN) = Labe	110	Ge	53.50N	9.00 E
Elbe-Lübeck-Kanal	120	Gc	53.50N	10.36 E
Elbert, Mount-	174	If	39.07N	106.27W
Elberton	184	Fh	34.07N	82.52W
Elbe-Seitenkanal	120	Gd	52.22N	10.34 E
Elbeuf	122	Ge	49.17N	1.00 E
Elbeyl	144	Eb	36.41N	37.26 E
El Bierzo	126	Fb	42.40N	6.50W
Elbistan	146	Gc	38.13N	37.12 E
Elbląg	112	He	54.10N	19.25 E
Elbląg [2]	120	Pb	54.10N	19.25 E
Elbląski, Kanał-	120	Pc	53.43N	19.53 E
El Bolsón	206	Ff	41.58S	71.31W
El Bonillo	126	Jf	38.57N	2.32W
Elbow	188	La	51.07N	106.35W
Elbow Cays	194	Gb	23.57N	80.29W
Elbow Lake	186	Id	46.00N	95.58W
Elbrus	110	Kg	43.21N	42.26 E
Elbsandsteingebirge	120	Kf	50.50N	14.12 E
'Ēlbūr	168	He	4.40N	46.40 E
Elburg	122	Lb	52.26N	5.50 E
El Burgo de Osma	126	Ic	41.35N	3.04W
Elburgon	170	Gc	0.18S	35.49 E
El Burro	192	Ic	29.16N	101.55W
Elburz Mountains (EN) = Alborz, Reshteh-ye Kūhhā-ye-	140	Hf	36.00N	53.00 E
El Cajon	182	De	32.48N	116.58W
El Callao	202	Fb	7.21N	61.49W
El Calvario	196	Ch	8.59N	67.00W
El Campo	186	Hl	29.12N	96.16W
El Canelo	192	Ie	24.19N	100.23W
El Cármen	204	Cd	18.49S	58.33W
El Carmen de Bolívar	202	Cb	9.43N	75.07W
El Casco	192	Ge	25.34N	104.35W
El Castillo	194	Eh	11.01N	84.24W
El Centro	182	De	32.48N	115.34W
El Cerro	202	Fg	17.31S	61.34W
El Chaparro	196	Dh	9.10N	65.01W
Elche / Elx	126	Lf	38.15N	0.42W
Elcho Island	212	Hb	11.55S	135.45 E
El Cuy	206	Ge	39.56S	68.20W
Elda	126	Lf	38.29N	0.47W
Ēldab	168	Hd	8.58N	46.38 E
Elde	120	Ic	53.17N	12.40 E
'Ēl Ḍēre	160	Lh	3.55N	47.10 E
El Dere	168	Gd	5.07N	43.12 E
El Descanso	192	Aa	32.12N	116.55W
El Desemboque	190	Bb	30.30N	112.59W
El Dificil	194	Ji	9.51N	74.14W
Eldikan	138	Id	60.38N	135.07 E
El Djouf	158	Gf	21.25N	6.40W
El Doncello	202	Cc	1.43N	75.17W
Eldorado	186	Fk	30.52N	100.36W
El Dorado	190	Cd	24.17N	107.31W
Eldorado	206	Jc	26.24S	54.38W
El Dorado [Ar.-U.S.]	182	Ie	33.13N	92.40W
El Dorado [Ks.-U.S.]	182	Hd	37.49N	96.52W
El Dorado [Ven.]	200	Je	6.44N	61.38W
Eldorado Paulista	204	Hg	24.32S	48.06W
El Dorado Springs	186	Ih	37.52N	94.01W
Eldoret	170	Gb	0.31N	35.17 E
Eldsberga	116	Eh	56.36N	12.59 E
'Ēl Ḍubbo	168	Ge	3.52N	44.45 E
Eldžik	135	De	39.25N	63.01 E
Elefantes, Rio dos-	172	Ed	24.03S	32.40 E
El Eglab	158	Gf	26.30N	5.00W
Elēja/Eleja	114	Fh	56.28N	23.41 E
Eleja/Elēja	114	Fh	56.28N	23.41 E
Elektrėnai/Elektrenaj	116	Kj	54.46N	24.47 E
Elektrenaj/Elektrėnai	116	Kj	54.46N	24.47 E
Elektrostal	136	Dd	55.48N	38.29 E
Elele	166	Gd	5.06N	6.49 E
Elena	130	Ig	42.56N	25.53 E
El Encanto [Bol.]	204	Cc	16.57S	59.24W
El Encanto [Col.]	202	Dd	1.37S	73.13W
Elephant Butte Reservoir	186	Cj	33.19N	107.10W
Elephant Island	222	Re	61.10S	55.14W
Elephant Mountain	186	Ek	30.02N	103.30W
Elesbão Veloso	202	Je	6.13S	42.08W
El Escorial	126	Hd	40.35N	4.10W
Eleşkirt	146	Jc	39.49N	42.40 E
El Estor	194	Cf	15.32N	89.21W
Eleuthera	174	Lg	25.15N	76.20W
Elevsis	130	Gk	38.02N	23.32 E
Elevtheroúpolis	130	Hi	40.55N	24.15 E
El Fendek	126	Gi	35.34N	5.35W
El Ferrol	126	Da	43.29N	8.14W
El Fud	168	Gd	7.15N	42.51 E
El Fuerte [Mex.]	192	Hf	23.50N	103.06W
El Fuerte [Mex.]	190	Cc	26.25N	108.39W
Elgåhogna	116	Eb	62.09N	12.04 E
'Ēl Gāl	168	Ic	11.23N	50.23 E
El Galhak	168	Ec	11.03N	32.42 E
El Gassi	162	Ic	30.55N	5.50 E
Elgen	138	Kd	62.45N	150.40 E
Elgepiggen	114	Ce	62.10N	11.22 E
El Ghomri	126	Mi	35.41N	0.12 E
Elgi	138	Jd	64.20N	142.05 E
Elgin [Il.-U.S.]	182	Jc	42.02N	88.17W
Elgin [N.D.-U.S.]	186	Fc	46.24N	101.51W
Elgin [Or.-U.S.]	188	Gd	45.34N	117.55W
Elgin [Scot.-U.K.]	118	Jd	57.39N	3.20W
Elginski	138	Jd	64.48N	141.50 E
Elgjaij	138	Gd	62.28N	117.37 E
El Goléa	160	He	30.34N	2.53 E
Elgon, Mont-	158	Kh	1.08N	34.33 E
Elgoran	168	Gd	5.04N	44.22 E
El Grao, Castellón de la Plana-	126	Me	39.58N	0.01 E
El Grao, Valencia-	126	Le	39.27N	0.20W
El Grao de Gandia, Gandia-	126	Lf	38.59N	0.09W
El Guapo	196	Dg	10.09N	65.58W
El Guayabo	194	Ki	8.37N	72.20W
El Hadjar	128	Bn	36.48N	7.45 E
El Hajeb	162	Fc	33.42N	5.22W
El Ham	126	Qi	35.42N	4.52 E
El Hammam	126	Li	35.50N	0.15W

Index Symbols

- [1] Independent Nation
- [2] State, Region
- [3] District, County
- [4] Municipality
- [5] Colony, Dependency
- Continent
- Physical Region
- Historical or Cultural Region
- Mount, Mountain
- Volcano
- Hill
- Mountains, Mountain Range
- Hills, Escarpment
- Plateau, Upland
- Pass, Gap
- Plain, Lowland
- Delta
- Salt Flat
- Valley, Canyon
- Crater, Cave
- Karst Features
- Depression
- Polder
- Desert, Dunes
- Forest, Woods
- Heath, Steppe
- Oasis
- Cape, Point
- Coast, Beach
- Cliff
- Peninsula
- Isthmus
- Sandbank
- Island
- Atoll
- Rock, Reef
- Islands, Archipelago
- Rocks, Reefs
- Coral Reef
- Well, Spring
- Geyser
- River, Stream
- Waterfall, Rapids
- River Mouth, Estuary
- Lake
- Salt Lake
- Intermittent Lake
- Reservoir
- Swamp, Pond
- Canal
- Glacier
- Ice Shelf, Pack Ice
- Ocean
- Sea
- Gulf, Bay
- Strait, Fjord
- Lagoon
- Bank
- Seamount
- Tablemount
- Ridge
- Shelf
- Basin
- Escarpment, Sea Scarp
- Fracture
- Trench, Abyss
- National Park, Reserve
- Point of Interest
- Recreation Site
- Cave, Cavern
- Historic Site
- Ruins
- Wall, Walls
- Church, Abbey
- Temple
- Scientific Station
- Railway station
- Airport
- Port
- Military installation
- Lighthouse
- Mine
- Tunnel
- Dam, Bridge

'Ēl Hamurre 168 Hd 7.11N 48.55 E
El Hank 158 Gf 24.00N 6.30W
El Harrach, Al Jazā'ir- 126 Ph 36.43N 3.08 E
Elhotovo 132 Nh 43.20N 44.13 E
Elhovo 130 Jg 42.10N 26.34 E
El Hueců 206 Fe 37.37S 70.36W
Elida 186 Ej 33.57N 103.39W
Éliki, Vallée d'- 166 Gc 14.45N 7.15 E
Elila 170 Ec 2.43S 25.53 E
Elila 158 Ji 2.45S 25.53 E
Elimäki 116 Ld 60.43N 26.28 E
Elin Pelin 130 Gg 42.40N 23.36 E
Elisejna 130 Gf 43.05N 23.29 E
Elisenvaara 116 Mc 61.19N 29.47 E
Elista 112 Kf 46.16N 44.14 E
Elizabeth [Austl.] 210 Eh 34.45S 138.39 E
Elizabeth [N.J.-U.S.] 184 Je 40.40N 74.13W
Elizabeth, Cape- 188 Cc 47.22N 124.22W
Elizabeth City 182 Ld 36.18N 76.14W
Elizabeth Reef 208 Gg 29.55S 159.05 E
Elizabethton 184 Fg 36.21N 82.13W
Elizabethtown [Ky.-U.S.] 184 Eg 37.42N 85.52W
Elizabethtown [N.C.-U.S.] 184 Hh 34.38N 78.37W
El Jadida 160 Ge 33.15N 8.30W
El Jadida [3] 162 Fc 32.54N 8.30W
El Jícaro 194 Dg 13.43N 86.08W
'Ēl Jilib 168 He 3.48N 47.07 E
Elk 120 Sc 53.50N 22.22 E
Ełk 120 Sc 53.32N 22.47 E
El Kala 162 Ib 36.54N 8.27 E
El Kantara 162 Ib 35.13N 5.43 E
El Karimia 126 Nh 36.07N 1.33 E
Elk City [Id.-U.S.] 188 Hd 45.51N 115.29W
Elk City [Ok.-U.S.] 186 Gi 35.25N 99.25W
El Kelaa des Srarhna 162 Fc 32.03N 7.24W
El Kelaa des Srarhna [3] 162 Fc 32.03N 7.30W
El Kere 168 Gd 5.51N 42.06 E
Elkhart [In.-U.S.] 182 Jc 41.41N 85.58W
Elkhart [Ks.-U.S.] 186 Fh 37.00N 101.54W
El Khatt 162 Ef 19.00N 12.25W
Elkhead Mountains 186 Cf 40.50N 107.05W
El Khnâchîch 166 Ea 21.20N 3.45W
Elkhorn River 186 Hf 41.07N 96.19W
Elkins 184 Hf 38.56N 79.53W
Elk Lake 184 Gb 47.42N 80.11W
Elk Mountain 188 Lf 41.38N 106.32W
Elk Mountains 186 Cg 38.55N 106.50W
Elko 176 He 40.50N 115.46W
Elk Peak 188 Jc 46.27N 110.46W
Elk River 186 Jd 45.18N 93.35W
Elk River 184 Gf 38.21N 81.38W
Elku kalns 116 Kg 57.04N 25.23 E
Ell, Lake- 212 Fe 29.15S 127.45 E
Ellás=Greece (EN) [1] 112 Ih 39.00N 22.00 E
Ellé 122 Cg 47.52N 3.32W
Ellef Ringnes 174 Ib 78.30N 104.00W
Ellen, Mount- 182 Ed 38.07N 110.49W
Ellendale 186 Hc 46.06N 98.32W
Ellensburg 182 Cb 46.40N 120.32W
Ellenville 184 Je 41.43N 74.23W
Ellesmere 174 Kb 79.00N 82.00W
Ellesmere, Lake- 218 Ee 43.45S 172.30 E
Ellice 180 Hc 68.02N 103.25W
Ellice Islands → Tuvalu [1] 210 Ie 8.00S 178.00 E
Elliot [Austl.] 212 Gc 17.35S 133.35 E
Elliot [S.Afr.] 172 Df 31.18S 27.50 E
Elliot, Mount- 212 Jc 19.29S 146.58 E
Elliot Lake 180 Jg 46.23N 82.39W
Ellisras 172 Dd 23.40S 27.46 E
Elliston 212 Gf 33.39S 134.55 E
Ellisville 186 Lk 31.36N 89.12W
Ellmau 128 Gc 47.31N 12.18 E
Ellös 114 Cg 58.11N 11.27 E
Ellsworth [Ks.-U.S.] 186 Gg 38.44N 98.14W
Ellsworth [Me.-U.S.] 184 Mc 44.33N 68.26W
Ellsworth [Nb.-U.S.] 186 Ee 42.04N 102.15W
Ellsworth, Lake- 186 Gi 34.48N 98.20W
Ellsworth Land (EN) 222 Pf 75.30S 80.00W
Ellsworth Mountains 222 Pf 78.30S 85.00W
Ellwangen (Jagst) 120 Gh 48.57N 10.08 E
Elm 120 Gd 52.09N 10.53 E
El Macao 194 Md 18.46N 68.33W
Elmadağ 146 Ec 39.55N 33.15 E
Elma Dağı 130 Mk 38.46N 29.32 E
El Maestrat/El Maestrazgo 126 Ld 40.30N 0.10W
El Maestrazgo/El Maestrat 126 Ld 40.30N 0.10W
El Mahia 166 Ea 22.30N 2.30W
El Maitén 206 Ff 42.03S 71.10W
Elmaki 166 Gb 17.55N 8.20 E
El Malah 126 Ph 36.18N 3.14 E
Elmalı 146 Cd 36.44N 29.56 E
Elmalı 146 Ic 39.25N 40.35 E
El Manteco 196 Ei 7.27N 62.32W
El Marfil 204 Bb 15.35S 60.19W
El Marsa 126 Mh 36.24N 0.55 E
El Medo 168 Gd 5.41N 41.46 E
El Meghaier 162 Ic 33.57N 5.56 E
Elmhurst 186 Mf 41.53N 87.56W
El Milagro 206 Gd 31.01S 65.59W
Elmira 182 Lc 42.06N 76.50W
El Mrâyer 162 Fe 21.30N 8.10W
El Mreiti 162 Fe 23.29N 7.52W
El Mreyyé 158 Gg 19.30N 7.00W
Elmshorn 120 Fc 53.45N 9.39 E
Elmstein 124 Je 49.22N 7.56 E
Elne 122 Il 42.36N 2.58 E
El Nevado, Cerro- 206 Ge 35.35S 68.30W
El Niabo 168 Fe 4.33N 39.59 E
El Nihuil 206 Gd 34.58S 68.40W
El Novillo 192 Ec 28.40N 109.30W
El Novillo, Presa- 192 Ec 29.05N 109.45W
El Ochenta y Uno 192 Kg 21.35N 97.57W
Elorn 122 Bf 48.27N 4.16W
Elortondo 204 Bk 33.42S 61.37W
Elorza 202 Eb 7.03N 69.31W
Elota, Río- 192 Ff 23.52N 106.56W
El Oued 162 Ic 33.20N 6.53 E
Eloy 188 Jj 32.45N 111.33W
El Palmar 196 Fh 8.01N 61.53W
El Palmito 192 Ge 25.40N 104.59W
El Panadés/El Penedès 126 Nc 41.25N 1.30 E
El Pao [Ven.] 196 Eh 8.06N 62.33W
El Pao [Ven.] 196 Bh 9.38N 68.08W
El Paraiso 194 Dg 13.51N 86.34W
El Paraíso [3] 194 Df 14.10N 86.30W
El Páramo 126 Gb 42.25N 5.45W
El Pardo, Madrid- 126 Id 40.32N 3.46W
El Paso [Il.-U.S.] 186 Lf 40.44N 89.01W
El Paso [Tx.-U.S.] 176 If 31.45N 106.29W
El Penedès/El Panadés 126 Nc 41.25N 1.30 E
El Perú 196 Fi 7.19N 61.49W
El Pico 202 Fg 15.57S 64.42W
El Pilar 196 Eg 10.32N 63.09W
El Pintado 206 Hb 24.38S 61.27W
El Port / Puerto de Sóller 126 Oe 39.48N 2.41 E
El Porvenir [Hond.] 194 Df 15.41N 87.11W
El Porvenir [Pan.] 194 Hi 9.12N 80.08W
El Porvenir [Ven.] 196 Bi 6.55N 68.42W
El Potosí 192 Ie 24.51N 100.19W
el Prat de Llobregat / Prat de Llobregat 126 Oc 41.20N 2.06 E
El Priorat/El Priorato 126 Mc 41.10N 1.00 E
El Priorato/El Priorat 126 Mc 41.10N 1.00 E
El Progreso [3] 194 Cf 14.50N 90.00W
El Progreso [Guat.] 194 Bf 14.51N 90.04W
El Progreso [Hond.] 194 Df 15.21N 87.49W
El Puente del Arzobispo 126 Ge 39.48N 5.10W
El Puerto 192 Dc 28.45N 111.20W
El Puerto de Santa María 126 Fh 36.36N 6.13W
El Rastro 196 Ch 9.03N 67.27W
El Real de Santa María 194 Ii 8.08N 77.43W
El Reno 182 Hd 35.32N 97.57W
El Ribeiro 126 Db 42.25N 8.10W
Elrose 188 Ka 51.13N 108.01W
El Saler 126 Le 39.23N 0.20W
El Salto 190 Cd 23.47N 105.23W
El Salvador [1] 176 Kh 13.50N 88.55W
El Samán de Apure 196 Bi 7.55N 68.44W
El Sauce [Mex.] 192 De 24.34N 111.29W
El Sauce [Nic.] 194 Dg 12.53N 86.32W
El Sauz 192 Fc 29.03N 106.15W
Elsberry 186 Kg 39.10N 90.47W
Elsdorf 124 Id 50.56N 6.34 E
Else 124 Kb 52.12N 8.40 E
El Seibo 194 Md 18.46N 68.52W
Elsen, Paderborn- 124 Kc 51.44N 8.41 E
Elsen Nur 152 Fd 35.08N 92.20 E
'Ēl Shāma 168 Ge 2.46N 41.03 E
El Socorro 196 Dh 8.59N 65.44W
El Sombrero 202 Eb 9.23N 67.03W
Elst 124 Hc 51.55N 5.52 E
Elsterwerda 120 Je 51.27N 13.32 E
El Sueco 190 Ce 29.54N 106.24W
El Taht 126 Mi 35.27N 0.46 E
El Tala 206 Gc 26.07S 65.17W
Eltanin Bay 222 Pf 73.40S 82.00W
Eltham 218 Fc 39.26S 174.18 E
El Tigre 200 Je 8.55N 64.15W
El Tigre, Isla- 194 Dg 13.16N 87.38W
El Toboso 126 Ie 39.31N 3.00W
El Tocuyo 202 Eb 9.47N 69.48W
Elton 132 Oe 49.08N 46.50 E
Elton, ozero- 136 Ef 49.10N 46.40 E
El Torcal 126 Hh 36.55N 4.35W
El Toro / Toro, Monte- 126 Qe 39.59N 4.07 E
El Trébol 204 Bk 32.12S 61.42W
El Trigo 204 Cl 35.52S 59.24W
El Triunfo [Hond.] 194 Dg 13.06N 87.00W
El Triunfo [Mex.] 192 Df 23.47N 110.08W
El Tuito 192 Gg 20.19N 105.22W
El Turbio 206 Fh 51.41S 72.05W
Eltville am Rhein 124 Kd 50.02N 8.07 E
Eltz 124 Jd 50.12N 7.18 E
Elūru 148 Ge 17.05N 82.15 E
Elva 114 Gg 58.13N 26.25 E
El Valle 194 Gi 8.31N 30.08W
El Vallès / El Vallés 126 Oc 41.35N 2.15 E
Elvas 126 Ef 38.53N 7.10W
El Vejo, Cerro- 202 Db 7.30N 73.05W
El Venado, Isla- 194 Fh 11.57N 83.44W
Elverum 114 Cf 60.53N 11.34 E
El Viejo 194 Dg 12.40N 87.10W
El Viejo, Volcán- 174 Kh 12.38N 87.11W
El Vigía 194 Li 8.38N 71.39W
El Vigía, Cerro- 192 Gg 21.25N 104.00W
El Wak 170 Hb 2.49N 40.56 E
Elwell, Lake- 188 Jb 48.22N 111.17W
Elwood 184 Ee 40.17N 85.50W
Elx / Elche 126 Lf 38.15N 0.42W
Ely [Eng.-U.K.] 118 Ni 52.24N 0.16 E
Ely [Mn.-U.S.] 182 Ib 47.54N 91.51W
Ely [Nv.-U.S.] 176 Hf 39.15N 114.53W
Elyria 184 Fe 41.22N 82.06W
El Yunque 197a Cb 18.18N 65.47W
Elz 124 Kd 50.25N 8.02 E
Elzbach 124 Jd 50.12N 7.22 E
Emaé 219b Dc 17.04S 168.22 E
Ema jõgi / Emajygi 116 Lf 58.20N 27.15 E
Emajygi / Ema jõgi 116 Lf 58.20N 27.15 E
Emali 170 Gc 2.05S 37.28 E
Emāmshahr [Iran] 144 Hb 36.50N 54.29 E
Emāmshahr [Iran] 144 Ib 36.25N 55.01 E
Emāmzādeh 'Abbās 146 Lf 32.25N 47.55 E
Emān 114 Dh 57.08N 16.30 E
Emba 136 Ff 48.50N 58.10 E
Emba 110 Lf 46.38N 53.04 E
Embarcación, Rio- 204 Ff 23.27S 53.58W
Embarcación 206 Hb 23.13S 64.06W
Embarras Portage 180 Ge 58.25N 111.27W
Embarras River 186 Mg 38.39N 87.37W
Embrun 122 Mj 44.34N 6.30 E
Embu 170 Gc 0.32S 37.27 E
Emden 120 Dc 53.22N 7.13 E
Emeldžak 138 He 58.27N 126.57 E
Emerald 210 Fg 23.32S 148.10 E
Emerald 180 Ga 76.50N 114.00W
Emerson 186 Hb 49.00N 97.12W
Emet 146 Cc 39.20N 29.15 E
Emi Koussi 158 Ig 19.55N 18.30 E
Emiliano Zapata 192 Ni 17.45N 91.46W
Emilia-Romagna [2] 128 Ef 44.45N 11.00 E
Emilio R. Coni 204 Cj 30.04S 58.16W
Emily Rocu 198 Hh 29.40S 87.25W
Emin/Dorbiljin 152 Db 46.32N 83.39 E
Emine, Nos- 130 Kg 42.42N 27.54 E
Emira Island 214 Dh 1.40S 150.00 E
Emirdağ 146 Dc 39.01N 31.10 E
Emisu, Tarso- 158 If 21.13N 18.32 E
Emlichheim 120 Cd 52.37N 6.51 E
Emmaboda 114 Dh 56.38N 15.32 E
Emmaste 114 Fg 58.43N 22.36 E
Emme 128 Bd 47.10N 7.35 E
Emmeloord, Noordoostpolder- 124 Hb 52.42N 5.44 E
Emmelshausen 124 Jd 50.09N 7.34 E
Emmen 122 Mb 52.47N 6.55 E
Emmendingen 120 Dh 48.08N 7.51 E
Emmen-Emmer-Compascuum 124 Jb 52.49N 7.03 E
Emmen-Klazienaveen 124 Jb 52.44N 7.01 E
Emmen-Nieuw-Weerdinge 124 Jb 52.52N 7.01 E
Emmental 128 Bd 46.55N 7.45 E
Emmen-Weerdinge 124 Ib 52.49N 6.57 E
Emmer 124 Lb 52.03N 9.23 E
Emmer-Compascuum, Emmen- 124 Jb 52.49N 7.03 E
Emmerich 120 Ce 51.50N 6.15 E
Emmet 212 Id 24.40S 144.28 E
Emmetsburg 186 Ie 43.07N 94.41W
Emmett 188 Ge 43.52N 116.30W
Emmonak 178 Gd 62.46N 164.30W
Emőd 120 Qi 47.56N 20.49 E
Emory 188 Jf 41.05N 111.16W
Emory Peak 182 Gf 29.13N 103.17W
Empalme 190 Bc 27.58N 110.51W
Empangeni 172 Ee 28.50S 31.48 E
Empedrado 206 Ii 27.57S 58.48W
Emperor Seamounts (EN) 106 Je 40.00N 171.00 E
Empoli 128 Eg 43.43N 10.57 E
Empordà / Ampurdán 126 Ob 42.12N 2.45 E
Emporia [Ks.-U.S.] 182 Hd 38.24N 96.11W
Emporia [Va.-U.S.] 184 Ig 36.42N 77.33W
Emporium 184 He 41.31N 78.14W
Empress Augusta Bay 219a Bb 6.25S 155.05 E
Empress Mine 172 Dc 18.27S 29.27 E
Empúries / Ampurias 126 Pb 42.10N 3.05 E
Ems 122 Na 53.19N 7.03 E
Emsbach 124 Kd 50.24N 8.06 E
Emsdetten 120 Dd 52.11N 7.32 E
Ems-Jade-Kanal 120 Dc 53.30N 7.30 E
Emsland 120 Dd 52.50N 7.20 E
Emstek 124 Kb 52.50N 8.09 E
Emumägi/Emumjagi 116 Lf 58.54N 26.23 E
Emumjagi/Emumägi 116 Lf 58.54N 26.23 E
Ena 156 Ed 35.27N 137.24 E
Enånger 114 Df 61.32N 17.00 E
Enaratoli 150 Kg 3.55S 136.21 E
Enard Bay 118 Hc 58.06N 5.20W
Ena-San 156 Ed 35.26N 137.36 E
Enbetsu 154 Pb 44.44N 141.47 E
Encantada, Cerro de la- 174 Hf 31.00N 115.23W
Encantada, Sierra de la- 192 He 28.30N 102.20W
Encantadas, Serra das- 204 Fj 30.40S 53.00W
Encantado, Cerro- 190 Bc 27.03N 112.30W
Encarnación 200 Kh 27.20S 55.54W
Encarnación de Díaz 192 Hg 21.31N 102.14W
Enchi 166 Ed 5.49N 2.49W
Encinal 186 Gl 28.02N 99.21W
Encinasola 126 Ff 38.08N 6.52W
Encontrados 202 Db 8.46N 72.30W
Encounter Bay 212 Hg 35.35S 138.45 E
Encruzijada 194 Hb 22.37N 79.52W
Encruzilhada do Sul 204 Fj 30.32S 52.31W
Encs 120 Rh 48.20N 21.08 E
Ende 142 Oj 8.50S 121.39 E
Endeavour Strait 212 Ib 10.50S 142.15 E
Endelave 116 Di 55.45N 10.15 E
Enderbury Atoll 208 Je 3.08S 171.05W
Enderby 188 Fa 50.33N 119.08W
Enderby Land 222 Ee 67.30S 53.00 E
Endicott Mountains 178 Ic 67.50N 152.00W
Ené, Río- 202 Df 11.09S 74.19W
Energetik 136 Fe 51.44N 58.48 E
Enewetak Atoll 208 Hc 11.30N 162.15 E
Enez 146 Bb 40.44N 26.04 E
Enez Körfezi 130 Ii 40.45N 26.00 E
Enfer, Pointe d'- 197b Bc 14.24N 60.52W
Enfer, Portes d'- 170 Ed 5.05S 27.30 E
Enfield 184 Ig 36.11N 77.47W
Enfield, London- 124 Bc 51.40N 0.04W
Engadin/Engiadin'ota/Engadina 128 Dd 46.35N 10.00 E
Engadina/Engadin/Engiadin'ota 128 Dd 46.35N 10.00 E
Engaño, Cabo- 190 Ke 18.37N 68.20W
Engaru 154 Qb 44.03N 143.31 E
Engelberg 128 Cd 46.50N 8.24 E
Engelhard 184 Jh 35.31N 76.00W
Engels 112 Ke 51.30N 46.07 E
Engelskirchen 124 Jd 50.59N 7.24 E
Engenho 204 Db 15.10S 56.25W
Enger 124 Kb 52.08N 8.34 E
Engeren 116 Ec 61.35N 12.05 E
Engershatu 168 Fb 16.34N 38.15 E
Enggano, Pulau- 140 Mj 5.24S 102.16 E
Enghien/Edingen 124 Gd 50.42N 4.02 E
Engiadin'ota/Engadina/Engadin 128 Dd 46.35N 10.00 E
England [2] 118 Li 52.30N 1.30W
England 110 Fe 52.30N 1.30W
Englehart 180 Jg 47.49N 79.52W
Englewood 186 Dg 39.39N 104.59W
English 184 Df 38.20N 86.28W
English Channel 110 Fe 50.20N 1.00W
English Channel (EN)=La Manche 110 Fe 50.20N 1.00W
English Coast 222 Qf 73.30S 73.00W
English River 186 Kb 49.13N 90.58W
English River 186 Ia 50.12N 95.00W
Engozero, ozero- 114 Hd 65.45N 33.30 E
Enguera 126 Lf 38.59N 0.41W
Engure/Engures 116 Jg 57.09N 23.06 E
Engures/Engure 116 Jg 57.09N 23.06 E
Engures, ozero- / Engures ezers 116 Jg 57.15N 23.10 E
Engures ezers / Engures, ozero- 116 Jg 57.15N 23.10 E
Enh-Gajvan 152 Gb 48.05N 97.35 E
Enid 176 Jf 36.19N 97.48W
Enid Lake 186 Li 34.10N 89.50W
Eniwa 154 Pc 42.53N 141.14 E
Eniwa-Dake 156a Bb 42.47N 141.17 E
Enkenbach-Alsenborn 124 Je 49.29N 7.53 E
Enkhuizen 122 Lb 52.42N 5.17 E
Enklinge 116 Id 60.20N 20.45 E
Enköping 114 Dg 59.38N 17.04 E
Enna 128 Im 37.34N 14.16 E
Ennadai 180 Hd 61.10N 101.00W
Ennadai Lake 180 Hd 60.55N 101.20W
Enné 168 Bc 14.24N 18.45 E
Ennedi 158 Jg 17.15N 22.00 E
Ennell, Lough-/Loch Ainninn 118 Fh 53.28N 7.24W
Ennepetal 124 Jc 51.18N 7.21 E
Ennigerloh 124 Kc 51.50N 8.01 E
Enning 186 Ed 44.37N 102.31W
Ennis [Mt.-U.S.] 188 Jd 45.21N 111.44W
Ennis [Tx.-U.S.] 186 Hj 32.20N 96.38W
Ennis/Inis 118 Ei 52.50N 8.59W
Enniscorthy/Inis Córthaidh 118 Gi 52.30N 6.34W
Enniskillen/Inis Ceithleann 118 Fg 54.21N 7.38W
Ennistimon / Inis Díomáin 118 Di 52.57N 9.13W
Enns 128 Ib 48.12N 14.28 E
Enns 110 Hf 48.14N 14.30 E
Ennstaler Alpen 128 Ic 47.37N 14.35 E
Eno 114 He 62.48N 30.09 E
Enontekiö 114 Fb 68.23N 23.38 E
Enonvesi [Fin.] 116 Lc 61.20N 26.30 E
Enonvesi [Fin.] 116 Mb 62.10N 28.55 E
Enozero, ozero- 114 Jb 68.10N 38.00 E
Enrekang 150 Gg 3.34S 119.47 E
Enrique Carbó 204 Ck 33.08S 59.14W
Enriquillo 194 Le 17.54N 71.14W
Enriquillo, Lago- 190 Je 18.27N 71.39W
Enschede 122 Mb 52.12N 6.53 E
Ensenada [Arg.] 204 Dl 34.51S 57.55W
Ensenada [Mex.] 176 Hf 31.52N 116.37W
Enshi 152 Ie 30.16N 109.26 E
Enshū-Nada 156 Ed 34.30N 138.00 E
Entebbe 160 Kh 0.04N 32.28 E
Entenbühl 120 Ig 49.46N 12.24 E
Enterprise [Al.-U.S.] 184 Ej 31.19N 85.50W
Enterprise [N.W.T.-Can.] 180 Fd 60.39N 116.08W
Enterprise [Or.-U.S.] 188 Gd 45.25N 117.17W
Entinas, Punta- 126 Jh 36.41N 2.46W
Entrada, Punta- 190 Ab 30.22N 115.59W
Entraygues-sur-Truyère 122 Ij 44.39N 2.34 E
Entrecasteaux, Récifs d'- = D'Entrecasteaux Reefs (EN) 208 Hf 18.20S 163.00 E
Entrepeñas, Embalse de- 126 Jd 40.34N 2.42W
Entre Rios 202 Fh 21.32S 64.12W
Entre Rios [2] 206 Id 32.00S 59.00W
Entre Rios de Minas 204 Je 20.41S 44.04W
Entrevaux 122 Mk 43.57N 6.49 E
Entroncamento 126 De 39.28N 8.28W
Enugu 160 Hh 6.26N 7.29 E
Enugu Ezike 166 Gd 6.59N 7.27 E
Envermeu 124 De 49.54N 1.16 E
Envigado 202 Cb 6.08N 75.39W
Envira 202 De 7.18S 70.13W
Envira, Rio- 202 De 7.19S 70.15W
Enyamba 170 Dc 3.40S 24.58 E
Enyélé 170 Cb 2.49N 18.06 E
Enz 120 Fh 49.00N 9.10 E
Enza 128 Ef 44.54N 10.31 E
Enzan 154 Og 34.52N 138.44 E
Enzgau 124 Kf 48.48N 8.37 E
Eo 126 Ea 43.28N 7.03W
Eochaill/Youghal 118 Fj 51.57N 7.50W
Eolie o Lipari, Isole-=Lipari Islands (EN) 110 Hh 38.35N 14.55 E
Epanomi 130 Fi 40.26N 22.56 E
Epazote, Cerro- 190 Cd 24.35N 105.07W
Epe [Neth.] 124 Hb 52.21N 5.59 E
Epe [Nig.] 166 Fd 6.35N 3.59 E
Epéna 170 Cb 1.22N 17.29 E
Epernay 122 Je 49.03N 3.57 E
Epe-Vaassen 124 Hb 52.17N 5.58 E
Ephesus (EN)=Efes 130 Kl 37.55N 27.20 E
Ephraim 188 Jg 39.22N 111.35W
Ephrata 188 Fc 47.19N 119.33W
Epi, Île- 208 Hf 16.43S 168.15 E
Epidamnus 130 Ch 41.19N 19.26 E
Epidaurus (EN) = Epidhavros 130 Gl 37.38N 23.09 E
Epidhavros = Epidaurus (EN) 130 Gl 37.38N 23.09 E
Épila 126 Kc 41.36N 1.17W
Epinal 122 Mf 48.11N 6.27 E
Epirus (EN)=Ipiros 110 Ih 39.30N 20.40 E
Epirus (EN)=Ipiros 130 Dj 39.30N 20.40 E
Episkopi 146 Ee 34.40N 32.54 E
Eppelheim 124 Ke 49.24N 8.38 E
Epping 124 Cc 51.42N 0.07 E
Eppingen 124 Ke 49.08N 8.54 E
Epsom 118 Mj 51.20N 0.16W
Epte 122 He 49.04N 1.31 E
Epukiro 172 Bd 21.41S 19.08 E
Epukiro 172 Bd 21.28S 19.59 E
Epulu 170 Eb 1.15N 28.21 E
Eqlīd 144 Hc 30.55N 52.39 E
Équateur = Equator (EN) 170 Eb 1.00N 20.00 E
Equator (EN)=Equateur [2] 170 Eb 1.00N 20.00 E
Equatorial Guinea (EN)= Guinea Ecuatorial [1] 160 Hh 2.00N 9.00 E
Equinox Mountain 184 Kd 43.15N 73.10W
Era [It.] 128 Eg 43.40N 10.38 E
Era [Sud.] 168 Dd 5.30N 29.50 E
Eraclea 128 Kj 40.15N 16.40 E
Eraclea Minoa 128 Hm 37.25N 13.18 E
Eradaka 219b Dc 17.39S 168.08 E
Eräjärvi 116 Kc 61.35N 24.34 E
Eratini 130 Fk 38.22N 22.14 E
Erbaa 146 Kb 40.42N 36.36 E
Erbach 120 Eg 49.39N 9.00 E
Erbeskopf 120 Dg 49.44N 7.05 E
Erbil 142 Gf 36.11N 44.01 E
Erbil [3] 146 Je 36.10N 44.00 E
Ercek 146 Jc 38.39N 43.36 E
Erçek Gölü 146 Jc 38.39N 43.32 E
Erciş 146 Jc 39.00N 43.19 E
Erciyas Dağı 140 Ff 38.32N 35.28 E
Ercolano 128 Ij 40.48N 14.21 E
Ercsi 120 Oi 47.15N 18.54 E
Érd 120 Oi 47.22N 18.56 E
Erdaobaihe 152 Mc 42.28N 128.05 E
Erdao Jiang 154 Ic 42.35N 127.10 E
Erdek 146 Bb 40.24N 27.48 E
Erdek Körfezi 146 Bb 40.25N 27.45 E
Erdemli 146 Fd 36.37N 34.18 E
Erdene-Cagan 152 Kb 45.55N 115.30 E
Erdene-Dalaj 152 Hb 46.02N 104.55 E
Erdene-Mandal 152 Hb 48.30N 101.21 E
Erdi 158 Jg 19.05N 22.40 E
Erdi Ma 168 Cb 18.35N 23.30 E
Erding 120 Hh 48.18N 11.56 E
Erdinger Moos 120 Hh 48.20N 11.50 E
Erdre 122 Eg 47.13N 1.32W
Erebus, Mount- 222 Kf 77.32S 167.09 E
Erechim 206 Jc 27.38S 52.17W
Ereğli [Tur.] 144 Db 37.31N 34.04 E
Ereğli [Tur.] 144 Da 41.17N 31.25 E
Erei, Monti- 128 Im 37.35N 14.20 E
Ereke 150 Hg 4.45S 123.10 E
Eren 146 Dd 37.25N 30.05 E
Erenhot 142 Ne 43.35N 112.00 E
Erepecu, Lago do- 202 Gd 1.20S 56.35W
Eresma 126 Hc 41.26N 4.45W
Erétria 130 Gk 38.25N 23.48 E
Erfelek 146 Fb 41.55N 34.57 E
Erfengshan 154 Ag 35.50N 111.47 E
Erfoud 162 Gc 31.26N 4.14W
Erft 120 Ce 51.11N 6.44 E
Erftstadt 124 Id 50.48N 6.49 E
Erfurt 112 He 50.59N 11.02 E
Ergani 146 Hc 38.17N 39.46 E
Ergene 146 Bb 41.01N 26.22 E
Erges 126 Ee 39.40N 7.01W
Ergig, Bahr- 168 Bc 11.22N 15.24 E
Ergli/Ērgļi 114 Fh 56.55N 25.41 E
Ērgļi/Ergli 114 Fh 56.55N 25.41 E
Ergun He 140 Od 53.20N 121.28 E
Ergun Youqi (Labudalin) 152 La 50.16N 120.09 E
Ergun Zuoqi (Genhe) 142 Od 50.47N 121.32 E
Er Hai 152 Hf 25.45N 100.10 E
Eria 126 Gb 42.03N 5.44W
Eriba 168 Fb 16.37N 36.04 E
Eriboll, Loch- 118 Ic 58.30N 4.40W
Eric 180 Kf 51.52N 65.45W
Erice 129 Gl 38.02N 12.35 E
Ericeira 125 Cf 38.59N 9.25W
Erichsen Lake 180 Jb 70.36N 80.20W
Ericht, Loch- 118 Ie 56.50N 4.25W
Erick 186 Gi 35.13N 99.52W
Eridu 146 Lg 36.00N 44.00 E
Erie 176 Ke 42.08N 80.04W
Erie, Lake- 174 Ke 42.15N 81.00W
'Erigābo 168 Hc 10.37N 47.24 E
Erîgât 158 Gg 19.40N 4.50W
Erikoússa 130 Cj 39.53N 19.35 E
Eriksdale 186 Ga 50.52N 98.06W
Eriksenstretet 179 Oc 79.00N 26.00 E
Erikub Atoll 208 Id 9.08N 170.02 E
Erimanthos Óros 130 El 37.58N 21.50 E
Erimo-Misaki 152 Pc 41.55N 143.15 E
Eriskay 118 Fd 57.04N 7.13W
Eritrea [3] 168 Fb 15.00N 39.00 E
Eritrea 158 Kg 15.00N 40.00 E
Eritrea 168 Fb 15.00N 40.00 E
Erjas 126 Ee 39.40N 7.01W
Erkelenz 124 Ic 51.05N 6.19 E
Erken 116 He 59.50N 18.35 E
Erkowit 168 Fb 18.46N 37.07 E
Erlangdian → Dawu 154 Ci 31.33N 114.07 E
Erlangen 120 Hg 49.36N 11.01 E
Erlang Shan 152 Hf 29.58N 102.20 E
Erlauf 128 Jb 48.12N 15.11 E
Erldunda 212 Ge 25.14S 133.12 E
Erlenbach 124 Ke 49.48N 8.11 E
Erlong Shan 152 Mc 43.30N 128.44 E
Ermelo [Neth.] 124 Hb 52.19N 5.37 E
Ermelo [S.Afr.] 172 De 26.34S 29.58 E
Ermenek 146 Ed 36.38N 32.54 E
Ermenistan=Armenia (EN) 140 Gf 39.10N 43.00 E
Ermenistan=Armenia (EN) 144 Fb 39.10N 43.00 E
Ermenonville 124 Ee 49.08N 2.42 E
Ermesinde 126 Dc 41.13N 8.33W
Ermoúpolis 130 Hl 37.27N 24.56 E
Erndtebrück 124 Kd 50.59N 8.16 E
Erne/An Éirne 118 Eg 54.30N 8.15W
Ernée 122 Ff 48.18N 0.56W
Ernest Legouvé Reef 208 Lh 35.12S 150.35W

Index Symbols

[1] Independent Nation
[2] State, Region
[3] District, County
[4] Municipality
[5] Colony, Dependency
Continent
Physical Region
Historical or Cultural Region
Mount, Mountain
Volcano
Hill
Mountains, Mountain Range
Hills, Escarpment
Plateau, Upland
Pass, Gap
Plain, Lowland
Delta
Salt Flat
Valley, Canyon
Crater, Cave
Karst Features
Depression
Polder
Desert, Dunes
Forest, Woods
Heath, Steppe
Oasis
Cape, Point
Coast, Beach
Cliff
Peninsula
Isthmus
Sandbank
Island
Atoll
Rock, Reef
Islands, Archipelago
Rocks, Reefs
Coral Reef
Well, Spring
Geyser
River, Stream
Waterfall, Rapids
River Mouth, Estuary
Lake
Salt Lake
Intermittent Lake
Reservoir
Swamp, Pond
Canal
Glacier
Ice Shelf, Pack Ice
Ocean
Sea
Gulf, Bay
Strait, Fjord
Lagoon
Bank
Seamount
Tablemount
Ridge
Shelf
Basin
Escarpment, Sea Scarp
Fracture
Trench, Abyss
National Park, Reserve
Point of Interest
Recreation Site
Cave, Cavern
Historic Site
Ruins
Wall, Walls
Church, Abbey
Temple
Scientific Station
Railway station
Airport
Fort
Military installation
Lighthouse
Mine
Tunnel
Dam, Bridge

Ernici, Monti- ⛰	128	Hi	41.50N	13.20 E
Erode	148	Ff	11.21N	77.44 E
Eromanga	212	Ie	26.40S	143.16 E
Erongoberg ▲	172	Bd	21.40S	15.40 E
Erpengdianzi	154	Hd	41.12N	125.29 E
Errego	172	Fc	16.02S	37.10 E
Errigal/An Ea agail ▲	118	Ef	55.02N	8.07W
Erris Head/Ceann Iorrais ►	110	Fe	54.19N	10.00W
Erromango, Ile- ◆	208	Hf	18.48S	169.05 E
Erseka	130	Di	40.20N	20.41 E
Erstein	122	Nf	48.26N	7.40 E
Ertai	152	Fb	46.02N	90.10 E
Ertil	136	Ee	51.50N	40.51 E
Ertix He ∿	140	Ke	47.52N	84.16 E
Erts	172	De	25.08S	29.55 E
Ertvågøy ◆	116	Ca	63.15N	8.25 E
Eruh	146	Jd	37.46N	42.15 E
Erval, Serra do- ⛰	204	Fk	30.25S	51.55W
Ervânia	204	Ee	21.43S	55.32W
Erve ∿	122	Fg	47.50N	0.20W
Ervy-le-Châtel	122	Jf	48.02N	3.55 E
Erwin	184	Fg	36.09N	82.25W
Erwitte	124	Kc	51.37N	8.21 E
Eryuan	152	Gf	26.09N	99.56 E
Erzeni ∿	130	Ch	41.26N	19.27 E
Erzgebirge=Ore Mountains (EN) ⛰	110	He	50.30N	13.15 E
Erzin	138	Ef	50.17N	95.10 E
Erzincan	144	Eb	39.44N	39.29 E
Erzurum	142	Gf	39.55N	41.17 E
Esan-Misaki ►	154	Pd	41.48N	141.12 E
Esashi [Jap.]	154	Pd	41.52N	140.07 E
Esashi [Jap.]	154	Qb	44.56N	142.35 E
Esashi [Jap.]	154	Pe	39.12N	141.09 E
Esbjerg	112	Gd	55.28N	8.27 E
Esbo/Espoo	114	Ff	60.13N	24.40 E
Escalante	188	Jh	37.47N	111.36W
Escalante Desert ◢	188	Ih	37.50N	113.30W
Escalante River ∿	188	Jh	37.17N	110.53W
Escalaplano	128	Dk	39.37N	9.21 E
Escalón	190	Dc	26.45N	104.20W
Escalona	126	Hd	40.10N	4.24W
Escanaba	176	Ke	45.45N	87.04W
Escanaba River ∿	184	Dc	45.47N	87.04W
Escandón, Puerto de- ⌣	126	Ld	40.17N	1.00W
Escandorgue ▬	122	Jk	43.46N	3.14 E
Escarpada Point ►	140	Oh	18.31N	122.13 E
Escarpé, Cap- ►	219b	Ce	20.41S	167.13 E
Escatrón	126	Lc	41.17N	0.19W
Escaut=Schelde (EN) ∿	122	Kc	51.22N	4.15 E
Esch an der Alzette/Esch-sur-Alzette	122	Le	49.30N	5.59 E
Eschkopf ▲	124	Je	49.19N	7.51 E
Esch-sur-Alzette/Esch an der Alzette	122	Le	49.30N	5.59 E
Eschwege	120	Ge	51.11N	10.04 E
Eschweiler	120	Cf	50.49N	6.17 E
Escocesa, Bahía- ◧	194	Md	19.25N	69.45W
Escondida, Punta- ►	192	Kj	15.49N	97.03W
Escondido	188	Gj	33.07N	117.05W
Escondido, Río- ∿	194	Fg	12.04N	83.45W
Escravos	166	Gd	5.36N	5.11 E
Escudo, Puerto del- ⌣	126	Ia	43.05N	3.50W
Escudo de Veraguas, Isla- ◆	194	Gi	9.06N	81.33W
Escuinapa de Hidalgo	190	Cd	22.51N	105.48W
Escuintla [3]	194	Bf	14.10N	91.00W
Escuintla [Guat.]	190	Ff	14.18N	90.47W
Escuintla [Mex.]	192	Mj	15.20N	92.38W
Escuro, Rio- [Braz.] ∿	204	Ha	12.50S	49.28W
Escuro, Rio- [Braz.] ∿	204	Ic	17.31S	46.39W
Ese	170	Eb	4.04N	26.40 E
Ese-Hajja	138	Ic	67.35N	134.55 E
Eséka	166	He	3.39N	10.46 E
Eşen	146	Cd	36.27N	29.16 E
Esendere	146	Kd	37.46N	44.40 E
Ésera / Éssera ∿	126	Mb	42.06N	0.15 E
Eşfahān [3]	144	Hc	32.50N	51.50 E
Eşfahān=Isfahan (EN)	142	Hf	32.40N	51.38 E
Esfandārān	146	Og	31.52N	52.32 E
Esfarāyen, Reshteh-ye- ⛰	146	Qd	36.46N	57.10 E
Esgueva ∿	126	Hc	41.40N	4.43W
Eshowe	172	Ee	28.58S	31.29 E
Eshtehārd	146	Ne	35.44N	50.23 E
Esigodini	172	Dd	20.18S	28.56 E
Esino ∿	128	Hg	43.39N	13.22 E
Esk ∿	118	Jg	54.58N	3.04W
Eskifjörður	114a	Cb	65.04N	14.01W
Eskilstuna	114	Dg	59.22N	16.30 E
Eskimo Point	176	Jc	61.07N	94.03W
Eskinşehir	142	Ff	39.46N	30.32 E
Esla ∿	126	Fc	41.29N	6.03W
Eslāmābād	144	Gc	34.11N	46.35 E
Eşler Dağı ▲	130	Ml	37.24N	29.43 E
Eslohe (Sauerland)	124	Kc	51.15N	8.10 E
Eslöv	114	Ci	55.50N	13.20 E
Eşme	146	Cc	38.24N	28.59 E
Esmeralda [Braz.]	204	Gi	28.03S	51.12W
Esmeralda [Cuba]	194	Hc	21.51N	78.07W
Esmeralda, Isla- ◆	206	Eg	48.57S	75.25W
Esmeralda Bank (EN) ⊟	220b	Ab	14.57N	145.15 E
Esmeraldas	200	Ie	0.59N	79.42W
Es Mercadal / Mercadal	126	Qe	39.59N	4.05 E
Esnagami Lake ◘	186	Ma	50.21N	86.48W
Esneux	124	Hd	50.32N	5.34 E
Espada, Punta- ►	194	Lg	12.05N	71.07W
Espagnol Point ►	197n	Ba	13.22N	61.09W
Espalion	122	Ij	44.31N	2.46 E
Espalmador, Isla- / s'Espalmador, Illa- ◆	126	Nf	38.47N	1.26 E
España=Spain (EN) [1]	112	Fg	40.00N	4.00W
Espanola [N.M.-U.S.]	186	Ch	36.06N	106.02W
Espanola [Ont.-Can.]	184	Gb	46.15N	81.46W
Española, Isla- ◆	202a	Bb	1.25S	89.42W
Espardell, Isla- / s'Espardell, Illa- ◆	126	Nf	38.47N	1.27 E
Esparta	194	Ei	9.59N	84.40W
Espeland	116	Ad	60.23N	5.28 E
Espelkamp	120	Ed	52.25N	8.37 E
Esperance	210	Dh	33.51S	121.53 E
Esperance, Cape- ►	219a	Dc	9.15S	159.43 E
Esperance Bay ◧	212	Ef	33.50S	121.55 E
Esperance Harbour ◧	197k	Ba	14.04N	60.55W
Esperancita	204	Bc	16.55S	60.06W
Esperantina	202	Jd	3.54S	42.14W
Esperanza ⊗	222	Re	63.26S	57.00W
Esperanza [Arg.]	206	Hd	31.27S	60.56W
Esperanza [Mex.]	192	Ed	27.35N	109.56W
Esperanza [P.R.]	197a	Cb	18.06N	65.29W
Esperanza, Sierra la- ⛰	194	Ef	15.40N	85.45W
Espevær	114	Ag	59.36N	5.10 E
Espichel, Cabo- ►	126	Cf	38.25N	9.13W
Espiel	126	Gf	38.12N	5.01W
Espigão, Serra do- ⛰	204	Gh	26.55S	50.25W
Espinal [Bol.]	204	Cc	17.13S	58.43W
Espinal [Col.]	202	Dc	4.10N	74.54W
Espinazo del Diablo, Sierra- ⛰	192	Ff	24.00N	106.00W
Espinhaço, Serra do- ⛰	198	Lg	17.30S	43.30W
Espinho	126	Dc	41.01N	8.38W
Espinilho, Serra do- ⛰	204	Ei	28.30S	55.06W
Espinillo	204	Cg	24.58S	58.34W
Espino	196	Dh	8.34N	66.01W
Espinosa	202	Jf	14.56S	42.50W
Espinouse, Monts de l'- ⛰	122	Ik	43.32N	2.46 E
Espírito Santo [2]	202	Jg	20.00S	40.30W
Espiritu Santo, Bahía del- ◧	192	Ph	19.20N	87.35W
Espíritu Santo, Isla- ◆	192	De	24.30N	110.22W
Espita	192	Og	21.01N	88.19W
Esplanada	202	Kf	11.47S	37.57W
Espoo/Esbo	114	Ff	60.13N	24.40 E
Espoo-Tapiola	116	Kd	60.11N	24.49 E
Esposende	126	Dc	41.32N	8.47W
Espumoso	204	Fi	28.44S	52.51W
Espuña, Sierra de- ⛰	126	Kg	37.52N	1.34W
Espungabera	172	Ed	20.28S	32.46 E
Esquel	200	Ij	42.55S	71.20W
Esquina	206	Id	30.01S	59.32W
Esquipular	194	Cf	14.34N	89.21W
Essandsjøen ◘	116	Da	63.05N	12.00 E
Essaouira	160	Ge	31.31N	9.46W
Essaouira [3]	162	Fc	31.04N	9.03W
Essen [Bel.]	124	Gc	51.28N	4.28 E
Essen [Ger.]	112	Ge	51.27N	7.01 E
Essen (Oldenburg)	124	Jb	52.42N	7.55 E
Essendon, Mount- ▲	212	Ed	24.59S	120.28 E
Essequibo River ∿	198	Ke	6.50N	58.30W
Éssera / Ésera ∿	126	Mb	42.06N	0.15 E
Essex	188	Hi	34.42N	115.12W
Essex [3]	118	Nj	51.50N	0.35 E
Essex ▣	118	Nj	51.50N	0.30 E
Essex Mountain ▲	188	Ke	42.02N	109.13W
Esslingen am Neckar	120	Fh	48.45N	9.18 E
Esso	138	Ke	55.55N	158.40 E
Essonne [3]	122	If	48.36N	2.20 E
Essonne ∿	122	If	48.37N	2.29 E
Est [Burkina] [3]	166	Fc	12.00N	1.00 E
Est [Cam.] [3]	166	He	4.00N	14.00 E
Est, Canal de l'- ═	122	Lf	48.45N	5.35 E
Est, Cap- ►	172	Ic	15.16S	50.29 E
Est, Ile de l'- ◆	222	Ec	46.15S	52.05 E
Est, Pointe de l' - ►	180	Lg	49.08N	61.41W
Estaca de Bares, Punta de la- / Estaca de Vares, Punta de la- ►	110	Fg	43.46N	7.42W
Estaca de Vares, Punta de la- / Estaca de Bares, Punta de la- ►	110	Fg	43.46N	7.42W
Estados, Isla de los-= Staten Island (EN) ◆	198	Jk	54.47S	64.15W
Estados Unidos Mexicanos [1]	176	Ig	23.00N	102.00W
Estahbān	146	Ph	29.08N	54.04 E
Estaimpuis	124	Fd	50.42N	3.15 E
Estância	202	Kf	11.16S	37.26W
Estancias, Sierra de las- ⛰	126	Jg	37.35N	2.20W
Estanislao del Campo	204	Bg	25.03S	60.06W
Estarreja	126	Dd	40.45N	8.34W
Estats, Pica d'-/Estats, Pico d'- ▲	122	Hl	42.40N	1.24 E
Estats, Pic d'- ▲	122	Hl	42.40N	1.24 E
Estats, Pico d'-/Estats, Pica d'- ▲	122	Hl	42.40N	1.24 E
Estcourt	172	De	29.01S	29.52 E
Este	128	Fe	45.14N	11.39 E
Este, Punta- ►	197a	Cb	18.08N	65.16W
Este, Punta del- ►	206	Jd	34.59S	54.57W
Esteban Rams	204	Bi	29.47S	61.29W
Estelí	190	Gf	13.05N	86.23W
Estelí [3]	194	Dg	13.10N	86.20W
Estella	126	Jb	42.40N	2.02W
Estepa	126	Hg	37.18N	4.54W
Estepona	126	Gh	36.26N	5.08W
Esterel ⛰	122	Mk	43.30N	6.50 E
Esternay	124	Ff	48.44N	3.34 E
Esterri d'Àneu/Esterri de Aneu	126	Nb	42.38N	1.08 E
Esterri de Aneu / Esterri d'Àneu	126	Nb	42.38N	1.08 E
Esterwegen	124	Jb	52.59N	7.37 E
Estes Park	186	Df	40.23N	105.31W
Este Sudeste, Cayos del- ❋	190	Hf	12.26N	81.27W
Estevan	180	Hg	49.07N	103.05W
Estherville	186	Ie	43.24N	94.50W
Estissac	122	Jf	48.16N	3.49 E
Eston	188	Ka	51.10N	108.46W
Estonia (EN) ⧗	110	Id	59.00N	26.00 E
Estonian SSR (EN)=Eesti NSV [2]	136	Cd	59.00N	26.00 E
Estonskaja Sovetskaja Socialističeskaja Respublika [2]	136	Cd	59.00N	26.00 E
Estonskaja SSR/Eesti Nõukogude Socialistlik Vabarijk [2]	136	Cd	59.00N	26.00 E
Estoril	126	Cf	38.42N	9.24W
Estrées-Saint-Denis	124	Ee	49.26N	2.39 E
Estreito	204	Gj	31.50S	51.44W
Estreito, Represa do- ◚	204	Ie	20.15S	47.09W
Estrêla [Braz.]	204	Gj	31.15S	51.45W
Estrêla [Braz.]	204	Gi	29.29S	51.58W
Estrela, Arroyo- ∿	204	Df	22.05S	56.25W
Estrela, Serra da- ⛰	204	Fc	16.27S	53.24W
Estrêla, Serra da- ⛰	110	Fg	40.20N	7.38W
Estrêla do Sul	204	Id	18.21S	47.49W
Estrella ▲	126	If	38.28N	3.35W
Estrella, Punta- ►	192	Bb	30.55N	114.40W
Estrema, Serra da- ⛰	204	Jc	16.50S	45.07W
Estremadura ▣	126	Ce	39.15N	9.10W
Estremoz	126	Ef	38.51N	7.35W
Estrondo, Serra do- ⛰	202	Ie	9.00S	48.45W
Estry	124	Bf	48.54N	0.44W
Estuaire [3]	170	Ab	0.10N	10.00 E
Es Vedrà, Illa- / Vedrá, Isla- ◆	126	Nf	38.52N	1.12 E
Esztergom	120	Oi	47.48N	18.45 E
Etah	179	Ec	78.19N	72.38W
Étain	122	Le	49.13N	5.38 E
Etajima	156	Cd	34.15N	132.29 E
Etalle	124	He	49.41N	5.36 E
Étampes	122	If	48.26N	2.09 E
Étaples	122	Hd	50.31N	1.39 E
Etāwah	148	Fc	26.46N	79.02 E
Ethe, Virton-	124	He	49.35N	5.35 E
Ethel Reefs ✾	219d	Ab	16.56S	177.13 E
Ethiopia (EN)=Itiopya [1]	160	Kh	9.00N	39.00 E
Ethiopian Plateau (EN) ▬	158	Kg	10.00N	38.10 E
Etive, Loch- ⇌	118	He	56.35N	5.15W
Etna ◮	110	Hh	37.50N	14.55 E
Etna ∿	116	Dd	60.50N	10.03 E
Etna (Mongibello) ◮	110	Hh	37.50N	14.55 E
Etne	116	Ae	59.40N	5.56 E
Etoile Cay ❋	172b	Bb	5.53S	53.01 E
Etolin Island ◆	178	Me	56.08N	132.26W
Etolin Strait ⇌	178	Fd	60.20N	165.15W
Etomo-Misaki ►	156a	Bb	42.20N	140.55 E
Etorofu Tō / Iturup, ostrov- ◆	140	Qe	44.54N	147.30 E
Etosha Pan ◘	158	Ij	18.50S	16.20 E
Etoumbi	170	Bb	0.01N	14.57 E
Etrépagny	124	De	49.18N	1.37 E
Étretat	122	Ge	49.42N	0.12 E
Etropole	130	Gg	42.50N	24.00 E
Etruria	206	Hd	32.56S	63.15W
Etsch/Adige ∿	110	Hf	45.10N	12.20 E
Ettelbrüch/Ettelbruck	124	Ie	49.51N	6.07 E
Ettelbruck/Ettelbrüch	124	Ie	49.51N	6.07 E
Etten-Leur	124	Gc	51.35N	4.39 E
Ettersberg ▲	120	He	51.03N	11.15 E
Ettlingen	124	Kf	48.57N	8.24 E
Etzna Tixmucuy ⁖	192	Nh	19.35N	90.13W
Eu	122	Hd	50.03N	1.25 E
'Eua Iki ◆	221b	Bc	21.07S	174.59W
Eua Island ◆	216	Gd	21.22S	174.56W
Euboea (EN)=Évvoia ◆	110	Ih	38.30N	24.00 E
Eucla	210	Dh	31.43S	128.52 E
Euclid	184	Ge	41.34N	81.33W
Euclides da Cunha	202	Kf	10.31S	39.01W
Eucumbene, Lake- ◘	212	Jg	36.05S	148.45 E
Eudora	186	Kj	33.07N	91.16W
Eufaula	184	Ej	31.54N	85.09W
Eufaula Lake ◘	186	Ii	35.17N	95.31W
Euganei, Colli- ◭	128	Fe	45.19N	11.40 E
Eugene	176	Ge	44.02N	123.05W
Eugenia, Punta- ►	174	Hg	27.50N	115.03W
Eugênio Penzo	204	Ef	22.13S	55.53W
Eugmo ◆	114	Fe	63.49N	22.45 E
Eume ∿	126	Da	43.25N	8.08W
Eunice [La.-U.S.]	186	Jk	30.30N	92.26W
Eunice [N.M.-U.S.]	186	Ej	32.26N	103.09W
Eupen	122	Md	50.38N	6.02 E
Euphrates (EN)=Al Furāt ∿	140	Gf	30.00N	47.25 E
Euphrates (EN)=Firat ∿	140	Gf	30.00N	47.25 E
Eupora	186	Lj	33.32N	89.16W
Eura	114	Ff	61.08N	22.08 E
Eurajoki	116	Ic	61.12N	21.44 E
Eurasia Basin (EN) ⊌	224	Ge	87.00N	80.00 E
Eure [3]	122	Ge	49.10N	1.00 E
Eure ∿	122	He	49.18N	1.12 E
Eure-et-Loir [3]	122	Hf	48.30N	1.30 E
Eureka [Ca.-U.S.]	176	Ge	40.47N	124.09W
Eureka [Ks.-U.S.]	186	Hh	37.49N	96.17W
Eureka [Mt.-U.S.]	188	Hb	48.53N	115.03W
Eureka [Nv.-U.S.]	182	Dd	39.31N	115.58W
Eureka [N.W.T.-Can.]	180	Ia	80.00N	85.59W
Eureka [S.D.-U.S.]	186	Gd	45.46N	99.38W
Eureka [Ut.-U.S.]	188	Ig	39.57N	112.07W
Eureka Sound ⇌	180	Ia	79.00N	87.00W
Europa,Ile de l'- ◆	158	Lk	22.20S	40.22 E
Europa, Picos de- ▲	110	Fg	43.12N	4.48W
Europa, Punta de- ►	126	Gh	36.10N	5.22W
Europe (EN) ■	106	Fd	50.00N	20.00 E
Europoort ⚓	122	Jc	51.58N	4.00 E
Euskal Mendiak / Vascos, Montes- ⛰	126	Jb	42.50N	2.10W
Euskirchen	120	Cf	50.40N	6.47 E
Eustis	184	Gk	28.51N	81.41W
Eutaw	184	Di	32.50N	87.53W
Eutin	120	Gb	54.08N	10.37 E
Euzkadi / Vascongadas = Basque Provinces (EN) ▣	126	Ja	43.00N	2.30W
Evale	170	Cf	16.33S	15.44 E
Evans, Lac- ◘	180	Jf	50.50N	77.00W
Evans, Mount- ▲	188	Ic	46.05N	113.07W
Evans Strait ⇌	180	Jd	63.20N	82.00W
Evanston [Il.-U.S.]	186	Me	42.03N	87.42W
Evanston [Wy.-U.S.]	182	Ec	41.16N	110.58W
Evansville	176	Kf	37.58N	87.35W
Evant	186	Gk	31.29N	98.09W
Evart	184	Ed	43.54N	85.14W
Évaux-les-Bains	122	Ih	46.10N	2.29 E
Evaz	146	Oi	27.46N	53.59 E
Evciler [Tur.]	130	Mk	38.03N	29.54 E
Evciler [Tur.]	130	Jj	39.46N	26.46 E
Evelyn, Mount- ▲	212	Gb	13.36S	132.53 E
Evenkijski nacionalny okrug [3]	138	Ed	65.00N	98.00 E
Evensk	142	Rc	61.57N	159.14 E
Everard, Lake- ◘	212	Hf	31.25S	135.05 E
Everard Ranges ⛰	212	Ge	27.05S	132.30 E
Everest, Mount- (EN)= Qomolangma Feng ▲	140	Kg	27.59N	86.56 E
Everest, Mount- (EN)= Saragmatha ▲	140	Kg	27.59N	86.56 E
Everett	182	Cb	47.59N	122.13W
Everett Mountains ⛰	180	Kd	62.45N	67.10W
Evergem	124	Fc	51.07N	3.42 E
Evergem-Sleidinge	124	Fc	51.08N	3.41 E
Everglades City	184	Gm	25.52N	81.23W
Evergreen	184	Dj	31.26N	86.57W
Evertsberg	116	Ec	61.08N	13.57 E
Evesham	118	Li	52.05N	1.56W
Evesham, Vale of- ∨	118	Li	52.05N	1.50W
Évian-les-Bains	122	Mh	46.23N	6.35 E
Evijärvi	114	Fe	63.22N	23.29 E
Evinayong	166	He	1.27N	10.34 E
Évinos ∿	130	Ek	38.19N	21.32 E
Evje	114	Bg	58.36N	7.51 E
Évora	112	Fh	38.34N	7.54W
Évora [2]	126	Ef	38.35N	7.50W
Evoron	138	If	51.23N	136.23 E
Evowghlī	146	Kc	38.43N	45.13 E
Evre ∿	122	Eg	47.22N	1.02W
Evrecy	124	Be	49.06N	0.30W
Évreux	122	He	49.01N	1.09 E
Évron	122	Ff	48.10N	0.24W
Évros ∿	130	Ji	40.52N	26.12 E
Evrótas ∿	130	Fm	36.48N	22.41 E
Évry	122	If	48.38N	2.27 E
Évvoia=Euboea (EN) ◆	110	Ih	38.30N	24.00 E
Évvoia, Gulf of- (EN)= Vórios Evvoïkós Kólpos ◧	130	Gk	38.45N	23.10 E
Evzonoi	130	Fh	41.06N	22.33 E
Ewa Beach	221a	Cb	21.19N	158.00W
Ewing Seamount (EN) ⩚	158	Hk	23.20S	8.45 E
Ewo	170	Bc	0.55S	14.49 E
Excelsior Mountain ▲	188	Fg	38.02N	119.18W
Excelsior Mountains ⛰	188	Fg	38.10N	118.30W
Excelsior Springs	186	Ig	39.20N	94.13W
Exe ∿	118	Jk	50.37N	3.25W
Executive Committee Range ⛰	222	Nf	76.50S	126.00W
Exeter [Eng.-U.K.]	112	Fe	50.43N	3.31W
Exeter [N.H.-U.S.]	184	Ld	42.59N	70.56W
Exeter Sound ⇌	180	Lc	66.10N	62.00W
Exmoor ▲	118	Jj	51.10N	3.45W
Exmouth [Austl.]	212	Cd	21.55S	114.07 E
Exmouth [Eng.-U.K.]	118	Jk	50.37N	3.25W
Exmouth Gulf ◧	208	Cg	22.00S	114.20 E
Exmouth Plateau (EN) ⋀	212	Cc	16.00S	114.00 E
Expedition Range ⛰	212	Jd	24.30S	149.05 E
Explorer Tablemount (EN) ⊓	190	He	16.55N	83.15W
Externsteine ☉	124	Kc	51.52N	8.55 E
Extertal	124	Lb	52.04N	9.07 E
Extertal-Bösingfeld	124	Lb	52.04N	9.07 E
Extremadura [2]	126	Ge	39.00N	6.00W
Exuma Cays ⁂	190	Id	24.00N	76.20W
Exuma Sound ⇌	190	Id	24.15N	76.00W
Eyasi, Lake- ◘	158	Ki	3.40S	35.05 E
Eydehavn	116	Cf	58.31N	8.53 E
Eye	124	Db	52.19N	1.09 E
Eyemouth	118	Kf	55.52N	2.06W
Eye Peninsula ⊐	118	Gc	58.13N	6.05W
Eygurande	122	Ii	45.40N	2.28 E
Eyjafjallajökull ▲	114a	Bc	63.38N	19.36W
Eyl	160	Lh	8.00N	49.51 E
Eymoutiers	122	Hi	45.44N	1.44 E
Eyneuil	146	Hb	41.03N	39.08 E
Eyrarbakki	114a	Bc	63.52N	21.09W
Eyre	212	Ff	32.15S	126.18 E
Eyre, Lake- ◘	208	Eg	28.43S	137.11 E
Eyre Creek ∿	208	Eg	26.40S	139.00 E
Eyre Mountains ⛰	218	Cf	45.20S	168.20 E
Eyre North, Lake- ◘	212	He	28.40S	137.10 E
Eyre Peninsula ⊐	208	Ef	34.00S	135.45 E
Eyre South, Lake- ◘	212	He	29.30S	137.20 E
Eyrieux ∿	122	Kj	44.48N	4.48 E
Eystrup	124	Lb	52.47N	9.13 E
Eythorne	124	Dc	51.11N	1.17 E
Eyvānakī	146	Oe	35.24N	51.56 E
Eyzies-de-Tayac, Les-	122	Hj	44.56N	1.01 E
Ezequiel Ramos Mexia, Embalse- ◚	206	Ge	39.30S	69.00W
Ezere	116	Jh	56.27N	22.17 E
Ežerelis	116	Jj	54.50N	23.38 E
Ezine	146	Bc	39.47N	26.20 E
Eznas/Jieznas	116	Kj	54.34N	24.17 E
Ežva	134	Ef	61.47N	50.40 E

F

Faaa	221e	Fc	17.33S	149.36W
Faaite Atoll ◎	216	Lc	16.45S	145.14W
Fabens	186	Ck	31.30N	106.10W
Fåberg	116	Dc	61.10N	10.24 E
Faber Lake ◘	180	Fd	63.55N	117.15W
Fåborg	114	Ci	55.06N	10.15 E
Fabriano	128	Gg	43.20N	12.54 E
Făcăeni	130	Ke	44.34N	27.54 E
Facatativá	202	Dc	4.49N	74.22W
Facha	164	Cd	29.30N	17.20 E
Fachi	160	Ig	18.06N	11.34 E
Facpi Point ►	220c	Bb	13.20N	144.38 E
Fada	160	Jg	17.14N	21.33 E
Fada N'Gourma	160	Hg	12.04N	0.21 E
Faddeja, zaliv- ◧	138	Fa	76.30N	107.30 E
Faddejevski, ostrov- ◆	138	Ja	75.30N	144.00 E
Fadiffolu Atoll ◎	148a	Ba	5.25N	73.30 E
Fāḑilī	146	Mi	26.58N	49.15 E
Faeara, Pointe- ►	221e	Fc	17.52S	149.11W
Faenza	128	Ff	44.17N	11.53 E
Faeroe-Iceland Ridge (EN) ⋀	110	Fc	64.00N	10.00W
Faeroe Islands (EN)= Færøerne/Föroyar [5]	112	Fc	62.00N	7.00W
Faeroe Islands (EN)= Færøerne/Föroyar ⁂	110	Fc	62.00N	7.00W
Faeroe Islands (EN) = Föroyar/Færøerne [5]	112	Fc	62.00N	7.00W
Faeroe Islands (EN)= Föroyar/Færøerne ⁂	110	Fc	62.00N	7.00W
Færøerne/Föroyar=Faeroe Islands (EN) [5]	112	Fc	62.00N	7.00W
Færøerne/Föroyar=Faeroe Islands (EN) ⁂	110	Fc	62.00N	7.00W
Fafa ∿	168	Bd	7.18N	18.16 E
Fafe	126	Dc	41.27N	8.10W
Fafen ∿	158	Lh	5.47N	44.11 E
Faga ∿	166	Fc	13.45N	0.58 E
Fagaloa Bay ◧	221c	Ba	13.54S	171.28W
Fagamalo	221c	Aa	13.25S	172.21W
Făgăraş	130	Hd	45.51N	24.58 E
Făgăraşului, Munţii- ⛰	130	Hd	45.35N	25.00 E
Fagataufa Atoll ◎	208	Ng	22.14S	138.45W
Fågelmara	116	Fh	56.15N	15.57 E
Fagerhult	116	Fg	57.09N	15.40 E
Fagernes	114	Bf	60.59N	9.15 E
Fagersta	114	Df	60.00N	15.47 E
Făget	130	Fd	45.51N	22.11 E
Fagita	150	Jg	1.48S	130.25 E
Fagnano, Lago- ◘	206	Gh	54.38S	68.00W
Fagne ⧗	122	Kd	50.10N	4.25 E
Faguibine, Lac- ◘	158	Gg	16.45N	3.54W
Fahliān	146	Ng	30.12N	51.28 E
Fahner Höhe ▲	120	Ge	51.10N	10.45 E
Faial ◆	158	Ee	38.34N	28.42W
Fā'id	146	Eg	30.19N	32.19 E
Faïoa ◆	220h	Bc	13.23S	176.08W
Fairbairn Reservoir ◚	212	Jd	23.40S	148.00 E
Fairbanks	176	Ec	64.51N	147.43W
Fairborn	184	Ef	39.48N	84.03W
Fairbury	182	Hc	40.08N	97.11W
Fairchild	186	Kd	44.36N	90.58W
Fairfield [Al.-U.S.]	184	Di	33.29N	86.55W
Fairfield [Ca.-U.S.]	188	Dg	38.15N	122.01W
Fairfield [Ia.-U.S.]	186	Kf	40.59N	91.57W
Fairfield [Id.-U.S.]	188	He	43.21N	114.48W
Fairfield [Il.-U.S.]	186	Lg	38.23N	88.22W
Fair Isle ◆	118	Lb	59.30N	1.40W
Fairlie	218	Df	44.06S	170.50 E
Fairmont [Mn.-U.S.]	182	Ic	43.39N	94.28W
Fairmont [W.V.-U.S.]	182	Ld	39.28N	80.08W
Fair Ness ►	180	Kd	63.24N	72.05W
Fairview [Mt.-U.S.]	188	Mc	47.51N	104.03W
Fairview [Ok.-U.S.]	186	Gh	36.16N	98.29W
Fairview Peak ▲	188	De	43.35N	122.39W
Fairweather, Mount- ▲	174	Fd	58.54N	137.32W
Faisalabad (Lyallpur)	142	Jf	31.25N	73.05 E
Fais Island ◆	208	Fd	9.46N	140.31 E
Faistós = Phaistos (EN) ⁖	130	Hn	35.03N	24.48 E
Faith	182	Gb	45.02N	102.02W
Faizābād	148	Gc	26.47N	82.08 E
Fajardo	194	Od	18.20N	65.39W
Fajou, Ilet à- ◆	197e	Ab	16.21N	61.35W
Fakahina Atoll ◎	208	Mf	15.59S	140.08W
Fakaofo Atoll ◎	208	Je	9.22S	171.14W
Fakarava Atoll ◎	208	Mf	16.20S	145.37W
Fakaura	156	Fa	40.38N	139.55 E
Fakel	114	Mh	57.40N	53.05 E
Fakenham	124	Cb	52.50N	0.50 E
Fakfak	150	Jg	2.55S	132.18 E
Fakhr	146	Pg	31.25N	54.01 E
Fakse Bugt ◧	116	Ei	55.10N	12.15 E
Faksefjell ▲	116	Ec	61.20N	12.52 E
Fakse Ladeplads	116	Ei	55.15N	12.08 E
Faku	154	Gc	42.30N	123.24 E
Falaba	166	Cd	9.51N	11.19W
Fala-Beguets ◆	220d	Bb	7.21N	151.40 E
Falaise	122	Ff	48.54N	0.12W
Falaise de Tiguidit ◭	166	Gb	16.22N	7.45 E
Falakrón Óros ⛰	130	Gh	41.19N	24.00 E
Falalu ◆	220d	Ba	7.38N	151.41 E
Falam	148	Id	22.55N	93.41 E
Falas ◆	220d	Ba	7.32N	151.46 E
Fălciu	130	Lc	46.18N	28.08 E
Falcón [2]	202	Ea	11.00N	69.50W
Falcon, Cap- ►	126	Li	35.46N	0.48W
Falcon, Presa- ◚	186	Gm	26.37N	99.11W
Falconara Marittima	128	Hg	43.37N	13.24 E
Falcone, Punta- ►	128	Cj	40.58N	8.12 E
Falcon Reservoir ◚	182	Hf	26.37N	99.11W
Faléa	166	Cc	12.16N	11.15W
Faleallej Pass ⇌	220d	Bb	7.26N	151.34 E
Falealupo	221c	Aa	13.30S	172.48W
Falelima	221c	Aa	13.32S	172.41W
Falémé ∿	158	Fg	14.46N	12.14W
Falenki	114	Mg	58.23N	51.36 E
Falerum	116	Gf	58.09N	16.13 E
Falešty	132	Ef	47.35N	27.44 E
Falevai	221c	Ba	13.55S	171.59W
Falfurrias	182	Hf	27.14N	98.09W
Falkenberg	114	Ch	56.54N	12.28 E
Falkensee	120	Jd	52.34N	13.05 E
Falkirk	118	Jf	56.00N	3.48W
Falkland Islands/Malvinas, Islas- [5]	200	Kk	51.45S	59.00W
Falkland Islands/Malvinas, Islas- ⁂	198	Kk	51.45S	59.00W
Falkland Plateau (EN) ⋀	198	Lk	51.00S	50.00W
Falkland Sound ⇌	206	Ih	51.45S	59.25W
Falkonéra ◆	130	Gm	36.50N	23.53 E
Falköping	114	Cg	58.10N	13.31 E
Fallingbostel	120	Fd	52.52N	9.42 E
Fallon [Mt.-U.S.]	188	Mc	46.48N	105.00W
Fallon [Nv.-U.S.]	188	Fg	39.28N	118.47W

Index Symbols

[1] Independent Nation	▣ Historical or Cultural Region	⌣ Pass, Gap	⊔ Depression	≡ Coast, Beach	✱ Rock, Reef	⤵ Waterfall, Rapids	═ Canal	⊖ Lagoon	⊼ Escarpment, Sea Scarp	⛫ Historic Site	✈ Airport
[2] State, Region	▲ Mount, Mountain	▭ Plain, Lowland	▥ Polder	▐ Cliff	⁂ Islands, Archipelago	⋎ River Mouth, Estuary	❄ Glacier	⊟ Bank	⚡ Fracture	⁖ Ruins	⚓ Port
[3] District, County	◮ Volcano	◣ Delta	◢ Desert, Dunes	⊐ Peninsula	❋ Rocks, Reefs	◘ Lake	⧈ Ice Shelf, Pack Ice	⩚ Seamount	∇ Trench, Abyss	⊞ Wall, Walls	⊡ Military installation
[4] Municipality	△ Hill	▤ Salt Flat	♣ Forest, Woods	⋈ Isthmus	✾ Coral Reef	◙ Salt Lake	≈ Ocean	⊓ Tablemount	✪ National Park, Reserve	✝ Church, Abbey	⚑ Lighthouse
[5] Colony, Dependency	⛰ Mountains, Mountain Range	∨ Valley, Canyon	≋ Heath, Steppe	⩸ Sandbank	⊙ Well, Spring	◌ Intermittent Lake	∽ Sea	⋀ Ridge	☉ Point of Interest	⛩ Temple	⚒ Mine
■ Continent	◭ Hills, Escarpment	◡ Crater, Cave	✽ Oasis	◆ Island	⌶ Geyser	◚ Reservoir	◧ Gulf, Bay	⊏ Shelf	⛺ Recreation Site	⊗ Scientific Station	∩ Tunnel
⧗ Physical Region	▬ Plateau, Upland	✿ Karst Features	► Cape, Point	◎ Atoll	∿ River, Stream	⩩ Swamp, Pond	⇌ Strait, Fjord	⊌ Basin	⌓ Cave, Cavern	⊶ Railway station	⌒ Dam, Bridge

Index Symbols

① Independent Nation	▬ Historical or Cultural Region
② State, Region	▲ Mount, Mountain
③ District, County	▲ Volcano
④ Municipality	▲ Hill
⑤ Colony, Dependency	▲ Mountains, Mountain Range
⬤ Continent	▲ Hills, Escarpment
⬤ Physical Region	▬ Plateau, Upland
⊔ Pass, Gap	⬟ Depression
⬟ Plain, Lowland	⬟ Polder
⬟ Delta	⬟ Desert, Dunes
⬟ Salt Flat	⬟ Forest, Woods
⬟ Valley, Canyon	⬟ Heath, Steppe
⬟ Crater, Cave	⬟ Oasis
⬟ Karst Features	⬟ Cape, Point
▬ Coast, Beach	⬤ Rock, Reef
⬟ Cliff	⬤ Islands, Archipelago
⬟ Peninsula	⬤ River Mouth, Estuary
⬟ Isthmus	⬟ Lake
⬟ Sandbank	⬟ Salt Lake
⬟ Island	⬟ Intermittent Lake
⊙ Atoll	⬟ Reservoir
⬟ Waterfall, Rapids	⬟ Canal
⬟ River, Stream	⬟ Glacier
⬟ Swamp, Pond	⬟ Bank
⬟ Seamount	⬟ Lagoon
⬟ Tablemount	⬟ Escarpment, Sea Scarp
⬟ Ridge	⬟ Fracture
⬟ Shelf	⬟ Trench, Abyss
⬟ Basin	⬟ National Park, Reserve
⬟ Point of Interest	⬟ Historic Site
⬟ Recreation Site	⬟ Ruins
⬟ Scientific Station	⬟ Wall, Walls
⬟ Cave, Cavern	⬟ Church, Abbey
⬟ Temple	⬟ Airport
⬟ Port	⬟ Military installation
⬟ Lighthouse	⬟ Mine
⬟ Tunnel	⬟ Railway station
⬟ Dam, Bridge	

Flekkefjord 114 Bg 58.17N 6.41 E
Flémalle 124 Hd 50.36N 5.29 E
Flemish Bight 122 Ib 51.44N 2.30 E
Flemish Cap (EN) 174 Oe 47.00N 45.00W
Flemsøya 116 Bb 62.40N 6.20 E
Flen 114 Dg 59.04N 16.35 E
Flensborg Fjord 116 Cj 54.50N 9.45 E
Flensburg 112 Ge 54.47N 9.26 E
Flensburger Förde 116 Cj 54.50N 9.45 E
Flers 122 Ff 48.45N 0.34W
Flesberg 116 Ce 59.51N 9.27 E
Fleurance 122 Gk 43.50N 0.40 E
Fleury-sur-Andelle 124 De 49.22N 1.21 E
Fleuve [3] 166 Cb 16.00N 13.50W
Flevoland 122 Lb 52.25N 5.30 E
Flian 116 Ef 58.27N 13.05 E
Flims 128 Dd 46.50N 9.16 E
Flinders Bay 212 Df 34.25S 115.19 E
Flinders Island 208 Fi 40.00S 148.00 E
Flinders Passage 212 Jc 18.50S 149.00 E
Flinders Ranges 208 Eh 31.25S 138.45 E
Flinders Reefs 208 Ff 17.40S 148.30 E
Flinders River 208 Ff 17.36S 140.36 E
Flin Flon 176 Id 54.56N 101.53W
Flint [Mi.-U.S.] 176 Ke 43.01N 83.41W
Flint [Wales-U.K.] 118 Jh 53.15N 3.07W
Flint Hills 186 Hh 37.20N 96.35W
Flint Island 208 Lf 11.26S 151.48W
Flint River 182 Ke 30.52N 84.38W
Flisa 114 Cf 60.37N 12.04 E
Flisa 116 Ed 60.36N 12.01 E
Flisegga 116 Be 59.50N 7.50 E
Flitwick 124 Bb 52.00N 0.29W
Flix 126 Mc 41.14N 0.33 E
Flixecourt 124 Ed 50.01N 2.05 E
Flize 124 Ge 49.42N 4.46 E
Flobecq/Vloesberg 124 Fd 50.44N 3.44 E
Floby 116 Ef 58.08N 13.20 E
Floda [Swe.] 116 Fd 60.26N 14.49 E
Floda [Swe.] 116 Eg 57.48N 12.22 E
Flood Range 222 Nf 76.03S 134.00W
Flora [Il.-U.S.] 186 Lg 38.40N 88.29W
Flora [Nor.] 114 Af 61.36N 5.00 E
Florac 122 Jj 44.19N 3.36 E
Florala 184 Dj 31.00N 86.20W
Florange 124 Ie 49.20N 6.07 E
Florence [Al.-U.S.] 182 Je 34.49N 87.40W
Florence [Ks.-U.S.] 186 Hg 38.15N 96.56W
Florence [Or.-U.S.] 188 Cd 44.01N 124.07W
Florence [S.C.-U.S.] 182 Le 34.12N 79.44W
Florence (EN) = Firenze 112 Hg 43.46N 11.15 E
Florencia [Arg.] 204 Ci 28.02S 59.15W
Florencia [Col.] 200 Ie 1.36N 75.36W
Florencio Sánchez 204 Dk 33.53S 57.24W
Florennes 124 Gd 50.15N 4.37 E
Florentino Ameghino, Embalse- 206 Gf 43.48S 66.25W
Florenville 122 Le 49.42N 5.18 E
Flores 190 Ge 16.58N 89.50W
Flores [2] 204 Dk 33.35S 56.50W
Flores 158 De 39.26N 31.13W
Flores, Arroyo de las- 204 Cl 35.36S 59.01W
Flores, Laut- = Flores Sea (EN) 140 Oj 8.00S 121.00 E
Flores, Pulau- 140 Oj 8.30S 121.00 E
Flores Island 188 Bb 49.20N 126.10W
Flores Sea (EN) = Flores, Laut- 140 Oj 8.00S 121.00 E
Floreşty 132 Ff 47.55N 28.18 E
Floriano 200 Lf 6.47S 43.01W
Florianópolis 200 Lh 27.35S 48.34W
Florida [Braz.] 204 Ei 29.15S 54.36W
Florida [Cuba] 190 Id 21.32N 78.14W
Florida [Fl.-U.S.] [2] 182 Kf 28.00N 82.00W
Florida [Ur.] 206 Id 34.06S 56.13W
Florida [Ur.] [2] 204 Ek 33.50S 55.55W
Florida, Estrecho de- = Florida, Straits of- (EN) 174 Kg 24.00N 81.00W
Florida, Straits of- 174 Kg 24.00N 81.00W
Florida, Straits of- (EN) = Florida, Estrecho de- 174 Kg 24.00N 81.00W
Florida Bay 184 Gm 25.00N 80.45W
Floridablanca 202 Db 7.04N 73.06W
Florida City 184 Gm 25.27N 80.29W
Florida Islands 214 Gi 9.00S 160.10 E
Florida Keys 182 Kg 24.45N 81.00W
Floridia 128 Jm 37.05N 15.09 E
Florido, Río- 192 Gd 27.43N 105.10W
Flórina 130 Ei 40.47N 21.24 E
Flörsheim 124 ud 50.01N 8.26 E
Flotte, Cap de- 219b Ce 21.11S 167.24 E
Floydada 186 Fj 33.59N 101.20W
Fluessen 122 Lb 52.57N 5.30 E
Flumen 126 Lc 41.43N 0.09W
Flumendosa 128 Dk 39.26N 9.37 E
Fluminimaggiore 128 Ck 39.26N 8.30 E
Flumini Mannu 128 Ck 39.16N 9.00 E
Flums 128 Dc 47.05N 9.20 E
Fluvià / Fluvià 126 Pb 42.12N 3.07 E
Fluvià / Fluvià 126 Pb 42.12N 3.07 E
Flying Fish, Cape- 222 Of 72.06S 102.29W
Flying Fish Cove 150 Ei 10.25S 105.43 E
Fly River 208 Fe 8.00S 142.21 E
Fnideq 126 Gi 35.50N 5.22W
Fnjóská 114a Bb 65.54N 18.07W
Foa 221b Ba 19.45S 174.18W
Foam Lake 188 Na 51.39N 103.33W
Foča 128 Mg 43.31N 18.47 E
Foça 130 Jk 38.39N 26.46 E
Fochi 168 Bb 18.56N 15.57 E
Fochi 168 Bb 18.25N 15.40 E
Focşani 130 Kd 45.42N 27.11 E
Fodda 126 Nh 36.14N 1.33 E
Fodé 168 Cd 5.29N 23.18 E
Fœringehavn 179 Gf 63.45N 51.28W
Foga, Dallol- 166 Fc 12.05N 3.32 E
Foggaret ez Zoua 162 Hd 27.22N 2.50 E
Foggia 112 Hg 41.27N 15.34 E
Foggo 166 Gc 11.23N 9.57 E
Foglia 128 Gg 43.55N 12.54 E
Föglö 116 Ie 60.00N 20.25 E
Fogo [Can.] 180 Mg 49.40N 54.10W
Fogo [C.V.] 158 Eg 14.55N 24.25W
Fohnsdorf 128 Ic 47.12N 14.41 E
Föhr 120 Eb 54.45N 8.30 E
Föhren 124 Ie 49.51N 6.46 E
Foix 122 Hl 42.58N 1.36 E
Fojnica 128 Lg 43.58N 17.54 E
Fokino 132 Ic 53.27N 34.26 E
Folda 114 Dc 67.36N 14.50 E
Folégandros 130 Hm 36.38N 24.54 E
Foley 180 Kc 68.30N 75.00W
Foleyet 180 Jg 48.16N 82.30W
Folgefonni 114 Bf 60.00N 6.20 E
Foligno 128 Gh 42.57N 12.42 E
Folkestone 118 Oj 51.05N 1.11 E
Folkingham 124 Bb 52.52N 0.24W
Folkston 184 Fj 30.50N 82.01W
Folldals verk 114 Be 62.08N 10.00 E
Follebu 114 Cf 61.14N 10.17 E
Föllinge 114 De 63.40N 14.37 E
Follo 116 De 59.55N 10.55 E
Follonica 128 Eh 42.55N 10.45 E
Follonica, Golfo di- 128 Eh 42.55N 10.40 E
Folschviller 124 Ie 49.04N 6.41 E
Fomboni 172 Gb 12.16S 43.45 E
Fomento 194 Hb 22.06N 79.43W
Fond d'Or Bay 197k Bb 13.56N 60.54W
Fond-du-Lac 180 Ge 59.19N 107.10W
Fond du Lac 182 Jc 43.47N 88.27W
Fond-du-Lac 180 Ge 59.17N 106.00W
Fondi 128 Hi 41.21N 13.25 E
Fongen 116 Da 63.11N 11.38 E
Fongoro 168 Cc 11.30N 22.25 E
Fonni 128 Dj 40.07N 9.15 E
Fonoifua 221b Bb 20.17S 174.38W
Fonsagrada 126 Ea 43.08N 7.04W
Fonsei a 202 Da 10.53N 72.50W
Fonseca, Golfo de- 174 Kh 13.08N 87.40W
Fonsecas, Serra dos- 204 Jc 17.02S 44.13W
Fontaine-Bellenger 124 De 49.11N 1.16 E
Fontainebleau 122 If 48.24N 2.42 E
Fontaine-Henry, Château de- 124 Be 49.17N 0.27W
Fontaine-le-Dun 124 Ce 49.49N 0.51 E
Fontaine-l'Evêque 124 Gd 50.25N 4.19 E
Fontas 180 Fe 58.17N 121.46W
Fonte Boa 202 Ed 2.32S 66.01W
Fontenay-le-Comte 122 Fh 46.28N 0.49W
Fontenay-Trésigny 124 Ef 48.42N 2.52 E
Fontenelle Reservoir 188 Je 42.05N 110.06W
Fontevrault-l'Abbaye 122 Gg 47.11N 0.03 E
Fontur 110 Eb 66.23N 14.32W
Fonuafo'ou Falcon 216 Fd 20.19S 175.25W
Fonualei Island 208 Jf 18.01S 174.19W
Fonyód 120 Nj 46.44N 17.33 E
Foraker, Mount- 178 Id 62.56N 151.26W
Forbach 122 Me 49.11N 6.54 E
Forbes 212 Jf 33.23S 148.01 E
Forbes, Mount- 188 Ga 51.52N 116.56W
Forcados 166 Gd 5.21N 5.25 E
Forcados 166 Gd 5.23N 5.19 E
Forcalquier 122 Lk 43.58N 5.47 E
Forchheim 120 Hg 49.43N 11.04 E
Ford City 188 Fi 35.09N 119.27W
Førde 114 Af 61.27N 5.52 E
Førdefjorden 116 Ac 61.30N 5.40 E
Ford Ranges 222 Mf 77.00S 145.00W
Fordyce 186 Jj 33.49N 92.25W
Forécariah 166 Cd 9.26N 13.06W
Forel, Mont- 224 Mc 67.05N 36.55W
Forelshogna 116 Db 62.41N 10.47 E
Forest 186 Lj 32.22N 89.28W
Forest Park 184 Ei 33.37N 84.22W
Forestville 184 Ma 48.45N 69.06W
Forez, Monts du- 122 Ji 45.35N 3.48 E
Forez, Plaine du- 122 Ki 45.50N 4.10 E
Forfar 118 Ke 56.38N 2.54W
Forges-les-Eaux 122 He 49.37N 1.33 E
Forggensee 120 Gi 47.36N 10.44 E
Forks 188 Cc 47.57N 124.23W
Forlì 128 Gf 44.13N 12.03 E
Forlì, Bocca di- 128 Ii 41.45N 14.10 E
Formazza 128 Cd 46.22N 8.26 E
Formby Point 118 Jh 53.33N 3.06W
Formentera 110 Gh 38.42N 1.28 E
Formentor, Cabo de-/Formentor, Cap de- 126 Pe 39.58N 3.12 E
Formentor, Cap de-/Formentor, Cabo de- 126 Pe 39.58N 3.12 E
Formerie 124 De 49.39N 1.44 E
Formia 128 Hi 41.15N 13.37 E
Formiga 202 Ih 20.27S 45.25W
Formigas 162 Cb 37.16N 24.47W
Formosa [2] 206 Ib 25.00S 60.00W
Formosa 166 Bc 11.45N 16.05W
Formosa [Arg.] 200 Kh 26.10S 58.11W
Formosa [Braz.] 202 Ig 15.32S 47.20W
Formosa → Taiwan [1] 142 Og 23.30N 121.00 E
Formosa, Serra- 198 Kg 12.00S 55.00W
Formosa Bay 170 Hc 2.45S 40.20 E
Formoso [Braz.] 204 Ha 13.37S 48.54W
Formoso [Braz.] 204 Ib 14.57S 46.14W
Formoso, Rio- [Braz.] 202 If 10.34S 49.59W
Formoso, Rio- [Braz.] 204 Fd 18.25S 52.28W
Formoso, Rio- [Braz.] 204 Ja 13.26S 44.14W
Fornæs 114 Ch 56.27N 10.58 E
Fornosovo 116 Ne 59.31N 30.45 E
Fornovo di Taro 128 Ef 44.42N 10.06 E
Föroyar/Færøerne = Faeroe Islands (EN) [5] 112 Fc 62.00N 7.00W
Föroyar/Færøerne = Faeroe Islands (EN) 110 Fc 62.00N 7.00W
Forres 118 Jd 57.37N 3.38W
Forrest 212 Ff 30.51S 128.06 E
Forrest City 186 Ki 35.01N 90.47W
Forrester Island 222 Nf 74.06S 132.00W
Forsayth 212 Ic 18.35S 143.36 E
Forserum 116 Fg 57.42N 14.28 E
Forshaga 114 Cg 59.32N 13.28 E
Forsnäs 114 Ec 66.14N 18.39 E
Forssa 114 Ff 60.49N 23.38 E
Forst/Baršć 120 Ke 51.44N 14.38 E
Forsyth 188 Lc 46.16N 106.41W
Fort Albany 176 Kd 52.15N 81.37W
Fortaleza 200 Mf 3.43S 38.30W
Fortaleza, Ribeirão- 204 Fd 19.50S 53.25W
Fort Augustus 118 Id 57.09N 4.41W
Fort Beaufort 172 Df 32.46S 26.40 E
Fort Benton 182 Eb 47.49N 110.40W
Fort Bragg 182 Cd 39.26N 123.48W
Fort Bridger 188 Jf 41.19N 110.23W
Fort-Carnot [Mad.] 172 Hd 21.53S 48.26 E
Fort Chipewyan 180 Ge 58.42N 111.08W
Fort Cobb Reservoir 186 Gi 35.12N 98.29W
Fort Collins 182 Fc 40.35N 105.05W
Fort Collinson 180 Fb 71.37N 117.57W
Fort Coulogne 184 Ic 45.51N 76.44W
Fort Davis 186 Ek 30.35N 103.54W
Fort-de-France 176 Mh 14.36N 61.05W
Fort-de-France, Baie de- 197h Ab 14.34N 61.04W
Fort Dodge 182 Ic 42.30N 94.10W
Forte 204 Ib 14.16S 47.17W
Forte dei Marmi 128 Eg 43.57N 10.10 E
Fortescue River 208 Cg 21.00S 116.06 E
Fort Frances 176 Je 48.36N 93.24W
Fort Franklin 180 Fc 65.12N 123.26W
Fort Garland 186 Dh 37.26N 105.26W
Fort Gibson Lake 186 Ih 36.00N 95.18W
Fort Good Hope 176 Gc 66.15N 128.38W
Forth 118 Je 56.04N 3.42W
Forth, Firth of- 110 Fd 56.05N 2.55W
Fort Hall 170 Gc 0.43S 37.09 E
Fort Hope 180 If 51.32N 88.00W
Fortín Avalos Sánchez 204 Bf 23.28S 60.07W
Fortín Boquerón 204 Cf 22.47S 59.57W
Fortín Buenos Aires 204 Bf 22.57S 61.51W
Fortín Cadete Pastor Pando 204 Cg 24.20S 58.54W
Fortín Capitán Figari 204 Cf 23.12S 59.32W
Fortín Carlos A. López 204 Ce 21.19S 59.44W
Fortín Comandante Nowak 204 Cg 24.51S 58.15W
Fortín Coronel Bogado 204 Ce 20.46S 59.09W
Fortín Coronel Hermosa 204 Bf 22.33S 60.01W
Fortín Coronel Martínez 204 Cf 22.15S 59.09W
Fortín Florida 204 Ce 20.45S 59.17W
Fortín Galpón 204 Cd 19.51S 58.16W
Fortín Gaspar Rodríguez de Francia 204 Cf 23.01S 59.57W
Fortín General Caballero 204 Cg 24.08S 59.30W
Fortín General Delgado 204 Cg 24.28S 59.15W
Fortín General Diaz 206 Hb 23.31S 60.34W
Fortín Guaraní 204 Cf 22.44S 59.30W
Fortín Hernandarias 204 Be 21.58S 61.30W
Fortín José M. López 204 Be 20.07S 60.15W
Fortín Lagerenza 204 Be 20.06S 61.03W
Fortín Madrejón 204 Ce 20.38S 59.52W
Fortín Mariscal López 204 Cf 23.39S 59.44W
Fortín Max Paredes 204 Cd 19.16S 59.58W
Fortín May Alberto Gardel 204 Af 22.46S 62.12W
Fortín Mayor Long 204 Ae 20.33S 62.01W
Fortín Mayor R. Santacruz 204 Be 20.15S 60.37W
Fortín Nueva Asunción 204 Be 20.42S 61.55W
Fortín Pikyrenda 204 Be 20.05S 61.48W
Fortín Pilcomayo [Arg.] 204 Bf 23.52S 60.53W
Fortín Pilcomayo [Par.] 204 Bf 23.44S 60.51W
Fortín Pratts Gill 204 Bf 22.41S 61.33W
Fortín Presidente Ayala 204 Cf 23.30S 59.46W
Fortín Ravelo 204 Bd 19.18S 60.35W
Fortín Suárez Arana 204 Bd 18.40S 60.09W
Fortín Teniente 1 Alfredo Stroessner 204 Bf 22.45S 61.32W
Fortín Teniente 1 H. Mendoza 204 Cd 19.54S 59.47W
Fortín Teniente 1 M. Cabello 204 Bf 23.28S 61.19W
Fortín Teniente 1 Ramiro Espinola 204 Be 21.28S 61.18W
Fortín Teniente Acosta 204 Bf 22.41S 60.32W
Fortín Teniente Agripino Enciso 204 Be 21.12S 61.34W
Fortín Teniente Américo Picco 204 Cd 19.35S 59.43W
Fortín Teniente Aristigueta 204 Bf 22.21S 60.38W
Fortín Teniente E. Ochoa 204 Be 21.42S 61.02W
Fortín Teniente Esteban Martínez 204 Cg 24.02S 59.51W
Fortín Teniente Juan E. López 204 Be 21.05S 61.48W
Fortín Teniente Montanía 204 Cf 22.04S 59.57W
Fortín Teniente R. Rueda 204 Be 21.49S 60.49W
Fortín Toledo 204 Bf 22.20S 60.21W
Fortín Torres 204 Ce 21.01S 59.30W
Fortín Vanguardia 204 Cd 19.39S 58.10W
Fortín Vitiones 204 Cd 19.30S 58.06W
Fortín Zenteno 204 Cf 23.10S 59.59W
Fort Jeuedy, Point of- 197p Bb 12.00N 61.42W
Fort Kent 184 Mb 47.15N 68.36W
Fort Knox 184 Eg 37.53N 85.55W
Fort-Lamy → N'Djamena 160 Ig 12.07N 15.03 E
Fort Lauderdale 182 Kf 26.07N 80.08W
Fort Liard 176 Gc 60.15N 123.28W
Fort-Liberté 194 Ld 19.38N 71.57W
Fort MacKay 180 Ge 57.08N 111.42W
Fort Macleod 180 Gg 49.43N 113.25W
Fort Mac Mahon 162 Hd 29.46N 1.37 E
Fort Madison 186 Kf 40.38N 91.21W
Fort-Mahon-Plage 124 Dd 50.21N 1.34 E
Fort McMurray 176 Hd 56.44N 111.23W
Fort McPherson 176 Fc 67.27N 134.53W
Fort Miribel 162 Hd 29.26N 3.00 E
Fort Morgan 186 Ef 40.15N 103.48W
Fort Myers 176 Kg 26.37N 81.54W
Fort Myers Beach 184 Gl 26.27N 81.57W
Fort Nelson 176 Gd 58.49N 122.39W
Fort Nelson 180 Fe 59.33N 124.01W
Fort Norman 180 Ed 64.56N 125.22W
Fortore 128 Ji 41.55N 15.17 E
Fort Payne 184 Eh 34.27N 85.43W
Fort Peck 188 Lb 48.01N 106.27W
Fort Peck Lake 182 Fb 47.45N 106.50W
Fort Pierce 182 Kf 27.27N 80.20W
Fort Pierre 182 Gc 44.21N 100.22W
Fort Portal 170 Fb 0.39N 30.17 E
Fort Providence 176 Hc 61.21N 117.39W
Fort Qu'Appelle 188 Na 50.56N 103.09W
Fort Resolution 180 Gd 61.10N 113.40W
Fortrose 218 Cg 46.34S 168.48 E
Fort Saint James 180 Ff 54.26N 124.15W
Fort Saint John 176 Gd 56.15N 120.51W
Fort Sandenam 148 Db 31.20N 69.27 E
Fort Saskatchewan 180 Gf 53.43N 113.13W
Fort Scott 186 Ih 37.50N 94.42W
Fort-Ševčenko 136 Fg 44.30N 50.14 E
Fort Severn 176 Kd 56.00N 87.38W
Fort Simpson 176 Gc 61.52N 121.23W
Fort Smith [Ar.-U.S.] 176 Jf 35.23N 94.25W
Fort Smith [N.W.T.-Can.] 176 Hd 60.00N 111.53W
Fort Stockton 182 Ge 30.53N 102.53W
Fort Sumner 186 Di 34.28N 104.15W
Fortuna 188 Cf 40.36N 124.09W
Fortuna, Río de la- 204 Cc 16.36S 58.46W
Fortune Bay 180 Lg 47.15N 55.40W
Fortuneswell 118 Kk 50.33N 2.27W
Fort Vermilion 180 Fe 58.24N 116.00W
Fort Walton Beach 182 Je 30.25N 86.36W
Fort Washakie 188 Ke 43.00N 108.53W
Fort Wayne 176 Ke 41.04N 85.09W
Fort William 118 He 56.49N 5.07W
Fort Worth 176 Jf 32.45N 97.20W
Fort Yates 186 Fc 46.05N 100.38W
Fort Yukon 176 Ec 66.34N 145.17W
Forūr, Jazīreh-ye- 146 Pi 26.17N 54.32 E
Foshan 142 Ng 22.59N 113.05 E
Fosheim Peninsula 180 Ja 80.00N 84.30W
Fosnavåg 116 Ab 62.21N 5.39 E
Fosnøy 116 Ad 60.45N 4.55 E
Fossacesia 128 Ih 42.15N 14.29 E
Fossa Magna (EN) 156 Fc 36.00N 138.08 E
Fossano 128 Bf 44.33N 7.43 E
Fossato, Colle di- 128 Gg 43.20N 12.49 E
Fossberg 116 Cc 61.50N 8.34 E
Fossil 188 Ed 44.59N 120.13W
Fossil Bluff 222 Qf 71.20S 68.17W
Fossombrone 128 Gg 43.41N 12.48 E
Fosston 186 Ic 47.35N 95.45W
Fos-sur-Mer 122 Kk 43.26N 4.57 E
Foster 212 Jg 38.39S 146.12 E
Foster, Mount- 178 Le 59.48N 135.29W
Foster Bugt 179 Jd 73.40N 21.40W
Fostoria 184 Fe 41.10N 83.25W
Fotuha'a 221b Ba 19.49S 174.44W
Foucarmont 124 De 49.51N 1.34 E
Fougamou 170 Bc 1.13S 10.36 E
Fougères 122 Ef 48.21N 1.12W
Foul, Khalīj- 164 Ge 23.30N 35.40 E
Foula 118 Ka 60.10N 2.05W
Foul Bay 197q Bb 13.06N 59.27W
Fouligny 124 Ie 49.06N 6.30 E
Foulness Island 118 Nj 51.36N 0.55 E
Foulness Point 124 Cc 51.37N 0.57 E
Foulwind, Cape- 218 Dd 41.45S 171.28 E
Foumban 166 Hd 5.43N 10.55 E
Foumbouni 172 Gb 11.50S 43.30 E
Foum Zguid 162 Fc 30.05N 6.52W
Foundation Ice Stream 222 Qg 83.15S 60.00W
Fountains Abbey 118 Lg 54.07N 1.34W
Fouquet Island 172b Bb 5.25S 53.20 E
Fourchambault 122 Jg 47.01N 3.05 E
Fourchue, Ile- 197b Bc 17.57N 62.55W
Fourmies 122 Kd 50.01N 4.03 E
Four Mountains, Islands of the- 178a Db 52.50N 170.00W
Foúrnoi 130 Jl 37.34N 26.30 E
Fouron/Voeren 124 Hd 50.45N 5.48 E
Fours 122 Jh 46.49N 3.43 E
Fourth Cataract (EN) = Rabī', Ash Shallāl ar- 158 Kg 18.47N 32.03 E
Fous, Pointe des- 197g Bb 15.12N 61.20W
Fouta 166 Cb 16.18N 14.48W
Fouta Djalon 158 Fg 11.30N 12.30W
Foutouna, Ile- 208 If 19.32S 170.13 E
Foux, Cap-à- 194 Kd 19.45N 73.27W
Fouzon 122 Hg 47.16N 1.27 E
Foveaux Strait 208 Hi 46.40S 168.10 E
Fowler [Co.-U.S.] 186 Eg 38.08N 104.00W
Fowler [In.-U.S.] 184 De 40.37N 87.19W
Fowlers Bay 212 Gf 32.00S 132.25 E
Fowman 146 Md 37.13N 49.19 E
Foxe Basin 174 Lc 68.25N 77.00W
Foxe Channel 174 Lc 64.30N 80.00W
Foxen 116 De 59.25N 11.55 E
Foxe Peninsula 174 Lc 65.00N 76.00W
Foxford/Béal Easa 118 Dh 53.59N 9.07W
Fox Glacier 216 Ch 43.28S 170.00 E
Fox Islands 174 Cd 54.00N 168.00W
Fox Peak 218 De 43.50S 170.47 E
Fox River 186 Lf 41.21N 88.50W
Foxton 218 Fd 40.28S 175.17 E
Fox Valley 188 Ka 50.29N 109.28W
Foyle / An Feabhal 118 Ff 55.04N 7.15W
Foyle, Lough-/Loch Feabhail 118 Ff 55.05N 7.10W
Foz do Cunene 170 Bf 17.15S 11.48 E
Foz do Iguaçu 200 Kh 25.33S 54.35W
Fraga 126 Mc 41.31N 0.21 E
Fragoso, Cayo 194 Hb 22.44N 79.30W
Fraire, Walcourt- 124 Gd 50.16N 4.30 E
Fram 204 Eh 27.06S 55.58W
Fram Basin (EN) 224 He 88.00N 80.00 E
Framlingham 124 Db 52.13N 1.20 E
Franca 206 Kb 20.32S 47.24W
Français, Récif des- 216 Bc 19.30S 163.45 E
Franca-Josifa, zemlja- = Franz Joseph Land (EN) 140 Ha 81.00N 55.00 E
Francavilla al Mare 128 Ih 42.25N 14.17 E
Francavilla Fontana 128 Lj 40.32N 17.35 E
France [1] 112 Gf 46.00N 2.00 E
Frances 180 Ed 60.16N 129.11W
Francés, Punta- 194 Fc 21.38N 83.12W
Francesi, Punta di li- 128 Di 41.08N 9.02 E
Francés Viejo, Cabo- 194 Md 19.39N 69.55W
Franceville 160 Ii 1.38S 13.35 E
Franche-Comté 122 Lh 47.00N 6.00 E
Franches Montagnes 128 Ac 47.15N 7.00 E
Francia 204 Dk 32.34S 36.38W
Francis Case, Lake- 174 Je 43.15N 99.00W
Francisco Beltrão 206 Jc 26.05S 53.04W
Francisco Escárcega 192 Nh 18.37N 90.43W
Francisco I. Madero 192 Ge 24.32N 104.22W
Francisco Madero 204 Al 35.52S 62.03W
Francisco Morazán [3] 194 Df 14.15N 87.15W
Francisco Sá 202 Jg 16.28S 43.30W
Franciscus Bay 172 Ae 25.00S 14.50 E
Francistown 160 Jk 21.09S 27.31 E
Francofonte 128 Im 37.14N 14.53 E
Franconian Jura (EN) = Fränkische Alb 110 Hf 49.00N 11.30 E
Francs Peak 182 Fc 43.58N 109.20W
Franeker 122 La 53.11N 5.32 E
Frankenau 124 Kc 51.06N 8.56 E
Frankenberg (Eder) 120 Ee 51.04N 8.40 E
Frankenhöhe 120 Gg 49.15N 10.15 E
Frankenthal (Pfalz) 124 Ke 49.32N 8.21 E
Frankenwald 120 Hf 50.18N 11.36 E
Frankfort [In.-U.S.] 184 De 40.17N 86.31W
Frankfort [Ky.-U.S.] 176 Kf 38.12N 84.52W
Frankfort [Mi.-U.S.] 184 Dc 44.38N 86.14W
Frankfort on the Main (EN) = Frankfurt am Main 112 Ge 50.07N 8.41 E
Frankfort on the Oder (EN) = Frankfurt (Oder) 120 Kd 52.21N 14.33 E
Frankfurt (Oder) = Frankfort on the Oder (EN) 120 Kd 52.21N 14.33 E
Frankfurt am Main = Frankfort on the Main (EN) 112 Ge 50.07N 8.41 E
Fränkische Alb = Franconian Jura(EN) 110 Hf 49.00N 11.30 E
Fränkische Saale 120 Ff 50.03N 9.42 E
Fränkische Schweiz 120 Hg 49.45N 11.20 E
Franklin [In.-U.S.] 184 Df 39.29N 86.03W
Franklin [Ky.-U.S.] 184 Dg 36.43N 86.35W
Franklin [La.-U.S.] 186 Kl 29.48N 91.30W
Franklin [N.C.-U.S.] 184 Fh 35.11N 83.23W
Franklin [N.H.-U.S.] 184 Ld 43.27N 71.39W
Franklin [Pa.-U.S.] 184 He 41.24N 79.49W
Franklin [Tn.-U.S.] 184 Dh 35.55N 86.52W
Franklin Bay 174 Gc 68.45N 125.35W
Franklin Delano Roosevelt Lake 182 Db 48.20N 118.10W
Franklin Island 222 Kf 76.05S 168.11 E
Franklin Lake [Nv.-U.S.] 188 Hf 40.24N 115.12W
Franklin Lake [N.W.T.-Can.] 180 Hc 66.55N 96.05W
Franklin Mountains 174 Gc 63.15N 123.30W
Franklin Strait 180 Hb 71.30N 96.30W
Fransfontein 172 Bd 20.12S 15.01 E
Fränsta 116 Gb 62.30N 16.09 E
Franz Josef Glacier 218 De 43.23S 170.11 E
Franz Joseph Land (EN) = Franca-Josifa, zemlja- 140 Ha 81.00N 55.00 E
Frascati 128 Gi 41.48N 12.41 E
Fraser [Can.] 174 Ge 49.09N 123.12W
Fraser [Newf.-Can.] 180 Le 56.39N 63.08W
Fraserburg 172 Cf 31.55S 21.30 E
Fraserburgh 118 Ld 57.42N 2.00W
Fraserdale 180 Jg 49.51N 81.38W
Fraser Island 208 Gg 25.15S 153.10 E
Fraser Plateau 174 Gd 51.30N 122.00W
Fraser Range 212 Ef 32.03S 122.48 E
Frasertown 218 Gc 38.58S 177.24 E
Frasnes-les-Anvaing 124 Fd 50.40N 3.36 E
Frauenfeld 128 Cc 47.35N 8.54 E
Fray Bentos 206 Id 33.08S 58.18W
Frechen 124 Id 50.55N 6.49 E
Frechilla 126 Hb 42.08N 4.50W
Fredericia 114 Bi 55.35N 9.46 E
Frederick [Md.-U.S.] 184 If 39.25N 77.25W
Frederick [Ok.-U.S.] 186 Gi 34.23N 99.01W
Frederick E. Hyde Fjord 179 Jb 82.40N 25.45W
Frederick Reef 208 Gg 21.00S 154.25 E
Fredericksburg [Tx.-U.S.] 186 Gk 30.17N 98.52W
Fredericksburg [Va.-U.S.] 184 If 38.18N 77.30W
Fredericktown 186 Kh 37.33N 90.18W
Frederico Westphalen 204 Fh 27.22S 53.24W
Fredericton 176 Me 45.58N 66.39W
Frederiksborg [2] 116 Ei 55.55N 12.15 E
Frederiksdal 179 Hf 60.15N 45.30W
Frederikshåb/Pâmiut 179 Hf 62.00N 49.45W
Frederikshabs Bank (EN) 179 Gf 62.16N 49.45W
Frederikshavn 112 Hd 57.26N 10.32 E
Frederikssund 116 Ei 55.50N 12.04 E
Fréderiksted 196 Dd 17.42N 64.48W
Frederiksværk 116 Ei 55.58N 12.02 E
Fredonia 188 Ih 36.57N 112.32W
Fredrika 114 Ed 64.05N 18.24 E
Fredriksberg 114 Df 60.08N 14.23 E
Fredrikshamn/Hamina 114 Gf 60.34N 27.12 E
Fredrikstad 114 Cg 59.13N 10.57 E
Fredvang 114 Cb 68.05N 13.10 E
Freeling Heights 212 Hf 30.10S 139.25 E
Freels, Cape - 180 Mg 49.13N 53.29W
Freeport [Bah.] 190 Ic 26.30N 78.45W
Freeport [Il.-U.S.] 182 Jc 42.17N 89.36W

Index Symbols

[1] Independent Nation
[2] State, Region
[3] District, County
[4] Municipality
[5] Colony, Dependency
Continent
Physical Region
Historical or Cultural Region
Mount, Mountain
Volcano
Hill
Mountains, Mountain Range
Hills, Escarpment
Plateau, Upland
Pass, Gap
Plain, Lowland
Delta
Salt Flat
Valley, Canyon
Crater, Cave
Karst Features
Depression
Polder
Desert, Dunes
Forest, Woods
Heath, Steppe
Oasis
Cape, Point
Coast, Beach
Cliff
Peninsula
Isthmus
Sandbank
Island
Atoll
Rock, Reef
Islands, Archipelago
Rocks, Reefs
Coral Reef
Well, Spring
Geyser
River, Stream
Waterfall, Rapids
River Mouth, Estuary
Lake
Salt Lake
Intermittent Lake
Reservoir
Swamp, Pond
Canal
Glacier
Ice Shelf, Pack Ice
Ocean
Sea
Gulf, Bay
Strait, Fjord
Lagoon
Bank
Seamount
Tablemount
Ridge
Shelf
Basin
Escarpment, Sea Scarp
Fracture
Trench, Abyss
National Park, Reserve
Point of Interest
Recreation Site
Cave, Cavern
Historic Site
Ruins
Wall, Walls
Church, Abbey
Temple
Scientific Station
Railway station
Airport
Port
Military installation
Lighthouse
Mine
Tunnel
Dam, Bridge

Freeport [N.Y.-U.S.] 184 Ke 40.40N 73.35W
Freeport [Tx.-U.S.] 182 Hf 28.55N 95.22W
Freer 186 Gm 27.53N 98.37W
Freetown [Atg.] 197d Bb 17.03N 61.42W
Freetown [S.L.] 160 Fh 8.30N 13.15W
Fregenal de la Sierra 126 Ff 38.10N 6.39W
Fregene 128 Gi 41.51N 12.12 E
Fréhel, Cap- 122 Df 48.42N 2.19W
Frei 116 Ba 63.01N 7.48 E
Freiberg 120 Jf 50.55N 13.22 E
Freiberger Mulde 120 Ie 51.10N 12.48 E
Freiburg/Fribourg 128 Bd 46.50N 7.10 E
Freiburg/Fribourg [2] 128 Bd 46.40N 7.10 E
Freiburg im Breisgau 112 Gf 48.00N 7.51 E
Freilassing 120 Ii 47.51N 12.59 E
Freirina 206 Fc 28.30S 71.06W
Freisen 124 Je 49.33N 7.15 E
Freising 120 Hh 48.24N 11.44 E
Freistadt 128 Ib 48.30N 14.30 E
Freital 120 Je 51.01N 13.39 E
Fréjus 122 Mk 43.26N 6.44 E
Fréjus, Col de- 122 Mi 45.07N 6.40 E
Fréjus, Colle del- 122 Mi 45.07N 6.40 E
Fremantle, Perth- 212 Df 32.03S 115.45 E
Fremont [Ca.-U.S.] 182 Cd 37.34N 122.01W
Fremont [Nb.-U.S.] 182 Hc 41.26N 96.30W
Fremont [Oh.-U.S.] 184 Fe 41.21N 83.08W
Fremont River 188 Jg 38.24N 110.42W
French Frigate Shoals 208 Kb 23.45N 166.10W
French Guiana (EN) = Guyane Française [5] 200 Ke 4.00N 53.00W
French Lick 184 Df 38.33N 86.37W
Frenchman Creek 186 Ff 40.13N 100.50W
Frenchman River 182 Fb 48.24N 107.05W
French Pass 218 Ed 40.55S 173.50 E
French Plain (EN) 110 Gf 47.00N 1.00 E
French Polynesia (EN) = Polynésie Française [5] 210 Mf 16.00S 145.00W
French River 184 Gc 45.56N 80.54W
Frenda 162 Hb 35.04N 1.02 E
Frentani, Monti dei- 128 Ii 41.55N 14.30 E
Freren 124 Jb 52.29N 7.33 E
Fresco 166 Dd 5.05N 5.34W
Fresco, Rio- 202 He 6.39S 52.00W
Freshfield, Cape- 222 Je 68.22S 151.05 E
Fresnes-en-Woëvre 124 He 49.06N 5.37 E
Fresnillo de González Echevarría 190 Dd 23.10N 102.53W
Fresno 176 Hf 36.45N 119.45W
Fresno River 188 Eh 37.05N 120.33W
Fresquel 122 Ik 43.14N 2.24 E
Fresvikbreen 116 Bc 61.02N 6.45 E
Freu, Cabo- / Freu, Cap des- 126 Pe 39.45N 3.27 E
Freu, Cap des- / Freu, Cabo- 126 Pe 39.45N 3.27 E
Freudenberg 124 Jd 50.54N 7.52 E
Freudenstadt 120 Eh 48.26N 8.25 E
Frévent 122 Id 50.16N 2.17 E
Freycinet Estuary 212 Ce 26.25S 113.45 E
Freycinet Peninsula 212 Jh 42.15S 148.20 E
Freyming-Merlebach 124 Ie 49.09N 6.47 E
Freyre 204 Aj 31.10S 62.02W
Freyung 120 Jh 48.48N 13.33 E
Fri 130 Jn 35.25N 26.56 E
Fria 166 Cc 10.27N 13.32W
Fria, Cape- 158 Ij 18.27S 12.01 E
Frias 206 Gc 28.39S 65.09W
Fribourg/Freiburg 128 Bd 46.50N 7.10 E
Fribourg/Freiburg [2] 128 Bd 46.40N 7.10 E
Fridtjof Nansen, Mount- 222 Lg 85.21S 167.33W
Friedberg 128 Kc 47.26N 16.03 E
Friedberg (Hessen) 120 Ef 50.21N 8.46 E
Friedrichshafen 120 Fi 47.39N 9.29 E
Friedrichsthal 124 Je 49.19N 7.06 E
Friesach 128 Id 46.57N 14.24 E
Friese Gat 124 Ia 53.30N 6.05 E
Friese Wad 124 Ha 53.24N 5.45 E
Friesische Inseln/ Waddeneilanden = Frisian Islands (EN) 110 Hc 54.00N 6.00 E
Friesland [3] 124 Ha 53.03N 5.45 E
Friesland 110 Ge 53.05N 6.00 E
Friesland 122 La 53.05N 6.00 E
Friesoythe 120 Dc 53.01N 7.51 E
Frigate Island 197p Cb 12.25N 61.29W
Friggesund 116 Gc 61.54N 16.32 E
Frignano 128 Ef 44.20N 10.50 E
Frindsbury Reef 219a Da 5.00S 159.07 E
Frinnaryd 116 Fg 57.56N 14.49 E
Frinton-on-Sea 124 Dc 51.50N 1.15 E
Frio, Cabo- 198 Lh 22.53S 42.00W
Frio, Rio- 194 Eh 11.08N 84.46W
Frio Draw 186 Ei 34.50N 102.08W
Friona 186 Ei 34.38N 102.43W
Frio River 186 Gl 28.30N 98.10W
Frisco Peak 188 Ig 38.31N 113.14W
Frisian Islands (EN) = Friesische Inseln/ Waddeneilanden 110 Hc 54.00N 6.00 E
Frisian Islands (EN) = Waddeneilanden/ Friesische Inseln 110 Hc 54.00N 6.00 E
Fristad 116 Eg 57.50N 13.01 E
Fritsla 116 Eg 57.33N 12.47 E
Fritzlar 120 Fe 51.08N 9.17 E
Friuli 128 Ge 46.00N 13.00 E
Friuli-Venezia Giulia 128 Gd 46.00N 13.00 E
Frobisher Bay 174 Mc 62.30N 66.00W
Frobisher Lake 180 Ge 56.20N 108.20W
Froidchapelle 124 Gd 50.09N 4.20 E
Froissy 124 Ee 49.34N 2.13 E
Frolovo 136 Ef 49.45N 43.39 E
Fromberg 188 Kd 45.23N 108.54W
Frombork 120 Pb 54.22N 19.41 E
Frome 118 Kj 51.14N 2.20W
Frome, Lake- 208 Eh 30.50S 139.50 E
Fröndenberg 124 Jc 51.28N 7.46 E
Fronteira 126 Ee 39.03N 7.39W
Fronteiras 202 Je 7.05S 40.37W
Frontera 192 Mh 18.32N 92.38W
Frontera, Punta- 192 Mh 19.36N 92.42W
Fronteras 192 Eb 30.56N 109.31W
Frontignan 122 Jk 43.27N 3.45 E
Frontino, Páramo- 202 Cb 6.28N 76.04W
Front Range 174 If 39.45N 105.45W
Front Royal 184 Hf 38.56N 78.13W
Frosinone 128 Hi 41.38N 13.19 E
Frösö 116 Fa 63.11N 14.32 E
Frostburg 184 Hf 39.39N 78.56W
Frost Glacier 222 Ie 67.05S 129.00 E
Frövi 116 Fe 59.28N 15.22 E
Frøya 114 Be 63.43N 8.42 E
Frøysjøen 116 Ac 61.50N 5.05 E
Fruges 122 Id 50.31N 2.08 E
Frunze [Kirg.-U.S.S.R.] → Pišpek 142 Je 42.54N 74.36 E
Frunze [Kirg.-U.S.S.R.] 135 Hd 40.06N 71.45 E
Frunzovka 130 Mb 47.20N 29.37 E
Fruška Gora 130 Cd 45.10N 19.35 E
Frutal 202 Ih 20.02S 48.55W
Frutigen 128 Bd 46.35N 7.40 E
Fry Canyon 188 Jh 37.38N 110.08W
Frýdek Mistek 120 Og 49.41N 18.22 E
Frylinckspan 172 Ce 26.46S 22.28 E
Fteri 130 Ej 39.09N 21.33 E
Fua'amotu 221b Ac 21.15S 175.08W
Fua Mulaku Island 148a Bc 0.15S 73.30 E
Fu'an 152 Kf 27.10N 119.44 E
Fu-chien Sheng → Fujian Sheng = Fukien (EN) [2] 152 Kf 26.00N 118.00 E
Fuchskauten 120 Ef 50.40N 8.05 E
Fuchū [Jap.] 156 Cd 34.34N 133.14 E
Fuchū [Jap.] 156 Fd 35.41N 139.28 E
Fuchun-Jiang 154 Fi 30.15N 120.15 E
Fuchunjiang-Shuiku 154 Ej 29.29N 119.31 E
Fucino, Conca del- 128 Hh 42.01N 13.31 E
Fudai 156 Ga 40.01N 141.52 E
Fuding 152 Lf 27.19N 120.08 E
Fuengirola 126 Hh 36.32N 4.37W
Fuente de Cantos 126 Ff 38.15N 6.18W
Fuente del Maestre 126 Ff 38.32N 6.27W
Fuente Obejuna 126 Gf 38.16N 5.25W
Fuentesaúco 126 Gc 41.14N 5.30W
Fuentes de Andalucía 126 Gg 37.28N 5.21W
Fuerte 190 Cc 25.54N 109.22W
Fuerte, Isla- 194 Ii 9.23N 76.11W
Fuerte, Sierra del- 192 Hd 27.30N 102.45W
Fuerte Olimpo 206 Ib 21.02S 57.54W
Fuerteventura 158 Ff 28.20N 14.00W
Fuga 150 Hc 18.52N 121.22 E
Fugong 152 Gf 27.03N 98.57 E
Fugou 154 Cg 34.04N 114.23 E
Fugu 152 Jd 39.02N 111.03 E
Fuguo → Zhanhua 154 Ef 37.42N 118.08 E
Fuhai/Burultokay 152 Eb 47.06N 87.23 E
Fuhayri, Wādi- 144 Hf 16.04N 52.11 E
Fu He 154 Dj 28.21N 116.04 E
Fuji 154 Og 35.09N 138.38 E
Fujian Sheng (Fu-chien Sheng) = Fukien (EN) [2] 152 Kf 26.00N 118.00 E
Fujieda 156 Fd 34.51N 138.15 E
Fuji-Gawa 156 Fd 35.07N 138.38 E
Fujin 152 Nb 47.15N 132.01 E
Fujinomiya 156 Fd 35.12N 138.38 E
Fujioka 156 Fc 36.15N 139.03 E
Fuji-San 140 Pf 35.26N 138.43 E
Fujisawa 156 Fd 35.21N 139.27 E
Fujiyoshida 156 Fd 35.29N 138.47 E
Fukagawa 152 Pc 43.43N 142.03 E
Fūkah 146 Bg 31.04N 27.55 E
Fukang 152 Ec 44.10N 87.59 E
Fuka-Shima 156 Be 32.43N 131.56 E
Fukiage 156 Bf 31.30N 130.20 E
Fukien (EN) = Fu-chien Sheng → Fujian Sheng [2] 152 Kf 26.00N 118.00 E
Fukien (EN) = Fujian Sheng (Fu-chien Sheng) [2] 152 Kf 26.00N 118.00 E
Fukuchiyama 154 Mg 35.18N 135.07 E
Fukue 154 Jh 32.41N 128.50 E
Fukueichiao 152 Lf 25.19N 121.34 E
Fukue-Jima 154 Jh 32.41N 128.48 E
Fukui 152 Od 36.04N 136.13 E
Fukui Ken [2] 154 Ng 36.00N 136.20 E
Fukuma 156 Be 33.47N 130.28 E
Fukuoka 142 Pf 33.35N 130.24 E
Fukuoka Ken [2] 154 Kh 33.28N 130.45 E
Fukuroi 156 Ed 34.45N 137.54 E
Fukushima [Jap.] 152 Pd 37.45N 140.28 E
Fukushima [Jap.] 152 Pc 41.29N 140.15 E
Fukushima Ken [2] 154 Pf 37.25N 140.10 E
Fukuyama 152 Ne 34.29N 133.22 E
Fukuyama-Matsunaga 156 Cd 34.27N 133.16 E
Fūlādī, Kūh-e- 144 Kc 34.38N 67.32 E
Fūlād Mahalleh 146 Od 36.02N 53.44 E
Fulanga 219d Cc 19.08S 178.34W
Fulda 120 Ff 50.33N 9.40 E
Fulda 110 Ge 51.25N 9.39 E
Fuliji 154 Dh 33.47N 116.59 E
Fulin → Hanyuan 152 Hf 29.25N 102.12 E
Fuling 152 If 29.40N 107.21 E
Fullerton 186 Hf 41.22N 97.58W
Fulton [Arg.] 204 Cm 37.25S 58.48W
Fulton [Il.-U.S.] 186 Kf 41.52N 90.11W
Fulton [Ky.-U.S.] 184 Cg 36.30N 88.53W
Fulton [Mo.-U.S.] 186 Kg 38.52N 91.57W
Fulton [N.Y.-U.S.] 184 Id 43.20N 76.26W
Fulufjället 116 Ec 61.33N 12.43 E
Fumaiolo 128 Gg 43.47N 12.04 E
Fumay 122 Kd 50.00N 4.42 E
Fumel 122 Gj 44.30N 0.58 E
Funabashi 154 Og 35.42N 139.59 E
Funabiki 156 Gc 37.26N 140.35 E
Funafuti 210 Ie 8.01S 178.00 E
Funafuti Atoll 208 Ie 8.31S 179.08 E
Funagata 156 Gb 38.42N 140.18 E
Funagata-Yama 156 Gb 38.27N 140.37 E
Funakoshi-Wan 156 Hb 39.25N 142.00 E
Funan 154 Ch 32.38N 115.35 E
Funäsdalen 114 Ce 62.32N 12.33 E
Funchal 160 Fe 32.38N 16.54W
Fundación 202 Da 10.29N 74.12W
Fundão 126 Ed 40.08N 7.30W
Fundy, Bay of- 174 Me 45.00N 66.00W
Funeral Peak 188 Gh 36.08N 116.37W
Fungalei 220h Bb 13.17S 176.07W
Funhalouro 172 Ed 23.05S 34.24 E
Funing [China] 152 Ig 23.39N 105.33 E
Funing [China] 154 Eh 33.48N 119.47 E
Funing [China] 154 Ee 39.56N 119.15 E
Funiu Shan 152 Je 33.40N 112.10 E
Funtua 166 Gc 11.32N 7.19 E
Fuping 154 Ce 38.49N 114.15 E
Fuqing 152 Kf 25.47N 119.24 E
Furancungo 172 Eb 14.54S 33.37 E
Furano 154 Qc 43.21N 142.23 E
Füren 156a Ca 44.17N 142.25 E
Furenai 156a Cb 42.43N 142.15 E
Füren-Ko 156a Db 43.20N 145.20 E
Fürg 146 Ph 28.18N 55.13 E
Fur Jiang 154 Hc 42.37N 125.33 E
Furmanov 114 Jh 57.16N 41.07 E
Furnas, Reprêsa de- 202 Ih 21.20S 45.50W
Furnas, Serra das- 204 Fb 15.45S 53.20W
Furneaux Group 208 Fi 40.10S 148.05 E
Furnes/Veurne 122 Ic 51.04N 2.40 E
Furqlus 146 Ge 34.36N 37.05 E
Furrīyānah 162 Ic 34.57N 8.34 E
Fürstenau 124 Jb 52.31N 7.43 E
Fürstenauer Berge 124 Jb 52.35N 7.45 E
Fürstenfeld 128 Kc 47.03N 16.05 E
Fürstenfeldbruck 120 Hh 48.11N 11.15 E
Fürstenlager 124 Ke 49.42N 8.38 E
Fürstenwalde 120 Kd 52.22N 14.04 E
Furtado, Rio- → Feijão Prêto, Rio- 204 Dc 17.33S 57.23W
Fürth [Ger.] 120 Gg 49.28N 11.00 E
Fürth [Ger.] 124 Ke 49.39N 8.47 E
Furth im Wald 120 Ig 49.18N 12.51 E
Furubira 156a Bb 43.16N 140.39 E
Furudal 114 Df 61.10N 15.08 E
Furukawa 152 Pd 38.34N 140.58 E
Furusund 116 He 59.40N 18.55 E
Fury and Hecla Strait 180 Jc 69.55N 84.00W
Fushan [China] 154 Ag 35.58N 111.51 E
Fushan [China] 154 Ff 37.30N 121.15 E
Fushë-Arëzi 130 Dg 42.04N 20.02 E
Fushë-Lura 130 Dh 41.48N 20.13 E
Fu Shui 154 Cj 29.52N 115.26 E
Fushun 142 Oe 41.46N 123.56 E
Fusong 152 Mc 42.20N 127.17 E
Füsselberg 124 Je 49.32N 7.14 E
Füssen 120 Gi 47.34N 10.42 E
Futa, Passo della- 128 Ff 44.05N 11.17 E
Futago-Yama 156 Be 33.35N 131.38 E
Futaoi-Jima 156 Bd 34.06N 130.47 E
Futog 130 Cd 45.15N 19.42 E
Futuna, Ile- 208 Jf 14.17S 178.09W
Fuwah 146 Dg 31.12N 30.33 E
Fuxian (Wafangdian) 152 Ld 39.38N 121.59 E
Fuxian Hu 152 Hg 24.30N 102.55 E
Fuxin 142 Oe 41.59N 121.38 E
Fuxin Monggolzu Zizhixian 154 Fc 42.06N 121.46 E
Fuyang 152 Ke 32.47N 115.46 E
Fuyang He 154 Dg 38.14N 116.05 E
Fuyang Zhan 154 Ch 32.56N 115.53 E
Fuyu [China] 152 Lb 45.10N 124.52 E
Fuyu [China] 152 Lb 47.48N 124.26 E
Fuyuan [China] 152 Nb 48.21N 134.18 E
Fuyuan [China] 152 Lc 42.44N 124.57 E
Fuyuan [China] 152 Hf 25.43N 104.20 E
Fuyun/Koktokay 142 Ke 47.13N 89.39 E
Füzesabony 120 Qi 47.45N 20.25 E
Fuzhou [China] 142 Ng 26.10N 119.20 E
Fuzhou [China] 152 Kf 27.58N 116.20 E
Fuzhou He 154 Fe 39.36N 121.35 E
Fyllas Bank (EN) 179 Gf 64.00N 53.00W
Fyn [2] 116 Di 55.20N 10.30 E
Fyn 110 Hd 55.20N 10.30 E
Fyne, Loch- 118 He 56.10N 5.20W
Fyresdal 114 Bg 59.11N 8.06 E
Fyresvatn 116 Ce 59.05N 8.10 E
Fzâra, Gara'et- 128 Bn 36.47N 7.30 E

G

Gaasbeek 124 Gd 50.48N 4.10 E
Gaasterland 124 Hb 52.54N 5.36 E
Gaasterland 124 Hb 52.53N 5.35 E
Gaasterland-Balk 124 Hb 52.54N 5.36 E
Gabaru Reef 220a Bb 7.53N 134.31 E
Gabas 122 Fk 43.46N 0.42W
Gabba' 168 Id 8.02N 50.08 E
Gabbs 188 Gg 38.52N 117.55W
Gabela 160 Ij 10.52S 14.23 E
Gabès, Gulf of-(EN)=Qābis, Khalīj- 158 Ie 34.00N 10.25 E
Gabon [1] 160 Ii 1.00S 11.45 E
Gabon 170 Ab 0.25N 9.20 E
Gaborone 160 Jk 24.40S 25.55 E
Gabras 168 Dc 10.16N 26.14 E
Gabriel Strait 180 Kd 61.50N 65.40W
Gabriel y Galán, Embalse de- 126 Fd 40.15N 6.15W
Gabrovo 130 Ig 42.52N 25.19 E
Gabrovo [2] 130 Ig 42.52N 25.19 E
Gacé 122 Gf 48.48N 0.18 E
Gachsārān 146 Ng 30.12N 50.47 E
Gackle 186 Gc 46.38N 99.09W
Gacko 128 Mg 43.10N 18.32 E
Gadag 148 Fe 15.25N 75.37 E
Gäddede 114 Dd 64.30N 14.09 E
Gadê 152 Ge 34.13N 99.29 E
Gadjač 132 Id 50.22N 34.01 E
Gádor, Sierra de- 126 Jh 36.55N 2.45W
Gadsden 182 Je 34.02N 86.02W
Gadūk, Gardaneh-ye- 146 Oe 35.55N 52.55 E
Gadzi 168 Be 4.47N 16.42 E
Gael Hamkes Bugt 179 Jd 74.00N 22.00W
Găeşti 130 Ie 44.43N 25.19 E
Gaeta 128 Hi 41.12N 13.35 E
Gaeta, Golfo di- 128 Hi 41.05N 13.30 E
Gaferut Island 208 Fd 9.14N 145.23 E
Gaffney 184 Gh 35.05N 81.39W
Gag, Pulau- 150 Ig 0.25S 129.53 E
Gagan 219a Ba 5.14S 154.37 E
Gagarin [R.S.F.S.R.] 136 Dd 55.35N 35.01 E
Gagarin [Uzb.-U.S.S.R.] 135 Gd 40.40N 68.05 E
Gagévésouva, Pointe- 219b Ca 13.04S 166.32 E
Gaggenau 124 Kf 48.48N 8.20 E
Gagnef 114 Df 60.35N 15.04 E
Gagnoa 160 Gh 6.08N 5.56W
Gagnoa [3] 166 Dd 6.03N 6.00W
Gagnon 180 Kf 51.55N 68.10W
Gagra 136 Eg 43.17N 40.15 E
Gahkom 146 Ph 28.12N 55.52 E
Gahkom, Kūh-e- 146 Ph 28.10N 55.57 E
Gaiba, Laguna- 204 Dc 17.45S 57.43W
Gail 128 Hd 46.36N 13.53 E
Gaillac 122 Hk 43.54N 1.55 E
Gaillefontaine 124 De 49.39N 1.37 E
Gaillimh/Galway 112 Fe 53.16N 9.03W
Gaillimh/Galway [2] 118 Eh 53.20N 9.00W
Gaillon 124 De 49.10N 1.20 E
Gailtaler Alpen 128 Gd 46.40N 13.00 E
Gaiman 206 Gf 43.17S 65.29W
Găineşti 130 Ib 47.25N 25.55 E
Gainesville [Fl.-U.S.] 176 Kg 29.40N 82.20W
Gainesville [Ga.-U.S.] 182 Ke 34.18N 83.50W
Gainesville [Mo.-U.S.] 186 Jh 36.36N 92.26W
Gainesville [Tx.-U.S.] 182 He 33.37N 97.08W
Gainsborough 118 Mh 53.24N 0.46W
Gairdner, Lake- 208 Eh 31.35S 136.00 E
Gairloch 118 Hd 57.43N 5.40W
Gai Xian 152 Lc 40.24N 122.17 E
Gaiziņa kalns / Gajzinkalns 116 Kh 56.50N 25.59 E
Gaj 136 Fe 51.31N 58.30 E
Gajny 136 Fc 60.20N 54.15 E
Gajsin 136 Cf 48.50N 29.27 E
Gajvoron 132 Fe 48.22N 29.52 E
Gajzinkalns / Gaiziņa kalns 116 Kh 56.50N 25.59 E
Galaasija 135 Ee 39.52N 64.27 E
Gălăbovo 130 Ig 42.08N 25.51 E
Gala Gölü 130 Ji 40.45N 26.12 E
Galaico, Macizo- 126 Eb 42.30N 7.20W
Galán, Cerro- 206 Gc 25.55S 66.52W
Galana 158 Li 3.09S 40.08 E
Galanta 120 Nh 48.12N 17.44 E
Galap 220a Bb 7.38N 134.39 E
Galápagos, Islas-/Colón, Archipiélago de-= Galapagos Islands (EN) 198 Gf 0.30S 90.30W
Galapagos Fracture Zone (EN) 106 Mi 0.00 100.00W
Galapagos Islands (EN)= Colón, Archipiélago de-/ Galápagos, Islas- 198 Gf 0.30S 90.30W
Galapagos Islands (EN)= Galápagos, Islas-/Colón, Archipiélago de- 198 Gf 0.30S 90.30W
Galarza 204 Di 28.06S 56.41W
Galashiels 118 Kf 55.37N 2.49W
Galaţi 112 If 45.27N 28.03 E
Galaţi [2] 130 Kd 45.33N 27.56 E
Galatina 128 Mj 40.10N 18.10 E
Galatone 128 Mj 40.09N 18.04 E
Galatzó 126 Oe 39.38N 2.29 E
Galdar 162 Dd 28.09N 15.39W
Galdhøpiggen 114 Bf 61.37N 8.17 E
Galeana [Mex.] 192 Fb 30.07N 107.38W
Galeana [Mex.] 192 Ie 24.50N 100.04W
Galeh Dār 146 Oi 27.38N 52.42 E
Galela 150 If 1.50N 127.50 E
Galena [Ak.-U.S.] 178 Hd 64.44N 156.57W
Galena [Il.-U.S.] 186 Ke 42.25N 90.26W
Galeota Point 196 Fg 10.08N 60.59W
Galera, Punta- 206 Fe 39.59S 73.43W
Galera, Rio- 204 Bb 14.25S 60.07W
Galera Point 196 Fg 10.49N 60.55W
Galesburg 182 Ic 40.57N 90.22W
Galga 120 Pi 47.33N 19.43 E
Gal Gaduud [3] 168 Hd 5.00N 47.00 E
Galheirão, Rio- 204 Ja 12.23S 45.05W
Galheiros 204 Ia 13.18S 46.25W
Gali 132 Lh 42.36N 41.42 E
Galič [R.S.F.S.R.] 136 Ed 58.23N 42.21 E
Galič [Ukr.-U.S.S.R.] 132 De 49.06N 24.43 E
Galicea Mare 130 Ge 44.06N 23.18 E
Galicia 110 Fg 43.00N 8.00W
Galicia / Galiza [2] 126 Eb 43.00N 8.00W
Galicia (EN)=Galicija 110 If 49.50N 21.00 E
Galicia (EN)=Galicija [Eur.] 120 Qg 49.50N 21.00 E
Galicia (EN)=Galicja 110 If 49.50N 21.00 E
Galicia (EN)=Galicja 120 Qg 49.50N 21.00 E
Galicija [Eur.] =Galicia (EN) 120 Qg 49.50N 21.00 E
Galicija [Ukr.-U.S.S.R.] 120 Tg 49.00N 24.00 E
Galicija=Galicia (EN) 110 If 49.50N 21.00 E
Galicja=Galicia (EN) 110 If 49.50N 21.00 E
Galicja=Galicia (EN) 120 Qg 49.50N 21.00 E
Galilee, Lake- 212 Jd 22.20S 145.55 E
Galimy 138 Kd 62.19N 156.00 E
Galina Point 194 Id 18.24N 76.53W
Galion 184 Fe 40.44N 82.46W
Galion, Baie du- 197h Bb 14.44N 60.57W
Galiton 128 Cm 37.30N 8.52 E
Galiuro Mountains 188 Jj 32.40N 110.20W
Galiza / Galicia [2] 126 Eb 43.00N 8.00W
Gálka'yo 160 Lh 6.49N 47.23 E
Galkino 134 Ki 55.40N 62.55 E
Gallarate 128 Ce 45.40N 8.47 E
Gallatin 184 Dg 36.24N 86.27W
Gallatin Range 188 Jd 45.15N 111.05W
Gallatin River 188 Jd 45.56N 111.29W
Galle 142 Ki 6.02N 80.13 E
Gállego 126 Lc 41.39N 0.51W
Gallegos, Río- 198 Jk 51.36S 68.59W
Gallinas, Punta- 198 Id 12.25N 71.40W
Gallinas Peak 186 Di 34.15N 105.45W
Gallipoli 128 Lj 40.03N 17.58 E
Gallipoli Peninsula (EN) = Gelibolu Yarımadası 130 Ji 40.20N 26.30 E
Gallipolis 184 Ff 38.49N 82.14W
Gällivare 112 Ib 67.08N 20.42 E
Galljaaral 135 Fd 40.02N 67.35 E
Gällö 114 De 62.55N 15.14 E
Gallo 126 Jd 40.48N 2.09W
Gallo, Capo- 128 Hl 38.15N 13.19 E
Gallo Mountains 186 Bi 34.00N 108.15W
Galloway 118 If 55.00N 4.25W
Galloway, Mull of- 118 Ig 54.38N 4.50W
Gallup 176 If 35.32N 108.44W
Gallur 126 Kc 41.52N 1.19W
Gallura 128 Dj 41.00N 9.15 E
Galmaarden/Gammerages 124 Fd 50.45N 3.58 E
Galole 170 Hc 1.30S 40.02 E
Galt 128 Gd 43.22N 80.19W
Gal Tardo 168 He 3.37N 45.58 E
Galtasen 116 Eg 57.48N 13.30 E
Galty Mountains/Na Gaibhlte 118 Ei 52.23N 8.11W
Galut 152 Hb 46.43N 100.08 E
Galveston 176 Jg 29.18N 94.48W
Galveston Bay 174 Jg 29.36N 94.57W
Galveston Island 186 Il 29.13N 94.55W
Gálvez 206 Hd 32.02S 61.13W
Galway/Gaillimh 112 Fe 53.16N 9.03W
Galway/Gaillimh [2] 118 Eh 53.20N 9.00W
Galway Bay/Cuan na Gaillimhe 110 Fe 53.10N 9.15W
Gamaches 124 De 49.59N 1.33 E
Gamagōri 156 Ed 34.49N 137.13 E
Gamarra 202 Db 8.19N 73.44W
Gamba [China] 152 Ef 28.17N 88.31 E
Gamba [Gabon] 170 Ac 2.37S 10.00 E
Gambaga 166 Ec 10.32N 0.26W
Gambela 160 Kh 8.15N 34.36 E
Gambell 178 Ed 63.46N 171.46W
Gambia [1] 160 Fg 13.25N 16.00W
Gambia 158 Fg 13.28N 16.34W
Gambia (EN)=Gambie 166 Bc 13.28N 16.34W
Gambie=Gambia (EN) 166 Bc 13.28N 16.34W
Gambier, Iles-=Gambier Islands (EN) 208 Ng 23.09S 134.58W
Gambier Islands (EN)= Gambier, Iles- 208 Ng 23.09S 134.58W
Gambo 168 Ce 4.39N 22.16 E
Gamboma 170 Cc 1.53S 15.51 E
Gamboula 168 Be 4.09N 15.09 E
Gamda → Zamtang 152 He 32.23N 101.05 E
Gamelão 204 Db 15.29S 57.50W
Gamkonora, Gunung- 150 If 1.21N 127.31 E
Gamlakarleby/Kokkola 112 Ic 63.50N 23.07 E
Gamla Uppsala 116 Ge 59.54N 17.38 E
Gamleby 114 Dh 57.54N 16.24 E
Gammerages/Galmaarden 124 Fd 50.45N 3.58 E
Gamo Gofa [3] 168 Fd 5.45N 37.20 E
Gamua 220h Bb 13.15S 176.08W
Gamud 168 Fe 4.05N 38.06 E
Gamvik 114 Ga 71.03N 28.14 E
Ganāne, Webi- = Juba (EN) 158 Lh 0.15S 42.38 E
Gananoque 184 Ic 44.20N 76.10W
Ganāveh 146 Nh 29.32N 50.31 E
Gancedo 204 Bh 27.30S 61.42W
Gancevići 132 Ec 52.45N 26.29 E
Gand/Gent=Ghent (EN) 122 Jc 51.03N 3.43 E
Ganda 170 Be 12.59S 14.40 E
Gandadiwata, Bulu- 150 Gg 2.42S 119.27 E
Gandajika 170 Dd 6.45S 23.57 E
Gandak 148 Hc 25.39N 85.13 E
Gander 176 Ne 48.57N 54.34W
Ganderkesee 124 Ka 53.03N 8.33 E
Gandesa 126 Mi 41.03N 0.26 E
Gandhinagar 142 Jg 23.21N 72.40 E
Gāndhi Sāgar 148 Fd 24.30N 75.30 E
Gandia / Gandía 126 Lf 38.58N 0.11W
Gandía / Gandia 126 Lf 38.58N 0.11W
Gandia-El Grao de Gandia 126 Lf 38.59N 0.09W
Gandu 202 Kf 13.45S 39.30W
Ganetti 168 Eb 17.58N 31.13 E
Ganga=Ganges (EN) 140 Lg 23.20N 90.30 E
Gangaw 148 Id 22.10N 94.08 E
Gangca (Shaliuhe) 152 Hd 37.30N 100.14 E
Gangdisê Shan 140 Kf 31.00N 83.00 E
Ganges 122 Jk 43.56N 3.42 E
Ganges (EN)=Ganga 140 Lg 23.20N 90.30 E
Ganges, Mouths of the- (EN) 140 Lg 23.20N 90.30 E
Gangi 128 Im 37.48N 14.12 E
Gango 170 Cd 9.48S 15.40 E
Gangtok 142 Kg 27.20N 88.37 E
Gangu 152 Ie 34.45N 105.12 E
Gangziyao 154 Cf 36.17N 114.06 E
Ganhe 152 La 50.43N 123.00 E
Gan He 152 Mb 49.12N 125.14 E
Gani 150 Ig 0.47S 128.13 E
Ganjgah 146 Md 37.42N 48.16 E
Gan Jiang 140 Ng 29.12N 116.00 E
Ganjig → Horqin Zuoyi Houqi 152 Lc 42.57N 122.14 E
Gannan 152 Lb 47.53N 123.26 E
Gannat 122 Jh 46.06N 3.12 E
Gannett Peak 174 Ie 43.10N 109.40W
Gansbaai 172 Bf 34.35S 19.22 E

Index Symbols

1 Independent Nation
2 State, Region
3 District, County
4 Municipality
5 Colony, Dependency
Continent
Physical Region
Historical or Cultural Region
Mount, Mountain
Volcano
Hill
Mountains, Mountain Range
Hills, Escarpment
Plateau, Upland
Pass, Gap
Plain, Lowland
Delta
Salt Flat
Valley, Canyon
Crater, Cave
Karst Features
Depression
Polder
Desert, Dunes
Forest, Woods
Heath, Steppe
Oasis
Cape, Point
Coast, Beach
Cliff
Peninsula
Isthmus
Sandbank
Island
Atoll
Rock, Reef
Islands, Archipelago
Rocks, Reefs
Coral Reef
Well, Spring
Geyser
River, Stream
Waterfall, Rapids
River Mouth, Estuary
Lake
Salt Lake
Intermittent Lake
Reservoir
Swamp, Pond
Canal
Glacier
Ice Shelf, Pack Ice
Ocean
Sea
Gulf, Bay
Strait, Fjord
Lagoon
Bank
Seamount
Tablemount
Ridge
Shelf
Basin
Escarpment, Sea Scarp
Fracture
Trench, Abyss
National Park, Reserve
Point of Interest
Recreation Site
Cave, Cavern
Historic Site
Ruins
Wall, Walls
Church, Abbey
Temple
Scientific Station
Railway station
Airport
Port
Military installation
Lighthouse
Mine
Tunnel
Dam, Bridge

Gansu Sheng (Kan-su Sheng)=Kansu (EN) [2] 152 Hd 38.00N 102.00 E
Ganta 166 Dd 7.14N 8.59W
Gantang → Taiping 154 Ei 30.18N 118.07 E
Ganyu (Qingkou) 154 Eg 34.50N 119.07 E
Ganzhou 142 Ng 25.49N 114.56 E
Gao [3] 166 Eb 18.15N 1.00W
Gao [Mali] 160 Hg 16.15N 0.01 E
Gao [Niger] 166 Gb 15.25N 5.45 E
Gao'an 152 Kf 28.27N 115.24 E
Gaocheng 154 Ce 39.20N 115.50 E
Gaocheng 154 Ce 38.02N 114.50 E
Gaolan (Shidongsi) 152 Hd 36.23N 103.55 E
Gaoliangjian → Hongze 154 Ke 33.10N 119.58 E
Gaoligong Shan [▲] 152 Gf 25.45N 98.45 E
Gaolou Ling [▲] 152 Ig 24.47N 106.48 E
Gaomi 154 Ef 36.23N 119.45 E
Gaoping 152 Jd 35.46N 112.55 E
Gaoqing (Tianzhen) 154 Df 37.10N 117.50 E
Gaotai 152 Gd 39.20N 99.58 E
Gaotingzhen → Daishan 154 Gi 30.15N 122.13 E
Gaoua 166 Ec 10.20N 3.11W
Gaoual 166 Cc 11.45N 13.12W
Gaoyang 154 Ce 38.42N 115.47 E
Gaoyi 154 Cf 37.37N 114.37 E
Gaoyou 154 Ke 32.46N 119.27 E
Gaoyou Hu [≋] 152 Ke 32.50N 119.15 E
Gaozhou 152 Jg 21.56N 110.47 E
Gap 122 Mj 44.34N 6.05 E
Gar 152 Ce 32.12N 79.57 E
Gara, Lough-/Loch Uí Ghadhra 118 Eh 53.55N 8.30W
Gara'ad 168 Hd 6.54N 49.20 E
Garabato 204 Bi 28.56S 60.09W
Garachiné 194 Hi 8.04N 78.22W
Garachiné, Punta- [►] 194 Hi 8.06N 78.25W
Gara Dragoman 130 Fg 42.55N 22.56 E
Ga'raet el Oubeira [≋] 128 Cn 36.50N 8.23 E
Gara Kostenec 130 Gg 42.18N 23.52 E
Garalo 166 Dc 11.00N 7.26W
Gara Muleta [▲] 168 Gd 9.05N 41.43 E
Garapan 220b Ba 15.12N 145.43 E
Garapuava 204 Ic 16.06S 46.33W
Garavuti 135 Gf 37.36N 68.29 E
Garba 168 Gd 9.12N 20.30 E
Garbahärrel 168 Ge 3.20N 42.17 E
Garberville 188 Df 40.06N 123.48W
Gârbosh, Küh-e- [▲] 146 Nf 32.36N 50.04 E
Garça 204 Hf 22.14S 49.37W
Garças, Rio das- [≋] 204 Fb 15.54S 52.16W
Garcias 204 Fe 20.34S 52.13W
Gard [3] 122 Jj 44.00N 4.00 E
Garda 128 Ee 45.34N 10.42 E
Garda, Lago di- (Benaco) = Garda Lake- (EN) [≋] 110 Hf 45.35N 10.35 E
Garda, Lake- (EN) = Garda, Lago di- (Benaco) 110 Hf 45.35N 10.35 E
Gardabani 132 Ni 41.29N 45.05 E
Garde, Cap de- [►] 128 Bn 36.58N 7.47 E
Gardelegen 120 Hd 52.32N 11.22 E
Garden City [Ga.-U.S.] 184 Gi 32.06N 81.09W
Garden City [Ks.-U.S.] 182 Fd 37.58N 100.53W
Garden Grove 188 Gj 33.46N 117.57W
Garden Peninsula [►] 184 Dc 45.40N 86.35W
Gardermoen 116 Dd 60.13N 11.06 E
Gardey 204 Cm 37.17S 59.22W
Gardēz 144 Kc 33.37N 69.07 E
Gardiner 188 Jd 45.02N 110.42W
Gardiner Range [▲] 212 Fc 19.15S 128.50 E
Gardner → Nikumaroro Atoll [●] 208 Je 4.40S 174.32W
Gardner Pinnacles [⛰] 208 Kb 25.00N 167.55W
Gardno, Jezioro- [≋] 120 Nb 54.43N 17.05 E
Gardon → Gard [≋] 122 Kk 43.51N 4.37 E
Gardone Riviera 128 Ee 45.37N 10.34 E
Gard ou Gardon [≋] 122 Kk 43.51N 4.37 E
Gareloi [●] 178a Cb 51.47N 178.48W
Garessio 128 Cf 44.12N 8.02 E
Garfagnana [▼] 128 Ef 44.05N 10.30 E
Gargaliánoi 130 El 37.04N 21.38 E
Gargano [►] 110 Hg 41.50N 16.00 E
Gargano, Testa del- [►] 128 Ki 41.35N 16.12 E
Gargantua, Cape- [►] 184 Kb 47.36N 85.02W
Gargždai/Gargžciai 114 Ei 55.43N 21.24 E
Gargždai/Gargžciai 114 Ei 55.43N 21.24 E
Gari 136 Gd 59.28N 62.25 E
Garibaldi 204 Oi 27.12S 53.04W
Garibaldi, Mount- [▲] 188 Db 49.51N 123.01W
Garies 172 Bf 30.30S 18.02 E
Garigliano [≋] 128 Hi 41.13N 13.45 E
Garimpo 204 Ed 18.41S 54.50W
Garissa 160 Ki 0.28S 39.38 E
Garkida 166 Ki 10.25N 12.34 E
Garland 182 Jd 32.54N 96.39W
Garlasco 128 Ce 45.12N 8.55 E
Garliava/Garljava 116 Jj 54.46N 23.55 E
Garljava/Garliava 116 Jj 54.46N 23.55 E
Garm 135 He 39.02N 70.18 E
Garmisch-Partenkirchen 135 He 47.30N 11.06 E
Garmsar 146 Oe 35.20N 52.13 E
Garnet Bank (EN) [≋] 184 Kh 33.05S 49.25W
Garnet Range [▲] 188 Ic 46.45N 113.15W
Garnett 186 Ig 38.17N 95.14W
Garonne [≋] 110 Ff 45.02N 0.36W
Garonne, Canal latéral à la- [≋] 122 Fj 44.34N 0.09 E
Garopába 204 Hh 28.04S 48.40W
Garoua 160 Ad 9.18N 13.24 E
Garoua Boulaï 160 Ad 5.53N 14.33 E
Garöwe 160 Lh 8.25N 48.33 E
Garpenberg 116 Gd 60.16N 16.04 E
Garphyttan 116 Fe 59.19N 14.56 E
Garrel 124 Kb 52.57N 8.01 E
Garreru [≋] 220a Bc 7.20N 134.33 E
Garri, Küh-e- [▲] 146 Mf 33.59N 48.25 E
Garrigues [▼] 122 Kj 44.10N 4.30 E
Garrison 186 Fc 47.40N 101.25W

Garron Point/An Gearrán [►] 118 Hf 55.05N 5.58W
Garrovillas 126 Fe 39.43N 6.33W
Garruchos 204 Ei 28.11S 55.39W
Garry [≋] 118 Je 56.45N 3.45W
Garry Bay [◄] 180 Ic 69.00N 85.10W
Garry Lake 174 Gc 66.00N 100.00W
Garsen 170 Hc 2.16S 40.07 E
Gartar/Qianning 152 He 30.27N 101.29 E
Gartempe [≋] 122 Gh 46.47N 0.50 E
Gartog → Markam 152 Gf 29.32N 98.33 E
Garut 150 Eh 7.13S 107.54 E
Garuva 204 Hh 26.01S 48.51W
Garve 148 Qd 24.11N 83.49 E
Garwa 148 Gd 24.11N 83.49 E
Garwolin 120 Re 51.54N 21.37 E
Gary 182 Jc 41.36N 87.20W
Garyarsa 152 De 31.40N 80.26 E
Garzê 152 Ge 31.42N 99.58 E
Garzón [Col.] 202 Cc 2.13N 75.38W
Garzón [Ur.] 206 Jd 34.36S 54.33W
Gasan-Kuli 136 Fh 37.29N 53.59 E
Gascogne = Gascony (EN) [▣] 122 Gk 43.30N 0.10 E
Gascogne, Golfe de- = Biscay, Bay of- (EN) [◄] 110 Fg 43.50N 2.30W
Gasconade River [≋] 186 Kg 38.40N 91.33W
Gascony (EN) = Gascogne [▣] 122 Gk 43.30N 0.10 E
Gascoyne Junction 212 De 25.03S 115.12 E
Gascoyne River [≋] 208 Dg 24.52S 113.37 E
Gasefjord [◄] 179 Je 70.00N 27.30W
Gaseland [◄] 179 Jd 70.20N 29.00W
Gash [≋] 168 Gb 16.48N 35.51 E
Gas Hu [≋] 152 Fd 38.00N 90.45 E
Gashua 160 Ig 12.52N 11.03 E
Gaspar Strait (EN)=Kelasa, Selat- [►] 150 Eg 2.40S 107.15 E
Gaspé 174 Me 48.50N 64.29W
Gaspé, Cap de - [►] 180 Lg 48.45N 64.10W
Gaspé, Péninsule de- = Gaspé Peninsula (EN) [►] 174 Me 48.30N 65.00W
Gaspé Peninsula (EN) = Gaspé, Péninsule de- [►] 174 Me 48.30N 65.00W
Gassan [▲] 156 Gb 38.34N 140.01 E
Gassol 166 Hd 8.32N 10.28 E
Gaston, Lake- [≋] 184 Ig 36.35N 78.00W
Gastonia 182 Kd 35.16N 81.11W
Gastoúni 130 El 37.51N 21.15 E
Gastre 206 Gf 42.17S 69.14W
Gästrikland [▣] 116 Gd 60.30N 16.30 E
Gata, Akra- [►] 146 Ee 34.34N 33.02 E
Gata, Cabo de- [►] 110 Fh 36.43N 2.12W
Gata, Sierra de- [▲] 126 Fd 40.15N 6.45W
Gataia 130 Ed 45.26N 21.26 E
Gatchina 136 Dd 59.34N 30.09 E
Gate 186 Fh 36.51N 100.01W
Gate City 184 Hg 36.38N 82.37W
Gateshead 118 Lg 54.58N 1.37W
Gateshead [◄] 180 Hb 70.35N 100.15W
Gathemo 124 Bf 48.46N 0.58 E
Gâtinais [▼] 122 If 48.00N 2.20 E
Gâtine, Hauteurs de- [▲] 122 Fh 46.38N 0.30W
Gatineau, Rivière- [≋] 180 Jg 45.27N 75.42W
Gatlinburg 184 Fh 35.43N 83.31W
Gato, Cumbres del- [▲] 192 Fd 27.00N 106.35W
Gattinara 128 Ce 45.37N 8.22 E
Gatún, Lago- = Gatun Lake [≋] 190 Ig 9.12N 79.55W
Gatun Lake (EN)=Gatún, Lago- [≋] 190 Ig 9.12N 79.55W
Gatvand 146 Mf 32.15N 48.50 E
Gatwick Airport [✈] 124 Bc 51.08N 0.12W
Gaucín 126 Gk 36.31N 5.19W
Gauhati → Guwāhāti 142 Lg 26.11N 91.44 E
Gauiena/Gaujiena 116 Lg 57.25N 26.28 E
Gauja/Gaujena [≋] 114 Fh 57.10N 24.16 E
Gaujiena/Gauiena 116 Lg 57.25N 26.28 E
Gaula [Nor.] [≋] 116 Da 63.21N 10.14 E
Gaula [Nor.] [≋] 116 Ac 61.22N 5.41 E
Gauldalen [▣] 116 Da 63.00N 11.00 E
Gauley River [≋] 184 Gf 38.10N 81.12W
Gau-Odernheim 124 Ke 49.46N 8.12 E
Gaurdak 146 Qc 37.49N 66.01 E
Gauri Phanta 148 Gc 28.41N 80.33 E
Gausdal [◄] 116 Cc 61.00N 10.10 E
Gausta [▲] 116 Bd 59.50N 8.39 E
Gåvbandī 146 Oi 27.12N 53.04 E
Gävbūs, Küh-e- [▲] 146 Oi 27.10N 54.00 E
Gavdhopoúla [●] 130 Go 34.50N 24.00 E
Gávdhos [●] 110 Ii 34.50N 24.05 E
Gavere 146 Le 35.00N 46.58 E
Gävle 116 Gd 60.56N 17.10 E
Gävleborg [2] 114 Df 61.30N 16.15 E
Gävlebukten [◄] 116 Gd 60.40N 17.20 E
Gavorrano 128 Eh 42.55N 10.54 E
Gavri 116 Le 56.49N 27.58 E
Gavrilov-Jam 114 Jh 57.19N 39.51 E
Gavrilov Posad 132 Ia 56.33N 40.07 E
Gãw Koshi 144 Id 28.38N 57.12 E
Gawler 212 Hf 34.37S 138.44 E
Gawler Ranges [▲] 208 Gg 32.30S 136.00 E
Gaxun Nur [≋] 140 Me 42.25N 101.00 E
Gaya [India] 142 Jg 24.47N 85.00 E
Gaya [Niger] 166 Fc 11.53N 3.27 E
Gaya Ni [●] 154 Cf 36.47N 43.00 E
Gaylord 184 Ec 45.02N 84.40W
Gayndah 212 Ke 25.37S 151.36 E
Gaz 172 Nf 23.30S 33.00 E
Gaza [3] 172 Nf 23.30S 33.00 E
Gaza → Ghazzah 146 Ef 31.30N 34.28 E
Gaz-Ačak 136 Ji 41.11N 61.27 E
Gazalkent 135 Gd 41.33N 69.46 E
Gazaoua 166 Gc 13.32N 7.55 E
Gazelle, Récif de la- [≋] 219b Be 20.11S 165.27 E

Gaziantep 142 Ff 37.05N 37.22 E
Gaziemir 130 Kk 38.19N 27.10 E
Gazimağusa = Famagusta (EN) 144 Dc 35.07N 33.57 E
Gazimurskij Zavod 138 Hf 52.57N 120.22 E
Gazipaşa 146 Ed 36.17N 32.20 E
Gazli 136 Gg 40.09N 63.23 E
Gazojak 136 Ji 41.50N 61.23 E
Gbarnga 160 Gh 7.00N 9.29W
Gboko 166 Gd 7.21N 8.58 E
Gbon 166 Dd 9.50N 6.27W
Gdańsk [2] 120 Ob 54.25N 18.40 E
Gdańsk (Danzig) 112 He 54.23N 18.40 E
Gdansk, Gulf of- (EN) = Gdańska, Zatoka- [◄] 110 He 54.40N 19.15 E
Gdov 114 Gg 58.47N 27.54 E
Gdynia 112 He 54.32N 18.33 E
Gearhart Mountain [▲] 188 Ee 42.30N 120.53W
Géba [≋] 166 Bc 11.58N 15.00W
Gebe, Pulau- [●] 150 Ig 0.05S 129.20 E
Gebze 146 Cb 40.48N 29.25 E
Gecha 168 Fd 7.29N 35.25 E
Geçitkale 148 Ee 35.15N 33.45 E
Gedinne 124 Ge 49.59N 4.56 E
Gediz 146 Cc 39.02N 29.25 E
Gediz [≋] 144 Cb 38.39N 26.45 E
Gedo 168 Fd 9.00N 37.29 E
Gedo [3] 168 Ge 3.00N 42.00 E
Gedo [▲] 168 Ge 2.20N 41.20 E
Gedser, Sydfalster- 114 Ci 54.35N 11.57 E
Gedser Odde- [►] 116 Dj 54.34N 11.59 E
Geel 122 Ld 51.10N 5.00 E
Geelong 210 Fh 38.08S 144.21 E
Geelvink Channel [≋] 212 Ce 28.30S 114.10 E
Geer [≋] 124 Hd 50.51N 5.42 E
Geeste 124 Jb 52.36N 7.16 E
Geesthacht 120 Gc 53.26N 10.22 E
Gê'gyai 152 De 32.29N 80.52 E
Ge Hu [≋] 154 Ei 31.36N 119.51 E
Geidam 166 Hc 12.53N 11.56 E
Geiger 168 Ec 11.59N 32.46 E
Geihoku 156 Cd 34.44N 132.17 E
Geikie [≋] 180 Hc 57.48N 103.46W
Geilo 114 Bf 60.31N 8.12 E
Geiranger 116 Bb 62.06N 7.12 E
Geisenheim 124 Je 49.59N 7.58 E
Geislingen an der Steige 120 Fh 48.37N 9.51 E
Geita 170 Fc 2.52S 32.10 E
Geithus 114 Bg 59.57N 9.57 E
Geiyo-Shotō [●] 156 Cd 34.15N 132.45 E
Gejiu 142 Jg 23.22N 103.14 E
Gel [Sud.] [≋] 158 Fh 7.46N 29.36 E
Gel [Sud.] [≋] 168 Ed 6.08N 31.17 E
Gela 128 Im 37.05N 14.15 E
Gela, Golfo di- [◄] 128 Im 37.00N 14.10 E
Geladi 168 Hd 6.57N 46.25 E
Geldenaken/Jodoigne 124 Gd 50.43N 4.52 E
Gelderland [3] 124 Hb 52.10N 5.50 E
Geldermalsen 124 Gc 51.53N 5.19 E
Geldern 120 Ce 51.31N 6.20 E
Geldrop 124 Hc 51.25N 5.33 E
Geleen 122 Ld 50.58N 5.52 E
Gelembé 130 Kj 39.10N 27.50 E
Gelemso 168 Gd 8.48N 40.32 E
Gelendžik 132 Gd 44.33N 38.06 E
Gélengdeng 168 Bc 10.56N 15.32 E
Gelgaudiškis 116 Ji 55.02N 22.58 E
Gelibolu 144 Bb 40.24N 26.40 E
Gelibolu Yarımadası = Gallipoli Peninsula (EN) [►] 130 Ji 40.20N 26.30 E
Gélise [≋] 122 Gj 44.11N 0.17 E
Gelinsör 168 Hd 6.24N 46.46 E
Gelnhausen 120 Ff 50.12N 9.11 E
Gelsenkirchen 120 De 51.31N 7.06 E
Gemas 150 Ih 2.35N 102.37 E
Gemena 160 Ih 3.15N 19.46 E
Gemerek 146 Ic 39.11N 36.05 E
Gemert 124 Hc 51.33N 5.41 E
Gemi, Jabal- [▲] 168 Ed 9.01N 34.09 E
Gemlik 146 Cb 40.26N 29.09 E
Gemlik Körfezi [◄] 146 Cb 40.26N 28.55 E
Gemona del Friuli 128 Hd 46.16N 13.09 E
Gemünden (Felda) 124 Ke 50.42N 9.03 E
Gemünden (Wohra) 124 Ke 50.58N 8.58 E
Gemünden am Main 120 Ff 50.03N 9.42 E
Genale [≋] 158 Lh 0.15S 42.38 E
Genç 146 Ic 38.46N 40.35 E
Gendringen-Ulft 124 Ic 51.52N 6.23 E
Genemuiden 124 Ib 52.38N 6.02 E
General Acha 206 Hc 37.23S 64.36W
General Alvear [Arg.] 206 Ha 35.58S 67.42W
General Alvear [Arg.] 206 Hc 36.03S 60.01W
General Arenales 204 Bl 34.18S 61.18W
General Artigas 204 Dh 26.53S 56.17W
General Belgrano 206 Jc 35.46S 58.30W
General Belgrano Station [⛺] 222 Af 77.50S 38.00W
General Bernardo O'Higgins [⛺] 222 Re 63.19S 57.54W
General Bravo 192 Jd 25.48N 99.10W
General Cabrera 206 Hb 32.48S 63.52W
General Capdevila 204 Bh 27.06S 61.28W
General Carneiro 204 Gc 15.42S 52.46W
General Carrera, Lago- [≋] 206 Fg 46.30S 72.00W
General Cepeda 192 Id 25.23N 101.27W
General Conesa [Arg.] 206 Jc 35.56S 57.20W
General Conesa [Arg.] 206 Hd 40.06S 64.25W
General Enrique Martínez 204 Fk 33.12S 53.50W
General Eugenio A. Garay 204 Cf 20.31S 62.08W
General Galarza 204 Cl 32.43S 59.24W
General Güemes 204 Ah 24.40S 65.00W
General Guido 206 Jc 36.40S 57.46W
General José de San Martín 204 Ch 26.33S 59.21W
General Juan Madariaga 206 Jc 37.00S 57.09W
General Lamadrid 206 Hc 37.16S 61.17W
General Lavalle 206 Jc 36.24S 56.58W
General Levalle 206 Hb 34.00S 63.55W
General Manuel Belgrano, Cerro- [▲] 198 Jh 29.01S 67.49W
General O'Brien 204 Bl 34.54S 60.45W
General Pico 206 Hc 35.40S 63.44W

General Pinedo 206 Hc 27.19S 61.17W
General Pinto 204 Bl 34.46S 61.53W
General Pirán 204 Dm 37.16S 57.45W
General Roca 206 Ge 39.02S 67.35W
General Salgado 204 Ge 20.39S 50.22W
General Santos 142 Oi 6.05N 125.10 E
General Sarmiento 204 Cl 34.33S 58.43W
General Terán 192 Je 25.16N 99.41W
General-Toševo 130 Lf 43.42N 28.02 E
General Treviño 192 Jd 26.14N 99.29W
General Trías 192 Fc 28.21N 106.22W
General Vargas 204 Ei 29.42S 54.40W
General Viamonte 204 Bl 35.01S 61.01W
General Villegas 206 Hc 35.03S 63.01W
Geneseo 184 Id 42.46N 77.49W
Geneva [Al.-U.S.] 184 Ej 31.02N 85.52W
Geneva [Nb.-U.S.] 186 Hf 40.32N 97.36W
Geneva [N.Y.-U.S.] 184 Id 42.53N 76.59W
Geneva (EN) = Genève 112 Gf 46.10N 6.10 E
Geneva, Lake- (EN) = Léman, Lac- [≋] 110 Gf 46.25N 6.30 E
Genève [2] 128 Ad 46.10N 6.15 E
Genève = Geneva (EN) 112 Gf 46.10N 6.10 E
Genevois [▼] 122 Mh 46.00N 6.10 E
Genhe → Ergun Zuoqi 142 Od 50.47N 121.32 E
Geni [≋] 168 Ed 8.31N 33.10 E
Geničesk 136 Ed 46.12N 34.48 E
Genil [≋] 126 Gj 37.42N 5.19W
Genk 122 Ld 50.58N 5.30 E
Genoa (EN) = Genova 112 Gf 44.25N 8.57 E
Genoa, Gulf of- (EN) = Genova, Golfo di- [◄] 110 Gg 44.10N 8.55 E
Genova = Genoa (EN) 112 Gf 44.25N 8.57 E
Genova, Golfo di- = Genoa, Gulf of- (EN) [◄] 110 Gg 44.10N 8.55 E
Genova-Nervi 128 Df 44.23N 9.02 E
Genova-Voltri 128 Cf 44.26N 8.45 E
Genovesa, Isla- [●] 202a Ba 0.20N 89.58W
Genrietty, ostrov- [●] 138 Ka 77.00N 157.00 E
Gennargentu [▲] 110 Gg 40.00N 9.20 E
Gennep 124 Hc 51.42N 5.59 E
Genthin 120 Id 52.24N 12.10 E
Gent/Gand = Ghent (EN) 124 Fc 51.03N 3.43 E
Gentbrugge, Gent- 124 Fc 51.03N 3.45 E
Gent-Gentbrugge 124 Fc 51.03N 3.45 E
Genzano di Lucania 128 Kj 40.51N 16.02 E
Genzano di Roma 128 Fi 41.42N 11.41 E
Geographe Bay [◄] 208 Ch 33.35S 115.15 E
Geographe Channel [≋] 212 Cd 24.40S 113.20 E
Geographical Society Øer [●] 179 Jd 72.40N 22.20W
Geokčaj 132 Oi 40.40N 47.42 E
Geok-Tepe 136 Fh 38.10N 57.58 E
Geomagnetic Pole (1975) (EN) 222 Hf 78.40S 109.33 E
Georga, zemlja- [●] 140 Ga 80.30N 49.00 E
George 172 Cf 33.58S 22.24 E
George [≋] 174 Md 58.30N 66.00W
George, Lake- [Austl.] 212 Jg 35.05S 149.25 E
George, Lake- [Fl.-U.S.] 184 Fk 29.17N 81.36W
George, Lake- [Ug.] 170 Fc 0.00N 30.12 E
George, Lake- [U.S.] 184 Kd 43.35N 73.35W
George Gill Range [▲] 212 Gd 24.15S 131.35 E
Georges Bank (EN) [≋] 182 Nc 41.15N 67.30W
George Sound [◄] 218 Bf 44.50S 167.20 E
Georgetown [Austl.] 210 Fc 41.06S 146.50 E
Georgetown [Austl.] 210 Hc 18.18S 143.33 E
Georgetown [Bah.] 194 Hd 23.30N 75.46W
Georgetown [Cay.Is.] 190 Ic 19.18N 81.23W
Georgetown [Del.-U.S.] 184 Jf 38.42N 75.23W
Georgetown [Gam.] 160 Cg 13.32N 14.46W
Georgetown [Guy.] 198 Ka 6.48N 58.10W
Georgetown [Ky.-U.S.] 184 Ef 38.13N 84.33W
Georgetown [Oh.-U.S.] 184 Ff 38.52N 83.54W
Georgetown [S.C.-U.S.] 184 If 33.23N 79.17W
Georgetown [St.Hel.] 160 Fi 7.56S 14.25W
Georgetown [St.Vin.] 196 Hk 13.16N 61.08W
Georgetown [Tx.-U.S.] 186 Hk 30.38N 97.41W
George Town (Pinang) 142 Mi 5.25N 100.20 E
George V Coast 222 Je 68.30S 147.30 E
George VI Sound [≋] 222 Qf 71.00S 68.00W
George West 186 Gl 28.20N 98.07W
Georgia [2] 182 Ke 32.50N 83.15W
Georgia, Strait of - [≋] 180 Fg 49.00N 123.20W
Georgia del Sur/South Georgia 222 Ad 54.15S 36.45W
Georgian Bay [◄] 174 Ke 45.15N 80.50W
Georgian SSR (EN) = Gruzinskaja SSR [2] 136 Eg 42.00N 44.00 E
Georgijevka [Kaz.-U.S.S.R.] 136 Ig 42.43N 74.43 E
Georgijevka [Kaz.-U.S.S.R.] 136 If 49.19N 81.35 E
Georgijevsk 132 Kd 44.09N 43.28 E
Georgina River [≋] 208 Ee 23.30S 139.47 E
Georgsmarienhütte 120 Ed 52.16N 8.02 E
Gera 120 Id 50.53N 12.05 E
Geraardsbergen/Grammont 124 Fd 50.46N 3.52 E
Gerais, Chapadão dos- [▲] 204 Jc 17.40S 45.35W
Geral, Serra- [Braz.] 204 Gi 29.10S 50.15W
Geral, Serra- [Braz.] 204 Gf 23.54S 50.15W
Geral, Serra- [Braz.] 198 Kg 13.00S 41.00W
Geral de Goiás, Serra- [▲] 198 Lg 13.00S 46.00W
Geral do Paraná, Serra- [▲] 204 Ib 15.00S 47.30W
Geraldine 218 Cf 44.05S 171.15 E
Geraldton [Austl.] 210 Cf 28.46S 114.36 E
Geraldton [Ont.-Can.] 180 Ig 49.44N 86.57W
Gérardmer 122 Mf 48.04N 6.53 E
Gerash 146 Pi 27.41N 54.06 E
Gerbici, gora- [▲] 138 Lc 66.39N 105.02 E
Gerca 130 Ja 48.10N 26.17 E
Gercüş 146 Ic 37.34N 41.23 E

Gerecse [▲] 120 Oi 47.41N 18.29 E
Gerede 146 Eb 40.48N 32.12 E
Gerede [≋] 146 Eb 40.52N 32.39 E
Gerês, Serra do- [▲] 126 Ec 41.48N 8.00W
Gereshk 144 Jc 31.48N 64.34 E
Gérgal 126 Jg 37.07N 2.33W
Gering 186 Ef 41.50N 103.40W
Gerlachovský štít [▲] 120 Qg 49.12N 20.09 E
Gerlogubi 168 Hd 6.56N 45.03 E
Gerlovo [≋] 130 Jf 43.03N 26.35 E
German Democratic Republic = Germany [1] 112 Ge 51.00N 10.00 E
Germania 204 Bl 34.34S 62.03W
Germania Land 179 Kc 76.50N 20.00W
Germany, Federal Republic of = Germany 112 Ge 51.00N 10.00 E
Germencik 130 Kl 37.51N 27.37 E
Germersheim 124 Ke 49.13N 8.22 E
Germi 144 Mc 32.53N 54.58 E
Germiston 172 De 26.15S 28.05 E
Gernika-Lumo / Guernica y Luno 126 Ja 43.19N 2.41W
Gernsbach 124 Kf 48.46N 8.19 E
Gernsheim 124 Ke 49.45N 8.29 E
Gero 154 Id 35.48N 137.14 E
Gerolstein 124 Ie 50.13N 6.40 E
Gerona/Girona 126 Oc 41.59N 2.49 E
Gerona / Girona [3] 126 Ob 42.10N 2.40 E
Gerpinnes 124 Gd 50.20N 4.31 E
Gers [3] 122 Gj 43.40N 0.30 E
Gers [≋] 122 Gj 44.09N 0.39 E
Gersprenz [≋] 124 Le 49.59N 9.04 E
Gerze 146 Fb 41.48N 35.12 E
Gêrzê 152 De 32.20N 84.04 E
Gescher 124 Jc 51.57N 7.00 E
Geseke 124 Kd 51.39N 8.31 E
Geser 150 Jg 3.53S 130.54 E
Gesunda 116 Fd 60.54N 14.32 E
Gesunden [≋] 116 Fa 63.10N 15.55 E
Geta 114 Ef 60.23N 19.50 E
Getafe 126 Id 40.18N 3.43W
Gete [≋] 122 Ld 50.55N 5.08 E
Getinge 114 Ci 56.49N 12.44 E
Gettysburg 186 Gd 45.01N 99.57W
Gettysburg Seamount (EN) [≋] 162 Eb 36.32N 11.37W
Getúlio Vargas 204 Fh 27.52S 52.16W
Getz Ice Shelf [≋] 222 Nf 74.15S 125.00W
Geul [≋] 124 Hd 50.40N 5.43 E
Gevaş 146 Jc 38.16N 43.05 E
Gévaudan [▣] 122 Jj 44.27N 3.30 E
Gevelsberg 124 Jc 51.19N 7.20 E
Gevgelija 130 Fh 41.08N 22.31 E
Gévora [≋] 126 Ff 38.53N 6.57W
Gevsjön [≋] 116 Ea 63.25N 12.40 E
Gewane 168 Gc 10.10N 40.39 E
Gex 122 Mh 46.20N 6.04 E
Gexianzhuang → Qinghe 154 Cf 37.03N 115.39 E
Geyersberg [▲] 120 Fg 49.50N 9.30 E
Geyik Dağı [▲] 146 Ed 36.54N 32.10 E
Geyikli 130 Jj 39.48N 26.12 E
Geyser, Banc du- [≋] 172 Hb 12.25S 46.25 E
Geysir [▲] 110 Da 64.19N 20.18W
Geyve 146 Db 40.30N 30.18 E
Ghābāri, Darb al- [≋] 146 Cj 25.10N 29.50 E
Ghadāmis 160 He 30.08N 9.30 E
Ghadduwah 164 Bd 26.26N 14.18 E
Ghaghara [≋] 142 Kg 24.52N 84.55 E
Ghaghe [●] 219a Db 7.23S 158.12 E
Ghallah, Wâdî al- [≋] 158 Jg 10.25N 27.32 E
Ghamrah, Wâdî al- [≋] 146 Hj 25.47N 38.45 E
Ghana [1] 160 Gh 8.00N 2.00W
Ghanzi 160 Jk 21.42S 21.38 E
Ghanzi [3] 172 Cd 22.00S 23.00 E
Ghâr ad Dimā' 128 Cn 36.27N 8.26 E
Gharaqābād 146 Mf 35.06N 49.50 E
Gharbi, Al Hajar al- [▲] 148 Fi 24.10N 56.15 E
Gharbīyah, Aş Şaḩrā' al- = Western Desert [▲] 158 Jf 27.30N 28.00 E
Ghardaïa 160 He 32.29N 3.40 E
Ghârib, Jabal- [▲] 164 Fd 28.07N 32.54 E
Gharrāf, Shaṭṭ al- [≋] 146 Kf 32.30N 45.48 E
Gharsah, Shaṭṭ al- [≋] 162 Ic 34.06N 7.50 E
Gharyān 164 Bc 32.10N 13.01 E
Gharyān [3] 164 Bc 30.35N 12.00 E
Ghāt 160 If 24.58N 10.11 E
Ghatere 219a Db 7.58S 159.01 E
Ghaṭṭ 146 Gj 31.16N 37.31 E
Ghazal, Baḩr al- [≋] 168 Bd 9.31N 30.25 E
Ghazal, Bahr el- [≋] 158 Ig 13.01N 15.28 E
Ghazaouet 162 Gb 35.06N 1.51W
Ghaziabad 148 Ec 28.40N 77.25 E
Ghazipur 148 Gd 25.35N 83.34 E
Ghazni 142 Ke 33.33N 68.26 E
Ghaznī [3] 144 Kc 33.00N 68.00 E
Ghazzah = Gaza (EN) 146 Dc 31.30N 34.28 E
Ghent (EN) = Gent/Gand 122 Ld 51.03N 3.43 E
Gheorghe Gheorghiu-Dej 130 Ic 46.16N 26.46 E
Gheorghieni 130 Ic 46.43N 25.37 E
Gherghiu-Dej 136 Eg 50.00N 39.31 E
Gherla 130 Gc 46.50N 23.54 E
Ghidigeni 130 Kc 46.03N 27.30 E
Ghidole (EN) = Gidole 168 Fd 5.37N 37.26 E
Ghilarza 128 Cj 40.07N 8.50 E
Ghimeş, Pasul- [▲] 130 Jc 46.33N 26.05 E
Ghisonaccia 122a Ba 42.00N 9.24 E
Ghiznibeana Islands [●] 219a Db 7.33S 158.45 E
Ghowr [3] 144 Jc 34.00N 65.00 E
Ghriss 126 Ni 35.15N 0.10 E
Ghubbat al Qamar [◄] 140 Fh 16.00N 52.32 E
Ghudāf, Wādī al- [≋] 146 Jf 32.56N 43.30 E
Ghurāb, Jabal al- [▲] 146 Hf 34.18N 38.42 E
Ghūrīān 144 Jc 34.21N 61.30 E

Index Symbols

Symbol	Meaning	Symbol	Meaning	Symbol	Meaning	Symbol	Meaning
[1]	Independent Nation	[▣]	Historical or Cultural Region	Pass, Gap	Depression	Coast, Beach	Rock, Reef	Waterfall, Rapids	Canal
[2]	State, Region	Mount, Mountain	Plain, Lowland	Polder	Cliff	Islands, Archipelago	River Mouth, Estuary	Glacier
[3]	District, County	Volcano	Delta	Desert, Dunes	Peninsula	Rocks, Reefs	Lake	Ice Shelf, Pack Ice
[4]	Municipality	Hill	Salt Flat	Forest, Woods	Isthmus	Coral Reef	Salt Lake	Ocean
[5]	Colony, Dependency	Mountains, Mountain Range	Valley, Canyon	Heath, Steppe	Sandbank	Well, Spring	Intermittent Lake	Sea
Continent	Hills, Escarpment	Crater, Cave	Oasis	Island	Geyser	Reservoir	Gulf, Bay
Physical Region	Plateau, Upland	Karst Features	Cape, Point	Atoll	River, Stream	Swamp, Pond	Strait, Fjord

Lagoon	Escarpment, Sea Scarp	Historic Site	Airport
Bank	Fracture	Ruins	Port
Seamount	Trench, Abyss	Wall, Walls	Military installation
Tableland	National Park, Reserve	Church, Abbey	Lighthouse
Ridge	Point of Interest	Temple	Mine
Shelf	Recreation Site	Scientific Station	Tunnel
Basin	Cave, Cavern	Railway station	Dam, Bridge

Ghurraḥ, Jabal al- 128 Cn 36.36N 8.23 E
Ghuzayyil, Sabkhat- 164 Dd 29.50N 19.45 E
Giaginskaja 132 Lg 44.47N 40.05 E
Giala, Jabal- 146 Ei 27.20N 32.57 E
Gialo Oasis (EN)=Jālū, Wāḥāt- 158 Jf 29.00N 21.20 E
Gia Nghia 148 Lf 11.59N 107.42 E
Giannutri 128 Fh 42.15N 11.05 E
Giant's Causeway/Clochán an Aifir 118 Gf 55.15N 6.35W
Giarre 128 Jm 37.43N 15.11 E
Gibara 194 Ic 21.07N 76.08W
Gibbon Point 197b Bb 18.14N 63.00W
Gibb River 212 Fc 16.25S 126.25 E
Gibbs Islands 222 Re 61.30S 55.31W
Gibellina 128 Gm 37.47N 12.58 E
Gibeon 172 Be 25.09S 17.43 E
Gibeon [3] 172 Bd 25.00S 18.30 E
Gibostad 114 Db 69.21N 18.00 E
Gibraleón 126 Fg 37.23N 6.58W
Gibraltar 112 Fh 36.11N 5.22W
Gibraltar [5] 112 Fh 36.11N 5.22W
Gibraltar, Estrecho de-= Gibraltar, Strait of- (EN) 110 Fh 35.57N 5.36W
Gibraltar, Strait of- (EN)= Djebel Ṭāriq, El Bōghāz- 110 Fh 35.57N 5.36W
Gibraltar, Strait of- (EN)= Gibraltar, Estrecho de- 110 Fh 35.57N 5.36W
Gibson Desert 208 Dg 24.30S 126.00 E
Gidami 168 Ed 8.58N 34.40 E
Giddings 186 Hk 30.11N 96.56W
Gidigič 130 Lb 47.04N 28.38 E
Gidole=Ghidole (EN) 168 Fd 5.37N 37.29 E
Gien 122 Ig 47.42N 2.38 E
Giens, Presqu'île de- 122 Mk 43.02N 6.08 E
Gier 122 Ki 45.35N 4.46 E
Gießen 120 Ef 50.35N 8.39 E
Gieten 124 Ia 53.01N 6.48 E
Giethoorn 124 Ib 52.43N 6.07 E
Gifford 180 Jb 70.21N 83.05W
Gifford Seamount (EN) 198 Ii 39.00S 82.00W
Gifhorn 120 Gd 52.29N 10.33 E
Gift Lake 180 Fe 55.49N 115.57W
Gifu 142 Pf 35.25N 136.45 E
Gifu Ken [2] 154 Ng 35.50N 137.00 E
Gigant 132 Lf 46.29N 41.20 E
Giganta, Cerro- 190 Bc 26.07N 111.36W
Giganta, Sierra de la- 190 Bc 26.18N 111.39W
Gigante 202 Cc 2.24N 75.34W
Gigen 130 Hf 43.42N 24.29 E
Gigha 118 Hf 55.41N 5.44W
Giglio 128 Eh 42.20N 10.55 E
Gijón 112 Fg 43.32N 5.40W
Gikongoro 170 Ec 2.30S 29.35 E
Gila Bend 188 Ij 32.57N 112.43W
Gila Bend Mountains 188 Ij 33.10N 113.10W
Gilān [3] 144 Gb 37.00N 49.50 E
Gilān-e-Gharb 146 Ke 34.08N 45.55 E
Gila River 182 Ee 32.43N 114.33W
Gilbert, Mount- 188 Ca 50.51N 124.20W
Gilbert River 212 Ic 16.35S 141.15 E
Gilbert Seamount (EN) 178 If 52.50N 150.10W
Gilbués 202 Ie 9.50S 45.21W
Gilé 172 Fc 16.09S 38.19 E
Giles Meterological Station 212 Fc 25.02S 128.18 E
Gilford Island 188 Ba 50.45N 126.25W
Gilgandra 212 Jf 31.42S 148.39 E
Gilgău 130 Gb 47.17N 23.43 E
Gilgil 170 Gc 0.30S 36.19 E
Gilgit 142 Jf 35.55N 74.18 E
Gilgit 148 Ea 35.44N 74.38 E
Giljuj 138 Hf 54.17N 127.05 E
Gillam 180 Ie 56.21N 94.43W
Gilleleje 116 Eh 56.07N 12.19 E
Gillen, Lake- 212 Ee 26.10S 124.40 E
Gillenfeld 124 Id 50.07N 6.54 E
Gillette 182 Fc 44.18N 105.30W
Gillian, Lake- 180 Jc 69.30N 75.30W
Gillingham 118 Nj 51.24N 0.33 E
Gilo 168 Ed 8.10N 33.15 E
Gilort 130 Ge 44.36N 23.27 E
Gilroy 188 Eh 37.00N 121.34W
Giluwe, Mount- 214 Ci 6.04S 143.53 E
Gilvān 146 Md 36.47N 49.08 E
Gimån 116 Gb 62.28N 16.20 E
Gimbi 168 Fd 9.10N 35.51 E
Gimie, Mount- 196 Ff 13.52N 61.01W
Gimli 180 Hf 50.39N 97.00W
Gimo 116 Hd 60.11N 18.11 E
Gimolskoje, ozero- 114 He 63.00N 32.15 E
Gimone 122 Hk 44.00N 1.06 E
Ginda 168 Fb 15.27N 39.06 E
Ginetu 219a Ac 9.30S 152.43 E
Gingin 212 Df 31.21S 115.42 E
Gin Gin 212 Kd 25.00S 151.58 E
Gingoog 150 Ie 8.50N 125.07 E
Ginir 168 Gd 7.08N 40.43 E
Ginosa 128 Kj 40.35N 16.45 E
Ginowan 156b Ab 26.17N 127.45 E
Giofra Oasis (EN)=Jufrah, Wāḥāt al- 158 If 29.10N 16.00 E
Gioia, Golfo di- 128 Jl 38.30N 15.45 E
Gioia del Colle 128 Kj 40.48N 16.55 E
Gioia Tauro 128 Jl 38.25N 15.54 E
Gion 168 Fd 8.24N 37.55 E
Gióna Óros 130 Fk 38.35N 22.15 E
Giovi, Passo dei- 128 Cf 44.33N 8.57 E
Giraltovce 120 Rg 49.07N 21.31 E
Girardot 202 Dc 4.18N 74.49W
Girdle Ness 118 Kd 57.08N 2.02W
Giresun 144 Ea 40.55N 38.24 E
Giresun Dağları 146 Hb 40.40N 38.10 E
Giri 170 Cb 0.28N 17.59 E
Giridih 148 Hd 24.11N 86.18 E
Giriftu 170 Gb 2.00N 39.45 E
Girne 146 Ee 35.20N 33.19 E
Girón 202 Cd 3.10S 79.09W
Girona/Gerona 126 Oc 41.59N 2.49 E
Girona / Gerona [3] 126 Ob 42.10N 2.40 E
Gironde [3] 122 Fj 44.55N 0.30W
Gironde 110 Ff 45.35N 1.03W
Gironella 126 Nb 42.02N 1.53 E
Girou 122 Hk 43.46N 1.23 E
Girvan 118 If 55.15N 4.51W
Girvas 114 He 62.31N 33.44 E
Gisborne 210 Ih 38.39S 178.01 E
Gisenyi 170 Ec 1.42S 29.15 E
Gislaved 116 Eg 57.18N 13.32 E
Gisors 122 He 49.17N 1.47 E
Gissar 135 Ge 38.31N 68.36 E
Gissarski hrebet 135 Ge 39.00N 68.40 E
Gistad 116 Ff 58.27N 15.55 E
Gistel 124 Ec 51.10N 2.57 E
Gistral 126 Ea 43.28N 7.35W
Gitarama 170 Ec 2.05S 29.16 E
Gitega 170 Ec 3.26S 29.56 E
Gitu 146 Me 35.20N 48.05 E
Giudicarie, Valli- 128 Ed 46.00N 10.40 E
Giulianova 128 Hh 42.45N 13.57 E
Giumalău, Vîrful- 130 Ib 47 26N 25.29 E
Giurgeni 130 Ke 44.35N 27.48 E
Giurgiu 130 If 43.53N 25.58 E
Giurgiu [2] 130 Ie 44.13N 26.00 E
Give 116 Ci 55.51N 9.15 E
Givet 122 Kd 50.08N 4.50W
Givors 122 Ki 45.35N 4.46 E
Givry-en-Argonne 124 Gf 48.57N 4.53 E
Givry Island 220d Bb 7.07N 151.53 E
Giwa 166 Gc 11.18N 7.27 E
Giza (EN)=Al Jīzah 160 Ke 30.01N 31.13 E
Gižduvan 136 Gg 40.06N 64.40 E
Gižiga 138 Ld 62.03N 160.30 E
Gižiginskaja guba 138 Kd 61.10N 158.30 E
Gizo 214 Fi 8.06S 156.51 E
Gizo 219a Cc 8.07S 156.50 E
Giżycko 120 Rb 54.03N 21.47 E
Gjalicës, Mali i- 130 Dg 42.01N 20.28 E
Gjamyš, gora- 132 Oi 40.20N 46.25 E
Gjandža = Kirovabad 112 Kg 40.40N 46.22 E
Gjerstad 116 Cf 58.52N 9.00 E
Gjevilvatn 116 Cb 62.40N 9.25 E
Gjirokastra 130 Di 40.05N 20.10 E
Gjoa Haven 176 Jc 68.38N 95.57W
Gjøvik 112 Hc 60.48N 10.42 E
Gjuhës, Kep i- 130 Ci 40.25N 19.18 E
Glace Bay 180 Lg 46.12N 59.57W
Glacier Bay 178 Le 58.40N 136.00W
Glacier Peak 182 Cb 48.07N 121.07W
Glacier Strait 180 Ja 76.15N 79.00W
Gladbeck 124 Ic 51.34N 6.59 E
Gladenbach 124 Kd 50.46N 8.34 E
Gladewater 186 Ij 32.33N 94.56W
Gladstone [Austl.] 210 Gg 23.51S 151.16 E
Gladstone [Man.-Can.] 186 Ga 50.15N 98.50W
Gladstone [Mi.-U.S.] 184 Dc 45.51N 87.03W
Gladstone [Mo.-U.S.] 186 Ig 39.13N 94.34W
Glafsfjorden 116 Ee 59.35N 12.35 E
Glåma 114a Ab 65.48N 23.00W
Glåma 110 Hd 59.12N 10.57 E
Glamis Castle 118 Ke 56.37N 3.00W
Glamoč 128 Kf 44.03N 16.51 E
Glan 114 Dg 58.35N 15.55 E
Glan [Aus.] 128 Id 46.36N 14.25 E
Glan [Ger.] 120 Dg 49.47N 7.43 E
Glan-Münchweiler 124 Je 49.28N 7.26 E
Glarner Alpen 128 Cd 46.55N 9.00 E
Glärnisch 128 Cd 47.00N 9.00 E
Glarus 128 Dc 47.03N 9.04 E
Glarus [2] 128 Dd 46.55N 9.05 E
Glasgow [Ky.-U.S.] 184 Eg 37.00N 85.55W
Glasgow [Mt.-U.S.] 182 Fb 48.12N 106.38W
Glasgow [Scot.-U.K.] 112 Fd 55.53N 4.15W
Glashütte 120 Jf 50.51N 13.47 E
Glass 118 Id 57.25N 4.30W
Glassboro 184 Jf 39.42N 75.07W
Glass Mountains 186 Ek 30.25N 103.15W
Glastonbury 118 Kj 51.09N 2.43W
Glauchau 120 If 50.49N 12.32 E
Glava 116 Ee 59.33N 12.34 E
Glazov 112 Ld 58.09N 52.40 E
Gleann Dá Loch/Glendalough 118 Gh 53.00N 6.20W
Gledićske Planine 130 Df 43.49N 20.55 E
Gleinalpe 128 Jc 47.10N 15.05 E
Gleisdorf 128 Jc 47.06N 15.43 E
Glen 124 Bb 52.50N 0.07W
Glénan, Iles de- 122 Cg 47.43N 4.00W
Glen Arbor 184 Ec 44.53N 85.58W
Glenavy 218 Df 44.55S 171.06 E
Glen Canyon 188 Jh 37.05N 111.41W
Glencoe [Mn.-U.S.] 186 Id 44.46N 94.03W
Glencoe [S.Afr.] 172 Ee 28.12S 30.07 E
Glendale [Az.-U.S.] 182 Ee 33.32N 112.11W
Glendale [Ca.-U.S.] 182 De 34.10N 118.17W
Glendalough/Gleann Dá Loch 118 Gh 53.00N 6.20W
Glendive 182 Fb 47.06N 104.43W
Glendo Reservoir 188 Me 42.31N 104.58W
Glenhope 216 Dh 41.39S 172.39 E
Glen Innes 210 Gg 29.44S 151.44 E
Glennallen 178 Jd 62.07N 145.33W
Glenner 128 Dd 46.46N 9.12 E
Glenns Ferry 188 He 42.57N 115.18W
Glenorchy 218 Cf 44.52S 168.24 E
Glenrock 188 Me 42.52N 105.52W
Glen Rose 186 Hj 32.14N 97.45W
Glenrothes 118 Je 56.12N 3.05W
Glens Falls 184 Kd 43.17N 73.41W
Glenville 184 Gf 38.57N 80.51W
Glenwood [Ia.-U.S.] 186 If 41.03N 95.45W
Glenwood [Mn.-U.S.] 186 Ic 45.39N 95.23W
Glenwood Springs 182 Fd 39.32N 107.19W
Glibokaja 130 Ja 48.05N 26.00 E
Glina 128 Ke 45.20N 16.06 E
Glinjany 120 Ug 49.46N 24.33 E
Glittertinden 110 Gc 61.39N 8.33 E
Gliwice 120 Of 50.17N 18.40 E
Globe 182 Ee 33.24N 110.47W
Globino 132 He 49.24N 33.18 E
Głogów 120 Me 51.40N 16.05 E
Glomfjord 114 Cc 66.49N 13.58 E
Glommersträsk 114 Ed 65.16N 19.38 E
Glonn 120 Hh 48.11N 11.45 E
Glorieuses, Iles- 158 Lj 11.30S 47.20 E
Glottof, Mount- 178 Ie 57.30N 153.30W
Gloucester 118 Kj 51.55N 2.15W
Gloucester [Eng.-U.K.] 118 Kj 51.53N 2.14W
Gloucester [Ma.-U.S.] 184 Ld 42.41N 70.39W
Gloucester, Cape- 214 Di 5.27S 148.25 E
Gloucestershire [3] 118 Lj 51.50N 1.55W
Glover Island 197p Bb 11.59N 61.47W
Glover's Reef 194 De 16.49N 87.48W
Gloversville 184 Jd 43.03N 74.21W
Głowno 120 Pe 51.58N 19.44 E
Głubczyce 120 Nf 50.13N 17.49 E
Glubokoje [Bye.-U.S.S.R.] 136 Cd 55.08N 27.41 E
Glubokoje [Kaz.-U.S.S.R.] 136 Ie 50.06N 82.19 E
Glubokoje, ozero- 116 Md 60.30N 29.25 E
Głuchołazy 120 Nf 50.20N 17.22 E
Glücksburg 120 Fb 54.50N 9.33 E
Glückstadt 120 Fc 53.47N 9.25 E
Gluhov 136 De 51.43N 33.57 E
Gluša 132 Fc 53.06N 28.52 E
Glyngøre 116 Ch 56.46N 8.52 E
Gmünd [Aus.] 128 Ib 48.46N 14.59 E
Gmünd [Aus.] 128 Hd 46.54N 13.32 E
Gmunden 128 Hc 47.55N 13.48 E
Gnarp 114 De 62.03N 17.16 E
Gnesta 114 Dg 59.03N 17.18 E
Gniben 116 Dh 56.01N 11.18 E
Gniew 120 Oc 53.51N 18.49 E
Gniewkowo 120 Od 52.54N 18.25 E
Gniezno 120 Nd 52.31N 17.37 E
Gnjilane 130 Eg 42.28N 21.29 E
Gnosjö 114 Ch 57.22N 13.44 E
Gnowangerup 212 Df 33.56S 117.50 E
Goa, Damān and Diu [3] 148 Ee 15.35N 74.00 E
Goageb 172 Be 26.44S 17.15 E
Goālpāra 148 Ic 26.10N 90.37 E
Goat 219b Dd 18.42S 169.17 E
Goat Island 197d Ba 17.44N 61.51W
Goat Point 197d Ba 17.44N 61.51W
Goba 160 Kh 7.01N 39.59 E
Gobabis 160 Ik 22.30S 18.58 E
Gobabis [3] 172 Bd 22.00S 19.00 E
Göbel 130 Lj 40.00N 28.09 E
Gober 166 Gc 13.48N 6.51 E
Gobernador Gregores 206 Fg 48.46S 70.15W
Gobernador Ingeniero Valentin Virasoro 206 Ic 28.03S 56.02W
Gobernador Mansilla 204 Ck 32.33S 59.22W
Gobi Altai (EN) = Gov'altajn Nuruu 140 Me 44.00N 102.00 E
Gobi Desert (EN) = Gov' 140 Me 43.00N 106.00 E
Gobō 154 Mh 33.53N 135.10 E
Göçbeyli 130 Kj 39.13N 27.25 E
Goceano 128 Dj 40.30N 9.15 E
Goce Delčev 130 Gh 41.33N 23.42 E
Goch 120 Ce 51.40N 6.10 E
Gochas 172 Bd 24.55S 18.55 E
Goczałkowickie, Jezioro- 120 Og 49.53N 18.50 E
Göd 120 Pi 47.42N 19.08 E
Godafoss 114a Cb 65.41N 17.33W
Godalming 124 Bc 51.11N 0.36W
Godār 146 Qh 29.45N 57.30 E
Godār-e Shah 146 Me 34.45N 48.10 E
Godāvari 140 Kh 17.00N 81.45 E
Godbout, Rivière- 184 Na 49.21N 67.42W
Gode 168 Gd 5.55N 43.40 E
Godeč 130 Gf 43.01N 23.03 E
Godelbukta 222 Df 70.00S 20.58 E
Goderich 184 Gd 43.45N 81.43W
Goderville 124 Ce 49.39N 0.22 E
Godhavn/Qeqertarssuaq 224 Nc 69.20N 53.35W
Godhra 148 Ed 22.45N 73.38 E
Godinlabe 168 Hd 5.54N 46.40 E
Gödöllő 120 Pi 47.36N 19.22 E
Godoy Cruz 206 Gd 32.55S 68.50W
Gods Lake 180 If 54.40N 94.09W
Gods Lake 180 If 54.40N 94.20W
Gods Mercy, Bay of- 180 Id 63.30N 86.10W
Gods River 180 Ie 56.22N 92.52W
Godthåb/Nûk 179 Nc 64.15N 51.40W
Godthåbfjord 179 Gf 64.20N 51.30W
Godwin Austen (EN) = Qogir Feng 140 Jf 35.53N 76.30 E
Godwin Austen → K2 140 Jf 35.53N 76.30 E
Goedereede 124 Fc 51.49N 3.58 E
Goéland, Lac au- 180 Jg 49.45N 76.50W
Goélands, Lac aux- 180 Le 55.30N 64.30W
Goële 124 Ee 49.10N 2.40 E
Goelette Island 172b Bc 10.13S 51.08 E
Goeree 122 Jc 51.50N 3.55 E
Goes 122 Jc 51.30N 3.54 E
Gogama 184 Jg 47.40N 81.43W
Gō-Gawa 156 Cd 35.01N 132.13 E
Gogebic Range 184 Ch 46.45N 89.25W
Gogland, ostrov- 114 Gf 60.05N 27.00 E
Gog Magog Hills 124 Cb 52.09N 0.11 E
Gogounou 166 Fc 10.50N 2.50 E
Gogrial 168 Dd 8.32N 28.07 E
Gogu, Vîrful- 130 Fd 45.12N 22.30 E
Gogui 166 Db 15.39N 9.21W
Gohelle 124 Ed 50.28N 2.45 E
Goiandira 202 Ig 18.08S 48.06W
Goianésia 202 Ig 15.19S 49.04W
Goiânia 200 Lg 16.40S 49.16W
Goianinha 202 Ke 6.16S 35.12W
Goiás 202 Hg 15.56S 50.08W
Goiás [2] 202 If 12.00S 48.00W
Goiatuba 202 Ig 18.01S 49.22W
Goikul 220a Bc 7.22N 134.36 E
Göinge 116 Eh 56.20N 13.50 E
Goio-Erê 206 Jb 24.12S 53.01W
Goioxim 204 Gg 25.14S 52.01W
Goirle 124 Hc 51.34N 5.05 E
Góis 126 Dd 40.09N 8.07W
Goito 128 Ee 45.15N 10.40 E
Gojam [3] 168 Fc 10.33N 37.35 E
Gojō 156 Dd 34.21N 135.42 E
Gojōme 156 Gb 39.56N 140.07 E
Gojra 148 Eb 31.09N 72.41 E
Gojthskij, pereval- 132 Kg 44.15N 39.18 E
Gokase-Gawa 156 Be 32.35N 131.42 E
Gokasho-Wan 156 Ed 34.20N 136.40 E
Gökbel Dağı 130 Kl 37.28N 28.00 E
Gökçay 146 Ed 36.36N 33.23 E
Gökçeada 144 Ca 40.10N 25.50 E
Gökçeören 130 Lk 38.35N 28.32 E
Gökçeyazi 130 Kj 39.38N 27.39 E
Gökdere 146 Ed 36.39N 33.35 E
Gökırmak 146 Fb 41.24N 35.08 E
Göksu [Tur.] 146 Fd 37.37N 35.35 E
Göksu [Tur.] 146 Fd 36.20N 34.05 E
Göksu [Tur.] 130 Mi 40.23N 29.58 E
Göksun 146 Gc 38.03N 36.30 E
Göktepe 130 Ll 37.16N 28.36 E
Gök Tepe 130 Mm 36.53N 29.17 E
Gokwe 172 Dc 18.13S 28.55 E
Gol 114 Bf 60.42N 8.57 E
Golāghāt 148 Ic 26.31N 93.58 E
Golaja Pristan 132 Hf 46.29N 32.31 E
Gołańcz 120 Nd 52.57N 17.18 E
Golconda [Il.-U.S.] 186 Lh 37.22N 88.29W
Golconda [Nv.-U.S.] 188 Gf 40.57N 117.30W
Gölcük 146 Cb 40.44N 29.44 E
Golčův Jeníkov 120 Lg 49.49N 15.30 E
Gołdap 120 Sb 54.19N 22.19 E
Gold Beach 188 Ce 42.25N 124.25W
Gold Coast 210 Gg 27.58S 153.25 E
Gold Coast 158 Gh 5.20N 0.45W
Golden [B.C.-Can.] 180 Ff 51.18N 116.58W
Golden [Co.-U.S.] 186 Dg 39.46N 105.13W
Golden Bay 218 Ed 40.50S 172.50 E
Goldendale 188 Ed 45.49N 120.50W
Goldene Aue 120 Ge 51.25N 11.00 E
Golden Gate 188 Dh 37.49N 122.29W
Golden Hinde 180 Eg 49.40N 125.45W
Golden Meadow 186 Kl 29.23N 90.16W
Golden Vale/Machaire na Mumhan 118 Fi 52.30N 8.00W
Goldfield 188 Gh 37.42N 117.14W
Gold River 188 Bb 49.41N 126.08W
Goldsboro 182 Ld 35.23N 77.59W
Goldsworthy 212 Dd 20.20S 119.30 E
Göle 146 Jb 40.48N 42.36 E
Golegã 126 De 39.24N 8.29W
Goleniów 120 Kc 53.36N 14.50 E
Golešnica 130 Eh 41.42N 21.33 E
Goleta, Cerro- 192 Ih 18.38N 100.04W
Golfito 190 Hg 8.38N 83.11W
Golfo Aranci 128 Dj 41.00N 9.37 E
Gölgeli Dağları 130 Ml 37.15N 29.06 E
Gölhisar 130 Ml 37.08N 29.30 E
Goliad 186 Hl 28.40N 97.23W
Golija [Yugo.] 130 Df 43.19N 20.18 E
Golija [Yugo.] 130 Bf 43.02N 18.47 E
Goljak 130 Eg 42.44N 21.31 E
Goljama Kamčija 130 Kf 43.03N 27.29 E
Goljama Sjutkja 130 Hh 41.54N 24.01 E
Goljamo Konare 130 Hg 42.16N 24.33 E
Goljam Perelik 130 Hh 41.36N 24.34 E
Goljam Persenk 130 Hh 41.49N 24.33 E
Gölköy 146 Gb 40.15N 37.26 E
Gölkük 130 Kj 39.19N 27.59 E
Göllheim 124 Ke 49.35N 8.03 E
Gölmarmara 130 Kk 38.42N 27.56 E
Golmud 142 Lf 36.22N 94.55 E
Golmud He 152 Gd 36.54N 95.11 E
Golo 122a Ba 42.31N 9.32 E
Goloby 120 Ve 51.06N 25.06 E
Gologory 120 Ug 49.35N 24.30 E
Gololcha 168 Gd 8.12N 40.05 E
Golovin 178 Gd 64.33N 163.02W
Golovnin Seamount (EN) 138 Kg 46.50N 157.00 E
Golpāyegan 144 Hc 33.27N 50.18 E
Gölpazarı 146 Db 40.17N 30.19 E
Golšanka 120 Zb 54.00N 26.16 E
Golspie 118 Jd 57.58N 3.58W
Gol Tappeh 146 Kd 36.35N 45.45 E
Golubac 130 Ee 44.39N 21.38 E
Golub-Dobrzyń 120 Pc 53.08N 19.02 E
Golungo Alto 170 Bd 9.08S 14.47 E
Golyšmanovo 136 Gd 56.23N 68.23 E
Goma 160 Ji 1.37S 29.12 E
Gómara 126 Jc 41.37N 2.13W
Gombe 160 Ig 10.17N 11.10 E
Gombi 166 Hc 10.10N 12.44 E
Gomel 112 Je 52.25N 31.00 E
Gomelskaja oblast [3] 136 Ce 52.20N 29.40 E
Gomera 158 Ff 28.06N 17.08W
Gómez Farías 192 Ie 24.57N 101.02W
Gómez Palacio 190 Dc 25.34N 103.30W
Gomo 152 Ee 33.26N 85.21 E
Gomo Co 152 Ee 33.45N 85.35 E
Goms 128 Cd 46.25N 8.10 E
Gonābād 144 Ic 34.20N 58.42 E
Gonaïves 190 Je 19.27N 72.43W
Gonam 138 Ie 57.18N 131.20 E
Gonâve, Golfe de la- 190 Je 19.00N 73.30W
Gonâve, Ile de la- 190 Je 18.51N 73.03W
Gonbad-e Qābūs 144 Ib 37.15N 55.09 E
Gonda 148 Gc 27.08N 81.56 E
Gonder 160 Kg 12.38N 37.27 E
Gonder [3] 168 Fc 12.00N 38.00 E
Gondia 148 Gd 21.27N 80.12 E
Gondo 158 Gg 14.20N 3.10W
Gondomar 126 Dc 41.09N 8.32W
Gondwana 140 Kg 23.00N 81.00 E
Gönen 146 Bb 40.06N 27.39 E
Gönen 146 Bb 40.06N 27.36 E
Gonfreville-l'Orcher 124 Ce 49.30N 0.14 E
Gong'an (Doushi) 152 Je 30.05N 112.12 E
Gongbo'gyamda 152 Ff 29.59N 93.25 E
Gonggar 152 Ff 29.17N 90.50 E
Gongga Shan 140 Mg 29.34N 101.53 E
Gonghe 152 Hd 36.21N 100.47 E
Gongliu/Tokkuztara 152 Dc 43.30N 82.15 E
Gongola [2] 166 Hd 8.40N 11.20 E
Gongola 158 Ih 9.30N 12.04 E
Gongpoquan 152 Gc 41.50N 97.00 E
Gongshan 152 Gf 27.39N 98.35 E
Gongxian (Xiaoyi) 154 Bg 34.46N 112.57 E
Gongzhuling → Huaide 152 Lc 43.30N 124.52 E
Goñi 204 Dk 33.31S 56.24W
Goniądz 120 Sc 53.30N 22.45 E
Gonīshān 146 Pd 37.04N 54.06 E
Gonjo 152 Ge 30.52N 98.20 E
Gonohe 156 Ga 40.31N 141.19 E
Go-no-ura 156 Ae 33.45N 129.41 E
Gonūk 146 Ic 39.00N 40.41 E
Gonzales 186 Hl 29.30N 97.27W
Gonzáles, Riacho- 204 Df 22.48S 57.54W
González 192 Jf 22.50N 98.27W
Goodenough, Cape- 222 Ie 66.16S 126.10 E
Goodenough Bay 212 Ja 9.55S 150.00 E
Goodenough Island 214 Ei 9.22S 150.16 E
Good Hope, Cape of- / Groeie Hoop, Kaap die- 158 Il 34.21S 18.28 E
Goodhouse 172 Be 28.57S 18.13 E
Gooding 188 He 42.56N 114.43W
Goodland 182 Gd 39.21N 101.43W
Goodnews Bay 178 Ge 59.07N 161.35W
Goodsir, Mount- 188 Ga 51.12N 116.20W
Good Spirit Lake 188 Na 51.34N 102.40W
Goodwin Sands 124 Dc 51.15N 1.35 E
Goodyear 188 Ij 33.26N 112.21W
Goole 118 Mh 53.42N 0.52W
Goomalling 212 Df 31.19S 116.49 E
Goondiwindi 210 Gg 28.32S 150.19 E
Goonyella 212 Jd 21.43S 147.58 E
Goor 124 Ib 52.14N 6.37 E
Goose Lake 182 Cc 41.57N 120.25W
Goose River 182 Hc 47.28N 96.52W
Gopło, Jezioro- 120 Od 52.35N 18.20 E
Göppingen 120 Fh 48.42N 9.40 E
Góra 120 Me 51.40N 16.33 E
Gora 130 Di 40.40N 20.30 E
Góra Kalwaria 120 Re 51.59N 21.12 E
Gorakhpur 142 Kg 26.45N 83.22 E
Goransko 130 Bf 43.07N 18.50 E
Gorata 130 Ih 41.45N 25.55 E
Goražde 128 Mg 43.40N 18.59 E
Gorda 188 Ei 35.55N 121.27W
Gorda, Cayo- 194 Ff 15.56N 82.15W
Gorda, Punta- [Ca.-U.S.] 188 Cf 40.16N 124.20W
Gorda, Punta- [Cuba] 154 Fb 22.24N 82.10W
Gorda, Punta- [Nic.] 194 Ff 14.21N 83.12W
Gördes 130 Lk 38.54N 28.18 E
Gördes 130 Kj 38.46N 27.58 E
Gordil 163 Cd 9.44N 21.35 E
Gordion 146 Ec 39.37N 32.00 E
Gordon [Nb.-U.S.] 186 Ee 42.48N 102.12W
Gordon [Wi.-U.S.] 186 Kc 46.15N 91.47W
Gordon, Lake- 212 Jh 43.05S 146.05 E
Gordon Horne Peak 188 Fa 51.46N 118.50W
Gordonvale 212 Jc 17.05S 145.47 E
Goré 168 Bd 7.55N 16.38 E
Gore 168 Fd 8.09N 35.34 E
Gore 218 Cg 46.06S 168.56 E
Görele 146 Hb 41.02N 39.00 E
Görenez Dağı 130 Lk 39.00N 28.01 E
Gorenjsko 128 Id 46.20N 14.10 E
Gorey/Guaire 118 Gi 52.40N 6.18W
Gorgān 146 Hf 36.50N 54.29 E
Gorgān 146 Pd 36.59N 54.05 E
Gorgān, Khalīj-e- 146 Od 36.40N 53.50 E
Gorgany 120 Uh 48.30N 24.15 E
Gorgin 146 Ld 36.15N 47.55 E
Gorgin 146 Ld 36.16N 47.52 E
Gorgol [3] 162 Ff 15.45N 13.00W
Gorgol el Abiod 162 Ef 16.14N 12.58W
Gorgona 128 Dg 43.25N 9.55 E
Gorgona, Isla- 202 Cc 2.59N 78.12W
Gorgora 168 Fc 12.14N 37.17 E
Gorham 184 Lc 44.23N 71.11W
Gori 136 Eg 42.00N 44.02 E
Gorinchem 122 Kc 51.50N 5.00 E
Goring 124 Ac 51.31N 1.08W
Goris 132 Oj 39.31N 46.22 E
Gorizia 128 He 45.57N 13.38 E
Gorj [2] 130 Gd 45.00N 23.20 E
Gorjačegorsk 138 De 55.24N 88.55 E
Gorjači Ključ 132 Kg 44.36N 39.07 E
Gorjanci 128 Je 45.45N 15.20 E
Gorki [Bye.-U.S.S.R.] 132 Gb 54.17N 31.00 E
Gorki [R.S.F.S.R.] → Nižnij Novgorod 6 Kd 57.38N 45.05 E
Gorki [R.S.F.S.R.] 20 Bc 65.05N 65.15 E
Gorkovskaja oblast [3] 136 Ed 56.15N 44.45 E
Gorkovskoje vodohranilišče = Gorky Reservoir (EN) 110 Kd 57.00N 43.10 E
Gorkum 120 Hf 50.10N 11.08 E
Gorky Reservoir (EN) = Gorkovskoje vodohranilišče 110 Kd 57.00N 43.10 E
Gørlev 116 Di 55.32N 11.14 E
Gorlice 120 Rg 49.40N 21.10 E
Görlitz 120 Ke 51.10N 15.00 E
Gorlovka 112 Jf 48.18N 38.03 E
Gornalunga 128 Jm 37.24N 15.03 E
Gorna Orjahovica 130 If 43.07N 25.41 E
Gornjak [R.S.F.S.R.] 138 Df 51.00N 81.29 E
Gornjak [Ukr.-U.S.S.R.] 120 Uf 50.16N 24.13 E
Gornji Milanovac 130 De 44.02N 20.27 E
Gornji Vakuf 128 Lg 43.56N 17.36 E

Index Symbols

[1] Independent Nation
[2] State, Region
[3] District, County
[4] Municipality
[5] Colony, Dependency
Continent
Physical Region
Historical or Cultural Region
Mount, Mountain
Volcano
Hill
Mountains, Mountain Range
Hills, Escarpment
Plateau, Upland
Pass, Gap
Plain, Lowland
Delta
Salt Flat
Valley, Canyon
Crater, Cave
Karst Features
Depression
Polder
Desert, Dunes
Forest, Woods
Heath, Steppe
Oasis
Cape, Point
Coast, Beach
Cliff
Peninsula
Isthmus
Sandbank
Island
Atoll
Rock, Reef
Islands, Archipelago
Rocks, Reefs
Coral Reef
Well, Spring
Geyser
River, Stream
Waterfall, Rapids
River Mouth, Estuary
Lake
Salt Lake
Intermittent Lake
Reservoir
Swamp, Pond
Canal
Glacier
Ice Shelf, Pack Ice
Ocean
Sea
Gulf, Bay
Strait, Fjord
Lagoon
Bank
Seamount
Tablemount
Ridge
Shelf
Basin
Escarpment, Sea Scarp
Fracture
Trench, Abyss
National Park, Reserve
Point of Interest
Recreation Site
Cave, Cavern
Historic Site
Ruins
Wall, Walls
Church, Abbey
Temple
Scientific Station
Railway station
Airport
Port
Military installation
Lighthouse
Mine
Tunnel
Dam, Bridge

Gorno-Altajsk 142 Kd 51.58N 85.58 E
Gorno-Altajskaja avtonomnaja oblast [3] 138 Df 51.00N 87.00 E
Gorno-Badahšanskaja avtonomnaja oblast [3] 136 Hh 38.15N 73.00 E
Gorno-Čujski 138 Ge 57.40N 111.40 E
Gornozavodsk [R.S.F.S.R.] 134 Ig 58.25N 58.20 E
Gornozavodsk [R.S.F.S.R.] 138 Jg 46.30N 141.55 E
Gorny [R.S.F.S.R.] 138 Ih 44.50N 133.56 E
Gorny [R.S.F.S.R.] 138 If 50.48N 136.26 E
Gorny [R.S.F.S.R.] 132 Pd 51.45N 48.34 E
Gornyje Ključi 154 Lb 45.15N 133.30 E
Gorochan 168 Fd 9.26N 37.05 E
Gorodec [R.S.F.S.R.] 136 Ed 56.40N 43.30 E
Gorodec [R.S.F.S.R.] 116 Mf 58.30N 29.55 E
Gorodenka 132 De 48.42N 25.32 E
Gorodišče [Bye.-U.S.S.R.] 120 Vc 53.16N 26.03 E
Gorodišče [R.S.F.S.R.] 132 Nc 53.16N 45.42 E
Gorodišče [Ukr.-U.S.S.R.] 132 Ge 49.17N 31.27 E
Gorodnica 132 Ed 50.49N 27.22 E
Gorodnja 132 Gd 51.55N 31.31 E
Gorodok [Bye.-U.S.S.R.] 136 Cd 55.26N 29.59 E
Gorodok [Ukr.-U.S.S.R.] 132 Ce 49.47N 23.39 E
Gorodok [Ukr.-U.S.S.R.] 132 Ee 49.10N 26.31 E
Gorodovikovsm 136 Ef 46.05N 41.59 E
Gorohov 120 Uf 50.28N 24.47 E
Gorohovec 114 Kh 56.12N 42.42 E
Goroka 210 Fe 6.02S 145.22 E
Gorom Gorom 166 Ec 14.26N 0.14W
Gorong, Kepulauan- 150 Jg 4.05S 131.20 E
Gorongosa, Serra da- 172 Ec 18.24S 34.06 E
Gorontalo 142 Oi 0.33N 123.03 E
Goroual 166 Fc 14.42N 0.53 E
Goroubi 166 Fc 13.07N 2.18 E
Górowo Iławeckie 120 Qb 54.17N 20.30 E
Gorron 122 Ff 48.25N 0.49W
Goršečnoje 132 Kd 51.33N 38.09 E
Gorski Kotar 128 Ie 45.26N 14.40 E
Gorssel 124 Ib 52.12N 6.13 E
Gort 118 Eh 53.04N 8.50W
Goru, Vîrful- 130 Jd 45.48N 26.25 E
Görükle 130 Li 40.14N 28.50 E
Goryn 136 Ce 52.09N 27.17 E
Gorzów [2] 120 Ld 54.25N 15.15 E
Gorzów Wielkopolski 120 Ld 52.44N 15.15 E
Goschen Strait 212 Kb 10.09S 150.56 E
Gosen 154 Of 37.44N 139.11 E
Gosford 212 Kf 33.26S 151.21 E
Goshen 184 Ee 41.35N 85.50W
Goshogawara 154 Pd 40.48N 140.27 E
Gosier 197e Bb 16.12N 61.30W
Goslar 120 Ge 51.54N 10.26 E
Gospić 128 Jf 44.33N 15.23 E
Gosport 118 Lk 50.48N 1.08W
Gossen 116 Bb 62.50N 6.55 E
Gossi 166 Eb 15.47N 1.15W
Gossinga 168 Dd 8.39N 25.59 E
Gostivar 130 Dh 41.48N 20.54 E
Gostyń 120 Me 51.53N 17.00 E
Gostynin 120 Pd 52.26N 19.29 E
Gota älv 110 Hd 57.42N 11.52 E
Göta Kanal 110 Hd 58.50N 13.58 E
Götaland 110 Hd 57.30N 14.30 E
Götaland 114 Dh 57.30N 14.30 E
Göteborg 112 Hd 57.43N 11.58 E
Göteborg och Bohus [2] 114 Cg 58.30N 11.30 E
Gotel Mountains 158 Ih 7.00N 11.40 E
Gotemba 156 Fd 35.18N 138.56 E
Götene 114 Cg 58.32N 13.29 E
Gotha 120 Gf 50.57N 10.43 E
Gothenburg 186 Ff 40.56N 100.09W
Gothèye 166 Fc 13.52N 1.34 E
Gotland [2] 114 Eh 57.30N 18.30 E
Gotland 110 Hd 57.30N 18.30 E
Gotō-Nada 156 Ae 32.45N 129.30 E
Gotō-Rettō 152 Me 32.50N 129.00 E
Gotowasi 150 If 0.38N 128.26 E
Gotska Sandön 114 Eg 58.25N 19.15 E
Götsu 154 Lg 35.00N 132.14 E
Göttingen 120 Fe 51.32N 9.56 E
Gottwaldov 120 Ng 49.13N 17.39 E
Goubangzi 154 Fd 41.23N 121.48 E
Gouda 122 Kc 52.01N 4.43 E
Goudiri 166 Cc 14.11N 12.43W
Gouet 122 Df 48.32N 2.45W
Gough Island 158 Gm 40.20S 10.00W
Gough Lake 188 Ia 52.02N 112.28W
Gouin, Réservoir- 180 Kg 48.35N 74.50W
Goulbin Kaba 166 Gc 13.42N 6.19 E
Goulburn 210 Fh 34.45S 149.43 E
Goulburn Islands 212 Gb 11.50S 133.30 E
Gould Bay 222 Rf 78.10S 44.00W
Gould Coast 222 Mg 84.30S 150.00W
Goulia 166 Dc 10.01N 7.11W
Goulimine 162 Ed 28.59N 10.04W
Gouménissa 130 Fi 40.57N 22.27 E
Gouna 166 Hd 8.32N 13.34 E
Gounda 168 Cd 9.25N 20.57 E
Goundam 166 Eb 16.24N 3.38W
Goundi 168 Bd 9.22N 17.22 E
Goundoumaria 166 Hc 13.42N 11.10 E
Gounou Gaya 168 Bd 9.38N 15.31 E
Gourara 162 Hd 29.30N 0.40 E
Gouraya 126 Nh 36.34N 1.55 E
Gourcy 166 Ec 13.13N 2.21W
Gourdon 122 Hj 44.44N 1.23 E
Gouré 160 Ig 13.58N 10.18 E
Gourin 122 Cf 48.08N 3.36W
Gourma [Burkina] 158 Hg 12.20N 1.30 E
Gourma [Mali] 158 Gg 15.45N 2.00W
Gourma-Rharous 166 Eb 16.52N 1.55W
Gournay-en-Bray 122 He 49.29N 1.44 E
Gourniá 130 In 35.06N 25.48 E
Gouro 168 Bb 19.40N 19.28 E
Gourrama 162 Gc 32.20N 4.05W
Goussainville 124 Ee 49.01N 2.28 E
Gouyave 197p Bb 12.10N 61.44W
Gouzeaucourt 124 Fd 50.03N 3.07 E
Gouzon 122 Ih 46.11N 2.14 E
Gov' = Gobi Desert (EN) 140 Me 43.00N 106.00 E
Gov'altajn Nuruu = Gobi Altai (EN) 140 Me 44.00N 102.00 E
Govena, mys- 138 Le 59.47N 166.02 E
Gove Peninsula 212 Hb 13.02S 136.50 E
Goverla, gora- 136 Cf 48.10N 24.32 E
Governador Valadares 200 Lg 18.51S 41.56W
Governor's Harbour 190 Ic 25.10N 76.14W
Gowanda 184 Hd 42.28N 78.57W
Gower 118 Ij 51.36N 4.10W
Gowganda 184 Gb 47.38N 80.46W
Goya 200 Kh 29.10S 59.20W
Goyave 197e Ab 16.08N 61.34W
Goyaves, Ilets à- 197e Ab 16.10N 61.48W
Goyder River 212 Hb 12.38S 135.05 E
Göynücek 146 Fb 40.24N 35.32 E
Göynük 146 Db 40.24N 30.47 E
Göynük 130 Ni 40.20N 30.05 E
Goyōmai-Kaikyō 156a Db 43.24N 145.50 E
Goz Arian 168 Bc 14.35N 20.00 E
Goz Beïda 168 Cc 12.13N 21.25 E
Gozha Co 152 De 34.59N 81.06 E
Goz Kerki 168 Bb 15.30N 18.50 E
Gözlü Baba Dağı 130 Lk 38.15N 28.28 E
Gozo 110 Hh 36.05N 14.15 E
Graaff-Reinet 172 Cf 32.14S 24.32 E
Graafschap 122 Mb 52.05N 6.30 E
Graben Neudorf 124 Ke 49.10N 8.28 E
Grabia 120 Oe 51.26N 18.56 E
Grabière Point 197g Bb 15.30N 61.29W
Grabo 166 De 4.55N 7.30W
Grabowa 120 Mb 54.26N 16.20 E
Gračac 128 Jf 44.18N 15.51 E
Gračanica 128 Mf 44.42N 18.18 E
Gračanica, Manastir- 130 Eg 42.36N 21.12 E
Gracias 194 Cf 14.35N 88.35W
Gracias a Dios [3] 194 Ef 15.20N 84.20W
Gracias a Dios, Cabo- 174 Kh 15.00N 83.08W
Graciosa [Azr.] 158 Ee 39.04N 28.00W
Graciosa [Can.Is.] 162 Ed 29.15N 13.30W
Gradačac 128 Mf 44.53N 18.26 E
Gradaús, Serra dos- 198 Kf 8.00S 50.45W
Grado [It.] 128 He 45.40N 13.23 E
Grado [Sp.] 126 Fa 43.23N 6.04W
Grænalon 114a Cb 64.10N 17.24W
Grænlandshaf = Greenland Sea (EN) 224 Ld 77.00N 1.00W
Grafenau 120 Jh 48.51N 13.24 E
Grafham Water 124 Bb 52.19N 0.10W
Grafing bei München 120 Hh 48.03N 11.58 E
Grafschaft Bentheim 124 Jb 52.30N 7.05 E
Grafton [Austl.] 212 Ke 29.41S 152.56 E
Grafton [N.D.-U.S.] 182 Hb 48.25N 97.25W
Grafton [W.V.-U.S.] 184 Hf 39.21N 80.00W
Grafton, Mount- 188 Hg 38.40N 114.45W
Graham [Can.] 182 Ef 53.40N 132.30W
Graham [N.C.-U.S.] 184 Hg 36.05N 79.25W
Graham [N.W.T.-Can.] 180 Ia 77.17N 90.50W
Graham [Tx.-U.S.] 186 Gj 33.06N 98.35W
Graham, Mount- 182 Fe 32.42N 109.52W
Graham Land (EN) 222 Qe 66.00S 63.30W
Graham Moore, Cape- 180 Jb 72.51N 76.05W
Grahamstown 160 Jl 33.19S 26.31 E
Grain Coast 158 Gh 5.00N 9.00W
Graisivaudan 122 Li 45.15N 5.50 E
Grajaú 202 Ie 5.49S 46.08W
Grajaú, Rio- 202 Jd 3.41S 44.48W
Grajewo 120 Sc 53.39N 22.27 E
Gram 116 Ci 55.17N 9.04 E
Gramalote 194 Kj 7.54N 72.48W
Gramat 122 Hj 44.47N 1.43 E
Gramat, Causse de- 122 Hj 44.40N 1.50 E
Graminha, Represa da- 204 Ie 21.33S 46.38W
Grammichele 128 Im 37.13N 14.38 E
Grammont/Geraardsbergen 124 Fd 50.46N 3.52 E
Grámmos Óros 130 Di 40.20N 20.45 E
Grampian [3] 118 Kd 57.25N 2.35W
Grampian Mountains 110 Fd 56.45N 4.00W
Gramshi 130 Di 40.52N 20.11 E
Gran 116 Dd 60.22N 10.34 E
Granada [Col.] 202 Dc 3.33N 73.44W
Granada [Nic.] 190 Gf 11.56N 85.57W
Granada [Nic.] [3] 194 Eh 11.50N 86.00W
Granada [Sp.] 110 Fh 37.13N 3.41W
Granada [Sp.] [3] 126 Ig 37.15N 3.15W
Granada, Vega de- 126 Ig 37.15N 4.00W
Granard/Gránard 118 Fh 53.47N 7.30W
Gránard/Granard 118 Fh 53.47N 7.30W
Granby 180 Kg 45.24N 72.43W
Gran Canaria 158 Ff 28.00N 15.36W
Gran Chaco 198 Jh 23.00S 60.00W
Grand Anse Bay 197p Bb 12.02N 61.45W
Grand Bahama 174 Lg 26.40N 78.20W
Grand Ballon 122 Ng 47.55N 7.08 E
Grand Bank 180 Lg 47.06N 55.47W
Grand Banks (EN) 174 Oe 45.00N 50.00W
Grand Bassa [3] 166 Dd 6.10N 9.40W
Grand-Bassam 160 Gh 5.12N 3.44W
Grand Bay 197p Cb 12.29N 61.23W
Grand Bay 197g Bb 15.14N 61.19W
Grand-Béréby 166 De 4.38N 6.55W
Grand-Bourg 196 Fe 15.53N 61.19W
Grand Caille Point 197k Ab 13.52N 61.05W
Grandcamp-Maisy 124 Ae 49.23N 1.02W
Grand Canal 118 Gh 53.21N 6.14W
Grand Canal (EN) = Da Yunhe 140 Nf 39.54N 116.44 E
Grand Canyon 182 Ed 36.03N 112.09W
Grand Canyon 174 Hf 36.10N 112.45W
Grand' Case 197b Ab 18.06N 63.03W
Grand Cayman 190 He 19.20N 81.15W
Grand Cess 166 De 4.24N 8.13W
Grand Colombier 122 Li 45.54N 5.46 E
Grand-Combe, La- 122 Kj 44.13N 4.02 E
Grand Coulee 188 Fc 47.56N 119.00W
Grand-Couronne 124 De 49.21N 1.01 E
Grandcourt 124 De 49.55N 1.30 E
Grand Cul de Sac Bay 197k Ab 13.59N 61.02W
Grand Cul-de-Sac Marin 197e Ab 16.20N 61.35W
Grande, Arroyo- 204 Dm 37.32S 57.34W
Grande, Bahía- 198 Jk 50.45S 68.45W
Grande, Boca- 202 Fb 8.45N 60.35W
Grande, Cachoeira- 204 Gb 15.37S 51.48W
Grande, Cerro- 192 If 23.40N 100.40W
Grande, Ciénaga- 194 Ji 9.13N 75.46W
Grande, Corixa- 204 Cc 17.10S 58.20W
Grande, Cuchilla- [Arg.] 204 Cj 31.45S 58.35W
Grande, Cuchilla- [Ur.] 198 Ki 33.15S 55.07W
Grande, Ile- 122 Cf 48.48N 3.35W
Grande, Ilha- 202 Jh 23.10S 44.10W
Grande, Rio- 202 Fb 8.39N 60.59W
Grande, Rio- 174 Jg 25.57N 97.09W
Grande, Rio- 174 Jg 25.57N 97.09W
Grande, Rio- [Braz.] 198 Kh 20.06S 51.04W
Grande, Rio- [Braz.] 198 Lg 11.05S 43.09W
Grande, Rio- (EN) = Bravo del Norte, Rio- 174 Jg 25.57N 97.09W
Grande, Rio- o Guapay, Rio- 198 Jg 15.51S 64.39W
Grande, Serra- 198 Lf 6.00S 40.52W
Grande, Sierra- 192 Gc 29.40N 104.55W
Grande Anse 197k Ba 14.01N 60.54W
Grande-Anse 197e Bb 16.18N 61.04W
Grande Brière 122 Dg 47.22N 2.15W
Grande Cache 180 Ff 53.14N 119.00W
Grande Casse, Pointe de la- 122 Mi 45.24N 6.50 E
Grande Cayemite 194 Kd 18.37N 73.45W
Grande Chartreuse 122 Li 45.22N 5.50 E
Grande Comore/Njazidja 158 Lj 11.35S 43.20 E
Grande de Santa Marta, Ciénaga- 194 Jh 10.50N 74.25W
Grande de Santiago, Rio- 174 Ig 21.36N 105.26W
Grande Inferior, Cuchilla- 204 Dk 33.50S 56.10W
Grande Kabylie 126 Ph 36.45N 4.00 E
Grande-Motte, La- 122 Kk 43.34N 4.07 E
Grande ou Sete Quedas, Ilha- 204 Ef 23.45S 54.03W
Grande Pointe [Guad.] 197e Ac 15.59N 61.38W
Grande Pointe [Guad.] 197b Bc 17.50N 62.50W
Grande Prairie 176 Hd 55.10N 118.48W
Grand Erg de Bilma 158 Ig 18.30N 13.50 E
Grand Erg Occidental 158 He 30.20N 0.01 E
Grand Erg Oriental 158 He 30.00N 7.00 E
Grande Rivière à Goyaves 197e Ab 16.18N 61.37W
Grande Rivière de la Baleine 174 Ld 55.15N 77.45W
Grande Rivière du Nord 194 Kd 19.35N 72.11W
Grande Ronde River 188 Gc 46.05N 116.59W
Grandes, Salinas- 198 Ji 30.05S 65.05W
Grande Sebkha d'Oran 126 Li 35.32N 0.48W
Grandes Rousses, Les- 122 Mi 45.06N 6.07 E
Grande-Synthe 124 Ec 51.01N 2.17 E
Grand Etang 197p Bb 12.06N 61.42W
Grande-Terre 196 Fd 16.20N 61.25W
Grande Vigie, Pointe de la- 197e Ba 16.31N 61.28W
Grand Falls [N.B.-Can.] 180 Kg 47.03N 67.44W
Grand Falls [Newf.-Can.] 176 Ne 48.56N 55.40W
Grand Forks [B.C.-Can.] 188 Fb 49.02N 118.27W
Grand Forks [N.D.-U.S.] 176 Je 47.55N 97.03W
Grand Found, Anse du- 197d Ba 17.53N 62.49W
Grand Gedeh [3] 166 Dd 5.45N 8.05W
Grand Haven 184 Dd 43.04N 86.10W
Grand Ilet 197e Ac 15.50N 61.36W
Grand Island 176 Je 40.55N 98.21W
Grand Junction 176 If 39.05N 108.33W
Grand-Lahou 166 Dd 5.08N 5.01W
Grand Lake [La.-U.S.] 186 Kl 29.55N 91.35W
Grand Lake [La.-U.S.] 186 Jl 29.55N 92.47W
Grand Lake [N.B.-Can.] 184 Nc 45.42N 66.05W
Grand Lake [Newf.-Can.] 180 Lg 49.00N 57.20W
Grand Lake [Oh.-U.S.] 184 Ee 40.30N 84.32W
Grand Lake Victoria 184 Ib 47.35N 77.33W
Grand-Lieu, Lac de- 122 Eg 47.05N 1.40W
Grand Manan Channel 184 Nc 44.45N 66.52W
Grand Manan Island 180 Kh 44.40N 66.50W
Grand Marais [Mi.-U.S.] 184 Eb 46.40N 85.59W
Grand Marais [Mn.-U.S.] 186 Kc 47.45N 90.20W
Grand-Mère 184 Kb 46.37N 72.41W
Grand Morin 122 If 48.54N 2.50 E
Grândola 126 Df 38.10N 8.34W
Grândola, Serra de- 126 Df 38.06N 8.38W
Grand Passage 219b Ad 18.45S 163.10 E
Grand-Popo 166 Fd 6.17N 1.50 E
Grand Portage 186 Lc 47.58N 89.41W
Grand Prairie 182 He 32.45N 96.59W
Grandpré 124 Ge 49.20N 4.52 E
Grand Rapids [Man.-Can.] 180 Hf 53.10N 99.17W
Grand Rapids [Mi.-U.S.] 176 Ke 42.58N 85.40W
Grand Rapids [Mn.-U.S.] 182 Ib 47.14N 93.31W
Grand Récif Sud 216 Cd 22.38S 167.00 E
Grand River [Mi.-U.S.] 184 Dd 43.04N 86.15W
Grand River [Mo.-U.S.] 186 Jg 39.23N 93.06W
Grand River [Ont.-Can.] 184 Hd 42.51N 79.34W
Grand River [S.D.-U.S.] 186 Fd 45.40N 100.32W
Grand'Rivière 197h Ab 14.52N 61.11W
Grand Roy 197p Bb 12.08N 61.45W
Grand Saint Bernard, Col du- 128 Be 45.50N 7.10 E
Grand-Sans-Toucher 197e Ab 16.06N 61.41W
Grand Teton 182 Ec 43.44N 110.48W
Grand Traverse Bay 182 Jb 45.02N 85.30W
Grand Turk 190 Jd 21.28N 71.09W
Grand Turk 194 Lc 21.30N 71.10W
Grand Union Canal 124 Bc 51.30N 0.02W
Grand Valley 186 Bg 39.27N 108.03W
Grand Veymont, Le- 122 Lj 44.52N 5.32 E
Grandview [Man.-Can.] 186 Fa 51.10N 100.45W
Grandview [Mo.-U.S.] 186 Ig 38.53N 94.31W
Grandvilliers 124 De 49.40N 1.56 E
Grand Wash Cliffs 188 Ii 35.45N 113.45W
Granger 188 Ee 46.21N 120.11W
Grängesberg 116 Fd 60.05N 14.59 E
Grangeville 188 Gd 45.56N 116.07W
Gran Guardia 206 Ic 25.52S 58.53W
Granite City 186 Kg 38.42N 90.09W
Granite Falls 186 Id 44.49N 95.33W
Granite Pass 188 Ld 44.38N 107.30W
Granite Peak [Nv.-U.S.] 182 Dc 41.40N 117.35W
Granite Peak [U.S.] 182 Fb 45.10N 109.48W
Granite Range 188 Ff 41.00N 119.35W
Granitola, Punta- 128 Gm 37.34N 12.41 E
Grankulla/Kauniainen 116 Kd 60.13N 24.45 E
Granma [3] 194 Ic 20.30N 77.00W
Gran Malvina, Isla-/West Falkland 198 Kk 51.40S 60.00W
Gran Morelos [Mex.] 192 Fc 28.15N 106.30W
Gran Morelos [Mex.] 192 Eb 30.40N 108.35W
Gränna 116 Ff 58.01N 14.28 E
Granollers/Granollérs 126 Oc 41.37N 2.18 E
Granollérs/Granollers 126 Oc 41.37N 2.18 E
Gran Paradis/Gran Paradiso 128 Be 45.32N 7.16 E
Gran Paradiso/Gran Paradis 128 Be 45.32N 7.16 E
Gran Pilastro/Hochfeiler 128 Fd 46.58N 11.44 E
Gran San Bernardo, Colle del- 128 Be 45.50N 7.10 E
Gran Sasso d'Italia 110 Hg 42.25N 13.40 E
Grant 186 Ff 40.50N 101.56W
Grant, Mount- 188 Fg 38.34N 118.48W
Gran Tarajal 162 Ed 28.12N 14.01W
Grantham 118 Mi 52.54N 0.38W
Grant Island 222 Nf 74.24S 131.20W
Grantown-on-Spey 118 Jd 57.20N 3.38W
Grant Range 188 Hg 38.25N 115.30W
Grants 182 Fd 35.09N 107.52W
Grantsburg 186 Jd 45.47N 92.41W
Grants Pass 182 Cc 42.26N 123.19W
Granville 122 Ef 48.50N 1.36W
Granville Lake 180 He 56.00N 100.20W
Granvin 116 Bd 60.33N 6.43 E
Grao de Sagunto, Sagunto-Grau 126 Le 39.40N 0.16W
Grappa, Monte- 128 Fe 45.52N 11.48 E
Grappler Bank (EN) 197a Cc 17.48N 65.55W
Graskop 172 Ed 24.58S 30.49 E
Gräsmark 116 Ee 59.57N 12.55 E
Gräsö 114 Ef 60.25N 18.25 E
Grasse 122 Mk 43.40N 6.55 E
Grasset, Lac- 184 Ha 49.58N 78.10W
Grassrange 188 Kc 47.01N 108.48W
Gråsten 114 Bi 54.55N 9.36 E
Grästorp 116 Ef 58.20N 12.40 E
Graubünden / Grigioni / Grischun [2] 128 Dd 46.35N 9.35 E
Grau-du-Roi, Le- 122 Kk 43.32N 4.08 E
Graulhet 122 Hk 43.46N 2.00 E
Graus 126 Mb 42.11N 0.20 E
Grave 124 Hc 51.45N 5.45 E
Grave, Pointe de- 122 Ei 45.34N 1.04W
Gravedona 128 Dd 46.09N 9.18 E
Gravelbourg 180 Gg 49.53N 106.34W
Gravelines 122 Id 50.59N 2.07 E
Gravenhage, 's- /Den Haag = The Hague (EN) 112 Ge 52.06N 4.18 E
Gravenhage-Scheveningen, 's- 122 Kb 52.06N 4.18 E
Gravenhurst 184 Hc 44.55N 79.22W
Gravenor Bay 197d Ba 17.33N 61.45W
Graves 122 Fj 44.35N 0.30W
Gravesend 118 Nj 51.27N 0.24 E
Gravesend-Tilbury 118 Nj 51.28N 0.23 E
Gravina in Puglia 128 Kj 40.49N 16.25 E
Gravone 122a Ab 41.55N 8.47 E
Gray 122 Lg 47.27N 5.35 E
Gray Feather Bank (EN) 214 Df 8.00N 148.40 E
Grayling 184 Ec 44.40N 84.43W
Grays 118 Nj 51.28N 0.20 E
Grays Harbor 188 Cc 46.56N 124.05W
Grayson 184 Ff 38.20N 82.57W
Grays Peak 182 Fd 39.37N 105.45W
Graz 112 Hf 47.04N 15.27 E
Grazalema 126 Gh 36.46N 5.22W
Grdelica 130 Fg 42.54N 22.04 E
Greåker 116 De 59.16N 11.02 E
Great 197p Bb 12.10N 61.38W
Great Artesian Basin 208 Fg 25.00S 143.00 E
Great Astrolabe Reef 219d Bc 18.52S 178.31 E
Great Australian Bight 208 Eh 35.00S 130.00 E
Great Bacolet Point 197p Bb 12.05N 61.37W
Great Bahama Bank (EN) 174 Lg 23.15N 78.00W
Great Bardfield 124 Cc 51.56N 0.29 E
Great Barrier Island 208 Ih 36.10S 175.25 E
Great Barrier Reef 208 Ff 19.10S 149.00 E
Great Basin 174 Hf 40.00N 117.00W
Great Bay 184 Jf 39.30N 74.23W
Great Bear 180 Ed 64.54N 125.35W
Great Bear Lake 174 Hc 66.00N 120.00W
Great Belt (EN) = Store Bælt 110 Hd 55.30N 11.00 E
Great Bend 182 Hd 38.22N 98.46W
Great Blasket/An Blascaod Mór 118 Ci 52.05N 10.32W
Great Britain 110 Fd 54.00N 3.00W
Great Central Lake 188 Cb 49.27N 125.12W
Great Channel 140 Li 6.00N 94.00 E
Great Chesterford 124 Cb 52.04N 0.12 E
Great Dismal Swamp 184 Ig 36.30N 76.30W
Great Dividing Range 208 Fg 25.00S 147.00 E
Great Dunmow 124 Cc 51.53N 0.22 E
Greater Accra [3] 166 Fd 5.45N 0.10 E
Greater Antilles (EN) = Antillas Mayores 174 Lh 20.00N 74.00W
Greater Khingan Range (EN) = Da Hinggan Ling 140 Oe 49.00N 122.00 E
Greater London [3] 118 Mj 51.35N 0.05W
Greater Manchester [3] 118 Kh 53.35N 2.10W
Greater Sunda Islands (EN) 140 Nj 3.52S 111.20 E
Great Exhibition Bay 216 Df 34.40S 173.00 E
Great Exuma Island 190 Id 23.32N 75.50W
Great Falls 176 He 47.30N 111.17W
Great Fisher Bank (EN) = Storefiskbank 118 Qe 56.50N 4.00 E
Great Fish River 158 Ik 17.11S 28.08 E
Great Guana Cay 194 Ia 24.00N 76.20W
Great Harbour Cay 184 Im 25.45N 77.52W
Great Inagua 174 Lg 21.02N 73.20W
Great Indian Desert/Thar 140 Jg 27.00N 70.00 E
Great Karasberge (EN) = Groot-Karasberge 158 Ik 27.20S 18.45 E
Great Karroo (EN) = Groot Karoo 158 Jl 33.00S 22.00 E
Great Lake 212 Jh 41.52S 146.45 E
Great Lyakhov (EN) = Bolšoj Ljahovski, ostrov- 138 Jb 73.35N 142.00 E
Great Namaland/Groot Namaland 172 Be 26.00S 17.00 E
Great Nicobar 140 Li 7.00N 93.50 E
Great North East Channel 212 Ia 9.30S 143.25 E
Great Ormes Head 118 Jh 53.21N 3.52W
Great Ouse 118 Ni 52.44N 0.23 E
Great Plain of the Koukdjuak 180 Kc 66.25N 72.50W
Great Plains 174 Je 42.00N 100.00W
Great Reef 219c Bb 10.14S 166.02 E
Great Ruaha 158 Ki 7.56S 37.52 E
Great Sacandaga Lake 184 Jd 43.08N 74.10W
Great Sale Cay 184 Hl 27.00N 78.12W
Great Salt Lake 174 He 41.10N 112.30W
Great Salt Lake Desert 182 Ec 40.40N 113.30W
Great Salt Plains Lake 186 Gh 36.44N 98.12W
Great Salt Pond 197c Ab 17.15N 62.38W
Great Sandy Desert [Austl.] 208 Dg 21.30S 125.00 E
Great Sandy Desert [U.S.] 182 Cc 43.35N 120.15W
Great Sea Reef 219d Bb 16.15S 178.33 E
Great Shelford 124 Cb 52.07N 0.08 E
Great Sitkin 178a Cb 52.03N 176.07W
Great Slave Lake 174 Hc 61.30N 114.00W
Great Smoky Mountains 184 Fh 35.35N 83.30W
Great Stour 118 Oj 51.19N 1.15 E
Great Valley [U.S.] 184 Ie 40.15N 76.50W
Great Valley [U.S.] 182 Kd 36.30N 82.00W
Great Victoria Desert 208 Dg 28.30S 127.45 E
Great Yarmouth 118 Oi 52.37N 1.44 E
Grebbestad 114 Cg 58.42N 11.15 E
Grebenka 132 Hd 50.07N 32.25 E
Gréboun, Mont- 166 Gb 20.00N 8.35 E
Greci 130 Ld 45.11N 28.14 E
Gredos, Sierra de- 126 Gd 40.20N 5.05W
Greece (EN) = Elläs [1] 112 Ih 39.00N 22.00 E
Greeley [Co.-U.S.] 182 Gc 40.25N 104.42W
Greeley [Nb.-U.S.] 186 Gf 41.33N 98.32W
Greely Fiord 180 Ja 80.40N 85.00W
Greem-Bell, ostrov- 140 Ia 81.10N 64.00 E
Green 188 De 43.07N 123.28W
Green Bay 176 Ke 44.30N 88.01W
Green Bay 182 Jb 45.00N 87.30W
Greencastle 184 Df 39.38N 86.52W
Green Cay 194 Ia 24.02N 77.11W
Greeneville 184 Fg 36.10N 82.50W
Greenfield [In.-U.S.] 184 Ef 39.47N 85.46W
Greenfield [Ma.-U.S.] 184 Kd 42.36N 72.36W
Greenhorn Mountain 186 Dh 37.57N 105.00W
Green Island 218 Df 45.54S 170.26 E
Green Island [Atg.] 197d Bb 17.03N 61.40W
Green Island [Gren.] 197p Bb 12.14N 61.35W
Green Islands 208 Ge 4.30S 154.10 E
Greenland 197q Ab 13.15N 59.34W
Greenland (EN) = Grønland/Kalaallit Nunaat [5] 224 Nd 70.00N 40.00W
Greenland (EN) = Grønland/Kalaallit Nunaat 174 Pb 70.00N 40.00W
Greenland (EN) = Kalaallit Nunaat/Grønland [5] 224 Nd 70.00N 40.00W
Greenland (EN) = Kalaallit Nunaat/Grønland 174 Pb 70.00N 40.00W
Greenland Basin (EN) 224 Ld 77.00N 0.00
Greenland Sea (EN) = Grænlandshaf 224 Ld 77.00N 1.00W
Greenland Sea (EN) = Grønlandshavet 224 Ld 77.00N 1.00W
Green Lookout Mountain 188 Dd 45.52N 122.08W
Green Mountains 174 Le 43.45N 72.45W
Greenock 118 If 55.57N 4.45W
Greenough River 212 Ce 28.51S 114.38 E
Green Peter Lake 188 Dd 44.28N 122.30W
Green River [U.S.] 184 Dg 37.55N 87.30W
Green River [U.S.] 174 If 38.11N 109.53W
Green River [Ut.-U.S.] 182 Ed 38.59N 110.10W
Green River [Wy.-U.S.] 182 Fc 41.32N 109.28W
Green River Lake 184 Eg 37.15N 85.15W
Greensboro 176 Lf 36.04N 79.47W
Greensburg [In.-U.S.] 184 Ef 39.20N 85.29W
Greensburg [Ks.-U.S.] 186 Gh 37.36N 99.18W
Greensburg [La.-U.S.] 186 Kk 30.51N 90.42W
Greenstone Point 118 Hd 57.55N 5.40W
Greenvale 212 Jc 18.55S 145.05 E
Greenville [Al.-U.S.] 184 Dj 31.50N 86.38W
Greenville [Il.-U.S.] 186 Lg 38.53N 89.25W
Greenville [Lbr.] 160 Gh 4.59N 9.02W
Greenville [Me.-U.S.] 184 Mc 45.28N 69.35W
Greenville [Ms.-U.S.] 182 Ie 33.25N 91.05W
Greenville [N.C.-U.S.] 182 Ld 35.37N 77.23W
Greenville [Oh.-U.S.] 184 Ee 40.06N 84.37W
Greenville [Pa.-U.S.] 184 Ge 41.24N 80.24W
Greenville [S.C.-U.S.] 176 Kf 34.51N 82.23W
Greenville [Tx.-U.S.] 182 He 33.08N 96.07W
Greenwich 184 Fe 41.02N 82.32W
Greenwich, London- 118 Mj 51.28N 0.00
Greenwood [Ms.-U.S.] 182 Ie 33.31N 90.11W
Greenwood [S.C.-U.S.] 184 Fh 34.12N 82.10W
Greenwood, Lake- 184 Gh 34.15N 82.05W
Greer 184 Fh 34.55N 82.14W
Greers Ferry Lake 186 Ji 35.30N 92.10W
Greeson, Lake- 186 Ji 34.10N 93.45W

Index Symbols

[1] Independent Nation
[2] State, Region
[3] District, County
[4] Municipality
[5] Colony, Dependency
Continent
Physical Region
Historical or Cultural Region
Mount, Mountain
Volcano
Hill
Mountains, Mountain Range
Hills, Escarpment
Plateau, Upland
Pass, Gap
Plain, Lowland
Delta
Salt Flat
Valley, Canyon
Crater, Cave
Karst Features
Depression
Polder
Desert, Dunes
Forest, Woods
Heath, Steppe
Oasis
Cape, Point
Coast, Beach
Cliff
Peninsula
Isthmus
Sandbank
Island
Atoll
Rock, Reef
Islands, Archipelago
Rocks, Reefs
Coral Reef
Well, Spring
Geyser
River, Stream
Waterfall, Rapids
River Mouth, Estuary
Lake
Salt Lake
Intermittent Lake
Reservoir
Swamp, Pond
Canal
Glacier
Ice Shelf, Pack Ice
Ocean
Sea
Gulf, Bay
Strait, Fjord
Lagoon
Bank
Seamount
Tablemount
Ridge
Shelf
Basin
Escarpment, Sea Scarp
Fracture
Trench, Abyss
National Park, Reserve
Point of Interest
Recreation Site
Cave, Cavern
Historic Site
Ruins
Wall, Walls
Church, Abbey
Temple
Scientific Station
Railway station
Airport
Port
Military installation
Lighthouse
Mine
Tunnel
Dam, Bridge

Grefrath 124 Ic 51.18N 6.19 E
Gregoria Pérez de Denis 204 Bi 28.14S 61.32W
Gregorio, Rio- 202 De 6.50S 70.46W
Gregório, Rio- 204 Ha 13.42S 49.58W
Gregory, Lake- 212 He 28.55S 139.00 E
Gregory Lake 212 Fd 20.10S 127.20 E
Gregory Range 208 Ff 19.00S 143.00 E
Gregory River 212 Hc 17.53S 139.17 E
Greifenburg 128 Hd 46.45N 13.11 E
Greifswald 120 Jb 54.06N 13.23 E
Greifswalder Bodden 120 Jb 54.15N 13.35 E
Greifswalder Oie 120 Jb 54.14N 13.55 E
Grein 128 Ib 48.13N 14.51 E
Greiz 120 If 50.39N 12.12 E
Grěko, Akra- 146 Fe 34.56N 34.05 E
Gremiha 112 Jb 68.03N 39.29 E
Gremjačinsk 134 Hg 58.34N 57.51 E
Grenå 114 Ch 56.25N 10.53 E
Grenada 186 Lj 33.47N 89.55W
Grenada [1] 176 Mh 12.07N 61.40W
Grenada 174 Mh 12.07N 61.40W
Grenada Basin (EN) 190 Lf 13.30N 62.00W
Grenada Lake 186 Lj 33.50N 89.40W
Grenadines 190 Lf 12.40N 61.15W
Grenchen 128 Bc 47.11N 7.25 E
Grenen 110 Hd 57.44N 10.40 E
Grenfell 186 Ea 50.25N 102.56W
Grenoble 112 Gf 45.10N 5.43 E
Grenora 186 Eb 48.37N 103.56W
Grense-Jakobselv 114 Hb 69.47N 30.50 E
Grenville 196 Ff 12.07N 61.37W
Grenville, Cape- 212 Ib 12.00S 143.15 E
Gréoux-les-Bains 122 Lk 43.45N 5.53 E
Gresham 188 Dd 45.30N 122.26W
Gresik 150 Fh 7.09S 112.38 E
Gressoney-la-Trinité 128 Be 45.50N 7.49 E
Gretas klackar 116 Gc 61.34N 17.50 E
Gretna 186 Kl 29.55N 90.03W
Grevelingen 124 Fc 51.45N 4.00 E
Greven 120 Dd 52.06N 7.37 E
Grevená 130 Ei 40.05N 21.25 E
Grevenbroich 120 Ce 51.05N 6.35 E
Grevenbrück, Lennestadt- 124 Kc 51.08N 8.01 E
Grevenmacher 124 Ie 49.41N 6.27 E
Grevesmühlen 120 Hc 53.52N 11.11 E
Grey 218 De 42.26S 171.11 E
Greybull 188 Kd 44.30N 108.03W
Greybull River 188 Kd 44.28N 108.03W
Grey Islands 180 Lf 50.50N 55.35W
Greymouth 216 Dh 42.27S 171.12 E
Grey Range 208 Fg 27.00S 143.35 E
Greystones/Ná Clocha Liatha 118 Gh 53.09N 6.04W
Greytow 172 Ee 29.07S 30.30 E
Greytown 218 Fd 41.05S 175.28 E
Gribanovski 132 Ld 51.29N 41.58 E
Gribb Bank (EN) 222 Ge 63.00S 90.30 E
Gribës, Mali i- 130 Ci 40.34N 19.34 E
Gribingui [3] 168 Bd 7.00N 19.30 E
Gribingui 168 Bd 8.33N 19.05 E
Griend 124 Ha 53.15N 5.20 E
Griesheim 124 Ke 49.52N 8.33 E
Grieskirchen 128 Hb 48.14N 13.50 E
Griffin 182 Ke 33.15N 84.16W
Griffith 212 Jf 34.17S 146.03 E
Grigioni / Grischun / Graubünden [2] 128 Dd 46.35N 9.35 E
Grigoriopol 130 Mb 47.09N 29.13 E
Grijalva 174 Jh 18.36N 92.39W
Grijalva, Rio- 192 Mh 18.36N 92.38W
Grim, Cape- 212 Ih 40.41S 144.41 E
Grimari 168 Cd 5.44N 20.03 E
Grimbergen 124 Gd 50.56N 4.23 E
Grimma 120 Ie 51.14N 12.43 E
Grimmen 120 Jb 54.06N 13.03 E
Grimsby 118 Mh 53.35N 0.05W
Grimsey 114a Ca 66.33N 18.00W
Grimsstadir 114a Cb 65.39N 16.07W
Grimstad 114 Bg 58.20N 8.36 E
Grimsvotn 114a Cb 64.24N 17.22W
Grindavik 114a Ac 63.50N 22.30W
Grindelwald 128 Cd 46.38N 8.03 E
Grindsted 114 Bi 55.45N 8.56 E
Grinnell 186 Jf 41.45N 92.43W
Grinnel Peninsula 180 Ia 76.40N 95.00W
Grintavec 128 Id 46.22N 14.32 E
Griquatown 172 Ce 28.49S 23.15 E
Grischun / Graubünden / Grigioni [2] 128 Dd 46.35N 9.35 E
Grise Fiord 176 Kb 76.10N 83.15W
Gris-Nez, Cap- 122 Hd 50.52N 1.35 E
Grisslehamn 116 Hd 60.06N 18.50 E
Grjazi 136 De 52.29N 39.57 E
Grjazovec 136 Ed 58.53N 40.15 E
Grmeč 128 Kf 44.43N 16.15 E
Grobiņa/Grobinja 114 Eh 56.33N 21.11 E
Grobinja/Grobiņa 114 Eh 56.33N 21.11 E
Groblersdal 172 De 25.15S 29.25 E
Grocka 130 De 44.41N 20.43 E
Grodk/Spremberg 120 Ke 51.33N 14.22 E
Grodków 120 Nf 50.43N 17.22 E
Grodnenskaja oblast [3] 136 Ce 53.45N 25.10 E
Grodno 112 Ie 53.42N 23.50 E
Grodzisk Mazowiecki 120 Qd 52.07N 20.37 E
Grodzjanka 132 Fc 53.34N 28.48 E
Groeie Hoop, Kaap die- / Good Hope, Cape of- 158 Il 34.21S 18.28 E
Groenlo 124 Ib 52.04N 6.39 E
Groesbeek 124 Hc 51.47N 5.56 E
Grofa, gora- 130 Ha 48.34N 24.03 E
Groix 122 Cg 47.38N 3.28W
Groix, Ile de- 122 Cg 47.38N 3.28W
Grójec 120 Qe 51.52N 20.52 E
Gröll Seamount (EN) 202 Lf 14.00S 32.00W
Gromnik 120 Nf 50.42N 17.07 E
Gronau (Westfalen) 120 Dd 52.12N 7.02 E
Grong 114 Cd 64.30N 12.27 E
Groningen [3] 124 Ia 53.13N 6.33 E
Groningen [Neth.] 112 Ge 53.13N 6.33 E
Groningen [Sur.] 202 Gb 5.48N 55.28W
Groningerwad 124 Ia 53.27N 6.25 E
Grønland/Kalaallit Nunaat = Greenland (EN) [5] 224 Nd 70.00N 40.00W
Grønland/Kalaallit Nunaat = Greenland (EN) 174 Pb 70.00N 40.00W
Grønlandshavet = Greenland Sea (EN) 224 Ld 77.00N 1.00W
Grønnedal 179 Hf 61.20N 47.45W
Grönskara 116 Fg 57.05N 15.44 E
Groot 158 Jl 33.45S 24.58 E
Groot Baai 197b Ab 18.01N 63.04W
Groote Eylandt 208 Ef 14.00S 136.40 E
Grootfontein 160 Ij 19.32S 18.05 E
Grootfontein [3] 172 Bc 19.00S 19.00 E
Groot-Karasberge = Great Karasberg (EN) 158 Ik 27.20S 18.45 E
Groot Karoo = Great Karroo (EN) 158 Jl 33.00S 22.00 E
Grootlaagte 172 Cd 20.55S 21.27 E
Groot Namaland/Great Namaland 172 Be 26.00S 17.00 E
Grootvloer 172 Ce 30.00S 20.40 E
Gropeni 130 Kd 45.05N 27.54 E
Gros Caps, Pointe des- 197e Bb 16.28N 61.25W
Gros Islet Bay 197k Ba 14.05N 60.58W
Gros Islets 197k Ba 14.05N 60.58W
Gros-Morne 197h Ab 14.43N 61.01W
Gros-Morne 180 Lg 49.00N 57.22W
Grosne 122 Kh 46.42N 4.56 E
Gros Piton 197k Ab 13.49N 61.04W
Große Aa 124 Jb 52.25N 7.23 E
Große Aue 124 Kb 52.30N 8.38 E
Großefehn 124 Ja 53.24N 7.33 E
Große Laaber 120 Ih 48.50N 12.30 E
Großenhain 120 Je 51.17N 13.33 E
Großenkneten 124 Kb 52.57N 8.16 E
Grosse Pointe 197e Bb 16.01N 61.17W
Großer Arber 120 Jg 49.07N 13.07 E
Großer Feldberg 124 Kd 50.13N 8.28 E
Großer Gleichberg 120 Gf 50.23N 10.35 E
Großer Inselsberg 120 Gf 50.52N 10.28 E
Grosseto 128 Fh 42.46N 11.08 E
Grosseto, Formiche di- 128 Eh 42.40N 10.55 E
Groß-Gerau 120 Eg 49.55N 8.29 E
Großglockner 110 Hf 47.04N 12.42 E
Großräschen 120 Je 51.35N 14.00 E
Groß-Umstadt 124 Ke 49.52N 8.56 E
Großvenediger 128 Gc 47.06N 12.21 E
Grostenquin 124 If 48.59N 6.44 E
Gros Ventre Range 188 Je 43.30N 110.15W
Groswater Bay 174 Nd 54.20N 57.30W
Grøtavær 114 Db 68.58N 16.16 E
Grote Nete 124 Gc 51.07N 4.34 E
Grotli 114 Be 62.01N 7.40 E
Grottaglie 128 Lj 40.32N 17.26 E
Grottammare 128 Hh 42.59N 13.52 E
Groumania 166 Ed 7.55N 4.00W
Groundhog River 184 Ga 49.43N 81.58W
Grouse Creek Mountains 188 If 41.55N 113.50W
Grove Mountains 222 Ff 72.53S 74.53 E
Groves 186 Jl 29.57N 93.55W
Grovfjord 114 Db 68.41N 17.09 E
Grow, Idaarderadeel- 124 Ha 53.06N 5.30 E
Grozny 112 Kg 43.20N 45.42 E
Grubišno Polje 128 Le 45.42N 17.10 E
Grudovo 130 Kg 42.21N 27.10 E
Grudziądz 120 Oc 53.29N 18.45 E
Grumento Nova 128 Jj 40.17N 15.53 E
Grumo Appula 128 Ki 41.01N 16.42 E
Grums 116 Ee 59.21N 13.06 E
Grünau 172 Be 27.47S 18.23 E
Grünberg 124 Kd 50.36N 8.57 E
Gründau 124 Ld 50.14N 9.05 E
Grundkallegrund 116 Hd 60.40N 18.45 E
Grundy 184 Fg 37.17N 82.06W
Gruñidera 192 Ie 24.15N 101.58W
Grünstadt 124 Ke 49.34N 8.10 E
Gruppo di Brenta 128 Ed 46.10N 10.55 E
Gruyère 128 Bd 46.40N 7.10 E
Gruža 130 Df 43.54N 20.47 E
Gruzinskaja Sovetskaja Socialističeskaja Respublika [2] 136 Eg 42.00N 44.00 E
Gruzinskaja SSR/ Sakartvelos Sabčata Socialisturi Respublika [2] 136 Eg 42.00N 44.00 E
Gruzinskaja SSR = Georgian SSR (EN) [2] 136 Eg 42.00N 44.00 E
Grybów 120 Qg 49.38N 20.56 E
Grycksbo 116 Fd 60.41N 15.28 E
Gryfice 120 Lc 53.56N 15.12 E
Gryfino 120 Kc 53.15N 14.30 E
Grythyttan 116 Fe 59.42N 14.32 E
Grytviken 222 Ad 54.17S 36.31W
Gstaad, Saanen- 128 Bd 46.28N 7.17 E
Guacanayabo, Golfo de- 190 Id 20.28N 77.30W
Guacara 196 Cg 10.14N 67.53W
Guaçu 204 Ef 22.11S 54.31W
Guadaira 126 Fg 37.20N 6.01W
Guadajoz 126 Hg 37.50N 4.51W
Guadalajara [3] 126 Jd 40.50N 2.30W
Guadalajara [Mex.] 176 Ig 20.40N 103.20W
Guadalajara [Sp.] 126 Id 40.38N 3.10W
Guadalaviar 126 Kd 40.21N 1.08W
Guadalbullón 126 Ig 37.59N 3.47W
Guadalcanal 126 Gf 38.06N 5.49W
Guadalcanal Island 208 He 9.32S 160.12 E
Guadalén 126 If 38.05N 3.32W
Guadalentin o Sangonera 126 Kg 37.59N 1.04W
Guadalete 126 Fh 36.35N 6.13W
Guadalfeo 126 Ih 36.43N 3.35W
Guadalimar 126 Ig 37.59N 3.44W
Guadalmanzor / Almanzora 126 Kg 37.14N 1.46W
Guadalmena 126 Jf 38.20N 2.55W
Guadalmez 126 Gf 38.46N 5.04W
Guadalop / Guadalope 126 Lc 41.15N 0.03W
Guadalope / Guadalop 126 Lc 41.15N 0.03W
Guadalquivir 110 Fh 36.47N 6.22W
Guadalupe [Mex.] 190 Dc 25.41N 100.15W
Guadalupe [Mex.] 192 Hf 22.45N 102.31W
Guadalupe [Mex.] 192 Id 26.12N 101.23W
Guadalupe [Sp.] 126 Ge 39.27N 5.19W
Guadalupe, Isla de- 174 Hg 29.00N 118.16W
Guadalupe, Laguna de- → Setúbal 204 Bj 21.33S 60.35W
Guadalupe, Sierra de- 126 Ge 39.25N 5.25W
Guadalupe Bravos 192 Fb 31.23N 106.07W
Guadalupe Mountains 186 Dj 32.20N 105.00W
Guadalupe Peak 182 Ge 31.50N 104.52W
Guadalupe River 186 Hl 28.30N 96.53W
Guadalupe Victoria, Presa- 192 Gf 23.50N 104.55W
Guadalupe y Calvo 192 Fd 26.06N 106.58W
Guadarrama 126 He 39.53N 4.10W
Guadarrama, Puerto de- 126 Hd 40.43N 4.10W
Guadarrama, Sierra de- 126 Id 40.55N 4.00W
Guadazaón 126 Ke 39.42N 1.36W
Guadeloupe [5] 176 Mh 16.15N 61.35W
Guadeloupe 174 Mh 16.15N 61.35W
Guadeloupe, Canal de la- = Guadeloupe Passage (EN) 190 Le 16.40N 61.50W
Guadeloupe Passage 196 Fd 16.40N 61.50W
Guadeloupe Passage (EN) = Guadeloupe, Canal de la- 190 Le 16.40N 61.50W
Guadiana 110 Fh 37.14N 7.22W
Guadiana, Canal del- 126 Ie 39.20N 3.20W
Guadiana, Ojos del- 126 Ie 39.08N 3.31W
Guadiana Menor 126 Ig 37.56N 3.15W
Guadiaro 126 Gh 36.17N 5.17W
Guadiela 126 Jd 40.22N 2.49W
Guadix 126 Ig 37.18N 3.08W
Guafo, Boca del- 206 Ff 43.40S 74.15W
Guafo, Isla- 206 Ff 43.36S 74.43W
Guaiba 206 Jd 30.06S 51.19W
Guaiba, Rio- 204 Gj 30.15S 51.12W
Guaimaca 194 Df 14.52N 86.51W
Guaimorato, Laguna de- 194 Ef 15.58N 85.55W
Guainia [3] 202 Ec 2.30N 69.00W
Guainia, Rio- 198 Je 2.01N 67.07W
Guaiquinima, Cerro- 202 Fb 5.49N 63.40W
Guaira [3] 204 Dg 25.45S 56.30W
Guaira [Braz.] 206 Jb 24.04S 54.15W
Guaira [Braz.] 204 He 20.19S 48.18W
Guaira Falls (EN) = Sete Quedas, Saltos das- 206 Jb 24.02S 54.16W
Guairas 204 Ja 12.39S 44.16W
Guaire/Gorey 118 Gi 52.40N 6.18W
Guaitecas, Islas- 206 Ff 43.57S 73.50W
Guajaba, Cayo- 194 Ic 21.50N 77.30W
Guajará Mirim 200 Jg 10.48S 65.22W
Guajira, Peninsula de la- 198 Id 12.00N 71.30W
Guajolotes, Sierra del- 192 Ge 26.00N 105.15W
Guakolak, Tanjung- 150 Eh 6.50S 105.14 E
Gualaco 194 Df 15.06N 86.07W
Gualán 194 Cf 15.08N 89.22W
Gualdo Tadino 128 Gg 43.14N 12.47 E
Gualeguay 204 Ck 33.09S 59.20W
Gualeguay, Rio- 204 Ck 33.19S 59.39W
Gualeguaychu 206 Id 33.01S 58.31W
Gualeguaychú, Rio- 204 Ck 33.05S 58.25W
Gualicho, Salina del- 206 Gf 40.24S 65.15W
Guam [5] 210 Fc 13.28N 144.47 E
Guam 208 Fc 13.28N 144.47 E
Guamini 206 He 37.02S 62.25W
Guampi, Sierra de- 202 Eb 6.00N 65.35W
Guamuchil 190 Cc 25.22N 108.22W
Gua Musang 150 Df 4.53N 101.58 E
Gu'an 154 De 39.24N 116.10 E
Guanabacoa 194 Fb 23.07N 82.18W
Guanabara, Baia de- 204 Kf 22.50S 43.10W
Guanacaste [3] 194 Eh 10.30N 85.15W
Guanacaste, Cordillera de- 194 Eh 10.45N 85.05W
Guanacevi 192 Ge 25.56N 105.57W
Guanahacabibes, Golfo de- 194 Eb 22.08N 84.35W
Guanahacabibes, Peninsula de- 194 Ec 21.57N 84.35W
Guana Island 197a Db 18.29N 64.34W
Guanaja 194 Ee 16.27N 85.54W
Guanaja, Isla de- 194 Ee 16.30N 85.55W
Guanajay 194 Fb 22.55N 82.42W
Guanajibo 197a Ab 18.10N 67.09W
Guanajibo, Punta- 197a Ab 18.12N 67.10W
Guanajuato 190 Dd 21.01N 101.15W
Guanajuato [2] 190 Dd 21.00N 101.00W
Guanambi 202 Jf 14.13S 42.47W
Guanare 202 Eb 9.03N 69.45W
Guanare, Rio- 196 Ch 8.13N 67.46W
Guanare Viejo, Rio- 194 Mi 8.19N 68.10W
Guanarito 196 Bh 8.42N 69.12W
Guandacol 206 Gc 29.31S 68.32W
Guandi Shan 152 Jd 38.09N 111.27 E
Guane 190 Hd 22.12N 84.05W
Guangde 152 Ke 30.51N 119.26 E
Guangdong Sheng (Kuang-tung Sheng) = Kwangtung (EN) [2] 152 Jg 23.00N 113.00 E
Guangfeng 154 Ej 28.27N 118.12 E
Guanghua 152 Je 32.18N 111.45 E
Guangji (Wuxue) 154 Kf 29.58N 115.32 E
Guangling 154 Ce 39.46N 114.16 E
Guangmao Shan 152 Hf 26.48N 100.56 E
Guangming Ding 154 Ei 30.09N 118.11 E
Guangnan 152 Ig 24.02N 105.04 E
Guangrao 154 Ef 37.03N 118.25 E
Guangshan 154 Ci 32.02N 114.53 E
Guangshui 154 Ci 31.37N 114.01 E
Guangxi Zhuangzu Zizhiqu (Kuang-hsi-chuang-tsu Tzu-chih-ch'ü) = Kwangsi Chuang (EN) [2] 152 Ig 24.00N 109.00 E
Guangyuan 142 Mf 32.27N 105.55 E
Guangzhou = Canton (EN) 142 Ng 23.07N 113.18 E
Guan He 154 Ch 32.18N 115.44 E
Guánica 197a Bc 17.59N 66.56W
Guanipa, Rio- 196 Eh 9.56N 62.26W
Guannan (Xin'anzhen) 154 Eg 34.04N 119.21 E
Guantánamo 176 Lg 20.08N 75.12W
Guantánamo [3] 194 Jc 20.10N 75.00W
Guantánamo, Bahia de- 194 Jd 20.00N 75.10W
Guantánamo Bay 190 Id 20.00N 75.10W
Guantánamo Bay Naval Station 194 Jd 20.00N 75.08W
Guantao (Nanguantao) 154 Cf 36.33N 115.18 E
Guanting Shuiku 154 Cd 40.13N 115.36 E
Guanxian 142 Mf 31.00N 103.38 E
Guanyun (Dayishan) 154 Eg 34.18N 119.14 E
Guapay, Rio- → Grande, Rio- 198 Jg 15.51S 64.39W
Guapé 204 Je 20.47S 45.55W
Guapi 202 Cc 2.35N 77.55W
Guápiles 194 Fh 10.13N 83.46W
Guapó 204 Hc 16.51S 49.33W
Guaporé 206 Jc 28.51S 51.54W
Guaporé 204 Gi 29.10S 51.54W
Guaporé, Rio- 198 Jg 11.55S 65.04W
Guaqui 202 Eg 16.35S 68.51W
Guará 204 Gg 25.23S 51.17W
Guara, Sierra de- 126 Lb 42.17N 0.10W
Guarabira 202 Ke 6.51S 35.29W
Guaranda 202 Cd 1.35S 78.59W
Guaraniaçu 206 Jc 25.06S 52.52W
Guarani de Goiás 204 Ia 13.57S 46.28W
Guarapiche, Rio- 196 Eh 9.57N 62.52W
Guarapuava 206 Jc 25.23S 51.27W
Guaraqueçaba 204 Hg 25.17S 48.21W
Guararapes 204 Ge 21.15S 50.38W
Guaratinguetá 204 Jf 22.49S 45.13W
Guaratuba 204 Hg 25.54S 48.34W
Guarayos, Rio- 204 Bb 14.38S 62.11W
Guarda 126 Ed 40.32N 7.16W
Guarda [2] 126 Ed 40.40N 7.10W
Guardafui, Cape-(EN) = 'Asayr 158 Mg 11.49N 51.15 E
Guardal 126 Jg 37.36N 2.45W
Guarda-Mor 204 Ic 17.47S 47.06W
Guardiagrele 128 Ih 42.11N 14.13 E
Guardian Seamount (EN) 174 Ki 9.32N 87.40W
Guardo 126 Hb 42.47N 4.50W
Guardunha, Serra da- 126 Ed 40.05N 7.31W
Guarei, Rio- 204 Ff 22.40S 53.34W
Guareña 126 Gc 41.29N 5.23W
Guarenas 196 Cg 10.28N 66.37W
Guaribas, Rio- 204 Jc 16.22S 45.03W
Guaribe, Rio- 196 Dh 9.53N 65.11W
Guárico [2] 202 Eb 8.40N 66.35W
Guárico, Embalse del- 196 Ch 9.00N 67.20W
Guárico, Rio- 202 Eb 7.40N 67.23W
Guariquito, Rio- 196 Ci 7.40N 66.18W
Guarita, Rio- 204 Fh 27.11S 53.44W
Guaritico, Caño- 196 Bi 7.52N 68.53W
Guaritire, Rio- 204 Ba 13.43S 60.38W
Guarujá 204 If 24.00S 46.16W
Guarulhos 206 Kb 23.28S 46.32W
Guasave 190 Cc 25.34N 108.27W
Guasdualito 202 Db 7.15N 70.44W
Guasipati 202 Fb 7.28N 61.54W
Guasopa 219a Ac 9.14S 152.55 E
Guastalla 128 Ef 44.55N 10.39 E
Guatemala 176 Jh 14.38N 90.31W
Guatemala [1] 176 Jh 14.38N 90.31W
Guatemala [3] 194 Bf 14.40N 90.30W
Guatemala Basin (EN) 106 Mh 11.00N 95.00W
Guateque 202 Db 5.05N 73.30W
Guatimozin 204 Ak 33.27S 62.27W
Guatisimiña 202 Fc 4.33N 63.57W
Guatraché 206 He 37.40S 63.32W
Guaviare [2] 202 Dc 2.00N 72.00W
Guaviare, Rio- 198 Je 4.03N 67.44W
Guaviravi 204 Di 29.22S 56.50W
Guaxupé 204 Ie 21.18S 46.42W
Guayabal [Cuba] 194 Ic 20.42N 77.36W
Guayabal [Ven.] 196 Ci 8.00N 67.24W
Guayabero, Rio- 202 Ec 4.03N 67.44W
Guayalejo, Rio- 192 Kf 22.13N 97.52W
Guayama 192 Ne 17.59N 66.07W
Guayana, Macizo de la- = Guaiana Highlands (EN) 198 Ke 5.00N 60.00W
Guayana Basin (EN) 106 Ci 10.00N 52.00W
Guayaneco, Archipiélago- 206 Eg 47.45S 75.10W
Guayanés, Punta- 197a Cb 18.04N 65.48W
Guayanilla 197a Bb 18.02N 66.47W
Guayanilla, Bahia de- 197a Bc 17.58N 66.45W
Guayape, Rio- 194 Df 14.26N 86.02W
Guayaquil 200 If 2.10S 79.50W
Guayaquil, Golfo de- 198 Hf 3.00S 80.30W
Guaycurú, Rio- 204 Ch 27.19S 58.45W
Guaymas 176 Hg 27.56N 110.54W
Guayquiraró, Rio- 204 Cj 30.10S 58.34W
Guba [Eth.] 168 Fc 11.15N 35.20 E
Guba [Zaire] 170 Ee 10.38S 26.25 E
Guba Dolgaja 136 Fa 70.19N 58.45 E
Gubaha 136 Fd 58.52N 57.36 E
Guban 158 Lg 10.15N 44.26 E
Gubbio 128 Gg 43.21N 12.35 E
Gubdor 134 Hf 60.15N 56.35 E
Guber 120 Rb 54.13N 21.02 E
Gubin 120 Ke 51.56N 14.45 E
Gubio 166 Hc 12.30N 12.47 E
Gubkin 136 De 51.17N 37.33 E
Gúdar, Sierra de- 126 Ld 40.27N 0.42W
Gudara 136 Hh 38.23N 72.42 E
Gudauta 132 Lh 43.07N 40.37 E
Gudbrandsdalen 114 Bf 61.30N 10.00 E
Gudenå 116 Dh 56.29N 10.13 E
Gudermes 136 Eg 43.22N 46.08 E
Gudivāda 148 Ge 16.27N 80.59 E
Gudiyāttam 148 Ff 12.57N 78.52 E
Gudou Shan 152 Jg 22.12N 112.57 E
Güdül 146 Eb 40.13N 32.15 E
Güdür 148 Ff 14.08N 79.51 E
Gudvangen 116 Bd 60.52N 6.50 E
Guebwiller 122 Ng 47.55N 7.12 E
Guéckédou 166 Cd 8.33N 10.09W
Guelma 162 Ib 36.28N 7.26 E
Guelma [3] 162 Ib 36.15N 7.30 E
Guelph 180 Jh 43.33N 80.15W
Guelta Zemmur 162 Ed 25.08N 12.22W
Guemar 162 Ic 33.29N 6.48 E
Guémené-Penfao 122 Eg 47.38N 1.50W
Guénange 124 Ie 49.18N 6.11 E
Guéné 166 Fc 11.44N 3.13 E
Guer 122 Dg 47.54N 2.07W
Güera 162 De 20.52N 17.03W
Guéra [3] 168 Bc 11.30N 18.30 E
Guéra, Massif de- 158 Ig 11.55N 18.12 E
Guérande 122 Dg 47.20N 2.26W
Guerara 162 Hc 32.48N 4.30 E
Guerche-sur-l'Aubois, La- 122 Ih 46.57N 2.57 E
Guercif 162 Gc 34.14N 3.22W
Guerdjoumane, Djebel- 126 Oh 36.25N 2.51 E
Güere, Rio- 196 Dh 9.50N 65.08W
Guéréda 166 Cc 14.31N 22.05 E
Guéret 122 Hh 46.10N 1.52 E
Guérin-Kouka 166 Fd 9.41N 0.37 E
Guernica y Luno / Gernika-Lumo 126 Ja 43.19N 2.41W
Guernsey 118 Kl 49.27N 2.35W
Guerrero 192 Ic 28.20N 100.26W
Guerrero [2] 190 De 17.40N 100.00W
Guessou-Sud 166 Fc 10.03N 2.38 E
Guest Peninsula 222 Mf 76.18S 148.00W
Guge 168 Fd 6.12N 37.30 E
Gügerd, Kūh-e- 146 Oe 34.50N 53.00 E
Guglionesi 128 Ii 41.55N 14.55 E
Guguan Island 208 Fc 17.19N 145.51 E
Guia 204 Db 15.22S 56.14W
Guia Lopes da Laguna 204 De 21.26S 56.07W
Guiana (EN) = Guyana [1] 200 Ke 5.00N 59.00W
Guiana Highlands (EN) = Guayana, Macizo de la- 198 Ke 5.00N 60.00W
Guiana Island 197d Bb 17.06N 61.44W
Guichi (Chizhou) 152 Ke 30.38N 117.29 E
Guichón 204 Dk 32.21S 57.12W
Guide 152 Hd 36.00N 101.30 E
Guider 166 Hd 9.56N 13.57 E
Guidimaka [3] 162 Ef 15.30N 12.00W
Guidimouni 166 Gc 13.42N 9.30 E
Guiding 152 If 26.33N 107.16 E
Guidong 152 Jf 26.11N 113.58 E
Guiers 122 Li 45.37N 5.37 E
Guiglo 166 Dd 6.33N 7.29W
Guiglo [3] 166 Dd 6.30N 7.40W
Guijá 172 Ed 24.29S 33.00 E
Güija, Lago de- 194 Cf 14.17N 89.34W
Gui Jiang 140 Ng 23.28N 111.18 E
Guijk en Sint Agatha 124 Hc 51.44N 5.52 E
Guijuelo 126 Gd 40.33N 5.40W
Guil 122 Mj 44.40N 6.36 E
Guildford 118 Mj 51.14N 0.35W
Guiler Gol 154 Ga 46.03N 122.06 E
Guilin 142 Ng 25.21N 110.15 E
Guillaume Delisle, Lac- 180 Je 56.25N 76.00W
Guillestre 122 Mj 44.40N 6.39 E
Guilvinec 122 Bg 47.47N 4.17W
Guimarães [Braz.] 202 Jd 2.08S 44.36W
Guimarães [Port.] 126 Dc 41.27N 8.18W
Guimaras 150 Hd 10.35N 122.37 E
Guinchos Cay 194 Hb 22.45N 78.06W
Guinea (EN) = Guinée [1] 160 Fg 11.00N 10.00W
Guinea, Gulf of- 158 Hh 2.00N 2.30 E
Guinea, Gulf of- (EN) = Guinée, Golfe de- 158 Hh 2.00N 2.30 E
Guinea Basin (EN) 106 Di 0.00 5.00W
Guinea-Bissau (EN) = Guiné-Bissau [1] 160 Fg 12.00N 15.00W
Guinea Ecuatorial = Equatorial Guinea (EN) [1] 160 Hh 2.00N 9.00 E
Guinea Rise (EN) 106 Dj 4.00S 0.00
Guiné-Bissau = Guinea-Bissau (EN) [1] 160 Fg 12.00N 15.00W
Guinée = Guinea (EN) [1] 160 Fg 11.00N 10.00W
Guinée, Kolfe de- = Guinea, Gulf of- (EN) 158 Hh 2.00N 2.30 E
Guinée Forestière [3] 166 Dd 8.40N 9.50W
Guinée Maritime [3] 166 Cc 10.00N 14.00W
Güines 190 Hd 22.50N 82.02W
Guînes 124 Dd 50.52N 1.52 E
Guingamp 122 Cf 48.33N 3.09W
Guinguinéo 166 Bc 14.16N 15.57W
Guiones, Punta- 194 Ei 9.54N 85.41W
Guiping 152 Ig 23.23N 110.00 E
Guipúzcoa [3] 126 Ja 43.10N 2.10W
Guir 162 Gc 30.29N 2.18W
Guir, Hamada du- 153 Ge 31.00N 3.20W
Güira de Melena 194 Fb 22.48N 82.30W
Guiratinga 202 Hg 16.21S 53.45W
Güiria 202 Fa 10.34N 62.18W
Guiscard 124 Fe 49.39N 3.03 E
Guise 122 Je 49.54N 3.38 E
Guitiriz 126 Ea 43.11N 7.54W
Guiuan 150 Id 11.02N 125.43 E
Guixi 152 Kf 28.18N 117.15 E
Guixian 152 Ig 23.10N 109.35 E
Guiyang 142 Mg 26.38N 106.43 E
Guizhou Sheng (Kuei-chou Sheng) = Kweichow (EN) [2] 152 If 27.00N 107.00 E
Gujan-Mestras 122 Ej 44.38N 1.04W
Gujarāt [3] 148 Ed 22.51N 71.30 E
Gujarāt 140 Jg 22.51N 71.30 E
Gujranwala 142 Jf 32.09N 74.11 E

Index Symbols

- [1] Independent Nation
- [2] State, Region
- [3] District, County
- [4] Municipality
- [5] Colony, Dependency
- Continent
- Physical Region
- Historical or Cultural Region
- Mount, Mountain
- Volcano
- Hill
- Mountains, Mountain Range
- Hills, Escarpment
- Plateau, Upland
- Pass, Gap
- Plain, Lowland
- Delta
- Salt Flat
- Valley, Canyon
- Crater, Cave
- Karst Features
- Depression
- Polder
- Desert, Dunes
- Forest, Woods
- Heath, Steppe
- Oasis
- Cape, Point
- Coast, Beach
- Cliff
- Peninsula
- Isthmus
- Sandbank
- Island
- Atoll
- Rock, Reef
- Islands, Archipelago
- Rocks, Reefs
- Coral Reef
- Well, Spring
- Geyser
- River, Stream
- Waterfall, Rapids
- River Mouth, Estuary
- Lake
- Salt Lake
- Intermittent Lake
- Reservoir
- Swamp, Pond
- Canal
- Glacier
- Ice Shelf, Pack Ice
- Ocean
- Sea
- Gulf, Bay
- Strait, Fjord
- Lagoon
- Bank
- Seamount
- Tablemount
- Ridge
- Shelf
- Basin
- Escarpment, Sea Scarp
- Fracture
- Trench, Abyss
- National Park, Reserve
- Point of Interest
- Recreation Site
- Cave, Cavern
- Historic Site
- Ruins
- Wall, Walls
- Church, Abbey
- Temple
- Scientific Station
- Railway station
- Airport
- Port
- Military installation
- Lighthouse
- Mine
- Tunnel
- Dam, Bridge

Gujrāt	148	Eb	32.34N	74.05 E
Gukovo	132	Ke	48.04N	39.58 E
Gulang	152	Hd	37.30N	102.54 E
Gulbarga	142	Jh	17.20N	76.50 E
Gulbene	136	Cd	57.12N	26.49 E
Gulča	136	Hg	40.19N	73.33 E
Gulf	204	Ad	19.08S	62.01W
Gulf Breeze	184	Dj	30.22N	87.07W
Gulf Coastal Plain (EN)	174	Jf	31.00N	92.00W
Gulfport	182	Je	30.22N	89.06W
Gulian	152	La	52.58N	122.09 E
Gulin	152	If	28.02N	105.47 E
Gulistan	136	Gg	40.30N	68.45 E
Guliya Shan	152	Lb	49.48N	122.25 E
Gulja	138	Hf	54.43N	121.03 E
Gulja/Yining	152	Dc	43.54N	81.21 E
Guljajpole	132	Jf	47.37N	36.18 E
Gulkana	178	Jd	62.16N	145.23W
Gulkeviči	132	Lg	45.19N	40.44 E
Gull Bay	186	Lb	49.47N	89.02W
Gulleråsen	116	Fc	61.04N	15.11 E
Gullfoss	114a	Bb	64.20N	20.08W
Gullkronafjärd	116	Jd	60.05N	22.15 E
Gull Lake	180	Gf	50.08N	108.27W
Gullringen	116	Fg	57.48N	15.42 E
Gull River	186	Lb	49.50N	89.04W
Gullspång	116	Ff	58.59N	14.06 E
Güllü	130	Mk	38.16N	29.07 E
Güllük	146	Bd	37.14N	27.36 E
Gülpinar	130	Jj	39.32N	26.07 E
Gülşehir	146	Fc	38.45N	34.38 E
Gulstav	116	Dj	54.43N	10.41 E
Gulu	160	Kh	2.47N	32.18 E
Guma /Pishan	152	Cd	37.38N	78.19 E
Gumbiri, Jabal-	168	Ee	4.18N	30.57 E
Gumel	166	Gc	12.38N	9.23 E
Gummersbach	120	De	51.02N	7.33 E
Gummi	166	Gc	12.09N	5.07 E
Gümüşçey	130	Ki	40.17N	27.17 E
Gümüşhacıköy	146	Fb	40.53N	35.14 E
Gümüşhane	144	Ea	40.27N	39.29 E
Gümüşsu	130	Nk	38.14N	30.01 E
Guna	148	Fd	24.19N	77.19 E
Guna	168	Fc	11.44N	38.15 E
Gundagai	212	Jg	35.04S	148.07 E
Gundji	170	Db	2.05N	21.27 E
Gündoğdu	130	Ki	40.15N	27.07 E
Gündoğmuş	146	Ed	36.48N	32.01 E
Güney	130	Mk	38.09N	29.05 E
Güney Doğu Toroslar	140	Gf	38.30N	41.00 E
Gungu	170	Cd	5.44S	19.19 E
Gunma Ken	154	Of	36.20N	139.05 E
Gunnar	180	Ge	59.23N	108.53W
Gunnbjørns Fjeld	224	Mc	68.55N	29.20W
Gunnedah	212	Kf	30.59S	150.15 E
Gunnison	182	Fd	38.33N	106.56W
Gunnison River	186	Bg	39.04N	108.33W
Gunt	135	Hf	37.30N	71.03 E
Guntakal	148	Fe	15.10N	77.23 E
Guntersville	184	Dh	34.21N	86.18W
Guntersville Lake	184	Dh	34.45N	86.03W
Guntūr	142	Kh	16.18N	80.27 E
Gunungapi, Pulau-	150	Ih	6.38S	126.40 E
Gunungsitoli	150	Cf	1.17N	97.37 E
Günz	120	Gh	48.27N	10.16 E
Günzburg	120	Gh	48.27N	10.16 E
Gunzenhausen	120	Gg	49.06N	10.45 E
Guo He	154	Dh	32.58N	117.13 E
Guojiadian	154	Hc	43.20N	124.37 E
Guoyang	154	Dh	33.31N	116.12 E
Guozhen	154	Bj	29.24N	113.09 E
Gurahonţ	130	Fc	46.16N	22.21 E
Gura Humorului	130	Ib	47.33N	25.54 E
Gurban Obo	152	Jc	43.06N	112.28 E
Gurbantünggüt Shamo	152	Eb	45.30N	87.30 E
Gurdžaani	132	Ni	41.43N	45.48 E
Güre	130	Mk	38.39N	29.10 E
Gurgei, Jabal-	168	Cc	13.50N	24.19 E
Gurghiului, Munţii-	130	Ic	46.41N	25.12 E
Gurgueia, Rio-	198	Lf	6.50S	43.24W
Guri → Raúl Leoni, Represa-	202	Fb	7.30N	63.00W
Gurjev	112	Lf	47.07N	51.56 E
Gurjevsk	138	Df	54.20N	86.00 E
Gurjevskaja oblast	136	Ff	47.30N	52.00 E
Gurk	128	Id	46.52N	14.18 E
Gurk	128	Id	46.36N	14.31 E
Gurktaler Alpen	128	Hd	46.55N	14.00 E
Guro	172	Ec	17.26S	33.20 E
Gürpınar	146	Jc	38.18N	43.25 E
Gurskoje	138	If	50.20N	138.05 E
Gurskøy	114	Ae	62.15N	5.40 E
Gürsu	130	Mi	40.13N	29.12 E
Gurué	172	Fc	15.28S	36.59 E
Gurumeti	170	Fc	2.05S	33.57 E
Gürün	146	Gc	38.43N	37.17 E
Gurupá	202	Hd	1.25S	51.39W
Gurupá, Ilha Grande do-	202	Hd	1.00S	51.30W
Gurupi	200	Lg	11.43S	49.04W
Gurupi, Rio-	198	Lf	1.13S	46.06W
Gurupi, Serra do-	202	Id	5.00S	47.30W
Guru Sikhar	148	Ed	24.39N	72.46 E
Gus	114	Ji	55.00N	41.12 E
Gusau	160	Hg	12.10N	6.40 E
Gusev	136	Ce	54.37N	22.12 E
Gushan	154	Ge	39.54N	123.36 E
Gushi	152	Ke	32.02N	115.39 E
Gushikawa	156b	Ab	26.21N	127.52 E
Gūshk	146	Ph	28.13N	55.52 E
Gus-Hrustalny	114	Ji	55.38N	40.40 E
Gusinaja, guba-	138	Kb	72.00N	150.00 E
Gusinaja Zemlja, poluostrov-	136	Fa	71.50N	52.00 E
Gusinje	130	Cg	42.34N	19.50 E
Gusinoozersk	138	Ff	51.17N	106.30 E
Guspini	128	Ck	39.32N	8.37 E
Güssing	128	Kc	47.04N	16.20 E
Gustav Holm, Kap-	179	Ie	66.45N	34.00W
Gustavia	197b	Bc	17.54N	62.52W
Gustavs/Kustavi	116	Id	60.33N	21.21 E
Gustavs/Kustavi	116	Id	60.30N	21.25 E
Gustavsfors	116	Ee	59.12N	12.06 E
Gustavus	178	Le	58.25N	135.44W
Güstrow	120	Ic	53.48N	12.10 E
Gusum	116	Gf	58.16N	16.29 E
Gütersloh	120	Ee	51.54N	8.23 E
Guthrie [Ok.-U.S.]	186	Hi	35.53N	97.25W
Guthrie [Tx.-U.S.]	186	Fj	33.37N	100.19W
Gutian	152	Kf	26.40N	118.42 E
Gutiérrez Zamora	192	Kg	20.27N	97.05W
Gutii, Vîrful-	130	Gb	47.42N	23.52 E
Guting → Yutai	154	Dg	35.00N	116.40 E
Gutu	172	Ec	19.39S	31.10 E
Guwāhāti	142	Lg	26.11N	91.44 E
Guyana = Guiana (EN)	200	Ke	5.00N	59.00W
Guyane Française = French Guiana (EN)	200	Ke	4.00N	53.00W
Guyang	152	Jc	41.02N	110.04 E
Guyenne	122	Gj	44.35N	1.00 E
Guymon	182	Gd	36.41N	101.29W
Guyonneau, Anse-	197e	Ab	16.14N	61.47W
Guyuan	152	Id	36.01N	106.17 E
Guyuan (Pingdingbu)	154	Cd	41.40N	115.41 E
Guzar	135	Fe	38.37N	66.18 E
Güzelyurt	146	Ee	35.12N	32.59 E
Güzelyurt Körfezi	146	Ee	35.15N	32.50 E
Gūzhān	146	Le	34.20N	46.57 E
Guzhen	154	Dh	33.20N	117.19 E
Guzhou → Rongjiang	152	If	25.58N	108.30 E
Guzmán, Laguna de-	192	Fb	31.20N	107.30W
Gvardejsk	114	Ei	54.40N	21.03 E
Gvardejskoje	132	Hg	45.06N	33.59 E
Gvary	116	Ce	59.23N	9.09 E
Gwa	148	Ie	17.36N	94.35 E
Gwadabawa	166	Gc	13.22N	5.14 E
Gwādar	142	Ig	25.07N	62.19 E
Gwai	172	Dc	19.17S	27.39 E
Gwai	158	Jj	17.59S	26.52 E
Gwalior	142	Jg	26.13N	78.10 E
Gwanda	172	Dd	20.56S	29.00 E
Gwane	170	Eb	4.43N	25.50 E
Gwda	120	Mc	53.04N	16.44 E
Gweebarra Bay/Béal an Bheara	118	Eg	54.52N	8.20W
Gwent	118	Kj	51.45N	2.55W
Gweru	160	Jj	19.27S	29.49 E
Gweta	172	Dd	20.13S	25.14 E
Gwydir River	212	Je	29.27S	149.48 E
Gwynedd	118	Ji	52.50N	3.50W
Gyaca	152	Ff	29.09N	92.38 E
Gya'gya → Saga	152	Ef	29.22N	85.15 E
Gyai Qu	152	Fe	31.30N	94.40 E
Gyaisi/Jiulong	152	Hf	28.58N	101.33 E
Gya La	152	Df	28.42N	84.35 E
Gyala Shankou	152	Df	28.42N	84.35 E
Gyangzê	152	Ef	29.00N	89.38 E
Gyaring Co	152	Ee	31.10N	88.15 E
Gyaring Hu	152	Ge	34.55N	98.00 E
Gyda	138	Cb	70.52N	78.30 E
Gydanskaja guba	138	Cb	71.20N	76.30 E
Gydanski poluostrov = Gyda Peninsula (EN)	140	Jb	70.50N	79.00 E
Gyda Peninsula (EN) = Gydanski poluostrov	140	Jb	70.50N	79.00 E
Gyigang → Zayü	152	Gf	28.43N	97.25 E
Gyirong (Zongga)	152	Ef	28.57N	85.12 E
Gyldenløves Fjord	179	Hf	64.10N	40.30W
Gyldenløves Høj	116	Di	55.33N	11.52 E
Gympie	210	Gg	26.11S	152.40 E
Gyoma	120	Qj	46.56N	20.50 E
Gyöngyös	120	Pi	47.47N	19.56 E
Győr	112	Hf	47.41N	17.38 E
Győr	120	Ni	47.40N	17.39 E
Győr-Sopron	120	Ni	47.40N	17.15 E
Gypsumville	180	Hf	51.45N	98.35W
Gysinge	116	Gd	60.17N	16.53 E
Gyttorp	116	Fe	59.31N	14.58 E
Gyula	120	Rj	46.39N	21.17 E

H

Haacht	124	Gd	50.59N	4.38 E
Häädemeeste/Hjademeste	116	Kf	58.00N	24.28 E
Ha'afeva	221b	Ba	19.57S	174.43W
Haafusia	220h	Bb	13.18S	176.09W
Haag, Mount-	222	Qf	77.40S	79.00W
Haaksbergen	124	Ib	52.09N	6.45 E
Haamstede, Westerschouwen-	124	Fc	51.42N	3.45 E
Haanja Kõrgustik	116	Lg	57.30N	27.30 E
Ha'ano	221b	Ba	19.40S	174.17W
Ha'apai Group	208	Jf	19.47S	174.27W
Haapajärvi	114	Fe	63.45N	25.20 E
Haapamäki	116	Kb	62.15N	24.28 E
Haapasaari	116	Ld	60.15N	27.10 E
Haapaselkä [Fin.]	116	Mb	62.10N	28.10 E
Haapaselkä [Fin.]	116	Mc	61.35N	28.15 E
Haapiti	221e	Fc	17.34S	149.52W
Haapsalu	136	Cd	58.57N	23.32 E
Ha'arava	146	Fg	30.58N	32.24 E
Haardt	120	Dg	49.15N	8.00 E
Haardtkopf	124	Je	49.51N	7.04 E
Haaren, Wünnenberg-	124	Kc	51.34N	8.44 E
Haarlem	122	Kb	52.23N	4.38 E
Haarlemmermeer	124	Gb	52.20N	4.41 E
Haarlerberg	124	Ib	52.20N	6.25 E
Haarstrang	124	Kc	51.30N	8.20 E
Haast	210	Hi	43.52S	169.01 E
Haast Pass	218	Cf	44.06S	169.21 E
Habahe/Kaba	152	Eb	47.53N	86.12 E
Habarovsk	142	Pe	48.27N	135.06 E
Habarovski kraj	138	If	53.00N	137.00 E
Ḩabarūt	144	Hf	17.22N	52.42 E
Ḩabashīyah, Jabal-	168	Ib	16.45N	50.05 E
Habaswein	170	Gb	1.01N	39.29 E
Habay [Alta.-Can.]	180	Fe	58.52N	118.45W
Habay [Bel.]	124	He	49.45N	5.38 E
Habay [Som.]	168	Ge	1.08N	43.46 E
Ḩabbān	168	Hc	14.21N	47.05 E
Ḩābbānīyah	146	Jf	33.22N	43.35 E
Ḩabbānīyah, Hawr al-	146	Jf	33.17N	43.29 E
Habbārīyah, Bi'r al-	146	Jf	32.17N	42.12 E
Habibas, Iles-	126	Ki	35.44N	1.08W
Habichtswald	120	Fe	51.20N	9.25 E
Habo	116	Fg	57.55N	14.04 E
Haboro	152	Pc	44.22N	141.42 E
Ḩabshān	146	Ok	23.50N	53.37 E
Hache	120	Ec	53.05N	8.50 E
Hachenburg	124	Jd	50.39N	7.50 E
Hachijō	156	Fe	35.15N	139.45 E
Hachijō-Fuji	156	Fe	33.08N	139.46 E
Hachijō-Jima	152	Oe	33.05N	139.50 E
Hachiman	156	Ed	35.46N	136.57 E
Hachimori	156	Fa	40.22N	140.00 E
Hachinohe	142	Qe	40.30N	141.29 E
Hachiōji	156	Fd	35.39N	139.18 E
Hachiro-Gata	156	Fa	40.00N	140.00 E
Hacibey De	146	Kd	36.58N	44.18 E
Hackås	114	De	62.55N	14.31 E
Håckren	116	Ea	63.10N	13.35 E
Hačmas	136	Eg	41.25N	48.52 E
Hadagang	154	Kb	45.24N	131.12 E
Hadamar	124	Kd	50.27N	8.03 E
Ḩaḑan, Ḩarrat-	164	He	21.30N	41.23 E
Hadano	156	Fd	35.22N	139.14 E
Ḩadāribah, Ra's al-	168	Fa	22.04N	36.54 E
HaDarom	146	Fg	30.40N	34.50 E
Hadd, Ra's al-	140	Hg	22.32N	59.59 E
Haddad	158	Ig	14.40N	18.46 E
Ḩadded	168	Hc	10.10N	48.28 E
Haddington	118	Kf	55.58N	2.47W
Haddummati Atoll	148a	Bb	1.45N	73.30 E
Hadejia	166	Hc	12.27N	10.03 E
Hadejia	166	Hc	12.50N	10.51 E
Hadeland	116	Dd	60.25N	10.35 E
Hadeln	120	Ec	53.45N	8.45 E
Hadera	146	Ff	32.26N	34.55 E
Haderslev	114	Bi	55.15N	9.30 E
Hadīboh	144	Hg	12.39N	54.02 E
Hadım	146	Ed	36.59N	32.28 E
Hadimköy	146	Cb	41.09N	28.37 E
Ḩadīyah	144	Ed	25.34N	38.41 E
Hadjer el Hamis	168	Ac	12.51N	14.50 E
Hadjout	126	Oh	36.31N	2.25 E
Hadleigh	124	Cb	52.03N	0.56 E
Hadley Bay	180	Gb	72.30N	108.30W
Ha Dong	148	Ld	20.58N	105.46 E
Ḩaḑramawt	140	Gh	15.00N	50.00 E
Hadrian's Wall	118	Kg	54.59N	2.26W
Hadsten	116	Dh	56.20N	10.03 E
Hadsund	116	Dh	56.43N	10.07 E
Hadytajaha	134	Nc	66.57N	69.12 E
Hadyžensk	132	Kg	44.25N	39.31 E
Hadzibeisui liman	130	Nc	46.40N	30.30 E
Haedo, Cuchilla de-	204	Dj	31.40S	56.18W
Haeju	154	He	38.02N	125.42 E
Haena	214	Oc	22.13N	159.34W
Ḩafar al 'Atk	146	Lj	25.56N	46.47 E
Ḩafar al Bātin	144	Gd	28.27N	46.00 E
Haffner Bjerg	179	Fc	76.30N	63.00W
Ḩaffūz	128	Do	35.38N	9.40 E
Hafik	146	Gc	39.52N	37.24 E
Ḩafīrat al 'Aydā	144	Ed	26.26N	39.12 E
Ḩafīt	146	Pk	23.59N	55.49 E
Ḩafīt, Jabal-	146	Pj	24.03N	55.46 E
Hafnarfjörður	114a	Bb	64.04N	21.57W
Haft Gel	146	Mg	31.27N	49.27 E
Hāfūn	168	Ic	10.10N	51.05 E
Hāfūn, Rās- = Hafun, Ras-(EN)	158	Mg	10.27N	51.24 E
Hafun, Ras-(EN) = Hāfūn, Rās-	158	Mg	10.27N	51.24 E
Hāfūn Bay North	168	Ic	10.37N	51.15 E
Hāfūn Bay South	168	Ic	10.15N	51.05 E
Hagadera	170	Hb	0.02N	40.17 E
Hagby	116	Gh	56.33N	16.10 E
Hageland	124	Gd	50.55N	4.45 E
Hagemeister	178	Ge	58.40N	161.00W
Hagen	120	De	51.21N	7.28 E
Hagenow	120	Hc	53.26N	11.12 E
Hagere Hiywet	168	Fd	8.58N	37.53 E
Hagerman	188	He	42.49N	114.54W
Hagerstown	182	Ld	39.39N	77.43W
Hagetmau	122	Fk	43.40N	0.35W
Hagfors	114	Cf	60.02N	13.42 E
Häggenås	116	Fa	63.24N	14.55 E
Hagi	154	Kg	34.24N	131.25 E
Ha Giang	148	Kd	22.50N	104.59 E
Hagman, Puntan-	220b	Ba	15.09N	145.48 E
Hagondange	122	Me	49.15N	6.10 E
Hags Head/Ceanna Caillighe	118	Di	52.57N	9.28W
Hague, Cap de la-	110	Ff	49.43N	1.57W
Haguenau	122	Nf	48.49N	7.47 E
Hagunia	162	Ed	27.26N	12.24W
Hahajima-Rettō	214	Cb	26.37N	142.10 E
Hahns Peak	186	Cf	40.56N	107.01W
Hahót	120	Mj	46.38N	16.56 E
Hai'an	154	Fh	32.33N	120.26 E
Haicheng	152	Lc	40.51N	122.43 E
Haidenaab	120	Ig	49.35N	12.08 E
Hai Duong	148	Ld	20.56N	106.19 E
Haifa (EN) = Ḩefa	142	Ff	32.50N	35.00 E
Haifeng	152	Kg	22.58N	115.21 E
Haiger	124	Kd	50.45N	8.13 E
Hai He	154	De	38.57N	117.43 E
Haikakan Sovetakan Socialistakan Respublika/Armjanskaja SSR	136	Eg	40.00N	45.00 E
Haikang (Leizhou)	152	Jg	20.56N	110.06 E
Haikou	142	Ng	20.05N	110.20 E
Ḩā'il	142	Gg	27.33N	41.42 E
Hailang He	154	Jb	44.33N	129.33 E
Hailar	142	Ne	49.14N	119.42 E
Hailar He	140	Ne	49.30N	117.50 E
Hailin	152	Mc	44.35N	129.22 E
Hailong (Meihekou)	152	Mc	42.32N	125.37 E
Hailsham	124	Cd	50.52N	0.16 E
Hailun	152	Mb	47.29N	126.55 E
Hailuoto/Karlö	110	Ib	65.02N	24.42 E
Haima Tan	150	Gd	10.52N	116.53 E
Haimen [China]	154	Fi	31.53N	121.10 E
Haimen [China]	154	Fj	28.40N	121.27 E
Haina	124	Kc	51.03N	8.56 E
Hainan Dao	140	Mh	19.00N	109.00 E
Hainaut	124	Fd	50.30N	4.00 E
Hainaut	122	Jd	50.20N	3.50 E
Hainburg an der Donau	128	Kb	48.09N	16.56 E
Haines	176	Fd	59.14N	135.27W
Haines Junction	180	Dd	60.45N	137.30W
Hainich	120	Ge	51.05N	10.27 E
Hainleite	120	Ge	51.20N	10.48 E
Hai Phong	142	Mg	20.52N	106.41 E
Haïti = Haiti (EN)	176	Lh	19.00N	72.25W
Haiti (EN) = Haïti	176	Lh	19.00N	72.25W
Haixing (Suji)	154	De	38.10N	117.29 E
Haixin Shan	152	Hd	37.00N	100.03 E
Haiyan (Sanjiaocheng)	152	Hd	36.58N	100.50 E
Haiyan (Wuyuanzhen)	154	Fi	30.31N	120.56 E
Haiyang (Dongoun)	154	Ff	36.46N	121.09 E
Haiyang Dao	154	Ge	39.03N	123.12 E
Haiyou → Sanmen	152	Lf	29.08N	121.22 E
Haiyuan	152	Id	36.35N	105.40 E
Haizhou	154	Eg	34.34N	119.08 E
Haizhou Wan	140	Nf	35.00N	119.30 E
Ḩajar Banga	168	Cc	11.30N	23.00 E
Hajdarken	136	Hh	39.55N	71.24 E
Hajdú-Bihar	120	Ri	47.25N	21.30 E
Hajdúböszörmény	120	Ri	47.40N	21.31 E
Hajdúdorog	120	Ri	47.49N	21.30 E
Hajdúhadház	120	Ri	47.41N	21.40 E
Hajdúnánás	120	Ri	47.51N	21.26 E
Hajdúság	120	Ri	47.35N	21.30 E
Hajdúszoboszló	120	Ri	47.27N	21.24 E
Hajihi-Zaki	156	Fb	38.19N	138.31 E
Ḩājjīābād [Iran]	146	Ph	28.21N	54.27 E
Ḩājjīābād [Iran]	146	Ph	28.19N	55.55 E
Ḩājjīābād-e Māsīleh	146	Ne	34.49N	51.13 E
Hajla	130	Dg	42.43N	20.10 E
Hajnówka	120	Td	52.45N	23.36 E
Hajós	120	Pj	46.24N	19.07 E
Hajpudyrskaja guba	134	Ib	68.40N	59.30 E
Hakase-Yama	156	Fc	37.22N	139.43 E
Hakasskaja avtonomnaja oblast	138	Df	53.30N	90.00 E
Hakata-Wan	156	Be	33.40N	130.20 E
Hakefjord	116	Dg	57.41N	11.44 E
Hakha	148	Id	22.39N	93.37 E
Hakkâri	144	Fb	37.34N	43.45 E
Hakken-Zan	156	Dd	34.10N	135.54 E
Hakkōda San	156	Ga	40.40N	140.53 E
Hako-Dake	156a	Ca	44.40N	142.25 E
Hakodate	142	Qe	41.45N	140.43 E
Hakone-Yama	156	Fd	35.13N	139.00 E
Hakui	154	Nf	36.53N	136.47 E
Hakupu	220k	Bb	19.06S	169.50W
Haku-San	156	Ec	36.09N	136.45 E
Hal/Halle	122	Kd	50.44N	4.14 E
Halab	146	Md	36.17N	48.03 E
Ḩalab = Aleppo (EN)	142	Ff	36.12N	37.10 E
Ḩalabjah	146	Ke	35.10N	45.59 E
Halač	136	Gh	39.04N	64.53 E
Halachó	192	Ng	20.29N	90.05W
Halahei	154	Ga	46.11N	122.46 E
Ḩalā'ib	160	Kf	22.13N	36.38 E
Halalii Lake	221a	Ab	21.52N	160.11W
Halangingie Point	220k	Bb	19.03S	169.58W
Hålaveden	116	Ff	58.05N	14.45 E
Halawa	221a	Eb	21.10N	156.44W
Halawa, Cape-	221a	Eb	21.10N	156.43W
Ḩalbā	146	Ge	34.33N	36.05 E
Halberstadt	120	He	51.54N	11.03 E
Halcon, Mount-	150	Hd	13.16N	121.00 E
Haldean-Sogotyn-Daba	152	Gb	49.05N	97.55 E
Halden	114	Cg	59.09N	11.23 E
Haldensleben	120	Hd	52.18N	11.25 E
Haldia	148	Hd	22.08N	88.05 E
Haldwani	148	Fc	29.13N	79.31 E
Hale, Mount-	212	De	26.00S	117.10 E
Haleakala Crater	221a	Ec	20.43N	156.12W
Haleiwa	221a	Cb	21.36N	158.06W
Halemaumau	221a	Fd	19.24N	155.17W
Hale River	212	Hd	24.56S	135.53 E
Halesworth	124	Db	52.21N	1.30 E
Haleyville	184	Dh	34.14N	87.37W
Ḩalfā al Gadida	160	Kg	15.19N	35.34 E
Half Assini	166	Ed	5.03N	2.53W
Halfeti	146	Gd	37.15N	37.52 E
Halfway	180	Fe	56.13N	121.26W
Halh-Gol	152	Kb	48.01N	118.10 E
Ḩalī	168	Gb	18.38N	41.22 E
Haliburton	184	Hc	45.03N	78.33W
Halifax	176	Me	44.39N	63.36W
Halifax, Mount-	212	Jc	19.05S	146.20 E
Halifax Bay	212	Jc	18.50S	146.30 E
Hālil	144	Id	27.28N	58.44 E
Halīleh, Ra's-e-	146	Nh	28.46N	50.56 E
Halilovo	132	Ud	51.27N	58.10 E
Ḩalin	168	Hd	9.08N	48.47 E
Haliut → Urad Zhonghou Lianheqi	152	Ic	41.34N	108.32 E
Haljala	116	Le	59.22N	26.09 E
Haljasavej	138	Cd	63.20N	78.30 E
Hall	178	Ed	60.40N	173.05W
Halladale	118	Jc	58.30N	3.50W
Hallam Peak	188	Fa	52.11N	118.46W
Halland	114	Ch	56.45N	13.00 E
Halland	116	Eh	57.00N	12.45 E
Hallandsås	116	Eh	56.23N	13.00 E
Halla-san	154	Ih	33.22N	126.32 E
Ḩallat 'Ammār	146	Gh	29.08N	36.02 E
Hall Beach	180	Jc	68.10N	81.56W
Halle	120	He	51.30N	12.00 E
Halle/Hal	122	Kd	50.44N	4.14 E
Halle (Westfalen)	124	Kb	52.05N	8.22 E
Halleberg	116	Ef	58.23N	12.25 E
Hällefors	116	Fe	59.47N	14.30 E
Hälleforsnäs	116	Ge	59.10N	16.30 E
Hallein	128	Hc	47.41N	13.06 E
Hällekis	116	Ef	58.38N	13.25 E
Hallen	114	De	63.11N	14.05 E
Hallenberg	124	Kc	51.07N	8.38 E
Hallencourt	124	De	49.59N	1.53 E
Halle-Neustadt	120	He	51.31N	11.53 E
Hallertau	120	Hh	48.35N	11.50 E
Hällestad	116	Ff	58.44N	15.34 E
Hallettsville	186	Hl	29.27N	96.57W
Halley Bay	222	Af	75.31S	26.38W
Halli	116	Kc	61.52N	24.50 E
Hallie-Jackson Bank (EN)	219c	Ba	9.45S	166.10 E
Halligen	120	Eb	54.35N	8.35 E
Hallingdal	114	Bf	60.40N	9.15 E
Hallingdalselva	116	Cd	60.23N	9.35 E
Hallingskarvet	110	Gc	60.37N	7.45 E
Hall in Tirol (Solbad Hall in Tirol)	128	Fc	47.17N	11.31 E
Hall Islands	208	Gd	8.37N	152.00 E
Halliste jõgi	116	Kf	58.23N	24.25 E
Hall Lake	180	Jc	68.40N	82.20W
Hall Land	179	Fb	81.12N	61.10W
Hallock	186	Hb	48.47N	96.57W
Hall Peninsula	174	Mc	63.30N	66.00W
Hallsberg	114	Dg	59.04N	15.07 E
Halls Creek	210	Df	18.13S	127.40 E
Hallstahammar	114	Dg	59.37N	16.13 E
Hallstatt	128	Hc	47.33N	13.39 E
Hallstavik	114	Ef	60.03N	18.36 E
Halluin	124	Fd	50.47N	3.08 E
Halmahera	208	Dd	1.00N	128.00 E
Halmahera, Laut- = Halmahera Sea (EN)	208	De	1.00S	129.00 E
Halmahera Sea (EN) = Halmahera, Laut-	208	De	1.00S	129.00 E
Halmer-Ju	136	Gb	67.58N	64.40 E
Halmeu	130	Gb	47.58N	23.01 E
Halmstad	112	Hd	56.39N	12.50 E
Haloze	128	Jd	46.20N	15.50 E
Ḩalq al Wādī	162	Jb	36.49N	10.18 E
Hals	114	Ch	57.00N	10.19 E
Hälsingland	116	Gc	61.30N	17.00 E
Halsön	116	Ib	62.50N	21.10 E
Halstead	124	Cc	51.57N	0.38 E
Halsteren	124	Gc	51.32N	4.16 E
Haltang He	152	Fd	39.00N	94.40 E
Halten Bank (EN)	114	Bd	64.45N	8.45 E
Haltern	124	Jc	51.44N	7.11 E
Haltiatunturi	114	Eb	69.18N	21.16 E
Haltom City	186	Hj	32.48N	97.16W
Halturin	136	Ed	58.35N	48.55 E
Hālūl	146	Oj	25.40N	52.25 E
Halver	124	Jc	51.12N	7.29 E
Ham	122	Je	49.45N	3.04 E
Ham, Roches de-	124	Ae	49.02N	1.02W
Hamada	156	Cd	34.53N	132.03 E
Hamadān	142	Gf	34.48N	48.30 E
Hamadān	144	Gb	35.00N	48.40 E
Hamadia	126	Ni	35.28N	1.52 E
Hamaguir	162	Gc	30.54N	3.02W
Ḩamāh	144	Eb	35.08N	36.45 E
Hamakita	156	Ed	34.49N	137.45 E
Hamamasu	156a	Bb	43.36N	141.21 E
Hamamatsu	152	Oe	34.42N	137.44 E
Hamanaka	156a	Db	43.05N	145.05 E
Hamanaka-Wan	156a	Db	43.07N	145.10 E
Hamana-Ko	156	Ed	34.45N	137.34 E
Hamanen, Oued el-	162	Hd	25.52N	1.26 E
Hamaoka	156	Fd	34.39N	138.07 E
Hamar	112	Hc	60.48N	11.06 E
Hamar-Daban, hrebet-	138	Ff	51.10N	105.00 E
Hamasaka	156	Dd	35.38N	134.27 E
Ḩamāţah, Jabal-	164	Ge	24.12N	35.00 E
Hamatonbetsu	154	Qb	45.07N	142.23 E
Hambantota	148	Gg	6.10N	81.07 E
Hambre, Cayos del-	194	Fb	22.15N	82.47W
Hamburg	120	Fc	53.35N	10.00 E
Hamburg [Ger.]	112	Ge	53.33N	10.00 E
Hamburg [S.Afr.]	172	Df	33.18S	27.28 E
Hamburg-Altona	120	Fc	53.33N	9.57 E
Hamburg-Harburg	120	Fc	53.28N	10.00 E
Hamburgsund	116	Df	58.33N	11.16 E
Ḩamḑ, Wādī al-	140	Fg	25.58N	36.42 E
Ḩamḑah	164	Hf	19.02N	43.36 E
Häme	114	Ff	61.30N	24.30 E
Häme	116	Kc	61.30N	25.30 E
Hämeenkangas	116	Jc	61.45N	22.40 E
Hämeenlinna/Tavastehus	114	Ff	61.00N	24.27 E
Hämeenselkä	116	Kb	62.30N	25.00 E
Hamelin Pool	212	Ce	26.15S	114.05 E
Hameln	120	Fd	52.06N	9.21 E
HaMerkaz	146	Fg	32.05N	34.55 E
Hamero Hadad	168	Gd	7.28N	42.13 E
Hamersley Range	212	Dd	21.55S	116.45 E
Hamgyŏng-Namdo	154	Id	40.00N	127.30 E
Hamgyŏng-Pukto	154	Jd	41.45N	129.50 E
Hamgyŏng-Sanmaek	154	Jd	41.00N	128.45 E
Hamhŭng	142	Of	39.54N	127.32 E
Hami/Kumul	142	Le	42.48N	93.27 E
Ḩamīdīyeh	146	Mg	31.29N	48.26 E
Hamilton [Austl.]	212	Ig	37.45S	142.02 E
Hamilton [Ber.]	176	Mf	32.17N	64.46W
Hamilton [Mt.-U.S.]	182	Eb	46.15N	114.09W
Hamilton [N.Z.]	210	Ih	37.47S	175.17 E
Hamilton [Oh.-U.S.]	182	Kd	39.23N	84.33W
Hamilton [Ont.-Can.]	176	Le	43.15N	79.51W
Hamilton [Scot.-U.K.]	118	If	55.47N	4.03W
Hamilton [Tx.-U.S.]	186	Gk	31.42N	98.07W

Index Symbols

- 1 Independent Nation
- 2 State, Region
- 3 District, County
- 4 Municipality
- 5 Colony, Dependency
- Continent
- Physical Region
- Historical or Cultural Region
- Mount, Mountain
- Volcano
- Hill
- Mountains, Mountain Range
- Hills, Escarpment
- Plateau, Upland
- Pass, Gap
- Plain, Lowland
- Delta
- Salt Flat
- Valley, Canyon
- Crater, Cave
- Karst Features
- Depression
- Polder
- Desert, Dunes
- Forest, Woods
- Heath, Steppe
- Oasis
- Cape, Point
- Coast, Beach
- Cliff
- Peninsula
- Isthmus
- Sandbank
- Island
- Atoll
- Rock, Reef
- Islands, Archipelago
- Rocks, Reefs
- Coral Reef
- Well, Spring
- Geyser
- River, Stream
- Waterfall, Rapids
- River Mouth, Estuary
- Lake
- Salt Lake
- Intermittent Lake
- Reservoir
- Swamp, Pond
- Canal
- Glacier
- Ice Shelf, Pack Ice
- Ocean
- Sea
- Gulf, Bay
- Strait, Fjord
- Lagoon
- Bank
- Seamount
- Tablemount
- Ridge
- Shelf
- Basin
- Escarpment, Sea Scarp
- Fracture
- Trench, Abyss
- National Park, Reserve
- Point of Interest
- Recreation Site
- Cave, Cavern
- Historic Site
- Ruins
- Wall, Walls
- Church, Abbey
- Temple
- Scientific Station
- Railway station
- Airport
- Port
- Military installation
- Lighthouse
- Mine
- Tunnel
- Dam, Bridge

Hamilton, Lake-	186	Ji	34.30N	93.05W
Hamilton, Mount-	188	Hg	39.14N	115.32W
Hamilton River	212	Hd	23.30S	139.47 E
Hamīn, Wādī al-	164	Dc	30.28N	22.00 E
Hamina/Fredrikshamn	114	Gf	60.34N	27.12 E
Hamm	120	De	51.41N	7.48 E
Ḥammām al 'Alīl	146	Jd	36.10N	43.16 E
Ḥammām al Anf	162	Jb	36.44N	10.20 E
Ḥammāmāt	162	Jb	36.24N	10.37 E
Ḥammāmāt, Khalīj-	162	Jb	36.05N	10.40 E
Hammam Bou Hadjar	126	Li	35.23N	0.58W
Hammami	158	Ff	23.03N	11.30W
Hammam Righa	126	Oh	36.23N	2.24 E
Hammār, Hawr al-	144	Gc	30.50N	47.10 E
Hammarstrand	116	Ga	63.06N	16.21 E
Hamme	124	Gc	51.06N	4.08 E
Hammelburg	120	Ff	50.07N	9.54 E
Hammerdal	114	De	63.36N	15.21 E
Hammeren	116	Fi	55.18N	14.47 E
Hammerfest	112	Ia	70.40N	23.45 E
Hamminkeln	124	Ic	51.44N	6.35 E
Hamminkeln-Dingden	124	Ic	51.46N	6.37 E
Hammond [In.-U.S.]	184	De	41.36N	87.30W
Hammond [La.-U.S.]	182	Ie	30.30N	90.28W
Hammonton	184	Jf	39.38N	74.48W
Hamont, Hamont-Achel-	124	Hc	51.15N	5.33 E
Hamont-Achel	124	Hc	51.15N	5.33 E
Hamont-Achel-Hamont	124	Hc	51.15N	5.33 E
Hamoyet, Jabal-	158	Kg	17.33N	38.02 E
Hampden	218	Df	45.20S	170.49 E
Hampshire [3]	118	Lk	51.00N	1.10W
Hampshire Downs	118	Lj	51.15N	1.15W
Hampton [Ia.-U.S.]	186	Je	42.45N	93.12W
Hampton [Va.-U.S.]	184	Ig	37.02N	76.23W
Hampton Butte	188	Ee	43.46N	120.17W
Hamp'yong	154	Ig	35.04N	126.31 E
Ḥamrā'	168	Dc	10.54N	29.54 E
Hamra [R.S.F.S.R.]	138	Gd	60.17N	114.10 E
Hamra [Swe.]	116	Fc	61.39N	15.00 E
Ḥamrā', Al Ḥamādah al-	158	If	29.30N	12.00 E
Hamra, Saguia el-	158	Ff	27.24N	13.43W
Hamrān	146	Kd	36.22N	45.44 E
Ḥamrat ash Shaykh	168	Dc	14.35N	27.58 E
Ḥamrīn, Jabal-	146	Ke	34.30N	44.30 E
Hāmūn-e Hirmand, Daryācheh-ye-	144	Jc	31.30N	61.20 E
Han	166	Ec	10.41N	2.27W
Hana	214	Oc	20.45N	155.59W
Hanahan	184	Hi	32.55N	80.00W
Hanaizum	156	Gb	38.51N	141.12 E
Ḥanak	144	Ed	25.33N	36.56 E
Hanalei	221a	Ba	22.13N	159.30W
Hanamaki	154	Pe	39.23N	141.07 E
Hanang	158	Ki	4.26S	35.24 E
Hanaoka	156	Ga	40.21N	140.34 E
Hanapepe	221a	Bb	21.55N	159.35W
Hanau	120	Ef	50.08N	8.55 E
Han-Bogdo	152	Ic	43.12N	107.10 E
Hanceville	180	Ff	51.55N	123.02W
Hancheng	152	Jd	35.30N	110.25 E
Hanchuan	154	Bi	30.39N	113.46 E
Hancock	184	Cb	47.07N	88.35W
Handa	156	Ed	34.53N	136.56 E
Handan	142	Nf	36.35N	114.28 E
Handen	116	He	59.10N	18.08 E
Handeni	170	Gd	5.26S	38.01 E
Handlová	120	Oh	48.44N	18.46 E
Handöl	116	Ea	63.16N	12.26 E
Handyga	142	Pc	62.40N	135.36 E
Hănegev=Negev Desert (EN)	146	Fg	30.30N	34.55 E
Hanford	188	Fh	36.20N	119.39W
Han-gang	152	Md	37.45N	126.11 E
Hanga Roa	221d	Ab	27.09S	109.26W
Hang'bu He	154	Di	31.33N	117.05 E
Hanggin Houqi (Xamba)	152	Ic	40.59N	107.07 E
Hanggin Qi (Xin Zhen)	152	Id	39.54N	108.55 E
Hangö/Hanko	114	Fg	59.50N	22.57 E
Hangöudde/Hankoniemi	116	Je	59.50N	23.10 E
Hangu	154	De	39.16N	117.50 E
Hangzhou	142	Of	30.18N	120.11 E
Hangzhou Wan	154	Fi	30.25N	121.00 E
Ḥanīsh	164	Hg	13.45N	42.45 E
Ḥanīsh al Kabīr, Jazīrat al-	164	Hg	13.43N	42.45 E
Hanja, vozvyšennost-	116	Lg	57.30N	27.30 E
Ḥanjūrah, Ra's-	146	Pj	24.44N	54.39 E
Hanka, ozero- = Khanka, Lake- (EN)	140	Pe	45.00N	132.24 E
Hankasalmi	116	Lb	62.23N	26.26 E
Hankensbüttel	120	Gd	52.44N	10.36 E
Hanko/Hangö	114	Fg	59.50N	22.57 E
Hankoniemi/Hangöudde	116	Je	59.50N	23.10 E
Hankou, Wuhan-	154	Ci	30.35N	114.16 E
Hanksville	188	Jg	38.25N	110.10W
Hanlar	132	Oi	40.34N	46.20 E
Hanmej, gora-	134	Lc	67.08N	66.00 E
Hanmer Springs	218	Ee	42.31S	172.50 E
Hann, Mount-	212	Fc	15.50S	125.50 E
Hanna [Alta.-Can.]	180	Gf	51.38N	111.54W
Hanna [Wy.-U.S.]	188	Lf	41.52N	106.34W
Hannah Bay	180	Jf	51.15N	79.50W
Hannibal	182	Id	39.42N	91.22W
Hanningfield Reservoir	124	Cc	51.37N	0.28 E
Hannō	156	Fd	35.53N	139.17 E
Hannover	112	Ge	52.22N	9.43 E
Hann River	212	Fc	17.10S	126.10 E
Hannuit/Hannut	124	Hd	50.40N	5.05 E
Hannut/Hannuit	124	Hd	50.40N	5.05 E
Hano	116	Fi	56.00N	14.50 E
Hanöbukten	116	Fi	55.45N	14.30 E
Ha Noi	142	Mg	21.02N	105.51 E
Hanover [N.H.-U.S.]	184	Kd	43.42N	72.17W
Hanover [Ont.-Can.]	184	Gc	44.09N	81.02W
Hanover [Pa.-U.S.]	184	If	39.47N	76.59W
Hanover [S.Afr.]	172	Cf	31.04S	24.29 E
Hanover, Isla-	206	Fh	51.00S	74.40W
Hanpan, Cape-	212	Ka	5.01S	154.37 E
Han Pijesak	128	Mf	44.05N	18.57 E
Hansen Mountains	222	Ee	68.16S	58.47 E
Hanshan	154	Ei	31.43N	118.07 E
Hanshou	154	Aj	28.55N	111.58 E
Han Shui	140	Nf	30.34N	114.17 E
Hanstholm	116	Cg	57.07N	8.38 E
Han Sum	154	Eb	44.33N	119.58 E
Han-sur-Lesse, Rochefort-	124	Hd	50.08N	5.11 E
Han-sur-Nied	124	If	48.59N	6.26 E
Hantau	136	Hg	44.13N	73.48 E
Hantengri Feng	152	Dc	42.03N	80.11 E
Hants	118	Lj	51.10N	1.10W
Hanty-Mansijsk	142	Ic	61.00N	69.06 E
Hanty-Mansijski nacionalny okrug [3]	136	Hc	62.00N	72.30 E
Hantzsch	180	Kc	67.32N	72.26W
Hanušovice	120	Mf	50.05N	16.55 E
Hanwang	152	He	31.25N	104.13 E
Hanyang	154	Ci	30.34N	114.01 E
Hanyang, Wuhan-	154	Ci	30.33N	114.16 E
Hanyū	156	Fc	36.11N	139.32 E
Hanyuan (Fulin)	152	Hf	29.25N	102.12 E
Hanzhong	142	Mf	32.59N	107.11 E
Hanzhuang	154	Dg	34.38N	117.23 E
Hao Atoll	208	Mf	18.15S	140.54W
Hāora	142	Kg	22.35N	88.20 E
Haoud el Hamra	162	Ic	31.58N	5.59 E
Hao Xi	154	Ej	28.26N	119.56 E
Haoxue	154	Bi	30.02N	112.25 E
Haparanda	114	Fd	65.50N	24.10 E
Hapčeranga	138	Kg	49.42N	112.20 E
Happy Valley-Goose Bay	176	Md	53.19N	60.24W
Hapsu	154	Jd	41.13N	128.51 E
Ḥaql	146	Fh	29.18N	34.57 E
Ḥaql al Burqān	146	Lh	28.55N	47.57 E
Ḥaql al Manāqish	146	Lh	29.02N	47.32 E
Ḥaql as Ṣābirīyah	146	Lh	29.48N	47.50 E
Hara, zaliv-/Hara laht	116	Ke	59.35N	25.30 E
Hara-Ajrag	152	Ib	45.50N	109.20 E
Harabali	136	Ef	47.25N	47.16 E
Ḥaraḍ	144	Ge	24.14N	49.11 E
Haraiki Atoll	208	Mf	17.28S	143.27W
Hara laht/Hara, zaliv-	116	Ke	59.35N	25.30 E
Haramachi	154	Pf	37.38N	140.58 E
Haram Dāgh	144	Gb	37.35N	46.43 E
Harami, pereval-	132	Oh	42.48N	46.12 E
Harand	146	Of	32.34N	52.26 E
Harani'ia Point	219a	Ed	10.21S	161.16 E
Hara Nur	152	Fb	48.05N	93.12 E
Ḥarardēre	168	He	4.32N	47.53 E
Harare	160	Kj	17.50S	31.10 E
Harat	168	Fb	16.05N	39.28 E
Hara-Tas, krjaž-	138	Fb	72.00N	107.00 E
Haratini	220n	Bc	10.28S	160.58W
Ḥarat Zuwayyah	160	Jf	24.14N	21.59 E
Hara-Us-Nur	152	Fb	48.00N	92.10 E
Haraz	168	Bc	13.57N	19.26 E
Harāz	146	Od	36.40N	52.43 E
Harāzah, Jabal-	168	Eb	15.03N	30.27 E
Haraze	168	Cd	9.55N	20.48 E
Harbel	166	Cd	6.16N	10.21W
Harbin	142	Oe	45.45N	126.37 E
Harbor Beach	184	Fd	43.51N	82.39W
Harbour Breton	180	Lg	47.29N	55.50W
Harbour Grace	180	Mg	47.41N	53.15W
Harburg, Hamburg-	120	Fc	53.28N	10.00 E
Harcourt	184	Ob	46.30N	65.15W
Harcuvar Mountains	188	Ii	34.00N	113.30W
Harcyzsk	132	Kf	47.59N	38.11 E
Hardanger	116	Bd	60.20N	6.30 E
Hardangerfjorden	110	Gc	60.10N	6.00 E
Hardangerjøkulen	116	Bd	60.35N	7.25 E
Hardangervidda	114	Bf	60.20N	7.30 E
Hardelot Plage, Neufchâtel Hardelot-	124	Dd	50.38N	1.35 E
Hardenberg	124	Ib	52.34N	6.37 E
Harderwijk	122	Lb	52.21N	5.36 E
Hardin	182	Fb	45.44N	107.37W
Harding	172	Df	30.34S	29.58 E
Hardinsburg	184	Dg	37.47N	86.28W
Hardler	124	Kc	51.06N	8.14 E
Hardoi	148	Gc	27.25N	80.07 E
Hardwār	148	Fc	29.58N	78.10 E
Hardy, Peninsula-	206	Gi	55.25S	68.30W
Hareid	116	Bb	62.22N	6.02 E
Hareidlandet	114	Ae	62.20N	5.55 E
Hare Indian	180	Ec	66.18N	128.38W
Harelbeke	124	Fd	50.51N	3.18 E
Haren	124	Ja	53.11N	6.38 E
Haren (Ems)	124	Jb	52.47N	7.14 E
Harer	160	Lh	9.18N	42.08 E
Harerge [3]	168	Gd	9.00N	41.30 E
Harerī Mālinwarfā	168	He	4.34N	47.21 E
Harewa	168	Gd	9.54N	41.58 E
Harfleur	124	Ce	49.30N	0.12 E
Harg	116	Hd	60.11N	18.24 E
Hargeysa	160	Lh	9.30N	44.03 E
Harghita [2]	130	Ic	46.25N	25.45 E
Harghita, Munții-	130	Ic	46.31N	25.33 E
Harghita, Vîrful-	130	Ic	46.27N	25.35 E
Hargla	116	Lg	57.31N	26.25 E
Harhorin	152	Hb	47.13N	102.50 E
Har Hu	152	Gd	38.15N	97.40 E
Harīb	144	Gg	14.56N	45.30 E
Haridwār	148	Fc	29.58N	78.10 E
Harihari	218	De	43.09S	170.34 E
Hari kurk	116	Je	59.00N	22.50 E
Harim	146	Gd	36.12N	36.31 E
Harim, Jabal al-	146	Qj	25.58N	56.14 E
Harima-Nada	156	Dd	34.30N	134.35 E
Haringey, London-	124	Bc	51.36N	0.06W
Haringvliet	124	Gc	51.49N	4.12 E
Harīrūd	140	If	37.24N	60.38 E
Härjångsfjället	116	Ea	63.01N	12.35 E
Harjavalta	114	Ff	61.19N	22.08 E
Härjedalen	116	Eb	62.20N	13.05 E
Härjehågna	116	Ec	61.44N	12.08 E
Hårkan	116	Fa	63.20N	14.55 E
Harkov	112	Je	50.00N	36.15 E
Harkovskaja oblast [3]	136	Df	49.40N	36.30 E
Harlan [Ia.-U.S.]	186	If	41.39N	95.19W
Harlan [Ky.-U.S.]	184	Fg	36.51N	83.19W
Harlan County Lake	186	Gf	40.04N	99.16W
Harlech Castle	118	Ii	52.52N	4.07W
Harlem	188	Kb	48.32N	108.47W
Harleston	124	Db	52.24N	1.18 E
Harlingen [Neth.]	122	La	53.10N	5.24 E
Harlingen [Tx.-U.S.]	182	Hf	26.11N	97.42W
Harlovka	114	Ib	68.47N	37.15 E
Harlovka	114	Ib	68.47N	37.20 E
Harlow	118	Nj	51.47N	0.08 E
Harlowton	188	Kc	46.26N	109.50W
Harlu	114	Hf	61.51N	30.54 E
Hărman	130	Id	45.43N	25.41 E
Harmancık	146	Cc	39.41N	29.10 E
Harmånger	114	Df	61.56N	17.13 E
Harmanli	130	Ih	41.56N	25.54 E
Harmil	168	Gb	16.30N	40.12 E
Harmony	186	Ke	43.33N	91.59W
Harnai	148	Ee	17.48N	73.06 E
Harney Basin	174	Ge	43.15N	120.40W
Harney Lake	182	Dc	43.14N	119.07W
Harney Peak	182	Gc	44.00N	103.30W
Harnön	116	Gb	62.35N	18.00 E
Härnösand	112	Hc	62.38N	17.56 E
Haro	126	Jb	42.35N	2.51W
Haro, Cabo-	192	Dd	27.50N	110.52W
Harovsk	136	Ed	59.59N	40.11 E
Harøya	116	Bb	62.45N	6.25 E
Harøyfjorden	116	Bb	62.45N	6.35 E
Harpenden	124	Bc	51.48N	0.21W
Harper [Ks.-U.S.]	186	Gh	37.17N	98.01W
Harper [Lbr.]	160	Gh	4.22N	7.43W
Harper, Mount-	178	Kd	64.14N	143.50W
Harper Pass	218	De	42.44S	171.53 E
Harpling	116	Eh	56.45N	12.43 E
Harqin Qi (Jinshan)	154	Ed	41.57N	118.40 E
Harqin Zuoyi Monggolzu Zizhixian	154	Ed	41.05N	119.40 E
Ḥarrat al 'Uwayrid	144	Ed	27.00N	37.30 E
Harricana	180	Jf	51.10N	79.47W
Harricana, Rivière-	184	Ha	51.10N	79.45W
Harrington-Harbour	180	Lf	50.26N	59.30W
Harris	197c	Bc	16.28N	62.10W
Harris	118	Gd	57.53N	6.55W
Harris, Lake-	184	Gk	28.46N	81.49W
Harris, Sound of-	118	Fd	57.45N	7.08W
Harrisburg	176	Le	40.16N	76.52W
Harrismith	172	De	28.18S	29.03 E
Harrison [Ar.-U.S.]	186	Jh	36.14N	93.07W
Harrison [Mi.-U.S.]	184	Ec	44.01N	84.48W
Harrison [Nb.-U.S.]	186	Ee	42.41N	103.53W
Harrison, Cape-	180	Lf	54.56N	57.55W
Harrison Bay	178	Ib	70.30N	151.30W
Harrisonburg	184	Hf	38.27N	78.54W
Harrison Lake	188	Eb	49.31N	121.59W
Harrison Point	197q	Ab	13.18N	59.38W
Harrisonville	186	Ig	38.39N	94.21W
Harrisville [Mi.-U.S.]	184	Fc	44.39N	83.17W
Harrisville [W.V.-U.S.]	184	Gf	39.13N	81.04W
Harrodsburg	184	Eg	37.46N	84.51W
Harrogate	118	Lh	54.00N	1.33W
Harrow, London-	124	Bc	51.36N	0.20W
Harry S. Truman Reservoir	186	Jg	38.00N	93.45W
Har Sai Shan	152	Gd	35.26N	97.41 E
Harsewinkel	124	Kc	51.58N	8.14 E
Harshō	168	Hc	11.17N	47.30 E
Harsim	146	Lf	33.48N	46.50 E
Harsin	146	Le	34.16N	47.35 E
Harstad	114	Db	68.47N	16.30 E
Harsvik	114	Cd	64.03N	10.02 E
Hart	184	Dd	43.42N	86.22W
Hart	180	Dc	65.51N	136.22W
Hartao	154	Gc	42.30N	122.08 E
Hartbees	158	Jk	28.45S	20.33 E
Hartberg	128	Jc	47.17N	15.58 E
Hårteigen	116	Bd	60.12N	7.04 E
Hartford [Ct.-U.S.]	176	Le	41.46N	72.41W
Hartford [Ky.-U.S.]	184	Dg	37.27N	86.55W
Hartford City	184	Ee	40.29N	85.23W
Hartington	186	He	42.37N	97.16W
Hartland	184	Nb	46.18N	67.32W
Hartland Point	118	Ij	51.02N	4.31W
Hartlepool	118	Lg	54.42N	1.11W
Hartmannberge	172	Ac	17.30S	12.23 E
Hartola	114	Gf	61.35N	26.01 E
Harts	158	Jk	28.24S	24.18 E
Hartselle	184	Dh	34.27N	86.56W
Harts Range	212	Gd	23.05S	134.55 E
Hartsville	184	Gh	34.23N	80.04W
Hartwell	184	Fh	34.21N	82.56W
Hartwell Lake	184	Fh	34.30N	82.55W
Harun, Bukit-	150	Gf	4.06N	115.46 E
Haruno	156	Ce	33.30N	133.30 E
Harves Bank (EN)	197c	Ac	16.52N	62.35W
Harvey [Austl.]	212	Df	33.05S	115.54 E
Harvey [N.D.-U.S.]	182	Hb	47.47N	99.56W
Harvey Bay	212	Kd	25.00S	153.00 E
Harwich	118	Oj	51.57N	1.17 E
Haryana [3]	148	Fc	29.30N	76.30 E
Harz	110	He	51.45N	10.30 E
Hasaki	156	Gd	35.44N	140.48 E
Hasama	156	Gb	38.42N	141.13 E
Hasan	138	Ih	42.26N	130.39 E
Ḥasanābād [Iran]	146	Ph	28.47N	54.19 E
Ḥasanābād [Iran]	146	Nd	36.28N	50.17 E
Hasan Dağı	144	Db	38.08N	34.12 E
Ḥasan Langī	146	Qi	27.22N	56.52 E
Hasavjurt	132	Oh	43.16N	46.35 E
Ḥasb, Sha'īb-	146	Kg	31.45N	44.17 E
Hāsbayyā	146	Ff	33.43N	33.52 E
Hasdo	148	Hd	21.44N	82.44 E
Hase	120	Dd	52.41N	7.18 E
Hasekijata	130	Kg	42.08N	27.30 E
Hasenkamp	204	Cj	31.31S	59.51W
Hashaf-Rūd	144	Jb	35.58N	61.07 E
Hashimoto	156	Dd	34.19N	135.37 E
Hashtpar	146	Md	37.48N	48.55 E
Hasi Hausert	162	Ee	22.35N	14.18W
Haskell	182	He	33.10N	99.44W
Haskerland	124	Hb	52.58N	5.47 E
Haskerland-Joure	124	Hb	52.58N	5.47 E
Haskovo	130	Ih	41.56N	25.33 E
Haskovo [2]	130	Ih	41.50N	25.55 E
Hasle	116	Fi	55.11N	14.43 E
Haslemere	118	Mj	51.06N	0.43W
Haslev	116	Di	55.20N	11.58 E
Hăşmaşu Mare, Vîrful-	130	Ic	46.30N	25.50 E
Haspengouws Plateau/Hesbaye	122	Ld	50.35N	5.10 E
Haspres	124	Fd	50.15N	3.25 E
Hassa	146	Gd	36.50N	36.29 E
Hassan	148	Ff	13.00N	76.05 E
Hassberge	120	Gf	50.12N	10.29 E
Hassela	114	De	62.07N	16.42 E
Hassel Sound	180	Ha	78.30N	99.00W
Hasselt	122	Ld	50.56N	5.20 E
Hassi Bel Guebbour	162	Id	28.30N	6.41 E
Hassi el Ghella	126	Ki	35.27N	1.03W
Hassi Mameche	126	Mi	35.51N	0.04 E
Hassi Messaoud	160	He	31.43N	6.03 E
Hassi R'mel	162	Hc	32.55N	3.16 E
Hassi Serouenout	162	Ie	24.00N	7.50 E
Hässleholm	114	Ch	56.09N	13.46 E
Hasslö	116	Fh	56.05N	15.25 E
Haßloch	124	Ke	49.23N	8.16 E
Hastière	124	Gd	50.13N	4.50 E
Hastière-Hastière par-delà	124	Gd	50.13N	4.50 E
Hastière-par-delà, Hastière	124	Gd	50.13N	4.50 E
Hastings [Bar.]	197q	Ab	13.04N	59.35W
Hastings [Eng.-U.K.]	118	Nk	50.51N	0.36 E
Hastings [Mi.-U.S.]	184	Ed	42.39N	85.17W
Hastings [Mn.-U.S.]	186	Jd	44.44N	92.51W
Hastings [Nb.-U.S.]	182	Hc	40.35N	98.23W
Hastings [N.Z.]	216	Eg	39.38S	176.50 E
Hästveda	116	Eh	56.16N	13.56 E
Hašuri	132	Mi	41.59N	43.33 E
Hasvik	114	Fa	70.29N	22.09 E
Ḥasy al Qaṭṭār	164	Ec	30.14N	27.11 E
Ḥasy Hague	164	Bd	26.17N	10.31 E
Hat'ae-Do	154	Hg	34.23N	125.17 E
Hatanga	142	Mb	71.58N	102.30 E
Hatanga	140	Mb	72.55N	106.00 E
Hatch	186	Cj	32.40N	107.09W
Hatches Creek	212	Hd	20.56S	135.12 E
Haţeg	130	Fd	45.37N	22.57 E
Hatgal	152	Ha	50.26N	100.09 E
Ḥaṭibah, Ra's-	144	Ee	21.59N	38.55 E
Ha Tien	148	Kf	10.23N	104.29 E
Ha Tinh	148	Le	18.20N	105.54 E
Hato Mayor	194	Md	18.46N	69.15W
Ḥattā, Jabal-	146	Qj	24.45N	56.04 E
Hattem	124	Ib	52.28N	6.06 E
Hatten	124	Ka	53.03N	8.23 E
Hatteras, Cape-	174	Lf	35.13N	75.32W
Hatteras Inlet	184	Jh	35.00N	75.40W
Hatteras Island	182	Ld	35.25N	75.30W
Hattfjelldal	114	Cd	65.36N	14.00 E
Hattiesburg	182	Je	31.19N	89.16W
Hattingen	124	Jc	51.24N	7.10 E
Hatu Iti, Ile-	216	Ma	8.42S	140.43W
Hatutaa, Ile-	208	Me	7.55S	140.38W
Hatvan	120	Pi	47.40N	19.41 E
Hat Yai	148	Kg	7.01N	100.27 E
Hatyrka	138	Md	62.03N	175.05 E
Haubourdin	124	Ed	50.36N	2.59 E
Hauge	114	Bg	58.21N	6.17 E
Haugesund	112	Gd	59.25N	5.18 E
Hauho	116	Kc	61.10N	24.33 E
Hauhungaroa Range	218	Fc	38.40S	175.35 E
Haukeligrend	114	Bg	59.51N	7.11 E
Haukipudas	114	Fd	65.15N	25.28 E
Haukivesi	110	Ic	62.05N	28.30 E
Haukivuori	116	Lb	62.01N	27.13 E
Hauraha	219a	Ed	10.49S	161.57 E
Hauraki Gulf	216	Eg	36.35S	175.00 E
Hauroko, Lake-	218	Bf	45.55S	167.20 E
Hausa	162	Ed	27.06N	11.01W
Hausruck	128	Hb	48.07N	13.35 E
Haut, Isle au-	184	Mc	44.03N	68.38W
Haut Atlas=High Atlas (EN)	158	Ge	32.00N	6.00W
Haute-Champagne	124	Ge	49.18N	4.15 E
Haute-Corse [3]	122a	Aa	42.30N	9.00 E
Haute-Garonne [3]	122	Hk	43.25N	1.30 E
Haute-Guinée [3]	166	Dc	11.30N	10.00W
Haute-Kotto [3]	168	Cd	7.00N	23.00 E
Haute-Loire [3]	122	Ji	45.05N	3.50 E
Haute-Marne [3]	122	Lf	48.05N	5.10 E
Hauterive	184	Ma	49.11N	68.16W
Hautes-Alpes [3]	122	Mj	44.40N	6.30 E
Haute-Sangha [3]	168	Be	4.30N	16.00 E
Haute-Saône [3]	122	Mg	47.40N	6.10 E
Haute-Saône, Plateau de-	122	Lg	47.50N	6.00 E
Haute-Savoie [3]	122	Mi	46.00N	6.20 E
Hautes Fagnes/Hoge Venen	120	Bf	50.30N	6.00 E
Hautes-Pyrénées [3]	122	Gk	43.00N	0.10 E
Haute-Vienne [3]	122	Hi	45.50N	1.10 E
Haut-Mbomou [3]	168	Dd	6.00N	26.00 E
Hautmont	122	Jd	50.15N	3.56 E
Haut-Ogooué [3]	170	Bc	2.00S	14.00 E
Haut-Rhin [3]	122	Ng	48.00N	7.20 E
Hauts-Bassins [3]	166	Ec	12.30N	4.30W
Hauts-de-Seine [3]	122	If	48.50N	2.11 E
Hauts Plateaux	158	He	34.00N	0.01 E
Haut-Zaïre [2]	170	Eb	2.30N	25.30 E
Hauula	221a	Db	21.36N	157.54W
Hauz-Han	135	Cf	37.16N	61.15 E
Hauz-Hanskoje vodohranilišče	135	Cf	37.10N	61.20 E
Havana	186	Kf	40.18N	90.04W
Havana (EN)=La Habana	176	Kg	23.08N	82.22W
Havant and Waterloo	118	Mk	50.51N	0.59W
Havast	135	Gd	40.16N	68.51 E
Havasu, Lake-	188	Hi	34.30N	114.20W
Havel	120	Hd	52.53N	11.58 E
Havelange	124	Hd	50.23N	5.14 E
Havelange-Méan	124	Hd	50.22N	5.20 E
Havelberg	120	Id	52.49N	12.05 E
Havelland	120	Id	52.25N	12.45 E
Havelländisches Luch	120	Id	52.40N	12.40 E
Havelock [N.C.-U.S.]	184	Ih	34.53N	76.54W
Havelock [N.Z.]	218	Ed	41.17S	173.46 E
Havelock North	218	Gc	39.40S	176.53 E
Havelte	124	Ib	52.46N	6.16 E
Haverfordwest	118	Ij	51.49N	4.58W
Haverhill [Eng.-U.K.]	118	Ni	52.05N	0.26 E
Haverhill [Ma.-U.S.]	184	Ld	42.47N	71.05W
Havering, London-	124	Cc	51.36N	0.11 E
Havířov	120	Og	49.48N	18.27 E
Havlíčkův Brod	120	Lg	49.36N	15.34 E
Havøysund	114	Fa	71.03N	24.40 E
Havran	146	Bc	39.33N	27.06 E
Havre	176	Ie	48.33N	109.41W
Havre, Le-	112	Gf	49.30N	0.08 E
Havre-Saint-Pierre	176	Md	50.15N	63.36W
Havsa	130	Jh	41.33N	26.49 E
Havza	146	Fb	41.05N	35.45 E
Hawaii [2]	176	Cg	24.00N	167.00W
Hawaiian Islands	208	Kb	24.00N	167.00W
Hawaiian Ridge (EN)	106	Kg	24.00N	165.00W
Hawaii Island	208	Lc	19.30N	155.30W
Ḥawallī	144	Gd	29.19N	48.02 E
Ḥawār	146	Nj	25.40N	50.45 E
Hawarden	218	Ee	42.56S	172.39 E
Ḥawāshīyah, Wādī-	146	Eh	28.31N	32.58 E
Hawaymī, Sha'īb al-	146	Kg	30.58N	44.15 E
Hawd	158	Lh	7.40N	47.43 E
Ḥawḍ Al Waqf	146	Ei	26.33N	32.22 E
Hawea, Lake-	218	Cf	44.30S	169.20 E
Hawera	216	Dg	39.35S	174.17 E
Hawi	210	Lb	20.14N	155.50W
Hawick	118	Kf	55.25N	2.47W
Ḥawīzah, Hawr al-	146	Lg	31.35N	47.38 E
Hawkdun Range	218	Cf	44.50S	170.00 E
Hawke Bay	216	Eg	39.25S	177.20 E
Hawke Harbour	180	Lf	53.01N	55.50W
Hawker	212	Hf	31.53S	138.25 E
Hawkes, Mount-	222	Rg	83.55S	56.05W
Hawke's Bay [2]	218	Gc	39.30S	176.40 E
Hawkesbury	184	Jc	45.36N	74.37W
Hawkhurst	124	Cc	51.02N	0.30 E
Hawkinsville	184	Fi	32.17N	83.28W
Hawksbill	184	Hf	38.33N	78.23W
Hawk Springs	188	Mf	41.48N	104.09W
Ḥawmat as Sūq	162	Jc	33.53N	10.51 E
Hawng Tuk	148	Jd	20.28N	99.56 E
Ḥawrā'	168	Hb	15.43N	48.18 E
Hawrān, Wādī-	144	Fc	33.58N	42.34 E
Hawsh 'Īsā	146	Dg	30.55N	30.17 E
Hawthorne	182	Dd	38.32N	118.38W
Hawthorne, Mount-	222	Pf	72.10S	98.39W
Haxtun	186	Ef	40.39N	102.38W
Hay	210	Fh	34.30S	144.51 E
Hay	174	Hc	60.51N	115.44W
Hayachine-San	156	Gb	39.34N	141.29 E
Hayakita	156a	Bb	42.45N	141.48 E
Hayange	122	Me	49.20N	6.03 E
Hayasaki-Seto	156	Be	32.34N	130.10 E
Hayasui-no-Seto	154	Kh	33.20N	132.00 E
Hayato	156	Bf	31.45N	130.43 E
Haybān	168	Ec	11.13N	30.31 E
Haybān, Jabal-	168	Ec	11.15N	30.31 E
Hayden	188	Jj	33.00N	110.47W
Hayes [Man.-Can.]	180	Ie	57.00N	92.15W
Hayes [N.W.T.-Can.]	178	Hc	67.20N	95.02W
Hayes, Mount-	178	Jd	63.37N	146.43W
Hayes Halvø=Hayes Peninsula (EN)	224	Od	77.40N	64.30W
Hayes Peninsula (EN)=Hayes Halvø	224	Od	77.40N	64.30W
Ḥayl	146	Qj	24.33N	56.06 E
Hayl, Wādī al-	146	He	34.47N	39.18 E
Hayling Island	124	Bd	50.48N	0.58W
Haymana	146	Ec	39.27N	32.30 E
Haymana Platosu	146	Ec	39.25N	32.45 E
Hayrabolu	146	Bb	41.12N	27.06 E
Ḥayrān	164	Hf	16.02N	42.49 E
Hay River	176	Hc	60.51N	115.40W
Hay River	212	Hd	25.00S	138.00 E
Hayrūt	168	Ib	15.59N	52.09 E
Hays	182	Hd	38.53N	99.20W
Hay Springs	186	Ee	42.41N	102.41W
Haystack Peak	188	Ig	39.50N	113.55W
Hayward [Ca.-U.S.]	188	Dh	37.40N	122.05W
Hayward [Wi.-U.S.]	186	Kc	46.01N	91.29W
Haywards Heath	124	Bc	51.00N	0.06W
HaẒafon [3]	146	Ff	32.50N	35.20 E
Ḥazar, Wādī-	168	Hb	17.50N	49.07 E
Hazarasp	135	Cd	41.19N	61.08 E
Hazard	184	Fg	37.15N	83.12W
Hazar Gölü	146	Hc	38.30N	39.25 E
Hazāribāgh	148	Hd	23.59N	85.21 E
Hazebrouck	122	Id	50.43N	2.32 E
Hazelton	180	Ee	55.15N	127.40W
Hazen	186	Fc	47.18N	101.38W
Hazen Strait	180	Ga	77.15N	110.00W
Ḥaẓeva	146	Fg	30.48N	35.15 E
Hazlehurst [Ga.-U.S.]	184	Fj	31.52N	82.36W
Hazlehurst [Ms.-U.S.]	186	Kk	31.52N	90.24W
Hazleton	184	Je	40.58N	76.00W
Hazlett, Lake-	212	Fd	21.30S	128.50 E
Hazrah, Ra's al-	146	Nj	24.22N	51.36 E
Hazro	146	Ic	38.15N	40.47 E
Heacham	124	Cb	52.55N	0.29 E
Headley	124	Bc	51.07N	0.49W
Healdsburg	188	Dg	38.37N	122.52W
Heanor	124	Aa	53.00N	1.18W
Heard Island	222	Fd	53.00S	73.35 E

Index Symbols

- [1] Independent Nation
- [2] State, Region
- [3] District, County
- [4] Municipality
- [5] Colony, Dependency
- Continent
- Physical Region
- Historical or Cultural Region
- Mount, Mountain
- Volcano
- Hill
- Mountains, Mountain Range
- Hills, Escarpment
- Plateau, Upland
- Pass, Gap
- Plain, Lowland
- Delta
- Salt Flat
- Valley, Canyon
- Crater, Cave
- Karst Features
- Depression
- Polder
- Desert, Dunes
- Forest, Woods
- Heath, Steppe
- Oasis
- Cape, Point
- Coast, Beach
- Cliff
- Peninsula
- Isthmus
- Sandbank
- Island
- Atoll
- Rock, Reef
- Islands, Archipelago
- Rocks, Reefs
- Coral Reef
- Well, Spring
- Geyser
- River, Stream
- Waterfall, Rapids
- River Mouth, Estuary
- Lake
- Salt Lake
- Intermittent Lake
- Reservoir
- Swamp, Pond
- Canal
- Glacier
- Ice Shelf, Pack Ice
- Ocean
- Sea
- Gulf, Bay
- Strait, Fjord
- Lagoon
- Bank
- Seamount
- Tablemount
- Ridge
- Shelf
- Basin
- Escarpment, Sea Scarp
- Fracture
- Trench, Abyss
- National Park, Reserve
- Point of Interest
- Recreation Site
- Cave, Cavern
- Historic Site
- Ruins
- Wall, Walls
- Church, Abbey
- Temple
- Scientific Station
- Railway station
- Airport
- Port
- Military installation
- Lighthouse
- Mine
- Tunnel
- Dam, Bridge

Hearne 186 Hk 30.53N 96.36W
Hearst 180 Jg 49.41N 83.40W
Heart River 186 Fc 46.47N 100.51W
Heathrow Airport London 124 Bc 51.28N 0.30W
Hebbronville 186 Gm 27.18N 98.41W
Hebei Sheng (Ho-pei Sheng) =Hopeh (EN) [2] 152 Kd 39.00N 116.00 E
Heber City 188 Jf 40.30N 111.25W
Hebi 152 Jd 35.53N 114.09 E
Hebian 152 Jd 38.35N 113.06 E
Hebiji 154 Cf 36.00N 114.08 E
Hebrides 110 Fd 57.00N 6.30W
Hebrides, Sea of the- 118 Ge 57.00N 7.00W
Hebron [N.D.-U.S.] 186 Ec 46.54N 102.03W
Hebron [Newf.-Can.] 180 Le 58.15N 62.35W
Heby 116 Ge 59.56N 16.53 E
Hecate Strait 180 Ef 53.20N 131.00W
Hecelchakán 192 Ng 20.10N 90.08W
Hechi (Jnchengjiang) 152 Ig 24.44N 108.02 E
Hechingen 120 Eh 48.21N 8.59 E
Hechuan 152 Ie 30.07N 106.15 E
Hecla 186 Gd 45.43N 98.09W
Hecla and Griper Bay 180 Ga 76.00N 111.30W
Hecla Island 186 Ha 51.08N 96.45W
Heddalsvatnet 116 Ce 59.30N 9.15 E
Hede 114 Ce 62.25N 13.30 E
Hede → Sheyang 154 Fh 33.47N 120.15 E
Hedemarken 116 Dd 60.50N 11.20 E
Hedemora 114 Df 60.17N 15.59 E
Hedensted 116 Ci 55.46N 9.42 E
Hedesunda 114 Df 60.25N 17.00 E
Hedesunda fjärdarna 116 Gd 60.20N 17.00 E
Hedmark [2] 114 Cf 61.30N 11.45 E
Hedo-Misaki 156b Bb 26.52N 128.16 E
Heemskerk 124 Gb 52.30N 4.42 E
Heemstede 124 Gb 52.21N 4.37 E
Heerenberg, Bergh 's- 124 Ic 51.53N 6.16 E
Heerenveen 122 Lb 52.57N 5.55 E
Heerhugowaard 124 Gb 52.40N 4.50 E
Heerlen 122 Ld 50.54N 5.59 E
Hefa [3] 146 Ff 32.35N 35.00 E
Hefa = Haifa (EN) 142 Ff 32.50N 35.00 E
Hefei 142 Nf 31.47N 117.15 E
Hefeng 152 Jf 29.49N 110.01 E
Hegang 142 Pe 47.20N 130.12 E
Hegau 120 Ei 47.50N 8.45 E
Hegura Jima 152 Od 37.50N 136.55 E
Heide 120 Fb 54.12N 9.06 E
Heidelberg 120 Eg 49.25N 8.42 E
Heidenheim an der Brenz 120 Gh 48.41N 10.09 E
Heidenreichstein 128 Jb 48.52N 15.07 E
Hei-Gawa 156 Gb 39.38N 141.58 E
Heigun-Tō 156 Ce 33.47N 132.15 E
Hei He 152 Hd 38.15N 100.15 E
Heihe → Aihui 142 Od 50.13N 127.26 E
Heilbron 172 De 27.21S 27.58 E
Heilbronn 120 Fg 49.08N 9.13 E
Heiligenblut 128 Gd 47.02N 12.50 E
Heiligenhafen 120 Gb 54.22N 10.59 E
Heiligenhaus 124 Ic 51.19N 6.58 E
Heiligenstadt 120 Gd 51.23N 10.08 E
Heilinzi 154 Ib 44.33N 126.41 E
Heilong Jiang 140 Qd 52.56N 141.10 E
Heilongjiang Sheng (Hei-lung-chiang Sheng) = Heilungkiang (EN) [2] 152 Mb 48.00N 128.00 E
Heiloo 124 Gb 52.36N 4.43 E
Hei-lung-chiang Sheng → Heilongjiang Sheng = Heilungkiang (EN) [2] 152 Mb 48.00N 128.00 E
Heilungkiang (EN) = Heilongjiang Sheng (Hei-lung-chiang Sheng) [2] 152 Mb 48.00N 128.00 E
Heilungkiang (EN) = Hei-lung-chiang Sheng → Heilongjiang Sheng [2] 152 Mb 48.00N 128.00 E
Heimæy 114a Bc 63.26N 20.17W
Heimbach 124 Id 50.38N 6.29 E
Heimdal 114 Ce 63.21N 10.22 E
Heimsheim 124 Kf 48.48N 8.51 E
Heinävesi 114 Ge 62.26N 28.36 E
Heinola 114 Gf 61.13N 26.02 E
Heinsberg 124 Ic 51.04N 6.05 E
Heishan 154 Gd 41.42N 122.07 E
Heishan Xia 152 Hd 37.18N 104.39 E
Heishui [China] 154 Ec 42.06N 119.22 E
Heishui [China] 152 He 32.03N 103.05 E
Heist, Knokke- 122 Jc 51.21N 3.15 E
Heist-op-den-Berg 124 Gc 51.05N 4.43 E
Hei-Zaki 156 Hb 39.39N 142.00 E
Hejgijaha 134 Pd 65.27N 72.50 E
Hejian 154 De 38.27N 116.05 E
Hejing 152 Ec 42.18N 86.18 E
Hejjaha 134 Kb 68.18N 62.32 E
Hekimhan 146 Gc 38.49N 37.56 E
Hekinan 156 Ed 34.52N 136.58 E
Hekla 110 Ec 64.00N 19.40W
Hekou 154 Ci 31.20N 114.25 E
Hekou → Yanshan 154 Dj 28.18N 117.41 E
Hel 120 Ob 54.37N 18.48 E
Helagsfjället 114 Ce 62.55N 12.27 E
Helan 152 Id 38.35N 106.16 E
Helan Shan 152 Id 39.00N 106.00 E
Helden's Point 197c Ab 17.24N 62.50W
Helena [Ar.-U.S.] 182 Ie 34.32N 90.35W
Helena [Guy.] 202 Gb 6.41N 57.55W
Helena [Mt.-U.S.] 176 He 46.36N 112.01W
Helen Glacier 222 Ge 66.40S 93.55 E
Helen Reef 208 Ed 2.53N 131.47 E
Helensburgh 118 Ie 56.01N 4.44W
Helensville 218 Fb 36.40S 174.27 E
Helgaå 116 Fi 55.53N 14.08 E
Helgasjön 116 Fh 56.55N 14.45 E
Helgeland 114 Cd 66.15N 13.05 E
Helgoland 120 Db 54.12N 7.53 E
Helgoländer Bucht 120 Eb 54.10N 8.04 E
Helikón Óros 138 Fk 38.20N 22.50 E
Helixi 154 Ei 30.39N 119.01 E
Heljulja 116 Nc 61.37N 30.38 E
Hella 114a Bc 63.50N 20.24W
Hellberge 120 Hd 52.34N 11.17 E
Hëlleh 146 Nh 29.10N 50.40 E
Hellendoorn 122 Mb 52.24N 6.26 E
Hellendoorn-Nijverdal 124 Ib 52.22N 6.27 E
Hellenic Trough (EN) 110 Ii 35.00N 24.00 E
Hellental 124 Id 50.29N 6.26 E
Hellesylt 114 Be 62.05N 6.54 E
Hellin 126 Kf 38.31N 1.41W
Hells Canyon 180 Db 45.20N 116.45W
Hellweg 124 Kc 51.40N 8.00 E
Helmand [3] 144 Jc 31.00N 64.00 E
Helmand 140 If 31.12N 61.34 E
Helme 120 He 51.20N 11.20 E
Helmeringhausen 172 Be 25.54S 16.57 E
Helmond 122 Lc 51.29N 5.40 E
Helmsdale 118 Jc 58.07N 3.40W
Helmsdale 118 Jc 58.10N 3.40W
Helmstedt 120 Hd 52.14N 11.02 E
Helong 152 Mc 42.32N 129.00 E
Helpe Majeure 124 Fd 50.11N 3.47 E
Helpringham 124 Bb 52.56N 0.18W
Helpter Berge 120 Jc 53.30N 13.36 E
Helsingborg 112 Hd 56.03N 12.42 E
Helsinge 116 Eh 56.01N 12.12 E
Helsingfors/Helsinki 112 Ic 60.10N 24.58 E
Helsingør 114 Ch 56.02N 12.37 E
Helsinki/Helsingfors 112 Ic 60.10N 24.58 E
Helska, Mierzeja- 120 Ob 54.45N 18.39 E
Helston 118 Hk 50.05N 5.16W
Helvecia 204 Bj 31.06S 60.05W
Helwān (EN) = Ḩulwān 164 Fd 29.51N 31.20 E
Ḩemār 146 Qg 31.42N 57.31 E
Hemčik 138 Ef 51.40N 92.10 E
Hemel Hempstead 118 Mj 51.46N 0.28W
Hemer 124 Jc 51.23N 7.46 E
Hemnesberget 114 Cc 66.14N 13.38 E
Hemsby 124 Db 52.41N 1.42 E
Hemse 116 Hg 57.14N 18.22 E
Hemsedal 116 Cd 60.50N 8.40 E
Hemsö 114 Ee 62.45N 18.05 E
Hen 116 Dd 60.13N 10.14 E
Henan 152 He 34.33N 101.55 E
Hen and Chickens Islands 218 Fa 35.55S 174.45 E
Henan Sheng (Ho-nan Sheng) = Honan (EN) [2] 152 Je 34.00N 114.00 E
Henares 126 Id 40.24N 3.30W
Henashi-Zaki 156 Fa 40.37N 139.51 E
Henbury 212 Gd 24.35S 133.15 E
Hendaye 122 Ek 43.22N 1.47W
Hendek 146 Db 40.48N 30.45 E
Henderson [Arg.] 204 Bm 36.18S 61.43W
Henderson [Ky.-U.S.] 184 Dg 37.50N 87.35W
Henderson [N.C.-U.S.] 184 Hg 36.20N 78.25W
Henderson [Nv.-U.S.] 182 Dd 36.02N 115.01W
Henderson [Tx.-U.S.] 186 Ij 32.09N 94.48W
Henderson Island 208 Og 24.22S 128.19W
Henderson Seamount (EN) 182 Df 25.34N 119.33W
Hendersonville [N.C.-U.S.] 184 Fh 35.19N 82.28W
Hendersonville [Tn.-U.S.] 184 Dg 36.18N 86.37W
Hendījān 146 Mg 30.14N 49.43 E
Hendorābī, Jazireh-ye- 146 Oi 26.40N 53.37 E
Hendrik Verwderddam 172 Df 30.45S 25.33 E
Hengām, Jazireh-ye- 146 Pi 26.39N 55.53 E
Henguduan Shan 140 Lg 27.30N 99.00 E
Hengelo 122 Mb 52.15N 6.45 E
Hengshan [China] 152 Id 37.51N 109.20 E
Hengshan [China] 152 Jf 27.16N 112.51 E
Hengshan [China] 154 Kb 45.24N 131.01 E
Heng Shan [China] 152 Jf 27.18N 112.41 E
Heng Shan [China] 152 Jd 39.42N 113.45 E
Hengshui 152 Kd 37.39N 115.46 E
Hengxian 152 Ig 22.46N 109.15 E
Hengyang 142 Ng 26.56N 112.35 E
Henik Lakes 180 Hd 61.05N 97.20W
Hénin-Liétard 122 Id 50.25N 2.56 E
Henley-on-Thames 124 Bc 51.32N 0.54W
Hennan 114 De 62.02N 15.54 E
Hennan 116 Fb 62.05N 15.45 E
Hennebont 122 Cg 47.48N 3.17W
Hennef (Sieg) 124 Jd 50.47N 7.17 E
Hennigsdorf bei Berlin 120 Jd 52.38N 13.12 E
Henrietta Maria, Cape - 180 Je 55.09N 82.19W
Henry, Mount- 188 Hb 48.53N 115.31W
Henry Bay 222 Ie 66.40S 120.40 E
Henryetta 186 Ii 35.27N 95.59W
Henry Kater Peninsula 180 Kc 69.15N 67.30W
Henry Mountains 188 Jh 37.55N 110.50W
Henrys Fork River 188 Je 43.45N 111.56W
Henslow, Cape- 219a Ec 9.56S 160.38 E
Hentej 140 Me 48.50N 109.00 E
Hentiesbaai 172 Ad 22.08S 14.18 E
Henzada 142 Lh 17.38N 95.28 E
Heping → Yanhe 152 If 28.31N 108.28 E
Heppenheim (Bergstraße) 124 Ke 49.38N 8.39 E
Heppner 188 Fd 45.21N 119.33W
Hepu (Lianzhou) 152 Ig 21.40N 109.12 E
Hequ 152 Jd 39.22N 111.15 E
Herakol Dağı 146 Id 37.45N 42.35 E
Heralds Cays 212 Jc 16.55S 149.10 E
Herāt 142 If 34.20N 62.12 E
Herāt [3] 144 Jc 34.30N 62.00 E
Hérault [3] 122 Jk 43.40N 3.30 E
Hérault 122 Jk 43.17N 3.26 E
Herbert [N.Z.] 218 Df 45.13S 170.46 E
Herbert [Sask.-Can.] 188 La 50.26N 107.12W
Herberton 212 Jc 17.23S 145.23 E
Herbert River 212 Jc 18.32S 146.17 E
Herbiers, Les- 122 Eh 46.52N 1.01W
Herborn 122 Ef 50.41N 8.19 E
Herby 120 Of 50.45N 18.40 E
Hercegnovi 130 Bg 42.27N 18.32 E
Hercegovina 110 Hg 43.00N 17.50 E
Hercegovina 128 Lg 43.00N 17.50 E
Herdubreid 114a Cb 65.11N 16.21W
Heredia 190 Hf 10.00N 84.07W
Heredia [3] 194 Fh 10.30N 84.00W
Hereford 118 Ki 52.15N 2.50W
Hereford [Eng.-U.K.] 118 Ki 52.04N 2.43W
Hereford [Tx.-U.S.] 182 Ge 34.49N 102.24W
Hereford and Worcester [3] 118 Ki 52.10N 2.35W
Hereheretue Atoll 208 Mf 19.54S 144.58W
Hereke 130 Mi 40.48N 29.39 E
Herekino 218 Ea 35.16S 173.13 E
Herent 124 Gd 50.54N 4.40 E
Herentals 124 Gc 51.11N 4.50 E
Herfølge 116 Ei 55.25N 12.10 E
Herford 120 Ed 52.08N 8.41 E
Héricourt 122 Mg 47.35N 6.45 E
Herington 186 Hg 38.40N 96.57W
Heriot 216 Ci 45.51S 169.16 E
Heris 146 Lc 38.14N 47.07 E
Herisau 128 Dc 47.24N 9.16 E
Herk 124 Hd 50.58N 5.07 E
Herk-de-Stad 124 Hd 50.56N 5.10 E
Herkimer 184 Jd 43.02N 74.59W
Herlen He 152 Kb 48.48N 117.00 E
Hermagor 128 Hd 46.37N 13.22 E
Hermanas 192 Id 27.14N 101.14W
Hermana Ness 118 Ma 60.50N 0.54W
Hermano Peak 186 Bh 37.17N 108.48W
Hermansverk 116 Cc 61.11N 6.51 E
Hermanus 172 Bf 34.25S 19.16 E
Hermeskeil 124 Ie 49.39N 6.57 E
Hermiston 188 Fd 45.51N 119.17W
Hermitage 218 De 43.44S 170.05 E
Hermit Islands 208 Fe 1.32S 145.05 E
Hermosa de Santa Rosa, Sierra- 192 Id 28.00N 101.45W
Hermosillo 176 Hg 29.04N 110.58W
Hermoso Campo 204 Bh 27.36S 61.21W
Hernád 120 Qh 48.00N 20.58 E
Hernandarias 206 Jc 25.22S 54.45W
Hernández [Arg.] 204 Bk 32.21S 60.02W
Hernández [Mex.] 192 Hf 23.02N 102.02W
Hernani 126 Ka 43.16N 1.58W
Herne 120 De 51.33N 7.13 E
Herne Bay 118 Oj 51.23N 1.08 E
Herning 112 Gd 56.08N 8.59 E
Heroica Alvarado 192 Lh 18.46N 95.46W
Heroica Tlapacoyan 192 Kh 19.58N 97.13W
Heroica Zitácuaro 192 Ih 19.24N 100.22W
Hérouville-Saint-Clair 124 Be 49.12N 0.19W
Herowābād 146 Md 37.37N 48.32 E
Herradura 204 Ch 26.29S 58.18W
Herre 116 Ce 59.06N 9.34 E
Herrera 204 Ck 32.26S 58.38W
Herrera [3] 194 Gj 7.54N 80.38W
Herrera del Duque 126 Ge 39.10N 5.03W
Herrera de Pisuerga 126 Hb 42.36N 4.20W
Herrero, Punta- 192 Ph 19.10N 87.30W
Herrljunga 116 Ef 58.05N 13.02 E
Hers 122 Hk 43.18N 1.33 E
Herschel 180 Dc 69.35N 139.05W
Herselt 124 Gc 51.03N 4.53 E
Herserange 124 He 49.31N 5.47 E
Hershey 184 Ie 40.17N 76.39W
Hersilia 204 Bj 30.00S 61.51W
Herson 112 Jf 46.38N 32.35 E
Hersonesski, mys- 132 Hg 44.33N 33.25 E
Hersonskaja oblast [3] 136 Df 46.40N 33.30 E
Herstal 122 Ld 50.40N 5.38 E
Herten 124 Jc 51.36N 7.08 E
Hertford 118 Mj 51.48N 0.05W
Hertford 118 Mj 51.50N 0.05W
Hertfordshire [3] 118 Mj 51.45N 0.20W
Hertogenbosch, 's- /Den Bosch 122 Lc 51.41N 5.19 E
Hertugen Af Orleans Land 179 Jc 78.15N 21.12W
Hervás 126 Gd 40.16N 5.51W
Herve 124 Hd 50.38N 5.48 E
Herve, Plateau van-/Herveland 124 Hd 50.40N 5.50 E
Herveland/Herve, Plateau van- 124 Hd 50.40N 5.50 E
Hervey Bay 212 Ke 25.15S 152.50 E
Herzberg 120 Je 51.41N 13.14 E
Herzberg am Harz 120 Ge 51.39N 10.20 E
Herzebrock 124 Kc 51.53N 8.15 E
Herzele 124 Fd 50.53N 3.53 E
Herzliyya 146 Ff 32.10N 34.51 E
Herzogenrath 124 Id 50.52N 6.06 E
Herzog-Ernst-Bucht (Vahsel Bay) 222 Af 77.48S 34.39W
Hesāmābād 146 Me 35.52N 48.25 E
Hesbaye/Haspengouws Plateau 122 Ld 50.35N 5.10 E
Hesdin 122 Id 50.22N 2.02 E
Hesel 124 Ja 53.18N 7.36 E
Heshī 146 Md 37.30N 48.15 E
Heshun 152 Jd 37.18N 113.32 E
Hesse (EN) = Hessen [2] 120 Ff 50.30N 9.15 E
Hesselberg 120 Gg 49.05N 10.35 E
Hesselø 116 Dh 56.10N 11.45 E
Hessen = Hesse (EN) [2] 120 Ff 50.30N 9.15 E
Hess Tablemount (EN) 208 Jc 17.50N 174.15W
Heta 138 Eb 71.35N 99.45 E
Heta 140 Mb 71.54N 102.00 E
Hettange-Grande 124 Ie 49.24N 6.09 E
Hettinger 186 Ec 46.00N 102.39W
Heuberg 120 Eh 48.06N 8.55 E
Heuchin 124 Ed 50.28N 2.16 E
Heuru 219a Ed 10.12S 161.25 E
Hève, Cap de la- 122 Ge 49.31N 0.04 E
Heves 120 Qi 47.36N 20.17 E
Heves [2] 120 Qi 47.50N 20.15 E
Hexham 118 Kg 54.58N 2.06W
Hexi 152 Hf 27.44N 102.09 E
Hexian 154 Ei 31.43N 118.22 E
Hexian (Babu) 152 Jg 24.28N 111.34 E
Hexigten Qi (Jingfeng) 152 Kc 43.15N 117.31 E
Heydarābād 146 Kd 37.06N 45.27 E
Heysham 118 Kg 54.02N 2.54W
Heyuan 152 Jg 23.41N 114.43 E
Heywood 212 Ig 38.08S 141.38 E
Heze (Caozhou) 152 Kd 35.14N 115.28 E
Hezuo 152 Hd 35.02N 102.57 E
Hialeah 184 Gm 25.49N 80.17W
Hiawatha 186 Ig 39.51N 95.32W
Hibara-Ko 156 Gc 37.42N 140.03 E
Hibbing 182 Ib 47.25N 92.56W
Hibernia Reef 212 Eb 12.00S 123.25 E
Hibiki-Nada 156 Bd 34.15N 130.40 E
Hibiny 114 Hc 67.40N 33.35 E
Hiburi-Jima 156 Ce 33.10N 132.18 E
Hickman 184 Cg 36.34N 89.11W
Hickory 184 Gh 35.44N 81.21W
Hick's Cay 194 Ce 17.39N 88.08W
Hida-Gawa 156 Ed 35.25N 137.03 E
Hidaka [Jap.] 154 Qc 42.53N 142.28 E
Hidaka [Jap.] 156 Dd 35.28N 134.47 E
Hidaka-Gawa 156 De 33.53N 135.08 E
Hidaka Sanmyaku 154 Qc 42.25N 142.50 E
Hidalgo [2] 190 Ed 20.30N 99.00W
Hidalgo [Mex.] 190 Ed 24.15N 99.26W
Hidalgo [Mex.] 192 Jd 27.47N 99.52W
Hidalgo del Parral 176 Ig 26.56N 105.40W
Hida-Sanchi 156 Ec 36.20N 137.00 E
Hida-Sanmyaku 154 Nf 36.10N 137.30 E
Hiddensee 120 Jb 54.33N 13.07 E
Hidra 116 Bf 58.15N 6.35 E
Hidrolândia 204 Hc 16.58S 49.16W
Hidrolina 204 Hb 14.37S 49.25W
Hieflau 128 Ic 47.36N 14.44 E
Hiei-Zan 156 Dd 35.05N 135.50 E
Hienghène 216 Cd 20.35S 164.56 E
Hierro 158 Ff 27.45N 18.00W
Higashi 156b Bb 26.38N 128.08 E
Higashihiroshima 156 Cd 34.25N 132.43 E
Higashi-izu 156 Fd 34.48N 139.02 E
Higashi-matsuyama 156 Fc 36.02N 139.22 E
Higashimuroran 156a Bb 42.21N 141.02 E
Higashine 154 Pe 38.26N 140.24 E
Higashiōsaka 156 Dd 34.40N 135.37 E
Higashi Rishiri 156a Ba 45.16N 141.15 E
Higashi-Shina-Kai = East China Sea (EN) 140 Og 29.00N 125.00 E
Higgins 186 Fh 36.07N 100.02W
Higham Ferrers 124 Bb 52.18N 0.35W
High Atlas (EN) = Haut Atlas 158 Ge 32.00N 6.00W
Highland [3] 118 Id 57.30N 5.00W
Highland Park 186 Me 42.11N 87.48W
High Level 180 Fe 58.30N 117.05W
Highmore 186 Gd 44.31N 99.27W
High Plains 174 If 38.30N 103.00W
High Point 182 Ld 35.58N 79.59W
High Prairie 180 Fe 55.27N 116.30W
High River 180 Gf 50.35N 113.52W
Highrock Lake 180 He 55.49N 100.23W
High Springs 184 Fk 29.50N 82.36W
High Tatra (EN) = Vysoké Tatry 120 Pg 49.10N 20.00 E
High Willhays 118 Jk 50.41N 3.59W
Highwood Mountains 188 Jc 47.25N 110.30W
High Wycombe 118 Mj 51.38N 0.46W
Higuera de Zaragoza 192 Ee 25.59N 109.16W
Higüero, Punta- 194 Nd 18.22N 67.16W
Higuerote 196 Cg 10.29N 66.06W
Higüey 194 Md 18.37N 68.43W
Hiidenvesi 116 Kd 60.20N 24.10 E
Hii-Gawa 156 Cd 35.26N 132.52 E
Hiiraan [3] 168 He 4.00N 45.30 E
Hiitola 114 Gf 61.16N 29.42 E
Hiiumaa/Hiiuma 110 Id 58.50N 22.40 E
Hijar 126 Lc 41.10N 0.27W
Hijāz, Jabal al- 164 Hf 19.45N 41.55 E
Hiji 156 Be 33.22N 131.32 E
Hiji-Gawa 156 Ce 33.36N 132.29 E
Hikami 156 Dd 35.11N 135.02 E
Hikari 154 Kh 33.58N 131.56 E
Hiketa 156 Dd 34.13N 134.24 E
Hikiā 116 Kd 60.45N 24.55 E
Hiki-Gawa 156 De 33.35N 135.26 E
Ḩikmah, Ra's al- 146 Bg 31.17N 27.44 E
Hikone 154 Ng 35.15N 136.15 E
Hiko-San 156 Be 33.29N 130.56 E
Hikueru Atoll 216 Mc 17.36S 142.37W
Hikurangi 218 Fa 35.36S 174.17 E
Hikurangi 218 Hb 37.55S 178.04 E
Hila 150 Ih 7.35S 127.24 E
Hilāl, Ra's al- 164 Dc 32.55N 22.11 E
Hiland 188 Le 43.08N 107.18W
Hilchenbach 124 Kc 51.00N 8.06 E
Hildburghausen 120 Gf 50.25N 10.45 E
Hilden 124 Ic 51.10N 6.56 E
Hildesheim 120 Fd 52.09N 9.58 E
Hillaby, Mount- 196 Gf 13.12N 59.35W
Hillared 116 Eg 57.38N 13.09 E
Hillary Coast 222 Kf 79.00S 161.00 E
Hill Bank 194 Ce 17.35N 88.42W
Hill City 186 Gg 39.22N 99.51W
Hillcrest Center 188 Fi 35.23N 118.57W
Hille 124 Kb 52.20N 8.45 E
Hillegom 124 Gb 52.18N 4.35 E
Hillekrog 116 Dj 54.36N 11.30 E
Hillerød 116 Ei 55.56N 12.19 E
Hillerstorp 116 Eg 57.19N 13.52 E
Hillesheim 124 Id 50.19N 6.41 E
Hillingdon, London- 124 Bc 51.31N 0.27W
Hillsboro [Il.-U.S.] 186 Lg 39.09N 89.29W
Hillsboro [N.D.-U.S.] 186 Hc 47.26N 97.03W
Hillsboro [Oh.-U.S.] 184 Ff 39.12N 83.37W
Hillsboro [Or.-U.S.] 188 Dd 45.31N 122.59W
Hillsboro [Tx.-U.S.] 186 Hj 32.01N 97.08W
Hillsborough 197p Cb 12.29N 61.26W
Hillsdale 184 Ee 41.55N 84.38W
Hillsville 184 Gg 36.46N 80.44W
Hillswich 118 La 60.28N 1.30W
Hilo 210 Lc 19.44N 155.05W
Hilo Bay 221a Fd 19.44N 155.05W
Hilok 138 Gf 51.22N 110.30 E
Hilok 140 Md 51.19N 106.59 E
Hilton Head Island 184 Gi 32.12N 80.45W
Hiltrup, Münster- 124 Jc 51.54N 7.38 E
Hilvan 146 Hd 37.30N 38.58 E
Hilvarenbeek 124 Hc 51.29N 5.08 E
Hilversum 122 Lb 52.14N 5.10 E
Himāchal Prādesh [3] 148 Fb 31.00N 78.00 E
Himalaya=Himalayas (EN) 140 Kg 29.00N 83.00 E
Himalayas (EN)=Himalaya 140 Kg 29.00N 83.00 E
Himara 130 Ci 40.07N 19.44 E
Himeji 152 Ne 34.49N 134.42 E
Hime-Jima 156 Be 33.43N 131.40 E
Hime-Kawa 156 Ec 37.02N 137.50 E
Hime-Shima 156 Ae 32.49N 128.41 E
Hime-Zaki 156 Fb 38.05N 138.34 E
Himi 154 Nf 36.51N 136.59 E
Himki 114 Ii 55.56N 37.28 E
Himmelbjerget 116 Ch 56.06N 9.42 E
Himmerfjärden 116 Ge 59.00N 17.43 E
Himmerland 116 Ch 56.50N 9.45 E
Himo 170 Gc 3.23S 37.33 E
Ḩimş = Homs (E) 142 Ff 34.44N 36.43 E
Hims, Bahrat- 146 Ge 34.39N 36.34 E
Hinai 156 Ga 40.13N 140.35 E
Ḩinākiyah, Wādī al- 146 Ij 24.30N 40.30 E
Hinca Renancó 206 Hd 34.50S 64.23W
Hinche 194 Kd 19.09N 72.01W
Hinchinbrook 178 Jd 60.22N 146.30W
Hinchinbrook Island 212 Jc 18.25S 146.15 E
Hinckley 124 Ab 52.32N 1.22W
Hindås 116 Eg 57.42N 12.27 E
Hindhead 124 Bc 51.06N 0.44W
Hindi, Badwëynta- = Indian Ocean (EN) 106 Gl 21.00S 82.00 E
Hindmarsh, Lake- 212 Ig 36.05S 141.55 E
Hinds 218 Df 44.00S 171.34 E
Hindsholm 116 Di 55.33N 10.40 E
Hindukush 140 Jf 35.00N 71.00 E
Hindustan 140 Jg 25.00N 79.00 E
Hinesville 184 Gj 31.51N 81.36W
Hinganghāt 148 Fd 20.34N 78.50 E
Hinis 146 Ic 39.22N 41.44 E
Hinis 146 Jc 39.18N 42.12 E
Hinlopenstretet 179 Oc 79.15N 21.00 E
Hinnøya 110 Hb 68.30N 16.00 E
Hino-Gawa 156 Cd 35.27N 133.22 E
Hinojosa del Duque 126 Gf 38.30N 5.09W
Hinokage 156 Be 32.39N 131.24 E
Hi-no-Misaki 156 Cd 35.26N 132.38 E
Hino-Misaki 156 De 33.53N 135.04 E
Hinterrhein 128 Dd 46.49N 9.25 E
Hinton 180 Ff 53.25N 117.34W
Hi-Numa 156 Gc 36.16N 140.30 E
Hinzir Burun 146 Fb 36.22N 35.45 E
Hiou 219b Ca 13.08S 166.33 E
Hipólito 192 Ie 25.41N 101.26W
Hippolytushoef, Wieringen- 124 Gb 52.54N 4.59 E
Hippone 128 Bn 36.52N 7.44 E
Hirado 154 Jh 33.22N 129.33 E
Hirado-Shima 154 Jh 33.19N 129.32 E
Hiraka 156 Gb 39.16N 140.29 E
Hirakata 156 Dd 34.48N 135.38 E
Hirākud 148 Gd 21.15N 84.15 E
Hiraman 170 Gc 1.07S 39.55 E
Hiranai 156a Bc 40.54N 140.57 E
Hirara 152 Mg 24.48N 125.17 E
Hira-Shima 156 Ae 33.01N 129.15 E
Hirata 156 Cd 35.26N 132.49 E
Hiratsuka 156 Fd 35.19N 139.19 E
Hirfanlı barajı Gölü 146 Ec 39.10N 33.32 E
Hirgis 152 Fb 49.32N 93.48 E
Hirgis-Nur 140 Le 49.12N 93.24 E
Hirhafok 162 Ie 23.29N 5.45 E
Hîrlău 130 Jb 47.26N 26.54 E
Hiromi 156 Ce 33.15N 132.38 E
Hiroo 152 Pc 42.17N 143.19 E
Hirosaki 152 Pc 40.35N 140.28 E
Hiroshima 142 Pf 34.24N 132.27 E
Hiroshima Ken [2] 154 Lg 34.35N 132.50 E
Hiroshima-Wan 156 Cd 34.10N 132.20 E
Hirschhorn (Neckar) 124 Ke 49.27N 8.54 E
Hirson 122 Ke 49.55N 4.05 E
Hîrşova 130 Ke 44.41N 27.56 E
Hirtibaciu 130 Hd 45.44N 24.14 E
Hirtshals 114 Bh 57.35N 9.58 E
Hirvensalmi 116 Lc 61.38N 26.48 E
His 168 Hc 10.50N 46.54 E
Hisai 156 Ed 34.40N 136.28 E
Hisaka-Shima 156 Ae 32.48N 128.52 E
Hisar 148 Fc 29.10N 75.43 E
Hisar 130 Jg 42.35N 27.00 E
Hisarcik 130 Mj 39.15N 29.15 E
Hisarja 130 Hg 42.30N 24.42 E
Ḩismā 146 Fh 28.30N 35.50 E
Ḩişn al 'Abr 164 If 16.08N 47.14 E
Ḩişn aş Şahābī 164 Dc 30.01N 20.48 E
Hispaniola (EN) = La Española 174 Lh 19.00N 71.00W
Histon 124 Cb 52.15N 0.06 E
Histria 130 Le 44.30N 28.45 E
Hit 146 Jf 33.38N 42.49 E
Hita 154 Kh 33.19N 130.56 E
Hitachi 154 Pf 36.36N 140.39 E
Hitachi-ōta 156 Gc 36.32N 140.31 E
Hitchin 124 Bc 51.57N 0.16W
Hitiaa 221e Fc 17.36S 149.18W
Hitotsuse-Gawa 156 Be 32.03N 131.31 E
Hitoyoshi 154 Kh 32.15N 130.45 E
Hitra 110 Gc 63.30N 8.45 E
Hiuchi-ga-Take 156 Fc 36.57N 139.17 E
Hiuchi-Nada 156 Cd 34.05N 133.15 E
Hiuma/Hiiumaa 110 Id 58.50N 22.40 E

Index Symbols

[1] Independent Nation
[2] State, Region
[3] District, County
[4] Municipality
[5] Colony, Dependency
Continent
Physical Region
Historical or Cultural Region
Mount, Mountain
Volcano
Hill
Mountains, Mountain Range
Hills, Escarpment
Plateau, Upland
Pass, Gap
Plain, Lowland
Delta
Salt Flat
Valley, Canyon
Crater, Cave
Karst Features
Depression
Polder
Desert, Dunes
Forest, Woods
Heath, Steppe
Oasis
Cape, Point
Coast, Beach
Cliff
Peninsula
Isthmus
Sandbank
Island
Atoll
Rock, Reef
Islands, Archipelago
Rocks, Reefs
Coral Reef
Well, Spring
Geyser
River, Stream
Waterfall, Rapids
River Mouth, Estuary
Lake
Salt Lake
Intermittent Lake
Reservoir
Swamp, Pond
Canal
Glacier
Ice Shelf, Pack Ice
Ocean
Sea
Gulf, Bay
Strait, Fjord
Lagoon
Bank
Seamount
Tablemount
Ridge
Shelf
Basin
Escarpment, Sea Scarp
Fracture
Trench, Abyss
National Park, Reserve
Point of Interest
Recreation Site
Cave, Cavern
Historic Site
Ruins
Wall, Walls
Church, Abbey
Temple
Scientific Station
Railway station
Airport
Port
Military installation
Lighthouse
Mine
Tunnel
Dam, Bridge

Hiv 132 Oi 41.46N 47.57 E
Hiva 136 Gg 41.25N 60.23 E
Hiva Oa, Ile- 208 Ne 9.45S 139.00W
Hiw 146 Ei 26.01N 32.16 E
Hjademeste/Häädemeeste 116 Kf 58.00N 24.28 E
Hjallerup 116 Dg 57.10N 10.09 E
Hjälmare kanal 116 Fe 59.25N 15.55 E
Hjälmaren 110 Hd 59.15N 15.45 E
Hjelm 116 Dh 56.10N 10.50 E
Hjelmelandsvågen 114 Bg 59.15N 6.10 E
Hjelmsøya 114 Fa 71.05N 24.43 E
Hjeltefjorden 116 Ad 60.40N 4.55 E
Hjerkinn 116 Cb 62.13N 9.32 E
Hjo 116 Ef 58.18N 14.17 E
Hjørring 114 Bh 57.28N 9.59 E
Hlatikulu 172 Ee 26.58S 31.19 E
Hlavní město Praha [3] 120 Kf 50.05N 14.25 E
Hlavní město SSR Bratislava [3] 120 Nh 48.10N 17.10 E
Hlinsko 120 Lg 49.46N 15.54 E
Hlohovec 120 Nh 48.25N 17.48 E
Hluhluwe 172 Ee 28.02S 32.17 E
Hmelnickaja oblast [3] 136 Cf 49.30N 27.00 E
Hmelnicki 136 Cf 49.24N 26.57 E
Hmelnik 132 Ee 49.33N 27.59 E
Hnilec 120 Rh 48.53N 21.01 E
Ho 166 Fd 6.36N 0.28 E
Hoa Binh 148 Ld 20.50N 105.20 E
Hoanib 172 Ac 19.23S 13.06 E
Hoare Bay 180 Lc 65.30N 63.10W
Hoback Peak 188 Je 43.10N 110.33W
Hobart [Austl.] 210 Fi 42.53S 147.19 E
Hobart [Ok.-U.S.] 186 Gi 35.01N 99.06W
Hobbs 182 Ge 32.42N 103.08W
Hobbs Coast 222 Nf 74.50S 131.00W
Hobda 132 Sd 50.55N 54.38 E
Hoboken, Antwerpen- 124 Gc 51.10N 4.21 E
Hoboksar 152 Eb 46.47N 85.43 E
Hobq Shamo 152 Ic 40.30N 108.00 E
Hobro 114 Bh 56.38N 9.48 E
Hoburgen 114 Eh 56.55N 18.07 E
Hobyā 160 Lh 5.20N 48.38 E
Hocalar 130 Mk 38.37N 29.57 E
Hochalmspitze 128 Hc 47.01N 13.19 E
Hochfeiler/Gran Pilastro 128 Fd 46.58N 11.44 E
Hochgolling 128 Hc 47.16N 13.45 E
Hochschwab 128 Jc 47.36N 15.05 E
Höchstadt an der Aisch 120 Gg 49.42N 10.44 E
Hochstetters Forland 179 Kc 75.45N 20.00W
Höchst im Odenwald 124 Ke 49.48N 9.00 E
Hochtor 128 Gc 47.05N 12.48 E
Hockenheim 124 Ke 49.19N 8.33 E
Hodaka-Dake 156 Ec 36.17N 137.39 E
Hodda 168 Ic 11.30N 50.45 E
Hoddesdon 124 Cc 51.45N 0.00
Hodgenville 184 Eg 37.34N 85.44W
Hodh 158 Gg 16.10N 8.40W
Hodh ech Chargui [3] 162 Ff 17.00N 7.15W
Hodh el Gharbi [3] 162 Ff 16.30N 10.00W
Hódmezővásárhely 120 Qj 46.25N 20.20 E
Hodna, Chott el- 162 Hb 35.25N 4.45 E
Hodna, Monts du- 162 Hb 35.50N 4.50 E
Hodna, Plaine du- 126 Qi 35.35N 4.35 E
Hodonín 120 Nh 48.52N 17.08 E
Hodorov 132 De 49.25N 24.18 E
Hodžambas 135 Ee 38.06N 65.01 E
Hodža-Pirjah, gora- 135 Fe 38.47N 67.35 E
Hodžejli 136 Fg 42.23N 59.20 E
Hœdic, Ile de- 122 Dg 47.20N 2.52W
Hoegaarden 124 Gd 50.47N 4.53 E
Hoei/Huy 122 Ld 50.31N 5.14 E
Hoë Karoo 158 Jl 30.00S 21.30 E
Hoekse Waard 124 Gc 51.45N 4.25 E
Hoek van Holland 122 Kc 51.59N 4.09 E
Hoeselt 124 Hd 50.51N 5.29 E
Hof 120 Hf 50.19N 11.55 E
Höfdakaupstadur 114a Bb 65.50N 20.19W
Hofgeismar 120 Fe 51.29N 9.24 E
Hofheim 124 Kd 50.05N 8.27 E
Hofmeyr 172 Df 31.39S 25.50 E
Höfn 114a Cb 64.15N 15.13W
Hofors 114 Df 60.33N 16.17 E
Hofsjökull 110 Ec 64.49N 18.48W
Hōfu 154 Kg 34.03N 131.34 E
Höganäs 116 Eh 56.12N 12.33 E
Hogarth, Mount- 212 Hd 21.48S 136.58 E
Hogback Mountain 188 Id 44.54N 112.07W
Hog Cliffs 197d Ba 17.38N 61.44W
Hoge Venen/Hautes Fagnes 120 Bf 50.30N 6.00 E
Högfors/Karkkila 114 Ff 60.32N 24.11 E
Hog Island 197p Bb 12.00N 61.44W
Hogne, Somme-Leuze- 124 Hd 50.15N 5.17 E
Hog Point 197d Ba 17.43N 61.48W
Högsby 114 Dh 57.10N 16.02 E
Høgste Breakulen 116 Bc 61.41N 7.02 E
Høgstegia 116 Db 62.23N 10.08 E
Hogsty Reef 194 Kc 21.41N 73.49W
Hōhang-nyōng 154 Jd 41.48N 128.20 E
Hohe Acht 120 Cf 50.23N 7.03 E
Hohe Eifel 124 Id 50.16N 6.50 E
Hohenau 204 Eh 27.05S 55.45W
Hohenems 128 Dc 47.22N 9.41 E
Hohenloher Ebene 120 Fg 49.20N 9.40 E
Hohes Venn 120 Bf 50.30N 6.00 E
Hohe Tauern 128 Gc 47.10N 12.30 E
Hohhot 142 Ne 40.51N 111.38 E
Hohneck, Le- 122 Nf 48.02N 7.01 E
Hōhoku 156 Bd 34.17N 130.57 E
Höhr-Grenzhausen 124 Jd 50.26N 7.40 E
Höhtiäinen 116 Mb 62.50N 29.40 E
Hoh Xil Hu 152 Fd 35.35N 91.06 E
Hoh Xil Shan 140 Lf 35.20N 91.00 E
Hoi An 148 Le 15.52N 108.19 E
Hoima 170 Fb 1.26N 31.21 E
Hoisington 186 Gg 38.31N 98.47W
Hoj, vozvyšennost- 134 Ob 68.50N 71.30 E
Højer 116 Cj 54.58N 8.43 E
Hojniki 136 Ce 51.54N 29.56 E
Hōjō 154 Lh 33.58N 132.46 E
Hökensås 116 Ff 58.11N 14.08 E
Hokianga Harbour 218 Ea 35.30S 173.20 E
Hokitika 210 Ii 42.43S 170.58 E
Hok-Kai=Okhotsk, Sea of- (EN) 140 Qd 53.00N 150.00 E
Hokkaidō 140 Qe 43.00N 143.00 E
Hokkaidō Ken [2] 154 Qc 43.00N 143.00 E
Hokksund 114 Bg 59.47N 9.59 E
Hokmābād 146 Qd 36.37N 57.36 E
Hokota 156 Gc 36.10N 140.30 E
Hol 116 Cd 60.36N 8.22 E
Holap 220d Ba 7.39N 151.54 E
Holbæk 116 Di 55.43N 11.43 E
Holbeach 124 Cb 52.48N 0.01 E
Holbeach Marsh 124 Cb 52.52N 0.02 E
Holbox, Isla- 192 Pg 21.33N 87.15W
Holbrook 182 Ee 34.54N 110.10W
Holdenville 186 Hi 35.05N 96.24W
Holderness 118 Mh 53.47N 0.10W
Holdrege 186 Gf 40.26N 99.22W
Hold With Hope 179 Jd 73.40N 21.45W
Hole in the Wall 184 Im 25.51N 77.12W
Hølen 116 De 59.32N 10.45 E
Holešov 120 Ng 49.20N 17.33 E
Holetown 197q Ab 13.11N 59.39W
Holguín 176 Lg 20.53N 76.15W
Holguín [3] 194 Jc 20.40N 75.50W
Hol-Hol 168 Gc 11.20N 42.50 E
Holitna 178 Hd 61.40N 157.12W
Höljes 114 Cf 60.54N 12.36 E
Hollabrunn 128 Kb 48.33N 16.05 E
Holland 184 Dd 42.47N 86.07W
Holland [Eng.-U.K.] 124 Bb 52.52N 0.10W
Holland [Neth.] 110 Ge 52.20N 4.45 E
Hollandale 186 Kj 33.10N 90.58W
Hollandsbird Island 172 Ad 24.45S 14.34 E
Hollands Diep 124 Gc 51.40N 4.30 E
Hollesley Bay 124 Db 52.04N 1.33 E
Hollick-Kenyon Plateau 222 Pf 79.00S 97.00W
Hollis 186 Gi 34.41N 99.55W
Hollister [Ca.-U.S.] 188 Eh 36.51N 121.24W
Hollister [Id.-U.S.] 188 He 42.23N 114.35W
Hollola 116 Kc 61.03N 25.26 E
Höllviksnäs 116 Ei 55.25N 12.57 E
Holly Springs 186 Li 34.41N 89.26W
Hollywood 182 Kf 26.00N 80.09W
Holm 114 Hh 57.09N 31.12 E
Holma 166 Hd 9.54N 13.06 E
Holman Island 180 Fb 70.40N 117.35W
Hólmavík 114a Bb 65.43N 21.41W
Holmes Reefs 208 Ff 16.30S 148.00 E
Holmestrand 116 De 59.29N 10.18 E
Holm Land 179 Kb 80.16N 18.20W
Holms 179 Gd 74.30N 57.00W
Holmsjö 116 Fh 56.25N 15.32 E
Holmsjön [Swe.] 114 De 62.25N 15.20 E
Holmsjön [Swe.] 116 Gb 62.40N 16.35 E
Holmsk 138 Jg 47.00N 142.03 E
Holmski 132 Kg 44.50N 38.24 E
Holmsland Klit 116 Ch 56.00N 8.10 E
Holmsund 114 Ee 63.42N 20.21 E
Holmsveden 116 Gc 61.07N 16.43 E
Holmudden 116 Hg 57.57N 19.21 E
Holod 130 Fc 46.47N 22.08 E
Holohit, Punta- 192 Og 21.37N 88.08W
Holothuria Banks (EN) 212 Fb 13.25S 126.00 E
Holsnøy 116 Ad 60.35N 5.05 E
Holstebro 114 Bh 56.21N 8.38 E
Holsted 116 Ci 55.30N 8.55 E
Holstein 186 Ie 42.29N 95.33W
Holsteinsborg/Sisimiut 224 Nc 67.05N 53.45W
Holt 124 Db 52.54N 1.05 E
Holten 124 Ib 52.17N 6.27 E
Holton 186 Ig 39.28N 95.44W
Holtoson 138 Ff 50.18N 103.23 E
Holtyn-Daba 152 Ib 47.40N 107.20 E
Holwerd, Westdongeradeel- 124 Ha 53.22N 5.54 E
Holy Cross 178 Hd 62.12N 159.47W
Holyhead 118 Ih 53.20N 4.36W
Holy Island [Eng.-U.K.] 118 Lf 55.41N 1.48W
Holy Island [Wales-U.K.] 118 Ih 53.18N 4.37W
Holyoke [Co.-U.S.] 186 Ef 40.35N 102.18W
Holyoke [Ma.-U.S.] 184 Kd 42.12N 72.37W
Holyšov 120 Jg 49.36N 13.07 E
Homa Bay 170 Fc 0.31S 34.27 E
Homalin 148 Id 24.52N 94.55 E
Homathko River 188 Ca 50.55N 124.50W
Homberg (Ohm) 124 Kd 50.44N 8.59 E
Hombori 166 Eb 15.17N 1.42W
Hombre Muerto, Salar del- 206 Gc 25.23S 67.06W
Homburg 120 Dg 49.19N 7.20 E
Home Bay 174 Mc 68.45N 67.10W
Homécourt 124 He 49.14N 5.59 E
Home Hill 212 Jc 19.40S 147.25 E
Homer [Ak.-U.S.] 176 Dd 59.39N 151.33W
Homer [La.-U.S.] 186 Jj 32.48N 93.04W
Homert 124 Jc 51.16N 8.06 E
Homerville 184 Fj 31.02N 82.45W
Homestead 184 Gm 25.29N 80.29W
Homewood 184 Di 33.29N 86.48W
Hommelstø 114 Cd 65.25N 12.30 E
Hommersåk 116 Af 58.55N 5.50 E
Homoine 172 Fd 23.52S 35.08 E
Homoljske Planina 130 Ee 44.20N 21.45 E
Homonhon 150 Id 10.44N 125.43 E
Homosassa 184 Fk 28.47N 82.37W
Homs (EN)=Ḥimṣ 142 Ff 34.44N 36.43 E
Honan (EN)=Henan Sheng (Ho-nan Sheng) [2] 152 Je 34.00N 114.00 E
Honan (EN)=Ho-nan Sheng→Henan Sheng [2] 152 Je 34.00N 114.00 E
Ho-nan Sheng→Henan Sheng=Honan (EN) [2] 152 Je 34.00N 114.00 E
Honaz 130 Ml 37.45N 29.17 E
Honaz Dağı 130 Ml 37.41N 29.18 E
Honbetsu 154 Qc 43.18N 143.33 E
Honda 202 Db 5.13N 74.45W
Honda, Bahia- 194 Lg 12.21N 71.47W
Hondeklipbaai 172 Bf 30.20S 17.18 E
Hòn Diên, Núi- 148 Lf 11.33N 108.38 E
Hondo 190 Ge 18.29N 88.19W
Hondo [Jap.] 154 Kh 32.27N 130.12 E
Hondo [N.M.-U.S.] 186 Dj 33.23N 105.16W
Hondo [Tx.-U.S.] 186 Gl 29.21N 99.09W
Hondo, Rio- 186 Dj 33.22N 104.24W
Hondschoote 124 Ed 50.59N 2.35 E
Hondsrug 122 Mb 52.50N 6.50 E
Honduras [1] 176 Kh 15.00N 86.30W
Honduras, Cabo de- 194 De 16.01N 86.01W
Honduras, Golfo de-=Honduras, Gulf of- (EN) 174 Kh 16.10N 87.50W
Honduras, Gulf of- 174 Kh 16.10N 87.50W
Honduras, Gulf of- (EN)=Honduras, Golfo de- 174 Kh 16.10N 87.50W
Hønefoss 114 Cf 60.10N 10.18 E
Honey Lake 188 Ef 40.16N 120.19W
Honfleur 122 Ge 49.25N 0.14 E
Hông, Sông- [Asia] =Red River (EN) 140 Mg 20.17N 106.34 E
Hong'an (Huang'an) 154 Ci 31.17N 114.37 E
Hongch'ŏn 154 If 37.41N 127.52 E
Hong-Do 154 Hg 34.41N 125.13 E
Hong He 154 Ch 32.24N 115.32 E
Honghton Lake 184 Ec 44.22N 84.43W
Hong Hu 152 Je 30.00N 113.25 E
Honghu (Xindi) 154 Bj 29.50N 113.28 E
Hongshui 152 Id 36.46N 105.05 E
Hong Kong/Xianggang [5] 142 Ng 22.15N 114.10 E
Hongliuyuan 152 Gc 41.02N 95.24 E
Hongluoxian 154 Fd 41.01N 120.52 E
Hongning → Wulian 154 Eg 35.45N 119.13 E
Hongor 154 Bb 45.48N 112.45 E
Hongqizhen 152 Ih 18.48N 109.30 E
Hongshui He 140 Mg 23.47N 109.33 E
Hongsŏng 154 If 36.36N 126.40 E
Hongtong 154 Af 36.15N 111.41 E
Hongū 156 De 33.50N 135.46 E
Honguedo, Détroit d' - 180 Lg 49.30N 65.00W
Hongwansi → Sunan 152 Gd 38.59N 99.25 E
Hongwŏn 154 Id 40.02N 127.58 E
Hongyuan (Hurama) 152 He 32.45N 102.38 E
Hongze (Gaoliangjian) 152 Ke 33.10N 119.58 E
Hongze Hu 152 Ke 33.20N 118.40 E
Honiara 210 Ge 9.27S 159.57 E
Honikulu, Passe- 220h Ac 13.03S 176.11W
Honiton 118 Jk 50.48N 3.13W
Honjō 154 Pe 39.23N 140.03 E
Honkajoki 116 Jb 61.59N 22.16 E
Hon-kawane 156 Fd 35.07N 138.06 E
Honningsvåg 114 Ga 70.59N 26.01 E
Honō 116 Dg 57.42N 11.39 E
Honokaa 221a Fc 20.05N 155.28W
Honokohau 221a Eb 21.01N 156.37W
Honolulu 210 Lb 21.19N 157.52W
Honomu 221a Fd 19.52N 155.07W
Honrubia 126 Je 39.37N 2.16W
Honshū 140 Pf 36.00N 136.00 E
Hontenisse 124 Gc 51.23N 4.00 E
Hontenisse-Kloosterzande 124 Gc 51.23N 4.00 E
Honuapo Bay 221a Fd 19.05N 155.33W
Honuu 138 Jc 66.27N 143.06 E
Honyō 156 Fc 36.14N 139.10 E
Hood 180 Gc 67.25N 108.53W
Hood, Mount- 174 Ge 45.23N 121.41W
Hood Point 212 Df 34.23S 119.34 E
Hood River 188 Ed 45.43N 121.31W
Hoogeveen 122 Mb 52.43N 6.29 E
Hoogezand-Sappemeer 124 Ia 53.09N 6.48 E
Hooglede 124 Fd 50.59N 3.05 E
Hoogstraten 124 Gc 51.24N 4.46 E
Hooker 186 Fh 36.52N 101.13W
Hooker, Cape- 222 Kf 70.38S 166.45 E
Hook Head/Rinn Dúain 118 Gi 52.07N 6.55W
Hook Island 212 Jc 20.10S 148.55 E
Hoolehua 221a Db 21.10N 157.05W
Hoonah 178 Le 58.07N 135.26W
Hooper, Cape - 180 Kc 68.24N 66.43W
Hooper Bay 178 Fd 61.31N 166.06W
Hoopeston 186 Mf 40.28N 87.40W
Höör 116 Ei 55.56N 13.32 E
Hoorn 122 Lb 52.38N 5.04 E
Hoornaar 124 Gc 51.53N 4.57 E
Hoover Dam 188 Hi 36.00N 114.27W
Hopa 146 Ib 41.25N 41.24 E
Hope [Ar.-U.S.] 186 Jj 33.40N 93.36W
Hope [Az.-U.S.] 188 Ij 33.44N 113.42W
Hope [B.C.-Can.] 188 Eb 49.23N 121.26W
Hope, Ben- 118 Ic 58.24N 4.36W
Hope, Lake- 212 Ef 32.50S 121.40 E
Hope, Point- 174 Cc 68.21N 166.50W
Hopedale 180 Le 55.50N 60.10W
Hopefield 172 Bf 33.04S 18.21 E
Hopeh (EN)=Hebei Sheng (Ho-pei Sheng) [2] 152 Kd 39.00N 116.00 E
Hopeh (EN)=Ho-pei Sheng→Hebei Sheng [2] 152 Kd 39.00N 116.00 E
Hopeh (EN)=Hu-pei Sheng→Hubei Sheng [2] 152 Je 31.00N 112.00 E
Ho-pei Sheng→Hebei Sheng=Hopeh (EN) [2] 152 Kd 39.00N 116.00 E
Hopelchén 192 Oh 19.46N 89.51W
Hopen 179 Oc 76.35N 25.10 E
Hopër 110 Kf 49.36N 42.19 E
Hopes Advance, Cap - 180 Kd 61.05N 69.33W
Hopetoun [Austl.] 212 Ig 35.44S 142.22 E
Hopetoun [Austl.] 210 Dh 33.57S 120.07 E
Hopetown 172 Ce 29.34S 24.03 E
Hopewell 184 Ig 37.17N 77.19W
Hopewell Islands 180 Je 58.20N 78.10W
Hopin 148 Jd 24.59N 96.31 E
Hopkins, Lake- 212 Fd 24.15S 128.50 E
Hopkinsville 182 Jd 36.52N 87.29W
Hopsten 124 Jb 52.23N 7.37 E
Hoptrup 116 Ci 55.11N 9.28 E
Hoquiam 182 Cb 46.59N 123.53W
Hor 138 Ig 47.55N 135.01 E
Hor 138 Ig 47.48N 134.43 E
Hōrai 156 Ed 34.55N 137.34 E
Hōrai-San 156 Dd 35.13N 135.53 E
Horasan 146 Jb 40.03N 42.11 E
Horaždovice 120 Jg 49.20N 13.42 E
Horb am Neckar 120 Eh 48.26N 8.41 E
Hörby 116 Ei 55.51N 13.39 E
Horconcitos 194 Fi 8.19N 82.10W
Hordaland [2] 114 Bf 60.15N 6.30 E
Hordogoj 138 Gd 62.32N 115.38 E
Horezmskaja oblast [3] 136 Gg 41.30N 60.40 E
Horezu 130 Hd 45.09N 24.01 E
Horgen 128 Cc 47.15N 8.36 E
Horgoš 130 Cc 46.09N 19.58 E
Horgos 136 Ig 44.10N 80.20 E
Hořice 120 Lf 50.22N 15.38 E
Horinger 154 Ad 40.24N 111.46 E
Horizon Tablemount (EN) 208 Kc 19.40N 168.30W
Horizontina 204 Eh 27.37S 54.19W
Horley 124 Bc 51.10N 0.11W
Horlick Mountains 222 Og 85.23S 121.00W
Hormigas 192 Gc 29.12N 105.45W
Hormoz 144 Id 27.06N 56.28 E
Hormoz, Kūh-e- 144 Id 27.27N 55.10 E
Hormoz, Tangeh-ye-=Hormuz, Strait of- (EN) 140 Hg 26.34N 56.15 E
Hormozgān [3] 144 Id 27.30N 56.00 E
Hormūd-e Bāgh 146 Pi 27.30N 54.18 E
Hormuz, Strait of- (EN)=Hormoz, Tangeh-ye- 140 Hg 26.34N 56.15 E
Horn 110 Db 66.28N 22.30W
Horn 180 Fd 61.30N 118.00W
Horn [Aus.] 128 Jb 48.39N 15.39 E
Horn [Swe.] 116 Fg 57.54N 15.50 E
Horn, Cape- (EN)=Hornos, Cabo de- 198 Jk 55.59S 67.16W
Hornád 120 Qh 48.00N 20.58 E
Hornaday 180 Fc 69.22N 123.56W
Hornavan 114 Dc 66.14N 17.30 E
Hornbach 124 Je 49.12N 7.22 E
Horn-Bad Meinberg 124 Kc 51.54N 8.57 E
Hornby Bay 180 Fc 66.35N 117.50W
Horncastle 118 Mh 53.13N 0.07W
Horndal 116 Gd 60.18N 16.25 E
Horndean 124 Bd 50.55N 0.59W
Horne, Iles de- = Horn Islands (EN) 208 Jf 14.19S 178.05W
Hörnefors 114 Ee 63.38N 19.54 E
Hornell 184 Id 42.19N 77.39W
Hornepayne 180 Jg 49.13N 84.47W
Hornindalsvatn 116 Bc 61.55N 6.25 E
Hornisgrinde 120 Eh 48.36N 8.12 E
Horn Islands (EN) = Horne, Iles de- 208 Jf 14.19S 178.05W
Hörnli 128 Cc 47.23N 8.56 E
Hornomoravský úval 120 Ng 49.25N 17.20 E
Hornos, Cabo de-=Horn, Cape- (EN) 198 Jk 55.59S 67.16W
Hornoy-le-Bourg 124 De 49.51N 1.54 E
Horn Plateau 180 Fd 62.10N 119.30W
Hornsea 118 Mh 53.55N 0.10W
Hornslandet 116 Gc 61.40N 17.30 E
Horns Rev 116 Bi 55.30N 7.45 E
Hornsund 179 Nc 76.58N 15.28 E
Hornsundtind 179 Nc 76.55N 16.10 E
Horog 142 Jf 37.31N 71.33 E
Horoizumi 156a Cb 42.01N 143.07 E
Horokanai 156a Ca 44.02N 142.09 E
Horol 132 He 49.29N 33.49 E
Horol [R.S.F.S.R.] 154 Lb 44.30N 132.03 E
Horol [Ukr.-U.S.S.R.] 132 He 49.47N 33.16 E
Horonobe 154 Pb 45.00N 141.51 E
Hořovice 120 Jg 49.50N 13.54 E
Horqin Youyi Qianqi (Ulan Hot) 142 Oe 46.04N 122.00 E
Horqin Youyi Zhongqi (Bayan Huxu) 152 Lb 45.04N 121.27 E
Horqin Zuoyi Houqi (Ganjig) 152 Lc 42.57N 122.14 E
Horqin Zuoyi Zhongqi (Baokang) 152 Lc 44.06N 123.19 E
Horqueta 206 Ib 23.24S 56.53W
Horred 116 Eg 57.21N 12.28 E
Horse Creek [Co.-U.S.] 186 Eg 38.05N 103.19W
Horse Creek [U.S.] 188 Nf 41.57N 103.58W
Horsehead Lake 186 Gc 47.02N 99.47W
Horsens 114 Bi 55.52N 9.52 E
Horsham [Austl.] 210 Fh 36.43S 142.13 E
Horsham [Eng.-U.K.] 118 Mj 51.04N 0.21W
Hørsholm 116 Ei 55.53N 12.30 E
Horšovský Týn 120 Ig 49.32N 12.57 E
Horst 124 Ic 51.28N 6.03 E
Horst 124 Gd 50.56N 4.47 E
Hörstel 124 Jb 52.19N 7.35 E
Horstmar 124 Jb 52.05N 7.19 E
Horsunlu 130 Ll 37.55N 28.36 E
Horta 162 Bb 38.32N 28.28W
Horta [3] 162 Bb 38.35N 28.40W
Horta, Cap de l'- / Huertas, Cabo de- 126 Lf 38.21N 0.24W
Horten 116 De 59.25N 10.30 E
Horton 180 Ec 70.01N 126.42W
Hörvik 116 Fh 56.03N 14.46 E
Horvot 'Avedat 146 Fg 30.48N 34.46 E
Horvot Mezada 146 Fg 31.19N 35.21 E
Horwood Lake 184 Fa 48.03N 82.20W
Hosaina 168 Fd 7.33N 37.52 E
Hose Mountains 150 Ff 2.00N 114.10 E
Hosenofu 164 De 23.34N 21.15 E
Hoseynābād [Iran] 146 Ne 34.30N 50.59 E
Hoseynābād [Iran] 146 Le 35.33N 47.08 E
Hoseynīyeh 146 Mg 32.42N 48.14 E
Hoshāb 146 Cc 26.01N 63.56 E
Hosingen 124 Id 50.01N 6.05 E
Hoskins 214 Ei 5.30S 150.32 E
Hospet 148 Fe 15.16N 76.24 E
Hospital, Cuchilla del- 204 Ej 31.40S 54.53W
Hospitalet del Infante / l'Hospitalet de l'Infant 126 Md 40.59N 0.56 E
Hospitalet de Llobregat 126 Oc 41.22N 2.08 E
Hoste, Isla- 198 Jk 55.15S 69.00W
Hot 148 Je 18.06N 98.35 E
Hotagen 114 De 63.53N 14.29 E
Hotaka 156 Ec 36.20N 137.53 E
Hotan 142 Jf 37.07N 79.55 E
Hotan He 140 Ke 40.30N 80.48 E
Hotazel 172 Ce 27.15S 23.00 E
Hotin 132 Ee 48.29N 26.29 E
Hoting 114 Dd 64.07N 16.10 E
Hotkovo 114 Ih 56.18N 38.00 E
Hotont 152 Hb 47.23N 102.30 E
Hot Springs 182 Gc 43.26N 103.29W
Hot Springs→Truth or Consequences 182 Fe 33.08N 107.15W
Hot Springs National Park 176 Jf 34.30N 93.03W
Hot Springs Peak 188 Gf 41.22N 117.26W
Hotspur Seamount (EN) 202 Kg 18.00S 36.00W
Hottah Lake 180 Fc 65.05N 118.36W
Hottentot Bay 172 Ae 26.07S 14.57 E
Hotton 124 Hd 50.16N 5.27 E
Hottstedt 124 He 51.39N 11.30 E
Houailou 216 Cd 21.17S 165.38 E
Houat, Ile de- 122 Dg 47.24N 2.58W
Houdan 122 Hf 48.47N 1.36 E
Houeillès 122 Gj 44.12N 0.02 E
Houffalize 124 Hd 50.08N 5.47 E
Houghton 182 Jb 47.06N 88.34W
Houillères, Canal des- 124 If 48.42N 6.55 E
Houji → Liangshan 154 Dg 35.48N 116.07 E
Houlgate 124 Be 49.18N 0.04W
Houlton 182 Nb 46.08N 67.51W
Houma [China] 152 Jd 35.36N 111.23 E
Houma [La.-U.S.] 182 If 29.36N 90.43W
Houndé 166 Ec 11.30N 3.31W
Hourn, Loch- 118 Hd 57.10N 5.40W
Hourtin, Étang d'- 122 Ei 45.10N 1.06W
House Range 188 Ig 39.30N 113.15W
Houston [Mo.-U.S.] 186 Kh 37.22N 91.58W
Houston [Tx.-U.S.] 176 Jg 29.46N 95.22W
Houthalen-Helchteren 124 Hc 51.02N 5.22 E
Houthulst 124 Ed 50.59N 2.57 E
Houthulst-Merkem 124 Ed 50.57N 2.51 E
Houtman Abrolhos 212 Ce 28.40S 113.50 E
Houtskär/Houtskari 116 Id 60.15N 21.20 E
Houtskari/Houtskär 116 Id 60.15N 21.20 E
Houyet 124 Hd 50.11N 5.01 E
Houyet-Celles 124 Hd 50.19N 5.01 E
Hov 116 Di 55.55N 10.16 E
Hova 116 Ff 58.52N 14.13 E
Hovden 116 Be 59.32N 7.21 E
Hovden 116 Ac 61.40N 4.50 E
Hove 118 Mk 50.49N 0.10W
Hovgaard 179 Kc 80.00N 18.45W
Hovmantorp 116 Fh 56.47N 15.08 E
Hovu-Aksy 138 Ef 51.01N 93.43 E
Howa 168 Db 17.30N 27.08 E
Howar 158 Jg 17.30N 27.08 E
Howard 186 Hd 44.01N 97.32W
Howe, Cape- 208 Fh 37.31S 149.59 E
Howell 184 Fd 42.36N 83.55W
Howick [N.Z.] 218 Fb 36.54S 174.56 E
Howick [S.Afr.] 172 Ee 29.28S 30.14 E
Howland 184 Mc 45.14N 68.40W
Howland Island 208 Jd 0.48N 176.38W
Howrah → Hāora 142 Kg 22.35N 88.20 E
Howth 118 Gh 53.23N 6.04W
Howz Soltān 146 Ne 35.06N 51.06 E
Hoxie 186 Fg 39.21N 100.26W
Höxter 120 Fe 51.46N 9.23 E
Hoxud 152 Ec 42.16N 86.51 E
Hoy 118 Jc 58.52N 3.18W
Hoya 124 Lb 52.48N 9.09 E
Høyanger 114 Bf 61.13N 6.05 E
Hoyerswerda/Wojerecy 120 Ke 51.26N 14.15 E
Hoyos 126 Fd 40.10N 6.43W
Hōyo-Shotō 156 Ce 33.50N 132.30 E
Hoytiäinen 114 Ge 62.48N 29.39 E
Hozat 146 Hc 39.07N 39.14 E
Hpunhpu 148 Jc 26.42N 97.17 E
Hradec Králové 120 Lf 50.13N 15.50 E
Hradiště 120 Jf 50.13N 13.08 E
Hrami 132 Ni 41.20N 45.07 E
Hrastnik 128 Jd 46.09N 15.06 E
Hřebeny 120 Kg 49.50N 14.10 E
Hristinovka 132 Fe 48.53N 29.56 E
Hroma 138 Jb 71.30N 144.49 E
Hromtau 136 Fe 50.18N 58.35 E
Hron 120 Oi 47.49N 18.45 E
Hrubieszów 120 Tf 50.49N 23.55 E
Hrubý Jeseník 120 Nf 50.05N 17.10 E
Hrustalny 138 Ih 44.24N 135.06 E
Hrvatska = Croatia (EN) [2] 128 Jf 45.00N 15.30 E
Hrvatska = Croatia (EN) [2] 110 Hf 45.00N 15.30 E
Hrvatska = Croatia (EN) [2] 128 Je 45.00N 15.30 E
Hrvot Shivta 146 Fg 30.53N 34.38 E
Hsin-chiang-wei-wu-erh-Tzu-chih-ch'ü→Xinjiang Uygur Zizhiqu [2] 152 Ec 42.00N 86.00 E
Hsinchu 152 Lg 24.48N 120.58 E
Hsinying 152 Lg 23.25N 120.20 E
Hsipaw 148 Jd 22.37N 97.18 E
Hsi-tsang Tzu-chih-ch'ü→Xizang Zizhiqu [2] 152 Ee 32.00N 90.00 E
Hsuphāng 148 Jd 20.18N 98.42 E
Huab 172 Ad 20.49S 13.24 E
Huabei Pingyuan 143 Nf 37.00N 117.00 E
Huachacalla 202 Eg 18.45S 68.17W
Huachinera 192 Eb 30.15N 108.50W
Huacho 202 Cf 11.07S 77.37W
Huaco 206 Gd 30.09S 68.31W
Huacrachuco 202 Ce 8.39S 77.05W
Huade 152 Jc 41.50N 114.00 E
Huadian 152 Mc 42.59N 126.38 E

Index Symbols

[1] Independent Nation
[2] State, Region
[3] District, County
[4] Municipality
[5] Colony, Dependency
Continent
Physical Region
Historical or Cultural Region
Mount, Mountain
Volcano
Hill
Mountains, Mountain Range
Hills, Escarpment
Plateau, Upland
Pass, Gap
Plain, Lowland
Delta
Salt Flat
Valley, Canyon
Crater, Cave
Karst Features
Depression
Polder
Desert, Dunes
Forest, Woods
Heath, Steppe
Oasis
Cape, Point
Coast, Beach
Cliff
Peninsula
Isthmus
Sandbank
Island
Atoll
Rock, Reef
Islands, Archipelago
Rocks, Reefs
Coral Reef
Well, Spring
Geyser
River, Stream
Waterfall, Rapids
River Mouth, Estuary
Lake
Salt Lake
Intermittent Lake
Reservoir
Swamp, Pond
Canal
Glacier
Ice Shelf, Pack Ice
Ocean
Sea
Gulf, Bay
Strait, Fjord
Lagoon
Bank
Seamount
Tablemount
Ridge
Shelf
Basin
Escarpment, Sea Scarp
Fracture
Trench, Abyss
National Park, Reserve
Point of Interest
Recreation Site
Cave, Cavern
Historic Site
Ruins
Wall, Walls
Church, Abbey
Temple
Scientific Station
Railway station
Airport
Port
Military Installation
Lighthouse
Mine
Tunnel
Dam, Bridge

Hua Hin 148 Jf 12.34N 99.58 E
Huahine, Iles- 208 Lf 16.45S 151.00W
Huahine Iti 221e Eb 16.45S 151.00W
Huahine Nui 221e Eb 16.43S 151.00W
Huahuapán 192 Ge 24.31N 105.57W
Huai'an 154 Eh 33.30N 119.08 E
Huai'an (Chaigoubu) 154 Cd 40.40N 114.25 E
Huaibei 152 Ke 33.56N 116.48 E
Huaibin (Wulongji) 154 Ci 32.27N 115.23 E
Huaide (Gongzhuling) 152 Lc 43.30N 124.52 E
Huaidian → Shenqiu 152 Ke 33.27N 115.05 E
Huai He 140 Nf 33.12N 118.33 E
Huaiji 152 Jg 23.57N 112.12 E
Huailai (Shacheng) 152 Kc 40.29N 115.30 E
Huainan 142 Nf 32.32N 116.59 E
Huaining (Shipai) 154 Di 30.25N 116.39 E
Huairen 152 Jd 39.50N 113.07 E
Huairou 154 Dd 40.20N 116.37 E
Huaiyang 154 Ch 33.44N 114.52 E
Huaiyin (Wangying) 154 Eh 33.35N 119.02 E
Huaiyuan 154 Dh 32.58N 117.10 E
Huajuapán de León 190 Ee 17.48N 97.46W
Hualalai 221a Fd 19.41N 155.52W
Hualapai Mountains 188 Ii 34.40N 113.45W
Hualien 152 Lg 23.58N 121.36 E
Huallaga, Río- 198 If 5.07S 75.30W
Huallanca 202 Ce 8.49S 77.52W
Huamachuco 202 Ce 7.48S 78.04W
Huamahuaca 206 Gb 23.13S 65.23W
Huambo 160 Ij 12.47S 15.43 E
Huambo [3] 170 Ce 12.30S 15.40 E
Huanan 152 Nb 46.14N 130.33 E
Huancabamba [Peru] 202 Ce 5.14S 79.28W
Huancabamba [Peru] 202 Cf 10.21S 75.32W
Huancané 202 Eg 15.12S 69.46W
Huancapi 202 Df 13.41S 74.04W
Huancavelica 200 Ig 12.46S 75.02W
Huancavelica [3] 202 Df 13.00S 75.00W
Huancayo 200 Ig 12.04S 75.14W
Huanchaca, Serrania- 204 Bb 14.30S 60.39W
Huang'an → Hong'an 154 Ci 31.17N 114.37 E
Huangcaoba → Xingyi 152 Hf 25.03N 104.55 E
Huangchuan 152 Ke 32.00N 115.02 E
Huanggang 154 Ci 30.27N 114.53 E
Huanggangliang 152 Kc 43.33N 117.32 E
Huanggang Shan 152 Kf 27.50N 117.47 E
Huanggi Hai 154 Bd 40.51N 113.17 E
Huang Hai=Yellow Sea (EN) 140 Of 36.00N 124.00 E
Huang He=Yellow River (EN) 140 Nf 37.32N 118.19 E
Huanghe Kou 154 Ef 37.54N 118.48 E
Huangheyan → Madoi 142 Lf 35.00N 98.56 E
Huanghua 154 De 38.23N 117.21 E
Huanghuashi 154 Bj 28.14N 113.11 E
Huangliu 152 Ih 18.41N 108.46 E
Huangmao Jian 152 Kf 27.55N 119.11 E
Huangmei 154 Ci 30.05N 115.56 E
Huangnihe 154 Ic 43.33N 127.28 E
Huangpi 154 Ci 30.53N 114.22 E
Huangpu 152 Jg 23.05N 113.25 E
Huang Shan 152 Ke 30.10N 118.10 E
Huangshi 142 Nf 30.12N 115.00 E
Huang Shui 152 Hd 36.05N 103.20 E
Huangtu Gaoyuan 140 Mf 37.00N 108.00 E
Huanguelén 204 Bm 37.02S 61.57W
Huangxian 152 Ld 37.32N 120.30 E
Huangyan 152 Lf 28.39N 121.17 E
Huangyan Dao 150 Gc 15.05N 117.45 E
Huangyuan 152 Hd 36.40N 101.12 E
Huangzhai → Yangqu 154 Be 38.05N 112.37 E
Huangzhong 152 Hd 36.30N 101.30 E
Huanren 152 Mc 41.16N 125.22 E
Huan Shui 154 Ci 30.40N 114.21 E
Huanta 202 Df 12.56S 74.15W
Huantai (Suozhen) 154 Ef 36.57N 118.05 E
Huánuco 200 If 9.55S 76.14W
Huánuco [3] 202 Ce 9.30S 75.50W
Huanxian 152 Id 36.36N 107.06 E
Huaraz 200 If 9.32S 77.32W
Huarmey 202 Cf 10.04S 78.10W
Huarong 154 Bj 29.31N 112.33 E
Huascarán, Nevado- 198 If 9.07S 77.37W
Huasco 206 Fc 28.28S 71.14W
Hua Shan 152 Je 34.27N 110.05 E
Huatabampo 190 Cc 26.50N 109.38W
Huatong 154 Fd 40.03N 121.56 E
Huatusco de Chicuéllar 192 Kh 19.09N 96.57W
Huauchinango 192 Jg 20.11N 98.03W
Huautla de Jiménez 192 Kh 18.08N 96.51W
Huaxian (Daokou) 154 Cg 35.33N 114.30 E
Huayllay 202 Cf 11.01S 76.21W
Huaynamota, Río- 192 Gg 21.51N 104.42W
Huaytará 202 Cf 13.36S 75.22W
Hubbard Creek Lake 186 Gj 32.45N 99.00W
Hubbard Lake 184 Fc 44.49N 83.34W
Hubei Sheng (Hu-pei Sheng) = Hupeh (EN) 152 Je 31.00N 112.00 E
Hubli-Dhārwār 142 Jh 15.21N 75.10 E
Hubsugul Nur (Chövsgöl Nuur) 140 Md 51.00N 100.30 E
Hückelhoven 124 Ic 51.03N 6.13 E
Hückeswagen 124 Jc 51.09N 7.21 E
Hucknall 118 Lh 53.02N 1.11W
Hucqueliers 124 Dd 55.03N 1.54 E
Huczwa 120 Tf 50.49N 23.59 E
Hudat [Abz.-U.S.S.R.] 132 Pi 41.34N 48.43 E
Hudat [Eth.] 168 Fe 4.45N 39.27 E
Huddersfield 118 Lh 53.39N 1.47W
Huddinge 116 Ge 59.14N 17.59 E
Ḥuddun 168 Hd 9.08N 47.32 E
Huddur Hadama 168 Ge 4.07N 43.55 E
Hude (Oldenburg) 124 Ka 53.07N 8.28 E
Huder 152 Lb 49.59N 121.30 E
Hudiksvall 112 Hc 61.44N 17.07 E
Hudson 174 Le 40.42N 74.02W
Hudson [Fl.-U.S.] 184 Fk 28.22N 82.42W
Hudson [N.Y.-U.S.] 184 Kd 42.15N 73.47W
Hudson, Lake- 186 Ih 36.20N 95.05W
Hudson Bay 180 Hf 52.52N 102.23W
Hudson Bay 174 Kd 60.00N 86.00W
Hudson Canyon (EN) 184 Kf 39.27N 72.12W
Hudson Hope 180 Fe 56.02N 121.55W
Hudson Land 179 Jd 73.45N 22.30W
Hudson Mountains 222 Pf 74.32S 99.20W
Hudson Strait 174 Li 62.30N 72.00W
Hudžirt 152 Hb 47.05N 102.45 E
Hue 142 Mh 16.28N 107.36 E
Huebra 126 Fc 41.02N 6.48W
Huechucuicui, Punta- 206 Ff 41.47S 74.02W
Hueco Mountains 186 Dj 32.05N 105.55W
Huedin 130 Gc 46.52N 23.03 E
Huehuetenango 190 Fe 15.20N 91.28W
Huehuetenango [3] 194 Bf 15.40N 91.35W
Huejutla de Reyes 192 Jg 21.08N 98.25W
Huelgoat 122 Cf 48.22N 3.45W
Huelma 126 Ig 37.39N 3.27W
Huelva 112 Fh 37.16N 6.57W
Huelva [3] 126 Fg 37.40N 7.00W
Huelva, Ribera de- 126 Gg 37.27N 6.00W
Huércal-Overa 126 Kg 37.23N 1.57W
Huerfano Mountain 186 Bh 36.30N 108.10W
Huertas, Cabo de- / Horta, Cap de l'- 126 Lf 38.21N 0.24W
Huerva 126 Lc 41.39N 0.52W
Huesca 126 Lb 42.08N 0.05W
Huesca [3] 126 Lb 42.10N 0.10W
Huéscar 126 Jg 37.49N 2.32W
Hueso, Sierra del- 192 Gb 30.15N 105.20W
Huesos, Arroyo de los- 204 Cm 36.30S 59.09W
Huetamo de Núñez 192 Ih 18.35N 100.53W
Huete 126 Jd 40.08N 2.41W
Huez 122 Mi 45.06N 6.04 E
Ḥufrat an Naḥās 168 Cd 9.45N 24.19 E
Huftarøy 116 Ad 60.05N 5.15 E
Hugh Butler Lake 186 Ff 40.22N 100.42W
Hughenden 210 Fg 20.51S 144.12 E
Hughes 178 Ic 66.03N 154.16W
Hughes Range 188 Hb 49.55N 115.28W
Hugo 186 Ii 34.01N 95.31W
Huguan 154 Bf 36.05N 113.12 E
Huhur He 154 Fc 43.55N 120.47 E
Hui'an 154 Dk 25.07N 118.47 E
Huiarau Range 218 Gc 38.35S 177.10 E
Huib-Hochplato 172 Be 27.10S 16.50 E
Huichang 152 Kf 25.33N 115.45 E
Huicheng → Shexian 154 Ej 29.53N 118.27 E
Huicholes, Sierra de los- 192 Gf 22.00N 104.00W
Huich'ŏn 152 Mc 40.10N 126.17 E
Huifa He 154 Ic 43.06N 126.53 E
Hui He [China] 154 Be 39.21N 112.37 E
Hui He [China] 152 Kb 48.51N 119.12 E
Huiji He 154 Ch 33.53N 115.37 E
Huila 202 Cc 2.30N 75.45W
Huila [3] 170 Ce 15.00S 15.00 E
Huila, Nevado del- 198 Ie 3.00N 76.00W
Huilai 152 Kg 23.05N 116.18 E
Huili 152 Hf 26.37N 102.19 E
Huimanguillo 192 Mi 17.51N 93.23W
Huimin 152 Kd 37.29N 117.30 E
Huinan (Chaoyang) 154 Ic 42.41N 126.03 E
Huisne 122 Gg 47.59N 0.11 E
Huissen 124 Hc 51.56N 5.55 E
Huiten Nur 152 Fd 35.30N 91.55 E
Huittinen 116 Jc 61.11N 22.42 E
Huivulay, Isla de- 192 Dd 27.03N 110.01W
Huixian [China] 152 Ie 33.46N 106.06 E
Huixian [China] 154 Bg 35.27N 113.47 E
Huixtla 190 Fe 15.09N 92.28W
Huize 152 Hf 26.28N 103.18 E
Huizen 124 Hb 52.18N 5.16 E
Huizhou 152 Jg 23.02N 114.28 E
Hukou 154 Dj 29.44N 116.14 E
Hu Kou 152 Jd 36.09N 110.20 E
Hŭksan-Chedo 152 Me 34.30N 125.20 E
Hukuntsi 172 Cd 23.59S 21.44 E
Hulah Lake 186 Hh 36.58N 96.10W
Hulan 152 Mb 46.03N 126.36 E
Hulan He 152 Mb 45.54N 126.42 E
Ḥulayfā' 144 Fd 26.00N 40.47 E
Hulett 188 Md 44.41N 104.36W
Hulga 134 Jd 64.15N 60.58 E
Hulin 152 Nb 45.52N 132.58 E
Hulin He 154 Hb 45.19N 124.06 E
Hull 180 Jg 45.26N 75.43W
Hull → Kingston upon Hull 112 Fe 53.45N 0.20W
Hull → Orona Atoll 208 Je 4.29S 172.10W
Hull Bay 222 Nf 74.55S 137.40W
Hull Glacier 222 Nf 75.05S 137.15W
Hull Mountain 188 Dg 39.31N 122.59W
Hüls, Krefeld- 124 Ic 51.22N 6.31 E
Hulst 124 Gc 51.17N 4.04 E
Hultsfred 114 Dh 57.29N 15.50 E
Huludao 152 Lc 40.44N 120.59 E
Hulun Nur 140 Ne 49.00N 117.30 E
Ḥulwân=Helwân (EN) 164 Fd 29.51N 31.20 E
Hulwat, Qūr al- 146 Hh 28.49N 38.50 E
Huma [China] 152 Ma 51.44N 126.36 E
Huma [Ton.] 221b Bc 21.19S 174.56W
Humacao 194 Od 18.09N 65.50W
Huma He 152 Ma 51.42N 126.42 E
Humaitá [Braz.] 200 Jf 7.31S 63.02W
Humaitá [Par.] 206 Ic 27.03S 58.33W
Humansdorp 172 Cf 34.02S 24.46 E
Humbe 170 Bf 16.42S 14.54 E
Humber 110 Fe 53.40N 0.10W
Humberside [3] 118 Mh 53.55N 0.30W
Humberto de Campos 202 Jd 2.37S 43.27W
Humboldt 216 Cd 21.53S 166.25 E
Humboldt [Ia.-U.S.] 186 Ie 42.43N 94.13W
Humboldt [Nb.-U.S.] 186 If 40.10N 95.57W
Humboldt [Sask.-Can.] 180 Gf 52.12N 105.07W
Humboldt [Tn.-U.S.] 184 Ch 35.49N 88.55W
Humboldt Gletscher 179 Fc 79.40N 63.45W
Humboldt Range 188 Ff 40.15N 118.10W
Humboldt River 174 He 40.02N 118.31W
Hume, Lake- 212 Jg 36.05S 147.05 E
Humenné 120 Rh 48.56N 21.55 E
Hummelfjell 116 Db 62.27N 11.17 E
Hümmling, Der- 120 Dd 52.52N 7.31 E
Humphreys Peak 174 Hf 35.20N 111.40W
Humppila 114 Ff 60.56N 23.22 E
Humuya, Rio- 194 Df 15.13N 87.57W
Hūn 160 If 29.07N 15.56 E
Húnaflói 110 Db 65.50N 20.50W
Hunan Sheng (Hu-nan Sheng) [3] 152 Jf 28.00N 112.00 E
Hu-nan Sheng → Hunan Sheng [3] 152 Jf 28.00N 112.00 E
Hunchun 154 Kc 42.52N 130.21 E
Hundested 116 Di 55.58N 11.52 E
Hunedoara 130 Fd 45.45N 22.54 E
Hunedoara [2] 130 Fd 45.45N 22.52 E
Hünfeld 120 Ff 50.40N 9.46 E
Hünfelden 124 Kd 50.19N 8.11 E
Hunga Ha'apai 221b Ab 20.33S 175.24W
Hungary (EN)= Magyarország [1] 112 Hf 47.00N 20.00 E
Hunga Tonga 221b Ab 20.32S 175.23W
Hungen 124 Kd 50.28N 8.54 E
Hŭngnam 152 Md 39.50N 127.38 E
Hungry Horse Reservoir 188 Ib 48.15N 113.50W
Hun He [China] 154 Gd 40.41N 122.12 E
Hun He [China] 154 Be 39.47N 113.15 E
Hunish, Rubha- 118 Gd 57.43N 6.20W
Hunjiang 152 Mc 41.55N 126.27 E
Hun Jiang 154 Hd 40.52N 125.42 E
Hunneberg 116 Ef 58.20N 12.27 E
Hunnebostrand 116 Df 58.27N 11.18 E
Hunsrück 120 Dg 49.50N 7.10 E
Hunstanton 118 Ni 52.57N 0.30 E
Hunte 120 Ec 53.14N 8.20 E
Hunter, Ile- 208 Ig 22.24S 172.03 E
Hunter Island 212 Ih 40.30S 144.45 E
Hunter Ridge (EN) 208 Ig 21.30S 174.30 E
Hunter River 212 Kf 32.30S 151.42 E
Hunterville 218 Fc 39.56S 175.34 E
Huntingdon 118 Mi 52.30N 0.10W
Huntingdon [Eng.-U.K.] 118 Mi 52.20N 0.12W
Huntingdon [Pa.-U.S.] 184 He 40.31N 78.02W
Huntingdon [Que.-Can.] 184 Jc 45.05N 74.08W
Huntington [In.-U.S.] 184 Ee 40.53N 85.30W
Huntington [W.V.-U.S.] 182 Kd 38.24N 82.26W
Huntly [N.Z.] 218 Fb 37.33S 175.10 E
Huntly [Scot.-U.K.] 118 Kd 57.27N 2.47W
Huntsville [Al.-U.S.] 176 Kf 34.44N 86.35W
Huntsville [Ont.-Can.] 180 Jg 45.20N 79.13W
Huntsville [Tx.-U.S.] 182 He 30.43N 95.33W
Hunucmá 192 Og 21.01N 89.52W
Hünxe 124 Ic 51.39N 6.47 E
Hunyani 172 Ec 15.37S 30.39 E
Hunyuan 152 Jd 39.38N 113.44 E
Hunza → Baltit 148 Ea 36.20N 74.40 E
Hunze 122 Ma 53.13N 6.40 E
Huocheng (Shuiding) 152 Dc 44.03N 80.49 E
Huojia 154 Bg 35.16N 113.39 E
Huolongmen 152 Mb 49.49N 125.49 E
Huolu 154 Ce 38.05N 114.18 E
Huon, Ile- 208 Hf 18.01S 162.57 E
Huon Gulf 212 Ja 7.10S 147.25 E
Huon Peninsula 214 Di 6.25S 147.30 E
Huonville 212 Jh 43.01S 147.02 E
Huoqin 154 Dh 32.21N 116.17 E
Huoshan 152 Ke 31.19N 116.20 E
Huo Shan [China] 152 Ke 31.06N 116.12 E
Huo Shan [China] 152 Jd 37.00N 111.52 E
Huoxian 152 Jd 36.39N 111.47 E
Hupeh (EN)=Hubei Sheng (Hu-pei Sheng) [2] 152 Je 31.00N 112.00 E
Hu-pei Sheng → Hubei Sheng=Hopeh (EN) [2] 152 Je 31.00N 112.00 E
Hūr 146 Qg 30.50N 57.07 E
Hurama → Hongyuan 152 He 32.45N 102.38 E
Hurānd 146 Lc 38.40N 47.20 E
Hurd, Cape- 184 Gc 45.13N 81.44W
Hurdalssjøen 116 Dd 60.20N 11.05 E
Hurd Deep=La Grande Trench (EN) 118 Kl 49.40N 3.00W
Hurdiyo 168 Ic 10.32N 51.08 E
Hurepoix 122 If 48.30N 2.10 E
Hure Qi 154 Fc 42.44N 121.44 E
Hurkett 186 Lb 48.50N 88.29W
Hurmuli 138 If 51.01N 136.56 E
Huron 182 Hc 44.22N 98.13W
Huron, Lake- 174 Ke 44.30N 82.15W
Huron Mountains 184 Db 46.45N 87.45W
Hurricane 188 Ih 37.11N 113.17W
Hurricane Cliffs 188 Ih 37.00N 113.05W
Hurrungane 116 Bc 61.27N 7.51 E
Hursley 124 Ac 51.01N 1.24W
Hurst 186 Hj 32.49N 97.09W
Hurstpierpoint 124 Bd 50.55N 0.10W
Hürth 120 Cf 50.52N 6.52 E
Hurum 116 De 59.35N 10.35 E
Hurunui 218 Ee 42.54S 173.18 E
Hurup 116 Ch 56.45N 8.25 E
Húsavík 114a Ca 66.03N 17.21W
Hushan → Cixi 154 Fi 30.10N 121.14 E
Huşi 130 Lc 46.41N 28.04 E
Huskvarna 116 Fg 57.48N 14.16 E
Huslia 178 Hc 65.42N 156.25W
Husnes 116 Ae 59.52N 5.46 E
Husnesfjorden 116 Ae 59.50N 5.35 E
Hussigny-Godbrange 124 He 49.29N 5.52 E
Hust 132 Ce 48.10N 23.27 E
Hustadvika 116 Ba 63.00N 7.05 E
Husum [Ger.] 120 Fb 54.28N 9.03 E
Husum [Swe.] 114 Ee 63.20N 19.10 E
Hutag 152 Hb 49.23N 102.43 E
Hutchinson [Ks.-U.S.] 182 Hd 38.05N 97.56W
Hutchinson [Mn.-U.S.] 186 Id 44.54N 94.22W
Hutch Mountain 188 Ji 34.47N 111.22W
Ḥūth 164 Hf 16.14N 43.58 E
Hutou 152 Nb 46.00N 133.36 E
Hutte Sauvage, Lac de la- 180 Ke 55.57N 65.45W
Hutton, Mount- 212 Je 25.51S 148.20 E
Hutubi 152 Ec 44.07N 86.57 E
Hutuiti, Caleta- 221d Bb 27.07S 109.17W
Hutuo He 154 De 38.14N 116.05 E
Huvhojtun, gora- 138 Le 57.44N 160.45 E
Huxley, Mount- 218 Cf 44.04S 169.41 E
Huy 120 Ge 51.55N 10.55 E
Huy/Hoei 122 Ld 50.31N 5.14 E
Huzgan 146 Mg 31.27N 48.04 E
Huzhou → Wuxing 152 Le 30.47N 120.07 E
Hvaler 116 De 59.05N 11.00 E
Hvalynsk 136 Ee 52.30N 48.07 E
Hvammstangi 114a Bb 65.24N 20.57W
Hvannadalshnúkur 110 Ec 64.01N 16.41W
Hvar 128 Kg 43.11N 16.27 E
Hvar 128 Kg 43.07N 16.45 E
Hvarski kanal 128 Kg 43.15N 16.37 E
Hvatovka 132 Oc 52.21N 46.36 E
Hveragerdi 114a Bb 64.00N 21.12W
Hveravellir 114a Bb 64.54N 19.35W
Hvide Sande 116 Ci 55.59N 8.08 E
Hvítá [Ice.] 114a Bb 64.35N 21.46W
Hvítá [Ice.] 114a Bb 64.00N 20.58W
Hvittingfoss 116 De 59.29N 10.01 E
Hvojnaja 114 Ig 58.56N 34.31 E
Hwach'on-ni 154 Ie 38.58N 126.02 E
Hwange 160 Jj 18.21S 26.30 E
Hwang-Hae=Yellow Sea (EN) 140 Of 36.00N 124.00 E
Hwanghae-Namdo [2] 154 He 38.15N 125.30 E
Hwanghae-Pukto [2] 154 Ie 38.30N 126.25 E
Hwangju 154 He 38.40N 125.45 E
Hyannis [Ma.-U.S.] 184 Le 41.39N 70.17W
Hyannis [Nb.-U.S.] 186 Ff 42.00N 101.44W
Hybo 116 Gc 61.48N 16.12 E
Hyde Park 196 Gi 6.30N 58.16W
Hyderābād [India] 142 Jh 17.23N 78.28 E
Hyderābād [Pak.] 142 Ig 25.22N 68.22 E
Hyères 122 Mk 43.07N 6.07 E
Hyères, Iles d'- 122 Ml 43.00N 6.20 E
Hyesan 152 Mc 41.24N 128.10 E
Hyltebruk 114 Ch 57.00N 13.14 E
Hyndman Peak 188 He 43.50N 114.10W
Hyōgo Ken [2] 154 Mg 34.50N 134.48 E
Hyrov 120 Sg 49.32N 22.48 E
Hyrum 188 Jf 41.38N 111.51W
Hyrylä 116 Kd 60.24N 25.02 E
Hyrynsalmi 114 Gd 64.40N 28.32 E
Hysham 188 Lc 46.18N 107.14W
Hythe [Eng.-U.K.] 124 Ad 50.52N 1.24W
Hythe [Eng.-U.K.] 118 Oj 51.05N 1.05 E
Hyūga 154 Kh 32.25N 131.38 E
Hyūga-Nada 156 Be 32.25N 131.45 E
Hyvinge/Hyvinkää 114 Ff 60.38N 24.52 E
Hyvinkää/Hyvinge 114 Ff 60.38N 24.52 E

I

Iaco, Rio- 202 Ee 9.03S 68.35W
Iacobeni 130 Ib 47.26N 25.19 E
Iakora 172 Hd 23.08S 46.38 E
Ialomița [2] 130 Ke 44.30N 27.30 E
Ialomița 130 Ke 44.42N 27.51 E
Ialomiței, Balta- 130 Ke 44.30N 28.00 E
Iapó, Rio- 204 Gg 24.30S 50.24W
Iași 112 If 47.10N 27.36 E
Iași [2] 130 Kb 47.07N 27.39 E
Iba 150 Gc 15.20N 119.58 E
Ibadan 160 Hh 7.23N 3.54 E
Ibagué 200 Ie 4.27N 75.14W
Ibaiti 206 Jb 23.50S 50.10W
Iballja 130 Cg 42.11N 20.00 E
Ibañeta, Puerto de- → Roncesvalles, Puerto de- 126 Ka 43.01N 1.19W
Ibans, Laguna de- 194 Ef 15.53N 84.52W
Ibar 130 Df 43.44N 20.45 E
Ibara 156 Cd 34.36N 133.28 E
Ibaraki 156 Dd 34.49N 135.34 E
Ibaraki Ken [2] 154 Pf 36.25N 140.30 E
Ibaré 204 Ej 30.49S 54.16W
Ibarra 200 Ie 0.21N 78.07W
Ibarreta 206 Ic 25.13S 59.51W
Ibb 142 Gh 13.58N 44.12 E
Ibba 168 De 4.48N 29.06 E
Ibba 168 Dd 7.09N 28.41 E
Ibbenbüren 120 Dd 52.16N 7.44 E
Ibdekkene 166 Fb 18.28N 0.38 E
Ibembo 170 Db 2.38N 23.37 E
Ibenga 170 Cb 2.20N 18.08 E
Iberá, Esteros del- 204 Di 28.05S 57.05W
Iberá, Laguna- 204 Di 28.30S 57.09W
Iberian Basin (EN) 106 De 40.00N 16.00W
Iberian Mountains (EN) = Ibérica, Cordillera- 110 Fg 41.30N 2.30W
Iberian Peninsula (EN)= Península Ibérica 110 Fg 40.00N 4.00W
Ibérica, Cordillera- = Iberian Mountains (EN) 110 Fg 41.30N 2.30W
Iberville, Lac d'- 180 Ke 56.00N 73.10W
Ibestad 114 Db 68.48N 17.08 E
Ibi [Nig.] 166 Gd 8.11N 9.45 E
Ibi [Sp.] 126 Lf 38.38N 0.34W
Ibiá 202 Ig 19.29S 46.32W
Ibiagui 204 Ja 13.03S 44.12W
Ibiai 204 Jc 16.51S 44.55W
Ibibobo 204 Fh 21.35S 62.58W
Ibicaraí 202 Kf 14.51S 39.36W
Ibicuí, Rio- 198 Kh 29.25S 56.47W
Ibicuí da Armada, Rio- 204 Ej 30.16S 54.54W
Ibicuy 204 Ck 33.44S 59.10W
Ibicuy, Rio- 204 Ck 33.48S 59.10W
Ibigawa 156 Ed 35.29N 136.34 E
Ibipetuba 202 Jf 11.00S 44.32W
Ibiraiaras 204 Gi 28.22S 51.39W
Ibirama 204 Hh 27.04S 49.31W
Ibirapuitã, Rio- 204 Ei 29.22S 55.57W
Ibirocai, Arroio- 204 Di 29.26S 56.43W
Ibiruba 204 Fi 28.38S 53.06W
Ibitinga 204 He 21.45S 48.49W
Ibitinga, Represa- 204 He 21.41S 49.05W
Ibity 172 Hd 20.10S 46.58 E
Ibiza/Eivissa=Iviza (EN) 110 Gh 39.00N 1.25 E
Ibiza / La Vila d'Eivissa 126 Nf 38.54N 1.26 E
Iblei, Monti- 128 Im 37.10N 14.55 E
Ibn Hāni', Ra's- 146 Fe 35.35N 35.43 E
Ibn Qawrah 168 Ib 15.43N 50.32 E
Ibo 172 Gb 12.22S 40.36 E
Ibo-Gawa 154a Dd 34.46N 134.35 E
Iboundji, Mont- 170 Bc 1.08S 11.48 E
Ibrā' 144 Ie 22.38N 58.40 E
Ibrah 168 Dc 10.36N 25.20 E
Ibrāhīm, Jabal- 140 Gg 20.27N 41.09 E
Ibresi 114 Li 55.18N 47.05 E
'Ibrī 144 Ie 23.16N 56.32 E
Ibrim 164 Fe 22.39N 32.05 E
Ibshawāy 146 Dh 29.22N 30.41 E
Ibuki-Sanchi 156 Ed 35.35N 136.25 E
Ibuki-Yama 156 Ed 35.25N 136.24 E
Ibusuki 154 Ki 31.16N 130.39 E
Iča 138 Ke 55.28N 155.58 E
Ica 200 Ig 14.04S 75.42W
Ica [3] 202 Cf 14.20S 75.30W
Iça, Rio- 198 Jf 3.07S 67.58W
Icaiché 192 Oh 18.05N 89.10W
Içamaquã, Rio- 204 Ei 28.34S 56.00W
Icana, Rio- 202 Ec 0.26N 67.19W
Icara 204 Hi 28.42S 49.18W
Icaraima 204 Ff 23.23S 53.41W
İçel 144 Db 36.48N 34.38 E
Iceland (EN) = Island 110 Eb 65.00N 18.00W
Iceland Basin (EN) 110 Dc 60.00N 20.00W
Ichalkaranji 148 Ee 16.42N 74.28 E
Ichibusa-Yama 156 Be 32.19N 131.06 E
Ichihara 154 Pg 35.31N 140.05 E
Ichikawa 156 Fd 35.44N 139.55 E
Ichi-Kawa 156 Dd 34.46N 134.43 E
Ichinohe 154 Pd 40.13N 141.17 E
Ichinomiya 154 Ng 35.18N 136.48 E
Ichinoseki 154 Pe 38.55N 141.08 E
Ich'ŏn [N.Kor.] 154 Ie 38.29N 126.53 E
Ich'ŏn [S.Kor.] 154 If 37.17N 127.27 E
Ichtegem 124 Fc 51.06N 3.00 E
Ičigemski hrebet 138 Ld 63.30N 164.00 E
Ičinskaja Sopka, vulkan- 140 Rd 55.39N 157.40 E
Ičnja 136 De 50.52N 32.25 E
Icó 202 Ke 6.24S 38.51W
Icy Cape 178 Gb 70.20N 161.52W
Idaarderadeel 124 Ha 53.06N 5.50 E
Idaarderadeel-Grow 124 Ha 53.06N 5.50 E
Idabel 186 Ij 33.54N 94.50W
Idah 166 Gd 7.06N 6.44 E
Idaho [2] 182 Ec 45.00N 115.00W
Idaho Falls 176 He 43.30N 112.02W
Idalia 186 Eg 39.43N 102.14W
Idān 168 Hd 6.03N 49.01 E
Idanha-a-Nova 126 Ee 39.55N 7.14W
Idar-Oberstein 120 Dg 49.42N 7.18 E
Idarwald 124 Je 49.50N 7.13 E
Idel 114 Id 64.08N 34.12 E
Ideles 162 Ie 23.49N 5.55 E
Ider 152 Hb 49.16N 100.41 E
Idfū 164 Fe 24.58N 32.52 E
Idhi Óros 110 Ih 35.15N 24.45 E
Idhra 130 Gl 37.21N 23.28 E
Idhra 130 Gl 37.20N 23.30 E
Idhras, Kólpos- 130 Gl 37.22N 23.22 E
Idice 128 Ff 44.35N 11.49 E
Idil 146 Id 37.21N 41.54 E
Idini 162 Df 17.58N 15.40W
Idiofa 170 Cc 4.59S 19.36 E
Idjil, Kédia d'- 162 Ee 22.38N 12.33W
Idkerberget 116 Fd 60.23N 15.14 E
Idle 118 Mh 53.27N 0.48W
Idlib 144 Eb 35.55N 36.38 E
Idokogo 170 Ab 0.35N 9.19 E
Idolo, Isla del- 192 Kg 21.25N 97.27W
Idre 116 Ec 61.52N 12.43 E
Idrica 116 Mh 56.18N 28.55 E
Idrija 128 Id 46.00N 14.02 E
Idro, Lago d'- 128 Ee 45.47N 10.30 E
Idstein 120 Ef 50.14N 8.16 E
Idževan 132 Ni 40.52N 45.04 E
Iecava 116 Kh 56.33N 24.11 E
Iecava 116 Jh 56.40N 23.40 E
Iepê 204 Gf 22.40S 51.05W
Ieper/Ypres 122 Id 50.51N 2.53 E
Ierápetra 130 In 35.01N 25.45 E
Ierisós 130 Gi 40.24N 23.53 E
Ierisoú, Kólpos- 130 Gi 40.26N 23.55 E
Iernut 130 Hc 46.27N 24.15 E
Ie-Shima 156b Ab 26.43N 127.47 E
Ieshima-Shotō 156 Dd 34.40N 134.30 E
Iesolo 128 Ge 45.32N 12.38 E
Iezerul, Vîrful- 130 Hd 45.28N 24.57 E
Ifakara 170 Gd 8.08S 36.41 E
Ifaki 166 Gd 7.48N 5.14 E
'Ifāl, Wādī al- 146 Fh 28.07N 35.02 E
Ifalik Atoll 208 Fd 7.15N 144.27 E
Ifanadiana 172 Hd 21.17S 47.35 E
Ife 166 Fd 7.28N 4.34 E
Iferouâne 160 Hg 19.04N 8.24 E
Ifetesene 162 Hd 25.30N 4.33 E
Ifni 162 Ed 29.15N 10.08W
Ifon 166 Gd 6.58N 5.46 E
Iforas, Adrar des- 158 Hg 19.00N 2.00 E
Iga 156 Ed 34.49N 136.12 E
Igal 120 Nj 46.32N 17.57 E
Iganga 170 Fb 0.37N 33.29 E
Igara Paraná, Rio- 202 Dd 2.09S 71.47W

Index Symbols

- [1] Independent Nation
- [2] State, Region
- [3] District, County
- [4] Municipality
- [5] Colony, Dependency
- Continent
- Physical Region
- Historical or Cultural Region
- Mount, Mountain
- Volcano
- Hill
- Mountains, Mountain Range
- Hills, Escarpment
- Plateau, Upland
- Pass, Gap
- Plain, Lowland
- Delta
- Salt Flat
- Valley, Canyon
- Crater, Cave
- Karst Features
- Depression
- Polder
- Desert, Dunes
- Forest, Woods
- Heath, Steppe
- Oasis
- Cape, Point
- Coast, Beach
- Cliff
- Peninsula
- Isthmus
- Sandbank
- Island
- Atoll
- Rock, Reef
- Islands, Archipelago
- Rocks, Reefs
- Coral Reef
- Well, Spring
- Geyser
- River, Stream
- Waterfall, Rapids
- River Mouth, Estuary
- Lake
- Salt Lake
- Intermittent Lake
- Reservoir
- Swamp, Pond
- Canal
- Glacier
- Ice Shelf, Pack Ice
- Ocean
- Sea
- Gulf, Bay
- Strait, Fjord
- Lagoon
- Bank
- Seamount
- Tablemount
- Ridge
- Shelf
- Basin
- Escarpment, Sea Scarp
- Fracture
- Trench, Abyss
- National Park, Reserve
- Point of Interest
- Recreation Site
- Cave, Cavern
- Historic Site
- Ruins
- Wall, Walls
- Church, Abbey
- Temple
- Scientific Station
- Railway station
- Airport
- Port
- Military installation
- Lighthouse
- Mine
- Tunnel
- Dam, Bridge

Igarapava 204 Ie 20.03S 47.47W
Igarapé-Açu 202 Id 1.07S 47.37W
Igarapé-Miri 202 Id 1.59S 48.58W
Igarka 142 Kc 67.28N 86.35 E
Igatimi 206 Ib 24.05S 55.30W
Igawa 170 Fd 8.46S 34.23 E
Igbetti 166 Fd 8.45N 4.08 E
Iğdır 146 Kc 39.56N 44.02 E
Iggesund 114 Df 61.38N 17.04 E
Iglesias 128 Ck 39.19N 8.32 E
Iglesiente 128 Ck 39.20N 8.40 E
Igli 162 Gc 30.27N 2.18W
Iglino 134 Hi 54.50N 56.28 E
Igloolik 176 Kc 69.24N 81.49W
Ignace 180 Ig 49.26N 91.41W
Ignalina 114 Gi 55.22N 26.13 E
Ignatovo 114 If 60.49N 37.48 E
Iğneada 146 Bb 41.50N 27.58 E
Iğneada Burun 130 Lh 41.54N 28.03 E
Igombe 170 Fc 4.25S 31.58 E
Igoumenitsa 130 Dj 39.30N 20.16 E
Igra 136 Fd 57.33N 53.10 E
Igreja, Morro de- 204 Hi 28.08S 49.30W
Igren 132 Ie 48.29N 35.13 E
Igrim 136 Gc 63.12N 64.29 E
Iguaçu, Rio- 198 Kh 25.36S 54.36W
Igualada 128 Nc 41.35N 1.38 E
Iguala de la Independencia 190 Ee 18.21N 99.32W
Iguana, Sierra de la- 192 Id 26.30N 100.15W
Iguape 204 Ig 24.43S 47.33W
Iguariaça, Serra do- 204 Ei 29.03S 55.15W
Iguassu Falls (EN)=Iguazú, Cataratas del- 198 Kh 25.41S 54.26W
Iguatemi 202 Hh 23.35S 54.30W
Iguatemi, Rio- 204 Ef 23.55S 54.10W
Iguatu 200 Mf 6.22S 39.18W
Iguazú, Cataratas del- = Iguassu Falls (EN) 198 Kh 25.41S 54.26W
Iguéla 170 Ac 1.55S 9.19 E
Iguidi, 'Erg- 158 Gf 27.00N 6.00W
Iharagna 172 Ib 13.22S 50.00 E
Ihavandiffulu Atoll 148a Ba 7.00N 72.55 E
Iheya-Jima 156b Ab 27.03N 127.57 E
Ih-Hajrhan 152 Ib 46.56N 105.56 E
Ihiala 166 Gd 5.51N 6.51 E
Ihirene 166 Fe 20.28N 4.37 E
Ihnāsiyat al Madīnah 146 Dh 29.05N 30.56 E
Ih-Obo-Ula 152 Gc 44.55N 95.20 E
Ihosy 160 Lk 22.25S 46.07 E
Ihotry, Lac- 172 Gd 21.56S 43.41 E
Ihrhove, Westoverledingen- 124 Ja 53.10N 7.27 E
Ihsaniye 146 Dc 36.55N 34.46 E
Ihtiman 130 Gg 42.26N 23.49 E
Ih-Ula 152 Hb 49.27N 101.27 E
Ii 114 Fd 65.19N 25.27 E
Iida 154 Ng 35.31N 137.50 E
Iide-San 156 Fc 37.52N 139.41 E
Iijoki 114 Fd 65.20N 25.17 E
Iisaku/Isaku 116 Le 59.14N 27.41 E
Iisalmi 114 Ge 63.34N 27.11 E
Iisvesi 114 Lb 62.45N 26.50 E
Iittala 116 Kc 61.04N 24.10 E
Iivaara 114 Gd 65.47N 29.40 E
Iiyama 156 Fc 36.52N 138.20 E
Iizuka 156 Be 33.38N 130.41 E
Ija 138 Fe 55.02N 101.00 E
Ijebu Ode 166 Fd 6.49N 3.56 E
IJmuiden, Velsen- 124 Gb 52.28N 4.35 E
Ijoubbâne, 'Erg- 166 Da 22.30N 6.00W
IJssel 122 Lb 52.30N 5.50 E
IJsselmeer 122 Lb 52.45N 5.25 E
IJsselmuiden 124 Hb 52.34N 5.56 E
IJsselstein 124 Hb 52.01N 5.02 E
Ijui 206 Jc 28.23S 53.55W
Ijui, Rio- 204 Eh 27.58S 55.20W
Ijūin 156 Bf 31.37N 130.24 E
Ijuízinho, Rio- 204 Ei 28.20S 54.28W
Ijuw 220e Bb 0.31S 166.57 E
Ijzendijke 124 Fc 51.20N 3.37 E
IJzer 122 Ic 51.09N 2.43 E
Ik 110 Ld 55.55N 52.36 E
Ikaalinen 114 Ff 61.46N 23.03 E
Ikalamavony 172 Hd 21.10S 46.32 E
Ikamatua 218 De 42.17S 171.42 E
Ikaría 130 Jl 37.35N 26.10 E
Ikarion Pélagos 130 Jl 37.30N 26.35 E
Ikast 116 Ch 56.08N 9.10 E
Ikatski hrebet 138 Gf 54.00N 111.15 E
Ikawa 156 Fd 35.13N 138.14 E
Ikeda [Jap.] 156 Cd 34.01N 133.48 E
Ikeda [Jap.] 152 Pc 42.55N 143.27 E
Ikeda-Ko 156 Bf 31.14N 130.34 E
Ikej 138 Ff 54.12N 100.04 E
Ikeja 166 Fd 6.36N 3.21 E
Ikela 160 Ji 1.11S 23.16 E
Ikelemba 170 Cb 0.07N 18.17 E
Ikerre 166 Gd 7.30N 5.14 E
Ikerssuaq 179 Ie 65.10N 39.45W
Iki 156 Ae 33.45N 129.45 E
Iki-Kaikyō 154 Jh 33.45N 129.50 E
Ikitsuki-Shima 156 Ae 33.25N 129.25 E
Ikizdere 146 Ib 40.47N 40.33 E
Ikom 166 Gd 5.58N 8.42 E
Ikongo [Mad.] 172 Hd 21.53S 48.26 E
Ikongo [Tan.] 170 Gd 9.04S 36.51 E
Ikopa 172 Hc 16.50S 46.50 E
Ikot Ekpene 166 Gd 5.10N 7.43 E
Ikuno 156 Dd 35.10N 134.48 E
Ikurangi, Mount- 220p Bb 21.12S 159.45W
Ila 166 Fd 7.40N 4.40 E
Ilaferh 162 He 21.50N 1.20 E
Ilagan 142 Oh 17.10N 121.54 E
Ilām [3] 144 Gc 33.00N 47.00 E
Ilām [Iran] 144 Gc 33.38N 46.26 E
Ilām [Nep.] 146 Hc 26.54N 87.56 E
Ilan 152 Lg 24.45N 121.44 E
Ilanski 138 Ee 56.10N 96.03 E
Ilaro 166 Fd 6.53N 3.01 E
Iława 120 Pc 53.37N 19.33 E
Ilbengja 138 Hd 62.55N 124.10 E
Ile-à-la-Crosse 180 Ge 55.27N 107.53W
Ilebo 160 Ji 4.44S 20.33 E
Ile-de-France [5] 122 Ie 49.00N 2.20 E
Ile de France 179 Kc 77.45N 27.45W
Ile-de-France, Côte de l'- 122 Jf 48.55N 3.50 E
Ilek 136 Fe 51.32N 53.27 E
Ilek 110 Le 51.30N 53.20 E
Ileksa 114 Ie 62.30N 36.57 E
Ilerh 162 He 21.40N 2.22 E
Ile Rousse, L'- 122a Aa 42.38N 8.56 E
Ileša 114 Le 62.37N 46.35 E
Ilesha [Nig.] 166 Fd 8.55N 3.25 E
Ilesha [Nig.] 166 Fd 7.37N 4.44 E
Ilet 114 Li 55.57N 48.14 E
Ilfracombe 118 Ij 51.13N 4.08W
Ilgaz 146 Eb 40.56N 33.38 E
Ilgaz Dağları 146 Eb 41.00N 33.35 E
Ilgın 146 Dc 38.17N 31.55 E
Ilha Grande 202 Ed 0.27S 65.02W
Ilha Grande, Baia da- 204 Jf 23.09S 44.30W
Ílhavo 126 Dd 40.36N 8.40W
Ilhéus 200 Mg 14.49S 39.02W
Ili 140 Je 45.24N 74.08 E
Ilia 130 Fd 45.56N 22.39 E
Iliamna 178 Ie 59.45N 154.54W
Iliamna Lake 178 He 59.30N 155.00W
Ilič 135 Gd 40.55N 68.29 E
Iliç 146 Hc 39.29N 38.34 E
Ilica 130 Kj 39.52N 27.46 E
Iličevsk [Abz.-U.S.S.R.] 132 Nj 39.33N 44.59 E
Iličevsk [Ukr.-U.S.S.R.] 136 Df 46.18N 30.37 E
Ilidža 128 Mg 43.50N 18.19 E
Iligan 142 Oi 8.14N 124.14 E
Iligan Bay 150 He 8.25N 124.05 E
Ilim 138 Fe 56.50N 103.25 E
Ilimskoje vodohranilišče 138 Fe 57.20N 102.30 E
Ilinski [R.S.F.S.R.] 138 Jg 47.59N 142.21 E
Ilinski [R.S.F.S.R.] 114 Hf 61.02N 32.42 E
Ilinski [R.S.F.S.R.] 136 Gg 58.35N 55.41 E
Ilion 184 Jd 43.01N 75.04W
Ilio Point 221a Db 21.13N 157.16W
Ilir 138 Fe 55.13N 100.45 E
Ilirska Bistrica 128 Ie 45.34N 14.16 E
Iljaly 135 Bd 41.53N 59.40 E
Ilkal 148 Fe 15.58N 76.08 E
Ilkeston 124 Ab 52.58N 1.18W
Ill 122 Nf 48.40N 7.53 E
Illampu, Nevado del- 202 Eg 15.50S 68.34W
Illana Bay 150 He 7.25N 123.45 E
Illapel 206 Fd 31.38S 71.10W
Illa Sa Conillera / Isla Cunillera 126 Nf 38.59N 1.12 E
Illbillee, Mount- 212 Ge 27.02S 132.30 E
Ille 122 Ef 48.08N 1.40W
Ille-et-Vilaine [3] 122 Ef 48.10N 1.30W
Illéla 166 Gc 14.28N 5.15 E
Iller 120 Fh 48.23N 3.58 E
Illescas 126 Id 40.07N 3.50W
Ille-sur-Têt 122 Il 42.40N 2.37 E
Illi, Ba- 168 Bc 10.44N 16.21 E
Illimani, Nevado del- 198 Jg 16.39S 67.48W
Illingen 124 Je 49.22N 7.03 E
Illinois [2] 182 Jd 40.00N 89.00W
Illinois 174 Jf 38.58N 90.27W
Illinois Peak 188 Hc 47.02N 115.04W
Illizi 160 Hf 26.29N 8.28 E
Ilm 120 He 51.07N 11.40 E
Ilmajoki 116 Jb 62.44N 22.34 E
Ilmen, ozero- 110 Jd 58.20N 31.20 E
Ilmenau 120 Gf 50.41N 10.54 E
Ilmenau 120 Gc 53.23N 10.10 E
Il Montello 128 Ge 45.49N 12.07 E
Ilo 202 Dg 17.38S 71.20W
Iloilo 142 Oh 10.42N 122.34 E
Ilok 128 Ne 45.13N 19.23 E
Ilomantsi 114 He 62.40N 30.55 E
Ilorin 160 Hh 8.30N 4.33 E
Iloron, Cerro- 192 Gg 20.57N 104.22W
Ilova 128 Ke 45.25N 16.45 E
Ilovik 128 If 44.27N 14.33 E
Ilovlja 132 Ne 49.18N 44.01 E
Ilovlja 132 Me 49.14N 43.54 E
Ilpyrski 138 Le 59.52N 164.12 E
Ilski 132 Kg 44.51N 38.32 E
Iltin 138 Nc 67.52N 178.48W
Ilubabor [3] 168 Ed 7.50N 35.00 E
Iluksle/Ilūkste 116 Li 55.58N 26.26 E
Ilūkste/Iluksle 116 Li 55.58N 26.26 E
Ilulissat/Jakobshavn 224 Nc 69.20N 50.50W
Ilwaki 150 Ih 7.56S 126.26 E
Ilyč 134 He 62.32N 56.40 E
Ilz 120 Jh 48.35N 13.30 E
Iłżanka 120 Re 51.14N 21.47 E
Imabari 154 Lg 34.03N 133.00 E
Imagane 154 Pc 42.26N 140.01 E
Imaichi 154 Of 36.43N 139.41 E
Imán, Sierra del- 204 Eh 27.42S 55.28W
Imanburluk 154 Mj 53.40N 67.15 E
Imandra, ozero- 110 Jb 67.30N 33.00 E
Imano-Yama 156 Ce 32.51N 132.49 E
Imari 154 Jh 33.16N 129.53 E
Imarui 204 Hi 28.21S 48.49W
Imataca, Serrania de- 196 Fi 7.45N 61.00W
Imatra 114 Gf 61.10N 28.46 E
Imazu 156 Ed 35.24N 136.01 E
Imbabah, Al Qāhirah- 164 Fc 30.05N 31.13 E
Imbert 194 Ld 19.45N 70.50W
Imbituba 206 Kc 28.14S 48.40W
Imeni 26 Bakinskih Komissarov [Abz.-U.S.S.R.] 136 Eh 39.19N 49.12 E
Imeni 26 Bakinskih Komissarov [Tur.-U.S.S.R.] 136 Fh 39.21N 54.12 E
İmeni Gastello 138 Jd 61.35N 147.59 E
Imeni Karla Liebknechta 132 Id 51.38N 35.29 E
Imeni Mariny Raskovoj 138 Jd 62.05N 146.30 E
İmeni Poliny Osipenko 138 If 52.23N 136.25 E
Imi 160 Lh 6.28N 42.11 E
Imilili 162 De 22.50N 15.54W
Imi n'Tanout 162 Fc 31.03N 8.08W
Imišli 136 Eh 39.53N 48.03 E
Imjin-gang 154 If 37.47N 126.40 E
Imlay 188 Ff 40.42N 118.07W
Immenstadt im Allgäu 120 Gi 47.34N 10.13 E
Imo [2] 166 Gd 5.30N 7.20 E
Imola 128 Ff 44.21N 11.42 E
Imotski 128 Lg 43.27N 17.13 E
Imperatriz 200 Lf 5.32S 47.29W
Imperia 128 Cg 43.53N 8.03 E
Imperial 186 Ff 40.31N 101.39W
Imperial de Aragón, Canal- 126 Kb 42.02N 1.33W
Imperial Valley 188 Hj 32.50N 115.30W
Impfondo 160 Ih 1.37N 18.04 E
Imphāl 142 Lg 24.49N 93.57 E
Imphy 122 Jh 46.56N 3.15 E
Impilanti 114 Hf 61.41N 31.12 E
Imralı Adası 130 Li 40.32N 28.32 E
İmroz 146 Ab 40.11N 25.55 E
Imst 128 Ec 47.14N 10.44 E
Imtan 146 Gf 32.24N 36.49 E
Imuris 192 Db 30.47N 110.52W
Im-Zouren 126 Ii 35.04N 3.50W
Ina 154 Ng 35.50N 137.57 E
Ina 120 Kc 53.32N 14.38 E
I-n-Abanrherit 166 Gb 17.58N 6.05 E
Inabu 156 Ed 35.13N 137.30 E
Inaccessible Island 222 Re 37.15S 12.45W
Inaccessible Islands 222 Re 60.34S 46.44W
I-n-Afaleleh 162 Ie 23.34N 9.12 E
I Naftan, Puntan- 220b Ba 15.05N 145.45 E
Ina-Gawa 156 Fc 37.23N 139.18 E
I-n-Amenas 160 Hf 28.03N 9.33 E
Inami 156 De 33.48N 135.12 E
Inanba-Jima 156 Fe 33.39N 139.18 E
Inangahua Junction 218 Dd 41.52S 171.56 E
Inanwatan 150 Jg 2.08S 132.10 E
Iñapari 202 Ef 10.57S 69.35W
Inarajan 220c Bb 13.16N 144.45 E
I-n-Arhâta 166 Ea 21.09N 0.18W
Inari 112 Ib 68.54N 27.01 E
Inari, Lake- (EN)= Inarijärvi 110 Ib 69.00N 28.00 E
Inarijärvi=Inari, Lake- (EN) 110 Ib 69.00N 28.00 E
Inawashiro 156 Gc 37.34N 140.05 E
Inawashiro-Ko 154 Pf 37.30N 140.03 E
I-n-Azaoua 166 Ga 20.54N 7.28 E
I-n-Azaoua 166 Ga 20.47N 7.31 E
Inazawa 156 Ed 35.15N 136.47 E
Inca 126 Oe 39.43N 2.54 E
Inca de Oro 206 Gc 26.45S 69.54W
Incaguasi 206 Fc 29.13S 71.03W
İnce Burun [Tur.] 130 Ki 40.28N 27.16 E
İnce Burun [Tur.] 140 Fe 42.07N 34.56 E
İncekum Burun 146 Ed 36.13N 33.58 E
Inceler 130 Ml 37.42N 29.35 E
I-n-Chaouâg 166 Fb 16.23N 0.10 E
Inchcape (Bell Rock) 118 Ke 56.26N 2.24W
Inchiri [3] 162 Df 20.00N 15.00W
Inch'ŏn 142 Of 37.28N 126.38 E
Incirliova 130 Kl 37.50N 27.43 E
Incudine, Monte- 122a Bb 41.51N 9.12 E
Indaiá, Rio- 204 Jd 18.27S 45.22W
Indaia Grande, Ribeirão- 204 Fd 19.31S 52.29W
Indaiatuba 204 If 23.05S 47.14W
Indal 116 Gb 62.34N 17.06 E
Indalsälven 114 De 62.31N 17.27 E
Inda Selase 168 Fc 14.06N 38.17 E
Indawgyi 148 Jc 25.08N 96.20 E
Indefatigable Banks 118 Ph 53.35N 2.20 E
Independence [Ca.-U.S.] 188 Fh 36.48N 118.12W
Independence [Ia.-U.S.] 186 Ke 42.28N 91.54W
Independence [Ks.-U.S.] 182 Hd 37.13N 95.42W
Independence [Mo.-U.S.] 186 Ig 39.05N 94.04W
Independence [Va.-U.S.] 184 Gg 36.38N 81.11W
Independence Fjord 224 Me 82.00N 30.25W
Independence Mountains 188 Gf 41.15N 116.05W
Independência [Braz.] 204 Fa 13.34S 53.57W
Independência [Braz.] 202 Je 5.23S 40.19W
Independenta 130 Kd 45.29N 27.45 E
Inder → Jalaid Qi 152 Lb 46.41N 122.52 E
Inder, ozero- 132 Qe 48.25N 51.55 E
Inderborski 112 Lf 48.32N 51.47 E
India (EN) 140 Jh 20.00N 77.00 E
India (EN)=Bhārat Juktarashtra [1] 142 Jh 20.00N 77.00 E
India Muerta, Arroyo de la- 204 Fk 33.40S 54.04W
Indiana 184 He 40.39N 79.11W
Indiana [2] 182 Jc 40.00N 86.15W
Indianapolis 176 Kf 39.46N 86.09W
Indian Church 194 Ce 17.45N 88.40W
Indian Creek Point 197d Bb 17.00N 61.43W
Indian Harbour 180 Lf 54.27N 57.13W
Indian Head 180 Hf 50.32N 103.40W
Indian Ocean 106 Gl 21.00S 82.00 E
Indian Ocean (EN)=Hindi, Badwēynta- 106 Gl 21.00S 82.00 E
Indian Ocean (EN)=Indico, Oceano- 106 Gl 21.00S 82.00 E
Indian Ocean (EN)= Indien,Océan- 106 Gl 21.00S 82.00 E
Indian Ocean (EN) = Indiese Oseaan 106 Gl 21.00S 82.00 E
Indian Ocean (EN)= Indonesia, Samudera- 106 Gl 21.00S 82.00 E
Indianola 186 Kj 33.27N 90.39W
Indianópolis 204 Id 19.02S 47.55W
Indian Peak 188 Ig 38.16N 113.53W
Indian Rock 180 Ec 46.01N 120.49W
Indian Springs 182 Dd 36.34N 115.40W
Indiantown 184 Gl 27.01N 80.28W
Indian Town Point 197d Bb 17.06N 61.40W
Indiapora 204 Gd 19.57S 50.17W
Indias Occidentales=West Indies (EN) 190 Je 19.00N 70.00W
Indico, Oceano-=Indian Ocean (EN) 106 Gl 21.00S 82.00 E
Indien,Océan-=Indian Ocean (EN) 106 Gl 21.00S 82.00 E
Indiese Oseaan = Indian Ocean (EN) 106 Gl 21.00S 82.00 E
Indiga 136 Eb 67.41N 49.00 E
Indigirka 140 Qb 70.48N 148.54 E
Indigskaja guba 134 Dc 67.45N 48.20 E
Inđija 130 Dd 45.03N 20.05 E
Indio 182 De 33.43N 116.13W
Indio, Rio- 194 Fh 10.57N 83.44W
Indio Rico 204 Bn 38.19S 60.53W
Indispensable Reefs 208 Hf 12.40S 160.25 E
Indispensable Strait 219a Ec 9.00S 160.30 E
Indochina (EN) 140 Mh 16.00N 107.00 E
Indonesia [1] 142 Nj 5.00S 120.00 E
Indonesia, Samudera-= Indian Ocean (EN) 106 Gl 21.00S 82.00 E
Indore 142 Jg 22.43N 75.50 E
Indra 116 Li 55.53N 27.40 E
Indragiri 150 Dg 0.22S 103.26 E
Indramayu 150 Eh 6.20S 108.19 E
Indrāvati 148 Ge 18.44N 80.16 E
Indre [3] 122 Hh 46.50N 1.40 E
Indre 122 Gg 47.14N 0.11 E
Indre Arna 116 Ad 60.26N 5.30 E
Indre-et-Loire [3] 122 Gg 47.15N 0.45 E
Indus 140 Ig 24.20N 67.47 E
İnebolu 144 Da 41.58N 33.46 E
Inece 130 Kh 41.41N 27.04 E
Inecik 130 Ki 40.56N 27.16 E
İnegöl 144 Ca 40.05N 29.31 E
Inés Indart 204 Bl 34.24S 60.33W
Ineu 130 Ec 46.26N 21.51 E
Ineu, Virful- 130 Hb 47.32N 24.53 E
Inezgane 162 Fc 30.21N 9.32W
I-n-Ezzane 162 Je 23.29N 11.15 E
Inferior, Laguna- 192 Li 16.15N 94.45W
Infiernillo, Presa del- 190 De 18.35N 101.45W
Infiesto 126 Ga 43.21N 5.22W
Infreschi, Punta degli- 128 Jk 39.59N 15.25 E
Ingá 202 Ke 7.17S 35.36W
Inga 170 Bd 5.39S 13.39 E
Ingå/Inkoo 114 Ff 60.03N 24.01 E
Ingabu 148 Je 17.49N 95.16 E
Ingai, Rio- 204 Je 21.10S 44.52W
I-n-Gall 166 Gb 16.47N 6.56 E
Ingarö 116 He 59.15N 18.30 E
Ingavi 204 Bb 15.02S 60.29W
Ingelheim am Rhein 124 Ke 49.59N 8.02 E
Ingelmunster 124 Fd 50.55N 3.15 E
Ingelstad 116 Fh 56.45N 14.55 E
Ingende 170 Cc 0.15S 18.57 E
Ingeniero Guillermo N. Juárez 206 Hb 23.54S 61.51W
Ingeniero Jacobacci 208 Gf 41.18S 69.35W
Ingeniero Luiggi 206 He 35.25S 64.29W
Ingenio Santa Ana 206 Gc 27.28S 65.41W
Ingermanland (EN) 110 Id 59.00N 30.00 E
Ingham 210 Ff 18.39S 146.10 E
Ingička 135 Ee 39.47N 65.58 E
Inglefield Bredning 179 Fc 77.40N 65.00W
Inglefield Land 179 Fc 78.44N 68.20W
Inglewood [Austl.] 212 Ke 28.25S 151.05 E
Inglewood [Ca.-U.S.] 188 Fj 33.58N 118.21W
Inglewood [N.Z.] 218 Fc 39.09S 174.12 E
Ingoda 138 Gf 52.03N 113.30 E
Ingolf Fjord 179 Kb 80.35N 17.35W
Ingólfshöfdi 114a Cc 63.48N 16.39W
Ingolstadt 120 Hh 48.46N 11.26 E
Ingrāj Bāzār 148 Hc 25.00N 88.09 E
I-n-Guezzâm 160 Hg 19.32N 5.42 E
Ingul 132 Gf 47.02N 31.59 E
Ingulec 136 Df 47.43N 33.10 E
Ingulec 132 Hf 46.41N 32.48 E
Inguri 132 Lh 42.24N 41.32 E
Inhaca, Ilha da- 158 Kk 26.02S 32.58 E
Inhambane 160 Kk 23.52S 35.23 E
Inhambane [3] 172 Ed 23.00S 34.30 E
Inhambane, Baia de- 172 Fd 23.50S 35.20 E
Inhaminga 172 Fc 18.25S 35.01 E
Inhandui-Guaçu, Rio- 204 Fe 21.37S 52.59W
Inhanduizinho, Rio- 204 Fe 21.34S 53.36W
Inharrime 172 Fd 24.28S 35.01 E
Inhassoro 172 Fd 21.32S 35.12 E
Inhaúma 204 Ja 13.01S 44.39W
I-n-Hihaou 162 He 23.00N 2.00 E
Inhobi, Rio- 204 Ef 23.45S 54.40W
Inhumas 202 Ig 16.22S 49.30W
Inio 116 Id 60.25N 21.25 E
Inirida, Rio- 198 Je 3.55N 67.52W
Inis/Ennis 118 Ei 52.50N 8.59W
Inis Airc/Inishark 118 Ch 53.37N 10.16W
Inis Bó Finne/Inishbofin 118 Ch 53.38N 10.12W
Inis Ceithleann/Enniskillen 118 Fg 54.21N 7.38W
Inis Córthaidh/Enniscorthy 118 Gi 52.30N 6.34W
Inis Díomáin / Ennistimon 118 Di 52.57N 9.13W
Inis Eoghain/Inishowen Peninsula 118 Ff 55.15N 7.20W
Inishark/Inis Airc 118 Ch 53.37N 10.16W
Inishbofin/Inis Bó Finne 118 Ch 53.38N 10.12W
Inisheer/Inis Oirr 118 Dh 53.03N 9.31W
Inishkea 118 Cg 54.08N 10.11W
Inishmaan/Inis Meáin 118 Dh 53.05N 9.35W
Inishmore/Árainn 118 Dh 53.07N 9.45W
Inishmurray/Inis Muirigh 118 Eg 54.26N 8.40W
Inishowen Peninsula/Inis Eoghain 118 Ff 55.15N 7.20W
Inishtranull 118 Ff 55.27N 7.14W
Inishturk/Inis Toirc 118 Ch 53.43N 10.05W
Inis Meáin/Inishmaan 118 Dh 53.05N 9.35W
Inis Muirigh/Inishmurray 118 Eg 54.26N 8.40W
Inis Oirr/Inisheer 118 Dh 53.03N 9.31W
Inis Toirc/Inishturk 118 Ch 53.43N 10.05W
Inja 138 Je 59.22N 144.50 E
Inja [R.S.F.S.R.] 138 Df 50.27N 86.42 E
Inja [R.S.F.S.R.] 138 Je 59.30N 144.48 E
Injeŭp 154 Je 38.04N 128.10 E
Injibara 168 Fc 10.55N 36.58 E
Injune 212 Je 25.51S 148.34 E
I-n-Kak 166 Fb 16.20N 0.17 E
Inkisi 170 Bc 4.46S 14.52 E
Inkoo/Ingå 114 Ff 60.03N 24.01 E
Inland Kaikoura Range 218 Ee 42.00S 173.35 E
Inland Sea (EN)= Setonaikai 140 Pf 34.10N 133.00 E
Inn 110 Hf 48.35N 13.28 E
Innamincka 212 Ie 27.45S 140.44 E
Inner Hebrides 118 Ge 57.00N 6.45W
Inner Mongol a (EN)=Nei Monggol Zizhiqu (Nei-meng-ku Tzu-chih-ch'ü) [2] 152 Jc 44.00N 112.00 E
Inner Silver Pit 118 Nh 53.30N 0.40 E
Inner Sound 118 Hd 57.30N 5.55W
Innerste 120 Fd 52.15N 9.50 E
Innisfail [Alta.-Can.] 188 Ia 52.02N 113.57W
Innisfail [Austl.] 212 Jc 17.32S 146.02 E
Innokentjevka 138 Ig 49.42N 136.55 E
Innokentjevski 138 Jg 48.38N 140.12 E
Innoko 178 Hd 62.14N 159.45W
In'noshima 156 Cd 34.19N 133.10 E
Innsbruck 112 Hf 47.16N 11.24 E
Innuksuac 180 Je 58.27N 78.08W
Innviertel 128 Hb 48.15N 13.15 E
Innvikfjorden 116 Bc 61.50N 6.35 E
Inny/An Eithne 118 Fh 53.35N 7.50W
Ino 156 Ce 33.33N 133.26 E
Inobonto 150 Hf 0.52N 123.57 E
Inongo 160 Ii 1.57S 18.16 E
Inoni 170 Cc 3.04S 15.39 E
Inönü 130 Nj 39.48N 30.09 E
I-n-Ouagar 166 Gb 16.12N 6.54 E
I-n-Ouzzal 162 He 21.34N 1.59 E
Inowrocław 120 Od 52.48N 18.15 E
I-n-Salah 160 Hf 27.13N 2.28 E
Insar 114 Kj 53.52N 44.23 E
Insar 114 Ki 54.42N 45.18 E
Inscription, Cape- 208 Cg 25.30S 112.59 E
Insjön 116 Fd 60.41N 15.05 E
Insko 120 Lc 53.27N 15.33 E
Instanbul Boğazi = Bosporus (EN) 110 Ig 41.00N 29.00 E
Instruč 116 Ij 54.39N 21.48 E
Insurăței 130 Ke 44.55N 27.36 E
Inta 112 Mb 66.05N 60.08 E
I-n-Tebezas 166 Fb 17.54N 1.50 E
I-n-Tallak 166 Fb 16.19N 3.15 E
Intepe 130 Ji 40.00N 26.20 E
Interlaken 128 Bd 46.41N 7.52 E
International Falls 182 Ib 48.36N 93.25W
Interview 148 If 12.55N 92.43 E
Inthanon, Doi- 148 Je 18.35N 98.29 E
Intibucá [3] 194 Cf 14.20N 88.15W
Intiyaco 206 Hc 28.39S 60.05W
Intorsura Buzaului 130 Jd 45.41N 26.02 E
Intracoastal Waterway 186 Im 28.45N 95.40W
Inubō-Zaki 156 Gd 35.42N 140.52 E
Inukjuak 176 Ld 58.30N 78.15W
Inútil, Bahia- 206 Fh 52.45S 71.24W
Inuvik 176 Fc 68.25N 133.30W
Inuyama 156 Ed 35.23N 136.56 E
Inva 134 Gg 58.59N 55.40 E
Inveraray 118 He 56.13N 5.05W
Invercargill 210 Hi 46.25S 168.21 E
Inverell 212 Ke 29.47S 151.07 E
Inverness 112 Fd 57.27N 4.15W
Inverurie 118 Kd 57.17N 2.23W
Investigator Group 208 Eh 33.45S 134.30 E
Investigator Strait 212 Hg 35.25S 137.10 E
Inyangani 172 Ec 18.13S 32.46 E
Inyangani 158 Kj 18.18S 32.51 E
Inyati 172 Dc 19.40S 28.51 E
Inyazura 172 Ec 18.43S 32.10 E
Inyo Mountains 188 Gh 36.50N 117.45W
Inza 136 Ee 53.53N 46.28 E
Inzá 202 Cc 2.33N 76.04W
Inžavino 132 Mc 52.19N 42.31 E
Inzer 134 Hi 54.14N 57.34 E
Inzer 134 Hi 54.24N 56.28 E
Inzia 170 Cc 3.45S 17.57 E
Iō/Kazan-Rettō=Volcano Islands (EN) 140 Qg 25.00N 141.00 E
Ioánnina 112 Ih 39.40N 20.50 E
Ioanninon, Limni- 130 Dj 39.40N 20.53 E
Iokanga 114 Jb 68.03N 39.40 E
Iola 186 Ih 37.55N 95.24W
Iolotan 136 Gh 37.18N 62.21 E
Iona 170 Bf 16.52S 12.34 E
Iona 118 Ge 56.19N 6.25W
Ionava/Jonava 114 Fi 55.05N 24.17 E
Ion Corvin 130 Ke 44.07N 27.48 E
Ione 188 Eg 38.21N 120.56W
Ionia 184 Ed 42.59N 85.04W
Ionian Basin (EN) 110 Hh 36.03N 20.00 E
Ionian Islands (EN)=Iónioi Nisoi 110 Ih 38.30N 20.30 E
Ionian Sea (EN)=Ionio, Mar- 110 Hh 39.00N 19.00 E
Ionian Sea (EN)=Iónion Pélagos 110 Hh 39.00N 19.00 E
Ionio, Mar-=Ionian Sea (EN) 110 Hh 39.00N 19.00 E
Iónioi Nisoi [2] 130 Dk 38.40N 20.10 E
Iónioi Nisoi=Ionian Islands (EN) 110 Ih 38.30N 20.30 E
Iónion Pélagos=Ionian Sea (EN) 110 Hh 39.00N 19.00 E
Ioniškis/Joniškelis 116 Ki 56.00N 24.14 E
Ioniškis/Joniškis 114 Fh 56.16N 23.37 E
Iony, ostrov- 138 Je 56.15N 143.20 E
Iori 132 Ci 41.03N 46.27 E
Ios 130 Im 36.44N 25.18 E

Index Symbols

- [1] Independent Nation
- [2] State, Region
- [3] District, County
- [4] Municipality
- [5] Colony, Dependency
- Continent
- Physical Region
- Historical or Cultural Region
- Mount, Mountain
- Volcano
- Hill
- Mountains, Mountain Range
- Hills, Escarpment
- Plateau, Upland
- Pass, Gap
- Plain, Lowland
- Delta
- Salt Flat
- Valley, Canyon
- Crater, Cave
- Karst Features
- Depression
- Polder
- Desert, Dunes
- Forest, Woods
- Heath, Steppe
- Oasis
- Cape, Point
- Coast, Beach
- Cliff
- Peninsula
- Isthmus
- Sandbank
- Island
- Atoll
- Rock, Reef
- Islands, Archipelago
- Rocks, Reefs
- Coral Reef
- Well, Spring
- Geyser
- River, Stream
- Waterfall, Rapids
- River Mouth, Estuary
- Lake
- Salt Lake
- Intermittent Lake
- Reservoir
- Swamp, Pond
- Canal
- Glacier
- Ice Shelf, Pack Ice
- Ocean
- Sea
- Gulf, Bay
- Strait, Fjord
- Lagoon
- Bank
- Seamount
- Tablemount
- Ridge
- Shelf
- Basin
- Escarpment, Sea Scarp
- Fracture
- Trench, Abyss
- National Park, Reserve
- Point of Interest
- Recreation Site
- Cave, Cavern
- Historic Site
- Ruins
- Wall, Walls
- Church, Abbey
- Temple
- Scientific Station
- Railway station
- Airport
- Port
- Military installation
- Lighthouse
- Mine
- Tunnel
- Dam, Bridge

Index Symbols

[1] Independent Nation	◩ Historical or Cultural Region	)(Pass, Gap
[2] State, Region	▲ Mount, Mountain	▭ Plain, Lowland
[3] District, County	▲ Volcano	▽ Delta
[4] Municipality	⌂ Hill	▭ Salt Flat
[5] Colony, Dependency	⋀ Mountains, Mountain Range	▭ Valley, Canyon
■ Continent	⌂ Hills, Escarpment	★ Crater, Cave
⊠ Physical Region	▱ Plateau, Upland	✦ Karst Features

▭ Depression	▭ Coast, Beach	▨ Rock, Reef
▭ Polder	▭ Cliff	▨ Islands, Archipelago
▭ Desert, Dunes	▭ Peninsula	▨ Rocks, Reefs
▭ Forest, Woods	▭ Isthmus	▭ Coral Reef
▭ Heath, Steppe	▭ Sandbank	▭ Well, Spring
▭ Oasis	▭ Island	▭ Geyser
▭ Cape, Point	⊙ Atoll	▭ River, Stream

▨ Waterfall, Rapids	▭ Canal	▭ Lagoon
▨ River Mouth, Estuary	▭ Glacier	▭ Bank
▭ Lake	▭ Ice Shelf, Pack Ice	▭ Seamount
▭ Salt Lake	▭ Ocean	▭ Tablemount
▭ Intermittent Lake	▭ Sea	▭ Ridge
▭ Reservoir	▭ Gulf, Bay	▭ Shelf
▭ Swamp, Pond	▭ Strait, Fjord	▭ Basin

▨ Escarpment, Sea Scarp	▲ Historic Site	▭ Airport
▭ Fracture	▭ Ruins	▭ Port
▭ Trench, Abyss	▭ Wall, Walls	▭ Military installati...
▭ National Park, Reserve	▭ Church, Abbey	▭ Lighthouse
▭ Point of Interest	▭ Temple	▭ Mine
▭ Recreation Site	▭ Scientific Station	▭ Tunnel
▭ Cave, Cavern	▭ Railway station	▭ Dam, Bridge

Izobilny 132 Lg 45.19N 41.42 E
Izola 128 He 45.32N 13.40 E
Ižorskaja vozvyšennost 116 Me 59.35N 29.30 E
Izozog, Bañados del- 202 Fg 18.50S 62.10W
Izra' 146 Gf 32.51N 36.15 E
Izsák 120 Pj 46.48N 19.22 E
Iztočni Rodopi 130 Ih 41.44N 25.31 E
Izúcar de Matamoros 192 Jh 18.36N 98.28W
Izu-Hantō 154 Og 34.55N 138.55 E
Izuhara 154 Jg 34.12N 129.17 E
Izu Islands (EN) = Izu-Shotō 140 Pf 32.00N 140.00 E
Izumi [Jap.] 154 Kh 32.05N 130.22 E
Izumi [Jap.] 156 Gb 38.19N 140.51 E
Izumi [Jap.] 156 Dd 34.29N 135.26 E
Izumi-sano 156 Dd 34.24N 135.18 E
Izumo 154 Lg 35.22N 132.46 E
Izu-Shotō=Izu Islands (EN) 140 Pf 32.00N 140.00 E
Izvesti CIK, ostrova- = Izvestiya Tsik Islands (EN) 138 Da 75.55N 82.30 E
Izvestiya Tsik lulands (EN) = Izvesti CIK, ostrova- 138 Da 75.55N 82.30 E

J

Jaala 116 Lc 61.03N 26.29 E
Jaama/Jama 116 Lf 58.59N 27.45 E
Jääsjärvi 116 Lc 61.35N 26.05 E
Jaba 146 Qe 35.55N 56.35 E
Jabal, Baḥr al-=Mountain Nile (EN) 158 Kh 9.30N 30.30 E
Jabal Abū Rujmayn 146 Ge 34.50N 37.56 E
Jabal al Awliyā' 168 Eb 15.14N 32.30 E
Jabal az Zannah 146 Oj 24.11N 52.38 E
Jabal Lubnān [3] 146 Ff 33.50N 35.40 E
Jabalón 126 Hf 38.53N 4.05W
Jabalpur 142 Jg 23.10N 79.57 E
Jabal Şabāyā 164 Hf 18.35N 41.03 E
Jabālyah 146 Fg 31.32N 34.29 E
Jabal Zuqar, Jazīrat- 164 Hg 14.00N 42.45 E
Jabbārah 164 Hf 19.27N 40.03 E
Jabbeke 124 Fc 51.11N 3.05 E
Jabjabah, Wādī- 168 Ea 22.37N 33.17 E
Jablah 146 Fe 35.21N 35.55 E
Jablanac 128 If 44.43N 14.53 E
Jablanica 130 Dh 41.15N 20.30 E
Jablanica [Bul.] 130 Hf 43.01N 24.06 E
Jablanica [Yugo.] 128 Lg 43.39N 17.45 E
Jabločny 138 Jg 47.09N 142.03 E
Jablonec nad Nisou 120 Lf 50.44N 15.10 E
Jablonicki, pereval- 110 If 48.18N 24.28 E
Jablonovo 138 Gf 51.51N 112.50 E
Jablonovy hrebet = Yablonovy Range (EN) 140 Nd 53.30N 115.00 E
Jablunkovský průsmyk 120 Og 49.31N 18.45 E
Jaboatão 202 Ke 8.07S 35.01W
Jabotí 204 De 20.48S 56.23W
Jaboticabal 206 Kb 21.16S 48.19W
Jabrīn 146 Ni 27.51N 51.26 E
Jabuka 128 Jg 43.05N 15.28 E
Jabung, Tanjung- 150 Dg 1.01S 104.22 E
Jabuticatubas 204 Kd 19.30S 43.45W
Jaca 126 Lb 42.34N 0.33W
Jacaltenango 194 Bf 15.40N 91.44W
Jacaré, Rio- 204 Je 21.03S 45.16W
Jacareí 204 Jf 23.19S 45.58W
Jacarezinho 206 Kb 23.09S 49.59W
Jáchal, Río- 198 Ji 30.44S 68.08W
Jaciara [Braz.] 204 Ib 14.12S 46.41W
Jaciara [Braz.] 204 Eb 15.59S 54.57W
Jackman 184 Lc 45.38N 70.16W
Jack Mountain 188 Eb 48.47N 120.57W
Jackpot 188 Hf 41.59N 114.09W
Jacksboro 186 Gj 33.13N 98.10W
Jacks Mountain 184 Ie 40.45N 77.30W
Jackson [Al.-U.S.] 184 Dj 31.31N 87.53W
Jackson [Bar.] 197q Ab 13.10N 59.43W
Jackson [Ky.-U.S.] 184 Fg 37.33N 83.23W
Jackson [Mi.-U.S.] 182 Kc 42.15N 84.24W
Jackson [Mn.-U.S.] 186 Ie 43.37N 94.59W
Jackson [Mo.-U.S.] 186 Lh 37.23N 89.40W
Jackson [Ms.-U.S.] 176 Jf 32.18N 90.12W
Jackson [Oh.-U.S.] 184 Ff 39.03N 82.40W
Jackson [Tn.-U.S.] 182 Jd 35.37N 88.49W
Jackson [Wy.-U.S.] 188 Je 43.29N 110.38W
Jackson, Cape- 218 Fd 40.59S 174.19 E
Jackson, Mount- [Ant.] 222 Qf 71.23S 63.22W
Jackson, Mount- [Austl.] 212 Df 30.15S 119.16 E
Jackson Bay 218 Ce 43.55S 168.40 E
Jackson Head 218 Ce 43.58S 168.37 E
Jackson Lake 188 Je 43.55N 110.40W
Jacksonville [Ar.-U.S.] 186 Ji 34.52N 92.07W
Jacksonville [Fl.-U.S.] 176 Kf 30.20N 81.40W
Jacksonville [Il.-U.S.] 186 Kg 39.44N 90.14W
Jacksonville [N.C.-U.S.] 182 Le 34.45N 77.26W
Jacksonville [Tx.-U.S.] 182 He 31.58N 95.17W
Jacksonville Beach 182 Ke 30.18N 81.24W
Jacmel 190 Je 18.14N 72.32W
Jacobābad 148 Dc 28.17N 68.26 E
Jacobina 202 Jf 11.11S 40.31W
Jacob Lake 188 Ih 36.45N 112.13W
Jacobs 186 La 50.15N 89.46W
Jacona de Plancarte 192 Hh 19.57N 102.16W
Jacques-Cartier, Détroit de - 180 Lg 50.00N 63.30W
Jacques Cartier, Mont - 180 Kg 48.58N 65.57W
Jacuba, Rio- 204 Fd 18.25S 52.28W
Jacuí, Rio- 198 Ki 30.02S 51.15W
Jacuí-Mirim, Rio- 204 Fi 28.51S 53.07W
Jacundá 202 Id 4.33S 49.28W
Jacundá, Rio- 202 Hd 1.57S 50.26W
Jacupiranga 206 Kb 24.42S 48.00W
Jada 166 Hd 8.46N 12.09 E
Jadal 166 Fb 18.37N 5.00 E
Jadar 128 Nf 44.38N 19.16 E
Jaddi, Rās- 148 Cc 25.14N 63.31 E
Jade 120 Ec 53.25N 8.05 E
Jadebusen 120 Ec 53.30N 8.10 E
Jadīd Ra's al Fīl 168 Dc 12.40N 25.43 E
Jadito Wash 188 Ji 35.22N 110.50W
J.A.D. Jensens Nunatakker 179 Hf 62.45N 48.20W
Jädraås 116 Gd 60.51N 16.28 E
Jadransko More=Adriatic Sea (EN) 110 Hg 43.00N 16.00 E
Jadrin 114 Li 55.57N 46.11 E
Jādū 164 Bc 31.57N 12.01 E
Ja'ēl 168 Ic 10.56N 51.09 E
Jaén 126 Ig 37.46N 3.47W
Jaén [3] 126 If 38.00N 3.30W
Jæren 116 Af 58.45N 5.45 E
Jærens rev 116 Af 58.45N 5.29 E
Jaffa, Cape- 212 Hg 36.58S 139.40 E
Jaffna 142 Ji 9.40N 80.00 E
Jafr, Qā' al- 146 Gg 30.17N 36.20 E
Jägala jõgi 116 Ke 59.28N 25.04 E
Jagdalpur 142 Kh 19.04N 82.02 E
Jagdaqi 152 La 50.26N 124.02 E
Jagersfontein 172 De 29.44S 25.29 E
Jaghbūb, Wāḥāt al-= Jarabub Oasis (EN) 158 Jf 29.41N 24.43 E
Jagotin 132 Gd 50.17N 31.47 E
Jagst 120 Fg 49.14N 9.11 E
Jaguapitã 204 Gf 23.07S 51.33W
Jaguaquara 202 Kf 13.32S 39.58W
Jaguarão 206 Jd 32.34S 53.23W
Jaguarão, Rio- 204 Fk 32.39S 53.12W
Jaguarari 202 Jf 10.16S 40.12W
Jaguari 204 Ei 29.30S 54.41W
Jaguari, Rio- [Braz.] 204 Ei 29.42S 55.07W
Jaguari, Rio- [Braz.] 204 If 22.41S 47.17W
Jaguariaíva 206 Kb 24.15S 49.42W
Jaguaribe 202 Ke 5.53S 38.37W
Jaguaribe, Rio- 198 Mf 4.25S 37.45W
Jaguaruana 202 Kd 4.50S 37.47W
Jagüey Grande 194 Gb 22.32N 81.08W
Jahadyjaha 134 Pc 67.03N 72.01 E
Jahām, 'Irq- 146 Li 26.12N 47.00 E
Jahorina 128 Mg 43.42N 18.35 E
Jahrom 144 Hd 28.31N 53.33 E
Jahroma 114 Ih 56.20N 37.29 E
Jaice 128 Lf 44.21N 17.17 E
Jaicoa, Cordillera- 197a Ab 18.25N 67.05W
Jaicós 202 Je 7.21S 41.08W
Jailolo 150 If 1.05N 127.30 E
Jailolo, Selat- 150 If 0.05N 129.05 E
Jaina, Isla de- 192 Ng 20.14N 90.40W
Jaipur 142 Jg 26.55N 75.49 E
Jaisalmer 148 Ec 26.55N 70.54 E
Jaja 138 De 56.12N 86.26 E
Jājarm 146 Qd 36.58N 56.27 E
Jajere 166 Hc 11.59N 11.26 E
Jajpan 135 Hd 40.23N 70.50 E
Jajsan 132 Td 50.51N 56.14 E
Jajva 136 Fd 59.20N 57.16 E
Jajva 134 Hg 59.16N 56.42 E
Jakarta (Djakarta) 142 Mj 6.10S 106.46 E
Jakobshavn/Ilulissat 224 Nc 69.20N 50.50W
Jakobstad/Pietarsaari 114 Fe 63.40N 22.42 E
Jakoruda 130 Gg 42.02N 23.40 E
Jakupica 130 Eh 41.43N 21.26 E
Jakutsk 142 Oc 62.13N 129.49 E
Jakutskaja ASSR [3] 138 Hc 67.00N 130.00 E
Jal 186 Ej 32.07N 103.12W
Jalaid Qi (Inder) 152 Lb 46.41N 122.52 E
Jalājil 146 Kj 25.41N 45.28 E
Jalālābād 144 Lc 34.26N 70.28 E
Jalālah al Baḥrīyah, Jabal al- 146 Eh 29.20N 32.20 E
Jalālah al Qiblīyah, Jabal al- 146 Eh 28.42N 32.22 E
Jalán, Río- 194 Df 15.43N 87.34W
Jalandhar 142 Jf 31.19N 75.34 E
Jalapa [3] 194 Cf 14.35N 89.55W
Jalapa [Guat.] 190 Gf 14.38N 89.59W
Jalapa [Mex.] 192 Mi 17.43N 92.49W
Jalapa [Nic.] 190 Gf 13.55N 86.08W
Jalapa Enríquez 176 Jh 19.32N 96.55W
Jalasjarvi 114 Fe 62.30N 22.45 E
Jales 204 Ge 20.16S 50.33W
Jālgaon 148 Fd 21.01N 75.34 E
Jalhay 124 Hd 50.34N 5.58 E
Jalībah 146 Lg 30.35N 46.32 E
Jalib Shahab 146 Lg 30.23N 46.09 E
Jalingo 166 Hd 8.53N 11.22 E
Jalisco [2] 190 Dd 20.20N 103.40W
Jāliţah=La Galite (EN) 158 He 37.32N 8.56 E
Jāliţah, Canal de- 128 Cm 37.20N 9.00 E
Jalkot 148 Ea 35.15N 73.17 E
Jallas 126 Cb 42.54N 9.08W
Jālna 148 Fe 19.50N 75.53 E
Jalón 126 Kc 41.47N 1.04W
Jalostotitlán 192 Hg 21.12N 102.28W
Jalpa 192 Hg 21.38N 102.58W
Jalpaiguri 148 Hc 26.31N 88.44 E
Jalpan 192 Jg 21.14N 99.29W
Jalpug, ozero- 132 Fg 45.25N 28.40 E
Jalta 136 Dg 44.30N 34.10 E
Jaltepec, Río- 192 Li 17.26N 94.59W
Jālū 164 Dd 28.30N 21.05 E
Jālū, Wāḥāt-=Gialo Oasis (EN) 158 Jf 29.00N 21.20 E
Jaluit Atoll 208 Hd 6.00N 169.35 E
Jalūlā' 146 Ke 34.16N 45.10 E
Jalutorovsk 136 Gd 56.40N 66.18 E
Jam [Iran] 146 Pe 35.45N 55.02 E
Jam [Iran] 146 Oi 27.50N 52.22 E
Jama/Jaama 116 Lf 58.59N 27.45 E
Jamaari 158 Ig 12.06N 10.14 E
Jamaica 194 Jc 20.12N 75.09W
Jamaica [1] 176 Lh 18.15N 77.30W
Jamaica 174 Lh 18.15N 77.30W
Jamaica Channel 190 Ie 18.00N 75.30W
Jamaica Channel (EN)= Jamaïque, Canal de- 194 Jd 18.00N 75.30W
Jamaïque, Canal de-= Jamaica Channel (EN) 194 Jd 18.00N 75.30W
Jamal, poluostrov- = Yamal Peninsula (EN) 140 Ib 70.00N 70.00 E
Jamalo-Nenecki nacionalny okrug [3] 138 Cc 67.00N 75.00 E
Jamālpur 148 Hd 24.55N 89.56 E
Jamāme 160 Lh 0.04N 42.46 E
Jamantau, gora- 110 Le 54.15N 58.06 E
Jamanxim, Rio- 198 Kf 4.43S 56.18W
Jamari, Rio- 202 Fe 8.27S 63.30W
Jamarovka 138 Gf 50.38N 110.16 E
Jambi 142 Mj 1.38S 103.42 E
Jambi [3] 150 Dg 1.36S 103.37 E
Jambol 130 Jg 42.29N 26.30 E
Jambol [2] 130 Jg 42.15N 26.35 E
Jambongan, Pulau- 150 Ge 6.41N 117.25 E
Jambuair, Tanjung- 150 Ce 5.16N 97.30 E
Jambusar 148 Ed 22.03N 72.48 E
James Bay 174 Kd 51.00N 80.30W
Jameson Land 179 Jd 70.45N 23.45W
James River [U.S.] 174 Je 42.52N 97.18W
James River [U.S.] 184 Ig 36.56N 76.27W
James Ross 222 Re 64.15S 57.45W
James Ross Strait 180 Hc 69.50N 96.30W
Jamestown [Austl.] 212 Hf 33.12S 138.36 E
Jamestown [N.D.-U.S.] 182 Hb 46.54N 98.42W
Jamestown [N.Y.-U.S.] 182 Lc 42.05N 79.15W
Jamestown [St.Hel.] 160 Gj 15.56S 5.43W
Jamestown Reservoir 186 Gc 47.15N 98.40W
Jamm 116 Mf 58.24N 28.15 E
Jammer Bugt 114 Bh 57.20N 9.30 E
Jammu 142 Jf 32.44N 74.52 E
Jammu and Kashmir [3] 148 Fb 34.00N 76.00 E
Jāmnagar 142 Jg 22.28N 70.04 E
Jamno, Jezioro- 120 Mb 54.15N 16.10 E
Jampol 132 Fe 48.16N 28.17 E
Jämsä 114 Ff 61.52N 25.12 E
Jamsah 146 Ei 27.38N 33.35 E
Jämsänkoski 116 Kc 61.55N 25.11 E
Jamshedpur 142 Kg 22.48N 86.11 E
Jamsk 138 Ke 59.37N 154.10 E
Jämtland [2] 114 De 63.00N 14.40 E
Jämtland 116 Fa 63.25N 14.05 E
Janā 146 Mi 27.22N 49.54 E
Jana 140 Pb 71.31N 136.32 E
Janakpur 148 Hc 26.42N 85.55 E
Janaucu, Ilha- 202 Hc 0.30N 50.10W
Janaul 134 Gh 56.16N 54.59 E
Janda, Laguna de la- 126 Gh 36.15N 5.51W
Jandaia 204 Gc 17.06S 50.07W
Jandaq 146 Pe 34.02N 54.26 E
Jandiatuba, Rio- 202 Ed 3.28S 68.42W
Jandowae 212 Ke 26.47S 151.06 E
Jandula 126 Hf 38.03N 4.06W
Jane Peak 218 Cf 45.20S 168.19 E
Janesville 182 Jc 42.41N 89.01W
Jangada 204 Db 15.14S 56.29W
Jangada, Rio- 204 Db 15.12S 56.24W
Jangao Shan 152 Gf 25.31N 98.08 E
Jangijer 135 Gd 40.18N 68.50 E
Jangijul 136 Gg 41.07N 69.03 E
Jangirabad 135 Ed 40.03N 65.59 E
Jango 204 Ee 20.27S 55.29W
Jangy-Bazar 135 Hd 41.40N 70.52 E
Janikowo 120 Od 52.45N 18.07 E
Janīn 146 Ff 32.28N 35.18 E
Janisjarvi, ozero- 114 He 62.00N 31.00 E
Janja 128 Nf 44.40N 19.19 E
Jan Mayen 110 Fa 71.00N 8.30W
Jan Mayen Ridge (EN) 110 Fb 69.00N 8.00W
Jano-Indigirskaja nizmennost 138 Ib 71.00N 139.30 E
Janos 190 Cb 30.56N 108.08W
Jánoshalma 120 Pj 46.18N 19.20 E
Jánosháza 120 Ni 47.07N 17.10 E
Janów Lubelski 120 Sf 50.43N 22.24 E
Janów Podlaski 120 Td 52.11N 23.11 E
Jansenville 172 Cf 32.56S 24.40 E
Janski zaliv 140 Pb 72.00N 136.00 E
Jantarny 116 Hj 54.53N 19.55 E
Jantra 130 If 43.38N 25.34 E
Januária 202 Jg 15.29S 44.22W
Janūbīyah, Aş Şaḥrā' al-= Southern Desert (EN) 158 Jf 24.00N 30.00 E
Janykurgan 136 Gg 43.55N 67.14 E
Janzhang Ansha 150 Ge 9.30N 116.59 E
Japan (EN) 140 Pf 35.00N 135.00 E
Japan (EN)=Nippon [1] 142 Pf 38.00N 137.00 E
Japan, Sea of- (EN) = Japonskoje more 140 Pf 40.00N 134.00 E
Japan, Sea of- (EN) = Nippon-Kai 140 Pf 40.00N 134.00 E
Japan, Sea of- (EN)=Tong-Hae 140 Pf 40.00N 134.00 E
Japan Basin (EN) 152 Nc 40.00N 135.00 E
Japan Trench (EN) 106 If 37.00N 143.00 E
Japiim 202 De 7.37S 72.54W
Japonskoje more = Japan, Sea of- (EN) 140 Pf 40.00N 134.00 E
Jäppilä 116 Lb 62.23N 27.26 E
Japtiksale 134 Pb 69.25N 72.29 E
Japurá 202 Ed 1.24S 69.25W
Japurá, Rio- 198 Jf 3.08S 64.46W
Jaqué 194 Hj 7.31N 78.10W
Jaquet, Point- 197g Ba 15.38N 61.26W
Jaquirana 204 Gi 28.54S 50.23W
Jar 114 Mg 58.17N 52.06 E
Jarabub Oasis (EN)= Jaghbūb, Wāḥāt al- 158 Jf 29.41N 24.43 E
Jarābulus 146 Hd 36.49N 38.01 E
Jaraguá [Braz.] 204 Hh 26.29S 49.04W
Jaraguá [Braz.] 204 Hb 15.45S 49.20W
Jaraguá, Serra do- 204 Hh 26.40S 49.15W
Jaraguari 204 Ee 20.09S 54.25W
Jaraiz de la Vera 126 Gd 40.04N 5.45W
Jarama 126 Id 40.02N 3.39W
Jaramillo 206 Gg 47.11S 67.09W
Jarandilla 126 Gd 40.08N 5.39W
Jaransk 136 Ed 57.18N 47.55 E
Jarash 146 Ff 32.17N 35.54 E
Jarau, Cêrro do- 204 Dj 30.18S 56.32W
Jarbah 158 Ie 33.48N 10.54 E
Järbo 114 Df 60.43N 16.36 E
Jarcevo [R.S.F.S.R.] 132 Hb 55.05N 32.45 E
Jarcevo [R.S.F.S.R.] 138 Ed 60.15N 90.10 E
Jardāwīyah 146 Jj 25.24N 42.42 E
Jardim 202 Gh 21.28S 56.09W
Jardine River 212 Ib 11.10S 142.30 E
Jardines de la Reina, Archipiélago de los- 190 Id 20.50N 78.55W
Jardinópolis 204 Ie 21.02S 47.46W
Jarega 134 Fe 63.27N 53.31 E
Jaremča 132 De 48.31N 24.33 E
Jarenga 114 Le 62.08N 49.03 E
Järfälla 116 Ge 59.24N 17.50 E
Jargava 130 Lc 46.27N 28.27 E
Jari, Rio- 198 Kf 1.09S 51.54W
Jarīd, Shaţţ al- 158 He 33.42N 8.26 E
Jarīr, Wādī- 146 Jj 25.38N 42.30 E
Jarjīs 162 Jc 33.30N 11.07 E
Jarkovo 134 Mh 57.26N 67.05 E
Jarmah 164 Bd 26.32N 13.04 E
Järna 116 Ge 59.06N 17.34 E
Jarnac 122 Fi 45.41N 0.10W
Järnlunden 116 Ff 58.10N 15.40 E
Jarny 122 Le 49.09N 5.53 E
Jarocin 120 Ne 51.59N 17.31 E
Jaroměř 120 Lf 50.21N 15.55 E
Jaroměřice nad Rokytnou 120 Lg 49.06N 15.54 E
Jaroslavl 112 Jd 57.37N 39.52 E
Jaroslavskaja oblast [3] 136 Dd 57.45N 39.15 E
Jaroslavski 154 Lb 44.10N 132.13 E
Jarosław 120 Sf 50.02N 22.42 E
Järpen 116 Ea 63.21N 13.29 E
Jarrāḥī 146 Mg 30.44N 48.46 E
Jarroto, ozero- 134 Oc 67.55N 71.40 E
Jar-Sale 138 Cc 66.50N 70.50 E
Jartai 152 Id 39.45N 105.46 E
Jartai Yanchi 152 Id 39.45N 105.40 E
Jarudej 134 Od 65.50N 71.50 E
Jarud Qi (Lubei) 152 Lc 44.30N 120.55 E
Järva-Jaani/Jarva-Jani 116 Ke 59.00N 25.49 E
Jarva-Jani/Järva-Jaani 116 Ke 59.00N 25.49 E
Jarvakanbdi/Järvakandi 116 Kf 58.45N 24.44 E
Järvakandi/Jarvakanbdi 116 Kf 58.45N 24.44 E
Järvenpää 114 Ff 60.28N 25.06 E
Jarvis Island 208 Ke 0.23S 160.01W
Järvsö 114 Df 61.43N 16.10 E
Jaščera 116 Ne 59.05N 30.00 E
Jaselda 132 Ec 52.07N 26.29 E
Jasień 120 Le 51.46N 15.01 E
Jasikan 166 Fd 7.24N 0.28 E
Jasinja 120 Uh 48.14N 24.31 E
Jasinovataja 132 Je 48.05N 37.57 E
Jasiołka 120 Rg 49.47N 21.30 E
Jasīra 168 He 1.57N 45.16 E
Jasīred Mayḍ 168 Hc 11.12N 47.13 E
Jāsk 144 Id 25.38N 57.46 E
Jaškul 132 Nf 46.11N 45.17 E
Jaškul 132 Nf 46.17N 45.10 E
Jasło 120 Rg 49.45N 21.29 E
Jasmund 120 Jb 54.32N 13.35 E
Jasnogorsk 132 Jb 54.29N 37.42 E
Jasny [R.S.F.S.R.] 136 Fe 51.01N 59.59 E
Jasny [R.S.F.S.R.] 138 Hf 53.18N 128.03 E
Jason Islands 206 Hh 51.00S 61.00W
Jasper [Alta.-Can.] 176 Hd 52.53N 118.05W
Jasper [Al.-U.S.] 182 Je 33.50N 87.17W
Jasper [Fl.-U.S.] 184 Fj 30.31N 82.57W
Jasper [In.-U.S.] 184 Df 38.24N 86.56W
Jasper [Tn.-U.S.] 184 Eh 35.04N 85.38W
Jasper [Tx.-U.S.] 186 Jk 30.55N 93.59W
Jasper Seamount (EN) 174 Gf 30.32N 122.42W
Jaşşān 146 Kf 32.58N 45.53 E
Jastrowie 120 Mc 53.26N 16.49 E
Jastrzebie Zdrój 120 Og 49.58N 18.34 E
Jászapáti 120 Qi 47.31N 20.09 E
Jászárokszállás 120 Pi 47.38N 19.59 E
Jászberény 120 Pi 47.30N 19.55 E
Jászság 120 Pi 47.25N 20.00 E
Jat, Uad el- 158 Ff 26.47N 13.03W
Jataí 200 Kg 17.53S 51.43W
Jatapu, Rio- 202 Gd 2.30S 58.17W
Játiva/Xàtiva 126 Lf 38.59N 0.31W
Jatobá, Rio- 204 Ea 12.23S 54.07W
Jaú 206 Kb 22.18S 48.33W
Jaú, Rio- 202 Fd 1.55S 61.25W
Jaua, Cerro- 202 Fc 4.48N 64.26W
Jauaperi, Rio- 198 Jf 1.26S 61.35W
Jauja 202 Cf 11.48S 75.30W
Jaumave 192 Jf 23.25N 99.23W
Jaunanna 116 Lg 57.13N 27.10 E
Jaunelgava/Jaunjelgava 114 Fh 56.37N 25.06 E
Jaunfeld 128 Id 46.36N 14.45 E
Jaungulbene 116 Lh 57.00N 26.42 E
Jaunjelgava/Jaunelgava 114 Fh 56.37N 25.06 E
Jaunpiebalga 116 Lg 57.05N 26.03 E
Jaunpur 148 Gc 25.44N 82.41 E
Jauru 204 Ed 18.35S 54.17W
Jauru, Rio- [Braz.] 204 Dc 16.22S 57.46W
Jauru, Rio- [Braz.] 202 Hg 18.40S 54.36W
Java (EN)=Jawa 140 Mj 7.20S 110.00 E
Javaes → Araguaia, Braço Menor do- 202 He 9.50S 50.12W
Javalambre 126 Ld 40.06N 1.00W
Javalambre, Sierra de- 126 Ld 40.05N 1.00W
Javan 135 Ge 38.19N 69.01 E
Javānrūd 146 Le 34.48N 46.30 E
Javari, Rio- 198 If 4.21S 70.02W
Java Sea (EN)=Jawa, Laut- 140 Mj 5.00S 110.00 E
Java Trench (EN) 106 Hk 10.30S 110.00 E
Jávea / Xābia 126 Mf 38.47N 0.10 E
Javier / Xavier 126 Kb 42.36N 1.13W
Javor 128 Mf 44.07N 18.59 E
Javorie 120 Ph 48.27N 19.18 E
Javornik 120 Jg 49.08N 13.35 E
Javorníky 120 Og 49.20N 18.20 E
Javorov 132 Cd 50.00N 23.27 E
Javorová skála 120 Kg 49.31N 14.30 E
Jävre 114 Ed 65.09N 21.29 E
Jawa=Java (EN) 140 Mj 7.20S 110.00 E
Jawa, Laut-=Java Sea (EN) 140 Mj 5.00S 110.00 E
Jawa Barat [3] 150 Eh 7.00S 107.00 E
Jawa Tengah [3] 150 Eh 7.30S 110.00 E
Jawa Timur [3] 150 Fh 8.00S 113.00 E
Jawf, Wādī- 164 If 15.50N 45.30 E
Jawor 120 Me 51.03N 16.11 E
Jaworzno 120 Pf 50.13N 19.15 E
Jaya, Puncak- 208 Ee 4.10S 137.00 E
Jayapura 210 Fe 2.32S 140.42 E
Jayawijaya, Pegunungan- 150 Kg 4.30S 139.30 E
Jāyezān 146 Mg 30.50N 49.52 E
Jaypur 148 He 18.51N 82.35 E
Jazā'ir Siyāl 168 Fa 23.00N 36.02 E
Jaz Mūrīān, Hāmūn-e- 144 Id 27.20N 58.55 E
Jazva 134 Hf 60.23N 56.50 E
Jazvān 146 Md 36.58N 48.40 E
Jazykovo 114 Li 54.20N 47.22 E
Jazzīn 146 Ff 33.32N 35.34 E
Jdiouia 126 Mi 35.56N 0.50 E
Jean-Rabel 194 Kd 19.52N 73.11W
Jebala 126 Gi 35.25N 5.30W
Jebal Bārez, Kūh-e- 144 Id 28.30N 58.20 E
Jebba 166 Fd 9.08N 4.50 E
Jebel 130 Ed 45.33N 21.14 E
Jebha 126 Hi 35.13N 4.40W
Jedincy 132 Ee 48.06N 27.19 E
Jedisa 132 Nh 42.32N 44.14 E
Jędrzejów 120 Qf 50.39N 20.18 E
Jeetze 120 Hc 53.09N 11.04 E
Jefferson 186 Ie 42.01N 94.23W
Jefferson, Mount- [Nv.-U.S.] 182 Dd 38.46N 116.55W
Jefferson, Mount- [Or.-U.S.] 188 Ed 44.40N 121.47W
Jefferson City 176 Jf 38.34N 92.10W
Jefferson River 188 Jd 45.56N 111.30W
Jeffersonville 184 Ef 38.17N 85.44W
Jef-Jef el Kebir 168 Ca 20.30N 21.25 E
Jefremov 136 De 53.11N 38.07 E
Jega 166 Fc 12.13N 4.23 E
Jegorjevsk 114 Ji 55.25N 39.07 E
Jegorlyk 132 Lf 46.32N 41.52 E
Jegorlykskaja 132 Lf 46.34N 40.44 E
Jehegnadzor 132 Nj 39.47N 45.18 E
Jeja 132 Kf 46.39N 38.36 E
Jejsk 136 Df 46.40N 38.15 E
Jejuí Guazú, Río- 204 Dg 24.13S 57.09W
Jēkabpils/Jekabpils 136 Cd 56.30N 25.59 E
Jekabpils/Jēkabpils 136 Cd 56.30N 25.59 E
Jekaterinovka 132 Nc 52.04N 44.30 E
Jekkevarre 114 Eb 69.28N 20.00 E
Jelabuga 136 Fd 55.48N 52.05 E
Jelai 150 Fg 2.59S 110.45 E
Jelan 132 Md 50.57N 43.43 E
Jelancy 138 Ff 52.44N 106.27 E
Jelanec 132 Gf 47.42N 31.50 E
Jelcz 120 Ne 51.01N 17.18 E
Jelec 112 Je 52.37N 38.30 E
Jeleckj 134 Lc 67.03N 64.15 E
Jelenia Góra 120 Lf 50.55N 15.46 E
Jelenia Góra [2] 120 Lf 50.55N 15.45 E
Jelgava 136 Cd 56.39N 23.41 E
Jelica 130 Df 43.47N 20.20 E
Jelin vrh 130 Cf 43.02N 19.27 E
Jelizavety, mys- 140 Qd 54.30N 142.40 E
Jelizovo [Bye.-U.S.S.R.] 132 Fc 53.24N 29.00 E
Jelizovo [R.S.F.S.R.] 138 Kf 53.06N 158.20 E
Jelling 116 Ci 55.45N 9.26 E
Jelnja 132 Hb 54.35N 33.12 E
Jeloguj 138 Dd 63.10N 87.45 E
Jelow Gīr 146 Lf 32.58N 47.48 E
Jeløy 116 De 58.30N 10.40 E
Jelsk 132 Fd 51.49N 29.13 E
Jelva 134 Ee 63.05N 50.50 E
Jemaja, Pulau- 150 Ef 2.55N 105.45 E
Jemanželinsk 136 Ge 54.45N 61.20 E
Jember 150 Fh 8.10S 113.42 E
Jemca 114 Je 63.04N 40.18 E
Jemca 114 Je 63.32N 41.56 E
Jemeppe-sur-Sambre 124 Gd 50.28N 4.40 E
Jeminay 152 Eb 47.28N 85.48 E
Jemnice 120 Lg 49.01N 15.35 E
Jena 120 Hf 50.56N 11.35 E
Jenakijevo 132 Ke 48.12N 38.18 E
Jenašimski Polkan, gora- 138 Ee 59.50N 92.45 E
Jendyr 134 Mf 61.38N 67.20 E
Jeneponto 150 Gh 5.41S 119.42 E
Jenisej=Yenisey (EN) 140 Kb 71.50N 82.40 E
Jenisejsk 138 Ee 58.27N 92.10 E
Jenisejski krjaž = Yenisey Ridge (EN) 140 Ld 59.00N 92.30 E
Jenisejski zaliv = Yenisey Bay (EN) 138 Db 72.00N 81.00 E
Jennersdorf 128 Kd 46.56N 16.08 E
Jennings 186 Jk 30.13N 92.39W
Jenny Lind 180 Hc 68.50N 101.30W
Jenny Point 197g Bb 15.28N 61.15W
Jensen 188 Kf 40.22N 109.17W
Jens Munk 180 Jc 69.40N 79.40W
Jequié 200 Lg 13.51S 40.05W
Jequitaí 204 Jc 17.15S 44.28W
Jequitaí, Rio- 204 Jc 17.04S 44.50W
Jequitinhonha, Rio- 198 Mg 15.51S 38.53W
Jerada 162 Gc 34.19N 2.09W
Jeralijev 136 Fg 43.12N 51.43 E
Jerbogačën 138 Fd 61.15N 107.57 E
Jérémie 190 Je 18.39N 74.08W
Jeremoabo 202 Kf 10.04S 38.21W

Index Symbols

[1] Independent Nation
[2] State, Region
[3] District, County
[4] Municipality
[5] Colony, Dependency
Continent
Physical Region
Historical or Cultural Region
Mount, Mountain
Volcano
Hill
Mountains, Mountain Range
Hills, Escarpment
Plateau, Upland
Pass, Gap
Plain, Lowland
Delta
Salt Flat
Valley, Canyon
Crater, Cave
Karst Features
Depression
Polder
Desert, Dunes
Forest, Woods
Heath, Steppe
Oasis
Cape, Point
Coast, Beach
Cliff
Peninsula
Isthmus
Sandbank
Island
Atoll
Rock, Reef
Islands, Archipelago
Rocks, Reefs
Coral Reef
Well, Spring
Geyser
River, Stream
Waterfall, Rapids
River Mouth, Estuary
Lake
Salt Lake
Intermittent Lake
Reservoir
Swamp, Pond
Canal
Glacier
Ice Shelf, Pack Ice
Ocean
Sea
Gulf, Bay
Strait, Fjord
Lagoon
Bank
Seamount
Tablemount
Ridge
Shelf
Basin
Escarpment, Sea Scarp
Fracture
Trench, Abyss
National Park, Reserve
Point of Interest
Recreation Site
Cave, Cavern
Historic Site
Ruins
Wall, Walls
Church, Abbey
Temple
Scientific Station
Railway station
Airport
Port
Military installation
Lighthouse
Mine
Tunnel
Dam, Bridge

Jerer 168 Gd 7.40N 43.48 E
Jerevan 112 Kg 40.11N 44.30 E
Jerez, Punta- 192 Kf 22.54N 97.46W
Jerez de Garcia Salinas 190 Dd 22.39N 103.00W
Jerez de la Frontera 126 Fh 36.41N 6.08W
Jerez de los Caballeros 126 Ff 38.19N 6.46W
Jergeni 110 Kf 47.00N 44.00 E
Jericho 212 Jd 23.36S 146.08 E
Jermak 136 He 52.02N 76.55 E
Jermakovskoje 138 Ef 53.16N 92.24 E
Jermentau 136 He 51.38N 73.10 E
Jermolajevo 134 Gj 52.43N 55.48 E
Jeroaquara 204 Gb 15.23S 50.25W
Jerofej Pavlovič 138 Hf 53.58N 121.57 E
Jerome 188 He 42.43N 114.31W
Jersa 134 Fc 66.19N 52.32 E
Jersey 118 Kl 49.15N 2.10W
Jersey City 182 Mc 40.44N 74.04W
Jerseyville 186 Kg 39.07N 90.20W
Jeršov 136 Ee 51.20N 48.17 E
Jertarski 134 Lh 56.47N 64.25 E
Jerte 126 Fe 39.58N 6.17W
Jerusalem (EN) = Yerushalayim 142 Ff 31.46N 35.14 E
Jeruslan 132 Od 50.20N 46.25 E
Jervis Bay 212 Kg 35.05S 150.44 E
Jerzu 128 Dk 39.47N 9.31 E
Jesberg 124 Lc 51.00N 9.09 E
Jesenice [Yugo.] 128 Jf 44.14N 15.34 E
Jesenice [Yugo.] 128 Id 46.27N 14.04 E
Jesenik 120 Nf 50.14N 17.12 E
Jesi 128 Hg 43.31N 13.14 E
Jesil 136 Ge 51.58N 66.24 E
Jeskianhor, kanal- 135 Fe 39.15N 66.00 E
Jessej 138 Fc 68.29N 102.10 E
Jessentuki 132 Mg 44.03N 42.51 E
Jessheim 114 Cf 60.09N 11.11 E
Jessore 148 Hd 23.10N 89.13 E
Ještěd 120 Kf 50.42N 14.59 E
Jestro, Wabe- 158 Lh 4.11N 42.09 E
Jesup 182 Ke 31.36N 81.53W
Jesús Carranza 192 Li 17.26N 95.02W
Jesús Maria 206 Hd 30.59S 64.06W
Jesús Maria, Boca de- 192 Ke 24.29N 97.40W
Jesús Maria, Rio- 192 Gg 21.55N 104.30W
Jetmore 186 Gg 38.03N 99.54W
Jeumont 124 Gd 50.18N 4.06 E
Jever 120 Dc 53.35N 7.54 E
Jevgenjevka 135 Kc 43.27N 77.40 E
Jevišovka 120 Mh 48.52N 16.36 E
Jevlah 136 Eg 40.35N 47.10 E
Jevnaker 114 Cf 60.15N 10.28 E
Jevpatorija 134 Df 45.12N 33.18 E
Jevrejskaja avtonomnaja oblast 138 Ig 48.30N 132.00 E
Jeyḫūn 146 Pi 27.16N 55.12 E
Jeypore → Jaypur 148 He 18.51N 82.35 E
Jezercës 110 Hg 42.26N 19.49 E
Jezero 128 Lf 44.21N 17.10 E
Jeziorak, Jezioro- 120 Pc 53.50N 19.35 E
Jeziorany 120 Qc 53.58N 20.46 E
Jeziorka 120 Rd 52.10N 21.06 E
Jhang Sadar 148 Eb 31.16N 72.19 E
Jhānsi 142 Js 25.26N 78.35 E
Jhelum 148 Eb 32.56N 73.44 E
Jhelum 140 Jf 31.12N 72.08 E
Jiaji → Qionghai 152 Jh 19.25N 110.28 E
Jialing Jiang 140 Mg 29.34N 106.35 E
Jialu He 154 Ch 33.40N 115.01 E
Jiamusi 142 Pe 46.49N 130.21 E
Ji'an [China] 152 Mc 41.08N 126.10 E
Ji'an [China] 142 Ng 27.12N 114.59 E
Jianchang 154 Ed 40.49N 119.46 E
Jianchuan 152 Gf 26.32N 99.53 E
Jiande (Baisha) 152 Kf 29.31N 119.17 E
Jiang'an 152 If 28.40N 105.07 E
Jiangbiancun 152 Kf 27.13N 115.57 E
Jiangcheng 152 Hg 22.37N 101.48 E
Jiangdu (Xiannümiao) 154 Eh 32.30N 119.33 E
Jiange 152 Ie 31.59N 105.28 E
Jianghua (Shuikou) 152 Jg 24.58N 111.56 E
Jiangjin 152 If 29.15N 106.18 E
Jiangle 152 Kf 26.48N 117.29 E
Jiangling (Jingzhou) 152 Je 30.21N 112.10 E
Jiangmen 152 Jg 22.35N 113.02 E
Jiangpu 154 Eh 32.03N 118.37 E
Jiangshan 154 Ej 28.45N 118.37 E
Jiangsu Sheng (Chiang-su Sheng) = Kiangsu (EN) [2] 152 Ke 33.00N 120.00 E
Jiangxi Sheng (Chiang-hsi Sheng) = Kiangsi (EN) [2] 152 Kf 28.00N 116.00 E
Jiangyou (Zhongba) 152 He 31.48N 104.39 E
Jianhu 154 Eh 33.28N 119.47 E
Jianli 152 Jf 29.50N 112.55 E
Jian'ou 152 Kf 27.08N 118.20 E
Jianping 154 Ed 41.27N 119.37 E
Jianping (Yebaishou) 152 Kc 41.55N 119.37 E
Jianshi 152 Ie 30.32N 109.43 E
Jianshui 152 Hg 23.39N 102.46 E
Jianyang 152 Kf 27.23N 118.03 E
Jiaocheng 152 Jd 37.32N 112.09 E
Jiaoding Shan 152 Lc 41.11N 120.01 E
Jiaohe [China] 152 Mc 43.43N 127.20 E
Jiaohe [China] 154 De 38.01N 116.17 E
Jiaolai He [China] 154 Ef 37.07N 119.35 E
Jiaolai He [China] 154 Fc 43.02N 120.48 E
Jiaoliu He 154 Gb 45.21N 122.48 E
Jiaonan (Wanggezhuang) 154 Eg 35.53N 119.58 E
Jiaoxian 152 Kd 36.20N 120.00 E
Jiaozhou-Wan 154 Ff 36.10N 120.15 E
Jiaozuo 142 Nf 35.15N 113.18 E
Jiashan 154 Fi 30.51N 120.54 E
Jiashan (Mingguang) 154 Dh 32.47N 118.00 E
Jiashi/Payzawat 152 Cd 39.29N 76.39 E
Jiawang 154 Dg 34.27N 117.26 E
Jiaxian 154 Bh 33.58N 113.13 E
Jiaxing 152 Le 30.44N 120.46 E
Jiayin (Chaoyang) 152 Nb 48.52N 130.21 E
Jiayu 152 Jf 30.00N 113.57 E
Jiayuguan 152 Gd 39.49N 98.18 E
Jibalei 168 Ic 10.07N 50.47 E
Jibão, Serra do- 204 Jb 14.48S 45.15W
Jibiya 166 Gc 13.06N 7.14 E
Jibou 130 Gb 47.16N 23.15 E
Jicarón, Isla- 194 Gj 7.16N 81.47W
Jičín 120 Lf 50.26N 15.22 E
Jiddah 142 Fg 21.29N 39.12 E
Jiddat al Ḥarāsīs 144 Ie 20.05N 56.00 E
Jiehu → Yinan 154 Eg 35.33N 118.27 E
Jieshou 154 Ch 33.17N 115.22 E
Jiesjjavrre 114 Fb 69.40N 24.12 E
Jiexiu 152 Jd 37.00N 112.00 E
Jieyang 152 Kg 23.32N 116.25 E
Jieznas/Eznas 116 Kj 54.34N 24.17 E
Jifn, Wādī al- 146 Jj 25.48N 42.15 E
Jiftūn, Jazā'ir- 146 Ei 27.13N 33.56 E
Jīgley 168 He 4.25N 45.22 E
Jiguaní 194 Ic 20.22N 76.26W
Jigüey, Bahia de- 194 Hb 22.08N 78.05W
Jigzhi 152 He 33.28N 101.29 E
Jihlava 120 Lg 49.24N 15.34 E
Jihlava 120 Mh 48.55N 16.37 E
Jihlavské vrchy 120 Lg 49.15N 15.20 E
Jihočeský kraj [3] 120 Kg 49.05N 14.30 E
Jihomoravský kraj [3] 120 Mg 49.10N 16.40 E
Jijel 162 Ib 36.48N 5.46 E
Jijel [3] 162 Ib 36.45N 5.45 E
Jijia 120 Lc 46.54N 28.05 E
Jijiga 168 Gd 9.21N 42.48 E
Jijona / Xixona 126 Lf 38.32N 0.30W
Jikharrah 164 Dd 29.17N 21.38 E
Jilava 130 Je 44.20N 26.05 E
Jilf al Kabīr, Haḍabat al- 164 Ee 23.30N 26.00 E
Jilib 160 Lh 0.29N 42.47 E
Jilin 142 Oe 43.51N 126.33 E
Jilin Sheng (Chi-lin Sheng) = Kirin (EN) [2] 152 Mc 43.00N 126.00 E
Jiliu He 152 La 52.02N 120.41 E
Jiloca 126 Kc 41.21N 1.39W
Jima = Jimma (EN) 160 Kh 7.39N 36.49 E
Jimāl, Wādī- 154 Fj 24.40N 35.06 E
Jimani 194 Ld 18.28N 71.51W
Jimbe 170 De 11.05S 24.00 E
Jimbolia 130 Dd 45.48N 20.43 E
Jimena 126 Ig 37.50N 3.28W
Jimena de la Frontera 126 Gh 36.26N 5.27W
Jiménez 190 Dc 27.08N 104.55W
Jiménez de Teúl 192 Gf 23.10N 104.05W
Jimma (EN) = Jima 160 Kh 7.39N 36.49 E
Jimo 154 Ff 36.24N 120.27 E
Jimsar 152 Ec 43.59N 89.04 E
Jimulco 192 He 25.20N 103.10W
Jināh 146 Dj 25.20N 30.31 E
Jinan (Tsinan) 142 Nf 36.35N 117.00 E
Jincheng [China] 152 Jd 35.32N 112.53 E
Jincheng [China] 154 Fd 41.12N 121.25 E
Jinchuan /Quqên 152 He 31.02N 102.02 E
Jind 148 Fc 29.19N 76.19 E
Jindřichův Hradec 120 Kg 49.09N 15.00 E
Jinfo Shan 152 If 29.01N 107.14 E
Jing/Jinghe 152 Dc 44.39N 82.50 E
Jing'an 154 Cj 28.51N 115.21 E
Jingbian (Zhangjiapan) 152 Id 37.32N 108.45 E
Jingde 154 Ei 30.18N 118.30 E
Jingdezhen 142 Ng 29.18N 117.18 E
Jingfeng → Hexigten Qi 152 Kc 43.15N 117.31 E
Jinggang Shan 152 Jf 26.42N 114.07 E
Jinggu 152 Hg 23.28N 100.39 E
Jinghai 154 De 38.57N 116.56 E
Jinghe/Jing 152 Dc 44.39N 82.50 E
Jinghong (Yunjinghong) 152 Hg 21.59N 100.43 E
Jinghong Dao 150 Fe 9.45N 114.28 E
Jingjiang 154 Fh 32.01N 120.15 E
Jingle 154 Ae 38.22N 111.56 E
Jingmen 152 Je 31.00N 112.11 E
Jingning 152 Hd 35.30N 105.45 E
Jingping → Pinglu 154 Be 39.32N 112.14 E
Jingpo Hu 152 Mc 43.50N 128.53 E
Jingshan 154 Bi 31.04N 113.08 E
Jingtai 152 Hd 37.10N 104.08 E
Jingxian [China] 152 If 26.40N 109.37 E
Jingxian [China] 152 Ke 30.41N 118.29 E
Jingxing (Weishui) 154 Ce 38.03N 114.09 E
Jingyu 154 Ic 42.25N 126.48 E
Jingyuan 152 Hd 36.35N 104.40 E
Jingzhi 154 Ef 36.18N 119.22 E
Jingzhou → Jiangling 152 Je 30.21N 112.10 E
Jinhu (Licheng) 154 Eh 33.01N 119.01 E
Jinhua 152 Kf 29.09N 119.38 E
Jining [China] 142 Nf 35.26N 116.36 E
Jining [China] 142 Ne 41.02N 113.07 E
Jinja 160 Kh 0.26N 33.13 E
Jin Jiang 154 Cj 28.23N 115.48 E
Jinkou 154 Ci 30.20N 114.07 E
Jinotega 154 Gf 13.06N 86.00W
Jinotega [3] 194 Eg 14.00N 85.25W
Jinotepe 190 Gf 11.51N 86.12W
Jinping 152 Hg 22.45N 103.15 E
Jinsha 152 If 27.18N 106.16 E
Jinsha → Nantong 154 Fh 32.06N 120.52 E
Jinsha Jiang 140 Mg 28.46N 104.38 E
Jinshan 152 Lf 30.54N 121.09 E
Jinshan → Harqin Qi 154 Ed 41.57N 118.40 E
Jinshi 154 Aj 29.03N 111.52 E
Jinta 152 Gc 40.00N 99.00 E
Jintan 154 Ei 31.45N 119.34 E
Jinxi 154 Lc 40.46N 120.50 E
Jinxian [China] 152 Ld 39.06N 121.44 E
Jinxian [China] 154 Dj 28.21N 116.16 E
Jinxiang 154 Dg 35.04N 116.19 E
Jinyang 152 Hf 27.39N 103.12 E
Jinyun 154 Fj 28.39N 120.05 E
Jinzhai (Meishan) 154 Ci 31.40N 115.52 E
Jinzhou 142 Oe 41.09N 121.08 E
Jinzū-Gawa 156 Ec 36.45N 137.13 E
Jiparaná, Rio- 198 Jf 8.03S 62.52W
Jipijapa 202 Bd 1.22S 80.34W
Jiquilisco 194 Cg 13.19N 88.35W
Jiquilisco, Bahia de- 194 Cg 13.10N 88.28W
Jirjā 164 Fd 26.20N 31.53 E
Jishou 152 If 28.18N 109.43 E
Jishu 154 Ib 44.16N 126.50 E
Jisr ash Shughur 146 Ge 35.48N 36.19 E
Jiu 130 Gf 43.47N 23.48 E
Jiucai Ling 152 Jf 25.33N 111.18 E
Jiucheng → Wucheng 154 Df 37.12N 116.04 E
Jiuding Shan 152 He 31.30N 104.00 E
Jiujiang 142 Ng 29.39N 116.00 E
Jiuling Shan 152 Jf 28.55N 114.50 E
Jiulong/Gyaisi 152 Hf 28.58N 101.33 E
Jiuquan (Suzhou) 142 Lf 39.46N 98.34 E
Jiurongcheng 154 Gf 37.22N 122.33 E
Jiutai 152 Mc 44.10N 125.50 E
Jiwani, Rās- 148 Cc 25.01N 61.44 E
Jixi [China] 142 Pe 45.15N 130.55 E
Jixi [China] 154 Ei 30.04N 118.36 E
Jixian [China] 154 Cg 35.23N 114.04 E
Jixian [China] 154 Dd 40.03N 117.24 E
Jixian [China] 154 Cf 37.34N 115.34 E
Jiyang 154 Df 36.59N 117.11 E
Jiyuan 154 Bg 35.06N 112.35 E
Jiyun He 154 De 39.05N 117.45 E
Jīz, Wādī al- 168 Ib 16.12N 52.14 E
Jīzān 142 Gh 16.54N 42.32 E
Jize 154 Cf 36.54N 114.52 E
Jizera 120 Kf 50.10N 14.43 E
Jizerské Hory 120 Lf 50.50N 15.13 E
Jizl, Wādī al- 146 Hj 25.39N 38.25 E
Jizō-Zaki 154 Lg 35.33N 133.18 E
Jmbe 170 De 10.20S 16.40 E
Jnchengjiang → Hechi 152 Ig 24.44N 108.02 E
Joaçaba 204 Gh 27.10S 51.30W
Joal-Fadiout 166 Bc 14.10N 16.51W
João Câmara 202 Ke 5.32S 35.48W
João Monlevade 204 Kd 19.50S 43.08W
João Pessoa 200 Mf 7.07S 34.52W
João Pinheiro 202 Ig 17.45S 46.10W
Joaquin V. González 206 Hb 25.00S 64.11W
Jobado 194 Ic 20.54N 77.17W
Jódar 126 Ig 37.50N 3.21W
Jodhpur 142 Jg 26.17N 73.02 E
Jodoigne/Geldenaken 124 Gd 50.43N 4.52 E
Joensuu 112 Ic 62.36N 29.46 E
Joerg Plateau 222 Qf 75.00S 69.30W
Joes Hill 220g Bb 1.48N 157.19W
Jõetsu 152 Od 37.06N 138.15 E
Joeuf 124 Ie 49.14N 6.01 E
Jōf di Montasio 128 Hd 46.26N 13.26 E
Joffre, Mount- 188 Ha 50.32N 115.13W
Jogbani 148 Hc 26.25N 87.15 E
Jõgeva/Jygeva 114 Gg 58.46N 26.26 E
Joghatāy 146 Qd 36.36N 57.01 E
Joghatāy, Kūh-e- 146 Qd 36.30N 57.00 E
Jōhana 156 Ec 36.31N 136.54 E
Johannesburg 160 Jk 26.15S 28.00 E
Jōhen 156 Ce 32.57N 132.35 E
John Day 188 Fd 44.25N 118.57W
John Day River 182 Cb 45.44N 120.39W
John H. Kerr Reservoir 184 Hg 36.31N 78.18W
John Martin Reservoir 186 Eg 38.05N 103.02W
John o' Groat's 118 Jc 58.38N 3.05W
Johnson 186 Fh 37.34N 101.45W
Johnson, Pico de- 192 Cc 29.13N 112.07W
Johnson City [Tn.-U.S.] 182 Kd 36.19N 82.21W
Johnson City [Tx.-U.S.] 186 Gk 30.17N 98.25W
Johnsons Crossing 180 Ed 60.29N 133.17W
Johnsons Point 197d Bb 17.02N 61.53W
Johnston Atoll [5] 210 Kc 17.00N 168.30W
Johnston Atoll 208 Kc 17.00N 168.30W
Johnstone, Lake- 212 Ef 32.20S 120.40 E
Johnstone Strait 188 Ca 50.25N 126.00W
Johnstown [N.Y.-U.S.] 184 Jd 43.01N 74.22W
Johnstown [Pa.-U.S.] 182 Lc 40.20N 78.56W
Johor [3] 150 Df 2.00N 103.30 E
Johor Baharu 142 Mi 1.28N 103.45 E
Joia 204 Ei 28.39S 54.08W
Joigny 122 Jg 47.59N 3.24 E
Joinvile 200 Lh 26.18S 48.50W
Joinville 122 Lf 48.27N 5.08 E
Joinville Island 222 Re 63.15S 55.45W
Jokau 168 Ed 8.24N 33.49 E
Jokela 116 Kd 60.33N 24.59 E
Jokelbugten 179 Kc 78.25N 19.00W
Jokioinen 116 Jd 60.49N 23.28 E
Jokkmokk 114 Ec 66.36N 19.51 E
Jøkuleggi 116 Cc 61.03N 8.12 E
Jolfā 146 Kc 38.57N 45.38 E
Joliet 182 Jc 41.32N 88.05W
Joliette 180 Kg 46.01N 73.26W
Jolo 150 He 6.00N 121.00 E
Jolo Group 140 Oi 6.00N 121.09 E
Jølstravatnet 116 Bc 61.30N 6.15 E
Jomala 116 Hd 60.09N 19.58 E
Jombang 150 Fh 7.33S 112.14 E
Jomda 152 Ge 31.37N 98.20 E
Jönåker 116 Gf 58.44N 16.40 E
Jonava/Ionava 114 Fi 55.05N 24.17 E
Jonê 152 He 34.35N 103.32 E
Jones Bank 118 Fl 49.50N 8.00W
Jonesboro [Ar.-U.S.] 182 Id 35.50N 90.42W
Jonesboro [La.-U.S.] 186 Jj 32.15N 92.43W
Jones Mountains 222 Pf 73.32S 94.00W
Jones Sound 174 Kb 76.00N 85.00W
Jonesville 184 Fg 36.41N 83.06W
Jonglei 168 Ed 6.50N 31.18 E
Jonglei [3] 168 Ed 7.20N 32.00 E
Jonglei, Tur'ah- = Jonglei Canal (EN) 168 Ed 9.22N 31.30 E
Jonglei Canal (EN) = Jonglei, Tur'ah- 168 Ed 9.22N 31.30 E
Joniškėlis/Ioniškelis 116 Ki 56.00N 24.14 E
Joniškis/Ioniškis 114 Fh 56.16N 23.37 E
Jönköping 112 Hd 57.47N 14.11 E
Jönköping [2] 114 Dh 57.30N 14.30 E
Jonquière 180 Kg 48.25N 71.15W
Jonuta 192 Mh 18.05N 92.08W
Jonzac 122 Fi 45.27N 0.26W
Joplin 176 Jf 37.06N 94.31W
Jordan 182 Fb 47.19N 106.55W
Jordan 144 Ec 31.46N 35.33 E
Jordan (EN) = Al Urdun [1] 142 Ff 31.00N 36.00 E
Jordan Valley 188 Ge 42.58N 117.03W
Jordão, Rio- 204 Fg 25.46S 52.07W
Jorhāt 142 Lg 26.45N 94.13 E
Jörn 114 Ed 65.04N 20.02 E
Joroinen 114 Ge 62.11N 27.50 E
Jørpeland 114 Bg 59.01N 6.03 E
Jos 160 Hh 9.55N 8.54 E
José A. Guisasola 204 Bn 38.40S 61.05W
José Battle y Ordóñez 204 Ek 33.28S 55.07W
José Bonifácio 204 He 21.03S 49.41W
José de San Martin 206 Ff 44.02S 70.29W
Joselandia 204 Dc 16.32S 56.12W
José Otávio 204 Ej 31.17S 54.07W
José Pedro Varela 204 Ek 33.27S 54.32W
Joseph, Lake- 184 Hc 45.14N 79.45W
Joseph Bonaparte Gulf 208 Df 14.55S 128.15 E
Josephine Seamount (EN) 110 Eh 36.52N 14.20W
Joseph Lake 180 Kf 52.48N 65.17W
Joshimath 148 Fb 30.34N 79.34 E
Joškar-Ola 112 Kd 56.40N 47.55 E
Jos Plateau 158 Hh 10.00N 9.30 E
Josselin 122 Dg 47.57N 2.33W
Jostedalen 116 Bc 61.35N 7.20 E
Jostedalsbreen 114 Bf 61.40N 7.00 E
Jostefonn 116 Bc 61.26N 6.33 E
Jost Van Dyke 197a Db 18.28N 64.45W
Jotunheimen 114 Bf 61.40N 8.20 E
Joubertberge 172 Ac 18.45S 13.55 E
Joué-lès-Tours 122 Gg 47.21N 0.40 E
Jouquara, Rio- 204 Db 15.06S 57.06W
Joure, Haskerland- 124 Hb 52.58N 5.47 E
Joutsa 114 Gf 61.44N 26.07 E
Joutseno 114 Gf 61.06N 28.30 E
Jovan, Deli- 130 Fe 44.15N 22.13 E
Jovellanos 194 Gb 22.48N 81.12W
Joviânia 204 Hc 17.49S 49.30W
Jowhar 160 Lh 2.46N 45.32 E
Jow Kār 146 Me 34.26N 48.42 E
Jowzjān [3] 144 Kb 36.30N 66.00 E
Joya, Laguna de la- 192 Mi 15.55N 93.40W
Jreida 162 Df 18.19N 16.03W
Juan Aldama 190 Dd 24.19N 103.21W
Juana Ramirez, Isla- 192 Kg 21.50N 97.40W
Juan Blanquier 204 Cl 35.46S 59.18W
Juancheng 154 Cg 35.33N 115.30 E
Juan de Fuca, Strait of- 174 Ge 48.20N 124.00W
Juan de Nova, Ile- 158 Lj 17.03S 42.45 E
Juan E. Barra 204 Bm 37.48S 60.29W
Juan Fernández, Archipiélago- = Juan Fernández Islands (EN) 198 Ii 33.00S 80.00W
Juan Fernández Islands (EN) = Juan Fernández, Archipiélago- 198 Ii 33.00S 80.00W
Juan G. Bazán 204 Bg 24.33S 60.50W
Juangriego 196 Eg 11.05N 63.57W
Juanjuí 202 Ce 7.11S 76.45W
Juan L. Lacaze 204 Dl 34.26S 57.27W
Juárez [Arg.] 206 Ie 37.40S 59.48W
Juárez [Mex.] 192 Id 27.37N 100.44W
Juárez, Sierra de- 192 Bb 32.00N 115.50W
Juarzohn 166 Dd 5.20N 8.58W
Juàzeirinho 202 Ke 7.04S 36.35W
Juàzeiro 200 Lf 9.25S 40.30W
Juàzeiro do Norte 200 Mf 7.12S 39.20W
Jūbā 160 Kh 4.51N 31.37 E
Juba (EN) = Ganāne, Webi- 158 Lh 0.15S 42.38 E
Juba, Rio- 204 Db 14.59S 57.44W
Jūbāl, Maḍīq- 146 Ei 27.40N 33.55 E
Jubaland (EN) 158 Lh 1.00N 42.00 E
Jubayl [Eg.] 146 Eh 28.12N 33.38 E
Jubayl [Leb.] 146 Fe 34.07N 35.39 E
Jubayt [Sud.] 168 Fb 18.57N 36.50 E
Jubayt [Sud.] 168 Hg 20.59N 36.18 E
Jubbada Dhexe [3] 168 Ge 1.15N 42.30 E
Jubbada Hoose [3] 168 Gf 0.30S 42.00 E
Jubbah 146 Ih 28.02N 40.56 E
Jubilee Lake 212 Fe 29.10S 126.40 E
Juby, Cap- 158 Ff 27.57N 12.55W
Júcar/Xúquer 110 Fh 39.09N 0.14W
Juçara 204 Gb 15.53S 50.51W
Jucaro 194 Hc 21.37N 78.51W
Jüchen 124 Ic 51.06N 6.30 E
Juchipila 192 Hg 21.25N 103.07W
Juchipila, Rio- 192 Hg 21.03N 103.25W
Juchitán de Zaragoza 176 Jh 16.26N 95.01W
Jučjugej 138 Jd 63.20N 142.15 E
Judas, Punta- 194 Ei 9.31N 84.32W
Judayyidat 'Ar'ar 144 Fc 31.22N 41.26 E
Judenburg 128 Ic 47.10N 14.40 E
Judith Mountains 188 Kc 47.12N 109.15W
Judith River 188 Kc 47.44N 109.38W
Judoma 138 Ie 59.08N 135.03 E
Judomski hrebet 138 Jd 61.05N 141.30 E
Juegang → Rudong 154 Fh 32.19N 121.11 E
Juelsminde 116 Di 55.43N 10.01 E
Jufrah, Wāḥāt al- = Giofra Oasis (EN) 158 If 29.10N 16.00 E
Jug 134 Hh 57.43N 56.12 E
Jug 110 Kc 60.45N 46.20 E
Jugo-Osetinskaja avtonomnaja oblast [3] 136 Eg 42.20N 44.05 E
Jugorski poluostrov 134 Kb 69.30N 62.30 E
Jugorski Šar, proliv- 136 Gb 69.45N 60.35 E
Jugoslavija = Yugoslavia (EN) [1] 112 Hg 44.00N 19.00 E
Jugo-Tala 138 Kc 66.03N 151.05 E
Jugydjan 134 Gf 61.42N 54.58 E
Juhaym 146 Kh 29.36N 45.24 E
Juhnov 132 Ib 54.43N 35.12 E
Juhor 130 Ef 43.50N 21.15 E
Juhoslovenská nižina 120 Ph 48.10N 19.40 E
Juhua Dao 154 Fd 40.32N 120.48 E
Juigalpa 194 Eg 12.05N 85.24W
Juina, Rio- 204 Ca 12.36S 58.57W
Juine 122 If 48.32N 2.23 E
Juininha, Rio- 204 Ca 12.55S 59.13W
Juist 120 Cc 53.40N 7.00 E
Juiz de Fora 200 Lh 21.45S 43.20W
Jujuy [2] 206 Gb 23.00S 66.00W
Jukagirskoje ploskogorje 138 Kc 66.00N 155.30 E
Jukonda 134 Mg 59.38N 67.20 E
Juksejevo 134 Gg 59.52N 54.16 E
Jula 114 Ke 63.48N 44.44 E
Juldybajevo 134 Hj 52.20N 57.52 E
Julesburg 186 Ef 40.59N 102.16W
Juli 202 Eg 16.13S 69.27W
Juliaca 202 Dg 15.30S 70.08W
Julia Creek 212 Id 20.39S 141.45 E
Julian Alps (EN) = Julijske Alpe 128 Hd 46.20N 13.45 E
Juliana Top 202 Gc 3.41N 56.32W
Julianehåb/Qaqortoq 224 Nc 60.50N 46.10W
Jülich 120 Cf 50.56N 6.22 E
Jülicher Borde 124 Id 50.50N 6.30 E
Julijske Alpe = Julian Alps (EN) 128 Hd 46.20N 13.45 E
Julimes 192 Gc 28.25N 105.27W
Júlio de Castilhos 204 Fi 29.14S 53.41W
Jullundur → Jalandhar 142 Jf 31.19N 75.34 E
Julong/New Kowloon 142 Ng 22.20N 114.09 E
Julu 154 Cf 37.13N 115.02 E
Juma 114 Hd 65.05N 33.13 E
Juma He 154 De 39.31N 116.08 E
Jumaymah, Birkat al- 146 Jh 29.36N 43.36 E
Jumentos Cays 194 Jb 23.00N 75.50W
Jumet, Charleroi- 122 Kd 50.27N 4.26 E
Jumièges 124 Ce 49.26N 0.49 E
Jumilla 126 Kf 38.29N 1.17W
Jümme 124 Ja 53.13N 7.31 E
Junāgadh 148 Ed 21.31N 70.28 E
Junan (Shizilu) 154 Eg 35.10N 118.50 E
Junaynah, Ra's al- 146 Eh 29.01N 33.58 E
Juncal 192 De 24.50N 111.47W
Juncos 197a Cb 18.13N 65.55W
Junction [Tx.-U.S.] 186 Gk 30.29N 99.46W
Junction [Ut.-U.S.] 188 Ig 38.14N 112.13W
Junction City 182 Hd 39.02N 96.50W
Jundiai 206 Kb 23.11S 46.52W
Jundiai do Sul 204 Gf 23.27S 50.17W
Jundūbah 162 Ib 36.30N 8.45 E
Jundūbah [3] 162 Ib 36.28N 8.41 E
Juneau 176 Fd 57.20N 134.27W
Junee 212 Jf 34.52S 147.35 E
Jungar Qi (Shagedu) 152 Jd 39.37N 110.58 E
Jungfrau 128 Bd 46.32N 7.58 E
Junggar Pendi = Dzungarian Basin (EN) 140 Ke 45.00N 88.00 E
Junin [3] 202 Df 11.30S 75.00W
Junin [Arg.] 200 Ji 34.35S 60.57W
Junin [Peru] 202 Cf 11.10S 76.00W
Junin, Lago de- 202 Cf 11.02S 76.05W
Junin de los Andes 206 Fe 39.56S 71.05W
Juniville 124 Ge 49.24N 4.23 E
Jūniyah 146 Ff 33.59N 35.38 E
Junjaha 134 Jc 66.25N 62.00 E
Junlian 152 Hf 28.12N 104.34 E
Junsele 114 De 63.41N 16.54 E
Juntura 188 Fe 43.45N 118.05W
Junxian (Danjiang) 152 Je 32.31N 111.32 E
Juoduppé 116 Kh 56.03N 25.44 E
Juojärvi 116 Mb 62.45N 28.35 E
Juoksengi 114 Fc 66.34N 23.51 E
Jupiá, Represa de- 206 Jb 20.47S 51.39W
Juquiá 204 Ig 24.19S 47.38W
Juquiá, Rio- 204 Ig 24.22S 47.49W
Juquiá, Serra do- 204 Gg 25.10S 52.00W
Jur 138 Ie 59.48N 137.29 E
Jur 158 Jh 8.39N 29.18 E
Jura [2] 128 Ac 47.25N 6.15 E
Jura [3] 122 Lh 46.50N 5.50 E
Jura 110 Gf 46.45N 6.30 E
Jura 118 Hf 56.00N 5.50W
Jūra/Jura 114 Ff 55.03N 22.10 E
Jūra/Jūra 118 Fi 55.03N 22.10 E
Jura, Sound of- 118 Hf 55.55N 5.22W
Juradó 202 Cb 7.07N 77.46W
Juratiški 116 Kj 54.02N 26.00 E
Juraybỹ'āt 146 Kh 29.08N 45.30 E
Jurbarkas 114 Fi 55.08N 22.47 E
Jurdī, Wādī- 146 Ei 26.33N 32.44 E
Jurga 138 De 55.42N 84.55 E
Jurgamyš 134 Li 55.25N 64.28 E
Juribej 134 Nb 68.55N 69.05 E
Jurien Bay 212 Cf 30.15S 115.00 E
Jurigue, Rio- 204 Ec 16.29S 54.37W
Jurilovca 130 Le 44.46N 28.52 E
Jurja 114 Lg 59.03N 49.20 E
Jurjaha 134 Gc 66.42N 56.00 E
Jurjevec 134 Kh 57.22N 43.06 E
Jurjev-Polskí 114 Jh 56.31N 39.44 E
Jurjuzan 134 Ii 54.52N 58.28 E
Jurjuzan 134 Hi 55.43N 56.57 E
Jurla 134 Gg 59.20N 54.16 E
Jūrmala/Jurmala 136 Cd 56.59N 23.38 E
Jurmala/Jūrmala 136 Cd 56.59N 23.38 E
Jurmo 116 Ie 59.50N 21.35 E
Jurong 154 Ei 31.56N 119.10 E
Juruá 202 Ed 3.27S 66.03W
Juruá, Rio- 198 Jf 2.37S 65.44W
Juruena, Rio- 198 Kf 7.20S 58.03W
Jurumirim, Represa de- 206 Kb 23.20S 49.00W
Juruti 202 Gd 2.09S 56.04W
Jurva 116 Ib 62.41N 21.59 E
Jusan-Kō 156a Bc 41.00N 140.20 E
Jusayrah 146 Nj 25.53N 50.36 E

Index Symbols

[1] Independent Nation
[2] State, Region
[3] District, County
[4] Municipality
[5] Colony, Dependency
Continent
Physical Region
Historical or Cultural Region
Mount, Mountain
Volcano
Hill
Mountains, Mountain Range
Hills, Escarpment
Plateau, Upland
Pass, Gap
Plain, Lowland
Delta
Salt Flat
Valley, Canyon
Crater, Cave
Karst Features
Depression
Polder
Desert, Dunes
Forest, Woods
Heath, Steppe
Oasis
Cape, Point
Coast, Beach
Cliff
Peninsula
Isthmus
Sandbank
Island
Atoll
Rock, Reef
Islands, Archipelago
Rocks, Reefs
Coral Reef
Well, Spring
Geyser
River, Stream
Waterfall, Rapids
River Mouth, Estuary
Lake
Salt Lake
Intermittent Lake
Reservoir
Swamp, Pond
Canal
Glacier
Ice Shelf, Pack Ice
Ocean
Sea
Gulf, Bay
Strait, Fjord
Lagoon
Bank
Seamount
Tablemount
Ridge
Shelf
Basin
Escarpment, Sea Scarp
Fracture
Trench, Abyss
National Park, Reserve
Point of Interest
Recreation Site
Cave, Cavern
Historic Site
Ruins
Wall, Walls
Church, Abbey
Temple
Scientific Station
Railway station
Airport
Port
Military installation
Lighthouse
Mine
Tunnel
Dam, Bridge

Name	Page	Grid	Lat	Long
Jusheng	152	Mb	48.44N	126.37 E
Ju Shui [S]	154	Ci	31.09N	114.52 E
Juškozero	136	Dc	64.45N	32.08 E
Jussarö [◉]	116	Je	59.50N	23.35 E
Justo Daract	206	Gd	33.52S	65.11W
Jusva	134	Gg	58.59N	54.57 E
Jutaí	202	Ee	5.11S	68.54W
Jutaí, Rio- [S]	198	Jf	2.43S	66.57W
Jüterbog	120	Je	51.59N	13.05 E
Juti	204	Ef	22.52S	54.37W
Jutiapa [3]	194	Bf	14.10N	89.50W
Jutiapa [Guat.] ·	190	Gf	14.17N	89.54W
Jutiapa [Hond.]	194	Df	15.46N	86.34W
Juticalpa	190	Gf	14.42N	86.15W
Jutland (EN) = Jylland [◉]	110	Gd	56.00N	9.15 E
Juuka	114	Gg	63.14N	29.15 E
Juva	114	Gf	61.54N	27.51 E
Juventud, Isla de la- = Pines, Isle of- (EN) [◉]	174	Kg	21.40N	82.50W
Juxian	152	Kd	35.33N	118.45 E
Jūybār	146	Od	36.38N	52.53 E
Juye	154	Dg	35.23N	116.05 E
Jüyom	146	Oh	28.10N	54.02 E
Juža	114	Kh	56.36N	42.01 E
Južnaja Keltma [S]	134	Gd	60.30N	55.40 E
Južna Morava [S]	130	Ef	43.41N	21.24 E
Južni Rodopi [▲]	130	Ih	41.15N	25.30 E
Južnoje	138	Jg	46.13N	143.27 E
Južno-Jenisejski	138	Ee	58.48N	94.45 E
Južno-Kurilsk	138	Ah	44.05N	145.52 E
Južno-Sahalinsk	142	Qe	46.58N	142.42 E
Južno-Uralsk	136	Ge	54.26N	61.15 E
Južny, mys- [▶]	138	Ke	57.42N	156.55 E
Južny Bug [S]	110	Jf	46.59N	31.58 E
Južny Ural = Southern Urals (EN) [▲]	110	Le	54.00N	58.30 E
Jygeva/Jõgeva	114	Gg	58.46N	26.26 E
Jylland=Jutland (EN) [◉]	110	Gd	56.00N	9.15 E
Jylland Bank [◉]	116	Bh	56.55N	7.20 E
Jyske Ås [◉]	116	Bh	57.15N	10.14 E
Jyväskylä	112	Ic	62.14N	25.44 E

K

Name	Page	Grid	Lat	Long
K2 (Godwin Austen) [▲]	140	Jf	35.53N	76.30 E
Ka [S]	166	Fc	11.39N	4.11 E
Kaabong	170	Fb	3.31N	34.09 E
Kaahka	136	Fh	37.21N	59.38 E
Kaala [▲]	221a	Cb	21.31N	158.09W
Kaala-Gomén	219b	Be	20.40S	164.24 E
Kaalualu Bay [◀]	221a	Fe	18.58N	155.37W
Kaamanen	114	Gb	69.06N	27.12 E
Kaap Kruis	172	Ad	21.46S	13.58 E
Kaap Plateau (EN)= Kaapplato [◉]	158	Jk	27.30S	23.45 E
Kaapplato=Kaap Plateau (EN) [◉]	158	Jk	27.30S	23.45 E
Kaapprovinsie/Cape Province [3]	172	Cf	32.00S	22.00 E
Kaapstad / Cape Town	160	Il	33.55S	18.22 E
Kaarst	124	Ic	51.15N	6.37 E
Kaarta [◉]	166	Cc	14.35N	10.00W
Kaba/Habahe	152	Ie	47.53N	86.12 E
Kabaena, Pulau- [◉]	156	Hh	5.15S	121.55 E
Kabah [◉]	192	Og	20.07N	89.29W
Kabala	166	Cd	9.35N	11.33W
Kabale	170	Ec	1.15S	29.59 E
Kabalega Falls (Murchison Falls) [S]	170	Fb	2.17N	31.41 E
Kabalo	160	Ji	6.03S	26.55 E
Kabaman	219a	Aa	4.38S	152.42 E
Kabambare	170	Ec	4.16S	27.07 E
Kabamet	170	Gb	0.30N	35.45 E
Kabanjahe	150	Cf	3.06N	98.30 E
Kabardino-Balkarskaja ASSR [3]	136	Eg	43.30N	43.30 E
Kabare	170	Ec	2.29S	28.48 E
Kabasalan	156	He	7.48N	122.45 E
Kaba-Shima [Jap.] [◉]	156	Ae	32.34N	129.47 E
Kaba-Shima [Jap.] [◉]	156	Ae	32.45N	129.02 E
Kabba	166	Gd	7.50N	6.04 E
Kåbdalis	114	Ec	66.09N	20.00 E
Kaberamaido	170	Fb	1.45N	33.10 E
Kabetogama Lake [◉]	186	Jb	48.28N	92.59W
Kabhegy [▲]	120	Ni	47.03N	17.39 E
Kabinakagami Lake [◉]	184	Ea	48.58N	84.25W
Kabinda	160	Ji	6.08S	24.29 E
Kabir, Wâdi al- [S]	128	Dn	36.23N	9.52 E
Kabir Küh [▲]	146	Lf	33.25N	46.45 E
Kabkâbîyah	168	Cc	13.39N	24.05 E
Kableškovo	130	Kg	42.39N	27.34 E
Kabna	168	Eb	19.10N	32.41 E
Kabo	168	Bd	7.35N	18.38 E
Kåbol [3]	144	Kc	34.30N	69.00 E
Kåbol (Kabul)	142	If	34.31N	69.12 E
Kabompo	170	De	13.36S	24.12 E
Kabompo [S]	158	Jj	14.11S	23.11 E
Kabondo Dianda	170	Ed	8.53S	25.40 E
Kabongo	170	Ed	7.19S	25.35 E
Kabou	166	Fd	9.27N	0.49 E
Kabüdiyäh, Ra's- [▶]	162	Jb	35.14N	11.10 E
Kabül [S]	144	Me	35.12N	66.42 E
Kåbul [▲]	140	Jf	33.55N	72.14 E
Kabül → Kábol	142	If	34.31N	69.12 E
Kabunda	170	Ee	12.13S	29.23 E
Kaburuang, Pulau- [◉]	150	If	3.48N	126.48 E
Kabwe	160	Jj	14.27S	28.27 E
Kača	132	Hg	44.44N	33.32 E
Kačanik	130	Eg	42.14N	21.15 E
Kačergine	116	Jj	54.53N	23.49 E
Kachchh, Gulf of	140	Ig	22.36N	69.32 E
Kachchh, Rann of	148	Dd	23.51N	70.30 E
achia	166	Gd	9.52E	7.57 E
achikau	172	Cc	18.09S	24.29 E

Name	Page	Grid	Lat	Long
Kachin [2]	148	Jc	26.00N	97.30 E
Kačiry	136	He	53.04N	76.07 E
Kačkanar	136	Fd	58.42N	59.35 E
Kaçkar Dağı [▲]	144	Fa	41.10N	40.50 E
Kaczawa [S]	120	Me	51.18N	16.27 E
Kadada [S]	132	Oc	53.09N	46.01 E
Kadaň	120	Jf	50.23N	13.16 E
Kadan Kyun [◉]	148	Jf	12.30N	98.22 E
Kadaň [S]	158	Ih	3.31N	16.03 E
Kadijevka	136	Df	48.32N	38.40 E
Kadiköy	146	Bb	40.51N	26.50 E
Kadiköy, İstanbul-	130	Mi	40.59N	29.01 E
Kadina	212	Hf	33.58S	137.43 E
Kadınhanı	146	Ec	38.15N	32.14 E
Kadiolo	166	Dc	10.34N	5.45W
Kadiri	148	Ff	14.07N	78.10 E
Kadirli	144	Eb	37.23N	36.05 E
Kadja [S]	168	Cc	12.02N	22.28 E
Kadmat Island [◉]	148	Ei	11.14N	72.47 E
Kadnikov	114	Jg	59.30N	40.24 E
Kadoka	186	Fe	43.50N	101.31W
Kadoma	160	Jj	18.21S	29.55 E
Kaduj	114	Ig	59.14N	37.09 E
Kaduna	160	Hg	10.31N	7.26 E
Kaduna [2]	166	Gc	11.00N	7.30 E
Kaduna [S]	158	Hh	8.45N	5.48 E
Kāduqlī	160	Jg	11.01N	29.43 E
Kadykčan	138	Jd	63.05N	146.58 E
Kadzaran	132	Oj	39.11N	46.10 E
Kadzerom	134	Gd	64.4 N	55.54 E
Kadži-Saj	135	Kc	42.06N	77.10 E
Kaech'ŏn	154	Me	39.42N	125.53 E
Kaédi	160	Tg	16.08N	13.31W
Kaélé	166	Hc	10.07N	14.27 E
Kaena Point [▶]	221a	Cb	21.35N	158.17W
Kaeo	218	Ea	35.06S	173.47 E
Kaesŏng	142	Of	37.58N	126.33 E
Kaesŏng Si [2]	154	Ie	38.05N	126.30 E
Kāf	146	Gg	31.24N	37.29 E
Kafakumba	170	Dd	9.41S	23.44 E
Kafan	136	Eh	39.12N	46.28 E
Kafanchan	166	Gd	9.35N	8.18 E
Kaffrine	166	Bc	14.06N	15.33W
Kafia Kingi	168	Cd	9.16N	24.25 E
Kafirévs, Dhiékplous- [◉]	130	Hl	38.00N	24.40 E
Kafirévs, Ákra- [▶]	130	Hk	38.10N	24.35 E
Kafr ad Dawwār	146	Dg	31.08N	30.07 E
Kafr ash Shaykh	164	Fc	31.07N	30.56 E
Kafta	168	Fc	13.54N	37.11 E
Kafu [S]	170	Fb	1.39N	32.05 E
Kafue	160	Jj	15.47S	28.11 E
Kafue Dam [◉]	170	Ef	15.45S	28.28 E
Kafue Flats [◉]	170	Ef	15.40S	26.25 E
Kafufu [S]	170	Fd	7.12S	31.31 E
Kaga	154	Nf	36.18N	136.18 E
Kaga Bandoro	168	Bd	7.02N	19.13 E
Kagalaska [◉]	178a	Cb	51.47N	176.23W
Kagalnik [S]	132	Kf	47.04N	39.18 E
Kagami	156	Be	32.34N	130.40 E
Kagan	136	Gh	39.43N	64.32 E
Kagarlyk	132	Ge	49.50N	30.56 E
Kagawa Ken [2]	154	Mg	34.15N	134.15 E
Kagera [S]	158	Ki	0.57S	31.47 E
Kagizman	146	Jb	40.09N	43.07 E
Kagoshima	142	Pf	31.36N	130.33 E
Kagoshima Bay (EN)= Kagoshima-Wan [◀]	154	Ki	31.27N	130.40 E
Kagoshima Ken [2]	154	Ki	31.45N	130.40 E
Kagoshima-Taniyama	156	Bf	31.31N	130.31 E
Kagoshima-Wan = Kagoshima Bay (EN) [◀]	154	Ki	31.27N	130.40 E
Kagul	136	Cf	45.53N	28.14 E
Kahal Tabelbala [▲]	162	Jb	28.45N	2.15W
Kahama	170	Fc	3.50S	32.36 E
Kahayan [S]	160	Ii	7.17S	19.00 E
Kahemba	132	Oi	41.23N	46.59 E
Kahi	146	He	7.48N	122.45 E
Kahler Asten [▲]	120	Ee	51.11N	8.29 E
Kahnûj	146	Ng	31.43N	61.44 E
Kâhta	146	Ng	37.46N	38.36 E
Kahoku	156	Ng	36.30N	141.20 E
Kahoku-Gata	156	Ng	36.40N	136.40 E
Kahoolawe Island [◉]	208	Lb	20.33N	156.35W
Kahouanne, Ilet à- [◉]	197e	Ab	16.22N	61.47W
Kahovka	136	Df	46.47N	33.32 E

Name	Page	Grid	Lat	Long
Kain, Tournai-	124	Fd	50.38N	3.22 E
Kainach [S]	128	Jd	46.54N	15.31 E
Kainan [Jap.]	156	Be	33.36N	134.22 E
Kainan [Jap.]	156	Dd	34.09N	135.12 E
Kainantu	214	Di	6.15S	145.53 E
Kainji Dam [◉]	166	Fd	9.55N	4.40 E
Kainji Reservoir [◉]	166	Fc	10.30N	4.35 E
Kaipara Harbour [◀]	218	Fb	36.25S	174.15 E
Kaiparowits Plateau [◉]	188	Jh	37.20N	111.15W
Kaiser Franz Josephs Fjord	179	Jd	73.30N	24.00W
Kaisersesch	124	Jd	50.14N	7.09 E
Kaiserslautern	120	Dg	49.27N	7.45 E
Kaiserstuhl [▲]	120	Dh	48.06N	7.40 E
Kaishantun	146	Ec	42.43N	129.37 E
Kaišiadorys/Kajšjadoris	114	Fi	54.53N	24.31 E
Kaita	156	Cd	34.20N	132.32 E
Kaitaia	218	Ea	35.07S	173.14 E
Kaitangata	218	Cg	46.17S	169.51 E
Kaithal	148	Fc	29.48N	76.23 E
Kaitong → Tongyu	152	Lc	44.47N	123.05 E
Kaituma River [S]	196	Gh	8.31N	59.41W
Kaiwaka	216	Dg	36.10S	174.26 E
Kaiwi Channel [◉]	214	Oc	21.13N	157.30W
Kaixian	152	Ie	31.10N	108.25 E
Kaiyuan [China]	152	Hg	23.47N	103.15 E
Kaiyuan [China]	152	Lc	42.33N	124.04 E
Kaiyuh Mountains [▲]	178	Hd	64.00N	158.00W
Kaja [S]	158	Jg	12.02N	22.28 E
Kajaani	112	Ic	64.14N	27.41 E
Kajaapu	150	Dh	5.26S	102.24 E
Kajabbi	210	Fg	20.02S	140.02 E
Kajang	150	Df	2.59N	101.47 E
Kajdak, sor- [◉]	132	Kg	44.40N	53.30 E
Kajdan	138	Dc	69.25N	87.30 E
Kajerkan	138	Dc	69.25N	87.30 E
Kajiado	170	Gc	1.51S	36.47 E
Kajki	156	Bf	31.44N	130.40 E
Kajmakčalan [▲]	130	Ei	40.58N	21.48 E
Kajnar [S]	130	Kh	47.50N	28.06 E
Kajo Kaji	168	Ee	3.53N	31.40 E
Kajrakkumskoje vodohranilišče [◉]	135	Hd	40.20N	70.05 E
Kajrakty	136	Hf	48.31N	73.14 E
Kajšjadorys/Kaišiadorys	114	Fi	54.53N	24.31 E
Kajuru	166	Gc	10.19N	7.41 E
Kákä	168	Fd	10.36N	32.11 E
Kaka [▲]	168	Fd	7.28N	39.06 E
Kakagi Lake [◉]	186	Jb	49.13N	93.52W
Kakamas	172	De	28.45S	20.33 E
Kakamega	170	Fb	0.17N	34.45 E
Kakamigahara	156	Dd	35.25N	136.50 E
Kakanj	128	Mf	44.08N	18.05 E
Kaka Point [▶]	221a	Ec	20.32N	156.33W
Kakata	166	Cd	6.32N	10.21W
Kake	156	Cd	34.36N	132.19 E
Kakegawa	156	Dd	34.46N	138.00 E
Kakenge	170	Dc	4.51S	21.55 E
Kakeroma-Jima [◉]	156b	Ba	28.08N	129.15 E
Kakhovka Reservoir (EN) = Kahovskoje vodohranilišče [◉]	110	Jf	47.25N	34.10 E
Käki	146	Nh	28.19N	51.34 E
Kākināda	142	Nh	16.56N	82.13 E
Kakisa Lake [◉]	180	Fd	60.55N	117.40W
Kakizaki	156	Fc	37.16N	138.22 E
Kaklkan	146	Cd	36.15N	29.24 E
Kakogawa	156	Dd	34.46N	134.51 E
Kakpin	166	Ed	8.39N	3.48W
Kaktovik	178	Kb	70.08N	143.37W
Kakuda	156	Fc	37.58N	140.47 E
Kakuma	170	Fb	3.43N	34.52 E
Kakunodate	154	Pe	39.40N	140.32 E
Kakva [S]	134	Jc	59.37N	60.50 E
Kakya	170	Gc	1.36S	39.02 E
Kalaa	126	Mi	35.35N	0.20 E
Kalaa Khasba	128	Co	35.38N	8.36 E
Kalaallit Nunaat/Grønland = Greenland (EN) [5]	224	Nd	70.00N	40.00W
Kalaallit Nunaat/Grønland = Kreenland (EN)	174	Pb	70.00N	40.00W
Kalabahi	150	Hh	8.13S	124.31 E
Kalabáka	130	Ej	39.42N	21.38 E
Kalabera	220b	Ba	15.14N	145.48 E
Kalabo	170	De	14.58S	22.41 E
Kálábsha [◉]	164	Ee	23.33N	32.50 E
Kalač	136	Ee	50.23N	41.01 E
Kalačinsk	136	Hd	55.03N	74.34 E
Kalač-na-Donu	136	Ef	48.41N	43.32 E
Kaladan [S]	148	Ih	20.09N	92.57 E
Ka Lae [▶]	214	Od	18.55N	155.41W
Kalahari Desert [◉]	158	Jk	23.00S	22.00 E
Kalaheo	221a	Bb	21.56N	159.32W
Kalai-Mor	146	Ic	35.39N	62.31 E
Kalaj Humo	135	He	38.25N	70.47 E
Kalakan	138	Ge	55.08N	116.45 E
Kalaldi	166	Gd	6.30N	14.04 E
Kalâleh	146	Pd	37.25N	55.40 E
Kalámai	112	Hm	37.02N	22.07 E
Kalamákion	112	Ih	37.52N	25.40 E
Kalamazoo	182	Jc	42.17N	85.32W
Kalambo Falls [S]	170	Ed	8.36S	31.14 E
Kalamitski zaliv [◀]	132	Hg	45.30N	33.25 E
Ka amos [◉]	130	Dk	38.37N	20.55 E
Kalamunda, Perth-	213	Df	31.57S	116.03 E
Kalan	144	Fb	39.06N	39.33 E
Kalanshiyū, Sarīr- [◉]	164	Cd	27.00N	21.30 E
Kalao, Pulau- [◉]	156	Hh	7.18S	120.58 E
Kalaotoa, Pulau- [◉]	156	Hh	7.22S	121.47 E
Kalaraš	130	Kf	47.16N	28.16 E
Kalarski hrebet [▲]	138	Ge	56.30N	118.50 E
Kalasin [Indon.]	150	Df	0.12N	114.16 E
Kalasin [Thai.]	148	Ke	16.29N	103.31 E
Kalāt	148	Kd	29.02N	66.35 E
Kalāteh	146	Pd	36.29N	54.10 E

Name	Page	Grid	Lat	Long
Kalau [◉]	221b	Bc	21.28S	174.57W
Kalaupapa	221a	Eb	21.12N	156.59W
Kalaus [S]	132	Ng	45.43N	44.07 E
Kalavárdha	130	Km	36.20N	27.57 E
Kálavrita	130	Fk	38.02N	22.07 E
Kalbā'	146	Oj	25.03N	56.21 E
Kalbïyah, Sabkhat al- [◉]	128	Eo	35.51N	10.17 E
Kaldbakur [▲]	114a	Ab	65.49N	23.39W
Kaldygajty [S]	132	Re	49.20N	52.38 E
Kale [Tur.]	146	Cd	36.14N	29.59 E
Kale [Tur.]	146	Cd	37.26N	28.51 E
Kalecik	146	Eb	40.06N	33.25 E
Kalehe	170	Ec	2.06S	28.55 E
Kalemie	160	Ji	5.56S	29.12 E
Käl-e Shur [S]	144	Jb	35.05N	60.59 E
Kalevala	136	Db	65.12N	31.10 E
Kalewa	148	Id	23.12N	94.18 E
Kaleybar	146	Lc	38.47N	47.02 E
Kalgoorlie	210	Dh	30.45S	121.28 E
Kaliakoúdha [▲]	130	Ek	38.48N	21.46 E
Kaliakra, Nos- [▶]	130	Lf	43.18N	28.30 E
Kalibo	150	Hd	11.43N	122.22 E
Kali Limni [▲]	130	Kn	35.35N	27.08 E
Kalima	160	Ji	2.34S	26.37 E
Kalimantan/Borneo [◉]	140	Ni	1.00N	114.00 E
Kalimantan Barat [3]	150	Ff	0.01N	110.30 E
Kalimantan Selatan [3]	150	Gg	2.30S	115.30 E
Kalimantan Tengah [3]	150	Fg	2.00S	113.30 E
Kalimantan Timur [3]	150	Gf	1.30N	116.30 E
Kálimnos	130	Jm	36.57N	26.59 E
Kalin [R.S.F.S.R.] → Tver'	112	Jd	56.52N	35.55 E
Kalinin [Tur.-U.S.S.R.]	136	Fg	42.07N	59.40 E
Kalininabad	135	Gf	37.53N	68.57 E
Kaliningrad [R.S.F.S.R.]	112	Ie	54.43N	20.30 E
Kaliningrad [R.S.F.S.R.]	114	Ii	55.55N	37.57 E
Kaliningradskaja oblast [3]	114	Sa	54.45N	21.20 E
Kalinino [Arm.-U.S.S.R.]	132	Ni	41.08N	44.14 E
Kalinino [R.S.F.S.R.]	132	Qg	45.05N	38.59 E
Kalininsk [Mold.-U.S.S.R.]	130	Ka	48.07N	27.16 E
Kalininsk [R.S.F.S.R.]	132	Ni	50.10N	44.30 E
Kalininskaja oblast [3]	136	Dd	57.20N	34.40 E
Kalinkoviči	136	Ce	52.07N	29.23 E
Kalino	134	Ng	58.15N	57.35 E
Kalinovik	128	Mg	43.31N	18.26 E
Kalinovka	132	Fe	49.29N	28.32 E
Kaliro	170	Fb	0.54N	33.30 E
Kalispell	176	Eb	48.12N	114.19W
Kalisz	120	Oe	51.46N	18.06 E
Kalisz [2]	120	Of	51.45N	18.05 E
Kalisz Pomorski	120	Lc	53.19N	15.54 E
Kalitva [S]	132	Le	48.10N	40.46 E
Kaliua	170	Fd	5.04S	31.48 E
Kalix	114	Fd	65.47N	23.08 E
Kalixälven [S]	114	Fc	65.50N	22.50 E
Kalja	134	Jf	60.20N	60.01 E
Kaljazin	136	De	57.15N	37.55 E
Kalkandere	146	Ib	40.55N	40.28 E
Kalkar	124	Ic	51.44N	6.18 E
Kalkaska	184	Ec	44.44N	85.11W
Kalkfeld	172	Bd	20.53N	16.11 E
Kalkfontein	172	Cd	22.07S	20.54 E
Kalkim	130	Kj	39.46N	27.13 E
Kalkrand	172	Bd	24.03S	17.33 E
Kall	114	Cc	63.28N	13.15 E
Kållands Halvö [◉]	116	Ef	58.35N	13.05 E
Kållandsö [◉]	116	Ef	58.40N	13.10 E
Kallaste	114	Gg	58.40N	27.08 E
Kallavesi [◉]	114	Gg	62.50N	27.45 E
Kalletal	124	Kb	52.08N	8.57 E
Kallhäll	116	Gg	59.27N	17.48 E
Kallidhromon Óros [▲]	130	Fk	38.48N	22.34 E
Kallinge	116	Fh	56.14N	15.17 E
Kallonis, Kolpos- [◀]	130	Jj	39.07N	26.08 E
Kallsjön [◉]	114	Cc	63.35N	13.00 E
Kalmakkyrgan [S]	135	Fb	44.30N	64.30 E
Kalmar	112	Hd	56.40N	16.22 E
Kalmar [2]	114	Gh	57.20N	16.00 E
Kalmarsund [◉]	116	Gh	56.40N	16.25 E
Kalmit [▲]	124	Ke	49.19N	8.06 E
Kalmius [S]	132	Jf	47.03N	37.34 E
Kalmthout	124	Fc	51.23N	4.28 E
Kalmyckaja ASSR [3]	136	Ef	46.30N	45.20 E
Kalmykovo	132	Qe	49.05N	51.47 E
Kalnciems	116	Ig	56.48N	23.34 E
Kalnik [▲]	128	Kd	46.10N	16.13 E
Kalocsa	120	Og	46.32N	19.00 E
Kalofer	130	Ig	42.37N	24.59 E
Kalohi Channel [◉]	221a	Ec	21.00N	156.56W
Kaloko	170	Ec	6.47S	25.47 E
Kalole	170	Ec	3.42S	27.22 E
Kaloli Point [▶]	221a	Gd	19.43N	154.57W
Kalomo	170	Ef	17.02S	26.30 E
Kalpa	148	Fc	31.33N	78.10 E
Kalpákion	130	Dj	39.33N	20.35 E
Kalpeni Island [◉]	148	Eh	10.05N	73.38 E
Kalpin	152	Fd	40.31N	79.03 E
Kalsúbai [▲]	148	Eg	19.36N	73.43 E
Kaltern/Caldaro	124	Nf	46.25N	11.14 E
Kaltungo	166	Gd	9.49N	11.19 E
Kaluga	112	Jd	54.31N	36.16 E
Kalulushi	170	Ee	12.50S	28.05 E
Kalumburu Mission	212	Fb	14.18S	126.39 E
Kalundborg	114	Ci	55.41N	11.06 E
Kaluš	120	Cf	49.03N	24.22 E
Kalužskaja oblast [3]	136	Ce	54.15N	35.30 E
Kalvåg	114	Af	61.47N	4.52 E
Kalvarija	114	Fi	54.24N	23.14 E
Kalya	134	Hd	60.19N	57.08 E
Kalyan	148	Eg	19.15N	73.09 E
Kám [S]	120	Mi	47.06N	16.53 E
Kama	134	Hf	55.45N	52.04 E
Kama [R.S.F.S.R.] [S]	134	Ge	60.27N	69.00 E
Kama [U.S.S.R.] [S]	110	Le	55.30N	52.00 E
Kamae	156	Be	32.48N	131.56 E
Kamaing	148	Ic	25.31N	96.44 E

Name	Page	Grid	Lat	Long
Kamaishi	154	Pe	39.16N	141.53 E
Kamakou [▲]	221a	Eb	21.07N	156.52W
Kamakura	156	Fd	35.19N	139.32 E
Kamália	148	Eb	30.44N	72.39 E
Kamalo	221a	Eb	21.03N	156.53W
Kaman	146	Ec	39.25N	33.45 E
Kamand, Åb-e- [S]	146	Mf	33.28N	49.04 E
Kamanjab	172	Ac	19.35S	14.51 E
Kamanyola	170	Ec	2.46S	29.00 E
Kamárán [◉]	144	Ff	15.21N	42.35 E
Kamararg	202	Fb	5.53N	60.35W
Kama Reservoir (EN) = Kamskoje vodohralin.šče [◉]	110	Ld	58.50N	56.15 E
Kamáši	136	Gh	38.48N	66.29 E
Kamativi	172	Cc	18.19S	27.03 E
Kambalda	212	Ef	31.10S	121.37 E
Kambalnaja Sopka, vulkan- [▲]	138	Kf	51.17N	156.57 E
Kambara	156	Fd	35.07N	138.36 E
Kambara [◉]	219d	Cc	18.57S	178.57W
Kambia	114	Nb	56.18N	54.14 E
Kambja	166	Gd	9.07N	12.55W
Kambove	170	Ee	10.52S	26.35 E
Kamčatka [◉]	138	Le	56.10N	162.30 E
Kamčatka, poluostrov- = Kamchatka Peninsula (EN) [◉]	140	Rd	56.00N	160.00 E
Kamčatskaja oblast [3]	138	Kf	54.50N	159.00 E
Kamčatski zaliv [◀]	138	Le	55.30N	163.00 E
Kamchatka Peninsula (EN) = Kamčatka, poluostrov- [◉]	140	Rd	56.00N	160.00 E
Kamčija [S]	130	Kf	43.02N	27.53 E
Kamčijska Platc [▲]	130	Kg	42.56N	27.32 E
Kameda [Jap.]	156a	Bc	41.49N	140.46 E
Kameda [Jap.]	156	Fc	37.52N	139.06 E
Kameda-Hantō [◉]	156a	Bc	41.45N	141.00 E
Kámeiros [◉]	130	Km	36 .38N	27.56 E
Kamelik [S]	132	Pc	52.06N	49.30 E
Kamen	124	Jc	51.36N	7.40 E
Kaménai [◉]	130	Im	36.25N	25.25 E
Kamen	170	Dc	6.28S	24.33 E
Kamenec	120	Td	52.23N	23.49 E
Kamenec-Podolski	136	Cf	48.35N	26.33 E
Kamenjam Rt- [▶]	128	Hf	44.46N	13.56 E
Kamenka [Kaz.-U.S.S.R.]	132	Qd	51.07N	50.20 E
Kamenka [Mold.-U.S.S.R.]	136	Cf	48.03N	28.45 E
Kamenka [R.S.F.S.R.]	136	Se	53.13N	44.03 E
Kamenka [R.S.F.S.R.]	132	Kd	50.43N	39.25 E
Kamenka [R.S.F.S.R.]	154	Nb	44.28N	136.01 E
Kamenka [R.S.F.S.R.]	114	Kd	65.54N	44.04 E
Kamenka [Ukr.-U.S.S.R.]	136	Df	49.03N	32.06 E
Kamenka-Bugskaja	120	Uf	50.01N	24.25 E
Kamenka-Dneprovskaja	132	Jf	47.29N	34.29 E
Kamen-Kaširski	132	Dd	51.36N	24.59 E
Kamen-na-Obi	138	Df	53.47N	81.20 E
Kamennogorsk	114	Gf	60.59N	29.12 E
Kamennoje, ozero- [◉]	114	Hd	64.30N	30.15 E
Kamennomostski	132	Lg	44.17N	40.12 E
Kamen-Rybolov	154	Kb	44.45N	132.04 E
Kamenskoe	138	Ld	62.30N	166.12 E
Kamensk-Uralski	142	Jd	56.28N	61.54 E
Kamenz/Kamjenc	120	Ke	51.16N	14.06 E
Kameškovo	114	Jb	56.27N	41.01 E
Kameoka	156	Dd	35.00N	135.35 E
Kamet [▲]	148	Fb	30.55N	79.35 E
Kameyama	156	Ed	34.51N	136.27 E
Kamiah	188	Ge	46.14N	116.02W
Kamiagata	156	Ae	34.38N	129.25 E
Kamicharo	156a	Ca	43.11N	143.52 E
Kamienna [S]	120	Re	51.06N	21.47 E
Kamienna Góra	120	Mf	50.47N	16.01 E
Kamień Pomorski	120	Lc	53.58N	14.46 E
Kamiénsk	120	Pe	51.12N	19.33 E
Kamieskroon	172	Bf	30.09S	17.56 E
Kami-furano	156a	Cb	43.29N	142.27 E
Kamiita	154	Pd	41.49N	140.35 E
Kamiji	170	Dd	6.39S	23.17 E
Kamikawa	156a	Cb	43.28N	141.58 E
Kamikitayama	156	Dd	34.13N	136.00 E
Kami-Koshiki-Jima [◉]	156	Af	31.50N	129.55 E
Kamina	160	Ji	8.44S	24.59 E
Kaminak Lake [◉]	180	Id	62.13N	95.00W
Kaminokuni	156a	Bc	41.46N	140.07 E
Kamino-Shima [◉]	156	Ae	34.30N	129.25 E
Kaminuriak Lake [◉]	180	Id	63.00N	95.45W
Kamishihoro	156a	Cb	43.13N	143.18 E
Kamisunagawa	156a	Bb	43.28N	141.58 E
Kamitsushima	156	Ae	34.39N	129.28 E
Kamituga	170	Ec	3.04S	28.11 E
Kamiyama	156a	Ca	44.11N	143.34 E
Kami-yübetsu	156a	Ca	44.11N	143.34 E
Kamjenc/Kamenz	120	Ke	51.16N	14.06 E
Kamloops	176	Cb	50.40N	120.20W
Kamloops Plateau [▲]	188	Da	50.40N	120.35W
Kammersee → Attersee [◉]	128	Hc	47.55N	13.33 E
Kamnik	128	Ic	46.14N	14.37 E
Kamo [Jap.]	156	Fc	37.39N	139.03 E
Kamo [N.Z.]	218	Fa	35.41S	174.17 E
Kamōda-Misaki [▶]	156	Ce	33.41N	134.45 E
Kamogawa	156	Gd	35.06N	140.05 E
Kamok	130	Ja	48.28S	15.48 E
Kampala	160	Kh	0.19N	32.35 E
Kampar	150	Df	4.18N	101.09 E
Kampar [S]	150	Mi	0.32N	103.08 E
Kampen	122	Ga	52.33N	5.54 E
Kamphaeng Phet	148	Je	16.26N	99.33 E
Kamp-Lintort	124	Ic	51.30N	6.32 E
Kamp'o	154	Jg	35.48N	129.30 E
Kâmpóng Cham	142	Mh	12.00N	105.27 E
Kâmpóng Chhnáng	148	Kf	12.15N	104.40 E

Index Symbols

Symbol	Meaning	Symbol	Meaning
	Independent Nation		Historical or Cultural Region
	State, Region		Mount, Mountain
	District, County		Volcano
	Municipality		Hill
	Colony, Dependency		Mountains, Mountain Range
	Continent		Hills, Escarpment
	Physical Region		Plateau, Upland
	Pass, Gap		Depression
	Plain, Lowland		Polder
	Delta		Desert, Dunes
	Salt Flat		Forest, Woods
	Valley, Canyon		Heath, Steppe
	Crater, Cave		Oasis
	Karst Features		Cape, Point
	Coast, Beach		Rock, Reef
	Cliff		Islands, Archipelago
	Peninsula		Rocks, Reefs
	Isthmus		Coral Reef
	Sandbank		Well, Spring
	Island		Geyser
	Atoll		River, Stream
	Waterfall, Rapids		Canal
	River Mouth, Estuary		Glacier
	Lake		Ice Shelf, Pack Ice
	Salt Lake		Ocean
	Intermittent Lake		Sea
	Reservoir		Shelf
	Swamp, Pond		Strait, Fjord
	Lagoon		Escarpment, Sea Scarp
	Bank		Fracture
	Seamount		Trench, Abyss
	Tablemount		National Park, Reserve
	Ridge		Point of Interest
	Basin		Recreation Site
			Scientific Station
			Cave, Cavern
	Historic Site		Airport
	Ruins		Port
	Wall, Walls		Military installation
	Church, Abbey		Lighthouse
	Temple		Mine
			Tunnel
	Railway station		Dam, Bridge

Index Symbols

Symbol	Meaning
[1]	Independent Nation
[2]	State, Region
[3]	District, County
[4]	Municipality
[5]	Colony, Dependency
■	Continent
[X]	Physical Region
	Historical or Cultural Region
▲	Mount, Mountain
	Volcano
	Hill
	Mountains, Mountain Range
	Hills, Escarpment
	Plateau, Upland
	Pass, Gap
	Plain, Lowland
	Delta
	Salt Flat
	Valley, Canyon
	Crater, Cave
	Karst Features
	Depression
	Polder
	Desert, Dunes
	Forest, Woods
	Heath, Steppe
	Oasis
	Cape, Point
	Coast, Beach
	Cliff
	Peninsula
	Isthmus
	Sandbank
	Island
	Atoll
	Rock, Reef
	Islands, Archipelago
	Rocks, Reefs
	Coral Reef
	Well, Spring
	Geyser
	River, Stream
	Waterfall, Rapids
	River Mouth, Estuary
	Lake
	Salt Lake
	Intermittent Lake
	Reservoir
	Swamp, Pond
	Canal
	Glacier
	Ice Shelf, Pack Ice
	Ocean
	Sea
	Gulf, Bay
	Strait, Fjord
	Lagoon
	Bank
	Seamount
	Tablemount
	Ridge
	Shelf
	Basin
	Escarpment, Sea Scarp
	Fracture
	Trench, Abyss
	National Park, Reserve
	Point of Interest
	Recreation Site
	Cave, Cavern
	Historic Site
	Ruins
	Wall, Walls
	Church, Abbey
	Temple
	Scientific Station
	Railway station
	Airport
	Port
	Military install.
	Lighthouse
	Mine
	Tunnel
	Dam, Bridge

Kas-Ket

Name	Page	Grid	Lat.	Long.
Kašira	114	Ji	54.52N	38.11 E
Kasiruta, Pulau-	150	Ig	0.25S	127.12 E
Kasisty	138	Fb	73.40N	109.45 E
Kaškadarinskaja oblast [3]	136	Gh	38.50N	66.10 E
Kaškadarja	135	Ee	39.35N	64.38 E
Kaskaskia River	186	Lh	37.59N	89.56W
Kaskelen	136	Hg	43.09N	76.37 E
Kaskinen/Kaskö	114	Ee	62.23N	21.13 E
Kaskö/Kaskinen	114	Ee	62.23N	21.13 E
Kasli	134	Ji	55.53N	60.48 E
Kaslo	188	Gb	49.55N	116.55W
Kasongo	160	Ji	4.27S	26.40 E
Kasongo-Lunda	170	Cd	6.28S	16.49 E
Kásos	130	Jn	35.25N	26.55 E
Kásou, Stenón-	130	Jn	35.25N	26.35 E
Kaspi	132	Ni	41.58N	44.25 E
Kaspičan	130	Kf	43.18N	27.11 E
Kaspijsk	136	Eg	42.57N	47.35 E
Kaspijski	136	Ef	45.25N	47.22 E
Kaspijskoje more = Caspian Sea (EN)	110	Lg	42.00N	50.30 E
Kasplja	132	Gb	55.24N	30.43 E
Kasr, Ra's-	168	Fb	18.04N	38.33 E
Kassaar/Kassar	116	Jf	58.47N	22.40 E
Kassalā	168	Fc	15.28N	36.24 E
Kassalā [3]	168	Fc	14.40N	35.30 E
Kassándra	130	Gi	40.00N	23.30 E
Kassándras, Ákra-	130	Gj	39.57N	23.21 E
Kassándras, Kólpos- = Kassandra, Gulf of- (EN)	130	Gi	40.05N	23.30 E
Kassel	120	Fe	51.19N	9.30 E
Kassiópi	130	Cj	39.47N	19.55 E
Kastamonu	144	Da	41.22N	33.47 E
Kastanéai	130	Jh	41.39N	26.28 E
Kastellaun	124	Jd	50.04N	7.27 E
Kastéllion [Grc.]	130	Gn	35.30N	23.39 E
Kastéllion [Grc.]	130	In	35.12N	25.20 E
Kastéllos, Ákra-	130	Kn	35.23N	27.09 E
Kasterlee	124	Gc	51.15N	4.57 E
Kastlösa	116	Gh	56.28N	16.25 E
Kastoria	130	Ei	40.31N	21.16 E
Kastorias, Limni-	130	Ei	40.31N	21.18 E
Kastornoje	132	Kd	51.51N	38.07 E
Kastós	130	Dk	38.35N	20.55 E
Kasuga	156	Be	33.32N	130.27 E
Kasugai	156	Ed	35.14N	136.58 E
Kasulu	170	Fc	4.34S	30.06 E
Kasumbalesa	170	Ee	12.13S	27.48 E
Kasumi	156	Dd	35.38N	134.38 E
Kasumi-ga-Ura	154	Pf	36.00N	140.25 E
Kasumkent	132	Pi	41.42N	48.10 E
Kasungan	150	Fg	1.58S	113.24 E
Kasungu	170	Fe	13.02S	33.29 E
Kasupe	170	Gf	15.10S	35.18 E
Kasūr	148	Eb	31.07N	74.27 E
Kaszuby	120	Ob	54.10N	18.15 E
Kataba	160	Jj	16.05S	25.10 E
Katahdin, Mount-	182	Nb	45.55N	68.55W
Katajsk	134	Kh	56.18N	62.35 E
Katako-Kombe	170	Dc	3.24S	24.25 E
Katanga	170	Ed	10.00S	25.30 E
Katanga	138	Fd	60.10N	102.10 E
Katangli	138	Jf	51.43N	143.16 E
Katanning	212	Df	33.42S	117.33 E
Katav-Ivanovsk	134	Ii	54.47N	58.15 E
Katchall	148	Ig	7.57N	93.22 E
Katchi	162	Ef	17.00N	13.55W
Katchiungo	170	Ce	12.33S	16.14 E
Katende, Chutes de-	170	Dd	6.30S	22.10 E
Katerini	130	Fi	40.16N	22.30 E
Katesh	170	Gc	4.31S	35.23 E
Katete	170	Fe	14.06S	32.05 E
Katha	148	Jd	24.11N	96.21 E
Katherine	210	Ef	14.28S	132.16 E
Katherine River	212	Gb	14.39S	131.42 E
Kāthiāwār	140	Jg	21.58N	70.30 E
Kāthmāndāū = Kathmandu (EN)	142	Kg	27.43N	85.19 E
Kathmandu → Kāthmāndāū	142	Kg	27.43N	85.19 E
Kathua	170	Gc	1.17S	39.03 E
Kati	166	Dc	12.43N	8.05W
Katihār	148	Hc	25.32N	87.35 E
Katiki, Volcán-	221d	Bb	27.06S	109.16W
Katima Mulilo	170	Df	17.28S	24.14 E
Katiola	166	Dd	8.08N	5.06W
Katiola [3]	166	Dd	8.13N	5.02W
Katiu Atoll	216	Mc	16.26S	144.22W
Katla	114a	Bc	63.36N	18.58W
Katlabuh, ozero-	130	Ld	45.25N	29.00 E
Katlanovo	130	Eh	41.54N	21.41 E
Katmai, Mount-	178	Ie	58.17N	154.56W
Káto Akhaia	130	Ek	38.09N	21.33 E
Katofio	170	Ee	11.02S	28.01 E
Katompi	170	Ed	6.11S	26.20 E
Katonga	170	Fb	0.10N	30.40 E
Katon-Karagaj	136	If	49.11N	85.37 E
Káto Ólimbos	130	Fj	39.55N	22.28 E
Katoomba	212	Kf	33.42S	150.18 E
Katopasa, Gunung-	150	Hg	1.14S	121.25 E
Katowice	112	He	50.16N	19.00 E
Katowice [2]	120	Of	50.15N	19.00 E
Katrancık Dağı	146	Dd	37.27N	30.25 E
Kātrīnā, Dayr- = Saint Catherine, Monastery of- (EN)	164	Fd	28.31N	33.57 E
Kātrīnā, Jabal-	158	Kf	28.31N	33.57 E
Katrineholm	114	Dg	59.00N	16.12 E
Katsina	160	Hg	13.00N	7.36 E
Katsina Ala	166	Gd	7.48N	8.52 E
Katsumoto	156	Jh	33.51N	129.42 E
Katsuta	154	Pf	36.24N	140.32 E
Katsuura	154	Pg	35.08N	140.18 E
Katsuyama [Jap.]	154	Nf	36.03N	136.30 E
Katsuyama [Jap.]	156	Cd	35.06N	133.41 E
Kattakurgan	136	Gh	39.55N	66.15 E
Kattavia	130	Kn	35.57N	27.46 E
Kattegat	110	Hd	57.00N	11.00 E
Katthammarsvik	116	Hg	57.26N	18.50 E
Katulo, Lagh-	170	Hb	2.08N	40.56 E
Katumbi	170	Fe	10.49S	33.32 E
Katun	140	Kd	52.25N	85.05 E
Katwijk aan Zee	122	Kb	52.13N	4.24 E
Katwijk aan Zee, Katwijk-	124	Gb	52.12N	4.25 E
Katzenelnbogen	124	Jd	50.17N	7.57 E
Kau	150	If	1.11N	127.54 E
Kauai Channel	214	Oc	21.45N	158.50W
Kauai Island	208	Lb	22.03N	159.30W
Kaub	124	Jd	50.05N	7.46 E
Kauehi Atoll	216	Lc	15.51S	145.09W
Kaufbeuren	120	Gi	47.53N	10.37 E
Kauhajoki	114	Fe	62.26N	22.11 E
Kauhava	114	Fe	63.06N	23.05 E
Kauiki Head	214	Oc	20.46N	155.59W
Kaukauna	186	Ld	44.17N	88.17W
Kaukauveld	158	Jk	20.30S	21.50 E
Kaukonen	114	Fc	67.29N	24.54 E
Kaukura Atoll	208	Mf	15.45S	146.42W
Kaula Island	208	Kb	21.40N	160.32W
Kaulakahi Channel	221a	Ba	22.02N	159.53W
Kaumalapau	221a	Ec	20.47N	156.59W
Kaunakakai	214	Oc	21.05N	157.02W
Kaunas	112	Ie	54.54N	23.54 E
Kaunasskoje vodohranilišče / Kauno marios	116	Kj	54.50N	24.15 E
Kauniainen/Grankulla	116	Kd	60.13N	24.45 E
Kauno marios / Kaunasskoje vodohranilišče	116	Kj	54.50N	24.15 E
Kaunos	130	Lm	36.50N	28.35 E
Kaupanger	114	Bf	61.11N	7.14 E
Kau Paulatmada, Gunung-	150	Ig	3.15S	126.09 E
Kaura Namoda	166	Gc	12.36N	6.35 E
Kauriāla Ghāt	148	Gc	28.27N	80.59 E
Kaušany	132	Ff	46.39N	29.25 E
Kaustinen	114	Fe	63.32N	23.42 E
Kautokeino	114	Fb	68.59N	23.08 E
Kavacık	130	Lj	39.40N	28.30 E
Kavadarci	130	Fh	41.26N	22.01 E
Kavaja	130	Ch	41.11N	19.33 E
Kavak [Tur.]	130	Ji	40.36N	26.54 E
Kavak [Tur.]	146	Gb	41.05N	36.03 E
Kavaklıdere	130	Ll	37.26N	28.22 E
Kavála	112	Ig	40.56N	24.25 E
Kavála, Kólpos-	130	Hi	40.52N	24.25 E
Kavalerovo	138	Ih	44.19N	135.05 E
Kavali	148	Ff	14.55N	79.59 E
Kavār	146	Oh	29.11N	52.44 E
Kavaratti	142	Jh	10.33N	72.38 E
Kavaratti Island	148	Ef	10.33N	72.38 E
Kavarna	130	Lf	43.25N	28.20 E
Kavarskas/Kovarskas	116	Ki	55.24N	25.03 E
Kavendou, Mont-	158	Fg	10.41N	12.12W
Kavieng	214	Eh	2.34S	150.48 E
Kavir, Dasht-e-	140	Hf	34.40N	54.30 E
Kavkaz	132	Jg	45.21N	36.12 E
Kavkaz, Bolšoj- = Caucasus (EN)	110	Kg	42.30N	45.00 E
Kävlinge	116	Ei	55.48N	13.06 E
Kävlingeån	116	Ei	55.47N	13.05 E
Kawa	168	Eb	19.10N	30.39 E
Kawabe	156	Gb	39.39N	140.15 E
Kawachi-nagano	156	Dd	34.27N	135.34 E
Kawagoe	156	Fd	35.55N	139.28 E
Kawaguchi	156	Fd	35.48N	139.42 E
Kawaihae Bay	221a	Fc	20.02N	155.51W
Kawaihoa Point	221a	Ab	21.47N	160.12W
Kawakawa	218	Fa	35.23S	174.04 E
Kawalusu, Pulau-	150	If	4.15N	125.19 E
Kawamata	156	Gc	37.40N	140.36 E
Kawambwa	170	Ed	9.47S	29.05 E
Kawaminami	156	Be	32.12N	131.32 E
Kawamoto	156	Cd	34.59N	132.29 E
Kawanishi	156	Gc	37.59N	140.03 E
Kawanoe	156	Cd	34.01N	133.34 E
Kawartha Lakes	184	Hc	44.32N	78.30W
Kawasaki [Jap.]	156	Gb	38.10N	140.38 E
Kawasaki [Jap.]	154	Og	35.32N	139.43 E
Kawashiri-Misaki	156	Bd	34.26N	130.58 E
Kawauchi	156a	Bc	41.12N	141.00 E
Kawau Island	218	Fb	36.25S	174.50 E
Kawaura	156	Be	32.21N	130.05 E
Kawerau	218	Gc	38.05S	176.42 E
Kawhia	218	Fc	38.04S	174.49 E
Kawich Range	188	Gh	37.40N	116.30W
Kawio, Kepulauan-	150	If	4.30N	125.30 E
Kawkareik	148	Je	16.33N	98.14 E
Kawm Umbū	164	Fe	24.28N	32.57 E
Kawthaung	148	Jg	9.59N	98.33 E
Kaxgar He	140	Jf	39.46N	78.15 E
Kax He	152	Dc	43.37N	81.48 E
Kaya	166	Ec	13.05N	1.05W
Kayah [2]	148	Je	19.15N	97.30 E
Kayak Island	178	Ke	59.52N	144.30W
Kayalı Dağı	130	Jj	39.58N	26.38 E
Kayan	140	Ni	2.55N	117.35 E
Kayanga	166	Cc	11.58N	15.00W
Kayangel Islands	208	Ed	8.04N	134.43 E
Kayangel Passage	220a	Ba	8.01N	134.42 E
Kaycee	188	Le	43.43N	106.38W
Kayenta	188	Jh	36.44N	110.17W
Kayes	160	Fg	14.26N	11.27W
Kayes [3]	166	Cc	14.00N	11.00W
Kayin	148	Je	17.30N	97.45 E
Kayoa, Pulau-	150	Ig	0.05S	127.25 E
Kayseri	142	Ff	38.43N	35.30 E
Kayuagung	150	Dg	3.24S	104.50 E
Kayu Ara, Pulau-	150	Ef	1.31N	106.26 E
Kazačje	138	Ib	70.40N	136.13 E
Kazah	132	Ni	41.05N	45.22 E
Kazahskaja Sovetskaja Socialističeskaja Respublika [2]	136	Gf	48.00N	68.00 E
Kazahskaja SSR/Kazak Sovettik Socialistik Respublikasy [2]	136	Gf	48.00N	68.00 E
Kazahskaja SSR = Kazakh SSR (EN) [2]	136	Gf	48.00N	68.00 E
Kazahskij melkosopočnik = Kazakh Hills (EN)	140	Je	49.00N	73.00 E
Kazahskij zaliv	132	Rh	42.40N	52.25 E
Kazakh Hills (EN) = Kazahskij melkosopočnik	140	Je	49.00N	73.00 E
Kazakh SSR (EN) = Kazahskaja SSR [2]	136	Gf	48.00N	68.00 E
Kazakhstan (EN)	140	Hd	51.11N	52.52 E
Kazaklija	130	Lc	46.05N	28.38 E
Kazak Sovettik Socialistik Respublikasy [2]	136	Gf	48.00N	68.00 E
Kazalak	130	Ke	44.03N	27.24 E
Kazalinsk	136	Gf	45.46N	62.07 E
Kazan	112	Kd	55.45N	49.08 E
Kazan	174	Jc	64.02N	95.30W
Kazandžik	136	Fh	39.17N	55.34 E
Kazanka	132	Hf	47.50N	32.49 E
Kazanka	114	Li	55.48N	49.05 E
Kazanlăk	130	Ig	42.37N	25.24 E
Kazan-Rettō/Iō = Volcano Islands (EN)	140	Qg	25.00N	141.00 E
Kazanskoje	136	Gd	55.38N	69.14 E
Kazarman	136	Hg	41.20N	74.02 E
Kazatin	136	Cf	49.43N	28.50 E
Kazbegi	132	Nh	42.39N	44.39 E
Kazbek, gora-	110	Kg	42.42N	44.31 E
Kaz Dağı [Tur.]	130	Mk	38.35N	29.15 E
Kaz Dağı [Tur.]	144	Cb	39.42N	26.50 E
Kāzerūn	144	Hd	29.37N	51.38 E
Kažim	134	Ef	60.20N	51.32 E
Kazi-Magomed	132	Pi	40.02N	48.56 E
Kazimierza Wielka	120	Qf	50.16N	20.30 E
Kâzımkarabekir	146	Ed	37.14N	32.59 E
Kazincbarcika	120	Qh	48.15N	20.38 E
Kazinga Channel	170	Ec	0.13S	29.53 E
Kazlų-Rūda/Kazlu-Ruda	116	Jj	54.42N	23.32 E
Kazlu-Ruda/Kazlų-Rūda	116	Jj	54.42N	23.32 E
Kazo	156	Fc	36.08N	139.36 E
Kaztalovka	132	Pe	49.46N	48.44 E
Kazumba	170	Dd	6.25S	22.02 E
Kazuno	154	Pd	40.14N	140.48 E
Kazym	136	Gc	63.54N	65.50 E
Kazyr	138	Ef	53.50N	92.53 E
Kcynia	120	Nd	53.00N	17.30 E
Kdyně	120	Ig	49.24N	13.02 E
Ké	168	Bb	18.32N	17.55 E
Kéa	130	Hl	37.39N	24.20 E
Kéa	130	Hl	37.37N	24.20 E
Keaau	221a	Fd	19.37N	155.03W
Keahole Point	221a	Ed	19.44N	156.04W
Kealaikahiki Channel	221a	Ec	20.37N	156.50W
Kealaikahiki Point	221a	Ec	20.32N	156.42W
Kealakekua Bay	221a	Fd	19.28N	155.56W
Keams Canyon	188	Ji	35.49N	110.12W
Keanae	221a	Ec	20.52N	156.09W
Keanapapa Point	221a	Dc	20.54N	157.04W
Kearney	182	Hc	40.42N	99.05W
Kearns	188	Jf	40.39N	111.59W
Kéas, Stenón-	130	Hl	37.40N	24.12 E
Keats Bank (EN)	208	Id	5.23N	173.28 E
Keb	116	Mg	57.44N	28.38 E
Keban Baraji	146	Hc	38.53N	39.00 E
Kébémer	166	Bb	15.22N	16.27W
Kebir, Oued el-	128	Bn	36.51N	7.57 E
Kebnekaise	110	Hb	67.53N	18.33 E
Kebri Dehar	160	Lh	6.45N	44.17 E
Kebumen	150	Eh	7.40S	109.39 E
Kecel	120	Pj	46.32N	19.16 E
Kechika	180	Ee	59.38N	127.09W
Kecskemét	120	Pj	46.54N	19.42 E
Kedah [2]	150	De	6.00N	100.40 E
Kėdainiai/Kedajnjaj	114	Fi	55.18N	23.59 E
Kedajnjaj/Kėdainiai	114	Fi	55.18N	23.59 E
Kedgwick	184	Nb	47.39N	67.21W
Kediri	142	Nj	7.49S	112.01 E
Kédougou	166	Cc	12.33N	12.11W
Kedva	134	Fd	64.14N	53.30 E
Kędzierzyn-Koźle	120	Of	50.20N	18.10 E
Keele	180	Fd	64.24N	124.47W
Keele Peak	174	Fc	63.26N	130.19W
Keeling Islands → Cocos Islands [5]	142	Lk	12.10S	96.55 E
Keeling Islands → Cocos Islands	140	Lk	12.10S	96.55 E
Keelung	142	Og	25.08N	121.44 E
Keene	184	Kd	42.55N	72.17W
Keer-Weer, Cape-	212	Ib	13.58S	141.30 E
Keetmanshoop	160	Ik	26.36S	18.08 E
Keetmanshoop [3]	172	Be	26.30S	18.30 E
Keewatin	180	Ig	49.46N	94.34W
Kefa [3]	168	Fd	7.00N	36.00 E
Kefallinia = Cephalonia (EN)	110	Ih	38.15N	20.35 E
Kefamenanu	150	Hh	9.27S	124.29 E
Kefar Sava	146	Ff	32.10N	34.54 E
Keffi	166	Gd	8.51N	7.52 E
Keflavík	114a	Ab	64.01N	22.34W
Kegen	136	Hg	42.58N	79.12 E
Kegums	116	Kh	56.41N	24.44 E
Kehdingen	120	Fc	53.45N	9.20 E
Kehl	120	Dh	48.35N	7.49 E
Kehra	114	Fg	59.19N	25.18 E
Keighley	118	Lh	53.52N	1.54W
Keila/Kejla	114	Fg	59.19N	24.27 E
Keila jõgi / Kejla	116	Ke	59.25N	24.15 E
Keimoes	172	Ce	28.41S	21.00 E
Keipel Bank (EN)	212	Le	25.15S	159.30 E
Keita	166	Gc	14.46N	5.46 E
Keita, Bahr-	168	Bd	9.14N	18.21 E
Keitele	110	Ic	62.55N	26.00 E
Keith [Austl.]	212	Ig	36.06S	140.21 E
Keith [Scot.-U.K.]	118	Kd	57.32N	2.57W
Keith Arm	180	Fc	65.20N	122.00W
Keiyasi	219d	Ab	17.53S	177.45 E
Kejla/Keila	114	Fg	59.19N	24.27 E
Kejla / Keila jõgi	116	Ke	59.25N	24.15 E
Kejvy	114	Ic	67.30N	37.45 E
Kekaha	221a	Bb	21.58N	159.43W
Kekerengu	218	Ee	42.00S	174.00 E
Kékes	120	Qi	47.52N	20.01 E
Keklau	220a	Bb	7.35N	134.39 E
Kelafo	168	Gd	5.37N	44.13 E
Kelakam	166	Hc	13.35N	11.44 E
Kela Met	168	Fb	15.50N	38.23 E
Kelan	152	Jd	38.44N	111.34 E
Kelang	142	Mi	3.02N	101.27 E
Kelantan [2]	150	De	5.20N	102.00 E
Kelasa, Selat- = Gaspar Strait (EN)	150	Eg	2.40S	107.15 E
Kelberg	124	Id	50.18N	6.55 E
Kelcyra	130	Di	40.19N	20.11 E
Kelefesia	221b	Bb	20.30S	174.44W
Kelekçi	130	Ml	37.14N	29.28 E
Kelem	168	Fe	4.49N	35.59 E
Keles	130	Mj	39.55N	29.14 E
Keles	135	Gd	41.02N	68.37 E
Kelheim	120	Hh	48.55N	11.52 E
Kelifely, Causse du-	172	Hc	17.15S	45.30 E
Kelifskij uzboj	135	Ef	37.45N	64.40 E
Keli Hāji Ibrāhim	146	Kd	36.42N	45.00 E
Kelkheim	124	Kd	50.08N	8.27 E
Kelkit	146	Hb	40.08N	39.27 E
Kelkit	144	Ea	36.32N	40.46 E
Kellé	170	Bc	0.06S	14.33 E
Kellerberrin	212	Df	31.38S	117.43 E
Kellerwald	120	Fe	51.03N	9.10 E
Kellett, Cape-	180	Eb	72.57N	125.27W
Kellett Strait	180	Fa	75.50N	117.40W
Kellog	138	Dd	62.27N	86.35 E
Kellogg	182	Db	47.32N	116.07W
Kelloselkä	114	Gc	66.56N	29.00 E
Kells/Ceanannas Mór	118	Gh	53.44N	6.53W
Kelmė/Kelme	114	Fi	55.39N	22.58 E
Kelme/Kelmė	114	Fi	55.39N	22.58 E
Kelmency	130	Ja	48.27N	26.47 E
Kelmis/La Calamine	124	Hd	50.43N	6.00 E
Kélo	168	Bd	9.15N	15.48 E
Kelowna	176	He	49.53N	119.29W
Kelsey	180	He	56.00N	97.00W
Kelsey Bay	180	Ef	50.24N	125.57W
Kelso	188	Dc	46.09N	122.54W
Kelso Bank (EN)	212	Ld	24.10S	159.30 E
Kel Tepe [Tur.]	146	Eb	41.05N	32.27 E
Kel Tepe [Tur.]	130	Ni	40.39N	30.06 E
Keltie, Mount-	222	Jf	79.15S	159.00 E
Keluang	150	Df	2.02N	103.19 E
Kelvin Seamount (EN)	182	Od	38.50N	64.00W
Kelyeḥed	168	Hd	8.44N	49.10 E
Kem	136	Dc	64.57N	34.31 E
Kema	114	If	60.19N	37.15 E
Ké Macina	166	Dc	13.57N	5.23W
Kemah	146	Hc	39.36N	39.02 E
Kemaliye	146	Hc	39.16N	38.29 E
Kemalpaşa	130	Kk	38.25N	27.26 E
Kemalpaşa	146	Cc	40.00N	28.20 E
Kembé	168	Ce	4.36N	21.54 E
Kemer [Tur.]	146	Dd	36.36N	30.34 E
Kemer [Tur.]	130	Mm	36.28N	29.21 E
Kemer Barajı	130	Ll	37.30N	28.35 E
Kemeri/Ķemeri	116	Jh	56.56N	23.25 E
Ķemeri/Kemeri	116	Jh	56.56N	23.25 E
Kemerovo	142	Kd	55.20N	86.05 E
Kemerovskaja oblast [3]	138	De	55.00N	87.00 E
Kemi	112	Ib	65.44N	24.34 E
Kemi, Lake- (EN) = Kemijärvi	114	Gc	66.36N	27.24 E
Kemijärvi	114	Gc	66.40N	27.25 E
Kemijärvi = Kemi, Lake- (EN)	114	Gc	66.36N	27.24 E
Kemijoki	110	Ib	65.47N	24.30 E
Kemiö/Kimito	116	Jd	60.10N	22.40 E
Kemlja	114	Ki	54.43N	45.15 E
Kemmerer	188	Jf	41.48N	110.32W
Kémo-Gribingui [3]	168	Bd	6.00N	19.00 E
Kemp, Lake-	186	Gj	33.45N	99.13W
Kempaž	134	Jd	64.03N	61.02 E
Kempele	114	Fd	64.55N	25.30 E
Kempen	124	Ic	51.22N	6.25 E
Kempen/Campine	122	Lc	51.10N	5.20 E
Kempendjaj	138	Gd	62.02N	118.42 E
Kempenich	124	Jd	50.25N	7.08 E
Kemp Land	222	Ee	67.10S	58.00 E
Kemps Bay	194	Ia	24.02N	77.33W
Kempsey	212	Kf	31.05S	152.50 E
Kempston	124	Bb	52.06N	0.29W
Kempt, Lac-	184	Kg	47.25N	74.15W
Kempten/Allgäu	120	Gi	47.43N	10.19 E
Ken	148	Hc	25.46N	80.31 E
Ken, Loch-	118	If	55.02N	4.02W
Kena	114	Je	62.06N	39.05 E
Kenadsa	162	Gc	31.34N	2.26W
Kenai	176	Dc	60.33N	151.15W
Kenai Mountains	178	Ie	60.00N	150.00W
Kenai Peninsula	174	Ed	60.10N	150.00W
Kendal	118	Kg	54.20N	2.45W
Kendall	184	Gm	25.41N	80.19W
Kendall, Cape-	180	Id	63.36N	87.13W
Kendallville	184	Ee	41.27N	85.16W
Kendari	142	Oj	3.57S	122.35 E
Kendawangan	150	Fg	2.32S	110.12 E
Kenema	160	Fh	7.52N	11.12W
Kenge	160	Ii	4.52S	16.59 E
Kengere	170	Ee	11.10S	25.28 E
Keng Tung	148	Jd	21.17N	99.36 E
Kenhardt	172	Ce	29.19S	21.12 E
Kéniéba	166	Cc	12.50N	11.14W
Keningau	150	Ge	5.20N	116.10 E
Kenitra	160	Ge	34.16N	6.36W
Kenitra [3]	162	Fc	34.00N	6.00W
Kenli (Xishuanghe)	154	Ef	37.35N	118.30 E
Kenmare	182	Gb	48.40N	102.05W
Kenmare/Neidin	118	Dj	51.53N	9.35W
Kenmare River/An Ribhéar	118	Dj	51.50N	9.50W
Kennebunk	184	Ld	43.23N	70.33W
Kennedy Peak	148	Id	23.19N	93.46 E
Kennedy Range	212	Cd	24.30S	115.00 E
Kenner	186	Ki	29.59N	90.15W
Kennet	118	Mj	51.28N	0.57W
Kennett	186	Kh	36.14N	90.03W
Kennewick	188	Fc	46.12N	119.07W
Kennington	124	Cc	51.09N	0.53 E
Kenn Reef	208	Gg	21.10S	155.50 E
Kénogami	184	La	48.26N	71.14W
Kénogami, Lac-	184	La	48.21N	71.28W
Kenogami River	180	Jf	51.06N	84.29W
Keno Hill	180	Dd	63.54N	135.18W
Kenora	176	Je	49.47N	94.29W
Kenosha	182	Jc	42.35N	87.49W
Kent [3]	118	Nj	51.20N	0.55 E
Kent	118	Nj	51.10N	0.55 E
Kent [S.L.]	166	Cd	8.10N	13.10W
Kent [Wa.-U.S.]	188	Dc	47.23N	122.14W
Kent, Vale of-	118	Nj	51.10N	0.30 E
Kentau	136	Gg	43.32N	68.33 E
Kent Group	212	Jg	39.30S	147.20 E
Kenton	184	Fe	40.38N	83.38W
Kent Peninsula	180	Gc	68.30N	107.00W
Kentucky [2]	182	Jd	37.30N	85.15W
Kentucky Lake	182	Jd	36.25N	88.05W
Kentucky River	184	Ef	38.41N	85.11W
Kenya [1]	160	Kh	1.00N	38.00 E
Kenya, Mount-/Kirinyaga	158	Ki	0.10S	37.20 E
Keokea	221a	Ec	20.42N	156.21W
Keokuk	182	Ic	40.24N	91.24W
Keonjhargarh	148	Hd	21.38N	85.35 E
Keowee, Lake-	184	Fh	34.55N	82.50W
Kepe	114	Hd	65.09N	32.08 E
Kepi	150	Kh	6.32S	139.19 E
Kępno	120	Ne	51.17N	17.59 E
Kepsut	146	Cc	39.41N	28.09 E
Kerala [3]	148	Ff	11.00N	76.30 E
Kerama-Rettō	156b	Ab	26.10N	127.15 E
Kerang	212	Ig	35.44S	143.55 E
Keratéa	130	Gl	37.48N	23.59 E
Kerava/Kervo	116	Kd	60.24N	25.07 E
Kerč	112	Jf	45.22N	36.27 E
Kerčenski poluostrov	132	Ig	45.15N	36.00 E
Kerdhilion Óros	130	Gi	40.47N	23.39 E
Kerema	214	Di	7.58S	145.46 E
Keren	168	Fb	15.47N	38.27 E
Keret, ozero-	114	Hd	65.50N	32.50 E
Kerewan	166	Bc	13.29N	16.06W
Kerguelen	158	Nm	49.20S	69.30 E
Kerguelen, Iles-	158	Nm	49.15S	69.10 E
Kerguelen Plateau (EN)	106	Go	55.00S	75.00 E
Kericho	170	Gc	0.22S	35.17 E
Keri Kera	168	Ec	12.21N	32.46 E
Kerimäki	116	Mc	61.55N	29.17 E
Kerinci, Gunung-	140	Mj	1.42S	101.16 E
Kerio	158	Kh	2.59N	36.07 E
Kerion	130	Dl	37.40N	20.49 E
Keriya/Yutian	142	Kf	36.52N	81.42 E
Keriya He	152	Dd	38.30N	82.10 E
Keriya Shankou	152	Dd	35.12N	81.44 E
Kerka	120	Mj	46.28N	16.36 E
Kerken	124	Ic	51.27N	6.26 E
Kerkennah Islands (EN) = Qarqannah, Juzur-	158	Ie	34.44N	11.12 E
Kerketevs Óros	130	Jl	37.44N	26.38 E
Kerki	136	Gh	37.50N	65.13 E
Kerkíni Óros	130	Fh	41.21N	22.50 E
Kérkira	130	Cj	39.36N	19.55 E
Kérkira = Corfu (EN)	110	Hh	39.40N	19.45 E
Kerkiras, Stenón- = Corfu, Strait of- (EN)	130	Dj	39.35N	20.05 E
Kerkrade	124	Id	50.52N	6.04 E
Kerma (EN) = Karmah	168	Eb	19.38N	30.25 E
Kermadec Islands	208	Jh	30.00S	178.30W
Kermadec Ridge (EN)	208	Jh	30.30S	178.30W
Kermadec Trench (EN)	106	Km	30.00S	177.00W
Kermajärvi	116	Mb	62.30N	28.40 E
Kermān	142	Hf	30.17N	57.05 E
Kermān [3]	144	Ic	30.50N	57.50 E
Kermānshāhān	146	Pg	31.17N	54.55 E
Kerme	130	Kl	37.02N	28.00 E
Kerme Körfezi	146	Bd	36.50N	28.00 E
Kermit	186	Ek	31.51N	103.06W
Kern River	188	Fi	35.13N	119.17W
Kérouané	166	Dd	9.16N	9.01W
Kerpen	124	Id	50.52N	6.41 E
Kerrobert	180	Gf	51.55N	109.08W
Kerrville	182	He	30.03N	99.08W
Kerry/Ciarrai [2]	118	Di	52.10N	9.30W
Kerry, Mountains of-	118	Dj	51.55N	9.50W
Kertamulya	150	Eg	0.23N	109.09 E
Kerteh	150	Df	4.31N	103.27 E
Kerteminde	116	Di	55.27N	10.40 E
Kerulen (Cherlen)	140	Ne	48.48N	117.00 E
Kervo/Kerava	116	Kd	60.24N	25.07 E
Kerzaz	162	Gd	29.27N	1.25W
Keržeenec	114	Kh	56.04N	45.01 E
Kesagami Lake	180	Jf	50.23N	80.10W
Kesälahti	116	Mc	61.54N	29.50 E
Keşan	144	Ca	40.51N	26.37 E
Keşap	146	Hb	40.55N	38.31 E
Kesen'numa	154	Pe	38.54N	141.35 E
Kesen'numa-Wan	156	Gb	38.50N	141.35 E
Keshan	152	Mb	48.04N	125.51 E
Keskastel	124	Jf	48.58N	7.02 E
Keskin	146	Ec	39.41N	33.37 E
Keski-Suomi [2]	114	Fe	62.30N	25.30 E
Kestenga	114	Hd	65.53N	31.45 E
Keswick	118	Jg	54.37N	3.08W
Keszthely	120	Nj	46.46N	17.15 E
Ket	140	Kd	58.55N	81.32 E
Kéta	166	Fd	5.55N	0.59 E

Index Symbols

- [1] Independent Nation
- [2] State, Region
- [3] District, County
- [4] Municipality
- [5] Colony, Dependency
- Continent
- Physical Region
- Historical or Cultural Region
- Mount, Mountain
- Volcano
- Hill
- Mountains, Mountain Range
- Hills, Escarpment
- Plateau, Upland
- Pass, Gap
- Plain, Lowland
- Delta
- Salt Flat
- Valley, Canyon
- Crater, Cave
- Karst Features
- Depression
- Polder
- Desert, Dunes
- Forest, Woods
- Heath, Steppe
- Oasis
- Cape, Point
- Coast, Beach
- Cliff
- Peninsula
- Isthmus
- Sandbank
- Island
- Atoll
- Rock, Reef
- Islands, Archipelago
- Rocks, Reefs
- Coral Reef
- Well, Spring
- Geyser
- River, Stream
- Waterfall, Rapids
- River Mouth, Estuary
- Lake
- Salt Lake
- Intermittent Lake
- Reservoir
- Swamp, Pond
- Canal
- Glacier
- Ice Shelf, Pack Ice
- Ocean
- Sea
- Gulf, Bay
- Strait, Fjord
- Lagoon
- Bank
- Seamount
- Tablemount
- Ridge
- Shelf
- Basin
- Escarpment, Sea Scarp
- Fracture
- Trench, Abyss
- National Park, Reserve
- Point of Interest
- Recreation Site
- Cave, Cavern
- Historic Site
- Ruins
- Wall, Walls
- Church, Abbey
- Temple
- Scientific Station
- Railway station
- Airport
- Port
- Military installation
- Lighthouse
- Mine
- Tunnel
- Dam, Bridge

Keta, ozero- 138 Dc 68.45N 90.00 E
Ketanda 138 Jd 60.38N 141.30 E
Ketapang 142 Mj 1.52S 109.59 E
Ketchikan 176 Fd 55.21N 131.35W
Ketchum 182 Ec 43.41N 114.22W
Ketchum Mountain 186 Fk 31.15N 101.00W
Kete Krachi 166 Ed 7.46N 0.03W
Ketelmeer 124 Hb 52.35N 5.45 E
Ketli, Jbel- 126 Gi 35.22N 5.17W
Ketmen, hrebet- 135 Lc 43.20N 80.00 E
Kétou 166 Fd 7.22N 2.36 E
Kętrzyn 120 Rb 54.06N 21.23 E
Kettering [Eng.-U.K.] 118 Mi 52.24N 0.44W
Kettering [Oh.-U.S.] 184 Ef 39.41N 84.10W
Kettle River 188 Fb 48.42N 118.07W
Kettle River Range 188 Fb 48.30N 118.40W
Keuka Lake 184 Id 42.27N 77.10W
Keur Massène 162 Df 16.33N 16.14W
Keuruu 114 Fe 62.16N 24.42 E
Keuruunselkä 116 Kb 62.10N 24.40 E
Kevelaer 124 Ic 51.35N 6.15 E
Kew 194 Kc 21.54N 72.02W
Kewanee 182 Jc 41.14N 89.56W
Keweenaw Bay 184 Cb 46.56N 88.23W
Keweenaw Peninsula 182 Jb 47.12N 88.25W
Key, Lough-/Loch Ce 118 Eg 54.00N 8.15W
Keya Paha River 186 Ge 42.54N 99.00W
Keyhole Reservoir 188 Md 44.21N 104.51W
Key Largo 184 Gm 25.04N 80.28W
Keystone Lake 186 Hh 36.15N 96.25W
Key West 176 Kg 24.33N 81.48W
Kez 114 Mh 57.56N 53.43 E
Kezi 172 Dd 20.55S 28.29 E
Kežma 138 Fe 59.02N 101.09 E
Kežmarok 120 Qg 49.08N 20.25 E
Kgalagadi [3] 172 Ce 25.00S 22.00 E
Kgatleng [3] 172 Dd 24.28S 26.05 E
Kghoti 172 Cd 24.55S 21.59 E
Khabr, Kūh-e- 144 Id 28.50N 56.26 E
Khābūr, Nahr al- 146 Ie 35.08N 40.26 E
Khadari, Wādī al- 168 Dc 10.29N 27.00 E
Khādim, Shūshat al- 146 Bh 28.35N 27.43 E
Khadki (Kirkee) 148 Ee 18.34N 73.52 E
Khadra 126 Mh 36.15N 0.35 E
Khafs Banbān 146 Lj 25.31N 46.27 E
Khairōnia 130 Fk 38.30N 22.51 E
Khairpur 148 Dc 27.32N 68.46 E
Khāiz, Kūh-e- 146 Ng 30.27N 50.55 E
Khakhea 172 Cd 24.42S 23.30 E
Khalatse 148 Fb 34.20N 76.49 E
Khálki 130 Km 36.13N 27.37 E
Khálki 130 Km 36.14N 27.36 E
Khalkidhiki=Chalcidice (EN) 110 Ig 40.25N 23.25 E
Khalkis 130 Gk 38.28N 23.36 E
Khaluf 144 Ie 20.29N 57.59 E
Khambhāt 148 Ed 22.18N 72.37 E
Khambhāt, Gulf of- 140 Jg 21.00N 72.30 E
Khāmgaon 148 Fd 20.41N 76.34 E
Khamili 130 Jn 35.52N 26.14 E
Khamir 144 Ff 15.59N 43.57 E
Khāmis, Ash Shallāl al-=Fifth Cataract (EN) 158 Kg 18.23N 33.47 E
Khamis Mushayt 144 Ff 18.18N 42.44 E
Khammam 148 Ge 17.15N 80.09 E
Khamseh 146 Md 36.40N 48.50 E
Khān 146 Oj 24.13N 56.20 E
Khan 172 Ad 22.42S 14.54 E
Khānābād 144 Kb 36.41N 69.07 E
Khān al Baghdādī 146 Jf 33.51N 42.33 E
Khān al Hammād 146 Kf 32.19N 44.17 E
Khānaqīn 144 Gc 34.21N 45.22 E
Khān az Zabīb 146 Gg 31.28N 36.06 E
Khandwa 148 Fd 21.50N 76.20 E
Khāneh Sorkh, Gardaneh-ye- 146 Qh 29.49N 56.06 E
Khānewāl 148 Eb 30.18N 71.56 E
Khangai Mountains (EN) = Changajn Nuruu 140 Le 47.30N 100.00 E
Khánia 112 Ih 35.31N 24.02 E
Khanion, Kólpos- 130 Gn 35.35N 23.50 E
Khanka, Lake- (EN) = Hanka, ozero- 140 Pe 45.00N 132.24 E
Khanka Lake (EN)=Xingkai Hu 140 Pe 45.00N 132.24 E
Khānpur 148 Ec 28.39N 70.39 E
Khān Shaykhūn 146 Ge 35.26N 36.38 E
Khan Takhtī 146 Kc 38.09N 44.55 E
Khān Yūnus 146 Fg 31.21N 34.19 E
Khānzīr, Rās- 168 Hc 10.50N 45.50 E
Khao Laem 148 Kf 14.19N 101.11 E
Khao Miang 148 Ke 17.42N 101.01 E
Khao Mokochu 148 Je 15.56N 99.06 E
Khao Saming 148 Kf 12.16N 102.26 E
Khar 146 Me 35.53N 48.55 E
Kharagpur 142 Kg 22.20N 87.20 E
Khárakas 130 In 35.01N 25.07 E
Khārān 146 Qh 28.55N 57.09 E
Kharānaq 146 Pf 32.20N 54.39 E
Kharānaq, Kūh-e- 146 Pf 32.10N 54.39 E
Kharga Oasis (EN) = Khārijah, Wāḥāt al- 158 Kf 25.20N 30.35 E
Khārijah, Wāḥāt al-=Kharga Oasis (EN) 158 Kf 25.20N 30.35 E
Kharīt, Wādī al- 146 Ej 24.26N 33.03 E
Kharīṭah, Shiqqat al- 164 If 17.10N 47.50 E
Khārk 146 Nh 29.15N 50.20 E
Khārk, Jazīreh-ye- 146 Nh 29.15N 50.20 E
Khār Kūh 146 Og 31.39N 53.46 E
Kharmān, Kūh-e- 144 Hd 29.13N 53.35 E
Kharshah, Qārat al- 146 Bg 30.35N 27.25 E
Khartoum (EN) = Al Kharṭūm 160 Kg 15.36N 32.32 E
Khartoum (EN) = Al Kharṭūm [3] 168 Eb 15.50N 33.00 E
Khartoum North (EN) Al Kharṭūm Baḥrī 160 Kg 15.38N 32.33 E
Khāsh 144 Jc 31.31N 62.52 E
Khāsh 144 Jc 31.11N 62.05 E
Khashm al Qirbah 168 Fc 14.58N 35.55 E
Khāsi Jaintia 140 Lg 25.35N 91.38 E
Khatikhon, Yam-=Mediterranean Sea (EN) 110 Hh 35.00N 20.00 E
Khaṭṭ 164 Dd 28.40N 22.40 E
Khātūn, Kūh-e- 146 Og 30.25N 53.38 E
Khawr al Fakkān 146 Qk 25.21N 56.22 E
Khawr āl Juḥaysh 168 Ia 20.36N 50.59 E
Khawr al Mufattaḥ 146 Mh 28.40N 48.25 E
Khawr Umm Qasr 146 Lg 30.02N 47.56 E
Khay' 144 Ff 18.45N 41.24 E
Khaybar 144 Ed 25.42N 39.31 E
Khaybar, Ḥarrat- 146 Hj 25.30N 39.45 E
Khazzī, Qārat- 158 Jf 21.26N 24.30 E
Khemis 126 Qh 36.10N 4.04 E
Khemis Anjra 126 Gi 35.41N 5.32W
Khémis Beni Arouss 126 Gi 35.19N 5.38W
Khemis Miliana 162 Hb 36.16N 2.13 E
Khemisset 162 Fc 33.49N 6.04W
Khemisset [3] 162 Fc 33.49N 6.00W
Khemmarat 148 Ke 16.03N 105.11 E
Khenchela 162 Ib 35.26N 7.08 E
Khenifra 162 Fc 32.56N 5.40W
Khenifra [3] 162 Fc 33.00N 5.08W
Kherāmeh 146 Oh 29.32N 53.21 E
Khersan 146 Ng 31.33N 50.22 E
Khersónisos Akrotiri 130 Hn 35.35N 24.10 E
Kheyrābād [Iran] 146 Ph 29.26N 55.19 E
Kheyrābād [Iran] 146 Mg 31.49N 48.23 E
Khionótripa 130 Hh 41.18N 24.05 E
Khios 130 Jk 38.22N 26.08 E
Khios=Chios (EN) 110 Ih 38.22N 26.00 E
Khirbat Isrīyah 146 Ge 35.21N 37.46 E
Khirr, Nahr al- 146 Kf 33.17N 44.21 E
Khlomón Óros 130 Fk 38.36N 23.00 E
Khlong Yai 148 Kf 11.46N 102.53 E
Khokhropār 148 Ec 25.42N 70.12 E
Khok Kloi 148 Jg 8.17N 98.19 E
Khok Samrong 148 Ke 15.03N 100.44 E
Kholm 144 Kb 36.42N 67.41 E
Khomām 146 Md 37.22N 49.40 E
Khomas Highland (EN)=Khomas Hochland 158 Ik 22.40S 16.20 E
Khomas Hochland=Khomas Highland (EN) 158 Ik 22.40S 16.20 E
Khomeyn 146 Nf 33.38N 50.04 E
Khomeynīshahr 146 Nf 32.42N 51.27 E
Khonj 146 Oi 27.52N 53.27 E
Khon Kaen 148 Ke 16.26N 102.50 E
Khonsār 146 Nf 33.21N 50.19 E
Khóra 130 Ei 37.03N 21.43 E
Khor Anghar 168 Gc 12.27N 43.16 E
Khorāsān [3] 144 Ic 35.00N 58.00 E
Khorāsān 140 Hf 34.00N 56.00 E
Khorāsānī, Godār-e 146 Qg 30.44N 57.03 E
Khóra Sfakion 130 Hn 35.12N 24.09 E
Khorat Plateau 140 Mh 15.30N 102.50 E
Khormūj, Kūh-e- 146 Nh 28.43N 51.22 E
Khorof Harar 170 Hb 2.14N 40.44 E
Khorramābād 144 Gc 33.30N 48.20 E
Khorramshahr 144 Gc 30.25N 48.11 E
Khorsābād 146 Jd 36.38N 43.17 E
Khoshyeylāq 146 Pd 36.53N 55.15 E
Khosrowābād 146 Mg 30.00N 48.25 E
Khosrowshāh 146 Ld 37.57N 46.03 E
Khouribga 162 Fc 32.53N 6.54W
Khouribga [3] 162 Fc 32.56N 6.36W
Khowst 144 Kc 33.22N 69.57 E
Khrisí 130 Io 34.52N 25.42 E
Khrisoúpolis 130 Hi 40.59N 24.42 E
Khristianá 130 Im 36.14N 25.13 E
Khu Dağı 146 Jc 38.35N 43.40 E
Khuff [Lib.] 164 Cd 28.17N 18.20 E
Khuff [Sau.Ar.] 144 Ed 25.20N 37.20 E
Khulna 142 Kg 22.48N 89.33 E
Khūrān 146 Pi 26.50N 55.40 E
Khurays 144 Gd 25.05N 48.02 E
Khurayt 168 Dc 13.57N 26.02 E
Khurīyā Murīyā, Jazā'ir-=Kuria Muria Islands (EN) 140 Hh 17.30N 56.00 E
Khurr, Wādī al- 146 Jg 30.52N 42.10 E
Khursaniyah 146 Mi 27.18N 49.16 E
Khūshābar 146 Md 37.59N 48.54 E
Khutse 172 Cd 23.20S 24.34 E
Khuwayy 168 Dc 13.05N 29.14 E
Khuzdār 148 Dc 27.48N 66.37 E
Khūzestān [3] 144 Gc 32.00N 48.30 E
Khūzestān 146 Gf 30.33N 50.00 E
Khvojeh Lāk, Kūh-e- 146 Le 35.43N 46.29 E
Khvor 146 Pf 33.47N 55.03 E
Khvorāsgān 146 Nf 32.39N 51.45 E
Khvormūj 146 Nh 28.39N 51.23 E
Khvoshkūh 146 Qi 27.37N 56.41 E
Khvoy 146 Kc 38.33N 44.58 E
Khyber Pass 148 Eb 34.05N 71.10 E
Kia 219a Db 7.32S 158.26 E
Kia 219d Bb 16.14S 179.05 E
Kiamba 150 He 5.59N 124.37 E
Kiambi 170 Ed 7.20S 28.01 E
Kiamichi River 186 Ij 33.57N 95.14W
Kiangarow, Mount- 212 Ke 26.49S 151.33 E
Kiangsi (EN) = Jiangxi Sheng (Chiang-hsi Sheng) [2] 152 Kf 26.00N 116.00 E
Kiangsu (EN)=Chiang-su Sheng→Jiangsu Sheng [2] 152 Ke 33.00N 120.00 E
Kiangsu (EN)=Jiangsu Sheng (Chiang-su Sheng) [2] 152 Ke 33.00N 120.00 E
Kiantajärvi 114 Gd 65.03N 29.07 E
Kiáton 130 Fk 38.01N 22.45 E
Kibali 170 Eb 3.37N 28.34 E
Kibangou 170 Bc 3.27S 12.21 E
Kibartaj/Kybartai 116 Jj 54.38N 22.44 E
Kibasira Swamp 170 Gd 8.20S 36.18 E
Kibau 170 Gd 8.35S 35.17 E
Kibaya 170 Gd 5.18S 36.34 E
Kibbish 168 Fe 4.40N 35.53 E
Kiberg 114 Ha 70.17N 31.00 E
Kibikogen 156 Cd 34.45N 133.15 E
Kiboko 170 Gc 2.15S 37.42 E
Kibombo 170 Ec 3.54S 25.55 E
Kibondo 170 Fc 3.35S 30.42 E
Kibre Mengist 168 Fd 5.58N 39.00 E
Kıbrıs/Kypros=Cyprus (EN) [1] 142 Ff 35.00N 33.00 E
Kıbrıs/Kypros=Cyprus (EN) 140 Ff 35.00N 33.00 E
Kibungo 170 Fc 2.10S 30.32 E
Kibuye 170 Ec 2.03S 29.21 E
Kibwezi 170 Gc 2.25S 37.58 E
Kičevo 130 Dh 41.31N 20.58 E
Kichi Kichi 168 Bb 17.36N 17.19 E
Kicking Horse Pass 180 Ff 51.50N 116.30W
Kidal 160 Hg 18.26N 1.24 E
Kidapawan 150 Ie 7.01N 125.03 E
Kidatu 170 Gd 7.42S 36.57 E
Kidira 166 Cc 14.28N 12.13W
Kidnappers, Cape- 218 Gc 39.38S 177.06 E
Kiekie 221a Ab 21.53N 160.13W
Kiel 112 He 54.20N 10.08 E
Kiel Canal (EN) = Nord-Ostsee-Kanal 110 Ge 53.53N 9.08 E
Kielce 120 Qf 50.52N 20.37 E
Kielce [2] 120 Qf 50.50N 20.35 E
Kieler Bucht 120 Gb 54.35N 10.35 E
Kienge 170 Ee 10.33S 27.33 E
Kierspe 124 Jc 51.08N 7.35 E
Kieta 210 Ge 6.15S 155.37 E
Kietrz 120 Of 50.05N 18.01 E
Kiev (EN)=Kijev 112 Je 50.26N 30.31 E
Kiev Reservoir (EN) = Kijevskoje vodohranilišče 110 Je 51.00N 30.25 E
Kiffa 160 Fg 16.36N 11.23W
Kifisiá 130 Gk 38.04N 23.49 E
Kifisós 130 Gk 38.26N 23.15 E
Kifrī 146 Ke 34.42N 44.58 E
Kigač 132 Pf 46.28N 49.08 E
Kigali 160 Ki 1.57S 30.04 E
Kiğı 146 Ic 39.19N 40.21 E
Kigille 168 Ed 8.40N 34.02 E
Kigoma 160 Ji 4.52S 29.38 E
Kigoma [3] 170 Fc 4.50S 30.05 E
Kigosi 170 Fc 4.40S 31.27 E
Kihelkonna 116 If 58.20N 21.54 E
Kihniö 116 Jb 62.12N 23.11 E
Kihnu 114 Fg 58.10N 24.00 E
Kiholo 221a Fd 19.51N 155.55W
Kiholo Bay 221a Fd 19.52N 155.56W
Kihti/Skiftet 116 Id 60.15N 21.05 E
Kii-Hantō 152 Oe 34.00N 135.45 E
Kiikka 116 Jc 61.20N 22.46 E
Kiil 132 Se 49.27N 54.50 E
Kiiminki 114 Fd 65.08N 25.44 E
Kii-Sanchi 156 Dd 34.15N 135.50 E
Kii-Suido 154 Mh 34.00N 134.55 E
Kija 136 De 56.52N 86.40 E
Kijev=Kiev (EN) 112 Je 50.26N 30.31 E
Kijevka 136 He 50.16N 71.34 E
Kijevskaja oblast [3] 136 De 50.20N 30.45 E
Kijevskoje vodohranilišče = Kiev Reservoir (EN) 110 Je 51.00N 30.25 E
Kijma 136 Ge 51.35N 67.34 E
Kikai-Jima 152 Mf 28.15N 130.00 E
Kikerino 116 Me 59.23N 29.38 E
Kikinda 130 Dd 45.50N 20.29 E
Kikládhes = Cyclades (EN) 110 Ih 37.00N 25.10 E
Kikonai 154 Pd 41.40N 140.26 E
Kikori 210 Fe 7.25S 144.13 E
Kikori River 208 Fe 7.23S 144.16 E
Kikuchi 156 Be 32.59N 130.49 E
Kikuma 156 Cd 34.03N 132.51 E
Kikvidze 132 Md 50.44N 43.03 E
Kikwit 160 Ii 5.02S 18.49 E
Kil [Nor.] 116 Cf 58.52N 9.19 E
Kil [Swe.] 114 Cg 59.30N 13.19 E
Kilafors 114 Df 61.15N 16.33 E
Kilambé, Cerro- 194 Eg 13.34N 85.42W
Kilauea 221a Ba 22.13N 159.25W
Kilauea Crater 221a Fd 19.24N 155.17W
Kilauea Point 221a Ba 22.14N 159.24W
Kilbrannan Sound 118 Hf 55.40N 5.25W
Kilbuck Mountains 178 Hd 60.30N 159.45W
Kilchu 152 Mc 40.58N 129.20 E
Kilcoy 212 Ke 26.57S 152.33 E
Kildare/Cill Dara 118 Gh 53.10N 6.55W
Kildare/Cill Dara [2] 118 Gh 53.15N 6.45W
Kil'din, ostrov- 114 Ib 69.20N 34.10 E
Kilembe 170 Cd 5.42S 19.55 E
Kilgore 186 Ij 32.23N 94.53W
Kilgoris 170 Fc 1.00S 34.53 E
Kiliç 130 Mi 40.40N 29.23 E
Kilifi 170 Gc 3.38S 39.51 E
Kili Island 208 Hd 5.39N 169.04 E
Kilija 136 Cf 45.27N 29.14 E
Kilijskoje girlo 130 Md 45.13N 29.43 E
Kilimanjaro [3] 170 Gc 4.00S 37.40 E
Kilimanjaro, Mount- 158 Ki 3.04S 37.22 E
Kilimli 146 Db 41.29N 31.50 E
Kilinailau Islands 214 Fh 4.45S 155.20 E
Kilindoni 160 Ki 7.55S 39.39 E
Kilingi-Nõmme/Kilingi-Nymme 114 Fg 58.08N 24.59 E
Kilingi-Nymme/Kilingi-Nõmme 116 Kf 58.08N 24.59 E
Kilis 146 Gd 36.44N 37.05 E
Kilitbahir 146 Bb 40.12N 26.20 E
Kilkee/Cill Chaoi 118 Di 52.41N 9.38W
Kilkenny/Cill Chainnigh 118 Fi 52.39N 7.15W
Kilkenny/Cill Chainnigh [2] 118 Fi 52.40N 7.20W
Kilkieran Bay 118 Dh 53.15N 9.45W
Kilkis 130 Fi 41.00N 22.52 E
Killala Bay/Cuan Chill Ala 118 Dg 54.15N 9.10W
Killarney/Cill Airne 118 Di 52.03N 9.30W
Killary Harbour/An Caoláire Rua 118 Dh 53.38N 9.55W
Killdeer 186 Ec 47.22N 102.45W
Killeen 182 He 31.08N 97.44W
Killinek 180 Ld 60.25N 64.40W
Killini 130 Ei 37.56N 21.09 E
Killini Óros 130 Fl 37.55N 22.26 E
Kilmallock/Cill Mocheallóg 118 Ei 52.25N 8.35W
Kilmarnock 118 If 55.37N 4.30W
Kilmez 114 Mh 57.03N 51.24 E
Kilmez 114 Mh 56.58N 50.29 E
Kilmore 212 Ig 37.18S 144.57 E
Kilombero 170 Gd 8.31S 37.22 E
Kilosa 160 Ki 6.50S 36.59 E
Kilpisjärvi 114 Eb 69.03N 20.48 E
Kilp-Javr 114 Hb 69.07N 32.28 E
Kilrush/Cill Rois 118 Di 52.39N 9.29W
Kilsbergen 116 Fe 59.20N 14.45 E
Kiltān Island 148 Ef 11.29N 73.00 E
Kilwa 170 Ed 9.17S 28.20 E
Kilwa Kisiwani 160 Ki 8.58S 39.30 E
Kilwa Kivinje 170 Gd 8.45S 39.24 E
Kilwa Masoko 170 Gd 8.56S 39.31 E
Kilyos → Kumköy 130 Mh 41.15N 29.02 E
Kim 186 Eh 37.15N 103.21W
Kimamba 170 Gd 6.47S 37.08 E
Kimba 212 Hf 33.09S 136.25 E
Kimball [Nb.-U.S.] 186 Ef 41.14N 103.40W
Kimball [S.D.-U.S.] 186 Ge 43.45N 98.57W
Kimball, Mount- 178 Kd 63.14N 144.39W
Kimbe 212 Ka 5.31S 150.12 E
Kimbe Bay 210 Ei 5.30S 150.30 E
Kimberley 208 Df 16.00S 126.00 E
Kimberley [B.C.-Can.] 180 Fg 49.41N 115.59W
Kimberley [S.Afr.] 160 Jk 28.43S 24.46 E
Kimberley Plateau 212 Fc 17.00S 127.00 E
Kimch'aek (Sŏngjin) 152 Mc 40.41N 129.12 E
Kimch'ŏn 152 Md 36.07N 128.07 E
Kimhandu 158 Ki 7.05S 37.35 E
Kimi 130 Hk 38.38N 24.06 E
Kimito/Kemiö 116 Jd 60.10N 22.40 E
Kimje 154 Ig 35.48N 126.53 E
Kimobetsu 156a Bb 42.47N 140.56 E
Kimolos 130 Hm 36.48N 24.34 E
Kimongo 170 Bc 4.29S 12.58 E
Kimovsk 136 De 54.01N 38.36 E
Kimpu-San 156 Fd 35.52N 138.37 E
Kimry 136 Dd 56.52N 37.24 E
Kimvula 170 Cd 5.44S 15.58 E
Kinabalu, Gunong- 140 Ni 6.05N 116.33 E
Kinabatangan 150 Ge 5.42N 118.23 E
Kinango 170 Gc 4.08S 39.19 E
Kinaros 130 Jm 36.59N 26.17 E
Kincardine 180 Jh 44.11N 81.38W
Kind 116 Eg 57.35N 13.25 E
Kinda 170 Ed 9.18S 25.04 E
Kinda 116 Ff 58.05N 15.40 E
Kindamba 170 Bc 3.44S 14.31 E
Kinder 186 Jk 30.29N 92.51W
Kinder Scout 118 Lh 53.23N 1.52W
Kindersley 180 Gf 51.27N 109.10W
Kindi 166 Ec 12.26N 2.01W
Kindia 160 Fg 10.04N 12.51W
Kindu 160 Ji 2.57S 25.56 E
Kinel 114 Mj 53.14N 50.40 E
Kinesi 170 Fc 1.28S 33.52 E
Kinešma 136 Ed 57.28N 42.16 E
King 219a Aa 4.24S 152.43 E
King, Cayos- 194 Fg 12.45N 83.20W
Kingaroy 212 Ke 26.33S 151.50 E
King Christian 180 Ha 77.45N 102.00W
King Christian IX Land (EN) = Kong Christian IX Land 224 Mc 68.00N 36.30W
King Christian X Land (EN) = Kong Christian X Land 224 Md 72.20N 32.30W
King City 182 Cd 36.13N 121.08W
King Edward River 212 Fb 14.14S 126.35 E
Kingfisher 186 Hi 35.52N 97.56W
King Frederik VI Coast (EN) =Kong Frederik VI Kyst 224 Nc 63.00N 43.30W
King Frederik VIII Land (EN) = Kong Frederik VIII Land 224 Md 78.30N 28.00W
King George Island 222 Re 62.00S 58.15W
King George Islands 180 Je 57.15N 78.30W
King George Sound 212 Dg 35.10S 118.10 E
Kingisepp 114 Gg 59.23N 28.37 E
Kingisepp/Kingissepp 136 Cd 58.17N 22.29 E
King Island 208 Fh 39.50S 144.00 E
Kingissepp/Kingisepp 136 Cd 58.17N 22.29 E
King Lear Peak 188 Ff 41.12N 118.34W
King Leopold Ranges 212 Fc 17.30S 125.45 E
Kingman [Az.-U.S.] 182 Ed 35.12N 114.04W
Kingman [Ks.-U.S.] 186 Gh 37.39N 98.07W
Kingman Reef 208 Kd 6.19N 162.28W
Kingombe [Zaire] 170 Ec 3.52S 26.35 E
Kingombe [Zaire] 170 Ec 2.35S 26.37 E
Kingoome Inlet 188 Ba 50.49N 126.13W
Kingoonya 210 Eh 30.54S 135.18 E
King Peninsula 222 Of 73.12S 101.00W
Kingsclere 124 Ac 51.19N 1.15W
Kingscote 212 Hg 35.40S 137.38 E
King's Lynn 118 Ni 52.45N 0.24 E
King Sound 208 Df 17.00S 123.30 E
Kings Peak [Ca.-U.S.] 188 Cf 40.10N 124.08W
Kings Peak [U.S.] 174 He 40.46N 110.22W
Kingsport 182 Kd 36.32N 82.33W
Kings River 188 Fh 36.03N 119.49W
Kingston [Jam.] 176 Lh 18.00N 76.50W
Kingston [Nor.I.] 210 Hg 29.04S 167.58 E
Kingston [N.Y.-U.S.] 182 Mc 41.55N 74.00W
Kingston [N.Z.] 216 Ci 45.20S 168.43 E
Kingston [Ont.-Can.] 176 Le 44.14N 76.30W
Kingston Peak 188 Hi 35.42N 115.52W
Kingston South East 210 Eh 36.50S 139.51 E
Kingston upon Hull (Hull) 112 Fe 53.45N 0.20W
Kingston-upon-Thames, London- 118 Mj 51.28N 0.19W
Kingstown 176 Mh 13.09N 61.14W
Kingsville 182 Hf 27.31N 97.52W
Kings Worthy 124 Ac 51.05N 1.18W
Kingussie 118 Id 57.05N 4.04W
King William 174 Jc 69.00N 97.30W
King William's Town 160 Jl 32.51S 27.22 E
Kiniama 170 Ee 11.26S 28.19 E
Kınık 146 Bc 39.05N 27.23 E
Kinkala 170 Bc 4.22S 14.46 E
Kinlochleven 118 Ie 56.43N 4.58W
Kinna 116 Eg 57.30N 12.41 E
Kinnairds Head 118 Ld 57.42N 2.00W
Kinnared 116 Eg 57.02N 13.06 E
Kinnekulle 116 Ef 58.35N 13.23 E
Kinneret, Yam- 146 Ff 32.48N 35.35 E
Kino-Kawa 156 Dd 34.13N 135.08 E
Kinomoto 156 Ed 35.31N 136.13 E
Kinoosao 180 He 57.06N 102.01W
Kinós Kefalai 130 Fj 39.25N 22.34 E
Kinross 118 Je 56.13N 3.27W
Kinsale / Cionn tSáile 118 Ej 51.42N 8.32W
Kinsale, Old Head of-/An Seancheann 118 Ej 51.36N 8.32W
Kinsangire 170 Gd 7.26S 38.35 E
Kinsarvik 114 Bf 60.23N 6.43 E
Kinshasa [2] 170 Cc 4.00S 16.00 E
Kinshasa (Leopoldville) 160 Ii 4.18S 15.18 E
Kinsley 186 Gh 37.55N 99.25W
Kinston 182 Ld 35.16N 77.35W
Kintampo 166 Ed 8.03N 1.43W
Kintap 150 Gg 3.51S 115.13 E
Kintyre 118 Hf 55.32N 5.35W
Kin-Wan 156b Ab 26.25N 127.54 E
Kinyan 166 Dc 11.51N 6.01W
Kinyeti 158 Kh 3.57N 32.54 E
Kinzig [Eur.] 120 Dh 48.37N 7.49 E
Kinzig [Ger.] 120 Ef 50.08N 8.54 E
Kioa 219d Bb 16.39S 179.55 E
Kipaka 170 Ec 4.09S 26.30 E
Kiparissia 130 El 37.15N 21.40 E
Kiparissia, Gulf of- (EN) = Kiparissiakós Kólpos 130 El 37.30N 21.25 E
Kiparissiakós Kólpos = Kiparissia, Gulf of- (EN) 130 El 37.30N 21.25 E
Kipawa, Lac- 180 Jg 46.55N 79.00W
Kipembawe 170 Fd 7.39S 33.24 E
Kipengere Range 158 Ki 9.10S 34.15 E
Kiperčeny 130 Lb 47.32N 28.40 E
Kipili 170 Fd 7.26S 30.36 E
Kipini 170 Hc 2.32S 40.31 E
Kipling 186 Ea 50.10N 102.38W
Kippure 118 Gh 53.11N 6.20W
Kiprarenukk, mys- / Undva neem 116 If 58.25N 21.45 E
Kípros = Cyprus (EN) 144 Db 35.01N 33.00 E
Kipushi 170 Ee 11.46S 27.14 E
Kirakira 210 Hf 10.27S 161.56 E
Kiraz 146 Cc 39.21N 27.25 E
Kirazlı 146 Bb 40.01N 26.40 E
Kirbla 116 Jf 58.42N 23.49 E
Kircasalih 130 Jh 41.23N 26.48 E
Kirchberg (Hunsrück) 124 Je 49.57N 7.24 E
Kirchhain 124 Kd 50.49N 8.58 E
Kirchheimbolanden 124 Ke 49.40N 8.01 E
Kirchheim unter Teck 120 Fh 48.39N 9.27 E
Kirchhundem 124 Kc 51.06N 8.06 E
Kirchhundem-Rahrbach 124 Jc 51.02N 7.59 E
Kirchlengern 124 Kb 52.12N 8.38 E
Kirdimi 168 Bb 18.11N 18.38 E
Kireç 130 Lj 39.33N 28.22 E
Kirenga 140 Md 57.47N 107.59 E
Kirensk 142 Md 57.46N 108.08 E
Kirghiz SSR (EN)= Kirgizskaja SSR [2] 136 Hg 41.30N 75.00 E
Kirghiz Steppe (EN) 110 Lf 49.30N 50.30 E
Kirgizskaja Sovetskaja Socialističeskaja Respublika [2] 136 Hg 41.30N 75.00 E
Kirgizskaja SSR/Kyrgyz Sovetik Soi ialistik Respublikasy [2] 136 Hg 41.30N 75.00 E
Kirgizskaja SSR=Kirghiz SSR (EN) [2] 136 Hg 41.30N 75.00 E
Kirgizski hrebet 136 Hg 42.30N 74.00 E
Kiri 170 Cc 1.27S 19.00 E
Kiribati [1] 210 Je 0.01S 174.00W
Kirikhan 146 Gd 36.32N 36.19 E
Kırıkkale 144 Db 39.50N 33.31 E
Kirillov 114 Jg 59.54N 38.27 E
Kirillovskoje 116 Md 60.28N 29.28 E
Kirin (EN)=Chi-lin Sheng→Jilin Sheng [2] 152 Mc 43.00N 126.00 E
Kirin (EN)=Jilin Sheng (Chi-lin Sheng) [2] 152 Mc 43.00N 126.00 E
Kirinyaga/Kenya, Mount- 158 Ki 0.10S 37.20 E
Kirishima-Yama 156 Bf 31.56N 130.52 E
Kiriši 136 Dd 59.27N 32.02 E
Kiritimati Atoll (Christmas) [5] 208 Ld 1.52N 157.20W
Kirja 114 Li 55.05N 46.52 E
Kirkağaç 146 Bc 39.06N 27.40 E
Kirkby Lonsdale 118 Kg 54.13N 2.36W
Kirkcaldy 118 Je 56.07N 3.10W
Kirkcudbright 118 Ig 54.50N 4.03W
Kirkee→Khadki 148 Ee 18.34N 73.52 E
Kirkenær 114 Cf 60.28N 12.03 E
Kirkenes 112 Jb 69.43N 30.03 E
Kirkjubæjarklaustur 114a Bc 63.47N 18.04W
Kirkkonummi/Kyrkslätt 116 Kd 60.07N 24.26 E
Kirkland 188 Dc 47.41N 122.12W
Kirkland Lake 176 Ke 48.09N 80.02W

Index Symbols

[1] Independent Nation
[2] State, Region
[3] District, County
[4] Municipality
[5] Colony, Dependency
Continent
Physical Region
Historical or Cultural Region
Mount, Mountain
Volcano
Hill
Mountains, Mountain Range
Hills, Escarpment
Plateau, Upland
Pass, Gap
Plain, Lowland
Delta
Salt Flat
Valley, Canyon
Crater, Cave
Karst Features
Depression
Polder
Desert, Dunes
Forest, Woods
Heath, Steppe
Oasis
Cape, Point
Coast, Beach
Cliff
Peninsula
Isthmus
Sandbank
Island
Atoll
Rock, Reef
Islands, Archipelago
Rocks, Reefs
Coral Reef
Well, Spring
Geyser
River, Stream
Waterfall, Rapids
River Mouth, Estuary
Lake
Salt Lake
Intermittent Lake
Reservoir
Swamp, Pond
Canal
Glacier
Ice Shelf, Pack Ice
Ocean
Sea
Gulf, Bay
Strait, Fjord
Lagoon
Bank
Seamount
Tablemount
Ridge
Shelf
Basin
Escarpment, Sea Scarp
Fracture
Trench, Abyss
National Park, Reserve
Point of Interest
Recreation Site
Cave, Cavern
Historic Site
Ruins
Wall, Walls
Church, Abbey
Temple
Scientific Station
Railway station
Airport
Port
Military installat
Lighthouse
Mine
Tunnel
Dam, Bridge

Kırklareli 144 Ca 41.44N 27.12 E
Kirkpatrick, Mount- 222 Kg 84.20S 166.19 E
Kirkpınar Dağı 146 Fd 37.14N 34.15 E
Kirksville 182 Ic 40.12N 92.35W
Kirkük 142 Gf 35.28N 44.23 E
Kirkwall 118 Kc 58.59N 2.58W
Kirkwood [Mo.-U.S.] 186 Kg 38.35N 90.24W
Kirkwood [S.Afr.] 172 Df 33.22S 25.15 E
Kırlangıç Burun 146 Dd 36.13N 30.25 E
Kirn 120 Dg 49.47N 7.27 E
Kirobasi 146 Ed 36.43N 33.52 E
Kirov [R.S.F.S.R.] 136 De 54.03N 34.21 E
Kirov [R.S.F.S.R.] 112 Kd 58.33N 49.42 E
Kirova, zaliv- 132 Pj 39.05N 49.05 E
Kirovabad → Gjandža 112 Kg 40.40N 46.22 E
Kirovaken 136 Eg 40.48N 44.28 E
Kirovgrad 134 Jh 57.26N 60.04 E
Kirovo 135 Hd 40.28N 70.34 E
Kirovo-Čepeck 136 Fd 58.35N 50.03 E
Kirovograd 112 Jf 48.30N 32.18 E
Kirovogradskaja oblast [3] 136 Df 48.20N 31.50 E
Kirovsk [R.S.F.S.R.] 136 Db 67.37N 33.37 E
Kirovsk [R.S.F.S.R.] 114 Hg 59.53N 31.01 E
Kirovsk [Tur.-U.S.S.R.] 135 Cf 37.43N 60.24 E
Kirovskaja oblast [3] 136 Ed 58.30N 50.00 E
Kirovski [Kaz.-U.S.S.R.] 136 Hg 44.53N 78.12 E
Kirovski [R.S.F.S.R.] 132 Pg 45.48N 48.08 E
Kirovski [R.S.F.S.R.] 138 Kf 54.25N 155.37 E
Kirovski [R.S.F.S.R.] 138 Hf 54.26N 127.00 E
Kirovski [R.S.F.S.R.] 138 Ig 45.05N 133.27 E
Kirovskoje 135 Hc 42.39N 71.35 E
Kirpilski liman 132 Kg 45.50N 38.05 E
Kirriemuir 118 Je 56.41N 3.01W
Kirs 136 Fd 59.21N 52.18 E
Kirsanov 132 Mc 52.41N 42.45 E
Kırşehir 144 Db 39.09N 34.10 E
Kirthar Range 140 Ig 27.00N 67.20 E
Kirton 124 Bb 52.55N 0.03W
Kiruna 112 Ib 67.51N 20.13 E
Kirundu 170 Ec 0.44S 25.32 E
Kiryū 156 Fc 36.25N 139.20 E
Kiržač 114 Jh 56.11N 38.53 E
Kisa 114 Dh 57.59N 15.37 E
Kisabi 170 Ed 8.03S 29.11 E
Kisač 130 Cd 45.21N 19.44 E
Kisakata 156 Fb 39.14N 139.54 E
Kisaki 170 Gd 7.28S 37.36 E
Kisalföld 120 Mi 47.30N 17.00 E
Kisangani 160 Jh 0.25N 25.12 E
Kisarazu 156 Fd 35.23N 139.55 E
Kisbér 120 Oi 47.30N 18.02 E
Kiselevsk 138 Df 54.03N 86.49 E
Kiserawe 170 Gd 6.54S 39.05 E
Kishangarh 148 Ec 26.34N 74.52 E
Kishb, Harrat al- 146 He 22.47N 41.30 E
Kishi 166 Fd 9.05N 3.51 E
Kishiwada 154 Mg 34.28N 135.22 E
Kisii 170 Fc 0.41S 34.46 E
Kisiju 170 Gd 7.24S 39.20 E
Kišinev 112 If 46.59N 28.52 E
Kısır Dağı 146 Jb 40.58N 43.04 E
Kiska 178a Bb 52.00N 177.30 E
Kiska Volcano 178a Bb 52.07N 177.36 E
Kisko 116 Jd 60.14N 23.29 E
Kiskörei Víztároló 120 Qi 47.44N 20.40 E
Kiskőrös 120 Pj 46.37N 19.18 E
Kiskunfélegyháza 120 Pj 46.33N 19.51 E
Kiskunhalas 120 Pj 46.26N 19.30 E
Kiskunmajsa 120 Pj 46.29N 19.45 E
Kiskunság 120 Pj 46.35N 19.15 E
Kislovodsk 136 Eg 43.54N 42.42 E
Kismanyo 160 Li 0.22S 42.32 E
Kisofukushima 156 Ed 35.51N 137.41 E
Kiso-Gawa 154 Ng 35.05N 136.45 E
Kisoro 170 Ec 1.17S 29.41 E
Kiso-Sanmyaku 156 Ed 35.45N 137.45 E
Kisria, Daiet el- 126 Oi 35.44N 2.47 E
Kissámou, Kólpos- 130 Gn 35.35N 23.40 E
Kissidougou 166 Cd 9.11N 10.06W
Kissimmee 184 Gk 28.18N 81.24W
Kissimmee, Lake- 184 Gl 27.55N 81.16W
Kissū, Jabal- 168 Da 21.35N 25.09 E
Kistelek 120 Pj 46.28N 19.59 E
Kisterenye 120 Ph 48.01N 19.50 E
Kisújszállás 120 Qi 47.13N 20.46 E
Kisuki 156 Cd 35.17N 132.54 E
Kisumu 160 Ki 0.06S 34.45 E
Kisvárda 120 Sh 48.13N 22.05 E
Kita 160 Gg 13.03N 9.30W
Kitab 136 Gh 39.08N 66.54 E
Kita-Daitō-Jima 152 Nf 25.55N 131.20 E
Kitaibaraki 154 Pf 36.48N 140.45 E
Kita-lō-Jima 214 Cb 25.26N 141.17 E
Kitaj, ozero- 130 Md 45.35N 29.15 E
Kitakami 152 Pd 39.30N 141.10 E
Kitakami-Gawa 156 Gb 38.25N 141.19 E
Kitakami-Sanchi 156 Gb 39.30N 141.30 E
Kitakata 154 Of 37.39N 139.52 E
Kitakyūshū 142 Pf 33.53N 130.50 E
Kitale 160 Kh 1.01N 35.00 E
Kitami 152 Pc 43.48N 143.54 E
Kitamiaioi 156a Cb 43.33N 143.57 E
Kitami-Fuji 156a Cb 43.42N 143.14 E
Kitami-Sanchi 154 Qb 44.30N 142.30 E
Kitami Tōge 156a Cb 43.55N 142.55 E
Kitan-Kaikyō 156 Dd 34.15N 135.00 E
ita-Taiheyō=Pacific Ocean
(EN) 214 Ch 22.00N 179.00 E
ta-Ura 156 Gc 36.00N 140.34 E
Carson 186 Eg 38.46N 102.48W
chener 180 Jh 43.27N 80.29W
ee 116 He 62.06N 30.09 E
ssa 168 Dd 5.22N 25.22 E
um 170 Fb 3.19N 32.53 E
ra=Cythera (EN) 130 Fm 36.09N 23.00 E
ra=Kythera (EN) 110 Ih 36.15N 23.00 E
ra Channel (EN) =
iron, Dhiékplous- 130 Fm 36.00N 23.00 E
Kithiron, Dhiékplous-=
Kithira Channel (EN) 130 Fm 36.00N 23.00 E
Kithnos 130 Hl 37.25N 24.26 E
Kithnos 130 Hl 37.23N 24.25 E
Kithnou, Stenón- 130 Hl 37.25N 24.30 E
Kitimat 176 Gd 54.05N 128.38W
Kitimat Ranges 180 Ef 53.58N 128.39W
Kitoushi-Yama 156a Cb 43.27N 143.25 E
Kitriani 130 Hm 36.54N 24.44 E
Kitridge Point 197q Bb 13.09N 59.25W
Kitros 130 Fi 40.22N 22.35 E
Kitsuki 156 Be 33.25N 131.37 E
Kittanning 184 He 40.49N 79.31W
Kittery 184 Ld 43.05N 70.45W
Kittilä 114 Fc 67.40N 24.54 E
Kitui 160 Ki 1.22S 38.01 E
Kitunda 170 Fd 6.48S 33.13 E
Kitutu 170 Ec 3.17S 28.05 E
Kitwe-Nkana 160 Jj 12.49S 28.13 E
Kitzbühel 128 Gc 47.27N 12.23 E
Kitzbüheler Alpen 128 Gc 47.20N 12.20 E
Kitzingen 120 Gg 49.44N 10.10 E
Kiunga [Kenya] 170 Hc 1.45S 41.29 E
Kiunga [Pap.N.Gui.] 214 Ci 6.07S 141.18 E
Kiuruvesi 114 Ge 63.39N 26.37 E
Kivalina 178 Gc 67.59N 164.33W
Kivercy 132 Dd 50.50N 25.31 E
Kivijärvi [Fin.] 114 Fe 63.10N 25.09 E
Kivijärvi [Fin.] 116 Ld 60.55N 27.40 E
Kivik 114 Di 55.41N 14.15 E
Kiviöli/Kiviyli 114 Gg 59.23N 26.59 E
Kiviyli/Kiviöli 114 Gg 59.23N 26.59 E
Kivu [2] 170 Ec 2.30S 27.30 E
Kivu, Lac-=Kivu, Lake- (EN) 158 Ji 2.00S 29.10 E
Kivu, Lake- (EN)=Kivu, Lac- 158 Ji 2.00S 29.10 E
Kiwai Island 214 Ci 8.30S 143.25 E
Kiyāmaki Dāgh 146 Kc 38.47N 45.51 E
Kiyiköy 146 Cb 41.25N 28.01 E
Kiyosato 156a Db 43.51N 144.35 E
Kizel 136 Fd 59.03N 57.40 E
Kizema 114 Kf 61.09N 44.46 E
Kizilcabölük 130 Ml 37.37N 29.01 E
Kızılca Dağı 146 Cd 36.55N 29.52 E
Kızılcahaman 146 Eb 40.28N 32.39 E
Kızıl Dağ 146 Ed 36.25N 32.42 E
Kizilhisar 130 Ml 37.33N 29.18 E
Kızılırmak 146 Eb 40.22N 33.59 E
Kızılırmak 140 Fe 41.45N 35.59 E
Kiziljurt 132 Oh 43.13N 46.55 E
Kizilskoje 134 Ij 52.44N 58.54 E
Kızıltepe 146 Id 37.12N 40.36 E
Kizimen, vulkan- 138 Le 55.03N 160.27 E
Kižinga 138 Ff 51.51N 109.55 E
Kizir 138 Ef 54.10N 93.20 E
Kizljar 136 Eg 43.50N 46.42 E
Kizljarski zaliv 132 Og 44.35N 46.55 E
Kizukuri 156a Bc 40.48N 140.22 E
Kizyl-Arvat 136 Fh 39.01N 56.20 E
Kizyl-Atrek 136 Fh 37.38N 54.47 E
Kizyl-Su 136 Fh 39.46N 53.01 E
Kjahta 136 Ff 50.26N 106.25 E
Kjalvaz 132 Pj 38.38N 48.20 E
Kjardla/Kärdla 114 Fg 59.01N 22.42 E
Kjarevere/Kärevere 116 Lf 58.23N 26.30 E
Kjarla/Kärla 116 Jf 58.16N 22.05 E
Kjellerup 116 Ch 56.17N 9.26 E
Kjøllefjord 114 Ga 70.56N 27.27 E
Kjølur 114a Bb 64.50N 19.25W
Kjøpsvik 114 Db 68.06N 16.21 E
Kjubjume 138 Jd 63.28N 140.30 E
Kjurdamir 136 Eg 40.20N 48.07 E
Kjusjur 138 Hb 70.35N 127.45 E
Kjustendil 130 Fg 42.17N 22.41 E
Kjustendil [2] 130 Fg 42.17N 22.41 E
Kjyosumi-Yama 156 Gd 35.10N 140.09 E
Klabat, Gunung- 150 If 1.28N 125.02 E
Kladanj 128 Mf 44.14N 18.42 E
Kladno 120 Kf 50.09N 14.07 E
Kladovo 130 Fe 44.37N 22.37 E
Klagenfurt 112 Hf 46.38N 14.18 E
Klaipėda/Klajpeda 112 Id 55.43N 21.07 E
Klajpeda/Klaipėda 112 Id 55.43N 21.07 E
Klamath 188 Cf 41.32N 124.02W
Klamath Falls 176 Ge 42.13N 121.46W
Klamath Mountains 182 Cc 41.40N 123.20W
Klamath River 188 Cf 41.33N 124.04W
Klamono 150 Jg 1.08S 131.30 E
Klarälven 110 Hd 59.23N 13.32 E
Klaten 150 Fh 7.42S 110.35 E
Klatovy 120 Jg 49.24N 13.19 E
Klavreström 116 Fg 57.08N 15.08 E
Klawer 172 Bf 31.44S 18.36 E
Klazienaveen, Emmen- 124 Jb 52.44N 7.01 E
Kleck 132 Ec 53.03N 26.40 E
Klecko 120 Nd 52.38N 17.26 E
Kleinblittersdorf 124 Je 49.09N 7.02 E
Kleine Nete 124 Gc 51.08N 4.34 E
Kleine Sluis, Anna Paulowna- 124 Gb 52.52N 4.52 E
Klein-Karoo=Little Karroo (EN) 172 Cf 33.42S 21.20 E
Kleinsee 172 Be 29.40S 17.05 E
Klekovača 128 Kf 44.26N 16.31 E
Kléla 166 Dc 11.40N 5.40W
Kleppe 116 Af 58.46N 5.40 E
Klerksdorp 172 De 26.58S 26.39 E
Kletnja 136 De 53.27N 33.17 E
Kletski 132 Me 49.19N 43.04 E
Kleve 120 Ce 51.47N 6.09 E
Klibreck, Ben- 118 Ic 58.19N 4.30W
Klička 138 Gf 50.24N 118.01 E
Kljmoviči 136 De 53.37N 32.01 E
Klimovo 132 Hc 52.23N 32.16 E
Klin 136 Dd 56.20N 36.42 E
Klina 130 Dg 42.37N 20.35 E
Klincy 136 De 52.46N 32.17 E
Klingbach 124 Ke 49.11N 8.24 E
Klingenthal 120 If 50.22N 12.28 E
Klinovec 120 If 50.24N 12.58 E
Klintehamn 114 Eh 57.24N 18.12 E
Klippan 116 Eh 56.08N 13.06 E
Klipplaat 172 Cf 33.02S 24.21 E
Kliškovcy 130 Ja 48.23N 26.13 E
Klisura 130 Hg 42.42N 24.27 E
Klitmøller 116 Cg 57.02N 8.31 E
Kljazma 110 Kd 56.10N 42.58 E
Ključevskaja Sopka, vulkan- 140 Sd 56.04N 160.38 E
Ključi 138 Le 56.14N 160.58 E
Kłobuck 120 Of 50.55N 18.57 E
Kłodawa 120 Od 52.16N 18.55 E
Kłodzka, Kotlina- 120 Mf 50.30N 16.35 E
Kłodzko 120 Mf 50.28N 16.40 E
Kløfta 116 Dd 60.04N 11.09 E
Kłomnice 120 Pf 50.56N 19.21 E
Klondike Plateau 180 Dd 63.10N 139.55W
Klondike River 180 Dd 64.03N 139.26W
Klooga/Kloga 116 Ke 59.24N 24.10 E
Kloosteezande, Hontenisse- 124 Gc 51.23N 4.00 E
Klosi 130 Dh 41.29N 20.06 E
Klosterneuburg 128 Kb 48.18N 16.19 E
Klosters / Claustra 128 Dd 46.52N 9.52 E
Kloten 128 Cc 47.27N 8.35 E
Klotz, Lac- 180 Kd 60.40N 73.00W
Kluane Lake 180 Dd 61.15N 138.40W
Kluczbork 120 Of 50.59N 18.13 E
Knaben 116 Bf 58.39N 7.04 E
Knäred 116 Eh 56.32N 13.19 E
Kneža 130 Hf 43.30N 24.05 E
Knife River 186 Fc 47.20N 101.23W
Knin 128 Kf 44.02N 16.12 E
Knislinge 116 Fh 56.11N 14.05 E
Knittelfeld 128 Ic 47.13N 14.49 E
Knivskjellodden 114 Fa 71.11N 25.40 E
Knivsta 116 Ge 59.43N 17.48 E
Knjaževac 130 Ff 43.34N 22.15 E
Knobly Mountain 184 Hf 39.15N 79.05W
Knockmealdown Mountains/Cnoc Mhaoldonn 118 Fi 52.15N 8.00W
Knokke-Heist 122 Jc 51.21N 3.15 E
Knokke-Westkapelle 124 Fc 51.19N 3.18 E
Knolls grund 116 Gg 57.30N 17.30 E
Knøsen 116 Dg 57.12N 10.18 E
Knosós = Cnossus (EN) 130 In 35.18N 25.10 E
Knox, Cape- 180 Ef 54.11N 133.05W
Knox Coast 222 He 66.30S 105.00 E
Knoxville [Ia.-U.S.] 186 Jf 41.19N 93.06W
Knoxville [Tn.-U.S.] 176 Kf 35.58N 83.56W
Knud Rasmussen Land 224 Nd 80.00N 55.00W
Knüllgebirge 120 Ff 50.50N 9.30 E
Knutsholstind 116 Cc 61.26N 8.34 E
Knysna 160 Jl 34.02S 23.02 E
Koartac 180 Kd 60.50N 69.30W
Koba 150 Eg 2.29S 106.24 E
Koba, Pulau- 150 Jh 6.25S 134.28 E
Kobar Sink 168 Gc 14.00N 40.30 E
Kobayashi 154 Ki 31.59N 130.59 E
Kobdo 142 Le 48.01N 91.38 E
Kobdo (Chovd) 152 Fb 48.06N 92.11 E
Kōbe 142 Pf 34.41N 135.10 E
Kobeljaki 132 Ie 49.08N 34.12 E
København [2] 116 Ei 55.40N 12.10 E
København=Copenhagen (EN) 112 Hi 55.40N 12.35 E
Kobenni 162 Ff 15.55N 9.05W
Kobern-Gondorf 124 Jd 50.19N 7.28 E
Kobjaj 138 Hd 63.30N 126.26 E
Koblenz 120 Df 50.21N 7.36 E
Kobo 168 Fc 12.09N 39.39 E
Koboldo 138 If 52.58N 132.42 E
Kobra 114 Mg 59.19N 50.54 E
Kobrin 136 Ce 52.13N 24.23 E
Kobrinskoje 116 Ne 59.22N 30.14 E
Kobroor, Pulau- 150 Jh 6.12S 134.32 E
Kobuk 174 Cc 66.45N 161.00W
Kobuleti 132 Li 41.47N 41.45 E
Koca 146 Eb 41.41N 32.15 E
Kocabaş 146 Bb 40.22N 27.19 E
Koca Çay 146 Bb 40.08N 27.57 E
Koca Çay [Tur.] 146 Cd 36.17N 29.16 E
Koca Çay [Tur.] 130 Lj 38.43N 28.30 E
Koca Çay/Orhaneli 130 Lj 39.56N 28.32 E
Kočani 130 Fh 41.55N 22.25 E
Koçarlı 130 Kl 37.45N 27.42 E
Kocasu 130 Mi 39.42N 29.31 E
Kočečum 138 Fd 64.17N 100.10 E
Kočetovka 132 Lc 53.01N 40.31 E
Kočevje 128 Ie 45.39N 14.51 E
Kočevski Rog 128 Ie 45.41N 15.00 E
Koch 102 Jc 69.35N 78.20W
Kōch'ang 154 Ig 35.41N 127.55 E
Ko Chang 148 Kf 12.00N 102.23 E
Koch Bihār 148 Hc 26.19N 89.26 E
Kochi 152 Ne 33.33N 133.33 E
Kōchi Ken [2] 154 Lh 33.20N 133.30 E
Kochisar Ovası 146 Ec 38.50N 33.30 E
Kock 120 Se 51.39N 22.27 E
Kočkorka 135 Jc 42.11N 75.45 E
Kočmar 130 Kf 43.41N 27.28 E
Kočubej 136 Eg 44.23N 46.31 E
Kočubejevskoje 132 Lg 44.41N 41.50 E
Kodiak 174 Dd 57.48N 152.23W
Kodiak 174 Dd 57.30N 153.30W
Kodino 114 Je 63.44N 39.40 E
Kodok 168 Ed 9.53N 32.07 E
Kodomari 156a Bc 41.08N 140.18 E
Kodori 132 Lh 42.49N 41.10 E
Kodry 130 Lb 47.15N 28.15 E
Kodyma 130 Nb 48.01N 30.48 E
Kodža Balkan 130 Jg 42.50N 27.00 E
Koekenaap 172 Bf 31.29S 18.19 E
Koes 172 Be 25.59S 19.08 E
Kofa Mountains 188 Ij 33.20N 114.00W
Kofçaz 146 Bb 41.58N 27.12 E
Koffiefontein 172 Ce 29.30S 25.00 E
Kofiau, Pulau- 150 Ig 1.11S 129.50 E
Köflach 128 Jc 47.04N 15.05 E
Koforidua 160 Gh 6.05N 0.15W
Kōfu [Jap.] 156 Cd 35.18N 133.29 E
Kōfu [Jap.] 152 Od 35.39N 138.35 E
Koga 156 Fc 36.12N 139.42 E
Kogaluc 180 Je 59.38N 77.30W
Kōge 156 Dd 35.24N 134.15 E
Køge 114 Ci 55.27N 12.11 E
Køge Bugt 116 Ei 55.30N 12.20 E
Kogel 134 He 62.38N 57.07 E
Kogilnik (Kunduk) 130 Md 45.51N 29.38 E
Kogon 166 Cc 11.09N 14.42W
Kogota 156 Gb 38.32N 141.01 E
Kohala Mountains 221a Fc 20.05N 155.43W
Kohāt 148 Eb 33.35N 71.26 E
Kohila 116 Ke 59.11N 24.40 E
Kohima 148 Ic 25.40N 94.07 E
Koh-i Mārān 148 Dc 29.05N 66.50 E
Kohinggo 219a Cc 8.13S 157.10 E
Kohma 114 Jh 56.57N 41.07 E
Kohtla-Järve/Kohtla-Jarve 136 Cd 59.25N 27.14 E
Kohtla-Jarve/Kohtla-Järve 136 Cd 59.25N 27.14 E
Kohu Daği 130 Mm 36.30N 29.50 E
Kohunlich 192 Oh 18.30N 88.55W
Koide 156 Fc 37.14N 138.57 E
Koigi/Kojgi 116 Kf 58.49N 25.40 E
Koin 134 Ee 63.10N 51.15 E
Koindu 166 Cd 8.28N 10.20W
Koitere 114 He 62.58N 30.45 E
Kojā 144 Jd 25.34N 61.13 E
Kojandytau 135 Lb 44.20N 78.45 E
Kojda 114 Kc 66.23N 42.31 E
Koje-Do 154 Jg 34.52N 128.37 E
Kojetin 120 Ng 49.21N 17.20 E
Kojgi/Koigi 116 Kf 58.49N 25.40 E
Ko-Jima [Jap.] 156 Fe 33.07N 139.40 E
Ko-Jima [Jap.] 154 Od 41.22N 139.47 E
Kojō 152 Md 38.57N 127.52 E
Kojonup 212 Df 33.50S 117.09 E
Kojtaš 135 Fd 40.14N 67.22 E
Kojtezek, pereval- 135 If 37.29N 72.45 E
Kojur 146 Nd 36.23N 51.43 E
Kojva 134 Ig 58.15N 58.14 E
Kokab 168 Cc 10.03N 22.04 E
Kokai-Gawa 156 Gd 35.52N 140.08 E
Kokand 142 Je 40.33N 70.57 E
Kökar 114 Eg 59.55N 20.55 E
Kokarsfjärden 116 Ie 59.55N 20.45 E
Kokas 150 Jg 2.42S 132.26 E
Kokava nad Rimavicou 120 Ph 48.34N 19.50 E
Kokawa 156 Dd 34.17N 135.26 E
Kokčetav 142 Id 53.17N 69.25 E
Kokčetavskaja oblast [3] 136 He 53.30N 70.00 E
Kokemäenjoki 116 Ic 61.33N 21.42 E
Kokemäki/Kumo 114 Ff 61.15N 22.21 E
Kok-Jangak 136 Hg 40.59N 73.15 E
Kokkina 146 Ee 35.10N 32.36 E
Kokkola/Gamlakarleby 112 Ic 63.50N 23.07 E
Koko [Eth.] 168 Fc 10.20N 36.04 E
Koko [Nig.] 166 Fc 11.26N 4.30 E
Kokomo 182 Jc 40.29N 86.08W
Kokonau 150 Kg 4.43S 136.26 E
Kokong 172 Cd 24.27S 23.03 E
Koko Nor (EN)=Qinghai Hu 140 Mf 37.00N 100.20 E
Kokpekty 136 If 48.45N 82.24 E
Kokšaal-Tau, hrebet- 136 Hg 41.00N 78.00 E
Kokšenga 114 Kf 61.27N 42.38 E
Koksijde 124 Ec 51.06N 2.39 E
Koksoak 180 Ke 58.31N 68.11W
Kokstad 160 Jl 30.32S 29.29 E
Koktal 135 Lb 44.05N 79.44 E
Koktokay/Fuyun 142 Ke 47.13N 89.39 E
Kokubu 154 Ki 31.44N 130.46 E
Kola 136 Db 68.53N 33.01 E
Kola, Pulau- 150 Jh 5.30S 134.35 E
Kolahun 166 Cd 8.17N 10.05W
Kolaka 150 Hg 4.03S 121.36 E
Kolamadulu Atoll 148a Bb 2.25N 73.10 E
Kola Peninsula (EN) = Kolski poluostrov 110 Jb 67.30N 37.00 E
Kolār Gold Fields 148 Ff 12.55N 78.17 E
Kolari 114 Fc 67.20N 23.48 E
Kolárovo 120 Ni 47.55N 18.00 E
Kolbäck 116 Ge 59.34N 16.15 E
Kolbäcksån 116 Ge 59.32N 16.16 E
Kolbio 170 Hc 1.09S 41.12 E
Kolbuszowa 120 Rf 50.15N 21.47 E
Kolby 116 Di 55.48N 10.33 E
Kolčugino 114 Jh 56.16N 39.23 E
Kolda 166 Cc 12.53N 14.57W
Kolding 112 Gd 55.31N 9.29 E
Kole [Zaire] 170 Eb 2.07N 25.26 E
Kole [Zaire] 170 Dc 3.31S 22.27 E
Koléa 126 Oh 36.38N 2.46 E
Kolendo 138 Jf 53.43N 142.57 E
Kolente 166 Cd 8.55N 13.08W
Kolesnoje 130 Mc 46.04N 29.45 E
Kolga 116 Ke 59.28N 25.29 E
Kolga, zaliv-/Kolga laht 116 Ke 59.30N 25.15 E
Kolga laht/Kolga, zaliv- 116 Ke 59.30N 25.15 E
Kolgompja, mys- 116 Me 59.44N 28.35 E
Kolgujev, ostrov- 110 Kb 69.05N 49.15 E
Kolhāpur 142 Jh 16.42N 74.13 E
Kolhozabad 135 Gf 37.35N 68.39 E
Kolhozbentskoje, vodohranilišče- 135 Df 37.10N 62.30 E
Koli 114 Ge 63.06N 29.53 E
Kolimbiné 166 Cc 14.45N 11.00 E
Kolin 120 Lf 50.02N 15.13 E
Kolito 168 Fd 7.25N 38.07 E
Koljučinskaja guba 138 Nc 66.50N 174.30W
Kolka 116 Jg 57.44N 22.27 E
Kolkasrags 114 Fh 57.46N 22.37 E
Kolki 132 Dd 51.07N 25.42 E
Kollinai 130 Fl 37.17N 22.22 E
Kollumúli 114a Cb 65.47N 14.21W
Kolmården 116 Gf 58.41N 16.35 E
Köln=Cologne (EN) 112 Ge 50.56N 6.57 E
Köln-Lövenich 124 Id 50.57N 6.50 E
Kolno 120 Rc 53.25N 21.56 E
Köln-Porz 120 Df 50.53N 7.03 E
Koło 120 Od 52.12N 18.38 E
Koloa 221a Bb 21.54N 159.28W
Kołobrzeg 120 Lb 54.12N 15.33 E
Kolodnja 132 Hb 54.49N 32.11 E
Kologriv 114 Kg 58.51N 44.17 E
Kolokani 166 Dc 13.34N 8.03W
Koloko 166 Dc 11.05N 5.19W
Kolokolkova guba 134 Fb 68.30N 52.30 E
Kololo 168 Gd 7.27N 41.59 E
Kolombangara Island 214 Fi 8.00S 157.05 E
Kolomna 112 Jd 55.05N 38.49 E
Kolomyja 136 Cf 48.32N 25.01 E
Kolondiéba 166 Dc 11.06N 6.53W
Kolonga 221b Ac 21.08S 175.04W
Kolonodale 150 Hg 2.00S 121.19 E
Kolosovka 136 Hd 56.28N 73.36 E
Kolossa 166 Dc 13.52N 7.35W
Kolovai 221b Ac 21.06S 175.20W
Kolozero, ozero- 114 Hb 68.15N 33.15 E
Kolp 114 Ig 59.20N 36.50 E
Kolpaševo 142 Kd 58.20N 82.50 E
Kolpino 114 Hg 59.45N 30.33 E
Kolpny 132 Jc 52.16N 37.00 E
Kolski poluostrov = Kola Peninsula (EN) 110 Jb 67.30N 37.00 E
Koltubanovski 132 Rc 52.57N 52.02 E
Kolubara 130 De 44.40N 20.15 E
Koluszki 120 Pe 51.44N 19.49 E
Koluton 136 Ge 51.42N 69.25 E
Kolva [R.S.F.S.R.] 134 Hf 60.22N 56.33 E
Kolva [R.S.F.S.R.] 136 Fb 65.55N 57.20 E
Kolvickoje, ozero- 114 Hc 67.05N 33.30 E
Kolvrå 116 Ch 56.18N 9.08 E
Kolwezi 160 Jj 10.43S 25.28 E
Kolyma 140 Sc 69.30N 161.00 E
Kolyma Plain (EN) = Kolymskaja nizmennost 140 Rc 68.30N 154.00 E
Kolyma Range (EN) = Kolymskoje nagorje 140 Rc 62.30N 155.00 E
Kolymskaja nizmennost = Kolyma Plain (EN) 140 Rc 68.30N 154.00 E
Kolymskoje nagorje = Kolyma Range (EN) 140 Rc 62.30N 155.00 E
Kolyšlej 132 Nc 52.40N 44.31 E
Kolžat 136 Ig 43.29N 80.37 E
Kom 170 Gb 1.05N 38.02 E
Kom 130 Gf 43.10N 23.03 E
Komádi 120 Fj 47.00N 21.30 E
Komadugu Gana 166 Hc 13.05N 12.24 E
Komadugu Yobe 158 Ig 13.42N 13.24 E
Komagane 156 Ed 35.43N 137.54 E
Koma-ga-Take [Jap.] 156 Fc 35.45N 138.13 E
Koma-ga-Take [Jap.] 156 Gb 39.47N 140.50 E
Koma-ga-Take [Jap.] 156a Bb 42.04N 140.40 E
Komandorski Islands (EN) = Komandorskije ostrova 140 Sd 55.00N 167.00 E
Komandorskije ostrova = Komandorski Islands (EN) 140 Sd 55.00N 167.00 E
Komandorskiye Basin (EN) 138 Le 57.00N 168.00 E
Komarin 132 Gd 51.27N 30.32 E
Komárno 120 Oi 47.46N 18.09 E
Komarno 120 Tg 49.34N 23.43 E
Komárom 120 Oi 47.44N 18.07 E
Komárom [2] 120 Oi 47.40N 18.15 E
Komatipoort 172 Ee 25.25S 31.55 E
Komatsu 152 Od 36.24N 136.37 E
Komatsujima 156 Dd 34.01N 134.35 E
Komba, Pulau- 150 Hh 7.47S 123.35 E
Kombissiri 166 Ec 12.04N 1.20W
Kombolcha 168 Fc 11.05N 39.45 E
Komebail Lagoon 220a Ac 7.24N 134.27 E
Komen/Comines 124 Ed 50.46N 2.59 E
Komi ASSR [3] 136 Fc 64.00N 55.00 E
Komi-Permjacki nacionalny okrug [3] 136 Fd 60.00N 54.30 E
Komló 120 Oj 46.12N 18.16 E
Kommunarsk 132 Ke 48.27N 38.52 E
Kommunary 116 Nd 60.55N 30.10 E
Kommunizma, pik- = Communism Peak (EN) 140 Jf 38.57N 72.08 E
Komodo, Pulau- 150 Gh 8.36S 119.30 E
Komoé [3] 166 Ec 10.25N 4.20W
Komoé 158 Gh 5.12N 3.44W
Komono 170 Ec 3.15S 13.14 E
Komoran, Pulau- 150 Kh 8.18S 138.45 E
Komoro 156 Fc 36.19N 138.24 E
Komotini 130 Ih 41.07N 25.24 E
Komovi 130 Cg 42.41N 19.39 E
Kompasberg 158 Jl 31.46S 24.32 E
Komrat 132 Ff 46.17N 28.38 E
Komsa 138 Dd 61.40N 89.25 E
Komsomolec 134 Kj 53.45N 62.02 E
Komsomolec, ostrov- 140 La 80.30N 95.00 E
Komsomolec, zaliv- 132 Rg 45.30N 52.45 E
Komsomolsk [R.S.F.S.R.] 138 De 57.25N 86.02 E
Komsomolsk [R.S.F.S.R.] 114 Jh 57.02N 40.22 E
Komsomolsk [Tur.-U.S.S.R.] 136 Gh 39.02N 63.36 E
Komsomolski [Kaz.-U.S.S.R.] 136 Ff 47.20N 53.44 E
Komsomolski [R.S.F.S.R.] 136 Gb 67.35N 63.47 E
Komsomolski [R.S.F.S.R.] 132 Og 45.22N 46.01 E
Komsomolski [R.S.F.S.R.] 114 Ki 54.27N 45.45 E
Komsomolski [R.S.F.S.R.] 134 Kf 61.20N 63.15 E
Komsomolski [R.S.F.S.R.] 138 Mc 69.12N 172.55 E
Komsomolsk-na-Amure 142 Pd 50.36N 137.02 E
Komsomolsk-na-Ustjurte 136 Fg 44.07N 58.17 E
Komsomolskoje [Ukr.-U.S.S.R.] 132 Je 49.36N 36.33 E
Komsomolskoje [Ukr.-U.S.S.R.] 132 Kf 47.37N 38.05 E

ex Symbols

dependent Nation
ate, Region
strict, County
nicipality
ony, Dependency
tinent
sical Region
Historical or Cultural Region
Mount, Mountain
Volcano
Hill
Mountains, Mountain Range
Hills, Escarpment
Plateau, Upland
Pass, Gap
Plain, Lowland
Delta
Salt Flat
Valley, Canyon
Crater, Cave
Karst Features
Depression
Polder
Desert, Dunes
Forest, Woods
Heath, Steppe
Oasis
Cape, Point
Coast, Beach
Cliff
Peninsula
Isthmus
Sandbank
Island
Atoll
Rock, Reef
Islands, Archipelago
Rocks, Reefs
Coral Reef
Well, Spring
Geyser
River, Stream
Waterfall, Rapids
River Mouth, Estuary
Lake
Salt Lake
Intermittent Lake
Reservoir
Swamp, Pond
Canal
Glacier
Ice Shelf, Pack Ice
Ocean
Sea
Gulf, Bay
Strait, Fjord
Lagoon
Bank
Seamount
Tablemount
Ridge
Shelf
Basin
Escarpment, Sea Scarp
Fracture
Trench, Abyss
National Park, Reserve
Point of Interest
Recreation Site
Cave, Cavern
Historic Site
Ruins
Wall, Walls
Church, Abbey
Temple
Scientific Station
Railway station
Airport
Port
Military installation
Lighthouse
Mine
Tunnel
Dam, Bridge

Komsomolskoj Pravdy, ostrova- 138 Fa 77.15N 107.30 E
Kõmun-Do 154 Ig 34.02N 127.19 E
Kömür Burun 130 Jk 38.39N 26.25 E
Komusan 152 Mc 42.07N 129.42 E
Kona 166 Ec 14.57N 3.53W
Kona Coast 221a Fd 19.35N 155.56W
Konakovo 136 Dd 56.42N 36.46 E
Konar 144 Lc 34.25N 70.32 E
Konārak 148 Hh 19.54N 86.07 E
Konarha [3] 144 Lb 35.15N 71.00 E
Konda 136 Gc 60.40N 69.46 E
Kondagaon 148 Ge 19.36N 81.40 E
Kondinin 212 Df 32.30S 118.16 E
Kondinskoje 134 Mg 59.40N 67.25 E
Kondoa 160 Ki 4.54S 35.47 E
Kondopoga 112 Jc 62.13N 34.17 E
Kondratjevo 116 Md 60.36N 28.02 E
Kondrovo 136 De 54.49N 35.55 E
Kondurča 114 Mj 53.31N 50.24 E
Koné 216 Bd 21.04S 164.52 E
Konečnaja 136 He 50.45N 78.27 E
Konevic, ostrov- 116 Nd 60.50N 30.45 E
Kong 166 Ed 9.09N 4.37W
Kõng 148 Lf 13.32N 105.58 E
Kõng, Kaôh- 148 Kf 11.20N 103.00 E
Konga/Koonga 116 Jf 58.34N 24.00 E
Kongauru 220a Ac 7.04N 134.17 E
Kong Christian IX Land = King Christian IX Land (EN) 224 Mc 68.00N 36.30W
Kong Christian X Land = King Christian X Land (EN) 224 Md 72.20N 32.30W
Kongeå 116 Ci 55.23N 8.39 E
Kong Frederik VIII Land = King Frederik VIII Land (EN) 224 Md 78.30N 28.00W
Kong Frederik VI Kyst = King Frederik VI Coast (EN) 224 Nc 63.00N 43.30W
Konginkangas 116 Kb 62.46N 25.48 E
Kongju 154 If 36.27N 127.08 E
Kong Karls Land 179 Oc 78.50N 28.00 E
Kong Kong 168 Ed 7.26N 33.14 E
Kongolo 160 Ji 5.23S 27.00 E
Kongor 168 Ed 7.10N 31.21 E
Kong Oscars Fjord 224 Md 72.20N 23.00W
Kongoussi 166 Ec 13.19N 1.32W
Kongsberg 114 Bg 59.39N 9.39 E
Kongsøya 179 Oc 78.55N 28.40 E
Kongsvinger 114 Cf 60.12N 12.00 E
Kongur Shan 140 Jf 38.40N 75.21 E
Kongwa 170 Gd 6.12S 36.25 E
Kong Wilhelms Land 179 Jc 75.48N 23.15W
Koniecpol 120 Pf 50.48N 19.41 E
Königslutter am Elm 120 Gd 52.15N 10.49 E
Konigswinter 124 Jd 50.41N 7.11 E
Königs Wusterhausen 120 Jd 52.17N 13.37 E
Konin 120 Od 52.13N 18.16 E
Konin [2] 120 Od 52.15N 18.15 E
Konispoli 130 Dj 39.39N 20.10 E
Kónitsa 130 Di 40.03N 20.45 E
Konj 128 Kg 43.43N 16.55 E
Konjed Jān 146 Nf 33.30N 50.27 E
Konjic 128 Lg 43.39N 17.58 E
Konjuh 128 Mf 44.18N 18.33 E
Konkan 148 Ee 18.05N 73.25 E
Konkiep 172 Be 28.00S 17.23 E
Konko 170 Ed 10.12S 27.27 E
Konkouré 166 Cd 9.58N 13.42W
Konnevesi 116 Lb 62.37N 26.19 E
Konnevesi 116 Lb 62.40N 26.35 E
Konnivesi 116 Lc 61.10N 26.10 E
Konoša 112 Kc 60.58N 40.15 E
Kōnosu 156 Fc 36.04N 139.30 E
Konotop 112 Je 51.14N 33.12 E
Konqi He 140 Ke 41.48N 86.47 E
Konrei 220a Bb 7.43N 134.37 E
Konsei-Tōge 156 Fc 36.52N 139.22 E
Konsen-Daichi 156a Db 43.20N 144.50 E
Końskie 120 Qe 51.12N 20.26 E
Konstantinovka 132 Je 48.29N 37.43 E
Konstantinovsk 132 Lf 47.35N 41.05 E
Konstanz 120 Fi 47.40N 9.11 E
Kontagora 160 Hg 10.24N 5.29 E
Kontcha 166 Hd 7.58N 12.14 E
Kontich 124 Gc 51.08N 4.27 E
Kontiolahti 114 Ge 62.46N 29.51 E
Kontiomäki 114 Gd 64.21N 28.09 E
Kontum 148 Lf 14.21N 108.00 E
Kontum, Plateau de- 148 Lf 13.55N 108.05 E
Konušin, mys- 114 Kc 67.10N 43.50 E
Konušinski bereg 134 Bc 66.45N 44.40 E
Konya 142 Ff 37.52N 32.31 E
Konya Ovası 146 Ed 37.30N 33.20 E
Konz 124 Ie 49.42N 6.35 E
Konza 170 Gc 1.45S 37.07 E
Konžakovski Kamen, gora- 110 Ld 59.38N 59.08 E
Koocanusa, Lake- 188 Hb 48.45N 115.15W
Kook, Punta- 221d Ab 27.08S 109.26W
Koolau Range 221a Db 21.21N 157.47W
Koonga/Konga 116 Jf 58.34N 24.00 E
Koorda 212 Df 30.50S 117.29 E
Koosa 116 Lf 58.33N 27.07 E
Kootenay Lake 188 Gb 49.35N 116.50W
Kootenay River 174 He 49.15N 117.39W
Kopa 135 Jc 43.31N 75.48 E
Kopaonik 130 Df 43.15N 20.50 E
Kópasker 114a Ca 66.18N 16.27W
Kópavogur 114a Bb 64.06N 21.55W
Kopejsk 136 Gd 55.08N 61.39 E
Koper 128 He 45.33N 13.44 E
Kopervik 114 Ag 59.17N 5.18 E
Kopetdag, hrebet- 140 Hf 37.45N 58.15 E
Kop Geçidi 146 Ib 40.01N 40.28 E
Ko Phangan 148 Jg 9.45N 100.00 E
Köping 114 Dg 59.31N 16.00 E
Köpingsvik 116 Gh 56.53N 16.43 E
Kopjevo 138 Df 54.59N 89.55 E
Kopliku 130 Cg 42.13N 19.26 E
Köpmanholmen 114 Ee 63.10N 18.34 E
Koporje 116 Me 59.40N 29.08 E
Koporski zaliv 116 Me 59.45N 28.45 E
Koppal 148 Fe 15.21N 76.09 E
Koppang 114 Cf 61.34N 11.04 E
Koppány 120 Oj 46.35N 18.26 E
Kopparberg 116 Fe 59.52N 14.59 E
Kopparberg [2] 114 Df 61.00N 14.30 E
Kopparstenarna 116 Hf 58.32N 19.20 E
Koppom 116 Ee 59.43N 12.09 E
Koprivnica 128 Kd 46.10N 16.50 E
Kopru 146 Dd 36.49N 31.10 E
Köprüören 130 Mj 39.30N 29.47 E
Kor 144 Hd 29.36N 53.18 E
Korab 110 Ig 41.44N 20.32 E
Korablino 114 Jj 53.57N 40.00 E
Korahe 168 Gd 6.36N 44.16 E
Korak 220a Bc 7.21N 134.34 E
Koralpe 128 Id 46.45N 15.00 E
Koramlik 152 Ed 37.32N 85.42 E
Korana 128 Je 45.30N 15.35 E
Korangi 148 Dd 24.47N 67.08 E
Koraput 148 Ge 18.49N 82.43 E
Korba 148 Gd 22.21N 82.41 E
Korbach 120 Ee 51.17N 8.52 E
Korça 130 Di 40.37N 20.46 E
Korčula 128 Lh 42.58N 17.08 E
Korčula 128 Kh 42.57N 16.55 E
Korčulanski kanal 128 Kg 43.03N 16.40 E
Kordān 146 Ne 35.56N 50.50 E
Kordel 124 Ie 49.50N 6.38 E
Kordestān [3] 144 Gb 35.30N 47.00 E
Kord Küy 144 Hb 36.48N 54.07 E
Kordun 128 Je 45.10N 15.35 E
Korea Bay (EN) = Sŏjosŏn-man 140 Of 39.15N 125.00 E
Korean Peninsula (EN) 140 Of 35.30N 125.30 E
Korea Strait (EN) = Taehan-Haehyŏp 140 Of 34.40N 129.00 E
Korea Strait (EN) = Tsushima-Kaikyō 140 Of 34.40N 129.00 E
Korec 132 Ed 50.37N 27.10 E
Korem 168 Fc 12.30N 39.32 E
Korenovsk 136 Df 45.28N 39.28 E
Korf 138 Ld 60.18N 166.01 E
Korfovski 138 Ig 48.11N 135.04 E
Korgen 114 Cc 66.05N 13.50 E
Kõrgesaare/Kyrgesare 116 Jf 59.00N 22.25 E
Korhogo 160 Gh 9.27N 5.38W
Korhogo [3] 166 Dd 9.35N 5.55W
Koribundu 166 Cd 7.43N 11.42W
Korienzé 166 Eb 15.24N 3.47W
Korinthiakós Kólpos = Corinth, Gulf of- (EN) 110 Ih 38.12N 22.30 E
Kórinthos 130 Fl 37.55N 22.53 E
Kórinthos = Corinth (EN) 130 Fl 37.55N 22.53 E
Korinthou, Dhiórix- = Corinth Canal (EN) 130 Fl 37.57N 22.58 E
Koriolei 160 Lh 1.48N 44.30 E
Kőrishegy 120 Ni 47.12N 17.49 E
Koritnik 130 Dg 42.05N 20.34 E
Kōriyama 152 Pd 37.24N 140.23 E
Korjakskaja Sopka, vulkan- 140 Rd 53.20N 158.47 E
Korjakski nacionalny okrug [3] 138 Le 60.00N 163.00 E
Korjakskoje nagorje = Koryak Range (EN) 140 Tc 62.30N 172.00 E
Korjažma 136 Ec 61.18N 47.07 E
Korjukovka 132 Hd 51.47N 32.17 E
Korkino 134 Ji 54.54N 61.25 E
Korkodon 138 Kd 64.43N 154.05 E
Korkuteli 146 Dd 37.04N 30.13 E
Korla 142 Ke 41.44N 86.09 E
Körmend 120 Mi 47.01N 16.36 E
Kormy, gora- 138 Fd 62.15N 106.08 E
Kornati 128 Jg 43.49N 15.20 E
Kornejevka 134 Ni 54.01N 68.27 E
Kornešty 130 Kb 47.23N 28.00 E
Korneuburg 128 Kb 48.21N 16.20 E
Kórnik 120 Nd 52.17N 17.04 E
Kornsjø 114 Cg 58.57N 11.39 E
Koro 166 Ec 14.05N 3.04W
Koroba 212 Ia 5.40S 142.45 E
Koroča 132 Jd 50.50N 37.13 E
Köroğlu Dağları 144 Da 40.40N 32.35 E
Köroğlu Tepe 146 Db 40.31N 31.53 E
Korogwe 170 Gd 5.09S 38.29 E
Koro Island 208 If 17.32S 179.42 E
Koroit 212 Ig 38.17S 142.22 E
Korolevo 120 Th 48.08N 23.07 E
Korolevu 219d Ac 18.12S 177.53 E
Korom, Bahr 168 Bc 10.35N 19.45 E
Koromiri 220p Cc 21.15S 159.43W
Koronadal 150 He 6.12N 125.01 E
Korónia, Límni- 130 Gi 40.40N 23.10 E
Koronowo 120 Nc 53.19N 17.57 E
Koronowski e, Jezioro- 120 Nc 53.22N 17.55 E
Koror 210 Ed 7.20N 134.29 E
Koror 208 Ed 7.20N 134.30 E
Körös 120 Qj 46.43N 20.12 E
Koro Sea 216 Ec 18.00S 180.00
Korosten 112 Ie 50.57N 28.39 E
Korostyšev 132 Fd 50.18N 29.05 E
Korotaiha 134 Jb 68.55N 60.55 E
Koro Toro 160 Ig 16.05N 18.30 E
Korovin Volcano 178a Db 52.22N 174.10W
Korpijärvi 116 Lc 61.15N 27.10 E
Korpilahti 114 Fe 62.01N 25.33 E
Korpo/Korppoo 116 Id 60.10N 21.35 E
Korppoo/Korpo 116 Id 60.10N 21.35 E
Korsakov 138 Jg 46.37N 142.51 E
Korshäs 114 Ee 62.47N 21.12 E
Korsholm/Mustasaari 116 Ia 63.05N 21.43 E
Korso 116 Kd 60.21N 25.06 E
Korsør 114 Ci 55.20N 11.09 E
Korsun-Ševčenkovski 132 Ge 49.26N 31.18 E
Korsze 120 Rb 54.10N 21.09 E
Kortemark 124 Fc 51.02N 3.02 E
Kortrijk/Courtrai 122 Jd 50.50N 3.16 E
Korucu 130 Kj 39.28N 27.22 E
Koru Dağ 130 Ji 40.42N 26.45 E
Koryak Range (EN) = Korjakskoje nagorje 140 Tc 62.30N 172.00 E
Korzybie 120 Mb 54.18N 16.50 E
Kos 130 Km 36.53N 27.18 E
Kos 130 Km 36.50N 27.10 E
Kosa 134 Gg 59.56N 55.01 E
Kosa 134 Gf 60.11N 55.10 E
Kosai 156 Ed 34.43N 137.30 E
Kosaja Gora 132 Jb 54.09N 37.31 E
Kosaka 156 Ga 40.20N 140.44 E
Kō-Saki 156 Ad 34.05N 129.13 E
Ko Samui 148 Jg 9.30N 99.58 E
Kosan-ŭp 152 Md 38.51N 127.25 E
Koščagyl 132 Rf 46.52N 53.47 E
Kościan 120 Md 52.06N 16.38 E
Kościerzyna 120 Nb 54.08N 18.00 E
Kosciusko 186 Lj 32.58N 89.35W
Kosciusko, Mount- 208 Fh 36.27S 148.16 E
Kose/Koze 116 Ke 59.11N 25.05 E
Köse Dağ 146 Gb 40.06N 37.58 E
Kosha 168 Ea 20.49N 30.32 E
Koshigaya 156 Fd 35.55N 139.45 E
Koshiji 156 Fc 37.24N 138.45 E
Koshiki-Kaikyō 156 Bf 31.45N 130.05 E
Koshiki Rettō 152 Me 31.45N 129.45 E
Koshimizu 156a Db 43.51N 144.25 E
Kōshoku 154 Of 36.38N 138.06 E
Kōshyū Seamount (EN) 156 Df 31.35N 135.50 E
Košice 112 If 48.43N 21.15 E
Kosjerić 130 Cf 44.00N 19.55 E
Kosju 134 Id 65.38N 58.59 E
Kosju 134 Ic 66.18N 59.53 E
Köşk 130 Ll 37.51N 28.03 E
Koski 116 Jd 60.39N 23.09 E
Koskolovo 116 Me 59.34N 28.30 E
Koslan 136 Ec 63.29N 48.52 E
Kosma 134 Dd 65.43N 49.50 E
Kosmaj 130 De 44.28N 20.33 E
Kosŏng 152 Md 38.40N 128.19 E
Kosov 130 Ia 48.15N 25.08 E
Kosovo [3] 130 Dg 42.35N 21.00 E
Kosovo 130 Eg 42.40N 21.05 E
Kosovska Mitrovica 130 Dg 42.53N 20.52 E
Kosrae (Kusaie) 208 Hd 5.19N 162.59 E
Kossol Passage 220a Bb 7.52N 134.36 E
Kossol Reef 220a Bb 7.57N 134.41 E
Kossou, Barrage de- 166 Dd 7.01N 5.29W
Kossovo 132 Dc 52.47N 25.10 E
Kostajnica 128 Ke 45.13N 16.33 E
Kostenec 130 Gg 42.16N 23.49 E
Koster 172 De 25.57S 26.42 E
Kosteröarna 116 Df 58.55N 11.05 E
Kostjukoviči 132 Hc 53.23N 32.06 E
Kostjukovka 132 Gc 52.32N 30.58 E
Kostolac 130 Ee 44.44N 21.12 E
Kostopol 132 Ed 50.53N 26.29 E
Kostriževka 130 Ia 48.31N 25.45 E
Kostroma 112 Kd 57.47N 40.59 E
Kostromskaja oblast [3] 136 Ed 58.30N 44.00 E
Kostrzyń 120 Nd 52.25N 17.14 E
Kostrzyn 120 Kd 52.37N 14.39 E
Kosva 134 Hg 58.50N 56.45 E
Koszalin 120 Mb 54.12N 16.09 E
Koszalin [2] 120 Mb 54.10N 16.10 E
Kőszeg 120 Mi 47.23N 16.33 E
Kota 142 Jg 25.16N 75.55 E
Kotaagung 150 Dh 5.30S 104.38 E
Kota Baharu 142 Mi 6.08N 102.15 E
Kotabaru 150 Gg 3.14S 116.13 E
Kotabumi 142 Mj 4.50S 104.54 E
Kotadabok 150 Dg 0.30S 104.33 E
Kota Kinabalu 142 Ni 5.59N 116.04 E
Kotamobagu 150 Hf 0.46N 124.19 E
Ko Tao 148 Jf 10.05N 99.52 E
Kotari 128 Jf 44.05N 15.30 E
Ko Tarutau 148 Jg 6.35N 99.40 E
Kota Tinggi 150 Df 1.44N 103.54 E
Kotel 130 Jg 42.53N 26.27 E
Kotelnič 136 Ed 58.20N 48.20 E
Kotelnikovo 132 Mf 47.38N 43.09 E
Kotelny, ostrov- 140 Pb 75.45N 138.44 E
Kotelva 132 Id 50.03N 34.45 E
Köthen 120 He 51.45N 11.58 E
Kotido 170 Fb 3.00N 34.09 E
Kotjužany 156 Gb 47.50N 28.27 E
Kotka 114 Gf 60.28N 26.55 E
Kot Kapūra 148 Eb 30.35N 74.54 E
Kotlas 112 Kc 61.16N 46.35 E
Kotlenik 130 Df 43.51N 20.42 E
Kotlenski prohod 130 Jg 42.53N 26.27 E
Kotlik 178 Gd 63.02N 163.33W
Kotlin, ostrov- 116 Md 60.00N 29.45 E
Kotly 116 Me 59.30N 28.48 E
Kotobi 166 Ed 6.42N 4.08W
Kotohira 156 Cd 34.11N 133.48 E
Koton Karifi 166 Gd 8.06N 6.48 E
Kotor 130 Bg 42.25N 18.46 E
Kotorosl 114 Jh 57.38N 39.57 E
Kotorska, Boka- 130 Bg 42.25N 18.40 E
Kotor Varoš 128 Lf 44.37N 17.22 E
Kotouba 166 Ed 8.41N 3.12W
Kotovo 136 Ee 50.18N 44.48 E
Kotovsk [Mold.-U.S.S.R.] 132 Ff 46.49N 28.33 E
Kotovsk [R.S.F.S.R.] 136 Ee 52.35N 41.32 E
Kotovsk [Ukr.-U.S.S.R.] 136 Cf 47.43N 29.33 E
Kotra 120 Uc 53.32N 24.17 E
Kotri 148 Dc 25.22N 68.18 E
Kötschach 128 Gd 46.40N 13.00 E
Kottayam 148 Fg 9.35N 76.31 E
Kotto 158 Jh 4.14N 22.02 E
Kotton 168 Id 9.37N 50.32 E
Kotu 221b Ba 19.57S 174.48W
Kotu Group 208 Jg 20.00S 174.45W
Kotuj 140 Mb 71.55N 102.05 E
Kotujkan 138 Fb 70.40N 103.25 E
Koturdepe 132 Rj 39.26N 53.40 E
Kotzebue 176 Cc 66.53N 162.39W
Kotzebue Sound 174 Cc 66.20N 163.00W
Kouandé 166 Fc 10.20N 1.42 E
Kouango 168 Be 4.58N 19.59 E
Kouba Modounga 168 Bb 15.40N 18.15 E
Koudougou 160 Gg 11.44N 4.31W
Kouéré 166 Ec 10.27N 3.59W
Koufália 130 Fi 40.47N 22.35 E
Koufonision [Grc.] 130 Jo 34.56N 26.10 E
Koufonision [Grc.] 130 Im 36.55N 25.35 E
Koufonisiou, Stenón- 130 Jo 35.00N 26.10 E
Kouilou [3] 170 Bc 4.00S 12.00 E
Kouilou 158 Ii 4.28S 11.41 E
Koukdjuak 180 Kc 66.47N 73.10W
Kouki 168 Bd 7.10N 17.18 E
Koukourou 168 Cd 7.12N 20.02 E
Koulamoutou 170 Bc 1.08S 12.29 E
Koulikoro 166 Dc 12.51N 7.34W
Koulountou 166 Cc 13.15N 13.37W
Koumac 210 Hg 20.30S 164.12 E
Koumac, Grand Récif de- 219b Be 20.32S 164.04 E
Koumbi-Saleh 162 Ff 15.47N 7.58W
Koumi 156 Fc 36.05N 138.28 E
Koumpentoum 166 Cc 13.59N 14.34W
Koumra 168 Bd 8.55N 17.33 E
Koundara 160 Fg 12.29N 13.18W
Koundian 166 Cc 13.08N 10.42W
Kounoúpoi 130 Jm 36.32N 26.27 E
Kounradski 136 Hf 46.57N 75.01 E
Kounta 166 Eb 17.30N 0.40W
Koupéla 166 Ec 12.11N 0.21W
Kouqian → Yongji 154 Ic 43.40N 126.30 E
Kourou 202 Hb 5.09N 52.39W
Kouroussa 166 Dc 10.39N 9.53W
Koury 166 Ec 12.10N 4.48W
Koussané 166 Cc 14.52N 11.15W
Kousséri 166 Ic 12.05N 15.02 E
Koutiala 160 Gg 12.23N 5.27W
Koutoumo 219b Cf 22.40S 167.32 E
Koutous 166 Hc 14.30N 10.00 E
Kouvola 114 Gf 60.52N 26.42 E
Kouyou 170 Cc 0.45S 16.38 E
Kova 138 Fe 58.20N 100.20 E
Kovač 130 Cf 43.31N 19.07 E
Kovačica 130 Dd 45.06N 20.38 E
Koval 120 Pd 52.31N 19.10 E
Kovalevka 130 Nc 46.42N 30.31 E
Kovarskas/Kavarskas 116 Ki 55.24N 25.03 E
Kovdor 136 Db 67.33N 30.25 E
Kovdozero, ozero- 114 Hc 66.47N 32.00 E
Kovel 136 Ce 51.13N 24.43 E
Kovenskaja 134 Mf 61.24N 67.39 E
Kovinskaja grjada 138 Fe 57.15N 101.00 E
Kovozero, ozero- 114 Ic 67.50N 35.10 E
Kovrov 136 Ed 56.24N 41.20 E
Kovylkino 114 Ki 54.02N 43.58 E
Kowlī Kosh, Gardaneh-ye- 146 Og 30.47N 53.12 E
Kowŏn 152 Md 39.26N 127.15 E
Kowtal-e Do Rāh 144 Lb 36.07N 71.15 E
Kowt-e 'Ashrow 144 Kc 34.27N 68.48 E
Kōyama 156 Bf 31.19N 130.57 E
Kōya-San 156 Dd 34.13N 135.35 E
Köyceğiz 146 Cd 36.55N 28.43 E
Köycegiz Gölü 130 Lm 36.55N 28.40 E
Koyoshi-Gawa 156 Gb 39.24N 140.01 E
Koyuk 178 Gd 64.56N 161.08W
Koyukuk 174 Dc 64.56N 157.30W
Kozaklı 146 Fc 39.13N 34.49 E
Kozan 146 Fd 37.27N 35.49 E
Kozáni 130 Ei 40.18N 21.47 E
Kozara 128 Ke 45.00N 16.55 E
Kozawa 156a Bb 42.58N 140.40 E
Koze/Kose 116 Ke 59.11N 25.05 E
Kozelsk 136 De 54.01N 35.46 E
Koževnikovo 138 De 56.18N 84.00 E
Kozhikode → Calicut 142 Jh 11.19N 75.46 E
Kozienice 120 Re 51.35N 21.33 E
Kožim 134 Id 65.43N 59.31 E
Kožim 134 Id 65.45N 59.15 E
Kozjak 130 Eh 41.06N 21.54 E
Kozloduj 130 Gf 43.47N 23.44 E
Kozlovka 114 Li 55.52N 48.13 E
Kozlovščina 120 Vc 53.14N 25.20 E
Kozlu 146 Db 41.25N 31.46 E
Kozluk 146 Ic 38.11N 41.29 E
Koźmin 120 Ne 51.50N 17.28 E
Kozmodemjansk 114 Lh 56.20N 46.36 E
Kožozero, ozero- 114 Je 63.05N 38.05 E
Kożuchów 120 Le 51.45N 15.35 E
Kožuf 130 Fh 41.09N 22.10 E
Kōzu-Shima 152 Oe 34.15N 139.10 E
Kožva 134 Hd 65.07N 56.57 E
Kožva 134 Hd 65.10N 57.00 E
Kozyrevsk 138 Ke 55.59N 159.59 E
Kpalimé 166 Fd 6.54N 0.38 E
Kpandu 166 Fd 7.00N 0.18 E
Kpessi 166 Fd 8.04N 1.16 E
Kra, Isthmus of- (EN) = Kra, Khokhok- 140 Lh 10.20N 99.00 E
Kra, Khokhok- = Kra, Isthmus of- (EN) 140 Lh 10.20N 99.00 E
Kraba 130 Ch 41.12N 19.59 E
Krabbfjärden 116 Gf 58.45N 17.40 E
Krabi 148 Jg 8.05N 98.53 E
Krabit, Mali i- 130 Cg 42.07N 19.59 E
Kra Buri 148 Jf 10.24N 98.47 E
Krâchéh 142 Mh 12.29N 106.01 E
Kragerø 114 Bg 58.52N 9.25 E
Kragujevac 130 De 44.01N 20.55 E
Kraichbach 124 Ke 49.22N 8.31 E
Kraichgau 120 Eg 49.10N 8.50 E
Kraichtal 124 Ke 49.07N 8.46 E
Krajina 130 Fe 44.10N 22.30 E
Krajište 130 Fg 42.35N 22.25 E
Krajnovka 132 Oh 43.57N 47.24 E
Krakatau, Gunung- 140 Mj 6.07S 105.24 E
Krak des Chevaliers 146 Ge 34.46N 36.19 E
Krakovec 120 Tg 49.56N 23.13 E
Kraków 112 He 50.03N 19.58 E
Kraków [2] 120 Pf 50.05N 20.00 E
Kraków-Nowa Huta 120 Qf 50.04N 20.05 E
Krakowsko-Częstochowska, Wyżyna- 120 Pf 50.50N 19.15 E
Kralendijk 196 Bf 12.10N 68.16W
Kraljevica 128 Ie 45.16N 14.34 E
Kraljevo 130 Df 43.44N 20.43 E
Kralupy nad Vltavou 120 Kf 50.14N 14.19 E
Kramatorsk 132 Je 48.43N 37.32 E
Kramfors 114 De 62.56N 17.47 E
Krammer 124 Gc 51.38N 4.15 E
Kranenburg 124 Ic 51.47N 6.01 E
Kranídhion 130 Gl 37.23N 23.09 E
Kranj 128 Id 46.14N 14.22 E
Krapina 128 Jd 46.10N 15.53 E
Krapkowice 120 Nf 50.29N 17.56 E
Kras = Karst (EN) 110 Hf 45.48N 14.00 E
Krasavino 136 Ec 60.59N 46.28 E
Krasiczyn 120 Sg 49.48N 22.39 E
Krasilov 132 Ee 49.37N 26.59 E
Kraskino 154 Kc 42.44N 130.48 E
Kraslava/Krāslava 114 Gi 55.54N 27.10 E
Krāslava/Kraslava 114 Gi 55.54N 27.10 E
Krasnaja Poljana 132 Lh 43.40N 40.12 E
Kraśnik 120 Sf 50.56N 22.13 E
Kraśnik Fabryczny, Kraśnik- 120 Sf 50.58N 22.12 E
Kraśnik-Kraśnik Fabryczny 120 Sf 50.58N 22.12 E
Krasnoarmejsk [Kaz.-U.S.S.R.] 136 Ge 53.57N 69.43 E
Krasnoarmejsk [R.S.F.S.R.] 136 Ee 51.02N 45.42 E
Krasnoarmejsk [Ukr.-U.S.S.R.] 132 Je 48.11N 37.12 E
Krasnoarmejski 138 Mc 69.37N 172.02 E
Krasnodar 112 Jf 45.02N 39.00 E
Krasnodarski kraj [3] 136 Df 45.20N 39.30 E
Krasnodon 132 Ke 48.17N 39.44 E
Krasnogorodskoje 116 Mh 56.47N 28.18 E
Krasnogorsk [R.S.F.S.R.] 138 Jg 48.26N 142.10 E
Krasnogorsk [R.S.F.S.R.] 114 Ii 55.51N 37.20 E
Krasnogorski 134 Ji 54.36N 61.15 E
Krasnograd 136 Df 49.22N 35.27 E
Krasnogvardejsk 135 Fe 39.45N 67.16 E
Krasnogvardejskoje 132 Lg 45.49N 41.31 E
Krasnoholmski 134 Gh 56.02N 55.05 E
Krasnoilsk 130 Ia 48.02N 25.48 E
Krasnojarsk 142 Ld 56.01N 92.50 E
Krasnojarski 134 Ik 51.58N 59.57 E
Krasnojarski kraj [3] 138 Ee 57.30N 95.00 E
Krasnojarskoje vodohranilišče 138 Ee 55.05N 91.30 E
Krasnoje 120 Ug 49.49N 24.39 E
Krasnoje Selo 114 Hg 59.43N 30.03 E
Krasnoje Znamja 135 Df 36.50N 62.29 E
Krasnokamensk 138 Gf 50.00N 118.05 E
Krasnokamsk 136 Fd 58.04N 55.45 E
Krasnokutsk 136 He 52.59N 75.59 E
Krasnolesje 116 Jj 54.23N 22.25 E
Krasnolesny 132 Kd 51.52N 39.35 E
Krasnooktjabrski [Kirg.-U.S.S.R.] 135 Jc 42.45N 74.20 E
Krasnooktjabrski [R.S.F.S.R.] 114 Lh 56.43N 47.37 E
Krasnooskolskoje vodohranilišče 132 Je 49.25N 37.35 E
Krasnoostrovski 116 Md 60.12N 28.39 E
Krasnoperekopsk 136 Df 45.57N 33.47 E
Krasnorečenski 154 Mb 44.38N 135.15 E
Krasnoščelje 114 Ic 67.23N 37.02 E
Krasnoselki 120 Uc 53.14N 24.30 E
Krasnoselkup 138 Dc 65.41N 82.28 E
Krasnoslobodsk [R.S.F.S.R.] 114 Ki 54.27N 43.47 E
Krasnoslobodsk [R.S.F.S.R.] 132 Ne 48.40N 44.31 E
Krasnoturinsk 136 Gd 59.46N 60.18 E
Krasnoufimsk 136 Fd 56.37N 57.46 E
Krasnouralsk 136 Gd 58.24N 60.03 E
Krasnousolski 136 Fe 53.54N 56.29 E
Krasnovišersk 136 Fc 60.23N 57.03 E
Krasnovodkaja oblast [3] 136 Fh 39.50N 55.00 E
Krasnovodsk 142 He 40.00N 53.00 E
Krasnovodski poluostrov 110 Lg 40.30N 53.15 E
Krasnovodski zaliv 132 Rj 39.50N 53.15 E
Krasnozatonski 136 Fc 61.41N 51.01 E
Krasnozavodsk 114 Jh 56.29N 38.13 E
Krasnoznamensk [Kaz.-U.S.S.R.] 136 Ge 51.03N 69.30 E
Krasnoznamensk [R.S.F.S.R.] 116 Jj 54.52N 22.27 E
Krasny Čikoj 138 Ff 50.25N 108.45 E
Krasny Holm 114 Ig 58.04N 37.09 E
Krasny Jar [R.S.F.S.R.] 138 De 57.07N 84.40 E
Krasny Jar [R.S.F.S.R.] 136 Hd 55.14N 72.56 E
Krasnyje Barrikady 132 Of 46.13N 47.50
Krasnyje Okny 130 Mb 47.34N 29.23
Krasny Kut 136 Ee 50.58N 46.58
Krasny Liman 132 Je 48.59N 37.47
Krasny Luč 132 Ke 48.09N 38.57
Krasny Oktjabr 136 Gd 55.37N 64.48
Krasny Profintern 114 Jh 57.47N 40.2
Krasnystaw 120 Tf 50.59N 23.1
Krasny Sulin 132 Lf 47.53N 40.0
Kratovo 130 Fg 42.05N 22.1
Kraulshavn 179 Gd 74.10N 57.0
Krawang 150 Eh 6.19S 107.
Krefeld 120 Ce 51.20N 6.
Krefeld-Hüls 124 Ic 51.22N 6
Kremastá, Limni- 130 Ek 38.50N 21

Index Symbols

- [1] Independent Nation
- [2] State, Region
- [3] District, County
- [4] Municipality
- [5] Colony, Dependency
- Continent
- Physical Region
- Historical or Cultural Region
- Mount, Mountain
- Volcano
- Hill
- Mountains, Mountain Range
- Hills, Escarpment
- Plateau, Upland
- Pass, Gap
- Plain, Lowland
- Delta
- Salt Flat
- Valley, Canyon
- Crater, Cave
- Karst Features
- Depression
- Polder
- Desert, Dunes
- Forest, Woods
- Heath, Steppe
- Oasis
- Cape, Point
- Coast, Beach
- Cliff
- Peninsula
- Isthmus
- Sandbank
- Island
- Atoll
- Rock, Reef
- Islands, Archipelago
- Rocks, Reefs
- Coral Reef
- Well, Spring
- Geyser
- River, Stream
- Waterfall, Rapids
- River Mouth, Estuary
- Lake
- Salt Lake
- Intermittent Lake
- Reservoir
- Swamp, Pond
- Canal
- Glacier
- Ice Shelf, Pack Ice
- Ocean
- Sea
- Gulf, Bay
- Strait, Fjord
- Lagoon
- Bank
- Seamount
- Tablemount
- Ridge
- Shelf
- Basin
- Escarpment, Sea Scarp
- Fracture
- Trench, Abyss
- National Park, Reserve
- Point of Interest
- Recreation Site
- Cave, Cavern
- Historic Site
- Ruins
- Wall, Walls
- Church, Abbey
- Temple
- Scientific Station
- Railway station
- Airport
- Port
- Military inst
- Lighthouse
- Mine
- Tunnel
- Dam, Bridg

Kremenchug Reservoir (EN) = Kremenčugskoje vodohranilišče	110	Jf	49.20N	32.30 E
Kremenčug	112	Jf	49.04N	33.25 E
Kremenčugskoje vodohranilišče = Kremenchug Reservoir (EN)	110	Jf	49.20N	32.30 E
Kremenec	132	Dd	50.06N	25.43 E
Kremennaja	132	Ke	49.03N	38.14 E
Kremmling	186	Cf	40.03N	106.24W
Krems	128	Jb	48.25N	15.36 E
Krems an der Donau	128	Jb	48.25N	15.36 E
Kremsmünster	128	Ib	48.03N	14.08 E
Krenitzin Islands	178a	Eb	54.08N	166.00W
Kresta, zaliv-	138	Nc	65.30N	179.00W
Krestcy	114	Hg	58.15N	32.31 E
Krestovy, pereval-	132	Nh	42.32N	44.30 E
Kretek	150	Fh	7.59S	110.19 E
Kretinga	114	Ei	55.55N	21.17 E
Kreuzau	124	Id	50.45N	6.29 E
Kreuzberg	120	Ff	50.22N	9.58 E
Kreuzlingen	128	Dc	47.39N	9.10 E
Kreuztal	120	Df	50.58N	7.59 E
Kria Vrisi	130	Fi	40.41N	22.18 E
Kribi	160	Hh	2.57N	9.55 E
Kričev	136	De	53.43N	31.43 E
Kričim	130	Hg	42.08N	24.31 E
Krim	128	Ie	45.56N	14.28 E
Krimml	128	Gc	47.13N	12.11 E
Krimpen aan den IJssel	124	Gc	51.55N	4.35 E
Kriōs, Akra-	110	Ih	35.14N	23.35 E
Krishna	140	Kh	15.57N	80.59 E
Krishnanagar	148	Hd	23.24N	88.30 E
Kristdala	116	Gg	57.24N	16.11 E
Kristiansand	116	Gd	58.10N	8.00 E
Kristianstad	114	Dh	56.02N	14.08 E
Kristianstad [2]	114	Ch	56.15N	14.00 E
Kristiansund	112	Gc	63.07N	7.45 E
Kristiinankaupunki/Kristinestad	114	Ee	62.17N	21.23 E
Kristineberg	114	Ed	65.04N	18.35 E
Kristinehamn	114	Dg	59.20N	14.07 E
Kristinestad/Kristiinankaupunki	114	Ee	62.17N	21.23 E
Kríti = Crete (EN) [2]	130	Hn	35.35N	25.00 E
Kríti = Crete (EN)	110	Ih	35.15N	24.45 E
Kritikón Pélagos = Crete, Sea of- (EN)	130	Hn	36.00N	25.00 E
Krivaja	128	Mf	44.27N	18.10 E
Kriva Palanka	130	Fg	42.12N	22.21 E
Kriviči	116	Lj	54.44N	27.20 E
Krivodol	130	Gf	43.23N	23.29 E
Krivoje Ozero	132	Gf	47.57N	30.21 E
Krivoj Rog	112	Jf	47.54N	33.21 E
Križevci	128	Kd	46.02N	16.32 E
Krk	128	Ie	45.02N	14.35 E
Krk	128	Ie	45.05N	14.35 E
Krka [Yugo.]	128	Je	45.53N	15.26 E
Krka [Yugo.]	128	Jg	43.43N	15.51 E
Krkonoše	120	Lf	50.46N	15.35 E
Krn	128	Hd	46.16N	13.40 E
Krndija	128	Le	45.27N	17.55 E
Krnjača, Beograd-	130	De	44.52N	20.28 E
Krnov	120	Nf	50.05N	17.41 E
Krobia	120	Me	51.47N	16.58 E
Krøderen	116	Cd	60.15N	9.40 E
Krokeai	130	Fm	36.53N	22.33 E
Krokek	116	Gf	58.40N	16.24 E
Kroken	114	Dd	65.22N	14.16 E
Krokom	114	De	63.20N	14.28 E
Krolevec	132	Hd	51.32N	33.30 E
Kroměříž	120	Ng	49.18N	17.22 E
Krompachy	120	Qh	48.56N	20.52 E
Kronach	120	Hf	50.14N	11.19 E
Krông Kaôh Kŏng	148	Kf	11.37N	102.59 E
Kronoberg [2]	114	Dh	56.40N	14.40 E
Kronockaja Sopka, vulkan-	138	Lf	54.47N	160.35 E
Kronocki, mys-	138	Lf	54.43N	162.07 E
Kronocki zaliv	138	Lf	54.00N	161.00 E
Kronoki	138	Lf	54.33N	161.14 E
Kronprins Christian Land	179	Jb	80.45N	22.00W
Kronprinsesse Mærtha Kyst	222	Bf	72.00S	7.30W
Kronprins Frederiks Bjerge	179	Ie	67.20N	34.00W
Kronprins Olav Kyst	222	Ee	68.30S	42.30 E
Kronštadt	136	Cc	60.01N	29.44 E
Kroonstad	160	Jk	27.46S	27.12 E
Kropotkin [R.S.F.S.R.]	136	Ef	45.26N	40.34 E
Kropotkin [R.S.F.S.R.]	136	Ge	58.36N	115.27 E
Kroppefjäll	116	Ef	58.40N	12.13 E
Krośniewice	120	Pd	52.16N	19.10 E
Krosno	120	Rg	49.42N	21.46 E
Krosno [2]	120	Rg	49.40N	21.45 E
Krosno Odrzańskie	120	Ld	52.04N	15.05 E
Krossfjorden	116	Ad	60.10N	5.05 E
Krotoszyn	120	Ne	51.42N	17.26 E
Kroviga, gora-	138	Ed	60.40N	91.30 E
Krško	128	Je	45.58N	15.28 E
Krstača	130	Dg	42.58N	20.08 E
Krugersdorp	160	Jk	26.05S	27.35 E
Krui	150	Dh	5.11S	103.56 E
Kruibeke	124	Gc	50.10N	4.19 E
Kruiningen	124	Gc	51.27N	4.02 E
Kruja	130	Ch	41.30N	19.48 E
Kruklevščina	116	Li	55.03N	27.52 E
Krumbach	120	Gh	48.15N	10.22 E
Krumovgrad	130	Ih	41.28N	25.39 E
Krung Thep = Bangkok (EN)	142	Mh	13.45N	100.31 E
Krupanj	130	Ce	44.22N	19.22 E
Krupnica	120	Oh	48.05N	18.54 E
Krupinská vrchovina	120	Ph	48.20N	19.15 E
	116	Cj	54.50N	9.25 E
Kruşdol	130	Cd	45.07N	19.57 E
Kruševac	130	Ef	43.35N	21.20 E
Kruševo	130	Eh	41.22N	21.15 E
Krušné Hory = Ore Mountains (EN)	110	He	50.30N	13.15 E
Krustpils	116	Lh	56.29N	26.00 E
Kruzof	178	Le	57.10N	135.40W
Krym	132	Jg	45.23N	36.36 E
Krymsk	136	Dg	44.54N	37.57 E
Krymskaja oblast [3]	136	Dg	45.15N	34.20 E
Krymskije gory = Crimean Mountains (EN)	110	Jg	44.45N	34.30 E
Krymski poluostrov = Crimea (EN)	110	Jf	45.00N	34.00 E
Krynica	120	Qg	49.25N	20.56 E
Krzemieniucha	120	Sb	54.12N	22.54 E
Krzepice	120	Of	50.58N	18.44 E
Krzna	120	Td	52.08N	23.31 E
Krzywiń	120	Me	51.58N	16.49 E
Krzyż	120	Md	52.53N	16.01 E
Ksar el Boukhari	162	Hb	35.53N	2.45 E
Ksar el Kebir	162	Fc	35.00N	5.59W
Ksar es Srhir	126	Gi	35.51N	5.34W
Ksenjevka	138	Gf	53.34N	118.44 E
Kšenski	132	Jd	51.52N	37.44 E
Ksour, Monts des-	162	Gc	32.45N	0.10W
Kstovo	114	Kh	56.12N	44.11 E
Kū', Wādī al-	168	Dc	12.12N	25.43 E
Kuai He	154	Dh	33.03N	117.32 E
Kuala Belait	150	Ff	4.35N	114.11 E
Kuala Dungun	150	Df	4.47N	103.26 E
Kuala Kangsar	150	Df	4.46N	100.56 E
Kualakapuas	150	Fg	3.01S	114.21 E
Kuala Kerai	150	De	5.32N	102.12 E
Kualakurun	150	Fg	1.07S	113.53 E
Kualalangsa	150	Cf	4.32N	98.01 E
Kuala Lipis	150	Df	4.11N	102.03 E
Kuala Lumpur	142	Mi	3.10N	101.42 E
Kuala Lumpur [2]	150	Df	3.14N	101.40 E
Kuala Pilah	150	Df	2.44N	102.15 E
Kuala Rompin	150	Df	2.49N	103.29 E
Kuala Terengganu	142	Mi	5.20N	103.08 E
Kuancheng	154	Ed	40.37N	118.31 E
Kuandang	150	Hf	0.52N	122.55 E
Kuandian	152	Lc	40.45N	124.48 E
Kuang-hsi-chuang-tsu Tzu-chih-ch'ü → Guangxi Zhuangzu Zizhiqu [2]	152	Ig	24.00N	109.00 E
Kuang-tung Sheng → Guangdong Sheng [2]	152	Jg	23.00N	113.00 E
Kuantan	150	Df	3.48N	103.20 E
Kuba	136	Eg	41.20N	48.35 E
Kuban	110	Jf	45.20N	37.30 E
Kuba-Shima	156b	Ab	26.10N	127.15 E
Kubaysah	146	Jf	33.35N	42.37 E
Kubbum	168	Cc	11.47N	23.47 E
Kubena	114	Jg	59.37N	39.48 E
Kubenskoje, ozero-	114	Jg	59.40N	39.33 E
Kubnja	114	Li	55.32N	48.28 E
Kubokawa	154	Lh	33.12N	133.08 E
Kubolta	130	Lb	47.48N	28.03 E
Kubrat	130	Jf	43.48N	26.30 E
Kubumesaai	150	Gf	1.31N	115.06 E
Kučaj	130	Ef	43.53N	21.44 E
Kučevo	130	Ee	44.29N	21.41 E
Kuching	142	Ni	1.33N	110.20 E
Kuchinoerabu-Shima	154	Ki	30.28N	130.10 E
Kuchinotsu	156	Be	32.36N	130.12 E
Kuçukçekmece	130	Li	40.59N	28.46 E
Küçükkerekköy	146	Ee	35.22N	33.45 E
Küçükkuyu	130	Jj	39.32N	26.36 E
Küçük Menderes	130	Kl	37.57N	27.16 E
Kučurgan	130	Mc	46.35N	29.55 E
Kudaka-Jima	156b	Ab	26.10N	127.54 E
Kudamatsu	156	Bd	34.01N	131.53 E
Kudat	150	Ge	6.53N	116.50 E
Kudeb	116	Mg	57.30N	28.16 E
Kudirkos-Naumestis	116	Jj	54.43N	22.49 E
Kudowa Zdrój	120	Mf	50.27N	16.20 E
Kudremukh	148	Ff	13.08N	75.16 E
Kudus	150	Fh	6.48S	110.50 E
Kudymkar	136	Fd	59.01N	54.37 E
Kuee Ruins	221a	Fd	19.12N	155.23W
Kuei-chou Sheng → Guizhou Sheng = Kweichow (EN) [2]	152	If	27.00N	107.00 E
Kufi	146	Cc	38.10N	29.43 E
Kufrah, Wāḥāt al- = Kufra Oasis (EN)	158	Jf	24.10N	23.15 E
Kufra Oasis (EN) = Kufrah, Wāḥāt al-	158	Jf	24.10N	23.15 E
Kufstein	128	Gc	47.35N	12.10 E
Kuganavolok	114	Ie	62.16N	36.55 E
Kugmallit Bay	180	Ec	69.30N	133.20W
Kugojeja	132	Kf	46.33N	39.38 E
Kūh, Ra's al-	146	Qj	25.48N	57.19 E
Kuḥaylī	168	Eb	19.29N	32.49 E
Kūhbonān	146	Qg	31.23N	56.19 E
Kühdasht	146	Lf	33.32N	47.36 E
Kūh-e Būrh	146	Pi	27.22N	54.40 E
Kūh-e Gāvbūs	146	Oi	27.10N	54.00 E
Kūh-e Karkas	146	Nf	33.27N	51.48 E
Kūh-e Kārūn	146	Nq	31.27N	50.18 E
Kūhestak	146	Qi	26.47N	57.02 E
Kūhīn, Gardaneh-ye-	146	Md	36.23N	49.37 E
Kühlungsborn	120	Hb	54.09N	11.43 E
Kuhmo	114	Gd	64.08N	29.31 E
Kuhmoinen	116	Kc	61.34N	25.11 E
Kuhn	179	Kd	74.45N	19.45W
Kūhpāyeh	144	Ic	30.35N	57.15 E
Kūhpāyeh [Iran]	146	Og	30.43N	57.30 E
Kūhpāyeh [Iran]	146	Of	32.43N	52.26 E
Kūhrān, Kūh-e-	144	Id	26.46N	58.12 E
Kuhtuj	138	Je	59.23N	143.10 E
Kuhva	116	Mg	57.17N	28.17 E
Kuiseb	172	Ad	23.00S	14.33 E
Kuishan Ding	154	Fj	28.32N	109.52 E
Kuito	160	Ij	12.23S	16.56 E
Kuiu	178	Me	57.45N	134.10W
Kuivaniemi	114	Fd	65.35N	25.11 E
Kujang	152	Md	39.52N	126.01 E
Kujawy	120	Od	52.45N	18.30 E
Kujbyšev [R.S.F.S.R.] → Samara	112	Le	53.12N	50.09 E
Kujbyšev [R.S.F.S.R.]	138	Ce	55.27N	78.29 E
Kujbyševskaja oblast [3]	136	Fe	53.20N	50.30 E
Kujbyševski [Kaz.-U.S.S.R.]	136	Ge	53.15N	66.51 E
Kujbyševski [Taj.-U.S.S.R.]	135	Gf	37.53N	68.44 E
Kujbyševskoje vodohranilišče = Kuybyshev Resevoir (EN)	110	Ke	53.50N	49.00 E
Kujeda	134	Gh	56.26N	55.35 E
Kujgan	136	Hf	45.22N	74.10 E
Kuji	154	Pd	40.11N	141.46 E
Kuji-Gawa	156	Gi	36.30N	140.37 E
Kujtun	138	Ff	54.21N	101.35 E
Kujūkuri-Hama	156	Gd	35.40N	140.30 E
Kujū-San	154	Kh	33.09N	131.15 E
Kūkalār, Kūh-e-	146	Ng	31.50N	50.53 E
Kukalaya, Rio-	194	Fg	13.39N	83.37W
Kukës	130	Dg	42.05N	20.24 E
Kukkia	116	Kc	61.20N	24.40 E
Kukmor	114	Mh	56.13N	50.52 E
Kükürt Tepe	146	Ib	41.07N	41.27 E
Kül	144	Id	27.15N	55.52 E
Kula [Bul.]	130	Ff	43.53N	22.31 E
Kula [Tur.]	146	Cc	38.30N	28.40 E
Kula [Yugo.]	130	Cd	45.37N	19.32 E
Kulai	150	Df	1.40N	103.36 E
Kulanak	135	Jd	41.18N	75.34 E
Kulandy	136	Ff	46.08N	59.31 E
Kular	138	Ib	70.32N	134.26 E
Kular, hrebet-	138	Ic	69.00N	133.30 E
Kulata	130	Gh	41.23N	23.22 E
Kulautuva	116	Jj	54.55N	23.43 E
Kulbus	168	Cc	14.24N	22.31 E
Kuldīga/Kuldiga	136	Cd	56.59N	21.59 E
Kuldīga/Kuldiga	136	Cd	56.59N	21.59 E
Kuldur	138	Ig	49.10N	131.40 E
Kulebaki	114	Ki	55.26N	42.32 E
Kulenjin	146	Me	35.40N	49.30 E
Kulen Vakuf	128	Kf	44.33N	16.06 E
Kulgera	210	Eg	25.50S	133.18 E
Kulikov	120	Ug	49.55N	24.06 E
Kulim	150	De	5.22N	100.34 E
Kuljab	136	Gh	37.55N	69.47 E
Kuljabskaja oblast [3]	136	Gh	38.00N	69.40 E
Kullaa	116	Jc	61.28N	22.10 E
Kullen	114	Ch	56.18N	12.26 E
Kulmasa	166	Ed	9.35N	2.27W
Kulmbach	120	Hf	50.06N	11.27 E
Kuloj	114	Kf	61.03N	42.30 E
Kuloj [R.S.F.S.R.]	136	Eb	66.00N	43.30 E
Kuloj [R.S.F.S.R.]	114	Kf	61.01N	42.12 E
Kulp	146	Ic	38.30N	41.02 E
Kulsary	136	Ff	46.57N	54.02 E
Kultuk	138	Ff	51.44N	103.42 E
Kulu	138	Jd	62.15N	147.45 E
Kulu [India]	148	Fb	31.58N	77.06 E
Kulu [Tur.]	146	Ei	39.06N	33.05 E
Kulumadau	219a	Ac	9.03S	152.43 E
Kulunda	138	Cf	52.35N	78.57 E
Kulundinskaja step	138	Cf	52.45N	79.00 E
Kulundinskoje, ozero-	138	Cf	53.00N	79.30 E
Kum	146	Bc	38.38N	27.32 E
Kum, Kūh-e-	146	Oh	29.55N	53.45 E
Kuma	156	Ce	33.39N	132.54 E
Kuma [R.S.F.S.R.]	114	Hc	66.15N	31.02 E
Kuma [R.S.F.S.R.]	134	Mg	59.33N	66.40 E
Kuma [U.S.S.R.]	110	Kg	44.56N	47.00 E
Kumagaya	154	Of	36.08N	139.23 E
Kumai [Indon.]	150	Fg	3.23S	112.33 E
Kumai [Indon.]	150	Fg	2.44S	111.43 E
Kumaishi	156a	Ab	42.08N	139.59 E
Kumak	132	Vd	51.13N	60.08 E
Kumamoto	142	Pf	32.48N	130.43 E
Kumamoto Ken [2]	154	Kh	32.30N	130.50 E
Kumano	154	Nh	33.54N	136.05 E
Kumano-Gawa	156	De	33.45N	135.59 E
Kumano-Nada	156	Ee	34.00N	136.30 E
Kumanovo	130	Eg	42.08N	21.43 E
Kumara [N.Z.]	218	De	42.38S	171.11 E
Kumara [R.S.F.S.R.]	138	Hf	51.35N	126.45 E
Kumasi	160	Gh	6.41N	1.37W
Kumba	166	Ge	4.38N	9.25 E
Kumbakonam	148	Ff	10.58N	79.23 E
Kumbe	150	Lh	8.21S	140.13 E
Kumbo	166	Hd	6.12N	10.40 E
Kumboro Cape	219a	Cb	7.18S	157.32 E
Kŭmch'ŏn	154	Ie	38.10N	126.30 E
Kum-Dag	136	Fh	39.13N	54.40 E
Kumdah	164	Ie	20.23N	45.05 E
Kume-Jima	152	Mf	26.20N	126.45 E
Kumertau	136	Fe	52.46N	55.47 E
Kumhwa	154	Ie	38.17N	127.28 E
Kumihama	156	Dd	35.36N	134.54 E
Kuminski	136	Gd	58.40N	65.55 E
Kumköy (Kilyos)	130	Mh	41.15N	29.02 E
Kumkuduk	152	Fc	40.15N	91.55 E
Kumkurgan	135	Ff	37.50N	67.35 E
Kumla	114	Dg	59.08N	15.08 E
Kumlirge	116	Id	60.15N	20.45 E
Kumluca	146	Dd	36.22N	30.18 E
Kummerower See	120	Ic	53.49N	12.52 E
Kumo/Kokemäki	114	Ff	61.15N	22.21 E
Kumola	135	Fa	46.58N	64.30 E
Kumo-Manyčski kanal	132	Ng	45.27N	44.38 E
Kumon Taung	140	Lg	26.30N	96.50 E
Kumora	138	Ge	55.56N	111.13 E
Kumru	146	Gb	40.53N	37.17 E
Kumu	170	Eb	3.04N	25.09 E
Kumuh	132	Oh	42.11N	47.07 E
Kumukahi Cape-	214	Od	19.31N	154.49W
Kumul/Hami	142	Le	42.48N	93.27 E
Kümüx	152	Ec	42.15N	88.10 E
Kumzār	146	Qj	26.20N	56.25 E
Kunashiri-Tō / Kunašir, ostrov-	140	Qe	44.05N	145.51 E
Kunašir, ostrov- / Kunashiri-Tō	140	Qe	44.05N	145.51 E
Kunaširski proliv = Nemuro Strait (EN)	138	Jh	43.50N	145.30 E
Kunchaung	148	Jd	23.50N	96.35 E
Kunda	114	Gg	59.30N	26.30 E
Kunda jõgi	116	Le	59.25N	26.27 E
Kundelungu, Monts-	170	Ed	9.30S	28.00 E
Kundiawa	212	Ia	6.00S	145.00 E
Kunduchi	170	Gd	6.40S	39.13 E
Kunduk → Kogilnik	130	Md	45.51N	29.38 E
Kunduk → Sasyk, ozero-	132	Fg	45.45N	29.40 E
Kunene	158	Ij	17.20S	11.50 E
Kunene (EN) = Cunene	158	Ij	17.20S	11.50 E
Künes/Xinyuan	152	Dc	43.24N	83.18 E
Künes He	152	Dc	43.32N	82.29 E
Kungälv	114	Ch	57.52N	11.58 E
Kungej-Alatau, hrebet-	136	Hg	42.50N	77.15 E
Kŭngmiut	179	Ie	65.50N	36.45W
Kungrad	136	Fg	43.06N	58.54 E
Kungsbacka	114	Ch	57.29N	12.04 E
Kungsbackafjorden	116	Eg	57.25N	12.04 E
Kungshamn	116	Df	58.21N	11.15 E
Kungsör	116	Ge	59.25N	16.05 E
Kungu	170	Cb	2.47N	19.12 E
Kungur	136	Fd	57.25N	56.57 E
Kunhegyes	120	Qi	47.22N	20.38 E
Kunhing	148	Jd	21.18N	98.26 E
Kunigami-Misaki	156b	Bb	27.26N	128.43 E
Kunimi-Dake	156	Be	32.33N	131.02 E
Kunisaki	156	Be	33.34N	131.45 E
Kunisaki-Hantō	156	Be	33.30N	131.40 E
Kunja	114	Hh	57.09N	31.10 E
Kunja-Urgenč	136	Fg	42.20N	59.12 E
Kunlong	148	Jd	23.25N	98.39 E
Kunlun Guan	152	Ig	23.06N	108.40 E
Kunlun Shan	140	Kf	36.00N	84.00 E
Kunlun Shankou	152	Fd	35.40N	94.03 E
Kunming	142	Mg	25.08N	102.43 E
Kunnui	156a	Bb	42.26N	140.19 E
Kunovat	134	Ld	64.59N	65.35 E
Kunsan	152	Md	35.59N	126.43 E
Kunshan	154	Fi	31.22N	120.57 E
Kuntaur	166	Cc	13.40N	14.53W
Kununurra	212	Fc	15.47S	128.44 E
Kunyao	170	Gb	1.47N	35.03 E
Kunyu Shan	154	Ff	37.15N	121.46 E
Künzelsau	120	Fg	49.17N	9.41 E
Kuohijärvi	116	Kc	61.15N	24.55 E
Kuolimo	116	Lc	61.15N	27.35 E
Kuop Atoll	208	Gd	7.03N	151.56 E
Kuopio	112	Ic	62.54N	27.41 E
Kuopio [2]	114	Ge	63.20N	27.35 E
Kuorboaivi	114	Gb	69.41N	27.45 E
Kuortane	116	Jb	62.48N	23.30 E
Kupa	128	Ke	45.28N	16.24 E
Kupang	142	Ok	10.10S	123.35 E
Kupiano	214	Dj	10.10S	148.02 E
Kupičev	120	Uf	50.58N	24.52 E
Kupino	138	Cf	54.22N	77.18 E
Kupiškis	114	Fi	55.49N	25.01 E
Kupjansk	136	Df	49.42N	37.37 E
Kupjansk-Uzlovoj	132	Je	49.39N	37.45 E
Küplü [Tur.]	130	Jh	41.07N	26.21 E
Küplü [Tur.]	130	Mi	40.06N	30.00 E
Kuppenheim	124	Kf	48.50N	8.15 E
Kupreanof	178	Me	56.50N	133.30W
Kuqa	142	Ke	41.43N	82.57 E
Kura [R.S.F.S.R.]	132	Mh	44.05N	44.45 E
Kura [U.S.S.R.]	110	Kh	39.20N	49.25 E
Kuragaty	135	Ic	43.55N	73.34 E
Kuragino	138	Ef	53.53N	92.40 E
Kurahashi-Jima	156	Cd	34.08N	132.31 E
Kuraminski hrebet	135	Hd	40.50N	70.30 E
Kurashiki	154	Lg	34.35N	133.46 E
Kurashiki-Kojima	156	Cd	34.28N	133.48 E
Kurashiki-Tamashima	156	Cd	34.33N	133.40 E
Kura-Take	156	Be	32.27N	130.20 E
Kuraymah = Karima (EN)	160	Kg	18.33N	31.51 E
Kurayoshi	154	Lg	35.28N	133.49 E
Kurbneshi	130	Dh	41.47N	20.05 E
Kurčatov	132	Id	51.41N	35.42 E
Kurdaj	135	Jc	43.18N	74.59 E
Kurdistan	140	Gf	37.00N	44.00 E
Kurdistan	144	Fb	37.00N	44.00 E
Kurdufān	158	Jg	13.00N	30.00 E
Kurdufān al Janūbīyah [3]	168	Dc	11.00N	29.30 E
Kurdufān ash Shamālīyah [3]	168	Dc	14.50N	29.40 E
Kure	154	Lg	34.14N	132.34 E
Küre	146	Eb	41.48N	33.43 E
Kure Island	208	Jb	28.25N	178.25W
Kurejka	140	Kc	66.25N	87.12 E
Kurgaldžinski	136	He	50.30N	70.03 E
Kurgalski, mys-	116	Me	59.39N	28.03 E
Kurgan	142	Id	55.26N	65.18 E
Kurganinsk	132	Lg	44.57N	40.35 E
Kurganskaja oblast [3]	136	Gd	55.00N	65.00 E
Kurgan-Tjube	136	Gh	37.51N	68.46 E
Kurgan-Tjubinskaja oblast [3]	136	Gh	37.30N	68.30 E
Kuria Island	208	Id	0.14N	173.25 E
Kuria Muria Islands (EN) = Khurīyā Murīyā, Jazā'ir	140	Hh	17.30N	56.00 E
Kuri Bay	212	Ec	15.35S	124.50 E
Kurikka	114	Fe	62.37N	22.25 E
Kurikoma	156	Gb	38.50N	140.59 E
Kurikoma-Yama	156	Gb	38.57N	140.47 E
Kuril Basin (EN)	138	Jg	47.00N	150.00 E
Kuril Islands (EN) = Kurilskije ostrova	140	Re	46.10N	152.00 E
Kurilo	130	Gg	42.49N	23.21 E
Kurilsk	138	Jg	45.16N	147.58 E
Kurilskije ostrova = Kuril Islands (EN)	140	Re	46.10N	152.00 E
Kuril Trench (EN)	106	Je	47.00N	155.00 E
Kuring Kuru	172	Bc	17.38S	18.33 E
Kurino	156	Bf	31.57N	130.43 E
Kurinskaja kosa	132	Pj	39.05N	49.10 E
Kurinwás, Rio-	194	Fg	12.49N	83.41W
Kuriyama	156a	Bb	43.03N	141.45 E
Kūrkhūd, Kūh-e-	146	Qd	37.15N	56.30 E
Kurkosa	132	Pj	38.59N	49.08 E
Kurkūmā, Ra's-	146	Gj	25.51N	36.39 E
Kurkur	146	Ek	23.54N	32.19 E
Kurlovski	114	Ji	55.29N	40.39 E
Kurmuk	168	Ec	10.33N	34.17 E
Kurnool	142	Jh	15.50N	78.03 E
Kurobe	154	Nf	36.51N	137.26 E
Kurobe-Gawa	156	Ec	36.55N	137.26 E
Kurogi	156	Be	33.14N	130.40 E
Kuroishi	154	Pd	40.38N	140.36 E
Kuroiso	154	Pf	36.58N	140.03 E
Kuromatsunai	154	Pc	42.43N	140.20 E
Kurono-Seto	156	Be	32.05N	130.10 E
Kurort Družba	130	Kf	43.12N	28.00 E
Kurort Slănčev brjag	130	Kg	42.40N	27.42 E
Kurort Zlatni pjasăci	130	Lf	43.16N	28.02 E
Kuro-Shima	154	Ji	31.52N	129.58 E
Kurovskoje	114	Ji	55.35N	38.59 E
Kurów	120	Se	51.25N	22.10 E
Kurow	216	Dh	44.44S	170.28 E
Kurpiowska, Puszcza-	120	Rc	53.20N	21.30 E
Kuršenai/Kuršėnaj	136	Cd	56.03N	22.58 E
Kuršėnaj/Kuršenai	136	Cd	55.03N	22.58 E
Kuršiu užūrekis	116	Ii	55.05N	21.00 E
Kursk	112	Je	51.42N	36.12 E
Kurskaja kosa	114	Ei	55.18N	21.00 E
Kurskaja oblast [3]	136	De	51.45N	36.15 E
Kurski zaliv	114	Ei	55.05N	21.00 E
Kuršumlija	130	Ef	43.09N	21.16 E
Kurtalan	146	Id	37.57N	41.42 E
Kurtamyš	136	Ge	54.55N	64.27 E
Kürti	160	Kg	18.07N	31.33 E
Kurtistown	221	Fd	19.36N	155.04W
Kurty	135	Kb	44.19N	76.42 E
Kuru	168	Dd	9.08N	26.57 E
Kurucaşile	146	Eb	41.51N	32.43 E
Kuruktag	152	Ec	41.30N	89.00 E
Kuruman	160	Jk	27.28S	23.28 E
Kuruman	158	Jk	26.56S	20.39 E
Kurume	154	Kh	33.19N	130.31 E
Kurunegala	148	Gg	7.29N	80.22 E
Kurur, Jabal-	168	Ea	20.31N	31.32 E
Kurzeme = Courland (EN)	110	Id	56.50N	22.00 E
Kurzemes Augstiene / Kurzemskaja vozvyšennost	116	Jh	56.45N	22.15 E
Kurzemskaja vozvyšennost / Kurzemes Augstiene	116	Jh	56.45N	22.15 E
Kusa	134	Ii	55.20N	59.29 E
Kuşada Körfezi	130	Kl	37.50N	27.08 E
Kuşadası	130	Bd	37.51N	27.15 E
Kusagaki-Guntō	152	Me	31.00N	129.00 E
Kusaie → Kosrae	208	Hd	5.19N	162.59 E
Kusalu/Kuusalu	116	Ke	59.23N	25.25 E
Kusary	132	Pi	41.24N	48.29 E
Kusatsu [Jap.]	156	Fc	36.37N	138.35 E
Kusatsu [Jap.]	156	Dd	35.03N	135.59 E
Kuščevskaja	132	Kf	46.33N	39.37 E
Kuščinski	132	Oi	40.33N	46.06 E
Kusel	124	Je	49.33N	7.24 E
Kuş Gölü	146	Bb	40.10N	27.59 E
Kushida-Gawa	156	Ed	34.36N	136.34 E
Kushikino	154	Ki	31.44N	130.16 E
Kushima	154	Ki	31.29N	131.14 E
Kushimoto	154	Mh	33.28N	135.47 E
Kushiro	142	Qe	42.58N	144.23 E
Kushiro-Gawa	156a	Db	42.59N	144.23 E
Kushtia	148	Hd	23.55N	89.07 E
Kuška	135	Dg	35.16N	62.18 E
Kuskokwim	174	Cc	60.17N	162.27W
Kuskokwim Bay	174	Cd	59.45N	162.25W
Kuskokwim Mountains	174	Dc	62.30N	156.00W
Kušmurun	136	Ge	52.27N	64.40 E
Kušmurun, ozero-	136	Ge	52.40N	64.45 E
Kušnarenkovo	134	Gi	55.06N	55.22 E
Kušnica	132	Ce	48.29N	23.20 E
Kusŏng	152	Md	39.59N	125.16 E
Kussharo Ko	154	Rc	43.35N	144.15 E
Kustanaj	142	Id	53.10N	63.35 E
Kustanajskaja oblast [3]	136	Ge	53.00N	64.00 E
Kustavi/Gustavs	116	Id	60.33N	21.21 E
Kustavi/Gustavs	116	Id	60.30N	21.25 E
Küstenkanal	120	Dc	53.08N	7.40 E
Kūstī	160	Kg	13.10N	32.40 E
Kustvlakte = Coast Plain (EN)	122	Ic	51.00N	2.30 E
Kusu	156	Be	33.16N	131.09 E
Kušum	132	Qd	51.06N	51.18 E
Kušva	136	Fd	58.18N	59.45 E
Kut, Ko-	148	Kf	11.40N	102.35 E
Kut, Ko-	148	Kf	11.40N	102.35 E
Kūt 'Abdollāh	146	Mg	31.13N	48.39 E
Kutacane	150	Cf	3.30N	97.48 E
Kutahya	144	Cb	39.25N	29.59 E
Kutaisi	112	Kg	42.15N	42.40 E
Kutch, Gulf of- → Kachchh, Gulf of	140	Ig	22.36N	69.30 E
Kutch, Rann of-	148	Ed	24.05N	70.10 E
Kutchan	154	Pc	42.54N	140.45 E
Kutcharo-Ko	156a	Ca	45.10N	142.20 E
Kutina	128	Ke	45.29N	16.47 E
Kutkai	148	Jd	23.27N	97.56 E
Kutkašen	132	Oi	40.58N	47.52 E
Kutná Hora	120	Lg	49.57N	15.16 E
Kutno	120	Pd	52.15N	19.23 E
Kutse, gora- / Kuutse Mägi	116	Lg	57.58N	26.24 E
Kuttara-Ko	156a	Bb	42.30N	141.10 E
Kutu	160	Ii	2.44S	18.09 E
Kutum	168	Cc	14.12N	24.40 E
Kúty	120	Nh	48.40N	17.01 E
Kuty	130	Ia	48.13N	25.15 E
Kuujjuaq	176	Md	58.10N	68.30W
Kuuli-Majak	136	Fg	40.15N	52.45 E

Index Symbols

Independent Nation	Historical or Cultural Region	Pass, Gap	Depression	Coast, Beach	Rock, Reef	Waterfall, Rapids	Canal	Lagoon
State, Region	Mount, Mountain	Plain, Lowland	Polder	Cliff	Islands, Archipelago	River Mouth, Estuary	Glacier	Bank
District, County	Volcano	Delta	Desert, Dunes	Peninsula	Rocks, Reefs	Lake	Ice Shelf, Pack Ice	Seamount
Municipality	Hill	Salt Flat	Forest, Woods	Isthmus	Coral Reef	Salt Lake	Ocean	Tablemount
Colony, Dependency	Mountains, Mountain Range	Valley, Canyon	Heath, Steppe	Sandbank	Well, Spring	Intermittent Lake	Sea	Ridge
Continent	Hills, Escarpment	Crater, Cave	Oasis	Island	Geyser	Reservoir	Gulf, Bay	Shelf
Physical Region	Plateau, Upland	Karst Features	Cape, Point	Atoll	River, Stream	Swamp, Pond	Strait, Fjord	Basin

Escarpment, Sea Scarp	Historic Site	Airport
Fracture	Ruins	Port
Trench, Abyss	Wall, Walls	Military Installation
National Park, Reserve	Church, Abbey	Lighthouse
Point of Interest	Temple	Mine
Recreation Site	Scientific Station	Tunnel
Cave, Cavern	Railway station	Dam, Bridge

Kuurne 124 Fd 50.51N 3.17 E
Kuusalu/Kusalu 116 Ke 59.23N 25.25 E
Kuusamo 112 Ib 66.00N 29.11 E
Kuusankoski 116 Ld 60.54N 26.38 E
Kuutse Mägi / Kutse, gora- 116 Lg 57.58N 26.24 E
Kuvandyk 132 Td 51.29N 57.28 E
Kuvango 160 Ij 14.29S 16.18 E
Kuvdlorssuaq 179 Gd 74.38N 56.40W
Kuvšinovo 114 Ih 57.03N 34.13 E
Kuwait (EN) = Al Kuwayt 142 Gg 29.20N 47.59 E
Kuwait (EN)=Al Kuwayt 142 Gg 29.30N 47.45 E
Kuwana 156 Ed 35.04N 136.39 E
Kuybychev Reservoir (EN) = Kujbyševskoje vodohranilišče 110 Ke 53.50N 49.00 E
Kuytun 152 Dc 44.25N 84.58 E
Kuyucak 130 Ll 37.55N 28.28 E
Kuzey Kibris = North Cyprus (EN) 144 Db 35.15N 33.40 E
Kuzneck 136 Ee 53.07N 46.36 E
Kuznecki Alatau 140 Kd 54.45N 88.00 E
Kuznečnoje 116 Md 61.04N 29.58 E
Kuźnia Raciborska 120 Of 50.11N 18.15 E
Kuzomen 136 Db 66.18N 36.49 E
Kuzovatovo 114 Lj 53.33N 47.41 E
Kuzumaki 156 Ga 40.02N 141.26 E
Kuzuryū-Gawa 156 Ec 36.13N 136.08 E
Kvænangen 114 Ea 70.05N 21.13 E
Kvaløy 114 Eb 69.40N 18.30 E
Kvaløya 114 Fa 70.37N 23.52 E
Kvalsund 114 Fa 70.30N 24.00 E
Kvau 116 Cc 61.40N 9.42 E
Kvareli 132 Ni 41.57N 45.47 E
Kvarkeno 134 Ij 52.05N 59.40 E
Kvarnbergsvattnet 114 Dd 64.36N 14.03 E
Kvarner 128 If 44.45N 14.15 E
Kvarnerić 128 If 44.45N 14.35 E
Kvemo-Kedi 132 Oi 41.22N 46.31 E
Kvenna 116 Bd 60.01N 7.56 E
Kvichak 178 He 59.10N 156.40W
Kvichak Bay 178 He 58.48N 157.30W
Kvikkjokk 114 Dc 66.57N 17.47 E
Kvina 116 Bf 58.17N 6.56 E
Kvinesdal 114 Bg 58.19N 6.57 E
Kvissleby 116 Gb 62.17N 17.21 E
Kviteggja 116 Bb 62.05N 6.40 E
Kviteseid 116 Ce 59.24N 8.30 E
Kvitøya 224 Je 80.08N 32.35 E
Kwa 158 Ii 3.10S 16.11 E
Kwahu Plateau 166 Ed 6.30N 0.30W
Kwailibesi 219a Ec 8.20S 160.40 E
Kwajalein Atoll 208 Hd 9.05N 167.20 E
Kwakoegron 202 Gb 5.15N 55.20W
Kwale [Kenya] 170 Gc 4.11S 39.27 E
Kwale [Nig.] 166 Gd 5.45N 6.25 E
Kwamouth 170 Cc 3.10S 16.12 E
Kwa Mtoro 170 Gd 5.14S 35.26 E
Kwando 170 Df 18.27S 23.32 E
Kwangdae-ri 152 Mc 40.34N 127.33 E
Kwangju 142 Of 35.09N 126.55 E
Kwango 158 Ii 3.14S 17.22 E
Kwangsi Chuang (EN)= Guangxi Zhuangzu Zizhiqu (Kuang-hsi-chuang-tsu Tzu-chih-ch'ü) 152 Ig 24.00N 109.00 E
Kwangtung (EN)= Guangdong Sheng (Kuang-tung Sheng) 152 Jg 23.00N 113.00 E
Kwanmo-bong 154 Jd 41.42N 129.13 E
Kwara 166 Fd 8.30N 5.00 E
Kweichow (EN)=Guizhou Sheng (Kuei-chou Sheng) 152 If 27.00N 107.00 E
Kweichow (EN)=Kuei-chou Sheng→Guizhou Sheng 152 If 27.00N 107.00 E
Kwekwe 160 Jj 18.55S 29.49 E
Kweneng 172 Cd 24.00S 24.00 E
Kwenge 158 Ii 4.50S 18.44 E
Kwethluk 178 Gd 60.49N 161.27W
Kwidzyn 120 Oc 53.45N 18.56 E
Kwigillingok 178 Ge 59.51N 163.08W
Kwilu 158 Ii 3.22S 17.22 E
Kwisa 120 Le 51.35N 15.25 E
Kwoka, Gunung- 150 Jg 0.31S 132.27 E
Kyabé 160 Ih 9.27N 18.57 E
Kyabram 212 Jg 36.19S 145.03 E
Kyaikkami 148 Je 16.04N 97.34 E
Kyaikto 148 Je 17.18N 97.01 E
Kyaka 170 Fc 1.16S 31.25 E
Kyancutta 210 Eh 33.08S 135.34 E
Kyan-Zaki 156b Ab 26.05N 127.40 E
Kyaukpyu 148 Id 20.51N 92.58 E
Kyaukse 148 Jd 21.36N 96.08 E
Kybartai/Kibartaj 116 Jj 54.38N 22.44 E
Kyeintali 148 Ie 18.00N 94.29 E
Kyelang 148 Fb 32.35N 77.02 E
Kyffhauser 120 He 51.25N 11.10 E
Kyjov 120 Ng 49.01N 17.08 E
Kyle, Lake- 172 Ed 20.12S 31.00 E
Kyle of Lochalsh 118 Hd 57.17N 5.43W
Kyll 120 Cg 49.48N 6.42 E
Kyllburg 124 Id 50.02N 6.35 E
Kyma 124 Ld 64.48N 47.31 E
Kymi 114 Gf 61.00N 28.00 E
Kymijoki 116 Ld 60.30N 26.52 E
Kyn 134 Ih 57.52N 58.32 E
Kynnefjäll 116 Df 58.42N 11.41 E
Kynsivesi 116 Lb 62.25N 26.10 E
Kyoga, Lake- 158 Kh 1.30N 33.00 E
Kyōga-Dake 156 Be 33.00N 130.05 E
Kyōga-Misaki 154 Mg 35.45N 135.11 E
Kyonan 156 Fd 35.07N 139.49 E
Kyŏnggi-Do 154 If 37.30N 127.15 E
Kyŏnggi-man 154 Hf 37.25N 126.00 E
Kyŏngju 152 Md 35.50N 129.13 E
Kyŏngsang-Namdo 154 Jg 35.15N 128.30 E
Kyŏngsang-Pukto 154 Jf 36.20N 128.40 E
Kyŏngsŏng 154 Jd 41.40N 129.40 E
Kyōto 142 Pf 35.00N 135.45 E
Kyōto Fu 154 Mg 35.25N 135.15 E
Kypros → Kipros = Cyprus (EN) 144 Db 35.01N 33.00 E
Kyra 138 Gg 49.36N 111.58 E
Kyren 138 Ff 51.41N 102.10 E
Kyrenia 146 Ee 35.20N 33.19 E
Kyrgesara/Kõrgessaare 116 Je 59.00N 22.25 E
Kyrgyz Sovetik Socialistik Respublikasy/Kirgizskaja SSR 136 Hg 41.30N 75.00 E
Kyritz 120 Id 52.57N 12.24 E
Kyrkheden 116 Ed 60.10N 13.29 E
Kyrksæterora 114 Be 63.17N 9.06 E
Kyrkslätt/Kirkkonummi 116 Kd 60.07N 24.26 E
Kyrö 116 Jd 60.42N 22.45 E
Kyrönjoki 116 Ia 63.14N 21.45 E
Kyrösjärvi 116 Jc 61.45N 23.10 E
Kyröskoski 116 Jc 61.40N 23.11 E
Kyštym 136 Gd 55.42N 60.34 E
Kysucké Nové Mesto 120 Og 49.18N 18.48 E
Kythera (EN) = Kíthira 110 Ih 36.15N 23.00 E
Kythraia 146 Ee 35.15N 33.29 E
Kyuquot Sound 188 Bb 49.55N 127.25W
Kyūshū 140 Pf 32.50N 131.00 E
Kyushu-Palau Ridge (EN) 106 Ih 20.00N 136.00 E
Kyūshū-Sanchi 156 Be 32.40N 131.10 E
Kyyjärvi 116 Fe 63.02N 24.34 E
Kyyvesi 116 Lc 61.55N 27.05 E
Kyzıkos 146 Bb 40.28N 27.47 E
Kyzyl 142 Ld 51.42N 94.27 E
Kyzylart, pereval- 136 Hh 39.22N 73.20 E
Kyzyl-Kija 136 Hg 40.14N 72.12 E
Kyzylkum 140 Ie 42.00N 64.00 E
Kyzylrabot 136 Hh 37.28N 74.45 E
Kyzylsu [U.S.S.R.] 135 Gf 37.22N 69.22 E
Kyzylsu [U.S.S.R.] 135 He 39.17N 71.25 E
Kyzylžar 136 Gf 48.17N 69.49 E
Kzyl-Orda 142 Ie 44.48N 65.28 E
Kzyl-Ordinskaja oblast 136 Gf 45.00N 65.00 E
Kzyltu 136 He 53.41N 72.15 E

L

Laa an der Thaya 128 Kb 48.43N 16.23 E
Laakdal 124 Gc 51.05N 4.59 E
La Alberca 126 Fd 40.29N 6.06W
La Alcarria 126 Jd 40.31N 2.45W
La Almunia de Doña Godina 126 Kc 41.29N 1.22W
La Araucanía 206 Fe 37.50S 73.15W
La Ardilla, Cerro- 192 Hf 22.15N 102.40W
La Armuña 126 Gc 41.05N 5.35W
Laasphe 124 Kd 50.56N 8.24 E
La Asunción 202 Fa 11.02N 63.53W
Laau Point 221a Db 21.06N 157.16W
Layoune 126 Ni 35.42N 2.00 E
Lab 130 Eg 42.45N 21.01 E
Laba 132 Kg 45.10N 39.40 E
La Babia 192 Hc 28.34N 102.04W
Laba Dağı 130 Kl 37.22N 27.33 E
Labaddey 168 Ge 0.32N 42.45 E
Labadie Bank 118 Ek 50.30N 8.15W
La Banda 206 Hc 27.44S 64.15W
La Bañeza 126 Gb 42.18N 5.54W
La Barca 192 Hg 20.17N 102.34W
Labardén 204 Cm 36.57S 58.06W
La Barge 188 Je 42.16N 110.12W
La Barra, Punta- 194 Lh 11.30N 70.10W
La-Barre-en-Ouche 124 Cf 48.57N 0.40 E
Labbezanga 166 Fc 14.59N 0.43 E
Labé 160 Fg 11.19N 12.17W
Labe=Elbe (EN) 110 Ge 53.50N 9.00 E
Labelle 184 Jb 46.17N 74.45W
La Belle 184 Gl 26.46N 81.26W
La Berzosa 126 Fd 40.35N 6.40W
Labin 128 Ie 45.05N 14.08 E
Labinsk 136 Eg 44.35N 40.44 E
Labis 150 Df 2.23N 103.02 E
La Bisbal / la Bisbal d'Empordà 126 Pc 41.57N 3.03 E
la Bisbal d'Empordà/La Bisbal 126 Pc 41.57N 3.03 E
La Blanca, Laguna- 204 Bj 30.14S 60.38W
Laboe 120 Gb 54.24N 10.13 E
Laborec 120 Rh 48.31N 21.54 E
Laborie 197k Bb 13.45N 61.00W
Labota 150 Hg 2.52S 122.10 E
Labouheyre 122 Fj 44.13N 0.55W
Laboulaye 206 Hd 34.07S 63.24W
Labra, Peña- 126 Ha 43.03N 4.26W
Labrador 174 Md 55.00N 70.00W
Labrador Basin (EN) 174 Od 53.00N 48.00W
Labrador City 176 Md 52.57N 66.54W
Labrador Sea 174 Nd 57.00N 53.00W
Labrang→Xiahe 152 Ha 35.18N 102.30 E
Lábrea 200 Jf 7.16S 64.46W
Labrieville 184 Ma 49.19N 69.34W
Labrit 122 Fj 44.06N 0.33W
La Broye 128 Bd 46.55N 7.02 E
Labuan, Pulau- 150 Ge 5.19N 115.13 E
Labudalin→Ergun Youqi 152 La 50.16N 120.09 E
Labuha 150 Ig 0.37S 127.29 E
Labuhan 150 Eh 6.22S 105.50 E
Labuhanbajo 150 Gh 8.29S 119.54 E
Labuhanbilik 150 Df 2.31N 100.10 E
Labuk, Teluk- 150 Ge 6.10N 117.50 E
La Bureba 126 Ib 42.36N 3.24W
Labutta 148 Ie 16.09N 94.46 E
Labytnangi 142 Ic 66.39N 66.21 E
Lac 168 Ac 13.30N 14.20 E
Lača, ozero- 114 Jf 61.20N 38.50 E
La Cadena 192 Ge 25.53N 104.12W
La Calamine/Kelmis 124 Hd 50.43N 6.00 E
La Calandria 204 Cj 30.48S 58.39W
Lac Alard 180 Lf 50.30N 63.30W
La Campiña 126 Hg 37.45N 4.45W
Lacanau 122 Ej 44.59N 1.05W
Lacanau, Étang de- 122 Ej 44.58N 1.07W
Lacanau-Lacanau-Océan 122 Ei 45.00N 1.12W
Lacanau-Océan, Lacanau- 122 Ei 45.00N 1.12W
Lacantún, Río- 192 Ni 16.36N 90.39W
Laćarak 130 Ce 45.00N 19.34 E
La Carlota [Arg.] 206 Hd 33.26S 63.18W
La Carlota [Phil.] 150 Hd 10.25N 122.55 E
La Carlota [Sp.] 126 Hg 37.40N 4.56W
La Carolina 126 If 38.15N 3.37W
Lacaune 122 Ik 43.43N 2.42 E
Lacaune, Monts de- 122 Ik 43.40N 2.36 E
Lac du Bonnet 186 Ha 50.35N 96.05W
La Ceiba [Hond.] 176 Kh 15.47N 86.50W
La Ceiba [Ven.] 194 Li 9.28N 71.04W
Lacepede Bay 212 Hg 36.45S 139.45 E
Lacepede Islands 212 Ec 16.50S 122.10 E
La Cerdaña/La Cerdanya 126 Nb 42.24N 1.40 E
La Cerdanya/La Cerdaña 126 Nb 42.24N 1.40 E
Lacey 188 Dc 47.07N 122.49W
Lac Giao → Buon Me Thuot 148 Lf 12.40N 108.03 E
La Chaux-de-Fonds 128 Ac 47.06N 6.50 E
Lachay, Punta- 202 Cf 11.18S 77.39W
La China, Sierra- 204 Bm 36.47S 60.34W
Lachine 184 Kc 45.26N 73.40W
Lachlan River 208 Fh 34.21S 143.57 E
La Chorrera [Col.] 202 Dd 0.45S 73.00W
La Chorrera [Pan.] 190 Ig 8.53N 79.47W
Laçi 130 Ch 41.38N 19.43 E
Lačin 132 Oj 39.39N 46.33 E
La Ciutat de Mallorca / Palma 112 Gh 39.34N 2.39 E
Łąck 120 Pd 52.28N 19.40 E
Lackawanna 184 Hd 42.49N 78.49W
Lac La Biche 180 Gf 54.46N 111.58W
Lac la Martre 180 Fd 63.21N 117.00W
Lac Mégantic 180 Kg 45.35N 70.53W
La Colina 204 Bm 37.20S 61.32W
La Coloma 194 Fb 22.15N 83.34W
La Colorada 192 Dc 28.41N 110.25W
Lacombe 180 Gf 52.28N 113.44W
Lacon 186 Lf 41.02N 89.24W
La Concepción [Pan.] 194 Fi 8.31N 82.37W
La Concepción [Ven.] 194 Lh 10.48N 71.46W
La Concha 192 Gg 21.46N 105.29W
Laconi 128 Dk 39.51N 9.03 E
Laconia 182 Mc 43.32N 71.29W
Laconia, Gulf of- (EN) = Lakonikós Kólpos 130 Fm 36.35N 22.40 E
La Coronilla 204 Fk 33.44S 53.31W
La Coruña 126 Da 43.10N 8.25W
La Coruña / A Cruña 112 Fg 43.22N 8.23W
La Côte-Saint-André 122 Li 45.23N 5.15 E
Lacq 122 Fk 43.25N 0.38W
Lacroix-sur-Meuse 124 Hf 48.58N 5.31 E
La Crosse [Ks.-U.S.] 186 Gg 38.32N 99.18W
La Crosse [Wi.-U.S.] 176 Je 43.49N 91.15W
La Cruz [Arg.] 206 Ic 29.10S 56.38W
La Cruz [C.R.] 194 Eh 11.04N 85.39W
La Cruz [Mex.] 190 Cd 23.55N 106.54W
La Cruz [Ur.] 206 Id 33.56S 56.15W
La Cruz de Rio Grande 194 Eg 13.06N 84.10W
La Cruz de Taratara 194 Mh 11.03N 69.44W
La Cuesta 192 Hc 28.45N 102.25W
La Cumbre 206 Hd 30.58S 64.30W
Lac Yora 168 Cb 19.08N 20.35 E
Ladário 204 Dd 19.01S 57.35W
Ladbergen 124 Jb 52.08N 7.45 E
Lądek-Zdrój 120 Mf 50.21N 16.50 E
Ladenburg 124 Ke 49.28N 8.37 E
La Désirade 196 Fd 16.19N 61.03W
La Digue Island 172b Ca 4.21S 55.50 E
Lâdik 146 Fb 40.36N 36.45 E
Ladismith 172 Cf 33.30S 21.16 E
Ladispoli 128 Gi 41.56N 12.05 E
Lado, Jabal- 168 Ed 5.06N 31.35 E
Ladoga, Lake- (EN) = Ladožskoje ozero 110 Jc 61.00N 31.00 E
Ladong 152 Ig 24.49N 109.34 E
La Dorada 202 Db 5.22N 74.42W
Ladožskoje ozero = Ladoga, Lake- (EN) 110 Jc 61.00N 31.00 E
Ladrones, Islas- 194 Fj 7.52N 82.26W
Laduškin 116 Ij 54.35N 20.10 E
Ladva-Vetka 114 If 61.20N 34.29 E
Lady Ann Strait 180 Ja 75.45N 80.00W
Ladybrand 172 De 29.19S 27.25 E
Lady Evelyn Lake 184 Gb 47.20N 80.10W
Lady Newnes Ice Shelf 222 Kf 73.40S 167.30 E
Ladysmith [B.C.-Can.] 188 Db 48.58N 123.49W
Ladysmith [S.Afr.] 160 Jk 28.34S 29.45 E
Ladysmith [Wi.-U.S.] 182 Ib 45.28N 91.07W
Ladyžin 132 Fe 48.40N 29.13 E
Lae 210 Fe 6.43S 147.01 E
Lae Atoll 208 Hd 8.56N 166.14 E
La Eduvigis 204 Ch 26.50S 59.05W
Laem, Khao- 148 Kf 14.19N 101.11 E
Laer [Ger.] 124 Jb 52.04N 7.21 E
Laer [Ger.] 124 Kb 52.06N 8.05 E
Lærdalsøyri 114 Bf 61.06N 7.29 E
La Escala / l'Escala 126 Pb 42.07N 3.08 E
La Esmeralda 202 Ec 3.10N 65.33W
Læsø 114 Bh 57.15N 10.00 E
Læsø Rende 116 Dg 57.15N 10.45 E
La Española=Hispaniola (EN) 174 Lh 19.00N 71.00W
La Esperanza [Bol.] 202 Ff 14.34S 62.10W
La Esperanza [Hond.] 194 Cf 14.20N 88.10W
La Estrada 126 Db 42.41N 8.29W
Lafayette [Al.-U.S.] 184 Ei 32.54N 85.24W
Lafayette [In.-U.S.] 182 Jc 40.25N 86.53W
Lafayette [La.-U.S.] 176 Jf 30.14N 92.01W
La Fère 124 Fe 49.40N 3.22 E
La Ferrière-sur-Risle 124 Cf 48.59N 0.48 E
La Ferté-Frênel 124 Cf 48.50N 0.30 E
La Ferté-Milon 124 Fe 49.10N 3.07 E
Laffān, Ra's- 146 Nj 25.54N 51.35 E
Lafia 166 Gd 8.29N 8.31 E
Lafiagi 166 Gd 8.52N 5.15 E
Lafnitz 128 Kd 46.57N 16.16 E
La Foa 219b Be 21.43S 165.49 E
La Follette 184 Eg 36.23N 84.07W
La Fria 194 Ki 8.13N 72.15W
Laft 146 Pi 26.54N 55.46 E
La Fuente de San Esteban 126 Fd 40.48N 6.15W
Laga, Monti della- 128 Hh 42.45N 13.35 E
La Galite (EN)=Jāliṭah 158 He 37.32N 8.56 E
La Gallareta 204 Bi 29.34S 60.23W
Lagamar 204 Id 18.13S 46.48W
Lagan 116 Eh 56.55N 13.59 E
Lagan 116 Eh 56.33N 12.56 E
Lagan/Abhainn an Lagáin 118 Hg 54.37N 5.53W
Lagarina, Val- 128 Fe 45.50N 11.10 E
La Garita Mountains 186 Ch 38.00N 106.40W
Lagarto 202 Kf 10.54S 37.41W
Lagash 146 Lg 31.27N 46.13 E
Lagawe 150 Hc 16.49N 121.06 E
Lage 124 Kc 51.59N 8.48 E
Lågen [Nor.] 116 De 59.03N 10.05 E
Lågen [Nor.] 114 Cf 61.08N 10.25 E
Lagh Bogal 170 Gb 0.42N 40.55 E
Laghmān 144 Lb 35.00N 70.15 E
Laghouat 160 He 33.48N 2.53 E
Laghouat 162 Hc 33.30N 3.15 E
La Gloria 194 Ki 8.38N 73.48W
Lagny-sur-Marne 122 If 48.52N 2.43 E
Lagôa 204 Eb 14.08S 55.20W
Lagoa 126 Dg 37.08N 8.27W
Lagoa da Prata 204 Je 20.01S 45.33W
Lagoa Vermelha 206 Jc 28.13S 51.32W
Lagodehi 132 Oi 41.50N 46.14 E
La Gomera 194 Bf 14.05N 91.03W
Lagonegro 128 Jj 40.07N 15.46 E
Lagonoy Gulf 150 Hd 13.35N 123.45 E
Lágos 130 Ih 41.01N 25.07 E
Lagos 166 Fd 6.30N 3.30 E
Lagos [Nig.] 160 Hh 6.27N 3.23 E
Lagos [Port.] 126 Dg 37.06N 8.40W
Lagos, Baia de- 126 Dg 37.06N 8.39W
Lagosa 170 Ed 5.57S 29.53 E
Lagos de Moreno 190 Dd 21.21N 101.55W
La Grande 182 Db 45.20N 118.05W
La Grande Fosse 118 Kl 49.40N 3.00W
La Grande Rivière 174 Ld 53.50N 79.00W
La Grande Trench (EN)= Hurd Deep 118 Kl 49.40N 3.00W
Lagrange 184 Ee 41.39N 85.25W
La Grange [Ky.-U.S.] 184 Ef 38.24N 85.23W
La Grange [Ga.-U.S.] 182 Je 33.02N 85.02W
La Grange [Tx.-U.S.] 186 Hl 29.54N 96.52W
La Granja → San Ildefonso 126 Id 40.54N 4.00W
La Gran Sabana 202 Fb 5.30N 61.30W
La Grita 202 Db 8.08N 71.59W
Lagskär 116 He 59.50N 20.00 E
La Guaira 200 Jd 10.36N 66.56W
La Guajira 202 Da 11.30N 72.30W
Lagua Lichan, Puntan- 220b Ba 15.16N 145.50 E
Laguardia 126 Jb 42.33N 2.35W
La Guardia [Sp.] 126 Dc 41.54N 8.53W
La Guardia [Sp.] 126 Ie 39.47N 3.29W
La Guasima 192 Kg 21.06N 97.49W
Laguiole 122 Ij 44.41N 2.51 E
Laguna 206 Kc 28.29S 48.47W
Laguna Alsina 204 Am 36.49S 62.13W
Laguna Beach 188 Gj 33.33N 117.51W
Laguna Blanca 204 Cg 25.08S 58.15W
Laguna de Bay 150 Hd 14.23N 121.15 E
Laguna Limpia 204 Ch 26.29S 59.41W
Laguna Mountains 188 Gj 32.55N 116.25W
Laguna Paiva 206 Hd 31.19S 60.39W
Laguna Superior 190 Fe 16.20N 94.25W
Laguna Veneta 128 Ge 45.25N 12.20 E
Laguna Yema 204 Bg 24.15S 61.15W
Lagunillas [Bol.] 202 Fg 19.38S 63.43W
Lagunillas [Mex.] 192 Ii 17.50N 101.44W
Lagunillas [Ven.] 194 Lh 10.08N 71.16W
Lagunillas [Ven.] 194 Li 8.31N 71.24W
Laha 152 Lb 48.13N 124.36 E
La Habana 194 Fb 22.45N 82.10W
La Habana=Havana (EN) 176 Kg 23.08N 82.22W
Lahad Datu 150 Ge 5.02N 118.19 E
Laham 166 Fc 14.54N 4.25 E
Lahat 150 Dg 3.48S 103.32 E
Lahdenpohja 114 Hf 61.33N 30.13 E
Lahewa 150 Cf 1.24N 97.11 E
Lahij 144 Fg 13.04N 44.53 E
Lāhījān 144 Hb 37.12N 50.01 E
Lahn 120 Df 50.18N 7.37 E
Lahnstein 124 Jd 50.20N 7.29 E
Laholm 114 Ch 56.31N 13.02 E
Laholmsbukten 116 Eh 56.35N 12.50 E
Lahore 142 Jf 31.35N 74.18 E
Lahr 120 Dh 48.20N 7.52 E
Lahti 112 Ic 60.58N 25.40 E
Laï 160 Ih 9.24N 16.18 E
Laiagam 214 Ci 5.31S 143.39 E
Lai'an 154 Eh 32.28N 118.26 E
Lai Chau 148 Kd 22.02N 103.10 E
Laich o'Moray 118 Jd 57.40N 3.30W
Laie 221a Db 21.39N 157.56W
Laifeng 152 If 29.31N 109.23 E
Laighean/Leinster 118 Gh 53.00N 7.00W
Laignes 122 Kg 47.50N 4.22 E
Laihia 114 Fe 62.58N 22.01 E
Lainioälven 114 Fc 67.22N 22.39 E
Lairg 118 Ic 58.01N 4.25W
Laïri 168 Bc 10.49N 17.06 E
Laïri, Batha de- 168 Bc 12.28N 16.45 E
Lais 150 Dg 3.32S 102.03 E
La Isabela 194 Gb 22.57N 80.01W
Laisamis 170 Gb 1.36N 37.48 E
Laiševo 114 Li 55.26N 49.32 E
Laishui 154 Ce 39.23N 115.42 E
Laisvall 114 Dc 66.08N 17.10 E
Laitila 114 Ef 60.53N 21.41 E
Laiwu 154 Df 36.12N 117.40 E
Laiwui 150 Ig 1.22S 127.40 E
Laixi (Shuiji) 154 Ff 36.52N 120.31 E
Laiyang 152 Ld 36.59N 120.39 E
Laiyuan 152 Jd 39.19N 114.43 E
Laizhou Wan 154 Ef 37.30N 119.30 E
Laja 206 Fe 37.16S 72.42W
Laja 134 Hc 66.20N 56.16 E
La Jara 126 He 39.40N 4.55W
Lajeado 204 Gi 29.27S 51.58W
Lajeado, Serra do- 204 Hd 19.08S 49.56W
Lajes [Braz.] 200 Kh 27.48S 50.19W
Lajes [Braz.] 202 Ke 5.41S 36.14W
Lajes do Pico 162 Bb 38.23N 28.16W
Lajosmizse 120 Pi 47.01N 19.33 E
Lajta 128 Lc 47.52N 17.18 E
La Junta [Co.-U.S.] 182 Gd 37.59N 103.33W
La Junta [Mex.] 192 Fc 28.28N 107.20W
Lak Bor 170 Hb 1.18N 40.40 E
Lake Cargelligo 212 Jf 33.18S 146.23 E
Lake Charles 176 Jf 30.12N 93.12W
Lake City 182 Ke 30.12N 82.38W
Lake District 118 Jg 54.30N 3.10W
Lake Fork Creek 188 Jf 40.13N 110.07W
Lake Geneva 186 Le 42.36N 88.26W
Lake George 184 Kd 43.25N 73.45W
Lake Grace 212 Df 33.06S 118.28 E
Lake Harbour 180 Kd 62.51N 69.53W
Lake Havasu City 188 Hi 34.27N 114.22W
Lake Itasca 186 Ic 46.51N 95.13W
Lake Jackson 186 Il 29.02N 95.27W
Lake King 212 Df 33.05S 119.40 E
Lakeland 182 Kf 28.03N 81.57W
Lake Louise 188 Ga 51.26N 116.11W
Lakemba 219d Cc 18.13S 178.47W
Lakemba Passage 219d Cb 17.53S 178.32W
Lake Mills 186 Je 43.25N 93.32W
Lake Minchumina 178 Id 63.53N 152.19W
Lake Murray 214 Ci 6.54S 141.28 E
Lake Oswego 188 Dd 45.26N 122.39W
Lake Placid 184 Kc 44.18N 73.59W
Lake Providence 186 Kj 32.48N 91.11W
Lake Pukaki 218 Df 44.11S 170.08 E
Lake Range 188 Ff 40.15N 119.25W
Lake River 180 Jf 54.28N 82.30W
Lakes Entrance 212 Jg 37.53S 147.59 E
Lakeside 188 If 41.13N 112.57W
Lake Tekapo 218 Df 44.00S 170.29 E
Lakeview 182 Cc 42.11N 120.21W
Lakeville 186 Jd 44.39N 93.14W
Lake Wales 184 Gl 27.55N 81.35W
Lakewood [Co.-U.S.] 186 Dg 39.44N 105.06W
Lakewood [Oh.-U.S.] 184 Ge 41.29N 81.50W
Lake Worth 184 Gl 26.37N 80.03W
Lakhdar, Chergui Kef- 126 Pi 35.57N 3.16 E
Lakhdaria 126 Ph 36.34N 3.35 E
Lāki 130 Hh 41.50N 24.50 E
Lakin 186 Fh 37.58N 101.15W
Lakinsk 114 Jh 56.04N 39.58 E
Lákmos Óros 130 Ej 39.40N 21.07 E
Lakon, Île- 208 Hf 14.17S 167.30 E
Lakonikós Kólpos = Laconia, Gulf of- (EN) 130 Fm 36.35N 22.40 E
Lakota 166 Dd 5.53N 5.42W
Lakota [I.C.] 166 Dd 5.51N 5.41W
Lakota [N.D.-U.S.] 186 Gb 48.02N 98.21W
Laksefjorden 114 Ga 70.58N 27.00 E
Lakselv 114 Fa 70.03N 25.01 E
Lakshadweep 148 Ef 11.00N 72.00 E
Lakshadweep 140 Jh 11.00N 72.00 E
La Laguna 204 Bb 14.30S 61.06W
Lalanna 172 Hd 23.28S 45.05 E
Lalapaşa 130 Jh 41.50N 26.44 E
Lāleh Zār, Kūh-e- 130 Hg 29.24N 56.46 E
La Leonesa 204 Ch 27.03S 58.43W
Lālī 146 Mf 32.21N 49.06 E
Lalibela 168 Fc 12.00N 39.04 E
La Libertad 202 Ce 8.00S 78.30W
La Libertad [El Sal.] 190 Gf 13.29N 89.16W
La Libertad [Guat.] 194 Be 16.47N 90.07W
La Libertad [Guat.] 194 Bf 15.30N 91.50W
La Libertad [Hond.] 194 Df 14.43N 87.36W
La Ligua 206 Fd 32.27S 71.14W
Lalín 126 Db 42.39N 8.07W
La Línea 126 Gh 36.10N 5.19W
Lalin He 154 Hb 45.28N 125.43 E
Lalitpur 148 Fd 24.41N 78.25 E
Lalla Khedidja 126 Qh 36.27N 4.14 E
Lālmanir Hāt 148 Hc 25.54N 89.27 E
La Loche 180 Ge 56.29N 109.27W
La Louvière 122 Kd 50.29N 4.11
La Lucila 204 Bj 30.25S 61.01
Lalzit, Gjiri i- 130 Ch 41.31N 19.29
La Maddalena 128 Di 41.13N 9.24
La Maiella 128 Ih 42.05N 14.07
La Maladeta/Malditos, Montes- 126 Mb 42.40N 0.5
La Malbaie 180 Kg 47.39N 70.1
La Mancha 110 Fh 39.05N 3.
La Manche=English Channel (EN) 110 Fe 50.20N 1.
Lamap 216 Cc 16.26S 167
Lamar 182 Gd 38.05N 10
La Maragateria 126 Fb 42.25N
La Marina 126 Lf 38.35N
La Marmora 128 Dk 39.59N
La Marque 186 Il 29.22N
Lamas 202 Ce 6.25S
Lamastre 122 Kj 44.59N
Lamawan 154 Ad 40.05N
Lambach 128 Hb 48.05N
Lamballe 122 Df 48.28N
Lambar, Rio- 204 Jd 19.30S
Lambaréné 160 Ii 0.42S

Index Symbols

- Independent Nation
- State, Region
- District, County
- Municipality
- Colony, Dependency
- Continent
- Physical Region
- Historical or Cultural Region
- Mount, Mountain
- Volcano
- Hill
- Mountains, Mountain Range
- Hills, Escarpment
- Plateau, Upland
- Pass, Gap
- Plain, Lowland
- Delta
- Salt Flat
- Valley, Canyon
- Crater, Cave
- Karst Features
- Depression
- Polder
- Desert, Dunes
- Forest, Woods
- Heath, Steppe
- Oasis
- Cape, Point
- Coast, Beach
- Cliff
- Peninsula
- Isthmus
- Sandbank
- Island
- Atoll
- Rock, Reef
- Islands, Archipelago
- Rocks, Reefs
- Coral Reef
- Well, Spring
- Geyser
- River, Stream
- Waterfall, Rapids
- River Mouth, Estuary
- Lake
- Salt Lake
- Intermittent Lake
- Reservoir
- Swamp, Pond
- Canal
- Glacier
- Ice Shelf, Pack Ice
- Ocean
- Sea
- Gulf, Bay
- Strait, Fjord
- Lagoon
- Bank
- Seamount
- Tablemount
- Ridge
- Shelf
- Basin
- Escarpment, Sea Scarp
- Fracture
- Trench, Abyss
- National Park, Reserve
- Point of Interest
- Recreation Site
- Cave, Cavern
- Historic Site
- Ruins
- Wall, Walls
- Church, Abbey
- Temple
- Scientific Station
- Railway station
- Airport
- Port
- Military
- Lighthou
- Mine
- Tunnel
- Dam, B

Lam-Lav

Lambari	204	Je	21.58S	45.21W
Lambasa	216	Ec	16.26S	179.24 E
Lambay/Reachrainn	118	Gh	53.29N	6.01W
Lambayeque	202	Ce	6.42S	79.55W
Lambayeque [3]	202	Ce	6.20S	80.00W
Lambert Glacier	222	Ff	71.00S	70.00 E
Lambert Land	179	Jc	79.10N	21.00W
Lamberts Bay	160	Il	32.05S	18.17 E
Lambro	128	De	45.08N	9.32 E
Lambsheim	124	Ke	49.31N	8.17 E
Lambton, Cape -	180	Fb	71.04N	123.08W
Lamé	168	Ad	9.15N	14.32 E
Lame Deer	188	Ld	45.37N	106.40W
Lamego	126	Ec	41.06N	7.49W
Lamentin	197e	Ab	16.16N	61.38W
La Mesa	188	Gj	32.46N	117.01W
Lamesa	182	Ge	32.44N	101.57W
La Meta	128	Hi	41.41N	13.56 E
Lamezia Terme	128	Kl	38.59N	16.17 E
Lamezia Terme - Nicastro	128	Kl	38.59N	16.19 E
Lamezia Terme - Sambiase	128	Kl	38.58N	16.17 E
Lamezia Terme - Sant'Eufemia Lamezia	128	Kl	38.55N	16.15 E
Lamia	130	Fk	38.54N	22.26 E
Lamina	204	De	20.34S	56.14W
Lamlam, Mount-	220c	Bb	13.20N	144.40 E
Lammermuir Hills	118	Kf	55.52N	2.40W
Lammhult	116	Fg	57.10N	14.35 E
Lammi	114	Ff	61.05N	25.01 E
Lamoil	220d	Ba	7.39N	151.41 E
Lamon Bay	140	Oh	14.25N	122.00 E
Lamone	128	Gf	44.29N	12.08 E
Lamoni	186	Jf	40.37N	93.56W
Lamont	184	Fj	30.21N	83.50W
La Montaña	198	If	10.00S	72.50W
La Moraña	126	Hd	40.45N	4.55W
La Mosquitia	194	Ef	15.00N	84.20W
Lamotrek Atoll	208	Fd	7.30N	146.20 E
Lamotte-Beuvron	122	Ig	47.36N	2.01 E
La Moure	186	Gc	46.21N	98.18W
Lampang	148	Je	18.16N	99.34 E
Lampasas	186	Gk	31.03N	98.12W
Lampazos de Naranjo	192	Id	27.01N	100.31W
Lampedusa	128	Go	35.30N	12.35 E
Lampertheim	120	Eg	49.36N	8.28 E
Lampeter	118	Ii	52.07N	4.05W
Lamphun	148	Je	18.35N	99.00 E
Lampione	128	Go	35.35N	12.20 E
Lampung [3]	150	Dg	5.00S	105.00 E
Lamu	160	Li	2.16S	40.54 E
Lamud	202	Ce	6.09S	77.55W
Lan	132	Ec	52.09N	27.18 E
Lana	128	Fd	46.37N	11.09 E
Lana, Río de la-	192	Li	17.49N	95.09W
Lanai City	221a	Ec	20.50N	156.55W
Lanaihale	221a	Ec	20.49N	156.52W
Lanai Island	208	Lb	20.50N	156.55W
Lanaken	124	Hd	50.53N	5.39 E
Lanao, Lake-	150	He	7.50N	124.15 E
Lanark	118	Jf	55.41N	3.48W
Lanbi Kyun	148	Jf	10.50N	98.15 E
Lancang (Menglangba)	152	Gg	22.37N	99.57 E
Lancang Jiang = Mekong (EN)	140	Mh	10.15N	105.55 E
Lancashire [3]	118	Kh	53.55N	2.40W
Lancashire Plain	118	Kh	53.40N	2.45W
Lancaster	118	Kh	53.45N	2.50W
Lancaster [Ca.-U.S.]	182	De	34.42N	118.08W
Lancaster [Eng.-U.K.]	118	Kg	54.03N	2.48W
Lancaster [Mo.-U.S.]	186	Jf	40.31N	92.32W
Lancaster [N.H.-U.S.]	184	Lc	44.29N	71.34W
Lancaster [Oh.-U.S.]	184	Ff	39.43N	82.37W
Lancaster [Ont.-Can.]	184	Jc	45.12N	74.30W
Lancaster [Pa.-U.S.]	182	Lc	40.01N	76.19W
Lancaster [S.C.-U.S.]	184	Gh	34.43N	80.47W
Lancaster Sound	174	Kb	74.13N	84.00W
Lançeiro	204	Fe	20.59S	53.43W
Lancelin	212	Df	31.01S	115.19 E
Lanciano	128	Ih	42.14N	14.23 E
Lančin	130	Ha	48.31N	24.49 E
Lancun	154	Ff	36.25N	120.11 E
Łańcut	120	Sf	50.05N	22.13 E
Land	116	Cd	60.45N	10.00 E
Lândana	170	Bd	5.15S	12.10 E
Landau an der Isar	120	Ih	48.41N	12.41 E
Landau in der Pfalz	120	Eg	49.12N	8.07 E
Land Bay	222	Mf	75.25S	141.45W
Landeck	128	Ec	47.08N	10.34 E
Landen	124	Hd	50.45N	5.05 E
Lander	182	Fc	42.50N	108.44W
Landerneau	122	Bf	48.27N	4.15W
Lander River	212	Gd	20.25S	132.00 E
Landeryd	116	Eg	57.05N	13.16 E
Landes [3]	122	Fj	44.00N	0.50W
Landes	122	Fj	44.15N	1.00W
Landesbergen	124	Lb	52.34N	9.08 E
Landeta	204	Ak	32.01S	62.04W
Landete	126	Ke	39.54N	1.22W
Landfallis	148	If	13.40N	93.02 E
Land Glacier	222	Mf	75.40S	141.45W
Landi Kotal	148	Eb	34.06N	71.09 E
andless Corner	170	Ee	14.53S	28.04 E
andrecies	124	Fd	50.08N	3.42 E
andsberg am Lech	120	Gh	48.03N	10.52 E
andsbro	116	Fg	57.22N	14.54 E
and's End	110	Fe	50.03N	5.44W
nds End	180	Fa	76.25N	122.45W
ndshut	120	Ih	48.32N	12.09 E
ndskrona	114	Ci	55.52N	12.50 E
ndsort	116	Gf	58.45N	17.50 E
dsortsdjupet	116	Hf	58.40N	18.30 E
dstuhl	124	Je	49.25N	7.34 E
dusky	188	Kc	47.54N	108.37W
euve-Lyre	124	Cf	48.54N	0.45 E
eng → Lankao	154	Cg	34.49N	114.48 E
	188	Mb	49.56N	104.23W
a Co	152	De	30.41N	81.17 E
dhás	130	Gi	40.45N	23.04 E
Langádhia	130	Fl	37.39N	22.03 E
Långan	114	De	63.19N	14.44 E
Langano, Lake-	168	Fd	7.36N	38.43 E
Langara	150	Hg	4.02S	123.00 E
Langarfoss	114a	Cb	65.35N	14.15W
Langasian	150	Ie	8.16N	125.39 E
Langdon	186	Gb	48.46N	98.22W
Langeac	122	Ji	45.06N	3.29 E
Langeais	122	Gg	47.20N	0.24 E
Langeb	168	Fb	17.46N	36.41 E
Langebaan	172	Bf	33.06S	18.02 E
Langeberg	172	Cf	33.56S	20.45 E
Langedijk	124	Gb	52.42N	4.48 E
Langeland	114	Ci	55.00N	10.50 E
Langelands Bælt	116	Dj	54.50N	10.55 E
Längelmävesi	116	Kc	61.30N	24.20 E
Langen	124	Ke	49.59N	8.40 E
Langenberg	124	Kc	51.17N	8.34 E
Langenburg	186	Fa	50.50N	101.43W
Langenfeld (Rheinland)	124	Ic	51.06N	6.57 E
Langenhagen	120	Fd	52.27N	9.45 E
Langenselbold	124	Ld	50.11N	9.02 E
Langenthal	128	Bc	47.13N	7.49 E
Langeoog	120	Dc	53.46N	7.32 E
Langeri	138	Jf	50.08N	143.20 E
Langesund	116	Ce	59.00N	9.45 E
Langesundsfjorden	116	Cf	59.00N	9.48 E
Langevåg	116	Bb	62.27N	6.12 E
Langfang → Anci	152	Kd	39.29N	116.40 E
Långfjället	116	Eb	62.10N	12.20 E
Langfjorden	116	Bb	62.45N	7.30 E
Langhe	128	Bf	44.30N	8.00 E
Langholm	118	Kf	55.09N	3.00W
Langjökull	110	Ec	64.39N	20.00W
Langkawi, Pulau-	150	Ce	6.22N	99.48 E
Langkon	150	Ge	6.32N	116.42 E
Langlade	184	Ja	48.12N	75.57W
Langnau im Emmental	128	Bd	46.56N	7.46 E
Langogne	122	Jj	44.43N	3.51 E
Langon	122	Fj	44.33N	0.15W
Langorūd	146	Nd	37.11N	50.10 E
Langøya	114	Db	68.44N	14.50 E
Langreo	126	Ga	43.18N	5.41W
Langres	122	Lg	47.52N	5.20 E
Langres, Plateau de-	110	Gf	47.41N	5.03 E
Langrune-sur-Mer	124	Be	49.19N	0.22W
Langsa	142	Li	4.28N	97.58 E
Långsele	116	Ga	63.11N	17.04 E
Långshyttan	116	Gd	60.27N	16.01 E
Lang Son	148	Ld	21.50N	106.44 E
Lang Suan	148	Jg	9.55N	99.07 E
Languedoc	110	Gg	44.00N	4.00 E
Languedoc	122	Jj	44.00N	4.00 E
Langueyú, Arroyo-	204	Cm	36.39S	58.27W
Langwedel	124	Lb	52.58N	9.13 E
Langxi	154	Ei	31.08N	119.11 E
Langzhong	152	Ie	31.40N	106.04 E
Lan Hsu	152	Lg	22.00N	121.30 E
Laniel	184	Hb	47.06N	79.15W
Lanin, Volcán-	198	Ii	39.38S	71.30W
Lankao (Lanfeng)	154	Cg	34.49N	114.48 E
Länkipohja	116	Kc	61.44N	24.48 E
Lannemezan	122	Gk	43.08N	0.23 E
Lannemezan, Plateau de-	122	Gk	43.09N	0.27 E
Lannion	122	Cf	48.44N	3.28W
Lannion, Baie de-	122	Cf	48.43N	3.34W
La Noria	206	Gb	20.23S	69.53W
Lansdowne House	180	If	52.13N	87.53W
L'Anse	184	Cb	46.45N	88.27W
Lansing [Ia.-U.S.]	186	Ke	43.22N	91.13W
Lansing [Mi.-U.S.]	176	Ke	42.43N	84.34W
Lansjärv	114	Fc	66.39N	22.12 E
Łańskie, Jezioro-	120	Qc	53.33N	20.30 E
Lantar	138	Ie	56.05N	137.35 E
Lanta Yai, Ko-	148	Jg	7.35N	99.03 E
Lanteri	204	Ci	28.50S	59.39W
Lanterne	122	Mg	47.44N	6.03 E
Lanús	204	Cl	34.43S	58.24W
Lanusei	128	Dk	39.53N	9.32 E
Lanvaux, Landes de-	122	Dg	47.47N	2.36W
Lanxi [China]	154	Ej	29.13N	119.28 E
Lanxi [China]	154	Ha	46.15N	126.16 E
Lanxian (Dongcun)	154	Ae	38.17N	111.38 E
Lanyi He	154	Ae	38.40N	110.53 E
Lanzarote	158	Ff	29.00N	13.40W
Lanzhou	142	Mf	36.03N	103.41 E
Lanzo Torinese	128	Be	45.16N	7.28 E
Lao	128	Jk	39.47N	15.48 E
Laoag	142	Oh	18.12N	120.36 E
Laoang	150	Id	12.34N	125.00 E
Lao Cai	142	Mg	22.30N	103.57 E
Laocheng	154	Hc	42.37N	124.04 E
Laoha He	152	Lc	43.24N	120.39 E
Lao He	154	Cj	29.02N	115.47 E
Laohuanghe Kou	154	Ef	37.39N	119.02 E
Laois [2]	118	Fi	53.00N	7.30W
Laojunmiao → Yumen	142	Lf	39.50N	97.44 E
Laojun Shan	152	Je	33.45N	111.38 E
Lao Ling	154	Id	41.24N	126.10 E
Laon	122	Je	49.34N	3.37 E
Laona	186	Ld	45.34N	88.40W
Laonnois	124	Fe	49.35N	3.40 E
La Orchila, Isla-	202	Ea	11.48N	66.10W
La Oroya	200	Ig	11.32S	75.57W
Laos [1]	142	Mh	18.00N	105.00 E
Laoshan (Licun)	154	Ff	36.10N	120.25 E
Laotougou	154	Jc	42.54N	129.09 E
Laou	126	Gi	35.26N	5.05W
Laoye Ling	154	Kb	44.50N	130.10 E
Lapa	206	Kc	25.45S	49.42W
Lapai	166	Gd	9.03N	6.43 E
Lapalisse	122	Jh	46.15N	3.38 E
La Palma	158	Ff	28.40N	17.52W
La Palma [El Sal.]	194	Cf	14.19N	89.11W
La Palma [Pan.]	190	Ig	8.25N	78.09W
La Palma del Condado	126	Fg	37.23N	6.33W
La Paloma	204	El	34.40S	54.10W
La Pampa [2]	206	Ge	37.00S	66.00W
La Panne/De Panne	124	Ec	51.06N	2.35 E
La Paragua	202	Fb	6.50N	63.20W
La Partida, Isla-	192	De	24.30N	110.25W
La Paz [Arg.]	206	Gd	33.28S	67.33W
La Paz [Arg.]	206	Id	30.45S	59.39W
La Paz [Bol.]	200	Jg	16.30S	68.09W
La Paz [Bol.] [3]	202	Eg	15.00S	68.00W
La Paz [Col.]	194	Kh	10.23N	73.10W
La Paz [Hond.]	190	Gf	14.16N	87.40W
La Paz [Hond.] [3]	194	Df	14.15N	87.50W
La Paz [Mex.]	176	Hg	24.10N	110.18W
La Paz [Ur.]	204	Dl	34.46S	56.13W
La Paz [Ven.]	194	Lh	10.41N	72.00W
La Paz, Bahía de-	190	Bd	24.09N	110.25W
La Paz, Llano de-	192	De	24.00N	110.30W
La Paz Centro	194	Dg	12.20N	86.41W
La Pedrera	202	Ed	1.18S	69.40W
Lapeer	184	Fd	43.03N	83.19W
La Pelada	204	Bj	30.52S	60.59W
La Pérouse, Bahia-	221d	Bb	27.04S	109.18W
La Perouse Strait (EN) = Laperuza, proliv-	140	Qe	45.30N	142.00 E
La Perouse Strait (EN) = Sōya-Kaikyō	140	Qe	45.30N	142.00 E
Laperuza, proliv- = La Perouse Strait (EN)	140	Qe	45.30N	142.00 E
La Pesca	190	Ed	23.47N	97.47W
La Petite-Pierre	124	Jf	48.52N	7.19 E
La Picasa, Laguna-	204	Al	34.20S	62.14W
La Piedad Cavadas	192	Hg	20.21N	102.00W
La Pine	188	Ee	43.40N	121.30W
Lapinjärvi/Lappträsk	116	Ld	60.36N	26.09 E
Lapinlahti	114	Ge	63.22N	27.30 E
La Plaine	197g	Bb	15.20N	61.15W
La Plana	126	Ld	40.00N	0.05W
Lapland (EN) = Lappi	110	Ib	66.50N	22.00 E
Lapland (EN) = Lappland	110	Ib	66.50N	22.00 E
La Plant	186	Fd	45.10N	100.38W
La Plata	200	Ki	34.55S	57.57W
la Pobla de Lillet	126	Nb	42.15N	1.59 E
la Pobla de Segur / Pobla de Segur	126	Mb	42.15N	0.58 E
La Pocatièr	184	Lb	47.21N	70.02W
La Porte	184	De	41.36N	86.43W
Lapovo	130	Ee	44.11N	21.06 E
Lappajärvi	114	Fe	63.08N	23.40 E
Lappeenranta/Villmanstrand	112	Ic	61.04N	28.11 E
Lappfjärd/Lapväärtti	116	Ib	62.15N	21.32 E
Lappi	116	Ic	61.06N	21.50 E
Lappi [2]	114	Gc	67.40N	26.30 E
Lappi = Lapland (EN)	110	Ib	66.50N	22.00 E
Lappo/Lapua	114	Fe	62.57N	23.00 E
Lappträsk/Lapinjärvi	116	Ld	60.36N	26.09 E
Lapri	138	He	55.45N	124.59 E
Laprida	206	He	37.33S	60.49W
Lâpseki	146	Bb	40.20N	26.31 E
Lapta	146	Ee	35.20N	33.10 E
Laptev Sea (EN) = Laptevyh, more-	224	Fd	76.00N	126.00 E
Laptevyh, more- = Laptev Sea (EN)	224	Fd	76.00N	126.00 E
Lapua/Lappo	114	Fe	62.57N	23.00 E
La Puebla / Sa Pobla	126	Pe	39.46N	3.01 E
La Puebla de Cazalla	126	Gg	37.14N	5.19W
Lapuna	204	Ba	13.19S	60.28W
La Puntilla	198	Hf	2.11S	81.01W
La Purísima	192	Cd	26.10N	112.04W
Lăpuş	130	Hb	47.30N	24.01 E
Lăpuş	130	Gb	47.39N	23.24 E
La Push	188	Cc	47.55N	124.38W
Lapväärtti/Lappfjärd	116	Ib	62.15N	21.32 E
Łapy	120	Sd	53.00N	22.53 E
Laqīyat al Arba'in	168	Da	20.03N	28.02 E
La Quemada	192	Hf	22.27N	102.45W
La Quiaca	206	Gb	22.06S	65.37W
L'Aquila	112	Hg	42.22N	13.22 E
Lar	144	Hd	27.41N	54.17 E
Lara [2]	202	Ea	10.10N	69.50W
La Rábida, Monasterio de-	126	Fg	37.12N	6.55W
Larache	162	Fb	35.12N	6.09W
Laragne-Montéglin	122	Lj	44.19N	5.49 E
Lārak	144	Id	26.52N	56.22 E
La Rambla	126	Hg	37.36N	4.44W
Laramie	176	Ie	41.19N	105.35W
Laramie Mountains	182	Fc	42.00N	105.40W
Laramie Peak	188	Me	42.17N	105.27W
Laramie River	188	Me	42.12N	104.32W
Laranjal, Rio-	204	Ff	23.12S	53.45W
Laranjeiras do Sul	206	Jc	25.25S	52.25W
Larantuka	150	Hh	8.21S	122.59 E
Larat	150	Jh	7.09S	131.45 E
Larat, Pulau-	150	Jh	7.10S	131.50 E
La Raya	194	Ji	8.20N	74.34W
L'Arba	126	Ph	36.34N	3.09 E
L'Arbaa Naït Irathen	126	Qh	36.38N	4.12 E
Lärbro	114	Eh	57.47N	18.47 E
Larche, Col de-	122	Mj	44.25N	6.53 E
Larde	172	Fc	16.28S	39.43 E
Larderello	128	Eg	43.14N	10.53 E
Laredo [Sp.]	126	Ia	43.24N	3.25W
Laredo [Tx.-U.S.]	176	Jg	27.31N	99.30W
Laren	124	Hb	52.16N	5.16 E
Lārestān	140	Hg	27.00N	55.30 E
Lārestān	144	Id	27.00N	55.30 E
Large Island	197p	Cb	12.24N	61.30W
Largentière	122	Kj	44.32N	4.18 E
Largo, Cayo-	194	Gc	21.38N	81.28W
Largs	118	If	55.48N	4.52W
La Ribera	126	Kb	42.30N	2.00W
Larimore	186	Hc	47.54N	97.38W
Larino	128	Ii	41.48N	14.54 E
Lario → Como, Lago di-	128	Dd	46.00N	9.15 E
La Rioja	200	Jh	29.25S	66.50W
La Rioja	126	Jb	42.20N	2.20W
La Rioja [Arg.] [2]	206	Gc	30.00S	67.30W
La Rioja [Sp.] [2]	126	Jb	42.15N	2.30W
Lárisa	112	Ih	39.38N	22.25 E
La Rivière-Thibouville, Nassandres-	124	Ce	49.07N	0.44 E
Lārkāna	148	Dc	27.33N	68.13 E
Larmor-Plage	122	Cg	47.42N	3.23W
Larnaka/Lárnax	144	Dc	34.55N	33.38 E
Lárnax/Larnaka	144	Dc	34.55N	33.38 E
Larne/Latharna	118	Hg	54.51N	5.49W
Larned	186	Gg	38.11N	99.06W
La Robla	126	Gb	42.48N	5.37W
La Roche	219b	De	21.28S	168.02 E
La Roche-en-Ardenne	122	Ld	50.11N	5.35 E
La Rochefoucauld	122	Gi	45.44N	0.23 E
La Roche-Guyon	124	De	49.05N	1.38 E
La Roda	126	Je	39.13N	2.09W
La Romana	190	Ke	18.25N	68.58W
La Ronge	180	Ge	55.06N	105.17W
La Ronge, Lac-	174	Id	55.05N	104.59W
Larose	186	Kl	29.35N	90.23W
La Rosita	192	Ic	28.24N	101.43W
Larouco	126	Ec	41.56N	7.40W
Larreynaga	194	Dg	12.40N	86.34W
Larrey Point	212	Dc	20.00S	119.10 E
Larrimah	210	Ef	15.35S	133.12 E
Larsa	146	Kg	31.16N	45.49 E
Lars Christensen Kyst	222	Fe	69.30S	68.00 E
Larsen, Mount-	222	Kf	74.51S	162.12 E
Larsen Ice Shelf	222	Qe	68.30S	62.30W
La Rumorosa	192	Aa	32.34N	116.06W
Laruns	122	Fk	43.00N	0.25W
Larvik	114	Bg	59.04N	10.00 E
Larzac, Causse du-	122	Jk	43.57N	3.11 E
La Sabana [Arg.]	204	Ch	27.52S	59.57W
La Sabana [Col.]	202	Ec	2.20N	68.32W
Las Adjuntas, Presa de-	192	Jf	23.55N	98.45W
La Sagra	126	Jg	37.57N	2.34W
La Sagra	126	Id	40.05N	4.00W
La Salle	186	Lf	41.20N	89.06W
La Salle, Pic-	190	Je	18.22N	71.59W
La Sal Mountains	188	Kg	38.30N	109.10W
Las Alpujarras	126	Ih	36.50N	3.25W
La Sanabria	126	Fb	42.08N	6.30W
Las Animas	186	Eg	38.04N	103.13W
Lās 'ānōd	168	Hd	8.26N	47.24 E
La Sarre	180	Jg	48.48N	79.12W
Las Aves, Islas-	202	Ea	11.58N	67.33W
Las Avispas	204	Bi	29.53S	61.18W
Las Bardenas	126	Kb	42.10N	1.25W
Las Bonitas	196	Di	7.52N	65.40W
Las Breñas	206	Hc	27.05S	61.05W
Las Cabezas de San Juan	126	Gh	36.59N	5.56W
Lascahobas	194	Ld	18.50N	71.56W
Lascano	204	Ek	33.40S	54.12W
Las Casitas, Cerro-	190	Cd	23.31N	109.53W
Lascaux, Grotte de-	122	Hi	45.03N	1.11 E
Las Cejas	206	Hc	26.53S	64.44W
Las Chilcas, Arroyo-	204	Cm	37.16S	58.26W
Las Choapas	190	Fe	17.55N	94.05W
Las Cinco Villas	126	Kb	42.05N	1.07W
Las Cruces	182	Fe	32.23N	106.29W
Lāsdāred	168	Hc	10.10N	46.01 E
Lās Dawa'o	168	Hc	10.22N	49.03 E
La Segarra	126	Nc	41.30N	1.10 E
La Selva	126	Oc	41.40N	2.50 E
La Serena	200	Ih	29.54S	71.16W
La Serena	126	Gf	38.45N	5.30W
la Seu d'Urgell / Seo de Urgel	126	Nb	42.21N	1.28 E
Las Flores	206	Ie	36.03S	59.07W
Lāsh-e Joveyn	144	Jc	31.43N	61.37 E
Las Heras	206	Gd	32.51S	68.49W
Lashio	142	Lg	22.58N	97.48 E
Lashkar Gāh	142	If	31.35N	64.21 E
Las Hurdes	126	Fd	40.20N	6.20W
La Sila	110	Hh	39.15N	16.30 E
Łasin	120	Pc	53.32N	19.05 E
Lāsjerd	146	Oe	35.24N	53.04 E
Łask	120	Pe	51.36N	19.07 E
Las Lajas	206	Fe	38.31S	70.22W
Las Lomitas	206	Hb	24.42S	60.36W
Las Margaritas	192	Ni	16.19N	91.59W
Las Mariñas	126	Da	43.20N	8.15W
Las Marismas	126	Fg	37.00N	6.15W
Las Mercedes	202	Eb	9.07N	66.24W
Las Mesteñas	192	Gc	28.13N	104.35W
Las Minas, Cerro-	190	Gf	14.33N	88.39W
Las Minas, Sierra de-	190	Ge	15.05N	90.00W
Las Mixtecas, Sierra de-	192	Ki	17.45N	97.15W
La Sola, Isla-	202	Fa	11.20N	63.34W
La Solana	126	If	38.56N	3.14W
Lasolo	150	Hg	3.29S	122.04 E
La Sorcière	197k	Bb	13.59N	60.56W
Las Palmas [3]	162	Ed	28.20N	14.20W
Las Palmas de Gran Canaria	160	Ff	28.06N	15.24W
Las Palomas	192	Fb	33.03N	107.19W
Las Petas	204	Cc	16.23S	59.11W
La Spezia	112	Gg	44.07N	9.50 E
Las Piedras	206	Id	34.45S	56.13W
Las Plumas	200	Jj	43.40S	67.15W
Lās Qoray	168	Hc	11.15N	48.22 E
Las Rosas	204	Bk	32.28S	61.34W
Lassen Peak	182	Cc	40.29N	121.31W
Lassigny	124	Ee	49.35N	2.51 E
Laßnitz	128	Jd	46.46N	15.32 E
Lasso	220b	Ba	15.02N	145.38 E
Las Tablas	194	Gj	7.46N	80.17W
Last Mountain Lake	180	Gf	51.10N	105.15W
Las Toscas	204	Ci	28.21S	59.17W
Lastovo	128	Kh	42.46N	16.55 E
Lastovo	128	Kh	42.45N	16.50 E
Lastovski kanal	128	Kh	42.50N	16.59 E
Las Tres Vírgenes, Volcán-	190	Bc	27.27N	112.34W
Las Tunas [3]	194	Ic	21.00N	77.00W
Las Tunas, Punta-	197a	Bb	18.30N	66.37W
Las Varillas	206	Hd	31.52S	62.43W
Las Vegas [N.M.-U.S.]	182	Fd	35.36N	105.13W
Las Vegas [Nv.-U.S.]	176	Hf	36.11N	115.08W
Las Villuercas	126	Ge	39.33N	5.27W
Łaszczów	120	Tf	50.32N	23.40 E
Lata	221c	Db	14.14S	169.29W
Latacunga	202	Cd	0.55S	78.37W
La Tagua	202	Dd	0.03S	74.40W
Latakia (EN) = Al Lādhiqīyah	142	Ff	35.31N	35.07 E
Late Island	216	Gc	18.48S	174.39W
Laterza	128	Kj	40.37N	16.48 E
Latgale	116	Lh	56.45N	27.30 E
Latgales Augstiene / Latgalskaja vozvyšennost	116	Lh	56.10N	27.30 E
Latgalskaja vozvyšennost / Latgales Augstiene	116	Lh	56.10N	27.30 E
Latharna/Larne	118	Hg	54.51N	5.49W
Lathen	124	Jb	52.52N	7.19 E
La Tigra	204	Bh	27.06S	60.34W
Latina	128	Gi	41.28N	12.52 E
Latisana	128	Ge	45.47N	13.00 E
Latium (EN) = Lazio [2]	128	Gh	42.02N	12.23 E
La Toja	126	Db	42.27N	8.50W
La Toma	206	Gd	33.03S	65.37W
La Tontouta	219b	Ce	22.00S	166.15 E
Latorica	120	Rh	48.28N	21.50 E
La Tortuga, Isla-	202	Ea	10.56N	65.20W
La Trinidad	194	Dg	12.58N	86.14W
La Trinidad de Orichuna	196	Bi	7.07N	69.45W
La Trinité	196	Fe	14.44N	60.58W
Latronico	128	Kj	40.05N	16.01 E
Lattari, Monti-	128	Ij	40.40N	14.30 E
La Tuque	180	Kg	47.27N	72.47W
Lātūr	148	Fe	18.24N	76.35 E
Latvian SSR (EN) = Latvijas PSR [2]	136	Cd	57.00N	25.00 E
Latvijas Padomju Socialistiska Respublika / Latvijskaja SSR [2]	136	Cd	57.00N	25.00 E
Latvijas PSR = Latvian SSR (EN) [2]	136	Cd	57.00N	25.00 E
Latvijskaja Sovetskaja Socialističeskaja Respublika [2]	136	Cd	57.00N	25.00 E
Latvijskaja SSR/Latvijas Padomju Socialistiska Respublika [2]	136	Cd	57.00N	25.00 E
Lau	158	Kh	6.56N	30.16 E
Laubach	124	Kd	50.33N	8.59 E
Lauchert	120	Fh	48.05N	9.15 E
Lauchhammer	120	Je	51.30N	13.48 E
Lauenburg	120	Gc	53.22N	10.34 E
Lauf an der Pegnitz	120	Hg	49.31N	11.17 E
Laughlan Islands	219a	Ac	9.15S	153.40 E
Laughlin Peak	186	Dh	36.38N	104.12W
Lau Group	208	Jf	18.20S	178.30W
Lauhanvuori	116	Jb	62.10N	22.10 E
Laujar de Andarax	126	Jh	36.59N	2.51W
Laukaa	114	Fe	62.25N	25.57 E
Laukuva	116	Ji	55.35N	22.08 E
Laulau, Bahia-	220b	Ba	15.08N	145.46 E
Launceston [Austl.]	210	Fi	41.26S	147.08 E
Launceston [Eng.-U.K.]	118	Ik	50.38N	4.21W
La Unión [Bol.]	204	Bb	15.18S	61.05W
La Unión [Chile]	206	Ff	40.17S	73.05W
La Unión [Col.]	202	Cc	1.37N	77.08W
La Unión [El Sal.]	190	Gf	13.20N	87.51W
La Unión [Mex.]	192	Ii	17.58N	101.49W
La Unión [Peru]	202	Ce	9.46S	76.48W
La Unión [Sp.]	126	Lg	37.37N	0.52W
La Unión [Ven.]	194	Ni	8.13N	67.46W
Laura	212	Ic	15.34S	144.28 E
La Urbana	136	Ci	7.08N	66.56W
Laurel [Ms.-U.S.]	182	Je	31.42N	89.08W
Laurel [Mt.-U.S.]	182	Fb	45.40N	108.46W
Laureles	204	Ej	31.23S	55.52W
Laurel Hill	184	He	40.02N	79.17W
Laurel Mountain	184	Hf	39.20N	79.50W
Laurens	184	Fh	34.30N	82.01W
Laurentian Plateau (EN) = Laurentien, Plateau-	174	Md	50.00N	70.00W
Laurentian Scarp	184	Ic	45.50N	76.15W
Laurentide Scarp	184	Kb	46.38N	73.00W
Laurentien, Plateau- = Laurentian Plateau (EN)	174	Md	50.00N	70.00W
Lauria	128	Jj	40.02N	15.50 E
Lau Ridge (EN)	106	Kl	25.00S	179.00 E
Laurie River	180	He	56.00N	100.58W
Laurinburg	184	Hh	34.47N	79.27W
Laurium	184	Cb	47.14N	88.26W
Lauro Muller	204	Hi	28.24S	49.23W
Lausanne	112	Gf	46.30N	6.40 E
Lausitzer Gebirge	120	Kf	50.48N	14.40 E
Lausitzer Neiße	120	Kc	52.04N	14.46 E
Laut, Pulau-	150	Ef	4.43N	107.59 E
Laut, Pulau-	140	Nj	3.40S	116.10 E
Lautaret, Col du-	122	Mi	45.02N	6.24 E
Lautaro	206	Fe	38.31S	72.27W
Lautém	150	Ih	8.22S	126.54 E
Lauter	120	Eg	48.58N	8.11 E
Lauterbach	120	Ff	50.38N	9.24 E
Lauterbourg	124	Kf	48.59N	8.11 E
Lauterecken	124	Je	49.39N	7.36 E
Lauthala	219d	Cb	16.45S	179.41W
Laut Kecil, Kepulauan-	150	Gg	4.50S	115.45 E
Lautoka	216	Ec	17.37S	177.27 E
Lauvergne Island	220d	Cb	7.00N	152.00 E
Lauwersmeer	124	Ia	53.25N	6.15 E
Lauzerte	122	Hj	44.15N	1.08 E
Lauzon	184	Lb	46.50N	71.10W
Lava	120	Rb	54.37N	21.14 E
Lava, Nosy- [Mad.]	172	Hb	14.33S	47.36 E
Lava, Nosy- [Mad.]	172	Hb	12.49S	48.41 E
Lavaca River	186	Hl	28.50N	96.36W
Lava Flow	186	Bi	34.45N	108.20W
Laval	122	Ff	48.04N	0.46W
La Vall d'Uxó / Vall de Uxó	126	Le	39.49N	0.14W
Lavalle	204	Ci	29.01S	59.11W
Lavalleja [2]	204	El	34.00S	55.00W
Lāvān, Jazīreh-ye-	144	Hd	26.48N	53.00 E

ex Symbols

- dependent Nation
- ate, Region
- trict, County
- nicipality
- ony, Dependency
- tinent
- sical Region
- Historical or Cultural Region
- Mount, Mountain
- Volcano
- Hill
- Mountains, Mountain Range
- Hills, Escarpment
- Plateau, Upland
- Pass, Gap
- Plain, Lowland
- Delta
- Salt Flat
- Valley, Canyon
- Crater, Cave
- Karst Features
- Depression
- Polder
- Desert, Dunes
- Forest, Woods
- Heath, Steppe
- Oasis
- Cape, Point
- Coast, Beach
- Cliff
- Peninsula
- Isthmus
- Sandbank
- Island
- Atoll
- Rock, Reef
- Islands, Archipelago
- Rocks, Reefs
- Coral Reef
- Well, Spring
- Geyser
- River, Stream
- Waterfall, Rapids
- River Mouth, Estuary
- Lake
- Salt Lake
- Intermittent Lake
- Reservoir
- Swamp, Pond
- Canal
- Glacier
- Ice Shelf, Pack Ice
- Ocean
- Sea
- Gulf, Bay
- Strait, Fjord
- Lagoon
- Bank
- Seamount
- Tablemount
- Ridge
- Shelf
- Basin
- Escarpment, Sea Scarp
- Fracture
- Trench, Abyss
- National Park, Reserve
- Point of Interest
- Recreation Site
- Cave, Cavern
- Historic Site
- Ruins
- Wall, Walls
- Church, Abbey
- Temple
- Scientific Station
- Railway station
- Airport
- Port
- Military installation
- Lighthouse
- Mine
- Tunnel
- Dam, Bridge

Index Symbols

⌐1 Independent Nation	Historical or Cultural Region	Pass, Gap	Depression	Coast, Beach
[2] State, Region	▲ Mount, Mountain	Plain, Lowland	Polder	Cliff
[3] District, County	Volcano	Delta	Desert, Dunes	Peninsula
Municipality	Hill	Salt Flat	Forest, Woods	Isthmus
Colony, Dependency	Mountains, Mountain Range	Valley, Canyon	Heath, Steppe	Sandbank
Continent	Hills, Escarpment	Crater, Cave	Oasis	Island
Physical Region	Plateau, Upland	Karst Features	Cape, Point	Atoll

Rock, Reef	Waterfall, Rapids	Canal	Lagoon	Escarpment, Sea Scarp
Islands, Archipelago	River Mouth, Estuary	Glacier	Bank	Fracture
Rocks, Reefs	Lake	Ice Shelf, Pack Ice	Seamount	Trench, Abyss
Coral Reef	Salt Lake	Ocean	Tablemount	National Park, Reserve
Well, Spring	Intermittent Lake	Sea	Ridge	Point of Interest
Geyser	Reservoir	Gulf, Bay	Shelf	Recreation Site
River, Stream	Swamp, Pond	Strait, Fjord	Basin	Cave, Cavern

Historic Site	Airport
Ruins	Por:
Wall, Walls	Military installation
Church, Abbey	Lighthouse
Temple	Mine
Scientific Station	Tunnel
Railway station	Dam, Bridge

Liverpool [N.S.-Can.] 180 Lh 44.02N 64.43W
Liverpool, Cape - 180 Jb 73.38N 78.05W
Liverpool Bay [Can.] 180 Ec 70.00N 129.00W
Liverpool Bay [Eng.-U.K.] 118 Jh 53.30N 3.16W
Liverpool Range 212 Kf 31.40S 150.30 E
Liverpool River 212 Gb 12.00S 134.00 E
Livezi 130 Ge 44.14N 23.47 E
Livigno 128 Ed 46.32N 10.04 E
Livingston [Guat.] 194 Cf 15.50N 88.45W
Livingston [Mt.-U.S.] 182 Eb 45.40N 110.34W
Livingston [Newf.-Can.] 180 Kf 53.40N 66.10W
Livingston [Tn.-U.S.] 184 Eg 36.23N 85.19W
Livingston [Tx.-U.S.] 186 Ik 30.43N 94.56W
Livingston, Lake- 186 Ik 30.45N 95.15W
Livingstone, Chutes de-=
Livingstone Falls (EN) 158 Ii 4.50S 14.30 E
Livingstone Falls (EN)=
Livingstone, Chutes de- 158 Ii 4.50S 14.30 E
Livingstone Memorial 170 Fe 12.19S 30.18 E
Livingstone Mountains 170 Fd 9.45S 34.20 E
Livingstonia 170 Fe 10.36S 34.07 E
Livingston Island 222 Qe 62.36S 60.30W
Livno 128 Lg 43.50N 17.01 E
Livny 136 De 52.28N 37.37 E
Livonia 184 Fd 42.25N 83.23W
Livonia (EN)=Livonija 110 Id 57.30N 25.30 E
Livonija=Livonia (EN) 110 Id 57.30N 25.30 E
Livorno=Leghorn (EN) 112 Hg 43.33N 10.19 E
Livradois, Montu du- 122 Ji 45.30N 3.33 E
Livramento do Brumado 202 Jf 13.39S 41.50W
Livron-sur-Drôme 122 Kj 44.46N 4.51 E
Liwale 170 Gd 9.46S 37.56 E
Liwiec 120 Rd 52.35N 21.33 E
Liwonde 170 Gf 15.01S 35.13 E
Lixi 152 Hf 26.21N 102.03 E
Lixian [China] 152 Jf 29.40N 111.45 E
Lixian [China] 152 Ie 34.11N 105.02 E
Lixian [China] 154 Ce 38.29N 115.34 E
Lixin 154 Dh 33.09N 116.12 E
Lixoúrion 130 Dk 38.12N 20.26 E
Liyang 154 Ei 31.26N 119.29 E
Lizard 118 Hl 49.57N 5.13W
Lizard Point 110 Ff 49.56N 5.13W
Lizhu 154 Fj 29.58N 120.26 E
Lizy sur Ourcq 124 Fe 49.01N 3.02 E
Ljady 116 Mf 58.35N 28.55 E
Ljahoviči 132 Ec 53.04N 26.15 E
Ljahovskije ostrova =
Lyakhov Islands (EN) 140 Qb 73.30N 141.00 E
Ljalja 134 Jg 59.10N 61.30 E
Ljamin 134 Of 61.18N 71.45 E
Ljangar 136 Ed 40.23N 65.59 E
Ljangasovo 114 Lg 58.33N 49.29 E
Ljapin 134 Je 63.38N 61.58 E
Ljaskelja 116 Nc 61.39N 31.03 E
Ljaskovec 130 If 43.06N 25.43 E
Ljig 130 De 44.14N 20.15 E
Ljuban [Bye.-U.S.S.R.] 132 Ec 52.48N 27.59 E
Ljuban [R.S.F.S.R.] 116 Hg 59.22N 31.13 E
Ljubar 132 Ee 49.55N 27.44 E
Ljubaščevka 130 Nb 47.50N 30.07 E
Ljubeli 128 Id 46.26N 14.16 E
Ljubercy 136 Dd 55.40N 37.55 E
Ljubešov 120 Ve 51.45N 25.37 E
Ljubim 114 Jg 58.22N 40.41 E
Ljubimec 130 Jh 41.50N 26.05 E
Ljubinje 128 Mh 42.57N 18.06 E
Ljubišnja 130 Cf 43.20N 19.07 E
Ljubljana 112 Hf 46.02N 14.30 E
Ljuboml 132 Cd 51.15N 23.59 E
Ljubotin 132 Ie 49.59N 35.55 E
Ljubovija 130 Ce 44.12N 19.22 E
Ljubuški 128 Lg 43.12N 17.33 E
Ljubytino 114 Hg 58.50N 33.25 E
Ljudinovo 136 De 53.51N 34.28 E
Ljugarn 114 Eh 57.19N 18.42 E
Ljungan 110 Hc 62.19N 17.23 E
Ljungaverk 116 Gb 62.29N 16.03 E
Ljungby 114 Ch 56.50N 13.56 E
Ljungbyholm 116 Gh 56.38N 16.10 E
Ljungdalen 114 Ce 62.51N 12.47 E
Ljungsbro 116 Ff 58.31N 15.30 E
Ljungskile 116 Df 58.14N 11.55 E
Ljusdal 114 Df 61.50N 16.05 E
Ljusnan 116 Hc 61.12N 17.08 E
Ljusne 114 Df 61.13N 17.08 E
Ljusterö 116 He 59.30N 18.35 E
Ljuta 116 Mf 58.33N 28.45 E
Llandilo 118 Jj 51.53N 3.59W
Llandovery 118 Jj 51.59N 3.48W
Llandrindod Wellu 118 Ji 52.15N 3.23W
Llandudno 118 Jh 53.19N 3.49W
Llanelli 118 Ij 51.42N 4.10W
Llanes 126 Ha 43.25N 4.45W
Llangefni 118 Ih 53.16N 4.18W
Llangollen 118 Ji 52.58N 3.10W
Llano 186 Gk 30.45N 98.41W
Llano Estacado 174 If 33.30N 102.40W
Llano River 186 Gk 30.35N 98.25W
Llanos 198 Je 5.00N 70.00W
Llanos de Sonora 190 Bc 28.20N 111.00W
Llanquihue, Lago- 206 Ff 41.08S 72.48W
Llata 202 Ce 9.25S 76.47W
Lleida/Lérida 126 Mc 41.37N 0.37 E
Lleida / Lérida [3] 126 Nc 42.00N 1.10 E
Llerena 126 Ff 38.14N 6.01W
Lleyn 118 Ii 52.54N 4.30W
Llica 202 Eg 19.52S 68.16W
Lliria / Liria 126 Le 39.38N 0.36W
Llivia 126 Nb 42.28N 1.59 E
Llobregat 126 Oc 41.19N 2.09 E
Lloret de Mar 126 Oc 41.42N 2.51 E
Llorona, Punta- 194 Fi 8.37N 83.44W
Llorri / Orri, Pic de l'- 126 Nb 42.23N 1.12 E
Lloydminster 180 Gf 53.17N 110.00W
Llucena / Lucena del Cid 126 Ld 40.08N 0.17W
Lluchmayor/Llucmajor 126 Oe 39.29N 2.54 E
Llucmajor/Lluchmayor 126 Oe 39.29N 2.54 E
Llullaillaco, Volcán- 198 Jh 24.43S 68.33W
Lo 219b Ca 13.21S 166.38 E
Loa 188 Jg 38.24N 111.38W
Loa, Rio- 206 Fb 21.26S 70.04W
Loanatit, Pointe- 219b Dd 19.21S 169.14 E
Loange 158 Ji 4.17S 20.02 E
Loango 170 Bc 4.39S 11.48 E
Loano 128 Cf 44.08N 8.15 E
Loban 114 Mh 56.59N 51.12 E
Lobatse 160 Jk 25.13S 25.41 E
Löbau/Lubij 120 Ke 51.06N 14.40 E
Lobaye [3] 168 Be 4.00N 17.40 E
Lobaye 158 Ih 3.41N 18.35 E
Lobenstein 120 Hf 50.27N 11.39 E
Loberia 206 Ie 38.09S 58.47W
Łobez 120 Lc 53.39N 15.36 E
Lobito 160 Ij 12.22S 13.34 E
Lobo 150 Jg 3.45S 134.05 E
Lobo 166 Dd 6.02N 6.47W
Lobos 206 Ie 35.11S 59.06W
Lobos 162 Ed 28.45N 13.49W
Lobos, Cabo- 192 Cc 29.55N 112.45W
Lobos, Cay- 194 Ib 22.24N 77.32W
Lobos, Cayo- 192 Ph 18.22N 87.24W
Lobos, Isla- 192 Dd 27.20N 110.36W
Lobos, Islas de- 192 Kg 21.27N 97.15W
Lobos de Afuera, Islas- 202 Be 6.57S 80.42W
Lobos de Tierra, Isla- 202 Be 6.27S 80.52W
Lobva 136 Gd 59.12N 60.30 E
Łobżonka 120 Nc 53.07N 17.18 E
Locana 128 Be 45.25N 7.27 E
Locarno 128 Cd 46.10N 8.48 E
Loch Aillionn/Allen, Lough- 118 Eg 54.08N 8.08W
Loch Ainninn 118 Fh 53.28N 7.24W
Loch Ainninn/Ennell, Lough- 118 Fh 53.28N 7.24W
Loch Arabhach/Arrow, Lough- 118 Eg 54.05N 8.20W
Lochboisdale 118 Fd 57.09N 7.19W
Loch Cairlinn/Carlingford Lough 118 Gg 54.05N 6.14W
Loch Ce/Key, Lough- 118 Eg 54.00N 8.15W
Loch Coirib/Corrib, Lough- 118 Dh 53.05N 9.10W
Loch Con/Conn, Lough- 118 Dg 54.04N 9.20W
Loch Cuan/Strangford Lough 118 Hg 54.26N 5.36W
Loch Deirgeirt/Derg, Lough- 118 Ei 53.00N 8.20W
Lochearnhead 118 Ie 56.23N 4.18W
Loch Éirne Íochtair/Lower Lough Erne 118 Fg 54.30N 7.50W
Loch Éirne Uachtair/Upper Lough Erne 118 Fg 54.20N 7.30W
Lochem 124 Ib 52.10N 6.25 E
Loches 122 Gg 47.08N 1.00 E
Loch Feabhail/Foyle, Lough- 118 Ff 55.05N 7.10W
Loch Garman/Wexford 118 Fi 52.20N 6.27W
Loch Garman/Wexford [2] 118 Gi 52.20N 6.40W
Lochgilphead 118 He 56.03N 5.26W
Lochinver 118 Hc 58.09N 5.15W
Loch Katrine 118 Ie 56.18N 4.30W
Loch Lao/Belfast Lough 118 Hg 54.40N 5.50W
Loch Léin/Leane, Lough- 118 Di 52.05N 9.35W
Loch Leven 118 Je 56.13N 3.10W
Lochmaddy 118 Fd 57.36N 7.10W
Loch Measca/Mask, Lough- 118 Dh 53.35N 9.20W
Lochnagar 118 Je 56.55N 3.10W
Loch nEathach/Neagh, Lough- 110 Fe 54.38N 6.24W
Loch Ness 118 Id 57.15N 4.30W
Łochów 120 Rd 52.32N 21.48 E
Loch Pholl an Phúca / Poulaphouca Reservoir 118 Gh 53.10N 6.30W
Loch Ri/Ree, Lough- 118 Fh 53.35N 8.00W
Lochsa River 188 Hc 46.08N 115.36W
Loch Sileann/Sheelin, Lough- 118 Fh 53.48N 7.20W
Loch Suili/Swilly, Lough- 118 Ff 55.10N 7.38W
Loch Ui Ghadra/Gara, Lough- 118 Eh 53.55N 8.30W
Lochy 118 He 56.49N 5.06W
Lochy, Loch- 118 Ie 56.55N 4.55W
Lockerbie 118 Jf 55.07N 3.22W
Lockhart 186 Hl 29.53N 97.41W
Lock Haven 184 Ie 41.09N 77.28W
Löcknitz 120 Hc 53.07N 11.16 E
Lockport 184 Hd 43.11N 78.39W
Locminé 122 Dg 47.53N 2.50W
Locri 128 Kl 38.14N 16.16 E
Lod 146 Fg 31.58N 34.54 E
Lodalskåpa 114 Bf 61.47N 7.12 E
Loddon 124 Db 52.32N 1.29 E
Loddon River 212 Ig 36.41S 143.55 E
Lodejnoje Pole 136 Dc 60.44N 33.33 E
Lodève 122 Jk 43.43N 3.19 E
Lodi [Ca.-U.S.] 188 Eg 38.08N 121.16W
Lodi [It.] 128 De 45.19N 9.30 E
Lødingen 114 Db 68.25N 16.00 E
Lodja 160 Ji 3.29S 23.26 E
Lodosa 126 Jb 42.25N 2.05W
Lödöse 116 Ef 58.02N 12.08 E
Lodwar 160 Kh 3.07N 35.36 E
Łódź 112 He 51.46N 19.30 E
Łódź [2] 120 Pe 51.45N 19.30 E
Loei 148 Ke 17.32N 101.34 E
Loeriesfontein 172 Bf 30.56S 19.26 E
Lofanga 221b Ba 19.50S 174.33W
Loffa [3] 166 Dd 7.45N 10.00W
Loffa 158 Fh 6.36N 11.05W
Lofoten 110 Hb 68.30N 15.00 E
Lofoten Basin (EN) 110 Ga 70.00N 4.00 E
Lofsdalen 116 Eb 62.07N 13.16 E
Loftahammar 116 Gg 57.52N 16.40 E
Loga 166 Fc 13.37N 3.14 E
Logan [N.M.-U.S.] 186 Ei 35.22N 103.25W
Logan [Oh.-U.S.] 184 Ff 39.32N 82.24W
Logan [Ut.-U.S.] 182 Ec 41.44N 111.50W
Logan [W.V.-U.S.] 184 Gg 37.52N 81.58W
Logan, Mount- [Can.] 174 Ec 60.34N 140.24W
Logan, Mount- [Wa.-U.S.] 188 Eb 48.32N 120.57W
Logan Martin Lake 184 Di 33.40N 86.15W
Logan Mountains 180 Ed 61.00N 128.00W
Logansport 184 De 40.45N 86.21W
Loge 158 Ii 7.49S 13.06 E
Logojsk 116 Lj 54.12N 27.57 E
Logone 158 Ig 12.06N 15.02 E
Logone Birni 166 Ic 11.47N 15.06 E
Logone Occidental [3] 168 Bd 8.40N 16.00 E
Logone Occidental 168 Bd 9.07N 16.26 E
Logone Oriental [3] 168 Bd 8.20N 16.30 E
Logone Oriental 168 Bd 8.07N 16.26 E
Logroño [Arg.] 204 Bi 29.30S 61.42W
Logroño [Sp.] 126 Jb 42.28N 2.27W
Logrosán 126 Ge 39.20N 5.29W
Løgstør 114 Bh 56.58N 9.15 E
Logudoro 128 Cj 40.35N 8.40 E
Løgumkloster 116 Ci 55.03N 8.57 E
Løgurinn 114a Cb 65.15N 14.30W
Lohja/Lojo 114 Ff 60.15N 24.05 E
Lohjanjärvi 116 Jd 60.15N 23.55 E
Lohjanselkä/Lojo åsen 116 Kd 60.15N 24.10 E
Löhme 124 Kc 51.41N 8.42 E
Löhne 120 Ed 52.11N 8.41 E
Lohne (Oldenburg) 124 Kb 52.40N 8.14 E
Lohra 124 Kd 50.44N 8.38 E
Lohr am Main 114 Ff 49.59N 9.35 E
Lohusuu/Lokusu 116 Lf 58.53N 27.01 E
Lohvica 132 Hd 50.22N 33.15 E
Loi, Phou- 148 Kd 20.16N 103.12 E
Loiblpaß 128 Id 46.26N 14.16 E
Loi-Kaw 148 Je 19.41N 97.13 E
Loile 170 Dc 0.52S 20.12 E
Loimaa 114 Ff 60.51N 23.03 E
Loimijoki 116 Jc 61.13N 22.38 E
Loing 122 If 48.23N 2.48 E
Loir 122 Fg 47.33N 0.32W
Loire [3] 122 Ji 45.30N 4.00 E
Loire 110 Ff 47.16N 2.11W
Loire, Canal latéral à la- 122 Jh 46.29N 3.59 E
Loire, Val de- 122 Hg 47.40N 1.35 E
Loire-Atlantique [3] 122 Eg 47.15N 1.50W
Loiret [3] 122 Ig 47.55N 2.20 E
Loir-et-Cher [3] 122 Hg 47.30N 1.30 E
Loisach 120 Hi 47.56N 11.27 E
Loison 124 He 49.30N 5.17 E
Loja [Ec.] 200 If 4.00S 79.13W
Loja [Sp.] 126 Hg 37.10N 4.09W
Lojo/Lohja 114 Ff 60.15N 24.05 E
Lojo åsen/Lohjanselkä 116 Kd 60.15N 24.10 E
Loka 168 Ee 4.16N 31.01 E
Lokači 120 Uf 50.43N 24.44 E
Lokalahti 116 Id 60.41N 21.28 E
Lokandu 170 Ec 2.31S 25.47 E
Lokantekojärvi 114 Gc 68.56N 27.40 E
Lokbatan 132 Pi 40.21N 49.42 E
Lokčim 134 Ef 61.48N 51.45 E
Løken 116 De 59.48N 11.29 E
Lokeren 122 Jc 51.06N 4.00 E
Lokichar 170 Gb 2.23N 35.39 E
Lokichokio 170 Fb 4.12N 34.21 E
Lokitaung 170 Gb 4.16N 35.45 E
Løkken [Den.] 116 Cg 57.22N 9.43 E
Løkken [Nor.] 114 Be 63.05N 9.36 E
Loknja 114 Hh 56.49N 30.09 E
Loko 166 Gd 8.00N 7.50 E
Lokoja 166 Gd 7.48N 6.44 E
Lokolo 170 Cc 0.43S 19.40 E
Lokomo 166 Ie 2.41N 15.19 E
Lokoro 170 Cc 1.43S 18.23 E
Lokossa 166 Fd 6.38N 1.43 E
Lokot 132 Ic 52.33N 34.31 E
Lokoti 166 Hd 6.22N 14.20 E
Loksa 116 Fg 59.34N 25.44 E
Loks Land 180 Ld 62.27N 64.30W
Lokuru 219a Cc 8.35S 157.20 E
Lokusu/Lohusuu 116 Lf 58.53N 27.01 E
Lokwa Kangole 170 Gb 3.32N 35.54 E
Lol 158 Jh 9.13N 28.59 E
Lola 166 Dd 7.48N 8.32W
Lolimi 168 Ee 4.35N 33.59 E
Loliondo 170 Gc 2.03S 35.37 E
Lolland 110 He 54.45N 11.30 E
Lollar 124 Kd 50.38N 8.42 E
Lolo 170 Db 2.13N 23.00 E
Lolo 170 Bc 0.40S 12.28 E
Lolodorf 166 He 3.14N 10.44 E
Lolo Pass 186 Hc 46.40N 114.33W
Loloway 219b Cb 15.17S 167.58 E
Lom 130 Gf 43.49N 23.14 E
Lom [Afr.] 166 Hd 5.20N 13.24 E
Lom [Bul.] 130 Gf 43.50N 23.15 E
Loma Bonita 192 Lh 18.07N 95.53W
Lomaloma 219d Cb 17.17S 178.59W
Lomami 158 Jh 0.46N 24.16 E
Loma Mountains 158 Fh 9.10N 11.07W
Lomas de Vallejos 204 Dh 27.44S 57.56W
Loma Verde 204 Cl 35.16S 58.24W
Lomba 170 Df 15.36S 21.32 E
Lombarda, Serra- 202 Hc 2.50N 51.50W
Lombarde, Prealpi- 128 De 46.00N 9.30 E
Lombardia = Lombardy (EN) [2] 128 De 45.40N 9.30 E
Lombardy (EN) = Lombardia [2] 128 De 45.40N 9.30 E
Lomblen, Pulau- 140 Oj 8.25S 123.30 E
Lombok, Pulau- 140 Nj 8.45S 116.30 E
Lombok, Selat- 150 Gh 8.30S 115.50 E
Lomé 160 Hh 6.08N 1.13 E
Lomela 160 Ji 2.18S 23.17 E
Lomela 158 Ji 0.14S 20.42 E
Lomellina 128 Ce 45.15N 8.45 E
Loméméti 219b Dd 19.30S 169.27 E
Lomié 166 He 3.10N 13.37 E
Lomlom 219c Bb 10.19S 166.16 E
Lomma 116 Ei 55.41N 13.05 E
Lomme 124 Hd 50.08N 5.10 E
Lommel 122 Lc 51.14N 5.18 E
Lomnica 120 Ug 49.02N 24.47 E
Lomond, Loch- 118 Ie 56.08N 4.38W
Lomonosov 136 Cd 59.55N 29.40 E
Lomonosovki 136 Ge 52.50N 66.28 E
Lomonosov Ridge (EN) 224 De 88.00N 140.00 E
Lomont 122 Mg 47.21N 6.36 E
Lompobatang, Gunung- 150 Gh 5.20S 119.55 E
Lompoc 182 Ce 34.38N 120.27W
Lomsegga 116 Cc 61.49N 8.22 E
Łomża 120 Sc 53.11N 22.05 E
Łomża [2] 120 Sc 53.10N 22.05 E
Lønahorg 116 Bd 60.42N 6.25 E
Loncoche 206 Fe 39.22S 72.38W
Londa 148 Ee 15.28N 74.31 E
Londerzeel 124 Gc 51.01N 4.18 E
Londiani 170 Gc 0.10S 35.36 E
Londinières 124 De 49.50N 1.24 E
London [Eng.-U.K.] 112 Fe 51.30N 0.10W
London [Kir.] 220g Bb 1.58N 157.29W
London [Ky.-U.S.] 184 Eg 37.08N 84.05W
London [Ont.-Can.] 176 Ke 42.59N 81.14W
London-Barnet 124 Bc 51.39N 0.12W
London-Bexley 124 Cc 51.26N 0.09 E
London Bridge 197p Bb 12.17N 61.35W
London-Bromley 124 Cc 51.25N 0.01 E
London-Croydon 118 Mj 51.23N 0.07W
Londonderry / Derry 112 Fd 55.00N 7.19W
Londonderry, Cape- 212 Fb 13.45S 126.55 E
London-Ealing 124 Bc 51.30N 0.19W
London-Enfield 124 Bc 51.40N 0.04W
London-Greenwich 118 Mj 51.28N 0.00
London-Haringey 124 Bc 51.36N 0.06W
London-Harrow 124 Bc 51.36N 0.20W
London-Havering 124 Cc 51.36N 0.11 E
London-Hillingdon 124 Bc 51.31N 0.27W
London-Kingston-upon-Thames 118 Mj 51.28N 0.19W
London-Redbridge 124 Cc 51.35N 0.08 E
London-Sutton 124 Bc 51.21N 0.12W
London-Wandsworth 124 Bc 51.27N 0.12W
London-Westminster 124 Bc 51.30N 0.07W
Londrina 200 Kh 23.18S 51.09W
Londuimbali 170 Ce 12.15S 15.19 E
Lone Pine 188 Fh 36.36N 118.04W
Long, Loch- 118 Ie 56.04N 4.50W
Longa 170 Ce 14.41S 18.29 E
Longa [Ang.] 170 Be 10.15S 13.30 E
Longa [Ang.] 170 Cf 16.25S 19.04 E
Longa, proliv- = De Long Strait (EN) 140 Tb 70.20N 178.00 E
Longá, Rio- 202 Jd 3.09S 41.56W
Long Akah 150 Ff 3.19N 114.47 E
Longarone 128 Gd 46.16N 12.18 E
Longbangun 150 Gf 0.36N 115.11 E
Long Bay [Bar.] 197q Bb 13.04N 59.29W
Long Bay [S.C.-U.S.] 182 Le 33.35N 78.45W
Long Beach [Ca.-U.S.] 176 Hf 33.46N 118.11W
Long Beach [N.Y.-U.S.] 184 Ke 40.35N 73.40W
Long Beach [Wa.-U.S.] 188 Cc 46.21N 124.03W
Long Branch 182 Mc 40.17N 73.59W
Long Buckby 124 Ab 52.18N 1.04W
Long Cay 194 Jb 22.37N 74.20W
Longchuan 152 Kg 24.10N 115.17 E
Long Creek 188 Nb 49.07N 103.00W
Long Eaton 124 Ab 52.54N 1.16W
Longfeng 154 Ha 46.31N 125.02 E
Longford / An Longfort 118 Fh 53.44N 7.47W
Longford / An Longfort [2] 118 Fh 53.40N 7.40W
Long Forties 118 Nd 57.10N 0.05 E
Long Hu 154 Dj 29.37N 116.12 E
Longhua 154 Dd 41.18N 117.44 E
Longido 170 Gc 2.44S 36.41 E
Long Island [Atg.] 197d Bb 17.08N 61.45W
Long Island [Bah.] 174 Lg 23.10N 75.10W
Long Island [Can.] 180 Jf 54.50N 79.20W
Long Island [Can.] 180 Nc 44.20N 66.15W
Long Island [Pap.N.Gui.] 208 Fe 5.20S 147.05 E
Long Island [U.S.] 174 Le 40.50N 73.00W
Long Island Sound 184 Ke 41.05N 72.58W
Longjiang 152 Lb 47.20N 123.09 E
Longjuzhai→Danfeng 152 Je 33.44N 110.22 E
Longkou 152 Ld 37.39N 120.20 E
Longlac 180 Ig 49.50N 86.32W
Long Lake [N.D.-U.S.] 186 Fc 46.43N 100.07W
Long Lake [Ont.-Can.] 186 Mb 49.32N 86.45W
Longmalinau 150 Gf 3.30N 116.31 E
Long Men 152 Je 34.40N 110.30 E
Longmont 186 Df 40.10N 105.06W
Longnan 152 Jg 24.54N 114.48 E
Longobucco 128 Kk 39.27N 16.37 E
Longoz 130 Kf 43.02N 27.41 E
Longping→Luodian 152 If 25.26N 106.47 E
Long Point 184 Gd 42.34N 80.15W
Long Point Bay 184 Gd 42.40N 80.14W
Longpujungan 150 Gf 2.34N 115.40 E
Longquan 152 Kf 28.06N 119.05 E
Long Range Mountains 180 Lg 48.00N 58.30W
Longreach 210 Fg 23.26S 144.15 E
Long Sand 124 Dc 51.37N 1.10 E
Longs Peak 174 Ie 40.15N 105.37W
Long Sutton 124 Cb 52.47N 0.08 E
Longtan 154 Eh 32.10N 119.03 E
Longtown 118 Kf 55.01N 2.58W
Longueau 124 Ee 49.52N 2.21 E
Longué-Jumelles 122 Fg 47.23N 0.07W
Longueville-sur-Scie 124 De 49.48N 1.06 E
Longuyon 122 Le 49.26N 5.36 E
Long Valley 188 Ji 34.37N 111.16W
Longview [Tx.-U.S.] 182 Ie 32.30N 94.44W
Longview [Wa.-U.S.] 182 Cb 46.08N 122.57W
Longwu 152 Hg 24.07N 102.18 E
Longwy 122 Le 49.31N 5.46 E
Longxi 152 Hd 35.01N 104.38 E
Longxian 152 Id 35.00N 106.53 E
Longxian → Wengyuan 152 Jg 24.21N 114.13 E
Longxi Shan 152 Kf 26.35N 117.17 E
Long Xuyen 148 Lf 10.23N 105.25 E
Longyan 152 Kf 25.06N 117.01 E
Longyao 154 Cf 37.21N 114.46 E
Longyearbyen 224 Kd 78.13N 15.38 E
Longyou 154 Ej 29.01N 119.10 E
Longzhou 152 Ig 22.23N 106.49 E
Lonigo 128 Fe 45.23N 11.23 E
Löningen 120 Dd 52.44N 7.46 E
Lonja 128 Ke 45.27N 16.41 E
Lonjsko Polje 128 Ke 45.24N 16.42 E
Lönsboda 116 Fh 56.24N 14.19 E
Lons-le-Saunier 122 Lh 46.40N 5.33 E
Lontra, Ribeirão- 204 Fe 21.28S 53.37W
Lookout, Cape- [N.C.-U.S.] 182 Le 34.35N 76.32W
Lookout, Cape- [Or.-U.S.] 188 Dd 45.20N 124.00W
Lookout Mountain 184 Eh 34.40N 85.20W
Lookout Pass 182 Db 47.27N 115.42W
Loolmalasin 170 Gc 3.03S 35.49 E
Loop Head/Ceann Léime 118 Di 52.34N 9.56W
Loosdrechtse Plassen 124 Hb 52.10N 5.08 E
Lop 152 Dd 37.01N 80.16 E
Lopatina, gora- 140 Qd 50.52N 143.10 E
Lopatino 132 Nc 52.37N 45.47 E
Lopatka, mys- 140 Rd 50.52N 156.40 E
Lop Buri 148 Kf 14.48N 100.37 E
Lopča 138 He 55.44N 122.45 E
Lopévi 219b Dc 16.30S 168.21 E
Lopez, Cap-=Lopez, Cape-(EN) 158 Hi 0.37S 8.43 E
Lopez, Cape-(EN)=Lopez, Cap- 158 Hi 0.37S 8.43 E
Lop Nur 140 Le 40.30N 90.30 E
Lopnur/Yuli 152 Ec 41.22N 86.09 E
Lopori 158 Ih 1.14N 19.49 E
Loppersum 124 Ia 53.19N 6.45 E
Lopphavet 114 Ea 70.25N 22.00 E
Loppi 116 Kd 60.43N 24.27 E
Lopud 128 Lh 42.41N 17.57 E
Łopuszno 120 Qf 50.57N 20.15 E
Lora del Río 126 Gg 37.39N 5.32W
Lorain 182 Kc 41.28N 82.11W
Lorán, Boca- 196 Fh 9.00N 60.45W
Lorca 126 Kg 37.40N 1.42W
Lorch 124 Jd 50.03N 7.49 E
Lord Howe Island 208 Gh 31.35S 159.05 E
Lord Howe Rise (EN) 106 Jm 32.00S 162.00 E
Lord Mayor Bay 180 Ic 69.45N 92.00W
Lordsburg 186 Bj 32.21N 108.43W
Loreley 124 Jd 50.08N 7.43 E
Lorena 204 Jf 22.44S 45.08W
Lorengau 214 Dh 2.01S 147.17 E
Lorestān [3] 144 Gc 33.30N 48.40 E
Loreto [3] 202 Dd 5.00S 75.00W
Loreto [Arg.] 204 Dh 27.46S 57.17W
Loreto [Bol.] 202 Fg 15.13S 64.40W
Loreto [Braz.] 202 Ie 7.05S 45.09W
Loreto [It.] 128 Hg 43.26N 13.36 E
Loreto [Mex.] 192 If 22.16N 101.58W
Loreto [Mex.] 190 Bc 26.01N 111.21W
Loreto [Par.] 206 Ib 23.16S 57.11W
Loreto Aprutino 128 Hh 42.26N 13.59 E
Lorica 202 Cb 9.14N 75.49W
Lorient 112 Ff 47.45N 3.22W
Lőrinci 120 Pi 47.44N 19.41 E
Lorn, Firth of- 118 He 56.20N 5.40W
Lorne 212 Ig 38.33S 143.59 E
Lörrach 120 Di 47.37N 7.40 E
Lorrain, Plateau- 122 Me 49.00N 6.30 E
Lorrain, Rivière du- 197h Ab 14.50N 61.03W
Lorraine 122 Lf 49.00N 6.00 E
Lorraine, Plaine- 122 Lf 48.10N 5.50 E
Lorsch 124 Ke 49.39N 8.34 E
Los 114 Df 61.44N 15.10 E
Los, Iles de-=Los Islands (EN) 166 Cd 9.30N 13.48W
Los Alamos 176 If 35.53N 106.19W
Los Amates 194 Cf 15.16N 89.06W
Los Amores 204 Ci 28.06S 59.59W
Los Ángeles 200 Ii 37.28S 72.21W
Los Angeles 176 Hf 34.03N 118.15W
Los Angeles Aqueduct 188 Fi 35.22N 118.05W
Losap Atoll 208 Gd 6.54N 152.44 E
Los Banos 188 Eh 37.04N 120.51W
Los Blancos 206 Hb 23.36S 62.36W
Los Charrúas 204 Cj 31.10S 58.11W
Los Chiles 194 Eh 11.02N 84.43W
Los Conquistadores 204 Cj 30.36S 58.28W
Los Frailes, Islas- 196 Eg 11.12N 63.45W
Los Frentones 204 Bh 26.25S 61.25W
Los Gatos 188 Eh 37.14N 121.59W
Losheim 124 Ie 49.31N 6.45 E
Los Hermanos, Islas- 202 Fa 11.45N 64.25W
Łosice 120 Sd 52.14N 22.43 E
Lošinj 128 If 44.35N 14.28 E
Los Islands (EN)=Los, Iles de- 166 Cd 9.30N 13.48W
Los Juries 204 Ai 28.28S 62.06W
Los Lagos 206 Fe 39.51S 72.50W
Los Lagos [2] 206 Ff 41.20S 73.00W
Los Llanos de Aridane 162 Dd 28.39N 17.54W
Los Médanos, Istmo de- 194 Mh 11.35N 69.45W
Los Mochis 176 Ig 25.45N 108.53W
Los Monegros 126 Lc 41.29N 0.03W
Los Monjes, Islas- 202 Da 12.25N 70.55W
Los Navalmorales 126 He 39.43N 4.38W
Loso 170 Ec 1.10S 27.10 E
Los Palacios 194 Fb 22.35N 83.12W
Los Palacios y Villafranca 126 Gg 37.10N 5.56W
Los Pedroches 126 Hf 38.27N 4.45W
Los Pirpintos 204 Ah 26.08S 62.05W
Los Remedios, Río de- 192 Fe 24.41N 106.28W
Los Reyes de Salgado 192 Hh 19.35N 102.29W
Los Roques, Islas- 202 Ea 11.50N 66.45W

Index Symbols

[1] Independent Nation
[2] State, Region
[3] District, County
[4] Municipality
[5] Colony, Dependency
Continent
Physical Region
Historical or Cultural Region
Mount, Mountain
Volcano
Hill
Mountains, Mountain Range
Hills, Escarpment
Plateau, Upland
Pass, Gap
Plain, Lowland
Delta
Salt Flat
Valley, Canyon
Crater, Cave
Karst Features
Depression
Polder
Desert, Dunes
Forest, Woods
Heath, Steppe
Oasis
Cape, Point
Coast, Beach
Cliff
Peninsula
Isthmus
Sandbank
Island
Atoll
Rock, Reef
Islands, Archipelago
Rocks, Reefs
Coral Reef
Well, Spring
Geyser
River, Stream
Waterfall, Rapids
River Mouth, Estuary
Lake
Salt Lake
Intermittent Lake
Reservoir
Swamp, Pond
Canal
Glacier
Ice Shelf, Pack Ice
Ocean
Sea
Gulf, Bay
Strait, Fjord
Lagoon
Bank
Seamount
Tablemount
Ridge
Shelf
Basin
Escarpment, Sea Scarp
Fracture
Trench, Abyss
National Park, Reserve
Point of Interest
Recreation Site
Cave, Cavern
Historic Site
Ruins
Wall, Walls
Church, Abbey
Temple
Scientific Station
Railway station
Airport
Port
Military installa
Lighthouse
Mine
Tunnel
Dam, Bridge

Los Roques Basin (EN) 196 Cf 12.20N 67.40W
Los Santos 194 Gj 7.56N 80.25W
Los Santos [3] 194 Gj 7.45N 80.30W
Losser 124 Jb 52.16N 7.01 E
Lossiemouth 118 Jd 57.43N 3.18W
Lossnen 116 Eb 62.30N 12.50 E
Los Taques 194 Lh 11.50N 70.16W
Los Telares 206 Hc 28.59S 63.26W
Los Teques 202 Ea 10.21N 67.02W
Los Testigos, Islas- 202 Fa 11.23N 63.06W
Lost River 188 Ef 41.56N 121.30W
Lost River Range 188 Id 44.10N 113.35W
Lost Trail Pass 182 Eb 45.41N 113.57W
Los Vilos 206 Fd 31.55S 71.31W
Lot [3] 122 Hj 44.30N 1.30 E
Lot 110 Gg 44.18N 0.20 E
Lota 206 Fe 37.05S 73.10W
Lotagipi Swamp 168 Ee 4.36N 34.55 E
Løten 116 Dd 60.49N 11.19 E
Lot-et-Garonne [3] 122 Gj 44.20N 0.30 E
Lothair 172 Ee 26.26S 30.27 E
Lothian [3] 118 Jf 55.55N 3.30W
Lothian 118 Jf 55.55N 3.05W
Loto 170 Dc 2.47S 22.30 E
Lotofaga 221c Ba 13.59S 171.50W
Lotoi 170 Cc 1.35S 18.30 E
Lotru 130 Hd 45.20N 24.16 E
Lotrului, Munţii- 130 Gd 45.30N 23.52 E
Lotta 114 Hb 68.39N 30.20 E
Lottefors 116 Gc 61.25N 16.24 E
Löttorp 116 Gg 57.10N 16.59 E
Lotuke, Jabal- 168 Ee 4.07N 33.48 E
Louang Namtha 148 Kd 20.57N 101.25 E
Louangphrabang 142 Mh 19.52N 102.08 E
Loubomo 160 Ii 4.12S 12.41 E
Loučná 120 Lf 50.06N 15.48 E
Loudéac 122 Df 48.10N 2.45W
Loudima 170 Bc 4.07S 13.04 E
Loudon 184 Eh 35.44N 84.20W
Loudun 122 Gh 47.00N 0.04 E
Loué 122 Fg 48.00N 0.09W
Loue 122 Lg 47.01N 5.27 E
Loufan 154 Ae 38.04N 111.47 E
Louga 166 Bb 15.37N 16.13W
Louga [3] 166 Bb 15.00N 15.30W
Louge 122 Hk 43.27N 1.20 E
Loughborough 118 Li 52.47N 1.11W
Lougheed 180 Ha 77.30N 105.00W
Loughrea/Baile Locha Riach 118 Eh 53.12N 8.34W
Louhans 122 Lh 46.38N 5.13 E
Louhi 136 Db 66.04N 33.01 E
Louisa 184 Ff 38.07N 82.36W
Louiseville 184 Kb 46.16N 72.57W
Louisiade Archipelago 208 Kf 11.00S 153.00 E
Louisiana 186 Kg 39.27N 91.03W
Louisiana [2] 182 Ie 31.15N 92.15W
Louis Trichardt 172 Dd 23.01S 29.43 E
Louisville [Ky.-U.S.] 176 Kf 38.16N 85.45W
Louisville [Ms.-U.S.] 186 Lj 33.07N 89.03W
Louis-XIV, Pointe - 180 Jf 54.50N 79.30W
Loukoléla 170 Cc 1.02S 17.07 E
Loulan Yiji 152 Ec 40.32N 89.50 E
Loulé 126 Dg 37.08N 8.02W
Loum 166 Ge 4.43N 9.44 E
Lount Lake 186 Ia 50.10N 94.20W
Louny 120 Jf 50.22N 13.49 E
Loup City 186 Gf 41.17N 98.58W
Loupe, La- 182 Hf 48.28N 1.01 E
Loup River 182 Hc 41.24N 97.19W
Loups Marins, Lacs des - 180 Ke 56.40N 74.00W
Lourdes 122 Fk 43.06N 0.03W
Lourenço Marques → Maputo 160 Kk 25.58S 32.34 E
Lousa, Serra da- 126 Dd 40.04N 8.13W
Loushan Guan 152 If 28.02N 106.51 E
Louštín 120 Jf 50.12N 13.48 E
Louth [Austl.] 212 Jf 30.32S 145.07 E
Louth [Eng.-U.K.] 118 Mh 53.22N 0.01W
Louth/Lú [2] 118 Gh 53.55N 6.30W
Loutrá Aidhipsoú 130 Gk 38.51N 23.03 E
Loutrá Killinis 130 El 37.52N 21.07 E
Loutrákion 130 Fl 37.59N 23.00 E
Louvain/Leuven 122 Kd 50.53N 4.42 E
Louvet Point 197b Bb 13.58N 60.53W
Louviers 122 He 49.13N 1.10 E
Lövånger 114 Ed 64.22N 21.18 E
Lovászi 120 Mj 46.33N 16.34 E
Lovat 110 Jd 58.14N 31.28 E
Lovćen 130 Bg 42.24N 18.49 E
Loveč 130 Hf 43.08N 24.43 E
Loveč [2] 130 Hf 43.08N 24.43 E
Loveland 186 Df 40.24N 105.05W
Lovell 182 Fc 44.50N 108.24W
Lovelock 182 Dc 40.11N 118.28W
Lövenich, Köln- 124 Id 50.57N 6.50 E
Lovere 128 Ee 45.49N 10.04 E
Loviisa/Lovisa 114 Gf 60.27N 26.14 E
Loving 186 Dj 32.17N 104.06W
Lovington 182 Ge 33.27N 103.21W
Lovisa/Loviisa 114 Gf 60.27N 26.14 E
Lovoi 170 Ed 8.05S 26.40 E
Lovosice 120 Kf 50.31N 14.03 E
Lovozero 114 Ib 68.01N 35.01 E
Lövstabruk 116 Gd 60.24N 17.53 E
Lövstabukten 116 Gd 60.35N 17.45 E
ovua 170 De 11.31S 23.35 E
ovua 170 Dd 6.07S 20.35 E
ow, Cape - 180 Id 63.06N 85.18W
owa 158 Ji 1.24S 25.52 E
owell 182 Mc 42.39N 71.18W
wemberg/Mark 120 Jd 52.53N 13.09 E
wer Arrow Lake 188 Fb 49.40N 118.08W
wer Austria (EN) = iederösterreich [2] 128 Jb 48.30N 15.45 E
ver California (EN) = ja California, Peninsula - 174 Hg 28.00N 112.00W
er Hutt 218 Fd 41.13S 174.55 E
Lower Lake 188 Dg 38.55N 122.36W
Lower Lake 188 Ef 41.15N 120.02W
Lower Lough Erne/Loch Éirne Íochtair 118 Fg 54.30N 7.50W
Lower Post 180 Ee 59.55N 128.30W
Lower Red Lake 186 Ic 48.00N 94.50W
Lower Rhine (EN) = Neder-Rijn 122 Mc 51.59N 6.20 E
Lower Saxony (EN) = Niedersachsen [2] 120 Fd 52.00N 10.00 E
Lower Trajan's Wall (EN) = Nižni Trajanov val 130 Ld 45.45N 28.30 E
Lower Tunguska (EN) = Nižnjaja Tunguska 140 Kc 65.48N 88.04 E
Lowestoft 118 Oi 52.29N 1.45 E
Lowestoft Ness 118 Oi 52.28N 1.44 E
Lowgar [3] 144 Kc 33.50N 69.00 E
Łowicz 120 Pd 52.07N 19.56 E
Lowlands 118 Jf 56.00N 4.00W
Lowrah 140 If 31.33N 66.33 E
Lowshān 146 Md 36.39N 49.32 E
Low Tatra (EN) = Nízke Tatry 120 Ph 48.54N 19.40 E
Lowther 180 Hb 74.35N 97.40W
Lowville 184 Jd 43.47N 75.30W
Loxton [Austl.] 212 If 34.27S 140.35 E
Loxton [S.Afr.] 172 Cf 31.30S 22.22 E
Loyalty Islands (EN) = Loyauté, Iles- 208 Hg 21.00S 167.00 E
Loyauté, Iles- = Loyalty Islands (EN) 208 Hg 21.00S 167.00 E
Loyoro 170 Fb 3.21N 34.17 E
Lozère [3] 122 Jj 44.30N 3.30 E
Lozère, Mont- 122 Jj 44.25N 3.46 E
Loznica 130 Ce 44.32N 19.13 E
Lozovaja 136 Df 48.53N 36.15 E
Lozva 136 Gd 59.36N 62.20 E
Lú/Louth [2] 118 Gh 53.55N 6.30W
Lua 170 Cb 2.46N 18.26 E
Luacano 170 De 11.16S 21.38 E
Luachimo 170 Dd 6.33S 20.59 E
Luaha-Sibuha 150 Cg 0.31S 98.28 E
Luahoko 221b Ba 19.40S 174.24W
Luala 172 Fc 17.57S 36.30 E
Lualaba 158 Jh 0.26N 25.20 E
Luama 170 Ec 4.46S 26.53 E
Lua Makika 221a Ec 20.35N 156.34W
Luampa 170 De 14.32S 24.10 E
Lu'an 152 Ke 31.44N 116.30 E
Luanda 160 Ii 8.48S 13.14 E
Luanda [3] 170 Bd 9.00S 13.15 E
Luando 158 Ij 10.19S 16.40 E
Luang, Khao- 148 Jg 8.31N 99.47 E
Luang, Thale- 148 Kg 7.30N 100.15 E
Luang Chiang Dao, Doi- 148 Je 19.23N 98.54 E
Luanginga 158 Jj 15.11S 22.55 E
Luang Prabang Range 148 Ke 18.30N 101.15 E
Luangue 170 Dc 4.17S 20.01 E
Luangwa 158 Kj 15.36S 30.25 E
Luan He 140 Nf 39.20N 119.10 E
Luaniva 220h Bb 13.16S 176.07W
Luannan (Bencheng) 154 Ee 39.30N 118.42 E
Luanping (Anjiangying) 154 Dd 40.55N 117.19 E
Luanshya 160 Jj 13.08S 28.25 E
Luanxian 152 Kd 39.45N 118.44 E
Luanza 170 Ed 8.40S 28.40 E
Luapula [3] 170 Ee 10.40S 29.15 E
Luapula 158 Ji 9.26S 28.33 E
Luarca 126 Fa 43.32N 6.32W
Luashi 170 De 10.56S 23.37 E
Luau 170 De 10.42S 22.12 E
Luba 166 Ge 3.28N 8.40 E
Lubaantum 194 Ce 16.17N 88.58W
Lubaczów 120 Tf 50.10N 23.07 E
Lubaczówka 120 Sf 50.08N 22.35 E
Lubalo 170 Cd 9.07S 19.15 E
Lubalo 170 Cd 7.22S 19.20 E
Lubamba 170 Ed 5.14S 26.02 E
Lubań 120 Le 51.08N 15.18 E
Lubāna/Lubana 116 Lh 56.49N 26.49 E
Lubāna/Lubana 116 Lh 56.49N 26.49 E
Lubānas, ozero- / Lubānas ezers 116 Lh 56.40N 27.00 E
Lubānas ezers / Lubanas, ozero- 116 Lh 56.40N 27.00 E
Lubang Islands 150 Hd 13.45N 120.15 E
Lubango 160 Ij 14.55S 13.28 E
Lubao 160 Ji 5.22S 25.45 E
Lubartów 120 Se 51.28N 22.46 E
Lubawa 120 Pc 53.30N 19.45 E
Lübbecke 120 Ed 52.18N 8.37 E
Lubbeek 124 Gd 50.53N 4.50 E
Lübben (Spreewald)/Lubin 120 Je 51.57N 13.54 E
Lübbenau/Lubnjow 120 Je 51.52N 13.58 E
Lubbock 176 If 33.35N 101.51W
Lübeck 112 He 53.52N 10.42 E
Lübecker Bucht 120 Gb 54.00N 10.55 E
Lübeck-Travemünde 120 Gc 53.57N 10.52 E
Lubefu 170 Dc 4.43S 24.25 E
Lubefu 170 Dc 4.10S 23.00 E
Lubei → Jarud Qi 152 Lc 44.30N 120.55 E
Lubelska, Wyżyna- 120 Sf 51.00N 23.00 E
Lubenec 120 Jf 50.08N 13.20 E
Lubenka 132 Sd 50.28N 54.06 E
Lubero 170 Ec 0.06S 29.06 E
Lubéron, Montagne du- 122 Lk 43.48N 5.22 E
Lubi 170 Dc 4.59S 23.26 E
Lubie, Jezioro- 120 Lc 53.30N 15.50 E
Lubień Kujawski 120 Pd 52.25N 19.10 E
Lubij/Löbau 120 Ke 51.06N 14.40 E
Lubilash 158 Ji 6.02S 23.45 E
Lubin 120 Me 51.24N 16.13 E
Lubin/Lübben (Spreewald) 120 Je 51.57N 13.54 E
Lublin 112 Ie 51.15N 22.35 E
Lublin [2] 120 Se 51.15N 22.35 E
Lubliniec 120 Of 50.40N 18.41 E
Lubnān = Lebanon (EN) [1] 142 Ff 33.50N 35.50 E
Lubnān, Jabal- = Lebanon Mountains (EN) 144 Ec 34.00N 36.30 E
Lubnjow/Lübbenau 120 Je 51.52N 13.58 E
Lubny 136 De 50.01N 33.00 E
Luboń 120 Md 52.23N 16.54 E
Lubraniec 120 Od 52.33N 18.50 E
Lubsko 120 Ke 51.46N 14.59 E
Lubsza 120 Ke 51.55N 14.45 E
Lubudi 170 Ed 9.57S 25.58 E
Lubudi 158 Ji 9.13S 25.38 E
Lubue 170 Cc 4.10S 19.53 E
Lubuklinggau 150 Dg 3.10S 102.52 E
Lubuksikaping 150 Df 0.08N 100.10 E
Lubumba 170 Ec 3.58S 29.06 E
Lubumbashi 160 Jj 11.40S 27.30 E
Lubuskie, Pojezierze- 120 Ld 52.18N 15.20 E
Lubutu 160 Ji 0.44S 26.35 E
Lucala 170 Cd 9.16S 15.16 E
Lucala 170 Bd 6.38S 12.34 E
Lucania, Mount- 180 Dd 61.01N 140.29W
Lucas 204 Ea 13.05S 55.56W
Lucca 128 Eg 43.50N 10.29 E
Lucea 194 Hd 18.27N 78.10W
Luce Bay 118 Ig 54.47N 4.50W
Lucedale 186 Lk 30.55N 88.35W
Lučegorsk 138 Ig 46.25N 134.20 E
Lucélia 204 Ge 21.44S 51.01W
Lucena [Phil.] 150 Hd 13.56N 121.37 E
Lucena [Sp.] 126 Hg 37.24N 4.29W
Lucena del Cid / Llucena 126 Ld 40.08N 0.17W
Luc-en-Diois 122 Lj 44.37N 5.27 E
Lučenec 120 Ph 48.20N 19.41 E
Lucera 128 Ji 41.30N 15.20 E
Lucerne (EN) = Luzern 128 Cc 47.05N 8.20 E
Lucerne, Lake- (EN) = Vierwaldstätter See 128 Cc 47.00N 8.30 E
Lucero 192 Fb 30.49N 106.30W
Lucheng 154 Bf 36.18N 113.15 E
Lucheringo 172 Fb 11.43S 36.15 E
Lucheux 124 Ed 50.12N 2.25 E
Luchico 170 Cd 6.12S 19.42 E
Lüchow 120 Hd 52.58N 11.09 E
Lüchun 152 Hg 23.02N 102.19 E
Lucipara, Kepulauan- 150 Ih 5.30S 127.33 E
Lucira 170 Be 13.52S 12.32 E
Luck 136 Ce 50.47N 25.20 E
Luckau 120 Je 51.51N 13.43 E
Luckenwalde 120 Jd 52.05N 13.10 E
Lucknow 142 Kg 26.51N 80.55 E
Luçon 122 Eh 46.27N 1.10W
Lucrecia, Cabo- 194 Jc 21.04N 75.37W
Luc-sur-Mer 124 Be 49.18N 0.21W
Lucunga 170 Bd 6.49S 14.35 E
Lucusse 170 De 12.33S 20.51 E
Lüda → Dalian 142 Of 38.55N 121.39 E
Luda Kamčija 130 Kg 43.03N 27.29 E
Ludbreg 128 Kd 46.15N 16.37 E
Lüdenscheid 120 De 51.13N 7.37 E
Lüderitz 160 Ik 26.38S 15.10 E
Lüderitz [3] 172 Be 26.00S 15.00 E
Lüderitz Bay 172 Be 26.35S 15.10 E
Ludhiāna 142 Jf 30.54N 75.51 E
Lüdinghausen 120 De 51.46N 7.28 E
Ludington 182 Jc 43.57N 86.27W
Ludlow 118 Ki 52.22N 2.43W
Ludogorije 130 Jf 43.46N 26.56 E
Ludogorsko Plato 130 Kf 43.36N 27.03 E
Luduş 130 Hc 46.29N 24.06 E
Ludvika 114 Df 60.09N 15.11 E
Ludwigsburg 120 Fh 48.54N 9.11 E
Ludwigshafen am Rhein 120 Eg 49.29N 8.27 E
Ludwigslust 120 Hc 53.19N 11.30 E
Ludza 114 Gh 56.32N 27.45 E
Luebo 160 Ji 5.21S 21.25 E
Lueki 170 Ec 3.22S 25.51 E
Lueki 170 Ec 3.24S 25.57 E
Luele 170 Dd 7.55S 20.00 E
Luembe 170 Dd 6.37S 21.06 E
Luembé 170 Dd 6.37S 21.05 E
Luena [Ang.] 160 Ij 11.48S 19.55 E
Luena [Ang.] 170 De 12.31S 22.34 E
Luena [Zaire] 170 Ed 9.27S 25.47 E
Luena [Zam.] 170 Df 15.20S 23.30 E
Luengué 170 Df 16.54S 21.52 E
Luenha 172 Ec 16.24S 33.48 E
Luera Peak 186 Cj 33.47N 107.49W
Lueta 170 Dd 7.04S 21.40 E
Lueyang 152 Ie 33.25N 106.14 E
Lufeng 152 Kg 22.57N 115.41 E
Lufico 170 Bd 6.22S 13.30 E
Lufira 158 Ji 8.16S 26.27 E
Lufira, Chutes de la- 170 Ed 9.50S 27.30 E
Lufkin 182 Ie 31.20N 94.44W
Lug 130 De 44.23N 20.45 E
Luga 136 Cd 58.44N 29.50 E
Luga 136 Cd 59.43N 28.18 E
Lugano 128 Cd 46.00N 8.57 E
Lugano, Lago di- (Ceresio) 128 Cd 46.00N 9.00 E
Lugansk = Vorošilovgrad 112 Jf 48.34N 39.20 E
Lugenville 210 Hf 15.32S 167.10 E
Lügde 124 Lc 51.57N 9.15 E
Lugela 172 Fc 16.26S 36.39 E
Lugenda 158 Kj 11.26S 38.33 E
Lugnaquillia 110 Fe 52.58N 6.27W
Lugo [3] 126 Eb 43.00N 7.30W
Lugo [It.] 128 Ff 44.25N 11.54 E
Lugo [Sp.] 126 Ea 43.00N 7.34W
Lugoj 130 Ed 45.41N 21.55 E
Lugovoj [Kaz.-U.S.S.R.] 136 Hg 42.55N 72.47 E
Lugovoj [R.S.F.S.R.] 136 Gd 59.44N 65.55 E
Lugovski 138 Ge 58.05N 112.55 E
Lugulu 170 Ec 2.17S 26.32 E
Luh 174 Kh 56.14N 42.28 E
Luhe 154 Eh 32.21N 118.50 E
Luhe 120 Gc 53.18N 10.11 E
Luhin Sum 152 Kb 46.41N 118.38 E
Luhit 148 Jc 27.48N 95.28 E
Luhovicy 114 Ji 54.59N 39.02 E
Luhuo 152 He 31.21N 100.40 E
Lui 170 Cd 8.41S 17.56 E
Luia 170 Dd 8.26S 21.45 E
Luiana 170 Df 17.22S 22.59 E
Luiana 158 Jj 17.27S 23.14 E
Luie 170 Cc 4.33S 17.41 E
Luik/Liège 112 Ge 50.38N 5.34 E
Luilaka 158 Ji 0.52S 20.12 E
Luilu 170 Dd 6.22S 23.50 E
Luimneach/Limerick 112 Fe 52.40N 8.38W
Luimneach/Limerick [2] 118 Ei 52.30N 9.00W
Luing 118 He 56.13N 5.39W
Luino 128 Cd 46.00N 8.44 E
Luio 170 De 13.15S 21.39 E
Lui Pătru, Vîrful- 130 Gd 45.30N 23.30 E
Luis Correia 202 Jd 2.53S 41.40W
Luishia 170 Ee 11.13S 27.07 E
Luitpold Coast 222 Af 78.30S 32.00W
Luiza 170 Dd 7.12S 22.25 E
Luján [Arg.] 206 Gd 32.22S 65.57W
Luján [Arg.] 206 Id 34.34S 59.07W
Lujiang 154 Di 31.15N 117.17 E
Lukafu 170 Ee 10.30S 27.33 E
Lukanga Swamp 170 Ee 14.25S 27.45 E
Lukavac 128 Mf 44.33N 18.32 E
Lukengo 170 Ed 5.46S 29.06 E
Lukenie 158 Ii 2.44S 18.09 E
Lukeville 188 Ik 31.57N 112.50W
Lukojanov 136 Ed 55.02N 44.30 E
Lukolela 170 Cc 1.03S 17.12 E
Lukonzolwa 170 Ed 8.47S 28.39 E
Lukov 120 Ue 51.14N 24.25 E
Lukovit 130 Hf 43.12N 24.10 E
Łuków 120 Se 51.56N 22.23 E
Lukuga 158 Ji 5.40S 26.55 E
Lukula 170 Bd 5.23S 12.57 E
Lukulu 170 De 14.23S 23.15 E
Lukusashi 170 Fe 14.38S 30.00 E
Luleå 112 Ib 65.34N 22.10 E
Luleälven 110 Ib 65.35N 22.03 E
Lüleburgaz 144 Ca 41.24N 27.21 E
Lüliang Shan 140 Nf 37.45N 111.25 E
Lulimba 170 Ec 4.42S 28.38 E
Luling 186 Hl 29.41N 97.39W
Lulong 154 Ee 39.53N 118.52 E
Lulonga 170 Cb 0.37N 18.23 E
Lulonga 158 Ih 0.43N 18.23 E
Lulua 158 Ji 5.02S 21.07 E
Lulu Fakahega, Mount- 220h Bb 13.16S 176.10W
Luma 221c Db 14.14S 169.32W
Lumajang 150 Fh 8.08S 113.13 E
Lumajangdong Co 152 De 34.00N 81.37 E
Lumbala Kaquengue 160 Jj 14.06S 21.25 E
Lumbala N'guimbo 170 De 12.39S 22.32 E
Lumberton 182 Le 34.37N 79.00W
Lumbo 172 Gc 15.00S 40.44 E
Lumbrales 126 Fd 40.56N 6.43W
Lumbres 124 Ed 50.42N 2.08 E
Lumby 188 Fa 50.15N 118.58W
Lumding 148 Ic 25.45N 93.10 E
Lumege 170 De 11.34S 20.48 E
Lumesule 170 Ge 11.14S 38.06 E
Lumi 214 Ch 3.29S 142.03 E
Lummen 124 Hd 50.59N 5.15 E
Lumparland 116 Id 60.10N 20.15 E
Lumphăt 148 Lf 13.30N 106.59 E
Lumsden [N.Z.] 218 Cf 45.44S 168.26 E
Lumsden [Sask.-Can.] 188 Ma 50.34N 104.53W
Lumuna 170 Ec 3.46S 26.24 E
Lumut 150 Df 4.14N 100.38 E
Luna 126 Gb 42.40N 5.49W
Luna, Laguna de- 204 Di 28.05S 56.46W
Lunan Shan 152 Hf 27.00N 102.30 E
Lunayyir, Harrat- 146 Gj 25.10N 37.50 E
Lunca Ilvei 130 Hb 47.22N 24.59 E
Lund 114 Ci 55.42N 13.11 E
Lunda [3] 170 Cd 9.30S 20.00 E
Lundazi 160 Kj 12.19S 33.13 E
Lunde 116 Gb 62.53N 17.51 E
Lundevatn 116 Bf 58.20N 6.35 E
Lundi 158 Kk 21.19S 32.24 E
Lundu 150 Ef 1.40N 109.51 E
Lundy Island 118 Ij 51.10N 4.40W
Lüneburg 120 Gc 53.15N 10.24 E
Lüneburger Heide 120 Gc 53.10N 10.20 E
Lunel 122 Kk 43.41N 4.08 E
Lünen 120 De 51.37N 7.31 E
Lunéville 122 Mf 48.36N 6.30 E
Lunga 158 Jj 14.34S 26.26 E
Lungué-Bungo 158 Jj 14.19S 23.14 E
Lungwebungu 170 De 14.19S 23.14 E
Lūni 148 Ec 26.00N 73.00 E
Lūni 148 Ed 24.41N 71.14 E
Lunigiana 128 Df 44.20N 9.55 E
Luninec 136 Ce 52.16N 26.50 E
Lunino 132 Nc 53.35N 45.14 E
Lunsemfwa 170 Fe 14.54S 30.12 E
Luntai/Bügür 152 Dc 41.46N 84.10 E
Luobei (Fengxiang) 152 Nb 47.36N 130.58 E
Luobuzhuang 152 Ed 39.30N 88.15 E
Luocheng 152 Ig 24.51N 108.53 E
Luodian (Longping) 152 If 25.26N 106.47 E
Luoding 152 Jg 22.43N 111.33 E
Luohe 152 Je 33.30N 114.08 E
Luo He 152 Id 32.18N 109.12 E
Luoma Hu 154 Eg 34.10N 118.12 E
Luonteri 116 Lc 61.35N 27.45 E
Luoping 152 Hg 24.58N 104.19 E
Luopioinen 116 Kc 61.22N 24.40 E
Luoshan 154 Ch 32.13N 114.32 E
Luotian 154 Ci 30.48N 115.23 E
Luoxiao Shan 152 Jf 26.35N 114.00 E
Luoyang 142 Nf 34.41N 112.25 E
Luoyuan 152 Kf 26.31N 119.32 E
Luozi 170 Bc 4.57S 14.08 E
Lupa 170 Fd 8.39S 33.12 E
Lupane 172 Dc 18.56S 27.48 E
Łupawa 120 Nb 54.42N 17.07 E
Lupeni 130 Gd 45.21N 23.14 E
Luperón 194 Ld 19.54N 70.57W
Łupków 120 Sg 49.12N 22.06 E
Luputa 170 Dd 7.10S 23.42 E
Lūq 160 Lh 3.56N 42.32 E
Luqiao 154 Fj 28.39N 120.05 E
Luqu 152 He 34.36N 102.30 E
Luque 206 Ic 25.16S 57.34W
Luquillo 197a Cb 18.22N 65.43W
Luray 184 Hf 38.40N 78.28W
Lure 122 Mg 47.41N 6.30 E
Lure, Montagne de- 122 Lj 44.07N 5.47 E
Luremo 170 Cd 8.30S 17.51 E
Lurgan/An Lorgain 118 Gg 54.28N 6.20W
Lurín 202 Cf 12.17S 76.52W
Lúrio 172 Gb 13.32S 40.30 E
Lúrio 158 Lj 13.31S 40.42 E
Lusaka 160 Jj 15.25S 28.17 E
Lusambo 160 Ji 4.58S 23.27 E
Lusanga 170 Cc 4.44S 18.58 E
Lusangi 170 Ec 4.37S 27.08 E
Lu Shan 152 Kf 29.30N 115.55 E
Lushan [China] 154 Cj 29.33N 115.58 E
Lushan [China] 154 Bh 33.44N 112.54 E
Lushi 152 Je 34.04N 111.02 E
Lushiko 170 Cd 6.12S 19.42 E
Lushnja 130 Ci 40.56N 19.42 E
Lushoto 170 Gc 4.47S 38.17 E
Lu Shui 154 Bj 29.54N 113.39 E
Lushui (Luzhangjie) 152 Gf 26.00N 98.50 E
Lüshun (Port Arthur) [China] 152 Ld 38.50N 121.13 E
Lusignan 122 Gh 46.26N 0.07 E
Lusk 182 Gc 42.46N 104.27W
Lussac-les-Châteaux 122 Gh 46.24N 0.43 E
Lustrafjorden 116 Bc 61.20N 7.20 E
Lūt, Dasht-e- = Lut, Dasht-i- (EN) 140 Hf 33.00N 57.00 E
Lut, Dasht-i- (EN) = Lūt, Dasht-e- 140 Hf 33.00N 57.00 E
Lu Tao 152 Lg 22.35N 121.30 E
Lutembo 170 De 13.28S 21.22 E
Luti 219a Cb 7.14S 157.00 E
Lütjenburg 120 Gb 54.17N 10.35 E
Luton 118 Mj 51.53N 0.25W
Luton Airport 124 Bc 51.50N 0.22W
Lutong 150 Ff 4.29N 114.00 E
Lutshima 170 Cd 5.22S 18.59 E
Lutshima 170 Cd 5.22S 18.59 E
Lutterworth 124 Ab 52.27N 1.12W
Lutuai 170 De 12.40S 20.12 E
Lutugino 132 Ke 48.23N 39.13 E
Lützow-Holmbukta 222 De 69.10S 37.30 E
Lutzputs 172 Ce 28.22S 20.37 E
Luuk 150 He 5.58N 121.18 E
Luverne 186 He 43.39N 96.13W
Luvidjo 170 Ed 6.26S 26.59 E
Luvua 158 Ji 6.46S 26.58 E
Luvuei 170 De 13.06S 21.12 E
Luwegu 158 Ki 8.31S 37.23 E
Luwingu 170 Ee 10.16S 29.54 E
Luwuk 150 Hg 0.56S 122.47 E
Luxembourg [3] 124 He 50.00N 5.30 E
Luxembourg/Luxemburg 112 Gf 49.45N 6.05 E
Luxembourg/Luxemburg [1] 112 Gf 49.45N 6.05 E
Luxemburg/Luxembourg 112 Gf 49.45N 6.05 E
Luxemburg/Luxembourg [1] 112 Gf 49.45N 6.05 E
Luxeuil-les-Bains 122 Mg 47.49N 6.23 E
Luxi 152 Hg 24.29N 103.44 E
Luxi (Mangshi) 142 Lg 24.29N 98.40 E
Luxor (EN) = Al Uqşur 164 Fd 25.41N 32.39 E
Luy 122 Ek 43.39N 1.08W
Luy de Béarn 122 Fk 43.39N 0.47W
Luy de France 122 Fk 43.38N 0.47W
Luyi 154 Ch 33.51N 115.28 E
Luz 204 Jd 19.48S 45.41W
Luz, Costa de la- 126 Fh 36.40N 6.20W
Luza 136 Ec 60.39N 47.15 E
Luza 110 Kc 60.40N 46.25 E
Luzarches 124 Ee 49.07N 2.25 E
Luzern [2] 128 Cc 47.05N 8.10 E
Luzern = Lucerne (EN) 128 Cc 47.05N 8.20 E
Luzhai 152 Ig 24.31N 109.46 E
Luzhangjie → Lushui 152 Gf 26.00N 98.50 E
Luzhou 142 Mg 28.55N 105.20 E
Luziânia 202 Ig 16.15S 47.56W
Lužická Nisa 120 Kd 52.04N 14.46 E
Lužické Hory 120 Kf 50.48N 14.40 E
Luzilândia 202 Jd 3.28S 42.22W
Lužnice 120 Kg 49.16N 14.25 E
Luzon 140 Oh 16.00N 121.00 E
Luzon Strait (EN) 140 Cg 21.00N 122.00 E
Luz-Saint-Sauveur 122 Gl 42.52N 0.01 E
Lužskaja guba 116 Me 59.35N 28.25 E
Lužskaja vozvyšennost 116 Mf 58.15N 28.45 E
Luzy 122 Jh 46.47N 3.58 E
Łużyca 120 Oe 51.33N 18.15 E
Lvov 112 If 49.50N 24.00 E
Lvovskaja oblast [3] 136 Cf 49.45N 24.00 E
Lwowa 214 Hj 10.44S 165.45 E
Lwówek 120 Md 52.28N 16.10 E
Lwówek Śląski 120 Le 51.07N 15.35 E
Lyakhov Islands (EN) = Ljahovskije ostrova 140 Qb 73.30N 141.00 E
Lyall, Mount- 218 Bf 45.17S 167.33 E
Lyallpur → Faisalabad 142 Jf 31.25N 73.05 E
Lycksele 114 Ed 64.36N 18.40 E
Lycia 130 Mm 36.30N 29.30 E
Lyckeby 116 Fh 56.12N 15.39 E
Lyckebyån 116 Fh 56.11N 15.40 E
Lyčkovo 114 Hh 57.57N 32.24 E
Lydd 118 Nk 50.57N 0.55 E
Lydd Airport 124 Cd 50.58N 0.56 E
Lydenburg 172 Ee 25.10S 30.29 E
Lydia 130 Lk 38.35N 28.30 E
Lygna 116 Bf 58.10N 7.02 E
Lygnern 116 Eg 57.29N 12.20 E

ex Symbols

ndependent Nation
tate, Region
istrict, County
unicipality
olony, Dependency
ntinent
ysical Region
Historical or Cultural Region
Mount, Mountain
Volcano
Hill
Mountains, Mountain Range
Hills, Escarpment
Plateau, Upland
Pass, Gap
Plain, Lowland
Delta
Salt Flat
Valley, Canyon
Crater, Cave
Karst Features
Depression
Polder
Desert, Dunes
Forest, Woods
Heath, Steppe
Oasis
Cape, Point
Coast, Beach
Cliff
Peninsula
Isthmus
Sandbank
Island
Atoll
Rock, Reef
Islands, Archipelago
Rocks, Reefs
Coral Reef
Well, Spring
Geyser
River, Stream
Waterfall, Rapids
River Mouth, Estuary
Lake
Salt Lake
Intermittent Lake
Reservoir
Swamp, Pond
Canal
Glacier
Ice Shelf, Pack Ice
Ocean
Sea
Gulf, Bay
Strait, Fjord
Lagoon
Bank
Seamount
Tablemount
Ridge
Shelf
Basin
Escarpment, Sea Scarp
Fracture
Trench, Abyss
National Park, Reserve
Point of Interest
Recreation Site
Cave, Cavern
Historic Site
Ruins
Wall, Walls
Church, Abbey
Temple
Scientific Station
Railway station
Airport
Port
Military Installation
Lighthouse
Mine
Tunnel
Dam, Bridge

Lyme Bay ◧	118	Kk	50.38N	3.00W
Lyminge	124	Dc	51.07N	1.05 E
Lymington	118	Lk	50.46N	1.33W
Łyna ∿	120	Rb	54.37N	21.14 E
Lynchburg	182	Ld	37.24N	79.09W
Lynd	210	Ff	18.56S	144.30 E
Lynden	188	Db	48.57N	122.27W
Lyndon River ∿	212	Cd	23.29S	114.06 E
Lyngdal	114	Bg	58.08N	7.05 E
Lyngen ⇌	114	Eb	69.58N	20.30 E
Lyngør	116	Cf	58.38N	9.10 E
Lyngseidet	114	Eb	69.35N	20.13 E
Lynn	184	Ld	42.28N	70.57W
Lynnaj, gora- ▲	138	Ld	62.55N	163.58 E
Lynn Canal ◧	178	Le	58.50N	135.15W
Lynn Deeps ⊍	124	Cb	52.58N	0.20 E
Lynn Lake	176	Id	56.51N	101.03W
Lyntupy	116	Li	55.02N	26.27 E
Lynx Lake ◒	180	Gd	62.25N	106.20W
Lyon	112	Gf	45.45N	4.51 E
Lyon Inlet ◧	180	Jc	66.20N	83.40W
Lyonnais, Monts du- ⛰	122	Ki	45.40N	4.30 E
Lyon River ∿	212	De	25.00S	115.20 E
Lyons [Ga.-U.S.]	184	Fi	32.12N	82.19W
Lyons [Ks.-U.S.]	186	Gg	38.21N	98.12W
Lyons, Forêt de- ♣	124	De	49.25N	1.30 E
Lyons-la-Forêt	124	De	49.24N	1.28 E
Lyra Reef ✺	214	Eh	1.50S	153.35 E
Lys ∿	122	Jc	51.03N	3.43 E
Łysa Góra ▲	120	Nd	52.07N	17.33 E
Lysaja, gora- ▲	116	Lj	54.12N	27.40 E
Lysá nad Labem	120	Kf	50.12N	14.50 E
Lysefjorden ⇌	116	Be	59.00N	6.14 E
Lysekil	114	Cf	58.16N	11.26 E
Lyskovo	136	Ed	56.03N	45.03 E
Lyss	128	Bc	47.04N	7.19 E
Lysva	136	Fd	58.07N	57.47 E
Lytham Saint Anne's	118	Jh	53.45N	3.01W
Lyttelton	218	Ee	43.36S	172.43 E
Lytton	188	Ea	50.14N	121.34W
Lyža ∿	134	Hd	65.42N	56.40 E

M

Ma, Oued el- ∿	162	Fe	24.03N	9.10W
Ma, Song ∿	148	Le	19.45N	105.55 E
Maâdis, Djebel- ▲	126	Qi	35.52N	4.44 E
Maalaea Bay ◧	221a	Ec	20.47N	156.29W
Ma'āmīr	146	Mg	30.04N	48.20 E
Ma'ān	144	Ec	30.12N	35.44 E
Ma'Ān [3]	146	Gg	30.20N	35.35 E
Maanselka	114	Ge	63.54N	28.30 E
Maanselkä ⌒	110	Ib	68.07N	28.29 E
Ma'anshan	152	Ke	31.38N	118.30 E
Maardu	116	Ke	59.28N	24.56 E
Maarianhamina/Mariehamn	114	Ef	60.06N	19.57 E
Ma 'arrat an Nu 'mān	146	Ge	35.38N	36.40 E
Maarssen	124	Hb	52.08N	5.03 E
Maas=Meuse (EN) ∿	110	Ge	51.49N	5.01 E
Maaseik	122	Lc	51.06N	5.48 E
Maaseik-Neeroeteren	124	Hc	51.05N	5.42 E
Maasin	150	Hd	10.08N	124.50 E
Maasmechelen/Mechelen	124	Hd	50.57N	5.40 E
Maassluis	124	Gc	51.55N	4.17 E
Maastricht	122	Ld	50.52N	5.43 E
Maasupa	219a	Ec	9.18S	161.15 E
Ma'āzah, Al Haḍabat al- ⌓	164	Fd	27.44N	31.44 E
Mabalane	172	Ed	23.38S	32.31 E
Mabaruma	196	Gh	8.12N	59.47W
Mabechi-Gawa ∿	156	Ga	40.31N	141.31 E
Mabella	186	Lb	48.37N	89.58W
Mabel Lake ◒	188	Fa	50.35N	118.44W
Mablethorpe	118	Nh	53.21N	0.15 E
Mabote	172	Ed	22.03S	34.08 E
Ma'būs Yūsuf	160	Jf	25.45N	21.00 E
Maçaão	126	Ee	39.33N	8.00W
McAdam	180	Kg	45.36N	67.20W
Macaé	202	Jh	22.23S	41.47W
Macajaí, Rio- ∿	202	Fc	2.25N	60.50W
McAlester	182	He	34.56N	95.46W
McAllen	182	Hf	26.12N	98.15W
Macaloge	172	Fb	12.25S	35.25 E
Mac Alpine Lake ◒	180	Hc	66.40N	102.50W
Macambará	204	Di	29.08S	56.03W
Macamic	184	Ha	48.48N	79.01W
Macamic, Lac- ◒	184	Ha	48.46N	79.00W
Macao (EN)=Aomen/Macau	152	Jg	22.12N	113.33 E
Macao (EN)=Aomen/Macau [5]	142	Ng	22.10N	113.33 E
Macao (EN)=Macau/Aomen	152	Jg	22.12N	113.33 E
Macao (EN)=Macau/Aomen [5]	142	Ng	22.10N	113.33 E
Macapá	200	Ke	0.02N	51.03W
Macará	202	Cd	4.21S	79.56W
Macaracas	194	Gj	7.44N	80.33W
Macareo, Caño- ∿	202	Fb	9.47N	61.36W
McArthur	184	Ff	39.14N	82.29W
Mc Arthur River ∿	212	Hc	15.54S	136.40 E
Macas	202	Cd	2.18S	78.06W
Maçãs ∿	126	Fc	41.29N	6.39W
Macatete, Sierra de- ⛰	192	Dd	28.00N	110.05W
Macau	200	Mf	5.07S	36.38W
Macau/Aomen=Macao (EN)	152	Jg	22.12N	113.33 E
Macau/Aomen=Macao (EN) [5]	142	Ng	22.10N	113.33 E
Macaúbas	202	Jf	13.02S	42.42W
Macauley Island ◆	208	Ih	30.13S	178.33W
Macaya, Pic de- ▲	190	Je	18.23N	74.02W
McBeth Fiord ◧	180	Kc	69.43N	69.20W
McCamey	186	Ek	31.08N	102.13W
McCammon	188	Ie	42.39N	112.12W
Mc Carthy	178	Kd	61.26N	142.55W
McClellanville	184	Hi	33.06N	79.28W
MacClenny	184	Fj	30.18N	82.07W
Macclesfield	118	Kh	53.16N	2.07W
Macclesfield Bank (EN) ▦	150	Fc	15.50N	114.20 E
McClintock	180	Ie	57.48N	94.12W
McClintock, Mount- ▲	222	Jg	80.13S	157.26 E
McClintock Channel ⇌	174	Ib	71.00N	101.00W
McCluer Gulf (EN)=Berau, Teluk- ◧	150	Jg	2.30S	132.30 E
McClure Strait ⇌	174	Hb	74.30N	116.00W
McClusky	186	Fc	47.29N	100.27W
McComb	182	Ie	31.14N	90.27W
McConaughy, Lake- ◒	186	Ff	41.18N	101.46W
McConnelsville	184	Gf	39.39N	81.51W
McCook	182	Gc	40.12N	100.38W
McCormick	184	Fi	33.55N	82.19W
McDame	180	Ee	59.13N	129.14W
McDermitt	188	Gf	41.59N	117.36W
Macdhui, Ben- ▲	118	Jd	57.04N	3.40W
Macdonald, Lake- ◒	212	Fd	23.30S	129.00 E
Mc Donald Islands ❖	222	Fd	52.59S	72.50 E
McDonald Peak [Ca.-U.S.] ▲	188	Ef	40.58N	120.26W
McDonald Peak [Mt.-U.S.] ▲	188	Ic	47.29N	113.46W
Macdonald Range ⛰	188	Hb	49.12N	114.46W
Macdonnell Ranges ⛰	208	Eg	23.45S	132.20 E
McDouglas Sound ⇌	180	Hd	75.15N	97.30W
Macduff	118	Kd	57.40N	2.29W
Macedo de Cavaleiros	126	Fc	41.32N	6.58W
Macedonia (EN)=Makedhonia ⧗	110	Ig	41.00N	23.00 E
Macedonia (EN)=Makedhonia ▣	130	Fh	41.00N	23.00 E
Macedonia (EN) = Makedonija [2]	130	Eh	41.50N	22.00 E
Macedonia (EN)=Makedonija ⧗	110	Ig	41.00N	23.00 E
Macedonia (EN)=Makedonija ▣	130	Fh	41.00N	23.00 E
Maceió	200	Mf	9.40S	35.43W
Macenta	166	Dd	8.33N	9.28W
Macerata	128	Hg	43.18N	13.27 E
McGehee	186	Kj	33.38N	91.24W
McGill	188	Hg	39.23N	114.47W
Macgillycuddy's Reeks/Na Cruacha Dubha ▲	118	Di	52.00N	9.50W
McGrath	178	Hd	62.58N	155.38W
MacGregor	186	Gb	49.57N	98.49W
McGregor	186	Jc	46.36N	93.19W
McGregor Lake ◒	188	Ia	50.31N	112.53W
Mc Gregor Range ⛰	212	Ie	26.40S	142.45 E
McGuire, Mount- ▲	188	Hd	45.10N	114.36W
Machachi	202	Cd	0.30S	78.34W
Machado	204	Je	21.41S	45.56W
Machagai	206	Hc	26.56S	60.03W
Machaíla	172	Ed	22.15S	32.58 E
Machaire na Mumhan/Golden Vale ⧗	118	Fi	52.30N	8.00W
Machaire Rátha/Maghera	118	Gg	54.51N	6.40W
Machakos	170	Gc	1.31S	37.16 E
Machala	202	Cd	3.16S	79.58W
Machaneng	172	Dd	23.12S	27.30 E
Machareti	202	Fh	20.49S	63.24W
Machar Marshes ⋯	168	Ed	9.20N	33.10 E
Machattie, Lake- ◒	212	Hd	24.50S	139.48 E
Machault	124	Ge	49.21N	4.30 E
Macheke	172	Ec	18.05S	31.51 E
Macheng	152	Je	31.10N	115.00 E
Machias	184	Nc	44.43N	67.28W
Machida	156	Fd	35.32N	139.27 E
Machilipatnam (Bandar)	148	Ge	16.10N	81.08 E
Machine, La-	122	Jh	46.53N	3.28 E
Machiques	202	Da	10.04N	72.34W
Machmi, Al- ⚘	146	Jg	31.32N	42.28 E
Machona, Laguna- ⊖	192	Mh	18.20N	93.40W
Machów	120	Rf	50.34N	21.40 E
Machupicchu ⁙	200	Ig	13.07S	72.34W
Macia	172	Ef	25.02S	33.06 E
Mc Ilwraith Range ⛰	212	Ib	13.45S	143.20 E
Măcin	130	Ld	45.15N	28.09 E
Macina ⧗	158	Gg	14.30N	5.00W
McIntosh	186	Fd	45.55N	101.21W
Macintyre River ∿	212	Je	29.25S	148.45 E
Maçka	146	Hb	40.50N	39.38 E
Mackay [Austl.]	210	Fg	21.09S	149.11 E
Mackay [Id.-U.S.]	188	Ie	43.55N	113.37W
Mackay, Lake- ◒	208	Dg	22.30S	129.00 E
McKay Lake ◒	186	Mb	49.35N	86.22W
McKean Atoll ◎	208	Je	3.36S	174.08W
McKeand ∿	180	Kd	63.00N	65.05W
McKeesport	184	He	40.21N	79.52W
McKenzie	184	Cg	36.08N	88.31W
Mackenzie ∿	174	Fc	69.15N	134.08W
Mackenzie Bay [Ant.] ◧	222	Fe	68.20S	71.15 E
Mackenzie Bay [Can.] ◧	174	Fc	69.00N	136.30W
McKenzie Island	180	If	51.05N	93.48W
Mackenzie King ◆	174	Hb	77.45N	111.00W
Mackenzie Mountains ⛰	174	Gc	64.00N	130.00W
McKenzie River ∿	188	Dd	44.07N	123.06W
Mackenzie River ∿	212	Jd	24.00S	149.55 E
McKerrow, Lake- ◒	218	Cf	44.30S	168.05 E
Mackinac, Straits of- ⇌	182	Kb	45.49N	82.45W
Mackinaw City	184	Ec	45.47N	84.44W
McKinley, Mount- ▲	174	Dc	63.30N	151.00W
McKinley Park	178	Jd	63.44N	148.54W
McKinney	186	Hj	33.12N	96.37W
Mackinnon Road	170	Gc	3.44S	39.03 E
McLaughlin	186	Fd	45.49N	100.49W
McLean	186	Fi	35.14N	100.36W
McLeans Town	184	Il	26.39N	77.59W
Maclean Strait ⇌	180	Ha	77.30N	103.10W
Maclear	172	Df	31.02S	28.23 E
Macleay River ∿	212	Kf	30.52S	153.01 E
Mc Leod, Lake- ◒	208	Cg	24.10S	113.35 E
McLeod Bay ◧	180	Gd	62.53N	110.15W
McLeod Lake	180	Ff	54.59N	123.02W
McLoughlin, Mount- ▲	188	De	42.27N	122.19W
McLure	188	Ea	51.03N	120.14W
Macmillan ∿	180	Dd	62.52N	135.55W
McMillan, Lake- ◒	186	Dj	32.40N	104.20W
Macmillan Pass ⩂	180	Ed	63.00N	130.00W
McMinnville [Or.-U.S.]	188	Dd	45.13N	123.12W
McMinnville [Tn.-U.S.]	184	Eh	35.41N	85.46W
McMurdo ⚗	222	Kf	77.51S	166.37 E
McNaughton Lake ◒	180	Ff	52.40N	117.50W
Macomb	186	Kf	40.27N	90.40W
Macomer	128	Cj	40.16N	8.47 E
Macomia	172	Gb	12.15S	40.08 E
Mâcon	122	Kh	46.18N	4.50 E
Macon	176	Kf	32.50N	83.38W
Macon [Mo.-U.S.]	186	Jg	39.44N	92.28W
Macon [Ms.-U.S.]	186	Lj	33.07N	88.34W
Macondo	170	De	12.36S	23.43 E
Mâconnais, Monts du- ⛰	122	Kh	46.18N	4.45 E
Macoris, Cabo- ►	194	Ld	19.47N	70.28W
Macouba	197h	Ab	14.52N	61.09W
McPherson	182	Hd	38.22N	97.40W
Mc Pherson Range ⛰	212	Ke	28.20S	153.00 E
Macquarie ◆	222	Jd	54.30S	158.30 E
Macquarie Harbour ◧	212	Jh	42.20S	145.25 E
Macquarie Ridge (EN) ⋀	106	Jo	57.00S	159.00 E
Macquarie River ∿	208	Fh	30.07S	147.24 E
Mac Robertson Land ⧗	222	Fe	70.00S	65.00 E
Macroom/Maigh Chromtha	118	Ej	51.54N	8.57W
Macugnaga	128	Be	45.58N	7.58 E
Macujer	202	Dc	0.24N	73.07W
Macuro	196	Fg	10.39N	61.56W
Macusani	202	Df	14.05S	70.26W
Macuspana	192	Mi	17.48N	92.36W
Mačva ⧗	130	Ce	44.49N	19.30 E
McVicar Arm ◧	180	Fc	65.10N	120.30W
Ma'dabā	146	Fg	31.43N	35.48 E
Madagali	166	Hc	10.53N	13.38 E
Madagascar ◆	158	Lj	20.00S	47.00 E
Madagascar (EN)=Madagasikara [1]	160	Lj	19.00S	46.00 E
Madagascar Basin (EN) ⊍	106	Fl	27.00S	53.00 E
Madagascar Plateau (EN) ⊓	106	Fm	30.00S	45.00 E
Madagasikara=Madagascar (EN) [1]	160	Lj	19.00S	46.00 E
Madā'in Şāliḩ	146	Gi	26.48N	37.53 E
Madalai	220a	Ac	7.20N	134.28 E
Madama	166	Ha	21.58N	13.39 E
Madan	130	Hh	41.30N	24.57 E
Madang	210	Fe	5.13S	145.48 E
Madanīyīn	160	Ie	33.21N	10.30 E
Madanīyīn [3]	162	Jc	33.00N	10.45 E
Madaoua	166	Gc	14.05N	5.58 E
Madara	130	Kf	43.17N	27.06 E
Madara-Shima ◆	156	Ae	33.35N	129.45 E
Madaroumfa	166	Gc	13.18N	7.09 E
Madau ◆	219a	Ac	9.00S	152.26 E
Madawaska Highlands ⌒	184	Hc	45.20N	78.15W
Maddalena ◆	128	Di	41.15N	9.25 E
Maddalena, Colle della- ⩂	122	Mj	44.25N	6.53 E
Maddaloni	128	Ii	41.02N	14.23 E
Made, Made en Drimmelen-	124	Gc	51.41N	4.48 E
Made en Drimmelen	124	Gc	51.41N	4.48 E
Made en Drimmelen-Made	124	Gc	51.41N	4.48 E
Madeir	168	Dd	7.50N	29.12 E
Madeira [5]	160	Fe	32.40N	16.45W
Madeira ◆	158	Fe	32.44N	17.00W
Madeira, Arquipélago da-=Madeira Islands (EN) ❖	158	Fe	32.40N	16.45W
Madeira, Rio- ∿	198	Kf	3.22S	58.45W
Madeira Islands (EN)=Madeira, Arquipélago da- ❖	158	Fe	32.40N	16.45W
Madeleine, Ile de la - ❖	180	Lg	47.26N	61.44W
Madeleine, Monts de la- ⛰	122	Jh	46.03N	3.50 E
Maden	146	Hc	38.23N	39.40 E
Madenassa Veld ⧗	158	Jj	19.00N	25.30 E
Madera [Ca.-U.S.]	188	Eh	36.57N	120.03W
Madera [Mex.]	190	Cc	29.12N	108.07W
Mader-Chih ∿	126	Ri	35.26N	5.07 E
Madero, Puerto del- ⩂	126	Jc	41.48N	2.05W
Madesimo	128	Dd	46.26N	9.21 E
Madgaon	148	Ee	15.22N	73.49 E
Madhya Pradesh [3]	148	Fd	22.00N	79.00 E
Madimba	170	Cc	4.58S	15.08 E
Madina do Boé	166	Cc	11.45N	14.13W
Madinani	166	Dd	9.37N	6.57W
Madīnat al Abyār	164	Dc	32.11N	20.36 E
Madīnat ash Sha'b	142	Gh	12.50N	44.56 E
Madingo-Kayes	170	Bc	4.10S	12.18 E
Madingou	170	Bc	4.09S	13.34 E
Madirovalo	172	Hc	16.29S	46.30 E
Madison [Fl.-U.S.]	184	Fj	30.28N	83.25W
Madison [In.-U.S.]	184	Ef	38.44N	85.23W
Madison [Mn.-U.S.]	186	Hd	45.01N	96.11W
Madison [S.D.-U.S.]	186	He	44.00N	97.07W
Madison [Wi.-U.S.]	176	Ke	43.05N	89.22W
Madison [W.V.-U.S.]	184	Gf	38.03N	81.50W
Madison Range ⛰	188	Jd	45.15N	111.20W
Madison River ∿	188	Jd	45.56N	111.30W
Madisonville	182	Jd	37.20N	87.30W
Madiun	150	Fh	7.37S	111.31 E
Mado Gashi	170	Gb	0.44N	39.10 E
Madoi (Huangheyan)	142	Lf	35.00N	98.56 E
Madon ∿	122	Mf	48.36N	6.06 E
Madona	114	Gh	56.53N	26.20 E
Madra Dağı ▲	130	Kj	39.23N	27.12 E
Madrakah, Ra's al- ►	144	If	18.59N	57.45 E
Madranbaba Dağı ▲	130	Ll	37.38N	28.12 E
Madras [India]	142	Kh	13.05N	80.17 E
Madras [Or.-U.S.]	188	Ed	44.38N	121.08W
Madre, Laguna- [Mex.] ⊖	190	Ed	25.00N	97.40W
Madre, Laguna- [Tx.-U.S.] ⊖	182	Hf	27.00N	97.35W
Madre, Sierra- [N.Amer.] ⛰	174	Jh	15.20N	92.20W
Madre, Sierra- [Phil.] ⛰	140	Oh	16.20N	122.00 E
Madre de Dios	202	Df	12.36S	69.59W
Madre de Dios [3]	202	Df	12.00S	70.15W
Madre de Dios, Isla- ◆	198	Ik	50.15S	75.05W
Madre de Dios, Río- ∿	198	Jg	10.59S	66.08W
Madre del Sur, Sierra-=Southern Sierra Madre (EN) ⛰	174	Jj	17.00N	100.00W
Madre de Oaxaca, Sierra- ⛰	192	Ki	17.30N	96.30W
Madre Occidental, Sierra-=Western Sierra Madre (EN) ⛰	174	Ig	25.00N	105.00W
Madre Oriental, Sierra-=Eastern Sierra Madre (EN) ⛰	174	Jg	22.00N	99.30W
Madrid	112	Fg	40.24N	3.41W
Madrid [2]	126	Id	40.30N	3.40W
Madrid-Aravaca	126	Id	40.27N	3.47W
Madridejos	126	Ie	39.28N	3.32W
Madrid-El Pardo	126	Id	40.32N	3.46W
Madrid-Vallecas	126	Id	40.23N	3.37W
Madrid-Villaverde	126	Id	40.21N	3.42W
Madrigal de las Altas Torres	126	Hc	41.05N	5.00W
Mad River ∿	188	Cf	40.57N	124.07W
Madriz [3]	194	Dg	13.30N	86.30W
Madrona, Sierra- ⛰	126	Hf	38.25N	4.10W
Madula	170	Eb	0.28N	25.23 E
Madura, Palau- ◆	140	Nj	7.00S	113.20 E
Madurai	142	Ji	9.56N	78.07 E
Madvār, Kūh-e- ▲	144	Hc	30.36N	54.52 E
Madwīn	164	Cd	28.42N	17.31 E
Madyan ⧗	140	Fg	27.40N	35.35 E
Madžalis	132	Oh	42.08N	47.50 E
Maebara	156	Be	33.34N	130.13 E
Maebashi	152	Od	36.23N	139.04 E
Mae Hong Son	148	Je	19.16N	97.56 E
Mæl	116	Ce	59.56N	8.48 E
Mae Nam Khong=Mekong (EN) ∿	140	Mh	10.15N	105.55 E
Maesawa	156	Gb	39.03N	141.07 E
Mae Sot	148	Je	16.40N	98.35 E
Maestra, Sierra- ⛰	174	Lh	20.00N	76.45W
Maevatanana	172	Hc	16.56S	46.49 E
Maéwo, Ile- ◆	208	Hf	15.10S	168.10 E
Mafeteng	172	De	29.45S	27.18 E
Mafia Channel ⇌	170	Gd	7.50S	39.35 E
Mafia Island ◆	158	Ki	7.50S	39.50 E
Mafikeng	160	Jk	25.53S	25.39 E
Mafra [Braz.]	206	Kc	26.07S	49.49W
Mafra [Port.]	126	Cf	38.56N	9.20W
Magadan	142	Rd	59.34N	150.48 E
Magadanskaja oblast [3]	138	Kd	62.30N	154.00 E
Magadi	170	Gc	1.54S	36.17 E
Magallanes, Estrecho de- = Magellan, Strait of- (EN) ⇌	198	Ik	54.00S	71.00W
Magallanes y Antártica Chilena [2]	206	Fh	51.30S	73.30W
Magangué	202	Db	9.14N	74.46W
Maganik ⛰	130	Cg	42.44N	19.16 E
Maganoy	150	He	6.51N	124.31 E
Magaria	166	Gc	12.59N	8.50 E
Magazine Mountain ▲	186	Ji	35.10N	93.38W
Magdagači	138	Hf	53.29N	125.55 E
Magdala	204	Bm	36.06S	61.42W
Magdalena [3]	202	Db	10.00N	74.15W
Magdalena [Arg.]	204	Dl	35.04S	57.32W
Magdalena [Bol.]	202	Ff	13.20S	64.08W
Magdalena [Mex.]	190	Bb	30.38N	110.57W
Magdalena [N.M.-U.S.]	186	Ci	34.07N	107.14W
Magdalena, Bahía- ◧	192	Ce	24.35N	112.00W
Magdalena, Isla- ◆	190	Bd	24.55N	112.15W
Magdalena, Llano de la- ▭	190	Bd	24.30N	111.40W
Magdalena, Río- [Col.] ∿	198	Id	11.06N	74.51W
Magdalena, Río- [Mex.] ∿	192	Cb	30.48N	112.32W
Magda Plateau ⌓	180	Jb	72.18N	82.55W
Magdeburg	112	He	52.10N	11.40 E
Magdeburger Börde ▭	120	Hd	52.00N	11.30 E
Magdelaine Cays ✺	208	Gf	16.35S	150.15 E
Magee	186	Lk	31.52N	89.44W
Magelang	150	Fh	7.28S	110.13 E
Magellan, Strait of- (EN) = Magallanes, Estrecho de- ⇌	198	Ik	54.00S	71.00W
Magellan Seamounts (EN) ⊼	208	Gc	17.30N	152.00 E
Magenta	128	Ce	45.28N	8.53 E
Magerøya ◆	114	Fa	71.03N	25.45 E
Magetan	150	Fh	7.39S	111.20 E
Maggiorasca ▲	128	Df	44.33N	9.29 E
Maggiore, Lago- (Verbano) ◒	128	Ce	45.55N	8.40 E
Maghāghah	164	Fd	28.39N	30.50 E
Maghama	162	Ef	15.31N	12.50W
Maghera/Machaire Rátha	118	Gg	54.51N	6.40W
Maghnia	162	Gc	34.51N	1.44W
Magic Reservoir ⊡	188	He	43.20N	114.18W
Mágina, Sierra de- ⛰	126	Ig	37.45N	3.30W
Magistralny	138	Fe	56.03N	107.35 E
Maglaj	128	Mf	44.33N	18.06 E
Măglenik ⛰	130	Ih	41.20N	25.45 E
Maglie	128	Mj	40.07N	18.18 E
Măgliž	130	Ig	42.36N	25.33 E
Magnetawan River ∿	184	Gc	45.46N	80.37W
Magnetic Island ◆	212	Jc	19.10S	146.50 E
Magnitka	134	Ii	55.21N	59.43 E
Magnitnaja, gora- ▲	134	Ij	53.10N	59.10 E
Magnitogorsk	112	Le	53.27N	59.04 E
Magnolia	186	Jj	33.16N	93.14W
Magnor	114	Cg	59.57N	12.12 E
Magny-en-Vexin	122	He	49.09N	1.47 E
Mago	138	Jf	53.18N	140.20 E
Mágoé	172	Ec	15.48S	31.43 E
Magoebaskloof ⩂	172	Ed	23.51S	30.02 E
Magog	184	Kc	45.16N	72.09W
Magosa/Ammokhostos=Famagusta (EN)	144	Dc	35.07N	33.57 E
Magra [Alg.] ∿	126	Qi	35.29N	4.58 E
Magra [It.] ∿	128	Df	44.03N	9.58 E
Magtá Lahjar	162	Ef	17.50N	13.20W
Maguarinho, Cabo- ►	202	Id	0.20S	48.20W
Magude	172	Ee	25.02S	32.40 E
Magumeri	166	Hc	12.07N	12.49 E
Magura, gora- ▲	120	Th	48.50N	23.44 E
Magway	148	Jd	20.00N	95.00 E
Magway	142	Lg	20.09N	94.55 E
Magyarország = Hungary (EN) [1]	112	Hf	47.00N	20.00 E
Mahābād	144	Gb	36.45N	45.53 E
Mahabalipuram ⁙	148	Gf	12.37N	80.12 E
Mahabe	172	Hc	17.05S	45.20 E
Mahabo	172	Gd	20.21S	44.39 E
Mahačkala	112	Kg	42.58N	47.30 E
Mahadday Wēyne	168	He	3.00N	45.32 E
Mahādeo Range ⛰	148	Ee	17.50N	74.15 E
Mahafaly, Plateau- ⌓	172	Gd	24.30S	44.00 E
Mahagi	170	Fb	2.18N	30.59 E
Mahajamba ∿	172	Hc	15.33S	47.08 E
Mahājan	148	Ec	28.47N	73.50 E
Mahajanga	160	Lj	15.17S	46.43 E
Mahajanga [3]	172	Hc	16.30S	47.00 E
Mahajilo ∿	172	Hc	19.42S	45.22 E
Mahakam ∿	140	Nj	0.35S	117.17 E
Mahalapye	172	Dd	23.07S	26.46 E
Mahalevona	172	Hc	15.26S	49.55 E
Mahallāt	146	Nf	33.55N	50.27 E
Mahamid ⧗	168	Cb	15.09N	20.25 E
Māhān	146	Qg	30.05N	57.19 E
Mahānadi ∿	140	Kg	20.19N	86.45 E
Mahanoro	172	Hc	19.53S	48.49 E
Maharadze	136	Eg	41.53N	42.01 E
Mahārāshtra [3]	148	Ee	18.00N	75.00 E
Mahārlū, Daryācheh-ye- ◒	146	Oh	29.25N	52.50 E
Maḩās	168	He	4.24N	46.07 E
Maha Sarakham	148	Ke	16.12N	103.16 E
Mahavavy ∿	158	Lj	15.57S	45.54 E
Mahbés	162	Fd	27.10N	9.50W
Maḩḑah	146	Pj	24.24N	55.59 E
Mahdia	202	Gb	5.16N	59.09W
Mahe	148	Ff	11.42N	75.32 E
Mahébourg	172a	Bb	20.24S	57.42 E
Mahé Island ◆	158	Mi	4.40S	55.28 E
Mahendra Giri ▲	148	Ge	18.58N	84.21 E
Mahenge	160	Ki	8.41S	36.43W
Maheno	218	Df	45.10S	170.50 E
Mahesāna	148	Ed	23.36N	72.24 E
Mahi ∿	148	Ed	22.16N	72.58 E
Mahia Peninsula ▬	216	Eg	39.10S	177.55 E
Mahmūdābād	146	Od	36.38N	52.15 E
Mahmudābād	146	Lc	39.25N	47.15 E
Mahmūd-e 'Erāqī	144	Kb	35.01N	69.20 E
Mahmudiye	146	Dc	39.30N	31.00 E
Mahmutşevketpaşa	130	Mh	41.09N	29.11 E
Māhneshān	146	Ld	36.45N	47.38 E
Mahnevo	134	Jg	58.27N	61.42 E
Mahnomen	186	Ic	47.19N	95.59W
Mahón / Maó	126	Qe	39.53N	4.15 E
Mahoré/Mayotte ◆	158	Lj	12.50S	45.10 E
Mahrāt, Jabal- ⛰	168	Ib	17.00N	52.00 E
Mahuan Dao ◆	150	Gd	10.50N	115.47 E
Mahua Point ►	219a	Fd	10.28S	162.05 E
Maiana Atoll ◎	208	Id	0.55N	173.00 E
Maïao, Ile- (Tubai-Manu) ◆	208	Lf	17.34S	150.35W
Maicao	202	Da	11.23N	72.15W
Maicasagi, Lac- ◒	184	Ia	49.52N	76.48W
Maîche	122	Mg	47.15N	6.48 E
Maicuru, Rio- ∿	202	Hd	2.10S	54.17W
Maidenhead	124	Bc	51.31N	0.42W
Maidstone	118	Nj	51.17N	0.32 E
Maiduguri	160	Ig	11.51N	13.09 E
Măieruş	130	Id	45.54N	25.32 E
Maigh Chromtha/Macroom	118	Ej	51.54N	8.57W
Maigudo ▲	168	Fd	7.26N	37.10 E
Maihara	156	Ed	35.20N	136.18 E
Maikala Range ⛰	148	Gd	22.30N	81.30 E
Maiko ∿	170	Eb	0.14N	25.33 E
Maikona	170	Gb	2.56N	37.38 E
Maikoor, Pulau- ◆	150	Jh	6.15S	134.15 E
Main ∿	120	Ef	50.00N	8.18 E
Maínalon Óros ▲	130	Fl	37.40N	22.15 E
Main Barrier Range ⛰	212	If	31.25S	141.25 E
Mainburg	120	Hh	48.39N	11.47 E
Main Camp	220g	Ba	2.01N	157.25W
Main Channel ⇌	184	Gc	45.22N	81.50W
Mai-Ndombe, Lac- ◒	158	Ii	2.10S	18.15 E
Main-Donau-Kanal ═	120	Gg	49.55N	10.50 E
Maindong → Coqên	152	Ee	31.15N	85.13 E
Maine [2]	182	Nb	45.15N	69.15W
Maine ▣	122	Ff	48.15N	0.10W
Maine [Fr.] ∿	122	Eg	47.09N	1.27W
Maine [Fr.] ∿	122	Fg	47.25N	0.37W
Maine, Gulf of- ◧	174	Me	43.00N	68.00W
Maine-et-Loire [3]	122	Fg	47.30N	0.20W
Maïné-Soroa	166	Hc	13.18N	12.02 E
Mainistir Fhear Maí/Fermoy	118	Ei	52.08N	8.16W
Mainistir na Búille/Boyle	118	Eh	53.58N	8.18W
Mainistir na Corann/Midleton	118	Ej	51.55N	8.10W
Mainistir na Féile/Abbeyfeale	118	Di	52.24N	9.18W
Mainit, Lake- ◒	150	Ie	9.26N	125.32 E
Mainland [Scot.-U.K.] ◆	110	Fd	59.00N	3.10W
Mainland [Scot.-U.K.] ◆	110	Fc	60.20N	1.22W
Maintal	124	Kd	50.08N	8.51
Maintenon	122	Hf	48.35N	1.35
Maintirano	160	Lj	18.03S	44.03
Mainz	120	Eg	50.00N	8.15
Maio	162	Cf	23.10N	15.10
Maio ◆	158	Eg	15.15N	23.1[illegible]
Maipo, Volcán- ♨	198	Ji	34.10S	69.5[illegible]
Maipú	206	Ie	36.52S	57.5[illegible]
Maiquetía	202	Ea	10.36N	66.5[illegible]
Maira ∿	128	Bf	44.49N	7.[illegible]
Mairi	202	Jf	11.43S	40.[illegible]
Mairipotaba	204	Hc	17.21S	49.[illegible]
Maisān [3]	146	Lg	32.00N	47[illegible]
Maisí, Punta- ►	190	Jd	20.15N	74[illegible]
Maišiagala/Maišjagala	116	Kj	54.51N	25[illegible]
Maišjagala/Maišiagala	116	Kj	54.51N	25[illegible]
Maïter ∿	126	Qi	35.23N	[illegible]

Index Symbols

[1] Independent Nation	▣ Historical or Cultural Region	⩂ Pass, Gap	⊔ Depression	⌇ Coast, Beach	✳ Rock, Reef	⫽ Waterfall, Rapids	═ Canal	⊖ Lagoon	⟋ Escarpment, Sea Scarp	♜ Historic Site	✈ Airport
[2] State, Region	▲ Mount, Mountain	▭ Plain, Lowland	⊟ Polder	▌ Cliff	❖ Islands, Archipelago	⊰ River Mouth, Estuary	❄ Glacier	▦ Bank	ϟ Fracture	⁙ Ruins	⚓ Port
[3] District, County	♨ Volcano	◣ Delta	∴ Desert, Dunes	▬ Peninsula	❋ Rocks, Reefs	◒ Lake	❅ Ice Shelf, Pack Ice	⊼ Seamount	▽ Trench, Abyss	▥ Wall, Walls	⚔ Military ins
[4] Municipality	◠ Hill	▤ Salt Flat	♣ Forest, Woods	⋈ Isthmus	✺ Coral Reef	⊜ Salt Lake	≈ Ocean	⊓ Tablemount	♤ National Park, Reserve	✝ Church, Abbey	☨ Lighthouse
[5] Colony, Dependency	⛰ Mountains, Mountain Range	⋁ Valley, Canyon	Ѡ Heath, Steppe	⩰ Sandbank	⊙ Well, Spring	◌ Intermittent Lake	≃ Sea	⋀ Ridge	✪ Point of Interest	⛩ Temple	⚒ Mine
■ Continent	⌒ Hills, Escarpment	◡ Crater, Cave	⚘ Oasis	◆ Island	⇑ Geyser	⊡ Reservoir	◧ Gulf, Bay	⊏ Shelf	⚑ Recreation Site	⚗ Scientific Station	∩ Tunnel
⧗ Physical Region	⌓ Plateau, Upland	⁜ Karst Features	► Cape, Point	◎ Atoll	∿ River, Stream	⋯ Swamp, Pond	⇌ Strait, Fjord	⊍ Basin	⌂ Cave, Cavern	⊷ Railway station	⌐ Dam, Brid

Name	Page	Grid	Lat.	Long.
Maitland [Austl.]	212	Hf	34.22S	137.40 E
Maitland [Austl.]	210	Gh	32.44S	151.33 E
Maíz, Isla Grande del-	194	Fg	12.10N	83.03W
Maíz, Isla Pequeña del-	194	Fg	12.18N	82.59W
Maíz, Islas del-	190	Hf	12.15N	83.00W
Maizhokunggar	152	Ff	29.50N	91.40 E
Maizières-lès-Metz	124	Ie	49.13N	6.09 E
Maizuru	154	Mg	35.27N	135.20 E
Maizuru-Nishimaizuru	156	Dd	35.28N	135.19 E
Maizuru-Wan	156	Dd	35.30N	135.20 E
Maja [R.S.F.S.R.]	140	Pd	60.17N	134.41 E
Maja [R.S.F.S.R.]	138	If	54.37N	134.50 E
Majagual	194	Ji	8.35N	74.37W
Majakovski	132	Mh	42.02N	42.47 E
Majangat	152	Fb	48.20N	91.58 E
Majardah, Wādī-	128	Em	37.07N	10.13 E
Majāz al Bāb	128	Dn	36.39N	9.37 E
Majdanpek	130	Ee	44.25N	21.56 E
Majene	142	Nj	3.33S	118.57 E
Majërtën=Mijirtein (EN)	158	Lh	9.00N	50.00 E
Majevica	128	Mf	44.40N	18.40 E
Maji	168	Fd	6.10N	35.35 E
Majia He	152	Kd	38.09N	117.53 E
Majja	138	Id	61.38N	130.25 E
Majkain	136	He	51.27N	75.52 E
Majkamys	135	Ka	46.34N	77.37 E
Majkop	112	Kg	44.35N	40.07 E
Majli-Saj	135	Id	41.15N	72.30 E
Majma'ah	146	Kj	25.54N	45.20 E
Majmak	136	Hg	42.40N	71.14 E
Majmakan	138	Ie	57.30N	135.23 E
Majmeča	138	Fb	71.20N	104.15 E
Majn	138	Mc	65.03N	172.10 E
Majna [R.S.F.S.R.]	114	Li	54.09N	47.37 E
Majna [R.S.F.S.R.]	138	Ef	53.00N	91.28 E
Major, Puig-/Mayor, Puig-	126	Oe	39.48N	2.48 E
Majorca (EN)=Mallorca	110	Gh	39.30N	3.00 E
Majrur	168	Db	16.40N	26.53 E
Majski [R.S.F.S.R.]	138	Hf	52.18N	129.38 E
Majski [R.S.F.S.R.]	132	Nh	43.36N	44.03 E
Maju, Pulau-	150	If	1.20N	126.25 E
Majuro Atoll	208	Id	7.09N	171.12 E
Makabana	160	Ii	3.28S	12.36 E
Makaha	221a	Cb	21.29N	158.13W
Makahuena Point	221a	Bb	21.52N	159.27W
Makalamabedi	172	Cd	20.20S	23.53 E
Makale	150	Gg	3.06S	119.51 E
Makallé	206	Ic	27.13S	59.17W
Makalondi	166	Fc	12.50N	1.41 E
Makamby, Nosy-	172	Hc	15.42S	45.54 E
Makanči	136	If	46.51N	81.57 E
Makanza	170	Cb	1.36N	19.07 E
Makapala	221a	Fc	20.13N	155.45W
Makapu Point	220k	Ba	18.59S	169.55W
Makapuu Head	221a	Db	21.18N	157.39W
Makara, prohod-	130	Ih	41.16N	25.26 E
Makarene, Irhazer-	166	Gb	18.07N	7.35 E
Makares	130	Il	37.05N	25.42 E
Makarfi	166	Gc	11.23N	7.53 E
Makari	166	Hc	12.35N	14.28 E
Makari Mountains	170	Ed	6.05S	29.50 E
Makarjev	114	Kh	57.57N	43.49 E
Makarov	138	Jg	48.39N	142.51 E
Makarov Basin (EN)	224	Ce	87.00N	170.00 E
Makarov Seamount (EN)	208	Gb	29.30N	153.30 E
Makarska	128	Lg	43.18N	17.02 E
Makā Rūd	146	Nd	36.21N	51.16 E
Makasar → Ujung Pandang	142	Nj	5.07S	119.24 E
Makasar, Selat-=Makassar Strait (EN)	140	Nj	2.00S	117.30 E
Makassar Strait (EN)= Makasar, Selat-	140	Nj	2.00S	117.30 E
Makat	112	Lf	47.40N	53.28 E
Makatea, Ile-	208	Mf	15.50S	148.15W
Makaw	136	Jc	26.27N	96.42 E
Makawao	221a	Ec	20.51N	156.19W
Makay, Massif du-	172	Hd	21.15S	45.15 E
Makedhonía	130	Fi	40.40N	22.30 E
Makedhonía=Macedonia (EN)	110	Ig	41.00N	23.00 E
Makedhonía=Macedonia (EN)	130	Fh	41.00N	23.00 E
Makedonija = Macedonia (EN)	130	Eh	41.50N	22.00 E
Makedonija=Macedonia (EN)	110	Ig	41.00N	23.00 E
Makedonija=Macedonia (EN)	130	Fh	41.00N	23.00 E
Makejevka	132	Jf	48.00N	37.58 E
Makelulu, Mount-	220a	Bb	7.34N	134.35 E
Makemo Atoll	208	Mf	16.35S	143.40W
Makeni	160	Fh	8.53N	12.03W
Makgadikgadi Pans	158	Jk	20.50S	25.30 E
Makhfar al Buşayyah	146	Lg	30.08N	46.07 E
Makhfar al Hammām	146	Hh	35.51N	38.45 E
Makhmūr	146	Je	35.46N	43.35 E
Makhyah, Wādī-	144	Gf	17.40N	49.01 E
aki	156	Fc	37.45N	138.52 E
akian, Pulau-	150	If	0.20N	127.25 E
akikihi	218	Df	44.38S	171.09 E
akinsk	136	He	52.40N	70.26 E
akkah=Mecca (EN)	142	Fg	21.27N	39.49 E
akkovik	180	Le	55.05N	59.11W
aknassy	162	Ic	34.37N	9.36 E
kó	120	Qj	46.13N	20.29 E
okou	160	Ih	0.34N	12.52 E
ongai	219d	Bb	17.27S	178.58 E
ongolosi	170	Fd	8.24S	33.09 E
orako	218	Gi	39.09S	176.03 E
oua	160	Ih	0.01N	15.39 E
ura	219b	Dc	17.08S	168.26 E
v	120	Og	49.22N	18.29 E
w Mazowiecki	120	Rd	52.52N	21.06 E
	130	Im	36.16N	25.53 E
n	140	Hg	26.00N	60.00 E
Makrónisos	130	Hl	37.42N	24.07 E
Maksatiha	114	Ih	57.48N	35.55 E
Makteir	158	Ff	21.50N	11.40W
Makthar	162	Ib	35.51N	9.12 E
Makthar	128	Do	35.50N	9.13 E
Mākū	146	Kc	39.17N	44.31 E
Mākū	144	Hd	27.52N	52.26 E
Makubetsu	156a	Cb	42.54N	143.19 E
Makumbato	170	Fd	9.51S	34.50 E
Makumbi	170	Dd	5.51S	20.41 E
Makunduchi	170	Gd	6.25S	39.33 E
Makung	152	Kg	23.35N	119.35 E
Makurazaki	154	Ki	31.16N	139.19 E
Makurdi	160	Hh	7.44N	8.32 E
Makushin Volcano	178a	Eb	53.53N	166.50W
Makušino	136	Gd	55.13N	67.13 E
Makuyuni	170	Gc	3.33S	36.06 E
Malå	114	Ed	65.11N	18.44 E
Mala/Mallow	118	Ei	52.08N	8.39W
Mala, Punta-	190	Ig	7.28N	80.00W
Malabang	150	He	7.38N	124.03 E
Malabar Coast	140	Jh	10.00N	76.15 E
Malabo	160	Hh	3.45N	8.47 E
Malabrigo	204	Ci	29.20S	59.58W
Malacca, Strait of- (EN)= Melaka, Selat-	140	Mi	2.30N	101.20 E
Malacky	120	Nh	48.27N	17.01 E
Malad City	188	Ie	42.12N	112.15W
Maladeta / Malditos, Montes-	126	Mb	42.40N	0.50 E
Malá Fatra	120	Og	49.08N	18.50 E
Málaga	126	Hh	36.48N	4.45W
Málaga [Col.]	202	Db	6.42N	72.44W
Málaga [Sp.]	112	Fh	36.43N	4.25W
Malagarasi	158	Ji	5.12S	29.47 E
Malagón	126	Ie	39.10N	3.51W
Malaimbandy	172	Hd	20.20S	45.36 E
Malaita Island	208	He	9.00S	161.00 E
Malaja Kuonamka	138	Gb	70.50N	113.20 E
Malaja Ob	138	Bc	66.08N	65.50 E
Malaja Sosva	136	Gc	63.10N	64.22 E
Malaja Višera	136	Dd	58.52N	32.14 E
Malaja Viska	132	Ge	48.39N	31.38 E
Malakāl	160	Kh	9.31N	31.39 E
Malakal Harbor	220a	Ac	7.20N	134.26 E
Malakal Pass	220a	Ac	7.17N	134.28 E
Mala Kapela	128	Jf	44.55N	15.28 E
Malakobi	219a	Db	7.19S	158.07 E
Malang	142	Nj	7.59S	112.37 E
Malangen	114	Eb	69.30N	18.20 E
Malanje	160	Ii	9.33S	16.22 E
Malanje	170	Cd	9.30S	16.30 E
Malanville	166	Fc	11.52N	3.23 E
Malao	219b	Cb	15.10S	166.51 E
Mała Panew	120	Nf	50.44N	17.52 E
Mälaren	110	Hd	59.30N	17.15 E
Malargüe	206	Ge	35.28S	69.35W
Malartic, Lac-	184	Ha	48.15N	78.05W
Malaspina Glacier	178	Ke	59.50N	140.30W
Malatya	142	Ff	38.21N	38.19 E
Malâvi	146	Lf	33.10N	47.50 E
Malawi	160	Kj	13.30S	34.00 E
Malawi, Lake-	158	Kj	12.00S	34.30 E
Malaya	150	Df	4.00N	102.00 E
Malaybalay	150	Hd	8.09N	125.05 E
Malāyer	144	Gc	34.17N	48.50 E
Malāyer	146	Me	34.16N	48.12 E
Malay Peninsula (EN)	140	Mi	6.00N	102.00 E
Malay Peninsula (EN)= Malaysia, Semenanjung-	150	Df	4.00N	102.00 E
Malaysia	142	Mi	4.00N	102.00 E
Malaysia, Semenanjung-= Malay Peninsula (EN)	150	Df	4.00N	102.00 E
Malazgirt	146	Jc	39.09N	42.31 E
Malberg	124	Id	50.03N	6.35 E
Malbon	118	Nj	51.45N	0.40 E
Malbork	120	Pb	54.02N	19.01 E
Malbrán	206	Hc	29.21S	62.27W
Malchin	152	Ic	53.44N	12.47 E
Maldegem	124	Fc	51.13N	3.27 E
Malden	186	Lh	36.34N	89.57W
Malden Island	208	Le	4.03S	154.59W
Malditos, Montes- / Maladeta	126	Mb	42.40N	0.50 E
Maldive Islands	140	Ji	3.15N	73.00 E
Mal di Ventre	128	Ck	40.00N	8.20 E
Maldives	142	Ji	3.15N	73.00 E
Maldon	118	Nj	51.45N	0.40 E
Maldonado	206	Jd	34.54S	54.57W
Maldonado	204	El	34.40S	54.55W
Maldonado, Punta-	192	Ji	16.20N	98.35W
Malé	128	Ed	46.21N	10.55 E
Male	142	Ji	4.10N	73.30 E
Mâle, Lac du-	184	Ja	48.30N	75.30W
Malea, Cape- (EN) = Maléas, Ákra-	130	Gm	36.26N	23.12 E
Maléas, Ákra- = Malea, Cape- (EN)	130	Gm	36.26N	23.12 E
Male Atoll	140	Ji	4.29N	73.30 E
Malebo, Pool-	158	Ii	4.17S	15.20 E
Mālegaon	148	Ed	20.33N	74.32 E
Maléha	166	Dc	11.48N	9.43W
Malek	168	Ed	6.04N	31.36 E
Malé Karpaty = Little Carpathians (EN)	120	Nh	48.30N	17.20 E
Malek Kandī	146	Ld	37.09N	46.06 E
Malékoula, Ile-	208	Hf	16.15S	167.30 E
Malema	172	Fb	14.57S	37.25 E
Malemba Nkulu	170	Ed	8.02S	26.48 E
Malenga	114	Ie	63.50N	36.25 E
Malesherbes	122	If	48.18N	2.25 E
Malgobek	132	Nh	43.32N	44.34 E
Malgomaj	114	Dd	64.47N	16.12 E
Malhada	204	Kb	14.21S	43.47W
Malhanski hrebet	138	Ff	50.30N	109.00 E
Malhão da Estrêla	126	Ed	40.19N	7.37W
Malha Wells	168	Db	15.08N	26.12 E
Malheur Lake	182	Dc	43.20N	118.45W
Malheur River	188	Gd	44.03N	116.59W
Mali	166	Cc	12.05N	12.18W
Mali	160	Gg	17.00N	4.00W
Mali	219d	Bb	16.20S	179.21 E
Mali	148	Jc	25.42N	97.30 E
Mália	130	In	35.17N	25.28 E
Maliakós Kólpos	130	Fk	38.52N	22.38 E
Malik, Wādī al-	158	Kg	18.02N	30.58 E
Mali kanal	130	Cd	45.42N	19.19 E
Malik Sīah, Kūh-i-	144	Jd	29.51N	60.52 E
Malili	150	Hg	2.38S	121.06 E
Målilla	116	Fg	57.23N	15.48 E
Mali Lošinj	128	If	44.32N	14.28 E
Malimba, Monts-	170	Ed	7.32S	29.30 E
Malin	132	Fd	50.46N	29.14 E
Malinalco	192	Jh	18.57N	99.30W
Malinaltepec	192	Ji	17.03N	98.40W
Malindi	160	Li	3.13S	40.07 E
Malines/Mechelen	122	Kc	51.02N	4.29 E
Malin Head/Cionn Mhálanna	110	Fd	55.23N	7.24W
Malino, Bukit-	150	Hf	0.45N	120.47 E
Malinovoje Ozero	138	Cf	51.40N	79.55 E
Malinyi	170	Gd	8.56S	36.08 E
Malipo	152	Hg	23.07N	104.42 E
Maliqi	130	Di	40.43N	20.41 E
Malita	150	Ie	6.25N	125.36 E
Maljen	130	De	44.07N	20.03 E
Maljovica	130	Gg	42.11N	23.22 E
Malka	132	Nh	43.44N	44.15 E
Malkara	146	Bb	40.53N	26.54 E
Malki Lom	130	Jf	43.39N	26.04 E
Malko Tărnovo	130	Kh	41.59N	27.32 E
Mallacoota	212	Jg	37.30S	149.50 E
Mallaig	118	Hd	57.00N	5.50W
Mallamalla Range	148	Fe	16.17N	79.29 E
Mallāq, Wādī-	128	Cn	36.32N	8.51 E
Mallawī	164	Fd	27.44N	30.50 E
Mallery Lake	180	Hd	64.00N	98.00W
Malles Venosta / Mals in Vinschgau	128	Ed	46.41N	10.32 E
Mallet	204	Gg	25.55S	50.50W
Mallnitz	128	Hd	46.59N	13.10 E
Mallorca=Majorca (EN)	110	Gh	39.30N	3.00 E
Mallow/Mala	118	Ei	52.08N	8.39W
Malm	114	Cd	64.04N	11.13 E
Malmbäck	116	Fg	57.35N	14.28 E
Malmberget	114	Ec	67.10N	20.40 E
Malmédy	122	Md	50.26N	6.02 E
Malmesbury	172	Bf	33.28S	18.44 E
Malmö	112	Hd	55.36N	13.00 E
Malmöhus	114	Ci	55.45N	13.30 E
Malmön	116	Df	58.21N	11.20 E
Malmslätt	116	Ff	58.25N	15.30 E
Malmyž	136	Fd	56.31N	50.41 E
Malo	219b	Cb	15.41S	167.10 E
Maloarhangelsk	132	Jc	52.26N	36.29 E
Maloelap	208	Id	8.45N	171.03 E
Maloggia/Malojapaß	128	Dd	46.24N	9.41 E
Malojapaß/Maloggia	128	Dd	46.24N	9.41 E
Malojaroslavec	132	Jb	55.02N	36.28 E
Maloje Polesje	120	Uf	50.10N	24.30 E
Malolo	219d	Ab	17.45S	177.10 E
Malolos	150	Hd	14.51N	120.49 E
Malombe, Lake-	170	Ge	14.38S	35.12 E
Malone	184	Jc	44.52N	74.19W
Malonga	170	De	10.24S	23.10 E
Małopolska	120	Pf	50.45N	20.00 E
Malorita	132	Dd	51.48N	24.05 E
Malošujka	114	Ie	63.47N	37.22 E
Måløy	114	Af	61.56N	5.07 E
Malozemelskaja tundra	134	Ec	68.00N	52.00 E
Malpaso	192	Mi	17.20N	93.30W
Malpelo, Isla de-	198	He	3.59N	81.35W
Malprabha	148	Fe	16.12N	76.03 E
Malsch	124	Kf	48.53N	8.20 E
Malše	120	Kh	48.59N	14.29 E
Mals in Vinschgau / Malles Venosta	128	Ed	46.41N	10.32 E
Malta	112	Hh	35.50N	14.30 E
Malta	110	Hh	35.54N	14.31 E
Malta [Lat.-U.S.S.R.]	116	Lh	56.18N	27.15 E
Malta [Mt.-U.S.]	182	Fb	48.21N	107.52W
Malta, Canale di-=Malta Channel (EN)	128	In	36.30N	14.30 E
Malta Channel (EN)=Malta, Canale di-	128	In	36.30N	14.30 E
Maltahöhe	160	Ik	24.50S	17.00 E
Maltahöhe	172	Bd	25.00S	16.30 E
Maltepe	130	Mi	40.55N	29.08 E
Malton	118	Mg	54.08N	0.48W
Maltsch	120	Kh	48.59N	14.29 E
Maluku	150	Ig	4.00S	128.00 E
Maluku, Kepulauan-= Moluccas (EN)	208	De	2.00S	128.00 E
Maluku, Laut-=Molucca Sea (EN)	140	Oj	0.05S	125.00 E
Malumfashi	166	Gc	11.48N	7.37 E
Malunda	150	Gg	3.00S	118.50 E
Malung	114	Cf	60.40N	13.44 E
Malungsfors	116	Ed	60.44N	13.33 E
Malūţ	168	Ec	10.26N	32.12 E
Maluu	219a	Ec	8.21S	160.38 E
Malvern [Ar.-U.S.]	186	Ji	34.22N	92.49W
Malvern [Eng.-U.K.]	118	Ki	52.07N	2.19W
Malvinas	204	Ci	29.37S	58.59W
Malvinas, Islas-/Falkland Islands	200	Kk	51.45S	59.00W
Malvinas, Islas-/Falkland Islands	198	Kk	51.45S	59.00W
Maly, ostrov-	116	Ld	60.02N	27.58 E
Malya	170	Fc	2.59S	33.31 E
Maly Anju	138	Lc	68.35N	161.03 E
Maly Čeremšan	114	Mi	54.20N	50.01 E
Maly Duna	120	Nh	48.08N	17.09 E
Malygina, proliv-	138	Cb	73.00N	70.30 E
Maly Jenisej	138	Ef	51.40N	94.26 E
Maly Kavkaz=Lesser Caucasus (EN)	110	Kg	41.00N	44.35 E
Maly Ljahovski, ostrov-	138	Jb	74.07N	140.36 E
Maly Tajmyr, ostrov-	138	Fa	78.08N	107.08 E
Maly Tjuters, ostrov-	116	Le	59.45N	26.53 E
Maly Uzen	110	Kf	48.50N	49.38 E
Mama	138	Ge	58.20N	112.54 E
Mamadyš	114	Mi	55.45N	51.24 E
Mamagota	219a	Bb	6.46S	155.24 E
Mamaia	130	Le	44.17N	28.37 E
Mamakan	138	Ge	57.48N	114.05 E
Mamantel	192	Nh	18.33N	91.05W
Mamanutha Group	219d	Ab	17.34S	177.04 E
Mamaqān	146	Kd	37.51N	45.59 E
Mambaj	204	Ib	14.28S	46.07W
Mambajao	150	He	9.15N	124.43 E
Mambasa	170	Eb	1.21N	29.03 E
Mambéré	168	Be	3.31N	16.03 E
Mambili	170	Cb	0.07N	16.08 E
Mamborê	204	Fg	24.18S	52.32W
Mambova	170	Ef	17.44S	25.11 E
Mambrui	170	Hc	3.07S	40.09 E
Mamburao	150	Hd	13.14N	120.35 E
Mamedkala	132	Ph	42.12N	48.06 E
Mamer	124	Ie	49.38N	6.02 E
Mamers	122	Gf	48.21N	0.23 E
Mamfe	166	Gd	5.46N	9.17 E
Mamiá, Lago-	202	Fd	4.15S	63.05W
Mamisonski, pereval-	132	Mh	42.43N	43.45 E
Mamljutka	136	Ge	54.57N	68.35 E
Mammoth Cave	184	Dg	37.10N	86.08W
Mammoth Hot Springs	188	Jd	44.59N	110.43W
Mamonovo	120	Pb	54.28N	19.57 E
Mamoré, Rio-	198	Jg	10.23S	65.53W
Mamou	160	Fg	10.23N	12.05W
Mamoutzou	172	Hb	12.47S	45.14 E
Mampikony	172	Hc	16.05S	47.37 E
Mampodre, Picos de-	126	Ga	43.02N	5.12W
Mampong	166	Ed	7.04N	1.24W
Mamry, Jezioro-	120	Rb	54.08N	21.42 E
Mamuju	150	Gg	2.41S	118.54 E
Mamuno	172	Cd	22.17S	20.02 E
Ma'mūrah, Ra's al-	128	En	36.27N	10.49 E
Mamurokawa	156	Gb	38.54N	140.15 E
Man	160	Gh	7.24N	7.33W
Man	166	Dd	7.13N	7.41W
Man, Calf of-	118	Ig	54.03N	4.48W
Man, Isle of-	110	Fe	54.15N	4.30W
Mana	214	Oc	22.02N	159.46W
Mana	138	Ee	55.57N	92.28 E
Manacapuru	202	Fd	3.18S	60.37W
Manacor	126	Pe	39.34N	3.12 E
Manado	142	Oi	1.29N	124.51 E
Managua	176	Kh	12.09N	86.17W
Managua	194	Dg	12.05N	86.20W
Managua, Lago de-	190	Gf	12.20N	86.20W
Manakara	160	Lk	22.07S	48.00 E
Manama (EN)=Al Manāmah	142	Hg	26.13N	50.35 E
Manambolo	172	Gc	19.19S	44.17 E
Manam Island	208	Fe	4.05S	145.03 E
Manamo, Caño-	202	Fb	9.55N	62.16W
Mananara	172	Hc	16.10S	49.45 E
Mananara	172	Hd	23.21S	47.42 E
Mananjary	160	Lk	21.14S	48.17 E
Manankoro	166	Dc	10.28N	7.25W
Manantenina	172	Hd	24.17S	47.18 E
Manaoba	219a	Ec	8.19S	160.47 E
Manapire, Río-	196	Ci	7.42N	66.07W
Manapouri	210	Hi	45.34S	167.36 E
Manapouri, Lake-	218	Bf	45.30S	167.30 E
Manār, Jabal-	164	Hg	14.10N	44.17 E
Manas	142	Ke	44.18N	86.13 E
Manas, gora-	135	Hc	42.18N	71.06 E
Manas He	152	Eb	45.38N	85.12 E
Manas Hu	152	Eb	45.45N	85.55 E
Manasija, Manastir-	130	Ee	44.06N	21.28 E
Manati	194	Ic	21.19N	76.56W
Manati	194	Nd	18.26N	66.29W
Manatuto	150	Ih	8.30S	126.01 E
Manaure	194	Kh	11.46N	72.28W
Manaus	200	Jf	3.08S	60.01W
Manavgat	146	Dd	36.47N	31.26 E
Manbij [Syr.]	146	Gd	36.31N	37.57 E
Manbij [Syr.]	146	Gd	36.30N	37.50 E
Manbūbnagar	148	Fe	16.44N	77.59 E
Mancelona	184	Ec	44.54N	85.04W
Mancha Real	126	Ig	37.47N	3.37W
Manche	122	Ee	50.00N	1.10W
Mancheng	154	Ce	38.57N	115.19 E
Manchester [Ct.-U.S.]	184	Ke	41.47N	72.31W
Manchester [Eng.-U.K.]	112	Fe	53.30N	2.15W
Manchester [Ia.-U.S.]	186	Ke	42.29N	91.27W
Manchester [Ky.-U.S.]	184	Fg	37.09N	83.46W
Manchester [N.H.-U.S.]	182	Mc	42.59N	71.28W
Manchester [Tn.-U.S.]	184	Dh	35.29N	86.05W
Manchok	166	Gd	9.40N	8.31 E
Manchuria (EN)	140	Oe	47.00N	125.00 E
Manciano	128	Fh	42.35N	11.31 E
Mand	144	Hd	28.11N	51.17 E
Manda [Chad]	168	Bd	9.11N	18.13 E
Manda [Tan.]	170	Fe	10.28S	34.35 E
Manda, Jabal-	168	Cd	8.39N	24.27 E
Mandabe	172	Gd	21.02S	44.56 E
Mandaguari	206	Jb	23.32S	51.42W
Manda Island	170	Hc	2.17S	40.57 E
Mandal	114	Bg	58.02N	7.27 E
Mandalay	142	Lg	22.00N	96.05 E
Mandalay	148	Jd	21.00N	96.00 E
Mandal-Gobi	152	Ib	45.50N	106.12 E
Mandalī	146	Kf	33.45N	45.32 E
Mandalselva	116	Bf	58.02N	7.28 E
Mandalt → Sonid Zuoqi	152	Jc	43.50N	113.45 E
Mandalya körfezi	146	Bd	37.12N	27.20 E
Mandan	182	Gb	46.50N	100.54W
Mandaon	150	Hd	12.13N	123.17 E
Mandara, Monts-=Mandara Mountains (EN)	166	Hc	10.45N	13.40 E
Mandara Mountains (EN)= Mandara, Monts-	166	Hc	10.45N	13.40 E
Mandas	128	Dk	39.38N	9.07 E
Mandasor	148	Fd	24.04N	75.04 E
Mandera	160	Lh	3.56N	41.52 E
Manderscheid	124	Id	50.06N	6.49 E
Mandeville	194	Id	18.02N	77.30W
Mandi	148	Fb	31.43N	76.55 E
Mandiana	166	Dc	10.38N	8.41W
Mandimba	172	Fb	14.21S	35.39 E
Mandingues, Monts-	166	Cc	13.00N	11.00W
Mandioli, Pulau-	150	Ig	0.44S	127.14 E
Mandioré, Laguna-	204	Dd	18.08S	57.33W
Mandirituba	204	Hg	25.46S	49.19W
Mandji	170	Bc	1.42S	10.24 E
Mandla	148	Gd	22.36N	80.23 E
Mandø	116	Ci	55.15N	8.35 E
Mandoúdhion	130	Gk	38.48N	23.29 E
Mandrákion	130	Km	36.36N	27.08 E
Mandritsara	172	Hc	15.49S	48.48 E
Mandurah	212	Df	32.32S	115.43 E
Manduria	128	Lj	40.24N	17.38 E
Māndvi	148	Dd	22.50N	69.22 E
Mandya	148	Ff	12.33N	76.54 E
Mâne	116	Ce	59.56N	8.48 E
Mâneciu Ungureni	130	Id	45.19N	25.59 E
Manendragarh	148	Gd	23.10N	82.35 E
Maneromango	170	Gd	7.16S	38.46 E
Manevići	132	Dd	51.19N	25.33 E
Manfalūţ	164	Fd	27.19N	30.58 E
Manfredonia	128	Ji	41.38N	15.55 E
Manfredonia, Golfo di-	128	Ki	41.35N	16.05 E
Manga [Afr.]	153	Ig	15.00N	14.00 E
Manga [Braz.]	202	Jf	14.46S	43.56W
Mangabeiras, Chapada das-	198	Lg	10.00S	46.30W
Mangai	170	Cc	4.03S	19.35 E
Mangaia Island	218	Lg	21.55S	157.55W
Mangakino	218	Fc	38.22S	175.46 E
Mangalia	130	Lf	43.48N	28.35 E
Mangalmé	168	Bc	12.21N	19.37 E
Mangalore	142	Jh	12.52N	74.53 E
Mangareva, Ile-	208	Ng	23.07S	134.57W
Mangfall	120	Ii	47.51N	12.08 E
Manggar	150	Eg	2.53S	108.16 E
Manggautu	219a	Dd	11.30S	159.59 E
Mangin Yoma	148	Jd	24.20N	95.42 E
Mangistau	132	Qg	44.03N	51.57 E
Mangit	136	Gg	42.07N	60.01 E
Mangkalihat, Tanjung-	150	Gf	1.02N	118.59 E
Manglares, Cabo-	202	Cc	1.36N	79.02W
Mangnai	152	Fd	37.48N	91.55 E
Mangniu He	154	Ib	45.10N	128.58 E
Mango [Fiji]	219d	Cb	17.27S	179.09W
Mango [Ton.]	221b	Bb	20.20S	174.43W
Mangoche	170	Ge	14.28S	35.16 E
Mangoky [Mad.]	158	Lk	21.29S	43.41 E
Mangoky [Mad.]	172	Hd	23.27S	45.13 E
Mangole, Pulau-	150	Ig	1.53S	125.50 E
Mangonui	218	Ea	34.59S	173.32 E
Mangrove Cay	194	Ia	24.51N	76.14W
Mangrullo, Cuchilla-	204	Fk	32.27S	53.50W
Mangshi → Luxi	142	Lg	24.29N	98.40 E
Mangualde	126	Ed	40.36N	7.46W
Mangueira, Lagoa-	206	Jd	33.06S	52.48W
Mangueni, Plateau de-	158	If	22.35N	12.40 E
Mangui	152	La	52.03N	122.09 E
Mangula	172	Ec	16.52S	30.08 E
Mangum	186	Gi	34.53N	99.30W
Manguredjipa	170	Eb	0.21N	28.44 E
Mangyšlak	135	Fg	43.40N	51.15 E
Mangyšlak, plato-	136	Fg	43.25N	53.00 E
Mangyšlakskaja oblast	136	Fg	44.00N	53.30 E
Mangyšlakski zaliv	132	Qg	44.45N	51.00 E
Manhattan	182	Hd	39.11N	96.35W
Manhica	172	Ee	25.24S	32.48 E
Mani	170	Ed	6.27S	25.20 E
Mani	202	Dc	4.49N	72.17W
Mānī', Wādī al-	146	Ie	34.16N	41.02 E
Mania	172	Hc	19.42S	45.22 E
Maniago	128	Gd	46.10N	12.43 E
Manica	172	Ec	18.56S	32.53 E
Manica	172	Ec	19.00S	33.20 E
Manicaland	172	Ec	19.00S	32.30 E
Manicoré	200	Jf	5.49S	61.17W
Manicoré, Rio-	202	Fe	5.51S	61.19W
Manicouagan	180	Kf	51.00N	68.20W
Manicouagan	180	Kg	49.10N	68.15W
Manicouagan, Réservoir-	174	Md	51.30N	68.19W
Manigotagan	186	Ha	51.06N	96.18W
Manihi Atoll	208	Mf	14.24S	145.56W
Manihiki Anchorage	220n	Ab	10.23S	161.03W
Manihiki Atoll	208	Kf	10.24S	161.01W
Manika, Plateau de la-	170	Ed	10.00S	25.00 E
Manila [Phil.]	142	Oh	14.35N	121.00 E
Manila [Ut.-U.S.]	188	Kf	40.59N	109.43W
Manila Bay	150	Oh	14.30N	120.45 E
Manilaid/Manilajd	116	Kf	58.08N	24.03 E
Manilajd/Manilaid	116	Kf	58.08N	24.03 E
Manily	138	Ld	62.30N	165.20 E
Maningrida Settlement	212	Gb	12.05S	134.10 E
Maniouro, Pointe-	219b	Dc	17.41S	168.35 E
Manipa, Selat-	150	Ig	3.20S	127.23 E
Manipur	148	Id	25.00N	94.00 E
Manipur	148	Id	22.52N	94.05 E
Manisa	144	Cb	38.36N	27.26 E
Manisa Dağı	130	Kk	38.33N	27.26 E
Manises	126	Le	39.29N	0.27W
Manissau a-Missu, Rio-	202	Hf	10.58S	53.20W
Manistee	184	Dc	44.15N	86.18W
Manistee River	184	Dc	44.15N	86.21W
Manistique	182	Jb	45.57N	86.15W
Manistique Lake	184	Eb	46.15N	85.45W
Manitoba	180	Hf	55.00N	97.00W
Manitoba, Lake-	174	Jd	51.00N	98.45W
Manitou Islands	184	Ec	45.10N	86.00W
Manitou Lake	184	Gc	45.48N	82.00W
Manitoulin Island	180	Jg	45.45N	82.30W

x Symbols

- ependent Nation
- te, Region
- rict, County
- icipality
- ny, Dependency
- inent
- ical Region
- Historical or Cultural Region
- Mount, Mountain
- Volcano
- Hill
- Mountains, Mountain Range
- Hills, Escarpment
- Plateau, Upland
- Pass, Gap
- Plain, Lowland
- Delta
- Salt Flat
- Valley, Canyon
- Crater, Cave
- Karst Features
- Depression
- Polder
- Desert, Dunes
- Forest, Woods
- Heath, Steppe
- Oasis
- Cape, Point
- Coast, Beach
- Cliff
- Peninsula
- Isthmus
- Sandbank
- Island
- Atoll
- Rock, Reef
- Islands, Archipelago
- Rocks, Reefs
- Coral Reef
- Well, Spring
- Geyser
- River, Stream
- Waterfall, Rapids
- River Mouth, Estuary
- Lake
- Salt Lake
- Intermittent Lake
- Reservoir
- Swamp, Pond
- Canal
- Glacier
- Ice Shelf, Pack Ice
- Ocean
- Sea
- Gulf, Bay
- Strait, Fjord
- Lagoon
- Bank
- Seamount
- Tablemount
- Ridge
- Shelf
- Basin
- Escarpment, Sea Scarp
- Fracture
- Trench, Abyss
- National Park, Reserve
- Point of Interest
- Recreation Site
- Cave, Cavern
- Historic Site
- Ruins
- Wall, Walls
- Church, Abbey
- Temple
- Scientific Station
- Railway station
- Airport
- Port
- Military installation
- Lighthouse
- Mine
- Tunnel
- Dam, Bridge

Manitou Springs 186 Dg 38.52N 104.55W
Manitouwadge 186 Nb 49.08N 85.47W
Manitowoc 182 Jc 44.06N 87.40W
Manitsoq/Sukkertoppen 186 Md 65.25N 53.00W
Maniwaki 180 Jg 46.23N 75.58W
Manizales 200 Ie 5.05N 75.32W
Manja 172 Gd 21.23S 44.20 E
Manja [S] 134 Jd 64.23N 60.50 E
Manjaća [M] 128 Lf 44.35N 17.05 E
Manjacaze 172 Ed 24.42S 33.33 E
Manjakandriana 172 Hc 18.55S 47.47 E
Manji 156a Bb 43.09N 141.59 E
Manjil 144 Gb 36.44N 49.24 E
Manjimup 212 Df 34.14S 116.09 E
Mänjra [S] 148 Fe 18.49N 77.52 E
Män Kät 148 Jd 22.05N 98.01 E
Mankato [Ks.-U.S.] 186 Gg 39.47N 98.12W
Mankato [Mn.-U.S.] 182 Ic 44.10N 94.01W
Mankono 166 Dd 8.04N 6.12W
Mankono [3] 166 Dd 7.58N 6.02W
Mankoya 160 Jj 14.50S 25.00 E
Manley Hot Springs 178 Ic 65.00N 150.37W
Manlleu 126 Ob 42.00N 2.17 E
Manmad 148 Ed 20.15N 74.27 E
Manmanoc, Mount- [M] 150 Hc 17.40N 121.06 E
Manna 150 Dh 4.27S 102.55 E
Mannahill 212 Hf 32.26S 139.59 E
Mannar 148 Fg 8.59N 79.54 E
Mannar, Gulf of- [C] 140 Ji 8.30N 79.00 E
Mannheim 112 Gf 49.29N 8.28 E
Manning [Alta.-Can.] 180 Fe 56.55N 117.33W
Manning [S.C.-U.S.] 184 Gi 33.42N 80.12W
Manning, Cape- [E] 220g Ba 2.02N 157.26W
Manning Strait [C] 219a Db 7.24S 158.04 E
Manningtree 124 Dc 51.57N 1.04 E
Mann Ranges [M] 212 Fe 26.00S 129.30 E
Mann River [S] 212 Gb 12.20S 134.07 E
Mannu, Capo- [E] 128 Cj 40.02N 8.22 E
Mannu, Rio- [It.] [S] 128 Cj 40.50N 8.23 E
Mannu, Rio- [It.] [S] 128 Cj 40.41N 8.59 E
Mano [S] 166 Cd 6.56N 11.31W
Mano [Jap.] 156 Fc 37.58N 138.20 E
Mano [S.L.] 166 Cd 7.55N 12.00W
Manoa 202 Ee 9.40S 65.27W
Man of War, Cayos- [E] 194 Fg 13.02N 83.22W
Manokwari 210 Ee 2.30S 134.36 E
Manombo [S] 172 Gd 22.55S 43.28 E
Manonga [S] 170 Fc 4.08S 34.12 E
Manono 160 Ji 7.18S 27.25 E
Manono [S] 221c Aa 13.50S 172.05W
Manouane, Lac- [S] 180 Kf 50.40N 70.45W
Mano-Wan [C] 156 Fc 37.55N 138.15 E
Manp'ojin 154 Id 41.09N 126.17 E
Manra Atoll (Sydney) [C] 208 Je 4.27S 171.15W
Manresa 126 Nc 41.44N 1.50 E
Mans, Le- 112 Gf 48.00N 0.12 E
Mansa 160 Jj 11.12S 28.53 E
Mansa Konko 166 Bc 13.28N 15.33W
Mansel [E] 174 Lc 62.00N 79.50W
Mansfield [Austl.] 212 Jg 37.03S 146.05 E
Mansfield [Eng.-U.K.] 118 Lh 53.09N 1.11W
Mansfield [La.-U.S.] 186 Jj 32.02N 93.43W
Mansfield [Oh.-U.S.] 182 Kc 40.46N 82.31W
Mansfield [Pa.-U.S.] 184 Ie 41.47N 77.05W
Mansfield, Mount- [M] 184 Kc 44.33N 72.49W
Mansle 122 Gi 45.52N 0.11 E
Manso, Rio- [S] 204 Db 14.42S 56.16W
Manso, Rio- ou Mortes, Rio das- [S] 198 Kg 11.45S 50.44W
Mansôa 166 Bc 12.04N 15.19W
Mansourah 126 Qh 36.04N 4.28 E
Mansourah, Djebel- [M] 126 Qh 36.02N 4.28 E
Manta 202 Bd 0.57S 80.42W
Manta, Bahia de- [C] 202 Bd 0.50S 80.40W
Mantalingajan, Mount- [M] 150 Ge 8.48N 117.40 E
Manteca 188 Eh 37.48N 121.13W
Mantecal [Ven.] 196 Bi 7.33N 69.09W
Mantecal [Ven.] 196 Di 6.52N 65.38W
Manteigas 126 Ed 40.24N 7.32W
Manteo 184 Jh 35.55N 75.40W
Mantes-la-Jolie 122 Hf 48.59N 1.43 E
Manti 188 Jg 39.16N 111.38W
Mantiqueira, Serra da- [M] 198 Lh 22.00S 44.45W
Manto 194 Df 14.55N 86.23W
Manton 184 Ec 44.24N 85.24W
Mantova 128 Ee 45.09N 10.48 E
Mäntsälä 116 Kd 60.38N 25.20 E
Mänttä 114 Kd 62.02N 24.38 E
Mantua 194 Eb 22.17N 84.17W
Manturovo 136 Gd 58.22N 44.44 E
Mäntyharju 114 Gf 61.25N 26.53 E
Mäntyluoto 116 Jc 61.35N 21.29 E
Manu 202 Ed 12.15S 70.50W
Manuae Atoll [Cook] [C] 208 Lf 19.21S 158.56W
Manuae Atoll [Fr.Poly.] [C] 208 Kf 16.32S 154.38W
Manua Islands [C] 208 Kf 14.13S 169.35W
Manuangi Atoll [C] 208 Mf 19.12S 141.16W
Manübah 128 En 36.48N 10.06 E
Manuel 192 Jf 22.44N 98.19W
Manuel Alves, Rio- [S] 202 If 11.19S 48.28W
Manuel Benavides 192 Hc 29.05N 103.55W
Manuel Derqui 204 Dc 27.50S 58.48W
Manuel J. Cobo 204 Dl 35.49S 57.54W
Manuel Ocampo 196 Bb 33.46S 60.39W
Manuga Reefs [E] 219Ad 10.23S 153.21 E
Manui [S] 150 Mg 3.35S 123.08 E
Manuján 146 Qi 27.24N 57.32 E
Mänük, Tell- [M] 146 Hf 33.10N 38.50 E
Manukau 210 Ih 36.56S 174.56 E
Manulu Lagoon [C] 220g Ba 1.57S 157.20W
Manus Island [C] 208 Fe 2.05S 147.00 E
Many 186 Jk 31.34N 93.29W
Manyara, Lake- [S] 170 Gc 3.35S 35.50 E
Manyas 146 Bb 40.02N 27.58 E
Manyč [S] 110 Kf 47.15N 40.00 E
Manyč-Gudilo, ozero- [S] 110 Kf 46.25N 42.35 E

Manyoni 170 Fd 5.45S 34.50 E
Manzanal, Puerto del- [E] 126 Fb 42.32N 6.10W
Manzanares 126 Ie 39.00N 3.22W
Manzaneda, Cabeza de- [M] 126 Eb 42.20N 7.15W
Manzanilla 126 Fg 37.23N 6.25W
Manzanillo [Cuba] 176 Lg 20.21N 77.07W
Manzanillo [Mex.] 176 Ih 19.03N 104.20W
Manzanillo, Bahia de- [Dom.Rep.] [C] 194 Ld 19.45N 71.46W
Manzanillo, Bahia de- [Mex.] [C] 192 Gh 19.04N 104.25W
Manzano Mountains [M] 186 Ci 34.45N 106.20W
Manzhouli 142 Ne 49.33N 117.28 E
Manzilah, Bubayrat al- [S] 146 Eg 31.15N 32.00 E
Manzil Bü Ruqaybah 162 Ib 37.10N 9.48 E
Manzil bü Zalafah 128 En 36.41N 10.35 E
Manzil Tamin 128 En 36.47N 10.59 E
Manzini 172 Ee 26.29S 31.22 E
Mao [+] 219bDc 17.29S 168.29 E
Mao [Chad] 160 Ig 14.07N 15.19 E
Mao [Dom.Rep.] 190 Je 19.34N 71.05W
Maó / Mahón 126 Qe 39.53N 4.15 E
Maoke, Pegunungan- [M] 150 Kg 4.00S 138.00 E
Maomao Shan [M] 152 Hd 37.12N 103.10 E
Maoming 142 Mg 21.41N 110.52 E
Maoniu Shan [M] 152 He 32.50N 104.12 E
Maotou Shan [M] 152 Hg 24.31N 100.38 E
Maouri, Dallol- [S] 166 Fc 12.05N 3.32 E
Mapai 172 Ee 22.51S 31.58 E
Mapam Yumco [S] 144 Kk 30.40N 81.20 E
Mapanda 170 Dd 9.32S 24.16 E
Mapati 170 Bc 3.38S 13.21 E
Mapi 210 Ee 7.07S 139.23 E
Mapi [S] 150 Kh 7.00S 139.16 E
Mapia, Kepulauan- [C] 208 Ed 0.50N 134.20 E
Mapimí, Bolsón de- [S] 174 Ig 27.30N 103.15W
Mapinhane 172 Fd 22.15S 35.07 E
Mapire 196 Di 7.45N 64.42W
Mapiri 202 Eg 15.15S 68.10W
Maple Creek 180 Gg 49.55N 109.27W
Maprik 214 Dh 3.38S 143.03 E
Mapuera, Rio- [S] 202 Gd 1.05S 57.02W
Maputo [3] 172 Ee 26.00S 32.30 E
Maputo (Lourenço Marques) 160 Kk 25.58S 32.34 E
Maputo, Baia de- [C] 158 Kk 26.05S 33.00 E
Maqên (Dawu) 152 He 34.29N 100.01 E
Maqran, Wädï al- [S] 164 Ie 20.55N 47.12 E
Maqu 152 He 34.05N 101.45 E
Maquan He/Damqog Kanbab [S] 152 Df 29.36N 84.09 E
Maquela do Zombo 160 Ii 6.03S 15.08 E
Maquinchao 206 Gf 41.15S 68.44W
Maquoketa 186 Ke 42.04N 90.40W
Mar, Serra do- [M] 198 Lh 25.00S 48.00W
Mara [3] 170 Fc 2.30S 34.00 E
Mara [S] 170 Fc 1.31S 33.56 E
Maraã 202 Ed 1.50S 65.22W
Marab [S] 168 Fc 14.54N 37.55 E
Marabá 202 Ie 5.21S 49.07W
Marabahan 150 Ff 3.00S 114.45 E
Marabá Paulista 204 Gf 22.06S 51.56W
Maracá, Ilha de- [C] 202 Hc 2.05N 50.25W
Maracaibo 200 Id 10.40N 71.37W
Maracaibo, Lago de- = 198 Ie 9.50N 71.30W
Maracaibo, Lake- (EN) [S] 198 Ie 9.50N 71.30W
Maracaibo, Lago de- [S] 198 Ie 9.50N 71.30W
Maracaju 202 Gg 21.38S 55.09W
Maracaju, Serra de- [Braz.] [M] 198 Kh 21.00S 55.00W
Maracaju, Serra de- [S.Amer.] [M] 204 Eb 23.57S 55.01W
Maracanã 202 Id 0.46S 47.27W
Maracás 202 Jf 13.26S 40.27W
Maracay 200 Jd 10.15N 67.36W
Maradah 164 Cd 29.14N 19.13 E
Maradi 166 Gc 14.15N 7.15 E
Maradi [2] 166 Gc 14.15N 7.06 E
Marägheh 144 Gb 37.23N 46.40 E
Märäh 144 Gd 25.04N 45.28 E
Maraho [S] 168 Bb 18.21N 17.28 E
Marahuaca, Cerro- [M] 198 Je 3.34N 65.27W
Marajó, Baia de- [C] 198 Lf 1.00S 48.30W
Marajó, Ilha de- [C] 198 Lf 1.00S 49.30W
Marakei Atoll [C] 208 Id 1.58N 173.25 E
Maralal 170 Gb 1.06N 36.42 E
Maralinga 212 Ff 30.13S 131.35 E
Maralwexi/Bachu 152 Cd 39.46N 78.15 E
Maramag 150 Mf 7.46N 125.00 E
Maramasike Island [C] 214 Gi 9.30S 161.25 E
Maramba 160 Jj 17.51S 25.52 E
Marampa 166 Cd 8.41N 12.28W
Maranchón 144 Ie 41.03N 2.12W
Maränd 144 Gb 38.26N 45.46 E
Marandellas 172 Ec 18.10S 31.36 E
Marang 150 Cg 5.12N 103.13 E
Maranhão, Rio- [S] 202 If 14.34S 49.02W
Marano, Laguna di- [S] 128 Ge 45.44N 13.10 E
Maranoa River [S] 212 Je 27.50S 148.37 E
Marañón, Rio- [S] 198 If 4.30S 73.35W
Marans 122 Fh 46.18N 1.00W
Marão 126 Ec 41.15N 7.55W
Marão, Serra do- [M] 126 Ec 41.15N 7.55W
Marari 202 Ee 10.55S 69.27W
Märäşeşti 130 Kd 45.53N 27.14 E
Märätea 128 Ji 39.59N 15.43 E
Marau 204 Fi 28.27S 52.12W

Maravari 219a Cb 7.54S 156.44 E
Maräveh Tappeh 146 Pd 37.55N 55.57 E
Maravilha 204 Fh 26.47S 53.09W
Maravillas Creek [S] 186 El 29.34N 102.47W
Maravovo 219aDc 9.17S 159.38 E
Marawah 164 Dc 32.29N 21.25 E
Marawi 150 He 8.13N 124.15 E
Maräwiti 168 Eh 18.29N 31.49 E
Maräwiti [+] 146 Oj 24.18N 53.18 E
Marayes 206 Gd 31.29S 67.20W
Marbella 126 Hh 36.31N 4.53W
Marble Bar 212 Dd 21.11S 119.44 E
Marble Canyon [V] 188 Jh 36.30N 111.50W
Marble Falls 186 Gk 30.34N 98.17W
Marble Hall 172 Dd 24.57S 29.13 E
Marburg 120 Ef 50.49N 8.46 E
Marca, Ponta da- [E] 158 Ij 16.31S 11.42 E
Marcal [S] 120 Kf 47.38N 17.32 E
Marcala 194 Df 14.07N 88.00W
Marçal Daglari [M] 130 Kl 37.09N 28.00 E
Marcali 120 Kf 46.35N 17.25 E
March 118 Ni 52.33N 0.06 E
March [S] 120 Ke 48.10N 16.59 E
Marche 122 Hh 46.10N 1.30 E
Marche = Marches (EN) [2] 128 Hh 43.30N 13.15 E
Marche, Plateau de la- [M] 122 Hh 46.16N 1.30 E
Marche-en-Famenne 124 Ld 50.14N 5.20 E
Marchena 126 Gg 37.20N 5.24W
Marchena, Isla- [C] 202aAa 0.20N 90.30W
Marches (EN) = Marche [2] 128 Hh 43.30N 13.15 E
Marchesato [M] 128 Kk 39.05N 17.00 E
Marchfeld [M] 120 Ke 48.15N 16.40 E
Marcigny 122 Kh 46.16N 4.02 E
Marcilly-sur-Eure 122 Hf 48.49N 1.21 E
Marcinelle, Charleroi- 124 Gd 50.25N 4.28 E
Marck 124 Hd 50.57N 1.57 E
Marcoing 124 Fd 50.07N 3.11 E
Marcos Juárez 206 Hd 32.42S 62.06W
Marcus Baker, Mount- [M] 178 Id 61.26N 147.45W
Marcus Island (EN) = Minami-Tori-Shima [+] 208 Gb 26.32N 142.09 E
Marcy, Mount- [M] 182 Mc 44.07N 73.56W
Mardakjan 130 Qi 40.29N 50.12 E
Mardän 148 Eb 34.09N 71.52 E
Mardarovka 130 Md 47.55N 29.40 E
Mar del Plata 200 Ki 38.01S 57.35W
Marden 124 Cc 51.10N 0.30 E
Mardin 144 Fb 37.18N 40.44 E
Mardin Daglari [M] 146 Jd 37.20N 41.00 E
Maré, Ile- [C] 208 Hg 21.30S 168.00 E
Mare, Muntele- [M] 130 Gc 46.29N 23.14 E
Marecal Cándido Rondon 204 Eg 24.34S 54.04W
Maree, Loch- [S] 118 Fc 57.40N 5.30W
Mareeba 212 Jc 17.00S 145.26 E
Märeg 168 Ih 3.47N 47.18 E
Maremma [M] 128 Fh 42.30N 11.30 E
Marennes 122 Ei 45.49N 1.07W
Marettimo [C] 128 Gm 37.56N 12.05 E
Mareuil-en-Brie 124 Ff 48.57N 3.45 E
Marfa 182 Bb 30.18N 104.01W
Marfil, Laguna- [S] 204 Bb 15.30S 60.20W
Margai Caka [S] 152 Ee 35.10N 86.55 E
Marganec 136 Df 47.38N 34.40 E
Margaret River 212 Df 33.57S 115.04 E
Margarida 204 De 21.41S 56.44W
Margarita, Isla- [C] 204 Fa 11.00N 64.00W
Margarita Belén 204 Em 27.16S 58.58W
Margarition 130 Dj 39.21N 20.26 E
Margate [Eng.-U.K.] 118 Oj 51.24N 1.24 E
Margate [S.Afr.] 172 Ef 30.55S 30.15 E
Margeride, Monts de la- [M] 122 Jj 44.50N 3.25 E
Marghera, Venezia- 128 Fe 45.28N 12.14 E
Margherita di Savoia 128 Ki 41.22N 16.09 E
Margherita Peak [M] 158 Jh 0.22N 29.51 E
Marghine, Catena del- [M] 128 Cj 40.20N 8.50 E
Marghita 130 Fb 47.21N 22.20 E
Marghüb, Küh-e- [M] 146 Qf 33.06N 57.30 E
Margilan 148 Fa 40.28N 71.46 E
Margina 130 Fd 45.51N 22.16 E
Marguerite Bay [C] 224 Qe 68.30S 68.30W
Margut 124 Ld 49.35N 5.16 E
Marha [S] 140 Nc 60.35N 123.10 E
Marha 168 Hc 15.43N 49.09 E
Mari 146 Ee 34.44N 33.18 E
Maria Atoll [Fr.Poly.] [C] 208 Ng 22.00S 136.10W
Maria Atoll [Fr.Poly.] [C] 208 Lg 21.48S 154.41W
Maria Cleofas, Isla- [C] 192 Fg 21.16N 106.14W
Maria Elena 206 Gb 22.21S 69.40W
Mariager 116 Ch 56.39N 10.00 E
Mariager Fjord [C] 116 Dh 56.40N 10.20 E
Maria Ignacia 204 Dm 37.24S 59.30W
Maria Island [Austl.] [C] 212 Kh 42.40S 148.05 E
Maria Island [Austl.] [C] 212 Hb 14.55S 135.40 E
Maria Island [St.Luc.] [C] 197bBb 13.44N 60.56W
Mariakani 170 Gc 3.52S 39.28 E
Maria Laach 124 Dd 50.24N 7.15 E
Maria Madre, Isla- [C] 192 Fg 21.35N 106.33W
Maria Magdalena, Isla- [C] 192 Fg 21.25N 106.25W
Marianao 190 Hb 23.05N 82.26W
Mariana Islands [C] 208 Fb 16.00N 145.30 E
Mariana Trench (EN) [V] 106 Ih 14.00N 147.30 E
Marianna [Fl.-U.S.] 184 Fj 30.47N 85.14W
Marianna [Ar.-U.S.] 116 Cg 34.46N 90.46W
Mariano I. Loza 204 Eh 29.21S 58.12W
Mariánské Lázné 120 Je 49.58N 12.43 E
Marias, Islas- [C] 192 Fg 21.25N 106.28W
Marias Pass [S] 188 Ib 48.19N 113.21W
Maria Theresa Reef [S] 208 Lh 36.58S 151.23W
Mariato, Punta- [E] 190 Hg 7.13N 80.53W
Maria van Diemen, Cape- [E] 218 Ha 34.29S 172.39 E

Mariazell 128 Jc 47.46N 15.19 E
Maribo 116 Dj 54.46N 11.31 E
Maribor 128 Jd 46.33N 15.39 E
Marica 130 Ig 42.02N 25.50 E
Marica [S] 110 Ig 42.00N 26.12 E
Maricao 197aBb 18.10N 66.58W
Maricopa 188 Ij 33.04N 112.03W
Maridi 168 De 4.55N 29.28 E
Marié, Rio- [S] 202 Ed 0.25S 66.26W
Mariehamn/Maarianhamina 114 Ef 60.06N 19.57 E
Mariembourg, Couvin- 124 Gd 50.06N 4.31 E
Marienburg 124 Jd 50.08N 7.08 E
Marienmünster 124 Lc 51.50N 9.13 E
Marienstatt [M] 124 Jd 50.40N 7.49 E
Mariental 160 Ik 24.36S 17.59 E
Mariestad 114 Cg 58.43N 13.51 E
Marietta [Ga.-U.S.] 182 Jd 33.57N 84.33W
Marietta [Oh.-U.S.] 184 Gf 39.26N 81.27W
Mariga [S] 166 Gd 9.36N 5.57 E
Marignac 122 Gl 42.55N 0.39 E
Marignane 122 Lk 43.25N 5.13 E
Marigot [Dom.] 196 Fe 15.32N 61.18W
Marigot [Guad.] 196 Ec 18.04N 63.06W
Marigot [Haiti] 194 Kd 18.14N 72.19W
Marigot [Mart.] 197bAb 14.49N 61.02W
Marigot [St.Luc.] 197bAb 13.58N 61.02W
Mariinsk 138 Dc 56.13N 87.45 E
Mariinski Posad 114 Lh 56.08N 47.48 E
Mariinskoje 138 Jf 51.43N 140.19 E
Marijovo [M] 130 Eh 41.04N 21.45 E
Marijskaja ASSR [3] 136 Ed 56.40N 48.00 E
Marília 206 Jb 22.13S 50.01W
Mariluz 204 Fg 24.02S 53.13W
Marimba 170 Cd 8.25S 18.46 E
Marimbondo, Cachoeira do- 204 Hd 20.18S 49.10W
Marin 126 Db 42.23N 8.42W
Marín, Cul-de-Sac du- 197bBc 14.27N 60.53W
Marina di Catanzaro, Catanzaro- 128 Kl 38.49N 16.36 E
Marina di Gioiosa Ionica 128 Kl 38.18N 16.20 E
Marina di Leuca, Castrignano del Capo- 128 Mk 39.48N 18.21 E
Marina di Pisa 128 Eg 43.40N 10.16 E
Marina di Ravenna 128 Gf 44.29N 12.17 E
Marina Gorka 136 Cc 53.31N 28.12 E
Marinduque [C] 150 Hd 13.24N 121.58 E
Marineland 184 Gk 29.43N 81.12W
Marines 124 Ie 49.09N 1.59 E
Marinette 182 Jb 45.06N 87.38W
Maringá 200 Kh 23.25S 51.55W
Maringa [S] 158 Ih 1.48N 19.48 E
Marinha Grande 126 De 39.45N 8.56W
Marino [It.] 128 Gi 41.46N 12.39 E
Marino [Van.] 219bDc 14.59S 168.03 E
Marins, Pico dos- [M] 204 Jf 22.27S 45.10W
Marinsko 116 Mf 58.46N 28.39 E
Marion [Al.-U.S.] 184 Df 32.32N 87.20W
Marion [Ia.-U.S.] 186 Ke 42.02N 91.36W
Marion [Il.-U.S.] 186 Lh 37.44N 88.56W
Marion [In.-U.S.] 184 Ee 40.33N 85.40W
Marion [Oh.-U.S.] 182 Kc 40.35N 83.08W
Marion [S.C.-U.S.] 184 Hh 34.11N 79.23W
Marion [Va.-U.S.] 184 Gg 36.51N 81.30W
Marion, Lake- [S] 184 Gi 33.30N 80.25W
Marion Reefs [S] 208 Gf 19.10S 152.20 E
Maripa 202 Eb 7.26N 65.09W
Maripasoula 202 Hc 3.39N 54.02W
Mariposa 188 Fh 37.29N 119.58W
Mariquita, Cerro- [M] 192 Jf 23.13N 98.22W
Marisa 150 Mf 0.28N 121.56 E
Mariscal Estigarribia 206 Hb 22.02S 60.38W
Marismas, Puerto de las- [M] 126 Ff 38.02N 6.12W
Maritime [3] 166 Ff 6.30N 1.20 E
Maritsa [S] 130 Ig 41.44N 26.18 E
Mariupol 112 Jf 47.06N 37.33 E
Mariusa, Caño- [S] 196 Fh 9.43N 61.24W
Mariusa, Isla- [C] 196 Fh 9.39N 61.19W
Marivan 146 Lf 35.31N 46.10 E
Marj 146 Ee 34.39N 40.53 E
Marjamaa/Märjamaa 116 Kf 58.54N 24.21 E
Märjamaa/Marjamaa 116 Kf 58.54N 24.21 E
Marjanovka [R.S.F.S.R.] 138 Ce 54.58N 72.38 E
Marjanovka [Ukr.-U.S.S.R.] 120 Uf 53.03N 24.55 E
Mark [S] 124 Jc 51.39N 4.39 E
Mark [Ger.] 124 Jc 51.33N 7.36 E
Mark [Swe.] 116 Eg 57.35N 12.35 E
Marka 168 Hf 1.43N 44.46 E
Markako, ozero- [S] 136 Lf 48.45N 85.50 E
Markala 166 Dc 13.39N 6.05W
Markam (Gartog) 152 Gf 29.32N 98.33 E
Markaryd 116 Fh 56.26N 13.36 E
Markazi [3] 146 Nf 34.00N 49.30 E
Marken [C] 124 Ic 52.27N 5.05 E
Markermeer [S] 124 Ib 52.31N 5.15 E
Market Deeping 124 Bb 52.40N 0.18W
Market Harborough 124 Bb 52.29N 0.55W
Markham, Mount- [M] 222 Jf 82.51S 161.21 E
Markham Bay [C] 180 Kd 63.30N 71.40W
Markham River [S] 214 Eh 6.45S 146.45 E
Marki 120 Rb 52.20N 21.07 E
Markit 152 Cd 38.53N 77.35 E
Markounda 168 Bd 7.38N 17.00 E
Markovac 130 Ee 44.14N 21.06 E
Markovka 136 Fe 49.31N 39.32 E
Markovo 138 Lb 64.40N 170.25 E
Markoye 166 Fc 14.39N 0.02 E
Marksburg [M] 124 Jd 50.16N 7.40 E
Marksville 186 Jk 31.08N 92.04W

Marktoberdorf 120 Gi 47.47N 10.37 E
Marktredwitz 120 If 50.00N 12.05 E
Markulešty 130 Lb 47.51N 28.07 E
Marl 120 Ce 51.39N 7.05 E
Marlagne [S] 124 Gd 50.33N 4.54 E
Marlborough [2] 218 Ed 41.50S 173.40 E
Marlborough [Austl.] 212 Jd 22.49S 149.53 E
Marlborough [Guy.] 196 Gi 7.29N 58.38W
Marle 122 Je 49.44N 3.46 E
Marlin 186 Hk 31.18N 96.53W
Marlinton 184 Gf 38.14N 80.06W
Marlow [Eng.-U.K.] 124 Bc 51.34N 0.46W
Marlow [Ok.-U.S.] 186 Hi 34.39N 97.57W
Marmande 122 Gj 44.30N 0.10 E
Marmara 146 Bb 40.35N 27.33 E
Marmara, Sea of- (EN) = Marmara Denizi [S] 110 Ig 40.40N 28.15 E
Marmara Adasi [C] 146 Bb 40.36N 27.37 E
Marmara Denizi = Marmara, Sea of- (EN) [S] 110 Ig 40.40N 28.15 E
Marmara Ereglisi 130 Ki 40.58N 27.57 E
Marmaris 130 Lk 36.37N 28.02 E
Marmarica (EN) = Barqah al Bahriyah [S] 158 Je 31.40N 24.30 E
Marmelos, Rio dos- [S] 202 Fe 6.08S 61.47W
Marmion Lake [S] 186 Kb 48.54N 91.30W
Marmolada [M] 128 Fd 46.26N 11.51 E
Marmora 184 Ic 44.29N 77.41W
Marmore, Cascata delle- [S] 128 Gh 42.35N 12.45 E
Marne 120 Dc 53.57N 9.00 E
Marne [3] 122 Kf 48.55N 4.10 E
Marne [S] 110 Gf 48.49N 2.24 E
Marne à la Saône, Canal de la- = 122 Kf 48.44N 4.36 E
Marne au Rhin, Canal de la- [S] 122 Nf 48.35N 7.47 E
Märnes 114 Dc 67.09N 14.06 E
Marneuli 132 Ni 41.29N 44.45 E
Maro 168 Bd 8.25N 18.46 E
Maro [S] 168 Bd 8.23N 18.38 E
Maroa 202 Ec 2.43N 67.33W
Maroantsetra 160 Lj 15.27S 49.44 E
Marokau Atoll [C] 216 Mc 18.02S 142.17W
Marolambo 172 Hd 20.04S 48.08 E
Maromandia 172 Hb 14.11S 48.06 E
Maromme 122 He 49.28N 1.02 E
Maromokotro [M] 172 Hb 14.01N 48.58 E
Maroni, Fleuve- [S] 198 Ke 5.45N 53.58W
Marónia 130 Ii 40.55N 25.31 E
Maroochydore 212 Ke 26.39S 153.06 E
Maro Reef [S] 208 Jb 25.25N 170.35W
Maros [S] 150 Lg 5.00S 119.34 E
Maros 150 Lg 5.00S 119.34 E
Marovoay 172 Hc 16.06S 46.37 E
Marowijne River [S] 202 Hb 5.45N 53.58W
Marqädah 146 Ke 35.44N 40.46 E
Marquard 172 De 28.54S 27.28 E
Marquenterre [M] 124 Dd 50.20N 1.41 E
Marquesas Islands (EN) = Marquises, Iles- [C] 208 Ne 9.00S 139.30W
Marquette 182 Jb 46.33N 87.24W
Marquion 124 Fd 50.13N 3.05 E
Marquis [Gren.] 197bBb 12.06N 61.37W
Marquis [St.Luc.] 197bBb 14.02N 60.55W
Marquis, Cape- [E] 197bBa 14.03N 60.54W
Marquises, Iles- = Marquesas Islands (EN) [C] 208 Ne 9.00S 139.30W
Marra, Jabal- [M] 158 Jf 13.04N 24.21 E
Marrak [E] 164 Hf 16.26N 41.54 E
Marrakech 158 Fc 31.38N 8.00W
Marrakech [3] 162 Fc 32.00N 8.00W
Marrawah 212 Ih 40.56S 144.41 E
Marree 210 Gf 29.15S 52.20 E
Marreh, Küh-e- [M] 146 Oh 29.15N 52.20 E
Marresalskije Koški, ostrova- [C] 134 Mb 69.44N 66.59 E
Marromeu 172 Fc 18.17S 35.56 E
Marrupa 172 Fb 13.12S 37.30 E
Marsá al 'Alam 164 Ff 25.05N 34.54 E
Marsá al Burayqah 164 Cc 30.25N 19.35 E
Marsá Ben Mehidi 126 Ki 35.05N 2.11W
Marsabit 168 Ge 2.20N 37.59 E
Marsala 128 Gm 37.48N 12.26 E
Marsá Matrüh 164 Ec 31.21N 27.14 E
Marsá Sha'b 168 Gb 22.52N 35.47 E
Marsá Umm Ghayj 146 Fj 25.38N 34.30 E
Marsberg 124 Kc 51.27N 8.51 E
Marsciano 128 Gh 42.54N 12.20 E
Marseille = Marseilles (EN) 112 Gg 43.18N 5.23 E
Marseille-en-Beauvaisis 122 Ie 49.35N 1.58 E
Marseilles (EN) = Marseille 112 Gg 43.18N 5.23 E
Marshall [Ak.-U.S.] 178 Fd 61.52N 162.03W
Marshall [Il.-U.S.] 186 Mg 39.23N 87.42W
Marshall [Lbr.] 166 Cd 6.09N 10.23W
Marshall [Mn.-U.S.] 186 Hd 44.27N 95.47W
Marshall [Mo.-U.S.] 186 Jg 39.07N 93.12W
Marshall [Tx.-U.S.] 186 Ij 32.33N 94.23W
Marshall Islands [5] 208 Hc 10.00N 165.00 E
Marshall River [S] 212 Gd 22.59S 136.59 E
Marshalltown 182 Ic 42.03N 92.55W
Marshfield 186 Kd 44.40N 90.10W
Marsh Harbour 190 Ic 26.33N 77.03W
Märshinän, Küh-e- [M] 146 Of 32.53N 52.02 E
Marsh Island [C] 186 Kl 29.35N 91.53W

Index Symbols

[1] Independent Nation	Historical or Cultural Region	Pass, Gap	Depression
[2] State, Region	Mount, Mountain	Plain, Lowland	Polder
[3] District, County	Volcano	Delta	Desert, Dunes
[4] Municipality	Hill	Salt Flat	Forest, Woods
[5] Colony, Dependency	Mountains, Mountain Range	Valley, Canyon	Heath, Steppe
Continent	Hills, Escarpment	Crater, Cave	Oasis
Physical Region	Plateau, Upland	Karst Features	Cape, Point

Coast, Beach	Rock, Reef	Waterfall, Rapids	Canal
Cliff	Islands, Archipelago	River Mouth, Estuary	Glacier
Peninsula	Rocks, Reefs	Lake	Ice Shelf, Pack Ice
Sandbank	Coral Reef	Salt Lake	Ocean
Island	Well, Spring	Intermittent Lake	Sea
Islands, Archipelago	Geyser	Reservoir	Gulf, Bay
Atoll	River, Stream	Swamp, Pond	Strait, Fjord

Lagoon	Escarpment, Sea Scarp	Historic Site	Airport
Bank	Fracture	Ruins	Port
Seamount	Trench, Abyss	Wall, Walls	Military Installation
Tablemount	National Park, Reserve	Church, Abbey	Lighthouse
Ridge	Point of Interest	Temple	Mine
Shelf	Recreation Site	Scientific Station	Tunnel
Basin	Cave, Cavern	Railway station	Dam, Br

Marsica	128	Hi	41.55N	13.35 E
Marsico Nuovo	128	Jj	40.25N	15.44 E
Marsjaty	134	Jf	60.05N	60.29 E
Marsland	186	Ee	42.29N	103.16W
Mars-la-Tour	124	He	49.06N	5.54 E
Marson	124	Gf	48.55N	4.32 E
Märsta	116	Ge	59.37N	17.51 E
Marstal	116	Dj	54.51N	10.31 E
Marstrand	116	Dg	57.53N	11.35 E
Marta	128	Fh	42.14N	11.42 E
Martaban	148	Je	16.32N	97.37 E
Martaban, Gulf of- (EN)	140	Lh	16.30N	97.00 E
Martap	166	Hd	6.54N	13.03 E
Martapura [Indon.]	150	Dg	4.19S	104.22 E
Martapura [Indon.]	150	Fg	3.25S	114.51 E
Martelange/Martelingen	124	He	49.50N	5.44 E
Martelingen/Martelange	124	He	49.50N	5.44 E
Martés, Sierra de-	126	Le	39.20N	0.57W
Martha's Vineyard	182	Mc	41.25N	70.40W
Martigny	128	Bd	46.06N	7.05 E
Martigues	122	Lk	43.24N	5.03 E
Martil	126	Gi	35.37N	5.17W
Martim Vaz, Ilhas-	198	Nh	20.30S	28.51W
Martín	126	Lc	41.18N	0.19W
Martin [Czech.]	120	Og	49.04N	18.55 E
Martin [S.D.-U.S.]	182	Gc	43.10N	101.44W
Martin [Tn.-U.S.]	184	Cg	36.21N	88.51W
Martina Franca	128	Lj	40.42N	17.20 E
Martinez de Hoz	204	Bl	35.19S	61.37W
Martínez de la Torre	192	Kg	20.04N	97.03W
Martín García, Isla-	204	Cl	34.11S	58.15W
Martin Hills	222	Pg	82.04S	88.01W
Martinho Campos	204	Jd	19.20S	45.13W
Martinique [5]	176	Mh	14.40N	61.00W
Martinique	174	Mh	14.40N	61.00W
Martinique, Canal de la-= Martinique Passage (EN)	190	Le	15.10N	61.20W
Martinique Passage	196	Fe	15.10N	61.20W
Martinique Passage (EN)= Martinique, Canal de la-	190	Le	15.10N	61.20W
Martin Lake	184	Ei	32.50N	85.55W
Martin Peninsula	222	Of	74.25S	114.10W
Martinsburg	184	If	39.28N	77.59W
Martins Ferry	184	Ge	40.07N	80.45W
Martinsville [In.-U.S.]	184	Df	39.26N	86.25W
Martinsville [Va.-U.S.]	182	Ld	36.43N	79.53W
Marton	218	Fd	40.05S	175.23 E
Martos	126	Ig	37.43N	3.58W
Martre, Lac la-	180	Fd	63.20N	118.00W
Martuk	136	Fe	50.47N	56.31 E
Martuni	132	Ni	40.06N	45.18 E
Maru	166	Gc	12.21N	6.24 E
Marud	148	Ee	18.19N	72.58 E
Marudi	150	Ff	4.11N	114.19 E
Marudu, Teluk-	150	Ge	6.45N	116.55 E
Marugame	156	Cd	34.18N	133.47 E
Maruko	156	Fc	36.19N	138.15 E
Mārūn	146	Mg	31.02N	49.36 E
Marungu, Monts-	158	Ji	7.42S	30.00 E
Maruoka	156	Ec	36.09N	136.16 E
Maruseppu	156a	Ca	44.01N	143.19 E
Marutea Atoll [Fr.Poly.]	208	Ng	21.30S	135.34W
Marutea Atoll [Fr.Poly.]	208	Mf	17.00S	143.10W
Maruyama-Gawa	156	Dd	35.40N	134.50 E
Marvão	126	Ee	39.24N	7.23W
Marvast	146	Pg	30.30N	54.15 E
Marvast, Kavīr-e-	146	Pg	30.20N	54.25 E
Mårvatn	116	Cd	60.10N	8.15 E
Marv-Dasht	144	Hd	29.50N	52.40 E
Marvejols	122	Jj	44.33N	3.17 E
Marvine, Mount-	188	Jg	38.40N	111.39W
Marx	132	Od	51.42N	46.46 E
Mary	142	If	37.36N	61.50 E
Maryborough [Austl.]	210	Gg	25.32S	152.42 E
Maryborough [Austl.]	212	Ig	37.03S	143.45 E
Marydale	172	Ce	29.23S	22.05 E
Maryjskaja oblast [3]	136	Gh	37.15N	62.30 E
Maryland [2]	182	Ld	39.00N	76.45W
Maryland [3]	166	De	4.45N	8.00W
Maryport	118	Jg	54.43N	3.30W
Mary River	212	Gb	12.53S	131.38 E
Marysville [Ca.-U.S.]	188	Eg	39.09N	121.35W
Marysville [Ks.-U.S.]	186	Hg	39.51N	96.39W
Marysville [N.B.-Can.]	184	Nc	45.59N	66.35W
Marysville [Oh.-U.S.]	184	Fe	40.13N	83.22W
Marysville [Wa.-U.S.]	188	Db	48.03N	122.11W
Maryville [Mo.-U.S.]	182	Ic	40.21N	94.52W
Maryville [Tn.-U.S.]	184	Fh	35.46N	83.58W
Marzūq	160	If	25.55N	13.55 E
Marzūq, Ḩamādat-	164	Bd	26.00N	12.30 E
Marzūq, Ṣaḩrā'-	158	If	24.30N	13.00 E
Masachapa	194	Dh	11.47N	86.31W
Masāhīm, Kūh-e-	146	Pg	30.21N	55.20 E
Masai Steppe	158	Ki	4.45S	37.00 E
Masaka	170	Fc	0.20S	31.44 E
Masākin	162	Jb	35.44N	10.35 E
Masalembo, Kepulauan-	150	Fh	5.30S	114.26 E
Masally	136	Eh	39.01N	48.40 E
Masalog, Puntan-	220b	Ba	15.01N	145.41 E
Masamba	150	Hg	2.33S	120.20 E
Masan	152	Md	35.11N	128.24 E
Masasi	160	Kj	10.43S	38.48 E
Masaya	190	Gf	11.58N	86.06W
Masaya [3]	194	Dh	12.00N	86.10W
Masbate	150	Hd	12.10N	123.35 E
Masbate	140	Oh	12.15N	123.30 E
Mascara	162	Hb	35.24N	0.08 E
Mascara [3]	162	Hb	35.30N	0.15 E
Mascareignes, Iles-/ Mascarene Islands	158	Mk	21.00S	57.00 E
Mascarene Basin (EN)	106	Fk	15.00S	56.00 E
Mascarene Islands/ Mascareignes, Iles-	158	Mk	21.00S	57.00 E
Mascarene Plateau (EN)	106	Gk	10.00S	60.00 E
Mascota	192	Gg	20.32N	104.49W
Mas-d'Azil, Le-	122	Hk	43.05N	1.22 E
Masee, Island-/Oileán Mhic Aodha	118	Hg	54.50N	5.50W
Masela, Pulau-	150	Ih	8.09S	129.50 E
Maseru	160	Jk	29.28S	27.29 E
Maşfūţ	146	Qk	24.48N	56.06 E
Mashābih	146	Gj	25.37N	36.32 E
Mashan	154	Kb	45.12N	130.32 E
Mashava	172	Ed	20.02S	30.29 E
Mashhad	142	Hf	36.18N	59.36 E
Mashike	154	Pc	43.51N	141.31 E
Mashiki	156	Be	32.47N	130.50 E
Mashīz	146	Qh	29.56N	56.37 E
Mashkel	144	Jd	28.02N	63.25 E
Mashonaland North [3]	172	Ec	17.00S	31.00 E
Mashonaland South [3]	172	Ec	18.00S	31.00 E
Mashra' ar Raqq	168	Dd	8.25N	29.16 E
Mashū-Ko	156a	Db	43.35N	144.30 E
Masiaca	192	Ed	26.45N	109.18W
Masīlah, Wādī al-	140	Hh	15.10N	51.08 E
Masi-Manimba	170	Cc	4.46S	17.55 E
Masindi	170	Fb	1.42N	31.43 E
Maşīrah, Jazīrat-	140	Hg	20.29N	58.33 E
Maşīrah, Khalīj-	140	Hg	20.15N	57.40 E
Masisi	170	Ec	1.24S	28.49 E
Masjed-Soleymān	144	Gc	31.58N	49.18 E
Mask, Lough-/Loch Measca	118	Dh	53.35N	9.20W
Maskanah	146	Hd	36.01N	38.05 E
Maskelynes, Iles-	219b	Cc	16.32S	167.49 E
Maşloc	130	Ed	46.00N	21.27 E
Maslovare	128	Lf	44.34N	17.33 E
Masoala, Cap-	158	Mj	15.59S	50.13 E
Masoala, Presqu'île de-	172	Ic	15.40S	50.12 E
Mason	186	Gk	30.45N	99.14W
Mason Bay	218	Bg	46.55S	167.45 E
Mason City	176	Je	43.09N	93.12W
Masovia (EN)= Mazowsze	110	Ie	52.40N	20.20 E
Masparro, Río-	194	Mi	8.04N	69.26W
Masqaţ=Muscat (EN)	142	Hg	23.29N	58.33 E
Massa	128	Ef	44.01N	10.09 E
Massachusetts [2]	182	Mc	42.15N	71.50W
Massachusetts Bay	184	Ld	42.20N	70.50W
Massaciuccoli, Lago di-	128	Eg	43.50N	10.20 E
Massafra	128	Lj	40.35N	17.07 E
Massaguet	168	Bc	12.28N	15.26 E
Massakori	168	Bc	13.00N	15.44 E
Massa Marittima	128	Eg	43.03N	10.53 E
Massangano	170	Bd	9.37S	14.17 E
Massangena	172	Ed	21.32S	32 57 E
Massapê	202	Jd	3.31S	40.19W
Massawa (EN)=Mitsiwa	160	Kg	15.37N	39.39 E
Massena	182	Mc	44.56N	74.57W
Massénya	168	Bc	11.24N	16.10 E
Masset	180	Ef	54.02N	132.09W
Masseube	122	Gk	43.26N	0.35 E
Massey Sound	180	Ia	78.00N	94.00W
Massiac	122	Ji	45.15N	3.13 E
Massiaru	116	Kg	57.52N	24.27 E
Massillon	184	Ge	40.48N	81.32W
Massinga	172	Fd	23.20S	35.22 E
Masson Island	222	Ge	66.08S	96.34 E
Massuma	170	De	14.05S	22.00 E
Mastābah	164	Ge	20.49N	39.26 E
Maštaga	132	Pi	40.32N	49.59 E
Masterton	216	Eh	40.57S	175.39 E
Mastūrah	164	Ge	23.06N	38.50 E
Masuda	152	Ne	34.40N	131.51 E
Māsūleh	146	Md	37.10N	48.59 E
Masurai, Gunung-	150	Dg	2.30S	101.51 E
Masuria (EN)	110	Ie	53.50N	21.30 E
Masurian Lakes (EN)	110	Ie	53.45N	21.45 E
Masvingo	160	Kk	20.05S	30.50 E
Masvingo [3]	172	Ed	21.00S	31.00 E
Maşyāf	146	Ge	35.03N	36.21 E
Maszewo	120	Lc	53.29N	15.02 E
Mataabé, Cap-	219b	Cb	15.38S	166.46 E
Matabeleland North [3]	172	Dc	19.00S	27.30 E
Matabeleland South [3]	172	Dd	21.00S	29.30 E
Matachel	126	Ff	38.50N	6.17W
Matachewan	180	Jg	47.56N	80.39W
Matacu	204	Bc	17.21S	61.28W
Matadi	160	Ii	5.49S	13.27 E
Matador	186	Fi	34.01N	100.49W
Matagalpa	176	Kh	12.53N	85.57W
Matagalpa [3]	194	Eg	13.00N	85.30W
Matagami	180	Jg	49.45N	77.35W
Matagami, Lac-	184	Ia	49.54N	77.32W
Mata Gassile	168	Ge	2.30N	42.16 E
Matagorda Bay	186	Hl	28.35N	96.20W
Matagorda Island	182	Hf	28.15N	96.30W
Matagorda Peninsula	186	Hl	28.32N	96.07W
Mataiea	221e	Fc	17.46S	149.25W
Mataiva Atoll	208	Mf	14.53S	148.40W
Mataj	136	Hf	45.51N	78.43 E
Matak, Pulau-	150	Ef	3.18N	106.16 E
Matakana Island	218	Kb	37.35S	176.05 E
Matala	170	Ce	14.43S	15.02 E
Matalaa, Pointe-	220h	Bc	13.20S	176.08W
Matale	148	Gg	7.28N	80.37 E
Mataliele	172	Df	30.24S	28.43 E
Matam	166	Cb	15.40N	13.15W
Matamey	166	Gc	13.26N	8.28 E
Matamoros [Mex.]	176	Jg	25.53N	97.30W
Matamoros [Mex.]	190	Dc	25.32N	103.15W
Matana, Danau-	150	Hg	2.28S	121.20 E
Ma'ṭan as Sarra	164	De	21.41N	21.52 E
Matancita	192	De	25.09N	111.59W
Matane	180	Kg	48.51N	67.32W
Matankari	166	Fc	13.46N	4.01 E
Matanza	204	Cl	34.33S	58.35W
Matanzas	176	Kg	23.03N	81.35W
Matanzas [3]	194	Gb	22.40N	81.10W
Matão	204	He	21.35S	48.22W
Matapalo, Cabo-	194	Fi	8.23N	83.19W
Matapan, Cape- (EN)= Tainaron, Ákra-	110	Ih	36.23N	22.29 E
Matape, Río-	192	Dc	28.17N	110.41W
Mata Point	220k	Bb	19.07S	169.50W
Matara	148	Gg	5.56N	80.33 E
Matara	168	Fc	14.35N	39.28 E
Mataram	142	Nj	8.35S	116.07 E
Mataranka	212	Gb	14.56S	133.07 E
Mataró	126	Oc	41.32N	2.27 E
Matarraña/Matarranya	126	Mc	41.14N	0.22 E
Matarranya/Matarraña	126	Mc	41.14N	0.22 E
Mataso	219b	Dc	17.15S	168.25 E
Matatula, Cape-	221c	Cb	14.15S	170.34W
Mataura	218	Cg	46.12S	168.52 E
Mataura	218	Cg	46.34S	168.44 E
Mata-Utu	210	Jf	13.17S	176.08W
Mata-Utu, Baie de-	220h	Bb	13.19S	176.07W
Matavai	216	Gb	13.28S	172.35W
Matavera	220p	Cb	21.13S	159.44W
Mataverj	221d	Ab	27.10S	109.27W
Matawai	218	Gc	38.21S	177.32 E
Matawin, Réservoir-	184	Kb	46.45N	73.50W
Matawin, Rivière-	184	Kb	46.55N	72.55W
Maţāy	146	Dh	28.25N	30.46 E
Maţbakhayn	164	Hf	17.29N	41.48 E
Matca	130	Kd	45.51N	27.32 E
Matehuala	190	Dd	23.39N	100.39W
Matemo, Ilha-	172	Gb	12.13S	40.36 E
Matera	128	Kj	40.40N	16.36 E
Matese	128	Ii	41.25N	14.20 E
Mátészalka	120	Si	47.57N	22.20 E
Matfors	114	De	62.21N	17.02 E
Matha	122	Fi	45.52N	0.19W
Mathematicians Seamounts (EN)	190	Be	15.30N	111.00W
Matheson	184	Ga	48.32N	80.28W
Mathis	186	Hl	28.06N	97.50W
Mathrákion	130	Cj	39.46N	19.31 E
Mathura	148	Fc	27.30N	77.41 E
Mati	150	Ie	6.57N	126.13 E
Mati	130	Ch	41.39N	19.34 E
Matias Cardoso	204	Kb	14.52S	43.56W
Matías Romero	190	Ee	16.53N	95.02W
Maticora, Río-	194	Lh	11.01N	71.09W
Matina	194	Fh	10.05N	83.17W
Matinha	202	Id	3.06S	45.02W
Māţir	162	Ib	37.03N	9.40 E
Matiyure, Río-	196	Ci	7.36N	67.39W
Matkaselkja	116	Nc	61.57N	30.33 E
Mātmāţah	162	Ic	33.33N	9.58 E
Matnog	150	Hd	12.35N	124.05 E
Mato, Cerro-	196	Di	7.15N	65.14W
Mato, Río-	196	Di	7.09N	65.07W
Matočkin Šar, proliv-	136	Fa	73.30N	54.55 E
Mato Grosso [2]	202	Gf	14.00S	56.00W
Mato Grosso [Braz.]	204	Dd	18.18S	57.20W
Mato Grosso [Braz.]	200	Kg	15.00S	59.57W
Mato Grosso, Planalto do- = Mato Grosso, Plateau of- (EN)	198	Kg	15.30S	56.00W
Mato Grosso, Plateau of- (EN) = Mato Grosso, Planalto do-	198	Kg	15.30S	56.00W
Mato Grosso do Sul [2]	202	Hg	20.00S	55.00W
Matos Costa	204	Gh	26.27S	51.09W
Matosinhos	126	Dc	41.11N	8.42W
Matou	154	Cj	29.50N	115.32 E
Matou → Qiuxian	154	Cf	36.50N	115.10 E
Mátra	110	If	47.53N	19.57 E
Maţrah	144	Ie	23.29N	58.31 E
Matrei in Osttirol	128	Gc	47.00N	12.32 E
Matsiatra	172	Hd	21.25S	45.33 E
Matsudo	154	Og	35.48N	139.55 E
Matsue	152	Nd	35.28N	133.04 E
Matsukawa [Jap.]	156	Ed	35.36N	137.53 E
Matsukawa [Jap.]	156	Gc	37.40N	140.28 E
Matsu Liehtao	152	Kf	26.05N	119.56 E
Matsumae	156a	Bc	41.26N	140.07 E
Matsumae-Hantō	156a	Bc	41.40N	140.15 E
Matsumoto	152	Od	36.14N	137.58 E
Matsunaga, Fukuyama-	156	Cd	34.27N	133.16 E
Matsuo	156	Gb	39.58N	141.02 E
Matsu-Ōminato	156a	Bc	41.16N	141.09 E
Matsusaka	154	Ng	34.34N	136.32 E
Matsushima	156	Gb	38.22N	141.04 E
Matsutō	156	Ec	36.31N	136.33 E
Matsuura	156	Ae	33.22N	129.42 E
Matsuyama	142	Pf	33.50N	132.45 E
Matsuzaki	156	Fd	34.44N	138.45 E
Mattagami Lake	184	Gb	47.57N	81.35W
Mattagami River	180	Jf	50.43N	81.30W
Mattawa	180	Jg	46.19N	78.42W
Matterhorn [Eur.]	128	Be	45.58N	7.39 E
Matterhorn [Nv.-U.S.]	188	Hf	41.49N	115.23W
Matthew, Ile-	208	Ig	22.20S	171.20 E
Matthews Ridge	202	Fb	7.30N	60.10W
Matthew Town	190	Jd	20.57N	73.40W
Maţţī, Sabkhat-	168	Ia	23.30N	52.00 E
Mattighofen	128	Hb	48.06N	13.09 E
Mattoon	186	Lg	39.29N	88.22W
Matua, ostrov-	138	Kg	48.00N	153.10 E
Matucana	202	Cf	11.51S	76.24W
Matuku Island	216	Ec	19.10S	179.46 E
Matundu	170	Db	4.21N	23.40 E
Matundu	170	Gd	8.50S	39.30 E
Maturín	200	Je	9.45N	63.11W
Matvejev Kurgan	132	Kf	47.34N	38.55 E
Maúa	172	Fb	13.52S	37.09 E
Maubeuge	122	Jd	50.17N	3.58 E
Ma-ubin	148	Je	16.44N	95.39 E
Maudheimvidda	222	Bf	74.00S	8.00W
Maud Seamount (EN)	222	Ce	65.00S	2.35 E
Maués	202	Gd	3.24S	57.42W
Maués, Rio-	202	Gd	3.22S	57.44W
Mau Escarpment	170	Gc	0.40S	36.02 E
Mauges, Les-	122	Fg	47.10N	1.00W
Maug Islands	208	Fb	20.01N	145.13 E
Maui Island	208	Lb	20.45N	156.20W
Mauke Island	208	Lg	20.09S	157.23W
Mau Kyun	148	Jf	12.45N	98.20 E
Mauldre	124	Df	48.59N	1.49 E
Maule [2]	206	Fe	35.45S	72.15W
Mauléon	122	Fh	46.55N	0.45W
Mauléon-Licharre	122	Fk	43.14N	0.53W
Maullín	206	Ff	41.38S	73.37W
Maumee	184	Fe	41.34N	83.39W
Maumere	150	Hh	8.37S	122.14 E
Maun	160	Jj	19.58S	23.26 E
Maun	128	If	44.26N	14.55 E
Mauna Kea	208	Lc	19.50N	155.28W
Maunaloa	221a	Db	21.08N	157.13W
Mauna Loa	221a	Fd	19.28N	155.36W
Maunath	148	Gc	25.40N	82.38 E
Maunawili	221a	Db	21.21N	157.47W
Maunga Roa	220p	Bb	21.13S	159.48W
Maungdaw	148	Id	20.49N	92.22 E
Maunoir, Lac -	180	Fc	67.30N	125.00W
Maupihaa Atoll (Mopelia, Atoll-)	208	Lf	16.50S	153.55W
Maupin	188	Ed	45.11N	121.05W
Maupiti, Ile-	208	Lf	16.27S	152.15W
Maurepas, Lake-	186	Kk	30.15N	90.30W
Maures, Massif des-	122	Mk	43.16N	6.23 E
Mauriac	122	Ii	45.13N	2.20 E
Maurice, Lake-	212	Ge	29.30S	131.00 E
Maurienne	122	Mi	45.13N	6.30 E
Mauritania (EN)= Mūrītāniyā [1]	160	Fg	20.00N	12.00W
Mauriti	202	Ke	7.23S	38.46W
Mauritius [1]	160	Mj	18.00S	57.40 E
Mauritius	158	Mk	20.17S	57.33 E
Mauron	122	Df	48.05N	2.18W
Maurs	122	Ij	44.43N	2.12 E
Mauston	186	Ke	43.48N	90.05W
Mauthausen	128	Ib	48.14N	14.31 E
Mauzé-sur-le-Mignon	122	Fh	46.12N	0.40W
Mavinga	170	Df	15.47S	20.24 E
Mavita	172	Ec	19.32S	33.09 E
Mavrovoúni [Grc.]	130	Fj	39.37N	22.47 E
Mavrovoúni [Grc.]	130	Gh	41.07N	23.08 E
Mawchi	148	Je	18.49N	97.09 E
Mawei	152	Kf	26.02N	119.30 E
Mawlaik	148	Id	23.38N	94.25 E
Mawlamyine	142	Le	16.30N	97.38 E
Mawqaq	146	Ii	27.25N	41.08 E
Mawson	222	Fe	67.36S	62.53 E
Mawson Coast	222	Fe	67.40S	63.30 E
Mawson Escarpment	222	Ff	73.05S	68.10 E
Maxcanú	190	Fd	20.35N	90.01W
Maxixe	172	Fd	23.51S	35.21 E
Maxwell Bay	180	Ib	74.32N	89.00W
May, Isle of-	118	Ke	56.10N	2.30W
Maya, Pulau-	150	Eg	1.10S	109.35 E
Mayaguana Island	190	Jd	22.23N	72.57W
Mayaguana Passage	194	Kb	22.32N	73.15W
Mayagüez	190	Ke	18.12N	67.09W
Mayahi	166	Gc	13.58N	7.40 E
Mayama	170	Bc	3.51S	14.54 E
Mayāmey	146	Pd	36.24N	55.42 E
Maya Mountains	190	Ge	16.40N	88.50W
Mayapán	190	Gd	20.38N	89.27W
Mayarí	194	Jc	20.40N	75.41W
Maybell	186	Bf	40.31N	108.05W
Maychew	168	Fc	12.46N	39.34 E
Mayḑ	168	Hc	10.57N	47.06 E
Maydān	146	Ke	34.55N	45.37 E
Maydena	212	Jh	42.55S	146.30 E
Maydī	144	Ff	16.18N	42.48 E
Mayen	120	Df	50.20N	7.13 E
Mayenne	122	Ff	48.18N	0.37W
Mayenne [3]	122	Ff	48.05N	0.40W
Mayenne	122	Fg	47.30N	0.32W
Mayfa'ah	168	Hc	14.16N	47.35 E
Mayfield	184	Cg	36.44N	88.38W
May Glacier	222	Ie	67.00S	130.00 E
Mayi He	154	Jb	45.52N	128.46 E
Maymyo	148	Jd	22.02N	96.28 E
Maynas	202	Dd	3.00S	75.00W
Mayo	176	Fc	63.35N	135.54W
Mayo/Muigheo [2]	118	Dh	53.50N	9.30W
Mayo, Mountains of-	118	Dg	54.05N	9.30W
Mayo, Río-	192	Ed	26.45N	109.47W
Mayo Darlé	166	Hd	6.30N	11.55 E
Mayo-Kébbi [3]	168	Bd	10.00N	15.30 E
Mayo-Kébbi	168	Ad	9.18N	13.33 E
Mayoko	170	Bc	2.18S	12.49 E
Mayon, Mount-	140	Oh	13.15N	123.41 E
Mayor, Puig-/Major, Puig-	126	Oe	39.48N	2.48 E
Mayor Island	218	Gb	37.15S	176.15 E
Mayor Pablo Lagerenza	206	Ha	19.58S	60.45W
Mayotte [5]	160	Lj	12.50S	45.10 E
Mayotte/Mahoré	158	Lj	12.50S	45.10 E
May Pen	190	Ie	17.58N	77.14W
Mayraira Point	150	Hc	18.39N	120.51 E
Mayran, Laguna de-	192	He	25.45N	102.45W
Mayreau Island	197n	Bb	12.39N	61.23W
May-sur-Orne	124	Be	49.06N	0.22W
Maysville	184	Ff	38.39N	83.46W
Mayumba [Gabon]	160	Ii	3.25S	10.39 E
Mayumba [Zaire]	170	Ed	7.16S	27.03 E
Mayum La	152	De	30.35N	82.27 E
Mayville	184	Hd	42.15N	79.32W
Mayyit, Al Baḩr al-=Dead Sea (EN)	140	Ff	31.30N	35.30 E
Mazabuka	170	Ef	15.51S	27.46 E
Mazagão	202	Hd	0.07S	51.17W
Mazamet	122	Ik	43.30N	2.24 E
Māzandarān [3]	144	Hb	36.00N	54.00 E
Māzandarān, Daryā-ye-= Caspian Sea (EN)	110	Lg	42.00N	50.30 E
Mazar	152	Cd	36.27N	77.03 E
Mazara del Vallo	128	Gm	37.39N	12.35 E
Mazār-e Sharīf	142	If	36.42N	67.06 E
Mazarrón, Golfo de-	126	Kg	37.30N	1.18W
Mazartag	152	Dd	38.29N	80.50 E
Mazaruni River	202	Gb	6.25N	58.38W
Mazatenango	190	Ff	14.32N	91.30W
Mazatlán	176	Ig	23.13N	106.25W
Mažeikiai/Mažejkjaj	114	Fh	56.20N	22.22 E
Mažejkjaj/Mažeikiai	114	Fh	56.20N	22.22 E
Mazḩafah, Jabal-	146	Fh	28.48N	34.57 E
Maẕhūr, 'Irq al-	146	Ji	27.25N	43.55 E
Mazinga	197c	Ab	17.29N	62.58W
Mazirbe	116	Jg	57.40N	22.10 E
Mazoe	172	Ec	17.30S	30.58 E
Mazoe	158	Kj	16.32S	33.25 E
Mazomeno	170	Ec	4.55S	27.13 E
Mazong Shan	152	Gc	41.33N	97.10 E
Mazowsze	120	Qd	52.40N	20.20 E
Mazowsze=Masovia (EN)	110	Ie	52.40N	20.20 E
Mazsalaca	116	Kg	57.45N	24.59 E
Mazunga	172	Dd	21.44S	29.52 E
Mazurskie, Pojezierze-	120	Qc	53.40N	21.00 E
Mazzarino	128	Im	37.18N	14.13 E
Mba	219d	Ab	17.32S	177.42 E
Mbabane	160	Kk	26.18S	31.07 E
Mbabo, Tchabal-	166	Hd	7.16N	12.09 E
Mbacké	166	Bc	14.48N	15.55W
Mbaéré	168	Be	3.47N	17.31 E
Mbaïki	160	Ih	3.53N	18.00 E
Mbakaou	166	Hd	6.19N	12.49 E
Mbakaou, Barrage de-	166	Hd	6.25N	13.00 E
Mbala	160	Ki	8.50S	31.22 E
Mbalam	166	He	2.13N	13.49 E
Mbale	160	Kh	1.05N	34.10 E
Mbali	168	Be	4.27N	18.20 E
Mbalmayo	166	He	3.31N	11.30 E
Mbam	158	Ih	4.24N	11.17 E
Mbamba Bay	170	Fe	11.17S	34.46 E
Mbandaka	160	Ih	0.04N	18.16 E
Mbanga	166	Ge	4.30N	9.34 E
Mbanika	219a	Dc	9.05S	159.12 E
M'banza Congo	170	Bd	6.16S	14.15 E
Mbanza-Ngungu	160	Ii	5.35S	14.47 E
Mbarangandu	170	Gd	8.57S	37.24 E
Mbarara	170	Fc	0.36S	30.38 E
Mbari	168	Ce	4.34N	22.43 E
Mbatiki	219d	Bb	17.46S	179.08 E
Mbava	219a	Cb	7.49S	156.37 E
Mbé	166	Hd	7.51N	13.36 E
Mbengga	219d	Bc	18.23S	178.08 E
Mbengwi	166	Hd	6.01N	10.00 E
Mbéré	168	Bd	9.07N	16.26 E
Mbeya	160	Ki	8.54S	33.27 E
Mbeya [3]	170	Fd	8.00S	33.30 E
Mbi	168	Be	4.28N	18.07 E
Mbigou	170	Bc	1.53S	11.56 E
Mbinda	160	Ii	2.07S	12.52 E
Mbinga	170	Ge	10.56S	35.01 E
Mbingué	166	Dc	10.00N	5.54W
Mbini	166	Ge	1.34N	9.37 E
Mbini [3]	166	He	1.30N	10.00 E
Mbini	158	Ih	1.30N	10.30 E
Mbini	166	He	1.40N	9.45 E
Mboki	168	Dd	5.19N	25.58 E
Mbokonimbeti	219a	Ec	8.57S	160.05 E
Mbomo	170	Bb	0.24N	14.44 E
Mbomou=Bomu (EN) [3]	168	Cd	5.30N	23.30 E
Mbomou=Bomu (EN)	158	Jh	4.08N	22.26 E
Mborokua	219a	Dc	9.02S	158.44 E
Mbour	166	Bc	14.24N	16.58W
Mbout	162	Ef	16.01N	12.35W
Mbozi	170	Fd	9.02S	32.56 E
Mbrés	168	Bd	6.40N	19.48 E
M'Bridge	170	Bd	7.14S	12.52 E
Mbua	219d	Bb	16.48S	178.37 E
Mbuji-Mayi	160	Ji	6.09S	23.33 E
Mbulo	219a	Dc	8.46S	158.21 E
Mbulu	170	Gc	3.51S	35.32 E
Mburucuyá	204	Ci	28.03S	58.14W
Mbutha	219d	Bb	16.39S	179.51 E
Mbuyuni	170	Gd	7.23S	36.32 E
Mbwemburu	170	Gd	9.29S	39.39 E
Mcensk	136	De	53.17N	36.32 E
M'Chedallah	126	Qh	36.22N	4.16 E
Mcherrah	162	Gd	27.00N	4.30W
Mchinga	170	Gd	9.44S	39.42 E
Mchinji	170	Fe	13.48S	32.54 E
Mdandu	170	Fd	9.09S	34.42 E
M'Daourouch	128	Bn	36.05N	7.49 E
Mdennah	162	Gd	25.00N	4.50W
Mdiq	126	Gi	35.41N	5.19W
Mead	184	Fa	49.29N	83.50W
Mead, Lake-	182	Ed	36.05N	114.25W
Meade	186	Fh	37.17N	100.20W
Meade	178	Hb	70.50N	156.25W
Meade Peak	188	Je	42.30N	111.15W
Meadow Lake	180	Gf	54.07N	108.20W
Meadville	184	Ge	41.38N	80.10W
Me-akan-Dake	156a	Cb	43.23N	143.59 E
Mealhada	126	Dd	40.22N	8.27W
Mealy Mountains	180	Lf	53.20N	59.30W
Meama	221b	Ba	19.45S	174.34W
Méan, Havelange-	124	Hd	50.22N	5.20 E
Meander Reef	150	Ge	8.09N	119.14 E
Meander River	180	Fe	59.02N	117.42W
Meanguera, Isla-	194	Dg	13.12N	87.43W
Mearim, Rio-	198	Lf	3.04S	44.35W
Meath/An Mhí [2]	118	Gh	53.35N	6.40W
Meaux	122	If	48.57N	2.52 E
Mecca (EN)=Makkah	142	Fg	21.27N	39.49 E
Mechara	168	Gd	8.34N	40.28 E
Mechelen/Maasmechelen	124	Hd	50.57N	5.40 E
Mechelen/Malines	122	Kc	51.02N	4.29 E
Mecheraa-Asfa	126	Ni	35.24N	1.03 E
Mecheria	162	Gc	33.33N	0.17W
Mechernich	124	Id	50.36N	6.39 E
Mechongué	204	Cn	38.09S	58.13W
Mecidiye	130	Ji	40.38N	26.32 E
Mecitözü	146	Fb	40.31N	35.19 E
Mecklemburgischer Höhenrücken	120	Ic	53.40N	12.10 E
Mecklenburg	120	Hc	53.30N	12.00 E
Mecklenburger Bucht	120	Hb	54.20N	11.40 E
Mecklenburger Schweiz	120	Ic	53.45N	12.35 E

Index Symbols

[1] Independent Nation
[2] State, Region
[3] District, County
[4] Municipality
[5] Colony, Dependency
Continent
Physical Region

Historical or Cultural Region
Mount, Mountain
Volcano
Hill
Mountains, Mountain Range
Hills, Escarpment
Plateau, Upland

Pass, Gap
Plain, Lowland
Delta
Salt Flat
Valley, Canyon
Crater, Cave
Karst Features

Depression
Polder
Desert, Dunes
Forest, Woods
Heath, Steppe
Oasis
Cape, Point

Coast, Beach
Cliff
Peninsula
Isthmus
Sandbank
Island
Atoll

Rock, Reef
Islands, Archipelago
Rocks, Reefs
Coral Reef
Well, Spring
Geyser
River, Stream

Waterfall, Rapids
River Mouth, Estuary
Lake
Salt Lake
Intermittent Lake
Reservoir
Swamp, Pond

Canal
Glacier
Ice Shelf, Pack Ice
Ocean
Sea
Gulf, Bay
Strait, Fjord

Lagoon
Bank
Seamount
Tablemount
Ridge
Shelf
Basin

Escarpment, Sea Scarp
Fracture
Trench, Abyss
National Park, Reserve
Point of Interest
Recreation Site
Cave, Cavern

Historic Site
Ruins
Wall, Walls
Church, Abbey
Temple
Scientific Station
Railway station

Airport
Port
Military installation
Lighthouse
Mine
Tunnel
Dam, Bridge

Index Symbols

[1] Independent Nation
[2] State, Region
[3] District, County
[4] Municipality
[5] Colony, Dependency
Continent
Physical Region

Historical or Cultural Region
Mount, Mountain
Volcano
Hill
Mountains, Mountain Range
Hills, Escarpment
Plateau, Upland

Pass, Gap
Plain, Lowland
Delta
Salt Flat
Valley, Canyon
Crater, Cave
Karst Features

Depression
Polder
Desert, Dunes
Forest, Woods
Heath, Steppe
Cape, Point

Coast, Beach
Cliff
Peninsula
Isthmus
Sandbank
Island
Atoll

Rock, Reef
Islands, Archipelago
Rocks, Reefs
Coral Reef
Well, Spring
Geyser
River, Stream

Waterfall, Rapids
River Mouth, Estuary
Lake
Salt Lake
Intermittent Lake
Sea
Gulf, Bay
Strait, Fjord

Canal
Glacier
Ice Shelf, Pack Ice
Ocean
Tablemount
Ridge
Shelf
Basin

Lagoon
Bank
Fracture
Seamount
Trench, Abyss
National Park, Reserve
Point of Interest
Recreation Site
Cave, Cavern

Escarpment, Sea Scarp
Ruins
Wall, Walls
Church, Abbey
Temple
Scientific Station
Railway station

Historic Site
Airport
Port
Military ins...
Lighthouse
Mine
Tunnel
Dam, Brid...

Mezcalapa, Río-	192	Mh	18.36N	92.39W
Mezdra	130	Gf	43.09N	23.42 E
Meždurečenski	136	Gd	59.36N	65.53 E
Meždušarski, ostrov-	136	Fa	71.20N	53.00 E
Mèze	122	Jk	43.25N	3.36 E
Mezen	112	Kb	65.50N	44.13 E
Mezen	110	Kb	66.00N	43.59 E
Mézenc, Mont-	122	Kj	44.55N	4.11 E
Meženin	120	Sc	53.07N	22.29 E
Mezenskaja guba	110	Kb	66.40N	43.45 E
Mezenskaja Pižma	114	Ld	64.30N	48.32 E
Mežgorje	120	Th	48.30N	23.37 E
Mežica	128	Id	46.31N	14.52 E
Mézidon-Canon	124	Be	49.05N	0.04W
Mézin	122	Gj	44.03N	0.16 E
Mezőberény	120	Rj	46.49N	21.02 E
Mezőcsát	120	Qi	47.49N	20.55 E
Mezőföld	120	Oj	46.55N	18.35 E
Mezőkovácsháza	120	Qj	46.24N	20.55 E
Mezőkövesd	120	Qi	47.49N	20.35 E
Mezőtúr	120	Qi	47.00N	20.38 E
Mežozerny	134	Ii	54.10N	59.25 E
Mežpjanje	114	Ki	55.25N	45.00 E
Mezquital	192	Gf	23.29N	104.23W
Mezquital, Río-	192	Gf	22.55N	104.54W
Mezquitic	192	Hf	22.23N	103.41W
Mgači	138	Jf	51.02N	142.18 E
Mglin	132	Hc	53.04N	32.53 E
Mhow	148	Fd	22.33N	75.46 E
Miahuatlán de Porfirio Díaz	192	Ki	16.20N	96.36W
Miajadas	126	Ge	39.09N	5.54W
Miaméré	168	Bd	9.02N	19.55 E
Miami [Az.-U.S.]	188	Jj	33.24N	110.52W
Miami [Fl.-U.S.]	176	Kg	25.46N	80.12W
Miami [Ok.-U.S.]	182	Id	36.53N	94.53W
Miami Beach	182	Kf	25.47N	80.08W
Miānābād	146	Qd	37.02N	57.27 E
Miāndowāb	144	Gb	36.58N	46.06 E
Miandrivazo	172	Hc	19.30S	45.28 E
Miānduhe	152	Lb	49.12N	121.09 E
Miāneh	144	Gb	37.26N	47.42 E
Miang, Khao-	148	Ke	17.42N	101.01 E
Miangas, Pulau-	150	Ie	5.35N	126.35 E
Mianning	152	Hf	28.31N	102.10 E
Miānwāli	148	Eb	32.35N	71.33 E
Mianyang	152	Ie	31.23N	104.49 E
Mianyang (Xiantaozhen)	154	Bi	30.22N	113.27 E
Miaodao Qundao	152	Ld	38.10N	120.45 E
Miao'er Shan	152	Jf	25.50N	110.22 E
Miao Ling	152	If	26.05N	108.00 E
Miarinarivo	172	Hc	18.56S	46.54 E
Miass	136	Gd	55.01N	60.06 E
Miass	136	Gd	56.06N	64.30 E
Miasskoje	134	Ji	55.15N	61.55 E
Miasteczko Krajeńskie	120	Nc	53.06N	17.01 E
Miastko	120	Mb	54.01N	17.00 E
Michael, Mount-	212	Ja	6.25S	145.20 E
Michajlova Island	222	Ge	66.30S	85.00 E
Michalovce	120	Rh	48.46N	21.55 E
Michelstadt	124	Le	49.41N	9.01 E
Miches	194	Md	18.59N	69.03W
Michigan [2]	182	Jc	44.00N	85.00W
Michigan, Lake-	174	Ke	44.00N	87.00W
Michigan City	182	Jc	41.43N	86.54W
Michipicoten Bay	184	Eb	47.55N	84.56W
Michipicoten Island	180	Ig	47.45N	85.45W
Michoacán [2]	190	De	19.10N	101.50W
Michów	120	Se	51.32N	22.19 E
Mico, Río-	194	Eg	12.11N	84.16W
Micoud	197k	Bb	13.50N	60.54W
Micronesia	208	Gc	11.00N	159.00 E
Micronesia,Federated States of- [5]	210	Gd	6.30N	152.00 E
Mičurin	130	Kg	42.10N	27.51 E
Mičurinsk	112	Ke	52.54N	40.31 E
Midai, Pulau-	150	Ef	3.00N	107.47 E
Midar	162	Gc	34.57N	3.32W
Mid-Atlantic Ridge (EN)	106	Di	0.00	20.00W
Middelburg [Neth.]	122	Jc	51.30N	3.37 E
Middelburg [S.Afr.]	172	Cf	31.30S	25.00 E
Middelburg [S.Afr.]	172	De	25.47S	29.28 E
Middelfart	114	Bi	55.30N	9.45 E
Middelharnis	124	Gc	51.45N	4.12 E
Middelkerke	124	Ec	51.11N	2.49 E
Middelkerke-Westende	124	Ec	51.10N	2.46 E
Middle Alkali Lake	188	Ef	41.28N	120.04W
Middle America Trench (EN)	106	Mh	15.00N	95.00W
Middle Andaman	148	If	12.30N	92.50 E
Middle Atlas (EN)=Moyen Atlas	158	Ge	33.30N	4.30W
Middlebury	184	Kc	44.01N	73.10W
Middle Caicos	194	Lc	21.47N	71.43W
Middle Fork Feather River	188	Eg	38.47N	121.36W
Middle Island	172b	Ab	9.22S	46.21 E
Middle Loup River	186	Gf	41.17N	98.23W
Middlemarch	218	Df	45.30S	170.07 E
Middle Reef	219a	Ee	12.35S	160.30 E
Middlesboro	182	Kd	36.36N	83.43W
Middlesbrough	112	Fe	54.35N	1.14W
Middlesex	194	Ce	17.02N	88.31W
Middlesex	124	Bc	51.35N	0.10W
Middlesex	118	Mj	51.30N	0.05W
Middleton	178	Je	59.25N	146.25W
Middleton Reef	208	Gg	29.30S	159.10 E
Middletown [Ct.-U.S.]	184	Ke	41.33N	72.39W
Middletown [N.Y.-U.S.]	184	Je	41.26N	74.26W
Middletown [Oh.-U.S.]	184	Ef	39.31N	84.25W
Midelt	162	Gc	32.41N	4.45W
Mid Glamorgan [3]	118	Jj	51.35N	3.35W
Midhordland	116	Ad	60.15N	5.55 E
Midhurst	124	Bd	50.59N	0.44W
Midi, Canal du-	110	Gg	43.36N	1.25 E
Midi de Bigorre, Pic du-	122	Gl	42.56N	0.08 E
Midi d'Ossau, Pic du-	122	Fl	42.51N	0.26W
Mid-Indian Basin (EN)	106	Gj	10.00S	80.00 E
Mid-Indian Ridge (EN)	106	Gj	3.00S	75.00 E
Midland [Mi.-U.S.]	184	Ed	43.37N	84.14W
Midland [Ont.-Can.]	180	Jh	44.45N	79.53W
Midland [S.D.-U.S.]	186	Fd	44.04N	101.10W
Midland [Tx.-U.S.]	182	Ge	32.00N	102.05W
Midlands [3]	172	Dc	19.00S	30.00 E
Midlands	118	Li	52.40N	1.50W
Midleton/Mainistir na Corann	118	Ej	51.55N	8.10W
Midnapore → Medinīpur	148	Hd	22.26N	87.20 E
Midongy du Sud	172	Hd	23.34S	47.01 E
Midou	122	Fk	43.54N	0.30W
Midouze	122	Fk	43.48N	0.51W
Mid-Pacific Mountains (EN)	106	Jg	20.00N	170.00 E
Midway Islands [5]	210	Jb	28.13N	177.22W
Midway Islands	208	Jb	28.13N	177.22W
Midwest	188	Le	43.25N	106.16W
Midwest City	186	Hi	35.27N	97.24W
Midyat	146	Id	37.25N	41.23 E
Midžor	110	Ig	43.24N	22.40 E
Miechów	120	Qf	50.23N	20.01 E
Miedwie, Jezioro-	120	Kc	53.15N	14.55 E
Międzychód	120	Ld	52.36N	15.53 E
Międzylesie	120	Mf	50.10N	16.40 E
Międzyrzec Podlaski	120	Se	52.00N	22.47 E
Międzyrzecz	120	Ld	52.27N	15.34 E
Międzyrzecze Łomżyńskie	120	Rd	52.45N	21.45 E
Miehikkälä	116	Ld	60.40N	27.42 E
Mie Ken [2]	154	Ng	34.35N	136.25 E
Miekojärvi	114	Fc	66.36N	24.23 E
Miélan	122	Gk	43.26N	0.19 E
Mielec	120	Rf	50.18N	21.25 E
Mielno	120	Mb	54.16N	16.01 E
Mien	116	Fh	56.25N	14.50 E
Mier	192	Jd	26.26N	99.09W
Miercurea Ciuc	130	Ic	46.21N	25.48 E
Mieres	126	Ga	43.15N	5.46W
Miersig	130	Ec	46.53N	21.51 E
Mier y Noriega	192	If	23.25N	100.07W
Miesbach	120	Hi	47.47N	11.50 E
Mieso	168	Gd	9.15N	40.45 E
Mifune	156	Be	32.43N	130.48 E
Migang Shan	152	Id	35.32N	106.13 E
Miguel Alamán, Presa-	192	Kh	18.13N	96.32W
Miguel Auza	192	He	24.18N	103.25W
Miguel Hidalgo, Presa-	192	Ed	26.40N	108.45W
Miha Chakaja	136	Eg	42.17N	42.02 E
Mihăilesti	130	Ie	44.20N	25.54 E
Mihail Kogălniceanu	130	Le	44.22N	28.27 E
Mihajlov	136	De	54.16N	39.03 E
Mihajlovgrad	130	Gf	43.25N	23.13 E
Mihajlovgrad [2]	130	Gf	43.25N	23.13 E
Mihajlovka [Kaz.-U.S.S.R.]	135	Hc	43.01N	71.31 E
Mihajlovka [R.S.F.S.R.]	136	Ee	50.05N	43.15 E
Mihajlovsk	134	Ih	56.29N	59.07 E
Mihalıççık	146	Dc	39.52N	31.30 E
Mihara	156	Cd	34.24N	133.05 E
Mihara-Yama	156	Fd	34.43N	139.23 E
Mi He	154	Ef	37.12N	119.10 E
Mihonoseki	156	Cd	35.34N	133.18 E
Miho-Wan	156	Cd	35.30N	133.20 E
Miiraku	156	Ae	32.45N	128.40 E
Mijaly	132	Re	48.54N	53.50 E
Mijares/Millars	126	Le	39.55N	0.01W
Mijdaḥah	168	Hc	14.00N	48.26 E
Mijdrecht	124	Gb	52.12N	4.52 E
Mijirtein (EN)=Majērtēn	158	Lh	9.00N	50.00 E
Mikasa	154	Pc	43.20N	141.40 E
Mikata	156	Dd	35.34N	135.54 E
Miki	156	Dd	34.17N	134.07 E
Mikinai = Mycenae (EN)	130	Fl	37.43N	22.45 E
Mikindani	170	Ge	10.17S	40.07 E
Mikkeli [2]	114	Ge	62.00N	27.30 E
Mikkeli/Sankt Michel	112	Ic	61.41N	27.15 E
Mikomoto-Jima	156	Fd	34.34N	138.56 E
Mikonos	130	Il	37.27N	25.20 E
Mikonos	130	Il	37.27N	25.23 E
Mikonou, Stenón-	130	Il	37.30N	25.20 E
Mikrá Préspa, Límni-	130	Ei	40.45N	21.06 E
Mikre	130	Hf	43.02N	24.31 E
Mikró Sofráno	130	Jm	36.05N	26.24 E
Mikulkin, mys-	134	Cc	67.48N	46.40 E
Mikulov	120	Mh	48.49N	16.39 E
Mikumi	170	Gd	7.24S	36.59 E
Mikun	136	Fc	62.21N	50.05 E
Mikuni	156	Ec	36.13N	136.09 E
Mikuni-Sanmyaku	154	Of	36.15N	138.40 E
Mikuni-Tōge	156	Fc	36.46N	138.50 E
Mikuni-Yama	156	Dd	35.21N	134.01 E
Mikura-Jima	156	Oe	33.50N	139.35 E
Milaca	186	Jd	45.45N	93.39W
Miladummadulu Atoll	148a	Ba	6.15N	73.15 E
Milagro	202	Cd	2.07S	79.36W
Milājerd	146	Me	34.37N	49.12 E
Milan [Mo.-U.S.]	186	Jf	40.12N	93.07W
Milan [Tn.-U.S.]	184	Ch	35.55N	88.46W
Milan (EN) = Milano	112	Gf	45.28N	9.12 E
Milange	172	Fc	16.05S	35.47 E
Milano = Milan (EN)	112	Gf	45.28N	9.12 E
Milâs	146	Bd	37.19N	27.47 E
Milazzo	128	Jl	38.13N	15.14 E
Milazzo, Capo di-	128	Jl	38.16N	15.14 E
Milazzo, Golfo di-	128	Jl	38.15N	15.20 E
Milbank	182	Hb	45.13N	96.38W
Mildenhall	124	Cb	52.21N	0.31 E
Mildura	210	Fh	34.12S	142.09 E
Mile	152	Hg	24.28N	103.26 E
Mile	168	Gc	11.08N	40.55 E
Miléai	130	Gj	39.20N	23.09 E
Miles	210	Gg	26.40S	150.11 E
Miles City	182	Fb	46.25N	105.51W
Milet = Miletus (EN)	130	Kl	37.30N	27.16 E
Miletus (EN) = Milet	130	Kl	37.30N	27.16 E
Milevec	130	Fg	42.34N	22.27 E
Milevsko	120	Kg	49.27N	14.22 E
Milford	188	Ig	38.24N	113.01W
Milford Haven	118	Hj	51.44N	5.02W
Milford Lake	186	Hg	39.15N	97.00W
Milford Sound	216	Ch	44.40S	167.55 E
Milford Sound	218	Bf	44.35S	167.50 E
Milgis	170	Gb	1.48N	38.06 E
Milḥ, Baḥr al-	144	Fc	32.40N	43.35 E
Milḥ, Ra's al-	164	Ec	31.55N	25.02 E
Miliana	126	Oh	36.17N	2.14 E
Mili Atoll	208	Id	6.08N	171.55 E
Milicz	120	Ne	51.32N	17.17 E
Milkovo	138	Kf	54.43N	158.43 E
Milk River	188	Ib	49.09N	112.05W
Milk River	182	Eb	49.09N	112.05W
Milkūh	144	Jc	32.45N	61.55 E
Mill	180	Jd	63.57N	78.00W
Millars/Mijares	126	Le	39.55N	0.01W
Millau	122	Jj	44.06N	3.05 E
Milledgeville	184	Fi	33.04N	83.14W
Mille Lacs, Lac des-	180	Ig	48.50N	90.30W
Mille Lacs Lake	182	Ib	46.15N	93.40W
Millen	184	Gi	32.48N	81.57W
Miller [Nb.-U.S.]	186	Gf	40.57N	99.26W
Miller [S.D.-U.S.]	186	Gd	44.31N	98.59W
Millerovo	136	Ef	48.52N	40.25 E
Miller Seamount (EN)	178	Kf	53.30N	144.20W
Millerton	218	Dd	41.38S	171.52 E
Millevaches, Plateau de-	122	Ii	45.45N	2.11 E
Millicent	212	Ig	37.36S	140.22 E
Millington	184	Ch	35.20N	89.54W
Millinocket	184	Mc	45.39N	68.43W
Mill Island	222	He	65.30S	100.40 E
Millmerran	212	Ke	27.52S	151.16 E
Mills Lake	180	Fd	61.28N	118.15W
Millstatt	128	Hd	46.48N	13.35 E
Millville	184	Jf	39.24N	75.02W
Millwood Lake	186	Jj	33.45N	94.00W
Milne Land	179	Jd	71.20N	27.30W
Milo	158	Gg	11.04N	9.14W
Milolii	221a	Fd	19.11N	155.55W
Milos	130	Hm	36.45N	24.26 E
Milos = Milos (EN)	130	Hm	36.41N	24.25 E
Milos (EN) = Milos	130	Hm	36.41N	24.25 E
Milparinka	212	Ie	29.44S	141.53 E
Miltenberg	120	Fg	49.42N	9.15 E
Milton [Fl.-U.S.]	184	Dj	30.38N	87.03W
Milton [N.Z.]	218	Cg	46.07S	169.58 E
Milton-Freewater	188	Fd	45.56N	118.23W
Milton Keynes	118	Mi	52.03N	0.42W
Miltou	168	Bc	10.14N	17.26 E
Milumbe, Monts-	170	Ed	8.00S	27.30 E
Miluo	154	Bj	28.51N	113.05 E
Miluo Jiang	152	Jf	28.51N	112.59 E
Milwaukee	176	Ke	43.02N	87.55W
Milwaukee Depth (EN)	106	Bh	19.30N	67.45W
Milwaukee Seamounts (EN)	208	Ia	32.28N	171.55 E
Milwaukie	188	Dd	45.27N	122.38W
Mimi-Gawa	156	Be	32.20N	131.37 E
Mimizan	122	Ej	44.12N	1.14W
Mimoń	120	Kf	50.40N	14.44 E
Mimongo	170	Bc	1.38S	11.39 E
Mimoso	204	Hb	15.10S	48.05W
Min	152	Kf	26.05N	119.32 E
Mina	126	Mi	35.58N	0.31 E
Mina [Mex.]	192	Id	26.01N	100.32W
Mina [Nv.-U.S.]	188	Fg	38.24N	118.07W
Mina, Cerro-	194	Ki	8.21N	73.10W
Mīnā' Abd Allāh	146	Mh	29.01N	48.10 E
Mīnā' al Aḥmadī	146	Mh	29.04N	48.09 E
Mīnāb	146	Qi	27.09N	57.05 E
Mīnāb	146	Qi	27.01N	56.53 E
Mīnā' Barānis	164	Ge	23.55N	35.28 E
Minahassa = Minahassa Peninsula (EN)	140	Oi	1.00N	124.35 E
Minahassa Peninsula (EN) = Minahassa	140	Oi	1.00N	124.35 E
Minakuchi	156	Ed	34.59N	136.11 E
Minamata	154	Kh	32.13N	130.24 E
Minami-Daitō-Jima	152	Nf	25.50N	131.15 E
Minami-furano	156a	Cb	43.10N	142.32 E
Minami-Iō-Jima	214	Cc	24.14N	141.28 E
Minami-kayabe	156a	Bc	41.53N	141.01 E
Minami-Tori-Shima = Marcus Island (EN)	208	Gb	26.32N	142.09 E
Minas [Cuba]	194	Ic	21.29N	77.37W
Minas [Indon.]	150	Df	0.50N	101.29 E
Minas [Ur.]	200	Ki	34.23S	55.14W
Minas de Riotinto	126	Fg	37.42N	6.35W
Minas Gerais [2]	202	Jg	18.00S	44.30W
Minā' Su'ūd	146	Mh	28.44N	48.24 E
Minatitlán [Mex.]	190	Fe	17.59N	94.31W
Minatitlán [Mex.]	192	Gh	19.22N	104.04W
Minaya	126	Je	39.17N	2.19W
Minbu	148	Id	20.11N	94.53 E
Minbya	148	Id	20.22N	93.16 E
Minchinmávida, Volcán-	206	Ff	42.49S	72.28W
Mincio	128	Ee	45.04N	10.59 E
Mindanao	140	Oi	8.00N	125.00 E
Mindanao Sea	140	Oi	9.15N	123.40 E
Mindel	120	Gh	48.31N	10.23 E
Mindelheim	120	Gh	48.03N	10.29 E
Mindelo	160	Eg	16.53N	25.00W
Minden [Ger.]	120	Ed	52.17N	8.55 E
Minden [La.-U.S.]	186	Jj	32.37N	93.17W
Minden [Nb.-U.S.]	186	Gf	40.30N	98.57W
Mindif	166	Hc	10.24N	14.26 E
Mindoro	140	Oh	12.50N	121.05 E
Mindoro Strait	150	Hd	12.20N	120.40 E
Minduli	170	Bc	4.17S	14.21 E
Mindszent	120	Qj	46.32N	20.12 E
Mine	156	Bd	34.12N	131.11 E
Minehead	118	Jj	51.13N	3.29W
Mine Head	118	Fj	52.00N	7.35W
Mineiros	202	Hg	17.34S	52.34W
Mineral del Monte	192	Jg	20.08N	98.40W
Mineral'nyje Vody	136	Eg	44.12N	43.08 E
Mineral Wells	182	He	32.48N	98.07W
Minerva Reefs	208	Jg	23.50S	179.00W
Minervino Murge	128	Ki	41.05N	16.05 E
Minervois	122	Ik	43.25N	2.45 E
Minfeng/Niya	152	Dd	37.04N	82.46 E
Minga	170	Ee	11.08S	27.56 E
Mingala	168	Cd	5.06N	21.49 E
Mingan	180	Lf	50.18N	64.01W
Mingečaur	132	Oi	40.46N	47.02 E
Mingečaurskoje vodohranilišče	132	Oi	40.55N	46.45 E
Mingenew	212	De	29.11S	115.26 E
Minggang	154	Ch	32.27N	114.02 E
Mingguang → Jiashan	154	Dh	32.47N	118.00 E
Ming He	154	Cf	37.14N	114.47 E
Minglanilla	126	Ke	39.32N	1.36W
Mingoyo	170	Ge	10.06S	39.38 E
Mingshui	152	Mb	47.15N	125.53 E
Mingshui → Zhangqiu	154	Df	36.44N	117.33 E
Mingteke	152	Bd	37.09N	74.58 E
Mingteke Daban	152	Bd	37.00N	74.50 E
Minguez, Puerto-	126	Ld	40.50N	0.59W
Mingulay	118	Fe	56.50N	7.40W
Mingyuegou	154	Jc	43.08N	128.55 E
Minhe	152	Hd	36.20N	102.50 E
Minho	126	Dc	41.40N	8.30W
Minho	126	Dc	41.52N	8.51W
Minicoy Island	140	Ji	8.17N	73.02 E
Minigwal, Lake-	212	Ee	29.35S	123.10 E
Minija	116	Ii	55.20N	21.12 E
Minilya	212	Cd	23.51S	113.58 E
Minilya River	212	Cd	23.56S	113.51 E
Minipi Lake	180	Lf	52.28N	60.50W
Ministra, Sierra-	126	Jc	41.07N	2.30W
Minjar	134	Hi	55.04N	57.33 E
Min Jiang	140	Mg	28.46N	104.38 E
Minmaya	154	Pd	41.10N	140.28 E
Minna	160	Hh	9.37N	6.33 E
Minna Bluff	222	Kf	78.32S	166.30 E
Minneapolis [Ks.-U.S.]	186	Hg	39.08N	97.42W
Minneapolis [Mn.-U.S.]	176	Je	44.59N	93.13W
Minnedosa	180	Hf	50.14N	99.51W
Minnedosa River	186	Fb	49.53N	100.08W
Minnesota [2]	182	Ib	46.00N	94.15W
Minnesota River	182	Ic	44.54N	93.10W
Mino	156	Ed	35.32N	136.54 E
Miño	110	Fg	41.52N	8.51W
Minobu	156	Fd	35.22N	138.24 E
Minobu-Sanchi	156	Fd	35.15N	138.20 E
Minokamo	156	Ed	35.26N	137.00 E
Mino-Mikawa-Kōgen	156	Ed	35.10N	137.25 E
Minorca (EN) = Menorca	110	Gg	40.00N	4.00 E
Minot	176	Ie	48.14N	101.18W
Minqin	152	Hd	38.42N	103.11 E
Minqing	152	Kf	26.15N	118.52 E
Minquan	154	Cg	34.39N	115.08 E
Minquiers, les-	118	Km	48.58N	2.08W
Min Shan	152	He	33.35N	103.00 E
Minsk	112	Ie	53.54N	27.34 E
Minskaja oblast [3]	136	Ce	53.50N	27.40 E
Minskaja vozvyšennost	116	Lj	54.00N	27.10 E
Mińsk Mazowiecki	120	Rd	52.11N	21.34 E
Minta	166	He	4.35N	12.48 E
Minto, Lac-	180	Ke	57.15N	74.50W
Minto, Mount-	222	Kf	71.47S	168.45 E
Minto Inlet	180	Fb	71.19N	117.00W
Minto Reef	208	Gd	8.08N	154.17 E
Minturn	186	Cg	39.35N	106.26W
Minūdasht	146	Pd	37.10N	55.25 E
Minuf	146	Dg	30.28N	30.56 E
Minusinsk	138	Ef	53.43N	91.48 E
Minvoul	170	Bb	2.09N	12.08 E
Minwakh	168	Hb	16.48N	48.06 E
Minxian	152	He	34.26N	104.02 E
Miory	114	Gi	55.39N	27.41 E
Mios Num	150	Kg	1.30S	135.10 E
Miquan	152	Ec	44.05N	87.33 E
Miquelon	180	Jg	49.00N	76.00W
Miquelon	174	Ne	47.03N	56.20W
Mira	126	Dg	37.43N	8.47W
Mira [It.]	128	Ge	45.26N	12.08 E
Mira [Port.]	126	Dd	40.26N	8.44W
Mira, Peña-	126	Fc	41.55N	6.28W
Mīrābād	144	Jc	30.25N	61.50 E
Mirabela	204	Jc	16.15S	44.11W
Miracatu	204	Ig	24.17S	47.28W
Miracema	202	Jh	21.25S	42.11W
Mirador, Serra do-	204	Hh	26.45S	49.50W
Miraflores [Col.]	202	Dc	1.30N	72.16W
Miraflores [Col.]	202	Db	5.12N	73.12W
Mīrah, Wādī al-	146	If	32.26N	41.42 E
Miraj	148	Ee	16.50N	74.38 E
Miramar	206	Ie	38.16S	57.51W
Miramar, Laguna-	192	Ni	16.20N	91.20W
Miramas	122	Lk	43.35N	5.00 E
Mirambeau	122	Fi	45.22N	0.34W
Miramichi Bay	180	Kg	47.07N	65.10W
Miramont-de-Guyenne	122	Gj	44.36N	0.22 E
Miran	152	Ed	39.15N	88.50 E
Miranda [2]	202	Ea	10.15N	66.25W
Miranda [Arg.]	204	Cm	36.32S	59.09W
Miranda [Braz.]	202	Gh	20.14S	56.22W
Miranda de Corvo	126	Dd	40.06N	8.20W
Miranda de Ebro	126	Jb	42.41N	2.57W
Miranda do Douro	126	Fc	41.30N	6.16W
Mirande	122	Gk	43.31N	0.25 E
Mirandela	126	Ec	41.29N	7.11W
Mirandola	128	Ff	44.53N	11.04 E
Mirandópolis	204	Ge	21.09S	51.06W
Mirante do Paranapanema	204	Gf	22.17S	51.54W
Mira Por Vos	194	Jb	22.04N	74.38W
Mirapuxi, Rio-	204	Ga	13.06S	51.10W
Mirassol	204	He	20.46S	49.28W
Miravalles	126	Fb	42.45N	6.53W
Miravalles, Volcán-	174	Kh	10.45N	85.10W
Miravete, Puerto de-	126	Ge	39.43N	5.43W
Mir-Bašir	132	Oi	40.19N	46.58 E
Mirbāṭ	144	Hf	16.58N	54.50 E
Mirdita	130	Ch	41.49N	19.56 E
Mirebalais	194	Kd	18.50N	72.06W
Mirebeau	122	Gh	46.47N	0.11 E
Mirecourt	122	Mf	48.18N	6.08 E
Mirepoix	122	Hk	43.05N	1.53 E
Mirgorod	136	Df	50.00N	33.40 E
Miri	142	Ni	4.23N	113.59 E
Miria	166	Gc	13.43N	9.07 E
Mirim, Lagoa-	198	Ki	32.45S	52.50W
Mirina	130	Ij	39.52N	25.04 E
Miriñay, Esteros del-	204	Di	28.49S	57.10W
Miriñay, Río-	204	Dj	30.10S	57.39W
Mirny	142	Nc	62.33N	113.53 E
Mirny	222	Ge	66.33S	93.01 E
Mironovka	132	Ge	49.40N	31.01 E
Mirosławiec	120	Mc	53.21N	16.05 E
Mirpur	148	Eb	33.11N	73.46 E
Mīrpur Khās	142	Ig	25.32N	69.00 E
Mirqah Sūr	146	Kd	36.50N	44.19 E
Mirsāle	168	Hd	5.58N	47.54 E
Mirşani	130	He	44.01N	24.01 E
Mirtóon Pélagos	130	Gm	37.00N	24.00 E
Miryang	154	Jg	35.29N	128.45 E
Mirzāpur	148	Gc	25.09N	82.35 E
Misaki	156	Ce	33.23N	132.07 E
Misawa	154	Pd	40.41N	141.24 E
Misery, Mount-	197c	Ab	17.22N	62.48W
Mishan	152	Nb	45.34N	131.50 E
Mishawaka	184	De	41.40N	86.11W
Mishima	156	Fd	35.07N	138.54 E
Mi-Shima	154	Kg	34.47N	131.10 E
Mishraq, Khashm-	146	Lj	24.13N	46.18 E
Misilmeri	128	Hl	38.02N	13.27 E
Misima Island	214	Ej	10.40S	152.45 E
Misiones [2]	206	Jc	27.00S	55.00W
Misiones [3]	204	Dh	27.00S	57.00W
Misiones, Sierra de-	204	Eh	26.45S	54.20W
Miskah	146	Jj	24.53N	42.58 E
Miski, Enneri-	168	Bb	18.10N	17.45 E
Miškino	134	Ki	55.20N	63.55 E
Miskitos, Cayos-	190	Hf	14.23N	82.46W
Miskolc	112	If	48.06N	20.47 E
Miskolc [2]	120	Qh	48.06N	20.43 E
Mismār	168	Fb	18.13N	35.38 E
Misool, Pulau-	208	Ee	1.52S	130.10 E
Misquah Hills	182	Ib	47.17N	92.00W
Miṣr = Egypt (EN) [1]	160	Jf	27.00N	30.00 E
Miṣr al Jadīdah, Al Qāhirah-	164	Fc	30.06N	31.20 E
Miṣrātah	160	Ie	32.23N	15.06 E
Miṣrātah [3]	164	Cd	29.00N	16.00 E
Miṣrātah, Ra's-	158	Ie	32.25N	15.05 E
Misserghin	126	Li	35.37N	0.44W
Missinaibi	180	Jf	50.44N	81.30W
Missinaibi Lake	184	Fa	48.23N	83.40W
Missinipe	180	He	55.36N	104.45W
Mission [S.D.-U.S.]	186	Fe	43.18N	100.40W
Mission [Tx.-U.S.]	186	Gn	26.13N	98.20W
Mission	188	Db	49.08N	122.18W
Mission Range	188	Ic	47.30N	113.55W
Mississippi [2]	182	Je	32.50N	89.30W
Mississippi	174	Kg	29.00N	89.15W
Mississippi Delta	174	Kg	29.10N	89.15W
Mississippi Fan (EN)	182	Jf	26.45N	88.30W
Mississippi River	184	Ic	45.26N	76.16W
Mississippi Sound	186	Lk	30.15N	89.00W
Misso	116	Lg	57.33N	27.23 E
Missoula	176	He	46.52N	114.01W
Missour	162	Gc	33.03N	3.59W
Missouri [2]	182	Id	38.30N	93.30W
Missouri	174	Jf	38.50N	90.08W
Missouri, Coteau du-	186	Gc	46.00N	99.30W
Missouri Valley	186	If	41.33N	95.53W
Mistassini	180	Kf	50.30N	74.00W
Mistassini	184	Ka	48.58N	72.40W
Mistassini, Lac-	174	Ld	51.00N	73.00W
Mistassini, Rivière-	180	Kg	48.42N	72.20W
Mistelbach an der Zaya	128	Kb	48.34N	16.34 E
Misterhult	116	Gg	57.28N	16.33 E
Mistrás	130	Fl	37.04N	22.22 E
Mistretta	123	Im	37.56N	14.22 E
Misugi	156	Ed	34.33N	136.15 E
Misumi [Jap.]	156	Bd	34.46N	131.58 E
Misumi [Jap.]	156	Be	32.37N	130.29 E
Mita, Punta-	192	Gg	32.04N	105.33W
Mitare, Río-	194	Mh	11.28N	69.56W
Mitchell [Austl.]	212	Je	26.29S	147.58 E
Mitchell [Or.-U.S.]	188	Ed	44.34N	120.09W
Mitchell [S.D.-U.S.]	182	Hc	43.40N	98.01W
Mitchell, Mount-	174	Kf	35.46N	82.16W
Mitchell Range	212	Hb	12.50S	135.35 E
Mitchell River	208	Ff	15.12S	141.35 E
Mitchell River Mission	212	Ic	15.28S	141.44 E
Mitchelstown/Baile Mhistéala	118	Ei	52.16N	8.16W
Mithimna	130	Jj	39.22N	26.10 E
Mitiaro Island	208	Lf	19.49S	157.43W
Mitidja, Plaine de la-	126	Oh	36.36N	3.00 E
Mitilini	130	Jj	39.06N	26.33 E
Mitilinis, Stenón-	130	Jj	39.10N	26.35 E
Mitla	190	Ee	16.55N	96.17W
Mitla, Laguna-	192	Ii	17.03N	100.25W
Mito	152	Pd	36.22N	140.28 E
Mitomoni	170	Ge	11.32S	35.19 E
Mitsamiouli	172	Gb	11.23S	43.18 E
Mitsinjo	172	Hc	16.00S	45.52 E
Mitsio, Nosy-	172	Hb	12.54S	48.36 E
Mitsiwa = Massawa (EN)	160	Kg	15.37N	39.39 E
Mitsiwa Channel	168	Fb	15.30N	40.00 E
Mitsuishi	156a	Cb	42.15N	142.33 E
Mitsukaido	156	Fc	36.01N	139.59 E
Mitsuke	156	Fc	37.32N	138.56 E
Mitsushima	156	Ad	34.16N	129.20 E
Mittelfranken [3]	120	Gg	49.20N	10.40 E
Mittelland	128	Bd	46.50N	7.05 E
Mittellandkanal	110	He	52.16N	11.41 E
Mittelmark	120	Jd	52.20N	13.20 E
Mittenwald	120	Hi	47.27N	11.15 E
Mittersheim	124	If	48.52N	6.56 E
Mittersill	128	Gc	47.16N	12.29 E
Mittweida	120	If	50.59N	12.59 E
Mitú	200	Ie	1.08N	70.03W

Index Symbols

- Independent Nation
- State, Region
- District, County
- Municipality
- Colony, Dependency
- Continent
- Physical Region
- Historical or Cultural Region
- Mount, Mountain
- Volcano
- Hill
- Mountains, Mountain Range
- Hills, Escarpment
- Plateau, Upland
- Pass, Gap
- Plain, Lowland
- Delta
- Salt Flat
- Valley, Canyon
- Crater, Cave
- Karst Features
- Depression
- Polder
- Desert, Dunes
- Forest, Woods
- Heath, Steppe
- Oasis
- Cape, Point
- Coast, Beach
- Cliff
- Peninsula
- Isthmus
- Sandbank
- Island
- Atoll
- Rock, Reef
- Islands, Archipelago
- Rocks, Reefs
- Coral Reef
- Well, Spring
- Geyser
- River, Stream
- Waterfall, Rapids
- River Mouth, Estuary
- Lake
- Salt Lake
- Intermittent Lake
- Reservoir
- Swamp, Pond
- Canal
- Glacier
- Ice Shelf, Pack Ice
- Ocean
- Sea
- Gulf, Bay
- Strait, Fjord
- Lagoon
- Bank
- Seamount
- Tablemount
- Ridge
- Shelf
- Basin
- Escarpment, Sea Scarp
- Fracture
- Trench, Abyss
- National Park, Reserve
- Point of Interest
- Recreation Site
- Cave, Cavern
- Historic Site
- Ruins
- Wall, Walls
- Church, Abbey
- Temple
- Scientific Station
- Railway station
- Airport
- Port
- Military installation
- Lighthouse
- Mine
- Tunnel
- Dam, Bridge

Mitumba, Monts- = Mitumba Range (EN) 158 Ji 6.00S 29.00 E
Mitumba Range (EN) = Mitumba, Monts- 158 Ji 6.00S 29.00 E
Mituva 116 Jj 55.00N 22.45 E
Mitwaba 170 Ed 8.38S 27.20 E
Mitzic 170 Bb 0.47N 11.34 E
Miura 156 Fd 35.08N 139.37 E
Miura-Hantō 156 Fd 35.15N 139.40 E
Mixco Viejo 194 Bf 14.52N 90.40W
Mixian 154 Bg 34.31N 113.22 E
Mixteco, Río- 192 Jh 18.11N 98.30W
Miya-Gawa 156 Ed 34.32N 136.42 E
Miyagi Ken [2] 154 Pe 38.30N 140.50 E
Miyagusuku-Jima 156b Ab 26.22N 127.59 E
Miyāh, Wādī al- 146 Gi 26.06N 36.31 E
Miyāh, Wādī al- [Eg.] 146 Ej 25.00N 33.23 E
Miyāh, Wādī al- [Syr.] 146 He 34.44N 39.57 E
Miyake-Jima 152 Oe 34.05N 139.30 E
Miyako 152 Pd 39.38N 141.57 E
Miyako-Jima 152 Mg 24.45N 125.20 E
Miyakonojō 154 Ki 31.44N 131.04 E
Miyako-Rettō 152 Lg 24.25N 125.00 E
Miyako-Wan 156 Hb 39.40N 142.00 E
Miyama 156 Dd 35.17N 135.34 E
Miyanojō 156 Bf 31.54N 130.27 E
Miyanoura-Dake 154 Ki 30.20N 130.29 E
Miyata 156 Be 33.45N 130.45 E
Miyazaki 152 Ne 31.54N 131.26 E
Miyazaki Ken [2] 154 Kh 32.05N 131.20 E
Miyazu 154 Mg 35.32N 135.11 E
Miyazuka-Yama 156 Fd 34.24N 139.16 E
Miyazu-Wan 156 Dd 35.35N 135.13 E
Miyoshi 154 Lg 34.48N 132.51 E
Miyun 152 Kc 40.22N 116.53 E
Miyun Shuiku 154 Dd 40.31N 116.58 E
Mizan Teferi 168 Fd 6.53N 35.28 E
Mizdah 164 Bc 31.26N 12.59 E
Mizen Head/Carn Ui Néid 110 Fe 51.27N 9.49W
Mizhi 152 Jd 37.50N 110.03 E
Mizija 130 Gf 43.43N 23.51 E
Mizil 130 Je 45.01N 26.27 E
Mizorām [3] 148 Id 23.00N 93.00 E
Mizque 202 Eg 17.56S 65.19W
Mizuho 156 Cd 34.50N 132.29 E
Mizuho 222 Ef 70.43S 40.20 E
Mizunami 156 Ed 35.22N 137.15 E
Mizusawa 154 Pe 39.08N 141.08 E
Mjadel 116 Lj 54.54N 27.03 E
Mjakiševo 116 Mh 56.30N 28.54 E
Mjakit 138 Kd 61.23N 152.10 E
Mjällom 116 Ha 62.59N 18.26 E
Mjaundža 138 Jd 63.02N 147.13 E
Mjölby 114 Dg 58.19N 15.08 E
Mjøndalen 116 De 59.45N 10.01 E
Mjorn 116 Eg 57.54N 12.25 E
Mjøsa 110 Hc 60.40N 11.00 E
Mkoani 170 Gd 5.22S 39.39 E
Mkokotoni 170 Gd 5.52S 39.15 E
Mkushi Bona 170 Ee 13.37S 29.23 E
Mkushi River 170 Fe 13.33S 29.40 E
Mkuze 172 Ee 27.10S 32.00 E
Mladá Boleslav 120 Kf 50.21N 14.54 E
Mladenovac 130 De 44.26N 20.42 E
Mlava 130 Ee 44.45N 21.14 E
Mława 120 Qc 53.06N 20.23 E
Mljet 128 Lh 42.45N 17.30 E
Mljetski kanal 128 Lh 42.48N 17.35 E
Mmadinare 172 Dd 21.53S 27.45 E
Mnichovo Hradiště 120 Kf 50.32N 14.59 E
Mnogoveršinny 138 If 53.55N 139.50 E
Moa 194 Jc 20.40N 74.56W
Moa 166 Cd 6.59N 11.36W
Moa, Pulau- 150 Ih 8.10S 127.56 E
Moab 182 Fd 38.35N 109.33W
Moabi 170 Bc 2.24S 10.59 E
Moala 219d Bc 18.36S 179.53 E
Moamba 172 Ee 25.36S 32.15 E
Moanda [Gabon] 170 Bc 1.34S 13.11 E
Moanda [Zaire] 170 Bd 5.56S 12.21 E
Moatize 172 Ec 16.10S 33.46 E
Moba 160 Ji 7.03S 29.47 E
Mobara 156 Gd 35.25N 140.17 E
Mobārakeh 146 Nf 32.20N 51.30 E
Mobaye 160 Jh 4.19N 21.11 E
Mobayi-Mbongo 170 Db 4.18N 21.11 E
Mobeka 170 Cb 1.53N 19.46 E
Moberly 182 Id 39.25N 92.26W
Mobile 176 Kf 30.42N 88.05W
Mobile Bay 182 Je 30.25N 88.00W
Mobridge 182 Gb 45.32N 100.26W
Mobuto Sese Seko, Lac- = Albert, Lake- (EN) 158 Kh 1.40N 31.00 E
Moca 194 Ld 19.24N 70.31W
Moçambique = Mozambique (EN) 160 Lj 15.03S 40.45 E
Moçambique = Mozambique (EN) [1] 160 Kj 18.15S 35.00 E
Moçambique, Canal de- = Mozambique Channel (EN) 158 Lk 20.00S 43.00 E
Mocapra, Río- 196 Ci 7.56N 66.46W
Mocha, Isla- 206 Fe 38.22S 73.56W
Moc Hoa 148 Lf 10.46N 105.56 E
Mochudi 172 Dd 24.23S 26.08 E
Mocimboa da Praia 160 Lj 11.20S 40.21 E
Möckeln 116 Fh 56.40N 14.10 E
Mockfjärd 116 Fd 60.30N 14.58 E
Móco, Serra- 168 Lj 12.28S 15.10 E
Mocoa 202 Cc 1.09N 76.38W
Mococa 204 Ie 21.28S 47.01W
Mocovi 204 Ci 28.24S 59.42W
Moctezuma [Mex.] 192 If 22.45N 101.05W
Moctezuma [Mex.] 192 Fb 30.12N 106.26W
Moctezuma [Mex.] 190 Cc 29.48N 109.42W
Moctezuma, Río- [Mex.] 192 Jg 21.59N 98.34W
Moctezuma, Río- [Mex.] 192 Ec 29.09N 109.40W
Mocuba 160 Kj 16.51S 36.56 E
Mocubúri 172 Fb 14.39S 38.54 E
Močurica 130 Jg 42.31N 26.32 E
Modane 122 Mi 45.12N 6.40 E
Modderrivier 172 Ce 29.02S 24.37 E
Modena [It.] 128 Ef 44.40N 10.55 E
Modena [Ut.-U.S.] 188 Ih 37.49N 113.55W
Moder 122 Of 48.49N 8.06 E
Modesto 182 Cd 37.39N 120.59W
Modica 128 In 36.52N 14.46 E
Modjamboli 170 Db 2.28N 22.06 E
Modjigo 166 Hb 17.09N 13.12 E
Mödling 128 Kb 48.05N 16.28 E
Modriča 128 Mf 44.58N 18.18 E
Modum 116 Ce 59.55N 10.00 E
Moe 212 Jg 38.10S 146.15 E
Moelv 114 Cf 60.56N 10.42 E
Moen 220d Bb 7.26N 151.52 E
Moengo 202 Hb 5.37N 54.24W
Moen-jo-Daro 148 Dc 27.19N 68.12 E
Moenkopi Wash 188 Ji 35.54N 111.26W
Moerbeke 124 Fc 51.10N 3.56 E
Moers 120 Ce 51.27N 6.39 E
Moeskroen/Mouscron 122 Jd 50.44N 3.13 E
Moffat 118 Jf 55.20N 3.27W
Moga 170 Ec 2.21S 26.49 E
Mogadishu (EN) = Muqdisho 160 Lh 2.03N 45.22 E
Mogadouro 126 Fc 41.20N 6.43W
Mogadouro, Serra do- 126 Fc 41.19N 6.40W
Mogāl 146 Nd 36.35N 50.35 E
Mogalakwena 172 Dd 22.27S 28.55 E
Mogami 156 Gb 38.45N 140.30 E
Mogami-Gawa 154 Oe 38.54N 139.50 E
Mogami Trench (EN) 156 Fb 39.00N 139.00 E
Mogaung 148 Jc 25.18N 96.56 E
Mogho 168 Ge 4.49N 40.19 E
Mogielnica 120 Qe 51.42N 20.43 E
Mogilev 112 Je 53.56N 30.18 E
Mogilev-Podolski 132 Ee 48.27N 27.48 E
Mogilevskaja oblast [3] 136 De 53.45N 30.30 E
Mogilno 120 Nd 52.40N 17.58 E
Mogincual 172 Gc 15.34S 40.24 E
Mogoča 142 Nd 53.44N 119.44 E
Mogočin 138 De 57.43N 83.40 E
Mogogh 168 Ed 8.26N 31.19 E
Mogojto 138 Gf 54.25N 110.27 E
Mogojtuj 138 Gf 51.15N 114.58 E
Mogok 148 Jd 22.55N 96.30 E
Mogollon Rim 182 Ee 34.20N 111.00W
Mogotes, Punta- 204 Dn 38.06S 57.33W
Mogotón, Pico- 194 Dg 13.45N 86.23W
Mogrein 160 Ff 25.13N 11.34W
Mogroum 168 Bc 11.06N 15.25 E
Moguer 126 Fg 37.16N 6.50W
Mogzon 138 Gf 51.42N 111.59 E
Mohács 120 Ok 45.59N 18.42 E
Mohaka 218 Gc 39.07S 177.12 E
Mohaka 218 Gc 39.07S 177.12 E
Mohales Hoek 172 Df 30.15S 27.25 E
Mohall 186 Fb 48.46N 101.31W
Moḥammadābād 146 Pg 31.47N 54.27 E
Mohammadia 126 Mi 35.35N 0.04 E
Mohammedia 162 Fc 33.42N 7.24W
Mohanganj 162 Id 24.54N 90.59 E
Mohang-ni 154 If 36.46N 126.08 E
Mohave, Lake- 182 Ed 35.25N 114.38W
Mohawk Mountains 188 Ij 32.25N 113.25W
Mohe 142 Od 53.27N 122.18 E
Moheda 116 Fh 57.00N 14.34 E
Mohéli/Mwali 158 Lj 12.15S 43.45 E
Moher, Cliffs of-/Aillte an Mhothair 118 Di 52.58N 9.27W
Mohican, Cape- 178 Fd 60.12N 167.28W
Mohinora 174 Ig 26.06N 107.04W
Möhne 120 Ee 51.27N 8.00 E
Möhnesee 124 Kc 51.29N 8.05 E
Mohns Ridge (EN) 110 Ga 73.00N 5.00 E
Moholm 116 Ff 58.37N 14.02 E
Mohon, Charleville-Mézières- 124 Ge 49.46N 4.43 E
Mohon Peak 188 Ii 34.57N 113.15W
Mohoro 170 Gd 8.08S 39.10 E
Mohotani, Ile- 216 Na 9.59S 138.49W
Mohovaja 138 Kf 53.01N 158.38 E
Moi 116 Bf 58.28N 6.32 E
Moikovac 130 Cg 42.58N 19.35 E
Moimenta da Beira 126 Ed 40.59N 7.37W
Moindou 219b Be 21.42S 165.41 E
Moinești 130 Jc 46.28N 26.29 E
Moirai 130 Hn 35.03N 24.52 E
Mo i Rana 112 Hb 66.18N 14.08 E
Mõisaküla/Myjzakjula 114 Fg 58.07N 25.10 E
Moisés Ville 204 Bj 30.43S 61.29W
Moisie 180 Kf 50.11N 66.06W
Moisie 180 Kf 50.13N 66.06W
Moissac 122 Hj 44.06N 1.05 E
Moissala 168 Bd 8.21N 17.46 E
Moitaco 196 Dh 8.01N 61.21W
Möja 116 He 59.25N 18.55 E
Mojácar 126 Kg 37.08N 1.51W
Mojada, Sierra- 192 Hd 27.15N 103.45W
Mojana, Caño- 194 Ji 9.02N 74.46W
Mojave 182 Dd 35.03N 118.10W
Mojave Desert 174 Hf 35.00N 117.00W
Mojiguaçu, Rio- 204 He 20.53S 48.10W
Moji Mirim 204 If 22.26S 46.57W
Mojjero 138 Fc 68.44N 103.30 E
Mojo 168 Fd 8.36N 39.09 E
Mojo 168 Gd 8.00N 41.50 E
Mojos, Llanos de- 198 Jg 15.00S 65.00W
Moju, Rio- 202 Id 1.40S 48.25W
Mojynty 136 Hf 47.10N 73.18 E
Mokambo 170 Ee 12.25S 28.21 E
Mokapu Peninsula 221a Db 21.26N 157.45W
Mokau 216 Dg 38.41S 174.37 E
Mokau 218 Fc 38.42S 174.37 E
Mokhotlong 172 De 29.17S 29.05 E
Mokil Atoll 208 Gd 6.40N 159.47 E
Moklakan 138 Gf 54.48N 118.56 E
Möklinta 116 Gd 60.05N 16.32 E
Mokochu, Khao- 148 Je 15.56N 99.06 E
Mokohinau Islands 218 Fa 35.55S 175.05 E
Mokolo 166 Hc 10.45N 13.48 E
Mokp'o 142 Of 34.47N 126.23 E
Mokra Gora 130 Dg 42.50N 20.25 E
Mokrany 120 Ue 51.48N 24.23 E
Mokrin 130 Dd 45.56N 20.25 E
Mokša 110 Ke 54.44N 41.53 E
Mokwa 166 Gd 9.17N 5.03 E
Mol 122 Lc 51.11N 5.07 E
Mola di Bari 128 Lj 41.04N 17.05 E
Molango 192 Jg 20.47N 98.43W
Moláoi 130 Fm 36.48N 22.51 E
Molara 128 Dj 40.50N 9.45 E
Molas, Punta- 192 Pg 20.35N 86.44W
Molat 128 If 44.13N 14.50 E
Molatón 126 Kf 38.59N 1.24W
Molay-Littry, Le- 124 Be 49.15N 0.53W
Moldau (EN) = Vltava 110 He 50.21N 14.30 E
Moldava nad Bodvou 120 Qh 48.37N 21.00 E
Moldavia (EN) = Moldova 110 If 46.30N 27.00 E
Moldavia (EN) = Moldova 130 Jc 46.30N 27.00 E
Moldavian SSR (EN) = Moldavskaja SSR [2] 136 Cf 47.00N 29.00 E
Moldavskaja Sovetskaja Socialističeskaja Respublika [2] 136 Cf 47.00N 29.00 E
Moldavskaja SSR/ Respublika Sovetike Sočialiste Moldovenjaske [2] 136 Cf 47.00N 29.00 E
Moldavskaja SSR = Moldavian SSR (EN) [2] 136 Cf 47.00N 29.00 E
Molde 112 Gc 62.44N 7.11 E
Moldefjorden 116 Bb 62.45N 7.05 E
Moldotau, hrebet- 135 Jd 40.00N 74.50 E
Moldova 130 Jc 46.54N 26.58 E
Moldova = Moldavia (EN) 110 If 46.30N 27.00 E
Moldova = Moldavia (EN) 130 Jc 46.30N 27.00 E
Moldova Nouă 130 Ee 44.44N 21.41 E
Moldoveanu, Vîrful- 110 If 45.36N 24.44 E
Moldovița 130 Ib 47.41N 25.32 E
Mole 124 Bc 51.24N 0.20W
Moléne, Ile de- 122 Bf 48.24N 4.58W
Molens van Kinderdijk 122 Gc 51.52N 4.40 E
Molepolole 160 Jk 24.25S 25.30 E
Môle Saint-Nicolas 194 Kd 19.47N 73.22W
Molėtai / Moletaj 116 Ki 55.13N 25.36 E
Moletaj / Molėtai 116 Ki 55.13N 25.36 E
Molfetta 128 Ki 41.12N 16.36 E
Molihong Shan 154 Hc 42.11N 124.43 E
Molina, Parameras de- 126 Jd 40.55N 2.01W
Molina de Aragón 126 Kd 40.51N 1.53W
Molina de Segura 126 Kf 38.03N 1.12W
Moline 186 Kf 41.30N 90.31W
Moliniere Point 197p Bb 12.05N 61.45W
Molise [2] 128 Ii 41.40N 14.30 E
Molkābād 146 Oe 34.32N 52.35 E
Molkom 116 Ee 59.36N 13.43 E
Moll 204 Cl 35.04S 59.39W
Möll 128 Hd 46.50N 13.26 E
Mollafeneri 130 Mi 40.54N 29.30 E
Mölle 116 Eh 56.17N 12.29 E
Mollendo 202 Dg 17.02S 72.01W
Molliens-Dreuil 124 Ee 49.52N 2.01 E
Mölln 120 Gc 53.38N 10.41 E
Möllösund 116 Df 58.04N 11.28 E
Mölndal 114 Ch 57.39N 12.01 E
Mölnlycke 116 Eg 57.39N 12.09 E
Moločansk 132 If 47.10N 35.36 E
Moločny, liman- 132 If 46.30N 35.20 E
Molócuè 172 Fc 17.03S 38.52 E
Molodečno 136 Ce 54.19N 26.53 E
Molodežnaja 222 Ee 67.40S 45.51 E
Molodi 116 Mf 58.00N 28.52 E
Molodogvardejskoje 136 He 54.07N 70.50 E
Mologa 110 Jd 58.50N 37.11 E
Molokai Island 208 Lb 21.08N 157.00W
Moloma 114 Lg 58.20N 48.28 E
Molong 212 Jf 33.06S 148.52 E
Molopo 158 Jk 28.31S 20.13 E
Moloundou 166 Ie 2.02N 15.13 E
Molteno 172 Df 31.24S 26.22 E
Molu, Pulau- 150 Jh 6.45S 131.33 E
Moluccas (EN) = Maluku, Kepulauan- 208 De 2.00S 128.00 E
Molucca Sea (EN) = Maluku, Laut- 140 Oj 0.05S 125.00 E
Molygino 138 Ee 58.11N 94.45 E
Moma 172 Fc 16.44S 39.14 E
Moma 138 Jc 66.20N 143.06 E
Mombaça 202 Ke 5.45S 39.28W
Mombasa 160 Ki 4.03S 39.40 E
Mombo 170 Gc 4.53S 38.17 E
Momboyo 170 Cc 0.16S 19.00 E
Mombuca, Serra da- 204 Fd 18.15S 52.26W
Momčilgrad 130 Ih 41.32N 25.25 E
Mömling 124 Le 49.50N 9.09 E
Momotombo, Volcán- 194 Dg 12.26N 86.33W
Mompono 170 Db 0.04N 21.48 E
Mompós 202 Db 9.14N 74.27W
Momskí hrebet 138 Jc 66.00N 145.00 E
Mon [2] 148 Je 17.22N 97.20 E
Møn 114 Ci 55.00N 12.20 E
Mona, Canal de la- = Mona Passage (EN) 174 Mh 18.30N 67.45W
Mona, Isla- 190 Ke 18.05N 67.54W
Mona, Punta- 194 Fi 9.38N 82.37W
Monach Islands 118 Fd 57.32N 7.40W
Monaco [1] 112 Gg 43.42N 7.23 E
Monadhliath Mountains 118 Id 57.15N 4.10W
Monagas [2] 202 Fb 9.20N 63.00W
Monaghan/Muineachán 118 Gg 54.15N 6.58W
Monaghan/Muineachán [2] 118 Gg 54.10N 7.00W
Monahans 186 Ek 31.36N 102.54W
Mona Passage (EN) = Mona, Canal de la- 174 Mh 18.30N 67.45W
Monapo 172 Gb 14.55S 40.18 E
Monarch Mountain 180 Ef 51.54N 125.54W
Monashee Mountains 180 Ff 51.00N 118.43W
Monastyrščina 132 Gb 54.19N 31.48 E
Monatélé 166 He 4.16N 11.12 E
Monbetsu [Jap.] 154 Qc 42.28N 142.07 E
Monbetsu [Jap.] 152 Pc 44.21N 143.22 E
Monbetsu-Shokotsu 156a Ca 44.23N 143.16 E
Moncalieri 128 Be 45.00N 7.41 E
Moncalvo 128 Ce 45.03N 8.16 E
Monção [Braz.] 202 Id 3.30S 45.15W
Monção [Port.] 126 Db 42.05N 8.29W
Moncayo 126 Kc 41.46N 1.50W
Moncayo, Sierra del- 126 Kc 41.45N 1.50W
Mončegorsk 136 Db 67.56N 32.58 E
Mönchengladbach 120 Ce 51.12N 6.26 E
Mönchengladbach-Rheydt 124 Ic 51.10N 6.27 E
Mönchengladbach-Wickrath 124 Ic 51.08N 6.25 E
Mönchgut 120 Jb 54.20N 13.40 E
Monchique 126 Dg 37.19N 8.33W
Monchique, Serra de- 126 Dg 37.19N 8.36W
Monclova 176 Ig 26.54N 101.25W
Moncton 176 Me 46.06N 64.07W
Monda 204 Fh 27.05S 53.25W
Mondego 126 Dd 40.09N 8.52W
Mondego, Cabo- 126 Cd 40.11N 8.55W
Mondeville 124 Be 49.10N 0.19W
Mondjoko 170 Dc 1.41S 21.12 E
Mondo 168 Bc 13.43N 15.32 E
Mondoñedo 126 Ea 43.26N 7.22W
Mondorf-les-Bains/Bad Mondorf 124 Ie 49.30N 6.17 E
Mondoubleau 122 Gg 47.59N 0.54 E
Mondovì 128 Bf 44.23N 7.49 E
Mondragone 128 Hi 41.07N 13.53 E
Mondy 138 Ff 51.40N 100.59 E
Monédières, Les- 122 Hi 45.30N 1.52 E
Monemvasia 130 Gm 36.41N 23.03 E
Monessen 184 He 40.09N 79.53W
Monett 186 Jh 36.55N 93.55W
Monfalcone 128 He 45.49N 13.32 E
Monferrato 128 Cf 44.55N 8.05 E
Monforte 126 Ee 39.03N 7.26W
Monforte de Lemos 126 Eb 42.31N 7.30W
Monga 170 Db 4.12N 22.49 E
Mongala 170 Cb 1.53N 19.46 E
Mongalla 168 Ed 5.12N 31.46 E
Mongbwalu 170 Eb 1.57N 30.02 E
Mong Cai 148 Ld 21.32N 107.58 E
Monger, Lake- 212 De 29.15S 117.05 E
Mongga 219a Cb 7.57S 156.59 E
Monggolküre/Zhaosu 152 Dc 43.10N 81.07 E
Monghyr → Munger 148 Hc 25.23N 86.28 E
Mongibello 110 Hh 37.50N 14.55 E
Mongibello → Etna 110 Hh 37.50N 14.55 E
Monginevro, Colle del- 122 Mj 44.56N 6.44 E
Mongo 160 Ig 12.11N 18.42 E
Mongo 166 Cd 9.34N 12.11W
Mongol Altajn Nuruu = Mongolian Altai (EN) 140 Le 46.30N 93.00 E
Mongol Ard Uls = Mongolia (EN) [1] 142 Me 47.00N 104.00 E
Mongolia (EN) = Mongol Ard Uls [1] 142 Me 47.00N 104.00 E
Mongolian Altai (EN) = Mongol Altajn Nuruu 140 Le 46.30N 93.00 E
Mongonu 166 Hc 12.41N 13.36 E
Mongororo 166 Cc 12.01N 22.28 E
Mongoumba 168 Be 3.38N 18.36 E
Mong Pan 148 Jd 20.19N 98.22 E
Mongrove, Punta- 192 Hi 17.56N 102.11W
Mongu 160 Jj 15.17S 23.08 E
Monguel 162 Ef 16.25N 13.08W
Mong Yai 148 Jd 22.25N 98.02 E
Monheim 124 Ic 51.05N 6.53 E
Mönichkirchen 128 Kc 47.30N 16.02 E
Mon Idée, Auvillers-lès-Forges- 124 Ge 49.52N 4.21 E
Monigotes 204 Bj 30.30S 61.39W
Moni Hosiou Louká 130 Fk 38.24N 22.49 E
Monistrol-sur-Loire 122 Ki 45.17N 4.10 E
Monito, Isla- 197a Ab 18.09N 67.56W
Monitor Peak 188 Gg 38.50N 116.32W
Monitor Range 188 Gg 38.45N 116.40W
Monjolos 204 Jd 18.18S 44.05W
Monkayo 150 Ie 7.50N 126.00 E
Monkey Bay 170 Fe 14.05S 34.55 E
Monkey Point 194 Fg 11.36N 83.39W
Monkey River 194 Ce 16.22N 88.29W
Monki 120 Sc 53.24N 22.49 E
Monkoto 170 Dc 1.38S 20.39 E
Monmouth 118 Kj 51.45N 3.00W
Monmouth [Il.-U.S.] 186 Kf 40.55N 90.39W
Monmouth [Or.-U.S.] 188 Dd 44.51N 123.14W
Monmouth [Wales-U.K.] 118 Kj 51.50N 2.43W
Monmouth Mountain 188 Da 51.00N 123.47W
Mönne 120 De 51.28N 7.30 E
Monnikendam 124 Hb 52.27N 5.02 E
Monnow 118 Kj 51.48N 2.42W
Mono [3] 166 Fd 6.45N 1.50 E
Mono 219a Bb 7.20S 155.35 E
Monobe-Gawa 156 Ce 33.32N 133.42 E
Mono Lake 182 Dd 38.00N 119.00W
Monólithos 130 Km 36.07N 27.45 E
Monopoli 128 Lj 40.57N 17.18 E
Monor 120 Pi 47.21N 19.27 E
Monou 168 Cb 16.24N 22.11 E
Monòvar / Monóver 126 Lf 38.26N 0.50W
Monóver / Monòvar 126 Lf 38.26N 0.50W
Monowai, Lake- 218 Bf 45.55S 167.25 E
Monreal del Campo 126 Kd 40.47N 1.21W
Monreale 128 Hl 38.05N 13.17 E
Monroe [Ga.-U.S.] 184 Fi 33.47N 83.43W
Monroe [La.-U.S.] 176 Jf 32.33N 92.07W
Monroe [Mi.-U.S.] 184 Fe 41.55N 83.24W
Monroe [N.C.-U.S.] 184 Gh 34.59N 80.33W
Monroe [Or.-U.S.] 188 Dd 44.19N 123.18W
Monroe [Wi.-U.S.] 186 Le 42.36N 89.38W
Monroe, Lake- 184 Df 39.05N 86.25W
Monroe City 186 Kg 39.39N 91.44W
Monroeville 184 Dj 31.31N 87.20W
Monrovia 160 Fh 6.19N 10.48W
Mons/Bergen 122 Jd 50.27N 3.56 E
Monsanto 126 Ed 40.02N 7.07W
Monschau 120 Cf 50.33N 6.15 E
Monselice 128 Fe 45.14N 11.45 E
Monserrate, Isla- 192 De 25.41N 111.05W
Monsheim 124 Ke 49.38N 8.12 E
Møns Klint 116 Ej 54.58N 12.33 E
Mönsterås 114 Dh 57.02N 16.26 E
Montabaur 120 Df 50.26N 7.50 E
Montagna Grande 128 Gm 37.56N 12.44 E
Montagne 122 Jh 46.10N 3.40 E
Montagu 222 Ad 58.25S 26.20W
Montague 178 Je 60.00N 147.30W
Montague, Isla- 192 Bb 31.45N 114.48W
Montaigu 122 Eh 46.59N 1.19W
Montalbán 126 Ld 40.50N 0.48W
Montalbano Ionico 128 Kj 40.17N 16.34 E
Montalcino 128 Fg 43.03N 11.29 E
Montalegre 126 Ec 41.49N 7.48W
Montalto di Castro 128 Fh 42.21N 11.37 E
Montalto Uffugo 128 Kk 39.24N 16.09 E
Montalvânia 204 Jb 14.28S 44.32W
Montana 128 Bd 46.18N 7.30 E
Montana [2] 182 Eb 47.00N 110.00W
Montana-Vermala 128 Bd 46.18N 7.30 E
Montánchez 126 Fe 39.13N 6.09W
Montánchez, Sierra de- 126 Ge 39.15N 5.55W
Montargis 122 Ig 48.00N 2.45 E
Montataire 124 Ee 49.16N 2.26 E
Montauban [Fr.] 122 Df 48.12N 2.03W
Montauban [Fr.] 122 Hj 44.01N 1.21 E
Montauk Point 184 Le 41.04N 71.52W
Montbard 122 Kg 47.37N 4.20 E
Montbéliard 122 Mg 47.31N 6.48 E
Montblanc 126 Nc 41.22N 1.10 E
Montbrison 122 Ki 45.36N 4.03 E
Montceau-les-Mines 122 Kh 46.40N 4.22 E
Mont Cenis, Col du- 110 Gf 45.15N 6.54 E
Montchanin 122 Kh 46.45N 4.27 E
Mont Darwin 172 Ec 16.46S 31.35 E
Mont-de-Marsan 122 Fk 43.53N 0.30W
Montdidier 122 Ie 49.39N 2.34 E
Mont-Dore [Fr.] 122 Ii 45.34N 2.49 E
Mont-Dore [N.Cal.] 219b Cf 22.17S 166.35 E
Monte, Laguna del- 204 Am 37.00S 62.28W
Monteagudo 202 Fg 19.49S 63.59W
Monte Albán 176 Jh 17.02N 96.45W
Monte Alegre 202 Hd 2.01S 54.04W
Monte Alegre, Rio- 204 Gc 17.16S 50.41W
Monte Alegre de Goiás 204 Ia 13.14S 47.10W
Montealegre del Castillo 126 Kf 38.47N 1.19W
Monte Alegre de Minas 204 Hd 18.52S 48.52W
Monte Azul 202 Jg 15.09S 42.53W
Montebello 184 Jc 45.39N 74.56W
Monte Bello Islands 212 Dd 20.25S 115.30 E
Monte-Carlo 122 Nk 43.44N 7.25 E
Montecarlo 204 Eh 26.34S 54.47W
Monte Carmelo 204 Id 18.43S 47.29W
Monte Caseros 206 Id 30.15S 57.39W
Montecatini Terme 128 Eg 43.53N 10.46 E
Montecchio Maggiore 128 Fe 45.30N 11.24 E
Monte Comán 206 Gd 34.36S 67.54W
Montecristi 194 Ld 19.52N 71.39W
Monte Cristo 204 Bb 14.43S 61.14W
Montecristo 128 Eh 42.20N 10.20 E
Monte Ermoso 204 Bn 38.55S 61.33W
Monte Escobedo 192 Hf 22.18N 103.35W
Montefalco 128 Gh 42.52N 12.39 E
Montefeltro 128 Gg 43.55N 12.15 E
Montefiascone 128 Gh 42.32N 12.02 E
Montefrio 126 Hg 37.19N 4.01W
Montego Bay 176 Lh 18.30N 77.55W
Monteiro 202 Ke 7.53S 37.07W
Montelíbano 194 Ji 8.02N 75.29W
Montélimar 122 Kj 44.34N 4.45 E
Monte Lindo, Arroyo- 204 Cg 25.28S 59.25W
Monte Lindo, Rio- 206 Ib 23.56S 57.12W
Monte Lindo Chico, Riacho- 204 Dg 25.53S 57.53W
Monte Lindo Grande, Riacho- 204 Cg 25.45S 58.06W
Montello [Nv.-U.S.] 188 Hf 41.16N 114.12W
Montello [Wi.-U.S.] 186 Le 43.48N 89.20W
Montemorelos 190 Ec 25.12N 99.49W
Montemor-o-Novo 126 Df 38.39N 8.13W
Montemor-o-Velho 126 Dd 40.10N 8.41W
Montemuro, Serra de- 126 Dc 40.58N 8.01W
Montenegro 206 Jc 29.42S 51.28W
Montenegro (EN) = Crna Gora [2] 130 Cg 42.30N 19.18 E
Montenegro (EN) = Crna Gora [2] 130 Cg 42.30N 19.18 E
Monte Plata 194 Md 18.48N 69.47W
Montepuez 172 Fb 13.07S 39.00 E
Montepuez 172 Gb 12.32S 40.27 E
Montepulciano 128 Fg 43.05N 11.4
Monte Quemado 206 Hc 25.48S 62.52W
Monte Real 126 De 39.51N 8.52W
Montereale, Passo di- 128 Hh 42.31N 13.13
Montereau-faut-Yonne 122 If 48.23N 2.57
Monterey 182 Cd 36.37N 121.55
Monterey Bay 182 Cd 36.45N 121.55
Monteria 200 Ie 8.46N 75.5
Montero 202 Fg 17.20S 63.1
Monteros 206 Gc 27.10S 65.3
Monterotondo 128 Gh 42.03N 12.3
Monterrey 176 Ig 25.40N 100.1
Montesano 188 Dc 46.59N 123.
Monte San Savino 128 Fg 43.20N 11.
Monte Sant'Angelo 128 Ji 41.42N 15.
Monte Santu, Capo di- 128 Dj 45.05N 9.

Index Symbols

[1] Independent Nation
[2] State, Region
[3] District, County
[4] Municipality
[5] Colony, Dependency
Continent
Physical Region
Historical or Cultural Region
Mount, Mountain
Volcano
Hill
Mountains, Mountain Range
Hills, Escarpment
Plateau, Upland
Pass, Gap
Plain, Lowland
Delta
Salt Flat
Valley, Canyon
Crater, Cave
Karst Features
Depression
Polder
Desert, Dunes
Forest, Woods
Heath, Steppe
Oasis
Cape, Point
Coast, Beach
Cliff
Peninsula
Isthmus
Sandbank
Island
Atoll
Rock, Reef
Islands, Archipelago
Rocks, Reefs
Coral Reef
Well, Spring
Geyser
River, Stream
Waterfall, Rapids
River Mouth, Estuary
Lake
Salt Lake
Intermittent Lake
Reservoir
Swamp, Pond
Canal
Glacier
Ice Shelf, Pack Ice
Ocean
Sea
Gulf, Bay
Strait, Fjord
Lagoon
Bank
Seamount
Tablemount
Ridge
Shelf
Basin
Escarpment, Sea Scarp
Fracture
Trench, Abyss
National Park, Reserve
Point of Interest
Recreation Site
Cave, Cavern
Historic Site
Ruins
Wall, Walls
Church, Abbey
Temple
Scientific Station
Railway station
Airport
Port
Military insta
Lighthouse
Mine
Tunnel
Dam, Bridge

Montes Claros 200 Lg 16.43S 43.52W
Montes Claros de Goiás 204 Gb 15.54S 51.13W
Montesilvano 128 Ih 42.31N 14.09 E
Montevarchi 128 Fg 43.31N 11.34 E
Montevideo [2] 204 Dl 34.50S 56.10W
Montevideo [Mn.-U.S.] 186 Id 44.57N 95.43W
Montevideo [Ur.] 200 Ki 34.53S 56.11W
Monte Vista 186 Ch 37.35N 106.09W
Montfaucon 124 He 49.17N 5.08 E
Montfort-l'Amaury 124 Df 48.47N 1.49 E
Montfort-sur-Risle 124 Ce 49.18N 0.40 E
Montgenèvre, Col de- 122 Mj 44.56N 6.44 E
Montgomery 176 Kf 32.23N 86.18W
Montgomery Pass 188 Fh 38.00N 118.20W
Montguyon 122 Fi 45.13N 0.11W
Monthermé 124 Ge 49.53N 4.44 E
Monthey 128 Ad 46.15N 6.56 E
Monthois 124 Ge 49.19N 4.43 E
Monticello [Ar.-U.S.] 186 Kj 33.38N 91.47W
Monticello [Fl.-U.S.] 184 Fj 30.33N 83.52W
Monticello [Ia.-U.S.] 186 Ke 42.15N 91.12W
Monticello [In.-U.S.] 184 De 40.45N 86.46W
Monticello [Ky.-U.S.] 184 Eg 36.50N 84.51W
Monticello [N.Y.-U.S.] 184 Je 41.39N 74.41W
Monticello [Ut.-U.S.] 182 Fd 37.52N 109.21W
Montiel 126 Jf 38.42N 2.52W
Montiel, Campo de- 126 Jf 38.46N 2.44W
Montiel, Cuchilla de- 204 Cj 31.05S 59.10W
Montignac 122 Hi 45.04N 1.10 E
Montigny-le-Roi 122 Lf 48.00N 5.30 E
Montigny-lès-Metz 122 Me 49.06N 6.09 E
Montigny-le-Tilleul 124 Gd 50.23N 4.22 E
Montijo [Pan.] 194 Gj 7.59N 81.03W
Montijo [Port.] 126 Df 38.42N 8.58W
Montijo [Sp.] 126 Ff 38.55N 6.37W
Montijo, Golfo de- 194 Gj 7.40N 81.07W
Montilla 126 Hg 37.35N 4.38W
Montividiu 204 Gc 17.24S 51.14W
Montivilliers 122 Ge 49.33N 0.12 E
Mont Joli 180 Kg 48.35N 68.11W
Mont-Laurier 180 Jg 46.33N 75.30W
Mont-Louis 122 Il 42.31N 2.07 E
Mont Louis 184 Oa 49.15N 65.43W
Montluçon 122 Ih 46.20N 2.36 E
Montmagny 180 Kg 46.59N 70.33W
Montmarault 122 Ih 46.19N 2.57 E
Montmédy 122 Le 49.31N 5.22 E
Montmirail 122 Jf 48.52N 3.32 E
Montmorency 124 Ef 49.00N 2.20 E
Montmorillon 122 Gh 46.26N 0.52 E
Montmort-Lucy 124 Ff 48.55N 3.49 E
Monto 212 Kd 24.52S 151.07 E
Montoire-sur-le-Loir 122 Gg 47.45N 0.52 E
Montone 128 Gf 44.24N 12.14 E
Montoro 126 Hf 38.01N 4.23W
Montpelier [Id.-U.S.] 182 Ec 42.19N 111.18W
Montpelier [Vt.-U.S.] 176 Le 44.16N 72.35W
Montpellier 112 Gg 43.36N 3.53 E
Montpon-Ménestérol 122 Gi 45.01N 0.10 E
Montréal 176 Le 45.31N 73.34W
Montreal Lake 180 Gf 54.20N 105.40W
Montreal River 184 Hb 47.08N 79.27W
Montréjeau 122 Gk 43.05N 0.35 E
Montreuil [Fr.] 124 Ef 48.52N 2.26 E
Montreuil [Fr.] 122 Hd 50.28N 1.46 E
Montreuil-l'Argillé 124 Cf 48.56N 0.29 E
Montreux 128 Ad 46.26N 6.55 E
Montrose [Co.-U.S.] 182 Fd 38.29N 107.53W
Montrose [Scot.-U.K.] 118 Ke 56.43N 2.29W
Monts, Pointe des- 184 Na 49.19N 67.23W
Mont-Saint-Aignan 124 De 49.28N 1.05 E
Mont-Saint-Michel, Baie du- 122 Ef 48.40N 1.40W
Mont-Saint-Michel, Le- 122 Ef 48.38N 1.30W
Montsalvy 122 Ij 44.42N 2.30 E
Montsant, Serra del-/ Montsant, Sierra de- 126 Mc 41.17N 0.50 E
Montsant, Sierra de-/ Montsant, Serra del- 126 Mc 41.17N 0.50 E
Montsec, Serra del-/ Montsech, Sierra del- 126 Mb 42.02N 0.50 E
Montsech, Sierra del-/ Montsec, Serra del- 126 Mb 42.02N 0.50 E
Montsent de Pallars/ Montseny 126 Nb 42.29N 1.02 E
Montseny/Pallars, Montsent de- 126 Nb 42.29N 1.02 E
Montseny, Macizo del- 126 Oc 41.48N 2.24 E
Montserrado [3] 166 Cd 6.35N 10.35W
Montserrat [5] 176 Mh 16.45N 62.12W
Montserrat, Monasterio de- / Montserrat, Monestir de- 126 Nc 41.35N 1.49 E
Montserrat, Monestir de- / Montserrat, Monasterio de- 126 Nc 41.35N 1.49 E
Montuosa, Isla- 194 Fj 7.28N 82.14W
Montville 124 De 49.33N 1.07 E
Monument Peak 188 He 42.07N 114.14W
Monument Valley 188 Jh 36.50N 110.20W
Monveda 170 Db 2.57N 21.27 E
Monviso 110 Gg 44.40N 7.07 E
Monywa 148 Jd 22.07N 95.08 E
Monza 128 De 45.35N 9.16 E
Monze 170 Ef 16.16S 27.29 E
Monzen 156 Ec 37.17N 136.46 E
Monzón 126 Mc 41.55N 0.12 E
Mo'oka 156 Fc 36.27N 139.59 E
Moonbeam 184 Fa 49.25N 82.11W
Moonie 212 Ke 27.40S 150.19 E
Moonie River 212 Je 29.19S 148.43 E
Moonta 212 Hf 34.04S 137.35 E
Moora 210 Ch 30.39S 116.00 E
Moorcroft 188 Md 44.16N 104.57W
Moore 186 Hi 35.20N 97.29W
Moore, Lake- 208 Cg 29.50S 117.35 E
Moorea, Ile- 208 Mf 17.32S 149.50W
Moore's Island 184 Il 26.18N 77.33W
Moorhead 182 Hb 46.53N 96.45W
Moormerland 124 Ja 53.18N 7.26 E
Moormerland-Neermoor 124 Ja 53.18N 7.26 E
Moorreesburg 172 Bf 33.09S 18.40 E
Moosburg an der Isar 120 Hh 48.28N 11.56 E
Moose 174 Kd 50.48N 81.18W
Moosehead Lake 182 Nb 45.40N 69.40W
Moose Jaw 176 Id 50.23N 105.32W
Moose Jaw River 188 Ma 50.34N 105.17W
Moose Lake 186 Jc 46.25N 92.45W
Mooselookmeguntic Lake 184 Lc 44.53N 70.48W
Moose Mountain 186 Eb 49.45N 102.37W
Moose Mountain Creek 186 Eb 49.12N 102.10W
Moosomin 180 Hf 50.09N 101.40W
Moosonee 176 Kd 51.17N 80.39W
Mopeia 172 Fc 17.59S 35.43 E
Mopelia, Atoll- → Maupihaa Atoll 208 Lf 16.50S 153.55W
Mopti 160 Gg 14.30N 4.12W
Mopti [3] 166 Ec 14.40N 4.15W
Moqokorei 168 He 4.04N 46.08 E
Moquegua 202 Dg 17.12S 70.56W
Moquegua [3] 202 Dg 16.50S 70.55W
Mór 120 Oi 47.23N 18.12 E
Mor, Glen- 118 Id 57.10N 4.40W
Mora [Cam.] 166 Hc 11.03N 14.09 E
Mora [Port.] 126 Df 38.56N 8.10W
Mora [Sp.] 126 Ie 39.41N 3.46W
Mora [Swe.] 114 Df 61.00N 14.33 E
Morača 130 Cg 42.16N 19.09 E
Morača, Manastir- 130 Cg 42.46N 19.24 E
Morādābād 142 Jg 28.50N 78.47 E
Morada Nova de Minas 204 Jd 18.25S 45.22W
Móra d'Ebre/Mora de Ebro 126 Mc 41.05N 0.38 E
Mora de Ebro/Móra d'Ebre 126 Mc 41.05N 0.38 E
Mora de Rubielos 126 Ld 40.15N 0.45W
Morafenobe 172 Gc 17.49S 44.55 E
Morąg 120 Pc 53.56N 19.56 E
Mórahalom 120 Pj 46.13N 19.53 E
Moraleda, Canal- 206 Ff 44.30S 73.30W
Moraleja 126 Fd 40.04N 6.39W
Morales [Col.] 194 Ki 8.17N 73.52W
Morales [Guat.] 194 Cf 15.29N 88.49W
Morales, Laguna- 192 Kf 23.35N 97.45W
Moramanga 172 Hc 18.57S 48.11 E
Moran 188 Je 43.50N 110.28W
Morane Atoll 208 Ng 23.10S 137.07W
Morangas, Ribeirão- 204 Fd 19.39S 52.19W
Morant Bay 194 Ie 17.53N 76.25W
Morant Cays 190 Ie 17.24N 75.59W
Morant Point 194 Ie 17.55N 76.10W
Morar, Loch- 118 He 56.58N 5.45W
Morarano 172 Hc 17.46S 48.10 E
Mora River 186 Di 35.44N 104.23W
Moraska, Góra- 120 Md 52.30N 16.52 E
Morata, Puerto de- 126 Kc 41.29N 1.31W
Moratalla 126 Kf 38.12N 1.53W
Moratuwa 148 Fg 6.46N 79.53 E
Morava 110 Hf 48.10N 16.59 E
Morava=Moravia (EN) 110 Hf 49.30N 17.00 E
Morava=Moravia (EN) 120 Mg 49.30N 17.00 E
Moravia (EN)=Morava 110 Hf 49.30N 17.00 E
Moravia (EN)=Morava 120 Mg 49.30N 17.00 E
Moravian Gate (EN) = Moravská brána 110 Hf 49.33N 17.42 E
Moravian Upland (EN)= Českomoravská Vrchovina 110 Hf 49.20N 15.30 E
Moravica 130 Df 43.51N 20.05 E
Moravská brána = Moravian Gate (EN) 110 Hf 49.33N 17.42 E
Moravské Budějovice 120 Lg 49.03N 15.49 E
Morawa 212 De 29.13S 116.00 E
Morawhanna 202 Gb 8.16N 59.45W
Moray Firth 110 Fd 57.50N 3.30W
Morbach 124 Je 49.49N 7.07 E
Morbihan [3] 122 Dg 47.55N 2.50W
Morbihan 122 Dg 47.35N 2.48W
Morbylånga 114 Dh 56.31N 16.23 E
Morcenx 122 Fj 44.02N 0.55W
Mordāb 146 Md 37.26N 49.25 E
Mordaga 152 La 51.14N 120.43 E
Morden 180 Hg 49.11N 98.05W
Mordovo 132 Lc 52.05N 40.46 E
Mordovskaja ASSR [3] 136 Ee 54.20N 44.30 E
Möre 116 Fh 56.25N 15.55 E
More, Ben- 118 Ie 56.23N 4.31W
Morea 172 Bd 22.41S 15.54 E
More Assynt, Ben- 118 Ic 58.07N 4.51W
Moreau River 182 Gb 45.18N 100.43W
Morecambe 118 Kg 54.04N 2.53W
Morecambe Bay 118 Kg 54.07N 3.00W
Moree 210 Fg 29.28S 149.51 E
Morehead [Ky.-U.S.] 184 Ff 38.11N 83.25W
Morehead [Pap.N.Gui.] 214 Ci 8.50S 141.57 E
Morehead City 176 Lf 34.43N 76.43W
Moreiz, gora- 136 Gb 69.30N 62.05 E
Moreju 134 Ib 68.20N 59.45 E
Morelia 176 Ih 19.42N 101.07W
Morella 126 Ld 40.37N 0.06W
Morelos 192 Ic 28.25N 100.53W
Morelos [2] 190 Ee 18.45N 99.00W
Morena, Sierra- 110 Fh 38.00N 5.00W
Moreni 130 Ie 44.59N 25.39 E
Møre og Romsdal [2] 114 Be 62.40N 7.50 E
Moresby 180 Ef 52.45N 131.50W
Moreton Bay 212 Ke 27.20S 153.15 E
Moreton Island 212 Ke 27.10S 153.25 E
Moret-sur-Loing 122 If 48.22N 2.49 E
Moreuil 122 Ie 49.46N 2.29 E
Morez 122 Mh 46.31N 6.02 E
Mörfelden 124 Ke 49.59N 8.34 E
Morgan City 186 Kl 29.42N 91.12W
Morganfield 184 Dg 37.41N 87.55W
Morganton 184 Gh 35.45N 81.41W
Morgantown [Ky.-U.S.] 184 Dg 37.14N 86.41W
Morgantown [W.V.-U.S.] 184 Hf 39.38N 79.57W
Morges 128 Ad 46.31N 6.30 E
Morghāb 144 Jb 38.18N 61.12 E
Morhange 122 Mf 48.55N 6.38 E
Mori [China] 152 Fc 43.49N 90.11 E
Mori [Jap.] 154 Pc 42.06N 140.35 E
Moriarty 186 Ci 34.59N 106.03W
Morichal Largo, Río- 196 Eh 9.27N 62.25W
Moriguchi 156 Dd 34.44N 135.34 E
Morin Dawa (Nirji) 152 Lb 48.30N 124.28 E
Morioka 142 Qf 39.42N 141.09 E
Moriyoshi 156 Ga 40.07N 140.22 E
Moriyoshi-Yama 156 Gb 39.59N 140.33 E
Morjärv 114 Fc 66.04N 22.43 E
Morki 114 Lh 56.28N 49.00 E
Morko 116 Gf 59.00N 17.40 E
Morkoka 138 Gc 65.03N 115.40 E
Mørkøv 116 Di 55.40N 11.32 E
Morlaix 122 Cf 48.35N 3.50W
Morlanwelz 124 Gd 50.27N 4.14 E
Mörlunda 116 Fg 57.19N 15.51 E
Mormanno 128 Jk 39.53N 15.59 E
Morne-à-l'Eau 196 Fd 16.21N 61.31W
Morne Diablotin 190 Le 15.30N 61.24W
Mornington, Isla- 206 Eg 49.45S 75.23W
Mornington Island 212 Hc 16.35S 139.24 E
Moro 188 Ed 45.29N 120.44W
Moro Almanzor, Plaza del- 126 Gd 40.15N 5.18W
Morobe 210 Fe 7.45S 147.37 E
Morocco (EN)=Al Maghrib [1] 160 Ge 32.00N 5.50W
Morogoro 160 Ki 6.49S 37.40 E
Morogoro [3] 170 Gd 8.20S 37.00 E
Moro Gulf 150 He 6.51N 123.00 E
Moroleón 192 Ig 20.08N 101.12W
Morombe 160 Lk 21.44S 43.23 E
Morón [Arg.] 204 Cl 34.39S 58.37W
Morón [Cuba] 190 Id 22.06N 78.38W
Morón [Ven.] 202 Ea 10.29N 68.11W
Morona, Río- 202 Cd 4.45S 77.04W
Morondava 160 Lk 20.15S 44.17 E
Morón de la Frontera 126 Gg 37.08N 5.27W
Morones, Sierra- 192 Hg 21.55N 103.05W
Moroni 160 Lj 11.41S 43.16 E
Moron Us He 140 Lf 34.42N 95.00 E
Morotai, Pulau- 208 Dd 2.20N 128.25 E
Moroto 160 Kh 2.32N 34.39 E
Moroviţa 130 Ed 45.16N 21.16 E
Morozov 130 Ig 42.30N 25.10 E
Morozovsk 136 Ef 48.20N 41.50 E
Morpeth 118 Lf 55.10N 1.41W
Morphou → Güzelyurt 146 Ee 35.12N 32.59 E
Morrilton 186 Ji 35.09N 92.45W
Morrinhos 202 Ig 17.44S 49.07W
Morrinsville 218 Fb 37.39S 175.32 E
Morris [Il.-U.S.] 186 Lf 41.22N 88.26W
Morris [Man.-Can.] 180 Hg 49.21N 97.22W
Morris [Mn.-U.S.] 186 Id 45.35N 95.55W
Morris, Mount- 212 Ge 26.09S 131.04 E
Morrisburg 184 Jc 44.54N 75.11W
Morris Jesup, Kap- 224 Me 83.45N 35.50W
Morrison Dennis Cays 194 Ff 14.28N 82.53W
Morristown 184 Fg 36.13N 83.18W
Morrito 194 Eh 11.37N 85.05W
Morro, Punta del- 192 Kh 19.51N 96.27W
Morro Bay 182 Cd 35.22N 120.51W
Morro do Chapéu 202 Jf 11.33S 41.09W
Morrosquillo, Golfo de- 194 Ji 9.35N 75.40W
Morro Vermelho, Serra do- 204 Jc 17.45S 45.20W
Mörrum 116 Fh 56.11N 14.45 E
Morrumbala 172 Fc 17.20S 35.35 E
Morrumbene 172 Fd 23.39S 35.20 E
Mörrumsån 116 Fh 56.09N 14.44 E
Mors 116 Ch 56.50N 8.45 E
Moršansk 136 Ee 53.26N 41.49 E
Morsbach 124 Jd 50.52N 7.45 E
Morsberg 124 Ke 49.43N 8.54 E
Mörsil 114 Ce 63.19N 13.38 E
Mörskom/Myrskylä 116 Kd 60.40N 25.51 E
Morsott 128 Co 35.40N 8.01 E
Mortagne 122 Mf 48.33N 6.27 E
Mortagne-au-Perche 122 Gf 48.31N 0.33 E
Mortagne-sur-Sèvre 122 Fg 47.00N 0.57W
Mortain 122 Ff 48.39N 0.56W
Mortara 128 Ce 45.15N 8.44 E
Mortcha 158 Jg 16.00N 21.10 E
Morteau 122 Mg 47.04N 6.37 E
Morteaux-Couliboeuf 124 Bf 48.56N 0.04W
Morteros 206 Hd 30.42S 62.00W
Mortes, Rio das- 204 Je 21.09S 44.53W
Mortes, Rio das- → Manso, Rio- 198 Kg 11.45S 50.44W
Mortesoro 168 Ec 10.12N 34.09 E
Mortlock Islands 208 Gd 5.27N 153.40 E
Morton 188 Dc 46.33N 122.17W
Mortsel 124 Gc 51.10N 4.28 E
Morumbi 204 Ef 23.46S 54.06W
Morvan 122 Jg 47.05N 4.00 E
Morven 212 Je 26.25S 147.07 E
Morvern 118 He 56.35N 5.50W
Morvi 148 Ed 22.49N 70.50 E
Morwell 210 Fh 38.14S 146.24 E
Morzine 122 Mh 46.11N 6.43 E
Moržovec, ostrov- 114 Kc 66.45N 42.35 E
Moša 114 Je 62.25N 39.48 E
Mosbach 120 Fg 49.21N 9.09 E
Mosby 116 Bf 58.14N 7.54 E
Moščny, ostrov- 114 Gg 60.00N 27.50 E
Mosconi 204 Bl 35.44S 60.34W
Moscos Islands 148 Jf 14.00N 97.45 E
Moscow [Id.-U.S.] 182 Db 46.44N 116.59W
Moscow (EN)=Moskva 110 Jd 55.08N 38.50 E
Moscow (EN)=Moskva [R.S.F.S.R.] 112 Jd 55.45N 37.35 E
Moscow Basin (EN)= Meščera 110 Kd 55.00N 40.30 E
Moscow Canal (EN) = Moskvy, kanal imeni- 110 Jd 56.43N 37.08 E
Moscow Upland (EN) = Moskovskaja vozvyšennost 110 Jd 56.30N 37.30 E
Mosel=Moselle (EN) 110 Ge 50.22N 7.36 E
Moselberge 124 Ie 49.57N 6.56 E
Moselle [3] 122 Me 49.00N 6.30 E
Moselle 110 Ge 50.22N 7.36 E
Moselle (EN)=Mosel 110 Ge 50.22N 7.36 E
Moses Lake 182 Db 47.08N 119.17W
Mosgiel 216 Di 45.53S 170.22 E
Moshi 160 Ki 3.21S 37.20 E
Mosina 120 Md 52.16N 16.51 E
Mosjøen 114 Cd 65.50N 13.12 E
Moskalvo 138 Jf 53.39N 142.37 E
Moskenesøy 114 Cc 67.59N 13.00 E
Moskovskaja oblast [3] 136 Dd 55.45N 37.45 E
Moskovskaja vozvyšennost = Moscow Upland (EN) 110 Jd 56.30N 37.30 E
Moskovski 135 Gf 37.40N 69.39 E
Moskva [R.S.F.S.R.] = Moscow (EN) 112 Jd 55.45N 37.35 E
Moskva [Tur.-U.S.S.R.] 135 Ee 38.27N 64.24 E
Moskva=Moscow (EN) 110 Jd 55.08N 38.50 E
Moskva, pik- 135 He 38.55N 71.52 E
Moskvy, kanal imeni- = Moscow Canal (EN) 110 Jd 56.43N 37.08 E
Moslavačka Gora 128 Ke 45.38N 16.42 E
Moso 219b Dc 17.32S 168.15 E
Mosomane 172 Dd 24.01S 26.19 E
Mosoni-Duna 120 Ni 47.44N 17.47 E
Mosonmagyaróvár 120 Ni 47.52N 17.17 E
Mosquero 186 Ei 35.47N 103.58W
Mosquito, Baie - 180 Jd 60.40N 78.00W
Mosquito, Riacho- 204 Cf 22.12S 57.57W
Mosquito Coast (EN) = Mosquitos, Costa de los- 174 Kh 13.00N 83.45W
Mosquitos, Costa de los- = Mosquito Coast (E) 174 Kh 13.00N 83.45W
Mosquitos, Golfo de los- 174 Ki 9.00N 81.20W
Moss 112 Hd 59.26N 10.42 E
Mossaka 170 Cc 1.13S 16.48 E
Mossâmedes 204 Gc 16.07S 50.11W
Mossbank 188 Mb 49.55N 105.59W
Mossburn 216 Ci 45.41S 168.15 E
Mosselbaai 160 Jl 34.11S 22.08 E
Mossendjo 170 Bc 2.57S 12.44 E
Mossman 210 Ff 16.28S 145.22 E
Mossø 116 Ch 56.05N 9.50 E
Mossoró 200 Mf 5.11S 37.20W
Moss Point 186 Lk 30.25N 88.29W
Mossuril 172 Gb 14.58S 40.40 E
Most 120 Jf 50.32N 13.39 E
Mostaganem 160 He 35.56N 0.05 E
Mostaganem [3] 162 Hb 35.40N 0.30 E
Mostar 128 Lg 43.21N 17.49 E
Mostardas 204 Gj 31.06S 50.57W
Møsting, Kap- 179 Hf 63.45N 41.00W
Mostiska 132 Ce 49.48N 23.09 E
Mostiştea 130 Je 44.15N 26.54 E
Mostovskoj 132 Lg 44.22N 40.48 E
Mosty 136 Ce 53.27N 24.33 E
Mosul (EN)=Al Mawşil 142 Gf 36.20N 43.08 E
Møsvatn 114 Bg 59.50N 8.05 E
Mota 168 Fc 11.05N 37.53 E
Mota 219b Ca 13.40S 167.42 E
Motaba 170 Cb 2.03N 18.03 E
Motacusito 204 Bc 17.35S 61.31W
Mota del Marqués 126 Gc 41.38N 5.10W
Motagua 174 Kh 15.44N 88.14W
Motajica 128 Le 45.04N 17.40 E
Motala 114 Dg 58.33N 15.03 E
Motala ström 116 Gf 58.38N 16.10 E
Motatán 194 Li 9.24N 70.36W
Motatán, Río- 194 Li 9.32N 71.02W
Motegi 156 Gc 36.32N 140.10 E
Mothe 219d Cc 18.40S 178.30W
Mothe-Achard, La- 122 Eh 46.37N 1.40W
Motherwell 118 Jf 55.48N 4.00W
Motīhāri 148 Gc 26.39N 84.55 E
Motilla del Palancar 126 Ke 39.34N 1.53W
Motiti Island 218 Gb 37.40S 176.25 E
Motlav 219b Ca 13.40S 167.40 E
Motobu 156b Ab 26.40N 127.55 E
Motol 120 Vd 52.17N 25.40 E
Motovski zaliv 114 Hb 69.30N 32.30 E
Motoyoshi 156 Gb 38.48N 141.31 E
Motozintla de Mendoza 192 Mj 15.22N 92.14W
Motril 126 Ih 36.45N 3.31W
Motru 130 Fe 44.48N 23.00 E
Motru 130 Ge 44.33N 23.27 E
Motsuta-Misaki 156a Ab 42.36N 139.49 E
Mott 186 Ec 46.22N 102.20W
Motteville 124 Ce 49.38N 0.51 E
Motu 218 Gb 37.51S 177.35 E
Motueka 218 Ed 41.07S 173.01 E
Motuhora Island 218 Gb 37.50S 177.00 E
Motu-Iti 221d Ac 27.11S 109.27W
Motu-Iti → Tupai Atoll 216 Kc 16.17S 151.50W
Motul 190 Gd 21.06N 89.17W
Motu-Nui 221d Ac 27.12S 109.28W
Motu One Atoll 208 Lf 15.48S 154.33W
Motupae 220n Ac 10.27S 161.02W
Motupena Point 219a Bb 6.32S 155.09 E
Moturiki 219d Bb 17.46S 178.45 E
Mototapu 220p Cb 21.14S 159.43W
Motu Tautara 221d Ab 27.05S 109.26W
Motutunga Atoll 208 Mf 17.06S 144.22W
Moubray Bay 222 Kf 72.11S 170.15 E
Mouchard 122 Lh 46.58N 5.48 E
Mouchoir Bank (EN) 190 Jd 20.57N 70.42W
Mouchoir Passage 194 Lc 21.10N 71.00W
Moudjéria 162 Ef 17.52N 12.20W
Mouila 160 Ii 1.52S 11.01 E
Mouka 168 Cd 7.16N 21.52 E
Moul 166 Hb 15.03N 13.18 E
Mould Bay 176 Hb 76.15N 119.30W
Moule 196 Fd 16.20N 61.21W
Moule à Chique, Cap- 197k Bb 13.43N 60.57W
Moulins 122 Jh 46.34N 3.20 E
Moulmein → Mawlamyine 142 Le 16.30N 97.38 E
Moulouya 158 Ge 35.06N 2.20W
Moult 124 Be 49.07N 0.10W
Moultrie 184 Fj 31.11N 83.47W
Moultrie, Lake- 184 Gi 33.20N 80.05W
Mouly, Pointe de- 219b Ce 20.43S 166.23 E
Moúnda, Ákra- 130 Dk 38.03N 20.47 E
Moundou 160 Ih 8.34N 16.05 E
Moundsville 184 Gf 39.54N 80.44W
Mo'unga'one 221b Ba 19.38S 174.29W
Moungoudou 170 Bc 2.40S 12.41 E
Mountainair 186 Ci 34.31N 106.15W
Mountain Grove 186 Jh 37.08N 92.16W
Mountain Home [Ar.-U.S.] 186 Jh 36.21N 92.23W
Mountain Home [Id.-U.S.] 182 Dc 43.08N 115.41W
Mountain Nile (EN)=Jabal, Baḩr al- 158 Kh 9.30N 30.30 E
Mountain Village 178 Gd 62.05N 163.44W
Mount Airy 184 Gg 36.31N 80.37W
Mount Barker 212 Df 34.38S 117.40 E
Mount Carmel 186 Mg 38.25N 87.46W
Mount Desert Island 184 Mc 44.20N 68.20W
Mount Douglas 210 Fg 21.30S 146.50 E
Mount Eba 212 Hf 30.12S 135.40 E
Mount Forest 184 Gd 43.59N 80.44W
Mount Frere 172 Df 31.00S 28.58 E
Mount Gambier 210 Fh 37.50S 140.46 E
Mount Hagen 214 Ci 5.52S 144.13 E
Mount Hope 212 Hf 34.07S 135.23 E
Mount Isa 210 Eg 20.44S 139.30 E
Mountlake Terrace 188 Dc 47.47N 122.18W
Mount Lebanon 184 Ge 40.23N 80.03W
Mount Lofty Ranges 212 Hg 35.15S 138.50 E
Mount Magnet 210 Cg 28.04S 117.49 E
Mount Maunganui 216 Eg 37.38S 176.12 E
Mount Morgan 212 Kd 23.39S 150.23 E
Mountnorris Bay 212 Gb 11.20S 132.45 E
Mount Peck 188 Ha 50.10N 115.02W
Mount Pleasant [Ia.-U.S.] 186 Kf 40.58N 91.33W
Mount Pleasant [Mi.-U.S.] 184 Ed 43.35N 84.47W
Mount Pleasant [S.C.-U.S.] 184 Hi 32.47N 79.52W
Mount Pleasant [Tx.-U.S.] 186 Ij 33.09N 94.58W
Mount Pleasant [Ut.-U.S.] 188 Jg 39.33N 111.27W
Mount's Bay 118 Hk 50.03N 5.25W
Mount Somers 218 De 43.42S 171.25 E
Mount Sterling [Il.-U.S.] 186 Kg 39.59N 90.45W
Mount Sterling [Ky.-U.S.] 184 Ff 38.04N 83.56W
Mount Vancouver 180 Dd 60.20N 139.41W
Mount Vernon [Al.-U.S.] 184 Cj 31.05N 88.01W
Mount Vernon [Austl.] 212 Dd 24.13S 118.14 E
Mount Vernon [Il.-U.S.] 182 Jd 38.19N 88.55W
Mount Vernon [In.-U.S.] 184 Dg 37.56N 87.54W
Mount Vernon [Ky.-U.S.] 184 Eg 37.21N 84.20W
Mount Vernon [Oh.-U.S.] 184 Fe 40.23N 82.30W
Mount Vernon [Wa.-U.S.] 182 Cb 48.25N 122.20W
Moura [Austl.] 212 Jd 24.35S 150.00 E
Moura [Port.] 126 Ef 38.08N 7.27W
Mourão 126 Ef 38.23N 7.21W
Mourdi 168 Cb 17.50N 22.25 E
Mourdi, Dépression du-= Mourdi Depression (EN) 158 Jg 18.10N 23.00 E
Mourdiah 166 Dc 14.26N 7.31W
Mourdi Depression (EN)= Mourdi, Dépression du- 158 Jg 18.10N 23.00 E
Mourmelon-le-Grand 124 Ge 49.08N 4.22 E
Mourne Mountains/Beanna Boirche 118 Gg 54.10N 6.04W
Mouscron/Moeskroen 122 Jd 50.44N 3.13 E
Moussoro 160 Ig 13.39N 16.29 E
Moustiers-Sainte-Marie 122 Mk 43.51N 6.13 E
Moutier/Münster 128 Bc 47.16N 7.22 E
Moutiers 122 Mi 45.29N 6.32 E
Moutong 150 Hf 0.28N 121.13 E
Mouy 124 Ee 49.19N 2.19 E
Mouydir 158 Hf 25.00N 4.10 E
Mouyondzi 170 Bc 3.58S 13.57 E
Mouzaia 126 Oh 36.28N 2.41 E
Mouzon 124 He 49.36N 5.05 E
Movas 192 Ec 28.10N 109.25W
Moxico 170 De 11.51S 20.01 E
Moxico [3] 170 De 12.00S 20.00 E
Moy/An Mhuaidh 118 Dg 54.12N 9.08W
Moyahua 192 Hg 21.16N 103.10W
Moyale [Eth.] 160 Kh 3.32N 39.04 E
Moyale [Kenya] 170 Gb 3.32N 39.03 E
Moyamba 166 Cd 8.10N 12.26W
Moÿ-de-l'Aisne 124 Fe 49.45N 3.22 E
Moyen Atlas=Middle Atlas (EN) 158 Ge 33.30N 4.30W
Moyen-Chari [3] 163 Bd 9.00N 18.00 E
Moyenne Guinée [3] 166 Cc 11.15N 12.30W
Moyenneville 124 Dd 50.04N 1.45 E
Moyen-Ogooué [3] 170 Bc 0.30S 10.30 E
Moyeuvre-Grande 124 Ie 49.15N 6.02 E
Moyo 170 Fb 3.40N 31.43 E
Moyo, Pulau- 150 Gh 8.15S 117.34 E
Moyobamba 200 If 6.02S 76.58W
Moyowosi 170 Fc 4.50S 31.24 E
Moyto 168 Bc 12.35N 16.33 E
Moyu/Karakax 152 Cd 37.17N 79.42 E
Možajsk 114 Ii 55.32N 36.02 E
Mozambique (EN)= Moçambique 160 Lj 15.03S 40.45 E
Mozambique (EN)= Moçambique [1] 160 Kj 18.15S 35.00 E
Mozambique, Canal de-= Mozambique Channel (EN) 158 Lk 20.00S 43.00 E
Mozambique Channel (EN) =Moçambique, Canal de- 158 Lk 20.00S 43.00 E

Index Symbols

[1] Independent Nation
[2] State, Region
[3] District, County
[4] Municipality
[5] Colony, Dependency
Continent
Physical Region
Historical or Cultural Region
Mount, Mountain
Volcano
Hill
Mountains, Mountain Range
Hills, Escarpment
Plateau, Upland
Pass, Gap
Plain, Lowland
Delta
Salt Flat
Valley, Canyon
Crater, Cave
Karst Features
Depression
Polder
Desert, Dunes
Forest, Woods
Heath, Steppe
Oasis
Cape, Point
Coast, Beach
Cliff
Peninsula
Isthmus
Sandbank
Island
Atoll
Rock, Reef
Islands, Archipelago
Rocks, Reefs
Coral Reef
Well, Spring
Geyser
River, Stream
Waterfall, Rapids
River Mouth, Estuary
Lake
Salt Lake
Intermittent Lake
Reservoir
Swamp, Pond
Canal
Glacier
Ice Shelf, Pack Ice
Ocean
Sea
Gulf, Bay
Strait, Fjord
Lagoon
Bank
Seamount
Tablemount
Ridge
Shelf
Basin
Escarpment, Sea Scarp
Fracture
Trench, Abyss
National Park, Reserve
Point of Interest
Recreation Site
Cave, Cavern
Historic Site
Ruins
Wall, Walls
Church, Abbey
Temple
Scientific Station
Railway station
Airport
Port
Military installation
Lighthouse
Mine
Tunnel
Dam, Bridge

Name	Page	Grid	Lat	Long
Mozambique Channel (EN) =Mozambique, Canal de-				
Mozambique Plateau (EN)	158	Kl	32.00 S	35.00 E
Mozdok	136	Eg	43.44 N	44.38 E
Mozga	136	Fd	56.28 N	52.13 E
Mozuli	116	Mh	56.32 N	28.14 E
Mozyr	136	Ce	52.02 N	29.16 E
Mpala	170	Ed	6.45 S	29.31 E
Mpanda	160	Ki	6.22 S	31.02 E
Mpigi	170	Fb	0.15 N	32.20 E
Mpika	160	Kj	11.50 S	31.27 E
Mpoko	168	Be	4.19 N	18.33 E
Mporokoso	170	Fd	9.23 S	30.08 E
Mpouia	170	Cc	2.37 S	16.13 E
Mpui	170	Fd	8.21 S	31.50 E
Mpulungu	170	Fd	8.46 S	31.07 E
Mpwapwa	170	Gd	6.21 S	36.29 E
Mragowo	120	Rc	53.52 N	21.19 E
Mrakovo	134	Hj	52.43 N	56.38 E
Mrkonjić Grad	128	Lf	44.25 N	17.06 E
Mrocza	120	Nc	53.14 N	17.36 E
Mroga	120	Pd	52.09 N	19.42 E
Msangesi	170	Ge	11.40 S	36.45 E
Msid, Djebel-	128	Ce	36.25 N	8.04 E
Msif	126	Qi	35.23 N	4.45 E
M'Sila	162	Hb	35.42 N	4.33 E
M'Sila	162	Hb	35.00 N	4.30 E
M'Sila	126	Qi	35.31 N	4.30 E
Mšinskaja	116	Nf	58.55 N	30.03 E
Msta	110	Jd	58.25 N	31.20 E
Mstislavl	132	Gc	53.59 N	31.45 E
Mszana Dolna	120	Qg	49.42 N	20.05 E
Mtakuja	170	Fd	7.22 S	30.37 E
Mtama	170	Ge	10.18 S	39.22 E
Mtelo	170	Gb	1.39 N	35.23 E
Mtera Reservoir	170	Gd	7.01 S	35.55 E
Mtito Andei	170	Gc	2.41 S	38.10 E
Mtubatuba	172	Ee	28.30 S	32.08 E
Mtwara	160	Lj	10.16 S	40.11 E
Mtwara	170	Ge	10.40 S	39.00 E
Mu, Cerro-	194	Kj	9.29 N	73.07 W
Mua	220h	Ac	13.21 S	176.10 W
Mu'a	221b	Ac	21.11 S	175.07 W
Mua, Baie de-	220h	Bc	13.23 S	176.09 W
Muaná	202	Id	1.32 S	49.13 W
Muang Huon	148	Kd	20.09 N	101.27 E
Muang Khammouan	148	Ke	17.24 N	104.48 E
Muang Không	148	Lf	14.07 N	105.51 E
Muang Khôngxédôn	148	Le	15.34 N	105.49 E
Muang Khoua	148	Kd	21.05 N	102.31 E
Muang Pak Lay	148	Ke	18.12 N	101.25 E
Muang Pakxan	148	Ke	18.22 N	103.39 E
Muang Pakxong	148	Le	15.11 N	106.14 E
Muang Sing	148	Kd	21.11 N	101.09 E
Muang Tahoi	148	Le	16.10 N	106.38 E
Muang Thai=Thailand (EN)	142	Mh	15.00 N	100.00 E
Muang Vangviang	148	Ke	18.56 N	102.27 E
Muang Xaignabouri	148	Ke	19.15 N	101.45 E
Muang Xay	148	Kd	20.42 N	101.59 E
Muang Xépôn	148	Le	16.41 N	106.14 E
Muanzanza	170	Dd	6.32 S	20.51 E
Muar	150	Df	2.02 N	102.34 E
Muaraaman	150	Dg	3.07 S	102.12 E
Muarabungo	150	Dg	1.28 S	102.07 E
Muaraenim	150	Dg	3.39 S	103.48 E
Muaralasan	150	Gf	1.48 N	117.12 E
Muarapajang	150	Gf	1.32 S	115.48 E
Muarasiberut	150	Cg	1.36 S	99.11 E
Muarasiram	150	Gg	0.46 S	116.11 E
Muaratebo	150	Dg	1.30 S	102.26 E
Muaratewe	150	Fg	0.57 S	114.53 E
Muarawahau	150	Gf	1.02 N	116.52 E
Mubarek	135	Ee	39.16 N	65.07 E
Mubende	170	Fb	0.35 N	31.23 E
Mubi	160	Ig	10.16 N	13.16 E
Much	124	Jd	50.55 N	7.24 E
Muchinga Escarpment	170	Fc	13.40 S	30.00 E
Muchinga Mountains	158	Kj	12.00 S	31.45 E
Muck	118	Ge	56.50 N	6.14 W
Mücke	124	Ld	50.37 N	9.02 E
Mucojo	172	Gb	12.04 S	40.28 E
Muconda	170	Dd	10.34 S	21.20 E
Mucua	172	Ec	18.09 S	34.58 E
Mucubela	172	Fc	16.54 S	37.49 E
Mucuchies	194	Ki	8.45 N	70.55 W
Mucumbura	172	Ec	16.10 S	31.42 E
Mucur	146	Fc	39.04 N	34.23 E
Mucusso	170	Df	18.00 S	21.25 E
Mudanjiang	140	Oe	44.35 N	129.34 E
Mudan Jiang	140	Oe	46.18 N	129.31 E
Mudanya	146	Db	40.22 N	28.52 E
Muddy Gap	188	Le	42.22 N	107.27 W
Mudgee	212	Jf	32.36 S	149.35 E
Mud Lake	188	Gh	43.53 N	112.24 W
Mud Lake	188	Gh	37.55 N	117.05 W
Mudon	148	Je	16.15 N	97.44 E
Mudug	168	Hd	6.30 N	48.00 E
Mudug	168	Hd	6.20 N	47.00 E
Mudurnu	146	Db	40.28 N	31.13 E
Muecate	172	Fb	14.53 S	39.38 E
Mueda	172	Fb	11.39 S	39.33 E
Muerto, Cayo-	194	Ff	14.34 N	82.44 W
Muerto, Mar-	192	Ni	16.10 N	94.10 W
Mufulira	160	Jj	12.33 S	28.14 E
Mufu Shan	152	Jf	29.00 N	113.50 E
Mufu Shan	152	Jf	29.15 N	114.20 E
Mugello	128	Fg	43.55 N	11.25 E
Múggia	128	Gf	45.36 N	13.46 E
Mughshin, Wādī-	168	Ib	19.44 N	55.00 E
Mugi	156	De	33.40 N	134.25 E
Mu Gia, Monts-	148	Le	17.40 N	105.47 E
Mugila, Monts-	170	Ee	6.49 S	29.08 E
Mugla	144	Cb	37.12 N	28.22 E
Mugodžary	140	He	49.00 N	58.40 E
Mugur an Na'ām	146	Ig	31.56 N	40.30 E
Muhaiwir	146	If	33.28 N	40.59 E
Muḥammad, Ra's-	164	Fd	27.42 N	34.13 E
Muḥammad Qawl	168	Fa	20.54 N	37.05 E
Muhen	138	Ig	48.10 N	136.08 E
Muheza	170	Gd	5.10 S	38.47 E
Muhit, Al Baḥr al-=Atlantic Ocean (EN)	106	Di	2.00 N	25.00 W
Mühlacher	120	Eh	48.57 N	8.50 E
Mühldorf am Inn	120	Ih	48.15 N	12.32 E
Mühlhausen in Thüringen	120	Ge	51.13 N	10.27 E
Mühlig-Hofmann Gebirge	222	Cf	72.00 S	5.20 E
Mühlviertel	128	Ib	48.30 N	14.10 E
Muhoršibir	138	Ff	51.01 N	107.50 E
Muhos	114	Gd	64.50 N	26.01 E
Muhu	116	Jf	58.37 N	23.05 E
Muhu	114	Fg	58.35 N	23.15 E
Muhu, Proliv- / Muhu Väin	116	Jf	58.45 N	23.15 E
Muhulu	170	Ec	1.03 S	27.17 E
Muhu Väin / Muhu, Proliv-	116	Jf	58.45 N	23.15 E
Muhuwesi	170	Ge	11.16 S	37.58 E
Muiderslot	124	Hb	52.20 N	5.06 E
Muigheo/Mayo	118	Dh	53.50 N	9.30 W
Muikamachi	154	Of	37.04 N	138.53 E
Muineachán/Monaghan	118	Gg	54.15 N	6.58 W
Muineachán/Monaghan	118	Gg	54.16 N	7.00 W
Muine Bheag	118	Gi	52.42 N	6.57 W
Muir Bhreatan=Saint George's Channel (EN)	110	Fe	52.00 N	6.00 W
Muiron Islands	212	Cd	21.35 S	114.20 E
Muir Seamount (EN)	174	Mf	33.41 N	63.32 W
Muite	172	Fb	14.02 S	39.02 E
Mujeres, Isla-	192	Pg	21.13 N	86.43 W
Mujezerski	116	He	63.57 N	32.01 E
Muji	152	Xf	37.27 N	78.33 E
Mujnak	136	Fg	43.44 N	59.02 E
Mujnakski zaliv	135	Bc	43.50 N	58.40 E
Mujunkum, peski-	140	Je	44.00 N	70.30 E
Mukačevo	136	Cf	48.26 N	22.45 E
Mukah	150	Ff	2.54 N	112.06 E
Mukawa	156a	Bb	42.34 N	141.55 E
Mu-Kawa	156a	Bb	42.33 N	141.53 E
Mukawwar	168	Fa	20.48 N	37.13 E
Mukdahan	148	Ke	16.31 N	104.42 E
Mukeru	220a	Bc	7.29 N	134.37 E
Mukho	154	Jf	37.33 N	129.07 E
Mukinbudin	212	Df	30.54 S	118.13 E
Mukojima-Rettō	214	Cb	27.37 N	142.10 E
Mukomuko	150	Dg	2.35 S	101.07 E
Muksu	135	He	39.17 N	71.25 E
Mula	126	Kf	38.03 N	1.30 W
Mula	148	Dc	27.57 N	67.36 E
Mulainagiri	148	Ff	13.24 N	75.43 E
Mulaku Atoll	148a	Bb	2.57 N	73.34 E
Mulaly	136	Hf	45.27 N	78.20 E
Mulan	152	Mb	46.00 N	128.02 E
Mulanje	170	Gf	16.02 S	35.30 E
Mulanje	158	Kj	16.03 S	35.31 E
Mulatre, Point-	197g	Bb	15.17 N	61.15 W
Mulatupo Sasardi	194	Ii	8.57 N	77.45 W
Mulchatna	188	Ce	59.39 N	157.08 W
Mulchén	206	Fe	37.34 S	72.14 W
Mulda	134	Kc	67.28 N	63.34 E
Mulde	120	Ie	51.48 N	12.10 E
Mulebreen	222	Ee	67.28 S	59.21 E
Mulhacén	110	Fh	37.03 N	3.19 W
Mülheim an der Ruhr	124	Jc	51.26 N	6.53 E
Mülheim-Kärlich	124	Jd	50.23 N	7.30 E
Mulhouse	112	Gf	47.45 N	7.20 E
Muli (Bowa)	152	Hf	27.55 N	101.13 E
Mulifanua	221c	Aa	13.50 S	172.02 W
Muling (Bamiantong)	154	Kb	44.34 N	130.12 E
Muling Guan	154	Kb	44.55 N	130.32 E
Muling He	154	Lb	45.53 N	133.30 E
Mull, Island of-	118	Fd	56.27 N	6.00 W
Mull, Sound of-	118	Ne	56.35 N	5.50 W
Mullen	186	Fe	42.03 N	101.01 W
Mullens	184	Gg	37.35 N	81.25 W
Müller, Pegunungan-	150	Ff	0.40 N	113.50 E
Mullet Peninsula/An Muirthead	118	Cg	54.15 N	10.04 W
Mullet Lake	184	Ec	45.30 N	84.30 W
Mullewa	212	De	28.33 S	115.31 E
Müllheim	120	Di	47.48 N	7.38 E
Mullingar/An Muileann gCearr	118	Fh	53.32 N	7.20 W
Mullsjö	114	Ef	57.59 N	13.53 E
Mulobezi	170	Ef	16.47 S	25.10 E
Mulock Glacier	222	Jf	79.03 S	159.10 E
Mulongo	170	Ed	7.50 S	26.57 E
Multán	142	Jf	30.11 N	71.29 E
Multé	192	Ni	17.41 N	91.24 W
Multia	116	Kb	62.25 N	24.47 E
Multien	124	Ib	49.05 N	2.55 E
Mulu, Gunong-	150	Ff	4.03 N	114.56 E
Mulvane	186	Hh	37.29 N	97.14 W
Mulyma	134	Lf	60.12 N	64.32 E
Mumbué	170	Ce	13.53 S	17.19 E
Mumbwa	170	Ee	14.59 S	27.04 E
Mumhan/Munster	118	Ei	52.30 N	9.00 W
Mumra	136	Ff	45.45 N	47.41 E
Muna	192	Og	20.29 N	89.43 W
Muna	110	Oc	67.52 N	123.10 E
Muna, Pulau-	150	Hg	5.00 S	122.30 E
Munábão	148	Ec	25.45 N	70.17 E
Munamägi/Munamjagi	116	Lg	57.38 N	27.10 E
Munamjagi/Munamägi	116	Lg	57.38 N	27.10 E
Munaybarah, Sharm-	164	Gi	26.04 N	36.38 E
Muncar	150	Fh	8.29 S	114.21 E
Münchberg	120	Hf	50.12 N	11.47 E
München=Munich (EN)	112	Hf	48.09 N	11.35 E
Münchhausen	124	Kd	50.57 N	8.43 E
Muncho Lake	180	Ee	58.56 N	125.46 W
Munch'ŏn	154	Ie	39.14 N	127.22 E
Muncie	182	Jc	40.11 N	85.23 W
Munda	219a	Cc	8.19 S	157.15 E
Mundaring, Perth-	212	Df	31.54 S	116.10 E
Munday	186	Gj	33.27 N	99.38 W
Mundemba	166	Ge	4.59 N	8.40 E
Mundesley	124	Db	52.52 N	1.25 E
Mundford	124	Cb	52.30 N	0.39 E
Mundiwindi	210	Dg	23.52 S	120.09 E
Mundo	126	Kf	38.19 N	1.40 W
Mundo Novo	202	Jf	11.52 S	40.28 W
Munelles, Mali i-	130	Dh	41.58 N	20.06 E
Munera	126	Je	39.02 N	2.28 W
Mungana	212	Ic	17.07 S	144.24 E
Mungbere	160	Jh	2.38 N	28.30 E
Munger	148	Hc	25.23 N	86.28 E
Mungindi	212	Je	28.58 S	148.59 E
Munhango	170	Ce	12.10 S	18.34 E
Munh-Hajrhan-Ula	140	Le	46.40 N	91.30 E
Muniesa	126	Lc	41.02 N	0.48 W
Munifah	144	Gd	27.38 N	49.00 E
Munising	184	Db	46.25 N	86.40 W
Munkedal	114	Cg	58.29 N	11.41 E
Munkfors	114	Cg	59.50 N	13.32 E
Munku-Sardyk, gora-	110	Md	51.45 N	100.20 E
Muñoz Gamero, Peninsula-	206	Fh	52.30 S	73.10 W
Munsan	154	If	37.55 N	126.22 E
Münsingen	120	Fh	48.25 N	9.30 E
Munster	122	Nf	48.03 N	7.08 E
Münster [Ger.]	120	De	51.58 N	7.38 E
Münster [Ger.]	124	Je	49.55 N	8.52 E
Münster/Moutier	128	Bc	47.16 N	7.22 E
Munster/Munhan	118	Ei	52.30 N	9.00 W
Münster-Hiltrup	124	Jc	51.54 N	7.38 E
Münsterland [Ger.]	120	De	52.00 N	7.30 E
Münsterland [Ger.]	124	Kb	52.45 N	8.10 E
Münstermaifeld	124	Jd	50.15 N	7.22 E
Muntenia	130	Ie	44.00 N	26.00 E
Munteni Buzău	130	Je	44.38 N	26.59 E
Muntok	150	Eg	2.04 S	105.11 E
Munzur Dağları	146	Hc	39.30 N	39.10 E
Muong Sen	148	Ke	19.24 N	104.08 E
Muonio	112	Ib	67.57 N	23.42 E
Muonioälven	110	Ib	67.11 N	23.34 E
Muonionjoki	110	Ib	67.11 N	23.34 E
Muping	154	Ff	37.23 N	121.36 E
Muqaddam	168	Eb	18.04 N	31.30 E
Muqayshiṭ	126	Oj	24.10 N	53.45 E
Muqdisho=Mogadishu (EN)	160	Lh	2.03 N	45.22 E
Mur	110	Hf	46.18 N	16.55 E
Mura	110	Hf	46.18 N	16.55 E
Muradiye [Tur.]	146	Jc	39.00 N	43.43 E
Muradiye [Tur.]	130	Kk	38.39 N	27.24 E
Murafa	132	Fe	48.13 N	28.14 E
Murakami	154	Oe	38.14 N	139.29 E
Murallón, Cerro-	198	Ij	49.48 S	73.25 W
Murán	120	Qh	48.45 N	20.02 E
Mur'anyo	168	Ic	11.41 N	50.27 E
Murashi	136	Fd	59.25 N	49.00 E
Murat	140	Ff	38.52 N	38.48 E
Murat Daği	144	Cb	39.20 N	29.43 E
Muratlı [Tur.]	146	Ib	41.29 N	41.41 E
Muratlı [Tur.]	146	Kh	41.10 N	27.30 E
Murau	128	Ic	47.06 N	14.10 E
Muravera	128	Dk	39.25 N	9.34 E
Murayama	156	Bb	38.29 N	140.23 E
Mürchen Khvort	146	Nf	33.06 N	51.30 E
Murchison	212	De	26.46 S	116.25 E
Murchison, Mount- [Austl.]	212	De	26.46 S	116.25 E
Murchison, Mount- [N.Z.]	218	De	43.01 S	171.17 E
Murchison Falls=Kabalega Falls	170	Fb	2.17 N	31.41 E
Murchison River	208	Cg	27.50 S	114.00 E
Murcia	112	Fh	37.59 N	1.07 W
Murcia	126	Kg	38.00 N	1.30 W
Mur-de-Barrez	126	Hf	44.51 N	2.39 E
Murdo	186	Fe	43.53 N	100.43 W
Mure, La-	122	Lj	44.54 N	5.47 E
Mureaux, Les-	124	Id	49.00 N	1.55 E
Mürefte	130	Ki	40.40 N	27.14 E
Muren	146	Me	49.38 N	100.12 E
Mureş	130	He	46.30 N	24.40 E
Mureş	130	If	46.15 N	20.12 E
Muret	112	Kk	43.28 N	1.21 E
Murfreesboro	182	Je	35.51 N	86.23 W
Murg	120	Eh	48.55 N	8.10 E
Murgab	140	If	38.18 N	61.12 E
Murgab [Taj.-U.S.S.R.]	135	Df	37.32 N	62.01 E
Murgab [Tur.-U.S.S.R.]	135	Df	38.18 N	73.59 E
Murgaš	130	Hg	42.50 N	23.42 E
Murgeni	130	Lc	46.12 N	28.01 E
Murgha Kibzai	148	Ec	30.44 N	69.25 E
Murgon	212	Ke	26.15 S	151.57 E
Muri	220b	Cc	21.15 S	159.43 W
Muriaé	202	Jh	21.08 S	42.22 W
Murici	202	Ke	9.19 S	35.56 W
Murihiti	220b	Cc	21.12 S	159.48 W
Murilo Atoll	208	Gd	8.40 N	152.11 E
Müritäniyä=Mauritania (EN)	160	Fg	20.00 N	12.00 W
Müritz	120	Hc	53.25 N	12.40 E
Murkong Selek	148	Jc	27.44 N	95.18 E
Murmansk	112	Jb	68.58 N	33.05 E
Murmanskaja oblast	136	Da	68.00 N	35.00 E
Murmaši	136	Db	68.49 N	32.49 E
Murnau	120	Hi	47.41 N	11.12 E
Muro / Muro de Mallorca	126	Pe	39.44 N	3.03 E
Muro, Capo di-	122a	Ab	41.44 N	8.40 E
Muro de Mallorca / Muro	126	Pe	39.44 N	3.03 E
Muro Lucano	128	Jj	40.45 N	15.29 E
Murom	112	Kd	55.34 N	42.02 E
Muromcevo	136	Hd	56.23 N	75.14 E
Muroran	154	Pd	42.18 N	140.59 E
Muros	126	Cb	42.47 N	9.02 W
Muroto	152	Ne	33.18 N	134.09 E
Muroto Zaki	154	Mh	33.16 N	134.10 E
Murowana Goślina	120	Nd	52.35 N	17.01 E
Murphy [Id.-U.S.]	188	Ge	43.13 N	116.33 W
Murphy [N.C.-U.S.]	184	Eh	35.05 N	84.01 W
Murphysboro	186	Lh	37.46 N	89.20 W
Murrah al Kubrá, Al Buḥayrah al-	146	Eg	30.20 N	32.23 E
Murray [Ky.-U.S.]	184	Cg	36.37 N	88.19 W
Murray [Ut.-U.S.]	188	Jf	40.40 N	111.53 W
Murray, Lake- [Pap.N.Gui.]	214	Ci	7.00 S	141.30 E
Murray, Lake- [S.C.-U.S.]	184	Gh	34.04 N	81.23 W
Murray Bridge	212	Hg	35.07 S	139.17 E
Murray Fracture zone (EN)	106	Lf	34.00 N	135.00 W
Murray Islands	212	Ia	9.55 S	144.05 E
Murray Ridge (EN)	106	Gg	21.00 N	61.50 E
Murray River	184	Eh	35.22 S	139.22 E
Murraysburg	172	Cf	31.58 S	23.47 E
Murro di Porco, Capo-	128	Jm	37.00 N	15.20 E
Murrumbidgee River	208	Fh	34.43 S	143.12 E
Murrupula	172	Fc	15.27 S	38.47 E
Murska Sobota	128	Jc	46.40 N	16.10 E
Murten	128	Bd	46.56 N	7.08 E
Murter	128	Jg	43.47 N	15.37 E
Murtle Lake	188	Fa	52.08 N	119.38 W
Murud, Gunong-	150	Gf	3.52 N	115.30 E
Murupara	218	Ib	38.27 S	176.42 E
Mururoa Atoll	208	Ng	21.52 S	138.55 W
Murwara	148	Gd	23.51 N	80.24 E
Murwillumbah	212	Ke	28.19 S	153.24 E
Mürz	128	Jc	47.24 N	15.17 E
Mürzzuschlag	128	Jc	47.36 N	15.41 E
Muş	144	Fb	38.44 N	41.30 E
Mūsa/Mūša	114	Fh	56.24 N	24.12 E
Mūsa/Mūša	114	Fh	56.24 N	24.12 E
Mūsa, Jabal-=Sinai, Mount- (EN)	146	Eh	28.32 N	33.59 E
Musa Ali	168	Gc	12.30 N	42.27 E
Musafi	164	Qk	25.18 N	56.10 E
Musa'id	164	Ed	31.36 N	25.03 E
Musala [Bul.]	112	If	42.12 N	23.42 E
Musallam	146	Lg	31.53 N	46.56 E
Musan	152	Mc	42.14 N	129.13 E
Musandam Peninsula	146	Qi	26.18 N	56.24 E
Musay'id	146	Nj	25.00 N	51.33 E
Muscat (EN)=Masqaṭ	142	Hg	23.29 N	58.33 E
Muscat and Oman (EN) = Oman (EN)	142	Hg	21.00 N	57.00 E
Muscatine	186	Kf	41.25 N	91.03 W
Musgrave	210	Ff	14.47 S	143.30 E
Musgrave Ranges	208	Eg	26.10 S	131.50 E
Mus-Haja, gora-	140	Qc	62.35 N	140.50 E
Mushâsh al 'Ashawî	146	Mj	24.12 N	48.50 E
Mushâsh Ramlân	146	Mj	24.25 N	49.15 E
Mushayrib, Ra's-	146	Nj	24.18 N	51.44 E
Mushie	170	Cc	3.01 S	16.54 E
Mūsi	148	Ge	15.20 N	80.06 E
Musi	150	Eg	2.20 S	104.56 E
Mūsiän	146	Lf	32.28 N	47.26 E
Musicians Seamounts (EN)	208	Kb	29.00 N	162.00 W
Muskegon	182	Jc	43.14 N	86.16 W
Muskegon Heights	184	Dd	43.12 N	86.12 W
Muskegon River	184	Dd	43.14 N	86.20 W
Muskö	116	He	59.00 N	18.05 E
Muskogee	182	He	35.45 N	95.22 W
Muskoka, Lake-	184	Fc	45.00 N	79.25 W
Musoma	160	Ki	1.30 S	33.48 E
Mussattabah, Al Jazirah al-	128	Em	37.11 N	10.20 E
Mussau Island	214	Ea	1.25 S	149.38 E
Musselkanaal, Stadskanaal-	124	Jb	52.56 N	7.02 E
Musselshell River	188	Le	47.21 N	107.58 W
Mussende	170	Ce	10.31 S	16.02 E
Mussidan	122	Gi	45.02 N	0.22 E
Mussoméli	128	Hm	37.35 N	13.45 E
Must	152	Fb	46.40 N	92.40 E
Muṣṭafá, Ra's-	146	Em	36.50 N	11.07 E
Mustafakemalpaşa	146	Cb	40.02 N	28.24 E
Mustahil	168	Gc	5.15 N	44.44 E
Mustang	148	Gc	29.11 N	83.58 E
Mustang Draw	186	Fj	32.00 N	101.40 W
Mustasaari/Korsholm	116	Ja	63.05 N	21.43 E
Musters, Lago-	206	Gg	45.27 S	69.13 W
Mustique Island	197h	Bb	12.53 N	61.11 W
Mustjala	116	Jf	58.25 N	22.04 E
Mustla	114	Gg	58.14 N	25.52 E
Mustvee	114	Gg	58.52 N	26.59 E
Musyna	120	Qg	49.21 N	20.54 E
Mut	164	Ed	25.30 N	28.59 E
Mūṭ	146	Ee	36.39 N	33.27 E
Muṭaf, Ra's al-	146	Nj	24.38 N	51.37 E
Mutalau	220ka	Ba	18.56 S	169.50 W
Mutare	160	Kj	18.57 S	32.40 E
Mutha	170	Gc	1.48 S	38.25 E
Muting	150	Lh	7.23 S	140.20 E
Mutis, Gunong-	150	Hh	9.34 S	124.14 E
Mutoko	172	Ec	17.24 S	32.13 E
Mutoraj	138	Fd	61.20 N	100.20 E
Mutsamudu	160	Lj	12.09 S	44.25 E
Mutshatsha	170	De	10.39 S	24.27 E
Mutsu	152	Pc	41.05 N	140.55 E
Mutsu-Wan	154	Pd	41.10 N	140.55 E
Muttaburra	212	Id	22.36 S	144.33 E
Mutterstadt	124	Ke	49.27 N	8.21 E
Mutton/Oiléan Coarach	118	Di	52.49 N	9.27 W
Mutton Bird Islands	218	Kg	47.15 S	167.25 E
Mutuali	172	Fb	14.53 S	37.00 E
Mutún	204	Dd	19.10 S	57.54 W
Mutunópolis	204	Ha	13.40 S	49.15 W
Mutusjärvi	114	Gb	69.31 N	26.57 E
Muurame	116	Kb	62.08 N	25.40 E
Mu Us Shamo=Ordos Desert	140	Mf	38.45 N	109.10 E
Muxima	170	Bd	9.32 S	13.57 E
Muy, Le-	122	Mk	43.28 N	6.33 E
Muyinga	170	Fc	2.51 S	30.20 E
Muy Muy	194	Eg	12.46 N	85.38 W
Muzaffarābād	148	Eb	34.22 N	73.28 E
Muzaffargarh	148	Eb	30.04 N	71.12 E
Muzaffarnagar	148	Fc	29.28 N	77.41 E
Muzaffarpur	148	Hc	26.07 N	85.24 E
Muzambinho	204	Ie	21.22 S	46.32 W
Muzat He	152	Dc	41.15 N	83.27 E
Muži	138	Ec	65.24 N	64.40 E
Muzillac	122	Dg	47.33 N	2.29 W
Mužlja	130	Ed	45.21 N	20.25 E
Muztag [China]	140	Kf	36.25 N	87.25 E
Muztag [China]	140	Kf	35.55 N	80.20 E
Muztagata	152	Cd	38.17 N	75.07 E
Mvolo	168	Db	6.03 N	29.56 E
Mvomero	170	Gd	6.20 S	37.25 E
Mvoung	170	Bb	0.04 N	12.18 E
Mwadingusha	170	Ee	10.45 S	27.15 E
Mwali/Mohéli	158	Lj	12.15 S	43.45 E
Mwanza	170	Fc	2.30 S	32.30 E
Mwanza [Mwi.]	170	Ff	15.37 S	34.31 E
Mwanza [Tan.]	160	Ki	2.31 S	32.54 E
Mwanza [Zaire]	170	Ed	7.54 S	26.45 E
Mwatate	170	Gc	3.30 S	38.23 E
Mweelrea	118	Dh	53.38 N	9.50 W
Mweka	160	Ji	4.51 S	21.34 E
Mwene Ditu	160	Ji	7.03 S	23.27 E
Mwenezi	172	Ed	21.22 S	30.45 E
Mwenga	170	Ec	3.02 S	28.26 E
Mweru, Lake-	158	Jj	9.00 S	28.45 E
Mweru Wantipa, Lake-	170	Fd	8.42 S	29.46 E
Mwimbi	170	Fd	8.39 S	31.40 E
Mwinilunga	170	De	11.44 S	24.26 E
Mya	158	He	31.40 N	5.15 E
Myanaung	148	Je	18.17 N	95.19 E
Myanmar-Nainggan-Daw→Burma (EN)	148	Ie	22.00 N	98.00 E
Myaungmya	148	Ie	16.36 N	94.56 E
Mycenae (EN) = Mikinai	130	Fl	37.43 N	22.45 E
Myebon	148	Id	20.03 N	93.22 E
Myingyan	148	Ia	21.28 N	95.23 E
Myinmoletkat Taung	148	Jf	13.28 N	98.48 E
Myitta	148	Jf	14.10 N	98.31 E
Myjava	120	Mh	48.45 N	17.34 E
Myjakula/Mõisaküla	114	Gg	58.07 N	25.10 E
Mylius Erichsens Land	118	Jb	81.40 N	24.00 W
Myltkyinä	142	Lg	25.23 N	97.24 E
Mymensingh	148	Id	24.45 N	90.24 E
Mynämäki	114	Ef	60.40 N	22.00 E
Mynaral	136	Hf	45.22 N	73.39 E
Myŏkŏ-Zan	156	Ac	36.52 N	138.06 E
Myrdalsjökull	114a	Bc	63.40 N	19.06 W
Myre	114	Db	68.51 N	15.05 E
Myrskylä/Mörskom	116	Kd	60.40 N	25.51 E
Myrtle Beach	182	Je	33.42 N	78.54 W
Myrtle Point	188	Ce	43.04 N	124.08 W
Mysen	114	Cg	59.33 N	11.20 E
Mysia	130	Kj	39.30 N	28.00 E
Myśla	120	Kc	52.40 N	14.29 E
Myślenice	120	Pg	49.51 N	19.56 E
Myślibórz	120	Kc	52.55 N	14.52 E
Mysore	142	Jh	12.18 N	76.39 E
Mysore → Karnataka	148	Fl	13.30 N	76.00 E
Mys Šmidta	138	Nc	68.45 N	178.40 W
Myszków	120	Pf	50.36 N	19.20 E
Myszyniec	120	Rc	53.24 N	21.21 E
My Tho	148	Kf	10.21 N	106.21 E
Mytišči	112	Jd	55.56 N	37.46 E
Mývatn	114a	Cb	65.36 N	17.00 W
Myzeqeja	130	Ci	40.50 N	19.36 E
M'Zab	162	Hc	32.35 N	3.20 E
Mže	120	Ig	49.46 N	13.24 E
Mziha	170	Gd	5.54 S	37.47 E
Mzimba	170	Fe	11.54 S	33.36 E
Mzuzu	160	Kj	11.27 S	33.55 E

N

Name	Page	Grid	Lat	Long
Naab	120	Ig	49.01 N	12.02 E
Naaldwijk	124	Gc	51.59 N	4.12 E
Naalehu	214	Od	19.04 N	155.35 W
Naantali/Nådendal	114	Ff	60.27 N	22.02 E
Naarden	124	Hb	52.18 N	5.10 E
Naas/An Nás	118	Gh	53.13 N	6.39 W
Nabā	126	Ng	38.48 N	43.29 E
Nabão	126	De	39.31 N	8.21 W
Naberera	170	Gc	4.12 S	36.56 E
Naberežnyje Čelny	112	Jh	55.42 N	52.19 E
Nābha	148	Fb	30.22 N	76.09 E
Nabire	160	Ib	3.21 S	135.29 E
Nabī Shu'ayb, Jabal an-	140	Gh	15.17 N	43.59 E
Nabq	146	Fh	28.04 N	34.25 E
Nābul	160	Ie	36.27 N	10.44 E
Nābul	162	Jb	36.45 N	10.45 E
Nābulus	146	Ff	32.13 N	35.16 E
Nābulus	146	Ff	32.18 N	35.17 E

Index Symbols

Symbol	Meaning
[1]	Independent Nation
[2]	State, Region
[3]	District, County
[4]	Municipality
[5]	Colony, Dependency
■	Continent
⊠	Physical Region

Historical or Cultural Region	Pass, Gap
Mount, Mountain	Plain, Lowland
Volcano	Delta
Hill	Salt Flat
Mountains, Mountain Range	Valley, Canyon
Hills, Escarpment	Crater, Cave
Plateau, Upland	Karst Features

Depression — Coast, Beach — Rock, Reef — Waterfall, Rapids — Canal — Lagoon — Escarpment, Sea Scarp — Historic Site — Airport
Polder — Cliff — Islands, Archipelago — River Mouth, Estuary — Glacier — Bank — Fracture — Ruins — Port
Forest, Dunes — Peninsula — Rocks, Reefs — Lake — Ice Shelf, Pack Ice — Seamount — Trench, Abyss — Wall, Walls — Military installation
Forest, Woods — Isthmus — Coral Reef — Salt Lake — Ocean — Tablemount — National Park, Reserve — Church, Abbey — Lighthouse
Heath, Steppe — Sandbank — Well, Spring — Intermittent Lake — Sea — Ridge — Point of Interest — Temple — Mine
Oasis — Island — Geyser — Reservoir — Gulf, Bay — Shelf — Recreation Site — Scientific Station — Tunnel
Cape, Point — Atoll — River, Stream — Swamp, Pond — Strait, Fjord — Basin — Cave, Cavern — Railway station — Dam, Bridge

Index Symbols

Symbol	Meaning
[1]	Independent Nation
[2]	State, Region
[3]	District, County
[4]	Municipality
[5]	Colony, Dependency
	Continent
	Physical Region
	Historical or Cultural Region
	Mount, Mountain
	Volcano
	Hill
	Mountains, Mountain Range
	Hills, Escarpment
	Plateau, Upland
	Pass, Gap
	Plain, Lowland
	Delta
	Salt Flat
	Valley, Canyon
	Crater, Cave
	Karst Features
	Depression
	Polder
	Desert, Dunes
	Forest, Woods
	Heath, Steppe
	Oasis
	Cape, Point
	Coast, Beach
	Cliff
	Peninsula
	Isthmus
	Sandbank
	Island
	Atoll
	Rock, Reef
	Islands, Archipelago
	Rocks, Reefs
	Coral Reef
	Well, Spring
	Geyser
	River, Stream
	Waterfall, Rapids
	River Mouth, Estuary
	Lake
	Salt Lake
	Intermittent Lake
	Reservoir
	Swamp, Pond
	Canal
	Glacier
	Ice Shelf, Pack Ice
	Ocean
	Sea
	Gulf, Bay
	Strait, Fjord
	Lagoon
	Bank
	Seamount
	Tablemount
	Ridge
	Shelf
	Basin
	Escarpment, Sea Scarp
	Fracture
	Trench, Abyss
	National Park, Reserve
	Point of Interest
	Recreation Site
	Cave, Cavern
	Historic Site
	Ruins
	Wall, Walls
	Church, Abbey
	Temple
	Scientific Station
	Railway station
	Airport
	Port
	Military installation
	Lighthouse
	Mine
	Tunnel
	Dam, Bridge

Natal [B.C.-Can.] 188 Hb 49.44N 114.50W
Natal [Braz.] 200 Mf 5.47S 35.13W
Natal [Indon.] 150 Cf 0.33N 99.07 E
Natal Basin (EN) 106 Fm 30.00S 40.00 E
Natanz 146 Nf 33.31N 51.54 E
Natashquan 180 Lf 50.11N 61.49W
Natashquan 180 Lf 50.09N 61.37W
Natchez 182 Ie 31.34N 91.23W
Natchitoches 182 Ie 31.46N 93.05W
Natewa Bay 219d Bb 16.35S 179.40 E
Nathorsts Land 179 Jd 72.20N 27.00W
Nathula 219d Ab 16.53S 177.25 E
Natitingou 160 Hg 10.19N 1.22 E
Natityāy, Jabal- 164 Fe 23.01N 34.22 E
Natividad, Isla- 192 Bd 27.55N 115.10W
Natividade 202 If 11.43S 47.47W
Natori 154 Pe 38.11N 140.58 E
Natron, Lake- 158 Ki 2.25S 36.00 E
Natrūn, Wādī an- 146 Dg 30.25N 30.13 E
Natsudomari-Zaki 156a Bc 41.00N 140.53 E
Nåttarö 116 Hf 58.50N 18.10 E
Nättraby 116 Fh 56.12N 15.31 E
Natuna, Kepulauan- = Natuna Islands (EN) 140 Mi 2.45N 109.00 E
Natuna Besar, Pulau- 150 Ef 4.00N 108.15 E
Natuna Islands (EN) = Natuna, Kepulauan- 140 Mi 2.45N 109.00 E
Naturaliste, Cape- 208 Ch 33.32S 115.01 E
Naturaliste Channel 212 Ce 25.25S 113.00 E
Naturita 186 Bg 38.14N 108.34W
Naturno / Naturns 128 Ed 46.39N 11.00 E
Naturns / Naturno 128 Ed 46.39N 11.00 E
Nau 135 Gd 40.09N 69.22 E
Nau, Cap de la-/Nao, Cabo de la- 110 Gh 38.44N 0.14 E
Naucelle 122 Ij 44.12N 2.21 E
Nauėji-Akmjane/Naujoji-Akmenė 114 Fh 56.21N 22.50 E
Naugo/Nauvo 116 Id 60.10N 21.50 E
Nauhcampatépetl → Cofre de Perote, Cerro- 192 Kh 19.29N 97.08W
Nauja Bay 180 Kc 68.58N 75.00W
Naujamiestis/Naujamestis 116 Ki 55.41N 24.09 E
Naujamestis/Naujamiestis 116 Ki 55.41N 24.09 E
Naujoji-Akmenė/Nauėji-Akmjane 114 Fh 56.21N 22.50 E
Naukluft 172 Bd 24.10S 16.10 E
Naumburg [Ger.] 124 Lc 51.15N 9.10 E
Naumburg [Ger.] 120 He 51.09N 11.49 E
Nā'ūr 146 Fg 31.53N 35.50 E
Nauru 208 He 0.31S 166.56 E
Nauru / Naoero 210 He 0.31S 166.56 E
Nauški 138 Ff 50.28N 106.07 E
Nausori 216 Ec 18.02S 178.32 E
Nauta 202 Dd 4.32S 73.33W
Nautanwa 148 Gc 27.26N 83.25 E
Nautla 192 Kg 20.13N 96.47W
Nauvo/Naugo 116 Id 60.10N 21.50 E
Nava 192 Ic 28.25N 100.45W
Navacerrada, Puerto de- 126 Id 40.47N 4.00W
Nava del Rey 126 Gc 41.20N 5.05W
Navahermosa 126 He 39.38N 4.28W
Navajo Mountain 188 Jh 37.02N 110.52W
Navajo Reservoir 186 Ch 36.55N 107.30W
Navalmoral de la Mata 126 Ge 39.54N 5.32W
Navan → An Uaimh 118 Gh 53.39N 6.41W
Navarin, mys- 140 Tc 62.16N 179.10 E
Navarino, Isla- 198 Jk 55.05S 67.40W
Navarra / Nafarroa 126 Kb 42.45N 1.40W
Navarro 204 Cl 35.01S 59.16W
Navarro Mills Lake 186 Hk 31.56N 96.45W
Navašino 114 Ki 55.33N 42.12 E
Navasota 186 Hk 30.23N 96.05W
Navasota River 186 Hk 30.20N 96.09W
Navassa 190 Ie 18.24N 75.01W
Navaste jõgi / Navesti 116 Kf 58.56N 24.58 E
Nävekvarn 116 Gf 58.38N 16.49 E
Naver 118 Ic 58.30N 4.15W
Navesti / Navaste jõgi 116 Kf 58.56N 24.58 E
Navia 126 Fa 43.32N 6.43W
Navia 126 Fa 43.33N 6.44W
Navidad, Bahia de- 192 Gh 19.10N 104.45W
Navidad Bank (EN) 194 Mc 20.00N 68.50W
Naviti 219d Ab 17.07S 177.15 E
Navlja 136 De 52.50N 34.31 E
Navlja 132 Ic 52.42N 34.03 E
Năvodari 130 Le 44.19N 28.36 E
Navoi 136 Gg 40.10N 65.15 E
Navoja 190 Cc 27.06N 109.26W
Navolato 192 Fe 24.47N 107.42W
Navoloki 114 Jh 57.28N 41.59 E
Návpaktos 130 Ek 38.24N 21.50 E
Návplion 130 Fl 37.34N 22.48 E
Navrongo 166 Ec 10.54N 1.06W
Navsāri 148 Ed 20.55N 72.55 E
Navtilos 130 Gn 35.57N 23.13 E
Navua 219d Bc 18.13S 178.10 E
Navy Board Inlet 180 Jb 73.30N 81.00W
Nawa 146 Gf 32.53N 36.03 E
Nawābshāh 148 Dc 26.15N 68.25 E
Nawāşif, Ḩarrat- 164 He 21.20N 42.10 E
Naws, Ra's- 144 If 17.18N 55.16 E
Náxos 130 Il 37.06N 25.23 E
Naxos 128 Jm 37.49N 15.15 E
Náxos = Naxos (EN) 110 Ih 37.02N 25.35 E
Naxos (EN) = Náxos 110 Ih 37.02N 25.35 E
Nayarit 190 Cd 22.00N 105.00W
Nayarit, Sierra de- 190 Dd 22.00N 103.50W
Nayau 219d Cb 17.58S 179.03W
Nāy Band [Iran] 146 Oi 27.23N 52.38 E
Nāy Band [Iran] 146 Qf 32.20N 57.34 E
Nāy Band, Kūh-e- 144 Ic 32.27N 57.23 E
Nāy Band, Ra's-e- 146 Oi 27.23N 52.34 E
Nayoro 152 Pc 44.21N 142.28 E
Nayyāl, Wādī- 146 Gh 28.58N 37.50 E
Nazaré [Braz.] 202 Kf 13.02S 39.00W
Nazaré [Port.] 126 Ce 39.36N 9.04W
Nazareth (EN) = Nazerat 146 Ff 32.42N 35.18 E
Nazarovo 138 Ee 56.01N 90.36 E
Nazas 192 Ge 25.14N 104.08W
Nazas, Rio- 174 Ig 25.35N 105.00W
Nazca 200 Ig 14.50S 74.55W
Nazca Ridge (EN) 106 Nl 22.00S 82.00W
Naze 152 Mf 28.23N 129.30 E
Nazerat = Nazareth (EN) 146 Ff 32.42N 35.18 E
Nazik Gölü 146 Jc 38.48N 42.15 E
Nazilli 144 Cb 37.55N 28.21 E
Nazimiye 146 Hc 39.11N 39.50 E
Nazimovo 138 Ee 59.30N 90.58 E
Nazino 138 Cd 60.15N 78.58 E
Nazlū 146 Kd 37.42N 45.16 E
Nazran 132 Nh 43.15N 44.46 E
Nazret 168 Fd 8.34N 39.18 E
Nazw'a 144 Ie 22.54N 57.31 E
Nazym 134 Nf 61.12N 68.57 E
Nazyvajevsk 136 Hd 55.34N 71.21 E
Nbâk 162 Ef 17.15N 14.59W
Nchanga 170 Ee 12.31S 27.52 E
Ncheu 170 Fe 14.49S 34.38 E
Ndala 170 Fc 4.46S 33.16 E
N'dalatando 170 Bd 9.18S 14.54 E
Ndali 166 Fd 9.51N 2.43 E
Ndélé 160 Jh 8.24N 20.39 E
Ndélélé 166 He 4.02N 14.56 E
Ndende 170 Bc 2.23S 11.23 E
Ndindi 170 Bc 3.46S 11.09 E
N'Djamena (Fort-Lamy) 160 Ig 12.07N 15.03 E
Ndola 160 Jj 12.58S 28.38 E
Ndouana, Pointe- 219b Dc 16.35S 168.09 E
Ndrhamcha, Sebkha de- 162 Df 18.45N 15.48W
Ndui Ndui 219b Cb 15.24S 167.46 E
Nduindui 214 Fi 9.48S 159.58 E
Né 122 Fi 45.40N 0.23W
Nea 219c Ab 10.51S 165.47 E
Nea 114 Ce 63.13N 11.02 E
Néa Alikarnassós 130 In 35.20N 25.09 E
Néa Artáki 130 Gk 38.31N 23.38 E
Neagari 156 Ec 36.26N 136.26 E
Neagh, Lough-/Loch nEathach 110 Fe 54.38N 6.24W
Neagră, Marea- = Black Sea (EN) 110 Jg 43.00N 35.00 E
Neah Bay 188 Cb 48.22N 124.37W
Néa Ionia 130 Fj 39.23N 22.56 E
Neajlov 130 Je 44.11N 26.12 E
Neale, Lake- 212 Fd 24.20S 130.00 E
Neamț 130 Jb 47.00N 26.20 E
Neápolis [Grc.] 130 Gm 36.31N 23.04 E
Neápolis [Grc.] 130 Ei 40.19N 21.23 E
Neápolis [Grc.] 130 In 35.15N 25.37 E
Near Islands 174 Bd 52.40N 173.30W
Neath 118 Jj 51.40N 3.48W
Neath 118 Jj 51.37N 3.50W
Néa Zíkhni 130 Gh 41.02N 23.50 E
Néba 219b Ae 20.09S 163.55 E
Nebaj 194 Bf 15.24N 91.08W
Nebbou 166 Ec 11.18N 1.53W
Nebesnaja, Gora- 135 Mc 43.15N 80.45 E
Nebit-Dag 142 Hf 39.30N 54.22 E
Neblina, Cerro de la- 198 Je 1.08N 66.10W
Nebo 212 Jd 21.40S 148.39 E
Nebo, Mount- 188 Jg 39.49N 111.46W
Nebolči 114 Hg 59.08N 33.21 E
Nebraska 182 Gc 41.30N 100.00W
Nebraska City 182 Hc 40.41N 95.52W
Nebrodi (Caronie) 128 Im 37.55N 14.35 E
Necedah 186 Kd 44.02N 90.03W
Nechako 180 Ff 53.55N 122.44W
Nechako Reservoir 180 Ef 53.00N 126.10W
Nechar, Djebel- 126 Qi 35.52N 4.59 E
Neches River 186 Jl 29.55N 93.52W
Nechi 194 Ji 8.07N 74.46W
Nechi, Rio- 194 Ji 8.08N 74.46W
Neckako Plateau 180 Ff 53.25N 124.40W
Neckar 120 Eg 49.31N 8.26 E
Neckargemünd 124 Ke 49.29N 8.50 E
Neckarsteinach 124 Ke 49.25N 8.50 E
Neckarsulm 120 Fg 49.11N 9.14 E
Necker Island 208 Kb 23.35N 164.42W
Necochea 200 Ki 38.34S 58.45W
Necy 124 Bf 48.50N 0.07W
Nedeley 168 Bb 15.34N 18.10 E
Nederland 186 Jl 29.58N 93.59W
Nederland = Netherlands (EN) 112 Ge 52.15N 5.30 E
Nederlandse Antillen [Neth.Ant.] = Netherlands Antilles (EN) 200 Jd 12.15N 69.00W
Nederlandse Antillen [Neth.Ant.] = Netherlands Antilles (EN) 200 Jd 18.06N 63.10W
Neder-Rijn = Lower Rhine (EN) 122 Mc 51.59N 6.20 E
Nêdong 142 Lg 29.14N 91.46 E
Nedstrand 116 Ae 59.21N 5.51 E
Nedstrandefjorden 116 Ae 59.20N 5.50 E
Neede 124 Ib 52.08N 6.37 E
Needham Market 124 Db 52.09N 1.02 E
Needham's Point 197q Ab 13.05N 59.36W
Needles 182 Ee 34.51N 114.37W
Neembucú 204 Dh 27.00S 58.00W
Neenah 186 Ld 44.11N 88.28W
Neepawa 186 Ga 50.13N 99.29W
Neermoor, Moormerland- 124 Ja 53.18N 7.26 E
Neeroeteren, Maaseik- 124 Hc 51.05N 5.42 E
Neerpelt 124 Hc 51.13N 5.25 E
Nefasit 168 Fb 15.18N 39.04 E
Nefedova 136 Hd 58.48N 72.34 E
Né Finn/Nephin 118 Dg 54.01N 9.22W
Neftah 162 Ic 33.52N 7.53 E
Neftečala 132 Pj 39.19N 49.13 E
Neftegorsk [R.S.F.S.R.] 136 Fe 52.45N 51.13 E
Neftegorsk [R.S.F.S.R.] 132 Kg 44.22N 39.42 E
Neftegorsk [R.S.F.S.R.] 138 Jf 53.00N 143.00 E
Neftejugansk 136 Hc 61.05N 72.45 E
Neftekamsk 136 Fd 56.06N 54.17 E
Neftekumsk 136 Eg 44.43N 44.59 E
Neftjanyje Kamin 132 Qi 40.15N 50.49 E
Negage 170 Cd 7.46S 15.18 E
Negara 150 Fh 8.22S 114.37 E
Negele = Neghelle (EN) 160 Kh 5.20N 39.37 E
Negeri Sembilan 150 Df 2.45N 102.10 E
Negev Desert (EN) = Ḥānegev 146 Fg 30.30N 34.55 E
Neghelle (EN) = Negele 160 Kh 5.20N 39.37 E
Negla, Arroyo- 204 Df 22.52S 56.41W
Negola 170 Be 14.10S 14.30 E
Negomano 172 Fb 11.26S 38.33 E
Negombo 148 Fg 7.13N 79.50 E
Negonego Atoll 208 Mf 18.47S 141.48W
Negotin 130 Fe 44.13N 22.32 E
Negra, Cordillera- 202 Ce 9.25S 77.40W
Negra, Coxilha- 204 Ej 31.02S 55.45W
Negra, Peña- 126 Fb 42.11N 6.30W
Negra, Ponta- 204 Jf 23.21S 44.36W
Negra, Punta- 198 Hf 6.06S 81.10W
Negra, Serra- 204 Fc 16.30S 52.10W
Negra o de los Difuntos, Laguna- 204 Fl 34.03S 53.40W
Negreira 126 Db 42.54N 8.44W
Negreni 130 He 44.34N 24.36 E
Negrești 130 Gb 47.52N 23.26 E
Negrine 130 Kc 34.29N 7.31 E
Negrinho, Rio- 204 Ed 19.20S 55.05W
Negro, Cabo- 126 Gi 35.41N 5.17W
Negro, Rio- [Arg.] 198 Ji 41.02S 62.47W
Negro, Rio- [Arg.] 204 Ch 27.27S 58.54W
Negro, Rio- [Bol.] 202 Ff 14.11S 63.07W
Negro, Rio- [Braz.] 206 Jc 26.01S 50.30W
Negro, Rio- [Braz.] 202 Gg 19.13S 57.17W
Negro, Rio- [Par.] 206 Ib 24.23S 57.11W
Negro, Rio- [S.Amer.] 204 Ce 20.11S 58.10W
Negro, Rio- [S.Amer.] 198 Kf 3.08S 59.55W
Negro, Rio- [Ur.] 198 Ki 33.24S 58.22W
Negro, Rio → Chixoy, Rio- 194 Be 16.28N 90.33W
Negros 140 Oi 10.00N 123.00 E
Negru, Rîu- 130 Id 45.45N 25.46 E
Negru Vodă 130 Lf 43.49N 28.12 E
Nehajevski 132 Ld 50.27N 41.46 E
Nehalem River 188 Dd 45.40N 123.56W
Nehāvand 146 Me 35.56N 49.31 E
Nehe 152 Lb 48.28N 124.53 E
Nehoiu 130 Jd 45.26N 26.17 E
Néhoué, Baie de- 219b Be 20.21S 164.09 E
Neiba 194 Ld 18.28N 71.25W
Neiba, Bahia de- 194 Ld 18.15N 71.02W
Neidin/Kenmare 118 Dj 51.53N 9.35W
Neige, Crêt de la- 122 Lh 46.16N 5.56 E
Neiges, Piton des- 155 Mk 21.05S 55.29 E
Neijiang 142 Mg 29.38N 104.58 E
Neilton 188 Dc 47.25N 123.52W
Nei-meng-ku Tzu-chih-ch'ü → Nei Monggol Zizhiqu 152 Jc 44.00N 112.00 E
Nei Monggol Gaoyuan 140 Ne 42.00N 111.00 E
Nei Monggol Zizhiqu (Nei-meng-ku Tzu-chih-ch'ü) = Inner Mongolia (EN) 152 Jc 44.00N 112.00 E
Neiqiu 154 Cf 37.17N 114.30 E
Neiva 200 Ie 2.56N 75.18W
Neja 136 Ed 58.19N 43.52 E
Nejanilini Lake 180 He 59.30N 97.50W
Nejdek 120 If 50.19N 12.44 E
Nejo 168 Fd 9.30N 35.32 E
Nejva 134 Kh 57.54N 62.18 E
Nekemt = Leqemt (EN) 166 Kh 9.05N 36.33 E
Neksø 116 Fi 55.04N 15.09 E
Nelemnoje 138 Kc 65.23N 151.08 E
Nelgese 138 Ic 66.40N 136.30 E
Nelichu 168 Ed 6.08N 34.25 E
Nelidovo 136 Dd 56.13N 32.50 E
Neligh 186 Ge 42.08N 98.02W
Neljaty 138 Ge 56.29N 115.50 E
Nelkan 138 Jd 64.15N 143.03 E
Nellore 142 Jh 12.56N 79.08 E
Nelma 138 Ig 47.40N 139.08 E
Nelson 218 Ed 41.45S 172.30 E
Nelson 174 Jd 57.04N 92.30W
Nelson [B.C.-Can.] 180 Fg 49.29N 117.17W
Nelson [N.Z.] 210 Ii 41.16S 173.15 E
Nelson, Cape- [Austl.] 208 Fh 38.26S 141.33 E
Nelson, Cape- [Pap.N.Gui.] 212 Ja 9.00S 149.15 E
Nelson Island 178 Gd 60.35N 164.45W
Nelson's Dockyard 197d Bb 17.00N 61.46W
Nelspruit 160 Kk 25.30S 30.58 E
Néma 160 Gg 16.36N 7.15W
Néma, Dahr- 162 Ff 16.14N 7.30W
Neman 114 Fi 55.03N 22.01 E
Neman 110 Id 55.18N 21.23 E
Nembrala 150 Hi 10.53S 122.50 E
Nemda 114 Kh 57.31N 43.15 E
Neméa 130 Fl 37.49N 22.39 E
Neméa 130 Fl 37.49N 22.40 E
Nemenčinė 116 Kj 54.50N 25.39 E
Nëmërçkës, Mali i- 130 Di 40.08N 20.24 E
Nemira, Vîrful- 130 Jc 46.15N 26.19 E
Nemirov [Ukr.-U.S.S.R.] 132 Fe 48.59N 28.50 E
Nemirov [Ukr.-U.S.S.R.] 120 Tf 50.08N 23.28 E
Némiscau 180 Jf 51.30N 77.00W
Nemjuga 114 Kd 65.29N 43.40 E
Nemours 122 If 48.16N 2.42 E
Nemrut Daği 146 Jc 38.40N 42.12 E
Nemunas 110 Id 55.18N 21.23 E
Nemunėlis 116 Kh 56.24N 24.10 E
Nemuro 152 Qc 43.20N 145.35 E
Nemuro-Hantō 156a Db 43.20N 145.35 E
Nemuro-Kaikyō = Nemuro Strait (EN) 138 Jh 43.50N 145.30 E
Nemuro Strait (EN) = Kunaširski proliv 138 Jh 43.50N 145.30 E
Nemuro Strait (EN) = Nemuro-Kaikyō 138 Jh 43.50N 145.30 E
Nemuro-Wan 156a Db 43.25N 145.25 E
Nenagh/An tAonach 118 Ei 52.52N 8.12W
Nenana 178 Jd 64.34N 149.07W
Nenana 178 Jd 64.30N 149.00W
Nendo Island 208 Hf 10.40S 165.54 E
Nene 118 Ni 52.48N 0.13 E
Nenecki nacionalny okrug 136 Fb 67.30N 54.00 E
Nenjiang 142 Oe 49.10N 125.12 E
Nen Jiang 140 Oe 45.26N 124.39 E
Neo 156 Ed 35.38N 136.37 E
Neodesha 186 Ih 37.25N 95.41W
Néon Karlovásion 130 Jl 37.47N 26.42 E
Neosho 186 Ih 36.52N 94.22W
Neosho River 186 Ih 35.48N 95.18W
Néouvielle, Massif de- 122 Gl 42.51N 0.07 E
Nepal 142 Kg 28.00N 84.00 E
Nepalganj 148 Gc 28.03N 81.37 E
Nephi 182 Ed 39.43N 111.50W
Nephin/Né Finn 118 Dg 54.01N 9.22W
Nepisiguit River 188 Ob 47.37N 65.38W
Nepoko 158 Jh 1.40N 27.01 E
Nepomuk 120 Jg 49.29N 13.34 E
Ner 120 Od 52.10N 18.40 E
Nera [It.] 128 Gh 42.26N 12.24 E
Nera [Rom.] 130 Ee 44.49N 21.22 E
Nérac 122 Gj 44.08N 0.21 E
Neratovice 120 Kf 50.16N 14.31 E
Nerău 130 Dd 45.58N 20.34 E
Nerbio / Nervión 126 Ja 43.14N 2.53W
Nerča 138 Gf 51.54N 116.30 E
Nerčinsk 138 Gf 51.58N 116.35 E
Nerčinski Zavod 138 Gf 51.17N 119.30 E
Nerehta 136 Ed 57.28N 40.34 E
Nereju 130 Jd 45.42N 26.43 E
Nereta 116 Kh 56.12N 25.24 E
Neretva 128 Lg 43.02N 17.27 E
Neretvanski kanal 128 Lg 43.03N 17.11 E
Nerica 134 Fd 65.20N 52.45 E
Neringa 114 Ei 55.24N 21.05 E
Neringa 114 Ei 55.18N 21.00 E
Neringa-Joudkrante/Neringa-Juodkrantė 116 Ii 55.35N 21.01 E
Neringa-Juodkrantė/Neringa-Joudkrante 116 Ii 55.35N 21.01 E
Neringa-Nida 116 Ii 55.18N 20.53 E
Neringa-Preila/Neringa-Prejla 116 Ii 55.20N 20.59 E
Neringa-Prejla/Neringa-Preila 116 Ii 55.20N 20.59 E
Neriquinha 170 Df 15.45S 21.33 E
Neris/Njaris 116 Kj 54.55N 25.45 E
Nerja 126 Ih 36.44N 3.52W
Nerjungri 138 He 56.40N 124.47 E
Nerl [R.S.F.S.R.] 114 Ih 57.07N 37.39 E
Nerl [R.S.F.S.R.] 114 Jh 56.11N 40.34 E
Nerpio 126 Jf 38.09N 2.18W
Nerussa 132 Hc 52.33N 33.47 E
Nerva 126 Fg 37.42N 6.32W
Nervi, Genova- 128 Df 44.23N 9.02 E
Nervión / Nerbio 126 Ja 43.14N 2.53W
Nes 116 Cd 60.34N 9.59 E
Nes, Ameland- 124 Ha 53.26N 5.48 E
Nesbyen 114 Bf 60.34N 9.06 E
Nesebăr 130 Kg 42.39N 27.44 E
Nesjøen 116 Db 63.00N 12.00 E
Neskaupstaður 114a Db 65.09N 13.42W
Nesle 124 Ee 49.46N 2.45 E
Nesna 114 Cc 66.12N 13.02 E
Ness City 186 Gg 38.27N 99.54W
Nesterov [R.S.F.S.R.] 114 Fi 54.42N 22.34 E
Nesterov [Ukr.-U.S.S.R.] 132 Cd 50.03N 24.00 E
Néstos 130 Hi 40.51N 24.44 E
Nesttun 116 Ad 60.19N 5.20 E
Nesviž 132 Ec 53.13N 26.39 E
Netanya 146 Ff 32.20N 34.51 E
Netcong 184 Je 40.54N 74.43W
Nete 122 Kc 51.10N 4.15 E
Nethe 124 Lc 51.44N 9.23 E
Netherdale 212 Jd 21.08S 148.32 E
Netherlands (EN) = Nederland 112 Ge 52.15N 5.30 E
Netherlands Antilles (EN) = Nederlandse Antillen [Neth.Ant.] 200 Jd 12.15N 69.00W
Netherlands Antilles (EN) = Nederlandse Antillen [Neth.Ant.] 200 Jd 18.06N 63.10W
Neto 128 Lk 39.12N 17.09 E
Netphen 124 Kd 50.55N 8.06 E
Nettebach 124 Jd 50.26N 7.28 E
Nettersheim 124 Id 50.30N 6.38 E
Nettetal 124 Ic 51.18N 6.12 E
Nettiling Lake 174 Lc 66.30N 70.40W
Nettuno 128 Gi 41.27N 12.39 E
Netzahualcóyotl, Presa- 192 Mi 17.00N 93.30W
Neubourg, Campagne du- 122 Ge 49.08N 1.00 E
Neubrandenburg 120 Jc 53.34N 13.16 E
Neuburg an der Donau 120 Hh 48.44N 11.11 E
Neuchâtel 128 Ac 47.05N 6.50 E
Neuchâtel/Neuenburg 128 Ad 46.59N 6.56 E
Neuchâtel, Lac de- 128 Ad 46.55N 6.55 E
Neuenbürg 124 Kf 48.50N 8.35 E
Neuenburg/Neuchâtel 128 Ad 46.59N 6.56 E
Neuenhaus 124 Ib 52.30N 6.58 E
Neuenkirchen 124 Jb 52.15N 7.22 E
Neuerburg 124 Id 50.01N 6.18 E
Neufchâteau [Bel.] 122 Le 49.51N 5.26 E
Neufchâteau [Fr.] 122 Lf 48.21N 5.42 E
Neufchâtel-en-Bray 122 He 49.44N 1.27 E
Neufchâtel Hardelot 124 Dd 50.37N 1.38 E
Neufchâtel Hardelot-Hardelot Plage 124 Dd 50.38N 1.35 E
Neufchâtel-sur-Aisne 124 Ge 49.26N 4.02 E
Neuffossé, Canal de- 124 Ed 50.45N 2.15 E
Neuhaus am Rennweg 120 Hf 50.31N 11.09 E
Neuilly-en-Thelle 124 Ee 49.13N 2.17 E
Neuilly-Saint-Front 124 Fe 49.10N 3.16 E
Neu-Isenburg 124 Kd 50.03N 8.42 E
Neukirchen-Vluyn 124 Ic 51.27N 6.35 E
Neum 128 Lh 42.55N 17.38 E
Neumagen-Dhron 124 Ie 49.51N 6.54 E
Neumarkter Sattel 128 Id 47.06N 14.22 E
Neumarkt in der Oberpfalz 120 Hg 49.17N 11.28 E
Neumünster 120 Fb 54.04N 9.59 E
Neunkirchen [Aus.] 128 Kc 47.43N 16.05 E
Neunkirchen [Ger.] 120 Dg 49.21N 7.11 E
Neunkirchen [Ger.] 124 Kd 50.48N 8.00 E
Neunkirchen [Ger.] 124 Jd 50.51N 7.20 E
Neuquén 200 Ji 39.00S 68.05W
Neuquén 206 Ge 39.00S 70.00W
Neuquén, Rio- 198 Ji 38.59S 68.00W
Neuruppin 120 Id 52.56N 12.48 E
Neuse River 184 Ih 35.06N 76.30W
Neusiedl am See 128 Kc 47.56N 16.50 E
Neusiedler See 120 Mi 47.50N 16.45 E
Neuss 120 Ce 51.12N 6.42 E
Neustadt (Hessen) 124 Ld 50.51N 9.07 E
Neustadt am Rübenberge 120 Fd 52.30N 9.28 E
Neustadt an der Aisch 120 Gg 49.35N 10.36 E
Neustadt an der Orla 120 Hf 50.44N 11.45 E
Neustadt an der Weinstraße 120 Eg 49.21N 8.09 E
Neustadt bei Coburg 120 Hf 50.19N 11.07 E
Neustadt in Holstein 120 Gb 54.06N 10.49 E
Neustrelitz 120 Jc 53.22N 13.05 E
Neu-Ulm 120 Gh 48.24N 10.01 E
Neuville-les-Dieppe 124 De 49.55N 1.06 E
Neuville-sur-Saône 122 Ki 45.52N 4.51 E
Neuwerk 120 Ec 53.55N 8.30 E
Neuwied 120 Df 50.26N 7.28 E
Neva 110 Jd 59.55N 30.15 E
Nevada 182 Dd 39.00N 117.00W
Nevada [Ia.-U.S.] 186 Je 42.01N 93.27W
Nevada [Mo.-U.S.] 182 Id 37.51N 94.22W
Nevada, Sierra- [Sp.] 110 Fh 37.05N 3.10W
Nevada, Sierra- [U.S.] 174 Hf 38.00N 119.15W
Nevada del Cocuy, Sierra- 198 Ie 6.10N 72.15W
Nevada de Santa Marta, Sierra- 198 Id 10.50N 73.40W
Nevado, Cerro- 198 Ie 3.59N 74.04W
Neve, Serra da- 158 Ij 13.52S 13.26 E
Nevel 136 Cd 56.02N 29.55 E
Nevele 124 Fc 51.02N 3.33 E
Nevelsk 138 Jg 46.37N 141.57 E
Neverkino 132 Oc 52.47N 46.48 E
Nevers 122 Jg 46.59N 3.10 E
Nevesinje 128 Mg 43.16N 18.07 E
Nevinnomyssk 136 Eg 44.38N 41.58 E
Nevis 190 Le 17.10N 62.34W
Nevis, Ben- 110 Fd 56.48N 5.01W
Nevis Peak 197c Ab 17.10N 62.34W
Nevjansk 136 Gd 57.32N 60.13 E
Nevşehir 144 Db 38.38N 34.43 E
Nevskoje 154 Lb 45.42N 133.40 E
Newala 170 Ge 10.56S 39.18 E
New Albany [In.-U.S.] 182 Jd 38.18N 85.49W
New Albany [Ms.-U.S.] 186 Li 34.29N 89.00W
New Alresford 124 Ac 51.05N 1.10W
New Amsterdam 200 Ke 6.17N 57.36W
Newark [De.-U.S.] 184 Jf 39.41N 75.45W
Newark [N.J.-U.S.] 182 Mc 40.44N 74.11W
Newark [N.Y.-U.S.] 184 Id 43.03N 77.06W
Newark [Oh.-U.S.] 182 Kc 40.03N 82.25W
Newark-on-Trent 118 Mh 53.05N 0.49W
New Bedford 182 Mc 41.38N 70.56W
New Bern 182 Ld 35.07N 77.03W
Newberry [Mi.-U.S.] 184 Eb 46.21N 85.30W
Newberry [S.C.-U.S.] 184 Gh 34.17N 81.37W
New Braunfels 182 Hf 29.42N 98.08W
New Britain 184 Ke 41.40N 72.47W
New Britain Island 208 Ge 5.40S 151.00 E
New Britain Trench (EN) 214 Ei 6.00S 153.00 E
New Brunswick 184 Je 40.29N 74.27W
New Brunswick 180 Kg 46.30N 66.45W
New Buckenham 124 Db 52.28N 1.05 E
New Buffalo 184 De 41.47N 86.45W
Newburgh 182 Mc 41.30N 74.00W
Newbury 118 Lj 51.25N 1.20W
New Caledonia (EN) = Nouvelle-Calédonie 210 Hg 21.30S 165.30 E
New Caledonia (EN) = Nouvelle-Calédonie 208 Hg 21.30S 165.30 E
New Caledonia Basin (EN) 208 Hg 30.00S 165.00 E
New Carlisle 184 Oa 48.01N 65.20W
New Castle (EN) = Castilla la Nueva 126 Id 40.00N 3.45W
Newcastle [Austl.] 210 Gh 32.56S 151.46 E
New Castle [In.-U.S.] 184 Ef 39.55N 85.22W
Newcastle [N.B.-Can.] 180 Kg 47.00N 65.34W
New Castle [Pa.-U.S.] 182 Kc 41.00N 80.22W
Newcastle [S.Afr.] 172 De 27.49S 29.55 E
Newcastle [St.C.N.] 197c Ab 17.13N 62.34W
Newcastle [Wy.-U.S.] 182 Gc 43.50N 104.11W
Newcastle/An Caisleán Nua 118 Hg 54.12N 5.54W
Newcastle Creek 212 Gc 17.20S 133.23 E
Newcastle-under-Lyme 118 Kh 53.00N 2.14W
Newcastle-upon-Tyne 112 Fd 54.59N 1.35W
Newcastle Waters 210 Ef 17.24S 133.24 E
Newcastle West/An Caisleán Nua 118 Di 52.27N 9.03W
New Delhi 142 Jg 28.36N 77.12 E
New Denver 188 Ga 50.00N 117.22W
Newell 186 Ed 44.43N 103.25W
Newell, Lake- 188 Ja 50.25N 111.56W
New England 174 Le 44.00N 71.20W
New England Range 208 Gh 30.00S 151.50 E
New England Seamounts (EN) 174 Mf 38.00N 61.00W
Newenham, Cape- 178 Ge 58.37N 162.12W
New Forest 118 Lk 50.55N 1.35W

Index Symbols

1 Independent Nation
2 State, Region
3 District, County
4 Municipality
5 Colony, Dependency
Continent
Physical Region
Historical or Cultural Region
Mount, Mountain
Volcano
Hill
Mountains, Mountain Range
Hills, Escarpment
Plateau, Upland
Pass, Gap
Plain, Lowland
Delta
Salt Flat
Valley, Canyon
Crater, Cave
Karst Features
Depression
Polder
Desert, Dunes
Forest, Woods
Heath, Steppe
Oasis
Cape, Point
Coast, Beach
Cliff
Peninsula
Isthmus
Sandbank
Island
Atoll
Rock, Reef
Islands, Archipelago
Rocks, Reefs
Coral Reef
Well, Spring
Geyser
River, Stream
Waterfall, Rapids
River Mouth, Estuary
Lake
Salt Lake
Intermittent Lake
Reservoir
Swamp, Pond
Canal
Glacier
Ice Shelf, Pack Ice
Ocean
Sea
Gulf, Bay
Strait, Fjord
Lagoon
Bank
Seamount
Tablemount
Ridge
Shelf
Basin
Escarpment, Sea Scarp
Fracture
Trench, Abyss
National Park, Reserve
Point of Interest
Recreation Site
Cave, Cavern
Historic Site
Ruins
Wall, Walls
Church, Abbey
Temple
Scientific Station
Railway station
Airport
Port
Military installation
Lighthouse
Mine
Tunnel
Dam, Bridge

Index Symbols

[1] Independent Nation
[2] State, Region
[3] District, County
[4] Municipality
[5] Colony, Dependency
[6] Continent
[7] Physical Region

Historical or Cultural Region
Mount, Mountain
Volcano
Hill
Mountains, Mountain Range
Hills, Escarpment
Plateau, Upland

Pass, Gap
Plain, Lowland
Delta
Salt Flat
Valley, Canyon
Crater, Cave
Karst Features

Depression
Polder
Desert, Dunes
Forest, Woods
Heath, Steppe
Oasis
Cape, Point

Coast, Beach
Cliff
Peninsula
Isthmus
Sandbank
Island
Atoll

Rock, Reef
Islands, Archipelago
Rocks, Reefs
Coral Reef
River, Stream

Waterfall, Rapids
River Mouth, Estuary
Lake
Salt Lake
Intermittent Lake
Reservoir
Swamp, Pond

Canal
Glacier
Ice Shelf, Pack Ice
Ocean
Sea
Gulf, Bay
Strait, Fjord

Lagoon
Bank
Fracture
Seamount
Tablemount
Ridge
Shelf
Basin

Escarpment, Sea Scarp
Trench, Abyss
National Park, Reserve
Point of Interest
Recreation Site
Cave, Cavern

Historic Site
Ruins
Wall, Walls
Church, Abbey
Temple
Scientific Station
Railway station

Airport
Port
Military installation
Lighthouse
Mine
Tunnel
Dam, Bridge

Njombe 158 Ki 6.56S 35.06 E
Njudung 116 Fg 57.25N 14.50 E
Njuja 138 Gd 60.32N 116.25 E
Njuk, ozero- 114 Hd 64.25N 31.45 E
Njuksenica 114 Kf 60.28N 44.15 E
Njukža 138 He 56.30N 121.40 E
Njunes 114 Eb 68.45N 19.30 E
Njurba 142 Nc 63.17N 118.20 E
Njurundabommen 114 De 62.16N 17.22 E
Njutånger 116 Gc 61.37N 17.03 E
Njuvčim 134 Ef 61.22N 50.42 E
Nkambe 166 Hd 6.38N 10.40 E
Nkawkaw 166 Ed 6.33N 0.46W
Nkayi [Con.] 160 Ii 4.05S 13.18 E
Nkayi [Zimb.] 172 Dc 19.00S 28.54 E
Nkhata Bay 170 Fe 11.36S 34.18 E
Nkongsamba 160 Hh 4.57N 9.56 E
Nkota Kota 160 Kj 12.55S 34.18 E
Nkululu 170 Fd 6.26S 32.49 E
Nkusi 170 Fb 1.07N 30.40 E
Nkwalini 172 Ee 28.45S 31.30 E
'Nmai 148 Jc 25.42N 97.30 E
Nnewi 166 Gd 6.01N 6.55 E
Nō 156 Ec 37.05N 137.59 E
Noailles 124 Ee 49.20N 2.12 E
Noākhāli 148 Id 22.49N 91.06 E
Noatak 178 Gc 67.34N 162.59W
Nobel 184 Gc 45.25N 80.06W
Nobeoka 152 Ne 32.35N 131.40 E
Noblesville 184 Ee 40.03N 86.00W
Noboribetsu 154 Pc 42.25N 141.11 E
Noce 128 Fd 46.09N 11.04 E
Nodaway River 186 Ig 39.54N 94.58W
Noën 152 Hc 43.15N 102.20 E
Noeux-les-Mines 124 Ed 50.29N 2.40 E
Nogajskaja step 132 Ng 44.15N 46.00 E
Nogales [Az.-U.S.] 182 Ee 31.21N 110.55W
Nogales [Mex.] 176 Hf 31.20N 110.56W
Nogaro 122 Fk 43.46N 0.02W
Nogat 120 Pb 54.11N 19.15 E
Nōgata 156 Be 33.44N 130.44 E
Nogent-le-Rotrou 122 Gf 48.19N 0.50 E
Nogent-sur-Marne 124 Ef 48.50N 2.29 E
Nogent-sur-Oise 124 Ee 49.16N 2.28 E
Nogent-sur-Seine 122 Jf 48.29N 3.30 E
Noginsk [R.S.F.S.R.] 136 Dd 55.54N 38.28 E
Noginsk [R.S.F.S.R.] 138 Ed 64.25N 91.10 E
Nogliki 138 Jf 51.45N 143.15 E
Nōgo-Hakusan 156 Ed 35.46N 136.31 E
Nogoyá 206 Id 32.24S 59.48W
Nogoya, Arroyo- 204 Ck 32.55S 59.59W
Nógrád [2] 120 Ph 48.00N 19.35 E
Nogueira, Serra da- 126 Fc 41.42N 6.52W
Noguera Pallaresa 126 Mb 42.15N 0.54 E
Noguera Ribagorçana/ Noguera Ribagorzana 126 Mc 41.40N 0.43 E
Noguera Ribagorzana/ Noguera Ribagorçana 126 Mc 41.40N 0.43 E
Noh, Laguna- 192 Nh 18.40N 90.20W
Nohain 122 Ig 47.24N 2.55 E
Noheji 154 Pd 40.52N 141.08 E
Nohfelden 124 Je 49.35N 7.09 E
Noia / Noya 126 Db 42.47N 8.53W
Noidore, Rio- 204 Fb 14.50S 52.34W
Noir, Causse- 122 Jj 44.09N 3.15 E
Noire, Montagne- 122 Ik 43.28N 2.18 E
Noires, Montagnes- 122 Cf 48.09N 3.40W
Noirétable 122 Ji 45.49N 3.46 E
Noirmoutier, Ile de- 122 Dh 46.58N 2.12W
Noirmoutier-en-l'Ile 122 Dg 47.00N 2.15W
Nojima-Zaki 156 Fd 34.54N 139.50 E
Nojiri-Ko 156 Fc 36.49N 138.13 E
Noka 219c Bb 10.40S 166.03 E
Nokaneng 172 Cc 19.40S 22.12 E
Nokia 114 Ff 61.28N 23.30 E
Nok Kundi 148 Cc 28.48N 62.46 E
Nokomis 188 Ma 51.30N 105.00W
Nokou 168 Ac 14.35N 14.47 E
Nokra 168 Fb 15.42N 39.56 E
Nol 116 Eg 57.55N 12.03 E
Nola 168 Be 3.32N 16.04 E
Nolin Lake 184 Dg 37.20N 86.10W
Nolinsk 136 Ed 57.33N 50.00 E
Nomad 210 Fe 6.21S 142.12 E
Noma Omuramba 172 Cc 19.10S 22.16 E
Noma-Zaki 156 Bf 31.25N 130.06 E
Nombre de Dios 192 Gf 23.51N 104.14W
Nome 176 Cc 64.30N 165.24W
Nomeny 124 If 48.54N 6.14 E
Nomozaki 156 Ae 32.35N 129.45 E
Nomo-Zaki 156 Ae 32.35N 129.45 E
Nomuka 221b Bb 20.15S 174.48W
Nomuka Group 174 Jg 20.20S 174.45W
Nomuka Iki 221b Bb 20.17S 174.49W
Nomwin Atoll 208 Gd 8.32N 151.47 E
Nonacho Lake 180 Gd 62.40N 109.30W
Nonancourt 124 Df 48.46N 1.12 E
Nonette 124 Ee 49.12N 2.24 E
Nong'an 152 Mc 44.24N 125.08 E
Nong Han 148 Ke 17.21N 103.06 E
Nong Khai 142 Mh 17.52N 102.45 E
Nongoma 172 Ee 27.53S 31.38 E
Nonoava 192 Fd 27.28N 106.44W
Nonouti Atoll 208 Ie 0.40S 174.21 E
Nonsan 154 If 36.12N 127.05 E
Nonsuch Bay 197d Bb 17.03N 61.42W
Nontron 122 Gi 45.32N 0.40 E
Noord-Beveland 124 Fc 51.35N 3.45 E
Noord-Brabant [3] 124 Gc 51.30N 5.00 E
Noord-Holland [3] 124 Gb 52.40N 4.50 E
Noordhollandskanaal 124 Kb 52.55N 4.50 E
Noordoewer 172 Be 28.45S 17.37 E
Noordoostpolder 124 Hb 52.42N 5.44 E
Noordoostpolder 122 Lb 52.42N 5.45 E
Noordoostpolder-Emmeloord 124 Hb 52.42N 5.44 E
Noordwijk aan Zee 122 Kb 52.14N 4.26 E
Noordwijk aan Zee, Noordwijk- 124 Gb 52.14N 4.26 E
Noordwijk-Noordwijk aan Zee 124 Gb 52.14N 4.26 E
Noordzee=North Sea (EN) 110 Gd 55.20N 3.00 E
Noordzeekanaal 122 Kb 52.30N 4.35 E
Noormarkku/Norrmark 116 Ic 61.35N 21.52 E
Noorvik 178 Gc 66.50N 161.12W
Nootka Island 188 Bb 49.32N 126.42W
Nootka Sound 188 Bb 49.33N 126.38W
Nōqui 170 Bd 5.50S 13.27 E
Nora 114 Dg 59.31N 15.02 E
Nora 168 Fc 15.40N 39.55 E
Nora 128 Dk 39.00N 9.02 E
Noranda 180 Jg 48.15N 79.01W
Noraskog 116 Fe 59.40N 14.50 E
Norberg 116 Fd 60.04N 15.56 E
Norcia 128 Hh 42.48N 13.05 E
Nord 179 Kb 81.45N 17.30W
Nord [Burkina] [3] 166 Ec 13.40N 2.50W
Nord [Cam.] [3] 166 Hd 9.00N 13.50 E
Nord [Fr.] [3] 122 Jd 50.30N 3.10 E
Nord, Canal du- 122 Id 49.57N 2.55 E
Nord, Mer du-=North Sea (EN) 110 Gd 55.20N 3.00 E
Nordausques 124 Ed 50.49N 2.05 E
Nordaustlandet 224 Jd 79.48N 22.24 E
Nordborg 116 Ci 55.03N 9.45 E
Nordby 116 Ci 55.27N 8.25 E
Norddeutsches Tiefland= North German Plain (EN) 110 He 53.00N 11.00 E
Norden 120 Dc 53.36N 7.12 E
Nordenham 120 Ec 53.39N 8.29 E
Nordenskiöld Archipelago (EN) = Nordenskjölda, ostrova- 138 Ea 76.50N 96.00 E
Nordenskjölda, ostrova- = Nordenskiöld Archipelago (EN) 138 Ea 76.50N 96.00 E
Norderney 120 Dc 53.42N 7.10 E
Norderstedt 120 Fc 53.41N 9.58 E
Nordfjord 116 Bc 61.50N 6.15 E
Nordfjord 114 Af 61.55N 5.10 E
Nordfjordeid 114 Af 61.54N 6.00 E
Nordfold 114 Dc 67.46N 15.12 E
Nordfriesische Inseln= North Frisian Islands (EN) 120 Ea 54.50N 8.30 E
Nordfriesland = North Friesland (EN) 120 Eb 54.40N 8.55 E
Nordgau 120 Hg 49.15N 11.50 E
Nordgrønland=North Greenland (EN) [2] 179 Gc 79.30N 50.00W
Nordhausen 120 Ge 51.31N 10.48 E
Nordhordland 116 Ad 60.50N 5.50 E
Nordhorn 120 Dd 52.26N 7.05 E
Nord-Jylland [2] 116 Cg 57.15N 10.00 E
Nordkapp [Nor.] =North Cape (EN) 110 Ia 71.11N 25.48 E
Nordkapp [Sval.] 179 Nb 80.31N 20.00 E
Nordkinn 110 Ia 71.08N 27.39 E
Nordkinnhalvøya 114 Ga 70.55N 27.45 E
Nord-Kvaløy 114 Ea 70.10N 19.11 E
Nordland [3] 114 Cc 67.06N 13.20 E
Nördlingen 120 Gh 48.51N 10.30 E
Nordloher Tief 124 Ja 53.10N 7.45 E
Nordmark 116 Fe 59.50N 14.06 E
Nordmøre 116 Ca 63.00N 8.30 E
Nordostrundingen 224 Le 81.30N 11.00W
Nord-Ostsee-Kanal = Kiel Canal (EN) 120 Ge 53.53N 9.08 E
Nord-Ouest [3] 166 Hd 6.30N 10.30 E
Nordøyane 116 Bb 62.40N 6.15 E
Nordreisa 114 Eb 69.46N 21.03 E
Nordre Rønner 116 Dg 57.22N 10.56 E
Nordrhein-Westfalen=North Rhine-Westphalia (EN) [2] 120 De 51.30N 7.30 E
Nordsee=North Sea (EN) 110 Gd 55.20N 3.00 E
Nordsjøen=North Sea (EN) 110 Gd 55.20N 3.00 E
Nordskjobotn 114 Eb 69.13N 19.34 E
Nordsøen=North Sea (EN) 110 Gd 55.20N 3.00 E
Nord Strand 120 Eb 54.30N 8.55 E
Nordtiroler Kalkalpen 120 Hi 47.30N 11.30 E
Nord-Trøndelag [2] 114 Cd 64.25N 12.00 E
Nordwestfjord 114 Jd 71.30N 26.30W
Nore/An Fheoir 118 Gi 52.25N 6.58W
Norefjell 116 Cd 60.16N 9.29 E
Norefjorden 116 Cd 60.10N 9.00 E
Norfolk [3] 118 Ni 52.45N 0.40 E
Norfolk 118 Oi 52.40N 1.05 E
Norfolk [Nb.-U.S.] 182 Hc 42.02N 97.25W
Norfolk [Va.-U.S.] 176 Lf 38.40N 76.14W
Norfolk Island [5] 210 Hg 29.05S 167.59 E
Norfolk Island 208 Hg 29.05S 167.59 E
Norfolk Ridge (EN) 208 Hg 29.00S 168.00 E
Norfolk Lake 186 Jh 36.25N 92.10W
Norg 124 Ia 53.04N 6.32 E
Norge=Norway (EN) [1] 112 Gc 62.00N 10.00 E
Norheimsund 114 Bf 60.22N 6.08 E
Norikura-Dake 156 Ec 36.06N 137.33 E
Norilsk 142 Kc 69.20N 88.06 E
Normal 186 Lf 40.31N 88.59W
Norman 182 Hd 35.15N 97.26W
Norman, Lake- 184 Gh 35.35N 81.00W
Normanby Island 214 Ej 10.00S 151.00 E
Normanby River 212 Ib 14.25S 144.08 E
Normand, Bocage- 122 Ef 49.00N 1.10W
Normandie=Normandy (EN) 110 Gf 49.00N 0.10 E
Normandie=Normandy (EN) 122 Gf 49.00N 0.10 E
Normandie, Collines de-=Normandy Hills (EN) 110 Ff 48.50N 0.40W
Normandin 184 Ka 48.52N 72.30W
Normandy (EN)= Normandie 110 Gf 49.00N 0.10 E
Normandy (EN)= Normandie 122 Gf 49.00N 0.10 E
Normandy Hills (EN)= Normandie, Collines de- 110 Ff 48.50N 0.40W
Norman Island 197a Db 18.20N 64.37W
Norman River 212 Ic 17.28S 140.39 E
Normanton 210 Ff 17.40S 141.05 E
Norman Wells 176 Gc 65.17N 126.51W
Norquinco 206 Ff 41.51S 70.54W
Norra Dellen 116 Gc 61.55N 16.40 E
Norrahammar 116 Fg 57.42N 14.06 E
Norrala 116 Gc 61.22N 16.59 E
Norra Midsjöbanken 116 Gh 56.10N 17.30 E
Norra Ny 114 Cf 60.24N 13.15 E
Norra Storfjället 114 Dd 65.53N 15.14 E
Norrbotten [2] 114 Ec 67.26N 19.35 E
Nørre Åby 116 Ci 55.27N 9.54 E
Nørre Alslev 116 Dj 54.54N 11.54 E
Nørre-Nebel 116 Ci 55.47N 8.18 E
Norrent-Fontes 124 Ed 50.35N 2.24 E
Nørresundby 114 Bh 57.04N 9.55 E
Norrhult 114 Dh 57.08N 15.10 E
Norris Lake 184 Fg 36.20N 83.55W
Norristown 184 Je 40.07N 75.20W
Norrköping 112 Hd 58.36N 16.11 E
Norrland 110 Hc 64.27N 17.20 E
Norrland 114 Dd 65.00N 18.00 E
Norrmark/Noormarkku 116 Ic 61.35N 21.52 E
Norrsundet 116 Gd 60.56N 17.08 E
Norrtälje 114 Eg 59.46N 18.42 E
Norseman 210 Dh 32.12S 121.46 E
Norsewood 218 Gd 40.04S 176.13 E
Norsjö 114 Ed 64.55N 19.29 E
Norsjø 116 Ce 59.20N 9.20 E
Norsk 138 Hf 52.20N 129.59 E
Norske Havet = Norwegian Sea (EN) 110 Gc 70.00N 2.00 E
Norske Øer 179 Kc 79.00N 18.00W
Norsoup 219b Cc 16.04S 167.23 E
Norte, Baia- 204 Hh 27.30S 48.35W
Norte, Cabo- [Braz.] 202 Ic 1.40N 50.00W
Norte, Cabo- [Pas.] 221d Ab 27.03S 109.24W
Norte, Canal do- 202 Hc 0.30N 50.30W
Norte, Punta- 206 Hf 42.04S 63.45W
Norte, Serra do- 202 Gf 11.00S 59.00W
Norte del Cabo San Antonio, Punta- 206 Ie 36.17S 56.47W
Norte de Santander [3] 202 Db 8.00N 73.00W
Nortelândia 202 Gf 14.25S 56.48W
North, Cape- 180 Lg 47.02N 60.25W
North Adams 184 Kd 42.42N 73.02W
Northallerton 118 Lg 54.20N 1.26W
Northam [Austl.] 210 Ch 31.39S 116.40 E
Northam [S.Afr.] 172 Dd 24.58S 27.11 E
North America (EN) 106 Me 40.00N 95.00W
North American Basin (EN) 106 Bf 30.00N 60.00W
Northampton 118 Mi 52.30N 1.00W
Northampton [Austl.] 212 Ce 28.21S 114.37 E
Northampton [Eng.-U.K.] 118 Mi 52.14N 0.54W
Northampton [Ma.-U.S.] 184 Kd 42.19N 72.38W
Northampton Seamounts (EN) 208 Jb 25.20N 172.04W
Northamptonshire [3] 118 Mi 52.25N 0.55W
North Andaman 148 If 13.15N 92.55 E
North Arm 180 Gd 62.00N 114.30W
North Astrolabe Reef 219d Bc 18.39S 178.32 E
North Augusta 184 Gi 33.30N 81.58W
North Aulatsivik 180 Le 59.45N 64.04W
North Australian Basin (EN) 106 Hk 14.30S 116.30 E
North Battleford 176 Id 52.47N 108.17W
North Bay 176 Le 46.19N 79.28W
North Belcher Islands 180 Je 56.45N 79.45W
North Berwick 118 Ke 56.04N 2.44W
North Bohemian Forest (EN) =Český Les 120 Ig 49.50N 12.30 E
North Bohemian Forest (EN) =Oberpfälzer Wald 120 Ig 49.50N 12.30 E
North Buganda [3] 170 Fb 0.50N 32.10 E
North Caicos 194 Lc 21.56N 71.59W
North Canadian River 182 Hd 35.17N 95.31W
North Cape 208 Ih 34.25S 173.03 E
North Cape (EN)=Nordkapp [Nor.] 110 Ia 71.11N 25.48 E
North Caribou Lake 180 If 52.48N 90.45W
North Carolina [2] 182 Ld 35.30N 80.00W
North Channel 180 Jg 46.02N 82.50W
North Channel/Sruth na Maoile 110 Fd 55.10N 5.40W
Northchapel 124 Bd 51.03N 0.38W
North Charleston 184 Hi 32.53N 80.00W
North Chicago 186 Me 42.20N 87.51W
North Cove 188 Cc 46.47N 124.06W
North Cyprus 142 Ff 35.15N 33.40 E
North Dakota [2] 182 Gb 47.30N 100.15W
North Downs 118 Nj 51.20N 0.10 E
North East 184 Hd 42.13N 79.51W
North-East [3] 172 Dd 21.00S 27.30 E
Northeast Cape 178 Fd 63.18N 168.42W
North-Eastern [3] 170 Hb 1.00N 40.15 E
Northeast Islands 220d Ba 7.36N 151.57 E
Northeast Pacific Basin (EN) 106 Lg 20.00N 140.00W
North East Point 220g Bb 1.57N 157.16W
Northeast Point [Bah.] 194 Kc 21.18N 72.54W
Northeast Point [Bah.] 194 Kb 22.43N 73.50W
Northeast Providence Channel 190 Ic 25.40N 77.09W
Northeim 120 Fe 51.42N 10.00 E
North Entrance 220a Bb 7.59N 134.37 E
Northern [Ghana] [3] 166 Ed 9.30N 1.00W
Northern [Mwi.] [3] 170 Fe 11.00S 34.00 E
Northern [S.L.] [3] 166 Cd 9.15N 11.45W
Northern [Ug.] [3] 170 Fb 2.45N 32.45 E
Northern [Zam.] [3] 170 Fe 11.00S 31.00 E
Northern Cay 194 De 17.27N 87.28W
Northern Cook Islands 208 Kf 10.00S 161.00W
Northern Dvina (EN)= Severnaja Dvina 110 Kc 64.32N 40.30 E
Northern Guinea (EN) 158 Gh 8.30N 1.00W
Northern Indian Lake 180 He 57.20N 97.17W
Northern Ireland [2] 118 Gg 54.40N 6.45W
Northern Mariana Islands [5] 210 Fc 16.00N 145.30 E
Northern Sporades (EN)= Vórioi Sporádhes, Nisoi- 110 Ih 39.15N 23.55 E
Northern Territory [3] 212 Gc 20.00S 134.00 E
Northern Urals (EN)= Severny Ural 110 Lc 62.00N 59.00 E
Northern Uvals (EN) = Severnyje Uvaly 110 Kd 59.30N 49.00 E
North Esk 118 Ke 56.45N 2.30W
Northfield 186 Jd 44.27N 93.09W
North Fiji Basin (EN) 106 Jk 16.00S 174.00 E
North Foreland 118 Oj 51.23N 1.27 E
North Fork Grand River 186 Ed 45.47N 102.16W
North Fork John Day River 188 Fd 44.45N 119.38W
North Fork Moreau River 186 Ed 45.09N 102.50W
North Fork Pass 180 Dd 64.00N 138.00W
North Fork Powder River 188 Le 43.40N 106.30W
North Fork Red 186 Gi 34.25N 99.14W
North Fort Myers 184 Gl 26.40N 81.54W
North Friesland (EN) = Nordfriesland 120 Eb 54.40N 8.55 E
North Frisian Islands (EN)= Nordfriesische Inseln 120 Ea 54.50N 8.30 E
North German Plain (EN)= Norddeutsches Tiefland 110 He 53.00N 11.00 E
North Greenland (EN) = Nordgrønland [2] 179 Gc 79.30N 50.00W
North Highlands 188 Eg 38.40N 121.23W
North Horr 170 Gb 3.19N 37.04 E
North Island [N.Z.] 208 Ih 39.00S 176.00 E
North Island [Sey.] 172b Bc 10.07S 51.11 E
North Kent 180 Ia 76.40N 90.15W
North Korea (EN)=Chosŏn M.I.K. [1] 142 Oe 40.00N 127.30 E
North Lakhimpur 148 Ic 27.14N 94.07 E
Northland [2] 218 Ea 35.30S 173.40 E
North Las Vegas 188 Hh 36.12N 115.07W
North Lincoln Land 180 Ja 76.15N 80.00W
North Little Rock 182 Ie 34.46N 92.14W
North Loup River 186 Gf 41.17N 98.23W
North Magnetic Pole (1980) (EN) 224 Qd 77.03N 101.08W
North Malosmadulu Atoll 148a Ba 5.35N 72.55 E
North Mamm Peak 186 Cg 39.23N 107.52W
North Mayreau Channel 197n Bb 12.41N 61.20W
North Miami 184 Gm 25.56N 80.09W
North Minch 110 Fd 58.05N 5.55W
North Palisade 188 Fh 37.10N 118.38W
North Pass [F.S.M.] 220d Ba 7.41N 151.48 E
North Pass [U.S.] 186 Ll 29.10N 89.15W
North Platte 182 Gc 41.08N 100.46W
North Platte 174 Ie 41.15N 100.45W
North Point [Bar.] 197q Ab 13.20N 59.36W
North Point [Cook] 220n Ab 10.22S 161.02W
North Pole (EN) 224 Ge 90.00N 0.00
Northport 184 Di 33.14N 87.35W
North Powder 188 Gd 45.03N 117.55W
North Raccoon River 186 Jf 41.35N 93.31W
North Reef 219a Ee 12.13S 160.04 E
North Rhine-Westphalia (EN)=Nordrhein-Westfalen [2] 120 De 51.30N 7.30 E
North Rim 188 Ih 36.12N 112.03W
North River 180 Ie 58.53N 94.42W
North Rona 118 Hb 59.10N 5.40W
North Ronaldsay 118 Kb 59.25N 2.30W
North Saskatchewan River 174 Id 53.15N 105.06W
North Sea 110 Gd 55.20N 3.00 E
North Sea (EN)= Noordzee 110 Gd 55.20N 3.00 E
North Sea (EN)=Nord, Mer du- 110 Gd 55.20N 3.00 E
North Sea (EN)= Nordsee 110 Gd 55.20N 3.00 E
North Sea (EN)= Nordsjøen 110 Gd 55.20N 3.00 E
North Sea (EN)= Nordsøen 110 Gd 55.20N 3.00 E
North Sentinel 148 If 11.33N 92.15 E
North Shoshone Peak 188 Gg 39.10N 117.29W
North Siberian Plain (EN) = Severo-Sibirskaja nizmennost 140 Mb 72.00N 104.00 E
North Sound 194 Gd 19.25N 81.26W
North Sound 197d Bb 17.07N 61.45W
North Stradbroke Island 212 Ke 27.35S 153.30 E
North Taranaki Bight 218 Fc 38.50S 174.25 E
North Thompson 180 Ff 50.41N 120.11W
North Tokelau Trough (EN) 106 Kj 3.00S 165.00W
North Tonawanda 184 Hd 43.02N 78.54W
North Trap 218 Bg 47.20S 167.55 E
North Tyne 118 Kg 54.59N 2.08W
North Uist 118 Fd 57.37N 7.22W
Northumberland 118 Kf 55.15N 2.10W
Northumberland 118 Kf 55.15N 2.05W
Northumberland Islands 208 Gg 21.40S 150.00 E
Northumberland Strait 180 Lg 46.00N 63.30W
North Umpqua River 188 De 43.16N 123.27W
North Vancouver 188 Db 49.19N 123.04W
North Walsham 124 Db 52.49N 1.23 E
Northway 178 Kd 62.59N 141.43W
North West Bluff 197c Bc 16.49N 62.12W
North West Cape 208 Cg 21.45S 114.10 E
North-Western [3] 170 Ee 13.00S 25.00 E
Northwest Frontier [3] 148 Eb 33.00N 70.30 E
North West Highlands 110 Fd 57.30N 5.00W
Northwest Pacific Basin (EN) 106 Je 40.00N 155.00 E
North West Point 220g Ab 2.02N 157.30W
Northwest Providence Channel 184 Hl 26.10N 78.20W
Northwest Reef 220a Bb 7.59N 134.33 E
North West River 180 Lf 53.32N 60.09W
Northwest Territories [3] 180 Hc 66.00N 102.00W
Northwich 118 Kh 53.16N 2.32W
North York Moors 118 Mg 54.25N 0.50W
North Yorkshire [3] 118 Lg 54.15N 1.40W
Norton [Ks.-U.S.] 182 Gd 39.50N 100.01W
Norton [Va.-U.S.] 184 Fg 36.56N 82.37W
Norton [Zimb.] 172 Ec 17.53S 30.41 E
Norton Bay 178 Gd 64.45N 161.15W
Norton Sound 174 Cc 64.45N 161.15W
Norvegia, Kapp- 222 Bf 71.25S 12.18W
Norwalk [Ct.-U.S.] 184 Ke 41.07N 73.27W
Norwalk [Oh.-U.S.] 184 Fe 41.14N 82.37W
Norway 184 Dc 45.47N 87.55W
Norway (EN)=Norge [1] 112 Gc 62.00N 10.00 E
Norway Bay 180 Hb 71.00N 104.35W
Norway House 180 Hf 53.58N 97.50W
Norwegian Basin (EN) 110 Fb 68.00N 2.00W
Norwegian Bay 180 Ia 77.45N 90.30W
Norwegian Sea (EN)= Norske Havet 110 Gc 70.00N 2.00 E
Norwegian Trench (EN) 110 Gd 59.00N 4.30 E
Norwich [Ct.-U.S.] 184 Ke 41.32N 72.05W
Norwich [Eng.-U.K.] 112 Ge 52.38N 1.18 E
Norwich [N.Y.-U.S.] 184 Jd 42.33N 75.33W
Norwich Airport 124 Db 52.40N 1.18 E
Norwood 184 Ef 39.10N 84.28W
Nosappu-Misaki 156a Db 43.23N 145.47 E
Noshappu-Misaki 156a Ba 45.27N 141.39 E
Noshiro 152 Pc 40.12N 140.02 E
Nosovaja 136 Fb 68.15N 54.31 E
Nosovka 136 De 50.55N 31.37 E
Nosratābād 144 Id 29.54N 59.59 E
Nossa Senhora das Candeias 202 Kf 12.40S 38.33W
Nossa Senhora do Livramento 204 Db 15.48S 56.22W
Noss Head 118 Jc 58.30N 3.05W
Nossob 158 Jk 26.55S 20.40 E
Nossop 172 Ce 26.55S 20.40 E
Nosy-Be 160 Lj 13.22S 48.16 E
Nosy-Be 158 Lj 13.20S 48.15 E
Nosy-Varika 172 Hd 20.35S 48.30 E
Nota 114 Hb 68.07N 30.10 E
Notch Peak 188 Ig 39.08N 113.24W
Noteć 120 Ld 52.44N 15.26 E
Notecka, Puszcza- 120 Ld 52.45N 16.00 E
Note Kemopla 219c Ab 10.55S 165.51 E
Notengo, Laguna de- 192 Ji 16.15N 98.10W
Notia Pindhos 130 Ej 39.30N 21.20 E
Nótioi Sporádhes = Dodecanese (EN) 110 Ih 36.00N 27.00 E
Nótios Evvoïkós Kólpos 130 Gk 38.20N 23.50 E
Nötö 116 Ie 60.00N 21.45 E
Noto [It.] 128 Jn 36.53N 15.04 E
Noto [Jap.] 154 Nf 37.18N 137.09 E
Noto, Golfo di- 128 Jn 36.50N 15.10 E
Notodden 114 Bg 59.34N 9.17 E
Noto-Hantō 152 Od 37.20N 137.00 E
Noto-Jima 156 Ec 37.07N 137.00 E
Notoro-Ko 156a Da 44.05N 144.10 E
Notoro-Misaki 156a Da 44.07N 144.15 E
Notranjsko 128 Ie 45.46N 14.26 E
Notre-Dame, Monts- 174 Me 48.00N 69.00W
Notre Dame Bay 180 Mg 49.50N 55.00W
Notre-Dame-de-Courson 124 Cf 48.59N 0.16 E
Notre-Dame-de-Gravenchon 124 Ce 49.29N 0.35 E
Notre Dame-du-Lac 184 Mb 47.38N 68.49W
Notre-Dame-du-Nord 184 Hb 47.36N 79.29W
Notsé 166 Fd 6.59N 1.12 E
Notsuke-Zaki 156a Db 43.34N 145.19 E
Nottawasaga Bay 184 Gc 44.40N 80.30W
Nottaway 174 Ld 51.25N 79.50W
Notterøy 116 De 59.15N 10.25 E
Nottingham 112 Fe 52.58N 1.10W
Nottingham 118 Mh 53.05N 1.00W
Nottingham 180 Jd 63.20N 78.00W
Nottinghamshire [3] 118 Mh 53.10N 0.55W
Nottoway River 184 Ig 36.33N 76.55W
Nottuln 124 Jc 51.56N 7.21 E
Notukeu Creek 188 Lb 49.55N 106.30W
Nouâdhibou 160 Ff 20.54N 17.01W
Nouâdhibou, Dahklet- 162 De 21.00N 16.50W
Nouâdhibou, Râs-=Blanc Cape- (EN) 158 Ff 20.46N 17.03W
Nouakchott 160 Fg 18.07N 15.59W
Nouakchott, District de- [3] 162 Df 18.06N 15.57W
Nouamrhar 162 Df 19.22N 16.31W
Nouméa 210 Hg 22.16S 166.26 E
Nouna 166 Ec 12.44N 3.52W
Noupoort 172 Cf 31.10S 24.57 E
Nouveau-Comptoir 180 Jf 52.35N 78.40W
Nouveau-Québec, Cratère du- = New Quebec Crater (EN) 180 Kd 61.30N 73.55W
Nouvelle-Calédonie = New Caledonia (EN) [5] 210 Hg 21.30S 165.30 E
Nouvelle-Calédonie=New Caledonia (EN) 208 Hg 21.30S 165.30 E
Nouvelle-France, Cap de- 180 Kd 62.33N 73.35W
Nouvelles-Hébrides / New Hebrides 208 Hf 16.01S 167.01 E
Nouvion 124 Dd 50.12N 1.47 E
Nouzonville 122 Ke 49.49N 4.45 E
Novabad 135 He 39.01N 70.09 E
Nová Baňa 120 Oh 48.26N 18.39 E
Nová Bystřice 120 Lg 49.02N 15.06 E
Novaci 130 Gd 45.11N 23.40 E
Nova Cruz 202 Ke 6.28S 35.26W
Nova Esperança 204 Ff 23.08S 52.13W
Nova Friburgo 202 Jh 22.16S 42.32W

Index Symbols

[1] Independent Nation
[2] State, Region
[3] District, County
[4] Municipality
[5] Colony, Dependency
Continent
Physical Region
Historical or Cultural Region
Mount, Mountain
Volcano
Hill
Mountains, Mountain Range
Hills, Escarpment
Plateau, Upland
Pass, Gap
Plain, Lowland
Delta
Salt Flat
Valley, Canyon
Crater, Cave
Karst Features
Depression
Polder
Desert, Dunes
Forest, Woods
Heath, Steppe
Oasis
Cape, Point
Coast, Beach
Cliff
Peninsula
Isthmus
Sandbank
Island
Atoll
Rock, Reef
Islands, Archipelago
Rocks, Reefs
Coral Reef
Well, Spring
Geyser
River, Stream
Waterfall, Rapids
River Mouth, Estuary
Lake
Salt Lake
Intermittent Lake
Reservoir
Swamp, Pond
Canal
Glacier
Ice Shelf, Pack Ice
Ocean
Sea
Gulf, Bay
Strait, Fjord
Lagoon
Bank
Seamount
Tablemount
Ridge
Shelf
Basin
Escarpment, Sea Scarp
Fracture
Trench, Abyss
National Park, Reserve
Point of Interest
Recreation Site
Cave, Cavern
Historic Site
Ruins
Wall, Walls
Church, Abbey
Temple
Scientific Station
Railway station
Airport
Port
Military installation
Lighthouse
Mine
Tunnel
Dam, Bridge

Nova Gaia 170 Ce 10.05S 17.32 E
Nova Gorica 128 He 45.57N 13.39 E
Nova Gradiška 128 Le 45.16N 17.23 E
Nova Granada 204 He 20.29S 49.19W
Nova Iguaçu 200 Lh 22.45S 43.27W
Novaja Igirma 138 Fe 57.10N 103.55 E
Novaja-Ivanovka 130 Md 45.59N 29.04 E
Novaja Kahovka 132 Hf 46.43N 33.23 E
Novaja Kazanka 132 Pe 48.58N 49.37 E
Novaja Ladoga 114 Hf 60.05N 32.16 E
Novaja Ljalja 136 Gd 59.03N 60.36 E
Novaja Odessa 132 Gf 47.18N 31.47 E
Novaja Sibir, ostrov- = New Siberia (EN) 140 Qb 75.00N 149.00 E
Novaja Vodolaga 132 Ie 49.45N 35.52 E
Novaja Zemlja = Novaya Zemlya (EN) 140 Hb 74.00N 57.00 E
Nova Lamego 166 Cc 12.17N 14.13W
Nova Lima 202 Jh 19.59S 43.51W
Nova Londrina 204 Ff 22.45S 53.00W
Nova Mambone 172 Fd 20.58S 35.00 E
Nova Olinda do Norte 202 Gd 3.45S 59.03W
Nová Paka 120 Lf 50.29N 15.31 E
Nova Prata 204 Gi 28.47S 51.36W
Novara 128 Ce 45.28N 8.38 E
Nova Roma 204 Ia 13.51S 46.57W
Nova Russas 202 Jd 4.42S 40.34W
Nova Scotia [2] 180 Lh 45.00N 63.00W
Nova Scotia 174 Me 45.00N 63.00W
Nova Sintra 162 Cf 14.54N 24.40W
Nova Sofala 172 Ed 20.10S 34.44 E
Novato 188 Dg 38.06N 122.34W
Nova Varoš 130 Cf 43.28N 19.49 E
Nova Venécia 202 Jg 18.43S 40.24W
Novaya Zemlya (EN) = Novaja Zemlja 140 Hb 74.00N 57.00 E
Nova Zagora 130 Jg 42.29N 26.01 E
Novelda 126 Lf 38.23N 0.46W
Novellara 128 Ef 44.51N 10.44 E
Nové Mesto nad Váhom 120 Nh 48.46N 17.50 E
Nové Zámky 120 Oi 47.59N 18.11 E
Novgorod 112 Jd 58.31N 31.17 E
Novgorodka 116 Mg 57.00N 28.37 E
Novgorod-Severski 136 De 52.01N 33.16 E
Novgorodskaja oblast [3] 136 Dd 58.20N 32.40 E
Novi Bečej 130 Dd 45.36N 20.08 E
Novigrad [Yugo.] 128 He 45.19N 13.34 E
Novigrad [Yugo.] 128 Jf 44.11N 15.33 E
Novi Kričim 130 Hg 42.03N 24.28 E
Novi Ligure 128 Cf 44.46N 8.47 E
Novillero 192 Gf 22.21N 105.39W
Novion-Porcien 124 Ge 49.36N 4.25 E
Novi Pazar [Bul.] 130 Kf 43.21N 27.12 E
Novi Pazar [Yugo.] 130 Df 43.08N 20.31 E
Novi Sad 112 Hf 45.15N 19.50 E
Novi Travnik 128 Lf 44.10N 17.39 E
Novi Vinodolski 128 Ie 45.08N 14.47 E
Novoaleksandrovsk 132 Lg 45.24N 41.14 E
Novoalekseevka [Kaz.-U.S.S.R.] 132 Sd 50.08N 55.42 E
Novoalekseevka [Ukr.-U.S.S.R.] 132 If 46.16N 34.39 E
Novoaltajsk 138 Df 53.24N 83.58 E
Novoanninski 132 Ee 50.31N 42.45 E
Novoarhangelsk 132 Ge 48.39N 30.50 E
Novo Aripuanã 202 Fe 5.08S 60.22W
Novoazovsk 132 Kf 47.05N 38.05 E
Novobirjusinski 138 Ee 56.58N 97.55 E
Novobogdanovka 132 If 47.05N 35.18 E
Novočeboksarsk 114 Lh 56.08N 47.29 E
Novočeremšansk 114 Mi 54.23N 50.10 E
Novočerkassk 136 Ef 47.25N 40.03 E
Novodevičje 114 Lj 53.35N 48.51 E
Novograd-Volynski 136 Ce 50.36N 27.36 E
Novogrudok 132 Dc 53.37N 25.50 E
Nôvo Hamburgo 206 Jc 29.41S 51.08W
Novohopërsk 132 Ld 51.06N 41.37 E
Novo Horizonte 204 He 21.28S 49.13W
Novoizborsk 116 Mg 57.43N 28.05 E
Novojenisejsk 138 Ee 58.19N 92.27 E
Novojerudinski 138 Ee 59.47N 93.30 E
Novokačalinsk 138 Ig 45.05N 131.59 E
Novokazalinsk 132 Ie 45.50N 62.10 E
Novokubansk 132 Lg 45.06N 41.01 E
Novokujbyševsk 136 Ee 53.08N 49.58 E
Novokuzneck 142 Kd 53.45N 87.06 E
Novolazarevskaja 222 Cf 70.46S 11.50 E
Novolukoml 114 Gi 54.38N 29.07 E
Novo Mesto 128 Je 45.48N 15.10 E
Novomičurinsk 114 Ji 54.02N 39.48 E
Novomihajlovka 138 Ih 44.17N 133.50 E
Novo Miloševo 130 Dd 45.43N 20.18 E
Novomirgorod 132 Ge 48.45N 31.39 E
Novomoskovsk [R.S.F.S.R.] 112 Je 54.05N 38.13 E
Novomoskovsk [Ukr.-U.S.S.R.] 136 Df 48.37N 35.16 E
Novonikolajevski 132 Md 50.55N 42.24 E
Novoorsk 136 Fe 51.24N 58.59 E
Novopokrovskaja 132 Lg 45.56N 40.42 E
Novopolock 136 Cd 55.31N 28.40 E
Novorossijsk 112 Jg 44.45N 37.45 E
Novorybnaja 138 Fb 72.50N 105.45 E
Novoržev 136 Cd 57.02N 29.20 E
Novošahtinsk 136 Df 47.47N 39.54 E
Novoselica 130 Ja 48.13N 26.17 E
Novoselje 116 Mf 58.05N 29.00 E
Novoselki 120 Ud 52.04N 24.25 E
Novoselovo 138 Ef 54.55N 91.00 E
Novosergijevka 136 Fe 52.03N 53.39 E
Novosibirsk 142 Kd 55.02N 82.55 E
Novosibirskaja oblast [3] 138 Ce 55.30N 80.00 E
Novosibirskije ostrova = New Siberian Islands (EN) 140 Qb 75.00N 142.00 E
Novosibirskoje vodohranilišče = Novosibirsk Reservoir (EN) 138 Df 54.40N 82.35 E
Novosibirsk Reservoir (EN) = Novosibirskoje vodohranilišče 138 Df 54.40N 82.35 E
Novosil 132 Jc 52.59N 37.01 E
Novosineglazovski 134 Ji 55.05N 61.25 E
Novosokolniki 136 Dd 56.19N 30.12 E
Novospasskoje 114 Lj 53.09N 47.44 E
Novotroick 136 Fe 51.12N 58.35 E
Novotroickoje 136 Hg 43.39N 73.45 E
Novoukrainka 132 Ge 48.19N 31.32 E
Novouljanovsk 114 Li 54.10N 48.23 E
Novouzensk 136 Ee 50.29N 48.08 E
Novovjatsk 114 Lg 58.31N 49.43 E
Novovolynsk 136 Ce 50.46N 24.09 E
Novovoronežski 132 Kd 51.17N 39.16 E
Novozybkov 136 De 52.32N 32.00 E
Novska 128 Ke 45.20N 16.59 E
Novy Bug 132 Hf 47.43N 32.29 E
Nový Bydžov 120 Lf 50.15N 15.29 E
Novy Jaričev 120 Ug 49.50N 24.21 E
Novyje Aneny 130 Mc 46.53N 29.13 E
Novyje Burasy 132 Od 52.06N 46.06 E
Nový Jičín 120 Og 49.36N 18.01 E
Novy Oskol 136 De 50.43N 37.54 E
Novy Pogost 116 Li 55.30N 27.32 E
Novy Port 142 Jc 67.40N 72.52 E
Novy Tap 114 Nh 56.55N 67.15 E
Novy Terek 132 Oh 43.37N 47.25 E
Novy Uzen 136 Fg 43.19N 52.55 E
Novy Vasjugan 138 Ce 58.34N 76.29 E
Novy Zaj 114 Mi 55.17N 52.02 E
Nowa Dęba 120 Rf 50.26N 21.46 E
Nowa Huta, Kraków- 120 Qf 50.04N 20.05 E
Nowa Ruda 120 Mf 50.35N 16.31 E
Nowa Sarzyna 120 Sf 50.23N 22.22 E
Nowa Sól 120 Le 51.48N 15.44 E
Now Bandegān 146 Oh 28.52N 53.53 E
Nowbarān 146 Me 35.08N 49.42 E
Nowdesheh 146 Le 35.11N 46.15 E
Nowe 120 Oc 53.40N 18.43 E
Nowe Miasto Lubawskie 120 Pc 53.27N 19.35 E
Nowe Miasto-nad-Pilicą 120 Qe 51.38N 20.35 E
Nowe Warpno 120 Kc 53.44N 14.20 E
Nowfel low Shātow 146 Ne 34.27N 50.55 E
Nowgong 148 Ic 26.21N 92.40 E
Nowogard 120 Lc 53.40N 15.08 E
Nowogród 120 Rc 53.15N 21.53 E
Nowood River 188 Ld 44.17N 107.58W
Nowra 212 Kf 34.53S 150.36 E
Now Shahr 146 Nd 36.39N 51.31 E
Nowy Dwór Gdański 120 Pb 54.13N 19.06 E
Nowy Dwór Mazowiecki 120 Qd 52.26N 20.43 E
Nowy Korczyn 120 Qf 50.20N 20.50 E
Nowy Sącz 120 Qg 49.38N 20.42 E
Nowy Sącz [2] 120 Qg 49.40N 20.40 E
Nowy Targ 120 Qg 49.29N 20.02 E
Nowy Tomyśl 120 Md 52.20N 15.07 E
Noya/Anoia 126 Nc 41.28N 1.56 E
Noya / Noia 126 Db 42.47N 8.53W
Noyant 122 Gg 47.31N 0.08 E
Noyon 122 Ie 49.35N 3.00 E
Nozaki-Jima 156 Ae 33.11N 129.08 E
Nozay 122 Eg 47.34N 1.38W
Nsanje 170 Gf 16.55S 35.16 E
Nsawan 166 Ed 5.48N 0.21W
Nsefu 170 Fe 13.03S 32.07 E
Nsukka 166 Gd 6.52N 7.23 E
Ntadembele 170 Cc 2.11S 17.08 E
Ntchisi 170 Fe 13.22S 34.00 E
Ntem 158 Hh 2.10N 9.57 E
Ntoum 170 Ab 0.22N 9.47 E
Ntui 166 He 4.27N 11.39 E
Ntusi 170 Fb 0.03N 31.13 E
Nuageuses, Iles- 222 Fc 48.40S 68.58 E
Nuanetsi 158 Kk 22.40S 31.49 E
Nūbah, Jibāl an- 158 Kg 12.00N 30.45 E
Nubian Desert (EN) = Nūbiyah, Aş Şaḩrā' an- 158 Kf 20.30N 33.00 E
Nūbiyah, Aş Şaḩrā' an- = Nubian Desert (EN) 158 Kf 20.30N 33.00 E
Nucet 130 Fc 46.28N 22.35 E
Nudha 219a Ec 9.32S 160.48 E
Nueces Plain 182 Hf 28.30N 99.15W
Nueces River 182 Hf 27.50N 97.30W
Nueltin Lake 174 Jc 60.50N 99.30W
Nu'er He 154 Fd 41.06N 121.09 E
Nueva 206 Ei 55.15S 66.32W
Nueva Asunción [3] 204 Be 21.00S 60.20W
Nueva Ciudad Guerrero 192 Jd 26.35N 99.15W
Nueva Esparta [2] 202 Fa 11.00N 64.00W
Nueva Germania 204 Df 23.54S 56.34W
Nueva Gerona 190 Hd 21.53N 82.48W
Nueva Imperial 206 Fe 38.44S 72.57W
Nueva Italia de Ruiz 192 Hh 19.01N 102.06W
Nueva Ocotepeque 194 Cf 14.24N 89.13W
Nueva Palmira 204 Ck 33.53S 58.25W
Nueva Rosita 176 Ig 27.57N 101.13W
Nueva San Salvador 190 Gf 13.41N 89.17W
Nueva Segovia [3] 194 Dg 13.40N 86.10W
Nueve de Julio 206 He 35.27S 60.52W
Nuevitas 192 Id 21.33N 77.16W
Nuevitas, Bahia de- 194 Ic 21.30N 77.12W
Nuevo, Cayo- 192 Mg 21.51N 92.05W
Nuevo, Golfo- 198 Jj 42.42S 64.36W
Nuevo Berlín 204 Ck 32.59S 58.03W
Nuevo Casas Grandes 176 If 30.25N 107.55W
Nuevo Laredo 176 Jg 27.30N 99.31W
Nuevo León [2] 176 Ec 25.40N 100.00W
Nuevo Mundo, Cerro- 202 Eh 21.55S 66.53W
Nuevo Rocafuerte 202 Cd 0.56S 75.25W
Nugaal [3] 168 Hd 8.30N 48.00 E
Nugāl 168 Hd 9.30N 46.30 E
Nugālēd, Dēh- 158 Lh 7.58N 49.51 E
Nugālēd, Dōho- 168 Hd 8.35N 48.35 E
Nugātsiaq 190 Gd 71.39N 53.45W
Nugget Point 218 Cg 46.27S 169.49 E
Nūgssuaq 179 Gd 70.30N 51.30W
Nuguria Islands 208 Ge 3.20S 154.45 E
Nuguš 134 Gj 53.05N 56.00 E
Nuhaka 218 Gc 39.02S 177.45 E
Nui Atoll 208 Ie 7.15S 177.10 E
Nuijama 116 Md 60.58N 28.32 E
Nuiqsut 178 Ib 70.20N 151.00W
Nu Jiang 140 Lh 16.31N 97.37 E
Nûk/Godthåb 224 Nc 64.15N 51.40W
Nukapu 219c Ab 10.07S 165.59 E
Nukey Bluff 212 Hf 32.35S 135.40 E
Nukhayb 144 Fc 32.02N 42.15 E
Nukhaylak 160 Jg 19.08N 26.20 E
Nukiki 219a Cb 6.45S 156.29 E
Nukuaéta 220h Ac 13.22S 176.11W
Nuku'alofa 210 Jg 21.08S 175.12W
Nukufetau Atoll 208 Ie 8.00S 178.22 E
Nukufotu 220h Bb 13.11S 176.10W
Nukuhifala 220h Bb 13.17S 176.05W
Nukuhione 220h Bb 13.16S 176.06W
Nuku Hiva, Ile- 208 Me 8.54S 140.06W
Nukulaelae Atoll 208 Ie 9.23S 179.52 E
Nukuloa 220h Bb 13.11S 176.09W
Nukumanu Islands 208 Ge 4.35S 159.30 E
Nukumbasanga 219d Cb 16.18S 179.15W
Nukunonu Atoll 208 Je 9.10S 171.53W
Nukuoro Atoll 208 Gd 3.51N 154.58 E
Nukus 142 He 42.50N 59.29 E
Nukutapu 220h Bb 13.13S 176.08W
Nukuteatea 220h Bb 13.12S 176.08W
Nulato 178 Hd 64.43N 158.06W
Nules 126 Le 39.51N 0.09W
Nullagine 210 Dg 21.53S 120.06 E
Nullagine River 212 Ed 20.43S 120.33 E
Nullarbor 212 Gf 31.26S 130.55 E
Nullarbor Plain 208 Dh 31.00S 129.00 E
Nulu'erhu Shan 152 Kc 41.40N 119.50 E
Numakawa 156a Ba 45.15N 141.51 E
Numan 166 Hd 9.28N 12.02 E
Numancia 150 Ie 9.52N 125.58 E
Numancia 126 Jc 41.47N 2.30W
Numanohata 156a Bb 42.40N 141.41 E
Numata [Jap.] 156a Bb 43.49N 141.55 E
Numata [Jap.] 154 Of 36.38N 139.03 E
Numatinna 168 Dd 7.14N 27.37 E
Numazu 154 Og 35.06N 138.52 E
Nümbrecht 124 Jd 50.54N 7.33 E
Numedal 124 Bf 60.05N 9.05 E
Numena 170 Ee 11.46S 26.31 E
Número Cinco, Canal- 204 Cm 37.14S 58.06W
Número Doce, Canal- 204 Cm 36.30S 59.08W
Número Dos, Canal- 204 Cm 36.51S 58.03W
Número Nueve, Canal- 204 Cm 36.08S 58.36W
Número Once, Canal- 204 Bm 36.28S 60.01W
Número Quince, Canal- 204 Dl 35.55S 57.45W
Número Uno, Canal- 204 Cm 36.40S 58.35W
Numfoor, Pulau- 150 Jg 1.03S 134.54 E
Nuneaton 118 Li 52.32N 1.28W
Nungarin 212 Df 31.11S 118.06 E
Nungnain Sum 152 Kb 45.45N 118.56 E
Nungo 172 Fb 13.25S 37.46 E
Nunivak 174 Cd 60.00N 166.30W
Nunkirchen, Wadern- 124 Ie 49.32N 6.53 E
Nunn 186 Df 40.45N 104.46W
Nunspeet 124 Hb 52.22N 5.46 E
Nunukan Timur, Pulau- 150 Gf 4.05N 117.40 E
Nuomin He 152 Lb 48.21N 124.32 E
Nuorgam 114 Ga 70.05N 27.51 E
Nuoro 112 Gg 40.19N 9.20 E
Nupani 219c Ab 10.04S 165.40 E
Nūq 146 Pg 30.55N 55.35 E
Nuqayr 146 Mi 27.48N 48.21 E
Nuqrah 146 Ij 25.34N 41.24 E
Nuqruş, Jabal- 164 Fe 24.49N 34.36 E
Nuqui 202 Cb 5.43N 77.16W
Nūr 146 Pg 31.25N 54.20 E
Nūr 146 Od 36.15N 52.20 E
Nura 136 Gf 48.57N 62.20 E
Nura 140 Id 50.30N 69.59 E
Nūrābād 146 Ng 30.48N 51.27 E
Nuraghe Santu Antine 128 Cj 40.29N 8.45 E
Nurata 136 Gg 40.34N 65.35 E
Nur Dağları 146 Gd 36.45N 36.20 E
Nure 128 De 45.03N 9.49 E
Nurek 136 Gh 38.25N 69.20 E
Nurhak Dağı 144 Eb 38.04N 37.29 E
Nūrī 168 Eb 18.30N 32.02 E
Nurki 138 Ie 56.42N 128.28 E
Nurlat 136 Fe 54.28N 50.48 E
Nurlaty 114 Li 55.38N 48.17 E
Nurmes 114 Ge 63.33N 29.07 E
Nurmijärvi 116 Kd 60.28N 24.48 E
Nurmo 114 Jb 62.50N 22.54 E
Nürnberg 112 Hf 49.27N 11.05 E
Nurra 128 Cj 40.45N 8.15 E
Nurri, Mount- 212 Jf 31.42S 146.02 E
Nurugas 172 Bc 19.11S 18.54 E
Nurzec 120 Sd 52.33N 22.28 E
Nusa Tenggara Barat [3] 150 Gh 8.50S 117.30 E
Nusa Tenggara Timur [3] 150 Hh 9.30S 122.00 E
Nusaybin 146 Id 37.03N 41.13 E
Nushagak 178 He 58.57N 158.29W
Nushan 152 Gf 25.00N 99.00 E
Nu-Shima 156 Dd 34.10N 134.50 E
Nutak 180 Le 57.31N 62.00W
Nuttal 148 Dc 28.45N 68.08 E
Nutuele 221c Bb 14.02S 171.22W
Nuwākot 148 Gc 28.08N 83.53 E
Nuwara 148 Gg 6.58N 80.46 E
Nuwaybi 'al Muzayyinah 164 Fd 28.58N 34.39 E
Nyabing 212 Df 33.32S 118.09 E
Nyagquka/Yajiang 152 He 30.07N 100.58 E
Nyagrong/Xinlong 152 He 30.57N 100.12 E
Nyahanga 170 Fc 2.23S 33.33 E
Nyahua 170 Fc 4.58S 33.34 E
Nyainqêntanglha Feng 152 Fe 30.12N 90.33 E
Nyainqêntanglha Shan 140 Kf 30.10N 90.00 E
Nyakanazi 170 Fc 3.00S 31.15 E
Nyala 160 Jg 12.03N 24.53 E
Nyalam 152 Ef 28.15N 85.55 E
Ny-Ålesund 179 Nc 78.56N 11.57 E
Nyalikungu 170 Fc 3.11S 33.47 E
Nyamandhlovu 172 Dc 19.51S 28.16 E
Nyamapanda 172 Ec 16.55S 32.52 E
Nyamlell 168 Dd 9.07N 26.58 E
Nyamtumbo 170 Ge 10.30S 36.06 E
Nyanding 168 Ed 8.40N 32.41 E
Nyanga [3] 170 Bc 3.00S 11.00 E
Nyanga 158 Ii 2.58S 10.15 E
Nyanza [3] 170 Fc 0.30S 34.30 E
Nyanza-Lac 170 Ec 4.21S 29.36 E
Nyasa, Lake- (EN) = Niassa, Lago- 158 Kj 12.00S 34.30 E
Nyaunglebin 148 Je 17.57N 96.44 E
Nyborg 114 Ci 55.19N 10.48 E
Nybro 114 Dh 56.45N 15.54 E
Nyda 138 Cc 66.36N 72.54 E
Nyda 134 Pc 66.40N 72.50 E
Nyeboe Land 179 Gb 81.45N 56.40W
Nyêmo 152 Ff 29.30N 90.07 E
Nyeri 170 Gc 0.25S 36.57 E
Nyerol 168 Ed 8.41N 32.02 E
Ny Friesland 179 Nc 79.30N 17.00 E
Nyhammar 116 Fd 60.17N 14.58 E
Nyhem 116 Fb 62.54N 15.40 E
Nyika 158 Ki 2.37S 38.44 E
Nyika Plateau 158 Kj 10.40S 33.50 E
Nyikog Qu 152 He 30.24N 100.40 E
Nyimba 170 Fe 14.33S 30.48 E
Nyingchi 152 Ff 29.38N 94.23 E
Nyirbátor 120 Si 47.50N 22.08 E
Nyíregyháza 120 Ri 47.57N 21.43 E
Nyiri Desert 170 Gc 2.20S 37.20 E
Nyiro, Mount- 170 Gb 2.08N 36.51 E
Nyírség 120 Ri 47.50N 21.55 E
Nykøbing [Den.] 114 Ci 55.55N 11.41 E
Nykøbing [Den.] 116 Ch 56.48N 8.52 E
Nykøbing [Den.] 114 Ci 54.46N 11.53 E
Nyköping 114 Dg 58.45N 17.00 E
Nyköpingsån 116 Gf 58.45N 17.01 E
Nykroppa 116 Fe 59.38N 14.18 E
Nyland 116 Ga 63.00N 17.46 E
Nylstroom 172 Dd 24.42S 28.20 E
Nymburk 120 Lf 50.11N 15.03 E
Nymphe Bank (EN) 118 Fj 51.30N 7.05W
Nynäshamn 114 Dg 58.54N 17.57 E
Nyngan 210 Fh 31.34S 147.11 E
Nyon 128 Ad 46.23N 6.15 E
Nyong 158 Hh 3.17N 9.54 E
Nyonga 170 Fd 6.43S 32.04 E
Nyons 122 Lj 44.22N 5.08 E
Nyřany 120 Jg 49.43N 13.13 E
Nyrob 134 Hf 60.42N 56.45 E
Nyš 138 Jf 51.30N 142.49 E
Nysa 120 Nf 50.29N 17.20 E
Nysa Kłodzka 120 Nf 50.49N 17.50 E
Nysa Łużycka 120 Kd 52.04N 14.46 E
Nyslott/Savonlinna 114 Gf 61.52N 28.53 E
Nyssa 188 Ge 43.53N 117.00W
Nystad/Uusikaupunki 114 Ef 60.48N 21.25 E
Nysted 116 Dj 54.40N 11.45 E
Nytva 136 Fd 57.56N 55.20 E
Nyūdō-Zaki 154 Od 40.00N 139.35 E
Nyunzu 170 Ed 5.57S 28.01 E
Nyūzen 156 Ec 36.56N 137.30 E
Nzambi 170 Bc 3.58S 11.16 E
Nzara 168 De 4.40N 28.14 E
Nzega 170 Fc 4.13S 33.11 E
Nzérékoré 160 Gh 7.45N 8.49W
N'zeto 170 Bd 7.05S 12.50 E
Nzi 158 Gh 5.57N 4.50W
Nzilo, Barrage de- 170 Ee 10.35S 25.30 E
Nzo 166 Dd 6.16N 7.03W
Nzoro 170 Eb 3.18N 29.26 E
Nzwani/Anjouan 158 Lj 12.15S 44.25 E

O

Oa, Mull of- 118 Gf 55.35N 6.20W
Oahe, Lake- 174 Ie 45.30N 100.25W
Oahu Island 208 Lb 21.30N 158.00W
O-akan-Dake 156a Db 43.27N 144.10 E
Oakdale [Ca.-U.S.] 188 Eh 37.46N 120.51W
Oakdale [La.-U.S.] 186 Jk 30.49N 92.40W
Oakham 118 Mi 52.40N 0.44W
Oak Harbor 188 Db 48.18N 122.39W
Oak Lake 186 Fb 49.40N 100.45W
Oakland [Ca.-U.S.] 176 Gf 37.47N 122.13W
Oakland [Md.-U.S.] 184 Hf 39.25N 79.24W
Oakley [Id.-U.S.] 188 Ie 42.15N 113.53W
Oakley [Ks.-U.S.] 182 Gd 39.08N 100.51W
Oak Park 186 Mf 41.53N 87.48W
Oak Ridge 182 Kd 36.01N 84.16W
Oakridge 188 De 43.45N 122.28W
Oakville 184 Hd 43.27N 79.41W
Oamaru 216 Di 45.05S 170.59 E
Oancea 130 Ld 45.55N 28.06 E
Oani-Gawa 156 Ga 40.12N 140.16 E
Ōarai 156 Gc 36.18N 140.33 E
Oaro 218 Ee 42.31S 173.30 E
Oasis 188 Hf 41.01N 114.37W
Oasis 162 Hd 26.00N 5.00 E
Oates Coast 222 Jf 70.00S 160.00 E
Oaxaca [2] 190 Ee 17.00N 96.30W
Oaxaca de Juárez 176 Jh 17.03N 96.43W
Ob 140 Ic 66.45N 69.30 E
Oba 180 Jg 48.55N 84.17W
Obala 166 He 4.10N 11.32 E
Obama [Jap.] 156 Be 32.43N 130.13 E
Obama [Jap.] 154 Mg 35.30N 135.45 E
Obama-Wan 156 Dd 35.30N 135.40 E
Oban [N.Z.] 216 Cj 46.52S 168.10 E
Oban [Scot.-U.K.] 118 He 56.25N 5.29W
Obanazawa 154 Pe 38.36N 140.24 E
Obando 200 Je 4.07N 67.45W
Oban Hills 166 Gd 5.30N 8.35 E
Obeliai/Obeljaj 116 Ki 55.58N 25.59 E
Obeljaj/Obeliai 116 Ki 55.58N 25.59 E
Oberá 206 Ic 27.29S 55.08W
Oberbayern 120 Hi 47.50N 11.50 E
Oberderdingen 124 Ke 49.04N 8.48 E
Oberfranken 120 Hf 50.10N 11.30 E
Oberhausen 120 Ce 51.28N 6.51 E
Oberkirchen, Schmallenberg- 124 Kc 51.09N 8.18 E
Oberland [Switz.] 128 Bd 46.35N 7.30 E
Oberland [Switz.] 128 Dd 46.45N 9.05 E
Oberlausitz 120 Ke 51.15N 14.30 E
Oberlin 186 Fg 39.49N 100.32W
Obermoschel 124 Je 49.44N 7.46 E
Obernkirchen 124 Lb 52.16N 9.08 E
Oberösterreich = Upper Austria (EN) [2] 128 Hb 48.15N 14.00 E
Oberpfalz 120 Ig 49.30N 12.10 E
Oberpfälzer Wald = North Bohemian Forest (EN) 120 Ig 49.50N 12.30 E
Oberpullendorf 128 Kc 47.30N 16.31 E
Ober-Ramstadt 124 Ke 49.50N 8.45 E
Oberstdorf 120 Gi 47.24N 10.16 E
Oberursel (Taunus) 124 Kd 50.12N 8.35 E
Obervellach 128 Hd 46.56N 13.12 E
Oberwesel 124 Jd 50.06N 7.44 E
Ob Gulf (EN) = Obskaja guba 140 Jc 69.00N 73.00 E
Obi, Kepulauan- 150 Ig 1.30S 127.45 E
Obi, Pulau- 208 De 1.30S 127.45 E
Obi, Selat- 150 Ig 0.52S 127.33 E
Óbidos [Braz.] 200 Kf 1.55S 55.31W
Óbidos [Port.] 126 Ce 39.22N 9.09W
Obihiro 152 Pc 42.55N 143.12 E
Obilić 130 Eg 42.41N 21.05 E
Obira 156a Ba 44.01N 141.38 E
Obispos 194 Li 8.36N 70.05W
Obispo Trejo 206 Hd 30.46S 63.25W
Obitočnaja kosa 132 Jf 46.35N 36.15 E
Obluče 138 Ig 48.59N 131.05 E
Obninsk 136 Dd 55.05N 36.37 E
Obo 160 Jh 5.24N 26.30 E
Obock 168 Gc 11.57N 43.17 E
Obojan 136 De 51.13N 36.16 E
Obokote 170 Ec 0.52S 26.19 E
Obol 114 Gi 55.24N 29.01 E
Oborniki 120 Md 52.39N 16.51 E
Obouya 170 Cc 0.56S 15.43 E
Obozerski 136 Ec 63.28N 40.20 E
Obra 120 Ld 52.36N 15.28 E
Obrenovac 130 De 44.39N 20.12 E
Obrovac 128 Jf 44.12N 15.41 E
Obrovo 120 Vd 52.27N 25.43 E
Obruchev Rise (EN) 138 Lf 52.30N 166.00 E
Obruk Platosu 146 Ec 38.02N 33.30 E
Obšči Syrt 110 Le 51.50N 51.00 E
Obskaja guba = Ob Gulf (EN) 140 Jc 69.00N 73.00 E
Ob' Tablemount (EN) 158 Ln 52.30S 42.00 E
Ōbu 156 Ed 35.01N 136.58 E
Obuasi 166 Ed 6.12N 1.40W
Obudu 166 Gd 6.40N 9.10 E
Obuhov 132 Gd 50.07N 30.37 E
Obva 134 Gg 58.35N 55.25 E
Obzor 130 Kg 42.49N 27.53 E
Oca 126 Ib 42.46N 3.26W
Oca, Montes de- 126 Ib 42.20N 3.15W
Očakov 136 Df 46.38N 31.33 E
Ocala 182 Kf 29.11N 82.07W
Očamcira 132 Lh 42.46N 41.27 E
Ocampo [Mex.] 192 Ec 28.11N 108.23W
Ocampo [Mex.] 192 Hd 27.20N 102.21W
Ocaña [Col.] 202 Db 8.15N 73.20W
Ocaña [Sp.] 126 Ie 39.56N 3.31W
Occhito, Lago di- 128 Ii 41.35N 14.55 E
Occidental, Cordillera- [Co.] 198 Ie 5.00N 76.00W
Ocean Bight 194 Kc 21.15N 73.15W
Ocean City [Md.-U.S.] 182 Ld 38.20N 75.05W
Ocean City [N.J.-U.S.] 184 Jf 39.16N 74.35W
Ocean Falls 180 Ef 52.21N 127.40W
Oceania (EN) 208 Ie 5.00S 175.00 E
Ocean Point 184 Il 26.25N 77.03W
Oceanside 182 De 33.12N 117.23W
Ocean Springs 186 Lk 30.25N 88.50W
Ocejón, Pico- 126 Ic 41.07N 3.15W
Očenyrd, gora- 134 Mb 58.05N 66.20 E
Očer 136 Fd 57.53N 54.45 E
Ochagabia / Ochagavía 126 Kb 42.55N 1.05W
Ochagavía / Ochagabia 126 Kb 42.55N 1.05W
Ochiai 156 Cd 35.02N 133.45 E
Ochiishi-Misaki 156a Db 43.10N 145.28 E
Ochil Hills 118 Je 56.23N 3.35W
Och'onjang 154 Jd 40.55N 128.50 E
Ocho Rios 194 Id 18.25N 77.07W
Ochsenfurt 120 Gg 49.39N 10.05 E
Ochtrup 124 Jb 52.13N 7.11 E
Ockelbo 114 Df 60.53N 16.43 E
Öckerö 116 Dg 57.43N 11.39 E
Ocmulgee River 184 Fj 31.58N 82.32W
Ocna Mureș 130 Gc 46.23N 23.51 E
Ocna Sibiului 130 Hd 45.53N 24.03 E
Ocoa, Bahía de- 194 Ld 18.22N 70.39W
Oconee River 184 Fj 31.58N 82.32W
Oconto 186 Md 44.55N 87.52W
Ocosingo 192 Mi 17.04N 92.15W
Ocotal 194 Dg 13.38N 86.29W
Ocotepeque [3] 194 Cf 14.30N 89.00W
Ocotlán 190 Dd 20.21N 102.46W
Ocotlán de Morelos 192 Ki 16.48N 96.43W
Ocracoke Inlet 184 Ih 35.10N 76.05W
Ocracoke Island 184 Jh 35.09N 75.59W
Ocreza 126 Ee 39.32N 7.50W
Octeville-sur-Mer 124 Ce 49.33N 0.07 E
October Revolution Island (EN) = Oktjabrskoj Revoljuci, ostrov- 140 Lb 79.30N 97.00 E
Ocú 194 Gj 7.57N 80.47W

Index Symbols

[1] Independent Nation
[2] State, Region
[3] District, County
[4] Municipality
[5] Colony, Dependency
Continent
Physical Region
Historical or Cultural Region
Mount, Mountain
Volcano
Hill
Mountains, Mountain Range
Hills, Escarpment
Plateau, Upland
Pass, Gap
Plain, Lowland
Delta
Salt Flat
Valley, Canyon
Crater, Cave
Karst Features
Depression
Polder
Desert, Dunes
Forest, Woods
Heath, Steppe
Oasis
Cape, Point
Coast, Beach
Cliff
Peninsula
Isthmus
Sandbank
Island
Atoll
Rock, Reef
Islands, Archipelago
Rocks, Reefs
Coral Reef
Well, Spring
Geyser
River, Stream
Waterfall, Rapids
River Mouth, Estuary
Lake
Salt Lake
Intermittent Lake
Reservoir
Swamp, Pond
Canal
Glacier
Ice Shelf, Pack Ice
Ocean
Sea
Gulf, Bay
Strait, Fjord
Lagoon
Bank
Seamount
Tablemount
Ridge
Shelf
Basin
Escarpment, Sea Scarp
Fracture
Trench, Abyss
National Park, Reserve
Point of Interest
Recreation Site
Cave, Cavern
Historic Site
Ruins
Wall, Walls
Church, Abbey
Temple
Scientific Station
Railway station
Airport
Port
Military installation
Lighthouse
Mine
Tunnel
Dam, Bridge

Ocumare del Tuy	196	Cg	10.07N	66.46W
Ōda	154	Lg	35.11N	132.30 E
Oda [Ghana]	166	Ed	5.55N	0.59W
Oda [Jap.]	156	Ce	33.34N	132.48 E
Oda, Jabal-	168	Fa	20.21N	36.39 E
Ódáðahraun	114a	Cb	65.09N	17.00W
Ōdai	156	Ed	34.24N	136.24 E
Odaigahara-San	156	Ed	34.11N	136.06 E
Odalen	116	Dd	60.15N	11.40 E
Ōdate	154	Pd	40.16N	140.34 E
Odawara	154	Og	35.15N	139.10 E
Odda	114	Bf	60.04N	6.33 E
Odder	116	Di	55.58N	10.10 E
Odeleite	126	Eg	37.21N	7.27W
Odemira	126	Dg	37.36N	8.38W
Ödemiş	146	Bc	38.13N	27.59 E
Odendaalsrus	172	De	27.48S	26.45 E
Odense	112	Hd	55.24N	10.23 E
Odenthal	124	Jc	51.02N	7.07 E
Odenwald	120	Eg	49.40N	9.00 E
Oder [Eur.]	110	He	53.40N	14.33 E
Oder [Ger.]	120	Ge	51.40N	10.02 E
Oderbruch	120	Kd	52.40N	14.15 E
Oderské vrchy	120	Ng	49.40N	17.45 E
Oderzo	128	Ge	45.47N	12.29 E
Ödeshög	114	Dg	58.14N	14.39 E
Odessa [Tx.-U.S.]	176	If	31.51N	102.22W
Odessa [Ukr.-U.S.S.R.]	112	Jf	46.28N	30.44 E
Odessa [Wa.-U.S.]	188	Fc	47.20N	118.41W
Odesskaja oblast [3]	136	Df	46.45N	30.30 E
Odet	122	Bg	47.52N	4.06W
Odiel	126	Fg	37.10N	6.54W
Odienné	160	Gh	9.30N	7.34W
Odienné [3]	166	Dd	9.45N	7.45W
Odivelas	126	Df	38.12N	8.18W
Ödmården	116	Gc	61.05N	16.40 E
Odobeşti	130	Kd	45.46N	27.03 E
Ŏdŏngk	148	Kf	11.48N	104.45 E
Odoorn	124	Ib	52.51N	6.50 E
Odorheiu Secuiesc	130	Ic	46.18N	25.18 E
Ōdose-Zaki	156a	Bc	40.46N	140.03 E
Odra	110	He	53.40N	14.33 E
Ŏdwēyne	168	Hd	9.23N	45.04 E
Odžaci	130	Cd	45.31N	19.16 E
Odžak	128	Me	45.01N	18.18 E
Odzi	172	Ec	19.47S	32.24 E
Oeiras	126	Eg	37.38N	7.40W
Oeiras [Braz.]	202	Je	7.01S	42.08W
Oeiras [Port.]	126	Cf	38.41N	9.19W
Oelde	124	Kc	51.49N	8.09 E
Oelerbeek	124	Ib	52.21N	6.38 E
Oelrichs	186	Ee	43.15N	103.10W
Oelsnitz	120	If	50.25N	12.10 E
Oelwein	186	Ke	42.41N	91.55W
Oeno Island	208	Ng	23.56S	130.44W
Oer-Erkenschwick	124	Jc	51.38N	7.15 E
Oeste, Punta-	197a	Ab	18.05N	67.57W
Oeventrop, Arnsberg-	124	Kc	51.24N	8.08 E
Ōe-Yama	156	Dd	35.27N	135.06 E
Of	146	Ib	40.57N	40.16 E
O'Fallon Creek	188	Mc	46.50N	105.09W
Ofanto	128	Ki	41.21N	16.13 E
Ofaqim	146	Fg	31.17N	34.37 E
Offa	166	Fd	8.09N	4.43 E
Offaly/Uíbh Fhailí [2]	118	Fh	53.20N	7.30W
Offenbach am Main	120	Ef	50.06N	8.46 E
Offenbach-Hundheim	124	Je	49.37N	7.33 E
Offenburg	120	Dh	48.29N	7.56 E
Offida	128	Hh	42.56N	13.41 E
Offoué	170	Bc	0.04S	11.44 E
Offranville	124	De	49.52N	1.03 E
Oficina Pedro de Valdivia	206	Gb	22.37S	69.38W
Ofidhoúsa	130	Jm	36.33N	26.09 E
Ofolanga	221b	Ba	19.36S	174.27W
Ofu	221c	Db	14.11S	169.42W
Ōfunato	154	Pe	39.04N	141.43 E
Oga	154	Oe	40.43N	141.18 E
Ogachi	156	Gb	39.05N	140.28 E
Ogaden	158	Lh	7.30N	45.00 E
Oga-Hantō	154	Oe	39.55N	139.50 E
Ōgaki	154	Ng	35.21N	136.37 E
Ogallala	182	Gc	41.08N	101.43W
Ogasawara-Shotō = Bonin Islands (EN)	140	Qg	27.00N	142.10 E
Ogawara-Ko	156a	Bc	40.45N	141.20 E
Ogbomosho	160	Hh	8.08N	4.16 E
Ogden	176	He	41.14N	111.58W
Ogdensburg	184	Jc	44.42N	75.31W
Ogeechee River	184	Gj	31.51N	81.06W
Oghāsh	146	Lc	39.10N	46.55 E
Ogi	156	Fc	37.50N	138.16 E
Ogilvie Mountains	180	Dc	65.00N	140.00W
Ogi-no-Sen	156	Dd	35.26N	134.26 E
Oginski kanal	132	Dc	52.20N	25.55 E
Oglanly	132	Sj	39.50N	54.33 E
Oglethorpe	184	Ei	31.28N	84.04W
Ogliastra	128	Dk	39.55N	9.35 E
Oglio	128	Ee	45.02N	10.39 E
Ognon	122	Lg	47.20N	5.29 E
Ogo	168	Hd	9.48N	45.35 E
Ogoamas, Bulu-	150	Hf	0.40N	120.12 E
Ogodža	138	If	52.48N	132.40 E
Ogoja	166	Gd	6.40N	8.48 E
Ogoki	180	If	51.38N	85.56W
Ogoki	180	If	51.38N	85.55W
Ogoki Reservoir	180	If	51.35N	86.00W
Ogonëk	138	Ie	59.40N	138.01 E
Ogooué	158	Hi	0.49S	9.00 E
Ogooué-Ivindo [3]	170	Bb	0.30N	13.00 E
Ogooué-Lolo [3]	170	Bc	1.00S	13.00 E
Ogooué-Maritime [3]	170	Ac	2.00S	9.30 E
Ogōri [Jap.]	156	Bd	34.06N	131.25 E
Ogōri [Jap.]	156	Be	33.24N	130.34 E
Ogosta	130	Gf	43.45N	23.51 E
Ogražden	130	Fh	41.30N	22.55 E
Ogre	114	Fh	56.50N	24.39 E
Ogre	116	Kh	56.42N	24.33 E
Ogulin	128	Je	45.16N	15.14 E
Ogun [2]	166	Fd	7.00N	3.40 E
Oguni [Jap.]	156	Fb	38.04N	139.45 E
Oguni [Jap.]	156	Be	33.07N	131.04 E
Ogurčinski, ostrov-	132	Rj	38.55N	53.05 E
Oğuzeli	146	Gd	37.00N	37.30 E
Oha	142	Qd	53.34N	142.56 E
Ohai	218	Bf	45.56S	167.57 E
Ohakune	218	Fc	39.25S	175.25 E
Ohanet	162	Id	28.40N	8.50 E
Ohansk	134	Gh	57.42N	55.25 E
Ōhara	156	Gd	35.15N	140.23 E
Ōhasama	156	Gb	39.28N	141.17 E
Ōhata	154	Pd	41.24N	141.10 E
Ohau, Lake-	218	Cf	44.15S	169.50 E
Ohey	124	Hd	50.26N	5.08 E
O'Higgins, Cabo-	221d	Bb	27.05S	109.15W
Ohio [2]	182	Kc	40.15N	82.45W
Ohio	174	Kf	36.59N	89.08W
Ohm	120	Ef	50.51N	8.48 E
Ohmberge	120	Ge	51.30N	10.28 E
'Ohonua	221b	Bc	21.20S	174.57W
Ohopoho	160	Ij	18.03S	13.45 E
Ohota	138	Je	59.20N	143.05 E
Ohotsk	142	Qd	59.23N	143.18 E
Ohotskoje more = Okhotsk, Sea of- (EN)	140	Qd	53.00N	150.00 E
Ohře	120	Kf	50.32N	14.08 E
Ohre	120	Hd	52.18N	11.47 E
Ohrid	130	Dh	41.07N	20.48 E
Ohrid, Lake- (EN) = Ohridsko jezero	110	Ig	41.00N	20.45 E
Ohrid, Lake- (EN) = Ohrit, Liqen i-	110	Ig	41.00N	20.45 E
Ohridsko jezero = Ohrid, Lake- (EN)	110	Ig	41.00N	20.45 E
Öhringen	120	Fg	49.12N	9.30 E
Ohrit, Liqen i- = Ohrid, Lake- (EN)	110	Ig	41.00N	20.45 E
Ohura	218	Fc	38.51S	174.59 E
Oiapoque	202	Hc	3.50N	51.50W
Oich	118	Id	57.10N	4.45W
Oi-Gawa	156	Fd	34.46N	138.17 E
Oil City	184	He	41.26N	79.44W
Oildale	188	Fi	35.25N	119.01W
Oiléan Baoi/Dursey	118	Cj	51.36N	10.12W
Oileán Ciarraí/Castleisland	118	Di	52.14N	9.27W
Oiléan Coarach/Mutton	118	Di	52.49N	9.31W
Oiléan Mhic Aodha/Masee, Island-	118	Hg	54.50N	5.50W
Oinoúsai	130	Jk	38.32N	26.13 E
Oinoúsai, Nísoi-	130	Em	36.45N	21.43 E
Oirschot	124	Hc	51.30N	5.18 E
Oisans	122	Mi	45.02N	6.02 E
Oise [3]	122	Ie	49.30N	2.30 E
Oise	122	Ie	49.00N	2.04 E
Oise à l'Aisne, Canal de l'-	122	Je	49.36N	3.11 E
Oisemont	124	De	49.57N	1.46 E
Oissel	124	De	49.20N	1.06 E
Oisterwijk	124	Hc	51.35N	5.11 E
Oistins	197q	Ab	13.04N	59.32W
Oistins Bay	197q	Ab	13.03N	59.33W
Ōita	152	Ne	33.14N	131.36 E
Ōita Ken [2]	154	Kh	33.15N	131.20 E
Oíti Óros	130	Fk	38.49N	22.17 E
Oituz, Pasul-	130	Jc	46.03N	26.23 E
Oiwake	156a	Bb	42.52N	141.48 E
Ojat	114	Hf	60.31N	33.05 E
Öje	116	Ed	60.49N	13.51 E
Ojika-Jima	156	Ae	33.13N	129.03 E
O-Jima	156	Be	34.00N	130.45 E
Ojinaga	190	Dc	29.34N	104.25W
Ojiya	154	Of	37.18N	138.48 E
Ojmjakon	138	Jd	63.28N	142.49 E
Ojo Caliente	192	Fb	30.25N	106.33W
Ojocaliente	192	Hf	22.34N	102.15W
Ojos del Salado, Nevado-	198	Jh	27.06S	68.32W
Ojos Negros	126	Kd	40.44N	1.30W
Ojtal	136	Hg	42.54N	73.21 E
Ojuelos de Jalisco	192	Ig	21.50N	101.35W
Oka [R.S.F.S.R.]	140	Md	55.00N	102.03 E
Oka [U.S.S.R.]	110	Kd	56.20N	43.59 E
Okaba	150	Kh	8.06S	139.42 E
Okahandja	160	Ik	21.59S	16.58 E
Okahandja [3]	172	Bd	21.30S	17.30 E
Okahukura	218	Fc	38.47S	175.14 E
Okaihau	218	Ea	35.19S	173.46 E
Okąk Islands	180	Le	57.28N	61.48W
Okanagan Lake	180	Fg	49.55N	119.30W
Okano	170	Bc	0.05S	10.57 E
Okanogan River	182	Db	48.06N	119.43W
Okapa	212	Ja	6.31S	145.32 E
Okāra	148	Eb	30.49N	73.27 E
Okarem	136	Fh	38.07N	54.05 E
Okato	218	Ec	39.12S	173.53 E
Okaukuejo	172	Bc	19.10S	15.54 E
Okavango [3]	172	Cc	18.00S	21.00 E
Okavango	158	Jj	18.53N	22.24 E
Okavango Swamp	158	Jj	19.30S	23.00 E
Ōkawa	156	Be	33.12N	130.23 E
Okaya	154	Of	36.03N	138.03 E
Okayama	142	Pf	34.39N	133.55 E
Okayama Ken [2]	154	Lg	34.50N	133.45 E
Okazaki	154	Ng	34.57N	137.10 E
Okeechobee	184	Gl	27.15N	80.50W
Okeechobee, Lake-	174	Kg	26.55N	80.45W
Okefenokee Swamp	184	Fj	30.42N	82.20W
Okehampton	118	Jk	50.44N	4.00W
Okene	166	Gd	7.33N	6.14 E
Oker	120	Gd	52.30N	10.22 E
Oketo	156a	Cb	43.41N	143.32 E
Okha	148	Dd	22.27N	69.04 E
Ókhi Óros	130	Hk	38.04N	24.28 E
Okhotsk, Sea of- (EN) = Hok-Kai	140	Qd	53.00N	150.00 E
Okhotsk, Sea of- (EN) = Ohotskoje more	140	Qd	53.00N	150.00 E
Okhthonia, Ákra-	130	Hk	38.32N	24.14 E
Oki-Daitō-Jima	152	Ng	24.30N	131.00 E
Okiep	172	Be	29.39S	17.53 E
Okinawa	156b	Ab	26.20N	127.47 E
Okinawa Islands (EN) = Okinawa-Shotō	140	Og	26.40N	128.00 E
Okinawa-Jima	152	Mf	26.40N	128.20 E
Okinawa Ken [2]	156b	Ab	26.31N	127.59 E
Okinawa-Shotō = Okinawa Islands (EN)	140	Og	26.40N	128.00 E
Okinoerabu-Jima	152	Mf	27.20N	128.35 E
Okino-Shima [Jap.]	156	Ce	32.44N	132.33 E
Okino-Shima [Jap.]	156	Bd	34.15N	130.08 E
Okino-Tori-Shima	140	Pg	20.25N	136.00 E
Oki Ridge (EN)	154	Mf	37.00N	135.00 E
Oki-Shotō	152	Nd	36.00N	132.50 E
Okitipupa	166	Fd	6.30N	4.48 E
Oki Trench (EN)	156	Dc	37.00N	135.30 E
Oklahoma [2]	182	Hd	35.30N	98.00W
Oklahoma City	176	Jf	35.28N	97.32W
Okmulgee	186	Ii	35.37N	95.58W
Oknica	130	Ka	48.22N	27.24 E
Oko	168	Fa	22.20N	35.56 E
Okob	170	Fb	2.06N	33.53 E
Okolo	170	Fb	2.40N	31.09 E
Okolona	184	Ef	38.08N	85.41W
Okondja	170	Bc	0.41S	13.47 E
Okonek	120	Mc	53.33N	16.50 E
Okoppe	154	Qb	44.28N	143.08 E
Okotoks	188	Ia	50.44N	113.59W
Okoyo	170	Cc	1.28S	15.04 E
Okrzeika	120	Re	51.40N	21.30 E
Øksfjord	114	Fa	70.14N	22.22 E
Oksino	134	Fc	67.33N	52.10 E
Okstindane	110	Hb	66.02N	14.10 E
Oktemberjan	132	Ni	40.09N	44.03 E
Oktjabrsk [Kaz.-U.S.S.R.]	112	Lf	48.40N	57.11 E
Oktjabrsk [R.S.F.S.R.]	114	Lj	53.13N	48.40 E
Oktjabrski [Bye.-U.S.S.R.]	132	Fc	52.38N	28.54 E
Oktjabrski [Kaz.-U.S.S.R.]	134	Kj	52.37N	62.43 E
Oktjabrski [R.S.F.S.R.]	134	Hh	56.31N	57.12 E
Oktjabrski [R.S.F.S.R.]	138	Ee	56.05N	99.25 E
Oktjabrski [R.S.F.S.R.]	138	Hf	53.00N	128.42 E
Oktjabrski [R.S.F.S.R.]	136	Fe	54.31N	53.28 E
Oktjabrski [R.S.F.S.R.]	114	Kf	61.05N	43.08 E
Oktjabrski [R.S.F.S.R.]	138	Kf	52.38N	156.15 E
Oktjabrski [R.S.F.S.R.]	132	Mf	47.56N	43.38 E
Oktjabrskoje	136	Gc	62.28N	66.01 E
Oktjabrskoj Revoljuci, ostrov- = October Revolution Island (EN)	140	Lb	79.30N	97.00 E
Oku	156b	Bb	26.50N	128.17 E
Ōkuchi	154	Kh	32.04N	130.37 E
Okulovka	114	Hg	58.24N	33.18 E
Okushiri	154	Oc	42.09N	139.29 E
Okushiri-Kaikyō	156a	Ab	42.15N	139.40 E
Okushiri-Tō	152	Oc	42.10N	139.25 E
Okuta	166	Fd	9.13N	3.11 E
Oku Tango-Hantō	156	Dd	35.40N	135.10 E
Okwa	158	Jk	22.26S	22.58 E
Ola	138	Ke	59.37N	151.20 E
Ólafsfjördur	114a	Ba	66.04N	18.39W
Ólafsvík	114a	Ab	64.53N	23.43W
Ola Grande, Punta-	197a	Bc	17.55N	66.08W
Olaiņe/Olajne	114	Fh	56.49N	23.59 E
Olajne/Olaiņe	114	Fh	56.49N	23.59 E
Olancha	188	Gh	36.17N	117.59W
Olanchito	194	Df	15.30N	86.35W
Olancho [3]	194	Ef	14.45N	86.00W
Öland	110	Hd	56.45N	16.40 E
Ölands norra udde	116	Gg	57.22N	17.05 E
Ölands södra grund	116	Gh	55.40N	17.25 E
Ölands södra udde	116	Gh	56.11N	16.24 E
Olanga	114	Hc	66.08N	30.38 E
Olathe	186	Ig	38.53N	94.49W
Olavarría	200	Ji	36.53S	60.20W
Oława	120	Nf	50.57N	17.17 E
Oława	120	Nf	50.57N	17.17 E
Olbernhau	120	Jf	50.40N	13.20 E
Olbia	112	Gg	40.55N	9.31 E
Olbia, Golfo di-	128	Dj	40.55N	9.40 E
Old Bahama Channel	194	Ib	22.30N	78.05W
Old Bahama Channel (EN) = Bahamas, Canal Viejo de-	194	Ib	22.30N	78.05W
Old Castile (EN) = Castilla la Vieja	126	Lc	41.30N	4.00W
Old Crow	176	Fc	67.35N	139.50W
Oldeani	170	Gc	3.21S	35.33 E
Oldebroek	124	Hb	52.26N	5.53 E
Oldenburg	120	Ec	53.10N	8.12 E
Oldenburg in Holstein	120	Gb	54.18N	10.53 E
Oldenzaal	122	Mb	52.19N	6.56 E
Old Faithful Geyser	188	Jd	44.30N	110.45W
Old Fletton	124	Bb	52.34N	0.15W
Oldham	118	Kh	53.33N	2.07W
Old Hickory Lake	184	Dg	36.18N	86.30W
Oldman River	188	Jb	49.56N	111.42W
Old Marsh Bed	212	Gd	20.55S	130.30 E
Old Mkushi	170	Ee	14.22S	29.22 E
Old Road	197d	Bb	17.01N	61.50W
Old Road Town	197c	Ab	17.19N	62.48W
Olds	180	Gf	51.47N	114.06W
Old Town	184	Mc	44.56N	68.39W
Old Wives Lake	188	Ma	50.06N	106.00W
Olean	184	Hd	42.05N	78.26W
Olecko	120	Sb	54.03N	22.30 E
Olëkma	140	Oc	60.22N	120.42 E
Olëkminsk	142	Oc	60.30N	120.15 E
Olëkminski stanovik	138	Gf	54.00N	119.00 E
Ølen	114	Ag	59.36N	5.48 E
Olenegorsk	136	Db	68.10N	33.13 E
Olenëk	140	Nb	73.00N	119.55 E
Olenëkski zaliv	138	Hb	73.10N	121.00 E
Olenica	114	Ic	66.29N	35.19 E
Olenj, ostrov-	138	Cb	72.25N	77.45 E
Olenty	132	Re	49.45N	52.10 E
Oléron, Ile d'-	110	Ff	45.56N	1.18W
Olesko	120	Ug	49.53N	24.58 E
Oleśnica	120	Ne	51.13N	17.23 E
Olesno	120	Of	50.53N	18.25 E
Olevsk	132	Ed	51.13N	27.41 E
Olga	138	Ih	43.46N	135.21 E
Olga, Mount-	212	Ge	25.19S	130.46 E
Olgastretet	179	Oc	78.30N	24.00 E
Ølgod	116	Ci	55.49N	8.37 E
Olhão	126	Eg	37.02N	7.50W
Olhovatka	132	Kd	50.17N	39.17 E
Oli	166	Fd	9.40N	4.29 E
Oliana	126	Nb	42.04N	1.19 E
Olib	128	If	44.23N	14.47 E
Oliena	128	Dj	40.16N	9.24 E
Olifantshoek	172	Ce	27.57S	22.42 E
Olifants River [Afr.]	158	Kk	24.03S	32.40 E
Olifants River [Nam.]	172	Be	25.30S	19.30 E
Olimarao Atoll	208	Fd	7.42N	145.53 E
Olimbia	130	El	37.39N	21.38 E
Ólimbos	130	Kn	35.44N	27.13 E
Ólimbos, Óros- = Olympus, Mount- (EN)	110	Ig	40.05N	22.21 E
Ólimbos Óros [Grc.]	130	Jj	39.05N	26.20 E
Olímpia	204	He	20.44S	48.54W
Olinda	202	Le	8.01S	34.51W
Olite	126	Kb	42.29N	1.39W
Oliva [Arg.]	206	Hd	32.03S	63.34W
Oliva [Sp.]	126	Lf	38.55N	0.07W
Oliva, Monasterio de la-	126	Kb	42.20N	1.25W
Oliva de la Frontera	126	Ff	38.16N	6.55W
Oliveira	204	Je	20.41S	44.49W
Oliveira dos Brejinhos	202	Jf	12.19S	42.54W
Olivença	172	Fb	11.46S	35.13 E
Olivenza	126	Ef	38.41N	7.06W
Oliver	188	Fb	49.11N	119.33W
Olivet	122	Hg	47.52N	1.54 E
Olivia	186	Id	44.46N	94.59W
Olja	132	Og	45.47N	47.35 E
Olji Moron He	154	Fb	44.16N	121.42 E
Oljutorski, mys-	140	Td	59.55N	170.25 E
Oljutorski zaliv	138	Ld	60.00N	168.00 E
Olkusz	120	Pf	50.17N	19.35 E
Ollagüe	200	Jh	21.08S	68.45W
Ollan	220d	Bb	7.14N	151.38 E
Ollerton	124	Aa	53.13N	1.01W
Olmedo	126	Hc	41.17N	4.41W
Olmos	202	Ce	5.59S	79.46W
Olney [Eng.-U.K.]	124	Bb	52.09N	0.42W
Olney [Il.-U.S.]	186	Lg	38.44N	88.05W
Olney [Tx.-U.S.]	186	Gj	33.22N	98.45W
Oloči	138	Gf	51.20N	119.53 E
Olofström	114	Dh	56.16N	14.30 E
Oloitokitok	170	Gc	2.56S	37.30 E
Oloj	138	Kc	66.20N	159.29 E
Olojski hrebet	138	Lc	65.50N	162.30 E
Olombo	170	Cc	1.18S	15.53 E
Ólomburi	219a	Ec	8.59S	161.09 E
Olomouc	112	Hf	49.36N	17.16 E
Olona	128	De	45.06N	9.21 E
Olonec	136	Dc	61.01N	32.58 E
Olonešty	130	Mc	46.29N	29.52 E
Olongapo	142	Oh	14.50N	120.16 E
Oloron, Gave d'-	122	Ek	43.33N	1.05W
Oloron-Sainte-Marie	122	Fk	43.12N	0.36W
Olosega	221c	Db	14.11S	169.39W
Olot	126	Ob	42.11N	2.29 E
Olovjannaja	138	Gf	50.56N	115.35 E
Olovo	128	Mf	44.07N	18.35 E
Olpe	120	De	51.02N	7.51 E
Olpoy	219b	Cb	14.52S	166.33 E
Olroyd River	212	Ib	14.10S	141.50 E
Olsberg	124	Kc	51.21N	8.30 E
Olshammar	116	Ff	58.45N	14.48 E
Olst	124	Ib	52.20N	6.08 E
Olsztyn	112	Ie	53.48N	20.29 E
Olsztyn [2]	120	Qc	53.50N	20.30 E
Olsztynek	120	Qc	53.36N	20.17 E
Olt [2]	130	He	44.25N	24.30 E
Olt	110	If	43.43N	24.51 E
Oltedal	116	Bf	58.50N	6.02 E
Olten	128	Bc	47.22N	7.55 E
Olteni	130	Ie	44.11N	25.17 E
Oltenia	130	Ge	44.30N	23.30 E
Olteniţa	130	Je	44.05N	26.38 E
Olteţ	130	He	44.14N	24.27 E
Oltu	146	Ib	40.33N	41.59 E
Oluanpi	140	Og	21.54N	120.51 E
Olutanga	150	He	7.22N	122.52 E
Olvera	126	Gh	36.56N	5.16W
Olym	132	Kc	52.27N	38.05 E
Olympia	176	Ge	47.03N	122.53W
Olympic Mountains	188	Dc	47.50N	123.45W
Olympus, Mount- [U.S.]	174	Ge	47.48N	123.43W
Olympus, Mount- (EN) = Ólimbos, Óros-	110	Ig	40.05N	22.21 E
Om	138	Cf	54.59N	73.22 E
Ōma	156a	Bc	41.30N	140.55 E
Oma	134	Cc	66.45N	46.20 E
Ōmachi	154	Nf	36.30N	137.52 E
Omae-Zaki	156	Fd	34.36N	138.14 E
Ōmagari	154	Pe	39.27N	140.29 E
Omagh/An Omaigh	118	Fg	54.36N	7.18W
Omaha	176	Je	41.16N	95.57W
Omak	188	Fb	48.24N	119.31W
Omakau	218	Cf	45.06S	169.36 E
Omak Lake	188	Fb	48.16N	119.23W
Oman (EN) = 'Umān [1]	142	Hg	21.00N	57.00 E
Oman (EN) = 'Umān	140	Hg	22.10N	58.00 E
Oman, Gulf of- (EN) = 'Umān, Khalīj-	140	Hg	25.00N	58.00 E
Omarama	216	Ch	44.29S	169.58 E
Omar Gambon	168	He	3.10N	45.47 E
Omaru-Gawa	156	Be	32.07N	131.34 E
Omaruru	172	Bd	21.28S	15.56 E
Omaruru [3]	172	Bd	21.30S	15.00 E
Omatako	172	Bd	21.07S	16.43 E
Omatako, Omuramba-	158	Jj	17.57S	20.25 E
Omate	202	Dg	16.41S	70.59W
Ōma-Zaki	156a	Bc	41.32N	140.55 E
Ombai, Selat-	150	Hh	8.30S	125.00 E
Ombella-Mpoko [3]	168	Bd	5.00N	18.00 E
Omberg	116	Ff	58.20N	14.39 E
Ombo	116	Ae	59.15N	6.00 E
Omboué	170	Ac	1.34S	9.15 E
Ombrone	128	Fh	42.39N	11.01 E
Ombu	152	Ee	31.18N	86.33 E
Omčak	138	Jd	61.38N	147.55 E
Omdurman (EN) = Umm Durmān	160	Kg	15.38N	32.30 E
Ōme	156	Fd	35.47N	139.15 E
Omegna	128	Ce	45.53N	8.24 E
Omeo	212	Jg	37.06S	147.36 E
Ömerköy	130	Lj	39.50N	28.04 E
Ometepe, Isla de-	190	Gf	11.30N	85.35W
Ometepec	190	Ee	16.41N	98.25W
Omhajer	168	Fc	14.19N	36.40 E
Ōmihachiman	156	Ed	35.08N	136.05 E
Omihi	218	Ee	43.01S	172.51 E
Omineca	180	Fe	56.05N	124.05W
Omineca Mountains	180	Ee	56.35N	125.55W
Omiš	128	Kg	43.27N	16.42 E
Ōmi-Shima [Jap.]	156	Cd	34.15N	133.00 E
Ōmi-Shima [Jap.]	156	Bd	34.25N	131.15 E
Omitara	172	Bd	22.18S	18.01 E
Ōmiya	152	Od	35.54N	139.38 E
Ommanney Bay	180	Hb	73.00N	101.00W
Omme Å	116	Ci	55.55N	8.25 E
Ommen	124	Ib	52.31N	6.25 E
Omø	116	Di	55.10N	11.10 E
Omo	158	Kh	4.32N	36.04 E
Omoa, Bahía de-	194	Cf	15.50N	88.10W
Omodeo, Lago-	128	Cj	40.10N	8.55 E
Omoloj	138	Ib	71.08N	132.01 E
Omolon	138	Lc	65.12N	160.27 E
Omolon	140	Rc	68.42N	158.36 E
Omono-Gawa	156	Gb	39.44N	140.04 E
Omont	124	Ge	49.36N	4.44 E
Omoto-Gawa	156	Gb	39.51N	141.58 E
Omsk	142	Jd	55.00N	73.24 E
Omskaja oblast [3]	136	Hd	56.00N	72.30 E
Omsukčan	138	Kd	62.27N	155.50 E
Omsukčanski hrebet	138	Kd	63.00N	155.10 E
Ōmu	154	Qb	44.34N	142.58 E
Omu, Vîrful-	130	Id	45.26N	25.25 E
Omulew	120	Rc	53.05N	21.32 E
Ōmura	154	Jh	32.54N	129.57 E
Ōmura-Wan	156	Ae	33.00N	129.50 E
Omurtag	130	Jf	43.06N	26.25 E
Ōmuta	154	Kh	33.02N	130.27 E
Omutinski	136	Gd	56.31N	67.45 E
Omutninsk	136	Fd	58.43N	52.12 E
Oña	126	Ib	42.44N	3.24W
Onagawa	156	Gb	38.26N	141.27 E
Onakayale	172	Bc	17.30S	15.01 E
Onaman Lake	186	Ma	50.00N	87.29W
Onamia	186	Jc	46.04N	93.40W
Onamue	220d	Bb	7.21N	151.31 E
Onaping Lake	184	Gb	46.57N	81.30W
Onatchiway, Lac-	184	La	49.03N	71.03W
Onawa	186	He	42.02N	96.06W
Onch'ŏn	154	He	38.49N	125.13 E
Oncócua	170	Bf	16.40S	13.24 E
Onda	126	Le	39.58N	0.15W
Ondangua	160	Ij	17.55S	16.00 E
Ondarroa / Ondárroa	126	Ja	43.19N	2.25W
Ondárroa / Ondarroa	126	Ja	43.19N	2.25W
Ondava	120	Rh	48.27N	21.48 E
Ondjiva	160	Ij	17.03S	15.47 E
Ondo [2]	166	Gd	7.00N	5.00 E
Ondo [Jap.]	156	Cd	34.12N	132.32 E
Ondo [Nig.]	166	Fd	7.06N	4.50 E
Ondor Sum	154	Bc	42.30N	113.00 E
Ondozero, ozero-	114	He	63.40N	33.15 E
One and Half Degree Channel	140	Ji	1.30N	73.10 E
Oneata	219d	Cc	18.27S	178.29W
Oneata Passage	219d	Cc	18.32S	178.28W
Onega	112	Jc	63.57N	38.05 E
Onega	110	Jc	63.58N	37.55 E
Onega, Lake- (EN) = Onežskoje ozero	110	Jc	61.30N	35.45 E
Onega Peninsula (EN) = Onežski poluostrov	110	Jc	64.35N	38.00 E
One Hundred Mile House	180	Ff	51.38N	121.16W
Oneida	184	Jd	43.04N	75.40W
Oneida Lake	184	Jd	43.13N	76.00W
O'Neil	182	Hc	42.27N	98.39W
Ōnejime	156	Bf	31.14N	130.47 E
Onekotan, ostrov-	140	Re	49.25N	154.45 E
Oneonta [Al.-U.S.]	184	Di	33.57N	86.29W
Oneonta [N.Y.-U.S.]	184	Jd	42.28N	75.04W
Oneroa	220p	Cb	21.15S	159.43W
Onežskaja guba	110	Jc	64.20N	36.30 E
Onežski poluostrov = Onega Peninsula (EN)	110	Jc	64.35N	38.00 E
Onežskoje ozero = Onega, Lake- (EN)	110	Jc	61.30N	35.45 E
Ongea Levu	219d	Cc	19.08S	178.24W
Ongijn-Gol	152	Hc	44.30N	103.40 E
Ongjin	152	Md	37.56N	125.22 E
Ongniud Qi (Wudan)	152	Kc	42.58N	119.01 E
Ongole	148	Ge	15.30N	80.03 E
Ongon	152	Jb	45.49N	113.08 E
Onhaye	124	Gd	50.15N	4.50 E
Oni	132	Mh	42.35N	43.27 E
Onigajō-Yama	156	Ce	33.07N	132.41 E
Onilany	158	Lk	23.34S	43.45 E
Onishibetsu	156a	Ca	45.21N	142.06 E
Onitsha	160	Hh	6.10N	6.47 E
Ōno	154	Ng	35.59N	136.29 E
Ōno	156	Cd	34.18N	132.17 E
Ono	156	Dd	34.51N	134.57 E
Ono	219d	Bc	18.54S	178.29 E
Onoda	156	Be	33.59N	131.11 E
Ōno-Kawa	156	Be	33.15N	131.43 E
Ōnohara-Jima	156	Fd	34.02N	139.23 E
Onohoj	138	Ff	51.55N	108.01 E

Index Symbols

- [1] Independent Nation
- [2] State, Region
- [3] District, County
- [4] Municipality
- [5] Colony, Dependency
- Continent
- Physical Region
- Historical or Cultural Region
- Mount, Mountain
- Volcano
- Hill
- Mountains, Mountain Range
- Hills, Escarpment
- Plateau, Upland
- Pass, Gap
- Plain, Lowland
- Delta
- Salt Flat
- Valley, Canyon
- Crater, Cave
- Karst Features
- Depression
- Polder
- Desert, Dunes
- Forest, Woods
- Heath, Steppe
- Oasis
- Cape, Point
- Coast, Beach
- Cliff
- Peninsula
- Isthmus
- Sandbank
- Island
- Atoll
- Rock, Reef
- Islands, Archipelago
- Rocks, Reefs
- Coral Reef
- Well, Spring
- Geyser
- River, Stream
- Waterfall, Rapids
- River Mouth, Estuary
- Lake
- Salt Lake
- Intermittent Lake
- Reservoir
- Swamp, Pond
- Canal
- Glacier
- Ice Shelf, Pack Ice
- Ocean
- Sea
- Gulf, Bay
- Strait, Fjord
- Lagoon
- Bank
- Seamount
- Tablemount
- Ridge
- Shelf
- Basin
- Escarpment, Sea Scarp
- Fracture
- Trench, Abyss
- National Park, Reserve
- Point of Interest
- Recreation Site
- Cave, Cavern
- Historic Site
- Ruins
- Wall, Walls
- Church, Abbey
- Temple
- Scientific Station
- Railway station
- Airport
- Port
- Military installation
- Lighthouse
- Mine
- Tunnel
- Dam, Bridge

Ono-i-Lau Islands	208	Jg	20.39S	178.42W
Onojō	156	Be	33.34N	130.29 E
Onomichi	154	Lg	34.25N	133.12 E
Onon	140	Nd	51.42N	115.50 E
Onoto	196	Dh	9.36N	65.12W
Onotoa Atoll	208	Ie	1.52S	175.34 E
Ons, Isla de-	126	Db	42.23N	8.56W
Onsala	114	Ch	57.25N	12.01 E
Onseepkans	172	Be	28.45S	19.17 E
Onslow	210	Cg	21.39S	115.06 E
Onslow Bay	182	Le	34.20N	77.20W
On-Take	156	Bf	31.35N	130.39 E
Ontake-San	156	Ed	35.53N	137.29 E
Ontario [2]	180	If	50.00N	86.00W
Ontario [Ca.-U.S.]	188	Gi	34.04N	117.39W
Ontario [Or.-U.S.]	182	Dc	44.02N	116.58W
Ontario, Lake-	174	Le	43.40N	78.00W
Ontario Peninsula	174	Ke	43.50N	81.00W
Onteniente/Ontinyent	126	Lf	38.49N	0.37W
Ontinyent/Onteniente	126	Lf	38.49N	0.37W
Ontojärvi	114	Gd	64.08N	29.09 E
Ontonagon	184	Cb	46.52N	89.19W
Ontong Java Atoll	208	Ge	5.20S	159.30 E
Ō-Numa	156a	Bc	41.59N	140.41 E
Oodnadatta	210	Eg	27.33S	135.28 E
Ooidonk	124	Fc	51.01N	3.35 E
Ookala	221a	Fc	20.01N	155.17W
Ooldea	210	Eh	30.27S	131.50 E
Oologah Lake	186	Ih	36.39N	95.36W
Ooltgensplaat, Oostflakkee-	124	Gc	51.41N	4.21 E
Oostburg	124	Fc	51.20N	3.30 E
Oostelijk Flevoland	124	Hb	52.30N	5.40 E
Oostende/Ostende	122	Ic	51.14N	2.55 E
Oosterhout	122	Kc	51.38N	4.51 E
Oosterschelde=East Schelde (EN)	122	Jc	51.30N	4.00 E
Oosterwolde, Ooststellingwerf-	124	Ha	53.00N	6.18 E
Oosterzele	124	Fd	50.57N	3.48 E
Oostflakkee	124	Gc	51.41N	4.21 E
Oostflakkee-Ooltgensplaat	124	Gc	51.41N	4.21 E
Oostkamp	124	Fc	51.09N	3.14 E
Oost-Souburg, Vlissingen-	124	Fc	51.28N	3.36 E
Ooststellingwerf	124	Ib	53.00N	6.18 E
Ooststellingwerf-Oosterwolde	124	Ha	53.00N	6.18 E
Oost Vieland, Vieland-	124	Ha	53.17N	5.06 E
Oost-Vlaanderen = Flanders, East- (EN) [3]	124	Fc	51.00N	3.40 E
Ootmarsum	124	Ib	52.25N	6.54 E
Opala	170	Dc	0.37S	24.21 E
Opalenica	120	Md	52.19N	16.23 E
Opanake	148	Gg	6.36N	80.37 E
Opari	168	Ee	3.56N	32.03 E
Oparino	114	Lg	59.53N	48.25 E
Opasatika	184	Fa	49.31N	82.58W
Opasatika Lake	184	Fa	49.06N	83.08W
Opasatika River	184	Fa	50.15N	82.25W
Opatija	128	Ie	45.20N	14.19 E
Opatów	120	Rf	50.49N	21.26 E
Opatówka	120	Rf	50.42N	21.50 E
Opava	120	Ng	49.57N	17.54 E
Opava	120	Og	49.51N	18.17 E
Opelika	182	Je	32.39N	85.23W
Opelousas	186	Jk	30.32N	92.05W
Opémisca, Lac-	184	Ja	49.58N	74.57W
Opheim	188	Lb	48.51N	106.24W
Ophir	178	Hd	63.10N	156.31W
Ophthalmia Range	212	Dd	23.15S	119.30 E
Opienge	170	Eb	0.12N	27.30 E
Opihikao	221a	Gd	19.26N	154.53W
Opinaca	180	Jf	52.14N	78.02W
Opiscotéo, Lac-	180	Kf	53.09N	68.10W
Opladen, Leverkusen-	120	De	51.04N	7.01 E
Opobo	166	Ge	4.34N	7.27 E
Opočka	136	Cd	56.42N	28.41 E
Opoczno	120	Qe	51.23N	20.17 E
Opole	120	Nf	50.41N	17.55 E
Opole [2]	120	Nf	50.40N	17.55 E
Opole Lubelskie	120	Re	51.09N	21.58 E
Oporny	136	Ff	46.13N	54.29 E
Opotiki	218	Gc	38.01S	177.17 E
Opp	184	Dj	31.17N	86.22W
Oppa-Wan	156	Gb	38.35N	141.30 E
Oppdal	114	Be	62.36N	9.40 E
Oppenheim	120	Eg	49.51N	8.21 E
Oppland [2]	114	Bf	61.10N	9.40 E
Opportunity	188	Gc	47.39N	117.15W
Opsa	116	Li	55.31N	26.54 E
Opsterland	124	Ia	53.03N	6.04 E
Opsterland-Beetsterzwaag	124	Ia	53.03N	6.04 E
Opua	218	Dg	35.18S	174.07 E
Opunake	218	Ec	39.27S	173.51 E
Oputo	192	Eb	30.03N	109.20W
Oquossoc	184	Lc	45.04N	70.44W
Or	132	Ud	51.12N	58.33 E
Ōra	164	Cd	28.20N	19.35 E
Oradea	112	If	47.04N	21.56 E
Orahovac	130	Dg	42.24N	20.40 E
Orahovica	128	Le	45.32N	17.53 E
Orai	148	Fc	25.59N	79.28 E
Oraibi Wash	188	Ji	35.26N	110.49W
Oran	160	Ge	35.42N	0.38W
Oran [3]	162	Gb	36.00N	0.35W
Orange [Austl.]	210	Fh	33.17S	149.06 E
Orange [Fr.]	122	Kj	44.08N	4.48 E
Orange [Tx.-U.S.]	186	Ie	30.01N	93.44W
Orange [Va.-U.S.]	184	Hf	38.14N	78.07W
Orange/Oranje	158	Ik	28.38N	16.27 E
Orange, Cabo-	198	Ke	4.24N	51.33W
Orangeburg	182	Ke	33.30N	80.52W
Orange Free State/Oranje Vrystaat [2]	172	De	29.00S	26.00 E
Orange Lake	184	Fk	29.25N	82.13W
Orange Park	184	Gj	30.10N	81.42W
Orangeville	184	Gd	43.55N	80.06W
Orange Walk	190	Ge	18.06N	88.33W
Orange Walk [3]	194	Ce	17.44N	88.40W
Oranienburg	120	Jd	52.45N	13.14 E
Oranje/Orange	158	Ik	28.38N	16.27 E
Oranje Gebergte	202	Hc	3.00N	55.00W
Oranjemund	172	Be	28.38S	16.24 E
Oranjestad	202	Da	12.33N	70.06W
Oranje Vrystaat/Orange Free State [2]	172	De	29.00S	26.00 E
Oranžerei	132	Og	45.50N	47.36 E
Orapa	172	Dd	21.16S	25.22 E
Orăştie	130	Gd	45.50N	23.12 E
Orava	120	Pg	49.08N	19.10 E
Oravița	130	Ed	45.02N	21.42 E
Oravská Priehradni Nádrž	120	Pg	49.20N	19.35 E
Orb	122	Jk	43.15N	3.18 E
Orba	128	Cf	44.53N	8.37 E
Orba Co	152	De	34.33N	81.06 E
Ørbæk	116	Di	55.16N	10.41 E
Orbec	124	Ce	49.01N	0.25 E
Orbetello	128	Fh	42.27N	11.13 E
Orbetello, Laguna di-	128	Fh	42.25N	11.15 E
Órbigo	126	Gc	41.58N	5.40W
Orbiquet	124	Ce	49.09N	0.14 E
Orbost	212	Jg	37.42S	148.27 E
Örbyhus	116	Gd	60.14N	17.42 E
Orcadas	222	Re	60.40S	44.30W
Orcas Island	188	Db	48.39N	122.55W
Orchies	124	Fd	50.28N	3.14 E
Orchon→Orhon	140	Md	50.21N	106.05 E
Orcia	128	Fh	42.58N	11.21 E
Orco	128	Be	45.10N	7.52 E
Ord, Mount-	212	Fc	17.20S	125.35 E
Órdenes / Ordes	126	Da	43.04N	8.24W
Ordes / Órdenes	126	Da	43.04N	8.24W
Ordos Desert (EN)=Mu Us Shamo	140	Mf	38.45N	109.10 E
Ord River	208	Df	15.30S	128.21 E
Ordu	144	Ea	41.00N	37.53 E
Ordubad	132	Oj	38.55N	46.01 E
Ordynskoje	138	Df	54.22N	81.58 E
Ordžonikidze [Kaz.-U.S.S.R.]	134	Jj	52.25N	61.45 E
Ordžonikidze [R.S.F.S.R.] → Vladikavkaz	112	Kg	43.03N	44.40 E
Ordžonikidze [Ukr.-U.S.S.R.]	132	If	47.40N	34.04 E
Ordžonikidzeabad	136	Gh	38.34N	69.02 E
Ore älv	116	Fc	61.08N	14.35 E
Orebić	128	Lh	42.58N	17.11 E
Örebro	112	Hd	59.17N	15.13 E
Örebro [2]	114	Dg	59.30N	15.00 E
Oredež	116	Nf	58.50N	30.13 E
Oregon	184	Fe	41.38N	83.28W
Oregon [2]	182	Cc	44.00N	121.00W
Oregon City	182	Cb	45.21N	122.36W
Oregon Inlet	184	Jh	35.50N	75.35W
Öregrund	116	Hd	60.20N	18.26 E
Orehovo	132	If	47.36N	35.47 E
Orehovo-Zujevo	112	Jd	55.49N	38.59 E
Orel	112	Je	52.59N	36.05 E
Orel	132	Ie	48.31N	34.55 E
Orel, gora-	138	Jf	53.55N	140.01 E
Orellana [Peru]	202	Cd	4.40S	78.10W
Orellana [Peru]	202	Ce	6.54S	75.04W
Orem	182	Ec	40.19N	111.42W
Ore Mountains (EN)=Erzgebirge	110	He	50.30N	13.15 E
Ore Mountains (EN)=Krušné Hory	110	He	50.30N	13.15 E
Ören	146	Bd	37.18N	29.17 E
Orenbel	146	Hb	40.00N	39.10 E
Orenburg	112	Le	51.54N	55.06 E
Orenburgskaja oblast [3]	136	Fe	52.00N	55.00 E
Örencik	146	Cc	39.16N	29.34 E
Orense	206	Ie	38.40S	59.47W
Orense / Ourense	126	Eb	42.20N	7.51W
Orense / Ourense [3]	126	Eb	42.10N	7.30W
Oreón, Dhíavlos-	130	Fk	38.54N	22.55 E
Orepuki	218	Bg	46.17S	167.44 E
Orestiás	130	Jh	41.30N	26.31 E
Øresund	110	Hd	55.50N	12.40 E
Oreti	218	Cg	46.28S	168.17 E
Orewa	218	Fb	36.35S	174.42 E
Orford	124	Db	52.05N	1.32 E
Orford Ness	118	Oi	52.05N	1.34 E
Orgañá	126	Nb	42.13N	1.20 E
Organ Needle	186	Cj	32.21N	106.33W
Orgaz	126	Ie	39.39N	3.54W
Orgejev	136	Cf	47.23N	28.50 E
Orgelet	122	Lh	46.31N	5.37 E
Orgon Tal	154	Bc	43.20N	112.40 E
Orgosolo	128	Dj	40.12N	9.21 E
Orgün	144	Kc	32.57N	69.11 E
Orhaneli	130	Lj	39.54N	29.00 E
Orhaneli/Koca Çay	130	Lj	39.56N	28.22 E
Orhangazi	130	Mi	40.30N	29.18 E
Orhomenós	130	Fk	38.35N	22.54 E
Orhon (Orchon)	140	Md	50.21N	106.05 E
Orhy, Pico de-	126	La	42.59N	1.00W
Orichuna, Rio-	196	Bi	7.30N	68.13W
Orick	188	Cf	41.17N	124.04W
Oriental	192	Kh	19.22N	97.37W
Oriental, Cordillera- [Col.]	198	Ie	6.00N	73.00W
Oriental, Cordillera- [Dom.Rep.]	196	Md	18.55N	69.15W
Oriente	206	He	38.44S	60.37W
Orihuela	126	Lf	38.05N	0.57W
Oriku	130	Ci	40.17N	19.25 E
Ori Lekánis	130	Hh	41.08N	24.33 E
Orillia	180	Jh	44.37N	79.25W
Orimattila	114	Ff	60.48N	25.45 E
Orinoco, Delta del-	202	Fb	9.15N	61.30W
Orinoco, Rio-	198	Je	8.37N	62.15W
Oripää	116	Jd	60.51N	22.41 E
Orissa [3]	148	Gd	21.00N	84.00 E
Orissaare/Orissare	114	Fg	58.34N	23.05 E
Orissare/Orissaare	114	Fg	58.34N	23.05 E
Oristano	128	Ck	39.54N	8.36 E
Oristano, Golfo di-	128	Ck	39.50N	8.30 E
Orituco, Rio-	196	Ch	8.45N	67.27W
Orivesi	114	Ff	61.41N	24.21 E
Orivesi	110	Ic	62.15N	29.25 E
Oriximiná	202	Gd	1.45S	55.52W
Orizaba	176	Jh	18.51N	97.06W
Orizaba, Pico de- (Citlaltépetl, Volcán-)	174	Jh	19.01N	97.16W
Orizona	204	Hc	17.03S	48.18W
Orjahovo	130	Gf	43.44N	23.58 E
Ørje	116	De	59.29N	11.39 E
Orjen	130	Bg	42.34N	18.33 E
Orjiva	126	Ih	36.54N	3.25W
Orkanger	114	Be	63.19N	9.52 E
Orkdalen	116	Ca	63.15N	9.50 E
Örkelljunga	116	Eh	56.17N	13.17 E
Orkla	116	Ca	63.18N	9.50 E
Orkney	172	De	27.00S	26.39 E
Orkney [3]	118	Kb	59.00N	3.00W
Orkney Islands	110	Fd	59.00N	3.00W
Orla	120	Me	51.35N	16.40 E
Orlândia	204	Ie	20.43S	47.53W
Orlando	176	Kg	28.32N	81.23W
Orlando, Capo d'-	128	Il	38.10N	14.45 E
Orlanka	120	Td	52.52N	23.12 E
Orléanais	122	Hf	48.40N	1.20 E
Orléans	112	Gf	47.55N	1.54 E
Orlice	120	Lf	50.12N	15.49 E
Orlické Hory	120	Mf	50.10N	16.30 E
Orlik	138	Ef	52.30N	99.55 E
Orlovskaja oblast [3]	136	De	52.45N	36.30 E
Orlovski	132	Mf	46.52N	42.06 E
Orlovski, mys-	114	Jc	67.16N	41.18 E
Orly	122	If	48.45N	2.24 E
Ormāra	148	Cc	25.12N	64.38 E
Ormes	124	Ce	49.03N	0.59 E
Ormoc	150	Hd	11.00N	124.37 E
Ormond	218	Gc	38.33S	177.55 E
Ormond Beach	184	Gk	29.17N	81.02W
Ornain	122	Kf	48.46N	4.47 E
Ornans	122	Mg	47.06N	6.09 E
Ornäs	116	Fd	60.31N	15.32 E
Orne [3]	122	Gf	48.40N	0.05 E
Orne [Fr.]	122	Me	49.17N	6.11 E
Orne [Fr.]	122	Fe	49.19N	0.14W
Orne Seamount (EN)	216	Je	27.30S	157.30W
Orneta	120	Qb	54.08N	20.08 E
Ornö	116	Fe	59.05N	18.25 E
Örnsköldsvik	114	Ee	63.18N	18.43 E
Oro	154	Id	40.01N	127.27 E
Oro, Rio de-	204	Ch	27.04S	58.34W
Oro, Rio del-	192	Ge	25.35N	105.03W
Orocué	202	Dc	4.48N	71.20W
Orodara	166	Ec	10.59N	4.55W
Orofino	188	Gc	46.29N	116.15W
Orogrande	186	Cj	32.23N	106.08W
Orohena, Mont-	221e	Fc	17.31S	149.28W
Oroluk Atoll	208	Gd	7.32N	155.18 E
Orom	170	Fb	3.20N	33.40 E
Oromocto	180	Kg	45.51N	66.29W
Oron	166	Ge	4.50N	8.14 E
Orona Atoll (Hull)	208	Je	4.29S	172.10W
Orongo	221d	Ac	27.10S	109.26W
Oronsay	118	Ge	56.01N	6.14W
Orontes (EN) = 'Āşī, Nahr al-	144	Eb	36.02N	35.58 E
Oropesa	126	Ge	39.55N	5.10W
Oropesa / Orpesa	126	Md	40.06N	0.09 E
Oroqen Zizhiqi (Alihe)	152	La	50.35N	123.42 E
Oroquieta	150	He	8.29N	123.48 E
Orós	202	Ke	6.15S	38.55W
Orós, Açude-	202	Ke	6.15S	39.05W
Orosei	128	Dj	40.23N	9.42 E
Orosei, Golfo di-	128	Dj	40.15N	9.45 E
Orosháza	120	Qj	46.34N	20.40 E
Oro-Shima	156	Be	33.52N	130.02 E
Oroszlány	120	Oi	47.29N	18.19 E
Orote Peninsula	220c	Bb	13.26N	144.38 E
Orote Point	220c	Bb	13.27N	144.37 E
Orotukan	138	Kd	62.17N	151.50 E
Oroville [Ca.-U.S.]	188	Eg	39.31N	121.33W
Oroville [Wa.-U.S.]	188	Fb	48.56N	119.26W
Orpesa / Oropesa	126	Md	40.06N	0.09 E
Orp-Jauche	124	Gd	50.40N	4.57 E
Orqohan	152	Lb	49.36N	121.23 E
Orr	186	Jb	48.03N	92.50W
Orrefors	116	Fh	56.50N	15.45 E
Orri, Pic de l'- / Llorri	126	Nb	42.23N	1.12 E
Orsa	114	Df	61.07N	14.37 E
Orša	112	Je	54.30N	30.24 E
Orsasjön	116	Fc	61.10N	14.35 E
Orsay	124	Ef	48.42N	2.11 E
Orsjön	116	Gc	61.35N	16.20 E
Orsk	112	Le	51.12N	58.34 E
Orşova	130	Fe	44.42N	22.25 E
Ørsta	114	Be	62.12N	6.09 E
Örsundsbro	116	Ge	59.44N	17.18 E
Orta, Lago d'- (Cusio)	128	Ce	45.50N	8.25 E
Ortaca	146	Cd	36.49N	28.47 E
Ortakent	130	Kl	37.02N	27.21 E
Ortaklar	130	Kl	37.53N	27.30 E
Orta Nova	128	Ji	41.19N	15.42 E
Orte	128	Gh	42.27N	12.23 E
Ortegal, Cabo-	126	Ea	43.45N	7.53W
Ortenberg	124	Ld	50.21N	9.03 E
Orthez	122	Fk	43.29N	0.46W
Orthon, Rio-	202	Ef	10.50S	66.04W
Ortigueira [Braz.]	206	Jb	24.12S	50.55W
Ortigueira [Sp.]	126	Ea	43.34N	7.44W
Ortisei / Sankt Ulrich in Gröden	128	Fd	46.34N	11.40 E
Ortiz [Mex.]	192	Dc	28.15N	110.43W
Ortiz [Ven.]	196	Ch	9.37N	67.17W
Ortlergruppe/Ortles	128	Ed	46.30N	10.40 E
Ortles/Ortlergruppe	128	Ed	46.30N	10.40 E
Ortolo	122a	Ab	41.30N	8.55 E
Ortona	128	Ih	42.21N	14.24 E
Ortonville	186	Hd	45.19N	96.27W
Orto-Tokoj	135	Kc	42.20N	76.02 E
Örtze	120	Fd	52.40N	9.57 E
Orukuizu	220a	Ac	7.10N	134.17 E
Orūmīyeh	142	Gf	37.33N	45.04 E
Orūmīyeh, Daryācheh-ye-= Urmia, Lake- (EN)	140	Gf	37.40N	45.30 E
Oruro	200	Jg	17.59S	67.09W
Oruro [3]	202	Eg	18.40S	67.30W
Orust	116	Df	58.10N	11.38 E
Orūzgān	144	Kc	32.56N	66.38 E
Orūzgān [3]	144	Kc	33.15N	66.00 E
Orval, Abbaye d'-	124	He	49.38N	5.22 E
Orvault	122	Eg	47.16N	1.37W
Orvieto	128	Gh	42.43N	12.07 E
Orville Escarpment	222	Qf	75.45S	65.30W
Órvilos, Óros-	130	Gh	41.23N	23.36 E
Orwell	124	Dc	51.58N	1.18 E
Orxois	124	Fe	49.08N	3.12 E
Orz	120	Rd	52.50N	21.30 E
Orzinuovi	128	De	45.24N	9.55 E
Orzyc	120	Rd	52.47N	21.13 E
Orzysz	120	Rc	53.49N	21.56 E
Oš	136	Hg	40.32N	72.50 E
Os	114	Ce	62.30N	11.12 E
Osa	136	Fd	57.17N	55.26 E
Oša	116	Lh	56.21N	26.29 E
Osa	120	Oc	53.33N	18.45 E
Osa, Península de-	190	Hg	8.35N	83.33W
Osage	186	Je	43.17N	92.49W
Osage River	182	Id	38.35N	91.57W
Ōsaka	142	Pf	34.40N	135.30 E
Ōsaka	156	Ed	35.57N	137.14 E
Osaka Bay (EN)=Ōsaka-Wan	154	Mg	34.36N	135.27 E
Ōsaka-Fu [2]	154	Mg	34.45N	135.35 E
Osakarovka	136	He	50.32N	72.39 E
Ōsaka-Wan=Osaka Bay (EN)	154	Mg	34.36N	135.27 E
Osăm	130	Hf	43.42N	24.51 E
Osan	154	If	37.09N	127.04 E
Osasco	204	If	23.32S	46.46W
Osat	128	Nf	44.02N	19.20 E
Osawatomie	186	Ig	38.31N	94.57W
Osborne	186	Gg	39.26N	98.42W
Osburger Hochwald	124	Ie	49.40N	6.50 E
Osby	114	Ch	56.22N	13.59 E
Osceola [Ar.-U.S.]	186	Li	35.42N	89.58W
Osceola [Ia.-U.S.]	182	Ic	41.02N	93.46W
Osceola [Mo.-U.S.]	186	Jh	38.03N	93.42W
Oschatz	120	Je	51.18N	13.07 E
Oschersleben	120	Hd	52.02N	11.15 E
Oschiri	128	Dj	40.43N	9.06 E
Osen	114	Cd	64.18N	10.31 E
Osered	132	Ld	50.01N	40.48 E
Osetr	132	Kb	55.00N	38.41 E
Ōse-Zaki	154	Jh	32.38N	128.42 E
Oshamanbe	154	Pc	42.30N	140.22 E
Oshawa	180	Jh	43.54N	78.51W
Oshekehia Lake	172	Bc	18.08S	15.45 E
Oshika	156	Gb	38.17N	141.31 E
Oshika-Hantō	154	Pe	38.22N	141.27 E
Oshikango	172	Bc	17.22S	15.55 E
Ōshima	156	Fd	34.44N	139.20 E
Oshima	156	Ce	33.55N	132.11 E
Ōshima	156	Ae	33.04N	129.36 E
Ō-Shima [Jap.]	156	De	33.28N	135.50 E
Ō-Shima [Jap.]	154	Od	41.30N	139.15 E
Ō-Shima [Jap.]	154	Jh	32.04N	128.26 E
Ō-Shima [Jap.]	156	De	33.38N	134.30 E
Ō-Shima [Jap.]	156	Be	33.54N	130.27 E
Ō-Shima [Jap.]	156	Ae	32.34N	128.54 E
Ō-Shima [Jap.]	156	Ae	33.14N	129.33 E
Ō-Shima [Jap.]	156	Cd	34.10N	133.05 E
Ō-Shima [Jap.]	156	Bf	31.32N	131.25 E
Ō-Shima [Jap.]	152	Oe	34.45N	139.30 E
Oshima-Hantō	154	Pd	41.40N	140.30 E
Ōshima-Kaikyō	156b	Ba	28.10N	129.15 E
Oshkosh [Nb.-U.S.]	186	Ef	41.24N	102.21W
Oshkosh [Wi.-U.S.]	182	Jc	44.01N	88.33W
Oshnavīyeh	146	Kd	37.02N	45.06 E
Oshogbo	160	Hh	7.46N	4.34 E
Oshtorān Kūh	144	Gc	33.20N	49.16 E
Oshtorīnān	146	Me	34.01N	48.38 E
Oshwe	170	Cc	3.24S	19.30 E
Osich'ŏn-ni	154	Jd	41.25N	128.16 E
Osijek	112	Hf	45.33N	18.42 E
Osilo	128	Cj	40.45N	8.40 E
Osimo	128	Hg	43.28N	13.29 E
Osinki	114	Lj	52.52N	49.31 E
Osinniki	138	Df	53.37N	87.31 E
Osipaonica	130	Ee	44.33N	21.04 E
Osipoviči	132	Fc	53.19N	28.40 E
Osječenica	128	Kf	44.29N	16.17 E
Oskaloosa	186	Jf	41.18N	92.39W
Oskarshamn	114	Dh	57.16N	16.26 E
Oskarström	116	Eh	56.48N	12.58 E
Oskélanéo	184	Ja	48.08N	75.05W
Oskino	138	Fd	60.48N	107.58 E
Öskjuvatn	114a	Cb	65.02N	16.45W
Oskol	132	Je	49.06N	37.25 E
Oskū	146	Lc	37.55N	46.06 E
Oslava	120	Mg	49.05N	16.22 E
Ösling	122	Le	49.55N	6.00 E
Osljanka, gora-	134	Ig	59.10N	58.33 E
Oslo	112	Hd	59.55N	10.45 E
Oslo [2]	114	Cg	59.55N	10.45 E
Oslofjorden	110	Hd	59.20N	10.35 E
Osmānābād	148	Fe	18.10N	76.03 E
Osmancık	146	Fb	40.59N	34.49 E
Osmaneli	130	Ni	40.22N	30.01 E
Osmaniye	144	Eb	37.05N	36.14 E
Osmino	116	Mf	58.54N	29.15 E
Ošmjanskaja vozvyšennost	116	Kj	54.30N	26.00 E
Ošmjany	132	Db	54.27N	25.57 E
Ösmo	116	Gf	58.59N	17.54 E
Osmussaar/Osmussar	116	Je	59.20N	23.15 E
Osmussar/Osmussaar	116	Je	59.20N	23.15 E
Osnabrück	112	Ge	52.16N	8.03 E
Osning	124	Kb	52.10N	8.05 E
Oso, Sierra del-	192	Gd	26.00N	105.25W
Osobloga	120	Nf	50.27N	17.58 E
Osogovske Planine	130	Fg	42.10N	22.30 E
Osor	128	If	44.42N	14.24 E
Osório	206	Jc	29.54S	50.16W
Osorno	200	Ij	40.34S	73.09W
Osoyoos	180	Fg	49.02N	119.28W
Osøyra	114	Af	60.11N	5.28 E
Ospino	196	Bh	9.18N	69.27W
Osprey Reef	208	Ff	13.55S	146.40 E
Oss	122	Lc	51.46N	5.31 E
Ossa, Mount-	208	Fi	41.54S	146.01 E
Óssa, Óros-	130	Fj	39.49N	22.40 E
Ossabaw Island	184	Gj	31.47N	81.06W
Ossa de Montiel	126	Jf	38.58N	2.45W
Osse	122	Gj	44.07N	0.17 E
Ossining	184	Ke	41.10N	73.52W
Ossjøen	116	Dc	61.15N	11.55 E
Osškaja oblast [3]	136	Hg	40.45N	73.20 E
Ossora	138	Le	59.15N	163.02 E
Östanvik	116	Fc	61.10N	15.13 E
Ostaškov	136	Dd	57.09N	33.07 E
Ostbevern	124	Jb	52.03N	7.51 E
Oste	120	Fc	53.50N	9.05 E
Ostende/Oostende	122	Ic	51.14N	2.55 E
Oster	132	Gd	50.55N	30.57 E
Oster [Ukr.-U.S.S.R.]	132	Gd	50.53N	30.55 E
Oster [U.S.S.R.]	132	Gc	53.47N	31.45 E
Osterburg in der Altmark	120	Hd	52.47N	11.44 E
Österbybruk	116	Gd	60.12N	17.54 E
Österdalälven	114	Df	60.33N	15.08 E
Østerdalen	114	Cf	62.00N	10.40 E
Osterfjorden	116	Ad	60.30N	5.20 E
Österforse	116	Ga	63.09N	17.01 E
Östergarnsholm	116	Hg	57.25N	19.00 E
Östergötland [2]	114	Dg	58.25N	15.45 E
Östergötland	116	Ff	59.25N	15.35 E
Osterholz Scharmbeck	120	Ec	53.14N	8.48 E
Österlen	116	Fi	55.30N	14.10 E
Östermark/Teuva	114	Ee	62.29N	21.44 E
Osterode am Harz	120	Ge	51.44N	10.11 E
Osterøya	114	Af	60.35N	5.35 E
Österreich = Austria (EN) [1]	112	Hf	47.30N	14.00 E
Östersjön=Baltic Sea (EN)	110	Hd	57.00N	19.00 E
Østersøen=Baltic Sea (EN)	110	Hd	57.00N	19.00 E
Östersund	112	Hc	63.11N	14.39 E
Osterwick, Rosendahl-	124	Jb	52.01N	7.12 E
Østfold [2]	114	Cg	59.20N	11.30 E
Ostfriesische Inseln=East Frisian Islands (EN)	120	Dc	53.45N	7.25 E
Ostfriesland=East Friesland (EN)	120	Dc	53.20N	7.40 E
Østgrønland=East Greenland (EN) [2]	179	Id	72.00N	35.00W
Östhammar	114	Ed	60.16N	18.22 E
Osthofen	124	Ke	49.42N	8.20 E
Östmark	116	Ed	60.17N	12.45 E
Ostrach	120	Fh	48.05N	9.25 E
Östra Silen	116	Ee	59.15N	12.20 E
Ostrava	112	Hf	49.50N	18.17 E
Ostrhauderfehn	124	Ja	53.08N	7.37 E
Ostróda	120	Pc	53.43N	19.59 E
Ostrog	132	Ed	50.19N	26.32 E
Ostrogožsk	136	De	50.52N	39.05 E
Ostrołęka	120	Rc	53.06N	21.34 E
Ostrołęka [2]	120	Rc	53.05N	21.35 E
Ostrošički Gorodok	116	Lj	54.03N	27.46 E
Ostrov [Bye.-U.S.S.R.]	120	Vd	52.48N	26.01 E
Ostrov [Czech.]	120	If	50.18N	12.57 E
Ostrov [Rom.]	130	Ke	44.07N	27.22 E
Ostrov [R.S.F.S.R.]	136	Cd	57.23N	28.22 E
Ostrov [R.S.F.S.R.]	116	Mf	58.28N	28.44 E
Ostrovec	116	Lj	54.38N	26.06 E
Ostrovicës, Mali i-	130	Di	40.32N	20.27 E
Ostrovskoje	114	Kh	57.50N	42.13 E
Ostrowiec Świętokrzyski	120	Rf	50.57N	21.23 E
Ostrów Lubelski	120	Se	51.30N	22.52 E
Ostrów Mazowiecka	120	Rd	52.49N	21.54 E
Ostrów Wielkopolski	120	Ne	51.39N	17.49 E
Ostryna	120	Uc	53.41N	24.37 E
Ostrzeszów	120	Ne	51.25N	17.57 E
Ostsee=Baltic Sea (EN)	110	Hd	57.00N	19.00 E
Oststeirisches Hügelland	128	Jd	47.00N	15.45 E
Osttirol	128	Gd	46.55N	12.30 E
Ostuni	128	Lj	40.44N	17.35 E
Ōsumi	156	Bf	31.36N	130.59 E
Osumi	130	Ci	40.48N	19.52 E
Ōsumi-Hantō	156	Bf	31.15N	130.50 E
Ōsumi Islands (EN)=Ōsumi-Shotō	140	Pf	30.35N	130.59 E
Ōsumi-Shotō=Osumi Islands (EN)	140	Pf	30.35N	130.59 E
Osuna	126	Gg	37.14N	5.07W
Osveja	116	Mi	55.59N	28.10 E
Osvejskoje, ozero-	116	Mh	56.00N	28.15 E
Oswego	182	Lc	43.27N	76.31W
Oswestry	118	Ji	52.52N	3.04W
Oświęcim	120	Pf	50.03N	19.12 E
Osyka	186	Kk	31.00N	90.28W
Ōta	156	Fc	36.18N	139.22 E
Ōta	156	Ed	35.56N	136.03 E
Otago [2]	218	Cf	45.00S	169.10 E
Otago Peninsula	218	Df	45.50S	170.45 E
Ōtake	154	Lg	34.12N	132.13 E
Otakeho	218	Fc	39.33S	174.03 E
Otaki	218	Fd	40.45S	175.08 E
Ōtakime-Yama	156	Ce	37.22N	140.42 E
Otanoshike	156a	Db	43.01N	144.16 E
Otar	136	Hg	43.31N	75.12 E
Otaru	152	Pc	43.13N	141.00 E
Otautau	218	Bg	46.09S	168.00 E
Otava	116	Lc	61.39N	27.04 E
Otava	120	Kg	49.26N	14.12 E
Otavi	172	Bc	19.39S	17.20 E
Ōtawara	154	Pf	36.52N	140.02 E

Index Symbols

[1] Independent Nation
[2] State, Region
[3] District, County
[4] Municipality
[5] Colony, Dependency
Continent
Physical Region
Historical or Cultural Region
Mount, Mountain
Volcano
Hill
Mountains, Mountain Range
Hills, Escarpment
Plateau, Upland
Pass, Gap
Plain, Lowland
Delta
Salt Flat
Valley, Canyon
Crater, Cave
Karst Features
Depression
Polder
Desert, Dunes
Forest, Woods
Heath, Steppe
Oasis
Cape, Point
Coast, Beach
Cliff
Peninsula
Isthmus
Sandbank
Island
Atoll
Rock, Reef
Islands, Archipelago
Rocks, Reefs
Coral Reef
Well, Spring
Geyser
River, Stream
Waterfall, Rapids
River Mouth, Estuary
Lake
Salt Lake
Intermittent Lake
Reservoir
Swamp, Pond
Canal
Glacier
Ice Shelf, Pack Ice
Ocean
Sea
Gulf, Bay
Strait, Fjord
Lagoon
Bank
Seamount
Tablemount
Ridge
Shelf
Basin
Escarpment, Sea Scarp
Fracture
Trench, Abyss
National Park, Reserve
Point of Interest
Recreation Site
Cave, Cavern
Historic Site
Ruins
Wall, Walls
Church, Abbey
Temple
Scientific Station
Railway station
Airport
Port
Military installation
Lighthouse
Mine
Tunnel
Dam, Bridge

Otelu Roşu 130 Fd 45.32N 22.22 E
Otematata 218 Df 44.37S 170.11 E
Otepää/Otepja 114 Gg 58.03N 26.30 E
Otepää, vozvyšennost- / Otepää Kõrgustik 116 Lf 58.00N 26.40 E
Otepää Kõrgustik / Otepää, vozvyšennost- 116 Lf 58.00N 26.40 E
Otepja/Otepää 114 Gg 58.03N 26.30 E
Oteros 190 Cc 26.55N 108.30W
Othain 124 He 49.31N 5.23 E
Othello 188 Fc 46.50N 119.10W
Othonoi 130 Cj 39.50N 19.25 E
Óthris Óros 130 Fj 39.02N 22.37 E
Oti 158 Hh 7.48N 0.08 E
Otira 218 De 42.51S 171.33 E
Otish, Monts- 174 Md 52.45N 69.15W
Otjikondo 172 Bc 19.50S 15.23 E
Otjimbingwe 172 Bd 22.21S 16.08 E
Otjiwarongo 160 Ik 20.29S 16.36 E
Otjiwarongo [3] 172 Bd 20.30S 17.30 E
Otjosondjou, Omuramba- 158 Ij 19.55S 20.00 E
Otjosondu 172 Bd 21.12S 17.58 E
Otmuchowskie, Jezioro- 120 Nf 50.27N 17.15 E
Otnes 114 Cf 61.46N 11.12 E
Otobe 156a Bc 41.57N 140.08 E
Otočac 128 Jf 44.52N 15.14 E
Otofuke 156a Cb 42.59N 143.10 E
Otofuke-Gawa 156a Cb 42.56N 143.12 E
Otog Qi (Ulan) 152 Id 39.07N 108.00 E
Otoineppu 156a Ca 44.43N 142.16 E
Otok 128 Me 45.09N 18.53 E
Otorohanga 218 Fc 38.11S 175.12 E
Otorten, gora- 134 If 61.50N 59.13 E
Ōtoyo 156 Ce 33.46N 133.40 E
Otra 110 Gd 58.09N 8.00 E
Otradnaja 132 Lg 44.23N 41.31 E
Otradnoje, ozero- 116 Nd 60.50N 30.25 E
Otradny 114 Mj 53.23N 51.24 E
Otranto 128 Mj 40.09N 18.30 E
Otranto, Canale d'-= Otranto, Strait of- (EN) 110 Hg 40.00N 19.00 E
Otranto, Capo d'- 128 Mj 40.06N 18.31 E
Otranto, Strait of- (EN)= Otranto, Canale d'- 110 Hg 40.00N 19.00 E
Otranto, Strait of- (EN)= Otrantos, Kanali i- 130 Bi 40.00N 19.00 E
Otranto, Terra d'- 128 Mj 40.20N 18.15 E
Otrantos, Kanali i-=Otranto, Strait of- (EN) 130 Bi 40.00N 19.00 E
Ötscher 128 Jc 47.51N 15.12 E
Ōtsu 154 Mg 35.00N 135.52 E
Ōtsuchi 154 Pe 39.21N 141.54 E
Ōtsuki [Jap.] 156 Ce 32.50N 132.41 E
Ōtsuki [Jap.] 156 Fd 35.36N 138.54 E
Otta 114 Bf 61.46N 9.32 E
Otta 220d Bb 7.09N 151.54 E
Otta 116 Cc 61.46N 9.31 E
Ottadalen 116 Bc 61.55N 8.00 E
Ottana 128 Dj 40.15N 9.05 E
Otta Pass 220d Bb 7.09N 151.53 E
Ottawa [Il.-U.S.] 186 Lf 41.21N 88.51W
Ottawa [Ks.-U.S.] 182 Hd 38.37N 95.16W
Ottawa [Oh.-U.S.] 184 Ee 41.02N 84.03W
Ottawa [Ont.-Can.] 176 Le 45.25N 75.42W
Ottawa Islands 174 Kd 59.30N 80.10W
Ottawa River 174 Le 45.20N 73.58W
Ottawa River (EN) = Outaouais, Rivière- 184 Kc 45.20N 73.58W
Ottenby 114 Dh 56.16N 16.24 E
Otterberg 124 Je 49.30N 7.46 E
Otter Creek 184 Fk 29.19N 82.48W
Otterndorf 120 Ec 53.48N 8.54 E
Otterøy 116 Bb 62.40N 6.50 E
Otter Rapids 184 Ga 50.15N 81.45W
Otterup 116 Di 55.31N 10.24 E
Ottumwa 182 Ic 41.01N 92.25W
Ottweiler 124 Je 49.23N 7.10 E
Otukpa 166 Gd 7.05N 7.40 E
Otumpa 204 Ah 27.19S 62.13W
Otuquis, Bañados de- 202 Gg 19.20S 58.30W
Otuquis, Río- 204 Cd 19.41S 58.20W
Oturkpo 166 Gd 7.13N 8.09 E
Otu Tolu Group 221b Bb 20.21S 174.32W
Otuzco 202 Ce 7.54S 78.35W
Otway, Cape- 212 Ig 38.52S 143.31 E
Otwock 120 Rd 52.07N 21.16 E
Otynja 120 Uh 48.40N 24.57 E
Ötz 128 Ec 47.12N 10.54 E
Ötztaler Ache 128 Ec 47.14N 10.50 E
Ötztaler Alpen 120 Gj 46.45N 10.55 E
Ou 148 Kd 20.04N 102.13 E
Oua 219b Ce 21.14S 167.05 E
'O'ua 221b Bb 20.02S 174.41W
Ouachita, Lake- 186 Ji 34.40N 93.25W
Ouachita Mountains 174 Jf 34.40N 94.25W
Ouachita River 182 Ie 31.38N 91.49W
Ouadane 160 Ff 20.57N 11.35W
Ouadda 160 Jh 8.04N 22.24 E
Ouaddaï [3] 168 Cc 13.00N 21.00 E
Ouaddaï 158 Jg 13.00N 21.00 E
Ouagadougou 160 Gg 12.22N 1.31W
Ouahigouya 160 Gg 13.35N 2.25W
Ouaka [3] 168 Cd 6.00N 21.00 E
Ouaka 158 Ih 4.59N 19.56 E
Oualata 162 Ff 17.18N 7.00W
Oualata, Dahr- 162 Ff 17.48N 7.24W
Oualidia 162 Fc 32.44N 9.02W
Ouallam 166 Fc 14.19N 2.05 E
Ouallene 162 He 24.35N 1.17 E
Ouanda-Djallé 168 Cd 8.54N 22.48 E
Ouandjia 168 Cd 8.35N 23.12 E
Ouandjia 168 Cd 9.35N 23.15 E
Ouango 168 Ce 4.19N 22.33 E
Ouangolodougou 166 Dd 9.58N 5.09W
Ouanne 122 Ig 47.57N 2.47 E
Ouarane 158 Ff 21.00N 10.00W
Ouargaye 166 Fc 11.32N 0.01 E
Ouargla 160 He 31.57N 5.20 E
Ouargla [3] 162 Id 30.00N 6.30 E
Ouarkziz, Jbel- 158 Gf 28.00N 8.20W
Ouarra 158 Jh 5.05N 24.26 E
Ouarsenis, Djebel- 126 Ni 35.53N 1.38 E
Ouarsenis, Massif de l'- 162 Hb 35.50N 2.05 E
Ouarzazate 162 Fc 30.55N 6.55W
Ouarzazate [3] 162 Fc 31.00N 6.30W
Oubangui 158 Ii 0.30S 17.42 E
Ouborré, Pointe- 219b Dd 18.47S 169.16 E
Ouche, Pays d'- 122 Gf 48.55N 0.45 E
Ōuchi 156 Gb 39.27N 140.06 E
Oud Beijerland 124 Gc 51.50N 4.26 E
Oude IJssel 124 Ic 52.00N 6.10 E
Oudenaarde/Audenarde 122 Jd 50.51N 3.36 E
Oudenbosch 124 Gc 51.35N 4.34 E
Oude Rijn 122 Kb 52.05N 4.20 E
Oudon 122 Fg 47.37N 0.42W
Oudtshoorn 160 Jl 33.35S 22.14 E
Oued Ben Tili 162 Fd 25.48N 9.32W
Oued el Abtal 126 Mi 35.27N 0.41 E
Oued Fodda 126 Nh 36.11N 1.32 E
Oued Lili 126 Ni 35.31N 1.16 E
Oued Rhiou 162 Hb 35.58N 0.55 E
Oued Taria 126 Mi 35.07N 0.05 E
Oued Tlelat 126 Li 35.33N 0.27W
Oued Zem 160 Ge 32.52N 6.34W
Ouégoa 219b Be 20.21S 164.26 E
Ouéllé 166 Ed 7.18N 4.01W
Ouémé [3] 166 Fd 7.00N 2.35 E
Ouémé 158 Hh 6.29N 2.32 E
Ouen 219b Cf 22.26S 166.48 E
Ouenza 162 Ib 35.57N 8.07 E
Ouenza, Djebel- 128 Co 35.57N 8.05 E
Ouessa 166 Ec 11.03N 2.47W
Ouessant, Ile d'- 122 Af 48.28N 5.05W
Ouesso 160 Ih 1.37N 16.04 E
Ouest [3] 166 Hd 5.20N 10.30 E
Ouest, Baie de l'- 220h Ab 13.15S 176.13W
Ouezzane 162 Fc 34.48N 5.36W
Oughter, Lough- 118 Fg 54.00N 7.29W
Ouham [3] 168 Bd 7.00N 18.00 E
Ouham 158 Ih 9.18N 18.14 E
Ouham-Pendé [3] 168 Bd 7.00N 16.00 E
Ouidah 166 Fd 6.22N 2.05 E
Ouistreham 122 Fe 49.17N 0.15W
Ouistreham-Riva Bella 124 Be 49.17N 0.16W
Oujda 160 Ge 34.40N 1.54W
Oujda [3] 162 Gc 33.00N 2.00W
Oujeft 162 Ee 20.02N 13.03W
Oulainen 114 Fd 64.16N 24.57 E
Oulchy-le-Château 124 Fe 49.12N 3.21 E
Ouled Djellal 162 Ic 34.25N 5.04 E
Ouled Nail, Monts des- 162 Hc 34.40N 3.25 E
Oulou, Bahr- 168 Cd 9.48N 21.32 E
Oulu [2] 114 Gd 65.00N 27.00 E
Oulu/Uleåborg 112 Ib 65.01N 25.30 E
Oulu, Lake- (EN)= Oulujärvi 110 Ic 64.20N 27.15 E
Oulujärvi=Oulu, Lake- (EN) 110 Ic 64.20N 27.15 E
Oulujoki 110 Ib 65.01N 25.25 E
Oum Chalouba 160 Jg 15.48N 20.46 E
Oumé 166 Dd 6.23N 5.25W
Oumé [3] 166 Dd 6.25N 5.30W
Oum el Bouaghi 162 Ib 35.53N 7.07 E
Oum el Bouaghi [3] 162 Ib 35.30N 7.10 E
Oum er Rbia 158 Ge 33.19N 8.20W
Oum Hadjer 168 Bc 13.18N 19.41 E
Oumm ed Droûs Guebli, Sebkhet- 162 Ee 24.03N 11.45W
Oumm ed Droûs Telli, Sebkhet- 162 Ee 24.20N 11.30W
Ounasjoki 110 Ib 66.30N 25.45 E
Oundle 124 Bb 52.29N 0.28W
Ounianga 168 Cb 19.10N 20.30 E
Ounianga Kébir 160 Jg 19.04N 20.29 E
Ountivou 166 Fd 7.21N 1.34 E
Ouolossébougou 166 Dc 12.00N 7.55W
Oupeye 124 Hd 50.42N 5.39 E
Oupu 152 Ma 52.45N 126.00 E
Our 124 Ie 49.53N 6.18 E
Ouray 186 Cg 38.01N 107.40W
Ouray, Mount- 186 Cg 38.25N 106.14W
Ource 122 Kf 48.06N 4.23 E
Ourcq 122 Je 49.01N 3.01 E
Ourcq, Canal de l'- 122 If 48.51N 2.22 E
Ourém 202 Id 1.33S 47.06W
Ourense / Orense 126 Eb 42.20N 7.51W
Ourense / Orense [3] 126 Eb 42.10N 7.30W
Ouricuri 202 Je 7.35S 40.05W
Ourinhos 200 Lh 22.59S 49.52W
Ouro, Rio do- 204 Ha 13.20S 48.59W
Ouro Fino 204 If 22.17S 46.22W
Ouro Prêto 204 Jh 20.23S 43.30W
Ourthe 122 Ld 50.38N 5.35 E
Ourville-en-Caux 124 Ce 49.44N 0.36 E
Ous 136 Gc 60.55N 61.31 E
Ou-Sanmyaku 154 Pe 39.00N 141.00 E
Ouse [Eng.-U.K.] 118 Nk 50.47N 0.03 E
Ouse [Eng.-U.K.] 118 Mh 53.42N 0.41W
Oust 122 Dg 47.35N 2.06W
Outagouna 166 Fb 15.11N 0.43 E
Outaouais, Rivière- = Ottawa River (EN) 184 Kc 45.20N 73.58W
Outardes, Rivière aux- 180 Kg 49.05N 68.23W
Outat Oulad El Hajj 162 Gc 33.21N 3.42W
Outer Dowsing 118 Oh 53.25N 1.05 E
Outer Hebrides 118 Fd 57.50N 7.32W
Outer Santa Barbara Passage 188 Fj 33.10N 118.30W
Outer Silver Pit 118 Og 54.05N 2.00 E
Outjo 160 Ik 20.08S 16.08 E
Outjo [3] 172 Ac 19.30S 14.30 E
Outlook 188 La 51.30N 107.03W
Outokumpu 114 Ge 62.44N 29.01 E
Outram Mountain 188 Eb 49.19N 121.05W
Outreau 124 Dd 50.42N 1.35 E
Out Skerries 118 Ma 60.30N 0.50W
Outwell 124 Cb 52.37N 0.14 E
Ouvéa, Ile- 208 Hg 20.35S 166.35 E
Ouvèze 122 Kk 43.59N 4.51 E
Ouyen 212 Ig 35.04S 142.20 E
Ouyou Bézédinga 166 Hb 16.32N 13.15 E
Ouzera 126 Oh 36.15N 2.51 E
Ovacık [Tur.] 146 Hc 39.22N 39.13 E
Ovacık [Tur.] 146 Ed 36.11N 33.40 E
Ovada 128 Cf 44.38N 8.38 E
Ova Gölü 130 Mm 36.16N 29.22 E
Ovakent 130 Lk 38.06N 28.02 E
Ovalau Island 219d Bb 17.40S 178.48 E
Ovalle 200 Ii 30.36S 71.12W
Oval Peak 188 Eb 48.15N 120.25W
Ovamboland 172 Bc 18.00S 16.00 E
Ovamboland 172 Bc 18.30S 16.00 E
Ovan 170 Bb 0.30N 12.10 E
Ovanåker 114 Df 61.21N 15.54 E
Ovar 126 Dd 40.52N 8.38W
Ovau 219a Cb 6.48S 156.02 E
Ovejas 194 Ji 9.32N 75.14W
Overath 124 Jd 50.57N 7.18 E
Øverbygd 114 Eb 69.01N 19.18 E
Overflakkee 122 Kc 51.45N 4.10 E
Överhalla 114 Cd 64.30N 12.00 E
Overijse 124 Gd 50.46N 4.32 E
Overijssel [3] 124 Ib 52.25N 6.30 E
Överkalix 114 Fc 66.19N 22.50 E
Overland Park 186 Ig 38.59N 94.40W
Övermark/Ylimarkku 116 Ib 62.37N 21.28 E
Overpelt 124 Hc 51.12N 5.25 E
Overri 166 Gd 5.29N 7.02 E
Overton 188 Hh 36.33N 114.27W
Övertorneå 114 Fc 66.23N 23.40 E
Överum 116 Gg 57.59N 16.19 E
Ovidiu 130 Le 44.16N 28.34 E
Oviedo [Dom.Rep.] 194 Le 17.47N 71.22W
Oviedo [Sp.] 112 Fg 43.22N 5.50W
Oviši 116 Ig 57.34N 21.35 E
Ovo, Capo dell'- 128 Lj 40.18N 17.30 E
Øvre Årdal 114 Bf 61.19N 7.48 E
Övre Fryken 116 Ed 60.00N 13.05 E
Övre Soppero 114 Eb 68.05N 21.41 E
Ovruč 136 Ce 51.19N 28.50 E
Ovsjanka 138 Hf 53.32N 126.58 E
Owaka 218 Cg 46.27S 169.40 E
Owando 160 Ii 0.29S 15.55 E
Owani 154 Pd 40.31N 140.35 E
Owase 154 Ng 34.04N 136.12 E
Owatonna 182 Ic 44.05N 93.14W
Owego 184 Id 42.06N 76.16W
Owen, Mount- 218 Ed 41.33S 172.32 E
Owendo 170 Ab 0.17N 9.30 E
Owen Falls Dam 170 Fb 0.24N 33.11 E
Owensboro 182 Jd 37.46N 87.07W
Owens Lake 188 Gh 36.25N 117.56W
Owen Sound 180 Jh 44.34N 80.56W
Owens River 188 Gh 36.31N 117.57W
Owen Stanley Range 208 Fe 9.20S 148.00 E
Owl Creek Mountains 188 Ke 43.30N 108.35W
Ownay, Kowlal-e- 144 Kc 34.27N 68.22 E
Owo 166 Gd 7.11N 5.35 E
Owosso 184 Ed 43.00N 84.10W
Owyhee 188 Gf 41.57N 116.06W
Owyhee, Lake- 188 Ge 43.28N 117.20W
Owyhee Mountains 188 Ge 43.00N 116.45W
Owyhee River 182 Dc 43.40N 117.16W
Oxberg 116 Fc 61.07N 14.10 E
Oxbow 186 Eb 49.14N 102.11W
Oxelösund 114 Dg 58.40N 17.06 E
Oxford 118 Lj 51.50N 1.30W
Oxford [Eng.-U.K.] 112 Fe 51.46N 1.15W
Oxford [Ms.-U.S.] 186 Li 34.22N 89.32W
Oxford [N.C.-U.S.] 184 Hg 36.19N 78.35W
Oxford [N.Z.] 218 Ee 43.17S 172.11 E
Oxford Lake 180 Hf 54.50N 95.35W
Oxfordshire [3] 118 Lj 51.50N 1.20W
Oxia 130 Ek 38.18N 21.06 E
Oxkutzcab 192 Og 20.18N 89.25W
Oxnard 182 De 34.12N 119.11W
Ox or Slieve Gamph Mountains 118 Eg 54.10N 8.50W
Ox or Slieve Gamph Mountains/Sliabh Gamh 118 Eg 54.10N 8.50W
Oxted 124 Bc 51.14N 0.01W
Oyabe 156 Ec 36.40N 136.52 E
O-Yama 156 Fd 34.04N 139.31 E
Ōyama [Jap.] 156 Ec 36.35N 137.18 E
Oyama [Jap.] 154 Of 36.21N 139.50 E
Ōyano 156 Be 32.35N 130.27 E
Oyapock, Fleuve- 198 Ke 4.08N 51.40W
Oyem 160 Ih 1.37N 11.35 E
Oyen 188 Ja 51.22N 110.28W
Øyeren 116 De 59.50N 11.14 E
Oykel 118 Id 57.50N 4.25W
Oyo [2] 166 Fd 8.00N 3.50 E
Oyo [Nig.] 166 Fd 7.51N 3.56 E
Oyo [Sud.] 168 Fa 21.55N 36.06 E
Oyodo-Gawa 156 Bf 31.55N 131.23 E
Oyonnax 122 Lh 46.15N 5.40 E
Oyster Bay 212 Jh 42.10S 148.10 E
Øystese 116 Bd 60.23N 6.13 E
Özalp 146 Jc 38.39N 43.59 E
Ozamiz 150 He 8.08N 123.50 E
Ozark 184 Ej 31.28N 85.38W
Ozark Plateau 174 Jf 37.00N 93.00W
Ozark Reservoir 186 Ii 35.25N 94.05W
Ozarks, Lake of the- 182 Id 37.39N 92.50W
Ózd 120 Qh 48.13N 20.18 E
Ozeblin 128 Jf 44.35N 15.53 E
Ozernoj, zaliv- 138 Le 57.00N 163.20 E
Ozernovski 138 Kf 51.21N 156.32 E
Ozerny 132 Vd 51.08N 60.55 E
Ozersk 116 Ij 54.24N 21.59 E
Ozery [Bye.-U.S.S.R.] 120 Uc 53.38N 24.18 E
Ozery [R.S.F.S.R.] 114 Ji 54.54N 38.32 E
Ožezdy 136 Gf 48.03N 37.09 E
Ozieri 128 Dj 40.35N 9.00 E
Ozinki 136 Ee 51.12N 49.47 E
Ōzogina 138 Kc 66.12N 151.05 E
Ozona 182 Ge 30.43N 101.12W
Ozorków 120 Pe 51.58N 19.19 E
Ozouri 170 Ac 0.55S 8.55 E
Ozren [Yugo.] 130 Ef 43.36N 21.54 E
Ozren [Yugo.] 128 Mg 43.59N 18.30 E
Ozren [Yugo.] 128 Mf 44.37N 18.15 E
Ōzu [Jap.] 154 Lh 33.30N 132.23 E
Ōzu [Jap.] 156 Be 32.52N 130.52 E

P

Pääjärvi 116 Kb 62.50N 24.45 E
Paama 219b Dc 16.28S 168.13 E
Pa-an → Pha-an 148 Je 16.53N 97.38 E
Paar 120 Hh 48.45N 11.35 E
Paarl 160 Il 33.45S 18.56 E
Paauilo 221a Fc 20.03N 155.22W
Paavola 114 Fd 64.36N 25.12 E
Pabbay 118 Fd 57.47N 7.20W
Pabellón, Ensenada del- 192 Fe 24.27N 107.36W
Pabellón, Punta- 206 Ff 43.16S 74.23W
Pabianice 120 Pe 51.40N 19.22 E
Pābna 148 Hd 24.00N 89.15 E
Pabradė/Pabrade 114 Fi 54.59N 25.50 E
Pabradé/Pabradė 114 Fi 54.59N 25.50 E
Pacaás Novos, Serra dos- 202 Ff 10.50S 64.00W
Pacajá, Rio- 202 Hd 1.56S 50.55W
Pacajus 202 Kd 4.10S 38.28W
Pacaraima, Serra- 198 Je 4.30N 60.40W
Pacasmayo 202 Ce 7.24S 79.34W
Paceco 128 Gm 37.59N 12.33 E
Pachala 168 Ed 7.10N 34.06 E
Pacheco 192 Eb 30.06N 108.21W
Pachino 128 Jn 36.43N 15.05 E
Pachitea, Río- 202 De 8.46S 74.32W
Pachuca de Soto 190 Ed 20.07N 98.44W
Pacific-Antarctic Ridge (EN) 222 Md 62.00S 157.00W
Pacific City 188 Dd 45.12N 123.57W
Pacific Grove 188 Eh 36.38N 121.56W
Pacífico, Océano-=Pacific Ocean (EN) 106 Ki 5.00N 155.00W
Pacific Ocean 106 Ki 5.00N 155.00W
Pacific Ocean (EN)=Kita-Taiheiyō 214 Ch 22.00N 179.00 E
Pacific Ocean (EN)= Pacífico, Océano- 106 Ki 5.00N 155.00W
Pacific Ocean (EN)= Pacifique, Océan- 106 Ki 5.00N 155.00W
Pacific Ocean (EN)= Taiheiyō 106 Ki 5.00N 155.00W
Pacific Ocean (EN) = Tihi okean 106 Ki 5.00N 155.00W
Pacific Ranges 180 Ef 50.55N 125.10W
Pacifique, Océan-=Pacific Ocean (EN) 106 Ki 5.00N 155.00W
Packsattel 128 Id 46.58N 14.58 E
Pacui, Rio- 204 Jc 16.46S 45.01W
Pacuneiro, Rio- 204 Fa 13.02S 53.25W
Pacy-sur-Eure 124 De 49.01N 1.23 E
Paczków 120 Mf 50.27N 17.00 E
Padana, Pianura-=Po Valley (EN) 110 Gf 45.20N 10.00 E
Padang 142 Mj 0.57S 100.21 E
Padangpanjang 150 Dg 0.27S 100.25 E
Padangsidempuan 150 Cf 1.22N 99.16 E
Padangtikar, Pulau- 150 Eg 0.50S 109.30 E
Padany 114 He 63.19N 33.25 E
Padasjoki 116 Kc 61.21N 25.17 E
Padauiri, Rio- 202 Fd 0.15S 64.05W
Paddle Prairie 180 Fe 58.02N 117.50W
Paderborn 120 Ee 51.43N 8.46 E
Paderborn-Elsen 124 Kc 51.44N 8.41 E
Paderborn-Schloss Neuhaus 124 Kc 51.44N 8.42 E
Padeş, Vîrful- 130 Fd 45.40N 22.20 E
Padilla 202 Fg 19.19S 64.20W
Padina 130 Ke 44.50N 27.07 E
Padornelo, Portillo del- 126 Fb 42.03N 6.50W
Padova = Padua (EN) 128 Fe 45.25N 11.53 E
Padre, Morro do- 204 Ic 16.48S 47.35W
Padre Bernardo 204 Hb 15.21S 48.30W
Padre Island 182 Hf 27.00N 97.15W
Padrón 126 Db 42.44N 8.40W
Padua (EN) = Padova 128 Fe 45.25N 11.53 E
Paducah [Ky.-U.S.] 176 Kf 37.05N 88.36W
Paducah [Tx.-U.S.] 186 Fi 34.01N 100.18W
Padula 128 Jj 40.20N 15.39 E
Paea 221e Fc 17.41S 149.35W
Paegam-san 154 Id 40.35N 126.15 E
Paengnyong-Do 152 Ld 38.00N 124.40 E
Paeroa 216 Eg 37.23S 175.41 E
Paestum 128 Jj 40.25N 15.01 E
Paeu 219c Bb 11.22S 166.50 E
Pafuri 172 Ed 22.26S 31.20 E
Pag 128 Jf 44.27N 15.03 E
Pag 128 If 44.30N 15.00 E
Pagadian 150 He 7.49N 123.25 E
Pagai, Kepulauan-=Pagai Islands (EN) 140 Lj 2.45S 100.00 E
Pagai Selatan 150 Dg 3.00S 100.20 E
Pagai Utara 150 Cg 2.42S 100.07 E
Pagan Island 208 Fc 18.07N 145.46 E
Pagasitikós Kólpos 130 Fj 39.15N 23.00 E
Pagatan 150 Gg 3.36S 115.56 E
Pagat Point 220c Bb 13.30N 144.53 E
Page 188 Jh 36.57N 111.27W
Pagėgiai 116 Ii 55.09N 21.54 E
Paget, Mount- 222 Ad 54.26S 36.33W
Pagi Islands (EN)=Pagai, Kepulauan- 140 Lj 2.45S 100.00 E
Paglia 128 Gh 42.42N 12.11 E
Pago Bay 220c Bb 13.25N 144.48 E
Pagoda Point 140 Lh 15.57N 94.15 E
Pāgodār 146 Qh 28.10N 57.22 E
Pago Pago 210 Jf 14.16S 170.42W
Pago Pago Harbor 221c Cb 14.17S 170.40W
Pago Redondo 204 Ci 29.35S 59.13W
Pagosa Springs 186 Ch 37.16N 107.01W
Pagoua Bay 197g Ba 15.32N 61.17W
Pagwa River 186 Na 50.01N 85.10W
Pahači 138 Ld 60.30N 169.00 E
Pahala 221a Fd 19.12N 155.29W
Pahang [2] 150 Df 3.30N 102.45 E
Pāhara, Laguna- 194 Ff 14.18N 83.15W
Pahiatua 218 Fd 40.27S 175.50 E
Pahkaing Bum 140 Lg 26.00N 95.30 E
Pahoa 221a Gd 19.30N 154.57W
Pahokee 184 Gl 26.49N 80.40W
Pahtakor 135 Fd 40.16N 67.55 E
Pahute Mesa 188 Gh 37.20N 116.40W
Paia 219b Dc 16.35S 168.12 E
Paide/Pajde 114 Fg 58.57N 25.35 E
Paignton, Torbay- 118 Jk 50.28N 3.30W
Päijänne 110 Ic 61.35N 25.30 E
Páikon Óros 130 Fi 40.56N 22.21 E
Paila 192 He 25.39N 102.07W
Pailín 148 Kf 12.51N 102.36 E
Pailitas 194 Ki 8.58N 73.38W
Pailolo Channel 221a Eb 21.05N 156.42W
Paimio/Pemar 116 Jd 60.27N 22.42 E
Paimionjoki 116 Jd 60.25N 22.40 E
Paimpol 122 Cf 48.46N 3.03W
Painan 150 Dg 1.21S 100.34 E
Paine, Mount- 222 Mg 86.46S 147.32W
Painel 204 Gh 27.55S 50.06W
Painesville 184 Ge 41.43N 81.15W
Painted Desert 182 Ed 36.00N 111.20W
Paintsville 184 Fg 37.49N 82.48W
Pais do Vinho 126 Ec 41.15N 7.55W
Paisley 118 If 55.50N 4.26W
Paita 219b Cf 22.08S 166.22 E
Paita 202 Be 5.06S 81.07W
Paiva 126 Dc 41.04N 8.16W
Paj 114 If 61.43N 34.28 E
Pajala 114 Fc 67.12N 23.22 E
Pajares, Puerto de- 126 Ga 43.00N 5.46W
Pajaros, Farallon de- 208 Fb 20.32N 144.54 E
Pajaros, Punta- 192 Ph 19.36N 87.25W
Pajaros Point 197a Db 18.31N 64.18W
Pajatén 202 Ce 7.29S 77.22W
Pajde/Paide 114 Fg 58.57N 25.35 E
Pajęczno 120 Oe 51.09N 19.00 E
Pajer, gora- 136 Gb 66.40N 64.20 E
Paj-Hoj 110 Mb 69.00N 62.30 E
Pajule 170 Fb 2.58N 32.56 E
Pakanbaru 142 Mi 0.32N 101.27 E
Pakaraima Mountains 202 Fb 4.05N 61.30W
Pakharan 148 Ec 26.55N 71.55 E
Pakch'on 154 He 39.44N 125.35 E
Pakhna 146 Ee 34.46N 32.48 E
Pákhnes 130 Hn 35.18N 24.02 E
Paki 166 Gc 11.30N 8.09 E
Pakima 170 Dc 3.21S 24.06 E
Pakin Atoll 208 Gd 7.04N 157.48 E
Pakistan 142 Ig 30.00N 70.00 E
Pakleni Otoci 128 Kg 43.10N 16.23 E
Pakokku 148 Jd 21.17N 95.06 E
Pakowki Lake 188 Jb 49.22N 110.57W
Pak Phanang 148 Kg 8.21N 100.12 E
Pakrac 128 Le 45.26N 17.12 E
Pakruois/Pakruojis 114 Fi 55.57N 23.50 E
Pakruojis/Pakruois 114 Fi 55.57N 23.50 E
Paks 120 Oj 46.38N 18.52 E
Paktiā [3] 144 Kc 33.30N 69.30 E
Pakwach 170 Fb 2.28N 31.30 E
Pakxé 142 Mh 15.07N 105.47 E
Pakxèng 148 Kd 20.10N 102.40 E
Pala 168 Ad 9.22N 14.54 E
Palacca Point 194 Kc 21.15N 73.26W
Palacios [Arg.] 204 Bj 30.43S 61.37W
Palacios [Tx.-U.S.] 186 Hl 28.42N 96.13W
Palafrugell 126 Pc 41.55N 3.10 E
Palagruža 128 Kh 42.24N 16.15 E
Palaiokastritsa 130 Cj 39.40N 19.41 E
Palaiokhóra 130 Gn 35.14N 23.41 E
Palais, Le- 122 Cg 47.21N 3.09W
Palaiseau 124 Ef 48.43N 2.15 E
Palamás 130 Fj 39.28N 22.05 E
Palamós 126 Pc 41.51N 3.08 E
Palamuse/Palamuze 116 Lf 58.39N 26.35 E
Palamut 130 Kk 38.59N 27.41 E
Palamuze/Palamuse 116 Lf 58.39N 26.35 E
Palana 142 Rd 59.07N 159.58 E
Palancia / Palància 126 Le 39.40N 0.12W
Palància / Palancia 126 Le 39.40N 0.12W
Palanga 136 Cd 55.57N 21.05 E
Palangkaraya 150 Fg 2.16S 113.56 E
Pālanpur 148 Ed 24.10N 72.26 E
Palaoa Point 221a Ec 20.44N 156.58W
Palapye 160 Jk 22.33S 27.08 E
Palasa 150 Hf 0.29N 120.24 E
Palatka [Fl.-U.S.] 182 Kf 29.39N 81.38W
Palatka [R.S.F.S.R.] 138 Kd 60.05N 151.00 E
Palau (EN) = Belau 128 Di 41.11N 9.23 E
Palau [5] 210 Ed 7.30N 134.30 E
Palau Islands 208 Ed 7.30N 134.30 E
Palauli 221c Aa 13.44S 172.16W
Palauli Bay 221c Aa 13.47S 172.14W
Palau Trench (EN) 214 Af 6.30N 134.30 E
Palavas-les-Flots 122 Jk 43.32N 3.56 E
Palaw 148 Jf 12.58N 98.39 E
Palawan 140 Ni 9.30N 118.30 E
Palawan Passage 150 Gd 10.00N 118.00 E
Palayan 150 Hc 15.33N 121.06 E
Pālayankottai 148 Fg 8.43N 77.44
Palazzo, Punta- 122a Aa 42.22N 8.33
Palazzolo Acreide 128 Im 37.04N 14.54
Palazzolo sull'Oglio 128 De 45.36N 9.53

Index Symbols

- [1] Independent Nation
- [2] State, Region
- [3] District, County
- [4] Municipality
- [5] Colony, Dependency
- Continent
- Physical Region
- Historical or Cultural Region
- Mount, Mountain
- Volcano
- Hill
- Mountains, Mountain Range
- Hills, Escarpment
- Plateau, Upland
- Pass, Gap
- Plain, Lowland
- Delta
- Salt Flat
- Valley, Canyon
- Crater, Cave
- Karst Features
- Depression
- Polder
- Desert, Dunes
- Forest, Woods
- Heath, Steppe
- Oasis
- Cape, Point
- Coast, Beach
- Cliff
- Peninsula
- Isthmus
- Sandbank
- Island
- Atoll
- Rock, Reef
- Islands, Archipelago
- Rocks, Reefs
- Coral Reef
- Well, Spring
- Geyser
- River, Stream
- Waterfall, Rapids
- River Mouth, Estuary
- Lake
- Salt Lake
- Intermittent Lake
- Reservoir
- Swamp, Pond
- Canal
- Glacier
- Ice Shelf, Pack Ice
- Ocean
- Sea
- Gulf, Bay
- Strait, Fjord
- Lagoon
- Bank
- Seamount
- Tablemount
- Ridge
- Shelf
- Basin
- Escarpment, Sea Scarp
- Fracture
- Trench, Abyss
- National Park, Reserve
- Point of Interest
- Recreation Site
- Cave, Cavern
- Historic Site
- Ruins
- Wall, Walls
- Church, Abbey
- Temple
- Scientific Station
- Railway station
- Airport
- Port
- Military installa
- Lighthouse
- Mine
- Tunnel
- Dam, Bridge

Index Symbols

■ Independent Nation ▣ Historical or Cultural Region ⤫ Pass, Gap ▭ Depression ▭ Coast, Beach ▭ Rock, Reef 〰 Waterfall, Rapids ▭ Canal ▭ Lagoon ▭ Escarpment, Sea Scarp ▭ Historic Site ✈ Airport
▣ State, Region ▲ Mount, Mountain ▭ Plain, Lowland ▭ Polder ▭ Cliff ▭ Islands, Archipelago 〰 River Mouth, Estuary ▭ Glacier ▭ Bank ▭ Fracture ▭ Ruins ▭ Wall, Walls ▭ For:
▣ District, County ▲ Volcano ▭ Delta ▭ Salt Flat ▭ Peninsula ▭ Rocks, Reef ▭ Lake ▭ Ice Shelf, Pack Ice ▭ Seamount ▭ Trench, Abyss ▭ Church, Abbey ▭ Military installation
▣ Municipality ▲ Hill ▭ Forest, Woods ▭ Isthmus ▭ Coral Reef ▭ Salt Lake ▭ Ocean ▭ Tablemount ▭ National Park, Reserve ▭ Temple ▭ Lighthouse
▣ Colony, Dependency ▲ Mountains, Mountain Range ▭ Valley, Canyon ▭ Heath, Steppe ▭ Sandbank ▭ Well, Spring ▭ Intermittent Lake ▭ Sea ▭ Ridge ▭ Point of Interest ▭ Scientific Station ▭ Mine
▣ Continent ▲ Hills, Escarpment ▭ Crater, Cave ▭ Oasis ▭ Island ▭ Geyser ▭ Reservoir ▭ Gulf, Bay ▭ Shelf ▭ Recreation Site ▭ Railway station ▭ Tunnel
▣ Physical Region ▭ Plateau, Upland ▭ Karst Features ▭ Cape, Point ▭ Atoll ▭ River, Stream ▭ Swamp, Pond ▭ Strait, Fjord ▭ Basin ▭ Cave, Cavern ▭ Dam, Bridge

Paternò 128 Jm 37.34N 15.54 E
Paterson 182 Mc 40.55N 74.10W
Paterson Inlet 218 Bg 46.55S 168.00 E
Paterson Range 212 Ed 21.45S 122.05 E
Pathānkot 148 Fb 32.17N 75.39 E
Pathein 142 Lh 16.47N 94.44 E
Pathfinder Reservoir 188 Le 42.30N 106.50W
Pathfinder Seamount (EN) 178 Kf 50.55N 143.15W
Pathiu 148 Jf 10.41N 99.20 E
Patía, Río- 202 Cc 2.13N 78.40W
Patiāla 148 Fb 30.19N 76.24 E
Patiño, Estero- 204 Cg 24.05S 59.55W
Patio 221e Db 16.35S 151.29W
Pati Point 220c Ba 13.36N 144.57 E
Pătîrlagele 130 Jd 45.19N 26.21 E
Pativilca 202 Cf 10.42S 77.47W
Pátmos 130 Jl 37.19N 26.34 E
Pátmos 130 Jl 37.20N 26.33 E
Patna 142 Kg 25.36N 85.07 E
Patnos 146 Jc 39.14N 42.52 E
Pato Branco 206 Jc 26.13S 52.40W
Patom Plateau (EN) = Patomskoje nagorje 138 Ge 59.00N 115.30 E
Patomskoje nagorje = Patom Plateau (EN) 138 Ge 59.00N 115.30 E
Patos 200 Mf 7.01S 37.16W
Patos, Isla de- 196 Fg 10.38N 61.52W
Patos, Lagoa dos- 198 Ki 31.06S 51.15W
Patos, Laguna de los- 204 Aj 30.25S 62.15W
Patos, Ribeirão dos- 204 Gd 18.58S 50.30W
Patos, Rio dos- [Braz.] 204 Da 13.33S 56.29W
Patos, Rio dos- [Braz.] 204 Hb 14.59S 48.46W
Patos de Minas 200 Lg 18.35S 46.32W
Patosi 130 Ci 40.38N 19.39 E
Patquía 206 Gd 30.03S 66.53W
Pátrai 112 Ih 38.15N 21.44 E
Patrai, Gulf of- (EN) = Patraïkós Kólpos 130 Ek 38.15N 21.30 E
Patraïkós Kólpos = Patrai, Kulf of- (EN) 130 Ek 38.15N 21.30 E
Patricio Lynch, Isla- 206 Eg 48.36S 75.26W
Patricios 204 Bl 35.27S 60.42W
Patrocinio 202 Ig 18.57S 46.59W
Patta Island 158 Li 2.07S 41.03 E
Pattani 148 Kg 6.51N 101.16 E
Patteson, Passage- 219b Db 15.26S 168.09 E
Patti 128 Il 38.08N 14.58 E
Patti, Golfo di- 128 Jl 38.10N 15.05 E
Patton Seamount (EN) 174 Dd 54.40N 150.30W
Pattullo, Mount - 180 Ee 56.14N 129.39W
Patu 202 Ke 6.06S 37.38W
Patuākhāli 148 Id 22.16N 90.18 E
Patuca, Punta- 194 Ef 15.51N 84.18W
Patuca, Río- 190 He 15.50N 84.18W
Pătulele 130 Fe 44.21N 22.47 E
Patutahi 218 Gc 38.37S 177.53 E
Patuxent Range 222 Qg 84.43S 64.30W
Pátzcuaro 192 Ih 19.31N 101.36W
Pau 122 Fk 43.18N 0.22W
Pau, Gave de- 122 Ek 43.33N 1.12W
Paucartambo 202 Df 13.18S 71.40W
Paucerne, Río- 204 Ba 13.34S 61.14W
Pau dos Ferros 202 Ke 6.07S 38.10W
Pauillac 122 Fi 45.12N 0.45W
Pauini 202 Ee 7.40S 66.58W
Pauini, Rio- 202 Ee 7.47S 67.15W
Pauksa Taung 148 Ie 19.55N 94.18 E
Paulatuk 176 Gc 69.23N 124.00W
Paulaya, Río- 194 Ef 15.51N 85.06W
Paulding Bay 222 Ie 66.35S 123.00 E
Paulina Peak 188 Ee 43.41N 121.15W
Păuliş 130 Ec 46.07N 21.35 E
Paulistana 202 Je 8.09S 41.09W
Paulo Afonso 200 Mf 9.21S 38.14W
Paulo Afonso, Cachoeira de- 198 Mf 9.24S 38.12W
Pauls Valley 186 Hi 34.44N 97.13W
Paungde 148 Je 18.29N 95.30 E
Pavant Range 188 Ig 39.00N 112.15W
Pāveh 146 Le 35.03N 46.22 E
Pavia 128 De 45.10N 9.10 E
Pavilly 124 Ce 49.34N 0.58 E
Pavilosta/Pāvilosta 114 Eh 56.55N 21.13 E
Pāvilosta/Pavilosta 114 Eh 56.55N 21.13 E
Pavlikeni 130 If 43.14N 25.18 E
Pavlodar 142 Jd 52.18N 76.57 E
Pavlodarskaja oblast 136 He 52.00N 76.30 E
Pavlof Islands 178 Ge 55.15N 161.20W
Pavlof Volcano 178 Ge 55.24N 161.55W
Pavlograd 132 Ie 48.32N 35.53 E
Pavlovka 134 Hi 55.25N 56.33 E
Pavlovo 136 Ed 55.58N 43.04 E
Pavlov Seamount (EN) 138 Lf 50.40N 162.00 E
Pavlovsk 132 Ld 50.27N 40.08 E
Pavlovskaja 136 Df 46.06N 39.48 E
Pavullo nel Frignano 128 Ef 44.20N 10.50 E
Pavuvu 219a Dc 9.04S 159.08 E
Pawa 219a Ed 10.15S 161.44 E
Pawhuska 186 Hh 36.40N 96.20W
Pawnee 186 Hh 36.20N 96.48W
Pawnee River 186 Gg 38.10N 99.06W
Pawtucket 184 Le 41.53N 71.23W
Paximádhia, Nisídhes- 130 Ho 35.00N 24.35 E
Paxoí 130 Dj 39.12N 20.10 E
Paxson 178 Jd 63.02N 145.30W
Payakumbuk 150 Dg 0.14S 100.38 E
Payas, Cerro- 194 Ef 15.50N 85.00W
Payerne 128 Ad 46.49N 6.58 E
Payette 182 Dc 44.05N 116.56W
Payette 188 Gd 44.05N 116.57W
Payne, Baie- 180 Ke 59.55N 69.35W
Payne, Lac- 180 Ke 59.30N 74.00W
Paysandú 200 Ki 32.19S 58.05W
Paysandú 204 Dk 32.00S 57.15W
Pays de Léon 122 Bf 48.28N 4.30W
Pays d'Othe 122 Jf 48.06N 3.37 E
Payson [Az.-U.S.] 188 Ji 34.14N 111.20W
Payson [Ut.-U.S.] 188 Jf 40.03N 111.44W
Payzawat/Jiashi 152 Cd 39.29N 76.39 E
Pāzanān 146 Mg 30.35N 49.59 E
Pazar 146 Ib 41.11N 40.53 E
Pazarbası Burun 146 Db 41.13N 30.17 E
Pazarcık 146 Gd 37.31N 37.19 E
Pazardžik 130 Hg 42.12N 24.20 E
Pazardžik 130 Hg 42.12N 24.20 E
Pazarköy 130 Kj 39.51N 27.24 E
Pazaryeri 146 Cc 40.00N 29.54 E
Pazin 128 He 45.14N 13.56 E
Pčinja 130 Eh 41.49N 21.40 E
Pea 221b Ac 21.11S 175.14W
Peabirú 204 Ff 23.54S 52.20W
Peace Point 180 Ge 59.12N 112.33W
Peace River 176 Hd 56.14N 117.17W
Peace River [Can.] 174 Hd 56.14N 117.17W
Peace River [Fl.-U.S.] 184 Fl 26.55N 82.05W
Peachland 188 Fb 49.46N 119.44W
Peach Springs 188 Ii 35.32N 113.25W
Peacock Hills 180 Gc 66.05N 110.00W
Peak District 118 Lh 53.17N 1.45W
Peake Creek 212 He 28.05S 136.07 E
Peaked Mountain 184 Mb 46.34N 68.49W
Peale, Mount- 182 Fd 38.26N 109.14W
Pearl 186 Lb 48.42N 88.44W
Pearland 186 Il 29.34N 95.17W
Pearl and Hermes Reef 208 Jb 27.55N 175.45W
Pearl City 221a Db 21.23N 157.58W
Pearl Harbor 221a Cb 21.20N 158.00W
Pearl River 182 Je 30.11N 89.32W
Pearsall 186 Gl 28.53N 99.06W
Pearsoll Peak 188 De 42.18N 123.50W
Peary Channel 180 Ha 79.25N 101.00W
Peary Land 224 Me 82.40N 30.00W
Pease River 186 Gi 34.12N 99.07W
Pebane 172 Fc 17.14S 38.10 E
Pebas 202 Dd 3.20S 71.49W
Peć 130 Dg 42.39N 20.18 E
Peca 128 Id 46.29N 14.48 E
Peças, Ilha das- 204 Hg 25.26S 48.19W
Pecatonica River 186 Le 42.29N 89.03W
Pečenežskoje vodohranilišče 132 Jd 50.05N 36.50 E
Pečenga 112 Jb 69.33N 31.07 E
Pečenga 114 Hb 69.39N 31.27 E
Pechea 130 Kd 45.38N 27.48 E
Pechora (EN)=Pečora 112 Lb 65.10N 57.11 E
Pechora (EN)=Pečora 110 Lb 68.13N 54.10 E
Pechora Bay (EN) = Pečorskaja guba 136 Fb 68.40N 54.45 E
Pechora Sea (EN) = Pečorskoje more 136 Fb 69.45N 54.30 E
Pecica 130 Ec 46.10N 21.04 E
Peckelsheim, Willebadessen- 124 Lc 51.36N 9.08 E
Pečora=Pechora (EN) 112 Lb 65.10N 57.11 E
Pečora=Pechora (EN) 110 Lb 68.13N 54.10 E
Pecora, Capo- 128 Ck 39.27N 8.23 E
Pečorskaja guba = Pechora Bay (EN) 136 Fb 68.40N 54.45 E
Pečorskoje more = Pechora Sea (EN) 136 Fb 69.45N 54.30 E
Pečory 114 Gh 57.49N 27.38 E
Pecos 182 Ge 31.25N 103.30W
Pecos 174 Ig 29.42N 101.22W
Pecos Plain 182 Ge 33.20N 104.30W
Pécs 112 Hf 46.05N 18.14 E
Pécs 120 Oj 46.06N 18.15 E
Pedasí 194 Gj 7.32N 80.02W
Pedder, Lake- 212 Jh 43.00S 146.15 E
Peddie 172 Df 33.14S 27.07 E
Pededze 116 Lh 56.53N 27.01 E
Pedernales [Dom.Rep.] 194 Ld 18.02N 71.45W
Pedernales [Ven.] 196 Eh 9.58N 62.16W
Pedernales, Salar de- 206 Gc 26.15S 69.10W
Pedja jõgi 116 Lf 58.20N 26.10 E
Pêdo Shankou 152 Df 29.12N 83.26 E
Pedra Azul 202 Jg 16.01S 41.16W
Pedra Branca 202 Ke 5.27S 39.43W
Pedra do Sino 204 Kf 22.27S 43.03W
Pedra Lume 162 Cf 16.46N 22.54W
Pedras, Rio das- 204 Ia 13.30S 47.09W
Pedras Altas, Coxilha- 204 Fj 31.45S 53.35W
Pedregal 202 Da 11.01N 70.08W
Pedreiras 202 Jd 4.34S 44.39W
Pedriceña 192 He 25.06N 103.47W
Pedrizas, Puerto de las- 126 Hh 36.55N 4.30W
Pedro Afonso 202 Ie 8.59S 48.11W
Pedro Bank (EN) 194 He 17.00N 78.30W
Pedro Betancourt 194 Gb 22.44N 81.17W
Pedro Cays 190 Ie 17.00N 77.50W
Pedro Gomes 204 Ed 18.04S 54.32W
Pedro Gonzáles, Isla- 194 Hi 8.24N 79.06W
Pedro II 202 Jd 4.25S 41.28W
Pedro II, Ilha- 202 Ec 1.10N 66.44W
Pedro Juan Caballero 206 Ib 22.34S 55.37W
Pedro Leopoldo 204 Jd 19.38S 44.03W
Pedro Luro 206 He 39.29S 62.41W
Pedro Lustoza 204 Gg 25.49S 51.51W
Pedro Montoya 192 Jg 21.38N 99.49W
Pedro Osorio 206 Jd 31.51S 52.45W
Pedro R. Fernández 204 Ci 28.45S 58.39W
Pedro Severo 204 Ec 17.40S 54.02W
Pedroso, Sierra del- 126 Gf 38.35N 5.35W
Peebles 118 Jf 55.39N 3.12W
Pee Dee River 174 Lf 33.21N 79.16W
Peekskill 184 Ke 41.18N 73.56W
Peel 118 Ig 54.13N 4.40W
Peel 122 Lc 51.25N 5.50 E
Peel 174 Fc 67.37N 134.40W
Peel Sound 180 Hb 73.00N 96.00W
Peene 120 Jb 54.09N 13.46 E
Peer 124 Hc 51.08N 5.28 E
Peera Peera Poolanna Lake 212 He 26.30S 138.00 E
Peetz 186 Ef 40.58N 103.07W
Pegasus, Port- 218 Bg 47.10S 167.40 E
Pegasus Bay 216 Dh 43.20S 172.50 E
Pegnitz 120 Hg 49.45N 11.33 E
Pegnitz 120 Hg 49.29N 11.00 E
Pego 126 Lf 38.51N 0.07W
Pegtymel 138 Mc 69.47N 174.00 E
Pegu → Bago 142 Lh 17.30N 96.30 E
Pegu Yoma 140 Lh 19.00N 95.50 E
Pegwell Bay 124 Dc 51.18N 1.23 E
Pehčevo 130 Fh 41.46N 22.54 E
Pehlivanköy 130 Jh 41.21N 26.55 E
Pehuajó 206 He 35.48S 61.53W
Pei-ching Shih → Beijing Shi 152 Kc 40.15N 116.30 E
Peine 120 Gd 52.19N 10.14 E
Peipsi järv=Peipus, Lake- (EN) 110 Id 58.45N 27.30 E
Peipus, Lake- (EN) = Čudskoje ozero 110 Id 58.45N 27.30 E
Peipus, Lake- (EN)=Peipsi järv 110 Id 58.45N 27.30 E
Peixe 202 If 12.03S 48.32W
Peixe, Lagoa do- 204 Gj 31.18S 51.00W
Peixe, Rio do- [Braz.] 204 Gh 27.27S 51.54W
Peixe, Rio do- [Braz.] 204 Ge 21.31S 51.58W
Peixe, Rio do- [Braz.] 204 Gb 14.06S 50.51W
Peixe, Rio do- [Braz.] 204 Fc 16.32S 52.38W
Peixe, Rio do- [Braz.] 204 Hc 17.37S 48.29W
Peixe de Couro, Rio- 204 Ec 17.21S 55.29W
Peixes, Rio dos- 204 Hb 15.10S 49.30W
Peixian (Yunhe) 154 Dg 34.44N 116.56 E
Peixoto, Represa de- 202 Ih 20.30S 46.30W
Pejantan, Pulau- 150 Ef 0.07N 107.14 E
Pëjde/Pöide 116 Jf 58.30N 22.50 E
Pek 130 Ee 44.46N 21.33 E
Pekalongan 150 Eh 6.53S 109.40 E
Pekan 150 Df 3.30N 103.25 E
Pekin 182 Jc 40.35N 89.40W
Peking (EN) = Beijing 142 Nf 39.55N 116.23 E
Pekulnej, hrebet- 138 Mc 66.30N 176.00 E
Pelabuhanratu 150 Eh 6.59S 106.33 E
Pelagie, Isole- 110 Hh 35.40N 12.40 E
Pelagonija 130 Eh 41.05N 21.30 E
Pélagos 130 Hj 39.20N 24.05 E
Pelaihari 150 Fg 3.48S 114.45 E
Pelat, Mont- 122 Mj 44.16N 6.42 E
Pelawanbesar 150 Gf 1.10N 117.54 E
Pélé 219b Dc 17.30S 168.24 E
Peleaga, Vîrful- 130 Fd 45.22N 22.53 E
Peleduj 138 Ge 59.40N 112.38 E
Pelée, Montagne- 190 Le 14.48N 61.10W
Pelee, Point- 184 Fe 41.54N 82.30W
Pelee Island 184 Fe 41.46N 82.39W
Peleliu Island 208 Ed 7.01N 134.15 E
Peleng, Pulau- 150 Hg 1.20S 123.10 E
Pelhřimov 120 Lg 49.26N 15.13 E
Pelican Lake 186 Gb 49.20N 99.35W
Pelicanpunt 172 Ad 22.54S 14.26 E
Peligre, Lac de- 194 Ld 18.52N 71.56W
Pelinaion Óros 130 Ik 38.32N 26.00 E
Pelješac 128 Lh 42.55N 17.25 E
Pelkosenniemi 114 Gc 67.07N 27.30 E
Pella 186 Jf 41.25N 92.55W
Pélla 130 Fi 40.46N 22.34 E
Pellegrini 206 He 36.16S 63.09W
Pellice 128 Bf 44.50N 7.38 E
Pellinge/Pellinki 116 Kd 60.15N 25.50 E
Pellinki/Pellinge 116 Kd 60.15N 25.50 E
Pello 114 Fc 66.47N 24.01 E
Pellworm 120 Eb 54.30N 8.40 E
Pelly 174 Fc 62.47N 137.19W
Pelly Bay 176 Kc 68.52N 89.55W
Pelly Bay 180 Ic 68.50N 90.10W
Pelly Crossing 180 Dd 62.50N 136.35W
Pelly Mountains 180 Ed 61.30N 132.00W
Peloncillo Mountains 188 Kj 32.15N 109.10W
Pelón de Nado, Cerro- 192 Jg 20.05N 99.55W
Peloponnesus (EN)= Pelopónnisos 110 Ih 37.40N 22.00 E
Peloponnesus (EN) = Pelopónnisos 130 El 37.40N 22.00 E
Pelopónnisos 130 El 37.40N 22.00 E
Pelopónnisos= Peloponnesus (EN) 110 Ih 37.40N 22.00 E
Pelopónnisos = Peloponnesus (EN) 130 El 37.40N 22.00 E
Peloritani 128 Jl 38.05N 15.20 E
Peloro o Punta dl Faro, Capo- 128 Jl 38.16N 15.39 E
Pelotas 200 Ki 31.46S 52.20W
Pelotas, Rio- 206 Jc 27.28S 51.55W
Pelplin 120 Oc 53.56N 18.42 E
Pelvoux, Massif du- 110 Gg 44.55N 6.20 E
Pelym 136 Gd 59.40N 63.05 E
Pelymski Tuman, ozero- 134 Kf 60.05N 63.05 E
Pemalang 150 Eh 6.54S 109.22 E
Pemar/Paimio 116 Jd 60.27N 22.42 E
Pematangsiantar 142 Li 2.57N 99.03 E
Pemba 170 Hd 5.02S 40.00 E
Pemba [Moz.] 160 Lj 12.57S 40.30 E
Pemba [Zam.] 170 Ef 16.31S 27.22 E
Pemba Channel 170 Gd 5.10S 39.20 E
Pemba Island 158 Ki 5.10S 39.48 E
Pemberton [Austl.] 212 Df 34.28S 116.01 E
Pemberton [B.C.-Can.] 188 Da 50.20N 122.48W
Pembina 182 Hb 48.58N 97.15W
Pembina 180 Gf 54.45N 114.17W
Pembina River 182 Hb 48.56N 97.15W
Pembroke [Ont.-Can.] 180 Jg 45.49N 77.07W
Pembroke [Wales-U.K.] 118 Ij 51.41N 4.55W
Pembuang 150 Fg 3.24S 112.33 E
Peña, Sierra de la- 126 Lb 42.31N 0.38W
Peña de Francia, Sierra de la- 126 Fd 40.35N 6.05W
Penafiel 126 Dc 41.12N 8.17W
Peñafiel 126 Hc 41.36N 4.07W
Peñagolosa/Penyagolosa 126 Ld 40.13N 0.21W
Peña Gorda, Cerro- 192 Gg 20.40N 104.55W
Peñalara 126 Id 40.51N 3.57W
Penalva 202 Id 3.18S 45.10W
Penamacor 126 Ed 40.10N 7.10W
Peña Nevada, Cerro- 174 Jg 23.46N 99.52W
Penápolis 204 Ge 21.24S 50.04W
Peñaranda de Bracamonte 126 Gd 40.54N 5.12W
Peñarroya 126 Ld 40.28N 0.43W
Peñarroya-Pueblonuevo 126 Gf 38.18N 5.16W
Peñas, Cabo de- 110 Fg 43.39N 5.51W
Penas, Golfo de- 198 Ij 47.22S 74.50W
Peñas, Punta- 202 Fa 10.44N 61.51W
Peñasco, Rio- 186 Dj 32.45N 104.19W
Pendé 168 Bd 8.07N 16.26 E
Pendembu [S.L.] 166 Cd 9.06N 12.12W
Pendembu [S.L.] 166 Cd 8.06N 10.42W
Pendik 130 Mi 40.53N 29.13 E
Pendjari 166 Fc 10.54N 0.51 E
Pendle Hill 118 Kh 53.52N 2.17W
Pendleton 176 He 45.40N 118.47W
Pendolo 150 Hg 2.05S 120.42 E
Pend Oreille Lake 182 Db 48.10N 116.11W
Pend Oreille River 182 Db 49.04N 117.37W
Pendžikent 136 Gh 39.29N 67.38 E
Peneda 126 Dc 41.58N 8.15W
Penedo 202 Kf 10.17S 36.36W
Penetanguishene 184 Hc 44.47N 79.55W
Penganga 148 Fe 19.53N 79.09 E
Pengcheng 152 Jd 36.25N 114.08 E
Penge 170 Dd 5.31S 24.37 E
Pengho Jiao 150 Fc 16.03N 112.35 E
Penghu Liehtao= Pescadores (EN) 152 Kg 23.30N 119.30 E
Penglai (Dengzhou) 152 Ld 37.44N 120.45 E
Pengshui 152 If 29.17N 108.13 E
Pengze 152 Kf 29.52N 116.34 E
Penha 204 Hh 26.46S 48.39W
Penhalonga 172 Ec 18.54S 32.40 E
Penibética, Cordillera- 126 Ig 37.00N 3.30W
Peniche 126 Ce 39.21N 9.23W
Penicuik 118 Jf 55.50N 3.14W
Penida, Nusa- 150 Gh 8.44S 115.32 E
Peninsula Ibérica=Iberian Peninsula (EN) 110 Fg 40.00N 4.00W
Peníscola / Peñíscola 126 Md 40.21N 0.25 E
Peñíscola / Peníscola 126 Md 40.21N 0.25 E
Penitente, Serra do- 202 Ie 8.45S 46.20W
Pénjamo 192 Ig 20.26N 101.44W
Penju, Kepulauan- 150 Ih 5.22S 127.46 E
Penmarch, Pointe de- 122 Bg 47.48N 4.22W
Perne 128 Hh 42.27N 13.55 E
Penne, Punta- 128 Lj 40.41N 17.56 E
Pennell Coast 222 Kf 71.00S 167.00 E
Penner 140 Kh 14.35N 80.10 E
Penn Hills 184 He 40.28N 79.53W
Pennines 110 Fe 54.10N 2.05W
Pennsylvania 182 Lc 40.45N 77.30W
Penn Yan 184 Id 42.41N 77.03W
Penny Ice Cap 180 Kc 67.00N 65.10W
Penny Strait 180 Ha 76.35N 97.10W
Peno 114 Hh 56.57N 32.45 E
Penobscot Bay 184 Mc 44.15N 68.52W
Penobscot River 182 Nc 44.30N 68.50W
Penola 212 Ig 37.23S 140.50 E
Peñón del Rosario, Cerro- 192 Jh 19.40N 98.12W
Penong 210 Eh 31.55S 133.01 E
Penonomé 190 Hg 8.31N 80.22W
Pénot, Mont- 219b Cc 16.20S 167.31 E
Penrhyn Atoll 208 Le 9.00S 158.00W
Penrith 118 Kg 54.40N 2.44W
Penrith, Sydney- 212 Kf 33.45S 150.42 E
Pensacola 176 Kf 30.25N 87.13W
Pensacola Mountains 222 Rg 83.45S 55.00W
Pensacola Seamount (EN) 208 Lc 18.17N 157.20W
Pensamiento 204 Bb 14.44S 61.35W
Pensiangan 150 Gf 4.33N 116.19 E
Pentecôte, Ile- 208 Hf 15.45S 168.10 E
Penticton 180 Fg 49.30N 119.35W
Pentland 212 Jd 20.32S 145.24 E
Pentland Firth 118 Jc 58.44N 3.13W
Pentland Hills 118 Jf 55.48N 3.23W
Penwith 118 Hk 50.13N 5.40W
Penyagolosa/Peñagolosa 126 Ld 40.13N 0.21W
Penza 112 Ke 53.13N 45.00 E
Penzance 112 Ff 50.07N 5.33W
Penzenskaja oblast 136 Ee 53.15N 44.40 E
Penzhina Bay (EN) = Penžinskaja guba 138 Ld 61.00N 163.00 E
Penžina 140 Sc 62.28N 165.18 E
Penžinskaja guba = Penzhina Bay (EN) 138 Ld 61.00N 163.00 E
Penžinski hrebet 138 Ld 62.15N 166.35 E
Peoples Creek 188 Kb 48.24N 108.19W
Peoria 176 Ke 40.42N 89.36W
Pepa 170 Ed 7.42S 29.47 E
Pepel 166 Cd 8.35N 13.03W
Peperiguaçu, Rio- 204 Fh 27.10S 53.50W
Peqini 130 Ch 41.03N 19.45 E
Pequena, Lagoa- 204 Fj 31.36S 52.04W
Pequiri, Rio- 202 Gg 17.23S 55.38W
Perabumulih 150 Dg 3.27S 104.15 E
Perak 150 Df 5.00N 101.00 E
Perälä 116 Ib 62.28N 21.36 E
Perales, Puerto de- 126 Fd 40.15N 6.41W
Pérama 130 Hn 35.22N 24.42 E
Peräseinäjoki 116 Jb 62.34N 23.04 E
Perche, Col de la- 122 Il 42.30N 2.06 E
Perche, Collines du- 122 Gf 48.25N 0.40 E
Percival Lakes 212 Ed 21.25S 125.00 E
Percy Islands 212 Kd 21.40S 150.15 E
Perdasdefogu 128 Dk 39.41N 9.26 E
Perdida, Sierra- 192 Hd 27.30N 103.30W
Perdido, Monte- 110 Gg 42.40N 0.05 E
Perdido, Rio- 204 Df 22.10S 57.33W
Perdizes 204 Id 19.21S 47.17W
Perečin 120 Sh 48.44N 22.29 E
Pereginskoje 132 De 48.49N 24.12 E
Pereira 202 Cc 4.48N 75.42W
Pereira Barreto 206 Jb 20.38S 51.07W
Perejaslav-Hmelnicki 132 Gd 50.04N 31.27 E
Perejil, Isla de- 126 Gi 35.55N 5.26W
Pereljub 132 Qd 51.52N 50.20 E
Peremennyj, Cape- 222 He 66.08S 105.30 E
Peremyšliany 120 Ug 49.38N 24.35 E
Perenjori 212 De 29.26S 116.17 E
Pereščepino 132 Ie 48.59N 35.22 E
Pereslavl-Zalesski 114 Jh 56.45N 38.55 E
Peretu 130 Ie 44.03N 25.05 E
Peretyčiha 138 Ig 47.10N 138.35 E
Perevolocki 132 Sd 51.51N 54.15 E
Pergamino 206 Hd 33.53S 60.35W
Pergamon 130 Kj 39.08N 27.13 E
Perge 146 Dd 37.00N 30.10 E
Pergine Valsugana 128 Fd 46.04N 11.14 E
Pergola 128 Gg 43.34N 12.50 E
Perham 186 Ic 46.36N 95.34W
Perho 114 Fe 63.13N 24.25 E
Periam 130 Dc 46.03N 20.52 E
Péribonca, Rivière- 180 Kg 48.44N 72.06W
Perico 206 Hb 24.23S 65.00W
Pericos 192 Fe 25.03N 107.42W
Périgord 122 Gi 45.00N 0.30 E
Perigoso, Canal- 202 Ic 0.05N 49.40W
Périgueux 122 Gi 45.11N 0.43 E
Perijá, Sierra de- 198 Ie 10.00N 73.00W
Peristerá 130 Gj 39.12N 23.59 E
Perito Moreno 200 Ij 46.36S 70.56W
Perkam, Tanjung-=Urville, Cape d'- (EN) 150 Kg 1.28S 137.54 E
Perković 128 Kg 43.41N 16.06 E
Perlas, Archipiélago de las- 190 Ig 8.25N 79.00W
Perlas, Cayos de- 194 Fg 12.28N 83.28W
Perlas, Laguna de- 194 Fg 12.30N 83.40W
Perlas, Punta de- 194 Fg 12.23N 83.30W
Perleberg 120 Hc 53.04N 11.52 E
Perlez 130 Dd 45.12N 20.23 E
Perlis 150 De 6.30N 100.15 E
Perm 112 Ld 58.00N 56.15 E
Përmeti 130 Di 40.14N 20.21 E
Permskaja oblast 136 Fd 59.00N 57.00 E
Pernambuco 202 Ke 8.30S 37.30W
Pernik 130 Gg 42.36N 23.02 E
Pernik 130 Fg 42.35N 22.50 E
Perniö/Bjärnå 114 Ff 60.12N 23.08 E
Péronne 122 Ie 49.56N 2.56 E
Perote 192 Kh 19.34N 97.14W
Perpignan 112 Gg 42.41N 2.53 E
Perro, Laguna del- 186 Di 34.40N 105.57W
Perros-Guirec 122 Cf 48.49N 3.27W
Perry [Fl.-U.S.] 184 Fj 30.07N 83.35W
Perry [Ga.-U.S.] 184 Fi 32.27N 83.44W
Perry [Ia.-U.S.] 186 If 41.50N 94.06W
Perry [Ok.-U.S.] 186 Hh 36.17N 97.17W
Perry Lake 186 Ig 39.20N 95.30W
Perryton 186 Fh 36.24N 100.48W
Perryville 178 He 55.54N 159.10W
Persan 124 Ee 49.09N 2.16 E
Perşani, Munţii- 130 Id 45.40N 25.15 E
Persberg 116 Fe 59.45N 14.15 E
Persembe 146 Gb 41.04N 37.46 E
Persepolis 146 Oh 29.57N 52.52 E
Perseverancia 202 Ff 14.44S 62.48W
Persian Gulf (EN)=Al-Khalīj al-'Arabī 140 Hg 27.00N 51.00 E
Persian Gulf (EN) = Fārs, Khalīj-e- 140 Hg 27.00N 51.00 E
Perstorp 116 Eh 56.08N 13.23 E
Pertek 146 Hc 38.50N 39.22 E
Perth [Austl.] 210 Ch 31.56S 115.50 E
Perth [Ont.-Can.] 184 Ic 44.54N 76.15W
Perth [Scot.-U.K.] 118 Je 56.24N 3.28W
Perth Amboy 184 Je 40.32N 74.17W
Perth-Andover 184 Nb 46.44N 67.42W
Perth-Armadale 212 Df 32.09S 116.00 E
Perth-Fremantle 212 Df 32.03S 115.45 E
Perth-Kalamunda 212 Df 31.57S 116.03 E
Perth-Mundaring 212 Df 31.54S 116.10 E
Perthus, Col de-/Portús, Coll del- 126 Ob 42.28N 2.51 E
Perthus, Col du- 126 Ob 42.28N 2.51 E
Pertuis 122 Lk 43.41N 5.30 E
Pertusato, Capo- 122a Bb 41.21N 9.11 E
Perú 200 Ig 10.00S 76.00W
Peru [Il.-U.S.] 186 Lf 41.20N 89.08W
Peru [In.-U.S.] 184 De 40.45N 86.04W
Perú, Altiplano del- 202 Df 15.00S 72.00W
Peruaçu, Rio- 204 Jb 15.11S 44.07W
Peru Basin (EN) 106 Mk 17.00S 90.00W
Peru-Chile Trench (EN) 106 Nl 20.00S 73.00W
Perugia 112 Hg 43.08N 12.22 E
Perugorria 204 Ci 29.20S 58.37W
Peruibe 204 Ig 24.19S 47.00W
Perušić 128 Jf 44.39N 15.22 E
Péruwelz 124 Fd 50.31N 3.35 E
Pervari 146 Jd 37.54N 42.36 E
Pervomajsk [R.S.F.S.R.] 136 Ee 54.52N 43.48 E
Pervomajsk [Ukr.-U.S.S.R.] 136 Df 48.03N 30.52 E
Pervomajsk [Ukr.-U.S.S.R.] 132 Ke 48.36N 38.32 E
Pervomajski [Bye.-U.S.S.R.] 120 Vc 53.52N 25.33 E
Pervomajski [Kaz.-U.S.S.R.] 136 Ie 50.15N 81.59 E
Pervomajski [R.S.F.S.R.] 136 Ec 64.26N 40.48 E
Pervomajski [R.S.F.S.R.] 132 Sd 51.34N 54.59 E
Pervomajski [R.S.F.S.R.] 132 Lc 53.18N 40.15 E
Pervomajski [R.S.F.S.R.] 134 Ji 54.52N 61.08 E
Pervomajski [Ukr.-U.S.S.R.] 132 Je 49.24N 36.15 E
Pervouralsk 136 Fd 57.00N 60.00 E
Pervy Kurilski proliv 138 Kf 50.50N 156.50 E
Perwez/Perwijs 124 Gd 50.37N 4.49 E
Perwijs/Perwez 124 Gd 50.37N 4.49 E
Pes 114 Ig 59.10N 35.18 E
Peša 134 Cc 66.50N 47.32
Pesaro 128 Gg 43.54N 12.55
Pescadores (EN)=Penghu Liehtao 152 Kg 23.30N 119.30
Pescadores, Punta- 192 Ef 23.45N 109.45

Index Symbols

- 1 Independent Nation
- 2 State, Region
- 3 District, County
- 4 Municipality
- 5 Colony, Dependency
- Continent
- Physical Region
- Historical or Cultural Region
- Mount, Mountain
- Volcano
- Hill
- Mountains, Mountain Range
- Hills, Escarpment
- Plateau, Upland
- Pass, Gap
- Plain, Lowland
- Delta
- Salt Flat
- Valley, Canyon
- Crater, Cave
- Karst Features
- Depression
- Polder
- Desert, Dunes
- Forest, Woods
- Heath, Steppe
- Oasis
- Cape, Point
- Coast, Beach
- Cliff
- Peninsula
- Isthmus
- Sandbank
- Island
- Atoll
- Rock, Reef
- Islands, Archipelago
- Rocks, Reefs
- Coral Reef
- Well, Spring
- Geyser
- River, Stream
- Waterfall, Rapids
- River Mouth, Estuary
- Lake
- Salt Lake
- Intermittent Lake
- Reservoir
- Swamp, Pond
- Canal
- Glacier
- Ice Shelf, Pack Ice
- Ocean
- Sea
- Gulf, Bay
- Strait, Fjord
- Lagoon
- Bank
- Seamount
- Tablemount
- Ridge
- Shelf
- Basin
- Escarpment, Sea Scarp
- Fracture
- Trench, Abyss
- National Park, Reserve
- Point of Interest
- Recreation Site
- Cave, Cavern
- Historic Site
- Ruins
- Wall, Walls
- Church, Abbey
- Temple
- Scientific Station
- Railway station
- Airport
- Port
- Military installa
- Lighthouse
- Mine
- Tunnel
- Dam, Bridge

Pesčany, mys-	132	Qh	43.10N	51.18 E
Pesčany, ostrov-	138	Gb	74.20N	115.55 E
Pescara	112	Hg	42.28N	14.13 E
Pescara	128	Ih	42.28N	14.13 E
Pescasseroli	128	Hi	41.48N	13.47 E
Peschici	128	Ki	41.57N	16.01 E
Pescia	128	Eg	43.54N	10.41 E
Pescocostanzo	128	Ii	41.53N	14.04 E
Peshāwar	142	Jf	34.01N	71.33 E
Peshkopia	130	Dh	41.41N	20.26 E
Pesio	128	Bf	44.28N	7.53 E
Peskovka	114	Mg	59.03N	52.22 E
Pesmes	122	Lg	47.17N	5.34 E
Pesočny	116	Nd	60.05N	30.20 E
Peso da Régua	126	Ec	41.10N	7.47W
Pesqueira	202	Ke	8.22S	36.42W
Pesqueria, Río-	192	Je	25.54N	99.11W
Pessac	122	Fj	44.48N	0.37W
Pest [2]	120	Pi	47.25N	19.20 E
Pešter	130	Df	43.05N	20.02 E
Peštera	130	Hg	42.02N	24.18 E
Pestovo	136	Dd	58.36N	35.47 E
Petacalco, Bahía de-	190	De	17.57N	102.05W
Petah Tiqwa	146	Ff	32.05N	34.53 E
Petäjävesi	116	Kb	62.15N	25.12 E
Petal	186	Lk	31.21N	89.17W
Petalioí	130	Hl	38.01N	24.17 E
Petalioi, Gulf of- (EN) = Petalión, Kólpos-	130	Hk	38.00N	24.05 E
Petalión, Kólpos- = Petalioi, Gulf of- (EN)	130	Hk	38.00N	24.05 E
Petaluma	188	Dg	38.14N	122.39W
Pétange/Petingen	124	He	49.33N	5.53 E
Petare	202	Ea	10.29N	66.49W
Petatlán	192	Ii	17.31N	101.16W
Petatlán, Río-	192	Fd	26.09N	107.45W
Petauke	170	Fe	14.15S	31.20 E
Petén [3]	194	Be	16.50N	90.00W
Petén	190	Fe	16.15N	89.50W
Petén Itzá, Lago-	194	Ce	16.59N	89.50W
Petenwell Lake	186	Ld	44.05N	89.45W
Peterborough [Austl.]	212	Hf	32.58S	138.50 E
Peterborough [Eng.-U.K.]	118	Mi	52.35N	0.15W
Peterborough [Ont.-Can.]	180	Jh	44.18N	78.19W
Peterhead	118	Ld	57.30N	1.46W
Peter I, Øy-	222	Pe	68.47S	90.35W
Peter Island	197a	Db	18.22N	64.35W
Peterlee	118	Lg	54.46N	1.19W
Petermann Gletscher	179	Fb	80.45N	61.00W
Petermann Ranges	212	Fd	25.00S	129.45 E
Petermanns Bjerg	224	Md	73.10N	28.00W
Peter Pond Lake	180	Ge	55.55N	108.40W
Petersberg	120	He	51.35N	11.57 E
Petersburg [Ak.-U.S.]	178	Me	56.49N	132.57W
Petersburg [In.-U.S.]	184	Df	38.30N	87.16W
Petersburg [Va.-U.S.]	182	Ld	37.14N	77.24W
Petersburg [W.V.-U.S.]	184	Hf	39.01N	79.09W
Petersfield	118	Mk	51.00N	0.56W
Petershagen	124	Kb	52.23N	8.58 E
Peter the Great Bay (EN) = Petra Velikogo, zaliv-	140	Pe	42.40N	132.00 E
Petilia Policastro	128	Kk	39.07N	16.47 E
Petingen/Pétange	124	He	49.33N	5.53 E
Petit-Bourg	197e	Ab	16.12N	61.36W
Petit-Canal	197e	Bb	16.23N	61.29W
Petit Canouan	197n	Bb	12.47N	61.17W
Petit Cul-de-Sac Marin	197e	Ab	16.12N	61.33W
Petite Kabylie	126	Rh	36.35N	5.25 E
Petite Rivière de l'Artibonite	194	Kd	19.08N	72.29W
Petites Pyrénées	122	Hk	43.05N	1.10 E
Petite-Terre, Iles de la-	197e	Bb	16.10N	61.07W
Petit-Goâve	194	Kd	18.26N	72.52W
Petit Martinique Island	197p	Ca	12.32N	61.22W
Petit-Mécatina, Rivière du-	180	Lf	50.39N	59.25W
Petit Morin	122	Jf	48.56N	3.07 E
Petit Mustique Island	197n	Bb	12.51N	61.13W
Petit Nevis Island	197n	Bb	12.58N	61.15W
Petitot	180	Fd	60.14N	123.29W
Petit Saint-Bernard, Col du-	128	Ae	45.40N	6.55 E
Petit Saint Vincent Island	197n	Bb	12.33N	61.23W
Petit Savanne	197g	Bb	15.15N	61.17W
Petitsikapau Lake	180	Kf	54.40N	66.25W
Petkula	114	Gc	67.40N	26.41 E
Petlalcingo	192	Kh	18.05N	97.54W
Peto	190	Gd	20.08N	88.55W
Petorca	206	Fd	32.15S	71.00W
Petoskey	184	Ec	45.22N	84.57W
Petra	146	Fg	30.19N	35.29 E
Petralia Soprana	128	Im	37.47N	14.06 E
Petra Pervogo, hrebet-	135	He	39.00N	71.10 E
Petra Velikogo, zaliv- = Peter the Great Bay	140	Pe	42.40N	132.00 E
Petre, Point-	184	Id	43.50N	77.09W
Petre Bay	218	Je	43.55S	176.40W
Petrel	222	Re	63.28S	56.17W
Petrela	130	Ch	41.15N	19.51 E
Petrella Tifernina	128	Ii	41.41N	14.42 E
Petrič	130	Gh	41.24N	23.13 E
Pétrie, Récif-	216	Bc	18.30S	164.20 E
Petrikov	132	Fc	52.08N	28.31 E
Petrila	130	Gd	45.27N	23.25 E
Petrinja	128	Ke	45.27N	16.17 E
Petrodvorec	114	Gg	59.53N	29.50 E
Petrólea	202	Db	8.30N	72.35W
Petrolia	184	Fd	42.52N	82.09W
Petrolina	202	Je	9.24S	40.30W
Petrolina de Goiás	204	Hc	16.06S	49.20W
Petronanski prohod	130	Gf	43.08N	23.08 E
Petronell	128	Kb	48.07N	16.51 E
Petropavlovka	138	Ff	50.38N	105.19 E
Petropavlovsk	142	Id	54.54N	69.06 E
Petropavlovsk-Kamčatski	142	Rd	53.01N	158.39 E
Petrópolis	200	Lh	22.31S	43.10W
Petroşani	130	Gd	45.25N	23.22 E
Petrovac [Yugo.]	130	Bg	42.12N	18.57 E
Petrovac [Yugo.]	130	Ee	44.22N	21.25 E
Petrova Gora	128	Je	45.17N	15.47 E
Petrovaradin	130	Cd	45.15N	19.53 E
Petrovka	130	Nc	46.55N	30.40 E
Petrovsk	136	Ee	52.18N	45.23 E
Petrovski Jam	114	Ie	63.18N	35.15 E
Petrovsk-Zabajkalski	142	Md	51.17N	108.50 E
Petrov Val	132	Nd	50.10N	45.12 E
Petrozavodsk	112	Jc	61.47N	34.20 E
Petuhovo	136	Gd	55.06N	67.58 E
Petuški	114	Ji	55.59N	39.28 E
Petworth	124	Bd	50.59N	0.36W
Peuetsagoe, Gunung-	150	Cf	4.55N	96.20 E
Peumo	206	Fd	34.24S	71.10W
Peureulak	150	Cf	4.48N	97.53 E
Pevek	142	Tc	69.42N	170.17 E
Pevensey	124	Cd	50.48N	0.21 E
Pevensey Bay	124	Cd	50.48N	0.22 E
Peyia	146	Ee	34.53N	32.23 E
Peza	114	Kd	65.34N	44.33 E
Pézenas	122	Jk	43.27N	3.25 E
Pezinok	120	Nh	48.18N	17.16 E
Pfaffenhofen an der Ilm	120	Hh	48.32N	11.31 E
Pfaffenhoffen	124	Jf	48.51N	7.37 E
Pfalz	124	Je	49.20N	7.57 E
Pfalzel, Trier-	124	Ie	49.46N	6.41 E
Pfälzer Bergland	120	Dg	49.35N	7.30 E
Pfälzer Wald	120	Dg	49.15N	7.50 E
Pfarrkirchen	120	Ih	48.26N	12.52 E
Pfinz	124	Ke	49.11N	8.25 E
Pfinztal	124	Ke	49.02N	8.30 E
Pforzheim an der Enz	120	Eh	48.53N	8.42 E
Pfrimm	124	Ke	49.39N	8.22 E
Pfullendorf	120	Fi	47.55N	9.15 E
Pfunds	128	Ed	46.58N	10.33 E
Pfungstadt	124	Ke	49.48N	8.36 E
Pha-an	148	Je	16.53N	97.38 E
Phalaborwa	172	Ed	23.55S	31.13 E
Phalodi	148	Ec	27.08N	72.22 E
Phangan, Ko-	148	Jg	9.45N	100.00 E
Phangnga	148	Jg	8.28N	98.32 E
Phan Ly Cham	148	Lf	11.13N	108.31 E
Phanom	148	Jg	8.49N	98.50 E
Phan Rang	148	Lf	11.34N	108.59 E
Phan Thiet	148	Lf	10.56N	108.06 E
Pharr	186	Gm	26.12N	98.11W
Phatthalung	148	Kg	7.38N	100.04 E
Phayao	148	Ke	18.07N	100.11 E
Phenix City	182	Je	32.29N	85.01W
Phet Buri	148	Jf	13.06N	99.56 E
Phetchabun, Thiu Khao-	148	Ke	16.20N	100.55 E
Phichit	148	Ke	16.24N	100.21 E
Philadelphia [Ms.-U.S.]	186	Lj	32.46N	89.07W
Philadelphia [Pa.-U.S.]	176	Lf	39.57N	75.07W
Philae	164	Fe	23.35N	32.52 E
Philip	186	Fd	44.02N	101.40W
Philippeville	122	Kd	50.12N	4.33 E
Philippi	184	Gf	39.08N	80.03W
Philippi (EN) = Filippoi	130	Hh	41.02N	24.18 E
Philippi, Lake-	212	Hd	24.20S	139.00 E
Philippi Glacier	222	Ge	66.45S	88.20 E
Philippine Basin (EN)	106	Ih	17.00N	132.00 E
Philippine Islands (EN) = Pilipinas	140	Oh	13.00N	122.00 E
Philippines (EN) = Pilipinas [1]	142	Oh	13.00N	122.00 E
Philippine Sea (EN)	140	Oh	20.00N	130.00 E
Philippine Trench (EN)	106	Ii	9.00N	127.00 E
Philippsburg	124	Ke	49.14N	8.27 E
Philipsburg [Mt.-U.S.]	188	Ic	46.20N	113.08W
Philipsburg [Neth.Ant.]	196	Ec	18.01N	63.04W
Philip Smith Mountains	178	Jc	68.30N	148.00W
Philipstown	172	Cf	30.26S	24.29 E
Phillipsburg	186	Gg	39.45N	99.19W
Philpots	180	Jb	74.55N	80.00W
Phitsanulok	142	Mh	16.49N	100.15 E
Phnom Penh (EN) = Phnum Pénh	142	Mh	11.33N	104.55 E
Phnum Pénh = Phnom Penh (EN)	142	Mh	11.33N	104.55 E
Phoenix	176	Hf	33.27N	112.05W
Phoenix → Rawaki Atoll	208	Je	3.43S	170.43W
Phoenix Islands	208	Je	4.00S	172.00W
Phôngsali	148	Kd	21.41N	102.06 E
Phrae	148	Ke	18.07N	100.11 E
Phra Nakhom Si Ayutthaya	142	Mh	14.21N	100.33 E
Phrygia	130	Mk	38.30N	29.50 E
Phuket	142	Li	7.54N	98.24 E
Phuket, Ko-	140	Li	8.00N	98.20 E
Phulbani	148	Gd	20.28N	84.14 E
Phumĭ Mlu Prey	148	Lf	13.48N	105.16 E
Phumĭ Sâmraông	148	Kf	14.11N	103.31 E
Phu My	148	Lf	14.10N	109.03 E
Phuoc Binh	148	Lf	11.50N	106.58 E
Phu Quoc	148	Kf	10.13N	103.58 E
Phu Quoc, Dao-	148	Kf	10.12N	104.00 E
Phu Tho	148	Ld	21.24N	105.13 E
Piaanu Pass	220d	Ab	7.20N	151.26 E
Piacenza	128	De	45.01N	9.40 E
Piana degli Albanesi	128	Hm	37.59N	13.17 E
Piana Mwanga	170	Ed	7.40S	28.10 E
Piancó	202	Ke	7.12S	37.57W
Pianguan	152	Jd	39.28N	111.32 E
Pianosa [It.]	128	Eh	42.35N	10.05 E
Pianosa [It.]	128	Jh	42.15N	15.45 E
Piaseczno	120	Rd	52.05N	21.01 E
Piaski	120	Se	51.08N	22.51 E
Piątek	120	Pd	52.05N	19.28 E
Piatra	130	If	43.49N	25.10 E
Piatra Neamţ	130	Jc	46.55N	26.20 E
Piatra Olt	130	He	44.22N	24.16 E
Piauí [2]	202	Je	7.00S	43.00W
Piauí, Rio-	198	Lf	6.38S	42.42W
Piave	110	Hf	45.32N	12.44 E
Piaxtla, Punta-	192	Ff	23.38N	106.50W
Piaxtla, Río-	192	Ff	23.42N	106.49W
Piazza Armerina	128	Im	37.23N	14.22 E
Pibor	168	Ed	8.26N	33.13 E
Pibor Post	168	Ed	6.48N	33.08 E
Pica	206	Gb	20.30S	69.21W
Picardie = Picardy (EN)	122	Je	50.00N	3.30 E
Picardy (EN) = Picardie	122	Je	50.00N	3.30 E
Picayune	186	Lk	30.26N	89.41W
Piccolo San Bernardo, Colle del-	128	Ae	45.40N	6.55 E
Picentini, Monti-	128	Jj	40.45N	15.10 E
Pichanal	200	Jh	23.20S	64.15W
Pichilemu	206	Fd	34.23S	72.00W
Pichilingue	192	De	24.20N	110.20W
Pichna	120	Oe	51.50N	18.40 E
Pichones, Cayos-	194	Ff	15.45N	82.55W
Pichucalco	192	Mi	17.31N	93.04W
Pickering	118	Mg	54.14N	0.46W
Pickering, Vale of-	118	Mg	54.10N	0.45W
Pickle Lake	180	If	51.29N	90.10W
Pickwick Lake	184	Ch	34.55N	88.10W
Pico	158	Ee	38.28N	28.20W
Picos	200	Lf	7.05S	41.28W
Pico Truncado	206	Gg	46.48S	67.58W
Picquigny	122	Ie	49.57N	2.09 E
Picton	216	Dh	41.18S	174.00 E
Picton	206	Gi	55.04S	67.00W
Pictou	180	Lg	45.41N	62.43W
Picunda	132	Lh	43.12N	40.21 E
Pidurutalagala	140	Ki	7.00N	80.46 E
Piedecuesta	202	Db	6.59N	73.03W
Piedimonte Matese	128	Ii	41.20N	14.22 E
Piedmont	174	Kf	35.00N	81.00W
Piedmont [Al.-U.S.]	184	Ei	33.55N	85.37W
Piedmont [Mo.-U.S.]	186	Kh	37.09N	90.42W
Piedmont (EN) = Piemonte [2]	128	Be	45.00N	8.00 E
Piedra	126	Kc	41.19N	1.48W
Piedra, Monasterio de-	126	Kc	41.10N	1.50W
Piedrabuena	126	He	39.02N	4.10W
Piedrafita, Puerto de-	126	Fb	42.36N	6.57W
Piedrahíta	126	Gd	40.28N	5.19W
Piedras	202	Cd	3.38S	79.54W
Piedras, Punta-	206	Ie	35.25S	57.08W
Piedras, Río de las-	202	Ef	12.30S	69.14W
Piedras Negras	176	Ig	28.42N	100.31W
Piedras Negras	194	Be	17.12N	91.15W
Piedra Sola	206	Id	32.04S	56.21W
Piekary Śląskie	120	Of	50.24N	18.58 E
Pieksämäki	114	Ge	62.18N	27.08 E
Pielach	128	Jb	48.15N	15.22 E
Pielavesi	114	Ge	63.14N	26.45 E
Pielinen	110	Ic	63.15N	29.40 E
Piemonte = Piedmont (EN) [2]	128	Be	45.00N	8.00 E
Pieniężno	120	Qb	54.15N	20.08 E
Pieni Salpausselkä	116	Lc	61.10N	27.20 E
Piennes	124	He	49.19N	5.47 E
Pienza	128	Fg	43.04N	11.41 E
Pierce	188	Hc	46.29N	115.48W
Piéria Óri	130	Fi	40.12N	22.07 E
Pierre	176	Ie	44.22N	100.21W
Pierrefitte-sur-Aire	124	Hf	48.54N	5.20 E
Pierrefonds	124	Ee	49.21N	2.59 E
Pierrelatte	122	Kj	44.23N	4.42 E
Pieskehaure	114	Dc	66.57N	16.30 E
Piešt'ány	120	Nh	48.36N	17.50 E
Pietarsaari/Jakobstad	114	Fe	63.40N	22.42 E
Pietermaritzburg	160	Kk	29.37S	30.16 E
Pietersburg	160	Jk	23.54S	29.25 E
Pietraperzia	128	Im	37.25N	14.08 E
Pietrasanta	128	Eg	43.57N	10.14 E
Piet Retief	172	Ee	27.01S	30.50 E
Pietrii, Vîrful-	130	Fd	45.23N	22.40 E
Pietroşani	130	If	43.43N	25.38 E
Pietrosu, Vîrful- [Rom.]	130	Ib	47.08N	25.11 E
Pietrosu, Vîrful- [Rom.]	110	If	47.23N	25.33 E
Pieve di Cadore	128	Gd	46.26N	12.22 E
Pigeon Island	197k	Ba	14.06N	60.58W
Pigeon River	186	Lb	48.02N	89.41W
Piggott	186	Kh	36.23N	90.11W
Pigg's Peak	172	Ee	25.58S	31.15 E
Pigs, Bay of- (EN) = Cochinos, Bahía de-	194	Gb	22.07N	81.10W
Pigüé	204	Am	37.37S	62.25W
Pi He	154	Dh	32.26N	116.34 E
Pihkva järv = Pskov, Lake- (EN)	110	Id	58.00N	28.00 E
Pihlajavesi	114	Gf	61.45N	28.45 E
Pihlava	116	Ic	61.33N	21.36 E
Pihtipudas	114	Fe	63.23N	25.34 E
Piikkiö	116	Jd	60.26N	22.31 E
Piirisaar/Pirissar	116	Lf	58.23N	27.40 E
Pijijiapan	192	Mj	15.42N	93.14W
Pijol, Pico-	194	Df	15.06N	87.35W
Pikalevo	114	Ig	59.32N	34.03 E
Pikangikum	180	If	51.49N	94.00W
Pikelot Island	208	Fd	8.05N	147.38 E
Pikes Peak	182	Fd	38.51N	105.03W
Piketberg	172	Bf	32.54S	18.46 E
Pikiutdleq	179	Hf	64.45N	40.10W
Pikou	154	Ge	39.24N	122.21 E
Pikounda	170	Cb	0.33N	16.42 E
Pila	204	Cm	36.01S	58.08W
Piła	120	Mc	53.10N	16.44 E
Piła [2]	120	Mc	53.10N	16.45 E
Pila, Sierra de la-	126	Kf	38.16N	1.11W
Pilar [Arg.]	204	Bj	31.27S	61.15W
Pilar [Braz.]	202	Ke	9.36S	35.56W
Pilar [Par.]	206	Ic	26.52S	58.23W
Pilas Group	150	He	6.45N	121.35 E
Pilat, Mont-	122	Ki	45.23N	4.35 E
Pilatus	128	Cd	46.59N	8.20 E
Pilaya, Río-	202	Fh	20.55S	64.04W
Pilcaniyeu	206	Ff	41.08S	70.40W
Pilcomayo, Río-	198	Kh	25.21S	57.42W
Pile, Jezioro-	120	Mc	53.35N	16.30 E
Píli	130	Ej	39.28N	21.37 E
Pili	150	Hd	13.37N	123.17 E
Pilībhīt	148	Fc	28.38N	79.48 E
Pilica	120	Re	51.52N	21.17 E
Pílion Óros	130	Gj	39.24N	23.05 E
Pilipinas = Philippine Islands (EN)	140	Oh	13.00N	122.00 E
Pilipinas = Philippines (EN) [1]	142	Oh	13.00N	122.00 E
Pilis	120	Oi	47.41N	18.53 E
Pillahuincó, Sierra de-	204	Bn	38.18S	60.45W
Pillar, Cape-	212	Jh	43.15S	148.00 E
Pilna	114	Ki	55.33N	45.55 E
Pilões, Rio-	204	Gc	16.14S	50.54W
Pilões, Serra dos-	204	Ic	17.50S	47.13W
Pilón, Río-	192	Je	25.32N	99.32W
Pílos	130	Em	36.55N	21.42 E
Pílos = Pylos (EN)	130	Em	36.56N	21.40 E
Pilot Peak	188	Hf	41.02N	114.06W
Pilot Rock	188	Fd	45.29N	118.50W
Pilsen (EN) = Plzeň	112	Hf	49.45N	13.24 E
Piltene	114	Eh	57.15N	21.42 E
Pilzno	120	Rg	49.59N	21.17 E
Pim	136	Hc	61.18N	71.57 E
Pimba	212	Hf	31.15S	136.47 E
Pimenteiras	202	Je	6.14S	41.25W
Pimža jõgi	116	Lg	57.57N	27.59 E
Pina	126	Lc	41.29N	0.32W
Pinacate, Cerro-	192	Cb	31.45N	113.31W
Pinaki Atoll	208	Nf	19.22S	138.44W
Pinamar	204	Dm	37.07S	56.50W
Piñami, Arroyo-	192	Cd	27.44N	113.47W
Pinang → George Town	142	Mi	5.25N	100.20 E
Pinar	126	Gh	36.46N	5.26W
Pinarbaşi	146	Gc	38.50N	36.30 E
Pinar del Río	176	Kg	22.25N	83.42W
Pinar del Río [3]	194	Eb	22.35N	83.40W
Pinarhisar	130	Kh	41.37N	27.30 E
Pinchbeck	124	Bb	52.48N	0.09W
Pincher Creek	180	Gg	49.30N	113.48W
Pinçon, Mont-	122	Ff	48.58N	0.37W
Pîncota	130	Ec	46.20N	21.42 E
Pindaíba, Ribeirão	204	Gb	14.48S	52.00W
Pindaré, Rio-	202	Jd	3.17S	44.47W
Pindaré-Mirim	202	Id	3.37S	45.21W
Pindaval	204	Dc	17.08S	56.09W
Píndhos Óros = Pindus Mountains (EN)	110	Ih	39.45N	21.30 E
Pindus Mountains (EN) = Píndhos Óros	110	Ih	39.45N	21.30 E
Pine Bluff	182	Ie	34.13N	92.01W
Pine Bluffs	188	Mf	41.11N	104.04W
Pine Creek	212	Gb	13.49S	131.49 E
Pine Falls	180	Hf	50.35N	96.15W
Pinega	136	Ec	64.42N	43.22 E
Pinega	110	Kc	64.08N	41.54 E
Pine Island Glacier	222	Of	75.00S	101.00W
Pineland	186	Jk	31.15N	93.58W
Pine Mountain [Ga.-U.S.]	184	Ei	32.51N	84.47W
Pine Mountain [U.S.]	184	Fg	36.55N	83.20W
Pine Pass	180	Fe	55.50N	122.30W
Pine Point	176	Hc	61.01N	114.15W
Pine Ridge	186	Ee	43.02N	102.33W
Pinerolo	128	Bf	44.53N	7.21 E
Pines, Isle of- (EN) = Juventud, Isla de la-	174	Kg	21.40N	82.50W
Pines, Isle of- (EN) = Pins, Ile des-	208	Hg	22.37S	167.30 E
Pines, Lake O' The-	186	Ij	32.46N	94.35W
Pinetown	172	Ee	29.52S	30.46 E
Ping	140	Mh	15.42N	100.09 E
Pingbian	152	Hg	22.56N	103.46 E
Pingchang	152	Ie	31.38N	107.06 E
Pingding	154	Bf	37.48N	113.37 E
Pingdingbu → Guyuan	154	Cd	41.40N	115.41 E
Pingdingshan	152	Je	33.41N	113.27 E
Pingding Shan	152	Mb	46.39N	128.30 E
Pingdu	154	Ef	36.47N	119.57 E
Pingelap Atoll	208	Hd	6.13N	160.42 E
Pingelly	212	Df	32.32S	117.05 E
Pinggu	154	Dd	40.08N	117.07 E
Pingguo	152	Ig	23.21N	107.34 E
Pinghu	154	Fi	30.42N	121.02 E
Pingjiang	154	Bj	28.45N	113.37 E
Pingle	152	Jg	24.43N	110.42 E
Pingli	152	Ie	32.27N	109.21 E
Pingliang	142	Mf	35.32N	106.41 E
Pinglu (Jingping)	154	Be	39.32N	112.14 E
Pingluo	142	Mf	38.56N	106.34 E
Pingma → Tiandong	152	Ig	23.40N	107.09 E
Pingnan	152	Jg	23.38N	110.23 E
Pingouins, Ile des-	222	Ec	46.25S	50.19 E
Pingquan	152	Kc	41.00N	118.36 E
Pingshan	154	Ce	38.21N	114.01 E
Pingshun	154	Bf	36.12N	113.26 E
Pingtan	152	Kf	25.31N	119.48 E
Pingtung	152	Lg	22.40N	120.29 E
Pingüicas, Cerro-	192	Jg	21.10N	99.42W
Pingvallavatn	114a	Bb	64.15N	21.09W
Pingvellir	114a	Bb	64.17N	21.03W
Pingwu	152	He	32.27N	104.35 E
Pingxiang [China]	152	Ig	22.11N	106.46 E
Pingxiang [China]	152	Jf	27.43N	113.48 E
Pingyang	152	Lf	27.40N	120.30 E
Pingyao	152	Jd	37.12N	112.13 E
Pingyi	154	Dg	35.30N	117.38 E
Pingyin	154	Df	36.17N	116.26 E
Pingyu	154	Ch	32.58N	114.36 E
Pingyuan	154	Df	37.10N	116.25 E
Pinhal	204	If	22.12S	46.45W
Pinhão	204	Gg	25.43S	51.38W
Pinheiro Machado	204	Fj	31.34S	53.23W
Pinhel	126	Ed	40.46N	7.04W
Pini, Pulau-	150	Cf	0.08N	98.40 E
Piniós [Grc.]	130	Fj	39.53N	22.44 E
Piniós [Grc.]	130	El	37.48N	21.14 E
Pinipel	219a	Ba	4.24S	154.08 E
Pinjug	114	Lf	60.16N	47.54 E
Pinka	128	Kc	47.00N	16.35 E
Pink Mountain	180	Fe	56.06N	122.35W
Pinnaroo	212	Ig	35.16S	140.55 E
Pinneberg	120	Fc	53.39N	9.48 E
Pinnes, Ákra-	130	Hi	40.07N	24.18 E
Pinolosean	150	Hf	0.23N	124.07 E
Pinos	192	If	22.18N	101.34W
Pinos, Mount-	174	Hf	34.50N	119.09W
Pinos-Puente	126	Ig	37.15N	3.45W
Pinrang	150	Gg	3.48S	119.38 E
Pins, Cap des-	219b	Ce	21.04S	167.28 E
Pins, Ile des- = Pines, Isle of- (EN)	208	Hg	22.37S	167.30 E
Pins, Pointe aux-	184	Gd	42.15N	81.51W
Pinsk	136	Ce	52.08N	26.06 E
Pinta, Isla-	202a	Aa	0.35N	90.44W
Pintas, Sierra de las-	192	Bb	31.40N	115.10W
Pinto [Arg.]	206	Hc	29.09S	62.39W
Pinto [Sp.]	126	Id	40.14N	3.41W
Pintwater Range	188	Hh	36.55N	115.30W
Pio	219a	Ed	10.12S	161.42 E
Pioche	188	Hh	37.56N	114.27W
Piombino	128	Eh	42.55N	10.32 E
Piombino, Canale di-	128	Eh	42.55N	10.30 E
Pioneer Mountains	188	Id	45.40N	113.00W
Pioner, ostrov-	140	Lb	79.50N	92.30 E
Pionerski [R.S.F.S.R.]	136	Gc	61.12N	62.57 E
Pionerski [R.S.F.S.R.]	114	Ei	54.57N	20.13 E
Pionki	120	Re	51.30N	21.27 E
Piorini, Lago-	202	Fd	3.35S	63.15W
Piorini, Rio-	202	Fd	3.23S	63.30W
Piotrków [2]	120	Pe	51.25N	19.40 E
Piotrków Trybunalski	120	Pe	51.25N	19.42 E
Piove di Sacco	128	Ge	45.18N	12.02 E
Pipa Dingzi	152	Mc	43.57N	128.14 E
Pipéri	130	Hj	39.19N	24.21 E
Pipestone	186	Hd	44.01N	96.19W
Pipestone Creek	186	Fb	49.42N	100.45W
Pipi	168	Cd	7.27N	22.48 E
Pipinas	204	Dl	35.32S	57.20W
Pipmouacan, Réservoir -	180	Kg	49.40N	70.20W
Piqan → Shanshan	152	Fc	42.52N	90.10 E
Piqua	184	Ee	40.08N	84.14W
Piqueras, Puerto de-	126	Jb	42.03N	2.32W
Piquiri, Rio-	206	Jb	24.03S	54.14W
Piquiri, Serra do-	204	Fg	24.53S	52.25W
Piracanjuba	204	Hc	17.18S	49.01W
Piracanjuba, Rio- [Braz.]	204	Hc	17.18S	48.13W
Piracanjuba, Rio- [Braz.]	204	Hd	18.14S	48.48W
Piracema	204	Je	20.31S	44.29W
Piracicaba	206	Kb	22.43S	47.38W
Piracicaba, Rio-	204	Hf	22.36S	48.19W
Piraçununga	204	Ie	21.59S	47.25W
Piracuruca	202	Jd	3.56S	41.42W
Piraeus (EN) = Piraiévs	112	Ih	37.57N	23.38 E
Pirai do Sul	204	Hg	24.31S	49.56W
Piraiévs = Piraeus (EN)	112	Ih	37.57N	23.38 E
Piraju	204	Hf	23.12S	49.23W
Pirajuí	204	He	21.59S	49.29W
Pirámide, Cerro-	198	Ij	49.01S	73.32W
Piran	128	He	45.32N	13.34 E
Pirané	206	Ic	25.43S	59.06W
Piranhas	204	Gc	16.31S	51.51W
Piranhas, Rio-	204	Gc	16.01S	51.52W
Pīrān Shahr	146	Kd	36.40N	45.05 E
Pirapora	200	Lg	17.21S	44.56W
Pirarajá	206	Jd	33.44S	54.45W
Pirate Well	194	Kb	22.26N	73.04W
Piratini	204	Fj	31.27S	53.06W
Piratini, Rio-	204	Fk	32.01S	52.25W
Piratinim, Rio-	204	Ei	28.06S	55.27W
Pirdop	130	Hg	42.42N	24.11 E
Pirenópolis	204	Hb	15.51S	48.57W
Pires do Rio	202	Ig	17.18S	48.17W
Pirgós	130	Fi	40.38N	22.44 E
Pírgos	130	El	37.41N	21.27 E
Piriápolis	204	El	34.54S	55.17W
Pirin	130	Gh	41.40N	23.30 E
Pirineos = Pyrenees (EN)	110	Gg	42.40N	1.00 E
Pirineus, Serra dos-	204	Hc	16.15S	49.10W
Piripiri	202	Jd	4.16S	41.47W
Pirissar/Piirisaar	116	Lf	58.23N	27.40 E
Píritu	196	Bh	9.23N	69.12W
Píritu, Islas-	196	Dg	10.10N	64.56W
Pirizal	204	Dc	16.16S	56.23W
Pirjatin	132	Hd	50.14N	32.30 E
Pirmasens	120	Dg	49.12N	7.36 E
Pirna	120	Jf	50.58N	13.56 E
Piron	219a	Ad	11.20S	153.27 E
Pirón	126	Hc	41.23N	4.31W
Pirot	130	Ff	43.09N	22.36 E
Pirre, Cerro-	194	Ij	7.49N	77.43W
Pirrit Hills	222	Pg	81.17S	85.21W
Pirsagat	132	Pj	39.53N	49.19 E
Pīr Tāj	146	Me	35.45N	48.07 E
Pirttikyla/Pörtom	116	Ib	62.42N	21.37 E
Piru	150	Ig	3.04S	128.12 E
Pis	220d	Ba	7.41N	151.46 E
Pisa	128	Eg	43.43N	10.23 E
Pisa	120	Rc	53.15N	21.52 E
Pisagua	206	Fa	19.36S	70.13W
Pisano	128	Eg	43.46N	10.33 E
Pisar	220d	Cb	7.19N	152.01 E
Pisciotta	128	Jj	40.06N	15.14 E
Pisco	200	Ig	13.42S	76.13W
Pişcolt	130	Fb	47.35N	22.18 E
Písek	120	Kg	49.19N	14.10 E
Pishan/Guma	152	Cd	37.38N	78.19 E
Pīsh Qal'eh	146	Qd	37.35N	57.05 E
Pīshvā	146	Ne	35.18N	51.44 E
Piso Firme	204	Ba	13.41S	61.52W
Pišpek = Frunze	142	Je	42.54N	74.36 E
Pisshiri-Dake	156a	Ba	44.20N	141.55 E
Pista	114	Hd	65.28N	30.45 E
Pisticci	128	Kj	40.23N	16.33 E
Pistoia	128	Eg	43.55N	10.54 E
Pisuerga	126	Hc	41.33N	4.52W
Pisz	120	Rc	53.38N	21.49 E
Pita	166	Cc	11.05N	12.24W
Pitalito	202	Cc	1.53N	76.02W
Pitanga	206	Jb	24.46S	51.44W
Pitanga, Serra da-	204	Gg	24.52S	51.48W

Index Symbols

- [1] Independent Nation
- [2] State, Region
- [3] District, County
- [4] Municipality
- [5] Colony, Dependency
- Continent
- Physical Region
- Historical or Cultural Region
- Mount, Mountain
- Volcano
- Hill
- Mountains, Mountain Range
- Hills, Escarpment
- Plateau, Upland
- Pass, Gap
- Plain, Lowland
- Delta
- Salt Flat
- Valley, Canyon
- Crater, Cave
- Karst Features
- Depression
- Polder
- Desert, Dunes
- Forest, Woods
- Heath, Steppe
- Oasis
- Cape, Point
- Coast, Beach
- Cliff
- Peninsula
- Isthmus
- Sandbank
- Island
- Atoll
- Rock, Reef
- Islands, Archipelago
- Rocks, Reefs
- Coral Reef
- Well, Spring
- Geyser
- River, Stream
- Waterfall, Rapids
- River Mouth, Estuary
- Lake
- Salt Lake
- Intermittent Lake
- Reservoir
- Swamp, Pond
- Canal
- Glacier
- Ice Shelf, Pack Ice
- Ocean
- Sea
- Gulf, Bay
- Strait, Fjord
- Lagoon
- Bank
- Seamount
- Tablemount
- Ridge
- Shelf
- Basin
- Escarpment, Sea Scarp
- Fracture
- Trench, Abyss
- National Park, Reserve
- Point of Interest
- Recreation Site
- Cave, Cavern
- Historic Site
- Ruins
- Wall, Walls
- Church, Abbey
- Temple
- Scientific Station
- Railway station
- Airport
- Fort
- Military installation
- Lighthouse
- Mine
- Tunnel
- Dam, Bridge

Pitangui 204 Jd 19.40S 44.54W
Pitcairn [5] 210 Og 24.00S 129.00W
Pitcairn Island 208 Ng 25.04S 130.05W
Piteå 114 Ed 65.20N 21.30 E
Piteälven 110 Ib 65.14N 21.32 E
Pitești 112 Ig 44.51N 24.52 E
Pithiviers 122 If 48.10N 2.15 E
Pithorāgarh 148 Gc 29.35N 80.13 E
Piti 220c Bb 13.28N 144.41 E
Piti 170 Fd 7.00S 32.44 E
Pitiquito 192 Cb 30.42N 112.02W
Pitkjaranta 136 Dc 61.35N 31.31 E
Pitkkala 116 Jc 61.28N 23.34 E
Pitljar 138 Bc 65.52N 65.55 E
Pitlochry 118 Je 56.43N 3.45W
Pitomača 128 Le 45.57N 17.14 E
Piton, Pointe du- 197e Ba 16.30N 61.27W
Pit River 182 Cc 40.45N 122.22W
Pitrufquén 206 Fe 38.59S 72.39W
Pitt 180 Ef 53.40N 129.50W
Pitt Island 208 Ji 44.20S 176.10W
Pittsburg 182 Id 37.25N 94.42W
Pittsburgh 176 Le 40.26N 80.00W
Pittsfield [Il.-U.S.] 186 Kg 39.36N 90.48W
Pittsfield [Ma.-U.S.] 184 Kd 42.27N 73.15W
Pittsfield [Me.-U.S.] 184 Mc 44.47N 69.23W
Pitt Strait 218 Jf 44.10S 176.20W
Pitu 150 If 1.41N 128.01 E
Piūi 204 Je 20.28S 45.58W
Piura 200 Hf 5.12S 80.38W
Piura [3] 200 Be 5.00S 80.20W
Piuthān 148 Gc 28.06N 82.52 E
Piva 130 Bf 43.21N 18.51 E
Pivan 138 If 50.27N 137.05 E
Pivijay 194 Jh 10.28N 74.38W
Pižma [R.S.F.S.R.] 114 Lh 57.36N 48.58 E
Pižma [R.S.F.S.R.] 134 Fd 65.24N 52.05 E
Pizzo 128 Kl 38.44N 16.40 E
Pjakupur 138 Cd 65.00N 77.48 E
Pjalica 116 Jc 66.12N 39.32 E
Pjalma 136 Dc 62.27N 35.53 E
Pjana 114 Ki 55.37N 45.58 E
Pjandž 136 Gh 37.15N 69.07 E
Pjandž 140 If 37.06N 68.20 E
Pjaozero, ozero- 110 Jb 66.05N 30.55 E
Pjarnu/Pärnu 112 Id 58.24N 24.32 E
Pjarnu / Pärnu jõgi 114 Fg 58.23N 24.34 E
Pjarnu, zaliv- / Pärnu laht 114 Fg 58.15N 24.25 E
Pjarnu-Jagupi/Pärnu-Jaagupi 116 Kf 58.36N 24.25 E
Pjasina 140 Kb 73.47N 87.01 E
Pjasino, ozero- 138 Dc 69.45N 87.30 E
Pjasinski zaliv 138 Db 74.00N 85.00 E
Pjatigorsk 112 Kg 44.03N 43.04 E
Pjatihatki 132 He 48.27N 33.40 E
Pjórsá 110 Dc 63.45N 20.50W
Pjuhjajarvi, ozero- 116 Nc 61.50N 30.00 E
Pjussi/Püssi 116 Le 59.17N 26.57 E
Pkulagalid 220a Ba 7.36N 134.33 E
Pkulagasemieg 220a Ac 7.08N 134.23 E
Pkurengel 220a Ac 7.27N 134.28 E
Plá 204 Bl 35.07S 60.13W
Placentia 180 Mg 47.14N 53.58W
Placentia Bay 174 Ne 47.15N 54.30W
Placer 150 Hd 11.52N 123.55 E
Placerville 188 Eg 38.43N 120.48W
Placetas 190 Id 22.19N 79.40W
Plácido Rosas 204 Fk 32.45S 53.44W
Plačkovci 130 Ig 42.49N 25.28 E
Plačkovica 130 Fh 41.46N 22.32 E
Plainfield 184 Je 40.37N 74.25W
Plains [Mt.-U.S.] 188 Hc 47.27N 114.53W
Plains [Tx.-U.S.] 186 Ej 33.11N 102.50W
Plainview [Nb.-U.S.] 186 He 42.21N 97.47W
Plainview [Tx.-U.S.] 182 Ge 34.11N 101.43W
Plainville 186 Gg 39.14N 99.18W
Pláka, Ákra- 130 Ii 40.02N 25.25 E
Plake 130 Eh 41.14N 21.02 E
Plampang 150 Gh 8.48S 117.48 E
Planá 120 Ig 49.52N 12.44 E
Plana, Illa- / Plana o Nueva Tabarca, Isla- 126 Lf 38.10N 0.28 E
Plana Cays 194 Kb 22.37N 73.33W
Plana o Nueva Tabarca, Isla- / Plana, Illa- 126 Lf 38.10N 0.28 E
Planco, Peñón- 192 Ge 24.35N 104.15W
Plane, Ile- 126 Li 35.46N 0.54W
Planeta Rica 202 Cb 8.25N 75.35W
Planet Depth (EN) 106 Hj 10.20S 110.30 E
Planézes 122 Ij 45.00N 2.50 E
Plankinton 186 Ge 43.43N 98.29W
Plantation 184 Gl 26.05N 80.14W
Plantaurel 122 Hk 43.04N 1.30 E
Plant City 184 Fk 28.01N 82.08W
Plasencia 126 Fd 40.02N 6.05W
Plast 136 Ge 54.22N 60.55 E
Plaster Rock 184 Nb 46.54N 67.24W
Plastun 138 Ih 44.48N 136.17 E
Plasy 120 Jg 49.56N 13.24 E
Plata, Río de la- [P.R.] 197a Bb 18.30N 66.14W
Plata, Río de la- [S.Amer.] 198 Ki 35.00S 57.00W
Plataiai 130 Gk 38.13N 23.16 E
Platani 128 Hm 37.24N 13.16 E
Plateau [2] 166 Gd 8.50N 9.00 E
Plateau [3] 170 Cc 2.10S 15.00 E
Plateaux [3] 166 Fd 7.30N 1.10 E
Platen, Kapp- 179 Ob 80.31N 22.48 E
Plati 130 Fi 40.39N 22.32 E
Plato 202 Db 9.47N 74.47W
Platte 186 Ge 43.23N 98.51W
Platte 174 Je 41.00N 95.52W
Platte Island 158 Mi 5.52S 55.23 E
Platte River 186 Ig 39.16N 94.50W
Platteville 186 Ke 42.44N 90.29W
Plattsburgh 182 Mc 44.42N 73.29W
Plattsmouth 186 If 41.01N 95.53W
Plau 120 Ic 53.27N 12.16 E
Plauen 120 If 50.30N 12.08 E
Plauer See 120 Ic 53.30N 12.20 E
Plav 130 Cg 42.36N 19.57 E
Plavecký Mikuláš 120 Nh 48.30N 17.18 E
Pļaviņas/Pljavinjas 114 Fh 56.38N 25.46 E
Plavsk 132 Jc 53.43N 37.18 E
Playa Azul 190 De 17.59N 102.24W
Playa Noriega, Laguna- 192 Dc 29.10N 111.50W
Playa Vicente 192 Li 17.50N 95.49W
Playón Chico 194 Hi 9.18N 78.14W
Pleasanton [Ks.-U.S.] 186 Ig 38.11N 94.43W
Pleasanton [Tx.-U.S.] 186 Gl 28.58N 98.29W
Pleasant Point 218 Df 44.16S 171.08 E
Pleasant Valley 186 Fi 35.15N 101.48W
Plechý 120 Jh 48.49N 13.53 E
Pleiku 148 Lf 13.59N 108.00 E
Pleiße 120 Ie 51.20N 12.22 E
Plenița 130 Ge 44.13N 23.11 E
Plenty, Bay of- 208 Ih 37.45S 177.10 E
Plentywood 182 Gb 48.47N 104.34W
Pleščenicy 132 Eb 54.29N 27.55 E
Pleseck 132 Ec 62.44N 40.18 E
Plešivec 120 Qh 48.33N 20.25 E
Pleșu, Vîrful- 130 Fc 46.32N 22.11 E
Pleszew 120 Ne 51.54N 17.48 E
Plétipi, Lac- 180 Kf 51.42N 70.08W
Plettenberg 124 Jc 51.13N 7.53 E
Plettenbergbaai 172 Cf 34.03S 23.22 E
Pleven 112 Ig 43.25N 24.37 E
Pleven [2] 130 Hf 43.25N 24.37 E
Plibo 166 De 4.35N 7.40W
Pliska 130 Kf 43.22N 27.07 E
Pliszka 120 Kd 52.15N 14.40 E
Plitvice 128 Jf 44.54N 15.36 E
Pljavinjas/Pļaviņas 114 Fh 56.38N 25.46 E
Plješevica 128 Jf 44.45N 15.45 E
Pljevlja 130 Cf 43.21N 19.21 E
Pljusa 114 Gg 58.25N 29.20 E
Pljusa 114 Gg 59.13N 28.11 E
Ploča, Rt- 128 Jg 43.30N 15.58 E
Ploče 128 Lg 43.04N 17.26 E
Płock 120 Pd 52.33N 19.43 E
Płock [2] 120 Pd 52.35N 19.45 E
Plöckenstein 120 Jh 48.49N 13.53 E
Ploërmel 122 Dg 47.56N 2.24W
Ploiești 112 Ig 44.57N 26.01 E
Plomárion 130 Jk 38.59N 26.22 E
Plomb du Cantal 122 Ii 45.03N 2.46 E
Plön 120 Gb 54.10N 10.26 E
Płonia 120 Kc 53.25N 14.36 E
Płonka 120 Qd 52.37N 20.30 E
Płońsk 120 Qd 52.38N 20.23 E
Plopana 130 Kc 46.41N 27.13 E
Płoty 120 Lc 53.50N 15.16 E
Plouguerneau 122 Bf 48.36N 4.30W
Plovdiv 112 Ig 42.09N 24.45 E
Plovdiv [2] 130 Hg 42.09N 24.45 E
Plummer 188 Gc 47.20N 116.53W
Plumridge Lakes 212 Fe 29.30S 125.25 E
Plumtree 172 Dd 20.31S 27.48 E
Plungė/Plunge 114 Ei 55.56N 21.48 E
Plunge/Plungė 114 Ei 55.56N 21.48 E
Plymouth [Eng.-U.K.] 112 Fe 50.23N 4.10W
Plymouth [In.-U.S.] 184 De 41.21N 86.19W
Plymouth [Ma.-U.S.] 184 Le 41.58N 70.41W
Plymouth [Mont.] 190 Le 16.42N 62.13W
Plymouth Sound 118 Ik 50.25N 4.05W
Plzeň=Pilsen (EN) 112 Hf 49.45N 13.24 E
Plzeňská pahorkatina 120 Jg 49.50N 13.15 E
Pniewy 120 Md 52.31N 16.15 E
Pô 166 Ec 11.10N 1.09W
Po 110 Hg 44.57N 12.05 E
Po, Foci del-=Po, Mouths of the- (EN) 128 Gf 44.52N 12.30 E
Po, Mouths of the- (EN)= Po, Foci del- 128 Gf 44.52N 12.30 E
Poarta de Fier a Transilvaniei, Pasul- 130 Fd 45.25N 22.40 E
Poarta Orientală, Pasul- 130 Fd 45.08N 22.20 E
Poás, Volcán- 194 Eh 10.11N 84.13W
Pobé 166 Fd 6.58N 2.41 E
Pobeda, gora- 140 Qc 65.12N 146.12 E
Pobeda Ice Island 222 Ge 64.30S 97.00 E
Pobedy, pik- 140 Ke 42.02N 80.05 E
Pobla de Segur / la Pobla de Segur 126 Mb 42.15N 0.58 E
Pobla de Trives / Puebla de Trives 126 Eb 42.20N 7.15W
Poblet, Monasterio de- / Poblet, Monestir de- 126 Nc 41.20N 1.05 E
Poblet, Monestir de- / Poblet, Monasterio de- 126 Nc 41.20N 1.05 E
Pobrežije 130 Jf 43.56N 26.21 E
Pocahontas 186 Kh 36.16N 90.58W
Pocatello 176 He 42.52N 112.27W
Počep 132 Hc 52.57N 33.28 E
Pocerina 130 Ce 44.38N 19.35 E
Počinok 136 De 54.23N 32.29 E
Počitelj 128 Lg 43.08N 17.44 E
Pocito, Sierra del- 126 He 39.20N 4.05W
Pocito Casas 192 Dc 28.32N 111.06W
Pocklington Reef 214 Fj 11.00S 155.00 E
Poções 202 Jf 14.31S 40.21W
Poço Fundo, Cachoeira- 204 Jc 16.10S 45.51W
Poconé 202 Gg 16.15S 56.37W
Pocono Mountains 184 Je 41.10N 75.20W
Poços de Caldas 202 Ih 21.48S 46.34W
Pocri 194 Gj 7.40N 80.07W
Podborovje [R.S.F.S.R.] 114 Ig 59.32N 35.01 E
Podborovje [R.S.F.S.R.] 116 Mg 57.51N 28.46 E
Podbrezová 120 Ph 48.49N 19.31 E
Podčerje 134 He 63.55N 57.30 E
Poděbrady 120 Lf 50.09N 15.07 E
Podgajcy 120 Vg 49.12N 25.12 E
Podgorina 130 Ce 44.15N 19.56 E
Po di Volano 128 Gf 44.49N 12.15 E
Podjuga 114 Jf 61.07N 40.54 E
Podkamennaja Tunguska= Stony Tunguska (EN) 140 Lc 61.36N 90.18 E
Podlasie 120 Sd 52.30N 23.00 E
Podlaska, Nizina- 120 Sc 53.00N 22.45 E
Podlužje 120 Ce 44.45N 19.55 E
Podolia (EN) = Podolskaja vozvyšennost 110 If 49.00N 28.00 E
Podolsk 136 Dd 55.27N 37.33 E
Podolskaja vozvyšennost = Podolia (EN) 110 If 49.00N 28.00 E
Podor 166 Cb 16.40N 14.57W
Podporožje 136 Dc 60.54N 34.09 E
Podravina 128 Le 45.40N 17.40 E
Podravska Slatina 128 Le 45.42N 17.42 E
Podrima 130 Dg 42.24N 20.33 E
Podromanija 128 Mg 43.54N 18.46 E
Podsvilje 116 Mi 55.09N 28.01 E
Podujevo 130 Eg 42.55N 21.12 E
Podunajská nížina 120 Nh 48.00N 17.40 E
Podvološino 138 Fe 58.15N 108.25 E
Poel 120 Hb 54.00N 11.26 E
Poenița, Vîrful- 130 Gc 46.15N 23.20 E
Pofadder 172 Be 29.10S 19.22 E
Pogăniș 130 Ed 45.41N 21.21 E
Pogar 132 Hc 52.33N 33.16 E
Poggibonsi 128 Fg 43.28N 11.09 E
Pöggstall 128 Jb 48.19N 15.11 E
Pogibi 138 Jf 52.15N 141.45 E
Pogny 124 Gf 48.52N 4.29 E
Pogoanele 130 Je 44.55N 27.00 E
Pogórze Karpackie 120 Qg 49.52N 21.00 E
Pogradeci 130 Di 40.54N 20.39 E
Pograničny 138 Ih 44.26N 131.20 E
Pogrebišče 132 Fe 49.29N 29.14 E
Poguba Xoréu, Rio- 204 Ec 16.29S 54.58W
P'ohang 152 Md 36.02N 129.22 E
Pohja/Pojo 116 Jd 60.06N 23.31 E
Pohjankangas 116 Jc 62.00N 22.30 E
Pohjanlahti=Bothnia, Gulf of- (EN) 110 Hc 63.00N 20.00 E
Pohjanmaa 116 Jb 63.00N 22.30 E
Pohjois-Karjala [2] 114 Ge 63.00N 30.00 E
Pohlheim 124 Kd 50.32N 8.42 E
Pohorje 128 Jd 46.32N 15.28 E
Po Hu 154 Di 30.15N 116.32 E
Pohue Bay 221a Fd 19.01N 155.48W
Pohvistnevo 136 Fe 53.40N 52.08 E
Poiana Mare 130 Gf 43.55N 23.04 E
Poiana Ruscă, Munții 130 Fd 45.41N 22.30 E
Pöide/Pëjde 116 Jf 58.30N 22.50 E
Poie 170 Dc 2.55S 23.10 E
Poindimié 216 Cd 20.56S 165.20 E
Poindo → Lhünzhub 152 Fe 30.17N 91.20 E
Poinsett, Cape- 222 He 65.42S 113.18 E
Poinsett, Lake- 186 Hd 44.34N 97.05W
Point Arena 188 Dg 38.55N 123.41W
Point au Fer Island 186 Kl 29.15N 91.15W
Pointe-à-Pitre 190 Le 16.14N 61.32W
Pointe Duble 197e Bb 16.20N 61.00W
Pointe-Noire 197e Ab 16.14N 61.47W
Pointe Noire 160 Ii 4.48S 11.51 E
Point Hope 178 Fc 68.21N 166.41W
Point Lake 180 Gc 65.15N 113.00W
Point Lay 178 Gc 69.45N 163.03W
Point Pleasant [N.J.-U.S.] 184 Je 40.06N 74.02W
Point Pleasant [W.V.-U.S.] 184 Ff 38.53N 82.07W
Poisson-Blanc, Lac- 184 Jc 46.00N 75.44W
Poissonnier Point 212 Dc 20.00S 119.10 E
Poissy 122 If 48.56N 2.03 E
Poitevin, Marais- 122 Eh 46.22N 1.06W
Poitiers 112 Gf 46.35N 0.20 E
Poitou 122 Fh 46.40N 0.30W
Poitou, Plaine et Seuil du- 122 Gh 46.26N 0.17 E
Poivre Islands 172b Bb 5.46S 53.19 E
Poix-de-Picardie 122 He 49.47N 1.59 E
Poix-Terron 124 Ge 49.39N 4.39 E
Pojarkovo 138 Hg 49.42N 128.50 E
Pojkovski 136 Hc 60.59N 72.00 E
Pojo/Pohja 116 Jd 60.06N 23.31 E
Pojuba, Rio- 204 Ec 16.30S 54.59W
Pokhara 148 Gc 28.14N 83.59 E
Poko 170 Eb 3.09N 26.53 E
Pokoinu 220p Bb 21.12S 159.49W
Pokój 120 Nf 50.56N 17.50 E
Pokrovka 135 Lc 42.19N 78.01 E
Pokrovsk 138 Hd 61.29N 129.10 E
Pokrovskoje [R.S.F.S.R.] 132 Jc 52.38N 36.51 E
Pokrovskoje [Ukr.-U.S.S.R.] 132 Jf 47.59N 36.13 E
Pokšenga 114 Kd 64.01N 44.15 E
Pokutje 130 Ia 48.20N 25.05 E
Pola 114 Hg 58.05N 31.40 E
Polabí 120 Lf 50.10N 15.10 E
Polacca 188 Ji 35.50N 110.23W
Pola de Laviana 126 Ga 43.15N 5.34W
Pola de Lena 126 Ga 43.10N 5.49W
Pola de Siero 126 Ga 43.23N 5.40W
Poland 204 Ek 33.54S 55.09W
Poland 220g Ab 1.52N 157.33W
Poland (EN)=Polska [1] 112 He 52.00N 19.00 E
Polanów 120 Mb 54.08N 16.39 E
Polar Plateau 222 Cg 90.00S 0.00
Polar Urals (EN)=Poljarny Ural 110 Mb 66.55N 64.30 E
Polatlı 144 Db 39.36N 32.09 E
Polch 124 Jd 50.18N 7.19 E
Połczyn Zdrój 120 Mc 53.46N 16.06 E
Pol-e Khomrī 144 Kb 35.56N 68.43 E
Pole of Inaccessibility (EN) 222 Eg 82.06S 54.58 E
Pol-e-Safīd 146 Od 36.06N 53.01 E
Polesella 128 Ff 44.58N 11.45 E
Polesie Lubelskie 120 Te 51.30N 23.20 E
Polesine 128 Fe 45.00N 11.45 E
Polesje=Polesye (EN) 110 Ie 52.00N 27.00 E
Polessk 116 Ij 54.51N 21.02 E
Polesskoje 132 Fd 51.16N 29.27 E
Polesye (EN)=Polesje 110 Ie 52.00N 27.00 E
Polevskoj 136 Gd 56.28N 60.11 E
Polewali 150 Gg 3.25S 119.20 E
Poležan 130 Gh 41.43N 23.30 E
Polgár 120 Ri 47.52N 21.07 E
Pŏlgyo 154 Ig 34.51N 127.21 E
Poli 166 Hd 8.29N 13.15 E
Poliaigos 130 Hm 36.46N 24.38 E
Poličani 130 Di 40.08N 20.21 E
Policastro, Golfo di- 128 Jk 40.00N 15.35 E
Police 120 Kc 53.33N 14.35 E
Police - Trzebiez 120 Kc 53.39N 14.32 E
Policoro 128 Kj 40.13N 16.41 E
Poligny 122 Lh 46.50N 5.43 E
Poligus 138 Ed 61.58N 94.40 E
Polikastron 130 Fh 41.00N 22.34 E
Polikhnitos 130 Jj 39.05N 26.11 E
Polillo Islands 140 Oh 14.50N 122.05 E
Pólis 146 Ee 35.02N 32.25 E
Polist 114 Hg 58.07N 31.32 E
Polistena 128 Kl 38.24N 16.04 E
Políyros 130 Gi 40.23N 23.27 E
Poljarny [R.S.F.S.R.] 138 Mc 69.01N 178.45 E
Poljarny [R.S.F.S.R.] 136 Db 69.13N 33.28 E
Poljarny Ural=Polar Urals (EN) 110 Mb 66.55N 64.30 E
Polkowice 120 Me 51.32N 16.06 E
Pöllau 128 Jc 47.18N 15.50 E
Polle 220d Bb 7.20N 151.15 E
Pollença/Pollensa 126 Pe 39.53N 3.01 E
Pollensa/Pollença 126 Pe 39.53N 3.01 E
Pollino 110 Hh 39.55N 16.10 E
Polochic, Río- 194 Cf 15.28N 89.22W
Polock 136 Cd 55.29N 28.52 E
Pologi 130 Dh 42.00N 21.00 E
Pologi 136 Df 47.28N 36.15 E
Polonina 120 Jh 48.30N 23.30 E
Polonnaruwa 148 Gg 7.56N 81.00 E
Polonnoje 132 Ed 50.06N 27.29 E
Polousny krjaž 138 Jc 69.30N 144.00 E
Polska=Poland (EN) [1] 112 He 52.00N 19.00 E
Polski Gradec 130 Jg 42.11N 26.06 E
Polski Trămbeš 130 If 43.22N 25.38 E
Polson 188 Hc 47.41N 114.09W
Poltár 120 Ph 48.27N 19.48 E
Poltava 112 Jf 49.35N 34.34 E
Poltavka 136 He 54.22N 71.45 E
Poltavskaja oblast [3] 136 Df 49.45N 33.50 E
Põltsamaa/Pyltsamaa 114 Fg 58.39N 25.59 E
Põltsamaa/Pyltsamaa 116 Lf 58.23N 26.08 E
Poluj 138 Bc 66.30N 66.31 E
Polunočnoje 136 Gc 60.52N 60.25 E
Polūr 146 Oe 32.52N 52.03 E
Põlva/Pylva 114 Gg 58.04N 27.06 E
Polvijärvi 114 Ge 62.51N 29.22 E
Polynesia 208 Le 4.00S 156.00W
Polynésie Française=French Polynesia (EN) [5] 210 Mf 16.00S 145.00W
Pom, Laguna de- 192 Mh 18.35N 92.15W
Pomarance 128 Eg 43.18N 10.52 E
Pomarkku/Påmark 116 Ic 61.42N 22.00 E
Pombal [Braz.] 202 Ke 6.46S 37.47W
Pombal [Port.] 126 De 39.55N 8.38W
Pombo, Rio- 204 Fe 20.53S 52.23W
Pomerania (EN)= Pommern 110 He 54.00N 16.00 E
Pomerania (EN)= Pommern 120 Lc 54.00N 16.00 E
Pomeranian Bay (EN)= Pommersche Bucht 120 Kb 54.20N 14.20 E
Pomeranian Bay (EN)= Pomorska, Zatoka- 120 Kb 54.20N 14.20 E
Pomeroy 184 Ff 39.03N 82.03W
Pomio 210 Ge 5.32S 151.30 E
Pomme de Terre Reservoir 186 Jh 37.51N 93.19W
Pommern=Pomerania (EN) 110 He 54.00N 16.00 E
Pommern=Pomerania (EN) 120 Lc 54.00N 16.00 E
Pommersche Bucht= Pomeranian Bay (EN) 120 Kb 54.20N 14.20 E
Pommersfelden 120 Gg 49.46N 10.49 E
Pomona 188 Gi 34.04N 117.45W
Pomona Lake 186 Ig 38.40N 95.35W
Pomorije 130 Kg 42.33N 27.39 E
Pomorska, Zatoka-= Pomeranian Bay (EN) 120 Kb 54.20N 14.20 E
Pomorski bereg 114 Id 64.00N 36.15 E
Pomorskie, Pojezierze- 120 Mc 53.30N 16.30 E
Pomorski proliv 136 Eb 68.40N 50.00 E
Pomošnaja 132 Ge 48.14N 31.29 E
Pompano Beach 184 Gl 26.15N 80.07W
Pompei 128 Ij 40.45N 14.30 E
Pompeu 204 Jd 19.12S 44.59W
Ponape 210 Gd 6.52N 158.15 E
Ponape Island 208 Gd 6.55N 158.15 E
Ponca City 182 Hd 36.42N 97.05W
Ponce 176 Mh 18.01N 66.37W
Poncheville, Lac- 184 Ia 50.12N 76.55W
Pondcreek 186 Hh 36.40N 97.48W
Pondicherry 148 Ff 11.56N 79.53 E
Pondicherry [3] 148 Ff 11.55N 79.45 E
Pond Inlet 176 Lb 72.41N 78.00W
Pond Inlet 180 Jb 72.48N 77.00W
Ponea 220n Ac 10.28S 161.01W
Ponente, Riviera di- 128 Cf 44.10N 8.20 E
Ponérihouen 219b Be 21.05S 165.24 E
Pones 220d Bb 7.12N 151.59 E
Ponferrada 126 Fb 42.33N 6.35W
Pongaroa 218 Gd 40.33S 176.11 E
Pongo 158 Jh 8.42N 27.40 E
Pongola 172 Ee 26.52S 32.20 E
Pong Qu 152 Ef 26.49N 87.09 E
Poniatowa 120 Se 51.11N 22.05 E
Ponoj 112 Kb 67.05N 41.07 E
Ponoj 110 Kb 66.59N 41.10 E
Ponomarevka 132 Sc 53.09N 54.12 E
Ponorogo 150 Fh 7.52S 111.27 E
Pons 122 Fi 45.35N 0.33W
Pons/Ponts 126 Nc 41.55N 1.12 E
Ponsul 126 Ee 39.40N 7.31W
Pont-à-Celles 124 Gd 50.30N 4.21 E
Ponta Delgada 160 Ee 37.44N 25.40W
Ponta Delgada [3] 162 Bb 37.48N 25.30W
Ponta Grossa 200 Kh 25.05S 50.09W
Pont-à-Mousson 122 Mf 48.54N 6.04 E
Ponta Porã 200 Kh 22.32S 55.43W
Pontarlier 122 Mh 46.54N 6.22 E
Pontassieve 128 Fg 43.46N 11.26 E
Pont-Audemer 122 Ge 49.21N 0.31 E
Pontaut 204 Bm 37.44S 61.20W
Pontávert 124 Fe 49.25N 3.49 E
Pontchartrain, Lake- 182 Ie 30.10N 90.10W
Pontchâteau 122 Dg 47.26N 2.05W
Pont-de-Claix, Le- 122 Li 45.07N 5.42 E
Pont-de-l'Arche 124 De 49.18N 1.10 E
Pont de Suert 126 Mb 42.24N 0.45 E
Pont-de-Vaux 122 Kh 46.26N 4.56 E
Ponte Alta 204 Gh 27.29S 50.23W
Ponte Alta, Serra da- 204 Id 19.42S 47.40W
Ponteareas / Puenteareas 126 Db 42.11N 8.30W
Ponte Branca 204 Fc 16.27S 52.40W
Pontecorvo 128 Hi 42.27N 13.40 E
Ponte de Lima 126 Dc 41.46N 8.35W
Ponte de Pedrā 204 Da 13.35S 57.21W
Ponte de Pedra 204 Ec 17.06S 54.23W
Ponte de Pedra, Rio- → Sacuriuiná, Rio- 204 Da 13.58S 57.18W
Pontedera 128 Eg 43.40N 10.38 E
Ponte de Sor 126 De 39.15N 8.01W
Pontedeume / Puentedeume 126 Da 43.24N 8.10W
Ponte Firme, Chapada da- 204 Id 18.05S 46.25W
Ponteix 188 Lb 49.49N 107.30W
Ponte Nova 202 Jh 20.24S 42.54W
Pontés e Lacerda 204 Cb 15.11S 59.21W
Pontevedra 126 Db 42.26N 8.38W
Pontevedra [3] 126 Db 42.30N 8.30W
Pontevedra, Ría de- 126 Db 42.22N 8.45W
Ponte Vermelha 204 Ed 19.29S 54.25W
Pont-Farcy 124 Af 48.56N 1.02W
Pontfaverger-Moronvilliers 124 Ge 49.18N 4.19 E
Ponthieu 122 Hd 50.10N 1.55 E
Pontiac [Il.-U.S.] 186 Lf 40.53N 88.38W
Pontiac [Mi.-U.S.] 184 Fd 42.37N 83.18W
Pontianak 142 Mj 0.02S 109.20 E
Pontian Kechil 150 Df 1.29N 103.23 E
Pontine Islands (EN) = Ponziane, Isole- 128 Gj 40.55N 13.00 E
Pontivy 122 Df 48.04N 2.59W
Pontivy, Pays de- 122 Dg 48.00N 3.00W
Pont-l'Abbé 122 Bg 47.52N 4.13W
Pont-l'Evêque 124 Ce 49.18N 0.11 E
Pontoise 122 Ie 49.03N 2.06 E
Pontorson 122 Ef 48.33N 1.31W
Pontremoli 128 Df 44.22N 9.53 E
Pontresina 128 Dd 46.28N 9.53 E
Ponts/Pons 126 Nc 41.55N 1.12 E
Pont-Sainte-Maxence 124 Ee 49.18N 2.36 E
Pont-Saint-Esprit 122 Kj 44.15N 4.39 E
Pontypool 118 Jj 51.43N 3.02W
Ponza 128 Gj 40.54N 12.58 E
Ponza 128 Gj 40.55N 12.55 E
Ponziane, Isole- = Pontine Islands (EN) 128 Gj 40.55N 13.00 E
Pool [3] 170 Bc 3.30S 15.00 E
Poole 118 Lk 50.43N 1.59W
Pool Malebo 158 Ii 4.02S 16.03 E
Poona → Pune 142 Jh 18.32N 73.52 E
Poopó 202 Eg 18.23S 66.59W
Poopó, Lago de- = Poopó, Lake- (EN) 198 Jg 18.45S 67.07W
Poopó, Lake- (EN) = Poopó, Lago de- 198 Jg 18.45S 67.07W
Poor Knights Islands 218 Fa 35.30S 174.45 E
Pōōsaspea neem / Pyzaspea 116 Je 59.15N 23.25 E
Popa Taung 148 Jd 21.08N 95.12 E
Popayán 200 Ie 2.27N 76.36W
Poperinge 122 Id 50.51N 2.43 E
Poperinge-Watou 124 Ed 50.51N 2.37 E
Popigaj 138 Gb 71.55N 110.47 E
Popigaj 138 Fb 72.55N 106.00 E
Poplar 188 Mb 48.07N 105.12W
Poplar 180 Hf 53.00N 97.18W
Poplar Bluff 182 Id 36.45N 90.24W
Poplar River 188 Mb 48.05N 105.11W
Popocatépetl, Volcán- 174 Jh 19.02N 98.38W
Popokabaka 170 Cd 5.42S 16.35 E
Popoli 128 Hh 42.10N 13.50 E
Popomanaseu, Mount- 219a Ec 9.42S 160.03 E
Popondetta 214 Di 8.46S 148.14 E
Popovo 130 Jf 43.21N 26.14 E
Poppberg 120 Hg 49.20N 11.45 E
Poppel, Ravels- 124 Hc 51.27N 5.02 E
Poprad 112 If 49.03N 20.19 E
Poprad 120 Qg 49.38N 20.42 E
Poptún 194 Ce 16.21N 89.26W
Por 120 Tf 50.48N 23.01 E
Porangahau 218 Gd 40.18S 176.38 E
Porangatu 204 Ha 13.26S 49.10W
Porbandar 148 Dd 21.38N 69.36 E
Porcien 124 Ge 49.40N 4.20 E
Porcos, Rio dos- 204 Ja 12.42S 45.07W
Porcuna 126 Hg 37.52N 4.11W
Porcupine 184 Ga 48.32N 81.10W
Porcupine 174 Ec 66.35N 145.15W
Porcupine Bank (EN) 110 Ee 53.20N 13.30W
Porcupine Creek 188 Lb 48.09N 106.22W
Porcupine Hills 188 Ha 50.05N 114.10W
Porcupine Plain 180 Dc 67.30N 137.30W
Pordenone 128 Ge 45.57N 12.39 E
Poreč 128 He 45.13N 13.37 E
Poreč 130 Fe 44.20N 22.05 E
Porecatu 204 Gf 22.43S 51.24W

Index Symbols

[1] Independent Nation; [2] State, Region; [3] District, County; [4] Municipality; [5] Colony, Dependency; Continent; Physical Region; Historical or Cultural Region; Mount, Mountain; Volcano; Hill; Mountains, Mountain Range; Hills, Escarpment; Plateau, Upland; Pass, Gap; Plain, Lowland; Delta; Salt Flat; Valley, Canyon; Crater, Cave; Karst Features; Depression; Polder; Desert, Dunes; Forest, Woods; Heath, Steppe; Oasis; Cape, Point; Coast, Beach; Cliff; Peninsula; Isthmus; Sandbank; Island; Atoll; Rock, Reef; Islands, Archipelago; Rocks, Reefs; Coral Reef; Well, Spring; Geyser; River, Stream; Waterfall, Rapids; River Mouth, Estuary; Lake; Salt Lake; Intermittent Lake; Reservoir; Swamp, Pond; Canal; Glacier; Ice Shelf, Pack Ice; Ocean; Sea; Gulf, Bay; Strait, Fjord; Lagoon; Bank; Seamount; Tablemount; Ridge; Shelf; Basin; Escarpment, Sea Scarp; Fracture; Trench, Abyss; National Park, Reserve; Point of Interest; Recreation Site; Cave, Cavern; Historic Site; Ruins; Wall, Walls; Church, Abbey; Temple; Scientific Station; Railway station; Airport; Port; Military installation; Lighthouse; Mine; Tunnel; Dam, Bridge

Porećje	116	Kk	53.53N	24.08 E
Poreckoje	114	Li	55.13N	46.19 E
Porhov	136	Cd	57.45N	29.32 E
Pori/Björneborg	112	Ic	61.29N	21.47 E
Porion	130	Gn	35.58N	23.16 E
Porirua	216	Dh	41.08S	174.50 E
Pórisvatn	114a	Bb	64.20N	18.55W
Porjus	114	Ec	66.57N	19.49 E
Porkkala	116	Ee	59.55N	24.25 E
Porlamar	202	Fa	10.57N	63.51W
Porma	126	Gb	42.29N	5.28W
Pornic	122	Dg	47.07N	2.06W
Poronajsk	142	Qe	49.14N	143.04 E
Poronin	120	Qg	49.20N	20.04 E
Póros	130	Gl	37.30N	23.27 E
Póros	130	Gl	37.30N	23.31 E
Poroshiri-Dake	154	Qc	42.42N	142.35 E
Porosozero	114	He	62.44N	32.42 E
Porozovo	120	Ud	52.54N	24.27 E
Porpoise Bay	222	Ie	66.30S	128.30 E
Porquis Junction	184	Ga	48.43N	80.52W
Porrentruy / Pruntrut	128	Bc	47.25N	7.10 E
Porreras / Porreres	126	Oe	39.31N	3.00 E
Porreres / Porreras	126	Oe	39.31N	3.00 E
Porretta, Passo della-	128	Ef	44.02N	10.56 E
Porretta Terme	128	Ef	44.09N	10.59 E
Porsangen	110	Ia	70.50N	26.00 E
Porsangerhalvøya	114	Fa	70.50N	25.00 E
Porsgrunn	114	Bg	59.09N	9.40 E
Porsuk	146	Dc	39.42N	31.59 E
Portachuelo	202	Fg	17.21S	63.24W
Portadown/ Port an Dúnáin	118	Gg	54.26N	6.27W
Portage	186	Le	43.33N	89.28W
Portage la Prairie	180	Hg	49.57N	98.18W
Port Alberni	180	Fg	49.14N	124.48W
Portalegre	126	Ee	39.17N	7.26W
Portalegre [2]	126	Ee	39.15N	7.35W
Portales	182	Ge	34.11N	103.20W
Port Alfred	172	Df	33.36S	26.55 E
Port Alice	180	Ef	50.23N	127.27W
Port Allegany	184	He	41.48N	78.18W
Port an Dúnáin/Portadown	118	Gg	54.26N	6.27W
Port Angeles	182	Cb	48.07N	123.27W
Port Antonio	190	Ie	18.11N	76.28W
Port Arthur [Austl.]	212	Jh	43.09S	147.51 E
Port Arthur [Tx.-U.S.]	176	Jg	29.55N	93.55W
Port Arthur → Lüshun	152	Ld	38.50N	121.13 E
Port Augusta	210	Eh	32.30S	137.46 E
Port-au-Prince	176	Lh	18.32N	72.20W
Port-au-Prince, Baie de-	194	Kd	18.40N	72.30W
Port Austin	184	Fc	44.03N	83.01W
Port aux Français	222	Fc	49.25S	70.10 E
Porta Westfalica	124	Kb	52.15N	8.56 E
Port-Bergé-Vaovao	172	Hc	15.33S	47.38 E
Port-Bergé-Vao Vao	172	Hc	15.33S	47.38 E
Port Blair	142	Lh	11.36N	92.45 E
Portbou/Port-Bou	126	Pb	42.25N	3.10 E
Port-Bou/Portbou	126	Pb	42.25N	3.10 E
Port Burwell [Newf.-Can.]	176	Mc	60.25N	64.49W
Port Burwell [Ont.-Can.]	184	Gd	42.39N	80.49W
Port-Cartier	180	Kf	50.01N	66.53W
Port Chalmers	218	Df	45.49S	170.37 E
Port Charlotte	182	Kf	26.59N	82.06W
Port Clinton	184	Fe	41.30N	82.58W
Port Coquitlam	188	Db	49.16N	122.46W
Port-de-Bouc	122	Kk	43.24N	4.59 E
Port-de-Paix	194	Kd	19.57N	72.50W
Port Dickson	150	Df	2.31N	101.48 E
Port Edward	172	Ef	31.03S	30.13 E
Portel [Braz.]	202	Hd	1.57S	50.49W
Portel [Port.]	126	Ef	38.18N	7.42W
Port Elgin	184	Gc	44.26N	81.24W
Port Elizabeth [S.Afr.]	170	Jl	33.58S	25.40 E
Port Elizabeth [St.Vin.]	197n	Ba	13.00N	61.16W
Port Ellen	118	Gf	55.39N	6.12W
Port-en-Bessin-Huppain	122	Fe	49.21N	0.45W
Port Erin	118	Ig	54.05N	4.43W
Porter Point	197n	Ba	13.23N	61.11W
Porterville [Ca.-U.S.]	182	Dd	36.04N	119.01W
Porterville [S.Afr.]	172	Bf	33.00S	19.00 E
Portete, Bahia de-	194	Lg	12.13N	71.55W
Port Fairy	212	Ig	38.23S	142.14 E
Port Fitzroy	218	Fb	36.10S	175.21 E
Port-Gentil	160	Hi	0.43S	8.47 E
Port Gibson	186	Kk	31.58N	90.58W
Port Harcourt	160	Hh	4.46N	7.01 E
Port Hardy	180	Ef	50.43N	127.29W
Port Hawkesbury	180	Lg	45.37N	61.21W
Porthcawl	118	Jj	51.29N	3.43W
Port Hedland	210	Cg	20.19S	118.34 E
Port Heiden	178	He	56.55N	158.41W
Porthmadog	118	Ii	52.55N	4.08W
Port Hope Simpson	180	Lf	52.30N	56.17W
Port Huron	182	Kc	42.58N	82.27W
Portile de Fier = Iron Gate (EN)	110	Ij	44.41N	22.31 E
Port-Ilič	132	Pj	38.53N	48.51 E
Portimão	126	Dg	37.08N	8.32W
Port Isabel	186	Hm	26.04N	97.13W
Portitja	130	Me	44.41N	29.00 E
Port Láirge/Waterford	112	Fe	52.15N	7.06W
Port Láirge/Waterford [2]	118	Fi	52.10N	7.40W
Portland [Austl.]	212	Ig	38.21S	141.36 E
Portland [In.-U.S.]	184	Ee	40.26N	84.59W
Portland [Me.-U.S.]	176	Le	43.39N	70.17W
Portland [N.D.-U.S.]	186	Hc	47.30N	97.22W
Portland [N.Z.]	218	Fa	35.48S	174.20 E
Portland [Or.-U.S.]	176	Ge	45.33N	122.36W
Portland [Tx.-U.S.]	186	Hm	27.53N	97.20W
Portland, Bill of-	118	Kk	50.31N	2.28W
Portland, Promontoire -	180	Je	58.41N	78.33W
Portland Bight	194	Ie	17.57N	77.08W
Portland Island	218	Gc	39.20S	177.50 E
Portland Point	194	Ie	17.42N	77.11W
Port-la-Nouvelle	122	Jk	43.01N	3.03 E
Port Laoise/Portlaoise	118	Fh	53.02N	7.17W
Portlaoise/Port Laoise	118	Fh	53.02N	7.17W
Port Lavaca	182	Hf	28.37N	96.38W
Port Lincoln	210	Eh	34.44S	135.52 E
Port Loko	166	Cd	8.46N	12.47W
Port Louis	196	Fd	16.25N	61.32W
Port-Louis	160	Mk	20.10S	57.30 E
Port Macquarie	212	Kf	31.26S	152.44 E
Port Maria	194	Id	18.22N	76.54W
Port-Menier	180	Lg	49.49N	64.20W
Port Moller	178	Ge	55.59N	160.34W
Port Moody	188	Db	49.17N	122.51W
Port Moresby	210	Fe	9.30S	147.07 E
Port Nelson	180	Ie	57.04N	92.30W
Portneuf, Rivière-	184	Ma	48.37N	69.05W
Port Nolloth	160	Ik	29.17S	16.51 E
Port Nouveau-Québec	176	Md	58.35N	65.59W
Porto [2]	126	Dc	41.15N	8.20W
Porto [Fr.]	122a	Aa	42.16N	8.42 E
Porto [Port.]	112	Fg	41.09N	8.37W
Porto, Golfe de-	122a	Aa	42.16N	8.37 E
Porto Acre	202	Ee	9.34S	67.31W
Porto Alegre [Braz.]	200	Ki	30.04S	51.11W
Porto Alegre [Sao T.P.]	166	Ge	0.02N	6.32 E
Porto Amboim	160	Ij	10.44S	13.45 E
Porto Azzurro	128	Eh	42.46N	10.24 E
Portobelo	194	Hi	9.33N	79.39W
Porto Cedro	204	Ed	18.17S	55.02W
Porto Cervo	128	Di	41.08N	9.35 E
Porto Curupai	204	Ff	22.50S	53.53W
Porto de Moz	200	Kf	1.45S	52.14W
Porto Empedocle	128	Hm	37.17N	13.32 E
Porto Esperança [Braz.]	204	Db	14.02S	56.06W
Porto Esperança [Braz.]	204	Dd	19.37S	57.27W
Porto Esperança [Braz.]	204	Dc	17.47S	57.07W
Porto Esperidião	204	Cb	15.51S	58.28W
Porto Estrêla	204	Db	15.20S	57.14W
Portoferraio	128	Eh	42.49N	10.19 E
Port of Ness	118	Gc	58.30N	6.15W
Porto Franco	202	Ie	6.20S	47.24W
Port of Spain	200	Jd	10.39N	61.31W
Porto Fundação	204	Ea	13.39S	55.18W
Portogruaro	128	Ge	45.47N	12.50 E
Porto Lucena	204	Eh	27.51S	55.01W
Pörtom/Pirttikylä	116	Ib	62.42N	21.37 E
Portomaggiore	128	Ff	44.42N	11.48 E
Porto Mendes	204	Eg	24.30S	54.20W
Porto Moniz	162	Dc	32.51N	17.10W
Porto Moroco	204	Ea	13.24S	55.35W
Porto Morrinho	204	Dc	16.38S	57.49W
Porto Murtinho	200	Kh	21.42S	57.52W
Porto Novo [Ben.]	160	Hh	6.29N	2.37 E
Porto Novo [C.V.]	162	Bf	17.07N	25.04W
Port Orford	188	Ce	42.45N	124.30W
Porto San Giorgio	128	Hg	43.11N	13.48 E
Porto Santana	202	Hd	0.03S	51.11W
Porto Sant'Elpidio	128	Hg	43.15N	13.45 E
Porto Santo	158	Fe	33.04N	16.20W
Porto Santo Stefano	128	Fh	42.26N	11.07 E
Portoscuso	128	Ck	39.12N	8.23 E
Porto Seguro	202	Kg	16.26S	39.05W
Porto Tolle	128	Gf	44.56N	12.22 E
Porto Torres	128	Cj	40.50N	8.24 E
Porto União	204	Gh	26.15S	51.05W
Porto Válter	202	De	8.15S	72.45W
Porto Vecchio	122a	Bb	41.35N	9.17 E
Porto Velho	200	Jf	8.46S	63.54W
Portoviejo	200	Hf	1.03S	80.27W
Porto Xavier	204	Eh	27.54S	55.08W
Port Phillip Bay	212	Ig	38.05S	144.50 E
Port Pirie	210	Eh	33.11S	138.01 E
Portree	118	Gd	57.24N	6.12W
Port Renfrew	188	Cb	48.33N	124.25W
Port Rois/Portrush	118	Gf	55.12N	6.40W
Port Royal	184	If	38.10N	77.12W
Portrush/Port Rois	118	Gf	55.12N	6.40W
Port Said (EN) = Būr Sa'īd	160	Ke	31.16N	32.18 E
Port Saint Joe	182	Jf	29.49N	85.18W
Port Saint Johns	172	Df	31.38S	29.33 E
Port-Saint-Louis-du-Rhône	122	Kk	43.23N	4.48 E
Port-Salut	194	Kd	18.05N	73.55W
Port Saunders	180	Lf	50.39N	57.18W
Port Shepstone	160	Kl	30.46S	30.22 E
Portsmouth [Dom.]	196	Fe	15.35N	61.28W
Portsmouth [Eng.-U.K.]	118	Lk	50.48N	1.05W
Portsmouth [N.H.-U.S.]	182	Mc	43.03N	70.47W
Portsmouth [Oh.-U.S.]	182	Kd	38.45N	82.59W
Portsmouth [Va.-U.S.]	182	Ld	36.50N	76.26W
Portsmouth City Airport	124	Ad	50.46N	1.04W
Port Sudan (EN) = Būr Sūdān	160	Kg	19.37N	37.14 E
Port Sulphur	186	Ll	29.29N	89.42W
Port Talbot	118	Jj	51.35N	3.47W
Porttipahdantekojärvi	114	Gb	68.06N	26.33 E
Port Townsend	188	Db	48.07N	122.46W
Portugal [1]	112	Fh	39.30N	8.00W
Portugalete	126	Ia	43.19N	3.01W
Portuguesa [2]	202	Eb	9.10N	69.15W
Portuguesa, Río-	202	Eb	7.57N	67.32W
Portuguesa, Sierra de-	196	Bh	9.35N	69.45W
Portuguese Guinea (EN) → Guinea-Bissau (EN) [1]	160	Fg	12.00N	15.00W
Portús, Coll del-/Perthus, Col de-	126	Ob	42.28N	2.51 E
Port-Vendres	122	Jl	42.31N	3.07 E
Port-Vila	210	Hf	17.44S	168.19 E
Port Wakefield	212	Hf	34.11S	138.09 E
Port Washington	186	Me	43.23N	87.53W
Porvenir [Bol.]	204	Ba	13.59S	61.39W
Porvenir [Bol.]	202	Ef	11.15S	68.41W
Porvenir [Chile]	206	Fh	53.18S	70.22W
Porvenir [Ur.]	204	Dk	32.23S	57.59W
Porvoo/Borgå	114	Ff	60.24N	25.40 E
Porvoonjoki	116	Kd	60.23N	25.40 E
Porz, Köln-	120	Df	50.53N	7.03 E
Posada, Fiume di-	128	Dj	40.39N	9.45 E
Posadas [Arg.]	200	Kh	27.25S	55.50W
Posadas [Sp.]	126	Gg	37.48N	5.06W
Posavina	128	Le	45.00N	17.30 E
Poschiavo / Puschlav	128	Ed	46.20N	10.04 E
Pošehonje-Volodarsk	114	Jg	58.30N	39.08 E
Posets	126	Mb	42.39N	0.25 E
Posht-e Bādām	146	Pf	33.02N	55.23 E
Posio	114	Gc	66.06N	28.09 E
Posjet	154	Kc	42.39N	130.48 E
Poskam/Zepu	152	Cd	38.12N	77.18 E
Poso	142	Oj	1.23S	120.44 E
Poso, Danau-	150	Hg	1.52S	120.35 E
Posof	146	Jb	41.31N	42.42 E
Posŏng	154	Ig	34.46N	127.05 E
Pospeliha	138	Df	52.02N	81.56 E
Posse	202	If	14.05S	46.22W
Possession, Ile de la-	222	Ec	46.14S	49.55 E
Possession Island	172	Be	27.01S	15.30 E
Pößneck	120	Hf	50.42N	11.36 E
Post	186	Fj	33.12N	101.23W
Posta de San Martin	204	Bk	33.09S	60.31W
Postavy	136	Cd	55.07N	26.50 E
Poste-de-la-Baleine	180	Je	55.20N	76.50W
Poste Maurice Cortier/Bidon V	162	He	22.18N	1.05 E
Poste Weygand	162	He	24.29N	0.40 E
Postmasburg	172	Ce	28.18S	23.05 E
Postojna	128	Ie	45.47N	14.14 E
Posto Simões Lopes	204	Eb	14.14S	54.41W
Postville [Ia.-U.S.]	186	Ke	43.05N	91.34W
Postville [Newf.-Can.]	180	Lf	54.55N	59.58W
Potchefstroom	172	De	26.46S	27.01 E
Poteau	186	Ii	35.03N	94.37W
Potenza	128	Jj	40.38N	15.48 E
Potenza	128	Hg	43.25N	13.40 E
Poteriteri, Lake-	218	Bg	46.05S	167.05 E
Potes	126	Ha	43.09N	4.37W
Potgietersrus	172	Dd	24.15S	28.55 E
Potholes Reservoir	188	Fc	47.01N	119.19W
Poti	112	Kg	42.08N	41.39 E
Poti, Rio-	202	Je	5.02S	42.50W
Potigny	124	Bf	48.58N	0.14W
Potiskum	160	Ig	11.43N	11.04 E
Potnarhvin	219b	Dd	18.45S	169.12 E
Potomac	174	Lf	38.00N	76.18W
Potosí [3]	202	Eh	20.40S	67.00W
Potosí [Bol.]	200	Jg	19.35S	65.45W
Potosí [Mex.]	190	Dd	24.51N	100.19W
Potosí, Bahía-	192	Ii	17.35N	101.30W
Potosí, Cerro-	192	Ie	24.52N	100.13W
Pototan	150	Hd	10.55N	122.40 E
Potrerillos	206	Gc	26.26S	69.29W
Potrero, Río-	204	Bc	17.32S	61.35W
Potsdam [Ger.]	120	Jd	52.24N	13.04 E
Potsdam [N.Y.-U.S.]	184	Jc	44.40N	75.01W
Pott	219b	Ad	19.35S	163.36 E
Potters Bar	124	Bc	51.41N	0.10W
Pottstown	184	Je	40.15N	75.38W
Pottsville	184	Ie	40.42N	76.13W
Pouancé	122	Eg	47.45N	1.10W
Pouébo	219b	Be	20.24S	164.34 E
Pouembout	219b	Be	21.08S	164.54 E
Poughkeepsie	184	Ke	41.43N	73.56W
Poulaphouca Reservoir / Loch Pholl an Phúca	118	Gh	53.10N	6.30W
Poum	219b	Be	20.14S	164.01 E
Pourtalé	204	Bm	37.02S	60.36W
Pouso Alegre	202	Ih	22.13S	45.56W
Pouss	166	Ic	10.51N	15.03 E
Poutasi	221c	Bb	14.01S	171.41W
Poŭthĭsăt	148	Kf	12.32N	103.55 E
Poutrincourt, Lac-	184	Ja	49.13N	74.04W
Po Valley (EN) = Padana, Pianura-	110	Gf	45.20N	10.00 E
Považská Bystrica	120	Og	49.07N	18.28 E
Považský Inovec	120	Nh	48.35N	18.00 E
Povenec	114	Ie	62.51N	34.45 E
Poverty Bay	218	Gc	38.45S	178.00 E
Povlen	130	Ce	44.09N	19.44 E
Póvoa de Varzim	126	Dc	41.23N	8.46W
Povorino	132	Md	51.12N	42.17 E
Povungnituk	176	Lc	60.02N	77.10W
Povungnituk	180	Jd	60.03N	77.16W
Powassan	184	Hb	46.05N	79.22W
Powder River [Or.-U.S.]	188	Gd	44.45N	117.03W
Powder River [U.S.]	182	Fb	46.44N	105.26W
Powell	188	Kd	44.45N	108.46W
Powell, Lake-	182	Ed	37.25N	110.45W
Powell Lake	188	Ca	50.11N	124.25W
Powell River	180	Fg	49.52N	124.33W
Powers	184	Dc	45.39N	87.32W
Powers Lake	186	Eb	48.34N	102.39W
Powidzkie, Jezioro-	120	Nd	52.24N	17.57 E
Powys [3]	118	Ji	52.25N	3.20W
Poxoréu	202	Hg	15.50S	54.23W
Poxoréu, Rio- [Braz.]	204	Ec	16.32S	54.46W
Poxoréu, Rio- [Braz.]	204	Ec	16.08S	54.14W
Poya	219b	Be	21.21S	165.09 E
Poyang Hu	140	Ng	29.00N	116.25 E
Poza de la Sal	126	Ib	42.40N	3.30W
Pozanti	146	Fd	37.25N	34.52 E
Požarevac	130	Ee	44.37N	21.12 E
Poza Rica de Hidalgo	176	Jg	20.33N	97.27W
Požarskoje	154	Ma	46.16N	134.04 E
Požega	130	Df	43.51N	20.02 E
Poznań	120	Md	52.25N	16.55 E
Poznań [2]	120	Md	52.25N	16.30 E
Pozoblanco	126	Hf	38.22N	4.51W
Pozo Borrado	204	Bi	28.56S	61.41W
Pozo Colorado	204	Cf	23.22S	58.55W
Pozo del Mortero	204	Bg	24.24S	61.02W
Pozo del Tigre	204	Bc	17.34S	61.59W
Pozo Dulce	204	Ai	29.04S	62.02W
Pozos, Punta-	206	Gg	47.57S	65.47W
Pozuelos	202	Fa	10.11N	64.39W
Pozzallo	128	In	36.43N	14.51 E
Pozzuoli	128	Ij	40.49N	14.07 E
Pra [Ghana]	166	Ed	6.27N	1.47W
Pra [R.S.F.S.R.]	114	Ji	54.45N	41.01 E
Prabuty	120	Pc	53.46N	19.10 E
Prachatice	120	Jg	49.01N	14.00 E
Prachin Buri	148	Kf	14.02N	101.22 E
Prachuap Khiri Khan	148	Jf	11.48N	99.47 E
Praděd	120	Nf	50.06N	17.14 E
Prades	122	Il	42.37N	2.26 E
Prado	202	Kg	17.21S	39.13W
Præstø	116	Ei	55.07N	12.03 E
Prague (EN) = Praha	112	He	50.05N	14.26 E
Praha = Prague (EN)	112	He	50.05N	14.26 E
Prahova [2]	130	Id	45.10N	26.00 E
Prahova	130	Je	44.43N	26.27 E
Praia	160	Eg	14.55N	23.31W
Praia a Mare	128	Jk	39.54N	15.47 E
Praia da Rocha	126	Dg	37.07N	8.32W
Praia Rica	204	Eb	14.51S	55.33W
Praid	130	Ic	46.33N	25.08 E
Prainha	202	Hd	1.48S	53.29W
Prairie Dog Town Fork	186	Gi	34.26N	99.21W
Prairie du Chien	186	Ke	43.03N	91.09W
Prangli	116	Ke	59.38N	24.50 E
Prānhita	148	Fe	18.49N	79.55 E
Prapat	150	Cf	2.40N	98.56 E
Prasat	148	Kf	14.38N	103.24 E
Praslin	197k	Bb	13.53N	60.54W
Praslin, Port-	197k	Bb	13.53N	60.54W
Praslin Island	172b	Ca	4.19S	55.44 E
Prasonisíon	130	Kn	35.52N	27.46 E
Prat, Isla-	206	Fg	48.15S	75.00W
Prata	202	Ig	19.18S	48.55W
Prata, Rio da-	204	Hd	18.49S	49.54W
Pratapgarh	148	Ed	24.02N	74.47 E
Prat de Llobregat / el Prat de Llobregat	126	Oc	41.20N	2.06 E
Prato	128	Fg	43.53N	11.06 E
Pratomagno	128	Fg	43.40N	11.40 E
Pratt	182	Hd	37.39N	98.44W
Prättigau	128	Dd	46.55N	9.40 E
Pratt Seamount (EN)	178	Ke	56.10N	142.30W
Prattville	184	Di	32.28N	86.29W
Pratudinho, Rio-	204	Ja	13.58S	45.10W
Pravda	135	Cf	36.50N	60.33 E
Pravda Coast	222	Ge	67.00S	94.00 E
Pravdinsk [R.S.F.S.R.]	114	Kh	56.33N	43.33 E
Pravdinsk [R.S.F.S.R.]	116	Ij	54.26N	21.00 E
Pravia	126	Fa	43.29N	6.07W
Praxedis G. Guerrero	192	Gb	31.22N	106.00W
Praya	150	Gh	8.42S	116.17 E
Prealpi Venete	128	Fd	46.25N	11.50 E
Predazzo	128	Fd	46.19N	11.36 E
Predeal	130	Id	45.30N	25.34 E
Predeal, Pasul-	130	Id	45.28N	25.36 E
Predel	128	Hd	46.25N	13.35 E
Predil, Passo del-	128	Hd	46.25N	13.35 E
Predivinsk	138	Ee	57.04N	93.37 E
Predporožny	138	Jd	65.00N	143.20 E
Pré-en-Pail	122	Ff	48.27N	0.12W
Preetz	120	Gb	54.14N	10.17 E
Pregolja	114	Ei	54.42N	20.24 E
Pregradnaja	132	Lh	43.58N	41.12 E
Preiļi/Prejli	114	Gh	56.19N	26.48 E
Preissac, Lac-	184	Ha	48.25N	78.28W
Prejli/Preiļi	114	Gh	56.19N	26.48 E
Prekmurje	128	Kd	46.45N	16.15 E
Prekornica	130	Cg	42.40N	19.12 E
Prekule/Priekulė	116	Ii	55.36N	21.12 E
Přelouč	120	Lf	50.02N	15.33 E
Premià de Mar/Premiá de Mar	126	Oc	41.29N	2.22 E
Premiá de Mar/Premià de Mar	126	Oc	41.29N	2.22 E
Premnitz	120	Id	52.32N	12.20 E
Premuda	128	If	44.21N	14.37 E
Prenaj/Prienai	114	Fi	54.39N	23.59 E
Prenj	128	Lg	43.32N	17.52 E
Prenjasi	130	Dh	41.04N	20.32 E
Prentice	186	Kd	45.33N	90.17W
Prentiss	186	Lk	31.36N	89.52W
Prenzlau	120	Jc	53.19N	13.52 E
Preobraženije	138	Ih	42.58N	133.55 E
Preobraženka	138	Fd	60.04N	107.58 E
Preparis Island	148	If	14.52N	93.41 E
Preparis North Channel	148	Ie	15.27N	94.05 E
Preparis South Channel	150	Bd	14.45N	94.05 E
Přerov	120	Ng	49.27N	17.27 E
Prescott [Ar.-U.S.]	186	Jj	33.48N	93.23W
Prescott [Az.-U.S.]	182	Ee	34.33N	112.28W
Preseli, Mynydd-	118	Ij	51.58N	4.42W
Preševo	130	Eg	42.19N	21.39 E
Presho	186	Fe	43.53N	100.04W
Presicce	128	Mk	39.54N	18.16 E
Presidencia Roque Sáenz Peña	200	Jh	26.50S	60.30W
Presidente Epitácio	206	Jb	21.46S	52.06W
Presidente Frei	222	Re	62.12S	58.55W
Presidente Hayes [3]	204	Cf	24.00S	59.00W
Presidente Juscelino	204	Jd	18.39S	44.05W
Presidente Murtinho	204	Fb	15.39S	53.54W
Presidente Olegário	204	Id	18.25S	46.25W
Presidente Prudente	206	Jb	22.07S	51.22W
Presidente Venceslau	204	Ge	21.52S	51.50W
President Thiers Seamount (EN)	208	Mg	24.39S	145.51W
Presidio	182	Gf	29.33N	104.23W
Presidio, Rio del-	192	Ff	23.06N	106.17W
Preslav	130	Jf	43.10N	26.49 E
Presnovka	134	Mi	54.40N	67.09 E
Prešov	120	Rh	49.00N	21.14 E
Prespa	130	Hh	41.43N	24.53 E
Prespa, Lake- (EN) = Prespansko jezero	110	Ig	40.55N	21.00 E
Prespansko jezero = Prespa, Lake- (EN)	110	Ig	40.55N	21.00 E
Presque Isle	182	Nb	46.41N	68.01W
Prestea	166	Ed	5.26N	2.09W
Přeštice	120	Ig	49.35N	13.21 E
Preston [Eng.-U.K.]	118	Kh	53.46N	2.42W
Preston [Id.-U.S.]	182	Ec	42.06N	111.53W
Preston [Ont.-Can.]	184	Gd	43.23N	80.21W
Prestonsburg	184	Fg	37.40N	82.46W
Preststranda	116	Ce	59.06N	9.04 E
Prestwick	118	If	55.30N	4.37W
Prêto, Rio- [Braz.]	202	Jf	11.21S	43.52W
Prêto, Rio- [Braz.]	204	Ha	13.37S	48.06W
Prêto, Rio- [Braz.]	204	Ic	17.00S	46.12W
Prêto, Rio- [Braz.]	204	Gd	18.44S	50.23W
Preto do Igapó Açu, Rio-	202	Gd	4.26S	59.48W
Pretoria	160	Jk	25.45S	28.10 E
Pretty Rock Butte	186	Fc	46.10N	101.42W
Preußisch-Oldendorf	124	Kb	52.18N	8.30 E
Préveza	130	Dk	38.57N	20.45 E
Prey	124	Df	48.58N	1.13 E
Prey Vêng	148	Lf	11.29N	105.19 E
Priangarskoje plato	138	Ee	57.30N	97.00 E
Priargunsk	138	Gf	50.27N	119.00 E
Pribelski	134	Hi	54.24N	56.29 E
Pribilof Islands	174	Cd	57.00N	170.00W
Priboj	130	Cf	43.35N	19.32 E
Příbram	120	Kg	49.42N	14.01 E
Price [Que.-Can.]	184	Ma	48.39N	68.12W
Price [Ut.-U.S.]	188	Jg	39.36N	110.48W
Price River	188	Jg	39.10N	110.06W
Prichard	184	Cj	30.44N	88.05W
Prickly Pear Cays	197b	Ab	18.16N	63.11W
Prickly Point	197p	Bc	11.59N	61.45W
Pridneprovskaja vozvyšennost = Dnepr Upland (EN)	110	Jf	49.00N	32.00 E
Priego	126	Jd	40.27N	2.18W
Priego de Córdoba	126	Hg	37.26N	4.11W
Priei, Măgura-	130	Fc	46.58N	22.50 E
Priekule	114	Eh	56.29N	21.37 E
Priekulė/Prekule	116	Ii	55.36N	21.12 E
Prienai/Prenaj	114	Fi	54.39N	23.59 E
Priene	146	Bd	37.40N	27.13 E
Prieska	160	Jk	29.40S	22.42 E
Priest Lake	188	Gb	48.34N	116.52W
Prieta, Peña-	126	Ha	43.01N	4.44W
Prieta, Sierra-	192	Cb	31.15N	112.55W
Prievidza	120	Oh	48.46N	18.39 E
Prignitz	120	Hc	53.00N	12.00 E
Prijedor	128	Kf	44.59N	16.42 E
Prijepolje	130	Cf	43.24N	19.39 E
Prijutovo	136	Fe	53.58N	53.58 E
Prikaspijskaja nizmennost = Caspian Depression (EN)	110	Lf	48.00N	52.00 E
Prilenskoje plato = Lena Mountains (EN)	140	Oc	60.45N	125.00 E
Prilep	130	Eh	41.21N	21.34 E
Priluki	136	De	50.36N	32.24 E
Primavera	222	Qe	64.09S	60.57W
Primeira Cruz	202	Jd	2.30S	43.26W
Primorje	116	Hj	54.56N	20.00 E
Primorsk [R.S.F.S.R.]	114	Gf	60.22N	28.36 E
Primorsk [R.S.F.S.R.]	120	Pb	54.44N	19.59 E
Primorsk [Ukr.-U.S.S.R.]	132	Jf	46.43N	36.22 E
Primorski hrebet	138	Ff	52.30N	106.00 E
Primorski kraj [3]	138	Ig	45.30N	135.30 E
Primorsko	130	Kg	42.16N	27.46 E
Primorsko-Ahtarsk	136	Df	46.03N	38.11 E
Primorskoje [R.S.F.S.R.]	116	Ld	60.32N	27.56 E
Primorskoje [Ukr.-U.S.S.R.]	130	Nd	45.59N	30.15 E
Primošten	128	Jg	43.36N	15.55 E
Primrose Lake	180	Gf	54.55N	109.45W
Prims	120	Cg	49.20N	6.44 E
Prince Albert	176	Id	53.12N	104.46W
Prince Albert Mountains	222	Jf	76.00S	161.30 E
Prince Albert Peninsula	180	Fb	72.30N	116.00W
Prince Albert Road	172	Cf	33.13S	22.02 E
Prince Albert Sound	180	Gb	70.25N	115.00W
Prince Alfred, Cape -	180	Fb	74.05N	124.29W
Prince Charles	174	Lc	67.50N	76.00W
Prince Charles Mountains	222	Ff	72.00S	67.00 E
Prince-de-Galles, Cap -	180	Kd	61.36N	71.30W
Prince Edward	158	Km	46.33S	37.57 E
Prince Edward Island [2]	180	Lg	46.30N	63.00W
Prince EdKard Island	174	Me	46.30N	63.00W
Prince Edward Islands	158	Km	46.35S	37.56 E
Prince George	176	Gd	53.55N	122.49W
Prince Gustaf Adolf Sea	174	Ib	78.30N	107.00W
Prince of Wales [Ak.-U.S.]	178	Me	55.47N	132.50W
Prince of Wales [Can.]	174	Jb	72.40N	99.00W
Prince of Wales, Cape-	174	Cc	65.40N	168.05W
Prince of Wales Island	212	Ib	10.40S	142.10 E
Prince of Wales Mountains	180	Ja	77.45N	78.00W
Prince of Wales Strait	180	Fb	72.45N	118.00W
Prince Patrick	174	Hb	76.45N	119.30W
Prince Regent Inlet	180	Ib	72.45N	90.30W
Prince Rupert	176	Fd	54.19N	130.19W
Prince Rupert Bay	197g	Ba	15.34N	61.29W
Prince Rupert Bluff	197g	Ba	15.35N	61.29W
Princes Risborough	124	Bc	51.43N	0.49W
Princess Anne	184	Jf	38.12N	75.41W
Princess Charlotte Bay	212	Ib	14.25S	144.00 E
Princess Elizabeth Land	222	Ff	70.00S	80.00 E
Princess Margaret Range	180	Ia	79.00N	88.30W
Princess Royal	180	Ef	52.55N	128.50W
Princeton [B.C.-Can.]	180	Fg	49.27N	120.31W
Princeton [Il.-U.S.]	186	Lf	41.23N	89.28W
Princeton [In.-U.S.]	184	Df	38.21N	87.34W
Princeton [Ky.-U.S.]	184	Dg	37.07N	87.53W
Princeton [Mo.-U.S.]	186	Jf	40.24N	93.35W
Prince William Sound	174	Ec	60.40N	147.00W
Principe	158	Hh	1.37N	7.25 E
Prineville	188	Ed	44.18N	120.51W
Prineville Reservoir	188	Ed	44.08N	120.42W
Prins Christians Sund	179	Hf	60.00N	43.10W
Prinsesse Astrid Kyst	222	Cf	70.45S	12.30 E
Prinsesse Ragnhild Kyst	222	Df	70.15S	27.30 E
Prins Harald Kyst	222	De	69.30S	36.00 E
Prins Karls Forland	179	Nc	78.32N	11.10 E
Prinzapolka	190	Hf	13.24N	83.34W
Prinzapolka, Río-	194	Fg	13.24N	83.34W
Priora, Mount-	212	Ja	6.51S	145.58 E

Index Symbols

- [1] Independent Nation
- [2] State, Region
- [3] District, County
- [4] Municipality
- [5] Colony, Dependency
- Continent
- Physical Region
- Historical or Cultural Region
- Mount, Mountain
- Volcano
- Hill
- Mountains, Mountain Range
- Hills, Escarpment
- Plateau, Upland
- Pass, Gap
- Plain, Lowland
- Delta
- Salt Flat
- Valley, Canyon
- Crater, Cave
- Karst Features
- Depression
- Polder
- Desert, Dunes
- Forest, Woods
- Heath, Steppe
- Oasis
- Cape, Point
- Coast, Beach
- Cliff
- Peninsula
- Isthmus
- Sandbank
- Island
- Atoll
- Rock, Reef
- Islands, Archipelago
- Rocks, Reefs
- Coral Reef
- Well, Spring
- Geyser
- River, Stream
- Waterfall, Rapids
- River Mouth, Estuary
- Lake
- Salt Lake
- Intermittent Lake
- Reservoir
- Swamp, Pond
- Canal
- Glacier
- Ice Shelf, Pack Ice
- Ocean
- Sea
- Gulf, Bay
- Strait, Fjord
- Lagoon
- Bank
- Seamount
- Tablemount
- Ridge
- Shelf
- Basin
- Escarpment, Sea Scarp
- Fracture
- Trench, Abyss
- National Park, Reserve
- Point of Interest
- Recreation Site
- Cave, Cavern
- Historic Site
- Ruins
- Wall, Walls
- Church, Abbey
- Temple
- Scientific Station
- Railway station
- Airport
- Port
- Military installation
- Lighthouse
- Mine
- Tunnel
- Dam, Bridge

Priozersk 136 Dc 61.04N 30.07 E
Pripet Marshes (EN) 110 Ie 52.00N 27.00 E
Pripjat 110 Je 51.21N 30.09 E
Pripoljarny Ural=Subpolar Urals (EN) 110 Lb 65.00N 60.00 E
Prirečny 136 Db 69.02N 30.15 E
Prišib 132 Pj 39.06N 48.38 E
Prislop, Pasul- 130 Hb 47.37N 24.55 E
Pristan-Prževalsk 135 Lc 42.33N 78.18 E
Pristen 132 Jd 51.15N 36.42 E
Priština 130 Eg 42.40N 21.10 E
Pritzwalk 120 Ic 53.09N 12.11 E
Privas 122 Kj 44.44N 4.36 E
Priverno 128 Hi 41.28N 13.11 E
Privolžkaja vozvyšennost = Volga Hills (EN) 110 Ke 52.00N 46.00 E
Privolžsk 114 Jh 57.27N 41.16 E
Privolžski 132 Od 51.23N 46.02 E
Prizren 130 Dg 42.13N 20.45 E
Prizzi 128 Hm 37.43N 13.26 E
Prjaža 114 Hf 61.43N 33.37 E
Prnjavor 128 Lf 44.52N 17.40 E
Probolinggo 150 Fh 7.45 S 113.13 E
Prochowice 120 Me 51.17N 16.22 E
Procida 128 Hj 40.45N 14.00 E
Proctor Reservoir 186 Gj 32.02N 98.32W
Proddatur 148 Ff 14.44N 78.33 E
Profitis Ilías [Grc.] 130 Fm 36.53N 22.22 E
Profítis Ilías [Grc.] 130 Fj 39.50N 22.38 E
Profondeville 124 Gd 50.23N 4.52 E
Progonati 130 Ci 40.13N 19.56 E
Prograničnik 135 Dg 35.43N 63.12 E
Progreso [Mex.] 192 Id 27.28N 101.04W
Progreso [Mex.] 176 Kg 21.17N 89.40W
Progress 138 Hg 49.41N 129.40 E
Prohladny 132 Nh 43.45N 44.01 E
Prohorovka 132 Jd 51.02N 36.42 E
Prokopjevsk 142 Kd 53.53N 86.45 E
Prokuplje 130 Ef 43.15N 21.36 E
Proletari 114 Hg 58.26N 31.43 E
Proletarsk [R.S.F.S.R.] 136 Ef 46.41N 41.44 E
Proletarsk [Taj.-U.S.S.R.] 135 Gd 40.10N 69.31 E
Proletarski 132 Id 50.51N 35.46 E
Proletarskoje vodohranilišče 132 Mf 46.30N 42.10 E
Prome 142 Lh 18.49N 95.13 E
Promissâe, Reprêsa- 206 Kb 21.32 S 49.52W
Promissão 204 He 21.32 S 49.52W
Promyšlenny 134 Kc 67.35N 63.55 E
Pronja [Bye.-U.S.S.R.] 132 Gc 53.27N 31.03 E
Pronja [U.S.S.R.] 132 Lb 54.21N 40.24 E
Pronsfeld 124 Id 50.10N 6.20 E
Prophet 180 Fe 58.46N 122.45W
Propriá 202 Kf 10.13 S 36.51W
Propriano 122a Ab 41.40N 8.54 E
Prorva 132 Rg 45.57N 53.13 E
Proserpine 212 Jd 20.24 S 148.34 E
Prosna 120 Nd 52.10N 17.39 E
Prosotsáni 130 Gh 41.11N 23.59 E
Prosperidad 150 Ie 8.34N 125.52 E
Prospihino 138 Ee 58.37N 99.20 E
Prosser 188 Fc 46.12N 119.46W
Prostějov 120 Ng 49.29N 17.07 E
Proszowice 120 Qf 50.12N 20.18 E
Próti 130 El 37.03N 21.33 E
Protoka 132 Jg 45.43N 37.46 E
Protva 114 Ii 54.51N 37.16 E
Provadija 130 Kf 43.11N 27.26 E
Prøven 179 Gd 72.15N 55.40W
Provence 110 Gg 44.00N 6.00 E
Provence 122 Lk 44.00N 6.00 E
Providence [Ky.-U.S.] 184 Dg 37.24N 87.39W
Providence [R.I.-U.S.] 176 Le 41.50N 71.25W
Providence, Cape- 218 Bg 46.01 S 166.28 E
Providence Bay 184 Fc 45.44N 82.18W
Providence Island 158 Mi 9.14 S 51.02 E
Providencia, Isla de- 190 Hf 13.21N 81.22W
Providenciales 194 Kc 21.49N 72.15W
Providenija 142 Uc 64.23N 173.18W
Provincetown 184 Ld 42.03N 70.11W
Provins 122 Jf 48.33N 3.18 E
Provo 176 He 40.14N 111.39W
Prozor 128 Lg 43.49N 17.37 E
Prudentópolis 204 Gg 25.12 S 50.57W
Prudhoe Bay 176 Eb 70.20N 148.25W
Prudnik 120 Nf 50.19N 17.34 E
Prüm 120 Cf 50.13N 6.25 E
Prüm 124 Ie 49.49N 6.28 E
Prune Island 197n Bb 12.35N 61.24W
Pruntrut / Porrentruy 128 Bc 47.25N 7.10 E
Prussia (EN) 120 Pc 53.45N 20.00 E
Pruszcz Gdański 120 Ob 54.16N 18.36 E
Pruszków 120 Qd 52.11N 20.48 E
Prut 110 If 45.28N 28.14 E
Pružany 136 Ce 52.36N 24.28 E
Prvić 128 If 44.54N 14.48 E
Prydz Bay 222 Fe 69.00 S 76.00 E
Pryor 186 Ih 36.19N 95.19W
Przasnysz 120 Qc 53.01N 20.55 E
Przedbórz 120 Pe 51.06N 19.53 E
Przemyśl 120 Sg 49.47N 22.47 E
Przemyśl [2] 120 Sg 49.45N 22.45 E
Prževalsk 142 Je 42.29N 78.24 E
Przeworsk 120 Sf 50.05N 22.29 E
Przysucha 120 Qe 51.22N 20.38 E
Psakhná 130 Gk 38.35N 23.38 E
Psará 130 Ik 38.35N 25.37 E
Psathoúra 130 Hj 39.30N 24.11 E
Pščišč 132 Kg 45.03N 39.25 E
Psebaj 132 Lg 44.07N 40.47 E
Psël 110 Jf 49.05N 33.30 E
Psérimos 130 Km 36.56N 27.09 E
Psina 120 Of 50.02N 18.16 E
Pšiš, gora- 132 Lh 43.24N 41.14 E
Pskem 135 Hd 41.38N 70.01 E
Pskent 135 Gd 40.54N 69.23 E
Pskov 112 Id 57.50N 28.20 E
Pskov, Lake- (EN)=Pihkva järv 110 Id 58.00N 28.00 E
Pskov, Lake- (EN) = Pskovskoje ozero 110 Id 58.00N 28.00 E
Pskova 116 Mg 57.47N 28.30 E
Pskovskaja oblast [3] 136 Cd 57.20N 29.20 E
Pskovskoje ozero = Pskov, Lake- (EN) 110 Id 58.00N 28.00 E
Psunj 128 Le 45.24N 17.20 E
Ptič 132 Fc 52.09N 28.52 E
Ptolemaïs 130 Ei 40.31N 21.41 E
Ptuj 128 Jd 46.25N 15.52 E
Pua-a, Cape- 221c Aa 13.26 S 172.43W
Puah, Pulau- 150 Hg 0.30 S 122.34 E
Puapua 221c Aa 13.34 S 172.09W
Pucallpa 200 If 8.20 S 74.30W
Pučež 114 Kh 56.59N 43.11 E
Pucheng [China] 152 Kf 27.55N 118.30 E
Pucheng [China] 152 Id 35.00N 109.38 E
Pucho 170 Cf 17.35 S 16.30 E
Pucioasa 130 Id 45.05N 25.25 E
Pučišća 128 Kg 43.21N 16.44 E
Puck 120 Ob 54.44N 18.27 E
Pucka, Zatoka- 120 Ob 54.40N 18.35 E
Pudasjärvi 114 Gd 65.23N 27.00 E
Pudož 136 Dc 61.50N 36.32 E
Pudukkottai 148 Ff 10.23N 78.49 E
Puebla [2] 190 Ee 18.50N 98.00W
Puebla, Sierra de- 192 Kh 19.50N 97.00W
Puebla de Alcocer 126 Gf 38.59N 5.15W
Puebla de Don Fabrique 126 Jg 37.58N 2.26W
Puebla de Guzmán 126 Eg 37.37N 7.15W
Puebla de Sanabria 126 Fb 42.03N 6.38W
Puebla de Trives / Pobla de Trives 126 Eb 42.20N 7.15W
Puebla de Zaragoza 176 Jh 19.03N 98.12W
Pueblo 176 If 38.16N 104.37W
Pueblo Libertador 204 Cj 30.13 S 59.23W
Pueblo Nuevo [Mex.] 192 Gf 23.23N 105.23W
Pueblo Nuevo [Ven.] 194 Mh 11.58N 69.55W
Pueblo Nuevo Tiquisate 194 Bf 14.17N 91.22W
Pueblo Viejo, Laguna de- 192 Kf 22.10N 97.55W
Puelches 206 Ge 38.09 S 65.55W
Puente Alto 206 Fd 33.37 S 70.35W
Puenteareas / Ponteareas 126 Db 42.11N 8.30W
Puentedeume / Pontedeume 126 Da 43.24N 8.10W
Puente-Genil 126 Hg 37.23N 4.47W
Puente la Reina 126 Kb 42.40N 1.49W
Puentelarrá 126 Ib 42.45N 3.03W
Pueo Point 221a Ab 21.54N 160.04W
Pu'er 152 Hg 23.00N 101.00 E
Puerca, Punta- 197a Cb 18.15N 65.35W
Puerco, Rio- 186 Ci 34.22N 107.50W
Puerco River 188 Ji 34.52N 110.05W
Puerto Abente 204 Df 22.55 S 57.43W
Puerto Acosta 202 Eg 15.32 S 69.15W
Puerto Adela 204 Eg 24.33 S 54.22W
Puerto Aisén 200 Ij 45.24 S 72.42W
Puerto Alegre 202 Ff 13.53 S 61.36W
Puerto Ángel 190 Ee 15.40N 96.29W
Puerto Arista 192 Mj 15.56N 93.48W
Puerto Armuelles 190 Hg 8.17N 82.52W
Puerto Asís 202 Cc 0.29N 76.32W
Puerto Ayacucho 200 Je 5.40N 67.35W
Puerto Ayora 202a Ab 0.45 S 90.23W
Puerto Barrios 176 Kh 15.43N 88.36W
Puerto Bermejo 204 Ch 26.56 S 58.30W
Puerto Berrío 202 Db 6.30N 74.25W
Puerto Boyacá 202 Db 5.45N 74.29W
Puerto Caballo 204 Ce 20.12 S 58.12W
Puerto Cabello 200 Jd 10.28N 68.01W
Puerto Cabezas 190 Hf 14.02N 83.23W
Puerto Carreño 200 Je 6.12N 67.22W
Puerto Casado 206 Ib 20.20 S 57.55W
Puerto Colombia 194 Jh 10.59N 74.57W
Puerto Colón 204 Df 23.11 S 57.33W
Puerto Constanza 204 Ck 33.50 S 59.03W
Puerto Cooper 206 Ib 23.03 S 57.43W
Puerto Cortés [C.R.] 194 Fi 8.58N 83.32W
Puerto Cortés [Hond.] 176 Kh 15.48N 87.56W
Puerto Cumarebo 202 Ea 11.29N 69.21W
Puerto de Eten 202 Ce 6.56 S 79.52W
Puerto de la Cruz 162 Dd 28.23N 16.33W
Puerto de Lajas, Cerro- 190 Cc 28.59N 107.02W
Puerto del Rosario 162 Ed 28.30N 13.52W
Puerto de Mazarrón 126 Kg 37.34N 1.15W
Puerto de San José 190 Ff 13.55N 90.49W
Puerto Deseado 200 Jj 47.45 S 65.55W
Puerto de Sóller / El Port 126 Oe 39.48N 2.41 E
Puerto Escondido [Mex.] 190 Ee 15.48N 96.57W
Puerto Escondido [Mex.] 192 De 25.48N 111.20W
Puerto Esperanza [Arg.] 204 Eh 26.01 S 54.39W
Puerto Esperanza [Par.] 204 Ce 20.26 S 58.06W
Puerto Estrella 194 Lg 12.14N 71.13W
Puerto Fonciere 204 Df 22.29 S 57.48W
Puerto Francisco de Orellana 202 Cd 0.27 S 76.57W
Puerto Frey 204 Bb 14.42 S 61.10W
Puerto Gaitán 202 Dc 4.20N 72.10W
Puerto General Diaz 204 Eg 25.12 S 54.32W
Puerto Goya 204 Ci 29.09 S 59.20W
Puerto Grether 202 Fg 17.12 S 64.21W
Puerto Guaraní 204 De 21.18 S 57.55W
Puerto Heath 202 Ef 12.30 S 68.40W
Puerto Huitoto 202 Dc 0.18N 74.03W
Puerto Iguazú 206 Jc 25.34 S 54.34W
Puerto Indio 204 Eg 24.52 S 54.29W
Puerto Ingeniero Ibáñez 206 Fg 46.18 S 71.56W
Puerto Isabel 204 Dd 18.11 S 57.37W
Puerto Jesús 194 Eh 10.07N 85.16W
Puerto Juárez 176 Kg 21.11N 86.49W
Puerto la Concordia 202 Dc 2.38N 72.47W
Puerto la Cruz 200 Jd 10.13N 64.38W
Puerto Leguizamo 200 If 0.12 S 74.46W
Puerto Lempira 194 Ff 15.15N 83.46W
Puerto Libertad 190 Bc 29.55N 112.43W
Puerto Limón [Col.] 202 Dc 3.23N 73.30W
Puerto Limón [Col.] 202 Cc 1.02N 76.32W
Puertollano 126 Hf 38.41N 4.07W
Puerto López [Col.] 202 Dc 4.06N 72.58W
Puerto López [Col.] 194 Lh 11.56N 71.17W
Puerto Lumbreras 126 Kg 37.34N 1.49W
Puerto Madero 192 Mj 14.44N 92.25W
Puerto Madryn 206 Gf 42.46 S 65.03W
Puerto Magdalena 192 Ce 24.35N 112.05W
Puerto Maldonado 200 Jg 12.36 S 69.11W
Puerto Marangatú 204 Eg 24.39 S 54.21W
Puerto Mayor Otaño 204 Eh 26.19 S 54.44W
Puerto Mihanovich 204 De 20.52 S 57.59W
Puerto Montt 200 Ij 41.28 S 72.57W
Puerto Morelos 192 Pg 20.50N 86.52W
Puerto Mutis 202 Cb 6.14N 77.25W
Puerto Naranjito 204 Eh 26.57 S 55.18W
Puerto Nariño 202 Ec 4.56N 67.48W
Puerto Natales 200 Ik 51.44 S 72.31W
Puerto Nuevo 204 Ce 20.33 S 58.03W
Puerto Nuevo, Punta- 197a Bb 18.30N 66.21W
Puerto Ordaz 202 Fb 8.22N 62.41W
Puerto Padre 194 Ic 21.12N 76.36W
Puerto Páez 202 Eb 6.13N 67.28W
Puerto Peñasco 190 Bb 31.20N 113.33W
Puerto Piña 194 Hj 7.35N 78.10W
Puerto Pinasco 206 Ib 22.43 S 57.50W
Puerto Píritu 196 Dg 10.04N 65.03W
Puerto Plata 190 Je 19.48N 70.41W
Puerto Presidente Stroessner 204 Eg 25.33 S 54.39W
Puerto Princesa 142 Ni 9.44N 118.44 E
Puerto Quijarro 204 Dc 17.47 S 57.46W
Puerto Real 126 Fh 36.32N 6.11W
Puerto Rico [5] 176 Mh 18.15N 66.30W
Puerto Rico 174 Mh 18.15N 66.30W
Puerto Rico [Arg.] 206 Jc 26.48 S 54.59W
Puerto Rico [Bol.] 202 Ef 11.05 S 67.38W
Puerto Rico [Col.] 202 Cc 1.54N 75.10W
Puerto Rico Trench (EN) 106 Bg 20.00N 66.00W
Puerto Rondón 202 Db 6.18N 71.06W
Puerto San José 204 Eh 26.32 S 54.50W
Puerto Santa Cruz 200 Jk 50.09 S 68.30W
Puerto Sastre 206 Ib 22.06 S 57.59W
Puerto Siles 202 Ef 12.48 S 65.05W
Puerto Suárez 200 Kg 18.57 S 57.51W
Puerto Tacurú Pytá 204 Df 23.49 S 57.09W
Puerto Tirol 204 Ch 27.23 S 59.05W
Puerto Tres Palmas 204 De 21.43 S 57.58W
Puerto Triunfo 204 Eh 26.45 S 55.06W
Puerto Vallarta 190 Cd 20.37N 105.15W
Puerto Varas 206 Ff 41.19 S 72.59W
Puerto Victoria 204 Eh 26.20 S 54.39W
Puerto Viejo 194 Eh 10.26N 83.59W
Puerto Villamizar 194 Ki 8.19N 72.26W
Puerto Villazón 204 Ba 13.32 S 61.57W
Puerto Wilches 202 Db 7.20N 73.54W
Puerto Ybapobó 204 Df 23.42 S 57.12W
Puesto Monte Lindo 204 Df 23.57 S 57.12W
Pueu 221e Fc 17.44 S 149.13W
Pugačev 136 Ee 52.03N 48.48 E
Puget Sound 188 Dc 48.00N 122.30W
Puglia = Apulia (EN) [2] 128 Ki 41.15N 16.15 E
Pu He 154 Gd 41.21N 122.47 E
Puhja 116 Lf 58.13N 26.17 E
Puigcerdà 126 Nb 42.26N 1.56 E
Puigmal 126 Ob 42.23N 2.07 E
Puir 138 Jf 53.10N 141.25 E
Puisaye, Collines de la- 122 Jg 47.35N 3.18 E
Puisieux 124 Ed 50.07N 2.42 E
Pujehum 166 Cd 7.21N 11.42W
Pujeşti 130 Kc 46.25N 27.29 E
Puji → Wugong 152 Ie 34.15N 108.14 E
Pujiang 154 Ei 29.28N 119.53 E
Pujili 202 Cd 0.57 S 78.42W
Puka 130 Cg 42.03N 19.54 E
Pukaki, Lake- 218 Df 44.05 S 170.10 E
Pukalani 221a Ec 20.50N 156.21W
Pukapuka Atoll [Cook] 208 Kf 10.53 S 165.49W
Pukapuka Atoll [Fr.Poly.] 208 Nf 14.49 S 138.48W
Pukaruha Atoll 208 Nf 18.20 S 137.02W
Pukatawagan 180 He 55.44N 101.19W
Pukchin 154 Hd 40.12N 125.45 E
Pukch'ŏng 152 Mc 40.14N 128.19 E
Pukega, Pointe- 220h Ab 13.17 S 176.13W
Pukekohe 218 Fb 37.12 S 174.54 E
Pukemiro 218 Fb 37.37 S 175.01 E
Pukeuri Junction 218 Df 45.02 S 171.02 E
Pukp'yong 152 Md 37.28N 129.08 E
Pukšenga 114 Je 63.36N 41.55 E
Puksoozero 136 Ec 62.38N 40.32 E
Puksubaek-san 154 Id 40.42N 127.15 E
Pula [It.] 128 Dk 39.01N 9.00 E
Pula [Yugo.] 128 Hf 44.52N 13.50 E
Pula, Capo di- 128 Dl 38.59N 9.01 E
Pulandian → Xinjin 152 Ld 39.24N 121.59 E
Pulap Atoll 208 Fd 7.39N 149.25 E
Pulaski [Tn.-U.S.] 184 Dh 35.12N 87.02W
Pulaski [Va.-U.S.] 184 Gg 37.03N 80.47W
Pulau 150 Kh 5.50 S 138.15 E
Pulau Halura 150 Hi 10.19 S 120.11 E
Pulau Irian/New Guinea 208 Fe 5.00 S 140.00 E
Pulau Pinang [2] 150 De 5.20N 100.20 E
Pulau Sapudi 150 Fh 7.06 S 114.20 E
Puławy 120 Re 51.25N 21.57 E
Pulborough 124 Bd 50.57N 0.31W
Pulheim 124 Ic 51.00N 6.48 E
Pulkau 128 Kb 48.43N 16.21 E
Pulkkila 114 Fd 64.16N 25.52 E
Pullman 182 Db 46.44N 117.10W
Pulo Anna Island 208 Ed 4.40N 131.58 E
Pulog, Mount- 140 Oh 16.36N 120.54 E
Pulpito, Punta- 192 Dd 26.30N 111.30W
Pulsano 128 Lj 40.23N 17.21 E
Pułtusk 120 Rd 52.43N 21.05 E
Pülümür 146 Hc 39.30N 39.54 E
Pulusuk Island 208 Fd 6.42N 149.19 E
Puluwat Atoll 208 Fd 7.22N 149.11 E
Puma Yumco 152 Ff 28.35N 90.20 E
Pumpėnai/Pumpenaj 116 Ki 55.53N 24.25 E
Pumpenaj/Pumpėnai 116 Ki 55.53N 24.25 E
Pumpkin Creek 188 Mc 46.15N 105.45W
Puná, Isla- 202 Bd 2.50 S 80.10W
Punākha 148 Hc 27.37N 89.52 E
Punaluu 221a Fd 19.08N 155.30W
Pūnch 148 Eb 33.46N 74.06 E
Punda Milia 172 Ed 22.40 S 31.05 E
Pune (Poona) 142 Jh 18.32N 73.52 E
Pūnel 146 Md 37.33N 49.07 E
Pungan 135 Hd 40.45N 70.50 E
P'unggi 154 Jf 36.52N 128.32 E
Púngoè 172 Ec 19.50 S 34.48 E
P'ungsan 154 Jd 40.40N 128.05 E
Punia 170 Ec 1.28 S 26.27 E
Punitaqui 206 Fd 30.50 S 71.16W
Punjab [3] 148 Fb 31.00N 76.00 E
Punjab 140 Jf 30.00N 74.00 E
Punjad [3] 148 Eb 30.00N 74.00 E
Punkaharju 116 Mc 61.48N 29.24 E
Punkalaidun 116 Jc 61.07N 23.06 E
Puno 200 Ig 15.50 S 70.02W
Puno [3] 202 Ef 15.00 S 70.00W
Punta, Cerro de- 190 Ke 18.10N 66.36W
Punta Alta 200 Ji 38.53 S 62.04W
Punta Arenas 200 Ik 53.09 S 70.55W
Punta Cardón 202 Da 11.38N 70.14W
Punta de Mata 196 Eh 9.43N 63.38W
Punta Gorda [Blz.] 190 Ge 16.07N 88.48W
Punta Gorda [Fl.-U.S.] 184 Fl 26.56N 82.03W
Punta Gorda [Nic.] 194 Fh 11.31N 83.47W
Punta Gorda, Bahía de- 194 Fh 11.15N 83.45W
Punta Gorda, Río- 194 Fh 11.30N 83.47W
Punta Indio 204 Dl 35.16 S 57.14W
Punta Prieta 190 Bc 28.58N 114.17W
Puntarenas 176 Ki 9.58N 84.50W
Puntarenas [3] 194 Ei 9.00N 83.15W
Punta Róbalo 194 Fi 9.02N 82.15W
Punto Fijo 202 Da 11.42N 70.13W
Puolanka 114 Gd 64.52N 27.40 E
Puolo Point 221a Bb 21.54N 159.36W
Puqi 152 Jf 29.43N 113.52 E
Puquio 202 Df 14.42 S 74.08W
Pur 140 Jc 67.29N 78.05 E
Puracé, Volcán- 202 Cc 2.21N 76.23W
Purari 214 Ci 7.52 S 145.10 E
Purcell Mountains 180 Fg 49.55N 116.15W
Purchena 126 Jg 37.21N 2.22W
Purdy Islands 208 Fe 2.53 S 146.20 E
Purgatoire River 186 Eg 38.04N 103.10W
Puri 148 He 19.48N 85.51 E
Purificación 190 Ed 23.58N 98.42W
Purikari neem / Purikarinem 116 Ke 59.36N 25.35 E
Purikarinem / Purikari neem 116 Ke 59.36N 25.35 E
Purmani/Puurmani 116 Lf 58.30N 26.14 E
Purmerend 122 Kb 52.31N 4.57 E
Purna [India] 148 Fd 21.05N 76.00 E
Purna [India] 148 Fe 19.07N 77.02 E
Purnač 114 Jc 67.00N 40.15 E
Pūrnia 148 Hc 25.47N 87.28 E
Purukcahu 150 Fg 0.35S 114.35 E
Puruliya 148 Hd 23.20N 86.22 E
Puruni River 196 Gi 6.00N 59.12W
Purús, Rio- 198 Jf 3.42 S 61.28W
Puruvesi 114 Gf 61.50N 29.25 E
Purwakarta 150 Eh 6.34 S 107.26 E
Purwokerto 150 Eh 7.25 S 109.14 E
Pusala Dağı 146 Ed 37.12N 32.54 E
Pusan 142 Of 35.06N 129.03 E
Pusan Si [2] 154 Jg 35.10N 129.05 E
Puschlav / Poschiavo 128 Ed 46.20N 10.04 E
Pushi He 154 Hd 40.17N 124.43 E
Puškin 136 Dd 59.43N 30.24 E
Puškino [Abz.-U.S.S.R.] 132 Pj 39.28N 48.33 E
Puškino [R.S.F.S.R.] 114 Ih 56.02N 37.53 E
Puškino [R.S.F.S.R.] 132 Od 51.14N 46.59 E
Puškinskije Gory 116 Mh 56.59N 28.59 E
Pušlahta 114 Id 64.48N 36.33 E
Püspökladány 120 Ri 47.19N 21.07 E
Püssi/Pjussi 116 Le 59.17N 26.57 E
Pusteci 130 Di 40.47N 20.54 E
Pusteria, Val-/Pustertal 128 Gd 46.45N 12.20 E
Pustertal/Pusteria, Val- 128 Gd 46.45N 12.20 E
Pustomyty 120 Tg 49.37N 23.59 E
Pustoška 114 Gh 56.20N 29.22 E
Putao 148 Jc 27.21N 97.24 E
Putaruru 218 Fc 38.03 S 175.47 E
Putian 152 Kf 25.32N 119.01 E
Putignano 128 Lj 40.51N 17.07 E
Putila 130 Ib 48.00N 25.07 E
Putivl 132 Hd 51.22N 33.55 E
Putjatin 154 Lc 42.52N 132.25 E
Putla de Guerrero 192 Ki 17.02N 97.56W
Putna 130 Ib 47.52N 25.37 E
Putna 130 Kd 45.34N 27.30 E
Putnok 120 Qh 48.18N 20.26 E
Puto 219a Ba 5.41 S 154.43 E
Putorana, plato- = Putoran Mountains (EN) 140 Lc 69.00N 95.00 E
Putoran Mountains (EN) = Putorana, plato- 140 Lc 69.00N 95.00 E
Puttalam 148 Fg 8.02N 79.49 E
Putte 124 Gc 51.04N 4.38 E
Puttelange-aux-Lacs 124 Ie 49.03N 6.56 E
Putten 124 Hb 52.16N 5.35 E
Putten 124 Gc 51.50N 4.15 E
Puttgarden, Burg auf Fehmarn- 120 Hb 54.30N 11.13 E
Püttlingen 124 Ie 49.17N 6.53 E
Putumayo [2] 202 Cc 0.30N 76.00W
Putumayo, Rio- 198 Jf 3.07 S 67.58W
Putuo (Shenjiamen) 154 Gj 29.57N 122.18 E
Putussibau 150 Ff 0.50N 112.56 E
Puu Kukui 221a Ec 20.54N 156.35W
Puulavesi 110 Ic 61.50N 26.40 E
Puumala 114 Gf 61.32N 28.11 E
Puu o Umi 221a Fc 20.05N 155.42W
Puurmani/Purmani 116 Lf 58.30N 26.14 E
Puurs 124 Gc 51.05N 4.17 E
Puuwai 221a Ab 21.54N 160.12W
Puy, Le- 122 Ji 45.02N 3.53 E
Puyallup 188 Dc 47.11N 122.18W
Puyang 152 Jd 35.41N 115.00 E
Puy-de-Dôme [3] 122 Ii 45.40N 3.00 E
Puy-l'Evêque 122 Hj 44.30N 1.08 E
Puymorens, Col de- 122 Hl 42.34N 1.49 E
Puyo 202 Cd 1.29 S 77.58W
Puysegur Point 218 Bg 46.10 S 166.37 E
Pwani [3] 170 Gd 7.30 S 39.00 E
Pweto 160 Ji 8.28 S 28.54 E
Pwllheli 118 Ii 52.53N 4.25W
Pyapon 148 Je 16.17N 95.41 E
Pyhäjärvi 114 Fe 63.40N 25.59 E
Pyhäjärvi [Fin.] 114 Fe 63.35N 25.57 E
Pyhäjärvi [Fin.] 114 Ff 61.00N 22.20 E
Pyhäjärvi [Fin.] 116 Kc 62.45N 25.25 E
Pyhäjärvi [Fin.] 116 Jc 61.30N 23.35 E
Pyhäjoki 114 Fd 64.28N 24.14 E
Pyhäjoki 114 Fd 64.28N 24.13 E
Pyhäntä 114 Gd 64.06N 26.19 E
Pyhäranta 116 Id 60.57N 21.27 E
Pyhaselkä 116 Mb 62.26N 29.58 E
Pyhäselkä 114 Ge 62.30N 29.40 E
Pyhätunturi 114 Gc 67.01N 27.09 E
Pyhävesi 116 Lc 61.25N 26.35 E
Pyhävuori 116 Ib 62.17N 21.38 E
Pyhrnpaß 128 Ic 47.38N 14.18 E
Pyhtää/Pyttis 114 Gf 60.29N 26.32 E
Pyinmana 142 Lh 19.44N 96.13 E
Pylos (EN) = Pilos 130 Em 36.56N 21.40 E
Pyltsamaa/Põltsamaa 114 Fg 58.39N 25.59 E
Pyltsamaa/Põltsamaa 116 Lf 58.23N 26.08 E
Pylva/Põlva 114 Gg 58.04N 27.06 E
Pymatuning Reservoir 184 Ge 41.37N 80.30W
P'yŏngan-Namdo [2] 154 Ie 39.20N 126.00 E
P'yŏngan-Pukto [2] 154 Hd 40.00N 125.15 E
P'yŏnggang 152 Md 38.25N 127.17 E
P'yŏngsan 152 Md 38.20N 126.24 E
P'yongt'aek 154 If 36.59N 127.05 E
P'yŏngyang 142 Of 39.01N 125.45 E
P'yŏngyang Si [2] 154 He 39.04N 125.50 E
Pyramiden 179 Nc 77.54N 16.41 E
Pyramid Lake 182 Dc 40.00N 119.35W
Pyramid Mountains 186 Bj 32.00N 108.30W
Pyrénées=Pyrenees (EN) 110 Gg 42.40N 1.00 E
Pyrenees (EN)=Pirineos 110 Gg 42.40N 1.00 E
Pyrenees (EN)= Pyrénées 110 Gg 42.40N 1.00 E
Pyrenees (EN)=Serralada Pirinenca 110 Gg 42.40N 1.00 E
Pyrénées-Atlantiques [3] 122 Fk 43.15N 0.50W
Pyrénées-Orientales [3] 122 Il 42.30N 2.20 E
Pyrzyce 120 Kc 53.10N 14.55 E
Pyšma 136 Gd 57.08N 66.18 E
Pytalovo 114 Gh 57.06N 27.59 E
Pyttegga 116 Bb 62.13N 7.42 E
Pyttis/Pyhtää 114 Gf 60.29N 26.32 E
Pyu 148 Je 18.29N 96.26 E
Pyzaspea / Pōōsaspea neem 116 Je 59.15N 23.25 E
Pyzdry 120 Nd 52.11N 17.41 E

Q

Qā', Wādī al- 146 Hi 27.04N 38.34 E
Qābis 160 Ie 33.53N 10.07 E
Qābis [3] 162 Ic 33.00N 9.30 E
Qābis, Khalīj-=Gabès, Gulf of-(EN) 158 Ie 34.00N 10.25 E
Qabr Hūd 168 Hb 16.09N 49.34 E
Qāderābād 146 Og 30.17N 53.16 E
Qādır Karam 146 Ke 35.12N 44.53 E
Qāḑub 144 Hg 12.38N 53.57 E
Qā'emshahr 146 Od 36.30N 52.55 E
Qafşah 160 He 34.25N 8.48 E
Qafşah [3] 162 Ic 34.30N 9.00 E
Qa'fūr 128 Dn 36.20N 9.19 E
Qagan 152 Kb 49.16N 118.04 E
Qagan Moron He 154 Ec 43.13N 119.02 E
Qagan Nur 152 Jc 43.20N 112.58 E
Qagan Nur [China] 154 Hb 45.14N 124.17 E
Qagan Nur [China] 154 Bd 41.33N 113.48 E
Qagan Nur [China] 152 Jc 43.25N 114.50 E
Qagan Nur → Zhengxiangbai Qi 152 Jc 42.16N 114.59 E
Qagan Us → Dulan 142 Lf 36.29N 98.29 E
Qagchêng/Xiangcheng 152 Gf 28.56N 99.46 E
Qahar Youyi Houqi (Bayan Qagan) 154 Bd 41.28N 113.10 E
Qahar Youyi Qianqi (Togrog Ul) 154 Bd 40.46N 113.13 E
Qahar Youyi Zhongqi 154 Bd 41.15N 112.36 E
Qahd, Wādī- 146 Ii 26.13N 40.49 E
Qaidam He 152 Gd 36.48N 95.50 E
Qaidam Pendi=Tsaidam Basin (EN) 152 Fd 37.00N 95.00 E
Qala'an Naḩl 168 Ec 13.38N 34.57 E
Qalāt 144 Kc 32.07N 66.54 E
Qal'at Abū Ghār 146 Lg 30.25N 46.09 E
Qal'at al Akhḑar 144 Ed 28.06N 37.05 E
Qal 'at al Marqab 146 Fe 35.09N 35.57 E
Qal'at al Mu'aẓẓam 146 Gi 27.45N 37.31 E
Qal'at aş Şanam 128 Co 35.46N 8.21 E
Qal'at Bīshah 142 Gh 20.00N 42.36 E
Qal'at Dīzah 146 Kd 36.11N 45.07 E
Qal'at Şāliḩ 146 Lg 31.31N 47.16 E
Qal'at Sukkar 146 Lg 31.53N 46.56 E
Qal'eh Asgar 146 Qh 29.30N 56.35 E
Qal'eh Kūh 146 Mf 33.00N 49.10 E
Qal'eh Mūreh 146 Pe 35.35N 55.58 E
Qal'eh-ye Now 144 Jc 34.59N 63.08 E
Qal'eh-ye Sahar 146 Mg 31.40N 48.33 E

Index Symbols

[1] Independent Nation
[2] State, Region
[3] District, County
[4] Municipality •
[5] Colony, Dependency
Continent
Physical Region
Historical or Cultural Region
Mount, Mountain
Volcano
Hill
Mountains, Mountain Range
Hills, Escarpment
Plateau, Upland
Pass, Gap
Plain, Lowland
Delta
Salt Flat
Valley, Canyon
Crater, Cave
Karst Features
Depression
Polder
Desert, Dunes
Forest, Woods
Heath, Steppe
Oasis
Cape, Point
Coast, Beach
Cliff
Peninsula
Isthmus
Sandbank
Island
Atoll
Rock, Reef
Islands, Archipelago
Rocks, Reefs
Coral Reef
Well, Spring
Geyser
River, Stream
Waterfall, Rapids
River Mouth, Estuary
Lake
Salt Lake
Intermittent Lake
Reservoir
Swamp, Pond
Canal
Glacier
Ice Shelf, Pack Ice
Ocean
Sea
Gulf, Bay
Strait, Fjord
Lagoon
Bank
Seamount
Tablemount
Ridge
Shelf
Basin
Escarpment, Sea Scarp
Fracture
Trench, Abyss
National Park, Reserve
Point of Interest
Recreation Site
Cave, Cavern
Historic Site
Ruins
Wall, Walls
Church, Abbey
Temple
Scientific Station
Railway station
Airport
Port
Military installation
Lighthouse
Mine
Tunnel
Dam, Bridge

Qalīb ash Shuyūkh 144 Gd 29.12N 47.55 E
Qallābāt 168 Fc 12.58N 36.09 E
Qalmarz, Godār-e- 146 Qf 33.26N 56.14 E
Qalyūb 146 Dg 30.11N 31.13 E
Qamata 172 Df 31.58S 27.24 E
Qamdo 142 Lf 31.15N 97.12 E
Qamīnis 164 Dc 31.40N 20.01 E
Qamsar 146 Nf 33.45N 51.26 E
Qamūdah 162 Ic 35.00N 9.21 E
Qamūdah [3] 162 Ic 34.50N 9.20 E
Qânâq/Thule 224 Od 77.35N 69.40W
Qandahār 142 If 31.35N 65.45 E
Qandahār [3] 144 Kc 31.00N 65.45 E
Qandala 168 Hc 11.23N 49.53 E
Qangdin Gol 154 Cc 43.27N 115.03 E
Qanţarat al Faḩş 128 Dn 36.23N 9.54 E
Qapqal 152 Dc 43.48N 80.47 E
Qaqortoq/Julianehåb 224 Nc 60.50N 46.10W
Qarā Dāgh 146 Lc 38.48N 47.13 E
Qārah 164 Ed 29.37N 26.30 E
Qarah Būlāq 146 Ke 34.32N 45.12 E
Qarah Dagh 146 Jd 37.00N 43.30 E
Qarah Tappah 146 Ke 34.25N 44.56 E
Qarānqū 146 Ld 37.23N 47.43 E
Qardo 160 Lh 9.30N 49.03 E
Qareh Āghāj 146 Ld 36.46N 48.46 E
Qareh Sū [Asia] 144 Gb 39.27N 47.30 E
Qareh Sū [Iran] 144 Hc 34.52N 51.25 E
Qareh Sū [Iran] 144 Ib 37.00N 56.50 E
Qareh Ẕīā'Od Dīn 146 Kc 38.53N 45.02 E
Qarkilik/Ruoqiang 142 Kf 39.02N 88.00 E
Qarnayn, Jazīrat al- 146 Oj 24.56N 52.52 E
Qarqan/Qiemo 142 Kf 38.08N 85.32 E
Qarqan He 140 Kf 39.30N 88.15 E
Qarqannah, Juzur-= Kerkennah Islands (EN) 158 Ie 34.44N 11.12 E
Qartājannah 128 En 36.51N 10.20 E
Qārūn, Birkat- 164 Fd 29.28N 30.40 E
Qaryat Abū Nujaym 164 Cc 30.35N 15.24 E
Qaryat al Gharab 146 Kg 31.27N 44.48 E
Qaryat al Qaddāḩīyah 164 Cc 31.22N 15.14 E
Qaryat al 'Ulyā 144 Gd 27.33N 47.42 E
Qaryat az Zarrūq 164 Cc 32.22N 15.09 E
Qaryat az Zuwaytīnah 164 Dc 30.58N 20.07 E
Qaryat Hubayn al Gharbīyah 146 Je 34.21N 42.05 E
Qaşabah, Ra's al- 146 Fh 28.02N 34.38 E
Qaşabāt, Hanshīr al- 128 Dn 36.24N 9.54 E
Qasigiánguit/Christianshåb 179 Ge 68.45N 51.30W
Qaşr al Azraq 146 Gg 31.53N 36.49 E
Qasr Al Hayr 146 Ge 34.23N 37.36 E
Qaşr al Qarahbullī 164 Bc 32.45N 13.43 E
Qaşr 'Amij 146 If 33.30N 41.45 E
Qaşr Bū Hādī 164 Cc 31.03N 16.40 E
Qaşr Burqu' 146 Gf 32.37N 37.58 E
Qasr-e Shīrīn 144 Gc 34.31N 45.35 E
Qaşr Farāfirah 160 Jf 27.15N 28.10 E
Qaşr Ḩamān 144 Ge 20.50N 45.50 E
Qaşr Qārūn 146 Dh 29.25N 30.25 E
Qaşş Abū Sa'īd 146 Bi 27.00N 27.35 E
Qatana 146 Gf 33.26N 36.05 E
Qaţar [1] 142 Hg 25.30N 51.15 E
Qaţar 140 Hg 25.30N 51.15 E
Qatlīsh 146 Qd 37.50N 57.19 E
Qaţrānī, Jabal- 146 Dh 29.41N 30.35 E
Qatrūyeh 146 Ph 29.09N 54.43 E
Qattara Depression (EN)= Qaţţārah, Munkhafaḑ al- 158 Je 30.00N 27.30 E
Qaţţārah, Munkhafaḑ al-= Qattara Depression (EN) 158 Je 30.00N 27.30 E
Qawām al Hamzah 146 Kg 31.43N 44.58 E
Qawz Abu Ḑulū' 168 Eb 16.55N 32.30 E
Qawz Rajab 168 Fb 16.04N 35.34 E
Qaysān 168 Ec 10.45N 34.48 E
Qayyārah 146 Je 35.48N 43.17 E
Qazvīn 142 Gf 36.16N 50.00 E
Qeqertarssuaq/Godhavn 224 Nc 69.20N 53.35W
Qeshm 146 Qi 26.58N 56.16 E
Qeshm 144 Id 26.45N 55.45 E
Qeydār 146 Md 36.07N 48.35 E
Qeys, Jazīreh-ye- 144 Hd 26.32N 53.58 E
Qezel 144 Gb 36.45N 49.22 E
Qian'an [China] 154 Ed 40.01N 118.42 E
Qian'an [China] 154 Hb 44.58N 124.01 E
Qianfangzi 154 Ad 40.01N 111.23 E
Qian Gorlos (Quianguozhen) 152 Lb 45.05N 124.52 E
Qian He 154 Dh 32.55N 117.10 E
Qianjiang [China] 154 Bi 30.25N 112.54 E
Qianjiang [China] 152 Ig 23.37N 108.58 E
Qianjiang [China] 152 If 29.30N 108.45 E
Qianning/Gartar 152 He 30.27N 101.29 E
Qianshan 154 Di 30.38N 116.35 E
Qian Shan 152 Lc 40.35N 123.00 E
Qiansuo 152 Hf 25.27N 100.41 E
Qianwei 152 Hf 29.08N 103.56 E
Qianxi [China] 152 If 27.03N 106.04 E
Qianxi [China] 154 Ed 40.08N 118.19 E
Qianyang (Anjiang) 152 Jf 27.19N 110.13 E
Qiaojia 152 Hf 27.00N 103.00 E
Qiaowan 152 Gc 40.36N 96.42 E
Qibilī 162 Ic 33.42N 8.58 E
Qichun (Caojiahe) 154 Ci 30.15N 115.26 E
Qidaogou 154 Id 41.31N 126.18 E
Qidong 154 Fi 31.48N 121.39 E
Qiemo/Qarqan 142 Kf 38.08N 85.32 E
Qift 146 Ei 26.00N 32.49 E
Qijiang 152 If 29.00N 106.39 E
Qijiaojing 152 Fc 43.28N 91.36 E
Qike → Xunke 152 Mb 49.34N 128.28 E
Qili → Shitai 154 Di 30.12N 117.28 E
Qilian (Babao) 152 Hd 38.14N 100.15 E
Qilian Shan 152 Gd 39.12N 98.35 E
Qilian Shan 140 Lf 38.30N 100.00 E
Qimantag 152 Fd 37.00N 91.00 E
Qimen 152 Kf 29.57N 117.39 E
Qinā 160 Kf 26.10N 32.43 E
Qinā, Wādī- 146 Ei 26.12N 32.44 E
Qin'an 152 Ie 34.50N 105.35 E
Qingchengzi 154 Gd 40.44N 123.36 E
Qingchuan 152 Ie 32.32N 105.11 E
Qingdao (Tsingtao) 142 Of 36.05N 120.21 E
Qingduizi 154 Fd 41.27N 121.52 E
Qingfeng 154 Cg 35.54N 115.07 E
Qinggang 152 Mb 46.41N 126.03 E
Qinggil/Qinghe 152 Fb 46.43N 90.24 E
Qinghai Hu=Koko Nor (EN) 140 Mf 37.00N 100.20 E
Qinghai Sheng (Ch'ing-hai Sheng)=Tsinghai (EN) [2] 152 Gd 36.00N 96.00 E
Qing He 154 Hc 42.16N 124.10 E
Qinghe/Qinggil 152 Fb 46.43N 90.24 E
Qinghe (Gexianzhuang) 154 Cf 37.03N 115.39 E
Qinghemen 154 Fd 41.45N 121.25 E
Qingjian 152 Jd 37.10N 110.09 E
Qingjiang 142 Nf 33.31N 119.03 E
Qing Jiang 152 Je 30.24N 111.30 E
Qingjiang (Zhangshuzhen) 152 Kf 28.02N 115.31 E
Qingkou → Ganyu 154 Eg 34.50N 119.07 E
Qinglong 154 Ed 40.26N 118.58 E
Qinglong He 154 Ee 39.51N 118.51 E
Qingshan 154 Ci 30.39N 114.27 E
Qingshuihe 152 Jd 39.56N 111.41 E
Qingshui Jiang 152 If 27.11N 109.48 E
Qingtian 152 Lf 28.12N 120.17 E
Qingxian 154 De 38.35N 116.48 E
Qingxu 154 Bf 37.36N 112.21 E
Qingyang [China] 154 Di 30.38N 117.50 E
Qingyang [China] 152 Id 36.01N 107.48 E
Qingyuan 152 Lc 42.06N 124.56 E
Qingyuan (Nandaran) 154 Ce 38.46N 115.29 E
Qingyun (Xiejiaji) 154 Df 37.46N 117.22 E
Qing Zang Gaoyuan=Tibet, Plateau of- (EN) 140 Kf 32.30N 87.00 E
Qin He 154 Bg 35.01N 113.25 E
Qinhuangdao 152 Kg 40.00N 119.32 E
Qin Ling 140 Mf 34.00N 108.00 E
Qinshui 154 Bg 35.41N 112.10 E
Qintong 154 Fh 32.39N 120.06 E
Qinxian 154 Bf 36.46N 112.42 E
Qinyang 154 Bg 35.05N 112.56 E
Qinyuan 154 Bf 36.29N 112.20 E
Qinzhou 152 Ig 22.02N 108.30 E
Qionghai (Jiaji) 152 Jh 19.25N 110.28 E
Qionglai 152 He 30.24N 103.28 E
Qiongzhou Haixia 140 Ng 20.10N 110.15 E
Qipan Guan 152 Ie 32.45N 106.11 E
Qiqihar 142 Oe 47.21N 123.58 E
Qīr 146 Oh 28.29N 53.04 E
Qira 152 Dd 37.02N 80.53 E
Qiryat Gat 146 Fg 31.36N 34.46 E
Qiryat Shemona 146 Ff 33.13N 35.34 E
Qiryat Yam 146 Ff 32.51N 35.04 E
Qishn 144 Hf 15.26N 51.40 E
Qi Shui 154 Ci 30.09N 115.22 E
Qishuyan 154 Fi 31.41N 120.04 E
Qitai 142 Ke 44.01N 89.28 E
Qitaihe 152 Nb 45.49N 130.51 E
Qiuxian (Matou) 154 Cf 36.50N 115.10 E
Qixia 154 Ff 37.18N 120.50 E
Qixian [China] 154 Cg 34.33N 114.46 E
Qixian [China] 154 Bf 37.23N 112.21 E
Qixian (Zhaoge) 154 Cg 35.35N 114.12 E
Qiyang 152 Jf 26.44N 111.50 E
Qizhou 154 Ci 30.04N 115.20 E
Qogir Feng=Godwin Austen (EN) 140 Jf 35.53N 76.30 E
Qog Qi 152 Ic 41.31N 107.00 E
Qog Ul 152 Kc 44.50N 116.19 E
Qohrūd, Kūhhā-ye- 140 Hf 32.40N 53.00 E
Qoltag 152 Ec 42.20N 88.45 E
Qom 142 Hf 34.39N 50.54 E
Qom 146 Ne 34.48N 51.02 E
Qomolangma Feng=Everest, Mount- (EN) 140 Kg 27.59N 86.56 E
Qomrud 146 Ne 34.43N 51.04 E
Qomsheh 144 Hc 32.00N 51.50 E
Qondūz 142 If 36.45N 68.51 E
Qondūz [3] 144 Kb 36.45N 68.30 E
Qondūz 144 Kb 37.00N 68.16 E
Qoqek/Tacheng 142 Ke 46.45N 82.57 E
Qôrnoq 179 Gf 64.30N 51.19W
Qorveh 146 Le 35.10N 47.48 E
Qoşbeh-ye Naşşār 144 Gc 30.02N 48.27 E
Qoţbābād [Iran] 146 Qi 27.46N 56.06 E
Qoţbābād [Iran] 146 Oh 28.39N 53.37 E
Qoţūr 146 Kc 38.28N 44.25 E
Qotūr 146 Kc 38.46N 45.16 E
Quadros, Lagoa dos- 204 Gi 29.42S 50.05W
Quairading 212 Df 32.01S 117.25 E
Quakenbrück 120 Dd 52.41N 7.57 E
Quanah 186 Gi 34.18N 99.44W
Quanbao Shan 152 Je 34.08N 111.26 E
Quang Ngai 148 Le 15.07N 108.48 E
Quang Tri 148 Le 21.02N 106.29 E
Quan He 154 Ch 32.55N 115.52 E
Quanjiao 154 Eh 32.09N 118.16 E
Quang Trach 148 Le 17.45N 106.27 E
Quanzhou [China] 152 Jf 26.01N 110.4 E
Quanzhou [China] 142 Ng 24.57N 118.35 E
Qu'Appelle River 180 Hf 50.27N 101.19W
Quaraí 206 Id 30.23S 56.27W
Quaraí, Rio- 204 Dj 30.12S 57.36W
Quaregnon 124 Fd 50.26N 3.51 E
Quartu Sant'Elena 128 Dk 39.14N 9.11 E
Quartz Lake 180 Jb 70.57N 80.40W
Quartz Mountain 188 De 43.10N 122.40W
Quartzsite 188 Hj 33.40N 114.13W
Quatre, Isle- 197n Bb 12.57N 61.15W
Quatsino Sound 188 Aa 50.25N 128.10W
Qūchān 142 Hf 37.06N 58.30 E
Qué 170 Ce 14.43S 15.06 E
Queanbeyan 212 Jg 35.21S 149.14 E
Québec 176 Le 46.49N 71.13W
Québec [2] 180 Kf 54.00N 72.00W
Quebó 204 Db 14.36S 56.04W
Quebra Anzol, Rio- 204 Id 19.09S 47.38W
Quebracho 204 Dj 31.57S 57.57W
Quebradillas 197a Bb 18.28N 66.56W
Quedas do Iguaçu 204 Fg 25.31S 52.54W
Quedlinburg 120 He 51.47N 11.09 E
Queen, Cape - 180 Jd 64.43N 78.18W
Queen Alexandra Range 222 Jg 84.00S 168.00 E
Queen Bess, Mount - 180 Ff 51.18N 124.33W
Queenborough 124 Cc 51.25N 0.46 E
Queen Charlotte Islands 174 Fd 51.30N 129.00W
Queen Charlotte Sound 180 Ef 51.30N 129.30W
Queen Charlotte Strait 174 Gd 50.40N 127.25W
Queen Elizabeth Islands 174 Ib 79.00N 105.00W
Queen Elizabeth Range 222 Kg 83.20S 162.00 E
Queen Mary Land 222 Ge 69.00S 96.00 E
Queen Maud Gulf 174 Ic 68.25N 102.30W
Queen Maud Land (EN) 222 Cf 72.30S 12.00 E
Queen Maud Range 222 Lg 86.00S 160.00W
Queens Channel [Austl.] 212 Fb 14.45S 129.25 E
Queens Channel [N.W.T.-Can.] 180 Ha 76.11N 96.00W
Queensland [2] 212 Id 22.00S 145.00 E
Queenstown [Austl.] 212 Jh 42.05S 145.33 E
Queenstown [Guy.] 196 Gi 7.12N 58.29W
Queenstown [N.Z.] 218 Cf 45.02S 168.40 E
Queenstown [S.Afr.] 160 Jl 31.52S 26.52 E
Queguay, Cuchilla del- 204 Dj 31.50S 57.30W
Queguay Grande, Río- 204 Ck 32.09S 58.09W
Queich 124 Ke 49.14N 8.23 E
Queimadas 202 Kf 10.58S 39.38W
Queiros 204 Ge 21.49S 50.13W
Quela 170 Cd 9.15S 17.05 E
Quelimane 160 Kj 17.51S 36.52 E
Quemado 186 Bi 34.20N 108.30W
Quemado de Güines 194 Gb 22.48N 80.15W
Quembo 170 De 14.57S 20.22 E
Quemoy (EN) = Chinmen 152 Kg 24.25N 118.25 E
Quemú-Quemú 206 He 36.03S 63.33W
Quepos 194 Ei 9.25N 84.09W
Quequén 206 Ie 38.32S 58.42W
Quequén Grande, Río- 204 Cn 38.34S 58.43W
Quequén Salado, Río- 204 Bn 38.56S 60.31W
Quercy 122 Hj 44.15N 1.15 E
Querétaro 176 Ig 20.36N 100.23W
Querétaro [2] 190 Ed 21.00N 99.55W
Querobabi 192 Db 30.03N 111.01W
Quesada [C.R.] 194 Eh 10.19N 84.26W
Quesada [Sp.] 126 Ig 37.51N 3.04W
Queshan 152 Je 32.42N 114.04 E
Quesnel 180 Ff 52.59N 122.30W
Quesnel Lake 180 Ff 52.32N 121.05W
Questa 186 Dh 36.42N 105.36W
Quetena 202 Eh 22.10S 67.25W
Quetico Lake 186 Kb 48.37N 91.52W
Quetta 142 If 30.12N 67.00 E
Quevas, Cerro- 192 Dc 29.15N 111.20W
Quevedo 202 Cd 1.02S 79.27W
Queyras 122 Mj 44.44N 6.49 E
Quezaltenango 176 Jh 14.50N 91.31W
Quezaltenango [3] 194 Bf 14.45N 91.40W
Quezon 150 Ge 9.14N 117.56 E
Quezon City 142 Oh 14.38N 121.00 E
Qufu 154 Dg 35.35N 116.59 E
Quianguozhen → Qian Gorlos 152 Lb 45.05N 124.52 E
Quibala 170 Be 10.44S 14.59 E
Quibaxe 170 Bd 8.30S 14.36 E
Quibdó 202 Cb 5.42N 76.39W
Quiberon 122 Cg 47.29N 3.07 E
Quiberon, Baie de- 122 Dg 47.32N 3.00W
Quiberon, Presqu'île de- 122 Cg 47.30N 3.08W
Quibor 194 Mi 9.56N 69.37W
Quiché [3] 194 Bf 15.30N 90.55W
Quierschied 124 Je 49.19N 7.03 E
Quiha 168 Fc 13.28N 39.33 E
Quiindy 204 Dh 25.58S 57.16W
Quijarro 204 Cd 19.26S 58.08W
Quilá 192 Fe 24.23N 107.13W
Quillabamba 202 Df 12.49S 72.43W
Quillacollo 202 Eg 17.26S 66.17W
Quillagua 206 Gb 21.39S 69.33W
Quillan 122 Il 42.52N 2.11 E
Quillebeuf-sur-Seine 124 Ce 49.28N 0.31 E
Quillota 206 Fd 32.53S 71.16W
Quilnes 206 Id 34.44S 58.16W
Quilon 148 Fg 8.53N 76.36 E
Quilpie 212 Ie 26.37S 144.15 E
Quilqué 206 Fd 33.03S 71.27W
Quimari, Alto de- 194 Ii 8.07N 76.23W
Quimbele 170 Cd 6.30S 16.14 E
Quimili 206 Hc 27.38S 62.25W
Quimome 204 Bc 17.42S 61.16W
Quimome, Río- 204 Bc 17.36S 61.09W
Quimper 122 Bf 48.00N 4.06W
Quimperlé 122 Cg 47.52N 3.33W
Quinault River 188 Cc 47.23N 124.18W
Quincy [Ca.-U.S.] 188 Eg 39.56N 120.57W
Quincy [Fl.-U.S.] 184 Ej 30.37N 84.32W
Quincy [Il.-U.S.] 182 Id 39.56N 91.23W
Quincy [Ma.-U.S.] 184 Ld 42.15N 71.01W
Quincy [Wa.-U.S.] 188 Fc 47.14N 119.51W
Quindío [3] 202 Cc 4.30N 75.40W
Quingey 122 Lg 47.06N 5.53 E
Quinhagak 178 Ge 59.45N 161.43W
Qui Nhon 142 Mh 13.46N 109.14 E
Quiñihual 204 Bm 37.47S 61.36W
Quiniluban Group 150 Hd 11.27N 120.48 E
Quinn River 188 Ff 40.25N 119.00W
Quiñones 192 De 24.22N 111.25W
Quintanar de la Orden 126 Ie 39.34N 3.03W
Quintana Roo [2] 190 Ge 19.40N 88.30W
Quinze, Lac des- 184 Hb 47.30N 79.00W
Quionga 172 Gb 10.35S 40.33 E
Quipungo 170 Be 14.45S 14.05 E
Quirigua 194 Cf 15.18N 89.07W
Quirihue 206 Fe 36.17S 72.32W
Quirima 170 Ce 10.48S 18.09 E
Quirinópolis 202 Hg 18.32S 50.30W
Quiroga 126 Eb 42.29N 7.16W
Quiros, Cap- 219b Cb 14.56S 167.01 E
Quisiro 194 Lh 10.53N 71.17W
Quissanga 172 Gb 12.25S 40.29 E
Quissico 172 Ed 24.43S 34.45 E
Quitasueño, Banco- 190 Hf 14.20N 81.15W
Quitengues 170 Be 14.06S 14.05 E
Quiterage 172 Gb 11.45S 40.27 E
Quitéria, Rio- 204 Ge 20.16S 51.08W
Quitilipi 204 Bh 26.52S 60.13W
Quitman [Ga.-U.S.] 184 Fj 30.47N 83.33W
Quitman [Ms.-U.S.] 186 Lj 32.03N 88.43W
Quito 200 If 0.13S 78.30W
Quitovac 192 Cb 31.32N 112.42W
Quixadá 202 Kd 4.58S 39.01W
Quixeramobim 202 Ke 5.12S 39.17W
Qujiang 154 Cj 28.14N 115.46 E
Qu Jiang [China] 152 Ie 30.01N 106.24 E
Qu Jiang [China] 152 Kf 29.32N 119.31 E
Qujing 152 Hf 25.31N 103.45 E
Qul'ān, Jazā'ir- 146 Fj 24.22N 35.23 E
Qulansiyah 144 Hg 12.41N 53.29 E
Qulaybīah 162 Jb 36.51N 11.06 E
Qulbān al 'Isāwīyah 146 Gg 30.38N 37.53 E
Qulbān an Nabk al Gharbī 146 Gg 31.15N 37.26 E
Qulbān Layyah 146 Lh 29.50N 46.03 E
Qumar He 140 Lf 34.42N 95.00 E
Qumarlêb 152 Ge 34.35N 95.18 E
Qunayfidhah, Nafūd- 146 Kj 24.45N 45.30 E
Quoi 220d Ba 7.32N 151.59 E
Quoich 180 Id 63.56N 93.25W
Quorn 212 Hf 32.21S 138.03 E
Quqên/Jinchuan 152 He 31.02N 102.02 E
Quraitu 146 Ke 34.36N 45.30 E
Qurayyāt, Juzur- 162 Jb 35.48N 11.02 E
Qurbah 128 En 36.35N 10.52 E
Qurdūd 168 Dc 10.17N 29.56 E
Qūr Laban 146 Cg 30.23N 28.59 E
Qurunbāliyah 128 En 36.36N 10.30 E
Qūş 164 Fd 25.55N 32.45 E
Qusaybah 146 Ie 34.24N 40.59 E
Quşay'ir 168 Ic 14.55N 50.20 E
Qutdligssat 179 Gd 70.12N 53.00W
Quthing 172 Df 30.24S 27.42 E
Quţū 164 Hf 18.30N 41.04 E
Quwaiz 164 He 20.27N 44.53 E
Quxian 152 Kf 28.54N 118.53 E
Qüxü 152 Ff 29.23N 90.45 E
Quyang 154 Ce 38.37N 114.41 E
Quy Chau 148 Le 19.33N 105.06 E
Quzhou 154 Cf 36.47N 114.56 E
Qyteti Stalin 130 Ci 40.48N 19.54 E

R

Ra'a as Saffānīyah 144 Gd 27.59N 48.37 E
Raab 120 Ni 47.41N 17.38 E
Raahe/Brahestad 114 Fd 64.41N 24.29 E
Rääkkylä 116 Mb 62.19N 29.37 E
Raalte 124 Ib 52.23N 6.17 E
Raamsdonk 124 Gc 51.41N 4.54 E
Raanes Peninsula 180 Ia 78.20N 86.20W
Raasay, Island of- 118 Gd 57.25N 6.04W
Raasay, Sound of- 118 Gd 57.25N 6.05W
Raasiku/Raziku 116 Ke 59.22N 25.11 E
Rab 128 If 44.45N 14.46 E
Rab 128 If 44.46N 14.46 E
Raba 142 Nj 8.27S 118.46 E
Rába 120 Ni 47.41N 17.38 E
Raba 120 Qf 50.09N 20.30 E
Rabāble 168 Hd 8.14N 48.18 E
Rabaçal 126 Ec 41.30N 7.12W
Rabat [Malta] 128 Io 35.50N 14.29 E
Rabat [Mor.] 160 Ge 34.02N 6.50W
Rabat-Salé [2] 162 Fc 34.02N 6.50W
Rabaul 210 Ge 4.12S 152.12 E
Rábca 120 Ni 47.41N 17.37 E
Rabenau 124 Kd 50.40N 8.52 E
Rabī', Ash Shallāl ar-= Fourth Cataract (EN) 158 Kg 18.47N 32.03 E
Rabiah 146 Jd 36.47N 42.07 E
Rābigh 144 Ee 22.48N 39.02 E
Rabinal 194 Bf 15.06N 90.27W
Rabka 120 Pg 49.36N 19.56 E
Rabočeostrovsk 114 Id 64.59N 34.44 E
Rabyānah, Şaḩrā'- 158 Jf 24.30N 21.00 E
Rabyānah, Wāḩāt al-= Rebiana Oasis (EN) 164 De 24.14N 21.59 E
Răcăciuni 130 Jc 46.20N 26.59 E
Racalmuto 128 Hm 37.24N 13.44 E
Răcăşdia 130 Ee 44.59N 21.38 E
Racconigi 128 Bf 44.46N 7.46 E
Race, Cape- 174 Ne 46.40N 53.10W
Race Point 184 Ld 42.04N 70.14W
Rach Gia 142 Mh 10.01N 105.05 E
Rachid 162 Ef 18.48N 11.41W
Raciąż 120 Qd 52.47N 20.06 E
Racibórz 120 Of 50.06N 18.13 E
Racine 182 Jc 42.43N 87.48W
Ráckeve 120 Oi 47.10N 18.57 E
Racos 130 Ic 46.03N 25.30 E
Råda 116 Ed 60.00N 13.36 E
Radama, Iles- 172 Hb 14.00S 47.47 E
Radan 130 Eg 43.02N 21.30 E
Rădăuţi 130 Ib 47.51N 25.55 E
Radbuza 120 Jg 49.46N 13.24 E
Radeberg 120 Je 51.07N 13.55 E
Radebeul 120 Je 51.06N 13.39 E
Radeče 128 Jd 46.04N 15.11 E
Radehov 120 Uf 50.13N 24.43 E
Radenthein 128 Hd 46.48N 13.43 E
Radevormwald 124 Jc 51.12N 7.22 E
Radew 120 Lb 54.07N 15.50 E
Radford 184 Gg 37.07N 80.34W
Radnevo 130 Ig 42.18N 25.56 E
Radolfzell 120 Ei 47.44N 8.58 E
Radom 112 Ie 51.25N 21.10 E
Radom [2] 120 Re 51.25N 21.10 E
Radomir 130 Fg 42.33N 22.58 E
Radomka 120 Re 51.43N 21.26 E
Radomsko 120 Pe 51.05N 19.25 E
Radomyšl 132 Fd 50.29N 29.14 E
Radomyśl Wielki 120 Rf 50.12N 21.16 E
Radoškoviči 116 Lj 54.12N 27.17 E
Radotín 120 Kg 49.59N 14.22 E
Radovanu 130 Je 44.12N 26.31 E
Radoviš 130 Fh 41.38N 22.28 E
Radøy 116 Ad 60.40N 5.00 E
Radstadt 128 Hc 47.23N 13.27 E
Radun 120 Vb 54.02N 25.07 E
Radunia 120 Ob 54.25N 18.45 E
Raduša 128 Lg 43.52N 17.29 E
Radvaniči 120 Ue 51.59N 24.09 E
Radviliškis 114 Fi 55.50N 23.33 E
Raḑwā, Jabal- 144 Ee 24.36N 38.18 E
Radymno 120 Sg 49.57N 22.48 E
Radziejów 120 Od 52.38N 18.32 E
Radzyń Podlaski 120 Se 51.48N 22.38 E
Rae 180 Fd 62.50N 116.00W
Rāe Bareli 148 Gc 26.13N 81.14 E
Rae Isthmus 180 Ic 66.55N 86.10W
Raesfeld 124 Ic 51.46N 6.51 E
Raeside, Lake- 212 Ee 29.30S 121.50 E
Raetihi 218 Fc 39.26S 175.17 E
Raevavae, Ile- 208 Mg 23.52S 147.40W
Raevski, Groupe- 216 Mc 16.45S 144.14W
Rāf, Jabal- 146 Hh 29.12N 39.48 E
Rafaela 200 Ji 31.17S 61.30W
Rafaï 168 Ce 4.58N 23.56 E
Rafḩā' 144 Fd 29.42N 43.30 E
Rafi 166 Fc 13.28N 4.10 E
Rāfkā 146 Qe 35.55N 57.36 E
Rafsanjān 144 Ic 30.24N 56.01 E
Räfsö/Reposaari 116 Ic 61.37N 21.27 E
Raga 160 Jh 8.28N 25.41 E
Ragay Gulf 150 Hd 13.30N 122.45 E
Ragged Island 194 Jb 22.12N 75.44W
Ragged Island Range 190 Id 22.42N 75.55W
Ragged Point 197q Bb 13.10N 59.25W
Raglan 218 Fb 37.48S 174.52 E
Ragueneau 184 Ma 49.04N 68.32W
Ragunda 114 De 63.04N 16.24 E
Ragusa 128 In 36.55N 14.44 E
Raguva 116 Ki 55.30N 24.45 E
Raha 150 Hg 4.51S 122.43 E
Raḩá, Ḩarrat ar- 146 Gi 27.40N 36.40 E
Rahad al Bardī 168 Cc 11.18N 23.53 E
Rahama 166 Gc 10.25N 8.41 E
Rahaţ, Ḩarrat- 164 He 23.00N 40.05 E
Rahat Dağı 130 Ml 37.08N 29.49 E
Rahden 124 Kb 52.26N 8.37 E
Rāhgāmāti 148 Id 22.38N 92.12 E
Rahīmyār Khan 148 Ec 28.25N 70.18 E
Rahmanovskije Ključi 136 If 49.35N 86.35 E
Rahmet 136 Gf 49.19N 65.16 E
Råholt 116 Dd 60.16N 11.11 E
Rahouia 126 Ni 35.32N 1.01 E
Rahov 132 De 48.02N 24.18 E
Rahrbach, Kirchhundem- 124 Jc 51.02N 7.59 E
Raia 126 Df 39.00N 8.17W
Raiatea, Ile- 208 Lf 16.50S 151.25W
Raices 204 Cj 31.54S 59.16W
Rāichūr 142 Jh 16.12N 77.22 E
Raiganj 148 Hc 25.37N 88.07 E
Raigarh 148 Gd 21.54N 83.24 E
Raijua, Pulau- 150 Hi 10.37S 121.36 E
Rainbow Peak 188 Hd 44.55N 115.17W
Rainier, Mount- 174 Ge 46.52N 121.46W
Rainy Lake 182 Ib 48.42N 93.10W
Rainy River 186 Ib 48.43N 94.29W
Rainy River 186 Ib 48.50N 94.41W
Raipur 142 Kg 21.14N 81.38 E
Raisi, Punta- 128 Hl 38.11N 13.06 E
Raisio/Reso 114 Ff 60.29N 22.11 E
Raita Bank (EN) 214 Mb 25.25N 169.30W
Raja Ampat, Kepulauan- 150 Jg 0.50S 130.25 E
Rājahmundry 142 Kh 16.59N 81.47 E
Rajakoski 114 Gb 68.59N 29.07 E
Rajang 140 Ni 2.07N 111.12 E
Rājapālaiyam 148 Fg 9.27N 77.34 E
Rājasthān [3] 148 Ec 26.00N 74.00 E
Rājasthān Canal 148 Eb 31.10N 75.00 E
Rajbiraj 148 Hc 26.30N 86.50 E
Raičihinsk 138 Hg 49.43N 129.27 E
Raievski 134 Gi 54.04N 54.56 E
Rājgarh 148 Fc 28.38N 75.23 E
Rajgródzkie, Jezioro- 120 Sc 53.45N 22.38 E
Rajka 120 Ni 48.00N 17.12 E
Rājkot 142 Jg 22.18N 70.47 E
Raj Nāndgaon 148 Gd 21.06N 81.02 E
Rajony respublikanskogo podčinenija [Kirg.-U.S.S.R.] [3] 136 Hg 42.30N 73.50 E
Rajony respublikanskogo podčinenija [Taj.-U.S.S.R.] [3] 136 Gh 38.50N 69.30 E
Rājshāhi 148 Hd 24.22N 88.36 E
Rakahanga Atoll 208 Ke 10.02S 161.05W
Rakaia 218 Ee 43.45S 172.01 E
Rakaia 218 Ee 43.54S 172.13 E
Rakan, Ra's- 146 Ni 26.10N 51.13 E
Rakata, Pulau- 150 Eh 6.10S 105.26 E
Raka Zangbo 152 Ef 29.24N 87.58 E
Rakhawt, Wādī- 168 Ib 18.16N 51.50 E
Rakht-e Shāh 146 Mf 33.17N 49.23 E
Rakitnoje 154 Mb 45.36N 134.17 E
Rakitovo 130 Hh 41.59N 24.05 E
Rakkestad 116 De 59.26N 11.21 E
Rakoniewice 120 Md 52.10N 16.16 E
Rakops 172 Cd 21.01S 24.20 E
Rakovnická panev 120 Jf 50.10N 13.30 E
Rakovník 120 Jf 50.06N 13.43 E
Rakovski 130 Hg 42.18N 24.58 E
Raków 120 Rf 50.42N 21.03 E

Index Symbols

[1] Independent Nation · [2] State, Region · [3] District, County · [4] Municipality · [5] Colony, Dependency · Continent · Physical Region · Historical or Cultural Region · Mount, Mountain · Volcano · Hill · Mountains, Mountain Range · Hills, Escarpment · Plateau, Upland · Pass, Gap · Plain, Lowland · Delta · Salt Flat · Valley, Canyon · Crater, Cave · Karst Features · Depression · Polder · Desert, Dunes · Forest, Woods · Heath, Steppe · Oasis · Cape, Point · Coast, Beach · Cliff · Peninsula · Isthmus · Sandbank · Island · Atoll · Rock, Reef · Islands, Archipelago · Rocks, Reefs · Coral Reef · Well, Spring · Geyser · River, Stream · Waterfall, Rapids · River Mouth, Estuary · Lake · Salt Lake · Intermittent Lake · Reservoir · Swamp, Pond · Canal · Glacier · Ice Shelf, Pack Ice · Ocean · Sea · Gulf, Bay · Strait, Fjord · Lagoon · Bank · Seamount · Tablemount · Ridge · Shelf · Basin · Escarpment, Sea Scarp · Fracture · Trench, Abyss · National Park, Reserve · Point of Interest · Recreation Site · Cave, Cavern · Historic Site · Ruins · Wall, Walls · Church, Abbey · Temple · Scientific Station · Railway station · Airport · Port · Military installation · Lighthouse · Mine · Tunnel · Dam, Bridge

Rakušečný, mys- 132 Qh 42.52N 51.55 E
Råkvåg 114 Ce 63.46N 10.05 E
Rakvere 114 Gg 59.22N 26.22 E
Raleigh [N.C.-U.S.] 176 Lf 35.47N 78.39W
Raleigh [Ont.-Can.] 186 Kb 49.31N 91.56W
Raleigh Bay 184 Ih 35.00N 76.20W
Ralik Chain 208 Hd 8.00N 167.00 E
Rama 190 Hf 12.09N 84.15W
Rama, Río- 194 Eg 12.08N 84.13W
Ramādah 162 Jc 32.19N 10.24 E
Ramaḑin, Wādī- 146 Ej 24.57N 32.34 E
Ramales de la Victoria 126 Ia 43.15N 3.27W
Ramalho, Serra do- 204 Ja 13.45S 44.00W
Ramapo Bank (EN) 208 Fb 27.15N 145.10 E
Ramatlabama 172 De 25.37S 25.30 E
Ramberg 120 He 51.45N 11.05 E
Rambervillers 122 Mf 48.21N 6.38 E
Rambi 219d Cb 16.30S 179.59W
Rambouillet 122 Hf 48.39N 1.50 E
Rambutyo Island 208 Fe 2.18S 147.48 E
Rāmhormoz 146 Mg 31.16N 49.36 E
Ramigala/Ramygala 116 Ki 55.28N 24.23 E
Ramis 168 Gd 8.02N 41.36 E
Ramla 146 Fg 31.55N 34.52 E
Ramlīyah, 'Aqabat ar- 146 Di 26.01N 30.42 E
Ramlu 168 Gc 13.20N 41.45 E
Ramm, Jabal- 146 Fh 29.35N 35.24 E
Rammāk, Ghurd ar- 146 Ch 29.40N 29.20 E
Rāmnagar 148 Fc 29.24N 79.07 E
Ramnäs 116 Ge 59.46N 16.12 E
Ramón Santamarina 204 Cn 38.26S 59.20W
Ramos 219a Ec 8.16S 160.11 E
Ramos, Río- 192 Ge 25.35N 105.03W
Ramotswa 172 Dd 24.52S 25.50 E
Rāmpur 148 Fc 28.49N 79.02 E
Ramree 148 Ie 19.06N 93.48 E
Rams 146 Qj 25.53N 56.02 E
Ramsele 114 De 63.33N 16.29 E
Ramsey [Eng.-U.K.] 124 Bb 52.27N 0.07W
Ramsey [I. of M.] 118 Ig 54.20N 4.21W
Ramsey [Ont.-Can.] 184 Fb 47.29N 82.24W
Ramsey Lake 180 Jg 47.20N 83.00W
Ramsgate 118 Oj 51.20N 1.25 E
Rāmshīr 146 Mg 30.50N 49.30 E
Ramsjö 114 De 62.11N 15.39 E
Ramstein-Miesenbach 124 Je 49.27N 7.32 E
Ramsund 114 Db 68.29N 16.32 E
Ramu 170 Hb 3.56N 41.13 E
Ramu 214 Di 4.02S 144.41 E
Ramvik 114 De 62.49N 17.51 E
Ramville, Ilet- 197b Bb 14.42N 60.53W
Ramygala/Ramigala 116 Ki 55.28N 24.23 E
Rana 114 Dc 66.20N 14.08 E
Rañadoiro, Sierra del- 126 Fa 43.20N 6.45W
Ranai 150 Ef 3.55N 108.23 E
Ranakah, Potjo- 150 Hh 8.38S 120.31 E
Rana Kao, Volcán- 221d Ac 27.11S 109.27W
Rana Roi, Volcán- 221d Ab 27.05S 109.23W
Rana Roraka, Volcán- 221d Bb 27.07S 109.18W
Ranau 150 Ge 5.58N 116.41 E
Rança 128 Lf 44.24N 17.22 E
Rancagua 200 Ii 34.10S 70.45W
Rance 122 Ef 48.31N 1.59W
Rance, Sivry-Rance- 124 Gd 50.09N 4.16 E
Rancharia 204 Gf 22.15S 50.55W
Rancheria, Río- 194 Kh 11.34N 72.54W
Rānchī 142 Kg 23.21N 85.20 E
Ranchos 204 Cl 35.32S 58.22W
Ranco, Lago- 206 Ff 40.15S 72.24W
Randa 168 Gc 11.51N 42.40 E
Randaberg 116 Ae 59.00N 5.36 E
Randazzo 128 Im 37.53N 14.57 E
Randers 114 Ch 56.28N 10.03 E
Randers Fjord 116 Dh 56.35N 10.20 E
Randijaure 114 Ec 66.42N 19.18 E
Randow 120 Kc 53.41N 14.04 E
Randsfjorden 114 Cf 60.25N 10.25 E
Ranérou 166 Cb 15.18N 13.58W
Ranfurly 218 Df 45.08S 170.06 E
Rangasa, Tanjung- 150 Gg 3.33S 118.56 E
Ranger 186 Gj 32.28N 98.41W
Rangiora 218 Ee 43.18S 172.36 E
Rangiroa Atoll 208 Mf 15.10S 147.35W
Rangitaiki 218 Gb 37.55S 176.53 E
Rangitata 218 Df 44.10S 171.30 E
Rangitikei 218 Fd 40.17S 175.13 E
Rangkasbitung 150 Eh 6.21S 106.15 E
Rangoon (EN) = Yangon 142 Lh 16.47N 96.10 E
Rangpur 148 Hc 25.44N 89.16 E
Rāniyah 146 Kd 36.15N 44.53 E
Rankin Inlet 176 Jc 62.45N 92.10W
Rankoshi 156a Bb 42.47N 140.31 E
Rannoch, Loch- 118 Ie 56.41N 4.20W
Ranobe 172 Gc 17.10S 44.08 E
Ranon 219b Dc 16.09S 168.07 E
Ranong 148 Jg 9.59N 98.40 E
Ranongga Island 214 Fi 8.05S 156.34 E
Ranova 132 Lb 54.07N 40.14 E
Ransaren 114 Dd 65.14N 14.59 E
Ransiki 150 Jg 1.27S 134.12 E
Rantabe 172 Hc 15.42S 49.39 E
Rantasalmi 116 Mb 62.04N 28.18 E
Rantaupanjang 150 Fg 1.23S 112.04 E
Rantauprapat 150 Cf 2.06N 99.50 E
Rantekombola, Bulu- 140 Oj 3.21S 120.01 E
Rantoul 186 Lf 40.19N 88.09W
Ranua 114 Gd 65.55N 26.32 E
Ranyah, Wādī- 164 He 21.18N 43.20 E
Raohe 152 Nb 46.48N 133.58 E
Raon-l'Étape 122 Mf 48.24N 6.51 E
Racui, Erg er- 162 Gd 29.15N 2.45W
Raoul Island 208 Jg 29.15S 177.52W
Raoyang 154 Ce 38.14N 115.44 E
Raoyang He 154 Gd 41.13N 122.12 E
Rapa, Ile- 208 Mg 27.36S 144.20W
Rapallo 128 Df 44.21N 9.14 E
Rapang 150 Gg 3.50S 119.48 E
Rapa Nui / Pascua, Isla de- = Easter Island (EN) 208 Qg 27.07S 109.22W
Raper, Cape - 180 Kc 69.41N 67.24W
Rapid City 176 Ie 44.05N 103.14W
Rapid Creek 186 Ee 43.54N 102.37W
Rapid River 184 Dc 45.58N 86.59W
Räpina/Rjapina 116 Lf 58.03N 27.35 E
Rapla 114 Fg 59.02N 24.47 E
Rappahannock River 184 Ig 37.34N 76.18W
Rápulo, Río- 198 Jg 13.43S 65.32W
Raqūbah 160 If 28.58N 19.02 E
Raraka Atoll 208 Mf 16.10S 144.54W
Raroia Atoll 208 Mf 16.05S 142.26W
Rarotonga Island 208 Lg 21.14S 159.46W
Rasa, Punta- 198 Jj 40.51S 62.19W
Ra's Abū Daraj 146 Eh 29.23N 32.33 E
Ra's Abū Rudays 146 Eh 28.53N 33.11 E
Ra's Abū Shajarah 168 Fa 21.04N 37.14 E
Ra's Ajdīr 164 Bc 33.09N 11.34 E
Ra's al 'Ayn 146 Id 36.51N 40.04 E
Ra's al-Barr 146 Dg 31.31N 31.50 E
Ra's al Ḥikmah 146 Bg 31.08N 27.50 E
Ra's al Jabal 128 Em 37.13N 10.08 E
Ra's al Khafjī 146 Mh 28.25N 48.30 E
Ra's al Khaymah 144 Id 25.47N 55.57 E
Ra's al Mish'āb 146 Mh 28.12N 48.37 E
Ra's al Unūf 164 Cc 30.31N 18.34 E
Ra's an Naqb 146 Fh 30.00N 35.29 E
Ra's as Sidr 146 Eh 29.36N 32.40 E
Ra's at Tannūrah 146 Ni 26.42N 50.10 E
Ras Beddouza 158 Ge 32.22N 9.18W
Ras Dashen Terara 158 Kg 13.19N 38.20 E
Raseiniai/Rasejnjaj 114 Fi 55.23N 23.07 E
Rasejnjaj/Raseiniai 114 Fi 55.23N 23.07 E
Ras-el-Ma 126 Ji 35.08N 2.29W
Râs el Mâ 166 Eb 16.37N 4.27W
Ras el Oued 126 Ri 35.57N 5.02 E
Ra's Ghārib 164 Fd 28.21N 33.06 E
Rashād 168 Ec 11.51N 31.04 E
Rāshayyā 168 Ff 33.30N 35.51 E
Rashīd=Rosetta (EN) 164 Fc 31.24N 30.25 E
Rashīd, Maşabb- 146 Dg 31.30N 30.20 E
Rasht 142 Gf 37.16N 49.36 E
Rāsiga 'Alūla 168 Ic 11.59N 50.50 E
Rās Jumbo 168 Gf 1.37S 41.31 E
Raška 130 Df 43.18N 20.38 E
Ra's Madhar, Jabal- 146 Gj 25.46N 37.32 E
Ra's Matārimah 146 Eh 29.27N 32.43 E
Rasmussen Basin 180 Hc 67.56N 95.15W
Rason Lake 212 Ee 28.45S 124.20 E
Rasskazovo 136 Ee 52.39N 41.57 E
Rasšua, ostrov- 138 Kg 47.40N 153.00 E
Rassvet 138 Ee 57.00N 91.32 E
Ras-Tarf, Cap- 126 Ii 35.17N 3.41W
Rastatt 120 Eh 48.51N 8.12 E
Rastede 124 Ka 53.15N 8.12 E
Rastigaissa 114 Ga 70.03N 26.18 E
Råstojaure 114 Eb 68.45N 20.30 E
Ra's Ţurunbī 146 Fj 25.40N 34.35 E
Rasūl 146 Pi 27.10N 55.30 E
Ra's Zayt 164 Fd 27.56N 33.31 E
Rat 178a Bb 51.55N 178.20 E
Ratak Chain 208 Id 9.00N 171.00 E
Ratangarh 148 Ec 28.05N 74.36 E
Ratansbyn 114 De 62.29N 14.32 E
Rat Buri 148 Jf 13.32N 99.49 E
Rathbun Lake 186 Jf 40.54N 93.05W
Ráth Droma/Rathdrum 118 Gi 52.56N 6.13W
Rathdrum/Ráth Droma 118 Gi 52.56N 6.13W
Rathenow 120 Id 52.36N 12.20 E
Rathlin Island / Reachlainn 118 Gf 55.18N 6.13W
Ráth Luirc/An Ráth 118 Ei 52.21N 8.41W
Rathor, pik- 135 If 37.55N 72.14 E
Rätikon 128 Dc 47.03N 9.40 E
Ratingen 124 Ic 51.18N 6.51 E
Rätische Alpen=Rhaetian Alps (EN) 128 Dd 46.30N 10.00 E
Rat Islands 174 Ad 52.00N 178.00 E
Ratlām 148 Fd 23.19N 75.04 E
Ratmanova, ostrov- 138 Lc 65.45N 169.00W
Ratnāgiri 148 Ee 16.59N 73.18 E
Ratnapura 148 Gg 6.41N 80.24 E
Ratno 132 Dd 51.42N 24.31 E
Raton 182 Gd 36.54N 104.24W
Ratqh, Wādī ar- 146 Ie 34.25N 40.55 E
Ratta 138 Dd 63.35N 84.05 E
Rattlesnake Hills 188 Le 42.45N 107.10W
Rattray Head 118 Ld 57.38N 1.46W
Rättvik 114 Df 60.53N 15.06 E
Ratz, Mount- 174 Fd 57.23N 132.19W
Ratzeburg 120 Gc 53.42N 10.46 E
Raub 150 Df 3.48N 101.52 E
Rauch 206 Ie 36.46S 59.06W
Raucourt-et-Flaba 124 Ge 49.36N 4.57 E
Raudeberg 116 Ab 61.59N 5.09 E
Rauer Islands 222 Fe 68.51S 77.50 E
Raufarhöfn 114a Ca 66.27N 15.57W
Raufjellet 116 Dc 61.15N 11.00 E
Raufoss 114 Cf 60.43N 10.37 E
Raukotaha 220n Ac 10.28S 161.01W
Raukumara Range 218 Gc 38.00S 178.00 E
Rauland 116 Be 59.44N 8.00 E
Raúl Leoni, Represa- (Guri) 202 Fb 7.30N 63.00W
Rauma 114 Be 62.33N 7.43 E
Rauma/Raumo 114 Ef 61.08N 21.30 E
Raumo/Rauma 114 Ef 61.08N 21.30 E
Rauna 116 Kg 57.14N 25.39 E
Raunds 124 Bb 52.20N 0.32W
Raurimu 218 Fc 39.07S 175.24 E
Raurkela 142 Kg 22.13N 84.53 E
Rausu 154 Rb 44.01N 145.12 E
Rausu-Dake 156a Da 44.06N 145.07 E
Rautalampi 116 Lb 62.38N 26.50 E
Ravahere Atoll 208 Mf 18.14S 142.09W
Ravan 128 Mf 44.15N 18.16 E
Ravanica, Manastir- 130 Ef 43.58N 21.30 E
Ravānsar 146 Le 34.43N 46.40 E
Ravanusa 128 Hm 37.16N 13.58 E
Rāvar 146 Qg 31.12N 56.53 E
Rava-Russkaja 132 Cd 50.13N 23.37 E
Ravels 124 Gc 51.22N 4.59 E
Ravelsbach 128 Jb 48.30N 15.50 E
Ravels-Poppel 124 Hc 51.27N 5.02 E
Ravenna [It.] 128 Gf 44.25N 12.12 E
Ravenna [Nb.-U.S.] 186 Gf 41.02N 98.55W
Ravensburg 120 Fi 47.47N 9.37 E
Ravenshoe 210 Ff 17.37S 145.29 E
Ravensthorpe 212 Ef 33.35S 120.02 E
Ravi 140 Jf 30.35N 71.49 E
Ravnina 136 Gh 37.57N 62.42 E
Rawaki Atoll (Phoenix) 208 Je 3.43S 170.43W
Rāwalpindi 142 Jf 33.35N 73.03 E
Rawa Mazowiecka 120 Qe 51.46N 20.16 E
Rawāndūz 146 Kd 36.37N 44.31 E
Rawdah 146 Ie 35.15N 41.05 E
Rawene 218 Ea 35.24S 173.30 E
Rawicz 120 Me 51.37N 16.52 E
Rawka 120 Qd 52.07N 20.08 E
Rawlinna 210 Dh 31.01S 125.20 E
Rawlins 182 Fc 41.47N 107.14W
Rawlinson Range 212 Fd 24.50S 128.00 E
Rawson [Arg.] 200 Jj 43.18S 65.06W
Rawson [Arg.] 204 Bl 34.36S 60.04W
Rawura, Ras- 170 He 10.20S 40.30 E
Raxaul 148 Gc 26.59N 84.51 E
Ray, Cape - 180 Lg 47.37N 59.19W
Raya, Bukit- 140 Nj 1.32S 111.05 E
Rayadrug 148 Ff 14.42N 76.52 E
Rayāt 146 Kd 36.40N 44.58 E
Rayleigh 124 Cc 51.35N 0.37 E
Raymond [Alta.-Can.] 188 Ib 49.27N 112.39W
Raymond [Wa.-U.S.] 188 Dc 46.41N 123.44W
Raymondville 182 Hf 26.29N 97.47W
Rayne 186 Jk 30.14N 92.16W
Rayón [Mex.] 192 Jg 21.51N 99.40W
Rayón [Mex.] 192 Dc 29.43N 110.35W
Rayones 192 Ie 25.01N 100.05W
Rayong 148 Kf 12.40N 101.17 E
Raysūt 144 Hf 16.54N 54.02 E
Raytown 186 Ig 39.00N 94.28W
Raz, Pointe du- 122 Bf 48.02N 4.44W
Razan 146 Me 35.23N 49.02 E
Razdan 132 Ni 40.28N 44.43 E
Razdelnaja 132 Gf 46.50N 30.05 E
Razdolinsk 138 Ee 58.25N 94.44 E
Razdolnaja 154 Kc 43.20N 131.49 E
Razdolnoje [R.S.F.S.R.] 154 Kc 43.33N 131.55 E
Razdolnoje [Ukr.-U.S.S.R.] 132 Hg 45.47N 33.30 E
Razgrad 130 Jf 43.32N 26.31 E
Razgrad [2] 130 Jf 43.32N 26.31 E
Razi 146 Mc 38.32N 48.08 E
Raziku/Raasiku 116 Ke 59.22N 25.11 E
Razlog 130 Gh 41.53N 23.28 E
Razo 162 Cf 16.37N 24.36W
Ré, Ile de- 110 Ff 46.12N 1.25W
Reachlainn/Rathlin Island 118 Gf 55.18N 6.13W
Reachrainn/Lambay 118 Gh 53.29N 6.01W
Read 180 Gc 69.12N 114.30W
Reading [Eng.-U.K.] 118 Mj 51.28N 0.59W
Reading [Pa.-U.S.] 184 Ic 40.20N 75.55W
Real, Cordillera- [Bol.] 202 Eg 16.30S 68.30W
Real, Cordillera- [Ec.] 198 If 3.00S 78.00W
Real Audiencia 204 Cm 36.11S 58.35W
Real del Castillo 192 Aa 31.58N 116.19W
Realicó 206 He 35.02S 64.15W
Réalmont 122 Ik 43.47N 2.12 E
Reao Atoll 208 Nf 18.31S 136.23W
Reatini, Monti- 128 Gh 42.35N 12.50 E
Rebais 124 Ff 48.51N 3.14 E
Rebecca, Lake- 212 Ee 29.55S 122.10 E
Rebiana Oasis (EN) = Rabyānah, Wāḩāt al- 164 De 24.14N 21.59 E
Rebollera 126 Hf 38.25N 4.02W
Reboly 114 He 63.52N 30.47 E
Rebord Manamblen 172 Hd 24.05S 46.30 E
Rebun 154 Pb 45.23N 141.02 E
Rebun-Dake 156a Ba 45.22N 141.01 E
Rebun-Suidō 156a Ba 45.15N 141.05 E
Rebun-Tō 152 Pb 45.23N 141.10 E
Recalde 204 Bm 36.39S 61.05W
Recanati 128 Hg 43.24N 13.32 E
Recaş 130 Ed 45.48N 21.30 E
Recherche, Archipelago of the- 208 Dh 34.06S 122.45 E
Rečica 136 De 52.22N 30.25 E
Recife 200 Mf 8.03S 34.54W
Recife, Cape- 158 Jl 34.02S 25.45 E
Recke 124 Jb 52.23N 7.43 E
Recklinghausen 120 De 51.37N 7.12 E
Recknitz 120 Ib 54.14N 12.28 E
Recoaro Terme 128 Fe 45.42N 11.13 E
Reconquista 206 Ic 29.09S 59.39W
Recovery Glacier 222 Ag 81.10S 28.00W
Recreo 206 Gc 29.16S 65.04W
Recz 120 Lc 53.16N 15.33 E
Reda 120 Ob 54.38N 18.30 E
Redange 124 He 49.46N 5.54 E
Red Bank 184 Eh 35.07N 85.17W
Red Bay 180 Lf 51.44N 56.25W
Red Bluff 182 Cc 40.11N 122.15W
Red Bluff Reservoir 186 Ek 31.57N 103.56W
Redbridge, London- 124 Cc 51.35N 0.08 E
Red Butte 188 Ii 35.55N 112.03W
Redcar 118 Lg 54.37N 1.04W
Redcliff 172 Dc 19.02S 29.50 E
Red Cliff 197c Ab 17.05N 62.32W
Redcliffe, Mount- 212 Ee 28.25S 121.32 E
Red Cloud 186 Gf 40.05N 98.32W
Red Deer 176 Hd 52.16N 113.48W
Red Deer [Can.] 174 Id 50.56N 109.54W
Red Deer [Can.] 180 Hf 52.55N 101.27W
Redding 176 Ge 40.35N 122.24W
Redditch 118 Li 52.19N 1.56W
Rede 118 Kf 55.08N 2.13W
Redenção 202 Kd 4.13S 38.43W
Redfield 182 Hc 44.53N 98.31W
Red Hill 221a Ec 20.43N 156.15W
Red Hills 186 Gh 37.25N 99.25W
Redkino 114 Ih 56.40N 36.19 E
Red Lake 180 If 51.03N 93.49W
Red Lake 180 If 51.05N 93.55W
Red Lake River 186 Hc 47.55N 97.01W
Red Lakes 188 Ib 48.05N 94.45W
Redlands 188 Gi 34.03N 117.11W
Red Lodge 188 Kd 45.11N 109.15W
Redmond 182 Cc 44.17N 121.11W
Red Mountain [Ca.-U.S.] 188 Df 41.35N 123.06W
Red Mountain [Mt.-U.S.] 182 Ic 47.07N 112.44W
Red Oak 186 If 41.01N 95.14W
Redon 122 Dg 47.39N 2.05W
Redonda 196 Ed 16.55N 62.19W
Redondela 126 Db 42.17N 8.36W
Redondo 126 Ef 38.39N 7.33W
Redondo Beach 188 Fj 33.51N 118.23W
Redoubt Volcano 174 Dc 60.29N 152.45W
Red River [N.Amer.] 174 Jd 50.24N 96.48W
Red River [U.S.] 174 Jf 31.00N 91.40W
Red River (EN)=Hông, Sông- [Asia] 140 Mg 20.17N 106.34 E
Red River (EN)=Yuan Jiang [Asia] 140 Mg 20.17N 106.34 E
Red Rock, Lake- 186 Jf 41.30N 93.20W
Red Rock River 188 Id 44.59N 112.52W
Redruth 118 Hk 50.13N 5.14W
Red Sea (EN)=Aḩmar, Al Baḩr al- 158 Kf 25.00N 38.00 E
Redstone 188 Da 52.08N 123.42W
Redstone 180 Fd 64.17N 124.33W
Red Volta (EN)=Volta Rouge 158 Gh 10.34N 0.30W
Redwater Creek 188 Mb 48.03N 105.13W
Red Wing 182 Ic 44.34N 92.31W
Redwood City 188 Dh 37.29N 122.13W
Redwood Falls 186 Id 44.32N 95.07W
Ree, Lough-/Loch Rí 118 Fh 53.35N 8.00W
Reed City 184 Ed 43.53N 85.31W
Reedley 188 Fh 36.24N 119.37W
Reeds Peak 186 Cj 33.09N 107.51W
Reedsport 182 Cc 43.42N 124.06W
Reedy Glacier 222 Ng 85.30S 134.00W
Reef Islands 208 Hf 10.15S 166.10 E
Reefton 218 De 42.07S 171.52 E
Reepham 124 Db 52.45N 1.07 E
Rees 124 Ic 51.46N 6.24 E
Reese River 188 Gf 40.39N 116.54W
Refahiye 146 Hc 39.54N 38.46 E
Reforma, Río- 192 Ed 26.56N 108.12W
Refteles 116 Eg 57.11N 13.35 E
Reftinski 134 Jh 57.10N 61.43 E
Refugio 186 Hl 28.18N 97.17W
Refugio, Punta- 192 Cc 29.30N 113.30W
Rega 120 Lb 54.10N 15.18 E
Regar 136 Gh 38.34N 68.13 E
Regen 120 Jh 48.58N 13.08 E
Regen 120 Ig 49.01N 12.06 E
Regensburg 112 Hf 49.01N 12.06 E
Reggane 160 Hf 26.42N 0.10 E
Regge 124 Ib 52.26N 6.29 E
Reggio di Calabria 112 Hh 38.06N 15.39 E
Reggio nell'Emilia 128 Ef 44.43N 10.36 E
Reghin 130 Hc 46.46N 24.42 E
Regina [Fr.Gui.] 202 Hc 4.19N 52.08W
Regina [Sask.-Can.] 176 Id 50.25N 104.39W
Registan (EN)=Rīgestān 140 If 31.00N 65.00 E
Registro 204 Ig 24.30S 47.50W
Registro do Araguaia 204 Gb 15.44S 51.50W
Regnitz 120 Gg 49.54N 10.49 E
Regocijo 192 Gf 23.35N 105.11W
Reguengos de Monsaraz 126 Ef 38.25N 7.32W
Rehburg-Loccum 124 Lb 52.28N 9.14 E
Rehoboth 172 Bd 23.18S 17.03 E
Rehoboth [3] 172 Bd 23.50S 17.00 E
Reḩovot 146 Fg 31.54N 34.49 E
Reichelsheim (Odenwald) 124 Ke 49.43N 8.51 E
Reichenbach 120 If 50.37N 12.18 E
Reichshof 124 Jd 50.55N 7.39 E
Reichshof-Denklingen 124 Jd 50.55N 7.39 E
Reichshoffen 124 Jf 48.56N 7.40 E
Reidsville 184 Hg 36.21N 79.40W
Reigate 118 Mj 51.14N 0.13W
Reims 112 Gf 49.15N 4.02 E
Rein=Rhine (EN) 110 Ge 51.52N 6.02 E
Reina Adelaida, Archipiélago- 198 Ik 52.10S 74.25W
Reindeer 180 He 55.34N 103.10W
Reindeer Bank (EN) 197p Ac 11.50N 62.05W
Reindeer Lake 174 Id 57.15N 102.40W
Reineskarvet 116 Cd 60.47N 8.13 E
Reinga, Cape- 218 Ea 34.25S 172.41 E
Reinhardswald 120 Fe 51.30N 9.30 E
Reinosa 126 Ha 43.00N 4.08W
Reisa 114 Eb 69.48N 21.00 E
Reitoru Atoll 208 Mf 17.52S 143.05W
Reitz 172 De 27.53S 28.31 E
Rejmyra 116 Ff 58.50N 15.55 E
Rejowiec Fabryczny 120 Te 51.08N 23.13 E
Reka Devnja 130 Kf 43.13N 27.36 E
Rekarne 116 Ge 59.20N 16.25 E
Reken 124 Jc 51.48N 7.03 E
Reliance 176 Ic 62.42N 109.08W
Relizane 162 Hb 35.45N 0.33 E
Remagen 124 Jd 50.34N 7.14 E
Remarkable, Mount- 212 Hf 32.48S 138.10 E
Rembang 150 Fh 6.42S 111.20 E
Remedios 194 Gi 8.14N 81.51W
Remedios, Punta- 194 Cg 13.31N 89.49W
Remedios, Río- 194 Mh 11.01N 69.15W
Remich 124 Ie 49.32N 6.22 E
Rémire 202 Hc 4.53N 52.17W
Remiremont 122 Mf 48.01N 6.35 E
Remire Reef 172b Bb 5.05S 53.22 E
Remontnoje 132 Mf 46.33N 43.40 E
Remoulins 122 Kk 43.56N 4.34 E
Remscheid 120 De 51.11N 7.12 E
Rena 114 Cf 61.08N 11.22 E
Rena 116 Dc 61.08N 11.23 E
Renaix/Ronse 122 Jd 50.45N 3.36 E
Renard Islands 219a Ad 10.50S 153.00 E
Renaud Island 222 Qe 65.40S 66.00W
Rende 128 Kk 39.20N 16.11 E
Rendezvous Bay 197b Ab 18.10N 63.07W
Rend Lake 186 Lg 38.05N 88.58W
Rendova Island 214 Fi 8.32S 157.20 E
Rendsburg 120 Fb 54.18N 9.40 E
Renfrew 180 Jg 45.28N 76.41W
Rengat 150 Dg 0.24S 102.33 E
Rengo 206 Fd 34.25S 70.52W
Reni 132 Fg 45.29N 28.18 E
Renko 116 Kd 60.54N 24.17 E
Renkum 124 Hc 51.58N 5.45 E
Renland 179 Jd 71.15N 27.20W
Renmark 210 Fh 34.11S 140.45 E
Rennell, Islas- 206 Fh 52.00S 74.00W
Rennell Island 208 Hf 11.40S 160.10 E
Rennes 112 Ff 48.05N 1.41W
Rennes, Bassin de- 122 Ef 48.05N 1.40W
Rennesøy 116 Ae 59.05N 5.40 E
Rennick Glacier 222 Kf 70.30S 161.45 E
Rennie Lake 180 Gd 61.10N 105.30W
Reno 176 Hf 39.31N 119.48W
Reno 128 Gf 44.38N 12.16 E
Renqiu 154 De 38.42N 116.06 E
Rensselaer [In.-U.S.] 184 De 40.57N 87.09W
Rensselaer [N.Y.-U.S.] 184 Kd 42.37N 73.44W
Renteria 126 Ka 43.19N 1.54W
Renton 188 Dc 47.30N 122.11W
Renwez 124 Ge 49.50N 4.36 E
Renxian 154 Cf 37.07N 114.41 E
Reo 150 Hh 8.19S 120.30 E
Réole, La- 122 Fj 44.35N 0.02W
Repartimento, Serra do- 204 Jc 17.40S 44.50W
Répce 120 Ni 47.41N 17.02 E
Repino 116 Md 60.10N 29.58 E
Repong, Pulau- 150 Ef 2.22N 105.53 E
Reposaari/Räfsö 116 Ic 61.37N 21.27 E
Republic 188 Fb 48.39N 118.44W
Republican River 174 Jf 39.03N 96.48W
Repulse Bay 176 Kc 66.32N 86.15W
Repulse Bay [Austl.] 212 Jd 20.35S 148.45 E
Repulse Bay [Can.] 180 Ic 66.20N 86.00W
Repvåg 114 Fa 70.45N 25.41 E
Requena [Peru] 202 Dd 5.00S 73.50W
Requena [Sp.] 126 Ke 39.29N 1.06W
Requin Bay 197b Bb 12.02N 61.38W
Réquista 122 Ij 44.02N 2.32 E
Reşadiye Yarımadası 130 Km 36.40N 27.45 E
Reschenpass/Resia, Passo di- 128 Ed 46.50N 10.30 E
Resen 130 Eh 41.05N 21.01 E
Reserva 204 Gg 24.38S 50.52W
Reserve 186 Bj 33.43N 108.45W
Rešetilovka 132 Ie 49.33N 34.05 E
Reshui 152 Hd 37.38N 100.30 E
Resia, Passo di-/Reschenpass 128 Ed 46.50N 10.30 E
Resistencia 200 Kh 27.30S 58.59W
Reşiţa 130 Ed 45.18N 21.55 E
Resko 120 Lc 53.47N 15.25 E
Reso/Raisio 114 Ff 60.29N 22.11 E
Resolute 176 Jb 74.41N 94.54W
Resolution 174 Mc 61.30N 65.00W
Resolution Island 180 Ld 61.35N 64.39W
Resolution Island 218 Bf 45.40S 166.35 E
Respublikai Soveth Socialisti Todžikiston/Tadžikskaja SSR [2] 136 Hh 39.00N 71.00 E
Respublika Sovetike Socialiste Moldovenjaske/Moldavskaja SSR [2] 136 Cf 47.00N 29.00 E
Ressa 132 Ib 54.45N 35.10 E
Ressons-sur-Matz 124 Ee 49.33N 2.45 E
Restigouche River 184 Na 48.02N 66.20W
Restinga de Sefton, Isla- 198 Hi 37.00S 83.50W
Restinga Sêca 204 Fi 29.49S 53.23W
Reszel 120 Rb 54.04N 21.09 E
Retalhuleu 190 Ff 14.32N 91.41W
Retalhuleu [3] 194 Bf 14.20N 91.50W
Retavas/Rietavas 116 Ii 55.43N 21.49 E
Retezatului, Munţii- 130 Fd 45.25N 23.00 E
Rethel 122 Ke 49.31N 4.22 E
Rethem (Aller) 124 Lb 52.47N 9.23 E
Réthimnon 130 Hn 35.22N 24.28 E
Retie 124 Hc 51.17N 5.05 E
Retourne 124 Ge 49.26N 4.02 E
Rétság 120 Pi 47.56N 19.08 E
Rettihovka 154 Lb 44.10N 132.45 E
Retz 128 Jb 48.45N 15.57 E
Retz, Pays de- 122 Eg 47.07N 1.58W
Réunion=Reunion (EN) [5] 160 Mk 21.06S 55.36 E
Réunion=Reunion (EN) 158 Mk 21.06S 55.36 E
Reunion (EN)=Réunion [5] 160 Mk 21.06S 55.36 E
Reunion (EN)=Réunion 158 Mk 21.06S 55.36 E
Reus 126 Nc 41.09N 1.07 E
Reusel 124 Hc 51.22N 5.10 E
Reuss 128 Cc 47.28N 8.14 E
Reut 132 Ff 47.15N 29.09 E
Reutlingen 120 Fh 48.29N 9.13 E
Reutte 128 Ec 47.29N 10.43 E
Revda [R.S.F.S.R.] 114 Ic 67.57N 34.32 E
Revda [R.S.F.S.R.] 134 Ih 56.48N 59.57 E
Revel 122 Hk 43.28N 2.00 E
Revellata, Punta di a- 122a Aa 42.35N 8.40 E
Revelstoke 180 Ff 50.59N 118.12W
Revermont 122 Lh 46.27N 5.25 E
Revillagigedo 178 Me 55.35N 131.23W
Revillagigedo, Islas- 174 Hh 19.00N 111.30W
Revin 122 Ke 49.56N 4.38 E
Revoljucii, pik- 135 Ie 38.33N 72.28 E
Revsundssjön 116 Fb 62.50N 15.15 E

Index Symbols

[1] Independent Nation
[2] State, Region
[3] District, County
[4] Municipality
[5] Colony, Dependency
Continent
Physical Region
Historical or Cultural Region
Mount, Mountain
Volcano
Hill
Mountains, Mountain Range
Hills, Escarpment
Plateau, Upland
Pass, Gap
Plain, Lowland
Delta
Salt Flat
Valley, Canyon
Crater, Cave
Karst Features
Depression
Polder
Desert, Dunes
Forest, Woods
Heath, Steppe
Oasis
Cape, Point
Coast, Beach
Cliff
Peninsula
Isthmus
Sandbank
Island
Atoll
Rock, Reef
Islands, Archipelago
Rocks, Reefs
Coral Reef
Well, Spring
Geyser
River, Stream
Waterfall, Rapids
River Mouth, Estuary
Lake
Salt Lake
Intermittent Lake
Reservoir
Swamp, Pond
Canal
Glacier
Ice Shelf, Pack Ice
Ocean
Sea
Gulf, Bay
Strait, Fjord
Lagoon
Bank
Seamount
Tablemount
Ridge
Shelf
Basin
Escarpment, Sea Scarp
Fracture
Trench, Abyss
National Park, Reserve
Point of Interest
Recreation Site
Cave, Cavern
Historic Site
Ruins
Wall, Walls
Church, Abbey
Temple
Scientific Station
Railway station
Airport
Port
Military installation
Lighthouse
Mine
Tunnel
Dam, Bridge

Rewa 148 Gd 24.32N 81.18 E
Rewa ≈ 219d Bc 18.08S 178.33 E
Rewāri 148 Fc 28.11N 76.37 E
Rex, Mount- ▲ 222 Qf 74.54S 75.57W
Rexburg 188 Je 43.49N 111.47W
Rexpoëde 124 Ed 50.56N 2.32 E
Rey 144 Hb 35.35N 51.25 E
Rey, Arroyo del- ≈ 204 Ci 29.12S 59.36W
Rey, Isla del- ◆ 190 Ig 8.22N 78.55W
Rey, Laguna del- ○ 192 Hd 27.00N 103.25W
Rey Bouba 166 Hd 8.40N 14.11 E
Reyes, Point- ► 188 Dg 38.00N 123.01W
Reyhanli 146 Gd 36.18N 36.32 E
Reykjalíd 114a Cb 65.39N 16.55W
Reykjanes ► 110 Dc 63.49N 22.43W
Reykjanes Ridge (EN) ⌃ 110 Dc 62.00N 27.00W
Reykjavík 112 Dc 64.09N 21.57W
Reynolds Range ⛰ 212 Gd 22.20S 132.50 E
Reynosa 176 Jg 26.07N 98.18W
Reyssouze ≈ 122 Kh 46.27N 4.54 E
Rež 134 Jh 57.23N 61.24 E
Rež ≈ 134 Kh 57.54N 62.20 E
Rezé 122 Eg 47.12N 1.34W
Rezekne/Rēzekne 112 Id 56.30N 27.19 E
Rēzekne/Rezekne 112 Id 56.30N 27.19 E
Rezelm, Lacul- ○ 130 Le 44.54N 28.57 E
Rezina 132 Ff 47.43N 28.58 E
Reznas, ozero- / Rēznas ezers ○ 116 Lh 56.20N 27.30 E
Rēznas ezers / Reznas, ozero- ○ 116 Lh 56.20N 27.30 E
Rezovo 130 Lh 41.59N 28.02 E
Rezvān 146 Qi 27.34N 56.06 E
Rezve ≈ 130 Lh 41.59N 28.01 E
Rgotina 130 Fe 44.01N 22.17 E
Rhaetian Alps (EN)=Alpi Retiche ⛰ 128 Dd 46.30N 10.00 E
Rhaetian Alps (EN)= Rätische Alpen ⛰ 128 Dd 46.30N 10.00 E
Rhallamane ⧗ 158 Ff 23.15N 10.00W
Rhauderfehn 124 Ja 53.08N 7.34 E
Rhaunen 124 Je 49.51N 7.21 E
Rheda-Wiedenbrück 120 Ee 51.51N 8.18 E
Rheden 124 Ib 52.01N 6.01 E
Rheden-Dieren 124 Ib 52.03N 6.08 E
Rheider Land ⧗ 124 Ja 53.13N 7.18 E
Rhein=Rhine (EN) ≈ 110 Ge 51.52N 6.02 E
Rheinberg 124 Ic 51.33N 6.36 E
Rheine 120 Dd 52.17N 7.27 E
Rheinfall ↯ 128 Cc 47.41N 8.38 E
Rheinfelden (Baden) 120 Di 47.34N 7.48 E
Rheingaugebirge ⛰ 120 Ef 50.05N 8.00 E
Rheinhessen ⧗ 124 Ke 49.52N 8.07 E
Rheinisches Schiefergebirge =Rhenish Slate Mountains (EN) ⛰ 110 Ge 50.25N 7.10 E
Rheinland-Pfalz=Rhineland-Palatinate (EN) [2] 120 Cf 50.00N 7.00 E
Rheinsberg / Mark 120 Ic 53.06N 12.53 E
Rheinstetten 124 Kf 48.58N 8.18 E
Rhenen 124 Hc 51.58N 5.35 E
Rhenish Slate Mountains (EN)=Rheinisches Schiefergebirge ⛰ 110 Ge 50.25N 7.10 E
Rheris ≈ 162 Gc 30.41N 4.57W
Rheydt, Mönchengladbach- 124 Ic 51.10N 6.27 E
Rhin=Rhine (EN) ≈ 110 Ge 51.52N 6.02 E
Rhine (EN)=Rein ≈ 110 Ge 51.52N 6.02 E
Rhine (EN)=Rhein ≈ 110 Ge 51.52N 6.02 E
Rhine (EN)=Rhin ≈ 110 Ge 51.52N 6.02 E
Rhine (EN)=Rijn ≈ 110 Ge 51.52N 6.02 E
Rhine Bank (EN) ▦ 206 Ji 50.30S 53.30W
Rhinelander 182 Jb 45.38N 89.25W
Rhineland-Palatinate (EN)= Rheinland-Pfalz [2] 120 Cf 50.00N 7.00 E
Rhinluch ⋓ 120 Id 52.50N 12.50 E
Rhino Camp 170 Fb 2.58N 31.24 E
Rhiou ≈ 126 Mi 35.59N 0.53 E
Rhir, Cap- ► 162 Fc 30.38N 9.54W
Rho 128 De 45.32N 9.02 E
Rhode Island [2] 182 Mc 41.40N 71.30W
Rhode Island Sound ⇌ 184 Le 41.25N 71.15W
Rhodes (EN) = Ródhos 112 Ih 36.26N 28.13 E
Rhodes (EN) = Ródhos ◆ 110 Ih 36.10N 28.00 E
Rhodesia → Zimbabwe [1] 160 Jj 20.00S 30.00 E
Rhodes Peak ▲ 188 Hc 46.41N 114.47W
Rhodope Mountains (EN) = Rodopi ⛰ 110 Ig 41.30N 24.30 E
Rhomara ⧗ 126 Hi 35.10N 4.57W
Rhön ⛰ 120 Gf 50.25N 10.05 E
Rhondda 118 Jj 51.40N 3.30W
Rhône [3] 122 Ki 46.00N 4.30 E
Rhône ≈ 110 Gg 43.20N 4.50 E
Rhône au Rhin, Canal du- ═ 122 Lg 47.06N 5.19 E
Rhourd el Baguel 162 Ic 31.24N 6.57 E
Rhue ≈ 122 Ii 45.23N 2.29 E
Rhum ◆ 118 Ge 57.00N 6.20W
Rhyl 118 Jh 53.19N 3.29W
Riaba 166 Ge 3.24N 8.42 E
Riacho de Santana 202 Jf 13.37S 42.57W
Riangnom 168 Ed 9.55N 30.01 E
Riaño 126 Gb 42.58N 5.01W
Riánsares ≈ 126 Ie 39.32N 3.18W
Rías Altas ≋ 126 Da 43.30N 8.30W
Rías Bajas ≋ 126 Db 42.30N 9.00W
Riau [3] 150 Df 1.00N 102.00 E
Riau, Kepulauan-=Riau Archipelago (EN) ❖ 140 Mi 1.00N 104.30 E
Riau Archipelago (EN)= Riau, Kepulauan- ❖ 140 Mi 1.00N 104.30 E
Riaza 126 Ic 41.17N 3.28W
Riaza ≈ 126 Ic 41.42N 3.55W
Ribadavia 126 Db 42.17N 8.08W
Ribadeo 126 Ea 43.32N 7.02W
Ribadesella 126 Ga 43.28N 5.04W
Ribagorça / Ribagorza ⧗ 126 Mb 42.15N 0.30 E
Ribagorza / Ribagorça ⧗ 126 Mb 42.15N 0.30 E
Ribamar 202 Jd 2.33S 44.03W
Ribas do Rio Pardo 204 Fe 20.27S 53.46W
Ribatejo ▣ 126 De 39.15N 8.30W
Ribáuè 172 Fb 14.57S 38.17 E
Ribble ≈ 118 Kh 53.44N 2.50W
Ribe 114 Bi 55.21N 8.46 E
Ribe [2] 116 Ci 55.35N 8.45 E
Ribécourt-Dreslincourt 124 Ee 49.31N 2.55 E
Ribeira 204 Hg 24.39S 49.00W
Ribeira → Santa Eugenia 126 Db 42.33N 9.00W
Ribeira, Rio- ≈ 204 Ig 24.40S 47.24W
Ribeira Brava 162 Cf 16.37N 24.18W
Ribeira Grande 162 Bf 17.11N 25.04W
Ribeirão Prêto 200 Lh 21.10S 47.48W
Ribeirãozinho 204 Fc 16.22S 52.36W
Ribeiro Gonçalves 202 Ie 7.32S 45.14W
Ribemont 124 Fe 49.48N 3.28 E
Ribera 128 Hm 37.30N 13.16 E
Ribérac 122 Gi 45.15N 0.20 E
Riberalta 200 Jg 10.59S 66.06W
Ribnica 128 Ie 45.44N 14.44 E
Ribnitz-Damgarten 120 Ib 54.15N 12.28 E
Ricardo Flores Magón 192 Fc 29.58N 106.58W
Riccia 128 Ii 41.29N 14.50 E
Riccione 128 Gg 43.59N 12.39 E
Rice Lake ○ 184 Hc 44.08N 78.13W
Rich 162 Gc 32.15N 4.30W
Richan 186 Jb 49.59N 92.49W
Richard Collinson Inlet ◐ 180 Gb 72.45N 113.00W
Richards ◆ 180 Ec 69.20N 134.35W
Richard's Bay 160 Kk 28.47S 32.06 E
Richardson 186 Hj 32.57N 96.44W
Richardson Mountains ⛰ 174 Fc 66.00N 135.20W
Richardson Seamount (EN) ⊼ 222 Cc 40.45S 14.10 E
Richard Toll 166 Bb 16.28N 15.41W
Rîchât, Guel er- ▲ 162 Ee 21.07N 11.24W
Richel ⋯ 124 Ha 53.18N 5.10 E
Richel Griend ○ 124 Ha 53.18N 5.15 E
Richelieu 122 Gg 47.01N 0.19 E
Richer 186 Hb 49.39N 96.28W
Richey 188 Mc 47.39N 105.04W
Richfield 182 Ed 38.46N 112.05W
Richibucto 184 Ob 46.41N 64.52W
Richland 182 Db 46.17N 119.18W
Richland Center 186 Ke 43.22N 90.21W
Richmond [Austl.] 212 Id 20.44S 143.08 E
Richmond [Ca.-U.S.] 182 Cd 37.57N 122.22W
Richmond [Eng.-U.K.] 118 Lg 54.24N 1.44W
Richmond [In.-U.S.] 182 Kd 39.50N 84.54W
Richmond [Ky.-U.S.] 182 Kd 37.45N 84.18W
Richmond [N.Z.] 218 Ed 41.21S 173.11 E
Richmond [S.Afr.] 172 Cf 31.23S 23.56 E
Richmond [Tx.-U.S.] 186 Il 29.35N 95.46W
Richmond [Va.-U.S.] 176 Lf 37.30N 77.28W
Richmond, Mount- ▲ 218 Ed 41.28S 173.24 E
Richmond Hill 184 Hd 43.52N 79.27W
Richmond Peak ▲ 197n Ba 13.17N 61.13W
Richthofen, Mount- ▲ 186 Df 40.29N 105.57W
Rickmansworth 124 Bc 51.38N 0.28W
Ricobayo, Embalse de- ⊖ 126 Gc 41.35N 5.50W
Ridā' 164 Hg 14.25N 44.50 E
Ridderkerk 124 Gc 51.52N 4.36 E
Ridgecrest 188 Gi 35.38N 117.36W
Ridgway 184 He 41.25N 78.45W
Riding Mountain ⛰ 186 Fa 50.55N 100.25W
Riecito, Río- ≈ 196 Bi 6.50N 68.51W
Ried ⧗ 124 Ke 49.50N 8.25 E
Ried im Innkreis 128 Hb 48.13N 13.30 E
Riedlingen 120 Fh 48.09N 9.28 E
Riemst 124 Hd 50.48N 5.36 E
Ries ⧗ 120 Gh 48.55N 10.40 E
Riesa 120 Je 51.18N 13.18 E
Riesco, Isla- ◆ 206 Fh 53.00S 72.30W
Riesi 128 Im 37.17N 14.05 E
Riet ≈ 158 Jk 29.00S 23.53 E
Rietavas/Retavas 116 Ii 55.43N 21.49 E
Rietberg 124 Kc 51.48N 8.26 E
Rietbron 172 Cf 32.54S 23.09 E
Rietfontein [Nam.] 172 Cd 21.58S 20.58 E
Rietfontein [S.Afr.] 172 Ce 26.44S 20.01 E
Rieti 128 Gh 42.24N 12.51 E
Rif ⛰ 158 Ge 35.00N 4.00W
Rifle 186 Cg 39.32N 107.47W
Rifstangi ► 110 Eb 66.32N 16.12W
Rift Valley [3] 170 Gb 0.30N 36.00 E
Rift Valley ⧗ 158 Kh 0.30N 36.00 E
Rīga/Riga 112 Id 56.57N 24.06 E
Riga/Rīga 112 Id 56.57N 24.06 E
Riga, Gulf of- (EN) = Rīgas jūŗas līcis ◐ 110 Id 57.30N 23.35 E
Riga, Gulf of- (EN) = Riia laht ◐ 110 Id 57.30N 23.35 E
Riga, Gulf of- (EN) = Rižski zaliv ◐ 110 Id 57.30N 23.35 E
Rigachikum 166 Gc 10.38N 7.28 E
Rīgas jūŗas līcis = Riga, Gulf of- (EN) ◐ 110 Id 57.30N 23.35 E
Rīgestān=Registan (EN) ⧗ 140 If 31.00N 65.00 E
Riggins 188 Gd 45.25N 116.19W
Rigolet 180 Lf 54.10N 58.26W
Rig-Rig 163 Ac 14.16N 14.21 E
Rihand Sagar ⊖ 148 Hd 24.05N 83.05 E
Riia laht = Riga, Gulf of- (EN) ◐ 110 Id 57.30N 23.35 E
Riihimäki 114 Ff 60.45N 24.46 E
Riiser-Larsen-Halvøya ⊟ 222 De 68.55S 34.00 E
Riito 192 Ba 32.10N 114.45W
Riječki zaljev = Rijeka, Gulf of- (EN) ◐ 128 Ie 45.15N 14.25 E
Rijeka 112 Hf 45.21N 14.24 E
Rijeka, Gulf of- (EN)= Riječki zaljev ◐ 128 Ie 45.15N 14.25 E
Rijksmuseum Kröller-Müller ✪ 124 Hb 52.06N 5.47 E
Rijn=Rhine (EN) ≈ 110 Ge 51.52N 6.02 E
Rijssen 124 Ib 52.18N 6.37 E
Rijswijk 124 Gb 52.03N 4.21 E
Rika ≈ 120 Th 48.08N 23.22 E
Rikā, Wādī ar- ≈ 164 He 22.25N 44.50 E
Rikubetsu 156a Cb 43.28N 143.43 E
Rikuzentakada 154 Pe 39.01N 141.38 E
Rila 130 Gg 42.08N 23.08 E
Rila ⛰ 130 Gg 42.08N 23.33 E
Riley 188 Fe 43.32N 119.29W
Riley, Mount- ▲ 186 Ck 31.58N 107.05W
Rilski Manastir ✝ 130 Gg 42.08N 23.20 E
Rima ≈ 158 Hg 13.04N 5.10 E
Rimatara, Ile- ◆ 208 Lg 22.38S 152.51W
Rimava ≈ 120 Qh 48.15N 20.21 E
Rimavská Şobota 120 Qh 48.23N 20.01 E
Rimbo 114 Eg 59.45N 18.22 E
Rimé ≈ 168 Bc 14.02N 18.03 E
Rimforsa 116 Ff 58.08N 15.40 E
Rimini 128 Gf 44.04N 12.34 E
Rimito/Rymättylä ◆ 116 Jd 60.25N 21.55 E
Rîmnic ≈ 130 Kd 45.32N 27.31 E
Rîmnicu Sărat 130 Kd 45.23N 27.03 E
Rîmnicu Vîlcea 130 Hd 45.06N 24.22 E
Rimouski 176 Me 48.27N 68.32W
Rimše/Rimšė 116 Li 55.30N 26.33 E
Rimšė/Rimše 116 Li 55.30N 26.33 E
Rinbung 152 Ef 29.15N 89.52 E
Rincón 197a Ab 18.21N 67.16W
Rincon 196 Bf 12.14N 68.20W
Rincón, Bahía de- ◐ 197a Bc 17.57N 66.19W
Rincón del Bonete, Lago Artificial de- ⊖ 206 Id 32.45S 56.00W
Rincón de Romos 192 Hf 22.14N 102.18W
Rindal 114 Be 63.03N 9.13 E
Ringe 116 Di 55.14N 10.29 E
Ringebu 116 Dc 61.31N 10.10 E
Ringerike ⧗ 116 Dd 60.05N 10.15 E
Ringgold Isles ❖ 208 Jf 16.15S 179.25W
Ringim 166 Gc 12.09N 9.10 E
Ringkøbing 114 Bh 56.05N 8.15 E
Ringkøbing [2] 116 Ch 56.10N 8.45 E
Ringkøbing Fjord ◛ 114 Bi 56.00N 8.15 E
Ringlades , 130 Dj 39.25N 20.04 E
Ringsjön ○ 116 Ei 55.50N 13.30 E
Ringsted 114 Ci 55.27N 11.49 E
Ringvassøy ◆ 114 Eb 69.55N 19.15 E
Rínia ◆ 130 Il 37.25N 25.13 E
Rinjani, Gunung- ▲ 150 Gh 8.24S 116.28 E
Rinn Chathóir/Cahore Point 118 Gi 52.34N 6.11W
Rinn Dúain/Hook Head ► 118 Gi 52.07N 6.55W
Rinteln 120 Fd 52.11N 9.05 E
Rinya ≈ 120 Nk 45.57N 17.27 E
Rio Azul 204 Gg 25.43S 50.47W
Riobamba 200 If 1.40S 78.38W
Río Branco 204 Fk 32.34S 53.25W
Rio Branco 200 Jf 9.58S 67.48W
Rio Branco do Sul 204 Hg 25.10S 49.18W
Rio Brilhante 202 Hh 21.48S 54.33W
Río Bueno 206 Ff 40.19S 72.58W
Río Caribe 202 Fa 10.42N 63.07W
Rio Chico 196 Dg 10.19N 65.59W
Rio Claro [Braz.] 204 If 22.24S 47.33W
Rio Claro [Trin.] 196 Fg 10.18N 61.11W
Rio Colorado 206 He 39.01S 64.05W
Río Cuarto 200 Ji 33.08S 64.20W
Rio de Janeiro 200 Lh 22.54S 43.15W
Rio de Janeiro [2] 202 Jh 22.30S 42.30W
Río de Jesús 194 Gj 7.59N 81.10W
Río de Oro 194 Ki 8.57N 73.23W
Río de Oro ▣ 162 Ee 24.00N 14.00W
Río de Oro, Bahía de- ◐ 162 De 23.45N 15.50W
Rio do Sul 206 Kc 27.13S 49.39W
Rio Fortuna 204 Hi 28.06S 49.07W
Río Gallegos 200 Jk 51.37S 69.10W
Rio Grande 200 Ki 32.02S 52.05W
Río Grande [Arg.] 206 Gh 53.47S 67.42W
Río Grande [Nic.] 194 Dg 12.59N 86.34W
Río Grande [P.R.] 197a Cb 18.23N 65.50W
Rio Grande City 186 Gm 26.23N 98.49W
Río Grande de Añasco ≈ 197a Ab 18.17N 67.10W
Río Grande de Manati ≈ 197a Bb 18.29N 66.32W
Río Grande de Matagalpa ≈ 190 Hf 12.54N 83.32W
Rio Grande do Norte [2] 202 Ke 5.40S 36.00W
Rio Grande do Sul [2] 206 Jc 30.00S 54.00W
Rio Grande Rise (EN) ⌃ 106 Cm 31.00S 35.00W
Riohacha 202 Da 11.32N 72.54W
Río Hato 194 Gi 8.23N 80.10W
Río Lagartos 192 Og 21.36N 88.10W
Rio Largo 202 Ke 9.29S 35.51W
Riom 122 Ji 45.54N 3.07 E
Rio Maior 126 De 39.20N 8.56W
Rio Mayo 206 Fg 45.41S 70.16W
Riom-és-Montagnes 122 Ii 45.17N 2.40 E
Rio Miranda ≈ 202 Gg 19.25S 57.20W
Río Mulatos 202 Eg 19.42S 66.47W
Ríon 130 Ek 38.18N 21.47 E
Río Negro 206 Ff 40.47S 73.14W
Río Negro [Arg.] [2] 206 Gf 40.00S 67.00W
Rio Negro [Braz.] 204 Dd 19.33S 56.12W
Rio Negro [Braz.] 206 Kc 26.06S 49.48W
Río Negro [Ur.] [2] 204 Dk 32.45S 57.20W
Rio Negro, Pantanal do- ⋒ 202 Gg 18.50S 56.00W
Rionero in Vulture 128 Jj 40.56N 15.40 E
Rioni ≈ 132 Lh 42.10N 41.38 E
Rio Novo 204 Dc 16.28S 56.30W
Rio Pardo 206 Jc 29.59S 52.22W
Rio Prêto, Serra do- ⛰ 204 Gd 18.18S 50.42W
Río San Juan [3] 194 Eh 11.10N 84.30W
Río Segundo 206 Hd 31.40S 63.55W
Riosucio 202 Cb 7.27N 77.07W
Río Tercero 206 Hd 32.11S 64.06W
Rio Tinto 202 Ke 6.48S 35.05W
Rioverde 190 Dd 21.56N 100.01W
Rio Verde 202 Hg 17.43S 50.56W
Rio Verde, Serra do- ⛰ 204 Fc 17.32S 52.25W
Rio Verde de Mato Grosso 202 Hg 18.56S 54.52W
Rio Verde do Sul 204 Ef 22.54S 55.27W
Rioz 122 Mg 47.25N 6.04 E
Řip ▲ 120 Kf 50.24N 14.18 E
Ripanj 130 De 44.38N 20.32 E
Ripley [Eng.-U.K.] 124 Aa 53.02N 1.24W
Ripley [Tn.-U.S.] 184 Ch 35.44N 89.33W
Ripley [W.V.-U.S.] 184 Gf 38.49N 81.44W
Ripoll 126 Ob 42.12N 2.12 E
Ripon 118 Lg 54.08N 1.31W
Riposto 128 Jm 37.44N 15.12 E
Ripple Mountain ▲ 188 Gb 49.02N 117.05W
Risan 130 Bg 42.31N 18.42 E
Risaralda [3] 202 Cb 5.00N 75.45W
Risbäck 114 Dd 64.42N 15.32 E
Rīshah, Wādī- ≈ 146 Kj 25.33N 44.05 E
Rī Shahr 146 Nh 28.55N 50.50 E
Rishiri 154 Pb 45.11N 141.15 E
Rishiri-Suidō ⇌ 156a Ba 45.10N 141.30 E
Rishiri-Tō ◆ 152 Pb 45.11N 141.15 E
Rishiri-Yama ▲ 156a Ba 45.11N 141.15 E
Rīshmūk 146 Ng 31.15N 50.20 E
Rishon Leẕiyyo 146 Fg 31.58N 34.48 E
Rising Star 186 Gj 32.06N 98.58W
Risle ≈ 122 Ge 49.26N 0.23 E
Risnjak ▲ 128 Ie 45.26N 14.37 E
Rîşnov 130 Id 45.35N 25.27 E
Risør 114 Bg 58.43N 9.14 E
Risoux, Mont- ▲ 122 Mh 46.36N 6.10 E
Risøyhamn 114 Db 69.00N 15.45 E
Riß ≈ 120 Fh 48.17N 9.49 E
Risti 114 Fg 59.03N 24.01 E
Ristiina 116 Lc 61.30N 27.16 E
Ristijarvi 114 Gd 64.30N 28.13 E
Ristna, mys- / Ristna neem ► 116 If 58.55N 21.55 E
Ristna neem / Ristna, mys- ► 116 If 58.55N 21.55 E
Rīsū ≈ 146 Qf 33.52N 57.28 E
Ritchie's Archipelago ❖ 148 If 12.14N 93.10 E
Ritidian Point ► 220c Ba 13.39N 144.51 E
Ritscher-Hochland ▬ 222 Bf 73.20S 9.30W
Ritter, Mount- ▲ 182 Dd 37.42N 119.20W
Ritterhude 124 Ka 53.11N 8.45 E
Rituerto ≈ 126 Jc 41.36N 2.22W
Ritzville 188 Fc 47.08N 118.23W
Riva-Bella, Ouistreham- 124 Be 49.17N 0.16W
Rivadavia [Arg.] 206 Gd 33.11S 68.28W
Rivadavia [Arg.] 206 Hb 24.11S 62.53W
Riva del Garda 128 Ee 45.53N 10.50 E
Rivas 176 Kh 11.26N 85.51W
Rivas [3] 194 Eh 11.25N 85.50W
Rive-de-Gier 122 Ki 45.22N 4.37 E
Rivera [2] 204 Ej 31.30S 55.15W
Rivera [Arg.] 206 He 37.12S 63.14W
Rivera [Ur.] 200 Ki 30.54S 55.31W
River Cess 166 Dd 5.27N 9.35W
Riverdale 186 Fc 47.30N 101.22W
Riverhead 184 Ke 40.55N 72.40W
Riverina ⧗ 212 Jg 35.25S 145.30 E
River Inlet 180 Ef 51.41N 127.15W
Rivers [2] 166 Ge 4.50N 6.30 E
Rivers, Lake of the- ○ 188 Mb 49.45N 105.45W
Riversdale [N.Z.] 218 Cf 45.54S 168.44 E
Riversdale [S.Afr.] 172 Cf 34.07S 21.15 E
Riverside 182 De 33.59N 117.22W
Riverton [N.Z.] 218 Bg 46.21S 168.00 E
Riverton [Wy.-U.S.] 182 Fc 43.02N 108.23W
Rivesaltes 122 Il 42.46N 2.52 E
Riviera Beach 184 Gl 26.47N 80.04W
Rivière-à-Pierre 184 Kb 46.58N 72.11W
Rivière-du-Loup 180 Kg 47.50N 69.32W
Rivière-Pilote 197h Bc 14.29N 60.54W
Rivière-Salée 197h Bb 14.32N 60.59W
Rivoli 128 Be 45.04N 7.31 E
Rivungo 170 Df 16.15S 22.00 E
Riwaka 218 Ed 41.05S 173.00 E
Riwoqê 152 Ge 31.13N 96.29 E
Rixensart 124 Gd 50.43N 4.35 E
Riyadh (EN)=Ar Riyāḑ 142 Gg 24.38N 46.43 E
Rize 144 Fa 41.02N 40.31 E
Rize, gora- ▲ 135 Bf 37.48N 58.13 E
Rıze Dağları ⛰ 146 Ib 40.30N 40.50 E
Rizhao 152 Kd 35.27N 119.28 E
Rizokarpásso → Dipkarpas 146 Fe 35.36N 34.23 E
Rižski zaliv = Riga, Gulf of- (EN) ◐ 110 Id 57.30N 23.35 E
Rizzuto, Capo- ► 128 Ll 38.53N 17.05 E
Rjabovo 116 Md 60.17N 29.01 E
Rjapina/Räpina 116 Lf 58.03N 27.35 E
Rjazan 112 Je 54.38N 39.44 E
Rjazanovski 114 Ji 55.08N 39.35 E
Rjazanskaja oblast [3] 136 Ee 54.30N 40.40 E
Rjažsk 112 Ke 53.43N 40.04 E
Rjukan 114 Bg 59.52N 8.34 E
Rjuven ◠ 116 Be 59.13N 7.10 E
Rkiz 162 Df 16.50N 15.20W
Roa [Nor.] 116 Dd 60.17N 10.37 E
Roa [Sp.] 126 Ic 41.42N 3.55W
Road Town 190 Le 18.27N 64.37W
Roag, Loch- ◐ 118 Gc 58.16N 6.50W
Roan Antelope 170 Ee 13.08S 28.24 E
Roannais ⧗ 122 Kh 46.05N 4.10 E
Roanne 122 Kh 46.02N 4.04 E
Roanoke ≈ 174 Lf 35.56N 76.43W
Roanoke [Al.-U.S.] 184 Ei 33.09N 85.22W
Roanoke [Va.-U.S.] 176 Lf 37.16N 79.57W
Roanoke Rapids 184 Ig 36.28N 77.40W
Roan Plateau ▬ 188 Kg 39.35N 108.55W
Roaringwater Bay ◐ 118 Dj 51.25N 9.30W
Roatán 194 De 16.18N 86.35W
Roatán, Isla de- ◆ 194 De 16.23N 86.30W
Robāţ 146 Qd 37.55N 57.42 E
Robāţ 146 Pg 30.04N 54.49 E
Robāt-e-Khān 144 Ic 33.21N 56.02 E
Robāt-e-Kord 146 Qf 33.45N 56.37 E
Robāt Karīm 146 Ne 35.28N 51.05 E
Robbie Bank (EN) ▦ 208 Jf 11.03S 176.53W
Robe, Mount- ▲ 212 If 31.40S 141.20 E
Röbel 120 Ic 53.23N 12.36 E
Robert Lee 186 Fk 31.54N 100.29W
Roberts 204 Bl 35.09S 61.57W
Roberts, Mount- ▲ 212 Ke 28.13S 152.28 E
Roberts Creek Mountain ▲ 188 Gg 39.52N 116.18W
Robertsfors 114 Ed 64.11N 20.51 E
Robert S. Kerr Lake ○ 186 Ii 35.25N 95.00W
Robertson 172 Bf 33.46S 19.50 E
Robertson Bay ◐ 222 Kf 71.25S 170.00 E
Robertson Range ⛰ 212 Ed 23.10S 121.00 E
Robertsport 166 Cd 6.45N 11.22W
Roberval 180 Kg 48.31N 72.13W
Robi 168 Fd 7.38N 39.52 E
Robinson Crusoe (EN) = Robinson Crusoe, Isla- ◆ 198 Ii 33.38S 78.52W
Robinson Crusoe, Isla- = Robinson Crusoe (EN) ◆ 198 Ii 33.38S 78.52W
Robinson Range ⛰ 212 De 25.45S 119.00 E
Robinson River ≈ 212 Hc 16.03S 137.16 E
Roboré 200 Kg 18.20S 59.45W
Rob Roy ◆ 219a Cb 7.23S 157.36 E
Robson, Mount- ▲ 174 Hd 53.07N 119.09W
Robstown 186 Hm 27.27N 97.40W
Roby 186 Fj 32.45N 100.23W
Roca, Cabo da- ► 110 Fh 38.47N 9.30W
Rocamadour 122 Hj 44.48N 1.38 E
Roca Partida, Isla- ✱ 190 Be 19.01N 112.02W
Roca Partida, Punta- ► 192 Lh 18.42N 95.10W
Rocas, Atol das- ◎ 198 Mf 3.52S 33.49W
Roccaraso 128 Ii 41.51N 14.05 E
Ročegda 136 Ec 62.42N 43.23 E
Rocha 206 Jd 34.29S 54.20W
Rocha [2] 204 Fk 34.00S 54.00W
Rochdale 118 Kh 53.38N 2.09W
Rochechouart 122 Gi 45.49N 0.49 E
Rochedo 204 Ed 19.57S 54.52W
Rochefort [Bel.] 122 Ld 50.10N 5.13 E
Rochefort [Fr.] 122 Fi 45.56N 0.59W
Rochefort-Han-sur-Lesse 124 Hd 50.08N 5.11 E
Rochelle 186 Lf 41.56N 89.04W
Rochelle, La- 112 Ff 46.10N 1.09W
Rocher River 180 Gd 61.23N 112.45W
Roche's Bluff ⊛ 197c Bc 16.42N 62.09W
Rochester [Eng.-U.K.] 118 Nj 51.24N 0.30 E
Rochester [In.-U.S.] 184 De 41.04N 86.13W
Rochester [Mn.-U.S.] 182 Ic 44.02N 92.29W
Rochester [N.H.-U.S.] 184 Ld 43.18N 70.59W
Rochester [N.Y.-U.S.] 176 Le 43.10N 77.36W
Roche-sur-Yon, La- 122 Eh 46.40N 1.26W
Rochlitzer Berg ▲ 120 Ie 51.05N 12.48 E
Rocigalgo ▲ 126 He 39.35N 4.35W
Rockall ◆ 110 Ed 57.35N 13.48W
Rockall Rise (EN) ⌃ 110 Ed 57.00N 14.00W
Rock Creek Butte ▲ 188 Fd 44.49N 118.07W
Rockefeller Plateau ▬ 222 Ng 80.00S 135.00W
Rockenhausen 124 Je 49.38N 7.50 E
Rockford 182 Jc 42.17N 89.06W
Rockglen 188 Mb 49.10N 105.57W
Rockhampton 210 Gg 23.23S 150.31 E
Rock Hill 182 Ke 34.55N 81.01W
Rockingham [Austl.] 212 Df 32.17S 115.44 E
Rockingham [N.C.-U.S.] 184 Hh 34.56N 79.46W
Rock Islands 182 Ic 41.30N 90.34W
Rockland 182 Nc 44.06N 69.06W
Rocklands Reservoir ⊖ 212 Ig 37.15S 142.00 E
Rockledge 184 Gk 28.20N 80.43W
Rockneby 116 Gh 56.49N 16.20 E
Rockport 186 Hl 28.01N 97.04W
Rock River ≈ 186 Kf 41.29N 90.37W
Rock Sound 184 Im 24.53N 76.09W
Rocksprings 186 Fk 30.01N 100.13W
Rock Springs 182 Fc 41.35N 109.13W
Rockville [In.-U.S.] 184 Df 39.45N 87.15W
Rockville [Md.-U.S.] 184 If 39.05N 77.09W
Rockwood 184 Eh 35.52N 84.41W
Rocky Ford 186 Eg 38.03N 103.43W
Rocky Island Lake ○ 184 Fb 46.56N 83.04W
Rocky Mount 182 Ld 35.56N 77.48W
Rocky Mountain ▲ 182 Eb 47.49N 112.49W
Rocky Mountain House 180 Gf 52.22N 114.55W
Rocky Mountains ⛰ 174 He 48.00N 116.00W
Rocky Point [Blz.] ► 194 Cd 18.22N 88.06W
Rocky Point [Nam.] ► 172 Ac 19.01S 12.29 E
Rocroi 124 Ge 49.55N 4.31 E
Rodach ≈ 120 Gf 50.08N 10.52 E
Rodalben 124 Je 49.14N 7.38 E
Roda Velha, Rio- ≈ 204 Ja 12.27S 45.33W
Rødberg 116 Cd 60.16N 8.58 E
Rødby 116 Dj 54.42N 11.24 E
Rødby Havn, Rødby- 114 Ci 54.39N 11.21 E
Rødby-Rødby Havn 114 Ci 54.39N 11.21 E
Roddickton 180 Lf 50.51N 56.07W
Rødding 116 Ci 55.22N 9.04 E
Rödeby 116 Fh 56.15N 15.36 E
Rodeio Bonito 204 Fh 27.28S 53.10W
Roden 124 Ia 53.09N 6.26 E
Rodeo [Arg.] 206 Gd 30.12S 69.06W
Rodeo [Mex.] 192 Ge 25.11N 104.34W
Rodeo [N.M.-U.S.] 186 Bk 31.50N 109.02W
Röder ≈ 120 Je 51.30N 13.25 E
Rodez 122 Ij 44.20N 2.34 E
Rodgau 124 Kd 50.01N 8.53 E
Rodholivos 130 Gi 40.56N 23.59 E
Ródhos = Rhodes (EN) 112 Ih 36.26N 28.13 E
Ródhos = Rhodes (EN) ◆ 110 Ih 36.10N 28.00 E
Rodi Garganico 128 Ji 41.55N 15.53 E
Roding ≈ 118 Nj 51.31N 0.06 E
Rodna 130 Hb 47.25N 24.49 E
Rodnei, Munţii- ⛰ 130 Hb 47.35N 24.40 E
Rodney, Cape- ► 178 Fd 64.39N 166.24W
Rodniki 114 Jh 57.07N 41.48 E
Roconit, Gjiri i- ◐ 130 Ch 41.35N 19.30 E
Roconit, Kep i- ► 130 Ch 41.35N 19.27 E
Rodopi=Rhodope Mountains (EN) ⛰ 110 Ig 41.30N 24.30 E
Rodrigues Island ◆ 158 Nj 19.42S 63.25 E
Roebourne 212 Dd 20.47S 117.09 E
Roebuck Bay ◐ 212 Ec 18.04S 122.15 E
Roer ≈ 124 Hc 51.12N 5.59 E
Roermond 122 Lc 51.12N 6.00 E
Roeselare/Roulers 122 Jd 50.57N 3.08 E
Roes Welcome Sound ⇌ 180 Id 64.30N 86.45W

Index Symbols

[1] Independent Nation
[2] State, Region
[3] District, County
[4] Municipality
[5] Colony, Dependency
■ Continent
⧗ Physical Region
▣ Historical or Cultural Region
▲ Mount, Mountain
⩓ Volcano
△ Hill
⛰ Mountains, Mountain Range
◠ Hills, Escarpment
▬ Plateau, Upland
◡ Pass, Gap
▭ Plain, Lowland
◣ Delta
▤ Salt Flat
∨ Valley, Canyon
◉ Crater, Cave
✲ Karst Features
▽ Depression
▥ Polder
◢ Desert, Dunes
♣ Forest, Woods
⋓ Heath, Steppe
⚘ Oasis
► Cape, Point
≋ Coast, Beach
▌ Cliff
⊟ Peninsula
⋈ Isthmus
⋯ Sandbank
◆ Island
◎ Atoll
✱ Rock, Reef
❖ Islands, Archipelago
⊛ Rocks, Reefs
❀ Coral Reef
⊙ Well, Spring
⊥ Geyser
≈ River, Stream
↯ Waterfall, Rapids
⊰ River Mouth, Estuary
○ Lake
◍ Salt Lake
◌ Intermittent Lake
⊖ Reservoir
⋒ Swamp, Pond
═ Canal
▼ Glacier
✶ Ice Shelf, Pack Ice
▒ Ocean
░ Sea
◐ Gulf, Bay
⇌ Strait, Fjord
◛ Lagoon
▦ Bank
⊼ Seamount
⊓ Tablemount
⌃ Ridge
⌐ Shelf
◟ Basin
⌒ Escarpment, Sea Scarp
⚡ Fracture
⩡ Trench, Abyss
⚑ National Park, Reserve
✪ Point of Interest
⇡ Recreation Site
⌓ Cave, Cavern
⌂ Historic Site
∴ Ruins
⊓⊓ Wall, Walls
✝ Church, Abbey
⛩ Temple
⊗ Scientific Station
⊞ Railway station
✈ Airport
⚓ Port
⊡ Military installation
⇑ Lighthouse
⚒ Mine
⊓̲ Tunnel
⟋ Dam, Bridge

Roetgen 124 Id 50.39N 6.12 E
Rogačev 132 Gc 53.09N 30.06 E
Rogačevka 132 Kd 51.31N 39.34 E
Rogagua, Laguna- 202 Ef 13.45S 66.55W
Rogaguado, Laguna- 202 Ef 12.55S 65.45W
Rogaland [2] 114 Bg 59.00N 6.15 E
Rogaška Slatina 128 Jd 46.15N 15.38 E
Rogatica 128 Ng 43.48N 19.01 E
Rogatin 120 Ug 49.19N 24.40 E
Rogers 186 Ih 36.20N 94.07W
Rogers, Mount- 184 Gg 36.39N 81.33W
Rogers City 184 Fc 45.25N 83.49W
Rogers Lake 188 Gi 34.52N 117.51W
Rogers Peak 188 Jg 38.04N 111.32W
Rogersville 184 Fg 36.25N 82.59W
Roggan 180 Jf 54.24N 79.30W
Roggeveldberge 172 Bf 31.50S 19.50 E
Roggewein, Cabo- 221d Bb 27.07S 109.15W
Rognan 114 Dc 67.06N 15.23 E
Rogozhina 130 Ch 41.05N 19.40 E
Rogozna 130 Df 43.04N 20.40 E
Rogoźno 120 Md 52.46N 17.00 E
Rogue River 188 Ce 42.26N 124.25W
Rohan, Plateau de- 122 Df 48.10N 2.50W
Rohl 168 Dd 7.05N 29.46 E
Rohrbach in Oberösterreich 128 Hb 48.34N 13.59 E
Rohrbach-lès-Bitche 124 Je 49.03N 7.16 E
Rohri 148 Dc 27.41N 68.54 E
Rohtak 148 Fc 28.54N 76.34 E
Roi, Le Bois du- 122 Kh 46.59N 4.02 E
Roi Et 148 Ke 16.05N 103.42 E
Roi Georges, Iles du- 208 Mf 14.32S 145.08W
Roine 116 Kc 61.25N 24.05 E
Roisel 124 Fe 49.57N 3.06 E
Roja 114 Fh 57.30N 22.51 E
Roja, Punta- / Rotja, Punta- 126 Nf 38.38N 1.34 E
Rojas 206 Hd 34.12S 60.44W
Rojo, Cabo- [Mex.] 190 Ed 21.33N 97.20W
Rojo, Cabo- [P.R.] 194 Nd 18.01N 67.15W
Rokan 150 Df 2.00N 100.52 E
Rokiškis 114 Fi 55.59N 25.37 E
Rokitnoje 132 Ed 51.21N 27.14 E
Rokkasho 156a Bc 40.58N 141.21 E
Rokycany 120 Jg 49.45N 13.36 E
Rokytná 120 Mg 49.05N 16.21 E
Rola Co 152 Ed 35.25N 88.25 E
Rolândia 204 Gf 23.18S 51.22W
Røldal 116 Be 59.49N 6.48 E
Rolla [Mo.-U.S.] 182 Id 37.57N 91.46W
Rolla [N.D.-U.S.] 186 Gb 48.52N 99.37W
Rolleston 218 Ee 43.35S 172.23 E
Rolvsøya 114 Fa 71.00N 24.00 E
Roma [Austl.] 210 Fg 26.35S 148.47 E
Roma [It.] = Rome (EN) 112 Hg 41.54N 12.29 E
Roma [Swe.] 114 Eh 57.32N 18.26 E
Romagna 128 Gf 44.30N 12.15 E
Romaine 180 Lf 50.18N 63.48W
Roman 130 Jc 46.55N 26.55 E
Romanche 122 Li 45.05N 5.43 E
Romanche Gap (EN) 106 Dj 0.10S 18.15W
Romang 204 Ci 29.30S 59.46W
Romang, Pulau- 150 Ih 7.35S 127.26 E
România = Romania (EN) [1] 112 If 46.00N 25.30 E
Romania (EN) = România [1] 112 If 46.00N 25.30 E
Romanija 128 Mg 43.51N 18.43 E
Roman-Koš, gora- 136 Dg 44.36N 34.16 E
Romano, Cayo- 194 Ib 22.04N 77.50W
Romanovka 138 Gf 53.14N 112.46 E
Romans-sur-Isère 122 Li 45.03N 5.03 E
Romanzof, Cape- 174 Cc 61.49N 166.09W
Romanzof Mountains 178 Kc 69.00N 144.00W
Rombas 124 Ie 49.15N 6.05 E
Romblon 150 Hd 12.35N 122.15 E
Rome [Ga.-U.S.] 182 Je 34.16N 85.11W
Rome [N.Y.-U.S.] 182 Lc 43.13N 75.28W
Rome [Or.-U.S.] 188 Ge 42.50N 117.37W
Rome (EN) = Roma [It.] 112 Hg 41.54N 12.29 E
Romeleåsen 116 Ei 55.34N 13.33 E
Romerike 116 Dd 60.05N 11.10 E
Romilly-sur-Seine 122 Jf 48.31N 3.43 E
Rommani 162 Fc 33.32N 6.36W
Romme 116 Fd 60.26N 15.30 E
Rommerskirchen 124 Ic 51.02N 6.41 E
Romney Marsh 124 Cc 51.02N 0.55 E
Romny 136 De 50.45N 33.29 E
Rømø 114 Bi 55.10N 8.30 E
Romodanovo 114 Ki 54.28N 45.18 E
Romont 128 Ad 46.42N 6.55 E
Romorantin-Lanthenay 122 Hg 47.22N 1.45 E
Romsdal 116 Bb 62.35N 7.50 E
Romsdalen 116 Be 62.30N 7.55 E
Romsdalsfjorden 116 Bb 62.40N 7.15 E
Romsdalshorn 116 Bd 62.29N 7.50 E
Romsey 118 Lk 50.59N 1.30W
Ronas Hill 118 La 60.38N 1.20W
Ronave 220e Ba 0.29S 166.56 E
Roncador, Cayos de- 190 Hf 13.32N 80.03W
Roncador, Serra do- 198 Kg 13.00S 51.50W
Roncador Reef 208 Ge 6.13S 159.22 E
Roncesvalles 126 Ka 43.01N 1.19W
Roncesvalles o de Ibañeta, Puerto de- 126 Ka 43.01N 1.19W
Ronciglione 128 Gh 42.17N 12.13 E
Ronco 128 Gf 44.24N 12.12 E
Ronda 126 Gh 36.44N 5.10W
Ronda, Serranía de- 126 Gh 36.45N 5.05W
Ronda do Sul 204 Cb 15.57S 59.42W
Rondane 114 Bf 61.55N 9.45 E
Rønde 114 Ch 56.18N 10.29 E
Ronde, Point- 197g Ba 15.33N 61.29W
Ronde Island 196 Ff 12.18N 61.31W
Rondeslottet 116 Cc 61.55N 9.46 E
Rondon 204 Ff 23.23S 52.48W
Rondón, Pico- 202 Fc 1.36N 63.08W
Rondônia 200 Jg 10.52S 61.57W
Rondônia [2] 202 Ff 11.00S 63.00W
Rondonópolis 200 Kg 16.28S 54.38W
Rong'an (Chang'an) 152 If 25.16N 109.23 E
Rongcheng 154 Ce 39.03N 115.52 E
Rongcheng (Yatou) 154 Gf 37.10N 122.25 E
Rongelap Atoll 208 Hc 11.09N 166.50 E
Rongerik Atoll 208 Hc 11.21N 167.26 E
Rongjiang (Guzhou) 152 If 25.58N 108.30 E
Rongxian 152 Jg 22.48N 110.30 E
Rongzhag/Danba 152 He 30.48N 101.54 E
Rønne 114 Di 55.06N 14.42 E
Ronne Bay 222 Qf 72.30S 74.00W
Ronneby 114 Dh 56.12N 15.18 E
Ronnebyån 116 Fh 56.10N 15.18 E
Ronne Ice Shelf 222 Qf 78.30S 61.00W
Ronse/Renaix 122 Jd 50.45N 3.36 E
Ronuro, Rio- 198 Kg 11.56S 53.33W
Roodepoort 172 De 26.11S 27.54 E
Roof Butte 182 Fd 36.28N 109.05W
Rooiboklaagte 172 Cd 20.20S 21.15 E
Roon, Pulau- 150 Jg 2.23S 134.33 E
Rooniu, Mont- 221e Fc 17.49S 149.12W
Roorkee 148 Fc 29.52N 77.53 E
Roosendaal 122 Kc 51.32N 4.28 E
Roosevelt [Az.-U.S.] 188 Jj 33.40N 111.09W
Roosevelt [Ut.-U.S.] 188 Kf 40.18N 109.59W
Roosevelt, Mount- 180 Ee 58.23N 125.04W
Roosevelt, Rio- 198 Jf 7.35S 60.20W
Roosevelt Island 222 Lf 79.30S 162.00W
Root Portage 186 Ka 50.53N 91.18W
Ropa 120 Rg 49.46N 21.29 E
Ropar 148 Fb 30.58N 76.20 E
Ropaži 116 Kh 56.58N 24.26 E
Ropczyce 120 Rf 50.03N 21.37 E
Rope, The- 220q Ab 25.04S 130.05W
Roper River 208 Ef 14.43S 135.27 E
Roquefort 122 Fj 44.02N 0.19W
Roque Pérez 204 Cl 35.25S 59.20W
Roquetas de Mar 126 Jh 36.46N 2.36W
Roraima, Monte- 198 Je 5.12N 60.44W
Roraima, Território de- [2] 202 Fc 1.30N 61.00W
Røros 114 Ce 62.35N 11.24 E
Rorschach 128 Dc 47.30N 9.30 E
Rørvik 114 Cd 64.51N 11.14 E
Ros 132 Ge 49.39N 31.35 E
Rosa, Cap- 128 Cn 36.57N 8.14 E
Rosa, Lake- 194 Kc 20.55N 73.20W
Rosa, Monte- 110 Gf 45.55N 7.53 E
Rošal 114 Ji 55.41N 39.55 E
Rosala 116 Je 59.50N 22.25 E
Rosalia 188 Gc 47.14N 117.22W
Rosalia, Punta- 221d Bb 27.03S 109.19W
Rosalie 197g Bb 15.22N 61.16W
Rosalind Bank (EN) 194 Ge 16.30N 80.30W
Rosamond Lake 188 Fi 34.50N 118.04W
Rosamorada 192 Gf 22.08N 105.12W
Rosana 204 Ff 22.36S 53.01W
Rosário 202 Jd 2.57S 44.14W
Rosario 200 Ji 32.57S 60.40W
Rosario [Mex.] 192 Dd 26.27N 111.38W
Rosario [Mex.] 190 Cd 23.00N 105.52W
Rosario [Par.] 206 Ib 24.27S 57.03W
Rosario [Ven.] 194 Kh 10.19N 72.19W
Rosario, Arroyo- 192 Bb 30.03N 115.45W
Rosario, Bahía- 192 Bc 29.50N 115.45W
Rosario, Cayo del- 194 Gc 21.38N 81.53W
Rosario, Islas del- 194 Jh 10.10N 75.46W
Rosario, Sierra del- 192 He 25.35N 103.50W
Rosario de Arriba 190 Ab 30.01N 115.40W
Rosario de la Frontera 206 Hc 25.48S 64.58W
Rosario de Lerma 206 Gb 24.59S 65.35W
Rosario del Tala 204 Ck 32.18S 59.09W
Rosário do Sul 206 Jd 30.15S 54.55W
Rosário Oeste 202 Gf 14.50S 56.25W
Rosarito 192 Bc 28.38N 114.04W
Rosarno 128 Jl 38.29N 15.58 E
Rosas/Roses 126 Pb 42.16N 3.11 E
Rosa Seamount (EN) 190 Bc 26.12N 114.58W
Rosa Zarate 202 Cc 0.18N 79.27W
Roščino 116 Md 60.13N 29.43 E
Roscoe Glacier 222 Ge 66.30S 95.20 E
Ros Comáin/Roscommon 118 Eh 53.38N 8.11W
Ros Comáin/Roscommon [2] 118 Eh 53.40N 8.30W
Roscommon 162 Ee 44.30N 84.35W
Roscommon/Ros Comáin 118 Eh 53.38N 8.11W
Roscommon/Ros Comáin [2] 118 Eh 53.40N 8.30W
Ros Cré/Roscrea 118 Fi 52.57N 7.47W
Roscrea/Ros Cré 118 Fi 52.57N 7.47W
Rose, Pointe de la- 197h Bb 14.33N 61.03W
Roseau [Dom.] 176 Mh 15.18N 61.24W
Roseau [Dom.] 197g Bb 15.18N 61.24W
Roseau [Mn.-U.S.] 186 Ib 48.51N 95.46W
Roseau [St.Luc.] 197k Ab 13.58N 61.02W
Roseau River 186 Hb 49.08N 97.14W
Rosebery 212 Jh 41.46S 145.32 E
Rosebud 188 Lc 46.16N 106.27W
Rosebud Creek 188 Lc 46.16N 106.28W
Rosebud River 188 Ia 51.25N 112.37W
Roseburg 182 Cc 43.13N 123.20W
Rosemary Bank (EN) 118 Cb 59.15N 10.10W
Rosenberg 188 Hf 29.33N 95.48W
Rosendahl 124 Jb 52.01N 7.12 E
Rosendahl-Osterwick 124 Jb 52.01N 7.12 E
Rosendal 114 Bf 59.59N 6.01 E
Rosenheim 120 Ii 47.51N 12.08 E
Rosental 128 Id 46.33N 14.15 E
Roses/Rosas 126 Pb 42.16N 3.11 E
Roses, Golf de- / Roses, Golfo de- 126 Pb 42.10N 3.15 E
Roses, Golfo de- / Roses, Golf de- 126 Pb 42.10N 3.15 E
Roseţi 130 Ke 44.13N 27.26 E
Roseto degli Abruzzi 128 Ih 42.41N 14.01 E
Rosetown 180 Gf 51.33N 108.00W
Rosetta (EN) = Rashīd 164 Fc 31.24N 30.25 E
Roseville 188 Eg 38.45N 121.17W
Roshage 114 Bh 57.07N 8.38 E
Rosica 130 If 43.15N 25.42 E
Rosières-en-Santerre 124 Ee 49.49N 2.43 E
Rosignano Solvay 128 Eg 43.23N 10.26 E
Rosignol 202 Gb 6.17N 57.32W
Roşiori de Vede 130 He 44.07N 24.59 E
Roskilde 114 Ci 55.39N 12.05 E
Roskilde [2] 116 Ei 55.35N 12.10 E
Roslagen 116 Hd 59.30N 18.40 E
Ros Láir/Rosslare 118 Gi 52.17N 6.23W
Roslavl 136 De 53.58N 32.53 E
Roslyn 188 Ec 47.13N 120.59W
Ros Mhic Thriúin/New Ross 118 Gi 52.24N 6.56W
Røsnæs 116 Di 55.45N 10.55 E
Rosny-sur-Seine 124 Df 49.00N 1.38 E
Rösrath 124 Jd 50.54N 7.12 E
Ross 180 Ed 62.00N 132.25W
Ross [Austl.] 212 Jh 42.02S 147.29 E
Ross [Bye.-U.S.S.R.] 120 Uc 53.16N 24.29 E
Ross [N.Z.] 218 De 42.54S 170.49 E
Ross, Cape- 150 Gd 10.56N 119.13 E
Ross, Mount- 222 Fc 49.25S 69.08 E
Rossano 128 Kk 39.34N 16.38 E
Rossan Point/Ceann Ros Eoghain 118 Eg 54.42N 8.48W
Ross Barnett Reservoir 186 Lj 32.30N 90.00W
Rosseau Lake 184 Hc 45.10N 79.35W
Rossel Island 208 Gf 11.26S 154.07 E
Rossell, Cap- 219b Ce 20.23S 166.36 E
Ross Ice Shelf 222 Lg 81.30S 175.00W
Rossijskaja Sovetskaja Federativnaja Socialističeskaja Respublika (RSFSR) [2] 136 Jc 60.00N 100.00 E
Ross Island 222 Kf 77.30S 168.00 E
Ross Lake 188 Eb 48.53N 121.04W
Rossland 188 Gb 49.05N 117.48W
Rosslare/Ros Láir 118 Gi 52.17N 6.23W
Roßlau 120 Ie 51.53N 12.15 E
Rosso 160 Fg 16.31N 15.49W
Ross-on-Wye 118 Kj 51.55N 2.35W
Rossoš 136 De 50.11N 39.39 E
Ross River 180 Ed 61.59N 132.27W
Ross Sea (EN) 222 Lf 76.00S 175.00W
Røssvatn 114 Cd 65.45N 14.00 E
Røst 114 Cc 67.31N 12.07 E
Rosta 114 Eb 69.02N 18.40 E
Rostamī 146 Nh 28.52N 51.02 E
Rostam Kalā 146 Od 36.42N 53.27 E
Rostāq 144 Hd 26.53N 53.52 E
Rösterkopf 124 Ie 49.40N 6.50 E
Rosthern 180 Gf 52.40N 106.20W
Rostock 118 Hc 54.05N 12.08 E
Rostock-Warnemünde 120 Ib 54.10N 12.05 E
Rostov 136 Dd 57.13N 39.25 E
Rostov-na-Donu 112 Jf 47.14N 39.42 E
Rostovskaja oblast [3] 136 Ef 47.45N 41.15 E
Roswell [Ga.-U.S.] 184 Eh 34.03N 84.22W
Roswell [N.M.-U.S.] 176 If 33.24N 104.32W
Rot 116 Fc 61.15N 14.02 E
Rota 126 Fh 36.37N 6.21W
Rota Island 208 Fc 14.10N 145.12 E
Rotenburg (Wümme) 120 Fc 53.07N 9.24 E
Rotenburg an der Fulda 120 Ff 50.59N 9.43 E
Roter Main 120 Hf 50.03N 11.27 E
Roth 120 Hg 49.15N 11.06 E
Rothaargebirge 124 Ee 51.05N 8.15 E
Rothenburg ob der Tauber 120 Gg 49.23N 10.11 E
Rother [Eng.-U.K.] 124 Bd 50.57N 0.22W
Rother [Eng.-U.K.] 118 Nk 50.57N 0.45 E
Rothera 222 Qe 67.46S 68.54W
Rotherham 118 Lh 53.26N 1.20W
Rothesay 118 Hf 55.51N 5.03W
Rothorn 128 Cd 46.47N 8.03 E
Rothschild Island 222 Qe 69.25S 72.30W
Rothwell 124 Bb 52.25N 0.48W
Roti, Pulau- 140 Ok 10.45S 123.10 E
Roti, Selat- 150 Hi 10.25S 123.25 E
Rotja, Punta- / Roja, Punta- 126 Nf 38.38N 1.34 E
Rotnes 116 Dd 60.04N 10.53 E
Roto 212 Jf 33.03S 145.29 E
Rotoiti, Lake- 218 Ed 41.50S 172.50 E
Rotondella 128 Kj 40.10N 16.31 E
Rotondo, Monte- 122a Ba 42.13N 9.03 E
Rotoroa, Lake- 218 Ed 41.50S 172.40 E
Rotorua 216 Eg 38.09S 176.15 E
Rotorua, Lake- 218 Gc 38.05S 176.15 E
Rotselaar 124 Gd 50.57N 4.43 E
Rott 120 Jh 48.25N 13.20 E
Rottenburg am Neckar 120 Eh 48.28N 8.56 E
Rotterdam 112 Ge 51.55N 4.28 E
Rottnaälven 116 Ed 59.48N 13.07 E
Rottnen 116 Fh 56.45N 15.05 E
Rottneros 116 Ee 59.48N 13.07 E
Rottnest Island 212 Df 32.00S 115.30 E
Rottumerplaat 124 Ia 53.35N 6.30 E
Rottweil 120 Eh 48.10N 8.37 E
Rotuma Island 208 If 12.30S 177.05 E
Roubaix 122 Jd 50.42N 3.10 E
Roubion 122 Kj 44.31N 4.42 E
Roudnice nad Labem 120 Kf 50.26N 14.16 E
Rouen 112 Gf 49.26N 1.05 E
Rouergue 122 Ij 44.30N 2.30 E
Rouge, Rivière- 184 Jc 45.38N 74.42W
Rouillac 122 Fi 45.47N 0.04W
Roulers/Roeselare 122 Jd 50.57N 3.08 E
Roumois 122 Ge 49.30N 0.30 E
Roundup 182 Fb 46.27N 108.33W
Rousay 118 Jb 59.01N 3.02W
Roussillon 122 Ik 45.22N 4.49 E
Roussillon 122 Il 42.30N 2.30 E
Roussin, Cap- 219b Ce 21.21S 167.59 E
Routot 124 Ce 49.23N 0.44 E
Rouyn 176 Le 48.14N 79.01W
Rovaniemi 112 Ib 66.30N 25.43 E
Rovenskaja oblast [3] 136 Ce 51.00N 26.30 E
Rovereto 128 Fe 45.53N 11.02 E
Rovigo 128 Fe 45.04N 11.47 E
Rovinari 130 Ge 44.55N 23.11 E
Rovinj 128 He 45.05N 13.38 E
Rovkulskoje, ozero- 114 Hd 64.00N 31.00 E
Rovno 112 Ie 50.37N 26.15 E
Rovnoje 132 Od 50.47N 46.05 E
Rovuma = Ruvuma (EN) 158 Lj 10.29S 40.28 E
Rowa, Iles- 219b Ca 13.37S 167.32 E
Rowley 180 Jc 69.05N 78.55W
Rowley Shoals 208 Cf 17.30S 119.00 E
Roxas [Phil.] 150 Gd 10.28N 119.30 E
Roxas [Phil.] 150 Hd 11.35N 122.45 E
Roxboro 184 Hg 36.24N 78.59W
Roxburgh 218 Cf 45.33S 169.19 E
Roxen 116 Ff 58.30N 15.40 E
Roxo, Cap- 158 Fg 12.20N 16.43W
Roy [N.M.-U.S.] 186 Di 35.57N 104.12W
Roy [Ut.-U.S.] 188 If 41.10N 112.02W
Roya 122 Nk 43.48N 7.35 E
Royal Canal 118 Gh 53.21N 6.15W
Royale, Isle- 182 Jb 48.00N 89.00W
Royal Leamington Spa 118 Li 52.18N 1.31W
Royal Society Range 222 Jf 78.10S 162.36 E
Royal Tunbridge Wells 118 Nj 51.08N 0.16 E
Royan 122 Ei 45.38N 1.02W
Royat 122 Ji 45.46N 3.03 E
Roye 122 Ie 49.42N 2.48 E
Roy Hill 212 Dd 22.38S 119.57 E
Røyken 116 De 59.45N 10.23 E
Royston 118 Mi 52.03N 0.01W
Rožaj 130 Dg 42.51N 20.10 E
Różan 120 Rd 52.53N 21.25 E
Rozdol 120 Ug 49.24N 24.08 E
Rozewie, Przylądek- 120 Ob 54.51N 18.21 E
Rožišče 120 Dd 50.54N 25.19 E
Rožňava 120 Qh 48.40N 20.32 E
Rožniatov 120 Uh 48.51N 24.14 E
Roznov 130 Jc 46.50N 26.31 E
Rožnov pod Radhoštěm 120 Og 49.28N 18.09 E
Rožnów 120 Qg 49.46N 20.42 E
Rožnowskie, Jezioro- 120 Qg 49.48N 20.45 E
Rozoy-sur-Serre 124 Ge 49.43N 4.08 E
Roztocze 110 Ie 50.30N 23.20 E
Rrësheni 130 Ch 41.47N 19.54 E
RSFSR = Russian SFSR (EN) [2] 136 Jc 60.00N 100.00 E
RSFSR → Rossijskaja Sovetskaja Federativnaja Socialističeskaja Respublika [2] 136 Jc 60.00N 100.00 E
Rtanj 130 Ef 43.47N 21.54 E
Rtiščevo 136 Ee 52.16N 43.52 E
Ruacana, Quedas- 158 Ij 17.23S 14.15 E
Ruahine Range 218 Gc 39.50S 176.05 E
Ruapehu 208 Ih 39.17S 175.34 E
Ruapuke Island 216 Ci 46.45S 168.30 E
Rua Sura 219a Ec 9.30S 160.36 E
Ruatahuna 218 Gc 38.38S 176.58 E
Rubbestadneset 116 Ae 59.49N 5.17 E
Rubcovsk 142 Kd 51.33N 81.10 E
Rubeho Mountains 170 Gd 6.55S 36.30 E
Rubeshibe 154 Qc 43.47N 143.38 E
Rubežnoje 132 Ke 48.59N 38.26 E
Rubi 170 Db 2.48N 23.54 E
Rubiataba 204 Hb 15.08S 49.48W
Rubiku 130 Ch 41.46N 19.45 E
Rubio 202 Db 7.43N 72.22W
Rubio 126 Ic 41.26N 3.47W
Ruby 178 Hd 64.44N 155.30W
Ruby Lake 188 Hf 40.15N 115.30W
Ruby Mountains 188 Hf 40.25N 115.35W
Ruby Range 188 Id 45.15N 112.15W
Rucăr 130 Id 45.24N 25.10 E
Rucava 116 Ih 56.10N 21.00 E
Ruciane Nida 120 Rc 53.39N 21.35 E
Ruda 120 Of 50.10N 18.18 E
Rudabánya 120 Qh 48.23N 20.38 E
Rūdak 146 Nh 35.51N 51.33 E
Rūdān 146 Qi 27.17N 57.13 E
Ruda Śląska 120 Of 50.18N 18.51 E
Rūdbār [Afg.] 144 Jc 30.09N 62.36 E
Rūdbār [Iran] 146 Md 36.48N 49.24 E
Rüdersdorf bei Berlin 120 Jd 52.27N 13.47 E
Rudesheim am Rhein 124 Je 49.59N 7.55 E
Rūdiškes/Rudiškes 116 Kj 54.30N 24.58 E
Rudiškes/Rūdiškes 116 Kj 54.30N 24.58 E
Rudki 120 Tg 49.34N 23.30 E
Rudkøbing 114 Ci 54.56N 10.43 E
Rudnaja-Pristan 138 Ih 44.25N 135.49 E
Rudničny 114 Mg 59.38N 52.29 E
Rudnik 130 De 44.08N 20.30 E
Rudnik [Bul.] 130 Kg 42.57N 27.46 E
Rudnik [Pol.] 120 Sf 50.28N 22.15 E
Rudnik [Yugo.] 130 De 44.08N 20.31 E
Rudnja [R.S.F.S.R.] 132 Nd 50.49N 44.36 E
Rudnja [R.S.F.S.R.] 136 De 54.57N 31.07 E
Rudno 120 Tg 49.44N 23.57 E
Rudny [Kaz.-U.S.S.R.] 136 Ge 52.57N 63.07 E
Rudny [R.S.F.S.R.] 154 Mb 44.28N 135.00 E
Rudolf, Lake- / Turkana, Lake- 158 Kh 3.30N 36.00 E
Rudolstadt 120 Hf 50.43N 11.20 E
Rudong (Juegang) 154 Fh 32.19N 121.11 E
Rudozem 130 Hh 41.29N 24.51 E
Rūd Sar 144 Hb 37.08N 50.18 E
Rudyard 188 Jb 48.34N 110.33W
Rue 122 Hd 50.16N 1.40 E
Ruecas 126 Ge 39.00N 5.55W
Ruelle 122 Gi 45.41N 0.14 E
Rufā'ah 168 Ec 14.46N 33.22 E
Ruffec 122 Gh 46.01N 0.12 E
Ruffing Point 197a Db 18.45N 64.25W
Rufiji 158 Ki 8.00S 39.20 E
Rufino 206 Hd 34.16S 62.42W
Rufisque 166 Bc 14.43N 17.17W
Rufunsa 170 Ef 15.05S 29.40 E
Rugao 154 Fh 32.24N 120.34 E
Rugby [Eng.-U.K.] 118 Li 52.23N 1.15W
Rugby [N.D.-U.S.] 182 Gb 48.22N 99.59W
Rügen 116 He 54.25N 13.24 E
Rugles 124 Cf 48.49N 0.42 E
Ru He 154 Ch 32.55N 114.24 E
Ruhea 148 Hc 26.10N 88.25 E
Ruhengeri 170 Ec 1.30S 29.38 E
Rühlertwist 124 Jb 52.39N 7.06 E
Ruhner Berge 120 Hc 53.17N 11.55 E
Ruhnu, ostrov- 114 Fh 57.50N 23.15 E
Ruhnu, ostrov- / Ruhnu saar 114 Fh 57.50N 23.15 E
Ruhnu saar / Ruhnu, ostrov- 114 Fh 57.50N 23.15 E
Ruhr 120 Ce 51.27N 6.44 E
Rui'an 152 Lf 27.48N 120.38 E
Ruichang 154 Cj 29.41N 115.38 E
Ruiena/Rūjiena 114 Fh 57.54N 25.17 E
Ruijin 152 Kf 25.59N 116.03 E
Ruili 152 Gg 24.03N 97.46 E
Ruiselede 124 Fc 51.03N 3.24 E
Ruiz 192 Gg 21.57N 105.09W
Ruiz, Nevado del- 202 Cc 4.54N 75.18W
Ruj 130 Fg 42.51N 22.35 E
Rūja/Ruja 116 Kg 57.38N 25.10 E
Ruja/Rūja 116 Kg 57.38N 25.10 E
Rujan 130 Eg 42.23N 21.49 E
Rujen 130 Fg 42.10N 22.31 E
Rūjiena/Ruiena 114 Fh 57.54N 25.17 E
Ruki 158 Ih 0.05N 18.17 E
Rukwa [3] 170 Fd 7.00S 31.20 E
Rukwa, Lake- 158 Ki 8.00S 32.15 E
Rūl Ḍadnah 146 Qk 25.33N 56.21 E
Rülzheim 124 Ke 49.10N 8.18 E
Ruma 130 Cd 45.01N 19.49 E
Rumaylah 168 Fc 12.57N 35.02 E
Rumbek 160 Jh 6.48N 29.41 E
Rumberpon, Pulau- 150 Jg 1.50S 134.15 E
Rum Cay 190 Jd 23.40N 74.53W
Rumes 124 Fd 50.33N 3.18 E
Rumford 184 Lc 44.33N 70.33W
Rumia 120 Ob 54.35N 18.25 E
Rumigny 124 Ge 49.48N 4.16 E
Rumija 130 Cg 42.06N 19.12 E
Rumilly 122 Li 45.52N 5.57 E
Rum Jungle 212 Gb 13.01S 131.00 E
Rummah, Wādī ar- 146 Ki 26.38N 44.18 E
Rumoi 152 Pc 43.56N 141.39 E
Rumphi 170 Fe 11.01S 33.52 E
Run 124 Hc 51.40N 5.20 E
Runan 154 Ci 33.00N 114.21 E
Runanga 218 De 42.24S 171.15 E
Runaway, Cape- 218 Gb 37.32S 177.59 E
Rundēni/Rundeni 116 Lh 56.14N 27.52 E
Rundeni/Rundēni 116 Lh 56.14N 27.52 E
Rundu 160 Ij 17.55S 19.45 E
Rungu 170 Eb 3.11N 27.52 E
Rungwa 160 Ki 6.57S 33.31 E
Rungwa 170 Fd 7.36S 31.50 E
Runnarö 116 He 59.55N 18.45 E
Runn 116 Fd 60.35N 15.40 E
Ruokolahti 114 Gf 61.17N 28.50 E
Ruoqiang/Qarkilik 142 Kf 39.02N 88.00 E
Ruo Shui 140 Le 40.20N 99.40 E
Ruotsalainen 116 Kc 61.15N 25.55 E
Ruotsinpyhtää/Strömfors 116 Ld 60.32N 26.27 E
Ruovesi 114 Ff 61.59N 24.05 E
Ruovesi 116 Kc 61.55N 24.10 E
Rupanco 206 Ff 40.46S 72.42W
Rupea 130 Ic 46.02N 25.13 E
Rupel 124 Gc 51.07N 4.19 E
Rupert 188 Ie 42.37N 113.41W
Rupert 180 Jf 51.30N 78.48W
Rupert, Baie de- 180 Jf 51.35N 79.00W
Ruppert Coast 222 Mf 75.45S 141.00W
Rur 120 Be 51.12N 5.59 E
Rurrenabaque 200 Jg 14.28S 67.34W
Rurstausee 124 Id 50.38N 6.24 E
Rurutu, Ile- 208 Lg 22.26S 151.20W
Rušan 136 Hh 37.57N 71.31 E
Rusape 172 Ec 18.32S 32.07 E
Ruşayriş, Khazzān ar- = Rusayris, Lake- (EN) 168 Ec 11.40N 34.20 E
Rusayris, Lake- (EN) = Ruşayriş, Khazzān ar- 168 Ec 11.40N 34.20 E
Ruse 112 Ig 43.50N 25.57 E
Ruse [2] 130 If 43.50N 25.57 E
Ruşeţu 130 Ke 44.57N 27.13 E
Rushan (Xiacun) 154 Ff 36.55N 121.30 E
Rushden 124 Bb 52.17N 0.35W
Rushville 186 Kf 40.07N 90.34W
Rusk 186 Ik 31.48N 95.09W
Rusken 116 Fg 57.17N 14.20 E
Rusne/Rusnė 116 Ii 55.19N 21.16 E
Rusnė/Rusne 116 Ii 55.19N 21.16 E
Russel 180 Hb 73.55N 98.35W
Russell [Ks.-U.S.] 186 Gg 38.54N 98.52W
Russell [Man.-Can.] 180 Hf 50.47N 101.15W
Russell [N.Z.] 218 Fa 35.16S 174.08 E
Russell Islands 214 Fi 9.04S 159.12 E
Russellville [Al.-U.S.] 184 Dh 34.30N 87.44W
Russellville [Ar.-U.S.] 186 Ji 35.17N 93.08W
Russellville [Ky.-U.S.] 184 Dg 36.51N 86.53W
Russel Range 212 Ef 33.25S 123.30 E
Rüsselsheim 120 Eg 50.00N 8.25 E
Russian River 188 Dg 38.27N 123.08W
Russian SFSR (EN) = RSFSR [2] 136 Jc 60.00N 100.00 E
Rust 128 Kc 47.48N 16.40 E
Rustavi 136 Eg 41.33N 45.02 E
Rustenburg 172 De 25.37S 27.08 E
Ruston 182 Ie 32.32N 92.38W
Rutaki Passage 220p Bc 21.15S 159.48W
Rutana 170 Fc 3.55S 30.00 E
Rutanzige, Lac- = Edward, Lake- (EN) 158 Ji 0.25S 29.30 E
Rute 126 Hg 37.19N 4.22W
Ruteng 150 Hh 8.36S 120.27 E
Rutenga 172 Ed 21.15S 30.44 E
Rüthen 124 Kc 51.29N 8.27 E
Ruthenia (EN) 130 Ga 48.20N 23.30 E

Index Symbols

[1] Independent Nation
[2] State, Region
[3] District, County
[4] Municipality
[5] Colony, Dependency
Continent
Physical Region
Historical or Cultural Region
Mount, Mountain
Volcano
Hill
Mountains, Mountain Range
Hills, Escarpment
Plateau, Upland
Pass, Gap
Plain, Lowland
Delta
Salt Flat
Valley, Canyon
Crater, Cave
Karst Features
Depression
Polder
Desert, Dunes
Forest, Woods
Heath, Steppe
Oasis
Cape, Point
Coast, Beach
Cliff
Peninsula
Isthmus
Sandbank
Island
Atoll
Rock, Reef
Islands, Archipelago
Rocks, Reefs
Coral Reef
Well, Spring
Geyser
River, Stream
Waterfall, Rapids
River Mouth, Estuary
Lake
Salt Lake
Intermittent Lake
Reservoir
Swamp, Pond
Canal
Glacier
Ice Shelf, Pack Ice
Ocean
Sea
Gulf, Bay
Strait, Fjord
Lagoon
Bank
Seamount
Tablemount
Ridge
Shelf
Basin
Escarpment, Sea Scarp
Fracture
Trench, Abyss
National Park, Reserve
Point of Interest
Recreation Site
Cave, Cavern
Historic Site
Ruins
Wall, Walls
Church, Abbey
Temple
Scientific Station
Railway station
Airport
Port
Military installation
Lighthouse
Mine
Tunnel
Dam, Bridge

Rutherfordton 184 Gh 35.22N 81.57W
Ruthin 118 Jh 53.07N 3.18W
Rutland 184 Kd 43.37N 72.59W
Rutland 118 Mi 52.40N 0.40W
Rutland 148 If 11.25N 92.10 E
Rutog 142 Jf 33.29N 79.42 E
Rutshuru 170 Ec 1.11S 29.27 E
Rutter 184 Gb 46.06N 80.40W
Rutul 132 Oi 41.33N 47.29 E
Ruutana 116 Kc 61.31N 24.02 E
Ruvo di Puglia 128 Ki 41.09N 16.29 E
Ruvu 170 Gd 6.48S 38.39 E
Ruvu → Pangani 170 Gc 5.26S 38.58 E
Ruvuma [3] 170 Ge 10.30S 35.50 E
Ruvuma 158 Lj 10.29S 40.28 E
Ruvuma (EN)=Rovuma 158 Lj 10.29S 40.28 E
Ruwayshid, Wādī- 146 Hf 32.41N 38.04 E
Ruwer 124 Ie 49.47N 6.42 E
Ruya 172 Ec 16.34S 33.12 E
Ruyang 154 Bg 34.10N 112.28 E
Ru'yas, Wādī ar- 164 Cd 27.06N 19.24 E
Ruyigi 170 Fc 3.29S 30.15 E
Ruza 114 Ii 55.39N 36.18 E
Ruzajevka [Kaz.-U.S.S.R.] 134 Mj 52.49N 67.01 E
Ruzajevka [R.S.F.S.R.] 136 Ee 54.05N 44.54 E
Ružany 120 Ud 52.48N 24.58 E
Ružomberok 120 Pg 49.05N 19.18 E
Rwanda [1] 160 Ji 2.30S 30.00 E
Ry 116 Ch 56.05N 9.46 E
Ryan 186 Hi 34.01N 97.57W
Rybachi Peninsula (EN) = Rybači, poluostrov- 110 Jb 69.45N 32.35 E
Rybači 116 Ii 55.09N 20.45 E
Rybači, poluostrov- = Rybachi Peninsula (EN) 110 Jb 69.45N 32.35 E
Rybačje 136 Hg 42.28N 76.11 E
Rybinsk 112 Jd 58.03N 38.52 E
Rybinskoje vodohranilišče = Rybinsk Reservoir (EN) 110 Jd 58.30N 38.25 E
Rybinsk Reservoir (EN) = Rybinskoje vodohranilišče 110 Jd 58.30N 38.25 E
Rybnica 132 Ff 47.45N 29.01 E
Rybnik 120 Of 50.06N 18.32 E
Rybnoje 136 De 54.46N 39.33 E
Rybnovsk 138 Jf 53.15N 141.55 E
Rychnov nad Kněžnou 120 Mf 50.10N 16.17 E
Rychwał 120 Od 52.05N 18.09 E
Ryd 116 Fh 56.28N 14.41 E
Rydaholm 116 Fh 56.59N 14.16 E
Ryde 124 Ad 50.43N 1.10W
Rye 118 Nk 50.57N 0.44 E
Rye 118 Mg 54.10N 0.45W
Rye Bay 124 Cd 50.55N 0.48 E
Ryegate 188 Kc 46.18N 109.15W
Rye Patch Reservoir 188 Ff 40.38N 118.18W
Ryes 124 Be 49.19N 0.37W
Ryfylke 116 Be 59.30N 6.30 E
Ryki 120 Re 51.39N 21.56 E
Rylsk 136 De 51.36N 34.43 E
Rymanów 120 Rg 49.34N 21.53 E
Rymättylä/Rimito 116 Jd 60.25N 21.55 E
Ryn 120 Rc 53.56N 21.33 E
Ryńskie, Jezioro- 120 Rc 53.53N 21.30 E
Ryōhaku-Sanchi 156 Ec 36.05N 136.45 E
Ryōsō-Yosui 156 Gd 35.22N 140.25 E
Ryōtsu 154 Oe 38.05N 138.26 E
Ryōtsu-Wan 156 Fb 38.10N 138.30 E
Ryō-Zen 156 Gc 37.46N 140.41 E
Rypin 120 Pc 53.05N 19.25 E
Ryškany 132 Ef 47.57N 27.32 E
Ryssby 116 Fh 56.52N 14.10 E
Rytterknægten 116 Fi 55.06N 14.54 E
Ryūgasaki 156 Gd 35.54N 140.10 E
Ryukyu Islands (EN)= Nansei-Shotō 140 Og 26.30N 128.00 E
Ryūkyū-Shotō 152 Mf 25.30N 126.30 E
Ryukyu Trench (EN) 106 Ig 25.45N 128.00 E
Rzepin 120 Kd 52.22N 14.50 E
Rzeszów 112 Ie 50.03N 22.00 E
Rzeszów [2] 120 Rf 50.05N 22.00 E
Ržev 112 Jd 56.16N 34.20 E

S

Šaa, gora- 132 Nh 42.39N 44.43 E
Sa'ādatābād [Iran] 146 Og 30.08N 52.38 E
Sa'ādatābād [Iran] 146 Og 30.06N 53.08 E
Sa'ādatābād [Iran] 146 Ph 28.02N 55.50 E
Sääksjarvi 116 Jc 61.24N 22.24 E
Saalbach 124 Ke 49.15N 8.27 E
Saale 120 He 51.57N 11.55 E
Saaler Bodden 120 Ib 54.20N 12.28 E
Saalfeld 120 Hf 50.39N 11.22 E
Saalfelden am Steinernen Meer 128 Gc 47.25N 12.51 E
Saaminki 116 Mc 61.52N 28.50 E
Saane 128 Bd 46.59N 7.16 E
Saâne 124 Ce 49.54N 0.56 E
Saanen 128 Bd 46.30N 7.15 E
Saanen-Gstaad 128 Bd 46.28N 7.17 E
Saar 120 Cg 49.42N 6.34 E
Saar-Bergland 124 Ie 49.27N 6.45 E
Saarbrücken 112 Gf 49.14N 7.00 E
Saarbrücken-Dudweiler 124 Je 49.17N 7.02 E
Saarburg 120 Cg 49.36N 6.33 E
Sääre/Sjare 116 Ig 57.57N 21.53 E
Saaremaa/Sarema 110 Id 58.25N 22.30 E
Saarijärvi 114 Fe 62.43N 25.16 E
Saaristomeri 116 Id 60.20N 21.10 E
Saarland [2] 120 Cg 49.20N 7.00 E
Saarlouis 120 Cg 49.19N 6.45 E
Šaartuz 136 Gh 37.16N 68.06 E
Saarwellingen 124 Ie 49.21N 6.49 E
Saas Fee 128 Bd 46.07N 7.55 E
Saatly 132 Pj 39.57N 48.26 E
Saavedra 204 Am 37.45S 62.22W
Sab, Tônlé- 150 Dd 11.34N 104.57 E
Saba 190 Le 17.38N 63.10W
Saba 116 Me 59.05N 29.10 E
Saba Bank (EN) 196 Ed 17.30N 63.30W
Šabac 130 Ce 44.45N 19.43 E
Sabadell 126 Oc 41.33N 2.06 E
Sabae 154 Ng 35.57N 136.11 E
Sabah [2] 150 Ge 5.30N 117.00 E
Sab'ah, Qārat as- 164 Cd 27.20N 17.10 E
Sabak Bernam 150 Df 3.46N 100.59 E
Sabalān, Kūhhā-ye- 140 Gf 38.15N 47.49 E
Sab'ān 146 Ii 27.04N 41.58 E
Sabana, Archipiélago de- 194 Hb 22.30N 79.00W
Sabana de la Mar 194 Md 19.04N 69.23W
Sabanagrande 194 Dg 13.50N 87.15W
Sabanalarga 202 Da 10.38N 74.56W
Sabancuy 192 Nh 18.58N 91.11W
Sabaneta 194 Ld 19.12N 70.58W
Sabaneta, Puntan- 220b Ba 15.17N 145.49 E
Sabang [Indon.] 150 Ce 5.55N 95.19 E
Sabang [Indon.] 150 Gf 0.11N 119.51 E
Şabanözü 146 Eb 40.29N 33.18 E
Săbăoani 130 Jb 47.01N 26.51 E
Sabarei 170 Gb 4.20N 36.55 E
Sab'Atayn, Ramlat as- 164 If 15.30N 46.10 E
Sabatini, Monti- 128 Gh 42.10N 12.15 E
Sabaudia 128 Hi 41.18N 13.01 E
Sabaudia, Lago di- 128 Hi 41.15N 13.05 E
Şabbāgh, Jabal- 146 Fh 28.12N 34.04 E
Sab 'Bi 'Ār 146 Gf 33.46N 37.41 E
Sa Bec 148 Lf 10.18N 105.46 E
Şabḩā 146 Gf 32.20N 36.30 E
Sabhā 160 If 27.02N 14.26 E
Sabhā [3] 164 Bd 26.00N 14.00 E
Sabhā, Wāḩāt- = Sebha Oasis (EN) 158 If 27.00N 14.25 E
Sabi 158 Kk 21.00S 35.02 E
Sabidana, Jabal- 168 Fb 18.04N 36.50 E
Sabile 116 Jg 57.05N 22.29 E
Sabina 128 Gh 42.20N 12.45 E
Sabinal 192 Fb 30.57N 107.30W
Sabinal, Península de- 194 Ic 21.40N 77.18W
Sabiñánigo 126 Lb 42.31N 0.22W
Sabinas 190 Dc 27.51N 101.07W
Sabinas, Río- 192 Id 27.37N 100.42W
Sabinas Hidalgo 190 Dc 26.30N 100.10W
Sabine Lake 186 Jl 29.50N 93.50W
Sabine Pass 186 Jl 29.44N 93.52W
Sabine Peninsula 180 Ga 76.25N 109.50W
Sabine River 182 Ie 30.00N 93.45W
Sabini, Monti- 128 Gh 42.15N 12.50 E
Şabir, Jabal- 144 Fg 13.30N 44.03 E
Sabirabad 132 Pj 39.59N 48.29 E
Šabla 130 Lf 43.32N 28.32 E
Sable, Anse de- 197e Ab 16.07N 61.34W
Sable, Cape- [Can.] 174 Me 43.25N 65.35W
Sable, Cape- [U.S.] 174 Kg 25.12N 81.05W
Sable, Ile de- 208 Gf 19.15S 159.56 E
Sable Island 174 Ne 43.55N 59.55W
Sables-d'Olonne, Les- 122 Eh 46.30N 1.47W
Sablé-sur-Sarthe 122 Fg 47.50N 0.20W
Sablūkah, Ash Shallāl as-= Sixth Cataract (EN) 158 Kg 16.20N 32.42 E
Sabonetau, Serra do- 204 Kb 15.20S 43.50W
Sabonkafi 166 Gc 14.38N 8.45 E
Sabór 126 Ec 41.10N 7.07W
Şabrātah 164 Bc 32.47N 12.29 E
Sabres 122 Fj 44.09N 0.44W
Sabrina Coast 222 He 67.00S 119.30 E
Sabtang 150 Hb 20.19N 121.52 E
Sabugal 126 Ed 40.21N 7.05W
Sabunči 132 Pi 40.27N 49.57 E
Şabyā 144 Ff 17.09N 42.37 E
Sabzevār 142 Hf 36.13N 57.42 E
Saca, Vîrful- 130 Ic 46.30N 25.15 E
Sacajawea Peak 182 Db 45.15N 117.17W
Sacalin, Insulă- 130 Me 44.50N 29.39 E
Sacandica 170 Cd 5.58S 15.56 E
Sacatepéquez [3] 194 Bf 14.35N 90.45W
Sacavém 126 Cf 38.46N 9.05W
Sac City 186 Ie 42.25N 95.00W
Sacco 128 Hi 41.31N 13.32 E
Sacedón 126 Jd 40.29N 2.43W
Săcel 130 Hb 47.38N 24.26 E
Săcele 130 Id 45.37N 25.41 E
Sachayoj 204 Bh 26.41S 61.50W
Sačhere 132 Mh 42.20N 43.22 E
Sachigo 180 Ie 55.05N 89.00W
Sachsen=Saxony (EN) 120 Ie 51.20N 13.30 E
Sachsenhagen 124 Lb 52.24N 9.16 E
Sachs Harbour 180 Eb 72.00N 125.08W
Šack [R.S.F.S.R.] 114 Ji 54.04N 41.42 E
Šack [Ukr.-U.S.S.R.] 120 Te 51.30N 24.00 E
Sackets Harbor 184 Id 43.57N 76.07W
Saco [Me.-U.S.] 184 Ld 43.29N 70.28W
Saco [Mt.-U.S.] 188 Lb 48.28N 107.21W
Sacramento 174 Gf 38.03N 121.56W
Sacramento [Braz.] 202 Ig 19.53S 47.27W
Sacramento [Ca.-U.S.] 176 Gf 38.35N 121.30W
Sacramento, Pampa del- 202 Ce 8.00S 75.50W
Sacramento Mountains 174 If 33.10N 105.50W
Sacramento Valley 182 Cd 39.15N 122.00W
Sacre ou Timalacia, Rio- 204 Ca 13.55S 58.02W
Săcueni 130 Fb 47.21N 22.06 E
Sacuriuiná ou Ponte de Pedra, Rio- 204 Da 13.58S 57.18W
Sádaba 126 Kb 42.17N 1.16W
Sa'dābād 146 Nh 29.23N 51.07 E
Şa'dah 142 Gh 16.57N 43.44 E
Sada-Misaki 156b Ce 33.22N 132.01 E
Sada-Misaki-Hantō 156 Ce 33.25N 132.15 E
Sadani 170 Gd 6.03S 38.47 E
Sadao 148 Kg 6.39N 100.31 E
Saddle Mountains 188 Fc 46.50N 119.55W
Saddle Peak [India] 148 If 13.09N 93.01 E
Saddle Peak [Mt.-U.S.] 188 Jd 45.57N 110.58W
Sad-e Eskandar 146 Pd 37.10N 55.00 E
Sadiya 148 Jc 27.50N 95.40 E
Sa'dīyah, Hawr as- 146 Lf 32.00N 46.45 E
Sad Kharv 146 Qd 36.19N 57.05 E
Sado 126 Df 38.29N 8.55W
Sado-Kaikyō 156 Fc 37.55N 138.40 E
Sado-Shima 140 Pf 38.00N 138.25 E
Sadowara 156 Be 32.04N 131.26 E
Sa Dragonera, Illa- / Dragonera, Isla- 126 Oe 39.35N 2.19 E
Šadrinsk 136 Gd 56.05N 63.38 E
Saeby 114 Ch 57.20N 10.32 E
Saeh, Teluk- 150 Gh 8.00S 117.30 E
Saengcheon 154 Ie 39.55N 126.34 E
Saerbeck 124 Jb 52.11N 7.38 E
Şafá, Wādī aş- 146 Pk 23.26N 55.41 E
Şafājah 146 Hi 26.30N 39.30 E
Safājah, Jazīrat- 146 Ei 26.45N 33.59 E
Safané 166 Ec 12.08N 3.13W
Şafāqis=Sfax (EN) 160 Ie 34.44N 10.46 E
Şafāqis=Sfax (EN) [3] 162 Jc 34.30N 10.30 E
Safata Harbour 221c Bb 14.00S 171.50W
Säffle 114 Cg 59.08N 12.56 E
Safford 182 Fe 32.50N 109.43W
Saffron Walden 118 Ni 52.01N 0.15 E
Safi 160 Ge 32.18N 9.14W
Safi [3] 162 Fc 31.55N 9.00W
Safia, Hamâda- 166 Ea 23.10N 4.15W
Şafiābād 146 Qd 36.45N 57.58 E
Safīd 144 Hb 37.23N 50.11 E
Safid, Kūh-e 146 Lf 33.55N 47.30 E
Safonovo [R.S.F.S.R.] 114 Ld 65.41N 47.43 E
Safonovo [R.S.F.S.R.] 136 Dd 55.06N 33.14 E
Şafrā' al Asyāḩ 146 Ji 26.50N 43.57 E
Şafrā' as Sark 146 Kj 25.25N 44.20 E
Safranbolu 146 Eb 41.15N 32.42 E
Şafwān 146 Lg 30.07N 47.43 E
Saga [Jap.] 152 Ne 33.15N 130.18 E
Saga [Jap.] 156 Ce 33.05N 133.06 E
Saga [Kaz.-U.S.S.R.] 136 Ge 50.30N 64.14 E
Saga (Gya'gya) 152 Ef 29.22N 85.15 E
Sagae 156 Gb 38.22N 140.17 E
Sagaing 148 Jd 21.52N 95.59 E
Sagaing [3] 148 Jd 23.30N 95.30 E
Saga Ken [2] 154 Kh 33.15N 130.15 E
Sagamihara 156 Fd 35.34N 139.22 E
Sagami-Nada 156 Fd 35.00N 139.30 E
Sagami-Wan 156 Fd 35.15N 139.20 E
Sagan 168 Fd 5.17N 36.57 E
Šagan 136 He 50.37N 79.15 E
Saganaga Lake 186 Kb 48.14N 90.52W
Saganoseki 156 Be 33.15N 131.53 E
Šagany, ozero- 130 Md 45.45N 29.55 E
Sāgar [India] 148 Ff 14.10N 75.02 E
Sāgar [India] 142 Jg 23.50N 78.42 E
Sagara 156 Fd 34.40N 138.12 E
Sagaredžo 132 Ni 41.43N 45.16 E
Sagavanirktok 178 Jb 70.20N 148.00W
Sagawa 156 Ce 33.29N 133.16 E
Sage 188 Jf 41.50N 110.56W
Saghād 146 Og 31.12N 52.30 E
Saginaw 182 Kc 43.25N 83.58W
Saginaw Bay 182 Kc 43.50N 83.40W
Sagiz 136 Ff 47.32N 53.45 E
Sagiz [Kaz.-U.S.S.R.] 136 Ff 48.12N 54.56 E
Sagiz [Kaz.-U.S.S.R.] 132 Rf 47.32N 53.27 E
Saglek Bay 180 Le 58.30N 63.00W
Saglouc 176 Lc 62.12N 75.38W
Šagonar 138 Ef 51.32N 92.51 E
Sagone, Golfe de- 122a Aa 42.06N 8.41 E
Sagres 126 Dg 37.01N 8.56W
Sagres, Ponta de- 126 Dh 37.00N 8.57W
Sagter Ems 124 Ja 53.10N 7.40 E
Şagu 130 Ec 46.03N 21.17 E
Sagu/Sauvo 116 Jd 60.21N 22.42 E
Saguache 186 Cg 38.05N 106.08W
Sagua de Tánamo 194 Jc 20.35N 75.14W
Sagua la Grande 190 Hd 22.49N 80.05W
Saguenay 174 Me 48.10N 69.45W
Saguia el-Hamra 162 Ed 26.50N 12.00W
Sagunto / Sagunt o Morvedre 126 Le 39.41N 0.16W
Sagunto-Grao de Sagunto 126 Le 39.40N 0.16W
Sagunt o Morvedre / Sagunto 126 Le 39.41N 0.16W
Sa'gya 152 Ef 28.53N 88.10 E
Sahagún [Col.] 202 Cb 8.57N 75.27W
Sahagún [Sp.] 126 Gb 42.22N 5.02W
Sahalin, ostrov- = Sakhalin (EN) 140 Qd 51.00N 143.00 E
Sahalinskaja oblast [3] 138 Jf 50.00N 143.30 E
Sahalinski zaliv 138 Jf 53.45N 141.30 E
Sahara 158 Hf 21.00N 6.00 E
Saharan Atlas (EN)=Atlas Saharien 158 He 34.00N 2.00 E
Sahāranpur 142 Jg 29.58N 77.23 E
Sahel [3] 166 Ec 14.10N 0.50W
Sahel 158 Gg 15.40N 8.30W
Şahin 130 Jh 41.01N 26.50 E
Sāhiwāl [Pak.] 148 Eb 30.41N 72.57 E
Sāhiwāl [Pak.] 148 Eb 31.58N 72.20 E
Sahlābād 144 Ic 32.10N 59.51 E
Sahneh 146 Le 34.29N 47.41 E
Sahnovščina 132 Ie 49.09N 35.57 E
Sahova Kosa, mys- 132 Qi 40.13N 50.22 E
Sahrihan 135 Id 40.40N 72.03 E
Šahrisabz 136 Gh 39.03N 66.41 E
Šahristan, pereval- 135 Ge 39.35N 68.38 E
Šahtersk [R.S.F.S.R.] 138 Jg 49.13N 142.09 E
Šahtersk [Ukr.-U.S.S.R.] 132 Ke 48.01N 38.32 E
Šahterski 138 Md 64.46N 177.47 E
Šahtinsk 136 Hf 49.40N 72.37 E
Šahty 136 Ef 47.42N 40.13 E
Sahuaripa 190 Cc 29.03N 109.14W
Sahuayo de Diaz 190 Dd 20.04N 102.43W
Šahunja 136 Ed 57.43N 46.35 E
Saḩūq, Wādī- 146 Jj 25.40N 42.30 E
Šahy 120 Oh 48.05N 18.58 E
Sahyadri/Western Ghats 140 Jh 14.00N 75.00 E
Sai Buri 148 Kg 6.42N 101.37 E
Saïda 160 He 34.50N 0.09 E
Saïda [3] 162 Hc 33.35N 0.30 E
Saïda, Monts de- 126 Mi 35.10N 0.30 E
Sa'īdābād 144 Id 29.28N 55.42 E
Saidaiji 156 Dd 34.39N 134.02 E
Said Bundas 168 Cd 8.35N 24.30 E
Saïdia 126 Ji 35.04N 2.13W
Saidor 214 Di 5.37S 146.28 E
Saidu 148 Eb 34.45N 72.21 E
Saigō 156 Cc 36.13N 133.20 E
Saigon → Thanh-pho Ho Chi Minh 142 Mh 10.45N 106.40 E
Saihan Tal → Sonid Youqi 152 Jc 42.45N 112.36 E
Saihan Toroi 152 Hc 41.54N 100.24 E
Saijō 156 Ce 33.55N 133.10 E
Saikai 156 Ae 33.03N 129.44 E
Sai-Kawa 156 Fc 36.37N 138.14 E
Saiki 154 Kh 32.57N 131.54 E
Saiki-Wan 156 Be 33.00N 131.55 E
Sail Rock 197n Bb 12.37N 61.16W
Saimaa 110 Ic 61.15N 28.15 E
Saimaa Canal (EN) = Sajmenski kanal 116 Mc 61.05N 28.18 E
Saín Alto 192 Hf 23.35N 103.15W
Sā īn Dezh 146 Ld 36.40N 46.33 E
Sains-Richaumont 124 Fe 49.49N 3.42 E
Saint Abb's Head 118 Kf 55.54N 2.09W
Saint-Affrique 122 Ik 43.57N 2.53 E
Saint Agnes Head 118 Hk 50.23N 5.07W
Saint-Agrève 122 Ki 45.01N 4.24 E
Saint Albans [Eng.-U.K.] 118 Mj 51.46N 0.21W
Saint Albans [Vt.-U.S.] 184 Kc 44.49N 73.05W
Saint Albans [W.V.-U.S.] 184 Gf 38.24N 81.53W
Saint Alban's Head → Saint Albhelm's Head 118 Kk 50.34N 2.04W
Saint Albert 180 Gf 53.38N 113.38W
Saint Albhelm's or Saint Alban's Head 118 Kk 50.34N 2.04W
Saint-Amand-les-Eaux 122 Jd 50.26N 3.26 E
Saint-Amand-Montrond 122 Ih 46.43N 2.31 E
Saint-André, Cap- 158 Lj 16.11S 44.27 E
Saint-André, Plaine de- 122 Hf 48.55N 1.10 E
Saint-André-de-Cubzac 122 Fi 45.00N 0.27W
Saint-André-de-l'Eure 124 Df 48.54N 1.17 E
Saint-André-sur-Cailly 124 De 49.33N 1.13 E
Saint Andrews [N.B.-Can.] 184 Nc 45.06N 67.02W
Saint Andrews [Scot.-U.K.] 118 Ke 56.20N 2.48W
Saint Anne 118 Kl 49.40N 2.10W
Saint Ann's Bay 194 Id 18.26N 77.16W
Saint Ann's Head 118 Hj 51.41N 5.10W
Saint Anthony [Id.-U.S.] 188 Je 43.58N 111.41W
Saint Anthony [Newf.-Can.] 180 Lf 51.22N 55.35W
Saint Arnaud 212 Ig 36.37S 143.15 E
Saint-Aubert 184 Lb 47.14N 70.15W
Saint-Aubin-sur-Mer 124 Be 49.20N 0.24W
Saint Augustine 182 Kf 29.51N 81.25W
Saint-Augustin-Saguenay 180 Lf 51.14N 58.39W
Saint Austell 118 Ik 50.20N 4.48W
Saint-Avold 122 Me 49.06N 6.42 E
Saint Barthélemy 190 Le 17.55N 62.50W
Saint Barthélemy, Canal de- 197b Bb 18.00N 63.00W
Saint Barthélemy, Kanaal Van- 197b Bb 18.00N 63.00W
Saint-Barthélemy, Pic de- 122 Hl 42.49N 1.45 E
Saint Bees Head 118 Jg 54.32N 3.38W
Saint-Benoit 172a Bb 21.02S 55.43 E
Saint-Benoît-sur-Loire 122 Ig 47.49N 2.18 E
Saint-Bonnet 122 Mj 44.41N 6.05 E
Saint-Brévin-les-Pins 122 Dg 47.15N 2.10W
Saint Brides Bay 118 Hj 51.48N 5.15W
Saint-Brieuc 122 Df 48.31N 2.47W
Saint-Brieuc, Baie de- 122 Df 48.38N 2.40W
Saint-Calais 122 Gg 47.55N 0.45 E
Saint-Camille 184 Lb 46.29N 70.12W
Saint Catharines 180 Jh 43.10N 79.15W
Saint Catherine, Monastery of- (EN) = Kātrīnā, Dayr- 164 Fd 28.31N 33.57 E
Saint Catherine, Mount- 197p Bb 12.10N 61.40W
Saint Catherines Island 184 Gj 31.38N 81.10W
Saint Catherine's Point 118 Lk 50.34N 1.15W
Saint-Céré 122 Hj 44.52N 1.54 E
Saint-Chamond 122 Ki 45.28N 4.30 E
Saint Charles 182 Id 38.47N 90.29W
Saint-Chély-d'Apcher 122 Jj 44.48N 3.17 E
Saint-Christol, Plateau de- 122 · Lj 44.00N 5.50 E
Saint Christopher/Saint Kitts 174 Mh 17.21N 62.48W
Saint Christopher-Nevis [1] 176 Mh 17.21N 62.48W
Saint-Cirq-Lapopie 122 Hj 44.28N 1.40 E
Saint Clair, Lake- 174 Ke 42.25N 82.41W
Saint Clair River 184 Fd 42.37N 82.31W
Saint Clair Shores 184 Fd 42.30N 82.54W
Saint-Clair-sur-l'Elle 124 Ae 49.12N 1.02W
Saint-Claud 122 Gi 45.54N 0.28 E
Saint-Claude 122 Lh 46.23N 5.52 E
Saint-Claude 197e Ab 16.02N 61.42W
Saint Claude 186 Gb 49.40N 98.22W
Saint Cloud 176 Je 45.33N 94.10W
Saint Croix 190 Le 17.45N 64.45W
Saint Croix Falls 186 Jd 45.24N 92.38W
Saint Croix River 182 Ic 44.45N 92.49W
Saint-Cyr-l'École 124 Ef 48.48N 2.04 E
Saint David Bay 197g Bb 15.26N 61.15W
Saint David's [Gren.] 197p Bb 12.04N 61.39W
Saint David's [Wales-U.K.] 118 Hj 51.54N 5.16W
Saint David's Head 118 Hj 51.55N 5.19W
Saint David's Point 197p Bb 12.01N 61.40W
Saint-Denis [Fr.] 122 If 48.56N 2.22 E
Saint-Denis [Reu.] 160 Mk 20.52S 55.28 E
Saint-Dié 122 Mf 48.17N 6.57 E
Saint-Dizier 122 Kf 48.38N 4.57 E
Sainte-Adresse 124 Ce 49.30N 0.05 E
Sainte-Anne [Guad.] 197e Bb 16.14N 61.23W
Sainte-Anne [Mart.] 197h Bc 14.26N 60.53W
Sainte-Anne-des-Monts 184 Na 49.07N 66.29W
Sainte-Baume, Chaîne de la- 122 Lk 43.20N 5.45 E
Sainte-Énimie 122 Jj 44.22N 3.25 E
Sainte Genevieve 186 Kh 37.59N 90.03W
Sainte-Geneviève 124 Ee 49.17N 2.12 E
Saint Elias, Mount- 174 Ec 60.18N 140.55W
Saint Elias Mountains 174 Fc 60.30N 139.30W
Saint-Elie 202 Hc 4.50N 53.17W
Sainte-Livrade-sur-Lot 122 Gj 44.24N 0.36 E
Saint-Éloy-les-Mines 122 Ih 46.09N 2.50 E
Sainte-Luce 197h Bc 14.28N 60.56W
Sainte Luce 172 Hd 24.46S 47.12 E
Sainte-Lucie, Canal de-= Saint Lucia Channel (EN) 196 Fe 14.09N 60.57W
Sainte-Marie [Guad.] 197e Ab 16.06N 61.34W
Sainte-Marie [Mart.] 197h Ab 14.47N 61.00W
Sainte-Marie, Cap-=Sainte-Marie, Cape- (EN) 158 Lk 25.36S 45.08 E
Sainte-Marie, Cape-(EN)= Sainte-Marie, Cap- 158 Lk 25.36S 45.08 E
Sainte-Marie, Ile- 158 Lj 16.50S 49.55 E
Sainte-Marie-aux-Mines 122 Nf 48.15N 7.11 E
Sainte-Maure-de-Touraine 122 Gg 47.06N 0.37 E
Sainte-Maxime 122 Mk 43.18N 6.38 E
Sainte-Menehould 122 Ke 49.05N 4.54 E
Sainte-Rose 197e Ab 16.20N 61.42W
Sainte-Rose-du-Dégelé 184 Mb 47.33N 68.39W
Sainte Rose du Lac 186 Ga 51.03N 99.32W
Saintes 122 Fi 45.45N 0.38W
Saintes, Canal des- 197e Ac 15.55N 61.40W
Saintes, Iles des- 196 Fe 15.52N 61.37W
Sainte-Savine 122 Kf 48.18N 4.03 E
Saintes-Maries-de-la-Mer 122 Kk 43.27N 4.26 E
Sainte-Thérèse 184 Kc 45.22N 73.15W
Saint-Étienne 112 Gf 45.26N 4.24 E
Saint-Étienne-du-Rouvray 122 He 49.23N 1.06 E
Sainte-Victoire, Montagne- 122 Lk 43.32N 5.39 E
Saint-Félicien 184 Ka 48.39N 72.28W
Saint-Florent 122a Ba 42.41N 9.18 E
Saint-Florent, Golfe de- 122a Ba 42.45N 9.16 E
Saint-Florentin 122 Jf 48.00N 3.44 E
Saint-Florent-sur-Cher 122 Ih 46.59N 2.15 E
Saint-Flour 122 Ji 45.02N 3.05 E
Saint Francis 186 Fg 39.46N 101.48W
Saint Francis River 186 Ki 34.38N 90.35W
Saint Francisville 186 Kk 30.47N 91.23W
Saint-François 197e Bb 16.15N 61.17W
Saint François Island 172b Bb 7.10S 52.44 E
Saint Francois Mountains 186 Kh 37.30N 90.35W
Saint-Gaudens 122 Gk 43.07N 0.44 E
Saint George 178 Fe 56.35N 169.35W
Saint George [Austl.] 212 Je 28.02S 148.35 E
Saint George [N.B.-Can.] 184 Nc 45.10N 66.48W
Saint George [Ut.-U.S.] 182 Ed 37.06N 113.35W
Saint George, Cape - [Newf.-Can.] 180 Lg 48.28N 59.16W
Saint George, Cape- [Pap.N.Gui.] 214 Eh 4.52S 152.52 E
Saint George, Point- 188 Cf 41.47N 124.15W
Saint George Harbour 184 Nd 43.15N 66.10W
Saint George Island 184 Ek 29.39N 84.55W
Saint-Georges 184 Lb 46.10N 70.38W
Saint George's 176 Mh 12.03N 61.45W
Saint George's Bay 180 Lg 48.20N 59.00W
Saint George's Channel 110 Fe 52.00N 6.00W
Saint George's Channel (EN) =Muir Bhreatan 110 Fe 52.00N 6.00W
Saint-Georges-du-Vièvre 124 Ce 49.15N 0.35 E
Saint-Germain-en-Laye 122 If 48.54N 2.05 E
Saint-Gervais-d'Auvergne 122 Ih 46.02N 2.49 E
Saint-Gervais-les-Bains 122 Mi 45.54N 6.43 E
Saint-Ghislain 124 Fd 50.27N 3.49 E
Saint-Ghislain-Baudour 124 Fd 50.29N 3.49 E
Saint-Gildas, Pointe de- 122 Dg 47.08N 2.15W
Saint-Gilles 122 Kk 43.41N 4.26 E
Saint-Gilles-Croix-de-Vie 122 Eh 46.41N 1.55W
Saint-Girons 122 Hl 42.59N 1.09 E
Saint-Gobain 124 Fe 49.36N 3.23 E
Saint Gotthard Pass (EN) = San Gottardo, Passo del- 110 Gf 46.30N 8.30 E
Saint Govan's Head 118 Ij 51.36N 4.55W
Saint Helena [5] 160 Gj 15.57S 5.42W
Saint Helena 158 Gj 15.57S 5.42W
Saint Helena Bay 158 Il 32.45S 18.05 E
Saint Helena Island 184 Gi 32.30N 80.30W
Saint Helena Sound 184 Gi 32.27N 80.25W
Saint Helens [Austl.] 212 Jh 41.20S 148.15 E
Saint Helens [Eng.-U.K.] 118 Kh 53.28N 2.44W
Saint Helens [Or.-U.S.] 188 Dd 45.52N 122.48W
Saint Helens, Mount- 188 Dc 46.12N 122.11W
Saint Helier 118 Kl 49.12N 2.07W
Saint-Hubert 124 Hd 50.03N 5.23 E
Saint-Hyacinthe 184 Kc 45.38N 72.57W
Saint Ignace 182 Kb 45.52N 84.43W
Saint Ignace Island 186 Mb 48.48N 87.55W
Saint Ignatius 188 Hc 47.19N 114.06W
Saint Ives [Eng.-U.K.] 124 Bb 52.18N 0.04W
Saint Ives [Eng.-U.K.] 118 Hk 50.12N 5.29W
Saint James 186 Ie 43.59N 94.38W
Saint James, Cape - 180 Ef 51.57N 131.01W
Saint-Jean 180 Kg 45.13N 73.15W
Saint-Jean, Baie de- 197b Bc 17.55N 62.51W
Saint-Jean, Lac- 174 Le 48.35N 72.00W
Saint-Jean-d'Angély 122 Fi 45.57N 0.31W
Saint-Jean-de-Luz 122 Ek 43.23N 1.40W
Saint-Jean-de-Maurienne 122 Mi 45.17N 6.21 E
Saint-Jean-de-Monts 122 Dh 46.47N 2.04W
Saint-Jean-du-Gard 122 Jj 44.06N 3.53 E
Saint-Jean-Pied-de-Port 122 Ek 43.10N 1.14W
Saint-Jérôme [Que.-Can.] 184 La 48.26N 71.52W
Saint-Jérôme [Que.-Can.] 180 Kg 45.46N 74.00W

Index Symbols

[1] Independent Nation
[2] State, Region
[3] District, County
[4] Municipality
[5] Colony, Dependency
Continent
Physical Region
Historical or Cultural Region
Mount, Mountain
Volcano
Hill
Mountains, Mountain Range
Hills, Escarpment
Plateau, Upland
Pass, Gap
Plain, Lowland
Delta
Salt Flat
Valley, Canyon
Crater, Cave
Karst Features
Depression
Polder
Desert, Dunes
Forest, Woods
Heath, Steppe
Oasis
Cape, Point
Coast, Beach
Cliff
Peninsula
Isthmus
Sandbank
Island
Atoll
Rock, Reef
Islands, Archipelago
Rocks, Reefs
Coral Reef
Well, Spring
Geyser
River, Stream
Waterfall, Rapids
River Mouth, Estuary
Lake
Salt Lake
Intermittent Lake
Reservoir
Swamp, Pond
Canal
Glacier
Ice Shelf, Pack Ice
Ocean
Sea
Gulf, Bay
Strait, Fjord
Lagoon
Bank
Seamount
Tablemount
Ridge
Shelf
Basin
Escarpment, Sea Scarp
Fracture
Trench, Abyss
National Park, Reserve
Point of Interest
Recreation Site
Cave, Cavern
Historic Site
Ruins
Wall, Walls
Church, Abbey
Temple
Scientific Station
Railway station
Airport
Port
Military installation
Lighthouse
Mine
Tunnel
Dam, Bridge

Saint Joe River	183	Gc	47.21N	116.42W
Saint John	196	Dc	18.20N	64.42W
Saint John [Can.]	174	Me	45.15N	66.04W
Saint John [Ks.-U.S.]	186	Gh	38.00N	98.46W
Saint John [Lbr.]	166	Cd	5.55N	10.05W
Saint John [N.B.-Can.]	176	Me	45.16N	66.03W
Saint John's [Atg.]	190	Le	17.06N	61.51W
Saint Johns [Az.-U.S.]	188	Ki	34.30N	109.22W
Saint Johns [Mi.-U.S.]	184	Ed	43.00N	84.33W
Saint John's [Mont.]	197c	Bc	16.48N	62.11W
Saint John's [Newf.-Can.]	176	Ne	47.34N	52.43W
Saint Johnsbury	184	Kc	44.25N	72.01W
Saint Johns River	184	Gj	30.24N	81.24W
Saint Joseph [Dom.]	197g	Bb	15.24N	61.26W
Saint Joseph [La.-U.S.]	186	Kk	31.55N	91.14W
Saint-Joseph [Mart.]	197h	Ab	14.40N	61.03W
Saint Joseph [Mi.-U.S.]	184	Dd	42.06N	86.29W
Saint Joseph [Mo.-U.S.]	182	Id	39.46N	94.51W
Saint-Joseph [N.Cal.]	219b	Ce	20.27S	166.36 E
Saint-Joseph [Reu.]	172a	Bb	21.22S	55.37 E
Saint Joseph, Lake-	180	If	51.06N	90.36W
Saint Joseph Island	184	Fb	46.13N	83.57W
Saint Joseph River	184	Dd	42.06N	86.29W
Saint-Junien	122	Gi	45.53N	0.54 E
Saint-Just-en-Chaussée	124	Ee	49.30N	2.26 E
Saint Kilda	118	Ed	57.49N	8.36W
Saint Kitts/Saint Christopher	174	Mh	17.21N	62.48W
Saint-Lary-Soulan	122	Gl	42.49N	0.19 E
Saint Laurent	200	Ke	5.30N	54.02W
Saint-Laurent = Saint Lawrence (EN)	174	Me	49.15N	67.00W
Saint Lawrence	174	Bc	63.30N	170.30W
Saint Lawrence	174	Me	49.15N	67.00W
Saint Lawrence (EN) = Saint-Laurent	174	Me	49.15N	67.00W
Saint Lawrence, Gulf of-	174	Me	48.00N	62.00W
Saint-Léger-en-Yvelines	124	Df	48.43N	1.46 E
Saint-Léonard	184	Nb	47.10N	67.56W
Saint-Léonard-de-Noblat	122	Hi	45.50N	1.29 E
Saint-Lewis	180	Lf	52.22N	55.58W
Saint-Lô	122	Ee	49.07N	1.05W
Saint-Louis [Guad.]	197e	Bc	15.57N	61.20W
Saint Louis [Mo.-U.S.]	176	Jf	38.38N	90.11W
Saint-Louis [Sen.]	160	Fg	16.02N	16.30W
Saint-Loup-sur-Semouse	122	Mg	47.53N	6.16 E
Saint Lucia	172	Ee	28.23S	32.25 E
Saint Lucia	176	Mh	13.53N	60.58W
Saint Lucia	176	Mh	13.53N	60.58W
Saint Lucia, Cape-	158	Kk	28.32S	32.24 E
Saint Lucia, Lake-	172	Ee	28.00S	32.30 E
Saint Lucia Channel	196	Fe	14.09N	60.57W
Saint Lucia Channel (EN) = Sainte-Lucie, Canal de-	196	Fe	14.09N	60.57W
Saint Magnus Bay	118	La	60.25N	1.35W
Saint-Maixent-l'Ecole	122	Fh	46.25N	0.12W
Saint-Malo	112	Ff	48.39N	2.01W
Saint-Malo, Golfe de-	110	Ff	48.45N	2.00W
Saint-Marc	190	Je	19.06N	72.43W
Saint-Marc, Canal de-	194	Kd	18.50N	72.45W
Saint-Marcellin	122	Li	45.09N	5.19 E
Saint Margaret's at Cliffe	124	Dc	51.09N	1.19 E
Saint Margaret's Hope	118	Kc	58.49N	2.57W
Saint Maries	188	Gc	47.19N	116.35W
Saint Martin	190	Le	13.04N	63.04W
Saint Martin, Cap-	197h	Ab	14.52N	61.13W
Saint-Martin-Boulogne	124	Dd	50.43N	1.40 E
Saint-Martin-de-Ré	122	Eh	46.12N	1.22W
Saint-Martin-des-Besaces	124	Be	49.01N	0.51W
Saint Martins	184	Oc	45.21N	65.32W
Saint-Martin-Vésubie	122	Nj	44.04N	7.15 E
Saint Mary, Cape-	184	Nc	44.05N	66.13W
Saint Mary Peak [Austl.]	212	Hf	31.30S	138.35 E
Saint Mary Peak [U.S.]	188	Hc	46.40N	114.20W
Saint Mary's	118	Gl	49.55N	6.20W
Saint Marys [Austl.]	212	Jh	41.35S	148.10 E
Saint Marys [Oh.-U.S.]	184	Ee	40.32N	84.22W
Saint Marys [W.V.-U.S.]	184	Gf	39.24N	81.13W
Saint Mary's, Cape-	180	Mg	46.49N	54.12W
Saint Mary's Bay [N.S.-Can.]	184	Nc	44.25N	66.10W
Saint Mary's Bay [N.W.T.-Can.]	180	Mg	46.50N	53.47W
Saint Marys River	184	Gj	30.45N	81.30W
Saint-Mathieu, Pointe de-	110	Ff	48.20N	4.46W
Saint Matthew	174	Bb	60.30N	172.45W
Saint Matthias Group	208	Fe	1.30S	149.48 E
Saint-Maur-des-Fossés	122	If	48.48N	2.30 E
Saint-Maurice, Rivière-	180	Kg	46.21N	72.31W
Saint Michael	178	Gd	63.29N	162.02W
Saint Michaels	188	Ki	35.46N	109.04W
Saint-Michel	124	Ge	49.55N	4.08 E
Saint-Mihiel	122	Lf	48.54N	5.33 E
Saint-Nazaire	122	Dg	47.17N	2.12W
Saint Neots	124	Bb	52.13N	0.16W
Saint-Nicolas/Sint Niklaas	122	Kc	51.10N	4.08 E
Saint-Nicolas-d'Aliermont	124	De	49.53N	1.13 E
Saint-Nicolas-de-Port	122	Mf	48.38N	6.18 E
Saint-Omer	122	Id	50.45N	2.15 E
Saintonge	122	Fi	45.50N	0.30W
Saint Patrick's	197c	Bc	16.41N	62.12W
Saint Paul	176	Je	44.58N	93.07W
Saint-Paul	158	Ol	38.55S	77.41 E
Saint Paul	178	Ee	57.07N	170.17W
Saint Paul	166	Cd	6.23N	10.48W
Saint Paul [Alta.-Can.]	178	Gf	53.59N	111.17W
Saint Paul [Nb.-U.S.]	186	Gf	41.13N	98.27W
Saint-Paul [Reu.]	172a	Bb	21.00S	55.16 E
Saint Paul, Cape-	166	Fd	5.49N	0.57 E
Saint-Paul-lès-Dax	122	Ek	43.44N	1.03W
Saint Paul's	197c	Ab	17.24N	62.49W
Saint Paul's Point	220q	Ab	25.04S	130.05W
Saint-Péray	122	Kj	44.57N	4.50 E
Saint Peter	186	Jd	44.17N	93.57W
Saint Peter Port	118	Kl	49.27N	2.32W
Saint Peter's	197c	Bc	16.46N	62.12W
Saint Petersburg	176	Kg	27.46N	82.38W
Saint Petersburg Beach	184	Fl	27.45N	82.45W
Saint-Pierre [Mart.]	196	Fe	14.45N	61.11W
Saint-Pierre [Reu.]	160	Mk	21.19S	55.29 E
Saint-Pierre [St.P.M.]	180	Lg	46.46N	56.12W
Saint-Pierre, Lac-	184	Kb	46.10N	72.50W
Saint Pierre and Miquelon (EN) = Saint-Pierre et Miquelon	176	Ne	46.55N	56.10W
Saint-Pierre-en-Port	124	Ce	49.48N	0.29 E
Saint-Pierre et Miquelon = Saint Pierre and Miquelon (EN)	176	Ne	46.55N	56.10W
Saint Pierre Island	172b	Bb	9.19S	50.43 E
Saint-Pierre-sur-Dives	124	Be	49.01N	0.02W
Saint-Pol-de-Léon	122	Cf	48.41N	3.59W
Saint-Pol-sur-Mer	124	Ec	51.02N	2.21 E
Saint-Pol-sur-Ternoise	122	Id	50.23N	2.20 E
Saint-Pons	122	Ik	43.29N	2.46 E
Saint-Pourçain-sur-Sioule	122	Jh	46.18N	3.17 E
Saint-Quentin	122	Je	49.51N	3.17 E
Saint-Quentin, Canal de-	124	Fe	49.36N	3.11 E
Saint-Raphaël	122	Mk	43.25N	6.46 E
Saint-Rémy-de-Provence	122	Kk	43.47N	4.50 E
Saint-Rigaux, Mont-	124	Kh	46.12N	4.29 E
Saint-Riquier	124	Dd	50.08N	1.57 E
Saint Roch Basin	180	Ic	68.50N	95.00W
Saint-Romain-de-Colbosc	124	Ce	49.32N	0.22 E
Saint-Saëns	124	De	49.40N	1.17 E
Saint Sauflieu	124	Ee	49.47N	2.15 E
Saint-Savin	122	Gh	46.34N	0.52 E
Saint-Sébastien, Cap-	172	Hb	12.26S	48.44 E
Saint-Seine-l'Abbaye	122	Kg	47.26N	4.47 E
Saint-Servais, Namur-	124	Gd	50.28N	4.50 E
Saint Simon	124	Fe	49.45N	3.10 E
Saint Simons Island	184	Gj	31.14N	81.21W
Saint Stanislas Bay	220g	Bb	1.53N	157.30W
Saint Stephen	180	Kg	45.12N	67.17W
Saint-Sylvain	124	Be	49.03N	0.13W
Saint Teresa Beach	184	Ek	29.58N	84.28W
Saint Thomas	184	Gd	42.47N	81.12W
Saint Thomas	190	Le	18.21N	64.55W
Saint-Trond/Sint-Truiden	122	Ld	50.49N	5.12 E
Saint-Tropez	122	Mk	43.16N	6.38 E
Saint-Tropez, Golfe de-	122	Mk	43.17N	6.38 E
Saint-Valéry-en-Caux	122	Ge	49.52N	0.44 E
Saint-Valéry-sur-Somme	122	Hd	50.11N	1.38 E
Saint-Vallier	122	Ki	45.10N	4.49 E
Saint-Venant	124	Ed	50.37N	2.33 E
Saint-Vincent	128	Be	45.45N	7.39 E
Saint Vincent	174	Mh	13.15N	61.12W
Saint-Vincent, Baie de-	219b	Cf	22.00S	166.05 E
Saint-Vincent, Cap-	158	Lk	21.57S	43.16 E
Saint Vincent, Gulf-	212	Hf	35.00S	138.05 E
Saint Vincent and the Grenadines	176	Mh	13.15N	61.12W
Saint-Vincent-de-Tyrosse	122	Ek	43.40N	1.18W
Saint Vincent Island	184	Ek	29.40N	85.07W
Saint Vincent Passage	196	Ff	13.30N	61.00W
Saint-Vith / Sankt-Vith	122	Md	50.17N	6.08 E
Saint-Wandrille-Rançon	124	Ce	49.32N	0.46 E
Saint-Yrieix-la-Perche	122	Hi	45.31N	1.12 E
Saipan	220a	Ad	6.54N	134.08 E
Saipan Channel	220b	Ba	15.05N	145.41 E
Saipan Island	208	Fc	15.12N	145.45 E
Saira	204	Ak	32.24S	62.06W
Sairecábur, Cerro-	202	Eh	22.43S	67.54W
Saitama Ken	154	Of	36.00N	139.50 E
Saito	154	Kh	32.06N	131.24 E
Sajak	136	Hf	46.55N	77.22 E
Sajama	202	Eg	18.07S	69.00W
Sajama, Nevado de-	198	Jg	18.06S	68.54W
Sajānan	128	Dm	37.03N	9.14 E
Sajat	135	De	38.49N	63.51 E
Sajīd	164	Hf	16.52N	41.55 E
Sajir, Ra's-	168	Ib	16.45N	53.35 E
Sajmenski kanal = Saimaa Canal (EN)	116	Mc	61.05N	28.18 E
Sajn-Sand	142	Ne	44.55N	110.11 E
Sajó	120	Ri	47.56N	21.08 E
Sajószentpéter	120	Qh	48.13N	20.43 E
Sajram	135	Gc	42.18N	69.45 E
Sajzī	146	Of	32.41N	52.07 E
Saka	170	Gc	0.09S	39.20 E
Sakai	154	Mg	34.35N	135.28 E
Sakaide	156	Cd	34.19N	133.51 E
Sakaiminato	156	Cd	35.33N	133.15 E
Sakākah	144	Fd	29.59N	40.06 E
Sakakawea, Lake-	182	Gb	47.50N	102.20W
Sakala, vozvyšennost- / Sakala Kõrgustik	116	Kf	58.00N	25.30 E
Sakala Kõrgustik / Sakala, vozvyšennost-	116	Kf	58.00N	25.30 E
Sakami	180	Jf	53.18N	76.45W
Sakami, lac-	180	Jf	53.15N	76.45W
Sakâne, 'Erg i-n-	166	Ea	20.40N	0.51W
Sakania	170	Ee	12.43S	28.33 E
Sakao	219b	Cb	14.58S	167.07 E
Sakar	135	De	38.59N	63.45 E
Sakar	130	Jh	41.59N	26.16 E
Sakaraha	172	Gd	22.54S	44.32 E
Sakar-Čaga	135	Cf	37.39N	61.40 E
Sakārinah, Jabal as-	128	Do	35.45N	9.05 E
Sakartvelos Sabčata Socialisturi Respublica / Gruzinskaja SSR	136	Eg	42.00N	44.00 E
Sakarya	144	Da	41.07N	30.39 E
Sakata	152	Od	38.55N	139.50 E
Sakchu	154	Hd	40.23N	125.02 E
Sakhalin (EN) = Sahalin, ostrov-	140	Qd	51.00N	143.00 E
Sakht Sar	146	Nd	36.53N	50.41 E
Saki	132	Hg	45.07N	33.37 E
Šakiai/Šakjaj	114	Fi	54.57N	23.01 E
Sakishima Islands (EN) = Sakishima-Shotō	140	Og	24.30N	125.00 E
Sakishima-Shotō = Sakishima Islands (EN)	140	Og	24.30N	125.00 E
Sakito	156	Ae	33.02N	129.34 E
Sakız Boğazı	130	Jk	38.20N	26.12 E
Šakjaj/Šakiai	114	Fi	54.57N	23.01 E
Sakmara	110	Le	51.46N	55.01 E
Sakon Nakhon	148	Ke	17.10N	104.01 E
Sakrivier	172	Cf	30.54S	20.28 E
Šakša	134	Hi	54.47N	56.15 E
Saksaulski	136	Gf	47.05N	61.13 E
Sakskøbing	116	Dj	54.48N	11.39 E
Saku	154	Of	36.09N	138.26 E
Sakuma	156	Ed	35.05N	137.47 E
Sakura	156	Gd	35.43N	140.13 E
Sakurai	156	Dd	34.31N	135.50 E
Sakura-Jima	156	Bf	31.35N	130.40 E
Säkylä	116	Jc	61.02N	22.20 E
Sal	158	Eg	16.45N	22.55W
Sal	136	Ef	47.31N	40.45 E
Sal, Cay-	194	Gb	23.42N	80.24W
Sal, Punta-	194	Df	15.53N	87.37W
Sala	114	Dg	59.55N	16.36 E
Šalá	120	Nh	48.09N	17.53 E
Sala	168	Cb	17.00N	20.53 E
Salabangka, Kepulauan-	150	Hg	3.02S	122.25 E
Salaca	116	Kg	57.39N	24.15 E
Salacgrīva/Salacgriva	114	Fh	57.46N	24.27 E
Salacgriva/Salacgrīva	114	Fh	57.46N	24.27 E
Sala Consilina	128	Jj	40.23N	15.36 E
Salada	192	Hc	28.36N	103.28W
Salada, Laguna-	192	Ba	32.20N	115.40W
Saladas	204	Ic	28.15S	58.38W
Saladillo	206	Ie	35.38S	59.46W
Saladillo, Arroyo-	204	Bj	31.22S	60.30W
Saladillo Amargo, Arroyo-	204	Bj	31.01S	60.19W
Saladillo Dulce, Arroyo-	204	Bj	31.01S	60.19W
Salado, Arroyo- [Arg.]	204	Bm	36.27S	61.06W
Salado, Arroyo- [Mex.]	192	De	24.25N	111.30W
Salado, Riacho-	204	Ch	26.30S	58.18W
Salado, Rio-	186	Ci	34.16N	106.52W
Salado, Rio-	190	Ec	26.52N	99.19W
Salado, Río- [Arg.]	198	Ki	35.44S	57.21W
Salado, Río- [Arg.]	198	Ji	31.42S	60.44W
Salado, Río- [Arg.]	206	Ge	38.49S	64.57W
Salado, Valle-	192	He	24.47N	102.50W
Salaga	166	Ed	8.33N	0.31W
Salagle	168	Ge	1.50N	42.18 E
Salāhuddīn	146	Je	34.40N	44.00 E
Salailua	221c	Aa	13.41S	172.34W
Salairski krjaž	138	Df	54.00N	85.00 E
Šalaj	130	Fb	47.10N	23.00 E
Salakuša	114	Je	62.15N	40.18 E
Salal	168	Bc	14.51N	17.13 E
Salālah [Oman]	142	Hh	17.05N	54.10 E
Salālah [Sud.]	168	Fa	21.19N	36.13 E
Salamá	194	Bf	15.06N	90.16W
Salamanca	126	Gd	40.50N	6.00W
Salamanca [Chile]	206	Fd	31.47S	70.58W
Salamanca [Mex.]	190	Dd	20.34N	101.12W
Salamanca [N.Y.-U.S.]	184	Hd	42.11N	78.43W
Salamanca [Sp.]	112	Fg	40.58N	5.39W
Salamat	168	Cc	11.00N	20.30 E
Salamat, Bahr-	168	Bd	9.27N	18.06 E
Salamina	194	Jh	10.30N	74.48W
Salamis	130	Gl	37.58N	23.29 E
Salamis	130	Gl	37.55N	23.30 E
Salamis	146	Ee	35.10N	33.54 E
Salamīyah, Sabkhat as-	146	Pj	24.00N	53.45 E
Sālang, Tūnel-e-	144	Kb	35.19N	69.02 E
Salani	221c	Bb	14.00S	171.34W
Salantai/Salantaj	116	Ih	56.05N	21.30 E
Salantaj/Salantai	116	Ih	56.05N	21.30 E
Salas	126	Fa	43.24N	6.16W
Salas de los Infantes	126	Ib	42.01N	3.17W
Salat	220d	Cb	7.14N	152.01 E
Salat	122	Gk	43.10N	0.58 E
Salatiga	150	Fh	7.19S	110.30 E
Salavat	112	Le	53.25N	55.58 E
Salawati, Pulau-	208	Ee	1.07S	130.52 E
Sala y Gómez	208	Qg	26.28S	105.28W
Sala y Gómez Ridge (EN)	198	Ff	25.00S	98.00W
Salazar	204	Am	36.18S	62.12W
Salbris	122	Ig	47.26N	2.03 E
Salcantay, Nevado de-	198	Ig	13.22S	72.34W
Šalčininkai/Šal'čininkaj	116	Kj	54.18N	25.30 E
Salčininkaj/Šalčininkai	116	Kj	54.18N	25.30 E
Salda Gölü	130	Ml	37.33N	29.42 E
Saldaña	126	Hb	42.31N	4.44W
Saldanha	160	Il	33.00S	17.56 E
Saldungaray	204	Bn	38.12S	61.47W
Saldus	136	Cd	56.40N	22.31 E
Salé	162	Fc	34.04N	6.48W
Sale	212	Jg	38.06S	147.04 E
Salebabu, Pulau-	150	If	3.55N	126.40 E
Şalehābād	146	Me	34.56N	48.20 E
Salehard	142	Ic	66.33N	66.40 E
Saleimoa	221c	Ba	13.48S	171.52W
Salelologa	221c	Aa	13.44S	172.10W
Salem [Fl.-U.S.]	184	Fk	29.58N	83.28W
Salem [Il.-U.S.]	186	Lg	38.38N	88.57W
Salem [India]	142	Jh	11.39N	78.10 E
Salem [In.-U.S.]	184	Df	38.36N	86.06W
Salem [Ma.-U.S.]	184	Ld	42.31N	70.55W
Salem [Mont.]	197c	Bc	16.45N	62.13W
Salem [Mo.-U.S.]	186	Kh	37.39N	91.32W
Salem [N.J.-U.S.]	184	Jf	39.35N	75.28W
Salem [Oh.-U.S.]	184	Ge	40.54N	80.52W
Salem [Or.-U.S.]	176	Ge	44.57N	123.01W
Salem [S.D.-U.S.]	186	He	43.44N	97.23W
Salem [Va.-U.S.]	184	Gg	37.17N	80.03W
Salemi	128	Gm	37.49N	12.48 E
Sälen	116	Ec	61.10N	13.16 E
Salentina, Penisola- = Salentine Peninsula (EN)	110	Hg	40.30N	18.00 E
Salentine Peninsula (EN) = Salentina, Penisola-	110	Hg	40.30N	18.00 E
Salerno	112	Hg	40.41N	14.47 E
Salerno, Golfo di-	128	Ij	40.30N	14.40 E
Salers	122	Ii	45.08N	2.30 E
Salève, Mont-	122	Mh	46.07N	6.10 E
Salgir	132	Ig	45.38N	35.01 E
Salgótarján	120	Ph	48.07N	19.49 E
Salgueiro	202	Ke	8.04S	39.06W
Salher	148	Ed	20.41N	73.52 E
Salhus	114	Af	60.30N	5.16 E
Šali	132	Nh	43.06N	45.56 E
Sali	128	Jg	43.56N	15.10 E
Salice Terme	128	Df	44.55N	9.01 E
Salida	182	Fd	38.32N	106.00W
Salies-de-Béarn	122	Fk	43.29N	0.55W
Salihli	144	Cb	38.29N	28.09 E
Salima	170	Fe	13.47S	34.26 E
Salīma, Wāḥāt- = Salimah Oasis (EN)	160	Jf	21.22N	29.19 E
Salimah Oasis (EN) = Salīma, Wāḥāt-	160	Jf	21.22N	29.19 E
Salina	128	Il	38.35N	14.50 E
Salina [Ks.-U.S.]	176	Jf	38.50N	97.37W
Salina [Ut.-U.S.]	188	Jg	38.58N	111.51W
Salina Cruz	190	Ee	16.10N	95.12W
Salinas [Ca.-U.S.]	176	Gf	36.40N	121.38W
Salinas [Ec.]	202	Bd	2.13S	80.58W
Salinas [P.R.]	197a	Be	17.59N	66.17W
Salinas, Bahía de-	194	Eh	11.03N	85.43W
Salinas, Cabo de-/Ses Salines, Cap de-	126	Pe	39.16N	3.03 E
Salinas, Punta- [Dom.Rep.]	194	Ld	18.12N	70.34W
Salinas, Punta- [P.R.]	197a	Bb	18.29N	66.10W
Salinas, Río-	194	Be	16.28N	90.33W
Salinas de Hidalgo	192	If	22.38N	101.43W
Salinas Peak	186	Cj	33.18N	106.31W
Saline, Point-	196	Fg	12.00N	61.48W
Saline Island	197p	Cb	12.26N	61.29W
Saline River [Ks.-U.S.]	186	Hg	38.51N	97.30W
Saline River [U.S.]	186	Jj	33.10N	92.08W
Salines, Pointe des-	197h	Bc	14.24N	60.53W
Salinópolis	202	Id	0.37S	47.20W
Salins-les-Bains	122	Lh	46.57N	5.53 E
Salisbury	180	Jd	63.35N	77.00W
Salisbury [Dom.]	197g	Bb	15.26N	61.27W
Salisbury [Eng.-U.K.]	118	Lj	51.05N	1.48W
Salisbury [Md.-U.S.]	182	Ld	38.22N	75.36W
Salisbury [N.C.-U.S.]	184	Gh	35.40N	80.29W
Salisbury Plain	118	Lj	51.15N	1.55W
Săliște	130	Gd	45.47N	23.53 E
Šalja	136	Fd	57.15N	58.43 E
Saljany	136	Eh	39.35N	48.59 E
Šalkar, ozero-	132	Qd	50.35N	51.40 E
Šalkar-Jega-Kara, ozero-	132	Vd	50.45N	60.55 E
Salkhad	146	Gf	32.29N	36.43 E
Salla	114	Gc	66.50N	28.40 E
Sallent de Gállego	126	Lb	42.46N	0.20W
Salling	116	Ch	56.40N	9.00 E
Salliqueló	206	He	36.45S	62.56W
Sallisaw	186	Ii	35.28N	94.47W
Sallūm	168	Fb	19.23N	37.06 E
Sallūm, Khalīj as- = Salum, Gulf of-(EN)	164	Ec	31.40N	25.20 E
Sallyana	148	Gc	28.22N	82.10 E
Salm	124	Ie	49.51N	6.51 E
Salmās	144	Fb	38.11N	44.47 E
Salmi	114	Hf	61.24N	31.54 E
Salmo	188	Gb	49.12N	117.17W
Salmon	182	Eb	45.11N	113.54W
Salmon Arm	180	Ff	50.42N	119.16W
Salmon Bank (EN)	214	Kb	26.56N	176.28W
Salmon Falls Creek Reservoir	188	He	42.05N	114.45W
Salmon Mountain	188	Hd	45.38N	114.50W
Salmon Mountains	188	Df	41.00N	123.00W
Salmon River	174	He	45.51N	116.46W
Salmon River Mountains	182	Dc	44.45N	115.30W
Salmtal	124	Ie	49.56N	6.48 E
Salmyš	132	Sc	52.01N	55.21 E
Salo	168	Be	3.12N	16.07 E
Salò	128	Ee	45.36N	10.31 E
Salo	114	Ff	60.23N	23.08 E
Salobra, Río-	204	De	20.12S	56.29W
Salobreña	126	Ih	36.44N	3.35W
Salomon, Cap-	197h	Ab	14.30N	61.06W
Salon-de-Provence	122	Lk	43.38N	5.06 E
Salonga	158	Ii	0.10S	19.50 E
Salonika (EN) = Thessaloníki	112	Ig	40.38N	22.56 E
Salonika, Gulf of- (EN) = Thermaïkós Kólpos	110	Ig	40.20N	22.45 E
Salonta	130	Ec	46.48N	21.39 E
Salop	118	Ki	52.40N	2.50W
Salor	126	Ee	39.39N	7.03W
Salou	126	Nc	41.04N	1.08 E
Salouël	124	Ee	49.52N	2.15 E
Saloum	166	Bc	13.50N	16.45W
Salpausselkä	110	Ic	61.00N	26.30 E
Sal-Rei	162	Cf	16.11N	22.55W
Salsbruket	114	Cd	64.48N	11.52 E
Salseleh-ye Safīd Kūh/ Paropamisus	140	If	34.30N	63.30 E
Salses, Étang de- → Leucate, Étang de-	122	Il	42.51N	3.00 E
Salsipuedes, Canal de-	192	Cc	28.40N	113.00W
Salsipuedes, Punta-	194	Fi	8.28N	83.37W
Salsk	136	Ef	46.28N	41.29 E
Šalski	114	If	61.48N	36.03 E
Salso [It.]	128	Im	37.39N	14.49 E
Salso [It.]	128	Hm	37.06N	13.57 E
Salsola	128	Ji	41.37N	15.40 E
Salsomaggiore Terme	128	Df	44.49N	9.59 E
Salt	126	Oc	41.59N	2.47 E
Salta	200	Jh	24.47S	65.24W
Salta	206	Hb	25.00S	64.30W
Saltash	118	Ik	50.24N	4.12W
Salt Basin	186	Dk	31.50N	105.00W
Saltburn-by-the-Sea	118	Mg	54.35N	0.58W
Salt Cay	194	Lc	21.20N	71.11W
Salt Creek	188	Gh	36.15N	116.49W
Salt Draw	186	Ek	31.19N	103.28W
Saltee Islands/Na Sailtí	118	Gi	52.07N	6.36W
Salten	114	Dc	67.45N	15.31 E
Salt Fork Brazos	186	Gj	33.15N	100.00W
Salt Fork of Arkansas River	186	Hh	36.36N	97.03W
Salt Fork Red	186	Gi	34.30N	99.22W
Saltholm	116	Ei	55.40N	12.45 E
Saltillo	176	Ig	25.25N	101.01W
Salt Lake City	176	He	40.46N	111.53W
Salto	204	Dj	31.25S	57.00W
Salto	128	Gh	42.23N	12.54 E
Salto [Arg.]	206	Hd	34.17S	60.15W
Salto [Ur.]	200	Ki	31.23S	57.58W
Salto da Divisa	202	Kg	16.00S	39.57W
Salto del Guairá	206	Jb	24.05S	54.15W
Salto Grande	204	Hf	22.54S	49.59W
Salton Sea	174	Hf	33.20N	115.50W
Salt River [Az.-U.S.]	182	Ee	33.23N	112.18W
Salt River [U.S.]	188	Je	43.07N	111.02W
Saltsjöbaden	116	He	59.17N	18.18 E
Saltvik	114	Ef	60.17N	20.03 E
Saluafata Harbour	221c	Ba	13.55S	171.38W
Saluda	184	Ig	37.36N	76.36W
Salum, Gulf of-(EN) = Sallūm, Khalīj as-	164	Ec	31.40N	25.20 E
Saluzzo	128	Bf	44.39N	7.29 E
Salvación, Bahía-	206	Eh	50.55S	75.05W
Salvador [Braz.]	200	Mg	12.59S	38.31W
Salvador [Niger]	166	Ha	23.14N	12.05 E
Salvador, Lake-	186	Kl	29.45N	90.15W
Salvador Mazza	206	Hb	22.10S	63.43W
Salvaterra de Magos	126	De	39.01N	8.48W
Salvatierra [Mex.]	192	Ig	20.13N	100.53W
Salvatierra [Sp.]	126	Jb	42.51N	2.23W
Salwa, Dawḥat as-	146	Nj	25.30N	50.40 E
Salwā Baḥrī	164	Fe	24.44N	32.56 E
Salween (EN) = Thanlwin	140	Lg	16.31N	97.37 E
Salyersville	184	Fg	37.45N	83.04W
Salza	128	Ic	47.40N	14.43 E
Salzach	120	Ih	48.12N	12.56 E
Salzburg	112	Hf	47.48N	13.02 E
Salzburg	128	Gc	47.20N	13.00 E
Salzburger Kalkalpen	128	Gc	47.35N	12.55 E
Salzgitter	120	Gd	52.05N	10.20 E
Salzkammergut	128	Hc	47.45N	13.30 E
Salzkotten	124	Kc	51.40N	8.36 E
Salzwedel	120	Hd	52.51N	11.09 E
Samadāy, Ra's-	146	Fj	25.00N	34.56 E
Samagaltaj	138	Ef	50.36N	95.03 E
Samaḥ [Lib.]	164	Cd	28.10N	19.10 E
Samaḥ [Sau.Ar.]	146	Kh	28.52N	45.30 E
Samaipata	202	Fg	18.09S	63.52W
Samalayuca	192	Fb	31.21N	106.28W
Samales Group	150	He	6.00N	121.45 E
Samalga Pass	178a	Eb	52.48N	169.25W
Samālūt	164	Fd	28.18N	30.42 E
Samambaia, Rio-	204	Ff	22.45S	53.21W
Samaná	194	Md	19.13N	69.19W
Samaná, Bahía de-	190	Ke	19.10N	69.25W
Samaná, Cabo-	194	Md	19.18N	69.09W
Samana Cay	194	Kb	23.06N	73.42W
Samandağı	146	Fd	36.07N	35.56 E
Samangān	144	Kb	36.15N	67.40 E
Samani	152	Pc	42.07N	142.56 E
Samanlı Dağları	130	Mi	40.32N	29.10 E
Samar	140	Oh	12.00N	125.00 E
Samara = Kujbyšev	112	Le	53.12N	50.09 E
Samara [R.S.F.S.R.]	110	Le	53.10N	50.04 E
Samarai	210	Gf	10.36S	150.39 E
Samarinda	142	Nj	0.30S	117.09 E
Samarkand	136	If	39.40N	66.58 E
Samarkandskaja oblast	136	Gg	40.10N	66.20 E
Sāmarrā'	144	Fc	34.12N	43.52 E
Samar Sea	150	Hd	11.50N	124.32 E
Samaru	166	Gc	11.10N	7.38 E
Samatan	122	Gk	43.30N	0.56 E
Samate	150	Jg	0.58S	131.04 E
Samba [Zaire]	170	Ec	4.38S	26.22 E
Samba [Zaire]	170	Db	0.14N	21.19 E
Samba Caju	170	Cd	8.45S	15.25 E
Sambalpur	148	Gd	21.27N	83.58 E
Sambar, Tanjung-	150	Fg	2.59S	110.19 E
Sambas	150	Ef	1.20N	109.15 E
Sambava	172	Ib	14.15S	50.10 E
Samber	122	Kd	50.28N	4.52 E
Sāmbhar	148	Fc	26.55N	75.12 E
Sambiase, Lamezia Terme-	128	Kl	38.58N	16.17 E
Samboja	150	Gg	1.02S	117.02 E
Sambor	136	Cf	49.32N	23.11 E
Samborombón, Bahía-	206	Ie	36.00S	57.12W
Samborombón, Río-	204	Dl	35.43S	57.20W
Sambre	122	Kd	50.28N	4.52 E
Sambre à l'Oise, Canal de la-	122	Je	49.39N	3.20 E
Samburg	138	Cc	67.00N	78.25 E
Samch'ŏnp'o	152	Me	34.55N	128.04 E
Samdi Dağı	146	Kd	37.19N	44.15 E
Samdŏng-ni	154	Ie	39.21N	126.14 E
Samdŭng	154	Ie	38.59N	126.11 E
Same [Indon.]	150	Ih	8.59S	125.40 E
Same [Tan.]	170	Gc	4.04S	37.44 E
Samer	124	Dd	50.38N	1.45 E
Sam Ford Fiord	180	Kb	70.40N	70.35W
Samfya	170	Ee	11.20S	29.32 E
Samhor	132	Oi	40.48N	46.01 E
Sámi	130	Dk	38.15N	20.39 E
Sāmī Ghar	144	Kc	31.43N	67.01 E
Samīrah	146	Ji	26.18N	42.05 E
Šamli	130	Kj	39.48N	27.51 E
Samnah, Jabal-	146	Ei	26.26N	33.34 E
Samoa I Sisifo = Western Samoa (EN)	210	Jf	13.40S	172.30W
Samoa Islands	208	Jf	14.00S	171.00W
Samobor	128	Je	45.48N	15.43 E
Samojlovka	132	Md	51.10N	43.43 E
Samokov	130	Gg	42.20N	23.33 E
Samolva	116	Lf	58.16N	27.45 E
Sámos	130	Jl	37.45N	26.58 E

Index Symbols

1 Independent Nation; 2 State, Region; 3 District, County; 4 Municipality; 5 Colony, Dependency; Continent; Physical Region; Historical or Cultural Region; Mount, Mountain; Volcano; Hill; Mountains, Mountain Range; Hills, Escarpment; Plateau, Upland; Pass, Gap; Plain, Lowland; Delta; Salt Flat; Valley, Canyon; Crater, Cave; Karst Features; Depression; Polder; Desert, Dunes; Forest, Woods; Heath, Steppe; Oasis; Cape, Point; Coast, Beach; Cliff; Peninsula; Isthmus; Sandbank; Island; Atoll; Rock, Reef; Islands, Archipelago; Rocks, Reefs; Coral Reef; Well, Spring; Geyser; River, Stream; Waterfall, Rapids; River Mouth, Estuary; Lake; Salt Lake; Intermittent Lake; Reservoir; Swamp, Pond; Canal; Glacier; Ice Shelf, Pack Ice; Ocean; Sea; Gulf, Bay; Strait, Fjord; Lagoon; Bank; Seamount; Tablemount; Ridge; Shelf; Basin; Escarpment, Sea Scarp; Fracture; Trench, Abyss; National Park, Reserve; Point of Interest; Recreation Site; Cave, Cavern; Historic Site; Ruins; Wall, Walls; Church, Abbey; Temple; Scientific Station; Railway station; Airport; Port; Military installation; Lighthouse; Mine; Tunnel; Dam, Bridge

Sámos 110 Ih 37.45N 26.48 E
Samosir, Pulau- 150 Cf 2.35N 98.50 E
Samothrace (EN) = Samothráki 130 Ii 40.27N 25.35 E
Samothráki 130 Ii 40.29N 25.31 E
Samothráki = Samothrace (EN) 130 Ii 40.27N 25.35 E
Sampacho 206 Hd 33.23S 64.43W
Sampaga 150 Gg 2.19S 119.07 E
Sampit 142 Nj 2.32S 112.57 E
Sampit 150 Fg 3.00S 113.03 E
Sampoku 156 Fb 38.30N 139.30 E
Sampwe 170 Ed 9.20S 27.23 E
Sam Rayburn Reservoir 186 Ik 31.27N 94.37W
Samro, ozero- 116 Mf 58.55N 28.50 E
Samsjøen 116 Da 63.05N 10.40 E
Samsø 114 Ci 55.50N 10.35 E
Samsø Bælt 116 Di 55.50N 10.45 E
Sam Son 148 Ld 19.44N 105.54 E
Samsun 142 Fe 41.17N 36.20 E
Samsun Daği 130 Kl 37.40N 27.15 E
Samtredia 132 Mh 42.11N 42.17 E
Samuel, Mount- 212 Gc 19.41S 134.09 E
Samuhú 204 Bh 27.31S 60.24W
Samui, Ko- 140 Li 9.30N 100.00 E
Samur 132 Pi 41.53N 48.32 E
Samur-Apšeronski kanal 132 Pi 40.35N 49.35 E
Samus 138 De 56.46N 84.44 E
Samut Prakan 148 Kf 13.36N 100.36 E
Samut Sakhon 148 Kf 13.31N 100.15 E
San 160 Gg 13.08N 4.53W
San [Asia] 148 Lf 13.32N 105.57 E
San [Pol.] 120 Rf 50.45N 21.51 E
Şan'ā' 142 Gh 15.23N 44.12 E
Sana 128 Ke 45.03N 16.23 E
Sanaag [3] 168 Hc 10.10N 47.50 E
Şanabū 146 Di 27.30N 30.47 E
Sanae 222 Bf 70.18S 2.22W
Sanāfir 146 Fi 27.55N 34.42 E
Sanāg 168 Hd 7.45N 48.00 E
Sanaga 158 Hh 3.35N 9.38 E
San Agustín 200 Ie 1.53N 76.16W
San Agustín 204 Cn 38.01S 58.21W
San Agustín, Cabo- 192 Bc 28.05N 115.20W
San Agustin, Cape- 150 Ie 6.16N 126.11 E
Sanak Islands 178 Gf 54.25N 162.35W
Sanalona, Presa- 192 Fe 24.53N 107.00W
San Ambrosio, Isla- 206 Ec 26.21S 79.52W
Sanana 150 Ig 2.04S 125.08 E
Sanana, Pulau- 150 Ig 2.12S 125.55 E
Sanandaj 144 Gb 35.19N 47.00 E
San Andreas 188 Eg 38.12N 120.41W
San Andrés [3] 190 Hf 12.35N 81.42W
San Andres, Cerro- 192 Ih 19.48N 100.36W
San Andrés, Isla de- 198 Hd 12.32N 81.42W
San Andrés, Laguna de- 192 Kf 22.40N 97.50W
San Andrés de Giles 204 Cl 34.27S 59.27W
San Andrés del Rabanedo 126 Gb 42.37N 5.36W
San Andres Mountains 182 Fe 32.55N 106.45W
San Andres Peak 186 Cj 32.43N 106.30W
San Andrés Tuxtla 190 Ee 18.27N 95.13W
San Andrés y Providencia [3] 202 Ba 12.30N 81.45W
Sanandua 204 Gh 27.57S 51.48W
San Angelo 182 Ge 31.28N 100.26W
San Antonio [Blz.] 194 Ce 16.30N 89.02W
San Antonio [Chile] 206 Fd 33.35S 71.38W
San Antonio [Tx.-U.S.] 176 Jg 29.28N 98.31W
San Antonio [Ur.] 204 Dj 31.20S 57.45W
San Antonio, Cabo- [Arg.] 198 Ki 36.40S 56.42W
San Antonio, Cabo- [Cuba] 174 Kg 21.52N 84.57W
San Antonio, Cabo de- / Sant Antoni, Cap de- 126 Mf 38.48N 0.12 E
San Antonio, Canal- 204 Aj 31.42S 62.15W
San Antonio, Punta- 192 Bc 29.45N 115.45W
San Antonio, Sierra de- 192 Db 30.00N 110.20W
San Antonio Abad / Sant Antoni de Portmany 126 Nf 38.58N 1.18 E
San Antonio Bay 186 Hl 28.20N 96.45W
San Antonio de Caparo 194 Lj 7.35N 71.27W
San Antonio de Cortés 194 Cf 15.05N 88.04W
San Antonio de los Baños 194 Fb 22.53N 82.30W
San Antonio de los Cobres 206 Gb 24.11S 66.21W
San Antonio del Táchira 202 Db 7.50N 72.27W
San Antonio de Tamanaco 196 Ch 9.14N 66.03W
San Antonio Oeste 200 Jj 40.44S 64.57W
San Antonio River 182 Hf 28.30N 96.50W
Sanare 194 Mi 9.45N 69.39W
Sanary-sur-Mer 122 Lk 43.07N 5.48 E
San Augustine 186 Ik 31.32N 94.07W
Sanāw 168 Ib 17.50N 51.05 E
San Bartolomeo in Galdo 128 Ji 41.24N 15.01 E
San Baudilio de Llobregat/ Sant Boi de Llobregat 126 Oc 41.21N 2.03 E
San Benedetto del Tronto 128 Hh 42.57N 13.53 E
San Benedetto Po 128 Ee 45.02N 10.55 E
San Benedicto, Isla- 190 Be 19.18N 110.49W
San Benito [Guat.] 194 Ce 16.55N 89.54W
San Benito [Tx.-U.S.] 186 Hm 26.08N 97.38W
San Benito, Islas- 192 Bc 28.20N 115.35W
San Benito Abad 194 Ji 8.56N 75.02W
San Benito Mountain 188 Eh 36.22N 120.38W
San Bernardino 176 Hf 34.06N 117.17W
San Bernardino, Passo del- 128 Dd 46.30N 9.10 E
San Bernardino Mountains 188 Gi 34.10N 117.00W
San Bernardino Strait 150 Hd 12.32N 124.10 E
San Bernardo [Arg.] 204 Bh 27.17S 60.42W
San Bernardo [Chile] 206 Fd 33.36S 70.43W
San Bernardo [Mex.] 192 De 25.32N 111.45W
San Bernardo, Islas de- 194 Ji 9.45N 75.50W
San Bernardo, Punta de- 194 Ji 9.42N 75.42W
San Bernardo del Viento 202 Cb 9.22N 75.57W
San Blas [3] 194 Hi 7.50N 81.10W
San Blas [Mex.] 190 Cd 21.31N 105.16W
San Blas [Mex.] 190 Cc 26.05N 108.46W
San Blas [Mex.] 192 Id 27.25N 101.40W
San Blas, Archipiélago de- 194 Hi 9.30N 78.30W
San Blas, Cape- 182 Jf 29.40N 85.22W
San Blas, Cordillera de- 194 Hi 9.18N 79.00W
San Blas, Golfo de- 194 Hi 9.30N 79.00W
San Blas, Punta- 194 Hi 9.34N 78.58W
San Borja 202 Ef 14.49S 66.51W
San Borjas, Sierra de- 192 Cc 28.40N 113.45W
San Buenaventura 192 Id 27.05N 101.32W
Sancai 168 Fc 10.43N 35.40 E
San Carlos [Arg.] 204 Eh 27.45S 55.54W
San Carlos [Chile] 206 Fe 36.25S 71.58W
San Carlos [Mex.] 192 Ic 29.01N 100.51W
San Carlos [Mex.] 192 Je 24.35N 98.56W
San Carlos [Nic.] 194 Eh 11.07N 84.47W
San Carlos [Pan.] 194 Hi 8.29N 79.57W
San Carlos [Par.] 204 Df 22.16S 57.18W
San Carlos [Phil.] 150 Hd 10.30N 123.25 E
San Carlos [Phil.] 150 Hc 15.55N 120.20 E
San Carlos [Ur.] 206 Jd 34.48S 54.55W
San Carlos [Ven.] 202 Eb 9.40N 68.39W
San Carlos, Bahía- 192 Cd 27.55N 112.45W
San Carlos, Mesa de- 192 Bc 29.40N 115.25W
San Carlos, Punta- 192 Cc 28.00N 112.45W
San Carlos, Riacho- 204 Df 22.49S 57.53W
San Carlos, Río- [C.R.] 194 Eh 10.47N 84.12W
San Carlos, Río- [Ven.] 196 Bh 9.07N 68.25W
San Carlos de Bariloche 200 Ij 41.08S 71.15W
San Carlos de Bolívar 206 He 36.15S 61.06W
San Carlos de la Rápita / Sant Carles de la Ràpita 126 Md 40.37N 0.36 E
San Carlos del Zulia 202 Db 9.01N 71.55W
San Carlos de Río Negro 202 Ec 1.55N 67.04W
San Carlos Reservoir 188 Jj 33.13N 110.24W
San Cataldo 128 Hm 37.29N 13.59 E
San Cayetano 204 Cn 38.20S 59.37W
Sancerre 122 Ig 47.20N 2.50 E
Sancerrois, Collines du- 122 Ig 47.20N 2.30 E
Sanchahe 154 Ib 44.59N 126.03 E
Sánchez 194 Md 19.14N 69.36W
Sánchez Magallanes 192 Mh 18.17N 93.59W
San Clemente [Ca.-U.S.] 182 De 33.26N 117.37W
San Clemente [Sp.] 126 Je 39.24N 2.26W
San Clemente del Tuyú 204 Dm 36.22S 56.43W
San Clemente Island 188 Fj 32.55N 118.30W
Sancois 122 Ih 46.50N 2.55 E
San Cosme 204 Ch 27.22S 58.31W
San Cristóbal [Arg.] 206 Hd 30.19S 61.14W
San Cristóbal [Bol.] 204 Ba 13.56S 61.50W
San Cristóbal [Cuba] 194 Fb 22.43N 83.03W
San Cristóbal [Dom.Rep.] 194 Ld 18.25N 70.06W
San Cristóbal [Mex.] 194 Li 17.49N 94.32W
San Cristóbal [Ven.] 230 Ie 7.46N 72.14W
San Cristóbal, Bahía de- 192 Bd 27.25N 114.40W
San Cristóbal, Isla- 198 Hf 0.50S 89.26W
San Cristóbal de las Casas 190 Fe 16.45N 92.38W
San Cristóbal Island 208 Hf 10.36S 161.45 E
San Cristóbal Verapaz 194 Bf 15.23N 90.24W
Sancti Spíritus 190 Id 21.56N 79.27W
Sancti Spíritus [3] 194 Hb 22.00N 79.30W
Sancy, Puy de- 122 Ii 45.32N 2.50 E
Sand 114 Bg 59.29N 6.15 E
Sand 172 Ed 22.25S 30.05 E
Sanda 156 Dd 34.53N 135.14 E
Sandai 150 Fg 1.15S 110.31 E
Sandakan 142 Ni 5.50N 118.07 E
Sandal, Baie de- 219b Ce 20.49S 167.10 E
Sandal, ozero- 114 Ie 62.25N 34.10 E
Sandane 114 Bf 61.46N 6.13 E
Sandanski 130 Gh 41.34N 23.17 E
Sandaré 166 Cc 14.42N 10.18W
Sandared 116 Eg 57.43N 12.47 E
Sandarne 116 Gc 61.16N 17.10 E
Sanday 118 Kb 59.15N 2.30W
Sande 116 De 59.36N 10.12 E
Sandefjord 114 Cg 59.08N 10.14 E
Sandégué 166 Ed 7.59N 3.33W
Sandeid 114 Ag 59.33N 5.50 E
Sanders 188 Ki 35.13N 109.20W
Sanderson 182 Ge 30.09N 102.24W
Sandersville 184 Fi 32.59N 82.48W
Sandfontein 172 Bd 22.11S 19.58 E
Sandgate 214 Dc 51.04N 1.09 E
Sandhammaren 116 Fi 55.23N 14.12 E
Sandhamn 116 He 59.17N 18.55 E
Sand Hills 182 Gc 41.45N 102.00W
Sandia 202 Ef 14.17S 69.26W
Sandia Crest 186 Ci 35.13N 106.27W
San Diego [Bol.] 204 Bc 16.04S 60.28W
San Diego [Ca.-U.S.] 176 Hf 32.43N 117.09W
San Diego, Cabo- 198 Jk 54.38S 65.07W
Sandikli 146 Dc 38.28N 30.17 E
San Dimitri Point 128 In 36.05N 14.05 E
Sand in Taufers / Campo Tures 128 Fd 46.55N 11.57 E
Sand Lake 186 Ia 50.05N 94.39W
Sand Mountain 186 Dh 34.20N 86.02W
Sandnes 114 Ag 58.51N 5.44 E
Sandnessjøen 114 Cc 66.01N 12.38 E
Sandoa 160 Ji 9.41S 22.52 E
Sando bank 116 Hf 58.10N 19.15 E
Sandomierska, Kotlina- 120 Rf 50.30N 22.00 E
Sandomierz 120 Rf 50.41N 21.45 E
San Domino 128 Jh 42.05N 15.30 E
Sandoná 202 Cc 1.18N 77.28W
San Donà di Piave 128 Ge 45.38N 12.34 E
Sandoval, Boca de- 192 Ke 24.58N 97.32W
Sandover River 212 Hd 21.43S 136.32 E
Sandoway 148 Ie 18.28N 94.22 E
Sandown 118 Lk 50.39N 1.09W
Sandpoint 182 Db 48.16N 116.33W
Sand Point 178 Ge 55.20N 160.30W
Sandras Daği 130 Ll 37.04N 28.51 E
Sandray 118 Fe 56.54N 7.25W
Sandspit 180 Ef 53.15N 131.50W
Sand Springs [Mt.-U.S.] 188 Lc 47.09N 107.27W
Sand Springs [Ok.-U.S.] 186 Hh 36.09N 96.07W
Sandstone [Austl.] 212 De 27.59S 119.17 E
Sandstone [Mn.-U.S.] 186 Jc 46.08N 92.52W
Sandu 152 Jf 26.08N 113.16 E
Sandusky [Mi.-U.S.] 184 Fd 43.25N 82.50W
Sandusky [Oh.-U.S.] 182 Kc 41.27N 82.42W
Sandveld 172 Cd 21.20S 20.10 E
Sandvig-Allinge 114 Di 55.15N 14.49 E
Sandvika 116 De 59.54N 10.31 E
Sandviken 114 Df 60.37N 16.46 E
Sandwich 118 Oj 51.17N 1.20 E
Sandwich Bay 180 Lf 53.35N 57.15W
Sandy 124 Bb 52.07N 0.17W
Sandy Cape [Austl.] 208 Gg 24.40S 153.15 E
Sandy Cape [Austl.] 212 Ih 41.25S 144.45 E
Sandy Desert 148 Cc 28.46N 62.30 E
Sandykači 136 Gh 36.32N 62.35 E
Sandy Lake 180 If 53.02N 93.14W
Sandy Lake 180 If 53.02N 92.55W
Sandy Point 184 Il 26.01N 77.24W
Sandy Point Town 196 Ed 17.22N 62.50W
Sandžak 130 Cf 43.10N 20.00 E
Sanem 124 He 49.33N 5.56 E
San Estanislao 206 Ib 24.39S 56.26W
San Esteban 194 Ef 15.17N 85.52W
San Esteban, Bahía de- 192 Ee 25.40N 109.15W
San Esteban, Isla- 192 Cc 28.42N 112.36W
San Esteban de Gormaz 126 Ic 41.35N 3.12W
San Felice Circeo 128 Hi 41.14N 13.05 E
San Felipe [Chile] 206 Fd 32.45S 70.44W
San Felipe [Col.] 202 Ec 1.55N 67.06W
San Felipe [Mex.] 190 Bb 31.00N 114.52W
San Felipe [Mex.] 192 Ig 21.29N 101.13W
San Felipe [Ven.] 202 Ea 10.20N 68.44W
San Felipe, Cayos de- 194 Fc 21.58N 83.30W
San Felipe, Cerro de- 126 Kd 40.24N 1.51W
San Felipe Creek 188 Hj 33.09N 115.46W
San Feliu de Llobregat / Sant Feliu de Llobregat 126 Oc 41.23N 2.03 E
San Félix, Isla- 206 Dc 26.17S 80.05W
San Fermín, Punta- 192 Bb 30.25N 114.40W
San Fernando [Chile] 206 Fd 34.35S 71.00W
San Fernando [Mex.] 190 Ed 24.51N 98.10W
San Fernando [Mex.] 192 Bb 29.59N 115.17W
San Fernando [Phil.] 150 Hc 15.01N 120.41 E
San Fernando [Phil.] 150 Hc 16.37N 120.19 E
San Fernando [Sp.] 126 Fh 36.28N 6.12W
San Fernando [Trin.] 202 Fa 10.17N 61.28W
San Fernando, Río- [Bol.] 204 Cc 17.13S 58.23W
San Fernando, Río- [Mex.] 192 Ke 24.55N 97.40W
San Fernando de Apure 200 Je 7.54N 67.28W
San Fernando de Atabapo 202 Ec 4.03N 67.42W
San Fernando del Valle de Catamarca 200 Jh 28.30S 65.45W
Sanford [Fl.-U.S.] 182 Kf 28.48N 81.16W
Sanford [Me.-U.S.] 184 Ld 43.26N 70.46W
Sanford [N.C.-U.S.] 184 Hh 35.29N 79.10W
Sanford, Mount- 178 Kd 62.13N 144.09W
San Francisco [Arg.] 206 Hd 31.26S 62.05W
San Francisco [Bol.] 204 Cc 17.42S 59.38W
San Francisco [Ca.-U.S.] 176 Gf 37.48N 122.24W
San Francisco [Pan.] 194 Gi 8.15N 80.58W
San Francisco, Isla- 192 De 24.50N 110.35W
San Francisco Bay 174 Gf 37.43N 122.17W
San Francisco Creek 186 El 29.53N 102.19W
San Francisco de Arriba 192 Hd 26.15N 102.50W
San Francisco de Bellocq 204 Bn 38.42S 60.01W
San Francisco de la Paz 194 Df 14.55N 86.14W
San Francisco del Laishi 204 Ch 26.14S 58.38W
San Francisco del Oro 190 Cc 26.52N 105.51W
San Francisco del Rincón 192 Ig 21.01N 101.51W
San Francisco de Macorís 190 Je 19.18N 70.15W
San Francisco Gotera 194 Cg 13.42N 88.06W
San Francisco Javier / Sant Francesc de Formentera 126 Nf 38.42N 1.25 E
San Francisco Mountains 188 Kj 33.45N 109.00W
San Francisco River 188 Kj 32.59N 109.22W
San Fratello 128 Il 38.01N 14.36 E
San Gabriel 204 Di 28.58S 57.12W
San Gabriel, Punta- 192 Cc 28.25N 112.50W
San Gabriel Mountains 188 Gi 34.20N 117.45W
San Gallán, Isla- 202 Cf 13.50S 76.28W
Sangamon River 186 Kf 40.07N 90.20W
Sangar [Iran] 146 Md 37.08N 49.02 E
Sangar [R.S.F.S.R.] 142 Oc 63.55N 127.31 E
Sangatte 124 Dd 50.56N 1.45 E
San Gavino Monreale 128 Ck 39.33N 8.47 E
Sangay, Volcán- 198 If 2.00S 78.20W
Sange 170 Ed 7.02S 28.21 E
Sangeang, Pulau- 150 Gh 8.12S 119.04 E
San Gemini 128 Gh 42.37N 12.33 E
Sanger 188 Fh 36.42N 119.27W
Sangerhausen 120 He 51.28N 11.18 E
San Germán [Cuba] 194 Ic 20.36N 76.08W
San Germán [P.R.] 194 Nd 18.05N 67.03W
Sanggan He 154 Cd 40.24N 115.18 E
Sanggau 150 Ff 0.08N 110.36 E
Sangha 158 Ii 1.13S 16.49 E
Sangha [C.A.R.] [3] 168 Be 3.30N 16.00 E
Sangha [Con.] [3] 170 Cb 2.00N 15.00 E
Sangihe, Kepulauan- = Sangihe Islands (EN) 140 Oi 3.00N 125.30 E
Sangihe, Pulau- 150 If 3.35N 125.32 E
Sangihe Islands (EN) = Sangihe, Kepulauan- 140 Oi 3.00N 125.30 E
San Gil 202 Db 6.32N 73.08W
San Gimignano 128 Fg 43.28N 11.02 E
San Giovanni in Fiore 128 Kk 39.15N 16.42 E
San Giovanni in Persiceto 128 Ff 44.38N 11.11 E
San Giovanni Rotondo 128 Ji 41.42N 15.44 E
San Giovanni Valdarno 128 Fg 43.34N 11.32 E
Sangju 154 Jf 36.25N 128.10 E
Sāngli 142 Jh 16.52N 74.34 E
Sangmélima 166 He 2.56N 11.59 E
Sangoli 146 Pd 37.25N 54.35 E
San Gorgonio 174 Hf 34.05N 116.50W
San Gottardo, Passo del- = Saint Gotthard Pass (EN) 110 Gf 46.30N 8.30 E
Sangradouro Grande, Rio- 204 Dc 16.24S 57.10W
Sangre de Cristo Mountains 174 If 37.30N 105.15W
San Gregorio 204 Al 34.19S 62.02W
Sangre Grande 196 Fg 10.35N 61.07W
Sangri 152 Ff 29.20N 92.15 E
Sangro 128 Ih 42.14N 14.32 E
Sangue, Rio do- 202 Gf 11.00S 58.40W
Sangüesa 126 Kb 42.35N 1.17W
Sanguinaires, Iles- 122a Ab 41.53N 8.35 E
San Gustavo 204 Cj 30.41S 59.23W
Sangyuan → Wuqiao 154 Df 37.38N 116.23 E
Sangzhi 152 Jf 29.23N 110.11 E
San He 154 Eh 33.00N 118.34 E
Sanhe [China] 154 Dd 40.00N 117.01 E
Sanhe [China] 152 La 50.30N 120.04 E
Sanhe-San 156 Cd 35.08N 132.37 E
Sanhezhen 154 Di 31.30N 117.15 E
San Hilario [Arg.] 204 Ch 26.02S 58.39W
San Hilario [Mex.] 192 De 24.22N 110.59W
San Hipólito, Bahía- 192 Cd 26.55N 113.55W
San Ignacio [Arg.] 204 Eh 27.16S 55.32W
San Ignacio [Blz.] 190 Ge 17.10N 89.04W
San Ignacio [Bol.] 202 Fg 16.23S 60.59W
San Ignacio [Bol.] 202 Ef 14.53S 65.36W
San Ignacio [Mex.] 190 Bc 27.27N 112.51W
San Ignacio [Mex.] 192 Ff 25.55N 106.25W
San Ignacio [Par.] 206 Ic 26.52S 57.03W
San Ignacio, Isla de- 192 Ee 25.25N 108.55W
San Ignacio, Laguna- 192 Cd 26.55N 113.15W
San Ildefonso (La Granja) 126 Id 40.54N 4.00W
San Ildefonso, Cape- 150 Hc 16.02N 121.59 E
San Ildefonso, Cerro- 194 Cf 15.31N 88.17W
Saniquellie 166 Dd 7.22N 8.43W
San Isidro [Arg.] 206 Id 34.27S 58.30W
San Isidro [Phil.] 150 Hd 11.24N 124.21 E
San Isidro de El General 190 Hg 9.22N 83.42W
Saniyah 146 If 33.49N 42.43 E
San Jacinto 194 Ji 9.50N 75.07W
San Jacinto Peak 188 Gj 33.49N 116.41W
San Jaime 204 Cj 30.20S 58.19W
San Javier [Arg.] 206 Id 30.35S 59.57W
San Javier [Sp.] 126 Lg 37.48N 0.51W
San Javier [Ur.] 204 Ck 32.41S 58.08W
San Javier, Rio- 204 Bj 31.30S 60.20W
San Javier de Loncomilla 206 Fe 35.36S 71.45W
San Jerónimo Taviche 192 Ki 16.44N 96.35W
Sanjiachang 152 Hg 24.45N 101.53 E
Sanjiaocheng → Haiyan 152 Hd 36.58N 100.50 E
Sanjō 154 Of 37.37N 138.57 E
San Joan de Labritja / San Juan Bautista 126 Ne 39.05N 1.30 E
San Joaquín 202 Ff 13.04S 64.49W
San Joaquín, Río- 202 Ff 13.08S 63.41W
San Joaquín, Sierra de- 204 Eg 24.48S 56.00W
San Joaquin River 188 Eh 36.43N 121.50W
San Joaquin Valley 174 Gf 36.50N 120.10W
San Jon 186 Ei 35.06N 103.20W
San Jorge 206 Hd 31.54S 61.52W
San Jorge, Bahía de- 192 Cb 31.10N 113.15W
San Jorge, Golfo- 198 Jj 46.00S 67.00W
San Jorge, Golfo de- / Sant Jordi, Golf de- 126 Md 40.53N 1.00 E
San Jorge, Rio- 194 Ji 9.07N 74.44W
San Jorge, Serranía- 204 Be 20.21S 60.59W
San Jorge Island 219a Dc 8.27S 159.35 E
San José [2] 204 Dl 34.15S 56.45W
San José [3] 194 Ei 9.40N 84.00W
San José [Arg.] 204 Eh 27.46S 55.47W
San José [Ca.-U.S.] 176 Gf 37.20N 121.53W
San José [C.R.] 176 Ki 9.56N 84.05W
San José [Mex.] 192 Dd 27.32N 110.09W
San José [Par.] 204 Dg 25.33S 56.45W
San Jose [Phil.] 150 Hd 12.21N 121.04 E
San Jose [Phil.] 150 Hc 15.48N 121.00 E
San José, Isla- [Mex.] 190 Bc 25.00N 110.38W
San José, Isla- [Pan.] 194 Hi 8.15N 79.07W
San José, Salinas de- 204 Bd 18.07S 60.54W
San José, Serranía de- 204 Bc 17.52S 60.49W
San Jose de Buenavista 150 Hd 10.46N 122.30 E
San José de Chiquitos 202 Fg 17.51S 60.47W
San José de Feliciano 204 Cj 30.23S 58.45W
San José de Gracia 192 Fd 26.08N 107.58W
San José de Guanipa 202 Fb 8.54N 64.09W
San José de Jáchal 206 Gd 30.14S 68.45W
San José de las Lajas 194 Fb 22.58N 82.09W
San José del Cabo 190 Cd 23.03N 109.41W
San José del Guaviare 200 Ie 2.35N 72.38W
San José del Rosario 204 Dg 24.12S 56.48W
San José de Mayo 206 Id 34.20S 56.42W
San José de Ocuné 202 Dc 4.15N 70.20W
San José de Tiznados 196 Ch 9.23N 67.33W
San Juan [2] 206 Gd 31.00S 69.00W
San Juan [Arg.] 200 Ji 31.30S 68.30W
San Juán [Bol.] 204 Cc 17.52S 59.59W
San Juan [Bol.] 204 Bd 18.23S 60.08W
San Juan [C.Amer.] 174 Kh 10.56N 83.42W
San Juan [Dom.Rep.] 190 Je 18.48N 71.14W
San Juan [P.R.] 176 Mh 18.28N 66.07W
San Juan [U.S.] 174 Hf 37.18N 110.28W
San Juan, Cabezas de- 197a Cb 18.23N 65.38W
San Juan, Cabo- 158 Hh 1.10N 9.21 E
San Juan, Muela de- 126 Kd 40.26N 1.44W
San Juan, Pico- 196 Hd 21.59N 80.09W
San Juan, Punta- 221d Ab 27.03S 109.22W
San Juan, Río- [Arg.] 206 Gd 32.17S 67.22W
San Juan, Río- [Mex.] 192 Jd 26.10N 99.00W
San Juan, Río- [Mex.] 192 Lh 18.36N 95.40W
San Juan, Río- [Ven.] 196 Eg 10.14N 62.39W
San Juan, Volcán- 192 Gg 21.30N 104.57W
San Juan Bautista / Sant Joan de Labritja 126 Ne 39.05N 1.30 E
San Juan Bautista de las Misiones 206 Ic 26.38S 57.10W
San Juan Bautista Tuxtepec 192 Kh 18.06N 96.07W
San Juan de Colón 194 Ki 8.02N 72.16W
San Juan de Guadalupe 192 He 24.38N 102.44W
San Juan de Cesar 194 Kh 10.46N 72.59W
San Juan de Lima, Punta- 192 Hh 18.36N 103.42W
San Juan del Norte 190 Hf 10.55N 83.42W
San Juan de los Cayos 202 Ea 11.10N 68.25W
San Juan de los Lagos 192 Hg 21.15N 102.14W
San Juan de los Morros 202 Ea 9.55N 67.21W
San Juan del Rio [Mex.] 192 Ge 24.47N 104.27W
San Juan del Rio [Mex.] 192 Jg 20.29N 100.00W
San Juan del Sur 190 Gf 11.15N 85.52W
San Juan de Payara 196 Ci 7.39N 67.36W
San Juanico, Isla- 192 Fg 21.55N 106.40W
San Juanico, Punta- 192 Cd 26.05N 112.15W
San Juan Island 188 Db 48.32N 123.05W
San Juan Mountains 182 Fd 37.35N 107.10W
San Juan Neembucú 204 Dh 26.39S 57.56W
San Juan Nepomuceno [Col.] 202 Cb 9.57N 75.05W
San Juan Nepomuceno [Par.] 204 Eh 26.06S 55.58W
San Juan y Martínez 194 Fb 22.16N 83.50W
San Julián 200 Jj 49.19S 67.40W
San Just, Sierra de- 126 Ld 40.46N 0.48W
San Justo 206 Hd 30.47S 60.35W
Sankarani 158 Gg 12.01N 8.19W
Sankt Anton am Arlberg 128 Ec 47.08N 10.16 E
Sankt Augustin 124 Jd 50.47N 7.11 E
Sankt Gallen 128 Dc 47.25N 9.25 E
Sankt Gallen [2] 128 Dc 47.20N 9.10 E
Sankt Goar 120 Df 50.09N 7.43 E
Sankt Goarshausen 124 Jd 50.09N 7.44 E
Sankt Ingbert 120 Dg 49.17N 7.07 E
Sankt Johann im Pongau 128 Hc 47.21N 13.12 E
Sankt Michael im Lungau 128 Hc 47.06N 13.38 E
Sankt Michel/Mikkeli 112 Ic 61.41N 27.15 E
Sankt Moritz 128 Dd 46.30N 9.52 E
Sankt Peter-Ording 120 Eb 54.18N 8.38 E
Sankt Pölten 128 Jb 48.12N 15.38 E
Sankt Ulrich in Gröden / Ortisei 128 Fd 46.34N 11.40 E
Sankt Veit an der Glan 128 Id 46.46N 14.22 E
Sankt-Vith / Saint-Vith 122 Md 50.17N 6.08 E
Sankt Wendel 120 Dg 49.28N 7.10 E
Sankt Wolfang im Salzkammergut 128 Hc 47.44N 13.27 E
Sankuru 158 Ji 4.17S 20.25 E
San Lázaro 206 Ib 22.10S 57.55W
San Lázaro, Cabo- 190 Bd 24.48N 112.19W
San Lázaro, Sierra de- 192 Df 23.25N 110.00W
San Leandro 188 Dh 37.43N 122.09W
San Lorenzo 190 Fe 17.44N 94.45W
San Lorenzo [Arg.] 204 Bk 32.45S 60.44W
San Lorenzo [Ec.] 200 Ie 1.17N 78.50W
San Lorenzo [Hond.] 194 Dg 13.25N 87.27W
San Lorenzo, Isla- [Mex.] 192 Cc 28.38N 112.51W
San Lorenzo, Isla- [Peru] 202 Cf 12.05S 77.15W
San Lorenzo, Rio- [Mex.] 192 Je 25.07N 98.32W
San Lorenzo, Rio- [Mex.] 192 Fe 24.15N 107.24W
San Lorenzo de El Escorial 126 Hd 40.35N 4.09W
Sanlúcar de Barrameda 126 Fh 36.47N 6.21W
Sanlúcar la Mayor 126 Fg 37.23N 6.12W
San Lucas [Mex.] 190 Cd 22.53N 109.54W
San Lucas [Mex.] 192 Gf 22.33N 104.24W
San Lucas, Cabo- 174 Ig 22.50N 109.55W
San Lucas, Serranía de- 202 Db 8.00N 74.20W
San Lucido 128 Kk 39.18N 16.03 E
San Luis [2] 206 Gd 34.00S 66.00W
San Luis [Arg.] 200 Ji 33.20S 66.20W
San Luis [Bol.] 204 Cc 17.39S 58.42W
San Luis [Cuba] 194 Jc 20.12N 75.51W
San Luis [Guat.] 194 Ce 16.14N 89.27W
San Luis [Mex.] 192 Dc 29.33N 111.05W
San Luis, Isla- 192 Bb 29.58N 114.26W
San Luis, Sierra de- 194 Mh 11.11N 69.42W
San Luis de la Paz 192 Ig 21.18N 100.31W
San Luis del Palmar 204 Ch 27.31S 58.34W
San Luis de Palenque 202 Db 5.25N 71.40W
San Luis Gonzaga, Bahía- 192 Bc 30.00N 114.25W
San Luis Obispo 176 Gf 35.17N 120.40W
San Luis Pass 186 Il 29.05N 95.08W
San Luis Peak 186 Ch 37.59N 106.56W
San Luis Potosí 176 Ig 22.09N 100.59W
San Luis Potosí [2] 190 Dd 22.30N 100.30W
San Luis Río Colorado 190 Bb 32.29N 114.48W
San Luis Valley 182 Fd 37.25N 106.00W
Sanluri 128 Ck 39.34N 8.54 E
San Manuel [Arg.] 204 Cm 37.47S 58.50W
San Manuel [Az.-U.S.] 188 Jj 32.36N 110.38W
San Marcial, Punta- 192 De 25.30N 111.00W
San Marco, Capo- 128 Hm 37.30N 13.01 E
San Marcos [3] 194 Bf 15.00N 91.55W
San Marcos [Col.] 202 Cb 8.39N 75.08W
San Marcos [Guat.] 194 Bf 14.58N 91.48W
San Marcos [Hond.] 194 Cf 14.24N 88.56W
San Marcos [Mex.] 192 Gg 20.47N 104.11W
San Marcos [Mex.] 192 Ji 16.48N 99.21W
San Marcos [Nic.] 194 Dh 11.55N 86.12W
San Marcos [Tx.-U.S.] 182 Hf 29.53N 97.57W
San Marcos, Isla- 192 Cd 27.13N 112.06W
San Marcos, Sierra de- 192 Hd 26.30N 101.55W
San Marino 128 Gg 43.55N 12.28 E
San Marino [1] 112 Hg 43.55N 12.28 E
San Martín 206 Gd 33.04S 68.28W
San Martín [3] 202 Ce 7.00S 76.50W
San Martín 192 Ab 30.30N 116.05W
San Martín 222 Qe 68.11S 67.00W
San Martín, Cerro- 192 Lh 18.19N 94.48W
San Martín, Lago- 206 Fg 48.52S 72.40W
San Martín, Río- 202 Ff 13.08S 63.43W
San Martín de los Andes 206 Ff 40.10S 71.21W
San Martín de Valdeiglesias 126 Hd 40.21N 4.24W
San Martino di Castrozza 128 Fd 46.16N 11.48 E
San Mateo [Ca.-U.S.] 188 Dh 37.35N 122.19W
San Mateo [Ven.] 196 Dh 9.45N 64.33W

Index Symbols

[1] Independent Nation
[2] State, Region
[3] District, County
[4] Municipality
[5] Colony, Dependency
Continent
Physical Region
Historical or Cultural Region
Mount, Mountain
Volcano
Hill
Mountains, Mountain Range
Hills, Escarpment
Plateau, Upland
Pass, Gap
Plain, Lowland
Delta
Salt Flat
Valley, Canyon
Crater, Cave
Karst Features
Depression
Polder
Desert, Dunes
Forest, Woods
Heath, Steppe
Oasis
Cape, Point
Coast, Beach
Cliff
Peninsula
Isthmus
Sandbank
Island
Atoll
Rock, Reef
Islands, Archipelago
Rocks, Reefs
Coral Reef
Well, Spring
Geyser
River, Stream
Waterfall, Rapids
River Mouth, Estuary
Lake
Salt Lake
Intermittent Lake
Reservoir
Swamp, Pond
Canal
Glacier
Ice Shelf, Pack Ice
Ocean
Sea
Gulf, Bay
Strait, Fjord
Lagoon
Bank
Seamount
Tablemount
Ridge
Shelf
Basin
Escarpment, Sea Scarp
Fracture
Trench, Abyss
National Park, Reserve
Point of Interest
Recreation Site
Cave, Cavern
Historic Site
Ruins
Wall, Walls
Church, Abbey
Temple
Scientific Station
Railway station
Airport
Port
Military installation
Lighthouse
Mine
Tunnel
Dam, Bridge

San-Sao

San Mateo/Sant Mateu del Maestrat	126	Md	40.28N	0.11 E
San Mateo Ixtatán	194	Bf	15.50N	91.29W
San Mateo Mountains	186	Cj	33.10N	107.20W
San Matías	204	Cc	16.22S	58.24W
San Matías, Golfo-	198	Jj	41.30S	64.15W
Sanmen (Haiyou)	152	Lf	29.08N	121.22 E
Sanmen Wan	154	Fj	29.00N	121.45 E
Sanmenxia	152	Je	34.44N	111.19 E
San Miguel [Arg.]	204	Dh	27.59S	57.36W
San Miguel [Bol.]	204	Bc	16.42S	61.01W
San Miguel [Ca.-U.S.]	188	Ei	35.45N	120.42W
San Miguel [El Sal.]	176	Kh	13.29N	88.11W
San Miguel [Pan.]	194	Hi	8.27N	78.56W
San Miguel, Golfo de-	194	Hi	8.22N	78.17W
San Miguel, Río- [Bol.]	198	Jg	13.52S	63.56W
San Miguel, Río- [Mex.]	192	Dc	29.16N	110.53W
San Miguel, Río- [Mex.]	192	Fd	26.59N	107.58W
San Miguel, Río- [S.Amer.]	204	Cd	19.25S	58.20W
San Miguel, Salinas de-	204	Bd	19.12S	60.45W
San Miguel, Volcán de-	190	Gf	13.26N	88.16W
San Miguel Bay	150	Hd	13.50N	123.10 E
San Miguel de Allende	192	Ig	20.55N	100.45W
San Miguel de Horcasitas	192	Dc	29.29N	110.45W
San Miguel del Monte	204	Cl	35.27S	58.48W
San Miguel del Padrón	194	Fb	23.05N	82.19W
San Miguel de Tucumán	200	Jh	26.49S	65.13W
San Miguel Island	188	Ei	34.02N	120.22W
San Miguel Islands	150	Ge	7.45N	118.28 E
San Miguelito	204	Bc	17.20S	63.10W
San Miguel River	186	Bg	38.23N	108.48W
San Miguel Sola de Vega	192	Ki	16.31N	96.59W
San Millán	126	Ib	42.18N	3.12W
Sanming	152	Kf	26.11N	117.37 E
San Miniato	128	Eg	43.41N	10.51 E
Sannan	156	Dd	35.04N	135.03 E
Sannār	160	Kg	13.33N	33.38 E
Sannicandro Garganico	128	Ji	41.50N	15.34 E
San Nicolás, Río- [Bol.]	204	Bc	17.08S	61.17W
San Nicolás, Río- [Mex.]	192	Gh	19.40N	105.14W
San Nicolás de los Arroyos	206	Hd	33.20S	60.13W
San Nicolás de los Garzas	192	Ie	25.45N	100.18W
San Nicolas Island	188	Fj	33.15N	119.31W
Sannikova, proliv-	138	Ib	74.30N	140.00 E
Sannio	128	Ii	41.20N	14.30 E
San'nohe	156	Ga	40.22N	141.15 E
San'nō-Tōge	156	Fc	37.06N	139.44 E
Sannūr, Wādī-	146	Dh	28.59N	31.03 E
Sanok	120	Sg	49.34N	22.13 E
Sanok-Zagórz	120	Sg	49.31N	22.17 E
San Onofre	202	Cb	9.45N	75.32W
San Pablo	142	Oh	14.04N	121.19 E
San Pablo, Punta-	192	Bd	27.15N	114.30W
San Pedro [3]	204	Dg	24.15S	56.30W
San Pedro [Arg.]	206	Jc	26.38S	54.08W
San Pedro [Arg.]	206	Hb	24.14S	64.52W
San Pedro [Arg.]	204	Ck	33.40S	59.40W
San-Pédro [I.C.]	166	De	4.44N	6.37W
San Pedro [Par.]	206	Ib	24.07S	56.59W
San Pedro, Río- [Guat.]	194	Be	17.46N	91.26W
San Pedro, Río- [Mex.]	192	Gg	21.45N	105.30W
San Pedro, Sierra de-	126	Fe	39.20N	6.35W
San Pedro Carchá	194	Bf	15.29N	90.16W
San Pedro Channel	188	Fj	33.43N	118.23W
San Pedro de Alcántara	126	Hh	36.29N	5.00W
San Pedro de Atacama	206	Gb	22.55S	68.13W
San Pedro de Lloc	202	Ce	7.26S	79.31W
San Pedro de Macorís	194	Md	18.27N	69.18W
San Pedro Mártir, Sierra de-	190	Ab	30.45N	115.13W
San Pedro Nolasco, Isla-	192	Dd	27.58N	111.25W
San Pedro Pochutla	192	Kj	15.44N	96.28W
San Pedros de las Colonias	190	Dc	25.45N	102.59W
San Pedro Sula	176	Kh	15.27N	88.02W
San Pedro Tapanatepec	192	Li	16.21N	94.12W
San Pedro Tututepec	192	Ki	16.09N	97.38W
San Pellegrino Terme	128	De	45.50N	9.40 E
San Pietro	128	Ck	39.10N	8.15 E
San Quintín	190	Ab	30.29N	115.57W
San Quintín, Bahía de-	192	Ab	30.20N	116.00W
San Rafael [Arg.]	200	Ji	34.40S	68.21W
San Rafael [Bol.]	204	Bc	16.45S	60.34W
San Rafael [Ca.-U.S.]	188	Dg	38.00N	122.31W
San Rafael [Mex.]	192	Ie	25.01N	100.33W
San Rafael [Mex.]	192	He	24.40N	102.01W
San Rafael [Ven.]	194	Lh	10.58N	71.44W
San Rafael, Cabo-	194	Md	19.01N	68.57W
San Rafael, Río-	204	Cd	18.26S	59.37W
San Rafael de Atamaica	196	Ci	7.32N	67.24W
San Rafael del Norte	194	Dg	13.12N	86.06W
San Rafael Knob	186	Jg	38.50N	110.48W
San Rafael Mountains	188	Fi	34.45N	119.50W
San Rafael River	188	Jg	38.47N	110.07W
San Ramón [Peru]	202	Cf	11.08S	75.20W
San Ramón [Ur.]	204	El	34.18S	55.58W
San Ramón, Río-	204	Bb	14.03S	61.35W
San Ramón de la Nueva Orán	206	Hb	23.08S	64.20W
San Raymundo, Arroyo-	192	Cd	26.21N	112.37W
San Remo	128	Bg	43.49N	7.46 E
Sanriku	156	Gb	39.08N	141.48 E
San Román, Cabo-	202	Ea	12.12N	70.00W
San Roque [Arg.]	204	Ci	28.34S	58.43W
San Roque [Sp.]	126	Gh	36.13N	5.24W
San Saba	186	Gk	31.12N	98.43W
Sansalé	166	Cc	11.07N	14.51W
San Salvador [Arg.]	204	Di	29.16S	57.31W
San Salvador [Arg.]	206	Id	31.37S	58.30W
San Salvador [El Sal.]	176	Kh	13.42N	89.12W
San Salvador [Par.]	204	Dg	25.51S	56.28W
San Salvador / Sant Salvador	126	Pe	39.27N	3.11 E
San Salvador (Watling)	190	Jd	24.02N	74.28W
San Salvador, Cuchilla-	204	Dk	33.56S	57.45W
San Salvador, Isla-	198	Gf	0.14S	90.45W
San Salvador, Río-	204	Ck	33.29S	58.23W
San Salvador de Jujuy	200	Jh	24.10S	65.20W
Sansanné-Mango	166	Fc	10.21N	0.28 E
San Sebastián [Col.]	194	Ji	9.13N	74.18W
San Sebastián [P.R.]	197a	Bb	18.21N	67.00W
San Sebastián / Donostia	112	Fg	43.19N	1.59W
San Sebastián, Bahía-	206	Gh	53.15S	68.23W
San Sebastián, Isla-	194	Cg	13.11N	88.26W
San Sebastián de la Gomera	162	Dd	28.06N	17.06W
Sansepolcro	128	Gg	43.34N	12.08 E
San Severo	128	Ji	41.41N	15.23 E
San Silvestre	194	Li	8.15N	70.02W
San Simeon	188	Ei	35.39N	121.11W
Sanski Most	128	Kf	44.46N	16.40 E
Santa Águeda	192	Cd	27.13N	112.20W
Santa Ana	219a	Fd	10.50S	162.28 E
Santa Ana [Arg.]	204	Eh	27.22S	55.34W
Santa Ana [Bol.]	204	Bc	16.37S	60.43W
Santa Ana [Bol.]	204	Cd	18.43S	58.44W
Santa Ana [Bol.]	202	Eg	15.31S	67.30W
Santa Ana [Ca.-U.S.]	182	De	33.43N	117.54W
Santa Ana [El Sal.]	176	Kh	13.59N	89.34W
Santa Ana [Mex.]	190	Bb	30.33N	111.07W
Santa Ana [Ven.]	196	Dh	9.19N	64.39W
Santa Ana, Río-	194	Li	9.30N	71.57W
Santa Ana, Volcán de-	174	Kh	13.50N	89.39W
Santa Bárbara [3]	194	Cf	15.10N	88.20W
Santa Barbara [Ca.-U.S.]	176	Hf	34.03N	118.15W
Santa Bárbara [Hond.]	194	Cf	14.53N	88.14W
Santa Bárbara [Mex.]	190	Cc	26.48N	105.49W
Santa Bárbara [Ven.]	194	Lj	7.47N	71.10W
Santa Bárbara, Puerto de-	126	Lb	42.30N	0.50W
Santa Bárbara, Serra de-	204	Fe	21.45S	53.23W
Santa Barbara Channel	188	Fi	34.15N	119.55W
Santa Barbara Island	188	Fj	33.23N	119.01W
Santa Catalina	219a	Fd	10.54S	162.27 E
Santa Catalina [Col.]	194	Jh	10.37N	75.33W
Santa Catalina [Ven.]	196	Fh	8.33N	61.51W
Santa Catalina, Gulf of-	188	Gj	33.20N	117.45W
Santa Catalina, Isla-	192	De	25.40N	110.45W
Santa Catalina Island	188	Fj	33.23N	118.24W
Santa Catarina	192	Ie	25.41N	100.28W
Santa Catarina [2]	206	Kc	27.00S	50.00W
Santa Catarina, Ilha de-	198	Lh	27.36S	48.30W
Santa Catarina, Sierra-	192	Fc	29.40N	107.30W
Santa Cecília	204	Gh	26.56S	50.27W
Santa Cesarea Terme	128	Mj	40.02N	18.28 E
Santa Clara [Ca.-U.S.]	188	Eh	37.21N	121.59W
Santa Clara [Cuba]	176	Lg	22.24N	79.58W
Santa Clara [Gabon]	170	Ab	0.34N	9.17 E
Santa Clara [Mex.]	192	Fc	29.17N	107.01W
Santa Clara [Ur.]	204	Ek	32.55S	54.58W
Santa Clara, Barragem do-	126	Dg	37.30N	8.20W
Santa Clara, Isla-	206	Ed	33.42S	79.00W
Santa Clara de Saguier	204	Bj	31.21S	61.50W
Santa Coloma de Farners/ Santa Coloma de Farnés	126	Oc	41.52N	2.40 E
Santa Coloma de Farnés/ Santa Coloma de Farners	126	Oc	41.52N	2.40 E
Santa Coloma de Gramenet	126	Oc	41.27N	2.13 E
Santa Coloma de Queralt	126	Nc	41.32N	1.23 E
Santa Comba	126	Da	43.02N	8.49W
Santa Croce Camerina	128	In	36.50N	14.31 E
Santa Cruz [2]	206	Gg	49.00S	70.00W
Santa Cruz [3]	202	Fg	17.30S	61.30W
Santa Cruz [Azr.]	162	Ab	39.27N	31.07W
Santa Cruz [Azr.]	162	Bb	39.05N	28.01W
Santa Cruz [Bol.]	200	Jg	17.48S	63.10W
Santa Cruz [Braz.]	204	Dd	18.32S	57.12W
Santa Cruz [Braz.]	202	Id	0.36S	49.11W
Santa Cruz [Ca.-U.S.]	188	Cd	36.58N	122.01W
Santa Cruz [Chile]	206	Fd	34.38S	71.22W
Santa Cruz [C.R.]	194	Eh	10.01N	84.02W
Santa Cruz [Phil.]	150	Hd	14.01N	121.21 E
Santa Cruz, Isla-	198	Gf	0.38S	90.23W
Santa Cruz, Isla de-	192	De	25.17N	110.43W
Santa Cruz, Río-	206	Gh	50.08S	68.20W
Santa Cruz, Serra da-	204	Jc	17.05S	45.17W
Santa Cruz Cabrália	202	Kg	16.17S	39.02W
Santa Cruz de la Palma	162	Dd	28.41N	17.45W
Santa Cruz de la Zarza	126	Ie	39.58N	3.10W
Santa Cruz del Quiché	194	Bf	15.02N	91.08W
Santa Cruz del Sur	190	Id	20.43N	78.00W
Santa Cruz de Mudela	126	If	38.38N	3.28W
Santa Cruz de Tenerife	160	Ff	28.27N	16.14W
Santa Cruz de Tenerife [3]	162	Dd	28.10N	17.20W
Santa Cruz do Rio Pardo	204	Hf	22.55S	49.37W
Santa Cruz do Sul	206	Jc	29.43S	52.26W
Santa Cruz Island	188	Fi	34.01N	119.45W
Santa Cruz Islands	208	Hf	10.45S	165.55 E
Santadi	128	Ck	39.05N	8.43 E
Santa Elena [Arg.]	206	Id	30.57S	59.48W
Santa Elena [Arg.]	204	Bm	37.21S	60.37W
Santa Elena [Ec.]	202	Bd	2.14S	80.52W
Santa Elena, Bahía de- [C.R.]	194	Eh	10.59N	85.50W
Santa Elena, Bahía de- [Ec.]	202	Bd	2.05S	80.55W
Santa Elena, Cabo-	194	Gf	10.55N	85.57W
Santa Elena de Uairén	202	Fc	4.37N	61.08W
Santa Eugenia (Ribeira)	126	Db	42.33N	9.00W
Santa Eulalia	126	Kd	40.34N	1.19W
Santa Eulalia del Río / Santa Eulària del Riu	126	Nf	38.59N	1.31 E
Santa Eulària del Riu / Santa Eulalia del Río	126	Nf	38.59N	1.31 E
Santa Fe [2]	206	Hd	31.00S	61.00W
Santa Fe [Arg.]	200	Ji	31.40S	60.40W
Santa Fé [Cuba]	194	Fc	21.45N	82.45W
Santa Fe [N.M.-U.S.]	176	If	35.42N	106.57W
Santafé [Sp.]	126	Ig	37.11N	3.43W
Santa Fé de Minas	204	Jc	16.41S	45.28W
Santa Fé do Sul	204	Ge	20.13S	50.56W
Sant'Agata di Militello	128	Il	38.04N	14.38 E
Santa Helena [Braz.]	204	Eg	24.56S	54.23W
Santa Helena [Braz.]	202	Id	2.14S	45.18W
Santa Helena de Goiás	202	Hg	17.43S	50.35W
Santa Inês	202	Id	3.39S	45.22W
Santa Inés	194	Mh	10.37N	69.18W
Santa Inés, Bahía de-	192	Dd	27.00N	111.55W
Santa Inés, Isla-	198	Ik	53.45S	72.45W
Santa Isabel [Arg.]	206	Ge	36.15S	66.56W
Santa Isabel [Arg.]	204	Bk	33.54S	61.42W
Santa Isabel [Braz.]	204	Ba	13.40S	60.44W
Santa Isabel [P.R.]	197a	Bc	17.58N	66.25W
Santa Isabel, Pico de-	166	Ge	3.35N	8.46 E
Santa Isabel Island	208	Ge	8.00S	159.00 E
Santa Izabel do Ivaí	204	Ff	22.58S	53.14W
Santa Juliana	204	Id	19.19S	47.32W
Santa Lucia [Arg.]	206	Gd	31.32S	68.29W
Santa Lucía [Ur.]	204	Dl	34.27S	56.24W
Santa Lucía, Esteros del-	204	Ci	28.15S	58.20W
Santa Lucía, Río- [Arg.]	204	Ci	29.05S	59.13W
Santa Lucía, Río- [Ur.]	204	Dl	34.48S	56.22W
Santa Lucia Cotzumalguapa	194	Bf	14.20N	91.01W
Santa Lucia Range	182	Cd	36.00N	121.20W
Santa Luzia	162	Cf	16.46N	24.45W
Santa Luzia, Ribeirão-	204	Fe	21.31S	53.53W
Santa Margarita	204	Bi	28.18S	61.33W
Santa Margarita, Isla de-	190	Bd	24.27N	111.50W
Santa Margherita Ligure	128	Df	44.20N	9.12 E
Santa Maria	158	Ee	36.58N	25.06W
Santa María	190	Cb	31.00N	107.14W
Santa María [Arg.]	206	Gc	26.41S	66.02W
Santa María [Bol.]	204	Cd	17.08S	61.01W
Santa Maria [Braz.]	200	Kh	29.41S	53.48W
Santa Maria [Ca.-U.S.]	182	Ce	34.57N	120.26W
Santa María, Bahía de-	192	Ee	25.05N	108.10W
Santa Maria, Cabo de- [Ang.]	158	Ij	13.25S	12.32 E
Santa Maria, Cabo de- [Port.]	126	Eh	36.58N	7.54W
Santa María, Cape-	194	Jb	23.41N	75.19W
Santa María, Cayo-	194	Hb	22.40N	79.00W
Santa María, Isla-	202a	Ab	1.15S	90.25W
Santa María, Isla-	206	Fe	37.02S	73.33W
Santa María, Laguna de-	192	Fb	31.10N	107.15W
Santa Maria, Rio- [Braz.]	204	Ee	21.50S	54.53W
Santa Maria, Rio- [Braz.]	204	Ib	14.19S	46.49W
Santa María, Río- [Mex.]	192	Jg	21.37N	99.15W
Santa María, Río- [Pan.]	194	Gi	8.06N	80.29W
Santa María Asunción Tlaxiaco	192	Ki	17.16N	97.41W
Santa Maria Capua Vetere	128	Ii	41.05N	14.15 E
Santa Maria da Vitória	204	Ja	13.24S	44.12W
Santa María de Cuevas	192	Fd	27.55N	106.23W
Santa María de Ipire	196	Dh	8.49N	65.19W
Santa María del Oro	192	Ge	25.56N	105.22W
Santa María del Río	192	Ig	21.48N	100.45W
Santa Maria di Leuca, Capo-	110	Hh	39.47N	18.22 E
Santa María la Real de Nieva	126	Hc	41.04N	4.24W
Santa María Zacatepec	192	Ki	16.46N	98.00W
Santa Marinella	128	Fh	42.02N	11.51 E
Santa Marta	200	Id	11.15N	74.13W
Santa Marta, Cabo de-	170	Be	13.52S	12.25 E
Santa Marta, Ría de-	126	Ea	43.42N	7.51W
Santa Marta, Serra de- → Divisões, Serra das-	202	Hg	16.40S	50.50W
Santa Marta Grande, Cabo de-	204	Hi	28.38S	48.45W
Santa Monica	182	De	34.01N	118.30W
Santan	150	Gg	0.03S	117.28 E
Santana	204	Ja	12.59S	44.03W
Santana, Coxilha de-	204	Ej	31.15S	55.15W
Santana, Rio-	204	Gd	19.43S	51.02W
Santana da Boa Vista	204	Fj	30.52S	53.07W
Santana do Livramento	206	Id	30.53S	55.31W
Santander [2]	202	Db	6.35N	73.20W
Santander [3]	126	Ia	43.10N	4.00W
Santander [Col.]	202	Cc	3.01N	76.29W
Santander [Phil.]	150	He	9.25N	123.20 E
Santander [Sp.]	112	Fg	43.28N	3.48W
Santander, Bahía de-	126	Ia	43.27N	3.48W
Santander Jiménez	190	Ed	24.13N	98.28W
Sant'Andrea	128	Lj	40.05N	17.55 E
Sant'Antioco	128	Ck	39.04N	8.27 E
Sant'Antioco	110	Gh	39.05N	8.25 E
Sant Antoni, Cap-/San Antonio, Cabo de-	126	Mf	38.48N	0.12 E
Sant Antoni de Portmany / San Antonio Abad	126	Nf	38.58N	1.18 E
Santanyi / Santañy	126	Pe	39.22N	3.07 E
Santañy / Santanyi	126	Pe	39.22N	3.07 E
Santa Olalla	126	Hd	40.01N	4.26W
Santa Olalla del Cala	126	Fg	37.54N	6.13W
Santa Paula	188	Fi	34.21N	119.04W
Santa Pola	126	Lf	38.11N	0.33W
Sant'Arcangelo	128	Kj	40.15N	16.16 E
Santarcangelo di Romagna	128	Gf	44.04N	12.27 E
Santarém [2]	126	De	39.15N	8.35W
Santarém [Braz.]	200	Kf	2.26S	54.42W
Santarém [Port.]	126	De	39.14N	8.41W
Santaren Channel	190	Id	24.00N	79.30W
Santa Rita [Braz.]	204	Cc	16.15S	59.00W
Santa Rita [Braz.]	202	Le	7.13S	35.02W
Santa Rita [Col.]	202	Ec	4.55N	68.20W
Santa Rita [Guam]	220c	Bb	13.23N	144.40 E
Santa Rita [Hond.]	194	Df	15.09N	87.53W
Santa Rita [Ven.]	196	Ch	8.08N	66.16W
Santa Rita [Ven.]	194	Lh	10.32N	71.32W
Santa Rita do Araguaia	204	Fc	17.20S	53.12W
Santa Rosa [3]	194	Bf	14.10N	90.18W
Santa Rosa [Arg.]	206	Gd	31.31S	65.04W
Santa Rosa [Arg.]	200	Ji	36.40S	64.15W
Santa Rosa [Braz.]	206	Jc	27.52S	54.29W
Santa Rosa [Ca.-U.S.]	182	Cd	38.26N	122.43W
Santa Rosa [Ec.]	202	Cd	3.27S	79.58W
Santa Rosa [N.M.-U.S.]	182	Ge	34.57N	104.41W
Santa Rosa [Par.]	204	Dh	26.52S	56.49W
Santa Rosa [Ven.]	194	Mi	8.26N	69.42W
Santa Rosa [Ven.]	196	Dh	9.38N	64.18W
Santa Rosa, Mount-	220c	Ba	13.32N	144.55 E
Santa Rosa de Copán	194	Cf	14.47N	88.46W
Santa Rosa de la Roca	204	Bc	16.04S	61.32W
Santa Rosa Island	188	Ej	33.58N	120.06W
Santa Rosalía	196	Bh	9.02N	69.01W
Santa Rosalía	176	Hg	27.19N	112.17W
Santa Rosalía, Punta-	192	Bc	28.40N	114.20W
Santa Rosa Range	188	Gf	41.00N	117.40W
Santa Rosa Wash	188	Ij	33.10N	112.05W
Šantarskije ostrova = Shantar Islands (EN)	140	Pd	55.00N	137.36 E
Santas Creus/Santes Creus	126	Nc	41.19N	1.18 E
Santa Sylvina	206	Hc	27.49S	61.09W
Santa Teresa [Arg.]	204	Bk	33.26S	60.47W
Santa Teresa [Mex.]	192	Ke	25.17N	97.51W
Santa Teresa [Peru]	202	Df	13.01S	72.39W
Santa Teresa, Rio-	204	Ha	12.40S	48.47W
Santa Teresa di Riva	128	Jm	37.57N	15.22 E
Santa Teresa Gallura	128	Di	41.14N	9.11 E
Santa Teresita	204	Dm	36.32S	56.41W
Santa Vitória	204	Gd	18.50S	50.08W
Santa Vitória do Palmar	206	Jd	33.31S	53.21W
Sant Boi de Llobregat/San Baudilio de Llobregat	126	Oc	41.21N	2.03 E
Sant Carles de la Ràpita/ San Carlos de la Rápita	126	Md	40.37N	0.36 E
Santee River	182	Le	33.14N	79.28W
Santeh	146	Ld	36.10N	46.32 E
San Telmo	192	Ab	30.58N	116.06W
San Telmo, Bahía de-	192	Hh	18.45N	103.40W
San Telmo, Punta-	190	De	18.19N	103.30W
Santerno	128	Ff	44.34N	11.58 E
Santerre	122	Ie	49.55N	2.30 E
Santes Creus/Santas Creus	126	Nc	41.19N	1.18 E
Sant'Eufemia, Golfo di-	128	Kl	38.50N	16.05 E
Sant'Eufemia Lamezia, Lamezia Terme-	128	Kl	38.55N	16.15 E
Sant Feliu de Guixols	126	Pc	41.47N	3.02 E
Sant Feliu de Llobregat / San Feliú de Llobregat	126	Oc	41.23N	2.03 E
Sant Francesc de Formentera / San Francisco Javier	126	Nf	38.42N	1.25 E
Santhià	128	Ce	45.22N	8.10 E
Santiago [2]	206	Fd	33.30S	70.50W
Santiago [Bol.]*	202	Gg	18.19S	59.34W
Santiago [Bol.]	204	Bd	19.22S	60.51W
Santiago [Braz.]	206	Jc	29.11S	54.53W
Santiago [Chile]	200	Ii	33.27S	70.40W
Santiago [Dom.Rep.]	176	Lh	19.27N	70.42W
Santiago [Mex.]	192	Cd	27.32N	112.49W
Santiago [Mex.]	192	Ie	25.25N	100.09W
Santiago [Pan.]	176	Ki	8.05N	80.59W
Santiago [Par.]	204	Dh	27.09S	56.47W
Santiago, Cerro-	194	Gi	8.33N	81.44W
Santiago, Rio-	202	Cd	4.27S	77.36W
Santiago, Río de-	192	Ge	25.11N	105.26W
Santiago, Serranía-	204	Cd	18.25S	59.25W
Santiago de Chuco	202	Ce	8.09S	78.11W
Santiago de Compostela	126	Db	42.53N	8.33W
Santiago de Cuba	176	Lg	20.01N	75.49W
Santiago de Cuba [3]	194	Ic	20.10N	76.10W
Santiago de la Ribera	126	Lg	37.48N	0.48W
Santiago del Estero	200	Jh	27.50S	64.15W
Santiago del Estero [2]	206	Hc	28.00S	63.30W
Santiago de Papasquiaro	192	Ge	25.03N	105.25W
Santiago do Cacém	126	Df	38.01N	8.42W
Santiago Ixcuintla	190	Cd	21.49N	105.13W
Santiago Mountains	186	El	29.40N	103.15W
Santiago Pinotepa Nacional	190	Ee	16.19N	98.01W
Santiaguillo, Isla-	192	Lh	19.05N	95.50W
Santiaguillo, Laguna de-	192	Ge	24.50N	104.50W
Santiam River	188	Dd	44.42N	123.55W
Santillana	126	Ha	43.23N	4.06W
San Timoteo	194	Li	9.48N	71.04W
Säntis	128	Dc	47.15N	9.20 E
Santisteban del Puerto	126	If	38.15N	3.12W
Sant Jordi, Golf de- / San Jorge, Golfo de-	126	Md	40.53N	1.00 E
Sant Mateu del Maestrat/ San Mateo	126	Md	40.28N	0.11 E
Santo, Ile-	208	Hf	15.15S	166.50 E
Santo Anastácio	204	Ge	21.58S	51.39W
Santo André	204	If	23.40S	46.31W
Santo Ângelo	206	Jc	28.18S	54.16W
Santo Antão	158	Eg	17.05N	25.10W
Santo Antônio	206	Jc	26.03S	53.12W
Santo Antonio	166	Ge	1.39N	7.25 E
Santo Antônio de Jesus	202	Kf	12.58S	39.16W
Santo Antônio do Içá	202	Ed	3.05S	67.57W
Santo Antônio do Leverger	202	Gg	15.52S	56.05W
Santo Corazón	200	Gg	17.59S	58.51W
Santo Corazón, Río-	204	Cc	17.23S	58.23W
Santo Domingo [Cuba]	194	Gb	22.35N	80.15W
Santo Domingo [Dom.Rep.]	176	Mh	18.28N	69.54W
Santo Domingo [Mex.]	192	Bc	28.12N	114.02W
Santo Domingo [Mex.]	192	Bb	30.43N	115.56W
Santo Domingo [Mex.]	192	If	23.20N	101.44W
Santo Domingo [Nic.]	194	Eg	12.16N	85.05W
Santo Domingo, Cay-	194	Jc	21.42N	75.46W
Santo Domingo, Punta-	192	Cd	26.20N	112.40W
Santo Domingo, Río- [Mex.]	192	Kh	18.10N	96.08W
Santo Domingo, Río- [Ven.]	194	Mi	8.01N	69.33W
Santo Domingo de la Calzada	126	Jb	42.26N	2.57W
Santo Domingo de los Colorados	202	Cd	0.15S	79.10W
Santo Domingo de Silos	126	Ic	41.58N	3.25W
Santo Domingo Pueblo	186	Ci	35.31N	106.22W
San Tomé	196	Dh	8.58N	64.08W
Santoña	126	Ia	43.27N	3.27W
Santos	200	Lh	23.57S	46.20W
Santos, Sierra de los-	126	Gf	38.15N	5.20W
Santos Dumont	204	Ke	21.28S	43.34W
Santos Unzué	204	Bl	35.45S	60.51W
Santo Tirso	126	Dc	41.21N	8.28W
Santo Tomás [Bol.]	204	Cc	17.46S	58.55W
Santo Tomás [Mex.]	192	Ab	31.33N	116.24W
Santo Tomás [Nic.]	194	Eg	12.04N	85.05W
Santo Tomás, Punta-	192	Ab	31.34N	116.42W
Santo Tomé	206	Ic	28.33S	56.03W
Sant Salvador / San Salvador	126	Pe	39.27N	3.11 E
Santu Lussurgiu	128	Cj	40.08N	8.39 E
Santurce-Antiguo / Santurtzi	126	Ia	43.20N	3.02W
Santurtzi / Santurce-Antiguo	126	Ia	43.20N	3.02W
Sant Vicent del Raspeig / San Vicente de Raspeig	126	Lf	38.24N	0.31 E
Sanuki-Sanmyaku	156	Cd	34.05N	134.00 E
San Valentín, Cerro-	198	Ij	46.36S	73.20W
San Vicente [Arg.]	204	Cl	35.01S	58.25W
San Vicente [Mex.]	192	Ab	31.20N	116.15W
San Vicente [Phil.]	150	Hc	18.30N	122.09 E
San Vicente, Sierra de-	126	Hd	40.10N	4.45W
San Vicente de Cañete	202	Cf	13.05S	79.24W
San Vicente de la Barquera	126	Ha	43.26N	4.24W
San Vicente del Caguán	202	Dc	2.07N	74.46W
San Vicente de Raspeig / Sant Vicent del Raspeig	126	Lf	38.24N	0.31 E
San Vincente	190	Gf	13.38N	88.48W
San Vincenzo	128	Eg	43.06N	10.32 E
San Vito [C.R.]	194	Fi	8.50N	82.58W
San Vito [It.]	128	Dk	39.26N	9.32 E
San Vito, Capo-	128	Gl	38.11N	12.44 E
Sanya→Yaxian	142	Mh	18.27N	109.28 E
Sanyati	172	Dc	16.49S	28.45 E
San'yō	156	Bd	34.03N	131.10 E
Sanza	128	Jj	40.15N	15.33 E
Sanza Pombo	170	Cd	7.20S	16.00 E
São Bartolomeu, Rio-	204	Ic	16.48S	47.55W
São Benedito	202	Jd	4.03S	40.53W
São Bento	202	Jd	2.42S	44.50W
São Bento do Sul	204	Hh	26.15S	49.23W
São Borja	206	Ic	28.39S	56.00W
São Brás de Alportel	126	Eg	37.09N	7.53W
São Caetano do Sul	206	Kb	23.36S	46.34W
São Carlos [Braz.]	206	Kb	22.01S	47.54W
São Carlos [Braz.]	204	Ej	33.47N	55.30W
São Carlos [Braz.]	204	Ej	30.11S	55.30W
São Domingos [Braz.]	204	Ia	13.24S	46.19W
São Domingos [Gui.Bis.]	166	Bc	12.24N	16.12W
São Domingos, Rio- [Braz.]	204	Gd	19.13S	50.44W
São Domingos, Rio- [Braz.]	204	Ib	15.37S	46.14W
São Domingos, Rio- [Braz.]	204	Ia	13.24S	47.12W
São Domingos, Rio- [Braz.]	204	Fe	20.03S	53.13W
São Felix	202	Hf	11.36S	50.39W
São Félix do Xingu	202	He	6.38S	51.59W
São Filipe	162	Cf	14.54N	24.31W
São Francisco [Braz.]	204	Dd	18.45S	56.55W
São Francisco [Braz.]	202	Jg	15.57S	44.52W
São Francisco, Ilha de-	198	Lh	26.18S	48.37W
São Francisco, Rio-	198	Mg	10.30S	36.24W
São Francisco de Assis	204	Ei	29.33S	55.08W
São Francisco de Paula	204	Gi	29.27S	50.35W
São Francisco de Sales	204	Hd	19.52S	49.46W
São Francisco do Sul	206	Kc	26.14S	48.39W
São Gabriel	206	Jd	30.20S	54.19W
São Gonçalo	202	Jh	22.51S	43.04W
São Gonçalo, Canal de-	204	Fk	32.10S	52.38W
São Gonçalo do Abaeté	204	Jd	18.20S	45.49W
São Gonçalo do Sapucaí	204	Je	21.54S	45.36W
São Gotardo	204	Id	19.19S	46.03W
Sao Hill	170	Gd	8.20S	35.12 E
São Jerônimo, Serra de-	204	Ec	16.20S	54.55W
São João da Barra	202	Jh	21.38S	41.03W
São João da Boa Vista	204	Ie	21.58S	46.47W
São João d'Aliança	204	Ib	14.42S	47.31W
São João da Madeira	126	Dd	40.54N	8.30W
São João da Ponte	204	Kb	15.56S	44.01W
São João del Rei	202	Jh	21.09S	44.16W
São João de Meriti	204	Kf	22.48S	43.22W
São João do Araguaia	202	Ie	5.23S	48.46W
São João do Piauí	202	Je	8.21S	42.15W
São João dos Patos	202	Je	6.30S	43.42W
São João do Triunfo	204	Gg	25.41S	50.18W
São Joaquim	206	Kc	28.18S	49.56W
São Joaquim da Barra	204	Ie	20.35S	47.53W
São Jorge	158	Ee	38.38N	28.03W
São José da Serra	204	Eb	15.40S	55.18W
São José do Cerrito	204	Gh	27.40S	50.35W
São José do Norte	204	Fk	32.01S	52.03W
São José do Rio Pardo	206	Kb	21.36S	46.54W
São José do Rio Prêto	200	Lh	20.48S	49.23W
São José dos Campos	206	Kb	23.11S	45.53W
São José dos Dourados, Rio-	204	Ge	20.22S	51.21W
Saolat, Buku-	150	If	0.45N	127.59 E
São Leopoldo	206	Jc	29.46S	51.09W
São Lourenço	204	Ec	16.32S	55.02W
São Lourenço, Pantanal de-	202	Gg	17.45S	56.15W
São Lourenço, Rio-	202	Gg	17.53S	57.27W
São Lourenço, Serra de-	204	Ec	17.30S	54.50W
São Lourenço do Sul	206	Jd	31.22S	51.58W
São Luís	200	Lf	2.31S	44.16W
São Luís Gonzaga	206	Jc	28.24S	54.58W
São Mamede, Serra de-	126	Ee	39.19N	7.19W
São Manuel	204	Hf	22.44S	48.34W
São Manuel, Rio-	198	Kf	7.21S	58.03W
São Marcos	204	Gi	28.58S	51.04W
São Marcos, Baía de-	198	Lf	2.30S	44.30W
São Marcos, Rio-	204	Id	18.15S	47.37W
São Mateus	202	Kg	18.44S	39.51W
São Mateus, Rio-	204	Ia	13.48S	46.54W
São Mateus do Sul	204	Gg	25.52S	50.23W
São Miguel	158	Ee	37.47N	25.30W
São Miguel, Rio-	204	Ic	16.03S	46.07W
São Miguel do Araguaia	204	Ga	13.19S	50.13W
São Miguel d'Oeste	204	Fh	26.45S	53.34W

Index Symbols

[1] Independent Nation
[2] State, Region
[3] District, County
[4] Municipality
[5] Colony, Dependency
Continent
Physical Region
Historical or Cultural Region
Mount, Mountain
Volcano
Hill
Mountains, Mountain Range
Hills, Escarpment
Plateau, Upland
Pass, Gap
Plain, Lowland
Delta
Salt Flat
Valley, Canyon
Crater, Cave
Karst Features
Depression
Polder
Desert, Dunes
Forest, Woods
Heath, Steppe
Oasis
Cape, Point
Coast, Beach
Cliff
Peninsula
Isthmus
Sandbank
Island
Atoll
Rock, Reef
Islands, Archipelago
Rocks, Reefs
Coral Reef
Well, Spring
Geyser
River, Stream
Waterfall, Rapids
River Mouth, Estuary
Lake
Salt Lake
Intermittent Lake
Reservoir
Swamp, Pond
Canal
Glacier
Ice Shelf, Pack Ice
Ocean
Sea
Gulf, Bay
Strait, Fjord
Lagoon
Bank
Seamount
Tablemount
Ridge
Shelf
Basin
Escarpment, Sea Scarp
Fracture
Trench, Abyss
National Park, Reserve
Point of Interest
Recreation Site
Cave, Cavern
Historic Site
Ruins
Wall, Walls
Church, Abbey
Temple
Scientific Station
Railway station
Airport
Port
Military installation
Lighthouse
Mine
Tunnel
Dam, Bridge

Name	Page	Grid	Lat.	Long.
Saona, Isla-	194	Md	18.09N	68.40W
Saône	110	Gf	45.44N	4.50 E
Saône-et-Loire [3]	122	Kh	46.40N	4.30 E
Saonek	150	Jg	0.28S	130.47 E
São Nicolau	204	Ei	28.11S	55.16W
São Nicolau	158	Eg	16.35N	24.15W
São Patricio, Rio-	204	Hb	15.02S	49.15W
São Paulo	200	Lh	23.32S	46.37W
São Paulo [2]	206	Kb	22.00S	49.00W
São Paulo de Olivença	202	Ed	3.27S	68.48W
São Pedro, Ribeirão-	204	Ic	16.54S	46.32W
São Pedro do Sul [Braz.]	204	Ei	29.37S	54.10W
São Pedro do Sul [Port.]	126	Dd	40.45N	8.04W
São Pedro e São Paulo, Penedos de-	198	Ne	0.56N	29.22W
São Raimundo Nonato	202	Je	9.01S	42.42W
São Romão [Braz.]	202	Ig	16.22S	45.04W
São Romão [Braz.]	204	Ed	18.33S	54.27W
São Roque	204	De	21.43S	57.46W
São Roque, Cabo de-	198	Mf	5.29S	35.16W
São Roque, Serra de-	204	Ib	14.40S	46.50W
São Sebastião	204	Jf	23.48S	45.25W
São Sebastião, Ilha de-	198	Lh	23.50S	45.18W
São Sebastião, Ponta-	158	Kk	22.05S	35.24 E
São Sebastião da Boa Vista	202	Id	1.42S	49.31W
São Sebastião do Paraiso	202	Ih	20.55S	47.00W
São Sepé	204	Fj	30.10S	53.34W
São Simão	202	Hg	18.56S	50.30W
São Tiago	158	Eg	15.05N	23.40W
São Tomé	160	Hh	0.20N	6.44 E
São Tomé	158	Hh	0.12N	6.39 E
São Tomé, Cabo de-	202	Jh	22.00S	40.59W
Sao Tome and Principe (EN) = São Tomé e Principe [1]	160	Hh	1.00N	7.00 E
São Tomé e Principe = Sao Tome and Principe (EN) [1]	160	Hh	1.00N	7.00 E
Saoura	162	Gd	27.50N	2.50W
Saoura	158	Gf	28.48N	0.50W
São Vicente	158	Eg	16.50N	25.00W
São Vicente [Braz.]	206	Kb	23.58S	46.23W
São Vicente [Braz.]	204	Ia	13.38S	46.31W
São Vicente, Cabo de-	110	Fh	37.01N	9.00W
São Xavier, Serra de-	204	Ei	29.15S	54.15W
Sápai	130	Ih	41.02N	25.42 E
Sapanca	130	Ni	40.41N	30.16 E
Sapanca Gölü	130	Ni	40.43N	30.15 E
Sape [Braz.]	202	Ke	7.06S	35.13W
Sape [Indon.]	150	Gh	8.34S	118.59 E
Sape, Selat-	150	Gh	8.39S	119.18 E
Sapele	166	Gd	5.55N	5.42 E
Sapelo Island	184	Gj	31.28N	81.15W
Şaphane	130	Mj	39.01N	29.14 E
Şaphane Daği	130	Mj	39.03N	29.16 E
Sapiéntza	130	Em	36.45N	21.42 E
Šapkina	134	Fc	66.44N	52.25 E
Sapo, Serrania del-	194	Hi	7.50N	78.17W
Sa Pobla / La Puebla	126	Pe	39.46N	3.01 E
Saponé	166	Ec	12.03N	1.36W
Sapopema	204	Gf	23.55S	50.35W
Saposoa	202	Ce	6.56S	76.48W
Sapphire Mountains	188	Ic	46.20N	113.45W
Sapporo	142	Qe	43.03N	141.21 E
Sapri	128	Jj	40.04N	15.38 E
Sapucaí, Rio-	204	He	20.08S	48.27W
Sapulpa	182	Hd	36.00N	96.06W
Sapulut	150	Gf	4.42N	116.29 E
Sāqand	146	Pf	32.33N	55.12 E
Sāqiyat Sīdī Yūsuf	128	Cn	36.13N	8.21 E
Saqqez	144	Gb	36.14N	46.16 E
Sarāb	144	Gb	37.56N	47.32 E
Saraburi	148	Kf	14.30N	100.55 E
Saraf Doungous	168	Bc	12.33N	19.42 E
Sarafjagān	146	Ne	34.28N	50.28 E
Saragmatha = Everest, Mount- (EN)	140	Kg	27.59N	86.56 E
Saragossa (EN) = Zaragoza [Sp.]	112	Fg	41.38N	0.53W
Sarai	114	Jj	53.44N	41.03 E
Sarajevo	112	Hg	43.50N	18.25 E
Saraji Mine	212	Jd	22.30S	148.20 E
Sarakhs	144	Jb	36.32N	61.11 E
Sarakiná	130	Hk	38.40N	24.37 E
Šarakol	134	Kj	52.03N	62.47 E
Saraktaš	136	Fe	51.47N	56.18 E
Saraland	184	Cj	30.49N	88.02W
Saramati	148	Jc	25.44N	95.02 E
Saran	136	Hf	49.46N	72.52 E
Saran, Gunung-	150	Fg	0.25S	111.18 E
Saranac Lake	184	Jc	44.20N	74.08W
Saranci	130	Gg	42.43N	23.46 E
Saranda	130	Dj	39.52N	20.00 E
Sarandi	204	Fh	27.56S	52.55W
Sarandí, Arroyo-	204	Cj	30.13S	59.19W
Sarandí del Yí	204	Ek	33.21S	55.38W
Sarandí Grande	204	Dk	33.44S	56.20W
Šaranga	114	Lh	57.12N	46.34 E
Sarangani Bay	150	Ie	5.57N	125.11 E
Sarangani Islands	150	Ie	5.25N	125.26 E
Saranley	168	Ge	2.23N	42.16 E
Saransk	112	Ke	54.11N	45.11 E
Sarapul	112	Ld	56.28N	53.48 E
Sarapulskoje	138	Ig	48.50N	135.58 E
Sarare	194	Mi	9.47N	69.10W
Sararé, Rio-	204	Cb	14.51S	59.58W
Sarasota	182	Kf	27.20N	82.34W
Sarata	132	Ff	46.01N	29.41 E
Sărăţel	130	Hb	47.03N	24.25 E
Saratoga	188	Lf	41.27N	106.48W
Saratoga Springs	182	Mc	43.04N	73.47W
Saratok	150	Ff	1.24N	111.31 E
Saratov	112	Ke	51.34N	46.02 E
Saratov Reservoir (EN) = Saratovskoje vodohranilišče	110	Ke	52.50N	47.50 E
Saratovskaja oblast [3]	136	Ee	51.30N	47.00 E
Saratovskoje vodohranilišče = Saratov Reservoir (EN)	110	Ke	52.50N	47.50 E
Saravan	148	Le	15.43N	106.25 E
Sarawak [2]	150	Ff	2.30N	113.30 E
Saray	146	Bb	41.26N	27.55 E
Sarāyā	146	Fe	35.47N	35.58 E
Saraya	166	Cc	12.50N	11.45W
Sarayköy	146	Cd	37.55N	28.56 E
Sarbāz	144	Jd	26.39N	61.15 E
Sárbogárd	120	Oj	46.53N	18.38 E
Sarca	128	Ee	45.52N	10.52 E
Sarcelle, Passe de la-	219b	Cf	22.28S	167.13 E
Sarcelles	124	Ef	49.00N	2.23 E
Sarcidano	128	Dk	39.40N	9.15 E
Sardara	128	Ck	39.37N	8.49 E
Sar Dasht [Iran]	146	Kd	36.09N	45.28 E
Sar Dasht [Iran]	146	Mf	32.32N	48.52 E
Sardegna [2]	128	Cj	40.00N	9.00 E
Sardegna = Sardinia (EN)	110	Gh	40.00N	9.00 E
Sardegna, Mar di-	128	Bk	40.00N	7.30 E
Sardes	130	Lk	38.29N	28.03 E
Sardinal	194	Eh	10.31N	85.39W
Sardinata	202	Db	8.07N	72.48W
Sardinia (EN) = Sardegna	110	Gh	40.00N	9.00 E
Sardis Lake	186	Li	34.27N	89.43W
Sarektjåkkå	114	Dc	67.25N	17.46 E
Sarema/Saaremaa	110	Id	58.25N	22.30 E
Sar-e Pol	144	Kb	36.14N	65.55 E
Sar Eskand Khān	146	Ld	37.29N	47.04 E
Sar-e Yazd	146	Pg	31.36N	54.35 E
Sargasso Sea	174	Mg	29.00N	65.00W
Sargatskoje	136	Hd	55.37N	73.30 E
Sargodha	148	Eb	32.05N	72.40 E
Šargun	135	Fe	38.31N	67.59 E
Sarh	160	Ih	9.09N	18.23 E
Sarhro, Jebel-	162	Fc	31.00N	6.00W
Sāri	142	Hf	36.34N	53.04 E
Saria	130	Kn	35.50N	27.15 E
Sariçakaya	146	Db	40.02N	30.31 E
Sarigan Island	208	Fc	16.42N	145.47 E
Sarigöl	146	Cc	38.14N	28.43 E
Sarıkamış	146	Jb	40.15N	42.35 E
Sarıkaya	146	Fc	39.48N	35.24 E
Sarikei	150	Ff	2.07N	111.31 E
Sariköy	130	Ki	40.12N	27.36 E
Sarina	212	Jd	21.26S	149.13 E
Sarine	128	Bd	46.59N	7.16 E
Sariñena	126	Lc	41.48N	0.10W
Sarıoğlan	146	Fc	39.05N	35.59 E
Sarīr	164	Dd	27.30N	22.30 E
Sariwŏn	152	Md	38.30N	125.45 E
Sarıyer	146	Cb	41.10N	29.03 E
Sarj, Jabal as-	128	Do	35.56N	9.32 E
Šarja	112	Kd	58.24N	45.30 E
Sark	118	Kl	49.26N	2.21W
Sarkad	120	Rj	46.45N	21.23 E
Sarkand	136	Hf	45.25N	79.54 E
Şarkikaraağaç	146	Dc	38.04N	31.23 E
Sarkışla	146	Gc	39.21N	36.26 E
Šarkovščina	116	Li	55.22N	27.32 E
Sarköy	146	Bb	40.37N	27.06 E
Sarlat-la-Canéda	122	Hj	44.53N	1.13 E
Šarlyk	132	Sc	52.54N	54.42 E
Sarmi	210	Ee	1.51S	138.44 E
Sarmiento	200	Jj	45.35S	69.05W
Sarmizegetuza	130	Fd	45.31N	22.47 E
Särna	116	Ec	61.41N	13.08 E
Sarnen	128	Cd	46.54N	8.15 E
Sărnena Gora	130	Ig	42.35N	25.30 E
Sarnia	180	Jh	42.58N	82.23W
Sarny	136	Ce	51.21N	26.36 E
Saroako	150	Hg	2.31S	121.22 E
Sarolangun	150	Dg	2.18S	102.42 E
Saroma	156a	Ca	44.02N	143.45 E
Saroma-Ko	154	Qb	44.10N	143.40 E
Šaromy	133	Kf	54.23N	158.14 E
Saronic Gulf (EN) = Saronikós Kólpos	130	Gl	37.45N	23.30 E
Saronikós Kólpos = Saronic Gulf (EN)	130	Gl	37.45N	23.30 E
Saronno	128	De	45.38N	9.02 E
Saros, Gulf of- (EN) = Saros Körfezi	146	Bb	40.30N	26.20 E
Saros Körfezi = Saros, Gulf of- (EN)	146	Bb	40.30N	26.20 E
Sárospatak	120	Rh	48.19N	21.35 E
Sar Passage	220a	Ac	7.12N	134.23 E
Sarpinskije ozera	132	Nf	47.45N	45.00 E
Šar Planina	130	Dg	42.05N	20.50 E
Sarpsborg	116	De	59.17N	11.07 E
Sarqaq	179	Gd	70.00N	51.39W
Sarrabus	128	Dk	39.20N	9.30 E
Sarralbe	122	Ne	49.00N	7.01 E
Sarrāţ, Wādī-	128	Co	35.59N	8.23 E
Sarre	120	Cg	49.42N	6.34 E
Sarrebourg	122	Nf	48.44N	7.03 E
Sarreguemines	122	Ne	49.06N	7.03 E
Sarre-Union	124	Jf	48.56N	7.05 E
Sarria	126	Eb	42.47N	7.24W
Sarstún, Río-	194	Cf	15.54N	88.54W
Sartang	138	Ic	67.30N	133.20 E
Sartène	122a	Ab	41.37N	8.59 E
Sarthe [3]	122	Gf	48.00N	0.05 E
Sarthe	122	Fg	47.32N	0.31W
Sartu → Anda	154	Ha	46.35N	125.00 E
Sarufutsu	156a	Ca	45.18N	142.13 E
Saru-Gawa	156a	Cb	42.30N	142.00 E
Saruhanlı	146	Bc	38.44N	27.34 E
Sarukaishi-Gawa	156	Gb	39.25N	141.08 E
Sārūq	146	Me	34.25N	49.30 E
Saruyama-Misaki	156	Ec	37.18N	136.43 E
Sárvár	120	Mi	47.15N	16.56 E
Sarvestān	146	Oh	29.16N	53.13 E
Sárviz	120	Oj	46.22N	18.48 E
Saryagač	135	Gd	41.28N	69.11 E
Sarybarak	135	Hc	43.24N	71.29 E
Sary-Bulak	135	Jd	41.54N	75.47 E
Saryč, mys-	110	Jg	44.23N	33.45 E
Saryg-Sep	138	Ef	51.30N	95.40 E
Sary-Išikotrau	135	Kb	45.15N	76.25 E
Sarykamys	136	Ff	46.00N	53.41 E
Sarykamyšskoje, ozero-	136	Fg	41.58N	57.58 E
Sarykolski hrebet	135	Je	38.30N	74.15 E
Šaryn-Gol	152	Ib	49.20N	106.30 E
Saryozek	136	Hg	44.22N	77.54 E
Saryšagan	136	Hf	46.05N	73.38 E
Saryšiganak, zaliv-	135	Ca	46.35N	61.25 E
Sarysu	140	Ie	45.12N	66.36 E
Sary-Taš	136	Hh	39.44N	73.16 E
Saryžaz	135	Lc	42.54N	79.31 E
Sarzana	128	Df	44.07N	9.58 E
Sasabe	192	Db	31.27N	111.31W
Sasabeneh	168	Gd	8.00N	43.44 E
Sasa-ga-Mine	156	Ce	33.49N	133.17 E
Sasago-Tōge	156	Fd	35.37N	138.45 E
Sasamungga	219a	Cb	7.02S	156.47 E
Sasarām	148	Gd	24.57N	84.02 E
Sasari, Mount-	219a	Dc	8.11S	159.33 E
Sascut	130	Kc	46.11N	27.04 E
Sásd	120	Oj	46.15N	18.07 E
Sasebo	152	Me	33.12N	129.44 E
Saseginaga, Lac-	184	Hb	47.05N	78.34W
Saskatchewan [2]	180	Gf	54.00N	106.00W
Saskatchewan	174	Jd	53.12N	99.16W
Saskatoon	176	Id	52.07N	106.38W
Saskylah	138	Gb	72.00N	114.00 E
Sasluya, Cerro-	194	Eg	13.45N	85.03W
Sasovo	136	Ee	54.22N	41.54 E
Sassafras Mountain	184	Fh	35.03N	82.48W
Sassandra	160	Gh	4.57N	6.05W
Sassandra [3]	166	Dd	5.20N	6.10W
Sassandra	158	Gh	4.58N	6.05W
Sassari	112	Gg	40.43N	8.34 E
Sassenberg	124	Kc	51.59N	8.03 E
Sassenheim	124	Gb	52.14N	4.33 E
Sassetot-le-Mauconduit	124	Ce	49.48N	0.32 E
Şaßnitz	120	Jb	54.31N	13.39 E
Sasso Marconi	128	Ff	44.24N	11.15 E
Sassuolo	128	Ef	44.33N	10.47 E
Sastobe	135	Hc	42.34N	70.03 E
Sastre	204	Bj	31.45S	61.50W
Sasyk, ozero- (Kunduk)	132	Fg	45.45N	29.40 E
Sasykkol, ozero-	136	If	46.40N	81.00 E
Sata	156	Bf	31.04N	130.42 E
Sata Cape- (EN) = Sata-Misaki	140	Pf	30.59N	130.37 E
Satakunta	116	Jc	61.30N	23.00 E
sa Talaiassa / Atalayasa	126	Nf	38.55N	1.15 E
Sata-Misaki = Sata, Cape- (EN)	140	Pf	30.59N	130.37 E
Satan, Pointe de-	219b	Dd	19.00S	169.17 E
Sātāra	148	Ee	17.41N	73.59 E
Sataua	221c	Aa	13.28S	172.40W
Satawal Island	208	Fd	7.21N	147.02 E
Satawan Atoll	208	Gd	5.25N	153.35 E
Satellite Bay	180	Fa	77.25N	117.15W
Säter	114	Df	60.21N	15.45 E
Satihaure	114	Ec	67.30N	18.45 E
Satipo	202	Df	11.16S	74.37W
Satīt	168	Fc	14.20N	35.50 E
Satka	136	Fd	55.03N	59.01 E
Šatki	114	Ki	55.11N	44.08 E
Sātmāla Range	148	Fe	19.30N	78.45 E
Satna	148	Gd	24.35N	80.50 E
Šator	128	Kf	44.09N	16.37 E
Sátoraljaújhely	120	Rh	48.24N	21.40 E
Sātpura Range	140	Jg	21.25N	76.10 E
Satsuma-Hantō	156	Bf	31.25N	130.25 E
Satsunai-Gawa	156a	Cb	42.55N	143.15 E
Satsunan-Shotō	152	Mf	29.00N	130.00 E
Sattahip	148	Kf	12.39N	100.54 E
Satulung	130	Gb	47.34N	23.26 E
Satu Mare	130	Fb	47.48N	22.53 E
Satu Mare [2]	130	Fb	47.46N	22.56 E
Satun	148	Kg	6.39N	100.03 E
Saturniná ou Papagaio, Rio-	204	Ca	13.55S	58.18W
Saualpe	128	Id	46.50N	14.40 E
Sauce	206	Ic	30.00S	58.46W
Sauce Corto, Arroyo-	204	Bm	36.55S	61.48W
Sauceda Mountains	188	Ij	32.30N	112.30W
Sauce Grande, Río-	204	Bn	38.59S	61.07W
Saucillo	190	Cc	28.01N	105.17W
Sauda	116	Be	59.39N	6.20 E
Saudade, Serra da- [Braz.]	204	Jd	19.20S	45.50W
Saudade, Serra da- [Braz.]	204	Fc	16.20S	53.53W
Sauðárkrókur	114a	Bb	65.45N	19.39W
Saudi Arabia (EN) = Al 'Arabīyah As-Su'ūdīyah [1]	142	Gg	25.00N	45.00 E
Sauer [Eur.]	120	Cg	49.44N	6.31 E
Sauer [Eur.]	124	Kf	48.55N	8.10 E
Sauerland	120	De	51.10N	8.00 E
Sauêruiná, Rio-	202	Gf	12.00S	58.40W
Sauga jõgi	116	Kf	58.19N	24.25 E
Saugatuck	184	Dd	42.40N	86.12W
Saugues	122	Jj	44.58N	3.33 E
Sauk Centre	186	Id	45.44N	94.57W
Sauk Rapids	186	Id	45.34N	94.09W
Saül	202	Hc	3.37N	53.12W
Šaulder	135	Gc	42.47N	68.24 E
Sauldre	122	Hg	47.16N	1.30 E
Saulieu	122	Kg	47.16N	4.14 E
Saulkrasti/Saulkrasty	114	Fh	57.17N	24.29 E
Saulkrasty/Saulkrasti	114	Fh	57.17N	24.29 E
Saulnois	124	If	48.52N	6.30 E
Sault	122	Lj	44.05N	5.25 E
Sault Sainte-Marie [Mi.-U.S.]	182	Kb	46.30N	84.21W
Sault Sainte-Marie [Ont.-Can.]	176	Ke	46.31N	84.20W
Saulx	122	Kf	48.45N	4.35 E
Saumarez Reefs	208	Gg	21.50S	153.40 E
Saumâtre, Étang-	194	Kd	18.35N	72.00W
Saumlaki	150	Jh	7.57S	131.19 E
Saumur	122	Fg	47.16N	0.05W
Saunders	222	Ad	57.47S	26.27W
Saunders Coast	222	Mf	77.45S	150.00W
Saurimo	160	Ji	9.38S	20.24 E
Sauro	128	Kj	40.18N	16.21 E
Sautar	170	Ce	11.09S	18.25 E
Sauteurs	197p	Bb	12.14N	61.38W
Sauveterre, Causse de-	122	Jj	44.22N	3.17 E
Sauveterre-de-Guyenne	122	Fj	44.42N	0.05W
Sauvo/Sagu	116	Jd	60.21N	22.42 E
Sauwald	128	Hb	48.28N	13.40 E
Sava	110	Ig	44.50N	20.28 E
Savage River	212	Jh	41.33S	145.09 E
Savai'i Island	208	Jf	13.35S	172.25W
Savala	132	Ld	51.06N	41.29 E
Savalou	166	Fd	7.56N	1.58 E
Savanes [3]	166	Fc	10.30N	0.30 E
Savan Island	197n	Bb	12.48N	61.12W
Savanna	186	Ke	42.05N	90.08W
Savannah	174	Kf	32.02N	80.53W
Savannah [Ga.-U.S.]	176	Kf	32.04N	81.05W
Savannah [Tn.-U.S.]	184	Ch	35.14N	88.14W
Savannah Beach	184	Gi	32.01N	80.51W
Savannakhét	142	Mh	16.33N	104.45 E
Savanna-la-Mar	190	Ie	18.13N	78.08W
Savanne	186	Kb	48.59N	90.12W
Savannes Bay	197k	Bb	13.45N	60.56W
Savant Lake	180	If	50.15N	90.42W
Savant Lake	186	Ka	50.30N	90.20W
Savaştepe	146	Bc	39.22N	27.40 E
Savdirī	168	Dc	14.25N	29.05 E
Savè	160	Hh	8.02N	2.29 E
Save [Afr.]	158	Kk	21.00S	35.02 E
Save [Fr.]	122	Hk	43.47N	1.17 E
Saveån	116	Dg	57.43N	11.59 E
Sāveh	144	Hb	35.01N	50.20 E
Săveni	130	Jb	47.57N	26.52 E
Saverdun	122	Hk	43.14N	1.35 E
Saverne	122	Nf	48.44N	7.22 E
Savigliano	128	Bf	44.38N	7.40 E
Savigsivik	179	Fc	76.00N	64.45W
Săvineşti	130	Jc	46.51N	26.28 E
Savinjske Alpe	128	Id	46.20N	14.30 E
Savinski	136	Ec	62.57N	40.13 E
Savio	128	Gf	44.19N	12.20 E
Săvîrşin	130	Fc	46.01N	22.14 E
Savitaipale	114	Gf	61.12N	27.42 E
Šavnik	130	Cg	42.57N	19.06 E
Savo	116	Lb	62.30N	27.30 E
Savo	219a	Dc	9.08S	159.48 E
Savoie [3]	122	Mi	45.30N	6.25 E
Savoie = Savoy (EN)	122	Mi	45.24N	6.30 E
Savona	128	Cf	44.17N	8.30 E
Savonlinna/Nyslott	114	Gf	61.52N	28.53 E
Savonranta	114	Ge	62.11N	29.12 E
Savonselkä	116	Lb	62.05N	27.20 E
Savoonga	178	Ed	63.42N	170.27W
Savoy (EN) = Savoie	122	Mi	45.24N	6.30 E
Şavşat	146	Jb	41.15N	42.20 E
Savsjö	114	Dh	57.25N	14.40 E
Savudrija, Rt-	128	He	45.30N	13.31 E
Savukoski	114	Gc	67.17N	28.10 E
Savur	146	Id	37.33N	40.53 E
Savusavu	216	Ec	17.34S	178.15 E
Savusavu Bay	219d	Bb	16.45S	179.15 E
Savu Sea (EN) = Sawu, Laut-	140	Oj	9.40S	122.00 E
Savuto	128	Kk	39.02N	16.06 E
Sawahlunto	150	Dg	0.40S	100.47 E
Sawai Mādhopur	148	Fc	25.59N	76.22 E
Sawākin	160	Kg	19.07N	37.20 E
Sawākin, Jazā'ir- = Suakin Archipelago (EN)	158	Kg	19.07N	37.20 E
Sawankhalok	148	Je	17.19N	99.54 E
Sawara	156	Gd	35.53N	140.29 E
Sawasaki-Hana	154	Of	37.47N	138.12 E
Sawatch Range	186	Cg	39.10N	106.25W
Sawbā = Sobat (EN)	158	Kh	9.45N	31.45 E
Sawbridgeworth	124	Cc	51.49N	0.09 E
Sawdā', Jabal as-	164	Cd	28.40N	15.30 E
Sawfajjīn	164	Cc	31.54N	15.07 E
Sawhāj = Sohag (EN)	160	Kf	26.33N	31.42 E
Sawkanah	164	Cd	29.04N	15.47 E
Sawla	166	Ed	9.17N	2.25W
Sawqirah	144	If	18.10N	56.30 E
Şawqirah, Ghubbat-	144	If	18.35N	56.45 E
Sawtooth Mountains	188	He	44.00N	115.00W
Sawu, Kepulauan-	150	Hi	10.30S	121.50 E
Sawu, Laut- = Savu Sea (EN)	140	Oj	9.40S	122.00 E
Sawu, Pulau-	140	Ok	10.30S	121.54 E
Şawwān, Ard as-	146	Gg	31.00N	37.00 E
Sax	126	Lf	38.32N	0.49W
Saxby River	212	Ic	18.25S	140.53 E
Saxmundham	124	Db	52.13N	1.30 E
Saxony (EN) = Sachsen	120	Ie	51.20N	13.30 E
Say	166	Fc	13.07N	2.21 E
Sayabec	184	Na	48.36N	67.37W
Saya de Malha Bank (EN)	158	Nj	11.00S	61.00 E
Sayago	126	Fc	41.20N	6.10W
Sayan	202	Cf	11.08S	77.12W
Sayang, Pulau-	150	If	0.18N	129.54 E
Sayaxché	194	Be	16.31N	90.10W
Saydā	144	Ec	33.33N	35.22 E
Sayḩūt	142	Hh	15.12N	51.14 E
Saylorville Lake	186	Jf	41.48N	93.46W
Säynätsalo	116	Kb	62.08N	25.46 E
Sayō	156	Dd	35.01N	134.22 E
Sayram Hu	152	Dc	44.35N	81.10 E
Sayula	192	Hh	19.52N	103.37W
Saywūn	168	Hb	15.56N	48.47 E
Sazanit, Ishull i-	130	Ci	40.30N	19.16 E
Sázava	120	Kg	49.52N	14.54 E
Sázava	120	Kg	49.53N	14.24 E
Sbaa	162	Gd	28.13N	0.10W
Sbisseb	126	Pi	35.42N	3.51 E
Sbruč	132	Ee	48.32N	26.25 E
Scaër	122	Cf	48.02N	3.42W
Scafell Pike	118	Jg	54.27N	3.12W
Scalea	128	Jk	39.49N	15.47 E
Scalone, Passo dello-	128	Jk	39.38N	15.57 E
Scammon, Laguna-	192	Bd	27.45N	114.15W
Scammon Bay	178	Fd	61.53N	165.38W
Scandinavia (EN)	110	Hc	65.00N	16.00 E
Scandinavian Highland (EN)	110	Hc	64.00N	13.00 E
Scanno	128	Hi	41.54N	13.53 E
Scansano	128	Fh	42.41N	11.20 E
Scapa Flow	118	Jc	58.54N	3.05W
Scapegoat Mountain	188	Ic	47.19N	112.50W
Ščapino	138	Ke	55.15N	159.25 E
Ščara	132	Dc	53.27N	24.44 E
Scaramia, Capo-	128	In	36.47N	14.29 E
Scarba	118	He	56.11N	5.42W
Scarborough [Eng.-U.K.]	118	Mg	54.17N	0.24W
Scarborough [Trin.]	202	Fa	11.11N	60.44W
Scarp	118	Fc	58.05N	7.05W
Scarpe	122	Jd	50.30N	3.27 E
Ščastje	132	Ke	48.44N	39.14 E
Sceaux	124	Ef	48.47N	2.17 E
Šćedro	128	Kg	43.05N	16.42 E
Ščekino	132	Jb	54.01N	37.29 E
Ščekurja	134	Jd	64.15N	60.52 E
Ščeljajur	136	Fb	65.21N	53.25 E
Scenic	186	Ee	43.47N	102.30W
Ščerbakty	136	He	52.29N	78.14 E
Schaalsee	120	Gc	53.35N	10.57 E
Schaarbeek/Schaerbeek	124	Gd	50.51N	4.23 E
Schaerbeek/Schaarbeek	124	Gd	50.51N	4.23 E
Schaffhausen	128	Cc	47.40N	8.40 E
Schaffhausen [2]	128	Cc	47.45N	8.40 E
Schagen	124	Gb	52.48N	4.48 E
Schärding	128	Hb	48.27N	13.26 E
Scharmützelsee	120	Kd	52.15N	14.03 E
Scharnhörn	120	Ec	53.57N	8.25 E
Scheeßel	124	La	53.10N	9.29 E
Schefferville	176	Md	54.47N	64.49W
Scheibbs	128	Jb	48.00N	15.10 E
Schelde	122	Kc	51.22N	4.15 E
Schelde (EN) = Escaut	122	Kc	51.22N	4.15 E
Schell Creek Range	182	Ed	39.10N	114.40W
Schenectady	182	Mc	42.48N	73.57W
Scheno	168	Fd	9.35N	39.25 E
Scherfede, Warburg-	124	Lc	51.32N	9.02 E
Scherpenheuvel-Zichem	124	Gd	50.59N	4.59 E
Scheveningen, 's-Gravenhage-	122	Kb	52.06N	4.18 E
Schiedam	122	Kc	51.55N	4.24 E
Schiermonnikoog	122	Ma	53.28N	6.15 E
Schifferstadt	124	Ke	49.23N	8.22 E
Schiffgraben	120	Hd	52.02N	11.10 E
Schifflange	124	Ie	49.30N	6.01 E
Schijndel	124	Hc	51.37N	5.28 E
Schiltigheim	122	Nf	48.36N	7.45 E
Schio	128	Fe	45.43N	11.21 E
Schipbeek	124	Ib	52.15N	6.14 E
Schladming	128	Hc	47.23N	13.41 E
Schlei	120	Fb	54.35N	9.50 E
Schleiden	120	Cf	50.32N	6.28 E
Schleiz	120	Hf	50.35N	11.49 E
Schleswig	120	Fb	54.31N	9.33 E
Schleswig-Holstein [2]	120	Gb	54.00N	10.30 E
Schlitz	120	Ff	50.40N	9.34 E
Schloß Holte-Stukenbrock	124	Kc	51.55N	8.38 E
Schloß Neuhaus, Paderborn-	124	Kc	51.44N	8.42 E
Schluchsee	120	Ei	47.49N	8.10 E
Schlüchtern	120	Ff	50.21N	9.31 E
Schmallenberg	124	Kc	51.09N	8.18 E
Schmallenberg-Bödefeld-Freiheit	124	Kc	51.15N	8.24 E
Schmallenberg-Oberkirchen	124	Kc	51.09N	8.18 E
Schmelz	124	Ie	49.26N	6.51 E
Schmida	128	Kb	48.20N	16.14 E
Schneeberg	120	If	50.36N	12.38 E
Schneeberg [Aus.]	128	Jc	47.46N	15.52 E
Schneeberg [Ger.]	120	Hf	50.00N	11.51 E
Schneifel	124	Id	50.16N	6.23 E
Schoberpaß	128	Ic	47.27N	14.40 E
Schoberspitze	128	Ic	47.17N	14.09 E
Schœlcher	197h	Ab	14.37N	61.06W
Schönebeck	120	Hd	52.01N	11.45 E
Schönecken	124	Id	50.10N	6.28 E
Schongau	120	Gi	47.49N	10.54 E
Schöningen	120	Gd	52.08N	10.57 E
Schoondijke	124	Fc	51.21N	3.33 E
Schoonebeek	124	Ib	52.40N	6.53 E
Schoonhoven	124	Gc	51.55N	4.51 E
Schorfheide	120	Jd	52.55N	13.35 E
Schoten	124	Gc	51.15N	4.30 E
Schotten	124	Ld	50.30N	9.08 E
Schouten Islands	208	Fe	3.30S	144.30 E
Schouwen	122	Jc	51.43N	3.50 E
Schramberg	120	Eh	48.14N	8.23 E
Schreiber	180	Ig	48.48N	87.15W
Schriesheim	124	Ke	49.29N	8.40 E
Schrobenhausen	120	Hh	48.33N	11.16 E
Schruns	128	Dc	47.04N	9.55 E
Schuls / Scuol	128	Ed	46.48N	10.17 E
Schultz Lake	180	Hd	64.45N	97.30W
Schurz	188	Fg	38.58N	118.46W
Schussen	120	Fi	47.37N	9.32 E
Schüttorf	124	Jb	52.19N	7.14 E
Schwabach	120	Hg	49.20N	11.02 E
Schwaben = Swabia (EN)	120	Gh	48.20N	10.30 E
Schwäbisch-Bayerisches Alpenvorland = Swabian-Bavarian Plateau (EN)	110	Hf	48.15N	10.30 E
Schwäbische Alb = Swabian Jura (EN)	110	Gf	48.25N	9.30 E
Schwäbisch Gmünd	120	Fh	48.48N	9.47 E
Schwäbisch Hall	120	Fg	49.06N	9.44 E
Schwalbach (Saar)	124	Ie	49.18N	6.49 E
Schwalm	120	Ff	50.45N	9.25 E
Schwalm	124	Lc	51.07N	9.24 E
Schwalmstadt	120	Ff	50.55N	9.12 E

Index Symbols

[1] Independent Nation
[2] State, Region
[3] District, County
[4] Municipality
[5] Colony, Dependency
Continent
Physical Region
Historical or Cultural Region
Mount, Mountain
Volcano
Hill
Mountains, Mountain Range
Hills, Escarpment
Plateau, Upland
Pass, Gap
Plain, Lowland
Delta
Salt Flat
Valley, Canyon
Crater, Cave
Karst Features
Depression
Polder
Desert, Dunes
Forest, Woods
Heath, Steppe
Oasis
Cape, Point
Coast, Beach
Cliff
Peninsula
Isthmus
Sandbank
Island
Atoll
Rock, Reef
Islands, Archipelago
Rocks, Reefs
Coral Reef
Well, Spring
Geyser
River, Stream
Waterfall, Rapids
River Mouth, Estuary
Lake
Salt Lake
Intermittent Lake
Reservoir
Swamp, Pond
Canal
Glacier
Ice Shelf, Pack Ice
Ocean
Sea
Gulf, Bay
Strait, Fjord
Lagoon
Bank
Seamount
Tablemount
Ridge
Shelf
Basin
Escarpment, Sea Scarp
Fracture
Trench, Abyss
National Park, Reserve
Point of Interest
Recreation Site
Cave, Cavern
Historic Site
Ruins
Wall, Walls
Church, Abbey
Temple
Scientific Station
Railway station
Airport
Port
Military installation
Lighthouse
Mine
Tunnel
Dam, Bridge

Index Symbols

[1] Independent Nation
[2] State, Region
[3] District, County
[4] Municipality
[5] Colony, Dependency
Continent
Physical Region

Historical or Cultural Region
Mount, Mountain
Volcano
Hill
Mountains, Mountain Range
Hills, Escarpment
Plateau, Upland

Pass, Gap
Plain, Lowland
Delta
Salt Flat
Valley, Canyon
Crater, Cave
Karst Features

Depression
Polder
Cliff
Desert, Dunes
Forest, Woods
Heath, Steppe
Oasis
Cape, Point

Coast, Beach
Peninsula
Isthmus
Sandbank
Island
Islands, Archipelago
Atoll

Rock, Reef
Rocks, Reefs
Coral Reef
Well, Spring
Geyser
River, Stream

Waterfall, Rapids
River Mouth, Estuary
Lake
Salt Lake
Intermittent Lake
Reservoir
Swamp, Pond

Canal
Glacier
Ice Shelf, Pack Ice
Ocean
Sea
Gulf, Bay
Strait, Fjord

Lagoon
Bank
Seamount
Tablemount
Ridge
Shelf
Basin

Escarpment, Sea Scarp
Fracture
Trench, Abyss
National Park, Reserve
Point of Interest
Recreation Site
Cave, Cavern

Historic Site
Ruins
Wall, Walls
Church, Abbey
Temple
Scientific Station
Railway station

Airport
Port
Military installation
Lighthouse
Mine
Tunnel
Dam, Bridge

Index Symbols

[1] Independent Nation	Historical or Cultural Region	Pass, Gap
[2] State, Region	Mount, Mountain	Plain, Lowland
[3] District, County	Volcano	Delta
[4] Municipality	Hill	Salt Flat
[5] Colony, Dependency	Mountains, Mountain Range	Valley, Canyon
[6] Continent	Hills, Escarpment	Crater, Cave
[7] Physical Region	Plateau, Upland	Karst Features

Depression	Coast, Beach	Rock, Reef
Polder	Cliff	River Mouth, Estuary
Desert, Dunes	Peninsula	Lake
Forest, Woods	Isthmus	Salt Lake
Heath, Steppe	Sandbank	Intermittent Lake
Oasis	Island	Reservoir
Cape, Point	Atoll	Swamp, Pond

Waterfall, Rapids	Canal	Lagoon
River, Stream	Glacier	Bank
Rocks, Reefs	Ice Shelf, Pack Ice	Seamount
Coral Reef	Ocean	Tablemount
Well, Spring	Sea	Ridge
Geyser	Gulf, Bay	Shelf
Islands, Archipelago	Strait, Fjord	Basin

Escarpment, Sea Scarp	Historic Site	Airport
Fracture	Church, Abbey	Port
Trench, Abyss	Temple	Wall, Walls
National Park, Reserve	Scientific Station	Lighthouse
Point of Interest	Railway station	Mine
Recreation Site		Tunnel
Scientific Station		Dam, Bridge
Cave, Cavern		

Shirakawa [Jap.]	156	Ec	36.17N	136.53 E
Shirane-San [Jap.] ▲	156	Fd	35.40N	138.13 E
Shirane-San [Jap.] ▲	152	Od	36.48N	139.22 E
Shirane-San [Jap.] ▲	156	Fc	36.38N	138.32 E
Shiranuka	154	Rc	42.57N	144.05 E
Shiraoi	154	Pc	42.31N	141.16 E
Shirase Coast ⌇	222	Mf	78.30S	156.00W
Shirataka	156	Gb	38.11N	140.06 E
Shirataki	156a	Cb	43.53N	143.09 E
Shīrāz	142	Hg	29.36N	52.32 E
Shirbīn	146	Dg	31.11N	31.32 E
Shire ◥	158	Kj	17.42S	35.19 E
Shiren	154	Id	41.54N	126.34 E
Shiretoko-Dake ▲	156a	Da	44.15N	145.14 E
Shiretoko-Hantō ▰	156a	Da	44.00N	145.00 E
Shiretoko-Misaki ►	152	Qc	44.21N	145.20 E
Shīrgāh	146	Od	36.17N	52.54 E
Shiribetsu-Gawa ◥	156a	Bb	42.52N	140.21 E
Shiriha-Misaki ►	156a	Db	42.56N	144.45 E
Shirikishinai	156a	Bc	41.48N	141.05 E
Shīrīn ◥	146	Qi	27.10N	56.41 E
Shīrīn sū	146	Me	35.29N	48.27 E
Shiriya-Zaki ►	152	Pc	41.26N	141.28 E
Shīr Kūh ▲	140	Hf	31.37N	54.04 E
Shirley Mountains ⛰	188	Le	42.15N	106.30W
Shiroishi	154	Pe	38.00N	140.37 E
Shirone	156	Fc	37.46N	139.00 E
Shirotori	156	Ed	35.53N	136.52 E
Shirouma-Dake ▲	156	Ec	36.45N	137.46 E
Shirshov Ridge (EN) ⋀	138	Me	57.30N	171.00 E
Shīrvān	144	Ib	37.24N	57.55 E
Shīrvān	146	Lf	33.33N	46.49 E
Shirwan Mazīn	146	Kd	37.03N	44.10 E
Shishaldin Volcano △	174	Cd	54.45N	163.57W
Shishi-Jima ◆	156	Be	32.17N	130.15 E
Shishmaref	178	Fc	66.14N	166.09W
Shishou	152	Jf	29.42N	112.23 E
Shitai (Qili)	154	Di	30.12N	117.28 E
Shitara	156	Ed	35.05N	137.34 E
Shithāthah	146	Jf	32.33N	43.29 E
Shitou Shan ▲	152	Ma	51.02N	125.12 E
Shivwits Plateau ▬	188	Ih	36.10N	113.40W
Shiwa	154	Pe	39.33N	141.35 E
Shiwan Dashan ⛰	152	Ig	21.45N	107.35 E
Shiwa Ngandu	170	Fe	11.12S	31.43 E
Shiwpuri	148	Fc	25.26N	77.39 E
Shixian	154	Jc	43.05N	129.46 E
Shiyan	152	Je	32.34N	110.48 E
Shiyang He ◥	152	Hd	39.00N	103.25 E
Shizilu → Junan	154	Eg	35.10N	118.50 E
Shizugawa	156	Gb	38.40N	141.28 E
Shizui	154	Ic	43.03N	126.09 E
Shizuishan (Dawukou)	152	Id	39.03N	106.24 E
Shizukuishi	156	Gb	39.42N	140.59 E
Shizunai	154	Qc	42.20N	142.22 E
Shizunai-Gawa ◥	156a	Cb	42.20N	142.22 E
Shizuoka	142	Pf	34.58N	138.23 E
Shizuoka Ken [2]	154	Og	35.00N	138.25 E
Shkodra = Scutari (EN)	112	Hg	42.05N	19.30 E
Shkodrës, Liqen i-=Scutari, Lake- (EN) ≈	110	Hg	42.10N	19.20 E
Shkumbini ◥	130	Ch	41.01N	19.26 E
Shoal Lake	186	Fa	50.26N	100.34W
Shoal Lake ≈	186	Ib	49.32N	95.00W
Shoal Lakes ≈	186	Ha	50.20N	97.40W
Shōbara	154	Lg	34.51N	133.01 E
Shodo-Shima ◆	156	Dd	34.30N	134.15 E
Shō-Gawa ◥	156	Ec	36.47N	137.04 E
Shokanbetsu-Dake ▲	156a	Bb	43.43N	141.31 E
Shokotsu-Gawa ◥	156a	Ca	44.23N	143.17 E
Sholāpur → Solāpur	142	Jh	17.41N	75.55 E
Shoqān	146	Qd	37.20N	56.58 E
Shoranūr	148	Ff	10.46N	76.17 E
Shoreham-by-Sea	118	Mk	50.49N	0.16W
Shortland Islands ◈	214	Fi	6.55S	155.53 E
Shosambetsu	156a	Ba	44.32N	141.46 E
Shoshone	188	He	42.56N	114.24W
Shoshone Mountains ⛰	182	Dd	39.15N	117.25W
Shoshone Peak ▲	188	Gh	36.56N	116.16W
Shoshone River ◥	188	Kd	44.52N	108.11W
Shoshong	172	Dd	23.02S	26.31 E
Shoshoni	188	Ke	43.14N	108.07W
Shotor Khūn ▲	144	Jc	34.20N	64.55 E
Shouchang	154	Ej	29.23N	119.12 E
Shouguang	154	Ef	36.53N	118.44 E
Shouxian (Shouyang)	154	Dh	32.35N	116.47 E
Shouyang → Shouxian	154	Dh	32.35N	116.47 E
Shōwa	156	Gb	39.51N	140.03 E
Show Low	188	Ji	34.15N	110.02W
Shqiperia=Albania (EN) [1]	112	Hg	41.00N	20.00 E
Shreveport	176	Jf	32.30N	93.45W
Shrewsbury	118	Ki	52.43N	2.45W
Shropshire [3]	118	Ki	52.40N	2.50W
Shuangcheng	152	Mb	45.21N	126.17 E
Shuangjiang → Tongdao	152	If	26.14N	109.45 E
Shuangliao	152	Lc	43.30N	123.30 E
Shuangyang	152	Mc	43.31N	125.28 E
Shuangyashan	142	Pe	46.37N	131.10 E
Shucheng	154	Di	31.28N	116.57 E
Shufu	152	Cd	39.27N	75.52 E
Shuguri Falls ⇊	170	Gd	8.31S	37.23 E
Shu He ◥	154	Eg	34.07N	118.30 E
Shuicheng	152	Hf	26.34N	104.52 E
Shuiding → Huocheng	152	Dc	44.03N	80.49 E
Shuiji → Laixi	154	Ff	36.52N	120.31 E
Shuijiahu → Changfeng	154	Dh	32.29N	117.10 E
Shuikou → Jianghua	152	Jg	24.58N	111.56 E
Shuiye	154	Cf	36.08N	114.06 E
Shuizhai → Xiangcheng	154	Ch	33.27N	114.53 E
Shūl ◥	146	Ng	30.10N	51.38 E
Shulan	152	Mc	44.26N	126.55 E
Shule	152	Cd	39.25N	76.06 E
Shule He ◥	140	Le	40.20N	92.50 E
Shulu (Xinji)	154	Cf	37.56N	115.14 E
Shumagin Islands ◈	178	He	55.07N	159.45W
Shumarinai-Ko ≈	156a	Ca	44.20N	142.13 E
Shunayn, Sabkhat- ≊	164	Dc	30.10N	21.00 E
Shungnak	178	Hc	66.53N	157.02W
Shunyi	154	Dd	40.09N	116.38 E
Shuolong	152	Ig	22.51N	106.55 E
Shuoxian	152	Jd	39.18N	112.25 E
Shūr [Iran] ◥	146	Oh	28.12N	52.09 E
Shūr [Iran] ◥	146	Oh	28.33N	53.12 E
Shūr [Iran] ◥	146	Ne	35.09N	51.30 E
Shūr [Iran] ◥	146	Pi	26.59N	55.47 E
Shurāb	144	Ic	33.07N	55.18 E
Shūr Āb ◥	146	Pg	31.45N	55.15 E
Shurugwi	172	Dc	19.40S	30.00 E
Shūsf	144	Jc	31.48N	60.01 E
Shūsh	146	Mf	32.12N	48.17 E
Shūsh = Susa (EN) ⁙	146	Mf	32.12N	48.17 E
Shushica ◥	130	Ci	40.34N	19.34 E
Shūshtar	144	Gc	32.03N	48.51 E
Shuswap Lake ≈	188	Fa	50.57N	119.15W
Shūt ◥	146	Oe	34.44N	52.53 E
Shuwak	168	Fc	14.23N	35.52 E
Shuyang	152	Ke	34.01N	118.52 E
Shuzenji	156	Fd	34.58N	138.55 E
Shwebo	148	Jd	22.34N	95.42 E
Shwell ◥	148	Jd	23.56N	96.17 E
Shyok ◥	148	Fa	35.13N	75.53 E
Sia	150	Jh	6.49S	134.19 E
Siagne ◥	122	Mk	43.32N	6.57 E
Siāh Band ▲	144	Jc	32.25N	62.35 E
Sīah-Chashmeh	146	Kc	39.04N	44.23 E
Sīāh-Kūh ⛰	146	Oe	34.38N	52.16 E
Siak ◥	150	Df	1.13N	102.09 E
Sialkot	142	Jf	32.30N	74.31 E
Sianów	120	Mb	54.15N	16.16 E
Siantan, Pulau- ◆	150	Ef	3.10N	106.15 E
Siargao ◆	150	Ie	9.53N	126.02 E
Šiaškotan, ostrov- ◆	140	Re	48.49N	154.06 E
Siátista	130	Ei	40.16N	21.33 E
Siau, Pulau- ◆	150	If	2.42N	125.24 E
Šiauliai	112	Id	55.53N	23.19 E
Šiauliai/Šjauljaj	112	Id	55.53N	23.19 E
Siavonga	170	Ef	16.32S	28.43 E
Siazan	136	Eg	41.04N	49.06 E
Sibā'ī, Jabal as- ▲	164	Fd	25.43N	34.09 E
Sibaj	136	Fe	52.42N	58.39 E
Sibari, Cassano allo Ionio-	128	Kk	39.45N	16.27 E
Sibasa	172	Ed	22.56S	30.29 E
Šibenik	128	Jg	43.44N	15.53 E
Siberimanua	150	Cg	2.09S	99.34 E
Siberut, Pulau- ◆	140	Lj	1.20S	98.55 E
Siberut, Selat- ⇌	150	Cg	0.42S	98.35 E
Sibi	148	Dc	29.33N	67.53 E
Sibigo	150	Cf	2.51N	95.55 E
Sibillini, Monti- ⛰	128	Hh	42.55N	13.15 E
Sibircatajaha ◥	134	Lb	69.05N	64.43 E
Sibircevo	138	Ih	44.16N	132.20 E
Sibirjakova, ostrov- ◆	138	Cb	72.50N	79.00 E
Sibiti	170	Bc	3.41S	13.21 E
Sibiu	112	If	45.48N	24.09 E
Sibiu [2]	130	Hd	45.46N	24.12 E
Sibolga	142	Li	1.45N	98.48 E
Sibsāgar	148	Ic	26.59N	94.38 E
Sibu	142	Ni	2.18N	111.49 E
Sibuguey Bay ◗	150	He	7.30N	122.40 E
Sibut	160	Ih	5.44N	19.05 E
Sibutu Islands ◈	150	Gf	4.45N	119.20 E
Sibutu Passage ⇌	150	Gf	4.56N	119.36 E
Sibuyan ◆	150	Hd	12.25N	122.34 E
Sibuyan Sea ▒	150	Hd	12.50N	122.40 E
Siby	166	Dc	12.22N	8.22W
Sibyllenstein ▲	120	Ke	51.12N	14.05 E
Sicani, Monti- ⛰	128	Hm	37.40N	13.15 E
Sicasica	202	Eg	17.22S	67.45W
Si Chon	148	Jg	9.00N	99.56 E
Sichuan Pendi ⊠	140	Mf	30.01N	105.00 E
Sichuan Sheng (Ssu-ch'uan Sheng)=Szechwan (EN) [2]	152	He	30.00N	103.00 E
Sicilia [2]	128	Im	37.45N	14.15 E
Sicilia = Sicily (EN) ◆	110	Hh	37.30N	14.00 E
Sicilia, Canale di-=Sicily, Strait of- (EN) ⇌	110	Hh	37.20N	11.20 E
Sicilia, Mar di- ▒	128	Gn	36.30N	13.00 E
Sicily (EN) = Sicilia ◆	110	Hh	37.30N	14.00 E
Sicily, Strait of- (EN)= Sicilia, Canale di- ⇌	110	Hh	37.20N	11.20 E
Sicily, Strait of- (EN)= Tūnis, Canal de- ⇌	110	Hh	37.20N	11.20 E
Sico Tinto, Río- ◥	194	Ef	15.58N	84.58W
Sicuani	200	Ig	14.15S	71.15W
Šid	130	Cd	45.08N	19.14 E
Sidamo [3]	168	Fd	5.48N	38.50 E
Siddipet	148	Fe	18.06N	78.51 E
Side ⁙	146	Dd	36.46N	31.22 E
Sidéradougou	166	Ec	10.40N	4.15W
Siderno	128	Kl	38.16N	16.18 E
Siders/Sierre	128	Bd	46.17N	7.32 E
Šiderty	136	He	51.40N	74.50 E
Šiderty ◥	136	He	52.32N	74.50 E
Sidheros, Ákra- ►	130	Jn	35.19N	26.19 E
Sidhirókastron	130	Gh	41.14N	23.23 E
Sīdī 'Abd ar Raḩmān	146	Cg	30.58N	28.44 E
Sidi Aïch	126	Qh	36.37N	4.41 E
Sidi Akacha	126	Nh	36.28N	1.18 E
Sidi Ali	126	Mh	36.06N	0.25 E
Sīdī'Alī al Makkī, Ra's- ►	128	Em	37.11N	10.17 E
Sīdī Barrānī	164	Ec	31.36N	25.55 E
Sidi Bel Abbes	162	Gb	35.12N	0.38W
Sidi Bel Abbes [3]	162	Gc	34.45N	0.35W
Sidi Bennour	162	Fc	32.39N	8.26W
Sidi di Daoud	126	Ph	36.51N	3.52 E
Sidi Ifni	160	Ff	29.33N	10.10W
Sidi Kacem	162	Fc	34.13N	5.42W
Sidikalang	150	Cf	2.45N	98.19 E
Sidi Lakhdar	126	Mh	36.10N	0.27 E
Sīdī Zayd, Jabal- ▲	128	En	36.29N	10.20 E
Sidlaw Hills ◬	118	Ke	56.30N	3.00W
Sidmouth	118	Jk	50.41N	3.15W
Sidney [B.C.-Can.]	180	Fg	48.39N	123.24W
Sidney [Mt.-U.S.]	182	Gb	47.43N	104.09W
Sidney [Nb.-U.S.]	182	Gc	41.09N	102.59W
Sidney [Oh.-U.S.]	184	Ee	40.16N	84.10W
Sidney Lanier, Lake- ≈	184	Fh	34.15N	83.57W
Sidobre ⊠	122	Ik	43.40N	2.30 E
Sidorovsk	138	Dc	66.35N	82.30 E
Sidra	120	Tc	53.33N	23.30 E
Sidra, Gulf of-(EN)=Surt, Khalīj- ◗	158	Ie	31.30N	18.00 E
Sidrolândia	204	Ee	20.55S	54.58W
Siedlce	120	Sd	52.11N	22.16 E
Siedlce [2]	120	Sd	52.10N	22.15 E
Siedlecka, Wysoczyzna- ▬	120	Sd	52.10N	22.15 E
Sieg [Ger.]	120	Df	50.45N	7.05 E
Sieg [Ger.]	124	Kd	50.55N	8.01 E
Siegburg	120	Df	50.48N	7.12 E
Siegen	120	Ef	50.52N	8.02 E
Siemiatycze	120	Sd	52.26N	22.53 E
Siĕmréab	148	Kf	13.22N	103.51 E
Siena	128	Fg	43.19N	11.21 E
Sieniawa	120	Sf	50.11N	22.36 E
Sienne ◥	122	Ee	49.00N	1.34W
Sieradz	120	Oe	51.36N	18.45 E
Sieradz [2]	120	Oe	51.35N	18.45 E
Sieradzka, Niecka- ⊠	120	Oe	51.35N	18.50 E
Sierck-les-Bains	124	Ie	49.26N	6.21 E
Sierpc	120	Pd	52.52N	19.41 E
Sierra Blanca	186	Dk	31.11N	105.21W
Sierra Blanca Peak ▲	182	Fe	33.23N	105.48W
Sierra Colorada	206	Gf	40.35S	67.48W
Sierra Leone [1]	160	Fh	8.30N	11.30W
Sierra Leone Basin (EN) ⊍	106	Di	5.00N	17.00W
Sierra Leone Rise (EN) ⋀	106	Di	5.30N	21.00W
Sierra Mojada	190	Dc	27.17N	103.42W
Sierre/Siders	128	Bd	46.17N	7.32 E
Siete Palmas	204	Cg	25.13S	58.20W
Siete Puntas, Río- ◥	204	Df	23.34S	57.20W
Şieu ◥	130	Hb	47.11N	24.13 E
Sifié	166	Dd	7.59N	6.55W
Sifnos ◆	130	Hm	37.00N	24.40 E
Sig	162	Gb	35.32N	0.11W
Siğacik Körfezi ◗	130	Jk	38.12N	26.45 E
Sigean	122	Ik	43.02N	2.59 E
Sighetu Marmaţiei	130	Gb	47.56N	23.53 E
Sighişoara	130	Hc	46.13N	24.48 E
Sigli	150	Ce	5.23N	95.57 E
Siglufjörður	114a	Ba	66.09N	18.55W
Sigmaringen	120	Fh	48.05N	9.13 E
Signal Peak ▲	188	Hj	33.22N	114.03W
Signy Island ⚗	222	Re	60.43S	45.38W
Signy-l'Abbaye	124	Ge	49.42N	4.25 E
Signy-le-Petit	124	Ge	49.54N	4.17 E
Sigtuna	114	Dg	59.37N	17.43 E
Siguanea, Ensenada de la- ◗	194	Fc	21.38N	83.05W
Siguatepeque	194	Df	14.32N	87.49W
Sigüenza	126	Jc	41.04N	2.38W
Siguiri	160	Gg	11.25N	9.10W
Sigulda	114	Fh	57.09N	24.53 E
Si He ◥	154	Dg	35.11N	116.42 E
Sihong	154	Eh	33.28N	118.13 E
Sihote-Alin ⛰	140	Pe	48.00N	138.00 E
Sihou → Changdao	154	Ff	37.56N	120.42 E
Sihuas	202	Ce	8.34S	77.37W
Siikainen	116	Ic	61.52N	21.50 E
Siilinjärvi	114	Ge	63.02N	27.40 E
Siirt	144	Fb	37.56N	41.57 E
Sijunjung	150	Dg	0.42S	100.58 E
Sikaiana ◆	219a	Fc	8.22S	162.45 E
Sikakap	150	Dg	2.46S	100.13 E
Sīkān	146	Lf	33.10N	47.39 E
Sikanni Chief ◥	180	Fe	58.17N	121.46W
Sīkar	148	Fc	27.37N	75.09 E
Sikasso	160	Gg	11.20N	5.40W
Sikasso [3]	166	Dc	10.55N	7.00W
Sikéa [Grc.]	130	Gi	40.03N	23.58 E
Sikéa [Grc.]	130	Fm	36.46N	22.56 E
Sikeston	182	Jd	36.53N	89.35W
Sikinos ◆	130	Im	36.50N	25.05 E
Sikkim [3]	148	Hc	27.50N	88.30 E
Siklós	120	Ok	45.51N	18.18 E
Sikonge	170	Fd	5.38S	32.46 E
Šikotan, ostrov- / Shikotan-Tō ◆	138	Jh	43.47N	146.45 E
Siktjah	138	Hc	69.55N	125.10 E
Sil ◥	126	Eb	42.27N	7.43W
Sila Grande ⛰	128	Kk	39.20N	16.30 E
Sila Greca ⛰	128	Kk	39.30N	16.30 E
Šilale/Šilalė	114	Fi	55.29N	22.12 E
Šilalė/Šilale	114	Fi	55.29N	22.12 E
Silao	192	Ig	20.56N	101.26W
Silaogou	154	Be	39.59N	113.03 E
Sila Piccola ⛰	128	Kk	39.05N	16.35 E
Silba ◆	128	If	44.23N	14.42 E
Silchar	148	Id	24.49N	92.48 E
Šilda	132	Ud	51.47N	59.50 E
Sildagapet ◗	116	Ab	62.05N	5.10 E
Şile	146	Cb	41.05N	29.35 E
Sile ◥	128	Ge	45.28N	12.35 E
Šilega	136	Ec	64.03N	44.02 E
Silesia (EN)=Śląsk ⊠	110	He	51.00N	16.45 E
Silesia (EN)=Śląsk ▣	120	Me	51.00N	16.45 E
Silet	162	He	22.39N	4.35 E
Silhouette Island ◆	172b	Ca	4.29S	55.14 E
Silifke	144	Db	36.22N	33.56 E
Siligir ◥	138	Gc	68.27N	114.50 E
Siling Co ≈	140	Kf	31.50N	89.00 E
Siling Jiao ✠	150	Ge	8.20N	115.27 E
Silisili, Mauga- ▲	221c	Aa	13.35S	172.27W
Silistra	130	Ke	44.07N	27.16 E
Silistra [2]	130	Kf	44.07N	27.16 E
Silivri	146	Cb	41.04N	28.15 E
Siljan ≈	114	Df	60.50N	14.45 E
Šilka	138	Gf	51.51N	116.02 E
Šilka ◥	140	Od	53.22N	121.32 E
Silkeborg	114	Bh	56.10N	9.34 E
Sillamäe/Sillamjae	114	Gg	59.24N	27.43 E
Sillamjae/Sillamäe	114	Gg	59.24N	27.43 E
Sillaro ◥	128	Ff	44.34N	11.51 E
Silleiro, Cabo- ►	126	Db	42.07N	8.54W
Sillé-le-Guillaume	122	Ff	48.12N	0.08W
Sillian	128	Gd	46.45N	12.25 E
Sillil	168	Gc	11.00N	43.26 E
Siloam Springs	186	Ih	36.11N	94.32W
Siloana Plains ▭	170	Df	17.15S	23.10 E
Šilovo	136	Ee	54.24N	40.52 E
Silsbee	186	Ik	30.21N	94.11W
Siltou	168	Bb	16.52N	15.43 E
Šilutė/Šilute	136	Cd	55.21N	21.30 E
Šilute/Šilutė	136	Cd	55.21N	21.30 E
Silvan	146	Ic	38.08N	41.01 E
Silvassa	148	Ed	20.20N	73.05 E
Silver Bank (EN) ⋒	194	Mc	20.30N	69.45W
Silver Bank Passage ⇌	194	Lc	21.00N	70.15W
Silver Bay	182	Ib	47.17N	91.16W
Silver City	182	Fe	32.46N	108.17W
Silverdalen	116	Fg	57.32N	15.44 E
Silver Lake ≈	188	Ee	43.06N	120.53W
Silver Spring	184	If	39.02N	77.03W
Silver Springs	188	Fg	39.25N	119.13W
Silverthrone Mountain ▲	188	Ba	51.31N	126.06W
Silverton [Co.-U.S.]	186	Ch	37.49N	107.40W
Silverton [Tx.-U.S.]	186	Fi	34.28N	101.19W
Silves [Braz.]	202	Gd	2.54S	58.27W
Silves [Port.]	126	Dg	37.11N	8.26W
Silvi	128	Ih	42.34N	14.06 E
Silvia	202	Cc	2.37N	76.24W
Silvies River ◥	188	Fe	43.22N	118.48W
Silvretta ⛰	128	Ed	46.50N	10.15 E
Silyānah	162	Ib	36.05N	9.22 E
Silyānah [3]	162	Ib	36.00N	9.30 E
Silyānah, Wādī- ◥	128	Dn	36.33N	9.25 E
Sim	134	Hi	54.59N	57.41 E
Sim ◥	134	Hi	54.32N	56.30 E
Sim, Cap- ►	162	Fc	31.23N	9.51W
Simanggang	150	Ff	1.15N	111.26 E
Šimanovsk	138	Hf	52.01N	127.36 E
Simao	152	Hg	22.40N	101.02 E
Simard, Lac- ≈	184	Hb	47.38N	78.40W
Sīmareh ◥	146	Mf	32.08N	48.03 E
Simav	146	Cc	39.05N	28.59 E
Simav ◥	144	Ca	40.23N	28.31 E
Simav Dağ ▲	130	Lj	39.04N	28.54 E
Simav Gölü ≈	130	Lj	39.09N	28.55 E
Simayama-Jima ◆	156	Ae	32.40N	128.38 E
Simba	170	Db	0.36N	22.55 E
Simbo	170	Fc	4.53S	29.44 E
Simbo ◆	219a	Cc	8.18S	156.34 E
Simbruini, Monti- ⛰	128	Hj	41.55N	13.15 E
Simcoe	184	Gd	42.50N	80.18W
Simcoe, Lake - ≈	180	Jh	44.27N	79.20W
Simen ⊠	168	Fc	13.25N	38.00 E
Simenti	166	Cc	13.00N	13.25W
Simeto ◥	128	Jm	37.24N	15.06 E
Simeulue, Pulau- ◆	140	Li	2.35N	96.05 E
Simferopol	112	Jf	44.57N	34.06 E
Sími	130	Km	36.36N	27.50 E
Sími ◆	130	Km	36.35N	27.50 E
Simití	194	Kj	7.58N	73.58W
Simitli	130	Gh	41.53N	23.06 E
Simla → Shimla	142	Jf	31.06N	77.10 E
Şimleu Silvaniei	130	Fb	47.14N	22.48 E
Simmental ∨	128	Bd	46.35N	7.25 E
Simmerath	124	Id	50.36N	6.18 E
Simmerbach ◥	124	Je	49.48N	7.31 E
Simmern (Hunsrück)	120	Dg	49.59N	7.31 E
Simmertal	124	Je	49.48N	7.33 E
Simnas	116	Jj	54.20N	23.45 E
Simo	114	Fd	65.39N	24.55 E
Simojärvi ≈	114	Gc	66.06N	27.03 E
Simojoki ◥	114	Fd	65.37N	25.03 E
Simojovel de Allende	192	Mi	17.12N	92.38W
Simonstown	172	Bf	34.14S	18.26 E
Simpele	114	Gf	61.26N	29.22 E
Simpelejärvi ≈	116	Mc	61.30N	29.25 E
Simplon Pass ⌓	128	Bd	46.15N	8.00 E
Simpson Desert ∴	208	Eg	25.00S	137.00 E
Simpson Hill ▲	212	Fe	26.30S	126.30 E
Simpson Peninsula ▰	180	Ic	68.45N	89.10W
Simrishamn	114	Di	55.33N	14.20 E
Simsonbaai	197b	Ab	18.02N	63.08W
Simušir, ostrov- ◆	140	Re	46.58N	152.02 E
Sina ◥	148	Fe	17.22N	75.54 E
Sīnā'=Sinai Peninsula (EN) ▰	158	Kf	29.30N	34.00 E
Sinabang	150	Cf	2.29N	96.23 E
Sinaḑaqo	168	Hd	5.22N	46.22 E
Sinai, Mount- (EN)=Mūsa, Jabal- ▲	146	Eh	28.32N	33.59 E
Sinaia	130	Id	45.21N	25.33 E
Sinai Peninsula (EN)= Sīnā' ▰	158	Kf	29.30N	34.00 E
Sinajana	220c	Bb	13.28N	144.45W
Sinaloa [2]	190	Cc	25.00N	107.30W
Sinaloa, Llanos de- ▭	190	Cc	25.00N	107.30W
Sinaloa, Río- ◥	192	Ee	25.18N	108.30W
Sinaloa de Leyva	192	Ee	25.50N	108.14W
Sinalunga	128	Fg	43.12N	11.44 E
Sinamaica	202	Da	11.05N	71.51W
Sinan	152	If	27.56N	108.11 E
Sinara ◥	134	Kh	56.17N	62.23 E
Sīnāwin	164	Bc	31.02N	10.36 E
Sinazongwe	170	Ef	17.15S	27.28 E
Şincai	130	Hc	46.39N	24.23 E
Sincanli	146	Dc	38.45N	30.15 E
Sincé	194	Ji	9.14N	75.06W
Sincelejo	200	Ie	9.18N	75.24W
Sinch'am	154	Jc	42.07N	129.25 E
Sinch'ang	154	Jd	40.07N	128.28 E
Sinch'on	154	He	38.28N	125.27 E
Sinclair, Lake- ≈	184	Fi	33.11N	83.16W
Sind [3]	148	Dc	25.30N	69.00 E
Sind ⊠	140	Ig	25.30N	69.00 E
Sindal	116	Dg	57.28N	10.13 E
Sindangbarang	150	Eh	7.27S	107.08 E
Sindara	170	Bc	1.02S	10.40 E
Sindfeld ⊠	124	Kc	51.32N	8.48 E
Sindi	114	Fg	58.24N	24.42 E
Sındırgı	146	Cc	39.14N	28.10 E
Sindirgi Geçidi ⌓	130	Lj	39.10N	28.04 E
Sîndominic	130	Ic	46.35N	25.47 E
Sindri	148	Hd	23.42N	86.29 E
Sinegorje	138	Kd	62.03N	150.25 E
Šine-Ider	152	Gb	48.56N	99.33 E
Sinekli	130	Lh	41.14N	28.12 E
Sinelnikovo	132	Ie	48.18N	35.31 E
Sines	126	Dg	37.57N	8.52W
Sines, Cabo de- ►	126	Dg	37.57N	8.53W
Sine-Saloum [3]	166	Bc	14.00N	15.50W
Singako	168	Bd	9.50N	19.29 E
Singapore / Singapura [1]	142	Mi	1.17N	103.51 E
Singapore Strait (EN)= Singapura, Selat- ⇌	150	Df	1.15N	104.00 E
Singapura / Singapore [1]	142	Mi	1.17N	103.51 E
Singapura, Selat-= Singapore Strait (EN) ⇌	150	Df	1.15N	104.00 E
Singaraja	150	Gh	8.07S	115.06 E
Singatoka	219d	Ac	18.08S	177.30 E
Sing Buri	148	Kf	14.53N	100.25 E
Singen	120	Ei	47.46N	8.50 E
Sîngeroz Băi	130	Hb	47.22N	24.41 E
Singida	160	Ki	4.49S	34.45 E
Singida [3]	170	Fd	5.30S	34.30 E
Singitic Gulf (EN) = Singitikós Kólpos ◗	130	Gi	40.10N	23.55 E
Singitikós Kólpos = Singitic Gulf (EN) ◗	130	Gi	40.10N	23.55 E
Singkaling Hkamti	148	Jc	26.00N	95.42 E
Singkang	150	Hg	4.08S	120.01 E
Singkawang	150	Ef	0.54N	109.00 E
Singkep, Pulau- ◆	150	Dg	0.30S	104.25 E
Singkil	150	Cf	2.17N	97.49 E
Singleton [Austl.]	212	Kf	32.34S	151.10 E
Singleton [Eng.-U.K.]	124	Bd	50.55N	0.44W
Singleton, Mount- ▲	212	De	29.28S	117.18 E
Singö ◆	116	Hd	60 10N	18.45 E
Siniscola	128	Dj	40.34N	9.41 E
Sini vrăh ▲	130	Ih	41.51N	25.01 E
Sinj	128	Kg	43.42N	16.38 E
Sinjah	168	Ec	13.09N	33.56 E
Sinjai	150	Hh	5.07S	120.15 E
Sinjaja ◥	116	Mg	57.05N	28.33 E
Sinjajevina ⛰	130	Cf	43.00N	19.18 E
Sinjār	146	Id	36.19N	41.52 E
Sinjār, Jabal- ⛰	146	Id	36.23N	41.52 E
Sinjuža ◥	132	Ge	48.03N	30.50 E
Sinkiang Uighur (EN) = Xinjiang Uygur Zizhiqu (Hsin-chiang-wei-wu-erh Tzu-chih-ch'ü) [2]	152	Ec	42.00N	86.00 E
Sin-le-Noble	124	Fd	50.22N	3.07 E
Sinmi-Do ◆	154	He	39.33N	124.53 E
Sinn	124	Kd	50.39N	8.20 E
Sinn al Kadhdhāb ◬	164	Fe	23.30N	32.05 E
Sinnamary	202	Hb	5.23N	53.00W
Sinni ◥	128	Kj	40.08N	16.41 E
Sînnicolau Mare	130	Dc	46.05N	20.38 E
Sinnūris	146	Dh	29.25N	30.52 E
Sinnyŏng	154	Jf	36.02N	128.47 E
Sinoe [3]	166	Dd	5.20N	8.40W
Sinoe, Lacul- ≈	130	Le	44.38N	28.53 E
Sinop	144	Ea	41.59N	35.09 E
Sinop Burun ►	146	Fa	42.02N	35.12 E
Sinp'o	154	Jd	40.02N	128.12 E
Sinsang	154	Ie	39.39N	127.25 E
Sinsheim	120	Eg	49.15N	8.53 E
Sint-Amandsberg, Gent-	124	Fc	51.04N	3.45 E
Sîntana	130	Ec	46.21N	21.30 E
Sint-Andries, Brugge-	124	Fc	51.12N	3.10 E
Sintang	150	Ff	0.04N	111.30 E
Sint Eustatius ◆	190	Le	17.30N	62.59W
Sint-Gillis-Waas	124	Gc	51.13N	4.08 E
Sint Kruis	196	Bf	12.18N	69.08W
Sint Laureins	124	Fc	51.15N	3.31 E
Sint Maarten ◆	190	Le	18.04N	63.04W
Sint Nicolaas	196	Bf	12.26N	69.55W
Sint Niklaas/Saint-Nicolas	122	Kc	51.10N	4.08 E
Sint-Oedenrode	124	Hc	51.34N	5.28 E
Sinton	186	Hl	28.02N	97.33W
Sint-Pieters-Leeuw	124	Gd	50.47N	4.14 E
Sintra	126	Cf	38.48N	9.23W
Sint-Truiden/Saint-Trond	122	Ld	50.49N	5.12 E
Sintu	168	Fd	8.12N	36.56 E
Sinú, Río- ◥	194	Ji	9.24N	75.49W
Sinŭiju	142	Oe	40.06N	124.24 E
Sinujīf	168	Hd	8.30N	48.59 E
Sinzig	124	Jd	50.33N	7.15 E
Sió ═	120	Oj	46.23N	18.40 E
Siocon	150	He	7.42N	122.08 E
Siófok	120	Oj	46.54N	18.03 E
Sioma	170	Df	16.40S	23.35 E
Sion/Sitten	128	Bd	46.15N	7.20 E
Siorapaluk	179	Ec	77.39N	71.00W
Sioule ◥	122	Jh	46.22N	3.19 E
Sioux City	176	Je	42.30N	96.23W
Sioux Falls	176	Je	43.32N	96.44W
Sioux Lookout	180	If	50.06N	91.55W
Sipalay	150	He	9.45N	122.24 E
Šipan ◆	128	Lh	42.43N	17.54 E
Siparia	196	Fg	10.08N	61.30W
Šipčenski prohod ⌓	130	Ig	42.46N	25.19 E
Siping	142	Oe	43.11N	124.24 E
Sipiwesk	180	He	55.27N	97.24W
Sipiwesk Lake ≈	180	He	55.05N	97.35W
Siple, Mount- ▲	222	Nf	73.15S	126.06W
Siple Coast ⌇	222	Mg	82.00S	153.00W
Siple Island ◆	222	Nf	73.39S	125.00W
Siple Station ⚗	222	Pf	75.55S	83.55W
Sipolilo	172	Ec	16.39S	30.42 E
Sipora, Pulau- ◆	150	Cg	2.12S	99.40 E
Sippola	116	Ld	60.44N	27.00 E
Siqueira Campos	204	Hf	23.42S	49.50W
Siquia, Río- ◥	194	Eg	12.09N	84.13W
Siquijor	150	He	9.13N	123.31 E
Siquisique	202	Ea	10.34N	69.42W

Index Symbols

- [1] Independent Nation
- [2] State, Region
- [3] District, County
- [4] Municipality
- [5] Colony, Dependency
- ■ Continent
- ⊠ Physical Region
- ▣ Historical or Cultural Region
- ▲ Mount, Mountain
- △ Volcano
- ◭ Hill
- ⛰ Mountains, Mountain Range
- ◬ Hills, Escarpment
- ▬ Plateau, Upland
- ⌓ Pass, Gap
- ▭ Plain, Lowland
- ◣ Delta
- ▤ Salt Flat
- ∨ Valley, Canyon
- ◌ Crater, Cave
- ✲ Karst Features
- ⌣ Depression
- ⊟ Polder
- ∴ Desert, Dunes
- ♣ Forest, Woods
- ⁂ Heath, Steppe
- ✽ Oasis
- ► Cape, Point
- ⌇ Coast, Beach
- ◧ Cliff
- ▰ Peninsula
- ⧖ Isthmus
- ⋯ Sandbank
- ◆ Island
- ○ Atoll
- ✠ Rock, Reef
- ◈ Islands, Archipelago
- ✣ Rocks, Reefs
- ✿ Coral Reef
- ◉ Well, Spring
- ⊙ Geyser
- ◥ River, Stream
- ⇊ Waterfall, Rapids
- ◩ River Mouth, Estuary
- ≈ Lake
- ≊ Salt Lake
- ≂ Intermittent Lake
- ⊜ Reservoir
- ⋍ Swamp, Pond
- ═ Canal
- ❄ Glacier
- ❅ Ice Shelf, Pack Ice
- ▓ Ocean
- ▒ Sea
- ◗ Gulf, Bay
- ⇌ Strait, Fjord
- ⊚ Lagoon
- ⋒ Bank
- ⌂ Seamount
- ⊓ Tablemount
- ⋀ Ridge
- ⊏ Shelf
- ⊍ Basin
- ◿ Escarpment, Sea Scarp
- ϟ Fracture
- ⊽ Trench, Abyss
- ♤ National Park, Reserve
- ✦ Point of Interest
- ☼ Recreation Site
- ◙ Cave, Cavern
- ♜ Historic Site
- ⁙ Ruins
- ▦ Wall, Walls
- ✝ Church, Abbey
- ⛩ Temple
- ⚗ Scientific Station
- ⊶ Railway station
- ✈ Airport
- ⚓ Port
- ⚔ Military installation
- ⛯ Lighthouse
- ⚒ Mine
- ⋂ Tunnel
- ⧸ Dam, Bridge

Šira	138	Ef	54.29N	90.02 E
Sira	114	Bg	58.25N	6.38 E
Sira	116	Bf	58.17N	6.24 E
Şīr Abū Nu'Ayr	146	Pj	25.13N	54.13 E
Si Racha	148	Kf	13.10N	100.57 E
Siracusa=Syracuse (EN)	112	Hh	37.04N	15.18 E
Sir Alexander, Mount -	180	Ff	53.56N	120.23W
Sirasso	166	Dd	9.16N	6.06W
Şirāţ, Jabal-	164	Hf	17.00N	43.50 E
Sirba	166	Fc	13.46N	1.40 E
Şīr Banī Yās	146	Oj	24.19N	52.37 E
Sirdalen	116	Bf	58.50N	6.40 E
Sirdalsvatn	116	Bf	58.35N	6.40 E
Sire [Eth.]	168	Fd	8.58N	37.00 E
Sire [Eth.]	168	Fd	8.16N	39.30 E
Sir Edward Pellew Group	212	Hc	15.40S	136.50 E
Siret	130	Jb	47.57N	26.04 E
Siret	110	If	45.24N	28.01 E
Sirevåg	114	Ag	58.30N	5.47 E
Şirhān, Wādī as-	144	Ec	30.30N	38.00 E
Şiria	130	Ec	46.16N	21.38 E
Sīrīk	144	Id	26.29N	57.09 E
Sirik, Tanjong-	150	Ff	2.46N	111.19 E
Sirina	130	Jm	36.21N	26.41 E
Sirino	128	Jj	40.07N	15.50 E
Sirius Seamount (EN)	178	Gf	52.00N	160.50W
Širjajevo	132	Gf	47.24N	30.13 E
Sir James Mac Brian, Mount-	180	Ed	62.08N	127.40W
Sirjān, Kavīr-e-	146	Ph	29.30N	55.30 E
Sirmione	128	Ee	45.29N	10.36 E
Şırnak	146	Jd	37.32N	42.28 E
Širokaja Pad	138	Jf	50.15N	142.11 E
Široki	138	Jd	63.04N	148.01 E
Širokoje	132	Hf	47.38N	33.14 E
Sironcha	148	Fe	18.50N	79.58 E
Siros	130	Hl	37.26N	24.55 E
Sirpsindiği	130	Jh	41.50N	26.29 E
Sirr, Nafūd as-	146	Kj	25.15N	44.45 E
Sirrayn	164	Hf	19.38N	40.36 E
Sirretta Peak	188	Fi	35.59N	118.20W
Sīrrī, Jazīreh-ye-	146	Pj	25.55N	54.32 E
Sirsa	148	Fc	29.32N	75.01 E
Sir Sandford, Mount-	188	Ga	51.40N	117.52W
Sirte Desert (EN)=As Sidrah	158	Ie	30.30N	17.30 E
Sir Thomas, Mount-	212	Fe	27.11S	129.46 E
Širvintos	114	Fi	55.03N	25.01 E
Sir Wilfrid Laurier, Mount -	180	Ff	52.48N	119.45W
Sisak	128	Ke	45.29N	16.22 E
Si Sa Ket	148	Ke	15.07N	104.19 E
Sīsakht	146	Ng	30.47N	51.33 E
Sisal	192	Ng	21.10N	90.02W
Sisante	126	Je	39.25N	2.13W
Sisargas, Islas-	126	Da	43.22N	8.50W
Šišchid-Gol	152	Ga	51.30N	97.10 E
Sishen	172	Ce	27.55S	22.59 E
Sishui	154	Dg	35.40N	117.17 E
Sisian	132	Oj	39.31N	46.03 E
Sisili	166	Ec	10.16N	1.15W
Sisimiut/Holsteinsborg	224	Nc	67.05N	53.45W
Siskiyou Mountains	188	Df	41.55N	123.15W
Sisŏphŏn	148	Kf	13.35N	102.59 E
Sissano	214	Ch	3.00S	142.03 E
Sisseton	186	Hd	45.40N	97.03W
Sissonne	124	Fe	49.34N	3.54 E
Sīstān=Seistan (EN)	140	If	30.30N	62.00 E
Sīstān-e Balūchestān [3]	144	Jd	28.30N	60.30 E
Sisteron	122	Lj	44.12N	5.56 E
Sisters	188	Ed	44.17N	121.33W
Sistranda	114	Be	63.43N	8.50 E
Sitāpur	148	Gc	27.34N	80.41 E
Sitasjaure	114	Dc	68.00N	17.25 E
Siteki	172	Ee	26.27S	31.57 E
Sitges	126	Nc	41.14N	1.49 E
Sithonia	130	Gi	40.05N	23.55 E
Sitia	130	Jn	35.12N	26.07 E
Sitio d'Abadia	204	Ib	14.48S	46.16W
Sitio Nuevo	194	Jh	10.46N	74.43W
Sitka	176	Fd	57.03N	135.14W
Sitkalidak	178	Ie	57.10N	153.14W
Sitna	130	Kb	47.30N	27.10 E
Sitnica	130	Dg	42.53N	20.52 E
Sitona	168	Fc	14.23N	37.22 E
Sitrah [Bhr.]	146	Ni	26.10N	50.40 E
Sitrah [Eg.]	146	Bh	28.42N	26.54 E
Sittard	122	Ld	51.00N	5.53 E
Sittee Point	194	Ce	16.48N	88.15W
Sitten/Sion	128	Bd	46.15N	7.20 E
Sittingbourne	124	Cc	51.20N	0.45 E
Sittoung	148	Je	17.10N	96.58 E
Sittwe (Akyab)	142	Lg	20.09N	92.54 E
Siuna	194	Eg	13.44N	84.46W
Siuslaw River	188	Cd	44.01N	124.08W
Siva	114	Mh	56.49N	53.55 E
Sivac	130	Cd	45.42N	19.23 E
Sivaki	138	Hf	52.38N	126.45 E
Sīvan	144	Hd	29.51N	52.46 E
Sivas	142	Ff	39.50N	37.03 E
Sivaš, ozero-	132	Ig	45.50N	34.40 E
Sivasli	130	Mk	38.30N	29.42 E
Šiveluč, vulkan-	138	Le	56.33N	161.25 E
Sivera, ozero- / Sivera ezers	116	Li	55.58N	27.25 E
Sivera ezers / Sivera, ozero-	116	Li	55.58N	27.25 E
Siverek	144	Eb	37.45N	39.19 E
Siverski	114	Hg	59.22N	30.02 E
Sivomaskinski	134	Kc	66.40N	62.31 E
Sivrice	146	Hc	38.27N	39.19 E
Sivrihisar	146	Dc	39.27N	31.34 E
Sivry-Rance	124	Gd	50.10N	4.16 E
Sivry Rance-Rance	124	Gd	50.09N	4.16 E
Sivry-sur-Meuse	124	He	49.19N	5.16 E
Sīwah	160	Jf	29.12N	25.31 E
Sīwah, Wāḩāt-=Siwa Oasis (EN)	158	Jf	29.10N	25.40 E
Siwalik Range	140	Jg	29.00N	80.00 E
Siwān	148	Gc	26.13N	84.22 E
Siwa Oasis (EN)=Sīwah, Wāḩāt-	158	Jf	29.10N	25.40 E
Sixaola, Río-	194	Fi	9.35N	82.34W
Six Cross Road	197q	Bb	13.07N	59.28W
Six-Fours-la-Plage	122	Lk	43.06N	5.51 E
Sixian	154	Dh	33.29N	117.53 E
Six Men's Bay	197q	Ab	13.16N	59.38W
Sixth Cataract (EN)=Sablūkah, Ash Shallāl as-	158	Kg	16.20N	32.42 E
Siyah-Chaman	146	Ld	37.35N	47.10 E
Siyang (Zhongxing)	154	Eh	33.43N	118.40 E
Siziwang Qi (Ulan Hua)	154	Ad	41.31N	111.41 E
Sjælland=Zealand (EN)	110	Hd	55.30N	11.45 E
Sjamozero, ozero-	114	Hf	61.55N	33.15 E
Sjare/Sääre	116	Ig	57.57N	21.53 E
Sjas	114	Hf	60.10N	32.31 E
Sjasstroj	114	Hf	60.09N	32.36 E
Šjašupe	114	Fi	55.00N	22.10 E
Šjauljaj	112	Id	55.53N	23.19 E
Šjauljaj/Šiauliai	112	Id	55.53N	23.19 E
Sjenica	130	Df	43.16N	20.00 E
Sjnjaja	138	Hd	61.00N	126.57 E
Sjoa	116	Cc	61.41N	9.33 E
Sjöbo	116	Ei	55.38N	13.42 E
Sjøholt	114	Be	62.29N	6.50 E
Sjujutlijka	130	Ig	42.17N	25.55 E
Sjun	134	Gi	55.43N	54.17 E
Sjuøyane	179	Ob	80.43N	20.45 E
Skadarsko jezero = Scutari, Lake- (EN)	110	Hg	42.10N	19.20 E
Skadovsk	136	Df	46.07N	32.56 E
Skælskør	116	Di	55.15N	11.19 E
Skærbæk	116	Ci	55.09N	8.46 E
Skagatá	114a	Ba	66.07N	20.06W
Skagen	114	Ch	57.44N	10.36 E
Skagern	116	Ff	59.00N	14.15 E
Skagerrak	110	Gd	57.45N	9.00 E
Skaget	116	Cc	61.17N	9.12 E
Skagit River	188	Db	48.20N	122.25W
Skagway	176	Fd	59.28N	135.19W
Skaidi	114	Fa	70.26N	24.30 E
Skaland	114	Db	69.27N	17.18 E
Skälderviken	116	Eh	56.20N	12.40 E
Skålevik	116	Bf	58.04N	8.00 E
Skalisty Golec, gora- [R.S.F.S.R.]	138	Ie	55.55N	130.35 E
Skalisty Golec, gora- [R.S.F.S.R.]	138	Ge	56.20N	119.10 E
Skanderborg	114	Bh	56.02N	9.56 E
Skåne	110	Hd	56.00N	13.30 E
Skånevik	116	Ae	59.44N	5.59 E
Skänninge	116	Ff	58.24N	15.05 E
Skanör	116	Ei	55.25N	12.52 E
Skántzoura	130	Hj	39.05N	24.07 E
Skara	114	Cg	58.22N	13.25 E
Skaraborg [2]	114	Cg	58.20N	13.30 E
Skärblacka	116	Ff	58.34N	15.54 E
Skārdu	148	Fa	35.18N	75.37 E
Skärhamn	116	Dg	57.59N	11.33 E
Skarnes	116	Dd	60.15N	11.41 E
Skärplinge	114	Df	60.28N	17.46 E
Skarsstind	116	Cb	62.03N	8.35 E
Skarsvåg	114	Fa	71.06N	25.56 E
Skarszewy	120	Ob	54.05N	18.27 E
Skarvdalsegga	116	Cb	62.09N	8.03 E
Skaryszew	120	Re	51.19N	21.15 E
Skarżysko-Kamienna	120	Qe	51.08N	20.53 E
Skasøy	116	Ca	63.20N	8.35 E
Skăt	130	Gf	43.44N	23.51 E
Skattkärr	116	Ee	59.25N	13.41 E
Skattungbyn	116	Fc	61.12N	14.52 E
Skaudvilė/Skaudvile	114	Fi	55.27N	22.33 E
Skaudvile/Skaudvilė	114	Fi	55.27N	22.33 E
Skaulen	116	Be	59.38N	6.35 E
Skawa	120	Pf	50.02N	19.26 E
Skawina	120	Pg	49.59N	19.49 E
Skee	116	Df	58.56N	11.19 E
Skeena	174	Fd	54.09N	130.02W
Skeena Mountains	180	Ee	56.45N	128.40W
Skegness	118	Nh	53.10N	0.21 E
Skeidararsandur	114a	Cc	63.54N	17.14W
Skeldon	202	Gb	5.53N	57.08W
Skeleton Coast	172	Ac	17.50S	12.45 E
Skellefteå	112	Ic	64.46N	20.57 E
Skellefteälven	110	Ic	64.42N	21.06 E
Skelleftehamn	114	Ed	64.41N	21.14 E
Skëndërbeut, Mali i-	130	Ch	41.35N	19.50 E
Skene	116	Eg	57.29N	12.38 E
Skerki Bank (EN)	162	Jb	37.45N	10.50 E
Skerries/Na Sceiri	118	Gh	53.35N	6.07W
Skerryvore	118	Fe	56.20N	7.05W
Skhiza	130	Em	36.44N	21.46 E
Skhoinoúsa	130	Im	36.50N	25.30 E
Ski	114	Cg	59.43N	10.50 E
Skiathos	130	Gj	39.10N	23.29 E
Skiathos	130	Gj	39.10N	23.28 E
Skibbereen/An Sciobairin	118	Dj	51.33N	9.15W
Skibotn	114	Eb	69.24N	20.16 E
Skidel	132	Dc	53.38N	24.17 E
Skien	112	Gd	59.12N	9.36 E
Skierniewice	120	Qe	51.58N	20.08 E
Skierniewice [2]	120	Qe	52.00N	20.10 E
Skiftet/Kihti	116	Id	60.15N	21.05 E
Skikda	160	He	36.52N	6.54 E
Skikda [3]	162	Ib	36.45N	6.50 E
Skillet Fork	186	Lg	38.08N	88.07W
Skillingaryd	116	Fg	57.26N	14.05 E
Skinári, Ákra-	130	Dl	37.56N	20.42 E
Skinnskatteberg	116	Fe	59.50N	15.41 E
Skipton	118	Kh	53.58N	2.01W
Skiptvet	116	De	59.28N	11.11 E
Skiropoúla	130	Hk	38.50N	24.21 E
Skiros	130	Hk	38.54N	24.34 E
Skiros	130	Hk	38.53N	24.32 E
Skive	114	Bh	56.34N	9.02 E
Skive Å	116	Ch	56.34N	9.04 E
Skjærhalden	116	De	59.02N	11.02 E
Skjåk	116	Cc	61.52N	8.22 E
Skjálfandafljót	114a	Cb	65.59N	17.38W
Skjeberg	116	De	59.14N	11.12 E
Skjern	114	Bi	55.57N	8.30 E
Skjern Å	114	Bi	55.55N	8.24 E
Skjervøy	114	Ea	70.02N	20.59 E
Skjoldungen	179	Hf	63.20N	41.20W
Sklad	138	Hb	71.52N	123.35 E
Šklov	132	Gb	54.14N	30.18 E
Skobeleva, pik-	135	Ie	39.51N	72.47 E
Skœrfjorden	179	Kc	77.30N	19.10W
Škofja Loka	128	Id	46.10N	14.18 E
Skog	116	Gc	61.10N	16.55 E
Skógafoss	114a	Bc	63.32N	19.31W
Skoghall	116	Ee	59.19N	13.26 E
Skogshorn	116	Cd	60.53N	8.42 E
Skokie	186	Me	42.02N	87.46W
Skole	120	Th	48.58N	23.32 E
Skópelos	130	Gj	39.07N	23.44 E
Skópelos	130	Gj	39.10N	23.40 E
Skopi	130	Jn	35.11N	26.02 E
Skopin	114	Jj	53.52N	39.37 E
Skopje	112	Ig	42.00N	21.29 E
Skórcz	120	Oc	53.48N	18.32 E
Skorovatn	114	Cd	64.39N	13.07 E
Skorpa	116	Ac	61.35N	4.50 E
Skørping	116	Ch	56.50N	9.53 E
Skorpiós	130	Dk	38.42N	20.45 E
Škotovo	154	Lc	43.20N	132.21 E
Skotselv	116	Ce	59.51N	9.53 E
Skoura	162	Fc	31.04N	6.43W
Skövde	114	Cg	58.24N	13.50 E
Skovorodino	142	Od	53.59N	123.55 E
Skowhegan	184	Mc	44.46N	69.43W
Skradin	128	Jg	43.49N	15.56 E
Skreia	116	Dd	60.39N	10.56 E
Skreia	116	Dd	60.34N	11.04 E
Skrekken	116	Bd	60.13N	7.49 E
Skridulaupen	116	Bc	61.55N	7.35 E
Skrimkolla	116	Cb	62.23N	9.04 E
Skriveri/Skrīveri	116	Kh	56.37N	25.10 E
Skrīveri/Skriveri	116	Kh	56.37N	25.10 E
Skrunda	114	Eh	56.41N	22.00 E
Skrwa	120	Pd	52.33N	19.32 E
Skudenesfjorden	116	Ae	59.05N	5.20 E
Skudeneshavn	114	Ag	59.09N	5.17 E
Skuodas	114	Eh	56.17N	21.31 E
Skurup	116	Ei	55.28N	13.30 E
Skutskär	116	Gd	60.38N	17.25 E
Skvira	132	Fe	49.44N	29.42 E
Skwierzyna	120	Ld	52.35N	15.30 E
Skye, Island of-	110	Fd	57.15N	6.10W
Slagelse	114	Ci	55.24N	11.22 E
Slagnäs	114	Ed	65.36N	18.10 E
Slamet, Gunung-	140	Mj	7.14S	109.12 E
Slaná	120	Ri	47.56N	21.08 E
Slancy	136	Cd	59.08N	28.02 E
Slaney/An tSláine	118	Gi	52.21N	6.30W
Slănic	130	Id	45.15N	25.56 E
Slănic Moldova	130	Jc	46.12N	26.26 E
Slannik	130	Jf	43.06N	26.13 E
Slano	128	Lh	42.47N	17.54 E
Slaný	120	Kf	50.14N	14.06 E
Śląsk=Silesia (EN)	110	He	51.00N	16.45 E
Śląsk=Silesia (EN)	120	Me	51.00N	16.45 E
Śląska, Wyżyna-	120	Of	50.28N	18.40 E
Slate Islands	186	Mb	48.34N	86.45W
Slatina	130	He	44.26N	24.22 E
Slatina	120	Ph	48.32N	19.10 E
Slaton	186	Fj	33.26N	101.39W
Slave Coast	158	Hh	6.00N	3.30 E
Slave Lake	180	Ge	55.17N	114.46W
Slave River	174	Hc	61.18N	113.39W
Slavgorod [Bye.-U.S.S.R.]	132	Gc	53.27N	31.01 E
Slavgorod [R.S.F.S.R.]	138	Cf	53.03N	78.48 E
Slavičín	120	Ng	49.06N	17.53 E
Slavjanka	138	Ih	42.55N	131.20 E
Slavjanka	130	Gh	41.23N	23.36 E
Slavjansk	112	Jf	48.52N	37.37 E
Slavjansk-na-Kubani	136	Df	45.15N	38.08 E
Slavkoje	120	Th	48.45N	23.31 E
Slavkoviči	116	Mg	57.37N	29.10 E
Slavonia (EN) = Slavonija	110	Hf	45.00N	18.00 E
Slavonia (EN)=Slavonija	128	Le	45.00N	18.00 E
Slavonija =' Slavonia (EN)	110	Hf	45.00N	18.00 E
Slavonija=Slavonia (EN)	128	Le	45.00N	18.00 E
Slavonska Požega	128	Le	45.20N	17.41 E
Slavonski Brod	128	Me	45.09N	18.02 E
Slavsk	116	Ii	55.01N	21.37 E
Slavuta	136	Ce	50.18N	26.52 E
Sława	120	Me	51.53N	16.04 E
Sławatycze	120	Te	51.43N	23.30 E
Sławno	120	Mb	54.22N	16.40 E
Slayton	186	Id	44.01N	95.45W
Sleaford	118	Mh	53.00N	0.24W
Slea Head/Ceann Sléibhe	118	Ci	52.06N	10.27W
Sleat, Sound of-	118	Hd	57.10N	5.50W
Sleen	124	Ib	52.47N	6.49 E
Sleeper Islands	180	Je	57.25N	79.50W
Sléibhte Chill Mhantáin/Wicklow Mountains	118	Gh	53.02N	6.24W
Sleidinge, Evergem-	124	Fc	51.08N	3.41 E
Slesin	120	Od	52.23N	18.19 E
Slessor Glacier	222	Af	79.50S	28.30W
Slessor Peak	222	Qe	66.31S	64.58W
Slettefjell	116	Cc	61.13N	8.44 E
Sletterhage	116	Dh	56.06N	10.31 E
Ślęża	120	Mf	50.52N	16.45 E
Ślęża	120	Me	51.10N	16.58 E
Sliabh Bearnach/Slieve Bernagh	118	Ei	52.50N	8.35W
Sliabh Bladhma/Slieve Bloom	118	Fh	53.10N	7.35W
Sliabh Eachtaí/Slieve Aughty	118	Eh	53.10N	8.30W
Sliabh Gamh	118	Eg	54.10N	8.50W
Sliabh Gamh/Ox or Slieve Gamph Mountains	118	Eg	54.10N	8.50W
Sliabh Mis/Slieve Mish	118	Di	52.10N	9.50W
Sliabh Speirin/Sperrin Mountains	118	Fg	54.50N	7.05W
Slidell	186	Lk	30.17N	89.47W
Slide Mountain	184	Jd	42.00N	74.23W
Slidre	116	Cc	61.10N	9.00 E
Sliedrecht	124	Gc	51.50N	4.46 E
Slieve Aughty/Sliabh Eachtai	118	Eh	53.10N	8.30W
Slieve Bernagh/Sliabh Bearnach	118	Ei	52.50N	8.35W
Slieve Bloom/Sliabh Bladhma	118	Fh	53.10N	7.35W
Slievekimalta	118	Ei	52.45N	8.15W
Slieve Mish/Sliabh Mis	118	Di	52.10N	9.50W
Sligeach/Sligo	112	Fe	54.17N	8.28W
Sligeach/Sligo [2]	118	Eg	54.10N	8.40W
Sligo/Sligeach	112	Fe	54.17N	8.28W
Sligo/Sligeach [2]	118	Eg	54.10N	8.40W
Sligo Bay/Cuan Shligigh	118	Eg	54.20N	8.40W
Slinge	124	Ib	52.08N	6.31 E
Slingebeek	124	Ic	51.59N	6.18 E
Slite	116	Hg	57.43N	18.48 E
Sliven	130	Jg	42.40N	26.19 E
Sliven [2]	130	Jg	42.40N	26.19 E
Slivnica	130	Gg	42.51N	23.02 E
Sljudjanka	138	Ff	51.38N	103.40 E
Slobodka	130	Mb	47.54N	29.12 E
Slobodskoj	136	Fd	58.47N	50.12 E
Slobodzeja	132	Ff	46.43N	29.43 E
Slobozia [Rom.]	130	Ke	44.34N	27.22 E
Slobozia [Rom.]	130	Ie	44.30N	25.11 E
Slochteren	124	Ia	53.12N	6.50 E
Slocum Mountain	188	Gi	35.18N	117.13W
Slonim	136	Ce	53.05N	25.18 E
Sloten	124	Hb	52.54N	5.40 E
Slotermeer	124	Hb	52.55N	5.40 E
Slough	118	Mj	51.31N	0.36W
Slovakia (EN)= Slovensko	110	Hf	48.45N	19.30 E
Slovakia (EN)= Slovensko	120	Ph	48.45N	19.30 E
Slovečna	132	Fd	51.41N	29.42 E
Slovenia (EN) = Slovenija [2]	128	Id	46.00N	15.00 E
Slovenia (EN) = Slovenija	110	Hf	46.00N	15.00 E
Slovenia (EN) = Slovenija	128	Id	46.00N	15.00 E
Slovenija=Slovenia (EN) [2]	128	Id	46.00N	15.00 E
Slovenija = Slovenia (EN)	110	Hf	46.00N	15.00 E
Slovenija = Slovenia (EN)	128	Id	46.00N	15.00 E
Slovenska Bistrica	128	Jd	46.24N	15.34 E
Slovenske Gorice	128	Jd	46.35N	15.55 E
Slovenské rudohorie	120	Ph	48.45N	20.00 E
Slovensko [2]	120	Ph	48.45N	19.30 E
Slovensko=Slovakia (EN)	110	Hf	48.45N	19.30 E
Slovensko=Slovakia (EN)	120	Ph	48.45N	19.30 E
Slovenský kras	120	Qh	48.35N	20.40 E
Słubice	120	Kd	52.20N	14.35 E
Sluč [Bye.-U.S.S.R.]	132	Ec	52.08N	27.32 E
Sluč [Ukr.-U.S.S.R.]	132	Ed	51.37N	26.38 E
Sluck	136	Ce	53.02N	27.31 E
Slunj	128	Je	45.07N	15.35 E
Słupca	120	Nd	52.19N	17.52 E
Słupia	120	Mb	54.35N	16.50 E
Słupsk	120	Nb	54.28N	17.01 E
Słupsk [2]	120	Mb	54.30N	17.00 E
Sly	126	Nh	36.06N	1.08 E
Småland	114	Dh	57.20N	15.05 E
Smålandsfarvandet	116	Di	55.06N	11.20 E
Smålandsstenar	116	Eg	57.10N	13.24 E
Smalininkai/Smalininkaj	116	Ji	55.01N	22.32 E
Smalininkaj/Smalininkai	116	Ji	55.01N	22.32 E
Smallingerland-Drachten	122	Ma	53.06N	6.05 E
Smallwood Reservoir	174	Md	54.00N	64.30W
Smederevo	130	De	44.39N	20.56 E
Smederevska Palanka	130	De	44.22N	20.58 E
Smedjebacken	114	Df	60.08N	15.25 E
Smela	136	Df	49.13N	31.53 E
Smidovič	138	Ig	48.36N	133.50 E
Šmidta, ostrov-	140	La	81.08N	90.48 E
Šmidta, poluostrov-	138	Jf	54.15N	142.40 E
Śmigiel	120	Md	52.01N	16.32 E
Smilde	124	Ib	52.56N	6.28 E
Smiltene	114	Fh	57.28N	25.56 E
Smirnovo	134	Ni	54.31N	69.28 E
Smirnyh	138	Jg	49.45N	142.53 E
Smith	204	Bl	35.30S	61.36W
Smith Arm	180	Fc	66.15N	124.00W
Smith Bay [Ak.-U.S.]	178	Ib	70.51N	154.25W
Smith Bay [Can.]	180	Ja	77.15N	79.00W
Smith Center	186	Gg	39.47N	98.47W
Smithers	180	Ef	54.47N	127.10W
Smithfield [S.Afr.]	172	Df	30.09S	26.30 E
Smithfield [Ut.-U.S.]	188	Jf	41.50N	111.50W
Smith Mountain Lake	184	Hg	37.10N	79.40W
Smith Peak	188	Gb	48.50N	116.39W
Smith River	188	Jc	47.25N	111.29W
Smiths Falls	180	Jh	44.54N	76.01W
Smith's Knoll	118	Pi	52.50N	2.10 E
Smith Sound	188	Ba	51.18N	127.48W
Smithton	210	Fi	40.51S	145.07 E
Smjadovo	130	Kf	43.04N	27.01 E
Smjörfjoll	114a	Cb	65.35N	14.46W
Smögen	116	Df	58.21N	11.13 E
Smoke Creek Desert	188	Ff	40.30N	119.40W
Smokey Dome	188	He	43.29N	114.56W
Smoky Bay	212	Gf	32.20S	133.45 E
Smoky Cape	212	Kf	30.56S	153.05 E
Smoky Falls	180	Jf	50.03N	82.10W
Smoky Hill	174	Jf	39.03N	96.48W
Smoky Hills	186	Gg	39.15N	99.00W
Smoky River	180	Fe	56.11N	117.19W
Smøla	114	Be	63.25N	8.00 E
Smolensk	112	Je	54.47N	32.03 E
Smolenskaja oblast [3]	136	De	55.00N	33.00 E
Smolenskaja vozvyšennost = Smolensk Upland (EN)	110	Je	54.40N	33.00 E
Smolensko, oblast de- (E) [3]	136	De	55.00N	33.00 E
Smolensk Upland (EN) = Smolenskaja vozvyšennost	110	Je	54.40N	33.00 E
Smoleviči	132	Fb	54.03N	28.02 E
Smolianica	120	Ud	52.40N	24.40 E
Smólikas Óros	110	Ig	40.06N	20.55 E
Smoljan	130	Hh	41.35N	24.41 E
Smoljan [2]	130	Hh	41.40N	24.40 E
Smooth Rock Falls	184	Ga	49.20N	81.39W
Smorgon	136	Ce	54.31N	26.23 E
Smørstabbtren	116	Cc	61.32N	8.06 E
Smrdeš	130	Fh	41.34N	22.28 E
Smygehamn	116	Ei	55.21N	13.22 E
Smygehuk	116	Ei	55.21N	13.23 E
Smyley, Cape-	222	Qf	72.00S	78.50W
Smyrna	184	Ei	33.53N	84.31W
Smyrna → İzmir	142	Ef	38.25N	27.09 E
Smyšljajevka	114	Mj	53.17N	50.24 E
Smythe, Mount-	174	Gd	57.50N	124.59W
Snacke Point	197b	Bb	18.17N	62.58W
Snæfell	114a	Cb	64.48N	15.34W
Snaefell	118	Ig	54.16N	4.27W
Snæfellsjökull	114a	Ab	64.49N	23.46W
Snag	180	Dd	62.23N	140.22W
Snake Bay Settlement	212	Gb	11.25S	130.40 E
Snake Range	188	Hg	39.00N	114.15W
Snake River [Can.]	180	Ec	65.57N	134.13W
Snake River [U.S.]	174	He	46.12N	119.02W
Snake River Plain	182	Ec	42.45N	114.30W
Snare	180	Fd	63.15N	116.08W
Snares Islands	216	Ci	48.00S	166.35 E
Snarumselva	116	Cd	59.57N	9.58 E
Snåsa	114	Cd	64.15N	12.22 E
Sneek	122	La	53.02N	5.40 E
Snekermeer	122	La	53.04N	5.40 E
Snežnaja, gora-	138	Lc	65.18N	165.30 E
Snežnik	128	Ie	45.26N	14.36 E
Snežnogorsk	138	Dc	68.15N	87.35 E
Šnežnoje	132	Kf	47.59N	38.50 E
Śniardwy, Jezioro-	120	Rc	53.46N	21.44 E
Śnieżka	110	He	50.45N	15.43 E
Śnieżnik	120	Mf	50.12N	16.50 E
Snigirevka	132	Hf	47.04N	32.45 E
Snillfjord	116	Ca	63.24N	9.30 E
Snina	120	Sh	48.59N	22.08 E
Snizort, Loch-	118	Gd	57.30N	6.25W
Snjatyn	132	De	48.29N	25.34 E
Snøhetta	110	Gc	62.20N	9.17 E
Snohomish	188	Dc	47.55N	122.06W
Snønuten	116	Be	59.31N	6.54 E
Snøonipa	116	Bc	61.42N	6.41 E
Snota	116	Cb	62.51N	9.06 E
Snov	132	Gd	51.32N	31.33 E
Snowbird Lake	180	Hd	60.40N	102.50W
Snowdon	110	Fe	53.04N	4.05W
Snowdonia	118	Jh	53.05N	3.55W
Snowdrift	180	Gd	62.23N	110.47W
Snowflake	188	Ji	34.30N	110.05W
Snow Hill	184	Jf	38.11N	75.24W
Snow Lake	180	Hf	54.53N	100.02W
Snow Mountain	182	Cd	39.23N	122.46W
Snowshoe Peak	188	Hb	48.13N	115.41W
Snowville	188	If	41.58N	112.43W
Snowy Mountain [N.Amer.]	188	Fb	49.02N	119.57W
Snowy Mountain [N.Y.-U.S.]	184	Jd	43.42N	74.23W
Snowy Mountains	212	Jg	36.30S	148.20 E
Snowy River	212	Jg	37.48S	148.32 E
Snudy, ozero-	116	Li	55.40N	27.15 E
Snug Corner	194	Kb	22.32N	73.53W
Snuŏl	148	Lf	12.04N	106.26 E
Snyder	182	Ge	32.44N	100.55W
Soalala	172	Hc	16.07S	45.21 E
Soalara	172	Gd	23.35S	43.44 E
Soanierana-Ivongo	172	Hc	16.54S	49.34 E
Soar	124	Ab	52.52N	1.17W
Şoarş	130	Hd	45.56N	24.55 E
Soavinandriana	172	Hc	19.10S	46.43 E
Sob [R.S.F.S.R.]	134	Mc	66.20N	66.02 E
Sob [Ukr.-U.S.S.R.]	132	Fe	48.41N	29.17 E
Soba	166	Gc	10.59N	8.04 E
Sobaek-Sanmaek	154	Jf	36.00N	128.00 E
Sobat (EN)=Sawbā	158	Kh	9.45N	31.45 E
Sobernheim	124	Je	49.48N	7.39 E
Soběslav	120	Kg	49.16N	14.44 E
Sōbetsu	156a	Bb	42.33N	140.51 E
Sobinka	114	Jh	56.01N	40.07 E
Sobolevo [R.S.F.S.R.]	132	Qd	51.59N	51.48 E
Sobolevo [R.S.F.S.R.]	138	Kf	54.17N	156.00 E
Sobolew	120	Re	51.41N	21.40 E
Sobo-San	156	Be	32.47N	131.21 E
Sobradinho	204	Fi	29.24S	53.03W
Sobral	200	Lf	3.42S	40.21W
Sobrarbe	126	Mb	42.20N	0.05 E
Soca	204	El	34.41S	55.41W
Soča=Isonzo (EN)	128	He	45.43N	13.33 E
Sochaczew	120	Qd	52.14N	20.14 E
Soči	112	Jg	43.35N	39.45 E
Société, Iles de la-=Society Islands (EN)	208	Lf	17.00S	150.00W
Society Islands (EN)= Société, Iles de la-	208	Lf	17.00S	150.00W
Socompa, Paso-	198	Jh	24.27S	68.18W
Socorro [Col.]	202	Db	6.27N	73.16W

Index Symbols

- [1] Independent Nation
- [2] State, Region
- [3] District, County
- [4] Municipality
- [5] Colony, Dependency
- Continent
- Physical Region
- Historical or Cultural Region
- Mount, Mountain
- Volcano
- Hill
- Mountains, Mountain Range
- Hills, Escarpment
- Plateau, Upland
- Pass, Gap
- Plain, Lowland
- Delta
- Salt Flat
- Valley, Canyon
- Crater, Cave
- Karst Features
- Depression
- Polder
- Desert, Dunes
- Forest, Woods
- Heath, Steppe
- Oasis
- Cape, Point
- Coast, Beach
- Cliff
- Peninsula
- Isthmus
- Sandbank
- Island
- Atoll
- Rock, Reef
- Islands, Archipelago
- Rocks, Reefs
- Coral Reef
- Well, Spring
- Geyser
- River, Stream
- Waterfall, Rapids
- River Mouth, Estuary
- Lake
- Salt Lake
- Intermittent Lake
- Reservoir
- Swamp, Pond
- Canal
- Glacier
- Ice Shelf, Pack Ice
- Ocean
- Sea
- Gulf, Bay
- Strait, Fjord
- Lagoon
- Bank
- Seamount
- Tablemount
- Ridge
- Shelf
- Basin
- Escarpment, Sea Scarp
- Fracture
- Trench, Abyss
- National Park, Reserve
- Point of Interest
- Recreation Site
- Cave, Cavern
- Historic Site
- Ruins
- Wall, Walls
- Church, Abbey
- Temple
- Scientific Station
- Railway station
- Airport
- Port
- Military installation
- Lighthouse
- Mine
- Tunnel
- Dam, Bridge

Socorro [N.M.-U.S.] 182 Fe 34.04N 106.54W
Socorro, Isla- 190 Be 18.45N 110.58W
Socotra (EN) = Suquṭrá 140 Hh 12.30N 54.00 E
Soc Trang 148 Lg 9.36N 105.58 E
Socuéllamos 126 Je 39.17N 2.48W
Sodankylä 114 Gc 67.25N 26.36 E
Soda Springs 188 Je 42.39N 111.36W
Söderåsen 116 Eh 56.04N 13.05 E
Söderfors 114 Df 60.23N 17.14 E
Söderhamn 114 Df 61.18N 17.03 E
Söderköping 116 Gf 58.29N 16.18 E
Södermanland [2] 114 Dg 59.15N 16.40 E
Södermanland 116 Ge 59.10N 16.50 E
Söderslätt 116 Ei 55.30N 13.15 E
Södertälje 114 Dg 59.12N 17.37 E
Södertörn 116 Ge 59.05N 18.00 E
Sodo 168 Fd 6.51N 37.45 E
Södra Dellen 116 Gc 61.50N 16.45 E
Södra Gloppet 116 Ia 63.05N 21.00 E
Södra Kvarken 116 Hd 60.20N 19.08 E
Södra-Midsjöbanken 116 Gi 55.40N 17.20 E
Södra Vi 116 Fg 57.45N 15.48 E
Soe 150 Hh 9.52S 124.17 E
Soekmekaar 172 Dd 23.28S 29.58 E
Soela, Proliv- / Soela Väin 116 Jf 58.40N 22.30 E
Soela Väin / Soela, Proliv- 116 Jf 58.40N 22.30 E
Soest [Ger.] 120 Ee 51.35N 8.07 E
Soest [Neth.] 124 Hb 52.10N 5.20 E
Soeste 124 Ja 53.10N 7.44 E
Soester Borde 124 Kc 51.38N 8.03 E
Soestwetering 124 Ib 51.30N 6.09 E
Sofádhes 130 Fj 39.20N 22.06 E
Sofala [3] 172 Ec 19.30S 34.40 E
Sofala, Baia de- 158 Kk 20.11S 34.45 E
Sofia [2] 130 Gg 42.43N 23.25 E
Sofia 172 Hc 15.27S 47.23 E
Sofia (EN)=Sofija 112 Ig 42.41N 23.19 E
Sofija=Sofia (EN) 112 Ig 42.41N 23.19 E
Sofijsk 138 If 52.20N 134.01 E
Sofporog 136 Db 65.48N 31.28 E
Sofrána, Nisídhes- 130 Jm 36.04N 26.24 E
Sōfu-Gan 152 Pf 29.50N 140.20 E
Sogamoso 202 Db 5.43N 72.56W
Soganlı 146 Eb 41.11N 32.38 E
Sogara, Lake- 170 Fd 5.15S 31.00 E
Sogda 138 If 50.24N 132.18 E
Sögel 120 Dd 52.51N 7.31 E
Sogeri 214 Di 9.10S 147.32 E
Sogn 116 Ac 61.05N 5.55 E
Sogndalsfjøra 116 Bc 61.14N 7.06 E
Søgne 116 Bf 58.05N 7.49 E
Sognefjell 116 Bc 61.35N 7.55 E
Sognefjorden 110 Gc 61.05N 5.10 E
Sognesjøen 116 Ac 61.05N 5.00 E
Sogn og Fjordane [2] 114 Bf 61.30N 6.50 E
Sogod 150 Hd 10.23N 124.59 E
Sogo Nur 152 Hc 42.20N 101.20 E
Sogoža 114 Jg 58.30N 39.06 E
Söğüt 130 Nj 40.00N 30.11 E
Söğütalan 130 Li 40.03N 28.34 E
Söğüt Gölü 146 Cd 37.03N 29.53 E
Sog Xian 152 Fe 31.51N 93.42 E
Soh 135 He 39.57N 71.08 E
Sohag (EN)=Sawhāj 160 Kf 26.33N 31.42 E
Sohano 214 Ei 5.29S 154.41 E
Sohŭksan-Do 154 Hg 34.04N 125.07 E
Soignies/Zinnik 122 Kd 50.35N 4.04 E
Soini 116 Kb 62.52N 24.13 E
Soisalo 116 Mb 62.40N 28.10 E
Soissonnais, Plateau du- 122 Je 49.20N 3.10 E
Soissons 122 Je 49.22N 3.20 E
Sōja 156 Cd 34.40N 133.44 E
Sojana 114 Kd 65.53N 43.30 E
Sojma 134 Ec 67.00N 51.00 E
Šojna 134 Bc 67.52N 44.08 E
Sŏjosŏn-man=Korea Bay (EN) 140 Of 39.15N 125.00 E
Sojuznoje 132 Vd 50.50N 60.10 E
Sojuz Sovetskih Socialističeskih Respublik (SSSR) [1] 142 Jd 60.00N 80.00 E
Sojuz Sovetskih Socialističeskih Respublik =USSR (EN) [1] 142 Jd 60.00N 80.00 E
Sok 136 Fe 53.25N 50.10 E
Sokal 132 Dd 50.29N 24.17 E
Šokalskogo, proliv- 138 Ea 79.00N 100.00 E
Sokch'o 152 Md 38.12N 128.36 E
Söke 144 Cb 37.45N 27.24 E
Sokele 170 Dd 9.55S 24.36 E
Sokirjany 132 Ee 48.28N 27.25 E
Sokna 114 Bf 60.14N 9.54 E
Soko Banja 130 Ef 43.39N 21.53 E
Sokodé 160 Hh 8.59N 1.08 E
Sokol 136 Ed 59.29N 40.13 E
Sokol 130 Ce 44.18N 19.25 E
Sokółka 120 Tc 53.25N 23.31 E
Sokolo 166 Dc 14.44N 6.07W
Sokolov 120 If 50.11N 12.38 E
Sokołów Podlaski 120 Sd 52.25N 22.15 E
Sokone 166 Bc 13.53N 16.22W
Sokosti 114 Gb 68.20N 28.01 E
Sokoto 160 Hg 13.04N 5.15 E
Sokoto [2] 166 Gc 12.20N 5.20 E
Sokoto 158 Hg 11.24N 4.07 E
Sokourala 166 Dd 9.13N 8.05W
Sōl 168 Hd 9.20N 49.25 E
Sol 168 Hd 9.40N 48.30 E
Sol, Costa del- 126 Ih 36.46N 3.55W
Sol, Pico do- 204 Ke 20.07S 43.28W
Sola 219b Ca 13.53S 167.33 E
Sola 120 Pf 50.04N 19.13 E
Solai 170 Gb 0.02N 36.09 E
Solakrossen 116 Af 58.53N 5.36 E
Solanet 204 Cm 36.51S 58.31W
Solāpur 142 Jh 17.41N 75.55 E
Solbad Hall in Tirol → Hall in Tirol 128 Fc 47.17N 11.31 E
Solcy 136 Dd 58.09N 30.20 E
Sölden 128 Ed 46.58N 11.00 E
Soldier Point 197d Bb 17.02N 61.41W
Soldotna 178 Id 60.29N 151.04W
Solec Kujawski 120 Oc 53.06N 18.14 E
Soledad [Arg.] 204 Bj 30.37S 60.55W
Soledad [Ca.-U.S.] 188 Eh 36.26N 121.19W
Soledad [Col.] 202 Da 10.55N 74.46W
Soledad [Ven.] 202 Fb 8.10N 63.34W
Soledad, Boca de- 192 Ce 25.17N 112.09W
Soledad, Isla-/East Falkland 198 Kk 51.45S 58.50W
Soledade 206 Jc 28.50S 52.30W
Sølen 116 Dc 61.55N 11.30 E
Sølensjøen 116 Dc 61.55N 11.35 E
Solentiname, Archipiélago de- 194 Fh 11.10N 85.00W
Solenzara 122a Bb 42.16N 9.24 E
Sole Pit 118 Oh 53.40N 1.30 E
Solesmes 124 Fd 50.11N 3.30 E
Solferino 128 Ee 45.23N 10.34 E
Solgen 116 Fg 57.33N 15.07 E
Solgne 124 Ie 48.58N 6.18 E
Soligalič 114 Kg 59.07N 42.13 E
Soligorsk 136 Ce 52.49N 27.31 E
Solihull 118 Li 52.25N 1.45W
Solikamsk 136 Fd 59.39N 56.47 E
Sol-Ileck 112 Le 51.12N 55.03 E
Solimán, Punta- 192 Ph 19.50N 87.27W
Solimoes → Amazonas, Rio- =Amazon (EN) 198 Lf 0.10S 49.00W
Solingen 120 De 51.11N 7.05 E
Solińskie, Jezioro- 120 Sg 49.22N 22.30 E
Solis, Presa- 192 Ig 20.05N 100.36W
Sollebrunn 116 Ef 58.07N 12.32 E
Sollefteå 114 De 63.10N 17.16 E
Sollentuna 116 Ge 59.28N 17.54 E
Sóller 126 Oe 39.46N 2.42 E
Sollerön 116 Fd 60.55N 14.37 E
Solling 120 Fe 51.45N 9.35 E
Solms 124 Kd 50.46N 8.36 E
Solna 116 He 59.22N 18.01 E
Solnečnogorsk 114 Ih 56.10N 37.00 E
Solnečny 138 Id 60.10N 137.35 E
Sologne 122 Hg 47.50N 2.00 E
Sologne Bourbonnaise 122 Jh 46.40N 3.30 E
Solok 150 Dg 0.48S 100.39 E
Sololá 194 Bf 14.46N 91.11W
Sololá [3] 194 Bf 14.40N 91.15W
Solomon Basin (EN) 214 Ei 7.00S 152.00 E
Solomon Islands 208 Ge 8.00S 159.00 E
Solomon Islands (British Solomon Islands) [1] 210 Ge 8.00S 159.00 E
Solomon River 182 Hd 38.54N 97.22W
Solomon Sea 208 Ge 8.00S 155.00 E
Solon Springs 186 Kc 46.22N 91.48W
Solør 116 Dd 60.30N 11.55 E
Solor, Kepulauan- 150 Hh 8.25S 123.30 E
Solothurn 128 Bc 47.15N 7.30 E
Solothurn [2] 128 Bc 47.20N 7.40 E
Solotvin 120 Uh 48.38N 24.31 E
Soloveckije ostrova 114 Id 65.05N 35.45 E
Solovjevka 116 Nd 60.44N 30.20 E
Solovjevsk [R.S.F.S.R.] 136 Gg 49.54N 115.43 E
Solovjevsk [R.S.F.S.R.] 138 Hf 54.15N 124.30 E
Sölöz 130 Mi 40.23N 29.25 E
Solre-le-Château 124 Gd 50.10N 4.05 E
Solsona 126 Nc 41.59N 1.31 E
Solt 120 Oj 46.48N 19.00 E
Šolta 128 Kg 43.23N 16.17 E
Solṭānābād [Iran] 146 Rd 36.23N 58.02 E
Solṭānābād [Iran] 146 Mg 31.03N 49.42 E
Solṭānī, Khowr-e- 146 Nh 29.00N 50.50 E
Solṭānīyeh 146 Md 36.26N 48.48 E
Soltau 120 Fd 52.59N 9.50 E
Soltvadkert 120 Pj 46.35N 19.23 E
Solvang 188 Ei 34.36N 120.08W
Sölvesborg 114 Dh 56.03N 14.33 E
Solvyčegodsk 114 Lf 61.21N 46.52 E
Solway Firth 118 Jg 54.50N 3.35W
Solwezi 160 Jj 12.11S 26.24 E
Soma 146 Bc 39.10N 27.36 E
Sōma 154 Pf 37.48N 140.57 E
Somain 124 Fd 50.22N 3.17 E
Somalia (EN)= Soomaaliya [1] 160 Lh 10.00N 49.00 E
Somali Basin (EN) 106 Fi 0.00 52.00 E
Sombo 170 Dd 8.42S 20.57 E
Sombor 130 Cd 45.46N 19.07 E
Sombrerete 190 Dd 23.38N 103.39W
Sombrero 190 Le 18.36N 63.26W
Sombrero Channel 148 Ig 7.41N 93.35 E
Sombrio 204 Hi 29.07S 49.40W
Sombrio, Lagoa do- 204 Hi 29.12S 49.42W
Somcuța Mare 130 Gb 47.31N 23.28 E
Someren 124 Hc 51.23N 5.43 E
Somero 116 Jd 60.37N 23.32 E
Somerset [3] 118 Jk 51.10N 3.00W
Somerset 118 Kj 51.00N 3.00W
Somerset 174 Jb 73.30N 93.30W
Somerset [Austl.] 212 Ib 10.35S 142.15 E
Somerset [Ky.-U.S.] 182 Kd 37.05N 84.36W
Somerset [Pa.-U.S.] 184 He 40.02N 79.05W
Somerset East 172 Df 32.42S 25.35 E
Somerton 188 Hj 32.36N 114.43W
Somerville Lake 186 Hk 30.18N 96.40W
Someş 130 Fa 48.07N 22.20 E
Someşu Mare 130 Gb 47.09N 23.55 E
Someşu Mic 130 Gb 47.09N 23.55 E
Somme [3] 122 Ie 49.55N 2.30 E
Somme 122 Hd 50.11N 1.39 E
Somme, Baie de- 124 Dd 50.14N 1.33 E
Somme, Bassurelle de la- 124 Dd 50.15N 1.10 E
Somme, Canal de la- 122 Hd 50.11N 1.39 E
Somme-Leuze 124 Hd 50.20N 5.22 E
Somme-Leuze-Hogne 124 Hd 50.15N 5.17 E
Sommen 116 Ff 58.08N 14.58 E
Sommen 114 Dh 58.00N 15.15 E
Sommepy-Tahure 124 Ge 49.15N 4.33 E
Sömmerda 120 He 51.09N 11.06 E
Somogy [2] 120 Nj 46.25N 17.35 E
Somontano Pirenaico 126 Lc 42.02N 0.20W
Somosierra, Puerto de- 126 Ic 41.09N 3.35W
Somosomo Strait 219d Bb 16.47S 179.58 E
Somotillo 194 Dg 13.02N 86.53W
Somoto 190 Gf 13.28N 86.35W
Somovo 132 Kd 51.45N 39.25 E
Sompolno 120 Od 52.24N 18.31 E
Somport, Puerto de- 126 Lb 42.48N 0.31W
Son 140 Kg 25.50N 84.55 E
Soná 194 Gi 8.01N 81.19W
Sona 120 Qd 52.33N 20.35 E
Sonaguera 194 Df 15.38N 86.20W
Sonári, Ákra 130 Lm 36.27N 28.13 E
Sŏnch'on 154 He 39.48N 124.55 E
Søndeled 116 Bg 58.46N 9.05 E
Sønderborg 114 Bi 54.55N 9.47 E
Sønder-Jylland [2] 116 Ci 55.00N 9.00 E
Sønder-Omme 116 Ci 55.50N 8.54 E
Sondershausen 120 Ge 51.22N 10.52 E
Søndre Strømfjord 224 Nc 66.59N 50.40W
Søndre Strømfjord 179 Ge 66.10N 53.10W
Søndre Upernavik 179 Gd 72.10N 55.38W
Sondrio 128 Dd 46.10N 9.52 E
Sonepat 148 Fc 28.59N 77.01 E
Song 166 Hd 9.50N 12.37 E
Songa 116 Be 59.47N 7.43 E
Songavatn 116 Be 59.50N 7.35 E
Song Cau 148 Lf 13.27N 109.13 E
Songe 116 Cf 58.41N 9.01 E
Songea 160 Kj 10.41S 35.39 E
Songeons 124 De 49.33N 1.52 E
Songhua Hu 154 Ic 43.30N 126.51 E
Songhua Jiang=Sungari (EN) 140 Pe 47.42N 132.30 E
Songjiang 152 Le 31.01N 121.14 E
Songjiang → Antu 154 Jc 42.33N 128.20 E
Songjianghe 154 Ic 42.10N 127.30 E
Sŏngjin → Kimch'aek 152 Mc 40.41N 129.12 E
Songjŏng 154 Ig 35.08N 126.48 E
Songkhla 142 Mi 7.13N 100.34 E
Songling 152 Lb 48.02N 121.08 E
Songnim 154 He 38.44N 125.38 E
Songo [Ang.] 170 Bd 7.21S 14.50 E
Songo [Moz.] 172 Ec 15.33S 32.48 E
Songololo 170 Bd 5.42S 14.02 E
Songpan (Sungqu) 152 He 32.37N 103.34 E
Songsa-dong 154 Hd 39.49N 124.49 E
Song Shan 152 Je 34.31N 113.00 E
Songshuzhen 154 Ic 42.01N 127.09 E
Songueur 126 Ni 35.11N 1.30 E
Songxian 154 Bg 34.12N 112.09 E
Songzi (Xinjiangkou) 154 Ai 30.10N 111.46 E
Sonid Youqi (Saihan Tal) 152 Jc 42.45N 112.36 E
Sonid Zuoqi (Mandalt) 152 Jc 43.50N 113.45 E
Sonkari 116 Lb 62.50N 26.35 E
Sonkël, ozero- 135 Jd 41.50N 75.10 E
Sonkovo 114 Ih 57.47N 37.09 E
Son La 148 Mj 21.19N 103.54 E
Sonmiāni Bay 148 Dc 25.15N 66.30 E
Sonneberg 120 Hf 50.21N 11.10 E
Sono, Rio do- [Braz.] 202 Ie 9.00S 48.11W
Sono, Rio do- [Braz.] 204 Jc 17.02S 45.32W
Sonobe 156 Dd 35.07N 135.28 E
Sonoita 190 Bb 31.51N 112.50W
Sonoma Peak 188 Gf 40.52N 117.36W
Sonora [2] 190 Bc 29.20N 110.40W
Sonora 190 Bc 28.48N 111.49W
Sonora [Ca.-U.S.] 188 Eh 37.59N 120.23W
Sonora [Tx.-U.S.] 186 Fk 30.34N 100.39W
Sonqor 146 Le 34.47N 47.36 E
Sonsbeck 124 Ic 51.37N 6.22 E
Sonsonate 190 Gf 13.43N 89.44W
Sonsorol Islands 208 Ed 5.20N 132.13 E
Sonthofen 120 Gi 47.31N 10.17 E
Sontra 120 Fe 51.04N 9.56 E
Soomaaliya=Somalia (EN) [1] 160 Lh 10.00N 49.00 E
Soomenlaht=Finland, Gulf of- (EN) 110 Ic 60.00N 27.00 E
Soonwald 124 Je 49.56N 7.35 E
Søorværøy 114 Cc 67.38N 12.40 E
Sopi, Tanjung- 150 If 2.39N 128.34 E
Sopo 168 Dd 8.51N 26.11 E
Sopockin 120 Tc 53.50N 23.42 E
Sopot [Bul.] 130 Hg 42.39N 24.45 E
Sopot [Pol.] 120 Ob 54.28N 18.34 E
Sopron 120 Mi 47.41N 16.36 E
Sopur 148 Eb 34.18N 74.28 E
Sor 126 De 39.00N 8.17W
Sora 128 Hi 41.43N 13.37 E
Sorachi-Gawa 156a Bb 43.32N 141.52 E
Soråker 116 Gb 62.31N 17.30 E
Sorak-san 152 Md 38.07N 128.28 E
Sorano 128 Fh 42.41N 11.43 E
Soratfeld 124 Kc 51.40N 8.55 E
Sorbas 126 Jg 37.07N 2.07W
Sorbe 126 Id 40.51N 3.08W
Sörberget 116 Gb 62.31N 17.22 E
Sore 122 Fj 44.19N 0.35W
Sorel 180 Kg 46.03N 73.07W
Sorell, Cape- 212 Jh 42.10S 145.10 E
Soresina 128 De 45.17N 9.51 E
Sorezaru Point 219a Cb 7.37S 156.38 E
Sørfjorden 116 Bd 60.25N 6.40 E
Sørfold 114 Dc 67.28N 15.28 E
Sorgues 122 Kj 44.00N 4.52 E
Sorgun 146 Fc 39.50N 35.19 E
Soria 126 Jc 41.46N 2.28W
Soria [3] 126 Jc 41.40N 2.40W
Soriano [2] 204 Dk 33.30S 57.45W
Sørkapp 224 Kd 76.28N 16.36 E
Sorkh, Godār-e- 146 Pf 33.05N 55.05 E
Sorkh, Kūh-e- 146 Pf 33.05N 55.05 E
Sorkheh 146 Oe 35.28N 53.13 E
Sorø 116 Di 55.26N 11.34 E
Sorocaba 200 Lh 23.29S 47.27W
Soroči Gory 114 Li 55.24N 49.55 E
Soročinsk 136 Fe 52.26N 53.10 E
Soroki 132 Fe 48.07N 28.16 E
Sorol Atoll 208 Fd 8.08N 140.23 E
Sorong 210 Ee 0.53S 131.15 E
Sorot 116 Mg 57.04N 28.50 E
Soroti 160 Kh 1.43N 33.37 E
Sørøya 110 Ia 70.36N 22.46 E
Sørøyane 116 Ab 62.20N 5.45 E
Sorraia 126 Df 38.56N 8.53W
Sørreisa 114 Eb 69.09N 18.10 E
Sorrentina, Penisola- 128 Ij 40.35N 14.30 E
Sorrento 128 Ij 40.37N 14.22 E
Sør Rondane 222 Df 72.00S 25.00 E
Sorsatunturi 114 Gc 67.24N 29.38 E
Sorsavesi 116 Lb 62.30N 27.35 E
Sorsele 114 Dd 65.32N 17.30 E
Sorsk 138 Ef 54.00N 90.20 E
Sorso 128 Cj 40.48N 8.34 E
Sorsogon 150 Hd 12.58N 124.00 E
Sort 126 Nb 42.24N 1.08 E
Šortandi 136 He 51.42N 71.05 E
Sortavala 136 Dc 61.44N 30.41 E
Sortland 114 Db 68.42N 15.24 E
Sør-Trøndelag [2] 114 Ce 63.00N 10.40 E
Sorum 134 Ne 63.50N 68.05 E
Sørumsand 116 De 59.58N 11.15 E
Šoša 114 Ih 56.33N 36.09 E
Sŏsan 154 If 36.47N 126.27 E
Sösdala 116 Eh 56.02N 13.40 E
Sos del Rey Católico 126 Kb 42.30N 1.13W
Sosna 132 Kc 52.42N 38.55 E
Sosnogorsk 112 Lc 63.37N 53.51 E
Sosnovka [R.S.F.S.R.] 132 Lc 53.14N 41.22 E
Sosnovka [R.S.F.S.R.] 114 Mh 56.18N 51.17 E
Sosnovka [R.S.F.S.R.] 114 Jc 66.31N 40.33 E
Sosnovka [Ukr.-U.S.S.R.] 132 Dd 50.15N 24.13 E
Sosnovo 116 Nd 60.31N 30.29 E
Sosnovo-Ozerskoje 138 Gf 52.31N 111.35 E
Sosnovy Bor 116 Me 59.48N 29.10 E
Sosnowiec 120 Pf 50.18N 19.08 E
Sospel 122 Nk 43.53N 7.27 E
Šostka 136 De 51.52N 33.31 E
Sosumav 172 Hb 13.03S 48.54 E
Sosva 136 Gd 59.32N 62.20 E
Sosva [R.S.F.S.R.] 136 Gd 59.10N 61.50 E
Sosva [R.S.F.S.R.] 136 Gc 63.40N 62.02 E
Sotavento [3] 162 Cf 14.40N 23.25W
Sotavento, Islas de- = Windward Islands (EN) 198 Jd 11.10N 67.00W
Sotik 170 Gc 0.41S 35.07 E
Sotkamo 114 Gd 64.08N 28.25 E
Soto la Marina 192 Jf 23.48N 98.13W
Soto la Marina, Rio- 192 Kf 23.45N 97.45W
Sotonera, Embalse de la- 126 Lb 42.05N 0.48W
Sotouboua 166 Fd 8.34N 0.59 E
Sotra 116 Ad 60.20N 5.05 E
Sotsudaka-Zaki 156b Ba 28.15N 129.10 E
Sottern 116 Fe 59.05N 15.30 E
Sotteville-lès-Rouen 122 He 49.25N 1.06 E
Sottrum 124 La 53.07N 9.14 E
Sottunga 116 Id 60.10N 20.40 E
Sotuf, Adrar- 162 De 21.42N 15.36W
Sotuta 192 Og 20.36N 89.01W
Souanké 170 Bb 2.05N 14.03 E
Soubré 166 Dd 5.47N 6.36W
Soubré [3] 166 Dd 5.47N 6.38W
Soúdha 130 Hn 35.29N 24.04 E
Souf 158 He 33.25N 6.50 E
Soufflenheim 124 Jf 48.50N 7.58 E
Souflíon 130 Jh 41.12N 26.18 E
Soufrière 196 Ff 13.52N 61.04W
Soufrière [Guad.] 190 Le 16.03N 61.40W
Soufrière [St.Vin.] 190 Lf 13.21N 61.11W
Soufrière Bay 197g Bb 15.13N 61.22W
Soufrière Hills 197c Bc 16.43N 62.10W
Souillac 122 Hj 44.54N 1.29 E
Souilly 122 Le 49.01N 5.17 E
Souk Ahras 162 Ib 36.17N 7.57 E
Souk el Arba du Rharb 162 Fc 34.41N 5.59W
Sŏul=Seoul (EN) 142 Of 37.34N 127.00 E
Soulac-sur-Mer 122 Ei 45.30N 1.06W
Sŏul Si [2] 154 If 37.35N 127.00 E
Soultz-sous-Forêts 124 Jf 48.56N 7.53 E
Soumagne 124 Hd 50.37N 5.45 E
Soummam 126 Rh 36.44N 5.04 E
Sounding Creek 188 Ja 52.06N 110.28W
Soúnion 130 Hl 37.39N 24.02 E
Soúnion, Ákra- 130 Hl 37.39N 24.01 E
Sources, Mont aux- 158 Jk 28.46S 28.52 E
Soure [Braz.] 202 Id 0.44S 48.31W
Soure [Port.] 126 Dd 40.03N 8.38W
Sour el Ghozlane 162 Hb 36.09N 3.41 E
Souris 180 Hg 49.38N 100.15W
Souris 174 Je 49.39N 99.34W
Sous 162 Fc 30.25N 9.30W
Sous 162 Fc 30.22N 9.37W
Sousa 200 Mf 6.45S 38.14W
Sousel 126 Ef 38.57N 7.40W
Sous le Vent, Iles-= Leeward Islands (EN) 208 Lf 16.38S 151.30W
Sousse (EN)=Sūsah [3] 162 Jb 35.45N 10.30 E
Sousse (EN)=Sūsah [Tun.] 160 Ie 35.49N 10.38 E
Sout 172 Cf 33.03S 23.29 E
Souterraine, La- 122 Hh 46.14N 1.29 E
South Africa/Suid-Afrika [1] 160 Jl 30.00S 26.00 E
South Alligator River 212 Gb 12.15S 132.24 E
Southam 124 Ab 52.15N 1.23W
South America (EN) 106 Ck 15.00S 60.00W
Southampton 174 Kc 64.20N 84.40W
Southampton [Eng.-U.K.] 112 Fe 50.55N 1.25W
Southampton [N.Y.-U.S.] 184 Ke 40.54N 72.23W
Southampton, Cape- 180 Jd 62.08N 83.44W
Southampton Airport 124 Ad 50.55N 1.23W
Southampton Water 124 Ad 50.52N 1.20W
South Andaman 148 If 11.45N 92.45 E
Southard, Cape- 222 Ie 66.33S 122.04 E
South Auckland-Bay of Plenty [2] 218 Fb 38.00S 176.00 E
South Aulatsivik 180 Le 56.47N 61.30W
South Australia [2] 212 Ge 30.00S 135.00 E
South Australian Basin (EN) 106 Im 40.00S 128.00 E
Southaven 186 Li 35.00N 90.00W
South Baldy 186 Cj 33.59N 107.11W
South Bay 180 Jd 64.00N 83.25W
South Bend 182 Jc 41.41N 86.15W
South Benfleet 124 Cc 51.32N 0.33 E
Southborough 124 Cc 51.09N 0.15 E
South Boston 184 Hg 36.42N 78.58W
Southbridge 218 Ee 43.48S 172.15 E
South Buganda [3] 170 Fc 0.30S 32.00 E
South Caicos 194 Lc 21.31N 71.30W
South Carolina [2] 182 Ke 34.00N 81.00W
South China Basin (EN) 106 Hh 15.00N 115.00 E
South China Sea (EN)=Bien Dong 140 Ni 10.00N 113.00 E
South China Sea (EN)=Cina Selatan, Laut- 140 Ni 10.00N 113.00 E
South China Sea (EN)=Nan Hai 140 Ni 10.00N 113.00 E
South Dakota [2] 182 Gc 44.15N 100.00W
South Downs 118 Mk 50.55N 0.25W
South-East [3] 172 De 25.00S 25.45 E
South East Cape 208 Fi 43.39S 146.50 E
Southeast Indian Ridge (EN) 106 Ho 50.00S 110.00 E
Southeast Pacific Basin (EN) 106 Mp 60.00S 115.00W
South East Point [Austl.] 208 Fh 39.00S 146.20 E
South East Point [Kir.] 220g Bb 1.40N 157.10W
Southend 180 He 56.20N 103.14W
Southend-on-Sea 118 Nj 51.33N 0.43 E
Southern [Bots.] [3] 172 Cd 24.45S 24.00 E
Southern [Mwi.] [3] 170 Gf 15.30S 35.00 E
Southern [S.L.] [3] 166 Cd 7.40N 12.15W
Southern [Ug.] [3] 170 Fc 0.30S 30.30 E
Southern [Zam.] [3] 170 Ef 16.00S 27.00 E
Southern Alps 208 Ii 43.30S 170.35 E
Southern Cook Islands 208 Lg 20.00S 159.00W
Southern Cross 210 Ch 31.13S 119.19 E
Southern Desert (EN)= Janūbīyah, Aş Şaḩrā' al- 158 Jf 24.00N 30.00 E
Southern Ghats 148 Ff 10.00N 76.50 E
Southern Gilbert Islands 214 Jh 1.30S 175.30 E
Southern Guinea (EN) 158 Ii 8.00S 14.00 E
Southern Indian Lake 174 Jd 57.10N 98.40W
Southern Pines 184 Hh 35.11N 79.24W
Southern Region (EN) = Al Iglim al Janūbīyah [2] 168 Dd 6.00N 30.00 E
Southern Sierra Madre (EN) =Madre del Sur, Sierra- 174 Jj 17.00N 100.00W
Southern Uplands 110 Fd 55.30N 3.30W
Southern Urals (EN)=Južny Ural 110 Le 54.00N 58.30 E
Southern Yemen (EN) → Yemen, People's Democratic Republic of- (EN) [1] 142 Gh 14.00N 46.00 E
South Esk 118 Ke 56.43N 2.28W
South Fiji Basin (EN) 106 Jl 26.00S 175.00 E
South Foreland 118 Oj 51.09N 1.23 E
South Fork 188 Ge 42.26N 116.53W
South Fork Flathead River 188 Ib 47.07N 113.45W
South Fork Grand River 186 Ed 45.43N 102.17W
South Fork Kern River 188 Fi 35.40N 118.27W
South Fork Moreau River 186 Ed 45.09N 102.50W
South Fork Powder River 188 Le 43.40N 106.30W
South Fork Republican River 186 Ff 40.03N 101.31W
South Georgia/Georgia del Sur 222 Ad 54.15S 36.45W
South Glamorgan [3] 118 Jj 51.30N 3.15W
South Haven 184 Dd 42.24N 86.16W
South Honshu Ridge (EN) 106 Ig 24.00N 142.00 E
South Horr 170 Gb 2.06N 36.55 E
South Indian Basin (EN) 222 Hd 60.00S 120.00 E
South Island [F.S.M.] 220d Bc 6.59N 151.59 E
South Island [Kenya] 170 Gb 2.38N 36.36 E
South Island [N.Z.] 208 Ii 44.00S 171.00 E
South Island [Sey.] 172b Ab 9.26S 46.23 E
South Island [Sey.] 172b Bc 10.10S 51.10 E
South Korea (EN)=Taehan-Min'guk [1] 142 Of 36.00N 127.30 E
South Lake Tahoe 188 Eg 38.57N 120.01W
Southland [2] 218 Bf 45.45S 168.00 E
South Loup River 186 Gf 41.04N 98.40W
South Lueti 170 Df 16.14S 23.12 E
South Magnetic Pole (1980) (EN) 222 Ie 65.08S 139.03 E
South Malosmadulu Atoll 148a Ba 5.10N 72.58 E
South Mountain 188 Ge 42.44N 116.54W
South Nahanni 180 Fd 61.03N 123.22W
South Negril Point 190 Ie 18.16N 78.22W
South Orkney Islands (EN) 222 Re 60.35S 45.30W
South Pass 174 Ie 42.22N 108.55W
South Pass [F.S.M.] 220d Bb 7.14N 151.48 E
South Pass [U.S.] 186 Ll 28.55N 89.20W
South Platte 174 Ie 41.15N 100.45W
South Point 197q Ab 13.02N 59.31W
South Pole (EN) 222 Bg 90.00S 0.00
South Porcupine 184 Ga 48.28N 81.13W
Southport [Eng.-U.K.] 118 Jh 53.39N 3.01W
Southport [N.C.-U.S.] 184 Hi 33.55N 78.01W
South Reef 219a Ee 13.00S 160.32 E
South Ronaldsay 118 Kc 58.46N 2.55W
South Rukuru 170 Fe 10.44S 34.14 E
South Saint Paul 186 Jd 44.52N 93.02W

Index Symbols

[1] Independent Nation
[2] State, Region
[3] District, County
[4] Municipality
[5] Colony, Dependency
Continent
Physical Region
Historical or Cultural Region
Mount, Mountain
Volcano
Hill
Mountains, Mountain Range
Hills, Escarpment
Plateau, Upland
Pass, Gap
Plain, Lowland
Delta
Salt Flat
Valley, Canyon
Crater, Cave
Karst Features
Depression
Polder
Desert, Dunes
Forest, Woods
Heath, Steppe
Oasis
Cape, Point
Coast, Beach
Cliff
Peninsula
Isthmus
Sandbank
Island
Atoll
Rock, Reef
Islands, Archipelago
Rocks, Reefs
Coral Reef
Well, Spring
Geyser
River, Stream
Waterfall, Rapids
River Mouth, Estuary
Lake
Salt Lake
Intermittent Lake
Reservoir
Swamp, Pond
Canal
Glacier
Ice Shelf, Pack Ice
Ocean
Sea
Gulf, Bay
Strait, Fjord
Lagoon
Bank
Seamount
Tablemount
Ridge
Shelf
Basin
Escarpment, Sea Scarp
Fracture
Trench, Abyss
National Park, Reserve
Point of Interest
Recreation Site
Cave, Cavern
Historic Site
Ruins
Wall, Walls
Church, Abbey
Temple
Scientific Station
Railway station
Airport
Port
Military installation
Lighthouse
Mine
Tunnel
Dam, Bridge

South Sandwich Islands (EN) 222 Ad 56.00S 26.30W
South Sandwich Trench (EN) 106 Do 56.30S 25.00W
South Saskatchewan River 174 Id 53.15N 105.05W
South Shetland Islands (EN) 222 Re 62.00S 58.00W
South Shields 118 Lg 55.00N 1.25W
South Sioux City 186 He 42.28N 96.24W
South Sister 188 Ed 44.12N 121.45W
South Taranaki Bight 218 Fc 39.40S 174.15 E
South Trap 218 Bg 47.30S 167.55 E
South Tyne 118 Kg 54.59N 2.08W
South Uist 118 Fd 57.15N 7.24W
South Umpqua River 188 De 43.20N 123.25W
Southwell 124 Ba 53.04N 0.57W
South Wellesley Islands 212 Hc 17.05S 139.25 E
South West Africa → Namibia [1] 160 Ik 22.00S 17.00 E
South West Cape 212 Jh 43.34S 146.02 E
Southwest Cape [N.Z.] 208 Hi 47.17S 167.27 E
Southwest Cape [V.I.U.S.] 197a Dc 17.42N 64.53W
Southwest Indian Ridge (EN) 106 Fm 32.00S 55.00 E
Southwest Miramichi River 184 Ob 46.50N 65.45W
Southwest Pacific Basin (EN) 106 Km 40.00S 150.00W
Southwest Pass 186 Ll 29.00N 89.20W
South West Point 197p Cb 12.27N 61.30W
South West Point 220g Ab 1.52N 157.33W
Southwest Point 194 Jb 22.10N 74.10W
Southwold 118 Oi 52.20N 1.40 E
South Yorkshire [3] 118 Lh 53.30N 1.25W
Soutpansberg 172 Dd 22.58S 29.50 E
Soverato 128 Kl 38.41N 16.33 E
Sovetabad 135 Gd 40.14N 69.42 E
Sovetsk [R.S.F.S.R.] 136 Cd 55.05N 21.52 E
Sovetsk [R.S.F.S.R.] 136 Ed 57.36N 48.58 E
Sovetskaja Gavan 142 Qe 48.58N 140.18 E
Sovetski [R.S.F.S.R.] 136 Gc 61.20N 63.29 E
Sovetski [R.S.F.S.R.] 114 Lh 56.47N 48.30 E
Sovetski [R.S.F.S.R.] 116 Md 60.29N 28.40 E
Sovetski, proliv- 156a Db 43.24N 145.50 E
Sovetski Sojuz = Soviet Union (EN) [1] 142 Jd 60.00N 80.00 E
Sovetski Sojuz → SSSR [1] 142 Jd 60.00N 80.00 E
Sovetskoje 136 Ef 47.17N 44.30 E
Soviet Union (EN) = Sovetski Sojuz [1] 142 Jd 60.00N 80.00 E
Soviet Union (EN) = Union of Soviet Socialist Republics (EN) [1] 142 Jd 60.00N 80.00 E
Sowghān 146 Qh 28.20N 56.54 E
Sowie, Góry- 120 Mf 50.38N 16.30 E
Sōya 156a Ba 45.28N 141.53 E
Sōya-Kaikyō = La Perouse Strait (EN) 140 Qe 45.30N 142.00 E
Sōya-Misaki 152 Pb 45.31N 141.56 E
Soyatita 192 Fe 25.45N 107.22W
Soyo 170 Bd 6.05S 12.20 E
Sož 110 Je 51.57N 30.48 E
Sozopol 130 Kg 42.25N 27.42 E
Spa 122 Ld 50.29N 5.52 E
Spain (EN) = España [1] 112 Fg 40.00N 4.00W
Špakovskoje 132 Mg 45.06N 42.00 E
Spalding 118 Mi 52.47N 0.10W
Spanish Fork 188 Jf 40.07N 111.39W
Spanish Peak 188 Fd 44.24N 119.46W
Spanish Point 197d Ba 17.33N 61.44W
Spanish Sahara (EN) → Western Sahara (EN) [5] 160 Ff 24.30N 13.00W
Spanish Town [B.V.I.] 197a Db 18.27N 64.26W
Spanish Town [Jam.] 190 Ie 17.59N 76.57W
Sparbu 114 Ce 63.55N 11.28 E
Spargi, Isola- 128 Di 41.15N 9.20 E
Sparks 182 Dd 39.32N 119.45W
Sparreholm 116 Ge 59.04N 16.49 E
Sparta [Il.-U.S.] 186 Lg 38.07N 89.42W
Sparta [N.C.-U.S.] 184 Gg 36.30N 81.07W
Sparta [Tn.-U.S.] 184 Eh 35.56N 85.29W
Sparta [Wi.-U.S.] 186 Ke 43.57N 90.47W
Sparta (EN) = Spárti 130 Fl 37.05N 22.26 E
Spartanburg 182 Ke 34.57N 81.55W
Spartel, Cap- 158 Ge 35.48N 5.56W
Spárti = Sparta (EN) 130 Fl 37.05N 22.26 E
Spartivento, Capo- [It.] 110 Hh 37.55N 16.04 E
Spartivento, Capo- [It.] 128 Cl 38.53N 8.50 E
Spas-Demensk 132 Ib 54.24N 34.01 E
Spas-Klepiki 114 Ji 55.10N 40.13 E
Spassk-Dalni 138 Ih 44.37N 132.48 E
Spassk-Rjazanski 114 Ji 54.27N 40.22 E
Spátha, Ákra- = Spatha, Cape- (EN) 130 Gn 35.42N 23.44 E
Spatha, Cape- (EN) = Spátha, Ákra- 130 Gn 35.42N 23.44 E
Spearfish 182 Gc 44.30N 103.52W
Spearman 186 Fh 36.12N 101.12W
Speedway 184 Df 39.47N 86.15W
Speicher 124 Ie 49.56N 6.38 E
Speightstown 196 Gf 13.15N 59.39W
Speke Gulf 170 Fc 2.20S 33.15 E
Spello 128 Gh 42.59N 12.40 E
Spenard 178 Jd 61.11N 149.55W
Spence Bay 176 Jc 69.32N 93.31W
Spencer [Ia.-U.S.] 182 Hc 43.09N 95.09W
Spencer [In.-U.S.] 184 Df 39.17N 86.46W
Spencer [Nb.-U.S.] 186 Ge 42.53N 98.42W
Spencer [W.V.-U.S.] 184 Gf 38.48N 81.22W
Spencer, Cape- 212 Hg 35.18S 136.53 E
Spencer Gulf 208 Eh 34.00S 137.00 E
Spenge 124 Kb 52.08N 8.29 E
Spenser Mountains 218 Ee 42.10S 172.35 E
Sperillen 116 Dd 60.30N 10.05 E
Sperkhiós 130 Fk 38.52N 22.34 E
Sperlonga 128 Hi 41.15N 13.26 E
Sperone, Capo- 128 Cl 38.55N 8.25 E
Sperrin Mountains/Sliabh Speirin 118 Fg 54.50N 7.05W
Spessart 120 Fg 49.55N 9.30 E
Spétsai 130 Gl 37.16N 23.09 E
Spétsai 130 Gl 37.16N 23.08 E
Spey 118 Jd 57.40N 3.06W
Spey Bay 118 Jd 57.40N 3.05W
Speyer 120 Eg 49.19N 8.26 E
Speyer-bach 124 Ke 49.19N 8.27 E
Speyside 196 Fg 11.18N 60.32W
Spezzano Albanese 128 Kk 39.40N 16.19 E
Spicer Islands 180 Jc 68.10N 79.00W
Spiekeroog 120 Dc 53.46N 7.42 E
Spiess Seamount (EN) 222 Cd 54.40S 0.15 E
Spiez 128 Bd 46.41N 7.42 E
Spijkenisse 124 Gc 51.51N 4.21 E
Spilimbergo 128 Gd 46.07N 12.54 E
Spilion 130 Hn 35.13N 24.32 E
Spilsby 124 Ca 53.11N 0.06 E
Spina 128 Gf 44.42N 12.08 E
Spinazzola 128 Kj 40.58N 16.05 E
Spincourt 124 He 49.20N 5.40 E
Spirit River 180 Fe 55.47N 118.50W
Spirovo 114 Ih 57.27N 35.01 E
Spiš 120 Qg 49.05N 20.30 E
Spišská Nová Ves 120 Qh 48.57N 20.34 E
Spitak 132 Ni 40.49N 44.14 E
Spitsbergen 224 Kd 78.45N 16.00 E
Spitsbergen 224 Kd 78.00N 19.00 E
Spittal an der Drau 128 Hd 46.48N 13.30 E
Spitzbergen Bank (EN) 179 Oc 76.00N 23.00 E
Spjelkavik 114 Ba 62.28N 6.23 E
Split 112 Hg 43.31N 16.26 E
Split Lake 180 He 56.10N 96.10W
Spluga, Passo dello- 128 Dd 46.29N 9.20 E
Splügenpaß 128 Dd 46.29N 9.20 E
Śpógi/Špogi 116 Lh 56.02N 26.52 E
Špogi/Śpógi 116 Lh 56.02N 26.52 E
Spokane 176 He 47.40N 117.23W
Spokane, Mount- 188 Gc 47.55N 117.07W
Spokane River 188 Fc 47.44N 118.20W
Špola 136 Df 49.01N 31.24 E
Spoleto 128 Gh 42.44N 12.44 E
Spooner 186 Kd 45.50N 91.53W
Spoon River 186 Kf 40.18N 90.04W
Sporovo 120 Vd 52.25N 25.27 E
Spotsylvania 184 If 38.12N 77.35W
Sprague 188 Gc 47.18N 117.59W
Sprague River 188 Ee 42.34N 121.51W
Spratly (EN) = NanKei Dao 150 Fe 8.42N 111.40 E
Spray 188 Fd 44.50N 119.48W
Spreča 128 Mf 44.44N 18.06 E
Spree 120 Jd 52.32N 13.13 E
Spreewald 120 Je 51.55N 14.00 E
Spremberg/Grodk 120 Ke 51.33N 14.22 E
Sprengisandur 114a Bb 64.40N 18.07W
Springbok 160 Ik 29.43S 17.15 E
Spring Creek 186 Fd 45.45N 100.18W
Springdale 186 Ih 36.11N 94.08W
Springe 120 Fd 52.13N 9.33 E
Springer 186 Dh 36.22N 104.36W
Springer, Mount- 184 Ja 49.48N 74.51W
Springerville 188 Ki 34.08N 109.17W
Springfield [Co.-U.S.] 186 Eh 37.24N 102.37W
Springfield [Il.-U.S.] 176 Kf 39.47N 89.40W
Springfield [Ma.-U.S.] 182 Mc 42.07N 72.36W
Springfield [Mn.-U.S.] 186 Id 44.14N 94.59W
Springfield [Mo.-U.S.] 176 Jf 37.14N 93.17W
Springfield [N.Z.] 218 De 43.20S 171.56 E
Springfield [Oh.-U.S.] 182 Kd 39.55N 83.48W
Springfield [Or.-U.S.] 182 Cc 44.03N 123.01W
Springfield [S.D.-U.S.] 186 He 42.49N 97.54W
Springfield [Tn.-U.S.] 184 Dg 36.31N 86.52W
Springfontein 172 Df 30.19S 25.36 E
Spring Garden 202 Gb 6.59N 58.31W
Spring Hall 197q Ab 13.19N 59.36W
Springhill [La.-U.S.] 186 Jj 33.00N 93.28W
Springhill [N.S.-Can.] 180 Lg 45.39N 64.03W
Spring Mountains 188 Hh 36.10N 115.40W
Springs 172 De 26.13S 28.25 E
Springsure 212 Jd 24.07S 148.05 E
Spring Valley 186 Je 43.41N 92.23W
Spring Valley 188 Hg 39.10N 114.30W
Springville 188 Jf 40.10N 111.37W
Spruce Knob 174 Lf 38.42N 79.32W
Spruce Mountain [Az.-U.S.] 188 Ii 34.28N 112.24W
Spruce Mountain [Nv.-U.S.] 188 Hf 40.33N 114.49W
Spulico, Capo- 128 Kk 39.58N 16.38 E
Spurn Head 118 Nh 53.34N 0.07 E
Squamish 180 Fg 49.42N 123.09W
Squillace 128 Kl 38.47N 16.31 E
Squillace, Golfo di- 128 Kl 38.45N 16.50 E
Squinzano 128 Mj 40.26N 18.02 E
Srbica 130 Dg 42.45N 20.47 E
Srbija = Serbia (EN) [2] 130 Df 44.00N 21.00 E
Srbija = Serbia (EN) 110 Ig 43.00N 21.00 E
Srbija = Serbia (EN) 130 Df 44.00N 21.00 E
Srbobran 130 Cd 45.33N 19.48 E
Srê Âmbĕl 148 Kf 11.07N 103.46 E
Sredinny hrebet 140 Rd 56.00N 158.00 E
Sredna Gora 130 Hg 42.30N 25.00 E
Srednekolymsk 138 Kc 67.27N 153.41 E
Srednerusskaja vozvyšennost = Central Russian Uplands (EN) 110 Je 52.00N 38.00 E
Srednesatyginski Tuman, ozero- 134 Lg 59.45N 65.25 E
Srednesibirskoje ploskogorje = Central Siberian Uplands (EN) 140 Mc 65.00N 105.00 E
Sredni Kujto, ozero- 114 Hd 65.05N 31.30 E
Sredni Ural = Central Urals (EN) 110 Ld 58.00N 59.00 E
Sredni Urgal 138 If 51.13N 132.58 E
Sredni Verecki, pereval- 132 Ce 48.49N 23.07 E
Srednjaja Ahtuba 132 Ne 48.43N 44.52 E
Srednjaja Olëkma 138 He 55.26N 120.40 E
Śrem 120 Nd 52.08N 17.01 E
Sremska Mitrovica 130 Ce 44.58N 19.37 E
Sremski Karlovci 130 Cd 45.12N 19.56 E
Sretensk 142 Nd 52.15N 117.43 E
Sri Gangānagar 148 Ec 29.55N 73.53 E
Sri Jayawardenepura 148 Gg 6.54N 80.02 E
Srijem 130 Cd 45.00N 19.40 E
Srikākulam 148 Ge 18.18N 83.54 E
Sri Lanka 140 Ki 7.30N 80.30 E
Sri Lanka (Ceylon) [1] 142 Ki 7.40N 80.50 E
Srīnagar 142 Jf 34.05N 74.49 E
Srivardhan 148 Ee 18.02N 73.01 E
Środa Śląska 120 Me 51.10N 16.36 E
Środa Wielkopolska 120 Nd 52.14N 17.17 E
Srpska Crnja 130 Dd 45.43N 20.42 E
Sruth na Maoile/North Channel 110 Fd 55.10N 5.40W
SSSR = Union of Soviet Socialist Republics (USSR) (EN) [1] 142 Jd 60.00N 80.00 E
SSSR → Sojuz Sovetskih Socialističeskih Respublik [1] 142 Jd 60.00N 80.00 E
Ssu-ch'uan Sheng → Sichuan Sheng = Szechwan (EN) [2] 152 He 30.00N 103.00 E
Staaten River 212 Ic 16.24S 141.17 E
Stabroek 124 Gc 51.20N 4.22 E
Stack Skerry 118 Ib 59.02N 4.30W
Stade 120 Fc 53.36N 9.29 E
Staden 124 Fd 50.59N 3.01 E
Stadhavet 116 Ab 62.15N 5.05 E
Stådjan 116 Ec 61.58N 12.52 E
Stadlandet 116 Ab 62.05N 5.20 E
Stadskanaal 122 Ma 53.00N 6.55 E
Stadskanaal-Musselkanaal 124 Jb 52.56N 7.02 E
Stadtallendorf 124 Ld 50.50N 9.00 E
Stadthagen 124 Lb 52.19N 9.12 E
Stadtkyll 124 Id 50.21N 6.32 E
Stadtlohn 124 Ic 51.59N 6.56 E
Stadtoldendorf 120 Fe 51.54N 9.39 E
Staffa 118 Ge 56.25N 6.10W
Staffanstorp 116 Ei 55.38N 13.13 E
Staffelsee 120 Hi 47.42N 11.10 E
Staffora 128 De 45.04N 9.01 E
Stafford 118 Ki 52.48N 2.07W
Stafford 118 Li 52.50N 2.00W
Staffordshire [3] 118 Li 52.55N 2.00W
Staicele/Stajcele 116 Kg 57.44N 24.39 E
Stainach 128 Ic 47.32N 14.06 E
Staines 124 Bc 51.26N 0.31W
Stakčin 120 Sg 49.00N 22.13 E
Stalać 130 Ef 43.40N 21.25 E
Stalham 124 Db 52.46N 1.31 E
Stalingrad → Volgograd 112 Kf 48.44N 44.25 E
Ställdalen 116 Fe 59.56N 14.56 E
Stalowa Wola 120 Sf 50.35N 22.02 E
Stamford [Ct.-U.S.] 184 Ke 41.03N 73.32W
Stamford [Eng.-U.K.] 118 Mi 52.39N 0.29W
Stamford [Tx.-U.S.] 186 Gj 32.57N 99.48W
Stamford, Lake- 186 Gj 33.05N 99.35W
Stampriet 172 Bd 24.20S 18.28 E
Stamsund 114 Cb 68.08N 13.51 E
Stanberry 186 If 40.13N 94.35W
Stancija Jakbabag 135 Fe 38.59N 66.42 E
Stancija-Karakul 136 Gh 39.30N 63.50 E
Standerton 172 De 26.58S 29.07 E
Standish 184 Fd 44.00N 83.57W
Stanford 188 Jc 47.09N 110.13W
Stånga 116 Hg 57.17N 18.28 E
Stångån 116 Ff 58.27N 15.37 E
Stange 116 Dd 60.43N 11.11 E
Stanger 172 Ee 29.27S 31.14 E
Stanke Dimitrov 130 Gg 42.16N 23.07 E
Stanley [Austl.] 212 Jh 40.46S 145.18 E
Stanley [Falk.Is.] 200 Kk 51.42S 57.51W
Stanley [N.D.-U.S.] 186 Eb 48.19N 102.23W
Stann Creek 190 Ge 16.59N 88.13W
Stann Creek [3] 194 Ce 16.50N 88.30W
Stanovoje nagorje = Stanovoy Upland (EN) 140 Nd 56.00N 114.00 E
Stanovoj hrebet = Stanovoy Range (EN) 140 Od 56.20N 126.00 E
Stanovoy Range (EN) = Stanovoj hrebet 140 Od 56.20N 126.00 E
Stanovoy Upland (EN) = Stanovoje nagorje 140 Nd 56.00N 114.00 E
Stans 128 Cd 46.58N 8.22 E
Stansted Airport 124 Cc 51.54N 0.13 E
Stansted Mountfitchet 124 Cc 51.54N 0.12 E
Stanthorpe 212 Ke 28.39S 151.57 E
Stanton Banks 118 Fe 56.15N 7.50W
Staphorst 124 Ib 52.38N 6.14 E
Staples 186 Ic 46.21N 94.48W
Stapleton 186 Ff 41.29N 100.31W
Stąporków 120 Qe 51.09N 20.34 E
Starachowice 120 Re 51.03N 21.04 E
Staraja Majna 114 Li 54.36N 48.59 E
Staraja Russa 136 Dd 57.59N 31.23 E
Staraja-Vyževka 120 Ue 51.27N 24.34 E
Stará L'ubovňa 120 Qg 49.18N 20.42 E
Stara Moravica 130 Cd 45.52N 19.28 E
Stara Pazova 130 De 44.59N 20.10 E
Stara Planina = Balkan Mountains (EN) 110 Ig 43.15N 25.00 E
Stara Zagora 112 Ig 42.25N 25.38 E
Stara Zagora [2] 130 Ig 42.25N 25.38 E
Starbuck Island 208 Le 5.37S 155.53W
Staretina 128 Kf 44.02N 16.43 E
Stargard Szczeciński 120 Lc 53.20N 15.02 E
Stari Begejski kanal 130 Dd 45.29N 20.25 E
Starica 114 Ih 56.30N 34.56 E
Starigrad 128 Kg 43.11N 16.36 E
Stari Vlah 130 Df 43.23N 20.10 E
Starke 184 Fk 29.57N 82.07W
Starkville 186 Lj 33.28N 88.48W
Starnberg 120 Hh 48.00N 11.21 E
Starnberger See (Würmsee) 120 Hi 47.55N 11.20 E
Starobelsk 136 Df 49.15N 38.58 E
Starodub 136 De 52.35N 32.46 E
Starogard Gdański 120 Oc 53.59N 18.33 E
Starokonstantinov 132 Ee 49.43N 27.13 E
Starominskaja 136 Df 46.31N 39.06 E
Staroščerbinovskaja 132 Kf 46.37N 38.42 E
Starosubhangulovo 134 Hj 53.06N 57.20 E
Starotimoškino 114 Lj 53.43N 47.32 E
Start Point 118 Jk 50.13N 3.38W
Staryje Dorogi 132 Fc 53.02N 28.17 E
Stary Krym 132 Ig 45.02N 35.05 E
Stary Oskol 136 De 51.18N 37.51 E
Stary Sambor 132 Ce 49.29N 23.01 E
Stary Terek 132 Og 44.01N 47.24 E
Staßfurt 120 He 51.52N 11.35 E
Staszów 120 Rf 50.34N 21.10 E
State College 184 Ie 40.48N 77.52W
Staten Island (EN) = Estados, Isla de los- 198 Jk 54.47S 64.15W
Statesboro 184 Gi 32.27N 81.47W
Statesville 184 Gh 35.47N 80.53W
Stathelle 116 Ce 59.03N 9.41 E
Stathmós Krioneriou 130 Ek 38.20N 21.35 E
Statland 114 Cd 64.30N 11.08 E
Staunton 182 Ld 38.10N 79.05W
Stavanger 112 Gd 58.58N 5.45 E
Stavelot 124 Hd 50.23N 5.56 E
Staveren 122 Lb 52.53N 5.22 E
Stavern 116 Df 59.00N 10.02 E
Stavnoje 120 Sh 48.59N 22.45 E
Stavropol 112 Kf 45.02N 41.59 E
Stavropolskaja vozvyšennost 132 Mg 45.10N 43.00 E
Stavropolski kraj [3] 136 Eg 45.00N 43.15 E
Stavrós [Grc.] 130 Fj 39.19N 22.14 E
Stavrós [Grc.] 130 Gi 40.40N 23.42 E
Stavroúpolis 130 Hh 41.12N 24.42 E
Stawell 212 Ig 37.04S 142.46 E
Stawiski 120 Sc 53.23N 22.09 E
Stawiszyn 120 Oe 51.55N 18.07 E
Stayton 188 Dd 44.48N 122.48W
Steamboat Springs 182 Fc 40.29N 106.50W
Stębark 120 Qc 53.30N 20.05 E
Stebnik 120 Tg 49.14N 23.34 E
Stedingen 124 Ka 53.10N 8.30 E
Steele 186 Gc 46.51N 99.55W
Steelpoort 172 Ed 24.48S 30.12 E
Steenbergen 124 Gc 51.35N 4.19 E
Steen River 180 Fe 59.38N 117.06W
Steensby Inlet 180 Jb 70.10N 78.25W
Steenstrups Gletscher 179 Gc 75.15N 57.30W
Steenvoorde 124 Ed 50.48N 2.35 E
Steenwijk 122 Mb 52.47N 6.08 E
Ştefăneşti 130 Kb 47.48N 27.12 E
Stefanie, Lake- (EN) = Chew Bahir 158 Kh 4.38N 36.50 E
Stefansson 180 Gb 73.30N 105.30W
Ştefleşti, Virful- 130 Gd 45.32N 23.48 E
Stege 116 Ej 54.59N 12.18 E
Steiermark = Styria (EN) [2] 128 Ic 47.15N 15.00 E
Steiermark = Styria (EN) 128 Ic 47.15N 15.00 E
Steigerwald 120 Gg 49.40N 10.20 E
Steilrandberge 172 Ac 17.53S 13.20 E
Steinach 128 Fc 47.05N 11.28 E
Steinbach 180 Hg 49.32N 96.41W
Steinen, Rio- 202 Hf 12.05S 53.46W
Steinfeld (Oldenburg) 124 Kb 52.36N 8.13 E
Steinfort/Steinfurt 124 Hd 49.40N 5.55 E
Steinfurt 120 Dd 52.09N 7.20 E
Steinfurt/Steinfort 124 He 49.40N 5.55 E
Steinfurt-Borghorst 124 Jb 52.08N 7.25 E
Steinhagen 124 Kb 52.01N 8.24 E
Steinhausen 172 Bd 21.49S 18.20 E
Steinheim 124 Lc 51.51N 9.06 E
Steinhuder Meer 120 Fd 52.28N 9.19 E
Steinkjer 114 Cd 64.01N 11.30 E
Steinkopf 172 Be 29.18S 17.43 E
Steinshamn 116 Bb 62.47N 6.29 E
Steinsøy 114 Af 61.00N 4.30 E
Steirisch-Niederösterreichische Kalkalpen 128 Jc 47.45N 15.30 E
Stekene 124 Gc 51.12N 4.02 E
Stekolny 138 Ke 60.00N 150.50 E
Stella 172 Ce 26.33S 24.53 E
Stellenbosch 172 Bf 33.58S 18.50 E
Stello 122a Ba 42.47N 9.25 E
Stelvio, Passo dello- / Stilfser Joch 128 Ed 46.32N 10.27 E
Stemwede 124 Kb 52.26N 8.26 E
Stenay 122 Le 49.29N 5.11 E
Stendal 120 Hd 52.36N 11.51 E
Stende 116 Jg 57.10N 22.28 E
Stende 116 Ig 57.40N 21.57 E
Stenhouse Bay 212 Hg 35.17S 136.56 E
Stenstorp 116 Ef 58.16N 13.43 E
Stenungsund 114 Cg 58.05N 11.49 E
Stepanakert 112 Kh 39.49N 46.44 E
Stepanavan 132 Ni 40.59N 44.20 E
Stephens, Cape- 218 Ed 40.42S 173.57 E
Stephens, Mount- 222 Rg 83.23S 51.27W
Stephens Passage 178 Me 57.50N 133.50W
Stephenville [Newf.-Can.] 180 Lg 48.33N 58.35W
Stephenville [Tx.-U.S.] 186 Gj 32.13N 98.12W
Steps Point 221c Cb 14.22S 170.45W
Sterea Ellás kai Évvoia [2] 130 Hk 38.20N 24.30 E
Sterkstroom 172 Df 31.32S 26.32 E
Sterlibaševo 134 Gj 53.28N 55.15 E
Sterling [Co.-U.S.] 182 Gc 40.37N 103.13W
Sterling [Il.-U.S.] 186 Lf 41.48N 89.42W
Sterling City 186 Fk 31.50N 100.59W
Sterlitamak 112 Le 53.37N 55.58 E
Šternberk 120 Ng 49.44N 17.19 E
Sterzing / Vipiteno 128 Fd 46.54N 11.26 E
Stettin → Szczecin 112 He 53.24N 14.32 E
Stettiner Haff 120 Kc 53.46N 14.14 E
Stettler 180 Gf 52.19N 112.43W
Steubenville 182 Kc 40.22N 80.39W
Stevenage 118 Mj 51.54N 0.11W
Stevenson Entrance 178 Ie 57.45N 152.20W
Stevens Point 182 Jc 44.31N 89.34W
Stewart 180 Ee 55.56N 129.59W
Stewart 180 Dd 63.18N 139.24W
Stewart Crossing 180 Dd 63.19N 136.33W
Stewart Island 208 Hi 47.00S 167.50 E
Stewart Islands 208 He 8.20S 162.40 E
Steyerberg 124 Lb 52.34N 9.02 E
Steyning 124 Bd 50.53N 0.20W
Steynsburg 172 Df 31.15S 25.49 E
Steyr 128 Ib 48.03N 14.25 E
Steyr 128 Ib 48.02N 14.25 E
Štiavnické vrchy 120 Oh 48.15N 18.50 E
Stidia 126 Li 35.50N 0.05W
Stiene 116 Kg 57.19N 24.28 E
Stiens, Leeuwarderadeel- 124 Ha 53.16N 5.46 E
Stigliano 128 Kj 40.24N 16.14 E
Stigtomta 116 Gf 58.48N 16.47 E
Stikine 174 Fd 56.40N 132.30W
Stikine Ranges 180 Ee 57.35N 131.00W
Stilfontein 172 De 26.50S 26.50 E
Stilfser Joch / Stelvio, Passo dello- 128 Ed 46.32N 10.27 E
Stilis 130 Fk 38.55N 22.37 E
Stillwater [Mn.-U.S.] 186 Jd 45.04N 92.49W
Stillwater [Ok.-U.S.] 182 Hd 36.07N 97.04W
Stillwater Range 188 Fg 39.50N 118.15W
Stilo 128 Kl 38.29N 16.28 E
Stilo, Punta- 128 Kl 38.27N 16.35 E
Štimlje 130 Eg 42.26N 21.03 E
Stînişoarei, Munţii- 130 Ib 47.20N 26.00 E
Stinnett 186 Fi 35.50N 101.27W
Štip 130 Fh 41.44N 22.12 E
Stirling 118 Je 56.07N 3.57W
Stirling Range 212 Df 34.25S 117.50 E
Stjernøya 114 Fa 70.18N 22.45 E
Stjørdalshalsen 114 Ce 63.28N 10.44 E
Stobi 130 Eh 41.33N 21.59 E
Stobrawa 120 Nf 50.50N 17.32 E
Stocka 116 Gc 61.54N 17.20 E
Stockach 120 Fi 47.51N 9.01 E
Stockbridge 124 Ac 51.06N 1.29W
Stockerau 128 Kb 48.23N 16.13 E
Stockholm 112 Hd 59.20N 18.03 E
Stockholm [2] 114 Dg 59.20N 18.00 E
Stockport 118 Kh 53.25N 2.10W
Stocks Seamount (EN) 198 Mg 12.15S 32.00W
Stockton [Ca.-U.S.] 176 Gf 37.57N 121.17W
Stockton [Mo.-U.S.] 186 Jh 37.42N 93.48W
Stockton Lake 186 Jh 37.40N 93.45W
Stockton-on-Tees 118 Lg 54.34N 1.19W
Stockton Plateau 182 Ge 30.30N 102.30W
Stoczek Łukowski 120 Re 51.58N 21.58 E
Stöde 114 De 62.25N 16.35 E
Stoĕng Trĕng 148 Lf 13.31N 105.58 E
Stoer, Point of- 118 Hc 58.20N 5.25W
Stogovo 130 Dh 41.29N 20.39 E
Stohod 120 Ve 51.52N 25.44 E
Stoholm 116 Ch 56.29N 9.10 E
Stoj, gora- 132 Ce 48.39N 23.15 E
Stojba 142 Pd 52.49N 131.43 E
Stoke-on-Trent 118 Kh 53.00N 2.10W
Stokksnes 114a Cb 64.14N 14.58W
Stokmarknes 114 Db 68.34N 14.55 E
Stol 130 Fe 44.11N 22.09 E
Stolac 128 Lg 43.05N 17.58 E
Stolbcy 132 Ec 53.31N 26.43 E
Stolberg (Rheinland) 122 Cf 50.46N 6.14 E
Stolbovo, ostrov- 138 Ib 74.05N 136.00 E
Stolin 132 Ed 51.57N 26.52 E
Stolzenau 124 Lb 52.31N 9.04 E
Ston 128 Lh 42.50N 17.42 E
Stone 118 Ki 52.54N 2.10W
Stonehaven 118 Ke 56.58N 2.13W
Stonehenge 212 Id 24.22S 143.17 E
Stonehenge 118 Lj 51.11N 1.49W
Stoner 186 Bh 37.37N 108.18W
Stonewall 186 Ha 50.09N 97.21W
Stony 178 Hd 61.45N 156.35W
Stony Rapids 180 Ge 59.16N 105.50W
Stony River 178 Hd 61.47N 156.41W
Stony Stratford 124 Bb 52.03N 0.51W
Stony Tunguska (EN) = Podkamennaja Tunguska 140 Lc 61.36N 90.18 E
Stör 120 Fc 53.50N 9.25 E
Storå 116 Fe 59.43N 15.08 E
Storå 116 Ch 56.19N 8.19 E
Storå/Isojoki 116 Ee 62.07N 21.58 E
Stora Gla 116 Ee 59.30N 12.30 E
Stora Le 116 De 59.05N 11.55 E
Stora Lulevatten 114 Ec 67.08N 19.20 E
Storavan 114 Ed 65.42N 18.12 E
Storby 116 Hd 60.13N 19.34 E
Stord 114 Ag 59.55N 5.25 E
Stordal 116 Bb 62.23N 7.01 E
Store Bælt = Great Belt (EN) 110 Hd 55.30N 11.00 E
Storebro 116 Fg 57.35N 15.51 E
Storefiskbank = Great Fisher Bank (EN) 118 Qe 56.50N 4.00 E
Store Heddinge 116 Ei 55.19N 12.25 E
Store Hellefiske Bank (EN) 179 Ge 67.30N 55.00W
Store Koldewey 179 Kc 76.20N 18.30W
Store Kvien 116 Dc 61.34N 10.33 E
Støren 114 Ce 63.02N 10.18 E
Store Nupsfonn 116 Be 59.54N 7.08 E
Store Sølnkletten 116 Dc 61.59N 10.18 E
Storfjorden [Nor.] 116 Bb 62.25N 6.30 E
Storfjorden [Sval.] 179 Nc 77.30N 20.00 E

Index Symbols

[1] Independent Nation · [2] State, Region · [3] District, County · [4] Municipality · [5] Colony, Dependency · Continent · Physical Region · Historical or Cultural Region · Mount, Mountain · Volcano · Hill · Mountains, Mountain Range · Hills, Escarpment · Plateau, Upland · Pass, Gap · Plain, Lowland · Delta · Salt Flat · Valley, Canyon · Crater, Cave · Karst Features · Depression · Polder · Desert, Dunes · Forest, Woods · Heath, Steppe · Oasis · Cape, Point · Coast, Beach · Cliff · Peninsula · Isthmus · Sandbank · Island · Atoll · Rock, Reef · Islands, Archipelago · Rocks, Reefs · Coral Reef · Well, Spring · Geyser · River, Stream · Waterfall, Rapids · River Mouth, Estuary · Lake · Salt Lake · Intermittent Lake · Reservoir · Swamp, Pond · Canal · Glacier · Ice Shelf, Pack Ice · Ocean · Sea · Gulf, Bay · Strait, Fjord · Lagoon · Bank · Seamount · Tablemount · Ridge · Shelf · Basin · Escarpment, Sea Scarp · Fracture · Trench, Abyss · National Park, Reserve · Point of Interest · Recreation Site · Cave, Cavern · Historic Site · Ruins · Wall, Walls · Church, Abbey · Temple · Scientific Station · Railway station · Airport · Port · Military installation · Lighthouse · Mine · Tunnel · Dam, Bridge

Storfors	116	Fe	59.32N	14.16 E
Storis Passage	180	Hc	67.40N	98.30W
Storkerson Bay	180	Fb	73.00N	124.00W
Storkerson Peninsula	180	Gb	73.00N	106.30W
Storlien	114	Ce	63.19N	12.06 E
Stormarn	120	Gc	53.45N	10.20 E
Storm Bay	212	Jh	43.10S	147.30 E
Storm Lake	182	Hc	42.39N	95.13W
Stornoway	118	Gc	58.12N	6.23W
Storøya	179	Ob	80.08N	27.50 E
Storožinec	132	De	48.10N	25.46 E
Storsjøen [Nor.]	116	Dd	61.35N	11.15 E
Storsjøen [Nor.]	116	Dd	60.25N	11.40 E
Storsjön [Swe.]	116	Gd	60.35N	16.45 E
Storsjön [Swe.]	110	Hc	63.15N	14.20 E
Storsteinfjellet	114	Db	68.14N	17.52 E
Storstrøm [2]	116	Dj	55.00N	11.50 E
Storstrømmen	179	Jc	77.20N	23.00W
Storsudret	116	Hh	57.00N	18.15 E
Storuman	112	Hb	65.06N	17.06 E
Storuman	114	Dd	65.14N	16.54 E
Storvätteshågna	116	Ed	62.07N	12.27 E
Storvigelen	116	Eb	62.32N	12.04 E
Storvik	116	Gd	60.35N	16.32 E
Storvreta	116	Ge	59.58N	17.42 E
Stöttingfjället	114	Dd	64.38N	17.44 E
Stoughton	188	Nb	49.41N	103.03W
Stour [Eng.-U.K.]	124	Dc	51.18N	1.22 E
Stour [Eng.-U.K.]	118	Lk	50.43N	1.47W
Stour [Eng.-U.K.]	118	Oj	51.52N	1.16 E
Stourbridge	118	Ki	52.27N	2.09W
Støvring	116	Ch	56.53N	9.51 E
Stowmarket	124	Cb	52.11N	0.59 E
Strabane/An Srath Bán	118	Fg	54.49N	7.27W
Stradella	128	De	45.05N	9.18 E
Straelen	124	Ic	51.27N	6.16 E
Strakonice	120	Jg	49.16N	13.55 E
Straldža	130	Jg	42.36N	26.41 E
Stralsund	112	He	54.18N	13.06 E
Strand	172	Bf	34.06S	18.50 E
Stranda	114	Be	62.19N	6.54 E
Strand Bay	180	Ia	79.00N	94.00W
Strangford Lough/Loch Cuan	118	Hg	54.26N	5.36W
Strängnäs	116	Ge	59.23N	17.02 E
Stranraer	118	Hg	54.54N	5.02W
Strasbourg [Fr.]	112	Gf	48.35N	7.45 E
Strasbourg [Sask.-Can.]	188	Ma	51.04N	104.57W
Strašeny	132	Ff	47.06N	28.34 E
Straßwalchen	128	Hc	47.59N	13.15 E
Stratford [N.Z.]	218	Fc	39.21S	174.17 E
Stratford [Ont.-Can.]	184	Gd	43.22N	80.57W
Stratford [Tx.-U.S.]	186	Eh	36.20N	102.04W
Stratford-upon-Avon	118	Li	52.12N	1.41W
Strathclyde [3]	118	If	55.50N	4.50W
Strathgordon	212	Jh	42.54S	146.10 E
Strathmore	188	Ia	51.03N	113.23W
Strathmore	118	Je	56.40N	3.05W
Strathroy	184	Gd	42.57N	81.38W
Strathy Point	118	Ic	58.35N	4.01W
Straubenhardt	124	Kf	48.50N	8.30 E
Straubing	120	Ih	48.53N	12.34 E
Straumnes	114a	Aa	66.26N	23.08W
Straumsjøen	114	Db	68.41N	14.30 E
Strausberg	120	Jd	52.35N	13.53 E
Strawberry Mountain	188	Fd	44.19N	118.43W
Strawberry River	188	Jf	40.10N	110.24W
Straža	120	Fg	42.15N	22.14 E
Stražica	130	If	43.14N	25.58 E
Strážiště	120	Kg	49.32N	14.58 E
Stražovské vrchy	120	Oh	48.55N	18.30 E
Streaky Bay	212	Gf	32.48S	134.13 E
Streaky Bay	212	Gf	32.35S	134.10 E
Streator	186	Lf	41.07N	88.50W
Středočeská pahorkatina	120	Kg	49.30N	14.15 E
Středočeský kraj [3]	120	Kg	49.55N	14.30 E
Středoslovenský kraj [3]	120	Ph	48.50N	19.10 E
Strehaia	130	Ge	44.37N	23.12 E
Strei	130	Gd	45.51N	23.03 E
Střela	120	Jg	49.54N	13.32 E
Strelasund	120	Jb	54.20N	13.05 E
Strelka	138	Ee	58.03N	93.05 E
Strelna	114	Jc	66.04N	38.39 E
Strenči	114	Fh	57.39N	25.38 E
Stresa	128	Ce	45.53N	8.32 E
Streževoj	138	Cd	60.42N	77.35 E
Stříbro	120	Ig	49.46N	13.00 E
Strickland River	212	Ia	6.00S	142.05 E
Strîmbeni	130	He	44.28N	24.58 E
Strimón	130	Gi	40.47N	23.51 E
Strimonikós Kólpos	130	Gi	40.40N	23.50 E
Strjama	130	Hg	42.10N	24.56 E
Strofádhes, Nisoi-	130	Dl	37.15N	21.00 E
Ströhen, Wagenfeld-	124	Kb	52.32N	8.39 E
Strohgäu	124	Kf	48.50N	9.00 E
Stromberg	124	Je	49.57N	7.46 E
Stromboli	128	Jl	38.47N	15.14 E
Strömfors/Ruotsinpyhtää	116	Ld	60.32N	26.27 E
Stromness	118	Jc	58.57N	3.18W
Strömsbro	116	Gd	60.42N	17.10 E
Strömsbruk	116	Dc	61.53N	17.19 E
Strömsnäsbruk	116	Eh	56.33N	13.43 E
Strömstad	116	Cg	58.56N	11.10 E
Strömsund	114	De	63.51N	15.35 E
Strongili	130	Hm	36.58N	24.55 E
Stròngoli	128	Lk	39.16N	17.03 E
Stronsay	118	Kb	59.08N	2.38W
Stropkov	120	Rg	49.12N	21.40 E
Stroud	118	Kj	51.45N	2.12W
Struer	114	Bh	56.29N	8.37 E
Struga	130	Dh	41.11N	20.41 E
Strugi-Krasnyje	114	Gg	58.17N	29.08 E
Strule	118	Fg	54.40N	7.20W
Struma	110	Ig	40.47N	23.51 E
Strumble Head	118	Hi	52.02N	5.04W
Strumica	130	Fh	41.26N	22.39 E
Stry	136	Cf	49.14N	23.49 E
Stry	132	De	49.24N	24.13 E
Strydenburg	172	Ce	29.58S	23.40 E
Stryn	114	Bf	61.55N	6.47 E
Strynsvatn	116	Bc	61.55N	7.05 E
Strzegom	120	Mf	50.57N	16.21 E
Strzegomka	120	Me	51.08N	16.50 E
Strzelce Krajeńskie	120	Ld	52.53N	15.32 E
Strzelce Opolskie	120	Of	50.31N	18.19 E
Strzelin	120	Nf	50.47N	17.03 E
Strzelno	120	Od	52.38N	18.11 E
Strzyzów	120	Rg	49.52N	21.47 E
Stuart	184	Gl	27.12N	80.16W
Stuart	178	Gd	63.35N	162.30W
Stuart, Mount-	188	Ec	47.29N	120.54W
Stuart Bluff Range	212	Gd	22.45S	132.15 E
Stuart Lake	180	Ff	54.33N	124.35W
Stuart Range	212	Ge	29.10S	134.55 E
Stubaier Alpen	128	Fc	47.10N	11.05 E
Stubbekøbing	116	Ej	54.53N	12.03 E
Stubbenkammer	120	Jb	54.35N	13.40 E
Stubbs Bay	197n	Ba	13.08N	61.10W
Štubik	130	Fe	44.18N	22.21 E
Stucka	114	Fh	56.36N	25.17 E
Studenica, Manastir-	130	Df	43.28N	20.37 E
Studholme Junction	218	Df	44.44S	171.08 E
Stugun	116	De	63.10N	15.36 E
Stuhr	124	Ka	53.02N	8.45 E
Stupino	114	Ji	54.57N	38.03 E
Stura di Demonte	128	Bf	44.40N	7.53 E
Stura di Lanzo	128	Be	45.06N	7.44 E
Sturge Island	222	Ke	67.27S	164.18 E
Sturgeon Bay	186	Md	44.50N	87.23W
Sturgeon Falls	184	Jg	46.22N	79.55W
Sturgeon Lake	186	Kb	50.00N	90.45W
Sturgis [Mi.-U.S.]	184	Ee	41.48N	85.25W
Sturgis [S.D.-U.S.]	186	Ed	44.25N	103.31W
Sturkö	116	Fh	56.05N	15.40 E
Sturt Creek	212	Fd	20.08S	127.24 E
Sturt Desert	212	Ie	28.30S	141.00 E
Stutterheim	172	Df	32.33S	27.28 E
Stuttgart [Ar.-U.S.]	186	Ki	34.30N	91.33W
Stuttgart [Ger.]	112	Gf	48.46N	9.11 E
Stviga	132	Ec	52.04N	27.55 E
Stykkishólmur	114a	Ab	65.04N	22.44W
Styr	132	Ce	52.07N	26.35 E
Styria (EN) = Steiermark [2]	128	Ic	47.15N	15.00 E
Styria (EN) = Steiermark	128	Ic	47.15N	15.00 E
Styrsö	116	Dg	57.37N	11.46 E
Suafa Point	219a	Ec	8.19S	160.41 E
Suai	150	Ih	9.21S	125.17 E
Suakin Archipelago (EN) = Sawākin, Jazā'ir-	158	Kg	19.07N	37.20 E
Suao	152	Lg	24.36N	121.51 E
Suardi	204	Bj	30.32S	61.58W
Suavanao	214	Fi	7.34S	158.44 E
Subačius/Subačjus	116	Ki	55.44N	24.53 E
Subačjus/Subačius	116	Ki	55.44N	24.53 E
Subang	150	Eh	6.34S	107.45 E
Subansiri	148	Jc	26.48N	93.49 E
Subao Ding	152	Jf	27.10N	110.18 E
Subarkuduk	136	Ff	49.09N	56.31 E
Šubarši	136	Fe	48.38N	57.12 E
Subate	116	Lh	56.01N	26.04 E
Subay', 'Urūq-	164	He	22.15N	43.05 E
Subaytilah	162	Ib	35.14N	9.08 E
Subbéticas, Cordillera-	126	Jf	38.30N	2.30W
Subei (Dangchengwan)	152	Fd	39.36N	94.58 E
Subi, Pulau-	150	Ef	2.55N	108.50 E
Subiaco	128	Hi	41.55N	13.06 E
Sublette	186	Fh	37.29N	100.50W
Subotica	130	Cc	46.06N	19.40 E
Subpolar Urals (EN) = Pripoljarny Ural	110	Lb	65.00N	60.00 E
Subugo	170	Gc	1.40S	35.49 E
Suceava	130	Jb	47.38N	26.15 E
Suceava [2]	130	Ib	47.40N	25.45 E
Suceava	130	Jb	47.32N	26.32 E
Sucha Beskidzka	120	Pg	49.44N	19.36 E
Süchbaatar → Suhe-Bator	142	Md	50.15N	106.12 E
Suchedniów	120	Qe	51.03N	20.51 E
Suchiapa, Rio-	192	Mi	16.36N	93.01W
Suchitepéquez [3]	194	Bf	14.25N	91.20W
Sucia, Bahia-	197a	Ac	17.57N	67.10W
Sucio, Rio-	194	Ij	7.27N	77.07W
Suck/An tSuca	118	Eh	53.16N	8.03W
Suckling, Mount-	212	Ja	9.45S	148.55 E
Sucre [3]	202	Fa	10.25N	63.30W
Sucre [3]	202	Db	9.00N	75.00W
Sucre [Bol.]	200	Jg	19.02S	65.17W
Sucre [Col.]	202	Db	8.50N	74.43W
Suçuarana, Serra da-	204	Jb	14.25S	45.00W
Sucunduri, Rio-	202	Ge	5.30S	59.40W
Sućuraj	128	Lg	43.08N	17.12 E
Sucuriú, Rio-	202	Hh	20.47S	51.38W
Sud, Canal du-	194	Kd	18.40N	73.05W
Sud, Massif du-	194	Kd	18.25N	73.55W
Suda	114	Ig	59.11N	37.33 E
Suda	114	Ig	59.12N	37.30 E
Sudak	136	Dg	44.50N	34.59 E
Sudan	158	Ig	11.30N	15.00 E
Sudan (EN) = As Sūdān [1]	160	Jg	15.00N	30.00 E
Sudbury [Eng.-U.K.]	118	Ni	52.02N	0.44 E
Sudbury [Ont.-Can.]	176	Ke	46.30N	81.00W
Suddie	196	Gi	7.07N	58.29W
Sude	120	Gc	53.22N	10.45 E
Sudeten (EN) = Sudety	110	He	50.30N	16.00 E
Sudety = Sudeten (EN)	110	He	50.30N	16.00 E
Sudirman, Pegunungan-	150	Kg	4.12S	137.00 E
Sudočje, ozero-	136	Bc	43.25N	58.30 E
Sudogda	114	Ji	55.59N	40.50 E
Sudost	132	Hc	52.19N	33.24 E
Sud-Ouest [Burkina] [3]	166	Ec	10.30N	3.15W
Sud-Ouest [Cam.] [3]	166	Gd	5.20N	9.20 E
Sudovaja Višnja	120	Tg	49.43N	23.26 E
Südradde	124	Jb	52.41N	7.34 E
Südtirol / Trentino-Alto Adige [2]	128	Fd	46.30N	11.20 E
Sudža	132	Id	51.13N	35.16 E
Sue	158	Jh	7.41N	28.03 E
Sueca	126	Le	39.12N	0.19W
Suess Land	179	Jd	72.45N	26.00W
Suez (EN) = As Suways	160	Kf	29.58N	32.33 E
Suez, Gulf of-(EN) = Suways, Khalij as-	158	Kf	28.10N	33.27 E
Suez Canal (EN) = Suways, Qanāt as-	158	Ke	29.55N	32.33 E
Suffolk	182	Lc	36.44N	76.37W
Suffolk [3]	118	Li	52.10N	1.05W
Suffolk	118	Ni	52.25N	1.00 E
Sufiān	146	Kc	38.17N	45.59 E
Sugana, Val-	128	Fd	46.00N	11.40 E
Sugana-no-Sen	156	Dd	35.22N	134.31 E
Sugar Island	184	Eb	46.25N	84.12W
Sugarloaf Mountain	184	Lc	45.01N	70.22W
Suğla Gölü	146	Ed	37.20N	32.02 E
Sugoj	138	Kd	64.15N	154.29 E
Suguta	170	Gb	2.03N	36.33 E
Suha	130	Ke	44.08N	27.36 E
Suhai Hu	152	Fd	38.55N	94.05 E
Şuḩār	144	Ie	24.22N	56.45 E
Suhe-Bator (Süchbaatar)	142	Md	50.15N	106.12 E
Suhiniči	132	Ib	54.06N	35.20 E
Suhl	120	Gf	50.36N	10.42 E
Suhodolskoje, ozero-	116	Nd	60.35N	30.30 E
Suhoj Log	134	Kh	56.55N	62.01 E
Suhona	116	Kc	60.46N	46.24 E
Suhr	128	Cc	47.25N	8.04 E
Suhumi	112	Kg	43.01N	41.02 E
Suhurlui	130	Kd	45.25N	27.35 E
Suiá-Missu, Rio-	202	Hf	11.13S	53.15W
Suibara	156	Fc	37.50N	139.12 E
Suichang	152	Kf	28.34N	119.15 E
Suid-Afrika/South Africa [1]	160	Jl	30.00S	26.00 E
Suide	152	Jd	37.28N	110.15 E
Suifenhe	152	Nc	44.25N	131.09 E
Suifen He	154	Kc	43.20N	131.49 E
Sui He	154	Eh	33.29N	118.06 E
Suihua	152	Mb	46.38N	126.57 E
Suijiang	152	Hf	28.37N	104.00 E
Suileng	152	Mb	47.17N	127.08 E
Suining [China]	152	Ie	30.30N	105.34 E
Suining [China]	154	Dh	33.54N	117.56 E
Suipacha	204	Cl	34.45S	59.41W
Suiping	154	Bh	33.09N	113.59 E
Suippe	122	Je	49.25N	3.57 E
Suippes	122	Ke	49.08N	4.32 E
Suir/An tSiúir	118	Gi	52.15N	7.00W
Suisse / Svizra / Svizzera / Schweiz = Switzerland (EN) [1]	112	Gf	46.00N	8.30 E
Suisse Normande	124	Bf	48.53N	0.50W
Suita	156	Dd	34.45N	135.32 E
Suixi	154	Dh	33.55N	116.47 E
Suixian	154	Cg	34.25N	115.04 E
Suiyang	154	Kb	44.26N	130.53 E
Suizhong	152	Lc	40.21N	120.20 E
Suj	152	Ic	42.12N	108.01 E
Šuja	114	If	61.54N	34.15 E
Šuja [R.S.F.S.R.]	136	Ed	56.52N	41.23 E
Šuja [R.S.F.S.R.]	114	If	61.59N	34.15 E
Sujer	134	Li	55.59N	65.47 E
Suji → Haixing	154	De	38.10N	117.29 E
Sujko Seamount (EN)	224	Ca	44.30N	170.20 E
Sujstamo	116	Nc	61.49N	31.05 E
Sukabumi	150	Eh	6.55S	106.56 E
Sukadana	150	Eg	1.15S	109.57 E
Sukagawa	154	Pf	37.17N	140.23 E
Sukaraja	150	Fg	2.23S	110.35 E
Sukeva	114	Ge	63.54N	27.26 E
Sukhothai	148	Je	17.01N	99.49 E
Suki	168	Ec	13.23N	33.58 E
Sukkertoppen/Manitsoq	179	Ge	65.25N	53.00W
Sukkozero	136	Dc	63.09N	32.23 E
Sukkur	142	Ig	27.42N	68.52 E
Sukon	150	Hg	0.56S	123.10 E
Sukses	172	Bd	21.01S	16.52 E
Suksun	134	Hh	57.07N	57.24 E
Sukumo	152	Ne	32.56N	132.44 E
Sukumo-Wan	156	Ce	32.55N	132.40 E
Sul, Baia-	204	Hh	27.40S	48.35W
Sul, Canal do-	202	Id	0.10S	49.30W
Sula [Nor.]	116	Bb	62.25N	6.10 E
Sula [Nor.]	114	Af	61.10N	4.55 E
Sula [R.S.F.S.R.]	134	Fc	67.16N	52.07 E
Sula [R.S.F.S.R.]	114	Ld	64.41N	47.46 E
Sula [Ukr.-U.S.S.R.]	132	He	49.40N	32.43 E
Sula, Kepulauan = Sulu Archipelago, (EN)	208	De	1.52S	125.22 E
Sulaimāniya	144	Gb	35.33N	45.26 E
Sulaimāniya [3]	146	Ke	35.40N	45.30 E
Sulaimān Range	140	Jf	30.30N	70.10 E
Sulak	132	Oh	43.17N	47.31 E
Sulak	136	Eg	43.17N	47.34 E
Sula Sgeir	118	Gb	59.05N	6.10W
Sulawesi/Celebes	140	Oj	2.00S	121.10 E
Sulawesi/Celebes Sea (EN)	140	Oi	3.00N	122.00 E
Sulawesi Selatan [3]	150	Gg	4.00S	120.00 E
Sulawesi Tengah [3]	150	Hg	1.00S	121.00 E
Sulawesi Tenggara [3]	150	Hg	4.00S	122.30 E
Sulawesi Utara [3]	150	Hf	1.00N	123.00 E
Sulaymān	128	En	36.42N	10.30 E
Sulb	168	Ea	20.26N	30.20 E
Sulcis	128	Ck	39.05N	8.40 E
Suldalsvatn	116	Be	59.35N	6.45 E
Süldeh	146	Od	36.34N	52.01 E
Sulechów	120	Ld	52.06N	15.37 E
Sulęcin	120	Ld	52.26N	15.08 E
Suleja	134	Ii	55.11N	58.50 E
Sulejów	120	Pe	51.22N	19.53 E
Süleoğlu	130	Jh	41.46N	26.55 E
Sule Skerry	118	Ib	59.10N	4.10W
Sulima	166	Cd	6.58N	11.35W
Sulina	130	Md	45.09N	29.40 E
Sulina, Braţul-	130	Md	45.09N	29.41 E
Sulingen	120	Ed	52.41N	8.48 E
Sulitjelma	114	Dc	67.09N	16.03 E
Sulitjelma	114	Dc	67.08N	16.24 E
Suljukta	136	Gh	39.56N	69.37 E
Sulkava	114	Gf	61.47N	28.23 E
Sullana	200	Hf	4.53S	80.42W
Süller	130	Mk	38.09N	29.29 E
Sullivan [In.-U.S.]	184	Df	39.06N	87.24W
Sullivan [Mo.-U.S.]	186	Kg	38.13N	91.10W
Sullivan Lake	188	Ja	52.00N	112.00W
Sully-sur-Loire	122	Ig	47.46N	2.22 E
Sulmona	128	Hh	42.03N	13.55 E
Sulphur [La.-U.S.]	186	Jk	30.14N	93.23W
Sulphur [Ok.-U.S.]	186	Hi	34.31N	96.58W
Sulphur Creek	186	Ed	44.46N	102.25W
Sulphur River	186	Jj	33.07N	93.52W
Sulphur Springs	186	Ij	33.08N	95.36W
Sulphur Springs Draw	186	Fj	32.12N	101.36W
Sultandağı	146	Dc	38.32N	31.14 E
Sultan Dağları	146	Dc	38.20N	31.20 E
Sultanhanı	146	Ec	38.15N	33.33 E
Sultanhisar	130	Ll	37.53N	28.10 E
Sultānpur	148	Gc	26.16N	82.04 E
Sulu Archipelago	140	Oi	6.00N	121.00 E
Sulu Archipelago (EN) = Sula Kepulauan	208	De	1.52S	125.22 E
Sulu Basin (EN)	150	Ge	8.00N	121.30 E
Suluova	146	Fb	40.47N	35.42 E
Sulūq	164	Dc	31.40N	20.15 E
Sulu Sea	140	Ni	9.00N	120.00 E
Sulz am Neckar	120	Eh	48.21N	8.37 E
Sulzbach/Saar	124	Je	49.18N	7.04 E
Sulzbach-Rosenberg	120	Hg	49.30N	11.45 E
Sulzberger Bay	222	Mf	77.00S	152.00W
Šumadija	130	De	44.20N	20.40 E
Sumalata	150	Hf	0.59N	122.30 E
Sumāmus	146	Nd	36.50N	50.30 E
Šumanaj	135	Bc	42.37N	58.55 E
Sumatera = Sumatra (EN)	140	Mj	0.01N	102.00 E
Sumatera Barat [3]	150	Dg	1.00S	100.30 E
Sumatera Selatan [3]	150	Dg	3.30S	104.00 E
Sumatera Utara [3]	150	Cf	2.00N	99.00 E
Sumatra (EN) = Sumatera	140	Mj	0.01N	102.00 E
Šumava = Bohemian Forest (EN)	110	Hf	49.00N	13.30 E
Sumayr	164	Hf	17.47N	41.26 E
Sumba, Pulau-	140	Nj	10.00S	120.00 E
Sumba, Selat- = Sumba Strait (EN)	150	Hh	9.05S	120.00 E
Sumbar	132	Sj	38.00N	55.15 E
Sumba Strait (EN) = Sumba, Selat-	150	Hh	9.05S	120.00 E
Sumbawa, Pulau-	140	Nj	8.40S	118.00 E
Sumbawa Besar	150	Gh	8.30S	117.26 E
Sumbawanga	170	Fd	7.58S	31.37 E
Sumbe	160	Ij	11.12S	13.51 E
Sumber	152	Ib	46.21N	108.20 E
Sumbi Point	219a	Cb	7.19S	157.04 E
Sumbu	170	Fd	8.31S	30.29 E
Sumburgh Head	118	Lb	59.51N	1.16W
Sumedang	150	Eh	6.52S	107.55 E
Šume'eh Sarā	146	Md	37.18N	49.19 E
Sümeg	120	Nj	46.59N	17.17 E
Šumen	130	Jf	43.16N	26.55 E
Šumen [2]	130	Jf	43.20N	27.00 E
Sumenep	150	Fh	7.01S	113.52 E
Šumerlja	112	Kd	55.30N	46.26 E
Sumgait	112	Kg	40.33N	49.40 E
Sumgait	132	Pi	40.37N	49.37 E
Sumidouro, Rio-	204	Da	13.28S	56.39W
Šumiha	136	Gd	55.14N	63.19 E
Sumisu-Jima	152	Oe	31.40N	140.00 E
Sumkino	136	Gd	58.09N	68.21 E
Summer, Lake- [N.M.-U.S.]	186	Di	34.38N	104.26W
Summer, Lake- [N.Z.]	218	Ee	42.40S	172.15 E
Summer Lake	188	Ee	42.50N	120.45W
Summerland	188	Fb	49.39N	119.33W
Summerside	184	Lg	46.24N	63.47W
Summersville	184	Gf	38.17N	80.52W
Summerville	184	Eh	34.29N	85.21W
Summit Lake	180	Fe	54.17N	122.38W
Summit Mountain	188	Gg	39.23N	116.28W
Summit Peak	186	Ch	37.21N	106.42W
Sumoto	156	Dd	34.20N	134.54 E
Šumperk	120	Mg	49.58N	16.59 E
Sumprabum	148	Jc	26.33N	97.34 E
Sumsar	135	Hd	41.13N	71.23 E
Sumskaja oblast [3]	136	De	51.00N	34.15 E
Šumšu, ostrov-	138	Kf	50.45N	156.20 E
Sumter	184	Gi	33.55N	80.20W
Sumustā al Waqf	146	Dh	28.55N	30.51 E
Sumy	112	Je	50.54N	34.48 E
Suna	114	Mh	57.53N	50.07 E
Suna	114	Ie	62.08N	34.12 E
Sunagawa	154	Pc	43.29N	145.55 E
Šunak, gora-	136	Hf	47.05N	72.35 E
Sunan	154	He	39.15N	125.40 E
Sunan (Hongwansi)	152	Gd	38.59N	99.25 E
Sunart, Loch-	118	He	56.45N	5.45W
Sunaysilah	146	Ie	35.35N	41.53 E
Sunburst	188	Jb	48.53N	111.55W
Sunbury	184	Ie	40.52N	76.47W
Sunchales	206	Hd	30.56S	61.34W
Suncho Corral	206	Hc	27.56S	63.27W
Sunch'ŏn [N.Kor.]	152	Md	39.25N	125.56 E
Sunch'ŏn [S.Kor.]	152	Me	34.57N	127.29 E
Sun City	188	Ij	33.36N	112.17W
Suncun → Xinwen	152	Kd	35.49N	117.38 E
Sunda, Selat- = Sunda Strait (EN)	140	Mj	6.00S	105.45 E
Sundance	188	Md	44.24N	104.23W
Sundarbans	148	Hd	22.00N	89.00 E
Sundargarh	148	Gd	22.07N	84.02 E
Sunda Strait (EN) = Sunda, Selat-	140	Mj	6.00S	105.45 E
Sunday Strait	212	Ec	16.20S	123.15 E
Sundborn	116	Fd	60.39N	15.46 E
Sundbron	116	Ha	63.01N	18.11 E
Sundbyberg	116	Ge	59.22N	17.58 E
Sunde	114	Ag	59.50N	5.43 E
Sunderland	118	Lg	54.55N	1.23W
Sundern (Sauerland)	124	Kc	51.20N	8.00 E
Sundgau	122	Ng	47.40N	7.15 E
Sündiken Dağları	146	Dc	39.55N	31.00 E
Sundridge	184	Hc	45.46N	79.24W
Sundsvall	112	Hc	62.23N	17.18 E
Sundsvallsbukten	116	Gb	62.20N	17.35 E
Sunflower, Mount-	186	Eg	39.04N	102.01W
Sungaidareh	150	Dg	0.58S	101.30 E
Sungaigerong	150	Dg	2.59S	104.52 E
Sungaiguntung	150	Df	0.18N	103.37 E
Sungai Kolok	148	Kg	6.02N	101.58 E
Sungai Lembing	150	Df	3.55N	103.02 E
Sungailiat	150	Eg	1.51S	106.08 E
Sungaipenuh	150	Dg	2.05S	101.23 E
Sungai Petani	150	De	5.39N	100.30 E
Sungai Siput	150	Df	4.49N	101.04 E
Sungari (EN) = Songhua Jiang	140	Pe	47.42N	132.30 E
Sungqu → Songpan	152	He	32.37N	103.34 E
Sungurlu	146	Fb	40.10N	34.23 E
Sunharon Roads	220b	Bb	14.57N	145.36 E
Suning	154	Ce	38.25N	115.50 E
Sunja	128	Ke	45.21N	16.33 E
Sunjiapuzi	154	Ic	42.02N	126.34 E
Sunkar, gora-	135	Ib	44.12N	73.55 E
Sun Kosi	148	Hc	26.55N	87.09 E
Sunndalsøra	114	Be	62.40N	8.33 E
Sunnan	114	Cd	64.04N	11.38 E
Sunndalen	116	Cb	62.40N	8.45 E
Sunndalsfjorden	116	Cb	62.45N	8.25 E
Sunne	114	Cg	59.50N	13.09 E
Sunnerbo	116	Eh	56.45N	13.50 E
Sunnersta	116	Ge	59.48N	17.39 E
Sunnfjord	116	Ac	61.25N	5.20 E
Sunnhordland	116	Ae	59.55N	6.00 E
Sunnmøre	116	Bb	62.20N	6.40 E
Sunnyside	188	Fc	46.20N	120.00W
Sunnyvale	188	Dh	37.23N	122.01W
Su-no-Saki	156	Fd	34.58N	139.45 E
Sun River	188	Jc	47.30N	111.25W
Sunsas, Serrania de-	204	Cc	17.57S	59.35W
Suntar	138	Gd	62.04N	117.40 E
Suntar-Hajata, hrebet- = Suntar-Khayata Range (EN)	140	Qc	62.00N	143.00 E
Suntar-Khayata Range (EN) = Suntar-Hajata, hrebet-	140	Qc	62.00N	143.00 E
Suntaži	116	Kh	56.49N	24.57 E
Sun Valley	182	Ec	43.42N	114.21W
Sunwu	152	Mb	49.27N	127.19 E
Sunyani	160	Gh	7.20N	2.20W
Sunža	132	Oh	43.26N	46.08 E
Suojarvi	136	Dc	62.04N	32.21 E
Suokonmäki	116	Kb	62.47N	24.30 E
Suolahti	114	Fe	62.34N	25.52 E
Suomenlahti = Finland, Gulf of- (EN)	110	Ic	60.00N	27.00 E
Suomenniemi	116	Lc	61.19N	27.27 E
Suomenselkä	110	Ic	62.55N	24.00 E
Suomi/Finland [1]	112	Ic	64.00N	26.00 E
Suomussalmi	114	Gd	64.54N	29.00 E
Suō-Nada	156	Be	33.50N	131.30 E
Suonenjoki	114	Ge	62.37N	27.08 E
Suontee	116	Lc	61.40N	26.35 E
Suordah	138	Ic	66.43N	132.04 E
Suozhen → Huantai	154	Ef	36.57N	118.05 E
Supamo, Rio-	196	Fi	6.48N	61.50W
Superior [Az.-U.S.]	188	Jj	33.18N	110.06W
Superior [Mt.-U.S.]	188	Hc	47.12N	114.53W
Superior [Nb.-U.S.]	186	Gf	40.01N	98.04W
Superior [Wi.-U.S.]	176	Je	46.44N	92.05W
Superior, Lake-	174	Ke	48.00N	88.00W
Supetar	128	Kg	43.23N	16.33 E
Suphan Buri	148	Kf	14.29N	100.10 E
Süphan Dağı	144	Fb	38.54N	42.48 E
Supiori, Pulau-	150	Kg	0.45S	135.30 E
Supoj	132	Ge	49.38N	31.50 E
Support Force Glacier	222	Rg	83.05S	47.30W
Suprasl	120	Tc	53.13N	23.20 E
Suprasl	120	Sc	53.12N	22.55 E
Sup'ung	152	Lc	40.27N	124.57 E
Sup'ung-chosuji	154	Hd	40.30N	125.05 E
Suq ash Shuyūkh	146	Lg	30.53N	46.28 E
Suqian	152	Ke	33.55N	118.13 E
Sūq Suwayq	146	Hj	24.23N	38.27 E
Suquṭrā = Socotra (EN)	140	Hh	12.30N	54.00 E
Sūr	142	He	22.31N	59.30 E
Şūr	144	Ec	33.16N	35.11 E
Sur, Cabo-	221d	Ac	27.12S	109.26W
Sur, Point-	188	Eh	36.18N	121.54W
Sura	132	Nc	53.53N	45.44 E
Sura	110	Kd	56.06N	46.00 E
Šurab	135	Hd	40.03N	70.33 E
Surabaya	142	Nj	7.15S	112.45 E
Surahammar	116	Ge	59.43N	16.13 E
Šurak	144	Id	25.43N	58.48 E
Surakarta	142	Nj	7.35S	110.50 E
Šurān	146	Ge	35.17N	36.45 E
Šurany	120	Oh	48.06N	18.11 E
Surar	168	Gd	7.29N	40.54 E
Surat	142	Jg	21.10N	72.50 E
Surat Thani	142	Li	9.06N	99.20 E
Suraž [Bye.-U.S.S.R.]	114	Hi	55.26N	30.43 E
Suraž [R.S.F.S.R.]	136	De	53.02N	32.29 E
Surčin	130	De	44.47N	20.17 E
Sur del Cabo San Antonio, Punta-	206	Ie	36.52S	56.40W
Surduc	130	Gb	47.15N	23.21 E
Süre	120	Cg	49.44N	6.31 E

Index Symbols

- [1] Independent Nation
- [2] State, Region
- [3] District, County
- [4] Municipality
- [5] Colony, Dependency
- Continent
- Physical Region
- Historical or Cultural Region
- Mount, Mountain
- Volcano
- Hill
- Mountains, Mountain Range
- Hills, Escarpment
- Plateau, Upland
- Pass, Gap
- Plain, Lowland
- Delta
- Salt Flat
- Valley, Canyon
- Crater, Cave
- Karst Features
- Depression
- Polder
- Desert, Dunes
- Forest, Woods
- Heath, Steppe
- Oasis
- Cape, Point
- Coast, Beach
- Cliff
- Peninsula
- Isthmus
- Sandbank
- Island
- Atoll
- Rock, Reef
- Islands, Archipelago
- Rocks, Reefs
- Coral Reef
- Well, Spring
- Geyser
- River, Stream
- Waterfall, Rapids
- River Mouth, Estuary
- Lake
- Salt Lake
- Intermittent Lake
- Reservoir
- Swamp, Pond
- Canal
- Glacier
- Ice Shelf, Pack Ice
- Ocean
- Sea
- Gulf, Bay
- Strait, Fjord
- Lagoon
- Bank
- Seamount
- Tablemount
- Ridge
- Shelf
- Basin
- Escarpment, Sea Scarp
- Fracture
- Trench, Abyss
- National Park, Reserve
- Point of Interest
- Recreation Site
- Cave, Cavern
- Historic Site
- Ruins
- Wall, Walls
- Church, Abbey
- Temple
- Scientific Station
- Railway station
- Airport
- Port
- Military installation
- Lighthouse
- Mine
- Tunnel
- Dam, Bridge

Surendranagar 148 Ed 22.42N 71.41 E
Surgères 122 Fh 46.06N 0.45W
Surgut 142 Jc 61.14N 73.20 E
Surgutiha 138 Dd 63.47N 87.20 E
Surhandarinskaja oblast [3] 136 Gh 38.00N 67.30 E
Surhandarja 135 Ff 37.14N 67.20 E
Surhob 136 Hh 38.54N 70.04 E
Surigao 150 Ie 9.45N 125.30 E
Surin 148 Kf 14.53N 103.30 E
Suriname = Surinam (EN) [1] 200 Ke 4.00N 56.00W
Suripá, Río- 194 Mj 7.47N 69.53W
Sūrīyah=Syria (EN) [1] 142 Ff 35.00N 38.00 E
Sūrmaq 146 Og 31.03N 52.48 E
Surmelin 124 Fe 49.04N 3.31 E
Sürmene 146 Ib 40.55N 40.07 E
Surna 116 Cb 62.59N 8.40 E
Surnadalsøra 116 Cb 62.59N 8.39 E
Surovikino 136 Ef 48.36N 42.54 E
Surovo 138 Fe 55.39N 105.36 E
Sur-Pakri/Suur-Pakri 116 Je 59.50N 23.45 E
Surprise, Ile- 219b Ad 18.32S 163.02 E
Surprise, Lac- 184 Ja 49.20N 74.57W
Surrey [3] 118 Mj 51.25N 0.30W
Surrey 118 Mj 51.20N 0.05W
Sursee 128 Cc 47.10N 8.07 E
Sursk 132 Nc 53.04N 45.42 E
Surskoje 114 Li 54.31N 46.44 E
Surt 160 Ie 31.13N 16.35 E
Surt, Khalīj-=Sidra, Gulf of-(EN) 158 Ie 31.30N 18.00 E
Surte 116 Eg 57.49N 12.01 E
Surtsey 114a Bc 63.20N 20.38W
Sürüç 146 Hd 36.58N 38.24 E
Surud Ad 158 Lg 10.42N 47.09 E
Suruga-Wan 154 Og 34.55N 138.35 E
Surulangun 150 Dg 2.37S 102.45 E
Survey Pass 178 Ic 67.52N 154.10W
Sur Vjajn / Suur Väin 116 Jf 58.30N 23.20 E
Surwold 124 Jb 52.57N 7.31 E
Šuša 132 Oj 39.43N 46.44 E
Suså 116 Di 55.11N 11.46 E
Susa [It.] 128 Be 45.08N 7.03 E
Susa [Jap.] 156 Bd 34.37N 131.36 E
Susa (EN) = Shūsh 146 Mf 32.12N 48.17 E
Susa, Val di- 128 Be 45.10N 7.10 E
Sušac 128 Kh 42.46N 16.30 E
Sūsah [Lib.] 164 Dc 32.54N 21.58 E
Sūsah [Tun.] =Sousse (EN) 160 Ie 35.49N 10.38 E
Sūsah=Sousse (EN) [3] 162 Jb 35.45N 10.30 E
Susak 128 If 44.31N 14.18 E
Susaki 152 Ne 33.22N 133.17 E
Susami 156 De 33.33N 135.29 E
Susamyr 135 Ic 42.09N 73.59 E
Susanville 182 Cc 40.25N 120.39W
Suşehri 146 Hb 40.11N 38.06 E
Suseja 116 Kh 56.23N 25.00 E
Šušenskoje 138 Ef 53.19N 92.01 E
Sušice 120 Jg 49.14N 13.30 E
Susitna 178 Id 61.16N 150.30W
Suslonger 114 Lh 56.18N 48.12 E
Susoh 150 Cf 3.43N 96.50 E
Susong 154 Di 30.10N 116.06 E
Suspiro 204 Ej 30.38S 54.22W
Suspiro del Moro, Puerto del- 126 Ig 37.08N 3.40W
Susquehanna River 182 Ld 39.33N 76.05W
Susques 206 Gb 23.25S 66.29W
Sussex 184 Oc 45.43N 65.31W
Sussex 118 Mk 50.55N 0.30W
Sussex, Vale of- 118 Mk 51.00N 0.15W
Susubona 219a Dc 8.19S 159.27 E
Susuman 142 Qc 62.47N 148.10 E
Susurluk 146 Cc 39.54N 28.10 E
Susuzmüsellim 130 •Kh 41.06N 27.03 E
Šušvė 116 Ji 55.08N 23.53 E
Susz 120 Pc 53.44N 19.20 E
Sütçüler 146 Dd 37.30N 30.59 E
Suţeşti 130 Kd 45.13N 27.26 E
Sutherland 172 Cf 32.24S 20.40 E
Sutherland Falls 218 Bf 44.48S 167.44 E
Sutherlin 188 De 43.25N 123.19W
Sutla 128 Je 45.51N 15.41 E
Sutlej 140 Jg 29.23N 71.02 E
Sutton 184 Gf 38.41N 80.43W
Sutton, London- 124 Bc 51.21N 0.12W
Sutton Bridge 124 Cb 52.46N 0.11 E
Sutton in Ashfield 124 Aa 53.07N 1.16W
Sutton Scotney 124 Ac 51.09N 1.20W
Suttor River 212 Jd 21.25S 147.45 E
Suttsu 154 Pc 42.48N 140.14 E
Sutwik 178 He 56.34N 157.05W
Su'uholo 219a Ec 9.46S 161.58 E
Suunduk 132 Ud 51.46N 58.46 E
Suure-Jaani 114 Fg 58.31N 25.29 E
Suur-Pakri/Sur-Pakri 116 Je 59.50N 23.45 E
Suur Väin / Sur-Vjajn 116 Jf 58.30N 23.20 E
Suva 210 If 18.08S 178.25 E
Suvadiva Atoll 140 Ji 0.30N 73.13 E
Suva Gora 130 Eh 41.51N 21.03 E
Suva Planina 130 Ff 43.08N 22.13 E
Suvasvesi 114 Ge 62.40N 28.10 E
Suvorov 132 Jb 54.08N 36.32 E
Suvorovo [Mold.-U.S.S.R.] 130 Mc 46.33N 29.35 E
Suvorovo [Ukr.-U.S.S.R.] 130 Ld 45.35N 29.00 E
Suvorovskaja 132 Mg 44.10N 42.38 E
Suwa 154 Of 36.02N 138.08 E
Suwa-Ko 156 Fc 36.03N 138.05 E
Suwałki 120 Sb 54.07N 22.56 E
Suwałki [2] 120 Sb 54.05N 22.55 E
Suwalskie, Pojezierze- 120 Sb 54.15N 23.00 E
Suwannee River 184 Fk 29.18N 83.09W
Suwanose-Jima 152 Mf 29.40N 129.45 E
Suwarrow Atoll 208 Kf 13.15S 163.05W
Suwayqīyah, Hawr as- 146 Lf 32.40N 46.03 E
Suways, Khalīj as-=Suez, Gulf of-(EN) 158 Kf 28.10N 33.27 E
Suways, Qanāt as-=Suez Canal (EN) 158 Ke 29.55N 32.33 E
Suwŏn 152 Md 37.16N 127.01 E
Suxian [China] 152 Ke 33.36N 116.58 E
Suxian [China] 152 Je 31.44N 113.25 E
Suzaka 156 Fc 36.39N 138.18 E
Suzdal 114 Jh 56.28N 40.27 E
Suzhou 142 Of 31.16N 120.37 E
Suzhou/Jiuquan 142 Lf 39.46N 98.34 E
Suzi He 154 Hd 41.56N 124.20 E
Suzu 152 Od 37.25N 137.17 E
Suzuka 156 Ed 34.51N 136.35 E
Suzuka-Sanmyaku 156 Ed 35.10N 136.20 E
Suzu-Misaki 154 Nf 37.28N 137.20 E
Suzun 138 Df 53.47N 82.19 E
Suzzara 128 Ef 45.00N 10.45 E
Sværholthalvøya 114 Ga 70.30N 26.05 E
Svågan 116 Gc 61.54N 16.33 E
Svalbard [5] 224 Kd 78.00N 20.00 E
Svaljava 132 Ce 48.32N 22.59 E
Svalöv 116 Ei 55.55N 13.06 E
Svaneholm 116 Ee 59.11N 12.33 E
Svaneke 114 Di 55.08N 15.09 E
Svängsta 116 Fh 56.16N 14.46 E
Svanøy 116 Ac 61.30N 5.05 E
Svapa 132 Id 51.44N 34.59 E
Svappavaara 114 Ec 67.39N 21.04 E
Svärdsjö 116 Fd 60.45N 15.55 E
Svartå 116 Fe 59.08N 14.31 E
Svartälven 116 Fe 59.20N 14.35 E
Svartån [Swe.] 116 Fe 59.17N 15.15 E
Svartån [Swe.] 116 Ge 59.37N 16.33 E
Svartån [Swe.] 116 Ff 58.28N 15.33 E
Svartenhuk Halvø= Svartenhuk Peninsula (EN) 179 Gd 71.30N 55.20W
Svartenhuk Peninsula (EN) =Svartenhuk, Halvø 179 Gd 71.30N 55.20W
Svartisen 114 Cc 66.38N 13.58 E
Svatovo 136 Df 49.24N 38.13 E
Svay Riĕng 148 Lf 11.05N 105.48 E
Sveabreen 222 Cf 72.08S 1.53 E
Sveagruva 179 Nc 78.39N 16.25 E
Svealand 110 Hc 60.30N 15.30 E
Svealand 114 Dg 59.55N 15.30 E
Svedala 116 Ei 55.30N 13.14 E
Sveg 114 De 62.02N 14.21 E
Švėkšna 116 Ii 55.32N 21.30 E
Svelgen 114 Af 61.45N 5.18 E
Svelvik 116 De 59.37N 10.24 E
Švenčėneljaj/Švenčioneliai 114 Gi 55.09N 26.02 E
Švenčėnis/Švenčionys 114 Gi 55.07N 26.12 E
Švenčioneliai/Švenčėneljaj 114 Gi 55.09N 26.02 E
Švenčionys/Švenčėnis 114 Gi 55.07N 26.12 E
Svendborg 114 Ci 55.03N 10.37 E
Svendsen Peninsula 180 Ja 77.50N 84.00W
Svenljunga 114 Ch 57.30N 13.07 E
Svenska högarna 116 He 59.35N 19.35 E
Svenskøya 179 Oc 78.43N 26.30 E
Svenstavik 114 De 62.46N 14.27 E
Šventoj/Šventoji 116 Ih 56.04N 20.59 E
Šventoji 114 Fi 55.05N 24.24 E
Šventoji/Šventoj 116 Ih 56.04N 20.59 E
Sverdlovsk 142 Id 56.51N 60.36 E
Sverdlovskaja oblast [3] 136 Gd 59.00N 62.00 E
Sverdrup, ostrov- 138 Cb 74.30N 79.35 E
Sverdrup Channel 180 Ha 80.00N 96.30W
Sverdrup Islands 174 Jb 79.00N 98.00W
Sverige=Sweden (EN) [1] 112 Hc 62.00N 15.00 E
Svetac 128 Jg 43.02N 15.45 E
Svete/Svēte 116 Jh 56.40N 23.38 E
Svēte/Svete 116 Jh 56.40N 23.38 E
Sveti Naum 130 Di 40.55N 20.45 E
Sveti Nikola, prohod- 130 Ff 43.27N 22.36 E
Sveti Nikole 130 Eh 41.52N 21.57 E
Sveti Stefan 130 Bg 42.16N 18.54 E
Svetlaja 138 Ig 46.31N 138.18 E
Svetli 138 Ge 58.34N 116.00 E
Svetlogorsk [Bye.-U.S.S.R.] 136 Ce 52.38N 29.42 E
Svetlogorsk [R.S.F.S.R.] 116 Ij 54.55N 20.08 E
Svetlograd 136 Ef 45.19N 42.40 E
Svetlovodsk 132 He 49.02N 33.15 E
Svetly [R.S.F.S.R.] 136 Ge 50.51N 60.53 E
Svetly [R.S.F.S.R.] 114 Ei 54.41N 20.08 E
Svetly Jar 132 Ne 48.29N 44.46 E
Svetogorsk 114 Gf 61.07N 28.58 E
Svetozarevo 130 Ef 43.59N 21.15 E
Sviča 120 Ug 49.04N 24.06 E
Svid 114 Jf 61.13N 38.45 E
Svidník 120 Rg 49.18N 21.35 E
Svidník 120 Kg 49.23N 14.58 E
Svijaga 136 Ed 55.39N 48.28 E
Svilaja 128 Kg 43.50N 16.26 E
Svilengrad 130 Jh 41.46N 26.12 E
Svincovy Rudnik 135 Ff 37.52N 66.28 E
Svinecea Mare, Vîrful- 130 Fe 44.48N 22.09 E
Svir 116 Lj 54.50N 26.34 E
Svir 110 Jc 60.30N 32.48 E
Svirica 114 Hf 60.30N 32.54 E
Svirsk 138 Ff 53.04N 103.18 E
Svisloč 132 Dc 53.03N 24.07 E
Svisloč 132 Fc 53.27N 28.59 E
Svištov 130 If 43.37N 25.20 E
Svit 120 Qg 49.03N 20.12 E
Svitava 120 Mg 49.11N 16.38 E
Svitavy 120 Mg 49.46N 16.27 E
Svizra / Svizzera / Schweiz / Suisse = Switzerland (EN) [1] 112 Gf 46.00N 8.30 E
Svizzera / Schweiz / Suisse / Svizra = Switzerland (EN) [1] 112 Gf 46.00N 8.30 E
Svjatoj Nos, mys- [R.S.F.S.R.] 110 Jb 68.10N 39.43 E
Svjatoj Nos, mys- [R.S.F.S.R.] 138 Jb 72.45N 140.45 E
Svobodny 142 Od 51.24N 128.07 E
Svoge 130 Gg 42.58N 23.21 E
Svolvær 114 Db 68.14N 14.34 E
Svratka 120 Mh 48.52N 16.38 E
Svrljig 130 Ff 43.25N 22.08 E
Svulrya 116 Ed 60.25N 12.24 E
Svytaya Anna Trough (EN) 224 He 80.00N 70.00 E
Swabia (EN)=Schwaben 120 Gh 48.20N 10.30 E
Swabian-Bavarian Plateau (EN)=Schwäbisch-Bayerisches Alpenvorland 110 Hf 48.15N 10.30 E
Swabian Jura (EN)= Schwäbische Alb 110 Gf 48.25N 9.30 E
Swaffham 124 Cb 52.39N 0.41 E
Swain Reefs 208 Gg 21.40S 152.15 E
Swains Atoll 208 Jf 11.03S 171.05W
Swainsboro 184 Fi 32.36N 82.20W
Swakop 172 Ad 22.41S 14.31 E
Swakopmund 160 Ik 22.41S 14.34 E
Swakopmund [3] 172 Ad 22.30S 15.00 E
Swale 118 Lg 54.06N 1.20W
Swalmen 124 Ic 51.14N 6.02 E
Swanage 118 Lk 50.37N 1.58W
Swan Hill 212 Ig 35.21S 143.34 E
Swan Range 188 Ic 47.50N 113.40W
Swan River 180 Hf 52.06N 101.16W
Swansboro 184 Ih 34.36N 77.07W
Swansea [Austl.] 212 Jh 42.08S 148.04 E
Swansea [Wales-U.K.] 112 Fe 51.38N 3.57W
Swansea Bay 118 Jj 51.35N 3.52W
Swans Island 184 Mc 44.10N 68.25W
Swanson Lake 186 Ff 40.09N 101.06W
Swan Valley 188 Je 43.28N 111.20W
Swartberge 158 Jl 33.23S 21.48 E
Swarzędz 120 Nd 52.26N 17.05 E
Swastika 184 Ga 48.07N 80.12W
Swaziland [1] 160 Kk 26.30S 31.10 E
Sweden (EN)=Sverige [1] 112 Hc 62.00N 15.00 E
Swedru 166 Ed 5.32N 0.42W
Sweet Grass Hills 188 Jb 48.55N 111.30W
Sweet Home 188 Dd 44.24N 122.44W
Sweetwater 182 Ge 32.28N 100.25W
Sweetwater River 182 Fc 42.31N 107.02W
Swellendam 172 Cf 34.02S 20.26 E
Świder 120 Rd 52.08N 21.12 E
Świdnica 120 Mf 50.51N 16.29 E
Świdnik 120 Se 51.14N 22.41 E
Świdwin 120 Lc 53.47N 15.47 E
Świebodzin 120 Ld 52.15N 15.32 E
Świecie 120 Oc 53.25N 18.28 E
Świętej Anny, Góra- 120 Of 50.28N 18.13 E
Świętokrzyskie, Góry- 120 Qf 50.55N 21.00 E
Swift Current 180 Gf 50.17N 107.50W
Swift Current Creek 188 La 50.40N 107.44W
Swift River 180 Ed 60.05N 131.11W
Swilly, Lough-/Loch Suilí 118 Ff 55.10N 7.38W
Swinburne, Cape - 180 Hb 71.14N 98.33W
Swindon 118 Lj 51.34N 1.47W
Swinford/Béal Átha na Muice 118 Eh 53.57N 8.57W
Świnoujście 120 Kc 53.53N 14.14 E
Swisttal 124 Id 50.44N 6.54 E
Switzerland (EN) = Schweiz / Suisse / Svizra / Svizzera [1] 112 Gf 46.00N 8.30 E
Switzerland (EN) = Suisse / Svizra / Svizzera / Schweiz [1] 112 Gf 46.00N 8.30 E
Switzerland (EN) = Svizra / Svizzera / Schweiz / Suisse [1] 112 Gf 46.00N 8.30 E
Switzerland (EN) = Svizzera / Schweiz / Suisse / Svizra [1] 112 Gf 46.00N 8.30 E
Syčevka 132 Ib 55.51N 34.15 E
Syców 120 Ne 51.19N 17.43 E
Sydfalster-Gedser 114 Ci 54.35N 11.57 E
Sydkap Ice Cap 180 Ja 76.30N 85.00W
Sydney [Austl.] 210 Gh 33.52S 151.13 E
Sydney [N.S.-Can.] 176 Me 46.09N 60.11W
Sydney→Manra Atoll 208 Je 4.27S 171.15W
Sydney-Campbelltown 212 Kf 34.04S 150.49 E
Sydney Lake 186 Ia 50.40N 94.24W
Sydney Mines 180 Lg 46.14N 60.12W
Sydney-Penrith 212 Kf 33.45S 150.42 E
Syktyvkar 112 Lc 61.40N 50.46 E
Sylacauga 184 Di 33.10N 86.15W
Sylane 114 Ce 63.02N 12.13 E
Sylarna 114 Ce 63.02N 12.13 E
Sylhet 148 Id 24.54N 91.52 E
Sylling 116 De 59.54N 10.17 E
Sylt 120 Eb 54.55N 8.20 E
Sylva 134 Hh 57.40N 56.57 E
Sylvania 184 Gi 32.45N 81.38W
Sylvania Tablemount (EN) 214 Ge 11.58N 165.00 E
Sylvan Pass 182 Ec 44.28N 110.08W
Sylvester 184 Fj 31.32N 83.49W
Sylvester, Lake- 212 Hc 18.50S 135.50 E
Sym 138 Ed 60.15N 90.02 E
Syndassko 138 Fb 73.14N 108.05 E
Synja 134 Ld 65.12N 64.45 E
Synnfjell 116 Cc 61.05N 9.45 E
Syowa 222 De 69.00S 39.35 E
Syracuse [Ks.-U.S.] 186 Fh 37.59N 101.45W
Syracuse [N.Y.-U.S.] 176 Le 43.03N 76.09W
Syracuse (EN)=Siracusa 112 Hh 37.04N 15.18 E
Syrdarinskaja oblast [3] 136 Gg 40.30N 68.40 E
Syrdarja 136 Gg 40.52N 68.38 E
Syrdarja=Syr Darya (EN) 140 Ie 46.03N 61.00 E
Syr Darya (EN)= Syrdarja 140 Ie 46.03N 61.00 E
Syria (EN) 140 Ff 35.00N 38.00 E
Syria (EN)=Sūrīyah [1] 142 Ff 35.00N 38.00 E
Syriam 148 Je 16.46N 96.15 E
Syrian Desert (EN) = Shām, Bādiyat ash- 140 Ff 32.00N 40.00 E
Syrkovoje, ozero- 134 Lf 60.40N 65.00 E
Syrski 132 Kc 52.36N 39.28 E
Sysert 134 Jh 56.31N 60.49 E
Sysmä 114 Ff 61.30N 25.41 E
Sysola 136 Fc 61.42N 50.58 E
Sysslebäck 116 Ed 60.44N 12.52 E
Sysulp, gora- 130 Ha 48.29N 24.17 E
Syverma, plato- 140 Lc 67.00N 99.00 E
Syzran 112 Ke 53.09N 48.27 E
Szabolcs-Szatmár [2] 120 Sh 48.00N 22.10 E
Szamocin 120 Nc 53.02N 17.08 E
Szamos 130 Fa 48.07N 22.20 E
Szamotuły 120 Md 52.37N 16.35 E
Szarvas 120 Qj 46.52N 20.33 E
Szczawnica Krościenko 120 Qg 49.26N 20.30 E
Szczebrzeszyn 120 Sf 50.42N 22.59 E
Szczecin [2] 120 Kc 52.35N 14.30 E
Szczecin (Stettin) 112 He 53.24N 14.32 E
Szczecinek 120 Mc 53.43N 16.42 E
Szczeciński, Zalew- 120 Kc 53.46N 14.14 E
Szczekociny 120 Pf 50.38N 19.50 E
Szczerców 120 Pe 51.18N 19.09 E
Szczucin 120 Rf 50.18N 21.04 E
Szczuczyn 120 Sc 53.34N 22.18 E
Szczytno 120 Qc 53.34N 21.00 E
Szechwan (EN)=Sichuan Sheng (Ssu-ch'uan Sheng) [2] 152 He 30.00N 103.00 E
Szechwan (EN)=Ssu-ch'uan Sheng→Sichuan Sheng [2] 152 He 30.00N 103.00 E
Szécsény 120 Ph 48.05N 19.31 E
Szeged 112 If 46.15N 20.10 E
Szeged [2] 120 Qj 46.16N 20.08 E
Szeghalom 120 Ri 47.02N 21.10 E
Székesfehérvár 112 Hf 47.12N 18.25 E
Szekszárd 120 Oj 46.21N 18.43 E
Szendrő 120 Qh 48.24N 20.44 E
Szentendre 120 Pi 47.40N 19.05 E
Szentes 120 Qj 46.39N 20.16 E
Szentgotthárd 120 Mj 46.57N 16.17 E
Szerencs 120 Rh 48.10N 21.12 E
Szeskie Wzgórza 120 Sb 54.14N 22.22 E
Szigetvár 120 Nj 46.03N 17.48 E
Szkwa 120 Rc 53.10N 21.45 E
Szlichtyngowa 120 Me 51.43N 16.15 E
Szob 120 Oi 47.49N 18.52 E
Szolnok 120 Qi 47.11N 20.12 E
Szolnok 1 120 Qi 47.15N 20.30 E
Szombathely 120 Mi 47.14N 16.37 E
Szprotawa 120 Le 51.34N 15.33 E
Szreniawa 120 Qf 50.10N 20.35 E
Sztum 120 Pc 53.56N 19.01 E
Szubin 120 Nc 53.00N 17.44 E
Szydłów 120 Rf 50.35N 21.01 E
Szydłowiec 120 Qe 51.14N 20.51 E

T

Taakoka 220p Cc 21.15S 159.43W
Taalintendas/Dalsbruk 116 Jd 60.02N 22.31 E
Taavetti 116 Ld 60.55N 27.34 E
Tab 120 Oj 46.44N 18.02 E
Tabacal 206 Hb 23.16S 64.15W
Ţābah 146 Ji 27.02N 42.08 E
Tabaqah 146 He 35.52N 38.34 E
Tabar Islands 208 Ge 2.50S 152.00 E
Ţabarqah 162 Ib 36.57N 8.45 E
Ţabas 146 Qf 33.36N 56.54 E
Tabasará, Serranía de- 194 Gi 8.33N 81.40W
Tabasco [2] 190 Fe 18.00N 92.40W
Tabasco y Campeche, Llanos de- 190 Fe 18.15N 91.00W
Tabašino 114 Lh 56.59N 47.43 E
Tābask, Kūh-e- 146 Nh 29.52N 51.49 E
Tabay 204 Ci 28.18S 58.17W
Tabelbala 162 Gd 29.24N 3.15W
Taber 180 Gg 49.47N 112.08W
Taberg 116 Fg 57.41N 14.05 E
Taberg 116 Fg 57.41N 14.05 E
Tabernacle 197c Ab 17.23N 62.46W
Tabernas 126 Jg 37.03N 2.23W
Tabernes de Valldigna / Tavernes de Valldigna 126 Le 39.04N 0.16W
Tabiteuea Atoll 208 Ie 1.20S 174.50 E
Tabla 166 Fc 13.46N 3.01 E
Tablas 150 Hd 12.24N 122.02 E
Tablas Strait 150 Hd 12.40N 121.48 E
Tablat 126 Ph 36.25N 3.19 E
Tablazo, Bahía del- 194 Lh 10.52N 71.35W
Table Cape 218 Gc 39.06S 178.00 E
Table Rock Lake 186 Jh 36.35N 93.30W
Tabocas 204 Jb 14.39S 45.28W
Taboco, Rio- 204 Ed 19.53S 55.58W
Tabola 132 Pg 45.53N 48.20 E
Tábor 120 Kg 49.25N 14.41 E
Tabora 160 Ki 5.01S 32.48 E
Tabora [3] 170 Fd 5.20S 32.30 E
Tabory 134 Lg 58.31N 64.33 E
Tabou 160 Gh 4.25N 7.21W
Tabrīz 142 Gf 38.05N 46.18 E
Tábua 126 Dd 40.21N 8.02W
Tabuaeran Atoll (Fanning) 208 Ld 3.52N 159.20W
Tabuk 150 Hc 17.24N 121.25 E
Tabūk 142 Fg 28.23N 36.35 E
Ţaburbah 128 Dn 36.50N 9.50 E
Tabursuq 128 Dn 36.28N 9.15 E
Tabursuq, Monts de- 128 Dn 36.25N 9.05 E
Tabusintac 184 Ob 47.24N 65.02W
Tabwemasana 219b Cb 15.22S 166.45 E
Täby 114 Eg 59.30N 18.03 E
Tacámbaro de Codallos 192 Ih 19.14N 101.28W
Tacarcuna, Cerro- 194 Ij 8.05N 77.17W
Tacarigua, Laguna de- 196 Dg 10.15N 65.50W
Tacheng/Qoqek 142 Ke 46.45N 82.57 E
Tachibana-Wan 156 Be 32.45N 130.05 E
Tachichilte, Isla de- 192 Ee 24.59N 108.04W
Tachikawa [Jap.] 156 Fb 38.48N 139.58 E
Tachikawa [Jap.] 156 Fd 35.42N 139.23 E
Táchira [2] 202 Db 7.50N 72.05W
Tachiumet 164 Bd 26.19N 10.03 E
Tachov 120 Ig 49.48N 12.40 E
Tachungnya 220b Bb 14.58N 145.36 E
Tacinski 132 Le 48.13N 41.17 E
Tacir 130 Mi 40.32N 29.44 E
Tacloban 142 Oh 11.15N 125.00 E
Tacna 200 Ig 18.01S 70.15W
Tacna [3] 202 Dg 17.40S 70.20W
Tacoma 176 Ge 47.15N 122.27W
Tacotalpa, Río- 192 Mi 17.50N 92.52W
Tacuaral 204 Cd 18.59S 58.07W
Tacuarembó 206 Id 31.44S 55.59W
Tacuarembó [2] 204 Ek 32.10S 55.30W
Tacuarembó, Río- 204 Ek 32.25S 55.29W
Tacuarí, Río- 204 Fk 32.46S 53.18W
Tacuati 204 Df 23.27S 56.35W
Tadami 156 Fc 37.21N 139.17 E
Tadami-Gawa 156 Fc 37.38N 139.45 E
Tadarimana, Rio- 204 Ec 16.29S 54.31W
Tademaït, Plateau du- 158 Hf 28.30N 2.15 E
Tadine 219b Ce 21.33S 167.53 E
Tadjeraout 162 He 21.17N 1.20 E
Tadjetaret 162 Ie 22.00N 7.30 E
Tadjourah 168 Gc 11.45N 42.54 E
Tadjourah, Golfe de- 168 Gc 11.45N 43.00 E
Tadoule Lake 180 He 58.35N 98.20W
Tadoussac 184 Ma 48.09N 69.43W
Tadžikskaja Sovetskaja Socialističeskaja Respublika [2] 136 Hh 39.00N 71.00 E
Tadžikskaja SSR/ Respublikai Soveth Socialisti Todžikiston [2] 136 Hh 39.00N 71.00 E
Tadžikskaja SSR = Tajik SSR (EN) [2] 136 Hh 39.00N 71.00 E
T'aebaek-Sanmaek 140 Of 37.40N 128.50 E
Taechon 154 If 36.21N 126.36 E
T'aech'on 154 He 39.55N 125.30 E
Taedong-gang 154 He 38.42N 125.15 E
Taegu 142 Of 35.52N 128.36 E
Taeha-dong 154 Kf 37.31N 130.48 E
Taehan-Haehyŏp=Korea Strait (EN) 140 Of 34.40N 129.00 E
Taehan-Min'guk=South Korea (EN) [1] 142 Of 38.00N 127.30 E
Taehuksan-Do 154 Hg 34.40N 125.25 E
Taejŏn 142 Of 36.20N 127.26 E
Tafahi Island 208 Jf 15.52S 173.55W
Tafalla 126 Kb 42.31N 1.40W
Tafassasset 158 If 21.56N 10.12 E
Tafassasset, Ténéré du- 166 Ha 21.20N 11.00 E
Taff 118 Jj 51.27N 3.09W
Tafilalt 162 Gc 31.18N 4.18W
Tafiré 166 Dd 9.04N 5.10W
Tafi Viejo 206 Gc 26.44S 65.16W
Taflan 146 Gb 41.25N 36.09 E
Tafna 126 Ki 35.18N 1.28W
Tafraout 162 Fd 29.43N 9.00W
Tafresh 146 Ne 34.41N 50.01 E
Taft 146 Pg 31.45N 54.14 E
Taftān, Kuh-e- 140 Ig 28.36N 61.06 E
Taftanāz 146 Ge 35.59N 36.47 E
Taga 221c Aa 13.46S 172.28W
Taga Dzong 148 Hc 27.04N 89.53 E
Tagajō 156 Gb 38.18N 140.58 E
Tagama 158 Hg 15.50N 8.12 E
Taganrog 112 Jf 47.12N 38.56 E
Taganrogski zaliv 132 Kf 46.50N 38.25 E
Tagant [3] 162 Ef 18.30N 10.30W
Tagant 158 Fg 17.31N 12.07W
Tagarev, gora- 135 Ae 38.19N 57.18 E
Tagawa 156 Be 33.39N 130.48 E
Tagbilaran 150 He 9.39N 123.51 E
Tageru, Jabal- 168 Db 16.25N 27.10 E
Taggia 128 Bg 43.52N 7.51 E
Taghit 162 Gc 30.55N 2.02W
Tagil 134 Kg 58.33N 62.30 E
Tagish Lake 180 Ed 60.00N 134.00W
Tagliamento 128 He 45.38N 13.06 E
Taglio di Po 128 Ge 45.00N 12.12 E
Tagomago, Illa- / Tagomago, Isla de- 126 Ne 39.02N 1.39 E
Tagomago, Isla de- / Tagomago, Illa- 126 Ne 39.02N 1.39 E
Tagounit 162 Fd 29.58N 5.35W
Tagpochau, Ogso- 220b Ba 15.11N 145.45 E
Tāgrifat 164 Cd 29.12N 17.21 E
Taguatinga 202 If 12.25S 46.26W
Taguersimet 162 De 24.09N 15.07W
Tagula 219a Ad 11.20S 153.00 E
Tagula Island 208 Gf 11.30S 153.30 E
Tagum 150 Ie 7.21N 125.50 E
Tagus (EN)=Tajo 110 Fh 38.40N 9.24W
Tagus (EN)=Tejo 110 Fh 38.40N 9.24W
Tah 162 Ed 27.37N 12.50W
Tahaa, Ile- 216 Kc 16.38S 151.30W
Tahakopa 218 Cg 46.31S 169.23 E
Tahan, Gunong- 140 Mi 4.39N 102.14 E
Tahanea Atoll 208 Mf 16.52S 144.45W
Tahat 158 Hf 23.18N 5.32 E
Tahe 152 La 52.22N 124.48 E
Ţāherī 146 Oi 27.42N 52.21 E
Tahgong, Puntan- 220b Ba 15.06N 145.39 E
Tahiataš 135 Bc 42.20N 59.33 E
Tahifet 162 Ie 22.56N 5.59 E
Tahir Geçidi 146 Jc 39.52N 42.20 E
Tahiti, Ile- 208 Mf 17.37S 149.27W
Tahkuna neem / Takuna, mys- 116 Je 59.05N 22.30 E
Tahlequah 186 Ii 35.55N 94.58W
Tahoe, Lake- 188 Fg 38.54N 120.00W
Tahoua 160 Hg 14.54N 5.16 E
Tahoua [2] 166 Gb 16.00N 5.30 E

Index Symbols

[1] Independent Nation
[2] State, Region
[3] District, County
[4] Municipality
[5] Colony, Dependency
Continent
Physical Region
Historical or Cultural Region
Mount, Mountain
Volcano
Hill
Mountains, Mountain Range
Hills, Escarpment
Plateau, Upland
Pass, Gap
Plain, Lowland
Delta
Salt Flat
Valley, Canyon
Crater, Cave
Karst Features
Depression
Polder
Desert, Dunes
Forest, Woods
Heath, Steppe
Oasis
Cape, Point
Coast, Beach
Cliff
Peninsula
Isthmus
Sandbank
Island
Atoll
Rock, Reef
Islands, Archipelago
Rocks, Reefs
Coral Reef
Well, Spring
Geyser
River, Stream
Waterfall, Rapids
River Mouth, Estuary
Lake
Salt Lake
Intermittent Lake
Reservoir
Swamp, Pond
Canal
Glacier
Ice Shelf, Pack Ice
Ocean
Sea
Gulf, Bay
Strait, Fjord
Lagoon
Bank
Seamount
Tablemount
Ridge
Shelf
Basin
Escarpment, Sea Scarp
Fracture
Trench, Abyss
National Park, Reserve
Point of Interest
Recreation Site
Cave, Cavern
Historic Site
Ruins
Wall, Walls
Church, Abbey
Temple
Scientific Station
Railway station
Airport
Port
Military installation
Lighthouse
Mine
Tunnel
Dam, Bridge

Index Symbols

- [1] Independent Nation
- [2] State, Region
- [3] District, County
- [4] Municipality
- [5] Colony, Dependency
- Continent
- Physical Region
- Historical or Cultural Region
- Mount, Mountain
- Volcano
- Hill
- Mountains, Mountain Range
- Hills, Escarpment
- Plateau, Upland
- Pass, Gap
- Plain, Lowland
- Delta
- Salt Flat
- Valley, Canyon
- Crater, Cave
- Karst Features
- Depression
- Polder
- Desert, Dunes
- Forest, Woods
- Heath, Steppe
- Oasis
- Cape, Point
- Coast, Beach
- Cliff
- Peninsula
- Isthmus
- Sandbank
- Island
- Atoll
- Rock, Reef
- Islands, Archipelago
- Rocks, Reefs
- Coral Reef
- Well, Spring
- Geyser
- River, Stream
- Waterfall, Rapids
- River Mouth, Estuary
- Lake
- Salt Lake
- Intermittent Lake
- Reservoir
- Swamp, Pond
- Canal
- Glacier
- Ice Shelf, Pack Ice
- Ocean
- Sea
- Gulf, Bay
- Strait, Fjord
- Lagoon
- Bank
- Fracture
- Seamount
- Tablemount
- Ridge
- Shelf
- Basin
- Escarpment, Sea Scarp
- Trench, Abyss
- National Park, Reserve
- Point of Interest
- Recreation Site
- Cave, Cavern
- Historic Site
- Ruins
- Wall, Walls
- Church, Abbey
- Temple
- Scientific Station
- Railway station
- Airport
- Port
- Military installation
- Lighthouse
- Mine
- Tunnel
- Dam, Bridge

Index Symbols

[1] Independent Nation	Historical or Cultural Region	Pass, Gap	Depression	Coast, Beach	Rock, Reef
[2] State, Region	Mount, Mountain	Plain, Lowland	Polder	Cliff	Islands, Archipelago
[3] District, County	Volcano	Delta	Desert, Dunes	Peninsula	Rocks, Reefs
[4] Municipality	Hill	Valley, Canyon	Forest, Woods	Isthmus	Coral Reef
[5] Colony, Dependency	Mountains, Mountain Range	Heath, Steppe	Sandbank	Well, Spring	Island
Continent	Hills, Escarpment	Crater, Cave	Oasis	Geyser	Atoll
Physical Region	Plateau, Upland	Karst Features	Cape, Point	River, Stream	

Waterfall, Rapids	Canal	Lagoon	Escarpment, Sea Scarp	Historic Site	Airport
River Mouth, Estuary	Glacier	Seamount	Fracture	Ruins	Port
Lake	Ice Shelf, Pack Ice	Tablemount	Trench, Abyss	Wall, Walls	Military installation
Salt Lake	Ocean	National Park, Reserve	Church, Abbey	Lighthouse
Intermittent Lake	Sea	Ridge	Point of Interest	Temple	Mine
Reservoir	Gulf, Bay	Basin	Recreation Site	Scientific Station	Tunnel
Swamp, Pond	Shelf		Cave, Cavern	Railway station	Dam, Bridge
Strait, Fjord					

Tepa [Indon.] 150 Ih 7.52S 129.31 E
Tepa [W.F.] 220h Bb 13.19S 176.09W
Te Pae Roa Ngake o Tuko 220n Bb 10.23S 161.00W
Tepako, Pointe- 220h Bb 13.16S 176.08W
Tepalcatepec, Río- 192 Ih 18.35N 101.59W
Tepa Point 220k Bb 19.07S 169.56W
Tepatitlán de Morelos 192 Hg 20.49N 102.44W
Tepehuanes 190 Cc 25.21N 105.44W
Tepehuanes, Río- 192 Ge 25.11N 105.26W
Tepehuanes, Sierra de- 190 Cc 25.00N 105.40W
Tepelena 130 Di 40.18N 20.01 E
Tepi 168 Fd 7.03N 35.30 E
Tepic 176 Ig 21.30N 104.54W
Teplá 120 Ig 49.59N 12.52 E
Teplá 120 If 50.14N 12.52 E
Teplice 120 Jf 50.39N 13.50 E
Tepoca, Bahía de- 192 Cb 30.15N 112.50W
Tepopa, Cabo- 192 Cc 29.20N 112.25W
Te Puka 220n Ac 10.26S 161.02W
Te Puke 218 Gb 37.47S 176.20 E
Tequepa, Bahía de- 192 Ii 17.17N 101.05W
Tequila 192 Hg 20.54N 103.47W
Tequisquiapan 192 Jg 20.31N 99.52W
Ter 126 Pb 42.01N 3.12 E
Téra 160 Hg 14.01N 0.45 E
Tera [Port.] 126 Df 38.56N 8.03W
Tera [Sp.] 126 Gc 41.54N 5.44W
Teradomari 156 Fc 37.38N 138.45 E
Terai 140 Kg 26.30N 85.15 E
Teraina Island (Washington) 208 Kd 4.43N 160.24W
Terakeka 168 Ed 5.26N 31.45 E
Teramo 128 Hh 42.39N 13.42 E
Terampa 150 Ef 3.14N 106.14 E
Ter Apel, Vlagtwedde- 124 Jb 52.52N 7.06 E
Terborg, Wisch- 124 Ic 51.55N 6.22 E
Tercan 146 Ic 39.47N 40.24 E
Terceira 158 Ee 38.43N 27.13W
Tercero, Río- 206 Hd 32.55S 62.19W
Terebovlja 132 De 49.18N 25.42 E
Terehovka 154 Kc 43.38N 131.55 E
Terek 132 Nh 43.29N 44.08 E
Terek 110 Kg 43.44N 47.30 E
Térékolé 166 Cb 15.07N 10.53W
Terek-Saj 135 Hd 41.29N 71.13 E
Terengganu [2] 150 De 5.00N 103.00 E
Terenos 204 Ee 20.26S 54.50W
Teresa Cristina 204 Gg 24.48S 51.07W
Teresina 200 Lf 5.05S 42.49W
Teresinha 202 Hc 0.58N 52.02W
Tereška 132 Od 51.50N 46.45 E
Terespol 120 Td 52.05N 23.36 E
Teressa 148 Ig 8.15N 93.10 E
Teresva 132 Cf 47.59N 23.15 E
Terevaka, Cerro- 221d Ab 27.05S 109.23W
Tergnier 122 Je 49.39N 3.18 E
Terhazza 166 Ea 23.36N 4.56W
Teriberka 114 Ib 69.10N 35.10 E
Teriberka 114 Ib 69.09N 35.08 E
Terlingua Creek 186 El 29.10N 103.36W
Termas de Río Hondo 206 Hc 27.29S 64.52W
Terme 146 Gb 41.12N 36.59 E
Termez 142 If 37.14N 67.16 E
Termini Imerese 128 Hm 37.59N 13.42 E
Termini Imerese, Golfo di- 128 Hl 38.00N 13.45 E
Terminillo 128 Hh 42.28N 13.01 E
Términos, Laguna de- 190 Fe 18.37N 91.33W
Termit, Massif de- 166 Hb 16.15N 11.17 E
Termit-Kaoboul 166 Hb 15.43N 11.37 E
Termoli 128 Ji 42.00N 15.00 E
Termonde/Dendermonde 124 Gc 51.02N 4.07 E
Termunten 124 Ja 53.18N 7.03 E
Ternaard, Westdongeradeel- 124 Ha 53.23N 5.58 E
Ternate 150 If 0.48N 127.24 E
Ternej 138 Ig 45.05N 136.35 E
Terneuzen 122 Jc 51.20N 3.50 E
Terni 128 Gh 42.34N 12.37 E
Ternitz 128 Kc 47.43N 16.02 E
Ternois 124 Ed 50.25N 2.19 E
Ternopol 112 If 49.34N 25.38 E
Ternopolskaja oblast [3] 136 Cf 49.20N 25.35 E
Terpenija, mys- 138 Jg 48.38N 144.40 E
Terpenija, zaliv- 140 Qe 49.00N 143.30 E
Terrace 180 Ef 54.31N 128.35W
Terrace Bay 186 Mb 48.47N 87.09W
Terracina 128 Hi 41.17N 13.15 E
Terra de Basto 126 Ec 41.25N 8.00W
Terra Firma 172 Ce 25.36S 23.24 E
Terråk 114 Cd 65.05N 12.25 E
Terralba 128 Ck 39.43N 8.39 E
Terra Rica 204 Ff 22.43S 52.38W
Terrassa 126 Oc 41.34N 2.01 E
Terrebonne Bay 186 Kl 29.09N 90.35W
Terre-de-Bas 197e Ac 15.51N 61.39W
Terre-de-Haut 197e Ac 15.58N 61.35W
Terre Haute 182 Jd 39.28N 87.24W
Terrell 186 Hj 32.44N 96.17W
Terre Plaine 122 Jg 47.25N 4.00 E
Terres Froides 122 Li 45.30N 5.30 E
Terril 126 Gh 37.00N 5.11W
Territoire de Belfort [3] 122 Mg 47.45N 6.55 E
Terry 188 Mc 46.47N 105.19W
Tersa 132 Nd 50.46N 44.42 E
Terschelling 124 Ha 53.21N 5.13 E
Terschelling 122 La 53.24N 5.20 E
Terschelling-West-Terschelling 124 Ha 53.21N 5.13 E
Tersef 168 Bc 12.55N 16.49 E
Terskej-Alatau, hrebet- 136 Hg 42.10N 78.45 E
Terski bereg 114 Jc 66.10N 39.30 E
Tersko-Kumski kanal 132 Ng 44.47N 44.37 E
Terter 132 Oi 40.27N 47.16 E
Teruel 126 Kd 40.21N 1.06W
Teruel [3] 126 Ld 40.40N 0.40W
Tervakoski 116 Kd 60.48N 24.37 E
Tervel 130 Kf 43.45N 27.24 E
Tervo 116 Lb 62.57N 26.45 E
Tervola 114 Fc 66.05N 24.48 E
Tes 152 Fa 50.27N 93.30 E
Teša 114 Ki 55.38N 42.10 E
Tesalia 202 Cc 2.29N 75.44W
Tesaret 162 Hd 25.40N 2.43 E
Tesdrero, Cerro- 192 Hf 22.47N 103.04W
Teseney 168 Fb 15.07N 36.40 E
Teshekpuk Lake 178 Ib 70.35N 153.30W
Teshikaga 154 Rc 43.29N 144.28 E
Teshio 154 Pb 44.53N 141.44 E
Teshio-Dake 154 Qc 43.58N 142.50 E
Teshio-Gawa 154 Pb 44.53N 141.44 E
Teshio-Sanchi 156a Ba 44.20N 142.00 E
Tesijn → Tesijn Gol 140 Ld 50.28N 93.04 E
Tesijn Gol (Tesijn) 140 Ld 50.28N 93.04 E
Teslić 128 Lf 44.37N 17.52 E
Teslin 180 Ed 60.09N 132.45W
Teslin 180 Ed 61.34N 134.50W
Teslin Lake 180 Ed 60.00N 132.30W
Teslui 130 He 44.09N 24.29 E
Tesocoma 192 Ed 27.41N 109.16W
Tesouras, Rio- 204 Gb 14.36S 50.51W
Tesouro 204 Fc 16.04S 53.34W
Tessala, Monts du- 126 Li 35.15N 0.45W
Tessalit 160 Hf 20.14N 0.59 E
Tessaoua 166 Gc 13.45N 7.59 E
Tessenderlo 124 Hc 51.04N 5.05 E
Test 118 Lk 50.55N 1.29W
Test, Tizi n'- 162 Fc 30.50N 8.20W
Testa, Capo- 128 Di 41.14N 9.08 E
Teste, La- 122 Ej 44.38N 1.09W
Têt 122 Jl 42.44N 3.02 E
Tetari, Cerro- 194 Ki 9.59N 72.55W
Tetas, Punta- 206 Fc 23.31S 70.38W
Tete 160 Kj 16.10S 33.36 E
Tete [3] 172 Ec 15.30S 33.00 E
Te Teko 218 Gc 38.02S 176.48 E
Tetepare I iland 219a Cc 8.45S 157.35 E
Téterchen 124 Ie 49.14N 6.34 E
Tetere 219a Ec 9.25S 160.15 E
Teterev 132 Gd 51.01N 30.08 E
Teterow 120 Ic 53.47N 12.34 E
Teteven 130 Hg 42.55N 24.16 E
Tetiaroa Atoll 208 Mf 17.05S 149.32W
Tetijev 132 Fe 49.23N 29.41 E
Tetjuši 114 Li 54.57N 48.49 E
Teton Peak 188 Ic 47.55N 112.48W
Teton Range 188 Je 43.50N 110.55W
Teton River 188 Jc 47.56N 110.31W
Tétouan 160 Ge 35.34N 5.22W
Tétouan [3] 162 Fb 35.35N 5.30W
Tetovo 130 Dg 42.01N 20.59 E
Tetri-Ckaro 132 Ni 41.33N 44.27 E
Teuco, Río- 204 Bg 25.38S 60.12W
Teufelskopf 124 Ie 49.36N 6.49 E
Teulada 128 Cl 38.58N 8.46 E
Teulada, Capo- 110 Gh 38.52N 8.38 E
Teul de Gonzáles Ortega 192 Hg 21.28N 103.29W
Teun, Pulau- 150 Ih 6.59S 129.08 E
Teupasenti 194 Df 14.13N 86.42W
Teuquito, Río- 204 Bg 24.22S 61.09W
Teuri-Tō 156a Ba 44.25N 141.20 E
Teutoburger Wald 120 Ee 52.10N 8.15 E
Teuva/Ostermark 114 Ee 62.29N 21.44 E
Teuz 130 Ec 46.39N 21.33 E
Tevai 219c Bb 11.37S 166.55 E
Tevaïtoa 221e Db 16.46S 151.28W
Tevere = Tiber (EN) 110 Hg 41.44N 12.14 E
Teverya 146 Ff 32.47N 35.32 E
Teviot 118 Kf 55.36N 2.26W
Tevli 120 Ud 52.19N 24.23 E
Tevriz 136 Hd 57.34N 72.24 E
Tevšruleh 152 Hb 47.25N 101.55 E
Te Waewae Bay 218 Bg 46.15S 167.30 E
Tewkesbury 118 Kj 51.59N 2.09W
Têwo (Dêngkagoin) 152 He 34.03N 103.21 E
Texada Island 188 Cb 49.40N 124.24W
Texarkana [Ar.-U.S.] 182 Ie 33.26N 94.02W
Texarkana [Tx.-U.S.] 176 Jf 33.26N 94.03W
Texas 212 Ke 28.51S 151.11 E
Texas [2] 182 He 31.30N 99.00W
Texas City 182 If 29.23N 94.54W
Texcoco 192 Jh 19.31N 98.53W
Texel 124 Ga 53.03N 4.47 E
Texel 122 Ka 53.05N 4.45 E
Texel-De Koog 124 Ga 53.07N 4.46 E
Texel-Den Burg 124 Ga 53.03N 4.47 E
Texoma, Lake- 182 He 33.55N 96.37W
Teyéa = Tegea (EN) 130 Fl 37.27N 22.25 E
Teza 114 Jh 56.32N 41.57 E
Teze-Jel 136 Gh 37.55N 60.22 E
Teziutlán 190 Ee 19.49N 97.21W
Tezpur 148 Ic 26.38N 92.48 E
Tha-anne 180 Id 60.31N 94.37W
Thabana Ntlenyana 158 Jk 29.30S 29.15 E
Thabazimbi 172 Dd 24.41S 27.21 E
Thai, Ao- = Thailand, Gulf of- (EN) 140 Mh 10.00N 102.00 E
Thai Binh 148 Ld 20.27N 106.20 E
Thailand (EN) = Muang Thai [1] 142 Mh 15.00N 100.00 E
Thailand, Gulf of- (EN) = Thai, Ao- 140 Mh 10.00N 102.00 E
Thai Nguyen 148 Ld 21.36N 105.50 E
Thal 148 Eb 31.30N 71.40 E
Thālith, Ash Shallāl ath- = Third Cataract (EN) 158 Kg 19.49N 30.19 E
Thamad Bū Ḩashīshah 164 Cd 25.50N 18.05 E
Thamarīd 168 Ib 17.39N 54.02 E
Thame 124 Bc 51.45N 0.59W
Thames 216 Eg 37.08S 175.33 E
Thames 110 Ge 51.28N 0.43 E
Thames River 184 Fd 42.19N 82.28W
Thamūd 144 Gf 17.15N 49.54 E
Thāna 142 Jh 19.12N 72.58 E
Thandaung 148 Je 19.04N 96.41 E
Thanh Hoa 142 Mh 19.48N 105.46 E
Thanh-pho Ho Chi Minh (Saigon) 142 Mh 10.45N 106.40 E
Thanjāvūr 148 Ff 10.48N 79.09 E
Thanlwin = Salween (EN) 140 Lg 16.31N 97.37 E
Thann 122 Ng 47.49N 7.05 E
Thaon-les-Vosges 122 Mf 48.15N 6.25 E
Thap Sakae 148 Jf 11.14N 99.31 E
Thar/Great Indian Desert 140 Jg 27.00N 70.00 E
Thargomindah 212 Ie 28.00S 143.49 E
Tharrawaddy 148 Je 17.39N 95.48 E
Tharros 128 Ck 39.54N 8.28 E
Tharthār, Baḩrath- 144 Fc 33.59N 43.12 E
Tharthār, Wādī ath- 146 Je 33.59N 43.12 E
Thasi Gang Dzong 148 Ic 27.19N 91.34 E
Thásou 130 Hi 40.47N 24.43 E
Thásos 110 Ig 40.49N 24.42 E
Thásou, Dhíavlos- 130 Hi 40.49N 24.42 E
Thathlīth, Wādī- 164 He 20.25N 44.55 E
Thaton 148 Je 16.56N 97.20 E
Thau, Bassin de- 122 Jk 43.23N 3.36 E
Thaxted 124 Cc 51.57N 0.22 E
Thaya 120 Mh 48.37N 16.56 E
Thayawthadangyi Kyun 148 Jf 12.20N 98.00 E
Thayetchaung 148 Jf 13.52N 98.16 E
Thayetmyo 148 Je 19.19N 95.11 E
The Alberga River 212 He 27.06S 135.33 E
The Aldermen Islands 218 Gb 37.00S 176.05 E
Thebai = Thebes (EN) 164 Fd 25.43N 32.35 E
Thebes (EN) = Thebai 164 Fd 25.43N 32.35 E
Thebes → Thívai 130 Gk 38.19N 23.19 E
The Black Sugarloaf 212 Kf 31.20S 151.33 E
The Borders 118 Kf 55.35N 2.50W
The Bottom 196 Ed 17.38N 63.15W
The Broads 118 Oi 52.40N 1.30 E
The Cheviot 118 Kf 55.28N 2.09W
The Cheviot Hills 118 Kf 55.30N 2.10W
The Crane 197q Bb 13.06N 59.26W
The Dalles 182 Cb 45.36N 121.10W
Thedford 182 Gc 41.59N 100.35W
The Entrance 212 Kf 33.21S 151.30 E
The Everglades 182 Kf 26.00N 81.00W
The Gap 188 Jh 36.25N 111.30W
The Granites 212 Gd 20.35S 130.21 E
The Hague (EN) = Den Haag /'s-Gravenhage 112 Ge 52.06N 4.18 E
The Knob 184 He 41.14N 78.22W
The Little Minch 118 Gd 57.35N 6.55W
Thelle 124 De 49.23N 1.51 E
Thelon 174 Jc 64.16N 96.05W
The Macumba River 208 Eg 27.45S 136.50 E
The Merse 118 Kf 55.50N 2.10W
The Naze 124 Di 51.42N 1.47 E
The Neales River 212 He 28.08S 136.47 E
The Needles 118 Lk 50.39N 1.34W
Theniet el Had 126 Oi 35.32N 2.01 E
Theodore 212 Kd 24.57S 150.05 E
Theológos 130 Hi 40.40N 24.42 E
The Pas 176 Id 53.50N 101.15W
The Pillories 197n Bb 12.54N 61.12W
Thérain 122 Ie 49.15N 2.27 E
Thermaïkós Kólpos = Salonika, Gulf of- (EN) 110 Ig 40.20N 22.45 E
Thermopílai = Thermopylae (EN) 130 Fk 38.48N 22.32 E
Thermopolis 182 Fc 43.39N 108.13W
Thermopylae (EN) = Thermopílai 130 Fk 38.48N 22.32 E
Thérouanne 124 Ed 50.38N 2.15 E
The Round Mountain 212 Kf 30.27S 152.16 E
The Sandlings 118 Oi 52.10N 1.30 E
Thesiger Bay 180 Fb 71.30N 124.00W
The Slot → New Georgia Sound 214 Fi 8.00S 158.10 E
The Solent Spithead 118 Lk 50.46N 1.20W
Thessalía [2] 130 Fj 39.30N 22.10 E
Thessalía = Thessaly (EN) 110 Ih 39.30N 22.10 E
Thessalía = Thessaly (EN) 130 Fj 39.30N 22.10 E
Thessalon 184 Fb 46.15N 83.34W
Thessaloníki = Salonika (EN) 112 Ig 40.38N 22.56 E
Thessaly (EN) = Thessalía 110 Ih 39.30N 22.10 E
Thessaly (EN) = Thessalía 130 Fj 39.30N 22.10 E
The Stevenson River 212 He 27.06S 135.33 E
Thet 124 Cb 52.24N 0.45 E
Thetford 118 Ni 52.25N 0.45 E
Thetford Mines 184 Lb 46.05N 71.18W
The Twins 218 Ed 41.14S 172.40 E
Theux 124 Hd 50.33N 5.49 E
The Valley 190 Le 18.03N 63.04W
The Warburton River 212 He 27.55S 137.28 E
The Wash 110 Ge 52.55N 0.15 E
The Weald 118 Nj 51.05N 0.05 E
The Witties 194 Ff 14.10N 82.45W
Thiaucourt-Regniéville 124 Hf 48.57N 5.52 E
Thiberville 124 Ce 49.08N 0.27 E
Thibodaux 186 Kl 29.48N 90.49W
Thief River Falls 182 Hb 48.07N 96.10W
Thiel Mountains 222 Pg 85.15S 91.00W
Thiene 128 Fe 45.42N 11.29 E
Thiérache, Collines de la- 122 Je 49.48N 3.55 E
Thiers 122 Ji 45.51N 3.34 E
Thiès 160 Fg 14.48N 16.56W
Thiès [3] 166 Bc 14.45N 16.50W
Thiesi 128 Cj 40.31N 8.43 E
Thika 170 Gc 1.03S 37.05 E
Thikombia 216 Fc 15.44S 179.55W
Thillot, Le- 122 Mg 47.53N 6.46 E
Thimerais 122 Hf 48.40N 1.20 E
Thimphu 142 Kg 27.28N 89.39 E
Thio 216 Cd 21.37S 166.14 E
Thionville 122 Me 49.22N 6.10 E
Thiou 166 Ec 13.48N 2.40W
Thíra 130 Im 36.25N 25.26 E
Thíra = Thira (EN) 130 Im 36.24N 25.26 E
Thira (EN) = Thíra 130 Im 36.24N 25.26 E
Thirasía 130 Im 36.25N 25.20 E
Third Cataract (EN) = Thālith, Ash Shallāl ath- 158 Kg 19.49N 30.19 E
Thirsk 118 Lg 54.14N 1.20W
Thisted 114 Bh 56.57N 8.42 E
Thithia 219d Cb 17.45S 179.18W
Thiu Khao Phetchabun 148 Ke 16.20N 100.55 E
Thívai (Thebes) 130 Gk 38.19N 23.19 E
Thiviers 122 Gi 45.25N 0.55 E
Thlewiaza 180 Id 60.28N 94.42W
Thoa 180 Gd 60.31N 109.45W
Tho Chu, Dao- 148 Kg 9.00N 103.50 E
Thoen 148 Je 17.41N 99.14 E
Tholen 124 Gc 51.32N 4.13 E
Tholen 122 Kc 51.35N 4.05 E
Tholey 124 Je 49.29N 7.04 E
Thomasset, Rocher- 208 Nf 10.21S 138.25W
Thomaston 184 Ei 32.54N 84.20W
Thomasville [Al.-U.S.] 184 Dj 32.18N 87.47W
Thomasville [Ga.-U.S.] 182 Ke 30.50N 83.59W
Thomasville [N.C.-U.S.] 184 Gh 35.53N 80.05W
Thompson 180 He 55.45N 97.45W
Thompson Falls 188 Hc 47.36N 115.21W
Thompson River [B.C.-Can.] 188 Ea 50.12N 121.34W
Thompson River [U.S.] 186 Jg 39.45N 93.36W
Thompson Sound 218 Bf 45.10S 167.00 E
Thomsen 180 Fb 73.40N 119.30W
Thomson 184 Fi 33.28N 82.30W
Thomson River 212 Ie 25.11S 142.53 E
Thomson's Falls 170 Gb 0.02N 36.22 E
Thon 124 Fe 49.53N 3.55 E
Thon Buri 142 Mh 13.43N 100.24 E
Thong Pha Phum 148 Jf 14.44N 98.38 E
Thongwa 148 Je 16.46N 96.32 E
Thonon-les-Bains 122 Mh 46.22N 6.29 E
Thoreau 186 Bi 35.24N 108.13W
Thornaby-on-Tees 118 Lg 54.34N 1.18W
Thornbury 216 Ci 46.17S 168.06 E
Thorney 124 Bb 52.37N 0.06W
Thornhill 118 Jf 55.18N 3.40W
Thorshavn 112 Fc 62.01N 6.46W
Thouars 122 Fh 46.58N 0.13W
Thouet 122 Fg 47.17N 0.06W
Thouquet-Paris-Plage, Le- 122 Hd 50.31N 1.35 E
Thrace (EN) = Thráki 110 Ig 41.20N 26.45 E
Thrace (EN) = Thráki 130 Jh 41.20N 26.45 E
Thrace (EN) = Trakya 110 Ig 41.20N 26.45 E
Thrace (EN) = Trakya 130 Jh 41.20N 26.45 E
Thráki [2] 130 Ih 41.10N 25.30 E
Thráki = Thrace (EN) 110 Ig 41.20N 26.45 E
Thráki = Thrace (EN) 130 Jh 41.20N 26.45 E
Thrakikón Pélagos 130 Hi 40.30N 25.00 E
Thrapston 124 Bb 52.24N 0.32W
Three Forks 182 Eb 45.54N 111.33W
Three Kings Islands 208 Ih 34.10S 172.10 E
Three Kings Trough (EN) 106 Jm 32.00S 170.30 E
Three Pagodas Pass 148 Je 15.18N 98.23 E
Three Points, Cape- 158 Gh 4.45N 2.06W
Three Rivers 184 Ee 41.57N 85.38W
Three Sisters Islands 219a Ed 10.10S 161.57 E
Throckmorton 186 Gj 33.11N 99.11W
Throssel, Lake- 212 Ee 27.25S 124.15 E
Thu Dau Mot 148 Lf 10.58N 106.39 E
Thuin 122 Kd 50.20N 4.17 E
Thule 222 Ad 59.27S 27.19W
Thule/Qânâq 224 Od 77.35N 69.40W
Thule, Mount - 180 Jb 73.00N 78.27W
Thun 128 Bd 46.45N 7.40 E
Thunder Bay 176 Ke 48.23N 89.15W
Thunder Bay [Ont.-Can.] 186 Lb 48.24N 89.00W
Thunder Bay [Ont.-Can.] 184 Fc 45.04N 83.25W
Thunder Butte 186 Fd 45.19N 101.53W
Thuner See 128 Bd 46.40N 7.45 E
Thung Song 148 Jg 8.11N 99.41 E
Thur 128 Cc 47.36N 8.35 E
Thurgau [2] 128 Dc 47.40N 9.10 E
Thüringen 120 Gf 50.40N 11.00 E
Thüringer Wald = Thuringian Forest (EN) 110 He 50.30N 11.00 E
Thuringian Forest (EN) = Thüringer Wald 110 He 50.30N 11.00 E
Thurles/Durlas 118 Fi 52.41N 7.49W
Thursday Island 212 Ib 10.35S 142.13 E
Thurso 112 Fd 58.35N 3.32W
Thurso 118 Jc 58.35N 3.30W
Thurston Island 222 Pf 72.06S 99.00W
Thury-Harcourt 124 Bf 48.59N 0.29W
Thusis/Tusaun 128 Dd 46.42N 9.26 E
Thuwayrāt, Nafūd ath- 146 Kj 26.00N 44.50 E
Thuy Phong 148 Lf 11.14N 108.43 E
Thwaites Iceberg Tongue 222 Of 74.00S 108.30W
Thy 116 Ch 57.00N 8.30 E
Thyborøn 116 Ch 56.42N 8.13 E
Tianbaoshan 154 Jc 42.57N 128.57 E
Tianchang 152 Ke 32.37N 119.00 E
Tiandong (Pingma) 152 Ig 23.40N 107.09 E
Tian'e (Liupai) 152 If 25.05N 107.12 E
Tianguá 202 Jd 3.44S 40.59W
Tianjin (Tientsin) 142 Nf 39.08N 117.12 E
Tianjin Shi (T'ien-chin Shih) [4] 152 Kd 39.08N 117.12 E
Tianjun (Xinyuan) 142 Lf 37.18N 99.15 E
Tianlin (Leli) 152 Ig 24.22N 106.11 E
Tian Ling 154 Kb 44.24N 130.10 E
Tianmen 152 Je 30.40N 113.10 E
Tianmu Shan 154 Ei 30.31N 119.36 E
Tianmu Xi 154 Ej 29.59N 119.24 E
Tianqiaoling 154 Jc 43.35N 129.35 E
Tian Shan 140 Ke 42.00N 80.01 E
Tianshan → Ar Horqin Qi 152 Lc 43.55N 120.05 E
Tianshifu 152 Lc 41.15N 124.20 E
Tianshui 142 Mf 34.35N 105.43 E
Tiantai 154 Fj 29.08N 121.00 E
Tianwangsi 154 Ei 31.45N 119.12 E
Tianyi → Ningcheng 152 Kc 41.34N 119.25 E
Tianzhen 154 Cd 40.24N 114.05 E
Tianzhen → Gaoqing 154 Df 37.10N 117.50 E
Tianzhuangtai 154 Gd 40.49N 122.06 E
Tiaraju 204 Ej 30.15S 54.23W
Tiarei 221e Fc 17.32S 149.20W
Tiaret 160 He 35.20N 1.14 E
Tiaret [3] 162 Hc 34.50N 1.30 E
Tiaret, Monts de- 126 Ni 35.26N 1.15 E
Tiassalé 166 Ed 5.54N 4.50W
Tiavea 221c Ba 13.57S 171.24W
Tīb, Ra's aţ- = Bon, Cape- (EN) 158 Ie 37.05N 11.03 E
Tibaji 204 Gg 24.30S 50.24W
Tibaji, Rio- 204 Kf 22.47S 51.01W
Tibasti, Sarīr- 158 If 24.00N 17.00 E
Tibati 160 Ih 6.28N 12.38 E
Tiber (EN) = Tevere 110 Hg 41.44N 12.14 E
Tiberina, Vai- 128 Gg 43.30N 12.10 E
Tibesti 158 If 21.30N 17.30 E
Tibet (EN) = Xizang Zizhiqu (Hsi-tsang Tzu-chih-ch'ü) [2] 152 Ee 32.00N 90.00 E
Tibet, Plateau of- (EN) = Qing Zang Gaoyuan 140 Kf 32.30N 87.00 E
Tibidabo 126 Oc 41.25N 2.07 E
Tibni 146 He 35.35N 30.49 E
Tibro 116 Ff 58.26N 14.10 E
Tibú 194 Ki 8.40N 72.42W
Tibugà, Golfo de- 202 Cb 5.45N 77.20W
Tiburón, Cabo- 194 Ii 8.42N 77.21W
Tiburón, Isla- 190 Bc 29.00N 112.25W
Ticao 150 Hd 12.31N 123.42 E
Tice 184 Gl 26.41N 81.49W
Tichá Orlice 120 Mf 50.09N 16.05 E
Tîchît 160 Gg 18.26N 9.31W
Tîchît, Dahr- 162 Ff 18.30N 9.25W
Tichka, Tizı n'- 162 Fc 31.17N 7.21W
Tichla 162 Ee 21.36N 14.58W
Ticinesi, Alpi- 128 Cd 46.20N 8.45 E
Ticino [2] 128 Cd 46.20N 9.00 E
Ticino 128 De 45.09N 9.14 E
Ticul 190 Gd 20.24N 89.32W
Tidaholm 114 Cg 58.11N 13.57 E
Tidan 116 Ef 58.42N 13.48 E
Tiddim 148 Id 23.22N 93.40 E
Tidikelt, Plaine du- 158 Hf 27.00N 1.30 E
Tidirhine 162 Gc 34.51N 4.31W
Tidjikja 160 Fg 18.32N 11.27W
Tidore 150 If 0.40N 127.26 E
Tidra, Ile- 158 Fg 19.44N 16.24W
Tiebissou 166 Dd 7.10N 5.13W
Tiechang 154 Id 41.40N 126.12 E
Tiel 122 Lc 51.54N 5.25 E
Tieli 152 Mb 47.04N 128.02 E
Tieling 154 Gc 42.18N 123.51 E
Tielongtan 152 Cd 35.10N 79.32 E
Tielt 122 Jc 51.00N 3.20 E
Tienba 166 Dd 8.30N 7.10W
T'ien-chin Shih → Tianjin Shi [4] 152 Kd 39.08N 117.12 E
Tienen/Tirlemont 124 Gd 50.48N 4.57 E
Tiengemeten 124 Gc 51.45N 5.20 E
Tientsin → Tianjin 142 Nf 39.08N 117.12 E
Tieroko, Tarso- 168 Ba 20.45N 17.52 E
Tierp 114 Df 60.20N 17.30 E
Tierra Amarilla [Chile] 206 Fc 27.29S 70.17W
Tierra Amarilla [N.M.-U.S.] 186 Ch 36.42N 106.33W
Tierra Blanca 190 Ee 18.27N 96.21W
Tierra Colorada 192 Ji 17.10N 99.35W
Tierra del Fuego [2] 206 Gh 54.00S 67.00W
Tierra del Fuego 198 Jk 54.00S 69.00W
Tierralta 202 Cb 8.10N 76.04W
Tiétar 126 Fe 39.50N 6.01W
Tietê, Rio- 198 Kh 20.40S 51.35W
Tietjerksteradeel 124 Ia 53.12N 6.00 E
Tietjerksteradeel-Bergum 124 Hb 52.17N 5.58 E
Tifariti 162 Ed 26.09N 10.33W
Tiffany Mountain 188 Fb 48.40N 119.56W
Tiffin 184 Fe 41.07N 83.11W
Tifton 182 Ke 31.27N 83.31W
Tiga 219b Ce 21.08S 167.49 E
Tigalda 178a Fb 54.05N 165.05W
Tigăneşti 130 If 43.54N 25.22 E
Tighennif 126 Mi 35.25N 0.15 E
Tigil 138 Ke 57.48N 158.40 E
Tigil 138 Ke 57.57N 158.20 E
Tignère 166 Hd 7.22N 12.39 E
Tigray [3] 168 Fc 14.00N 39.00 E
Tigre 192 Hh 19.53N 102.59W
Tigre, Cerro del- 192 Jf 23.03N 99.16W
Tigre, Río- [S.Amer.] 198 If 4.30S 74.10W
Tigre, Río- [Ven.] 196 Eh 9.20N 62.30W
Tigris (EN) = Dicle 140 Gf 31.00N 47.25 E
Tigris (EN) = Dijlah 140 Gf 31.00N 47.25 E
Tigrovy Hvost, mys- 135 Bc 43.57N 58.45 E
Tiguent 162 Df 17.15N 16.00W
Tiguentourine 162 Id 27.43N 9.33 E
Tigui 168 Bb 18.38N 18.47 E
Tigzirt 126 Qh 36.54N 4.07 E
Tīh, Jabal at- 164 Fd 29.35N 34.00 E
Tīh, Şaḩrā' at- = At Tīh Desert (EN) 164 Fc 30.05N 34.00 E
Tihāmat 144 Ff 18.30N 41.30 E
Tihāmat Ash Shām 164 Hf 19.15N 41.10 E
Tihāmat 'Asīr 164 Hf 17.30N 42.20 E
Tihi okean = Pacific Ocean (EN) 106 Ki 5.00N 155.00W
Tihoreck 112 Kf 45.51N 40.09 E
Tihuţa, Pasul- 130 Ib 47.15N 25.00 E
Tihvin 136 Dd 59.38N 33.31 E
Tiirismaa 116 Kc 61.01N 25.31 E
Tijī 164 Bc 32.01N 11.22 E
Tijirît 162 Ee 20.30N 15.00W
Tijuana 176 Hf 32.32N 117.01W
Tijucas 204 Hh 27.14S 48.38W
Tijucas, Baía do- 204 Hh 27.15S 48.31W
Tijucas, Rio- 204 Hh 27.15S 48.38W

Index Symbols

[1] Independent Nation	Historical or Cultural Region	Pass, Gap	Depression	Coast, Beach	Rock, Reef	Waterfall, Rapids	Canal	Lagoon	Escarpment, Sea Scarp	Historic Site	Airport
[2] State, Region	Mount, Mountain	Plain, Lowland	Polder	Cliff	Islands, Archipelago	River Mouth, Estuary	Glacier	Bank	Fracture	Ruins	Port
[3] District, County	Volcano	Delta	Desert, Dunes	Peninsula	Rocks, Reefs	Lake	Ice Shelf, Pack Ice	Seamount	Trench, Abyss	Wall, Walls	Military installation
[4] Municipality	Hill	Salt Flat	Forest, Woods	Isthmus	Coral Reef	Salt Lake	Ocean	Tablemount	National Park, Reserve	Church, Abbey	Lighthouse
[5] Colony, Dependency	Mountains, Mountain Range	Valley, Canyon	Heath, Steppe	Sandbank	Well, Spring	Intermittent Lake	Sea	Ridge	Point of Interest	Temple	Mine
Continent	Hills, Escarpment	Crater, Cave	Oasis	Island	Geyser	Reservoir	Gulf, Bay	Shelf	Recreation Site	Scientific Station	Tunnel
Physical Region	Plateau, Upland	Karst Features	Cape, Point	Atoll	River, Stream	Swamp, Pond	Strait, Fjord	Basin	Cave, Cavern	Railway station	Dam, Bridge

Name	Page	Grid	Lat	Long
Tijucas, Serra do-[▲]	204	Hh	27.16 S	49.10 W
Tijucas do Sul	204	Hg	25.56 S	49.10 W
Tijuco, Rio-[≈]	204	Gd	18.40 S	50.05 W
Tikal [∴]	176	Kh	17.20 N	89.39 W
Tikanlik	152	Ec	40.42 N	87.38 E
Tikchik Lakes [≈]	178	Hd	60.07 N	158.35 W
Tikehau Atoll [○]	216	Lb	15.00 S	148.10 W
Tikei, Ile-[●]	216	Mb	14.58 S	144.32 W
Tikitiki	218	Fc	37.47 S	178.25 E
Tikkakoski	116	Kb	62.24 N	25.38 E
Tikkurila	116	Kd	60.18 N	25.03 E
Tiko	166	Ge	4.05 N	9.22 E
Tikopia Island [●]	208	Hf	12.19 S	168.49 E
Tikrit	144	Fc	34.36 N	43.42 E
Tikšeozero, ozero-[≈]	114	Hc	66.15 N	31.45 E
Tiksi	142	Ob	71.36 N	128.48 E
Tiladummati Atoll [○]	148a	Ba	6.50 N	73.05 E
Tilamuta	150	Hf	0.30 N	122.20 E
Tilburg	122	Lc	51.34 N	5.05 E
Tilbury	118	Nj	51.28 N	0.23 E
Tilcara	206	Gb	23.34 S	65.22 W
Til-Châtel	122	Lg	47.31 N	5.10 E
Tileagd	130	Fb	47.04 N	22.12 E
Tilemsès	166	Fb	15.37 N	4.44 E
Tilemsi, Vallée du-[≈]	158	Hg	19.00 N	0.02 E
Tilia	162	Gd	27.22 N	0.02 W
Tiličiki	138	Ld	60.20 N	166.03 E
Tiligul [≈]	132	Gf	47.07 N	30.57 E
Tiligulski liman [≈]	132	Gf	46.50 N	31.10 E
Till [≈]	118	Kf	55.41 N	2.12 W
Tillabéry	166	Fc	14.13 N	1.27 E
Tillamook	188	Dd	45.27 N	123.51 W
Tillamook Bay [◗]	188	Dd	45.30 N	123.53 W
Tillanchong [●]	148	Ig	8.30 N	93.37 E
Tillberga	116	Ge	59.41 N	16.37 E
Tille [≈]	122	Lg	47.07 N	5.21 E
Tillia	166	Fb	16.08 N	4.47 E
Tillières-sur-Avre	124	Df	48.46 N	1.04 E
Tillingham	124	Cd	50.58 N	0.44 E
Tillsonburg	184	Gd	42.51 N	80.44 W
Tilly-sur-Seulles	124	Be	49.11 N	0.37 W
Tiloa	166	Fb	15.04 N	2.03 E
Tilos [●]	130	Me	36.25 N	27.25 E
Tilpa	212	Hf	30.57 S	144.24 E
Tim	132	Jd	51.37 N	37.11 E
Tim [≈]	132	Jc	52.15 N	37.22 E
Timâ	164	Fd	26.54 N	31.26 E
Timagami	184	Gb	47.00 N	80.05 W
Timagami, Lake- [≈]	180	Jg	46.57 N	80.05 W
Timalacia, Rio- → Sacre, Rio-[≈]	204	Ca	13.55 S	58.02 W
Timane, Rio-[≈]	204	Be	20.16 S	60.08 W
Timan Ridge (EN) = Timanski krjaž [▲]	110	Lc	65.00 N	51.00 E
Timanski bereg [▲]	134	Eb	68.20 N	51.45 E
Timanski krjaž = Timan Ridge (EN) [▲]	110	Lc	65.00 N	51.00 E
Timaru	210	Ii	44.24 S	171.15 E
Timaševsk	136	Df	45.35 N	38.58 E
Timbalier Bay [◗]	186	Kl	29.10 N	90.20 W
Timbalier Island [●]	186	Kl	29.04 N	90.28 W
Timbaúba	202	Ke	7.31 S	35.19 W
Timbédra	162	Ff	16.14 N	8.10 W
Timbó	204	Hh	26.50 S	49.18 W
Timbuktu (EN) = Tombouctou	160	Gg	16.46 N	2.59 W
Timedouine, Ras-[▲]	126	Qh	36.28 N	4.09 E
Timétrine	166	Eb	19.27 N	0.26 W
Timétrine [✕]	166	Eb	19.20 N	0.42 W
Timfi Óros [▲]	130	Ec	39.57 N	20.50 E
Timfristós [▲]	130	Ek	38.57 N	21.49 E
Timia	166	Gb	18.04 N	8.40 E
Timimoun	160	Hf	29.15 N	0.15 E
Timimoun, Sebkha de-[≈]	162	Hd	29.00 N	0.05 E
Timiris, Cap-[▲]	162	Df	19.23 N	16.32 W
Timirjazevo	136	Ge	53.45 N	66.33 E
Timiş [2]	130	Ed	45.38 N	21.13 E
Timiş [≈]	130	De	44.51 N	20.39 E
Timiskaming, Lake- [≈]	184	Hb	47.35 N	79.35 W
Timişoara	112	Hf	45.45 N	21.13 E
Ti-m-Merhsoi [≈]	166	Gb	18.00 N	5.40 E
Timmins	176	Ke	48.28 N	81.20 W
Timmoudi	162	Gd	29.19 N	1.08 W
Timms Hill [▲]	186	Kd	45.27 N	90.11 W
Timok [≈]	130	Fe	44.13 N	22.40 E
Timon	202	Je	5.06 S	42.49 W
Timor, Laut- = Timor Sea (EN) [≈]	208	Df	11.00 S	128.00 E
Timor, Pulau-[●]	210	Oj	9.30 S	126.00 E
Timor Sea (EN) = Timor, Laut-[≈]	208	Df	11.00 S	128.00 E
Timor Timur [3]	150	Ih	8.35 S	126.00 E
Timor Trough (EN) [≈]	106	Ij	9.50 S	126.00 E
Timote	206	He	35.21 S	62.14 W
Timotes	202	Db	8.59 N	70.44 W
Timpton [≈]	138	Ne	58.43 N	127.12 E
Timrå	114	De	62.29 N	17.18 E
Tims Ford Lake [≈]	184	Dh	35.15 N	86.10 W
Tin, Ra's at-[▲]	164	Dc	32.37 N	23.08 E
Tinaca Point [▲]	140	Gj	5.33 N	125.20 E
Tinaco	196	Bh	9.42 N	68.26 W
Tinakula [●]	219c	Ab	10.24 S	165.47 E
Ti-n-Alkoum	162	Je	24.34 N	10.11 E
Ti-n-Amzi [Alg.] [≈]	162	Ne	20.32 N	4.37 E
Ti-n-Amzi [Niger] [≈]	166	Fb	17.54 N	4.32 E
Tinaquillo	196	Bh	9.55 N	68.18 W
Tinchebray	124	Bf	48.46 N	0.44 W
Tindalo	168	Gd	5.39 N	31.03 E
Tindari [∴]	128	Jl	38.10 N	15.04 E
Tindila	166	Dc	10.16 N	8.15 W
Tindouf	160	Gf	27.42 N	8.09 W
Tindouf, Hamada de-[▲]	160	Ff	27.45 N	8.15 W
Tindouf, Sebkha de-[≈]	162	Fd	27.45 N	7.35 W
Tinée [≈]	122	Nk	43.55 N	7.11 E
Tineo	126	Fa	43.20 N	6.25 W
Ti-n-Essako	166	Fb	18.27 N	2.29 E
Tin Fouye	162	Id	28.15 N	7.45 E
Tinghert, Ḥamadat-[▲]	158	Hf	28.50 N	10.00 E
Tinglev	116	Cj	54.56 N	9.15 E
Tingmiarmiut	179	Hf	62.25 N	42.15 W
Tingo Maria	202	Ce	9.10 S	76.00 W
Tingri (Xêgar)	152	Ef	28.41 N	87.00 E
Tingsryd	114	Dh	56.32 N	14.59 E
Tingstäde	116	Hg	57.44 N	18.36 E
Tingvoll	114	Be	62.54 N	8.12 E
Tinharé, Ilha de-[●]	202	Kf	13.30 S	38.55 W
Tinian Channel [≈]	220b	Ba	14.54 N	145.37 E
Tinian Island [●]	208	Fc	15.00 N	145.38 E
Tini Wells	168	Cb	15.02 N	22.48 E
Tinkisso [≈]	166	Dc	11.21 N	9.10 W
Tinnelva [≈]	116	Ce	59.34 N	9.15 E
Tinniswood, Mount-[▲]	188	Da	50.19 N	123.50 W
Tinnoset	116	Ce	59.43 N	9.02 E
Tinnsjø [≈]	116	Ce	59.54 N	8.55 E
Tinogasta	206	Gc	28.04 S	67.34 W
Tinos	130	Il	37.32 N	25.10 E
Tinos [●]	130	Il	37.35 N	25.10 E
Tinou, Stenón-[≈]	130	Il	37.38 N	25.10 E
Tinrhert, Hamada de-[▲]	158	Hf	28.50 N	10.00 E
Tinsukia	148	Jc	27.30 N	95.22 E
Tintagel Head [▲]	118	Ik	50.41 N	4.46 W
Tintamarre, Ile-[●]	197b	Ba	18.07 N	63.00 W
Tintăreni	130	Ge	44.36 N	23.29 E
Tintina	206	Hc	27.02 S	62.43 W
Tinto [≈]	126	Fg	37.12 N	6.55 W
Ti-n-toumma [≈]	158	Ig	16.04 N	12.40 E
Tinwald	218	De	43.55 S	171.43 E
Ti-n-Zaouâtene	160	Hg	19.56 N	2.55 E
Tiobraid Árann/Tipperary	118	Ei	52.29 N	8.10 W
Tiobraid Árann/Tipperary [2]	118	Ei	52.40 N	8.20 W
Tioga	186	Eb	48.24 N	102.56 W
Tioman, Pulau-[●]	150	Df	2.48 N	104.11 E
Tione di Trento	128	Ed	46.02 N	10.43 E
Tioro, Selat- = Tioro, Strait (EN) [≈]	150	Hg	4.40 S	122.20 E
Tioro Strait (EN) = Tioro, Selat-[≈]	150	Hg	4.40 S	122.20 E
Tiotta	114	Cd	65.50 N	12.24 E
Tiouilit	162	Df	18.52 N	16.10 W
Tipasa	126	Pg	36.35 N	2.27 E
Tipitapa	190	Gf	12.12 N	86.06 W
Tipperary/Tiobraid Árann	118	Ei	52.29 N	8.10 W
Tipperary/Tiobraid Árann [2]	118	Ei	52.40 N	8.20 W
Tipton, Mount-[▲]	188	Hi	35.32 N	114.12 W
Tip Top Mountain [▲]	184	Nb	48.16 N	85.59 W
Tiptree	124	Ce	51.49 N	0.45 E
Tiracambu, Serra do-[▲]	202	Id	3.15 S	46.30 W
Tirahart [≈]	166	Ea	23.45 N	2.30 E
Tiran	146	Nf	32.42 N	51.09 E
Tirân, Maḍîq-[≈]	146	Fi	27.55 N	34.28 E
Tirana	112	Hj	41.20 N	19.50 E
Tirania [≈]	162	Ie	23.08 N	9.01 E
Tirano	128	Ed	46.13 N	10.10 E
Tiraspol	136	Cf	46.50 N	29.37 E
Tirat Karmel	146	Ff	32.46 N	34.58 E
Tire	144	Cc	38.04 N	27.45 E
Tirebolu	146	Hb	41.00 N	38.50 E
Tiree [●]	118	Ge	56.31 N	6.49 W
Tiree, Passage of-[≈]	118	Ge	56.30 N	6.30 W
Tirgovişte	130	Id	44.56 N	25.27 E
Tirgu Bujor	130	Kd	45.52 N	27.54 E
Tirgu Cărbuneşti	130	Gd	44.57 N	23.31 E
Tirgu Frumos	130	Jb	47.12 N	27.00 E
Tirgu Jiu	130	Gd	45.03 N	23.17 E
Tirgu Lăpuş	130	Gb	47.27 N	23.52 E
Tirgu Mureş	112	If	46.33 N	24.34 E
Tirgu Neamţ	130	Jb	47.12 N	26.22 E
Tirgu Ocna	130	Jc	46.17 N	26.37 E
Tirgu Secuiesc	130	Jc	46.00 N	26.08 E
Tirguşor	130	Le	44.27 N	28.25 E
Tirich Mir [▲]	147	Jf	36.15 N	71.50 E
Tiriça [≈]	130	Fl	37.36 N	22.48 E
Tiririca, Serra da-[▲]	204	Ic	17.06 S	47.06 W
Tîrnava Mare [≈]	130	Gc	46.09 N	23.42 E
Tîrnava Mică [≈]	130	Gc	46.11 N	23.55 E
Tîrnăveni	130	Gc	46.20 N	24.17 E
Tîrnavos	130	Fj	39.45 N	22.17 E
Tiro	166	Gd	9.45 N	10.39 W
Tirol/Tirolo = Tyrol (EN) [2]	128	Fd	47.00 N	11.20 E
Tirol/Tirolo = Tyrol (EN) [2]	128	Fc	47.10 N	11.25 E
Tirol/Tirol = Tyrol (EN) [2]	128	Fd	47.00 N	11.20 E
Tirreno, Mar- = Tyrrhenian Sea (EN) [≈]	110	Hh	40.00 N	12.00 E
Tirschenreuth	120	Ig	49.53 N	12.21 E
Tirso [≈]	128	Ck	39.53 N	8.32 E
Tirstrup	116	Be	56.18 N	10.42 E
Tirua Point [▲]	218	Fc	38.23 S	174.38 E
Tiruchchirappalli	148	Ff	10.49 N	78.41 E
Tiruliai/Tiruliaj	116	Ji	55.44 N	23.18 E
Tiruliaj/Tiruliai	116	Ji	55.44 N	23.18 E
Tirunelveli	142	Ji	8.44 N	77.42 E
Tirupati	148	Fg	13.39 N	79.25 E
Tirza [≈]	116	Lg	57.09 N	26.37 E
Tisa = Tisza (EN) [≈]	110	If	45.15 N	20.17 E
Tis Abay [≈]	168	Fc	11.20 N	37.40 E
Tisdale	180	Ef	52.51 N	104.04 W
Tisnaren [≈]	116	Ff	58.55 N	15.55 E
Tisovec	120	Ph	48.42 N	19.57 E
Tissemsilt	162	Mf	35.36 N	1.49 E
Tissø [≈]	116	Di	55.35 N	11.20 E
Tisza (EN) = Tisa [≈]	110	If	45.15 N	20.17 E
Tiszaföldvár	120	Qi	46.59 N	20.15 E
Tiszafüred	120	Qi	47.37 N	20.46 E
Tiszakécske	120	Qi	46.56 N	20.06 E
Tiszántúl [▲]	120	Qi	47.00 N	21.00 E
Tiszasüly	120	Qi	47.58 N	20.21 E
Tiszavasvári	120	Ri	47.58 N	21.21 E
Titao	166	Ec	13.46 N	2.04 W
Titarisios [≈]	130	Fj	39.47 N	22.23 E
Tit-Ary	138	Hb	71.55 N	127.01 E
Titicaca, Lago-[≈]	198	Jg	15.50 S	69.20 W
Titikaveka	220b	Bc	21.15 S	159.45 W
Titlagarh	148	Gd	20.18 N	83.09 E
Titlis [▲]	128	Cd	46.47 N	8.26 E
Titograd	112	Hg	42.26 N	19.16 E
Titova Korenica	128	Jf	44.45 N	15.42 E
Titovo Užice	130	Cf	43.52 N	19.51 E
Titov Veles	130	Eh	41.42 N	21.48 E
Titov vrh [▲]	130	Dh	41.58 N	20.50 E
Titran	114	Be	63.40 N	8.18 E
Titteri [▲]	126	Pi	35.59 N	3.15 E
Titu	130	Ie	44.39 N	25.32 E
Titule	170	Eb	3.17 N	25.32 E
Titusville [Fl.-U.S.]	182	Kf	28.37 N	80.49 W
Titusville [Pa.-U.S.]	184	Mf	41.37 N	79.42 W
Tiva [≈]	170	Gc	2.20 S	39.55 E
Tivaouane	166	Bc	14.57 N	16.49 W
Tiveden [✕]	116	Ff	58.45 N	14.40 E
Tiverton	118	Jk	50.55 N	3.29 W
Tivoli [Gren.]	197p	Bb	12.10 N	61.37 W
Tivoli [It.]	128	Gi	41.58 N	12.48 E
Tiwi	168	Cc	10.22 N	22.43 E
Ţiwāl [≈]	168	Cc	14.15 N	39.35 E
Tiyo	168	Gc	14.41 N	40.57 E
Tizatlán [∴]	192	Jh	19.21 N	98.15 W
Tizimín	192	Og	21.09 N	88.09 W
Tizi Ouzou	162	Hb	36.42 N	4.03 E
Tizi Ouzou [2]	162	Hb	36.35 N	4.05 E
Tiznados, Rio-[≈]	196	Ch	8.16 N	67.47 W
Tiznit	162	Fd	29.43 N	9.43 W
Tiznit [3]	162	Fd	29.07 N	9.04 W
Tjačev	120	Th	48.02 N	23.36 E
Tjanšan [▲]	152	Dc	42.00 N	80.01 E
Tjanšan [▲]	132	Me	49.03 N	32.50 E
Tjasmin [≈]	114	Dc	56.35 N	12.45 E
Tjeggelvas [≈]	114	Db	66.35 N	17.30 E
Tjeuemeer [≈]	122	Lb	52.54 N	5.50 E
Tjøme [●]	116	De	59.10 N	10.25 E
Tjørn [●]	118	Dl	58.00 N	11.38 E
Tjub-Karagan, mys-[▲]	132	Qg	44.38 N	50.20 E
Tjuleni, ostrov-[●]	134	Jh	56.03 N	60.58 E
Tjuhtet	138	Db	56.32 N	89.29 E
Tjukalinsk	132	Hd	55.52 N	72.12 E
Tjuleni, ostrov-[●]	132	Og	44.30 N	47.30 E
Tjuleni, ostrova-[●]	132	Qg	44.55 N	50.10 E
Tjulgan	136	Fe	52.22 N	56.12 E
Tjumen	142	Id	57.09 N	65.32 E
Tjumenskaja oblast [3]	138	Gd	63.00 N	69.00 E
Tjung [≈]	138	Hd	63.42 N	121.30 E
Tjup	135	Lc	42.44 N	78.20 E
Tjuri/Türi	114	Fg	58.50 N	25.27 E
Tjust [✕]	116	Gg	57.50 N	16.15 E
Tjuzašu, pereval-[≈]	135	Ic	42.19 N	73.50 E
Tkibuli	132	Mh	42.19 N	42.59 E
Tkvarčeli	136	Eg	42.51 N	41.40 E
Tlacolula	192	Ki	16.57 N	96.29 W
Tlacotalpan	192	Lh	18.37 N	95.40 W
Tlahualilo, Sierra del-[▲]	192	Hd	26.30 N	103.20 W
Tlalnepantla	192	Ji	19.33 N	99.12 W
Tlapa de Comonfort	192	Ji	17.33 N	98.33 W
Tlapaneco, Rio-[≈]	192	Jh	18.00 N	98.48 W
Tlaquepaque	192	Hg	20.39 N	103.19 W
Tlaxcala	190	Ee	19.25 N	98.14 W
Tlaxcala [2]	190	Ee	19.25 N	98.10 W
Tlemcen	162	Gc	34.53 N	1.21 W
Tlemcen [3]	162	Gc	34.45 N	1.30 W
Tleta Rissana	126	Gi	35.14 N	5.59 W
Tletat ed Douair	126	Nh	36.02 N	1.26 E
Tljarata	132	Oh	42.06 N	46.22 E
Tlumač	120	Vh	48.46 N	25.06 E
Tluszcz	120	Rd	52.26 N	21.26 E
Tmassah	164	Cd	26.22 N	15.48 E
Toaca, Vîrful-[▲]	130	Ic	46.55 N	25.57 E
Toagel Mlungui [≈]	220a	Ab	7.32 N	134.28 E
Toamasina	160	Lj	18.10 S	49.24 E
Toamasina [3]	172	Hc	18.00 S	48.30 E
Toau Atoll [○]	216	Lc	15.55 S	146.00 W
Toba	154	Ng	34.29 N	136.51 E
Toba, Danau- = Toba, Lake-(EN) [≈]	140	Li	2.35 N	98.50 E
Toba, Lake- (EN) = Toba, Danau-[≈]	140	Li	2.35 N	98.50 E
Tobago [●]	198	Jd	11.15 N	60.40 W
Tobago Basin (EN) [≈]	197n	Bb	12.39 N	61.22 W
Tobago Cays [●●]	197n	Bb	12.38 N	61.21 W
Toba Kākar Range [▲]	148	Bb	31.15 N	68.00 E
Tobarra	126	Kf	38.35 N	1.41 W
Tobarra, Isla-[●]	196	Fh	9.20 N	60.52 W
Tobelo	156	If	1.25 N	127.31 E
Tobermory [Ont.-Can.]	184	Gc	45.15 N	81.40 W
Tobermory [Scot.-U.K.]	118	Ge	56.37 N	6.04 W
Tobetsu	156a	Bb	43.14 N	141.29 E
Tobi Island [●]	208	Ed	3.00 N	131.10 E
Tobin, Mount-[▲]	188	Gf	40.22 N	117.32 W
Tobin Lake [Austl.] [≈]	212	Fd	21.45 S	125.50 E
Tobin Lake [Sask.-Can.] [≈]	180	Hf	53.40 N	103.20 W
Tobi-Shima [●]	156	Pb	39.12 N	139.32 E
Toblach / Dobbiaco	128	Gd	46.44 N	12.14 E
Toboali	150	Eg	3.00 S	106.30 E
Tobol	136	Ge	52.40 N	62.39 E
Tobol [≈]	142	Id	58.10 N	68.12 E
Tobolsk	142	Id	58.12 N	68.16 E
Tobruk (EN) = Ţubruq	160	Kf	32.05 N	23.59 E
Tobseda	134	Fb	68.36 N	52.22 E
Tobyš [≈]	134	Fb	65.30 N	51.00 E
Tocantinópolis	200	Lf	6.20 S	47.25 W
Tocantins, Rio-[≈]	198	Lf	1.45 S	49.10 W
Tocantinzinho, Rio-[≈]	204	Ha	13.57 S	48.20 W
Tocciea [≈]	128	Fh	44.35 N	8.29 E
Tochigi	154	Of	36.35 N	139.55 E
Tochigi Ken [2]	154	Of	36.50 N	139.50 E
Tochio	156	Fc	37.29 N	138.58 E
Töcksfors	116	De	59.31 N	11.50 E
Toco	196	Fg	10.50 N	60.57 W
Tocoa	194	Df	15.41 N	86.03 W
Toconao	206	Gb	23.11 S	68.01 W
Tocopilla	200	Ih	22.05 S	70.12 W
Tocumen	194	Hi	9.05 N	79.23 W
Tocuyo, Rio-[≈]	194	Mh	11.03 N	68.20 W
Todd Mountain [▲]	184	Nb	46.32 N	66.43 W
Todi	128	Gh	42.47 N	12.24 E
Tôdi [▲]	128	Cd	46.49 N	8.55 E
Todo-ga-Saki [▲]	152	Pd	39.33 N	142.05 E
Todos os Santos, Baía de-[◗]	198	Mg	12.48 S	38.38 W
Todos Santos	190	Bd	23.27 N	110.13 W
Todos Santos, Bahía-[◗]	192	Ab	31.48 N	116.42 W
Tofino	180	Eg	49.09 N	125.54 W
Tofte	116	De	59.33 N	10.34 E
Toftlund	116	Ci	55.11 N	9.04 E
Tofua Island [●]	216	Fc	19.45 S	175.05 W
Toga [●]	219b	Ca	13.26 S	166.41 E
Tōgane	156	Hc	35.33 N	140.21 E
Tog Ḍaror [≈]	168	Hd	9.01 N	47.07 E
Togdheer [3]	168	Hd	9.50 N	45.50 E
Tog-Dheer [3]	168	Hd	9.50 N	45.50 E
Togi	156	Ec	37.08 N	136.43 E
Togiak	178	Ge	59.04 N	160.24 W
Togian, Kepulauan- = Togian Islands (EN) [●●]	150	Hg	0.20 S	122.00 E
Togian Islands (EN) = Togian, Kepulauan-[●●]	150	Hg	0.20 S	122.00 E
Togliatti	112	Le	53.31 N	49.26 E
Togni	196	Ch	8.16 N	67.47 W
Togo [1]	160	Hh	8.00 N	1.10 E
Togog Ul → Qahar Youyi Qianqi	154	Bd	40.46 N	113.13 E
Togtoh	152	Jc	40.17 N	111.15 E
Togučin	138	Dc	55.16 N	84.33 E
Toguzak [≈]	134	Ki	53.54 N	62.48 E
Togwotee Pass [≈]	182	Ec	43.45 N	110.04 W
Tohen	168	Ic	11.44 N	51.15 E
Tohma [≈]	146	Hc	38.31 N	38.25 E
Tohmajärvi	114	Hc	62.11 N	30.23 E
Tohopekaliga, Lake-[≈]	184	Gk	28.12 N	81.23 W
Toi	156	Fd	34.54 N	138.47 E
Toijala	114	Ff	61.10 N	23.52 E
Toi-Misaki [▲]	154	Ki	31.26 N	131.19 E
Toisvesi [≈]	116	Jb	62.20 N	23.45 E
Tōjō	136	Cd	34.53 N	133.16 E
Tojtepa	135	Kd	41.04 N	69.22 E
Tok [▲]	178	Kd	63.20 N	142.59 W
Tok [≈]	132	Lc	52.46 N	52.22 E
Tokachi-Dake [▲]	156a	Cb	43.24 N	142.41 E
Tokachi-Gawa [≈]	156a	Cb	42.41 N	143.37 E
Tokachi-Heiya [▲]	156a	Cb	43.00 N	143.20 E
Tokachimitsumata	156a	Cb	43.31 N	143.07 E
Tōkai [Jap.]	154	Of	36.02 N	140.34 E
Tōkai [Jap.]	156	Ed	35.01 N	136.51 E
Tokaj	120	Rh	48.07 N	21.25 E
Tokaj [≈]	132	Ji	51.18 N	41.04 E
Tōkamachi	154	Of	37.08 N	138.46 E
Tokanui	218	Cg	46.34 S	168.57 E
Tokara Islands (EN) = Tokara-Rettō [●●]	140	Qg	29.35 N	129.45 E
Tokara-Kaikyō [≈]	154	Ki	30.10 N	130.15 E
Tokara-Rettō = Tokara Islands (EN) [●●]	140	Qg	29.35 N	129.45 E
Tokashiki-Jima [●]	156b	Ab	26.13 N	127.21 E
Tokat	144	Ec	40.19 N	36.34 E
Tōkch'ŏn	154	Ie	39.45 N	126.15 E
Tok-Do [●]	154	Kf	37.15 N	131.58 E
Tokelau [5]	210	Je	9.00 S	171.46 W
Tokelau/Union Islands [●●]	208	Je	9.00 S	171.45 W
Toki	156	Ed	35.21 N	137.11 E
Tokke	116	Ce	59.00 N	9.15 E
Tokke [≈]	116	Be	59.27 N	7.58 E
Tokkuztara/Gongliu	152	Dc	43.30 N	82.15 E
Tokmak [Kirg.-U.S.S.R.]	136	Hg	42.49 N	75.19 E
Tokmak [Ukr.-U.S.S.R.]	136	Df	47.13 N	35.43 E
Tokomaru Bay	218	Gb	38.08 S	178.20 E
Tokoname	156	Ed	34.53 N	136.49 E
Tokoro	156a	Da	44.08 N	144.03 E
Tokoro-Gawa [≈]	156a	Da	44.08 N	144.04 E
Toksovo	116	Nd	60.10 N	30.42 E
Toksu/Xinhe	152	Dc	41.34 N	82.38 E
Toksun	152	Ec	42.47 N	88.38 E
Toktogul	136	Hg	41.50 N	73.01 E
Toktogulskoje vodohranilišče [≈]	135	Id	41.45 N	73.00 E
Tokuji	156	Bd	34.11 N	131.39 E
Tokunoshima	156b	Bb	27.45 N	128.50 E
Toku-no-Shima [●]	152	Mf	27.45 N	128.50 E
Tokur	138	Mc	53.09 N	132.50 E
Tokushima	154	Ng	34.04 N	134.34 E
Tokushima Ken [2]	154	Ng	34.00 N	134.10 E
Tokuyama [Jap.]	154	Kg	34.03 N	131.49 E
Tokuyama [Jap.]	156	Ed	35.43 N	136.27 E
Tōkyō	154	Of	35.42 N	139.46 E
Tokyo (EN) = Tōkyō-Wan [◗]	154	Og	35.38 N	139.57 E
Tōkyō To [3]	154	Of	35.40 N	139.20 E
Tōkyō-Wan = Tokyo Bay (EN) [◗]	154	Og	35.38 N	139.57 E
Tolaga Bay	218	Gb	38.22 S	178.18 E
Tolbazy	134	Gi	54.00 N	55.54 E
Tolbuhin	130	Kf	43.34 N	27.50 E
Tolbuhin [3]	130	Kf	43.34 N	27.50 E
Toledo [Blz.]	193	Bb	16.15 N	88.55 W
Toledo [Blz.] [3]	194	Ce	16.15 N	88.58 W
Toledo → Dong'e	152	—	—	—
Toledo [Oh.-U.S.]	176	Ke	41.39 N	83.32 W
Toledo [Phil.]	156	Hh	10.23 N	123.38 E
Toledo [Sp.]	112	Fh	39.52 N	4.01 W
Toledo [Sp.] [3]	126	Ie	39.50 N	4.00 W
Toledo, Montes de-[▲]	126	He	39.35 N	4.20 W
Toledo Bend Reservoir [≈]	182	Id	31.30 N	93.45 W
Tolentino	128	Hg	43.12 N	13.17 E
Tolfa	128	Fh	42.09 N	11.56 E
Tolfa, Monti della-[▲]	128	Fh	42.10 N	11.55 E
Tolga	114	Ce	62.25 N	11.00 E
Toli	152	Bb	45.57 N	83.37 E
Toliara	160	Lk	23.21 S	43.39 E
Toliara [3]	172	Gd	22.00 S	44.00 E
Tolima [2]	202	Cc	3.45 N	75.15 W
Tolima, Nevado del-[▲]	198	Ie	4.40 N	75.19 W
Toling → Zanda	152	Ce	31.28 N	79.50 E
Tolitoli	150	Hf	1.02 N	120.49 E
Toll [▲]	220d	Bb	7.22 N	151.37 E
Tollarp	116	Ei	55.56 N	13.59 E
Tollja, zaliv-[◗]	138	Ea	76.40 N	100.00 E
Tolmačevo	116	Nf	46.10 N	30.01 E
Tolmezzo	128	Hd	46.24 N	13.01 E
Tolmin	128	Hd	46.11 N	13.44 E
Tolna	120	Oi	46.26 N	18.47 E
Tolna [2]	120	Oj	46.30 N	18.35 E
Tolo	170	Cc	2.56 S	18.34 E
Tolo, Gulf of-(EN) = Tolo, Teluk-[◗]	140	Oj	2.00 S	122.30 E
Tolo, Teluk- = Tolo, Gulf of-[◗]	140	Oj	2.00 S	122.30 E
Toločin	114	Gi	54.25 N	29.41 E
Tolosa	126	Ja	43.08 N	2.04 W
Tolstoj, mys-[▲]	140	Rd	59.10 N	155.05 E
Toltén	206	Ge	39.13 S	73.14 W
Tolú	202	Cb	9.32 N	75.34 W
Toluca, Nevado de-[▲]	174	Jh	19.08 N	99.44 W
Toluca ce Lerdo	176	Jh	19.17 N	99.40 W
Tom [≈]	140	Kd	56.50 N	84.27 E
Toma	166	Ec	12.46 N	2.53 W
Tomah	186	Kc	43.59 N	90.30 W
Tomakomai	152	Pc	42.38 N	141.36 E
Tomamae	156a	Ba	44.18 N	141.39 E
Tomanivi [▲]	219d	Bb	17.37 S	178.01 E
Tomar	126	De	39.36 N	8.25 W
Tómaros [▲]	130	Dj	39.32 N	20.45 E
Tomaševka	132	Ce	51.33 N	23.40 E
Tomás Young	204	Ai	28.36 S	62.11 W
Tomaszów Lubelski	120	Tf	50.28 N	23.25 E
Tomaszów Mazowiecki	120	Qe	51.32 N	20.01 E
Tomatlán	192	Gh	19.56 N	105.15 W
Tombador, Serra do-[▲]	202	Gf	12.00 S	57.40 W
Tombigbee River [≈]	182	Je	31.04 N	87.58 W
Tombcco	170	Bd	6.45 S	13.18 E
Tombouctou = Timbuktu (EN)	160	Gg	16.46 N	2.59 W
Tombstone	188	Jk	31.43 N	110.04 W
Tombua	160	Ij	15.48 S	11.52 E
Tomé	206	Fe	36.37 S	72.57 W
Tomé-Açu	202	Id	2.25 S	48.09 W
Tomelilla	114	Ci	55.33 N	13.57 E
Tomé loso	126	Ie	39.10 N	3.01 W
Tomichi Creek [≈]	186	Af	38.31 N	106.58 W
Tomie	156	Ae	32.37 N	128.46 E
Tominé [≈]	166	Cc	10.53 N	13.18 W
Tomini, Gulf of- (EN) = Tomini, Teluk-[◗]	140	Oj	0.20 S	121.00 E
Tomini, Teluk- = Tomini, Gulf of-(EN) [◗]	140	Oj	0.20 S	121.00 E
Tominian	166	Ec	13.17 N	4.35 W
Tomioka [Jap.]	156	Ec	36.15 N	138.52 E
Tomioka [Jap.]	156	Gc	37.20 N	140.59 E
Tomkinson Ranges [▲]	212	Fe	26.10 S	129.05 E
Tomma [●]	114	Cc	66.15 N	12.48 E
Tommot	138	Lc	58.58 N	126.19 E
Tomo, Rio-[≈]	202	Eb	5.20 N	67.48 W
Tomootu Neo [●]	219c	Bb	10.41 S	166.07 E
Tomootu Noi [●]	219c	Bb	10.50 S	166.02 E
Tom Price	212	Dd	22.40 S	117.55 E
Tomskaja oblast [3]	138	Db	58.20 N	81.30 E
Tomtabacken [▲]	116	Fh	57.30 N	14.28 E
Tomur Feng	140	Kf	42.02 N	80.05 E
Tom White, Mount-[▲]	178	Kd	60.40 N	143.40 W
Tonaki-Shima [●]	156b	Ab	26.21 N	127.09 E
Tonalá	190	Fe	16.04 N	93.45 W
Tcnale, Passo del-[≈]	128	Fd	46.16 N	10.35 E
Tcnami	156	Ec	36.38 N	136.57 E
Tonara	128	Ck	40.01 N	9.10 E
Tonasket	188	Fb	48.42 N	119.26 W
Tonb-e Bozorg	146	Pi	26.15 N	55.03 E
Tonbetsu-Gawa [≈]	156a	Ca	45.08 N	142.23 E
Tonbridge	118	Nj	51.12 N	0.16 E
Tondano	156	Hf	1.19 N	124.54 E
Tondela	126	Df	40.31 N	8.05 W
Tønder	114	Bi	56.44 N	8.54 E
Toney [▲]	222	Of	75.48 S	115.48 W
Tonga [●]	168	Ed	9.28 N	31.03 E
Tonga [1]	210	Jf	20.00 S	175.00 W
ʼonga [3]	172	—	29.37 S	31.03 E
Tongaat	172	Ee	29.37 S	31.03 E
Tonga Islands [●●]	208	Jf	20.00 S	175.00 W
Tonga Ridge (EN) [≈]	208	Ja	21.00 S	175.00 W
Tongariki [●]	219b	Dc	17.01 S	168.37 E
Tongatapu Group [●●]	208	Jg	21.10 S	175.10 W
Tongatapu Island [●]	216	Fz	21.10 S	175.10 W
Tonga Trench (EN) [≈]	106	Kl	20.00 S	173.00 W
Tongbai	154	Ce	32.21 N	113.24 E
Tongbai Shan [▲]	152	Jf	32.20 N	113.14 E
Tongbo [≈]	154	Bj	29.15 N	114.08 E
Tongcheng [China]	154	Ce	31.05 N	116.14 E
Tongcheng [China]	154	Bj	29.15 N	114.08 E
Tongchuan	154	Ad	35.10 N	109.03 E
Tongde (Shuangjiang)	152	If	35.16 N	100.35 E
Tongduchŏn	154	Ie	37.54 N	127.03 E
Tongeren/Tongres	122	Ld	50.47 N	5.28 E
Tonghae	154	Je	37.30 N	129.08 E
Tongguzbasti	152	Dd	38.23 N	82.00 E

Index Symbols

[1] Independent Nation	Historical or Cultural Region	Pass, Gap
[2] State, Region	Mount, Mountain	Plain, Lowland
[3] District, County	Volcano	Delta
[4] Municipality	Hill	Salt Flat
[5] Colony, Dependency	Mountains, Mountain Range	Valley, Canyon
Continent	Hills, Escarpment	Crater, Cave
Physical Region	Plateau, Upland	Karst Features

Depression	Coast, Beach	Rock, Reef
Polder	Islands, Archipelago	Islands, Archipelago
Cliff	Rocks, Reefs	Rocks, Reefs
Desert, Dunes	Peninsula	Coral Reef
Forest, Woods	Isthmus	Well, Spring
Heath, Steppe	Sandbank	Geyser
Cape, Point	Island	River, Stream
	Atoll	

Waterfall, Rapids	Canal	Lagoon
River Mouth, Estuary	Glacier	Bank
Lake	Ice Shelf, Pack Ice	Seamount
Salt Lake	Ocean	Tablemount
Intermittent Lake	Sea	Ridge
Reservoir	Gulf, Bay	Shelf
Swamp, Pond	Strait, Fjord	Basin

Escarpment, Sea Scarp	Historic Site	Airport
Fracture	Ruins	Port
Trench, Abyss	Wall, Walls	Military installation
National Park, Reserve	Church, Abbey	Lighthouse
Point of Interest	Temple	Mine
Recreation Site	Scientific Station	Tunnel
Cave, Cavern	Railway station	Dam, Bridge

Tonggu Zhang 152 Kg 24.12N 116.22 E
Tong-Hae=Japan, Sea of- (EN) 140 Pf 40.00N 134.00 E
Tonghai 142 Mg 24.15N 102.45 E
Tonghe 152 Mb 46.01N 128.42 E
Tonghua 142 Oe 41.43N 125.55 E
Tongjiang 152 Nb 47.39N 132.30 E
Tongjosŏn-man 140 Of 39.30N 128.00 E
Tongliao 142 Oe 43.37N 122.15 E
Tongling 152 Ke 30.49N 117.47 E
Tonglu 154 Ej 29.48N 119.39 E
Tongmun'gŏ-ri 152 Mc 40.58N 127.08 E
Tongoa 219b Dc 16.54S 168.33 E
Tongoy 206 Fd 30.15S 71.30W
Tongren [China] 152 Hd 35.40N 102.07 E
Tongren [China] 152 If 27.45N 109.09 E
Tongres/Tongeren 122 Ld 50.47N 5.28 E
Tongsa Dzong 148 Ic 27.31N 90.30 E
Tongshan 154 Cj 29.36N 114.30 E
Tongta 148 Jd 21.20N 99.16 E
Tongtian He/Zhi Qu 140 Lf 33.26N 96.36 E
Tongue 118 Ic 58.28N 4.25W
Tongue of the Ocean 194 Ia 24.12N 77.10W
Tongue River 182 Fb 46.24N 105.52W
Tongxian 152 Kd 39.52N 116.38 E
Tongxin 152 Id 36.59N 105.50 E
Tongxu 154 Cg 34.29N 114.27 E
Tongyu (Kaitong) 152 Lc 44.47N 123.05 E
Tongyu Yunhe 154 Fh 34.46N 119.51 E
Tongzi 152 If 28.09N 106.50 E
Tonichi 192 Ec 28.35N 109.34W
Tönisvorst 122 Ic 51.19N 6.28 E
Tonj 168 Dd 7.17N 28.45 E
Tonj 158 Jh 7.31N 29.25 E
Tonk 148 Fc 26.10N 75.47 E
Tonkin (EN)=Bac-Phan 140 Mg 22.00N 105.00 E
Tonkin, Gulf of- (EN)= Beibu Wan 140 Mh 20.00N 108.00 E
Tonkin, Gulf of- (EN)=Vinh Bac Phan 140 Mh 20.00N 108.00 E
Tônlé Sab, Bœng-=Tonle Sap (EN) 140 Mh 13.00N 104.00 E
Tonle Sap (EN)=Tônlé Sab, Bœng- 140 Mh 13.00N 104.00 E
Tonnay-Charente 122 Fi 45.57N 0.54W
Tonneins 122 Gj 44.23N 0.19 E
Tönning 120 Eb 54.19N 8.57 E
Tōno 154 Pe 39.19N 141.32 E
Tonopah 182 Dd 38.04N 117.14W
Tonoshō 156 Dd 34.29N 134.11 E
Tonosí 192 Gj 7.24N 80.27W
Tønsberg 114 Cg 59.17N 10.25 E
Tonstad 114 Bg 58.40N 6.43 E
Tonumeia 221b Bb 20.28S 174.46W
Tonya 146 Hb 40.53N 39.16 E
Tooele 182 Ec 40.32N 112.18W
Toora-Hem 138 Ef 52.28N 96.22 E
Tootsi 116 Kf 58.34N 24.43 E
Toowoomba 210 Gg 27.33S 151.57 E
Topalu 130 Le 44.33N 28.03 E
Topeka 176 Jf 39.03N 95.41W
Topki 138 De 55.18N 85.40 E
Topko, gora- 138 Ie 57.00N 137.23 E
Topl'a 120 Rh 48.45N 21.45 E
Toplet 130 Fe 44.48N 22.24 E
Toplica 130 Ef 43.13N 21.51 E
Toplița 130 Ic 46.55N 25.20 E
Topola 130 De 44.16N 20.42 E
Topol'čany 120 Oh 48.34N 18.10 E
Topolnica 130 Hg 42.11N 24.18 E
Topolobampo 190 Cc 25.36N 109.03W
Topolobampo, Bahia de- 192 Ee 25.30N 109.05W
Topolog 130 Hd 44.56N 24.16 E
Topolovgrad 130 Jg 42.05N 26.20 E
Topozero, ozero- 110 Jb 65.40N 32.00 E
Toppenish 188 Ec 46.23N 120.19W
Toprakkale 146 Gd 37.06N 36.07 E
Top Springs 212 Gc 16.38S 131.50 E
Toquepala 202 Eg 17.38S 69.56W
Tor 168 Ed 7.51N 33.36 E
Tora 220d Ba 7.39N 151.53 E
Toraigh/Tory Island 118 Ef 55.16N 8.13W
Tora Island Pass 220d Ba 7.39N 151.53 E
Toråker 116 Gd 60.31N 16.29 E
Torbalı 146 Bc 38.10N 27.21 E
Torbat-e Heydariyeh 142 Hf 35.16N 59.13 E
Torbat-e Jam 142 Jb 35.14N 60.36 E
Torbay 118 Jk 50.28N 3.30W
Torbay-Brixham 118 Jk 50.24N 3.30W
Torbay-Paignton 118 Jk 50.28N 3.30W
Torbay-Torquay 118 Jk 50.29N 3.29W
Torbert, Mount- 178 Id 61.25N 152.24W
Torch Lake 184 Ec 45.00N 85.19W
Torčin 120 Vf 50.44N 25.05 E
Tordesillas 126 Hc 41.30N 5.00W
Tordino 128 Hh 42.44N 13.59 E
Töre 114 Fd 65.54N 22.39 E
Töreboda 114 Dg 58.43N 14.08 E
Torekov 116 Eh 56.26N 12.37 E
Torenberg 122 Lb 52.15N 5.55 E
Torez 132 Kf 47.59N 38.41 E
Torgau 120 Ie 51.34N 13.00 E
Torgelow 120 Kc 53.38N 14.01 E
Torgun 132 Od 50.10N 46.20 E
Torhamn 116 Fh 56.05N 15.50 E
Torhout 122 Jc 51.04N 3.06 E
Toribulu 150 Hg 0.19S 120.01 E
Torigni-sur-Vire 124 Be 49.05N 0.59W
Tori-Tōge 156 Ed 35.59N 137.49 E
Torino = Turin (EN) 112 Gf 45.03N 7.40 E
Toriparu 204 Fc 16.20S 53.55W
Tori-Shima [Jap.] 156b Bb 27.52N 128.14 E
Tori-Shima [Jap.] 156b Ab 26.35N 126.50 E
Tori-Shima [Jap.] 152 Pe 30.25N 140.15 E
Torit 168 Ee 4.24N 32.34 E
Torixoreu 202 Hg 16.15S 52.26W
Torkovići 114 Hg 58.53N 30.20 E
Törmänen 114 Gb 68.36N 27.29 E
Tormes 126 Fc 41.18N 6.29W
Tornado Mountain 188 Hb 49.58N 114.39W
Tornavacas, Puerto de- 126 Gd 40.16N 5.37W
Torneå/Tornio 114 Fd 65.51N 24.08 E
Torneälven 110 Ib 65.48N 24.08 E
Torneträsk 114 Eb 68.22N 19.06 E
Torngat Mountains 174 Md 59.00N 64.00W
Tornio/Torneå 114 Fd 65.51N 24.08 E
Tornionjoki 110 Ib 65.48N 24.08 E
Tornquist 204 An 38.06S 62.14W
Toro 126 Gc 41.31N 5.24W
Torö 116 Gf 58.50N 17.50 E
Toro, Cerro del- 198 Jh 29.08S 69.48W
Toro, Isla del- 192 Kg 21.35N 97.32W
Toro, Monte- / El Toro 126 Qe 39.59N 4.07 E
Toroiaga, Vîrful- 130 Hb 47.44N 24.43 E
Torokina 219a Bb 6.14S 155.03 E
Tōro-Ko 156a Db 43.08N 144.30 E
Törökszentmiklós 120 Qi 47.11N 20.25 E
Torola, Rio- 194 Cg 13.52N 88.30W
Toronto 176 Le 43.39N 79.23W
Toropec 136 Dd 56.31N 31.39 E
Tororo 170 Fb 0.41N 34.11 E
Toros Dağları=Taurus Mountains (EN) 140 Ff 37.00N 33.00 E
Torquato Severo 204 Ej 31.02S 54.11W
Torquay, Torbay- 118 Jk 50.29N 3.29W
Torrá, Cerro- 198 Ie 4.38N 76.15W
Torrance 188 Fj 33.50N 118.19W
Torre Annunziata 128 Ij 40.45N 14.27 E
Torreblanca 126 Md 40.13N 0.12 E
Torrecilla 126 Hh 36.41N 5.00W
Torrecilla en Cameros 126 Jb 42.16N 2.37W
Torre del Greco 128 Ij 40.47N 14.22 E
Torre del Mar 126 Hh 36.44N 4.06W
Torredembarra 126 Nc 41.09N 1.24 E
Torre de Moncorvo 126 Ec 41.10N 7.03W
Torre de' Passeri 128 Hh 42.14N 13.56 E
Torredonjimeno 126 Ig 37.46N 3.57W
Torrejón de Ardoz 126 Id 40.27N 3.29W
Torrelaguna 126 Id 40.50N 3.32W
Torrelavega 126 Ha 43.21N 4.03W
Torre Miró, Port de- / Torre Miró, Puerto de- 126 Ld 40.42N 0.05W
Torre Miró, Puerto de- / Torre Miró, Port de- 126 Ld 40.42N 0.05W
Torremolinos 126 Hh 36.37N 4.30W
Torrens, Lake- 208 Eh 31.00S 137.50 E
Torrens Creek 212 Jd 20.46S 145.02 E
Torrent de l'Horta/Torrente 126 Le 39.26N 0.28W
Torrente/Torrent de l'Horta 126 Le 39.26N 0.28W
Torrenueva 126 If 38.38N 3.22W
Torreón 176 Ig 25.33N 103.26W
Torre-Pacheco 126 Lg 37.44N 0.57W
Torre Pellice 128 Bf 44.49N 7.13 E
Tôrres 206 Kc 29.21S 49.44W
Torres 220d Ab 7.19N 151.27 E
Torrès, Iles-=Torres Islands (EN) 208 Hf 13.15S 166.37 E
Torres Islands (EN)=Torrès, Iles- 208 Hf 13.15S 166.37 E
Torres Novas 126 De 39.29N 8.32W
Torres Strait 208 Ff 10.25S 142.10 E
Torres Vedras 126 Ce 39.06N 9.16W
Torrevieja 126 Lg 37.59N 0.41W
Torridon, Loch- 118 Hd 57.35N 5.50W
Torriglia 128 Df 44.31N 9.10 E
Torrijos 126 He 39.59N 4.17W
Torrington [Ct.-U.S.] 184 Ke 41.48N 73.08W
Torrington [Wy.-U.S.] 182 Gc 42.04N 104.11W
Torroella de Montgri 126 Pb 42.02N 3.08 E
Torröjen 114 Ce 63.55N 12.56 E
Torrox 126 Ih 36.46N 3.58W
Torsås 114 Dh 56.24N 16.00 E
Torsby 114 Cf 60.08N 13.00 E
Torshälla 116 Ge 59.25N 16.28 E
Torsken 114 Db 69.20N 17.06 E
Torsö 114 Cg 58.50N 13.50 E
Torto 128 Hm 37.58N 13.46 E
Tortola 190 Le 18.27N 64.36W
Tortoli 128 Dk 39.55N 9.39 E
Tortona 128 Cf 44.54N 8.52 E
Tortorici 128 Il 38.02N 14.49 E
Tortosa 126 Md 40.48N 0.31 E
Tortosa, Cabo de-/Tortosa, Cap de- 126 Md 40.43N 0.55 E
Tortosa, Cap de-/Tortosa, Cabo de- 126 Md 40.43N 0.55 E
Tortue, Ile de la- 190 Jd 20.04N 72.49W
Tortuga, Isla- 192 Dd 27.26N 111.55W
Tortum 146 Ib 40.19N 41.35 E
Torud 146 Pe 35.26N 55.07 E
Torugart, pereval- 140 Je 40.32N 75.24 E
Torul 146 Hb 40.35N 39.18 E
Toruń 120 Oc 53.02N 18.35 E
Toruń [2] 120 Oc 53.00N 18.35 E
Torunos 194 Li 8.30N 70.04W
Toruńska, Kotlina- 120 Oc 53.00N 18.30 E
Torup 114 Ch 56.58N 13.05 E
Tõrva/Tyrva 116 Kf 58.01N 25.59 E
Tory Island/Toraigh 118 Ef 55.16N 8.13W
Torysa 120 Rh 48.39N 21.21 E
Toržok 136 Dd 57.03N 35.01 E
Tosa 154 Lh 33.29N 133.25 E
Tosas, Puerto de- / Toses, Collada de- 126 Ob 42.20N 2.01 E
Tosashimizu 154 Lh 32.46N 132.57 E
Tosa-Wan 154 Lh 33.25N 133.35 E
Tosa-yamada 156 Ce 33.36N 133.40 E
Toscana = Tuscany (EN) [2] 128 Eg 43.25N 11.00 E
Toscano, Arcipelago- = Tuscan Archipelago (EN) 110 Hg 42.45N 10.20 E
Toses, Collada de- / Tosas, Puerto de- 126 Ob 42.20N 2.01 E
Toshibetsu-Gawa [Jap.] 156a Cb 42.54N 143.25 E
Toshibetsu-Gawa [Jap.] 156a Ab 42.25N 139.48 E
Tōshi-Jima 156 Ed 34.31N 136.52 E
To-Shima 156 Fd 34.31N 139.17 E
Tosno 114 Hg 59.34N 30.50 E
Toson-Cengel 152 Gb 48.47N 98.15 E
Toson Hu 152 Gd 37.08N 96.52 E
Töss 128 Cc 47.33N 8.33 E
Tossa 126 Oc 41.43N 2.56 E
Tostado 206 Hc 29.14S 61.46W
Tõstamaa/Tystama 116 Jf 58.17N 23.52 E
Tosu 156 Be 33.22N 130.30 E
Tosya 146 Fb 41.01N 34.02 E
Totak 116 Be 59.40N 7.55 E
Totana 126 Kg 37.46N 1.30W
Toten 116 Dd 60.40N 10.50 E
Toteng 172 Cd 20.23S 22.59 E
Tôtes 122 He 49.41N 1.03 E
Totes Gebirge 128 Hc 47.42N 13.55 E
Tōtias 168 Ge 3.57N 43.58 E
Totland 124 Ad 50.40N 1.32W
Totma 136 Ed 60.00N 42.45 E
Totness 202 Gb 5.53N 56.19W
Toto 170 Bd 7.10S 14.25 E
Totonicapán 190 Ff 14.55N 91.22W
Totonicapán [3] 194 Bf 15.00N 91.20W
Totora 202 Eg 17.42S 65.09W
Totoras 204 Bk 32.35S 61.11W
Totota 166 Dd 6.49N 9.56W
Totoya 219d Cc 18.57S 179.50W
Totten Glacier 222 He 66.45S 116.10 E
Totton 124 Ad 50.55N 1.29W
Tottori 152 Nd 35.30N 134.14 E
Tottori Ken [2] 154 Lg 35.25N 133.50 E
Tou, Motu- 220p Bb 21.11S 159.48W
Touâjil 162 Ee 21.45N 12.35W
Touat 158 Gf 27.40N 0.01W
Touba 166 Dd 8.17N 7.41W
Touba [3] 166 Dd 8.15N 7.45W
Toubkal, Jebel- 158 Ge 31.03N 7.55W
Touch 122 Hk 43.38N 1.24 E
Toucy 122 Jg 47.44N 3.18 E
Tougan 166 Ec 13.04N 3.04W
Touggourt 160 He 33.06N 6.04 E
Tougué 166 Cc 11.27N 11.41W
Touho 219b Be 20.47S 165.14 E
Toûîl 162 Hb 35.33N 2.36 E
Toukoto 166 Dc 13.28N 9.52W
Toul 122 Lf 48.41N 5.54 E
Touléplieu 166 Dd 6.35N 8.25W
Toulon 112 Gg 43.07N 5.56 E
Toulouse 112 Gg 43.36N 1.26 E
Toulumne River 188 Eh 37.36N 121.10W
Toumodi 166 Dd 6.33N 5.01W
Tounassine, Hamada- 162 Fd 28.36N 5.10W
Toungo 166 Hd 8.07N 12.03 E
Toungoo 142 Lh 18.56N 96.26 E
Touques 122 Ge 49.22N 0.06 E
Toura 168 Bc 10.30N 15.19 E
Touraine 122 Gg 47.12N 0.30 E
Touraine, Val de- 122 Hg 47.20N 1.30 E
Tourcoing 122 Jd 50.43N 3.09 E
Tour-du-Pin, La- 122 Li 45.34N 5.27 E
Touriñán, Cabo- 126 Ca 43.03N 9.18W
Tourine 162 Ee 22.00N 12.15W
Tournai/Doornik 122 Jd 50.36N 3.23 E
Tournai-Kain 124 Fd 50.38N 3.22 E
Tournon 122 Ki 45.04N 4.50 E
Tournus 122 Kh 46.34N 4.54 E
Touros 202 Ke 5.12S 35.28W
Tours 112 Gf 47.23N 0.41 E
Tourteron 124 Ge 49.32N 4.39 E
Toury 122 Hf 48.12N 1.56 E
Touside, Pic- 168 Ba 21.02N 16.25 E
Toussoro 168 Cd 9.02N 23.55 E
Toutouba 219b Cb 15.34S 167.16 E
Touwsrivier 172 Cf 33.20S 20.00 E
Toužim 120 If 50.04N 12.59 E
Tovar 194 Li 8.20N 71.46W
Tovarkovski 132 Kc 53.43N 38.13 E
Tovdalselva 116 Cf 58.12N 8.06 E
Tove 124 Bb 52.04N 0.50W
Tōwa 156 Gb 39.23N 141.15 E
Towada 154 Pd 40.35N 141.13 E
Towada-Kō 156 Fa 40.28N 140.55 E
Towanda 184 Ie 41.46N 76.27W
Tower 186 Jc 47.48N 92.17W
Towner 186 Fb 48.21N 100.25W
Townsend 188 Jc 46.19N 111.31W
Townshend, Cape- 212 Kd 22.15S 150.30 E
Townsville 210 Ff 19.16S 146.48 E
Towot 168 Ed 6.12N 34.25 E
Towson 184 If 39.24N 76.36W
Towuti, Danau- 150 Hg 2.45S 121.32 E
Toxkan He 152 Dc 41.08N 80.11 E
Tōya 156a Bb 42.39N 140.48 E
Toyah Creek 186 Ek 31.18N 103.27W
Tōya-Ko 154 Pc 42.33N 140.50 E
Toyama 142 Pf 36.41N 137.13 E
Toyama Ken [2] 154 Nf 30.40N 137.10 E
Toyama Trench (EN) 156 Ec 38.00N 138.00 E
Toyama-Wan 154 Nf 37.00N 137.15 E
Tōyō 154 Mh 33.22N 134.18 E
Toyohashi 152 Oe 34.46N 137.23 E
Toyokoro 156a Cb 42.48N 143.28 E
Toyonaka 156 Dd 34.47N 135.28 E
Toyo'oka 152 Od 35.33N 137.54 E
Toyosaka 156 Fc 37.55N 139.12 E
Toyota 154 Ng 35.05N 137.09 E
Toyotama 156 Ad 34.27N 129.19 E
Toyotomi 156a Ba 45.08N 141.47 E
Toyoura 156 Bd 34.10N 130.55 E
Trabancos 126 Gc 41.27N 5.11W
Traben Trabach 124 Je 49.57N 7.07 E
Trabzon 142 Fe 40.59N 39.43 E
Traer 186 Je 42.12N 92.28W
Trafalgar, Cabo- 126 Fh 36.11N 6.02W
Tragacete 126 Kd 40.21N 1.51W
Traiguén 206 Fe 38.15S 72.41W
Trail 176 He 49.06N 117.43W
Traill 179 Jd 72.45N 24.00W
Trairas, Rio- 204 Hb 14.07S 48.31W
Trairi 202 Kd 3.17S 39.15W
Traisen 128 Jb 48.22N 15.48 E
Trakai/Trakaj 114 Fi 54.38N 24.57 E
Trakaj/Trakai 114 Fi 54.38N 24.57 E
Trakt 134 Ee 62.44N 51.11 E
Trakya = Thrace (EN) 110 Ig 41.20N 26.45 E
Trakya = Thrace (EN) 130 Jh 41.20N 26.45 E
Tralee/Trá Lí 118 Di 52.16N 9.42W
Tralee Bay/Bá Thrá Lí 118 Di 52.15N 9.59W
Trá Lí/Tralee 118 Di 52.16N 9.42W
Trá Mhór/Tramore 118 Fi 52.10N 7.10W
Tramore/Trá Mhór 118 Fi 52.10N 7.10W
Tramping Lake 188 Ka 52.10N 108.48W
Trăn 130 Fg 42.50N 22.39 E
Tranås 114 Dg 58.03N 14.59 E
Trancoso 126 Ed 40.47N 7.21W
Tranebjerg 116 Di 55.50N 10.36 E
Tranemo 116 Eg 57.29N 13.21 E
Trang 142 Li 7.33N 99.36 E
Trangan, Pulau- 150 Jh 6.35S 134.20 E
Trani 128 Ki 41.17N 16.25 E
Transantarctic Mountains (EN) 222 Lg 85.00S 175.00W
Transcaucasia (EN) 110 Kg 41.00N 45.00 E
Transilvania = Transylvania (EN) 110 If 46.30N 25.00 E
Transilvania = Transylvania (EN) 130 Hc 46.30N 25.00 E
Transkei 158 Jl 31.30S 29.00 E
Transkei 172 Df 32.45S 28.30 E
Transtrand 116 Ec 61.05N 13.19 E
Transtrandsfjällen 116 Ec 61.15N 12.58 E
Transvaal [2] 172 Dd 25.00S 30.00 E
Transylvania (EN) = Transilvania 110 If 46.30N 25.00 E
Transylvania (EN) = Transilvania 130 Hc 46.30N 25.00 E
Transylvanian Alps (EN)= Carpații Meridionali 110 If 45.30N 24.15 E
Trants Bay 197c Bc 16.46N 62.09W
Trapani 112 Hh 38.01N 12.29 E
Trapper Peak 188 Hd 45.54N 114.18W
Trappes 124 Ef 48.47N 2.01 E
Traralgon 212 Jg 38.12S 146.32 E
Trarza [3] 162 Ef 18.00N 15.00W
Trarza 158 Fg 17.20N 14.40W
Trașcăului, Munții- 130 Gc 46.23N 23.33 E
Trasimeno, Lago- 128 Gg 43.10N 12.05 E
Träslövsläge 116 Eg 57.04N 12.16 E
Trás os Montes e Alto Douro 126 Ec 41.30N 7.15W
Trat 148 Kf 12.13N 102.16 E
Traun 128 Ib 48.13N 14.14 E
Traun 128 Ib 48.16N 14.22 E
Traunsee 128 Hc 47.52N 13.48 E
Traunstein 120 Ii 47.53N 12.39 E
Trave 120 Gc 53.54N 10.50 E
Travemünde, Lübeck- 120 Gc 53.57N 10.52 E
Travers, Mount- 216 Dh 42.01S 172.44 E
Traverse, Lake- 186 Hd 45.43N 96.40W
Traverse City 182 Jc 44.46N 85.37W
Traverse Islands 222 Ad 56.36S 27.43W
Travers Reservoir 188 Ia 50.14N 112.51W
Travesía 194 Df 15.20N 87.53W
Tra Vinh 148 Lg 9.56N 106.20 E
Travnik 128 Lf 44.14N 17.40 E
Travo 122a Bb 41.54N 9.24 E
Trbovlje 128 Jd 46.10N 15.03 E
Treasurers 219c Ba 9.53S 167.09 E
Treasury Islands 219a Bb 7.22S 155.37 E
Trebbia 128 De 45.04N 9.41 E
Třebíč 120 Lg 49.13N 15.53 E
Trebinje 128 Mh 42.43N 18.21 E
Trebisacce 128 Kk 39.52N 16.32 E
Trebišnjica 128 Lg 43.01N 17.47 E
Trebišov 120 Rh 48.40N 21.43 E
Treblinka 120 Sd 52.40N 22.03 E
Trebnje 128 Je 45.54N 15.01 E
Třeboň 120 Kg 49.01N 14.48 E
Třeboňska pánev 120 Kg 49.00N 14.50 E
Trégorrois 122 Cf 48.45N 3.15W
Tregrosse Islets 208 Gf 17.40S 150.45 E
Tréguier 122 Cf 48.47N 3.14W
Treherne 186 Gb 49.38N 98.41W
Treignac 122 Hi 45.32N 1.48 E
Treinta y Tres 206 Jd 33.14S 54.23W
Treinta y Tres [2] 204 Ek 33.00S 54.15W
Treis-Karden 124 Jd 50.11N 7.17 E
Trélazé 122 Fg 47.27N 0.28W
Trelew 206 Gf 43.15S 65.18W
Trelleborg 112 Hd 55.22N 13.10 E
Trélon 124 Gd 50.04N 4.06 E
Tremadog Bay 118 Ii 52.40N 4.10W
Tremblant, Mount- 174 Le 46.15N 74.34W
Tremiti, Isole-=Tremiti Islands (EN) 110 Hg 42.10N 15.30 E
Tremiti Islands (EN)= Tremiti, Isole- 110 Hg 42.10N 15.30 E
Tremonton 188 If 41.43N 112.10W
Tremp 126 Mb 42.10N 0.54 E
Třemšín 120 Jg 49.33N 13.48 E
Trenche, Rivière- 184 Kb 47.35N 72.58W
Trenčín 120 Oh 48.54N 18.04 E
Trenque Lauquen 206 He 35.58S 62.42W
Trent 118 Mh 53.42N 0.40W
Trent, Vale of- 118 Li 52.45N 1.50W
Trentino-Alto Adige / Südtirol [2] 128 Fd 46.30N 11.20 E
Trento 128 Fd 46.04N 11.08 E
Trenton [Mo.-U.S.] 186 Jf 40.05N 93.37W
Trenton [N.J.-U.S.] 176 Le 40.13N 74.45W
Trenton [Ont.-Can.] 184 Ic 44.06N 77.35W
Tréon 124 Df 48.41N 1.20 E
Trepassey 180 Mg 46.44N 53.22W
Tréport, Le- 122 Hd 50.04N 1.22 E
Tres Árboles 206 Id 32.24S 56.43W
Tres Arroyos 200 Ji 38.22S 60.15W
Tres Bocas 204 Ck 32.44S 59.45W
Tres Carações 202 Ih 21.42S 45.16W
Tres Cruces, Cerro- 192 Mj 15.28N 92.24W
Três de Maio 204 Eh 27.47S 54.14W
Tres Esquinas 202 Cc 0.43N 75.15W
Tres Isletas 204 Bh 26.21S 60.26W
Treska 130 Eh 41.59N 21.19 E
Treskavica 128 Mg 43.35N 18.24 E
Três Lagoas 200 Kh 20.48S 51.43W
Tres Marías, Represa- 202 Ig 18.15S 45.15W
Tres Montes, Peninsula- 206 Eg 46.50S 75.30W
Três Passos 206 Jc 27.27S 53.56W
Tres Picos, Cerro- 198 Ji 38.09S 61.57W
Tres Picos, Cerro- 192 Li 16.36N 94.13W
Três Pontas 204 Je 21.22S 45.31W
Tres Puntas, Cabo- [Arg.] 198 Jj 47.06S 65.53W
Tres Puntas, Cabo- [Guat.] 194 Cf 15.58N 88.37W
Três Ranchos 204 Id 18.22S 47.47W
Três Rios 204 Kf 22.07S 43.12W
Třešť 120 Lg 49.18N 15.28 E
Tres Valles 192 Kh 18.15N 96.08W
Tres Zapotes 190 Ee 18.28N 95.24W
Tretten 114 Cf 61.19N 10.19 E
Treuchtlingen 120 Gh 48.57N 10.55 E
Treuer Range 212 Gd 22.15S 130.50 E
Treungen 116 Ce 59.02N 8.33 E
Trêve, Lac la- 184 Ja 49.58N 75.31W
Trevi 128 Gh 42.52N 12.45 E
Trévières 124 Be 49.19N 0.54W
Treviglio 128 De 45.31N 9.35 E
Trevinca, Peña- 126 Fb 42.15N 6.46W
Treviño 126 Jb 42.44N 2.45W
Treviso 128 Ge 45.40N 12.15 E
Trevose Head 118 Hk 50.33N 5.01W
Trgovište 130 Fg 42.21N 22.06 E
Triagoz, Les- 122 Cf 48.53N 3.40W
Triánda 130 Lm 36.24N 28.10 E
Triangle 172 Ed 21.02S 31.28 E
Triángulos, Arrecifes- 192 Mg 20.57N 92.16W
Trianísia 130 Jm 36.18N 26.45 E
Tribeč 120 Oh 48.27N 18.15 E
Tribune 186 Fg 38.28N 101.45W
Tricarico 128 Kj 40.37N 16.09 E
Tricase 128 Mk 39.56N 18.22 E
Trichūr 148 Ff 10.31N 76.13 E
Tri City 188 De 43.02N 123.15W
Trie-Château 124 De 49.17N 1.50 E
Triel-sur-Seine 124 Ef 48.59N 2.01 E
Trier 120 Cg 49.45N 6.38 E
Trier-Ehrang 124 Ie 49.49N 6.41 E
Trier-Pfalzel 124 Ie 49.46N 6.41 E
Trieste 112 Hf 45.40N 13.46 E
Trieste, Golfo di- 128 He 45.40N 13.30 E
Trieux 122 Cf 48.50N 3.03W
Trifels 124 Je 49.11N 7.59 E
Triglav 110 Hf 46.23N 13.50 E
Trigno 128 Ih 42.04N 14.48 E
Trikala 130 Ej 39.33N 21.46 E
Trikhonis, Limni- 130 Ek 38.34N 21.30 E
Trikomo → Yeniboğaziçi 146 Ee 35.17N 33.52 E
Trikomon → Yeniboğaziçi 146 Ee 35.17N 33.52 E
Trikora, Puncak- 150 Kg 4.15S 138.45 E
Trilport 124 Ef 48.57N 2.57 E
Trim/Baile Átha Troim 118 Gh 53.34N 6.47W
Trimouille, La- 122 Hh 46.28N 1.03 E
Trincheras 192 Gc 28.55N 104.18W
Trincomalee 142 Ki 8.34N 81.14 E
Trindade 202 Ig 16.40S 49.30W
Trindade, Ilha da- 198 Nh 20.31S 29.19W
Třinec 120 Og 49.41N 18.42 E
Tring 124 Bc 51.47N 0.39W
Tringia 130 Ej 39.38N 21.25 E
Trinidad 198 Jd 10.30N 61.15W
Trinidad [Bol.] 200 Jg 14.47S 64.47W
Trinidad [Ca.-U.S.] 188 Cf 41.07N 124.07W
Trinidad [Co.-U.S.] 176 If 37.10N 104.31W
Trinidad [Cuba] 190 Id 21.48N 79.59W
Trinidad [Mex.] 192 Ec 28.25N 109.06W
Trinidad [Ur.] 206 Id 33.32S 56.54W
Trinidad, Golfo- 206 Eg 49.55S 75.25W
Trinidad, Isla- 204 Bn 39.08S 61.58W
Trinidad, Laguna- 204 Be 20.21S 61.35W
Trinidad and Tobago [1] 200 Jd 11.00N 61.00W
Trinidade Spur (EN) 106 Cl 21.00S 35.00W
Trinitapoli 128 Ki 41.21N 16.05 E
Trinity 186 Ik 30.57N 95.22W
Trinity 174 Jg 29.47N 94.42W
Trinity Bay [Austl.] 212 Jc 16.25S 145.35 E
Trinity Bay [Can.] 180 Mg 48.15N 53.10W
Trinity Islands 178 Ie 56.33N 154.25W
Trinity Range 188 Ff 40.20N 118.45W
Trinity River 188 Df 41.11N 123.42W
Trinkitat 168 Fb 18.41N 37.43 E
Trino 128 Ce 45.12N 8.18 E
Trionto 128 Kk 39.37N 16.45 E
Trionto, Capo- 128 Kk 39.37N 16.45 E
Triora 128 Bf 43.59N 7.46 E
Tripoli (EN)=Ṭarābulus 160 Ie 32.54N 13.11 E
Tripoli (EN)=Ṭarābulus 144 Ec 34.26N 35.51 E
Tripoli (EN)=Ṭarābulus [3] 164 Bc 32.40N 13.15 E
Tripolis 130 Fl 37.31N 22.22 E
Tripolitania (EN) = Ṭarābulus 158 Ie 31.00N 14.00 E
Tripolitania (EN)= Ṭarābulus 164 Bc 30.00N 15.00 E
Tripura [3] 148 Id 24.00N 92.00 E
Trisanna 128 Ec 47.07N 10.30 E
Tristan da Cunha 158 Fl 37.05S 12.17W
Tristan da Cunha Group 158 Fl 37.15S 12.30W
Triste, Golfo- 196 Bg 10.40N 68.10W
Triunfo 204 Ee 20.46S 55.47W
Trivandrum 142 Ji 8.29N 76.55 E
Trivento 128 Ii 41.47N 14.33 E
Trjavna 130 Ig 42.52N 25.30 E
Trnava 120 Nh 48.22N 17.35 E
Troarn 124 Be 49.11N 0.11W

Index Symbols

- [1] Independent Nation
- [2] State, Region
- [3] District, County
- [4] Municipality
- [5] Colony, Dependency
- Continent
- Physical Region
- Historical or Cultural Region
- Mount, Mountain
- Volcano
- Hill
- Mountains, Mountain Range
- Hills, Escarpment
- Plateau, Upland
- Pass, Gap
- Plain, Lowland
- Delta
- Salt Flat
- Valley, Canyon
- Crater, Cave
- Karst Features
- Depression
- Polder
- Desert, Dunes
- Forest, Woods
- Heath, Steppe
- Oasis
- Cape, Point
- Coast, Beach
- Cliff
- Peninsula
- Isthmus
- Sandbank
- Island
- Atoll
- Rock, Reef
- Islands, Archipelago
- Rocks, Reefs
- Coral Reef
- Well, Spring
- Geyser
- River, Stream
- Waterfall, Rapids
- River Mouth, Estuary
- Lake
- Salt Lake
- Intermittent Lake
- Reservoir
- Swamp, Pond
- Canal
- Glacier
- Ice Shelf, Pack Ice
- Ocean
- Sea
- Gulf, Bay
- Strait, Fjord
- Lagoon
- Bank
- Seamount
- Tablemount
- Ridge
- Shelf
- Basin
- Escarpment, Sea Scarp
- Fracture
- Trench, Abyss
- National Park, Reserve
- Point of Interest
- Recreation Site
- Cave, Cavern
- Historic Site
- Ruins
- Wall, Walls
- Church, Abbey
- Temple
- Scientific Station
- Railway station
- Airport
- Port
- Military installation
- Lighthouse
- Mine
- Tunnel
- Dam, Bridge

Tro-Tuz

Trobriand Islands 208 Ge 8.30S 151.05 E
Trödje 116 Gd 60.49N 17.12 E
Trofors 114 Cd 65.34N 13.25 E
Trögd 116 Ge 59.30N 17.15 E
Trogir 128 Kg 43.32N 16.15 E
Troglav [Yugo.] 128 Mg 43.02N 18.33 E
Troglav [Yugo.] 128 Kg 43.58N 16.36 E
Trøgstad 116 De 59.38N 11.18 E
Troia 128 Ji 41.22N 15.18 E
Troick [R.S.F.S.R.] 138 Ee 57.23N 94.55 E
Troick [R.S.F.S.R.] 142 Id 54.06N 61.35 E
Troickoje [R.S.F.S.R.] 138 Df 52.58N 84.45 E
Troickoje [R.S.F.S.R.] 138 Ig 49.30N 136.32 E
Troickoje [Ukr.-U.S.S.R.] 130 Nb 47.38N 30.12 E
Troicko Pečorsk 136 Fc 62.44N 56.06 E
Troina 128 Im 37.47N 14.36 E
Troisdorf 124 Jd 50.49N 7.10 E
Trois Fourches, Cap des- 162 Gb 35.26N 2.58W
Trois-Pistoles 184 Ma 48.07N 69.10W
Trois Pitons, Morne- 197g Bb 15.22N 61.20W
Trois-Ponts 124 Hd 50.22N 5.52 E
Trois-Rivières [Guad.] 197e Ac 15.59N 61.39W
Trois-Rivières [Que.-Can.] 176 Le 46.21N 72.33W
Troissereux 124 Ee 49.29N 2.03 E
Troisvierges/Ulflingen 124 Hd 50.07N 6.00 E
Trojan 130 Hg 42.53N 24.43 E
Trojanovka 120 Ve 51.21N 25.25 E
Trojanski Manastir 130 Hg 42.53N 24.48 E
Trojanski prohod 130 Hg 42.48N 24.40 E
Trojebratski 136 Ge 54.25N 66.03 E
Trollhättan 114 Cg 58.16N 12.18 E
Trollheimen 114 Be 62.50N 9.05 E
Trollhetta 116 Cb 62.51N 9.19 E
Trolltindane 116 Bd 62.29N 7.43 E
Tromba 204 Ha 13.28S 48.45W
Trombetas, Rio- 198 Kf 1.55S 55.35W
Tromelin 158 Mj 15.52S 54.25 E
Tromøya 116 Cf 58.30N 8.50 E
Troms [3] 114 Eb 69.07N 19.15 E
Tromsø 112 Hb 69.40N 19.00 E
Tron 116 Db 62.10N 10.43 E
Trona 188 Gi 35.46N 117.24W
Tronador, Monte- 198 Ij 41.10S 71.54W
Trondheim 112 Hc 63.25N 10.25 E
Trondheimsfjorden 110 Hc 63.40N 10.50 E
Tronto 128 Hh 42.54N 13.55 E
Troodos 144 Dc 34.55N 32.53 E
Tropea 128 Jl 38.41N 15.54 E
Tropeiros, Serra dos- 204 Jb 14.43S 44.33W
Tropoja 130 Dg 42.24N 20.10 E
Trosa 114 Dg 58.54N 17.33 E
Troškūnai/Troškunaj 116 Ki 55.32N 24.59 E
Troškunaj/Troškūnai 116 Ki 55.32N 24.59 E
Trostberg 120 Ih 48.02N 12.33 E
Trostjanec 132 Id 50.29N 34.59 E
Trotuş 130 Kc 46.03N 27.14 E
Trou Gras Point 197k Bb 13.52N 60.53W
Troumasse 197k Bb 13.49N 60.54W
Trout Lake [Mi.-U.S.] 184 Eb 46.12N 85.01W
Trout Lake [N.W.T.-Can.] 180 Fd 60.35N 121.10W
Trout Lake [Ont.-Can.] 180 If 53.54N 89.56W
Trout Lake [Ont.-Can.] 180 If 51.12N 93.19W
Trout Peak 188 Kd 44.36N 109.32W
Trout River 180 Lg 49.29N 58.08W
Trouville-sur-Mer 122 Ge 49.22N 0.05 E
Trowbridge 118 Kj 51.20N 2.13W
Troy [Al.-U.S.] 182 Je 31.48N 85.58W
Troy [Mo.-U.S.] 186 Kg 38.59N 90.59W
Troy [Mt.-U.S.] 188 Hb 48.28N 115.53W
Troy [N.Y.-U.S.] 182 Mc 42.43N 73.40W
Troy [Oh.-U.S.] 184 Ee 40.02N 84.12W
Troy (EN)=Truva [Tur.] 146 Bc 39.57N 26.15 E
Troyes 112 Gf 48.18N 4.05 E
Troy Peak 182 Dd 38.19N 115.30W
Trstenik 130 Df 43.37N 21.00 E
Trubčevsk 136 De 52.36N 33.46 E
Truchas Peak 186 Di 35.58N 105.39W
Trucial Coast (EN) 140 Hg 24.00N 53.00 E
Trucial States (EN) → United Arab Emirates (EN) [1] 142 Hg 24.00N 54.00 E
Truckee 188 Eg 39.20N 120.11W
Trudfront 132 Og 45.56N 47.41 E
Trudovoje 138 Ih 43.18N 132.05 E
Trufanova 114 Kd 64.29N 44.05 E
Trujillo [2] 202 Db 9.25N 70.30W
Trujillo [Hond.] 190 Ge 15.55N 86.00W
Trujillo [Peru] 200 If 8.10S 79.02W
Trujillo [Sp.] 126 Ge 39.28N 5.53W
Trujillo [Ven.] 202 Db 9.22N 70.26W
Trujillo, Rio- 192 Hf 23.39N 103.08W
Truk Islands 208 Gd 7.25N 151.47 E
Trumann 186 Ki 35.41N 90.31W
Trumbull, Mount- 182 Ed 36.25N 113.10W
Trun 124 Gf 48.51N 0.02 E
Trung Phan=Annam (EN) 140 Mh 15.00N 108.00 E
Truro [Eng.-U.K.] 118 Hk 50.16N 5.03W
Truro [N.S.-Can.] 176 Me 45.22N 63.16W
Truskavec 132 Ce 49.17N 23.34 E
Truth or Consequences (Hot Springs) 182 Fe 33.08N 107.15W
Trutnov 120 Lf 50.34N 15.54 E
Truva [Tur.] =Troy (EN) 146 Bc 39.57N 26.15 E
Truyère 122 Ij 44.38N 2.34 E
Trysil 114 Cf 61.18N 12.16 E
Trysil 116 Ec 61.25N 12.25 E
Trysilelva 116 Ee 59.23N 13.32 E
Trysilfjellet 116 Ec 61.18N 12.11 E
Trzcianka 120 Mc 53.03N 16.28 E
Trzcińsko Zdrój 120 Kd 52.58N 14.35 E
Trzebiatów 120 Lb 54.04N 15.14 E
Trzebiez, Police- 120 Kc 53.39N 14.32 E
Trzebinia-Siersza 120 Pf 50.11N 19.25 E
Trzebnica 120 Ne 51.19N 17.03 E
Trzebnicki, Wał- 120 Me 51.30N 16.20 E
Trzebnickie, Wzgórza- 120 Me 51.15N 17.00 E
Trzemeszno 120 Nd 52.35N 17.50 E
Tsaidam Basin (EN)= Qaidam Pendi 152 Fd 37.00N 95.00 E
Tsamandá, Óri- 130 Dj 39.48N 20.21 E
Tsarap 148 Fb 33.31N 76.56 E
Tsaratanana 172 Hc 16.46S 47.38 E
Tsaratanana (EN)= Tsaratanana, Massif du- 158 Lj 14.00S 49.00 E
Tsaratanana, Massif du-= Tsaratanana (EN) 158 Lj 14.00S 49.00 E
Tsau 172 Cd 20.10S 22.27 E
Tsavo 170 Gc 2.59S 38.28 E
Tses 172 Be 25.58S 18.08 E
Tsévié 166 Fd 6.25N 1.13 E
Tshabong 160 Jk 26.02S 22.06 E
Tshane 160 Jk 24.01S 21.43 E
Tshangalele, Lac- 170 Ee 10.55S 27.03 E
Tshela 160 Ii 4.59S 12.56 E
Tshesebe 172 Dd 20.43S 27.36 E
Tshibala 170 Dd 6.56S 21.28 E
Tshibamba 170 Dd 9.06S 22.34 E
Tshikapa 160 Ji 6.25S 20.48 E
Tshilenge 170 Dd 6.15S 23.46 E
Tshimbalanga 170 Dd 9.43S 23.06 E
Tshimbulu 170 Dd 6.29S 22.51 E
Tshinsenda 170 Ee 12.16S 27.55 E
Tshofa 170 Ed 5.14S 25.15 E
Tsholotsho 172 Dc 19.46S 27.45 E
Tshopo 170 Eb 0.33N 25.07 E
Tshuapa 158 Ji 0.14S 20.42 E
Tshwaane 172 Cd 22.38S 22.05 E
Tsiafajavona 172 Hc 19.21S 47.15 E
Tsihombe 172 He 25.17S 45.30 E
Tsimlyansk Reservoir (EN) = Cimljanskoje vodohranilišče 110 Kf 48.00N 43.00 E
Tsinan → Jinan 142 Nf 36.35N 117.00 E
Tsinghai (EN)=Ch'ing-hai Sheng→Qinghai Sheng [2] 152 Gd 36.00N 96.00 E
Tsinghai (EN)=Qinghai Sheng (Ch'ing-hai Sheng) [2] 152 Gd 36.00N 96.00 E
Tsingtao → Qingdao 142 Of 36.05N 120.21 E
Tsiribihina 172 Gc 19.42S 44.31 E
Tsiroanomandidy 172 Hc 18.50S 46.00 E
Tsis 220d Bb 7.18N 151.50 E
Tsjokkarassa 114 Fb 69.59N 24.32 E
Tsodilo Hill 172 Cc 18.50S 21.45 E
Tsu 152 Oe 34.43N 136.31 E
Tsubame 156 Fc 37.39N 138.56 E
Tsubata 154 Nf 36.40N 136.44 E
Tsubetsu 156a Db 43.43N 144.01 E
Tsuchiura 154 Pf 36.05N 140.12 E
Tsugaru-Hantō 156a Bc 41.00N 140.30 E
Tsugaru-Kaikyō=Tsugaru Strait (EN) 140 Qe 41.40N 140.55 E
Tsugaru Strait (EN)= Tsugaru-Kaikyō 140 Qe 41.40N 140.55 E
Tsuken-Jima 156b Ab 26.15N 127.57 E
Tsukidate 156 Gb 38.44N 141.01 E
Tsukigata 156a Bb 43.20N 141.39 E
Tsukumi 156 Be 33.04N 131.52 E
Tsukura-Se 156 Af 31.18N 129.47 E
Tsukushi-Sanchi 156 Be 33.25N 130.30 E
Tsumeb 160 Ij 19.13S 17.42 E
Tsumeb [3] 172 Bc 19.00S 17.30 E
Tsumkwe 172 Cc 19.32S 20.30 E
Tsuna 156 Dd 34.26N 134.54 E
Tsuno-Shima 156 Bd 34.22N 130.52 E
Tsuru 156 Fd 35.35N 138.50 E
Tsuruga 152 Od 35.39N 136.04 E
Tsuruga-Wan 156 Ed 35.45N 136.05 E
Tsurugi 156 Ec 36.26N 136.37 E
Tsurugi-San 156 De 33.51N 134.03 E
Tsurui 156a Db 43.14N 144.21 E
Tsurumi-Dake 156 Be 33.18N 131.27 E
Tsurumi-Saki 156 Ce 32.56N 132.05 E
Tsuruoka 154 Oe 38.44N 139.50 E
Tsuruta 156 Ga 40.44N 140.26 E
Tsushima 140 Of 34.30N 129.20 E
Tsushima [Jap.] 156 Ed 35.10N 136.43 E
Tsushima [Jap.] 156 Ce 33.07N 132.30 E
Tsushima-Kaikyō=Korea, Strait (EN) 140 Of 34.40N 129.00 E
Tsuwano 156 Bd 34.28N 131.46 E
Tsuyama 154 Lg 35.03N 134.00 E
TTPI → Pacific Islands, Trust Territory of the- [5] 210 Gc 10.00N 155.00 E
Tua 126 Ec 41.13N 7.26W
Tuai 218 Gc 38.49S 177.08 E
Tuaim/Tuam 118 Eh 53.31N 8.50W
Tuakau 218 Fb 37.15S 174.57 E
Tual 150 Jh 5.40S 132.45 E
Tuam/Tuaim 118 Eh 53.31N 8.50W
Tuamotu, Iles-=Tuamotu Archipelago (EN) 208 Mf 19.00S 142.00W
Tuamotu Archipelago (EN) =Tuamotu, Iles- 208 Mf 19.00S 142.00W
Tuamotu Ridge (EN) 106 Ll 20.00S 145.00W
Tuapa 220k Ba 18.57S 169.54W
Tuapse 112 Jg 44.07N 39.05 E
Tuaran 150 Ge 6.11N 116.14 E
Tuasivi 221c Aa 13.40S 172.07W
Tuasivi, Cape- 221c Aa 13.40S 172.07W
Tuatapere 216 Ci 46.08S 167.41 E
Tuba 138 Ef 54.00N 91.40 E
Tuba City 188 Jh 36.08N 111.14W
Tubai, Ile- 208 Mg 23.18S 149.30W
Tubai-Manu→Maïao, Ile- 208 Lf 17.34S 150.35W
Tubal, Wādī at- 146 Jf 32.19N 42.13 E
Tuban 150 Fh 6.54S 112.03 E
Tubarão 206 Kc 28.30S 49.01W
Ţubayq, Jabal at- 146 Gh 29.32N 37.30 E
Tubbataha Reefs 150 Ge 8.51N 119.56 E
Tubeke/Tubize 124 Gd 50.41N 4.12 E
Tübingen 120 Fh 48.32N 9.03 E
Tubize/Tubeke 124 Gd 50.41N 4.12 E
Ţubruq=Tobruk (EN) 160 Je 32.05N 23.59 E
Tubuai Islands (EN) = Tubuai ou Australes, Iles- 208 Lg 23.00S 150.00W
Tubuai ou Australes, Iles- = Tubuai Islands (EN) 208 Lg 23.00S 150.00W
Tubutama 192 Db 30.53N 111.29W
Tucacas 202 Ea 10.48N 68.19W
Tucacas, Punta- 194 Mh 10.52N 68.13W
Tucavaca 204 Cd 18.36S 58.55W
Tucavaca, Rio- 204 Cd 18.37S 58.59W
Tuchola 120 Nc 53.35N 17.50 E
Tucholska, Równina- 120 Oc 53.40N 18.30 E
Tuchów 120 Rg 49.54N 21.03 E
Tucker Glacier 222 Kf 72.35S 169.20 E
Tucson 176 Hf 32.13N 110.58W
Tucumán [2] 206 Gc 27.00S 65.30W
Tucumcari 182 Gd 35.10N 103.44W
Tucunui 202 Id 3.42S 49.27W
Tucupido 202 Eb 9.17N 65.47W
Tucupita 202 Fb 9.04N 62.03W
Tudela 126 Kb 42.05N 1.36W
Tudia, Sierra de- 126 Ff 38.05N 6.20W
Tudmur 144 Ec 34.33N 38.17 E
Tudora 130 Jb 47.31N 26.38 E
Tuela 126 Ec 41.30N 7.12W
Tuensang 148 Ic 26.17N 94.40 E
Tuerto 126 Gb 42.18N 5.53W
Tufanbeyli 146 Gc 38.18N 36.11 E
Tufi 210 Fe 9.08S 149.20 E
Tugela 158 Kk 29.14S 31.30 E
Tug Fork 184 Ff 38.25N 82.35W
Tuguegarao 142 Oh 17.37N 121.44 E
Tugulym 134 Lh 57.04N 64.39 E
Tugur 138 If 53.51N 136.52 E
Tuhai He 154 Ee 38.05N 118.13 E
Tujiabu → Yongxiu 152 Kf 29.05N 115.49 E
Tujmazy 136 Fe 54.36N 53.42 E
Tukan 134 Hj 53.50N 57.31 E
Tukangbesi, Kepulauan-= Tukangbesi Islands (EN) 150 Hh 5.40S 123.50 E
Tukangbesi Islands (EN)= Tukangbesi, Kepulauan- 150 Hh 5.40S 123.50 E
Tukayel 168 Hd 8.05N 45.20 E
Tukayyid 146 Kh 29.47N 45.36 E
Tukituki 218 Gc 39.36S 176.56 E
Tuko Village 220n Ab 10.22S 161.02W
Tükrah 164 Dc 32.32N 20.34 E
Tuktoyaktuk 176 Fc 69.27N 133.02W
Tukums 114 Fh 56.59N 23.11 E
Tukuringra, hrebet- 138 Hf 54.30N 126.00 E
Tukuyu 170 Fd 9.15S 33.39 E
Tula 170 Gc 0.50S 39.51 E
Tula 190 Ed 20.06N 99.19W
Tula [Mex.] 192 Jf 23.00N 99.43W
Tula [R.S.F.S.R.] 112 Je 54.12N 37.37 E
Tula de Allende 192 Jg 20.03N 99.21W
Tula Mountains 222 Ee 66.54S 51.06 E
Tulancingo 190 Ed 20.05N 98.22W
Tulare 188 Fh 36.13N 119.21W
Tulare Lake Bed 188 Fh 36.03N 119.49W
Tularosa 186 Cj 33.04N 106.01W
Tularosa Valley 186 Cj 32.45N 106.10W
Tulcán 202 Cc 0.48N 77.43W
Tulcea 130 Ld 45.10N 28.48 E
Tulcea [2] 130 Md 45.12N 29.10 E
Tulčin 132 Fe 48.39N 28.52 E
Tulelake 188 Ef 41.57N 121.29W
Tulemalu Lake 180 Hd 62.55N 99.25W
Tulgheş 130 Ic 46.57N 25.46 E
Tuli 172 Dd 21.55S 29.12 E
Tuli 172 Dd 21.48S 29.04 E
Tulia 186 Fi 34.32N 101.46W
Tulihe 152 La 50.30N 121.51 E
Tullahoma 184 Dh 35.22N 86.11W
Tullamore/An Tulach Mhór 118 Fh 53.16N 7.30W
Tulle 122 Hi 45.16N 1.46 E
Tulln 128 Kb 48.20N 16.03 E
Tulln 128 Kb 48.22N 16.03 E
Tullner Becken 128 Jb 48.25N 15.55 E
Tullow/An Tulach 118 Gi 52.48N 6.44W
Tullus 168 Cc 11.03N 24.33 E
Tully 212 Jc 17.56S 145.56 E
Ţulmaythah 164 Dc 32.43N 20.57 E
Tuloma 110 Jb 68.52N 32.49 E
Tulos, ozero- 114 He 63.35N 30.35 E
Tulsa 176 Jf 36.09N 95.58W
Tulskaja oblast [3] 136 De 54.00N 37.30 E
Tuluá 202 Cc 4.05N 76.12W
Tuluksak 178 Gd 61.06N 160.58W
Tulum 192 Pg 20.13N 87.28W
Tulum 190 Gd 20.15N 87.27W
Tulun 142 Md 54.35N 100.33 E
Tulungagung 150 Fh 8.04S 111.54 E
Tuma 114 Ji 55.10N 40.33 E
Tuma, Rio- 194 Eg 13.03N 84.44W
Tumaco 200 Ie 1.49N 78.46W
Tumaco, Rada de- 202 Cc 1.50N 78.45W
Tumacuari, Pico- 202 Fc 1.15N 64.40W
Tuman-gang 154 Kc 42.18N 130.41 E
Tumba 116 Ge 59.12N 17.49 E
Tumbarumba 212 Jg 35.47S 148.01 E
Tumbes 200 Hf 4.05S 80.35W
Tumbes [3] 202 Bd 3.50S 80.30W
Tumča 114 Hc 66.35N 31.45 E
Tumd Youqi 152 Jc 40.33N 110.32 E
Tumd Zuoqi 152 Jc 40.43N 111.06 E
Tumen 152 Mc 42.58N 129.49 E
Tumen Jiang 154 Kc 42.18N 130.41 E
Tumereng 202 Fb 7.18N 61.30W
Tumkur 148 Ff 13.21N 77.05 E
Tummel 118 Je 56.43N 3.44W
Tummo 164 Be 23.00N 14.10 E
Tumon Bay 220c Ba 13.31N 144.48 E
Tumpat 150 De 6.12N 102.10 E
Tumu 166 Ec 10.52N 1.59W
Tumucumaque, Serra- 198 Ke 2.20N 55.00W
Tumwater 188 Dc 47.01N 122.54W
Tuna, Punta- 197a Cc 18.00N 65.52W
Tunapuna 196 Fg 10.38N 61.23W
Tunas 204 Hg 24.58S 49.06W
Tunas, Sierra de las- 192 Fc 29.40N 107.15W
Tunas Chicas, Laguna- 204 Am 36.01S 62.20W
Tunaydah 146 Cj 25.31N 29.21 E
Tunçbilek 130 Mj 39.37N 29.29 E
Tunduma 170 Fd 9.18S 32.46 E
Tunduru 170 Ge 11.07S 37.21 E
Tundža 130 Jh 41.40N 26.34 E
Tunga 166 Gd 8.07N 9.12 E
Tungabhadra 148 Fe 15.57N 78.15 E
Tungaru 168 Ec 10.14N 30.42 E
Tungnaá 114a Bb 64.10N 19.34W
Tungokočen 138 Gf 53.33N 115.34 E
Tungsten 180 Ed 62.05N 127.42W
Tungua 221b Bb 20.01S 174.46W
Tuni 148 Ge 17.21N 82.33 E
Tūnis=Tunis (EN) 160 Ie 36.48N 10.11 E
Tūnis=Tunis (EN) [3] 162 Jb 36.30N 10.00 E
Tūnis=Tunisia (EN) [1] 160 He 34.00N 9.00 E
Tunis (EN)=Tūnis 160 Ie 36.48N 10.11 E
Tunis (EN)=Tūnis [3] 162 Jb 36.30N 10.00 E
Tunis, Canal de-=Sicily, Strait of- (EN) 110 Hh 37.20N 11.20 E
Tūnis, Khalīj- 162 Jb 37.00N 10.30 E
Tunisia (EN)=Tūnis [1] 160 He 34.00N 9.00 E
Tunja 200 Ie 5.31N 73.22W
Tunkhannock 184 Je 41.32N 75.57W
Tunliu 154 Bf 36.18N 112.53 E
Tunnhovdfjorden 116 Cd 60.25N 8.55 E
Tunø 116 Di 55.55N 10.25 E
Tunumuk 180 Ec 69.00N 134.57W
Tununak 178 Fd 60.35N 165.16W
Tunungayualok 180 Le 56.05N 61.05W
Tunxi 152 Kf 29.45N 118.15 E
Tuo He 154 Dh 33.16N 117.45 E
Tuo Jang 152 If 28.55N 105.26 E
Tuostah 138 Ic 67.50N 135.40 E
Tuotuo He 152 Fe 34.03N 92.46 E
Tuotuoheyan / Tanggulashanqu 142 Lf 34.15N 92.29 E
Tupã 206 Jb 21.56S 50.30W
Tupaciguara 204 Hd 18.35S 48.42W
Tupai Atoll (Motu-Iti) 216 Kc 16.17S 151.50W
Tupanciretã 206 Jc 29.05S 53.51W
Tupelo 182 Je 34.16N 88.43W
Tupik 138 Gf 54.28N 119.57 E
Tupinambaranas, Ilha- 202 Gd 3.00S 58.00W
Tupiraçaba 204 Hb 14.29S 48.34W
Tupiza 202 Eh 21.27S 65.43W
Tupper Lake 184 Jc 44.13N 74.29W
Tupungato, Cerro- 206 Gd 33.22S 69.47W
Tuquan 152 Lb 45.22N 121.33 E
Túquerres 202 Cc 1.06N 77.37W
Tur 130 Fa 48.04N 22.33 E
Tura 136 Gd 57.12N 66.56 E
Tura [India] 148 Ic 25.31N 90.13 E
Tura [R.S.F.S.R.] 142 Mc 64.17N 100.15 E
Turabah [Sau.Ar.] 144 Fe 21.13N 41.39 E
Turabah [Sau.Ar.] 144 Fd 28.13N 42.59 E
Turagua, Serranías- 196 Di 7.20N 64.35W
Turakina 218 Fd 40.02S 175.13 E
Turān 146 Qe 35.40N 56.50 E
Turan 138 Ef 52.08N 93.55 E
Turana, hrebet- 138 If 51.30N 132.00 E
Turangi 218 Fc 38.59S 175.48 E
Turano 128 Gh 42.26N 12.47 E
Turanskaja nizmennost 140 Ie 44.30N 63.00 E
Turawa 120 Of 50.45N 18.05 E
Turawskie, Jezioro- 120 Of 50.43N 18.10 E
Turbaco 194 Jh 10.19N 75.25W
Turbat 148 Cc 25.59N 63.04 E
Turbo 200 Ie 8.06N 76.43W
Turcoaia 130 Ld 45.07N 28.11 E
Turda 130 Gc 46.34N 23.47 E
Türeh 146 Me 34.02N 49.17 E
Tureia Atoll 208 Ng 20.50S 138.32W
Turek 120 Od 52.02N 18.30 E
Turenki 116 Kd 60.55N 24.38 E
Turfan Depression (EN)= Turpan Pendi 140 Ke 42.30N 89.30 E
Turgai Gates (EN) = Turgajskaja ložbina 140 Id 51.00N 64.30 E
Turgai Upland (EN) = Turgajskoje plato 140 Id 51.00N 64.00 E
Turgaj 136 Gf 49.38N 63.28 E
Turgaj 140 Ie 48.01N 62.45 E
Turgajskaja ložbina = Turgai Gates (EN) 140 Id 51.00N 64.30 E
Turgajskaja oblast [3] 136 Ge 50.30N 66.00 E
Turgajskoje plato = Turgai Upland (EN) 140 Id 51.00N 64.00 E
Turgeon, Rivière- 184 Ha 50.00N 78.55W
Turgutlu 146 Bc 38.30N 27.50 E
Turhal 146 Gb 40.24N 36.06 E
Türi/Tjuri 114 Fg 58.50N 25.27 E
Túria / Turia 126 Le 39.27N 0.19W
Túria / Turia 126 Le 39.27N 0.19W
Turiaçu, Baia de- 202 Id 1.30S 45.15W
Turiec 120 Og 49.06N 18.52 E
Turijsk 120 Ue 51.10N 24.37 E
Turimiquire, Cerro- 202 Fa 10.03N 64.00W
Turin (EN) = Torino 112 Gf 45.03N 7.40 E
Turinsk 136 Gd 58.03N 63.42 E
Turja 132 Dd 51.48N 24.52 E
Turka [R.S.F.S.R.] 138 Ff 52.57N 108.13 E
Turka [Ukr.-U.S.S.R.] 120 Tg 49.07N 23.01 E
Turkana 170 Gb 4.00N 35.30 E
Turkana, Lake-/Rudolf, Lake- 158 Kh 3.30N 36.00 E
Türkeli 146 Fb 41.57N 34.21 E
Turkestan 142 Ie 43.18N 68.15 E
Turkestanski hrebet 136 Gh 39.35N 69.00 E
Türkeve 120 Qi 47.06N 20.45 E
Turkey (EN)=Türkiye [1] 142 Ff 39.00N 35.00 E
Turkey Creek 212 Fc 17.02S 128.12 E
Turki 132 Mc 52.01N 43.16 E
Türkiye=Turkey (EN) [1] 142 Ff 39.00N 35.00 E
Turkmenistan Sovet Socialistik Respublikasy/ Turkmenskaja SSR [2] 136 Fh 40.00N 60.00 E
Turkmen-Kala 135 Df 37.26N 62.19 E
Turkmenskaja Sovetskaja Socialističeskaja Respublika [2] 136 Fh 40.00N 60.00 E
Turkmenskaja SSR/ Turkmenistan Sovet Socialistik Respublikasy [2] 136 Fh 40.00N 60.00 E
Turkmenskaja SSR= Turkmen SSR (EN) [2] 136 Fh 40.00N 60.00 E
Turkmenski zaliv 132 Rj 39.00N 53.30 E
Turkmen SSR (EN)= Turkmenskaja SSR [2] 136 Fh 40.00N 60.00 E
Türkoğlu 146 Gd 37.31N 36.49 E
Turks and Caicos Islands [5] 176 Lg 21.45N 71.35W
Turks Island Passage 194 Lc 21.25N 71.19W
Turks Islands 190 Jd 21.24N 71.07W
Turku/Åbo 112 Ic 60.27N 22.17 E
Turku-Pori [2] 114 Ff 61.00N 22.30 E
Turkwel 170 Gb 3.06N 36.06 E
Turlock 188 Eh 37.30N 120.51W
Turmantas 116 Li 55.42N 26.34 E
Turnagain, Cape- 218 Gd 40.30S 176.37 E
Turneffe Islands 190 Ge 17.22N 87.51W
Turnhout 122 Kc 51.19N 4.57 E
Turnov 120 Lf 50.35N 15.09 E
Turnu Măgurele 130 Hf 43.45N 24.52 E
Turnu Roşu, Pasul- 130 Hd 45.33N 24.16 E
Turočak 138 Df 52.16N 87.05 E
Turó de L'Home 126 Oc 41.45N 2.25 E
Turopolje 128 Ke 45.38N 16.07 E
Turpan 142 Ke 42.56N 89.10 E
Turpan Pendi=Turfan Depression (EN) 140 Ke 42.30N 89.30 E
Turquino, Pico- 190 Ie 19.59N 76.51W
Turrialba 194 Fi 9.54N 83.41W
Tursuntski Tuman, ozero- 134 Kf 60.35N 63.55 E
Turtas 134 Ng 58.57N 69.10 E
Turtas 134 Ng 59.06N 68.50 E
Turtkul 136 Gg 41.35N 61.00 E
Turtle Mountain 186 Fb 49.05N 100.15W
Turugart Shankou 140 Je 40.32N 75.24 E
Turuhan 138 Dc 65.56N 87.42 E
Turuhansk 138 Dc 65.49N 87.59 E
Turvânia 204 Gc 16.39S 50.09W
Turvo 204 Hi 28.56S 49.41W
Turvo, Rio- [Braz.] 204 Hd 19.56S 49.55W
Turvo, Rio- [Braz.] 204 Gc 17.46S 50.12W
Tusaun/Thusis 128 Dd 46.42N 9.26 E
Tuscaloosa 182 Je 33.13N 87.33W
Tuscan Archipelago (EN) = Toscano, Arcipelago- 110 Hg 42.45N 10.20 E
Tuscania 128 Fh 42.25N 11.52 E
Tuscany (EN) = Toscana [2] 128 Eg 43.25N 11.00 E
Tuscarora Mountain 184 Ie 40.10N 77.45W
Tuscarora Mountains 188 Gf 41.00N 116.20W
Tuščibas, zaliv- 135 Ba 46.10N 59.45 E
Tuscola 186 Lg 39.48N 88.17W
Tusenøyane 179 Oc 77.05N 22.00 E
Tuskar 132 Jd 51.40N 36.15 E
Tuskegee 184 Ei 32.26N 85.42W
Tuşnad Băi 130 Ic 46.09N 25.51 E
Tustna 116 Ca 63.10N 8.05 E
Tuszymka 120 Rf 50.09N 21.30 E
Tuszyn 120 Pe 51.37N 19.34 E
Tutajev 136 Dd 57.52N 39.32 E
Tutak 146 Jc 39.32N 42.46 E
Tuticorin 148 Fg 8.47N 78.08 E
Tutira 218 Gc 39.12S 176.53 E
Tutóia 202 Jd 2.45S 42.16W
Tutoko Peak 218 Bf 44.36S 167.58 E
Tutončana 138 Ed 64.05N 93.50 E
Tutova 130 Kc 46.06N 27.32 E
Tutrakan 130 Je 44.03N 26.37 E
Tuttle Creek Lake 186 Hg 39.22N 96.40W
Tuttlingen 120 Ei 47.59N 8.49 E
Tutuala 150 Ih 8.24S 127.15 E
Tutuila Island 208 Jf 14.18S 170.42W
Tutupaca, Volcán- 202 Dg 17.01S 70.22W
Tuupovaara 116 Nb 62.29N 30.36 E
Tuusniemi 114 Ge 62.49N 28.30 E
Tuvalu (Ellice Islands) [1] 210 Ie 8.00S 178.00 E
Tuvalu Islands 208 Ie 8.00S 178.00 E
Tuvana-i-Ra Island 216 Fd 21.00S 178.43W
Tuvana-i-Tholo Island 208 Ig 21.02S 178.49W
Tuvinskaja ASSR [3] 138 Ef 51.30N 94.00 E
Tuvutha 219d Cb 17.40S 178.48W
Ţuwayq, Jabal- 140 Gg 25.30N 46.20 E
Tuxer Alpen 128 Fc 47.10N 11.45 E
Tuxford 124 Ba 53.13N 0.53W
Tuxpan [Mex.] 190 Cd 21.57N 105.18W
Tuxpan [Mex.] 192 Hh 19.33N 103.22W
Tuxpan, Arrecife- 192 Kg 21.02N 97.13W
Tuxpan, Rio- 192 Kg 20.53N 97.18W
Tuxpan de Rodríguez Cano 190 Ed 20.57N 97.24W
Tuxtla Gutiérrez 176 Jh 16.45N 93.07W
Tuy 126 Db 42.03N 8.38W
Tuy, Rio- 196 Dg 10.24N 65.59W
Tuy An 148 Lf 13.17N 109.16 E
Tuy Hoa 148 Lf 13.05N 109.18 E
Tüyserkān 146 Me 34.33N 48.27 E
Tuz, Lake- (EN)=Tuz Gölü 140 Ff 38.45N 33.25 E
Tuz Gölü=Tuz, Lake- (EN) 140 Ff 38.45N 33.25 E
Tuzkan, ozero- 135 Fd 40.35N 67.30 E
Tüz Khurmātū 146 Ke 34.53N 44.38 E
Tuzla 128 Mf 44.33N 18.41 E
Tuzla Gölü 146 Fc 39.01N 35.50 E
Tuzlov 132 Lf 47.23N 40.08 E
Tuzluca 146 Jb 40.03N 43.39 E
Tuzly 130 Nd 45.56N 30.05 E

Index Symbols

[1] Independent Nation
[2] State, Region
[3] District, County
[4] Municipality
[5] Colony, Dependency
Continent
Physical Region
Historical or Cultural Region
Mount, Mountain
Volcano
Hill
Mountains, Mountain Range
Hills, Escarpment
Plateau, Upland
Pass, Gap
Plain, Lowland
Delta
Salt Flat
Valley, Canyon
Crater, Cave
Karst Features
Depression
Polder
Desert, Dunes
Forest, Woods
Heath, Steppe
Oasis
Cape, Point
Coast, Beach
Cliff
Peninsula
Isthmus
Sandbank
Island
Atoll
Rock, Reef
Islands, Archipelago
Rocks, Reefs
Coral Reef
Well, Spring
Geyser
River, Stream
Waterfall, Rapids
River Mouth, Estuary
Lake
Salt Lake
Intermittent Lake
Reservoir
Swamp, Pond
Canal
Glacier
Ice Shelf, Pack Ice
Ocean
Sea
Gulf, Bay
Strait, Fjord
Lagoon
Bank
Seamount
Tablemount
Ridge
Shelf
Basin
Escarpment, Sea Scarp
Fracture
Trench, Abyss
National Park, Reserve
Point of Interest
Recreation Site
Cave, Cavern
Historic Site
Ruins
Wall, Walls
Church, Abbey
Temple
Scientific Station
Railway station
Airport
Port
Military installation
Lighthouse
Mine
Tunnel
Dam, Bridge

Tvååker 116 Eg 57.03N 12.24 E
Tvărdica 130 Ig 42.42N 25.54 E
Tvedestrand 114 Bg 58.37N 8.55 E
Tver' = Kalinin 112 Jd 56.52N 35.55 E
Tweed 118 Lf 55.46N 2.00W
Tweedsmuir Hills 118 Jf 55.30N 3.22W
Tweerivier 172 Be 25.35S 19.37 E
Twello, Voorst- 124 Ib 52.14N 6.07 E
Twente 122 Mb 52.17N 6.40 E
Twentekanaal 124 Ib 52.13N 6.53 E
Twilight Cove 212 Ff 32.20S 126.00 E
Twin Buttes Reservoir 186 Fk 31.20N 100.35W
Twin Falls 176 He 42.34N 114.28W
Twin Islands 180 Jf 53.50N 80.00W
Twin Peaks 188 Hd 44.35N 114.29W
Twisp 188 Eb 48.22N 120.07W
Twiste 124 Lc 51.29N 9.09 E
Twistringen 120 Ed 52.48N 8.39 E
Two Butte Creek 186 Eg 38.02N 102.08W
Two Harbors 186 Kc 47.01N 91.40W
Two Rivers 186 Md 44.09N 87.34W
Two Thumb Range 218 De 43.45S 170.40 E
Tychy 120 Of 50.09N 18.59 E
Tyczyn 120 Sg 49.58N 22.02 E
Tydal 114 Ce 63.04N 11.34 E
Tygda 138 Hf 53.07N 126.20 E
Tyin 116 Cc 61.14N 8.14 E
Tyin 116 Cc 61.15N 8.15 E
Tyler 182 He 32.21N 95.18W
Tylertown 186 Kk 31.07N 90.09W
Tylösand 116 Eh 56.39N 12.44 E
Tylöskog 116 Ff 58.40N 15.10 E
Tym 138 De 59.30N 80.07 E
Tymovskoje 138 Jf 50.50N 142.41 E
Tympákion 130 Hn 35.06N 24.45 E
Tynda 142 Od 55.10N 124.43 E
Tyne 118 Lf 55.01N 1.26W
Tyne and Wear [3] 118 Lg 55.00N 1.35W
Tynemouth 118 Lf 55.01N 1.24W
Týn nad Vltavou 120 Kg 49.14N 14.26 E
Tynset 114 Ce 62.17N 10.47 E
Tyra, Cayos- 194 Fg 12.50N 83.20W
Tyrifjorden 116 De 60.05N 10.10 E
Tyringe 116 Eh 56.10N 13.35 E
Tyrma 138 If 50.01N 132.10 E
Tyrnyauz 132 Mh 43.23N 42.56 E
Tyrol (EN)=Tirol [2] 128 Fc 47.10N 11.25 E
Tyrol (EN)=Tirol/Tirolo 128 Fd 47.00N 11.20 E
Tyrol (EN)=Tirolo/Tirol 128 Fd 47.00N 11.20 E
Tyrone 184 He 40.41N 78.15W
Tyrrell, Lake- 212 Ig 35.20S 142.50 E
Tyrrel Lake 180 Gd 63.05N 105.30W
Tyrrhenian Basin (EN) 110 Hh 40.00N 13.00 E
Tyrrhenian Sea (EN)=
Tirreno, Mar- 110 Hh 40.00N 12.00 E
Tyrva/Tõrva 114 Fg 58.01N 25.59 E
Tyrvää 116 Jc 61.21N 22.53 E
Tysmenica 120 Uh 48.49N 24.56 E
Tyśmienica 120 Se 51.33N 22.30 E
Tysnesøy 114 Af 60.00N 5.35 E
Tysse 116 Ad 60.22N 5.45 E
Tyssedal 116 Bd 60.07N 6.34 E
Tystama/Tõstamaa 116 Jf 58.17N 23.52 E
Tystberga 116 Gf 58.52N 17.15 E
Tyszowce 120 Tf 50.36N 23.41 E
Tytuvėnai/Tituvenaj 116 Ji 55.33N 23.09 E
Tywyn 118 Ii 52.35N 4.05W
Tzanconeja, Río- 192 Ni 16.51N 91.47W
Tzaneen 172 Ed 23.50S 30.09 E
Tzintzuntzan 192 Ih 19.38N 101.34W
Tzucacab 192 Og 20.04N 89.05W

U

Uaboe 220e Ab 0.31S 166.54 E
Uacurizal, Ilha do- 204 Dc 16.25S 56.05W
Ua Huka, Ile- 208 Ne 8.54S 139.33W
Uanukuhahaki 221b Ba 19.58S 174.29W
Ua Pou, Ile- 208 Me 9.23S 140.03W
Uaroo 212 Dd 23.00S 115.10 E
Uatumã, Rio- 198 Kf 2.26S 57.37W
Uaupés 200 Jf 0.08S 67.05W
Uaupés, Rio- 198 Je 0.02N 67.16W
Uaxactún 190 Ge 17.25N 89.29W
Ub 130 De 44.27N 20.05 E
Ubá 202 Jh 21.07S 42.56W
Übach-Palenberg 120 Cf 50.56N 6.05 E
Ubagan 136 Ge 54.23N 64.40 E
Ubaila 146 If 33.06N 40.15 E
Ubaitaba 202 Kf 14.18S 39.20W
Ubajay 204 Cj 31.47S 58.18W
Ubangi 158 Ii 0.30S 17.42 E
Ubatuba 204 Jf 23.26S 45.04W
Ubay 150 Hd 10.03N 124.28 E
Ubaye 122 Mj 44.28N 6.18 E
Ubayyiḑ, Wādī al- 144 Fc 32.34N 43.48 E
Ube 154 Kh 33.56N 131.15 E
Úbeda 126 If 38.01N 3.22W
Ubekendt Ejland 179 Gd 71.10N 53.45W
Uberaba 200 Lg 19.45S 47.55W
Uberaba, Lagoa- 204 Dc 17.30S 57.45W
Uberlândia 200 Lg 18.56S 48.18W
Überlingen 120 Fi 47.46N 9.10 E
Ubiaja 166 Gd 6.39N 6.23 E
Ubiña, Peña- 126 Ga 43.01N 5.57W
Ubiratã 204 Fg 24.32S 52.56W
Ubon Ratchathani 142 Mh 15.15N 104.54 E
Ubort 132 Fc 52.06N 28.30 E
Ubrique 126 Gh 36.41N 5.27W
Ubsu-Nur (Uvs Nuur) 140 Ld 50.20N 92.45 E
Ubundu 160 Ji 0.21S 25.29 E
Učaly 136 Fe 54.20N 59.31 E
Učami 138 Ed 63.50N 96.39 E
Učaral 136 If 46.08N 80.52 E
Ucayali [3] 202 De 7.10S 75.15W
Ucayali, Rio- 198 If 4.30S 73.30W
Uccle/Ukkel 124 Gd 50.48N 4.19 E
Üçdoruk Tepe 146 Ib 40.45N 41.05 E
Ucero 126 Ic 41.31N 3.04W
Uchiko 156 Ce 33.34N 132.38 E
Uchi Lake 186 Ja 51.05N 92.35W
Uchinomi 156 Dd 34.30N 134.19 E
Uchinoura 156 Bf 31.16N 131.05 E
Uchiura-Wan 154 Pc 42.18N 140.35 E
Uchte 120 Ed 52.30N 8.55 E
Učka 128 Ie 45.17N 14.12 E
Uckange 124 Ie 49.18N 6.09 E
Uckermark 120 Jc 53.10N 13.35 E
Uckfield 124 Cd 50.58N 0.06 E
Učkuduk 136 Gg 42.10N 63.30 E
Učkurgan 135 Id 41.01N 72.04 E
Ucrainskaja Sovetskaja
Socialističeskaja
Respublika [2] 136 Df 49.00N 32.00 E
Ucross 188 Ld 44.33N 106.31W
Ucua 170 Bd 8.40S 14.12 E
Učur 140 Pd 58.48N 130.35 E
Uda [R.S.F.S.R.] 138 Ff 51.45N 107.25 E
Uda [R.S.F.S.R.] 140 Pd 54.42N 135.14 E
Uda [R.S.F.S.R.] 138 Ee 56.05N 99.34 E
Udačny 138 Gc 66.25N 112.20 E
Udaipur 142 Jg 24.35N 73.41 E
Udaj 132 Hd 50.05N 33.07 E
Udaquiola 204 Cm 36.34S 58.31W
Udbina 128 Jf 44.32N 15.46 E
Uddevalla 114 Cg 58.21N 11.55 E
Uddjaure 110 Hb 65.58N 17.50 E
Uden 124 Hc 51.40N 5.37 E
Udgīr 148 Fe 18.23N 77.07 E
Udhampur 148 Fb 32.56N 75.08 E
Udimski 114 Kf 61.09N 45.52 E
Udine 128 Hd 46.03N 13.14 E
Udipi 148 Ef 13.21N 74.45 E
Udmurtskaja ASSR [3] 136 Fd 57.20N 52.50 E
Udoha 116 Mg 57.58N 29.50 E
Udomlja 114 Ih 57.56N 35.02 E
Udone-Jima 156 Fd 34.28N 139.17 E
Udon Thani 148 Ke 17.25N 102.48 E
Udot 220d Bb 7.23N 151.43 E
Udskaja guba 140 Pd 55.00N 136.00 E
Udskoje 138 If 54.36N 134.30 E
Udy 132 Je 49.47N 36.35 E
Udžary 132 Oi 40.31N 47.40 E
Udzungwa Range 170 Gd 8.05S 35.50 E
Uebonti 150 Hg 0.55S 121.38 E
Uecker 120 Kc 53.45N 14.04 E
Ueckermünde 120 Kc 53.44N 14.03 E
Ueda 152 Od 36.24N 138.16 E
Uele 158 Jh 4.09N 22.26 E
Uelen 138 Oc 66.13N 169.48W
Uelzen 120 Gd 52.58N 10.34 E
Ueno 156 Ed 34.46N 136.06 E
Uere 158 Jh 3.42N 25.24 E
Ufa 112 Le 54.44N 55.56 E
Ufa 110 Le 54.40N 56.00 E
Uftjuga 114 Lf 61.28N 46.12 E
Ugab 158 Ik 21.12S 13.38 E
Ugāle/Ugale 116 Ig 57.19N 21.52 E
Ugale/Ugāle 116 Ig 57.19N 21.52 E
Ugalla 170 Fd 5.08S 30.42 E
Uganda [1] 160 Kh 1.00N 32.00 E
Ugărčin 130 Hf 43.06N 24.25 E
Ugashik 178 He 57.32N 157.25W
Ughelli 166 Gd 5.30N 5.59 E
Ugíjar 126 Ih 36.57N 3.03W
Uglegorsk 138 Jg 49.05N 142.06 E
Uglekamensk 138 Ih 43.18N 133.08 E
Ugleuralski 134 Hg 58.59N 57.38 E
Uglič 136 Dd 57.33N 38.23 E
Ugljan 128 Jf 44.05N 15.10 E
Uglovoje 154 Lc 43.20N 132.06 E
Ugnev 120 Tf 50.20N 23.45 E
Ugo 156 Gb 39.13N 140.23 E
Ugolnyje Kopi 138 Md 64.42N 177.50 E
Ugoma 170 Ec 4.55S 26.50 E
Ugra 136 De 54.30N 36.07 E
Ugtal-Cajdam 152 Ib 48.25N 105.30 E
Uh 120 Rh 48.33N 22.00 E
Uherské Hradiště 120 Ng 49.04N 17.27 E
Úhlava 120 Jg 49.45N 13.23 E
Uhlenhorst 172 Bd 23.45S 17.55 E
Uhta 112 Lc 63.33N 53.40 E
Uíbh Fhailí/Offaly [2] 118 Fh 53.20N 7.30W
Uig 118 Gd 57.30N 6.20W
Uíge 160 Ii 7.35S 15.04 E
Uíge [3] 170 Cd 7.00S 15.30 E
'Uiha 221b Ba 19.54S 174.25W
Uijec 220d Bb 7.10N 151.57 E
Ŭijŏngbu 154 If 37.44N 127.02 E
Uiju 154 Hd 40.12N 124.32 E
Uil 136 Ff 49.04N 54.42 E
Uil 136 Ff 48.36N 52.30 E
Uilpata, gora- 132 Mh 42.47N 43.44 E
Uinta Mountains 182 Ec 40.45N 110.05W
Uinta River 188 Kf 40.14N 109.51W
Uis 172 Ad 21.08S 14.49 E
Ŭisŏng 154 Jf 36.21N 128.42 E
Uitenhage 160 Jl 33.40S 25.28 E
Uithoorn 124 Gb 52.14N 4.52 E
Uithuizen 124 Ia 53.25N 6.42 E
Uithuizerwad 124 Ia 53.30N 6.40 E
Uj 136 Ge 54.20N 63.58 E
Ujae Atoll 208 Hd 9.05N 165.40 E
Ūjān 146 Og 30.45N 52.05 E
Ujandina 138 Jc 68.23N 145.50 E
Ujar 138 Ee 55.48N 94.20 E
Ujarrás 194 Fi 9.50N 83.40W
Ujedinenija, ostrov- 138 Da 77.30N 82.30 E
Ujelang Atoll 208 Hd 9.49N 160.55 E
Újfehértó 120 Ri 47.48N 21.41 E
Uji 156 Dd 34.53N 135.47 E
Uji-Guntō 154 Ji 31.10N 129.28 E
Ujiie 156 Fc 36.41N 139.57 E
Ujiji 160 Ji 4.55S 29.41 E
Ujjain 142 Jg 23.11N 75.46 E
Ujunglamuru 150 Gg 4.40S 119.58 E
Ujung Pandang=Makasar
(EN) 142 Nj 5.07S 119.24 E
Uk 138 Ee 55.04N 98.52 E
Ukata 166 Gc 10.50N 5.50 E
Ukeng, Bukit- 150 Gf 1.45N 115.08 E
Ukerewe Island 170 Fc 2.03S 33.00 E
Uke-Shima 156b Ba 28.02N 129.15 E
Ukhayḑir 146 Jf 32.26N 43.36 E
Ukiah [Ca.-U.S.] 182 Cd 39.09N 123.13W
Ukiah [Or.-U.S.] 188 Fd 45.08N 118.56W
Uki Ni Masi 219a Ed 10.15S 161.44 E
Ukkel/Uccle 124 Gd 50.48N 4.19 E
Ukmergė/Ukmerge 114 Fi 55.14N 24.47 E
Ukmerge/Ukmergė 114 Fi 55.14N 24.47 E
Ukraine (EN) 110 Jf 49.00N 35.00 E
Ukrainian SSR (EN)=
Ukrainskaja SSR [2] 136 Df 49.00N 32.00 E
Ukrainskaja SSR/Ukrainska
Radyanska Socialistična
Respublika [2] 136 Df 49.00N 32.00 E
Ukrainskaja SSR=Ukrainian
SSR (EN) [2] 136 Df 49.00N 32.00 E
Ukrainska Radyanska
Socialistična Respublika/
Ukrainskaja SSR [2] 136 Df 49.00N 32.00 E
Ukrina 128 Le 45.05N 17.56 E
Uku 170 Be 11.25S 14.18 E
Uku-Jima 156 Ae 33.16N 129.07 E
Ula 146 Cd 37.05N 28.26 E
Ula 120 Ub 54.06N 24.20 E
Ulaidh/Ulster 118 Gg 54.30N 7.00W
Ulalu 220d Bb 7.25N 151.40 E
Ulan (Xiligou) 152 Gd 36.55N 98.16 E
Ulan → Otog Qi 152 Id 39.07N 108.00 E
Ulanbaatar → Ulan-Bator 142 Me 47.55N 106.53 E
Ulan-Badrah 154 Ac 43.58N 110.37 E
Ulan-Bator (Ulaanbaatar) 142 Me 47.55N 106.53 E
Ulanbel 136 Hg 44.49N 71.10 E
Ulan-Burgasy, hrebet- 138 Ff 52.30N 108.30 E
Ulangom 142 Le 49.58N 92.02 E
Ulanhad/Chifeng 152 Kc 42.16N 118.57 E
Ulan Hol 136 Ef 45.27N 46.46 E
Ulan Hot/Horqin Youyi
Qianqi 142 Oe 46.04N 122.00 E
Ulan Hua → Siziwang Qi 154 Ad 41.31N 111.41 E
Ulan-Hus 152 Eb 49.02N 89.23 E
Ulanów 120 Sf 50.30N 22.16 E
Ulansuhai Nur 152 Ic 40.56N 108.49 E
Ulan-Tajga 152 Ga 50.45N 98.30 E
Ulan-Ude 142 Md 51.50N 107.37 E
Ulan Ul Hu 152 Fe 34.45N 90.25 E
Ulas 146 Gc 39.27N 37.03 E
Ulawa Island 214 Gi 9.46S 161.57 E
Ulbeja 138 Je 59.20N 144.25 E
Ulchin 154 Jf 36.59N 129.24 E
Ulcinj 130 Ch 41.56N 19.13 E
Uleåborg/Oulu 112 Ib 65.01N 25.30 E
Ulefoss 114 Bg 59.17N 9.16 E
Ulegej 142 Ke 48.56N 89.57 E
Ulety 138 Gf 51.22N 112.30 E
Uleza 130 Ch 41.40N 19.53 E
Ulfborg 116 Ch 56.16N 8.20 E
Ulflingen/Troisvierges 124 Hd 50.07N 6.00 E
Ulft, Gendringen- 124 Ic 51.54N 6.24 E
Ulgain Gol 152 Kb 45.31N 117.50 E
Ulhāsnagar 148 Ee 19.10N 73.07 E
Uliastai → Dong Ujimqin Qi 152 Kc 45.31N 116.58 E
Uliga 210 Id 7.09N 171.13 E
Ulindi 158 Ji 1.40S 25.52 E
Ulithi Atoll 208 Ed 9.58N 139.40 E
Ulja 138 Je 58.48N 141.40 E
Uljanovka [R.S.F.S.R.] 116 Ne 59.37N 30.55 E
Uljanovka [Ukr.-U.S.S.R.] 132 Ge 48.20N 30.13 E
Uljanovsk 112 Ke 54.20N 48.24 E
Uljanovskaja oblast [3] 136 Ee 54.00N 48.00 E
Uljanovski 136 He 50.05N 73.45 E
Uljasutaj 142 Le 47.45N 96.49 E
Ulkan 138 Fe 55.55N 107.55 E
Ulla 126 Db 42.39N 8.44W
Ullapool 118 Hd 57.54N 5.10W
Ullared 114 Ch 57.08N 12.43 E
Ulldecona 126 Md 40.36N 0.27 E
Ullsfjorden 114 Eb 69.58N 20.00 E
Ullswater 118 Kg 54.34N 2.54W
Ullŭng-Do 154 Kf 37.29N 130.52 E
Ullvettern 116 Fe 59.25N 14.15 E
Ulm 120 Fh 48.25N 10.00 E
Ulmen 124 Id 50.13N 6.59 E
Ulmeni 130 Jd 45.04N 26.39 E
Ulmu 130 Je 44.16N 26.55 E
Ulongwé 172 Eb 14.43S 34.21 E
Ulricehamn 114 Ch 57.47N 13.25 E
Ulrichstein 124 Ld 50.35N 9.12 E
Ulrum 124 Ia 53.22N 6.20 E
Ulrum-Zoutkamp 124 Ia 53.20N 6.18 E
Ulsan 152 Md 35.33N 129.19 E
Ulsteinvik 114 Ae 62.20N 5.53 E
Ulster 120 Ff 50.51N 9.59 E
Ulster/Ulaidh 118 Gg 54.30N 7.00W
Ulster Canal 118 Gg 54.27N 6.40W
Ulu 168 Ec 10.43N 33.29 E
Ulu/Uulu 116 Kf 58.13N 24.29 E
Ulua, Río- 190 Ge 15.56N 87.43W
Ulubat Gölü 146 Cb 40.10N 28.35 E
Ulubey 146 Cc 38.09N 29.33 E
Uludağ 144 Ca 40.04N 29.13 E
Uludere 146 Jd 37.27N 42.51 E
Ulugqat/Wuqia 152 Cd 39.40N 75.07 E
Ulukışla 146 Fd 37.33N 34.30 E
Ulungur He 140 Ke 46.58N 87.28 E
Ulungur Hu 152 Eb 47.20N 87.10 E
Ulus 146 Eb 41.35N 32.39 E
Ulus Dağ 130 Lj 39.18N 28.24 E
Ulva 118 Ge 56.28N 6.12W
Ulverston 118 Jg 54.12N 3.06W
Ulverstone 212 Jh 41.09S 146.10 E
Ulvik 116 Bd 60.34N 6.54 E
Ulvön 116 Ha 63.05N 18.40 E
Ulysses 186 Fh 37.35N 101.22W
Ulytau 136 Gf 48.35N 67.05 E
Ulytau, gora- 136 Gf 48.45N 67.00 E
Uly-Žilanšik 136 Gf 48.51N 63.47 E
Uma 152 La 52.36N 120.38 E
Umag 128 He 45.25N 13.32 E
Umala 202 Eg 17.24S 67.58W
Umán 192 Og 20.53N 89.45W
Uman 136 Df 48.47N 30.09 E
Uman 220d Bb 7.18N 151.53 E
'Umān=Oman (EN) [1] 142 Hg 21.00N 57.00 E
'Umān = Oman (EN) 140 Hg 22.10N 58.00 E
'Umān, Khalīj-=Oman, Gulf
of- (EN) 140 Hg 25.00N 58.00 E
Umanak 179 Gd 70.36N 52.15W
Ūmánarssuaq/Farvel, Kap-
224 Nb 59.50N 43.50W
Umatac 220c Bb 13.18N 144.40 E
Umba 136 Db 66.41N 34.17 E
Umbelasha 168 Cd 9.51N 24.50 E
Umbertide 128 Gg 43.18N 12.20 E
Umboi Island 208 Fe 5.36S 148.00 E
Umbozero, ozero- 114 Ic 67.45N 34.20 E
Umbria [2] 128 Gh 43.00N 12.30 E
Ume 172 Dc 17.15S 28.20 E
Umeå 112 Ic 63.50N 20.15 E
Umeälven 110 Ic 63.47N 20.16 E
Umm al Arānib 164 Bd 26.08N 14.45 E
Umm al Hayf, Wādī- 144 Hf 18.37N 53.59 E
Umm al Jamaājim 146 Ki 26.59N 45.19 E
Umm al Qaywayn 144 Id 25.35N 55.34 E
Ummanz 120 Jb 54.30N 13.10 E
Umm ar Rizam 164 Dc 32.32N 23.00 E
Umm as Samīm 144 Ie 21.30N 56.45 E
Umm aţ Ţūz 146 Je 34.47N 42.42 E
Umm Bāb 146 Nj 25.12N 50.48 E
Umm Bel 168 Dc 13.32N 28.04 E
Umm Buru 168 Cb 15.01N 23.36 E
Umm Dhibbān 168 Dc 14.14N 29.37 E
Umm Durmān=Omdurman
(EN) 160 Kg 15.38N 32.30 E
Umm Inderaba 168 Eb 15.12N 31.54 E
Umm Kaddādah 168 Dc 13.36N 26.42 E
Umm Lajj 144 Ed 25.04N 37.13 E
Umm Naqqāţ, Jabal- 146 Fj 25.30N 34.14 E
Umm Qam'ul 146 Pj 24.47N 54.42 E
Umm Ruwābah 160 Kg 12.54N 31.13 E
Umm Sayyālah 168 Ec 14.25N 31.00 E
Umm Urūmah 146 Gj 25.46N 36.33 E
Umnak 174 Cd 58.25N 168.10W
Umne-Gobi 152 Fb 49.06N 91.43 E
Umpqua River 188 Ce 43.42N 124.03W
Umpulu 170 Ce 12.42S 17.40 E
Umsini, Gunung- 150 Jg 1.35S 133.30 E
Umtata 160 Jl 31.35S 28.47 E
Umuarama 206 Jb 23.45S 53.20W
Umurbey 130 Ji 40.14N 26.36 E
Umvukwes 172 Ec 17.01S 30.52 E
Umvuma 172 Ec 19.19S 30.35 E
Umzingwani 172 Dd 22.12S 29.56 E
Una 128 Ke 45.16N 16.55 E
Unabetsu-Dake 156a Db 43.52N 144.51 E
Unac 128 Kf 44.29N 16.08 E
Unaí 202 Ig 16.23S 46.53W
Unalakleet 178 Gd 63.53N 160.47W
Unalaska 174 Cd 53.45N 166.45W
Unare, Río- 196 Dg 10.06N 65.12W
Unauna, Pulau- 150 Hg 0.10S 121.35 E
'Unayzah 146 Fg 30.29N 35.48 E
'Unayzah 142 Gg 26.06N 43.56 E
Uncía 202 Eg 18.27S 66.37W
Uncompahgre Peak 182 Fd 38.04N 107.28W
Uncompahgre Plateau 186 Bg 38.30N 108.25W
Unden 116 Ff 58.45N 14.25 E
Underberg 172 De 29.50S 29.22 E
Under-Han 142 Ne 47.19N 110.39 E
Undjuljung 138 Hc 66.20N 124.40 E
Undu Point 219d Cb 16.08S 179.57W
Undva neem 116 If 58.25N 21.45 E
Undva neem / Kiprarenukk,
mys- 116 If 58.25N 21.45 E
Uneča 132 Hc 52.50N 32.44 E
'Ung, Jabal al- 128 Dn 36.45N 9.35 E
Unga 178 Ge 55.15N 160.45W
Ungava, Péninsule d'-=
Ungava Peninsula (EN) 174 Lc 60.00N 74.00W
Ungava Bay 174 Md 59.30N 67.30W
Ungava Peninsula (EN)=
Ungava, Péninsule d'- 174 Lc 60.00N 74.00W
Ungeny 132 Ef 47.13N 27.50 E
Unggi 154 Kc 42.21N 130.23 E
Ungureni 130 Jb 47.53N 26.47 E
Ungwatiri 168 Fb 16.55N 36.05 E
União 202 Jd 4.35S 42.52W
União da Vitória 206 Jc 26.13S 51.05W
União dos Palmares 202 Ke 9.10S 36.02W
Uničov 120 Ng 49.49N 17.07 E
Uniejów 120 Oe 51.58N 18.49 E
Unije 128 If 44.38N 14.15 E
Unimak 174 Cd 54.50N 164.00W
Unimak Pass 178 Gf 54.35N 164.43W
Unini, Rio- 202 Fd 1.41S 61.30W
Union [Mo.-U.S.] 186 Kg 38.27N 91.00W
Union [S.C.-U.S.] 184 Gh 34.42N 81.37W
Union City 184 Cg 36.26N 89.03W
Uniondale 172 Cf 33.40S 23.08 E
Unión de Reyes 194 Gb 22.48N 81.32W
Unión de Tula 192 Gh 19.58N 104.16W
Union Island 196 Ff 12.36N 61.26W
Union Islands/Tokelau 208 Je 9.00S 171.45W
Union of Soviet Socialist
Republics (USSR) (EN)=
SSSR [1] 142 Jd 60.00N 80.00 E
Union Seamount (EN) 180 Eg 49.35N 132.45W
Union Springs 184 Ei 32.09N 85.49W
Uniontown 184 Hf 39.54N 79.44W
Unionville 186 Jf 40.29N 93.01W
United Arab Emirates (EN)
= Al Imārāt al 'Arabīyah
al Muttaḩidah [1] 142 Hg 24.00N 54.00 E
United Arab Republic (EN)
→ Egypt (EN) [1] 160 Jf 27.00N 30.00 E
United Kingdom [1] 112 Fe 54.00N 2.00W
United Kingdom of Great
Britain and Northern
Ireland [1] 112 Fe 54.00N 2.00W
United States [1] 176 Jf 38.00N 97.00W
United States of America [1] 176 Jf 38.00N 97.00W
Unity [Or.-U.S.] 188 Fd 44.29N 118.13W
Unity [Sask.-Can.] 180 Gf 52.27N 109.10W
University City 186 Kg 38.39N 90.19W
Unna 120 De 51.32N 7.41 E
Unnāb, Wādī al- 146 Gg 30.11N 36.39 E
Unnukka 116 Lb 62.25N 27.55 E
Unst 110 Fc 60.45N 0.55W
Unstrut 120 He 51.10N 11.48 E
Unterfranken 120 Fg 50.00N 10.00 E
Unterwalden nid dem
Wald [2] 128 Cd 46.55N 8.30 E
Unterwalden ob dem
Wald [2] 128 Cd 46.50N 8.20 E
Unuli Horog 152 Fd 35.12N 91.58 E
Ünye 144 Ea 41.08N 37.17 E
Unža 110 Kd 57.20N 43.08 E
Unzen-Dake 156 Be 32.45N 130.17 E
Uoleva 221b Ba 19.51S 174.24W
Uozu 154 Nf 36.48N 137.24 E
Úpa 120 Lf 50.22N 15.54 E
Upata 202 Fb 8.01N 62.24W
Upemba, Lac- 170 Ed 8.36S 26.26 E
Upernavik 179 Gd 72.20N 56.00W
Upin 150 Ig 2.56S 129.11 E
Upington 160 Jk 28.25S 21.15 E
Upland 124 Kc 51.18N 8.42 E
Upolu Island 208 Jf 13.55S 171.45W
Upolu Point 214 Oc 20.16N 155.52W
Upper [3] 166 Ec 10.30N 1.30W
Upper Arlington 184 Fe 40.01N 83.03W
Upper Arrow Lake 188 Ga 50.30N 117.55W
Upper Austria (EN) =
Oberösterreich [2] 128 Hb 48.15N 14.00 E
Upper Hutt 218 Fd 41.07S 175.04 E
Upper Klamath Lake 182 Cc 42.23N 122.00W
Upper Lake 188 Ef 41.44N 120.08W
Upper Lough Erne/Loch
Éirne Uachtair 118 Fg 54.20N 7.30W
Upper Red Lake 186 Ib 48.10N 94.40W
Upper Sandusky 184 Fe 40.48N 83.17W
Upper Sheik 168 Hd 9.57N 45.09 E
Upper Thames Valley 118 Lj 51.40N 1.40W
Upper Trajan's Wall (EN) =
Verhni Trajanov val 130 Lc 46.40N 29.00 E
Upper Volta (EN) →
Burkina Faso [1] 160 Gg 13.00N 2.00W
Uppingham 124 Bb 52.35N 0.43W
Uppland 116 Gd 60.00N 17.50 E
Upplands Väsby 116 Ge 59.31N 17.54 E
Uppsala 112 Hd 59.52N 17.38 E
Uppsala [2] 114 Df 60.00N 17.45 E
Upsala 186 Kb 49.02N 90.29W
Upshi 148 Fb 33.50N 77.49 E
Upton 188 Md 44.06N 104.38W
Uqbān 164 Hf 15.30N 42.23 E
'Uqlat aş Şuqūr 146 Jj 25.53N 42.15 E
Uqturpan/Wuski 152 Cc 41.10N 79.16 E
Ur 144 Gc 30.58N 46.06 E
Urabá, Golfo de- 202 Cb 8.25N 77.00W
Uracoa 196 Eh 9.00N 62.21W
Uracoa, Río- 196 Eh 9.08N 62.20W
Uradarja 135 Fe 38.51N 66.02 E
Urad Qianqi 152 Ic 40.49N 108.37 E
Urad Zhonghou Lianheqi
(Haliut) 152 Ic 41.34N 108.32 E
Uraga-Suido 156 Fd 35.15N 139.45 E
Ura-Guba 114 Hb 69.18N 32.48 E
Urahoro 156a Cb 42.48N 143.38 E
Urahoro-Gawa 156a Cb 42.44N 143.40 E
Uraj 136 Gc 60.08N 64.40 E
Urakawa 154 Qc 42.09N 142.47 E
Ural 110 Lf 47.00N 51.48 E
Ural Mountains (EN) =
Uralskije gory 110 Ld 57.00N 60.00 E
Uralsk 112 Le 51.14N 51.22 E
Uralskaja oblast [3] 136 Ff 49.45N 51.00 E
Uralskije gory = Ural
Mountains (EN) 110 Ld 57.00N 60.00 E
Urambo 170 Fd 5.04S 32.03 E
Uranium City 176 Id 59.34N 108.36W
Uraricoera 202 Fc 3.27N 60.59W
Uraricoera, Rio- 198 Je 3.02N 60.30W
Ura-Tjube 136 Gh 39.53N 69.01 E
Urawa 154 Og 35.51N 139.39 E
'Uray'irah 146 Mj 25.57N 48.53 E
Urayq, Nafūd al- 146 Jj 25.17N 42.25 E
Urbana [Il.-U.S.] 186 Lf 40.07N 88.12W
Urbana [Oh.-U.S.] 184 Fe 40.06N 83.45W
Urbandale 186 Jf 41.38N 93.48W
Urbania 128 Gg 43.40N 12.31 E
Urbano Santos 202 Jd 3.12S 43.23W
Urbino 128 Gg 43.43N 12.38 E
Urbino, Étang d'- 122a Ba 42.02N 9.28 E
Urbión, Picos de- 126 Jb 42.01N 2.52W
Urcel 124 Fe 49.30N 3.33 E
Urcos 202 Df 13.42S 71.38W
Urdinarrain 204 Ck 32.41S 58.53W
Urdoma 114 Lf 61.47N 48.29 E
Urdžar 136 If 47.05N 81.37 E
Uré 194 Jj 7.46N 75.31W
Ure 118 Lg 54.01N 1.12W
Uren 136 Ed 57.29N 45.48 E
Urenui 218 Fc 39.00S 174.23 E
Ures 190 Bc 29.26N 110.24W
Ureshino 156 Ab 33.06N 129.59 E
'Urf, Jabal al- 146 Ei 27.49N 32.55 E

Index Symbols

[1] Independent Nation
[2] State, Region
[3] District, County
[4] Municipality
[5] Colony, Dependency
Continent
Physical Region
Historical or Cultural Region
Mount, Mountain
Volcano
Hill
Mountains, Mountain Range
Hills, Escarpment
Plateau, Upland
Pass, Gap
Plain, Lowland
Delta
Salt Flat
Valley, Canyon
Crater, Cave
Karst Features
Depression
Polder
Desert, Dunes
Forest, Woods
Heath, Steppe
Oasis
Cape, Point
Coast, Beach
Cliff
Peninsula
Isthmus
Sandbank
Island
Atoll
Rock, Reef
Islands, Archipelago
Rocks, Reefs
Coral Reef
Well, Spring
Geyser
River, Stream
Waterfall, Rapids
River Mouth, Estuary
Lake
Salt Lake
Intermittent Lake
Reservoir
Swamp, Pond
Canal
Glacier
Ice Shelf, Pack Ice
Ocean
Sea
Gulf, Bay
Strait, Fjord
Lagoon
Bank
Seamount
Tablemount
Ridge
Shelf
Basin
Escarpment, Sea Scarp
Fracture
Trench, Abyss
National Park, Reserve
Point of Interest
Recreation Site
Cave, Cavern
Historic Site
Ruins
Wall, Walls
Church, Abbey
Temple
Scientific Station
Railway station
Airport
Port
Military installation
Lighthouse
Mine
Tunnel
Dam, Bridge

Index Symbols

[1] Independent Nation — Historical or Cultural Region — Pass, Gap — Depression — Coast, Beach — Waterfall, Rapids — Canal — Lagoon — Escarpment, Sea Scarp — Historic Site — Airport
[2] State, Region — Mount, Mountain — Plain, Lowland — Polder — Rock, Reef — River Mouth, Estuary — Glacier — Bank — Fracture — Ruins — Port
[3] District, County — Volcano — Delta — Cliff — Islands, Archipelago — Ice Shelf, Pack Ice — Seamount — Trench, Abyss — Wall, Walls — Military installation
[4] Municipality — Hill — Desert, Dunes — Peninsula — Rocks, Reefs — Ocean — Tableland — National Park, Reserve — Church, Abbey — Lighthouse
[5] Colony, Dependency — Mountains, Mountain Range — Salt Flat — Forest, Woods — Isthmus — Sandbank — Sea — Shelf — Point of Interest — Temple — Mine
Continent — Hills, Escarpment — Valley, Canyon — Heath, Steppe — Coral Reef — Intermittent Lake — Ridge — Recreation Site — Scientific Station — Tunnel
Physical Region — Plateau, Upland — Crater, Cave — Oasis — Well, Spring — Lake — Gulf, Bay — Basin — Cave, Cavern — Railway station — Dam, Bridge
— Karst Features — Cape, Point — Island — Reservoir — Geyser — Strait, Fjord — Atoll — River, Stream — Swamp, Pond

Viana do Castelo 126 Dc 41.42N 8.50W
Viana do Castelo [2] 126 Dc 41.55N 8.25W
Vianden 124 Ie 49.55N 6.16 E
Vianen 124 Hb 52.00N 5.05 E
Viangchan (Vientiane) 142 Mh 17.58N 102.36 E
Vianópolis 204 Hc 16.45 S 48.32W
Viar 126 Gg 37.36N 5.50W
Viareggio 128 Eg 43.52N 10.14 E
Viarmes 124 Ee 49.08N 2.22 E
Viaur 122 Hj 44.08N 1.58 E
Viborg 114 Bh 56.26N 9.24 E
Viborg [2] 116 Ch 56.30N 9.30 E
Vibo Valentia 128 Kl 38.40N 16.06 E
Vic 126 Oc 41.56N 2.15 E
Vicari 128 Hm 37.49N 13.34 E
Vicecomodoro Marambio 222 Re 64.16 S 56.44W
Vicente Guerrero 190 Dd 23.45N 103.59W
Vicenza 128 Fe 45.33N 11.33 E
Vichada [3] 202 Ec 5.00N 69.30W
Vichada, Río- 198 Je 4.55N 67.50W
Vichadero 204 Ej 31.48 S 54.43W
Vichy 122 Jh 46.07N 3.25 E
Vicksburg 182 Ie 32.14N 90.56W
Vico, Lago di- 128 Gh 42.19N 12.10 E
Vic-sur-Aisne 124 Fe 49.24N 3.07 E
Vic-sur-Cère 122 Ij 44.59N 2.37 E
Victor Bay 222 Ie 66.20 S 136.30 E
Victor Harbour 212 Hg 35.34 S 138.37 E
Victoria [2] 212 Ig 38.00 S 145.00 E
Victoria 174 Hb 71.00N 114.00W
Victoria [Arg.] 206 Hd 32.37 S 60.10W
Victoria [B.C.-Can.] 176 Ge 48.25N 123.22W
Victoria [Cam.] 166 Ge 4.01N 9.12 E
Victoria [Chile] 206 Fe 38.13 S 72.20W
Victoria [Gren.] 196 Ff 12.12N 61.42W
Victoria [Mala.] 150 Ge 5.17N 115.15 E
Victoria [Malta] 128 In 36.02N 14.14 E
Victoria [Rom.] 130 Hd 45.44N 24.41 E
Victoria [Sey.] 160 Mi 4.38 S 55.27 E
Victoria [Tx.-U.S.] 176 Jg 28.48N 97.00W
Victoria/Ying zhan 142 Ng 22.17N 114.09 E
Victoria, Lake- [Afr.] 158 Ki 1.00 S 33.00 E
Victoria, Lake- [Austl.] 212 If 34.00 S 141.15 E
Victoria, Mount- [Bur.] 140 Lg 21.14N 93.55 E
Victoria, Mount- [Pap.N.Gui.] 208 Fe 8.53 S 147.33 E
Victoria, Sierra de la- 204 Fg 25.55 S 54.00W
Victoria and Albert Mountains 180 Ka 79.00N 75.00W
Victoria de Durango 176 Ig 24.02N 104.40W
Victoria de las Tunas 190 Id 20.58N 76.57W
Victoria Falls 160 Jj 17.56 S 25.50 E
Victoria Falls 158 Jj 17.55 S 25.21 E
Victoria Fjord 179 Hb 82.20N 48.00W
Victoria Land (EN) 222 Jf 75.00 S 159.00 E
Victoria Nile 158 Kh 2.14N 31.26 E
Victoria Peak [B.C.-Can.] 188 Ba 50.03N 126.06W
Victoria Peak [Blz.] 194 Ce 16.48N 88.37W
Victoria River 208 Df 15.12 S 129.43 E
Victoria River Downs 212 Gc 16.24 S 131.00 E
Victoria Strait 180 Hc 69.30N 100.00W
Victoriaville 180 Kg 46.03N 71.58W
Victoria West 172 Cf 31.25 S 23.04 E
Victorville 188 Gi 34.32N 117.18W
Victory, Mount- 212 Ja 9.10 S 149.05 E
Vičuga 136 Ed 57.15N 42.00 E
Vicuña 206 Fc 29.59 S 70.44W
Vicuña Mackenna 206 Hd 33.54 S 64.23W
Vidå 116 Cj 54.58N 8.41 E
Vidal 188 Hi 34.11N 114.34W
Vidalia 186 Kk 31.34N 91.26W
Videbæk 116 Ch 56.05N 8.38 E
Videira 206 Jc 27.00 S 51.08W
Videla 204 Bj 30.56 S 60.39W
Videle 130 Ie 44.17N 25.31 E
Vidigueira 126 Ef 38.13N 7.48W
Vidin 130 Ff 43.59N 22.52 E
Vidin [2] 130 Ff 43.59N 22.52 E
Vidisha 148 Fd 23.42N 77.47 E
Vidlič 130 Ff 43.08N 22.47 E
Vidojevica 130 Ef 43.10N 21.32 E
Vidöstern 116 Fg 57.04N 14.01 E
Vidourle 122 Kk 43.32N 4.08 E
Vidra [Rom.] 130 Jd 45.55N 26.54 E
Vidra [Rom.] 130 Je 44.16N 26.09 E
Vidsel 114 Ed 65.49N 20.31 E
Viduša 128 Mh 42.54N 18.18 E
Vidzeme 116 Kg 57.10N 26.00 E
Vidzemes Augstiene / Vidzemskaja vozvyšennost 116 Kh 56.45N 26.00 E
Vidzemskaja vozvyšennost / Vidzemes Augstiene 116 Kh 56.45N 26.00 E
Vidzy 116 Li 55.23N 26.47 E
Vie 124 Be 49.09N 0.04W
Viechtach 120 Ig 49.05N 12.53 E
Viedma 200 Jj 40.50 S 63.00W
Viedma, Lago- 198 Ij 49.35 S 72.35W
Vieille Case 197g Ba 15.36N 61.24W
Vieja, Sierra- 186 Dk 30.30N 104.40W
Viejo, Cerro- 190 Bb 30.20N 112.15W
Viekšniai/Viekšnjai 116 Jh 56.14N 22.28 E
Viekšnjai/Viekšniai 116 Jh 56.14N 22.28 E
Vielha / Viella 126 Mb 42.42N 0.48 E
Viella / Vielha 126 Mb 42.42N 0.48 E
Vielsalm 124 Hd 50.17N 5.55 E
Viels-Maisons 124 Ff 48.54N 3.24 E
Vienna [Mo.-U.S.] 186 Kg 38.11N 91.57W
Vienna [W.V.-U.S.] 184 Gf 39.20N 81.33W
Vienna (EN) = Wien 112 Hf 48.12N 16.22 E
Vienna Woods (EN)= Wienerwald 128 Jb 48.10N 16.00 E
Vienne 122 Ki 45.31N 4.52 E
Vienne [3] 122 Gh 46.30N 0.30 E
Vienne 110 Gf 47.13N 0.05 E
Vientiane → Viangchan 142 Mh 17.58N 102.36 E
Vientos, Paso de los- = Windward Passage (EN) 174 Lh 20.00N 73.50W
Vieques, Isla de- 190 Ke 18.08N 65.25W
Vieques, Pasaje de- 197a Cb 18.08N 65.40W
Vieques, Sonda de- 197a Cb 18.17N 65.25W
Vierge Point 197k Bb 13.49N 60.53W
Viernheim 124 Ke 49.32N 8.35 E
Viersen 120 Ce 51.15N 6.23 E
Vierville-sur-Mer 124 Be 49.22N 0.54W
Vierwaldstätter See = Lucerne, Lake- (EN) 128 Cc 47.00N 8.30 E
Vierzon 122 Ig 47.13N 2.05 E
Viesca 192 He 25.21N 102.48W
Viesite/Viesīte 116 Kh 56.20N 25.38 E
Viesīte/Viesite 116 Kh 56.20N 25.38 E
Vieste 128 Ki 41.53N 16.10 E
Viet Nam = Vietnam (EN) [1] 142 Mh 13.00N 108.00 E
Vietnam (EN) = Viet Nam [1] 142 Mh 13.00N 108.00 E
Viet Tri 148 Ld 21.18N 105.26 E
Vieux Fort 196 Ff 13.44N 60.57W
Vieux-Fort, Pointe du- 197e Ac 15.57N 61.43W
Vieux Fort Bay 197k Bb 13.44N 60.58W
Vieux-Habitants 197e Ab 16.04N 61.46W
Vievis/Vevis 116 Kj 54.45N 24.58 E
Viga 114 Kg 59.15N 43.42 E
Vigala 116 Kf 58.43N 24.22 E
Vigan 150 Hc 17.34N 120.23 E
Vigan, Le- 122 Jk 43.59N 3.36 E
Vigeland 116 Bf 58.05N 7.18 E
Vigevano 128 Ce 45.19N 8.51 E
Vigia 202 Id 0.48 S 48.08W
Vigía Chico 192 Ph 19.46N 87.35W
Vignacourt 124 Ed 50.01N 2.12 E
Vignemale 126 Lb 42.46N 0.08W
Vigneulles-lès-Hattonchâtel 124 Hf 48.59N 5.43 E
Vignoble 122 Lh 46.50N 5.30 E
Vignola 128 Ef 44.29N 11.00 E
Vigny 124 De 49.05N 1.56 E
Vigo 112 Fg 42.14N 8.43W
Vigo, Ría de- 126 Db 42.15N 8.45W
Vigra 116 Bb 62.30N 6.05 E
Vigrestad 116 Af 58.34N 5.42 E
Vihanti 114 Fd 64.30N 25.00 E
Vihiers 122 Fg 47.09N 0.32W
Vihorevka 138 Fe 56.12N 101.09 E
Vihorlat 120 Sh 48.55N 22.10 E
Vihren 130 Gh 41.46N 23.24 E
Vihti 114 Ff 60.25N 24.20 E
Viiala 116 Jc 61.13N 23.47 E
Viinijärvi 116 Mb 62.39N 29.14 E
Viinijärvi 116 Mb 62.45N 29.15 E
Viitasaari 114 Fe 63.04N 25.52 E
Viivikonna/Vijvikonna 116 Le 59.14N 27.41 E
Vijayawāda 142 Kh 16.31N 80.37 E
Vijvikonna/Viivikonna 116 Le 59.14N 27.41 E
Vik 114a Bc 63.25N 19.01W
Vika 116 Fd 60.57N 14.27 E
Vikarbyn 116 Fd 60.55N 15.01 E
Vikbolandet 116 Gf 58.30N 16.40 E
Viken 116 Eh 56.09N 12.34 E
Viken 116 Ff 58.40N 14.20 E
Vikenara Point 219a Dc 8.34 S 159.53 E
Vikersund 116 De 59.59N 10.02 E
Vikingbanken 118 Pa 60.20N 2.30 E
Vikmanshyttan 116 Fd 60.17N 15.49 E
Vikna 114 Cd 64.53N 10.58 E
Vikna 114 Cd 64.54N 11.00 E
Viksoyri 114 Bf 61.05N 6.34 E
Viktorija 179 Pb 80.10N 36.45 E
Vila da Maganja 172 Fc 17.18 S 37.31 E
Vila de Rei 126 De 39.40N 8.09W
Vila do Bispo 126 Dg 37.05N 8.55W
Vila do Conde 126 Dc 41.21N 8.45W
Vila do Porto 162 Bb 36.56N 25.09W
Vila Flor 126 Ec 41.18N 7.09W
Vilafranca del Maestrat / Villafranca del Cid 126 Ld 40.25N 0.15W
Vilafranca del Penedès/ Villafranca del Panadés 126 Nc 41.21N 1.42 E
Vila Franca de Xira 126 Df 38.57N 8.59W
Vila Franca do Campo 162 Bb 37.43N 25.26W
Vila Franca do Save 172 Ed 21.09 S 34.32 E
Vila Gamito 172 Eb 14.10 S 32.59 E
Vilagarcía de Arousa / Villagarcía de Arosa 126 Db 42.36N 8.45W
Vila Gouveia 172 Ec 18.03 S 33.11 E
Vilaine 122 Dg 47.23N 2.27W
Viļaka/Viljaka 114 Gh 57.14N 27.46 E
Vila Machado 172 Ec 19.17 S 34.12 E
Vilanculos 160 Kk 22.00 S 35.19 E
Viļani/Viljani 114 Gh 56.33N 26.59 E
Vila Nova da Cerveira 126 Dc 41.56N 8.45W
Vila Nova de Famalicão 126 Dc 41.25N 8.32W
Vila Nova de Foz Côa 126 Ec 41.05N 7.12W
Vila Nova de Gaia 126 Dc 41.08N 8.37W
Vilanova i la Geltrú/ Villanueva y Geltrú 126 Nc 41.14N 1.44 E
Vila Paiva de Andrada 172 Ec 18.41 S 34.04 E
Vila Pouca de Aguiar 126 Ec 41.30N 7.39W
Vila Real 126 Ec 41.18N 7.45W
Vila Real [2] 126 Ec 41.35N 7.35W
Vila-Real / Villarreal de los Infantes 126 Le 39.56N 0.06W
Vila Real de Santo António 126 Eg 37.12N 7.25W
Vilar Formoso 126 Fd 40.37N 6.50W
Vila Velha 202 Jh 20.20 S 40.17W
Vila Velha de Ródão 126 Ee 39.40N 7.42W
Vila Viçosa 126 Ef 38.47N 7.25W
Vilcabamba 202 Df 13.05 S 73.01W
Vilcabamba, Cordillera- 202 Df 13.00 S 73.00W
Vîlcea [2] 130 He 45.10N 24.10 E
Vilches 126 If 38.12N 3.30W
Vildbjerg 116 Ch 56.12N 8.46 E
Viled 114 Lf 61.22N 47.15 E
Vilejka 136 Ce 54.30N 26.53 E
Vilhelmina 114 Dd 64.37N 16.39 E
Vilhena 200 Jg 12.43 S 60.07W
Vilija 132 Db 54.55N 25.40 E
Viljaka/Viļaka 114 Gh 57.14N 27.46 E
Viljandi 136 Cd 58.22N 25.35 E
Viljany/Viļani 114 Gh 56.33N 26.59 E
Viljuj 140 Oc 64.24N 126.26 E
Viljujsk 138 Hd 63.40N 121.33 E
Viljujskoje plato = Vilyui Range (EN) 140 Mc 66.00N 108.00 E
Viljujskoje vodohranilišče 138 Gd 62.30N 111.00 E
Vilkaviškis 114 Fi 54.43N 23.02 E
Vilkickogo, ostrov- [R.S.F.S.R.] 138 Cb 73.30N 76.00 E
Vilkickogo, ostrov- [R.S.F.S.R.] 138 Ka 75.40N 152.30 E
Vilkickogo, proliv- = Vilkitski Strait (EN) 140 Mb 77.55N 103.00 E
Vilkija 114 Fi 55.03N 23.35 E
Vilkitski Strait (EN) = Vilkickogo, proliv- 140 Mb 77.55N 103.00 E
Vilkovo 132 Fg 45.23N 29.35 E
Villa Aberastain 206 Gd 31.39 S 68.35W
Villa Ahumada 190 Cb 30.37N 106.31W
Villa Altagracia 194 Ld 18.40N 70.10W
Villa Ana 204 Ci 28.29 S 59.37W
Villa Ángela 206 Hc 27.35 S 60.43W
Villa Atuel 206 Gd 34.50 S 67.54W
Villa Berthet 204 Bh 27.17 S 60.25W
Villablino 126 Fb 42.56N 6.19W
Villa Bruzual 202 Eb 9.20N 69.06W
Villa Cañas 204 Bk 34.00 S 61.36W
Villacañas 126 Ie 39.38N 3.20W
Villacarrillo 126 If 38.07N 3.05W
Villacastín 126 Hd 40.47N 4.25W
Villach 128 Hd 46.36N 13.50 E
Villacidro 128 Ck 39.27N 8.44 E
Villa Clara 204 Cj 31.50 S 58.49W
Villaclara [3] 194 Hb 22.30N 80.00W
Villa Constitución [Arg.] 206 Hd 33.14 S 60.20W
Villa Constitución [Mex.] 190 Bc 25.09N 111.43W
Villa Coronado 192 Gd 26.45N 105.10W
Villada 126 Hb 42.15N 4.58W
Villa de Arriaga 192 Ig 21.54N 101.23W
Villa de Cos 192 Hf 23.17N 102.21W
Villa de Cura 196 Cg 10.02N 67.29W
Villa de María 206 Hc 29.54 S 63.43W
Villa de Reyes 192 Ig 21.48N 100.56W
Villa de San Antonio 194 Df 14.16N 87.36W
Villadiego 126 Ib 42.31N 4.00W
Villa Dolores 206 Gd 31.56 S 65.12W
Villa Elisa 204 Ck 32.10 S 58.24W
Villa Flores 192 Mi 16.14N 93.14W
Villa Florida 204 Dh 26.23 S 57.09W
Villafranca del Bierzo 126 Fb 42.36N 6.48W
Villafranca del Cid / Vilafranca del Maestrat 126 Ld 40.25N 0.15W
Villafranca de los Barros 126 Ff 38.34N 6.20W
Villafranca del Panadés/ Vilafranca del Penedès 126 Nc 41.21N 1.42 E
Villafranca di Verona 128 Ee 45.21N 10.50 E
Villa Frontera 190 Dc 26.56N 101.27W
Villagarcía de Arosa / Vilagarcía de Arousa 126 Db 42.36N 8.45W
Villa General Roca 206 Gd 32.39 S 66.28W
Villa Gesell 204 Dm 37.15 S 56.55W
Villagrán 192 Je 24.29N 99.29W
Villaguay 206 Id 31.51 S 59.01W
Villa Guillermina 204 Ci 28.14 S 59.28W
Villa Hayes 206 Ic 25.06 S 57.34W
Villa Hermandarias 204 Cj 31.13 S 59.59W
Villahermosa 176 Jh 17.59N 92.55W
Villa Hidalgo 192 Gd 26.16N 104.54W
Villa Huidobro 206 Hd 34.50 S 64.35W
Villajoyosa / La Vila Joiosa 126 Lf 38.30N 0.14W
Villalba 126 Ea 43.18N 7.41W
Villaldama 192 Id 26.30N 100.26W
Villalón de Campos 126 Gb 42.06N 5.02W
Villalpando 126 Gc 41.52N 5.24W
Villamalea 126 Ke 39.22N 1.35W
Villamanrique 126 Jf 38.33N 3.00W
Villa María 200 Ji 32.25 S 63.15W
Villamartín 126 Gh 36.52N 5.38W
Villa Matamoros 192 Gd 26.50N 105.35W
Villa Media Agua 206 Gd 31.59 S 68.25W
Villamil 202a Ab 0.56 S 91.01W
Villa Minetti 204 Bi 28.37 S 61.39W
Villa Montes 200 Jh 21.15 S 63.30W
Villandraut 122 Fj 44.28N 0.22W
Villa Nueva 206 Gd 32.54 S 68.47W
Villanueva 192 Hf 22.21N 102.53W
Villanueva [Col.] 194 Kh 10.37N 72.59W
Villanueva [N.M.-U.S.] 186 Di 35.17N 105.23W
Villanueva de Córdoba 126 Hf 38.20N 4.37W
Villanueva del Arzobispo 126 Jf 38.10N 3.00W
Villanueva de la Serena 126 Gf 38.58N 5.48W
Villanueva del Fresno 126 Ef 38.23N 7.10W
Villanueva de los Infantes 126 If 38.44N 3.01W
Villanueva del Río y Minas 126 Gg 37.39N 5.42W
Villanueva y Geltrú/Vilanova i la Geltrú 126 Nc 41.14N 1.44 E
Villa Ocampo [Arg.] 206 Ic 28.28 S 59.22W
Villa Ocampo [Mex.] 190 Cc 26.27N 105.31W
Villa Ojo de Agua 206 Hc 29.31 S 63.42W
Villa Oliva 204 Dh 26.01 S 57.53W
Villa Pesqueira 192 Ec 29.08N 109.58W
Villaputzu 128 Dk 39.26N 9.34 E
Villa Ramírez 204 Bk 32.11 S 60.12W
Villarcayo 126 Ib 42.56N 3.34W
Villar del Arzobispo 126 Le 39.44N 0.49W
Villa Regina 206 Ge 39.06 S 67.04W
Villa Rosario 202 Db 7.50N 72.29W
Villarreal de los Infantes / Vila-Real 126 Le 39.56N 0.06W
Villarrica [Chile] 206 Fe 39.16 S 72.16W
Villarrica [Par.] 200 Kh 25.45 S 56.26W
Villarrobledo 126 Je 39.16N 2.36W
Villasalto 128 Dk 39.29N 9.23 E
Villa San Giovanni 128 Jl 38.13N 15.38 E
Villa San Martín 206 Hc 28.18 S 64.12W
Villasimius 128 Dk 39.08N 9.31 E
Villatoro, Puerto de- 126 Gd 40.33N 5.10W
Villa Unión [Mex.] 192 Ic 28.15N 100.43W
Villa Unión [Mex.] 190 Cd 23.12N 106.16W
Villaverde, Madrid- 126 Id 40.21N 3.42W
Villavicencio 200 Ie 4.09N 73.37W
Villaviciosa 126 Ga 43.29N 5.26W
Villazón 202 Eh 22.06 S 65.36W
Ville-de-Laval 184 Kc 45.33N 73.44W
Ville de Paris [3] 122 If 48.52N 2.20 E
Ville de Toulouse Bank (EN) 174 Hh 11.30N 117.00W
Villedieu-les-Poêles 122 Ef 48.50N 1.13W
Ville-en-Tardenois 124 Fe 49.11N 3.48 E
Villefranche-de-Lauragais 122 Hk 43.24N 1.44 E
Villefranche-de-Rouergue 122 Ij 44.21N 2.03 E
Villefranche-sur-Saône 122 Ki 45.59N 4.43 E
Ville-Marie 184 Hb 47.20N 79.26W
Villemur-sur-Tarn 122 Hk 43.52N 1.31 E
Villena 126 Lf 38.38N 0.51W
Villeneuve d'Ascq 124 Fd 50.38N 3.09 E
Villeneuve-Saint-Georges 124 Ef 48.44N 2.27 E
Villeneuve-sur-Lot 122 Gj 44.24N 0.43 E
Villeneuve-sur-Yonne 122 Jf 48.05N 3.18 E
Ville Platte 186 Jk 30.42N 92.16W
Villers-Bocage [Fr.] 124 Ee 50.00N 2.20 E
Villers-Bocage [Fr.] 124 Be 49.05N 0.39W
Villers-Bretonneux 124 Ee 49.52N 2.31 E
Villers-Carbonnel 124 Ee 49.52N 2.54 E
Villers-Cotterêts 124 Fe 49.15N 3.05 E
Villers-la-Ville 124 Gd 50.35N 4.32 E
Villers-sur-Mer 124 Be 49.19N 0.01W
Villerupt 122 Le 49.28N 5.56 E
Villerville 124 Ce 49.24N 0.08 E
Ville-sur-Tourbe 124 Ge 49.11N 4.47 E
Villeurbanne 122 Ki 45.46N 4.53 E
Villiersdorp 172 Bf 33.59 S 19.17 E
Villingen-Schwenningen 120 Eh 48.04N 8.28 E
Villmanstrand/Lappeenranta 112 Ic 61.04N 28.11 E
Villmar 124 Kd 50.23N 8.12 E
Vilnius/Vilnjus 112 Ie 54.41N 25.19 E
Vilnjus/Vilnius 112 Ie 54.41N 25.19 E
Vilok 120 Sh 48.08N 22.50 E
Vilppula 116 Kb 62.01N 24.31 E
Vils [Ger.] 120 Hg 49.10N 11.59 E
Vils [Ger.] 120 Jh 48.35N 13.10 E
Vilsandi 116 If 58.20N 21.45 E
Vilsbiburg 120 Ih 48.27N 12.21 E
Vilshofen 120 Jh 48.38N 13.11 E
Vilusi 130 Bg 42.44N 18.36 E
Vilvoorde/Vilvorde 122 Kd 50.56N 4.26 E
Vilvorde/Vilvoorde 122 Kd 50.56N 4.26 E
Vilyui Range (EN) = Viljujskoje plato 140 Mc 66.00N 108.00 E
Vimeu 124 Dd 50.05N 1.35 E
Vimianzo 126 Ca 43.07N 9.02W
Vimmerby 114 Dh 57.40N 15.51 E
Vimoutiers 122 Gf 48.55N 0.12 E
Vimperk 120 Jg 49.03N 13.47 E
Vimy 124 Ed 50.22N 2.49 E
Vina 166 Id 7.45N 15.36 E
Viña del Mar 200 Ii 33.02 S 71.34W
Vinalhaven Island 184 Mc 44.05N 68.52W
Vinalopó 126 Lf 38.11N 0.36W
Vinaròs / Vinaroz 126 Md 40.28N 0.29 E
Vinaroz / Vinaròs 126 Md 40.28N 0.29 E
Vînători 130 Hc 46.14N 24.56 E
Vincennes 182 Jd 38.41N 87.32W
Vincennes Bay 222 He 66.30 S 109.30 E
Vincente, Puntan- 220b Bb 14.56N 145.40 E
Vinci 128 Eg 43.47N 10.55 E
Vindafjorden 116 Ae 59.20N 5.55 E
Vindelälven 114 Ee 63.54N 19.52 E
Vindeln 114 Ed 64.12N 19.44 E
Vinderup 116 Ch 56.29N 8.47 E
Vindhya Range 140 Jg 24.37N 77.00 E
Vindö 116 He 59.20N 18.40 E
Vineland 184 Jf 39.29N 75.02W
Vingåker 114 Dg 59.02N 15.52 E
Vingeanne 122 Lg 47.21N 5.29 E
Vinh 142 Mh 18.40N 105.40 E
Vinhais 126 Fc 41.50N 7.00W
Vinh Bac Phan=Tonkin, Gulf of- (EN) 140 Mh 20.00N 108.00 E
Vinh Linh 148 Le 17.04N 107.02 E
Vinica [Yugo.] 130 Fh 41.53N 22.30 E
Vinica [Yugo.] 128 Je 45.28N 15.15 E
Vinita 186 Ih 36.39N 95.09W
Vînju Mare 130 Fe 44.25N 22.52 E
Vinkovci 128 Me 45.17N 18.49 E
Vinnica 112 If 49.14N 28.29 E
Vinnickaja oblast [3] 136 Cf 49.00N 28.50 E
Vinniki 132 De 49.48N 24.11 E
Vino, Tierra del- 126 Gc 41.30N 5.30W
Vinogradov 132 Ce 48.09N 23.02 E
Vinslöv 116 Eh 56.06N 13.55 E
Vinson Massif 222 Pf 78.35 S 85.25W
Vinstervåtn 116 Cc 61.20N 9.00 E
Vinstra 114 Bf 61.36N 9.45 E
Vinstra 116 Cc 61.36N 9.45 E
Vintilă Vodă 130 Jd 45.28N 26.43 E
Vintjärn 116 Gd 60.50N 16.03 E
Vinton 186 Ke 42.10N 92.00W
Vintschgau/Venosta, Val- 128 Ed 46.40N 10.35 E
Vipiteno / Sterzing 128 Fd 46.54N 11.26 E
Vipya Plateau 170 Fe 11.09 S 34.00 E
Viqueque 150 Ih 8.52 S 126.22 E
Vir 128 Jf 44.18N 15.03 E
Virac 150 Hd 13.35N 124.15 E
Viramgām 148 Ed 23.07N 72.02 E
Virandozero 114 Id 64.01N 36.03 E
Viranşehir 146 Hd 37.13N 39.45 E
Virbalis 116 Jj 54.37N 22.49 E
Vircava 116 Jh 56.35N 23.43 E
Virden 180 Hg 49.51N 100.55W
Virdois/Virrat 114 Fe 62.14N 23.47 E
Vire 122 Ff 48.50N 0.53W
Vire 122 Ee 49.20N 1.07W
Virei 170 Bf 15.43 S 12.54 E
Vireux-Wallerand 124 Gd 50.05N 4.44 E
Vîrful, Curcubăta- 130 Fc 46.25N 22.35 E
Virgin Gorda 196 Dc 18.30N 64.25W
Virginia [2] 182 Ld 37.30N 78.45W
Virginia [Mn.-U.S.] 182 Ib 47.31N 92.32W
Virginia [S.Afr.] 172 De 28.12 S 26.49 E
Virginia Beach 182 Ld 36.51N 75.59W
Virginia City 188 Fg 39.19N 119.39W
Virgin Islands 174 Mh 18.20N 66.45W
Virgin Islands of the United States [5] 176 Mh 18.20N 64.52W
Virgin Mountains 188 Ih 36.40N 113.50W
Virgin Passage 197a Cb 18.20N 65.10W
Virgin River 188 Hh 36.35N 114.18W
Virihaure 114 Dc 67.22N 16.33 E
Virkby/Virkkala 116 Kd 60.13N 24.01 E
Virkkala/Virkby 116 Kd 60.13N 24.01 E
Virmasvesi 116 Lb 62.50N 26.55 E
Virôchey 148 Lf 13.59N 106.49 E
Viroin 122 Kd 50.05N 4.43 E
Viroinval 124 Gd 50.05N 4.33 E
Viroinval-Nismes 124 Gd 50.05N 4.33 E
Virojoki 114 Gf 60.35N 27.42 E
Viroqua 186 Ke 43.34N 90.53W
Virovitica 128 Le 45.50N 17.23 E
Virpazar 130 Cg 42.15N 19.06 E
Virrat/Virdois 114 Fe 62.14N 23.47 E
Virserum 114 Dh 57.19N 15.35 E
Virsko More 128 If 44.20N 15.00 E
Virton 122 Le 49.34N 5.32 E
Virton-Ethe 124 He 49.35N 5.35 E
Virtsu 114 Fg 58.37N 23.31 E
Virudunagar 148 Fg 9.36N 77.58 E
Virvičja/Virvyčia 116 Jh 56.14N 22.30 E
Virvyčia/Virvičja 116 Jh 56.14N 22.30 E
Vis 128 Kg 43.03N 16.12 E
Vis 128 Kg 43.02N 16.10 E
Visalia 182 Dd 36.20N 119.18W
Visayan Sea 150 Hd 11.35N 123.51 E
Visby 114 Eh 57.38N 18.18 E
Viscount Melville Sound 174 Hb 74.10N 113.00W
Visé/Wezet 124 Hd 50.44N 5.42 E
Višegrad 128 Ng 43.48N 19.17 E
Višegrad 130 Jh 41.59N 26.20 E
Višera [R.S.F.S.R.] 110 Lc 59.55N 56.50 E
Višera [R.S.F.S.R.] 136 Fc 61.57N 52.25 E
Viseu [2] 126 Ed 40.45N 7.50W
Viseu [Braz.] 202 Id 1.12 S 46.07W
Viseu [Port.] 126 Ed 40.39N 7.55W
Vişeu de Sus 130 Hb 47.43N 24.26 E
Vishākhapatnam 142 Kh 17.42N 83.18 E
Visingsö 116 Ff 58.03N 14.20 E
Viskafors 116 Eg 57.38N 12.50 E
Viskan 114 Ch 57.14N 12.12 E
Viški kanal 128 Kg 43.07N 16.17 E
Vislanda 116 Fh 56.47N 14.27 E
Vislinski zaliv 120 Pb 54.27N 19.40 E
Visnes 116 Ae 59.21N 5.14 E
Višnevka 130 Lc 46.22N 28.27 E
Visoki Dečani 130 Dg 42.33N 20.16 E
Visoko 128 Mg 43.59N 18.11 E
Visokoi 222 Ad 56.42 S 27.12W
Visonggo 219d Bb 16.13 S 179.40 E
Visp 128 Bd 46.17N 7.53 E
Vissefjärda 116 Fh 56.32N 15.35 E
Vista 188 Gj 33.12N 117.15W
Visten 116 Ee 59.40N 13.20 E
Vistonias, Órmos- 130 Ii 40.58N 25.05 E
Vistonis, Limni- 130 Ih 41.03N 25.07 E
Vistula (EN)=Wisła 110 He 54.22N 18.55 E
Vištytis 116 Jj 54.27N 22.44 E
Visuvisu Point 219a Cb 7.57 S 157.31 E
Vit 130 Hf 43.41N 24.45 E
Vitebsk 112 Jd 55.12N 30.11 E
Vitebskaja oblast [3] 136 Cd 55.20N 29.00 E
Viterbo 128 Gh 42.25N 12.06 E
Vithkuqi 130 Di 40.31N 20.35 E
Vitichi 202 Eh 20.13 S 65.29W
Vitigudino 126 Fc 41.01N 6.26W
Viti Levu 208 If 18.00 S 178.00 E
Vitim 138 Ge 59.33N 112.28 E
Vitim 140 Nd 59.26N 112.34 E
Vitimski 138 Ge 58.18N 113.18 E
Vitimskoje ploskogorje 138 Gf 54.00N 114.00 E
Vitinja → Cureski prohod 130 Gg 42.47N 23.45 E
Vitjaz Strait 214 Di 5.35 S 147.00 E
Vitolište 130 Eh 41.11N 21.50 E
Vitória 200 Lh 20.19 S 40.21W
Vitoria / Vitoria-Gasteiz 126 Jb 42.51N 2.40W
Vitória da Conquista 200 Lg 14.51 S 40.51W
Vitória de Santo Antão 202 Ke 8.07 S 35.18W
Vitoria-Gasteiz / Vitoria 126 Jb 42.51N 2.40W
Vitorog 128 Lf 44.08N 17.03 E
Vitosa 130 Gg 42.33N 23.15 E
Vitré 122 Ef 48.08N 1.12W
Vitry-en-Artois 124 Ed 50.20N 2.59 E
Vitry-le-François 122 Kf 48.44N 4.35 E
Vitsi 130 Ei 40.39N 21.23 E
Vittangi 114 Ec 67.41N 21.39 E
Vitteaux 122 Kg 47.24N 4.32 E
Vittel 122 Lf 48.12N 5.57 E
Vittinge 116 Ge 59.54N 17.04 E
Vittoria 128 In 36.57N 14.32 E
Vittorio Veneto 128 Ge 45.59N 12.18 E
Vityaz Depth (EN) 106 Je 44.00N 151.00 E
Vityaz I Depth (EN) 106 Ih 11.20N 141.30 E
Vityaz II Depth (EN) 106 Kl 23.27 S 175.00W
Vityaz III Depth (EN) 106 Km 32.00 S 178.00W
Vityaz Seamount (EN) 208 Jc 13.30N 173.15W
Vityaz Trench (EN) 106 Jj 10.00 S 170.00 E
Vivarais, Monts du- 122 Ki 44.55N 4.15 E
Vivarais, Plateaux du- 122 Kj 44.50N 4.45 E
Viver 126 Le 39.55N 0.36W

Index Symbols

- [1] Independent Nation
- [2] State, Region
- [3] District, County
- [4] Municipality
- [5] Colony, Dependency
- Continent
- Physical Region
- Historical or Cultural Region
- Mount, Mountain
- Volcano
- Hill
- Mountains, Mountain Range
- Hills, Escarpment
- Plateau, Upland
- Pass, Gap
- Plain, Lowland
- Delta
- Salt Flat
- Valley, Canyon
- Crater, Cave
- Karst Features
- Depression
- Polder
- Desert, Dunes
- Forest, Woods
- Heath, Steppe
- Oasis
- Cape, Point
- Coast, Beach
- Cliff
- Peninsula
- Isthmus
- Sandbank
- Island
- Atoll
- Rock, Reef
- Islands, Archipelago
- Rocks, Reefs
- Coral Reef
- Well, Spring
- Geyser
- River, Stream
- Waterfall, Rapids
- River Mouth, Estuary
- Lake
- Salt Lake
- Intermittent Lake
- Reservoir
- Swamp, Pond
- Canal
- Glacier
- Ice Shelf, Pack Ice
- Ocean
- Sea
- Gulf, Bay
- Strait, Fjord
- Lagoon
- Bank
- Seamount
- Tablemount
- Ridge
- Shelf
- Basin
- Escarpment, Sea Scarp
- Fracture
- Trench, Abyss
- National Park Reserve
- Point of Interest
- Recreation Site
- Cave, Cavern
- Historic Site
- Ruins
- Wall, Walls
- Church, Abbey
- Temple
- Scientific Station
- Railway station
- Airport
- Port
- Military installation
- Lighthouse
- Mine
- Tunnel
- Dam, Bridge

Vivero 126 Ea 43.40N 7.35W
Viverone, Lago di- 128 Ce 45.25N 8.05 E
Vivi 138 Ed 63.52N 97.50 E
Vivian 186 Jj 32.53N 93.59W
Viviers 122 Kj 44.29N 4.41 E
Vivo 172 Dd 23.03S 29.17 E
Vivoratá 204 Dm 37.40S 57.39W
Vivorillo, Cayos- 194 Ff 15.50N 83.18W
Viwa 219d Ab 17.08S 176.56 E
Vizcaíno, Desierto de- 190 Bc 27.40N 114.40W
Vizcaíno, Sierra- 192 Bd 27.20N 114.00W
Vizcaya / Bizkaia 126 Ja 43.15N 2.55W
Vizcaya, Golfo de- 110 Fg 44.00N 4.00W
Vizcaya, Golfo de- = Biscay, Bay of- (EN) 110 Fg 43.50N 2.30W
Vize 130 Kh 41.34N 27.45 E
Vize, ostrov- 140 Jb 79.30N 77.00 E
Vizianagaram 148 Ge 18.07N 83.25 E
Vizille 122 Li 45.05N 5.46 E
Vizinga 136 Fc 61.05N 50.10 E
Viziru 130 Kd 45.00N 27.42 E
Vižnica 132 De 48.14N 25.12 E
Vizzini 128 Im 37.10N 14.45 E
Vjaike-Maarja/Väike-Maarja 116 Le 59.04N 26.12 E
Vjajke-Pakri/Väike-Pakri 116 Je 59.50N 23.50 E
Vjajke-Vjajn / Väike Väin 116 Jf 58.30N 23.10 E
Vjalje, ozero- 116 Ne 59.00N 30.20 E
Vjalozero, ozero- 114 Ic 66.50N 35.10 E
Vjandra/Vändra 114 Fg 58.40N 25.01 E
Vjartsilja 114 He 62.10N 30.48 E
Vjatka 110 Ld 55.36N 51.30 E
Vjatskije Poljany 136 Fd 56.14N 51.04 E
Vjatski uval 114 Lg 58.00N 49.45 E
Vjazemski 138 Ig 47.31N 134.45 E
Vjazma 112 Jd 55.13N 34.18 E
Vjazniki 114 Kh 56.15N 42.12 E
Vjeio, Río- 194 Dg 12.17N 86.54W
Vjosa 130 Ci 40.37N 19.20 E
Vlaamse Banken 124 Ec 51.15N 2.30 E
Vlaamse Vlakte = Flanders Plain (EN) 122 Id 50.40N 2.50 E
Vlaanderen/Flandres= Flanders (EN) 122 Jc 51.00N 3.20 E
Vlaardingen 122 Kc 51.54N 4.21 E
Vlădeasa, Vîrful- 130 Fc 46.45N 22.48 E
Vlădeni 130 Kb 47.25N 27.20 E
Vladičin Han 130 Fg 42.43N 22.04 E
Vladikavkaz = Ordžonikidze [R.S.F.S.R.] 112 Kg 43.03N 44.40 E
Vladimir 112 Kd 56.10N 40.25 E
Vladimirskaja oblast 136 Ed 56.00N 40.40 E
Vladimirski Tupik 132 Hb 55.42N 33.18 E
Vladimir-Volynski 136 Ce 50.51N 24.22 E
Vladivostok 142 Pe 43.10N 131.56 E
Vlad Ţepeş 130 Ke 44.21N 27.05 E
Vlagtwedde 124 Ja 53.02N 7.08 E
Vlagtwedde-Ter Apel 124 Jb 52.52N 7.06 E
Vlahina 130 Fh 41.54N 22.52 E
Vlăhiţa 130 Ic 46.21N 25.31 E
Vlasenika 128 Mf 44.11N 18.57 E
Vlašić 128 Lf 44.19N 17.40 E
Vlašic 130 Ce 44.27N 19.35 E
Vlašim 120 Kg 49.42N 14.54 E
Vlasotince 130 Fg 42.58N 22.08 E
Vlasovo 138 Ib 70.40N 134.35 E
Vlieland 124 Ha 53.17N 5.06 E
Vlieland 122 Ka 53.15N 5.00 E
Vlieland-Oost Vlieland 124 Ha 53.17N 5.06 E
Vliestroom 124 Ha 53.17N 5.10 E
Vlissingen 122 Jc 51.26N 3.35 E
Vlissingen-Oost-Souburg 124 Fc 51.28N 3.36 E
Vloesberg/Flobecq 124 Fd 50.44N 3.44 E
Vlorë 112 Hg 40.27N 19.30 E
Vlorës, Gjiri i- 130 Ci 40.25N 19.25 E
Vlotho 124 Kb 52.10N 8.51 E
Vltava=Moldau (EN) 110 He 50.21N 14.30 E
Vöcklabruck 128 Hb 48.01N 13.39 E
Vodice 128 Jg 43.46N 15.47 E
Vodla 114 If 61.49N 36.00 E
Vodlozero, ozero- 114 Ie 62.20N 37.00 E
Vodňany 120 Kg 49.09N 14.11 E
Vodnjan 128 Hf 44.57N 13.51 E
Vodny 134 Fe 63.32N 53.20 E
Voerde (Niederrhein) 120 Ce 51.35N 6.41 E
Voeren/Fouron 124 Hd 50.45N 5.48 E
Vôge, La- 122 Mf 48.05N 6.05 E
Vogel Peak 166 Hd 8.24N 11.47 E
Vogelsberg 120 Ff 50.30N 9.15 E
Voghera 128 Df 44.59N 9.01 E
Vogtland 120 If 50.30N 12.05 E
Voh 219b Be 20.58S 164.42 E
Võhandu jõgi / Vyhandu 116 Lf 58.03N 27.40 E
Vohémar 172 Ib 13.22S 50.00 E
Vohipeno 172 Hd 22.20S 47.52 E
Vöhl 124 Kc 51.12N 8.56 E
Vohma 136 Ed 58.58N 46.45 E
Vohma 114 Lg 58.45N 46.36 E
Voi 160 Ki 3.23S 38.34 E
Voikoski 116 Lc 61.16N 26.48 E
Voinjama 160 Gh 8.25N 9.45W
Vóion Óros 130 Ei 40.15N 21.03 E
Voire 122 Kf 48.27N 4.25 E
Voiron 122 Li 45.22N 5.35 E
Voitsberg 128 Jc 47.02N 15.09 E
Voïviis, Límni- 130 Fj 39.32N 22.45 E
Vojens 116 Ci 55.15N 9.19 E
Vojkar 134 Ld 65.38N 64.40 E
Vojmsjön 114 Dd 65.00N 16.24 E
Vojnić 128 Je 45.19N 15.42 E
Vojnilov 120 Ug 49.04N 24.33 E
Vojvodina 130 Cd 45.00N 20.00 E
Voj-Vož 136 Fc 62.56N 54.59 E
Voknavolok 114 Hd 64.57N 30.31 E
Vokré, Hoséré- 158 Ih 8.21N 13.15 E
Volary 120 Jh 48.55N 13.54 E
Volcán 194 Fi 8.46N 82.38W
Volcánica, Cordillera- 174 Ih 18.00N 101.00W
Volcano 221a Fd 19.26N 155.20W
Volcano Islands (EN)=Iō/ Kazan-Rettō 140 Qg 25.00N 141.00 E
Volcano Islands (EN)= Kazan-Rettō/Iō 140 Qg 25.00N 141.00 E
Volčansk [R.S.F.S.R.] 134 Jg 59.59N 60.04 E
Volčansk [Ukr.-U.S.S.R.] 132 Jd 50.16N 37.01 E
Volčiha 138 Df 52.02N 80.23 E
Volda 114 Be 62.09N 6.06 E
Voldafjorden 116 Ab 62.10N 6.00 E
Volga 114 Jh 57.57N 38.25 E
Volga 110 Kf 45.55N 47.52 E
Volga-Baltic Canal (EN)= Volgo-Baltijski vodny put imeni V. I. Lenina 110 Jd 59.58N 37.10 E
Volga Delta (EN) 110 Kf 46.30N 47.00 E
Volga Hills (EN) = Privolžkaja vozvyšennost 110 Ke 52.00N 46.00 E
Volgo-Baltijski vodny put imeni V.I. Lenina=Volga-Baltic Canal (EN) 110 Jd 59.58N 37.10 E
Volgodonsk 136 Ef 47.33N 42.08 E
Volgo-Donskoj sudohodny kanal imeni V. I. Lenina= Lenin Canal (EN) 110 Kf 48.40N 43.37 E
Volgograd (Stalingrad) 112 Kf 48.44N 44.25 E
Volgograd Reservoir (EN) = Volgogradskoje vodohranilišče 110 Kf 49.20N 45.00 E
Volgogradskaja oblast 136 Ef 49.30N 44.30 E
Volgogradskoje vodohranilišče = Volgograd Reservoir (EN) 110 Kf 49.20N 45.00 E
Volhov 112 Jd 59.55N 32.20 E
Volhov 110 Jc 60.08N 32.20 E
Volhynia 110 Ie 51.00N 25.00 E
Volhynia (EN) 120 Uf 51.00N 25.00 E
Volissós 130 Ik 38.29N 25.55 E
Volja 134 Je 63.11N 61.16 E
Volka 120 Vd 52.43N 25.43 E
Völkermarkt 128 Id 46.39N 14.38 E
Völklingen 120 Cg 49.15N 6.51 E
Volkmarsen 124 Lc 51.24N 9.07 E
Volkovysk 132 Dc 53.10N 24.31 E
Volkovysskaja vozvyšennost 120 Uc 53.10N 24.30 E
Volksrust 172 De 27.24S 29.53 E
Vollenhove 124 Hb 52.40N 5.57 E
Vollsjö 116 Ei 55.42N 13.46 E
Volme 124 Jc 51.24N 7.27 E
Volmunster 124 Je 49.07N 7.21 E
Volna, gora- 138 Kd 63.30N 154.57 E
Volnjansk 132 If 47.54N 35.29 E
Volnovaha 132 Jf 47.37N 37.36 E
Voločajevka 2-ja 138 Ig 48.36N 134.36 E
Voločisk 132 Ee 49.31N 26.13 E
Volodarsk 114 Kh 56.14N 43.13 E
Volodarski 132 Pf 46.26N 48.31 E
Volodarskoje 136 Ge 53.18N 68.08 E
Vologda 112 Jd 59.12N 39.55 E
Vologodskaja oblast 136 Ed 60.00N 41.00 E
Volokolamsk 114 Ih 56.03N 35.58 E
Volokonovka 132 Jd 50.29N 37.52 E
Vólos 112 Ih 39.22N 22.57 E
Vološka 114 Jf 61.21N 40.03 E
Vološka 114 Jf 61.42N 39.15 E
Volosovo 114 Gg 59.28N 29.31 E
Volovec 120 Th 48.42N 23.17 E
Volovo 132 Kc 53.35N 38.01 E
Vol0žin 132 Eb 54.06N 26.32 E
Volquart Boons Kyst 179 Jd 70.20N 24.20W
Volsini, Monti- 128 Fh 42.40N 11.55 E
Volsk 136 Ee 52.02N 47.23 E
Volta 166 Fd 7.00N 0.30 E
Volta 158 Hh 5.46N 0.41 E
Volta, Lake- 158 Hh 7.30N 0.15 E
Volta Blanche=White Volta (EN) 158 Gh 8.38N 0.59W
Volta Noire=Black Volta (EN) 166 Ec 12.30N 4.00W
Volta Noire=Black Volta (EN) 158 Gh 8.38N 1.30W
Volta Redonda 200 Lh 22.32S 44.07W
Volta Rouge=Red Volta (EN) 158 Gh 10.34N 0.30W
Volterra 128 Eg 43.24N 10.51 E
Volţoya 126 Hc 41.13N 4.31W
Voltri, Genova- 128 Cf 44.26N 8.45 E
Volturino 128 Jj 40.25N 15.48 E
Volturno 128 Hi 41.01N 13.55 E
Volubilis 162 Fc 34.04N 5.33W
Vólvi, Límni- 130 Gi 40.41N 23.28 E
Volynskaja grjada 120 Ue 51.05N 25.00 E
Volynskaja oblast 136 Ce 51.10N 25.00 E
Volynskaja vozvyšennost 132 Dd 50.30N 25.00 E
Volžsk 136 Ed 55.55N 48.19 E
Volžski [R.S.F.S.R.] 112 Kf 48.48N 44.44 E
Volžski [R.S.F.S.R.] 114 Mj 53.28N 50.08 E
Voma 219d Bc 18.00S 178.08 E
Vomano 128 Ih 42.39N 14.02 E
Vonavona 219a Cc 8.12S 157.05 E
Vondrozo 172 Hd 22.47S 47.17 E
Von Frank Mountain 178 Id 63.33N 154.20W
Vónitsa 130 Dk 38.55N 20.53 E
Vonne 122 Gh 46.25N 0.15 E
Võnnu/Vynnu 116 Lf 58.15N 27.10 E
Voorne 124 Gc 51.52N 4.05 E
Voorschoten 124 Gb 52.08N 4.28 E
Voorst 124 Ib 52.10N 6.09 E
Voorst-Twello 124 Ib 52.14N 6.07 E
Vop 132 Hb 54.56N 32.44 E
Vopnafjörður 114a Cb 65.45N 14.50W
Vora 130 Ch 41.23N 19.40 E
Vörå/Vöyri 116 Ja 63.09N 22.15 E
Vorarlberg 128 Dc 47.15N 9.50 E
Vóras Óros 130 Ei 41.00N 21.50 E
Vorau 128 Jc 47.24N 15.53 E
Vorden 124 Ib 52.06N 6.20 E
Vorderrhein 128 Dd 46.49N 9.26 E
Vordingborg 114 Ci 55.01N 11.55 E
Voreifel 124 Jd 50.10N 7.00 E
Vorga Šor 134 Kc 67.35N 63.40 E
Voria Píndhos 130 Dj 40.20N 20.55 E
Vórioi Sporádhes, Nísoi-= Northern Sporades (EN) 110 Ih 39.15N 23.55 E
Vórios Evvoïkós Kólpos= Évvoia, Gulf of- (EN) 130 Gk 38.45N 23.10 E
Vorkuta 112 Mb 67.27N 63.58 E
Vorma 114 Cf 60.09N 11.27 E
Vormsi 116 Je 59.02N 23.05 E
Vormsi 114 Fg 59.00N 23.15 E
Vorniceni 130 Jb 47.59N 26.40 E
Vorogovo 138 Dd 60.58N 89.28 E
Vorona 132 Md 51.22N 42.03 E
Voroncovo [R.S.F.S.R.] 138 Db 71.40N 83.40 E
Voroncovo [R.S.F.S.R.] 116 Mg 57.15N 28.49 E
Voronež 112 Je 51.40N 39.10 E
Voronež 132 Kd 51.31N 39.05 E
Voronežskaja oblast 136 Ee 51.00N 40.15 E
Voronin Trough (EN) 224 Ge 80.00N 85.00 E
Voronja 114 Ib 69.09N 35.47 E
Voronovo 116 Kj 54.09N 25.19 E
Voropajevo 116 Li 55.07N 27.19 E
Vorošilograd → Lugansk 112 Jf 48.34N 39.20 E
Vorošilovgradskaja oblast 136 Df 49.00N 39.10 E
Vorotan 132 Oj 39.15N 46.43 E
Vorotynec 114 Kh 56.02N 45.52 E
Vorožba 132 Id 51.10N 34.11 E
Vorskla 132 Ie 48.52N 34.05 E
Vorsma 114 Ki 55.58N 43.17 E
Võrts järv / Vyrtsjarv, ozero- 114 Gg 58.15N 26.05 E
Võru/Vyru 136 Cd 57.52N 27.05 E
Voruh 135 He 39.52N 70.35 E
Vosges 122 Mf 48.10N 6.20 E
Vosges 110 Gf 48.30N 7.10 E
Voskresensk 114 Ji 55.22N 38.42 E
Voskresenskoje 114 Kh 56.51N 45.27 E
Voss 116 Bd 60.40N 6.30 E
Vossa 116 Ad 60.39N 5.42 E
Vossevangen 114 Bf 60.39N 6.26 E
Vostočno-Kazahstanskaja oblast 136 If 49.00N 84.00 E
Vostočno-Kounradski 136 Hf 46.58N 75.07 E
Vostočno Sibirskoje more = East Siberian Sea (EN) 224 Cd 74.00N 166.00 E
Vostočny [R.S.F.S.R.] 134 Jg 58.48N 61.52 E
Vostočny [R.S.F.S.R.] 138 Jg 48.19N 142.40 E
Vostočny, hrebet- 138 Lf 55.00N 160.30 E
Vostočny Sajan=Eastern Sayans (EN) 140 Ld 53.00N 97.00 E
Vostok 222 Hf 78.28S 106.48 E
Vostok Island 208 Lf 10.06S 152.23W
Vostrecovo 138 Ig 45.56N 134.59 E
Võsu/Vyzu 116 Ke 59.30N 25.50 E
Votkinsk 136 Fd 57.05N 53.59 E
Votkinskoje vodohranilišče = Votkinsk Reservoir (EN) 110 Ld 57.30N 55.10 E
Votkinsk Reservoir (EN) = Votkinskoje vodohranilišče 110 Ld 57.30N 55.10 E
Votuporanga 204 He 20.24S 49.59W
Vouga 126 Dd 40.41N 8.40W
Vouillé 122 Gh 46.38N 0.10 E
Voulgára 130 Ej 39.06N 21.54 E
Vouliagméni 130 Gl 37.49N 23.47 E
Voulte-sur-Rhône, La- 122 Kj 44.48N 4.47 E
Voúrinos Óros 130 Ei 40.11N 21.40 E
Voúxa, Ákra- 130 Gn 35.38N 23.36 E
Vouziers 122 Ke 49.24N 4.42 E
Voves 122 Hf 48.16N 1.38 E
Vovodo 168 Cd 5.40N 24.21 E
Voxna 116 Fc 61.21N 15.34 E
Voxnan 116 Gc 61.17N 16.26 E
Voyeykov Ice Shelf 222 Ie 66.20S 124.38 E
Vöyri/Vörå 116 Ja 63.09N 22.15 E
Vože, ozero- 114 Jf 60.35N 39.05 E
Vožega 114 Jf 60.30N 40.12 E
Vožega 114 Jf 60.33N 39.13 E
Voznesenje 114 If 61.01N 35.27 E
Voznesensk 136 Df 47.35N 31.20 E
Vozroždenija, ostrov- 135 Bb 45.05N 59.15 E
Vraca 130 Gf 43.12N 23.33 E
Vraca 130 Gf 43.12N 23.33 E
Vraca 130 Dh 41.54N 20.45 E
Vradijevka 132 Gf 47.51N 30.34 E
Vrakhiónas 130 Dl 37.48N 20.45 E
Vran 128 Lg 43.39N 17.27 E
Vrancea 130 Jd 45.50N 26.42 E
Vranica 128 Lg 43.57N 17.44 E
Vranje 130 Eg 42.33N 21.54 E
Vranov nad Topľou 120 Rh 48.54N 21.41 E
Vrăška čuka, prohod- 130 Ff 43.50N 22.23 E
Vratnica 130 Eg 42.08N 21.07 E
Vratnik, prohod- 130 Jg 42.49N 26.10 E
Vrbas 130 Cd 45.34N 19.39 E
Vrbas 128 Le 45.07N 17.31 E
Vrbno pod Pradědem 120 Nf 50.08N 17.23 E
Vrbovsko 128 Je 45.22N 15.05 E
Vrchlabí 120 Lf 50.38N 15.37 E
Vrede 172 De 27.30S 29.06 E
Vreden 124 Ib 52.02N 6.50 E
Vredenburg 172 Bf 32.54S 17.59 E
Vredendal 172 Bf 31.41S 18.35 E
Vresse, Vresse-sur-Semois- 124 Ge 49.52N 4.56 E
Vresse-sur-Semois 124 Ge 49.52N 4.56 E
Vresse-sur-Semois-Vresse 124 Ge 49.52N 4.56 E
Vretstorp 116 Fe 59.02N 14.52 E
Vrhnika 128 Ie 45.58N 14.18 E
Vries 124 Ia 53.05N 6.36 E
Vriezenveen 124 Ib 52.26N 6.36 E
Vrigstad 116 Fg 57.21N 14.28 E
Vron 124 Dd 50.19N 1.45 E
Vršac 130 Ed 45.07N 21.18 E
Vryburg 160 Jk 26.55S 24.45 E
Vryheid 172 Ee 27.52S 30.38 E
Vsetín 120 Ng 49.21N 18.00 E
Vsevidof, Mount- 178a Eb 53.07N 168.43W
Vsevoložsk 114 Hf 60.04N 30.41 E
Vstrečny 138 Lc 68.00N 165.58 E
Vtačnik 120 Oh 48.42N 18.37 E
Vuanggava 219d Cc 18.52S 178.54W
Vučitrn 130 Dg 42.49N 20.58 E
Vučjak 130 Fh 41.28N 22.20 E
Vuka 128 Me 45.21N 19.00 E
Vukovar 128 Me 45.21N 19.00 E
Vuktyl 136 Fc 63.50N 57.25 E
Vulavu 219a Dc 8.31S 159.48 E
Vulcan 130 Gd 45.23N 23.16 E
Vulcan, Vîrful- 130 Fc 46.14N 22.58 E
Vulcano 128 Il 38.25N 15.00 E
Vulkanešty 132 Fg 45.38N 28.27 E
Vulture 128 Jj 40.57N 15.38 E
Vung Tau 148 Lf 10.21N 107.04 E
Vunindawa 219d Bb 17.49S 178.19 E
Vunisea Station 216 Ec 19.03S 178.09 E
Vuohijarvi 116 Lc 61.10N 26.40 E
Vuoksa 116 Nd 60.35N 30.42 E
Vuoksa, ozero- [R.S.F.S.R.] 116 Mc 61.00N 30.00 E
Vuoksa, ozero- [R.S.F.S.R.] 116 Md 60.38N 29.55 E
Vuollerim 114 Ec 66.25N 20.36 E
Vuosjärvi 116 Ka 63.00N 25.30 E
Vuotso 114 Gb 68.06N 27.08 E
Vuranimala 219a Ec 9.05S 160.51 E
Vyborg 112 Ic 60.42N 28.45 E
Vyčegda 110 Kc 61.18N 46.36 E
Vyčegodski 114 Lf 61.17N 46.48 E
Vychodočeský kraj 120 Lf 50.10N 16.00 E
Východoslovenska nižina 120 Rh 48.35N 21.50 E
Východoslovenský kraj 120 Rg 49.00N 21.15 E
Vyg 114 Ie 63.17N 35.17 E
Vygoda [Ukr.-U.S.S.R.] 130 Nc 46.38N 30.24 E
Vygoda [Ukr.-U.S.S.R.] 120 Uh 48.52N 24.01 E
Vygozero, ozero- 110 Jc 63.35N 34.45 E
Vyhandu / Võhandu jõgi 116 Lf 58.03N 27.40 E
Vyja 114 Le 62.57N 46.42 E
Vyksa 136 Ed 55.20N 42.12 E
Vym 136 Fc 62.13N 50.25 E
Vynnu/Võnnu 116 Lf 58.15N 27.10 E
Vyrica 136 Dd 59.24N 30.19 E
Vyrnwy 118 Ki 52.45N 2.50W
Vyrtsjarv, ozero- / Võrts järv 114 Gg 58.15N 26.05 E
Vyru/Võru 136 Cd 57.52N 27.05 E
Vyša 132 Mb 54.03N 42.06 E
Vyšgorod 132 Gd 50.38N 30.29 E
Vyšgorodok 116 Mh 56.55N 28.05 E
Vyškov 120 Mg 49.17N 17.00 E
Vyškovski, pereval- 120 Th 48.38N 23.45 E
Vyšni Voloček 136 Dd 57.37N 34.32 E
Vysock 114 Gf 60.36N 28.36 E
Vysohé Tatry = Hight Tatra (EN) 120 Pg 49.10N 20.00 E
Vysokogorny 138 If 50.07N 139.10 E
Vysokogorsk 154 Mb 44.23N 135.23 E
Vysokoje 132 Cc 52.22N 23.26 E
Vysokovsk 114 Ih 56.21N 36.29 E
Vyšší Brod 120 Kh 48.37N 14.18 E
Vytebet 132 Ic 53.53N 35.38 E
Vytegra 136 Dc 61.01N 36.28 E
Vyvenka 138 Ld 60.10N 165.20 E
Vyzu/Võsu 116 Ke 59.30N 25.50 E
Vzmorje 138 Jg 47.45N 142.30 E

W

Wa 166 Ec 10.03N 2.29W
Waal 122 Kc 51.55N 4.30 E
Waalre 124 Hc 51.23N 5.27 E
Waalwijk 124 Hc 51.41N 5.04 E
Waar, Meos- 150 Jg 2.05S 134.23 E
Waardgronden 124 Ha 53.12N 5.05 E
Waarschoot 124 Fc 51.09N 3.36 E
Wabana 180 Mg 47.38N 52.57W
Wabao, Cap- 219b Ce 21.36S 167.51 E
Wabasca 180 Ge 56.00N 113.53W
Wabasca 180 Fe 58.21N 115.20W
Wabash 184 Ee 40.48N 85.49W
Wabash 174 Kf 37.46N 88.02W
Wabasha 186 Jd 44.23N 92.02W
Wabash River 186 Lh 37.46N 88.02W
Wabowden 180 Hf 54.55N 98.38W
Wąbrzeźno 120 Oc 53.17N 18.57 E
Wabu Hu 152 Ke 32.20N 116.55 E
Wachau 128 Jb 48.20N 15.25 E
Wachile 168 Fe 4.33N 39.03 E
Wachusett Seamount (EN) 208 Lh 32.00S 151.20W
Waco 176 Jf 31.55N 97.08W
Waconda Lake 186 Gg 39.30N 98.30W
Wadayama 156 Dd 35.20N 134.51 E
Wad Bandah 168 Dc 13.06N 27.57 E
Waddān 164 Cd 29.10N 16.08 E
Waddān, Jabal- 164 Cd 29.20N 16.20 E
Waddeneilanden/Friesische Inseln = Frisian Islands (EN) 110 Hc 54.00N 6.00 E
Waddeneilanden = West Frisian Islands (EN) 122 Ka 53.30N 5.00 E
Waddenzee 124 Ha 53.20N 5.30 E
Waddington, Mount- 174 Gd 51.23N 125.15W
Wadena 186 Ic 46.26N 95.08W
Wadern 124 Ie 49.32N 6.53 E
Wadern-Nunkirchen 124 Ie 49.32N 6.53 E
Wadersloh 124 Kc 51.44N 8.15 E
Wadersloh-Liesborn 124 Kc 51.43N 8.16 E
Wadesboro 184 Gh 34.58N 80.04W
Wadhams 188 Ba 51.30N 127.31W
Wādī Bīshah 144 Fe 21.24N 43.26 E
Wādī Fajr 144 Ec 30.17N 38.18 E
Wādī Ḩalfā' 160 Kf 21.56N 31.20 E
Wādī Jimāl, Jazīrat- 146 Fj 24.40N 35.10 E
Wādī Mūsá 146 Fg 30.19N 35.29 E
Wādī Shiḩan 168 Ib 18.10N 52.57 E
Wad Madanī 160 Kg 14.24N 33.32 E
Wad Nimr 168 Ec 14.32N 32.08 E
Wadowice 120 Pg 49.53N 19.30 E
Wadsworth 188 Fg 39.38N 119.17W
Wafangdian → Fuxian 152 Ld 39.38N 121.59 E
Wafrah 144 Gd 28.25N 47.56 E
Waga-Gawa 156 Gb 39.18N 141.07 E
Wagenfeld 124 Kb 52.33N 8.35 E
Wagenfeld-Ströhen 124 Kb 52.32N 8.39 E
Wageningen 124 Hc 51.57N 5.41 E
Wagēr, Qar- 168 Hc 10.01N 45.30 E
Wager Bay 174 Kc 65.26N 88.40W
Wagga Wagga 210 Fh 35.07S 147.22 E
Waghäusel 124 Ke 49.15N 8.30 E
Wagin 210 Ch 33.18S 117.21 E
Waginger See 120 Ii 47.58N 12.50 E
Wagoner 186 Ii 35.58N 95.22W
Wagon Mound 186 Dh 36.01N 104.42W
Wagontire Mountain 188 Fe 43.21N 119.53W
Wagrien 120 Gb 54.15N 10.45 E
Wągrowiec 120 Nd 52.49N 17.11 E
Wah 148 Eb 33.48N 72.42 E
Waha 160 If 28.10N 19.57 E
Wahai 150 Ig 2.48S 129.30 E
Wahiawa 214 Oc 21.30N 158.02W
Wahoo 186 Hf 41.13N 96.37W
Wahpeton 182 Hb 46.16N 96.36W
Waialeale, Mount- 221a Ba 22.04N 159.30W
Waialua 221a Cb 21.35N 158.08W
Waianae 221a Cb 21.27N 158.12W
Waiau 216 Dh 42.39S 173.03 E
Waiau 218 Ee 42.47S 173.22 E
Waiblingen 120 Fh 48.50N 9.18 E
Waibstadt 124 Ke 49.18N 8.56 E
Waidhofen/Ybbs 128 Ic 47.58N 14.46 E
Waidhofen an der Thaya 128 Jb 48.49N 15.17 E
Waigame 150 Ig 1.50S 129.49 E
Waigeo, Pulau- 208 Ee 0.14S 130.45 E
Waihi 218 Fb 37.24S 175.50 E
Waihou 218 Fb 37.10S 175.33 E
Waikabubak 150 Gh 9.38S 119.25 E
Waikare, Lake- 218 Fb 37.25S 175.10 E
Waikaremoana, Lake- 216 Eg 38.45S 177.05 E
Waikato 218 Fb 37.23S 174.43 E
Waikawa 218 Cg 46.38S 169.08 E
Waikouaiti 218 Df 45.36S 170.41 E
Wailangilala 219d Cb 16.45S 179.06W
Wailua 221a Ba 22.03N 159.20W
Wailuku 214 Oc 20.53N 156.30W
Waimamaku 218 Ea 35.34S 173.29 E
Waimanalo Beach 221a Db 21.20N 157.42W
Waimangaroa 218 Dd 41.43S 171.46 E
Waimate 218 Df 44.45S 171.03 E
Waimea [Hi.-U.S.] 221a Fc 20.02N 155.40W
Waimea [Hi.-U.S.] 221a Bb 21.57N 159.40W
Waimes 124 Id 50.25N 6.07 E
Wainfleet All Saints 124 Ca 53.06N 0.15 E
Wainganga 140 Jh 19.36N 79.48 E
Waingapu 150 Hh 9.39S 120.16 E
Waini Point 196 Gh 8.24N 59.49W
Waini River 196 Gh 8.24N 59.51W
Wainwright [Ak.-U.S.] 178 Gb 70.38N 160.01W
Wainwright [Alta.-Can.] 180 Gf 52.49N 110.52W
Waiouru 216 Eg 39.29S 175.40 E
Waipahu 221a Cb 21.23N 158.01W
Waipara 218 Ee 43.03S 172.45 E
Waipawa 218 Gc 39.56S 176.35 E
Waipiro 218 Hc 38.02S 178.20 E
Waipu 218 Fa 35.59S 174.26 E
Waipukurau 218 Gd 40.00S 176.33 E
Wairakei 218 Gc 38.37S 176.05 E
Wairarapa, Lake- 218 Fd 41.15S 175.15 E
Wairau 218 Fd 41.31S 174.03 E
Wairoa 216 Eg 39.03S 177.26 E
Wairoa 218 Fb 36.11S 174.02 E
Waitaki 218 Df 44.56S 171.09 E
Waitangi 216 Fh 43.56S 176.34W
Waitara 216 Dg 39.00S 174.14 E
Waitati 218 Df 45.45S 170.34 E
Waitemata 218 Fb 36.50S 174.40 E
Waitotara 218 Fc 39.48S 174.44 E
Waiuku 218 Fb 37.15S 174.44 E
Waiwerang 150 Hh 8.23S 123.09 E
Waiyevo 216 Fc 16.48S 179.59W
Wājid 168 Ge 3.50N 43.14 E
Wajima 154 Nf 37.24N 136.54 E
Wajir 160 Ih 1.42N 40.04 E
Waka [Eth.] 168 Fd 7.09N 37.19 E
Waka [Zaire] 170 Db 1.01N 20.13 E
Wakamatsu-Shima 156 Ae 32.54N 129.00 E
Wakasa-Wan 152 Od 35.45N 135.40 E
Wakatipu, Lake- 216 Ci 45.05S 168.35 E
Wakaya 219d Bb 17.37S 179.00 E
Wakayama 142 Pf 34.13N 135.11 E
Wakayama Ken 154 Mh 33.55N 135.20 E
Wake 156 Dd 34.48N 134.08 E
Wa Keeney 186 Gg 39.01N 99.53W
Wakefield [Eng.-U.K.] 118 Lh 53.42N 1.29W
Wakefield [N.Z.] 218 Ed 41.24S 173.03 E
Wake Island 210 Hc 19.18N 166.36 E
Wake Island 208 Hc 19.18N 166.36 E
Wakkanai 142 Qe 45.25N 141.40 E
Waku Kungo 170 Ce 11.25S 15.07 E
Wakunai 219a Ba 5.52S 155.13 E
Wakuya 156 Gb 38.33N 141.05 E
Wala 170 Fd 5.46S 32.04 E
Walachia (EN) = Valahia 110 Ig 44.00N 25.00 E
Walachia (EN) = Valahia 130 He 44.00N 25.00 E

Index Symbols

1 Independent Nation
2 State, Region
3 District, County
4 Municipality
5 Colony, Dependency
Continent
Physical Region

Historical or Cultural Region
Mount, Mountain
Volcano
Hill
Mountains, Mountain Range
Hills, Escarpment
Plateau, Upland

Pass, Gap
Plain, Lowland
Delta
Salt Flat
Valley, Canyon
Crater, Cave
Karst Features

Depression
Polder
Desert, Dunes
Forest, Woods
Heath, Steppe
Oasis
Cape, Point

Coast, Beach
Cliff
Peninsula
Isthmus
Sandbank
Island
Atoll

Rock, Reef
Islands, Archipelago
Rocks, Reefs
Coral Reef
Well, Spring
Geyser
River, Stream

Waterfall, Rapids
River Mouth, Estuary
Lake
Salt Lake
Intermittent Lake
Reservoir
Swamp, Pond

Canal
Glacier
Ice Shelf, Pack Ice
Ocean
Sea
Gulf, Bay
Strait, Fjord

Lagoon
Bank
Seamount
Tablemount
Ridge
Shelf
Basin

Escarpment, Sea Scarp
Fracture
Trench, Abyss
National Park, Reserve
Point of Interest
Recreation Site
Cave, Cavern

Historic Site
Ruins
Wall, Walls
Church, Abbey
Temple
Scientific Station
Railway station

Airport
Port
Military installation
Lighthouse
Mine
Tunnel
Dam, Bridge

Wałbrzych 112 He 50.46N 16.17 E
Wałbrzych [2] 120 Mf 50.45N 16.15 E
Walchensee 120 Hi 47.35N 11.20 E
Walcheren 122 Jc 51.33N 3.35 E
Walcott, Lake- 188 Ie 42.40N 113.23W
Walcourt 124 Gd 50.15N 4.25 E
Walcourt-Fraire 124 Gd 50.16N 4.30 E
Wałcz 120 Mc 53.17N 16.28 E
Waldböckelheim 124 Je 49.49N 7.43 E
Waldbröl 120 Df 50.53N 7.37 E
Waldeck 124 Lc 51.12N 9.05 E
Waldeck 124 Kc 51.17N 8.50 E
Waldems 124 Kd 50.15N 8.18 E
Walden 186 Cf 40.44N 106.17W
Waldfischbach-Burgalben 124 Je 49.17N 7.40 E
Waldkirchen 120 Jh 48.44N 13.36 E
Waldkraiburg 120 Ih 48.12N 12.25 E
Wald-Michelbach 124 Ke 49.34N 8.49 E
Waldnaab 120 Ig 49.35N 12.07 E
Waldorf 184 If 38.37N 76.54W
Waldrach 124 Ie 49.45N 6.45 E
Waldron 186 Ii 34.54N 94.05W
Waldshut-Tiengen 120 Ei 47.37N 8.13 E
Waldviertel 128 Jb 48.30N 15.30 E
Waleabahi, Pulau- 150 Hg 0.15S 122.20 E
Walej, Sha'īb al- 146 Hf 33.30N 39.15 E
Wales 178 Fc 65.36N 168.05W
Wales [2] 118 Ji 52.30N 3.30W
Wales 110 Fe 52.30N 3.30W
Wales 180 Ic 67.50N 86.40W
Walewale 166 Ec 10.21N 0.48W
Walferdange 124 Ie 49.39N 6.08 E
Walgett 210 Fh 30.01S 148.07 E
Walgreen Coast 222 Of 75.15S 105.00W
Walhalla 186 Hb 48.55N 97.55W
Walikale 170 Ec 1.25S 28.03 E
Walker 186 Ic 47.06N 94.35W
Walker Lake 182 Dd 38.40N 118.43W
Walkerston 212 Jd 21.10S 149.10 E
Wall 186 Ed 44.01N 102.14W
Wallace 188 Hc 47.28N 115.56W
Wallaceburg 184 Fd 42.36N 82.23W
Wallangarra 212 Ke 28.56S 151.56 E
Wallaroo 212 Hf 33.56S 137.38 E
Wallary Island 212 Ic 15.05S 141.50 E
Wallasey 118 Jh 53.26N 3.03W
Walla Walla 182 Db 46.08N 118.20W
Walldorf 124 Ke 49.20N 8.39 E
Wallenhorst 124 Kb 52.21N 8.01 E
Wallibu 197n Ba 13.19N 61.15W
Wallingford 124 Ac 51.36N 1.08W
Wallis / Valais [2] 128 Bd 46.15N 7.30 E
Wallis, Iles-=Wallis Islands (EN) 208 Jf 13.18S 176.10W
Wallis and Futuna (EN)= Wallis-et-Futuna [5] 210 Jf 14.00S 177.00W
Wallis-et-Futuna=Wallis and Futuna (EN) [5] 210 Jf 14.00S 177.00W
Wallis Islands (EN)=Wallis, Iles- 208 Jf 13.18S 176.10W
Wallowa 188 Gd 45.34N 117.32W
Wallowa Mountains 188 Gd 45.10N 117.30W
Walmer 124 Dc 51.12N 1.24 E
Walney, Isle of- 118 Jg 54.07N 3.15W
Walnut Ridge 182 Id 36.04N 90.57W
Walpole, Ile- 208 Hg 22.37S 168.57 E
Walrus Islands 178 Ge 58.45N 160.20W
Walsall 118 Li 52.35N 1.58W
Walsenburg 182 Gd 37.37N 104.47W
Walsrode 120 Fd 52.52N 9.35 E
Walterboro 184 Gi 32.54N 80.39W
Walter F. George Lake 184 Ej 31.49N 85.08W
Walters 186 Gi 34.22N 98.19W
Waltershausen 120 Gf 50.54N 10.34 E
Waltham 184 Ic 45.58N 76.57W
Walton-on-the-Naze 124 Dc 51.51N 1.17 E
Waltrop 124 Jc 51.38N 7.24 E
Walvisbaai/Walvis Bay [3] 172 Ad 23.00S 14.30 E
Walvisbaai=Walvis Bay (EN) 160 Ik 22.59S 14.31 E
Walvisbaai=Walvis Bay (EN) [5] 160 Ik 22.59S 14.31 E
Walvisbaai=Walvis Bay (EN) 158 Ik 22.57S 14.30 E
Walvis Bay/Walvisbaai [3] 172 Ad 23.00S 14.30 E
Walvis Bay (EN)= Walvisbaai 160 Ik 22.59S 14.31 E
Walvis Bay (EN)= Walvisbaai [5] 160 Ik 22.59S 14.31 E
Walvis Bay (EN)= Walvisbaai 158 Ik 22.57S 14.30 E
Walvis Ridge (EN) 106 El 28.00S 3.00 E
Wama 170 Ce 12.14S 15.34 E
Wamba 158 Ii 3.56S 17.12 E
Wamba [Kenya] 170 Gb 0.59N 37.19 E
Wamba [Nig.] 166 Gd 8.56N 8.36 E
Wamba [Zaire] 170 Eb 2.09N 28.00 E
Wamena 150 Kg 4.00S 138.57 E
Wami 158 Ki 6.08S 38.49 E
Wampusirpi 194 Ef 15.15N 84.37W
Wamsutter 188 Lf 41.40N 107.58W
Wan 150 Kh 8.23S 137.56 E
Wana 148 Db 32.17N 69.35 E
Wanaka 210 Hi 44.42S 169.08 E
Wanaka, Lake- 218 Cf 44.30S 169.10 E
Wan'an 152 Jf 26.32N 114.48 E
Wanapiri 150 Kg 4.33S 135.59 E
Wanapitei Lake 184 Gb 46.45N 80.45W
Wandel Hav=Wandel Sea (EN) 179 Kb 83.00N 15.00W
Wandel Sea (EN)=Wandel Hav 179 Kb 83.00N 15.00W
Wandsworth, London- 124 Bc 51.27N 0.12W
Wanganui 216 Eg 39.56S 175.02 E
Wanganui 218 Fc 39.58S 175.00 E
Wangaratta 212 Jg 36.22S 146.20 E
Wangcun [China] 152 Jd 39.58N 112.53 E
Wangcun [China] 154 Df 36.41N 117.42 E
Wangda/Zogang 152 Gf 29.37N 97.58 E
Wangdu 154 Ce 38.43N 115.09 E
Wangen im Allgäu 120 Fi 47.41N 9.50 E
Wangerooge 120 Dc 53.46N 7.55 E
Wanggameti, Gunung- 150 Hi 10.07S 120.14 E
Wanggezhuang → Jiaonan 154 Eg 35.53N 119.58 E
Wangiwangi, Pulau- 150 Hh 5.20S 123.35 E
Wangjiang 154 Di 30.08N 116.41 E
Wangkui 152 Mb 46.50N 126.29 E
Wangpan Yang 140 Of 30.33N 121.26 E
Wangping 152 Mc 43.18N 129.46 E
Wangying → Huaiyin 154 Eh 33.35N 119.02 E
Wani, Laguna- 194 Ff 14.50N 83.25W
Wanie-Rukula 170 Eb 0.14N 25.34 E
Wanitsuka-Yama 156 Bf 31.45N 131.17 E
Wanlewēyn 168 Ge 2.35N 44.55 E
Wān Namton 148 Jd 22.03N 99.33 E
Wannian (Chenying) 154 Dj 28.42N 117.04 E
Wanning 152 Jh 18.59N 110.24 E
Wanquan 154 Cd 40.52N 114.44 E
Wansbeck 118 Lf 55.10N 1.34W
Wan Shui 154 Di 30.30N 117.01 E
Wanxian 142 Mf 30.48N 108.21 E
Wanyuan 152 Ie 32.03N 108.04 E
Wanzai 154 Cj 28.06N 114.27 E
Wanzhi → Wuhu 154 Ei 31.21N 118.23 E
Wapato 188 Ec 46.27N 120.25W
Wapiti 188 Kd 44.28N 109.28W
Wapiti 180 Fe 55.08N 118.19W
Wapsipinicon River 186 Kf 41.44N 90.20W
Waqooyi Galbeed [3] 168 Gc 10.00N 44.00 E
Warangal 142 Jh 18.18N 79.35 E
Waratah Bay 212 Jg 38.50S 146.05 E
Warburg 120 Fe 51.30N 9.10 E
Warburger Borde 124 Lc 51.35N 9.12 E
Warburg-Scherfede 124 Lc 51.32N 9.02 E
Warburton Bay 180 Gd 63.50N 111.30W
Warburton Mission 212 Fe 26.10S 126.35 E
Warburton Range 212 Fe 26.10S 126.40 E
Ward 218 Fd 41.50S 174.08 E
Warden 172 De 27.56S 29.00 E
Wardenburg 124 Ka 53.04N 8.12 E
Wardha 148 Fd 20.45N 78.37 E
Ward Hunt Strait 212 Ja 9.25S 149.55 E
Ware [B.C.-Can.] 180 Ee 57.27N 125.38W
Ware [Eng.-U.K.] 124 Bc 51.49N 0.01W
Waregem 124 Fd 50.53N 3.25 E
Waremme/Borgworm 122 Ld 50.42N 5.15 E
Waren [Ger.] 120 Ic 53.31N 12.41 E
Waren [Indon.] 210 Ee 2.16S 136.20 E
Warendorf 120 De 51.57N 7.59 E
Warin Chamrap 148 Ke 15.14N 104.52 E
Warka 120 Re 51.47N 21.10 E
Warkworth 218 Fb 36.24S 174.40 E
Warmbad [3] 172 Be 28.00S 18.30 E
Warmbad [Nam.] 172 Be 28.29S 18.41 E
Warmbad [S.Afr.] 172 Dd 24.53S 28.17 E
Warming Land 179 Gb 81.50N 52.45W
Warmington 124 Ab 52.08N 1.24W
Warminster 118 Kj 51.13N 2.12W
Warm Springs [Nv.-U.S.] 183 Gg 38.13N 116.20W
Warm Springs [Or.-U.S.] 183 Ed 44.46N 121.16W
Warnemünde, Rostock- 120 Ib 54.10N 12.05 E
Warner, Mount- 188 Da 51.03N 123.12W
Warner Mountains 182 Cc 41.40N 120.20W
Warner Peak 188 Fe 42.27N 119.44W
Warner Robins 182 Ke 32.37N 83.36W
Warner Valley 188 Fe 42.30N 119.55W
Warnes 202 Fg 17.30S 63.10W
Warnow 120 Ib 54.06N 12.09 E
Waroona 212 Df 32.50S 115.55 E
Warragul 212 Jg 38.10S 145.56 E
Warrego Range 212 Je 25.00S 145.45 E
Warrego River 208 Fh 30.24S 145.21 E
Warren [Ar.-U.S.] 186 Jj 33.38N 92.05W
Warren [Mi.-U.S.] 184 Fd 42.28N 83.01W
Warren [Mn.-U.S.] 186 Hb 48.12N 96.46W
Warren [Oh.-U.S.] 182 Kc 41.15N 80.49W
Warren [Pa.-U.S.] 184 He 41.52N 79.09W
Warrenpoint/An Pointe 118 Gg 54.06N 6.15W
Warrensburg 186 Jg 38.46N 93.44W
Warrenton 172 Ce 28.09S 24.47 E
Warri 166 Gd 5.31N 5.45 E
Warrington [Eng.-U.K.] 118 Kh 53.24N 2.37W
Warrington [Fl.-U.S.] 184 Dj 30.23N 87.16W
Warrior Reefs 212 Ia 9.35S 143.10 E
Warrnambool 210 Fh 38.23S 142.29 E
Warroad 182 Hb 48.54N 95.19W
Warrumbungle Range 212 Jf 31.30S 149.40 E
Warsaw [In.-U.S.] 184 Ee 41.14N 85.51W
Warsaw [Mo.-U.S.] 186 Jg 38.15N 93.23W
Warsaw [N.Y.-U.S.] 184 Hd 42.45N 78.07W
Warsaw (EN)=Warszawa [Pol.] 112 Ie 52.15N 21.00 E
Warshīkh 168 He 2.18N 45.48 E
Warstein 124 Kc 51.27N 8.22 E
Warstein-Belecke 124 Kc 51.29N 8.20 E
Warszawa [2] 120 Qd 52.15N 21.00 E
Warszawa [Pol.] =Warsaw (EN) 112 Ie 52.15N 21.00 E
Warta 110 He 52.35N 14.39 E
Waru 150 Jg 3.24S 130.40 E
Warwick 212 Ke 28.13S 152.02 E
Warwick 118 Li 52.15N 1.30W
Warwick [Eng.-U.K.] 118 Li 52.17N 1.34W
Warwick [R.I.-U.S.] 184 Le 41.42N 71.23W
Warwickshire [3] 118 Li 52.10N 1.35W
Wasagu 166 Gc 11.22N 5.48 E
Wasatch Range 174 He 41.15N 111.30W
Wascana Creek 188 Ma 50.40N 104.55W
Wasco 188 Fi 35.36N 119.20W
Waseca 186 Jd 44.05N 93.30W
Washburn 186 Fc 47.17N 101.02W
Washess Bay 220g Ab 1.49N 157.31W
Wāshim 148 Fd 20.10N 76.58 E
Washington [2] 182 Cb 47.30N 120.30W
Washington [D.C.-U.S.] 176 Lf 38.54N 77.01W
Washington [Eng.-U.K.] 118 Lg 54.54N 1.31W
Washington [Ga.-U.S.] 184 Fi 33.44N 82.44W
Washington [Ia.-U.S.] 186 Kf 41.18N 91.42W
Washington [In.-U.S.] 184 Df 38.40N 87.10W
Washington [N.C.-U.S.] 184 Ih 35.33N 77.03W
Washington [Pa.-U.S.] 184 Ge 40.11N 80.16W
Washington → Teraina Island 208 Kd 4.43N 160.24W
Washington, Mount- 174 Le 44.15N 71.15W
Washington Court House 184 Ff 39.32N 83.29W
Washington Island 186 Md 45.23N 86.55W
Washington Land 179 Fb 80.15N 65.00W
Washita River 186 Hi 34.12N 96.50W
Washtucna 188 Fc 46.45N 118.19W
Wasile 150 If 1.04N 127.59 E
Wasilków 120 Tc 53.12N 23.12 E
Wasior 150 Jg 2.43S 134.30 E
Wāsiṭ [3] 146 Lf 32.35N 46.00 E
Waskaganish 176 Ld 51.25N 78.45W
Wąsosz 120 Me 51.34N 16.42 E
Waspán 190 Hf 14.44N 83.58W
Wassamu 156a Ca 44.02N 142.24 E
Wassenaar 124 Gb 52.09N 4.24 E
Wassenberg 124 Ic 51.06N 6.09 E
Wasserburg am Inn 120 Ih 48.04N 12.14 E
Wasserkuppe 120 Ff 50.30N 9.56 E
Wassigny 124 Fd 50.01N 3.36 E
Wassuk Range 188 Fg 38.40N 118.50W
Wassy 122 Kf 48.30N 4.57 E
Waswanipi, Lac- 184 Ia 49.32N 76.29W
Watampone 142 Oj 4.32S 120.20 E
Watansoppeng 150 Gg 4.21S 119.53 E
Watari 156 Gb 38.02N 140.51 E
Waterbeach 124 Cb 52.16N 0.12 E
Waterberg 172 Bd 20.25S 17.15 E
Waterbury 182 Mc 41.33N 73.02W
Water Cays 194 Ib 23.40N 77.45W
Wateree Pond 184 Gh 34.25N 80.50W
Waterford/Port Láirge 112 Fe 52.15N 7.06W
Waterford/Port Láirge [2] 118 Fi 52.10N 7.40W
Waterford Harbour/Cuan Phort Láirge 118 Gi 52.10N 6.57W
Wateringues 122 Id 50.55N 2.15 E
Waterloo [Bel.] 122 Kd 50.43N 4.24 E
Waterloo [Ia.-U.S.] 182 Ic 42.30N 92.20W
Waterloo [Il.-U.S.] 186 Kg 38.20N 90.09W
Waterlooville 124 Ad 50.52N 1.01W
Watersmeet 184 Cb 46.18N 89.11W
Watertown [N.Y.-U.S.] 184 Lc 43.57N 75.56W
Watertown [S.D.-U.S.] 182 Hc 44.54N 97.07W
Watertown [Wi.-U.S.] 186 Le 43.12N 88.43W
Waterville 182 Nc 44.33N 69.38W
Watford 118 Mj 51.40N 0.25W
Watford City 186 Ec 47.48N 103.17W
Wa'th 168 Ed 8.10N 32.07 E
Watheroo 212 Df 30.17S 116.04 E
Watīr, Wādī- 146 Fh 29.01N 34.40 E
Watkins Glen 184 Id 42.23N 76.53W
Watling → San Salvador 190 Jd 24.02N 74.28W
Watlington 124 Ac 51.38N 1.00W
Watonga 186 Gi 35.51N 98.25W
Watou, Poperinge- 124 Ed 50.51N 2.37 E
Watrous 180 Gf 51.40N 105.28W
Watsa 160 Jh 3.03N 29.32 E
Watseka 186 Mf 40.47N 87.44W
Watsi [C.R.] 194 Fi 9.37N 82.52W
Watsi [Zaire] 170 Dc 0.19S 21.04 E
Watsi Kengo 170 Dc 0.48S 20.33 E
Watson Lake 176 Gc 60.07N 128.48W
Watsonville 188 Eh 36.55N 121.45W
Watt, Morne- 197g Bb 15.19N 61.19W
Watton 124 Cb 52.34N 0.50 E
Watts Bar Lake 184 Eh 35.48N 84.39W
Wattwil 128 Dc 47.18N 9.05 E
Watubela, Kepulauan- 150 Jg 4.35S 131.40 E
Wau 212 Ja 7.20S 146.45 E
Waubay Lake 186 Hd 45.25N 97.25W
Wauchope 212 Kf 31.27S 152.44 E
Wauchula 184 Gl 27.33N 81.49W
Waucoba Mountain 188 Fh 37.00N 118.01W
Waukara, Gunung- 150 Gg 1.15S 119.42 E
Waukarlycarly, Lake- 212 Ed 21.25S 121.50 E
Waukegan 182 Jc 42.22N 87.50W
Waukesha 184 Le 43.01N 88.14W
Waupaca 186 Ld 44.21N 89.05W
Wausau 182 Jc 44.59N 89.39W
Wauseon 184 Ee 41.33N 84.09W
Wauwatosa 186 Me 43.03N 88.00W
Wave Hill 212 Gc 17.29S 130.57 E
Waveney 118 Oi 52.28N 1.45 E
Waver/Wavre 122 Kd 50.43N 4.37 E
Waverly [Ia.-U.S.] 186 Je 42.44N 92.29W
Waverly [Oh.-U.S.] 184 Ff 39.07N 82.59W
Waverly [Tn.-U.S.] 184 Dg 36.05N 87.48W
Waves 184 Jh 35.37N 75.29W
Wavre/Waver 122 Kd 50.43N 4.37 E
Wāw 160 Jh 7.42N 28.00 E
Wawa [Nig.] 166 Fd 9.55N 4.27 E
Wawa [Ont.-Can.] 180 Jg 47.59N 84.47W
Wawa, Río- 194 Fg 13.53N 83.28W
Wāw al Kabīr 160 If 25.20N 16.43 E
Wāw an Nāmūs 164 Ce 24.55N 19.45 E
Wāw Nahr 168 Dd 7.03N 27.13 E
Wawo 150 Hg 3.41S 121.02 E
Wawotobi 150 Hg 3.51S 122.06 E
Waxahachie 186 Hj 32.24N 96.51W
Waxweiler 124 Id 50.06N 6.22 E
Waxxari 152 Ed 38.37N 87.22 E
Way, Lake- 212 Ee 26.50S 120.20 E
Waya 219d Ab 17.18S 177.08 E
Wayabula 150 If 2.17N 128.12 E
Wayan 188 Je 43.00N 111.22W
Waycross 182 Ke 31.13N 82.21W
Wayne [Nb.-U.S.] 186 He 42.14N 97.01W
Wayne [W.V.-U.S.] 184 Ff 38.14N 82.27W
Waynesboro [Ga.-U.S.] 184 Fi 33.06N 82.01W
Waynesboro [Ms.-U.S.] 186 Lk 31.40N 88.39W
Waynesboro [Pa.-U.S.] 184 If 39.45N 77.36W
Waynesboro [Va.-U.S.] 184 Hf 38.04N 78.54W
Waynesville [Mo.-U.S.] 186 Jh 37.50N 92.12W
Waynesville [N.C.-U.S.] 184 Fh 35.29N 83.00W
Waynoka 186 Gh 36.35N 98.53W
Waziers 124 Fd 50.23N 3.07 E
Wda 120 Oc 53.25N 18.29 E
Wdzydze, Jezioro- 120 Nc 54.00N 17.50 E
Wé 216 Cd 20.55S 167.16 E
We, Pulau- 150 Ce 5.51N 95.18 E
Wear 118 Lg 54.55N 1.22W
Weatherford [Ok.-U.S.] 186 Gi 35.32N 98.42W
Weatherford [Tx.-U.S.] 182 He 32.46N 97.48W
Weaverville 188 Df 40.44N 122.56W
Weber 218 Gd 40.24S 176.20 E
Webster 186 Hd 45.20N 97.31W
Webster City 186 Je 42.28N 93.49W
Webster Springs 184 Gf 38.29N 80.25W
Weda 150 If 0.21N 127.52 E
Weda, Teluk- 150 If 0.20N 128.00 E
Weddell Island 206 Hh 51.50S 61.00W
Weddell Sea (EN) 222 Rf 72.00S 45.00W
Wedel 120 Fc 53.35N 9.41 E
Wedgeport 184 Od 43.44N 65.59W
Wedza 172 Ec 18.35S 31.35 E
Weed 188 Df 41.25N 122.27W
Weener 120 Dc 53.10N 7.21 E
Weerdinge, Emmen- 124 Ib 52.49N 6.57 E
Weert 122 Lc 51.15N 5.43 E
Weesp 124 Hb 52.18N 5.02 E
Wegberg 124 Ic 51.09N 6.16 E
Węgliniec 120 Le 51.17N 15.13 E
Węgorzewo 120 Rb 54.14N 21.44 E
Węgrów 120 Sd 52.25N 22.01 E
Wehni 168 Fc 12.40N 36.42 E
Weichang (Zhuizishan) 152 Kc 41.55N 117.39 E
Weida 120 If 50.46N 12.04 E
Weiden in der Oberpfalz 120 Ig 49.41N 12.10 E
Weifang 142 Nf 36.43N 119.06 E
Weihai 152 Ld 37.27N 122.02 E
Weihe 154 Jb 44.55N 128.23 E
Wei He 140 Nf 34.36N 110.10 E
Weil 124 Kd 50.28N 8.16 E
Weilburg 120 Ef 50.29N 8.15 E
Weilerbach 124 Je 49.29N 7.38 E
Weilerswist 124 Id 50.46N 6.50 E
Weilheim in Oberbayern 120 Hi 47.50N 11.09 E
Weilmünster 124 Kd 50.26N 8.21 E
Weimar [Ger.] 124 Kd 50.46N 8.43 E
Weimar [Ger.] 120 Hf 50.59N 11.19 E
Weinan 152 Ie 34.30N 109.34 E
Weingarten 120 Fi 47.48N 9.38 E
Weinheim 120 Eg 49.33N 8.40 E
Weining 152 Hf 26.46N 104.18 E
Weinsberger Wald 128 Ib 48.25N 15.00 E
Weinstraße 124 Ke 49.20N 8.05 E
Weinviertel 128 Kb 48.35N 16.30 E
Weipa 210 Ff 12.41S 141.52 E
Weirton 184 Ge 40.24N 80.37W
Weiser 188 Gd 44.15N 116.58W
Weiser River 188 Gd 44.15N 116.59W
Weishan Hu 152 Ke 34.35N 117.15 E
Weishi 154 Cg 34.25N 114.10 E
Weishui → Jingxing 154 Ce 38.03N 114.09 E
Weiße Elster 120 He 51.26N 11.57 E
Weißenberg 124 Je 49.15N 7.49 E
Weißenburg in Bayern 120 Gg 49.02N 10.59 E
Weißenfels 120 He 51.12N 11.58 E
Weißer Main 120 Hf 50.05N 11.24 E
Weißerstein 124 Id 50.24N 6.22 E
Weißkugel/Palla Bianca 128 Ed 46.48N 10.44 E
Weiss Lake 184 Eh 34.15N 85.35W
Weißwasser/Běła Woda 120 Ke 51.31N 14.38 E
Weitra 128 Ib 48.42N 14.53 E
Weixi 152 Gf 27.13N 99.19 E
Weixian (Zhaxi) 154 Cf 36.59N 115.15 E
Weixin (Zhaxi) 152 If 27.46N 105.04 E
Weiz 128 Jc 47.13N 15.37 E
Wejherowo 120 Ob 54.37N 18.15 E
Welbourn Hill 210 Eg 27.21S 134.06 E
Welch 184 Gg 37.26N 81.36W
Weldiya 168 Fc 11.48N 39.35 E
Weld Range 212 De 26.55S 117.25 E
Welega [3] 168 Fd 8.38N 35.40 E
Welel 168 Fd 8.56N 34.52 E
Weligama 148 Gg 5.58N 80.25 E
Welkenraedt 124 Hd 50.39N 5.58 E
Welker Seamount (EN) 178 Ke 55.07N 140.20W
Welkite 168 Fd 8.17N 37.49 E
Welkom 160 Jk 27.59S 26.45 E
Welland 180 Jh 42.59N 79.15W
Welland 118 Ni 52.53N 0.02 E
Welland Canal 184 Hd 43.14N 79.13W
Wellesley Islands 208 Ef 16.45S 139.30 E
Wellin 124 Hd 50.05N 5.07 E
Wellingborough 118 Mi 52.19N 0.42W
Wellington [2] 218 Fd 40.10S 175.30 E
Wellington [Austl.] 212 Jf 32.33S 148.57 E
Wellington [Eng.-U.K.] 118 Jk 50.59N 3.14W
Wellington [Ks.-U.S.] 186 Hh 37.16N 97.24W
Wellington [Nv.-U.S.] 188 Fg 38.45N 119.22W
Wellington [N.Z.] 210 Ii 41.17S 174.46 E
Wellington, Isla- 198 Ij 49.20S 74.40W
Wellington, Lake- 212 Jg 38.10S 147.15 E
Wellington Channel 180 Ia 75.10N 93.00W
Wells [Eng.-U.K.] 118 Kj 51.13N 2.39W
Wells [Eng.-U.K.] 118 Ni 52.58N 0.51 E
Wells [Nv.-U.S.] 182 Dc 41.07N 115.01W
Wells, Lake- 212 Ee 26.45S 123.15 E
Wells, Mount- 212 Fc 17.26S 127.14 E
Wellsboro 184 Ie 41.45N 77.18W
Wellsford 218 Fb 36.18S 174.31 E
Wellton 188 Hj 32.40N 114.08W
Welmel 168 Gd 5.35N 40.55 E
Welna 120 Md 52.36N 16.50 E
Welo [3] 168 Fc 12.00N 40.00 E
Wels 128 Ib 48.10N 14.02 E
Welshpool 118 Ji 52.40N 3.09W
Welver 124 Jc 51.37N 7.58 E
Welwitschia 172 Ad 20.21S 14.57 E
Welwyn Garden City 118 Mj 51.48N 0.13W
Wema 170 Dc 0.26S 21.38 E
Wemding 120 Gh 48.52N 10.43 E
Wen'an 154 De 38.52N 116.30 E
Wenatchee 182 Cb 47.25N 120.19W
Wenatchee Mountains 188 Ec 47.20N 120.45W
Wenchang 152 Jh 19.43N 110.44 E
Wenchi 166 Ed 7.44N 2.06W
Wenchit 168 Fc 10.03N 38.35 E
Wenden 124 Jd 50.58N 7.52 E
Wendeng 152 Ld 37.10N 122.01 E
Wendland 120 Gc 53.10N 11.00 E
Wendo 168 Fd 6.37N 38.25 E
Wendover 188 Hf 40.45N 114.02W
Wengyuan (Longxian) 152 Jg 24.21N 114.13 E
Wen He 154 Ef 37.06N 119.29 E
Wenling 152 Lf 28.23N 121.22 E
Wenquan 152 Fe 33.15N 91.55 E
Wenquan/Arixang 152 Dc 44.59N 81.04 E
Wenshan 152 Hg 23.22N 104.23 E
Wenshui 154 Bf 37.26N 112.01 E
Wensu 152 Dc 41.15N 80.14 E
Wensum 124 Db 52.37N 1.22 E
Wentworth 212 If 34.07S 141.55 E
Wenxian 152 He 32.52N 104.40 E
Wenzhou 142 Og 27.57N 120.38 E
Wenzhu 152 Jf 27.00N 114.00 E
Wepener 172 De 29.46S 27.00 E
Wépion, Namur- 124 Gd 50.25N 4.52 E
Werda 172 Ce 25.16S 23.17 E
Werder 160 Lh 7.00N 45.21 E
Werder 120 Jc 53.40N 13.25 E
Werdoh 124 Jc 51.16N 7.46 E
Were Ilu 168 Fc 10.38N 39.23 E
Werkendam 124 Gc 51.49N 4.55 E
Werl 124 Jc 51.33N 7.55 E
Werlte 124 Jb 52.51N 7.41 E
Wermelskirchen 124 Jc 51.09N 7.13 E
Werne 124 Jc 51.40N 7.38 E
Wernigerode 120 Ge 51.50N 10.47 E
Werra 110 Ge 51.26N 9.39 E
Werribee 212 Ig 37.54S 144.40 E
Werris Creek 212 Kf 31.21S 150.39 E
Werse 124 Jb 52.02N 7.41 E
Wertach 120 Gh 48.24N 10.53 E
Wertheim 120 Fg 49.45N 9.31 E
Wesel 120 Ce 51.40N 6.37 E
Weser 110 Ge 53.32N 8.34 E
Weserbergland 120 Fe 51.55N 9.30 E
Wesergebirge 120 Fd 52.15N 9.10 E
Weslaco 186 Gm 26.09N 98.01W
Wesley 197g Ba 15.34N 61.19W
Wesleyville 180 Mg 49.09N 53.34W
Wessel, Cape- 212 Hb 11.00S 136.45 E
Wesseling 124 Id 50.50N 6.59 E
Wessel Islands 208 Ef 12.00S 136.45 E
Wessington Springs 186 Gd 44.05N 98.34W
West Allis 186 Le 43.01N 88.00W
West Baines River 212 Gc 15.26S 130.08 E
West Bay 186 Ll 29.00N 89.30W
West Bend 186 Le 43.25N 88.11W
West Bengal [3] 148 Hd 24.00N 88.00 E
West Berlin = Berlin 112 He 52.31N 13.24 E
West Branch 184 Ec 44.17N 84.14W
West Bridgford 124 Ab 52.55N 1.07W
West Bromwich 118 Li 52.31N 1.59W
Westbrook 184 Ld 43.41N 70.21W
West Burra 118 La 60.05N 1.10W
West Caicos 194 Kc 21.47N 72.17W
West Cape 208 Hi 45.55S 166.26 E
West Caroline Basin (EN) 106 Ii 4.00N 138.00 E
West Carpathians (EN)= Zapadné Karpaty 120 Og 49.30N 19.00 E
West Des Moines 186 Jf 41.35N 93.43W
Westdongeradeel 124 Ha 53.23N 5.58 E
Westdongeradeel-Holwerd 124 Ha 53.22N 5.54 E
Westdongeradeel-Ternaard 124 Ha 53.23N 5.58 E
Westeinderplassen 124 Gb 52.15N 4.30 E
West Elk Mountains 186 Cg 38.40N 107.15W
West End 184 Hl 26.41N 78.58W
Westende, Middelkerke- 124 Ec 51.10N 2.46 E
West End Village 197b Ab 18.11N 63.09W
West Entrance 220a Bb 7.57N 134.30 E
Westerbork 124 Ib 52.51N 6.36 E
Westerburg 124 Jd 50.34N 7.59 E
Westerland 120 Eb 54.54N 8.18 E
Westerlo 124 Gc 51.05N 4.55 E
Western [Ghana] [3] 166 Ed 5.30N 2.30W
Western [Kenya] [3] 170 Fb 0.30N 34.35 E
Western [S.L.] [3] 166 Cd 8.20N 13.00W
Western [Ug.] [3] 170 Fb 1.00N 31.00 E
Western [Zam.] [3] 170 Df 15.00S 24.00 E
Western Australia [2] 212 Ed 25.00S 122.00 E
Western Desert (EN) = Gharbīyah, Aş Şaḩrā' al- 158 Jf 27.30N 28.00 E
Western Dvina (EN) = Daugava 136 Cd 57.04N 24.03 E
Western Dvina (EN)= Zapadnaja Dvina 110 Id 57.04N 24.03 E
Western Entrance 219a Bb 6.55S 155.40 E
Western Ghats/Sahyadri 140 Jh 14.00N 75.00 E
Western Isles [3] 118 Fd 57.40N 7.10W
Western Port 212 Jg 38.25S 145.10 E
Western River 180 Gc 66.22N 107.15W
Western Sahara (EN) [5] 160 Ff 24.30N 13.00W
Western Samoa (EN) = Samoa I Sisifo [1] 210 Jf 13.40S 172.30W
Western Sayans (EN)= Zapadny Sajan 140 Ld 53.00N 94.00 E
Western Sierra Madre (EN) =Madre Occidental, Sierra- 174 Ig 25.00N 105.00W
Western Turkistan (EN) 140 He 41.00N 60.00 E
Westerschelde=West Schelde (EN) 122 Jc 51.25N 3.45 E
Westerschouwen 124 Fc 51.41N 3.43 E

Index Symbols

[1] Independent Nation
[2] State, Region
[3] District, County
[4] Municipality
[5] Colony, Dependency
Continent
Physical Region
Historical or Cultural Region
Mount, Mountain
Volcano
Hill
Mountains, Mountain Range
Hills, Escarpment
Plateau, Upland
Pass, Gap
Plain, Lowland
Delta
Salt Flat
Valley, Canyon
Crater, Cave
Karst Features
Depression
Polder
Desert, Dunes
Forest, Woods
Heath, Steppe
Oasis
Cape, Point
Coast, Beach
Cliff
Peninsula
Isthmus
Sandbank
Island
Atoll
Rock, Reef
Islands, Archipelago
Rocks, Reefs
Coral Reef
Well, Spring
Geyser
River, Stream
Waterfall, Rapids
River Mouth, Estuary
Lake
Salt Lake
Intermittent Lake
Reservoir
Swamp, Pond
Canal
Glacier
Ice Shelf, Pack Ice
Ocean
Sea
Gulf, Bay
Strait, Fjord
Lagoon
Bank
Seamount
Tablemount
Ridge
Shelf
Basin
Escarpment, Sea Scarp
Fracture
Trench, Abyss
National Park, Reserve
Point of Interest
Recreation Site
Cave, Cavern
Historic Site
Ruins
Wall, Walls
Church, Abbey
Temple
Scientific Station
Railway station
Airport
Port
Military installation
Lighthouse
Mine
Tunnel
Dam, Bridge

Westerschouwen-Haamstede 124 Fc 51.42N 3.45 E
Westerstede 120 Dc 53.15N 7.56 E
Westerwald 120 Df 50.40N 7.55 E
Westerwoldse A 124 Ja 53.10N 7.10 E
West European Basin (EN) 106 De 47.00N 15.00W
West Falkland/Gran Malvina, Isla- 198 Kk 51.40S 60.00W
West Fayu Island 208 Fd 8.05N 146.44 E
West Fork Big Blue River 186 Hf 40.42N 96.59W
Westfriesland = West Friesland (EN) 122 Kb 52.45N 4.50 E
West Friesland (EN) = Westfriesland 122 Kb 52.45N 4.50 E
West Frisian Islands (EN) = Waddeneilanden 122 Ka 53.30N 5.00 E
Westgate-on-Sea 124 Dc 51.22N 1.21 E
West Glacier 188 Ib 48.30N 113.59W
West Glamorgan [3] 118 Jj 51.40N 3.55W
West Grand Lake 184 Nc 45.15N 67.52W
West Greenland (EN) = Vestgrønland [2] 179 He 69.00N 49.30W
West Helena 186 Ki 34.33N 90.39W
West Hollywood 184 Gm 25.59N 80.11W
Westhope 186 Fb 48.55N 101.01W
West Ice Shelf 222 Ge 67.00S 85.00 E
West Indies 190 Je 19.00N 70.00W
West Indies (EN) = Indias Occidentales 190 Je 19.00N 70.00W
West Island 172b Ab 9.22S 46.13 E
Westkapelle 124 Fc 51.31N 3.26 E
Westkapelle, Knokke- 124 Fc 51.19N 3.18 E
West Lafayette 184 De 40.27N 86.55W
Westland [2] 218 De 43.10S 170.30 E
West Liberty 184 Fg 37.55N 83.16W
Westlock 180 Gf 54.09N 113.52W
West Lunga 170 De 13.06S 24.39 E
Westmalle 124 Gc 51.18N 4.41 E
West Mariana Basin (EN) 106 Ih 15.00N 137.00 E
Westmeath/An Iarmhí [2] 118 Fh 53.30N 7.30W
West Melanesian Trench (EN) 214 Dh 1.00S 150.00 E
West Memphis 182 Id 35.08N 90.11W
West Mersea 124 Cc 51.46N 0.54 E
West Midlands [3] 118 Li 52.30N 2.00W
Westminster 184 If 39.35N 76.59W
Westminster, London- 124 Bc 51.30N 0.07W
West Monroe 186 Jj 32.31N 92.09W
Westmorland 118 Kg 54.30N 2.40W
West Nicholson 160 Jk 21.03S 29.22 E
West Nueces River 186 Gl 29.16N 99.56W
Weston [Mala.] 150 Ge 5.13N 115.36 E
Weston [W.V.-U.S.] 184 Gf 39.03N 80.28W
Weston [Wy.-U.S.] 188 Md 44.42N 105.18W
Weston-super-Mare 118 Kj 51.21N 2.59W
Westoverledingen 124 Ja 53.10N 7.27 E
Westoverledingen - Ihrhove 124 Ja 53.10N 7.27 E
West Palm Beach 176 Kg 26.43N 80.04W
West Pensacola 184 Dj 30.27N 87.15W
West Plains 182 Id 36.44N 91.51W
West Point [Ms.-U.S.] 186 Lj 33.36N 88.39W
West Point [Nb.-U.S.] 186 Hf 41.51N 96.43W
Westport 210 Ii 41.45S 171.36 E
Westport/Cathair na Mart 118 Dh 53.48N 9.32W
Westray 118 Kb 59.20N 3.00W
Westree 184 Gb 47.27N 81.32W
Westrich 124 Je 49.20N 7.25 E
West Road 124 Cd 50.52N 0.50 E
West Schelde (EN) = Westerschelde 122 Jc 51.25N 3.45 E
West Scotia Basin (EN) 198 Kk 57.00S 53.00W
West Siberian Plain (EN) = Zapadno-Sibirskaja ravnina 140 Jc 60.00N 75.00 E
Weststellingwerf 124 Ib 52.53N 6.00 E
Weststellingwerf-Wolvega 124 Ib 52.53N 6.00 E
West Sussex [3] 118 Mk 51.00N 0.40W
West Tavaputs Plateau 188 Jf 40.00N 110.25W
West-Terschelling, Terschelling- 124 Ha 53.21N 5.13 E
West Union [Ia.-U.S.] 186 Ke 42.57N 91.49W
West Union [Oh.-U.S.] 184 Ff 38.48N 83.33W
West Virginia [2] 182 Kd 38.45N 80.30W
West-Vlaanderen = Flanders, West- (EN) [3] 124 Ec 51.00N 3.00 E
Westwood 188 Ef 40.18N 121.00W
West Wyalong 212 Jf 33.55S 147.13 E
West Yellowstone 182 Ec 44.30N 111.05W
West Yorkshire [3] 118 Lh 53.40N 1.30W
Wetar, Pulau- 208 De 7.48S 126.18 E
Wetaskiwin 180 Gf 52.58N 113.22W
Wete 170 Gd 5.04S 39.43 E
Wětošow/Vetschau 120 Ke 51.47N 14.04 E
Wetter 124 Kd 50.18N 8.49 E
Wetter (Hessen) 124 Kd 50.54N 8.43 E
Wetter (Ruhr) 124 Jc 51.23N 7.24 E
Wetterau 120 Ef 50.15N 8.50 E
Wetteren 122 Jc 51.00N 3.53 E
Wetzlar 120 Ef 50.33N 8.30 E
Wetzstein 120 Hf 50.27N 11.27 E
Wevelgem 124 Fd 50.48N 3.10 E
Wewahitchka 184 Ej 30.07N 85.12W
Wewak 210 Fe 3.34S 143.38 E
Wexford/Loch Garman 112 Fe 52.20N 6.27W
Wexford/Loch Garman [2] 118 Gi 52.20N 6.40W
Wexford Harbour/Cuan Loch Garman 118 Gi 52.20N 6.25W
Wey 118 Mj 51.23N 0.28W
Weyburn 180 Hg 49.41N 103.52W
Weyhe 124 Kb 52.59N 8.52 E
Weyhe-Leeste 124 Kb 52.59N 8.50 E
Weymouth and Melcombe Regis 118 Kk 50.36N 2.28W
Wezet/Visé 124 Hd 50.44N 5.42 E
Whakatane 216 Eg 37.58S 177.00 E
Whale Cove 180 Id 62.14N 92.10W
Whalsay 118 Ma 60.22N 0.59W
Whangarei 210 Ih 35.43S 174.19 E
Wharfe 118 Lh 53.51N 1.07W
Wharton 186 Hl 29.19N 96.06W
Wharton Basin (EN) 106 Hk 19.00S 100.00 E
Wharton Lake 180 Hd 64.00N 99.55W
Whataroa 218 De 43.16S 170.22 E
Wheatland 188 Me 42.03N 104.57W
Wheat Ridge 186 Dg 39.46N 105.07W
Wheeler 188 Dd 45.42N 123.52W
Wheeler 180 Ke 57.02N 67.14W
Wheeler Lake 184 Dh 34.40N 87.05W
Wheeler Peak [N.M.-U.S.] 182 Fd 36.34N 105.25W
Wheeler Peak [U.S.] 174 Hf 38.59N 114.19W
Wheeling 182 Kc 40.05N 80.43W
Whidbey Island 188 Db 48.15N 122.40W
Whitby 118 Mg 54.29N 0.37W
Whitchurch [Eng.-U.K.] 118 Ki 52.58N 2.41W
Whitchurch [Eng.-U.K.] 124 Bc 51.53N 0.50W
Whitchurch [Eng.-U.K.] 124 Ac 51.13N 1.20W
White 180 Jc 65.50N 85.00W
White, Lake- 212 Fd 21.05S 129.00 E
White Bay 174 Nd 50.00N 56.30W
White Bear Lake 186 Jd 45.04N 93.01W
White Butte 186 Ec 46.23N 103.19W
White Carpathians (EN) = Bilé Karpaty 120 Nh 48.55N 17.50 E
White Cliffs 212 If 30.51S 143.05 E
White Cloud 184 Ed 43.33N 85.46W
Whitecourt 180 Ff 54.09N 115.41W
Whitefish 182 Eb 48.25N 114.20W
Whitefish Bay 182 Kb 46.40N 84.50W
Whitefish Point 184 Eb 46.45N 85.00W
Whitefish Range 188 Hb 48.40N 114.26W
Whitehall [Mi.-U.S.] 184 Dd 43.24N 86.21W
Whitehall [Mt.-U.S.] 188 Id 45.52N 112.06W
Whitehall [Oh.-U.S.] 184 Ff 39.58N 82.54W
Whitehall [Wi.-U.S.] 186 Kd 44.22N 91.19W
Whitehaven 118 Jg 54.33N 3.35W
Whitehorse 176 Fc 60.43N 135.03W
White Island [Ant.] 222 Ee 66.44S 48.35 E
White Island [N.Z.] 218 Gb 37.30S 177.10 E
White Lake 186 Jl 29.45N 92.30W
White Lake (EN) = Beloje ozero 110 Jc 60.11N 37.35 E
Whiteman Range 212 Ja 5.50S 149.55 E
Whitemark 212 Jh 40.07S 148.01 E
White Mountain 178 Gd 64.35N 163.04W
White Mountain Peak 182 Dd 37.38N 118.15W
White Mountains [Ak.-U.S.] 178 Jc 65.30N 147.00W
White Mountains [U.S.] 182 Mc 44.10N 71.35W
White Mountains [U.S.] 188 Fh 37.30N 118.15W
Whitemouth Lake 186 Ib 49.14N 95.40W
Whitemouth River 186 Ha 50.07N 96.02W
White Nile (EN) = Abyaḑ, Al Baḩr al- [3] 168 Ec 12.40N 32.30 E
White Nile (EN) = Abyaḑ, Al Baḩr al- 158 Kg 15.38N 32.31 E
White Pass [N.Amer.] 178 Le 59.37N 135.08W
White Pass [Wa.-U.S.] 188 Ec 46.38N 121.24W
White River 180 Ig 48.35N 85.17W
White River 186 Fe 43.34N 100.45W
Whiteriver 188 Kj 33.50N 109.58W
White River [In.-U.S.] 184 Df 38.25N 87.44W
White River [Nv.-U.S.] 188 Hh 37.18N 115.08W
White River [Tx.-U.S.] 186 Fj 33.14N 100.56W
White River [U.S.] 188 Kf 40.04N 109.41W
White River [U.S.] 182 Hc 43.45N 99.30W
White River [U.S.] 174 Jf 33.53N 91.03W
White River [Yuk.-Can.] 180 Dd 63.10N 139.32W
White Salmon 188 Ed 45.44N 121.29W
Whitesand Bay 118 Ik 50.20N 4.35W
White Sea (EN) = Beloje more 110 Kb 66.00N 44.00 E
White Sea-Baltic Canal (EN) = Belomorsko-Baltijski kanal 110 Jc 63.30N 34.48 E
White Settlement 186 Hj 32.45N 97.27W
White Sulphur Springs 188 Jc 46.33N 110.54W
Whiteville 184 Hh 34.20N 78.42W
White Volta 158 Gh 8.38N 0.59W
White Volta (EN) = Volta Blanche 158 Gh 8.38N 0.59W
Whitewater 186 Bg 38.59N 108.27W
Whitewater Baldy 186 Bj 33.20N 108.39W
Whitewater Bay 184 Gm 25.16N 81.00W
Whitewater Lake 186 La 50.50N 89.10W
Whitewood 186 Ea 50.20N 102.15W
Whitianga 218 Fb 36.50S 175.42 E
Whitmore Mountains 222 Og 82.35S 104.30W
Whitney 184 Hc 45.30N 78.14W
Whitney, Lake- 186 Hk 31.55N 97.23W
Whitney, Mount- 174 Hf 36.35N 118.18W
Whitstable 124 Dc 51.21N 1.06 E
Whitsunday Island 212 Jd 20.15S 149.00 E
Whittier 178 Jd 60.46N 148.41W
Whittlesea 212 Jg 37.31S 145.07 E
Whittlesey 124 Bb 52.33N 0.08W
Wholdaia Lake 180 Hd 60.45N 104.10W
Whyalla 212 Hf 33.02S 137.35 E
Wiarton 184 Gc 44.45N 81.09W
Wiawso 166 Ed 6.12N 2.29W
Wibaux 188 Mc 46.59N 104.11W
Wichita 176 Jf 37.41N 97.20W
Wichita Falls 176 Jf 33.54N 98.30W
Wichita Mountains 186 Gi 34.45N 98.40W
Wichita River 186 Gi 34.07N 98.10W
Wick 118 Jc 58.26N 3.06W
Wick 118 Jc 58.25N 3.05W
Wickenburg 188 Ij 33.58N 112.44W
Wickepin 212 Df 32.46S 117.30 E
Wickham 124 Ad 50.54N 1.10W
Wickham Market 124 Db 52.09N 1.22 E
Wickiup Reservoir 188 Ee 43.40N 121.43W
Wickliffe 184 Cg 36.58N 89.05W
Wicklow/Cill Mhantáin 118 Gi 52.59N 6.03W
Wicklow/Cill Mhantáin [2] 118 Gi 53.00N 6.30W
Wicklow Head/Ceann Chill Mhantáin 118 Hi 52.58N 6.00W
Wicklow Mountains/Sléibhte Chill Mhantáin 118 Gh 53.02N 6.24W
Wicko, Jezioro- 120 Mb 54.33N 16.35 E
Wickrath, Mönchengladbach- 124 Ic 51.08N 6.25 E
Widawa 120 Me 51.13N 16.55 E
Wide Bay 212 Ka 5.05S 152.05 E
Widefield 186 Dg 38.42N 104.40W
Widgiemooltha 212 Ef 31.30S 121.34 E
Wi-Do 154 Ig 35.38N 126.17 E
Więcbork 120 Nc 53.22N 17.30 E
Wied 124 Jd 50.27N 7.28 E
Wiehengebirge 120 Ed 52.20N 8.40 E
Wiehl 124 Jd 50.57N 7.32 E
Wieliczka 120 Qg 49.59N 20.04 E
Wielimie, Jezioro- 120 Mc 53.47N 16.50 E
Wielki Dział 120 Tf 50.18N 23.25 E
Wielkopolska 120 Ne 51.50N 17.20 E
Wielkopolskie-Kujawskie, Pojezierze- 120 Md 52.25N 16.30 E
Wieluń 120 Oe 51.14N 18.34 E
Wien [2] 128 Kb 48.15N 16.25 E
Wien = Vienna (EN) 112 Hf 48.12N 16.22 E
Wiener Becken 128 Kc 48.00N 16.28 E
Wiener Neustadt 128 Kc 47.48N 16.15 E
Wienerwald = Vienna Woods (EN) 128 Jb 48.10N 16.00 E
Wieprz 120 Re 51.32N 21.49 E
Wieprza 120 Mb 54.26N 16.22 E
Wieprz-Krzna, Kanał- 120 Se 51.56N 22.56 E
Wierden 124 Ib 52.22N 6.36 E
Wieringen 124 Hb 52.56N 5.02 E
Wieringen-Den Oever 124 Hb 52.56N 5.02 E
Wieringen-Hippolytushoef 124 Gb 52.54N 4.59 E
Wieringermeer 124 Hb 52.51N 5.01 E
Wieringermeer Polder 124 Gb 52.50N 5.00 E
Wieringermeer-Wieringerwerf 124 Hb 52.51N 5.01 E
Wieringerwerf, Wieringermeer- 124 Hb 52.51N 5.01 E
Wieruszów 120 Oe 51.18N 18.08 E
Wierzchowo, Jezioro- 120 Mc 53.50N 16.45 E
Wierzyca 120 Oc 53.51N 18.50 E
Wiesbaden 112 Ge 50.05N 8.15 E
Wiese 120 Di 47.35N 7.35 E
Wieslautern 124 Je 49.05N 7.49 E
Wiesloch 120 Eg 49.18N 8.42 E
Wietingsmoor 124 Kb 52.39N 8.39 E
Wietmarschen 124 Jb 52.32N 7.08 E
Wieżyca 120 Ob 54.17N 18.10 E
Wigan 118 Kh 53.32N 2.35W
Wigger 128 Bc 47.15N 7.55 E
Wiggins 186 Lk 30.51N 89.08W
Wight, Isle of- 110 Fe 50.40N 1.20W
Wigry, Jezioro- 120 Tb 54.05N 23.07 E
Wigston 124 Ab 52.35N 1.06W
Wigtown 118 Ig 54.52N 4.26W
Wigtown Bay 118 Ig 54.46N 4.15W
Wijchen 124 Hc 51.48N 5.44 E
Wijdefjorden 179 Nc 79.50N 15.30 E
Wijk bij Duurstede 124 Hc 51.59N 5.22 E
Wil 128 Dc 47.27N 9.05 E
Wilbur 188 Fc 47.46N 118.42W
Wilburton 186 Ii 34.55N 95.19W
Wilcannia 210 Fh 31.34S 143.23 E
Wild Coast 158 Jl 32.00S 29.50 E
Wildeshausen 120 Ed 52.54N 8.26 E
Wild Horse 188 Jb 49.01N 110.12W
Wildspitze 128 Ed 46.53N 10.52 E
Wilga 120 Re 51.50N 21.20 E
Wilhelm-II-Land 222 Ge 69.00S 90.00 E
Wilhelminakanaal 124 Gc 51.43N 4.53 E
Wilhelm-Pieck-Stadt-Guben 120 Ke 51.57N 14.43 E
Wilhelmshaven 120 Ec 53.31N 8.08 E
Wilhelmstal 172 Bd 21.54S 16.20 E
Wilkes-Barre 182 Lc 41.15N 75.50W
Wilkesboro 184 Gg 36.09N 81.09W
Wilkes Land (EN) 222 Hf 71.00S 120.00 E
Wilkins Coast 222 Qe 69.40S 63.00W
Wilkins Sound 222 Qf 70.15S 73.00W
Willamette River 188 Dd 45.39N 122.46W
Willandra Billabong Creek 212 If 33.08S 144.06 E
Willapa Bay 188 Dc 46.37N 124.00W
Willard 186 Ci 34.36N 106.02W
Willards, Punta- 192 Cc 28.50N 112.35W
Willcox 188 Kj 32.15N 109.50W
Willebadessen 124 Lc 51.38N 9.02 E
Willebadessen-Peckelsheim 124 Lc 51.36N 9.08 E
Willebroek 124 Gc 51.04N 4.22 E
Willemstad [Neth.] 124 Gc 51.41N 4.26 E
Willemstad [Neth.Ant.] 200 Jd 12.06N 68.56W
Willeroo 212 Gc 15.17S 131.35 E
William Bill Dannelly Reservoir 184 Di 32.15N 86.45W
Williams 182 Ed 35.15N 112.11W
Williamsburg [Ky.-U.S.] 184 Eg 36.44N 84.10W
Williamsburg [Va.-U.S.] 184 Ig 37.17N 76.43W
Williams Lake 180 Ff 52.08N 122.09W
Williamson Glacier 222 He 66.30S 114.30 E
Williamsport 182 Lc 41.16N 77.03W
Williamston 184 Ih 35.50N 77.06W
Williamstown 184 Ef 38.38N 84.34W
Willich 124 Ic 51.16N 6.33 E
Willikie's 197d Bb 17.03N 61.42W
Willingdon, Mount- 188 Ga 51.48N 116.17W
Willis Groúp 208 Gf 16.20S 150.00 E
Willis Islands 222 Ad 54.00S 38.11W
Williston [N.D.-U.S.] 182 Gb 48.09N 103.37W
Williston [S.Afr.] 172 Cf 31.20S 20.53 E
Williston Lake 174 Gd 50.57N 122.23W
Willits 188 Dg 39.25N 123.21W
Willmar 182 Hb 45.07N 95.03W
Willoughby Bay 197d Bb 17.02N 61.44W
Willow Bunch Lake 188 Mb 49.27N 105.28W
Willowlake 180 Fd 62.42N 123.08W
Willowmore 172 Cf 33.17S 23.29 E
Willows 188 Dg 39.31N 122.12W
Willow Springs 186 Kh 36.59N 91.58W
Wills, Lake- 212 Fd 21.20S 128.40 E
Wills Point 186 Ij 32.43N 95.57W
Wilma Glacier 222 Ee 67.12S 56.00 E
Wilmington [De.-U.S.] 182 Ld 39.44N 75.33W
Wilmington [N.C.-U.S.] 176 Lf 34.13N 77.55W
Wilmington [Oh.-U.S.] 184 Ff 39.28N 83.50W
Wilnsdorf 124 Kd 50.49N 8.06 E
Wilseder Berg 120 Fc 53.10N 9.56 E
Wilson 182 Ld 35.44N 77.55W
Wilson, Cape - 180 Jc 66.59N 81.27W
Wilson, Mount- 186 Ch 37.51N 107.59W
Wilson Bluff 222 Ff 74.20S 66.47 E
Wilson Lake [Al.-U.S.] 184 Dh 34.49N 87.30W
Wilson Lake [Ks.-U.S.] 186 Gg 38.57N 98.40W
Wilsons Promontory 212 Jg 38.55S 146.20 E
Wilton River 212 Gb 14.45S 134.33 E
Wilts 118 Lj 51.20N 2.00W
Wiltshire [3] 118 Lj 51.30N 2.00W
Wiltz 122 Le 49.58N 5.55 E
Wiluna 212 Ee 26.36S 120.13 E
Wimereux 124 Dd 50.46N 1.37 E
Winamac 184 De 41.03N 86.36W
Winburg 172 De 28.37S 27.00 E
Winchelsea 124 Cd 50.55N 0.43 E
Winchester [Eng.-U.K.] 118 Lj 51.04N 1.19W
Winchester [In.-U.S.] 184 Ee 40.10N 84.59W
Winchester [Ky.-U.S.] 184 Ef 38.01N 84.11W
Winchester [Va.-U.S.] 182 Ld 39.11N 78.12W
Windeck 124 Jd 50.49N 7.34 E
Windemin, Pointe- 219b Cc 16.34S 167.27 E
Winder 184 Fi 34.00N 83.47W
Windermere 118 Kg 54.22N 2.56W
Windermere [B.C.-Can.] 188 Ha 50.30N 115.58W
Windermere [Eng.-U.K.] 118 Kg 54.23N 2.54W
Windhoek 160 Ik 22.34S 17.06 E
Windhoek [3] 172 Bd 22.30S 17.00 E
Windischgarsten 128 Ic 47.43N 14.20 E
Wind Mountain 186 Dj 32.02N 105.34W
Windom 186 Ie 43.52N 95.07W
Windom Mountain 186 Ch 37.37N 107.35W
Windorah 212 Ie 25.26S 142.39 E
Window Rock 188 Ki 35.41N 109.03W
Wind River 188 Ke 43.08N 108.12W
Wind River Peak 188 Ke 42.42N 109.07W
Wind River Range 182 Fc 43.05N 109.25W
Windrush 118 Lj 51.42N 1.25W
Windsor [Eng.-U.K.] 118 Mj 51.29N 0.38W
Windsor [N.S.-Can.] 180 Lh 44.59N 64.09W
Windsor [Ont.-Can.] 180 Jh 42.18N 83.01W
Windsor Forest 184 Gj 31.58N 81.10W
Windward Islands 190 Lf 13.00N 61.00W
Windward Islands (EN) = Barlovento, Islas de- 174 Mh 15.00N 61.00W
Windward Islands (EN) = Sotavento, Islas de- 198 Jd 11.10N 67.00W
Windward Islands (EN) = Vent, Iles du- 208 Mf 17.30S 149.30W
Windward Passage (EN) = Vent, Canal du- 194 Lh 20.00N 73.50W
Windward Passage (EN) = Vientos, Paso de los- 174 Lh 20.00N 73.50W
Winfield [Al.-U.S.] 184 Di 33.56N 87.49W
Winfield [Ks.-U.S.] 182 Hd 37.15N 96.59W
Wingene 124 Fc 51.04N 3.16 E
Wingen-sur-Moder 124 Jf 48.55N 7.22 E
Winisk 176 Kd 55.15N 85.12W
Winisk 174 Kd 55.17N 85.05W
Winisk Lake 180 If 52.55N 87.20W
Winkler 186 Hb 49.11N 97.56W
Winklern 128 Gd 46.52N 12.52 E
Winneba 166 Ed 5.20N 0.37W
Winnebago, Lake- 182 Jc 44.00N 88.25W
Winnemucca 182 Dc 40.58N 117.44W
Winnemucca Lake 188 Ff 40.10N 119.20W
Winner 182 Hc 43.22N 99.51W
Winnett 188 Kc 47.00N 108.21W
Winnfield 186 Jk 31.55N 92.38W
Winnibigoshish, Lake- 186 Ic 47.27N 94.12W
Winnipeg 176 Je 49.53N 97.09W
Winnipeg 174 Jd 50.38N 96.19W
Winnipeg, Lake- 174 Jd 52.00N 97.00W
Winnipeg Beach 186 Ha 50.31N 96.58W
Winnipegosis 180 Hf 51.39N 99.56W
Winnipegosis, Lake- 174 Jd 52.30N 100.00W
Winnipesaukee, Lake- 184 Ld 43.35N 71.20W
Winnsboro 186 Kj 32.10N 91.43W
Winnweiler 124 Je 49.34N 7.51 E
Winona [Mn.-U.S.] 182 Ic 44.03N 91.39W
Winona [Mo.-U.S.] 186 Kh 37.06N 91.19W
Winona [Ms.-U.S.] 186 Lj 33.29N 89.44W
Winschoten 122 Na 53.08N 7.02 E
Winsen (Luhe) 120 Gc 53.22N 10.13 E
Winslow [Az.-U.S.] 182 Ed 35.01N 110.42W
Winslow [Eng.-U.K.] 124 Bc 51.57N 0.52W
Winslow Reef 208 Je 1.36S 174.57W
Winston-Salem 182 Kd 36.06N 80.15W
Winterberg 120 Ee 51.12N 8.32 E
Winter Harbour 180 Gb 75.00N 111.00W
Winter Harbour 180 Gb 74.46N 110.40W
Winter Haven 182 Kf 28.01N 81.44W
Winter Park [Co.-U.S.] 186 Dg 39.47N 105.45W
Winter Park [Fl.-U.S.] 184 Gk 28.36N 81.20W
Winters 186 Gk 31.57N 99.58W
Winterset 186 If 41.20N 94.01W
Winterswijk 122 Mc 51.58N 6.44 E
Winterthur 128 Cc 47.30N 8.45 E
Winton [Austl.] 210 Fg 22.23S 143.02 E
Winton [N.C.-U.S.] 184 Ig 36.24N 76.56W
Winton [N.Z.] 218 Cg 46.09S 168.20 E
Wipper [Ger.] 120 He 51.20N 11.10 E
Wipper [Ger.] 120 He 51.47N 11.42 E
Wisbech 118 Ni 52.40N 0.10 E
Wiscasset 184 Mc 44.00N 69.40W
Wisch 124 Ic 51.55N 6.22 E
Wisch-Terborg 124 Ic 51.55N 6.22 E
Wisconsin [2] 182 Jc 44.45N 89.30W
Wisconsin 174 Je 43.00N 91.15W
Wisconsin Range 222 Ng 85.45S 125.00W
Wisconsin Rapids 182 Jc 44.23N 89.49W
Wiseman 178 Ic 67.25N 150.06W
Wisła 120 Og 49.39N 18.50 E
Wisła = Vistula (EN) 110 He 54.22N 18.55 E
Wiślana, Mierzeja- 120 Pb 54.25N 19.30 E
Wiślane, Żuławy- 120 Ob 54.10N 19.00 E
Wiślany, Zalew- 120 Pb 54.27N 19.40 E
Wisłok 120 Sf 50.13N 22.32 E
Wisłoka 120 Rf 50.27N 21.23 E
Wismar 120 Hc 53.54N 11.28 E
Wismarbucht 120 Hc 53.57N 11.25 E
Wissant 124 Dd 50.53N 1.40 E
Wissembourg 122 Ne 49.02N 7.57 E
Wissen 120 Df 50.47N 7.45 E
Wissenkerke 124 Fc 51.35N 3.45 E
Wissey 124 Cb 52.34N 0.21 E
Witbank 160 Jk 25.56S 29.07 E
Witchekar Lake 186 Fb 49.15N 100.16W
Witdraai 172 Ce 26.58S 20.41 E
Witham 124 Cc 51.47N 0.38 E
Witham 118 Ni 52.56N 0.04 E
Withernsea 118 Nh 53.44N 0.02 E
Witkowo 120 Nd 52.27N 17.47 E
Witmarsum, Wonseradeel- 124 Ha 53.06N 5.28 E
Witney 118 Lj 51.48N 1.29W
Witnica 120 Kd 52.40N 14.55 E
Witputz 172 Be 27.37S 16.42 E
Witten 120 De 51.26N 7.20 E
Wittenberg [Ger.] 120 Ie 51.52N 12.39 E
Wittenberg [Wi.-U.S.] 186 Ld 44.49N 89.10W
Wittenberge 120 Hc 53.00N 11.45 E
Wittenoom 212 Dd 22.17S 118.19 E
Wittingen 120 Gd 52.44N 10.43 E
Wittlich 120 Cg 49.59N 6.53 E
Wittmund 120 Dc 53.34N 7.47 E
Wittow 120 Jb 54.38N 13.19 E
Wittstock 120 Ic 53.09N 12.30 E
Witu 170 Hc 2.23S 40.26 E
Witu Islands 214 Dh 4.40S 149.18 E
Witvlei 172 Bd 22.23S 18.32 E
Witzenhausen 120 Fe 51.20N 9.52 E
Wivenhoe 124 Cc 51.51N 0.58 E
Wizard Reef 158 Mi 8.57S 51.01 E
Wizna 120 Sc 53.13N 22.26 E
Wjdawka 120 Oe 51.32N 18.52 E
W. J. Van Blommestein Meer 202 Hc 4.45N 55.00W
Wkra 120 Qd 52.27N 20.44 E
Władysławowo 120 Ob 54.49N 18.25 E
Włocławek 120 Pd 52.39N 19.02 E
Włocławek [2] 120 Od 52.40N 19.00 E
Włodawa 120 Te 51.34N 23.32 E
Włoszczowa 120 Pf 50.25N 19.59 E
Wodonga 212 Jg 36.17S 146.54 E
Wodzisław Śląski 120 Of 50.00N 18.28 E
Woensdrecht 124 Gc 51.25N 4.18 E
Woerden 124 Gb 52.05N 4.52 E
Woerth 124 Jf 48.56N 7.45 E
Woëvre, Plaine de la- 122 Le 49.15N 5.45 E
Wohlthat-Massif 222 Cf 71.35S 12.20 E
Woippy 124 Ie 49.09N 6.09 E
Wojerecy/Hoyerswerda 120 Ke 51.26N 14.15 E
Wokam, Pulau- 150 Jh 5.37S 134.30 E
Woken He 154 Ja 46.19N 129.34 E
Woking 118 Mj 51.20N 0.34W
Wokingham 124 Bc 51.25N 0.50W
Wolbrom 120 Pf 50.24N 19.46 E
Wolcott 184 Id 43.13N 76.42W
Wołczyn 120 Oe 51.01N 18.03 E
Woldberg 124 Hb 52.25N 5.55 E
Woleai Atoll 208 Fd 7.21N 143.52 E
Woleu-Ntem [3] 170 Bb 2.00N 12.00 E
Wolf, Isla- 202a Aa 1.23N 91.49W
Wolf, Volcán- 202a Ab 0.01S 91.20W
Wolfach 120 Eh 48.18N 8.13 E
Wolf Creek 188 Ic 47.00N 112.04W
Wolf Creek 186 Gh 36.35N 99.30W
Wolfen 120 Ie 51.40N 12.17 E
Wolfenbüttel 120 Gd 52.10N 10.33 E
Wolfhagen 120 Fe 51.19N 9.10 E
Wolf Point 182 Fb 48.05N 105.39W
Wolfratshausen 120 Hi 47.54N 11.25 E
Wolf River 186 Ld 44.11N 88.48W
Wolfsberg 128 Id 46.50N 14.50 E
Wolfsburg 120 Gd 52.26N 10.48 E
Wolfstein 124 Je 49.35N 7.36 E
Wolgast 120 Jb 54.03N 13.46 E
Wolica 120 Tf 50.54N 23.12 E
Wolin 120 Kc 53.50N 14.35 E
Wolin 120 Kc 53.51N 14.38 E
Wollaston 124 Bb 52.15N 0.40W
Wollaston, Islas- 206 Gi 55.40S 67.30W
Wollaston Forland 179 Jd 74.35N 20.15W
Wollaston Lake 180 He 58.05N 103.38W
Wollaston Lake 174 Id 58.15N 103.20W
Wollaston Peninsula 174 Hc 70.00N 115.00W
Wollongong 210 Gh 34.25S 150.54 E
Wöllstein 124 Je 49.49N 7.58 E
Wolmaransstad 172 De 27.12S 26.13 E
Wołomin 120 Rd 52.21N 21.14 E
Wołów 120 Me 51.29N 16.55 E
Wolseley 180 Hf 50.25N 103.19W
Wolstenholme, Cap - 180 Jd 62.34N 77.30W
Wolstenholme Fjord 179 Ec 76.40N 69.45W
Wolsztyn 120 Md 52.08N 16.06 E
Wolvega, Weststellingwerf- 124 Ib 52.53N 6.00 E
Wolverhampton 118 Ki 52.36N 2.08W
Wolverton 118 Mi 52.04N 0.50W
Wŏnju 152 Md 37.21N 127.58 E
Wŏnsan 142 Of 39.10N 127.26 E
Wonseradeel 124 Ha 53.06N 5.28 E
Wonseradeel-Witmarsum 124 Ha 53.06N 5.28 E
Wonthaggi 212 Jg 38.36S 145.35 E
Woodall Mountain 186 Li 34.45N 88.11W
Woodbridge 118 Oi 52.06N 1.19 E

Index Symbols

[1] Independent Nation
[2] State, Region
[3] District, County
[4] Municipality
[5] Colony, Dependency
Continent
Physical Region
Historical or Cultural Region
Mount, Mountain
Volcano
Hill
Mountains, Mountain Range
Hills, Escarpment
Plateau, Upland
Pass, Gap
Plain, Lowland
Delta
Salt Flat
Valley, Canyon
Crater, Cave
Karst Features
Depression
Polder
Desert, Dunes
Forest, Woods
Heath, Steppe
Oasis
Cape, Point
Coast, Beach
Cliff
Peninsula
Isthmus
Sandbank
Island
Atoll
Rock, Reef
Islands, Archipelago
Rocks, Reefs
Coral Reef
Well, Spring
Geyser
River, Stream
Waterfall, Rapids
River Mouth, Estuary
Lake
Salt Lake
Intermittent Lake
Reservoir
Swamp, Pond
Canal
Glacier
Ice Shelf, Pack Ice
Ocean
Sea
Gulf, Bay
Strait, Fjord
Lagoon
Bank
Seamount
Tablemount
Ridge
Shelf
Basin
Escarpment, Sea Scarp
Fracture
Trench, Abyss
National Park, Reserve
Point of Interest
Recreation Site
Cave, Cavern
Historic Site
Ruins
Wall, Walls
Church, Abbey
Temple
Scientific Station
Railway station
Airport
Port
Military installation
Lighthouse
Mine
Tunnel
Dam, Bridge

Woodbridge Bay 197g Bb 15.19N 61.25W
Woodhall Spa 124 Ba 53.09N 0.13W
Woodland [Ca.-U.S.] 188 Eg 38.41N 121.46W
Woodland [Wa.-U.S.] 188 Dd 45.54N 122.45W
Woodlark Island 208 Ge 9.05S 152.50 E
Wood Mountain 188 Lb 49.14N 106.20W
Woodridge 186 Hb 49.17N 96.09W
Wood River 188 Lb 50.08N 106.10W
Wood River Lakes 178 He 59.30N 158.45W
Woodroffe, Mount- 212 Ge 26.20S 131.45 E
Woods, Lake- 212 Gc 17.50S 133.30 E
Woods, Lake of the- 174 Je 49.15N 94.45W
Woods Hole 184 Le 41.31N 70.40W
Woodside 188 Jg 39.21N 110.18W
Woodstock [Eng.-U.K.] 118 Lj 51.52N 1.21W
Woodstock [N.B.-Can.] 180 Kg 46.09N 67.34W
Woodstock [Ont.-Can.] 184 Gd 43.08N 80.45W
Woodstock [Vt.-U.S.] 184 Kd 43.37N 72.31W
Woodville [Ms.-U.S.] 186 Kk 31.01N 91.18W
Woodville [N.Z.] 218 Fd 40.20S 175.52 E
Woodville [Tx.-U.S.] 186 Ik 30.46N 94.25W
Woodward 182 Hd 36.26N 99.24W
Wooler 118 Kf 55.33N 2.01W
Woomera 212 Hf 31.11S 137.10 E
Wooramel River 212 Ce 25.47S 114.10 E
Wooster 184 Ge 40.46N 81.57W
Worcester 118 Ki 52.15N 2.10W
Worcester [Eng.-U.K.] 118 Ki 52.11N 2.13W
Worcester [Ma.-U.S.] 182 Mc 42.16N 71.48W
Worcester [S.Afr.] 160 Il 33.39S 19.27 E
Worcester Range 222 Jf 78.50S 161.00 E
Wörgl 128 Gc 47.29N 12.04 E
Workai, Pulau- 150 Jh 6.40S 134.40 E
Workington 118 Jg 54.39N 3.33W
Worksop 118 Lh 53.18N 1.07W
Workum 124 Hb 52.59N 5.27 E
Worland 182 Fc 44.01N 107.57W
Wormer 124 Gb 52.30N 4.52 E
Wormhout 124 Ed 50.53N 2.28 E
Worms 120 Eg 49.38N 8.21 E
Worms Head 118 Ij 51.34N 4.20W
Wörrstadt 124 Ke 49.50N 8.06 E
Wörth am Rhein 124 Ke 49.03N 8.16 E
Wörther-See 128 Id 46.37N 14.10 E
Worthing 118 Mk 50.48N 0.23W
Worthington 182 Hc 43.37N 95.36W
Wosi 150 Ig 0.11S 127.58 E
Wotho Atoll 208 Hc 10.06N 165.59 E
Wotje Atoll 208 Id 9.27N 170.02 E
Woudenberg 124 Hb 52.05N 5.25 E
Wounnioné, Pointe- 219b Db 14.54S 168.02 E
Wounta, Laguna de- 194 Fg 13.38N 83.34W
Wour 168 Ba 21.21N 15.57 E
Wousi 219b Cb 15.22S 166.39 E
Wowoni, Pulau- 150 Hg 4.08S 123.06 E
Woy Woy 212 Kf 33.30S 151.20 E
Wrangel, ostrov- = Wrangel Island (EN) 140 Tb 71.00N 179.30 E
Wrangel Island (EN) = Wrangel, ostrov- 140 Tb 71.00N 179.30 E
Wrangell 176 Fd 56.28N 132.23W
Wrangell, Cape- 178a Ab 52.50N 172.26 E
Wrangell Mountains 174 Ec 62.00N 143.00W
Wrath, Cape- 110 Fd 58.37N 5.01W
Wray 182 Gc 40.05N 102.13W
Wreake 124 Ab 52.41N 1.05W
Wreck Reef 208 Gg 22.15S 155.10 E
Wrecks, Bay of- 220g Bb 1.52N 157.17W
Wrexham 118 Kh 53.03N 3.00W
Wright Island 222 Of 74.03S 116.45W
Wright Patman Lake 186 Ij 33.16N 94.14W
Wrightson, Mount- 188 Jk 31.42N 110.50W
Wrigley 180 Fd 63.19N 123.38W
Wrigley Gulf 222 Nf 74.00S 129.00W
Wrocław [2] 120 Me 51.05N 17.00 E
Wrocław=Breslau (EN) 112 He 51.06N 17.00 E
Wronki 120 Md 52.43N 16.23 E
Wrotham 124 Cc 51.18N 0.19 E
Wroxham 124 Db 52.42N 1.24 E
Września 120 Nd 52.20N 17.34 E
Wschodnia 120 Rf 50.30N 21.18 E
Wschowa 120 Me 51.48N 16.19 E
Wu'an 154 Cf 36.42N 114.12 E
Wuchale 168 Fc 11.31N 39.37 E
Wuchang 154 Ib 44.55N 127.11 E
Wuchang, Wuhan- 154 Ci 30.32N 114.18 E
Wucheng (Jiucheng) 154 Df 37.12N 116.04 E
Wuchiu Hsu 152 Kg 25.00N 119.27 E
Wuchuan 154 Ad 41.08N 111.25 E
Wuchuan (Duru) 152 If 28.28N 107.57 E
Wuchuan (Meilü) 152 Jg 21.28N 110.44 E
Wuda 152 Id 39.30N 106.33 E
Wudan → Ongniud Qi 152 Kc 42.58N 119.01 E
Wudao 152 Ld 39.28N 121.30 E
Wudaoliang 152 Fd 35.15N 93.14 E
Wudi 154 Df 37.44N 117.36 E
Wudil 166 Gc 11.49N 8.51 E
Wuding 152 Hf 25.36N 102.27 E
Wudu 152 He 33.24N 105.00 E
Wugang 152 Jf 26.48N 110.32 E
Wugong (Puji) 152 Ie 34.15N 108.14 E
Wuhai 152 Id 39.32N 106.55 E
Wuhan 142 Nf 30.30N 114.20 E
Wuhan-Hankou 154 Ci 30.35N 114.16 E
Wuhan-Hanyang 154 Ci 30.33N 114.16 E
Wuhan- Wuchang 154 Ci 30.32N 114.18 E
Wuhe 152 Ke 33.08N 117.51 E
Wuhu 142 Nf 31.18N 118.27 E
Wuhu (Wanzhi) 154 Ei 31.21N 118.23 E
Wujia He 152 Ic 40.56N 108.52 E
Wujiang 154 Fi 31.09N 120.38 E
Wu Jiang 140 Mg 29.43N 107.24 E
Wukari 160 Hh 7.51N 9.47 E
Wukro 168 Fc 13.48N 39.37 E
Wular 148 Eb 34.30N 74.30 E
Wulff Land 179 Hb 82.19N 50.00W
Wulian (Hongning) 154 Eg 35.45N 119.13 E
Wuliang Shan 152 Hg 24.00N 101.00 E
Wuliaru, Pulau- 150 Jh 7.27S 131.04 E
Wuling Shan 140 Mg 28.20N 110.00 E
Wulongbei 154 Hd 40.15N 124.16 E
Wulongji → Huaibin 154 Ci 32.27N 115.23 E
Wulur 150 Ih 7.09S 128.39 E
Wum 166 Hd 6.23N 10.04 E
Wumei Shan 154 Cj 28.47N 114.50 E
Wümme 124 Ka 53.10N 8.40 E
Wuning 154 Cj 29.17N 115.05 E
Wünnenberg 124 Kc 51.31N 8.42 E
Wünnenberg-Haaren 124 Kc 51.34N 8.44 E
Wunnummin Lake 180 If 52.55N 89.10W
Wun Rog 168 Dd 9.00N 28.21 E
Wunstorf 120 Fd 52.26N 9.25 E
Wuntho 148 Jd 23.54N 95.41 E
Wupper 124 Ce 51.05N 7.00 E
Wuppertal 120 De 51.16N 7.11 E
Wuqi 152 Id 36.57N 108.15 E
Wuqia/Ulugqat 152 Cd 39.40N 75.07 E
Wuqiao (Sangyuan) 154 Df 37.38N 116.23 E
Wuqing 154 De 39.23N 117.04 E
Wuqing (Yangcun) 154 De 39.23N 117.04 E
Würm 124 Kf 48.53N 8.42 E
Würmsee → Starnberger See 120 Hi 47.55N 11.20 E
Wurno 166 Gc 13.18N 5.26 E
Würselen 124 Id 50.49N 6.08 E
Würzburg 112 Gf 49.48N 9.56 E
Wurzen 120 Ie 51.22N 12.44 E
Wu Shan 152 Ie 31.00N 110.00 E
Wushaoling 152 Hd 37.15N 102.50 E
Wusheng Guan 152 Je 31.45N 114.04 E
Wuski/Uqturpan 152 Cc 41.10N 79.16 E
Wusong 154 Fi 31.23N 121.29 E
Wüst Seamount (EN) 158 Gl 34.00S 3.40W
Wusuli Jiang 152 Ob 48.28N 135.02 E
Wutach 120 Ei 47.37N 8.15 E
Wutai [China] 154 Be 38.43N 113.14 E
Wutai [China] 152 Dc 44.38N 82.06 E
Wutai Shan 152 Jd 39.04N 113.28 E
Wuustwezel 124 Gc 51.23N 4.36 E
Wuvulu Island 208 Fe 1.43S 142.50 E
Wuwei 154 Di 31.17N 117.54 E
Wuwei (Liangzhou) 142 Mf 37.58N 102.48 E
Wuxi [China] 142 Of 31.32N 120.18 E
Wuxi [China] 152 Ie 31.27N 109.34 E
Wu Xia 152 Je 31.02N 110.10 E
Wuxiang (Duancun) 154 Bf 36.50N 112.51 E
Wuxing (Huzhou) 152 Le 30.47N 120.07 E
Wuxue → Guangji 152 Kf 29.58N 115.32 E
Wuyang [China] 152 Jd 36.29N 113.07 E
Wuyang [China] 154 Bh 33.26N 113.35 E
Wuyang → Zhenyuan 152 If 27.05N 108.26 E
Wuyi [China] 154 Ej 28.54N 119.50 E
Wuyi [China] 154 Cf 37.49N 115.54 E
Wuyiling 152 Mb 48.37N 129.20 E
Wuyi Shan 140 Ng 27.00N 117.00 E
Wuyuan [China] 142 Me 41.08N 108.17 E
Wuyuan [China] 152 Dj 29.15N 117.52 E
Wuyuanzhen → Haiyan 154 Fi 30.31N 120.56 E
Wuzhai 154 Ae 38.54N 111.49 E
Wuzhen 154 Ai 31.42N 112.00 E
Wuzhi Shan [China] 154 Ed 40.31N 118.02 E
Wuzhi Shan [China] 152 Ih 18.54N 109.40 E
Wuzhong 152 Id 38.00N 106.10 E
Wuzhou 142 Ng 23.32N 111.21 E
Wyalkatchem 212 Df 31.10S 117.22 E
Wyandotte 184 Fd 42.12N 83.10W
Wyandra 212 Je 27.15S 145.59 E
Wye 124 Cc 51.11N 0.56 E
Wye 118 Kj 51.37N 2.39W
Wyemandoo, Mount- 212 De 28.31S 118.32 E
Wyk auf Föhr 120 Eb 54.42N 8.34 E
Wylie, Lake- 184 Gh 35.07N 81.02W
Wymondham 118 Oi 52.34N 1.07 E
Wyndham [Austl.] 210 Df 15.28S 128.06 E
Wyndham [N.Z.] 218 Cg 46.20S 168.51 E
Wyndmere 186 Hc 46.16N 97.08W
Wynne 186 Ki 35.14N 90.47W
Wynniatt Bay 180 Gb 72.50N 111.00W
Wynyard [Austl.] 212 Jh 40.59S 145.41 E
Wynyard [Sask.-Can.] 186 Hf 51.47N 104.10W
Wyoming 184 Ed 42.54N 85.42W
Wyoming [2] 182 Fc 43.00N 107.30W
Wyoming Peak 186 Ec 42.36N 110.37W
Wyśmierzyce 120 Qe 51.38N 20.49 E
Wysoka 120 Nc 53.11N 17.05 E
Wysokie Mazowieckie 120 Sd 52.56N 22.32 E
Wyszków 120 Rd 52.36N 21.28 E
Wyszogród 120 Qd 52.23N 20.11 E
Wytheville 184 Gg 36.57N 81.07W
Wyvjlle Thomson Ridge (EN) 118 Fa 60.10N 8.00W
Wyvis, Ben- 118 Id 57.42N 4.30W

X

Xàbia / Jávea 126 Mf 38.47N 0.10 E
Xaintrie 122 Ii 45.00N 2.10 E
Xainza 152 Ee 30.50N 88.37 E
Xaitongmoin 152 Ef 29.26N 88.08 E
Xai-Xai 160 Kk 25.04S 33.39 E
Xamba → Hanggin Houqi 152 Ic 40.59N 107.07 E
Xam Nua 148 Kd 20.25N 104.02 E
Xá-Muteba 170 Cd 9.34S 17.50 E
Xangongo 160 Ij 16.46S 14.59 E
Xang Qu 152 Ef 29.22N 89.09 E
Xanten 120 Ce 51.40N 6.27 E
Xánthi 130 Hh 41.08N 24.53 E
Xanthos 146 Cd 36.20N 29.20 E
Xanxerê 206 Jc 26.53S 52.23W
Xapuri 202 Ef 10.39S 68.31W
Xar Hudag 152 Jb 45.06N 114.30 E
Xar Moron 154 Ac 42.37N 111.02 E
Xar Moron He 152 Lc 43.24N 120.39 E
Xarrama 126 Df 38.14N 8.20W
Xàtiva/Játiva 126 Lf 38.59N 0.31W
Xau, Lake- 172 Cd 21.15S 24.44 E
Xavantes, Represa de- 204 Hf 23.20S 49.35W
Xavantina 204 Fe 21.15S 52.48W
Xavier / Javier 126 Kb 42.36N 1.13W
Xayar 152 Dc 41.15N 82.50 E
Xebert 154 Fc 44.00N 122.00 E
Xêgar → Tingri 152 Ef 28.41N 87.00 E
Xenia 184 Ff 39.41N 83.56W
Xiachengzi 154 Kb 44.41N 130.26 E
Xiacun → Rushan 154 Ff 36.55N 121.30 E
Xiaguan 152 Hf 25.32N 100.12 E
Xiahe (Labrang) 152 Hd 35.18N 102.30 E
Xiajin 154 Cf 36.57N 116.00 E
Xiamen = Amoy (EN) 142 Ng 24.32N 118.06 E
Xi'an 142 Mf 34.15N 108.50 E
Xianbin Ansha 150 Ge 9.48N 116.38 E
Xianfeng 152 If 29.41N 109.09 E
Xiangcheng 154 Bh 33.51N 113.29 E
Xiangcheng/Qagchêng 152 Gf 28.56N 99.46 E
Xiangcheng (Shuizhai) 154 Ch 33.27N 114.53 E
Xiangfan 142 Nf 32.03N 112.05 E
Xianggang/Hong Kong [5] 142 Ng 22.15N 114.10 E
Xianghua Ling 152 Jf 25.26N 112.32 E
Xianghuang Qi (Xin Bulag) 152 Jc 42.12N 113.59 E
Xiang Jiang 140 Ng 29.26N 113.08 E
Xiangkhoang 148 Ke 19.20N 103.22 E
Xiangkhoang, Plateau de- 148 Ke 19.30N 103.10 E
Xiangquan He 152 Ce 32.05N 79.20 E
Xiangshan (Dancheng) 152 Lf 29.29N 121.52 E
Xiangshan Gang 154 Fj 29.35N 121.38 E
Xiangtan 142 Ng 27.54N 112.55 E
Xiangtang 154 Cj 28.26N 115.59 E
Xiangyin 154 Bj 28.41N 112.53 E
Xiangyuan 154 Bf 36.32N 113.02 E
Xianju 152 Lf 28.50N 120.42 E
Xianning 154 Cj 29.52N 114.17 E
Xiannümiao → Jiangdu 154 Eh 32.30N 119.33 E
Xiantaozhen → Mianyang 154 Bi 30.22N 113.27 E
Xianxia Ling 152 Kf 28.24N 118.40 E
Xianxian 154 De 38.12N 116.07 E
Xianyang 152 Ie 34.26N 108.40 E
Xiaobole Shan 152 La 51.46N 124.09 E
Xiao'ergou 152 Lb 49.10N 123.43 E
Xiaogan 152 Je 30.52N 113.58 E
Xiao He 154 Bf 37.38N 112.24 E
Xiao Hinggan Ling = Lesser Khingan Range (EN) 140 Oe 48.45N 127.00 E
Xiaoling He 154 Fd 40.55N 121.12 E
Xiaoluan He 154 Dd 41.36N 117.05 E
Xiaoqing He 154 Ef 37.19N 118.59 E
Xiaoshan 154 Fi 30.10N 120.16 E
Xiaowutai Shan 154 Ce 39.57N 114.59 E
Xiaoxian 154 Dg 34.11N 116.56 E
Xiaoyi 154 Af 37.07N 111.48 E
Xiaoyi → Gongxian 154 Bg 34.46N 112.57 E
Xiapu 152 Kf 26.57N 119.59 E
Xiawa 154 Fc 42.36N 120.33 E
Xiayi 154 Dg 34.14N 116.07 E
Xiazhuang → Linshu 154 Eg 34.56N 118.38 E
Xicalango, Punta- 192 Nh 19.41N 92.00W
Xichang 142 Mg 27.52N 102.15 E
Xicheng → Yangyuan 154 Cd 40.08N 114.10 E
Xicoténcatl 192 Jf 23.00N 98.56W
Xicotepec de Juárez 192 Kg 20.17N 97.57W
Xiejiaji → Qingyun 154 Df 37.46N 117.22 E
Xifei He 154 Dh 32.38N 116.39 E
Xifeng 154 Hc 42.45N 124.44 E
Xifengzhen 152 Id 35.40N 107.42 E
Xigazê 142 Kg 29.15N 88.52 E
Xi He [China] 154 Dj 29.38N 116.53 E
Xi He [China] 152 Hc 42.23N 101.03 E
Xiheying 154 Ce 39.53N 114.42 E
Xihua 154 Ch 33.48N 114.31 E
Xi Jang 140 Ng 23.05N 114.23 E
Xiji [China] 154 Ia 46.09N 127.08 E
Xiji [China] 152 Id 35.52N 105.35 E
Xi Jiang 152 Jg 23.05N 114.23 E
Xijir Ulan Hu 152 Fd 35.12N 90.18 E
Xikouzi 152 La 42.58N 120.29 E
Xiliao He 140 Oe 43.24N 123.42 E
Xiligou → Ulan 152 Gd 36.55N 98.16 E
Xilin 152 Ig 24.30N 105.05 E
Xilin Gol 154 Dc 43.55N 116.05 E
Xilin Hot → Abagnar Qi 142 Ne 43.58N 116.08 E
Xilitla 192 Jg 21.20N 98.58W
Xilókastron 130 Fk 38.05N 22.38 E
Ximiao 152 Hc 41.04N 100.14 E
Xin'an 154 Bg 34.43N 112.09 E
Xin'anjiang 154 Ei 29.27N 119.15 E
Xin'anjiang Shuiku 154 Ej 29.25N 119.05 E
Xin'anzhen → Guannan 154 Eg 34.04N 119.21 E
Xin'anzhen → Xinyi 152 Ke 34.17N 118.14 E
Xin Barag Youqi (Altan-Emel) 152 Kb 48.41N 116.47 E
Xin Barag Zuoqi (Amgalang) 152 Kb 48.13N 118.14 E
Xinbin 154 Hd 41.44N 125.02 E
Xin Bulag → Xianghuang Qi 152 Jc 42.12N 113.59 E
Xincai 152 Je 32.40N 114.57 E
Xinchang 154 Fj 29.30N 120.54 E
Xincheng [China] 152 Ig 24.04N 108.39 E
Xincheng [China] 154 Bf 37.57N 112.33 E
Xincheng [China] 152 Id 38.33N 106.10 E
Xincheng (Gaobeidian) 154 Ce 39.20N 115.50 E
Xindi → Honghu 154 Bj 29.50N 113.28 E
Xing'an → Ankang 142 Mf 32.37N 109.03 E
Xingcheng 154 Fd 40.38N 120.43 E
Xingguo 152 Kf 26.22N 115.21 E
Xinghai 152 Gd 35.45N 99.59 E
Xinghe 152 Jc 40.52N 113.56 E
Xinghua 154 Eh 32.56N 119.49 E
Xinghua Hu = Khanka Lake (EN) 140 Pe 45.00N 132.24 E
Xinglong 154 Dd 40.25N 117.31 E
Xinglongzhen 154 Ia 46.26N 127.03 E
Xingren 152 If 25.26N 105.08 E
Xingtai 142 Nf 37.00N 114.30 E
Xingtang 154 Ce 38.26N 114.33 E
Xingu, Rio- 198 Kf 1.30S 51.53W
Xingxingxia 152 Gc 41.47N 95.07 E
Xingyang 154 Bg 34.47N 113.21 E
Xingyi (Huangcaoba) 152 Hf 25.03N 104.55 E
Xingzi 154 Dj 29.28N 116.03 E
Xinhe 154 Cf 37.32N 115.14 E
Xinhe/Toksu 152 Dc 41.34N 82.38 E
Xin Hot → Abag Qi 152 Jc 44.01N 114.59 E
Xinhuai He 154 Fg 34.23N 120.05 E
Xinhui → Aohan Qi 154 Ec 42.18N 119.53 E
Xining 142 Mf 36.37N 101.46 E
Xinji → Shulu 154 Cf 37.56N 115.14 E
Xinjian 154 Cj 28.41N 115.50 E
Xin Jiang 154 Dj 28.37N 116.40 E
Xinjiangkou → Songzi 154 Ai 30.10N 111.46 E
Xinjiang Uygur Zizhiqu (Hsin-chiang-wei-wu-erh Tzu-chih-ch'ü) = Sinkiang Uighur (EN) [2] 152 Ec 42.00N 86.00 E
Xinjin 152 He 30.25N 103.46 E
Xinjin (Pulandian) 152 Ld 39.24N 121.59 E
Xinkai He 154 Gc 43.36N 122.31 E
Xinle 154 Ce 38.15N 114.40 E
Xinlin 154 Ec 43.58N 118.03 E
Xinlitun [China] 154 Gc 42.01N 122.11 E
Xinlitun [China] 152 Ma 50.58N 126.39 E
Xinlong/Nyagrong 152 He 30.57N 100.12 E
Xinmin 154 Gc 42.00N 122.50 E
Xinpu → Lianyungang 142 Nf 34.34N 119.15 E
Xinqing 152 Mb 48.15N 129.31 E
Xintai 154 Dg 35.54N 117.44 E
Xinwen (Suncun) 152 Kd 35.49N 117.38 E
Xinxian [China] 152 Jd 38.24N 112.43 E
Xinxian [China] 154 Ci 31.42N 114.50 E
Xinxiang 142 Nf 35.17N 113.50 E
Xinyang 152 Je 32.05N 114.07 E
Xinye 154 Bh 32.30N 112.22 E
Xinyi (Xin'anzhen) 152 Ke 34.17N 118.14 E
Xinyi He 154 Eg 34.29N 119.49 E
Xinyuan/Künes 152 Dc 43.24N 83.18 E
Xinyuan → Tianjun 142 Lf 37.18N 99.15 E
Xinzhan 154 Ic 43.52N 127.20 E
Xin Zhen → Hanggin Qi 152 Id 39.54N 108.55 E
Xinzheng 154 Bg 34.25N 113.46 E
Xinzhou 154 Ci 30.51N 114.49 E
Xinzo de Limia 126 Eb 42.03N 7.43W
Xiong Xian 154 De 38.59N 116.06 E
Xionyuecheng 154 Gd 40.12N 122.08 E
Xiping [China] 154 Bh 33.22N 114.00 E
Xiping [China] 154 Ej 28.27N 119.29 E
Xisha Qundao = Paracel Islands (EN) 140 Nh 16.30N 112.15 E
Xishuangbanna 152 Gg 22.15N 100.00 E
Xishuanghe → Kenli 154 Ef 37.35N 118.30 E
Xishui 154 Ci 30.28N 115.15 E
Xi Taijnar Hu 152 Fd 37.15N 93.30 E
Xitianmu Shan 152 Ke 30.21N 119.25 E
Xi Ujimqin Qi (Bayan Ul Hot) 152 Kc 44.31N 117.33 E
Xiuning 154 Ej 29.47N 118.11 E
Xiushui 152 Jf 29.02N 114.33 E
Xiu Shui 154 Cj 29.13N 116.00 E
Xiuwu 154 Bg 35.13N 113.27 E
Xiuyan 152 Lc 40.18N 123.10 E
Xiwanzi → Chongli 154 Cd 40.57N 115.12 E
Xixabangma Feng 152 Ef 28.21N 85.47 E
Xixian 154 Ch 32.21N 114.43 E
Xixiang 152 Ie 32.58N 107.45 E
Xixona / Jijona 126 Lf 38.32N 0.30W
Xiyang 154 Bf 37.38N 113.41 E
Xizang Zizhiqu (Hsi-tsang Tzu-chih-ch'ü) = Tibet (EN) [2] 152 Ee 32.00N 90.00 E
Xizhong Dao 154 Fe 39.25N 121.18 E
Xochicalco 192 Jh 18.45N 99.20W
Xochimilco 192 Jh 19.16N 99.06W
Xorkol 152 Fd 39.04N 91.05 E
Xpujil 192 Oh 18.35N 89.25W
Xuancheng 154 Ei 30.56N 118.44 E
Xuande Qundao 150 Fc 17.08N 111.30 E
Xuan'en 152 Ie 30.02N 109.30 E
Xuanhan 152 Ie 31.23N 107.39 E
Xuanhua 152 Kc 40.39N 115.05 E
Xuanwei 152 Hf 26.19N 104.05 E
Xuchang 142 Nf 34.00N 113.58 E
Xuecheng (Lincheng) 154 Dg 34.38N 117.14 E
Xuefeng Shan 152 Jf 27.35N 110.50 E
Xue Shan 152 Gf 27.30N 99.55 E
Xugezhuang → Fengnan 154 Ee 39.34N 118.05 E
Xugou 154 Eg 34.37N 119.08 E
Xugui 152 Gd 35.45N 96.08 E
Xuguit Qi (Yakeshi) 152 Lb 49.16N 120.41 E
Xümatang 152 Ge 33.57N 97.00 E
Xun Jiang 152 Jg 23.28N 111.18 E
Xunke (Qike) 152 Mb 49.34N 128.28 E
Xunwu 152 Kg 24.59N 115.33 E
Xunxian 154 Cg 35.40N 114.33 E
Xupu 152 Jf 27.54N 110.35 E
Xúquer/Júcar 110 Fh 39.09N 0.14W
Xushui 154 Ce 39.02N 115.40 E
Xuwen 152 Jg 20.22N 110.10 E
Xuyi 152 Ke 32.58N 118.33 E
Xuyong (Yongning) 152 If 28.13N 105.26 E
Xuzhou 142 Nf 34.12N 117.13 E

Y

Ya'an 142 Mg 30.00N 102.57 E
Yabassi 166 Ge 4.28N 9.58 E
Yabe 156 Be 32.42N 130.59 E
Yabebyry 204 Dh 27.24S 57.11W
Yabelo 168 Fe 4.53N 38.07 E
Yablonovy Range (EN) = Jablonovy hrebet 140 Nd 53.30N 115.00 E
Yabrai Shan 152 Hc 40.00N 103.10 E
Yabrīn 168 Ha 23.15N 48.59 E
Yabrūd 146 Gf 33.58N 36.40 E
Yabucoa 197a Cb 18.03N 65.53W
Yabuli 152 Mc 44.56N 128.37 E
Yabulu 212 Jc 19.00S 146.40 E
Yacaré Cururu, Cuchilla- 204 Dj 30.30S 56.33W
Yacaré Norte, Riacho- 204 Cf 22.43S 58.14W
Yacaré Sur, Riacho- 204 Cf 22.43S 58.14W
Yachats 188 Cd 44.20N 124.03W
Yacuma, Rio- 202 Ef 13.38S 65.23W
Yacyretá, Isla- 204 Dh 27.25S 56.30W
Yadé, Massif du- 168 Bd 7.00N 15.30 E
Yādgīr 148 Fe 16.46N 77.08 E
Yadong/Chomo 152 Ef 27.38N 89.03 E
Yae-Dake 156b Ab 26.38N 127.56 E
Yaeyama-Rettō 152 Lg 24.20N 124.00 E
Yafran 164 Bc 32.04N 12.31 E
Yağcilar 130 Lj 39.25N 28.23 E
Yagishiri-Tō 156a Ba 44.26N 141.25 E
Yagoua 166 Ic 10.20N 15.14 E
Yagradagzê Shan 152 Gd 35.09N 95.39 E
Yaguajay 194 Hb 22.19N 79.14W
Yaguari 204 Ej 31.31S 54.58W
Yaguari, Arroyo- 204 Di 29.44S 57.37W
Yahyalı 146 Fc 38.05N 35.25 E
Yahualica de González Gallo 192 Hg 21.08N 102.51W
Yahuma 170 Db 1.06N 23.10 E
Yaita 156 Fc 36.50N 139.55 E
Yaizu 156 Fd 34.51N 138.19 E
Yajiang/Nyagquka 152 He 30.07N 100.58 E
Yakacik 146 Ed 36.05N 32.45 E
Yake-Dake 156 Ec 36.14N 137.35 E
Yakeishi-Dake 156 Gb 39.10N 140.50 E
Yakeshi → Xuguit Qi 152 Lb 49.16N 120.41 E
Yake-Yama 156 Gb 39.58N 140.48 E
Yakima 176 Ge 46.36N 120.31W
Yakima River 188 Fc 46.15N 119.02W
Yako 166 Ec 12.58N 2.16W
Yakumo 152 Pc 42.15N 140.16 E
Yaku-Shima 152 Ne 30.20N 130.30 E
Yakutat 178 Le 59.33N 139.44W
Yakutat Bay 178 Ke 59.45N 140.45W
Yala 148 Kg 6.32N 101.19 E
Yalahán, Laguna de- 192 Pg 21.30N 87.15W
Yalcubul Punta- 192 Og 21.35N 88.35W
Yale Point 188 Kh 36.25N 109.48W
Yalewa Kalou 219d Ab 16.40S 177.46 E
Yalgoo 212 De 28.20S 116.41 E
Yalikavak 130 Kl 37.06N 27.18 E
Yaliköy 130 Lh 41.29N 28.17 E
Yalinga 168 Cd 6.31N 23.13 E
Yaloké 168 Bd 5.19N 17.05 E
Yalong Jiang 140 Mg 26.37N 101.48 E
Yalova 146 Cb 40.39N 29.15 E
Yalu Jiang 140 Of 39.55N 124.20 E
Yalvaç 146 Dc 38.17N 31.11 E
Yām, Ramlat- 164 If 17.42N 45.09 E
Yamada [Jap.] 156 Be 33.33N 130.45 E
Yamada [Jap.] 154 Pe 39.28N 141.57 E
Yamada-Wan 156 Hb 39.30N 142.00 E
Yamaga 156 Be 33.01N 130.41 E
Yamagata 152 Pd 38.15N 140.15 E
Yamagata Ken [2] 154 Pe 38.30N 140.00 E
Yamagawa 156 Bf 31.12N 130.39 E
Yamaguchi 152 Ne 34.10N 131.29 E
Yamaguchi Ken [2] 154 Kh 34.10N 131.30 E
Yamakuni 156 Be 33.24N 131.02 E
Yamal Peninsula (EN) = Jamal, poluostrov- 140 Ib 70.00N 70.00 E
Yamamoto 156 Ga 40.06N 140.03 E
Yamanaka 156 Ec 36.15N 136.22 E
Yamanashi Ken [2] 154 Og 35.30N 138.35 E
Yamashiro 156 Ce 33.57N 133.43 E
Yamato Rise (EN) 154 Me 39.30N 134.30 E
Yamatsuri 156 Gc 36.53N 140.25 E
Yamazaki 156 Dd 35.00N 134.33 E
Yambi, Mesa de- 202 Dc 1.30N 71.20W
Yambio 160 Jh 4.34N 28.23 E
Yambo 168 Fd 8.25N 36.00 E
Yambu Head 197n Ba 13.09N 61.09W
Yambuya 170 Db 1.16N 24.33 E
Yame 156 Be 33.13N 130.34 E
Yamethin 148 Jd 20.26N 96.09 E
Yamma Yamma, Lake- 212 Ie 26.20S 141.25 E
Yamoto 156 Gb 38.25N 141.13 E
Yamoussoukro 166 Dd 6.49N 5.17W
Yampa River 182 Fc 40.32N 108.59W
Yampi Sound 212 Ec 16.11S 123.40 E
Yamuna 140 Kg 25.30N 81.53 E
Yamunanagar 148 Fb 30.08N 76.59 E
Yamzho Yumco 152 Ff 29.00N 90.40 E
Yanagawa 156 Be 33.10N 130.24 E
Yanahara 156 Dd 34.57N 134.05 E
Yanahuanca 202 Cf 10.30S 76.30W
Yanai 156 Ce 33.58N 132.07 E
Yanam 148 Ge 16.51N 82.15 E
Yan'an 142 Mf 36.36N 109.30 E
Yanaoca 202 Df 14.13S 71.26W
Yanbian 152 Hf 26.51N 101.32 E
Yanbu' 144 Ee 24.05N 38.03 E
Yanchang 152 Jd 36.39N 110.03 E
Yancheng [China] 152 Le 33.16N 120.10 E
Yancheng [China] 154 Bh 33.35N 114.00 E
Yanchi 152 Id 37.47N 107.24 E
Yandé 219b Ae 20.03S 163.48 E
Yandina 219a Dc 9.07S 159.13 E
Yandja 170 Cc 1.41S 17.43 E
Yandua 219d Bb 16.49S 178.18 E
Yanfolila 166 Dc 11.11N 8.08W
Yangalia 168 Cd 6.58N 21.01 E
Yangambi 160 Jh 0.47N 24.28 E
Yangcheng 154 Bg 35.32N 112.36 E
Yangchun 152 Jg 22.11N 111.48 E
Yangcun 154 De 39.23N 117.04 E
Yangcun → Wuqing 154 De 39.23N 117.04 E
Yangdŏg-ŭp 154 Ie 39.13N 126.39 E
Yangganga 219d Bb 16.35S 178.35 E
Yanggang-Do [2] 154 Jd 41.15N 128.00 E

Index Symbols

[1] Independent Nation
[2] State, Region
[3] District, County
[4] Municipality
[5] Colony, Dependency
Continent
Physical Region
Historical or Cultural Region
Mount, Mountain
Volcano
Hill
Mountains, Mountain Range
Hills, Escarpment
Plateau, Upland
Pass, Gap
Plain, Lowland
Delta
Salt Flat
Valley, Canyon
Crater, Cave
Karst Features
Depression
Polder
Desert, Dunes
Forest, Woods
Heath, Steppe
Oasis
Cape, Point
Coast, Beach
Cliff
Peninsula
Isthmus
Sandbank
Island
Atoll
Rock, Reef
Islands, Archipelago
Rocks, Reefs
Coral Reef
Well, Spring
Geyser
River, Stream
Waterfall, Rapids
River Mouth, Estuary
Lake
Salt Lake
Intermittent Lake
Reservoir
Swamp, Pond
Canal
Glacier
Ice Shelf, Pack Ice
Ocean
Sea
Gulf, Bay
Strait, Fjord
Lagoon
Bank
Seamount
Tablemount
Ridge
Shelf
Basin
Escarpment, Sea Scarp
Fracture
Trench, Abyss
National Park, Reserve
Point of Interest
Recreation Site
Cave, Cavern
Historic Site
Ruins
Wall, Walls
Church, Abbey
Temple
Scientific Station
Railway station
Airport
Port
Military installation
Lighthouse
Mine
Tunnel
Dam, Bridge

Yanggao 152 Jc 40.21N 113.47 E
Yanggeta 219d Ab 17.01S 177.20 E
Yanggu 154 Cf 36.08N 115.48 E
Yang He 154 Cd 40.24N 115.18 E
Yangi 130 Mm 36.55N 29.01 E
Yangjiang 152 Jg 21.59N 111.59 E
Yangjiazhangzi 154 Fd 40.48N 120.30 E
Yangon = Rangoon (EN) 142 Lh 16.47N 96.10 E
Yangor 220e Ab 0.32S 166.54 E
Yangqu (Huangzhai) 154 Be 38.05N 112.37 E
Yangquan 152 Jd 37.49N 113.34 E
Yangquanqu 152 Jd 37.04N 111.30 E
Yangshuo 152 Jg 24.46N 110.28 E
Yang Sin, Chu- 148 Lf 12.24N 108.26 E
Yangtze Kiang → Chang Jiang 140 Of 31.48N 121.10 E
Yangxian 152 Ie 33.20N 107.35 E
Yangxin [China] 152 Kf 29.50N 115.11 E
Yangxin [China] 154 Df 37.39N 117.34 E
Yangyuan (Xicheng) 154 Cd 40.08N 114.10 E
Yangzhou 152 Ke 32.20N 119.25 E
Yanhe (Heping) 152 If 28.31N 108.28 E
Yanji 152 Mc 42.56N 129.30 E
Yanjin 154 Cg 35.09N 114.11 E
Yankton 182 Hc 42.53N 97.23W
Yanling 154 Cg 34.07N 114.11 E
Yanqi 142 Ke 42.04N 86.34 E
Yanqing 154 Cd 40.28N 115.57 E
Yan Shan 140 Ne 40.18N 117.36 E
Yanshan [China] 154 De 38.03N 117.12 E
Yanshan [China] 152 Hg 23.38N 104.24 E
Yanshan (Hekou) 154 Dj 28.18N 117.41 E
Yanshi 154 Bg 34.44N 112.47 E
Yanshou 154 Jb 45.28N 128.19 E
Yantai 142 Of 37.28N 121.24 E
Yanutha 219d Ac 16.14S 178.00 E
Yanweigang 154 Eg 34.28N 119.46 E
Yanyuan 152 Hf 27.26N 101.32 E
Yanzhou 152 Kd 35.33N 116.49 E
Yao [Chad] 168 Bc 12.51N 17.34 E
Yao [Jap.] 156 Dd 34.38N 135.36 E
Yaodu → Dongzhi 154 Di 30.06N 117.01 E
Yaoundé 160 Ih 3.52N 11.31 E
Yapacani 202 Fg 16.36S 64.18W
Yapei 166 Ed 9.10N 1.10W
Yapen, Pulau- 208 Ee 1.45S 136.15 E
Yapen, Selat- 150 Kg 1.30S 136.10 E
Yapeyú 204 Di 29.28S 56.49W
Yap Islands 208 Ed 9.32N 138.08 E
Yapraklı 146 Eb 40.46N 33.47 E
Yapu 148 Jf 14.51N 98.03 E
Yaqian → Yuexi 154 Di 30.51N 116.22 E
Yaque del Norte, Río- 194 Ld 19.51N 71.41W
Yaque del Sur, Río- 194 Ld 18.17N 71.06W
Yaqueling 154 Ai 30.40N 111.36 E
Yaqui 174 Hg 27.37N 110.39W
Yaracuy [2] 202 Ea 10.20N 68.45W
Yaraka 210 Fg 24.53S 144.04 E
Yaralıgöz 146 Fb 41.45N 34.10 E
Yare 118 Oi 52.35N 1.44 E
Yaren 220e Ab 0.33S 166.54 E
Yari, Río- 198 If 0.23S 72.16W
Yariga-Take 156 Ec 36.20N 137.39 E
Yarīm 144 Fg 14.21N 44.22 E
Yaritagua 202 Ea 10.05N 69.08W
Yarkant/Shache 142 Jf 38.24N 77.15 E
Yarkant He 140 Ke 40.28N 80.52 E
Yarlung Zangbo Jiang 140 Lg 24.02N 90.59 E
Yarmouth [Eng.-U.K.] 124 Ad 50.41N 1.30W
Yarmouth [N.S.-Can.] 176 Me 43.50N 66.07W
Yarram 212 Jg 38.33S 146.41 E
Yarumal 202 Cb 6.58N 75.25W
Yasawa 219d Ab 16.47S 177.31 E
Yasawa Group 208 If 17.00S 177.23 E
Yashi 166 Gc 12.22N 7.55 E
Yashima 156 Gb 39.09N 140.10 E
Ya-Shima 156 Ce 33.45N 132.10 E
Yashiro-Jima 156 Ce 33.55N 132.15 E
Yasothon 148 Ke 15.46N 104.12 E
Yass 212 Jf 34.50S 148.55 E
Yassiören 130 Lh 41.18N 28.35 E
Yasugi 156 Cd 35.26N 133.15 E
Yāsūj 144 Hc 30.45N 51.33 E
Yasun Burnu 146 Gb 41.09N 37.41 E
Yatağan 146 Cd 37.20N 28.09 E
Yatate Tōge 156 Gb 40.26N 140.37 E
Yatate-Yama 156 Ad 34.12N 129.14 E
Yatenga 166 Ec 13.48N 2.10W
Yaté-Village 216 Cd 22.09S 166.57 E
Yathata 219d Cb 17.15S 179.32W
Yathkyed Lake 180 Hd 62.40N 98.00W
Yatolema 170 Db 0.21N 24.33 E
Yatou → Rongcheng 154 Gf 37.10N 122.25 E
Yatsu-ga-Take 156 Fd 35.59N 138.23 E
Yatsushiro 152 Ne 32.30N 130.36 E
Yatsushiro-Kai 156 Be 32.20N 130.25 E
Yatta Plateau 170 Gc 2.00S 38.00 E
Yauco 194 Nd 18.02N 66.51W
Yauri 202 Df 14.47S 71.29W
Yauyos 202 Cf 12.24S 75.57W
Yavari, Río- 202 Dd 4.21S 70.02W
Yavi, Cerro- 202 Eb 5.32N 65.59W
Yaviza 194 Ii 8.11N 77.41W
Yawatahama 154 Lh 33.27N 132.24 E
Yaxchilán 190 Fe 16.54N 90.58W
Yaxian (Sanya) 142 Mh 18.27N 109.28 E
Yayladağı 146 Ge 35.56N 36.01 E
Yazd 142 Hf 31.53N 54.25 E
Yazd [3] 144 Hc 31.30N 54.30 E
Yazılıkaya 146 Dc 39.13N 30.45 E
Yazoo City 186 Kj 32.51N 90.28W
Yazoo River 186 Kj 32.22N 91.00W
Ybbs 128 Jb 48.10N 15.06 E
Ybbs an der Donau 128 Jc 48.10N 15.05 E
Yding Skovhøj 116 Ch 56.01N 9.48 E
Ydre 116 Fg 57.52N 15.15 E
Ydstebøhamn 116 Ae 59.03N 5.25 E
Ye 142 Lh 15.15N 97.51 E
Yebaishou → Jianping 152 Kc 41.55N 119.37 E
Yebbi Bou 168 Ba 20.58N 18.04 E
Yébigé 168 Ba 22.04N 17.49 E
Yecheng/Kargilik 142 Jf 37.54N 77.26 E
Yech'ŏn 154 Jf 36.39N 128.27 E
Yecla 126 Kf 38.37N 1.07W
Yécora 190 Cc 28.20N 108.58W
Yēd 168 Ge 4.48N 43.02 E
Yedi Burun 130 Mm 36.23N 29.05 E
Yedseram 166 Hc 12.16N 14.09 E
Yefira 130 Fi 40.44N 22.42 E
Yegros 204 Dh 26.24S 56.25W
Yeguas 126 Hf 38.02N 4.15W
Yeha 168 Fc 14.21N 39.05 E
Yei 168 Ee 4.05N 30.40 E
Yei 168 Ee 4.40N 30.30 E
Yeji [China] 154 Ci 31.51N 115.55 E
Yeji [Ghana] 166 Ed 8.13N 0.39W
Yekepa 166 Dd 7.35N 8.32W
Yelgu 168 Ec 10.01N 32.31 E
Yélimané 166 Cb 15.07N 10.36W
Yell 110 Fc 60.35N 1.05W
Yellice Dağı 130 Mj 39.23N 29.57 E
Yellowhead Pass 180 Ff 52.50N 117.55W
Yellowknife 176 Hc 62.27N 114.21W
Yellowknife 180 Gd 62.23N 114.20W
Yellow River (EN) = Huang He 140 Nf 37.32N 118.19 E
Yellow Sea (EN) = Huang Hai 140 Of 36.00N 124.00 E
Yellow Sea (EN) = Hwang-Hae 140 Of 36.00N 124.00 E
Yellowstone 174 Ie 47.58N 103.59W
Yellowstone Lake 174 He 44.25N 110.22W
Yellowstone National Park 188 Jd 44.58N 110.42W
Yell Sound 118 La 60.33N 1.15W
Yeltes 126 Fd 40.56N 6.31W
Yelwa [Nig.] 166 Gd 8.51N 9.37 E
Yelwa [Nig.] 166 Fc 10.50N 4.44 E
Yemen (EN) = Al Yaman 142 Gh 15.00N 44.00 E
Yemen, People's Democratic Republic of- (EN) → Al Yaman 142 Gh. 15.00N 44.00 E
Yenagoa 166 Ge 4.55N 6.16 E
Yenangyaung 148 Id 20.28N 94.53 E
Yen Bay 148 Kd 21.42N 104.52 E
Yendi 166 Ed 9.26N 0.01W
Yenge 170 Dc 0.55S 20.40 E
Yengisar 152 Cd 38.56N 76.09 E
Yengo 170 Cb 0.22N 15.29 E
Yeniboğaziçi 146 Ee 35.17N 33.52 E
Yenice [Tur.] 130 Kj 39.55N 27.18 E
Yenice [Tur.] 146 Fd 36.59N 35.03 E
Yeni Erenkoy 146 Fe 35.35N 34.15 E
Yenice [Tur.] 146 Eb 41.18N 32.08 E
Yenifoça 130 Jk 38.44N 26.51 E
Yenihisar 130 Kl 37.22N 27.15 E
Yenimahalle, Ankara- 146 Ec 39.56N 32.52 E
Yenipazar 130 Ll 37.48N 28.12 E
Yenişehir 146 Cb 40.16N 29.39 E
Yenisey (EN) = Jenisej 140 Kb 71.50N 82.40 E
Yenisey Bay (EN) = Jenisejski zaliv 138 Db 72.00N 81.00 E
Yenisey Ridge (EN) = Jenisejski krjaž 140 Ld 59.00N 92.30 E
Yennádhion 130 Km 36.01N 27.56 E
Yeo, Lake- 212 Ee 28.05S 124.25 E
Yeovil 118 Kk 50.57N 2.39W
Yepes 126 Ie 39.54N 3.38W
Yeppoon 212 Kd 23.08S 150.45 E
Yerákion 130 Fm 37.00N 22.42 E
Yerbabuena 192 Hf 23.00N 103.30W
Yerer 168 Gd 7.32N 42.05 E
Yerington 188 Fg 38.59N 119.10W
Yerkesik 130 Ll 37.07N 28.17 E
Yerköy 146 Fc 39.38N 34.29 E
Yerlisu 130 Ji 40.46N 26.39 E
Yermak Plateau (EN) 179 Mb 82.00N 6.00 E
Yeroham 146 Fg 31.00N 34.55 E
Yerres 122 If 48.43N 2.27 E
Yerupajá, Nevado- 198 Ig 10.16S 76.54W
Yerushalayim [3] 146 Fg 31.45N 35.00 E
Yerushalayim = Jerusalem (EN) 142 Ff 31.46N 35.14 E
Yerville 124 Ce 49.40N 0.54 E
Yerwa 166 Hc 11.13N 12.53 E
Yesa, Embalse de- 126 Kb 42.36N 1.09W
Yeşan 154 If 36.41N 126.51 E
Yeşilhisar 146 Fc 38.21N 35.06 E
Yeşilırmak 144 Ea 41.24N 36.35 E
Yeşilköy 146 Cb 40.57N 29.49 E
Yeşilova 130 Ml 37.30N 29.46 E
Yeşilyurt 130 Ll 37.11N 28.17 E
Yeso 204 Cj 30.56S 59.28W
Yeste 126 Jf 38.22N 2.18W
Yetti 158 Gf 26.10N 7.50W
Ye-u 148 Jd 22.46N 95.26 E
Yeu, Ile d'- 122 Dh 46.43N 2.20W
Yèvre 122 Ig 47.13N 2.04 E
Yexian [China] 154 Ef 37.11N 119.58 E
Yexian [China] 154 Bh 33.38N 113.21 E
Yguazú, Río- 204 Eg 25.20S 55.00W
Yhú 204 Eg 24.59S 55.59W
Yí, Río- 204 Dk 33.07S 57.08W
Yialí 130 Km 36.40N 27.05 E
Yi'an 152 Mb 47.53N 125.17 E
Yiannitsá 130 Fi 40.48N 22.25 E
Yiaros 130 Hl 37.37N 24.43 E
Yibin 142 Mg 28.47N 104.35 E
Yibug Caka 152 Ee 33.55N 87.05 E
Yichang 142 Nf 30.42N 111.22 E
Yicheng [China] 154 Ag 35.44N 111.43 E
Yicheng [China] 154 Bi 31.42N 112.16 E
Yichuan 152 Jd 36.00N 110.06 E
Yichun [China] 152 Jf 27.47N 114.25 E
Yichun [China] 152 Mb 47.41N 128.55 E
Yıdılzeli 146 Gc 39.52N 36.38 E
Yidu [China] 152 Je 30.23N 111.28 E
Yidu [China] 152 Kd 36.41N 118.29 E
Yidun (Dagxoi) 152 Ge 30.25N 99.28 E
Yifag 168 Fc 12.02N 37.41 E
Yifeng 154 Cj 28.25N 114.47 E
Yığılca 146 Db 40.58N 31.27 E
Yigo 220c Ba 13.32N 144.53W
Yi He [China] 154 Bg 34.41N 112.33 E
Yi He [China] 154 Eg 34.07N 118.15 E
Yilan 152 Mb 46.18N 129.33 E
Yıldız Dağı 144 Ea 40.08N 36.56 E
Yıldız Dağları 146 Bb 41.50N 27.10 E
Yiliang 152 Hg 24.59N 103.08 E
Yimianpo 154 Jb 45.04N 128.03 E
Yimin He 152 Kb 49.15N 119.42 E
Yinan (Jiehu) 154 Eg 35.33N 118.27 E
Yinchuan 142 Mf 38.28N 106.19 E
Yindarlgooda, Lake- 212 Ef 30.45S 121.55 E
Yingcheng [China] 154 Bi 30.57N 113.33 E
Yingcheng [China] 154 Hb 44.08N 125.54 E
Yingde 152 Jg 24.13N 113.24 E
Ying He 152 Ke 32.30N 116.31 E
Yingjiang 152 Gg 24.45N 97.58 E
Yingjin He 154 Ec 42.20N 119.19 E
Yingkou 142 Oe 40.40N 122.12 E
Yingkou (Dashiqiao) 154 Gd 40.39N 122.31 E
Yingshan 154 Ci 30.45N 115.40 E
Yingshang 154 Dh 32.38N 116.16 E
Yingshouyingzi 154 Dd 40.33N 117.37 E
Yingtan 154 Dj 28.13N 117.00 E
Yingxian 154 Be 39.33N 113.10 E
Ying zhan/Victoria 142 Ng 22.17N 114.09 E
Yining/Gulja 152 Dc 43.54N 81.21 E
Yinma He 154 Hb 44.50N 125.45 E
Yinqing Qunjiao 150 Fe 8.55N 112.35 E
Yin Shan 140 Me 41.30N 109.00 E
Yi'ong Zangbo 152 Gf 29.56N 95.10 E
Yioúra 130 Hj 39.24N 24.10 E
Yipinglang 152 Hf 25.13N 101.55 E
Yiquan → Meitan 152 If 27.48N 107.32 E
Yirga Alem 168 Fd 6.44N 38.24 E
Yirol 168 Ed 6.33N 30.30 E
Yirshi 152 Kb 47.17N 119.55 E
Yishui 154 Eg 35.47N 118.38 E
Yisra'el = Israel (EN) [1] 142 Ff 31.30N 35.00 E
Yithion 130 Fm 36.45N 22.34 E
Yitong 154 Hc 43.20N 125.17 E
Yitong He 154 Hb 44.45N 125.40 E
Yitulihe 152 La 50.41N 121.33 E
Yiwu 154 Fj 29.19N 120.04 E
Yiwu/Aratürük 152 Fc 43.15N 94.35 E
Yixian [China] 154 Dj 29.56N 117.56 E
Yixian [China] 154 Fd 41.33N 121.14 E
Yixian [China] 154 Ce 39.21N 115.30 E
Yixing 154 Ei 31.21N 119.48 E
Yixun He 154 Dd 41.00N 117.41 E
Yiyang [China] 154 Dj 28.24N 117.24 E
Yiyang [China] 154 Bg 34.30N 112.10 E
Yiyang [China] 152 Jf 28.41N 112.20 E
Yiyuan (Nanma) 154 Ef 36.11N 118.10 E
Yizheng 154 Eh 32.16N 119.10 E
Yläne 116 Jd 60.53N 22.25 E
Ylikitka 114 Gc 66.08N 28.30 E
Yli-Li 114 Fd 65.22N 25.50 E
Ylimarkku/Övermark 116 Ib 62.37N 21.28 E
Ylistaro 114 Fe 62.57N 22.31 E
Ylitornio 114 Fc 66.18N 23.40 E
Ylivieska 114 Fd 64.05N 24.33 E
Ylöjärvi 116 Jc 61.33N 23.36 E
Ymers 179 Jd 73.20N 25.00W
Yngaren 116 Gf 58.50N 16.35 E
Yngen 116 Fe 59.45N 14.20 E
Ynykčanski 138 Id 60.08N 137.47 E
Yoboki 168 Gc 11.28N 42.06 E
Yobuko 156 Ae 33.33N 129.54 E
Yodo-Gawa 156 Dd 34.41N 135.25 E
Yogoum 168 Bb 17.27N 19.31 E
Yoğuntaş 130 Kh 41.50N 27.04 E
Yogyakarta 142 Nj 7.48S 110.22 E
Yoichi 154 Pc 43.12N 140.41 E
Yojoa, Lago de- 194 Df 14.50N 88.00W
Yŏju 154 If 37.18N 127.38 E
Yokadouma 160 Ih 3.31N 15.03 E
Yōkaichi 156 Ed 35.07N 136.11 E
Yōkaichiba 156 Gd 35.40N 140.28 E
Yokkaichi 154 Ng 34.58N 136.37 E
Yoko 166 Hd 5.32N 12.19 E
Yokoate-Jima 152 Mf 28.50N 129.00 E
Yokohama 142 Pf 35.27N 139.39 E
Yokosuka 154 Og 35.18N 139.40 E
Yokote 152 Pd 39.18N 140.34 E
Yola 160 Ih 9.12N 12.29 E
Yolaina, Serranías de- 194 Fh 11.40N 84.20W
Yolombo 170 Dc 1.32S 23.15 E
Yom 148 Ke 15.52N 100.16 E
Yom 148 Ke 15.52N 100.16 E
Yŏmju 154 He 39.50N 124.33 E
Yomou 166 Dd 7.34N 9.16W
Yomra 146 Hb 40.58N 39.54 E
Yon 122 Eh 46.30N 1.18W
Yona 220c Bb 13.25N 144.47 E
Yonago 154 Lg 35.26N 133.20 E
Yonaguni-Jima 152 Lg 24.25N 123.00 E
Yonaha-Dake 156b Ab 26.43N 128.13 E
Yonan 154 If 37.55N 126.05 E
Yoneshiro-Gawa 156 Ga 40.13N 140.00 E
Yonezawa 152 Pd 37.55N 140.07 E
Yong 166 He 4.54N 13.12 E
Yong'an 152 Kf 25.58N 117.29 E
Yŏngan 152 Mc 41.15N 129.30 E
Yongchang 152 Hd 38.17N 102.07 E
Yongcheng 154 Dh 33.56N 116.21 E
Yongch'on 154 Jg 35.59N 127.59 E
Yongchuan 152 If 29.22N 105.59 E
Yongch'u-gap 154 Jf 37.03N 129.26 E
Yongdeng 152 Hd 36.44N 103.24 E
Yongding He 152 Kd 39.20N 117.04 E
Yŏngdŏk 154 Jf 36.24N 129.22 E
Yŏngdong 154 If 36.10N 127.47 E
Yonghung 154 Ie 39.33N 127.14 E
Yongji (Kouqian) 154 Ic 43.40N 126.30 E
Yongjing 152 Hd 36.00N 103.17 E
Yŏngju 152 Md 36.49N 128.37 E
Yongkang 152 Lf 28.51N 120.05 E
Yongle Qundao 150 Fc 16.35N 111.40 E
Yongnian (Linmingguan) 154 Cf 36.47N 114.30 E
Yongning → Xuyong 152 If 28.13N 105.26 E
Yongqing 154 De 39.19N 116.29 E
Yŏngsanp'o 154 Ig 35.00N 126.43 E
Yongsheng 152 Hf 26.41N 100.45 E
Yongshu Jiao 150 Fe 9.35N 112.50 E
Yŏngwŏl 154 Jf 37.11N 128.28 E
Yongxiu (Tujiabu) 152 Kf 29.05N 115.49 E
Yonibana 166 Cd 8.26N 12.14W
Yonkers 184 Ke 40.56N 73.54W
Yonne [3] 122 Jg 47.55N 3.45 E
Yonne 122 If 48.23N 2.58 E
Yopal 202 Db 5.21N 72.23W
Yopurga 152 Cd 39.15N 76.45 E
York 118 Lg 54.10N 1.30W
York [Al.-U.S.] 184 Ci 32.29N 88.18W
York [Austl.] 212 Df 31.53S 116.46 E
York [Eng.-U.K.] 118 Lh 53.58N 1.05W
York [Nb.-U.S.] 186 Hf 40.52N 97.36W
York [Pa.-U.S.] 182 Ld 39.57N 76.44W
York, Cape- 208 Ff 10.40S 142.30 E
York, Kap- 224 Od 76.05N 67.05W
York, Vale of- 118 Lg 54.10N 1.20W
Yorke Peninsula 212 Hf 35.00S 137.30 E
Yorkshire Dales 118 Kg 54.15N 2.10W
Yorkshire Wolds 118 Mh 54.00N 0.40W
York Sound 212 Fb 14.50S 125.05 E
Yorkton 176 Id 51.13N 102.28W
Yorktown 184 Ig 37.14N 76.32W
Yoro 194 Df 15.09N 87.07W
Yoro [3] 194 Df 15.15N 87.15W
Yoron-Jima 156b Bb 27.03N 128.26 E
Yoro-Shima 156b Ba 28.02N 129.10 E
Yorosso 166 Ec 12.21N 4.47W
Yorubaland Plateau 166 Fd 8.00N 4.30 E
Yörük 130 Ki 40.56N 27.04 E
Yosemite National Park 182 Dd 35.28N 119.33W
Yosemite Rock 198 Hi 31.58S 83.15W
Yoshida [Jap.] 156 Ce 33.16N 132.32 E
Yoshida [Jap.] 156 Cd 34.40N 132.42 E
Yoshii 156 Ae 33.18N 129.40 E
Yoshii-Gawa 156 Dd 34.36N 134.02 E
Yoshino-Gawa 156 Dd 34.05N 134.36 E
Yŏsu 152 Me 34.44N 127.44 E
Yotaú 202 Fg 16.03S 63.03W
Yōtei-Zan 156a Bb 42.49N 140.47 E
Yotvata 146 Fh 29.53N 35.03 E
Youghal/Eochaill 118 Fj 51.57N 7.50W
Youghal Harbour/Cuan Eochaille 118 Fj 51.52N 7.50W
You Jiang 140 Mg 22.50N 108.06 E
Youllemmedene 158 Hg 16.00N 1.00 E
Young [Austl.] 212 Jf 34.19S 148.18 E
Young [Ur.] 204 Dk 32.41S 57.38W
Young, Cape- 218 Je 43.42S 176.37W
Younghusband Peninsula 212 Hg 36.00S 139.30 E
Young Island 222 Ke 66.25S 162.30 E
Young's Island 197n Ba 13.08N 61.13W
Youngs Rock 220q Ab 25.03S 130.06W
Youngstown 182 Kc 41.05N 80.40W
Youshashan 152 Fd 38.04N 90.53 E
Youssoufia 162 Fc 32.15N 8.32W
Youyang 152 If 28.49N 108.45 E
Yozgat 144 Db 39.50N 34.48 E
Ypacaraí 206 Ic 25.23S 57.16W
Ypacaraí, Laguna- 204 Dg 25.17S 57.20W
Ypané, Río- 204 Df 23.29S 57.19W
Ypé Jhú 204 Ef 23.54S 55.20W
Ypoá, Lago- 204 Dg 25.48S 57.28W
Yport 124 Ce 49.44N 0.19 E
Ypres/Ieper 122 Id 50.51N 2.53 E
Yreka 182 Cc 41.44N 122.43W
Yser 122 Ic 51.09N 2.43 E
Yssingeaux 122 Ki 45.08N 4.07 E
Ystad 114 Ci 55.25N 13.49 E
Ytambey, Río- 204 Eg 24.46S 54.24W
Ythan 118 Ld 57.25N 2.00W
Ytre Arna 116 Ad 60.28N 5.26 E
Ytre Sula 116 Ac 61.05N 4.40 E
Ytterhogdal 116 Fb 62.11N 14.56 E
Ytterlännäs 114 De 63.01N 17.41 E
Yttermalung 116 Ed 60.35N 13.50 E
Ytyk-Kjuël 138 Id 62.28N 133.25 E
Yu 'Alliq, Jabal- 146 Eg 30.22N 33.31 E
Yuan'an 154 Ai 31.04N 111.39 E
Yuanbaoshan 154 Ec 42.19N 119.19 E
Yuanbao Shan 152 If 25.24N 109.11 E
Yuan Jiang [Asia] = Red River (EN) 140 Mg 20.17N 106.34 E
Yuanjiang [China] 154 Bj 28.50N 112.23 E
Yuanjiang [China] 152 Hg 23.22N 102.26 E
Yuan Jiang [China] 140 Ng 28.58N 111.49 E
Yuanling 152 Jf 28.30N 110.25 E
Yuanmou 152 Hf 25.45N 101.54 E
Yuanping 152 Jd 38.43N 112.42 E
Yuanqu (Liuzhangzhen)) 152 Jd 35.19N 111.44 E
Yuanshi 154 Cf 37.45N 114.30 E
Yuba City 182 Cd 39.08N 121.37W
Yūbari 152 Pc 43.04N 141.59 E
Yūbari-Dake 156a Cb 43.06N 142.15 E
Yūbari-Gawa 156a Bb 43.08N 141.35 E
Yūbari-Sanchi 156a Cb 43.10N 142.15 E
Yuba River 188 Eg 39.07N 121.36W
Yubdo 168 Fd 8.58N 35.27 E
Yūbetsu 154 Qb 43.13N 144.05 E
Yūbetsu-Gawa 156a Ca 44.14N 143.37 E
Yucatán [2] 190 Gd 20.50N 89.00W
Yucatán, Canal de- = Yucatan Channel (EN) 174 Kg 21.45N 85.45W
Yucatán, Península de- = Yucatan Peninsula (EN) 174 Kh 19.30N 89.00W
Yucatan Basin (EN) 190 Ge 20.00N 84.00W
Yucatan Channel (EN) = Yucatán, Canal de- 174 Kg 21.45N 85.45W
Yucatan Peninsula (EN) = Yucatán, Península de- 174 Kh 19.30N 89.00W
Yucheng 154 Df 36.56N 116.39 E
Yuci 152 Jd 37.41N 112.49 E
Yucuyácua, Cerro- 190 Ee 17.07N 97.40W
Yuda 156 Gb 39.19N 140.48 E
Yudi Shan 152 Lb 52.17N 121.52 E
Yueliang Pao 154 Gb 45.44N 123.55 E
Yueqing 152 Lf 28.08N 120.58 E
Yuexi 152 Hf 28.37N 102.36 E
Yuexi (Yaqian) 154 Di 30.51N 116.22 E
Yueyang 152 Jf 29.18N 113.12 E
Yufu-Dake 156 Be 33.17N 131.23 E
Yugan 152 Kf 28.42N 116.39 E
Yugoslavia (EN) = Jugoslavija [1] 112 Hg 44.00N 19.00 E
Yu He 154 Be 39.51N 113.26 E
Yuhuang Ding 154 Df 36.20N 117.01 E
Yuki 170 Cc 3.55S 19.25 E
Yukon 186 Hi 35.31N 97.44W
Yukon 174 Cc 62.33N 163.59W
Yukon Flats 178 Jc 66.35N 146.00W
Yukon Plateau 174 Fc 61.30N 135.40W
Yukon Territory [3] 180 Dd 63.00N 136.00W
Yüksekova 146 Kd 37.19N 44.10 E
Yukuhashi 156 Be 33.44N 130.58 E
Yule River 212 Dd 20.41S 118.17 E
Yuli/Iopnur 152 Ec 41.22N 86.09 E
Yulin [China] 142 Ng 22.39N 110.08 E
Yulin [China] 142 Mf 38.14N 109.48 E
Yuling Guan 152 Ke 30.04N 118.53 E
Yulin Jiao 140 Mh 17.50N 109.30 E
Yulongxue Shan 152 Hf 27.09N 100.12 E
Yuma [Az.-U.S.] 176 Hf 32.43N 114.37W
Yuma [Co.-U.S.] 186 Ef 40.08N 102.43W
Yuma, Bahía de- 194 Md 18.21N 68.35W
Yumare 196 Bg 10.37N 68.41W
Yumari, Cerro- 202 Ec 4.27N 66.50W
Yumbe 170 Fb 3.28N 31.15 E
Yumbi [Zaire] 170 Cc 1.53S 16.32 E
Yumbi [Zaire] 170 Ec 1.14S 26.14 E
Yumen (Laojunmiao) 142 Lf 39.50N 97.44 E
Yumenkou 152 Jd 35.42N 110.37 E
Yumenzhen 152 Gc 40.17N 97.12 E
Yumin 152 Db 45.59N 82.28 E
Yumurtalik 146 Fd 36.49N 35.45 E
Yuna, Río- 194 Md 19.12N 69.37W
Yunak 146 Dc 38.49N 31.45 E
Yunaska 178a Db 52.40N 170.50W
Yuncheng [China] 152 Jd 35.02N 111.00 E
Yuncheng [China] 154 Cg 35.35N 115.56 E
Yungas 198 Jg 16.20S 66.45W
Yungay 206 Fe 37.07S 72.01W
Yungui Gaoyuan 140 Mg 26.00N 105.00 E
Yunhe → Peixian 154 Dg 34.44N 116.56 E
Yuni 156a Bb 42.59N 141.46 E
Yunjinghong → Jinghong 152 Hg 21.59N 100.48 E
Yunkai Dashan 152 Jg 22.30N 111.00 E
Yunlin 152 Lg 23.43N 120.33 E
Yun Ling 152 Gf 27.00N 99.30 E
Yunmeng 154 Bi 31.01N 113.45 E
Yunnan Sheng (Yün-nan Sheng) [2] 152 Hg 25.00N 102.00 E
Yün-nan Sheng → Yunnan Sheng [2] 152 Hg 25.00N 102.00 E
Yunomae 156 Be 32.15N 130.57 E
Yunotsu 156 Cd 35.05N 132.21 E
Yun Shui 154 Bi 30.43N 113.57 E
Yunxian 152 Je 32.50N 110.50 E
Yunxiao 152 Kg 24.05N 117.18 E
Yunyang 152 Ie 31.00N 108.55 E
Yunzhong Shan 152 Jd 38.50N 112.27 E
Yuquan 154 Ib 45.27N 127.08 E
Yuquerí 204 Ci 28.53S 58.02W
Yura 202 Dg 16.12S 71.42W
Yura-Gawa 156 Dd 35.31N 135.17 E
Yurimaguas 200 If 5.54S 76.05W
Yuriria 192 Ig 20.12N 101.09W
Yuruarí, Río- 196 Fi 6.44N 61.40W
Yurungkax He 152 Dd 38.05N 80.20 E
Yuscarán 194 Dg 13.55N 86.51W
Yushan 154 Ej 28.41N 118.15 E
Yushan 140 Og 23.30N 121.00 E
Yu Shan 152 Kf 27.00N 116.00 E
Yushe 154 Bf 37.04N 112.58 E
Yushu [China] 154 Ib 44.50N 126.33 E
Yushu [China] 142 Lf 33.06N 96.48 E
Yushutun 152 Lb 47.06N 123.41 E
Yūsuf, Baḩr- 146 Dh 29.19N 30.50 E
Yusufeli 146 Ib 40.50N 41.33 E
Yutai (Guting) 154 Dg 35.00N 116.40 E
Yutian 154 De 39.53N 117.45 E
Yutian/Keriya 142 Kf 36.52N 81.42 E
Yuty 206 Ic 26.32S 56.18W
Yutz 124 Ie 49.21N 6.11 E
Yuwan-Dake 156b Ba 28.18N 129.19 E
Yuxi 152 Hg 24.27N 102.34 E
Yuxian [China] 152 Jd 39.49N 114.35 E
Yuxian [China] 152 Jd 38.03N 113.28 E
Yuxian [China] 154 Bg 34.09N 113.29 E
Yuxikou 154 Ei 31.26N 118.18 E
Yuyao 154 Fi 30.04N 121.10 E
Yuya-Wan 156 Bd 34.20N 130.55 E
Yuza 156 Fb 39.01N 139.53 E
Yuzawa [Jap.] 156 Fc 36.56N 138.47 E
Yuzawa [Jap.] 154 Pe 39.10N 140.30 E
Yvel 122 Dg 47.59N 2.23W
Yvelines [3] 122 Hf 48.50N 1.50 E
Yverdon 128 Ad 46.46N 6.40 E
Yvetot 122 Ge 49.37N 0.46 E
Yvette 124 Ef 48.40N 2.20 E
Yxlan 116 He 59.40N 18.50 E
Yxningen 116 Gf 58.15N 16.20 E

Index Symbols

[1] Independent Nation
[2] State, Region
[3] District, County
[4] Municipality
[5] Colony, Dependency
Continent
Physical Region
Historical or Cultural Region
Mount, Mountain
Volcano
Hill
Mountains, Mountain Range
Hills, Escarpment
Plateau, Upland
Pass, Gap
Plain, Lowland
Delta
Salt Flat
Valley, Canyon
Crater, Cave
Karst Features
Depression
Polder
Desert, Dunes
Forest, Woods
Heath, Steppe
Oasis
Cape, Point
Coast, Beach
Cliff
Peninsula
Isthmus
Sandbank
Island
Atoll
Rock, Reef
Islands, Archipelago
Rocks, Reefs
Coral Reef
Well, Spring
Geyser
River, Stream
Waterfall, Rapids
River Mouth, Estuary
Lake
Salt Lake
Intermittent Lake
Reservoir
Swamp, Pond
Canal
Glacier
Ice Shelf, Pack Ice
Ocean
Sea
Gulf, Bay
Strait, Fjord
Lagoon
Bank
Seamount
Tablemount
Ridge
Shelf
Basin
Escarpment, Sea Scarp
Fracture
Trench, Abyss
National Park, Reserve
Point of Interest
Recreation Site
Cave, Cavern
Historic Site
Ruins
Wall, Walls
Church, Abbey
Temple
Scientific Station
Railway station
Airport
Port
Military installation
Lighthouse
Mine
Tunnel
Dam, Bridge

Z

Zaajatskaja 134 Jj 52.53N 61.35 E
Zaalajski hrebet 135 Ie 39.25N 72.50 E
Zaanstad 122 Kb 52.26N 4.49 E
Žabaj 134 Nj 51.42N 68.22 E
Zabajkalsk 138 Gg 49.40N 117.21 E
Zabarjad 164 Ge 23.37N 36.12 E
Zāb-e Kūchek 146 Ke 36.00N 45.15 E
Zabīb, Ra's az- 128 Em 37.16N 10.04 E
Zabīd 144 Fg 14.12N 43.18 E
Zabīd, Wādī- 144 Fg 14.07N 43.06 E
Žabinka 132 Dc 52.13N 24.01 E
Ząbkowice Śląskie 120 Mf 50.36N 16.53 E
Žabljak 130 Cf 43.09N 19.08 E
Zabłudów 120 Tc 53.01N 23.20 E
Zabok 128 Jd 46.02N 15.55 E
Zābol 144 Jc 31.02N 61.30 E
Zābol [3] 144 Kc 32.00N 67.15 E
Zabolot 116 Kk 53.56N 24.46 E
Zabolotje 120 Ue 51.37N 24.26 E
Zabolotov 130 Ia 48.25N 25.23 E
Zabré 166 Ec 11.10N 0.38W
Zábřeh 120 Mg 49.53N 16.52 E
Zabrze 120 Of 50.18N 18.46 E
Zacapa 190 Gf 14.58N 89.32W
Zacapa [3] 194 Cf 15.00N 89.30W
Zacapu 192 Ih 19.50N 101.43W
Zacatecas 176 Ig 22.47N 102.35W
Zacatecas [2] 190 Dd 23.00N 103.00W
Zacatecoluca 194 Cg 13.30N 88.52W
Zacatepec 192 Jh 18.39N 99.12W
Zacatlán 192 Kh 19.56N 97.58W
Zaccar, Djebel- 126 Oh 36.20N 2.13 E
Zacoalco de Torres 192 Hg 20.14N 103.35W
Zacualtipán 192 Jg 20.39N 98.36W
Zaculeu 194 Bf 15.21N 91.29W
Zadar 112 Hg 44.07N 15.15 E
Zadarski kanal 128 Jf 44.10N 15.10 E
Zadetkyi Kyun 148 Jg 9.58N 98.13 E
Zadi 170 Bc 4.46S 14.52 E
Zadoi 152 Fe 33.10N 94.58 E
Zadonsk 132 Kc 52.23N 38.58 E
Za'farānah 164 Fd 29.07N 32.33 E
Zafferano, Capo- 128 Hl 38.07N 13.32 E
Ẓafīr 144 He 23.07N 53.46 E
Zafra 126 Ff 38.25N 6.25W
Żagań 120 Le 51.37N 15.19 E
Žagarė/Zagare 116 Jh 56.19N 23.14 E
Zagare/Žagarė 116 Jh 56.19N 23.14 E
Zāgheh 146 Mf 33.30N 48.42 E
Zāgh Marz 146 Od 36.47N 53.17 E
Zaghrah, Wādī- 146 Fh 28.40N 34.20 E
Zaghwān 162 Jb 36.24N 10.09 E
Zaghwān [3] 162 Jb 36.25N 10.10 E
Zaghwān, Jabal- 128 En 36.21N 10.07 E
Zagora 160 Ge 30.19N 5.50W
Zagora 128 Kg 43.40N 16.15 E
Zagória 130 Dj 39.45N 20.50 E
Zagorje 128 Jd 46.05N 16.00 E
Zagorodje 120 Vd 52.15N 25.30 E
Zagórów 120 Nd 52.11N 17.55 E
Zagorsk 112 Jd 56.18N 38.08 E
Zagórz, Sanok- 120 Sg 49.31N 22.17 E
Zagreb 112 Hf 45.48N 16.00 E
Zāgros, Kūhhā-ye-=Zagros Mountains (EN) 140 Gf 33.40N 47.00 E
Zagros Mountains (EN)=Zāğros, Kūhhā-ye- 140 Gf 33.40N 47.00 E
Žagubica 130 Ee 44.12N 21.48 E
Za'gya Zangbo 152 Ee 31.55N 88.58 E
Zagyva 120 Qi 47.10N 20.12 E
Zāhedān 142 Ig 29.30N 60.52 E
Zahlah 146 Ff 33.51N 35.53 E
Zahmet 136 Gh 37.48N 62.29 E
Ẓahrān 164 Hf 17.40N 43.30 E
Zahrez Chergúi 126 Pi 35.14N 3.32 E
Zailijski Alatau, hrebet- 135 Kc 43.00N 77.00 E
Žailma 136 Ge 51.32N 61.40 E
Zaire [3] 170 Bd 6.30S 13.30 E
Zaïre 158 Ii 6.04S 12.24 E
Zaire 158 Ii 6.04S 12.24 E
Zaïre (Congo, Democratic Republic of the-) [1] 160 Ji 1.00S 25.00 E
Zaisan, Lake- (EN) = Zajsan, ozero- 140 Ke 48.10N 83.50 E
Zaj 114 Mi 55.36N 51.40 E
Zaječar 130 Ff 43.54N 22.17 E
Zajsan 142 Ke 47.30N 84.55 E
Zajsan, ozero- = Zaisan, Lake- (EN) 140 Ke 48.10N 83.50 E
Zak 158 Jk 29.39S 21.11 E
Zaka 172 Ed 20.20S 31.29 E
Zakamensk 138 Ff 50.23N 103.20 E
Zakarpatskaja oblast [3] 136 Cf 48.20N 23.20 E
Zakataly 136 Eg 41.38N 46.37 E
Zakháro 130 El 37.29N 21.39 E
Zākhū 144 Fb 37.08N 42.41 E
Zákinthos 130 Dl 37.47N 20.54 E
Zákinthos=Zante (EN) 110 Ih 37.47N 20.47 E
Zakinthou Dhiavlos- 130 Dl 37.50N 21.00 E
Zakopane 120 Pg 49.19N 19.57 E
Zakouma 168 Bc 10.54N 19.49 E
Žaksy 136 Ge 51.53N 67.20 E
Zala [2] 120 Mj 46.40N 16.50 E
Zala 120 Nj 46.43N 17.16 E
Zālābıyah 146 He 35.39N 39.51 E
Zalaegerszeg 120 Mj 46.50N 16.51 E
Zalāf 146 Gf 32.55N 37.20 E
Zalalövő 120 Mj 46.51N 16.36 E
Zalamea de la Serena 126 Gf 38.39N 5.39W
Zalamea la Real 126 Fg 37.41N 6.39W
Zalantum → Butha Qi 152 Lb 48.02N 122.42 E
Zalari 138 Ff 53.36N 102.32 E
Zalaszentgrót 120 Nj 46.57N 17.05 E
Zălau 130 Gb 47.12N 23.03 E
Zaleščiki 132 De 48.39N 25.44 E
Ẓalim 144 Fe 22.43N 42.10 E
Zalingei 168 Cc 12.54N 23.29 E
Zalţan 164 Cd 28.55N 19.50 E
Zaltbommel 124 Hc 51.49N 5.17 E
Žaltidjal 130 Ih 41.30N 25.05 E
Žaltyr 136 Ge 51.35N 69.58 E
Žaltyr, ozero- 132 Qf 47.25N 51.05 E
Zamakh 144 Gf 16.28N 47.35 E
Zamami-Shima 156b Ab 26.15N 127.18 E
Zambeze=Zambezi (EN) 158 Kj 18.50N 36.17 E
Zambezi 158 Kj 18.50N 36.17 E
Zambezi (EN)=Zambeze 158 Kj 18.50N 36.17 E
Zambézia [3] 172 Fc 17.00S 37.00 E
Zambezi Escarpment 172 Ec 16.15S 30.10 E
Zambia [1] 160 Jj 15.00S 30.00 E
Zamboanga 142 Oi 6.54N 122.04 E
Zamboanga Peninsula 150 He 7.32N 122.16 E
Zambrah, Jazīrat- 162 Jb 37.08N 10.48 E
Zambrano 194 Ji 9.45N 74.49W
Zambrów 120 Sd 53.00N 22.15 E
Zambué 172 Ec 15.07S 30.49 E
Zamfara 166 Fc 12.02N 4.03 E
Zamkova, gora- 120 Vc 53.34N 25.53 E
Zamkowa, Góra- 120 Qb 54.25N 20.25 E
Zammar 146 Jd 36.47N 42.40 E
Zamora [3] 126 Gc 41.45N 6.00W
Zamora [Ec.] 202 Cd 4.04S 78.52W
Zamora [Sp.] 126 Gc 41.30N 5.45W
Zamora, Río- 202 Cd 2.59S 78.15W
Zamora de Hidalgo 190 De 19.59N 102.16W
Zamość 120 Tf 50.44N 23.15 E
Zamość [2] 120 Tf 50.44N 23.15 E
Zampa-Misaki 156b Ab 26.26N 127.43 E
Zamtang (Gamda) 152 He 32.23N 101.05 E
Zamuro, Punta- 194 Mh 11.26N 68.50W
Zamzam 164 Cc 31.24N 15.17 E
Zanaga 170 Bc 2.51S 13.50 E
Žanatas 136 Gg 43.36N 69.43 E
Zancara 126 Ie 39.18N 3.18W
Zanda (Toling) 152 Ce 31.28N 79.50 E
Zandvoort 122 Kb 52.22N 4.32 E
Zanesville 182 Kd 39.55N 82.02W
Zangelan 132 Oj 39.05N 46.38 E
Zanhuang 154 Cf 37.38N 114.26 E
Zanjān 144 Gb 36.40N 48.29 E
Zanjān [3] 144 Gb 36.35N 48.15 E
Zanjānrūd 146 Ld 37.08N 47.47 E
Žannetty, ostrov- 138 Ka 76.45N 158.25 E
Zannone 128 Hj 40.55N 13.05 E
Zante (EN)=Zákinthos 110 Ih 37.47N 20.47 E
Zanthus 212 Ef 31.02S 123.34 E
Zanzibar 160 Ki 6.10S 39.11 E
Zanzibar [2] 170 Gd 6.10S 39.20 E
Zanzibar [3] 170 Gd 6.00S 39.50 E
Zanzibar Channel 170 Gd 6.00S 39.00 E
Zanzibar Island 158 Ki 6.10S 39.20 E
Zaolin 152 Jd 39.09N 113.03 E
Zaō-San 156 Gb 38.08N 140.28 E
Zaouatallaz 162 Ie 24.52N 8.26 E
Zaoyang 152 Je 32.08N 112.45 E
Zaozerny 138 Ee 55.57N 94.42 E
Zaozhuang 152 Ke 34.58N 117.34 E
Zap 146 Jd 36.00N 43.21 E
Zapacos Norte, Río- 204 Ac 17.03S 62.23W
Zapacos Sur, Río- 204 Ac 17.03S 62.23W
Zapadnaja Dvina 114 Hh 56.17N 32.03 E
Zapadnaja Dvina=Western Dvina (EN) 110 Id 57.04N 24.03 E
Zapadna Morava 130 Ef 43.41N 21.24 E
Západné Karpaty=West Carpathians (EN) 120 Og 49.30N 19.00 E
Zapadni Rodopi 130 Hh 41.45N 24.05 E
Zapadno-Karelskaja vozvyšennost 114 He 63.40N 31.40 E
Zapadno-Sibirskaja ravnina = West Siberian Plain (EN) 140 Jc 60.00N 75.00 E
Zapadny Sajan = Western Sayans 140 Ld 53.00N 94.00 E
Západočeský kraj [3] 120 Ig 49.45N 13.00 E
Západoslovenský kraj [3] 120 Nh 48.20N 18.00 E
Zapala 200 Ii 38.55S 70.05W
Zapardiel 126 Gc 41.29N 5.02W
Zapata 186 Gm 26.52N 99.19W
Zapata, Peninsula de- 194 Gb 22.20N 81.35W
Zapatera, Isla- 194 Eh 11.45N 85.50W
Zapatosa, Cienaga de- 194 Ki 9.05N 73.50W
Zapljusje 116 Mf 58.24N 29.56 E
Zapoljarny 136 Db 69.26N 30.48 E
Zapopan 192 Hg 20.43N 103.24W
Zaporožje 112 Jf 47.50N 35.10 E
Zaporožskaja oblast [3] 136 Df 47.15N 35.50 E
Zapotitlàn, Punta- 192 Lh 18.33N 94.49W
Za Qu 152 Ge 32.00N 96.55 E
Zara 146 Gc 39.55N 37.48 E
Zarāf, Baḩr az- 168 Ed 9.25N 31.10 E
Zarafšan 136 Gg 41.39N 64.10 E
Zaragoza [3] 126 Lc 41.35N 1.00W
Zaragoza [Col.] 202 Db 7.30N 74.52W
Zaragoza [Mex.] 192 Jf 23.58N 99.46W
Zaragoza [Mex.] 192 If 22.02N 100.44W
Zaragoza [Mex.] 192 Ic 28.29N 100.55W
Zaragoza [Sp.] =Saragossa (EN) 112 Fg 41.38N 0.53W
Zarajsk 114 Ji 54.47N 38.53 E
Zarand [Iran] 146 Me 35.08N 49.00 E
Zarand [Iran] 146 Qg 30.48N 56.53 E
Zarand-e-Kohneh 146 Ne 35.17N 50.30 E
Zărandului, Munţii- 130 Fc 46.10N 22.15 E
Zaranj 142 If 31.06N 61.53 E
Zarasai/Zarasaj 114 Gi 55.43N 26.19 E
Zarasaj/Zarasai 114 Gi 55.43N 26.19 E
Zárate 200 Ki 34.05S 59.02W
Zarautz / Zarauz 126 Ja 43.17N 2.10W
Zarauz / Zarautz 126 Ja 43.17N 2.10W
Zaraza 202 Eb 9.21N 65.19W
Žarcovski 114 Hi 55.53N 32.16 E
Zard Kūh 140 Hf 32.22N 50.04 E
Zardob 132 Oi 40.14N 47.42 E
Zarečensk 114 Hc 66.40N 31.23 E
Zarghaţ 146 Ii 26.32N 40.29 E
Zarghun 148 Db 30.31N 68.50 E
Zarghūn Shahr 144 Kc 32.51N 68.25 E
Zaria 160 Hg 11.04N 7.42 E
Žarkamys 136 Ff 47.59N 56.29 E
Žarma 136 If 48.48N 80.55 E
Zărneşti 130 Id 45.33N 25.18 E
Zarqān 146 Oh 29.46N 52.43 E
Zarrīneh 146 Kd 37.05N 45.40 E
Zarrīnshahr 146 Nf 32.30N 51.25 E
Zaruma 202 Cd 3.42S 79.38W
Zarumilla 202 Bd 3.30S 80.16W
Żary 120 Le 51.38N 15.09 E
Žaryk 136 Hf 48.52N 72.54 E
Zarzaïtine 162 Id 28.05N 9.45 E
Zasa 116 Lh 56.15N 26.01 E
Zāskar 148 Fb 34.10N 77.20 E
Žaškov 132 Ge 49.15N 30.09 E
Zaslavl 116 Lj 54.00N 27.22 E
Zaslavskoje vodohranilišče 116 Lj 54.00N 27.30 E
Zastavna 130 Ia 48.25N 25.49 E
Zastron 172 Df 30.18S 27.07 E
Žatec 120 Jf 50.20N 13.33 E
Zatišje 130 Mb 47.47N 29.48 E
Zatobolsk 134 Kj 53.12N 63.43 E
Zatoka 130 Nc 46.07N 30.25 E
Zauche 120 Id 52.15N 12.35 E
Žavadovskogo Island 222 Ge 66.30S 86.00 E
Zavāreh 146 Of 33.30N 52.29 E
Zaventem 124 Gd 50.53N 4.28 E
Zavety Ilića 138 Jg 49.02N 140.19 E
Zavidovići 128 Mf 44.27N 18.09 E
Zavitinsk 138 Hf 50.01N 129.26 E
Zavodoukovsk 136 Gd 56.33N 66.32 E
Zavodovski 222 Ad 56.20S 27.35W
Zavolžje 114 Kh 56.38N 43.21 E
Zavolžsk 114 Kh 57.32N 42.10 E
Zawidów 120 Le 51.01N 15.02 E
Zawiercie 120 Pf 50.30N 19.25 E
Zawīlah 164 Cd 26.10N 15.07 E
Zāwiyat al Mukhaylá 164 Dc 32.10N 22.17 E
Zāwiyat Masūs 164 Dc 31.35N 21.01 E
Zāwiyat Qirzah 164 Bc 31.00N 14.20 E
Zāwiyat Shammās 146 Bg 31.31N 26.24 E
Zawr, Ra's az- 146 Mi 27.26N 49.19 E
Zaya 128 Kb 48.31N 16.55 E
Zāyandeh 146 Of 32.20N 52.50 E
Zaydūn, Wādī- 146 Ej 25.53N 33.04 E
Zayü (Gyigang) 152 Gf 28.43N 97.25 E
Zaza, Río- 194 Hc 21.37N 79.32W
Zazir 162 If 19.50N 5.13 E
Zbaraž 132 De 49.42N 25.47 E
Zbąszyń 120 Ld 52.16N 15.55 E
Zborov 120 Vg 49.37N 25.09 E
Ždanichý les 120 Mg 49.05N 16.50 E
Ždanov → Mariupol' 112 Jf 47.00N 37.33 E
Ždanovsk 132 Oj 39.45N 47.33 E
Žd'árské vrchy 120 Mg 49.35N 16.03 E
Ždiar 120 Qg 49.16N 20.15 E
Zdolbunov 132 Ed 50.33N 26.15 E
Zduńska Wola 120 Oe 51.36N 18.57 E
Zealand (EN)=Sjælland 110 Hd 55.30N 11.45 E
Zebediela 172 Dd 24.19S 29.16 E
Zebës, Mali i- 130 Dh 41.55N 20.14 E
Zebil 130 Le 44.57N 28.46 E
Zeča 128 If 44.46N 14.19 E
Zeddine 126 Nh 36.12N 1.50 E
Zedelgem 124 Fc 51.09N 3.08 E
Zeehan 210 Fi 41.53S 145.20 E
Zeeland [3] 124 Fc 51.27N 3.45 E
Zeeland 122 Jc 51.27N 3.45 E
Zeerust 172 De 25.33S 26.06 E
Zefat 146 Ff 32.58N 35.30 E
Zegrzyńskie, Jezioro- 120 Rd 52.30N 21.05 E
Zehdenick 120 Jd 52.59N 13.20 E
Zeil, Mount- 212 Gd 23.25S 132.25 E
Žeimelis/Zeimjalis 116 Jh 56.14N 23.58 E
Žeimena/Žejmena 114 Fi 54.54N 23.53 E
Zeimjalis/Žeimelis 116 Jh 56.14N 23.58 E
Zeist 122 Lb 52.05N 5.15 E
Zeitz 120 Ie 51.03N 12.09 E
Zeja 142 Od 53.45N 127.15 E
Zeja 140 Od 50.13N 127.35 E
Žejmena/Žeimena 114 Fi 54.54N 23.53 E
Zejskoje vodohranilišče 138 Hf 54.40N 127.30 E
Zêkog 152 Hd 35.00N 101.35 E
Želanija, mys- 140 Ib 76.57N 68.35 E
Zelaya [3] 194 Eg 13.00N 84.00W
Želča 116 Lf 58.18N 27.50 E
Zele 124 Gc 51.04N 4.02 E
Żelechów 120 Re 51.49N 21.54 E
Zelee, Cape- 219a Ec 9.44S 161.34 E
Zelenaja Rošča 116 Md 60.08N 29.14 E
Zelenčukskaja 132 Lh 43.51N 41.34 E
Zelengora 128 Mg 43.22N 18.35 E
Zelenoborsk 136 Gc 61.29N 63.59 E
Zelenoborski 136 Db 66.50N 32.18 E
Zelenodolsk 136 Ed 55.53N 48.31 E
Zelenogorsk 136 Cc 60.12N 29.42 E
Zelenograd 114 Ih 56.01N 37.12 E
Zelenogradsk 116 Ij 54.57N 20.27 E
Zelenokumsk 136 Eg 44.23N 43.53 E
Zeletin 130 Kc 46.03N 27.23 E
Železné hory 120 Lg 49.50N 15.45 E
Zeleznik 130 De 44.43N 20.23 E
Železnodorožny [R.S.F.S.R.] 138 Fe 57.55N 102.50 E
Železnodorožny [R.S.F.S.R.] 114 Ei 54.23N 21.19 E
Železnodorožny [R.S.F.S.R.] 136 Fc 62.37N 50.55 E
Železnogorsk 136 De 52.21N 35.23 E
Železnogorsk-Tlimski 138 Fe 56.40N 104.05 E
Železnovodsk 132 Mg 44.08N 43.00 E
Zelfana 162 Hc 32.24N 4.14 E
Želiezovce 120 Oh 48.03N 18.40 E
Zelivka 120 Lg 49.43N 15.06 E
Željin 130 Df 43.29N 20.48 E
Zell am See 128 Gc 47.19N 12.47 E
Zell am Ziller 128 Fc 47.14N 11.53 E
Zelów 120 Pe 51.28N 19.13 E
Želtau Ajtau 135 Ib 44.30N 74.00 E
Želtyje Vody 132 He 48.23N 33.31 E
Želudok 120 Vc 53.33N 25.07 E
Zelva 120 Uc 53.04N 24.54 E
Želva 116 Ki 55.13N 25.13 E
Zelzate 122 Jc 51.12N 3.49 E
Žemaičiu Aukštuma / Zemajtskaja vozvyšennost 116 Ji 55.45N 22.30 E
Žemaiciy-Naumiestis/Žemajčju-Naumiestis 116 Ii 55.21N 21.37 E
Žemaitija 116 Ji 55.55N 22.30 E
Žemajčju-Naumiestis/Žemaiciy-Naumiestis 116 Ii 55.21N 21.37 E
Zemajtskaja vozvyšennost / Žemaičiu Aukštuma 116 Ji 55.45N 22.30 E
Zembin 116 Mj 54.24N 28.19 E
Zembretta, Ile- 128 Em 37.07N 10.53 E
Zemetčino 132 Mc 53.31N 42.38 E
Zemgale 116 Kh 56.30N 25.00 E
Zémio 168 Dd 5.19N 25.08 E
Zemmora 126 Mi 35.43N 0.45 E
Zemmour 158 Ff 25.30N 12.00W
Zemplínska Sírava, údolná nádrž- 120 Sh 48.50N 22.02 E
Zempoala 190 Ee 19.27N 96.23W
Zempoaltepec 174 Jh 17.00N 96.50W
Zemra, Djebel- 126 Pi 35.14N 3.54 E
Zemst 124 Gd 50.59N 4.28 E
Zemun, Beograd- 130 De 44.53N 20.25 E
Zengfeng Shan 154 Jc 42.25N 128.44 E
Zenica 128 Lf 44.13N 17.55 E
Zenker Seamount (EN) 222 Bc 41.00S 6.00W
Zenkov 132 Id 50.13N 34.22 E
Zenne 124 Gc 51.04N 4.26 E
Zenobia Peak 186 Bf 40.40N 108.48W
Zentsūji 156 Cd 34.14N 133.47 E
Zenzach 126 Pi 35.21N 3.22 E
Zenza do Itombe 170 Bd 9.16S 14.13 E
Žepče 128 Mf 44.26N 18.03 E
Zepu/Poskam 152 Cd 38.12N 77.18 E
Zèralda 126 Oh 36.43N 2.50 E
Zeravšan 135 Ge 39.10N 68.40 E
Zeravšan 140 If 39.22N 63.45 E
Zeravšanski hrebet 136 Gh 39.15N 68.30 E
Zerbst 120 Ie 51.58N 12.05 E
Žerdevka 136 Ee 51.53N 41.28 E
Zerind 130 Ec 46.37N 21.31 E
Zermatt 128 Bd 46.02N 7.44 E
Zernez 128 Ed 46.42N 10.07 E
Zernograd 136 Ef 46.48N 40.19 E
Zeroua 126 Ph 36.22N 3.21 E
Žešart 134 De 62.05N 49.31 E
Zestafoni 132 Mh 42.07N 43.02 E
Zeta 130 Cg 42.28N 19.16 E
Zetland → Shetland Islands 110 Fc 60.30N 1.30W
Žetybaj 136 Fg 43.34N 52.04 E
Žetykol, ozero- 132 Vd 51.05N 60.55 E
Zeune Islands 219a Bb 6.18S 155.50 E
Zeven 120 Fc 53.18N 9.17 E
Zevenaar 124 Ic 51.55N 6.05 E
Zevenbergen 124 Gc 51.38N 4.36 E
Zeydābād 146 Ph 29.37N 55.33 E
Zeydār 146 Pd 36.20N 55.53 E
Zeytinbağı 130 Li 40.23N 28.47 E
Zeytindağ 130 Kk 38.58N 27.04 E
Zêzere 126 De 39.28N 8.20W
Žežmarjaj/Žiežmariai 116 Kj 54.47N 24.36 E
Zghartā 146 Fe 34.24N 35.54 E
Zgierz 120 Pe 51.52N 19.25 E
Zgorzelec 120 Le 51.12N 15.01 E
Zhabdun → Zhongba 142 Kg 29.41N 84.10 E
• Zhag'yab 152 Ge 30.40N 97.40 E
Zhangbei 152 Jc 41.13N 114.43 E
Zhangde → Anyang 142 Nf 36.01N 114.25 E
Zhangdian → Zibo 152 Kd 36.48N 118.04 E
Zhangguangcai Ling 154 Jb 45.00N 129.00 E
Zhang He 154 Cf 36.27N 114.42 E
Zhangjiakou 142 Ne 40.49N 114.57 E
Zhangjiapan → Jingbian 152 Id 37.32N 108.45 E
Zhangling 152 La 52.39N 123.31 E
Zhanglou 154 Dh 32.40N 116.47 E
Zhangping 152 Kf 25.25N 117.27 E
Zhangqiu (Mingshui) 154 Df 36.44N 117.33 E
Zhangshuzhen → Qingjiang 152 Kf 28.02N 115.31 E
Zhangwei Xinhe 154 Dg 38.13N 117.48 E
Zhangwu 152 Lc 42.23N 122.33 E
Zhangye 142 Mf 38.57N 100.28 E
Zhangzhou 142 Ng 24.38N 117.39 E
Zhangzi 152 Jd 36.04N 112.53 E
Zhan He 152 Mb 49.21N 128.07 E
Zhanhua (Fuguo) 154 Ef 37.42N 118.08 E
Zhanjiang 142 Ng 21.13N 110.23 E
Zhanyi 152 Hf 25.40N 103.46 E
Zhao'an 152 Kg 23.49N 117.10 E
Zhaodong 152 Mb 46.04N 125.56 E
Zhaoge → Qixian 154 Cg 35.35N 114.12 E
Zhaojue 152 Hf 28.02N 102.50 E
Zhaoqing 152 Jg 23.04N 112.28 E
Zhaosu/Monggolküre 152 Dc 43.10N 81.07 E
Zhaosutai He 154 Gc 42.42N 123.35 E
Zhaotong 142 Mg 27.20N 103.46 E
Zhaoxian 154 Cf 37.46N 114.46 E
Zhaoyang Hu 154 Dg 35.00N 116.48 E
Zhaoyuan [China] 154 Ff 37.22N 120.23 E
Zhaoyuan [China] 154 Hb 45.30N 125.06 E
Zhaozhou 154 Hb 45.42N 125.15 E
Zhari Namco 152 Ee 31.05N 85.35 E
Zhaxi → Weixin 152 If 27.46N 105.04 E
Zhaxi Co 152 Ee 32.12N 85.10 E
Zhecheng 154 Cg 34.05N 115.17 E
Zheduo Shankou 152 He 30.06N 101.48 E
Zhejiang Sheng (Che-Chiang Sheng) [2] 152 Kf 29.00N 120.00 E
Zhen'an 152 Ie 33.27N 109.10 E
Zhenba 152 Ie 32.37N 107.50 E
Zhenghe 152 Kf 27.20N 118.58 E
Zhenghe Qunjiao 150 Fd 10.20N 114.20 E
Zhenglan Qi (Dund Hot) 154 Cc 42.14N 115.59 E
Zhengxiangbai Qi (Qagan Nur) 152 Jc 42.16N 114.59 E
Zhengyang 154 Ci 32.36N 114.23 E
Zhengzhou 142 Nf 34.42N 113.41 E
Zhenhai 154 Fj 29.57N 121.43 E
Zhenjiang 152 Ke 32.03N 119.26 E
Zhenkang (Fengweiba) 152 Gg 23.54N 99.00 E
Zhenlai 152 Lb 45.50N 123.14 E
Zhenning 152 If 26.05N 105.46 E
Zhenping 154 Bh 33.02N 112.14 E
Zhenxiong 152 Hf 27.28N 104.52 E
Zhenyuan 152 Hg 23.52N 100.53 E
Zhenyuan (Wuyang) 152 If 27.05N 108.26 E
Zhicheng 152 Je 30.17N 111.29 E
Zhidan (Bao'an) 152 Id 36.48N 108.46 E
Zhidoi 152 Ge 34.46N 95.46 E
Zhijiang 152 If 27.32N 109.42 E
Zhi Qu/Tongtian He 140 Lf 33.26N 96.36 E
Zhiziluo → Bijiang 152 Gf 26.39N 99.00 E
Zhob 148 Db 32.04N 69.50 E
Zhongba (Zhabdun) 142 Kg 29.41N 84.10 E
Zhongba → Jiangyou 152 He 31.48N 104.39 E
Zhongdian 152 Gf 27.42N 99.41 E
Zhōngguó = China (EN) 140 Mg 35.00N 105.00 E
Zhonghua Renmin Gongheguo=China (EN) [1] 142 Mf 35.00N 105.00 E
Zhongjian Dao 150 Fc 15.52N 111.13 E
Zhongmou 154 Cg 34.45N 114.01 E
Zhongning 152 Id 37.28N 105.41 E
Zhongshan 152 Jg 22.31N 113.23 E
Zhongwei 142 Mf 37.30N 105.09 E
Zhongxian 152 Ie 30.20N 108.02 E
Zhongxiang 152 Je 31.10N 112.38 E
Zhongxing → Siyang 154 Eh 33.43N 118.40 E
Zhongye Qundao 150 Fd 11.20N 114.30 E
Zhoukoudianzhen 154 Ce 39.41N 115.55 E
Zhoukouzhen 152 Je 33.32N 114.40 E
Zhoushan Dao 154 Gi 30.00N 122.00 E
Zhoushan Qundao 140 Of 30.00N 122.00 E
Zhuanghe 152 Ld 39.42N 122.58 E
Zhucheng 152 Kd 35.58N 119.28 E
Zhu Dao 154 Fe 39.05N 121.10 E
Zhugqu 152 He 33.46N 104.18 E
Zhuhe 154 Bj 29.44N 113.07 E
Zhuizishan → Weichang 152 Kc 41.55N 117.39 E
Zhuji 154 Fj 29.43N 120.13 E
Zhuji → Shangqiu 152 Ke 34.24N 115.37 E
Zhujiang Kou 152 Jg 22.20N 113.45 E
Zhumadian 152 Je 32.54N 114.03 E
Zhuolu 154 Cd 40.23N 115.13 E
Zhuoxian 152 Kd 39.26N 116.00 E
Zhuozhang He 154 Bf 36.36N 113.10 E
Zhuozi 154 Bd 40.52N 112.33 E
Zhuozi Shan 152 Id 39.36N 107.00 E
Zhushan 152 Je 32.16N 110.12 E
Zhuzhou 142 Ng 27.52N 113.12 E
Ziama Mansouria 162 Ib 36.40N 5.29 E
Ziar nad Hronom 120 Oh 48.36N 18.52 E
Ẓibā' 144 Ed 27.21N 35.40 E
Zibo (Zhangdian) 152 Kd 36.48N 118.04 E
Zicavo 122a Bb 41.54N 9.08 E
Židačov 120 Ug 49.17N 24.12 E
Zielona Góra 120 Le 51.56N 15.31 E
Zielona Góra [2] 120 Le 51.55N 15.30 E
Zierikzee 122 Jc 51.38N 3.55 E
Žiežmariai/Žežmarjaj 116 Kj 54.47N 24.36 E
Ziftá 146 Dg 30.43N 31.15 E
Žigalovo 138 Ff 54.48N 105.08 E
Zigana Geçidi 146 Hb 40.38N 39.25 E
Žigansk 138 Hc 66.45N 123.30 E
Zigey 168 Bc 14.43N 15.47 E
Zīghan, Wāḩāt- 164 Dd 25.35N 22.06 E
Zigong 142 Mg 29.20N 104.48 E
Zigui 152 Je 31.01N 110.42 E
Ziguinchor 160 Fg 12.35N 16.16W
Žigulevsk 136 Ee 53.27N 49.29 E
Zihuatanejo 190 De 17.38N 101.33W
Zijing Shan 152 Jd 37.12N 112.50 E
Zijpenberg 124 Hb 52.04N 6.00 E
Zilâlet 166 Gb 18.28N 7.48 E
Zile 144 Ea 40.18N 35.54 E
Žilina 112 Hf 49.14N 18.45 E
Žilino 116 Ij 54.55N 21.48 E
Zillah 160 If 28.33N 17.35 E
Ziller 128 Fc 47.24N 11.50 E
Zillertaler Alpen 120 Hi 47.00N 11.55 E
Žiloj 132 Qi 40.19N 50.33 E
Zilupe 114 Gh 56.25N 28.07 E
Zima 142 Md 53.56N 102.04 E
Zimapán 192 Jg 20.45N 99.21W
Zimatlán de Álvarez 192 Ki 16.52N 96.47W
Zimba 170 Ef 17.02S 26.30 E
Zimbabwe 172 Ed 20.16S 30.55 E
Zimbabwe (Rhodesia) [1] 160 Jj 20.00S 30.00 E
Zimbor 130 Gc 47.00N 23.16 E
Zimi 166 Cd 7.19N 11.18W
Zimni Bereg 114 Jd 66.00N 40.45 E
Zimnicea 130 If 43.40N 25.22 E
Zimovniki 132 Mf 47.08N 42.29 E
Zina 166 Hc 11.16N 14.58 E
Zincirli 146 Gd 37.00N 36.41 E
Zinder 160 Hg 13.48N 8.59 E
Zinder [2] 166 Hb 15.00N 10.00 E
Zinga 168 Be 3.43N 18.35 E
Zingst 120 Ib 54.25N 12.50 E
Zinjibār 164 Ig 13.08N 45.23 E
Zinnik/Soignies 122 Kd 50.35N 4.04 E
Zinsel du Nord 124 Jf 48.49N 7.44 E
Zion [Il.-U.S.] 186 Me 42.27N 87.50W
Zion [St.C.N.] 197c Ab 17.09N 62.32W
Zipaquirá 202 Db 5.02N 74.01W
Zirc 120 Ni 47.16N 17.52 E

Index Symbols

[1] Independent Nation
[2] State, Region
[3] District, County
[4] Municipality
[5] Colony, Dependency
Continent
Physical Region
Historical or Cultural Region
Mount, Mountain
Volcano
Hill
Mountains, Mountain Range
Hills, Escarpment
Plateau, Upland
Pass, Gap
Plain, Lowland
Delta
Salt Flat
Valley, Canyon
Crater, Cave
Karst Features
Depression
Polder
Desert, Dunes
Forest, Woods
Heath, Steppe
Oasis
Cape, Point
Coast, Beach
Cliff
Peninsula
Isthmus
Sandbank
Island
Atoll
Rock, Reef
Islands, Archipelago
Rocks, Reefs
Coral Reef
Well, Spring
Geyser
River, Stream
Waterfall, Rapids
River Mouth, Estuary
Lake
Salt Lake
Intermittent Lake
Reservoir
Swamp, Pond
Canal
Glacier
Ice Shelf, Pack Ice
Ocean
Sea
Gulf, Bay
Strait, Fjord
Lagoon
Bank
Seamount
Tablemount
Ridge
Shelf
Basin
Escarpment, Sea Scarp
Fracture
Trench, Abyss
National Park, Reserve
Point of Interest
Recreation Site
Cave, Cavern
Historic Site
Ruins
Wall, Walls
Church, Abbey
Temple
Scientific Station
Railway station
Airport
Port
Military installation
Lighthouse
Mine
Tunnel
Dam, Bridge

Index Symbols

[1] Independent Nation	Pass, Gap	Depression	Coast, Beach
[2] State, Region	Plain, Lowland	Polder	Cliff
[3] District, County	Delta	Desert, Dunes	Peninsula
[4] Municipality	Salt Flat	Forest, Woods	Isthmus
[5] Colony, Dependency	Valley, Canyon	Heath, Steppe	Sandbank
Continent	Crater, Cave	Oasis	Island
Physical Region	Karst Features	Cape, Point	Atoll

Historical or Cultural Region	Rock, Reef	Waterfall, Rapids	Canal
Mount, Mountain	Islands, Archipelago	River Mouth, Estuary	Glacier
Volcano	Rocks, Reefs	Lake	Ice Shelf, Pack Ice
Hill	Well, Spring	Salt Lake	Ocean
Mountains, Mountain Range	Geyser	Intermittent Lake	Sea
Hills, Escarpment	River, Stream	Reservoir	Gulf, Bay
Plateau, Upland		Swamp, Pond	Strait, Fjord

Lagoon	Escarpment, Sea Scarp	Historic Site	Airport
Bank	Fracture	Ruins	Port
Seamount	Trench, Abyss	Wall, Walls	Military installation
Tablemount	National Park, Reserve	Church, Abbey	Lighthouse
Ridge	Point of Interest	Temple	Mine
Shelf	Recreation Site	Scientific Station	Tunnel
Basin	Cave, Cavern	Railway station	Dam, Bridge